THE LYLE OFFICIAL ARTS REVIEW 1988

While every care has been taken in the compiling of information contained in this volume the publishers cannot accept any liability for loss, financial or otherwise, incurred by reliance placed on the information herein.

All prices quoted in this book are obtained from a variety of auctions in various countries during the twelve months prior to publication and are converted to dollars at the rate of exchange prevalent at the time of sale.

British Library Cataloguing in Publication Data

The Lyle official arts review. – 1988-
1. Art auctions – Periodicals
2. Painting – Prices – Periodicals
338.4'375 N8670

ISBN 0-86248-101-5

SBN 0-86248-101-5

Printed by A. Wheaton & Co. Ltd., Exeter, Devon.
Bound by Dorstel Press, Harlow, Essex.

THE LYLE OFFICIAL ARTS REVIEW 1988

COMPILED & EDITED BY
TONY CURTIS

Auction Acknowledgements

Anderson & Garland, *Anderson House, Market Street, Newcastle-upon-Tyne NE1 6XA*
Australian Art Auctions, *62/65 Market Street, Sydney 2000*
Barbers Fine Art Auctioneers, *The Mayford Centre, Smarts Heath Rd., Mayford Green, Woking GU22 0PP*
Biddle & Webb, *Ladywood Middleway, Birmingham B16 0PP*
Bonhams, *Montpelier Galleries, Montpelier St., Knightsbridge, London SW7 1HH*
Bridgfords, *The Alderley Saleroom, 1 Heyes Lane, Alderley Edge, Cheshire SK9 7LA*
Capes, Dunn & Co., *The Auction Galleries, 38 Charles Street, Manchester*
Chancellors Hollingsworths, *31 High Street, Ascot*
Christie, Manson & Woods Int. Inc., *502 Park Avenue, New York*
Christie's, *8 King Street, St. James's, London*
Christie's, *219 East 67th Street, New York, NY10021*
Christie's (Monaco) S.A.M., *Park Palace, 98000 Monte Carlo*
Christie's & Edmiston's, *164/166 Bath Street, Glasgow*
Christie's (Hong Kong) Ltd., *3607 Edinburgh Tower, 15 Queen's Rd. Central, Hong Kong*
Christie's S. Kensington, *85 Old Brompton Road, London*
Dacre, Son & Hartley, *1-5 The Grove, Ilkley, Yorkshire*
Dee & Atkinson, *Chartered Surveyors, Auctioneers, Land & Estate Agents, The Exchange, Driffield*
Du Mouchelle Art Galleries, *409E Jefferson, Detroit, Michigan 48226*
Geering & Colyer, *22-24 High Street, Tunbridge Wells, Kent TN1 1XA*
Andrew Grant Fine Art Auctioneers, *59/60 Foregate Street, Worcester*
Graves, Son & Pilcher, *38 Holland Road, Hove, Sussex BN3 2EL*
Giles Haywood, *The Auction House, St. Johns Road, Stourbridge DY8 1EW*
Heathcote Ball & Co. Ltd., *Albion Auction Rooms, Commercial St., Northampton NN1 1PJ*
Hobbs & Chambers, *'At the Sign of the Bell', Market Place, Cirencester, Glos. GL7 1QQ*
Messrs. Jacobs & Hunt's, *Lavant Street, Petersfield*
Lalonde Fine Art, *The Auction Room, Oakfield Road, Bristol BS8 2BE*
W. H. Lane & Son, *64 Morrab Road, Penzance, Cornwall*
R. R. Leonard & Son, *512 Holderness Road, Hull HU9 3DS*
Lots Road Chelsea Auction Galleries, *71 Lots Road, London*
Lowery's, *24 Bridge Street, Northampton NN1 1NT*
Michael G. Matthews, *The Devon Fine Art Auction House, Dowell St., Honiton, Devon EX14 8LX*
Morphets, *4–6 Albert Street, Harrogate, Yorkshire HG1 1JL*
D. M. Nesbit & Co., *Southsea Salerooms, 7 Clarendon Road, Southsea, Hants PO5 2ED*
Onslow's Auctioneers, *123 Hursley, Winchester, Hants SO21 2LQ*
Osmond Tricks, *Regent Street Auction Rooms, Clifton, Bristol BS8 4HG*
Outhwaite & Litherland, *Kingsway Galleries, Fontenoy Street, Liverpool*
Parsons, Welch & Cowell, *49 London Road, Sevenoaks, Kent*
Phillips, *65 George Street, Edinburgh*
Phillips, *207 Bath Street, Glasgow*
Phillips, *98 Sauchiehall Street, Glasgow*
Phillips, *Blenstock House, 7 Blenheim Street, New Bond St., London W1Y 0AS*
Prudential Fine Art/Auctioneers, *Millmead Auction Rooms, Guildford, Surrey*
Reeds Rains, *Trinity House, 114 Northenden Road, Sale, Cheshire*
Robt. W. Skinner Inc., *Bolton Gallery, Route 117, Bolton, Mass.*
Taylor's, *Honiton Galleries, 205 High Street, Honiton, Devon*
Anthony Lipmann Walton (Fine Arts) Ltd., *1 Rydens Court, 9 Rydens Rd. Walton-on-Thames, Surrey KT12 3AA*
Warner's Wm. H. Brown, *The Warner Auction Rooms, 16-18 Halford St., Leicester LE1 1JB*
Woolley & Wallis, *The Castle Auction Mart, Castle Street, Salisbury SP1 3SU*
Worsfolds Auction Galleries, *40 Station Road West, Canterbury*

Introduction

Published annually and containing details of thousands of oil paintings, watercolours and prints, The Lyle Official Arts Review is the most comprehensively illustrated reference work on the subject available at this time.

Each entry is listed alphabetically under the Artist's name for easy reference and includes a description of the picture, its size, medium, auctioneer and the price fetched at auction during the twelve months prior to publication.

As regards authenticity of the works listed, this is often a delicate matter and throughout this book the conventional system has been observed:

The full Christian name(s) and surname of the artist denote that, in the opinion of the auctioneer listed, the work is by that artist.

The initials of the Christian name(s) and the surname denote that, in the opinion of the auctioneer listed, the work is of the period of the artist and may be wholly or partly his work.

The surname only of the artist denotes that, in the opinion of the auctioneer listed, the work is of the school or by one of the followers of the artist or painted in his style.

The word 'after' associated with the surname of the artist denotes that, in the opinion of the auctioneer listed, the picture is a copy of the work of the artist. The word 'signed' associated with the name of the artist denotes that, in the opinion of the auctioneer listed, the work bears a signature which is the signature of the artist.

The words 'bears signature' or 'traces of signature' denote that, in the opinion of the auctioneer listed, the work bears a signature or traces of a signature which may be that of the artist.

The word 'dated' denotes that the work is dated and that, in the opinion of the auctioneer listed, was executed at that date.

The words 'bears date' or 'inscribed' (with date) denotes that, in the opinion of the auctioneer listed, the work is so dated and may have been executed at about that date.

All pictures are oil on canvas unless otherwise specified. In the dimensions (sight size) given, the height precedes the breadth.

Although the greatest possible care has been taken to ensure that any statement as to authorship, attribution, origin, date, age, provenance and condition is reliable, all such statements can only be statement of opinion and are not to be taken as statements or representations of fact.

The Lyle Official Arts Review offers a unique opportunity for identification and valuation of paintings by an extremely broad cross section of artists of all periods and schools.

Unless otherwise stated descriptions are placed immmediately underneath the relevant illustrations.

We firmly believe that dealers, collectors and investors alike will treasure this and subsequent annual editions of the Lyle Official Arts Review (published in September each year) as changing trends in the fluctuating world of art values are revealed.

Tony Curtis

FRONT COVER

'Sunflowers' by VINCENT VAN GOGH *(Christie's)*
'Sonja In Green' by SIR HERBERT JAMES GUNN, R.A. *(Christie's)*
'Laugh Clown Laugh' by DAME LAURA KNIGHT, R.A. *(Christie's)*
'Off To School' by CHARLES BURTON BARBER *(Christie's)*
'Grandfather's Favourite' by KARL FRANZ EDOUARD VON GEBHARDT *(Christie's)*

SPINE

'Fillette Au Tablier Noir' by AMEDEO MODIGLIANI *(Christie's)*

BACK COVER

'Les Soleils' by ALBERT ANDRE *(Christie's)*
'The Toy Seller' by JOHN P. BURR *(Phillips)*
'Robert, The Artist's Son' by FRANZ VON DEFREGGER *(Christie's)*

The publishers wish to express their sincere thanks to the following for their involvement and assistance in the production of this volume:

KAREN DOUGLASS (Art Editor)
JANICE MONCRIEFF (Assistant Editor)
ANNETTE CURTIS
SUSAN CAMERON
NICHOLA FAIRBURN
TANYA FAIRBAIRN
SALLY DALGLIESH
ISHBELL MAC PHAIL
FRANK BURRELL
ROBERT NISBET
EILEEN BURRELL

ARTS REVIEW

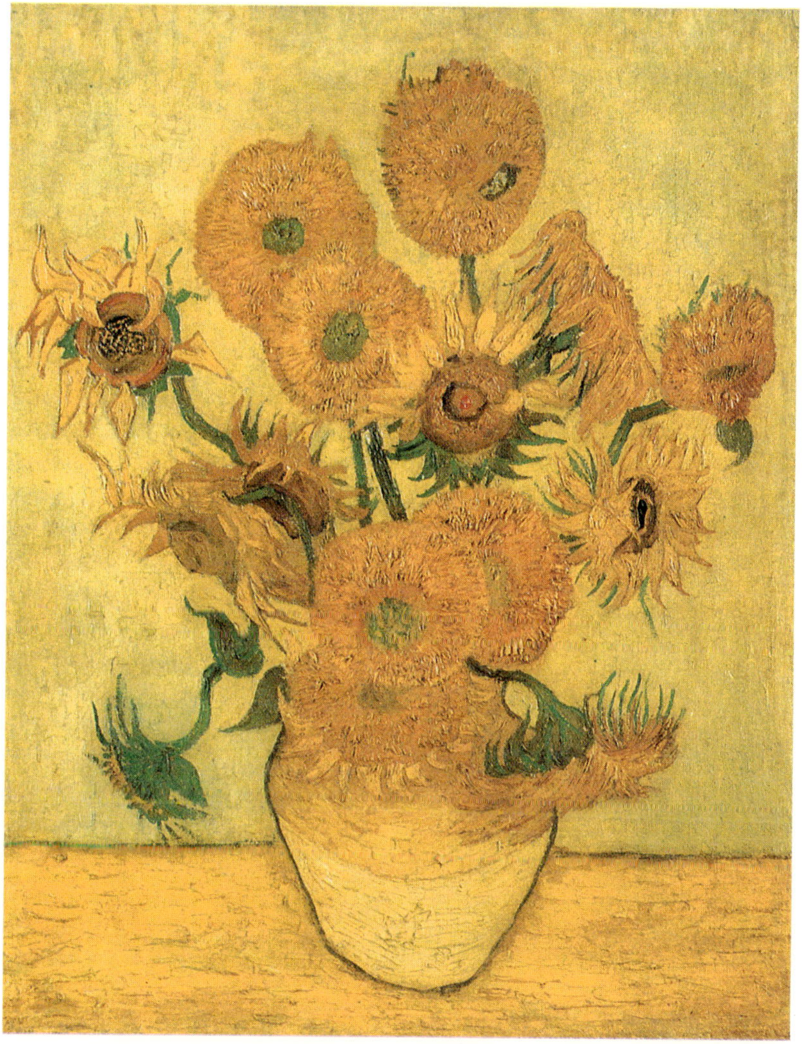

1987 will be remembered as the year the art market ran wild. In March, on the anniversary of the artist's birth, Christie's sold the largest of the seven paintings Vincent Van Gogh did of sunflowers for a truly astonishing £24,750,000. It was one of only two of Van Gogh's sunflower paintings still in private hands – Britain is lucky to possess one which can be seen in London's National Gallery. The record breaking picture was sent for sale from the American Beatty collection.

The Van Gogh tripled the record for a picture sold at auction which was previously held by Mantegna's "Adoration of the Magi", sold for £8.1 million in 1985.

The atmosphere in Christie's London rooms was literally breathtaking during the sale of the Van Gogh. Bids were stepped up in leaps of £500,000 at a time and the glamour was not diminished by the fact that the victor's identity was kept a close secret for several days afterwards although it was later disclosed that the buyer was the Yasuda Fire and Marine Insurance Company of Tokyo who plan to display the picture in their head office.

Among all the talk of millions, it is sobering to remember that Van Gogh only sold one painting in his lifetime and once despairingly wrote to his brother about his unfulfilled wish for someone to pay as little as £25 for an example of his work. Apart from the Van Gogh there were another forty-two major works of art sold on the same day including a Piet Mondrian 'Tableau No. 1' which sold for £1,320,000 and Amedeo Modigliani 'Fillette au Tablier Noir' for £2,640,000 and an Andre Derain 'Collioure le Port de Peche' which sold for £2,200,000. The salerooms have been literally raking in money for art this year and the boom started in late 1986 when Sotheby's in London secured over £40m for 106 works of Impressionist and Modern Art. This beat their own record of two weeks previously in New York when £29m was paid out.

Christie's were not lagging either for in the same week, they also got £20 million in 24 hours for paintings and their total was secured for half as many pictures as Sotheby's.

Significant among Christie's lots were Manet's 'La Rue Mosnier aux Paveurs', painted in 1878, which sold to a European millionaire for £7.7 million, a world record for a Modern Painting and double its estimate. Star of Sotheby's sales was Braque's 'Femme Lisant' which sold for

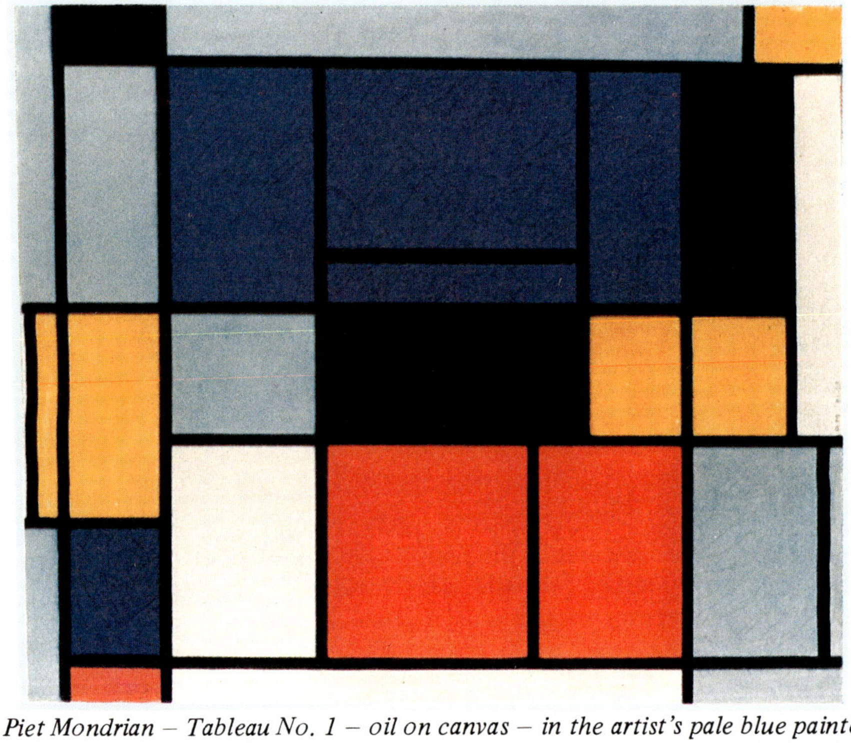

Piet Mondrian – Tableau No. 1 – oil on canvas – in the artist's pale blue painted frame – 29.5/8 x 25.5/8in. (Christie's) *£1,320,000*

Amedeo Modigliani – 'Fillette Au Tablier Noir' – oil on canvas – signed upper right – 36¼ x 23¾in. – painted in 1918. (Christie's) £2,640,000

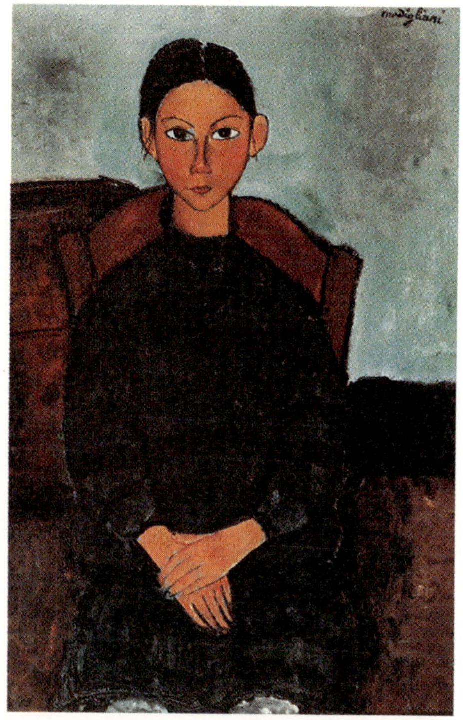

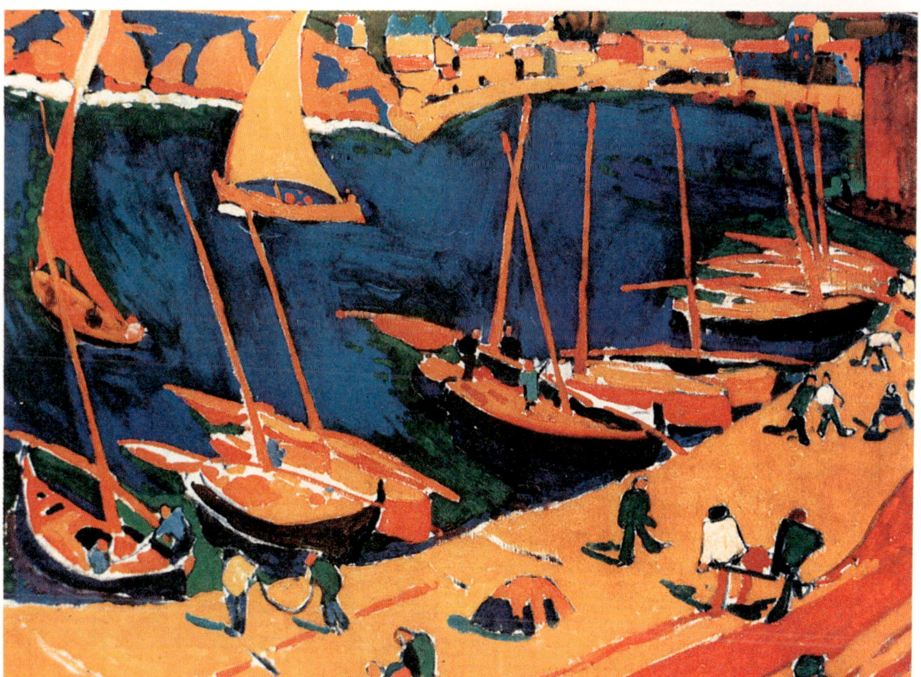

Andre Derain – 'Collioure, Le Port De Peche' – oil on canvas – 32 x 39in. (Christie's) £2,200,000

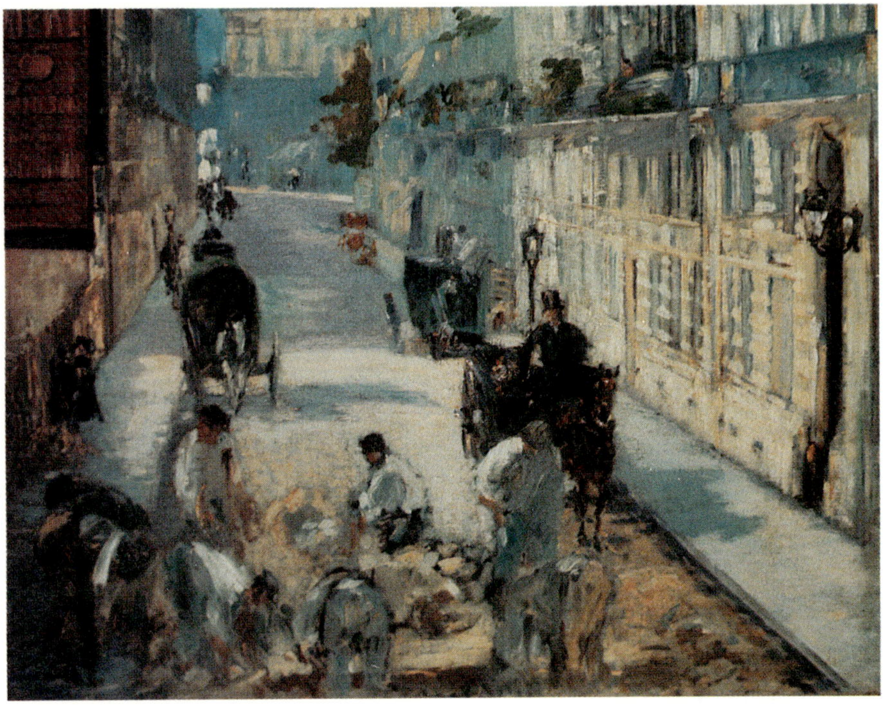

Edouard Manet – 'La Rue Mosnier Aux Paveurs' – oil on canvas – 25¼ x 31½in. (Christie's) £7,700,000

£6.6 million – an auction record for the artist and for any 20th century work of art.

The Impressionist boom has now been strong for two years but it really began in the 1970's when the Japanese started buying Impressionists, which they greatly admire. Perhaps more than any other category of collectors, the Japanese see paintings as things to deal in and recently have been attracted to buy in London because of the softness of sterling. In recognition of the interest, Christie's have increased the number of their Impressionist sales from four to five a year because of the pressure.

Americans too are paying extraordinary money for contemporary and 20th century art, for example Mondrian and Henry Moore. Moore sold recently for £1.2m in New York, and Christie's also secured £1.1m for a Leger of 1920; £811,00 for a Mondrian of the Houses of Parliament; and £220,000 for a Marie Laurencin 'Femme au Chat et au Chien'.

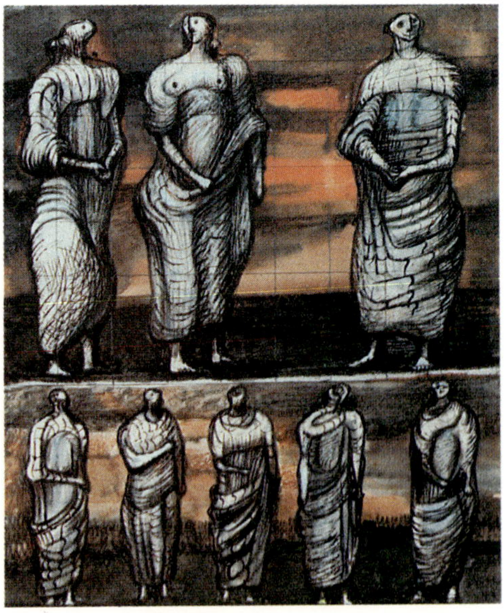

Henry Moore, O.M., C.H. – 'Standing Figures' – watercolour, pen and black ink, charcoal and white chalk. (Christie's) £55,000

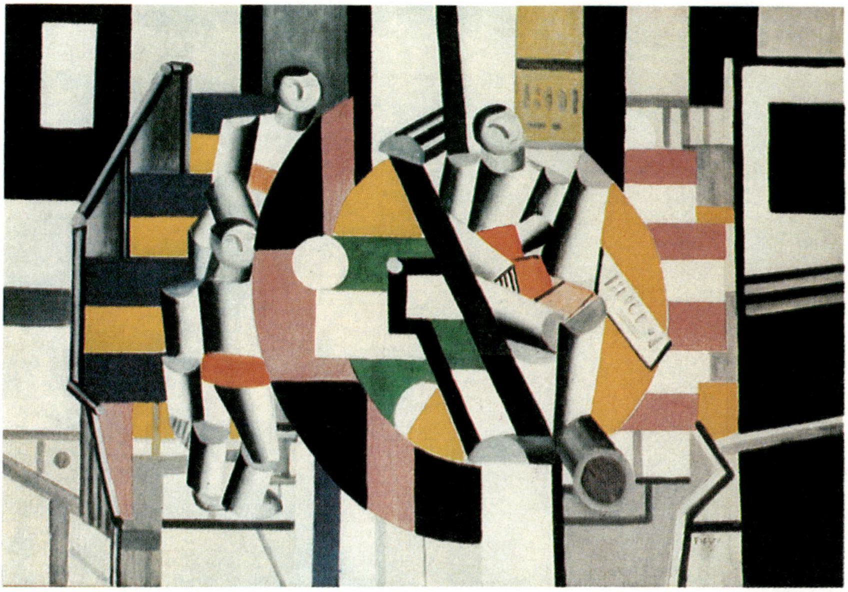

Fernand Leger – 'Les Trois Personnages' – oil on canvas – painted in 1920 – 25.5/8 x 36.5/8in. (Christie's) *£1,100,000*

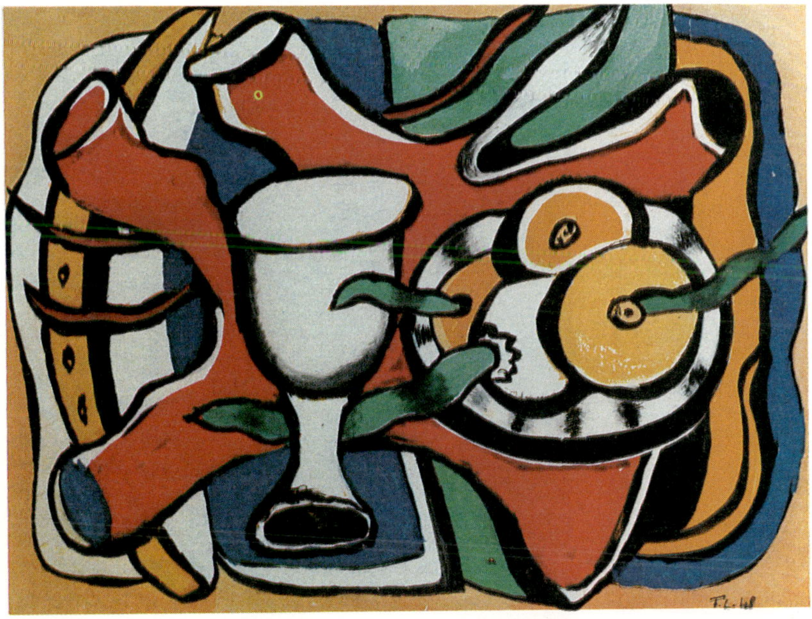

Fernand Leger – 'Nature Morte Aux Pommes' – gouache on paper – 10 x 13in. (Christie's) *£24,200*

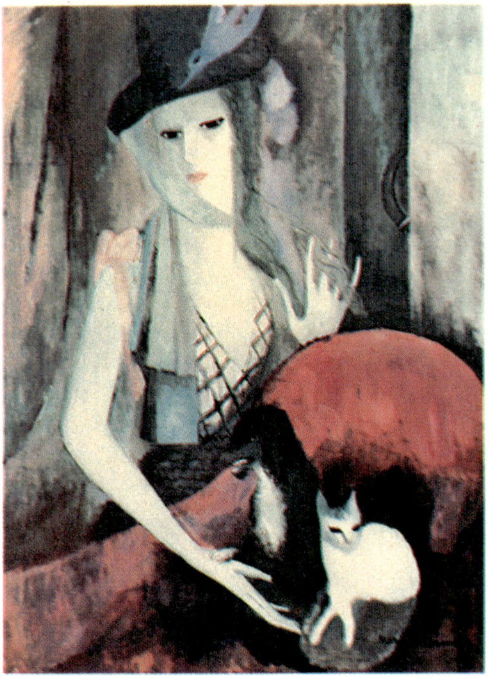

Marie Laurencin – 'Femme Au Chat Et Au Chien' – oil on canvas – 39½ x 28¾in. – painted in 1916. (Christie's) £220,000

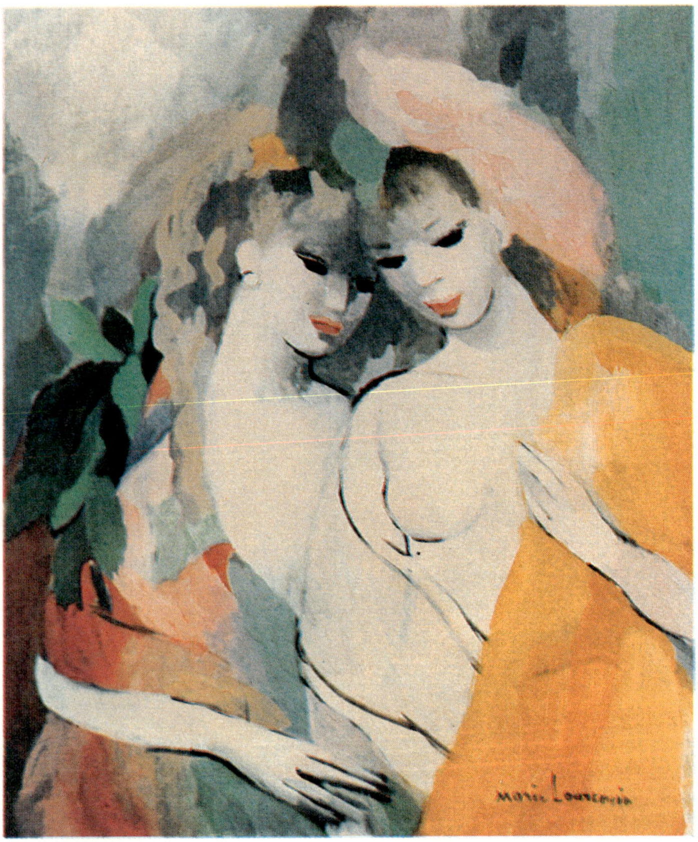

Marie Laurencin – 'Les Deux Femmes' – oil on canvas – painted circa 1930 – 24 x 19¾in. (Christie's) £165,000

The reason why Impressionists and Moderns are so popular is because they, especially the Impressionists, are easier to understand, decorate modern homes better, and usually demand less wall space than Old Masters. Also people with money to spend on pictures like to build up collections and there are more Impressionists about. As a result second rate Impressionists now fetch more than some Old Masters and Italian baroque painters of the 17th century.

Impressionist and Modern artists are behind the biggest increase in the Art Market for some time. Taking 1975 prices as the base level of 100, the art market index has gone up from 431 in December 1985 to 508 in December 1986. The Impressionist sector rose from 487 to 628 over that period and Modern Paintings rose from 467 to 656. All this activity has re-established London as the centre of the art world, having fought off the challenge from New York.

The booming stock market is one, but only one, of the factors behind the escalation in art prices. Everywhere in the world, at any one time, there is someone making money and not all the new rich are content to spend their money on yachts and houses. This means that there are enough new collectors to give the market a buzz and because the art world is international, there are always people making fortunes somewhere. There is even a rumour that the Mafia have been

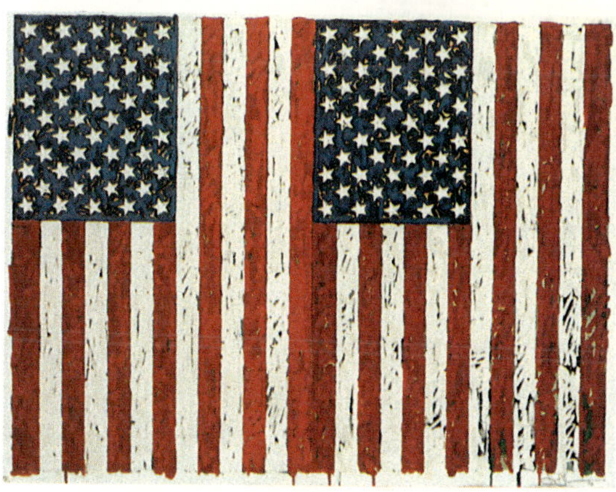

Jasper Johns – 'Flags 1 (Field 173)' – screen-print in colours – 27½ x 35in. (Christie's)

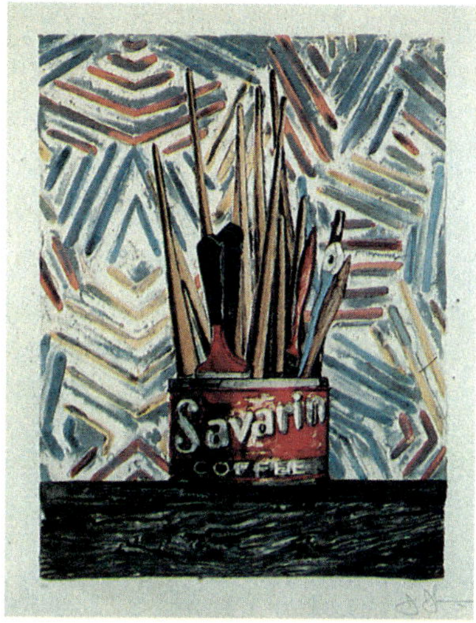

Jasper Johns – 'Savarin (Field 259)' – lithograph in colours – 45 x 34½in. (Christie's)

buying works of art in order to launder money and a painting by American artist Jasper Johns, which made $3.63m in New York recently (a record for a living artist), could be a case in point.

Records make records and while confidence is high, the buying looks set to continue as long as spiralling stock markets supply the cash.

The London art world boom also records the consequence of weakness of sterling against foreign currencies. It is noticeable that this year's top prices have been made in centres of weak currency – London, New York and Hong Kong. The buyers on the other hand have been using strong currency – the yen, the deutschmark and the Swiss franc.

It is interesting that only 20 per cent of works of art sold in London originated in this country.

Fifty per cent of the sellers are the connoisseurs of Europe and their paintings came here because London sales are still not liable for VAT as the EEC has been pressing for them to become. Owners, nervous that this loophole might be eliminated, have been sending a large number of works to London for sale while the going is good. At the moment however it looks as if we are in for a stay of execution because, through British government pressure, the EEC's moves have been shelved.

Another reason for the rush to sell by Continental owners is the fear that British export laws will soon be tightened up to come into line with those of France and Italy. There has also been a certain amount of selling ahead of incoming changes in the American tax laws which will tighten up tax concessions for donating works of art to museums or galleries. The current value of a donated work of art used to be deducted from the donor's tax bill for the year, a notable bonus and one which encouraged the escalation in art prices. The market has been rising too because of panic on the part of buyers as well as sellers who want to cash in while the going is so good. There are now so few major works available, and if they go to museums they stay there, that buyers, especially American and Japanese, are snapping up everything good that comes on the market. Soon the auction houses will have to worry about finding enough top quality goods.

Old Master paintings have for some time been out of favour but the past year has also shown a change which began in New York in November 1986 when 34 world records were set in a sale of 45 Old Masters. Top item was a single sheet from a Leonardo da Vinci sketchbook, showing a chubby

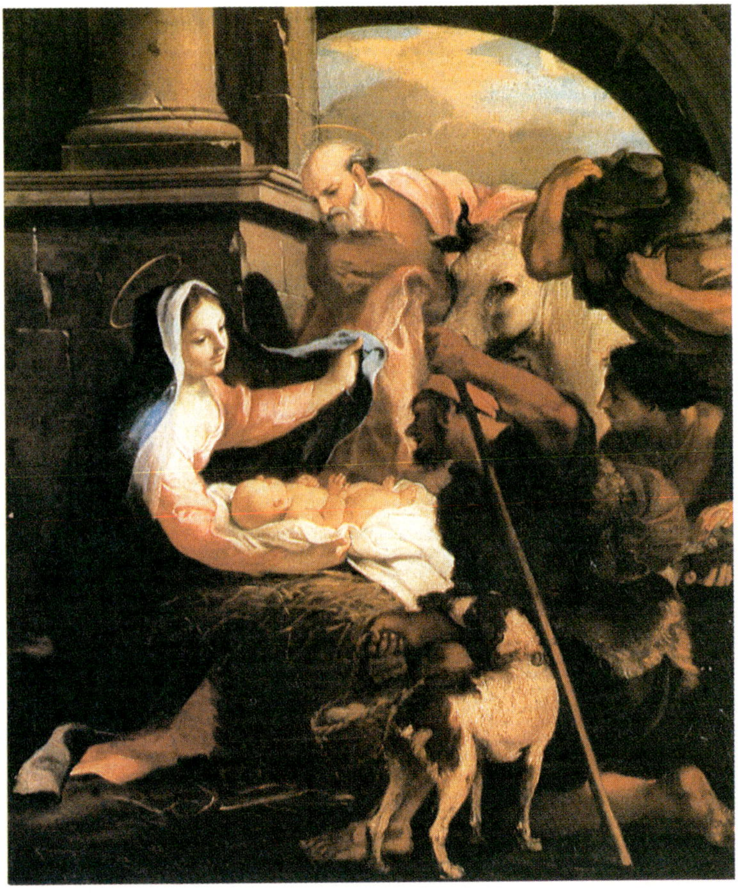

Circle of Ubaldo Gandolfi – 'The Adoration Of The Shepherds' – 24¾ x 17¼in. (Phillips)

Workshop of Niccol Di Pietro Gerini – 'The Madonna And Child' – 26¼ x 16¾in. (Phillips) £36,000

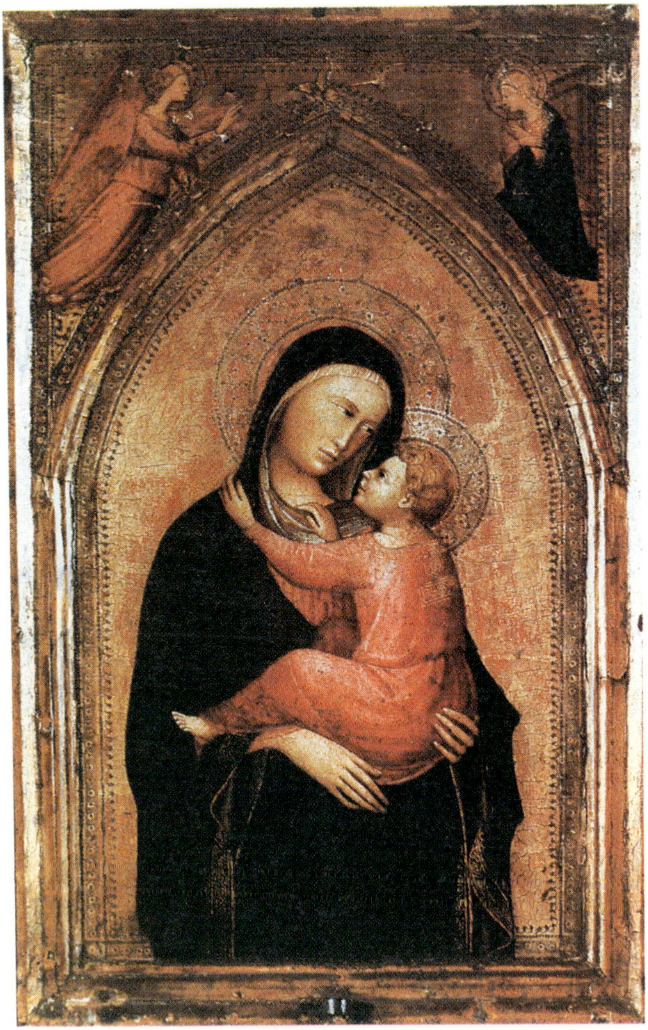

child clutching a lamb, which went for \$3.63m dollars.

Popular taste used to be against Old Masters and Japanese buyers frankly do not like or understand them. The farthest back in time they will go is to Fragonard or Boucher.

However, it is said that collectors come to Old Masters late in life, and among Americans today it is considered chic to collect them. Fervent religious imagery however is still not popular and even the new buyers of Old Masters tend to prefer Madonnas to scenes of the Crucifixion. Some fine Old Masters are still considered uninteresting by modern collectors and two Franz Hals offered for sale last autumn failed to reach their reserves because the sitters were stodgy looking Dutch burghers.

Reviving interest in this category however has meant that many aristocratic sellers are rushing to put family heirlooms on the market though many of them prefer to negotiate with trusted dealers, thus avoiding the publicity of putting their pictures on the open market. It is thought that prices even outstripping auction records have been secured in this way.

It is significant that the Duke of Devonshire is preparing another sale of his Rembrandt drawings – the last lot, offered to the British Museum for £5.25 million and refused, made £20 million at auction.

The British Rail pension fund, which put large sums of money into art in the 1970's, has now also been enticed into the market by the boom and, in a toss up between putting its Impressionists or its Old Master drawings on the market, the Old Masters won. They were valued at £40 million in September, 1986, and the big puzzle now is, how much will they make when the market for them is rising again?

Because there is a rapidly diminishing stock of Old Masters, little known names or categories are being pushed. Neapolitan painting began to rise in price about five years ago and buyers were particularly attracted after a major exhibition in the Royal Academy. The new interest is Bolognese painting although until recently Bolognese paintings were quite unpopular

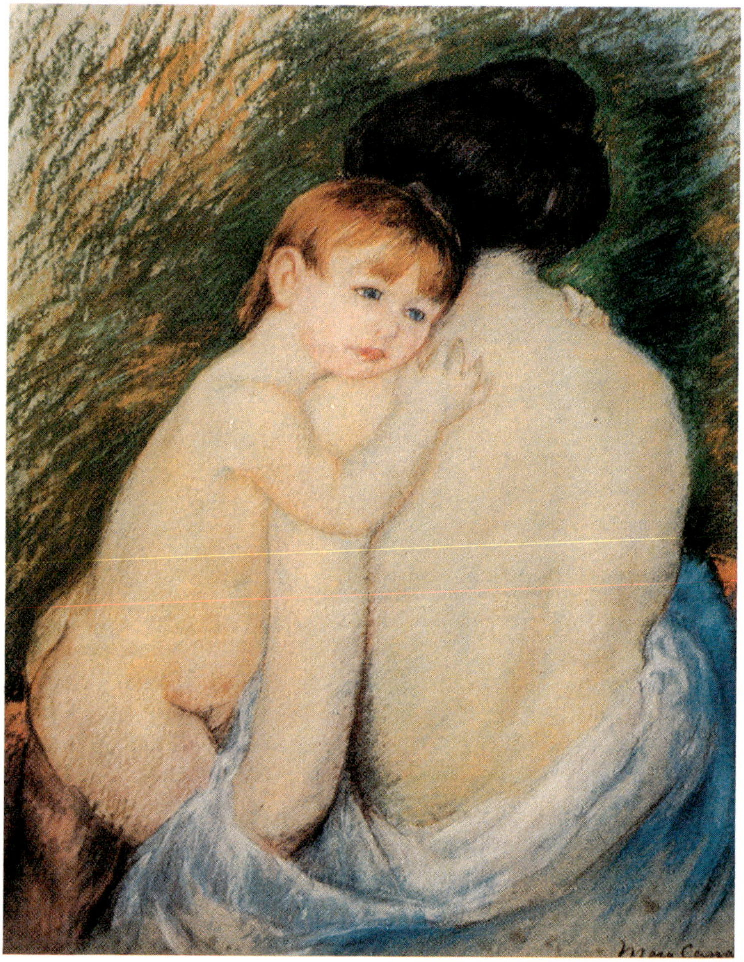

Mary Cassatt – Study For 'The Bare Back' – 1906 – pastel on board – 29 x 22½in. (Phillips) £990,000

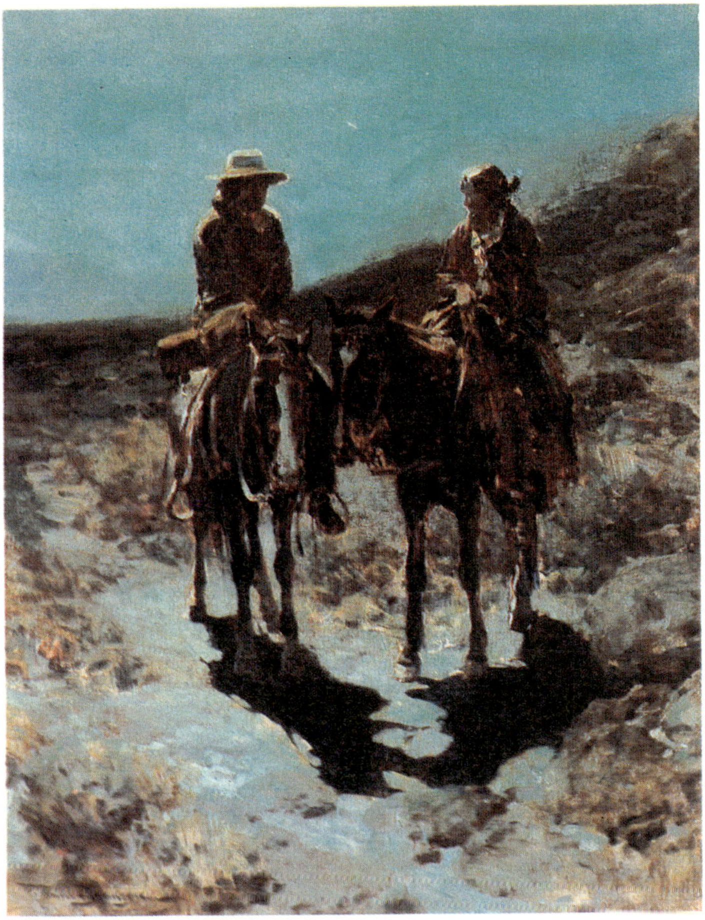

Frank Tenney Johnson – 'Lovers Of The Desert' – oil on canvas – 36 x 28in. (Christie's) $37,400

because of the tendency of the artists to depict pious virgins looking skywards. Buying interest however has been activated by exhibitions recently mounted in Italy, Oxford and in New York's Metropolitan Museum with a smaller one in London. The big names among the Bolognese are the Carracci brothers, with Annibale the best of the three. Lesser names include Tiarini, Elisabetta Sirani and Del Sole.

The Van Gogh sensation tended to overshadow the success of two portraits by Gustav Klimt which made a double record in March 1987. They were a portrait of Rose von Rosthorn-Friedmann painted between 1900-1901 and another of Egon Schiele, done in 1909. Both fetched £1,760,000 at Sotheby's Impressionist sale over estimates ranging between £1.3 million and £1.8 million. Klimt was one of the Secessionists, Austria's answer to the Art Nouveau movement. Another portrait success was the £1.815 million paid for Benjamin West's picture of Sir Joseph Banks which is thought to have been purchased by the Australian millionaire, Alan Bond.

For collectors outside the mammoth money bracket it is worth noting that one of the areas for making money in future could be early 20th century American art.

This category hit the highspots when Mary Cassatt's 1906 pastel study 'The Bare Back' made £990,000 although the estimate was £200,000. In the same early 20th century American category was Frank Tenney Johnson's oil, 'A Council on the Mesa' which Phillips sold in New York .

Another interesting new sector is Russian 20th century and Avant Garde art which the Communists used to dismiss as decadent but there has been a new wave of interest over the past five years and sales of these pictures will now become an annual event for Sotheby's.

They include drawings, paintings, prints and posters and names to look out for include Mikhail Larionov and Natalia Gontcharova from the early period; Alexander Rodchenko and Liobov Popova who were Constructivists. Designs for mobile stages were done by El Lissitsky and there are also collectors of architectural designs for Russian government buildings. Among the earlier Russian painters is Stephan Mikhailovich Shoukhvostov whose 'Interior of the Coronation Cathedral in Moscow's Kremlin', painted in 1851, was estimated at between £4,000 and £6,000. Equally rising are Indian and Persian miniatures dating from the 16th to the 19th centuries and showing scenes of courtly life and from popular myths. The Emperor Akbar, who lived around 1590, was a keen patron of art and many of the most attractive miniatures date from this time but there are also fine 17th century Rajasthani and Pahari pieces available illustrating the Bhagavata Purana. Prices range around £6,000 to £8,000.

English miniatures are also being collected at the moment and one by William Wood of Lieut. Gother Mann of the Royal Artillery, showing the sitter with powdered hair, a blue coat and gilt epaulettes, dated 1797 made £2,200 at Phillips.

Among British 20th century artists whose work is now fetching good prices is William Russell Flint. His print, 'Danza Montana' printed in colour from an edition of 750 in 1962 made a world record price of

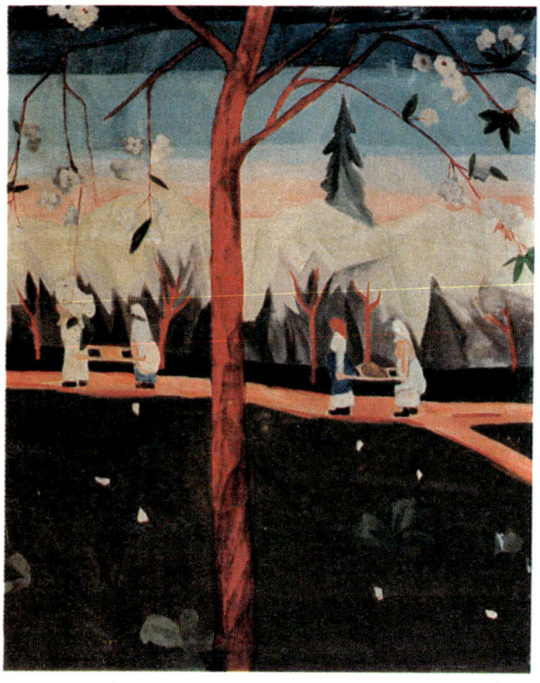

Natalia Gontcharova – 'Le Printemps' – oil on canvas – 36¼ x 29¼in. (Christie's)
£30,800

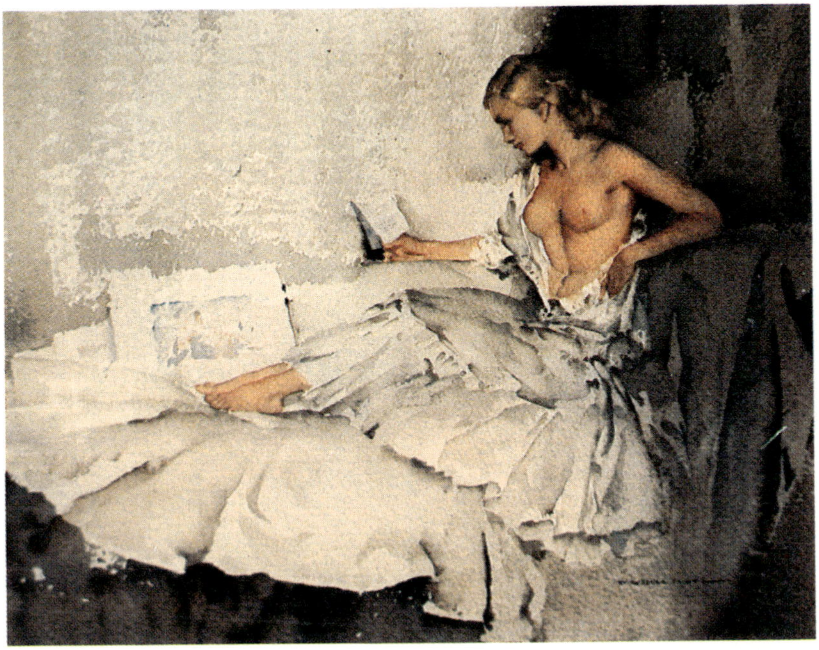

Sir William Russell Flint, R.A. – 'Primavera' – watercolour – 9½ x 11¾in. (Christie's)
£14,300

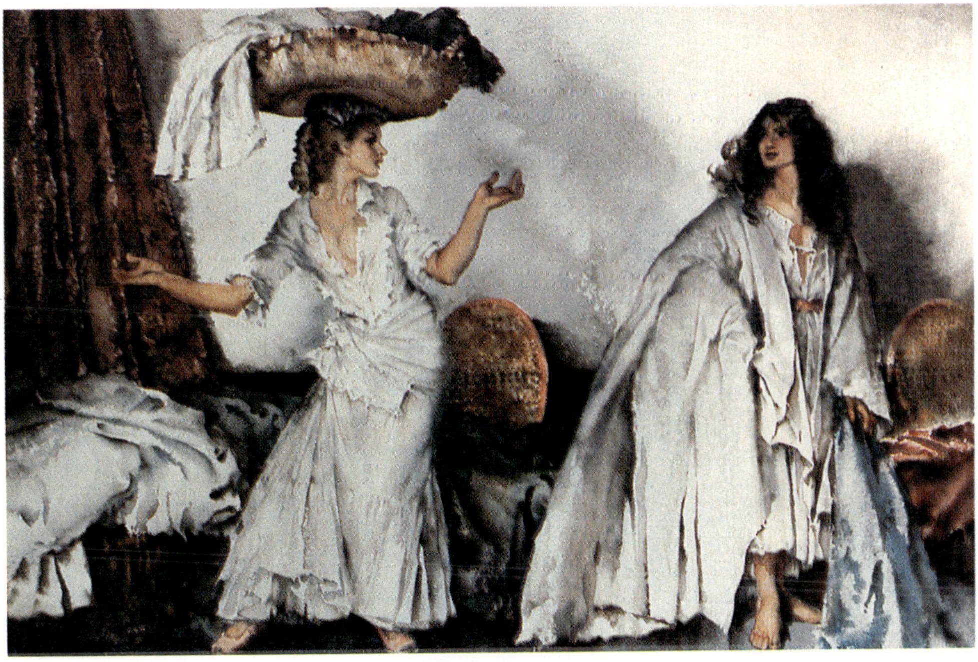

Sir William Russell Flint, R.A. – 'Balance' – signed, inscribed and dated on the reverse – 15¼ x 22¼in. (Christie's) *£26,400*

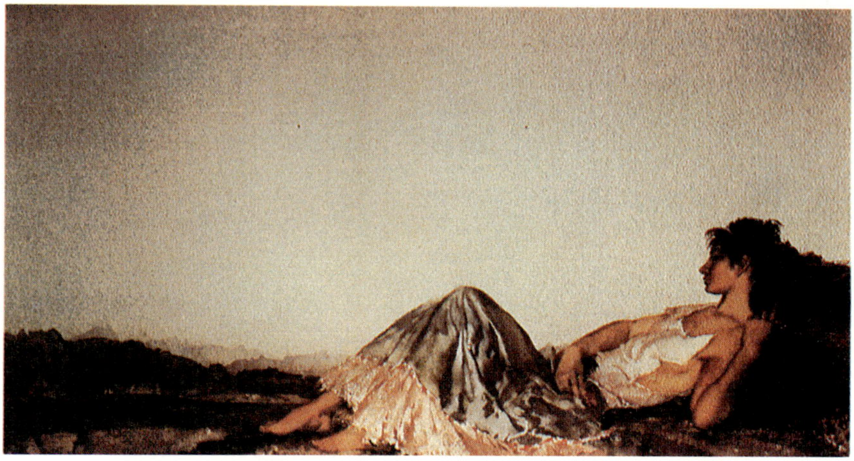

Sir William Russell Flint, R.A. – 'Lucilla' – watercolour – 13½ x 24½in. (Christie's)

£1,300 for the artist at Phillips in February, 1987. Six draped figures, in pen, ink and watercolour, done by Henry Moore, OM, in 1945, made £64,000 again at Phillips in the following month. In the same sale a 1902 oil painting by Sir John Lavery, RA, RSA, RHA, 'A Garden in France' made £42,000. At Phillips' Edinburgh office, a very attractive still life by London based Belgian artist Leon de Smet sold for £22,000 although the estimate was only around £3,000.

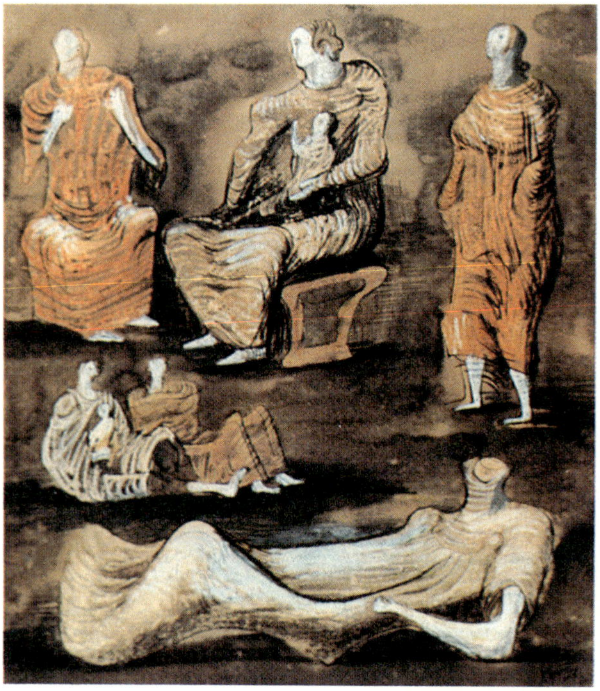

Henry Moore, O.M., C.H., 'Six Draped Figures - Ideas For Sculpture', ink and watercolour heightened with white over traces of pencil, 19¾ x 17in. (Phillips) £64,000

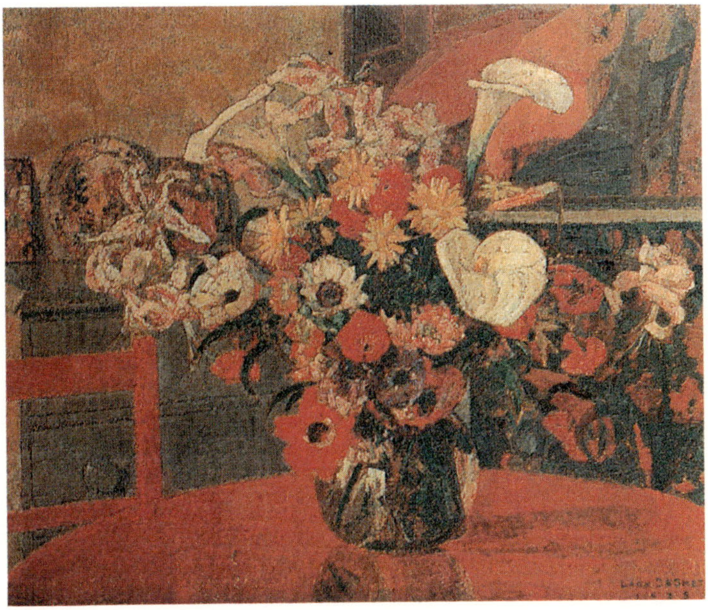

Leon De Smet – 'Bouquet De Fleurs' – oil on canvas – 28½ x 32¼in. (Christie's) *£33,000*

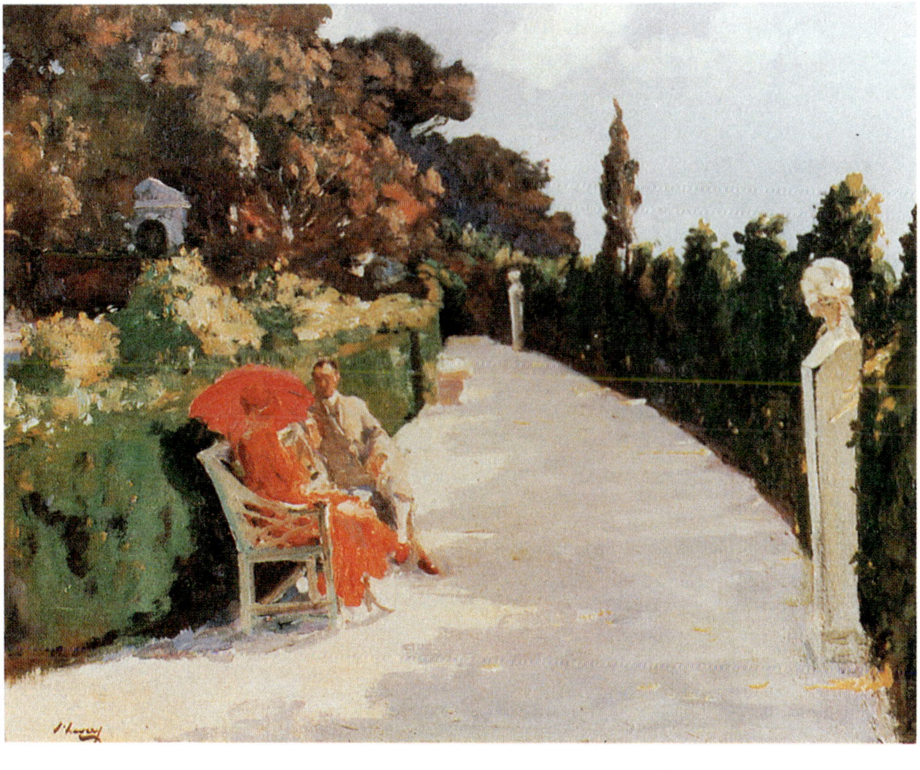

Sir John Lavery, R.A., R.S.A., R.H.A. – 'A Garden In France' – oil on canvas board – 20 x 24in. (Phillips) *£42,000*

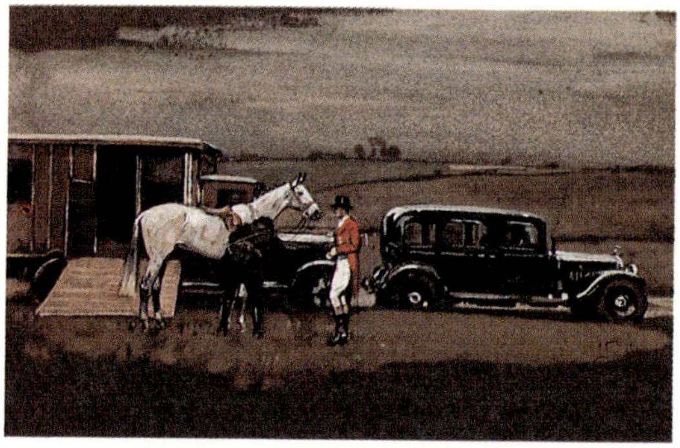

Lionel Edwards – 'Fox Hunting 20th Century' – pencil and watercolour – one of a set of six entitled 'Sport Through The Ages' – 18 x 27cm. (Phillips) *£7,000*

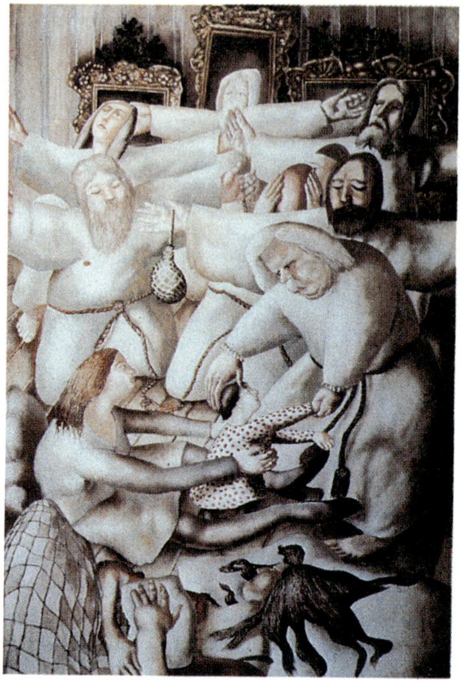

Sir Stanley Spencer, R.A. – 'The Coming Of The Wise Men' – 1940 – oil on canvas – 36 x 24in. (Christie's)

Popular artist Lionel Edwards' work made the good price of £6,400 for an unframed pen, ink and watercolour drawing of 'The Cambridgeshire, Newmarket 1953' at Phillips in January. Another equestrian artist who is very popular at the moment is Sir Alfred Munnings. His 'The Prince of Wales on Horseback' was sold by Sotheby's in November, 1987, for £187,000.

Tipped to make money over the past year was the St Ives school and Sir Stanley Spencer's 1937 view of rooftops at 'The Harbour St Ives' did just that when it fetched around £50,000. Another significant name for collectors is Walter Sickert, best known for nude studies and scenes of Venice

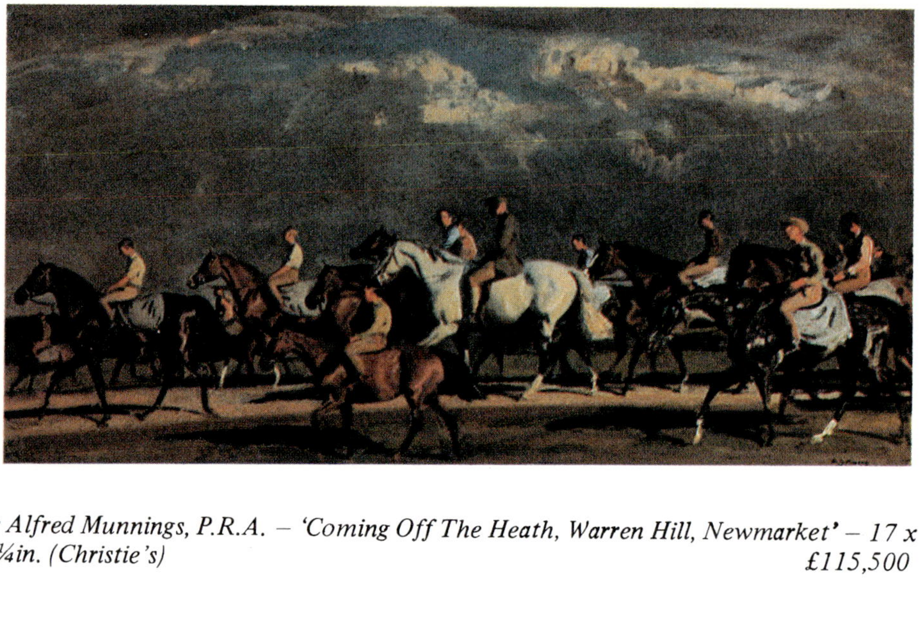

Sir Alfred Munnings, P.R.A. – 'Coming Off The Heath, Warren Hill, Newmarket' – 17 x 32¼in. (Christie's) *£115,500*

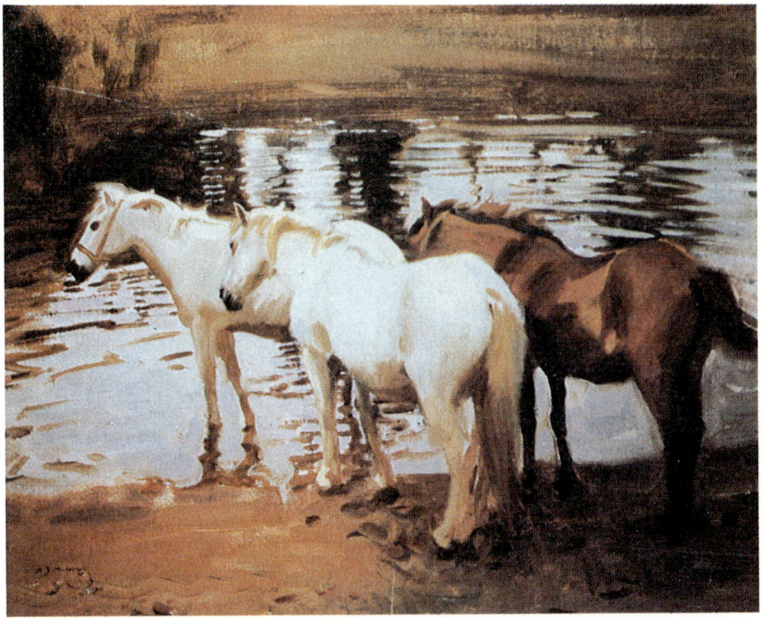

Sir Alfred Munnings, P.R.A. – 'The Ford' – oil on canvas – 20 x 24in. (Christie's)

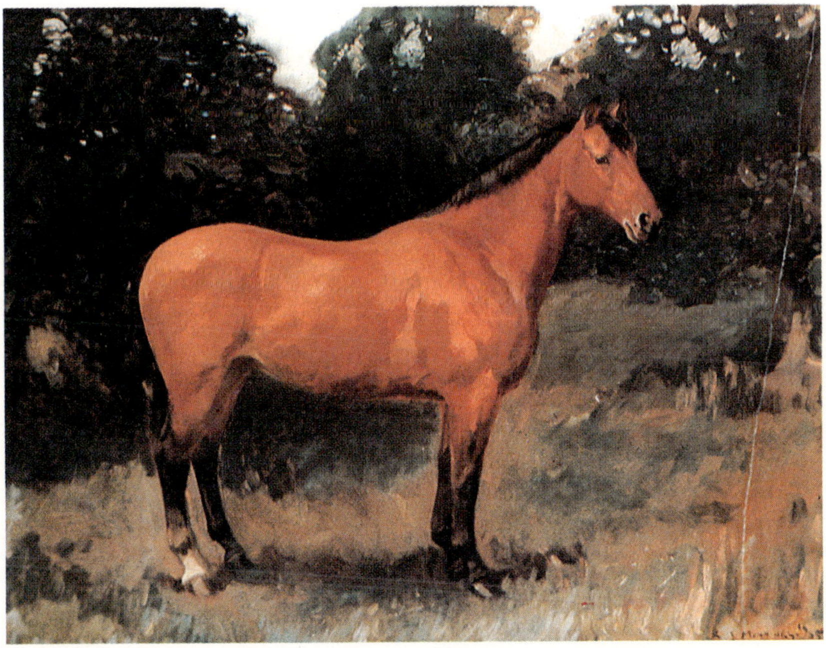

Sir Alfred Munnings, P.R.A. – 'A Chestnut Hunter In A Meadow' – oil on canvas – 20 x 25in. (Christie's) *£7,700*

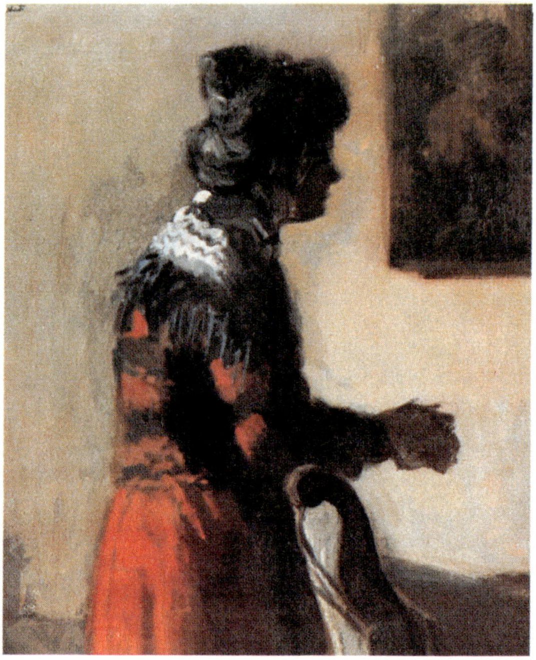

Walter Richard Sickert, A.R.A. – 'Carolina Dell 'Aqua In A Red Dress' – oil on canvas. (Christie's) £22,000

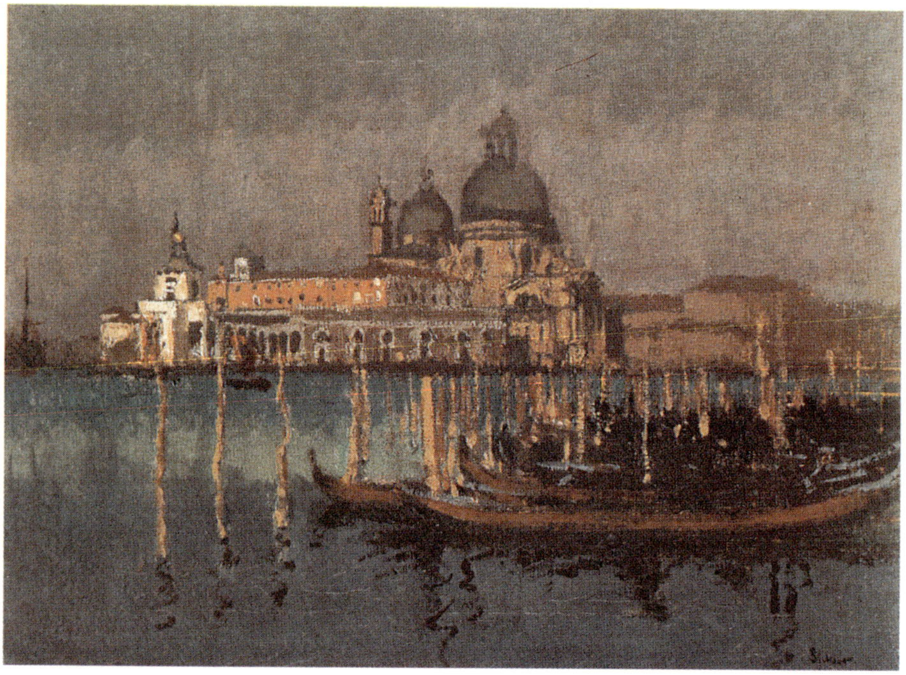

Walter Richard Sickert, A.R.A. – 'Nocturne: The Dogana And Santa Maria Della Salute, Venice' – oil on canvas. (Christie's) £33,000

in characteristic warm rich colours. His nocturne 'The Dogana and Santa Maria Della Salute, Venice, made £33,000 at Christies.

Watercolours by early Victorians, Neapolitan gouaches and Scottish Colourists all did well over the year. A red crayon drawing attributed to Polidoro di Caravaggio, 'Madonna and Child' sold for £12,000 at Phillips in February and four folios of David Roberts' 'The Holy Land' made £9,500 at Phillips in Knowle. William Callow, a mid 19th century watercolour artist whose work had never broken five figures before, reached star quality when his picture of Versailles made £16,000 at Phillips in Edinburgh. The same firm sold Stanhope

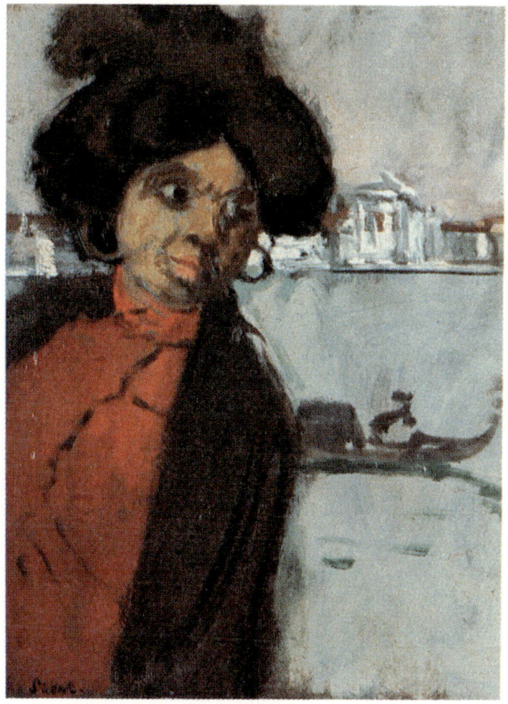

Walter Richard Sickert, A.R.A. – 'Inez On The Zattere' – oil on panel – 16 x 11¾in. (Christie's) £10,450

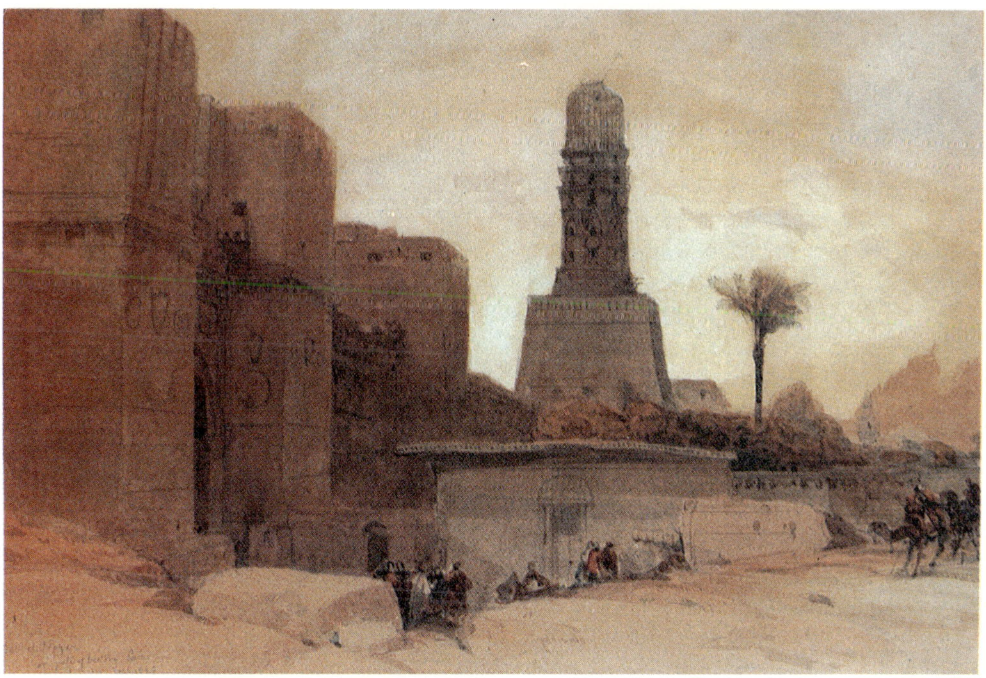

David Roberts, R.A. – 'Bab El Nazar' or 'Gate Of Victory, Cairo' – 9.1/8 x 13.1/8in. (Christie's) £6,600

A. Forbes, RA's 'Three Old Fishermen', an oil on canvas, for £34,000 in March 1987 and Edinburgh again scored a triumph with J. M. W. Turner's tiny watercolour of New Abbey, Dumfries which they sold for £24,000.

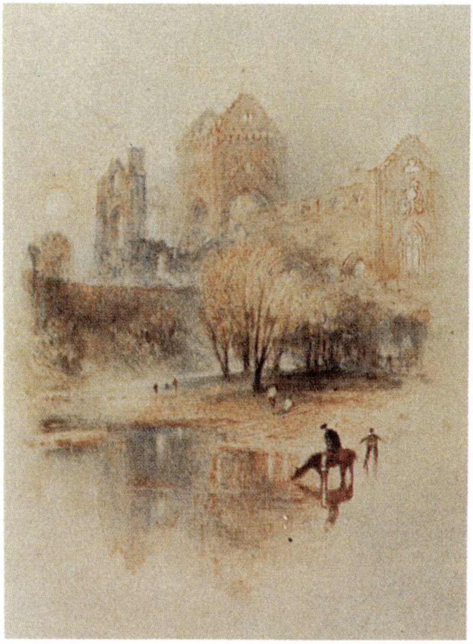

Joseph Mallord William Turner – 'New Abbey Near Dumfries' – watercolour. (Phillips) £14,000

The same saleroom scored a world record for Thomas Jones 'Naples', an 18th century oil on paper which sold for £50,000 and 'The Muse, Polymnia' an oil on canvas, from the studio of Francois Boucher also made £145,000 there. French 18th century pictures are currently being reassessed and Francois Boucher's 1730's study of a boy and girl blowing bubbles made a record $1,925,000 in New York while his 'Allegory of Painting', dated about 1750, made $880,000. A gouache of the gardens of the Villa D'Este by Fragonard sold for $193,500.

Bonhams, the smallest of the big four salerooms and one which is rumoured to be on the market for a possible takeover, continues to be the happy hunting ground of specialist and shorter pocketed collectors.

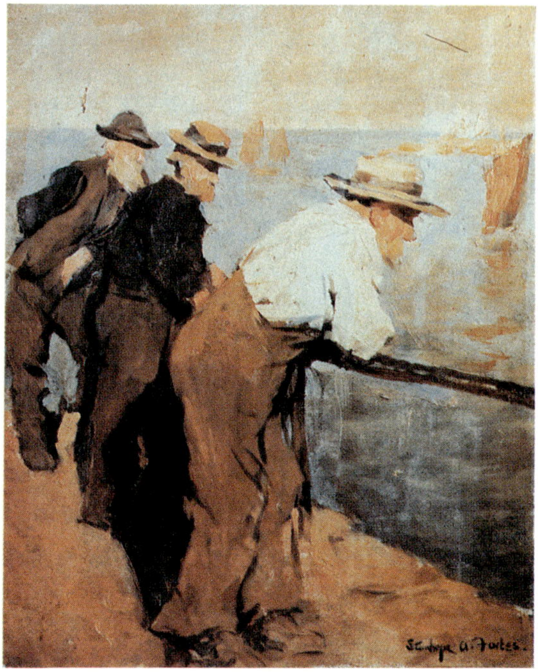

Stanhope A. Forbes, R.A. – 'Three Old Fishermen' – oil on canvas – 24 x 19in. (Phillips) £34,000

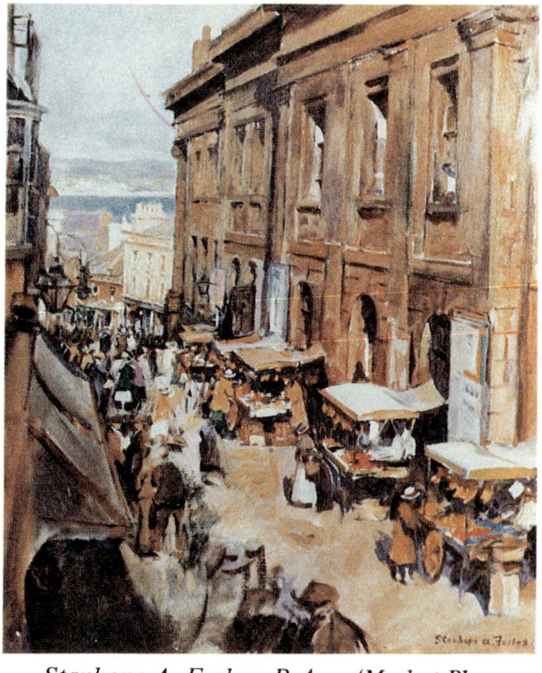

Stanhope A. Forbes, R.A. – 'Market Place, Penzance' – oil on canvas – 24 x 20in. (Phillips) £15,000

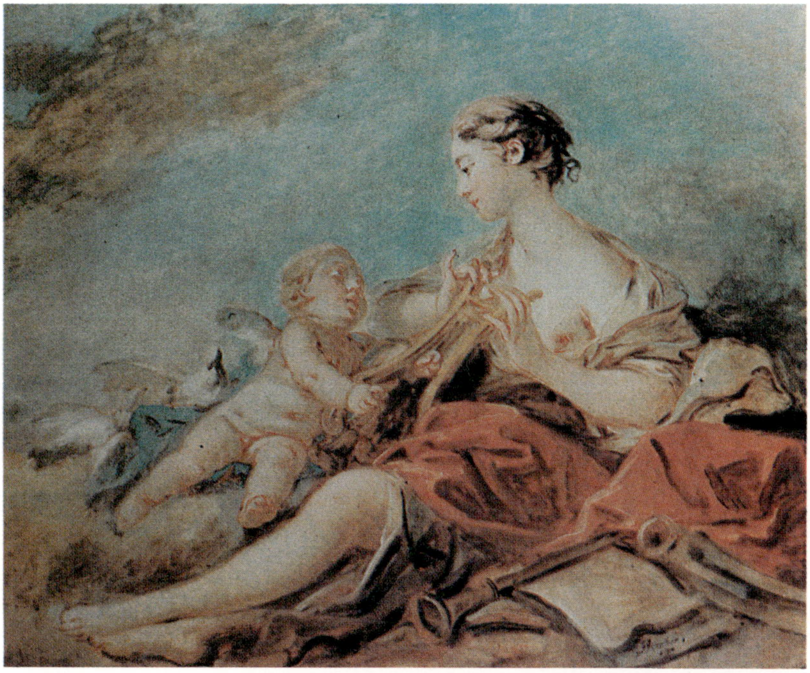

Francois Boucher – 'The Muse Polymnia' – oil on canvas – dated 1750. (Phillips) £145,000

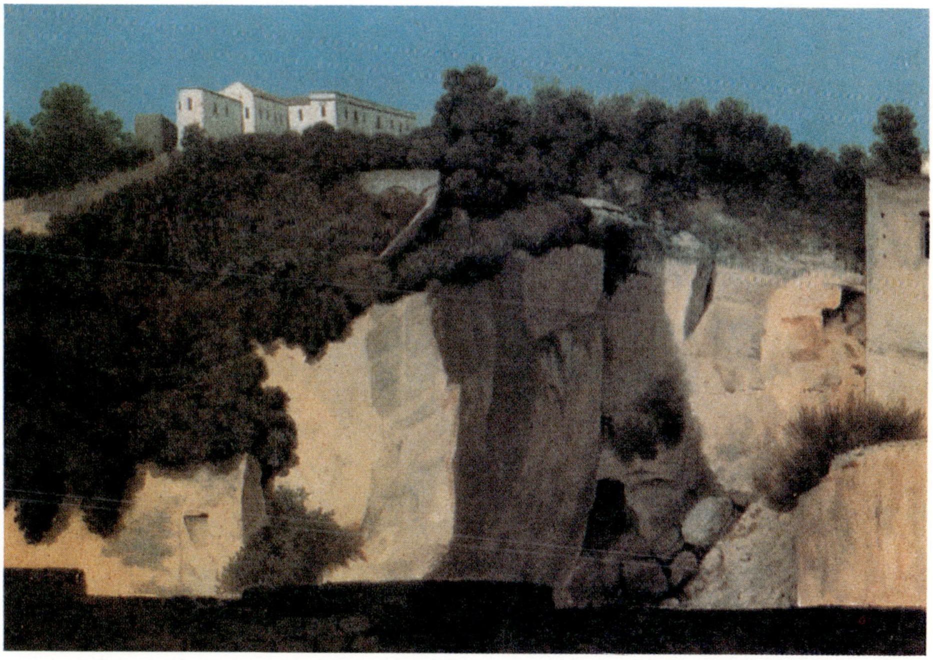

Thomas Jones – 'Naples' – oil painting on paper dated 1728. (Phillips) £50,000

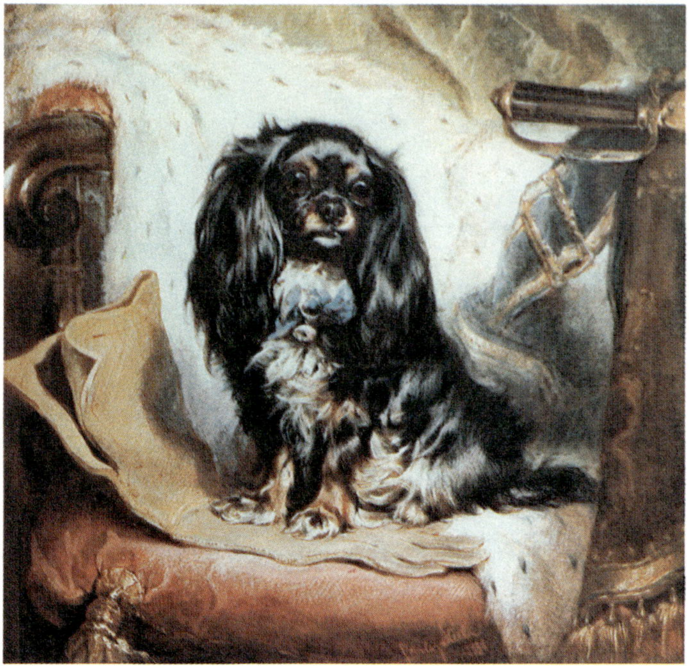

Gourlay Steell – 'Jeannie' – signed and dated 1858 – gouache – 19¾ x 20¾in. (Bonhams)
£3,800

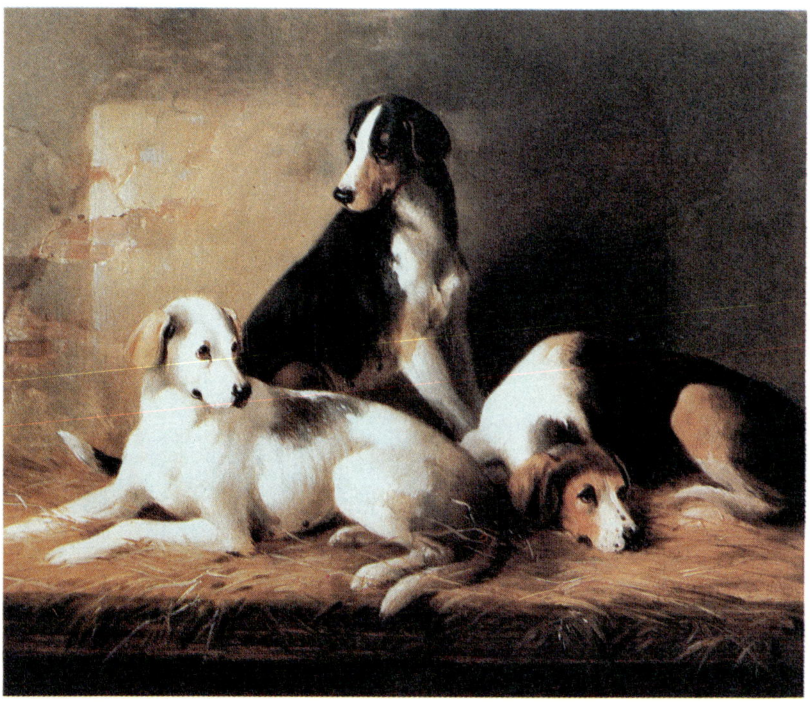

William Barraud – 'Dreaming Of The Chase – A Trio Of Foxhounds' – signed on board. (Bonhams)
£4,600

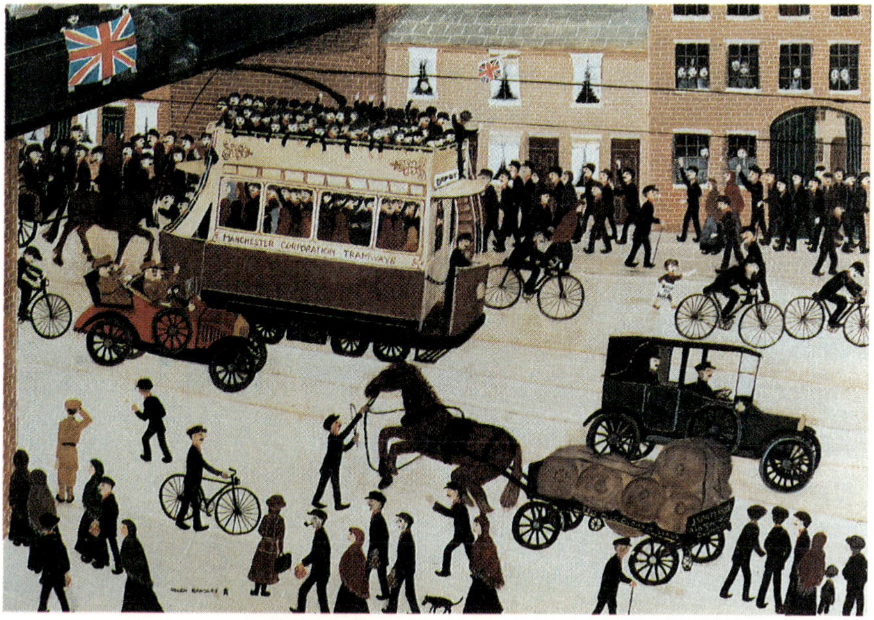

Helen Bradley – 'Armistice Day November 11th 1918' – oil on canvas board – 20¾ x 28¾in. (Christie's) *£8,250*

In the past year they put on their usual sales of ship pictures, flower works and studies of dogs as well as a highly publicised Erotica sale which did very well. Among the erotica were aquatints of French Folie Bergere dancers selling for around £300 a time.

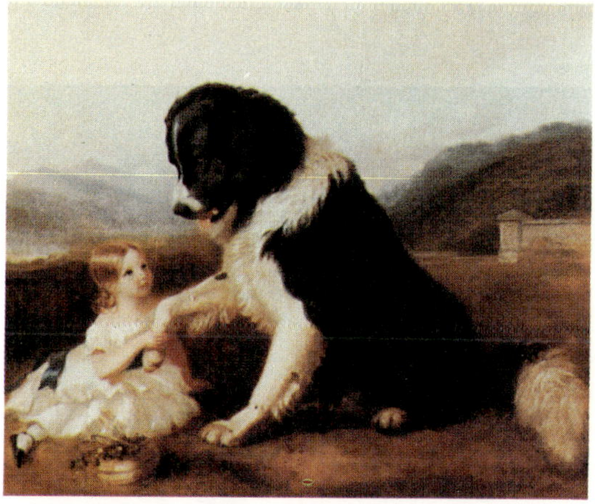

Byron Webb, 'A Newfoundland Proffering A Paw To An Elegant Young Lady, In A Highland Landscape', 30 x 36in. (Bonhams) *£5,800*

Dogs continue to be a Bonhams' speciality and they sold a rather simpering portrait of Queen Victoria's favourite spaniel 'Jeannie' by Gourlay Steell for £3,800. More curious was A. Butler's 'Tiny the Wonder', a 1948 lithograph of a rat-killing terrier which weighed just five and a half pounds and killed 250 rats in 54 minutes and 50 seconds. The estimate for this gory work was around £250. This year Bonhams also sold several pictures by Helen Bradley signed with her fly symbol. Mrs Bradley, a Yorkshire naive artist, started to paint in her 60's and her pictures often have narrative titles like 'Oh, look what's happening! Those bulls have got loose' which sold for £9,000.

Overall the art market looks healthy and prospects for the coming year are very bright. With plenty of cash around and the supply of top quality works dwindling, prices are set to rise and new categories can only increase in importance.

LIZ TAYLOR

THIS IS *THE* BOOK FOR THE PROFESSIONAL ANTIQUES DEALER 'THE LYLE BOOK' – WE'VE EVEN HEARD IT CALLED 'THE DEALER'S BIBLE'.

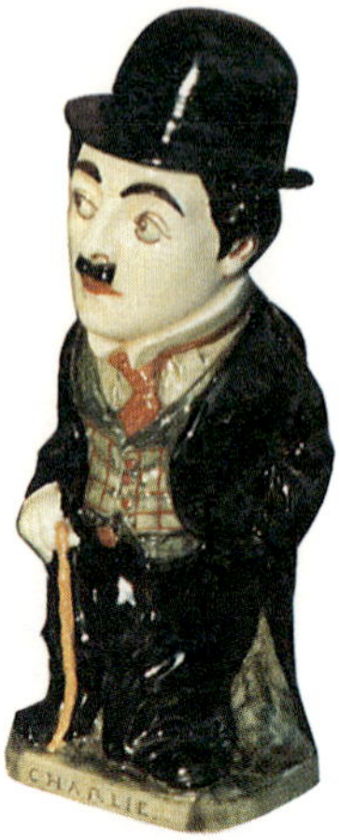

A brand new publication each year *The Lyle Official Antiques Review* is the most comprehensive, up-to-date price guide to antiques available.

Its 800 pages are packed with precisely the kind of profitable information the professional Dealer needs – including descriptions, photographs and values of thousands and thousands of individual items carefully selected to give a representative picture of the current market in antiques and collectibles –

ISBN 0-86248-100-7
800 Pages.
Size 10 x 7in. Hardback
32 Pages in Full Colour.
Eighteenth Edition.

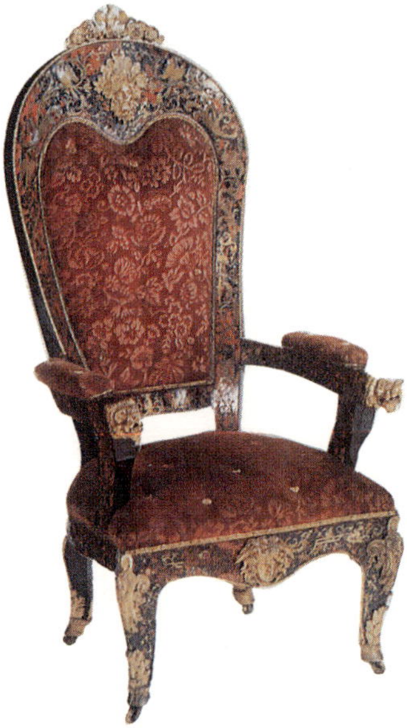

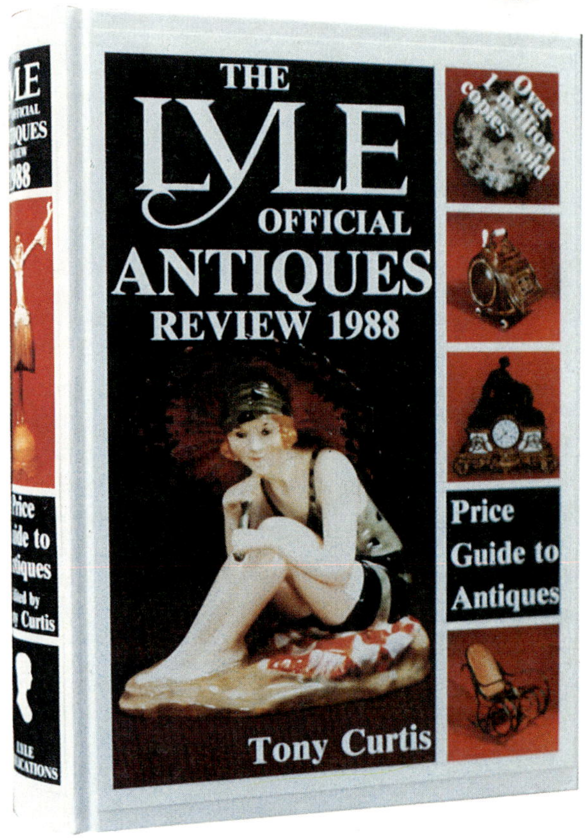

AND REMEMBER ALL VALUES ARE PRICES ACTUALLY PAID AT AUCTION THROUGHOUT THE TWELVE MONTHS PRIOR TO PUBLICATION – AND WITH SOURCES QUOTED.

JUST £12·95

'. . . . probably the world's foremost reference book on antiques.'
NEW YORK TIMES

ARTS
REVIEW 1988

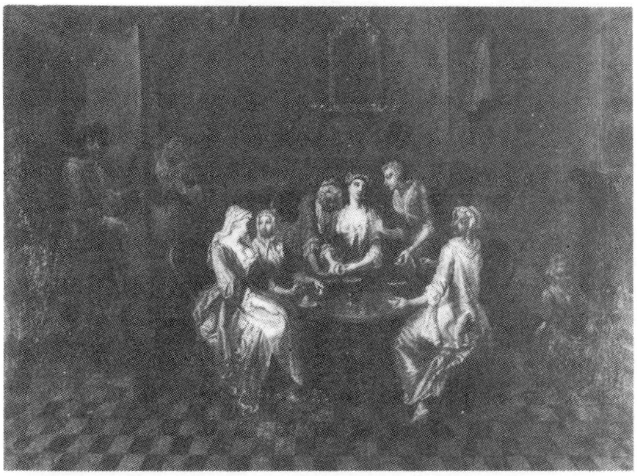

JOSEPH VAN AAKEN, Circle of – Women Of Pleasure Taking Refreshments – 21½ x 28¼in.
(Christie's) **$4,536 £3,024**

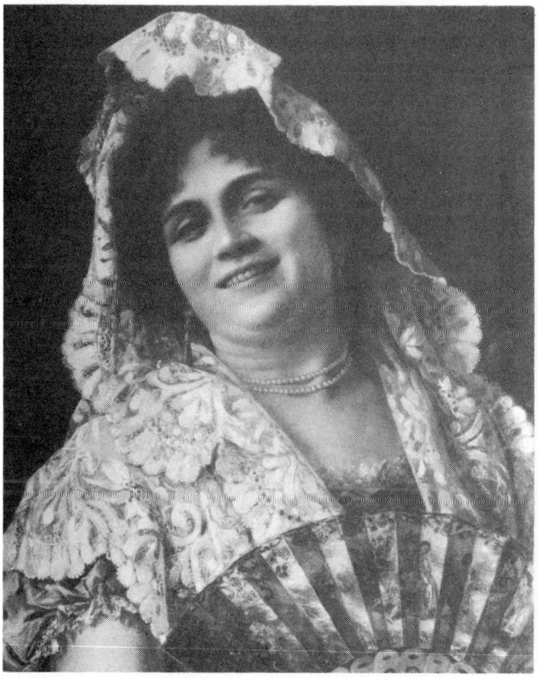

ADOLFO DD AGUITA ACUSTA – Head And Shoulder Portrait Study Of A Spanish Lady Holding A Fan – signed and dated 1909 – oil on canvas – 24 x 18in.
(Biddle & Webb) **$988 £650**

EDOUARD ADAM – Portrait Of The Tramp Steamer 'Trentham Hall' In A Strong Swell – signed and dated 1912 – oil on canvas – 24 x 36¼in.
(Phillips) **$734 £480**

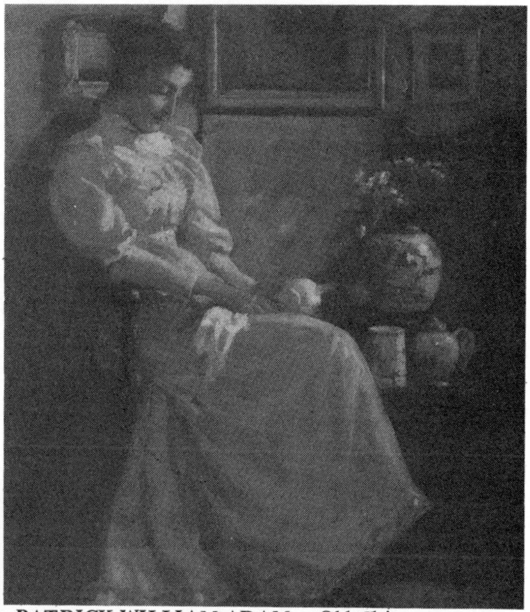

PATRICK WILLIAM ADAM – Old China – signed and dated 1893 – oil on canvas – 37 x 28½in.
(Phillips) **$4,970 £3,500**

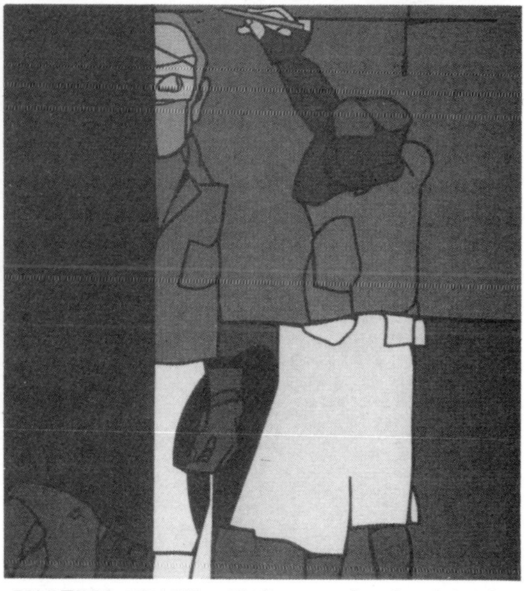

VALERIO ADAMI – L'Altezza – signed and dated 1975/76 on the reverse – acrylic on canvas – 50¾ x 37in.
(Christie's) **$10,296 £7,150**

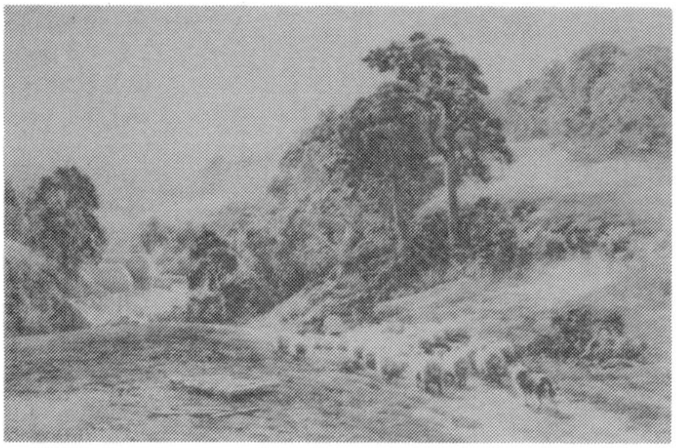

CHARLES JAMES ADAMS – The Bourne Valley Near Farnham – signed – watercolour heightened with white – 38 x 55.5 cm.
(Phillips) **$2,119** **£1,300**

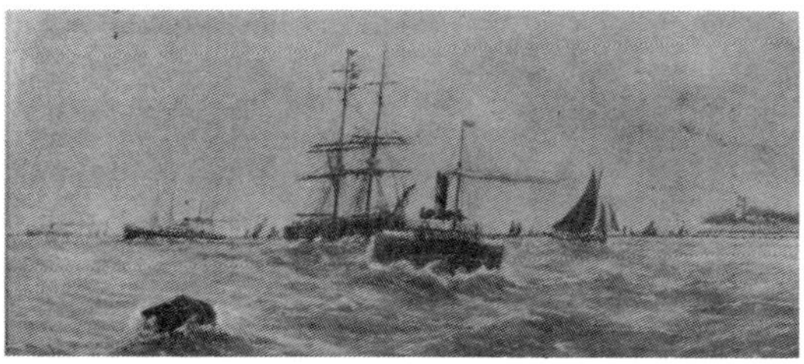

M. E. ADAMS – Seascape With Steamer And Sailing Vessel In Choppy Water – signed and dated 1902 – watercolour – 9½ x 20½in.
(Hobbs & Chambers) **$308** **£200**

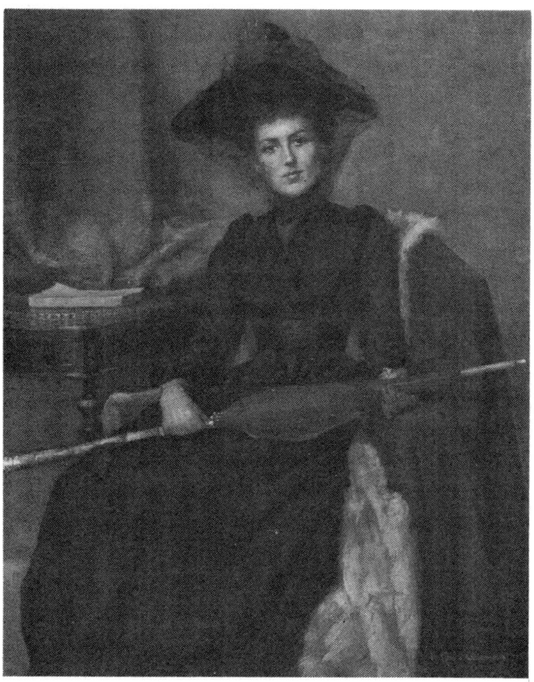

DAVID COMBA ADAMSON – The Scarlet Parasol – signed and inscribed – oil on canvas – 36 x 28in.
(Christie's) **$22,022** **£15,400**

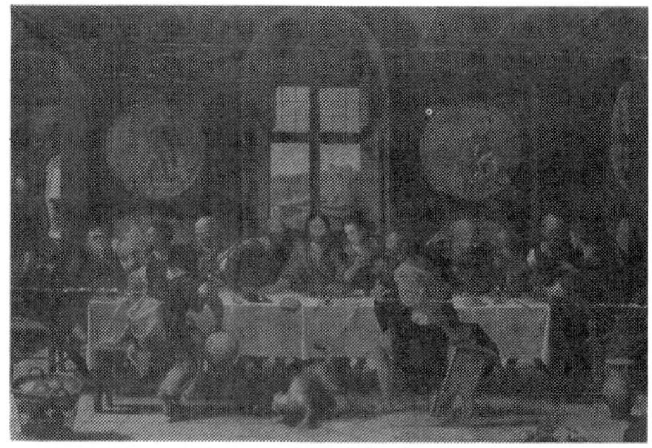

PIETER COECK VAN AELST, Studio of – The Last Supper – inscribed with the date Anno 1544 – on panel – 24¼ x 31¾in.
(Phillips) **$4,648** **£2,800**

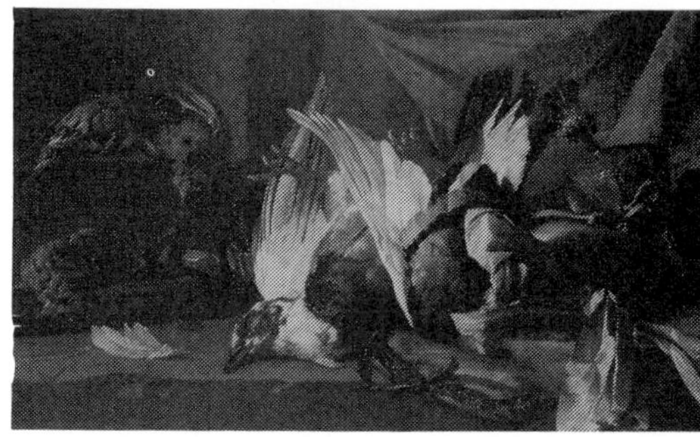

WILLIAM VAN AELST – Still Life Of Game – on canvas – 15¼ x 19¾in.
(Phillips) **$14,940** **£9,000**

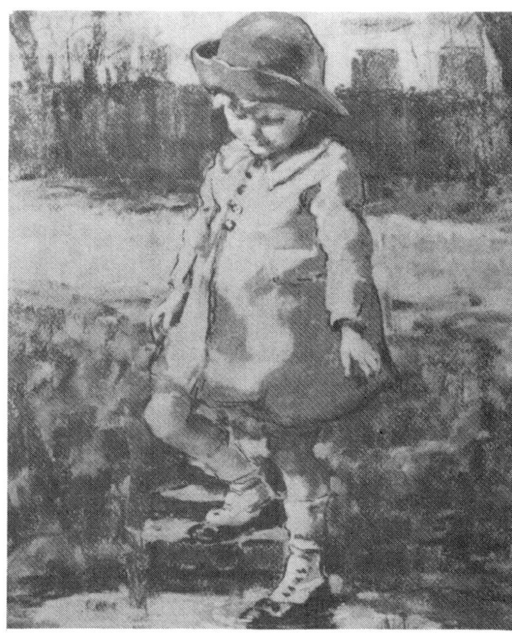

ANNA AIRY – The Puddle – signed and inscribed – pastel on buff paper – 35 x 26cm.
(Phillips) **$3,366** **£2,200**

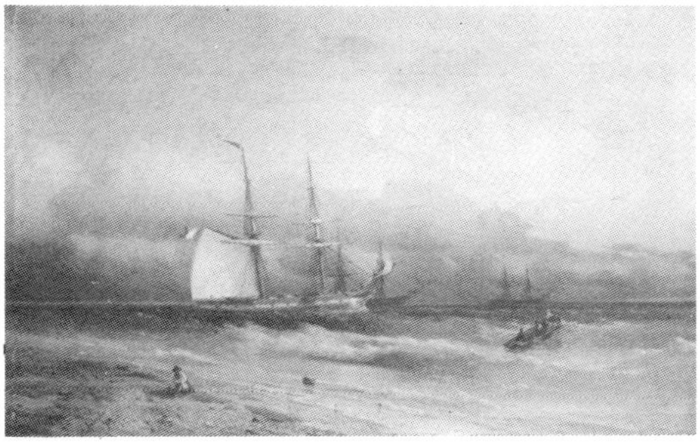

IVAN CONSTANTINOVICH AIVASOWSKY – Shipping Offshore In A Strong Breeze – signed and dated 1857 – 14½ x 23¼in.
(Christie's) **$20,592** **£14,300**

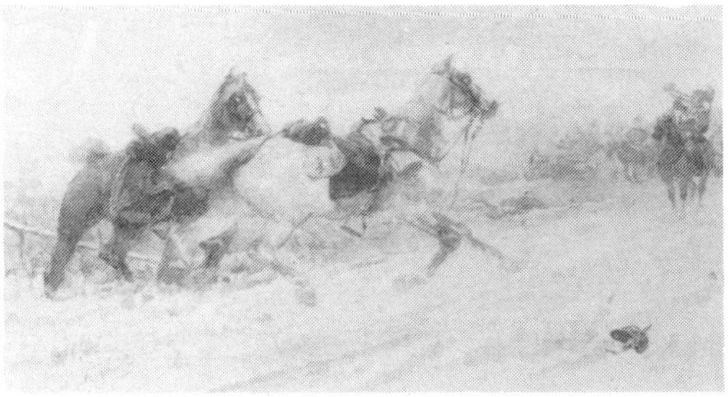

SEBASTIANO DE ALBERTIS – Cavalry Horses Returning From Battle – signed – watercolour – 6½ x 11½in.
(Christie's) **$2,373** **£1,430**

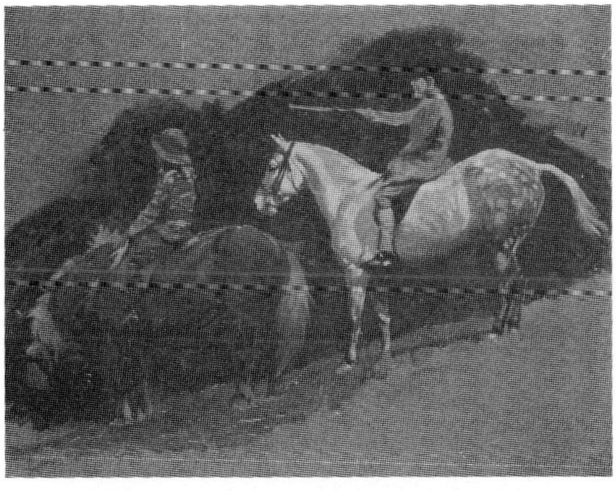

CECIL ALDIN – Study For Cloutsham Farm, With S. V. Hine Pointing Out To Miss Milrain The Huntsman And Tufters Drawing The Coombe Above Home Water – signed – oil on canvas – 18½ x 23¾in.
(Christie's) **$11,225** **£7,150**

CECIL CHARLES WINDSOR ALDIN – 'Jim' – signed and inscribed – coloured chalks on grey paper – 25 x 20in.
(Christie's) **$4,342** **£3,080**

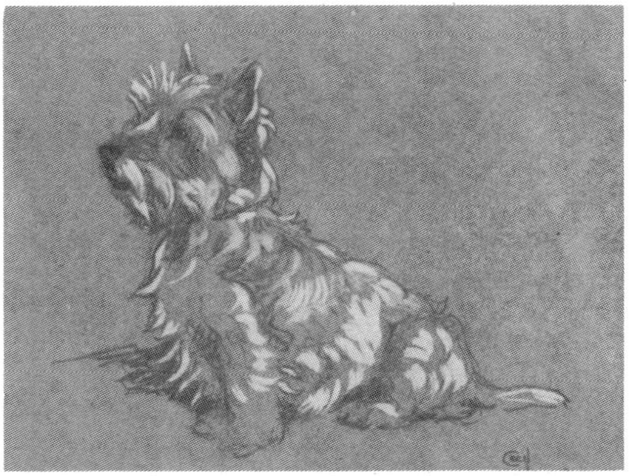

CECIL CHARLES WINDSOR ALDIN – A White West Highland Terrier – signed – black chalk heightened with white on Japan – 6 x 6½in.
(Christie's) **$3,888** **£2,592**

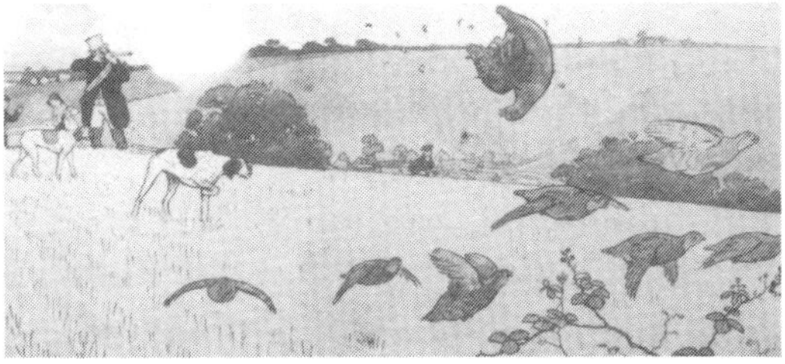

CECIL CHARLES WINDSOR ALDIN, After – The First; A Likely Spot; and In The Open – chromolithographs – 11 x 24in.
(Christie's) **$157** **£110 Three**

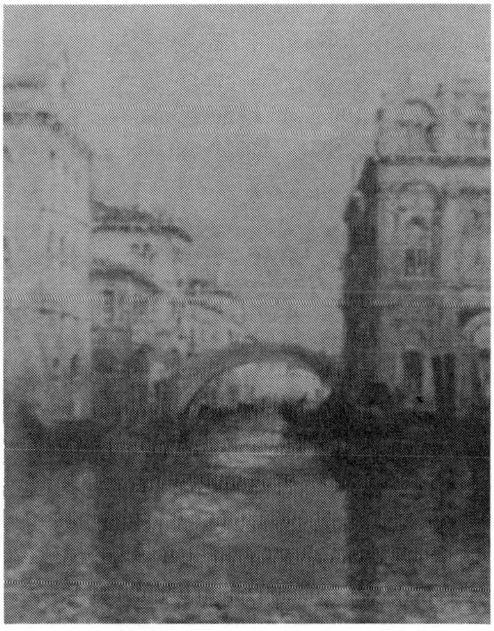

MARC ALDINE – Canal In Venice – signed and inscribed on the reverse – oil on canvas – 25½ x 19¾in.
(Robt. W. Skinner Inc.) **$650** **£398**

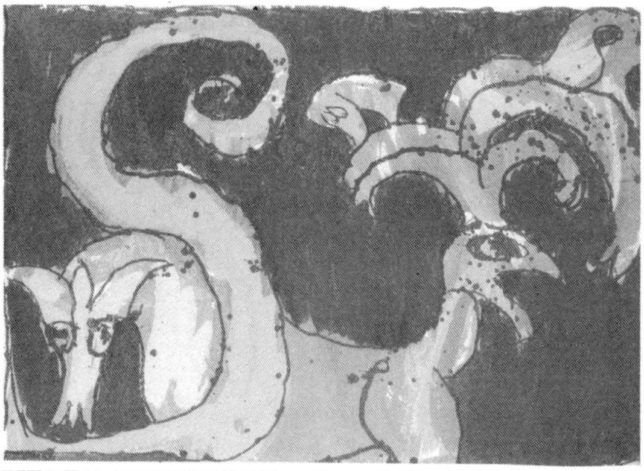

PIERRE ALECHINSKY – Regard En Arriere – signed, also signed, inscribed and dated 1973 on the reverse – acrylic on paper mounted on canvas – 44¾ x 60¼in.
(Christie's) **$31,680 £22,000**

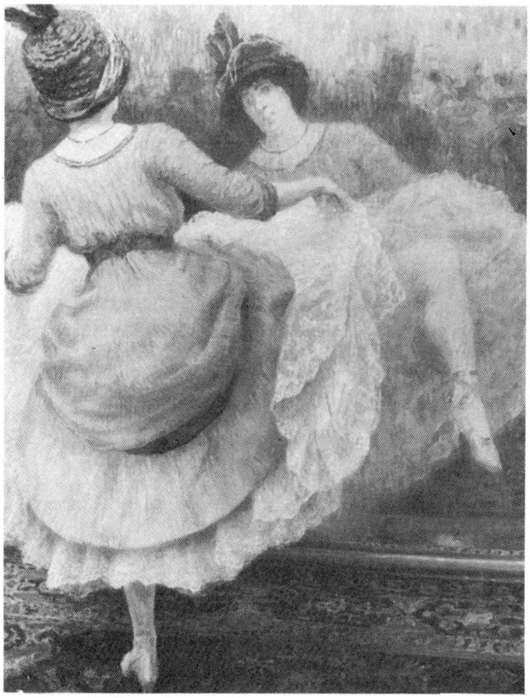

PEDRO YSERN Y ALIE – Le Can-Can – signed – oil on canvas – 57¼ x 45in.
(Christie's) **$7,920 £5,500**

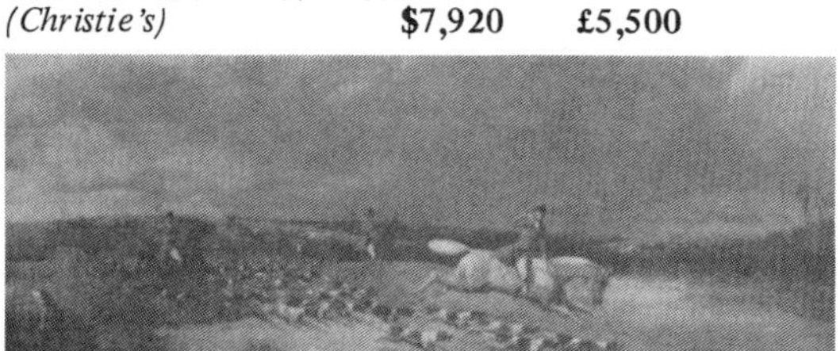

HENRY ALKEN, Circle of – Tally Ho!; and The Water Jump – 12 x 24in.
(Christie's) **$3,300 £2,200 Pair**

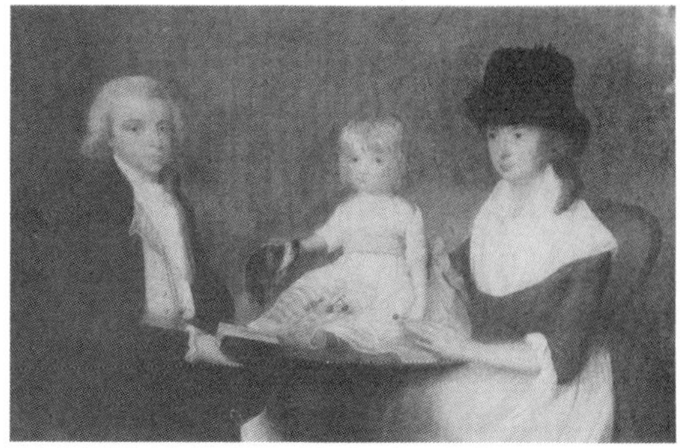

FRANCIS ALLEYNE, Circle of – A Group Portrait Of A Lady In A Brown And White Dress, And A Gentleman, Seated Small Three-Quarter Lengths, With Their Daughter Seated On A Table, A Dog Beside Her – 14 x 20¼in.
(Christie's) **$2,754 £1,836**

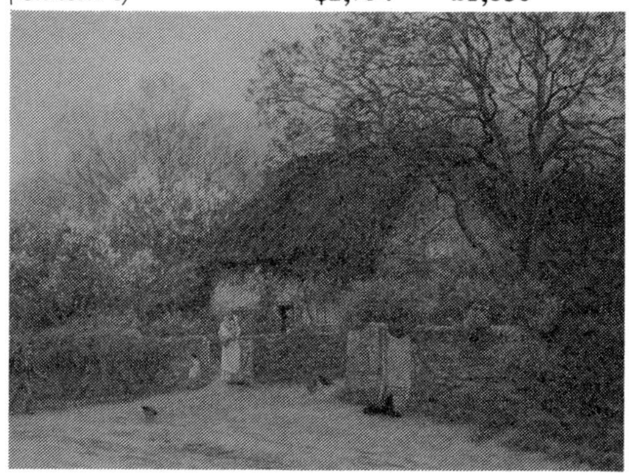

HELEN ALLINGHAM – Figures Outside A Cottage, A Woodman Passing By – signed – watercolour – 10½ x 14¼in.
(Christie's) **$11,869 £7,150**

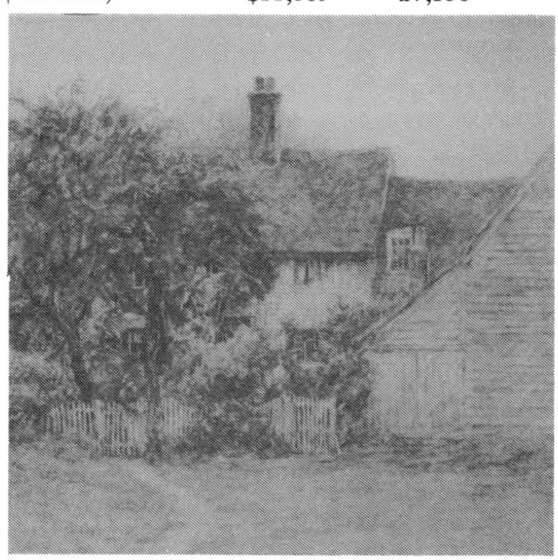

HELEN ALLINGHAM – Wylde's Farm, North End, Hampstead Heath – signed – watercolour – 7¾ x 8¾in.
(Lawrence Fine Art) **$5,478 £3,300**

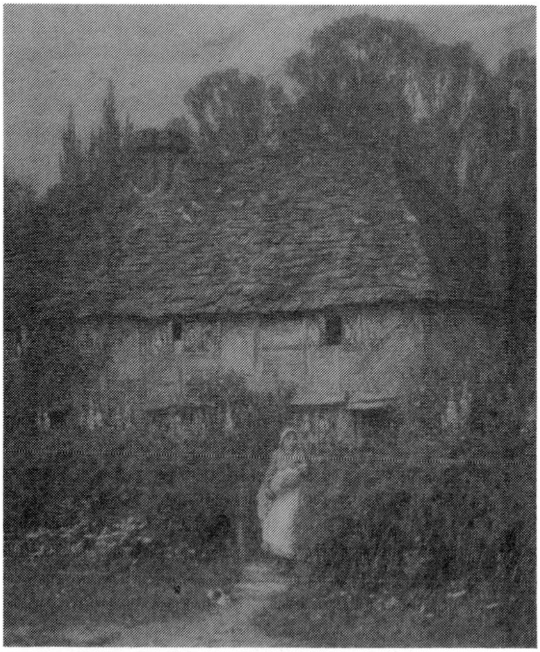

HELEN ALLINGHAM – A Mother With Her Child Outside A Cottage – signed – watercolour – 13 x 10in.
(Christie's) **$7,304** **£4,400**

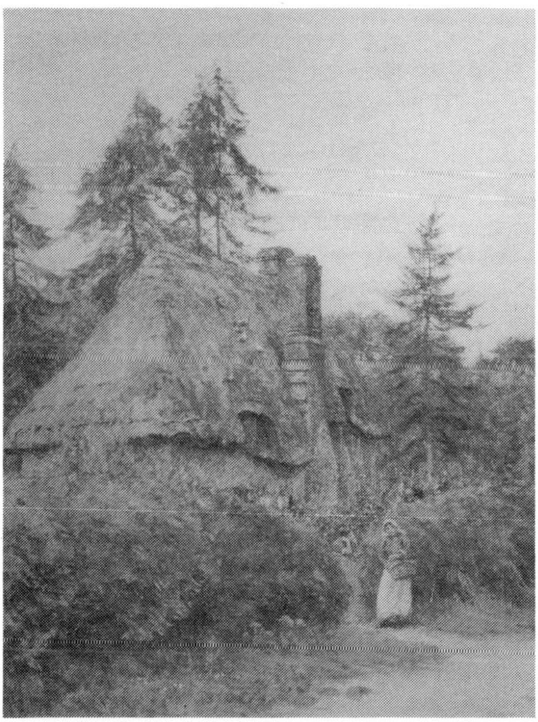

HELEN ALLINGHAM – A Cottage At Nunton, Wiltshire – signed, and inscribed on a label – watercolour – 8½ x 6½in.
(Christie's) **$6,573** **£3,960**

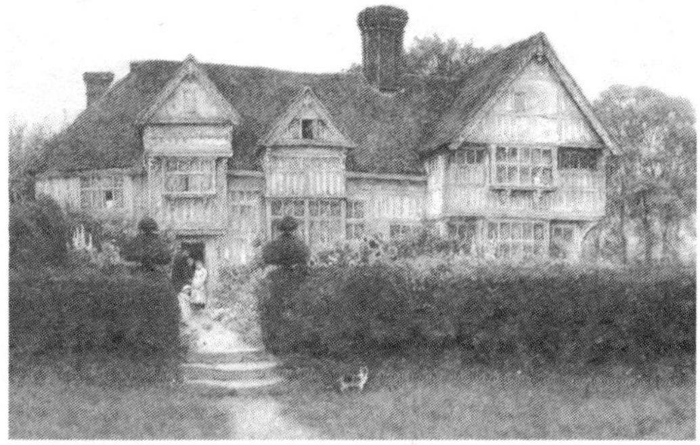

HELEN ALLINGHAM – Old Kentish Manor House – signed – watercolour – 14½ x 21¾in.
(Christie's) **$16,285** **£11,550**

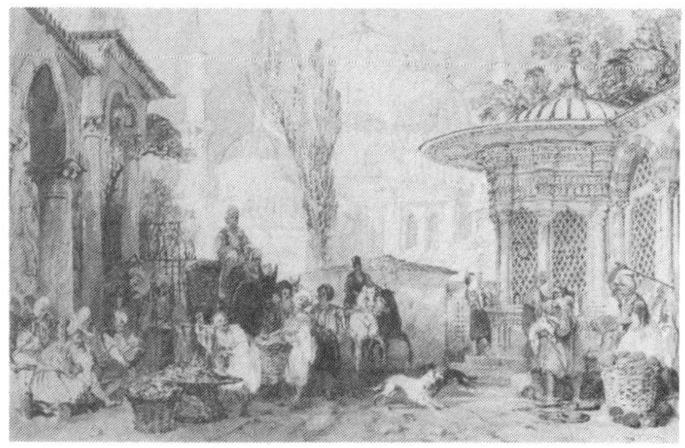

THOMAS ALLOM – The Mosque Of Shah-Za-Deh Djamesi, Constantinople – pencil, pen and brown ink and watercolour – 7¾ x 11¾in.
(Christie's) **$7,348** **£4,400**

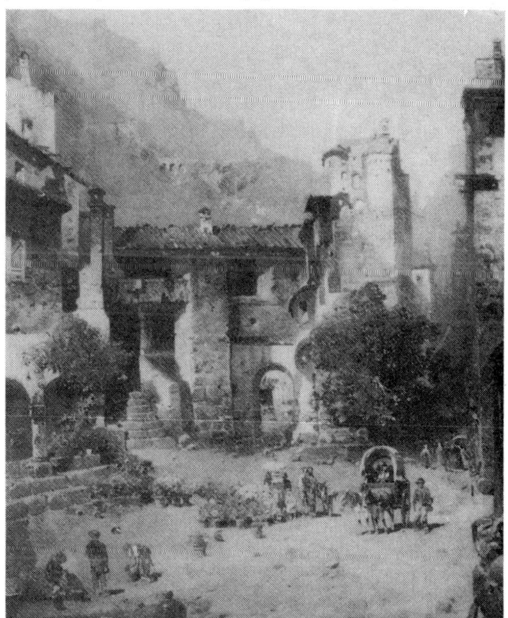

ROBERT ALOTT – A Market Square With Flower Sellers And A Covered Cart – signed – 39¼ x 29in.
(Christie's) **$2,508** **£1,650**

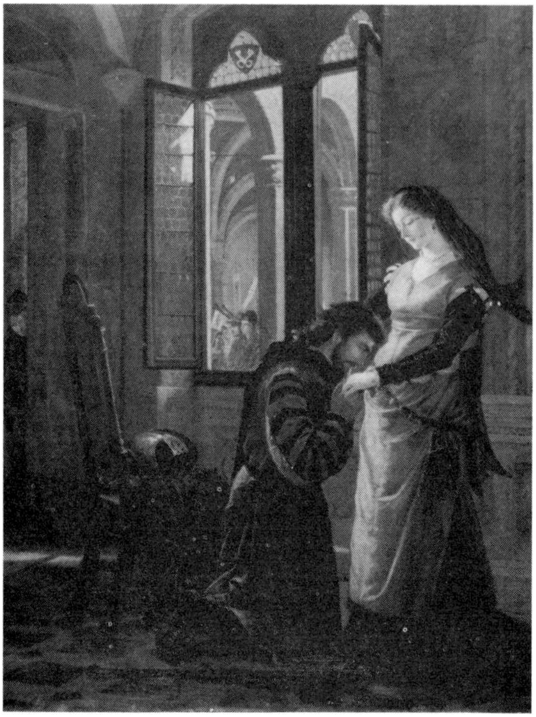

ALTAMURA – Interior Scene, With Lady Receiving A Knight, Figures In A Courtyard Through An Open Window – signed and dated – oil on canvas – 48 x 36½in.
(Morphets) **$1,627** **£1,050**

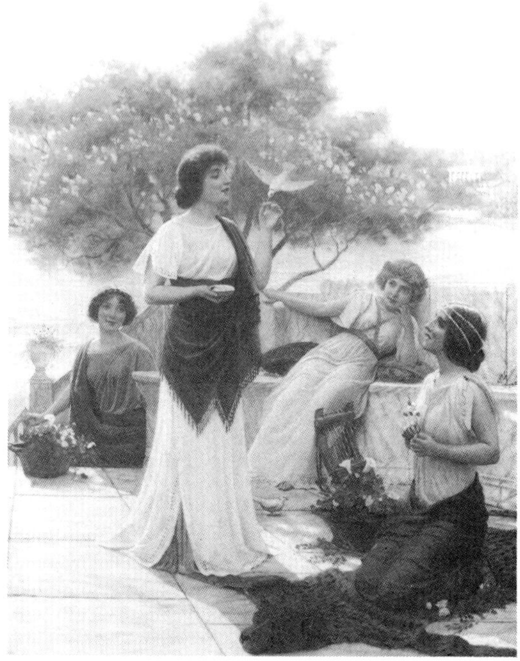

ABBEY ALTSON – On The Terrace – signed – 52 x 39in.
(Christie's) **$15,840** **£11,000**

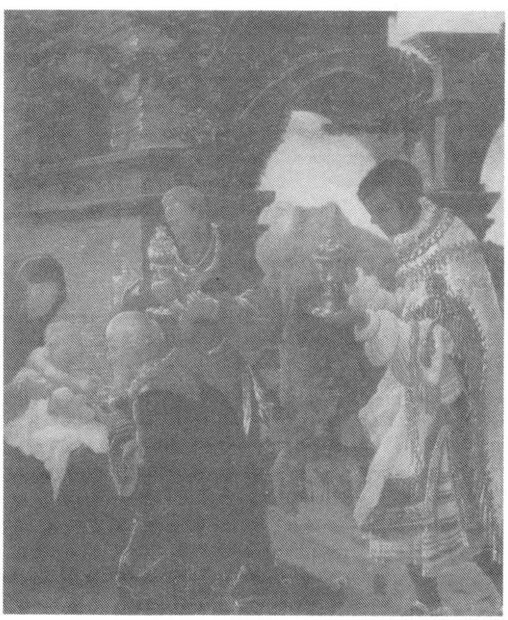

ALBRECHT ALTDORFER, Workshop of – The Adoration Of The Kings – on panel – 19¼ x 16¼in.
(Phillips) **$102,920** **£62,000**

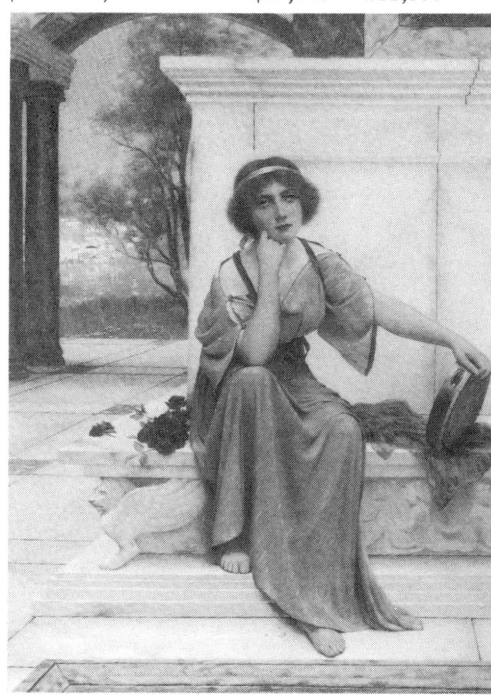

ABBEY ALTSON – Meditation – signed and dated 1904 – 21¼ x 15½in.
(Christie's) **$7,040** **£4,400**

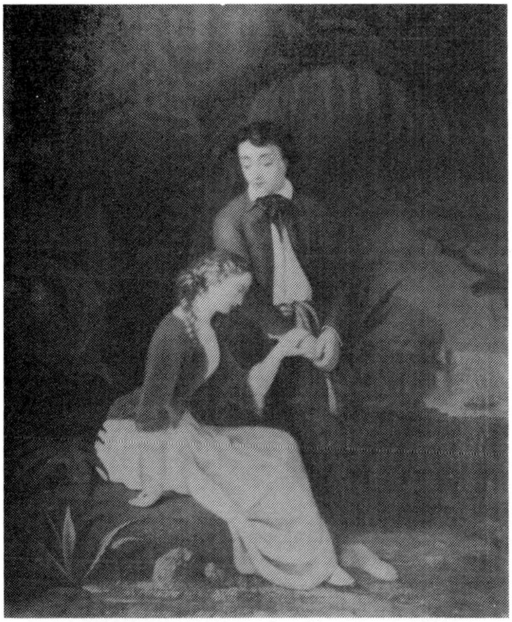

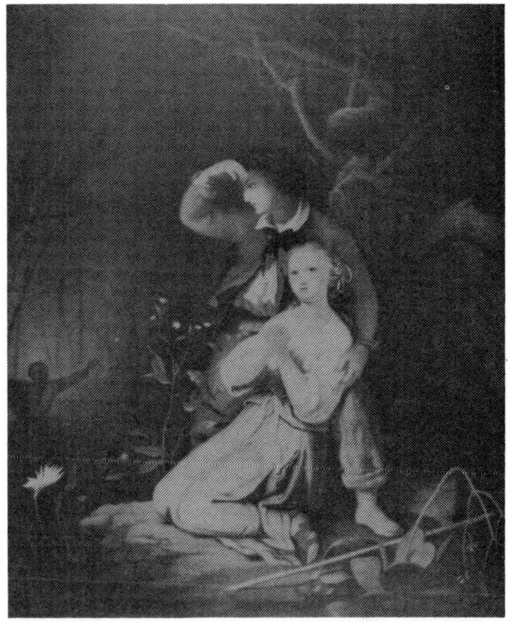

AMERICAN SCHOOL, 19th/20th century – Lost In The Woods – oil on canvas – 31¼ x 25 in.
(Christie's) **$1,600 £981 Pair**

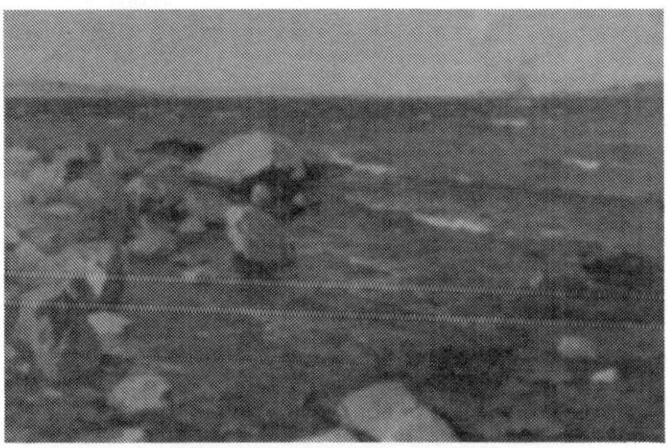

AMERICAN SCHOOL, 20th century – New England Seascape – indistinctly signed – oil on canvas – 30 x 40in.
(Robt. W. Skinner Inc.) **$2,300 £1,411**

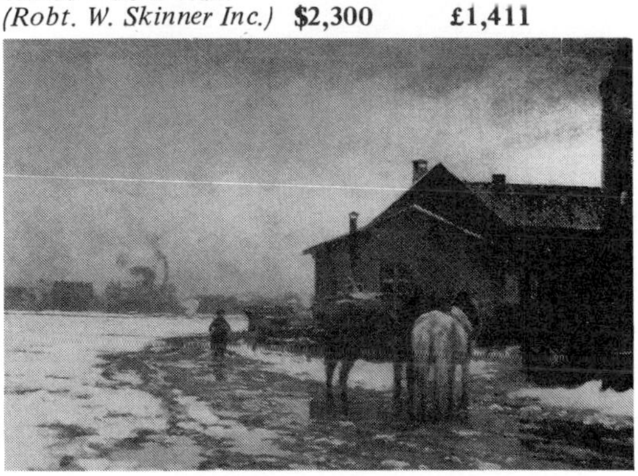

ANDERS ANDERSEN-LUNDBY – The City Outskirts, Winter – signed – 18½ x 25 in.
(Christie's) **$2,842 £1,870**

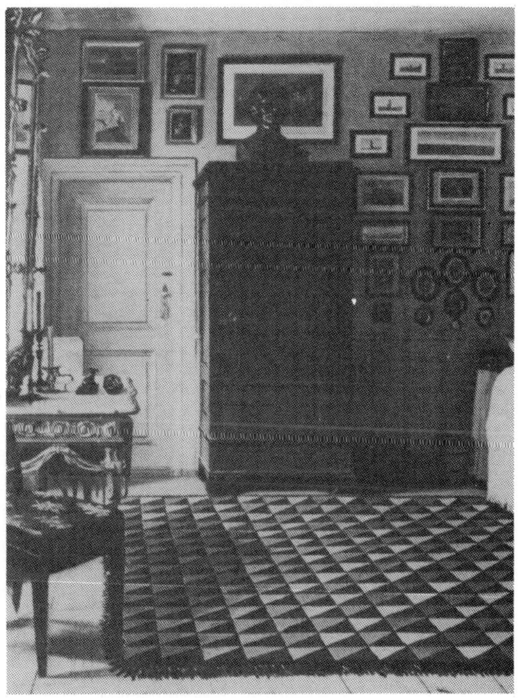

CARL CHRISTIAN ANDERSON – The Interior Of A Collector's Bedroom – signed and dated 1880 – oil on canvas – 44 x 35 cm.
(Phillips) **$1,510 £1,000**

JOHN ANDERSON – London, From Hungerford – 42¼ x 71¾in.
(Christie's) **$21,714 £15,400**

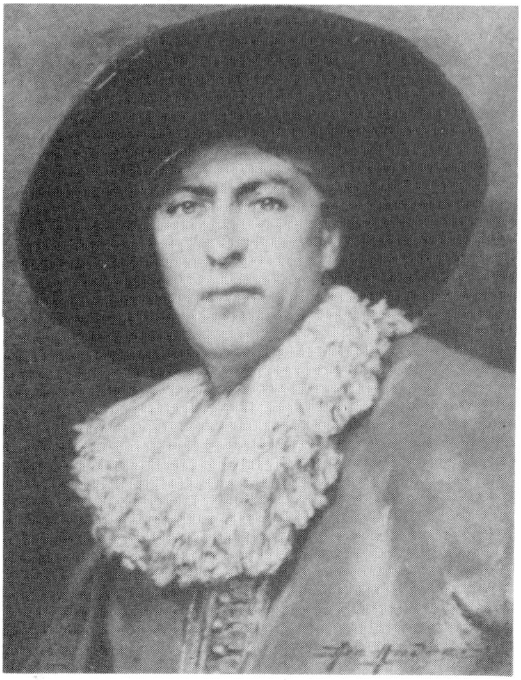

ALEX DE ANDREIS – Portraits Of Cavaliers, Head And Shoulders, Wearing Red Cloaks, White Ruffs And Black Hats – signed – oil on canvas – 13 x 10in.
(Christie's) **$871** **£605 Pair**

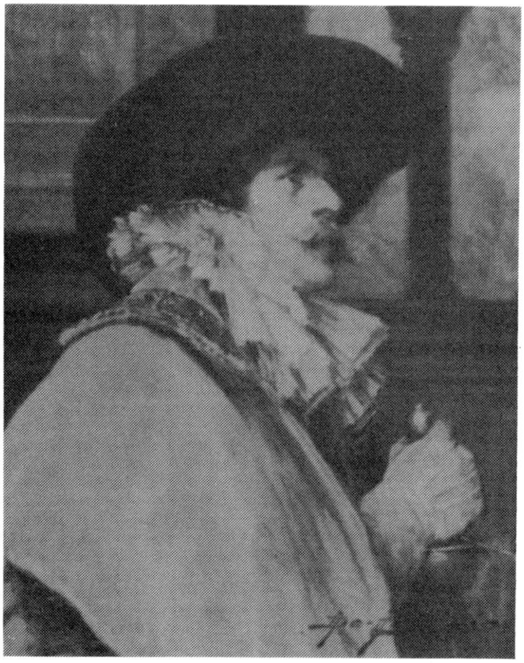

ALEX DE ANDREIS – Cavalier In A Red Cloak – signed – oil on canvas – 46 x 39cm.
(Phillips) **$1,503** **£900**

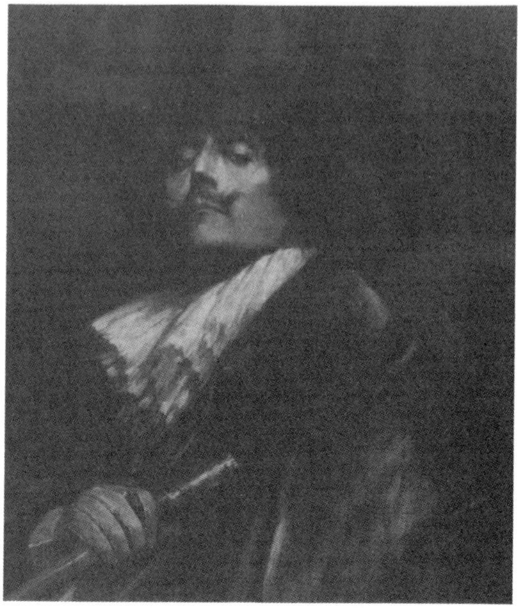

DE ANDRES – Portrait Of A Man In Regency Dress Holding A Cane – oil – 31 x 25in.
(Chancellors Hollingsworths) **$715** **£480**

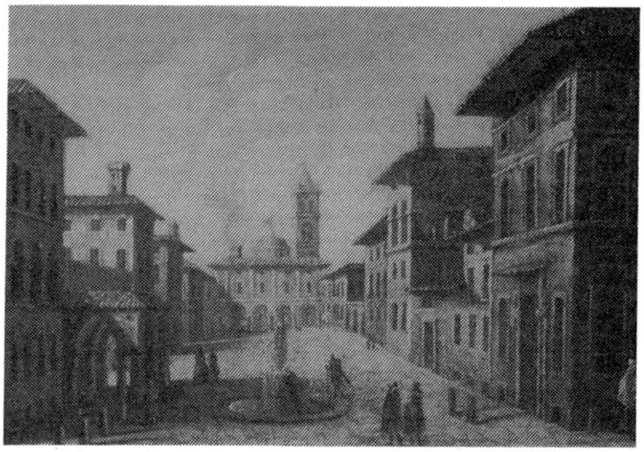

PAOLO ANESI, Circle of – A Town Square With A Fountain; and A Horse And Carriage In A Town – on canvas laid down on panel – 6¼ x 7¾in.
(Phillips) **$5,312** **£3,200 Pair**

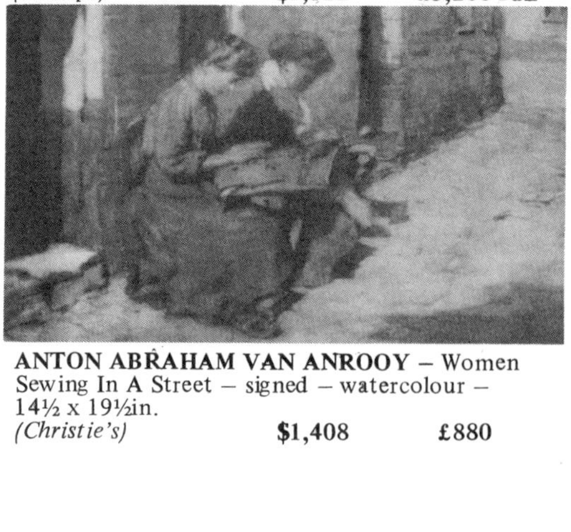

ANTON ABRAHAM VAN ANROOY – Women Sewing In A Street – signed – watercolour – 14½ x 19½in.
(Christie's) **$1,408** **£880**

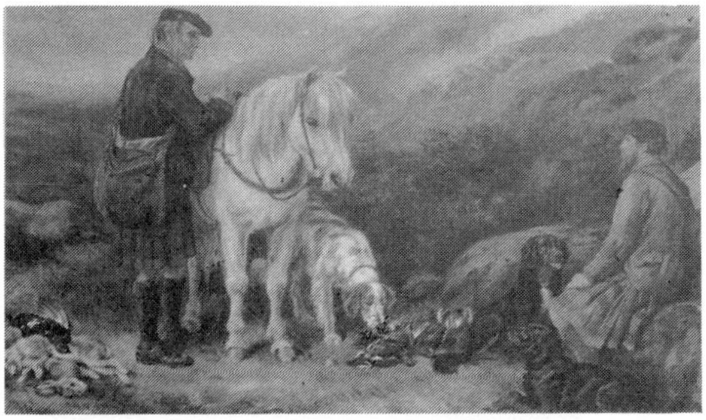

R. ANSDELL – Highland Scene With Figures, Pony And Dogs – oil on canvas – 27½ x 35½in.
(Michael G. Matthews) **$4,960** **£3,100**

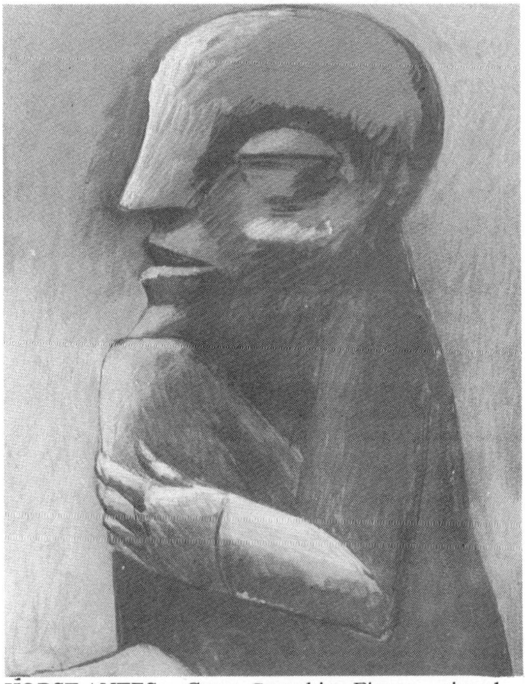

HORST ANTES – Green Crouching Figure – signed – gouache, chalk and oil on paper 42¼ x 23½in.
(Christie's) **$9,504** **£6,600**

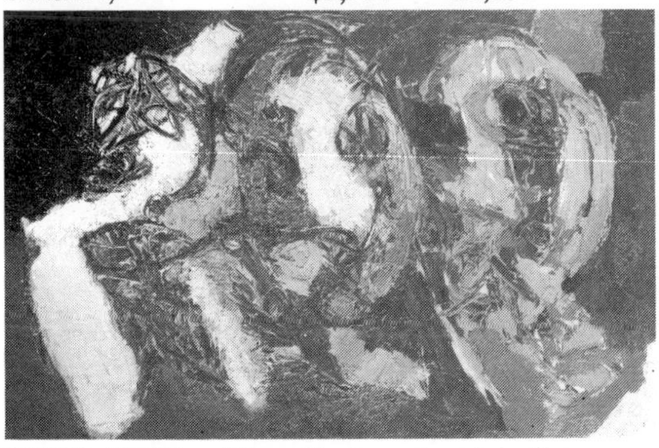

KAREL APPEL – Three Heads – signed – oil on canvas – 38¼ x 51¼in.
(Christie's) **$79,200** **£49,500**

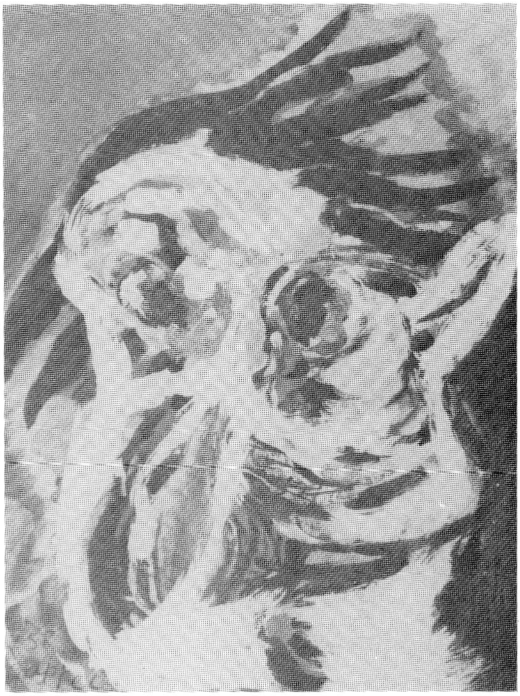

KAREL APPEL – Tete – signed and dated '58 – gouache and black chalk on paper – 25¾ x 19¾in.
(Christie's) **$9,152** **£5,720**

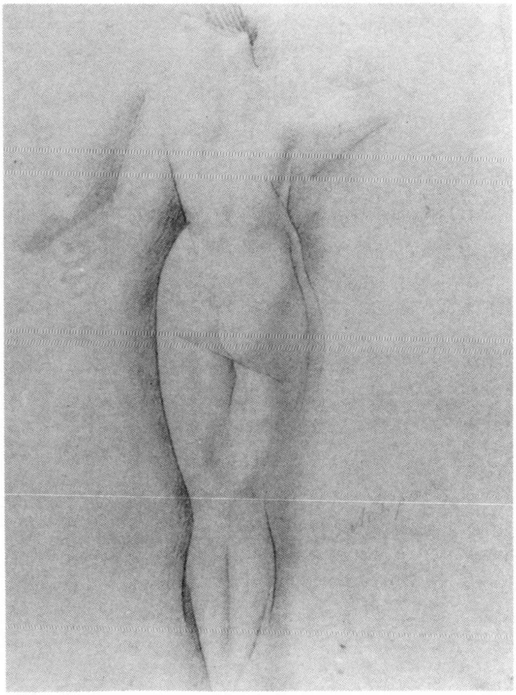

ALEXANDER ARCHIPENKO – Nu debout – signed – red chalk and pencil on paper – 13 x 9¾in.
(Christie's) **$6,652** **£4,620**

ARDIZZONE

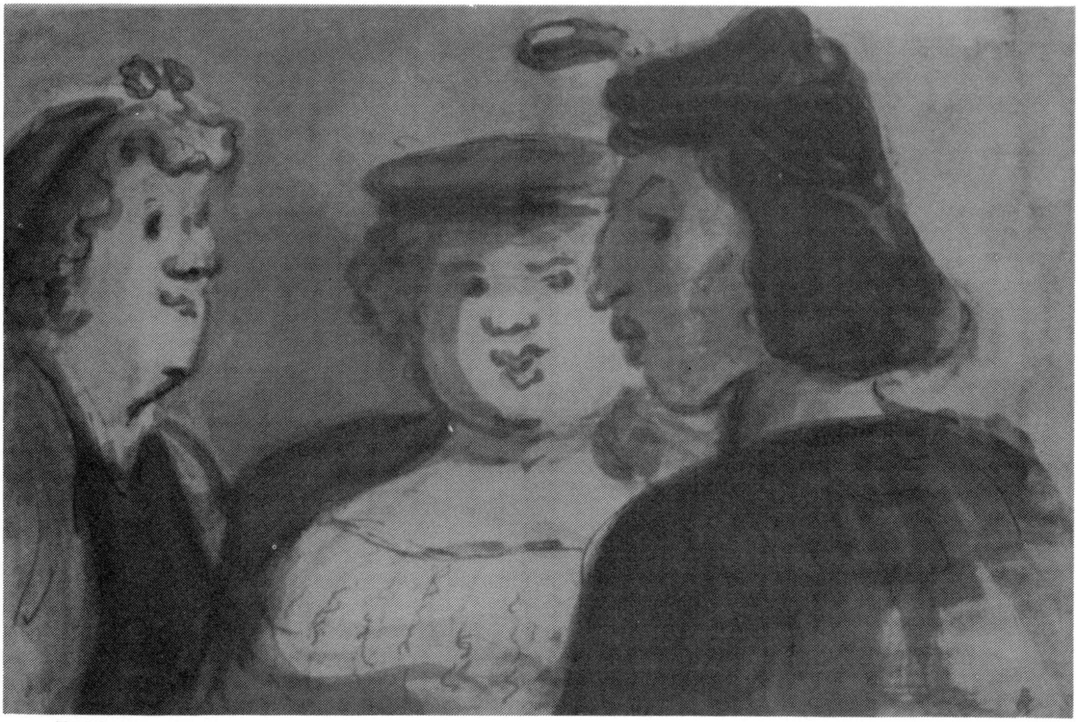

EDWARD ARDIZZONE – The Gossipers – signed with initials – pen, brush and indian ink – 18.5 x 27.5 cm. *(Phillips)* **$747 £450**

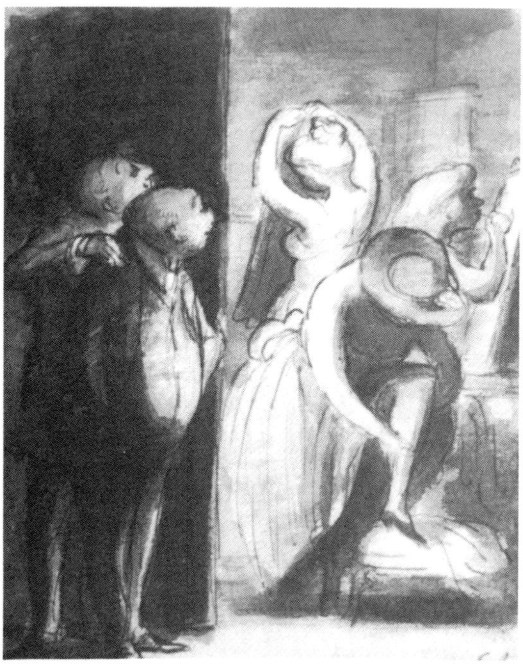

EDWARD ARDIZZONE – Two Gentlemen Spying On The Actresses Dressing-Room; and A Man And A Woman Dressing In A Bedroom – signed with initials – watercolour, pen and black ink – 8¾ x 7 in. and 7¾ x 10 in.
(Christie's) **$4,404** **£3,080** Two

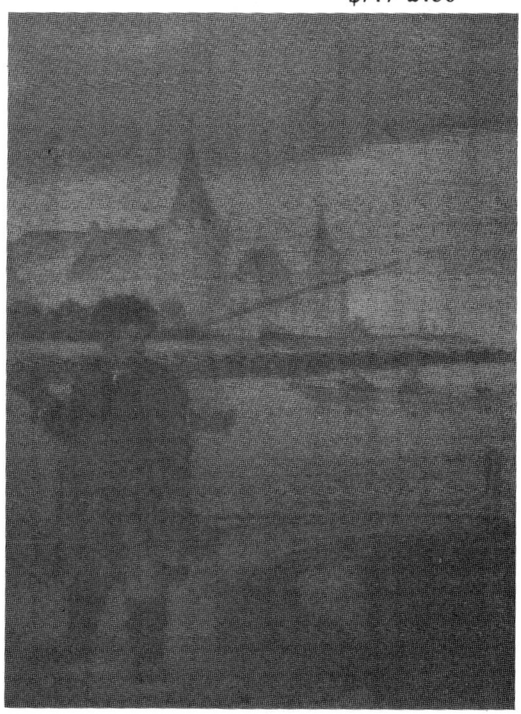

ARENT ARENTSZ, Called Cabel – A Fisherman – signed with monogram – on panel – 7¼ x 6¼in.
(Phillips) **$14,940** **£9,000**

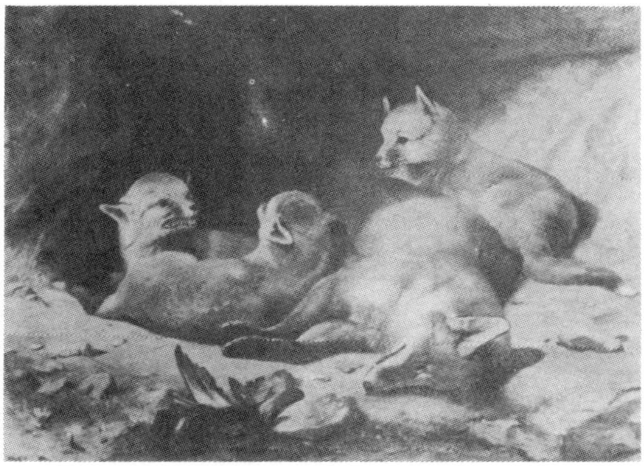

ELIZABETH ARKWRIGHT – Rest And Play – 28 x 36in.
(Christie's) **$1,240** **£880**

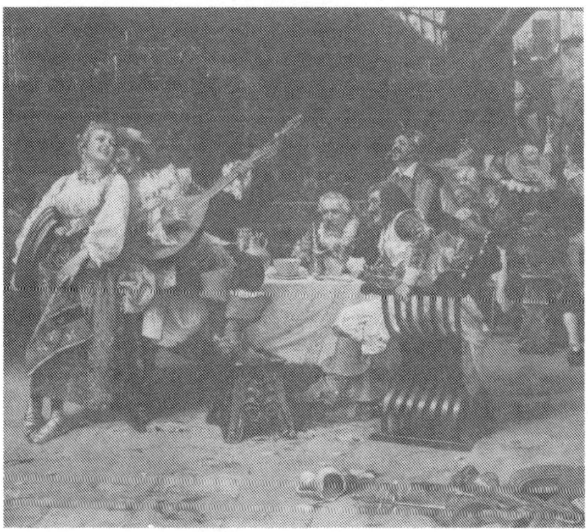

RAFFAELE ARMENISE – Cavaliers Merrymaking – signed and inscribed – 24½ x 33in.
(Christie's) **$10,956** **£6,600**

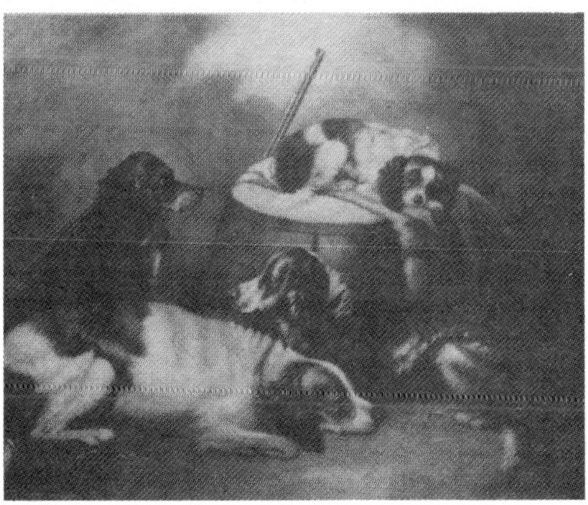

EDWARD ARMFIELD, Circle of – Gun Dogs Resting By A Barrel – oil on canvas – 23 x 29in.
(Christie's) **$633** **£440**

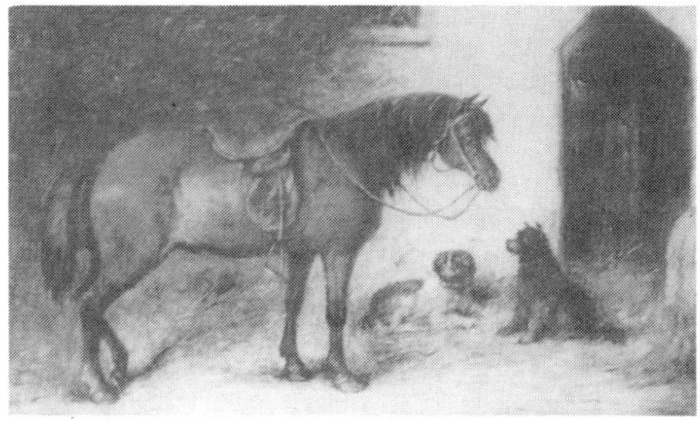

EDWARD ARMFIELD – Waiting For Master – signed – 16 x 24in.
(Christie's) **$1,430** **£935**

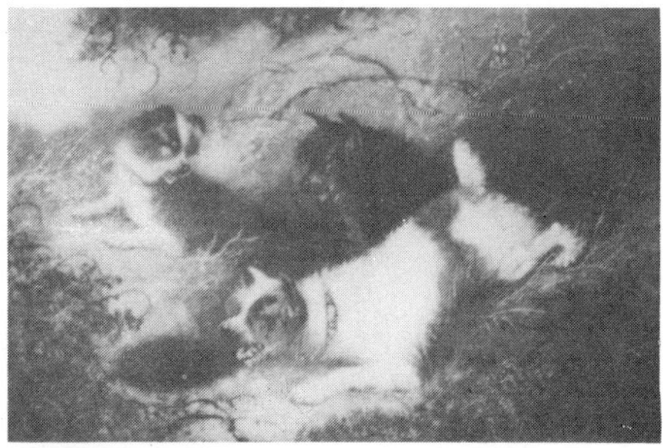

EDWARD ARMFIELD – Terriers Rabbiting signed – oil on canvas – 11½ x 15½in.
(Christie's) **$520** **£340**

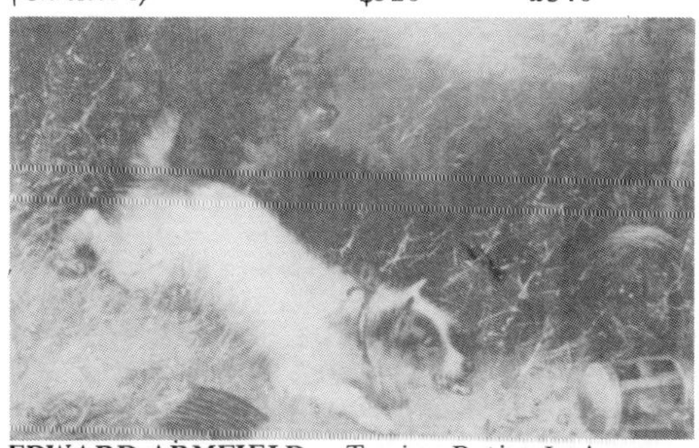

EDWARD ARMFIELD – Terriers Rating In A Barn – signed – oil on canvas – 11½ x 15½in.
(Christie's) **$896** **£550**

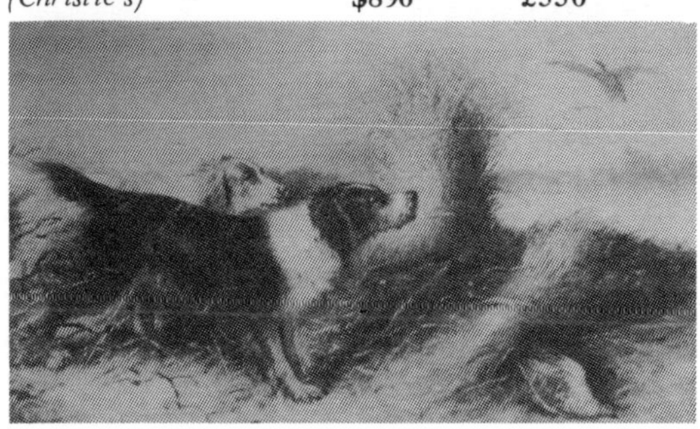

EDWARD ARMFIELD – Gundogs Putting Up Partridge – signed – on canvas – 20 x 30in.
(Phillips) **$1,690** **£1,050**

ARMFIELD

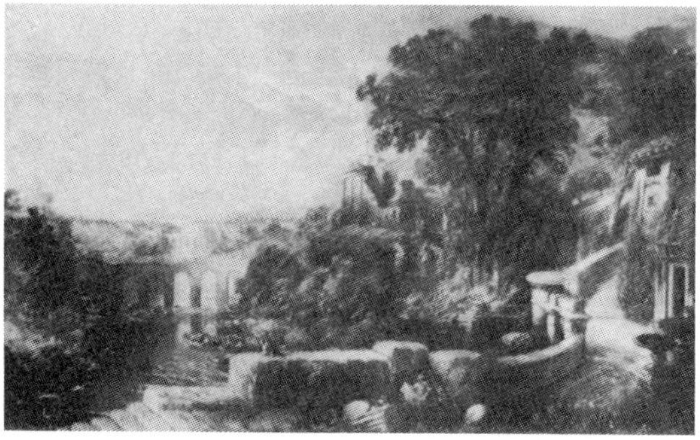

GEORGE ARMFIELD – An Extensive Wooded River Landscape With Viaducts And Classical Buildings – signed – oil on canvas – 26 x 40¼in.
(Phillips) **$2,448 £1,600**

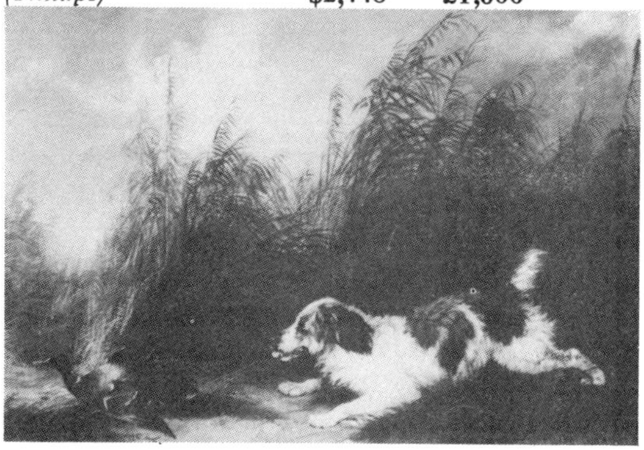

GEORGE ARMFIELD – A Spaniel Flushing A Duck From Reeds – signed and dated 1848 – oil on canvas – 17 x 21in.
(Phillips) **$2,754 £1,800**

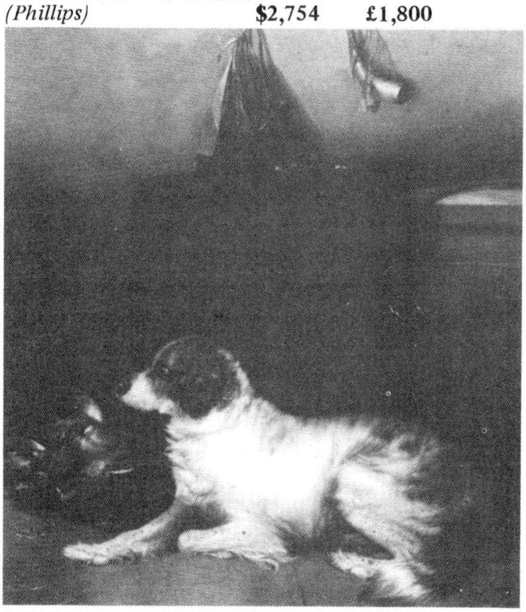

GEORGE ARMFIELD – Spaniel With The Day's Bag In An Interior – signed and dated 1862 – oil on canvas – 30 x 24in.
(Phillips) **$3,978 £2,600**

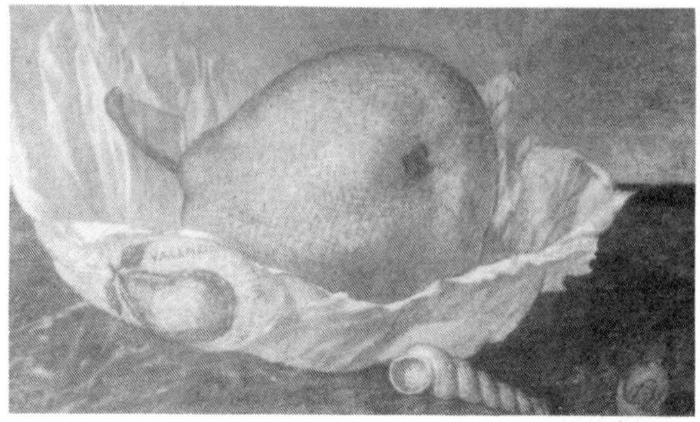

MAXWELL ARMFIELD – Souvenir Of Valencia – signed with monogram – tempera on board – 5¾ x 7¼in.
(Christie's) **$1,022 £715**

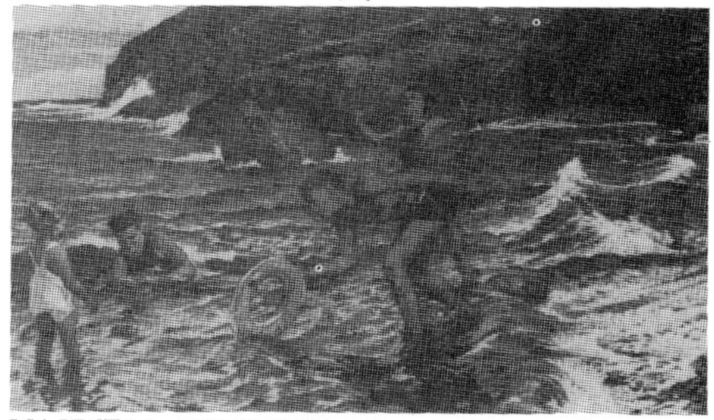

MAXWELL ARMFIELD – Beauty Preserved – signed with monogram and dated '32 – oil on board – 19 x 23in.
(Christie's) **$3,454 £2,200**

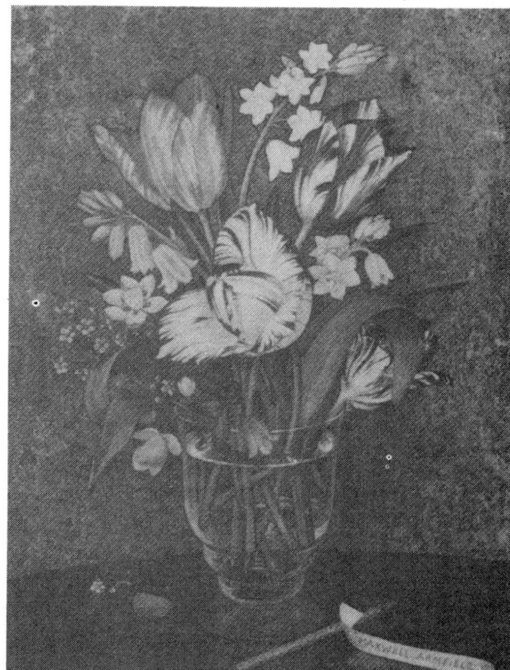

MAXWELL ARMFIELD – Beibloemen – signed and dated '36 – tempera – 31.5 x 23cm.
(Phillips) **$2,448 £1,600**

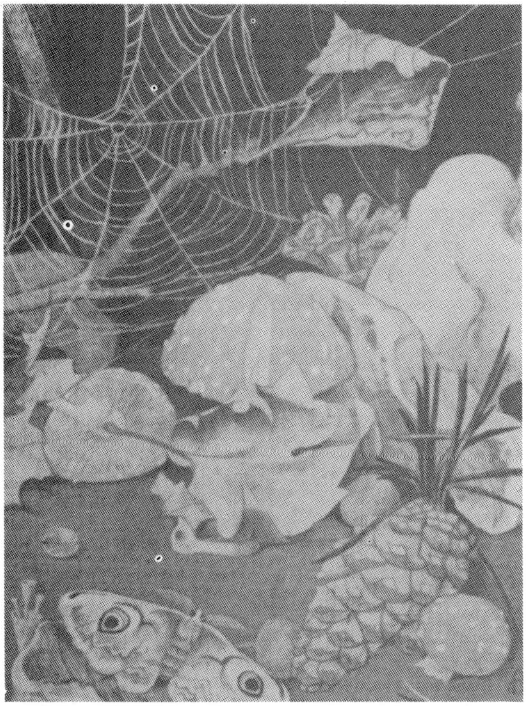

MAXWELL ARMFIELD – Winter Wood – signed with monogram, also signed and inscribed on the backboard – tempera on silk – 24 x 19cm.
(Phillips) **$1,562** **£1,100**

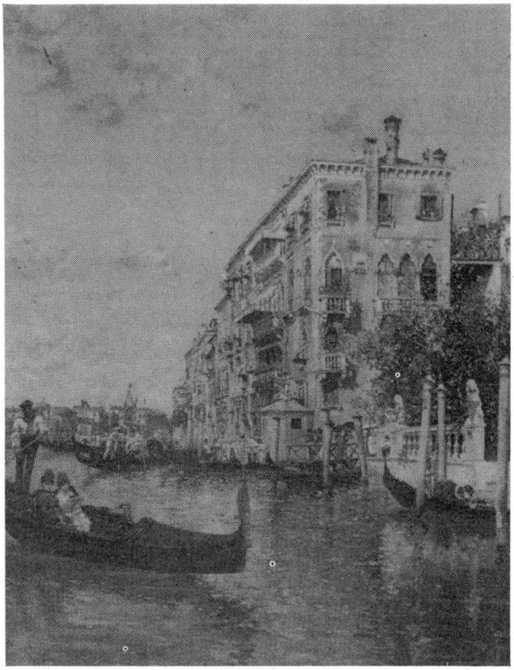

JOSE GALLEGOS Y ARNOSA – A Scene On The Grand Canal – signed and inscribed – oil on panel – 53 x 33cm.
(Phillips) **$23,040** **£16,000**

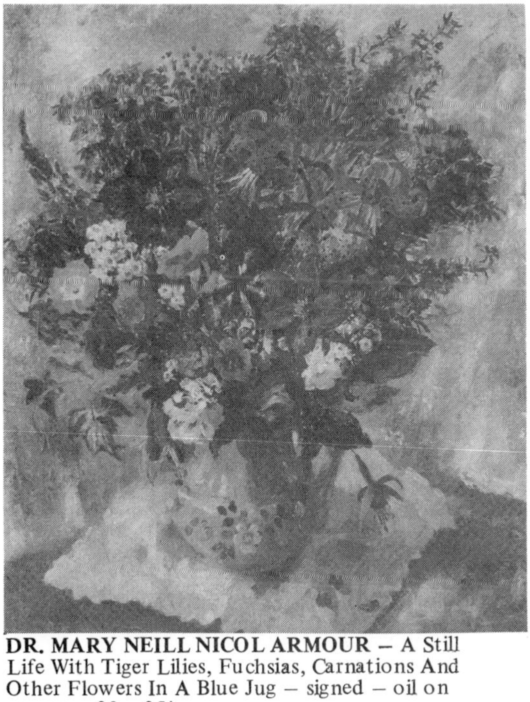

DR. MARY NEILL NICOL ARMOUR – A Still Life With Tiger Lilies, Fuchsias, Carnations And Other Flowers In A Blue Jug – signed – oil on canvas – 30 x 25in.
(Christie's) **$5,760** **£4,000**

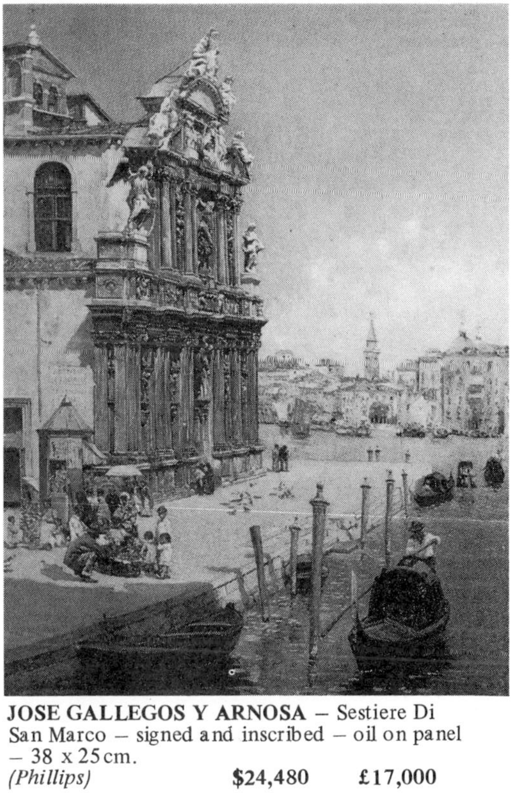

JOSE GALLEGOS Y ARNOSA – Sestiere Di San Marco – signed and inscribed – oil on panel – 38 x 25cm.
(Phillips) **$24,480** **£17,000**

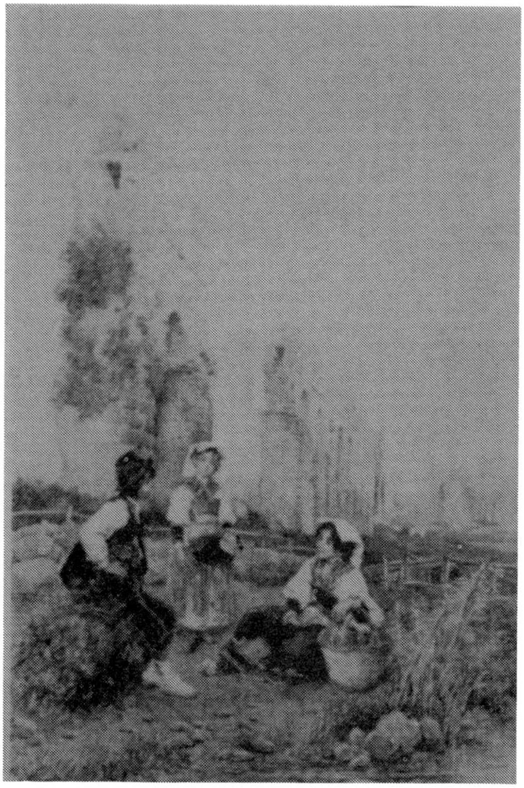

E. ASCENZI – Three Youths In An Italian Landscape – signed – watercolour on paper – 21 x 14in.
(Robt. W. Skinner Inc.) **$300** **£184**

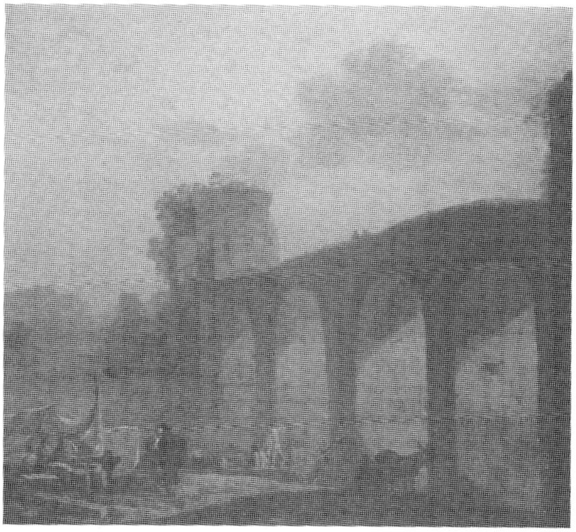

JAN ASSELIJN, Attributed to – A River Landscape With The Ponte Molle – bears signature and date 1646 – on panel – 19½ x 26in.
(Lawrence Fine Art) **$4,017** **£2,420**

SAMUEL ATKINS – Hotwells, Bristol – signed – watercolour – 14¼ x 19¼in.
(Christie's) **$3,240** **£2,160**

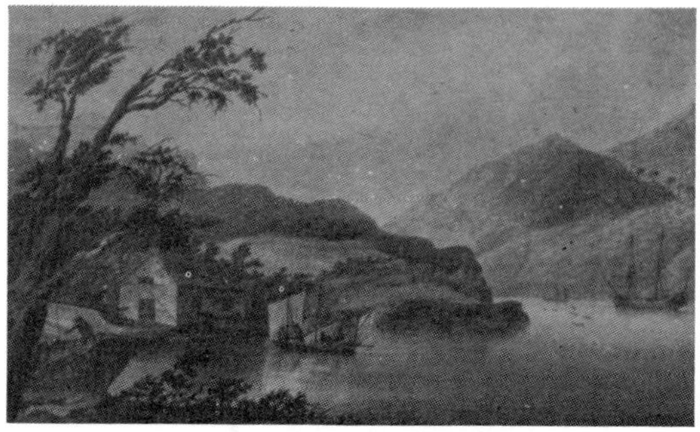

SAMUEL ATKINS – Fishing Boats And Cottage By Lake – signed – watercolour – 10 x 14in.
(Chancellors Hollingsworths) **$1,230** **£820**

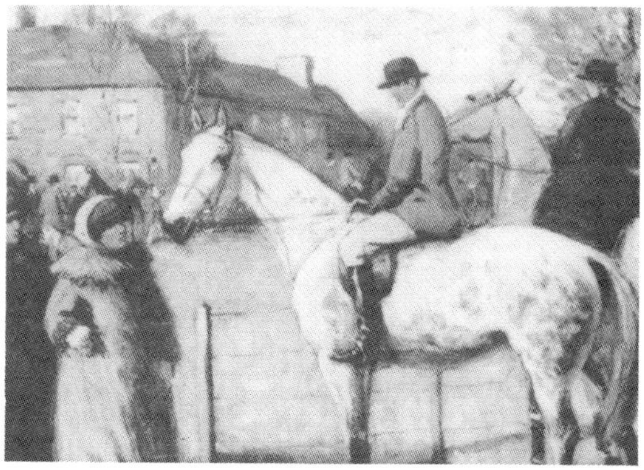

JOHN ATKINSON – Members Of The Carlisle Hunt Assembling In The Grounds Of A Country House – signed – oil on board – 13½ x 18½in.
(Anderson & Garland) **$1,430** **£1,000**

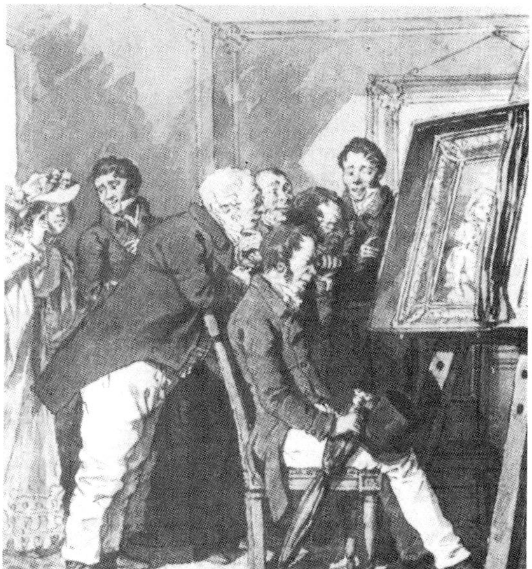

JOHN AUGUSTUS ATKINSON – The Connoisseurs – pen and black ink and watercolour on Whatman paper – 6¼ x 5¼in.
(Christie's) **$3,748** **£2,640**

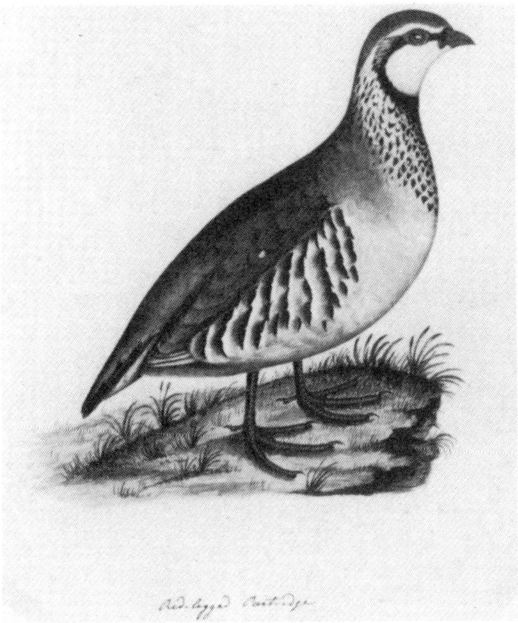

THE REV. CHRISTOPHER ATKINSON – The Red-Legged Partridge; and Anas Crecca, Teal – inscribed – pencil and watercolour heightened with bodycolour – the second signed, inscribed and dated 1786 – pen and ink and watercolour heightened with white – 11¼ x 8¾in.
(Christie's) **$1,874** **£1,320 Two**

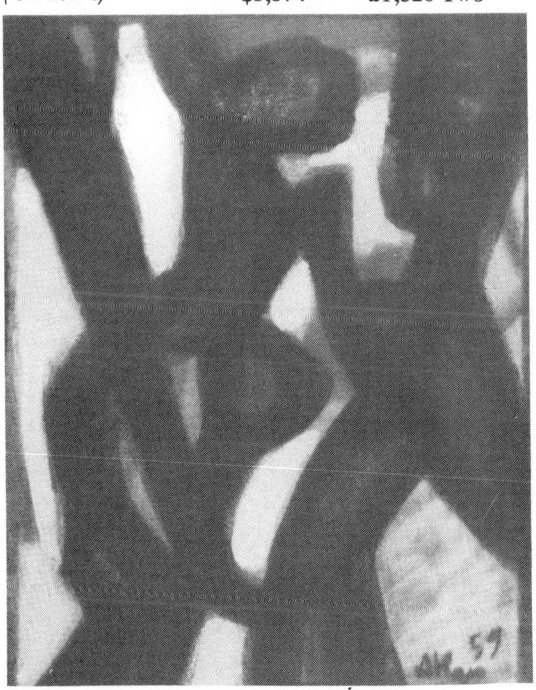

JEAN ATLAN – Californie – signed and dated '59 – pastel, charcoal and gouache on paper – 12¼ x 9½in.
(Christie's) **$6,160** **£3,850**

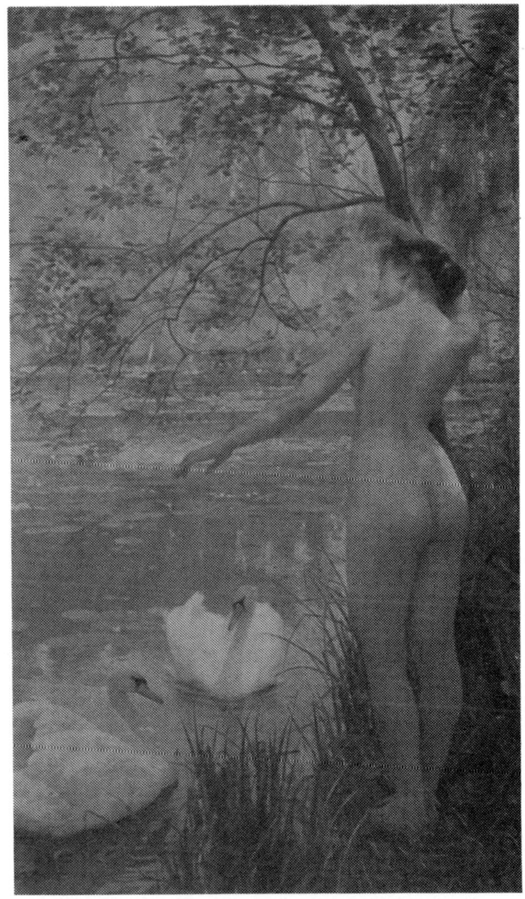

ALBERT AUBLET – A Nude Young Girl On The Banks Of A Sunlit Lake, Approached By A Swan – signed – oil on canvas – 165 x 101cm.
(Phillips) **$26,720** **£16,000**

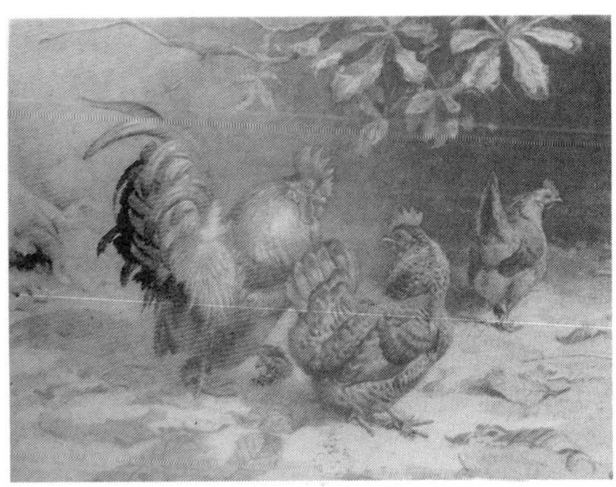

WINIFRED MARY LOUISE AUSTEN – Promenade: A Study Of Bantams – signed with monogram – pencil and watercolour heightened with white – 12¾ x 15¾in.
(Christie's) **$2,059** **£1,430**

AUSTRIAN SCHOOL

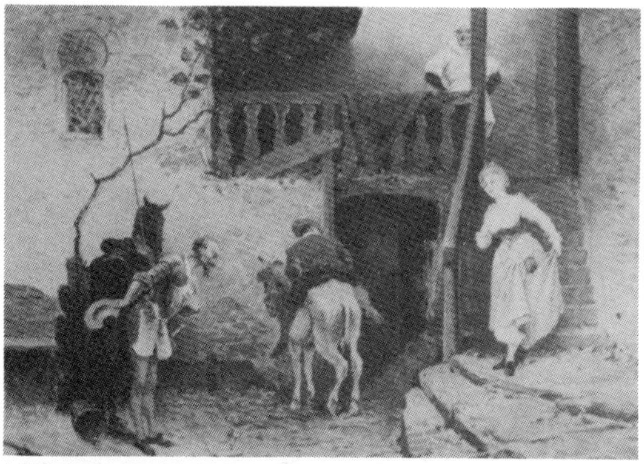

AUSTRIAN SCHOOL, 19th century – Don Quixote At The Inn – signed with monogram and dated 1888 – oil on panel – 23.5 x 31cm.
(Phillips) **$460** **£320**

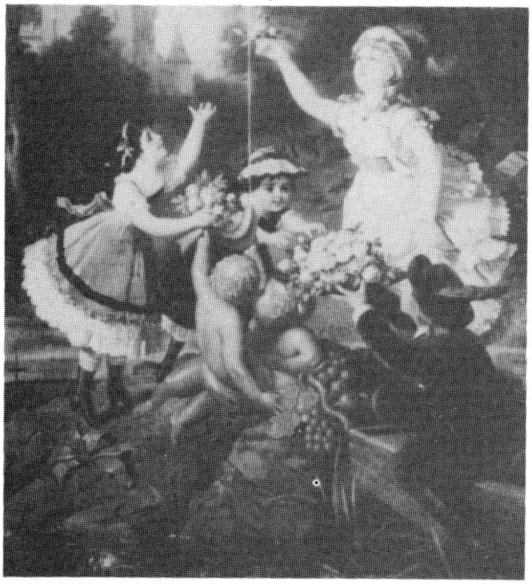

AUSTRIAN SCHOOL, 19th century – Children Playing At A Fountain – signed and inscribed – oil on canvas – 37½ x 30in.
(Robt. W. Skinner Inc.) **$3,400** **£2,236**

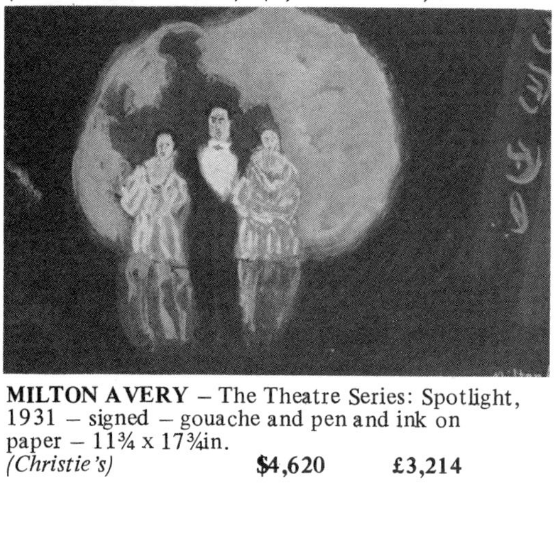

MILTON AVERY – The Theatre Series: Spotlight, 1931 – signed – gouache and pen and ink on paper – 11¾ x 17¾in.
(Christie's) **$4,620** **£3,214**

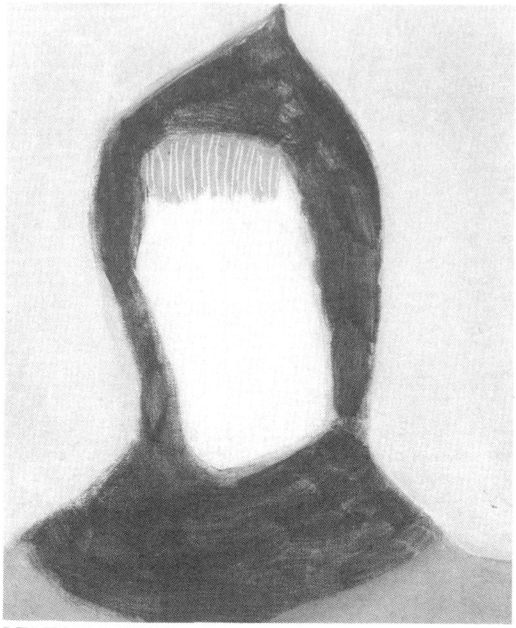

MILTON AVERY – Blue Hood – signed and dated 1961, inscribed on the reverse – oil on canvas board – 12 x 9in.
(Christie's) **$12,672** **£8,800**

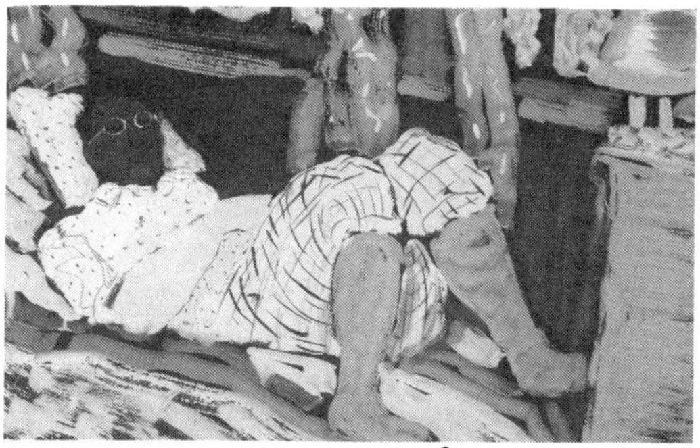

MILTON AVERY – Plaid Pants – signed – watercolour on black paper – 18 x 24in.
(Christie's) **$17,600** **£12,372**

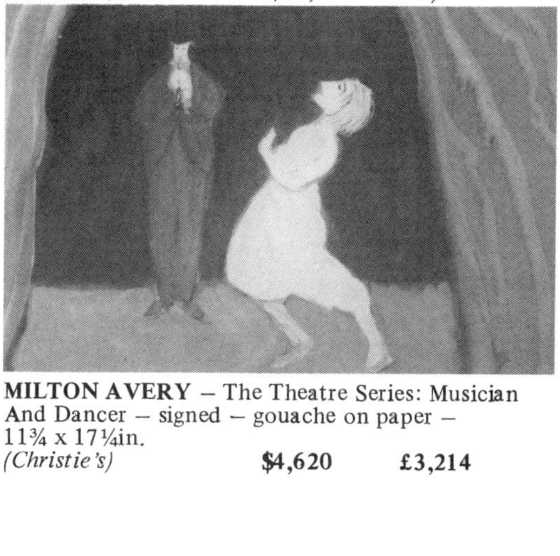

MILTON AVERY – The Theatre Series: Musician And Dancer – signed – gouache on paper – 11¾ x 17¼in.
(Christie's) **$4,620** **£3,214**

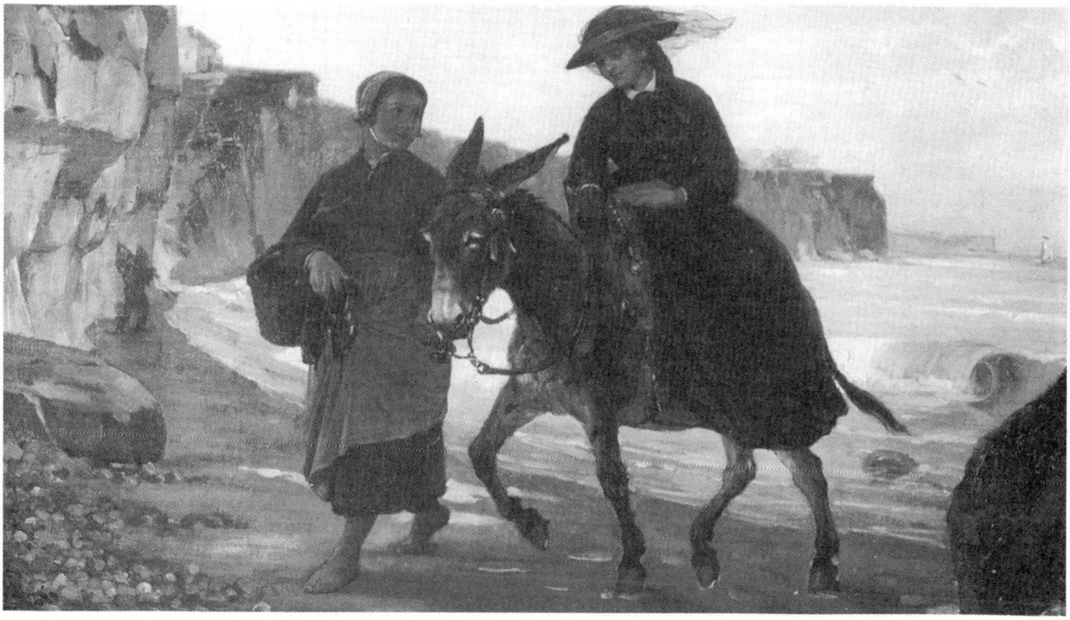

HENRY BACON – The Tourist And The Fisherwoman – signed and dated 1870 – oil on canvas – 13¾ x 17¾in. *(Christie's)* **$3,300 £2,319**

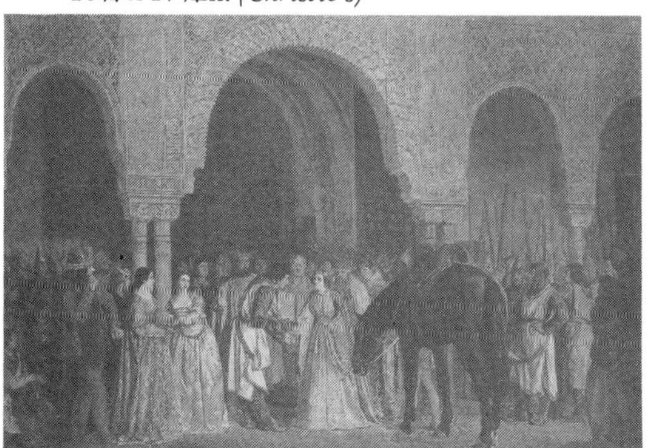

BERNARDO FERRANDIZ Y BADENES – The Knighting Of El Cid; and El Cid And The Lion – signed and dated 1869 – oil on panel. *(Phillips)* **$12,240 £8,500 Pair**

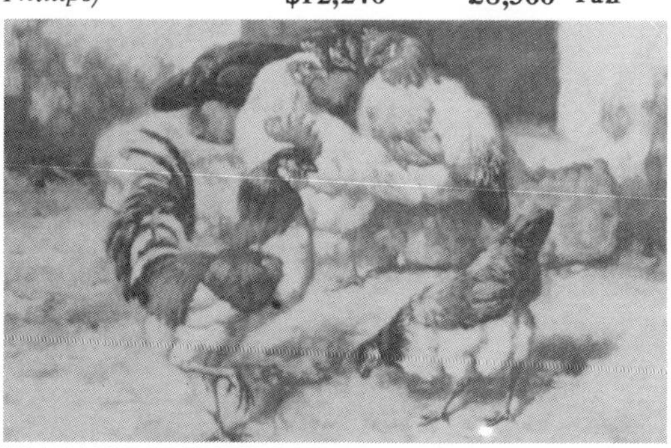

WILLIAM BAPTISTE BAIRD – Ruling The Roost – signed, also signed and inscribed on the reverse – oil on panel, the other oil on canvas – 15.6 x 22.1cm. and 15.6 x 22.8cm. *(Christie's)* **$770 £535** Two

THOMAS BAKER of Leamington – Cattle Grazing Beside A Stream – signed and dated 1843 – watercolour – 17 x 26cm. *(Phillips)* **$1,385 £850**

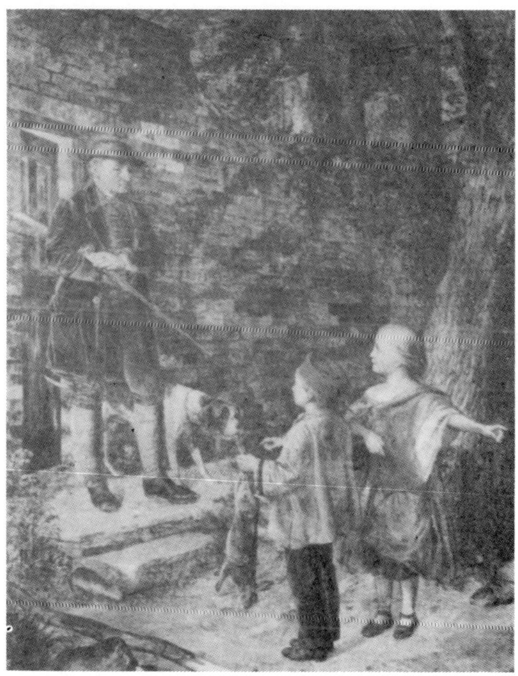

SAMUEL BALDWIN – A Gift For The Gamekeeper – signed and dated 1862 – 19½ x 15½in. *(Christie's)* **$1,584 £1,100**

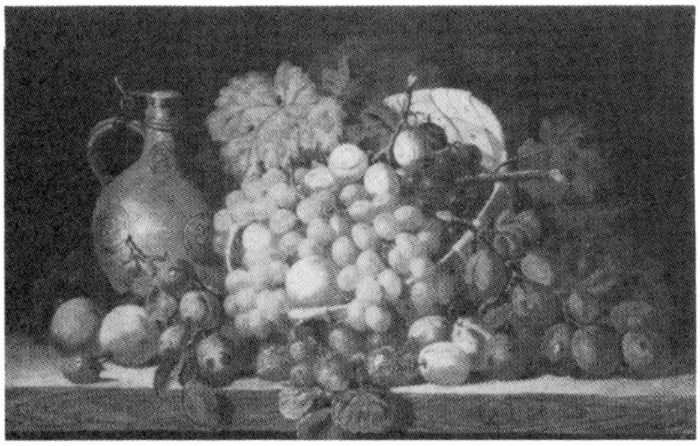

CHARLES THOMAS BALE – A Basket Of Grapes, And Plums With Strawberries And Other Fruit On A Wooden Table; and A Melon, Grapes, And Peaches On A Silver Salver On A Wooden Table – signed – 20 x 30in.
(Christie's) **$3,412** **£2,420 Pair**

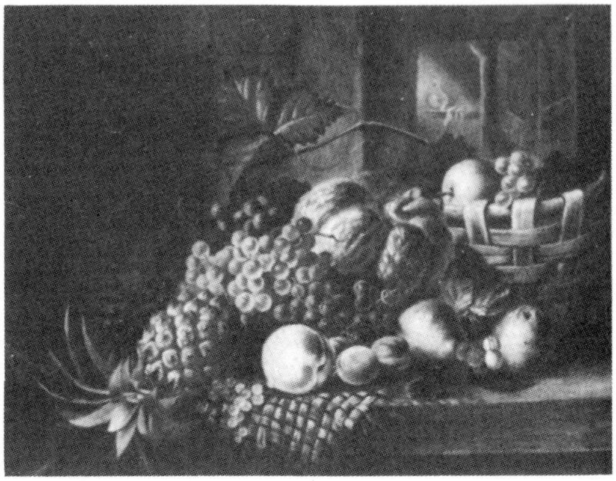

CHARLES THOMAS BALE – Still Life Of Fruit In A Basket And On A Ledge – oil on canvas – 23½ x 31½in.
(Phillips) **$1,377** **£900**

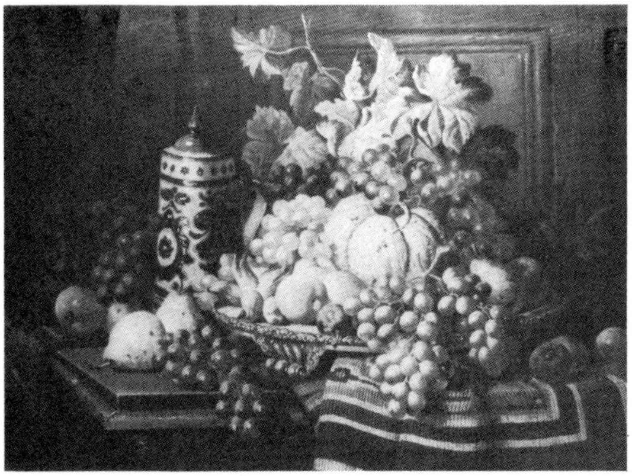

CHARLES THOMAS BALE – Grapes, Peaches, Pears And Other Fruit On A Tray On A Draped Table – signed and dated 1887 – 27¾ x 36in.
(Christie's) **$3,888** **£2,592**

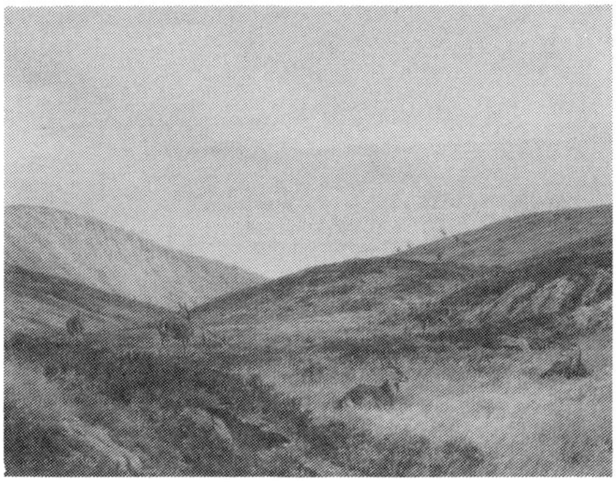

VINCENT R. BALFOUR-BROWNE – 'D-n said the Stalker in his quiet earnest way!' – signed with initials and dated 1925, and signed with initials, inscribed and dated 1925 on the reverse – pencil and watercolour – 12 x 18¼in.
(Christie's) **$9,306** **£6,600**

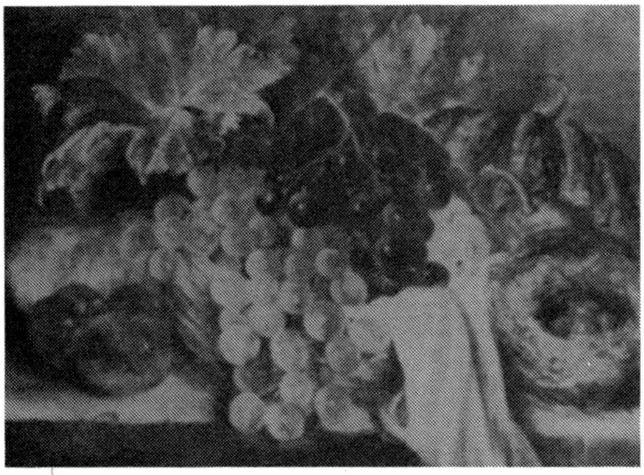

CHARLES THOMAS BALE – A Still Life Of A Bird's Nest Beside A Basket Of Grapes With Peaches And A Pumpkin On A Ledge – signed with monogram – on canvas – 12 x 16in.
(Phillips) **$966** **£600**

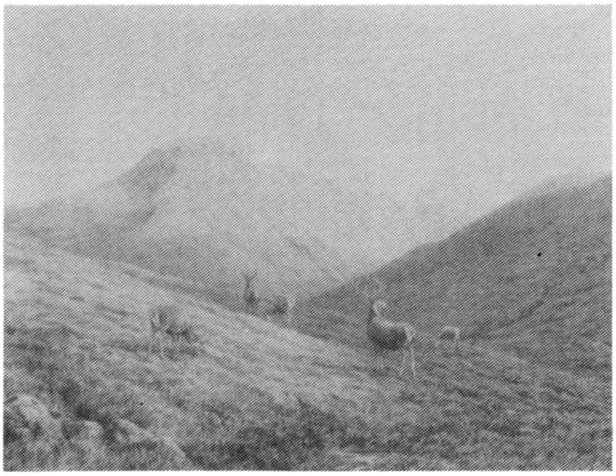

VINCENT R. BALFOUR-BROWNE – 'It so seldom happens like this!' – signed with initials and dated 1952 – pencil and watercolour with touches of white heightening – 9¼ x 13¼in.
(Christie's) **$6,514** **£4,620**

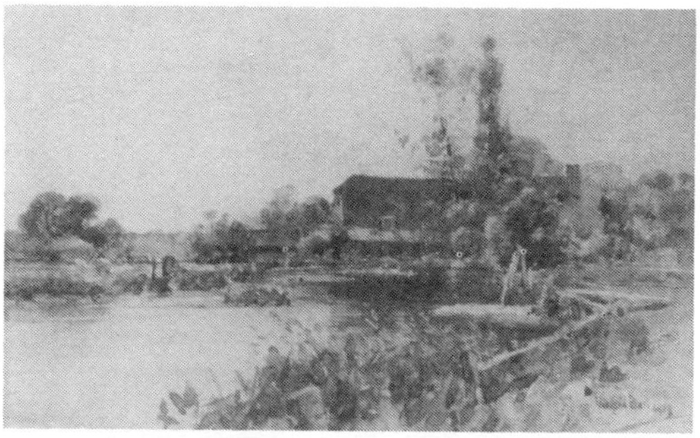

WILFRED WILLIAMS BALL – The Old Mill, Romney – signed and dated 1908, and inscribed on the reverse – watercolour on Whatman board – 7½ x 10½in.
(Christie's) **$821** **£495**

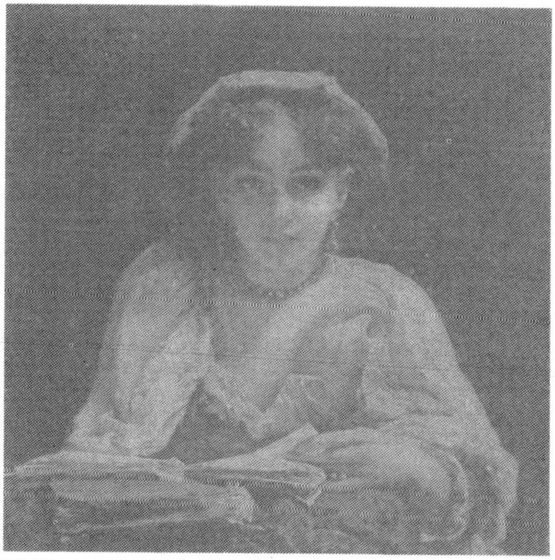

JOHN BALLANTYNE – A Pensive Moment – on canvas – 30 x 25in.
(Phillips) **$2,737** **£1,700**

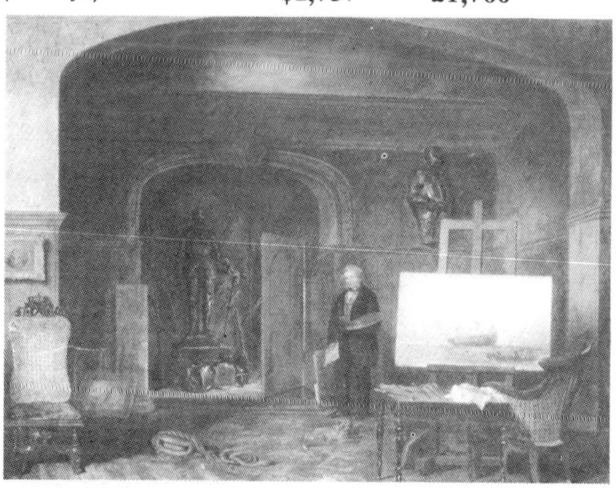

JOHN BALLANTYNE – Portrait Of William Clarkson Stanfield, Standing In His Studio – signed, and signed and inscribed on a label on the reverse – 24¾ x 30in.
(Christie's) **$7,128** **£4,950**

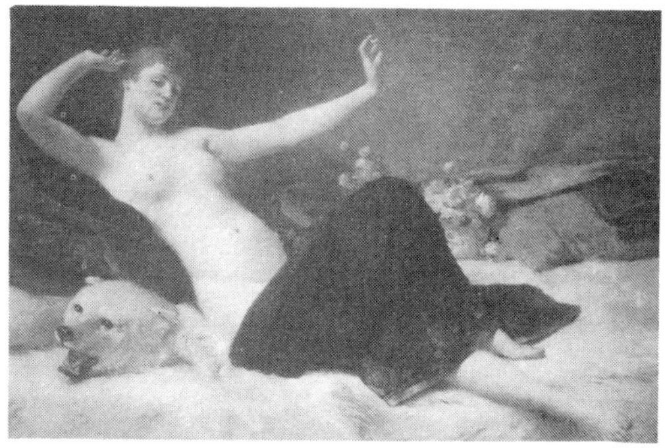

JULES FREDERIC BALLAVOINE – A Nude On A Bearskin – signed – 35 x 51in.
(Christie's) **$26,928** **£18,700**

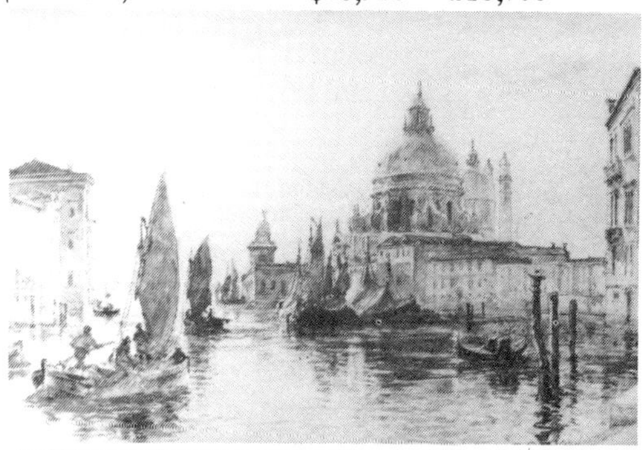

ALEXANDER BALLINGALL – 'Morning, The Grand Canal', Venetian Scene Busy With Boats – signed – oil – 13 x 20in.
(Capes, Dunn & Co.) **$554** **£340**

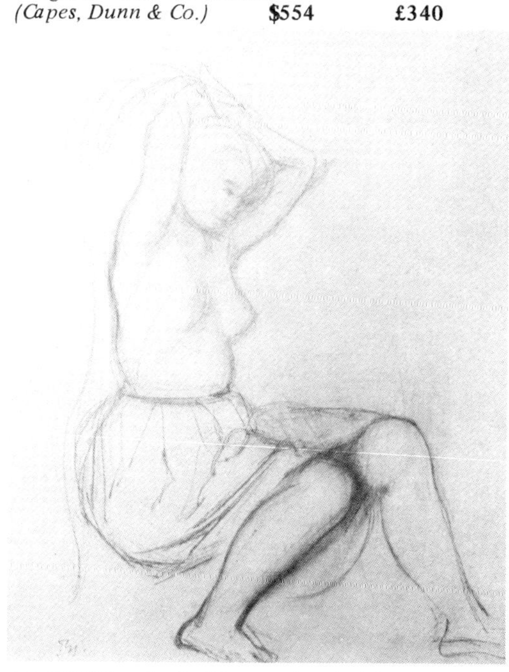

BALTHUS – La Coiffure – signed with monogram – pencil on paper – 21½ x 17in.
(Christie's) **$17,424** **£12,100**

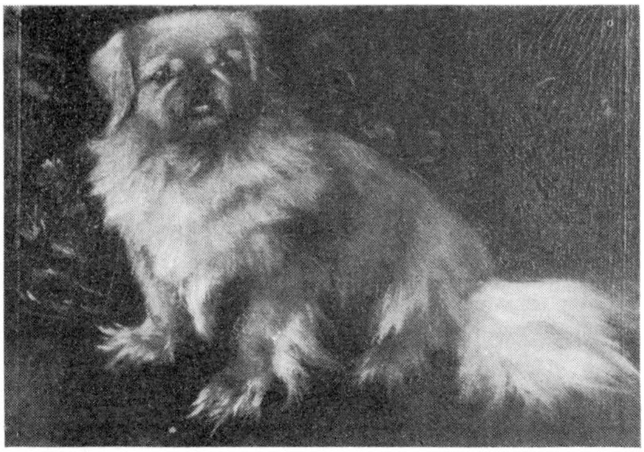

BETSY BAMBER – A Pekinese – signed with monogram – 22 x 16in.
(Christie's) **$3,366** **£2,200**

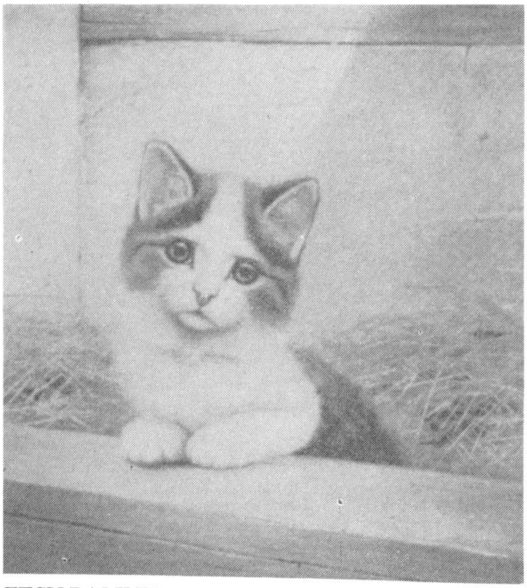

BETSY BAMBER – The Inquisitive Kitten – signed with initials – oil on panel – 11½ x 9½in.
(Christie's) **$844** **£528**

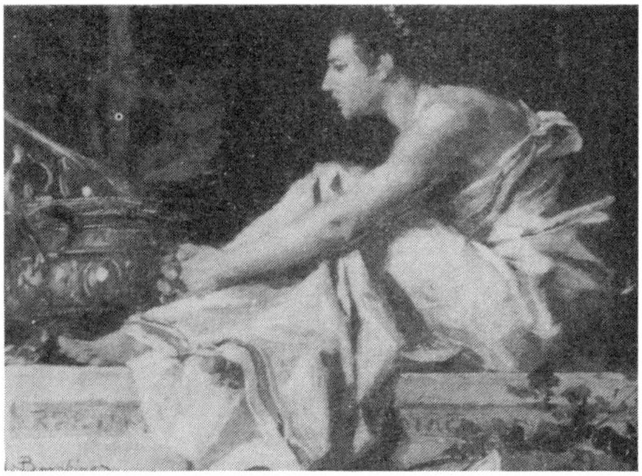

NICOLO BARABINO – A Roman Priestess – signed – on panel – 7½ x 9¾in.
(Christie's) **$2,739** **£1,650**

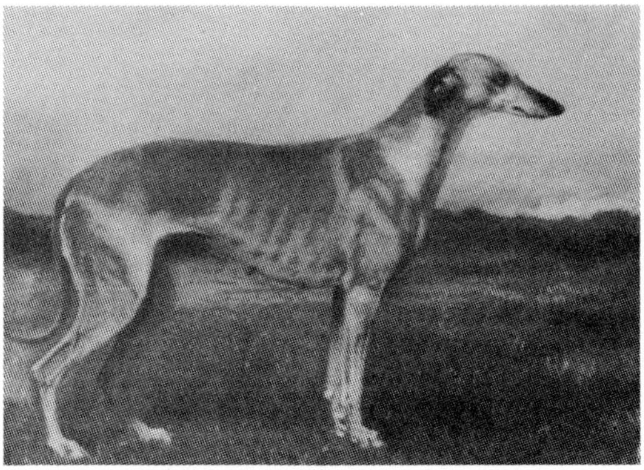

CHARLES BURTON BARBER – Snowflight, Winner Of The Waterloo Cup 1882 – signed and dated 1882 – 10¼ x 14¼in.
(Christie's) **$1,514** **£990**

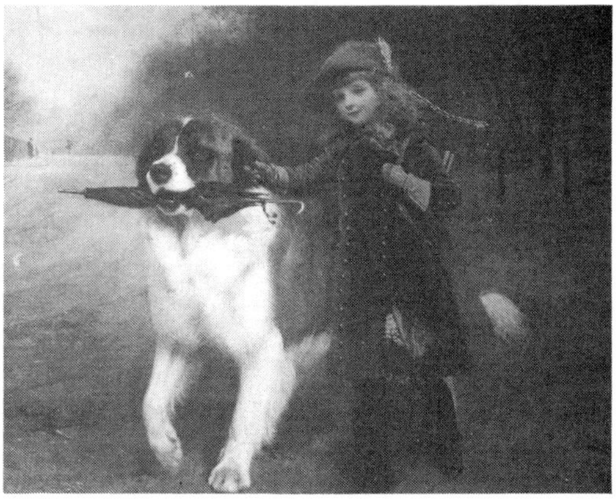

CHARLES BURTON BARBER – Off To School – signed and dated 1883 – 20 x 24in.
(Christie's) **$26,928** **£17,600**

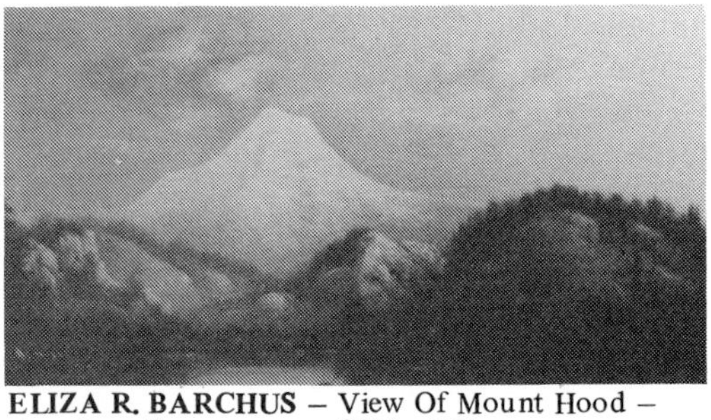

ELIZA R. BARCHUS – View Of Mount Hood – signed – oil on canvas – 21¾ x 36in.
(Robt. W. Skinner Inc.) **$1,400** **£858**

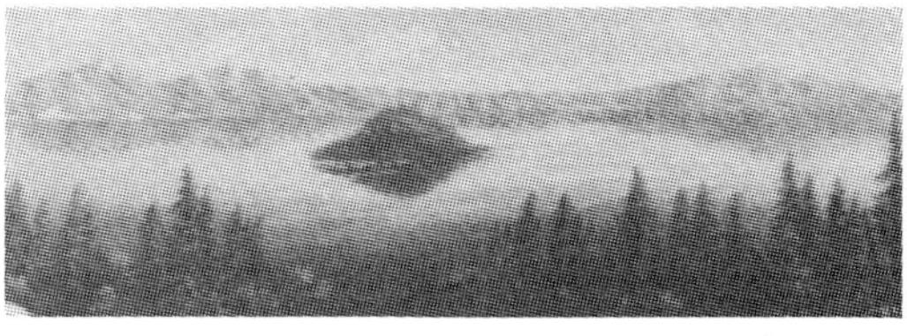

ELIZA R. BARCHUS – Crater Lake – signed – oil on canvas – 12 x 36in.
(Robt. W. Skinner Inc.) **$650** **£398**

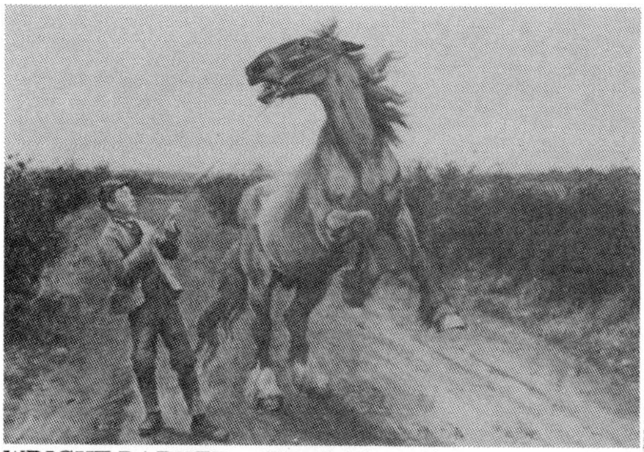

WRIGHT BARKER – The Frightened Horse – signed – on canvas – 37 x 48¼in.
(Phillips) **$2,254** **£1,400**

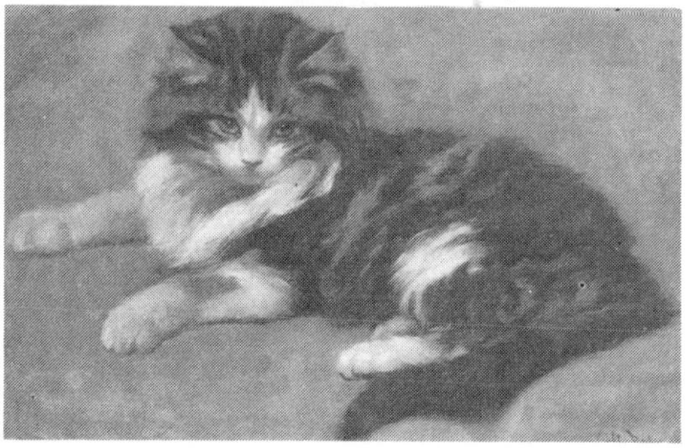

WRIGHT BARKER – A Siamese Cat – signed – oil – 16 x 20¾in.
(Bonhams) **$2,790** **£1,800**

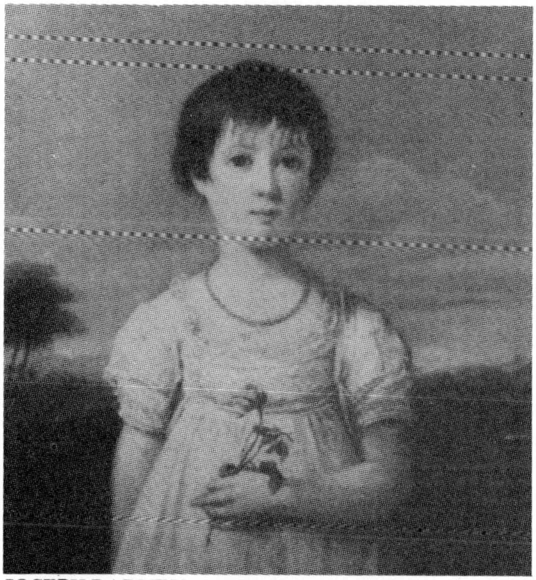

JOSEPH BARNEY, Attributed to – Portrait Of A Young Girl Wearing A White Gown And Holding A Pink Rose, An Extensive Landscape Beyond – with signature and dated 1801 – oil on canvas – 30 x 25in.
(Christie's) **$994** **£650**

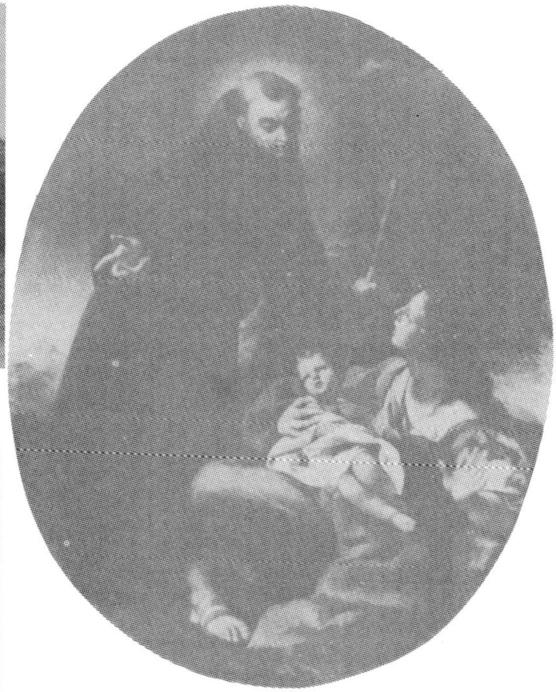

POMPEO BARONI, Circle of – Madonna And Child With St. Francis – oil on canvas – 32¼ x 25½in.
(Phillips) **$2,538** **£1,800**

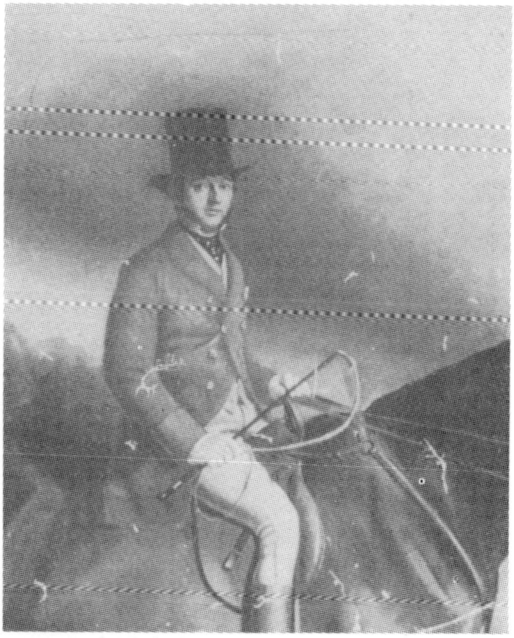

WILLIAM BARRAUD, Circle of – Portrait Of A Mounted Huntsman, Wearing Top Hat And Pink Coat, And Carrying A Whip – oil on canvas – 21 x 18½in.
(Phillips) **$796** **£480**

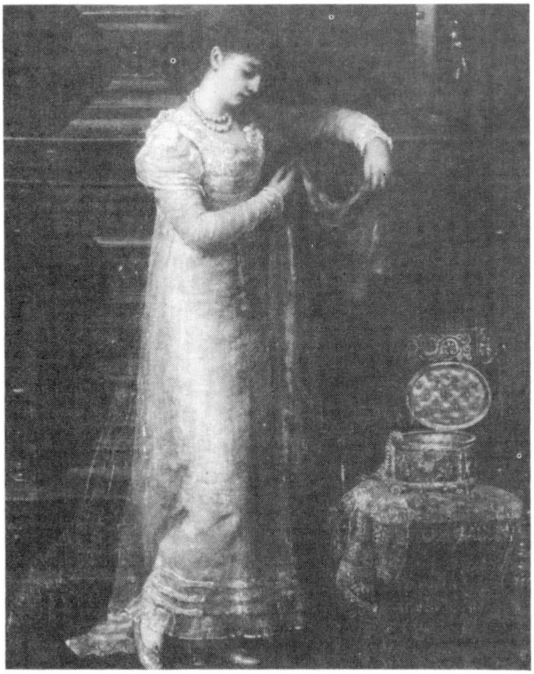

JERRY BARRETT – Portrait Study Of A Young Lady Wearing A White Lace Dress And Studying An Oval Shaped Jewellery Box – signed – oil on canvas – 20 x 15in.
(Biddle & Webb) **$2,128** **£1,400**

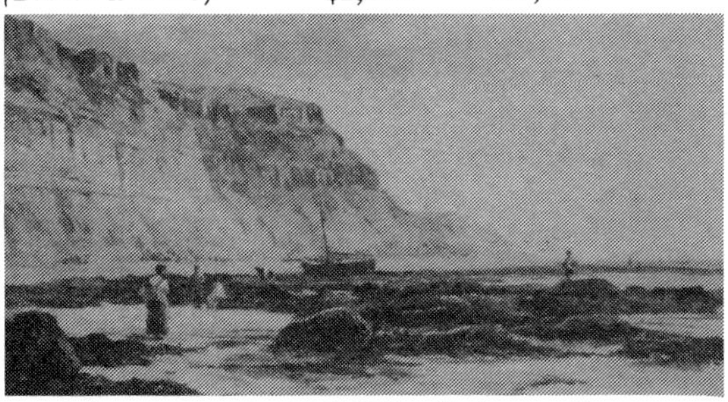

WILLIAM HENRY BARROW – Shrimpers On The Seashore – signed with initials and dated 1880 – 10½ x 16in.
(Lawrence Fine Art) **$1,095** **£660**

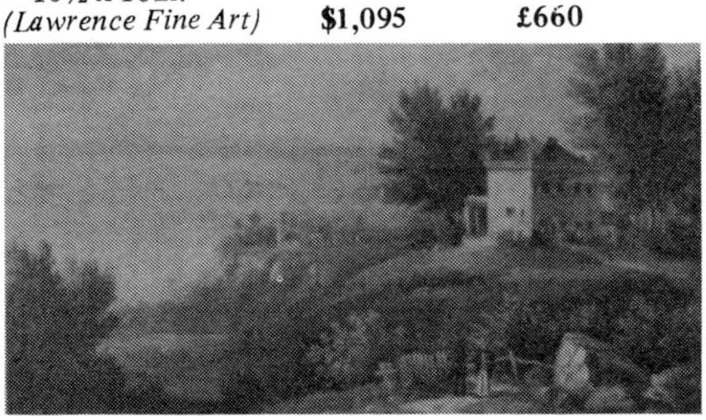

WILLIAM HENRY BARTLETT, After – View Of New York Bay From Gowanus Heights, Brooklyn – inscribed on the reverse – oil on board – 10¼ x 13in.
(Robt. W. Skinner Inc.) **$2,000** **£1,226**

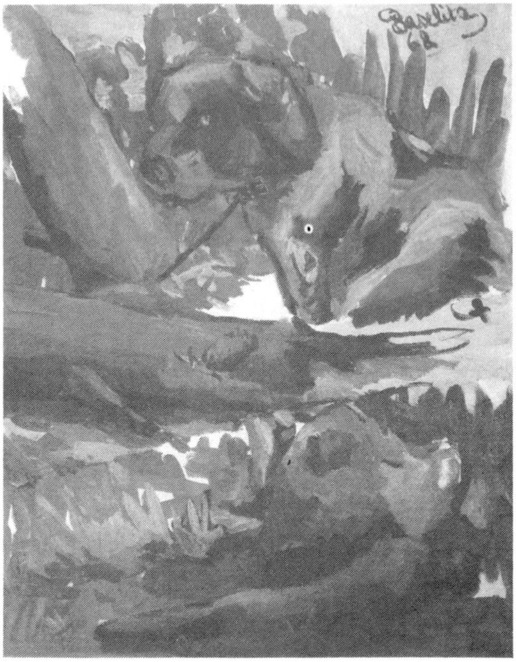

GEORG BASELITZ – Grosser Bernhard – signed and dated '68, also signed, inscribed and dated on the reverse – oil on canvas – 63¾ x 51¼in.
(Christie's) **$60,192** **£41,800**

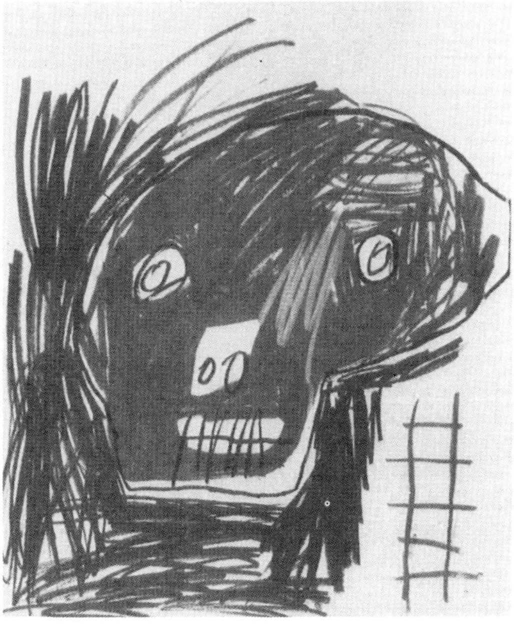

JEAN MICHEL BASQUIAT – Untitled – coloured crayons on card – 13¾ x 11in.
(Christie's) **$1,584** **£1,100**

GEORGE BASSETT – An Extensive Wooded River Valley – signed – on canvas – 20 x 30in.
(Phillips) **$998** **£620**

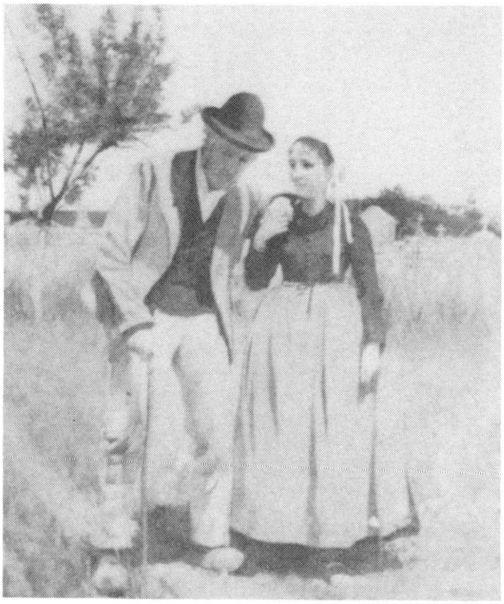

JULES BASTIEN-LEPAGE – A Helping Hand – signed and dated '81 – oil on canvas – 29 x 24in. *(Christie's)* **$7,530** **£4,620**

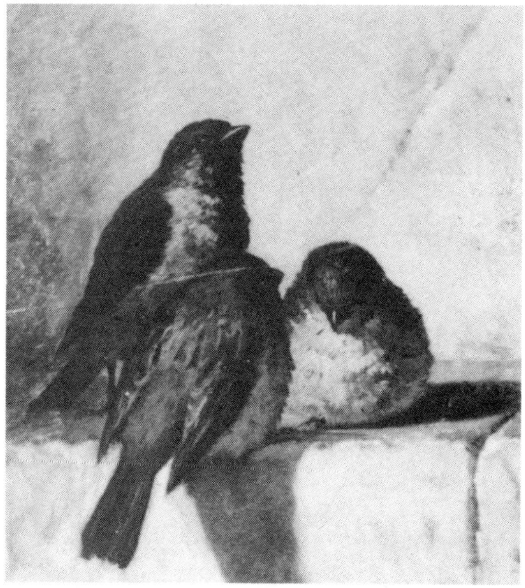

FREDERICK S. BATCHELLER – Three Sparrows – signed – oil on board – 10 x 8in. *(Robt. W. Skinner Inc.)* **$1,700** **£1,180**

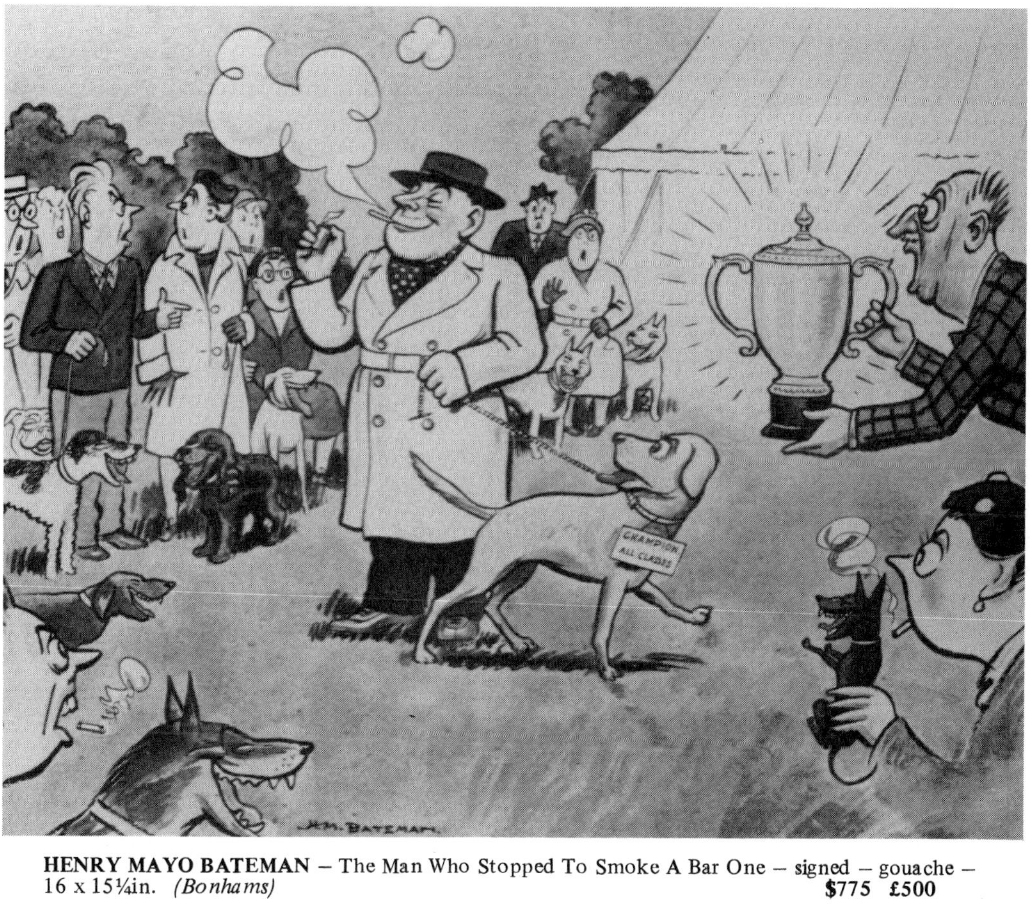

HENRY MAYO BATEMAN – The Man Who Stopped To Smoke A Bar One – signed – gouache – 16 x 15¼in. *(Bonhams)* **$775** **£500**

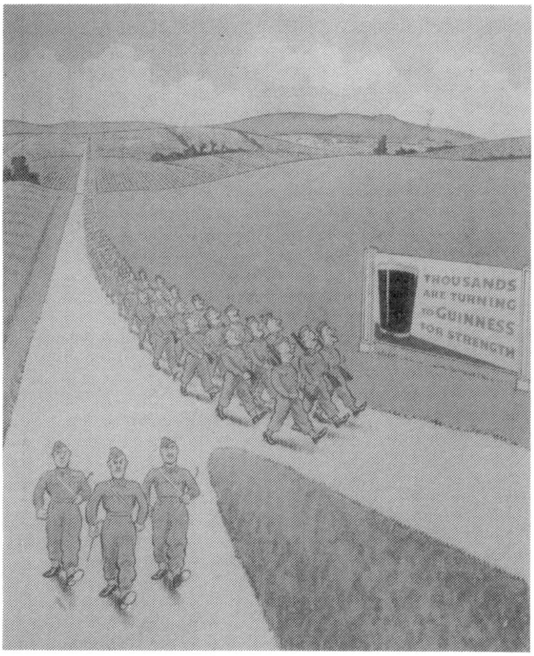

HENRY MAYO BATEMAN – 'Thousands Are Turning To Guinness For Strength' – signed and inscribed – pen and black ink and watercolour with touches of white heightening – 13¾ x 10¼in.
(Christie's) **$5,843** **£3,520**

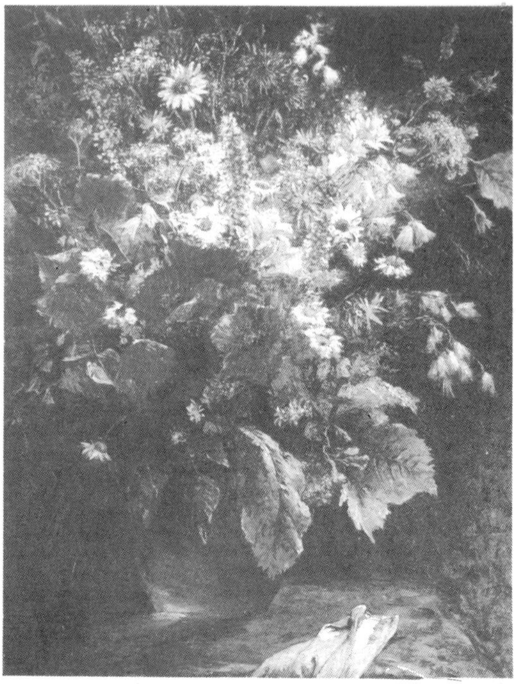

JEANNE MARIA CHARLOTTA BAUCK – Poppies, Daisies, Cowslips And Tulips In A Vase On A Ledge With A Pair Of Gloves – signed – 33½ x 26in.
(Christie's) **$4.752** **£3,300**

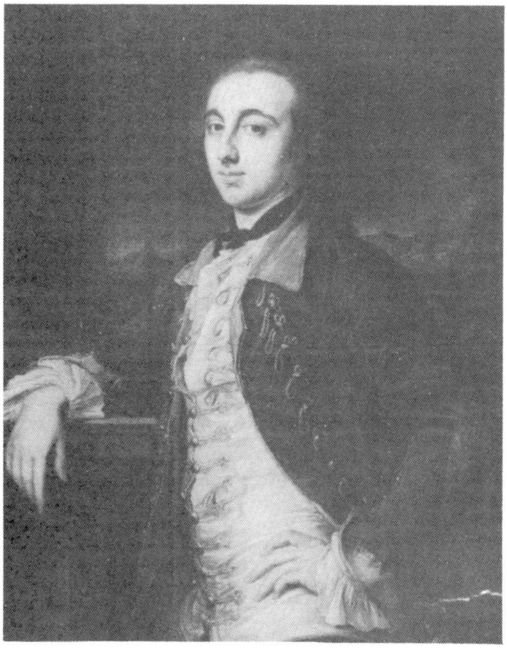

POMPEO GIROLAMO BATONI, Circle of – Portrait Of A Gentleman, Half Length, In A Green Coat, With Red Collar And Cuffs, Trimmed With Gold Braid, And A White Waistcoat, An Italianate Landscape Beyond – 38½ x 29in.
(Christie's) **$6,480** **£4,320**

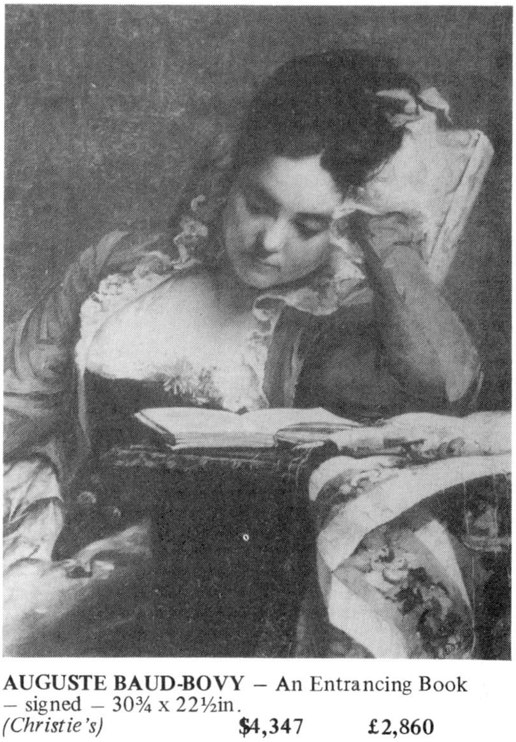

AUGUSTE BAUD-BOVY – An Entrancing Book – signed – 30¾ x 22½in.
(Christie's) **$4,347** **£2,860**

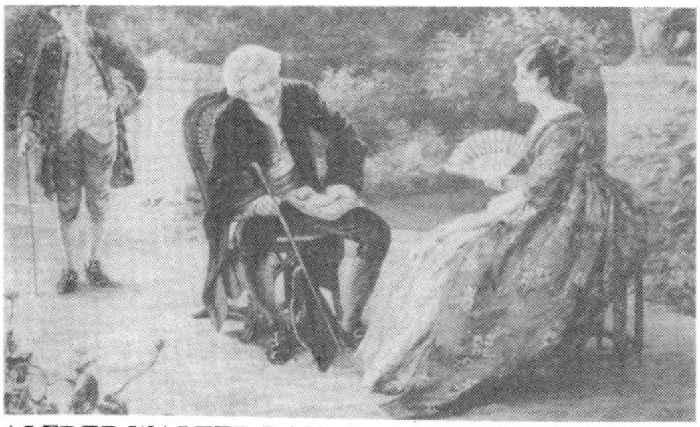

ALFRED WALTER BAYES – 'Sweet Was Her Smile But Not For Me . . .' – signed – oil on canvas – 19¼ x 23¾in.
(Christie's) **$1,524** **£935**

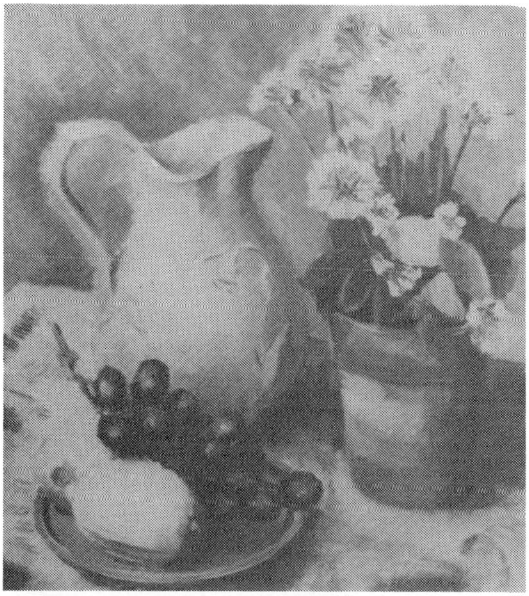

KEITH BAYNES – Still Life With Blue Jug – signed – oil on canvas – 51 x 40.5 cm.
(Phillips) **$381** **£230**

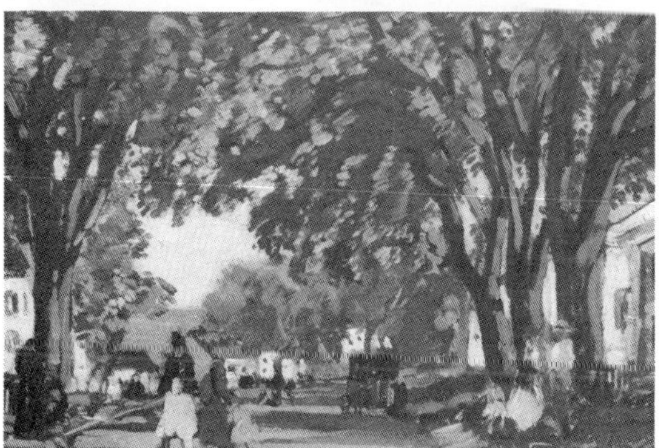

GIFFORD BEAL – New England Elms – signed – oil on board – 20 x 24in.
(Christie's) **$19,800** **£13,919**

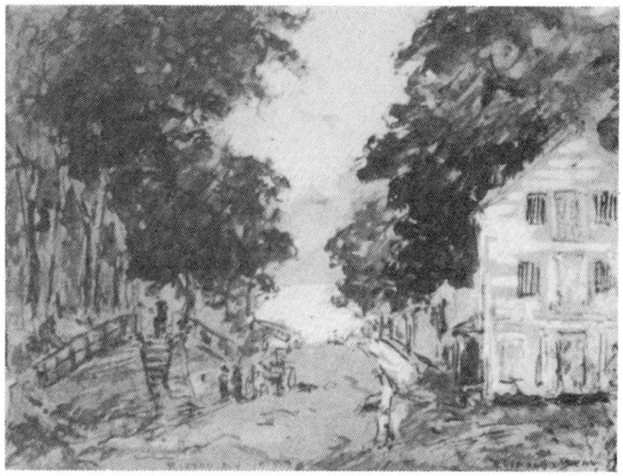

REYNOLDS BEAL – Rifton, New York – signed and dated 1915, also inscribed – watercolour, gouache and pencil on brown paper – 8½ x 11¾in.
(Christie's) **$1,650** **£1,147**

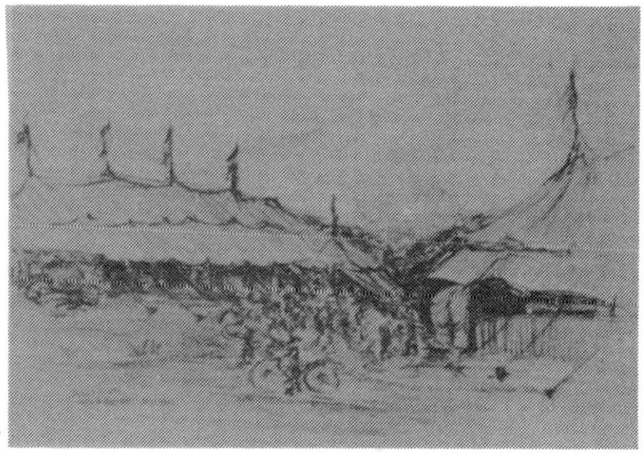

REYNOLDS BEAL – 'Sells Floto, Newburyport' – signed and dated 1928 – coloured crayon on paper – 10¾ x 15¼in.
(Robt. W. Skinner Inc.) **$500** **£306**

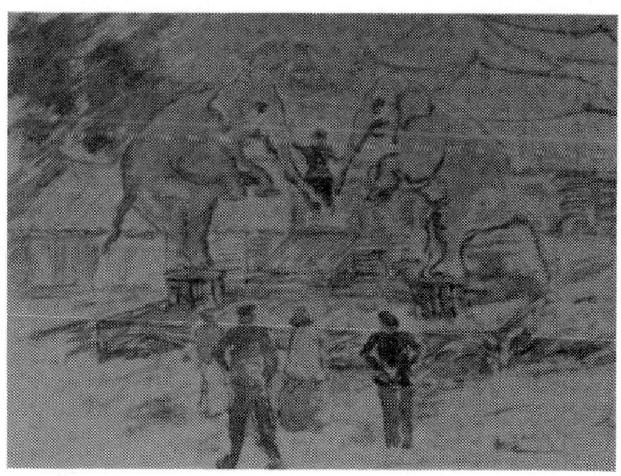

REYNOLDS BEAL – Elephants – signed – watercolour and graphite on paper – 8¾ x 12in.; 'Sells Floto Montreal' – signed and dated 1927 – watercolour and graphite on paper – 7 x 10in.; and 'Downey Bros. Gloucester' – signed and dated 1934 – graphite and crayon on paper – 9 x 12in.
(Robt. W. Skinner Inc.) **$1,500** **£920 Three**

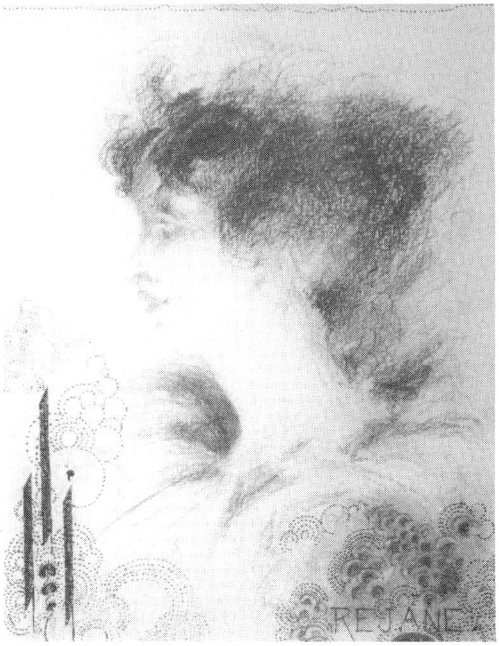

AUBREY BEARDSLEY – Rejane – signed and inscribed – red chalk, pen and ink on paper – 7¾ x 6¼in.
(Christie's) **$47,520 £33,000**

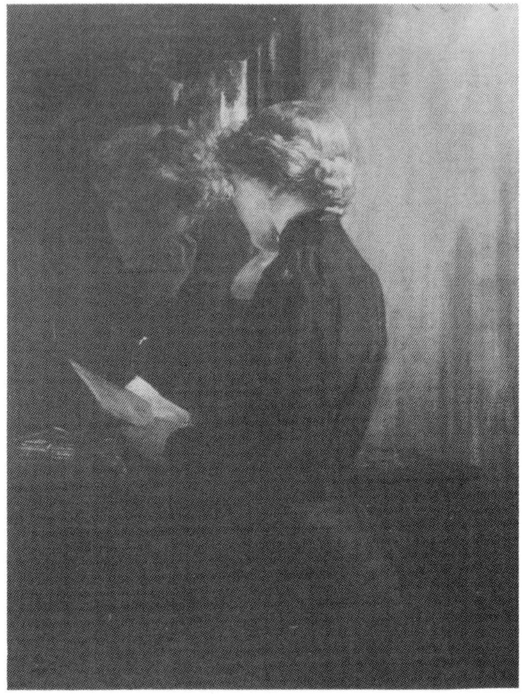

JAMES CARROLL BECKWITH – The Letter – signed – oil on canvas – 50 x 34¼in.
(Christie's) **$19,800 £13,919**

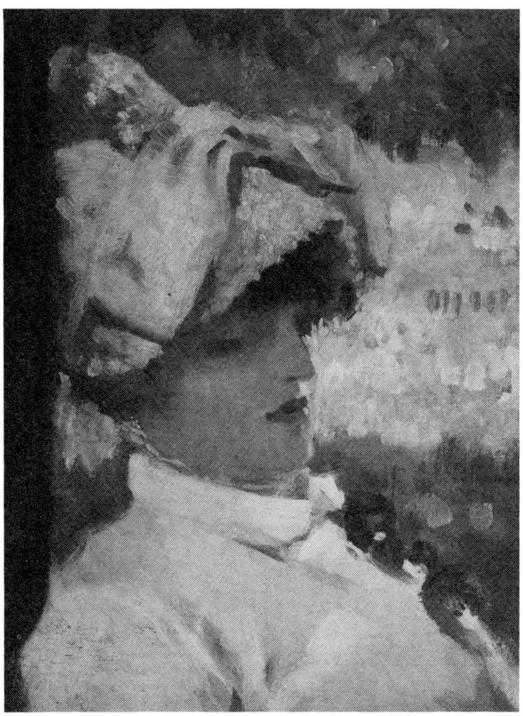

JAMES CARROLL BECKWITH – Celine In The Garden – signed, dated '82 and inscribed on the reverse – oil on panel – 13¾ x 10¼in.
(Christie's) **$8,800 £5,483**

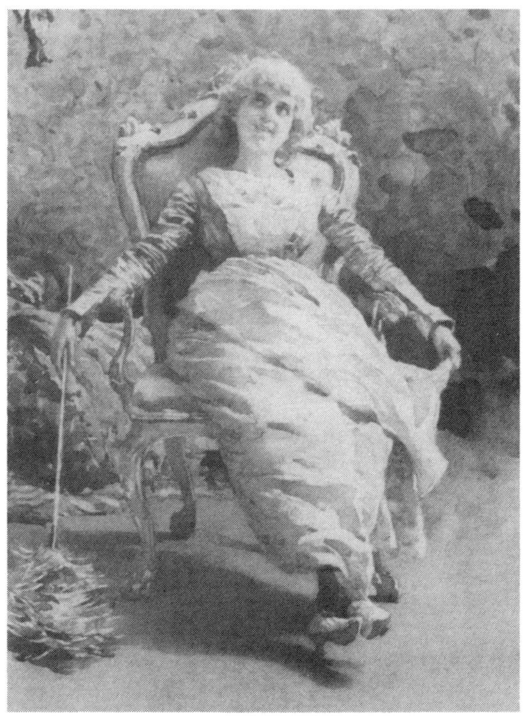

PAOLO BEDINI – Women In Interiors – signed – watercolour – 13¾ x 7¾in.
(Christie's) **$5,478 £3,300 Four**

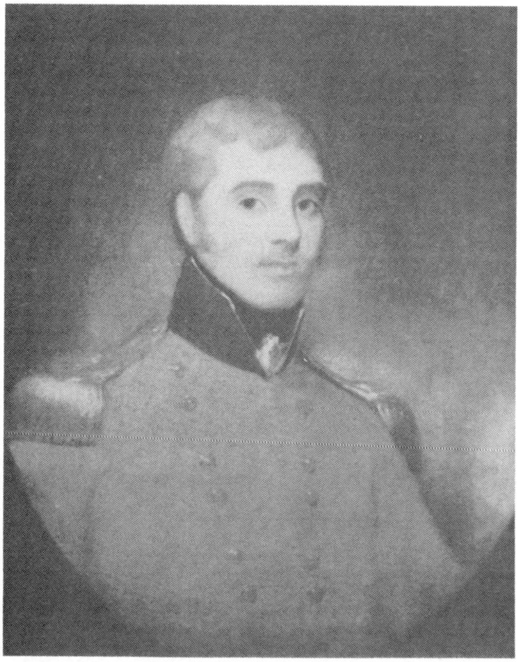

SIR WILLIAM BEECHY, Follower of – Portrait Of An Officer, Half Length, A Scarlet Frock Coat With Green Facings And Gold Epaulettes – oil on canvas – 30 x 25in.
(Christie's) **$645** **£396**

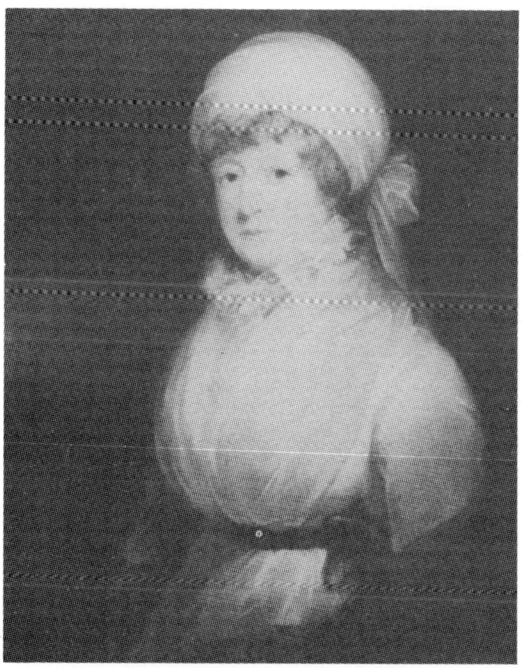

SIR WILLIAM BEECHEY – A Portrait Of Lady Pollock, Half-Length And Wearing White Dress And Headgear – oil on canvas – 30 x 25in.
(Phillips) **$1,328** **£800**

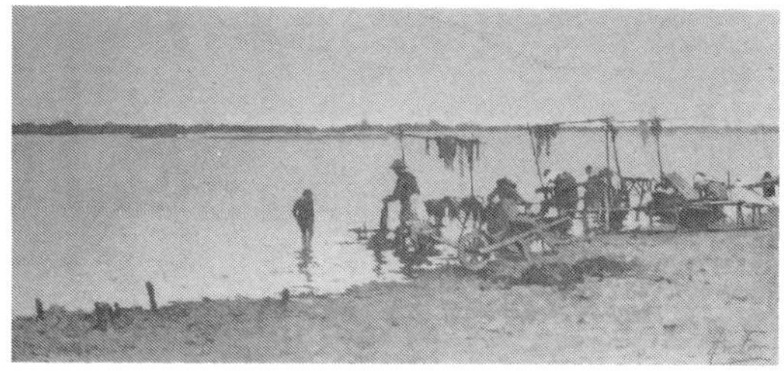

ACHILLE FORMIS BEFANI – Washerwomen At The Water's Edge – signed – on panel – 10½ x 21¾in.
(Christie's) **$36,520** **£22,000**

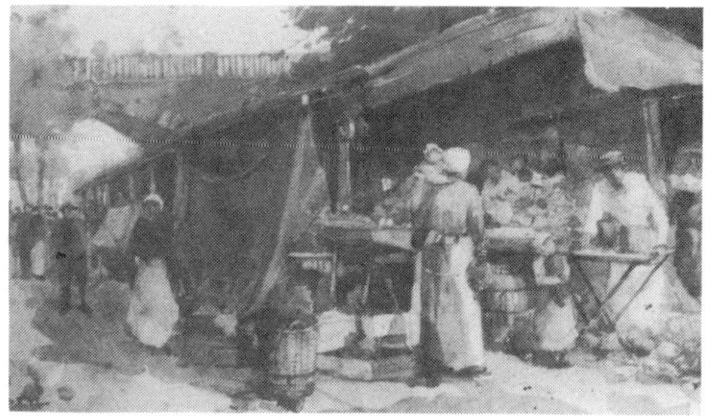

LILIAN RUSSELL BELL – French Street Scene – watercolour – 12 x 20in.
(Michael G. Matthews) **$672** **£420**

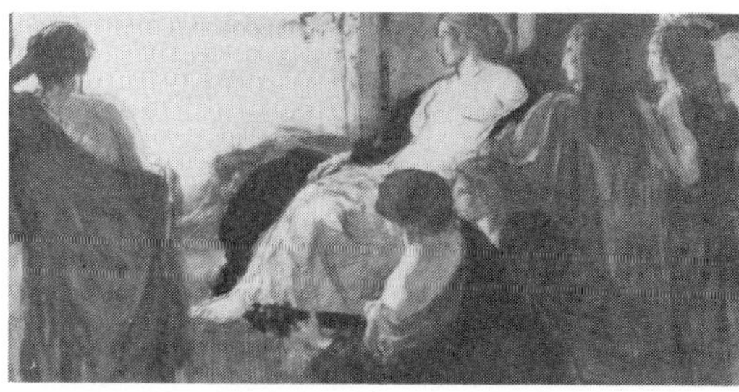

ROBERT ANNING BELL – Allegorical Scene – black chalk, brush and ink and watercolour and traces of pencil – 29 x 56cm.
(Phillips) **$664** **£400**

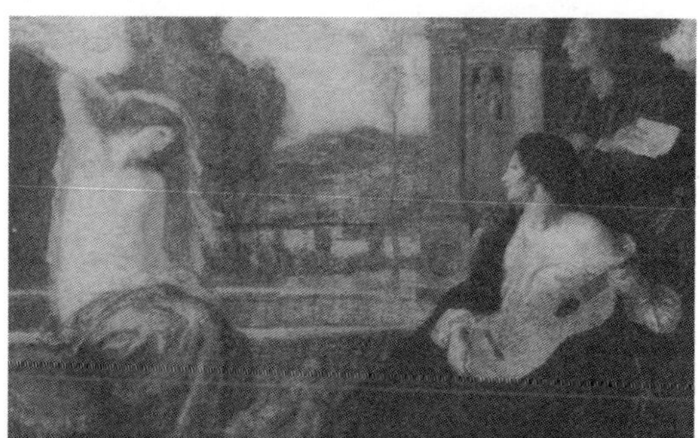

ROBERT ANNING BELL – Venus And The Dilettanti – signed and dated 1906 – oil on canvas – 14 x 21in.
(Christie's) **$1,415** **£990**

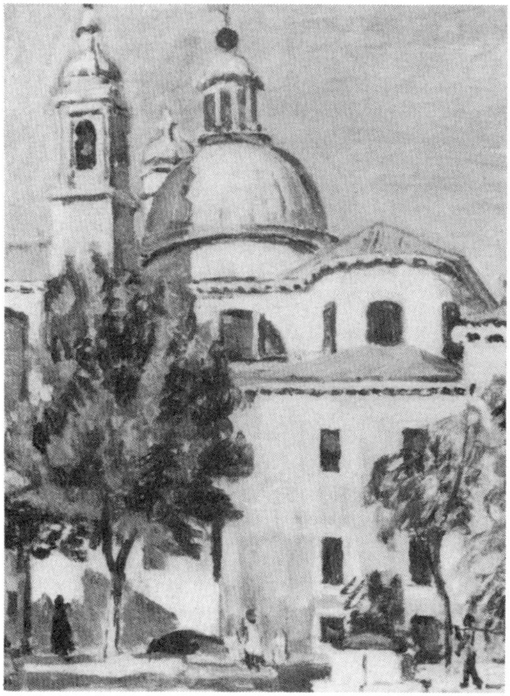

VANESSA BELL – The Church Of The Jesuati, Venice – signed with initials, and signed and inscribed on the reverse – oil on canvas – 16½ x 13in.
(Christie's) **$1,573** **£1,100**

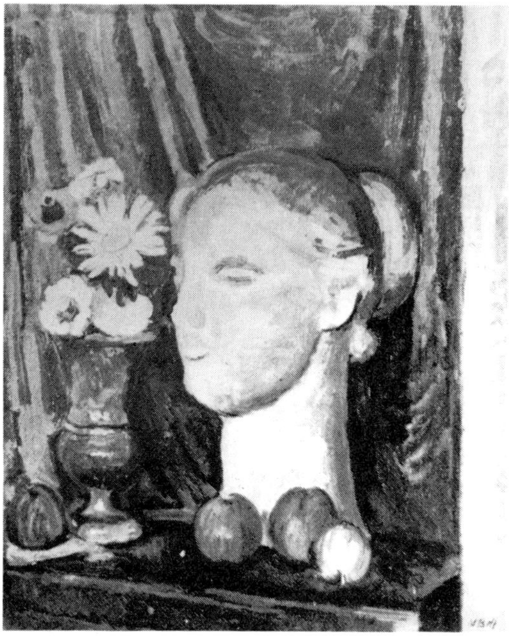

VANESSA BELL – Still Life At Charleston – signed – oil on canvas – 22 x 18¼in.
(Christie's) **$2,417** **£1,540**

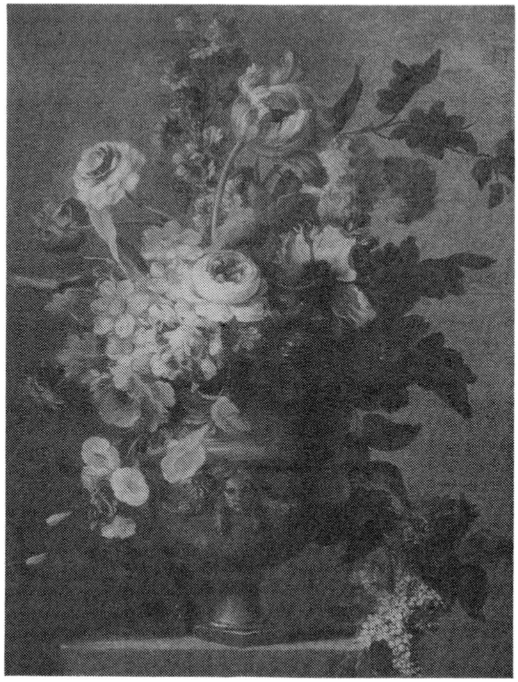

MICHEL BRUNO BELLENGE – An Ornamental Vase Of Flowers On A Stone Ledge – signed – on canvas – 33½ x 28in.
(Phillips) **$9,960** **£6,000**

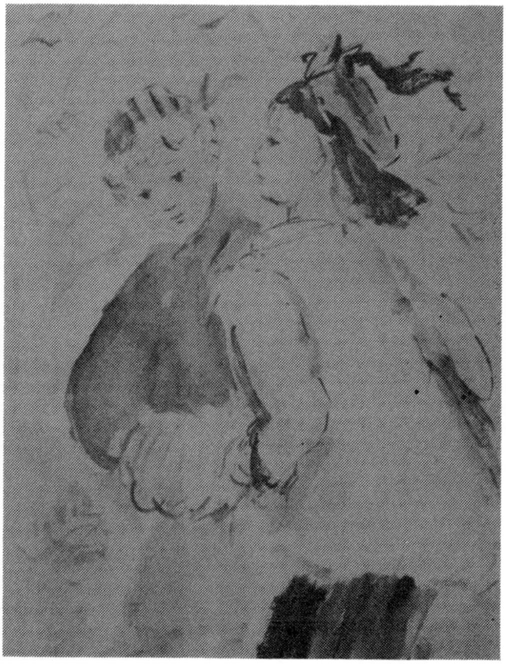

ELINOR BELLINGHAM-SMITH – A Wintry Day – signed with initials – watercolour on grey paper – 46 x 29cm.
(Phillips) **$332** **£200**

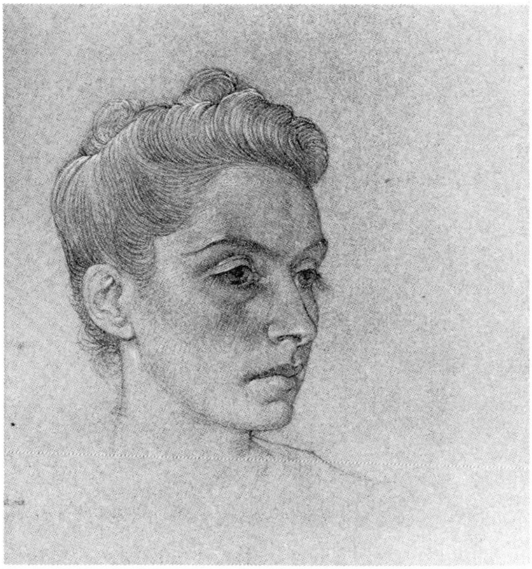

HANS BELLMER – Portrait de Madame Bellmer – recto – signed – pencil heightened with red crayon and white gouache on paper – 11¾ x 8¾in. – Sans Titre – verso – signed and dated 1943 – pencil heightened with white gouache – 12 x 9½in.
(Christie's) **$2,376 £1,650**

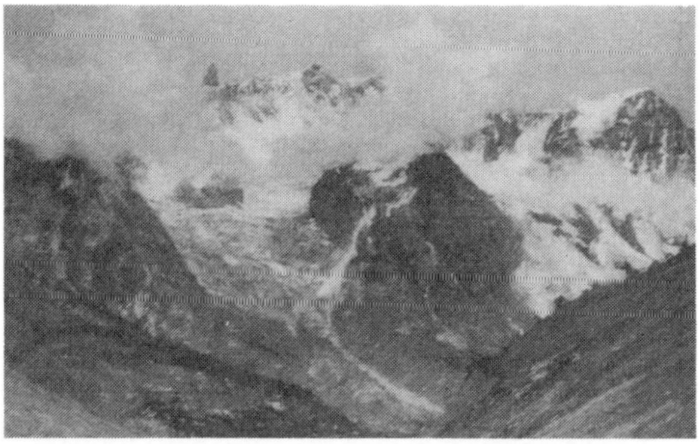

GIORGIO BELLONI – Landscape And Seascape Studies – signed – on board and panel – 11¾ x 15¾in. – 27.
(Christie's) **$40,172 £24,200**

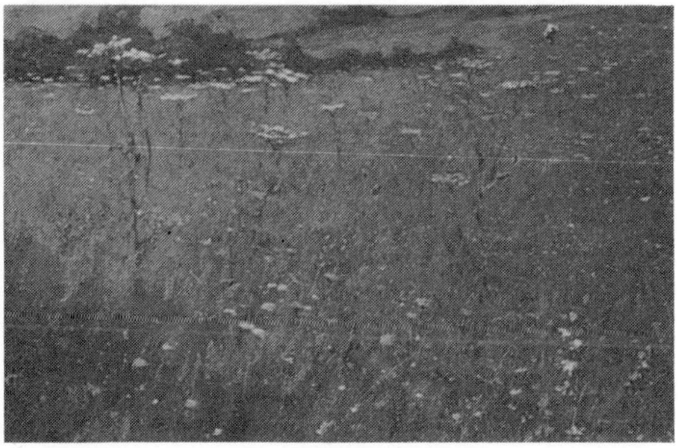

GIORGIO BELLONI – In The Meadows – signed – on panel – 10¼ x 13¾in.
(Christie's) **$5,843 £3,520**

GIORGIO BELLONI – Genoa; and Milan; and Landscape And Seascape Studies – signed – on panel and board – 10¼ x 14in. – 23.
(Christie's) **$30,129 £18,150**

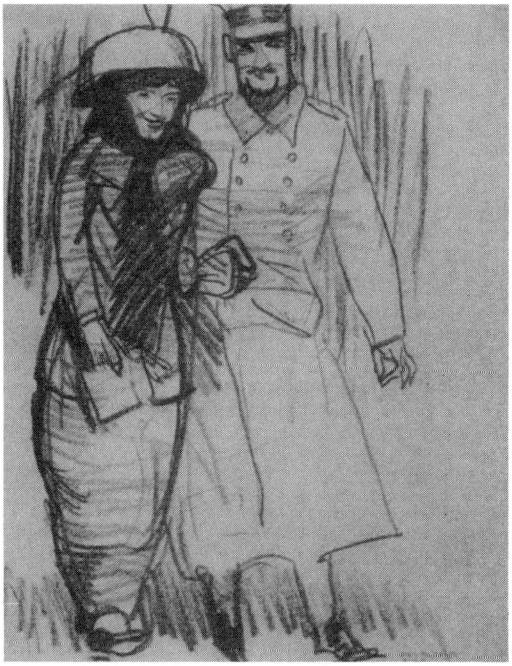

GEORGE BELLOWS – Walking Out – bears signature and initials – crayon on paper – 10 x 8in.
(Christie's) **$2,640 £1,644**

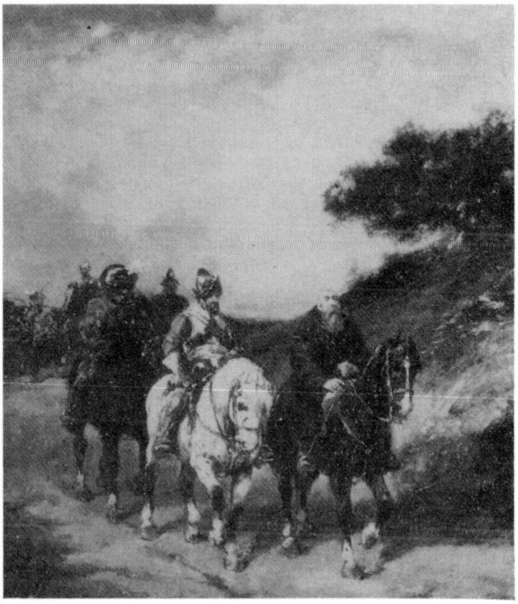

EMILE LOUIS BENASSIT – The Inquisitors – signed – on panel – 10¾ x 8½in.
(Christie's) **$1,170 £770**

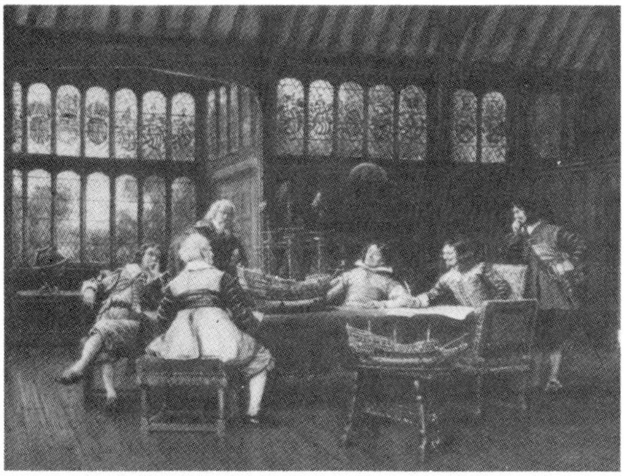

FRANK MOSS BENNETT – The Ship Designers – signed and dated 1946 – 15¼ x 19½in.
(Christie's) **$3,722 £2,640**

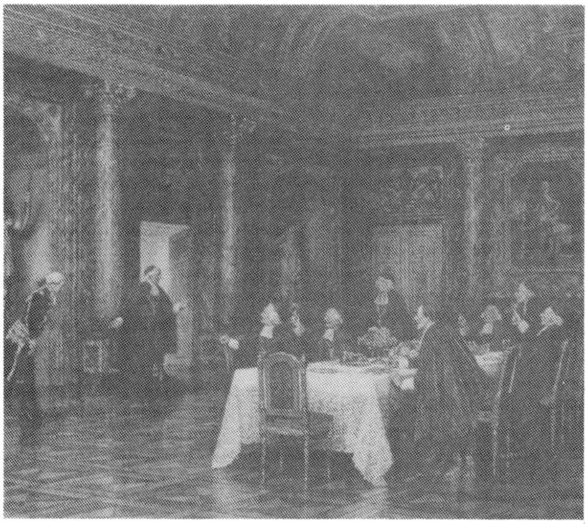

FRANK MOSS BENNETT – A Late Dinner Guest At The Vatican – signed and dated 1936 – on canvas – 24 x 30in.
(Phillips) **$22,540 £14,000**

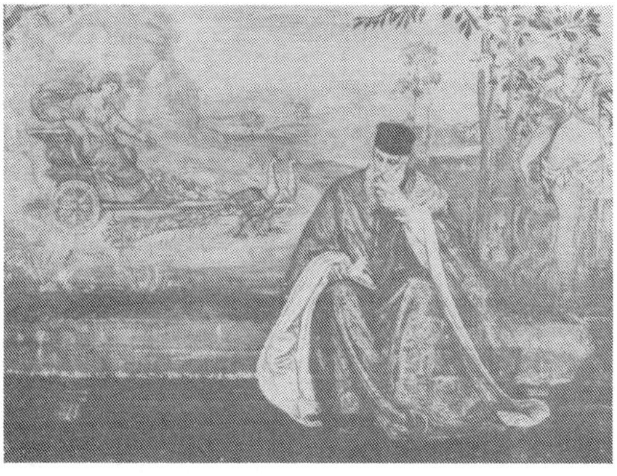

EUGENE BENSON – A State Secret, Of A Venetian Senator – signed, also signed, inscribed and dated '15 on reverse – on canvas – 15 x 21½in.
(Phillips) **$1,771 £1,000**

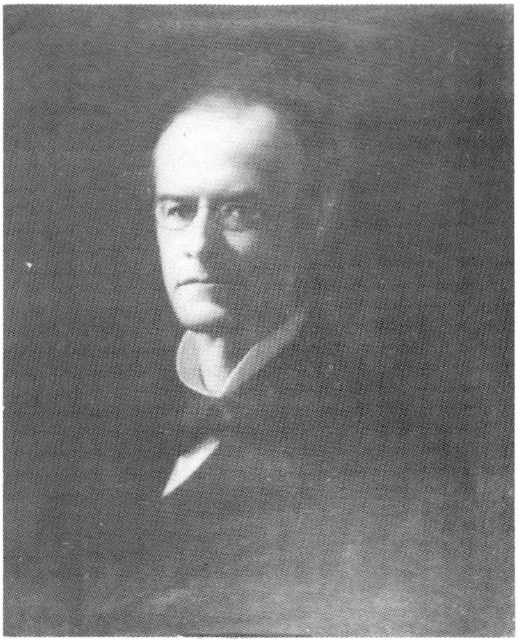

FRANK WESTON BENSON – Portrait Of Professor Charles Edward Hamlin – signed and dated '87 – oil on canvas – 27 x 22in.
(Robt. W. Skinner Inc.) **$800 £555**

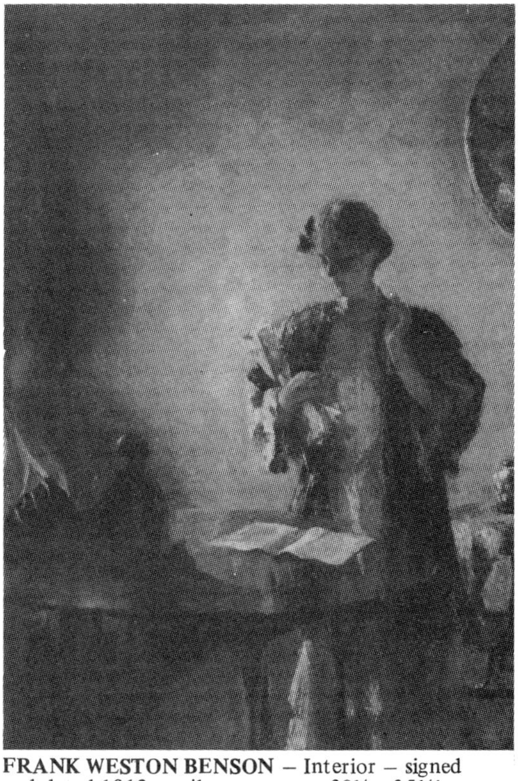

FRANK WESTON BENSON – Interior – signed and dated 1912 – oil on canvas – 30¼ x 25¼in.
(Christie's) **$38,500 £27,065**

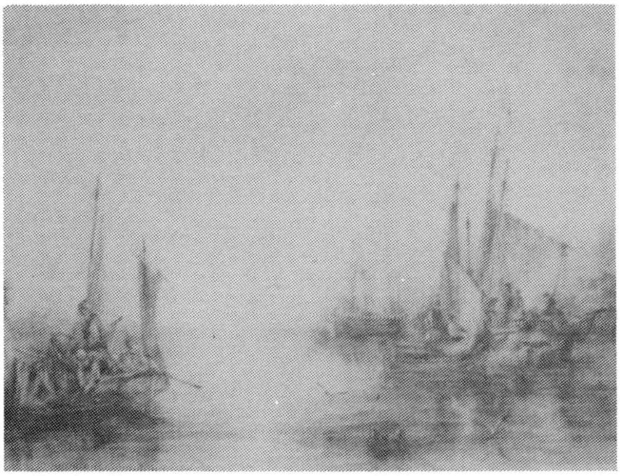

CHARLES BENTLEY – Pulling In The Nets – signed – watercolour – 37 x 49cm.
(Phillips) **$2,037** **£1,250**

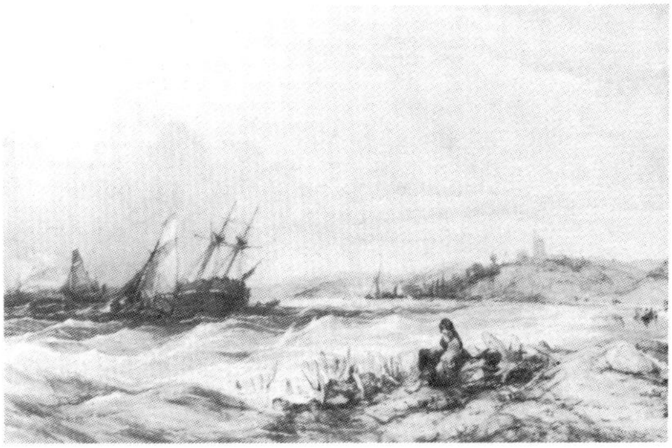

CHARLES BENTLEY – A Collier On A Sand Bank Off Leigh-on-Thames – signed and dated 1845 – pencil and watercolour heightened with white – 19¾ x 29¼in.
(Christie's) **$3,240** **£2,160**

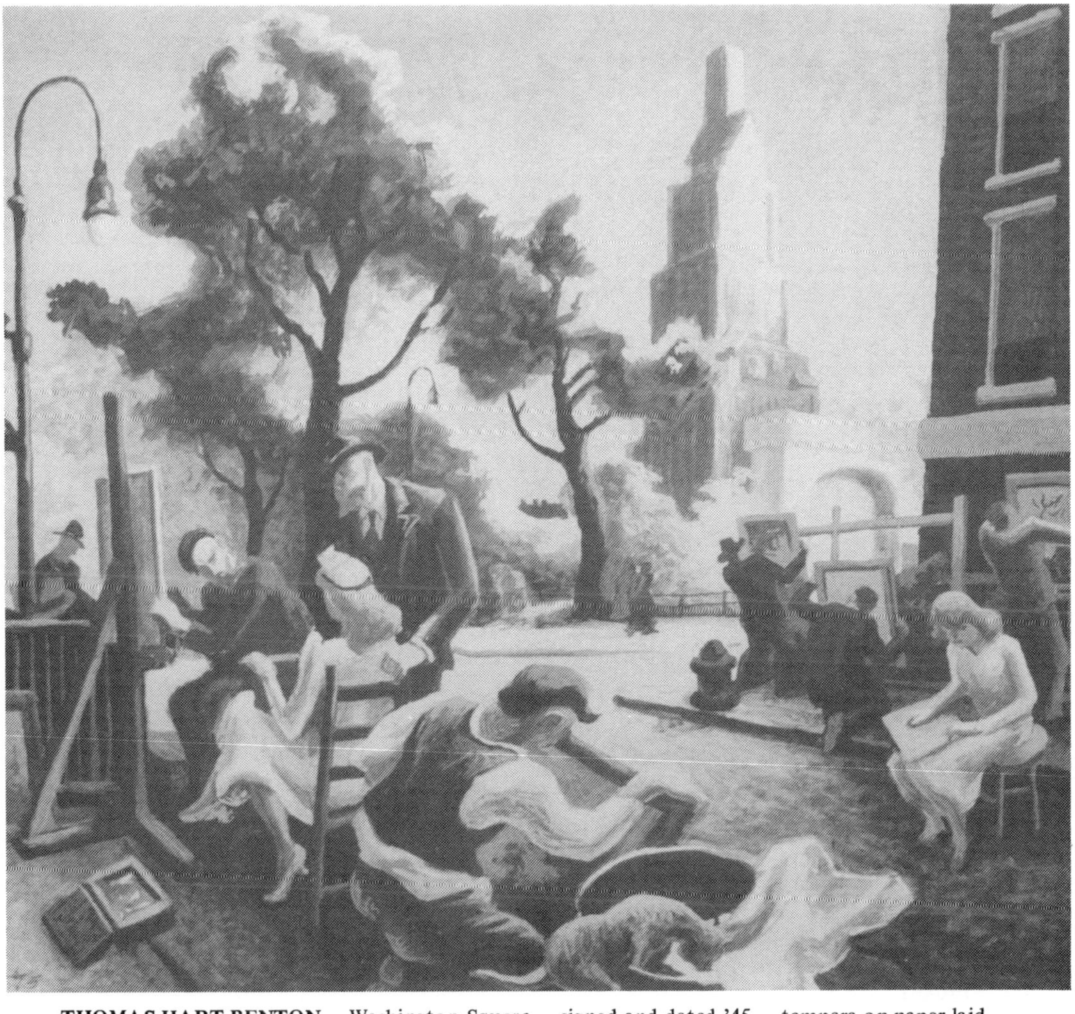

THOMAS HART BENTON – Washington Square – signed and dated '45 – tempera on paper laid down on board – 13¾ x 16¾in. *(Christie's)* **$88,000** **£54,832**

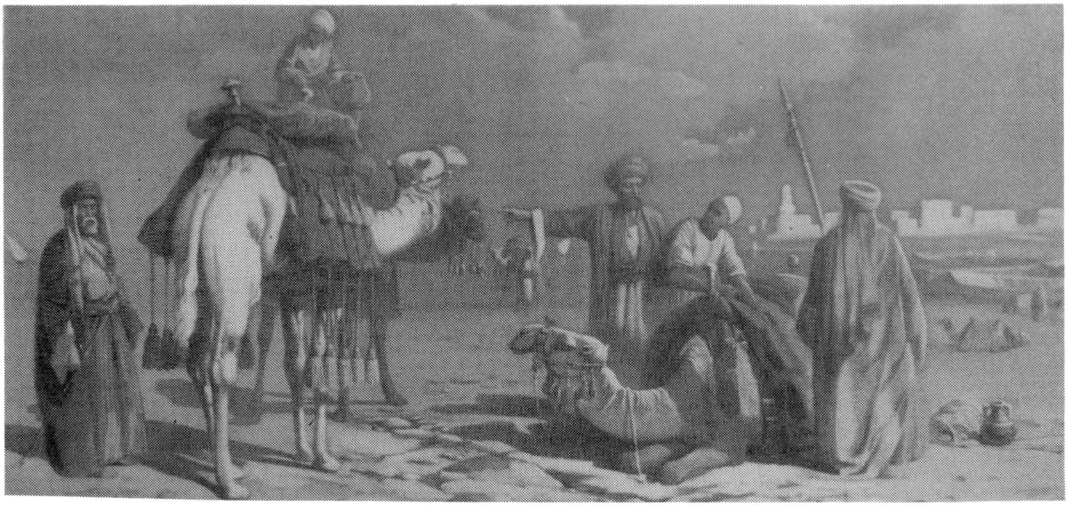

JOSEPH AUSTIN BENWELL – **A** Caravan On The Shore – signed – pencil and watercolour heightened with white on brown paper – 8¼ x 17in. *(Christie's)* **$766 £462**

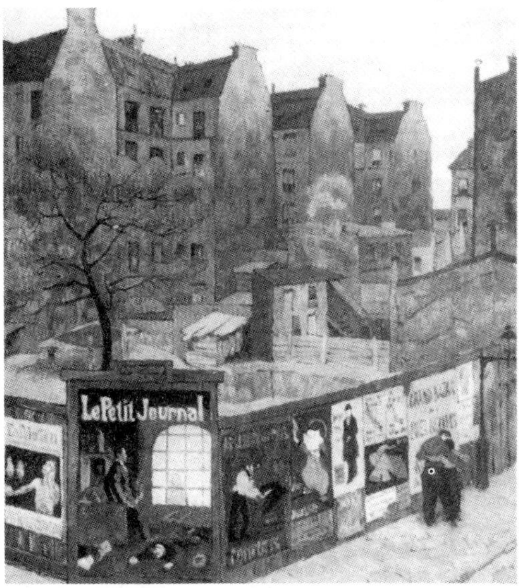

GINAR BERGSTEN – Le Petit Journal – signed and dated 1915 – oil on canvas – 25¼ x 21in. *(Christie's)* **$4,455 £3,080**

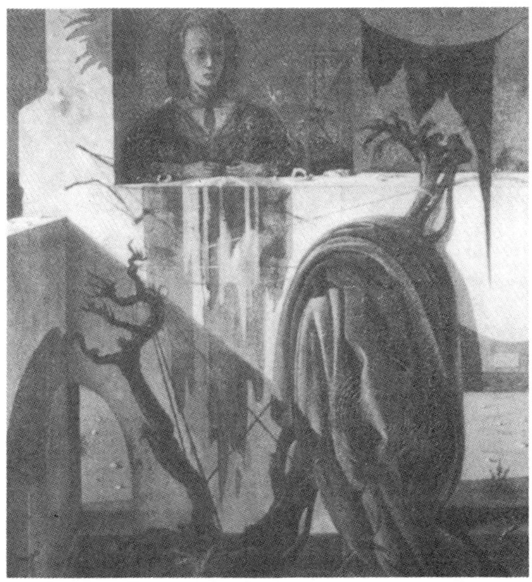

EUGENE BERMAN – Violetta – signed and dated 1942 on the reverse – oil on canvas – 52 x 38¼in. *(Christie's)* **$2,860 £1,989**

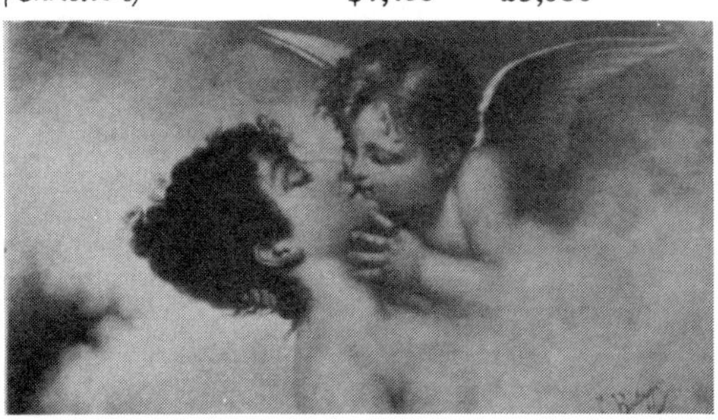

F. BERLINGIERI – **A** Visit From Cupid – signed – oil on canvas – 27½ x 37in. *(Christie's)* **$1,232 £770**

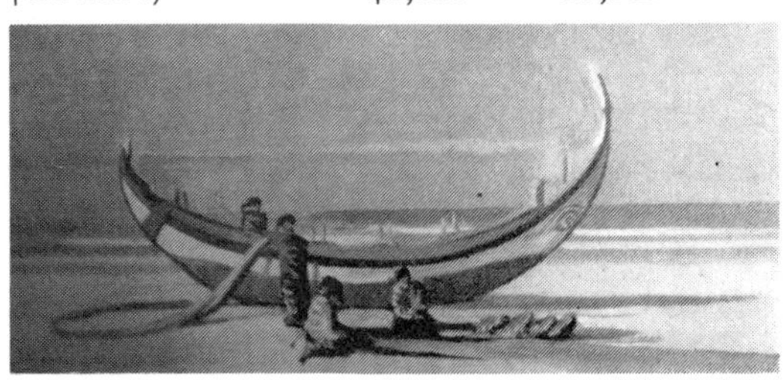

LEONID BERMAN – Barque de Caparica – signed with initial and dated '47, signed, dated and inscribed on the reverse – oil on canvas – 8½ x 16in. *(Christie's)* **$968 £605**

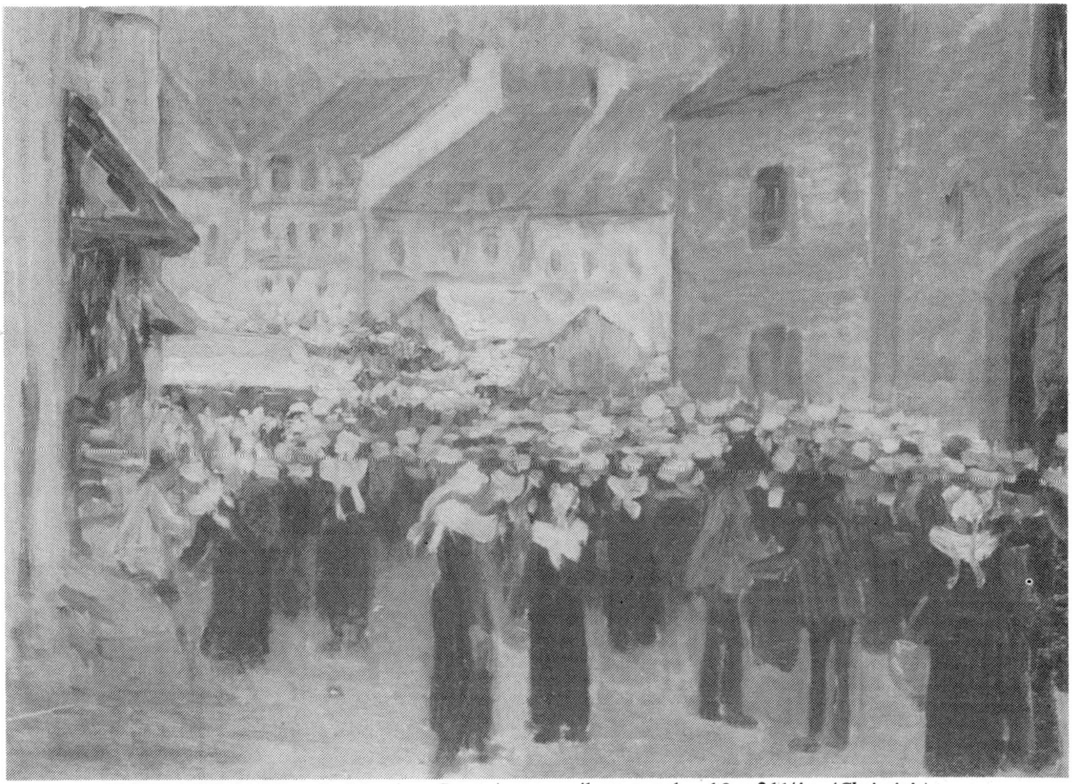

EMILE BERNARD – Le Marche a Pont-Aven – oil on panel – 18 x 21½in. *(Christie's)*
$47,762 £28,600

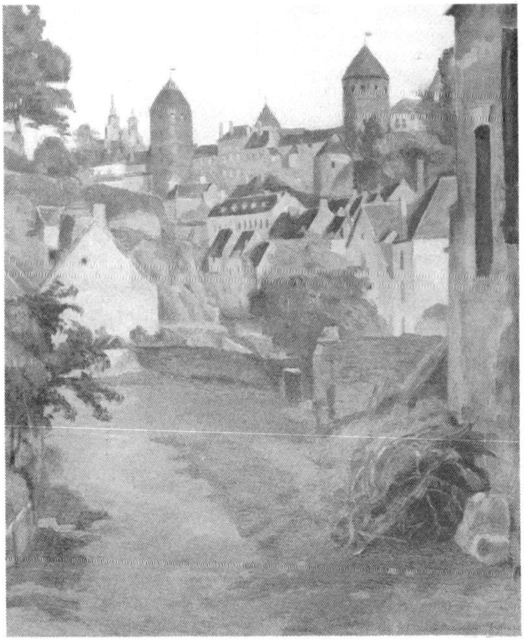

EMILE BERNARD – Vue de Semur avec Chateau – signed and inscribed – oil on canvas – 29 x 24in.
(Christie's) **$14,256 £9,900**

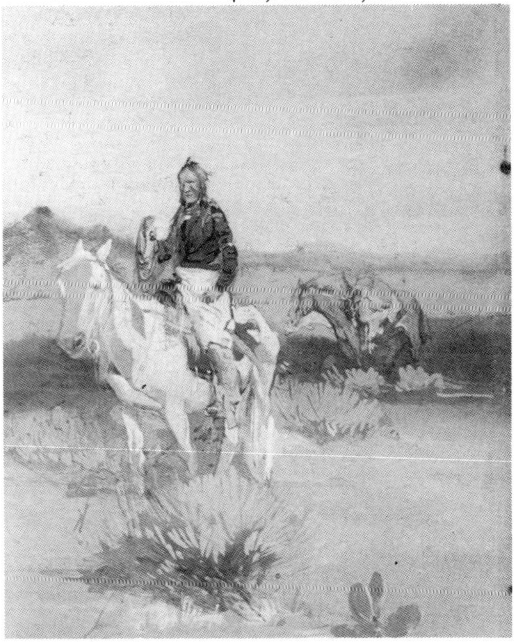

OSCAR EDMUND BERNINGHAUS – Indian With Packhorse – signed – watercolour on paper – 8½ x 5¾in.
(Christie's) **$9,900 £6,959**

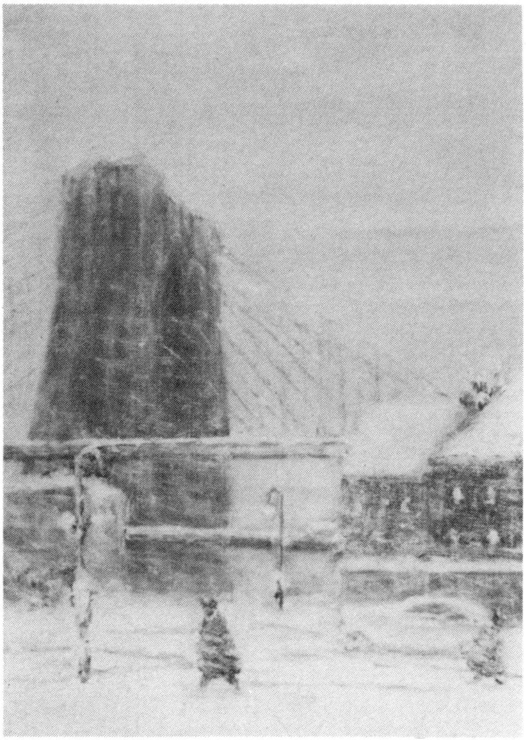

JOHANN BERTHELSEN – Snow On Brooklyn Bridge; and Outside The Ritz – signed – oil on canvas board – 15¾ x 12in., the other 15¾ x 11¾in.
(Christie's) **$4,400** **£3,061** Two

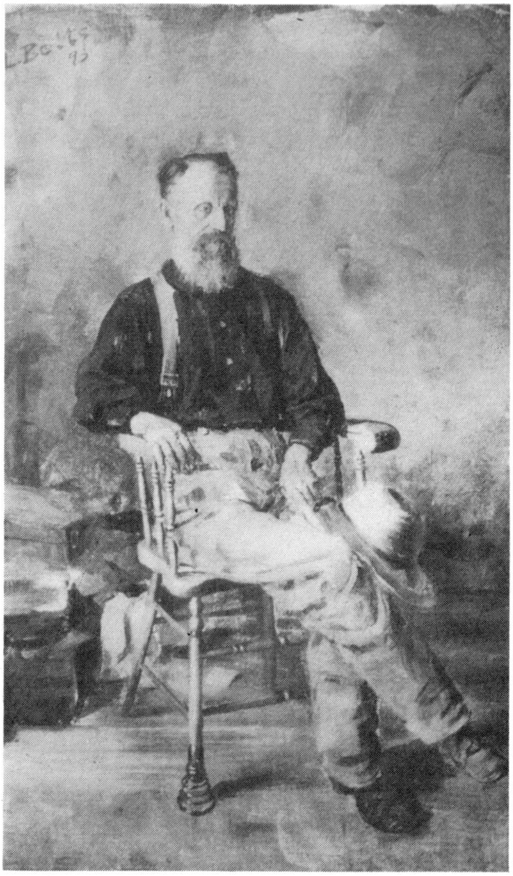

LOUIS BETTS – Old Man In A Spring Rocker – signed and dated '93 – oil on canvas – 11 x 14in.
(Christie's) **$4,180** **£2,604**

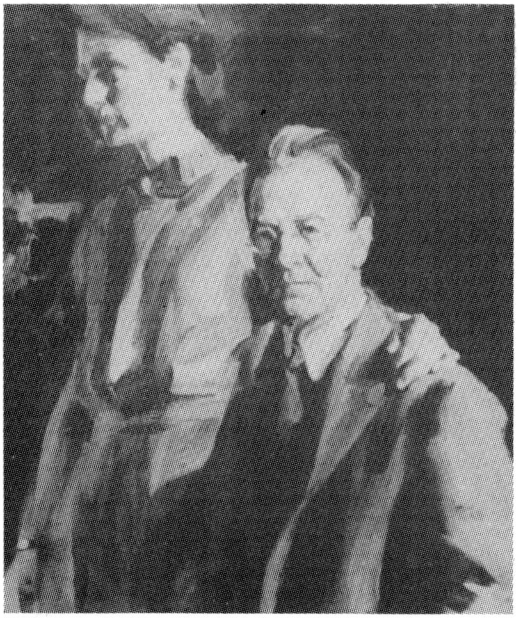

LOUIS BETTS – Portrait Of A Gentleman With His Daughter – signed – oil on canvas – 30 x 25in.
(Robt. W. Skinner Inc.) **$700** **£429**

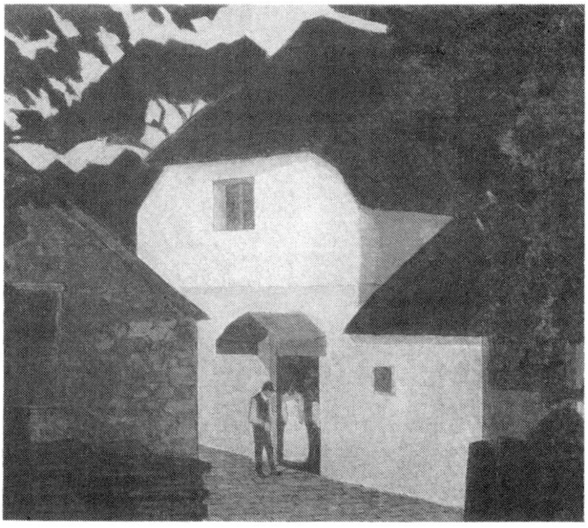

ROBERT BEVAN – Caller At The Mill – oil on canvas – 22 x 25¾in.
(Christie's) **$23,314** **£14,850**

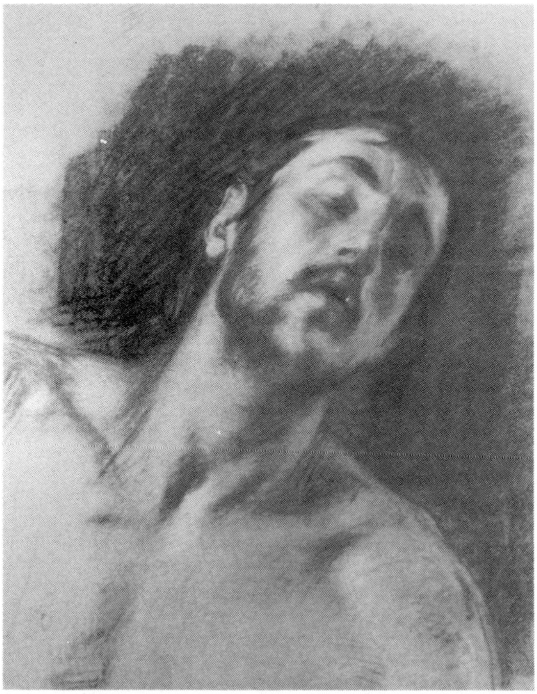

MOSE BIANCHI – Figure Studies – some pastel, the majority black chalk – 13¼ x 19¼in. – 21.
(Christie's) **$6,938** **£4,180**

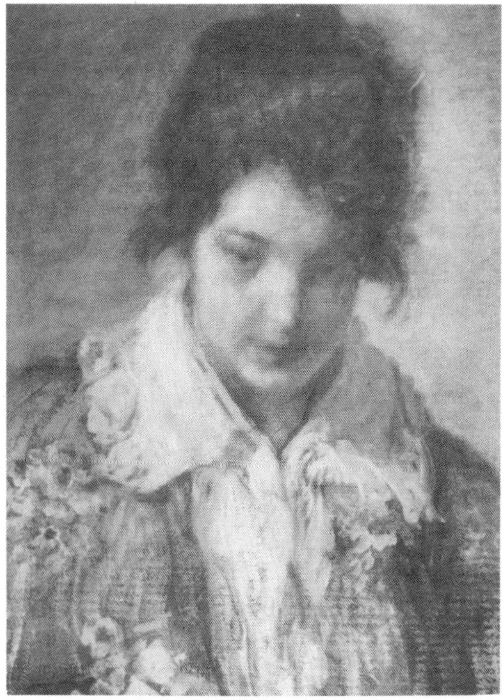

MOSE BIANCHI – Portrait Of A Lady – signed – on board – 19¾ x 13¾in.
(Christie's) **$11,869** **£7,150**

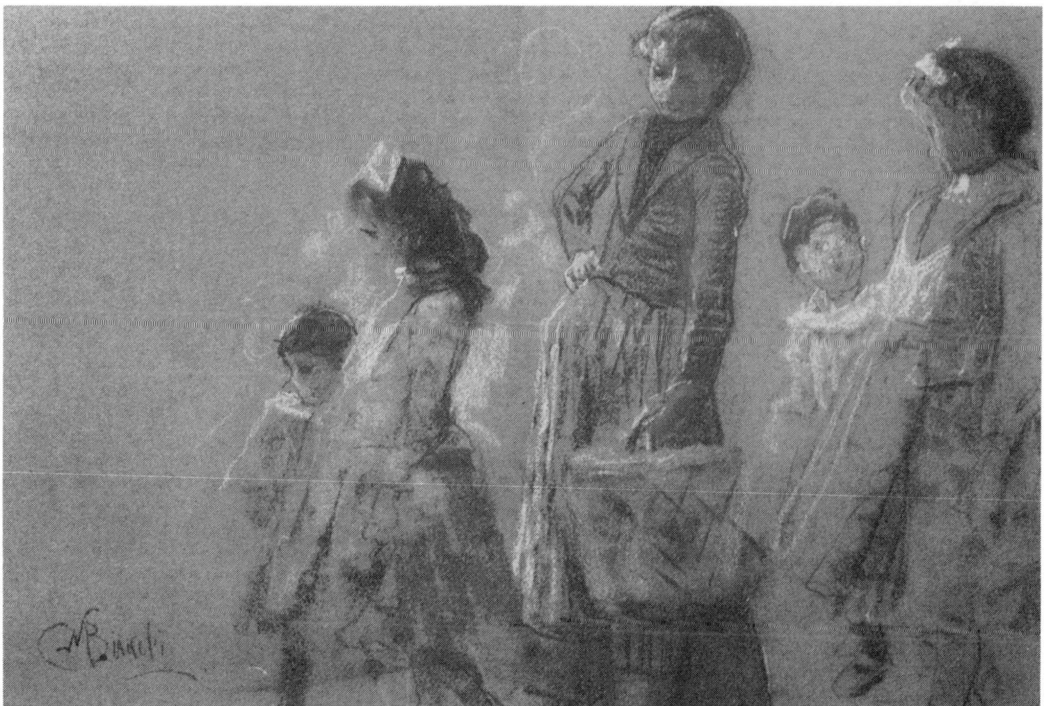

MOSE BIANCHI – Figure Studies – signed – pastels – 14¾ x 20¾in. – and two portraits.
(Christie's) **$18,260 £11,000 Three**

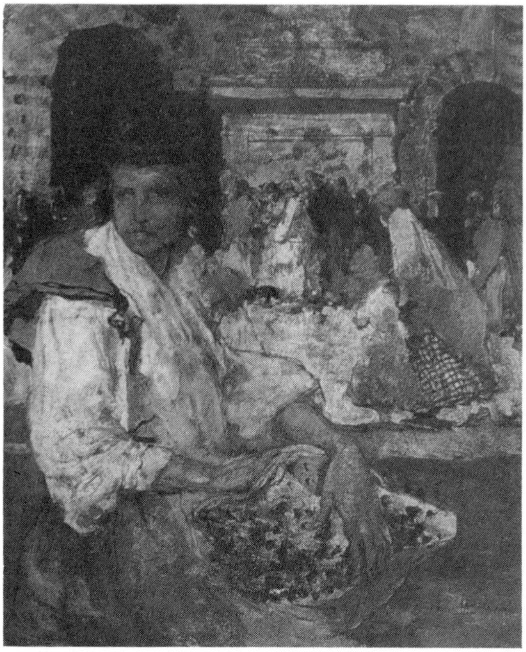

MOSE BIANCHI – The Flowerseller – signed, and signed with initials on the reverse – on board – 15¾ x 13in.
(Christie's) **$43,824** **£26,400**

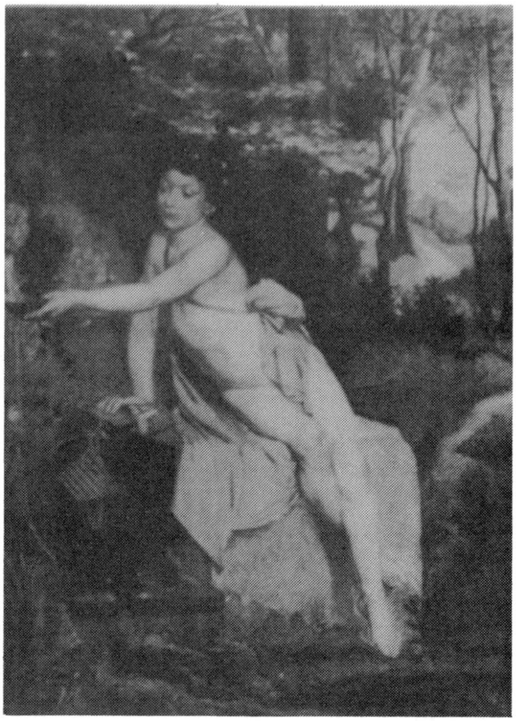

JULES VAN BIESBROECK – Pan – signed with monogram and dated 1872 – oil on canvas – 103 x 79cm.
(Phillips) **$2,171** **£1,300**

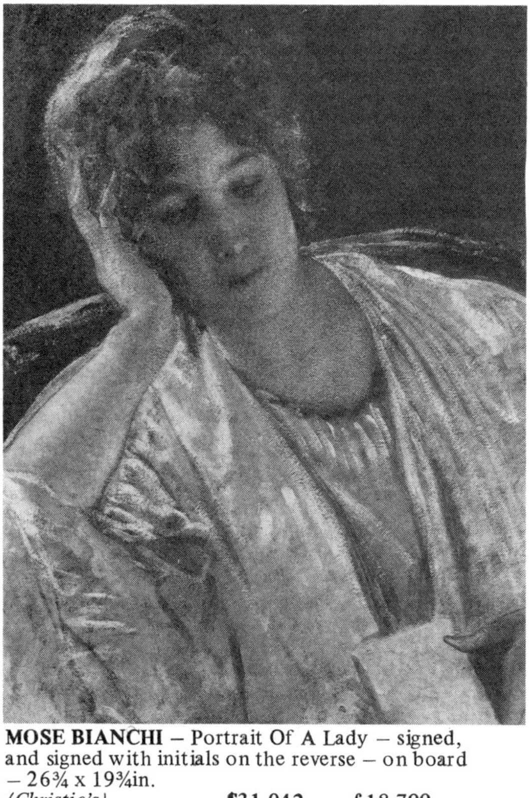

MOSE BIANCHI – Portrait Of A Lady – signed, and signed with initials on the reverse – on board – 26¾ x 19¾in.
(Christie's) **$31,042** **£18,700**

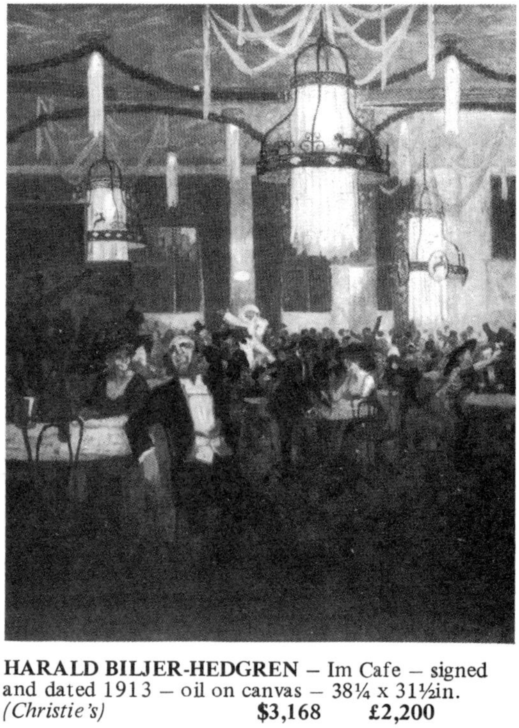

HARALD BILJER-HEDGREN – Im Cafe – signed and dated 1913 – oil on canvas – 38¼ x 31½in.
(Christie's) **$3,168** **£2,200**

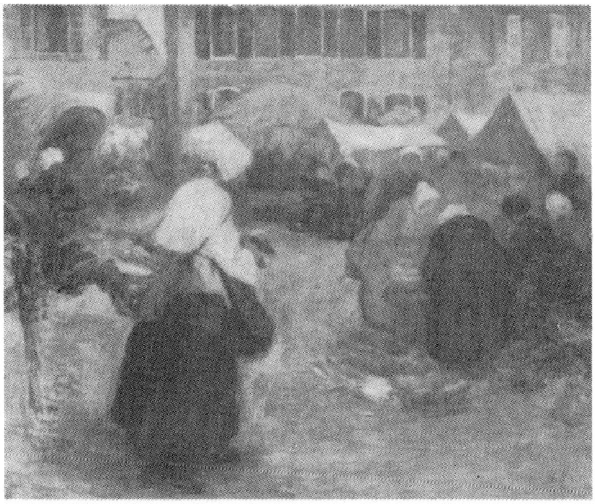

FLORENCE BILL – A Breton Market – signed – oil on canvas – 28 x 33½in.
(Christie's) **$1,022** **£715**

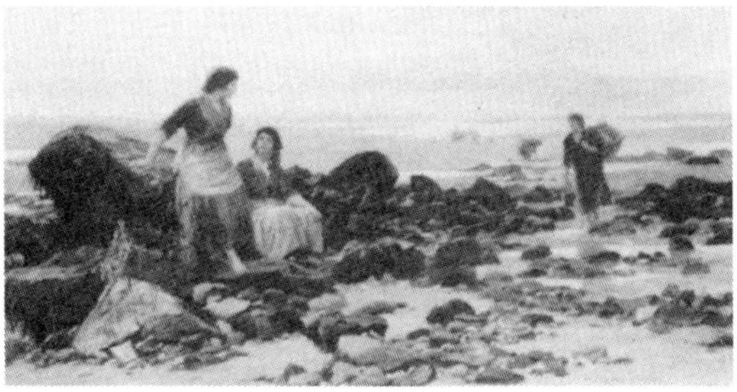

FRANK BINDLEY – 'Low Tide' – signed – oil on canvas – 28 x 51½in.
(Phillips) **$1,530** **£1,000**

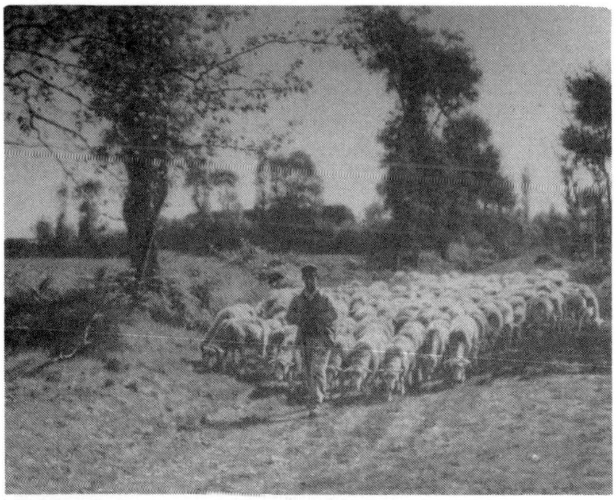

VICTOR JEAN BAPTISTE BINET – A Shepherd And His Flock In A Country Lane – signed – on canvas – 38 x 47cm.
(Phillips) **$4,032** **£2,800**

SAMUEL JOHN LAMORNA BIRCH – Summertime – signed, indistinctly inscribed on the reverse – oil on canvas – 20 x 24¼in.
(Christie's) **$3,799** **£2,420**

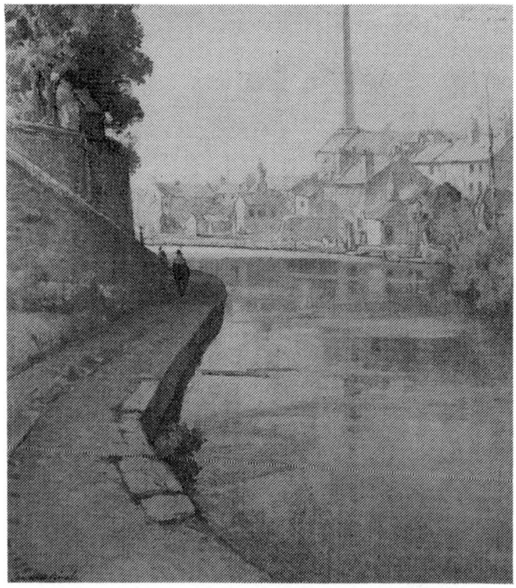

SAMUEL JOHN LAMORNA BIRCH – Lancaster Canal – signed – oil on canvas – 61 x 56cm.
(Phillips) **$5,760** **£3,600**

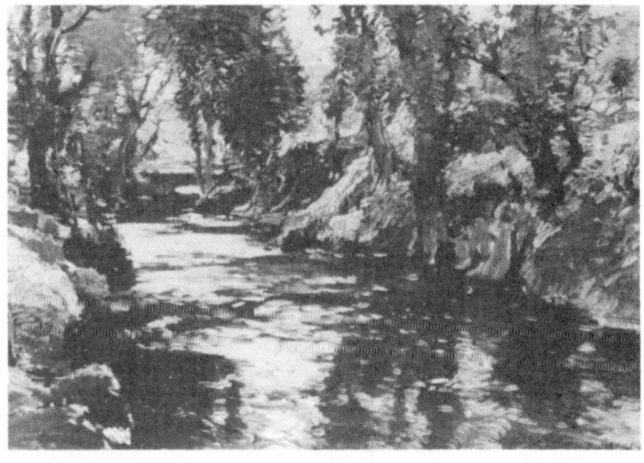

SAMUEL JOHN LAMORNA BIRCH – The Dappled River – signed – oil on canvas – 37.5 x 52.5cm.
(Phillips) **$6,426** **£4,200**

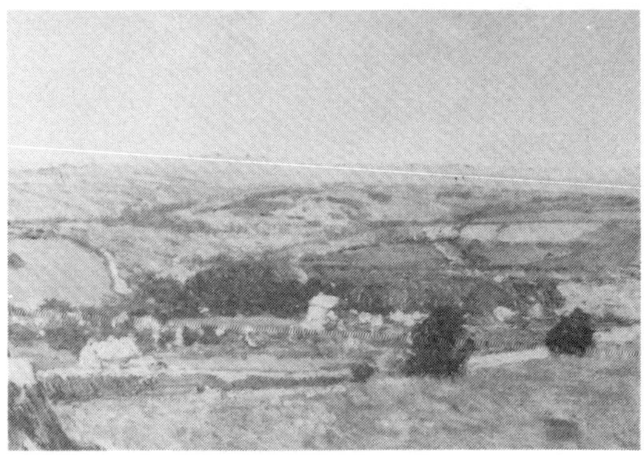

SAMUEL JOHN LAMORNA BIRCH – Extensive Landscape – oil on board – 25 x 35cm.
(Phillips) **$612** **£400**

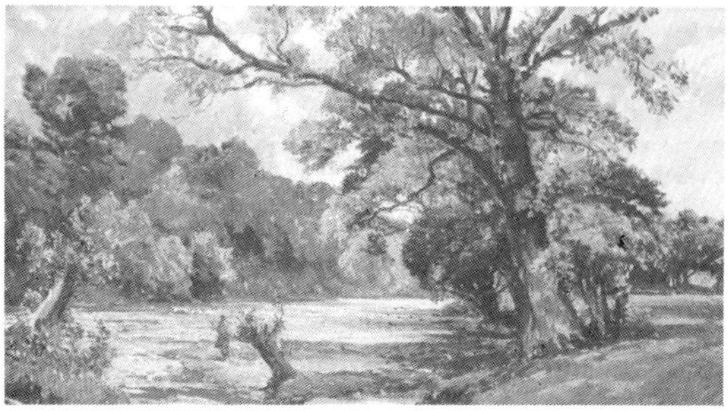

SAMUEL JOHN LAMORNA BIRCH – The Joy Of A June Day – signed and dated 1947, and signed and inscribed on a label on the frame – 22 x 30in.
(Christie's) **$4,719** **£3,300**

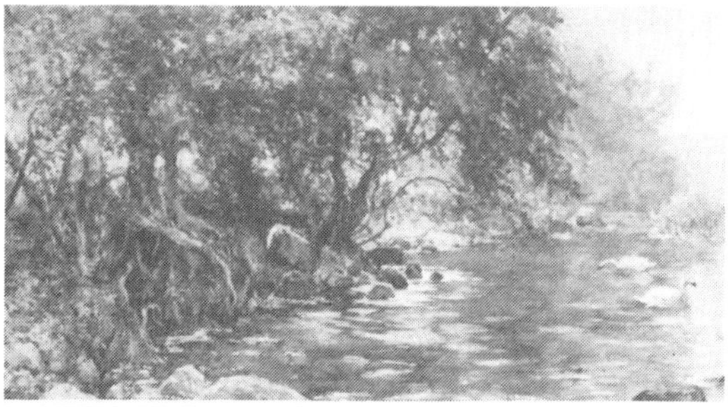

SAMUEL JOHN LAMORNA BIRCH – Swans In Summer – signed and dated 1895 – watercolour with white heightening – 27.5 x 42cm.
(Phillips) **$1,101** **£720**

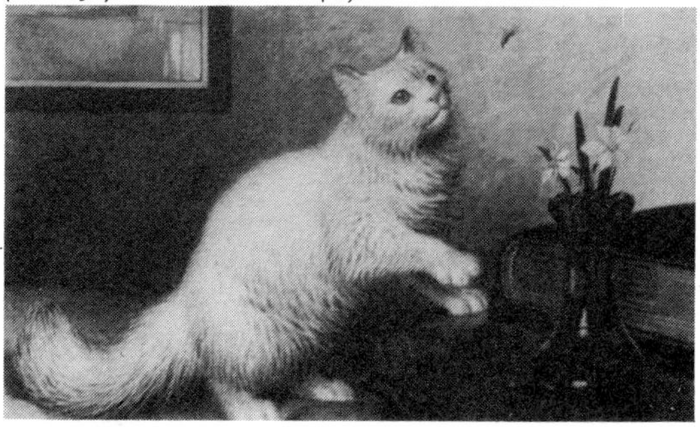

HARINGTON BIRD – Curiosity – signed – watercolour and bodycolour – 10¼ x 15in.
(Bonhams) **$775** **£500**

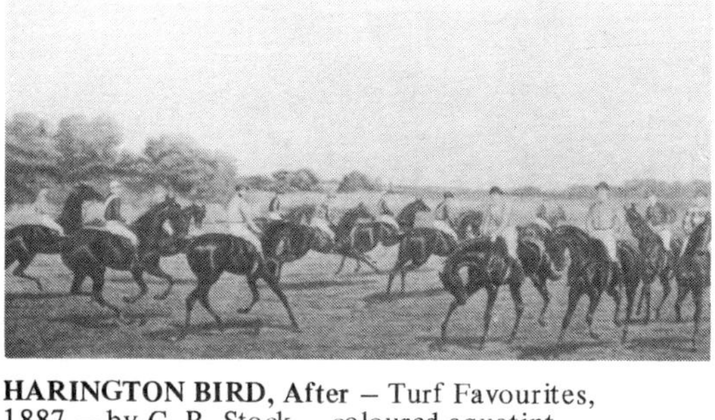

HARINGTON BIRD, After – Turf Favourites, 1887 – by C. R. Stock – coloured aquatint – 24 x 42in.
(Christie's) **$243** **£170**

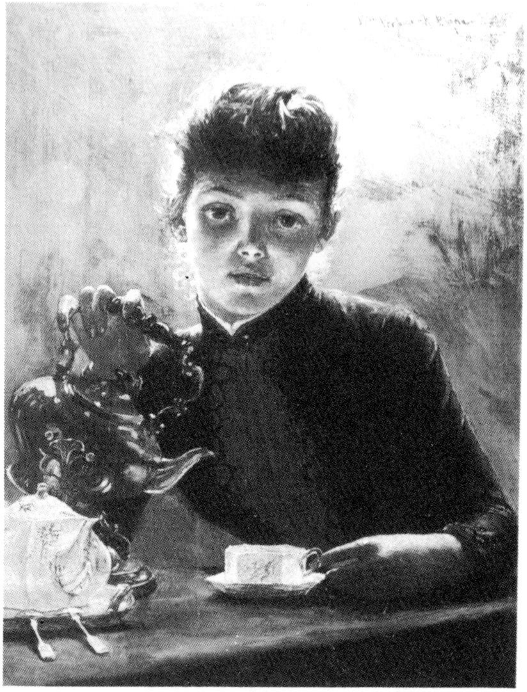

WILLIAM VERPLANCK BIRNEY – A Cup Of Tea – signed – oil on panel – 8¾ x 6¾in.
(Christie's) **$12,100** **£8,506**

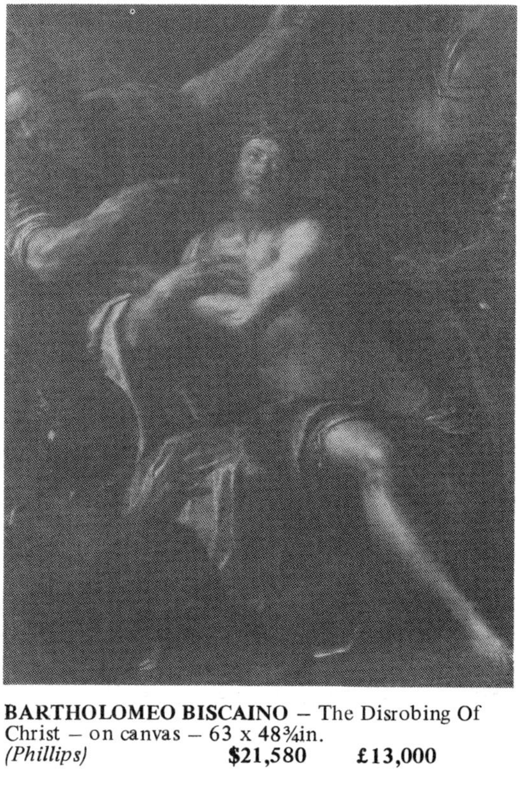

BARTHOLOMEO BISCAINO – The Disrobing Of Christ – on canvas – 63 x 48¾in.
(Phillips) **$21,580** **£13,000**

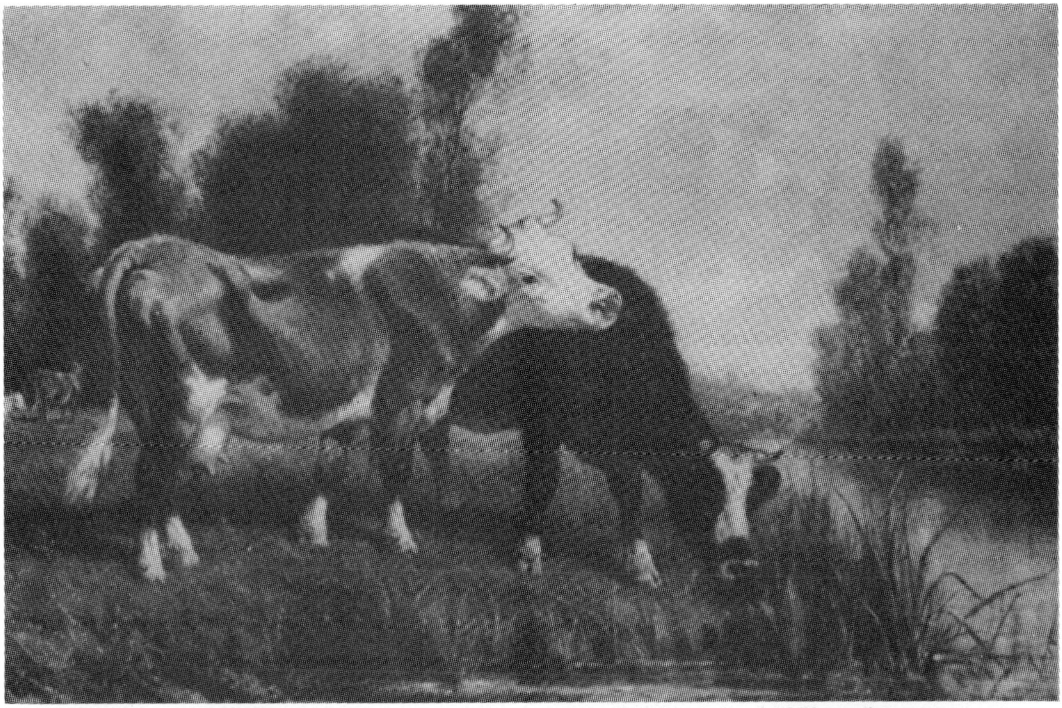

HENRY COLLIN BISPHAM – Cows In A Landscape – signed and dated 1880 – oil on canvas – 24 x 32in. *(Robt. W. Skinner Inc.)* **$900 £592**

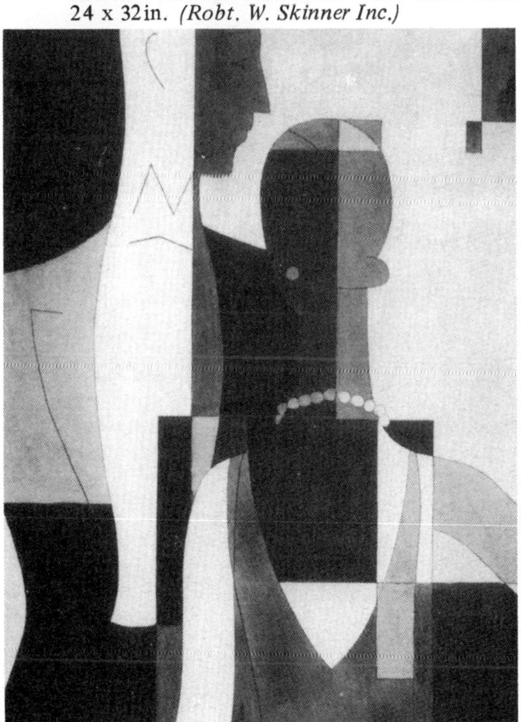

EMIL J. BISTTRAM – Couple – signed with initials – watercolour and pencil on paper – 17¼ x 12¼in.
(Christie's) **$1,210** **£850**

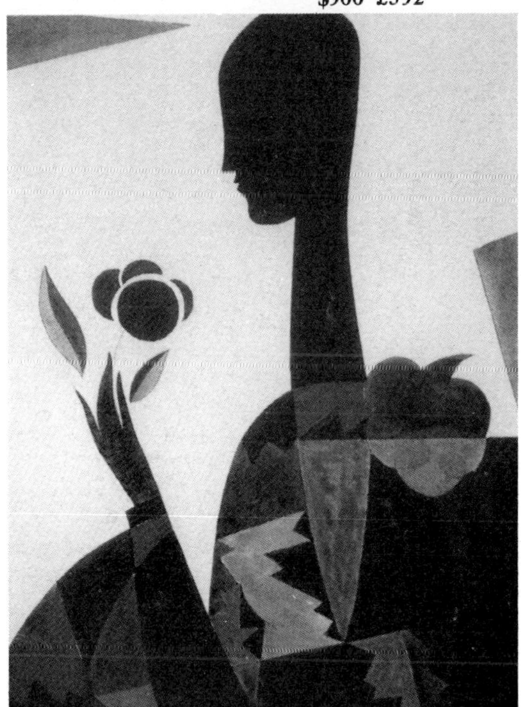

EMIL J. BISTTRAM – Lady With Flower – signed with initials – watercolour and pencil on paper – 17¼ x 12¼in.
(Christie's) **$1,210** **£850**

EMIL J. BISTTRAM – Duality – signed, also signed, dated 1938 and inscribed on the stretcher – oil on canvas – 36 x 48in.
(Christie's) **$18,700 £13,146**

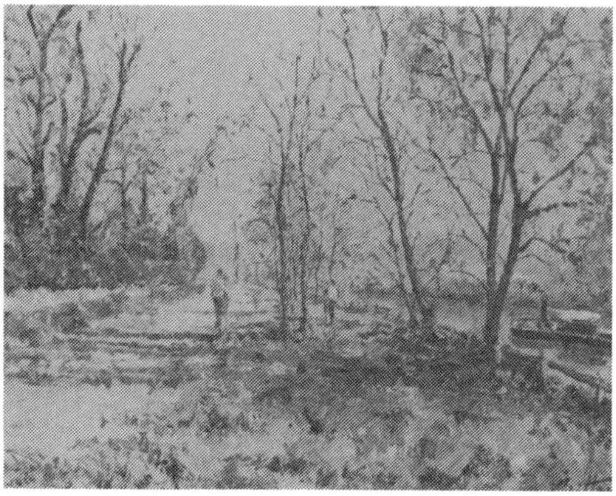

PIERRE BITTAR – Promenade A Croissy Sur Seine – signed – oil on canvas – 60 x 73cm.
(Phillips) **$2,015 £1,300**

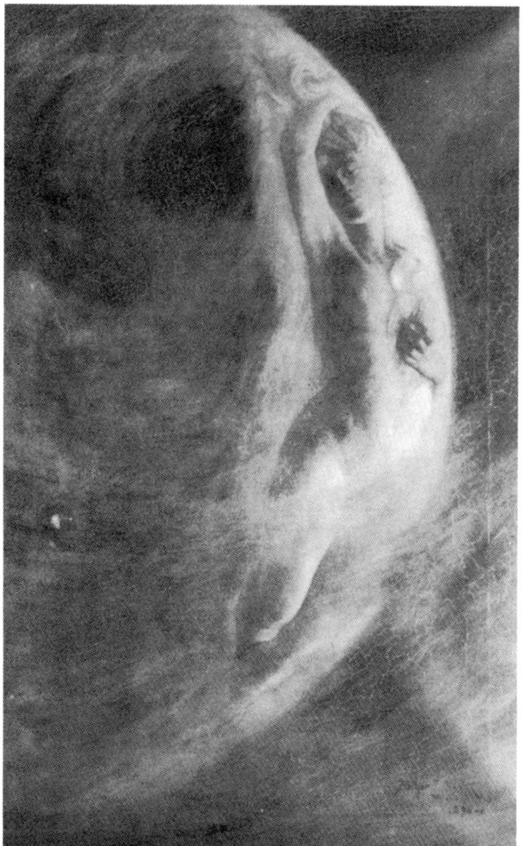

ARTHUR J. BLACK – The Awakening Moon – signed and dated 1890-1 – 55 x 34½in.
(Christie's) **$1,944 £1,296**

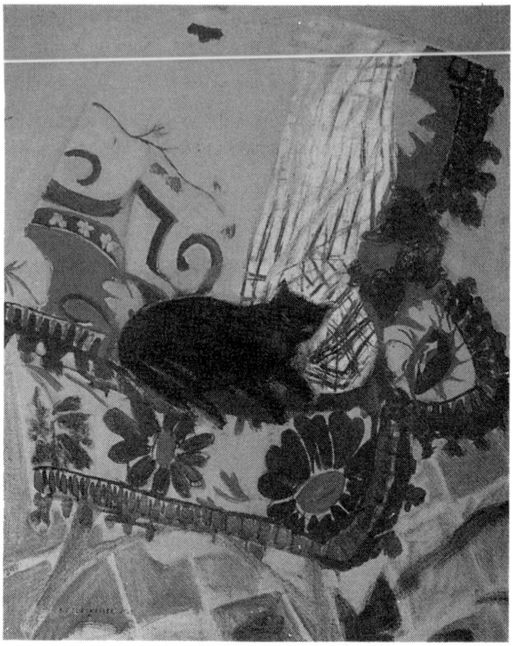

ELIZABETH BLACKADDER – Cat On A Rug – signed and dated 1969 – oil on canvas – 30 x 25in.
(Christie's) **$4,317 £2,750**

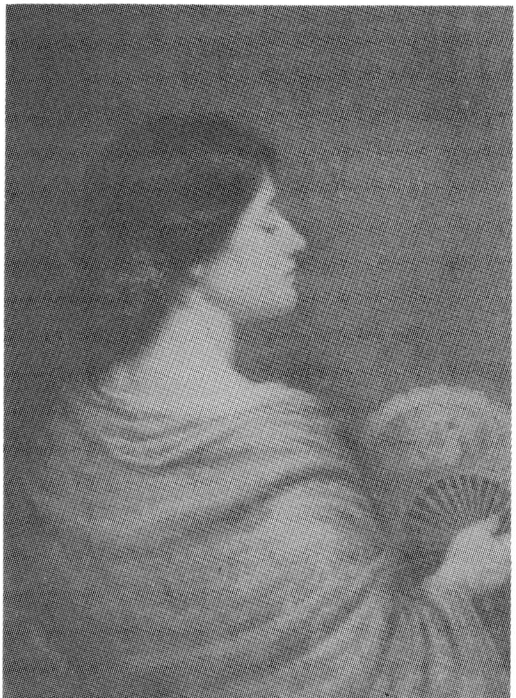

WILLIAM KAY BLACKLOCK – Head And Shoulder Study Of Cynthia, Niece Of The Artist – signed – watercolour – 29 x 22in.
(W. H. Lane & Son) **$6,864 £4,800**

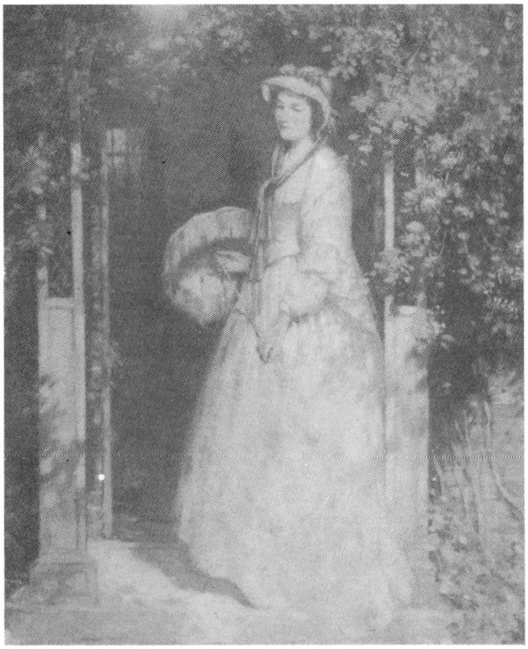

WILLIAM KAY BLACKLOCK – Full Length Portrait Of Mrs. Nellie Blacklock, The Artist's Wife – signed – oil on canvas – 28 x 20in.
(W. H. Lane & Son) **$6,006** **£4,200**

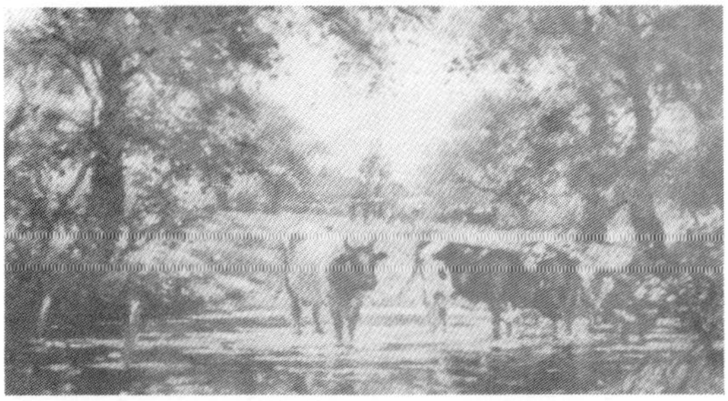

WILLIAM KAY BLACKLOCK – Cows In A Summer Landscape Drinking From A Stream In The Shade Of Trees – signed – oil on board – 9¾ x 13¼in.
(W. H. Lane & Son) **$1,001** **£700**

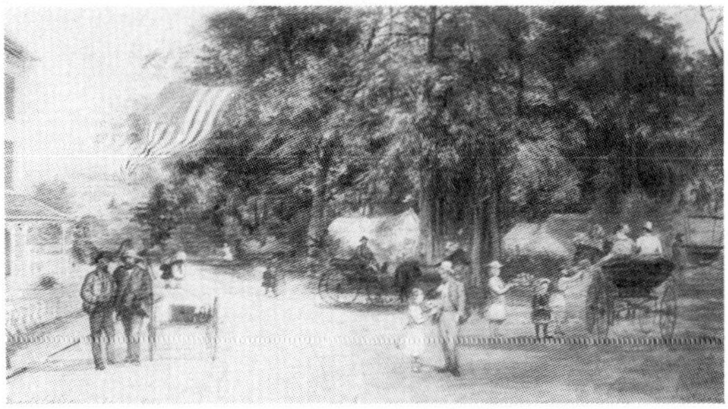

ALEXANDER BLAIKLEY – Montclair, New Jersey 1882 – signed and dated – gouache, watercolour, pen and black ink and pencil on paper – 12½ x 20½in.
(Christie's) **$8,250** **£5,799**

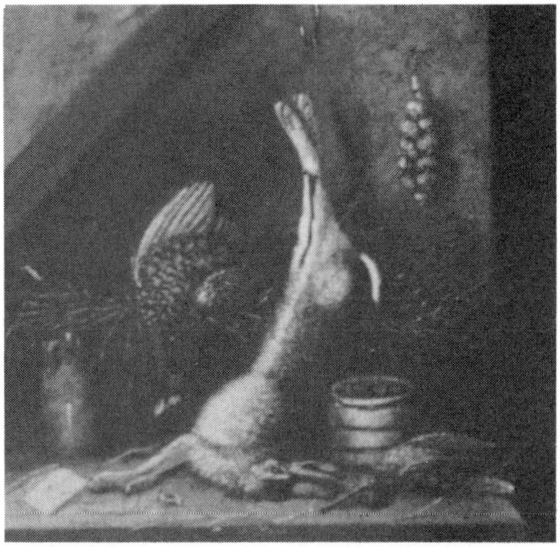

BENJAMIN BLAKE – Still Lives Of Game Larders – oil on canvas – 11 x 9½in.
(Christie's) **$1,430** **£935 Pair**

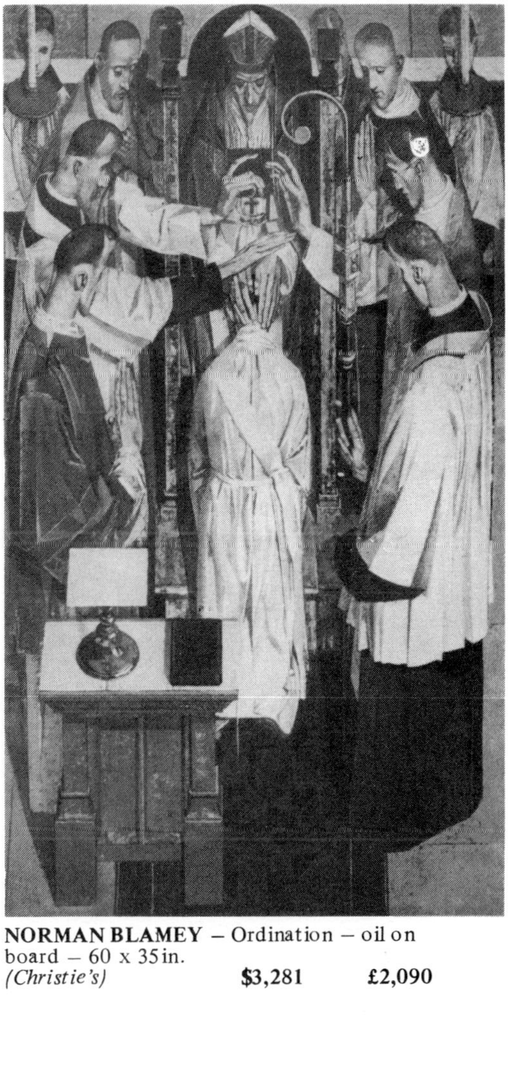

NORMAN BLAMEY – Ordination – oil on board – 60 x 35in.
(Christie's) **$3,281** **£2,090**

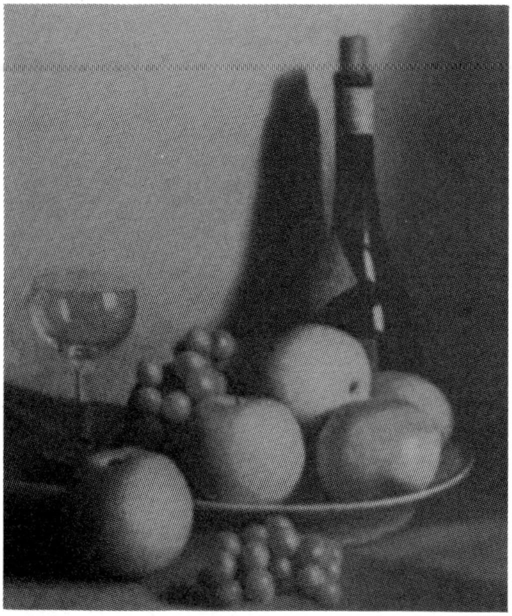

JACQUES BLANCHARD – Nature Morte – signed – oil on canvas – 41.25 x 33cm.
(Phillips) **$930** **£600**

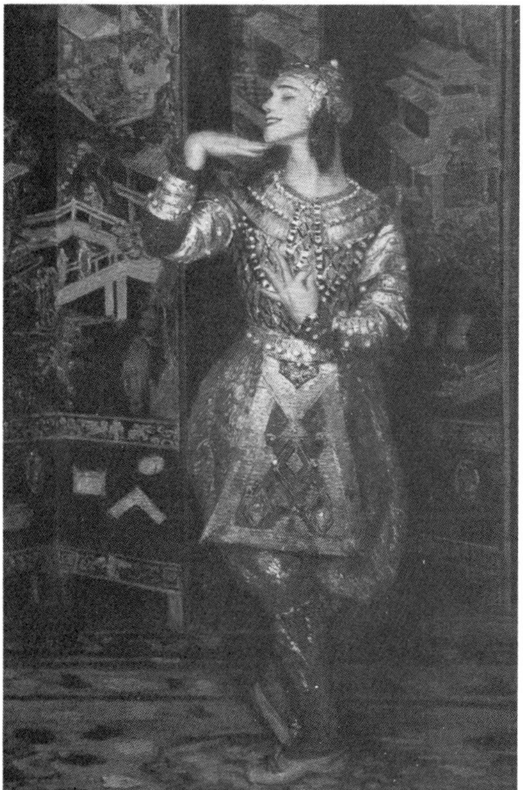

JACQUES EMILE BLANCHE – Vaslav Nijinsky In Danse Orientale – signed – 86½ x 47¼in.
(Christie's) **$158,400** **£110,000**

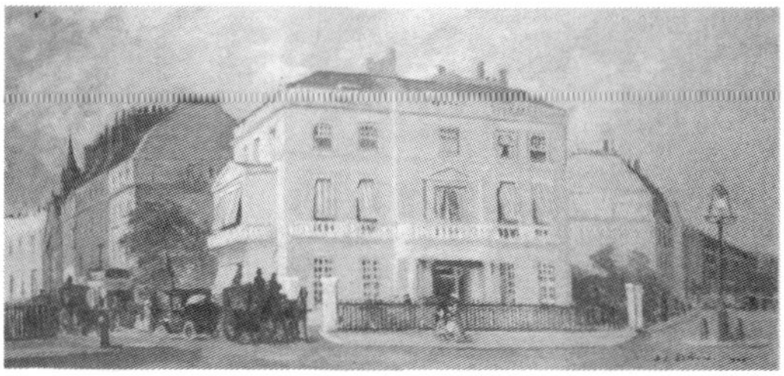

JACQUES EMILE BLANCHE – Belgrave Square, London, Looking North-West – signed and dated 1908, inscribed on the reverse – 19 x 41in.
(Christie's) **$38,016** **£26,400**

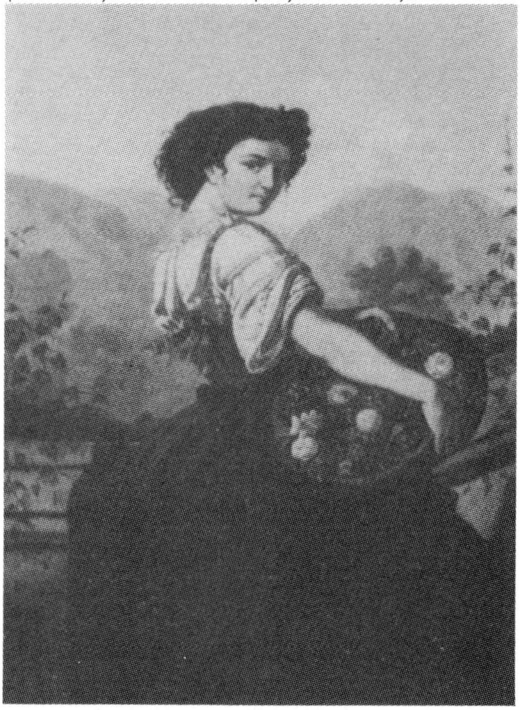

EUGENE DE BLAS – Portrait Of A Peasant Girl With A Basket Of Flowers – signed and dated 1879 – oil on canvas – 26½ x 21½in.
(Christie's) **$1,042** **£660**

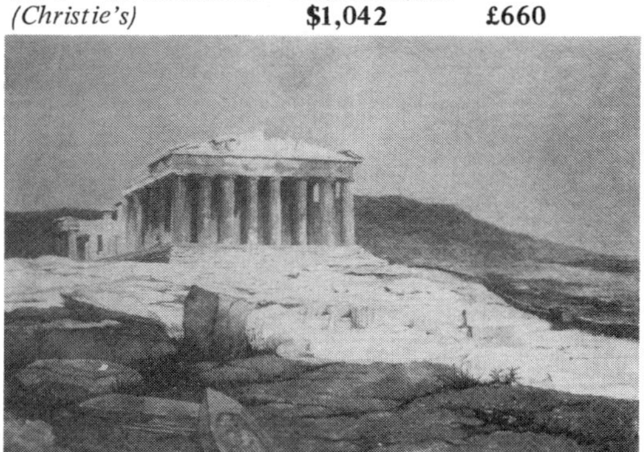

EDWIN HOWLAND BLASHFIELD – Parthenon At Athens – signed – oil on canvas – 28½ x 41½in.
(Christie's) **$6,600** **£4,112**

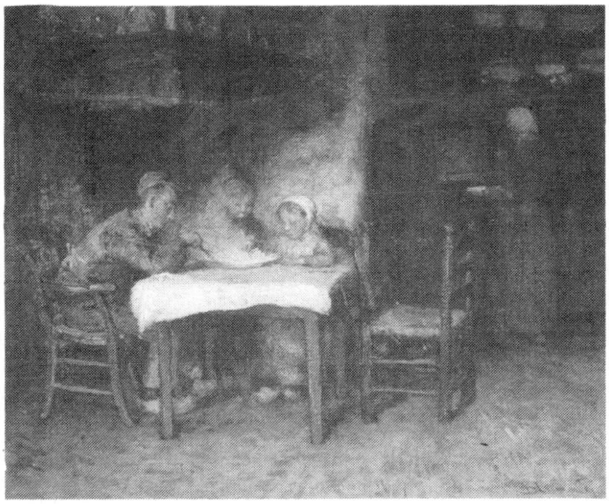

BERNARDUS JOHANNES BLOMMERS – A Family At Supper Time – signed – 16 x 19¼in.
(Christie's) **$7,920** **£4,950**

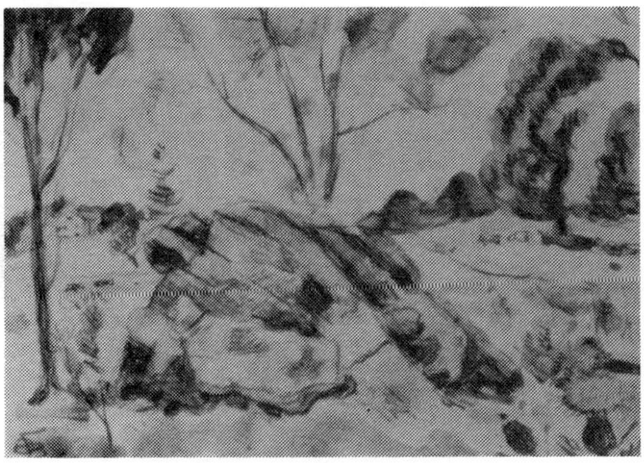

OSCAR FLORIANUS BLUEMNER – Rural Landscape – signed with monogram – watercolour on paper – 7 x 9½in.
(Robt. W. Skinner Inc.) **$800** **£490**

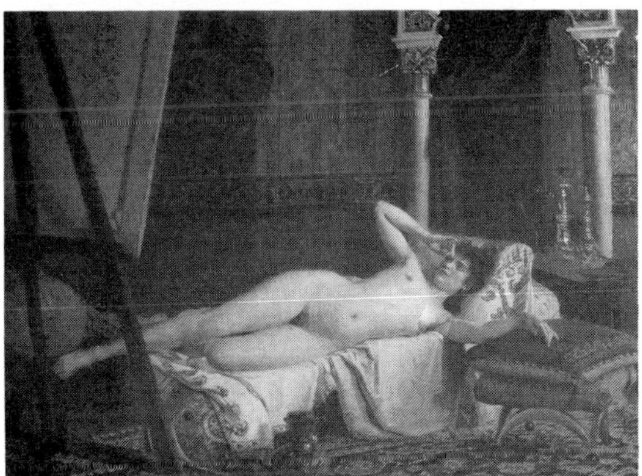

NIKOLAI CORNELOVICH BODAREVSKI – The Artist's Model – signed and dated 1886 – 22¾ x 31½in.
(Christie's) **$12,320** **£7,700**

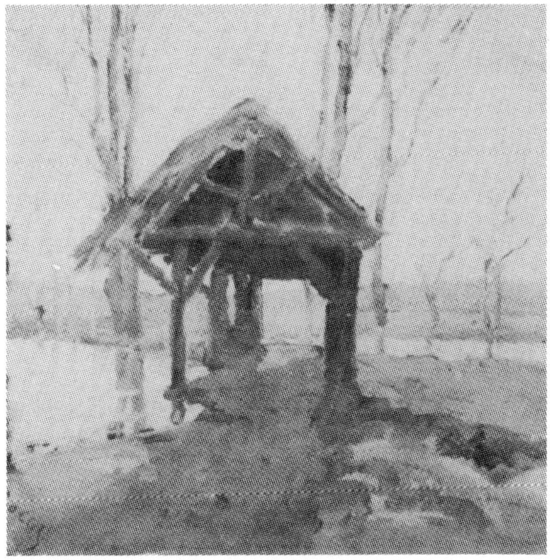

FRANK MYERS BOGGS – A Deserted Bridge – signed – oil on canvas – 15 x 18¼in.
(Christie's) **$2,200** **£1,530**

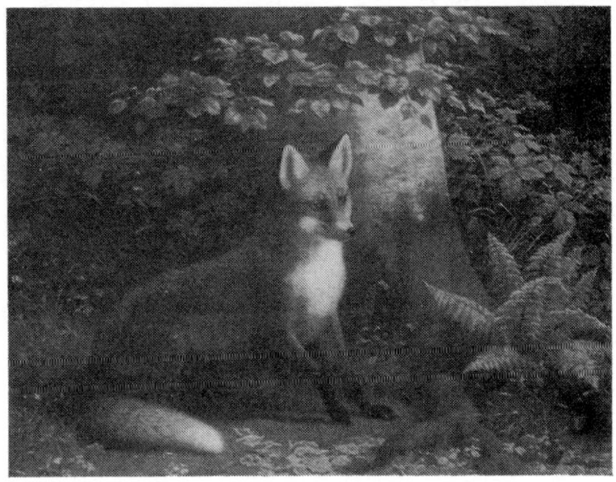

CARL BOGH – Waiting To Pounce – signed and dated 1871 – 32¼ x 43in.
(Christie's) **$4,681** **£3,080**

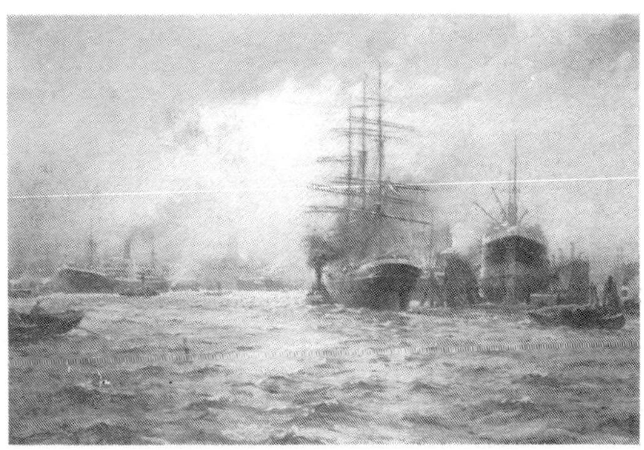

HANS BOHRDT – Hamburg Harbour – signed – on panel – 27½ x 40in.
(Christie's) **$4,752** **£3,300**

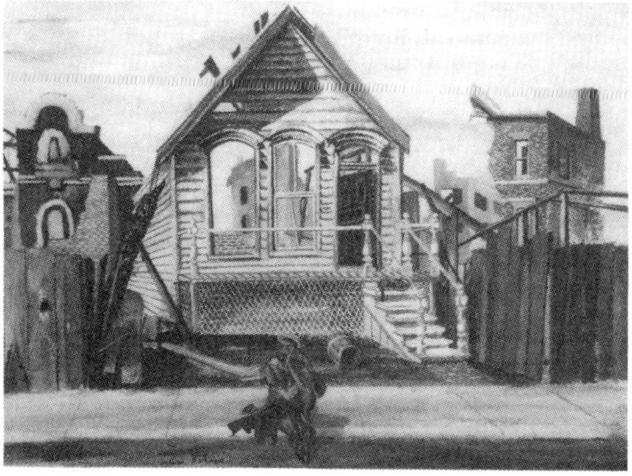

AARON BOHROD – Abandonment – signed – casein on paper – 14¾ x 19½in.
(Christie's) **$4,620** **£3,247**

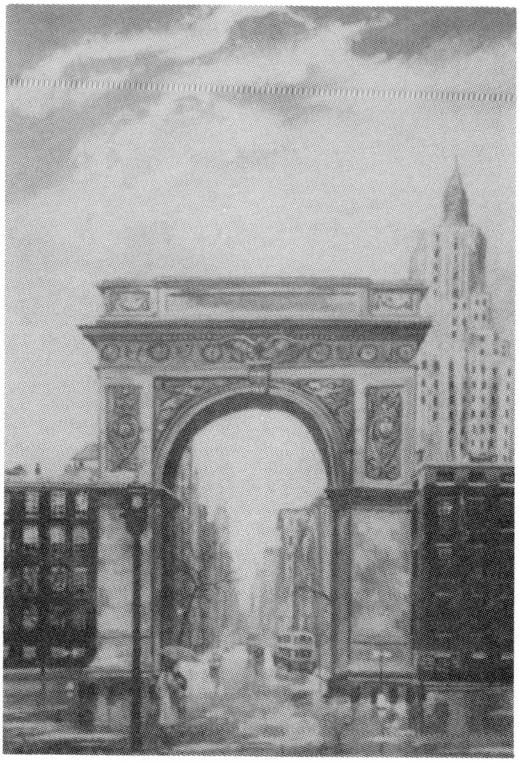

AARON BOHROD – Rainy Day Washington Square – signed – gouache on board – 20 x 15in.
(Christie's) **$1,870** **£1,165**

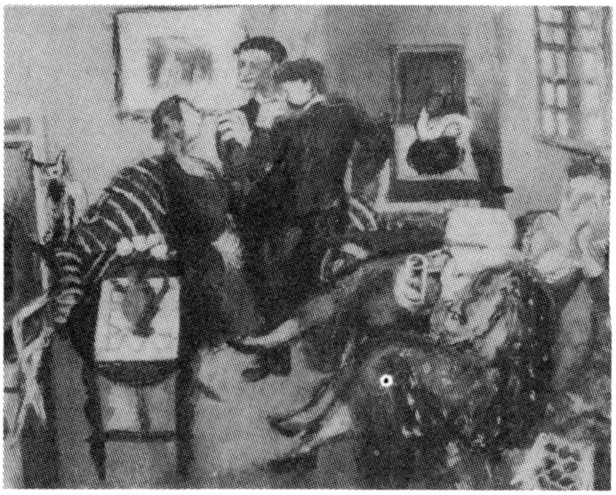

AARON BOHROD – The Studio Party – signed and dated '32 – oil on masonite – 18 x 24in.
(Christie's) **$3,300** **£2,319**

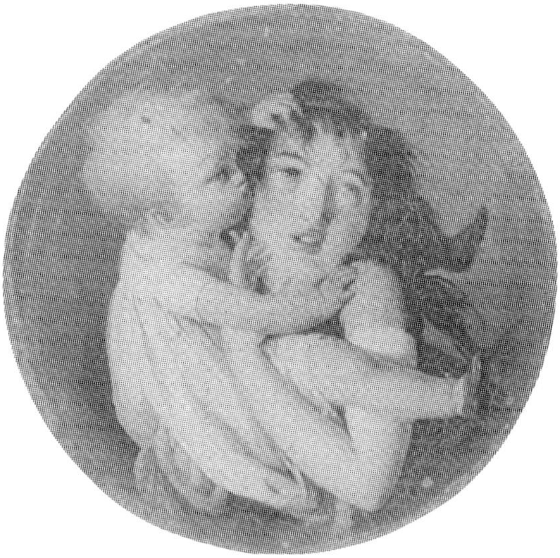

LEOPOLD LOUIS BOILLY – A Mother And Child – on metal – 3¼in. diam.
(Phillips) **$15,272** **£9,200**

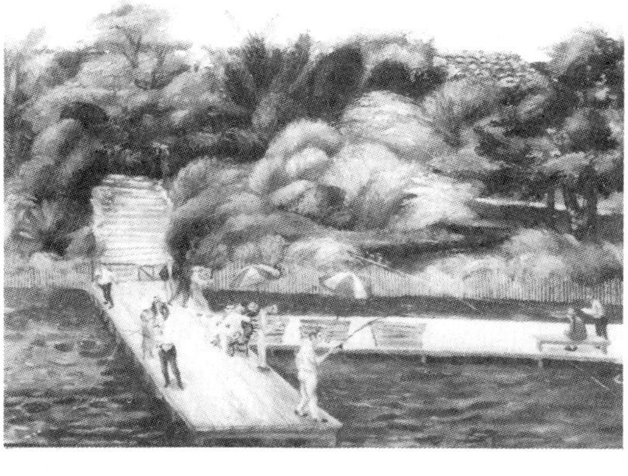

AARON BOHROD – Fishing From The Pier, Lincoln Park, Chicago – signed and dated '35 – oil on masonite – 19 x 24in.
(Christie's) **$3,300** **£2,319**

GUY PENE DU BOIS – Three Women – signed – pencil on paper – 11¾ x 17¾in.
(Christie's) **$2,640** **£1,836**

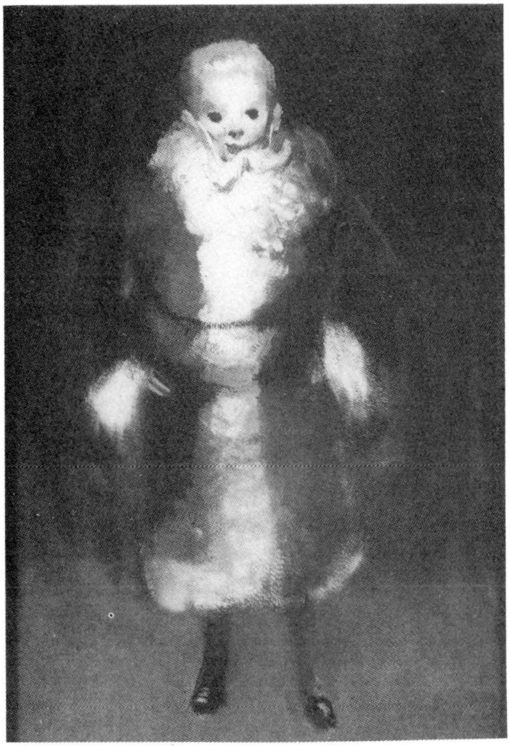

GUY PENE DU BOIS – The Santa Suit – signed – oil on board – 17¾ x 11¾in.
(Christie's) **$2,640** **£1,855**

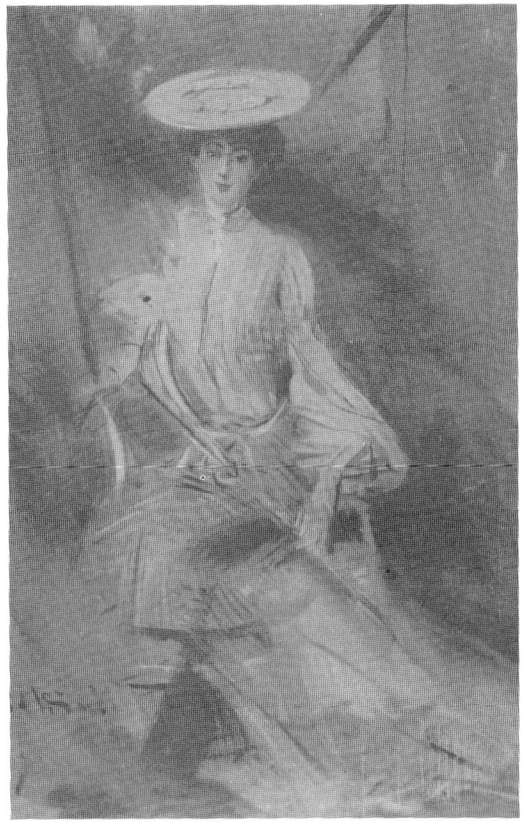

GIOVANNI BOLDINI –Portrait Of A Lady, Seated, With A Parasol – signed – 26 x 21in.
(Christie's) **$79,200** **£55,000**

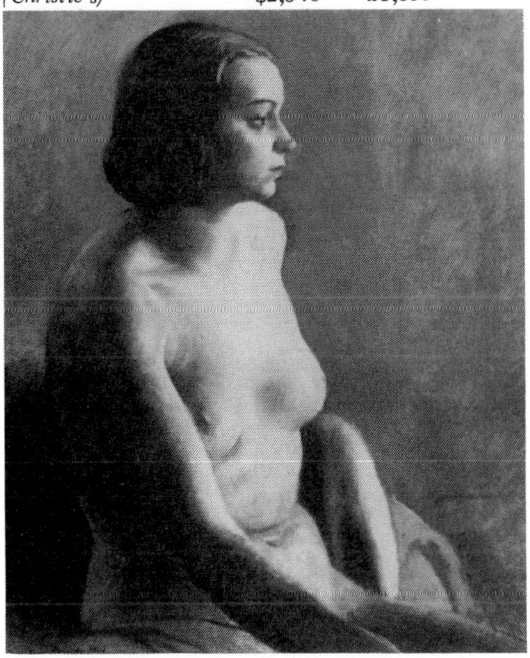

GUY PENE DU BOIS – Nanette – signed and dated 1932, inscribed on the reverse – oil on board – 20 x 15in.
(Christie's) **$4,620** **£3,247**

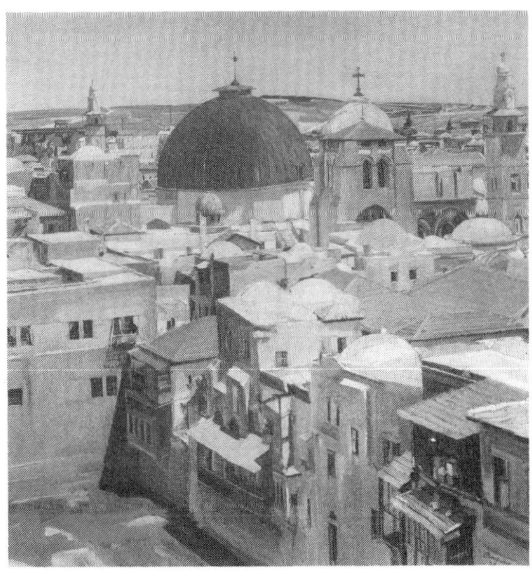

DAVID BOMBERG – The Church Of The Holy Sepulchre, Jerusalem – signed and dated '25 – oil on canvas – 20½ x 20in.
(Christie's) **$37,994** **£24,200**

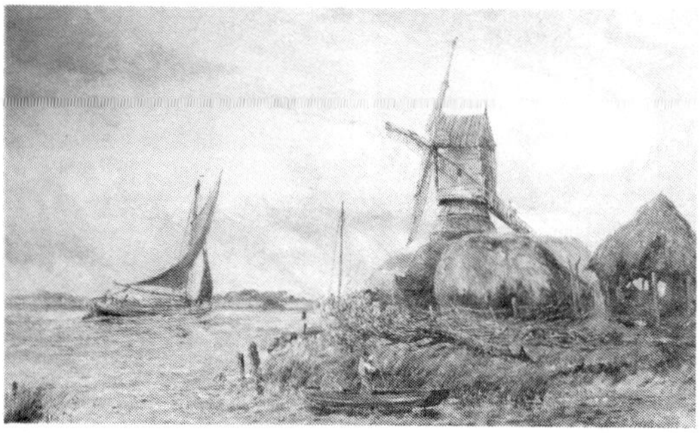

WILLIAM JOSEPH J. C. BOND – A Barge Sailing Past A Windmill And Hay Ricks – signed – oil on panel – 19¾ x 27in.
(Phillips) **$8,415** **£5,500**

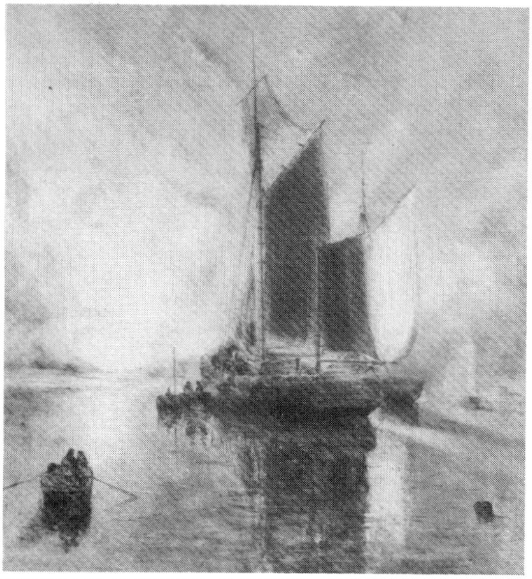

WILLIAM JOSEPH J. C. BOND – Fishing Boats At Sunrise – signed and dated 1900 – 30 x 24in.
(Christie's) **$4,207** **£2,750**

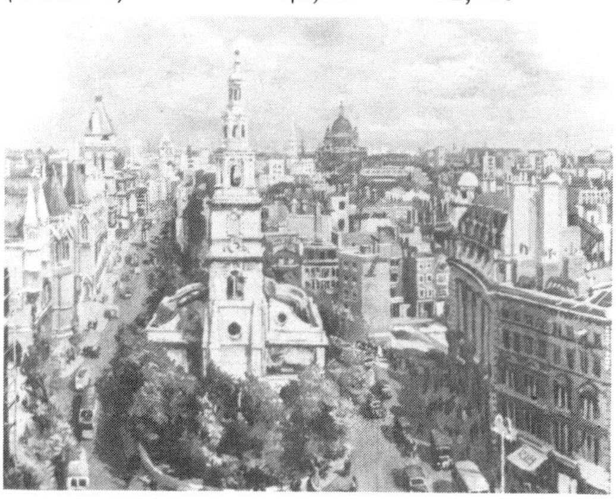

STEPHEN BONE – The Strand – signed – oil on canvas board – 51 x 63.5cm.
(Phillips) **$2,448** **£1,600**

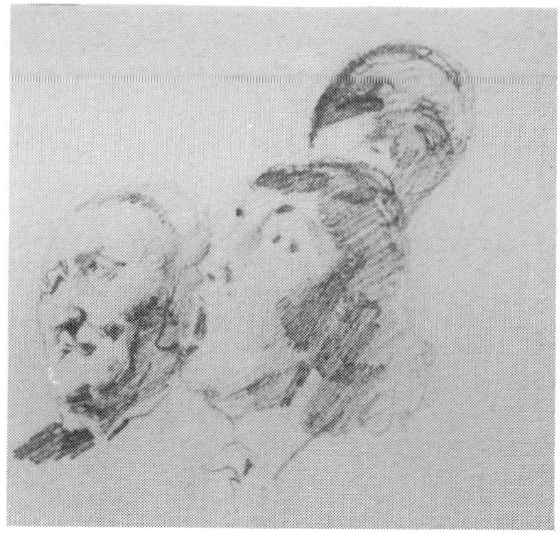

RICHARD PARKES BONINGTON – Study Of Three Heads – pencil – 9.5 x 10.5cm.
(Phillips) **$489** **£300**

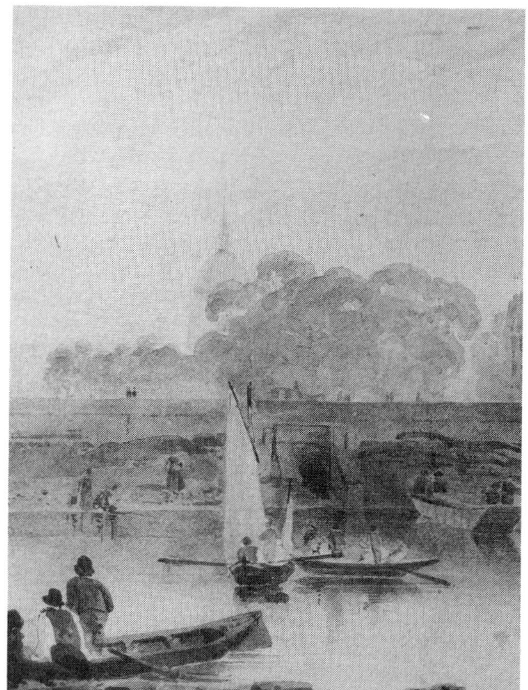

RICHARD PARKES BONINGTON – The Hotel Des Invalides, Paris – with signature and inscription on the reverse – pencil and watercolour – 6 x 4½in.
(Christie's) **$15,614** **£9,350**

PIERRE BONNARD – Le Port De Cannes – signed – gouache, watercolour and pencil on paper – 11 x 15in.
(Christie's) **$50,688** **£35,200**

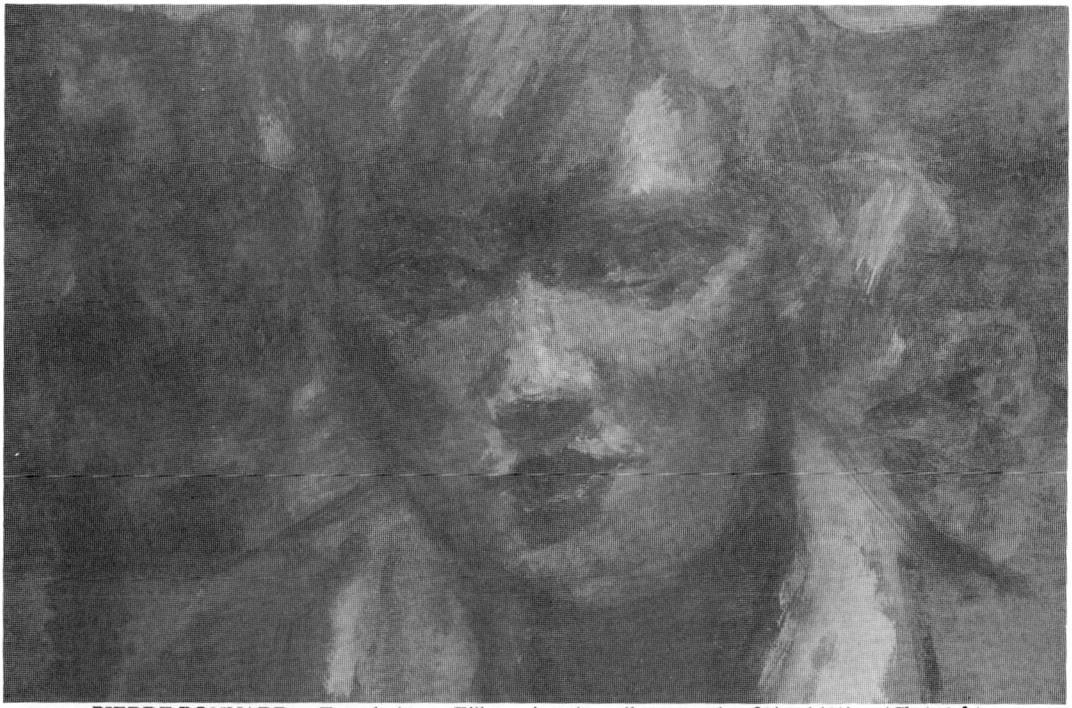

PIERRE BONNARD – Tete de jeune Fille – signed – oil on panel – 9½ x 11½in. *(Christie's)*
$66,528 £46,200

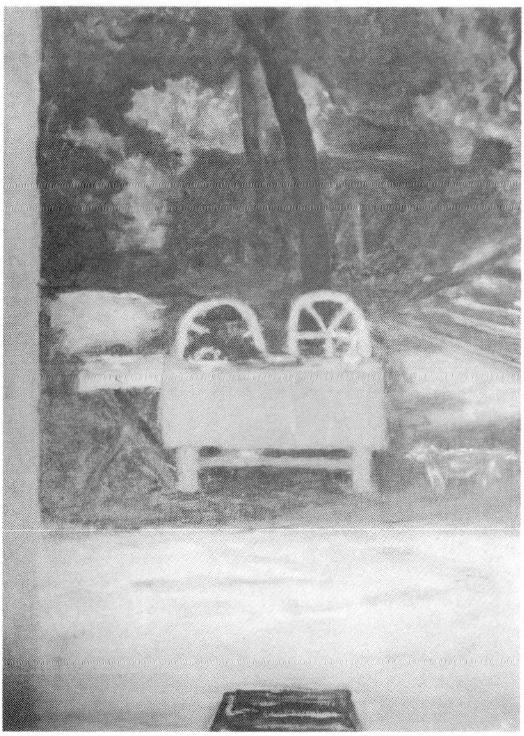

PIERRE BONNARD – Le Gouter au Jardin, Table jaune – oil on canvas – 24¾ x 16½in.
(Christie's) **$134,640 £93,500**

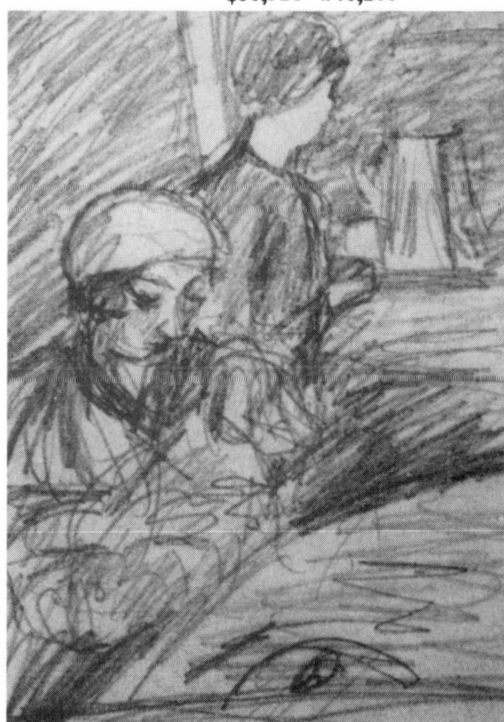

PIERRE BONNARD – Dans la Salle a Manger – pencil on buff paper – 6½ x 4¼in.
(Christie's) **$1,320 £825**

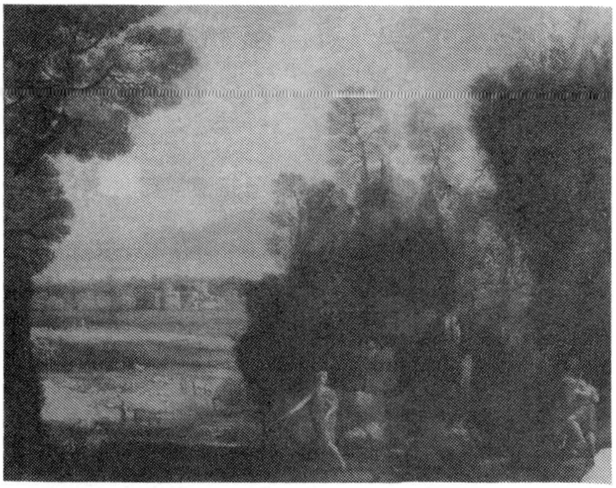

PIETRO PAOLO BONZI, Called Il Gobbo Dei Carracci – A Pastoral Landscape – on canvas – 22½ x 26¼in.
(Phillips) **$11,288** **£6,800**

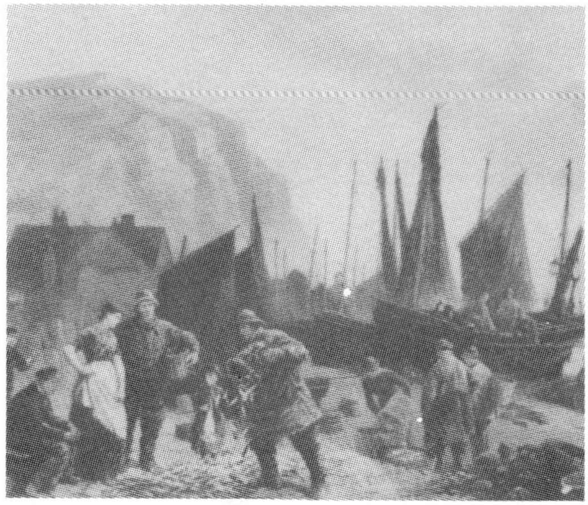

WILLIAM H. BORROW – Unloading The Catch, Hastings – signed and dated 1891 – oil on canvas – 32½ x 50½in.
(Phillips) **$3,978** **£2,600**

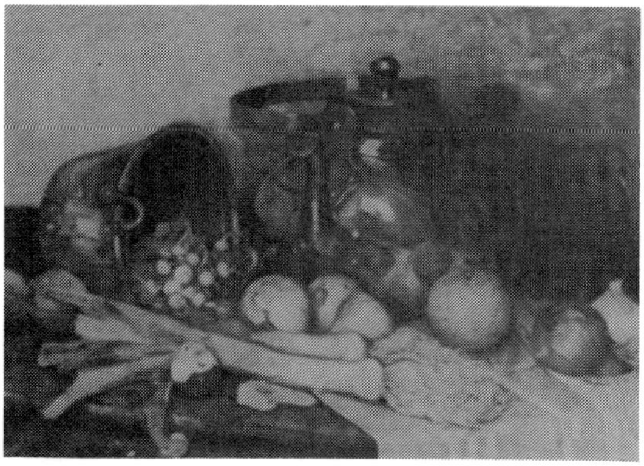

CHARLOTTE BOOM-POTHUIS – Still Life With Copper Kettle – signed – oil on canvas – 50 x 70.5cm.
(Phillips) **$744** **£480**

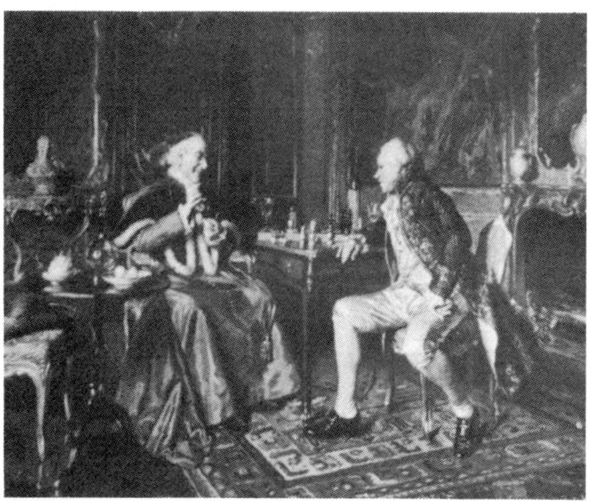

BERNARD LOUIS BORIONE – Checkmate? – signed and inscribed – on canvas – 38 x 46cm.
(Phillips) **$830** **£550**

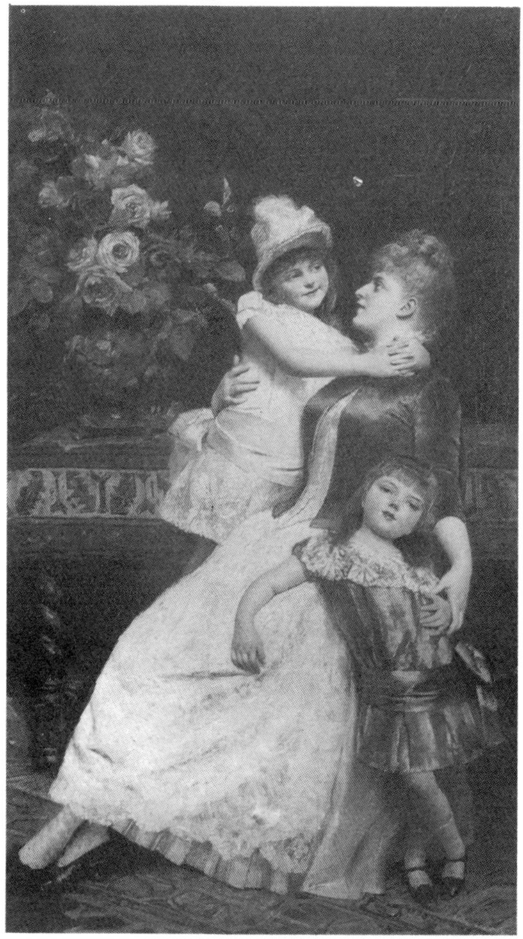

GEORGES P. M. VAN DEN BOS – Bonheur maternel – signed – 46½ x 28in.
(Christie's) **$17,600** **£11,000**

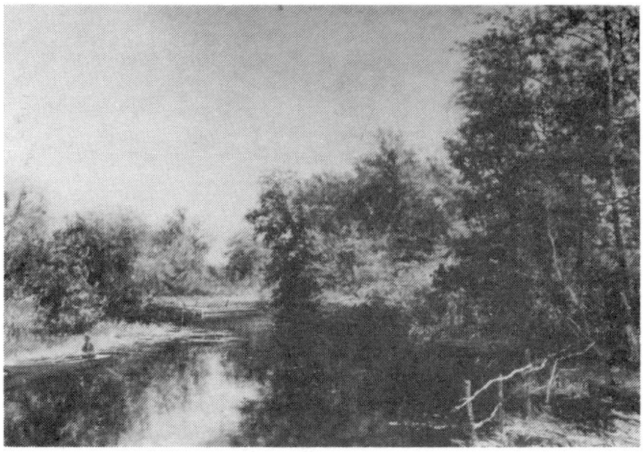

ROBERT WARD VAN BOSKERCK – Fisherman On The Hackensack River – signed – oil on canvas – 20 x 30in.
(Robt. W. Skinner Inc.) **$5,500** **£3,374**

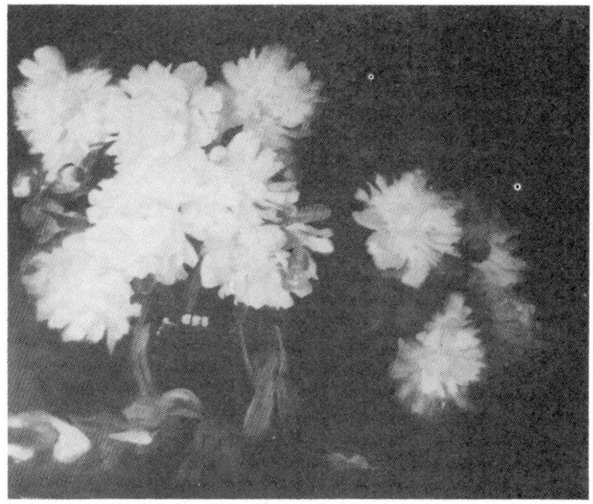

BOSTON SCHOOL, 19th/20th century – Still Life With Peonies – oil on canvas – 30¼ x 36in.
(Robt. W. Skinner Inc.) **$850** **£590**

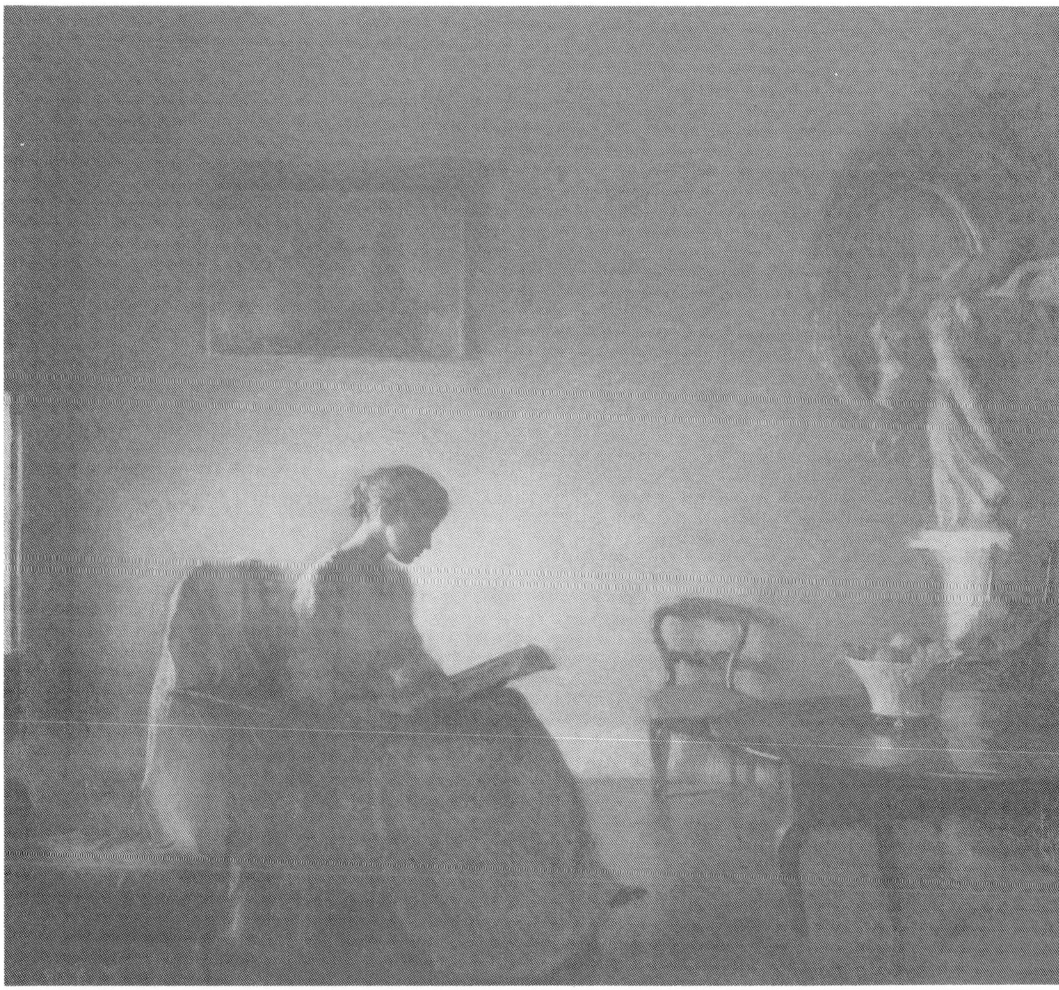

FREDERICK ANDREW BOSLEY – 'The Grey Room' – signed and dated 1921 – oil on canvas – 28½ x 30½in. *(Robt. W. Skinner Inc.)* **$34,000** **£20,858**

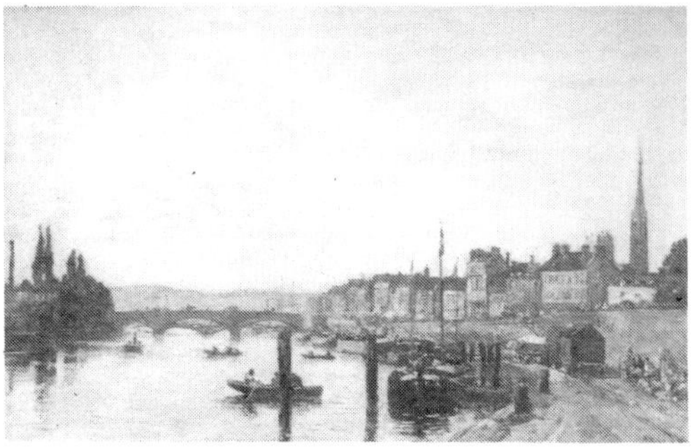

EUGENE BOUDIN – Rouen, La Seine et le Pont Corneille – signed, inscribed and dated '95 – oil on canvas – 20 x 30in.
(Christie's) **$183,700 £110,000**

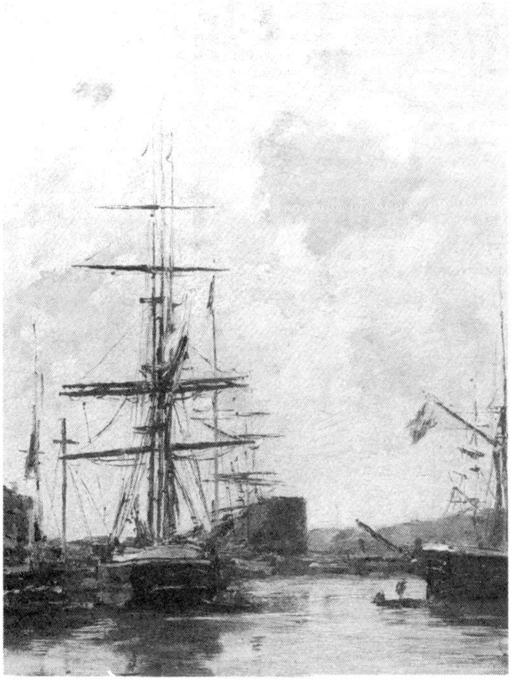

EUGENE BOUDIN – Bateaux a Quai – signed – oil on panel – 12¾ x 9¼in.
(Christie's) **$44,352 £30,800**

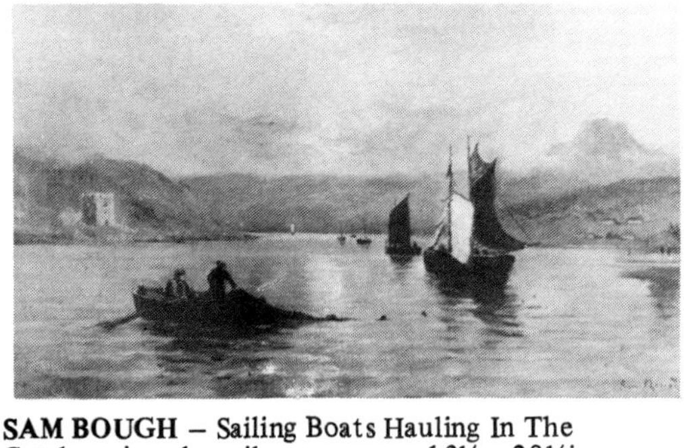

SAM BOUGH – Sailing Boats Hauling In The Catch – signed – oil on canvas – 13½ x 20½in.
(Worsfolds) **$666 £450**

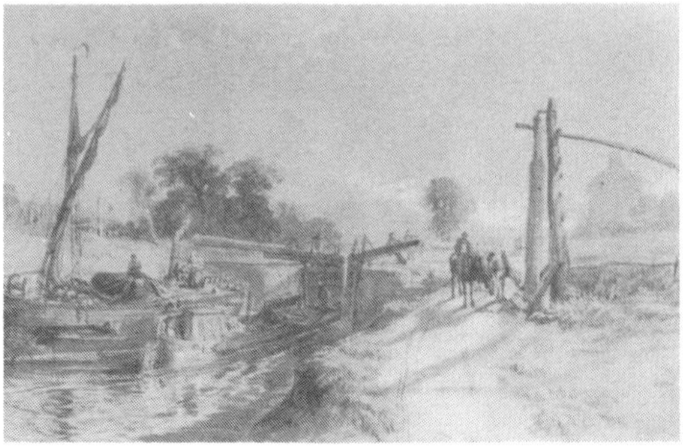

SAMUEL BOUGH – On The Bridgewater Canal, Near Manchester – signed, and signed and inscribed verso – watercolour, heightened with white – 10½ x 16½in.
(Christie's) **$1,584 £1,100**

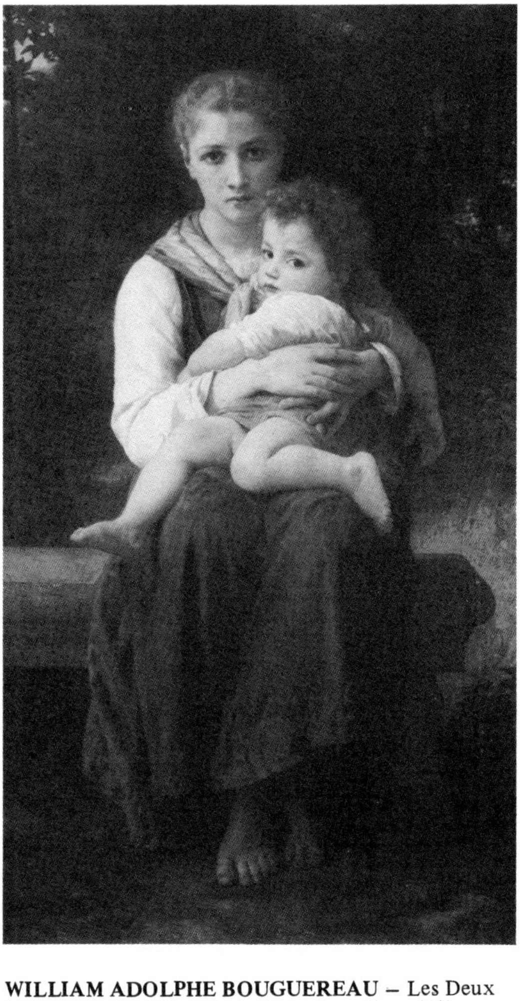

WILLIAM ADOLPHE BOUGUEREAU – Les Deux Soeurs – signed and dated 1877 – 53½ x 31½in.
(Christie's) **$82,368 £57,200**

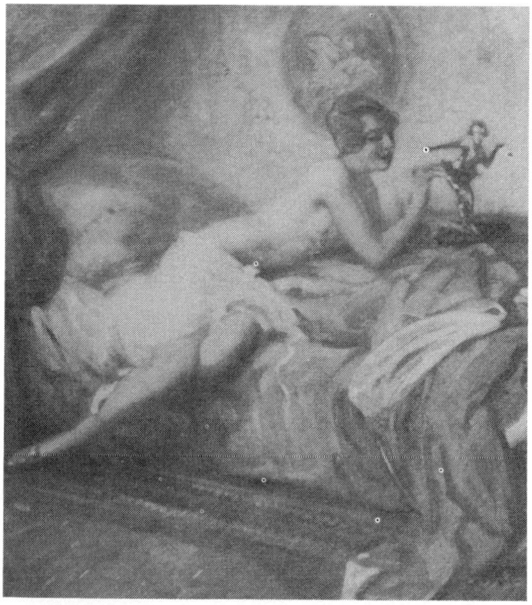

A. DE BOULBE – Portrait Of A Nude Reclining On A Bed Captivated By A Small Statue Of A Dancer – signed – 27½ x 23½in.
(Biddle & Webb) **$2,006** **£1,320**

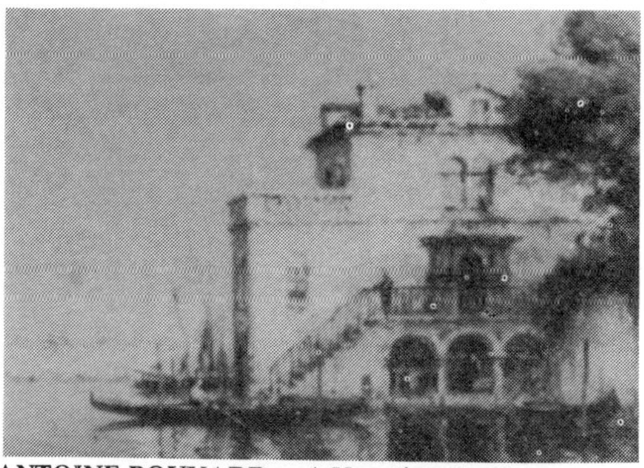

ANTOINE BOUVARD – A Venetian Canal At Dusk – signed – oil on canvas – 19.5 x 24cm.
(Phillips) **$3,676** **£2,800**

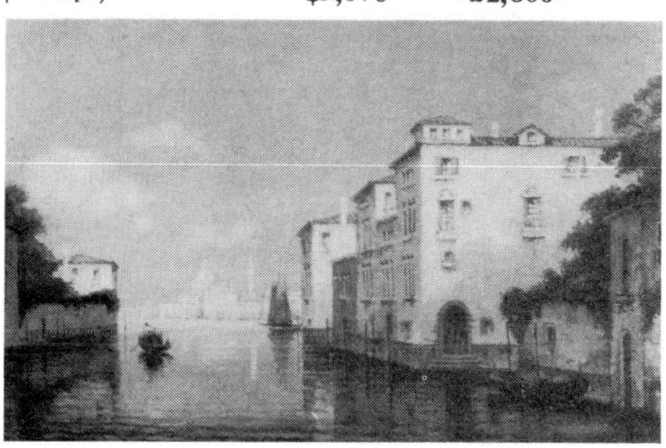

ANTOINE BOUVARD – A Venetian Canal – signed – 20 x 30in.
(Christie's) **$2,629** **£1,430**

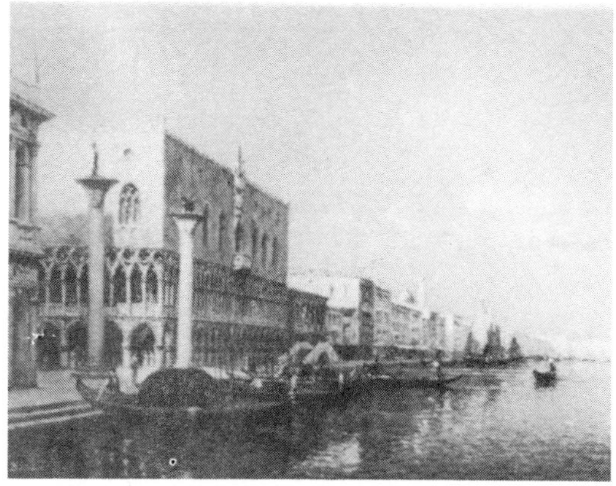

ANTOINE BOUVARD – The Grand Canal, Venice – signed – on canvas – 50 x 65cm.
(Phillips) **$4,832** **£3,200**

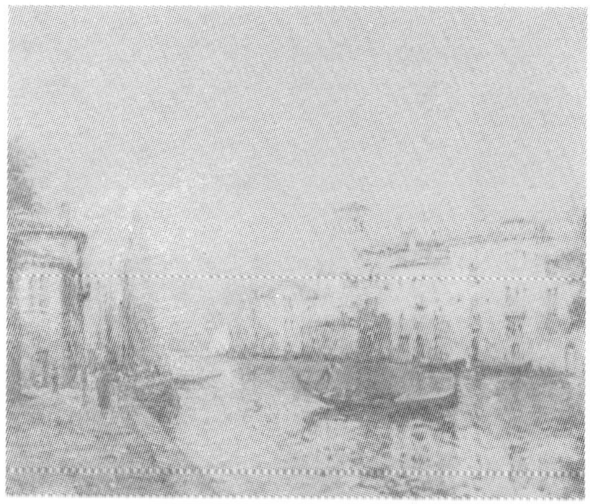

ANTOINE BOUVARD – A Venetian Backwater – signed – oil on canvas – 19 x 25in.
(Christie's) **$6,573** **£3,960**

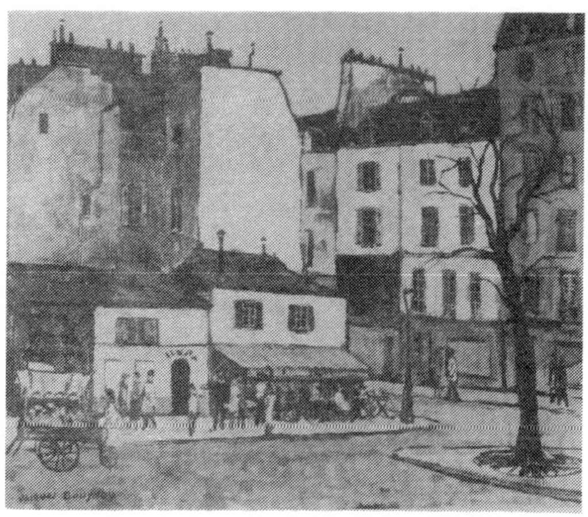

JACQUES BOUYSSOU – Rue St. Andre Des Arts – signed – oil on canvas – 60 x 71cm.
(Phillips) **$1,116** **£720**

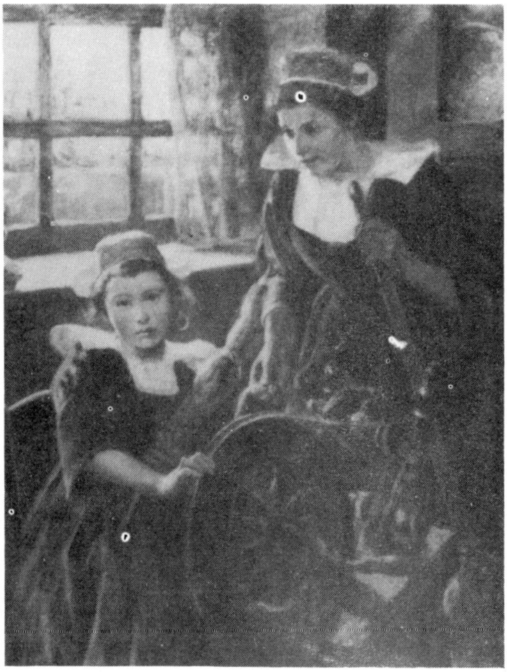

BENJAMIN JAMES BOWEN – Normandy Mother And Child – oil on canvas – 40 x 30in.
(Robt. W. Skinner Inc.) **$1,000** £657

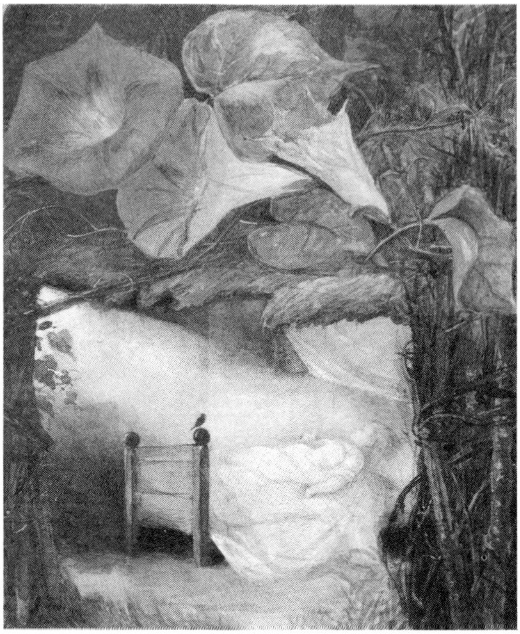

ELEANOR VERE BOYLE – 'In The Hut There Was Only A Bed – The Sunbeam Stole In To Kiss Him' – pencil and watercolour heightened with white – 6 x 5¼in.
(Christie's) **$15,510** **£11,000**

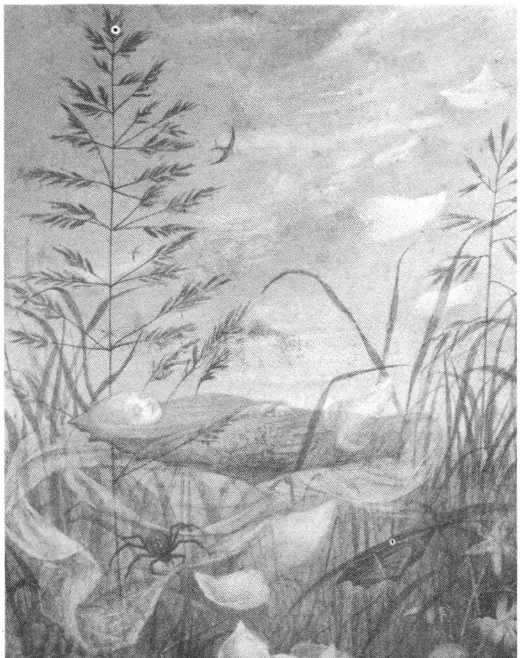

ELEANOR VERE BOYLE – 'Death But A Sleep / When The Spring Begins' – watercolour heightened with white – 6 x 4½in.
(Christie's) **$13,959** £9,900

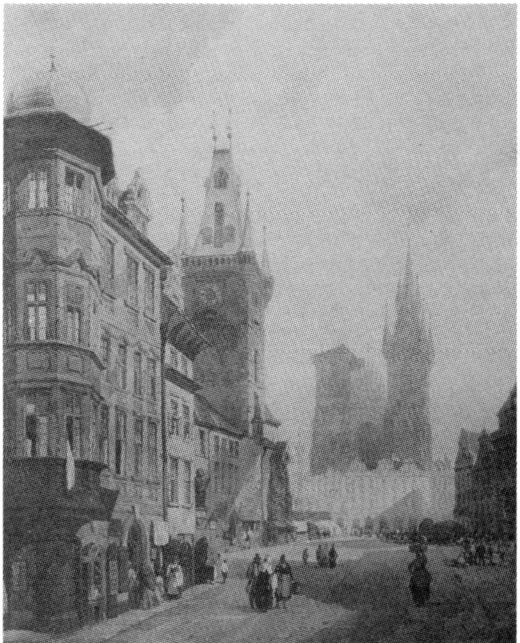

THOMAS SHOTTER BOYS – Rath Haus Thein Kirche, Prague – signed, inscribed and dated 1860 – pencil and watercolour – 18¼ x 14½in.
(Christie's) **$12,859** £7,700

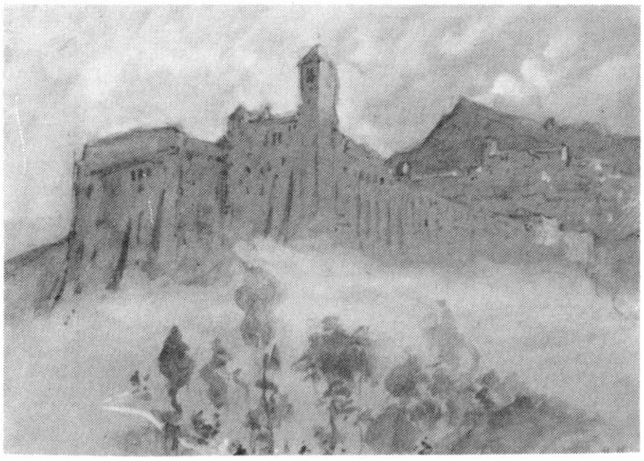

HERCULES BRABAZON BRABAZON – Assisi – signed with initials – pencil and watercolour heightened with white on pale grey-green paper – 8¼ x 11¼in.
(Christie's) **$2,791** **£1,980**

HERCULES BRABAZON BRABAZON – Venice: The Grand Canal With Santa Maria Della Salute – signed with initials – pencil and watercolour heightened with white – 7¼ x 10¾in.
(Christie's) **$1,186** **£715**

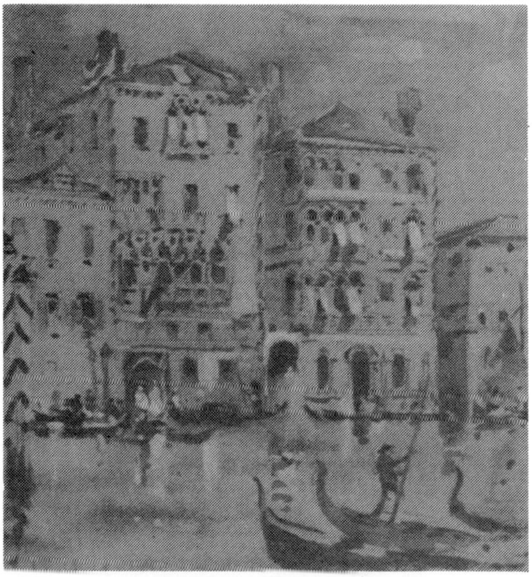

HERCULES BRABAZON BRABAZON – A Venetian Canal Scene – signed with initials – watercolour and bodycolour over pencil – 16.5 x 14.5cm.
(Phillips) **$1,548** **£950**

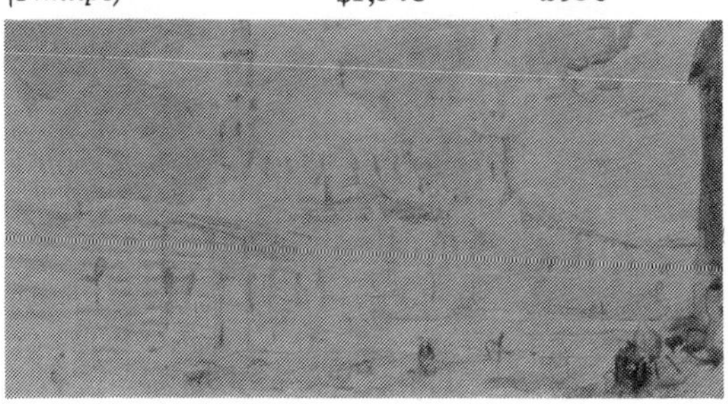

HERCULES BRABAZON BRABAZON – A Mosque, Cairo – inscribed – watercolour over pencil – 22 x 30cm.
(Phillips) **$2,282** **£1,400**

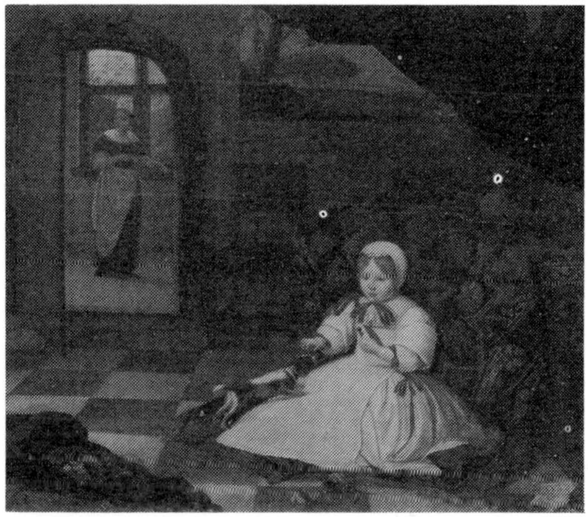

RICHARD BRACKENBERGH – A Child With Her Pet Spaniel – inscribed, signed and dated 1677 – on canvas – 22½ x 25½in.
(Phillips) **$26,560** **£16,000**

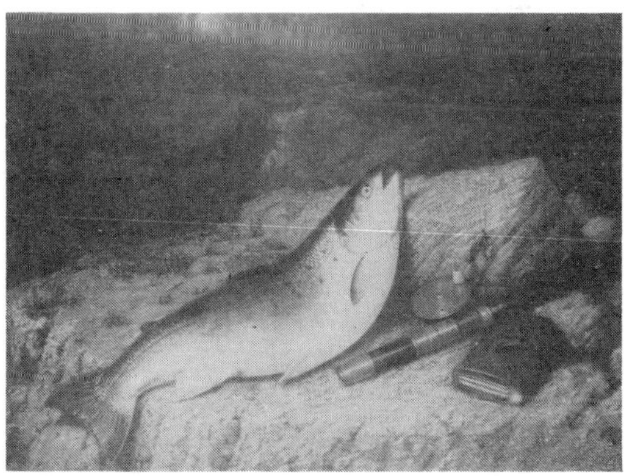

WALTER M. BRACKETT – The Fisherman's Catch – signed and dated 1869 – oil on canvas – 26 x 36¼in.
(Christie's) **$7,700** **£4,797**

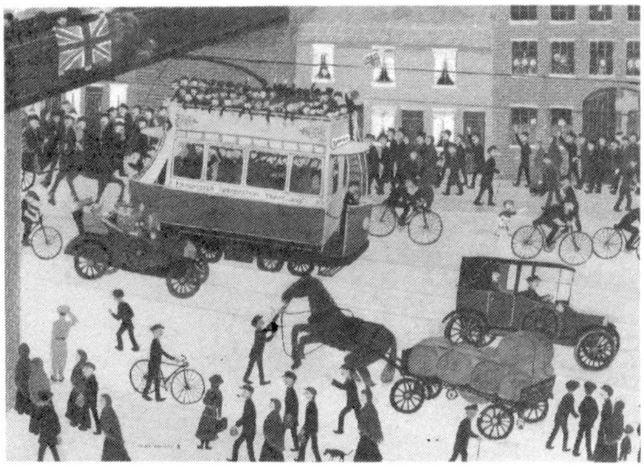

HELEN BRADLEY – Armistice Day, November 11th 1918 – signed – oil on canvas board – 20¾ x 28¾in.
(Christie's) **$11,797** **£8,250**

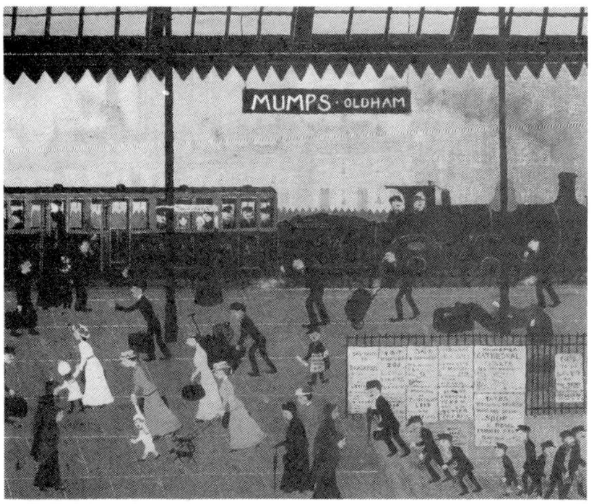

HELEN BRADLEY – 'Stop The Train' Called Father, 'We're Coming On It' – signed, and signed, inscribed and dated on a card on the reverse – oil on canvas board – 19½ x 23½in.
(Christie's) **$10,016** **£6,380**

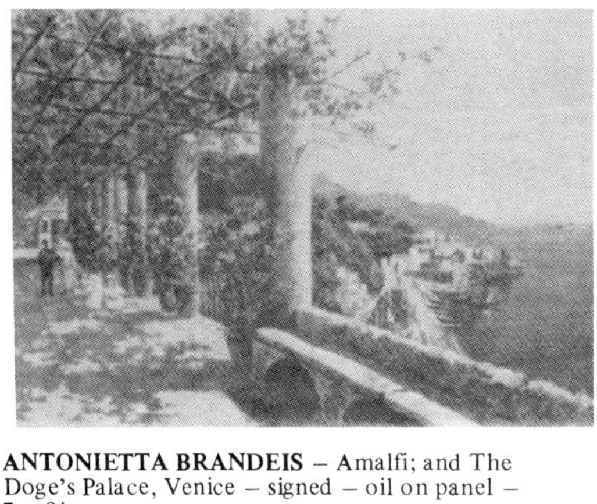

ANTONIETTA BRANDEIS – Amalfi; and The Doge's Palace, Venice – signed – oil on panel – 7 x 9in.
(Christie's) **$3,744** **£2,600 Pair**

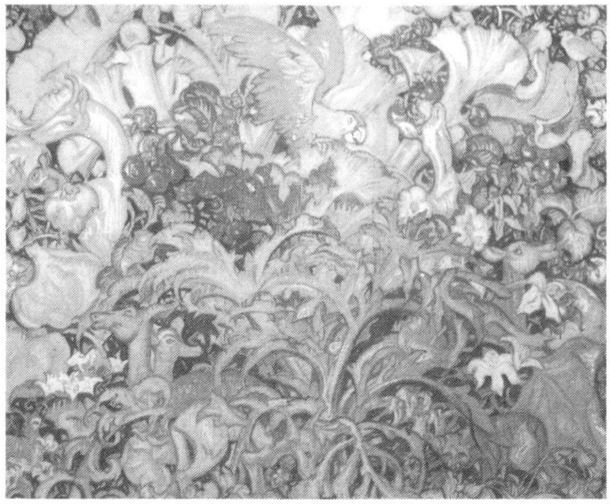

SIR FRANK BRANGWYN – Cartoon For The British Empire Panels House Of Lords – gouache and soft pencil on squared paper – 32½ x 38in.
(Christie's) **$6,292** **£4,400**

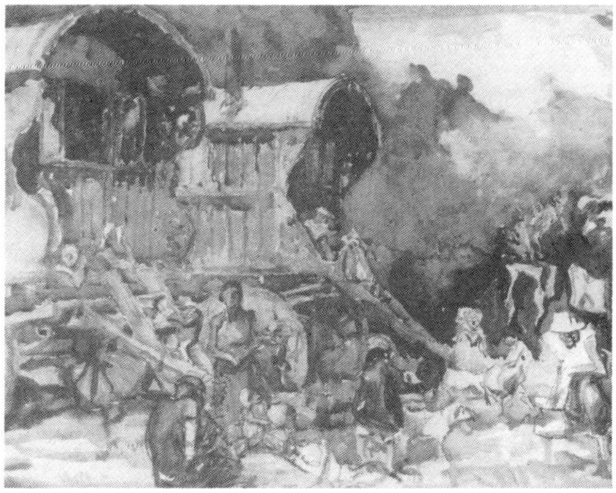

SIR FRANK BRANGWYN – Caravans And Gypsies – watercolour and bodycolour over soft pencil – 21¾ x 28¾in.
(Christie's) **$3,932** **£2,750**

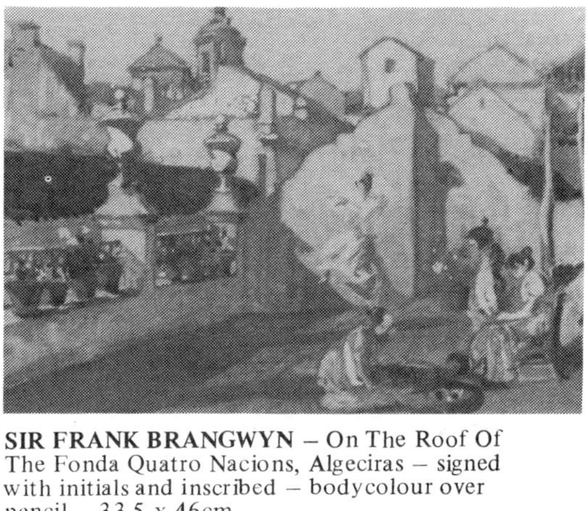

SIR FRANK BRANGWYN – On The Roof Of The Fonda Quatro Nacions, Algeciras – signed with initials and inscribed – bodycolour over pencil – 33.5 x 46cm.
(Phillips) **$1,460** **£880**

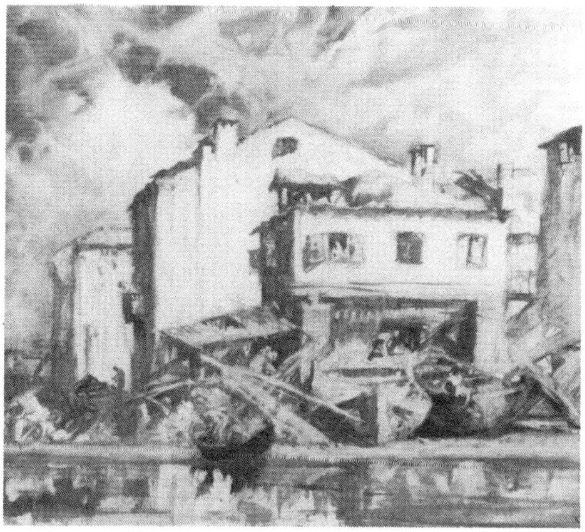

SIR FRANK BRANGWYN – Rio Della Abazia, Venice – signed with initials – watercolour and bodycolour over pencil – 15¾ x 17¼in.
(Christie's) **$3,460** **£2,420**

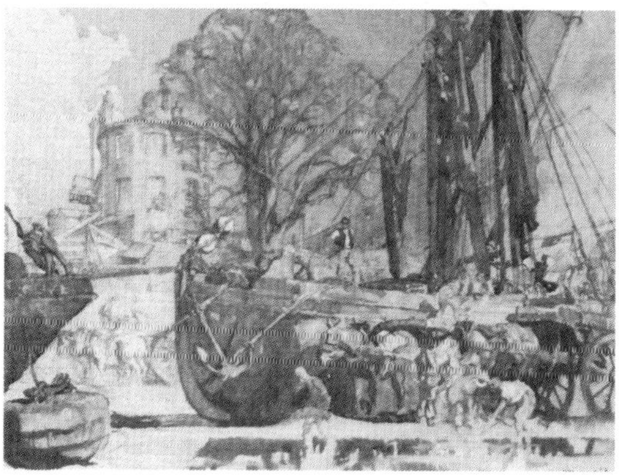

SIR FRANK BRANGWYN – Hammersmith Hard – signed with initials and inscribed – watercolour and bodycolour – 22 x 30in.
(Christie's) **$3,932** **£2,750**

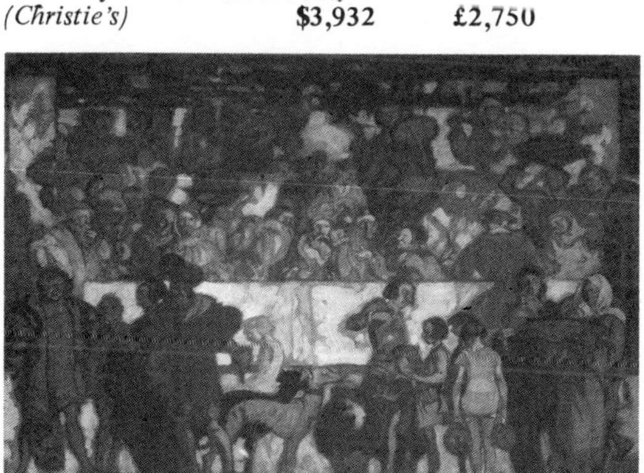

SIR FRANK BRANGWYN – The Feast – signed – oil on panel – 21½ x 30in.
(Christie's) **$6,292** **£4,400**

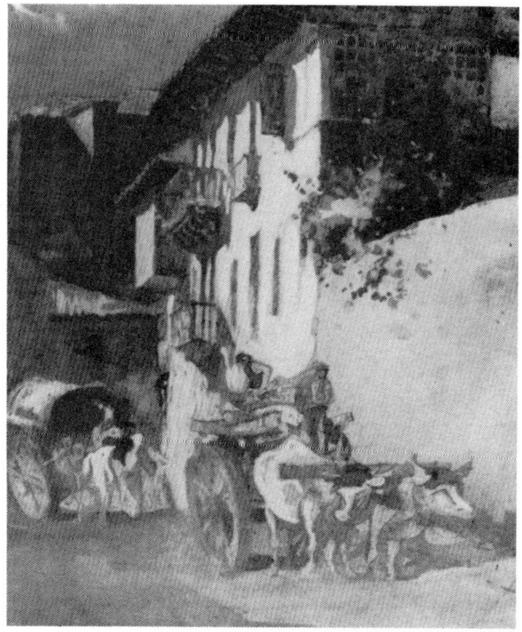

SIR FRANK BRANGWYN – Puerta De Passages – signed with initials, inscribed and dated '91 – watercolour and bodycolour over pencil – 22 x 16½in.
(Christie's) **$3,932** **£2,750**

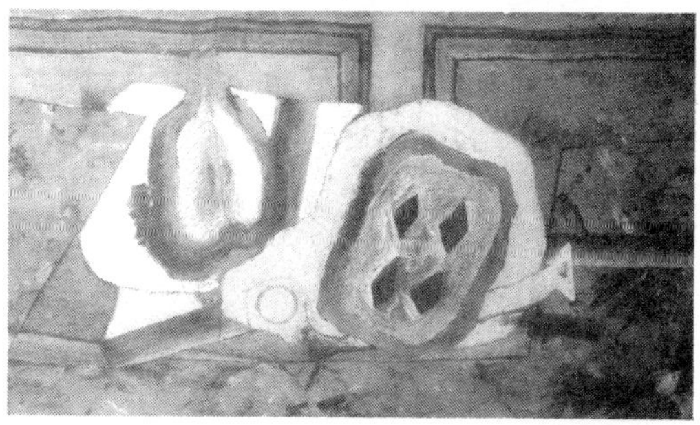

GEORGES BRAQUE – Le Quatre de Carreau – signed on the reverse – oil on canvas – 7½ x 13¼in.
(Christie's) **$50,688** **£35,200**

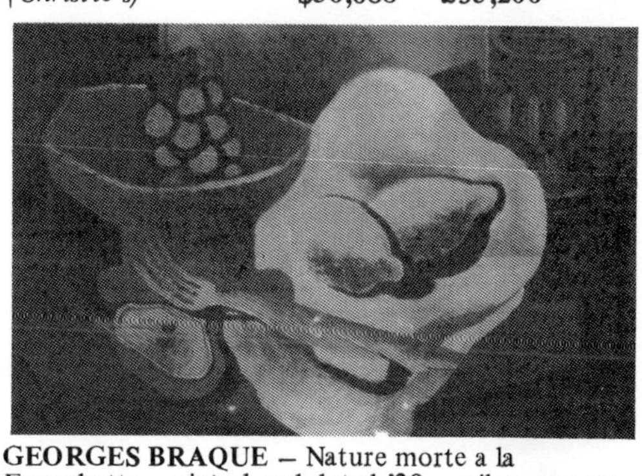

GEORGES BRAQUE – Nature morte a la Fourchette – signed and dated '29 – oil on canvas – 15 x 22in.
(Christie's) **$312,290** **£187,000**

BRAUER

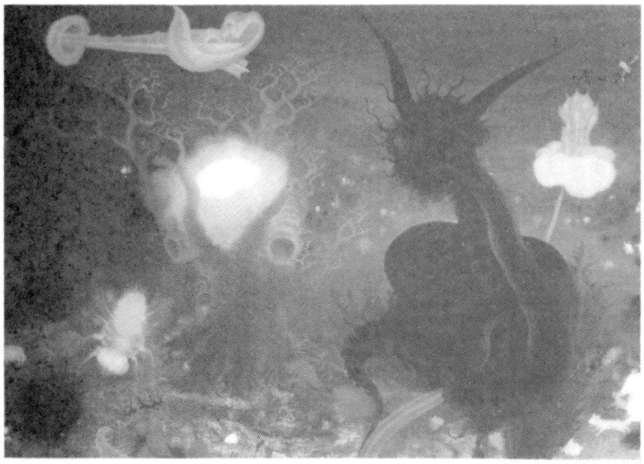

ERICH BRAUER – Schnecke – signed – oil on panel – 24 x 33¼in.
(Christie's) **$10,296** **£7,150**

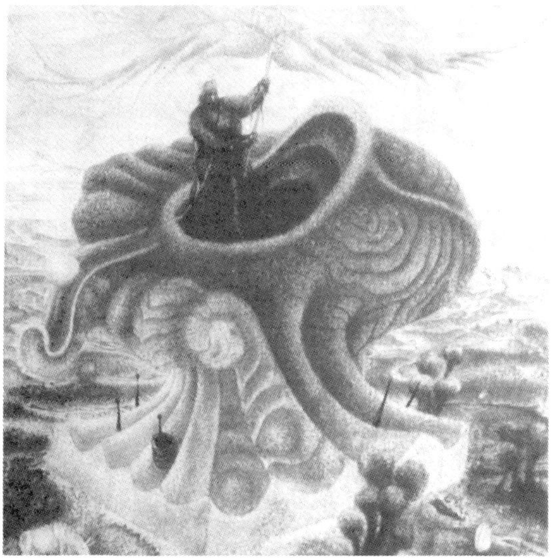

ERICH BRAUER – Eisener Turm – signed, inscribed and dated 1967 on the reverse – gouache on paper – 9 x 8½in.
(Christie's) **$2,059** **£1,430**

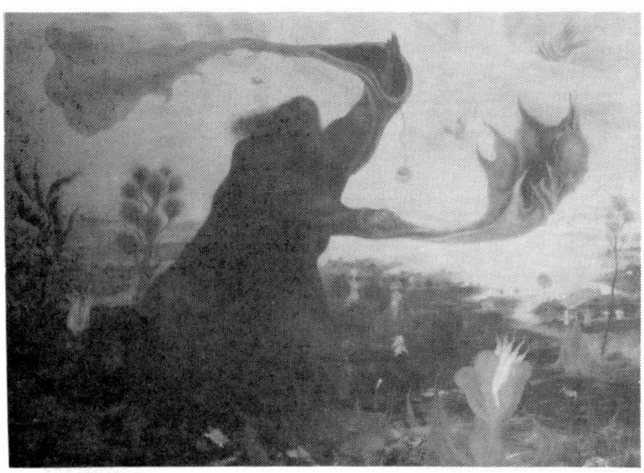

ERICH BRAUER – Der Windmacher – signed – oil on panel – 19¼ x 25in.
(Christie's) **$9,680** **£6,050**

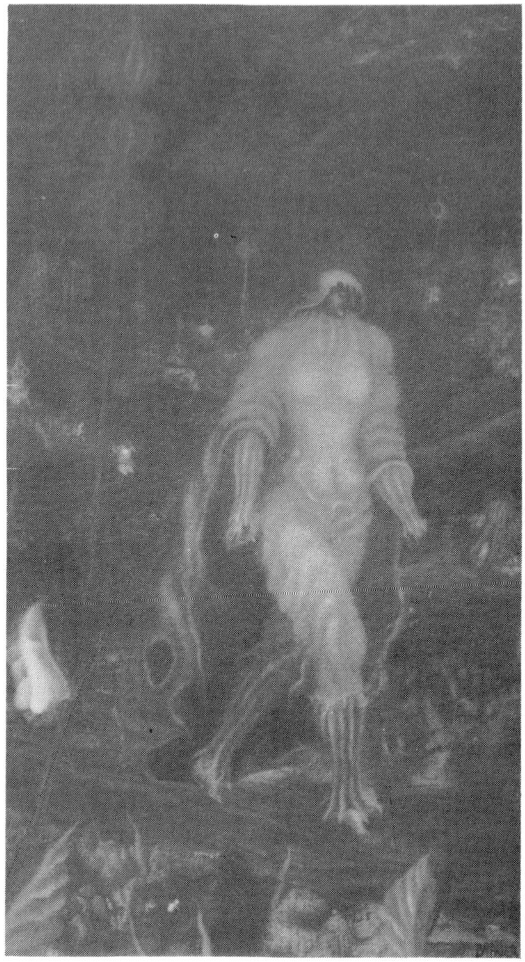

ERICH BRAUER – Nachtwandlerin – signed – oil on panel – 18¼ x 9½in.
(Christie's) **$5,632** **£3,520**

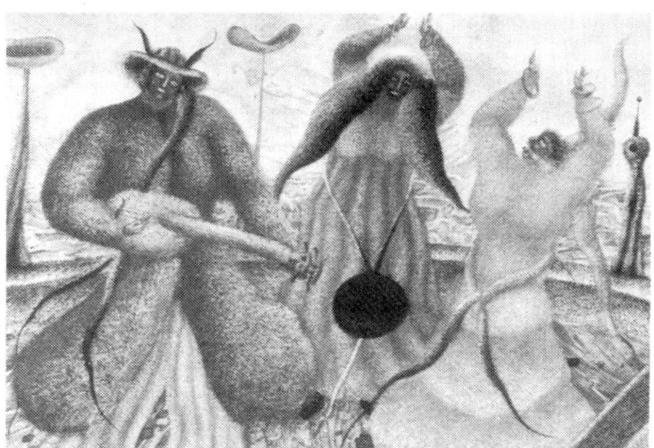

ERICH BRAUER – Flamenko Tanzer – signed and inscribed on the reverse – gouache on paper – 8 x 9¾in.
(Christie's) **$3,801** **£2,640**

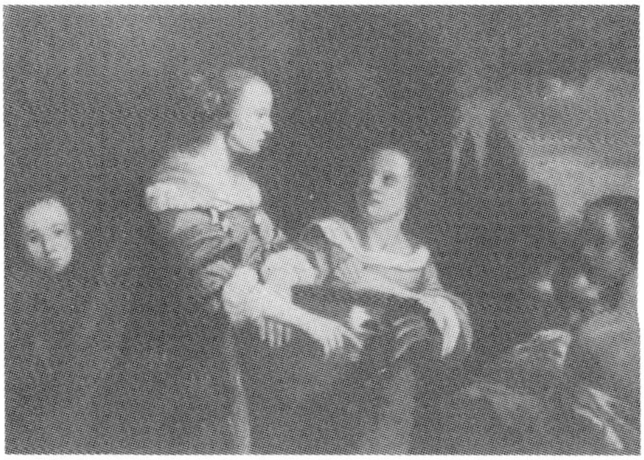

JAN DE BRAY, Circle of – The Finding Of Moses – oil on canvas – 47½ x 65in.
(Phillips) **$1,833** **£1,300**

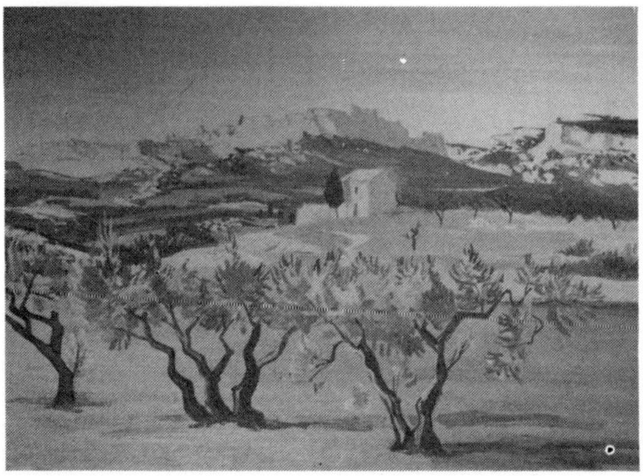

YVES BRAYER – Les Baux De Provence – signed – 20 x 24in.
(Lawrence Fine Art) **$3,652** **£2,200**

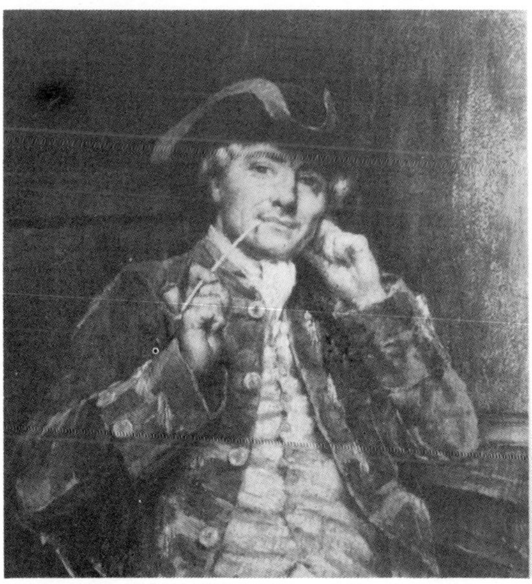

WILLIAM A. BREAKSPEARE – A Good Smoke – signed – on panel – 10 x 8¾in.
(Christie's) **$972** **£648**

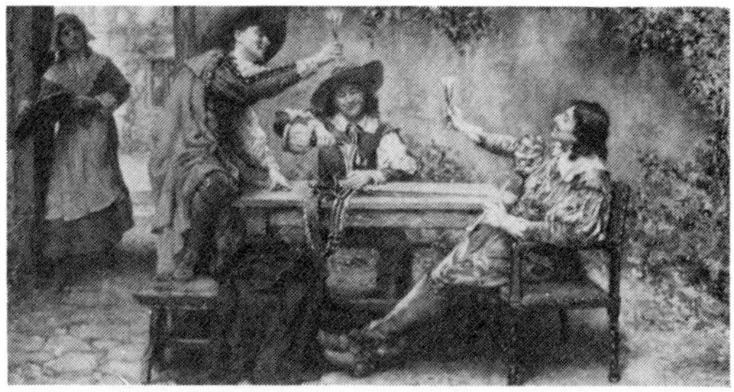

WILLIAM A. BREAKSPEARE – A Toast – signed – on panel – 12 x 18½in.
(Christie's) **$2,754** **£1,836**

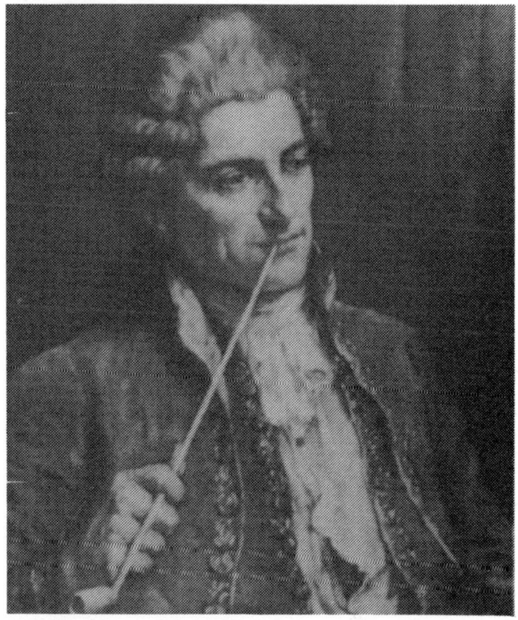

WILLIAM A. BREAKSPEARE – The Smoker – signed – on panel – 9¾ x 7in.
(Phillips) **$933** **£580**

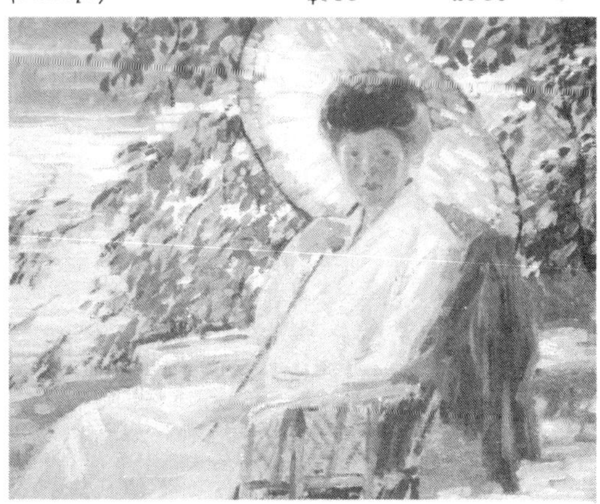

RAE SLOAN BREDIN – Sunlight And Shadow – signed, also signed on the reverse – oil on canvas – 12 x 14¼in.
(Christie's) **$15,400** **£10,826**

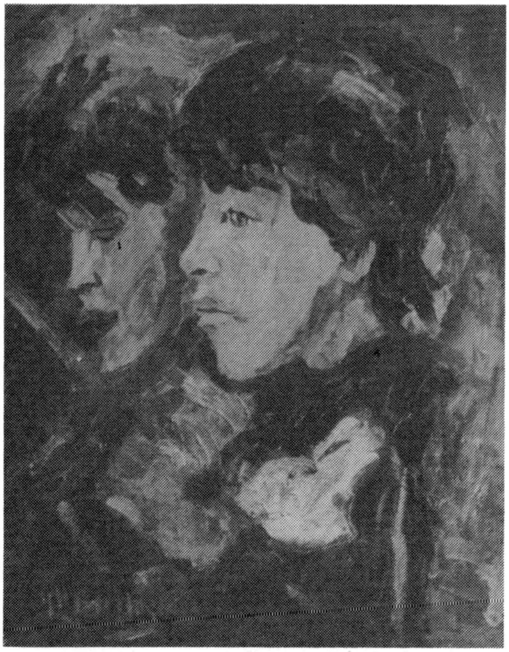

GEORG HENDRIK BREITNER – Dual Portrait – – signed – oil on panel – 55 x 45cm.
(Phillips) **$310** **£200**

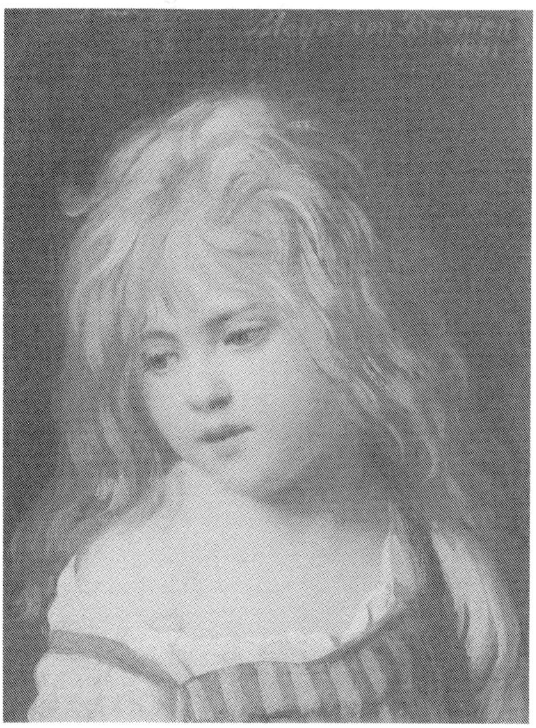

MEYER VON BREMEN – Portrait Of A Child – signed and dated 1881 – on panel – 14 x 12cm.
(Phillips) **$4,896** **£3,400**

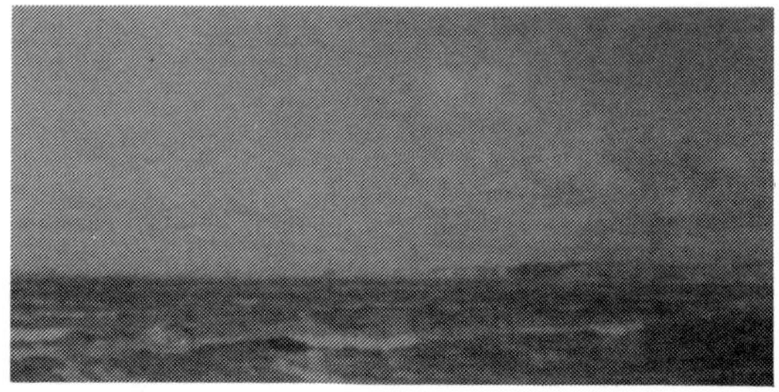

JOHN BRETT – 'Lands End' – inscribed and dated '81 – on canvas – 10 x 19in.
(Phillips) **$1,529** **£950**

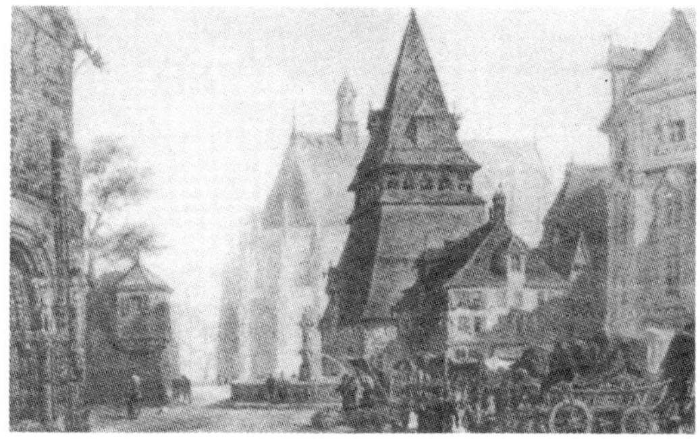

HENRY WILLIAM BREWER – The Church Of The Holy Cross, Schwabisch Grund, Wurtemburg – signed, signed and inscribed on a label on the reverse – oil on canvas – 19½ x 29½in.
(Christie's) **$2,851** **£1,980**

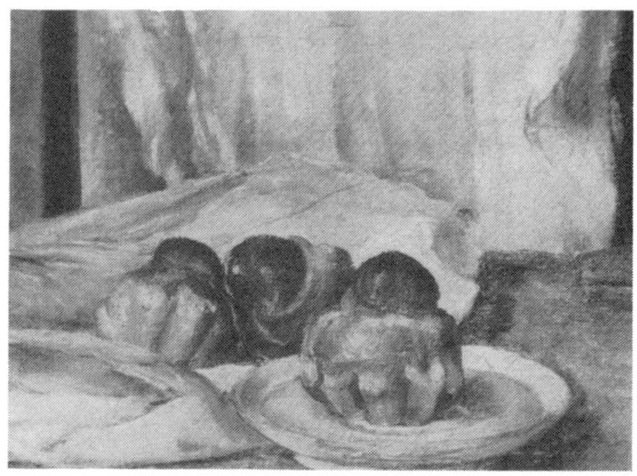

MAURICE BRIANCHON – Nature morte aux Brioches – signed – oil on board – 8½ x 10½in.
(Christie's) **$5,280** **£3,300**

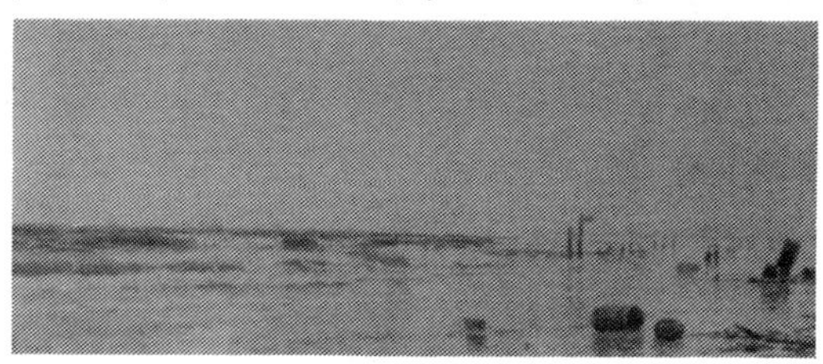

ALFRED THOMPSON BRICHER – Coastal View With Figures On The Beach – signed – watercolour on paper – 9½ x 21in.
(Robt. W. Skinner Inc.) **$3,300** **£2,024**

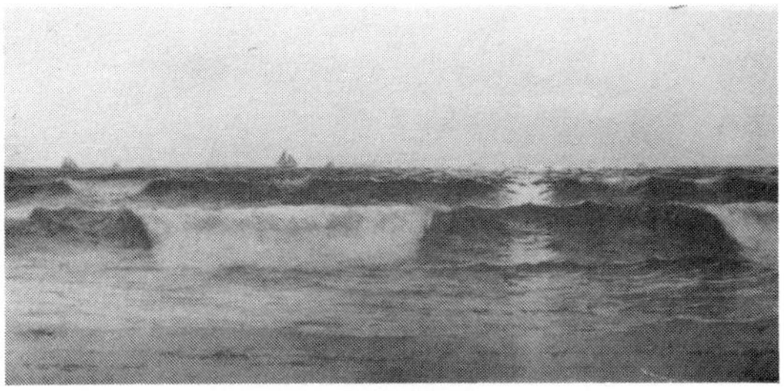

ALFRED THOMPSON BRICHER – Seascape – signed – watercolour on paper laid down on cardboard – 12¾ x 26¼in.
(Robt. W. Skinner Inc.) **$6,500** **£4,513**

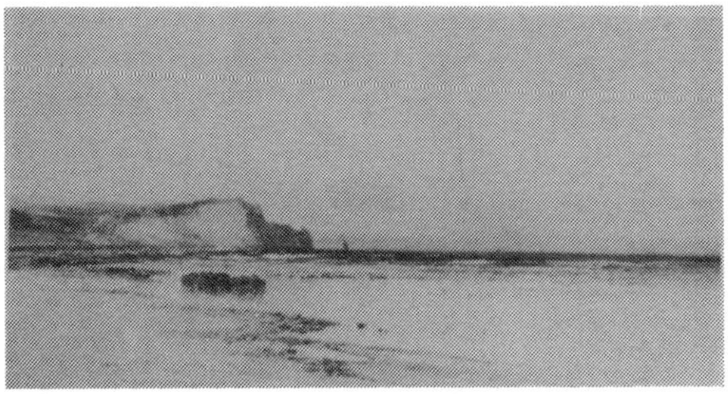

ALFRED THOMPSON BRICHER, Attributed to – Coastal View Of A Headland – signed – watercolour on paper – 10¾ x 19½in.
(Robt. W. Skinner Inc.) **$375** **£230**

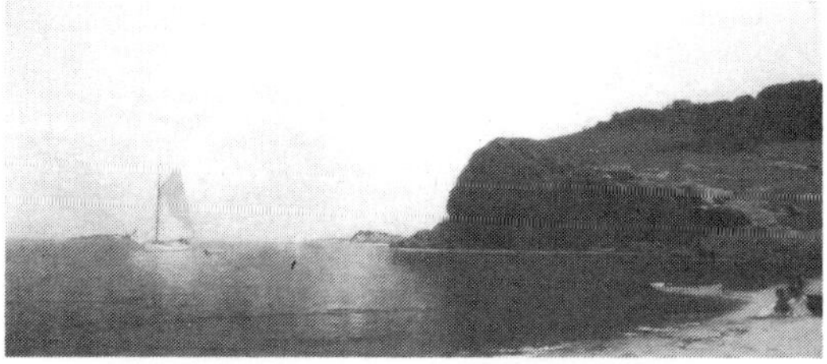

ALFRED THOMPSON BRICHER – Afternoon Calm – signed with initials in monogram – oil on canvas – 18 x 39in.
(Christie's) **$55,000** **£38,665**

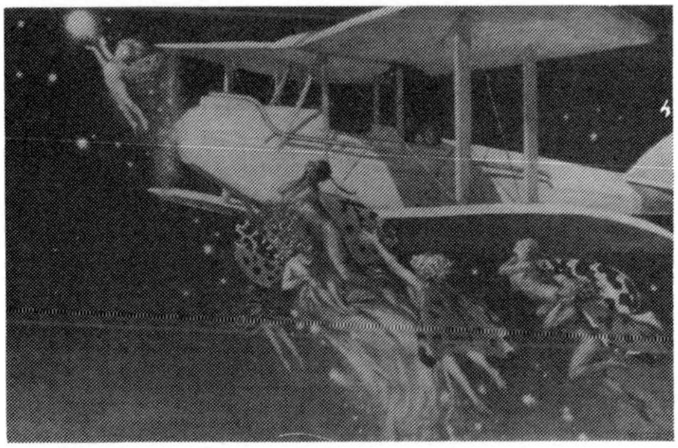

ELEANOR FORTESCUE BRICKDALE – The Moth – signed – watercolour heightened with bodycolour – 30 x 47cm.
(Phillips) **$3,586** **£2,200**

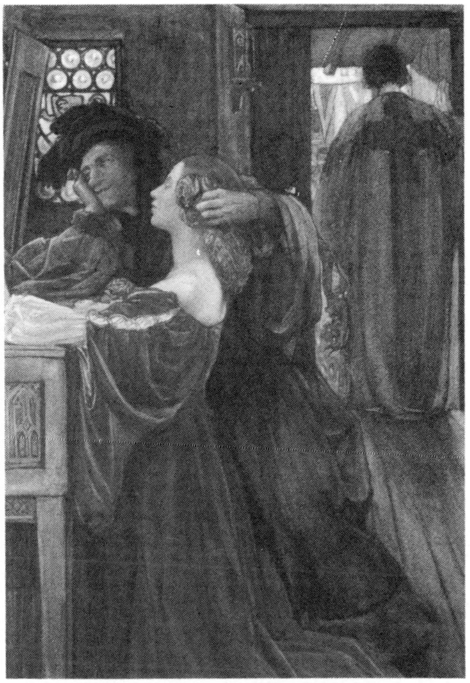

ELEANOR FORTESCUE BRICKDALE – 'One Said "I Have Married A Wife And Therefore I Cannot Come"' – signed and inscribed on the reverse – watercolour heightened with white on card – 15½ x 9in.
(Christie's) **$9,720** **£6,480**

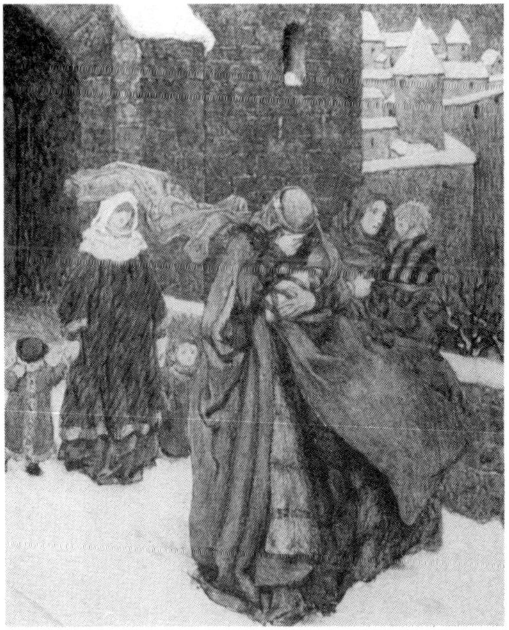

ELEANOR FORTESCUE BRICKDALE – The Departure In Winter – signed with initials – pencil and watercolour – 7¼ x 4¾in.
(Christie's) **$1,108** **£770**

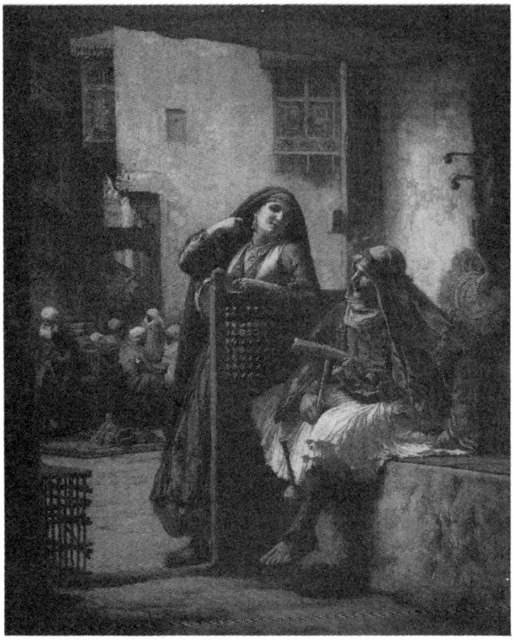

FREDERICK ARTHUR BRIDGMAN – A Visit From The Chieftain – signed – 21¼ x 17¾in.
(Christie's) **$21,120** **£13,200**

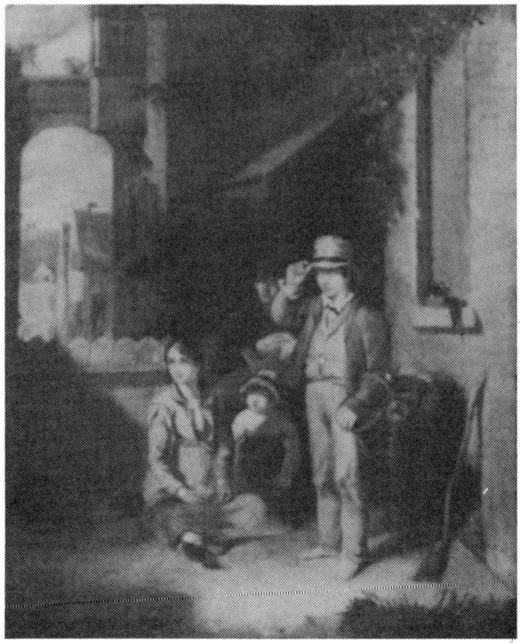

EDMUND BRISTOW, Follower of – Family Group Before A House – oil on canvas – 12 x 10in.
(Phillips) **$863** **£520**

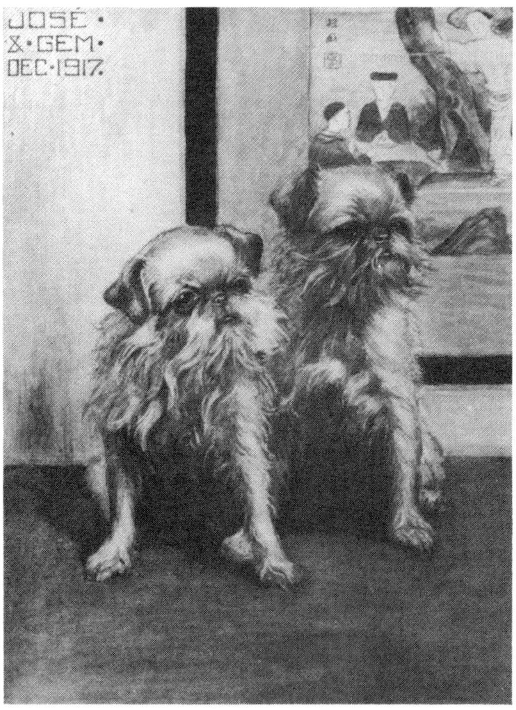

NINA K. BRISLEY – Study Of The Belgian Griffons 'Jose and Gem' – signed, inscribed and dated 1917 – watercolour – 13¾ x 10¼in.
(Bonhams) **$930** **£600**

CHARLES EDWARD BRITTAN – Animals In A Wayside Shed On The Continent – signed – watercolour heightened with white – 17½ x 23¼in.
(Christie's) **$1,008** **£715**

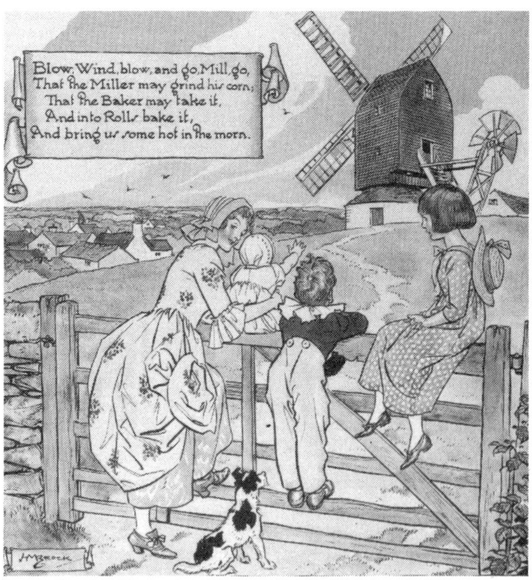

HENRY MATTHEW BROCK – 'Blow, Wind, Blow, And Go, Mill, Go' – signed and inscribed – pencil, pen and black ink and watercolour heightened with white on board – 12¼ x 10½in.
(Christie's) **$3,702** **£2,420**

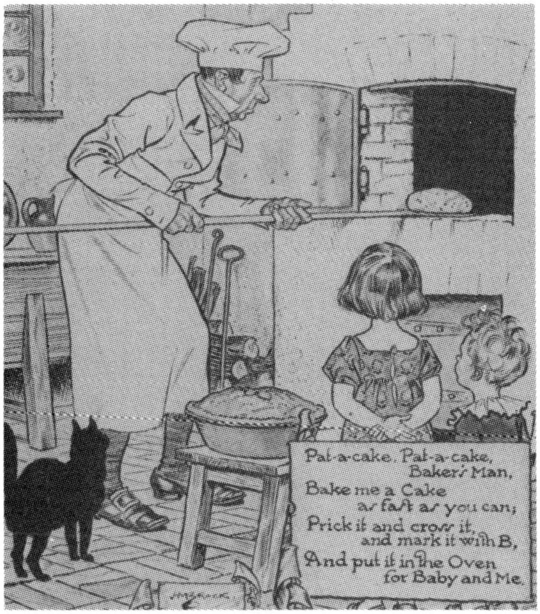

HENRY MATTHEW BROCK – 'Pat-a-Cake, Pat-a-Cake, Baker's Man' – signed and inscribed – pencil, pen and black ink and watercolour on Bristol board – 13¼ x 11½in.
(Christie's) **$2,861** **£1,870**

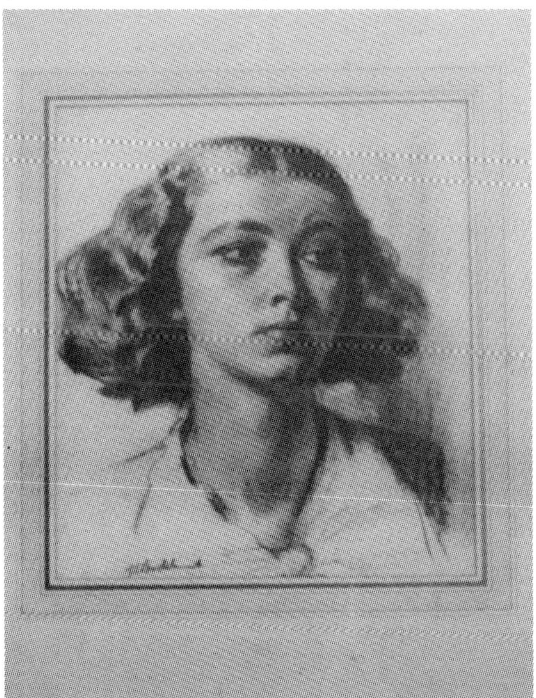

GERALD LESLEY BROCKHURST – Head – dated 1938 on verso – pastel – 16½ x 14in.
(Prudential Fine Art Auctioneers) **$1,195** **£720**

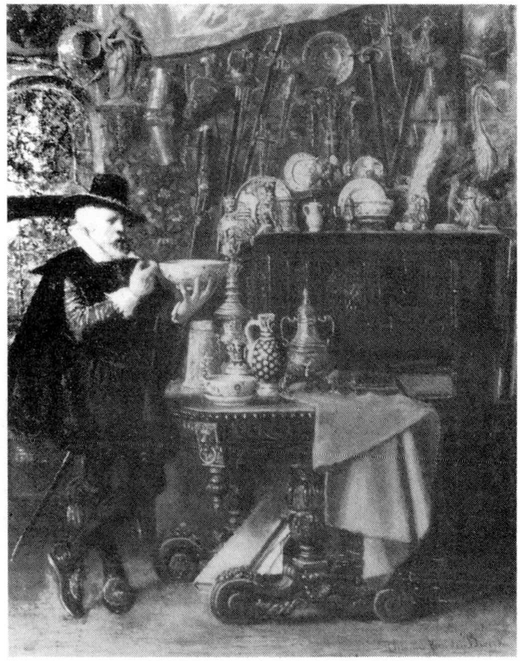

CLEMENCEUVAN DEN BROECK – The Connoisseur – signed – on panel – 15¾ x 12¾in.
(Christie's) **$1,421** **£935**

WILLIAM BROMLEY – Waiting For A Bite – signed – 14 x 18in.
(Christie's) **$10,098** **£6,600**

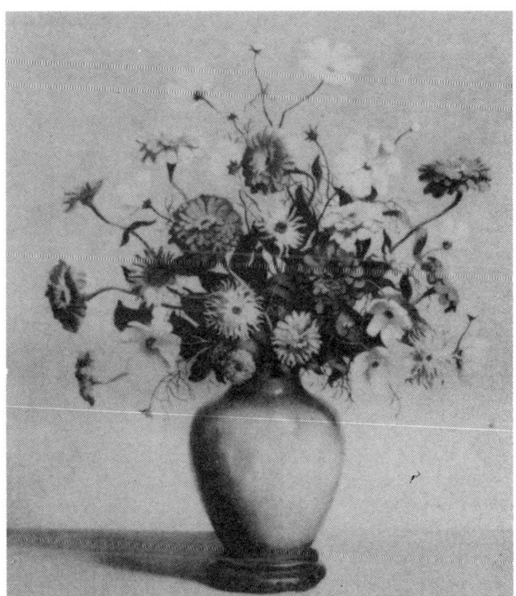

HENRY HOWARD BROOKS – Summer Flowers With Green Vase – signed – oil on canvas – 36¼ x 30¼in.
(Robt. W. Skinner Inc.) **$600** **£416**

BROWN

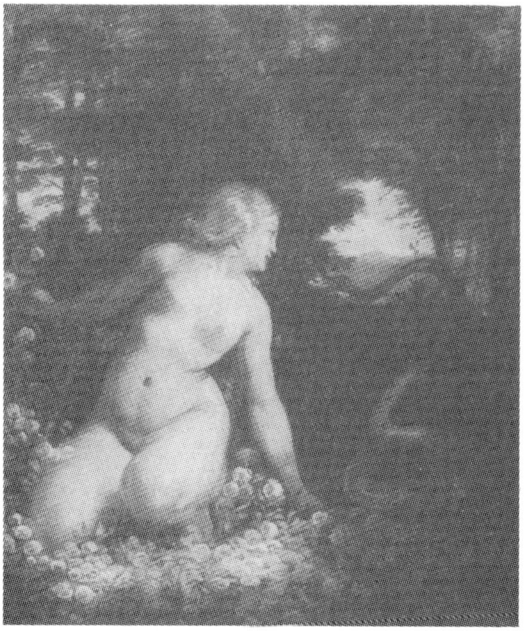

FORD MADOX BROWN, Attributed to – The Temptation Of Eve – 18 x 22in.
(Christie's) **$1,178** **£770**

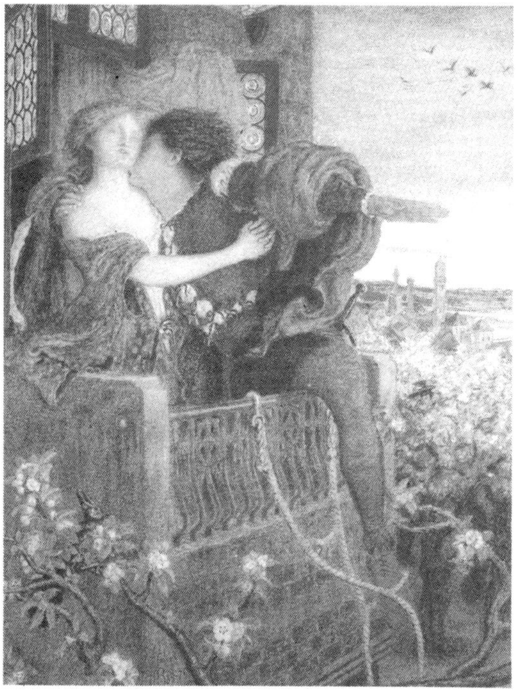

FORD MADOX BROWN – Romeo And Juliet – signed with monogram and dated 68-71 – watercolour, bodycolour and gum arabic – 12½ x 9½in.
(Christie's) **$41,184** **£28,600**

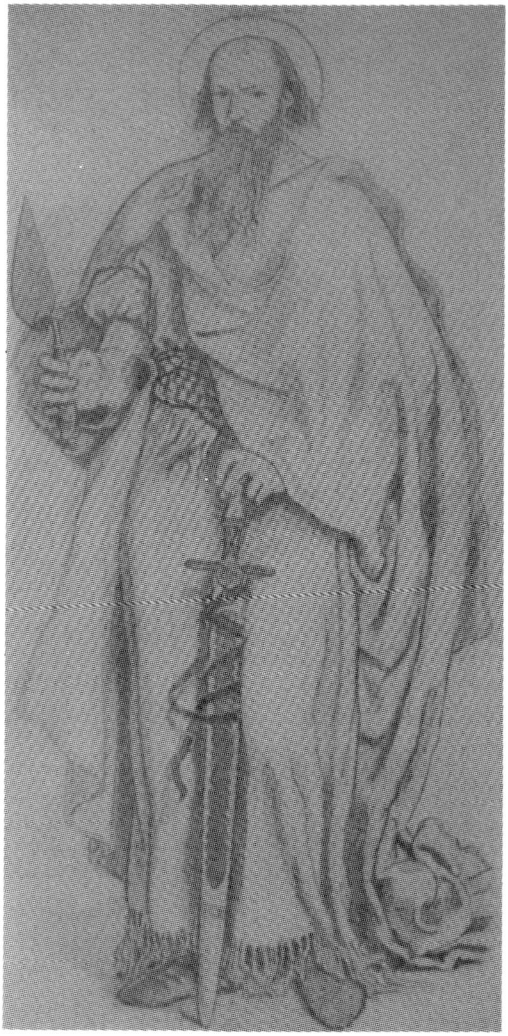

FORD MADOX BROWN – Nehemiah: A Design For A Figure In The East Window Of The Chancel Of St. John The Evangelist, Tuebrook – inscribed – pencil, grey and brown wash on board – 38 x 19½in.
(Christie's) **$3,104** **£1,870**

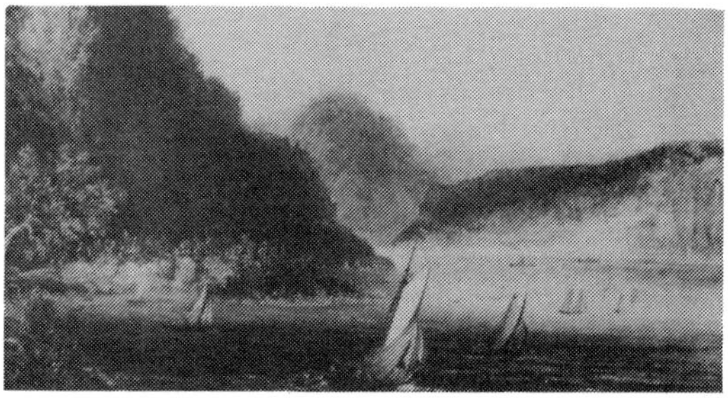

GEORGE LORING BROWN – A View Of The Hudson – signed and dated 1837 – oil on canvas – 16¾ x 21in.
(Robt. W. Skinner Inc.) **$1,900** **£1,165**

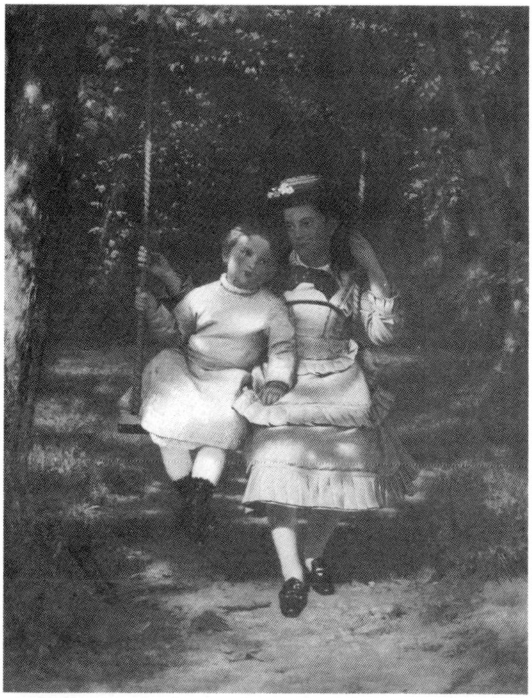

JOHN GEORGE BROWN – Two Girls On A Swing – signed and dated 1872 – oil on canvas – 17¾ x 13¾in.
(Christie's) **$38,500** **£27,065**

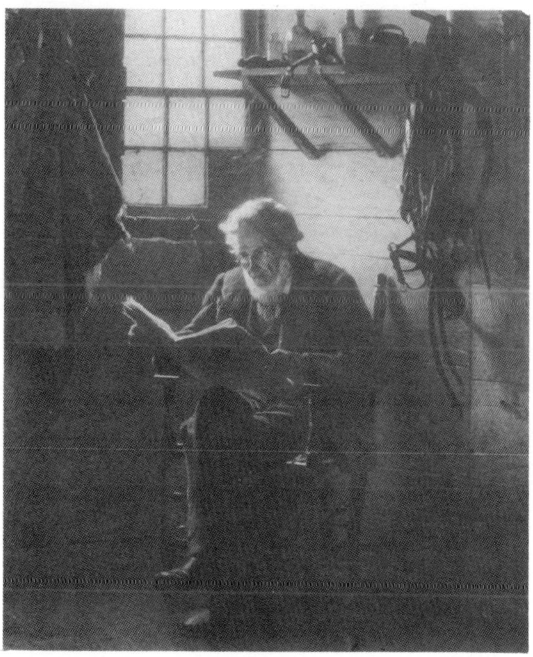

JOHN GEORGE BROWN – An Idle Hour – signed – oil on canvas – 30 x 25½in.
(Christie's) **$19,800** **£13,919**

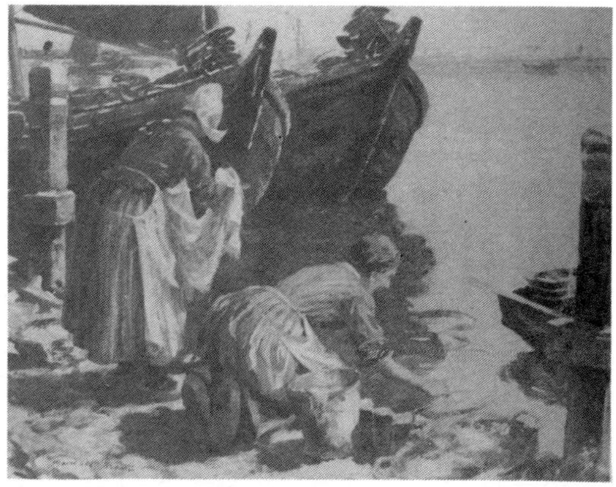

WILLIAM MARSHALL BROWN – Washerwomen, Volendam – signed, inscribed on a label verso – oil on canvas – 28 x 36in.
(Christie's) **$3,456** **£2,400**

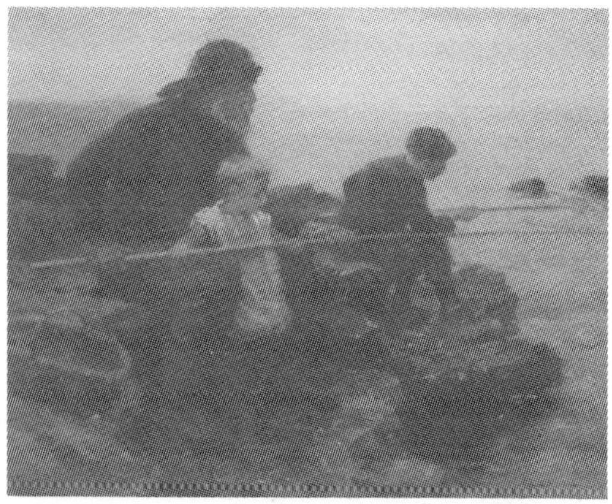

WILLIAM MARSHALL BROWN – The Fishing Lesson – signed – oil on canvas – 28 x 36in.
(Christie's) **$7,200** **£5,000**

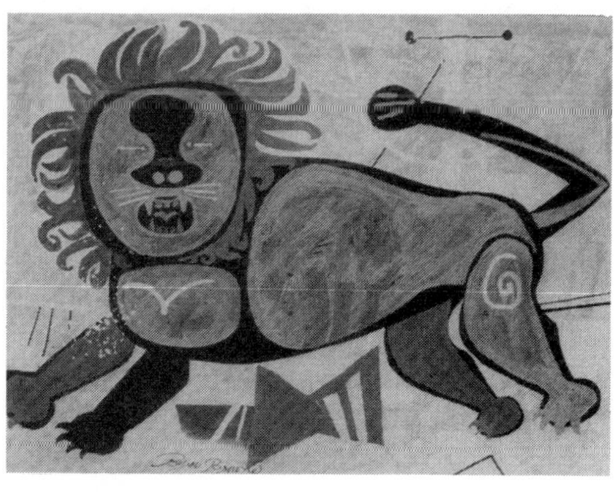

BYRON BROWNE – Lion Hunt – signed, also signed, dated 1947 and inscribed on the reverse – tempera and pen and black ink on paper – 19 x 25in.
(Christie's) **$880** **£548**

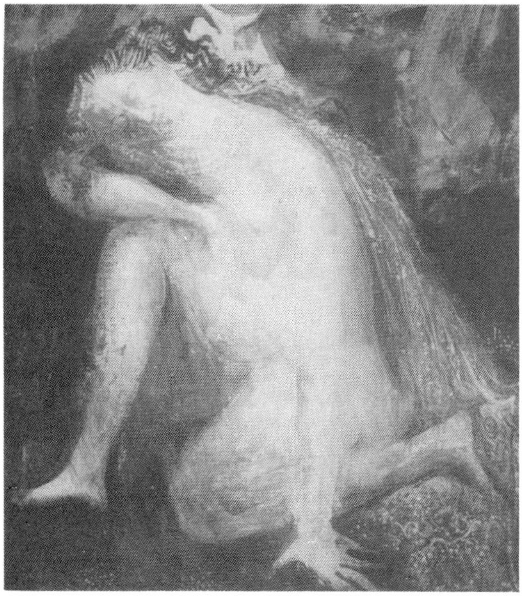

BYRON BROWNE – The Dream – signed and dated 1959, signed, dated and inscribed on the reverse – oil on canvas – 26¼ x 20in.
(Christie's) **$1,760** **£1,224**

GEORGE ELMER BROWNE – Marine Nocturne – signed – oil on canvas – 40 x 50in.
(Christie's) **$2,200** **£1,530**

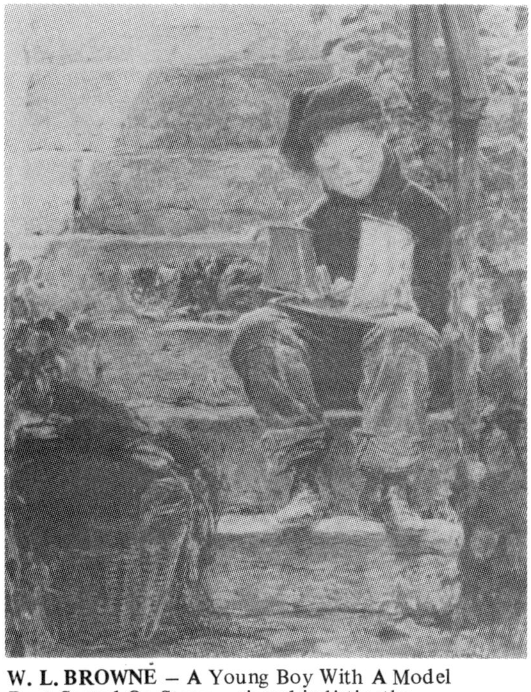

W. L. BROWNE – **A** Young Boy With **A** Model Boat Seated On Steps – signed indistinctly – watercolour and bodycolour heightened with gum arabic – 19 x 16cm.
(Phillips) **$1,430** **£1,000**

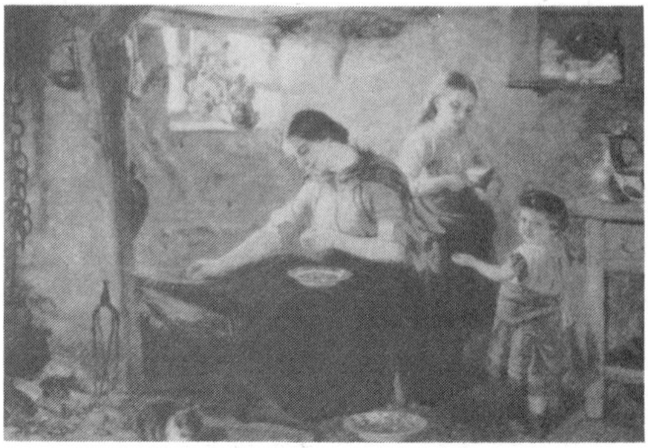

GEORGE WASHINGTON BROWNLOW – 'Baiting The Line', Scene In A Findon Fisherman's Cottage – signed, signed with initials and inscribed on the stretcher on the reverse – oil on canvas – 9¾ x 12¾in.
(Christie's) **$4,017** **£2,420**

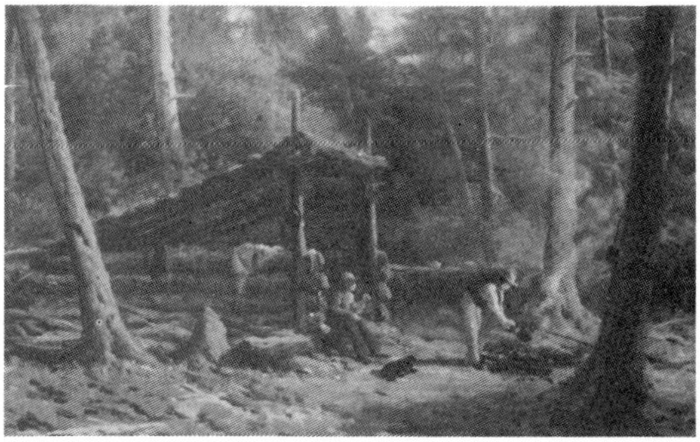

WILLIAM BLAIR BRUCE – A Man's Life – signed – oil on canvas – 15 x 22in.
(Christie's) **$2,640** **£1,836**

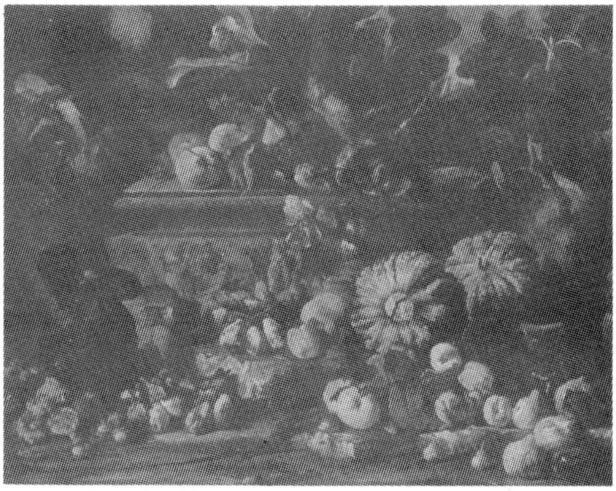

ABRAHAM BRUEGHEL – A Still Life Of Fruit – on canvas – 38 x 51¾in.
(Phillips) **$89,640** **£54,000**

PIETER BRUEGHEL, The Younger – The Wedding Feast – signed and dated 1626 – on panel – 15 x 19¾in.
(Phillips) **$332,000** **£200,000**

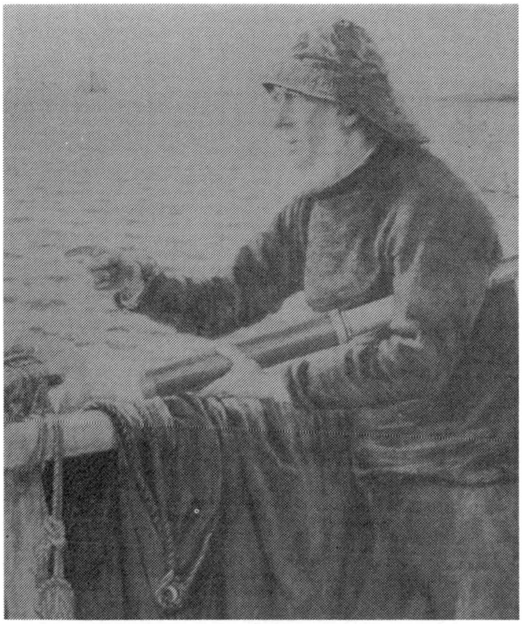

FRED BRUETON – An Old Cornish Fisherman – signed and dated 1911 – watercolour over traces of pencil – 53 x 36cm.
(Phillips) **$796** **£480**

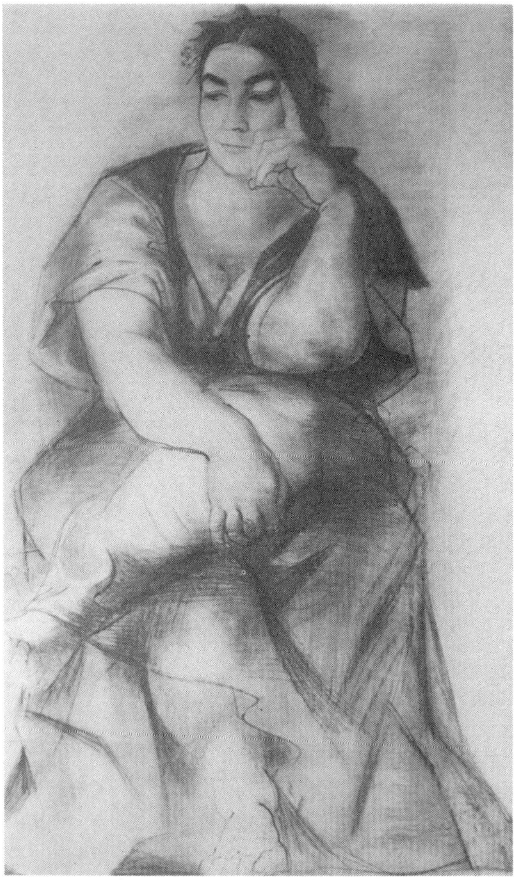

FREDERICO 'RICO' LE BRUN – Portrait Of Kate Lawson – signed and dated 1940 – chalk, pencil and tempera on paper – 58½ x 35½in.
(Christie's) **$2,640** **£1,836**

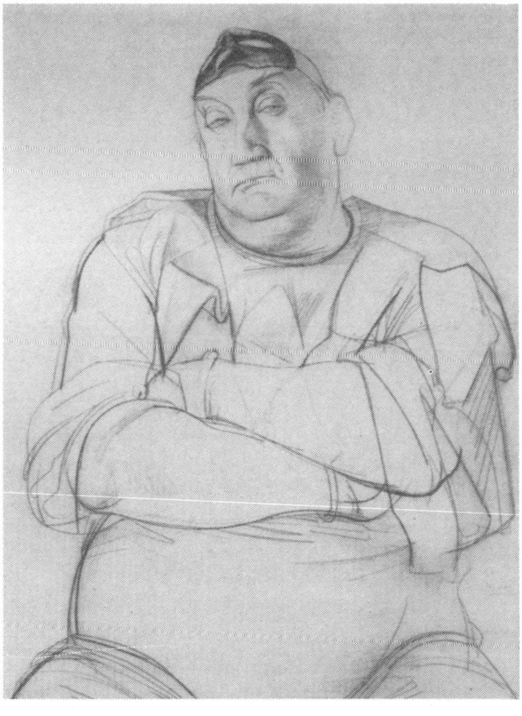

FREDERICO 'RICO' LE BRUN – The Great Petito, Pulcinella Napoletano – signed, dated 1940 and inscribed – pencil, charcoal and pen and black ink on tan paper – 40 x 30in.
(Christie's) **$4,620** **£3,214**

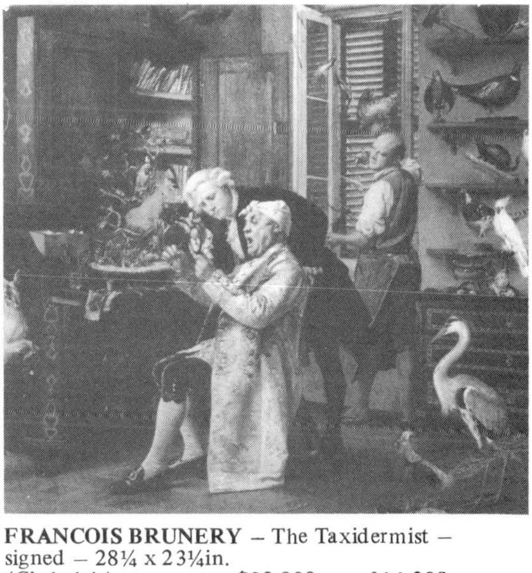

FRANCOIS BRUNERY – The Taxidermist – signed – 28¼ x 23¼in.
(Christie's) **$22,880** **£14,300**

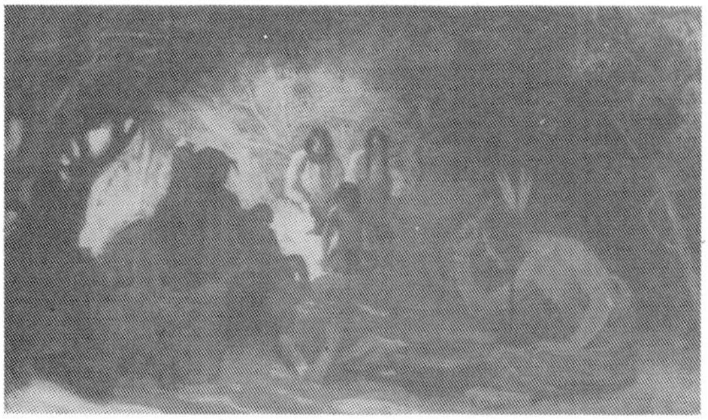

GEORGE DE FOREST BRUSH – Apache Medicine Man – oil en grisaille on board – 4¾ x 6¼in.
(Christie's) **$2,860** **£1,782**

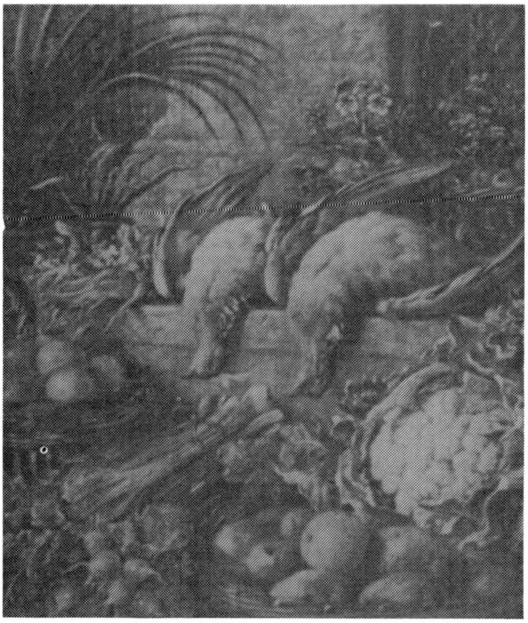

H. C. BRYANT – A Still Life Of Various Flowers, Vegetables And Game, Beside A Wall – signed – on canvas – 12 x 10in.
(Phillips) **$1,288** **£800**

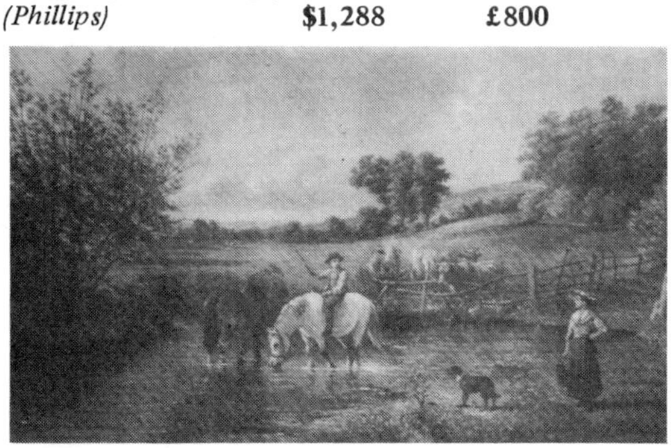

HENRY C. BRYANT – A Wooded River Landscape With A Boy On A Horse Talking To A Milkmaid – signed – 24 x 40½in.
(Christie's) **$4,207** **£2,750**

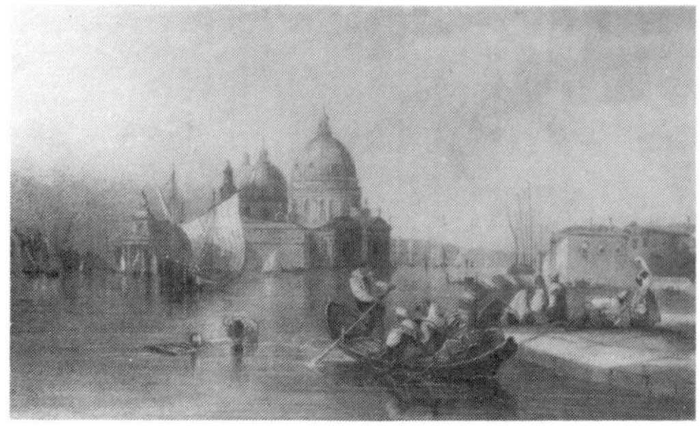

C. F. BUCKLEY – Figures In A Boat Near Santa Maria Della Salute, Venice – signed – pencil and watercolour heightened with white – 7¼ x 10¼in.
(Christie's) **$1,095** **£660**

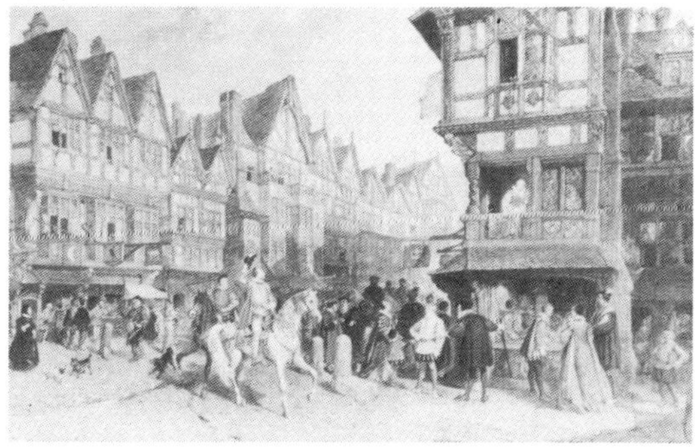

J. E. BUCKLEY – 'Old Rivals – London Street' – signed and dated 1865 – watercolour and bodycolour – 17 x 26½in.
(Christie's) **$1,318** **£935**

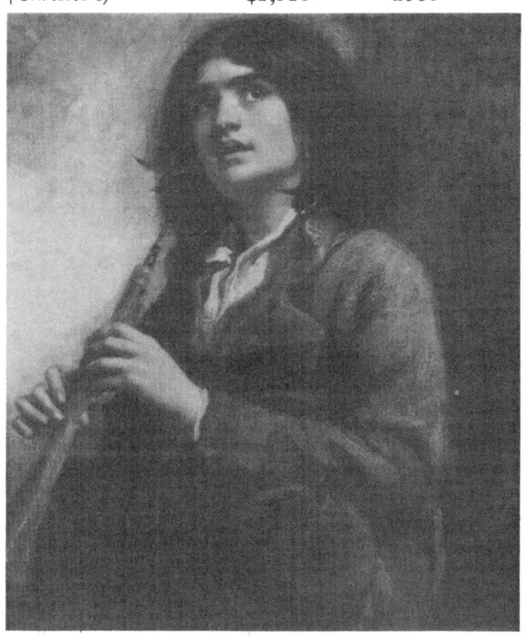

RICHARD BUCKNER – The Piper – signed – 31¼ x 25¼in.
(Christie's) **$615** **£410**

XAVIER BUENO – Due Bambini – signed – oil on canvas – 57¼ x 31½in.
(Christie's) **$3,484 £2,420**

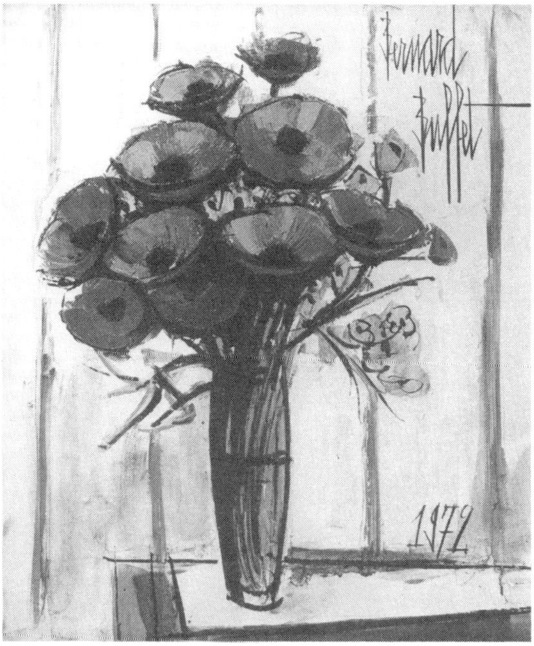

BERNARD BUFFET – Bouquet de Fleurs – signed and dated 1972 – oil on canvas – 21¼ x 25½in.
(Christie's) **$22,044 £13,200**

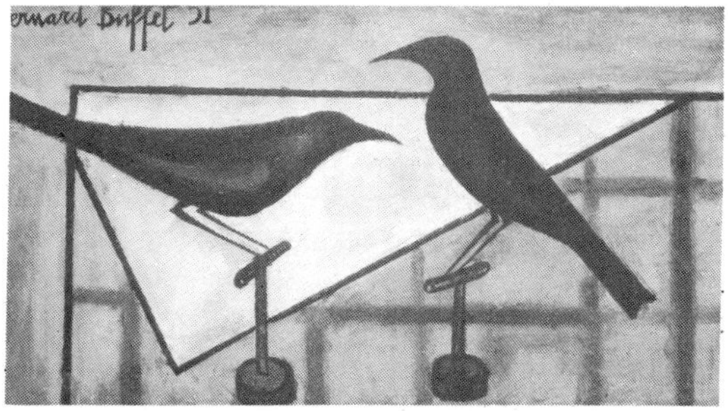

BERNARD BUFFET – Deux Oiseaux sur Perchoirs – signed and dated '51 – oil on canvas – 10¼ x 18in.
(Christie's) **$15,840 £11,000**

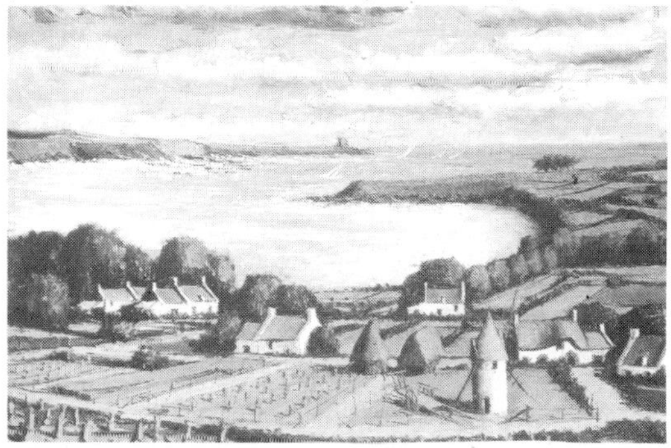

BERNARD BUFFET – Le Moulin de Sainte-Anne – signed and dated 1974, also inscribed on the reverse – oil on canvas – 39¼ x 51¼in.
(Christie's) **$33,264 £23,100**

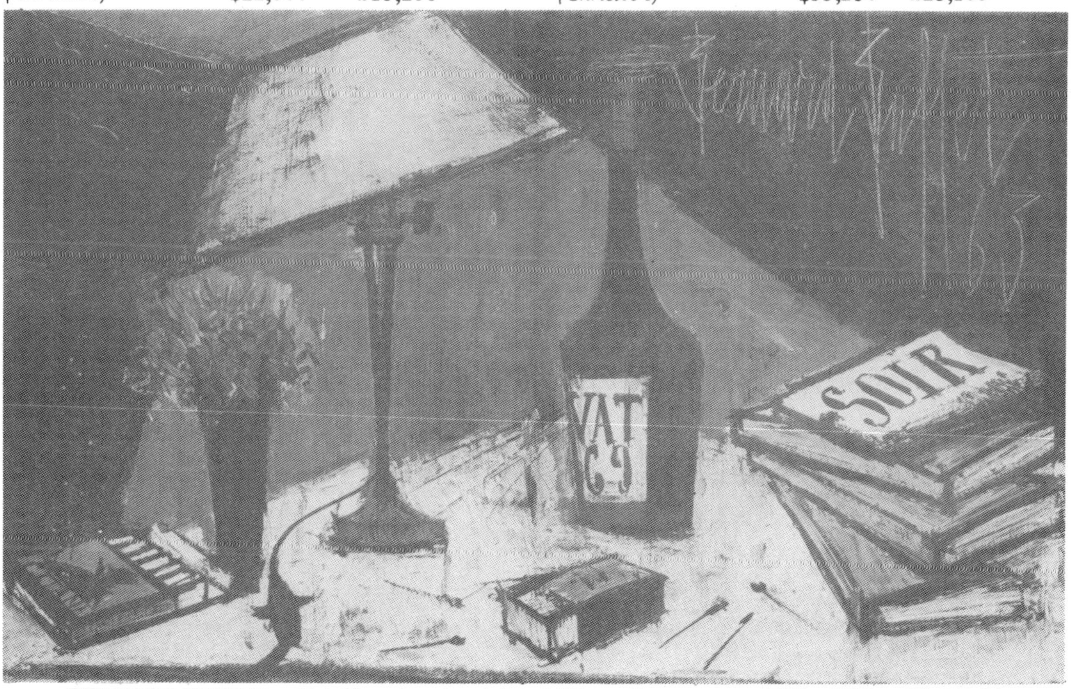

BERNARD BUFFET – Vat 69 – signed and dated '63 – oil on canvas – 23¾ x 36¼in. *(Christie's)*
$40,414 £24,200

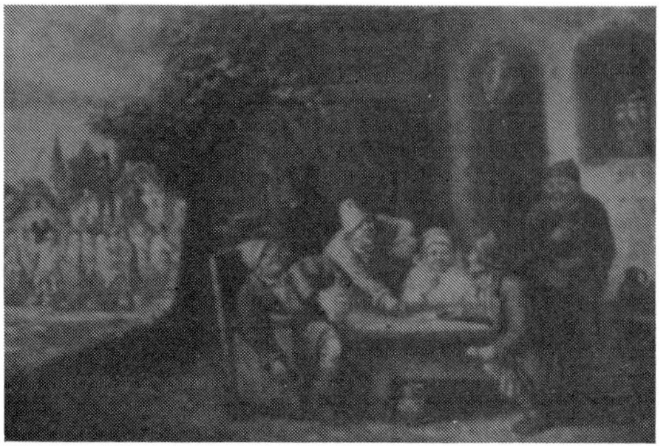

G. BUISSON – Peasants Carousing At A Village Festival – signed – oil on panel – 31 x 47cm.
(Phillips) **$1,753** **£1,050**

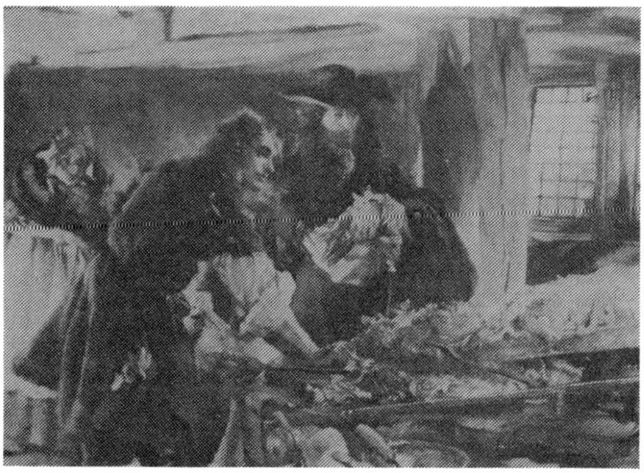

EDGAR BUNDY – The Violin Maker – signed and dated 1901 – on canvas – 16½ x 25½in.
(Phillips) **$1,610** **£1,000**

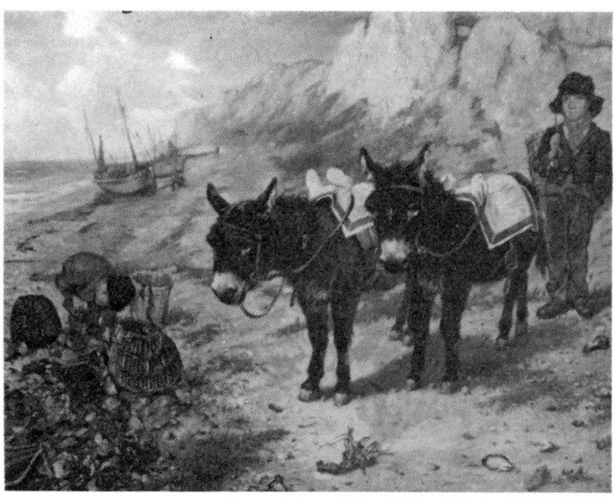

EDGAR BUNDY – Boy With Two Donkeys And Second Boy Checking Lobster Pots – signed and dated – oil on canvas – 27 x 35in.
(Morphets) **$6,200** **£4,000**

ANDREW FISHER BUNNER – Procession Of Sails – signed – oil on canvas – 17 x 27in.
(Christie's) **$2,200** **£1,530**

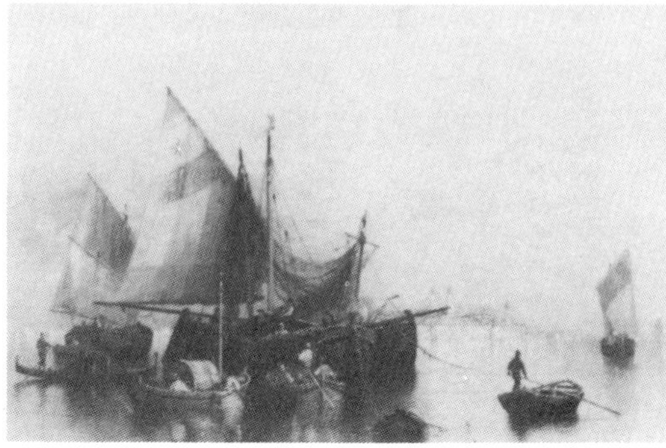

ANDREW FISHER BUNNER – 'Venetian Boats – San Lazarro' – signed, and signed on verso – oil on canvas – 22 x 32in.
(Robt. W. Skinner Inc.) **$1,500** **£1,041**

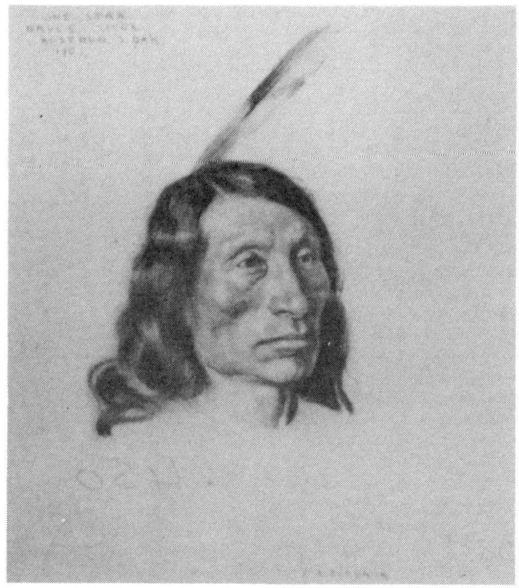

ELBRIDGE AYER BURBANK – Portrait Of The Indian 'One Star' – signed and inscribed, dated 1903 – conte crayon on paper laid down on board – 13¾ x 9¾in.
(Robt. W. Skinner Inc.) **$350** **£230**

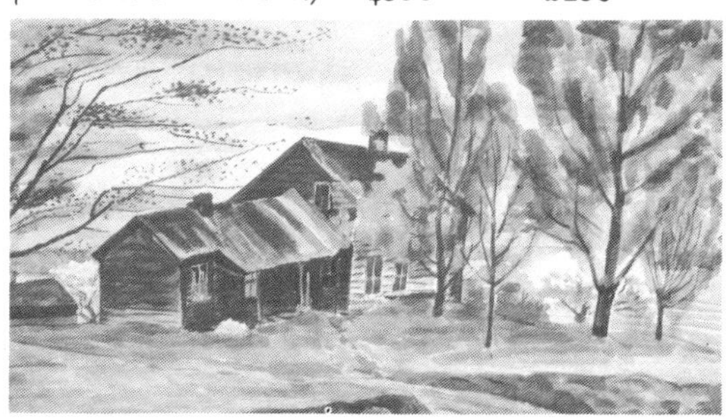

CHARLES EPHRAIM BURCHFIELD – Log Cabin – signed with monogrammed initials and dated 1933 – watercolour on paper – 18 x 27in.
(Christie's) **$9,350** **£6,504**

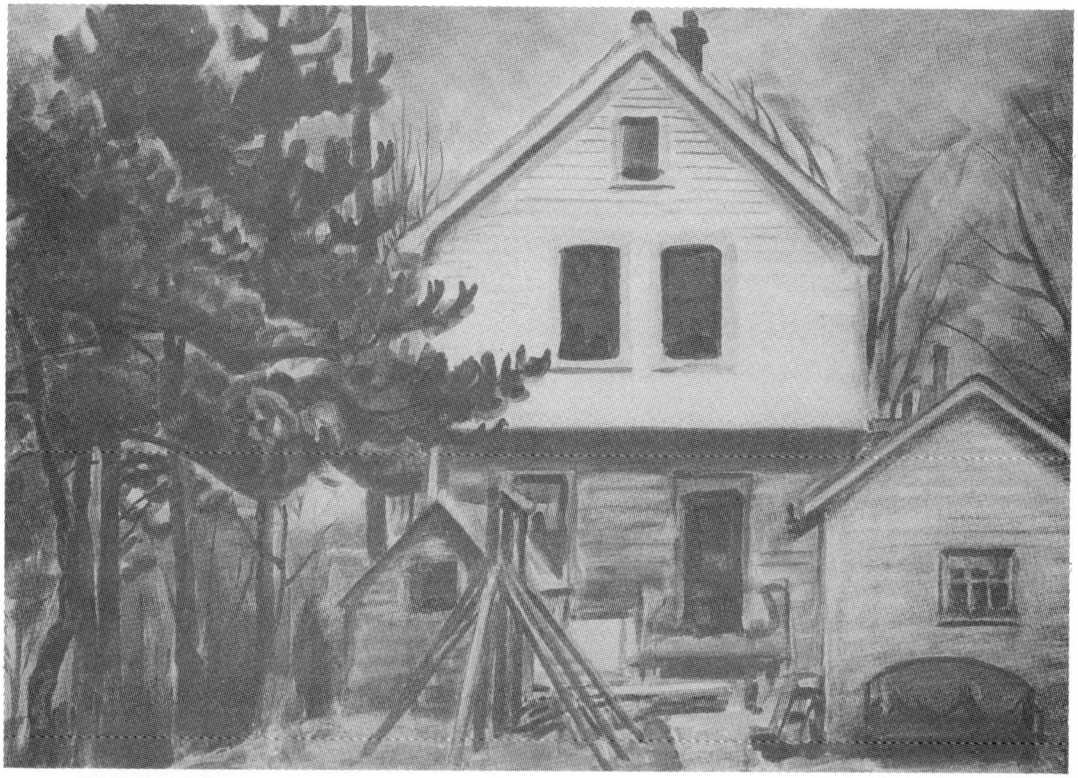

CHARLES EPHRAIM BURCHFIELD – Backyard – signed with monogrammed initials and dated 1938 – watercolour on paper – 22¾ x 27½in. *(Christie's)* **$16,500 £11,599**

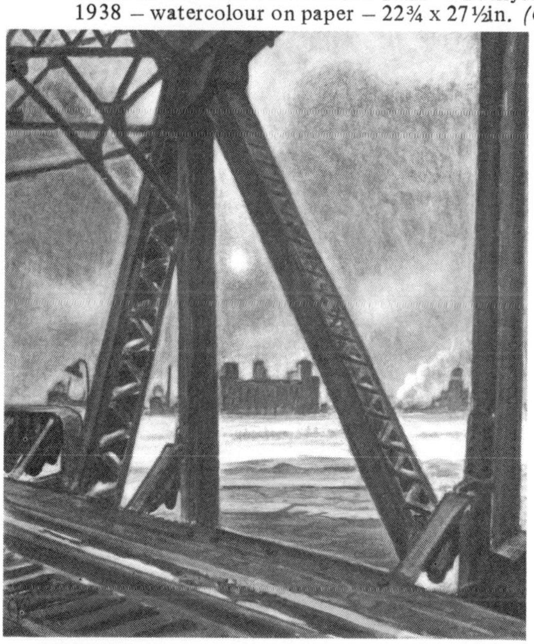

CHARLES EPHRAIM BURCHFIELD – Iron Bridge In Winter Sun – signed with monogrammed initials, dated 1943 – watercolour on paper laid down on board – 27¼ x 23½in.
(Christie's) $52,800 £37,118

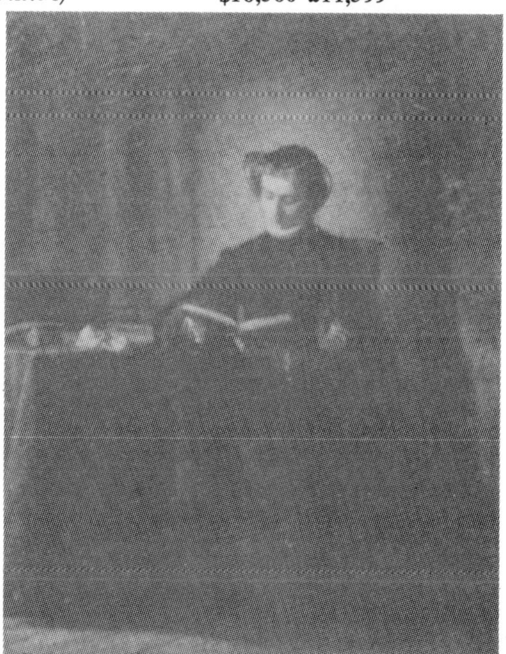

PAUL BURDE – The Reader – signed and dated '59 – oil on panel – 14 x 11in.
(Christie's) $539 £350

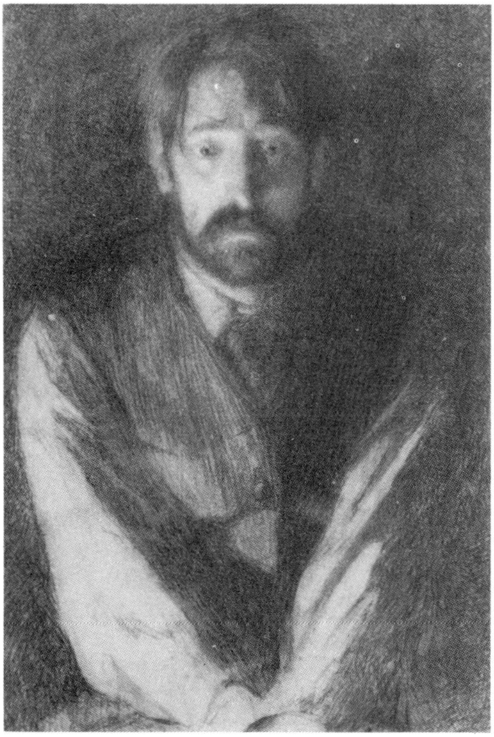

LEOPOLD BURGER – Portrat – signed and dated 1900 – charcoal with red chalk on paper – 29½ x 11½in.
(Christie's) **$1,108** **£770**

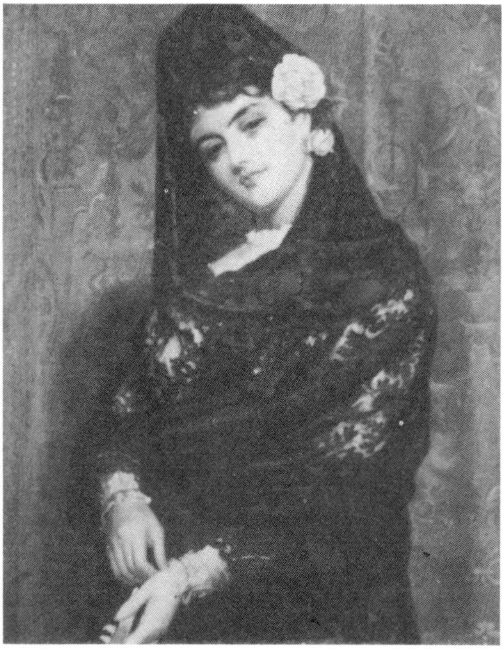

JOHN BAGNOLD BURGESS – A Spanish Beauty – signed and dated 1877 – 21¼ x 15in.
(Christie's) **$1,861** **£1,320**

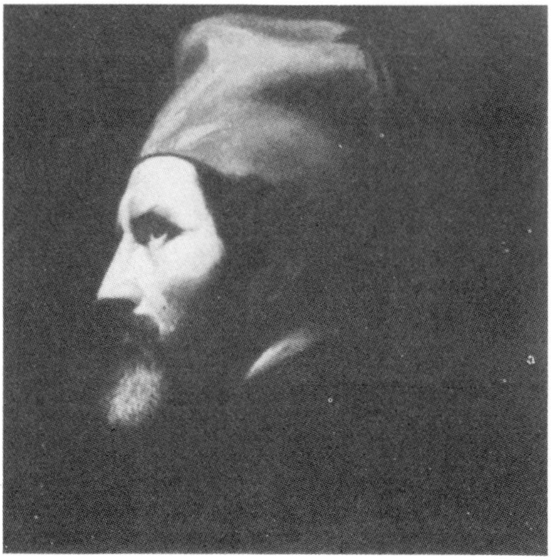

JOHN BAGNOLD BURGESS, Circle of – Portrait Of A Bearded Man Wearing A Red Fez – oil on board – 8¼ x 10¼in.
(Phillips) **$1,377** **£900**

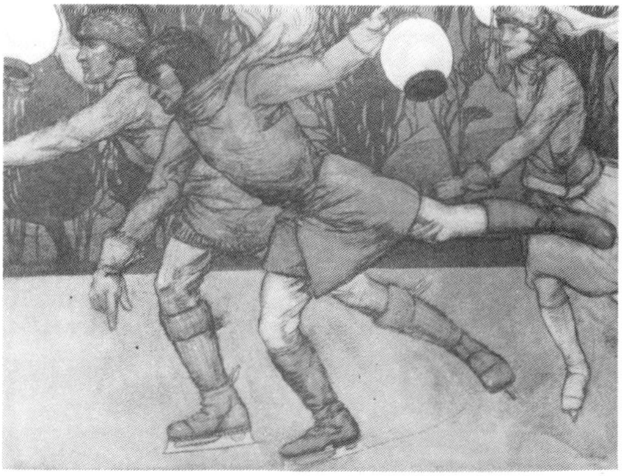

AVERIL BURLEIGH – Skating With Lanterns – signed – watercolour, bodycolour, black crayon, pencil and grey wash – 22 x 29½in.
(Christie's) **$1,887** **£1,320**

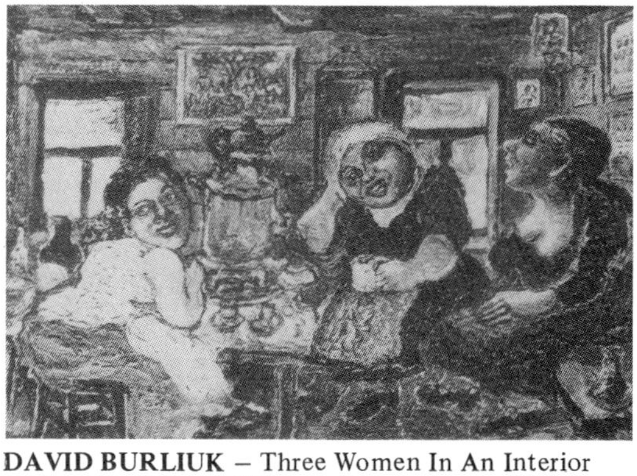

DAVID BURLIUK – Three Women In An Interior – signed and dated 1947 – oil on canvas – 13¼ x 16¾in.
(Christie's) **$1,760** **£1,096**

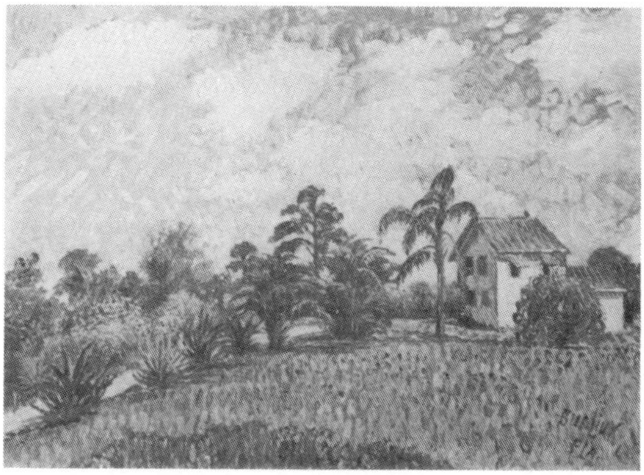

DAVID BURLIUK – A Tropical Yard In Florida – signed and inscribed – oil on canvas – 18 x 24in.
(Christie's) **$1,100** **£765**

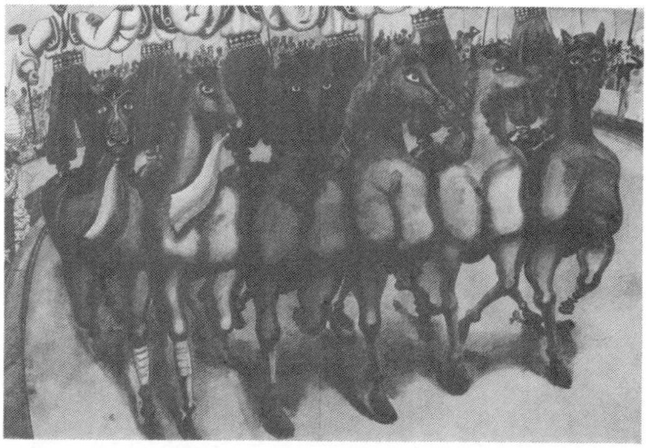

EDWARD BURRA – Circus Horses – signed and dated 1936 – watercolour – 31½ x 44in.
(Christie's) **$18,997** **£12,100**

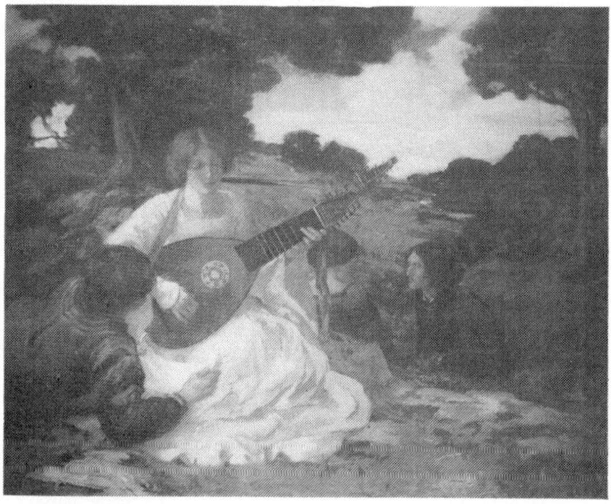

ROBERT BURNS – Music – signed and dated 1904 – 45 x 54in.
(Christie's) **$5,890** **£3,850**

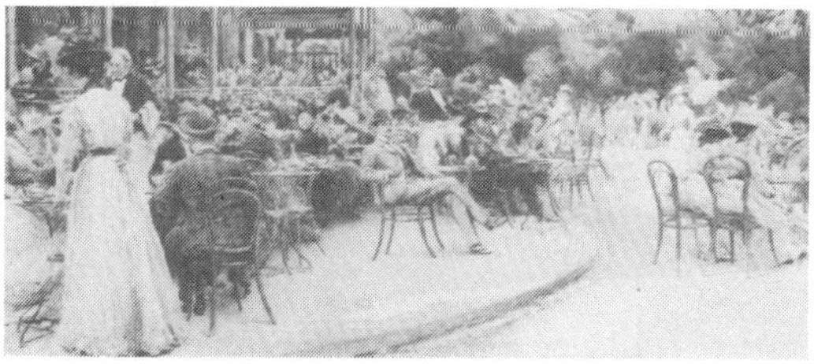

ARTHUR ALFRED BURRINGTON – Cafe De Paris, Monte Carlo – signed, also inscribed and dated 1899 on backboard – watercolour and bodycolour – 35.5 x 53cm.
(Phillips) **$6,864** **£4,800**

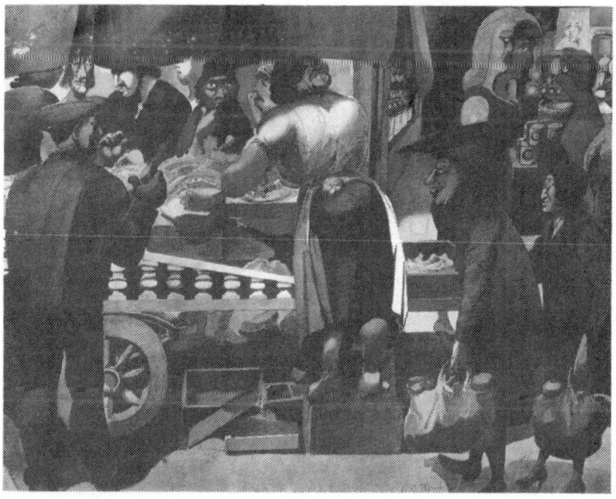

EDWARD BURRA – The Fish Stall – watercolour – 19¾ x 24½in.
(Christie's) **$22,022** **£15,400**

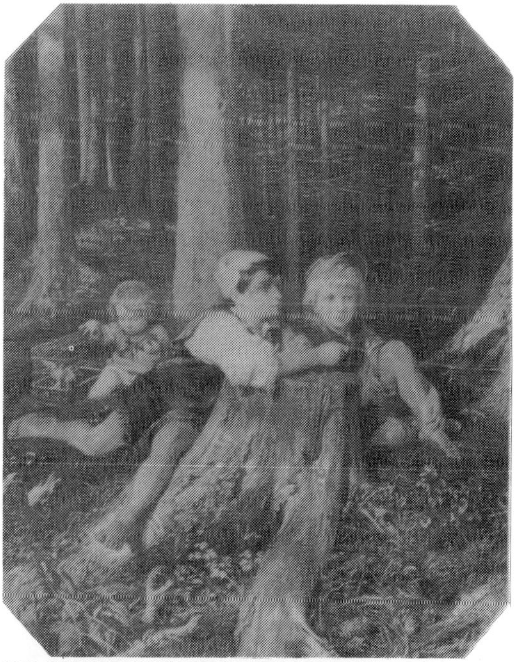

SIR FREDERICK WILLIAM BURTON – Tyrolese Boys Trapping Birds – signed and indistinctly dated (1858?) – watercolour heightened with white – 21 x 15¾in.
(Christie's) **$1,186** **£715**

BUTLER

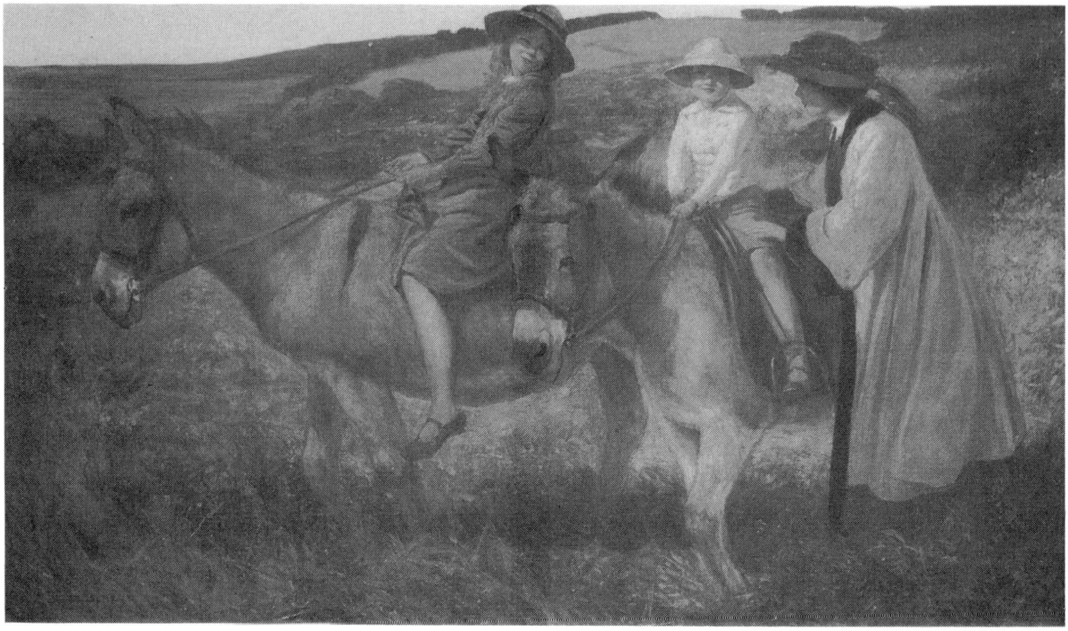

GEORGE BUTLER – Two Children Riding Donkeys On The Edge Of A Moor – signed and dated 1912 – oil on canvas – 36 x 40in.
(Christie's) **$12,089 £7,700**

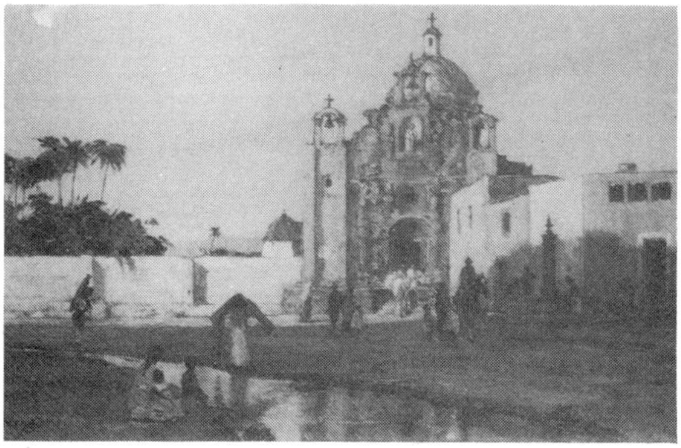

HOWARD RUSSELL BUTLER – Church At Agar Calientes – signed – oil on canvas – 21½ x 32¼in.
(Christie's) **$2,420 £1,507**

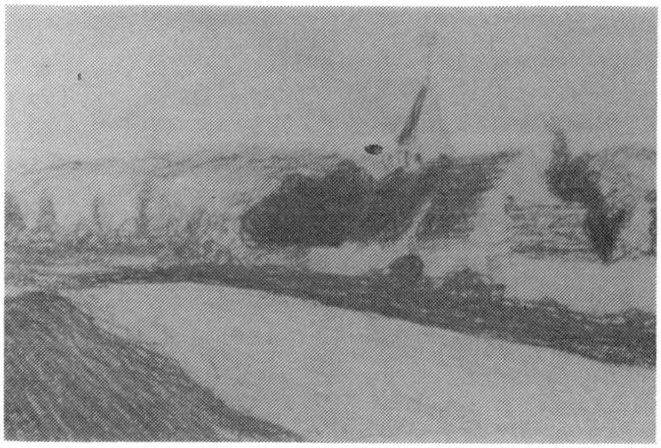

THEODORE EARL BUTLER – Cottage By Road – pastel on paper – 12½ x 19in.
(Robt. W. Skinner Inc.) **$1,200 £736**

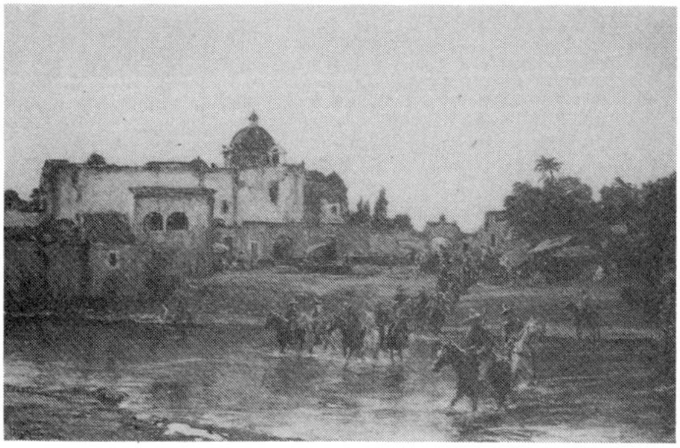

HOWARD RUSSELL BUTLER – Crossing The Yautepec – signed – oil on canvas – 21½ x 32¼in.
(Christie's) **$4,400 £2,741**

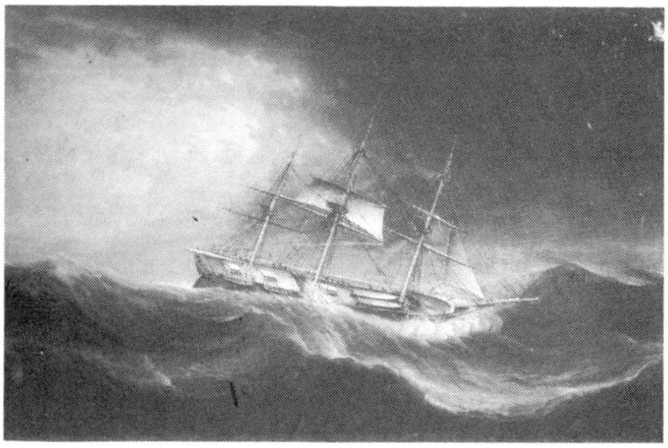

JAMES E. BUTTERSWORTH – Holding The Lines – signed – oil on canvas – 14 x 22in.
(Christie's) **$12,650 £8,800**

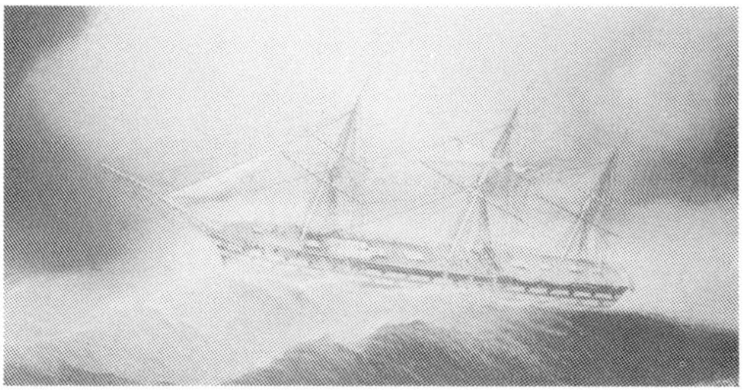

JAMES E. BUTTERSWORTH – Ship Of The Line U.S.S. Ohio – signed – oil on canvas – 36 x 50in.
(Christie's) **$28,600 £20,105**

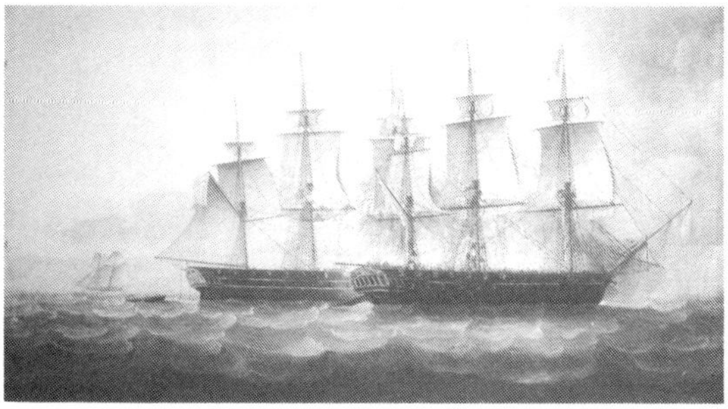

JAMES E. BUTTERSWORTH – The U.S.S. Chesapeake And The H.M.S. Shannon – signed – oil on canvas – 19½ x 32in.
(Christie's) **$46,200 £32,478**

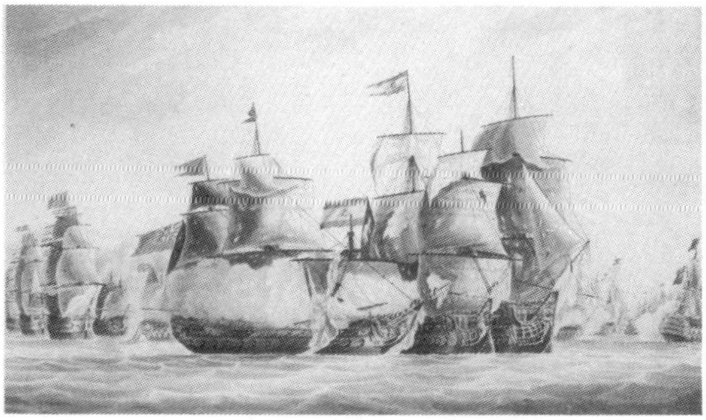

THOMAS BUTTERSWORTH – The Battle Of Cape St. Vincent, 14 February 1797 – signed and dated '97 – pencil and watercolour – 17½ x 29¼in.
(Christie's) **$4,212 £2,808**

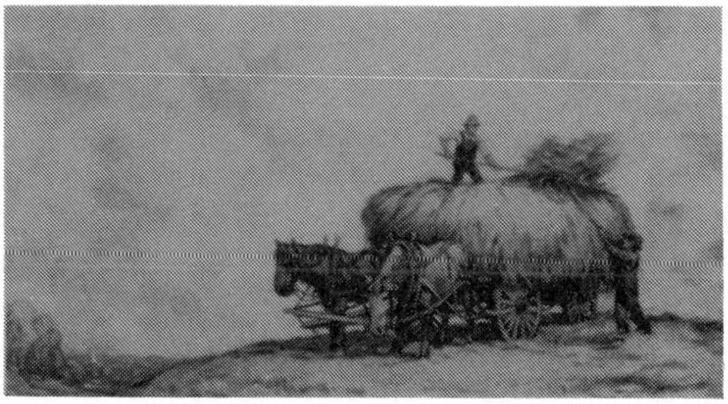

ALBERT PRENTICE BUTTON – Haying – signed – oil on canvas – 20 x 24in.
(Robt. W. Skinner Inc.) **$650 £398**

A. BUZZI – The Departure – signed – pencil and watercolour – 28 x 21in.
(Christie's) **$2,112 £1,320**

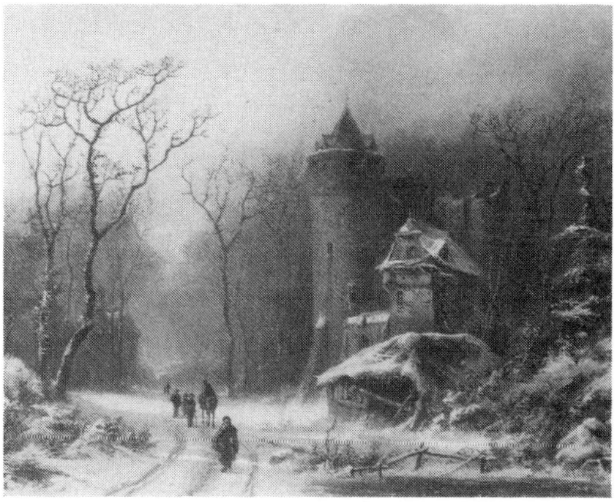

ALFRED EDOUARD VAN BYLANDT – A Winter Wooded Landscape With Figures On A Path By A Ruined Castle – signed and dated 1851 – on panel – 14 x 18in.
(Christie's) **$3,344 £2,200**

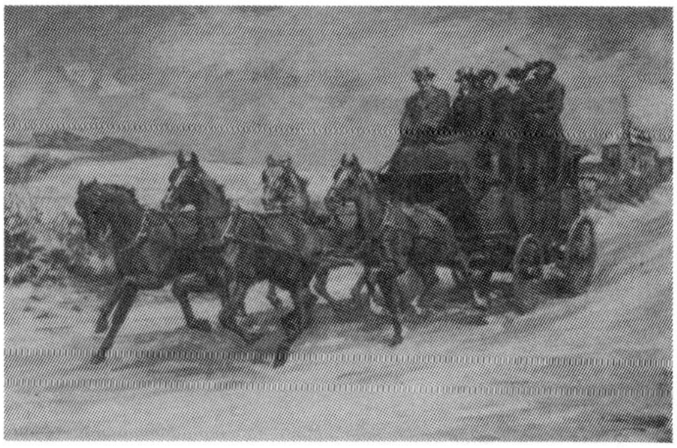

WILLIAM HOUNSOM BYLES – The Royal Mail Stagecoach Setting Out In A Winter Landscape – signed – on canvas – 20 x 30in.
(Phillips) **$3,059 £1,900**

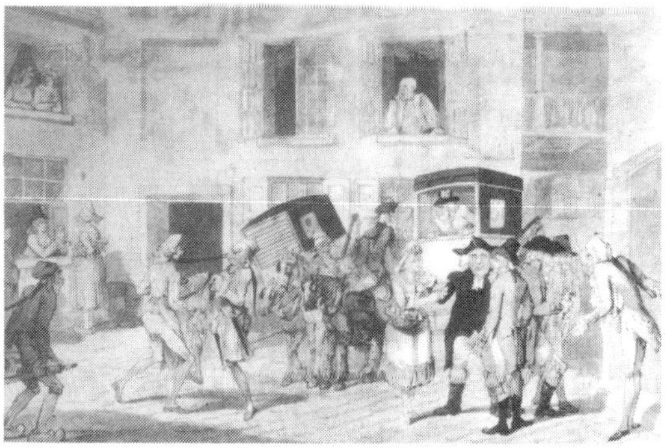

FREDERICK GEORGE BYRON – Inn Yard At Calais – signed – pencil, pen and grey ink and watercolour with touches of white heightening – 15¼ x 23¼in.
(Christie's) **$2,571 £1,540**

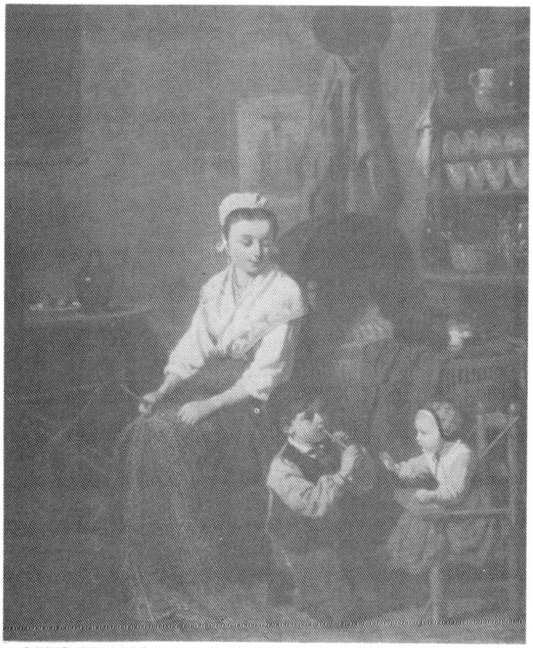

LOUIS SIMON CABAILLOT, Called Lassalle – A Nursery Recital – signed – on canvas – 41 x 32.5 cm.
(Phillips) **$3,624** **£2,400**

ADRIAEN VAN DER CABEL, Circle of – Figures Rolling Their Barrels Along A Path Before A Busy Mediterranean Port – oil on panel – 23¼ x 33in.
(Phillips) **$2,820** **£2,000**

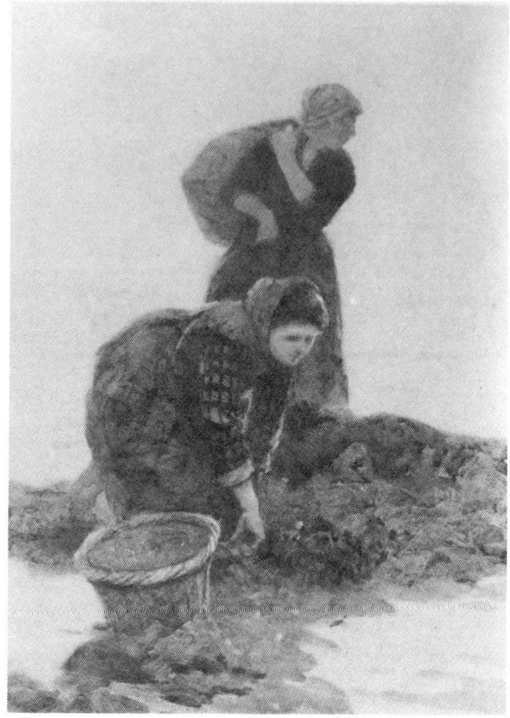

HECTOR CAFFIERI – The Seaweed Gatherers – signed – coloured chalk and watercolour heightened with white on board – 20 x 13¾in.
(Christie's) **$2,016** **£1,430**

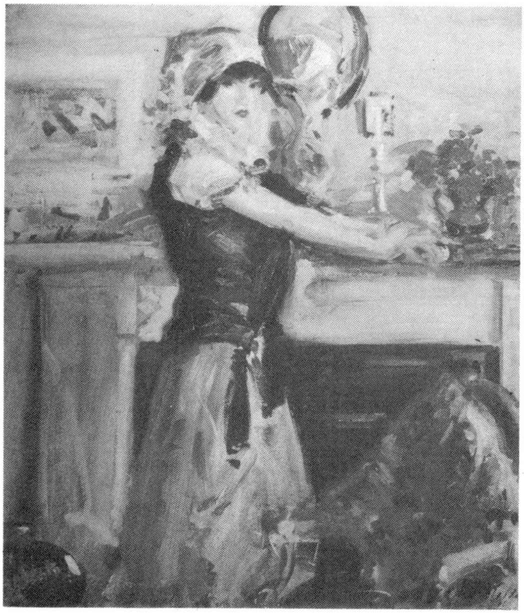

FRANCIS CAMPBELL BOILEAU CADELL – The Pink Scarf – signed and dated 1911 – oil on board – 27 x 23in.
(Christie's) **$24,480** **£17,000**

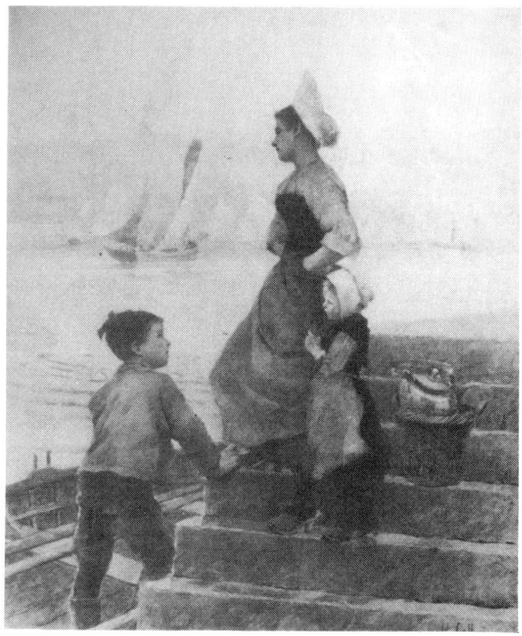

HECTOR CAFFIERI – On The Harbour Steps, Waiting For The Ferry – signed – watercolour heightened with white – 27 x 21¼in.
(Christie's) **$10,939** **£7,150**

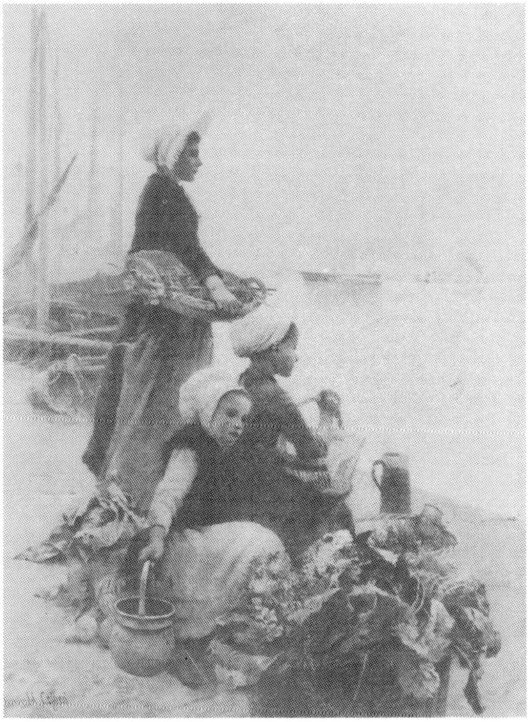

HECTOR CAFFIERI – Fishergirls On A Quay – signed – 39½ x 29½in.
(Christie's) **$13,770** **£9,180**

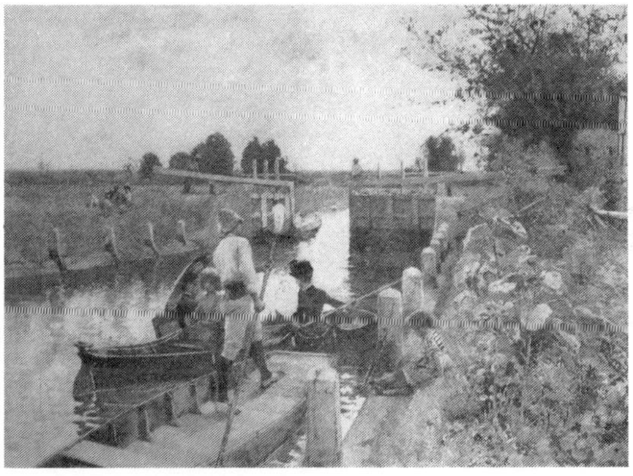

HECTOR CAFFIERI – Boaters In A Lock On The Thames – signed – watercolour heightened with white, laid on board – 22½ x 29½in.
(Christie's) **$13,183** **£9,350**

HECTOR CAFFIERI – Squally Weather – Boulogne Pier – signed, and inscribed on the reverse – watercolour heightened with white on card – 14¼ x 19½in.
(Christie's) **$6,204** **£4,400**

HECTOR CAFFIERI – A Young Woman With A Parasol Reading Beside A Brook – signed – watercolour heightened with white over pencil – 30 x 22.5cm.
(Phillips) **$4,075** **£2,500**

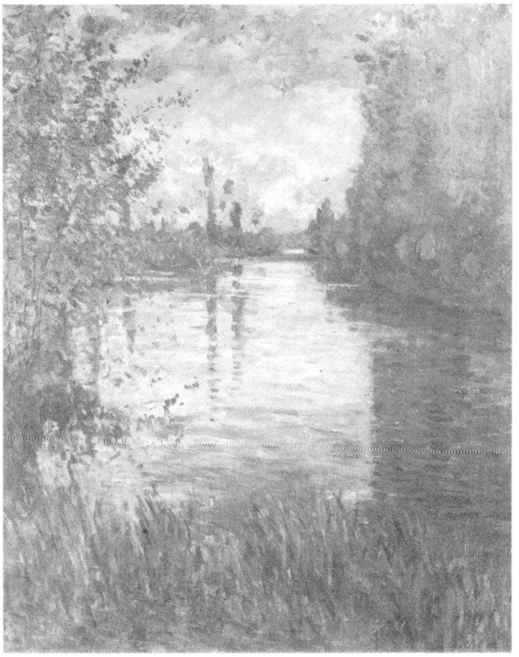

GUSTAVE CAILLEBOTTE – Le Petit Bras de la Seine en Automne – oil on canvas – 25½ x 21¼in.
(Christie's) **$150,480** **£104,500**

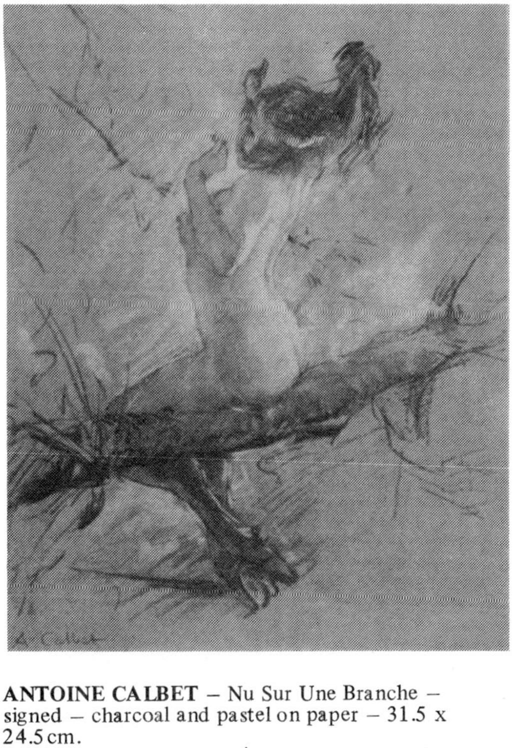

ANTOINE CALBET – Nu Sur Une Branche – signed – charcoal and pastel on paper – 31.5 x 24.5cm.
(Phillips) **$1,007** **£650**

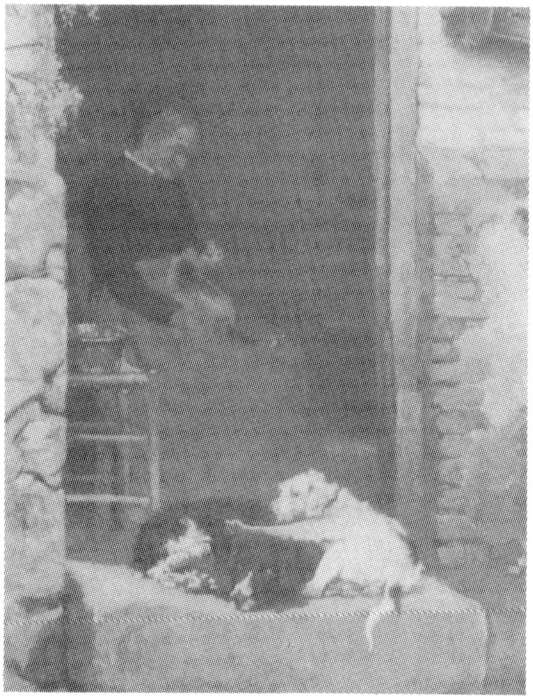

WILLIAM FRANK CALDERON – Resting – signed with initials and dated 1888 – 20½ x 14in.
(Christie's) **$4,039** **£2,640**

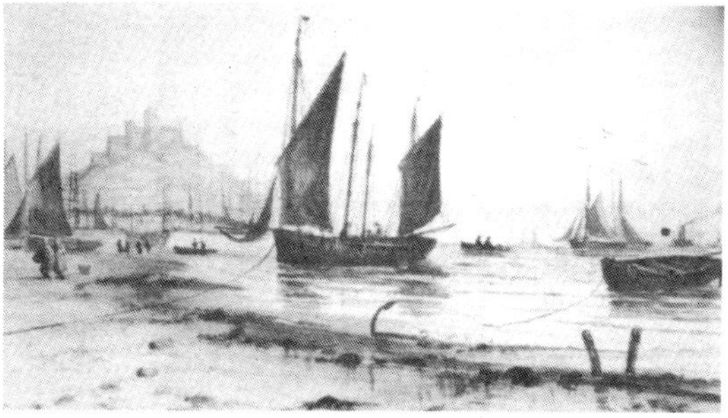

GEORGE CALLOW – Shipping Boats Before St. Michael's Mount, Mounts Bay, Cornwall – signed – watercolour – 10 x 16½in.
(W. H. Lane & Son) **$345** **£230**

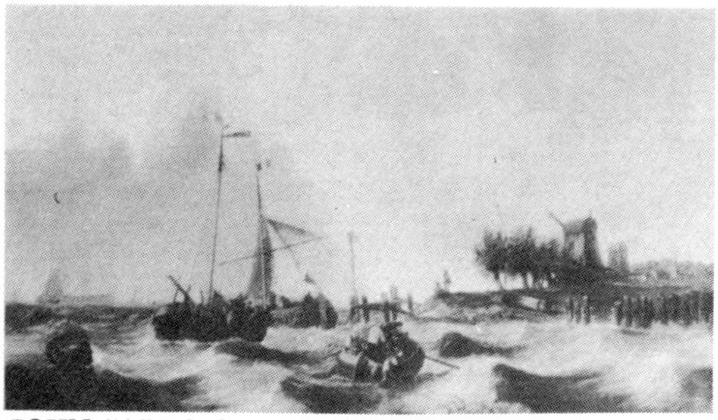

JOHN CALLOW, Circle of – A Coastal View With Fishing Vessels In A Choppy Sea – 27¼ x 41¼in.
(Christie's) **$4,342** **£3,080**

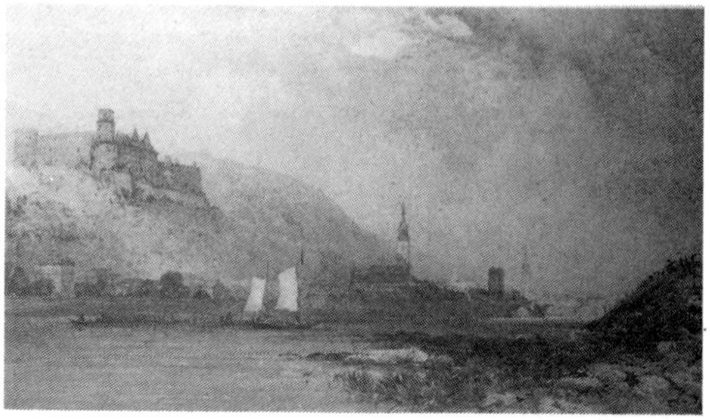

WILLIAM CALLOW – Heidelberg From Above The Bridge – signed and dated 1854 – watercolour – 10¾ x 19¾in.
(Christie's) **$9,185** **£5,500**

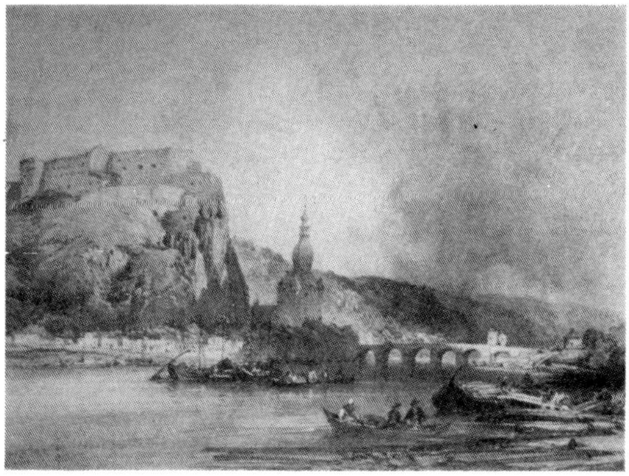

WILLIAM CALLOW – The Fortress And Town Of Dinant On The Meuse – signed and dated 1908 – pencil and watercolour – 15½ x 11¼in.
(Christie's) **$2,967** **£2,090**

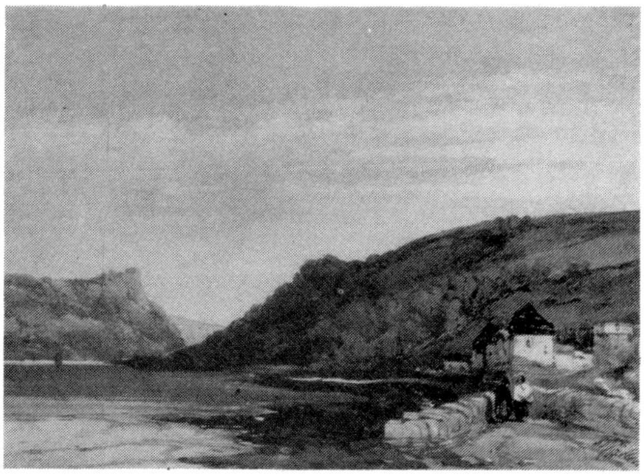

WILLIAM CALLOW – Figures On A Road Beside An Estuary – signed, and signed again with initials on the reverse – pencil and watercolour – 10¼ x 14¼in.
(Christie's) **$821** **£405**

WILLIAM CALLOW – Shipping Off A Coastline – signed – watercolour – 32 x 48cm.
(Phillips) **$2,526** **£1,550**

WILLIAM CALLOW – A Street Scene In Bologna: The Leaning Tower (Torre Garisenda) And San Bartolommeo – signed and dated 1844 – watercolour – 13¼ x 19¼in.
(Christie's) **$10,530** **£7,020**

WILLIAM CALLOW – Figures In The Street Of An English Country Town – pencil and watercolour – 7¼ x 10¾in.
(Christie's) **$781** **£550**

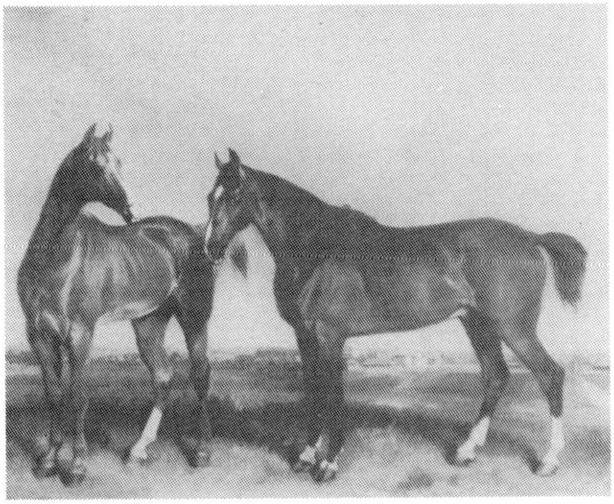

HENRY CALVERT – Hunters In A Paddock, A Town Beyond – 16½ x 22in.
(Christie's) **$1,782** **£1,188**

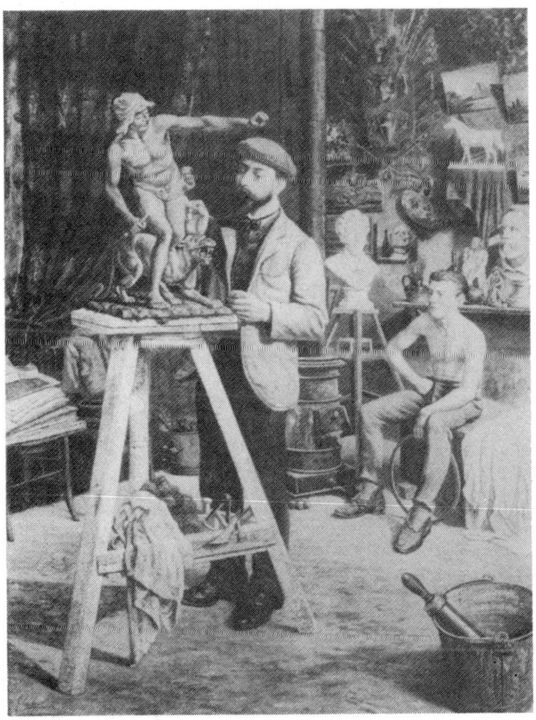

LOUIS CAMBIER – The Sculptor At Work – signed and dated 1891 – oil on canvas – 178 x 133.5cm.
(Phillips) **$5,760** **£4,000**

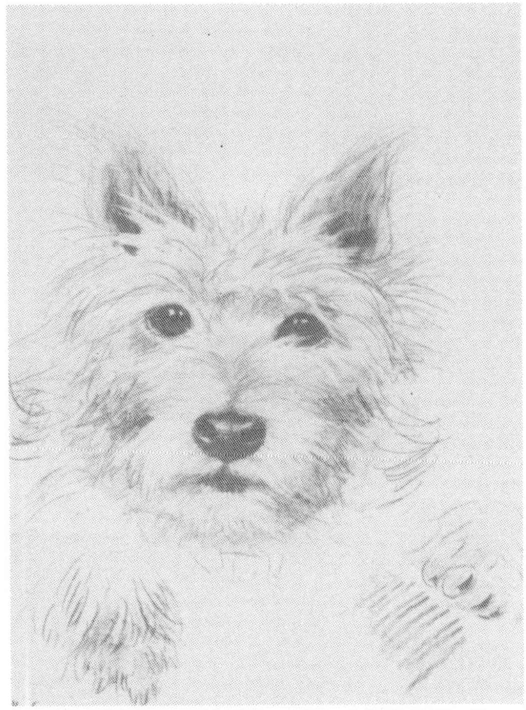

KATE CAMERON – 'After A Hard Rabbit Hunt' – signed, inscribed and dated '31 – coloured chalks – 23 x 35cm.
(Phillips) **$978** **£600**

CHARLES CAMOIN – La Plage a Tanger – signed – oil on canvas – 25½ x 32in.
(Christie's) **$19,288** **£11,550**

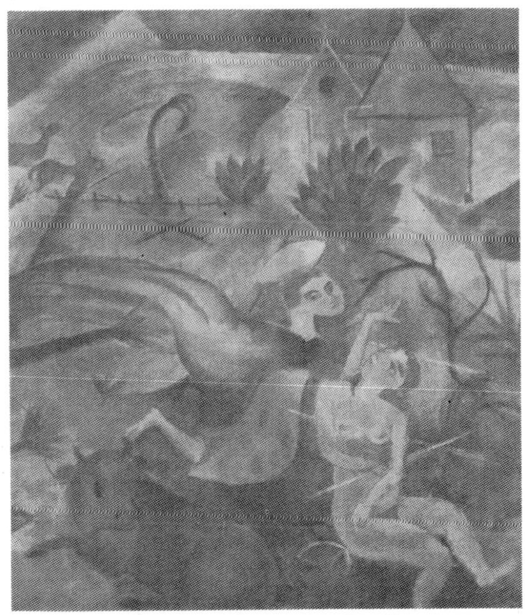

HEINRICH CAMPENDONK – Verkundigung – signed and dated '17 – oil on canvas – 22 x 22in.
(Christie's) **$202,070** **£121,000**

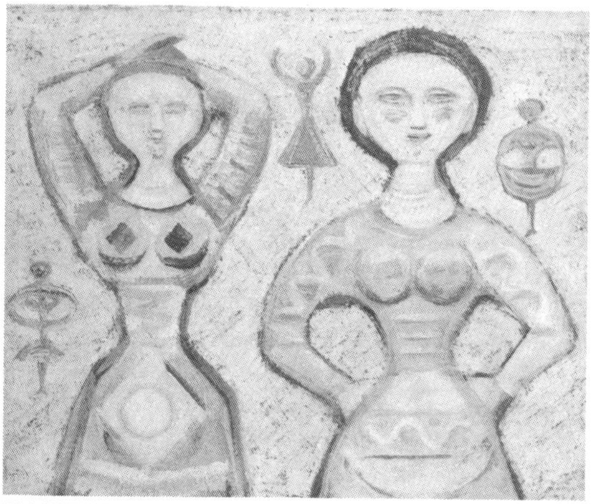

MASSIMO CAMPIGLI – Due Donna – signed and dated '65 – oil on canvas – 23½ x 28¾in.
(Christie's) **$44,352 £30,800**

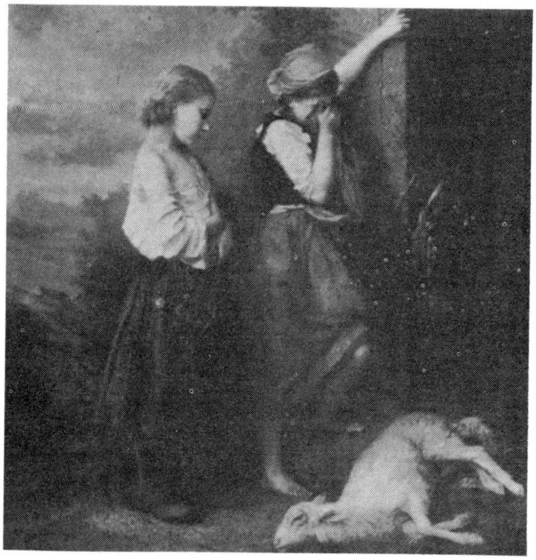

HENRY CAMPOTOSTO – The Pet Lamb – signed and dated 1872 – on panel – 44 x 34¼in.
(Christie's) **$4,712 £3,080**

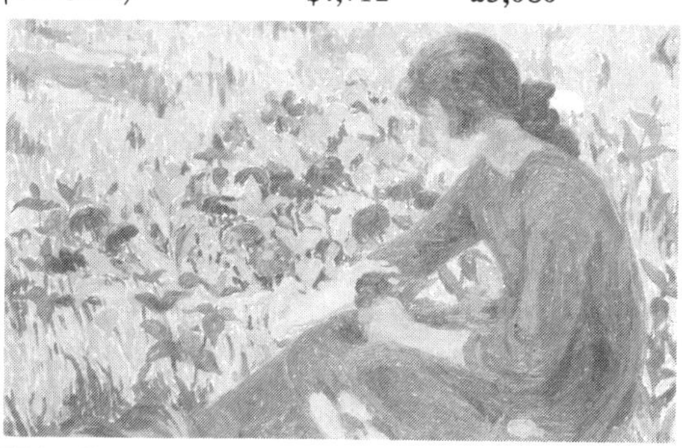

BLANCHE CAMUS – Jeune Fille cueuillant des Fleurs – signed – oil on canvas – 35 x 45½in.
(Christie's) **$9,680 £6,050**

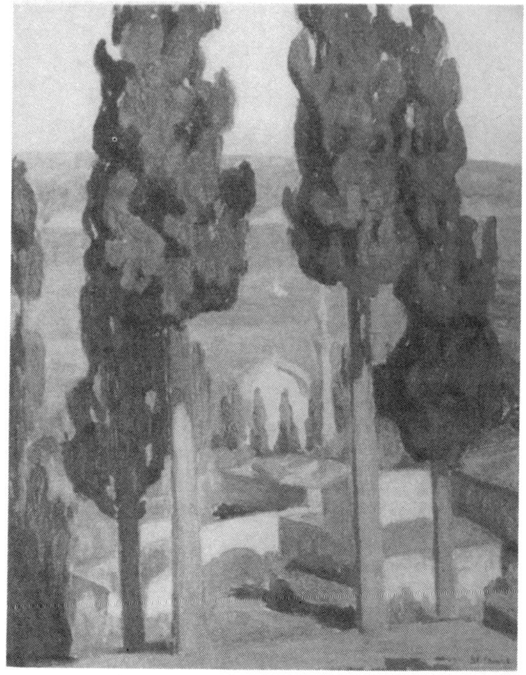

BLANCHE CAMUS – La Corne d'Or – signed – oil on canvas – 25½ x 21in.
(Christie's) **$3,168 £1,980**

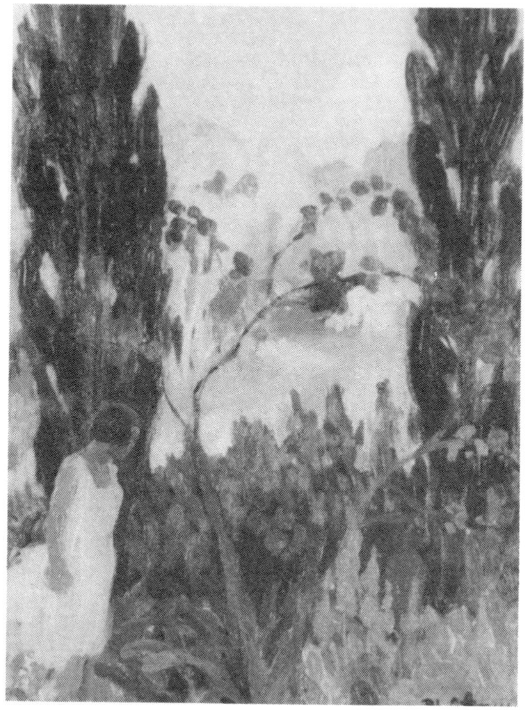

BLANCHE CAMUS – Jeune Fille dans la Campagne – signed, signed again on the reverse – oil on panel – 18 x 14¾in.
(Christie's) **$3,344 £2,090**

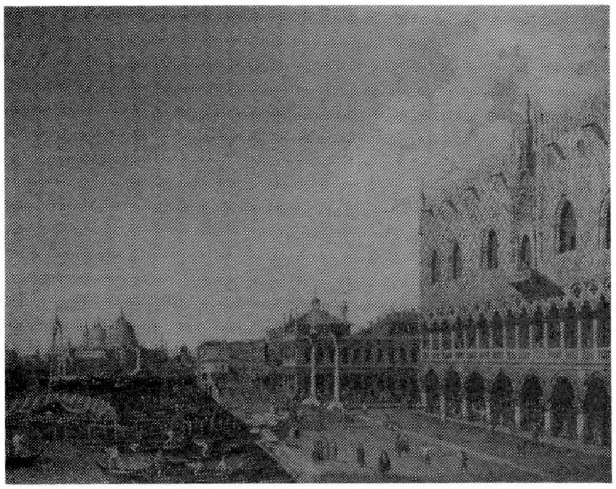

GIOVANNI ANTONIO CANALE, A Follower of, Called Canaletto – Venice – on canvas – 34½ x 43¾in.
(Phillips) **$29,880** **£18,000**

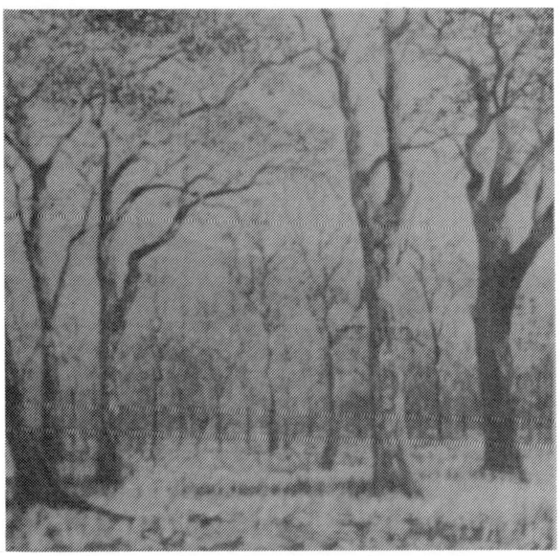

G. P. CANITZ – Landscape With Trees – signed – oil on canvas 74.5 x 74.5cm.
(Phillips) **$620** **£400**

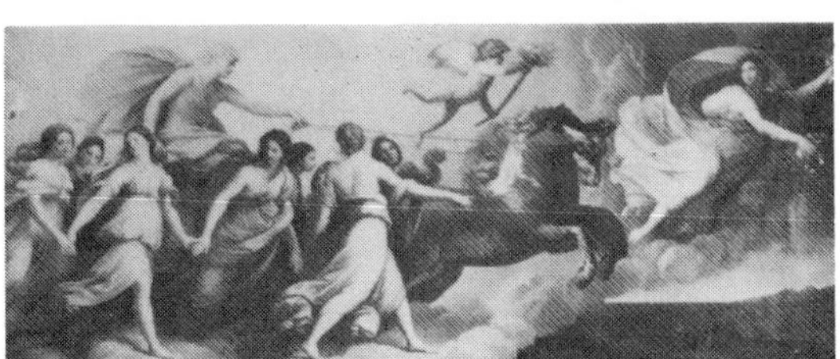

VINCENTIUS CAPOBIANCHI, Attributed to The Aurora After Guido Reni – inscribed, also inscribed on the reverse – oil on canvas – 13½ x 30½in.
(Robt. W. Skinner Inc.) **$750** **£493**

JOSEPH CARAUD – In The Boudoir – signed and dated 1895 – 22 x 17in.
(Christie's) **$10,296** **£7,150**

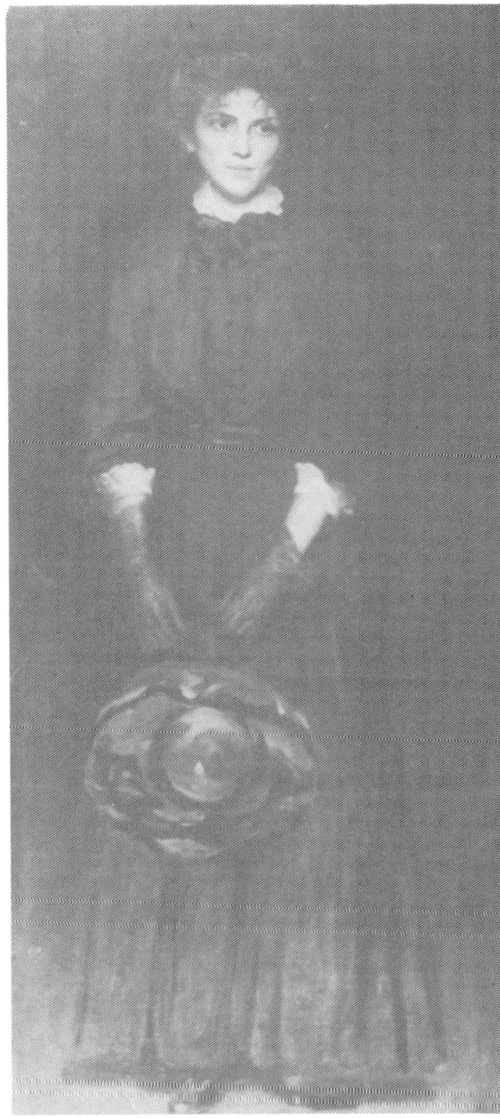

SCOTT CLIFTON CARBEE – Young Boston Woman With A Hat – signed – oil on canvas – 72 x 32in.
(Robt. W. Skinner Inc.) **$9,500** **£6,597**

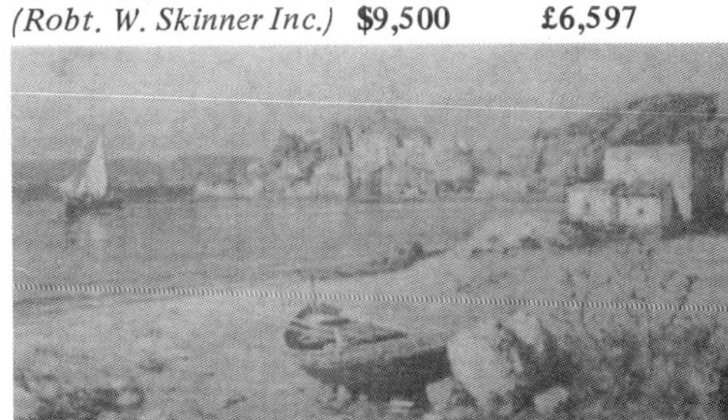

GABRIELLI CARELLI – 'On The Neapolitan Coast' – signed – oil on canvas – 12 x 17½in.
(Christie's) **$1,453** **£950 Pair**

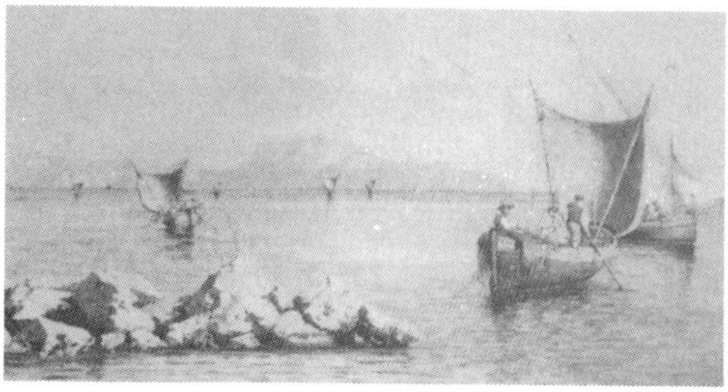

GIUSEPPE CARELLI – Capri – signed and inscribed – on panel – 10 x 16in.
(Christie's) **$1,950** **£1,300**

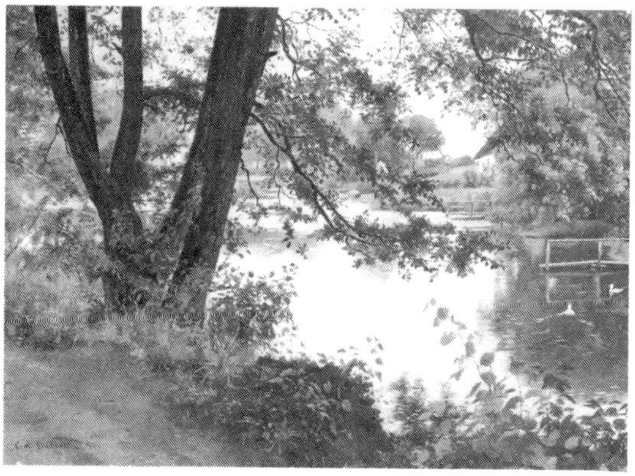

CARL CARLSEN – A Wooded River Landscape With Ducks And Horses – signed and dated '94 – 15¾ x 21¾in.
(Christie's) **$7,128** **£4,950**

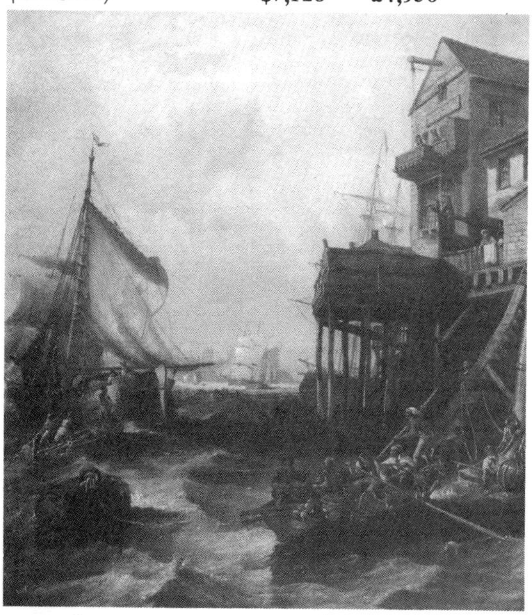

JOHN WILSON CARMICHAEL – The Custom House, Tynemouth – signed and dated 1838 – 33 x 25in.
(Christie's) **$11,632** **£8,250**

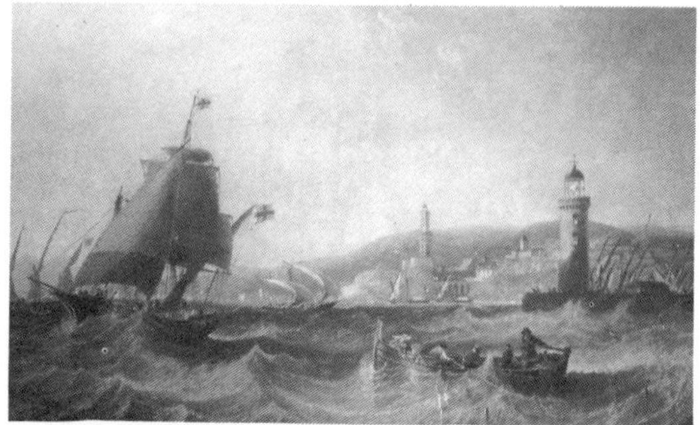

JOHN WILSON CARMICHAEL – Genoa – signed and dated 1862 – 23½ x 35¼in.
(Christie's) **$10,857** **£7,700**

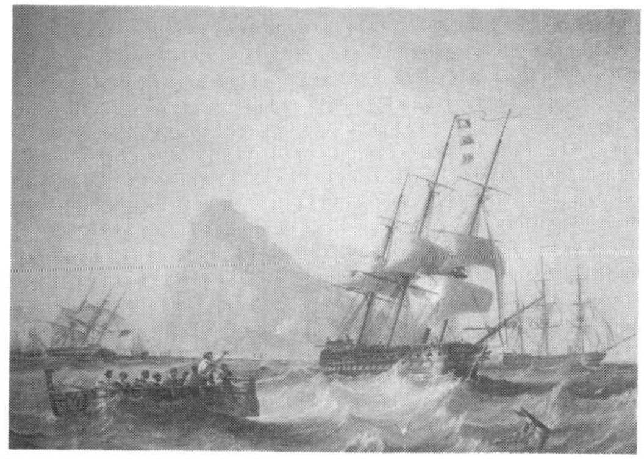

JOHN WILSON CARMICHAEL – British Men O' War Off Gribraltar – signed and dated 1855 – 35 x 47in.
(Christie's) **$26,400** **£16,500**

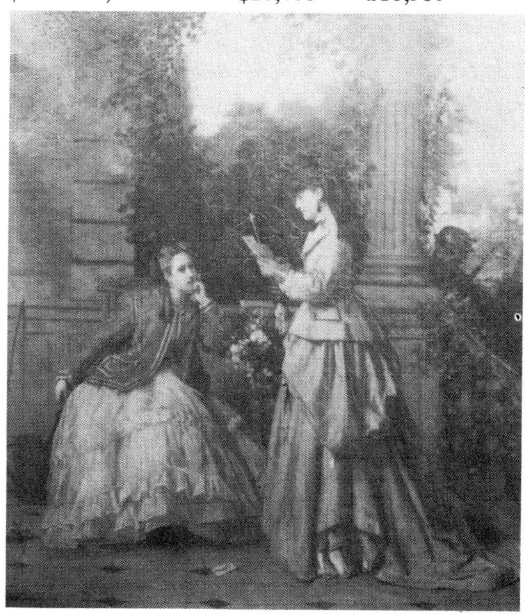

JEAN CAROLUS – The Confidente – signed and dated 1868, signed, inscribed and dated on the reverse – 28 x 23in.
(Christie's) **$4,752** **£3,300**

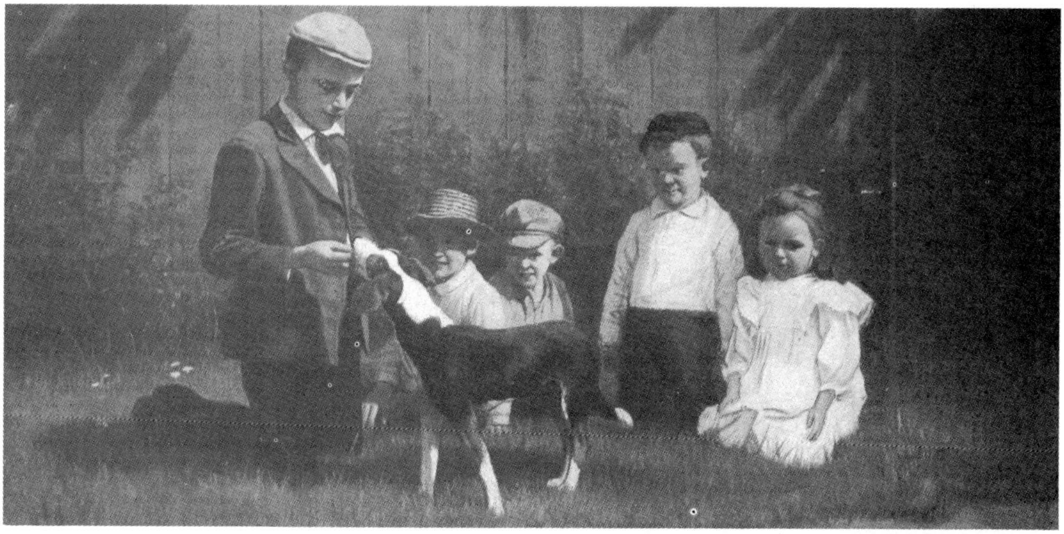

SAMUEL S. CARR – Dog Trainers – signed – oil on canvas – 12 x 18in. *(Christie's)* **$11,000 £7,733**

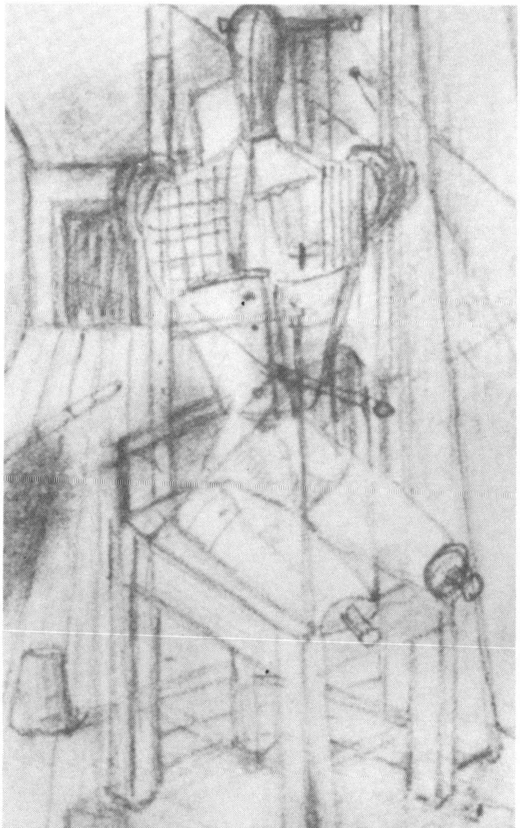

CARLO CARRA – Solitudine – signed and dated '916 – pencil on paper – 4¼ x 2¼in.
(Christie's) **$8,800 £5,500**

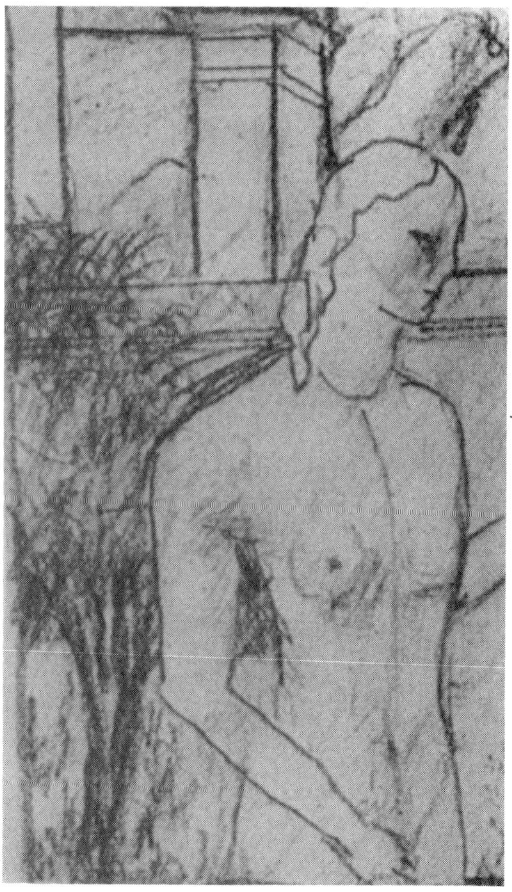

CARLO CARRA – La Statua – signed and dated 1918 – pencil on paper – 4½ x 2¼in.
(Christie's) **$1,672 £1,045**

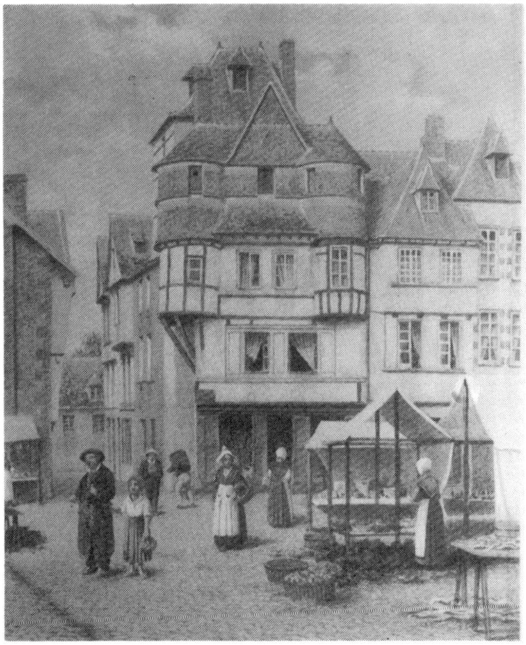

JOHN MULCASTER CARRICK – Old House In Market Place, Lannion, Brittany; and Street In Josselin Morbihan, Brittany – signed and one dated 1882, both signed, inscribed and dated on the reverse – on board – 10 x 8in.
(Christie's) **$2,692** **£1,760 Pair**

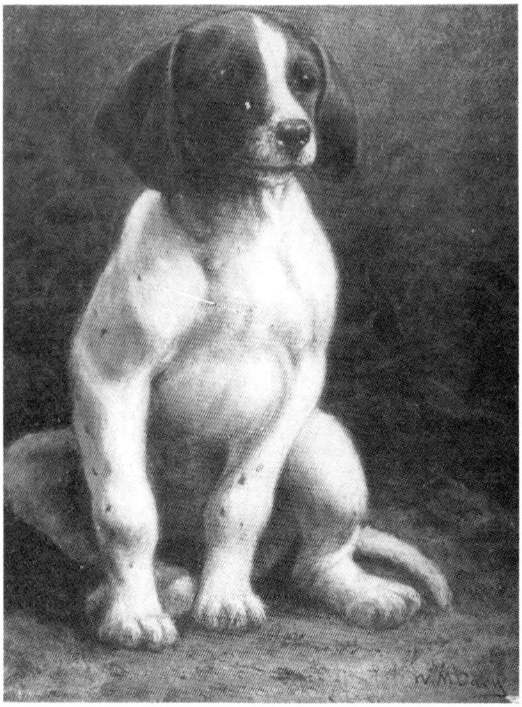

WILLIAM DE LA MONTAGNE CARY – Springer Spaniel – signed – oil on canvas – 11 x 8¼in.
(Christie's) **$3,080** **£2,165**

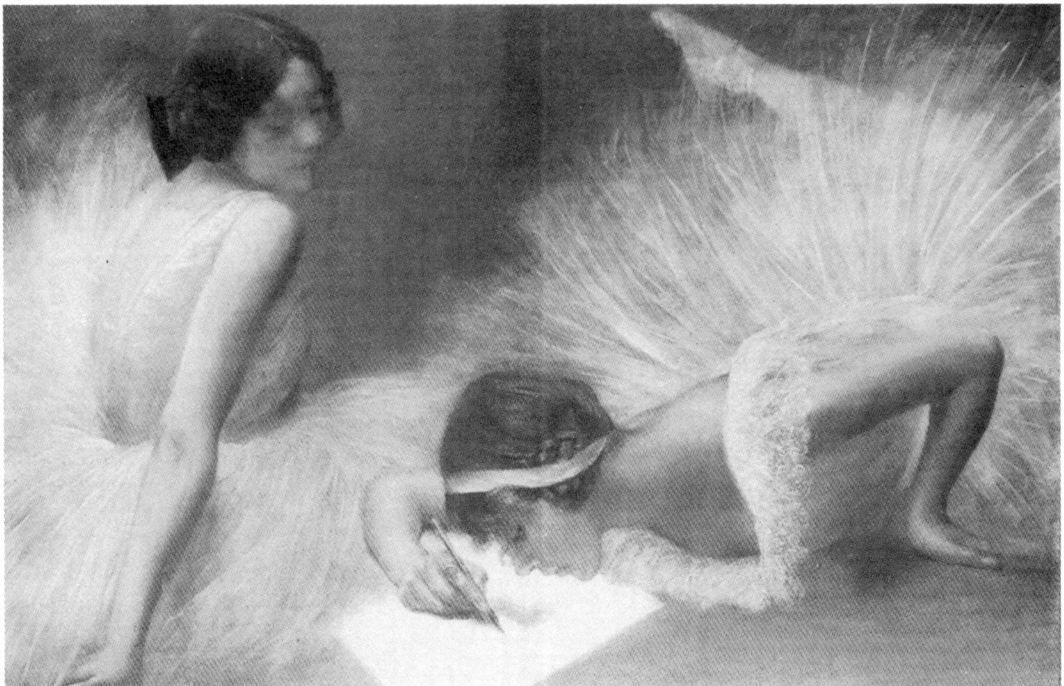

PIERRE CARRIER-BELLEUSE – La Lettre – signed and dated 1913 – pastel on paper laid on canvas – 35 x 46in. *(Christie's)* **$3,801** **£2,640**

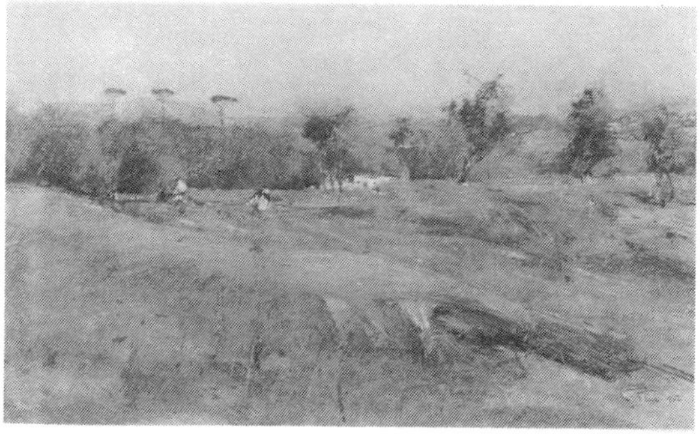

GIUSEPPE CASCIARO – Ble coupe; and An Extensive Landscape – one signed and dated 1902 and the other signed and dated '904 – pastels – 12 x 19¾in. and 12½ x 17¼in.
(Christie's) **$7,669** **£4,520 Two**

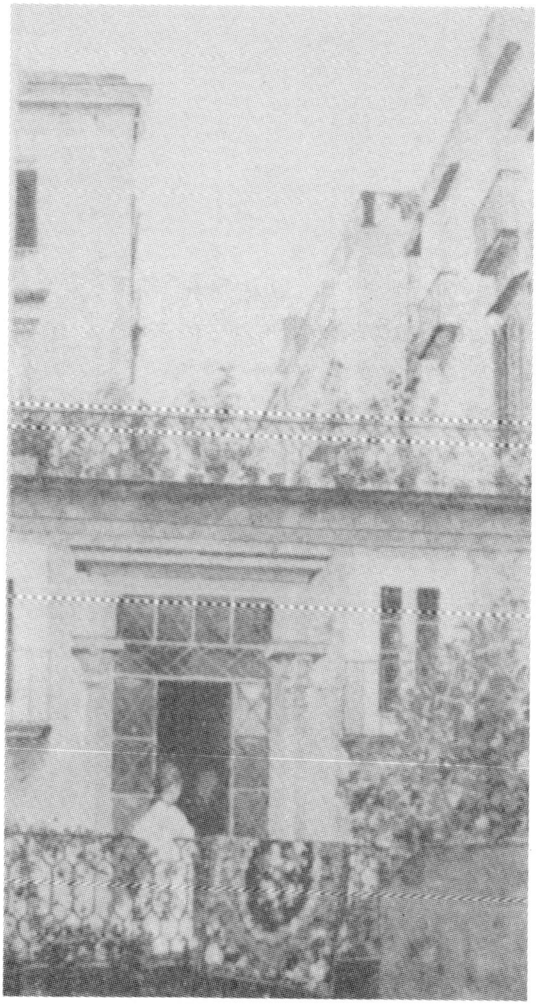

G. CASENZA – On The Balcony – signed and dated '76 – on panel – 12 x 16in.
(Christie's) **$1,500** **£1,000**

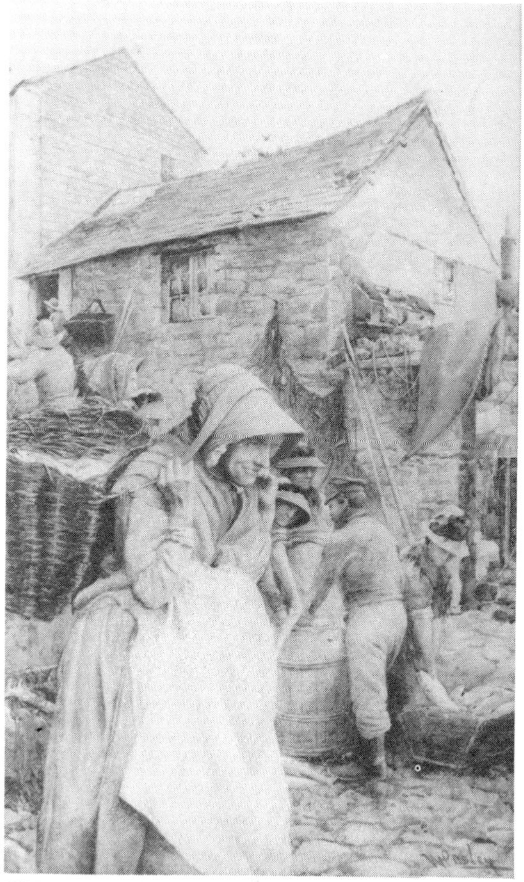

WILLIAM CASLEY – Mousehole, Cornwall, With Fisherfolk – signed – watercolour – 25¼ x 15¼in.
(Geering & Colyer) **$1,440** **£900**

PIETER CASTEELS – Flowers In A Wicker Basket – on canvas – 42¾ x 35in.
(Phillips) **$13,280** **£8,000**

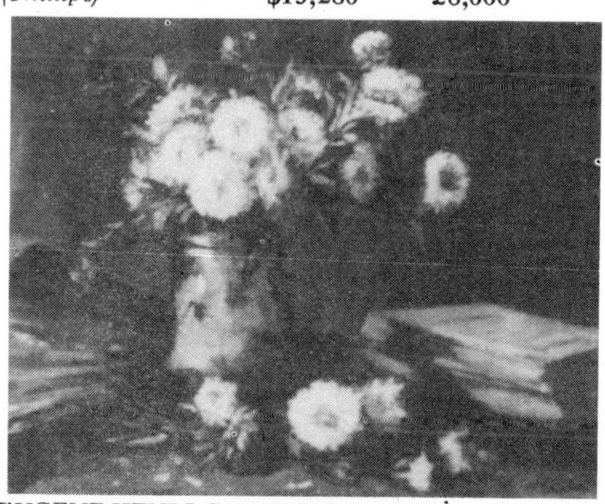

EUGENE-HENRI CAUCHOIS – Still Life Of A Vase Of Flowers, A Fan And A Book, All Arranged On A Table – signed – oil on canvas – 19 x 23½in.
(Christie's) **$986** **£605**

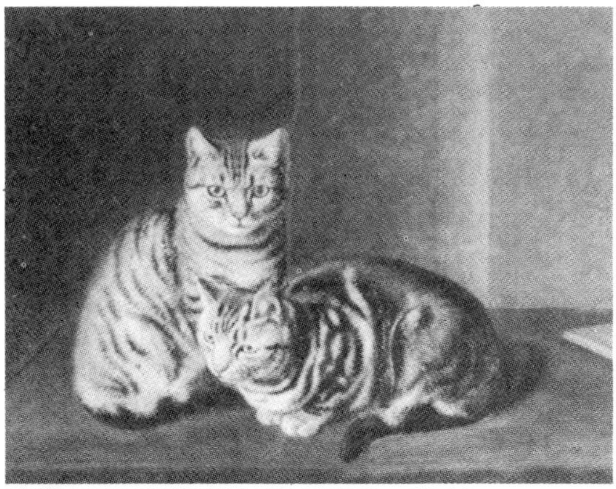

HORATIO HENRY CAULDERY – 'Waiting Patiently' – signed and dated '79 – oil on canvas – 15¾ x 12½in.
(Phillips) **$2,142** **£1,400**

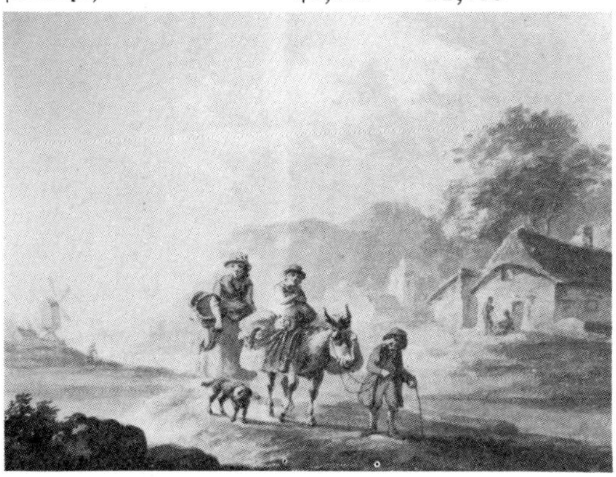

PETER LA CAVE – A Peasant Family On The Way To Market – pencil, pen and grey ink and watercolour – 7½ x 10in.; and a set of three watercolours – two signed.
(Christie's) **$891** **£594 Four**

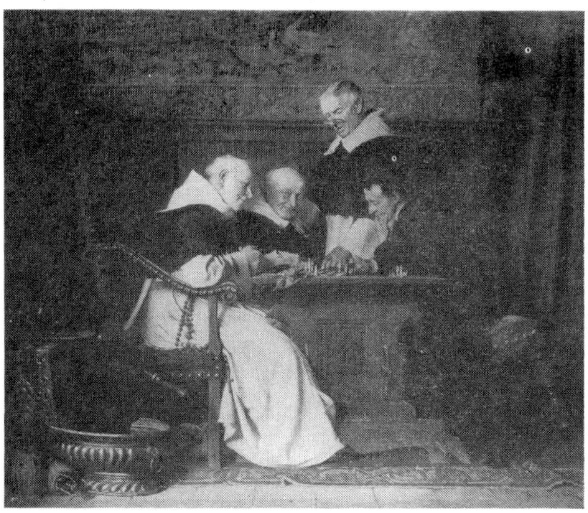

TURE NIKOLAUS CEDERSTROM – The Chess Players – signed – 21 x 26in.
(Christie's) **$8,025** £5,280

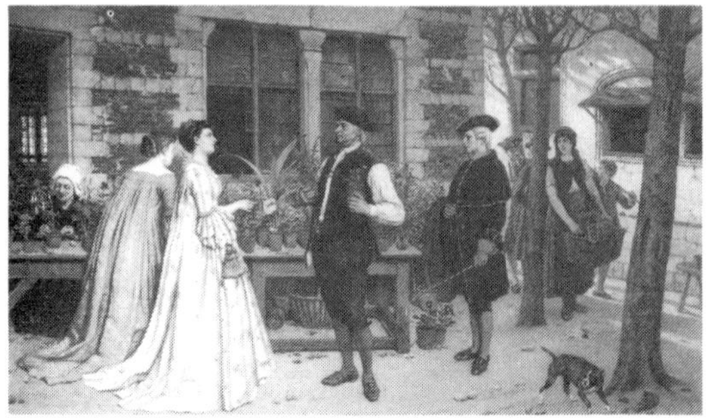

THEODORE CERIEZ – The Flower Seller – signed, and signed and inscribed on the reverse – on panel – 19½ x 31½in.
(Christie's) **$8,800** **£5,500**

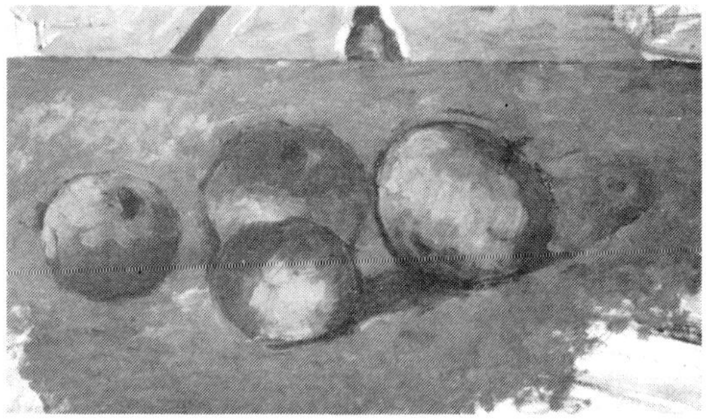

PAUL CEZANNE – Quatre Pommes – oil on canvas – 6¾ x 13¼in.
(Christie's) **$554,400** **£385,000**

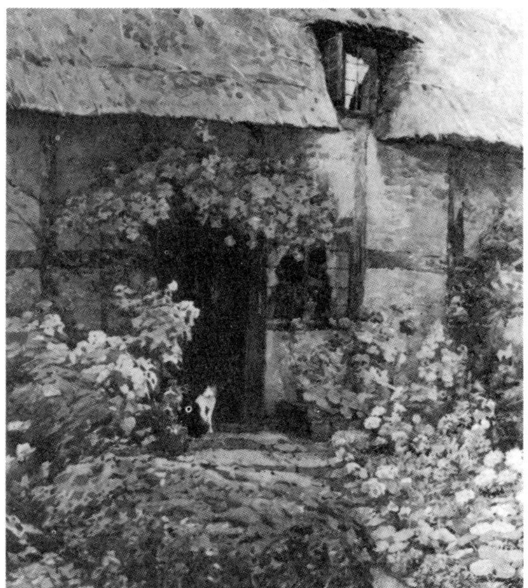

ERNEST A. CHADWICK – Study Of A Cat In A Cottage Doorway – signed – watercolour – 11 x 8in.
(Biddle & Webb) **$2,520** **£1,750**

ERNEST A. CHADWICK – Study Of Thatched Cottage – signed – watercolour – 10 x 14in.
(Biddle & Webb) **$2,016** **£1,400**

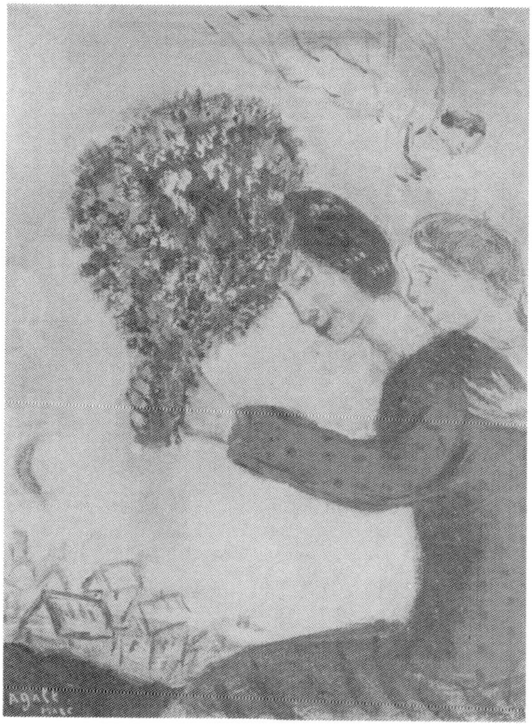

MARC CHAGALL – Jeune Femme au Bouquet de Fleurs – signed – oil on canvas – 10½ x 8½in.
(Christie's) **$87,120 £60,500**

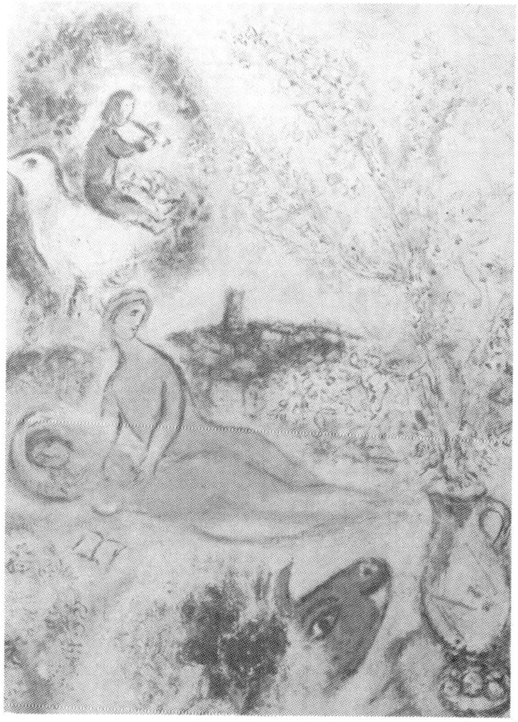

MARC CHAGALL – Les Amandiers – signed and dated 1955-56 – oil on canvas – 59 x 47¼in.
(Christie's) **$871,200 £605,000**

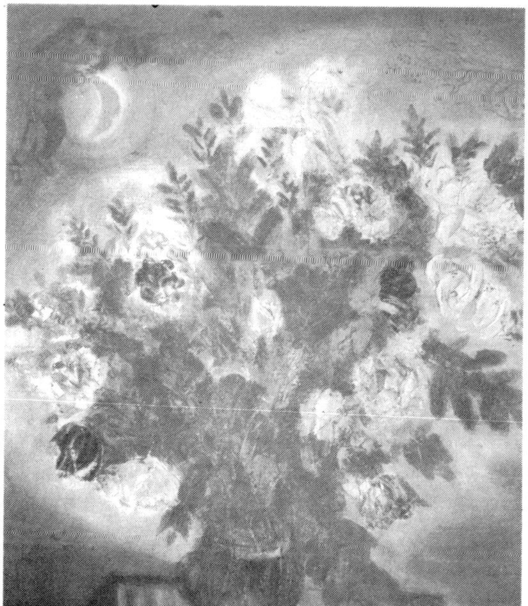

MARC CHAGALL – Bouquet de Fleurs avec Amoureux – signed – oil on canvas – 18 x 15in.
(Christie's) **$285,120 £198,000**

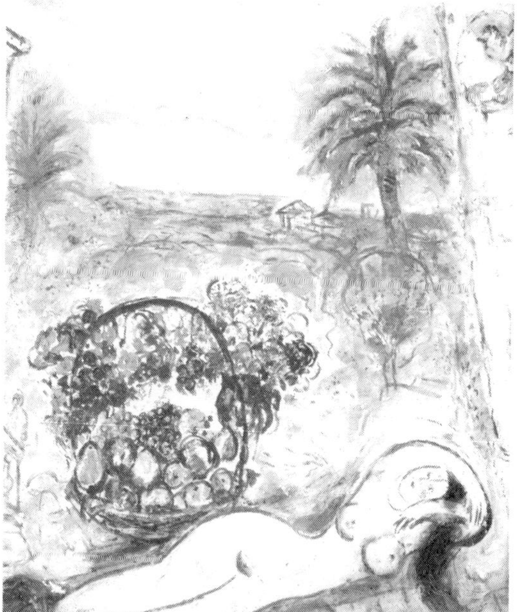

MARC CHAGALL – Le grand Nu a la Corbeille – signed and dated 1955, also signed and dated on the stretcher – oil on canvas – 59 x 47¼in.
(Christie's) **$665,280 £462,000**

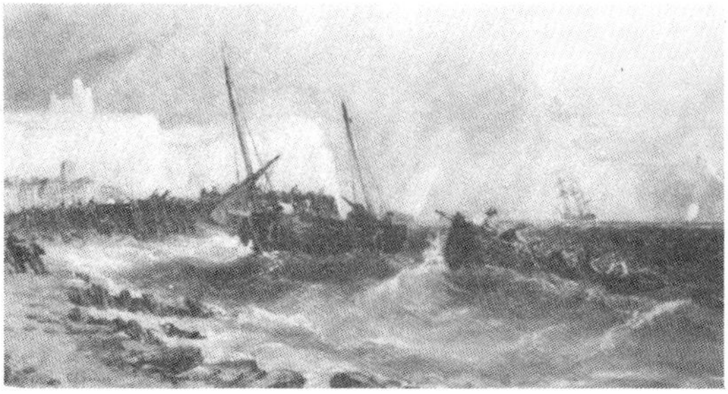

GEORGE CHAMBERS – Fishing Smacks Off Whitby – signed and dated 1856 – oil on canvas – 15½ x 23½in.
(Christie's) **$1,267** **£880**

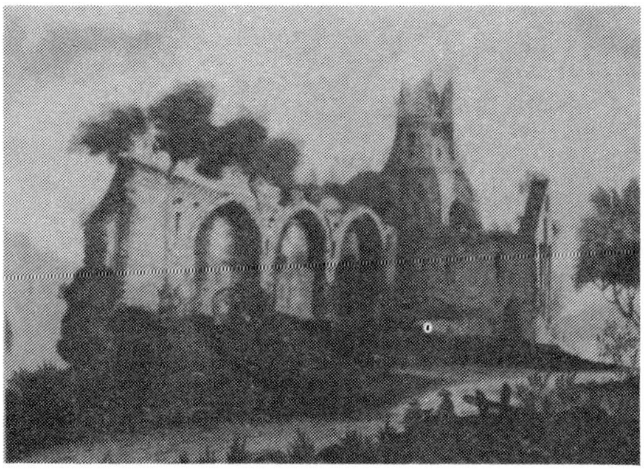

THOMAS CHAMBERS, Attributed to – The Ruined Abbey – oil on canvas – 14¼ x 18in.
(Robt. W. Skinner Inc.) **$650** **£398**

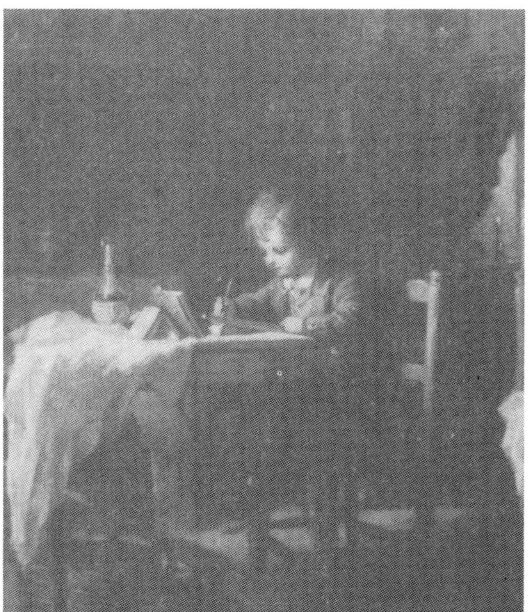

JAMES WELLS CHAMPNEY – Lessons – signed and dated '70 – oil on panel – 10½ x 8¼in.
(Christie's) **$6,050** **£3,769**

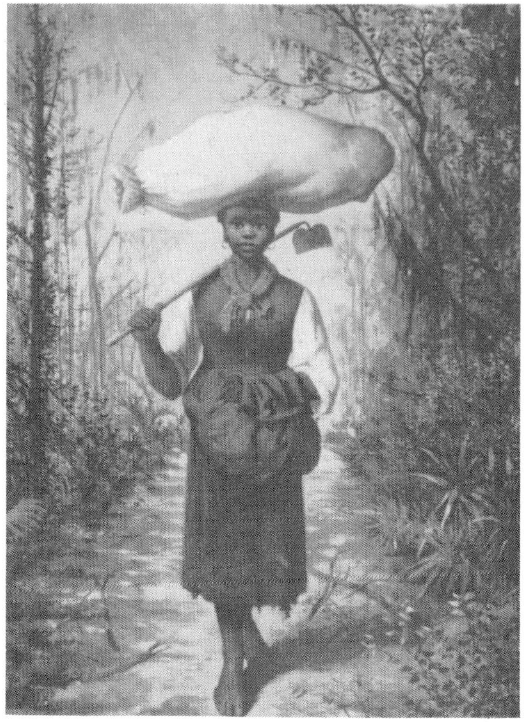

JAMES WELLS CHAMPNEY – In Florida – signed and dated '74 – oil on panel – 17¼ x 12½in.
(Christie's) **$2,860** **£1,989**

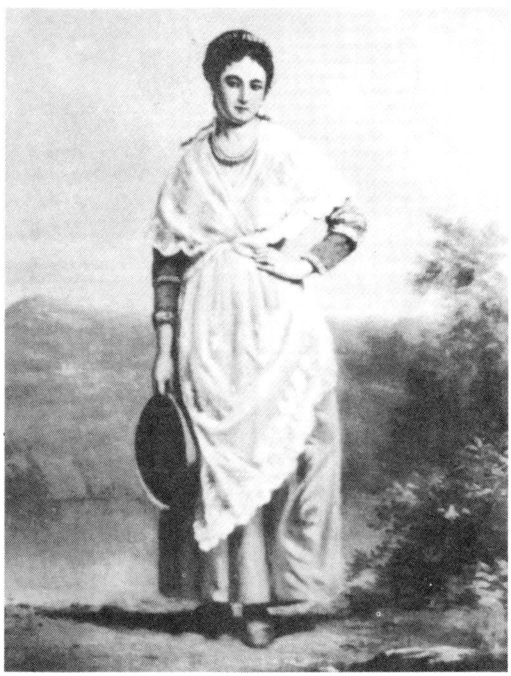

CONRAD WISE CHAPMAN – Woman By A Lake Shore – signed with monogram and dated 1902 – oil on canvas – 18 x 12in.
(Robt. W. Skinner Inc.) **$750** **£520**

MARY LOUISE CHAPMAN – Portrait Of An English Setter – signed with initials – oil on canvas – 29½ x 42in.
(Robt. W. Skinner Inc.) **$1,800** **£1,184**

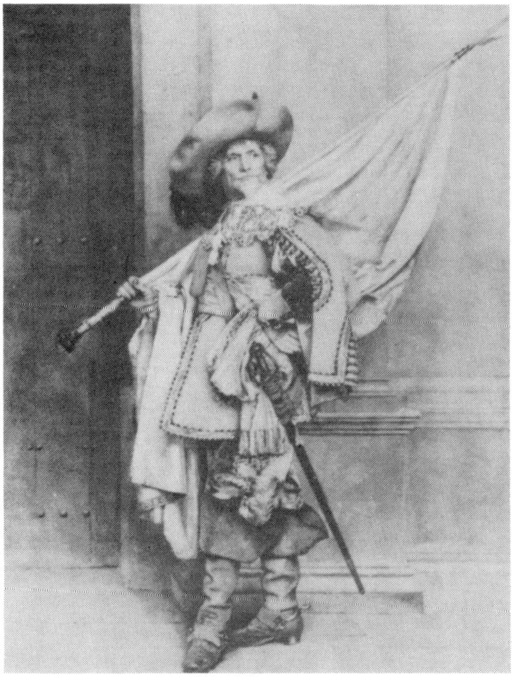

EDUARD CHARLEMONT – The Cavalier – signed and dated '93 – watercolour on paper laid down on cardboard – 20 x 14in.
(Robt. W. Skinner Inc.) **$550** **£361**

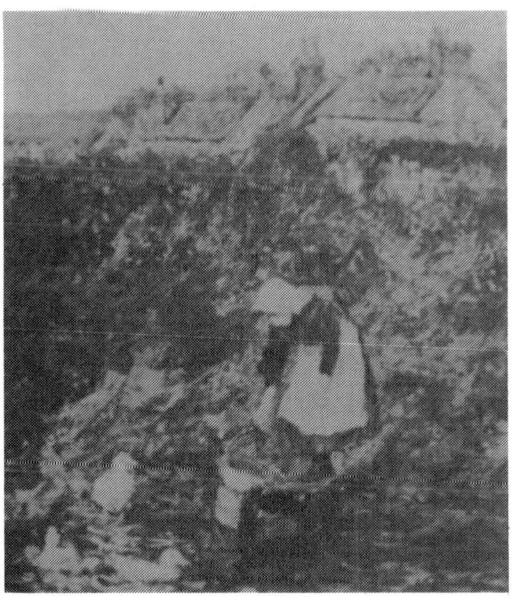

JAMES CHARLES – Feeding The Ducks – signed – on canvas – 12¾ x 9½in.
(Phillips) **$2,254** **£1,400**

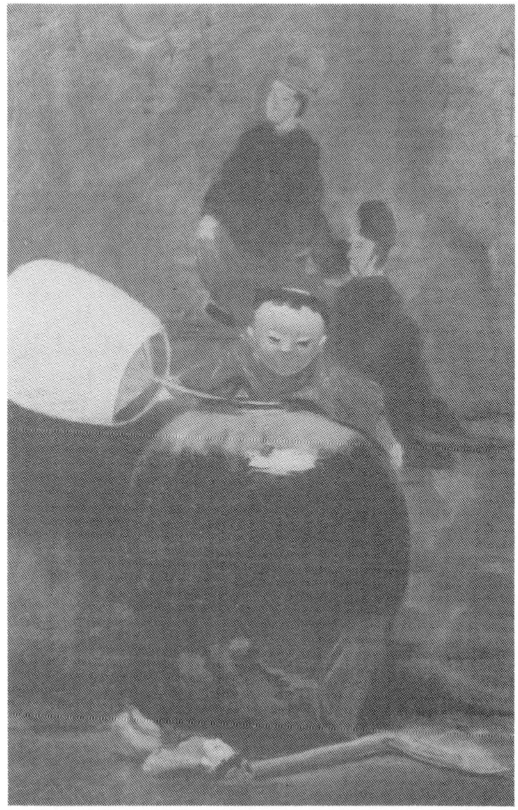

WILLIAM MERRITT CHASE – The Japanese Doll – signed – oil on canvas – 30 x 20in.
(Christie's) **$44,000** **£27,416**

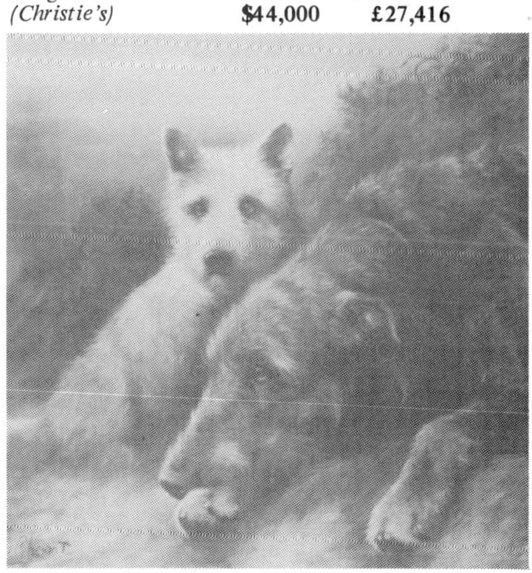

LILIAN CHEVIOT – The Best Of Friends – signed – 25 x 30in.
(Christie's) **$1,782** **£1,188**

EUGENE CHIGOT – Scene De Port – signed and inscribed – oil on canvas – 45.5 x 58cm.
(Phillips) **$930** **£600**

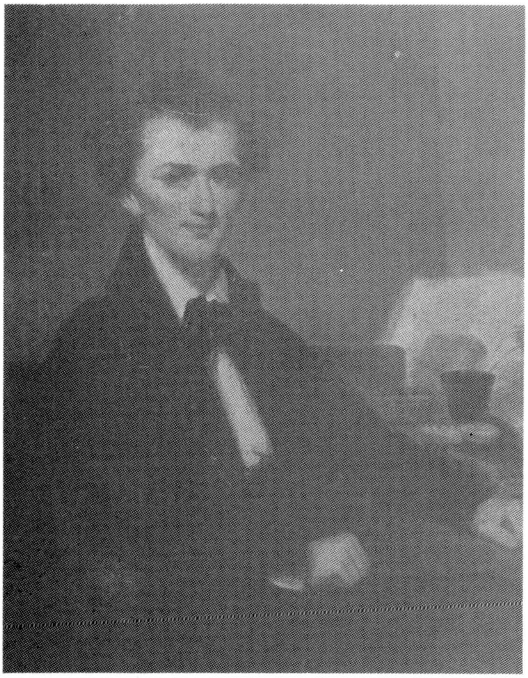

GEORGE CHINNERY – Portrait Of John Robert Morrison – circa 1835 – 10½ x 8in.
(Lawrence Fine Art) **$10,043** **£6,050**

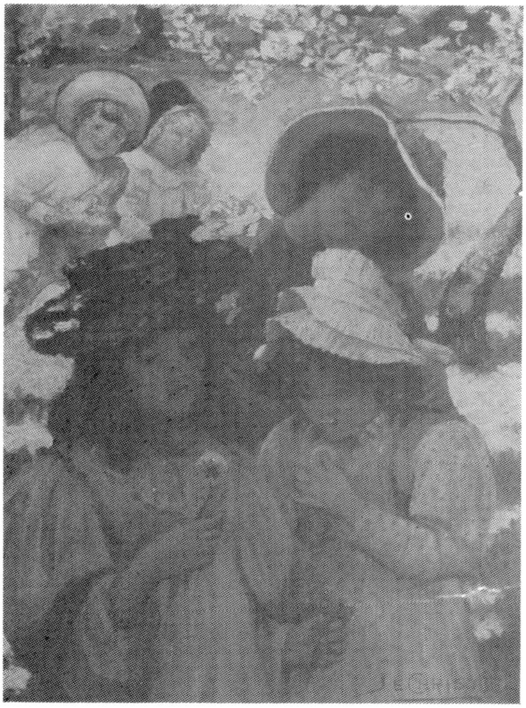

JAMES ELDER CHRISTIE – The Dandelion Clock – signed – oil on canvas – 18 x 14in.
(Christie's) **$7,920** **£5,500**

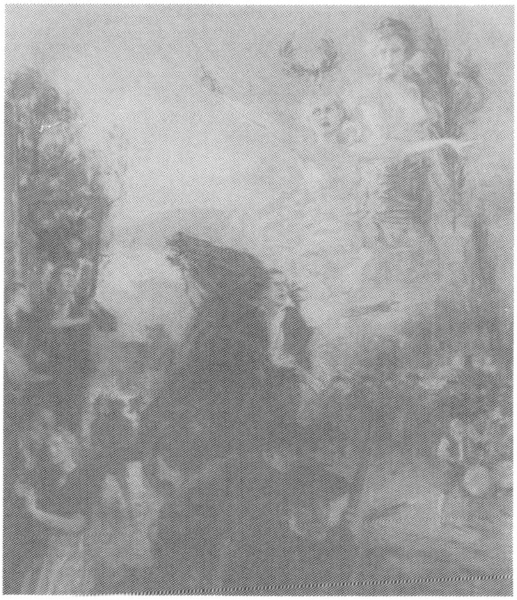

HOWARD CHANDLER CHRISTY – A Call To Arms – signed and dated 1927 – oil on canvas – 45 x 40in.
(Christie's) **$4,950** **£3,479**

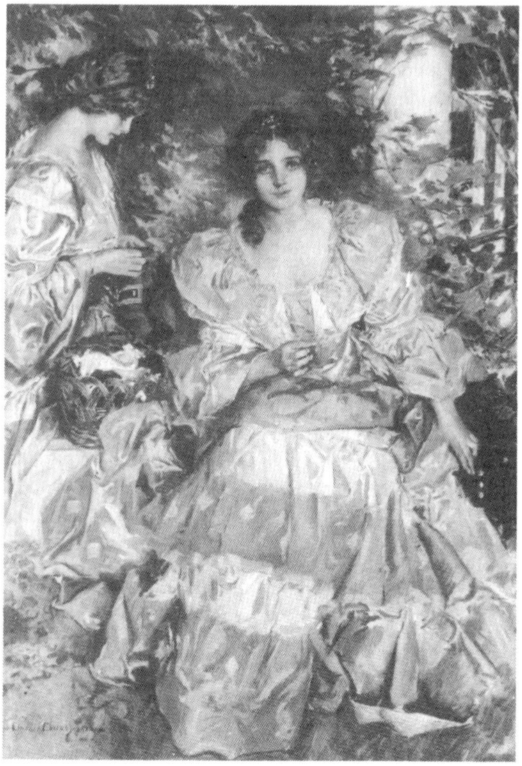

HOWARD CHANDLER CHRISTY – Far Away Thoughts – signed and dated 1912 – oil on canvas – 63 x 45in.
(Christie's) **$17,600** **£12,372**

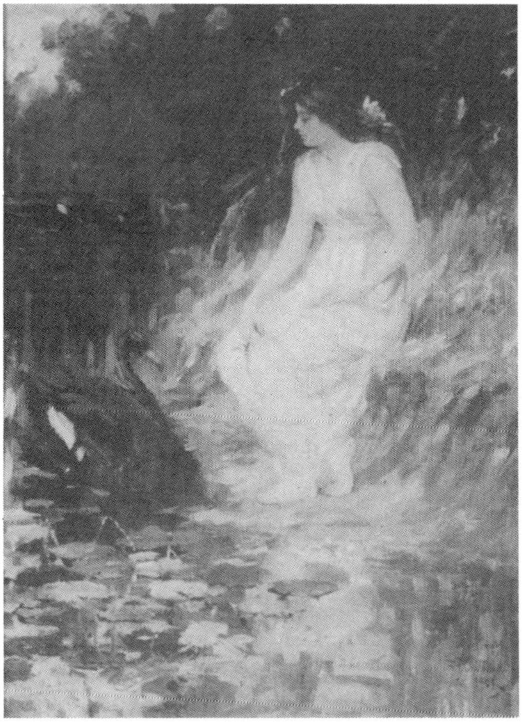

FREDERICK STUART CHURCH – The Black Swans – signed and dated 1905 – oil on canvas – 22 x 16¼in.
(Christie's) **$2,860** **£1,989**

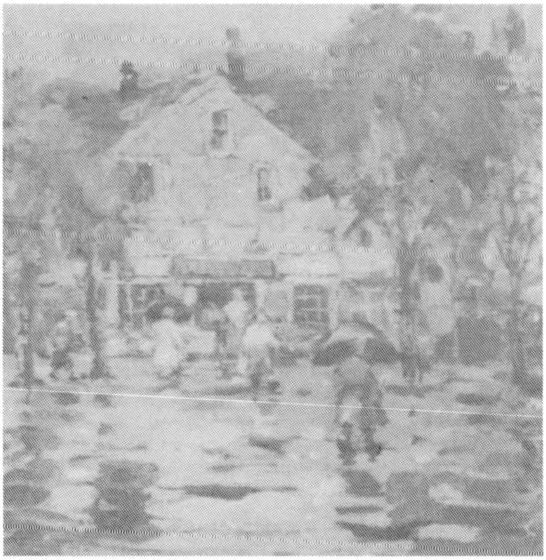

ANTONIO CIRINO – Dock Square – signed – oil on board – 8 x 9¾in.
(Robt. W. Skinner Inc.) **$1,500** **£920**

GEORGE CLARE – Gooseberries And Strawberries In Wicker Baskets With Other Fruit On A Mossy Bank – signed – 18 x 24in.
(Christie's) **$5,670** **£3,780**

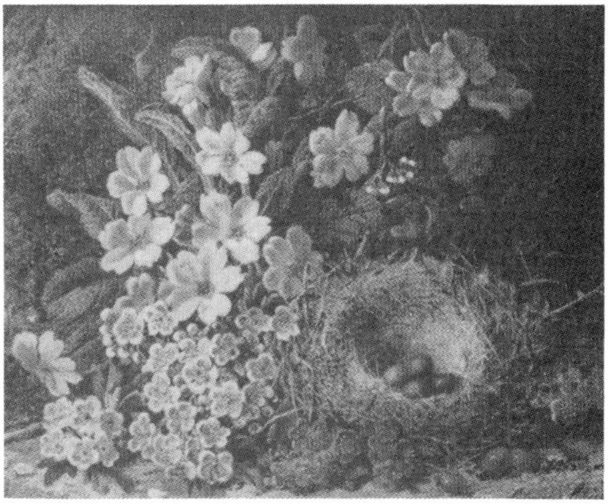

GEORGE CLARE – A Bird's Nest With Primroses And Other Flowers By A Mossy Bank; and Plums And Other Fruit By A Mossy Bank – signed – 10 x 12in.
(Christie's) **$4,032** **£2,860 Pair**

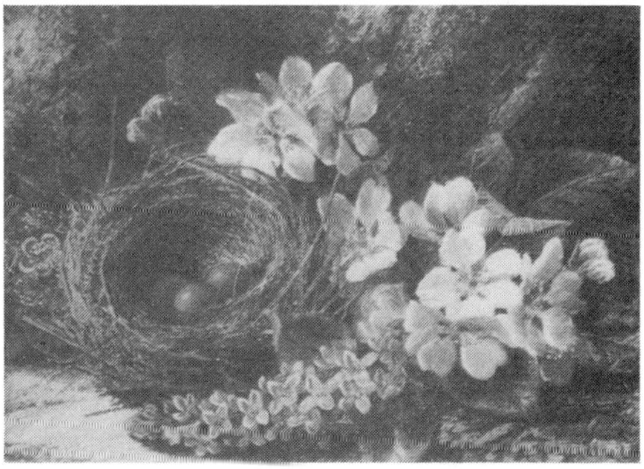

OLIVER CLARE – Blossom With A Bird's Nest On A Mossy Bank – signed – 7 x 9in.
(Christie's) **$1,514** **£990**

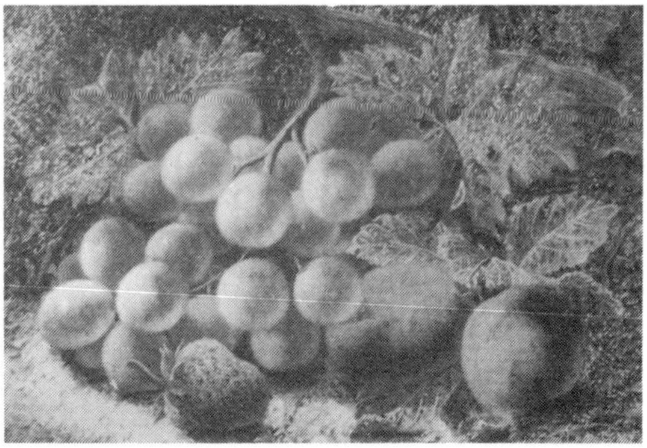

OLIVER CLARE – Still Life, Grapes, Plums And Strawberry – signed – oil on board – 12.5 x 17cm.
(W. H. Lane & Son) **$863** **£520**

OLIVER CLARE – Still Life, Peach, Raspberries And Gooseberries – signed – oil on board – 13 x 17cm.
(W. H. Lane & Son) **$1,029** **£620**

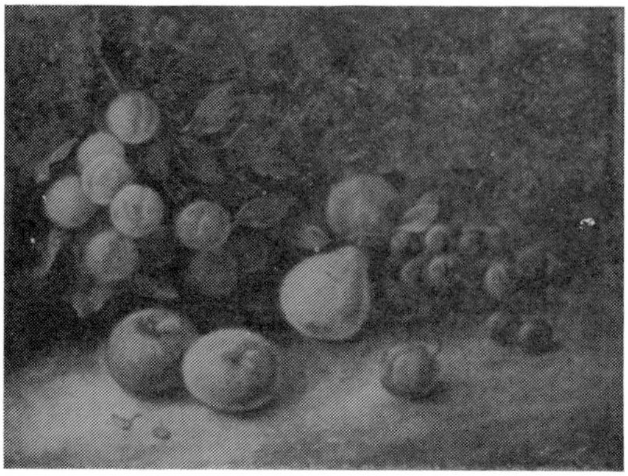

VINCENT CLARE – Still Life Summer Fruit – oil on board – 10 x 12½in.
(Prudential Fine Art Auctioneers) **$564** **£340**

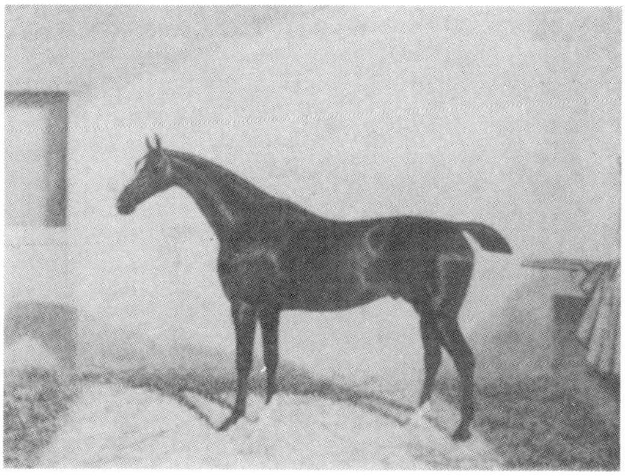

ALBERT CLARK – A Chestnut Hunter In A Loose Box – signed and dated 1889 – oil on canvas – 19 x 23in.
(Christie's) **$1,754** **£1,210**

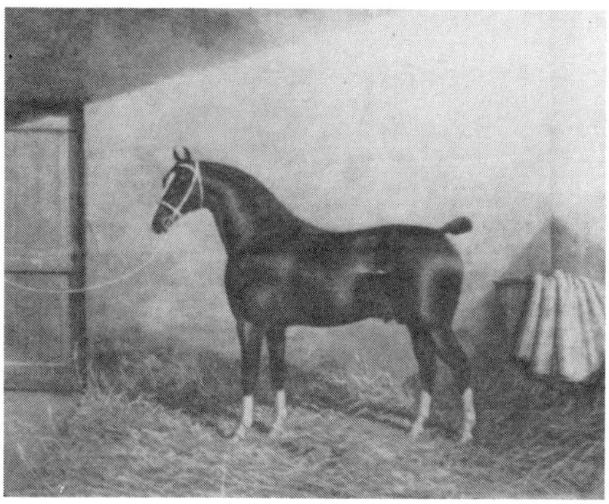

ALBERT CLARK – A Hunter Tethered In A Loose Box – signed – oil on canvas – 20 x 24in.
(Christie's) **$1,584** **£990**

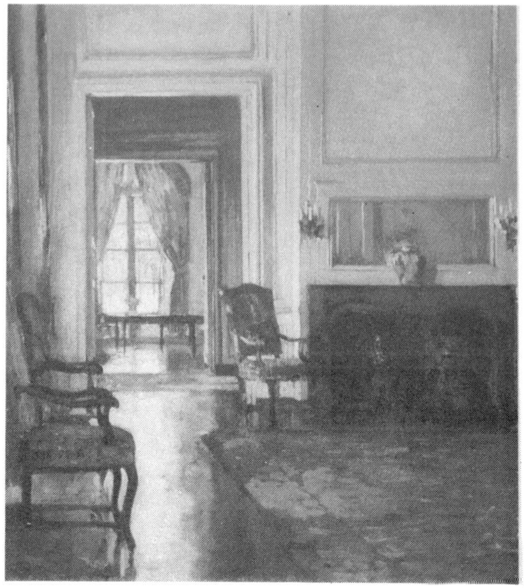

ALSON SKINNER CLARK – Some House – signed and dated '15 – oil on canvas – 25½ x 21¼in.
(Christie's) **$2,640** **£1,644**

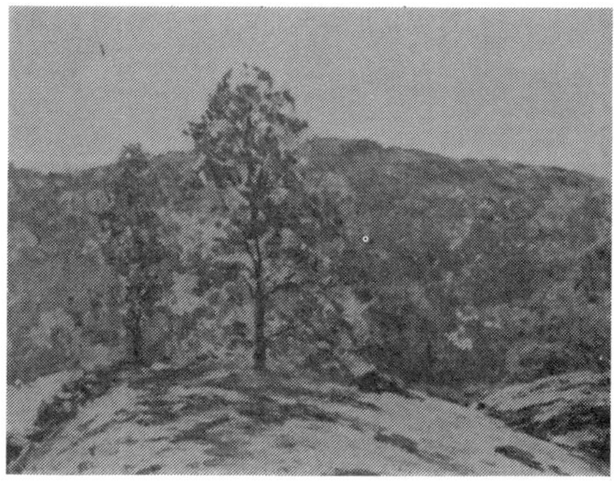

ELIOT CLARK – Autumn, Kent, Connecticut – signed, signed and dated 1923 on the reverse – oil on board – 13¾ x 16in.
(Robt. W. Skinner Inc.) **$550** **£337**

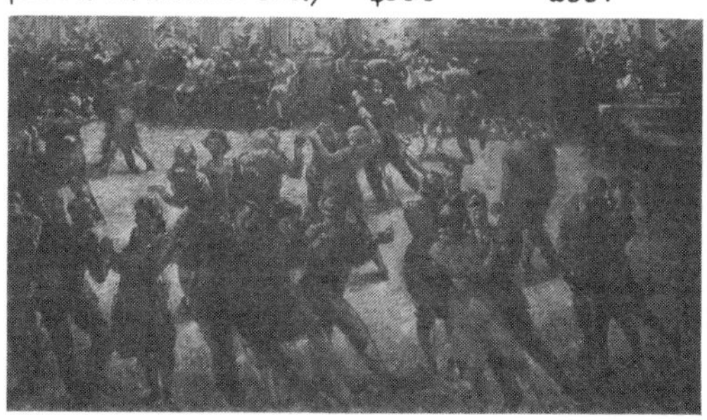

J. COSMO CLARK – Dancing In A South London Pub In Wartime – signed and dated 1945 – oil on canvas – 20 x 34¼in.
(Christie's) **$8,289** **£5,280**

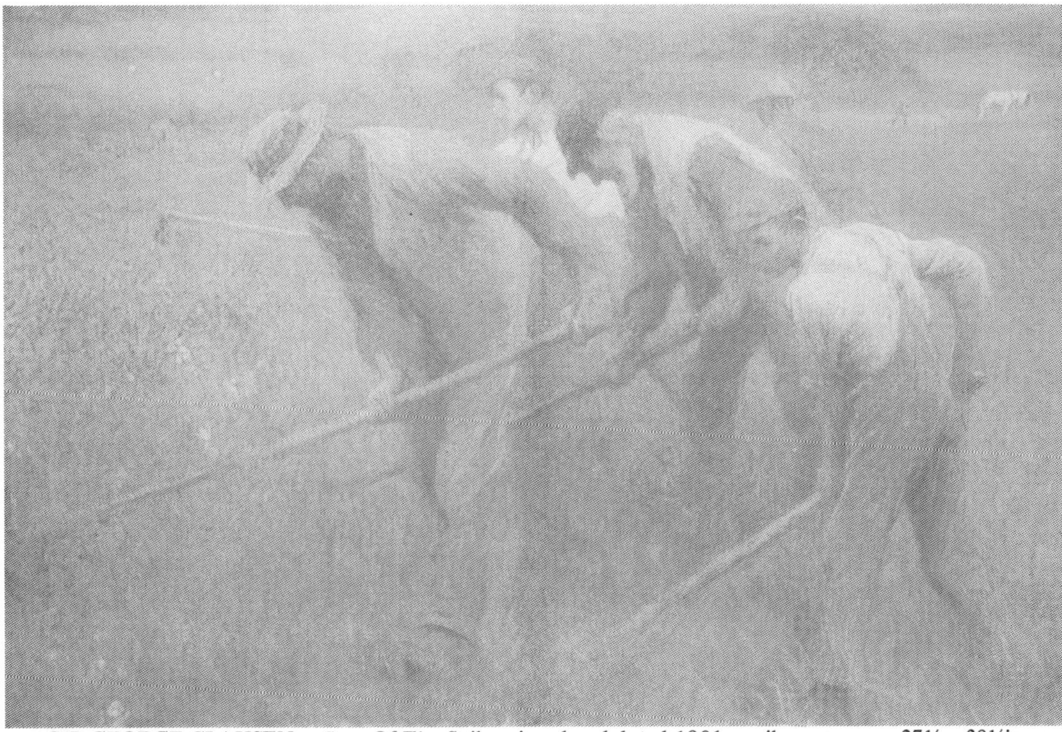

SIR GEORGE CLAUSEN – Sons Of The Soil – signed and dated 1901 – oil on canvas – 27¼ x 30¼in.
(Christie's) **$86,515 £60,500**

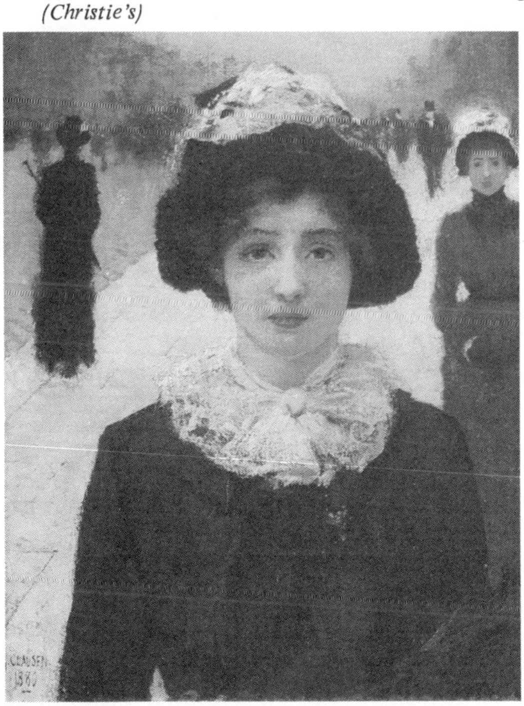

SIR GEORGE CLAUSEN – In The Street – signed and dated 1880, and signed, inscribed and dated on the reverse – oil on canvas – 9¾ x 6¾in.
(Christie's) **$42,471 £29,700**

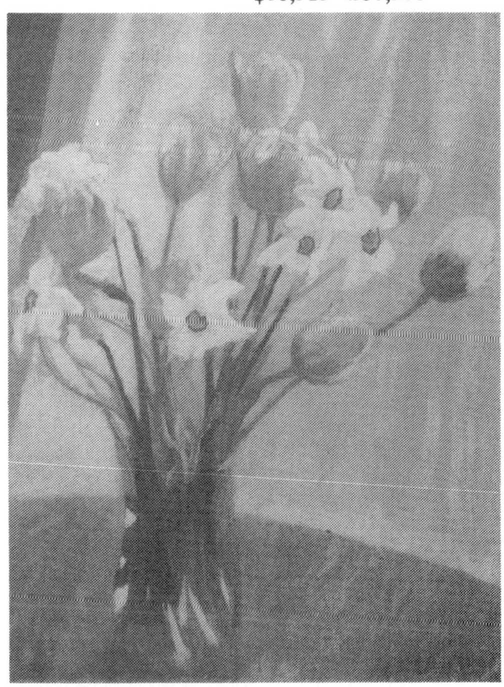

SIR GEORGE CLAUSEN – A Vase Of Tulips And Narcissi – signed – oil on canvas – 46 x 36cm.
(Phillips) **$3,680 £2,300**

CLAY

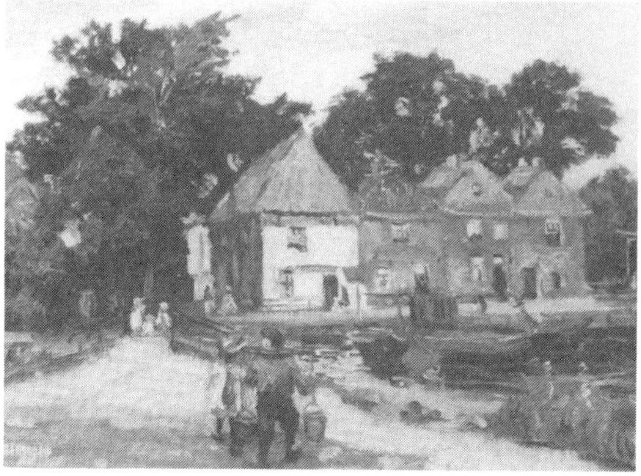

ELIZABETH C. FISHER CLAY – Fetching Water – signed – oil on canvas – 46 x 54cm.
(Phillips) **$2,130** **£1,500**

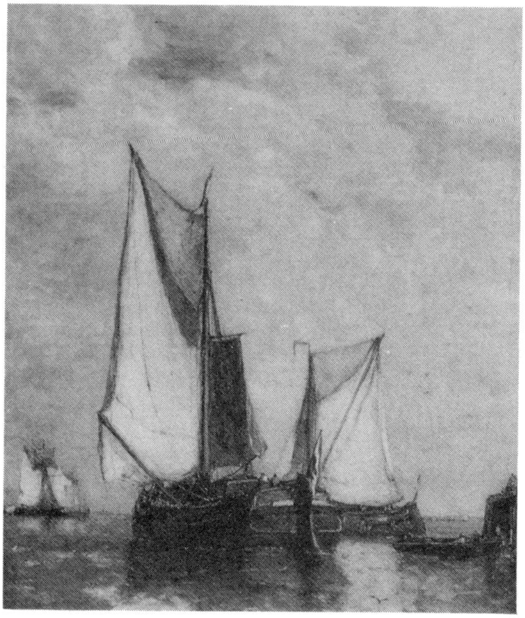

PAUL JEAN CLAYS – Shipping Off A Jetty – signed – on panel – 24 x 19in.
(Christie's) **$3,678** **£2,420**

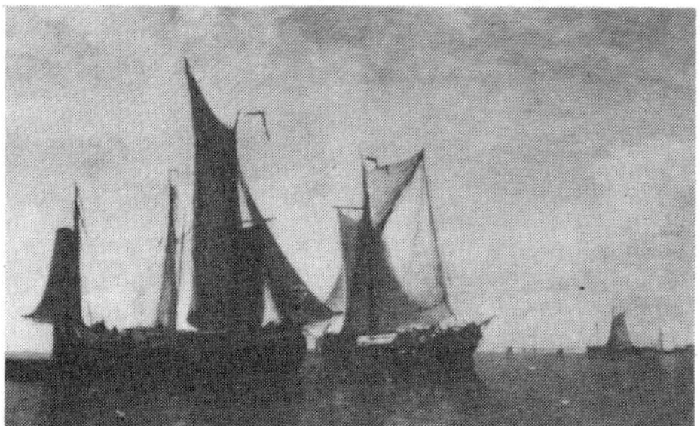

PAUL JEAN CLAYS – Fishing Vessels In A Calm – signed and dated 1870 – oil on canvas – 77 x 111cm.
(Phillips) **$2,505** **£1,500 Four**

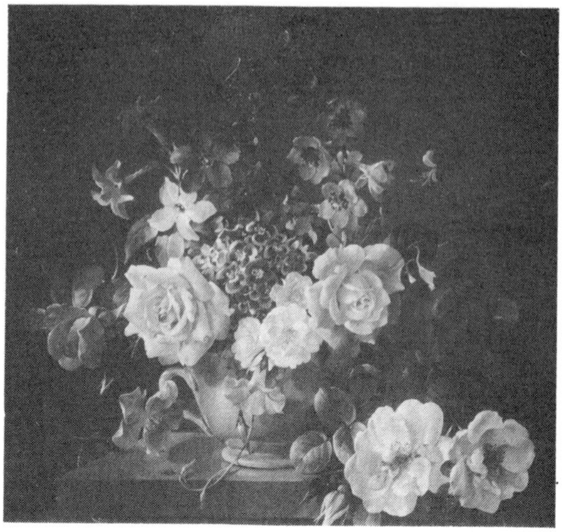

HAROLD CLAYTON – Roses, Delphiniums And Sweet William In A Vase On A Stone Ledge – signed – oil on board – 46 x 51cm.
(Phillips) **$8,804** **£6,200**

ROBERT CLEMINSON – At The End Of The Day; and Retrievers On A Moor – signed – oil on canvas – 16 x 24in.
(Christie's) **$1,440** **£1,000 Pair**

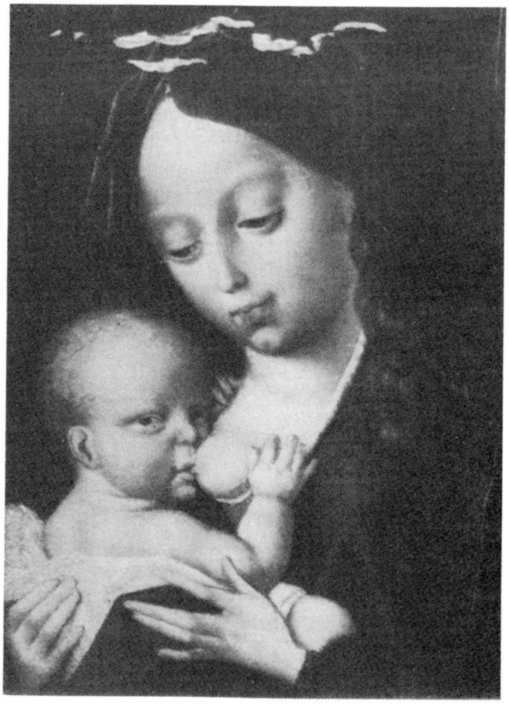

JOOS VAN CLEVE, Follower of – The Madonna And Child – oil on panel – 9½ x 7½in.
(Phillips) **$1,974** **£1,400**

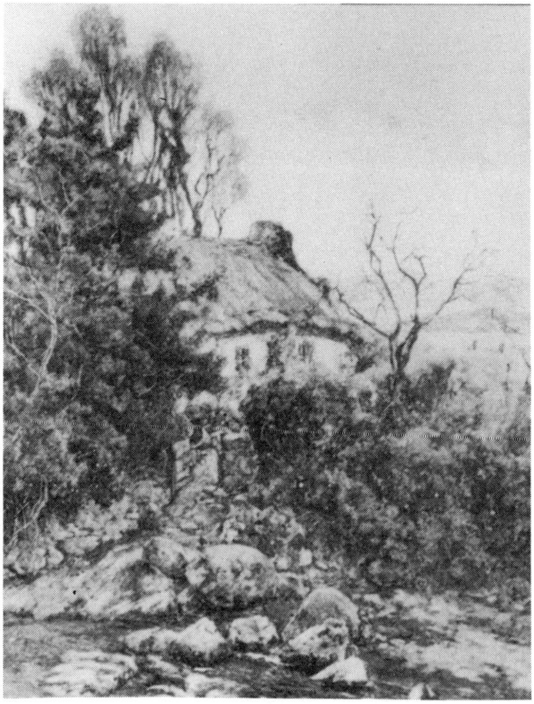

TOM CLOUGH – Rustic Scene, Secluded Thatched Cottage By A Stream, Distant Mountains – signed – watercolour – 24 x 17½in.
(Capes, Dunn & Co.) **$619** **£380**

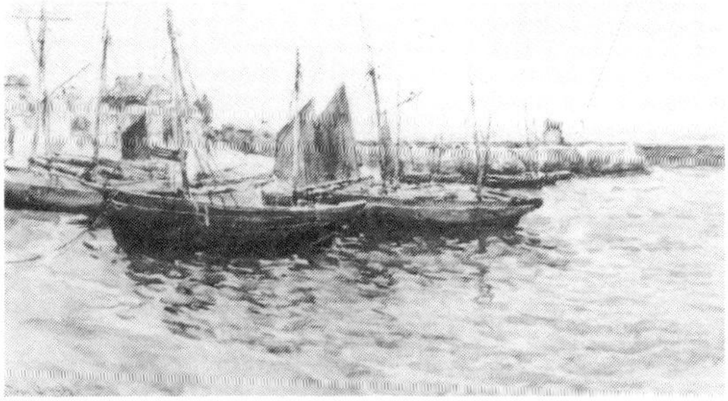

TOM CLOUGH – Coastal Village With Moored And Drawn-Up Fishing Boats In The Harbour – signed – watercolour – 14 x 24in.
(Capes, Dunn & Co.) **$978** **£600**

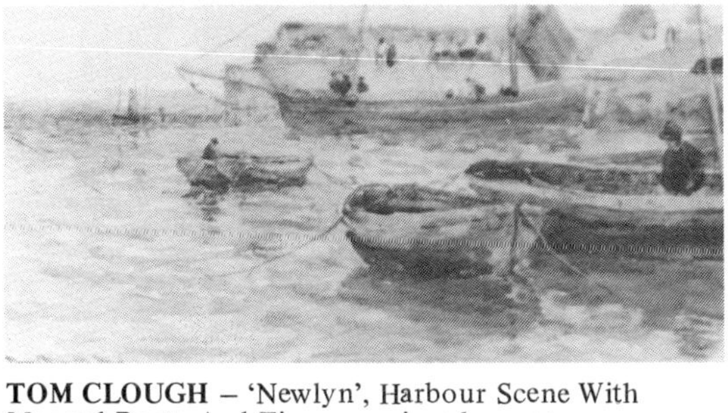

TOM CLOUGH – 'Newlyn', Harbour Scene With Moored Boats And Figures – signed – watercolour – 10 x 20in.
(Capes, Dunn & Co.) **$619** **£380**

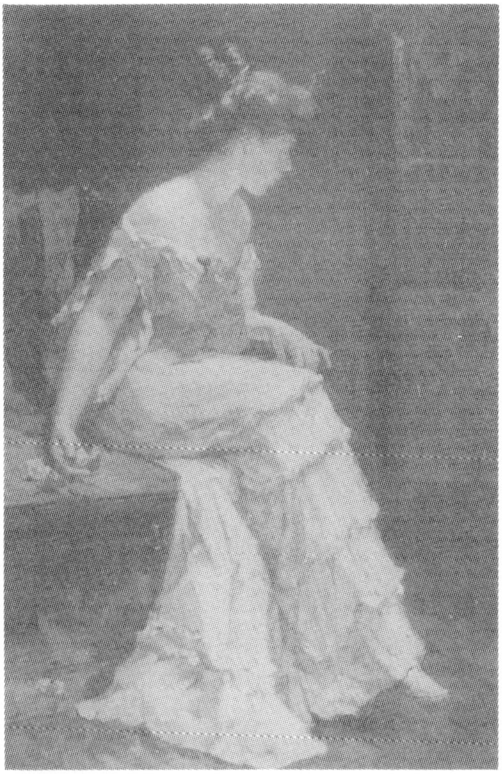

ANDRE CLUYSENAAR – The Fallen Rose – signed and dated 1906 – 31 x 19in.
(Christie's) **$4,681** **£3,080**

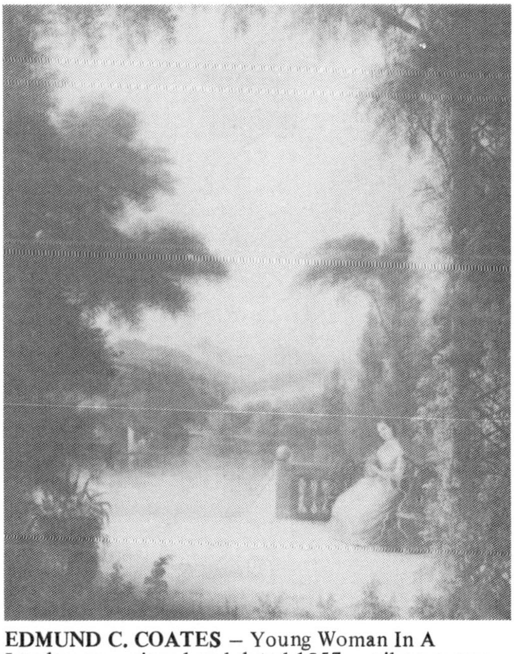

EDMUND C. COATES – Young Woman In A Landscape – signed and dated 1857 – oil on canvas – 33¾ x 27in.
(Robt. W. Skinner Inc.) **$2,200** **£1,447**

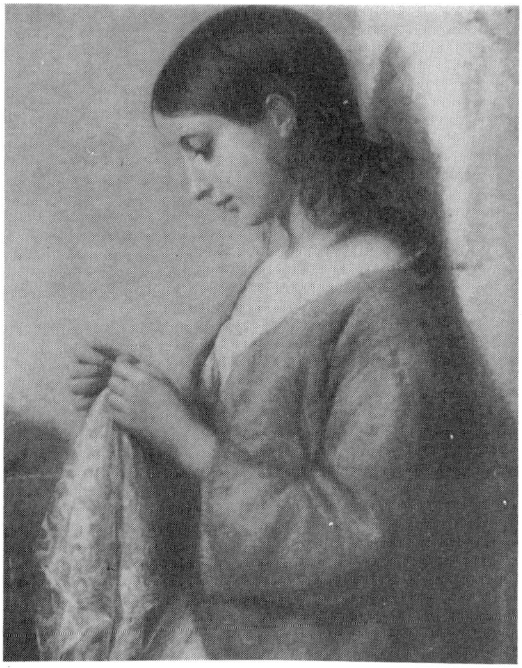

EDWARD JOHN COBBETT – Making Lace – partially signed – on board – 18½ x 12¾in.
(Christie's) **$2,019** **£1,320**

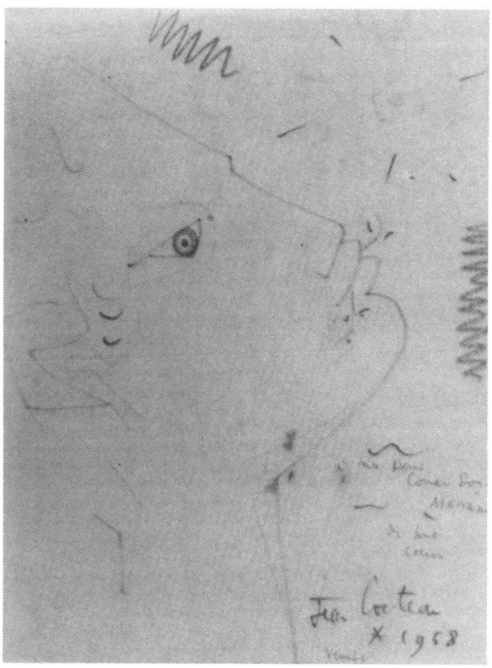

JEAN COCTEAU – Portrait de la Princess Nina Mdivani – signed, dated 1958 and inscribed – coloured crayon, felt pen, pastel and ballpoint pen on paper – 13¼ x 10in.
(Christie's) **$1,936** **£1,210**

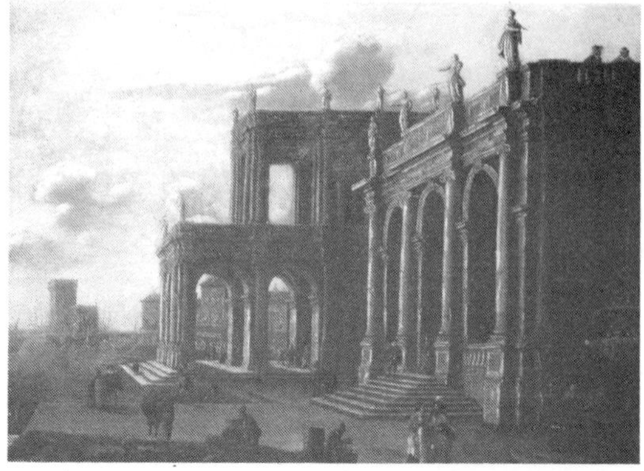

VIVIANO CODAZZI, Circle of – A Port Scene With Elegant Figures Strolling Before A Classical Building – bears monogram LB – oil on canvas – 38½ x 51½in.
(Phillips) **$4,512** **£3,200**

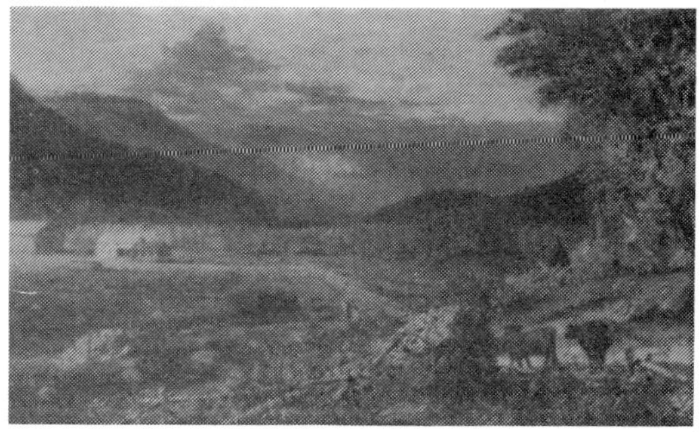

JOHN AMORY CODMAN – View Of Mount Washington Bowl – signed with initials and dated '64, also dated 1862 – oil on canvas – 16 x 24in.
(Robt. W. Skinner Inc.) **$1,500** **£920**

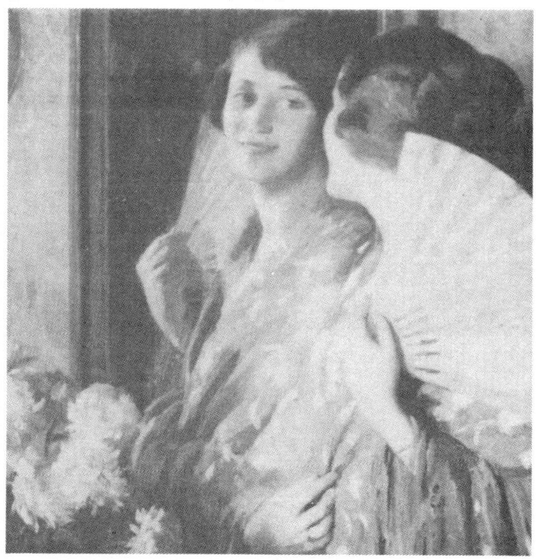

ALPHAEUS P. COLE – Young Woman Looking In The Mirror – signed and dated 1924 – oil on canvas – 30¼ x 24in.
(Christie's) **$5,500** **£3,826**

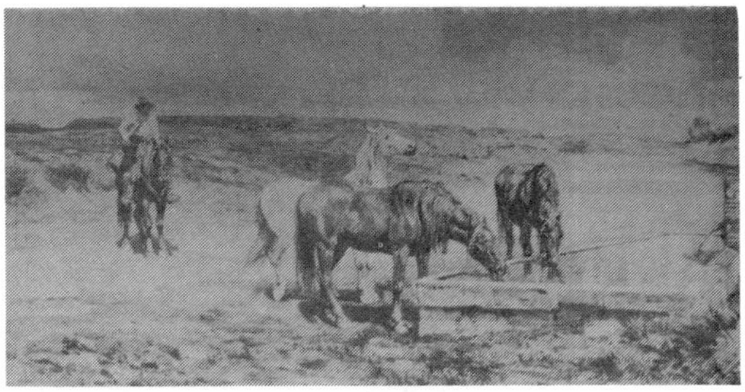

ENRICO COLEMAN – The Watering Place – signed and inscribed – watercolour – 11 x 21in.
(Lawrence Fine Art) **$5,295** **£3,190**

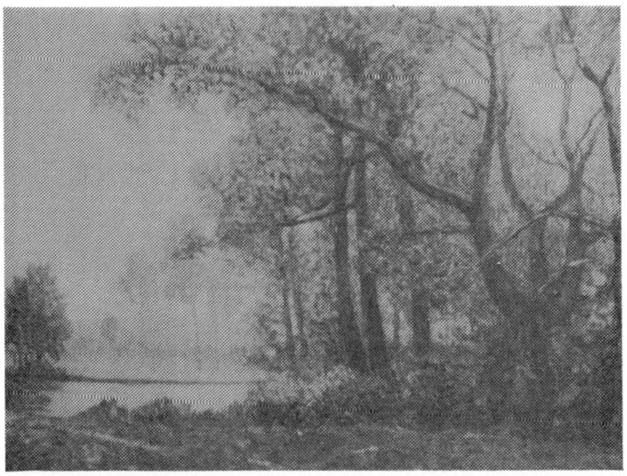

AUGUSTE-MICHEL COLLE – Au Bord De La Riviere – signed and dated '05 – oil on canvas – 72.5 x 92cm.
(Phillips) **$4,185** **£2,700**

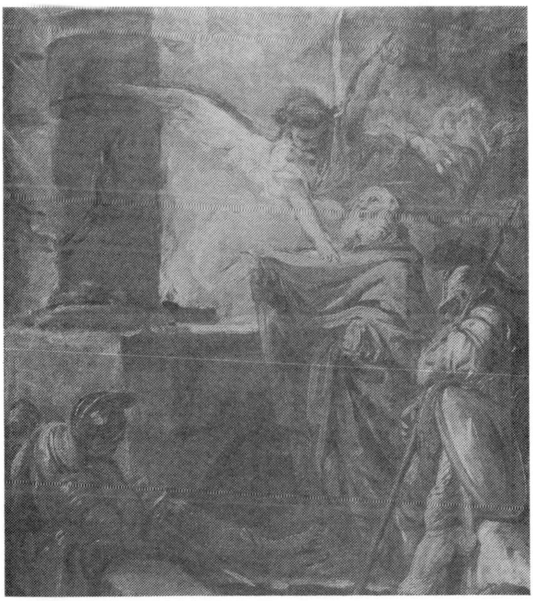

JEAN-BAPTISTE HENRI DESHAYS DE COLLEVILLE – Saint Peter Being Delivered From Prison – on canvas – 22¾ x 16½in.
(Phillips) **$16,600** **£10,000**

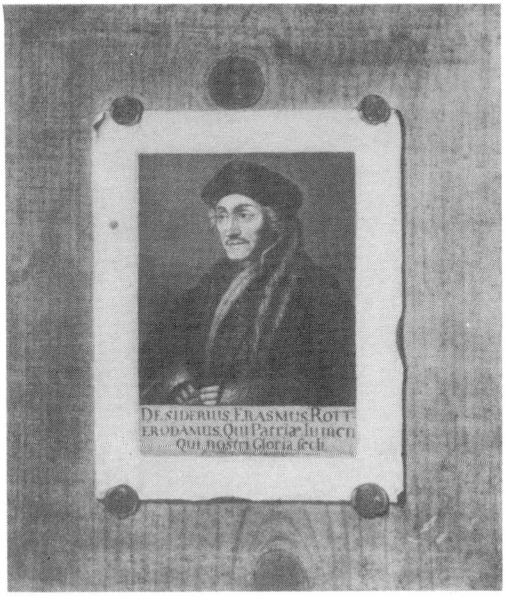

EVERT COLLIER – A Tromp L'Oeil With An Engraving Of Erasmus Attached To A Panel – signed, inscribed and dated 1695 – 14¼ x 12½in.
(Christie's) **$3,078** **£2,052**

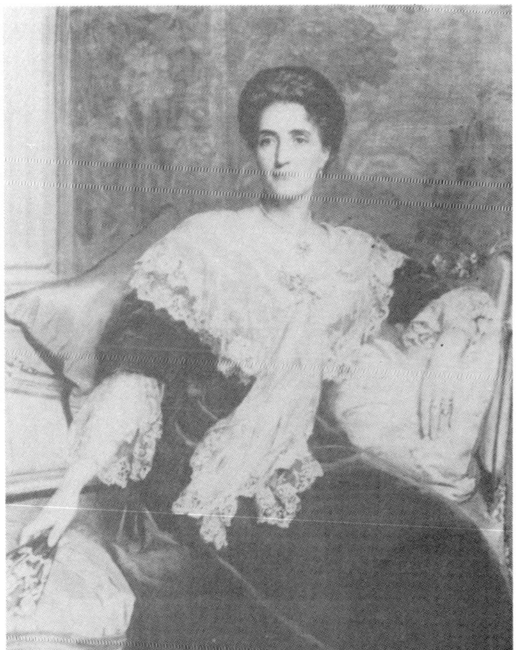

THE HON. JOHN COLLIER – Portrait Of Mrs. J. S. Wood, Seated Half Length Wearing A Red Dress; and Portrait Of Mr. J. S. Wood, Seated, Holding A Cigarette – one signed and dated 1903, the other signed – oil on canvas – 50 x 40in.
(Christie's) **$5,505** **£3,850 Pair**

COLLIER

THE HON. JOHN COLLIER – 'The Land Of Dreams' – signed – oil on canvas – 42 x 64in.
(Phillips) **$10,710 £7,000**

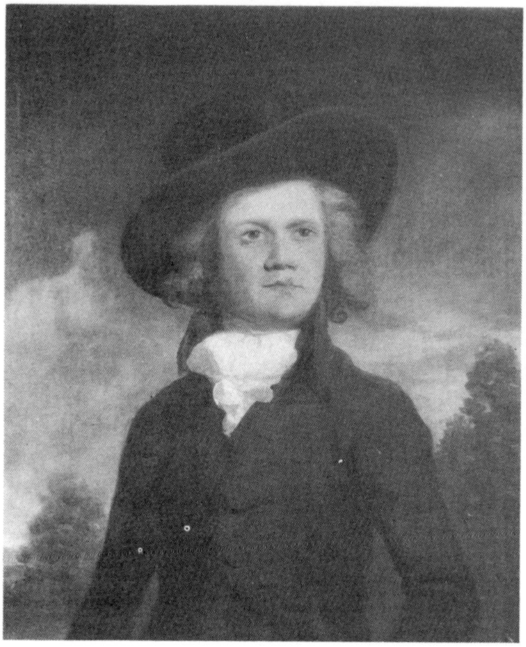

SAMUEL COLLINGS – Self-Portrait Of The Artist, Standing Half Length, Wearing A Dark Grey Coat And Hat, In A Wooded Landscape – 30¼ x 25¼in.
(Christie's) **$1,944 £1,296**

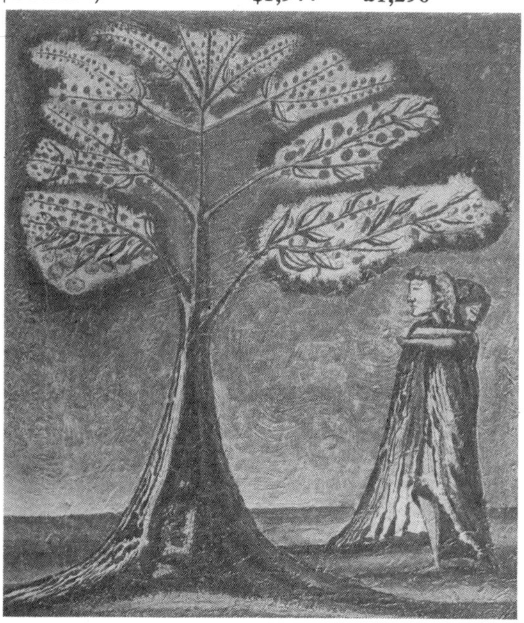

CECIL COLLINS – Morning – signed and dated 1943, and signed, dated and inscribed on a label on the stretcher – oil on canvas – 14 x 12in.
(Christie's) **$8,651 £6,050**

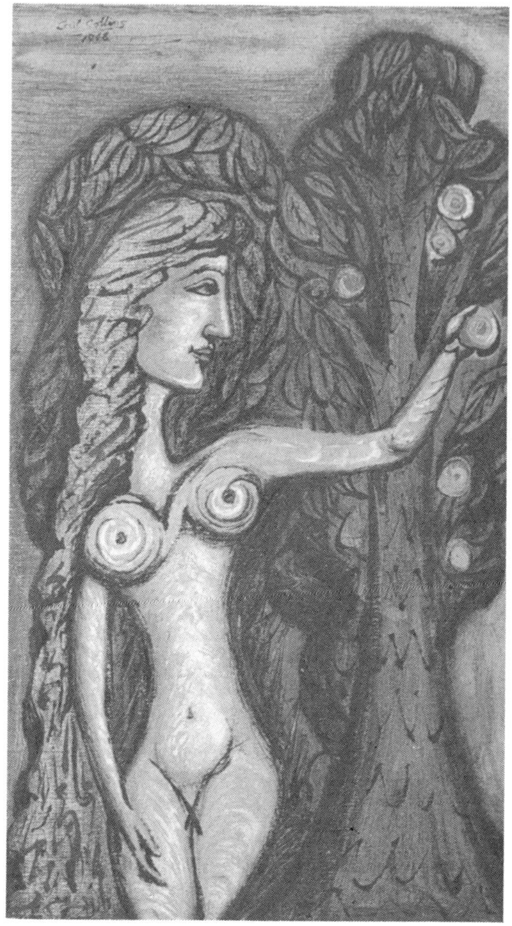

CECIL COLLINS – Eve In The Garden Of Paradise – signed and dated 1948, and signed and dated and inscribed on the reverse – oil on canvas – 18 x 10in.
(Christie's) **$6,606 £4,620**

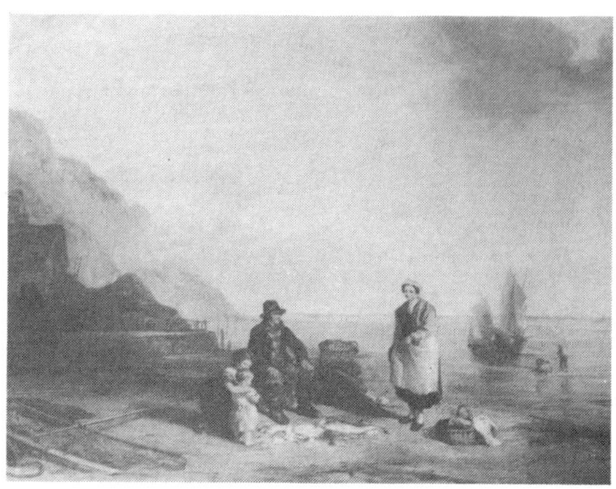

WILLIAM COLLINS – Buying Fish – dated 1826 – 34 x 47in.
(Christie's) **$23,562 £15,400**

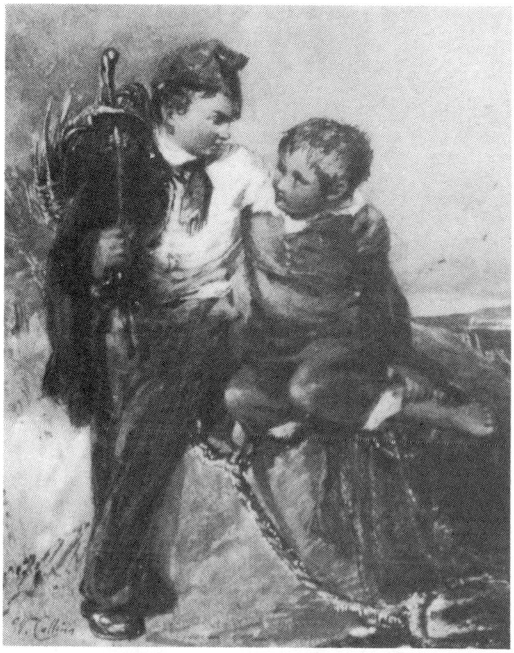

WILLIAM COLLINS – Fisherboys On A Sand Dune – signed – pencil and watercolour heightened with white – 11½ x 8½in.
(Christie's) **$1,296** **£864**

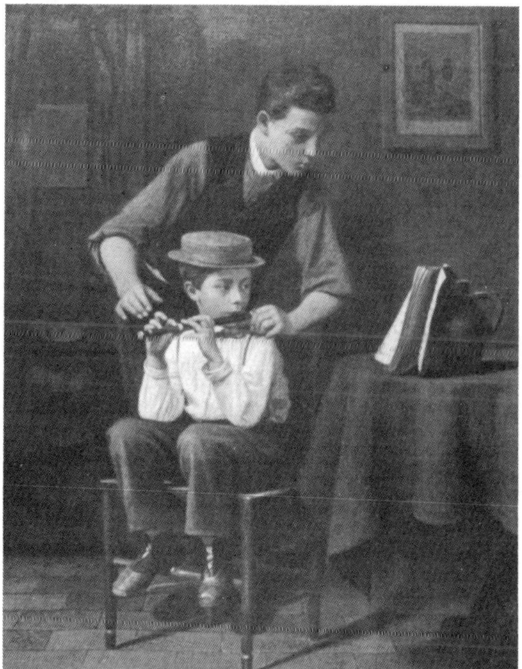

JAMES COLLINSON – Interior Scene With Boy Learning The Flute – signed and dated – oil – 14 x 10in.
(Graves Son & Pilcher) **$1,512** **£1,050**

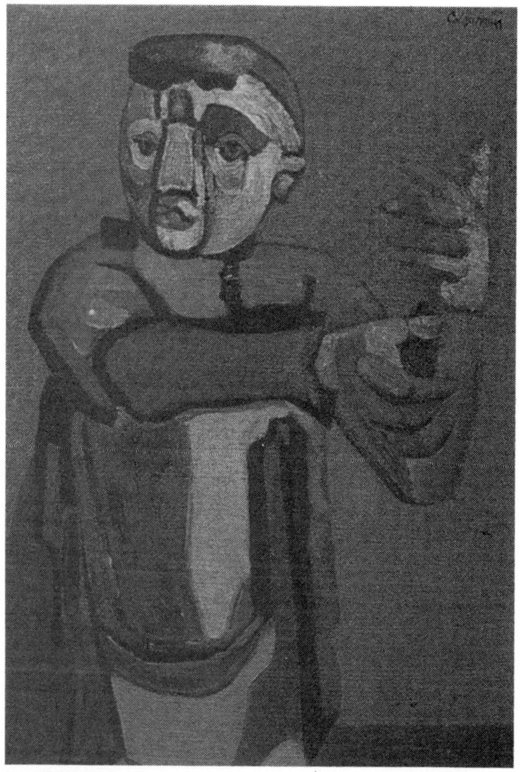

ROBERT COLQUHOUN – The Conjurer – signed – oil on canvas – 17 x 11½in.
(Christie's) **$6,562** **£4,180**

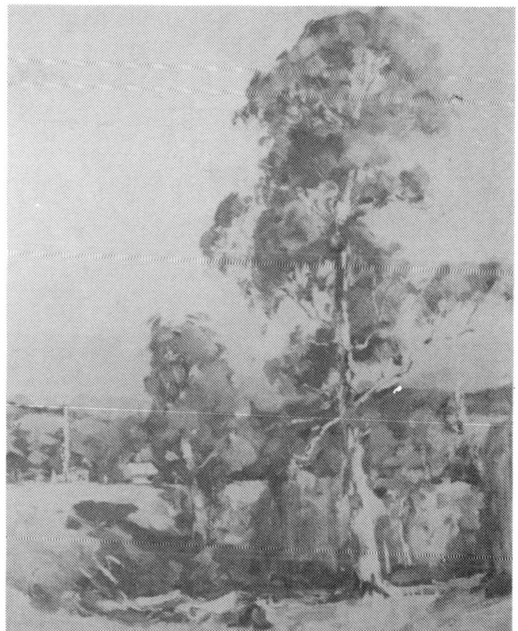

GEORGE COLVILLE – Australian Landscape – signed – oil on canvas board – 51 x 41cm.
(Phillips) **$913** **£550**

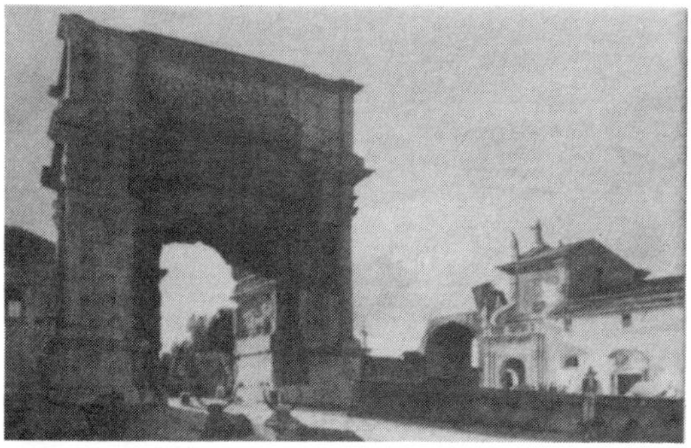

JOSE FALOFRE Y COMA – Vespasian's Arch, Rome – signed, inscribed and dated 1841 – watercolour – 12 x 18½in.
(Christie's) **$968** **£605**

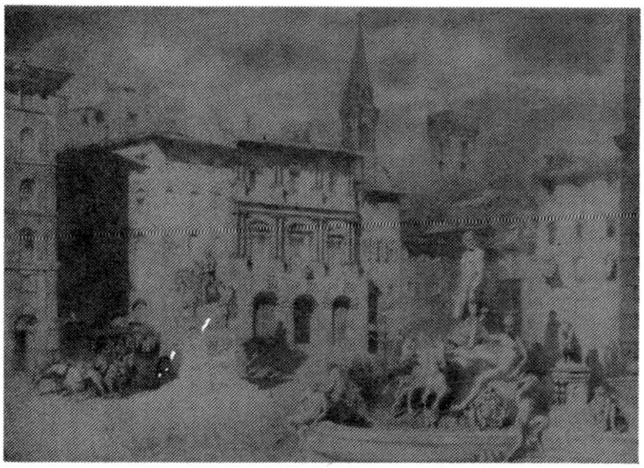

ALFRED CHARLES CONRADE – Piazza Della Signoria, Florence – signed, inscribed and dated 1928 – pencil and watercolour – 15 x 21in.
(Christie's) **$1,734** **£1,045**

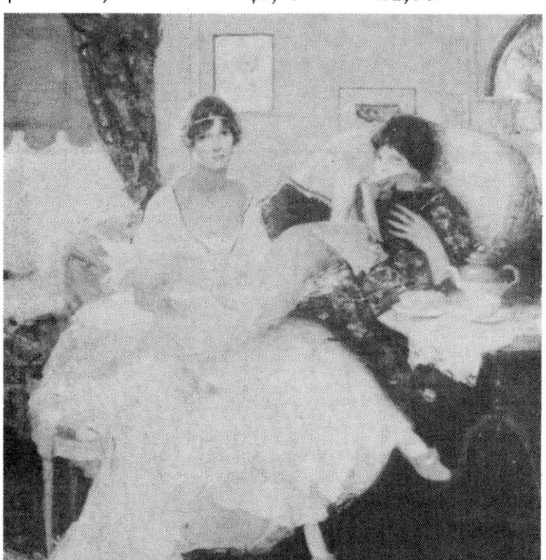

DANIEL CONTENT – Two Ladies At Leisure – signed – oil on canvas – 30 x 24¼in.
(Christie's) **$4,180** **£2,908**

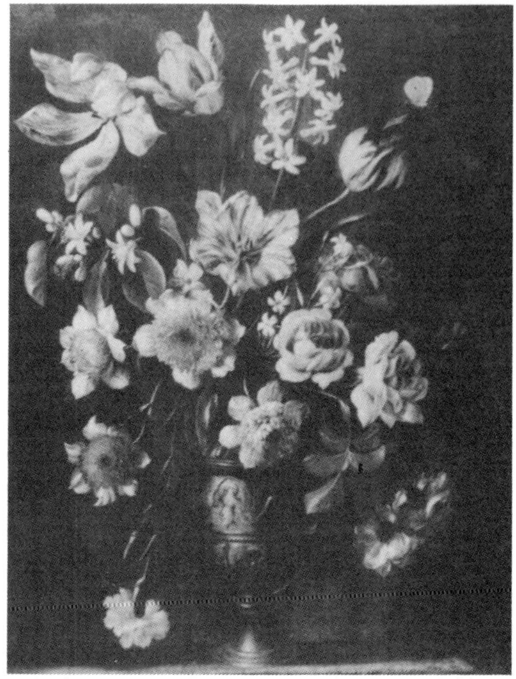

CONTINENTAL SCHOOL, 19th century – Floral Still Life – oil on canvas – 25½ x 19½in.
(Robt. W. Skinner Inc.) **$3,900** **£2,708 Pair**

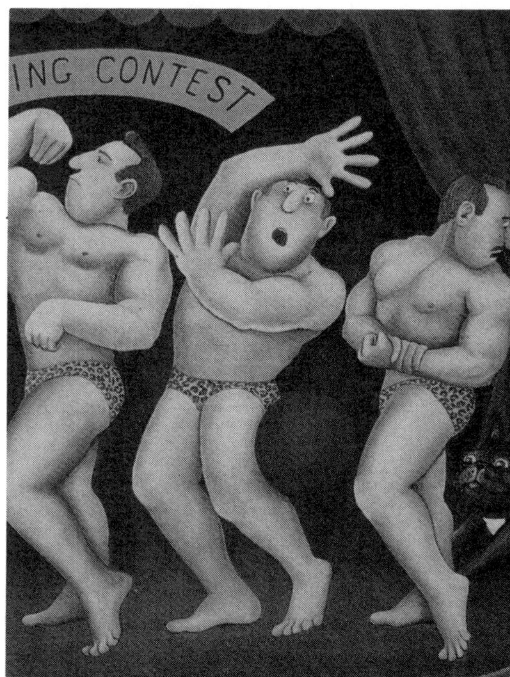

BERYL COOK – Body Building – oil on board – 19 x 14½in.
(Christie's) **$5,181** **£3,300**

COLIN CAMPBELL COOPER – New England Doorways – oil on canvas – 12¾ x 20in.
(Christie's) **$3,520** **£2,448**

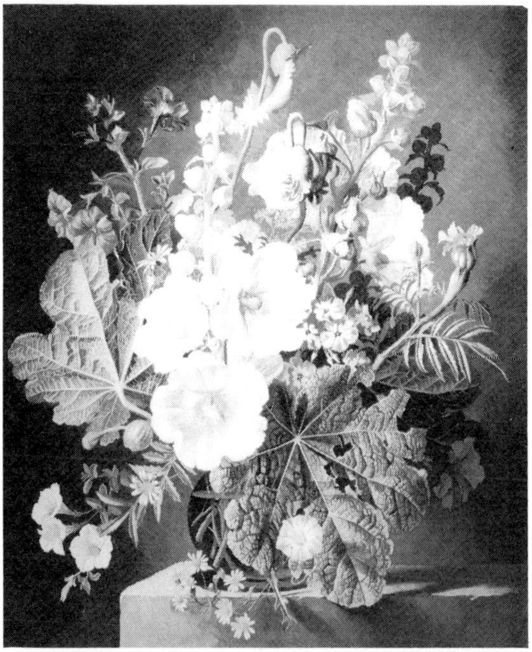

GERALD COOPER – Flowerpiece – signed – oil on board – 61 x 51cm.
(Phillips) **$7,810** **£5,500**

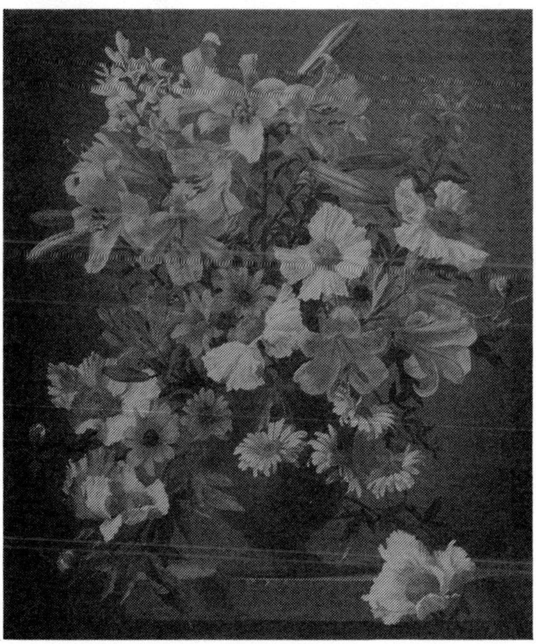

GERALD COOPER – Lilies And Californian Tree Poppies In A Vase On A Stone Ledge – signed – oil on canvas – 76 x 64cm.
(Phillips) **$4,800** **£3,000**

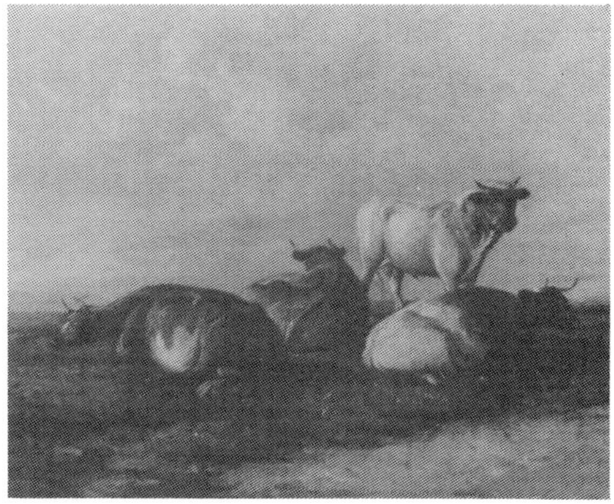

T. SIDNEY COOPER – In The Meadows, Cattle Reposing – signed and dated 1877 – oil on board – 9½ x 12½in.
(Worsfolds) **$1,500** **£1,000**

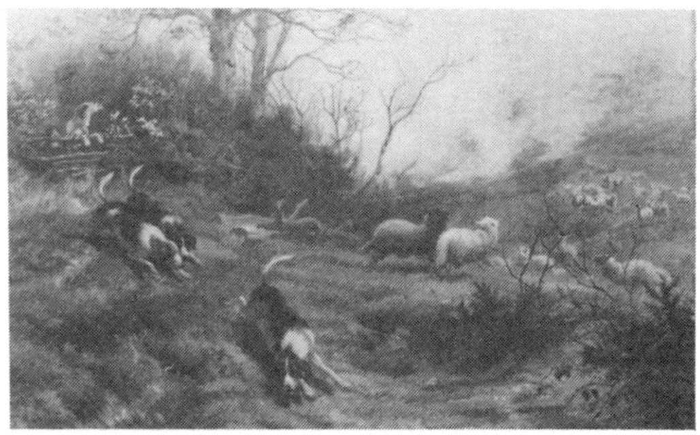

THOMAS GEORGE COOPER – On The Scent – signed and dated 1880 – 28 x 45in.
(Biddle & Webb) **$2,675** **£1,760**

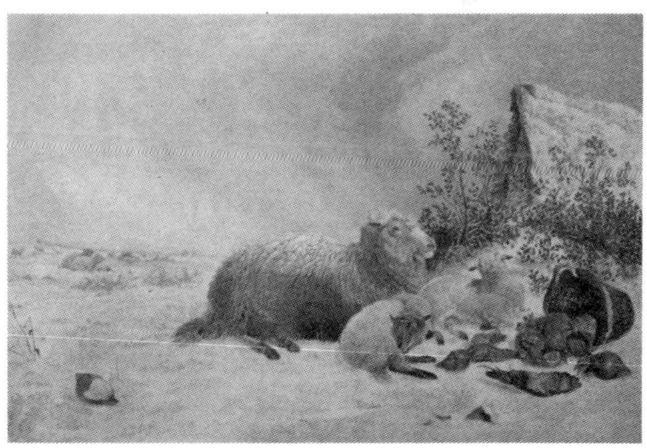

THOMAS SIDNEY COOPER – Sheep With Swedes In Snowy Landscape – signed – watercolour – 19 x 29in.
(Hobbs & Chambers) **$2,618** **£1,700**

THOMAS CRESWICK and THOMAS SIDNEY COOPER – A Wooded River Landscape With A Mother And Child By A Bridge And Cattle Watering – signed and dated 1860 – 26½ x 38in.
(Christie's) **$20,240** **£12,650**

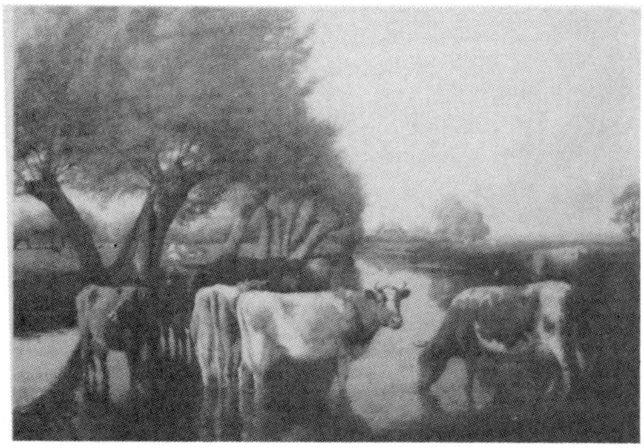

WILLIAM SIDNEY COOPER – An Extensive Wooded River Landscape With Cattle Watering In The Foreground – signed and dated 1916 – oil on canvas – 29 x 39in.
(Christie's) **$2,592** **£1,800**

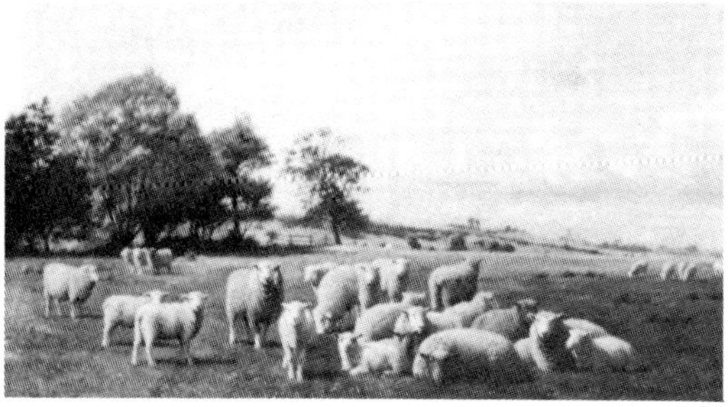

WILLIAM SIDNEY COOPER – Sheep Resting In An Open Pasture, A View Of Canterbury Beyond – signed and dated 1901 – oil on canvas – 20 x 36¼in.
(Phillips) **$1,530** **£1,000**

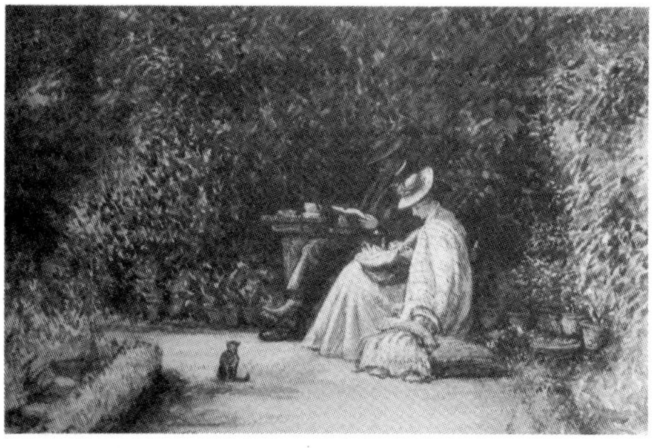

CHARLES WEST COPE – Mr. and Mrs. Auchmutz, The Son-In-Law And Daughter Of The Artist, And Their Son Kenneth, In The Garden Of Lucton School House – signed with initials – pencil and watercolour heightened with white – 6½ x 9½in.; and a sheet of chalk portraits of the Auchmutz children.
(Christie's) **$601** **£418**

ROGER DE LA CORBIERE – Claire De Lune En Bretagne – signed and inscribed on the reverse – oil on canvas – 61 x 92cm.
(Phillips) **$542** **£350**

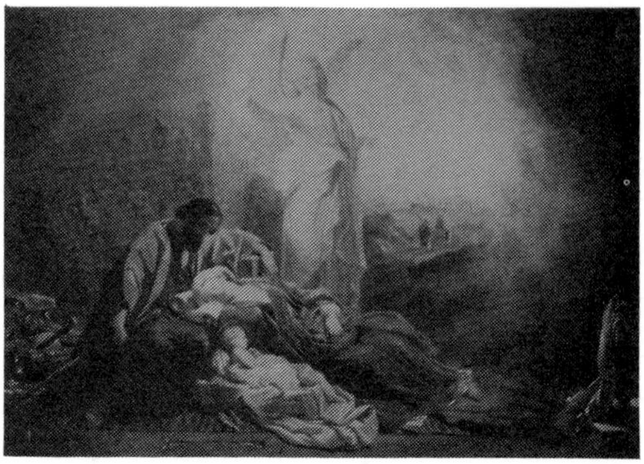

EDWARD HENRY CORBOULD – The Eve Of The Flight Into Egypt – watercolour – 14 x 20in.
(Lawrence Fine Art) **$474** **£286**

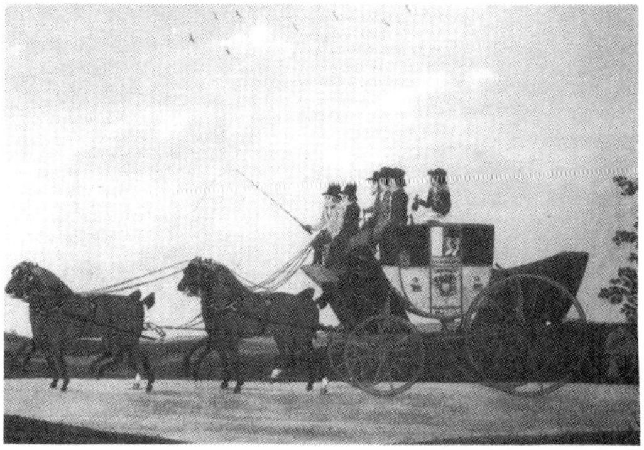

JOHN CORDREY – The London To Birmingham Coach – 20 x 23¾in.
(Christie's) **$4,212** **£2,808**

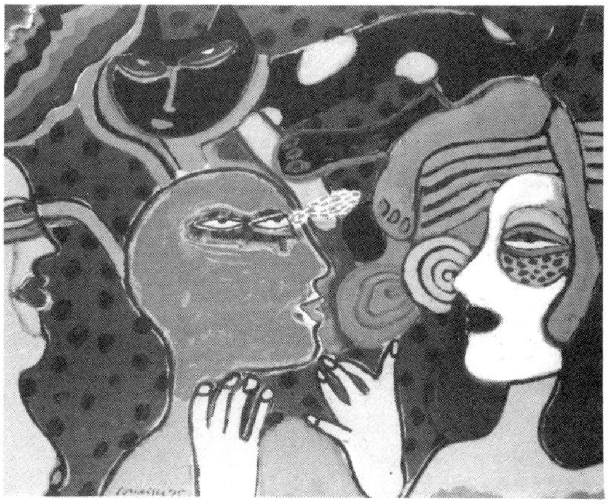

CORNEILLE (Cornelius Guillaume van Beverloo) – L'Heure du Reveil Le Chat – signed and dated '75, also signed, inscribed and dated on the reverse – acrylic on canvas – 23¾ x 28¾in.
(Christie's) **$14,256** **£9,900**

PAUL CORNOYER – Woman With Apple Blossoms – signed and dated '8* – oil on canvas – 10½ x 16½in.
(Christie's) **$6,600** **£4,639**

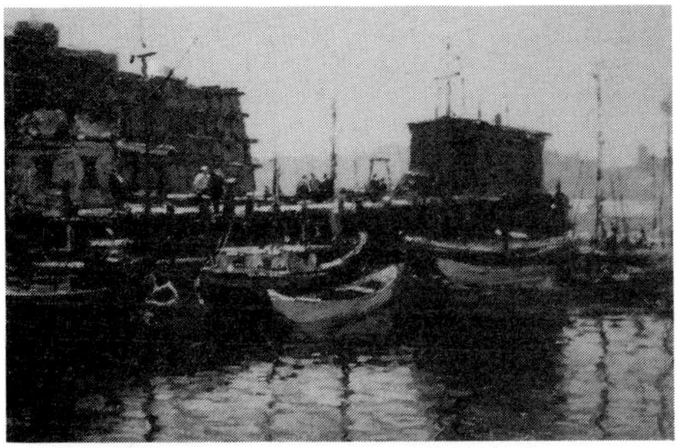

PAUL CORNOYER – Dusk – signed – oil on board – 12 x 15¾in.
(Christie's) **$5,500** **£3,427**

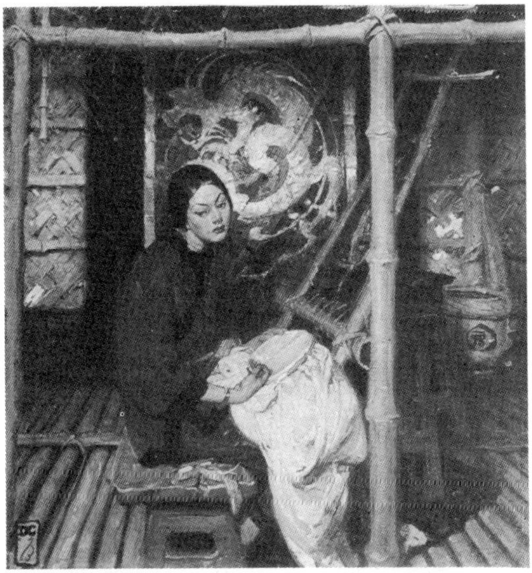

DEAN CORNWELL – Japanese Weaver – signed and dated '23 – oil on canvas – 32 x 30in.
(Christie's) **$6,600** **£4,639**

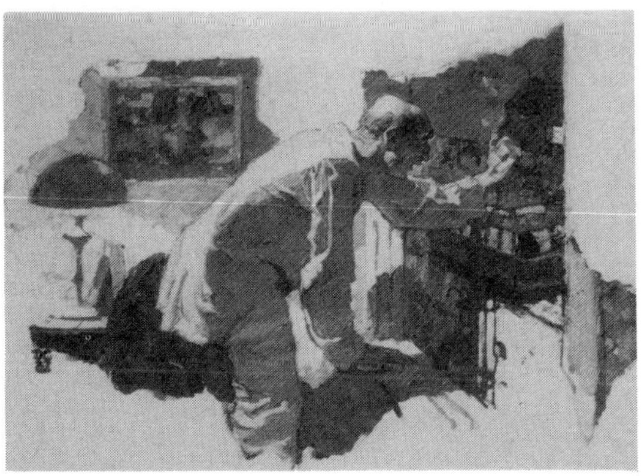

DEAN CORNWELL – A Noisy Streetcar – signed with initials and dated '27 – oil on canvas – 25¼ x 30¼in.
(Christie's) **$1,650** **£1,028**

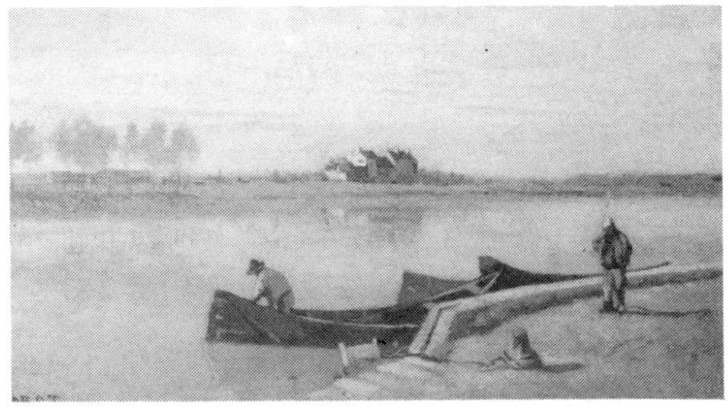

JEAN BAPTISTE CAMILLE COROT – Une Riviere avec une Barque sur le Bord et un Marinier longeant la Berge – signed – oil on panel – 10¾ x 15¾in.
(Christie's) **$134,640** **£93,500**

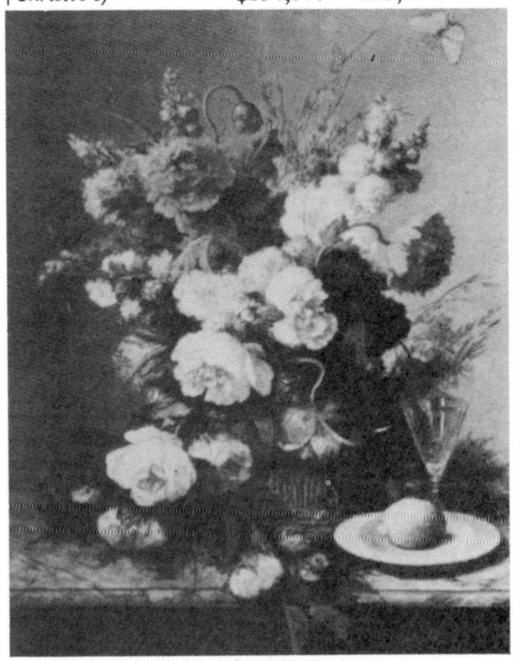

JEAN ALEXANDER RENY COUDER – A Still Life Of Poppies, Roses And Hollyhocks In A Basket On A Marble Topped Table – signed – on panel – 21.5 x 16cm.
(Phillips) **$3,624** **£2,400**

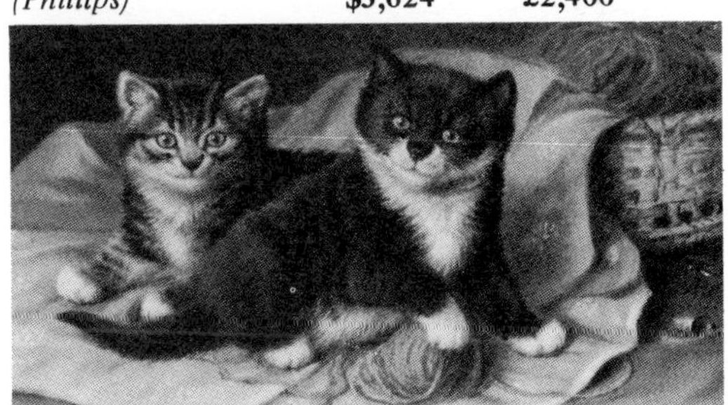

HORATIO H. COULDERY – Playmates – signed with a monogram – canvas laid down on board – 9½ x 12½in.
(Christie's) **$1,944** **£1,296**

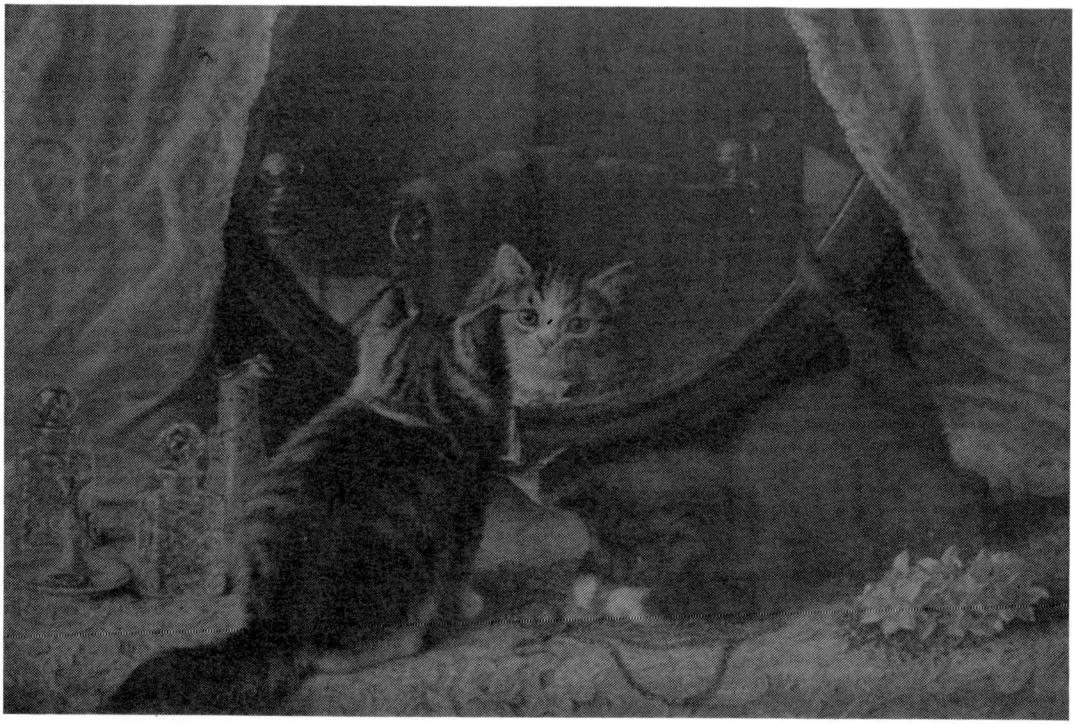

HORATIO HENRY COULDERY – 'Beauties Toilet' – signed with monogram – on canvas – 16½ x 22½in. *(Phillips)* **$16,100 £10,000**

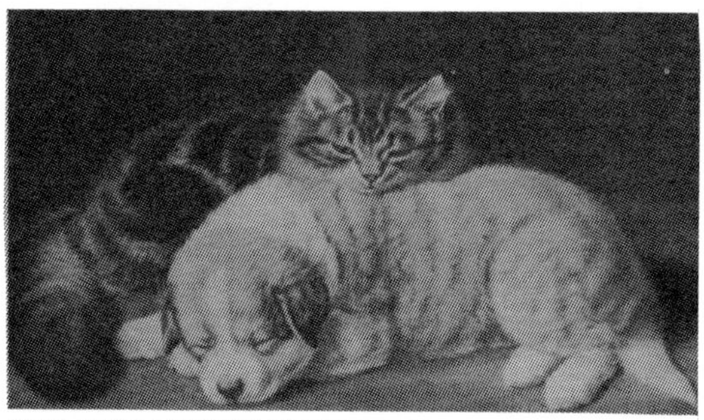

HORATIO HENRY COULDERY – 'Chums' – signed – on canvas – 13 x 19in. *(Phillips)* **$4,508 £2,800**

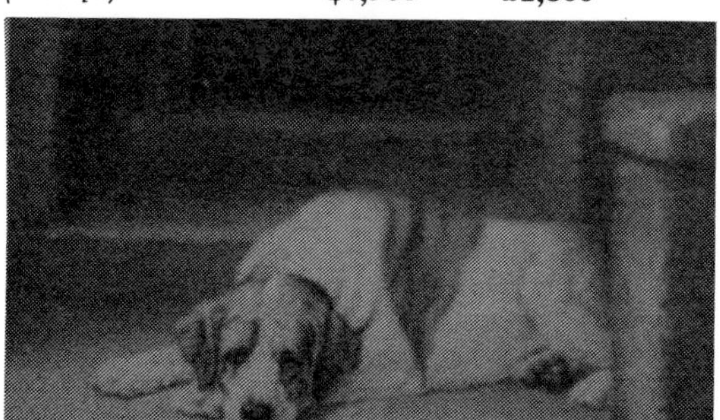

HORATIO HENRY COULDERY – 'The Midday Rest' – signed – on canvas – 13 x 19in. *(Phillips)* **$3,864 £2,400**

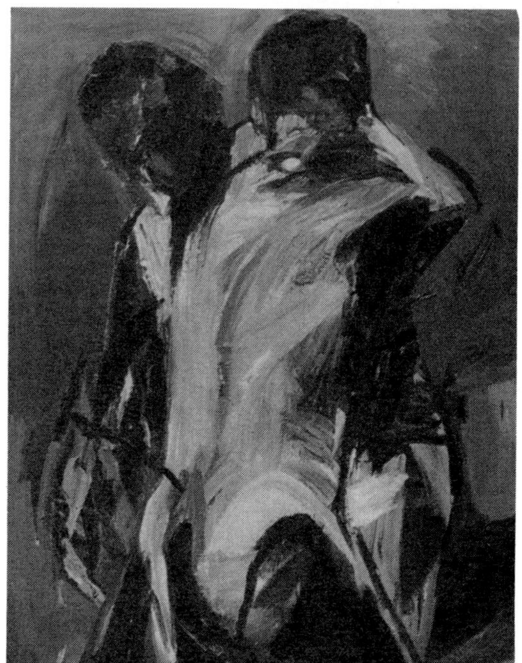

NICOLA COUNSELL – Wrestlers – signed and inscribed on the reverse – oil on canvas – 72 x 48in. *(Christie's)* **$2,417 £1,540**

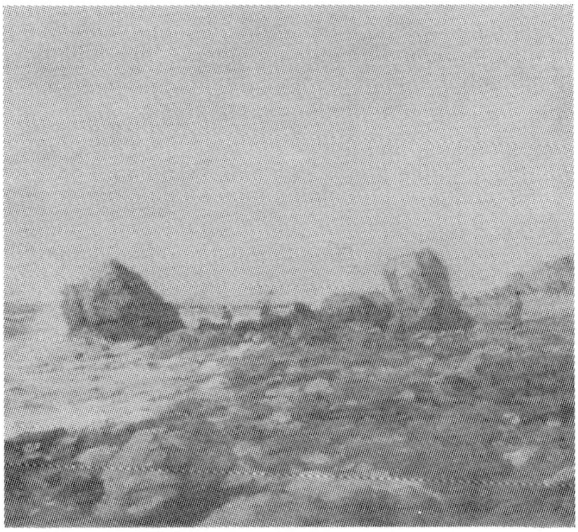

MAURICE COURANT – Les Ramasseurs des Moules – signed and dated 1896 – oil on canvas – 17 x 24in.
(Christie's) **$1,936** **£1,210**

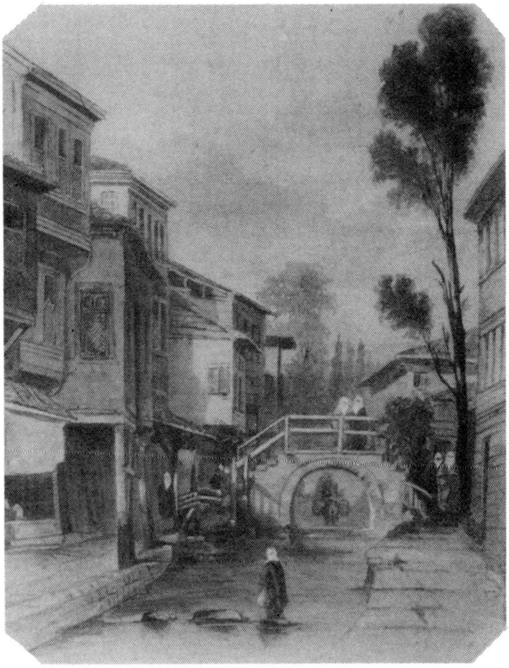

ALFRED DE COURVILLE – Kassim Pacha – signed with monogram and inscribed – pencil, watercolour and bodycolour – 13 x 10in.
(Christie's) **$3,344** **£2,090**

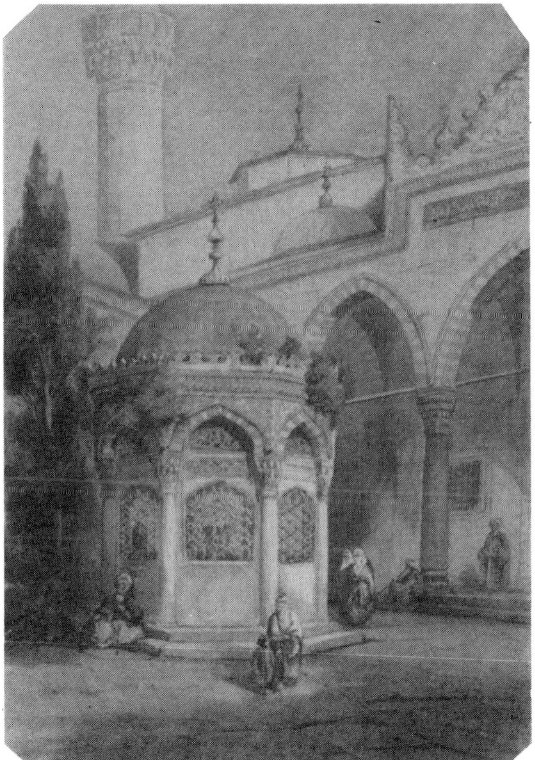

ALFRED DE COURVILLE – Fontaine de Yeni-Djenni – inscribed – pencil, watercolour and bodycolour – 14¼ x 9¾in.
(Christie's) **$4,224** **£2,640**

ALFRED DE COURVILLE – Eaux douces d'Asie – inscribed – pencil, watercolour and bodycolour – 9 x 15¼in.
(Christie's) **$4,224** **£2,640**

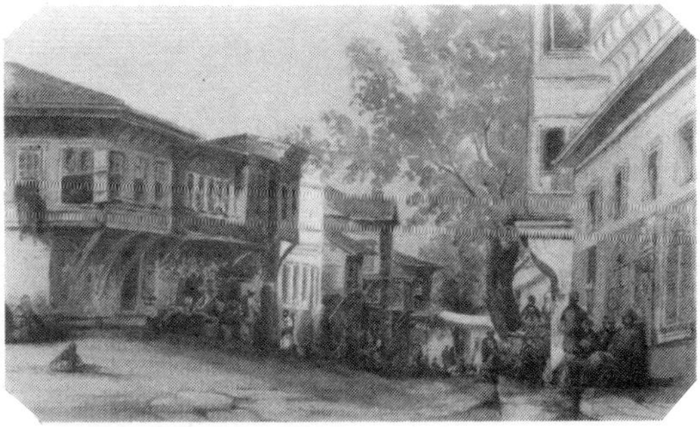

ALFRED DE COURVILLE – Bouadji-Keni – inscribed – pencil, watercolour and bodycolour – 9½ x 14¾in.
(Christie's) **$4,576** **£2,860**

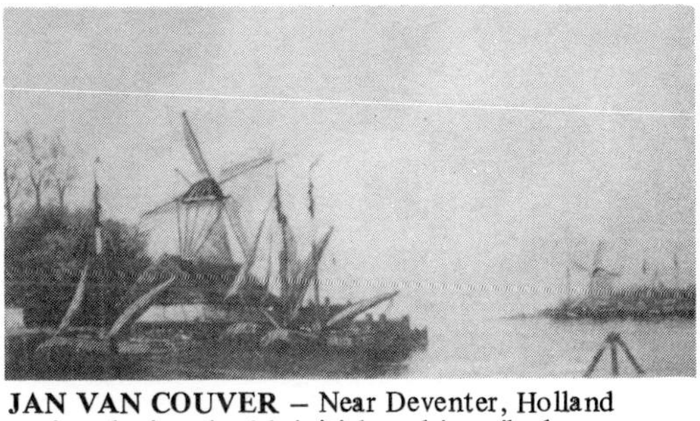

JAN VAN COUVER – Near Deventer, Holland – signed, signed with initials and inscribed on the reverse – oil on canvas – 20 x 30in.
(Christie's) **$2,217** **£1,540**

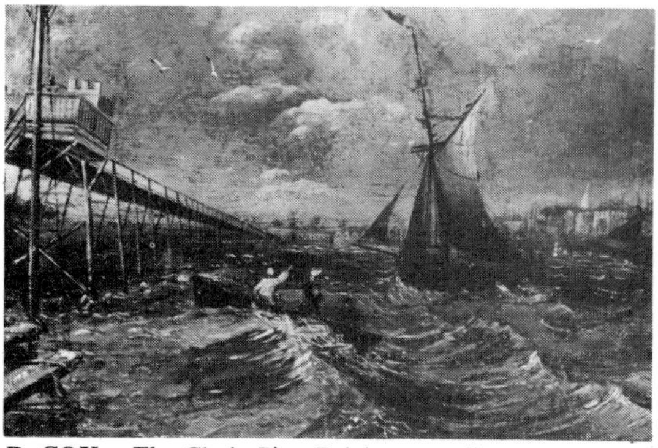

D. COX – The Chain Pier, Brighton – oil on panel.
(Lots Road Chelsea Auction Galleries) **$336** **£220**

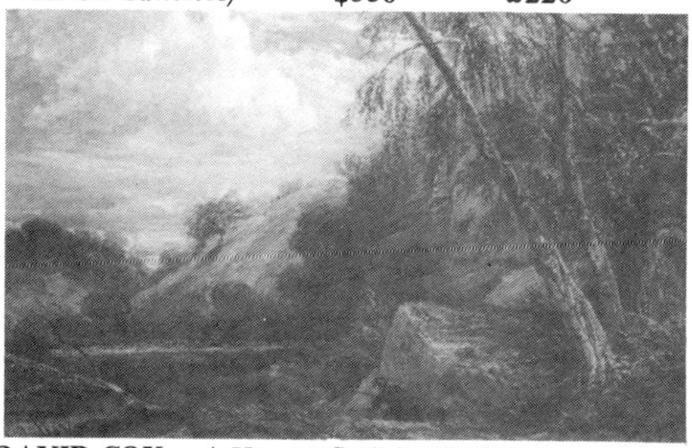

DAVID COX – A Hunter Stalking Red Deer – signed – watercolour – 23 x 33in.
(Christie's) **$9,185** **£5,500**

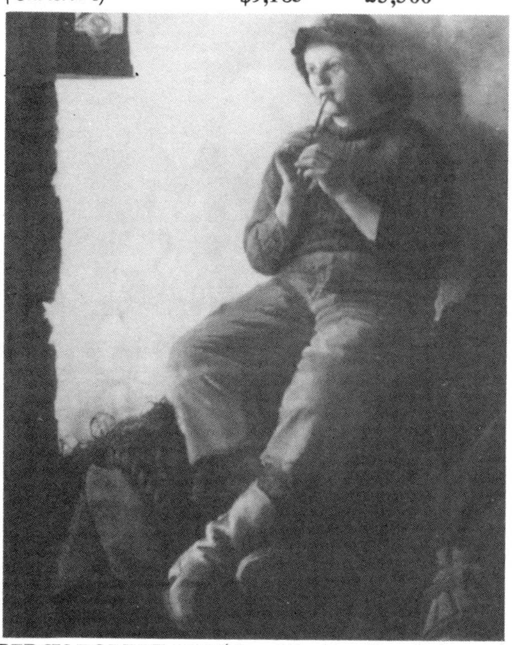

PERCY ROBERT CRAFT – 'The New Song' – signed and dated 1887 – oil on canvas – 77 x 51cm.
(W. H. Lane & Son) **$19,920** **£12,000**

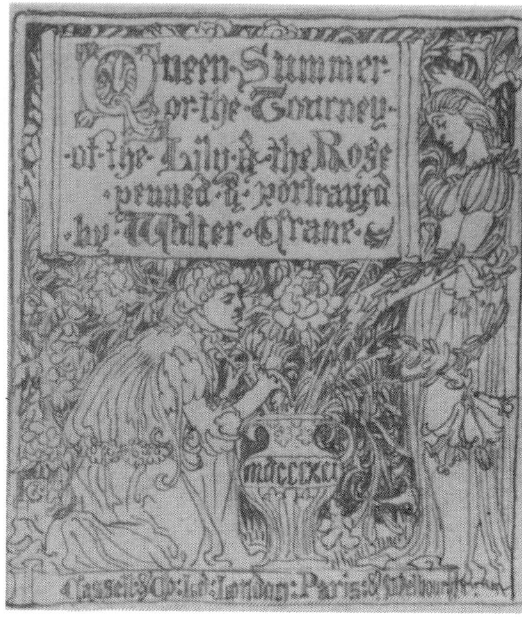

WALTER CRANE – Designs For Queen Summer of The Tourney Of The Lily And The Rose (1891): The front cover, the title page, and pages 2-11 – the majority signed with monogram – pencil – the title page with watercolour heightened with white on four sheets – 7¼ x 11in.
(Christie's) **$3,102** **£2,200 Four**

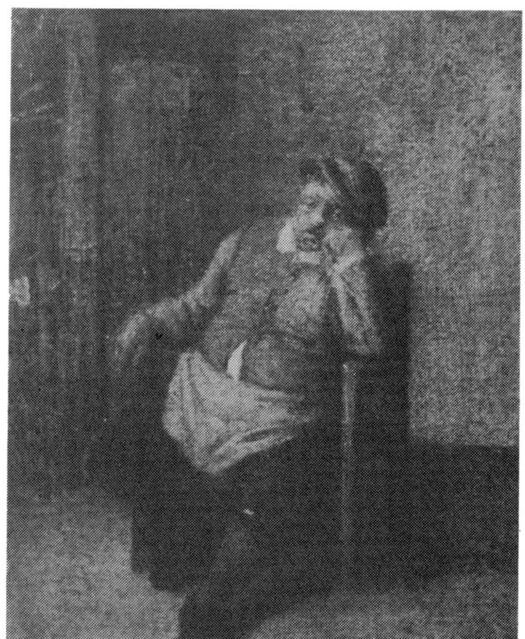

JOOS VAN CRASEBEECK, Circle of – **A Peasant** In An Interior – on paper laid on panel – 5 x 4in.
(Lawrence Fine Art) **$1,369** **£825**

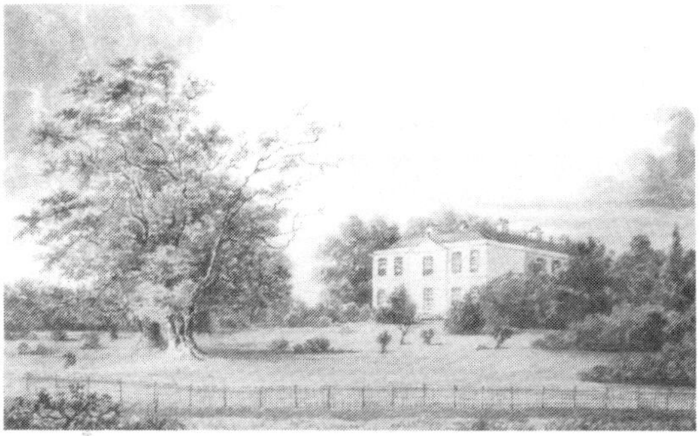

LADY LOUISA CRAVEN – An Album Including Views – one signed with initials and variously inscribed, the majority watercolour, 45 drawings loose or laid down in the album – 13½ x 10¼in.
(Christie's) **$2,019** **£1,320**

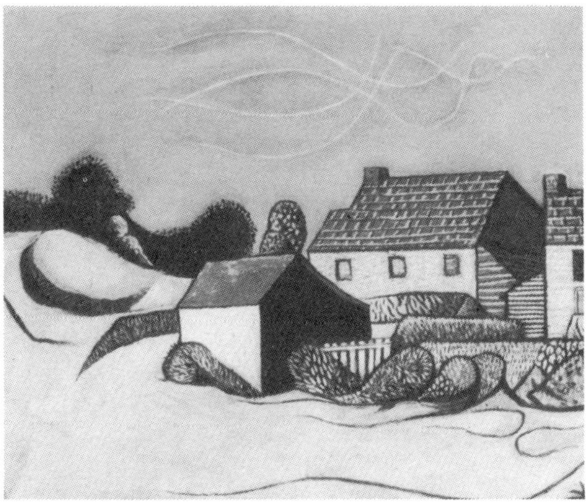

JOHN CRAXTON – The Mill House – signed and dated '44 – tempera and oil on paper – 17¾ x 21¼in.
(Christie's) **$2,674** **£1,870**

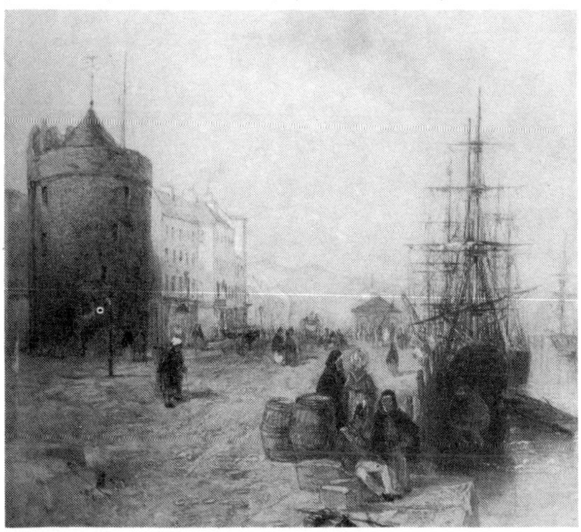

THOMAS CRESWICK – Figures On The Quay, Waterford; and Figures Resting Above Cove, Near Cork – oil on panel – 7 x 7in.
(Phillips) **$5,508** **£3,600 Pair**

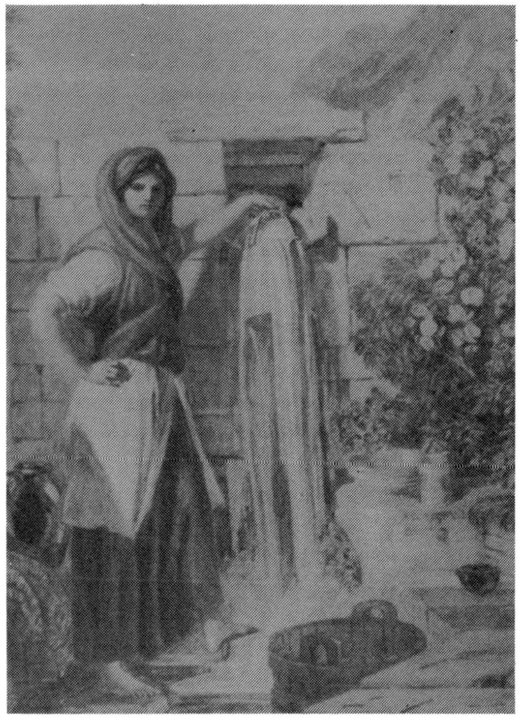

JOSHUA CRISTALL – A Welsh Girl At A Fountain – signed and dated 1857 – watercolour and bodycolour with scratching out – 43 x 33cm.
(Phillips) **$652** **£400**

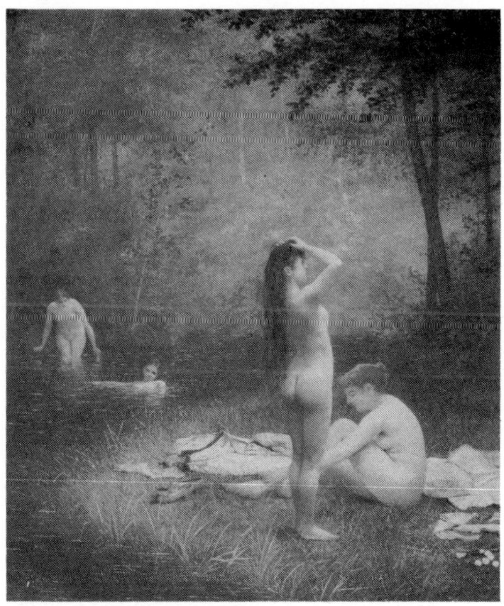

GEORGES CROEGAERT – Les Baigneuses signed – oil on panel – 26 x 20cm.
(Phillips) **$7,515** **£4,500**

GEORGES CROEGAERT – A Cardinal Seated At A Table In An Interior Cutting A Melon – signed and inscribed – oil on panel – 8½ x 6in.
(Christie's) **$2,871** **£1,980**

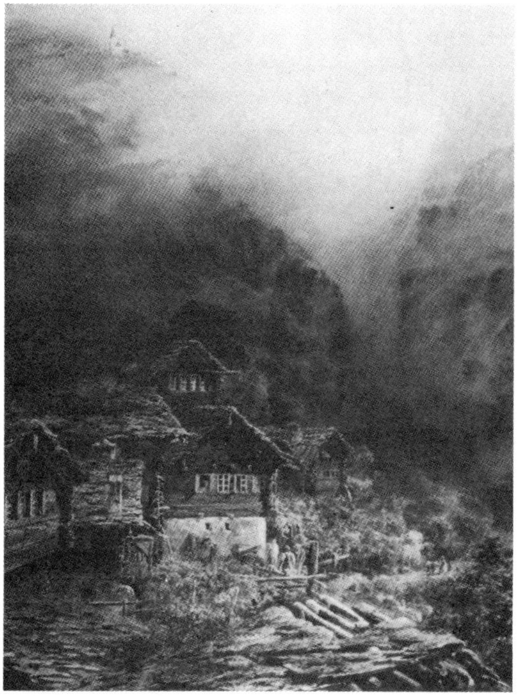

ARTHUR CROFT – Views Of Alpine Villages – signed and dated 1884 – pencil and watercolour, heightened with white – 27¾ x 21in.
(Christie's) **$1,163** **£825 Pair**

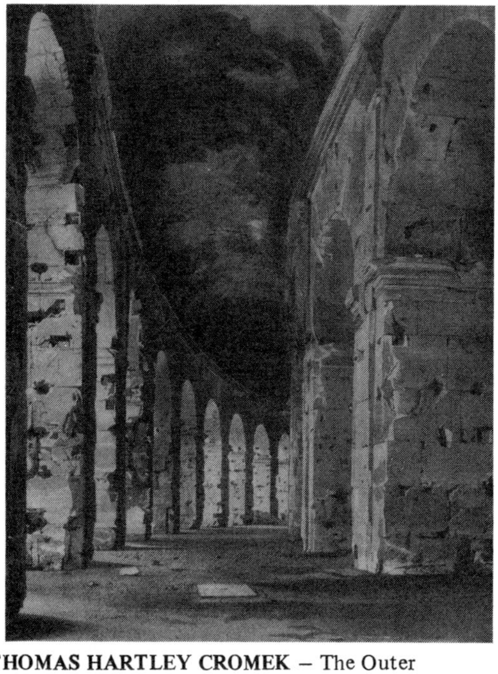

THOMAS HARTLEY CROMEK – The Outer Colonnade Of The Colosseum, Rome – signed, inscribed and dated 1848 – pencil and watercolour – 14¾ x 11½in.
(Christie's) **$3,674** **£2,200**

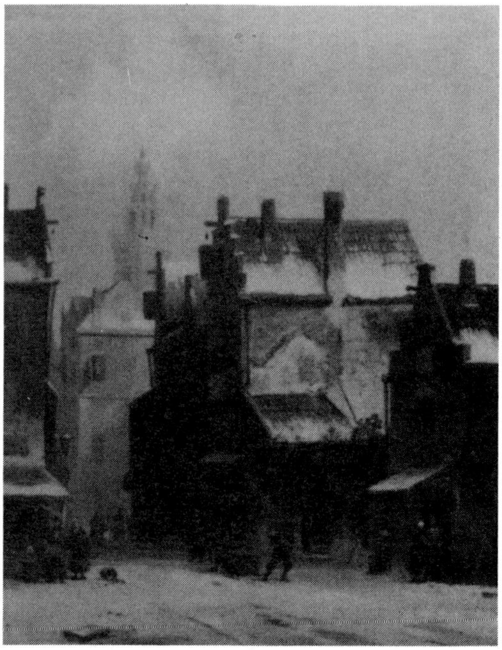

A. DE CROOTE – A Frozen Dutch Town Street With Figures – signed – oil on panel – 16 x 13in.
(Christie's) **$1,216** **£770**

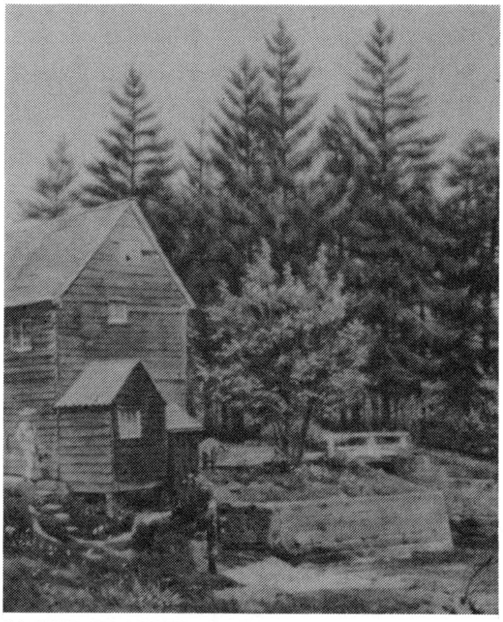

JASPER FRANCIS CROPSEY – Mill House By A Stream With Figures – signed and dated 1880 – watercolour on paper laid down on watercolour paper – 19¼ x 15¾in.
(Robt. W. Skinner Inc.) **$1,200** **£736**

JASPER FRANCIS CROPSEY – Winter In Switzerland – signed and dated 1860 – oil on canvas – 14 x 24¼in.
(Christie's) **$26,400** **£18,559**

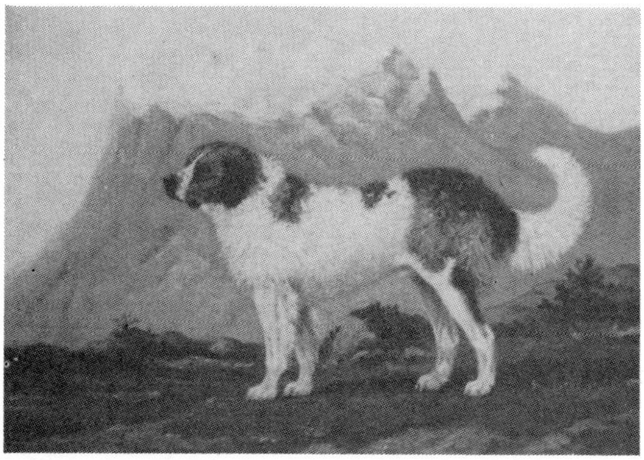

HENRY H. CROSS – Gladstone At 17 Months Old – signed, dated 1890 and inscribed, also signed, dated and inscribed on the reverse – oil on panel – 15¾ x 22in.
(Christie's) **$1,100** **£765**

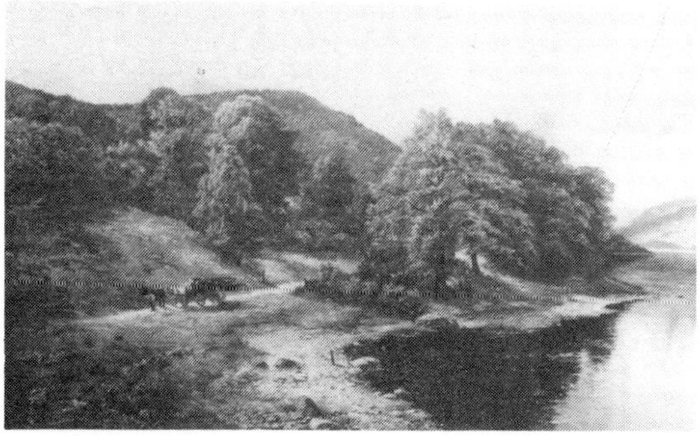

JAMES HENRY CROSSLAND – 'Windermere', Lake Scene With Horse Drawn Timber Wagon In The Left Foreground, Distant Yachts – signed – oil – 28 x 58in.
(Capes, Dunn & Co.) **$2,282** **£1,400**

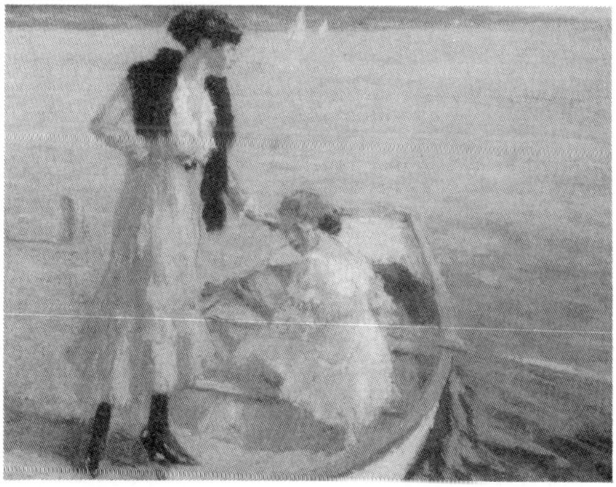

EDWARD CUCUEL – The White Boat – signed – oil on canvas – 17¼ x 22¾in.
(Christie's) **$8,250** **£5,799**

DOMINGO MUNOZ Y CUESTA – Happy Encounter – signed and inscribed – oil on canvas – 47 x 39cm.
(Phillips) **$10,855** **£6,500**

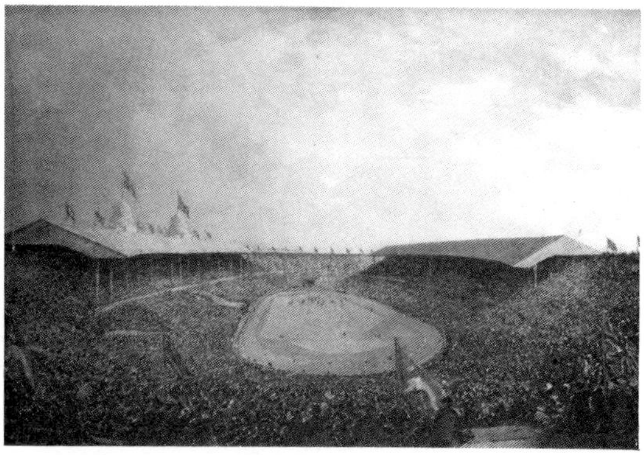

CHARLES CUNDALL – The 1936 F.A. Cup Final, Arsenal Versus Sheffield United At Wembley – signed and dated 1936 – oil on canvas – 25 x 36in.
(Christie's) **$20,449** **£14,300**

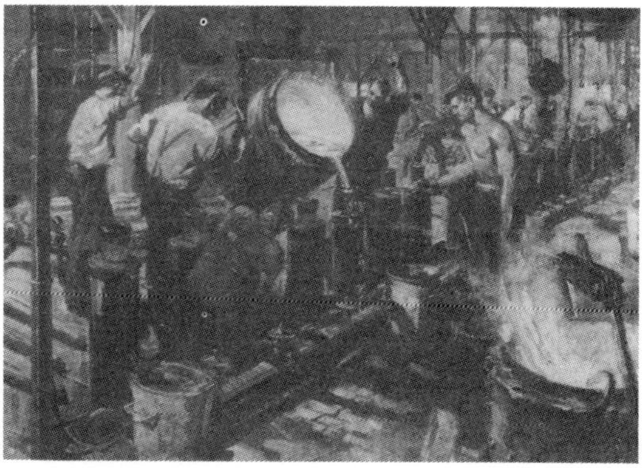

TERENCE CUNEO – The Casting Factory – signed and dated 1944 – oil on canvas – 24 x 30in.
(Christie's) **$3,932** **£2,750**

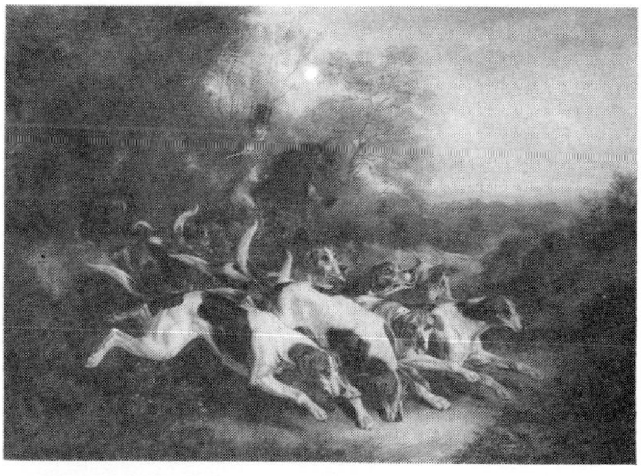

DAVID CUNLIFFE – The Berkeley Hunt, Drawing Cover – signed – oil on canvas – 28 x 36¼in.
(Christie's) **$14,300** **£9,333**

CHARLES COURTNEY CURRAN – Girl In A Bonnet – signed and dated '84 – oil on canvas – 7½ x 6½in.
(Christie's) **$2,200** **£1,546**

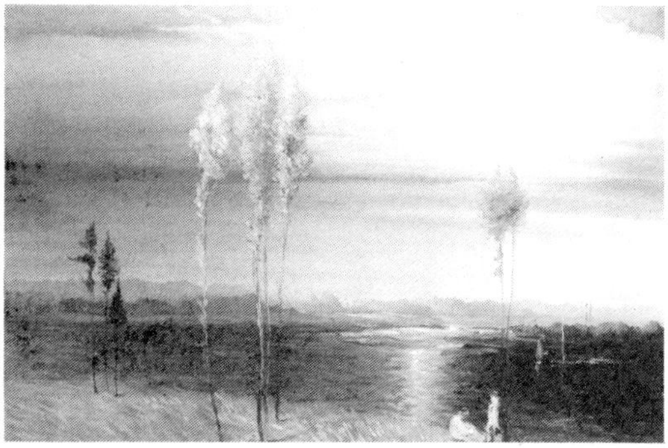

LEON DABO – Summer Idyll – signed and dated '16 – oil on canvas – 30 x 34¼in.
(Christie's) **$9,900** **£6,887**

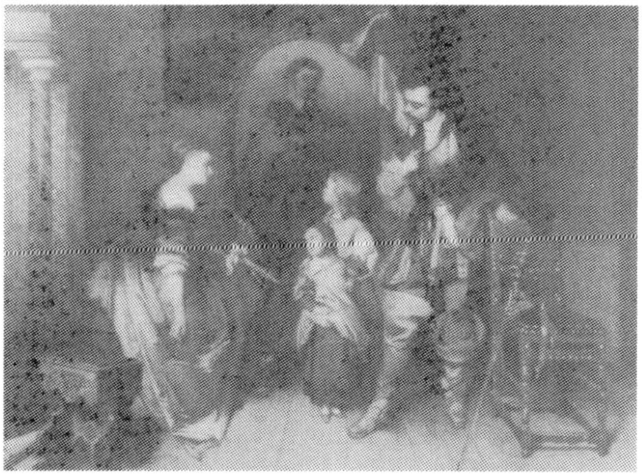

CHARLES VAN DEN DAELE – In The Studio – signed and dated 1871 – on panel – 27¾ x 37in.
(Christie's) **$4,347** **£2,860**

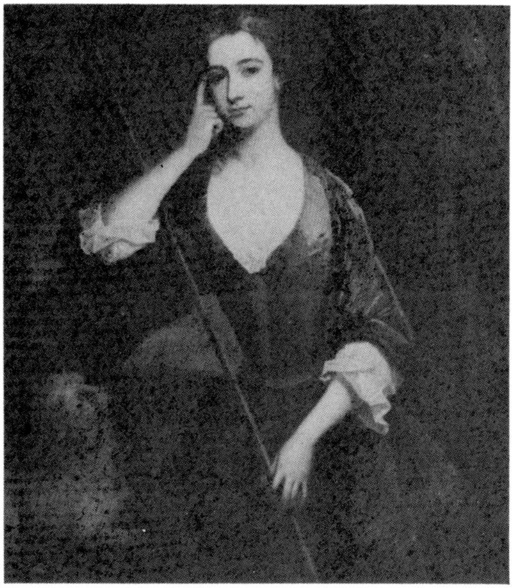

MICHAEL DAHL, Circle of – Portrait Of A Lady As Saint Agnes – 49¾ x 40¼in.
(Christie's) **$1,296** **£864**

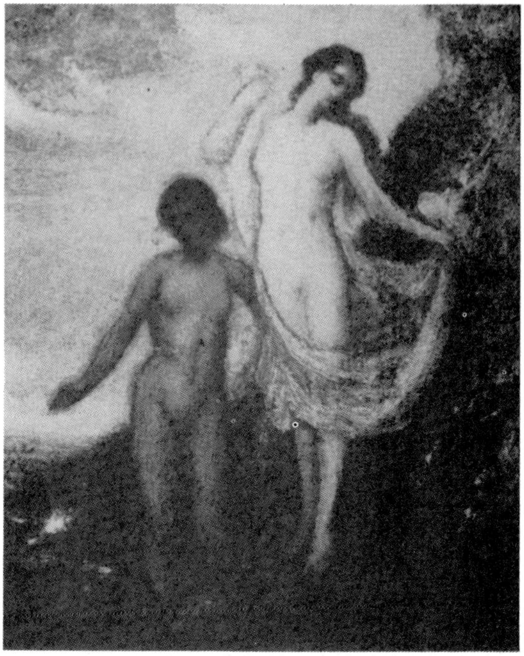

ELLIOTT DAINGERFIELD – Bathers On The Cliff – signed – oil on board – 16 x 12in.
(Christie's) **$2,750** **£1,913**

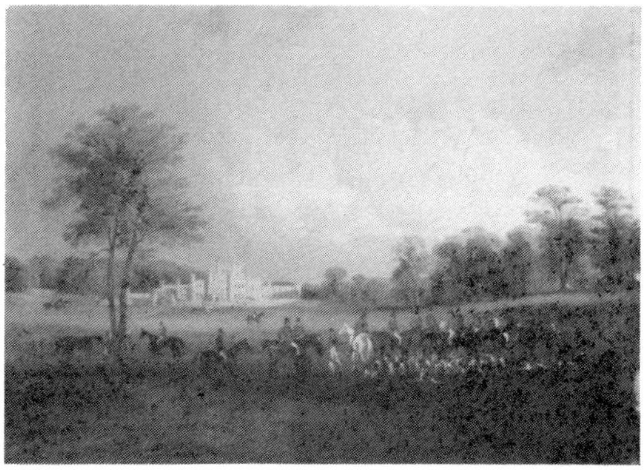

DALBY of York – The Meet At Lowther Hall – oil – 10 x 12in.
(Woolley & Wallis) **$6,486** **£4,600**

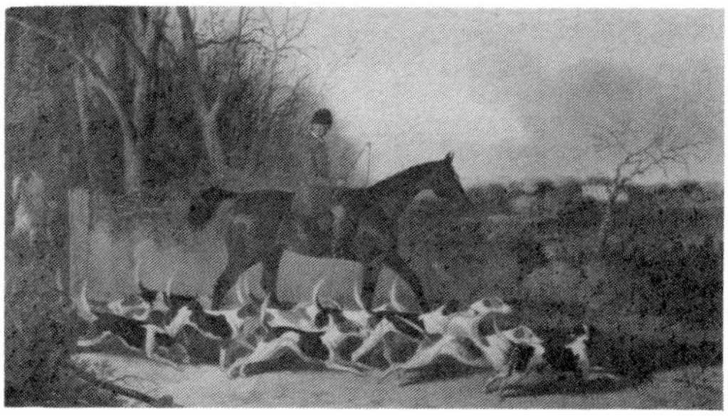

JOHN DALBY of York – Crocteth Harriers – inscribed on the reverse – oil on panel – 9 x 15in.
(Woolley & Wallis) **$18,330** **£13,000**

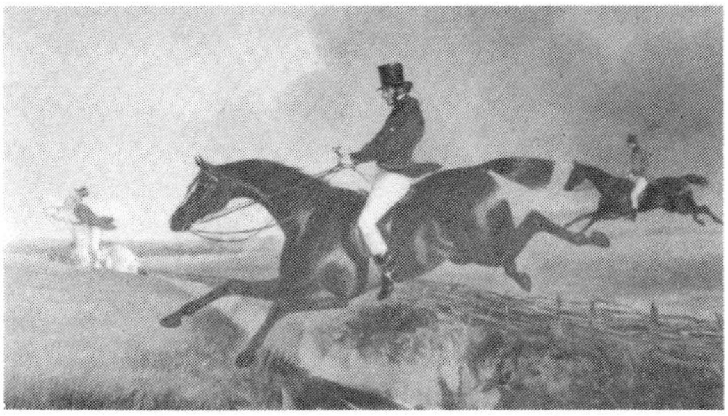

JOHN DALBY of York – Huntsmen In A Landscape – oil on board – 8.5 x 12in.
(Woolley & Wallis) **$12,126** **£8,600**

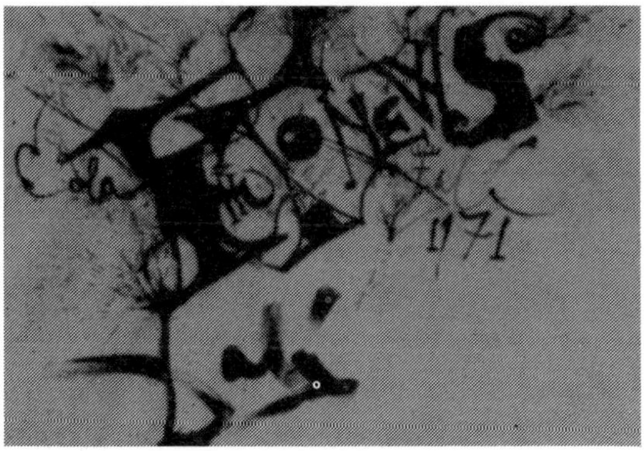

SALVADOR DALI – Foto News – signed and dated 1971 – brush and ink – 24 x 35 cm.
(Phillips) **$1,007** **£650**

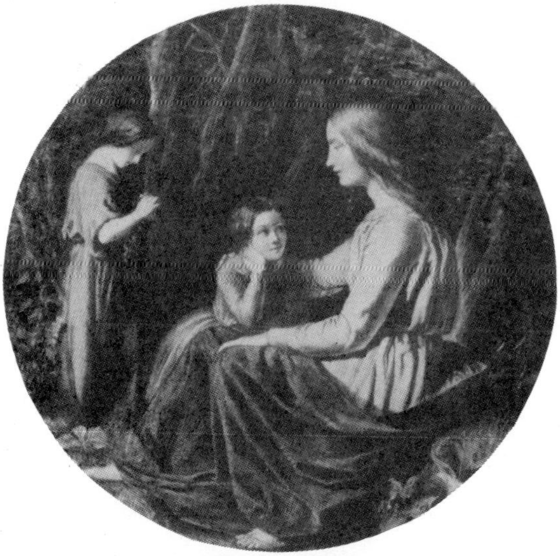

WILLIAM FREDERICK D'ALMAINE – The Evening Retreat – signed and dated 1849 – 23½in. diam.
(Christie's) **$1,163** **£825**

WILLIAM DANIELL – Mausoleum At Lucknow – pencil and watercolour with touches of white heightening – 3¾ x 5¾in.
(Christie's) **$1,944** **£1,296**

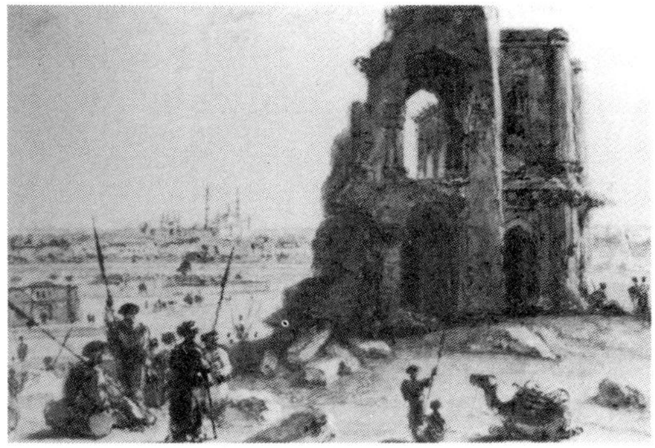

WILLIAM DANIELL – Shah Jehanabad, Near Delhi – pencil and watercolour with touches of white heightening – 3¾ x 5¾in.
(Christie's) **$2,916** **£1,944**

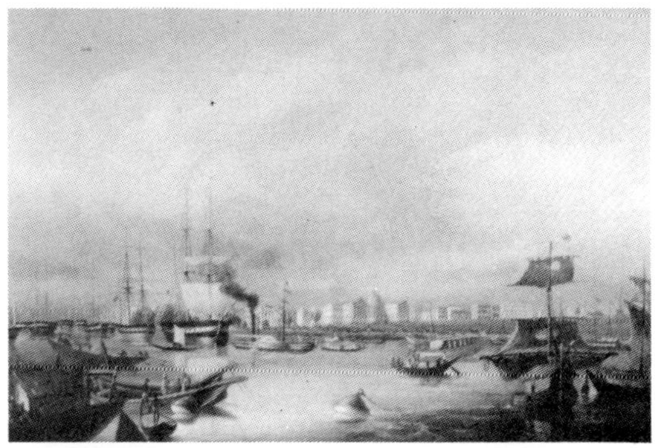

DANIELLS – 'Calcutta' – oil – 14½ x 19½in.
(Graves Son & Pilcher) **$4,896** **£3,400**

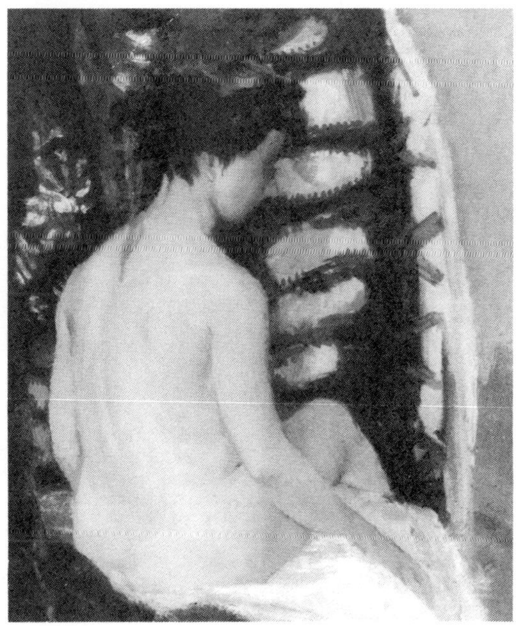

SIR ROBERT DARWIN – The Aztec Rug – signed and dated '47 – oil on canvas – 30 x 25in.
(Christie's) **$1,337** **£935**

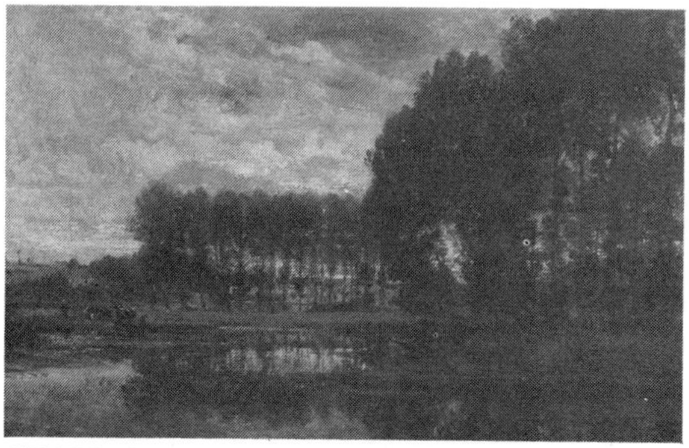

CHARLES FRANCOIS DAUBIGNY – A Wooded River Landscape – signed – 13¾ x 28¾in.
(Christie's) **$14,960** **£9,550**

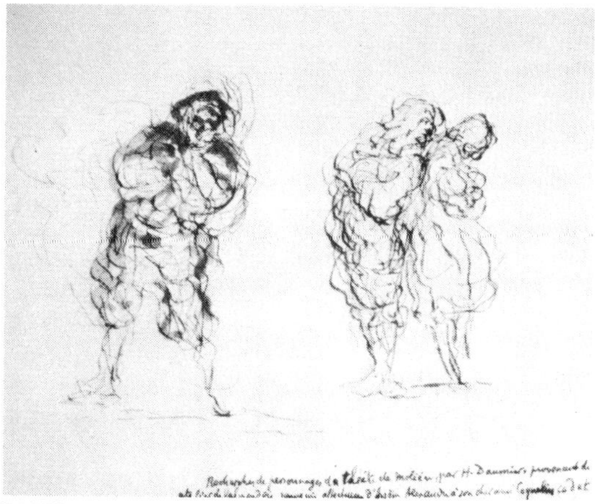

HONORE DAUMIER – Scene d'une Comedie de Moliere – inscribed – pen, ink, brush and grey wash – 4¾ x 5¾in.
(Christie's) **$8,712** **£6,050**

HONORE DAUMIER – Oedipe Et Le Berger – 25¾ x 19¾in.
(Christie's) **$34,848** **£24,200**

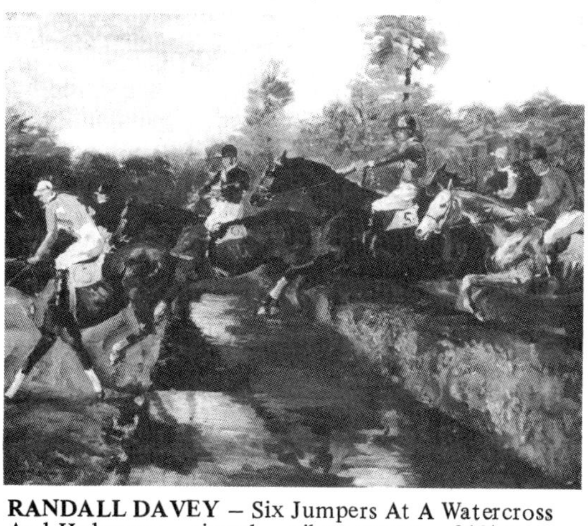

RANDALL DAVEY – Six Jumpers At A Watercross And Hedgerow – signed – oil on canvas – 31¾ x 40in.
(Christie's) **$16,500** **£11,599**

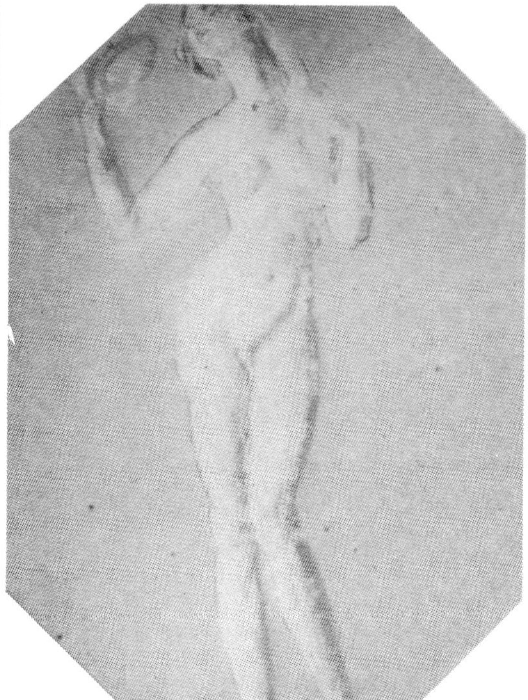

ARTHUR BOWEN DAVIES – Nude With A Mirror – signed – pastel on blue paper laid down on board – 14½ x 11in.
(Christie's) **$770** **£535**

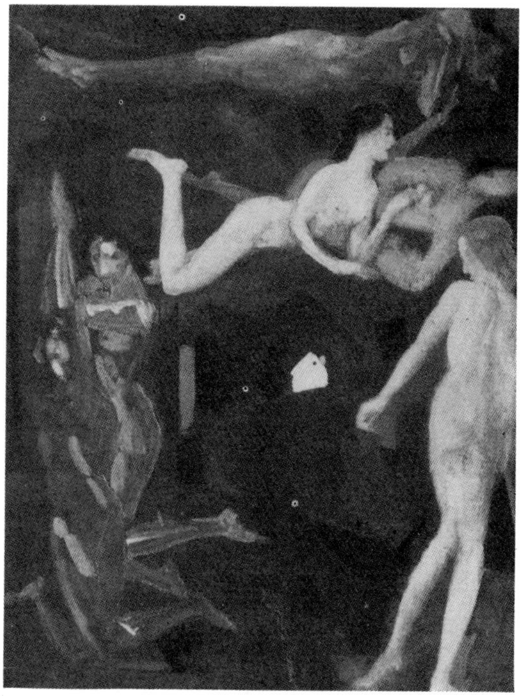

ARTHUR BOWEN DAVIES – Floating Figures In A Landscape – oil on canvas – 31¾ x 23½in.
(Christie's) **$3,300** **£2,319**

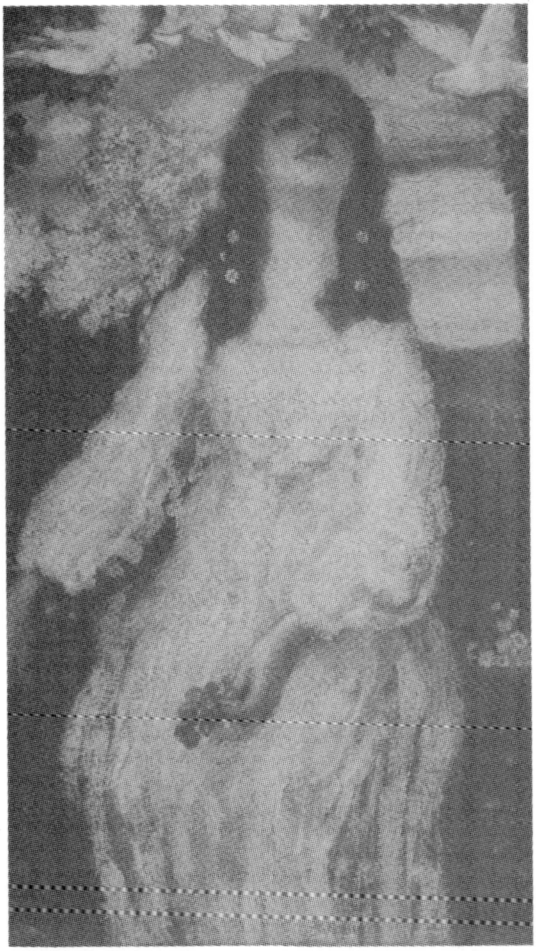

ARTHUR BOWEN DAVIES – Doves – signed with initials – oil on canvas – 13 x 7¾in.
(Christie's) **$4,180** **£2,604**

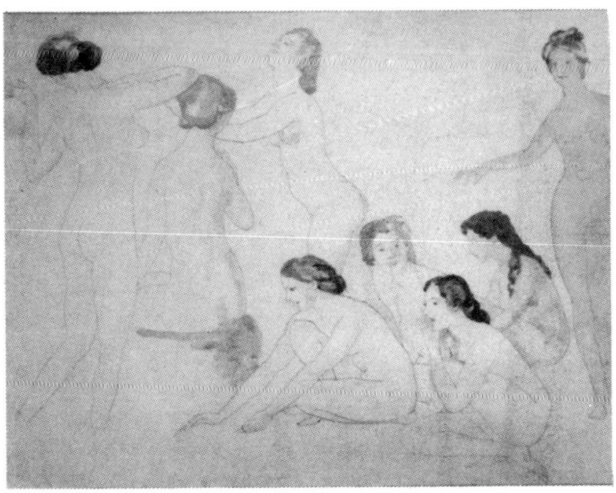

ARTHUR BOWEN DAVIES – Eight Female Nudes – watercolour and pencil on silk laid down on board – 16½ x 21¾in.
(Christie's) **$1,430** **£1,005**

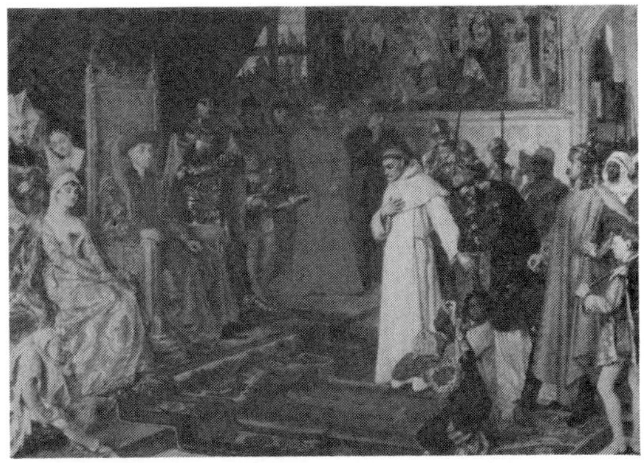

FREDERICK W. DAVIS – The Spoils Of War – 20 x 29in.
(Biddle & Webb) **$1,672** **£1,100**

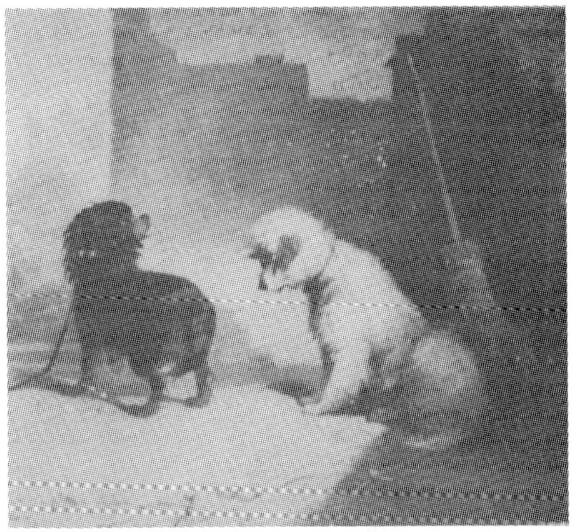

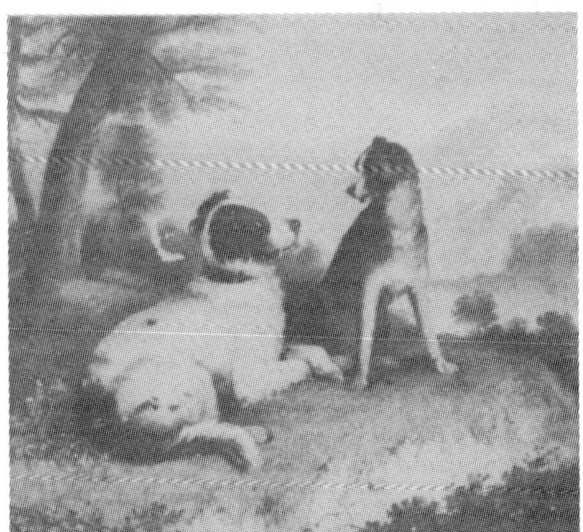

HENRY T. DAVIS – The Lost Dog; and Dogs In A Landscape – signed and inscribed – on canvas – 20 x 24in.
(Phillips) **$2,093** **£1,300 Pair**

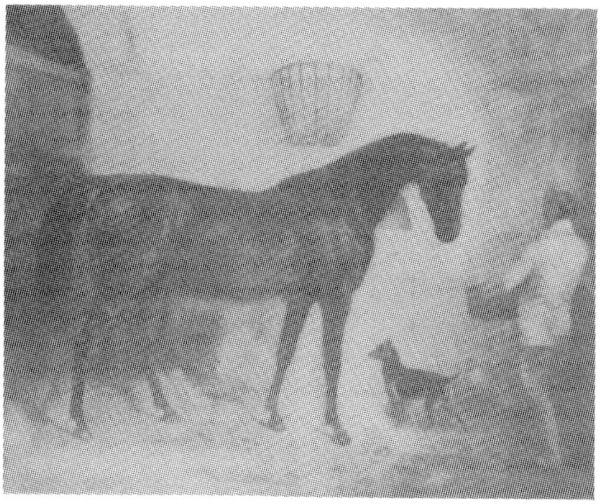

RICHARD BARRET DAVIS, Circle of – A Chestnut Racehorse With A Groom And Dog In A Stable Interior – oil on canvas – 22 x 28in.
(Christie's) **$1,254** **£820**

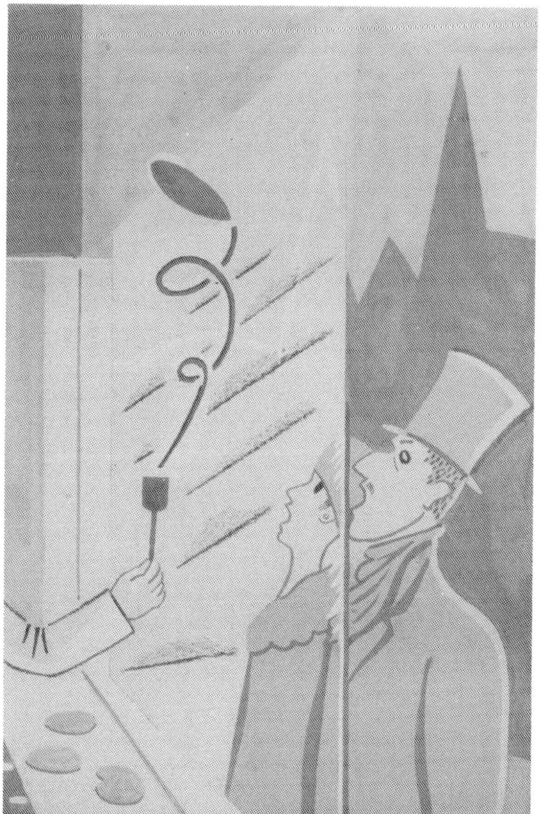

STUART DAVIS – Flap Jack – signed and dated '26 – gouache on board – 14¾ x 10in.
(Christie's) **$11,000** **£7,733**

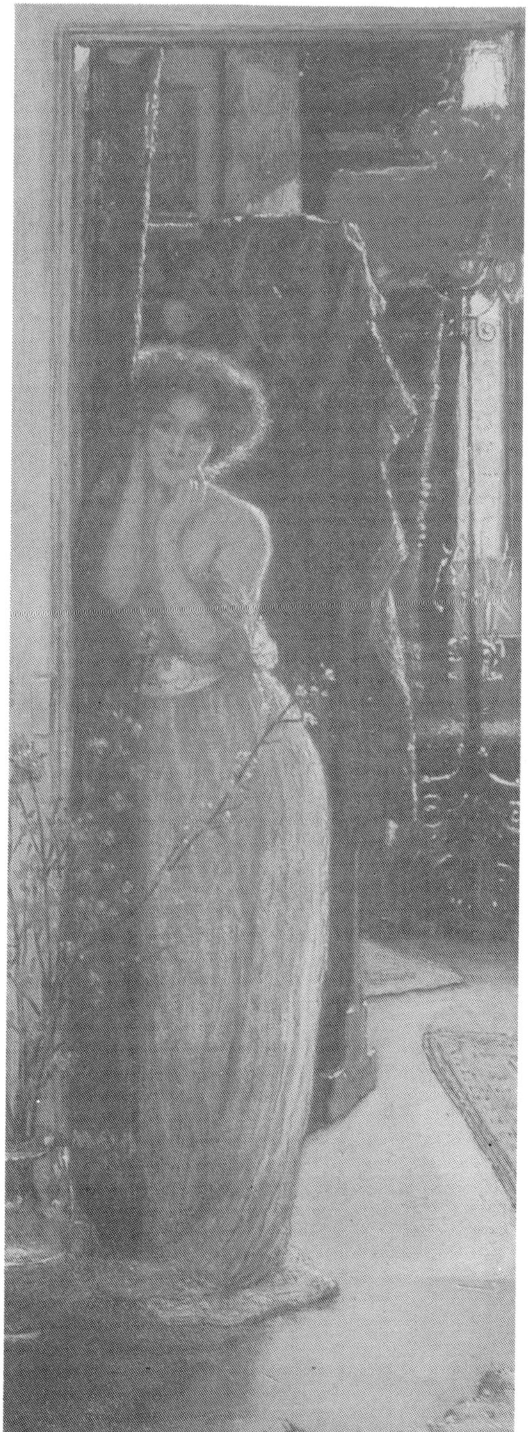

STUART C. DAVIS – 'Day Dream' – signed and dated 1903 – on panel – 13¼ x 5½in.
(Phillips) **$8,050** **£5,000**

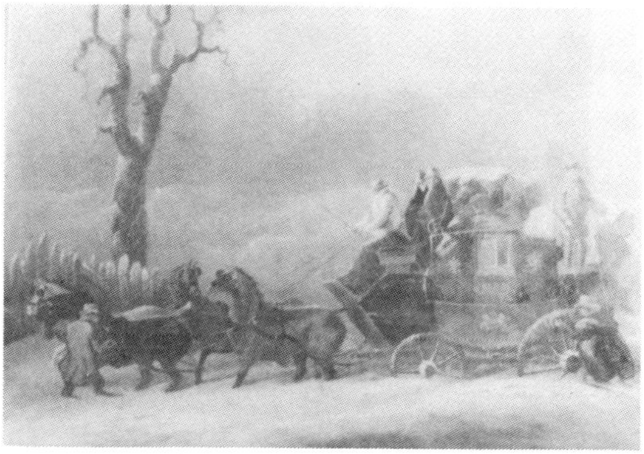

W. DAVIS – A Mail Coach; and The Arrival – oil on canvas – 19 x 26in.
(Christie's) **$2,871** **£1,980 Pair**

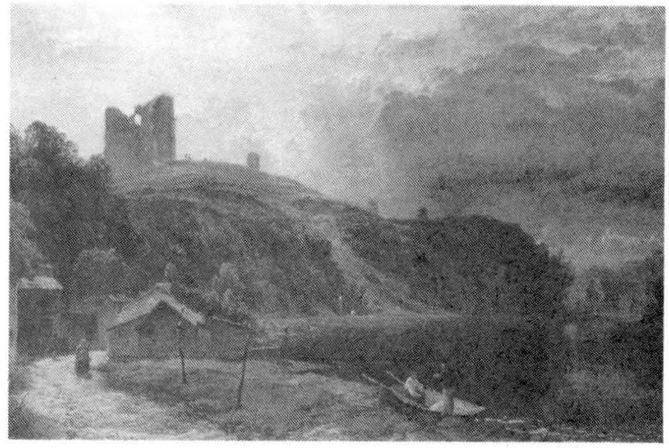

HENRY DAWSON – Figures In A Rowing Boat By A Riverside Village, A Ruined Tower Beyond – signed and dated 1866 – oil on canvas – 20¼ x 30¼in.
(Phillips) **$3,978** **£2,600**

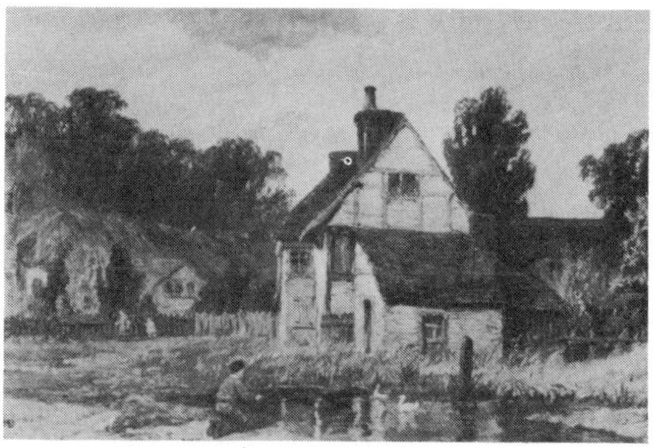

HENRY DAWSON – A Village Scene With A Boy By A Pond – signed with initials – 12¼ x 18½in.
(Christie's) **$841** **£550**

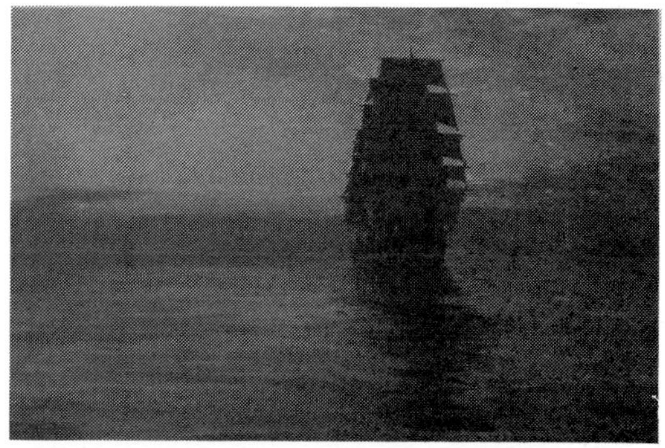

MONTAGUE DAWSON – Twilight Shadows – signed – oil on canvas – 71 x 108cm.
(Phillips) **$11,200** **£7,000**

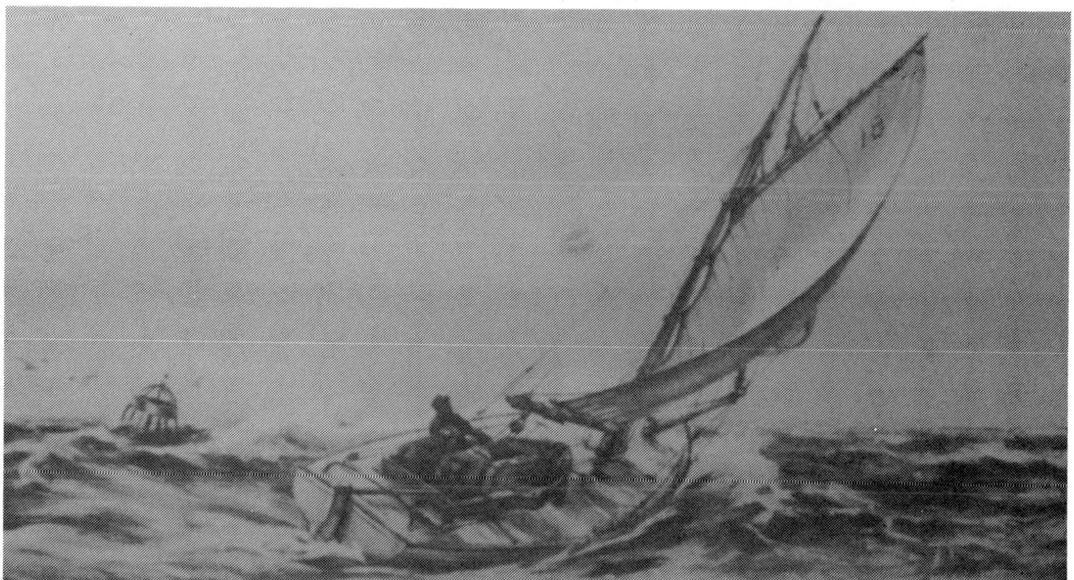

MONTAGUE DAWSON – Catching The Wind – signed – watercolour – 22 x 34cm. *(Phillips)*
$3,154 **£1,900**

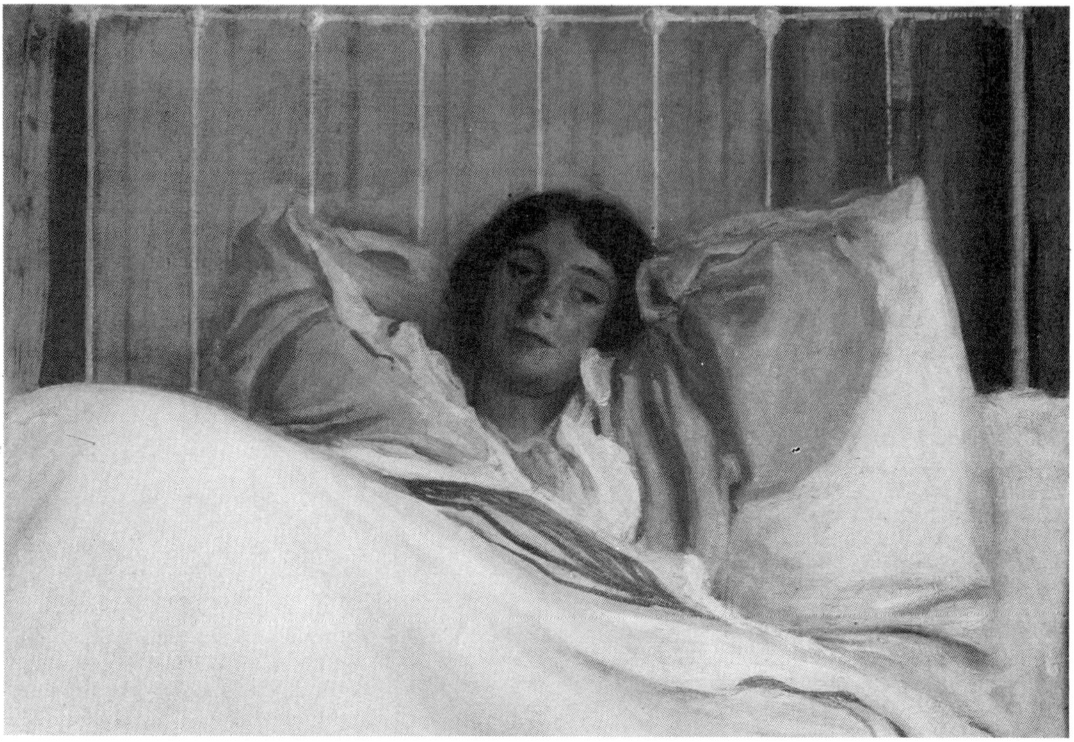

JOSEPH RODEFER DECAMP – Portrait Of The Artist's Wife Edith – oil on canvas – 24 x 21in.
(Christie's) **$55,000 £38,665**

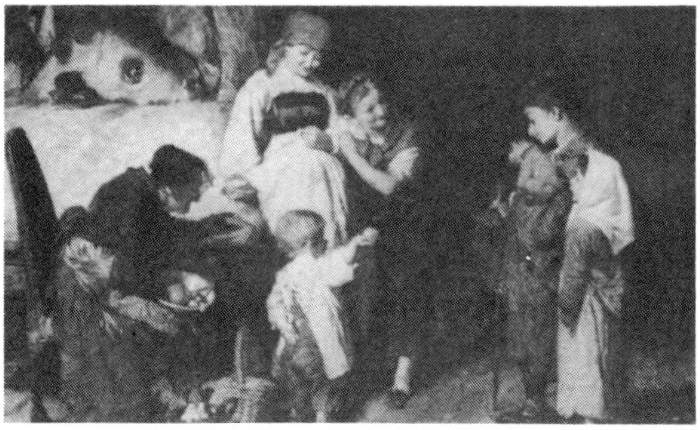

FRANZ VON DEFREGGER, Circle of – A New Addition To The Family? – on canvas – 44.5 x 34cm.
(Phillips) **$5,889 £3,900**

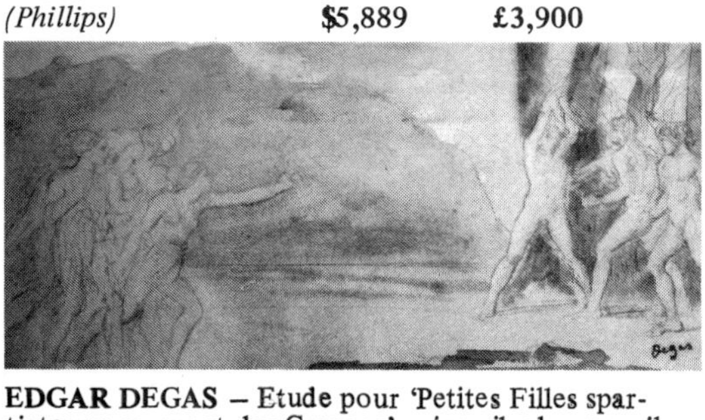

EDGAR DEGAS – Etude pour 'Petites Filles spartiates provoquant des Garcons' – inscribed – pencil, brush and brown wash on paper – 8¾ x 13¼in.
(Christie's) **$30,096 £20,900**

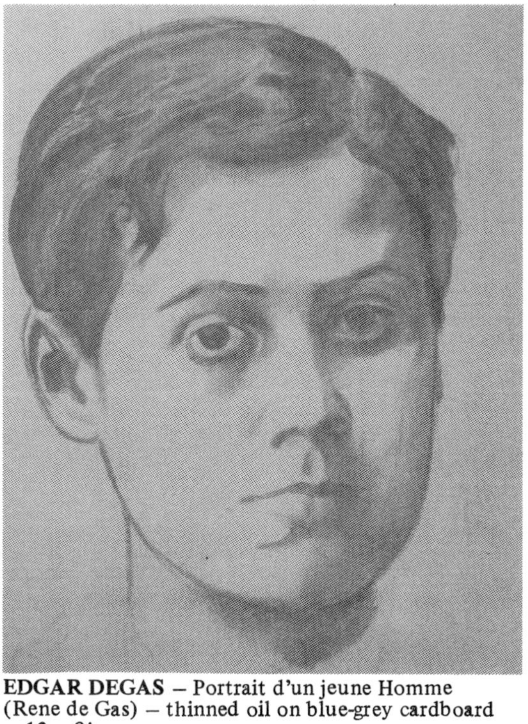

EDGAR DEGAS – Portrait d'un jeune Homme (Rene de Gas) – thinned oil on blue-grey cardboard – 12 x 9in.
(Christie's) **$31,680 £22,000**

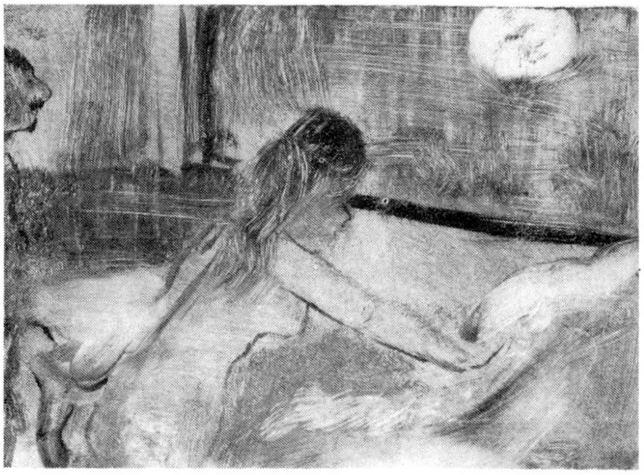

EDGAR DEGAS – Preparatifs – monotype, on Chine volant – 4¾ x 6¼in.
(Christie's) **$57,024 £39,600**

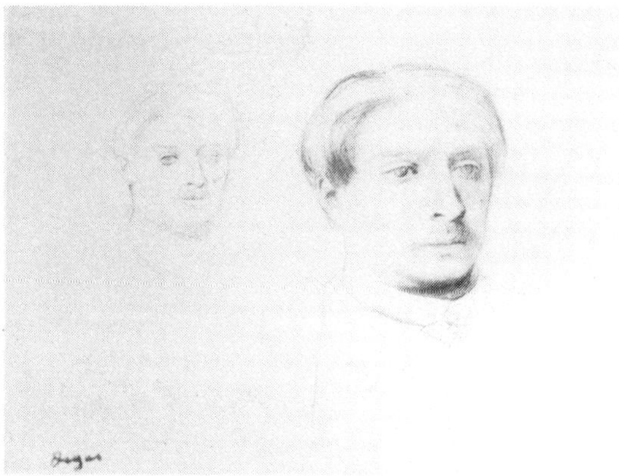

EDGAR DEGAS – Portraits de Tissot – indistinctly inscribed – pencil on paper – 7½ x 9½in.
(Christie's) **$22,880 £14,300**

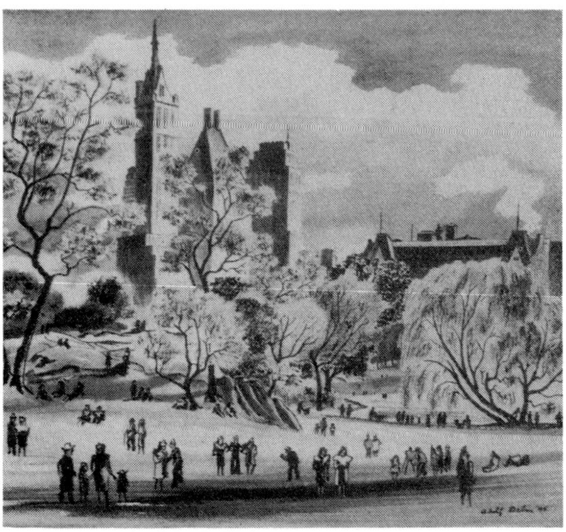

ADOLPH DEHN – In The Park – signed and dated '45 – pen and black ink and ink wash on paper – 19¼ x 21in.
(Christie's) **$825 £514**

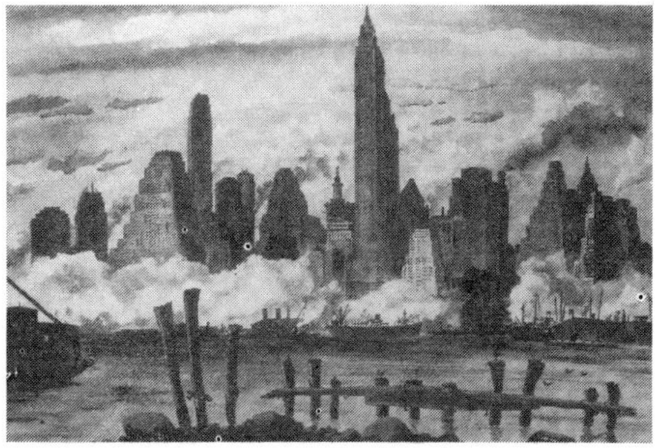

ADOLPH DEHN – Lower Manhattan From Under Brooklyn Bridge – signed and dated '46, also signed, dated and inscribed on the reverse – watercolour, gouache and pencil on paper – 22 x 30¼in.
(Christie's) **$4,180 £2,604**

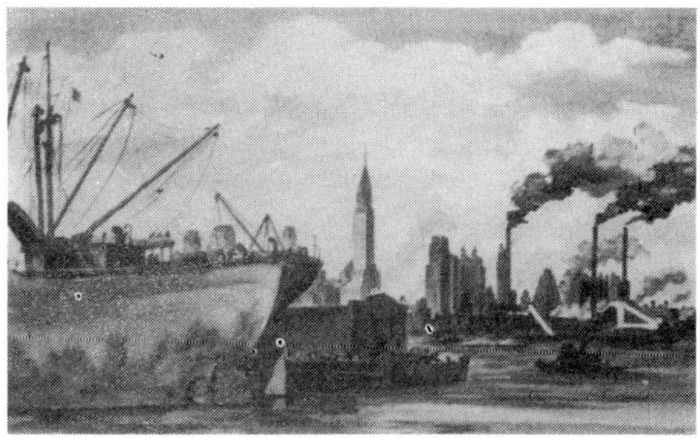

ADOLPH DEHN – East River Looking North From East River Drive At 18th Street – signed and dated 1946, also signed, dated and inscribed on the reverse – watercolour, gouache and pencil on paper – 20¾ x 30in.
(Christie's) **$1,320 £822**

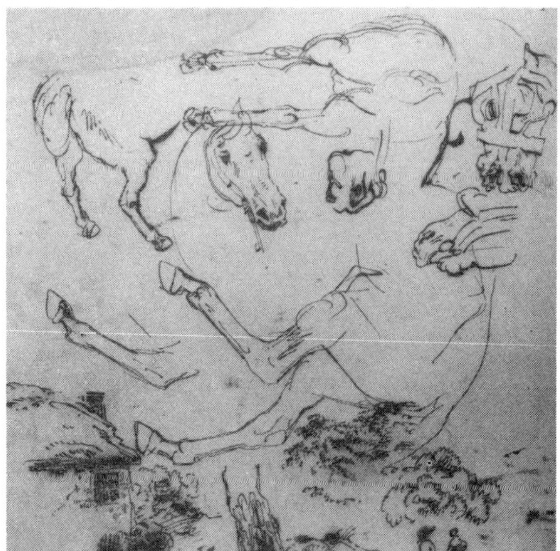

EUGENE DELACROIX – Paysage et Etudes de Chevaux – pen and ink on paper – 9½ x 8¾in.
(Christie's) **$3,520 £2,200**

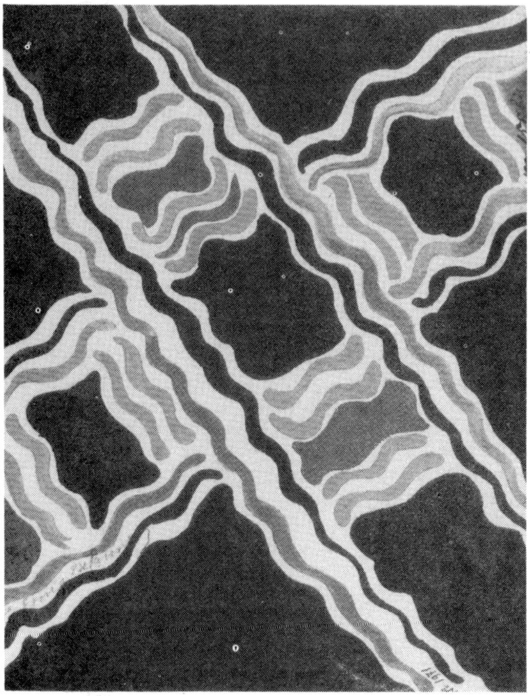

SONIA DELAUNAY – Sans Titre – signed and dated 1925, also inscribed – gouache and pencil on paper – 13½ x 10½in.
(Christie's) **$6,160** **£3,850**

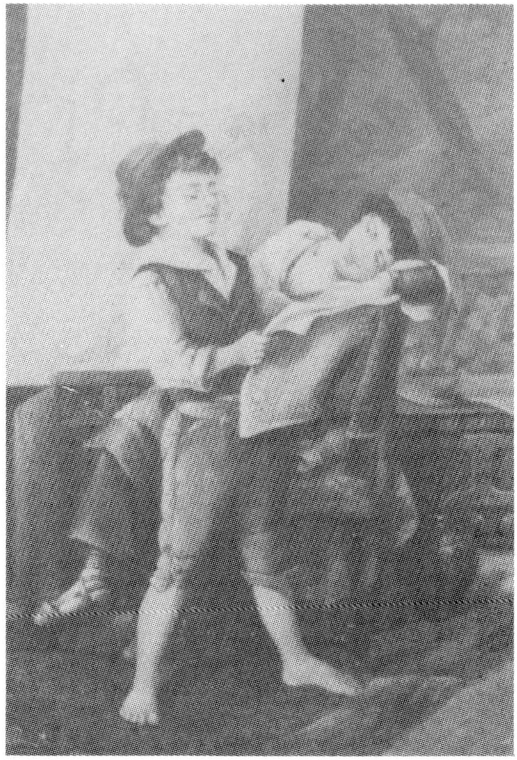

PAUL DELORME – 'Le Figaro' – signed and dated 1891 – 26¾ x 19½in.
(Christie's) **$1,071** **£700**

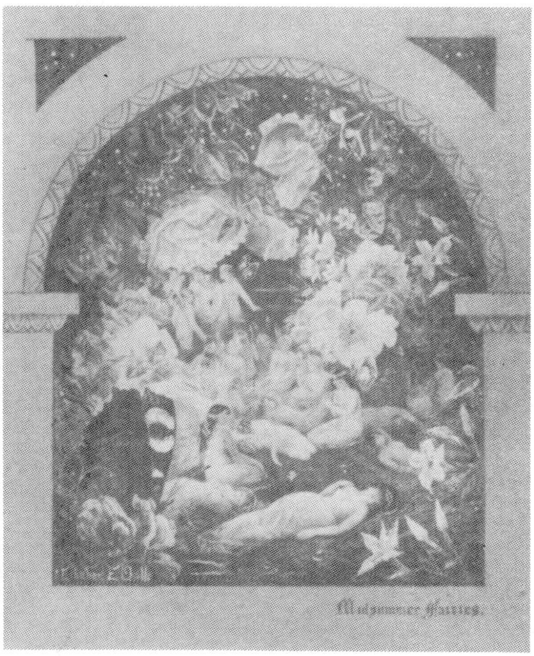

ETHELINE E. DELL – Midsummer Fairies – signed and inscribed – bodycolour – 7½ x 6¼in.
(Christie's) **$6,514** **£4,620**

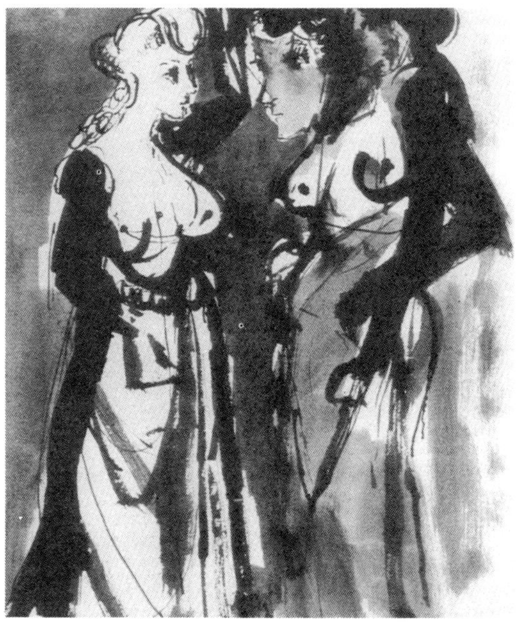

PAUL DELVAUX – La Conversation – signed and dated 1945 – brush and black ink on paper – 8½ x 6¾in.
(Christie's) **$5,702** **£3,960**

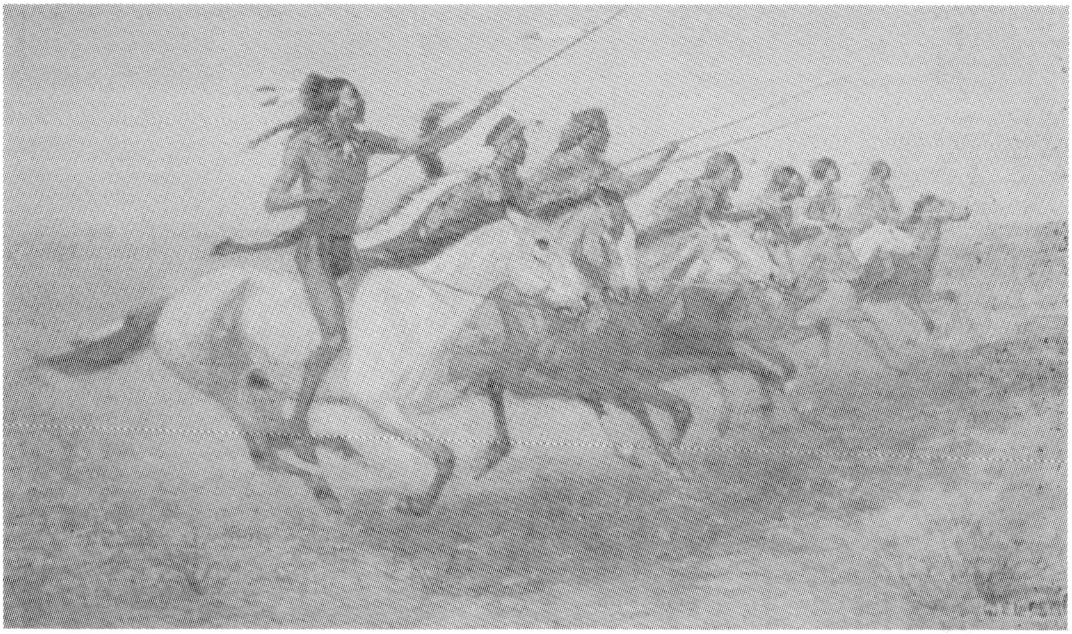

EDWIN WILLARD DEMING – Royal Reception – signed, inscribed on the reverse – oil on canvas laid down on board – 22 x 40¼in. *(Christie's)* **$7,700 £5,025**

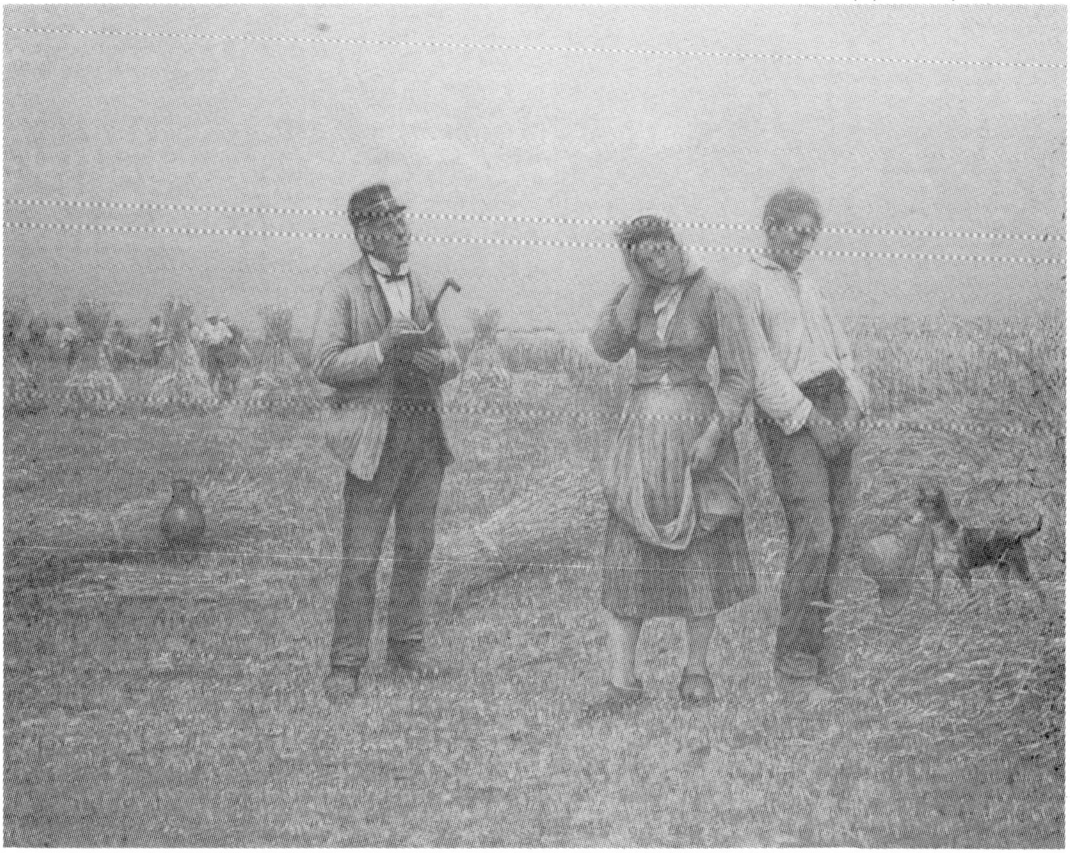

JULES DENNEULIN – Un reprouve – signed – 34½ x 44¾in. *(Christie's)* **$15,840 £9,900**

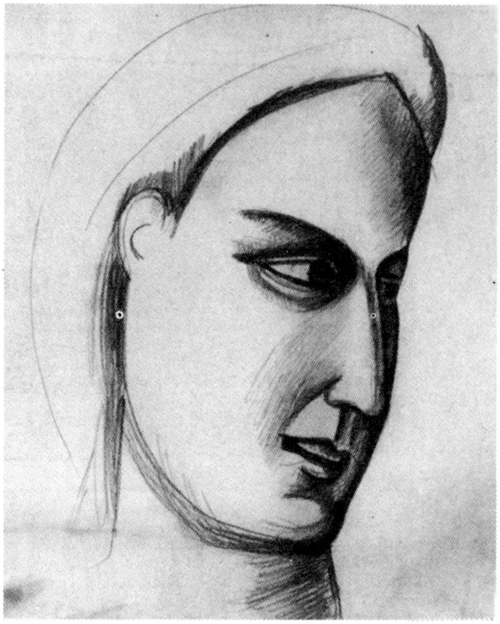

ANDRE DERAIN – Tete de jeune Femme – pencil on paper – 13½ x 9¾in.
(Christie's) **$2,217** **£1,540**

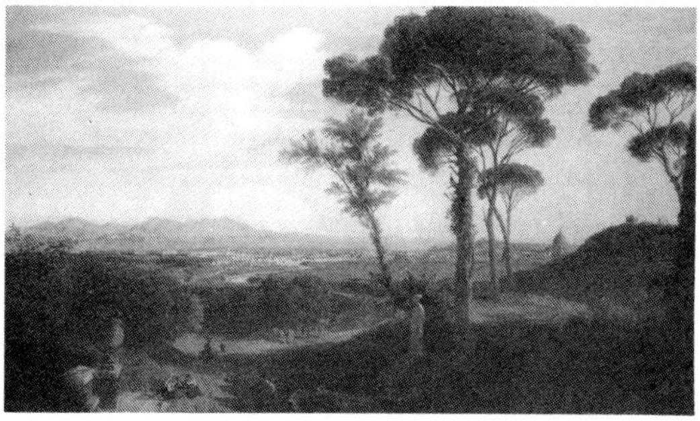

THOMAS DESSOULAVY – A View Of Rome – signed and dated 1841 – 33½ x 46½in.
(Christie's) **$23,760** **£16,500**

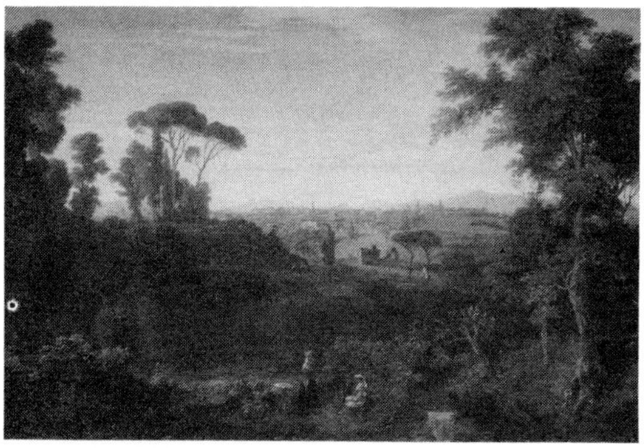

THOMAS DESSOULAVY – A View Of Rome And The Campagna – signed and dated 1844 – 33 x 47 in.
(Christie's) **$15,840** **£9,900**

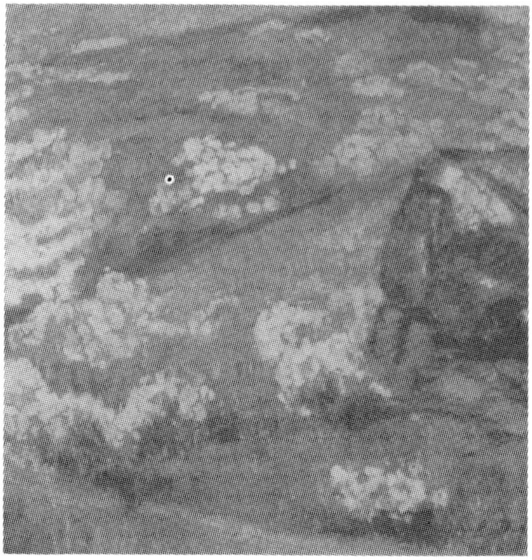

LEON DETROY – Les Genets – signed – oil on board – 14½ x 18in.
(Christie's) **$968** **£605**

LUDWIG DEUTSCH – The Koran School – signed and dated 1905 – on panel – 27½ x 31¾in.
(Christie's) **$52,800** **£33,000**

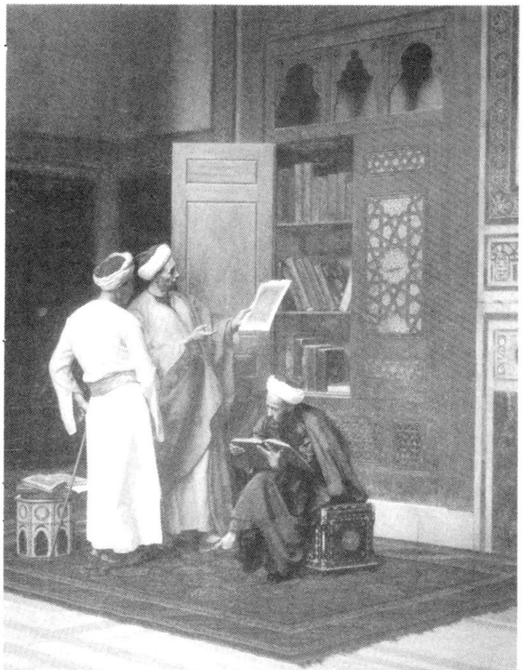

LUDWIG DEUTSCH – Arab Scholars In An Interior – signed and dated 1901 – on panel – 25½ x 19¾in.
(Christie's) **$118,800** **£82,500**

LUDWIG DEUTSCH – News From The Sudan – signed and dated 1885 – oil on panel – 33.5 x 46cm.
(Phillips) **$48,960** **£34,000**

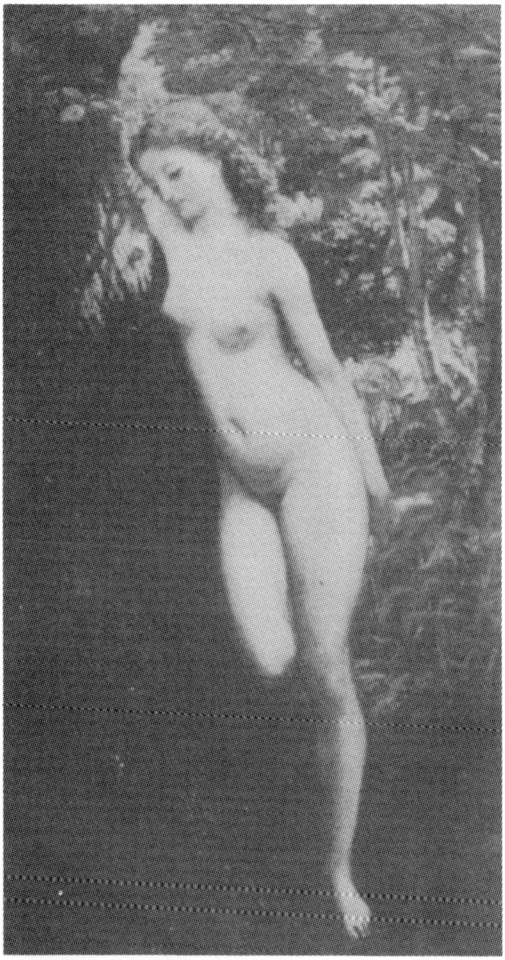

ALFRED DEVER – A Woodland Idyll – signed and dated 1865 – 20¼ x 9in.
(Christie's) **$2,946** **£2,090**

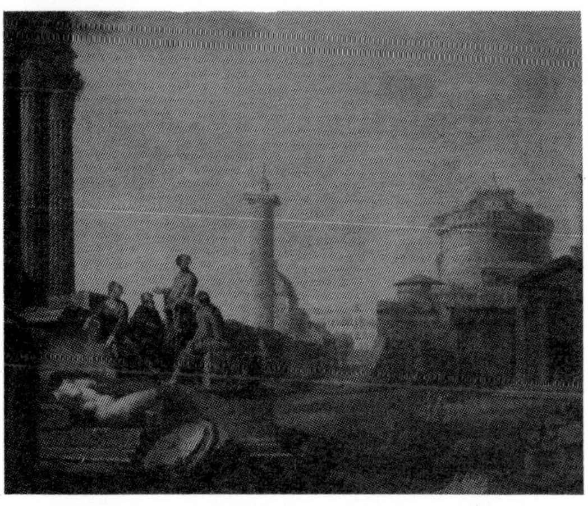

A. DEVIS – An Architectural Cappricio – signed and dated 1736 – on canvas – 24¼ x 29¼in.
(Phillips) **$19,920** **£12,000**

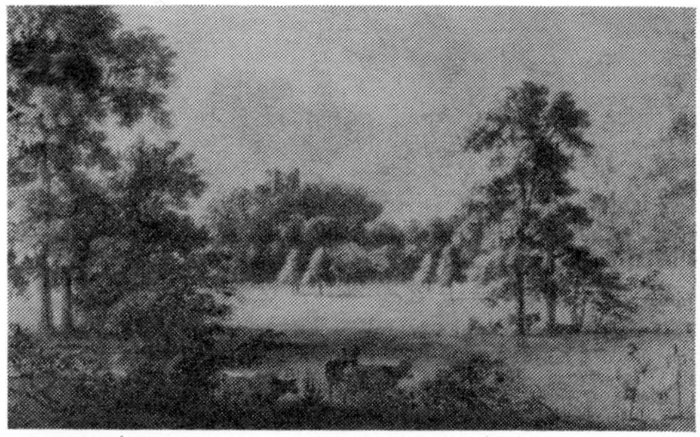

ANTHONY DEVIS – Figures And Cattle In A Landscape, A Castle Beyond – signed with initials and dated 1800 – pen and ink and wash – 22 x 31cm.
(Phillips) **$586** **£360**

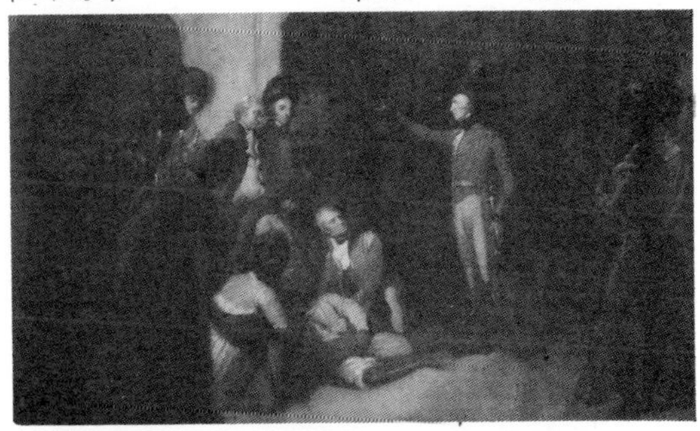

ARTHUR WILLIAM DEVIS – Major-General David Baird And Col. The Hon. Arthur Wellesley Discovering The Body Of Tippoo Sultan At Seringapatam On 4th May 1799 – 29½ x 39in.
(Christie's) **$6,480** **£4,320**

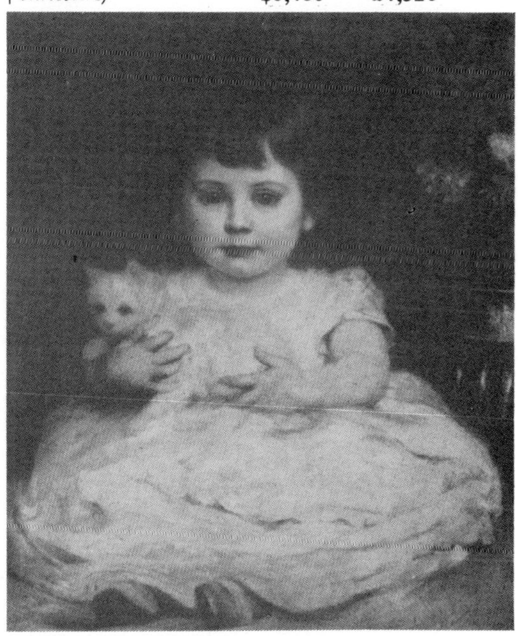

SIR FRANK DICKSEE – Ethel, Daughter Of Sidney Dicksee Esq. – 24 x 20in.
(Christie's) **$2,791** **£1,980**

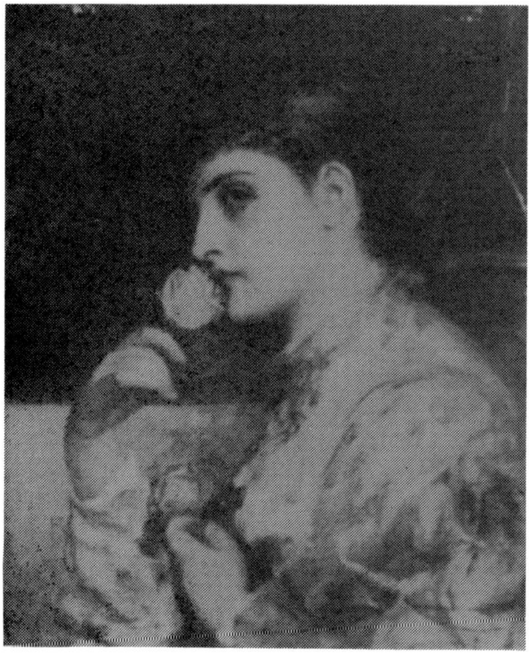

JOHN ROBERT DICKSEE – 'Contemplation' – canvas laid on board – 13¾ x 12in.
(Phillips) **$2,415** **£1,500**

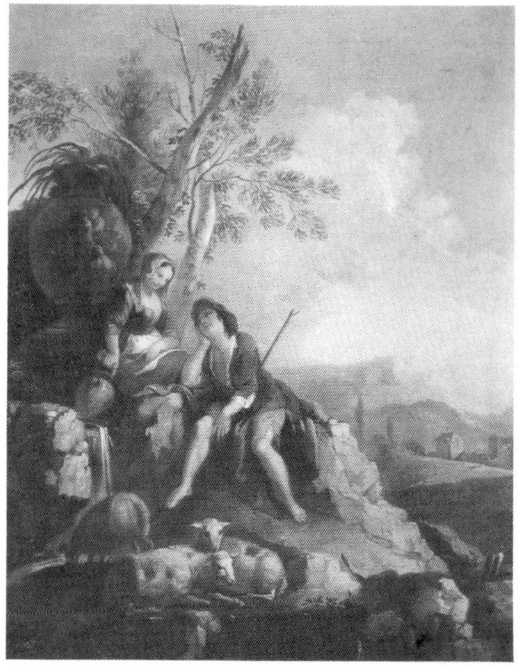

CHRISTIAN WILHELM ERNST DIETRICHY – A Shepherd And His Companion Seated In A Pastoral Landscape – oil on canvas – 20½ x 15½in.
(Phillips) **$3,948** **£2,800**

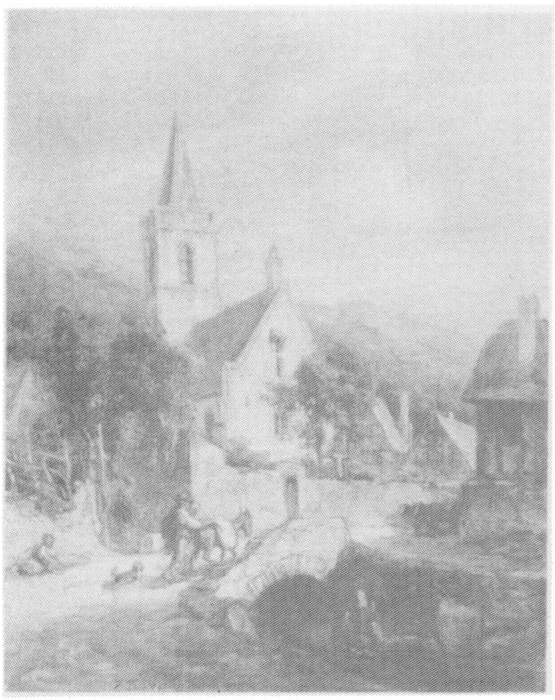

JAKOB FURCHTEGOTT DIELMANN – Figures By A Stream In A Mountain Village – signed – oil on panel – 27 x 23cm.
(Phillips) **$7,776** **£5,400**

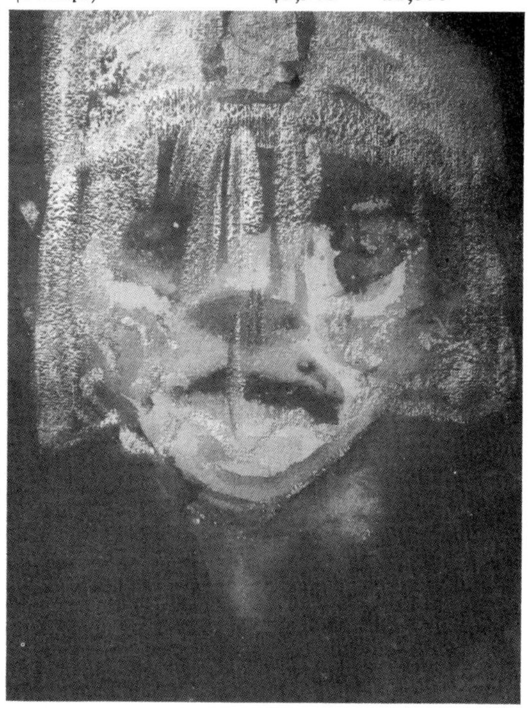

OTTO DIX – Nachtliche Erscheinung – signed – watercolour, gold leaf and silver paint on paper – 13¼ x 10in.
(Christie's) **$76,032** **£52,800**

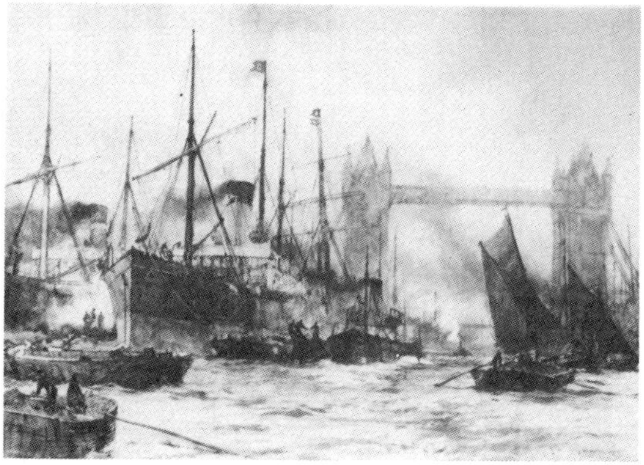

CHARLES DIXON – Tower Bridge, Looking West From Cherry Gardens Pier – signed, inscribed and dated '99 – watercolour heightened with white – 21½ x 30¼in.
(Christie's) **$7,290** **£4,860**

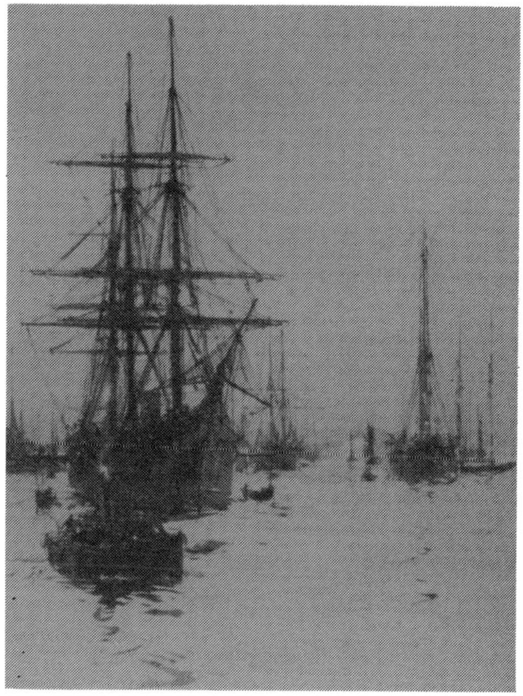

CHARLES EDWARD DIXON – Moonrise – signed and inscribed – watercolour heightened with white – 49 x 40cm.
(Phillips) **$3,912** **£2,400**

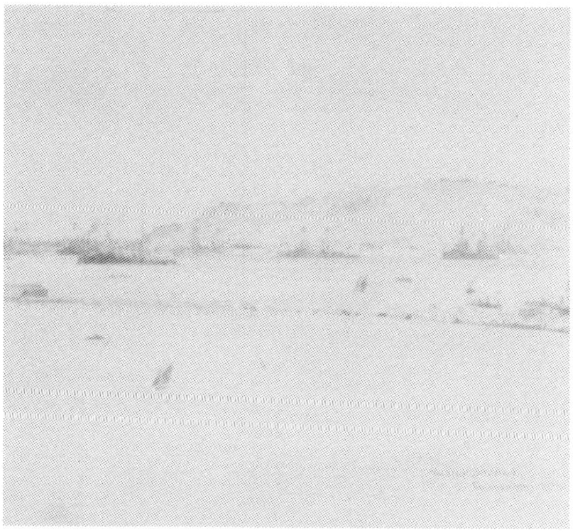

CHARLES EDWARD DIXON – The Fleet At Portland – signed, inscribed and dated 1912 – pencil and watercolour – 5¾ x 7¾in.
(Christie's) **$821** **£495**

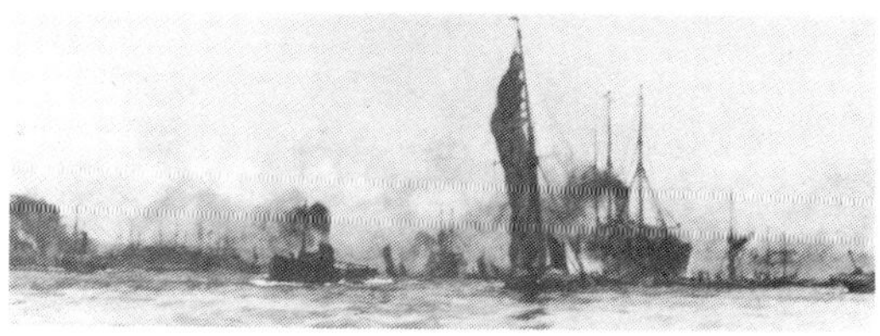

CHARLES EDWARD DIXON – The Lower Pool Of London – signed, inscribed and dated '05 – watercolour with touches of white heightening – 11¼ x 30½in.
(Christie's) **$3,722** **£2,640**

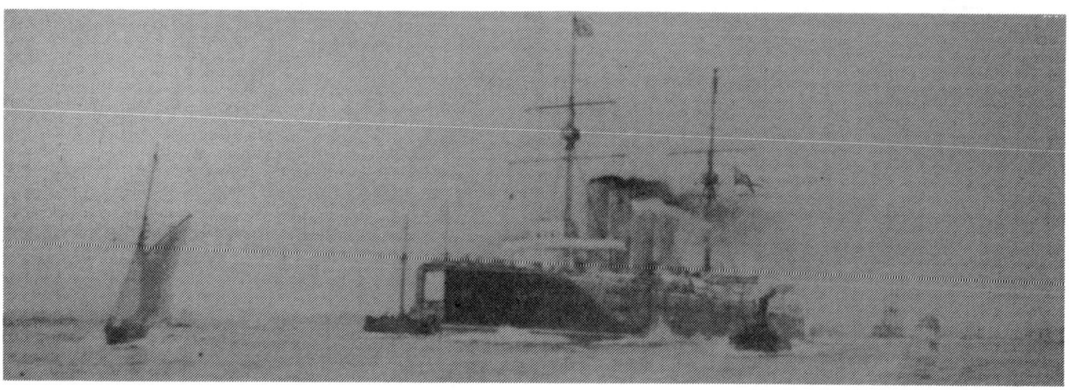

CHARLES EDWARD DIXON – 'H.M.S. Ariadne Leaving Portsmouth' – signed and inscribed – watercolour and bodycolour – 27 x 77cm. *(Phillips)* **$3,912 £2,400**

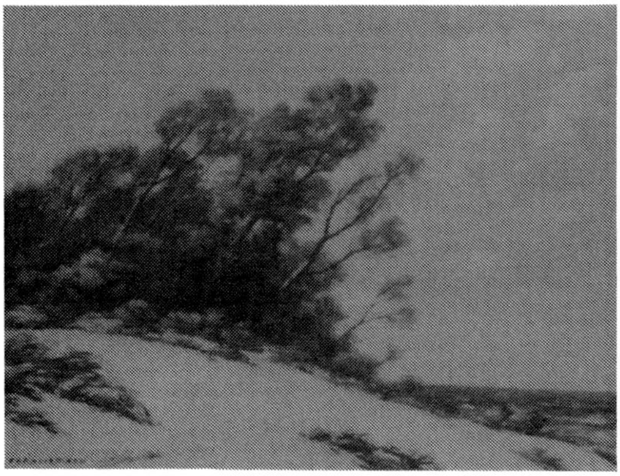

FRANCIS STILWELL DIXON – Winter Wind – signed – oil on canvas laid down on board – 8 x 10in.
(Robt. W. Skinner Inc.) **$250** **£153**

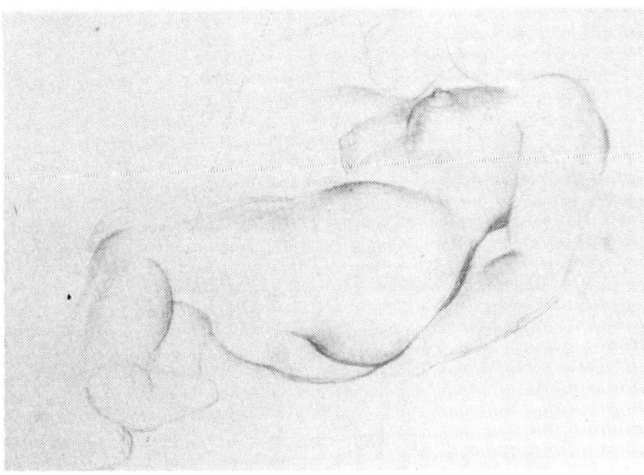

FRANK DOBSON – Reclining Nude – signed and dated '27 – red chalk drawing – 34 x 49cm.
(Phillips) **$795** **£520**

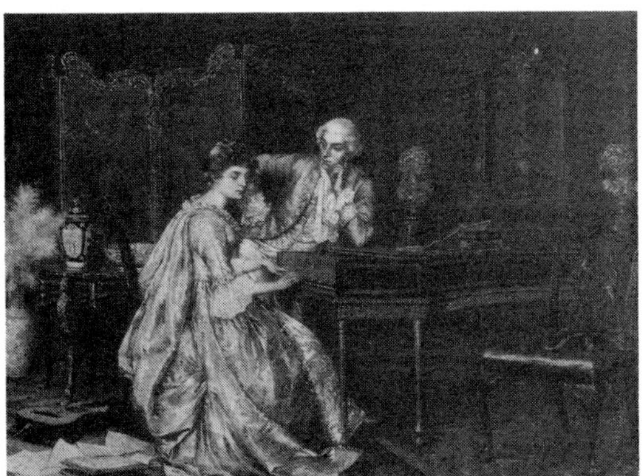

W. ANSTEY DOLLAND – Touches Of Sweet Harmony – signed – 20 x 26in.
(Christie's) **$2,861** **£1,870**

W. ANSTEY DOLLOND – Finishing Touches – signed, and inscribed on the reverse – pencil and watercolour – 19 x 12¼in.
(Christie's) **$1,826** **£1,100**

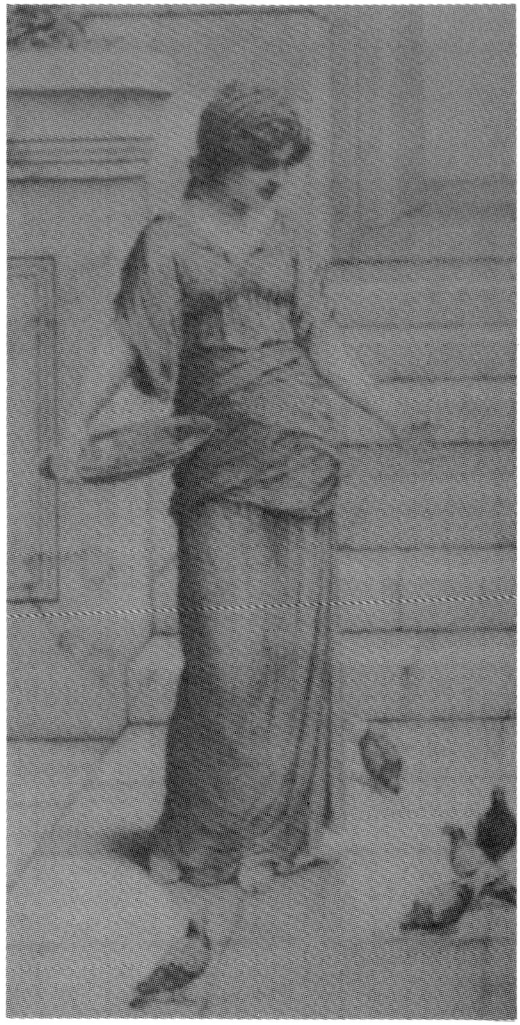

W. ANSTEY DOLLAND – Feeding The Pigeons – signed – watercolour – 45 x 20cm.
(Phillips) **$1,630** **£1,000**

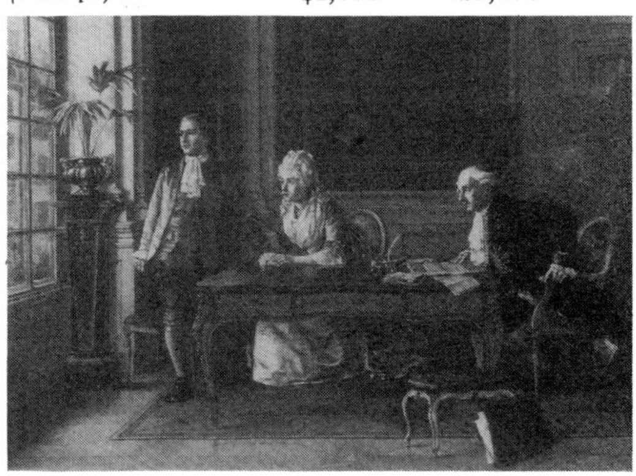

W. ANSTEY DOLLAND – The Growing Of The Cloud, Paris 1789 – signed – 22½ x 30in.
(Christie's) **$2,692** **£1,768**

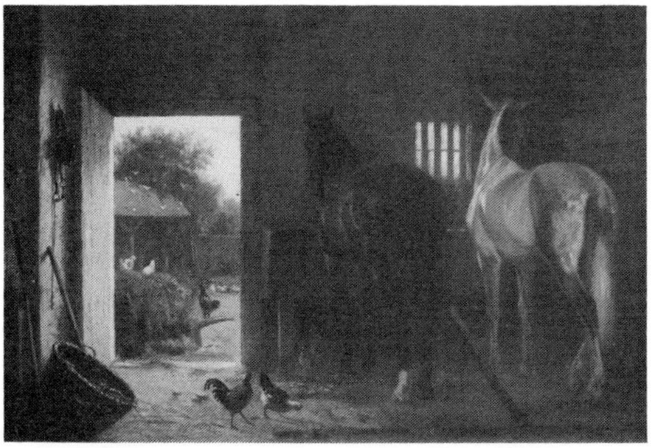

JOHN HENRY DOLPH – Interior Of A Stable – signed and dated 1875 – oil on canvas – 16 x 24¼in.
(Christie's) $7,700 £5,356

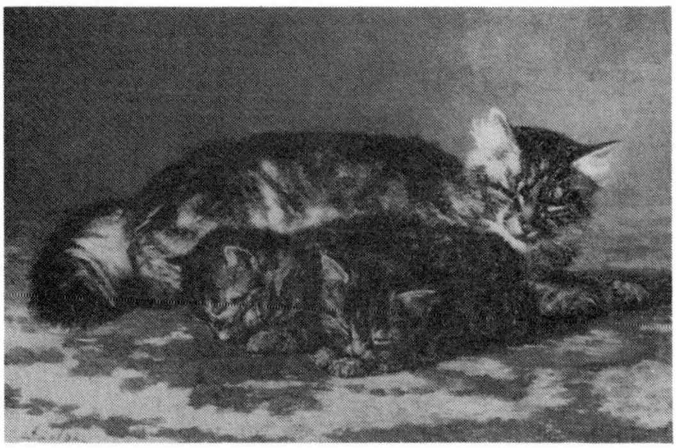

JOHN HENRY DOLPH – An After Dinner Nap – signed with initials – oil on canvas – 12½ x 18½in.
(Christie's) $3,300 £2,056

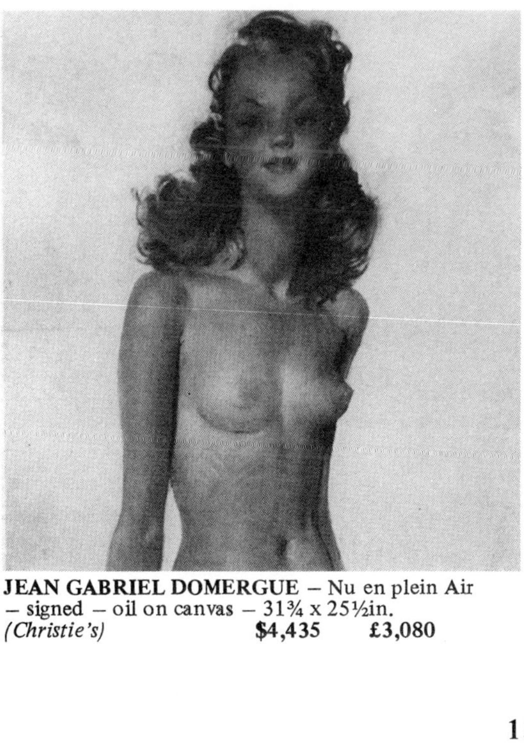

JEAN GABRIEL DOMERGUE – Nu en plein Air – signed – oil on canvas – 31¾ x 25½in.
(Christie's) $4,435 £3,080

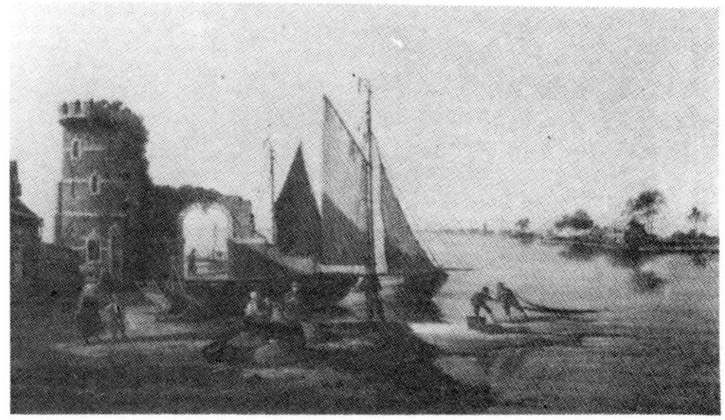

WILLIAM DOMMERSEN – Schiedam On The Scheldt – signed, signed and inscribed on the reverse – oil – 20 x 30in.
(Christie's) $1,377 £900

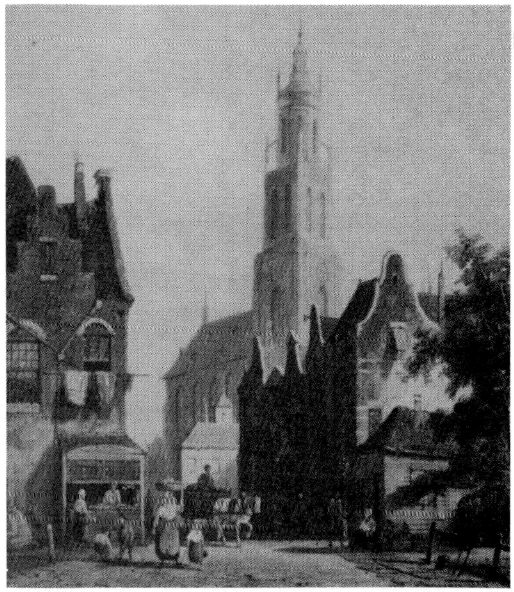

WILLIAM ROGERS DOMMERSEN – A Continental Town Scene – signed and dated 1883 – on panel – 31 x 26cm.
(Phillips) $2,736 £1,900

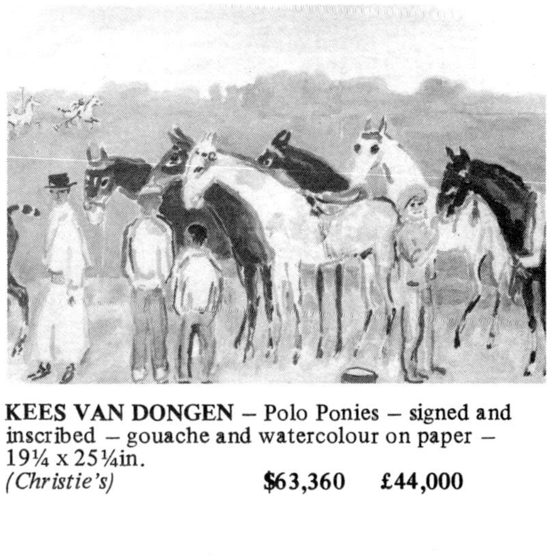

KEES VAN DONGEN – Polo Ponies – signed and inscribed – gouache and watercolour on paper – 19¼ x 25¼in.
(Christie's) $63,360 £44,000

DONGEN

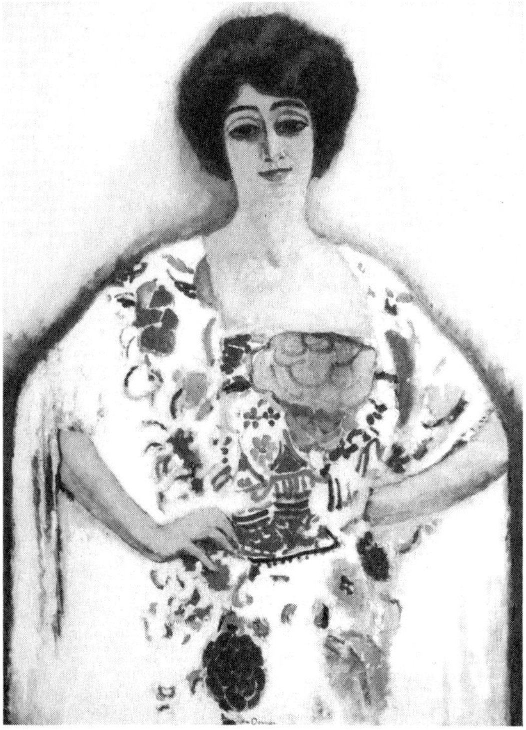

KEES VAN DONGEN – L'Espagnole – signed – oil on canvas – 51½ x 38¼in.
(Christie's) **$570,240 £396,000**

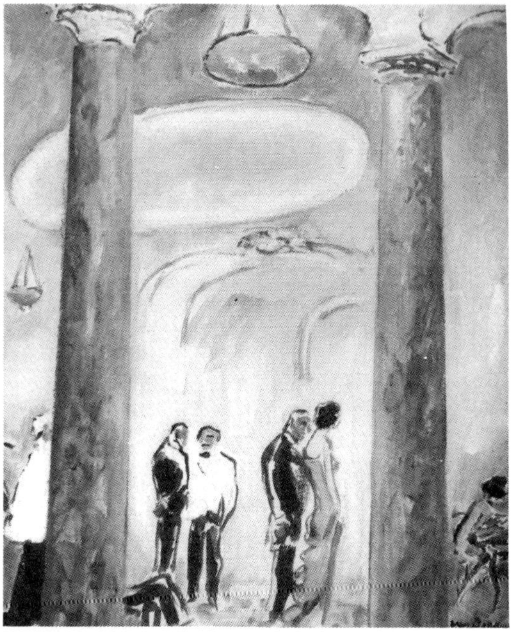

KEES VAN DONGEN – Hall de l'Hotel Normandy, Deauville – signed, and inscribed and dated on the reverse – 18 x 15in.
(Christie's) **$126,720 £88,000**

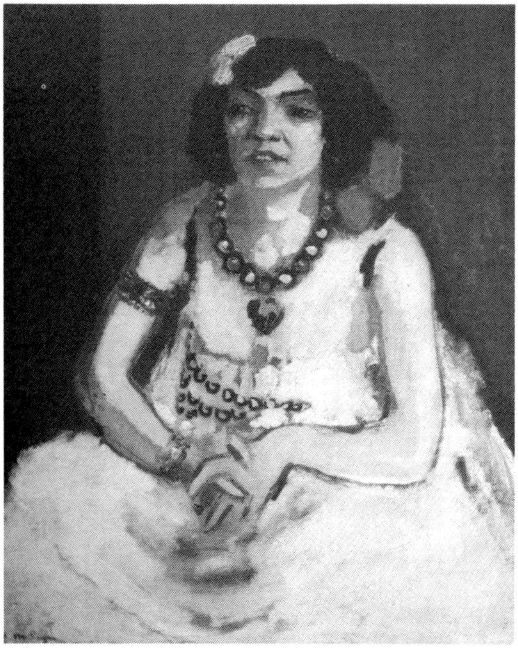

KEES VAN DONGEN – Anita au Coeur vert – signed – oil on canvas – 39½ x 32in.
(Christie's) **$443,520 £308,000**

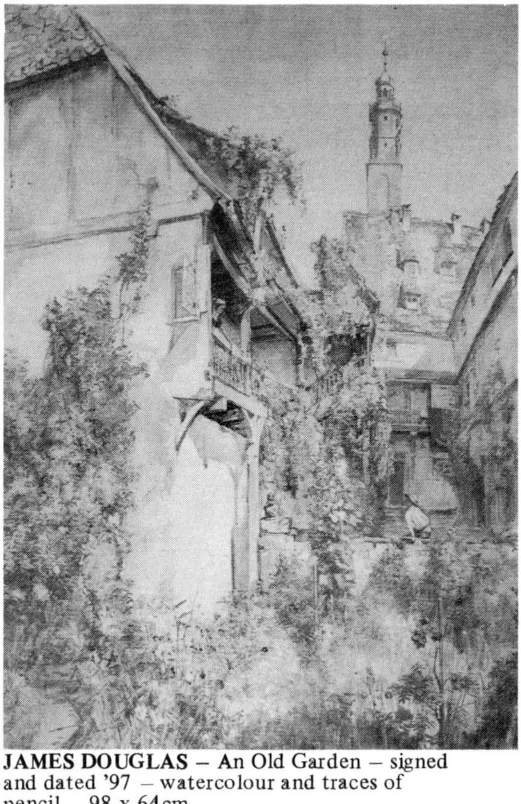

JAMES DOUGLAS – An Old Garden – signed and dated '97 – watercolour and traces of pencil – 98 x 64cm.
(Phillips) **$2,556 £1,800**

WALTER DOUGLAS – 'Sarah's Chickens' – signed – oil on panel – 8 x 10in.
(Robt. W. Skinner Inc.) **$550** **£361**

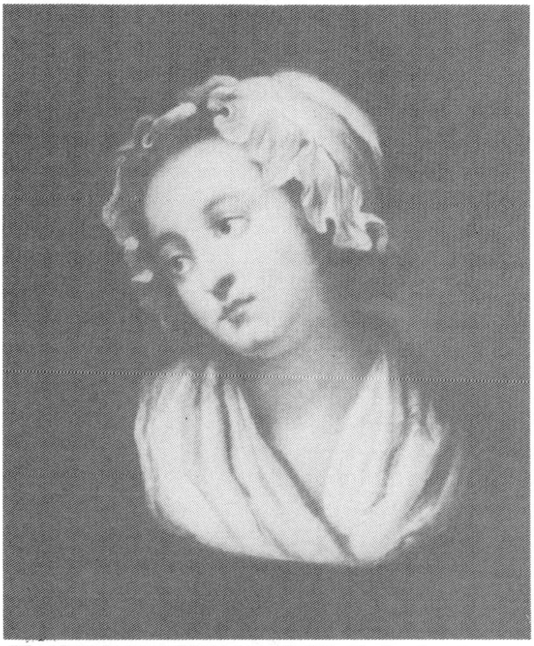

JEANNE PHILIBERTI LE DOUX, Circle of – A Young Girl, Half Length, Wearing A Mob Cap – oil on canvas – 18 x 15in.
(Phillips) **$451** **£320**

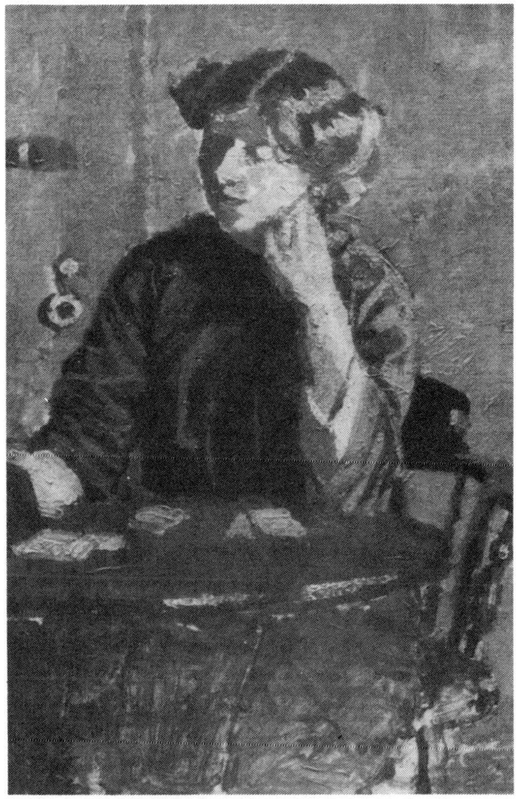

MALCOLM DRUMMOND – Girl At A Round Table – on canvas board – 15½ x 11¼in.
(Christie's) **$1,573** **£1,100**

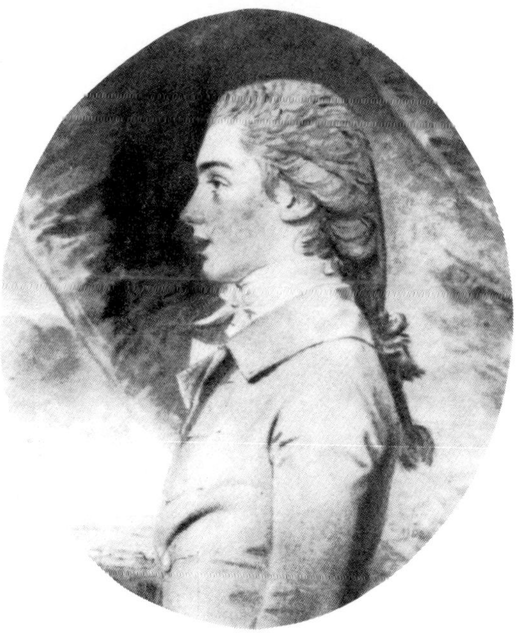

JOHN DOWNMAN – Portrait Of A Young Man, Facing To The Left, In A Landscape – signed with initials and dated 1782 – stump and watercolour heightened with white – 7¾ x 6¼in.
(Christie's) **$2,343** **£1,650**

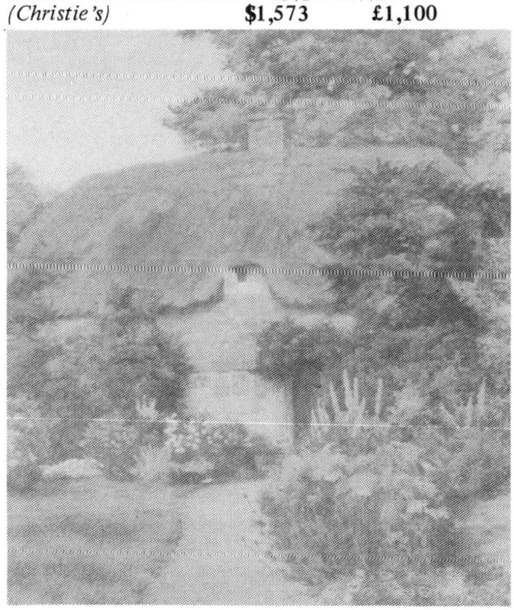

CURTIUS DUASSUT – An Old Cottage Near Buscombe, Wiltshire – signed, and inscribed on the reverse – pencil and watercolour heightened with white – 11 x 12¼in.
(Christie's) **$3,469** **£2,090**

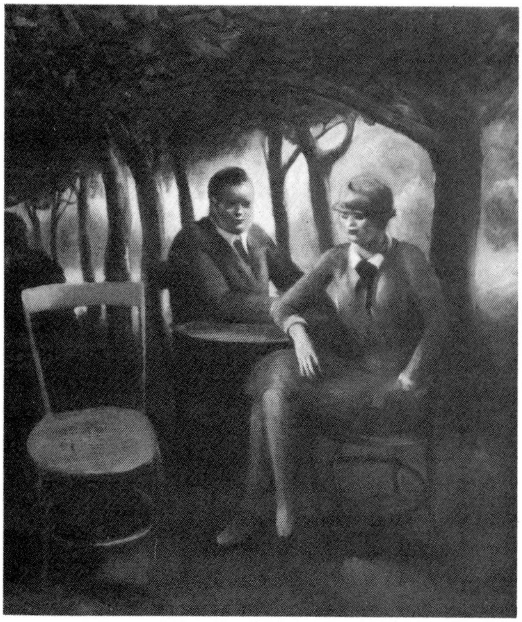

GUY PENE DUBOIS – Country Cafe, 1920 – signed – oil on canvas – 21½ x 18¼in.
(Christie's) **$20,900** **£14,692**

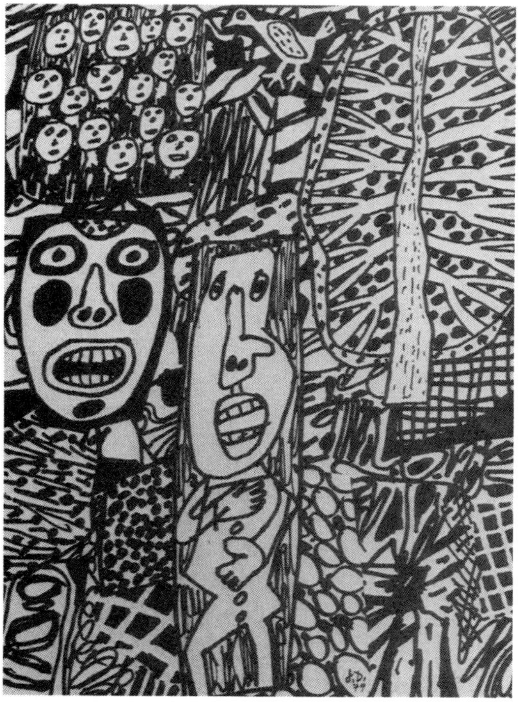

JEAN DUBUFFET – Situation LXXXCIII (Avec Arbre Et Oiseau) – signed with initials and dated '79 – black felt marker and collage on paper – 13¾ x 10in.
(Christie's) **$10,771** **£7,480**

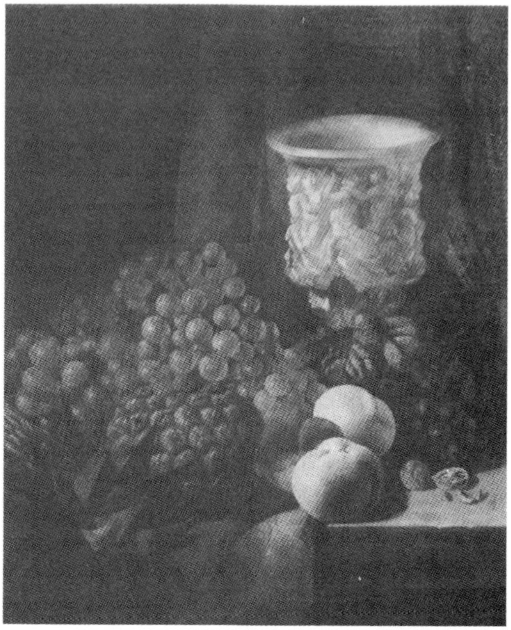

WILLIAM DUFFIELD – A Pineapple, Grapes, Gooseberries, Peaches And Walnuts By A Sculptured Urn On A Draped Ledge – signed – 24 x 20in.
(Christie's) **$2,481** **£1,760**

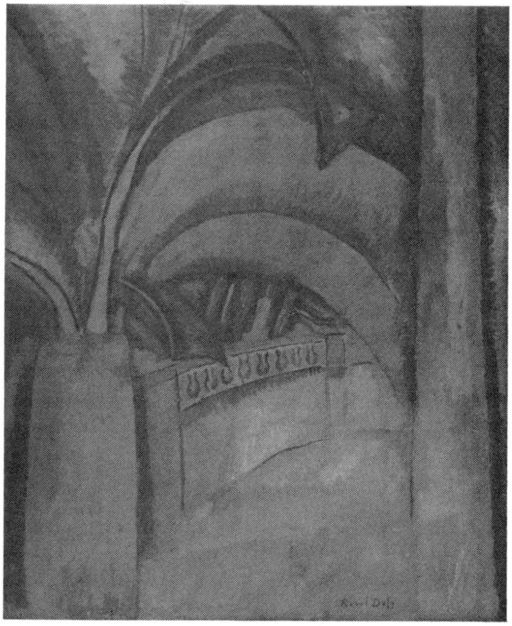

RAOUL DUFY – Palmier et Terrasse a l'Estaque – signed – oil on canvas – 28½ x 23½in.
(Christie's) **$47,762** **£28,600**

RAOUL DUFY – Les Explorateurs – pen, brush and indian ink heightened with white gouache on paper – 19¾ x 25½in.
(Christie's) **$8,651** **£6,050**

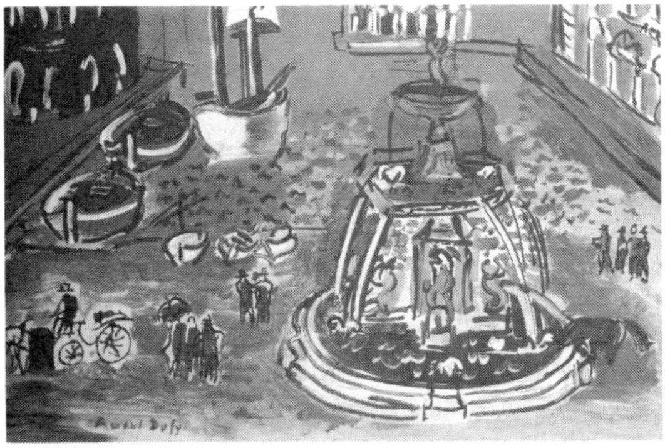

RAOUL DUFY – Hommage a Claude le Lorrain – signed – oil on canvas – 8¾ x 13in.
(Christie's) **$60,192** **£41,800**

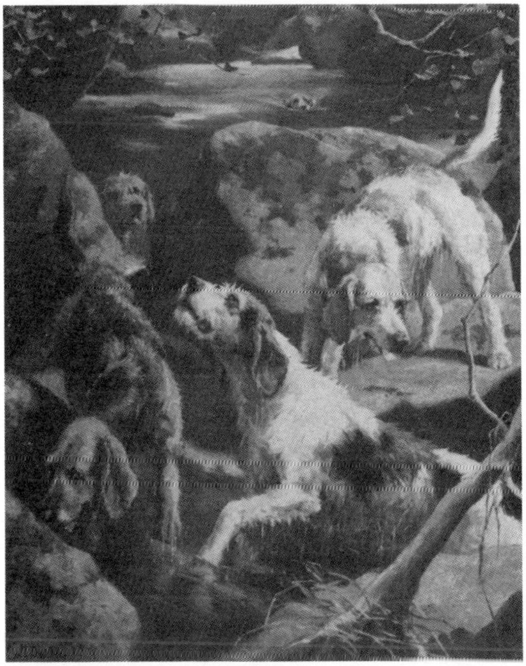

ALFRED DUKE – Other Hounds – signed – 23½ x 17½in.
(Christie's) **$1,240** **£880**

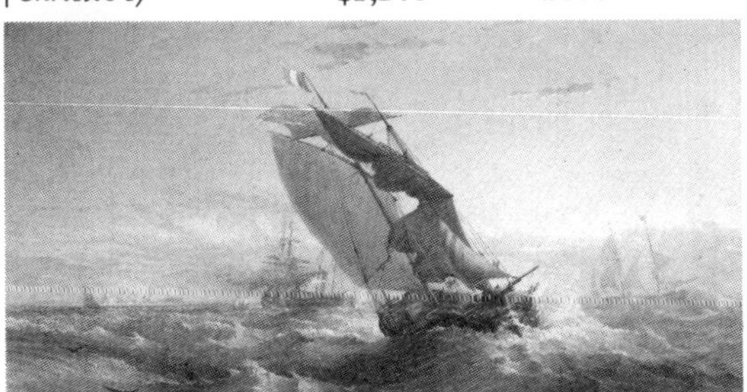

EDWARD DUNCAN – Shipping In A Squall – signed and dated 1856 – pencil and watercolour – 15¾ x 28in.
(Christie's) **$9,059** **£6,380**

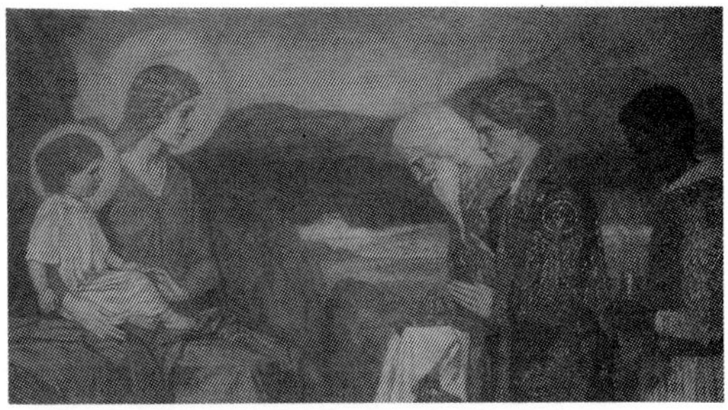

JOHN DUNCAN – Adoration Of The Magi – signed with initials and dated 1915 – on canvas – 27 x 48¾in.
(Phillips) **$8,855** **£5,500**

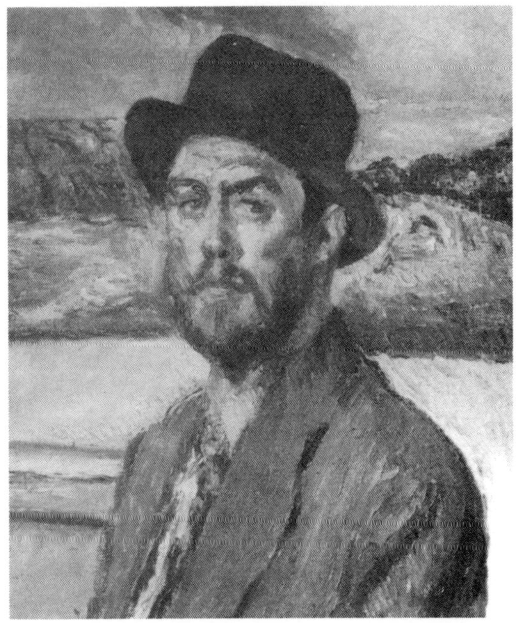

RONALD OSSORY DUNLOP – Portrait Of The Artist, Bust Length, Wearing A Hat – signed, and signed and inscribed on the reverse – oil on canvas – 23¼ x 19¼in.
(Christie's) **$2,072** **£1,320**

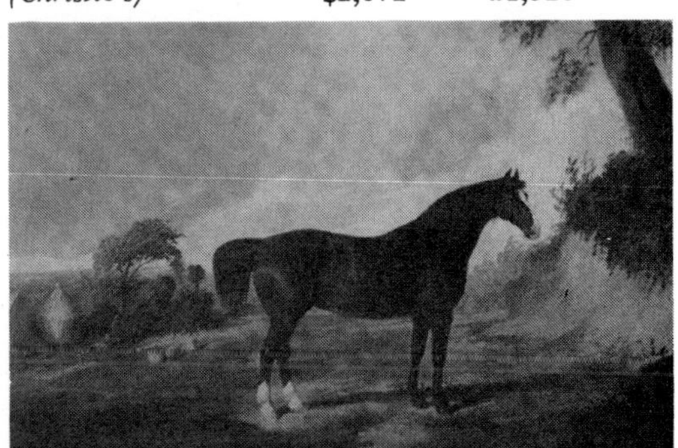

J. DUNN – A Hunter In A Landscape – signed – oil on canvas laid on board – 23½ x 29½in.
(Warners) **$2,720** **£1,700**

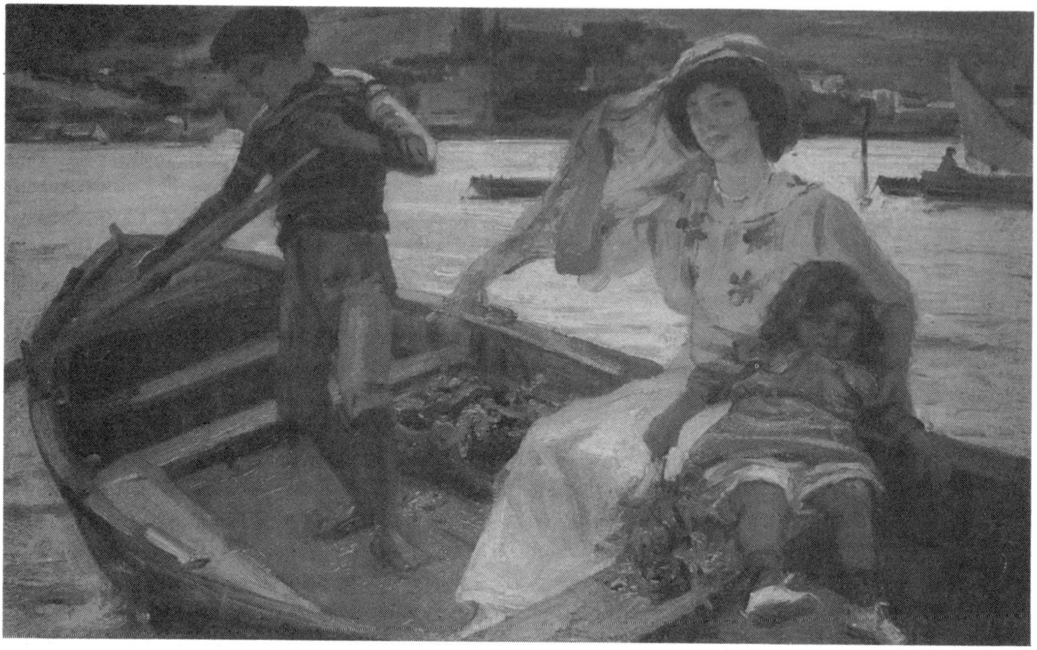

PAUL MICHEL DUPUY – A Mother And Child Being Ferried Across A River With A Town Beyond – signed and dated 1913 – 18 x 25½in. *(Christie's)* **$14,080 £8,800**

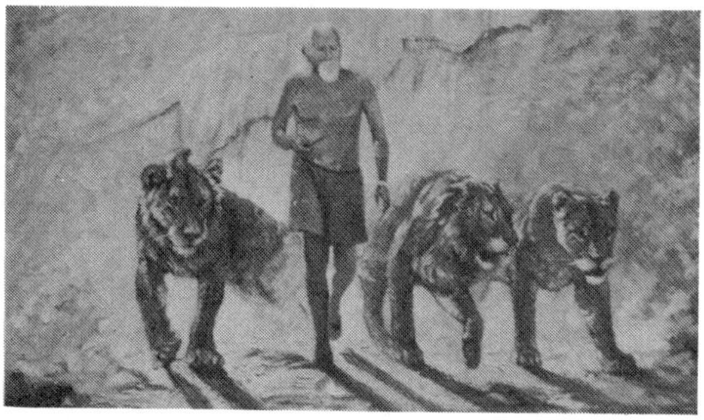

SILVIA DURAN – George Adamson And Lionesses – signed and dated 1986 – oil on canvas – 35½ x 39½in.
(Christie's) **$863 £550**

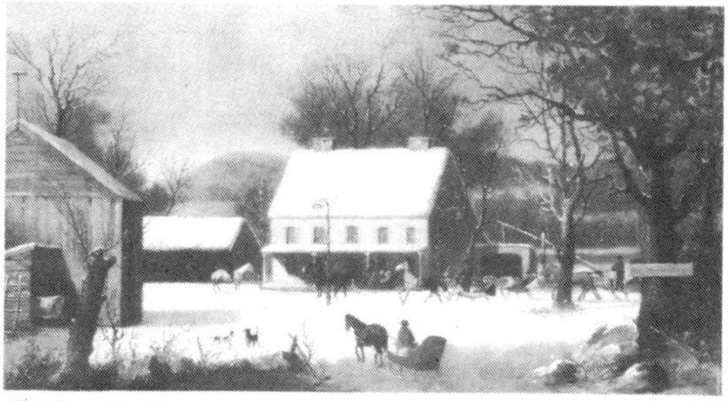

GEORGE HENRY DURRIE – Inn Scene, Seven Miles To New Haven – oil on canvas – 18¼ x 24in.
(Christie's) **$49,500 £34,798**

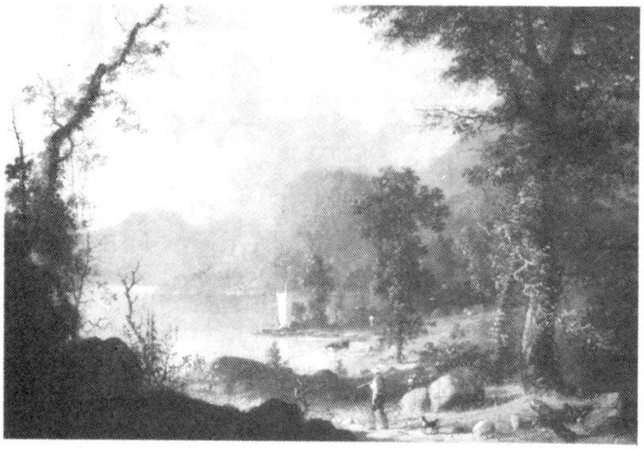

GEORGE HENRY DURRIE – Return From The Fields – oil on canvas – 17¾ x 24in.
(Christie's) **$16,500 £11,599**

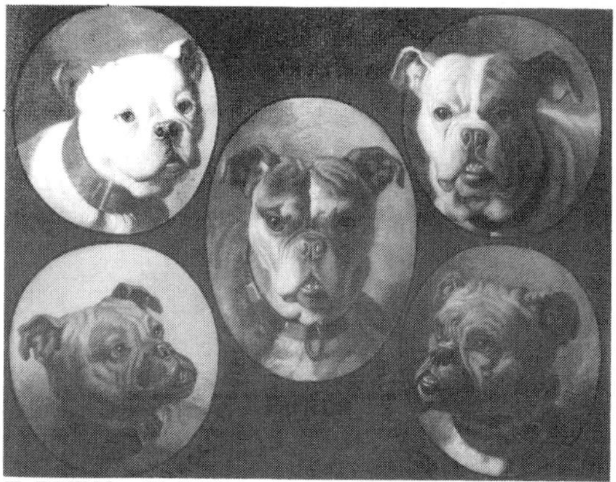

T. DURY – Nell, Dido, Punch, Maggie Lauder And Alexander, English Bulldogs – signed, inscribed and dated 1875 – oil – 26¼ x 32¼in.
(Bonhams) **$4,650 £3,000**

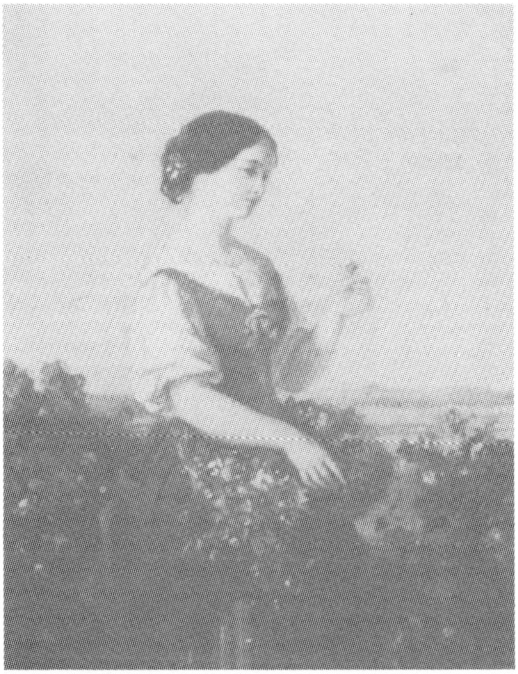

DUTCH SCHOOL, mid 19th century – The Flower Gatherer – indistinctly signed verso – oil on panel – 16 x 12.5 cm.; and 'Morning Of The Wedding.
(Phillips) **$1,336** **£800 Pair**

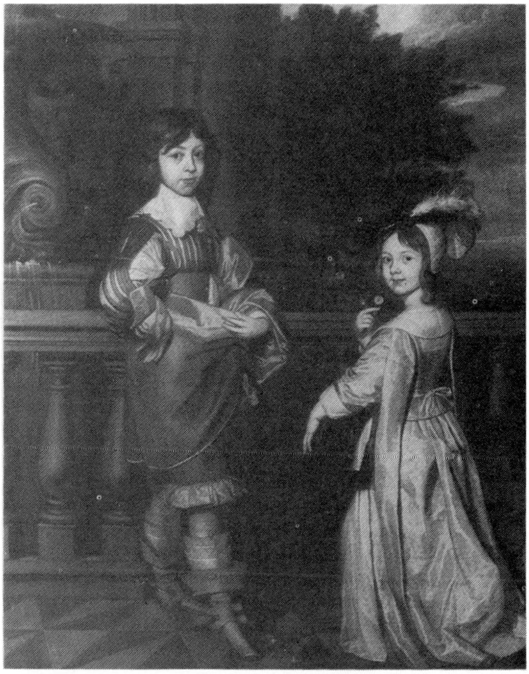

SIR ANTHONY VAN DYCK, Follower of – Portrait Of Prince Edward And Princess Amelia, As Children, Standing Full Length, With A Dog By Balustrading And A Fountain – 66½ x 49¼in.
(Christie's) **$5,184** **£3,456**

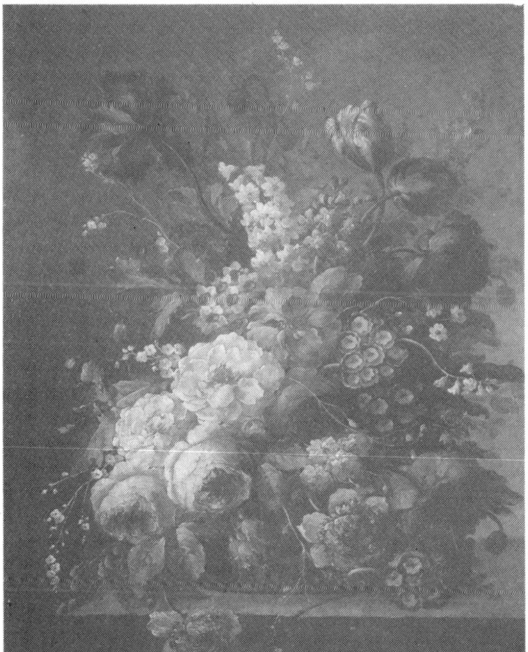

DUTCH SCHOOL, 19th century – Roses And Other Flowers In A Basket On A Ledge – 31 x 24in.
(Christie's) **$9,680** **£6,050**

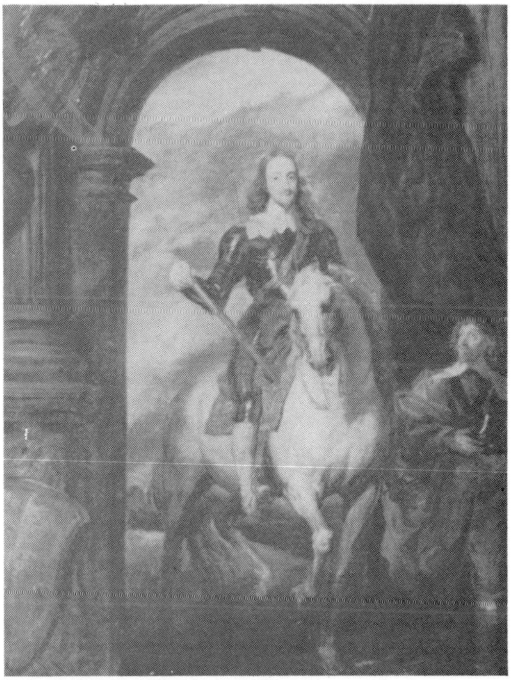

SIR ANTHONY VAN DYCK, After – Charles I On Horseback With M. De Antoine – oil on canvas – 28½ x 20½in.
(Christie's) **$896** **£550**

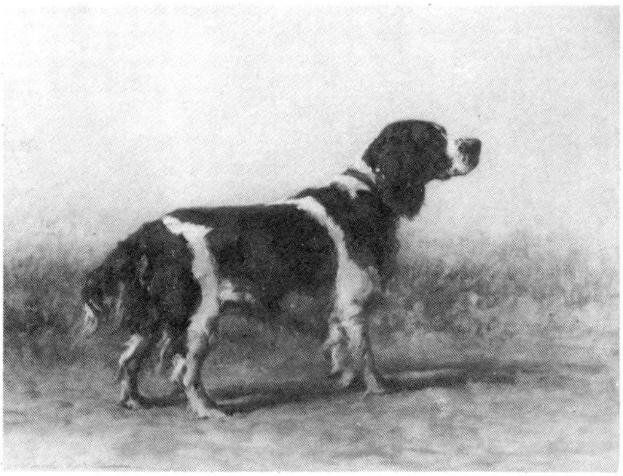

MAUD EARL – A Liver And White Cocker Spaniel – signed and dated 1910 – 18¼ x 24½in.
(Christie's) **$9,504** **£6,600**

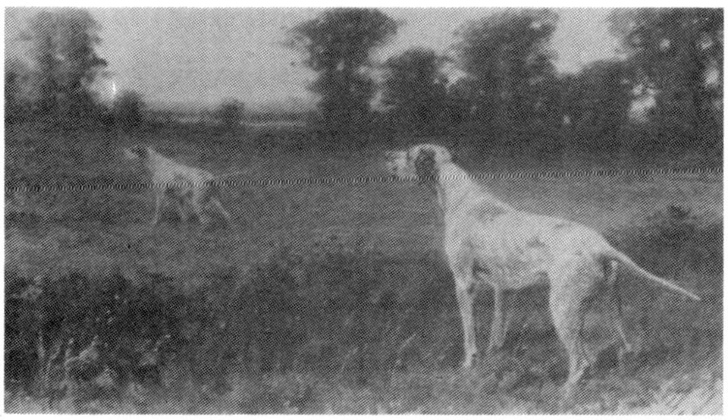

MAUD EARL – Catching The Scent – signed – 17½ x 29in.
(Christie's) **$6,514** **£4,620**

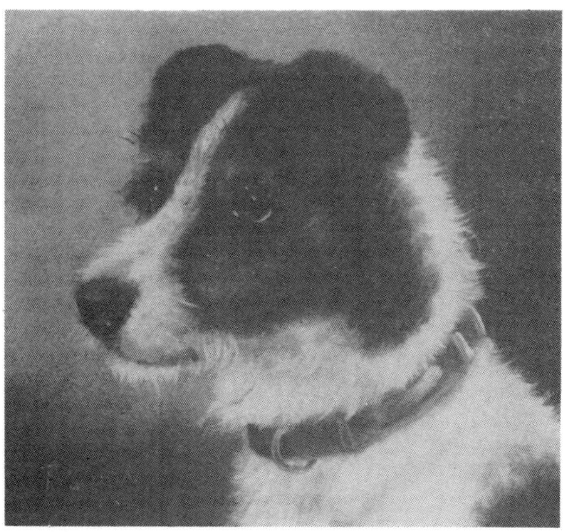

THOMAS EARL – A Wire-Haired Fox Terrier; and A Smooth-Haired Fox Terrier – signed – oil on board – 6 x 6½in.
(Christie's) **$620** **£440 Pair**

SIR ALFRED EAST – An Evening Song – signed – oil on canvas – 51¼ x 87¼in.
(Christie's) **$5,662** **£3,960**

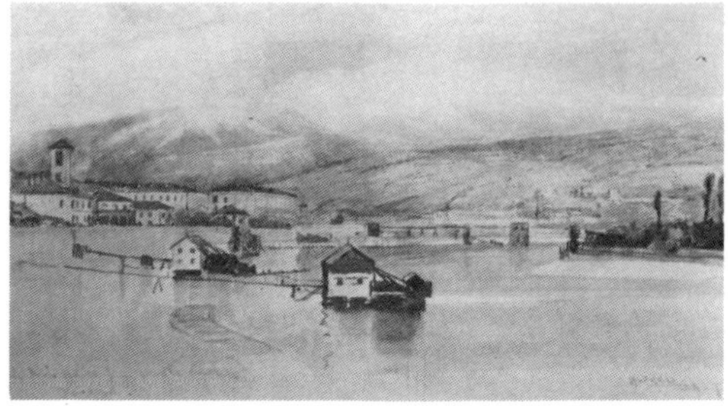

SIR ALFRED EAST – 'Verona' – signed and inscribed – watercolour – 10 x 15in.
(Worsfolds) **$725** **£500**

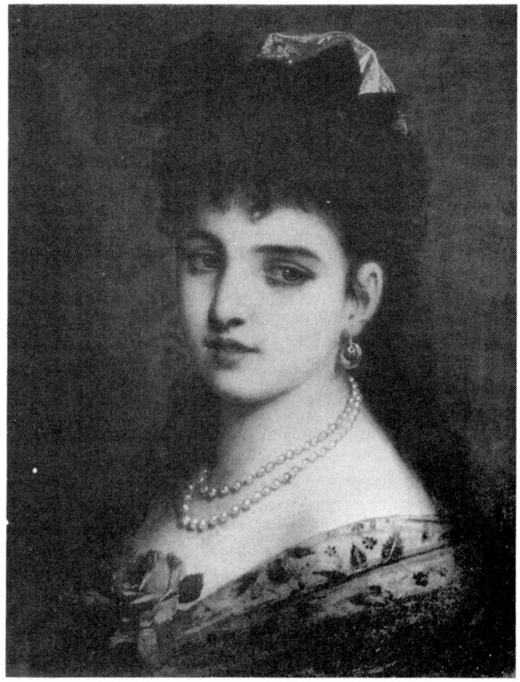

ANTON EBERT – Portrait Of A Lady Said To Be Adelina Patti, Bust Length – signed and inscribed – on panel – 20¾ x 16½in.
(Christie's) **$1,421** **£935**

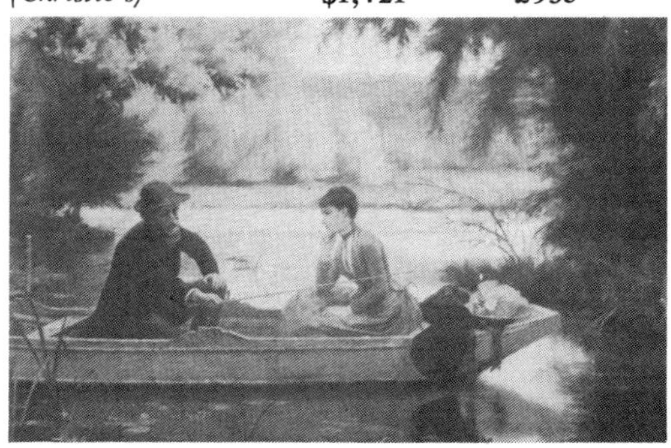

ALBERT JULES EDOUARD – A Quiet Afternoon On The River – signed – oil on canvas – 51 x 66cm.
(Phillips) **$2,567** **£1,700**

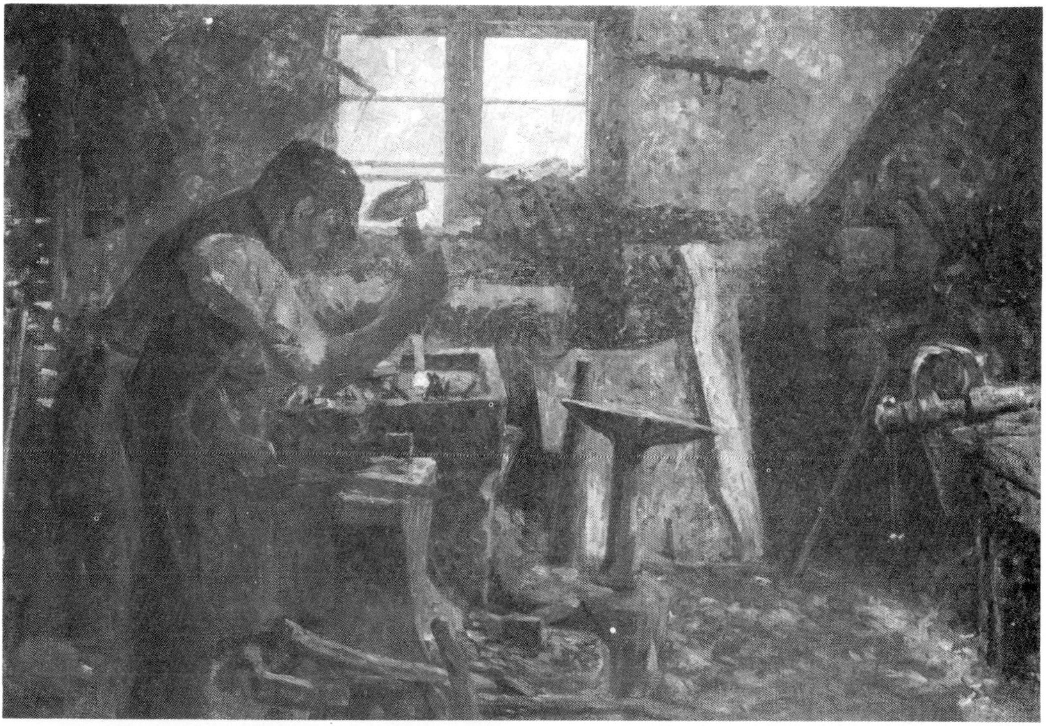

JULIUS VON EHREN – Schmiede – signed – oil on canvas – 26 x 32¼in. *(Christie's)*
£11,088 £7,700

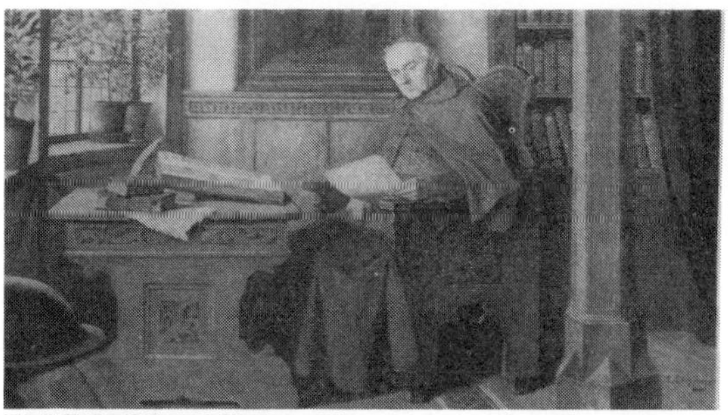

ERWIN EICHINGER – The Letter – signed – on panel – 10¼ x 12¾in.
(Christie's) **$1,839 £1,210**

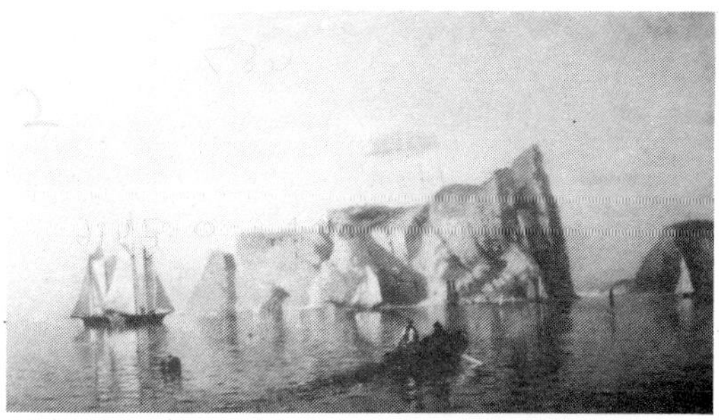

LEMEUL D. ELDRED – Bay Of Fundy – signed and dated 1879 – oil on canvas – 22 x 36in.
(Robt. W. Skinner Inc.) **$10,000 £6,944**

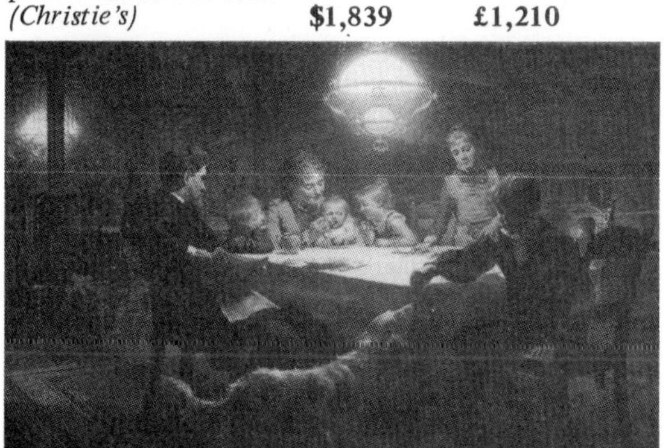

KNUT EKWALL – A Happy Family – signed – on panel – 31½ x 39½in.
(Christie's) **$19,008 £13,200**

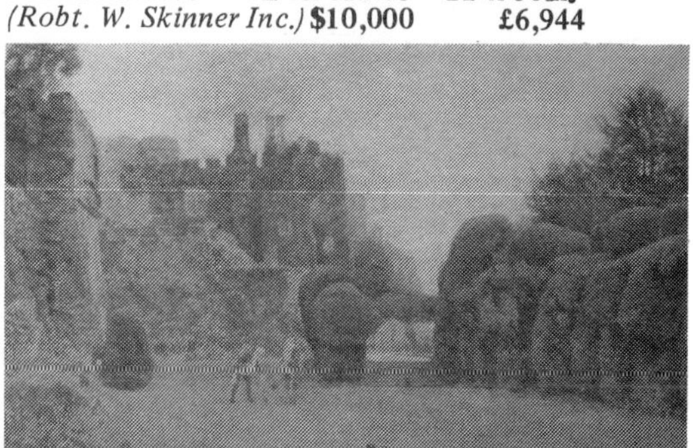

GEORGE SAMUEL ELGOOD – The Bowling Green, Berkley Castle – signed – watercolour – 39 x 59cm.
(Phillips) **$3,260 £2,000**

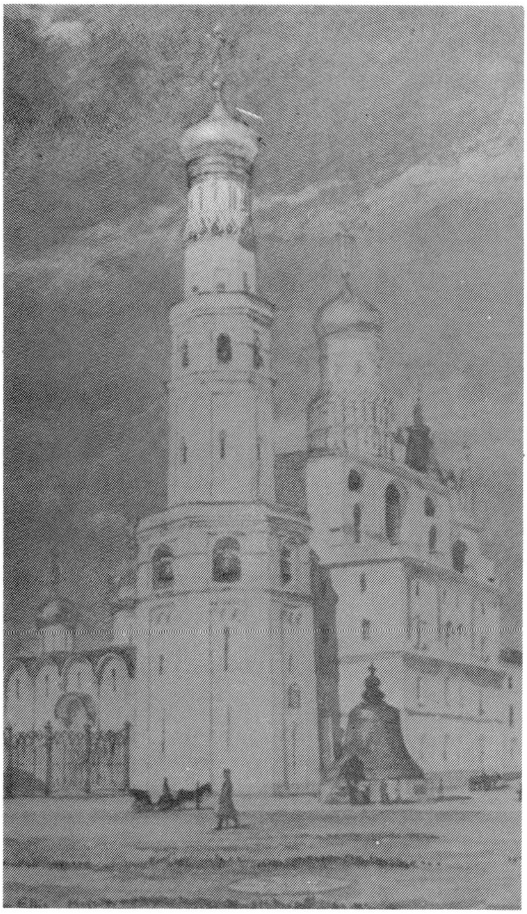

TRISTRAM JAMES ELLIS – The Tsar Bell In The Kremlin, Moscow – signed, inscribed and dated 1897 – pencil and watercolour heightened with white – 14¼ x 10½in.
(Christie's) **$504** **£330**

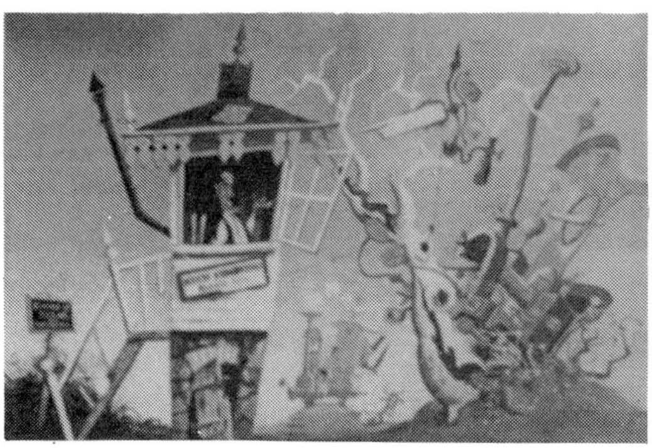

EMETT – Backdrop Design And Working Drawings For Prehistoric Complaint, Penny Plain – watercolour – 15¾ x 20in.
(Prudential Fine Art Auctioneers) **$1,660** **£1,000**

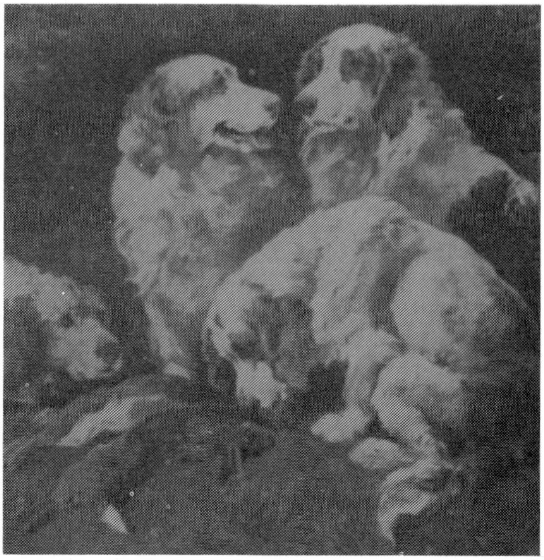

JOHN EMMS – The Day's Bag – signed and dated '83 – on canvas – 21 x 17in.
(Phillips) **$3,220** **£2,000**

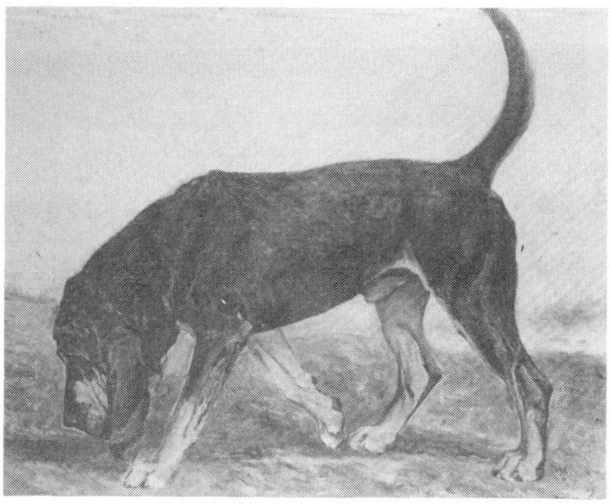

JOHN EMMS – Champion Chatley Blazer, A Bloodhound On The Scent – signed and dated 1905 – oil – 22¾ x 27in.
(Bonhams) **$2,015** **£1,300**

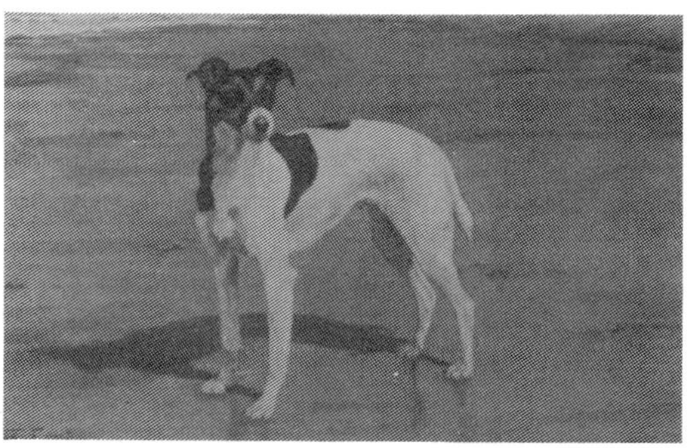

JOHN EMMS, Attributed to – A Fox Terrier On A Beach – with signature – on board – 17 x 23¼in.
(Christie's) **$620** **£440**

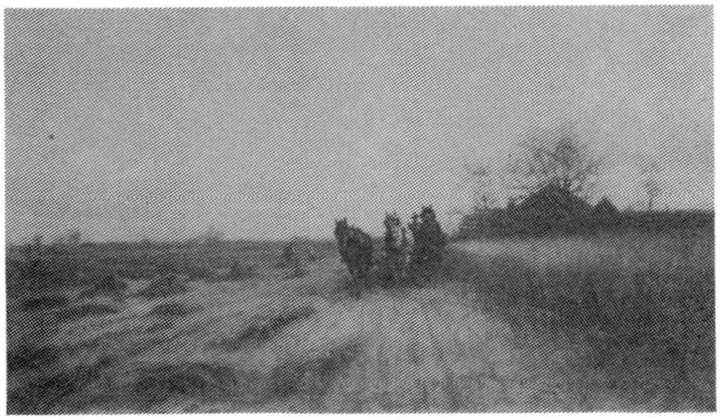

FRANK F. ENGLISH – Harvesting The Fields – signed – oil on canvas – 18 x 30in.
(Christie's) **$3,080** **£2,142**

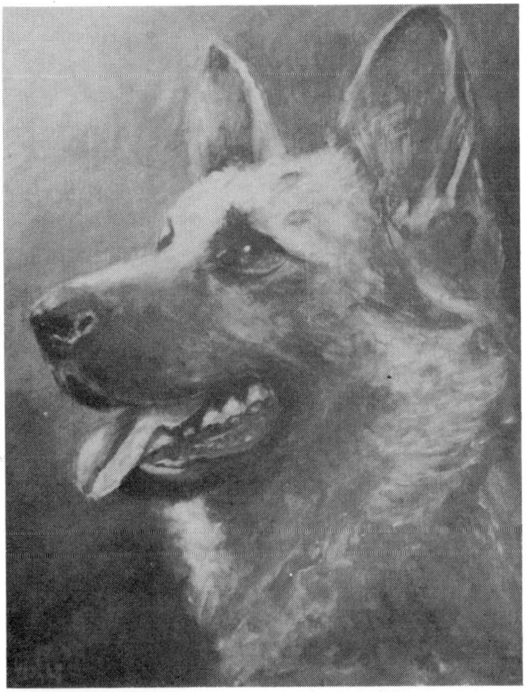

ENGLISH SCHOOL – A Head Of An Alsation – inscribed – oil on hardboard – 10 x 8in.
(Bonhams) **$248** **£160**

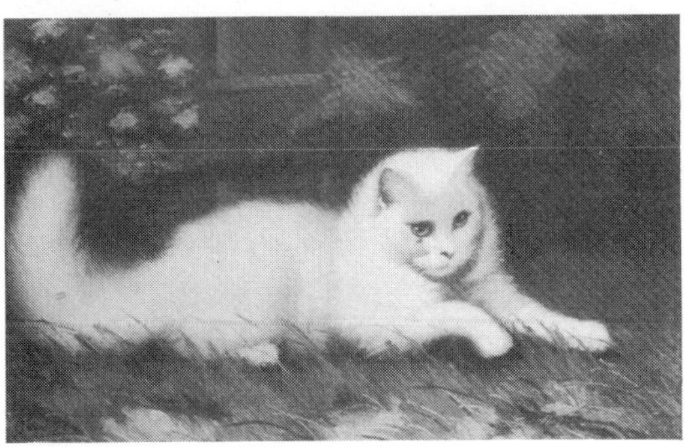

ENGLISH SCHOOL – A White Cat – 15½ x 19½in.
(Christie's) **$1,178** **£770**

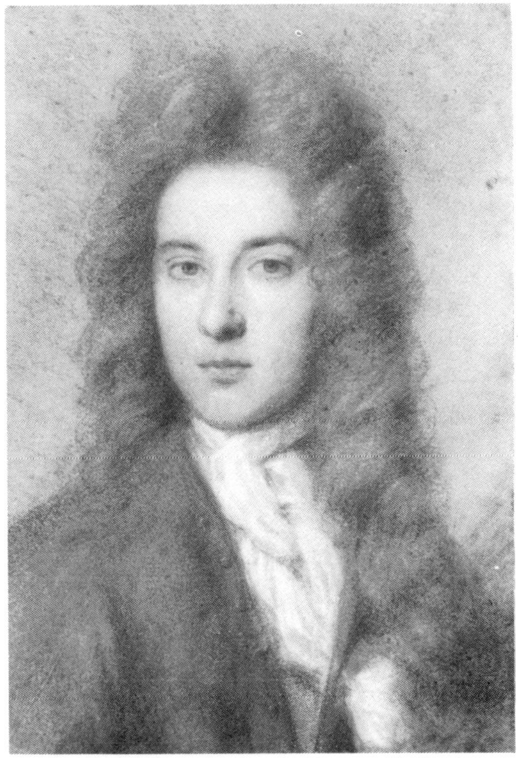

ENGLISH SCHOOL, circa 1700 – Portrait Of A Gentleman, Bust Length, In Flowing Wig, Dark Coat And White Stock – pastel on pale grey paper – 10¾ x 7½in.
(Christie's) **$1,171** **£825**

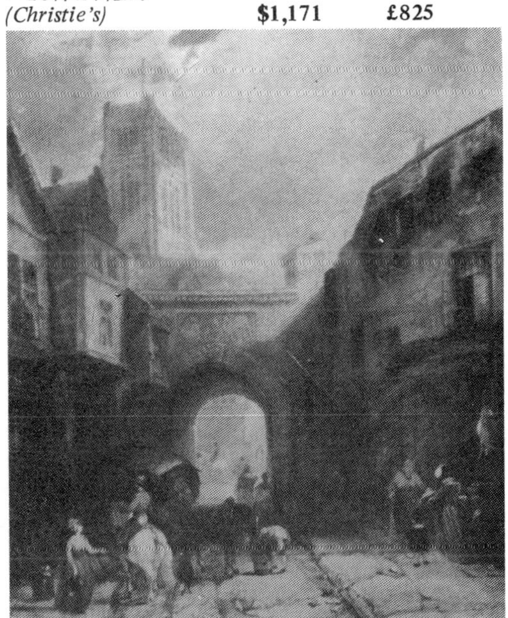

ENGLISH SCHOOL, mid 19th century – The Old Archway, Newcastle-Upon-Tyne – 30 x 25in.
(Christie's) **$1,008** **£715**

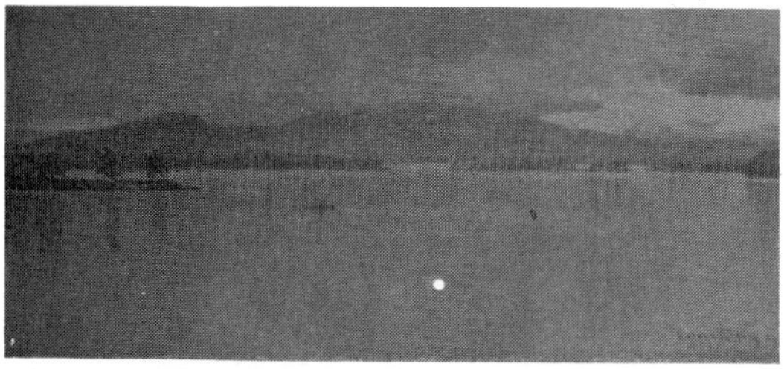

JOHN JOSEPH ENNEKING – Goose Hunting In Maine – signed and dated '92 – oil on board – 8¼ x 17½in.
(Robt. W. Skinner Inc.) **$25,000** **£15,337**

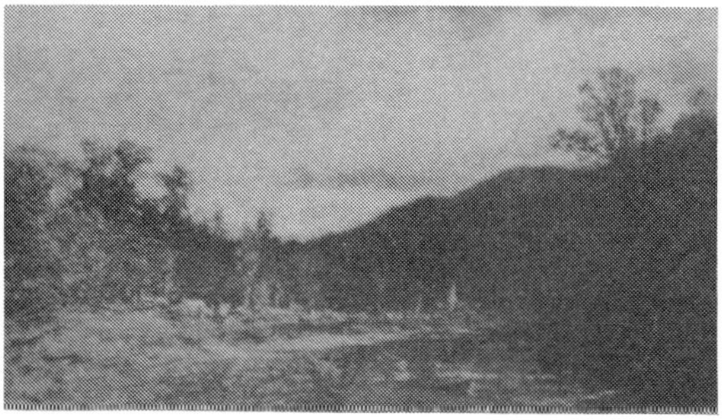

JOHN JOSEPH ENNEKING – River Landscape With Cows – oil on panel – 6½ x 9¼in.
(Robt. W. Skinner Inc.) **$700** **£429**

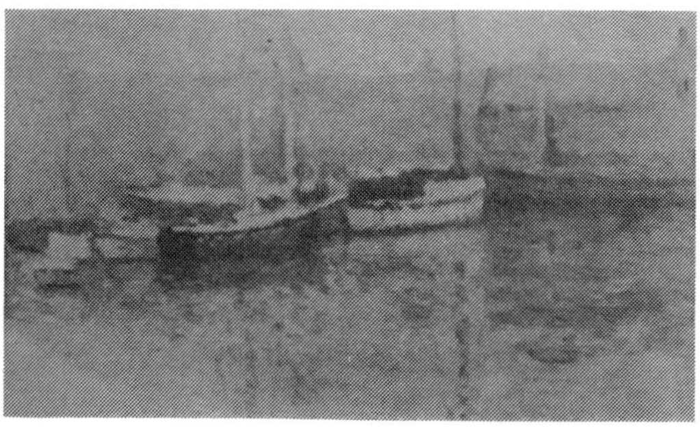

JOSEPH ELIOT ENNEKING – Schooners At Dock – signed – oil on board – 10 x 12in.
(Robt. W. Skinner Inc.) **$550** **£337**

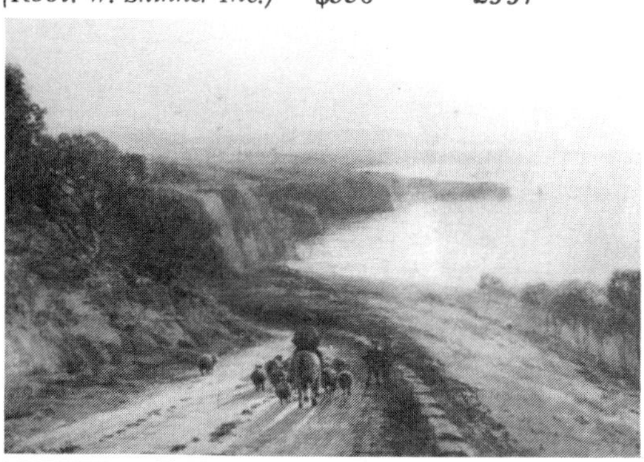

ARTHUR H. ENOCK – Coastal Scene With Shepherd On Horseback Herding Sheep Past Two Children On A Lane – signed – watercolour – 12 x 15in.
(Biddle & Webb) **$790** **£520**

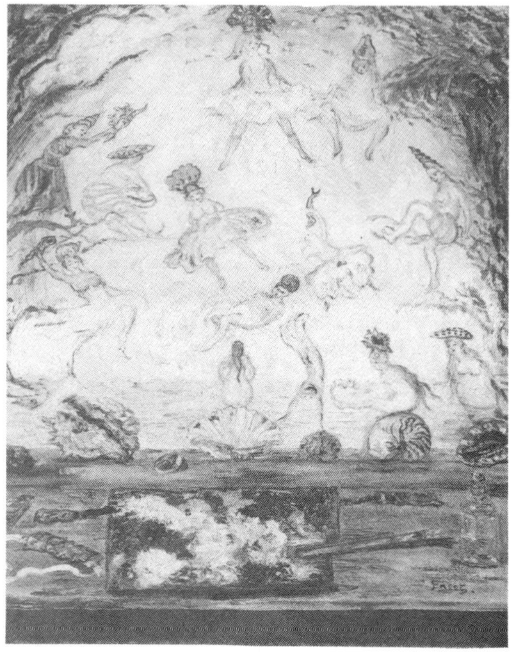

JAMES ENSOR – Crachats de Tubes, Caresses de Pinceau – signed, also signed on the reverse – oil on canvas – 23½ x 20in.
(Christie's) **$55,440** **£38,500**

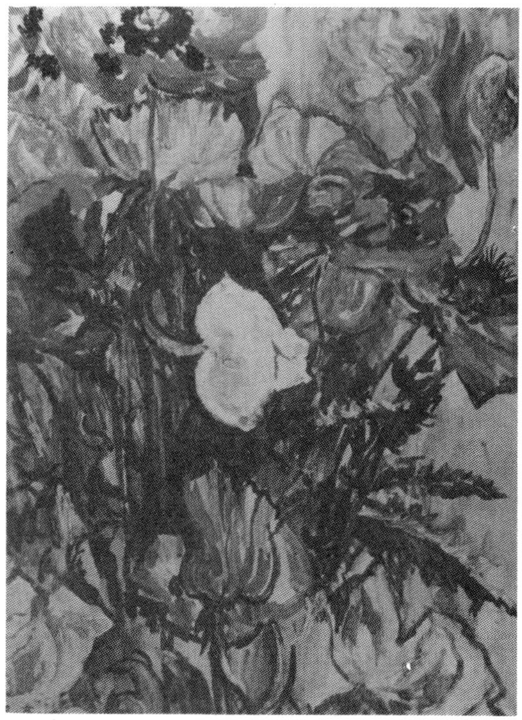

SIR JACOB EPSTEIN – Still Life With Poppies – signed – watercolour and bodycolour – 57 x 44cm.
(Phillips) **$3,519** **£2,300**

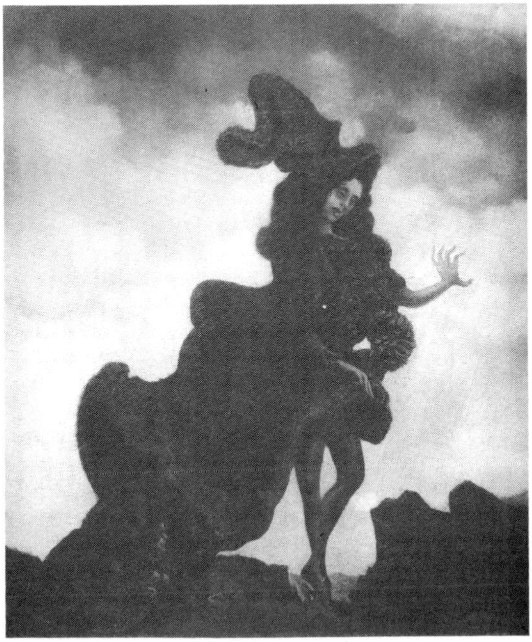

MAX ERNST – La Fuite – signed and dated '40, also signed, inscribed and dated on the reverse – oil on canvas – 21½ x 18¼in.
(Christie's) **$150,480 £104,500**

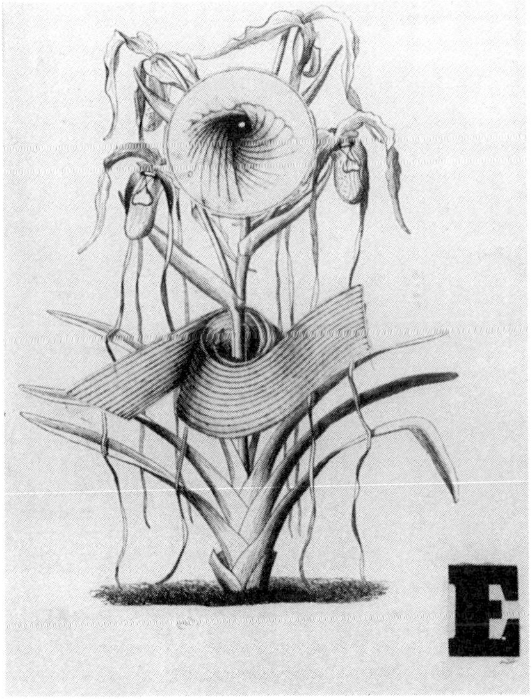

MAX ERNST – 'E' – signed – collage – 6¾ x 5¼in.
(Christie's) **$6,336 £4,400**

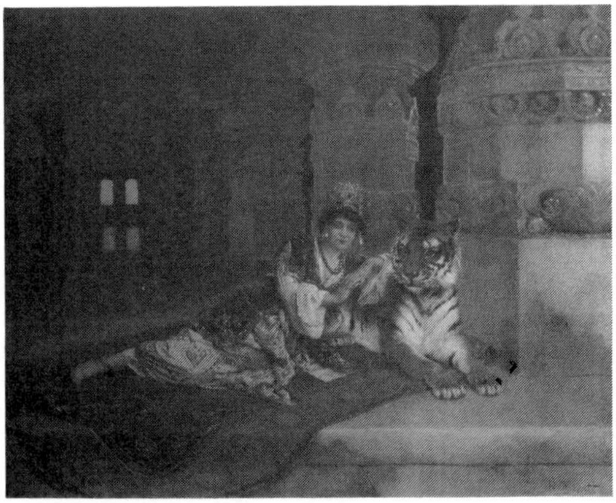

RUDOLPH ERNST – A Princess With Her Tiger – signed – oil on canvas – 38 x 46cm.
(Phillips) **$10,800 £7,500**

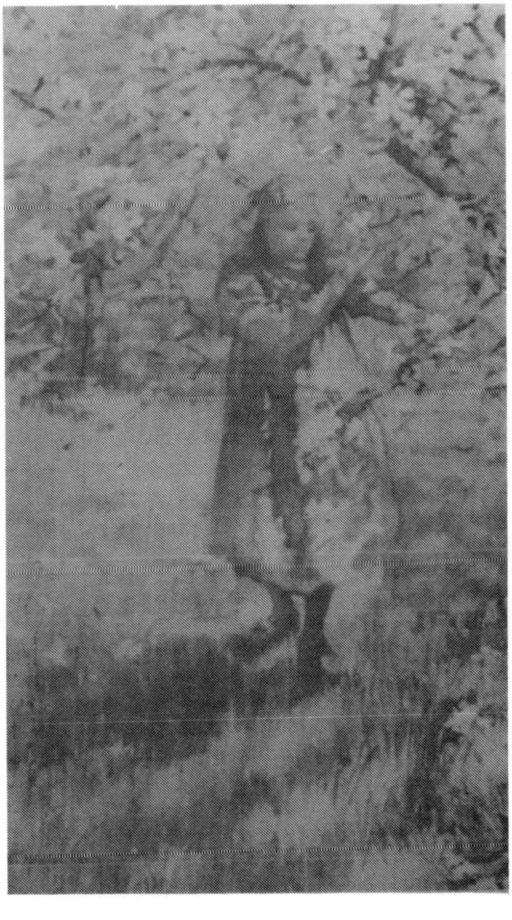

ETHEL HORSFALL ERTZ – A Young Girl In Blue Dress Before The Flowering Bough Of An Apple Tree – signed – 15½ x 9in.
(W. H. Lane & Son) **$886 £620**

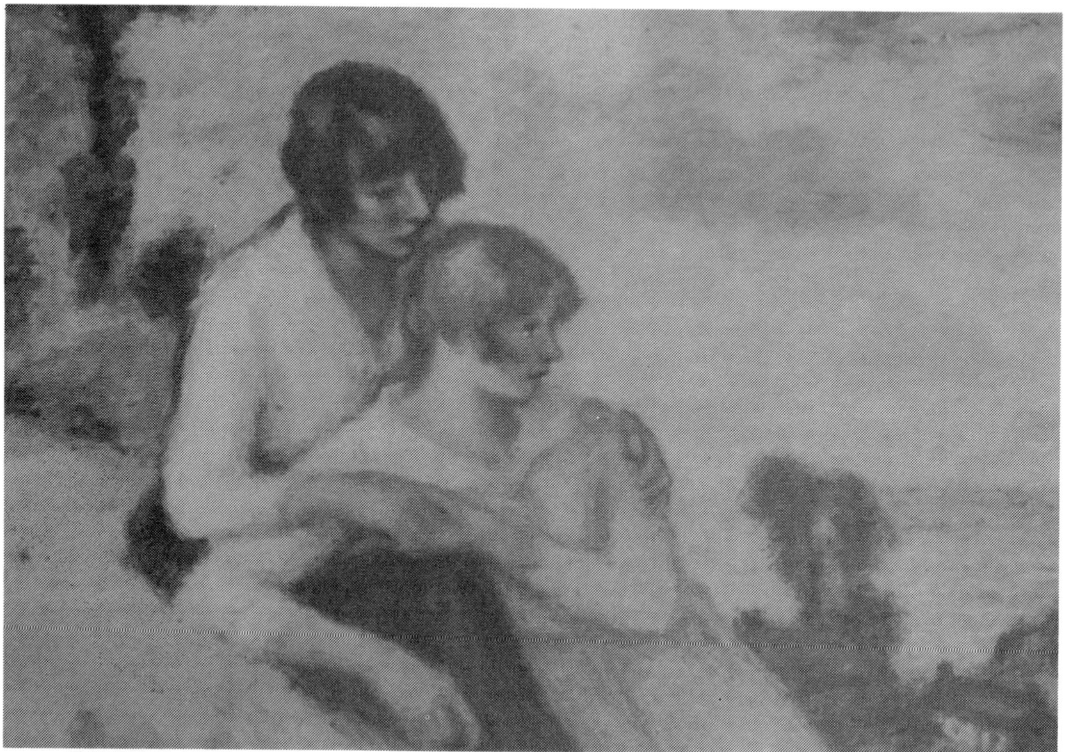

GEORGES d'ESPAGNAT – Jeunes Filles dan un Paysage – signed with initials – oil on canvas – 35 x 39¼in. *(Christie's)* **$12,859 £7,700**

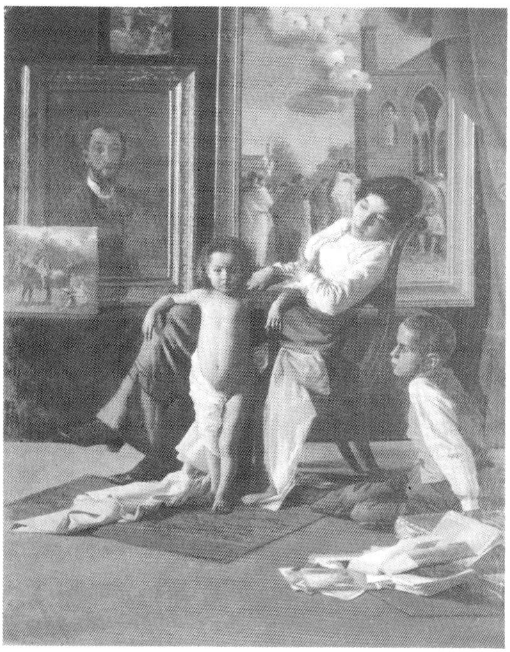

GAETANO ESPOSITO – In The Studio – 31 x 25in.
(Christie's) **$19,008 £13,200**

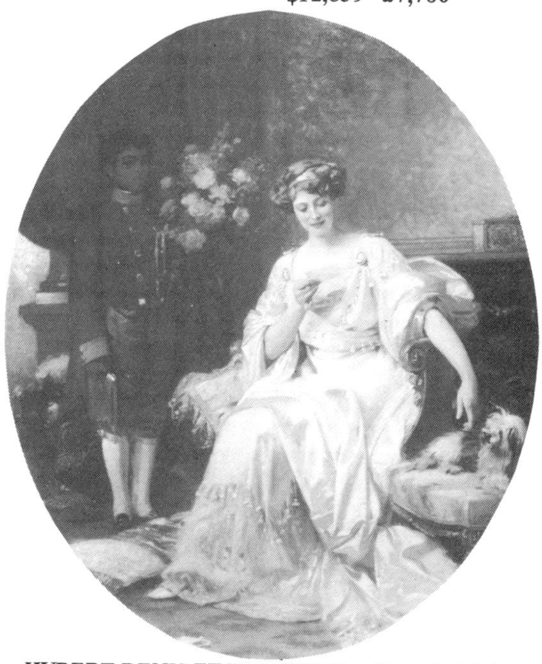

HUBERT DENIS ETCHEVERRY – Portrait Of A Lady, Said To Be Anna De Noailles, Seated, Full Length, With A Negro Page In An Interior – signed – 78 x 63in.
(Christie's) **$39,600 £27,500**

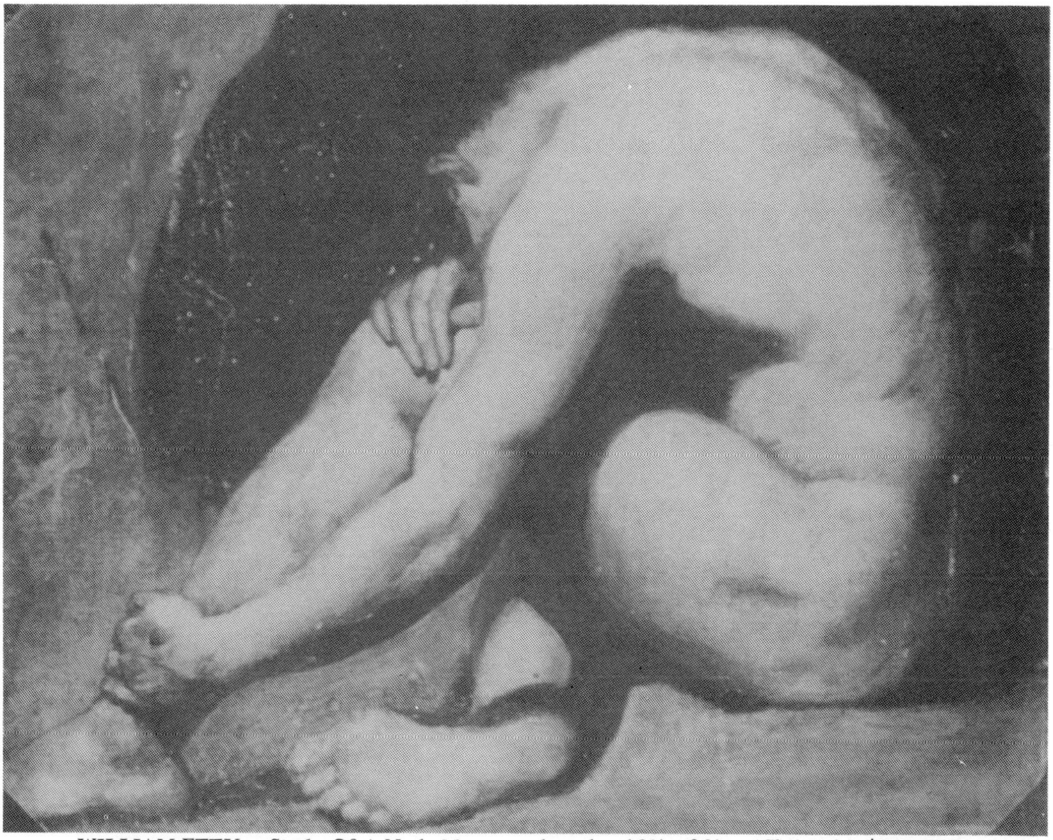

WILLIAM ETTY – Study Of A Nude Man – on board – 18¾ x 23in. *(Christie's)* **$648 £432**

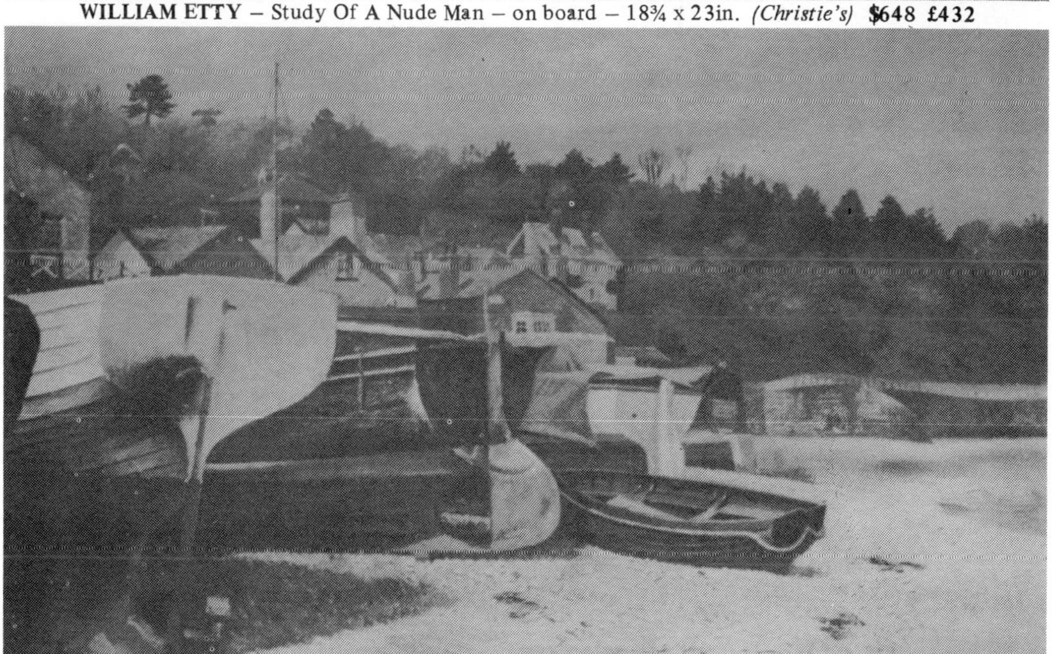

RICHARD EURICH – Moored Boats On A Beach – signed and dated '38 – oil on canvas – 15½ x 19½in. *(Christie's)* **$4,835 £3,080**

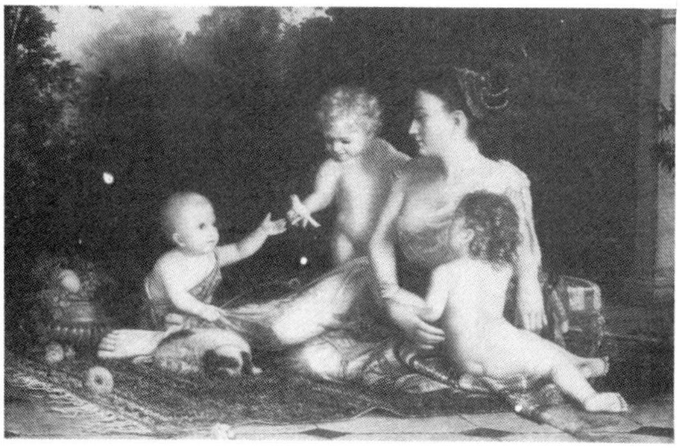

DE SCOTT EVANS – Roman Motherhood – signed and dated 1877-79 – oil on canvas – 53½ x 72½in.
(Christie's) **$6,600 £4,639**

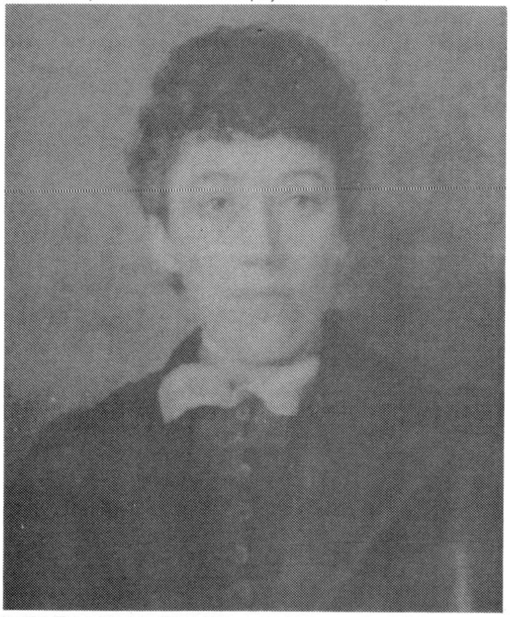

FREDERICK M. EVANS – Half Portrait Of An Attractive Lady In Blue Cravat And Jacket – signed – watercolour – 9¾ x 7in.
(W. H. Lane & Son) **$558 £360**

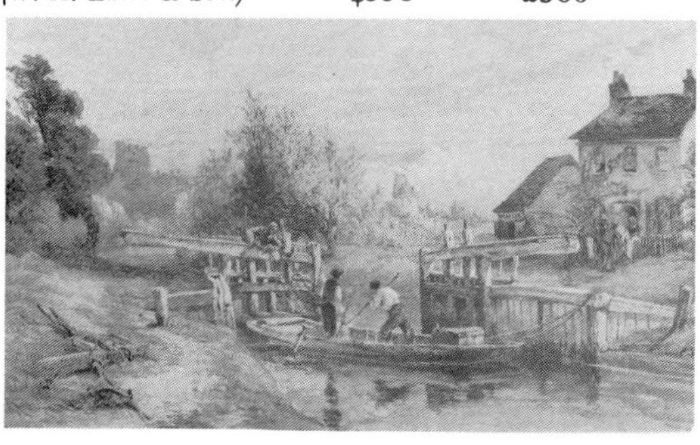

WILLIAM EVANS of Eton – Romney Lock, Near Windsor – pencil and watercolour heightened with white – 12¼ x 18¾in.
(Christie's) **$5,511 £3,300**

DAVID SHANKS EWART – These Shall Our Hearts Remember – signed and dated 1928 – oil on canvas – 171 x 80cm.
(Phillips) **$4,480 £2,800**

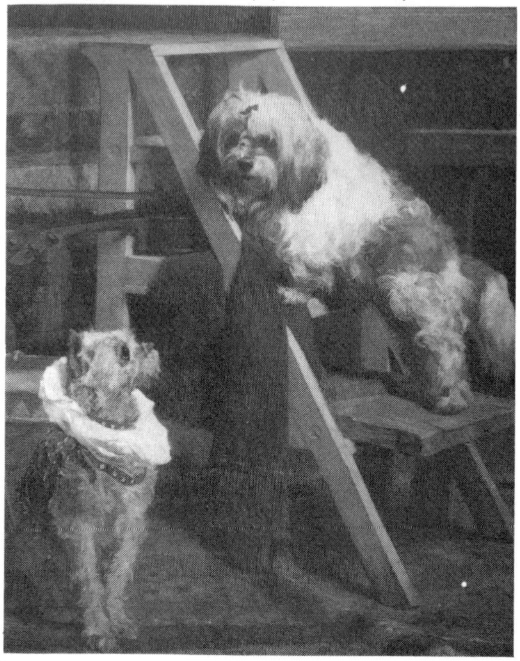

CHARLES H. VAN DEN EYCKEN – A Circus Romance – signed and dated 1889 – oil – 26 x 21¼in.
(Bonhams) **$4,650 £3,000**

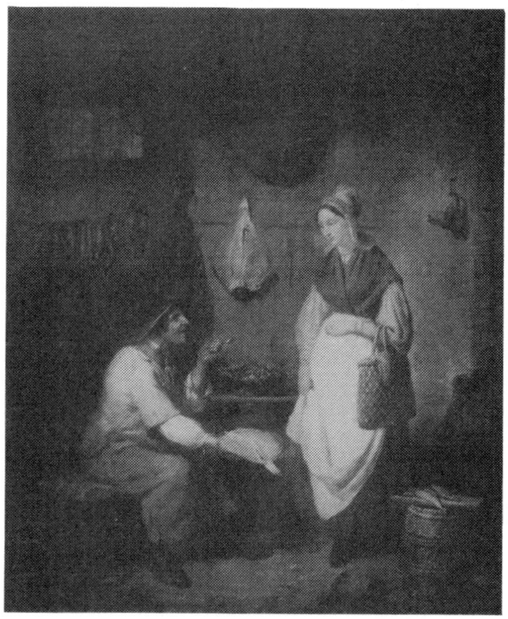

JEAN BAPTISTE VAN EYCKEN – In A Fishmonger's Shop – signed – oil on panel – 21½ x 18¼in.
(Christie's) **$2,420 £1,579**

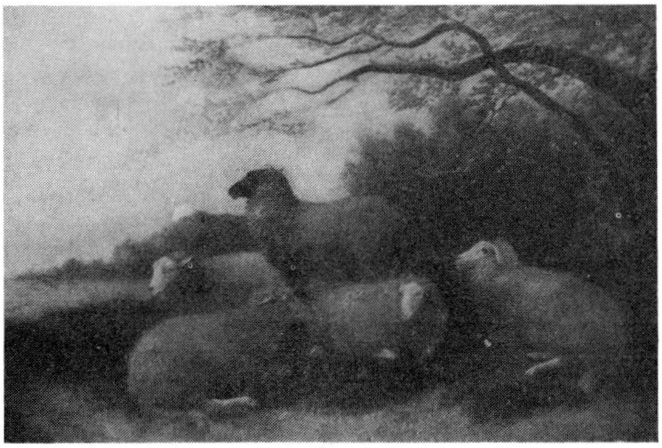

F.B. – Sheep In A Wooded Landscape – monogram and signed indistinctly – oil – 10 x 18in.
(Warners) **$736** **£460**

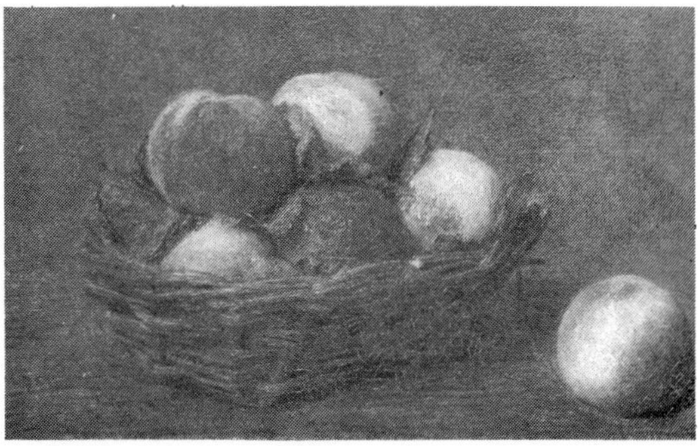

HENRI FANTIN-LATOUR – Nature morte aux Peches – signed and dated '96 – oil on canvas – 11¾ x 15¾in.
(Christie's) **$60,192** **£41,800**

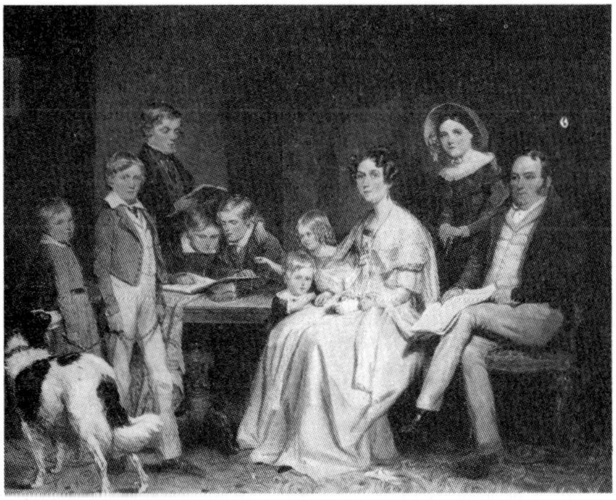

THOMAS FAED – The Leisham Family Of Tillicoultry, Clackmannanshire, Seated Round A Table – 40 x 49in.
(Christie's) **$8,712** **£6,050**

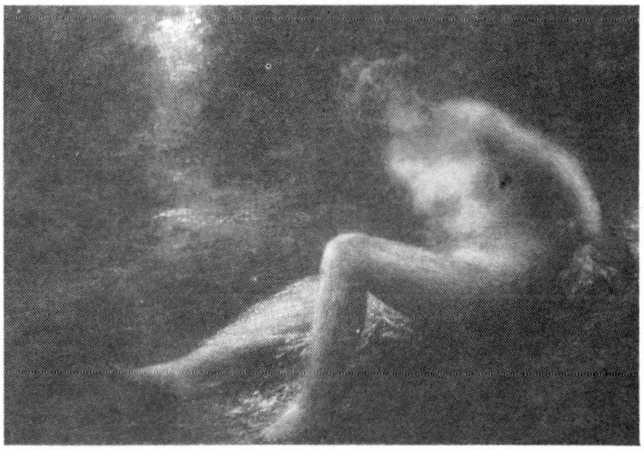

HENRI FANTIN-LATOUR – Chasseresse – signed – oil on canvas – 15½ x 18½in.
(Christie's) **$19,008** **£13,200**

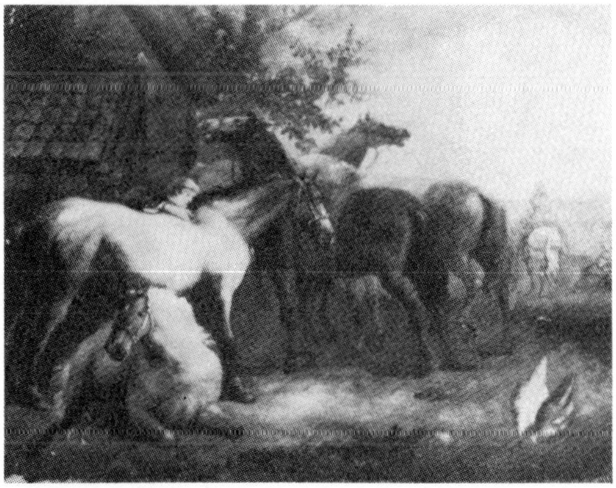

CAREL VAN FALENS, Circle of – A Groom Tending To Tethered Horses Before An Inn, A Mounted Traveller Rides Away – oil on copper – 5¼ x 6¾in.
(Phillips) **$846** **£600**

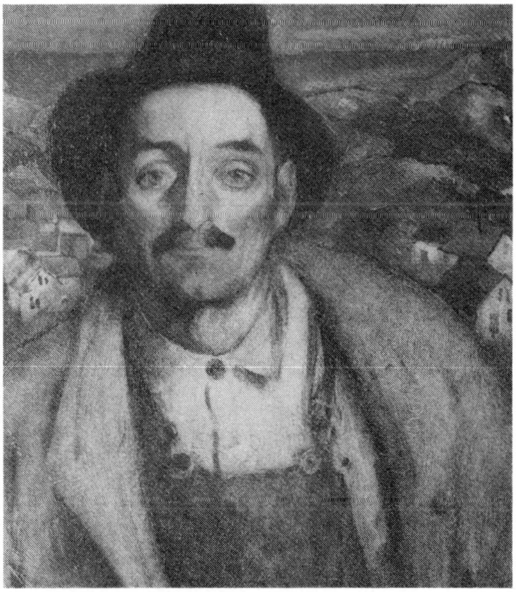

JERRY FARNSWORTH – Manuel – signed and dated '24 – oil on canvas – 22 x 18in.
(Christie's) **$1,210** **£753**

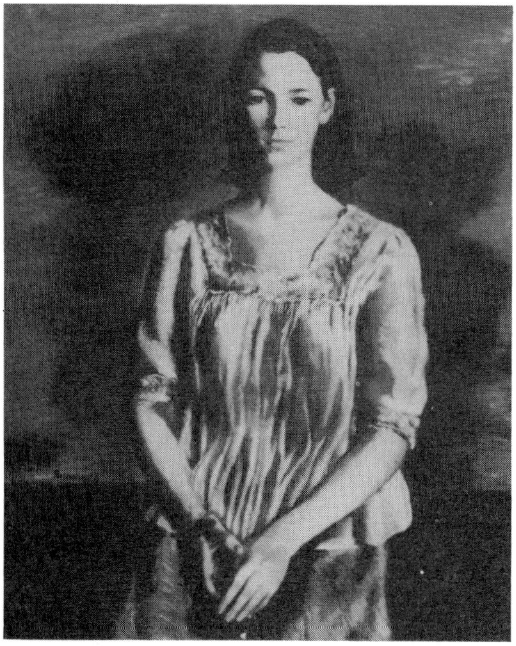

JERRY FARNSWORTH – The Young Girl – signed, also signed on the reverse – oil on canvas – 35 x 30in.
(Christie's) **$1,650 £1,028**

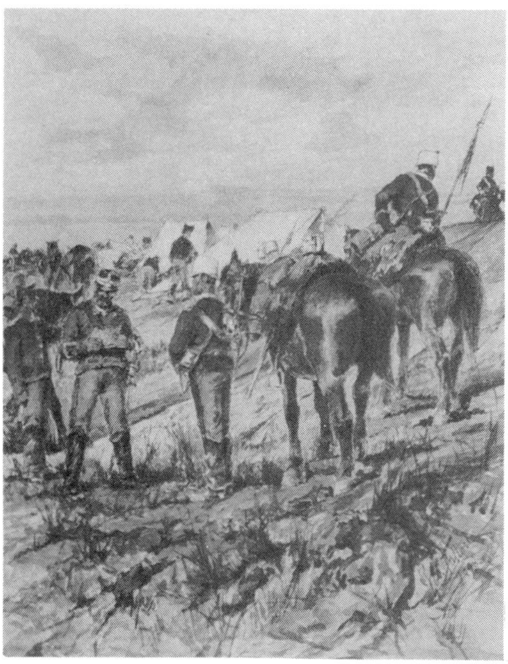

GIOVANNI FATTORI – A Military Encampment – signed and dated 1898 – pen, ink and watercolour – 17¾ x 13¾in.
(Christie's) **$65,736 £39,600**

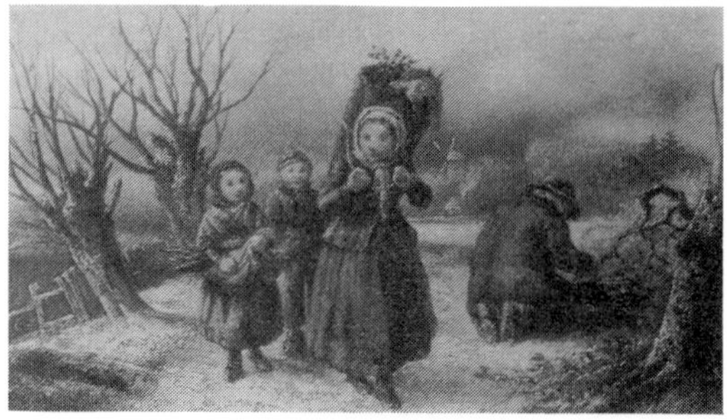

R. FAVELLE – Young Faggot Gatherers – signed and dated 1864 – on panel – 9 x 12in.
(Christie's) **$4,681 £3,080**

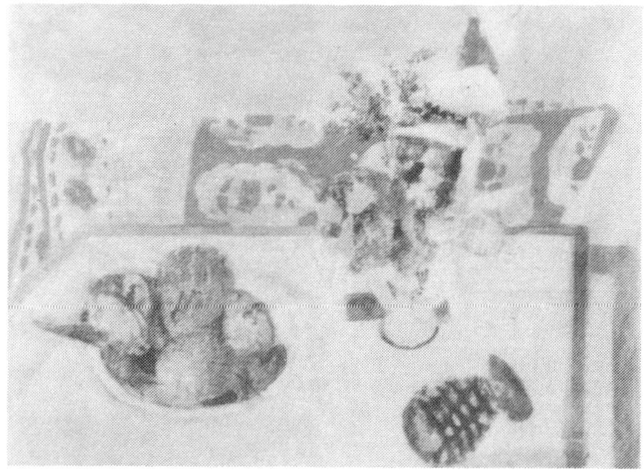

PIERRE FAVRE – Nature morte sur la Table – signed and dated '55 – oil on canvas – 32 x 39¼in.
(Christie's) **$880 £550**

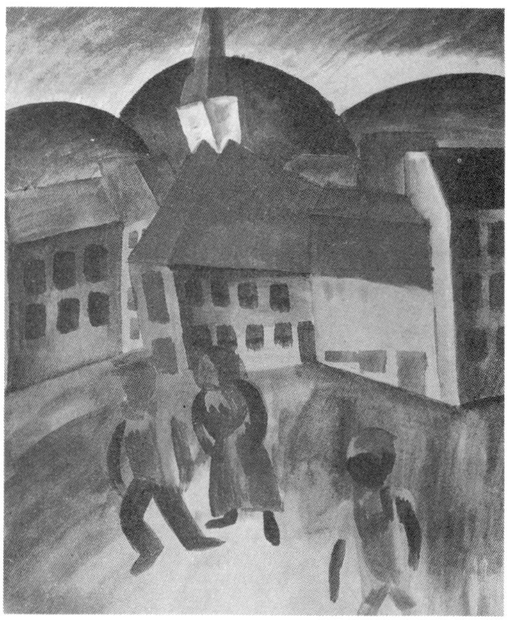

CONRAD FELIXMULLER – Sachsische kleine Stadt – signed, inscribed on the reverse – watercolour on paper – 23 x 18in.
(Christie's) **$34,848 £24,200**

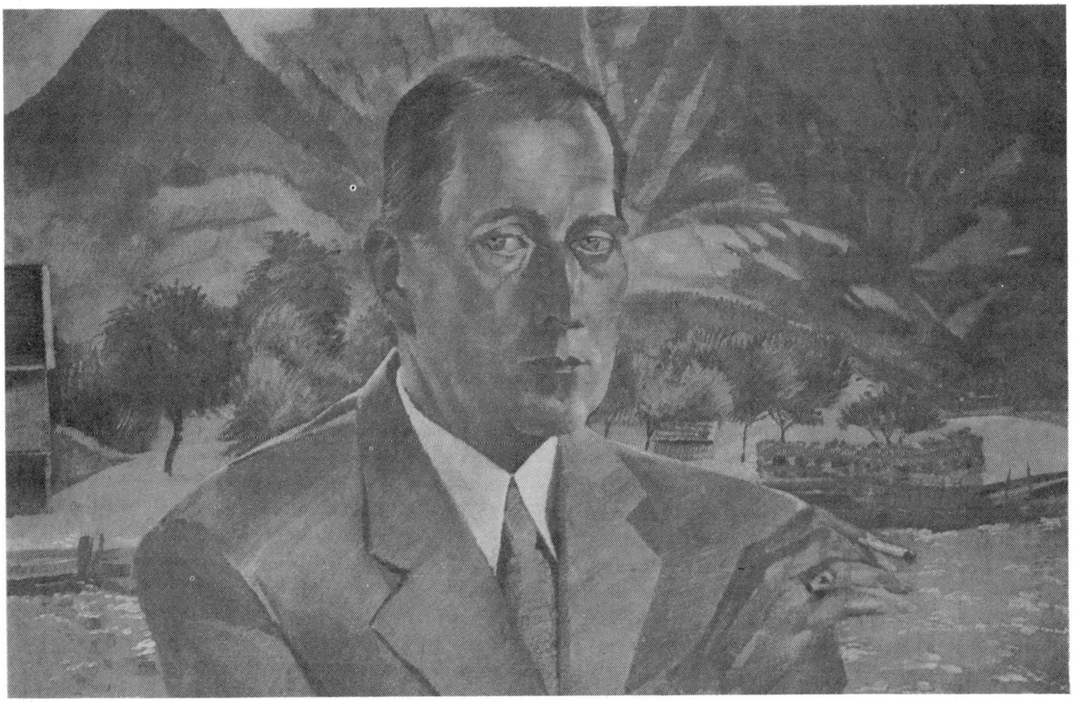

CONRAD FELIXMULLER – Bildnis des Baron Nicolaus von Hoting, im Hintergrund Berchtesgaden mit Watzmann – signed and dated 1930 – oil on canvas – 22¾ x 26½in. *(Christie's)* **$19,360 £12,100**

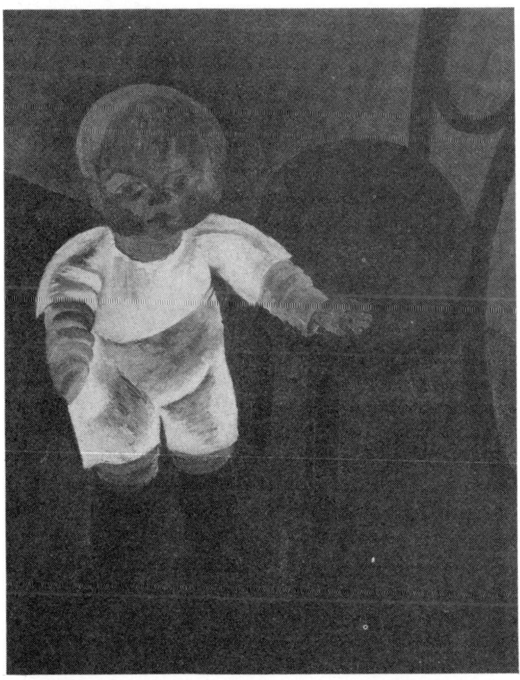

CONRAD FELIXMULLER – Luca Portrait – signed, and signed on the reverse – oil on canvas – 38 x 29¼in.
(Christie's) **$58,784 £35,200**

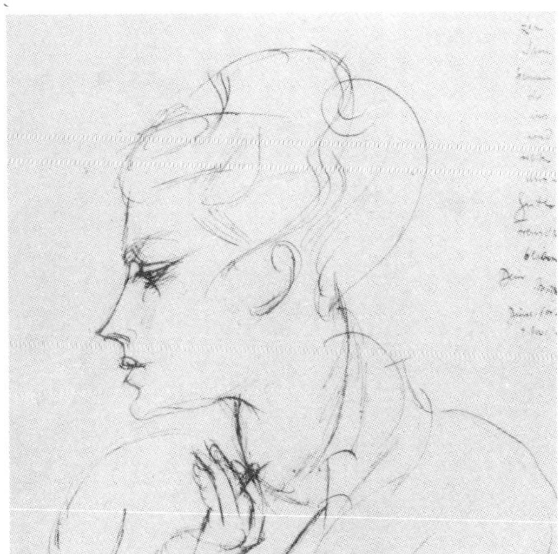

CONRAD FELIXMULLER – Frau mit einer Zigarette – signed and dated '18, and inscribed – pen and black ink on paper – 17 x 13in.
(Christie's) **$2,217 £1,540**

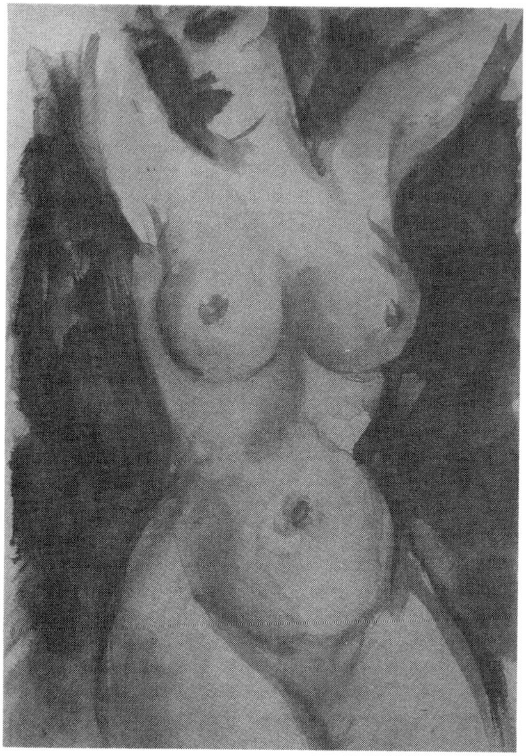

JOHN DUNCAN FERGUSSON – Seated Nude In A Landscape – watercolour – 7¼ x 5¼in.
(Christie's) **$5,040** **£3,500**

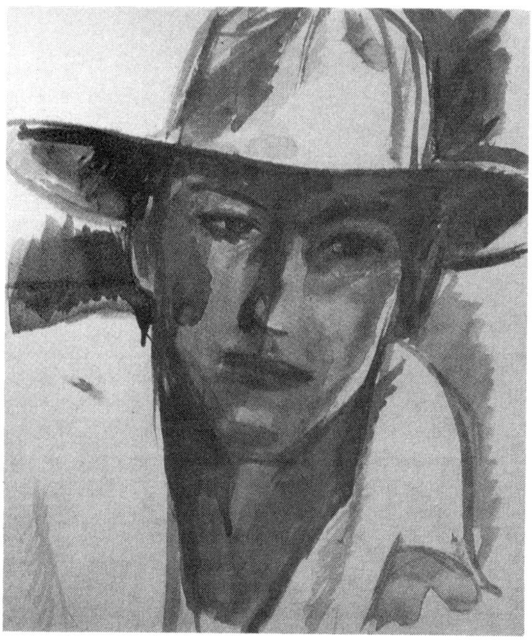

JOHN DUNCAN FERGUSSON – Self Portrait, 21st July 1929 – watercolour - 9¾ x 7¾in.
(Christie's) **$5,040** **£3,500**

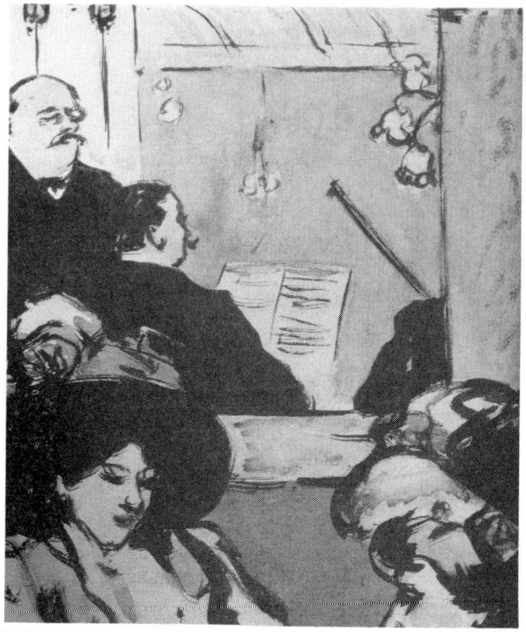

JOHN DUNCAN FERGUSSON – Cafe Dameseuil, Gare Montparnasse – signed, inscribed and dated 1907 verso – watercolour heightened with white – 15¾ x 12½in.
(Christie's) **$6,912** **£4,800**

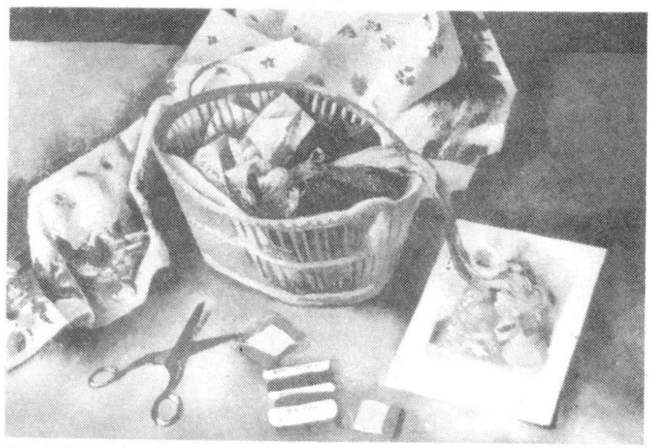

PAUL-ELIE FERNEZ – Nature morte au Neccessaire a Couture – signed – oil on canvas – 21½ x 28¾in.
(Christie's) **$5,280** **£3,300**

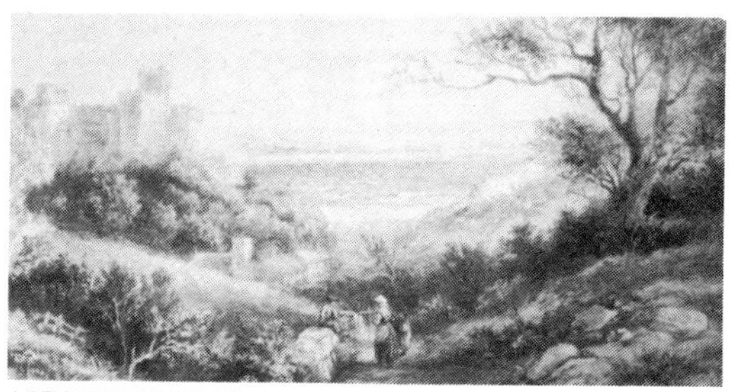

ANTHONY VANDYKE COPLEY FIELDING – View Of Donat's Castle – watercolour – 7 x 11in.
(Parsons, Welch & Cowell) **$483** **£320**

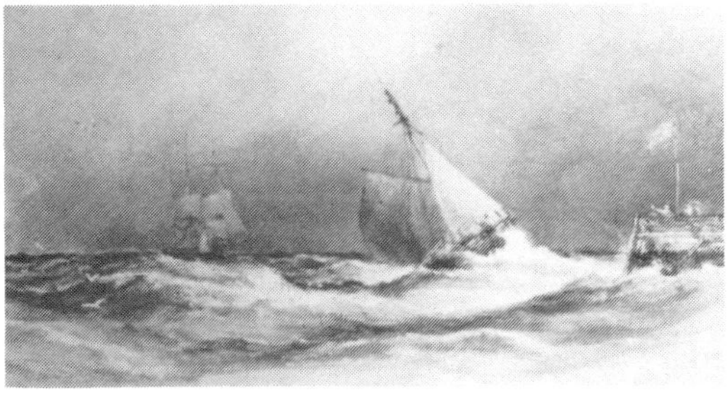

COPLEY FIELDING – 'A Stiff Breeze', Fishing Boat Approach Approaching A Breakwater On A Rough Day, Three-Master On The Skyline – signed and dated – oil – 8 x 12in.
(Capes, Dunn & Co.) **$733** **£450**

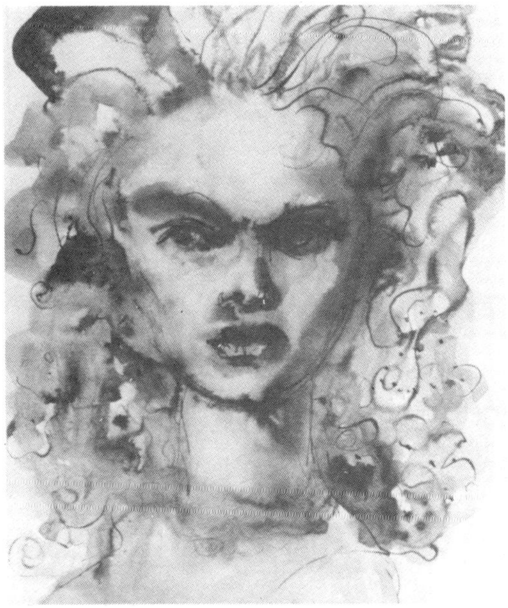

LEONOR FINI – Tete de Jeune Fille – signed and dated 1945 – watercolour and pen and ink on buff paper – 13½ x 10in.
(Christie's) **$2,534** **£1,760**

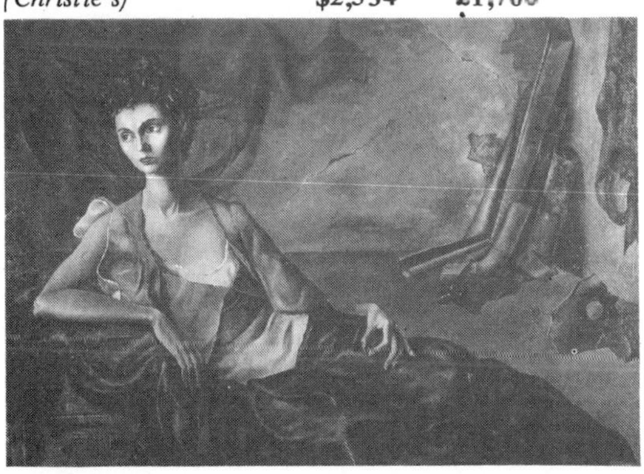

LEONOR FINI – La Marquise Miha Ferni (nee Princesse Colonna di Cesare) – signed – oil on canvas – 22¾ x 30¾in.
(Christie's) **$31,680** **£22,000**

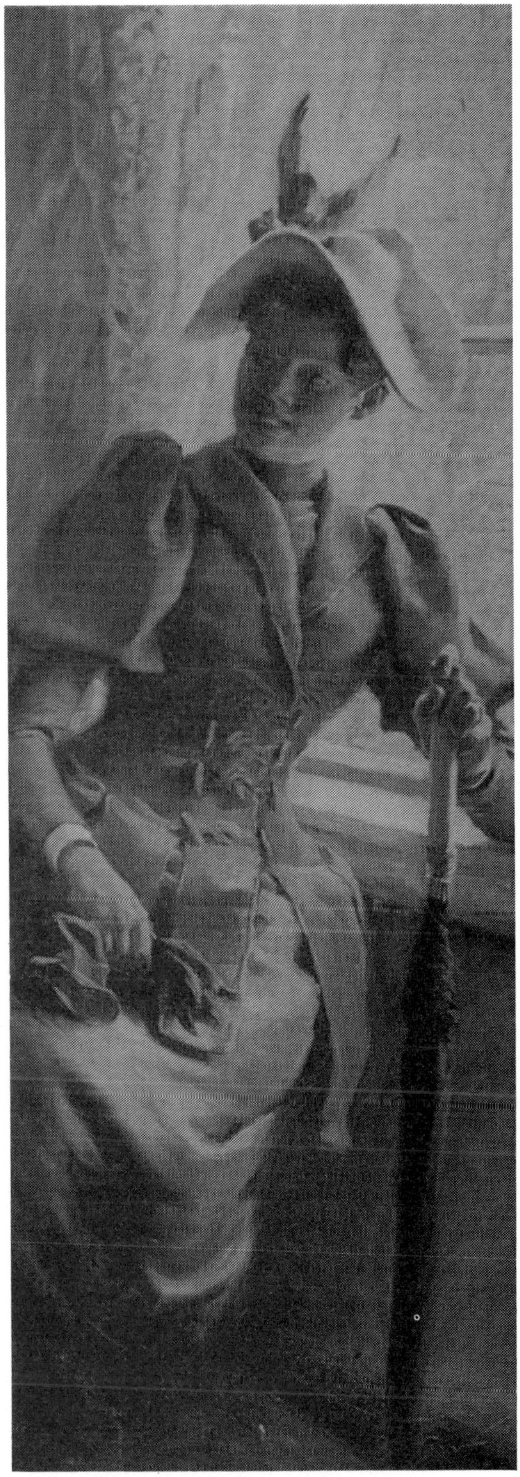

PAUL FISCHER – At The Window – signed and dated 1892 – 25½ x 11in.
(Christie's) **$10,560** **£6,600**

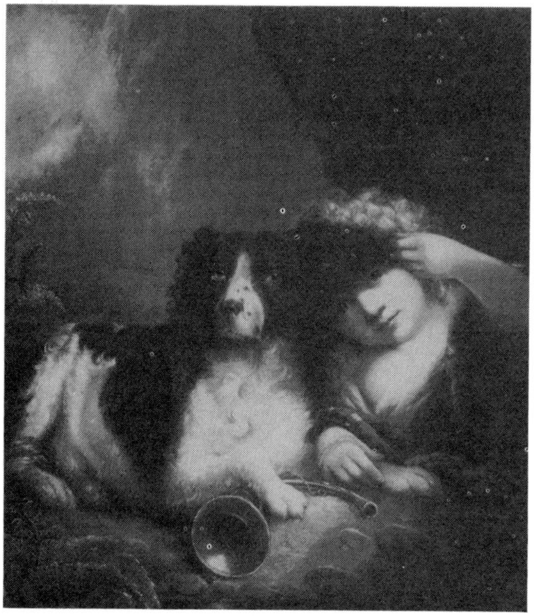

ALVAN FISHER – Chieftain's Son – signed and dated 1834 on the reverse – oil on canvas – 30 x 25¼in.
(Christie's) **$4,400** **£2,741**

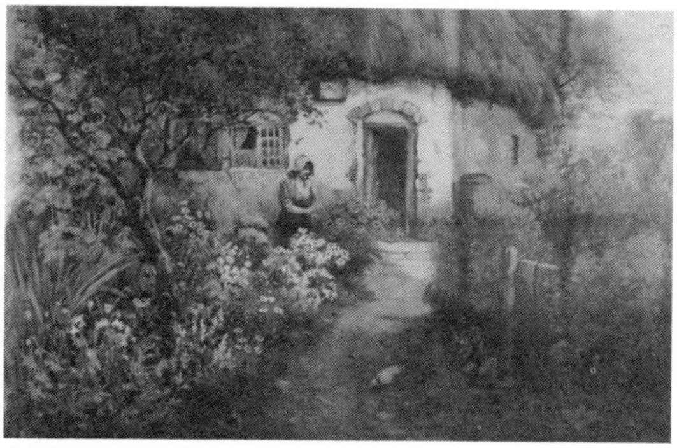

JOSHUA FISHER – Thatched Cottage Garden With Woman Picking Sunflowers – signed – watercolour – 11½ x 17¾in.
(Hobbs & Chambers) **$477** **£310**

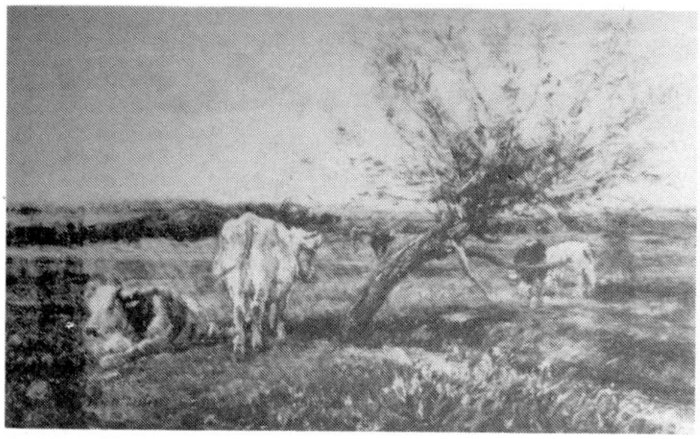

MARK FISHER – Cattle In A Landscape – signed – oil on canvas – 30 x 46cm.
(Phillips) **$688** **£450**

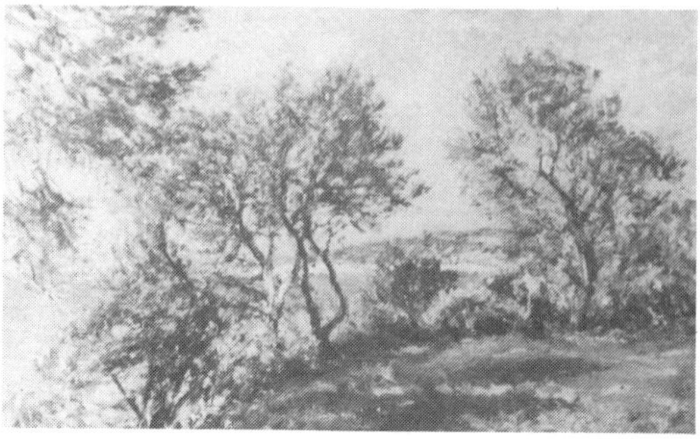

MARK FISHER – A Southern Bay – signed – oil on canvas – 46 x 66cm.
(Phillips) **$1,499** **£980**

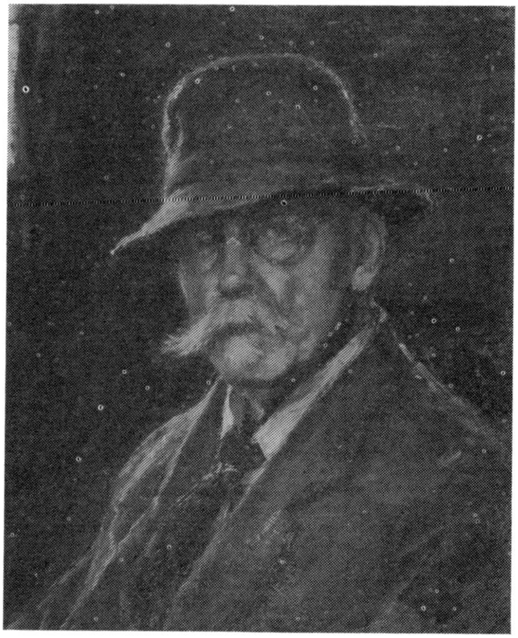

MARK FISHER – Self Portrait – oil on canvas – 51 x 41cm.
(Phillips) **$3,408** **£2,400**

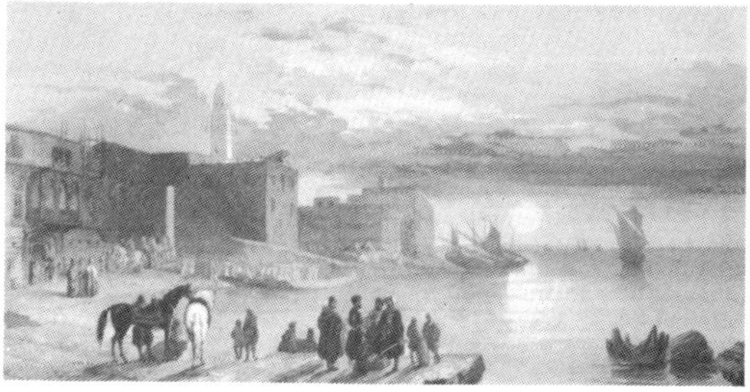

HENRY FITZCOOK, Attributed to – The Route Of The Overland Mail To India – An Album Of Watercolours Recording The Diorama Of 1850 – nine signed with monogram – pencil and watercolour heightened with white – 31 drawings – 8½ x 12½in., 23 x 20in. overall.
(Christie's) **$36,352** **£23,760**

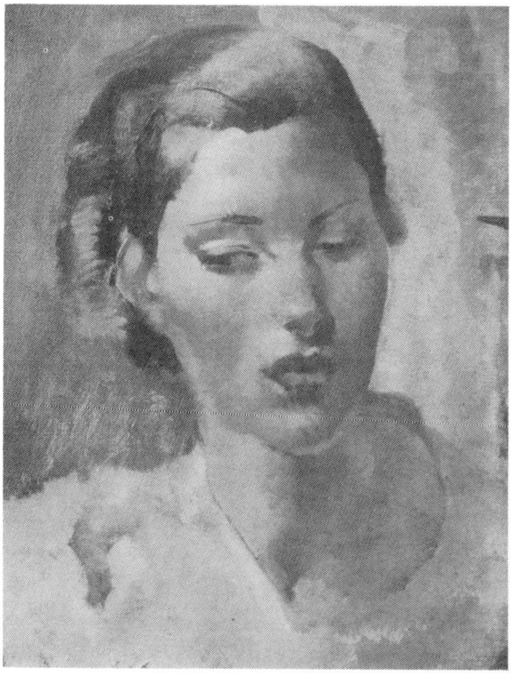

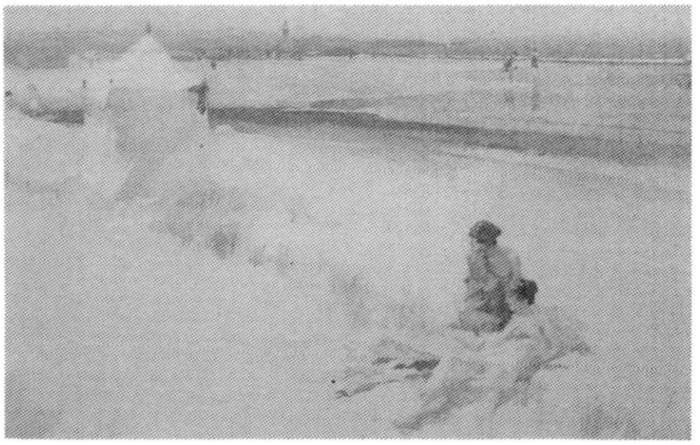

SIR WILLIAM RUSSELL FLINT – Afternoon Idleness, Bamburgh – signed – watercolour – 49 x 67 cm.
(Phillips) **$22,400** **£14,000**

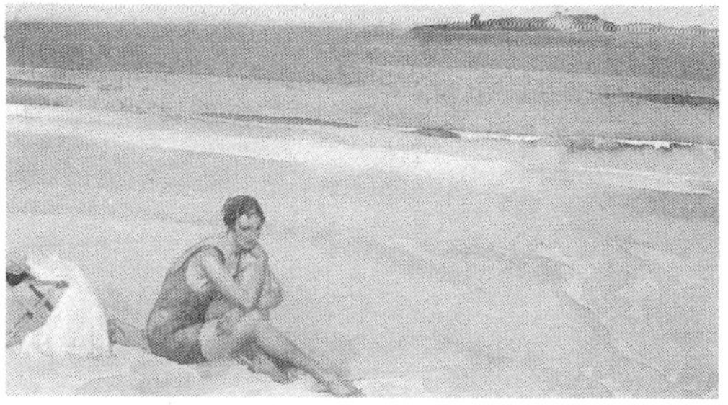

BERNARD FLEETWOOD-WALKER – Head Of A Girl – oil on canvas – 15½ x 12¼in.
(Christie's) **$943** **£660**

SIR WILLIAM RUSSELL FLINT – In View Of The Islands – signed, and signed and inscribed on the reverse – watercolour – 12¾ x 19½in.
(Christie's) **$4,719** **£3,300**

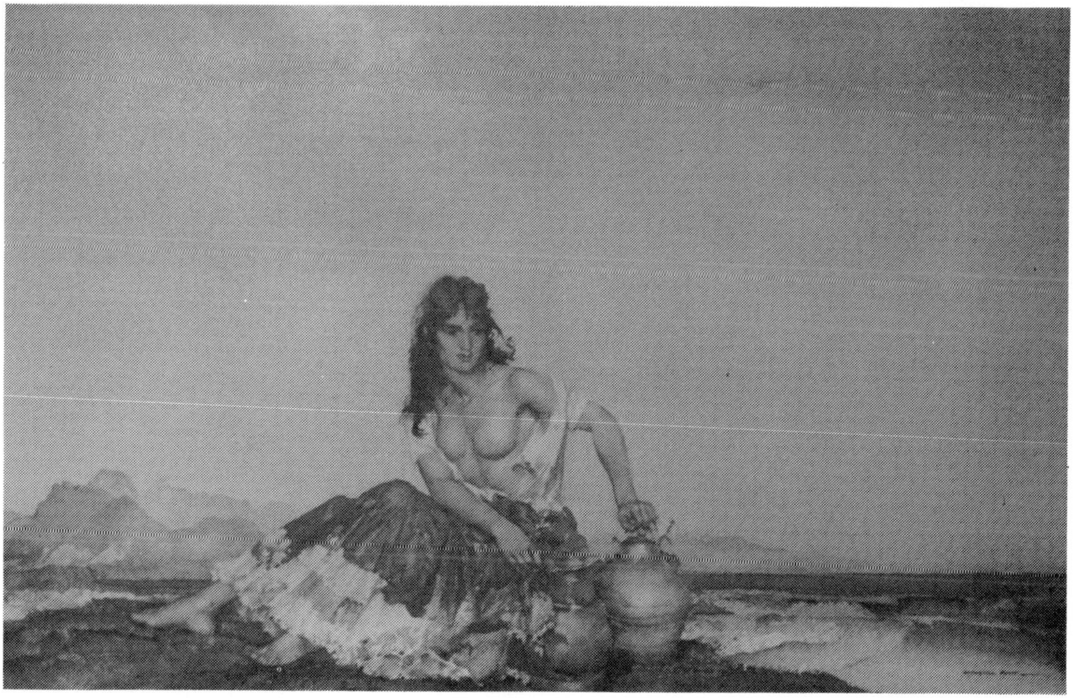

SIR WILLIAM RUSSELL FLINT – 'Sari' – 15½ x 25in. *(Parsons, Welch & Cowell)* **$739** **£490**

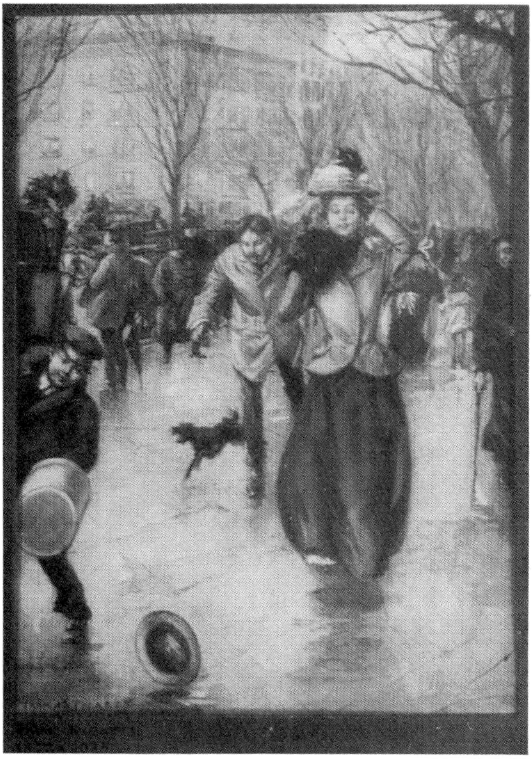

THOMAS FOGARTY – Windy Day – signed – brush and black ink and chinese white on tan paper laid down on board – 16 x 11in.
(Christie's) **$2,420** **£1,701**

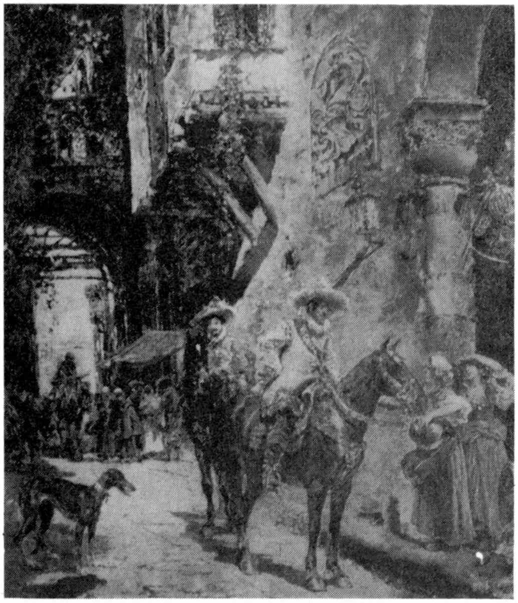

ARTURO MAS Y FONDEVILA – Cavaliers Conversing With Serving Girls – signed and inscribed – on panel – 18 x 13in.
(Christie's) **$10,868** **£7,150**

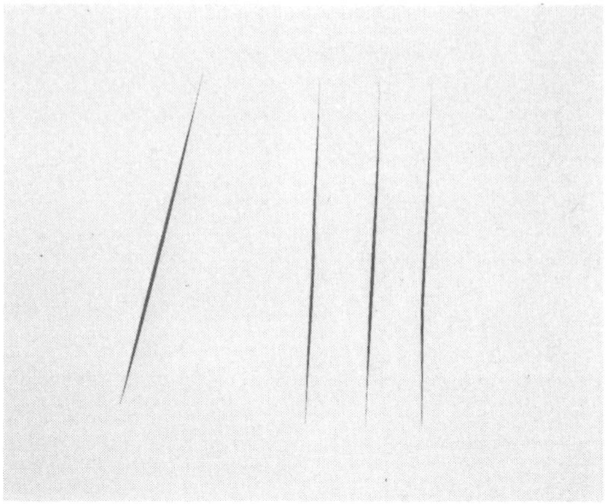

LUCIO FONTANA – Concetto Spaziale Attese – signed, inscribed on the reverse – oil on canvas – 18¼ x 21¾in.
(Christie's) **$34,848** **£24,200**

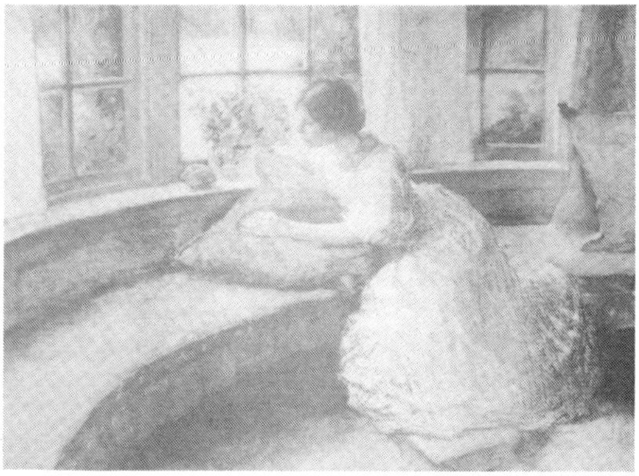

ELIZABETH A. FORBES – 'Girl On A Window Seat' – watercolour and charcoal – 18 x 24in.
(W. H. Lane & Son) **$10,850** **£7,000**

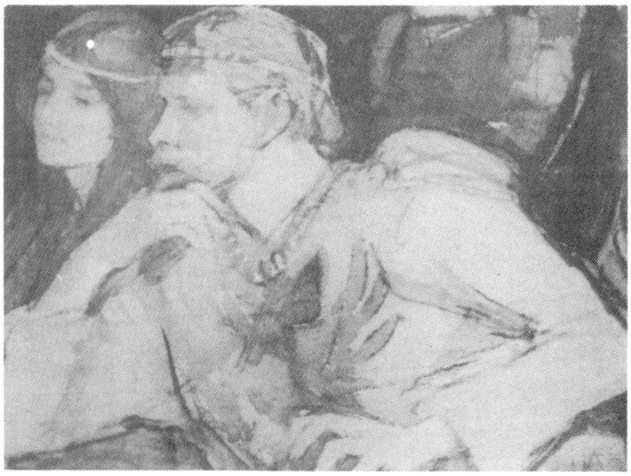

ELIZABETH ADELA FORBES – A Basis For An Illustration In The Artist's Book 'King Arthur's Wood' – inscribed – monogrammed – watercolour – 4¾ x 5¾in.
(W. H. Lane & Son) **$643** **£450**

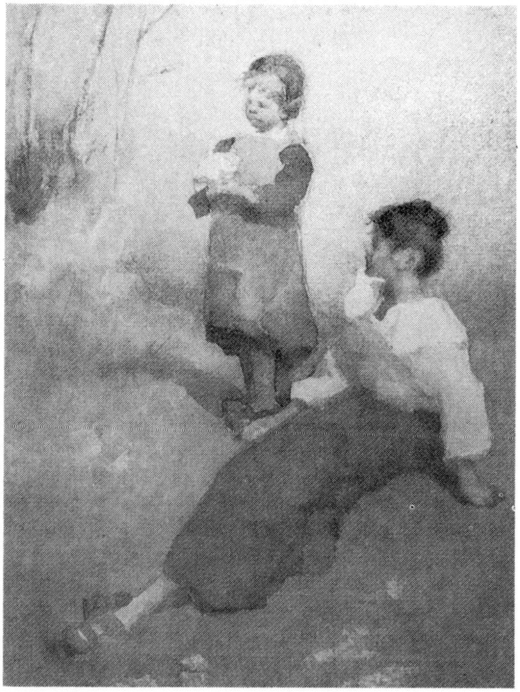

ELIZABETH ADELA STANHOPE FORBES – In The Spring – signed with monogram – watercolour over traces of pencil – 27.5 x 17.5cm.
(Phillips) **$5,396** **£3,800**

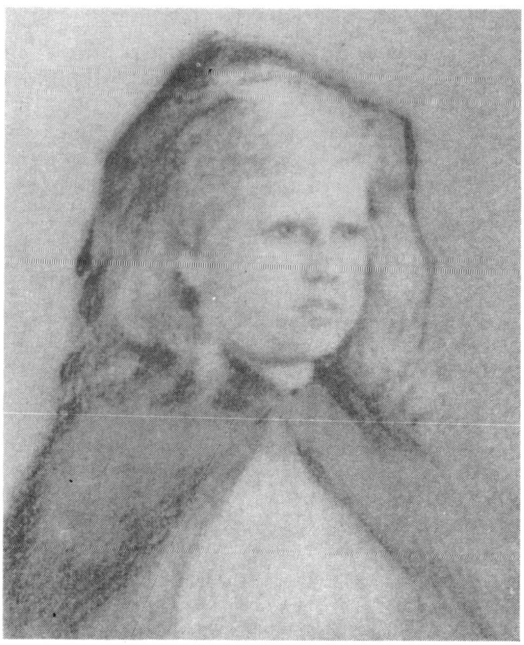

ELIZABETH ARMSTRONG FORBES – Half Portrait Of A Young Girl With Blonde Hair Wearing A Red Cape – signed – pastel – 18 x 14in.
(W. H. Lane & Son) **$961** **£620**

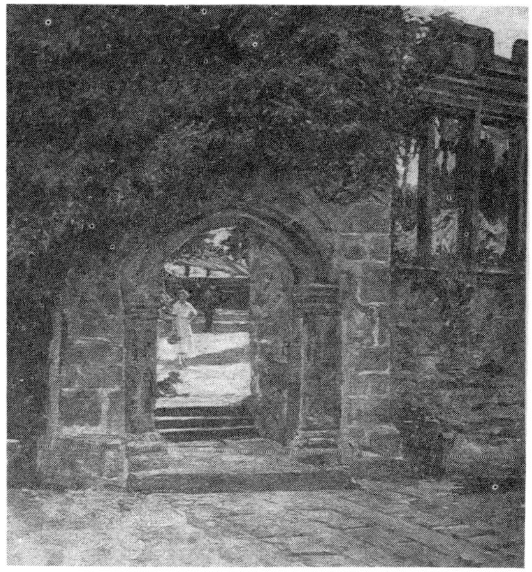

STANHOPE A. FORBES – Through The Garden Wall – signed and dated 1925 – oil on canvas – 61 x 51cm.
(Phillips) **$6,390** **£4,500**

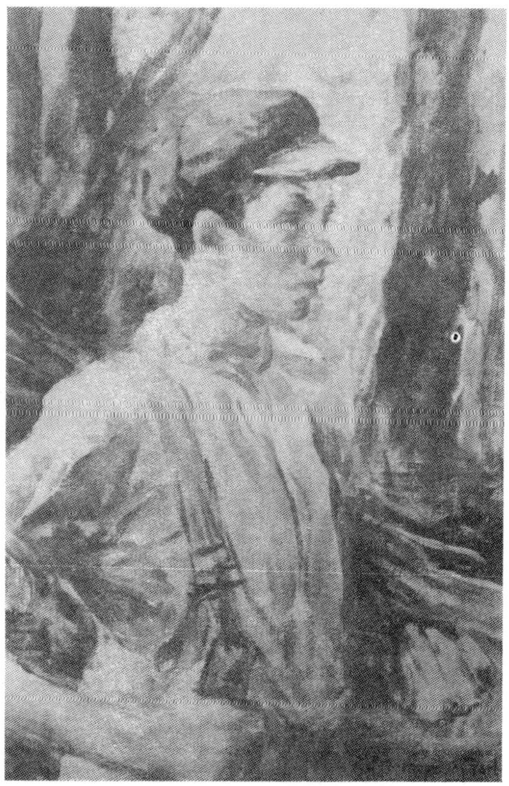

STANHOPE A. FORBES – Collecting Firewood – signed – oil on canvas laid down on board – 43 x 29.5cm.
(Phillips) **$3,442** **£2,250**

FORBES

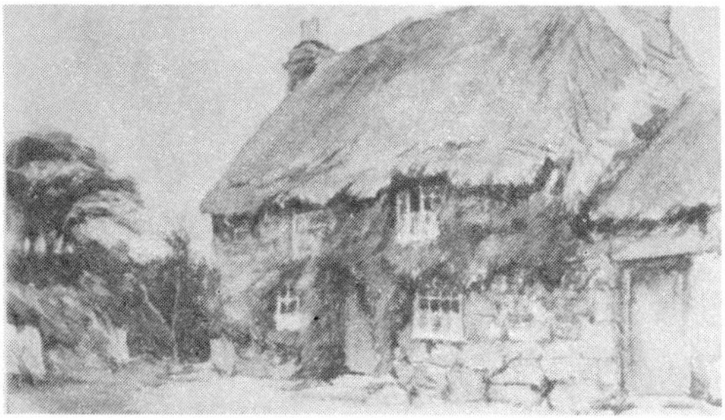

STANHOPE A. FORBES – The Blue Door – signed, also signed, inscribed and dated 1914 on the reverse – watercolour – 24 x 31cm.
(Phillips) **$996** **£600**

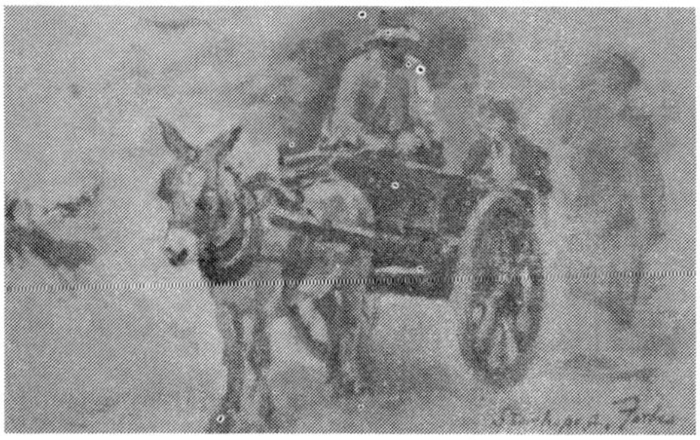

STANHOPE A. FORBES – The Donkey Cart – signed – oil on canvas board – 22 x 33cm.
(Phillips) **$3,840** **£2,400**

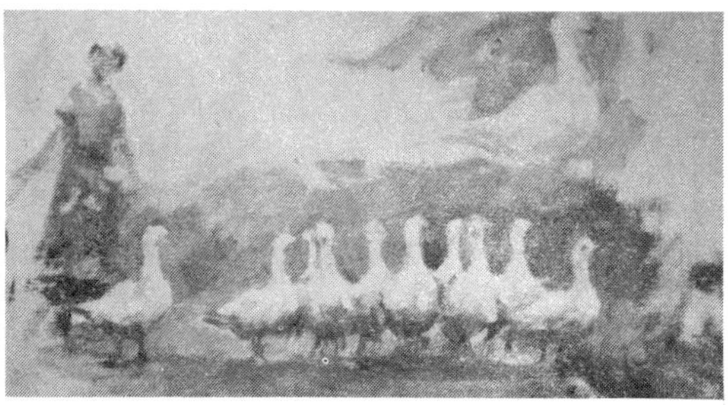

STANHOPE A. FORBES – A Goosegirl And Her Flock – oil on canvas board – 18 x 27.5cm.
(Phillips) **$2,324** **£1,400**

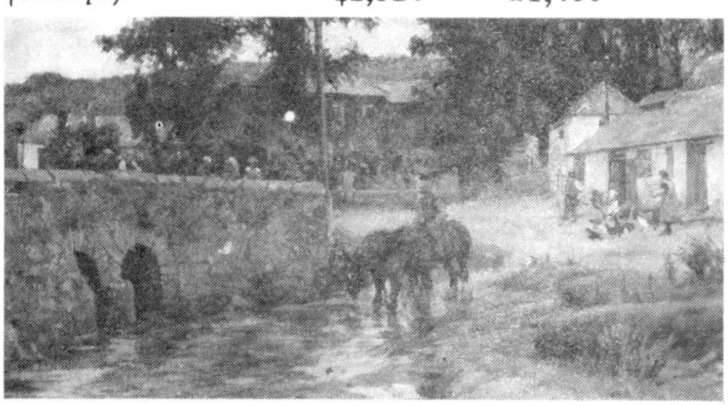

STANHOPE ALEXANDER FORBES – Watering The Horses In The Village Stream – signed and dated 1931 – oil on canvas – 24 x 30in.
(Christie's) **$34,606** £24,200

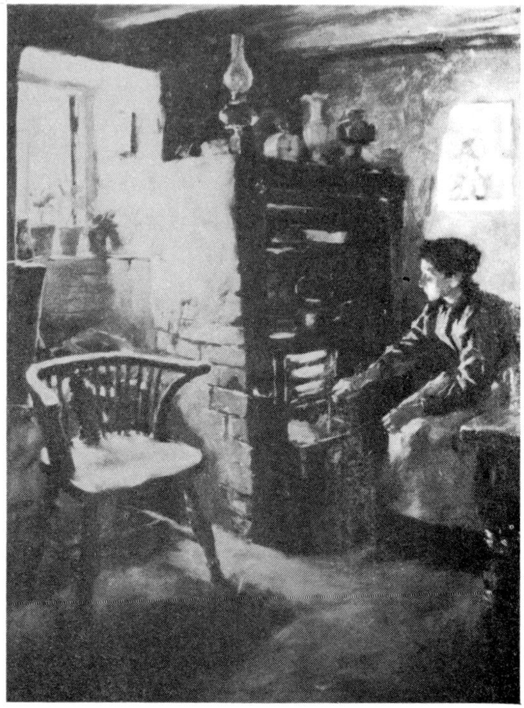

STANHOPE ALEXANDER FORBES – Fireside Reverie – signed and dated 1900 – 30 x 24½in.
(Lawrence Fine Art) **$23,738** **£14,300**

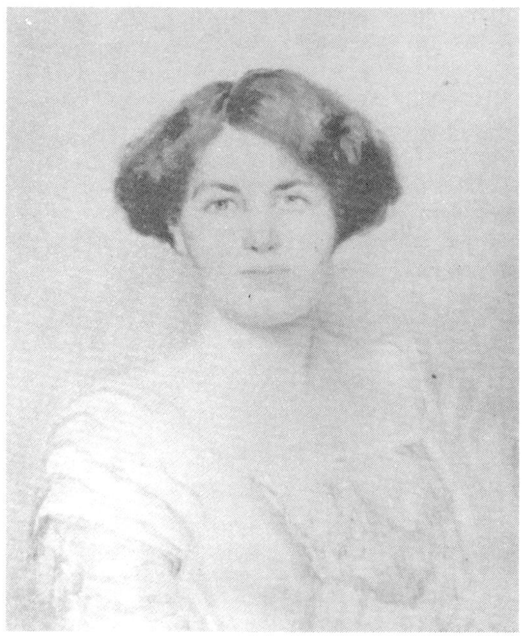

STANHOPE ALEXANDER FORBES – Half-Portrait Of Laura Semmens – signed and dated 1930 – oil on canvas – 23 x 19in.
(W. H. Lane & Son) **$1,725** **£1,150**

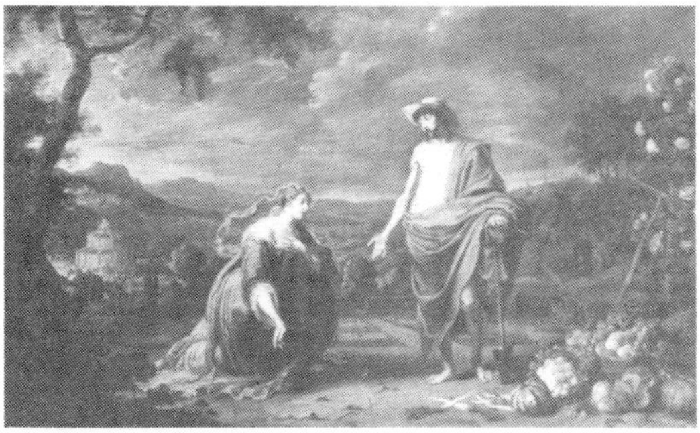

WILLEM FORCHOUDT – Noli Me Tangere – oil on copper – 16¼ x 25in.
(Phillips) **$4,230** **£3,000**

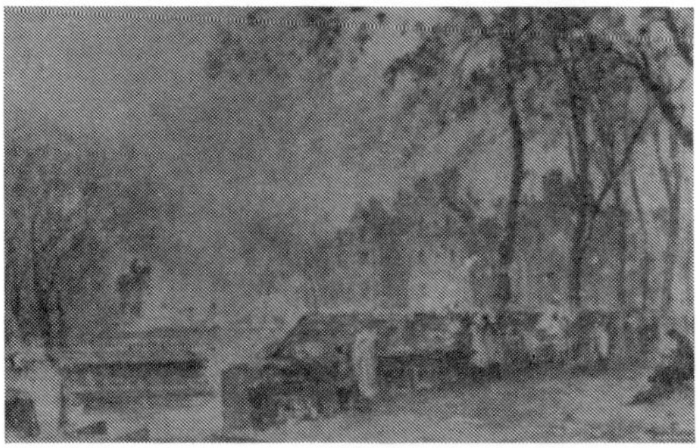

HENRI FOREAU – Les Bouquinistes – signed – watercolour and pencil on paper – 27.5 x 37.5cm.
(Phillips) **$496** **£320**

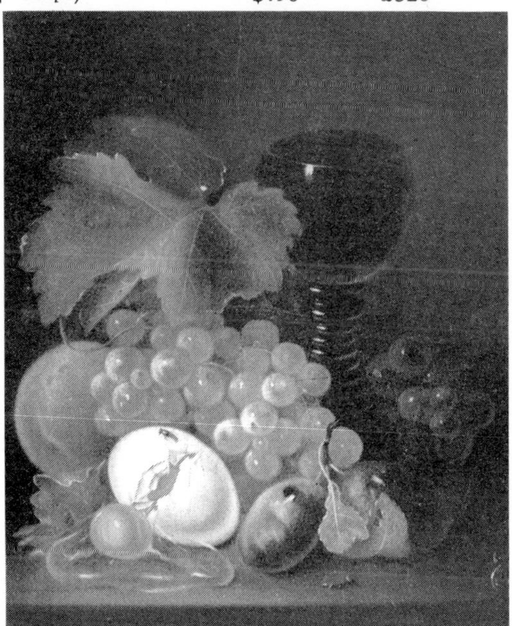

GEORGE FORSTER – Still Life With Broken Egg – signed and inscribed – oil on panel – 11¾ x 9¼in.
(Christie's) **$3,850** **£2,406**

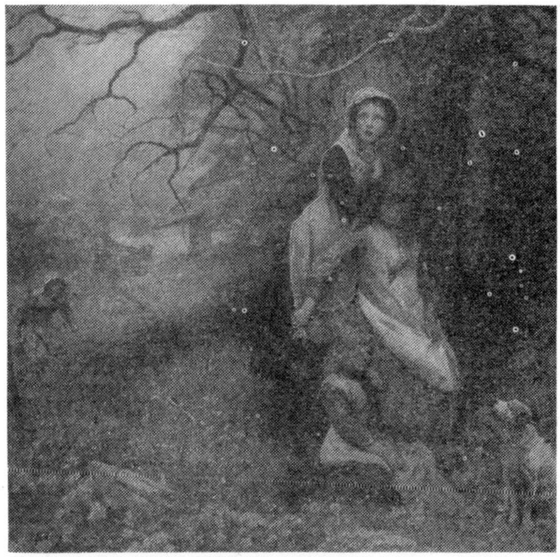

ELEANOR FORTESQUE-BRICKDALE – Picking Primroses – signed with monogram and dated 1890 – 36½ x 48¾in.
(Christie's) **$10,857** **£7,700**

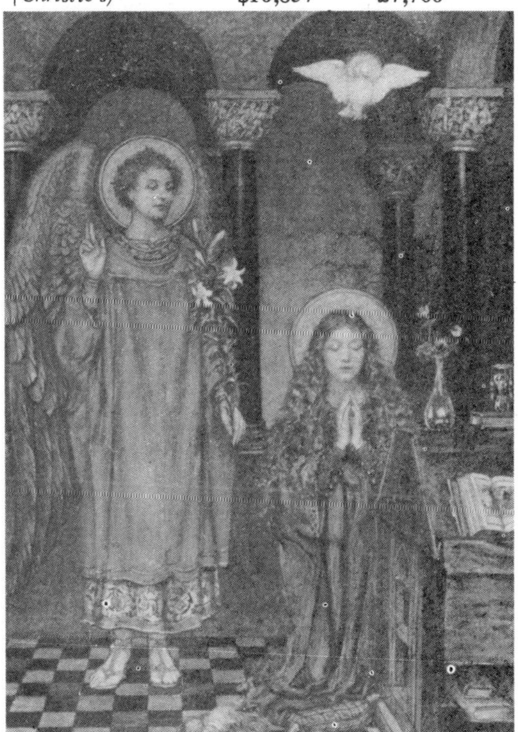

ELEANOR FORTESCUE-BRICKDALE – The Annunciation – watercolour – 14¼ x 6½in.
(Parsons, Welch & Cowell) **$302** **£200**

GILBERT FOSTER – A Mother And Child At The Gate Of A Cottage – signed – watercolour heightened with white – 21½ x 14¾in.
(Christie's) **$1,460** **£880**

FOSTER

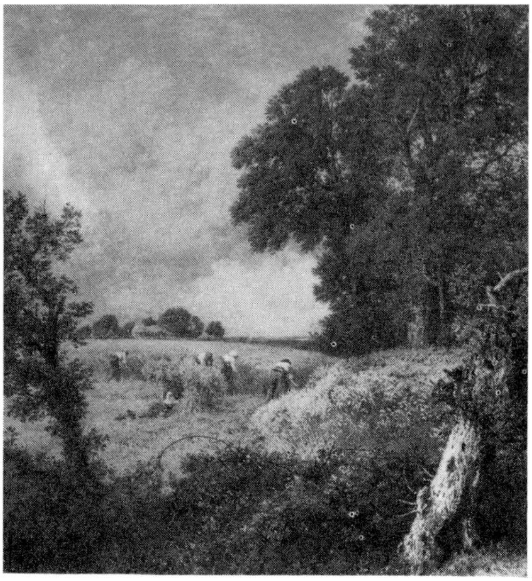

MYLES BIRKET FOSTER – The Reapers – signed with monogram – watercolour heightened with white – 30¼ x 26¼in.
(Christie's) **$38,346** **£23,100**

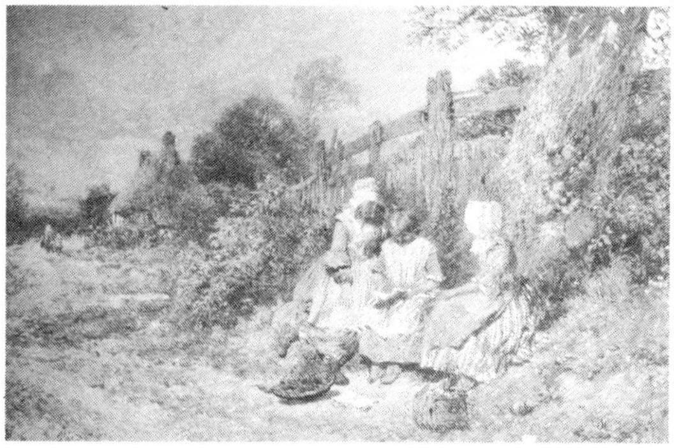

MYLES BIRKET FOSTER – Children Reading Beside A Country Lane – signed with monogram – pencil and watercolour heightened with white – 5¼ x 8¼in.
(Christie's) **$6,979** **£4,950**

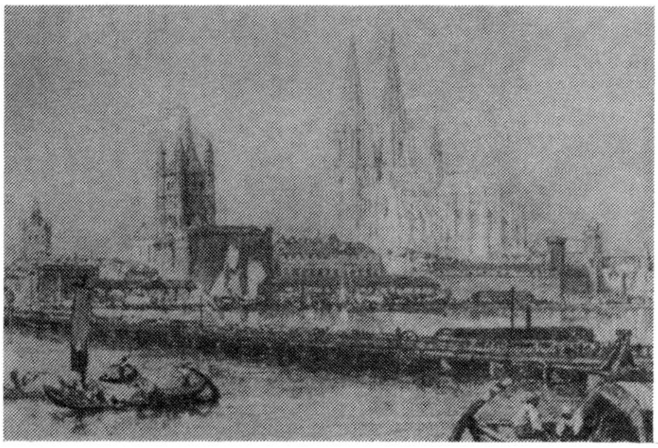

MYLES BIRKET FOSTER – Cologne – signed with monogram – watercolour heightened with white – 4 x 5½in.
(Lawrence Fine Art) **$4,565** **£2,750**

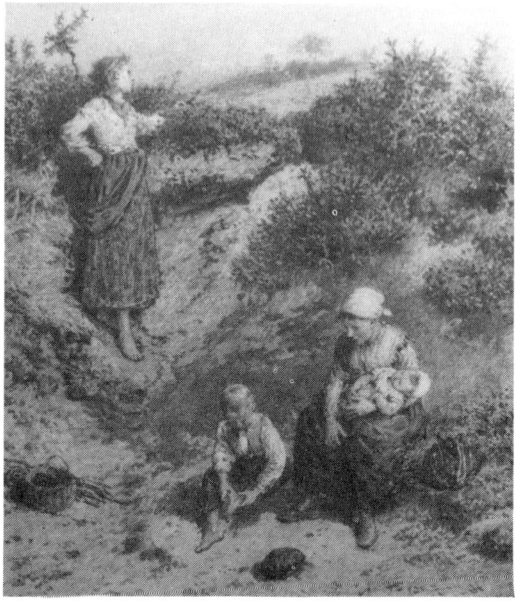

MYLES BIRKET FOSTER – 'The Blackberry Gatherers' – signed with monogram – watercolour – 8 x 6in.
(Geering & Colyer) **$7,056** **£4,900**

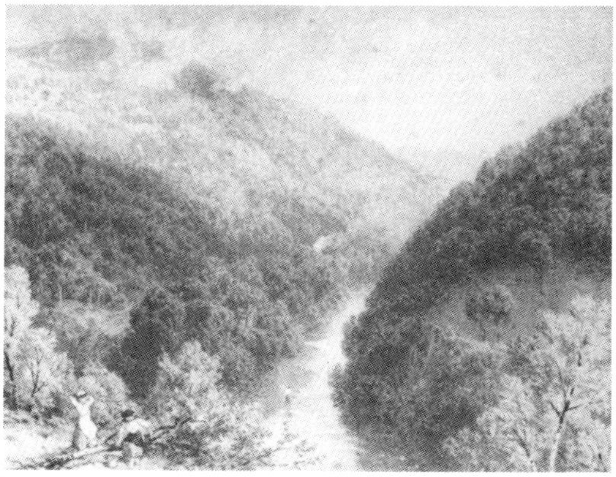

MYLES BIRKET FOSTER – The Pass Of Killiecrankie – signed with monogram – pencil and watercolour heightened with white – 6 x 8in.
(Christie's) **$3,412** **£2,420**

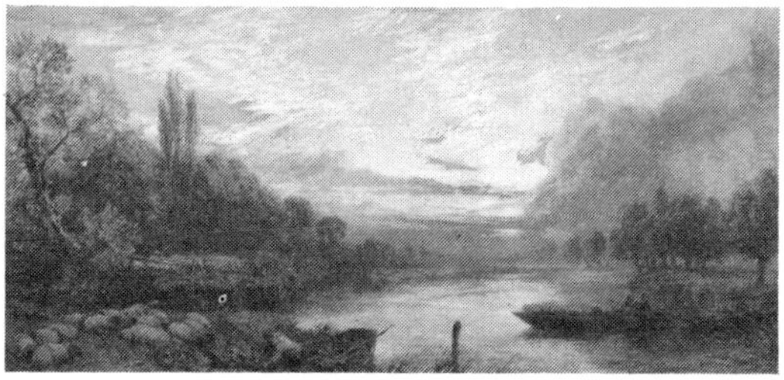

MYLES BIRKET FOSTER – The Ferry – signed with monogram – watercolour heightened with bodycolour – 17½ x 35½in.
(Christie's) **$32,571** **£23,100**

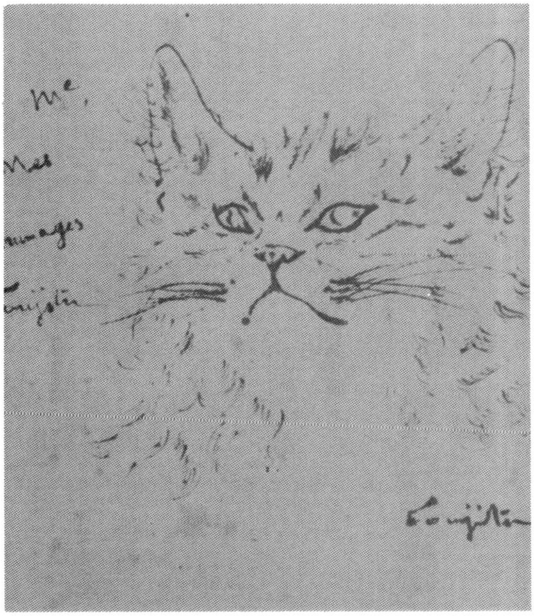

TSUGUHARO LEONARD FOUJITA – Le Chat – signed and inscribed – ink on sepia – 13 x 13cm.
(Phillips) **$2,015** **£1,300**

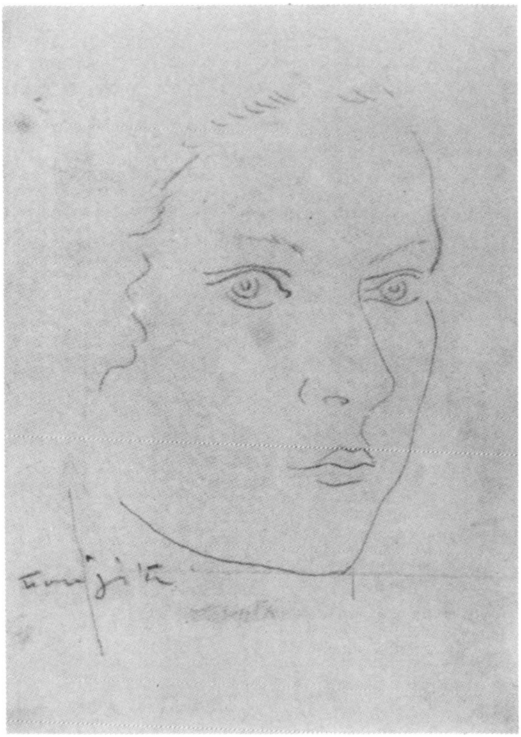

TSUGUJI FOUJITA – Tete de Femme – signed – pencil on paper – 7½ x 5½in.
(Christie's) **$1,504** **£1,045**

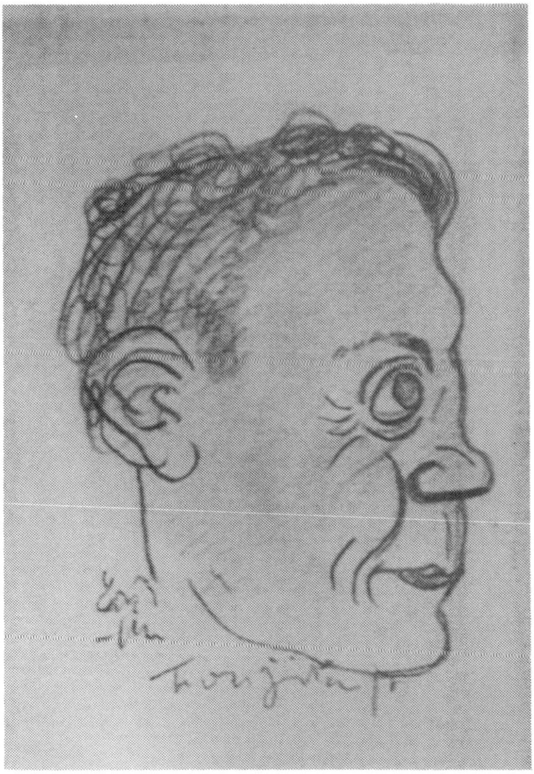

TSUGUJI FOUJITA – Caricature en Profil – signed – pencil on paper – 4¼ x 2½in.
(Christie's) **$475** **£330**

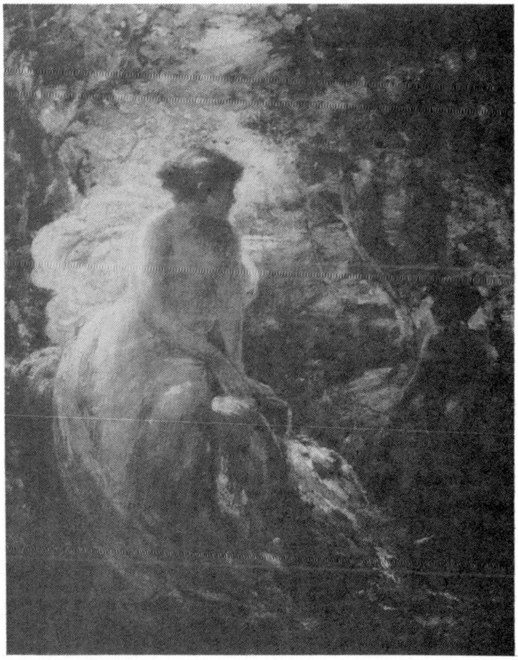

ROBERT FOWLER – The Nymph – signed – 30 x 24½in.
(Christie's) **$6,979** **£4,950**

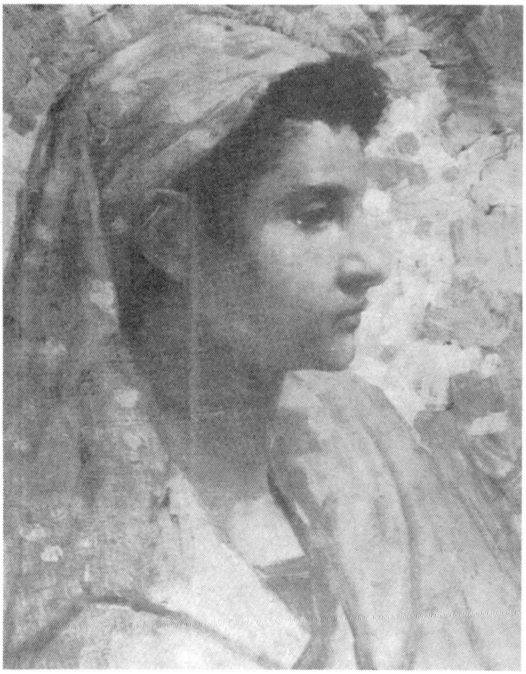

ROBERT FOWLER – Far Away Thoughts – signed with initials – on board – 20 x 14in.
(Christie's) **$729** **£486**

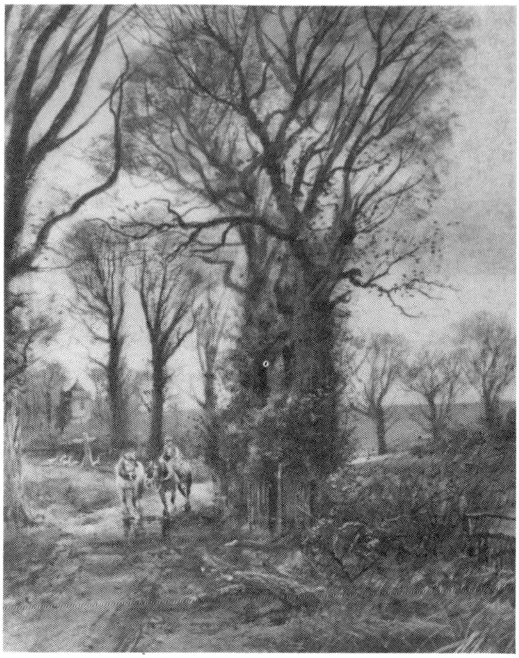

HENRY CHARLES FOX – Man With Two Shire Horses In Pastoral Landscape; and Shepherd Herding Sheep In A Woodland Scene – signed and dated 1924 – watercolour – 21½ x 14½in.
(Capes, Dunn & Co.) **$1,015** **£700 Pair**

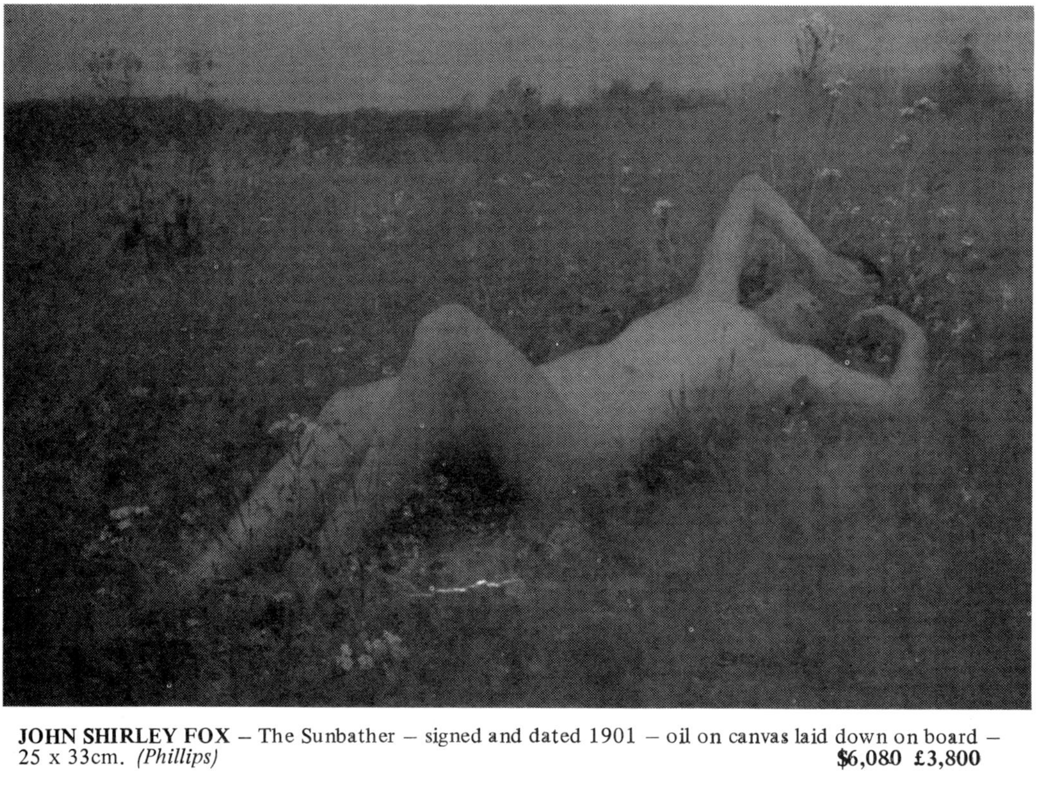

JOHN SHIRLEY FOX – The Sunbather – signed and dated 1901 – oil on canvas laid down on board – 25 x 33cm. *(Phillips)* **$6,080 £3,800**

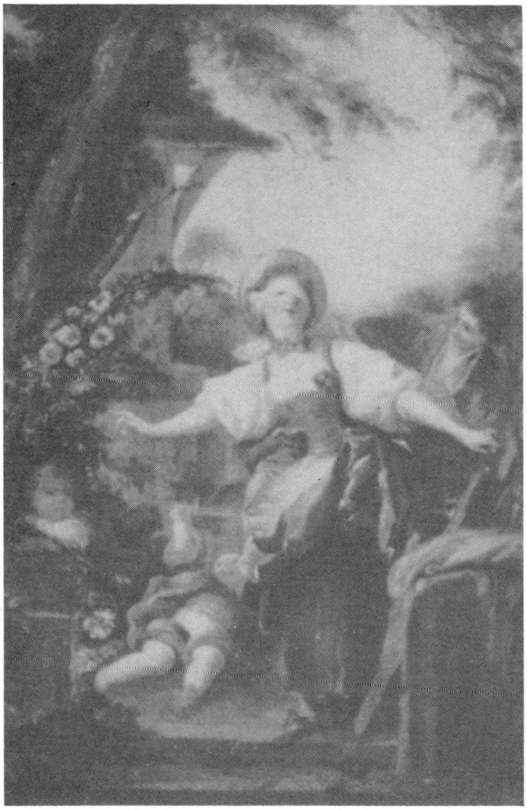

JEAN-HONORE FRAGONARD, After – Le Collin Millard – oil on panel – 16 x 12½in., together with an album of photographs.
(Christie's) $1,344 £825

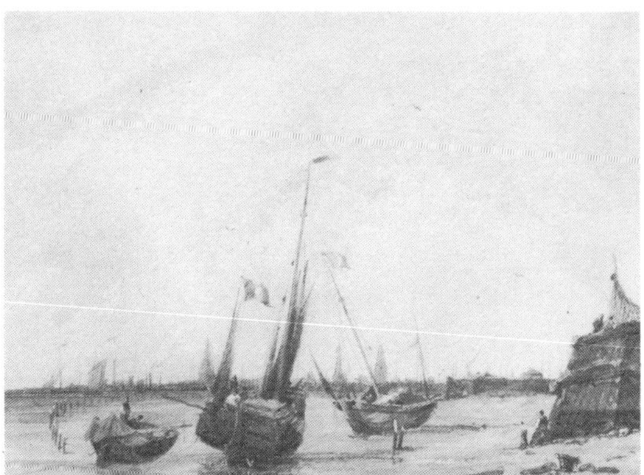

FRANCOIS LOUIS THOMAS FRANCIA – Low Tide, Calais – signed and dated 1832 – pen and brown ink and watercolour, on Whatman paper – 10 x 12in.
(Christie's) **$7,715** **£4,620**

AMBROSIUS FRANCKEN, Circle of – Balthasar's Feast – oil on panel – 28¾ x 41in.
(Phillips) **$4,230** **£3,000**

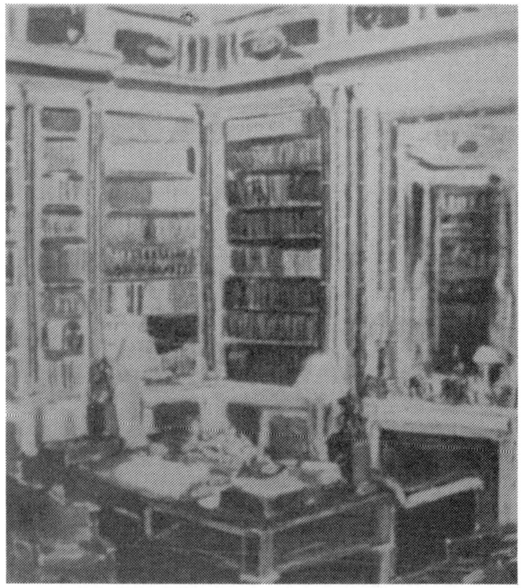

FRANK – Interior – signed and dated '46 – oil on canvas – 61 x 50cm.
(Phillips) **$387** **£250**

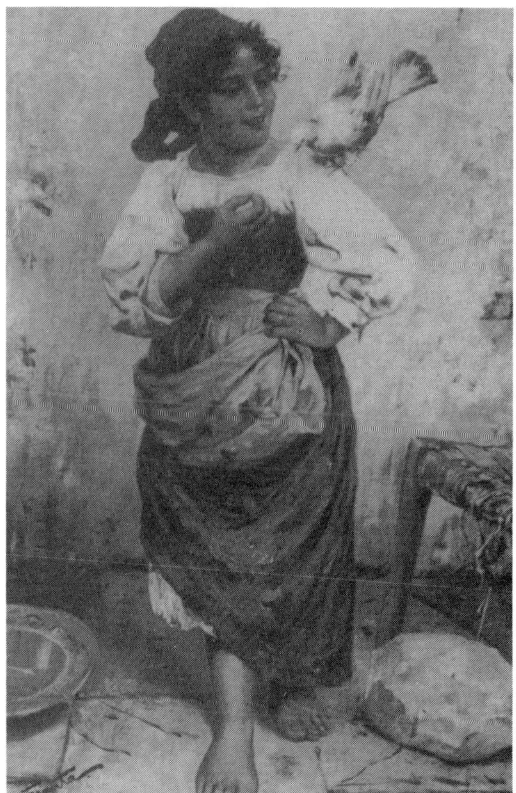

O. FRANTA – An Italian Peasant Girl With A White Dove – signed – 32½ x 19¾in.
(Christie's) **$3,009** **£1,980**

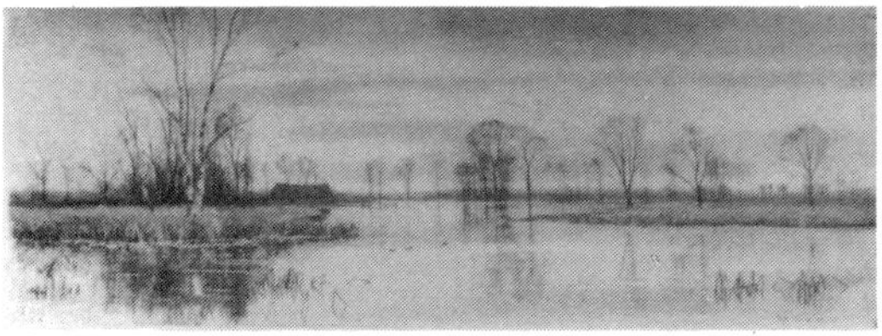

ROBERT WINCHESTER FRASER – In The Isle Of Ely, A Flooded Landscape – signed, inscribed and dated '90 – watercolour heightened with white – 8¼ x 27¼in.
(Christie's) **$1,278** **£770**

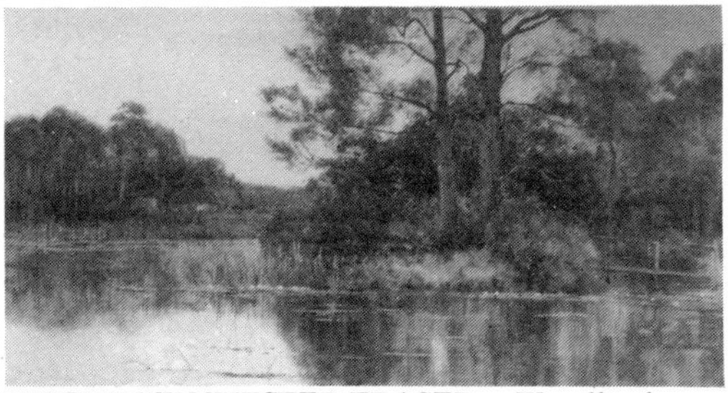

ROBERT WINCHESTER FRASER – Woodland Near St. Albans – signed, inscribed and dated '90 – watercolour heightened with white – 9¾ x 9¼in.
(Christie's) **$1,278** **£770**

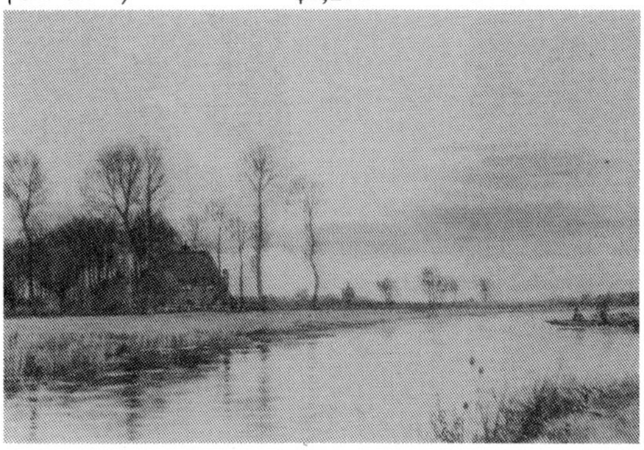

ROBERT WINCHESTER FRASER – Ditton On Cam, Children Punting – signed, inscribed and dated '93 – pencil and watercolour – 6¾ x 14¾in.
(Christie's) **$1,186** **£715**

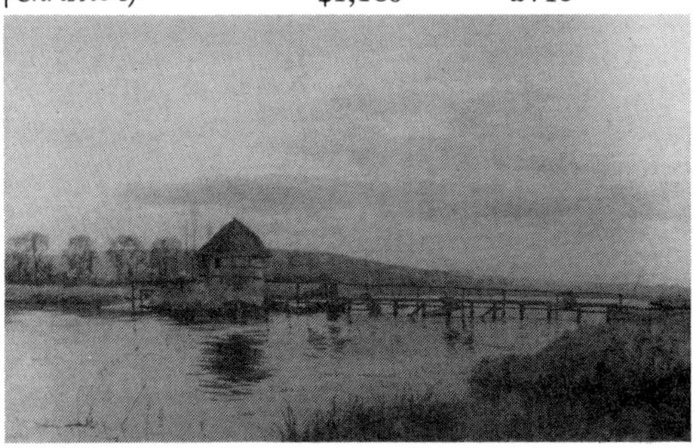

ROBERT WINCHESTER FRASER – Eel Traps Across A River – signed and dated '85 – pencil and watercolour – 16½ x 28¾in.
(Christie's) **$1,278** **£770**

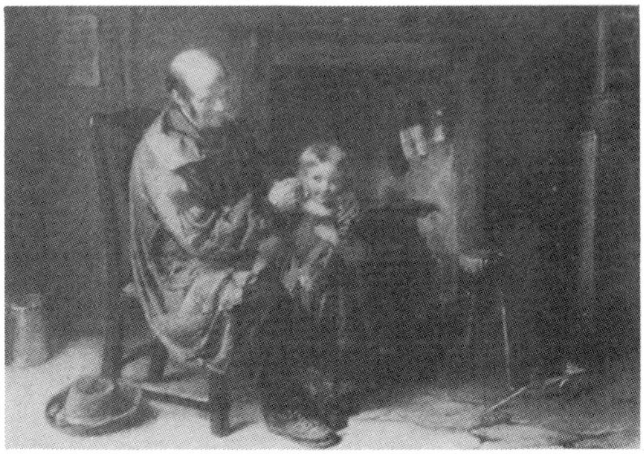

GEORGE AUGUSTUS FREEZOR – Grandfather's Watch – signed and dated '70 – on panel – 8¼ x 11¼in.
(Christie's) **$1,296** **£864**

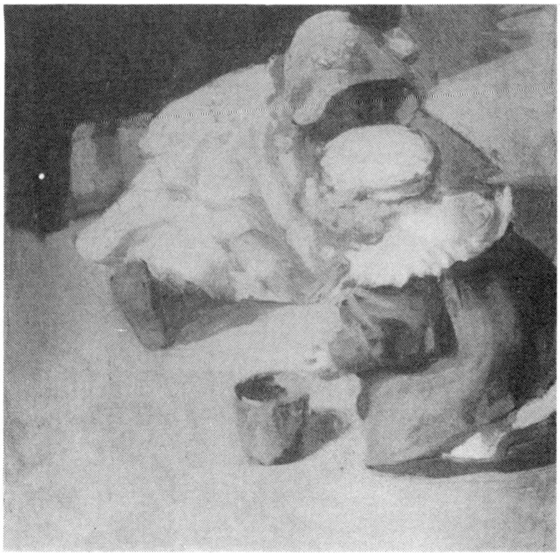

FRENCH SCHOOL, late 19th century – Playing In The Sand – 18 x 17¾in.
(Christie's) **$1,839** **£1,210**

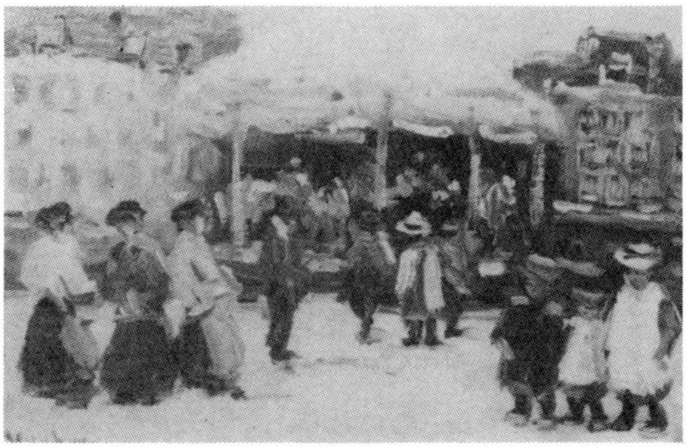

FRENCH SCHOOL, 20th century – Figures Before A Carousel – signed – oil on panel – 7 x 10½in.
(Robt. W. Skinner Inc.) **$1,000** **£694**

FRENCH SCHOOL – Sous Les Arbres – oil on canvas – 55 x 38cm.
(Phillips) **$403** **£260**

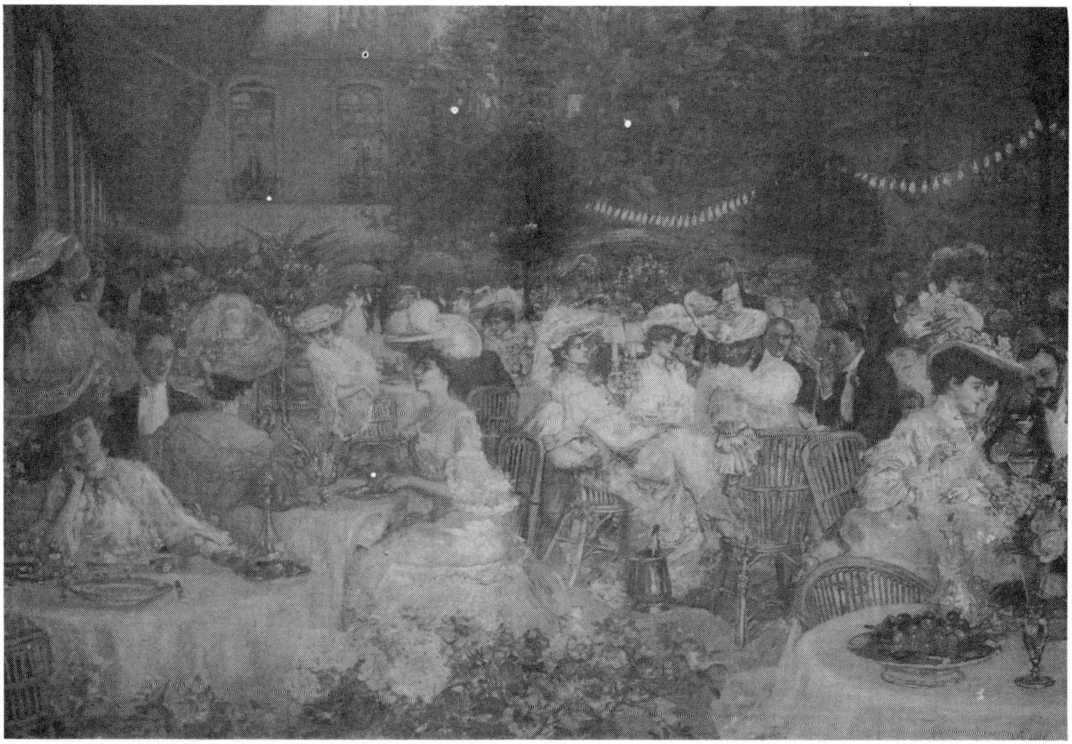

FRENCH SCHOOL – A Restaurant Terrace – signed indistinctly and dated 1904 – **44** x 31in.
(Christie's) **$28,424 £18,700**

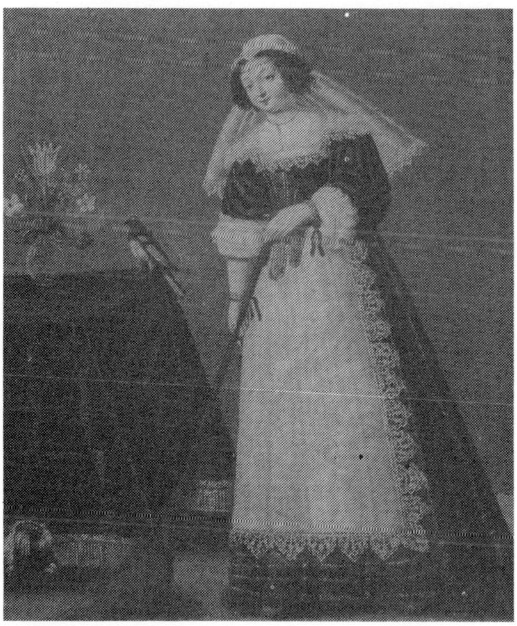

FRENCH SCHOOL, 17th century – A Maid, Standing By A Table, Holding A Broom – inscribed on the reverse and dated 1604 – on canvas – 23¼ x 18¾in.
(Phillips) **$7,636 £4,600**

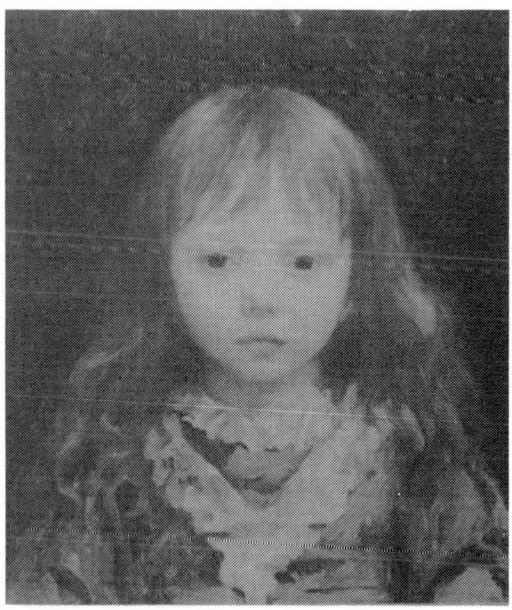

FRENCH SCHOOL, early 19th century – Portrait Of A Young Girl, Bust Length, Wearing A Blue Dress – on panel – 30.5 x 26cm.
(Phillips) **$1,080 £750**

FRENCH SCHOOL

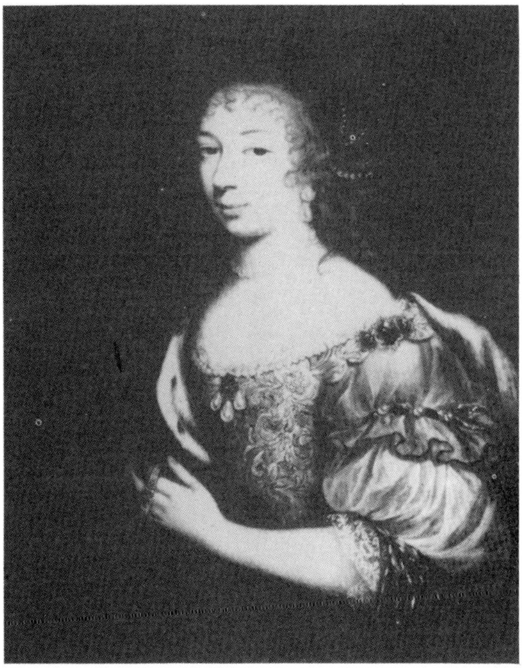

FRENCH SCHOOL, 17th century – A Portrait Of A Lady At The Court Of Charles II – oil – 28¼ x 23in.
(Anderson & Garland) **$886** **£620**

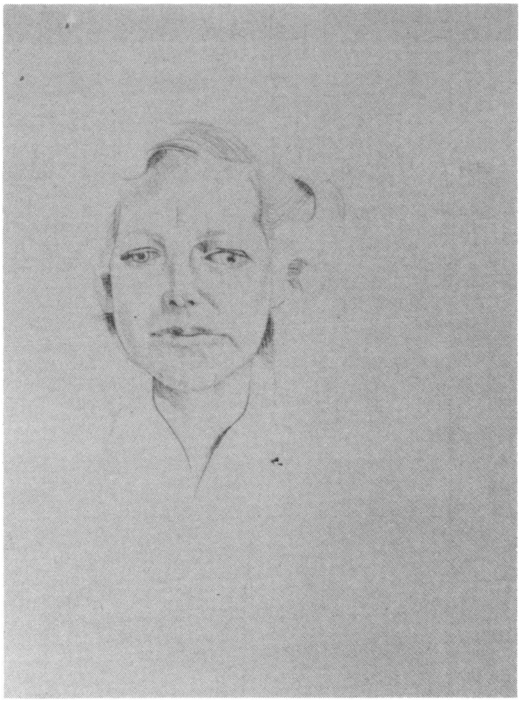

LUCIEN FREUD – Portrait Of Moyna Campbell, Lady Anderson – signed with initials – pencil – 14¼ x 9in.
(Christie's) **$6,044** **£3,850**

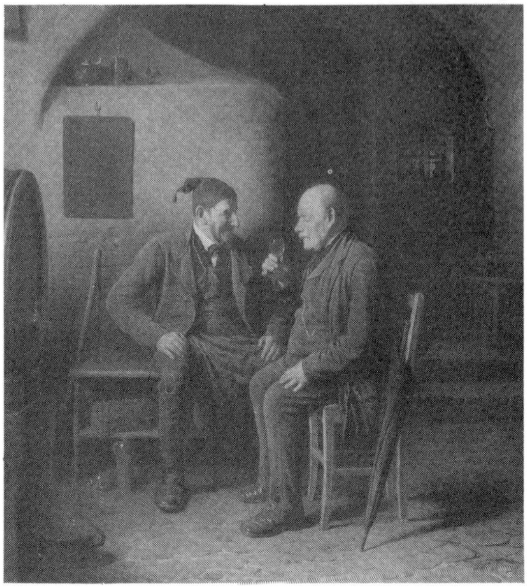

FRIEDRICH FRIEDLANDER – A Visit To The Cellars – signed – oil on panel – 52 x 41.5cm.
(Phillips) **$4,896** **£3,400**

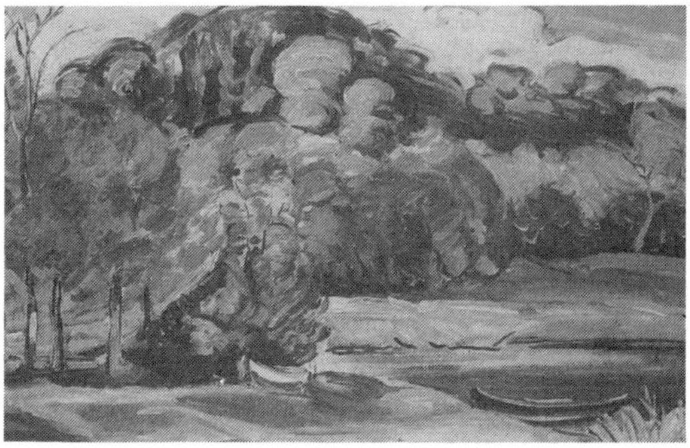

EMILE OTHON FRIESZ – Paysage au Bord du Lac – signed and dated 1935 – oil on canvas – 21½ x 25¾in.
(Christie's) **$8,448** **£5,280**

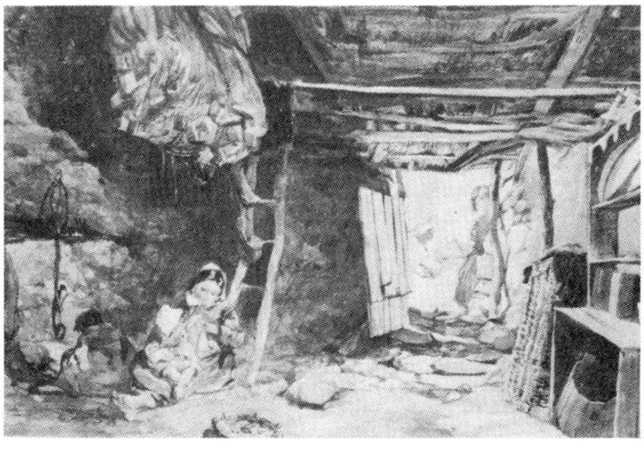

ALFRED DOWNING FRIPP – In A Fisherman's Hut – signed and dated '44 – pencil and watercolour heightened with white – 10½ x 14in.
(Christie's) **$1,126** **£756**

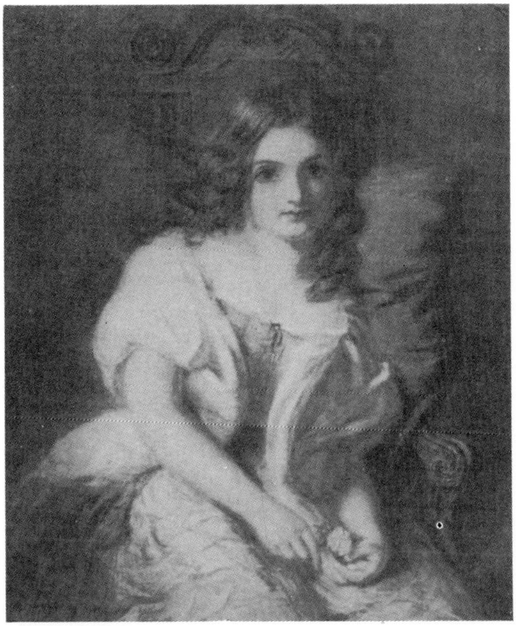

WILLIAM POWELL FRITH – Fair Beauties – signed – 7 x 6in.
(Christie's) **$1,085** **£770 Pair**

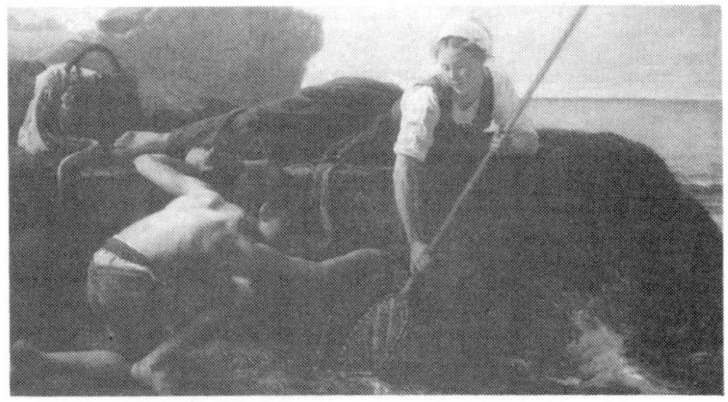

ALFRED FUILLOU – Jeunes Pecheurs – signed and dated 1874 – 47 x 83in.
(Christie's) **$18,216** **£12,650**

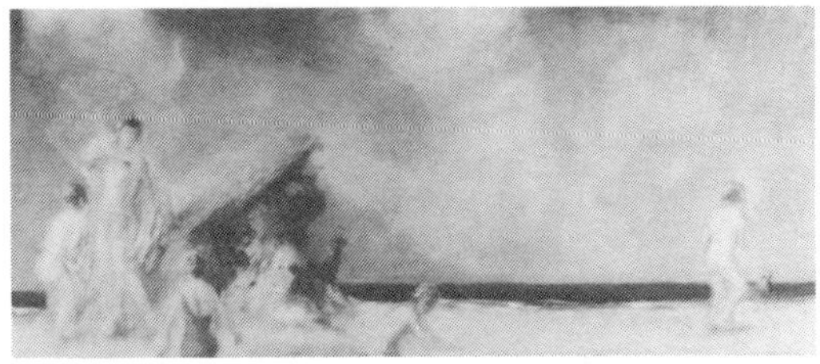

LEONARD J. FULLER – 'The Waters Edge' – signed – oil on canvas – 18 x 45cm.
(W. H. Lane & Son) **$1,162** **£700**

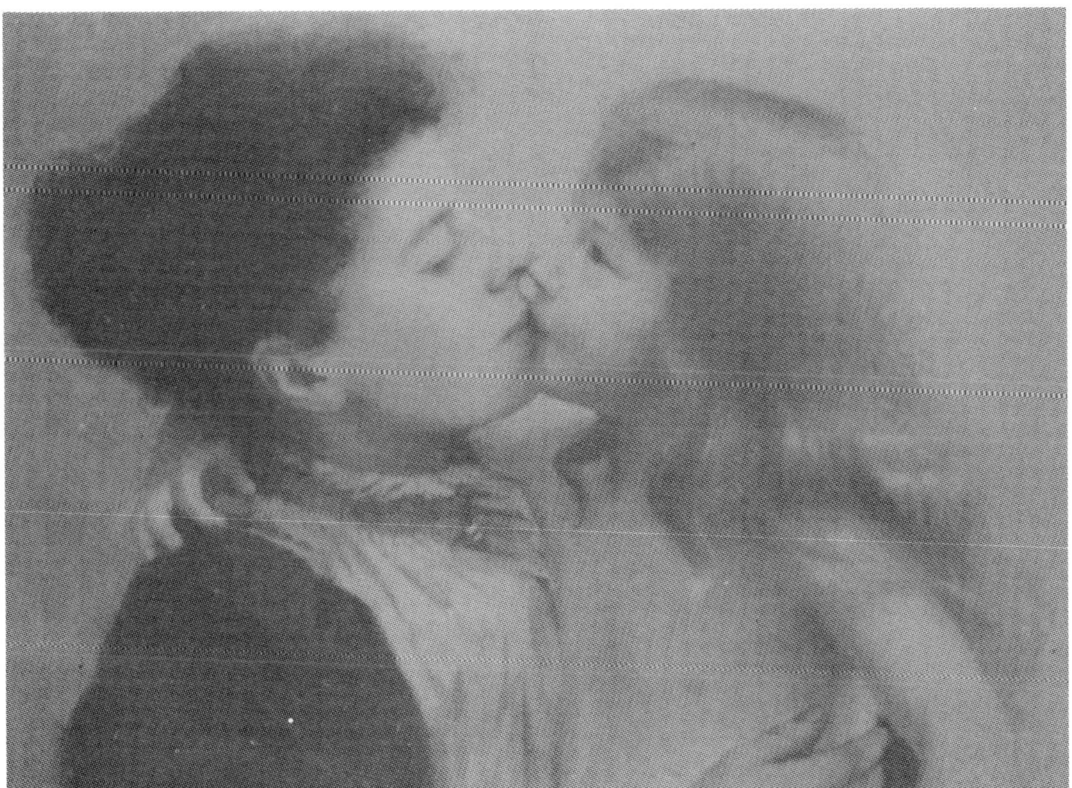

FLORENCE A. FULLER – An Elegant Mother Kissing Her Naked Auburn Haired Daughter – signed – oil on canvas – 17 x 24½in. *(Christie's)* **$792** **£495**

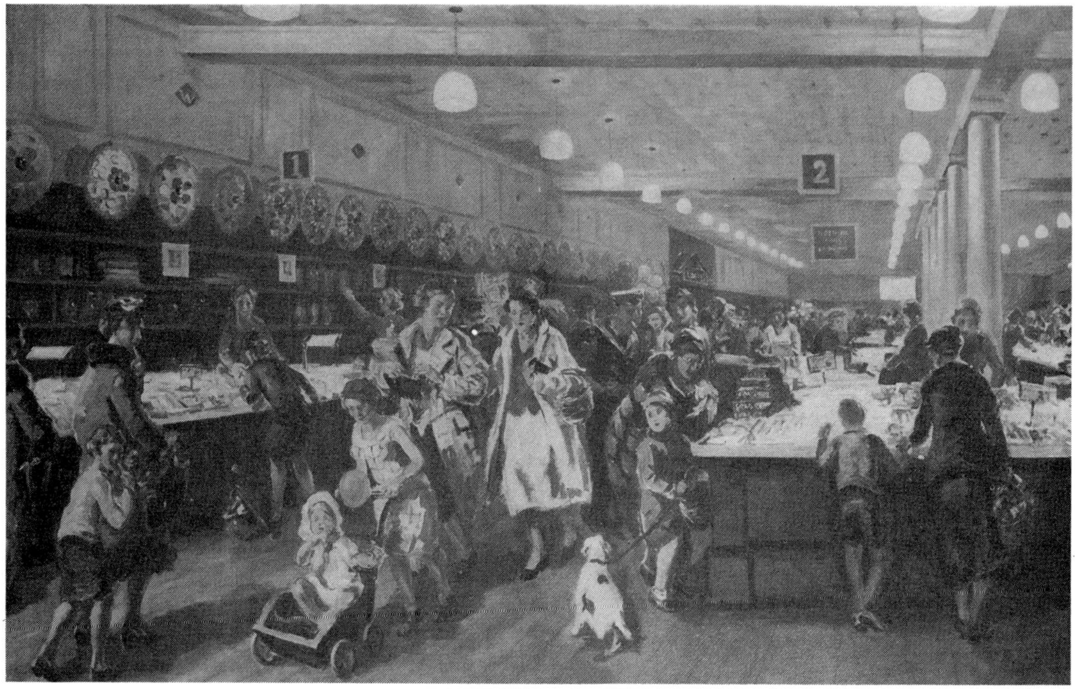

LEONARD JOHN FULLER – The People's Store, Threepence v. Sixpence, The Interior Of Woolworths – signed – oil on canvas – 40 x 50in. *(Christie's)* **$12,952 £8,250**

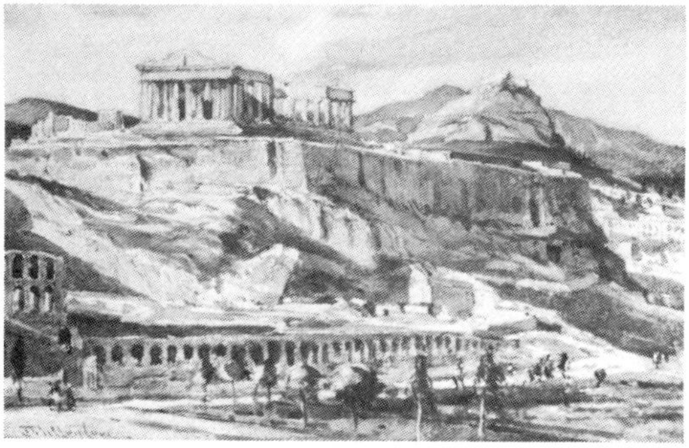

JOHN FULLEYLOVE – The Acropolis From The Lower Part Of The Philopappus Hill – signed – pencil and watercolour – 5¼ x 7¼in.
(Christie's) **$1,861 £1,320**

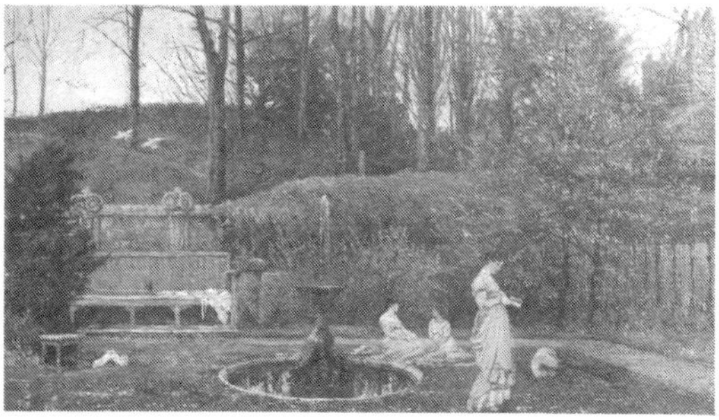

JOHN FULLEYLOVE – The Garden Of Love – signed – 12 x 18in.
(Christie's) **$4,118 £2,860**

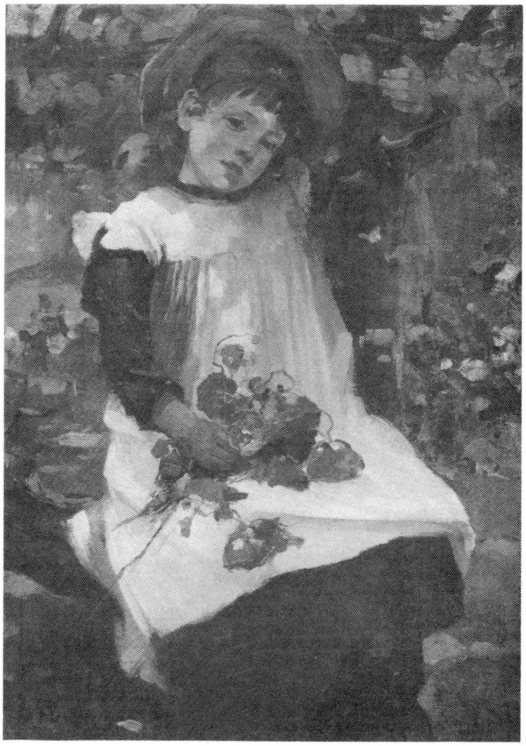

DAVID FULTON – The Poppy Gatherer – signed – oil on canvas – 21 x 14in.
(Christie's) **$20,449 £14,300**

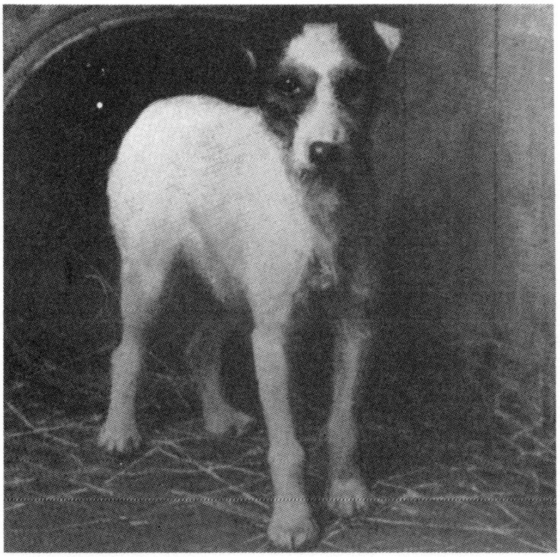

SAMUEL FULTON – A Terrier Puppy – signed – 19¾ x 16in.
(Christie's) **$1,085** **£770**

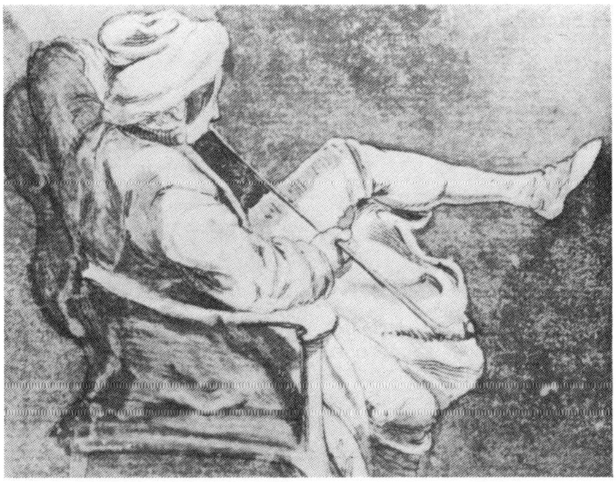

JOHANN HEINRICH FUSELI – Self-Portrait, In Dressing Gown And Night-Cap, Smoking A Pipe – grey wash, black chalk, pen and black ink – 4½ x 5in.
(Christie's) **$6,156** **£4,104**

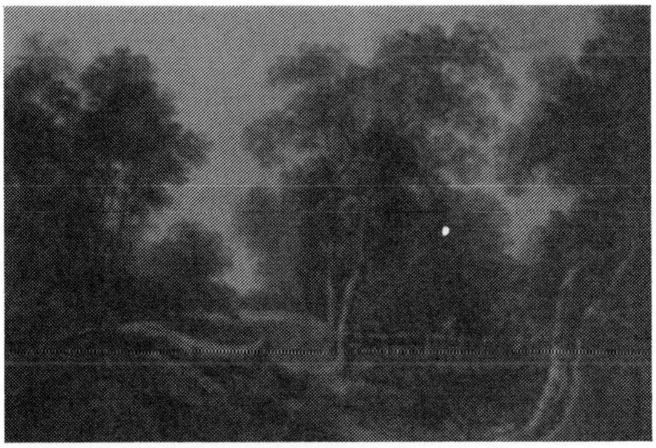

THOMAS GAINSBOROUGH, Follower of – Figure Crossing A Bridge In A Wooded Landscape – oil on canvas – 12¾ x 16¼in.
(Phillips) **$830** **£500**

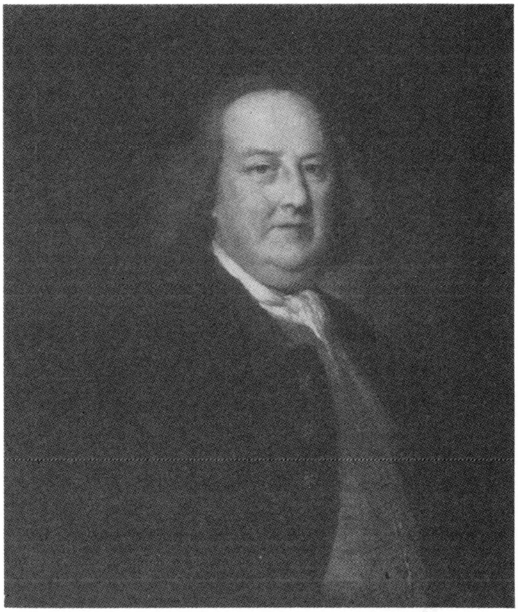

THOMAS GAINSBOROUGH, Circle of – Portrait Of Sir William Gould, Half Length, In A Blue Coat, A Red Waistcoat And A White Stock – 30 x 25in.
(Christie's) **$1,539** **£1,026**

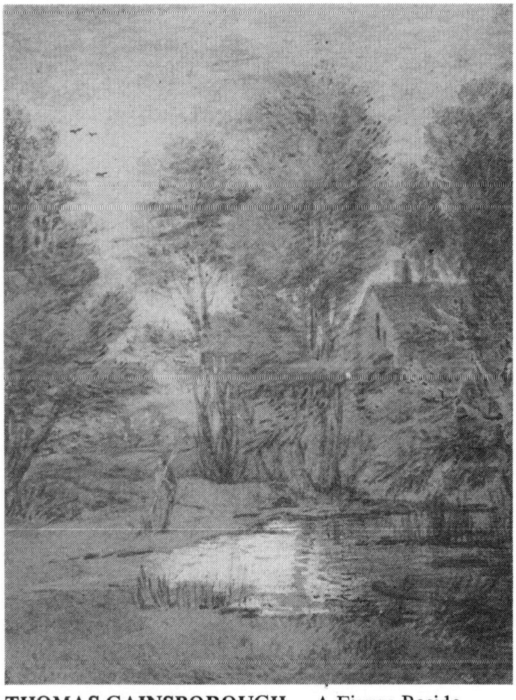

THOMAS GAINSBOROUGH – A Figure Beside A Pool In A Wood With A House Beyond – pencil, grey and pink wash, heightened with white (partly oxidized) on light brown prepared paper, ink framing lines – 9¾ x 7½in.
(Christie's) **$14,696** **£8,800**

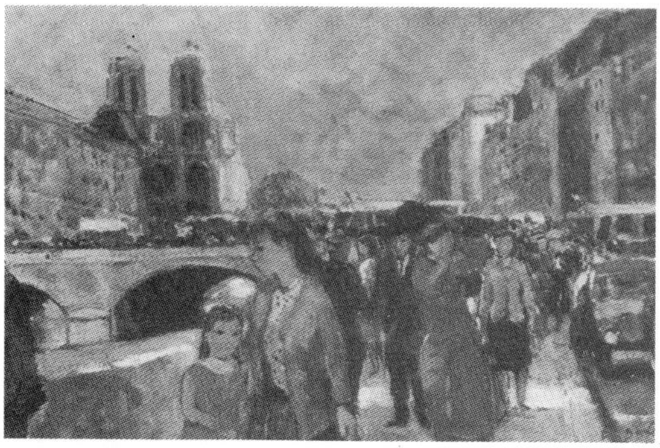

FRANCOIS GALL – La Rive Gauche – signed – oil on canvas – 13 x 16¼in.
(Christie's) **$2,851** **£1,980**

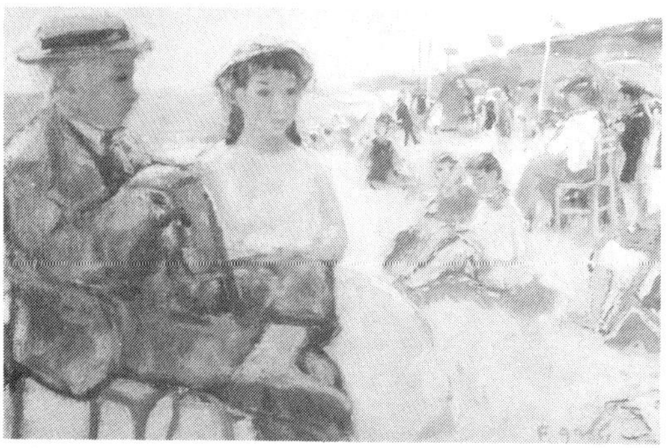

FRANCOIS GALL – Sur la Plage – signed – oil on canvas – 8¾ x 10½in.
(Christie's) **$3,168** **£1,980**

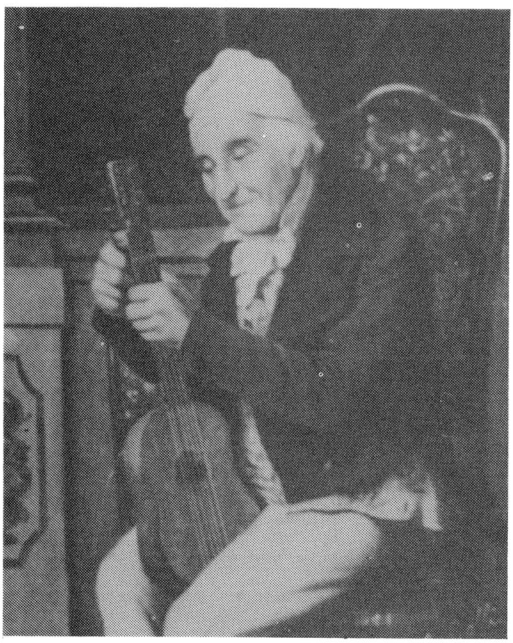

LUIGI GALLI – 'Preparing For Song' – signed – oil on canvas – 30.5 x 20.5cm.
(Phillips) **$751** **£450**

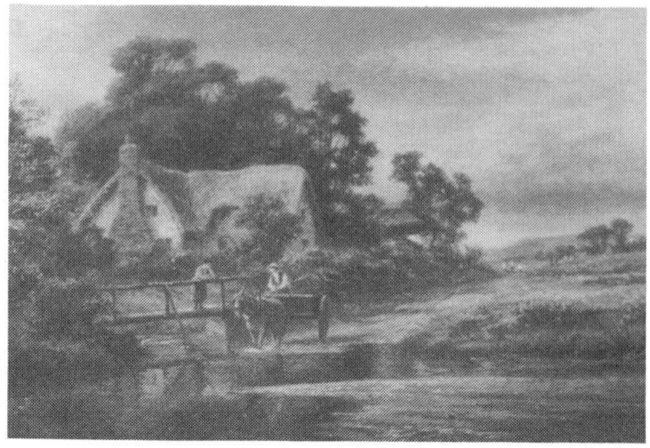

ROBERT GALLON – A Welsh Ford – signed – 12 x 18in.
(Christie's) **$2,019** **£1,320**

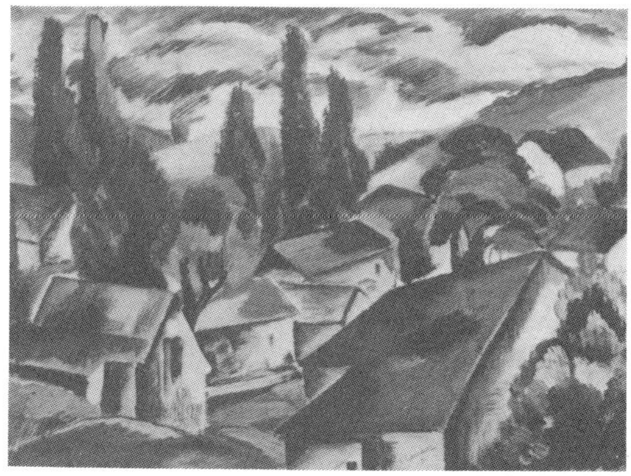

EMIL GANSO – Cubist Landscape – signed and dated '25 – gouache on paper – 12¼ x 17¼in.
(Christie's) **$1,320** **£918**

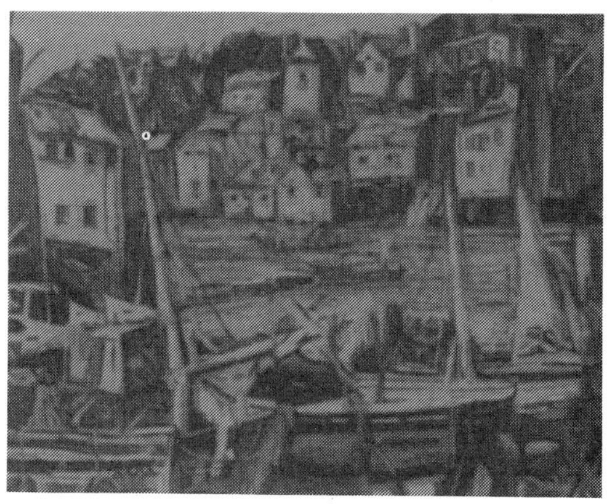

DIRAN GARABEDIAN – Boats In Harbour – signed – oil on canvas – 61 x 76cm.
(Phillips) **$542** **£350**

DANIEL GARDNER – Portrait Of The Countess Of Buckinghamshire – signed – gouache and pastel – 84 x 54cm.
(Phillips) **$11,736** **£7,200**

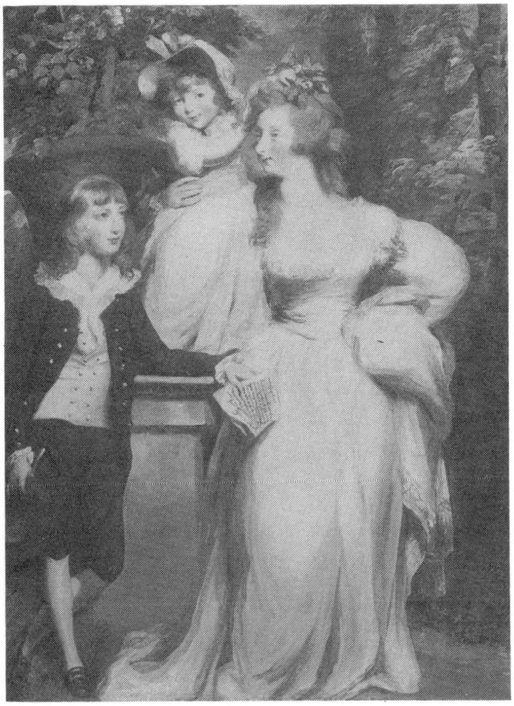

DANIEL GARDNER – Portrait Of Elizabeth Keck And Her Children, By An Urn In A Garden – pastel and bodycolour – 37¼ x 28¼in.
(Christie's) **$9,185** **£5,500**

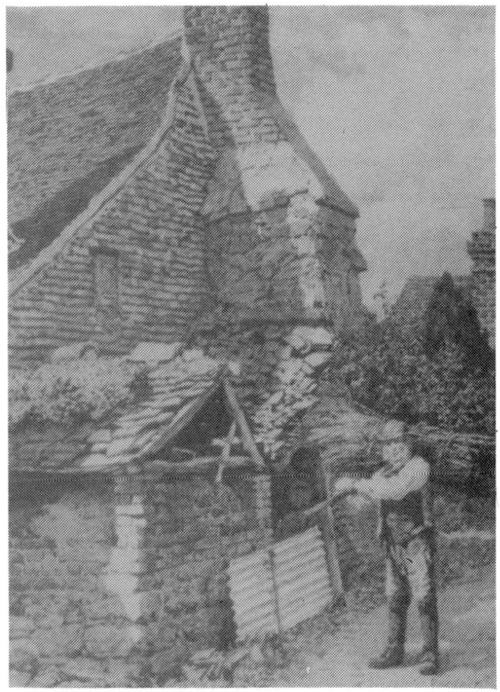

WILLIAM BISCOMBE GARDNER – A Man Carrying Faggots By A Farm House – signed – pencil and watercolour – 7¾ x 5¾in.
(Christie's) **$1,004** **£605**

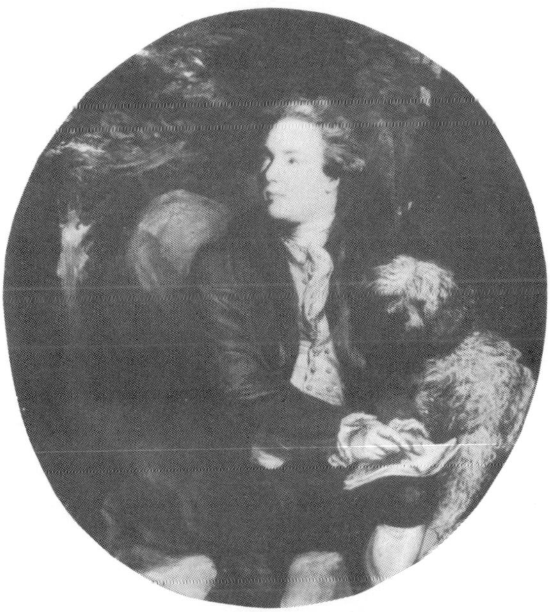

DANIEL GARDNER – A Young Man Seated By A Waterfall, Sketching, His Spaniel Beside Him – pastel and bodycolour – 21¾ x 18¾in.
(Christie's) **$6,156** **£4,104**

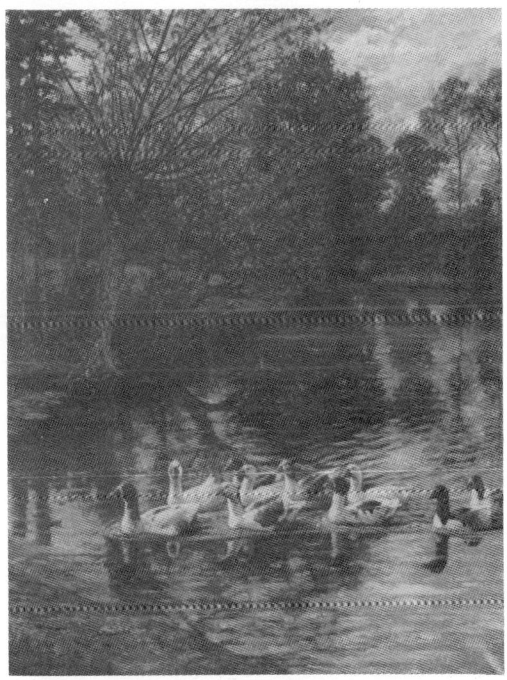

ANGELO GARINO – Geese On A Wooded River – signed and dated 1903 – 45½ x 34½in.
(Christie's) **$14,080** **£8,800**

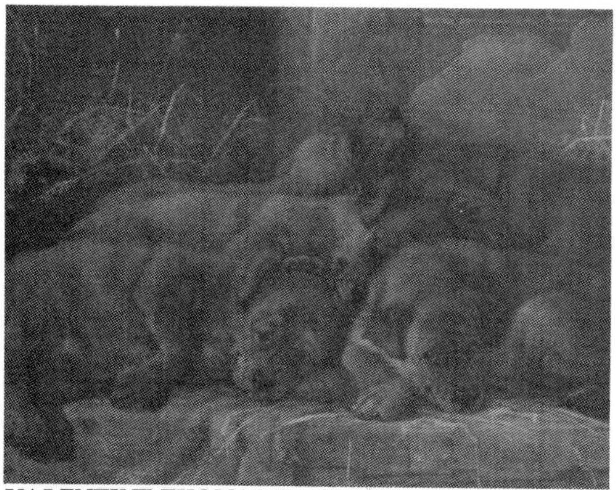

VALENTINE THOMAS GARLAND – Let Sleeping Pups Lie – inscribed on a label on the reverse – oil on panel – 12 x 18in.
(Bonhams) **$7,440** **£4,800**

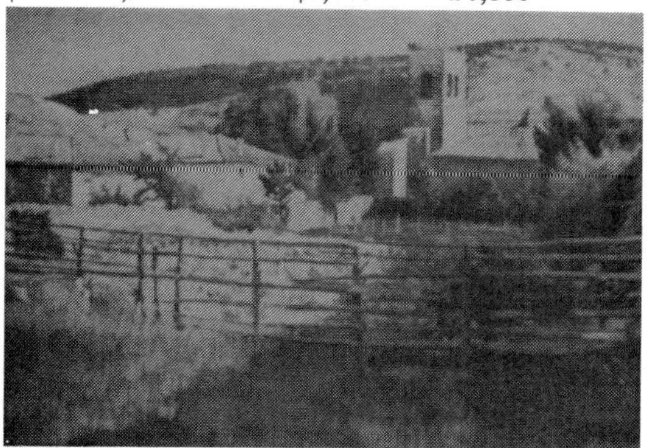

L. GARRALDA – Village And Landscape In Spain – signed, inscribed and dated 1925 – oil on canvas – 117 x 152cm.
(Phillips) **$1,054** **£680**

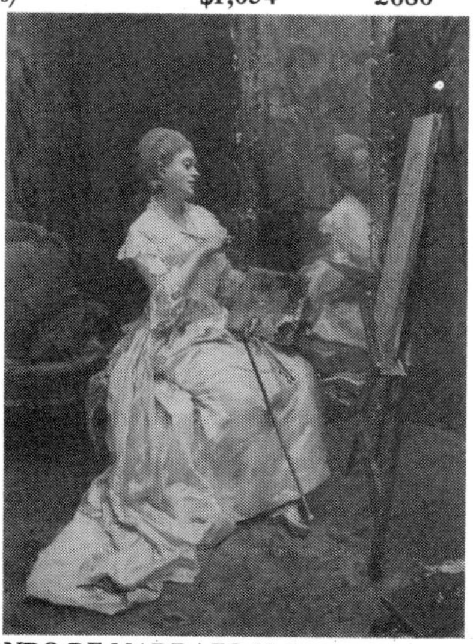

RAIMONDO DE MADRAZO Y GARRETA – Vanity – signed – oil on panel – 51.5 x 38cm.
(Phillips) **$60,120** **£36,000**

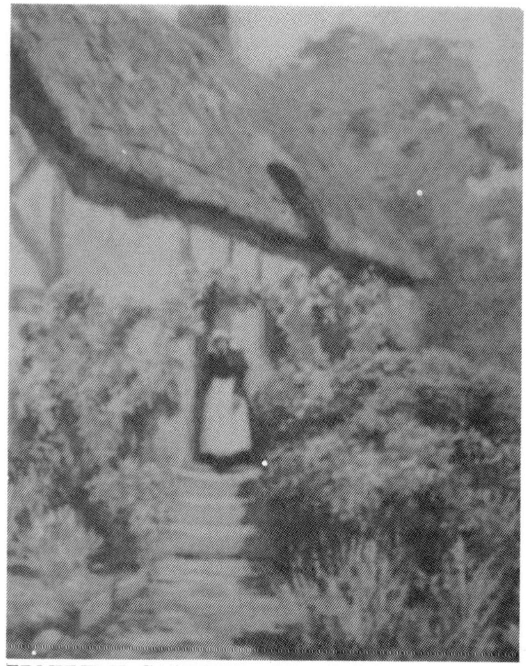

EDMUND H. GARRETT – Thatched Cottage In Spring – signed – oil on canvas – 21 x 27in.
(Robt. W. Skinner Inc.) **$1,900** **£1,250**

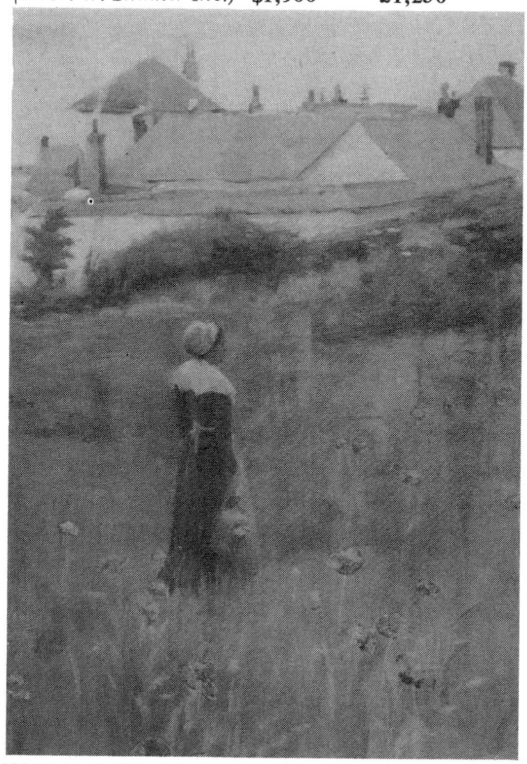

NORMAN GARSTIN – Poppies – signed – oil on canvas – 72.5 x 41cm.
(Phillips) **$15,620** **£11,000**

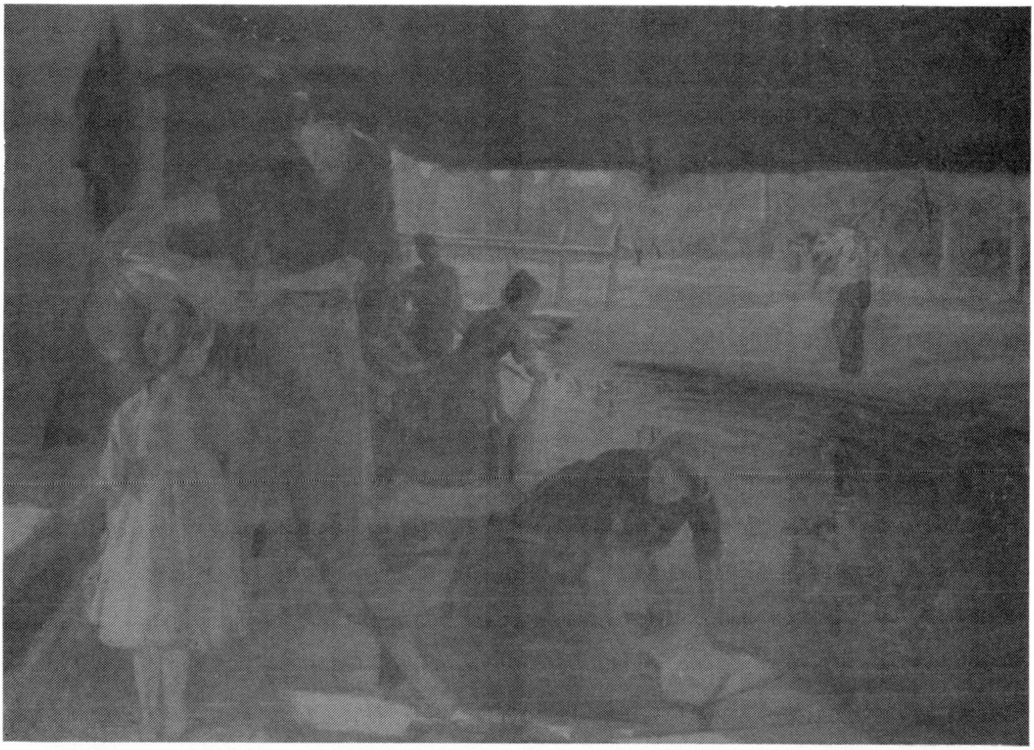

NORMAN GARSTIN, Attributed to – Washerwomen – oil on canvas – 102 x 127cm. *(Phillips)*
$6,400 £4,000

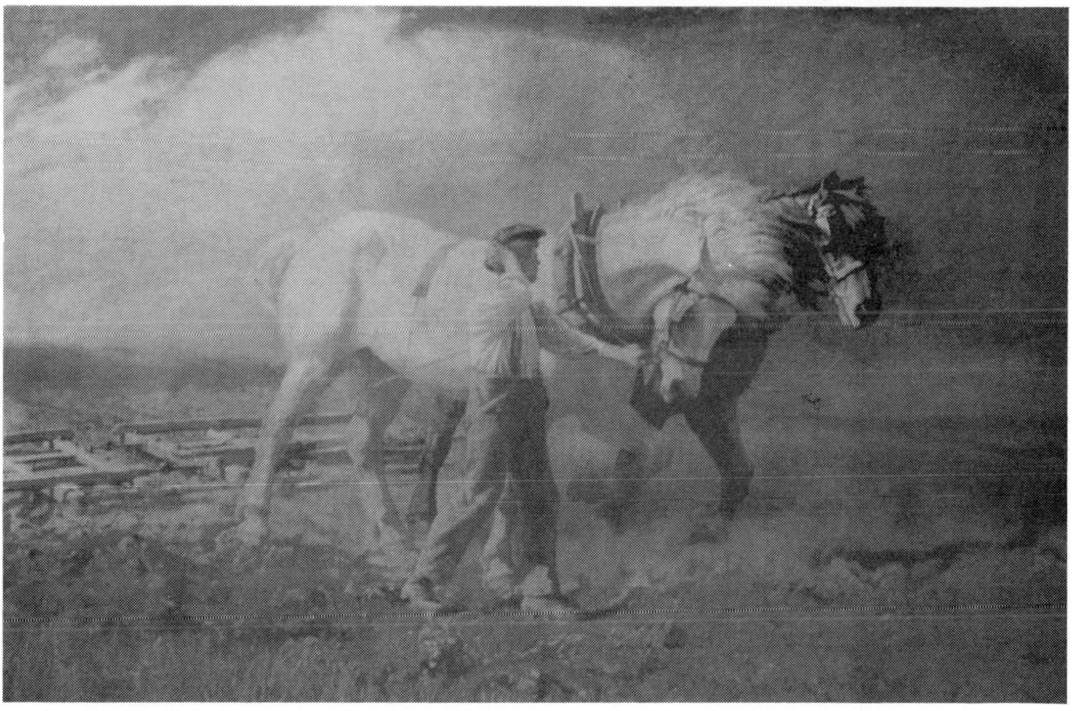

GEORGE GASCOYNE – The Harrow – signed, also signed, inscribed and dated 1887 on the reverse – oil on canvas – 101 x 152cm. *(Phillips)* **$5,680 £4,000**

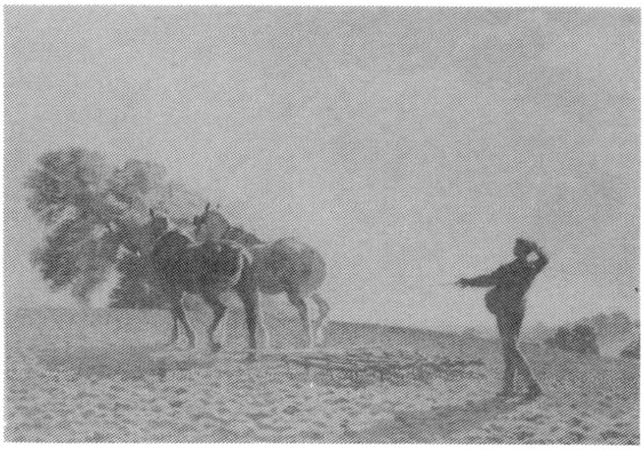

GEORGE GASCOYNE – Tilling The Upland – signed, inscribed and dated 1913 on the reverse – 85.5 x 122.5cm.
(Phillips) **$3,519** **£2,300**

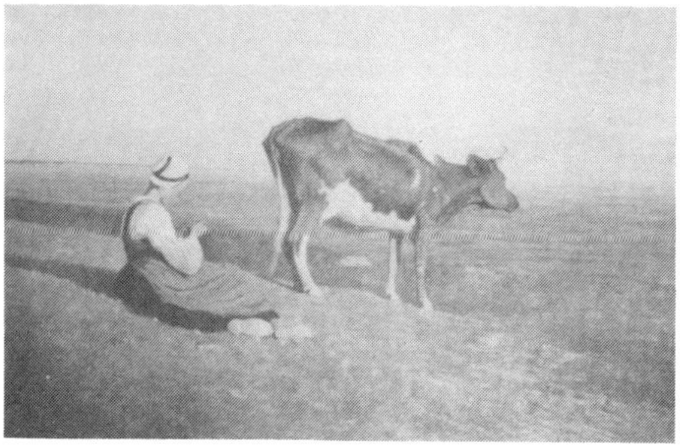

GEORGE GASCOYNE – Evening, Brittany – signed with initials and dated 1891, also signed, inscribed and dated on the reverse – oil on canvas – 30.5 x 48in.
(Christie's) **$1,434** **£880**

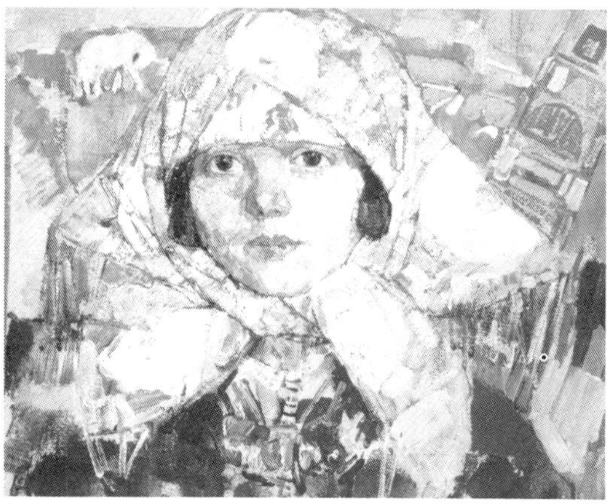

LEON SHULMAN GASPARD – The Pink Babushka – signed and dated 1921 – oil on board – 12½ x 15¼in.
(Christie's) **$30,800** **£21,652**

HENRY GASSER – Gloucester – signed – watercolour on paper laid down on board – 22½ x 30¾in.
(Christie's) **$1,100** **£765**

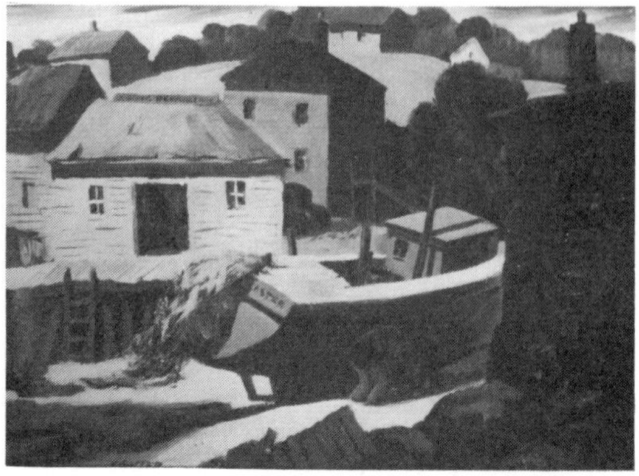

HENRY GASSER – Gloucester Inlet – signed, signed and inscribed on the stretcher – oil on canvas – 19 x 26¼in.
(Christie's) **$3,300** **£2,295**

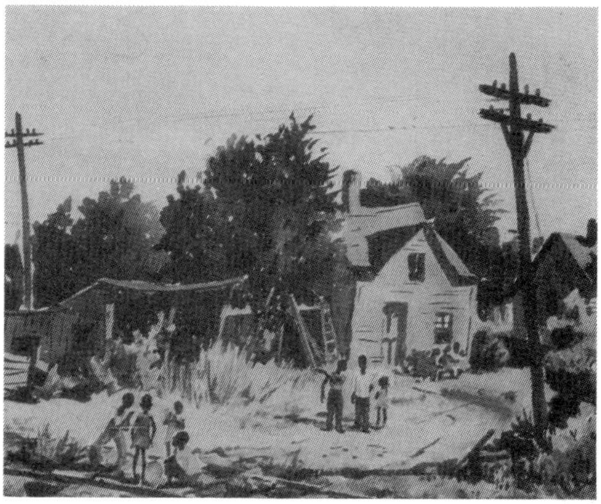

HENRY MARTIN GASSER – House By The Tracks – signed – watercolour on paper laid down on board – 19¼ x 24½in.
(Christie's) **$1,100** **£685**

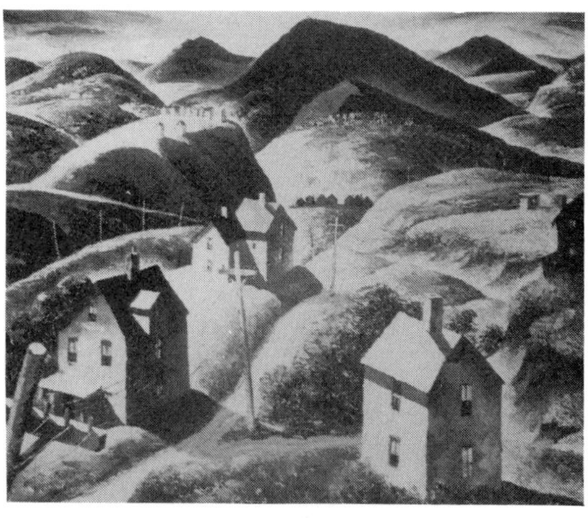

HENRY MARTIN GASSER – Mountain Road – signed – oil on canvas – 25 x 30in.
(Christie's) **$2,860** **£1,782**

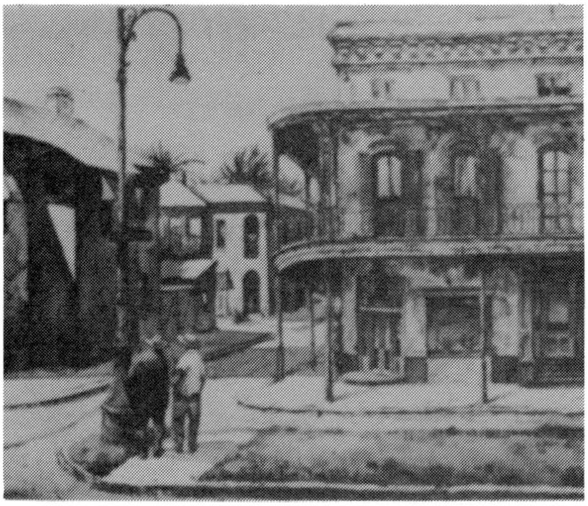

HENRY MARTIN GASSER – New Orleans Corner – signed and inscribed – watercolour on paper – 15 x 21½in.
(Robt. W. Skinner Inc.) **$800** **£526**

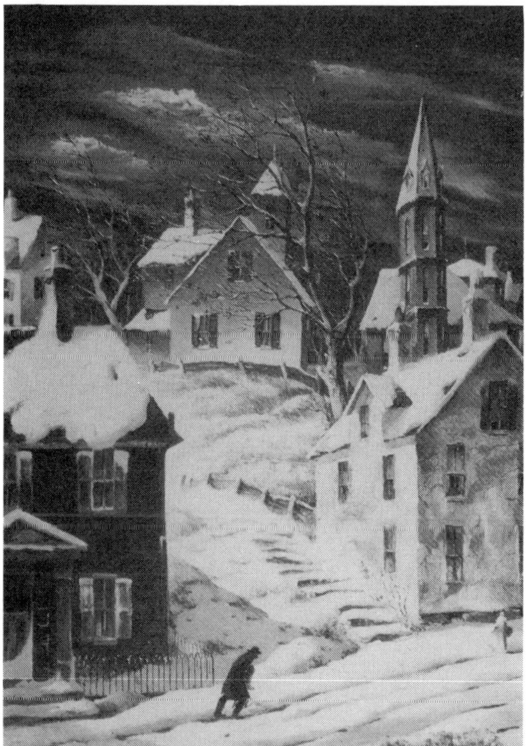

HENRY MARTIN GASSER – Winter Steps – signed, and signed and inscribed on the frame – oil on masonite – 36 x 25in.
(Christie's) **$3,300** **£2,056**

HENRI GAUDIER-BRZESKA – Eagle – inscribed – pen and ink – 19½ x 15½in.
(Christie's) **$6,908** **£4,400**

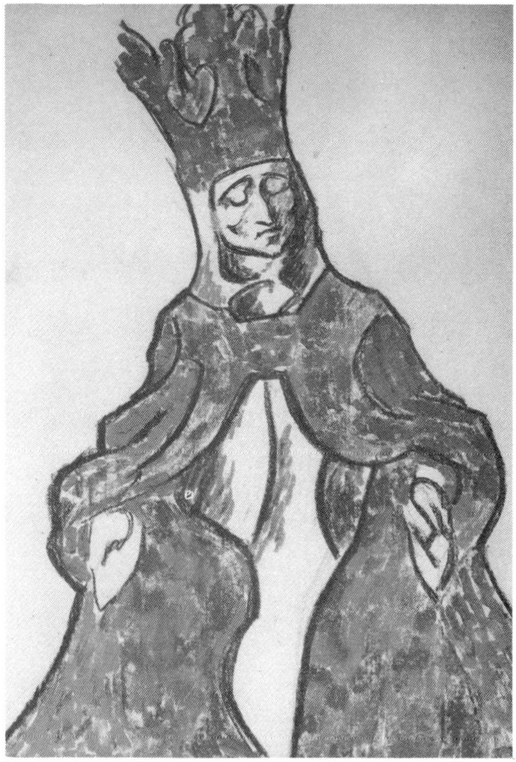

HENRI GAUDIER-BRZESKA – Maria Carmi As The Madonna In 'The Miracle' – signed and dated '12 – charcoal, gold paint and pastel on paper – 29 x 21½in.
(Christie's) **$15,840** **£11,000**

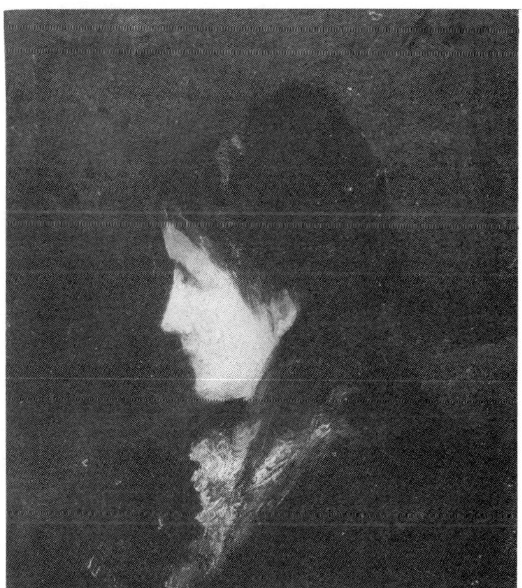

PAUL GAUGUIN – Portrait d'Ingeborg Thaulow – signed with initials – oil on board – 6 x 4¾in.
(Christie's) **$22,176** **£15,400**

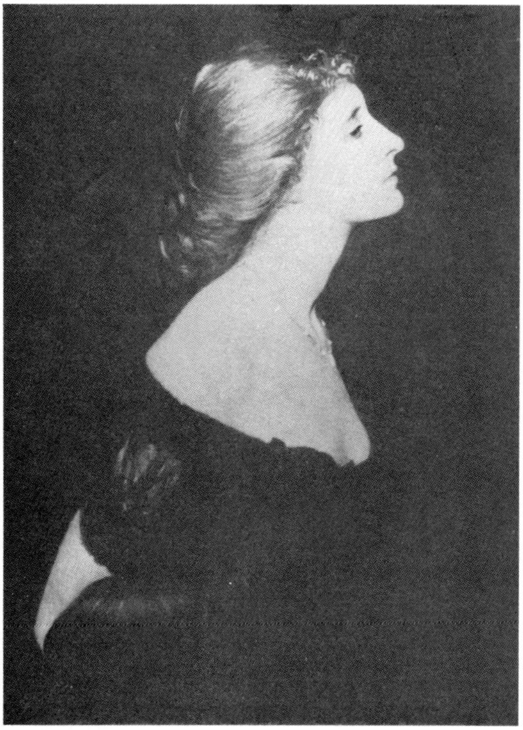

ROBERT DAVID GAULEY – The Lady In Black – signed and dated 1908 – oil on canvas – 32¼ x 24in.
(Christie's) **$2,200** **£1,530**

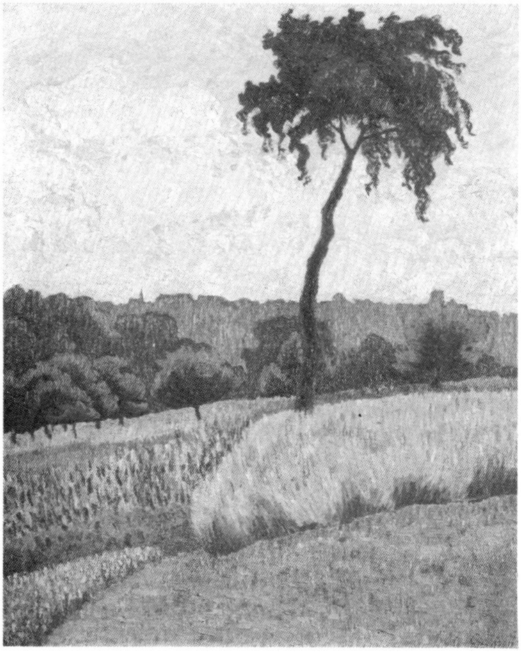

LEO GAUSSON – Paysage en Province – signed and dated '91 – oil on canvas – 21 x 18in.
(Christie's) **$17,424** **£12,100**

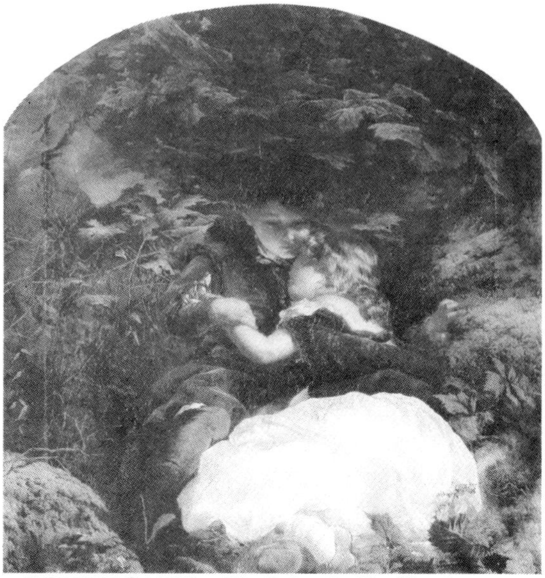

ROBERT GAVIN – The Babes In The Wood – signed and inscribed on an old label on the reverse – 31 x 26in.
(Christie's) **$17,061** **£12,100**

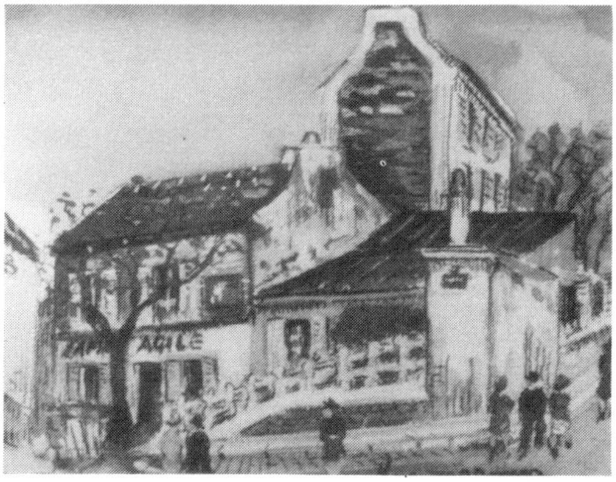

LUCIEN GENIN – Le Lapin Agile, Montmartre – signed – gouache, watercolour and charcoal on buff paper – 7½ x 9in.
(Christie's) **$1,144** **£715**

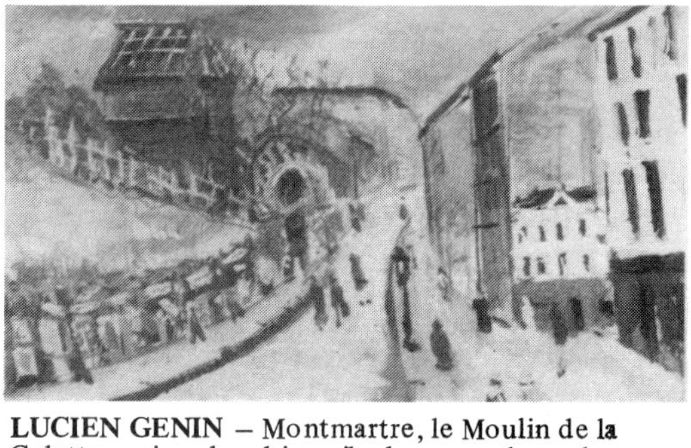

LUCIEN GENIN – Montmartre, le Moulin de la Galette – signed and inscribed – gouache and watercolour on paper – 12½ x 15¾in.
(Christie's) **$2,288** **£1,430**

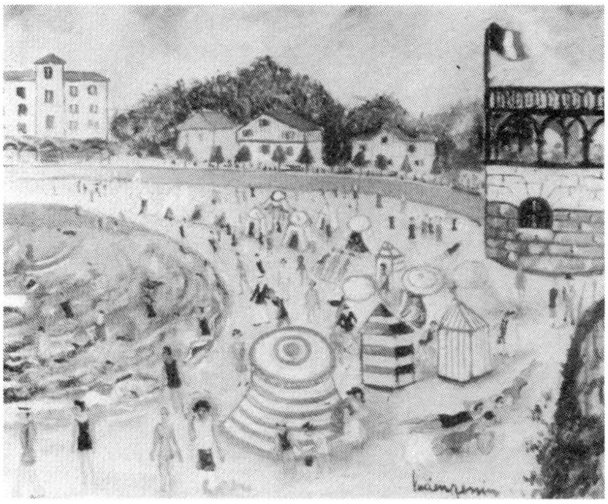

LUCIEN GENIN – La Plage au Tricolore – signed – oil on canvas – 28¼ x 23¼in.
(Christie's) **$3,801** **£2,640**

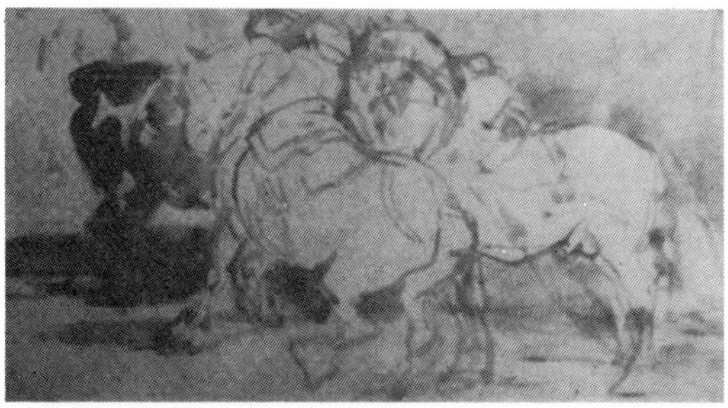

GERICAULT – Study Of Heavy Horses – colour wash – 12 x 9in.
(Michael G. Matthews) **$304** **£190**

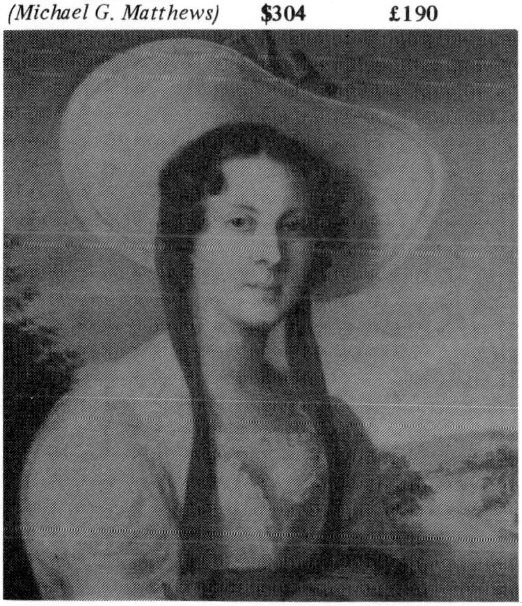

GERMAN SCHOOL, circa 1830 – Portrait Of A Young Lady Wearing A White Dress And Straw Bonnet With Blue Ribbons, An Extensive Landscape Beyond – pastel – 34 x 28cm.
(Phillips) **$684** **£420**

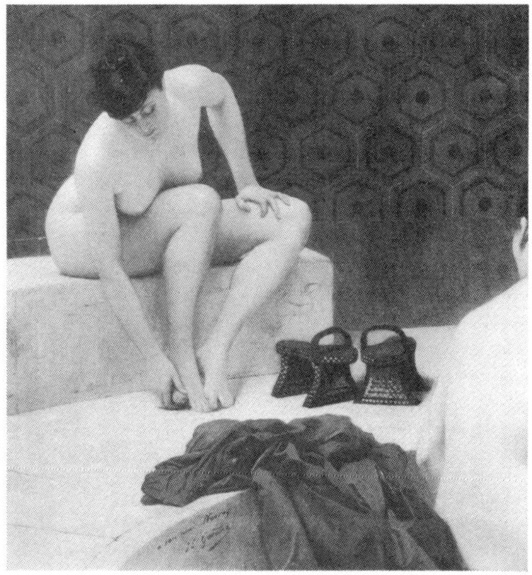

JEAN LEON GEROME – Two Ladies At The Baths – signed – 16¼ x 12¼in.
(Christie's) **$33,264** **£23,100**

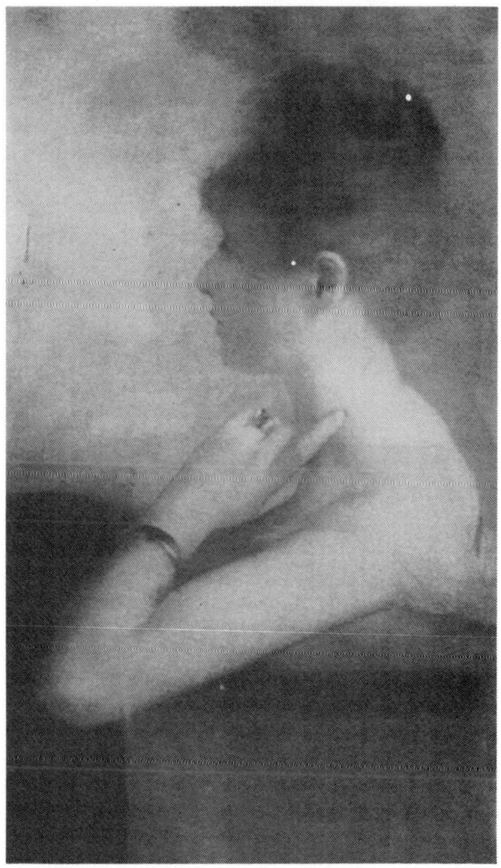

HENRI GERVEX – A Young Lady In An Interior – signed – pastel – 40½ x 17½in.
(Christie's) **$4,400** **£2,750**

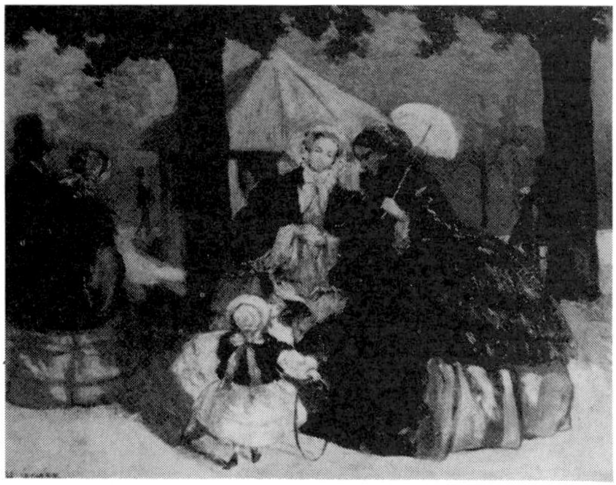

HENRI GERVEX, Attributed to – Aux Champs Elysees – signed – on board – 13 x 15¾in.
(Christie's) **$2,006** **£1,320**

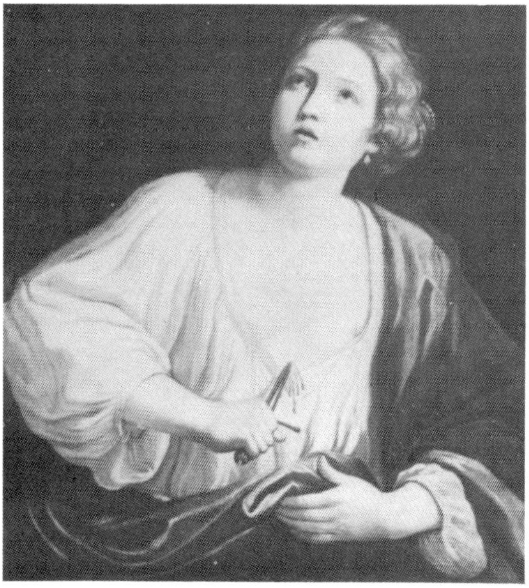

GIOVANNI FRANCESCO GESSI, Circle of – Lucretia – oil on canvas – 28¼ x 80in.
(Phillips) **$775** **£550**

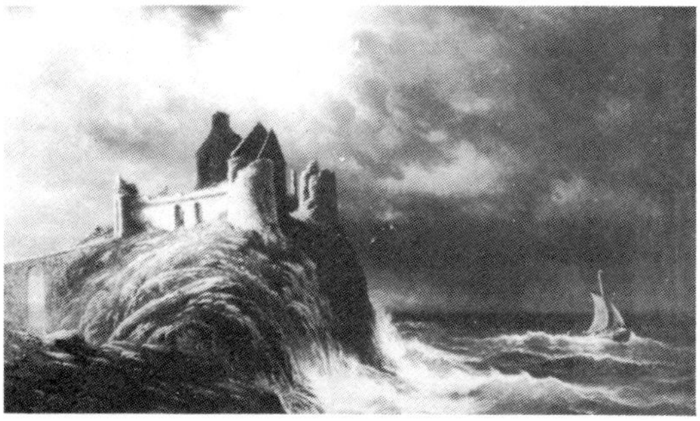

CHARLES HENRY GIFFORD – Irish Castle On A Precipice Overlooking The Sea – signed and dated 1881 – oil on canvas – 26 x 44in.
(Robt. W. Skinner Inc.) **$2,250** **£1,562**

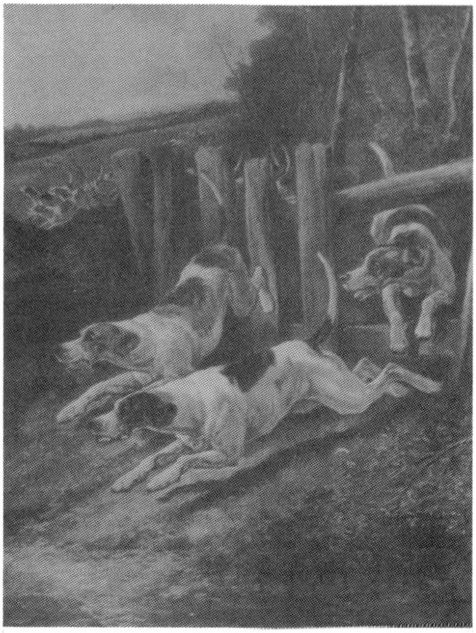

JOHN GIFFORD – Breaking Cover – signed – 35 x 27in.
(Christie's) **$2,356** **£1,540**

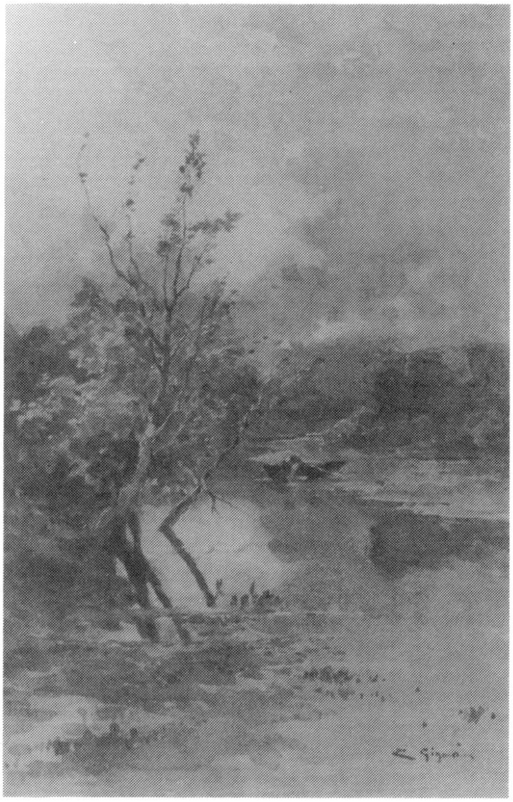

EUGENIO GIGNOUS – Lake Landscapes – signed – watercolour – 21¼ x 13½in.
(Christie's) **$10,956** **£6,600 Three**

EUGENIO GIGNOUS – An Italian Lake – signed – 19 x 28¾in.
(Christie's) **$58,432** **£35,200**

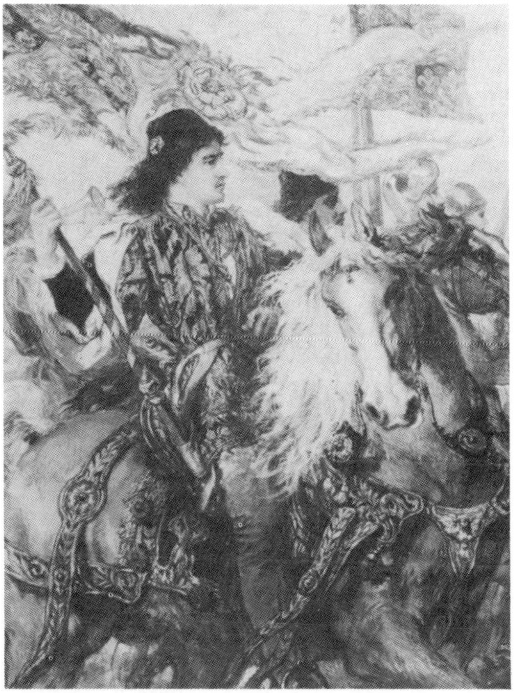

SIR JOHN GILBERT – The Standard-Bearer – signed and dated 1865 – watercolour and body-colour – 18¾ x 14¼in.
(Christie's) **$1,706** **£1,210**

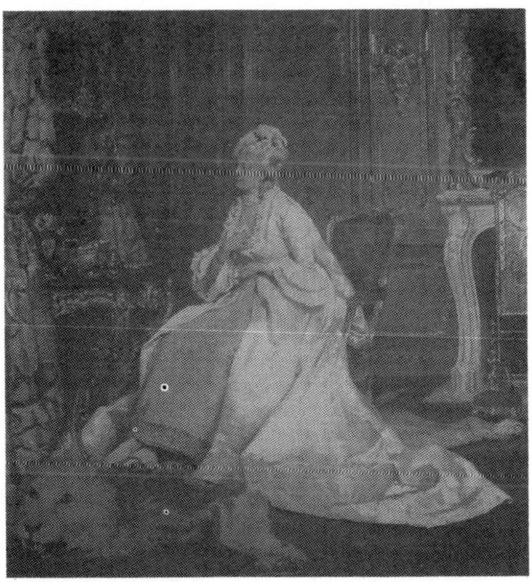

VICTOR GILBERT – In The Boudoir – signed and dated 1876 – 29½ x 26in.
(Christie's) **$16,720** **£10,450**

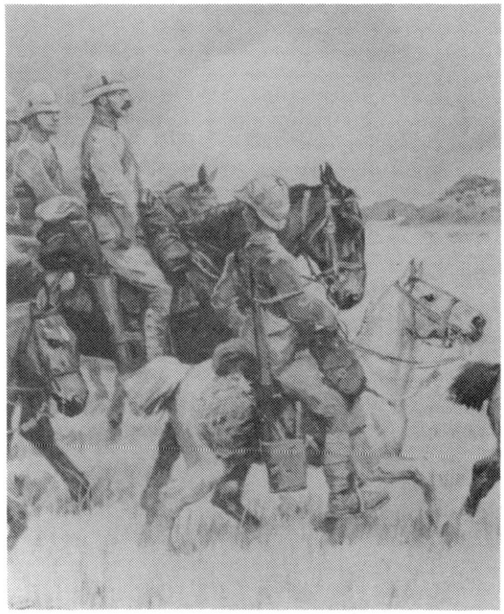

MAJOR GODFREY DOUGLAS GILES – Mounted Soldiers On The Veldt In The Boer War – signed and dated 1901 – oil on canvas – 24 x 20in.
(Phillips) **$841** **£550**

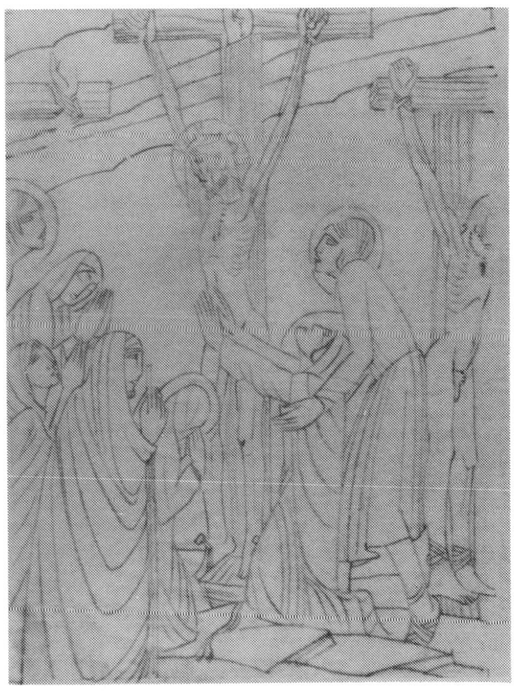

ERIC GILL – The Crucifixion – pencil on buff paper – 16 x 13cm.
(Phillips) **$581** **£350**

GILL

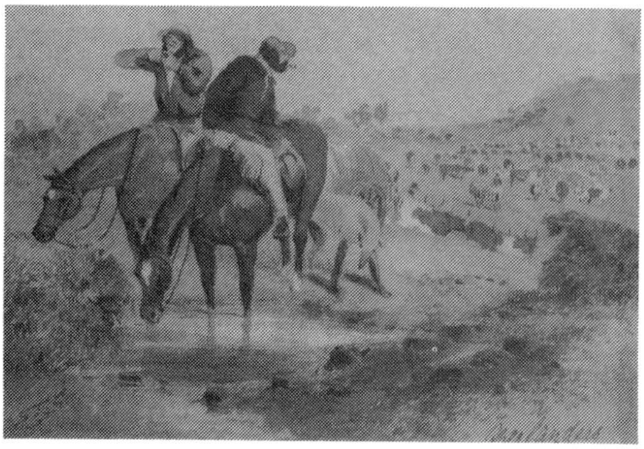

SAMUEL THOMAS GILL – The Overlanders – signed with initials and inscribed – watercolour heightened with gum arabic over pencil – 16.5 x 24cm.
(Phillips) **$7,335** **£4,500**

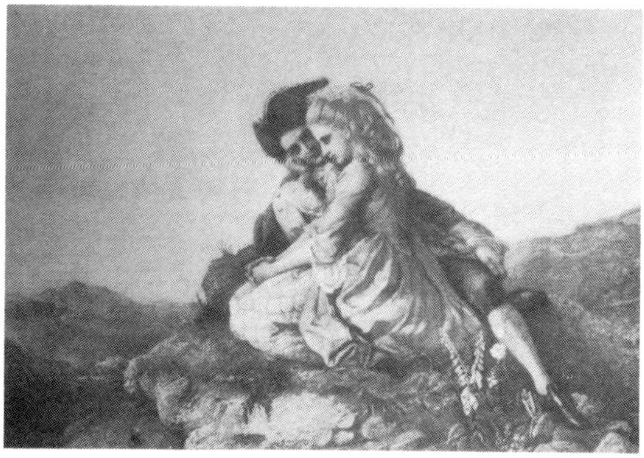

MARGARET GILLIES – An Idyll Of The Olden Time – signed and inscribed verso – watercolour – 15 x 20in.
(Christie's) **$936** **£650**

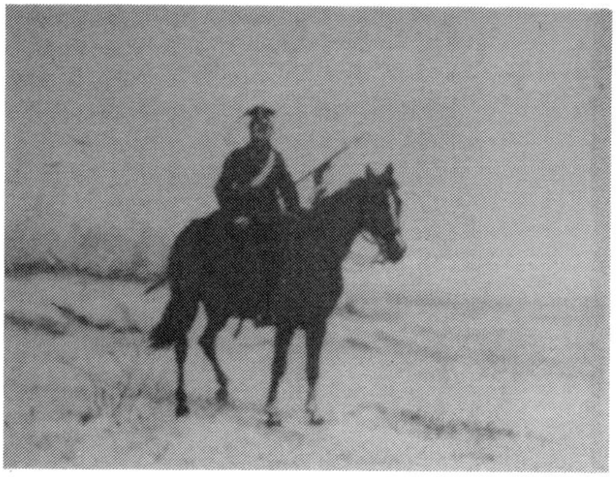

KARL GILLISSEN – A Prussian Lancer On His Horse In A Snowy Landscape – signed and dated 1879 – oil on panel – 14 x 17.5cm.
(Phillips) **$918** **£550**

JAMES GILLRAY, HENRY HEATH and others – A Collection Of Caricatures – coloured etchings, aquatints and lithographs – twenty-five.
(Christie's) **$743** **£520**

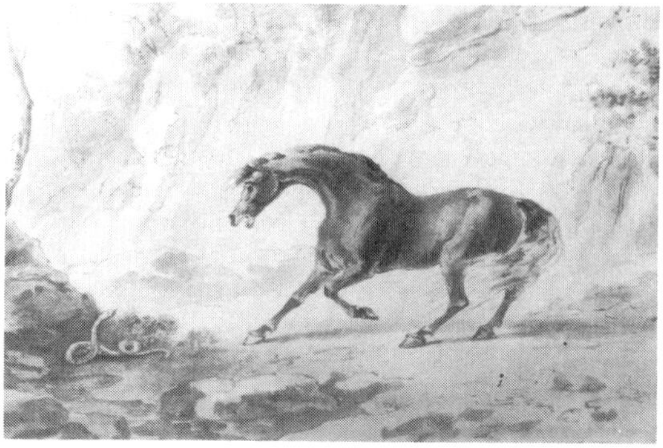

SAWREY GILPIN – A Horse Frightened By A Snake – inscribed and dated 1782 on the reverse – pencil, pen and brown ink and watercolour – 8½ x 11¼in.
(Christie's) **$3,122** **£1,870**

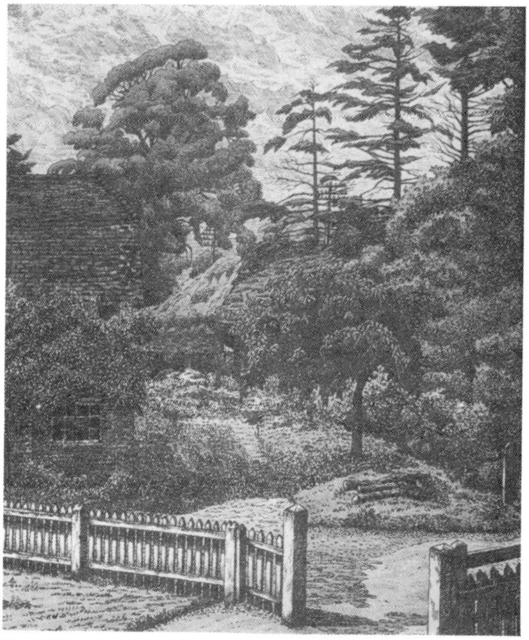

CHARLES GINNER – Durnsford Mill, Near Marlborough – signed – watercolour, pen and black ink – 15 x 11in.
(Christie's) **$3,460** **£2,420**

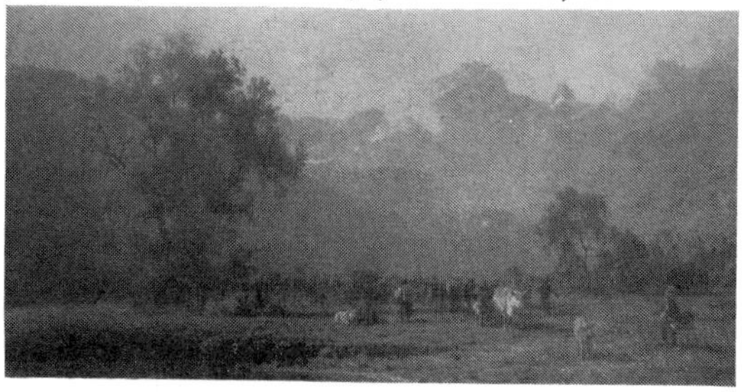

KARL GIRARDET – A Mountainous River Landscape With Cattle – signed – 13½ x 22in.
(Christie's) **$14,080** **£8,800**

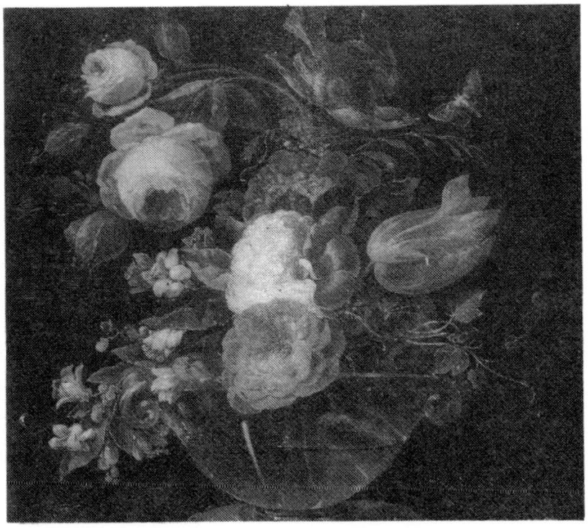

A. GIUSTI – Roses, Tulips And Other Flowers In Vases On Plinths – signed and dated 1852 – on panel – 16 x 17in.
(Christie's) **$4,681** **£3,080 Pair**

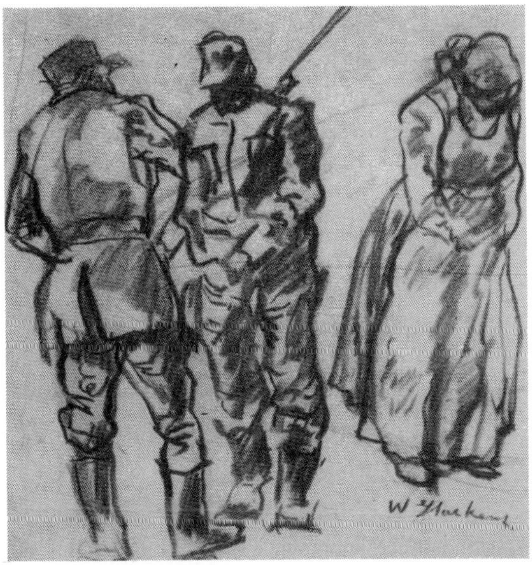

WILLIAM GLACKENS – Figure Studies; and Soldiers – signed – one charcoal on paper, the other charcoal and pencil on paper – one 11 x 14in., the other 11 x 9¾in.
(Christie's) **$880** **£548 Two**

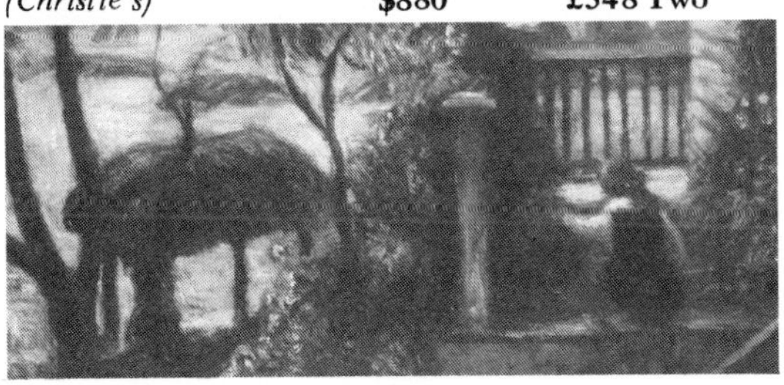

WILLIAM GLACKENS – Eastern Point, Gloucester – oil on canvas – 20 x 25¾in.
(Christie's) **$198,000** **£139,194**

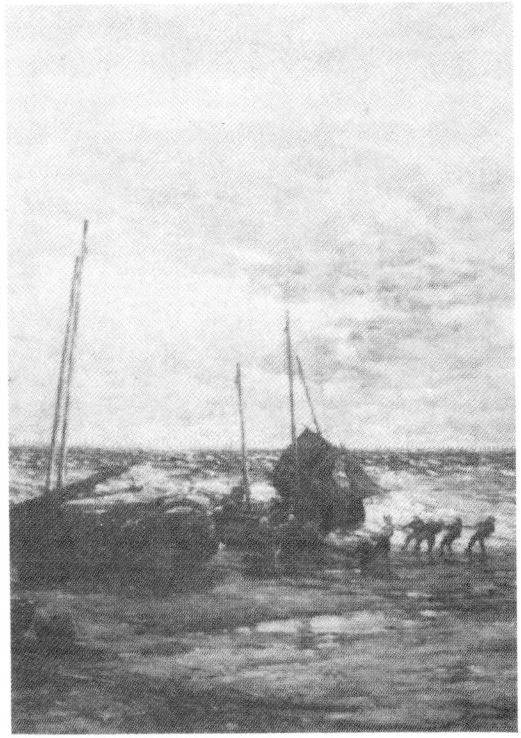

JOHN HAMILTON GLASS – Sunset On The Brittany Coast, Ebbing Tide – signed, inscribed on the reverse – oil on canvas – 36 x 26½in.
(Christie's) **$642** **£420**

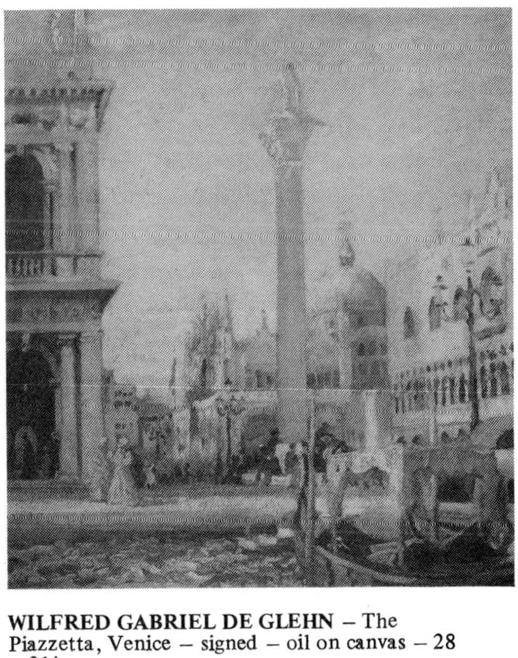

WILFRED GABRIEL DE GLEHN – The Piazzetta, Venice – signed – oil on canvas – 28 x 31in.
(Christie's) **$62,920** **£44,000**

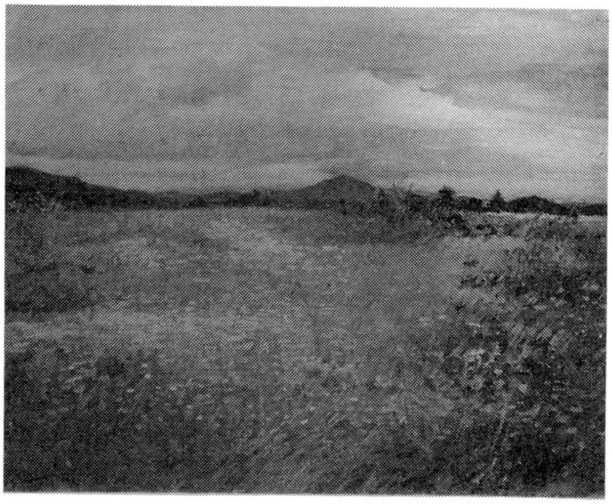

WILFRED GABRIEL DE GLEHN – A Meadow Of Wild Flowers – signed and dated 1903 – oil on canvas – 51 x 64cm.
(Phillips) **$5,760** **£3,600**

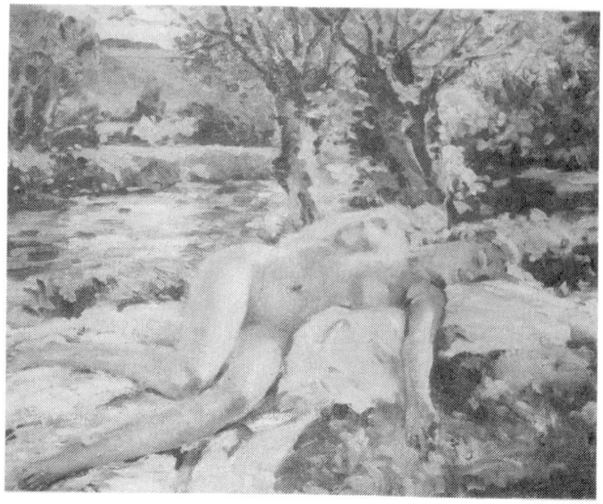

WILFRED GABRIEL DE GLEHN – Summer On The Avon – signed, inscribed on the reverse – oil on canvas – 21½ x 27¾in.
(Christie's) **$37,994** **£24,200**

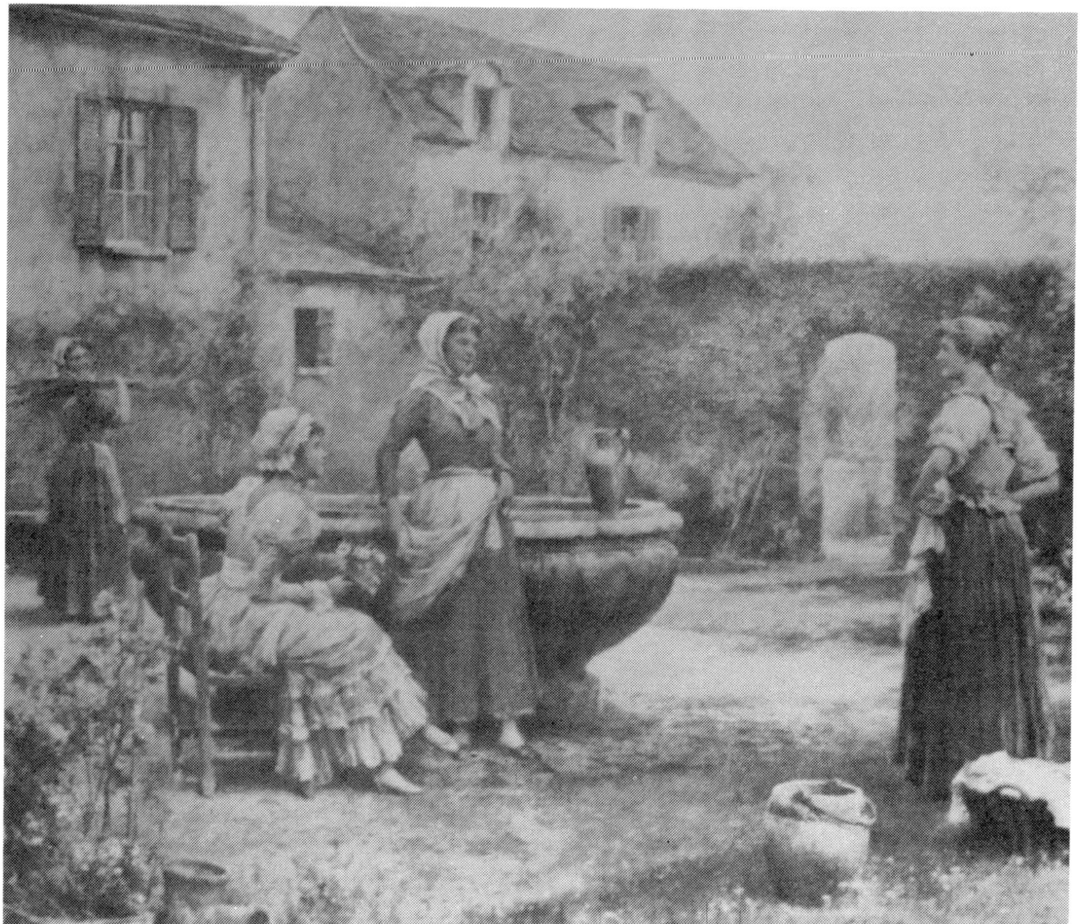

ALFRED AUGUSTUS GLENDENING – Young Women Laughing By A Well – signed with monogram – watercolour and bodycolour – 60 x 90cm. *(Phillips)* **$6,520** **£4,000**

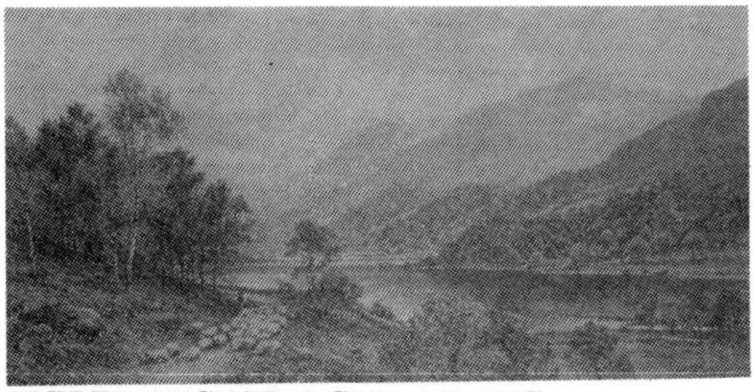

ALFRED AUGUSTUS GLENDENING – Thirlemere, A Shepherd With His Sheep Beside The Lake, Late Afternoon – signed and dated 1904 – oil on canvas – 24 x 42in.
(Phillips) **$27,370** **£17,000**

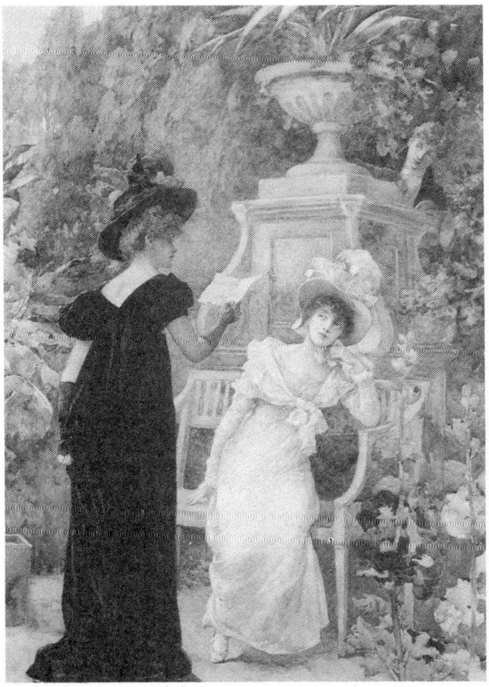

HENRY GILLARD GLINDONI – The Love Letter – signed and dated 1899 and inscribed – pencil and watercolour – 39 x 24in.
(Christie's) **$2,916** **£1,944**

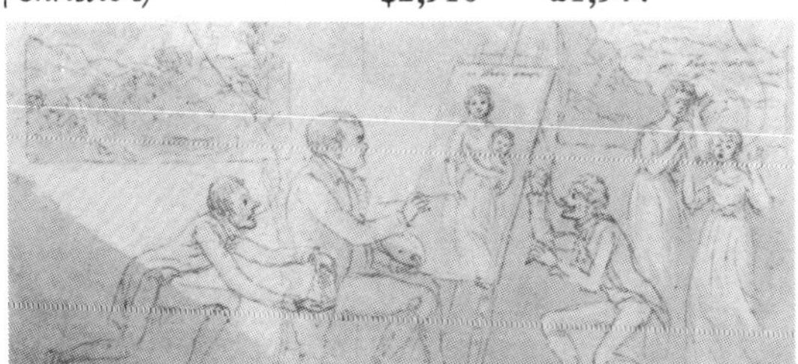

JOHN GLOVER – 'A Painter Studying The Beauties Of Nature' – signed and inscribed – pen and grey ink, grey wash – 7¾ x 11in., and four grey wash drawings of Ullswater, London and elsewhere, one dated 1829.
(Christie's) **$593** **£418 Five**

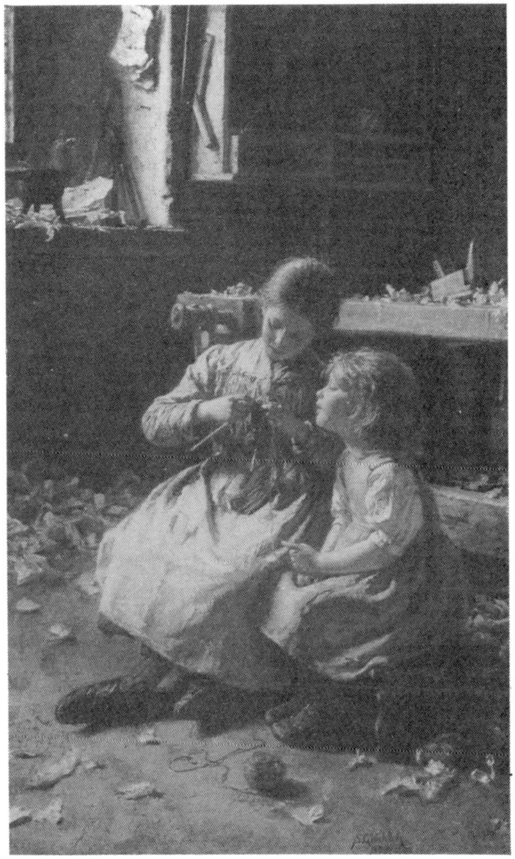

SIMON GLUCHLICK – The Knitting Lesson – signed and dated 1894 – 23¾ x 15in.
(Christie's) **$29,920** **£18,700**

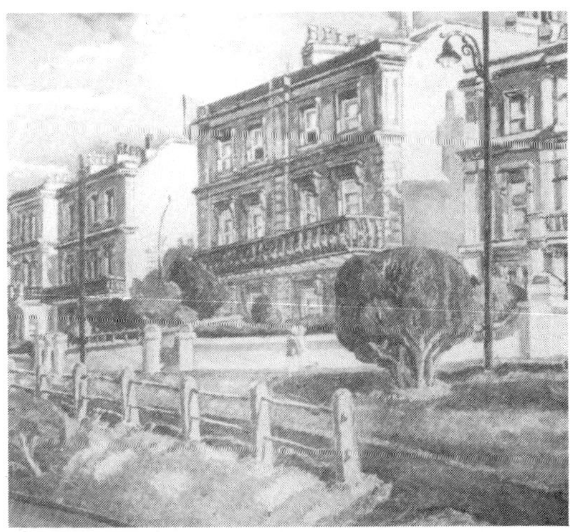

MARY GODWIN – Torquay – signed – oil on canvas – 64 x 76cm.
(Phillips) **$535** **£350**

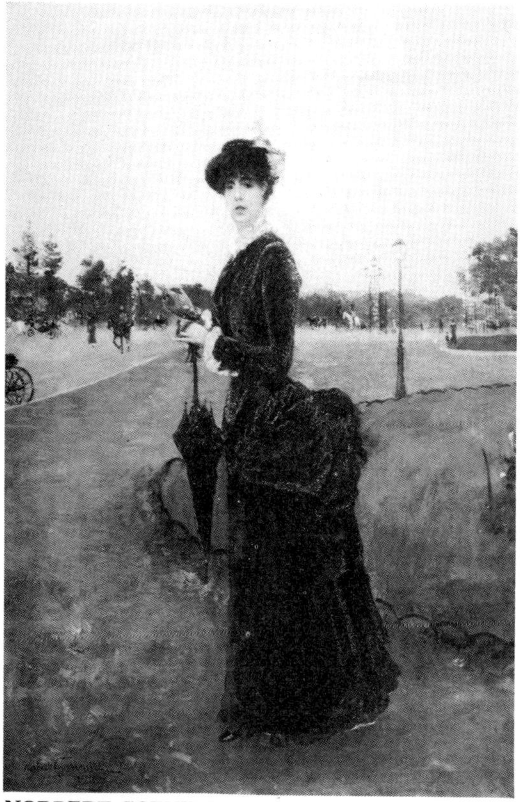

NORBERT GOENEUTTE – La Parisienne – signed and dated 1889(?) – 18¼ x 12¾in.
(Christie's) **$7,920** **£5,500**

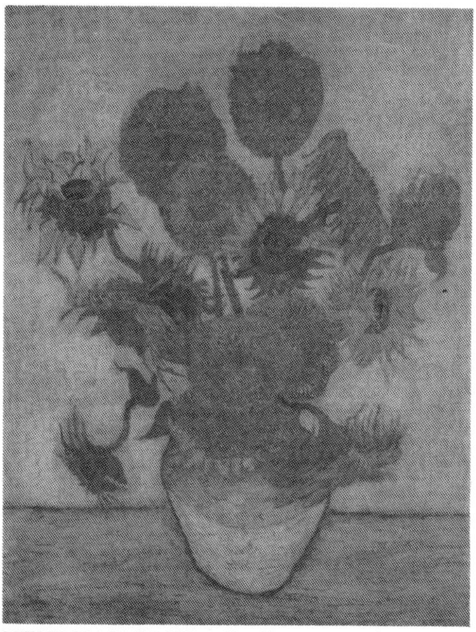

VINCENT VAN GOGH – Sunflowers – oil on extended canvas – 39½ x 30¼in.
(Christie's) **$41,332,500** **£24,750,000**

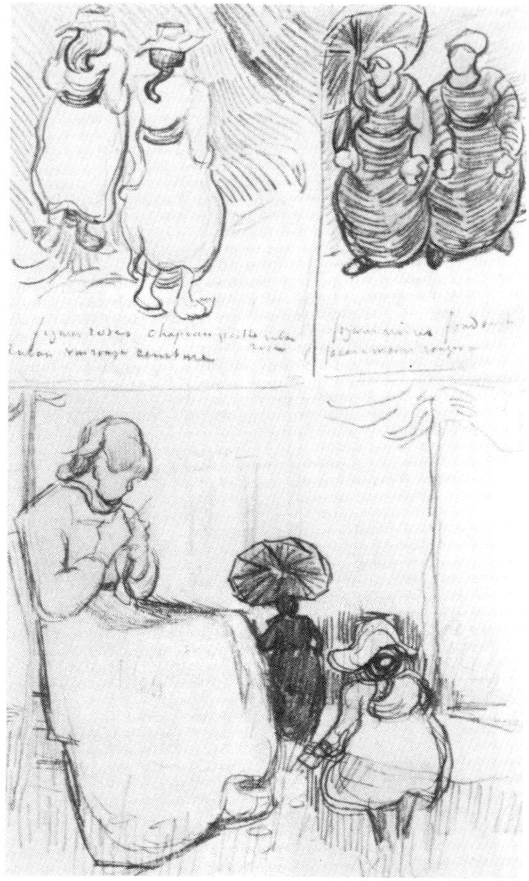

VINCENT VAN GOGH – Deux jeunes Filles en Chapeau de Paille; and Deux Paysannes marchant de Face; Jeune Fille assise dans un Jardin, tricotant en surveillant une petite Fille – inscribed – recto; Deux Hommes en Barque; Deux Femmes en Barque; Petit Bateau-a-Vapeur; and Paysanne en Coiffe – soft pencil on paper – verso – 16½ x 10½in.
(Christie's) **$134,640** **£93,500**

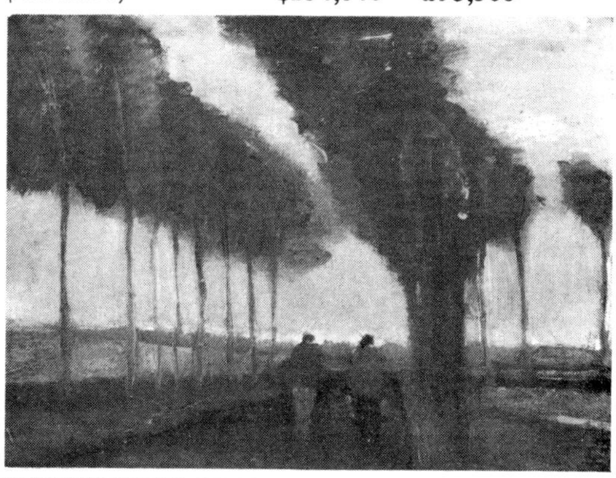

VINCENT VAN GOGH – L'Allee aux deux Promeneurs – oil on canvas laid on panel – 12½ x 15½in.
(Christie's) **$71,280** **£49,500**

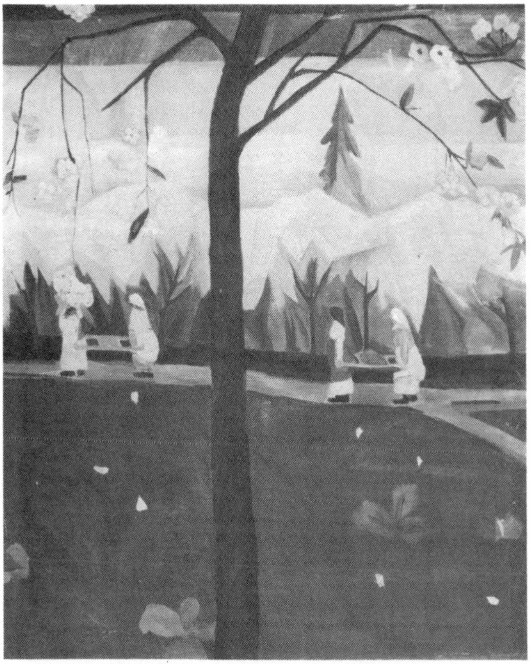

NATALIA GONTCHAROVA – Le Printemps – signed with initials – oil on canvas – 36¼ x 29¼in.
(Christie's) **$44,352 £30,800**

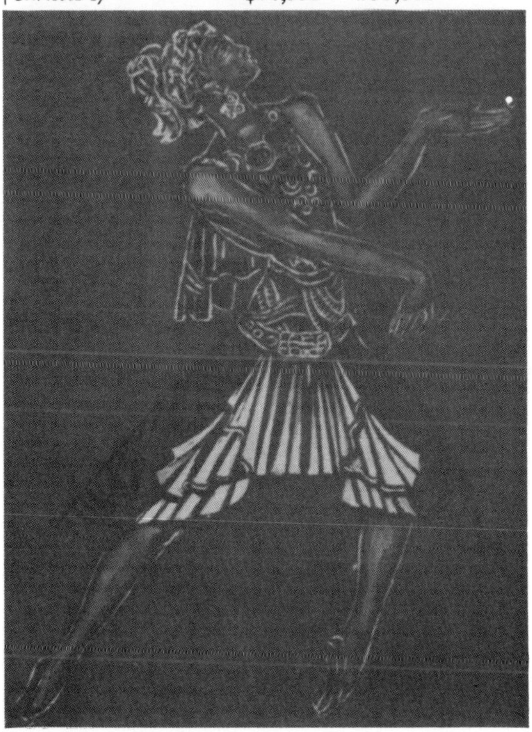

NATALIA GONTCHAROVA – Danseuse orientale – signed with initials – watercolour and gouache on green paper – 14½ x 10½in.
(Christie's) **$1,232 £770**

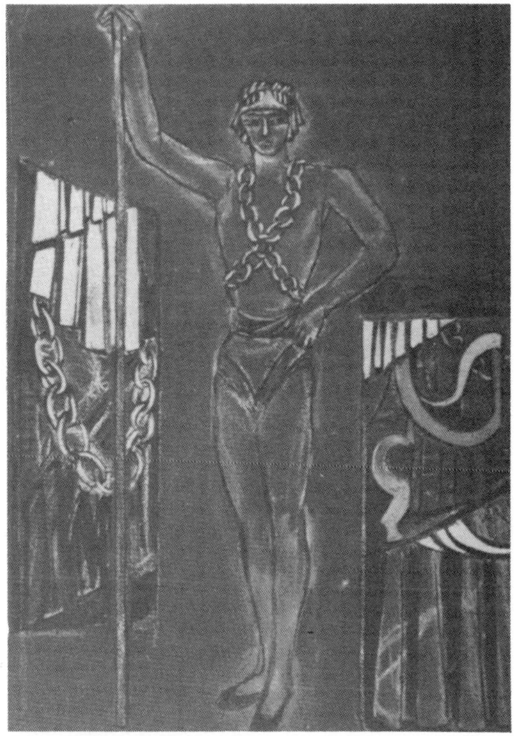

NATALIA GONTCHAROVA – Le Geolier – signed with initials – gouache, brush and indian ink heightened with white on mauve paper – 14½ x 10½in.
(Christie's) **$1,232 £770**

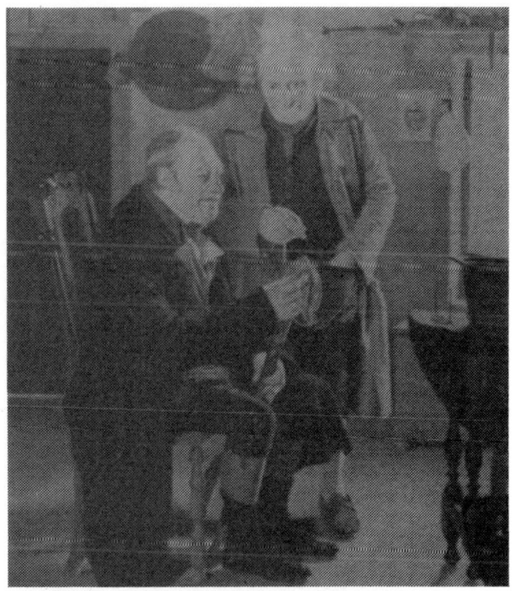

THOMAS SWORD GOOD – Two Old Men Reminiscing Over An Old Campaign Sabre (Survivors Of The Battle Of Minden) – signed and dated 1822 – on panel – 13 x 10½in.
(Phillips) **$4,025 £2,500**

GOODALL

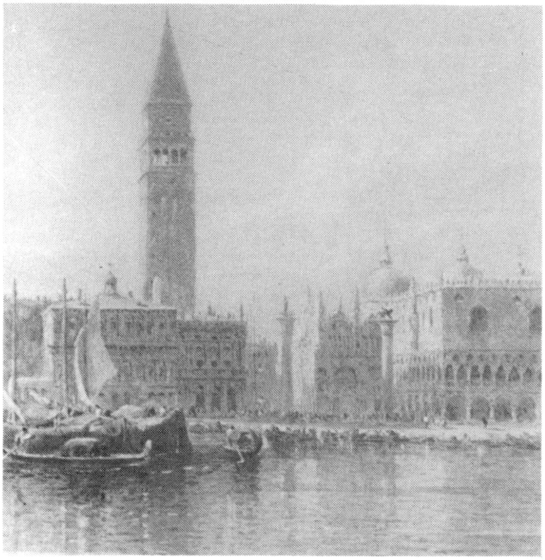

EDWARD ALFRED GOODALL – View Across The Basin Towards St. Mark's Square, Venice – signed and dated 1881 – 10¼ x 7¾in.
(Dacre, Son & Hartley) **$1,433** **£925**

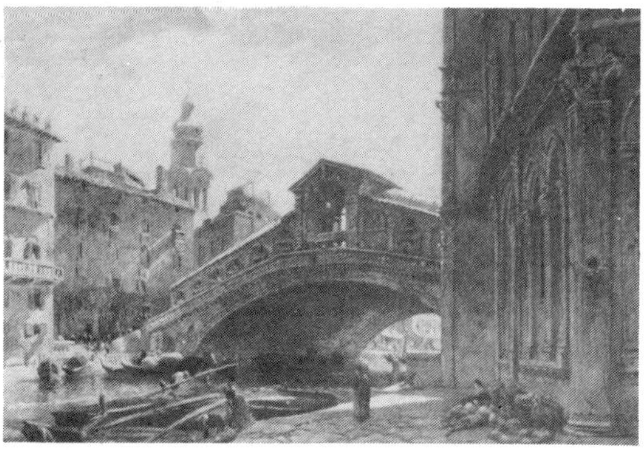

EDWARD ANGELO GOODALL – Venice: The Rialto Bridge From The Fruit Market – signed and dated 1880 – pencil and watercolour – 8 x 11½in.
(Christie's) **$1,008** **£715**

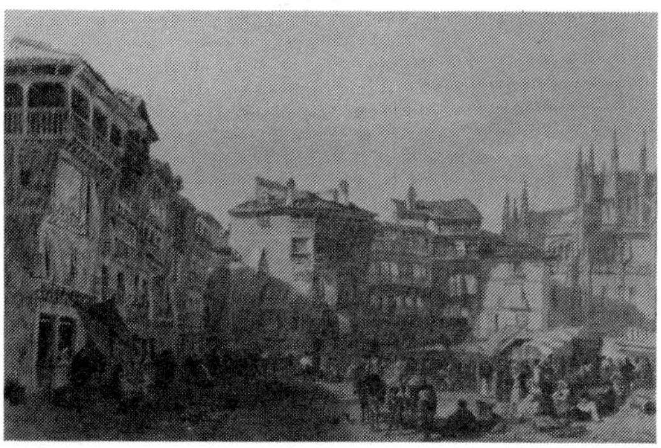

EDWARD ANGELO GOODALL – 'Segovia' – signed, inscribed and dated 1856 – watercolour over traces of pencil – 35.5 x 52.5cm.
(Phillips) **$3,260** **£2,000**

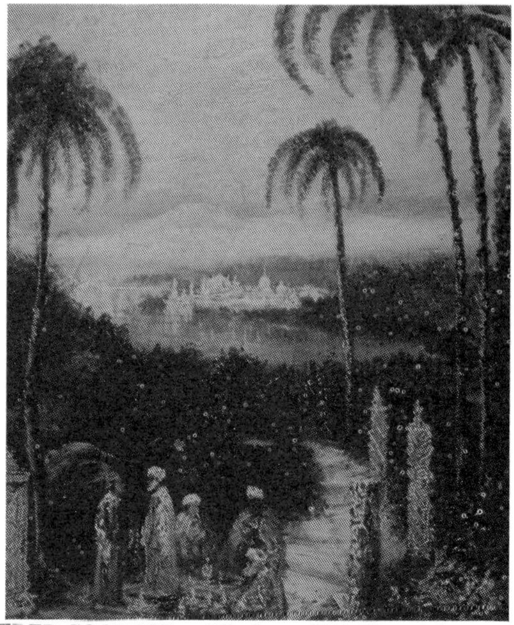

FRED GOODALL – Nile Scene With Figures In Foreground And Buildings In Background – initialled and dated – oil – 12 x 9in.
(Morphets) **$651** **£420**

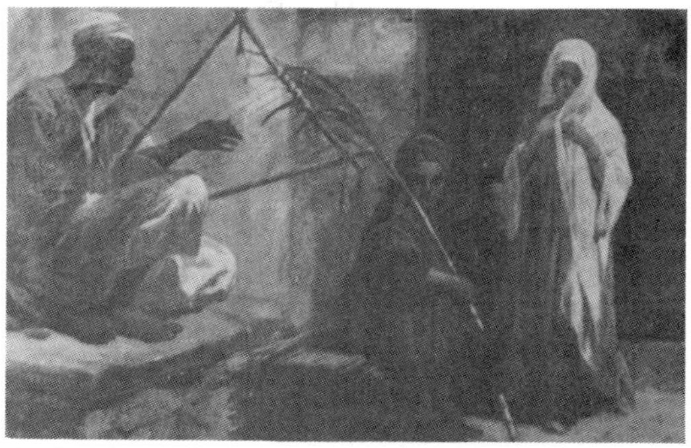

FREDERICK GOODALL – The Street Musician – signed and inscribed – oil on canvas – 15 x 21in.
(Christie's) **$1,377** **£900**

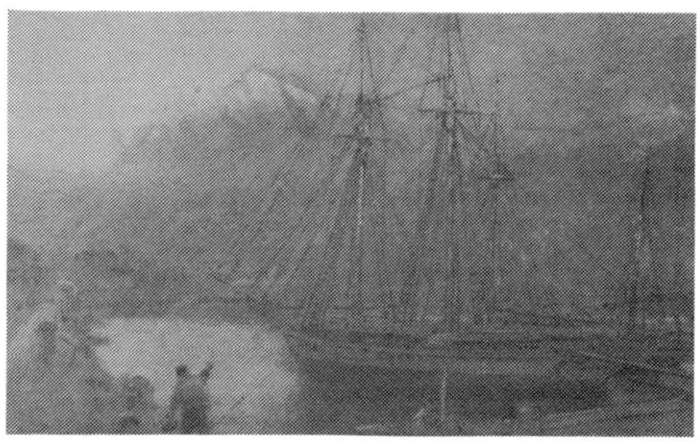

ALBERT GOODWIN – 'The Pool Of Solla, Majorca' – signed and inscribed – pen and ink and bodycolour – 23.5 x 35cm.
(Phillips) **$2,934** **£1,800**

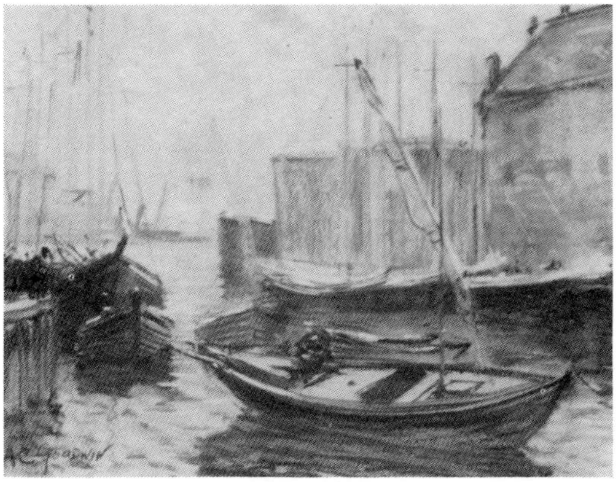

ARTHUR CLIFTON GOODWIN – Sailboats At A Wharf; and Feast Day, The North End – a double-sided painting – the first signed – pastel on paper – 17½ x 22½in.
(Robt. W. Skinner Inc.) **$1,900** **£1,319**

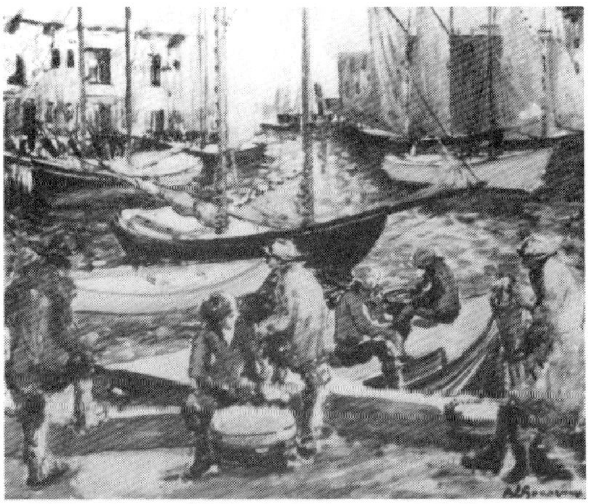

ARTHUR CLIFTON GOODWIN – Old Days, T Wharf – signed – oil on canvas – 33½ x 40½in.
(Robt. W. Skinner Inc.) **$7,250** **£4,769**

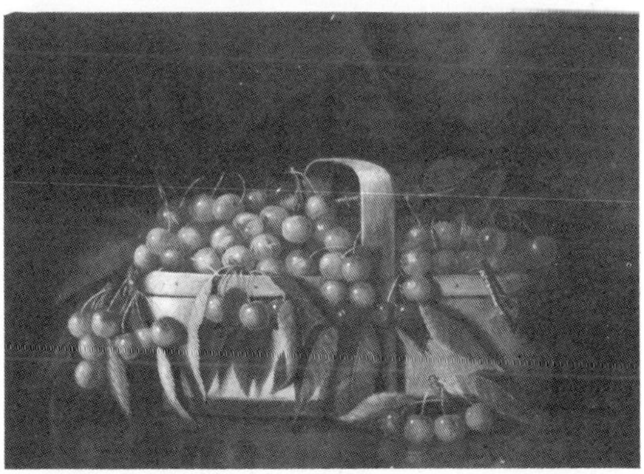

RICHARD LA BARRE GOODWIN – A Basket Of Cherries – signed – oil on canvas – 15¾ x 22in.
(Christie's) **$7,700** **£5,413**

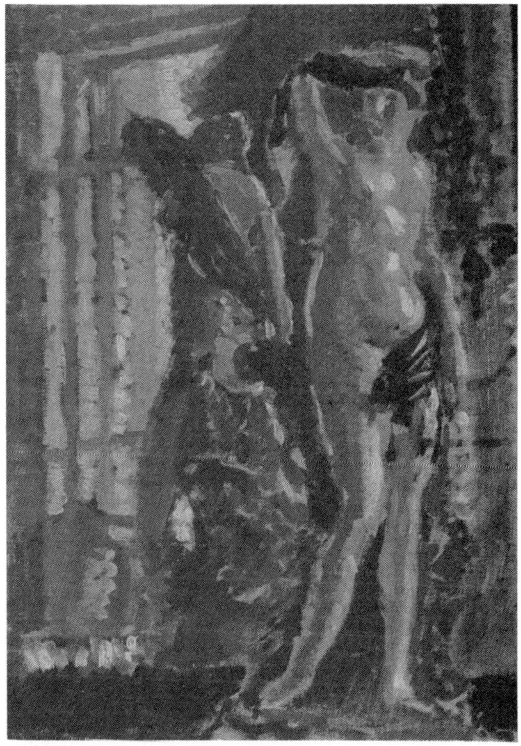

SPENCER FREDERICK GORE – A Porcelain Figurine By A Mirror – oil on canvas – 16 x 12in.
(Christie's) **$6,292** **£4,400**

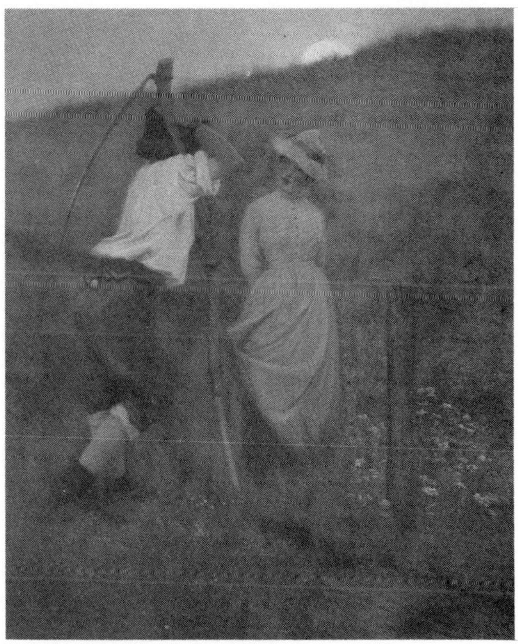

WILLIAM HENRY GORE – By Unfrequented Ways – signed, and signed and inscribed on a label on the stretcher – oil on canvas – 43½ x 33½in.
(Christie's) **$7,078** **£4,950**

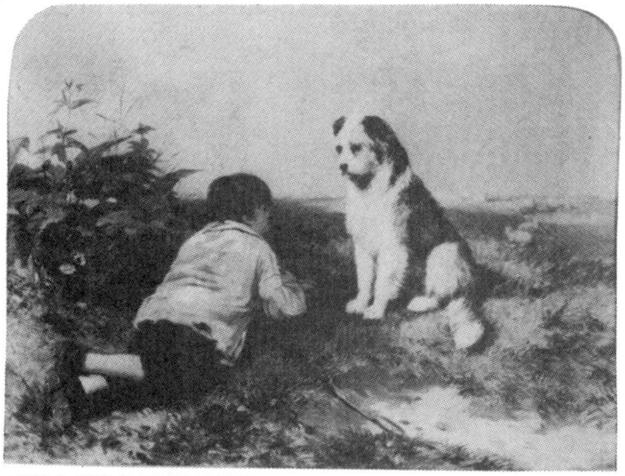

WILLIAM GOSLING – Break For Lunch: A Shepherd Boy And His Dog In A Summer Landscape – signed and dated on verso – oil – 12 x 16in.
(Woolley & Wallis) **$733** **£520**

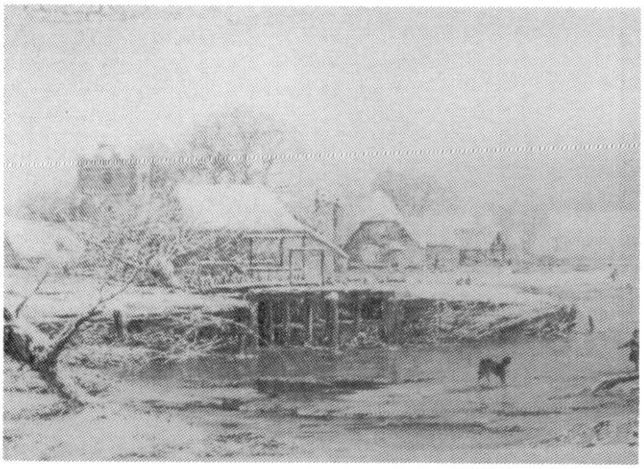

WILLIAM W. GOSLING – A Winter Landscape With Children Skating On A Lake Outside A Village – signed – pencil and watercolour heightened with white – 9 x 17¾in.
(Christie's) **$2,191** **£1,320**

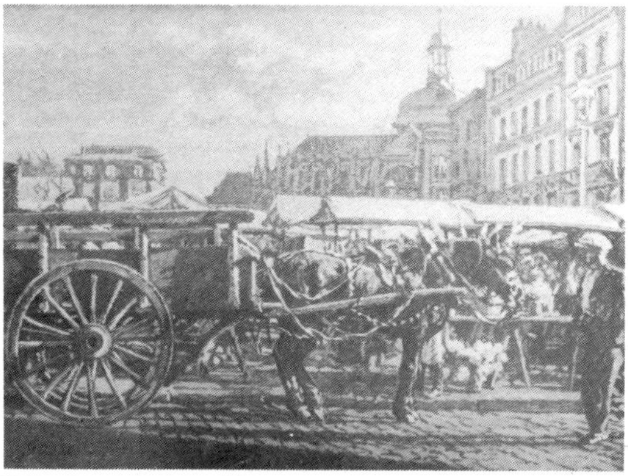

SYLVIA GOSSE – The Market Place, Dieppe – signed – oil on canvas – 30 x 40in.
(Christie's) **$3,799** **£2,420**

SYLVIA GOSSE – A Primula – signed – oil on canvas – 40.5 x 30.5cm.
(Phillips) **$962** **£580**

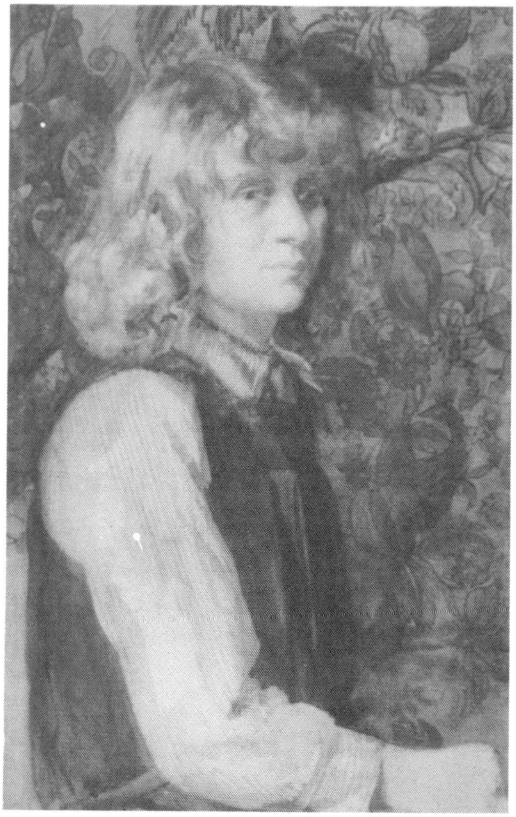

THOMAS COOPER GOTCH – Half Portrait Of A Young Girl With Blond Hair Wearing School Uniform – signed – watercolour – 55 x 34cm.
(W. H. Lane & Son) **$1,411** **£850**

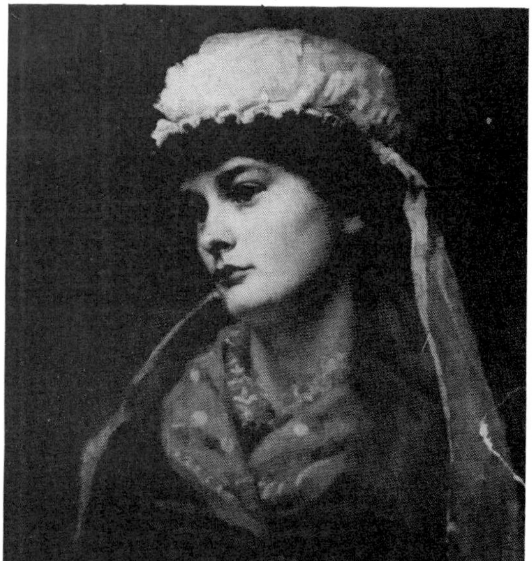

THOMAS COOPER GOTCH – A Newlyn Lass – signed and dated '89 – oil on canvas – 24 x 20in.
(Christie's) **$4,317** **£2,750**

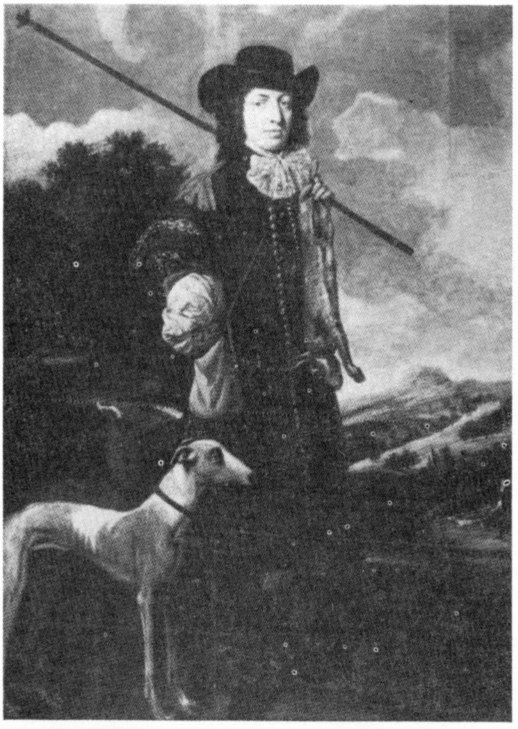

JAN GOTINGH – Portrait Of A Huntsman, Standing Full Length, In A Landscape With His Hounds, Holding A Dead Hare And Staff – signed and indistinctly dated – oil on panel – 32¼ x 22¾in.
(Phillips) **$2,820** **£2,000**

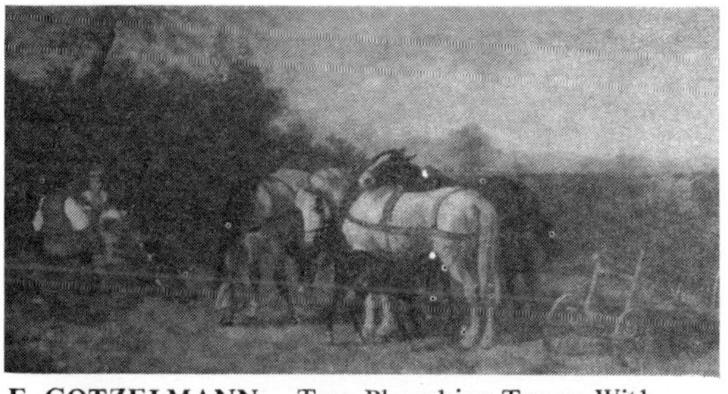

E. GOTZELMANN – Two Ploughing Teams With Figures And Dog In A Landscape – signed – oil – 19¾ x 32in.
(Warners) **$2,480** **£1,550**

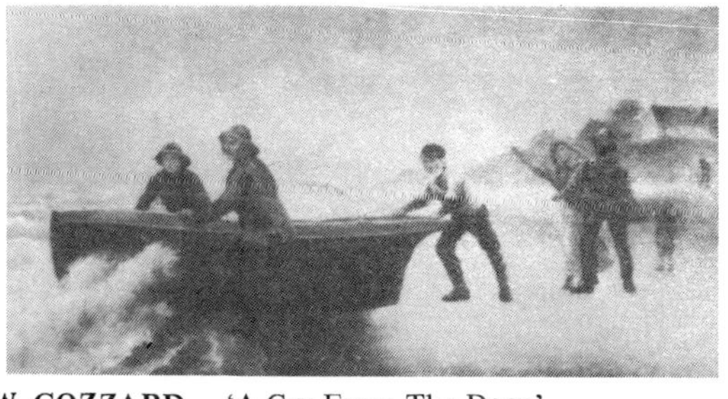

W. GOZZARD – 'A Cry From The Deep' – signed – oil on canvas – 49 x 74cm.
(W. H. Lane & Son) **$996** **£600**

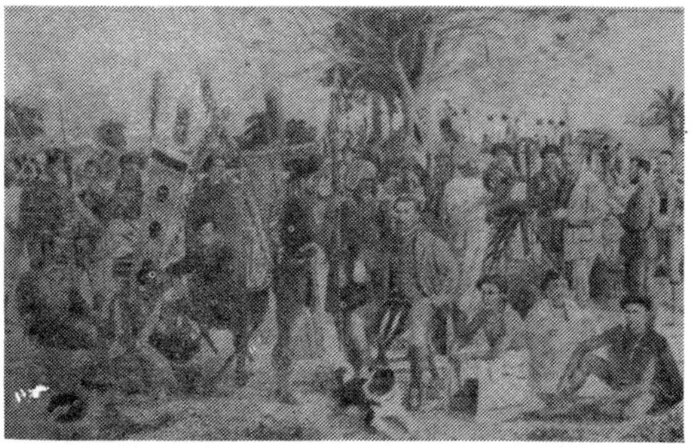

G. R. – Europeans Visiting And Photographing Naga Indians – signed with initials and dated 1875 – watercolour heightened with white – 31.5 x 51cm.
(Phillips) **$2,934** **£1,800**

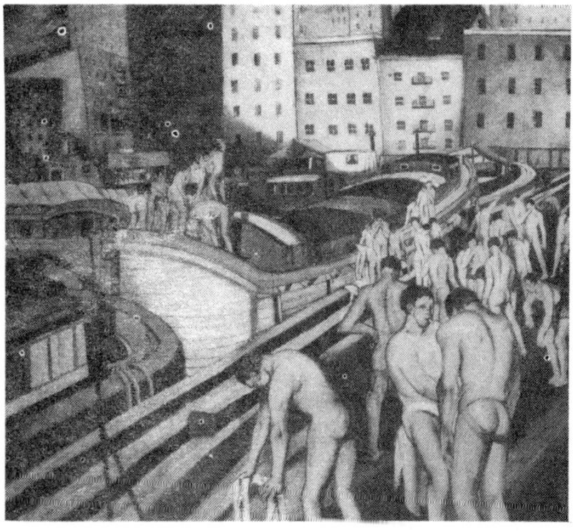

JOHN R. GRABACH – Urban Bathers – signed – oil on canvas – 42 x 48in.
(Christie's) **$15,400** **£9,595**

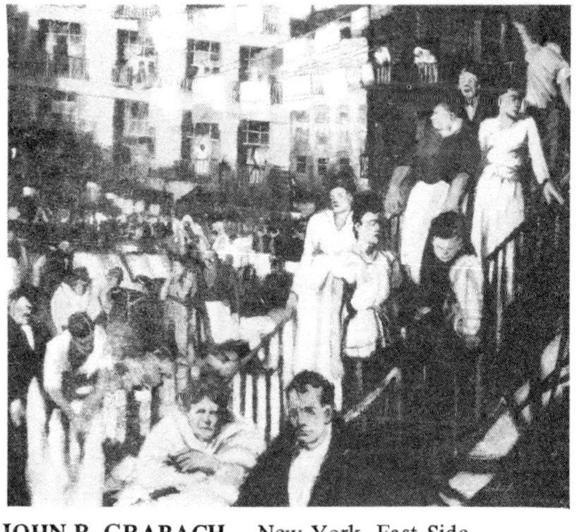

JOHN R. GRABACH – New York, East Side – signed and inscribed – oil on canvas – 36 x 42in.
(Christie's) **$28,600** **£20,105**

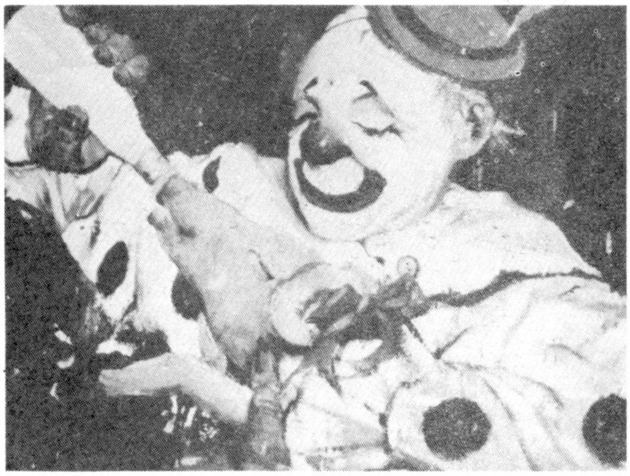

JOHN R. GRABACH – Clown – signed – oil on canvas laid down on wood panel – 12 x 15½in.
(Christie's) **$2,860** **£1,989**

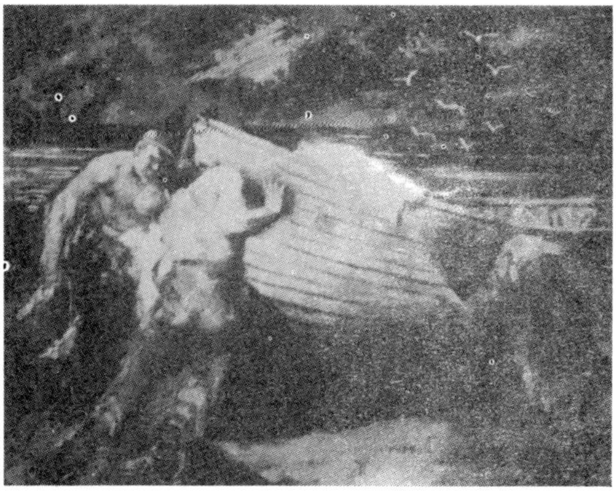

JOHN R. GRABACH – Boatmen – signed – oil on canvas laid down on panel – 14 x 17¼in.
(Christie's) **$2,420** **£1,683**

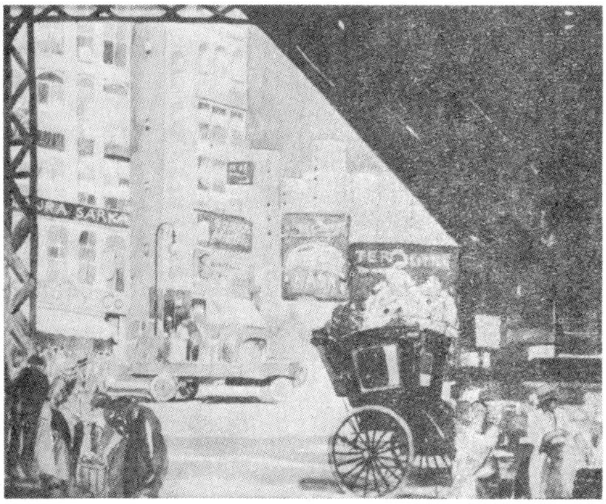

JOHN R. GRABACH – Chinatown – signed – watercolour and pencil on paper – 19 x 23¾in.
(Christie's) **$4,400** **£3,061**

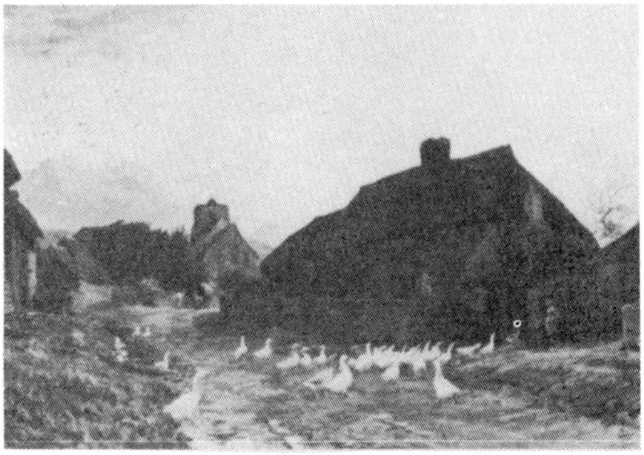

ALFRED FITZWALTER GRACE – Geese On A Village Street, A Horse And Covered Wagon Beyond, At Dusk – signed, indistinctly inscribed and dated 1883 – oil on canvas – 27½ x 40½in.
(Phillips) **$2,754** **£1,800**

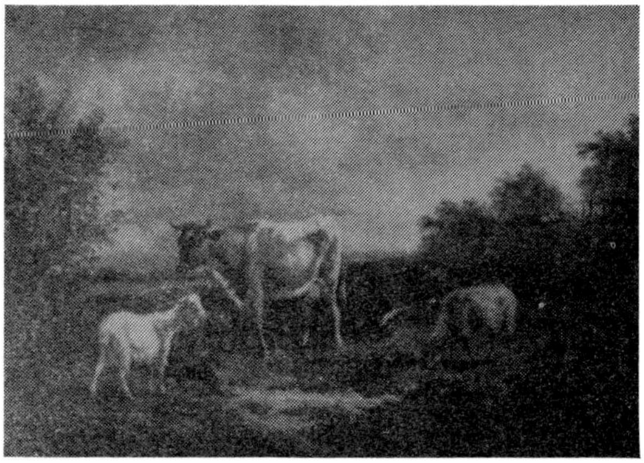

VICTOR DE GRAILLY – Cows And Sheep In A Farmyard – signed and dated 1859 – oil on canvas – 21 x 29in.
(Robt. W. Skinner Inc.) **$700** **£429**

CARLTON GRANT – Coastal View With Figure Gazing Wistfully Out To Sea – watercolour – 17 x 28½in.
(Prudential Fine Art Auctioneers) **$830** **£500**

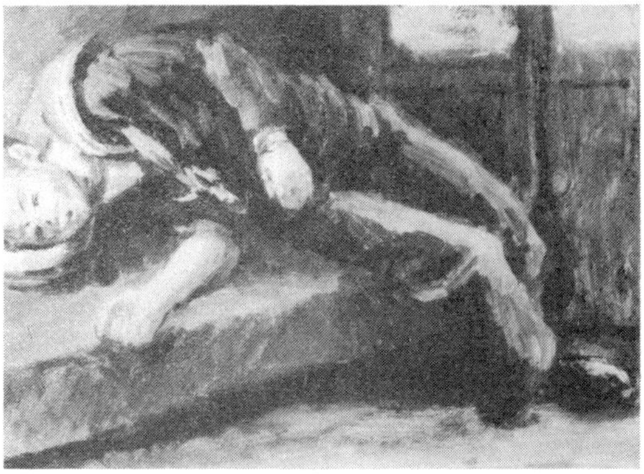

DUNCAN GRANT – Asleep In The Railway Carraige – oil on board – 9½ x 13¾in.
(Christie's) **$2,763** **£1,760**

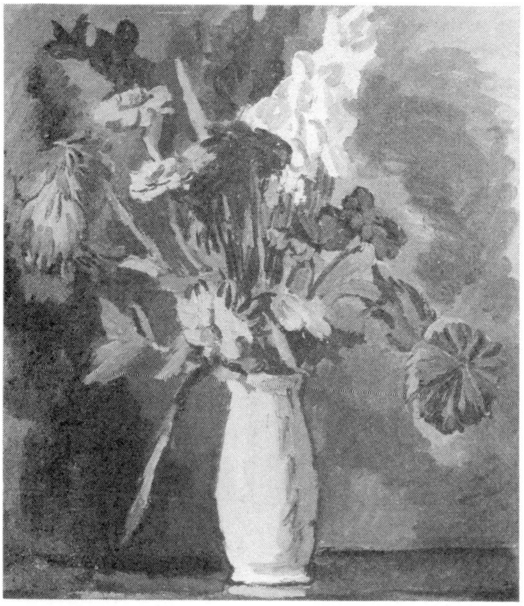

DUNCAN GRANT – Still Life With Gladioli And Chrysanthemums – signed – oil on canvas – 66 x 61cm.
(Phillips) **$3,976** **£2,800**

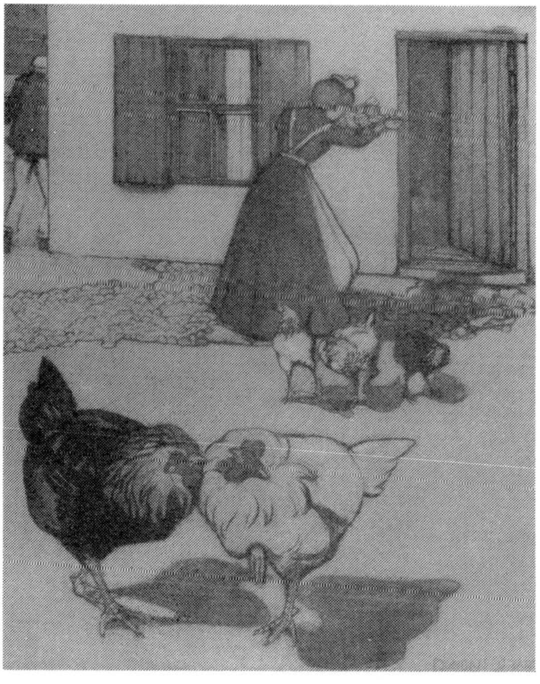

DUNCAN GRANT – A Cook And Cockerels Outside A Cottage – signed and dated 1902 – watercolour, soft pencil and bodycolour – 18½ x 16in.
(Christie's) **$4,719** **£3,300**

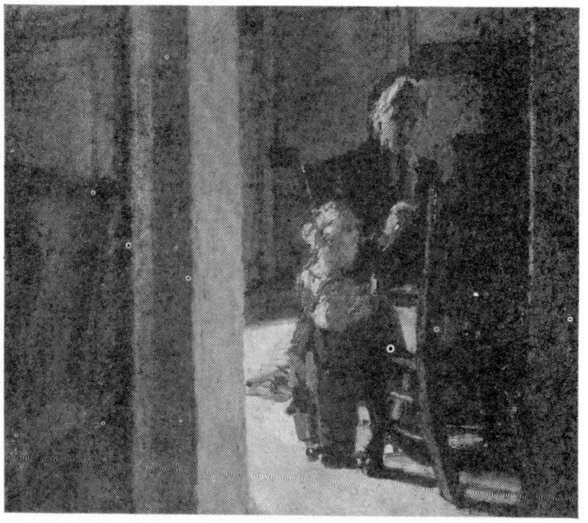

DUNCAN GRANT – Vanessa Bell Painting At Charleston With Angelica Bell Watching – signed – oil on canvas – 24¼ x 20in.
(Christie's) **$6,908** **£4,400**

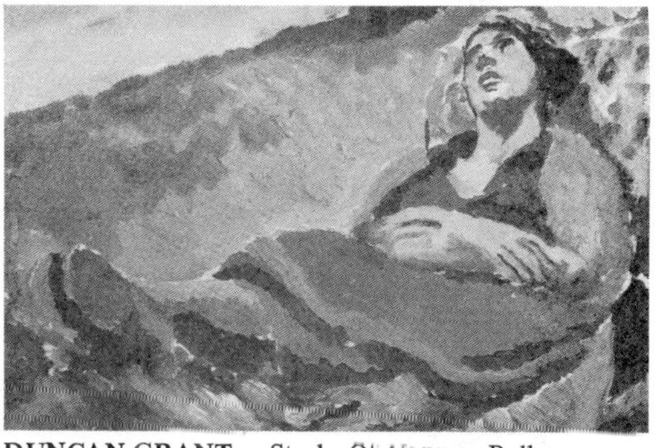

DUNCAN GRANT – Study Of Vanessa Bell Resting In A Hammock, Charleston – signed with initials on the reverse – oil on canvas board – 10¼ x 14in.
(Christie's) **$3,932** **£2,750**

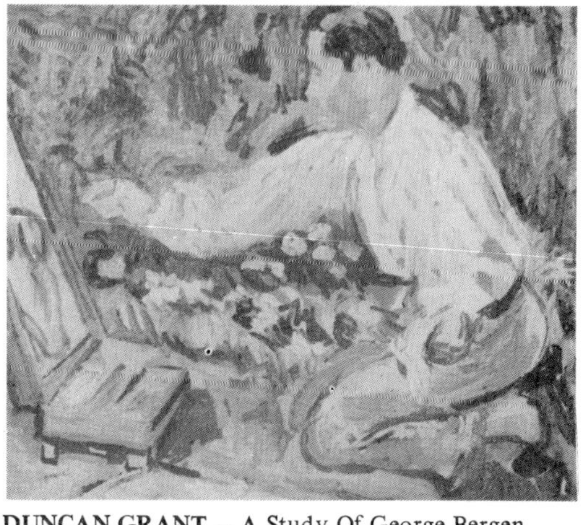

DUNCAN GRANT – A Study Of George Bergen Painting In The Garden At Charleston – oil on panel – 15 x 18in.
(Christie's) **$4,404** **£3,080**

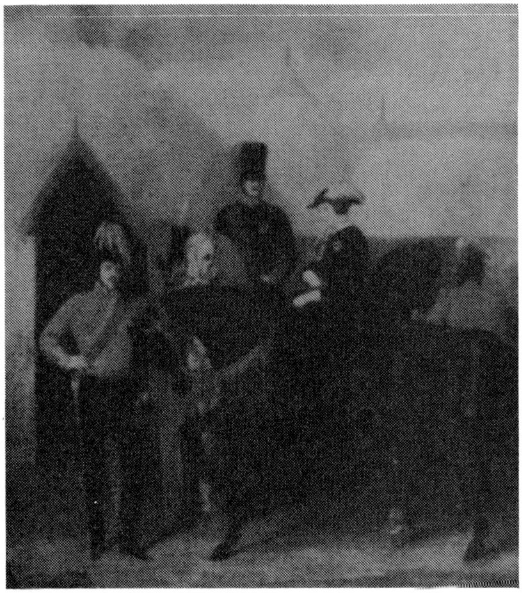

SIR FRANCIS GRANT, Circle of – Queen Victoria Preparing For A Review – oil on canvas – 36½ x 28in.
(Phillips) **$1,328** **£800**

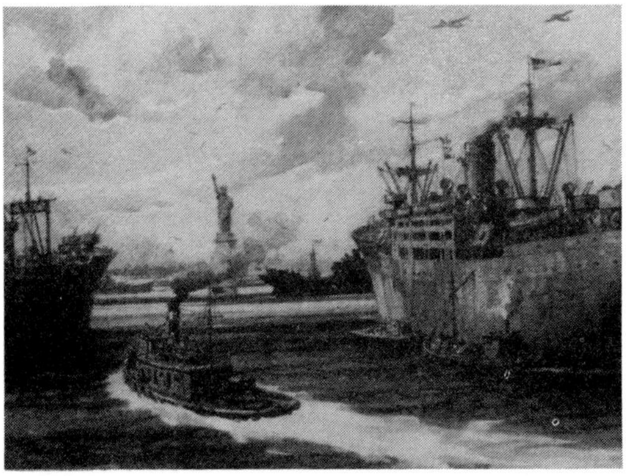

GORDON GRANT – New York Harbour – signed and dated '45 – brush and black ink, ink wash, chinese white, and pencil on board – 21½ x 25½in.
(Christie's) **$1,100** **£685**

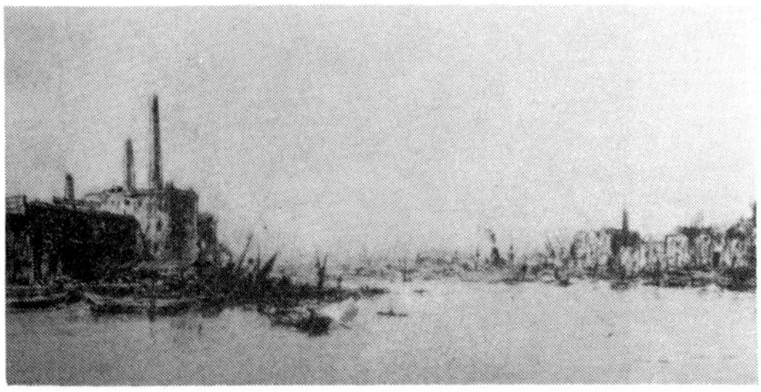

JOSEPH GRAY – A View Of The Thames – signed, inscribed and dated 1930 – pen, ink and wash over traces of pencil – 19 x 36cm.
(Phillips) **$382** **£250**

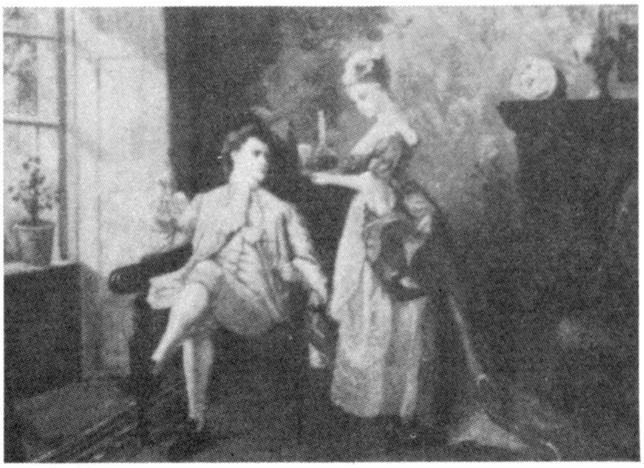

KATE GRAY – 'After Dinner Port' – oil on canvas – 16 x 20in.
(Christie's) **$797** **£550**

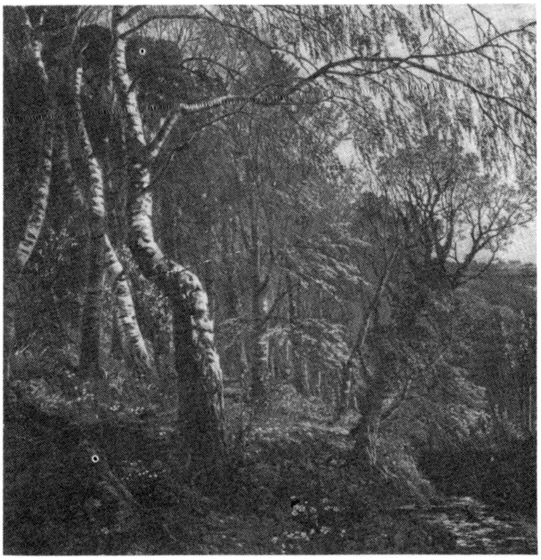

WILLIAM GRAY – Early Spring, North Devon – signed and dated 1876 – 30 x 24in.
(Christie's) **$2,016** **£1,430**

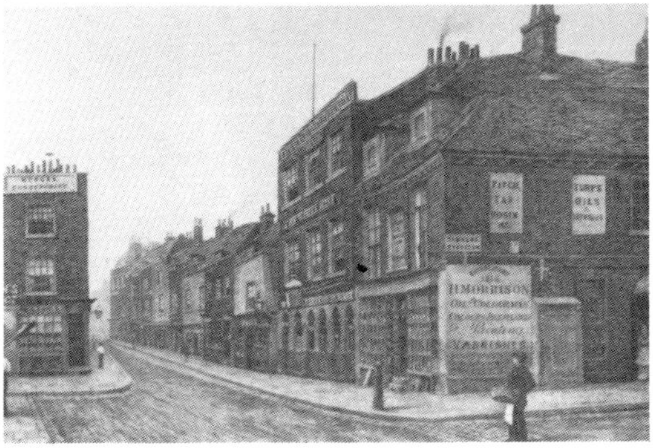

HENRY AND WALTER GREAVES – The White Hart At The Corner Of Danvers Street And Poulton Street Off Cheyne Walk – signed and dated 1858 – pen, black ink, grey wash and pencil – 19 x 24¼in.
(Christie's) **$4,719** **£3,300**

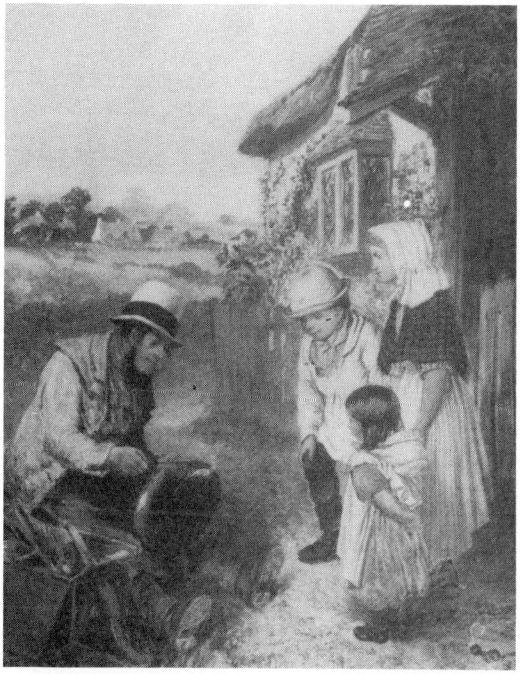

ALFRED H. GREEN – The Village Tinker; and The Travelling Salesman – signed with monogram – on panel – 10¼ x 8½in.
(Christie's) **$3,197** **£2,090 Pair**

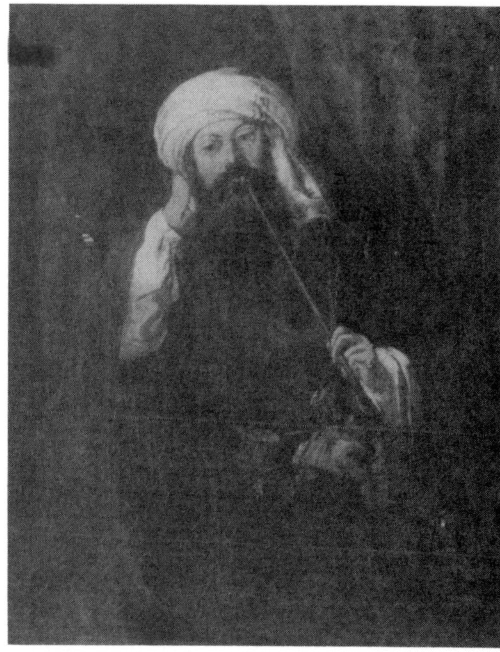

H. GREEN – A Turkish Merchant – indistincly signed – 24 x 20in.
(Christie's) **$8,078** **£5,280**

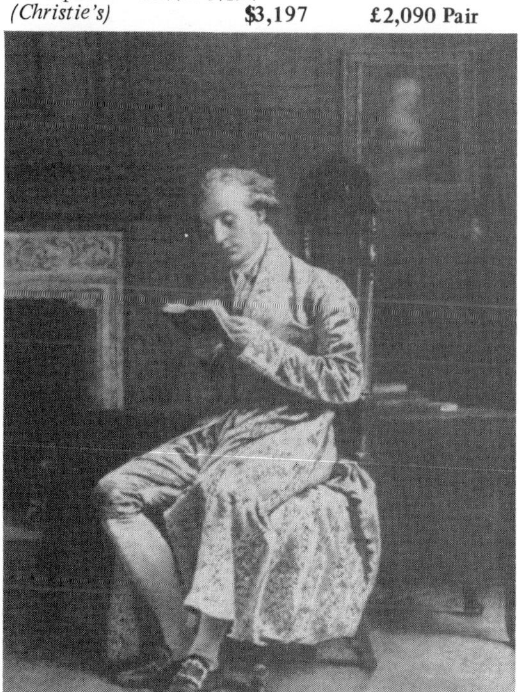

CHARLES GREEN – The Student – signed with initials and dated 1881 – watercolour – 6¾ x 9¾in.
(Christie's) **$891** **£594**

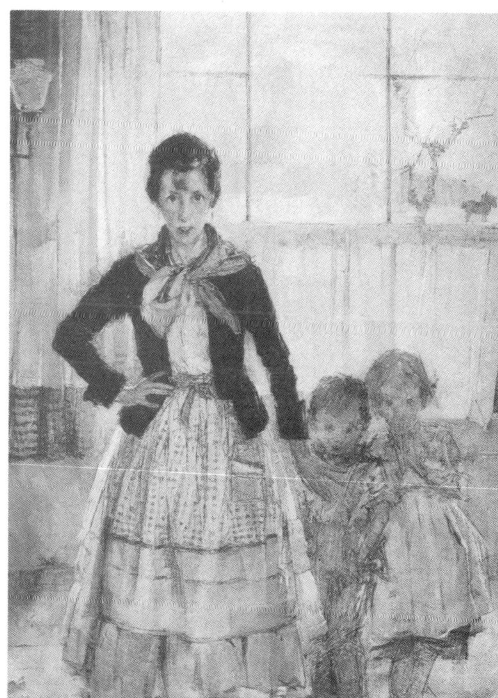

MADELINE GREEN – The Velvet Jacket – oil on canvas – 23 x 17½in.
(Christie's) **$11,011** **£7,700**

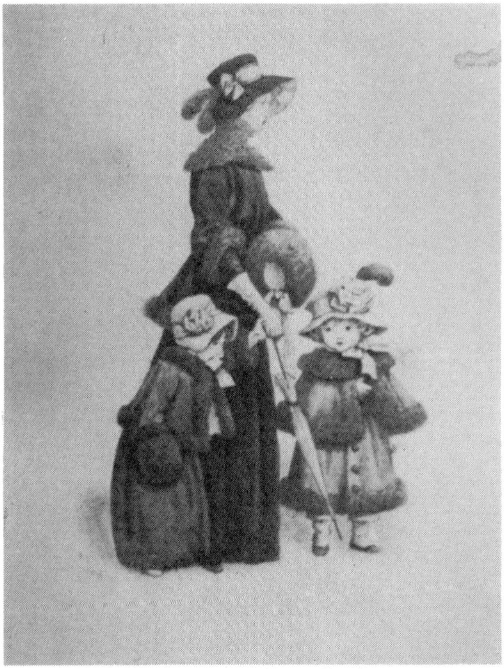

KATE GREENAWAY – A Winter Outing – signed with initials and dated 1900 – pencil and watercolour on stone-coloured paper – 6¼ x 4¼in.
(Christie's) **$5,049** **£3,300**

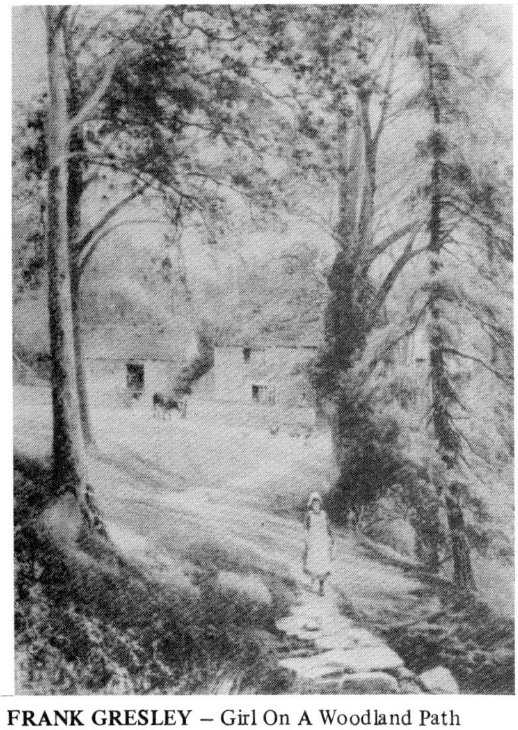

FRANK GRESLEY – Girl On A Woodland Path Before A Farmstead, Derbyshire – signed and dated 1892 – watercolour – 23½ x 15½in.
(W. H. Lane & Son) **$1,575** **£1,050**

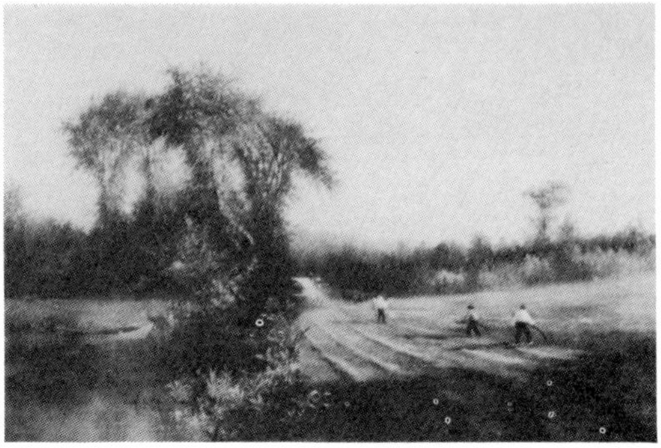

SAMUEL W. GRIGGS – Farmers In A Field – signed and dated 1867 – oil on canvas – 20 x 30in.
(Robt. W. Skinner Inc.) **$2,000** **£1,388**

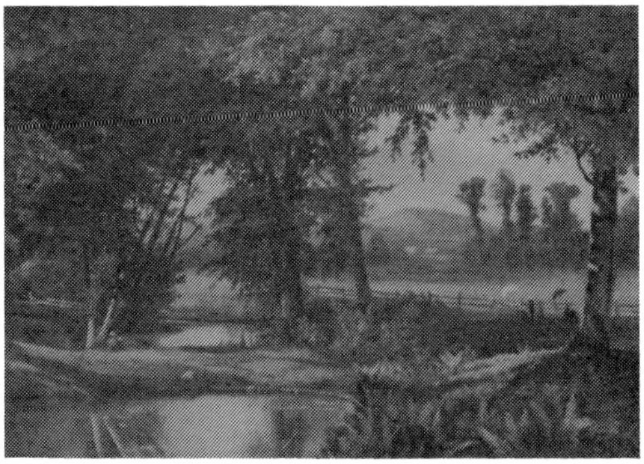

SAMUEL W. GRIGGS – Willey Brook, North Conway, New Hampshire – signed and dated 1861 – oil on canvas – 14¼ x 20¼in.
(Robt. W. Skinner Inc.) **$1,200** **£736**

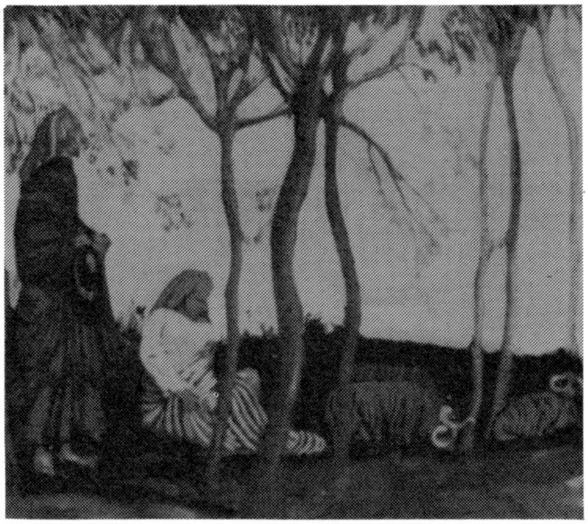

BORIS GRIGORIEV – Shepherds With Sheep – signed and dated '912 – gouache on paper – 35 x 40cm.
(Phillips) **$1,085** **£700**

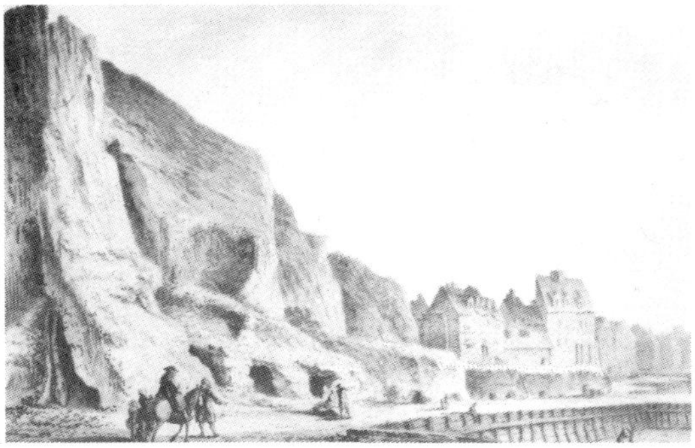

SAMUEL HIERONYMUS GRIMM – Dieppe – signed and dated 1770 – pen and grey ink and watercolour – 11¾ x 14¾in.
(Christie's) **$1,483** **£1,045**

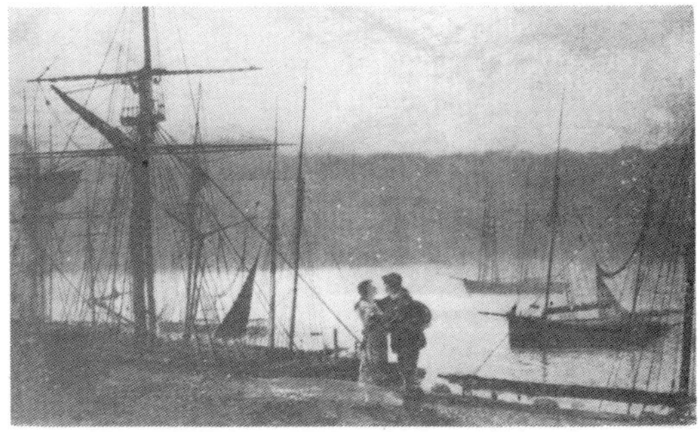

ATKINSON GRIMSHAW – Outward Bound – signed, inscribed and dated 1880(?) on the reverse – 18½ x 29¾in.
(Christie's) **$6,804** **£4,536**

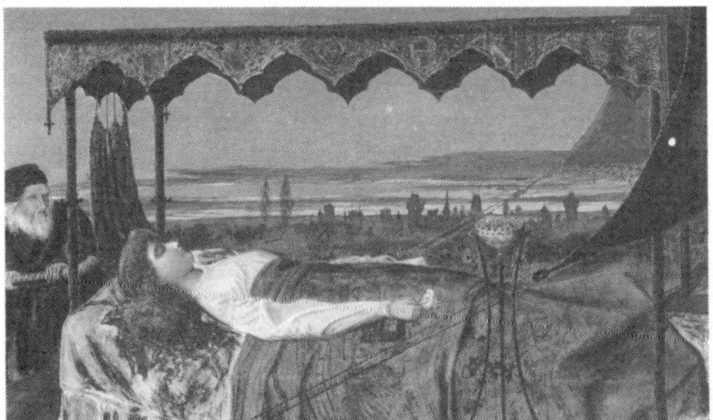

ATKINSON GRIMSHAW – Elaine – signed and dated 1864 – 18 x 24¼in.
(Christie's) **$8,800** **£5,500**

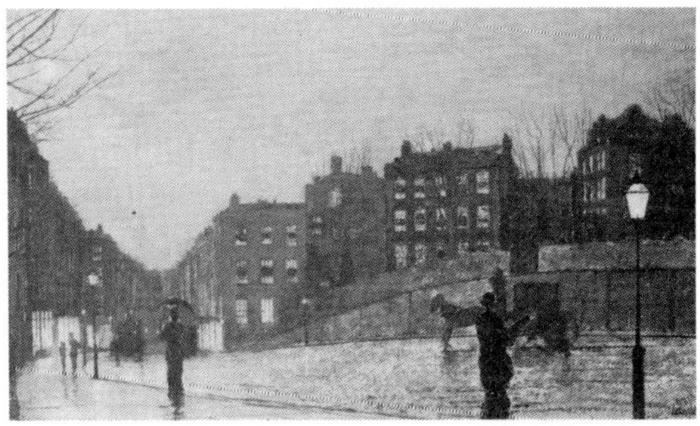

ATKINSON GRIMSHAW – Hampstead High Street – signed and dated 1881 – on board – 12 x 20in.
(Christie's) **$6,480** **£4,320**

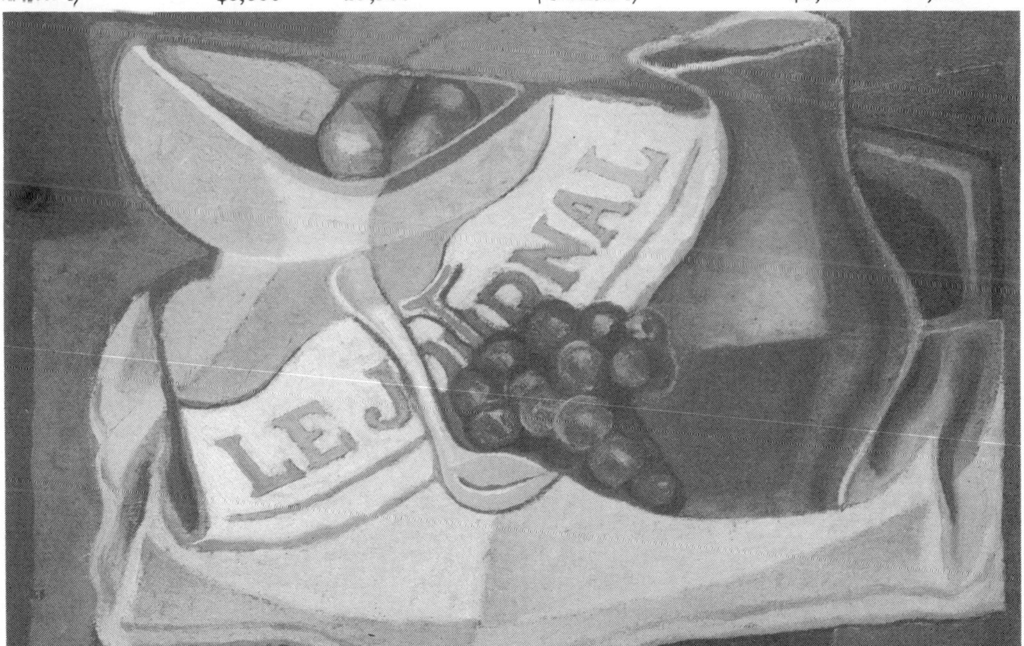

JUAN GRIS – La Grappe de Raisins – signed and dated '25 – oil on canvas – 15 x 18in. *(Christie's)*
$202,070 **£121,000**

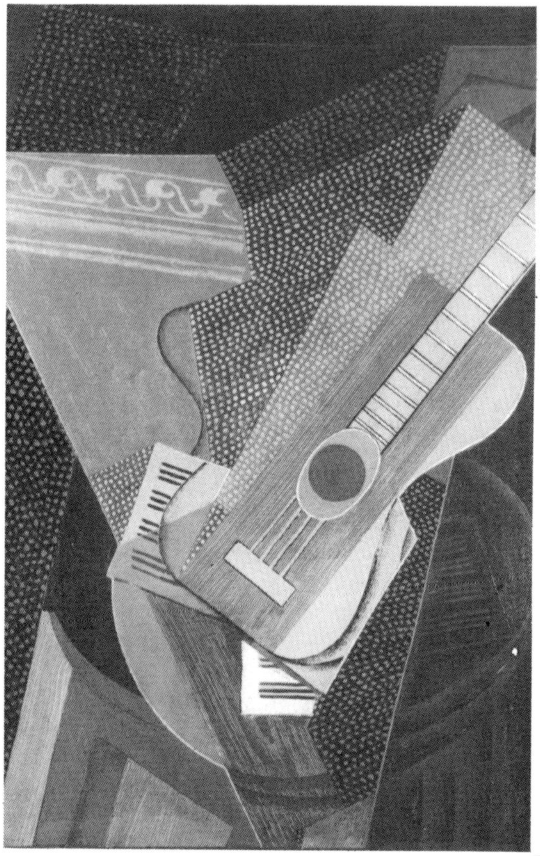

JUAN GRIS – Guitare sur une Table – signed and dated – oil on canvas – 36¼ x 23½in.
(Christie's) **$792,000 £550,000**

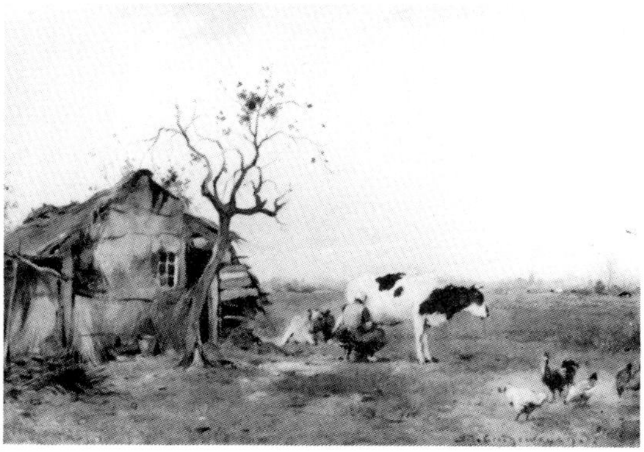

ADRIANUS JOHANNES GROENEWEGEN – 'Pastoral Scenes In Holland' – signed – watercolour – 7¾ x 11¼in.
(Graves Son & Pilcher) **$1,368 £950 Pair**

ADRIANUS JOHANNES GROENEWEGEN – Cattle By A River – signed – watercolour – 13½ x 20in.
(Graves Son & Pilcher) **$892 £620**

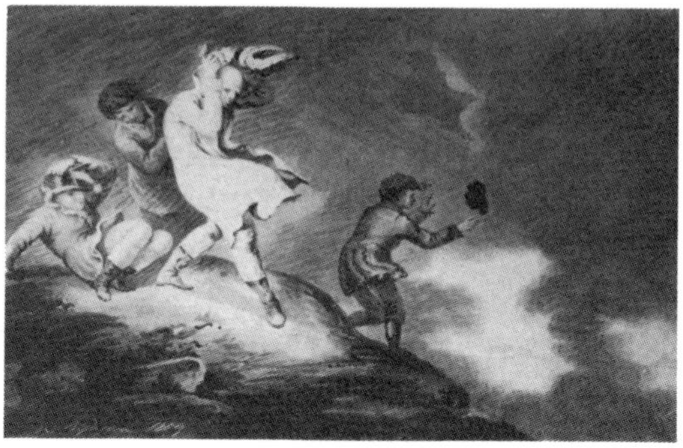

NATHANIEL GROGAN, Jnr. – A Windy Day On The Macgillycuddy Rocks; and Figures In A Wood – signed, the first dated 1809 – pencil, blue and grey wash – 9¾ x 15¼in. and 7¼ x 9¼in.; and another three, two by Wm. Payne.
(Christie's) **$406 £286 Five**

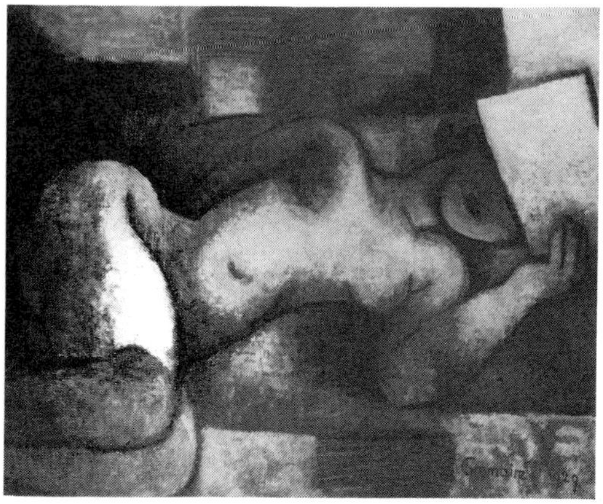

MARCEL GROMAIRE – Femme nue allongee, lisant – signed and dated 1929 – oil on canvas – 17¾ x 21½in.
(Christie's) **$40,480 £25,300**

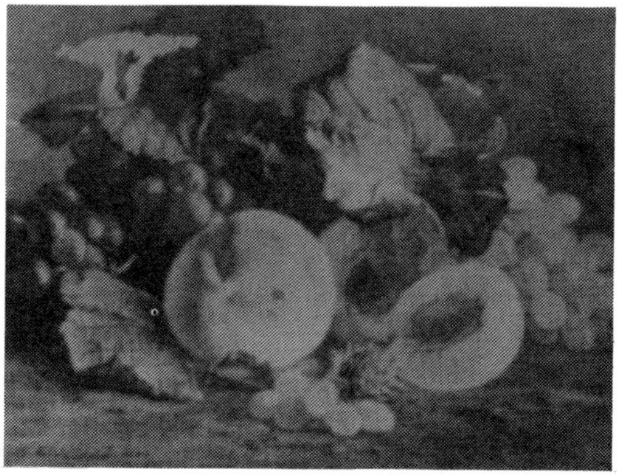

THEUDE GRONLAND – A Still Life Of Peaches And Grapes – signed and dated 1865 – oil on canvas – 27.5 x 35.5cm.
(Phillips) **$1,503 £900**

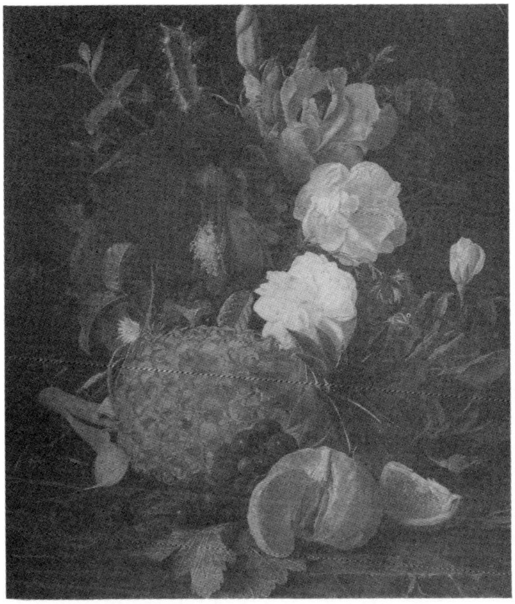

THEUDE GRONLAND – Flowers, A Pineapple And A Peeled Orange On A Ledge – signed and dated 1844 – 17½ x 14½in.
(Christie's) **$22,880** **£14,300**

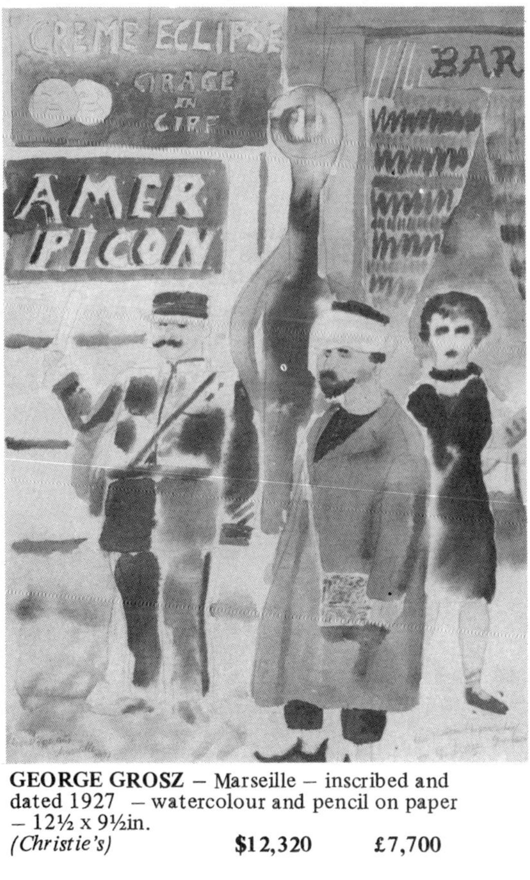

GEORGE GROSZ – Marseille – inscribed and dated 1927 – watercolour and pencil on paper – 12½ x 9½in.
(Christie's) **$12,320** **£7,700**

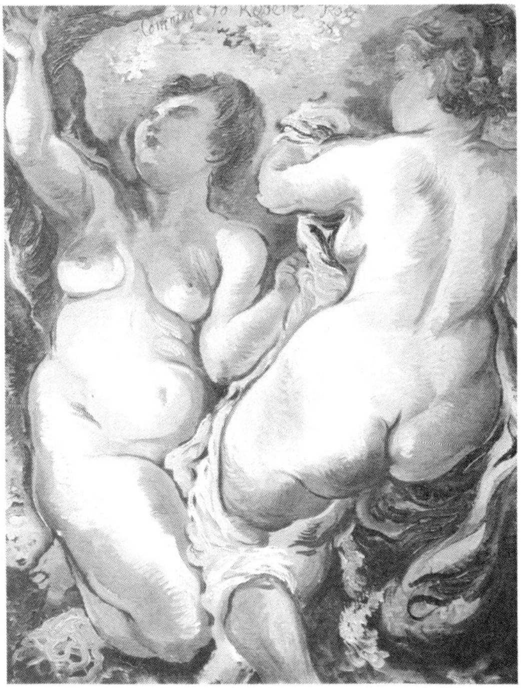

GEORGE GROSZ – Hommage to Rubens – signed, dated '38, and inscribed – oil on canvas – 27¼ x 21½in.
(Christie's) **$11,880** **£8,250**

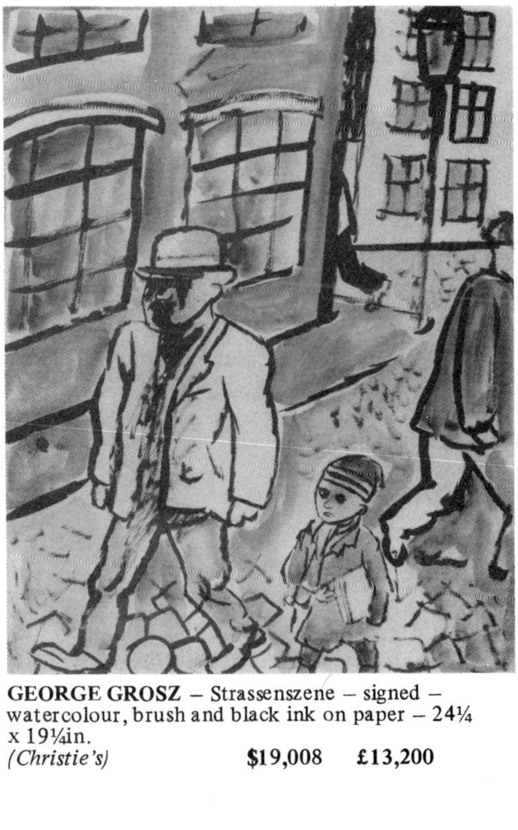

GEORGE GROSZ – Strassenszene – signed – watercolour, brush and black ink on paper – 24¼ x 19¼in.
(Christie's) **$19,008** **£13,200**

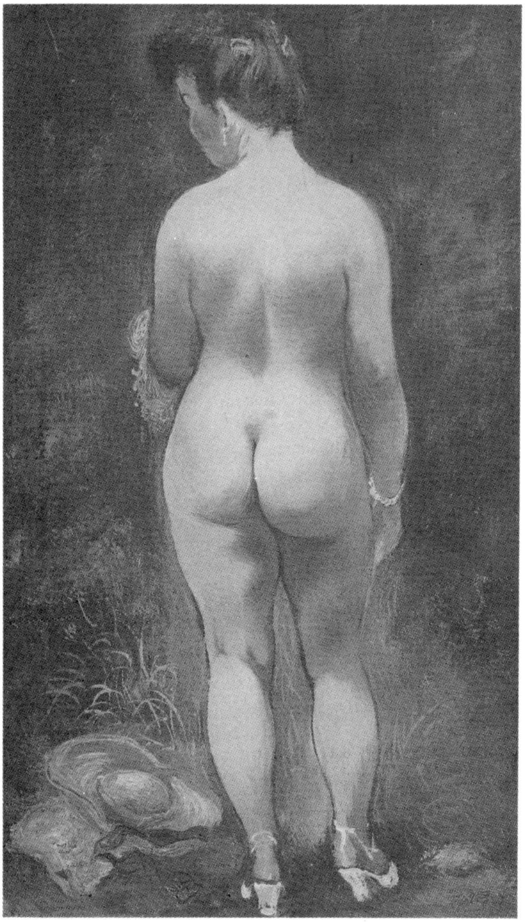

GEORGE GROSZ – Standing Nude – signed – oil on canvas – 25¼ x 15in.
(Christie's) **$9,504** **£6,600**

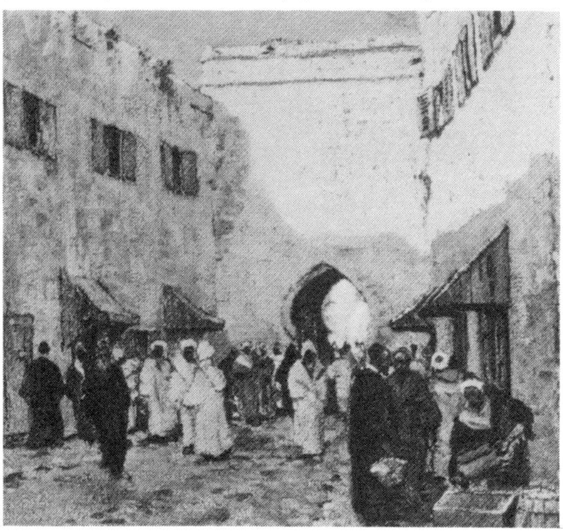

ROBERT E. GROVES – An Arab Market – signed – oil on board – 30.5 x 25.5cm.
(Phillips) **$1,300** **£850**

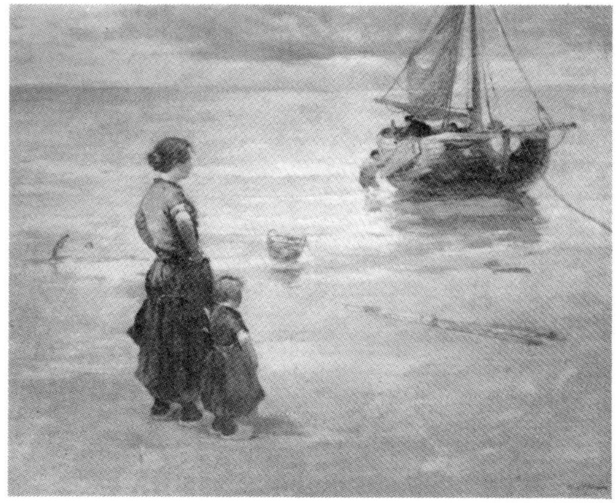

CHARLES PAUL GRUPPE – 'Farewell', Twilight On The Beach – signed, inscribed on an old label affixed to the stretcher – oil on canvas – 32 x 40in.
(Christie's) **$9,350** **£6,504**

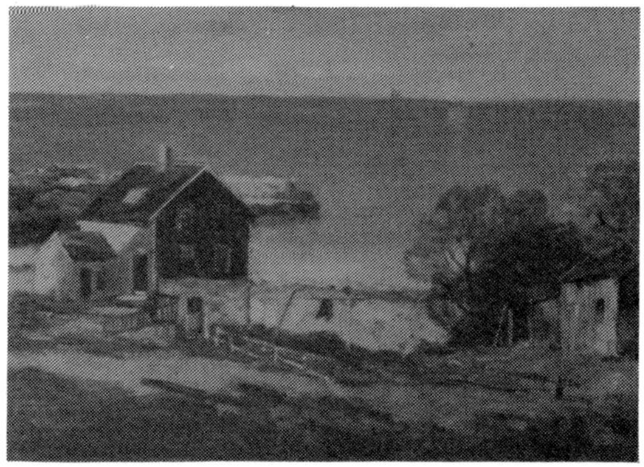

CHARLES PAUL GRUPPE – Cottage In A Seaside Landscape – signed – oil on paper – 12 x 16in.
(Robt. W. Skinner Inc.) **$1,500** **£920**

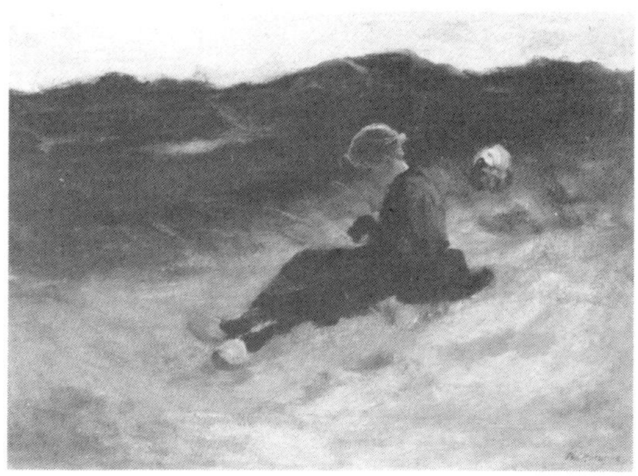

CHARLES PAUL GRUPPE – A Study In Grey In The Dunes, Holland – signed, inscribed on an old label attached to the stretcher – oil on canvas – 12¾ x 17¾in.
(Christie's) **$2,750** **£1,923**

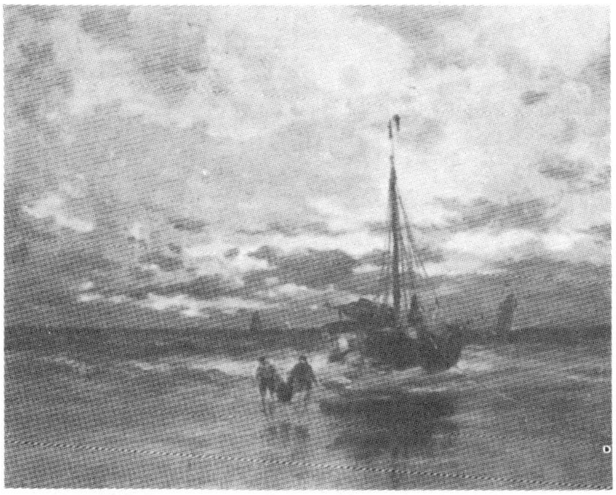

CHARLES PAUL GRUPPE – Sunset On The Dutch Coast – signed – oil on canvas – 16 x 20¼in.
(Christie's) **$4,520** **£3,214**

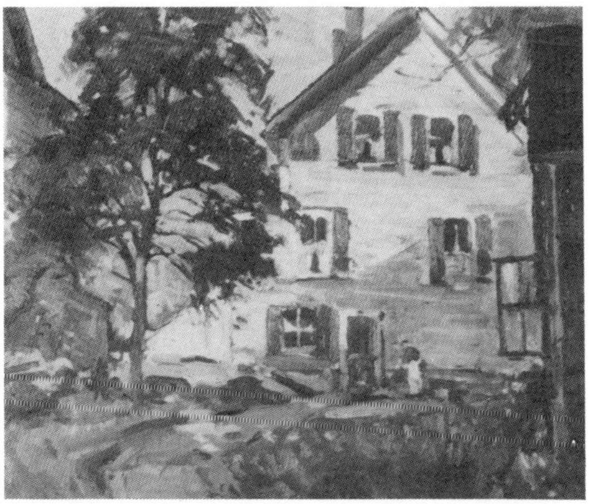

EMILE ALBERT GRUPPE – 'Afternoon Shadows' – signed – oil on canvas – 18 x 20in.
(Robt. W. Skinner Inc.) **$2,600** **£1,805**

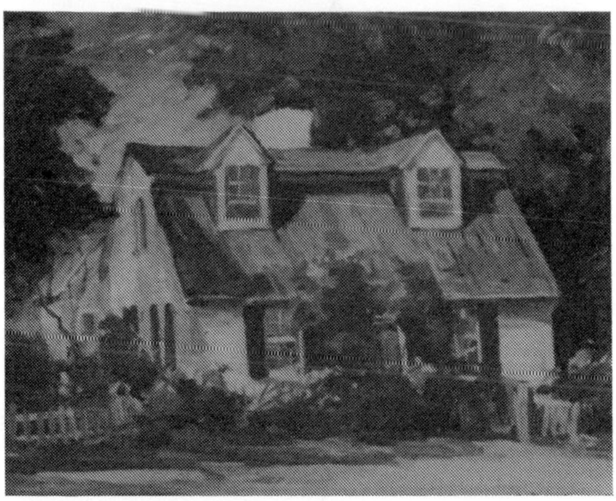

EMILE ALBERT GRUPPE – New England Cottage – signed, and signed and dated 1960 on the stretcher – oil on canvas – 16 x 20in.
(Robt. W. Skinner Inc.) **$1,400** **£858**

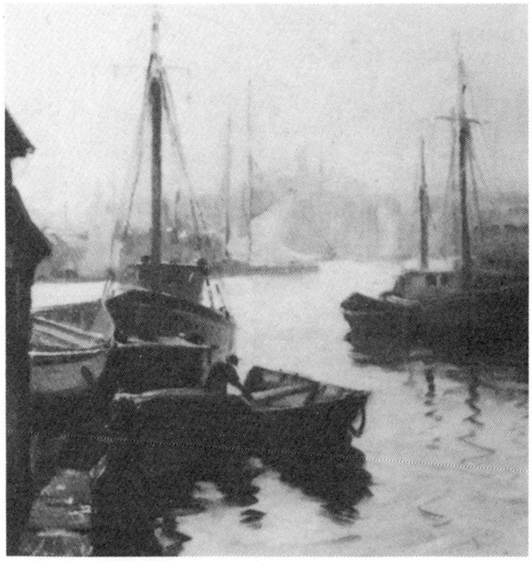

EMILE ALBERT GRUPPE – 'Afternoon Glow' – signed, also signed on the stretcher – oil on canvas – 24 x 20in.
(Robt. W. Skinner Inc.) **$3,400** **£2,361**

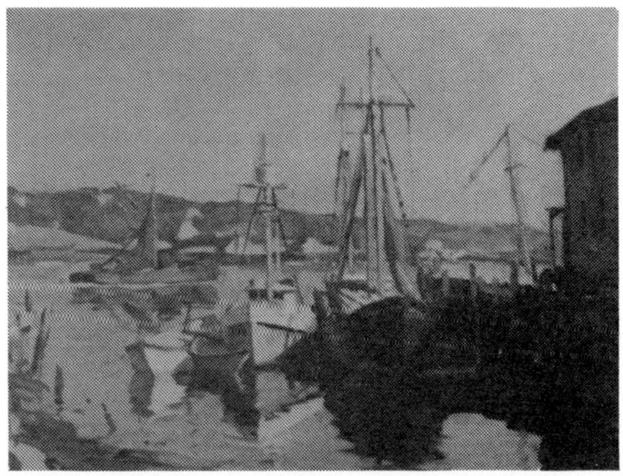

EMILE ALBERT GRUPPE – Fishing Boats At Dock – signed – oil on canvas – 25 x 30in.
(Robt. W. Skinner Inc.) **$6,000** **£3,680**

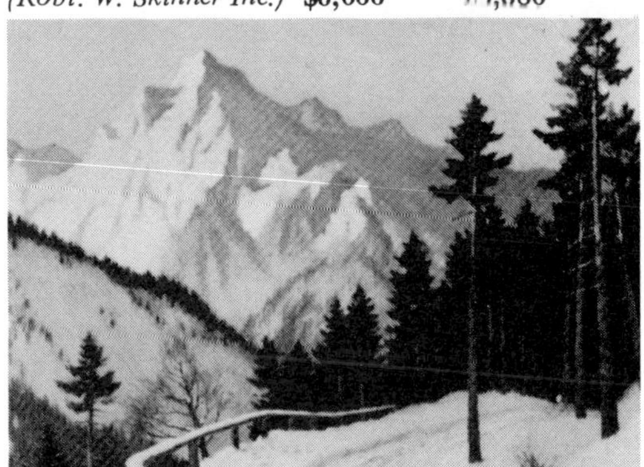

MICHAEL GUERMACHEFF – Winter Landscape – signed – oil on canvas – 21 x 26in.
(Robt. W. Skinner Inc.) **$700** **£460**

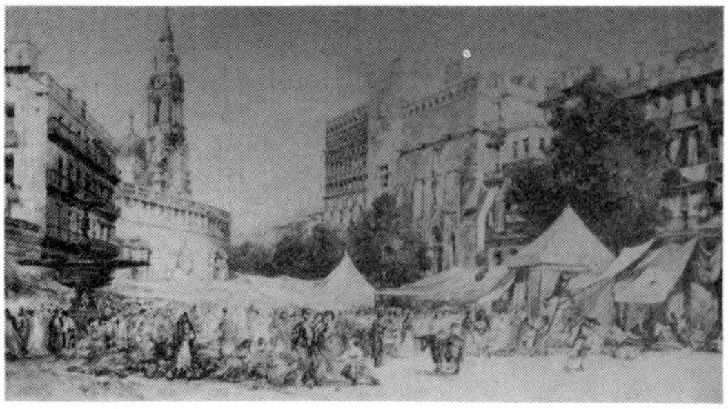

JACQUES GUIAUND – Lonja Del La Seda, Valencia – signed – watercolour – 20 x 35in.
(Lawrence Fine Art) **$2,191** **£1,320**

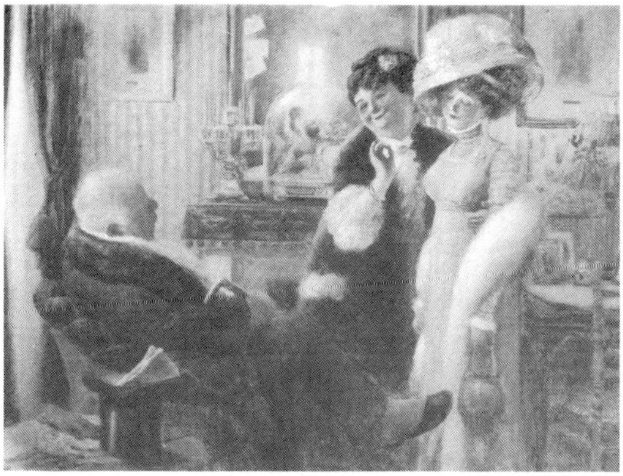

ALBERT GUILLAUME – A Choice Offering – signed – on panel – 21 x 25in.
(Christie's) **$8,236** **£5,720**

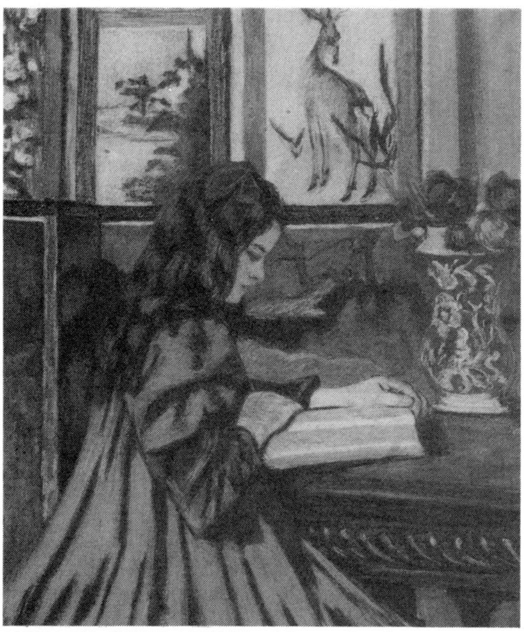

ARMAND GUILLAUMIN – Marguerite, la Fille de l'Artiste – signed and dated '98 – pastel on paper – 32 x 25½in.
(Christie's) **$69,806** **£41,800**

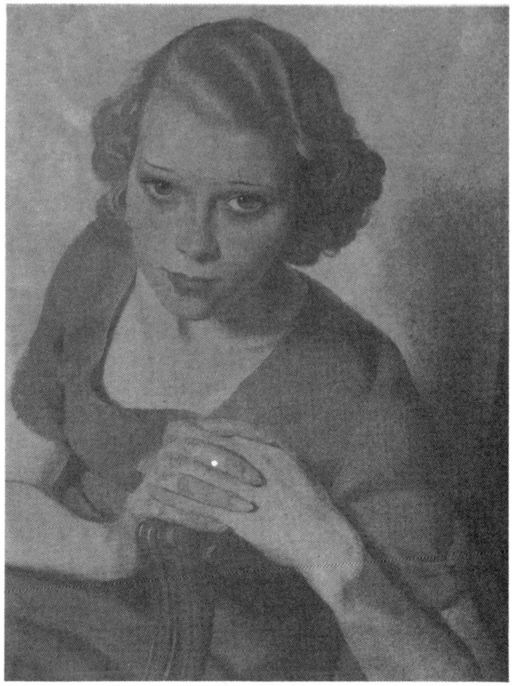

SIR HERBERT JAMES GUNN – Sonja In Green – signed – oil on canvas – 18 x 14in.
(Christie's) **$3,460** **£2,420**

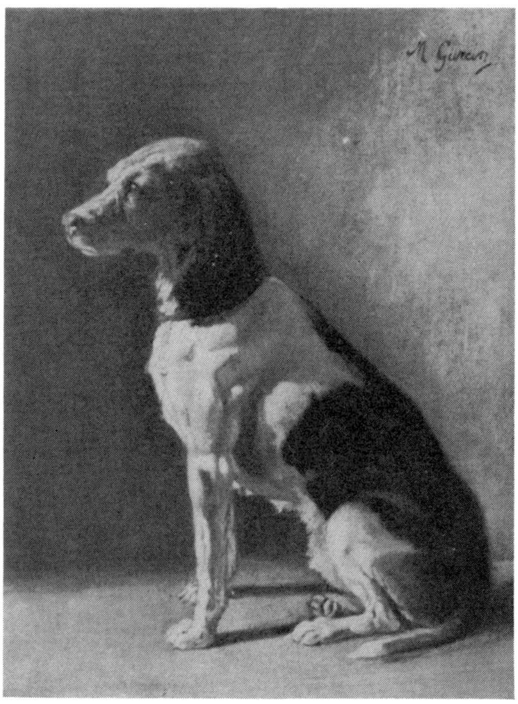

M. GURCIN – A Seated Hound – signed – oil on panel – 11½ x 15½in.
(Bonhams) **$775** **£500**

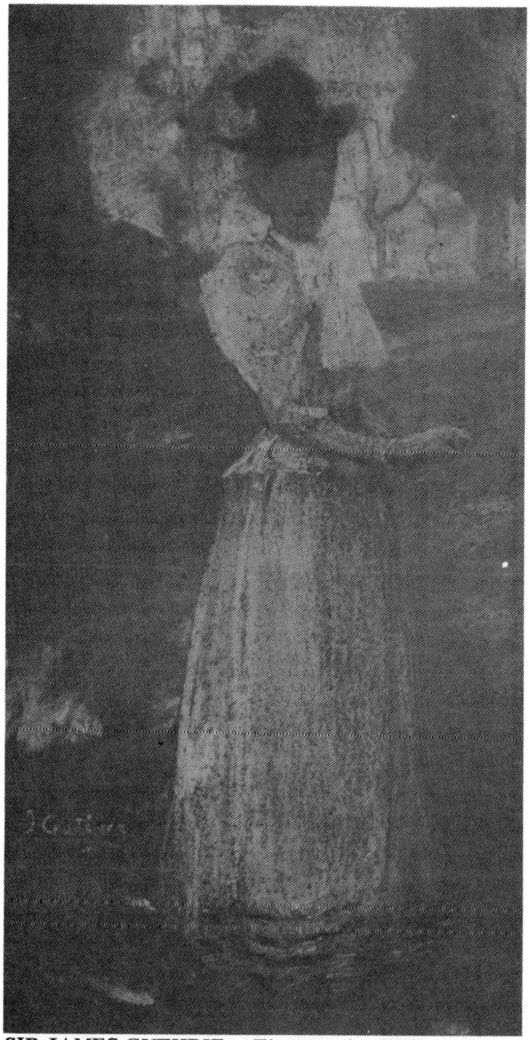

SIR JAMES GUTHRIE – The Morning Walk – signed – pastel on buff paper – 19½ x 9½in.
(Christie's) **$6,048** **£4,200**

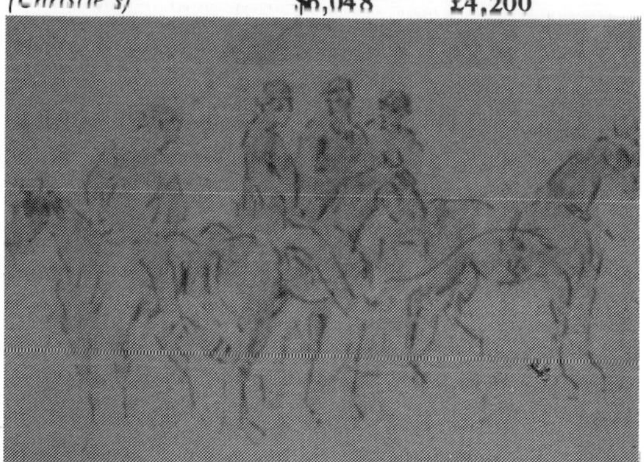

CONSTANTIN GUYS – Quatre Equestriens – pencil, pen and ink – 11.4 x 16.5cm.
(Phillips) **$310** **£200**

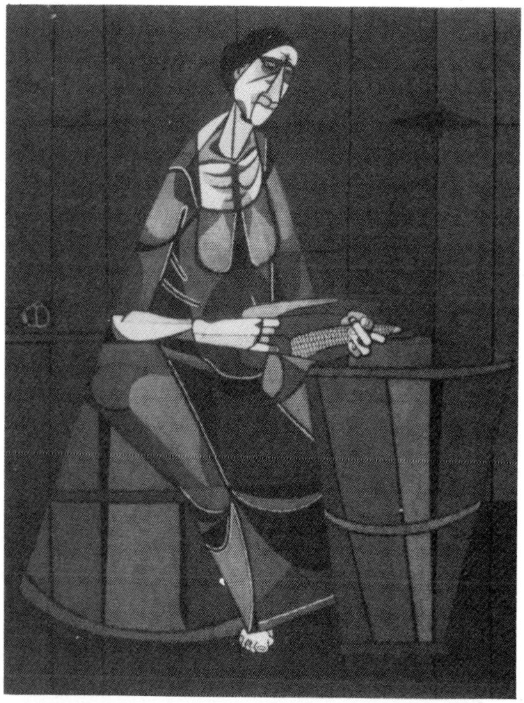

ROBERT GWATHMEY – Woman Husking Corn – signed – oil on canvas – 20¼ x 16¼in.
(Christie's) **$11,000** **£7,733**

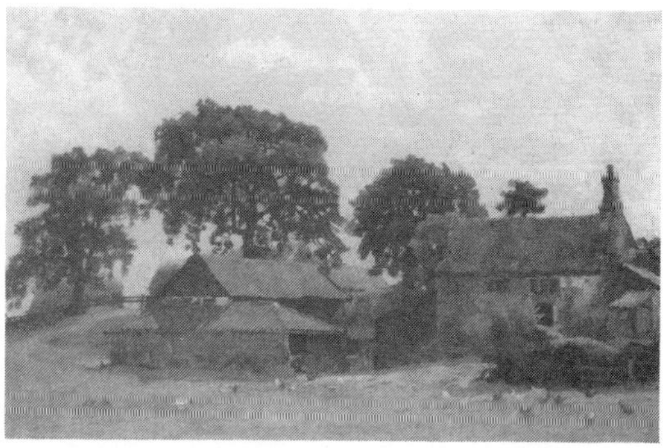

ALAN GWYNNE-JONES – The Farm – signed with initials and dated 1935 – oil on panel – 19½ x 25½in.
(Christie's) **$3,799** **£2,420**

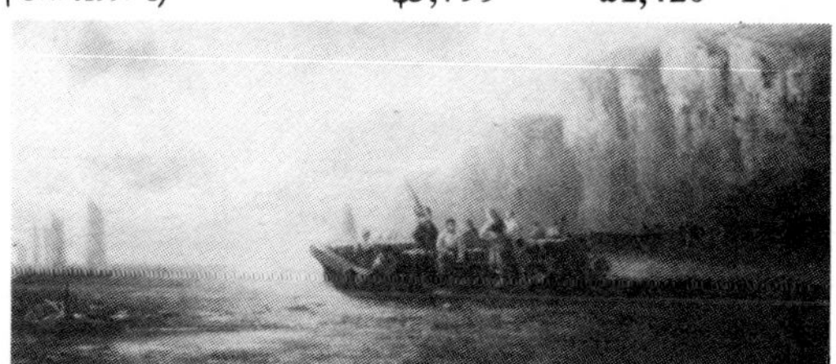

WARNER GYSELMAN – Fisher Folk Resting In An Extensive Coastal Landscape – signed – oil on canvas – 26¾ x 46in.
(Christie's) **$1,036** **£715**

PIETER GYSELS, Circle of – Travellers Passing Along A Path Overlooking An Extensive Landscape – oil on panel – 8¾ x 11in.
(Phillips) **$2,115 £1,500**

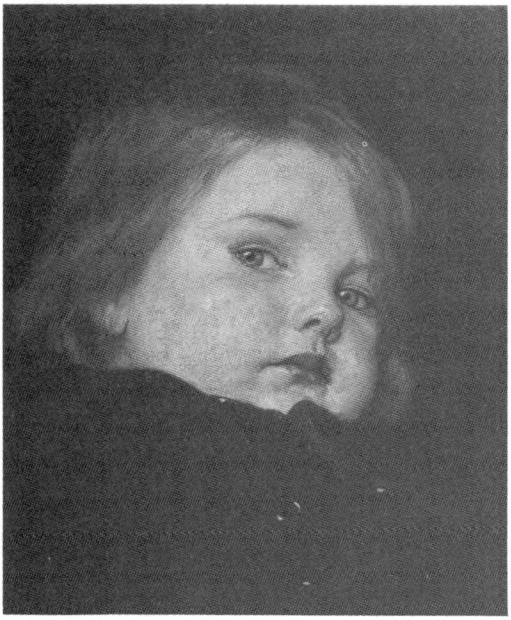

NICOLAS GYSIS – Portrait Of A Child – signed – 12 x 10in.
(Christie's) **$45,760 £28,600**

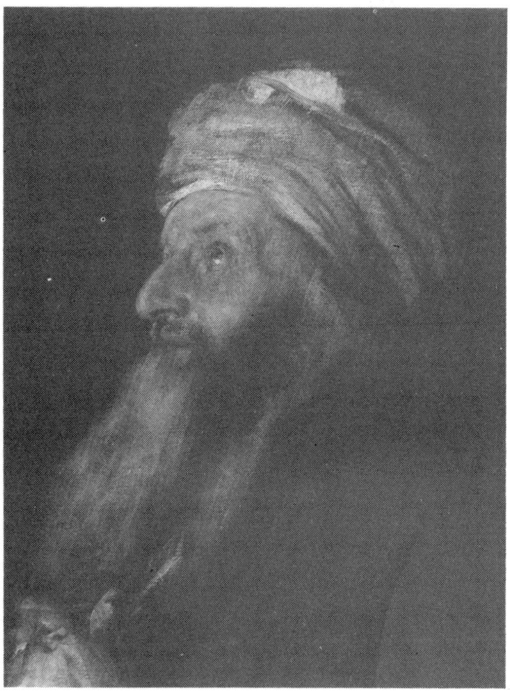

NICOLAS GYSIS – A Bearded Oriental – signed with initials – 18½ x 14in.
(Christie's) **$28,160 £17,600**

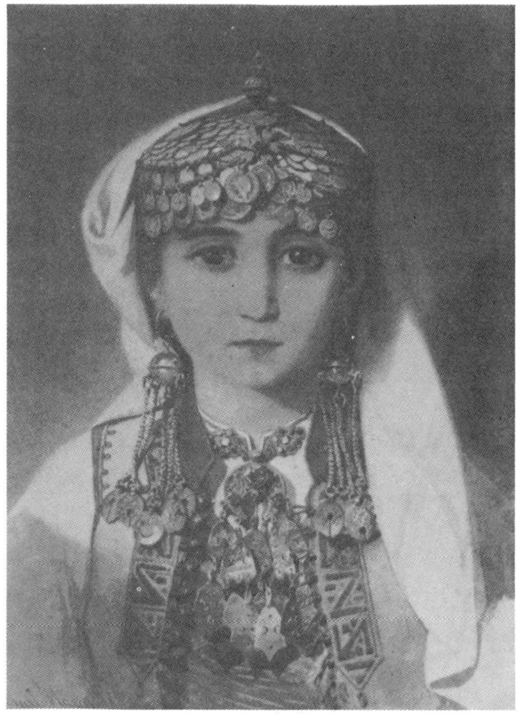

CARL HAAG – A Montenegrin Princess – signed and dated 1855, and inscribed on artist's label – pencil and watercolour heightened with white and gold on paper laid on canvas – 14¼ x 9¾in.
(Christie's) **$1,085 £770**

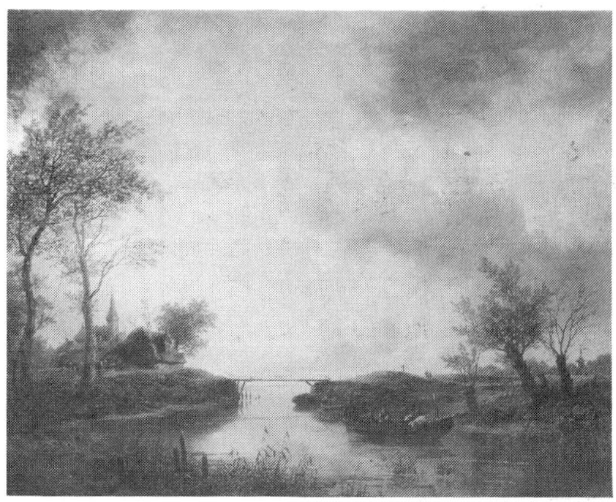

REMIGIUS ADRIANUS VAN HAANEN – A Wooded River Landscape With Figures In A Punt And A Town Beyond – signed and dated 1851(?) – 15 x 18in.
(Christie's) **$13,200 £8,250**

JOHN NICHOLS HAAPANEN – Camden, Maine – signed – oil on canvas – 20 x 24in.
(Robt. W. Skinner Inc.) **$1,500 £1,041**

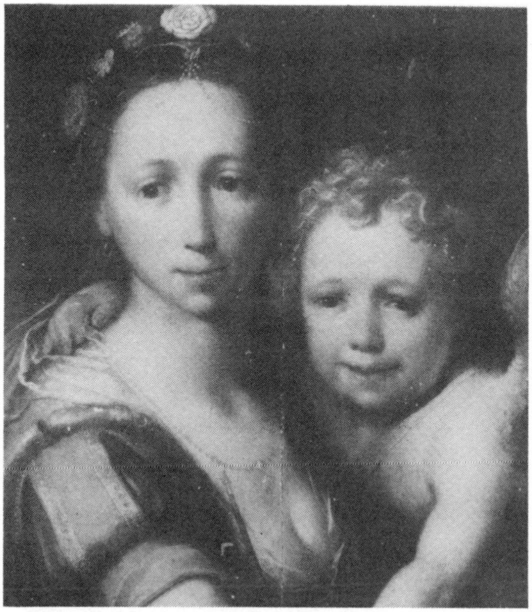

CORNELIS CORNELISZ VAN HAARLEM – Venus And Cupid (probably a portrait) – signed with conjoined initials and dated 1602 – oil on panel – 21½ x 15½in.
(Robt. W. Skinner Inc.) **$38,000** **£26,388**

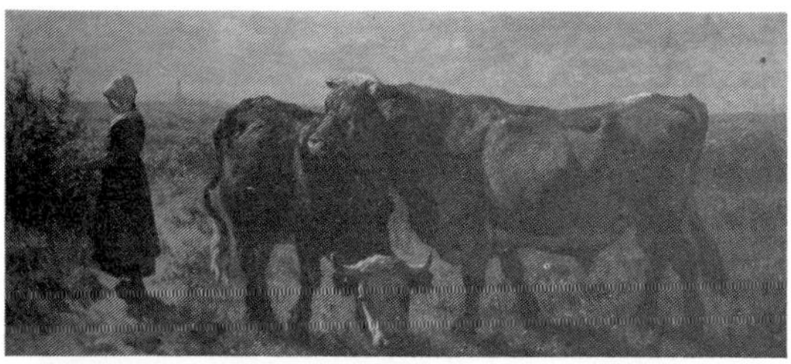

JOHANNES HUBERTUS LEONARDUS DE HAAS – Cows And Their Young Shepherdess In An Extensive Dutch Landscape – signed – on panel – 65 x 92cm.
(Phillips) **$3,020** **£2,000**

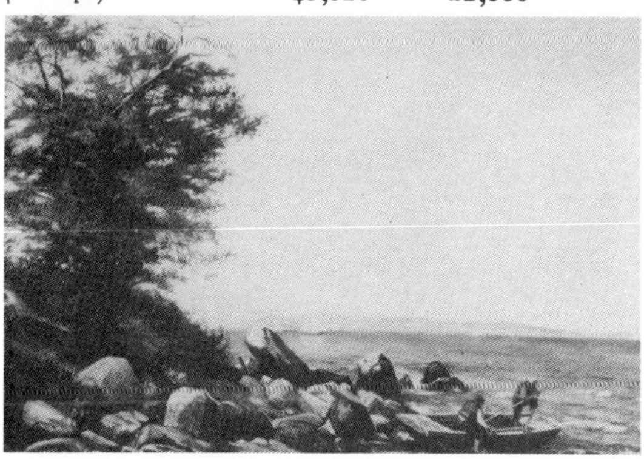

MAURITZ FREDERICK HENDRICK DE HAAS, Attributed to – Coast Of Massachusetts – oil on canvas – 14 x 20in.
(Robt. W. Skinner Inc.) **$1,200** **£833**

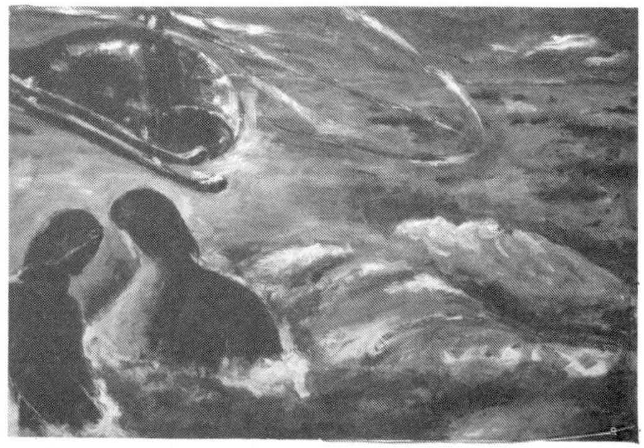

DIETER HACKER – Das Meer – signed, inscribed and dated 1984 on the reverse – oil on canvas – 75½ x 112½in.
(Christie's) **$14,256** **£9,900**

DAVID W. HADDON – Old Salts – signed and dated '98 and '96 – oil on panel – 11½ x 8½in.
(Christie's) **$612** **£400 Pair**

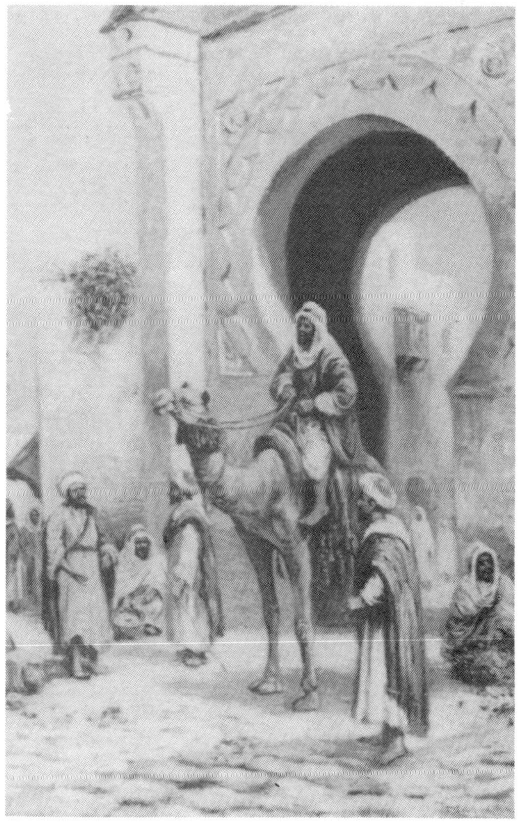

TREVOR HADDON – 'A Gateway, Algiers' – signed, inscribed on the reverse – oil – 29½ x 19¾in.
(Anderson & Garland) **$2,145** **£1,500**

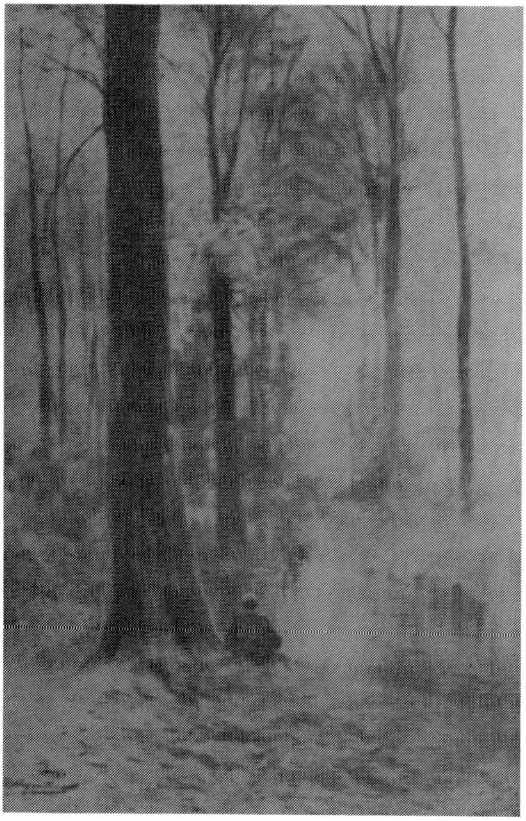

MAURICE HAGEMANS – Le Pecheur Au Bord De La Riviere – signed – watercolour on paper – 119 x 79.5cm.
(Phillips) **$775** **£500**

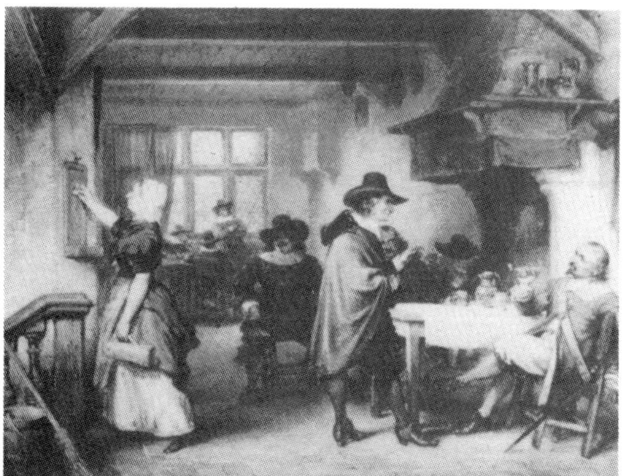

LOUIS HAGHE – Gentlemen Conversing In The Interior Of A 16th century Tavern – signed and dated 1835 – watercolour – 9¾ x 12½in.
(Anderson & Garland) **$1,787** **£1,250**

J. HAIER – Study Of A Family Group Resting On A Stepway – signed – oil on canvas – 30 x 40in.
(Biddle & Webb) **$1,185** **£750**

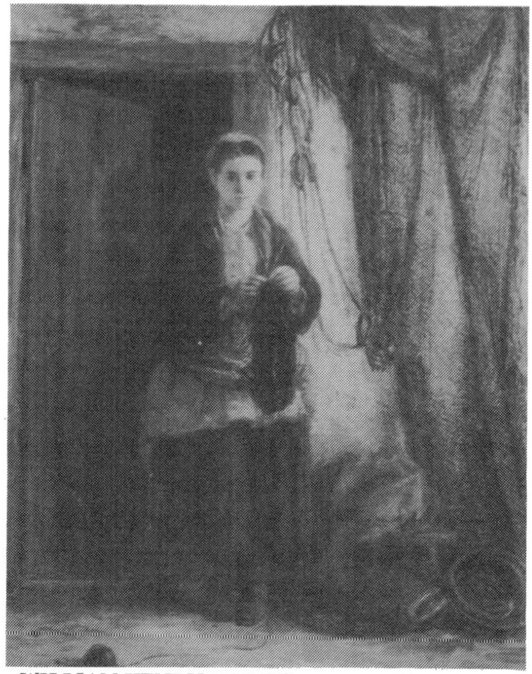

WILLIAM HENRY HAINES – Happy Thoughts – signed and dated 1867, and signed and inscribed on an old label on the reverse – on panel – 8 x 6in.
(Christie's) **$1,178** **£770**

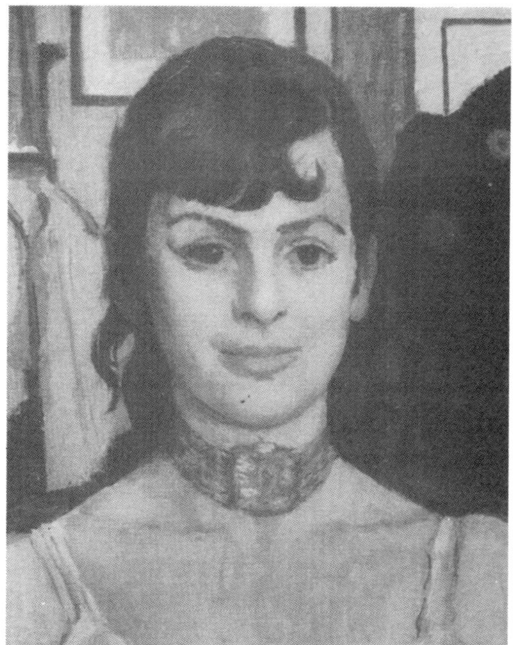

CLIFFORD HALL – Portrait Of Hannah Weil, Bust Length – signed and dated '51 – oil on board – 14 x 9½in.
(Christie's) **$755** **£528**

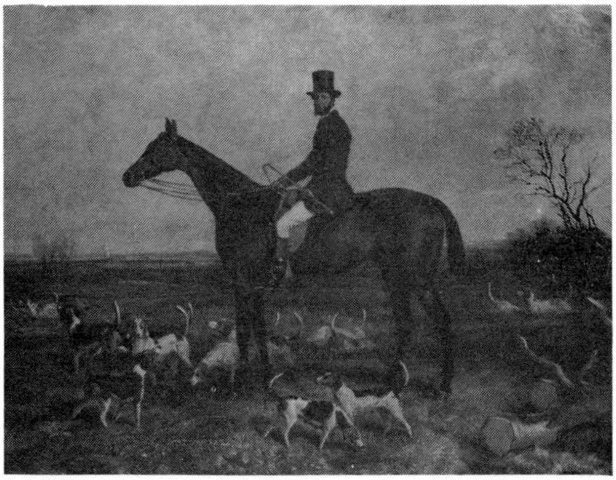

HARRY HALL, Attributed to – A Huntsman And Hounds – 22½ x 29½in.
(Lawrence Fine Art) **$10,956** **£6,600**

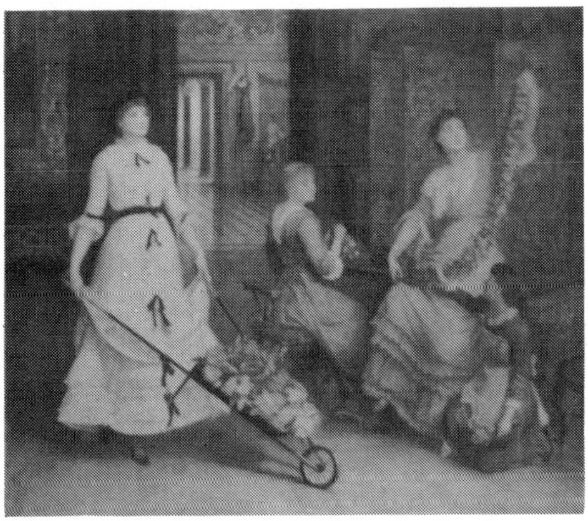

CHARLES EDWARD HALLE – Preparing For The Ball – signed with monogram – on panel – 24 x 27in.
(Christie's) **$11,340** **£7,560**

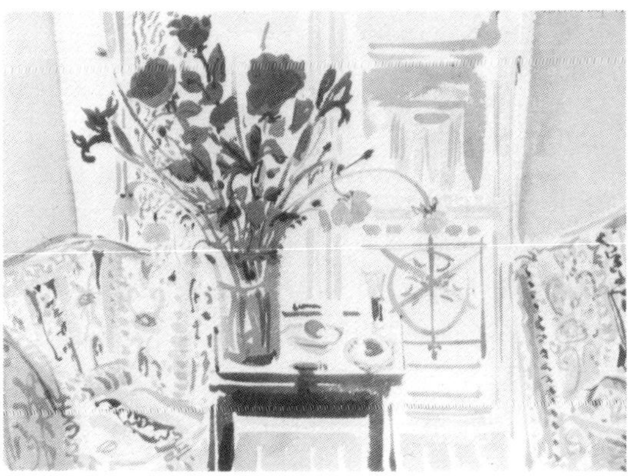

ALAN HALLIDAY – Atelier Artiste, Montmartre – signed and dated '85 – watercolour – 11¼ x 15in.
(Christie's) **$660** **£462**

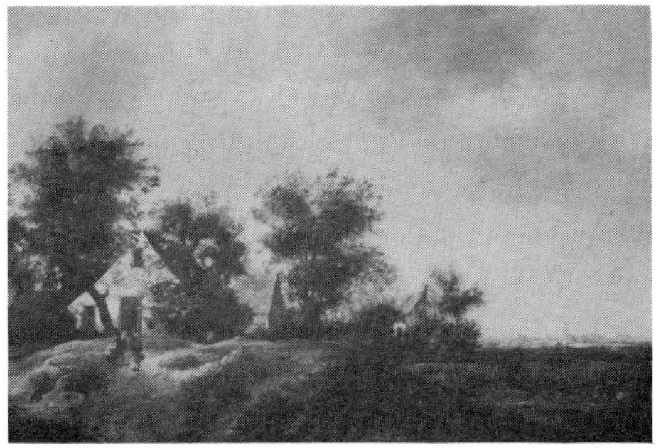

CLAES HALS, Attributed to – An Extensive Landscape With Peasants Conversing On A Track By A Cottage, A View To A Town Beyond – on panel – 23½ x 32¾in.
(Lawrence Fine Art) **$2,739** **£1,650**

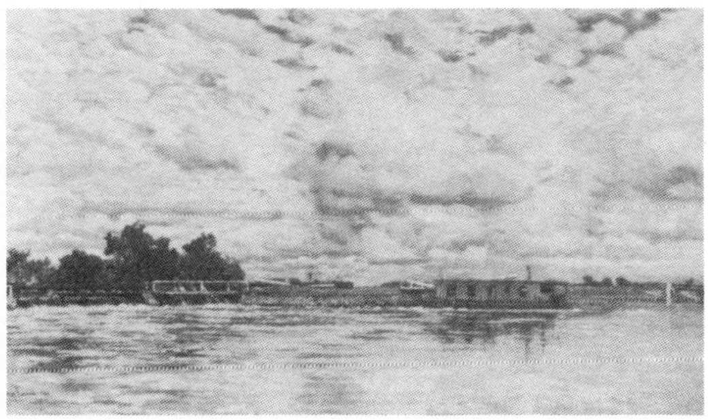

KEELEY HALSWELLE – The Keepie At Days Lock – signed and dated 1882 – 13¾ x 24in.
(Christie's) **$1,085** **£770**

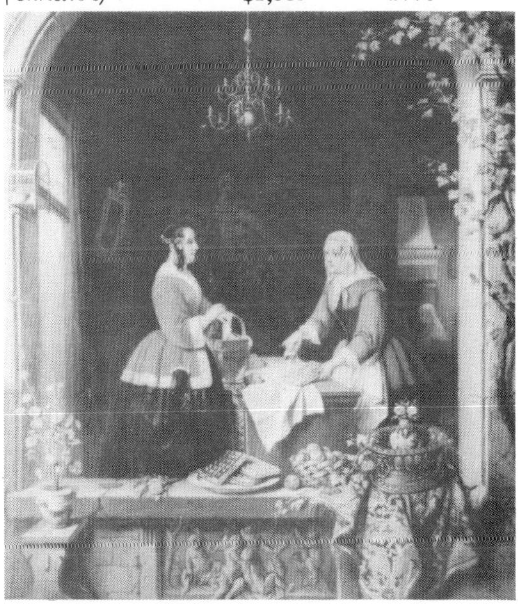

ALEXIS VAN HAMME – Preparing Belgian Waffles – signed and dated 1864 – oil on cradled panel – 28¾ x 22¼in.
(Robt. W. Skinner Inc.) **$5,500** **£3,819**

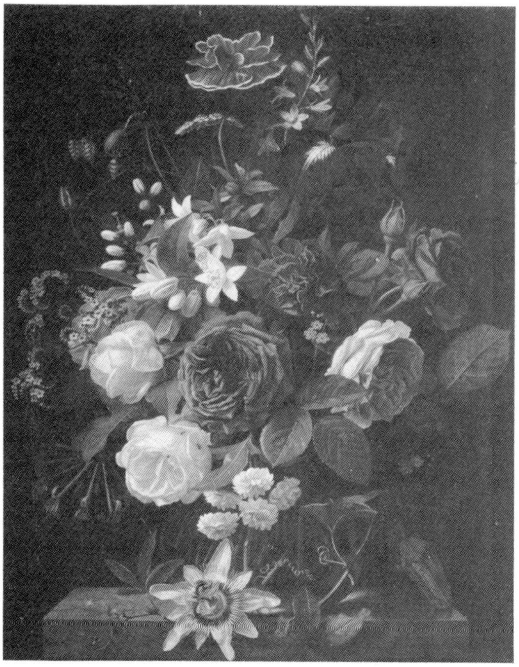

WILLIAM HAMMER – Roses, Fuchsias And Other Flowers In A Glass Vase On A Ledge – signed – 18½ x 14¾in.
(Christie's) **$12,672** **£8,800**

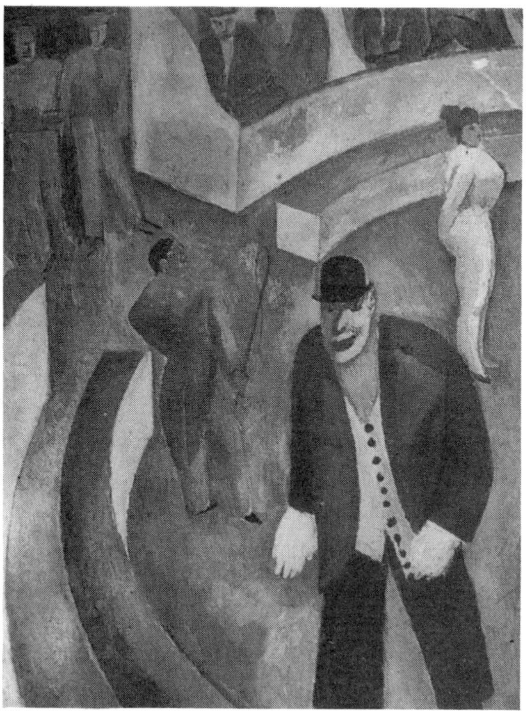

NINA HAMNETT – The Ringmaster – signed – oil on canvas – 29½ x 20in.
(Christie's) **$7,253** **£4,620**

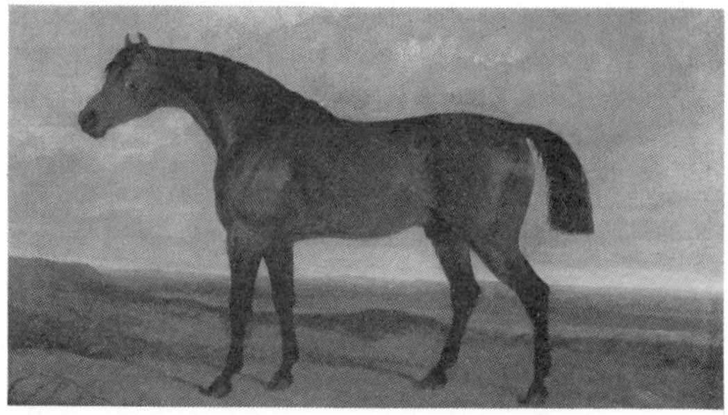

CHARLES HANCOCK – Philip Dauncey's Celebrated Thoroughbred Hunter 'Cashmere' – signed and dated 1829 – 27½ x 35¾in.
(Christie's) **$2,916** **£1,944**

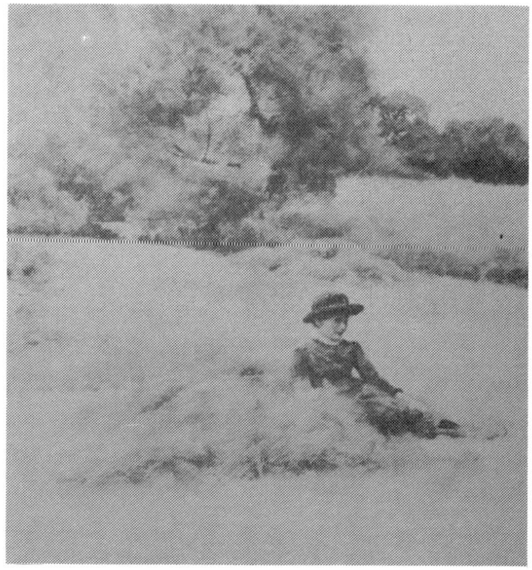

WILLIAM LEE HANKEY, Attributed to – In The Fields – watercolour – 9 x 7½in.
(Lawrence Fine Art) **$4,017** **£2,420**

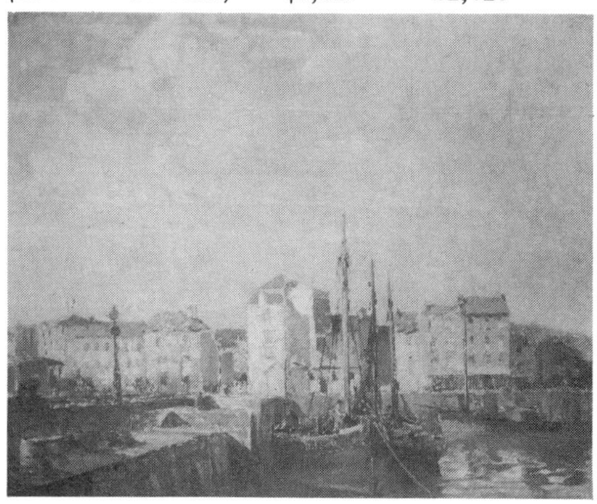

WILLIAM LEE HANKEY – The Inner Harbour, Dieppe – signed, signed and inscribed on the reverse – oil on canvas – 19½ x 23½in.
(Christie's) **$7,253** **£4,620**

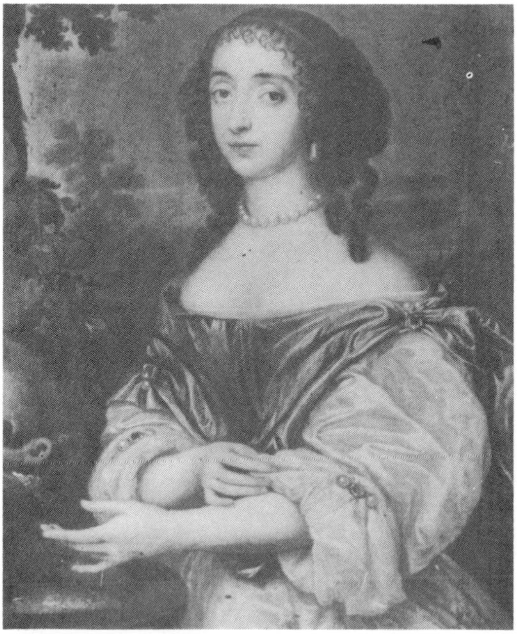

ADRIAEN HANNEMAN, Follower of – Portrait Of A Lady, Said To Be Mary Of Orange – on panel – 17 x 13in.
(Christie's) **$2,592 £1,728**

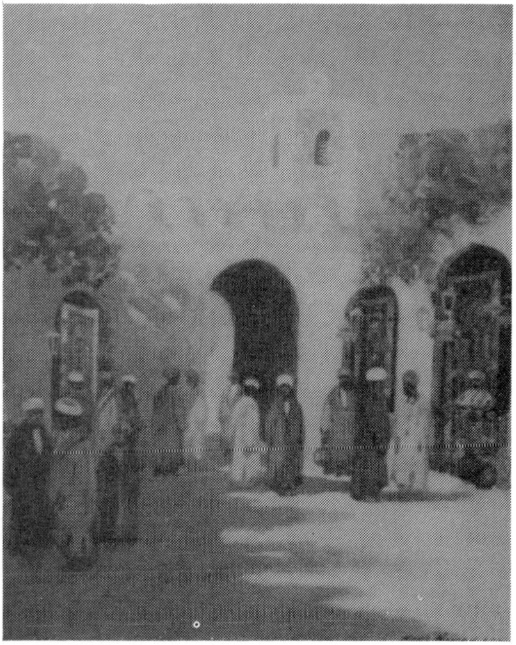

HANS HANSEN – Arab Figures – watercolour – 15½ x 12½in.
(Parsons, Welch & Cowell) **$143 £95**

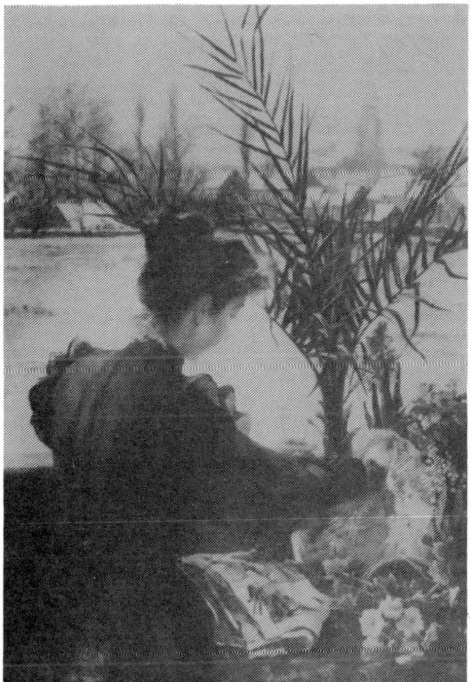

THEODORE HANNON – 'Dans La Serre' (In The Greenhouse) – signed – oil on canvas – 50 x 31in.
(Robt. W. Skinner Inc.) **$27,000 £18,750**

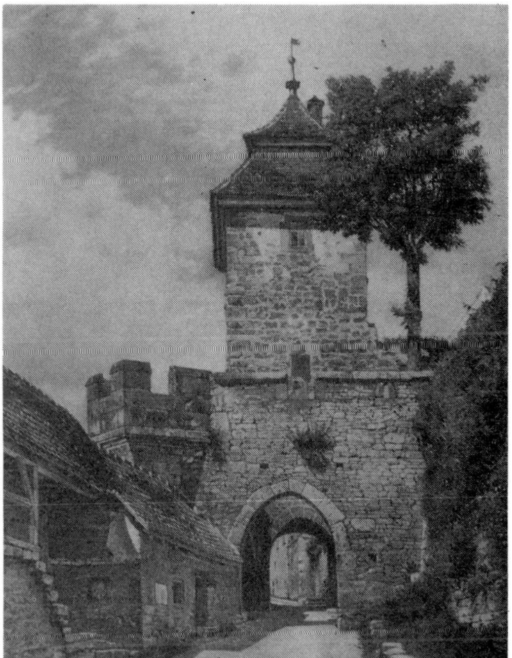

JOSEF THEODOR HANSEN – The Kobolzellertor, Rothenburg Castle – signed and dated 1910 – 15¼ x 11¼in.
(Christie's) **$1,337 £880**

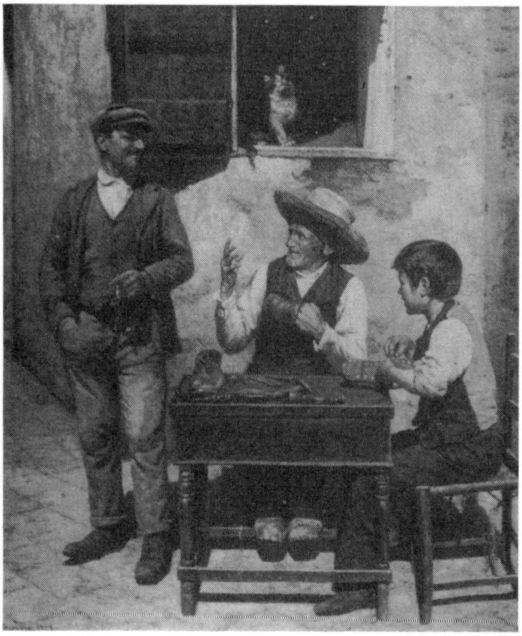

NIELS CHRISTIAN HANSEN – Sicilian Cobblers – signed and dated 1907 – 26 x 21¾in.
(Christie's) **$3,678** **£2,420**

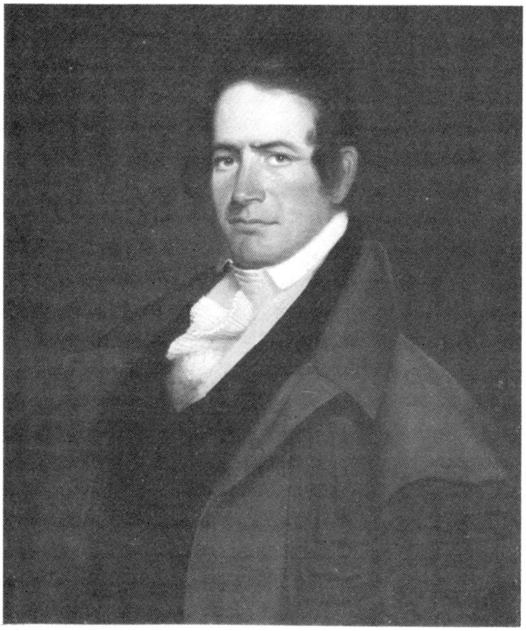

CHESTER HARDING – Major Benjamin O'Fallon – oil on canvas – 26 x 22in.
(Christie's) **$8,800** **£6,186**

JAMES DUFFIELD HARDING – In The Highlands, Sportsmen By A Burn – signed and indistinctly dated – watercolour heightened with white – 17½ x 22in.
(Lawrence Fine Art) **$1,552** **£935**

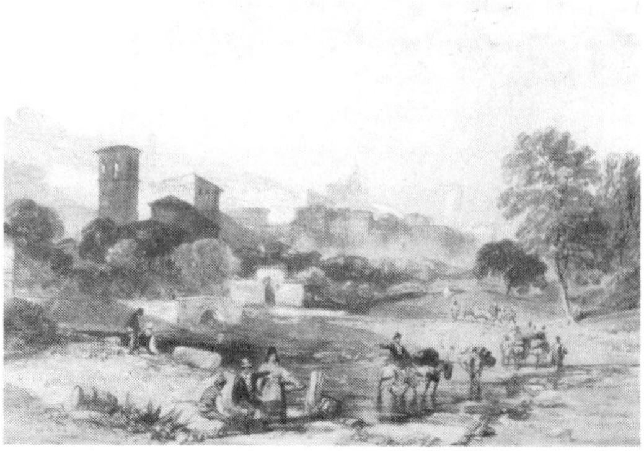

JAMES DUFFIELD HARDING – Spoleto – pencil and watercolour heightened with white – 7¾ x 11½in.
(Christie's) **$2,967** **£2,090**

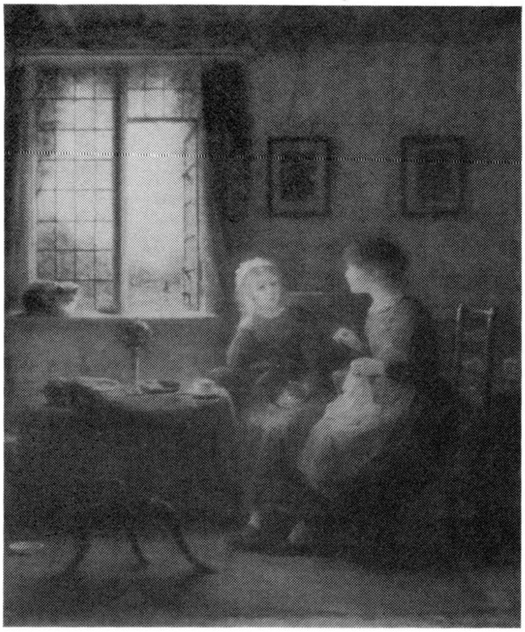

FREDERICK DANIEL HARDY – The Sisters – signed and dated 1898 – 10½ x 8½in.
(Christie's) **$5,890** **£3,850**

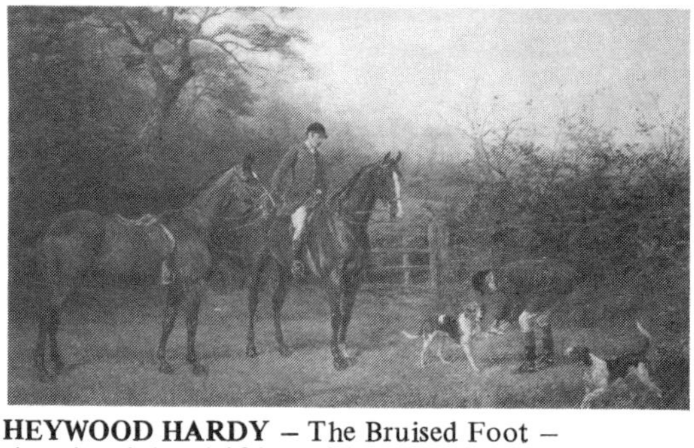

HEYWOOD HARDY – The Bruised Foot – signed and dated 1905 – 24 x 34in.
(Christie's) **$33,660** **£22,000**

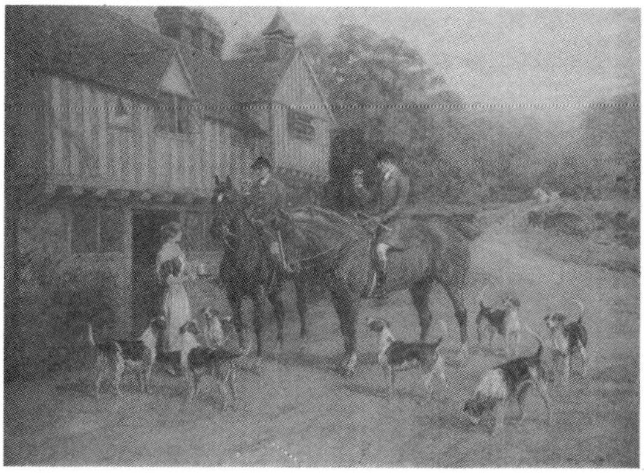

HEYWOOD HARDY – The Stirrup Cup – signed – 17½ x 23½in.
(Christie's) **$17,836** **£12,650**

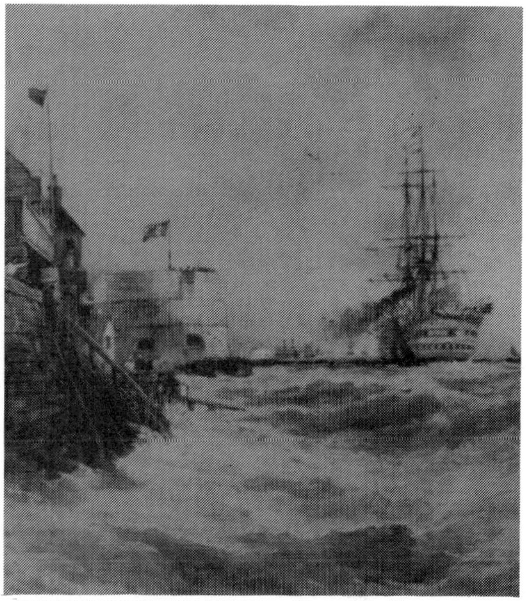

THOMAS BUSH HARDY – 'Entrance To Portsmouth Harbour . . .' – watercolour.
(Parsons, Welch & Cowell) **$1,117** **£740**

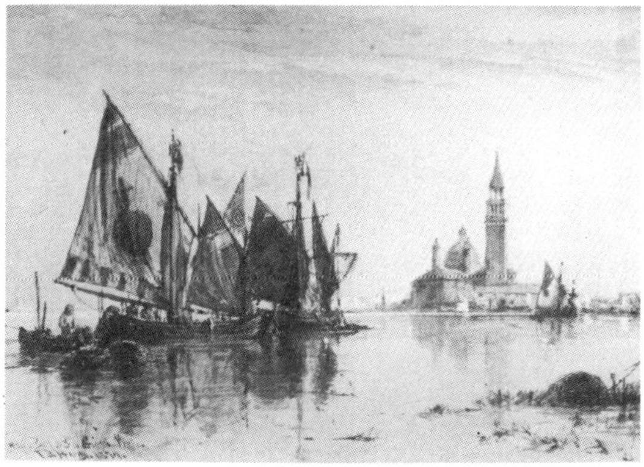

THOMAS BUSH HARDY – Venice: Chioggia Boats Off San Giorgio Maggiore – signed, inscribed and dated 1879 – watercolour heightened with white – 4¾ x 7¼in.
(Christie's) **$2,268** **£1,512**

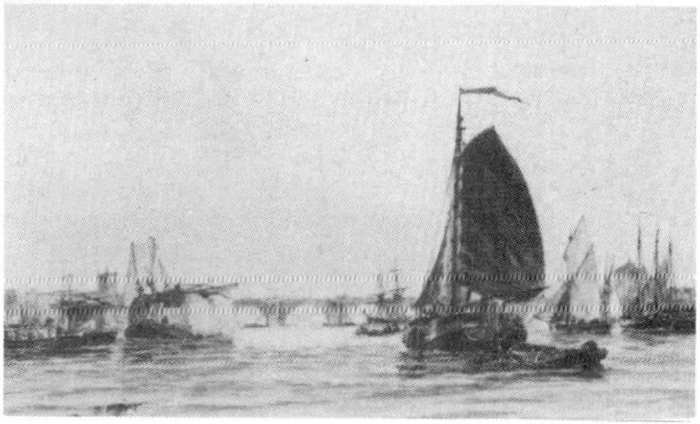

THOMAS BUSH HARDY – The Pool Of London Looking Towards London Bridge – signed, inscribed and dated 1875 – pencil and watercolour heightened with white – 13¼ x 18¾in.
(Christie's) **$2,481** **£1,760**

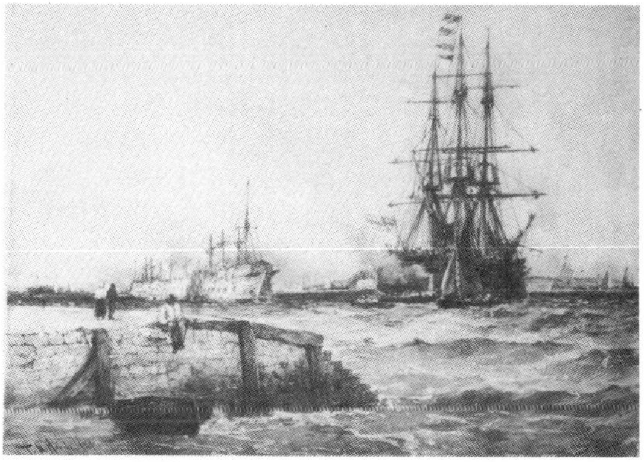

THOMAS BUSH HARDY – Portsmouth Harbour: H.M.S. Victory And Moored Hulks – signed, inscribed and dated 1889 – watercolour heightened with bodycolour – 9½ x 13in.
(Christie's) **$1,458** **£972**

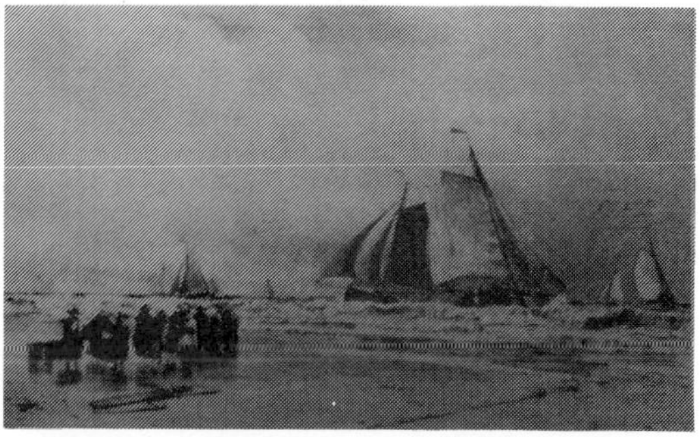

THOMAS BUSH HARDY – 'Dutch Pincks Getting Under Way Scheveningen, Tide Going Out' – signed, inscribed and dated 1881 – watercolour and bodycolour – 32 x 49cm.
(Phillips) **$2,934** **£1,800**

HARE

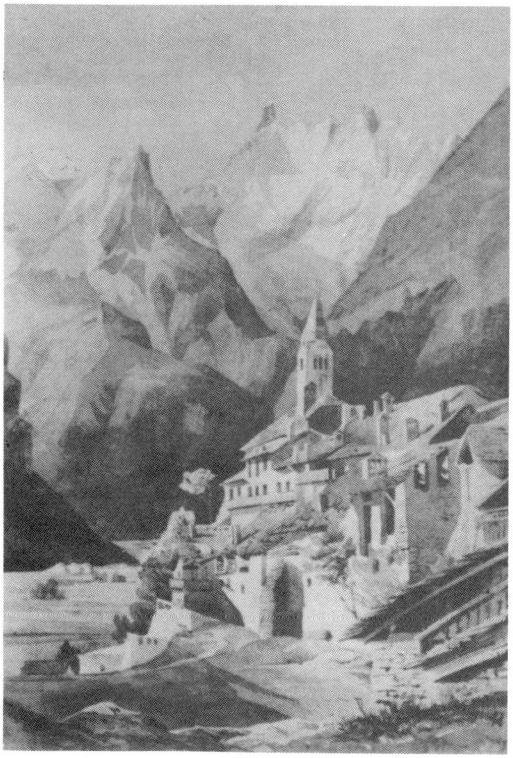

AUGUSTUS JOHN CUTHBERT HARE – Mont Blanc From Courmayeur – watercolour – 13.5 x 9.2in.
(Woolley & Wallis) **$480** **£320 Three**

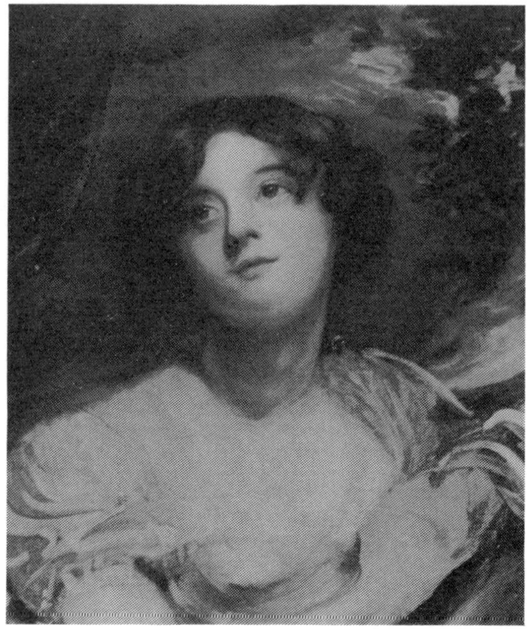

GEORGE HENRY HARLOW, Circle of – Portrait Of A Young Lady, Bust Length, Wearing A White Dress, By A Red Draped Curtain – 22½ x 19¾in.
(Christie's) **$648** **£432**

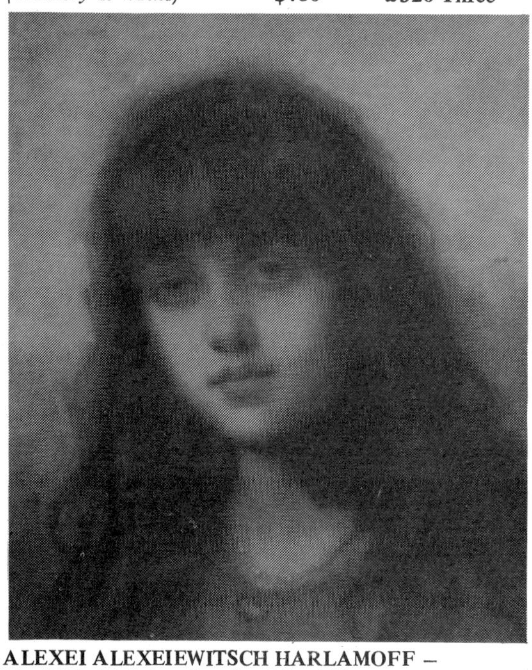

ALEXEI ALEXEIEWITSCH HARLAMOFF – My Little Model – signed – 16 x 13in.
(Christie's) **$10,560** **£6,600**

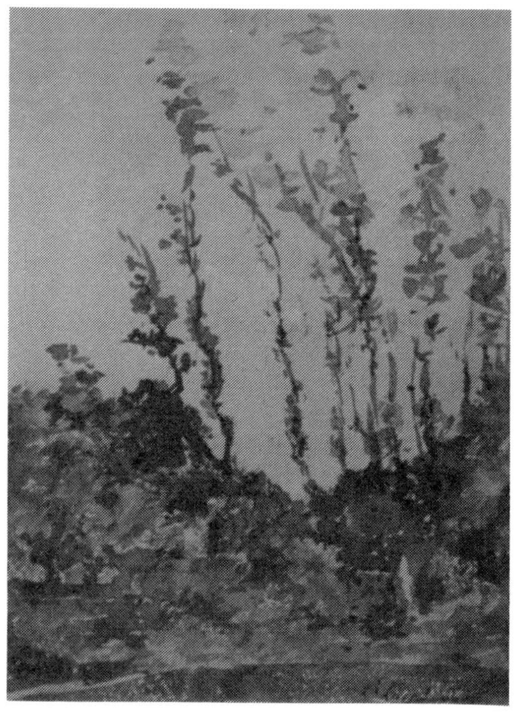

HENRI HARPIGNIES – Paysage – signed – watercolour – 30 x 22.5 cm.
(Phillips) **$697** **£450**

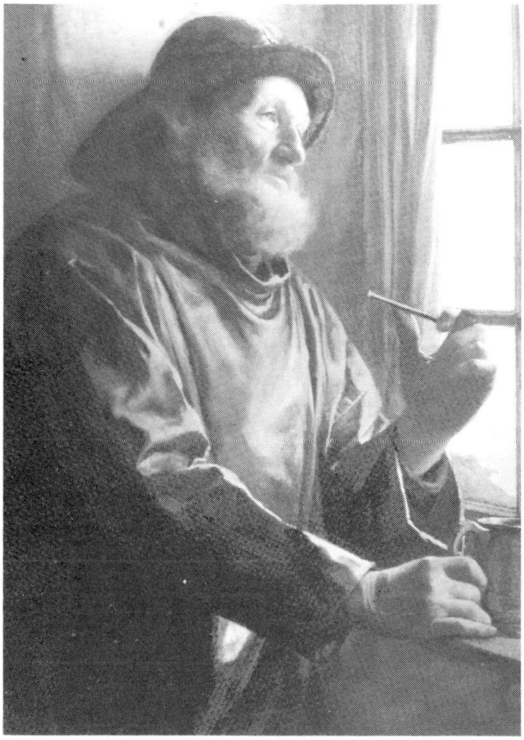

EDWIN HARRIS – Remembering The Old Fishing Days – signed and dated 1890 – oil on canvas – 91 x 61cm.
(Phillips) **$7,810** **£5,500**

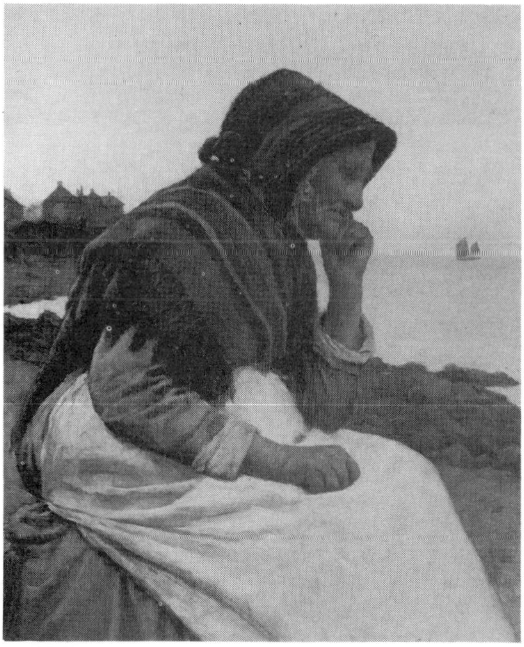

EDWIN HARRIS – A Newlyn Fishwife – signed – oil on canvas – 15¼ x 12¼in.
(Christie's) **$6,562** **£4,180**

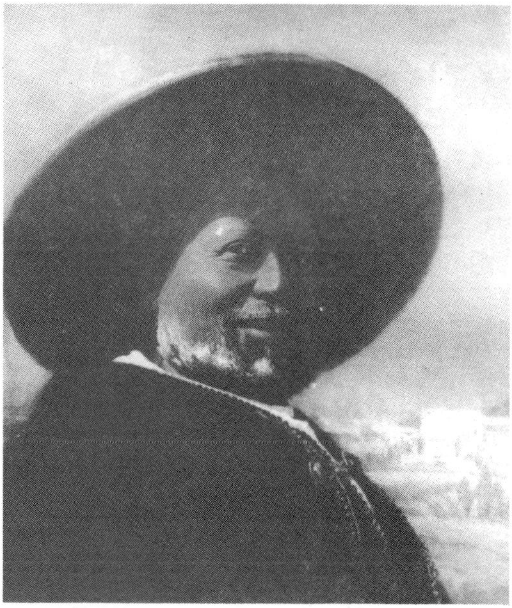

G. F. HARRIS – Portrait Study Of The Emperor Of Merelik – signed and dated 1913 – oil on canvas – 30 x 25in.
(Biddle & Webb) **$491** **£330**

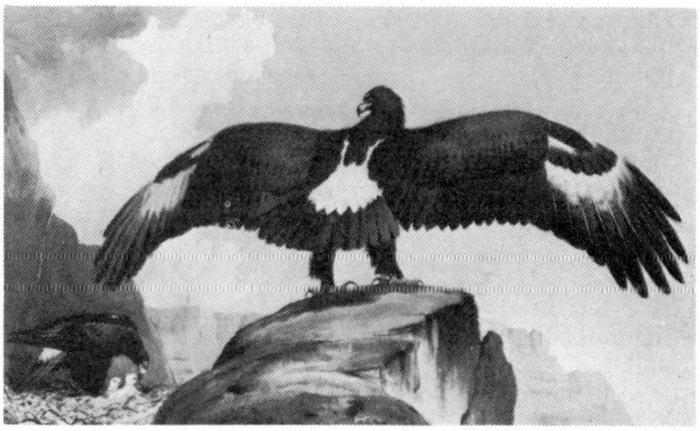

JOHN CYRIL HARRISON – Black Eagles, Drakensburg Mountains, South Africa – signed – pencil and watercolour – 26 x 39½in.
(Christie's) **$1,134** **£756**

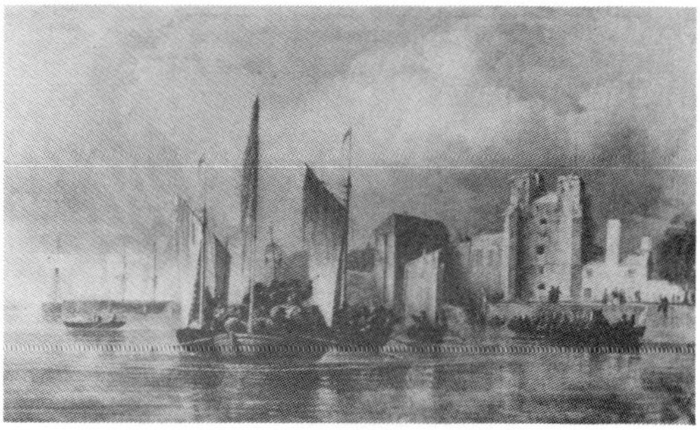

THOMAS HART – Civic Ceremony, With A View Of Gods House Tower, Southampton, On The Left In The Distance The Town Quay – signed and dated – oil – 17.7 x 27.2in.
(Woolley & Wallis) **$958** **£680**

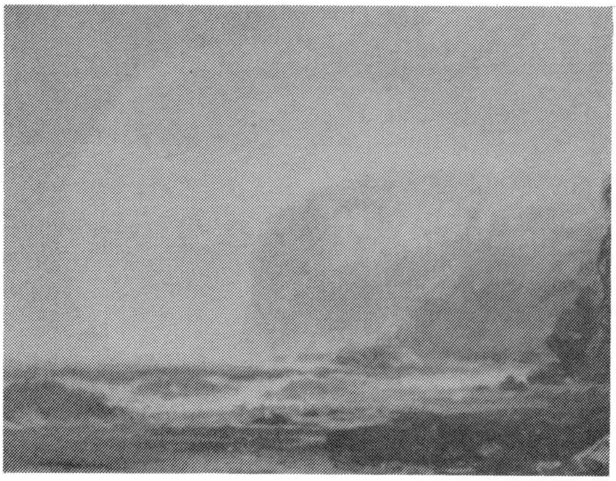

WILLIAM M. HART – Coastal Landscape, Mt. Desert, Maine – signed, also inscribed and dated 1858 on the reverse – oil on board – 5 x 7¾in.
(Robt. W. Skinner Inc.) **$800** **£490**

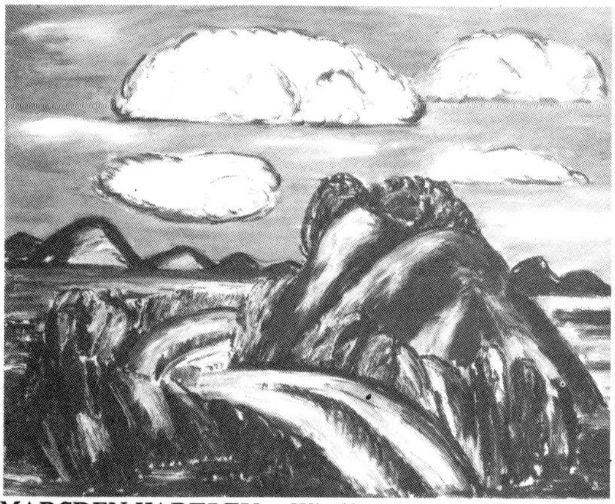

MARSDEN HARTLEY – Winding Road – oil on canvas – 32 x 39½in.
(Christie's) **$77,000** **£54,131**

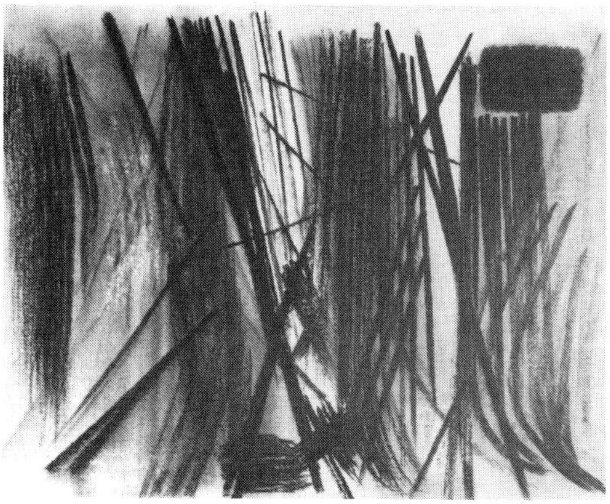

HANS HARTUNG – Composition – signed and dated '53 – coloured crayons and charcoal on buff paper – 18½ x 25½in.
(Christie's) **$13,728** **£8,580**

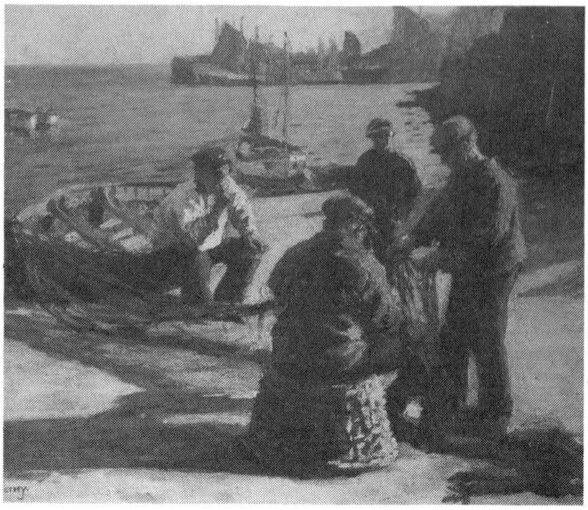

HAROLD HARVEY – Mending The Nets, Newlyn – signed – oil on canvas – 15 x 18in.
(Christie's) **$31,086** **£19,800**

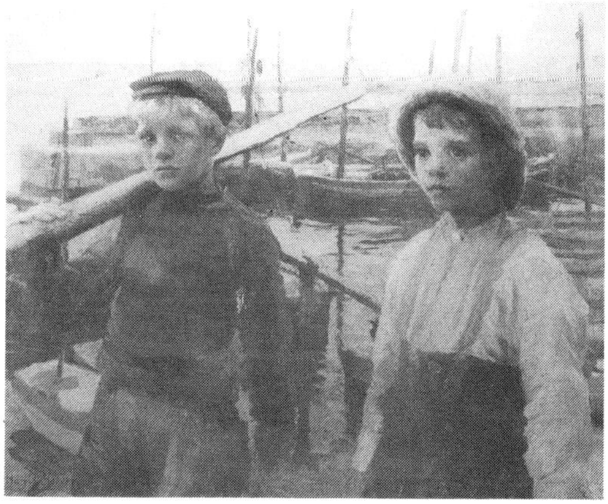

HAROLD HARVEY – Carrying The Oars – signed and dated '06 – 34 x 41cm.
(Phillips) **$38,340** **£27,000**

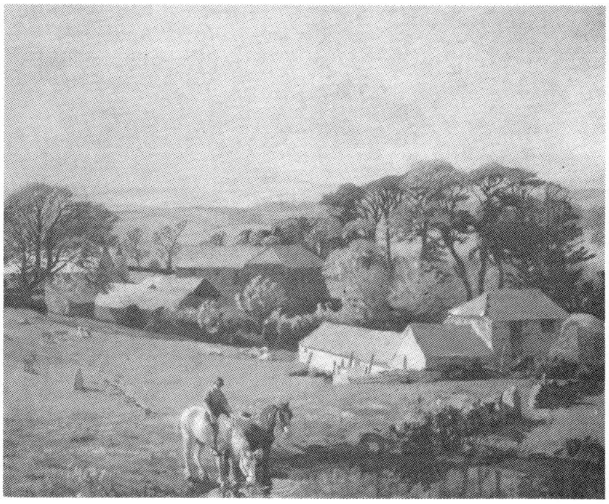

HAROLD HARVEY – A Cornish Homestead – signed and dated '35 – oil on canvas – 25 x 30in.
(Christie's) **$25,954** **£18,150**

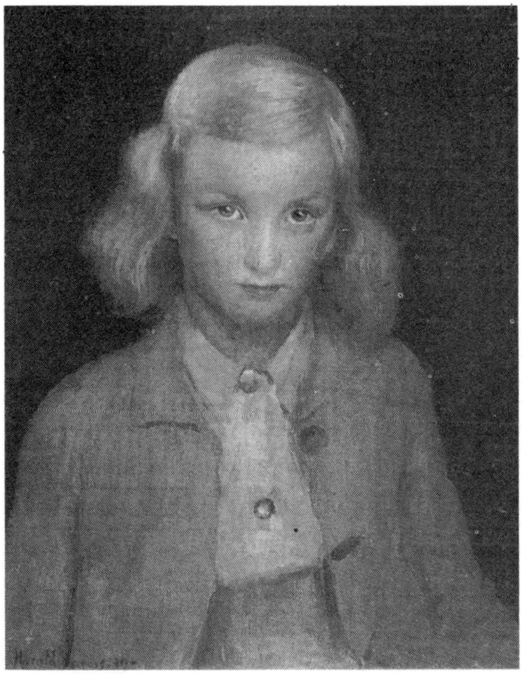

HAROLD HARVEY – The Yellow Blouse – signed and dated '39 – oil on canvas – 19¼ x 15in.
(Christie's) **$3,775** **£2,640**

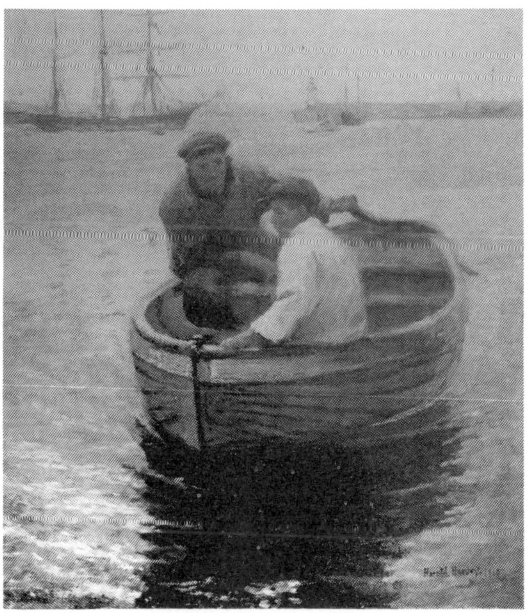

HAROLD HARVEY – Whiffling Outer Harbour – signed and dated 1910 – oil on canvas – 41 x 36cm.
(Phillips) **$16,000** **£10,000**

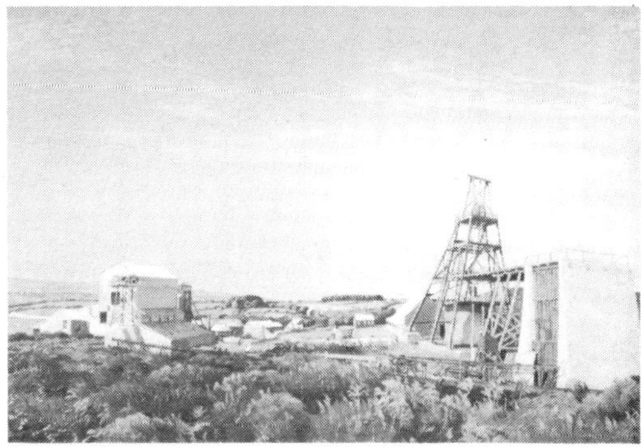

HAROLD HARVEY – The Lady, A Cornish Tin Mine – signed and dated '34 – oil on canvas – 34 x 50in.
(Christie's) **$3,932** **£2,750**

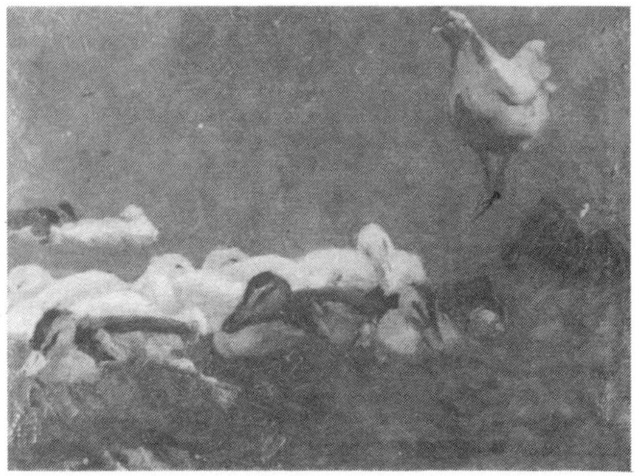

HAROLD HARVEY, Attributed to – Hen And Ducklings Basking In The Sun – oil on canvas 25 x 35cm.
(W. H. Lane & Son) **$1,245** **£750**

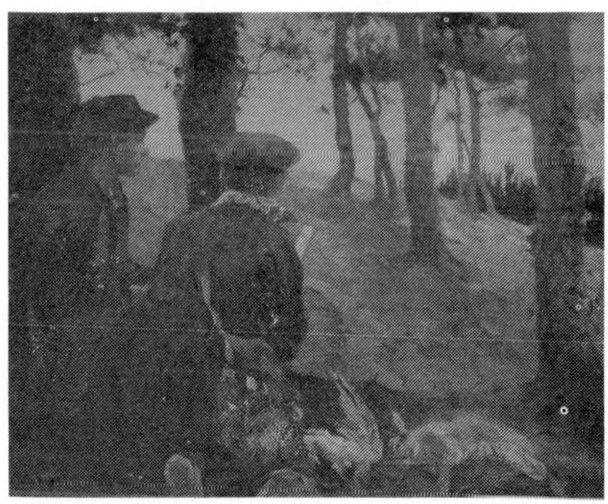

HAROLD HARVEY – The Poachers – signed and dated '16 – oil on canvas – 61 x 76cm.
(Phillips) **$24,000** **£15,000**

HAROLD HARVEY, Attributed to – Ducks Swimming And Seated At The Edge Of A Pond – oil on canvas – 25 x 35cm.
(W. H. Lane & Son) **$1,452** **£875**

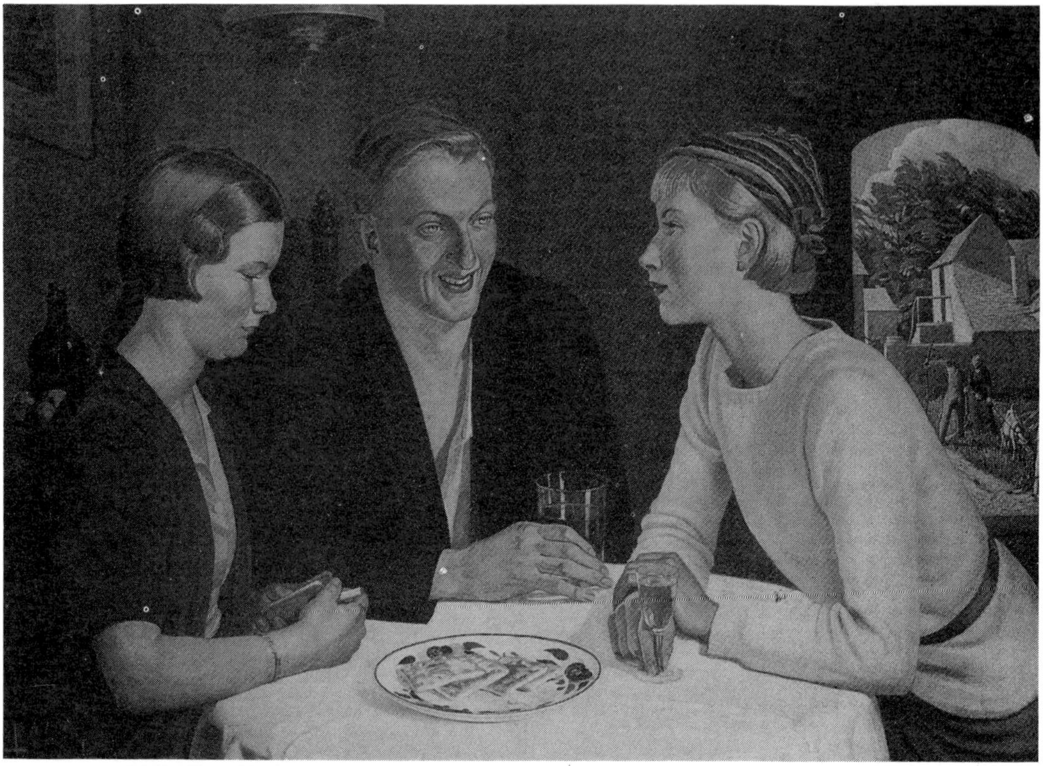

HILDA MARY HARVEY – Holidays In Cornwall – signed – oil on canvas – 30 x 40in.
(Christie's) **$6,908 £4,400**

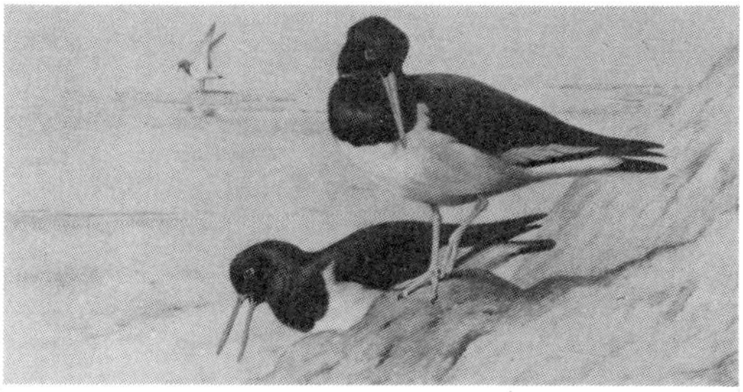

JOHN HAMMOND HARWOOD – Roseate Terns; and Oyster-Catchers – signed and dated 1923 – watercolour heightened with white – 8¼ x 10¾in.
(Christie's) **$1,318 £935 Pair**

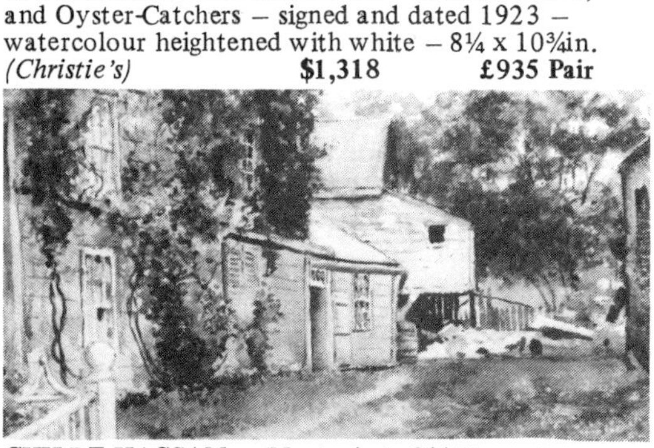

CHILDE HASSAM – 'Nantucket, Old Houses' – signed and inscribed – watercolour on paper, laid down on cardboard – 9 x 11¼in.
(Robt. W. Skinner Inc.) **$18,000 £12,500**

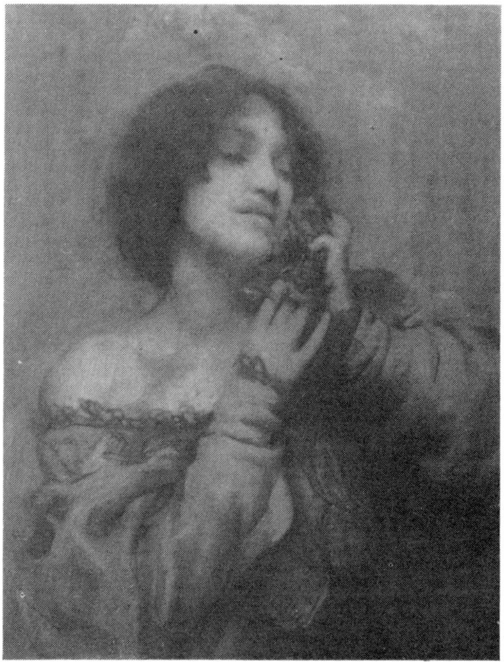

FRANK HAVILAND – Portrait Of The Artist's Wife – 30 x 22in.
(Worsfolds) **$592 £400**

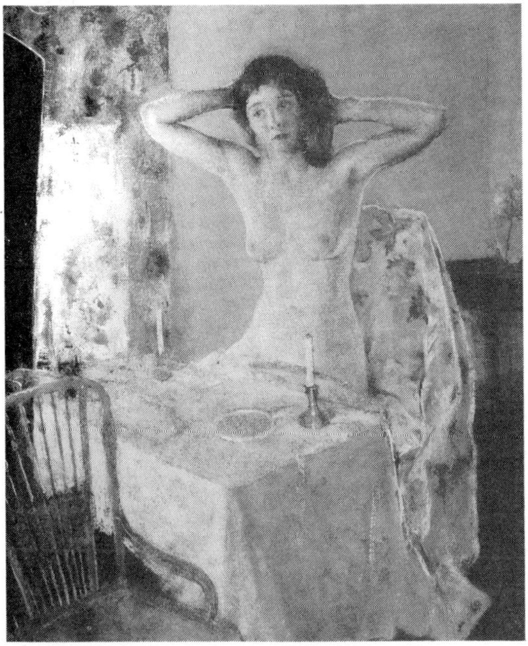

CHARLES WEBSTER HAWTHORNE – The Dressing Table – signed – oil on canvas – 29½ x 24¾in.
(Christie's) **$9,900** **£6,168**

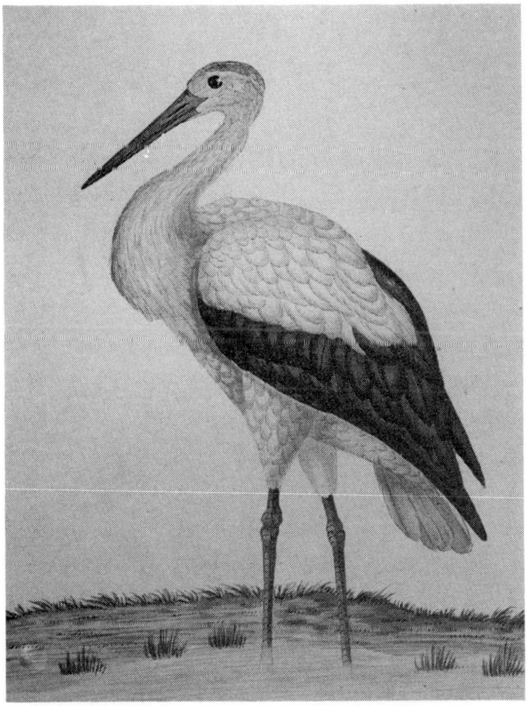

WILLIAM HAYES – A Stork; A Spoonbill; and A Female Crane – the first and second signed, inscribed and dated 1872 – pen and grey or brown ink and watercolour – 13¼ x 9½in. and smaller.
(Christie's) **$4,776** **£2,860 Three**

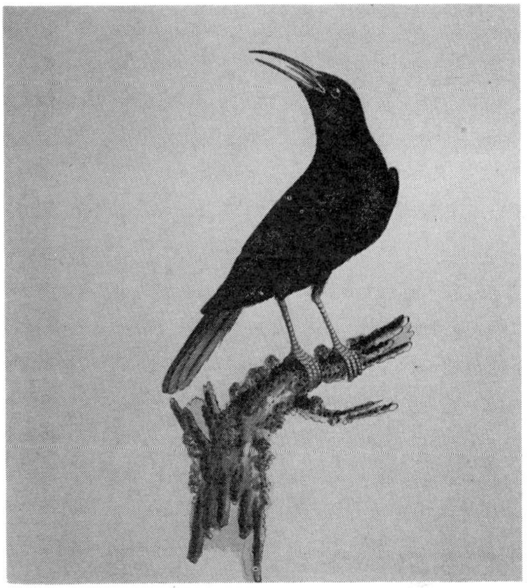

WILLIAM HAYES – A Creeper From Sandwich Island; A Blue-Headed Parakeet From Sandwich Island; A Cape Pigeon; and A Ghillan Sparrow In Winter – two signed and dated 1782 and 1785, the last signed and dated 1782 – 9½ x 12¼in.
(Christie's) **$4,408** **£2,640 Four**

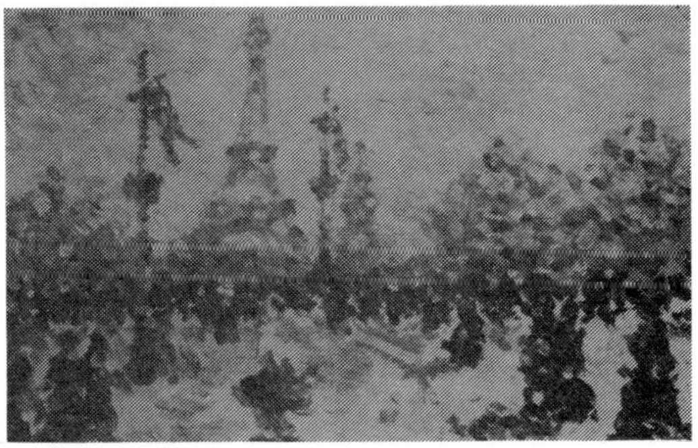

LOUIS HAYET – Vue De Paris – signed – oil on board – 27 x 36cm.
(Phillips) **$15,500** **£10,000**

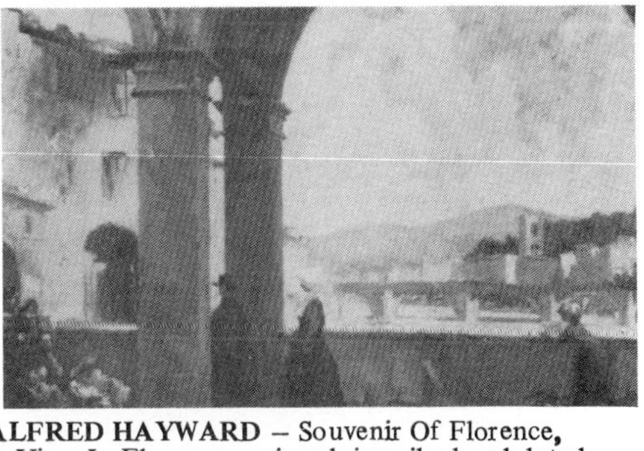

ALFRED HAYWARD – Souvenir Of Florence, A View In Florence – signed, inscribed and dated 1906, and signed and inscribed on a label on the frame.
(Christie's) **$1,730** **£1,210**

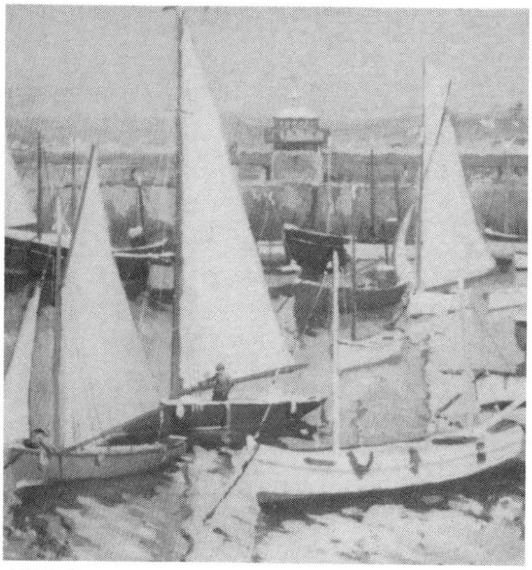

ALFRED HAYWARD – Yachts And Fishing Boats In A Harbour – signed – oil on panel – 10 x 8½in.
(Christie's) **$2,516** **£1,760**

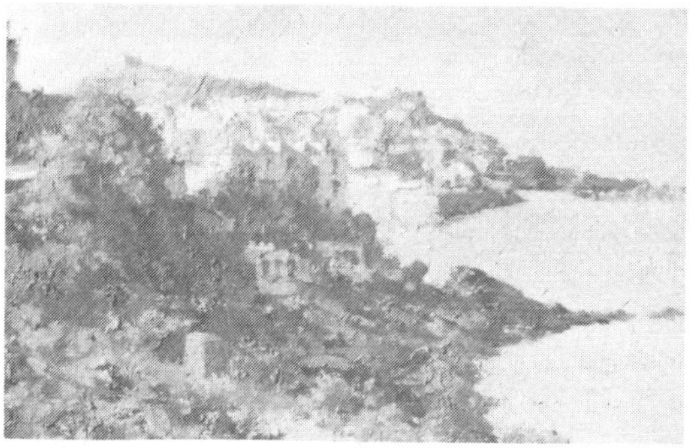

ARTHUR HAYWARD – St. Ives From Porthminster – signed, inscribed on the reverse – oil on board – 24 x 34cm.
(Phillips) **$1,224** **£800**

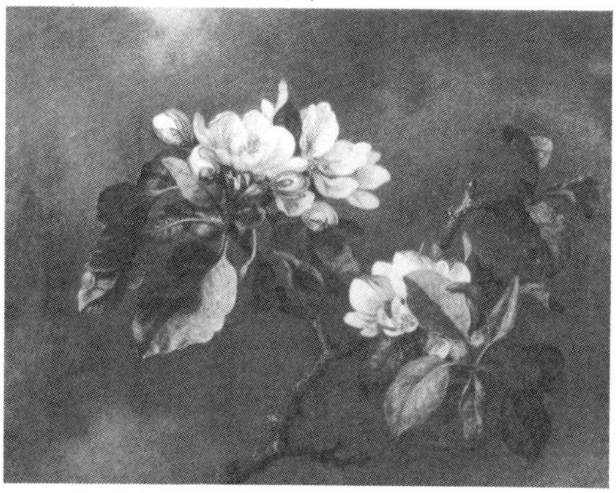

MARTIN JOHNSON HEADE – Apple Blossom – signed and dated 1875 – oil on canvas – 10 x 12in.
(Christie's) **$46,200** **£32,478**

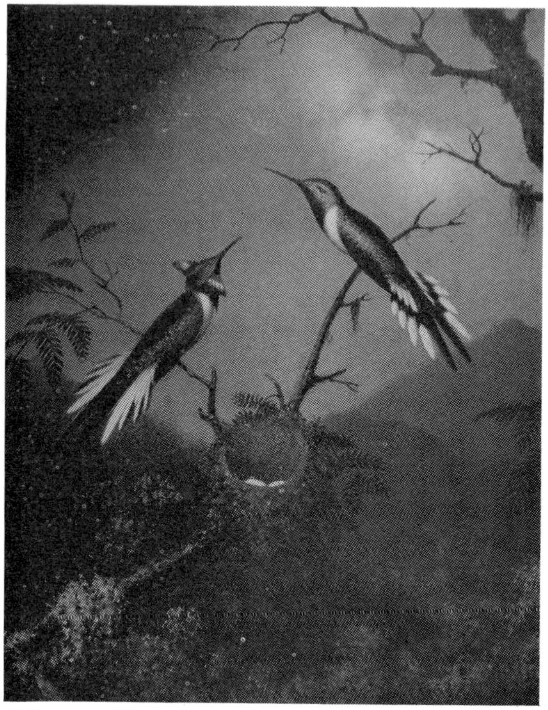

MARTIN JOHNSON HEADE – Hummingbirds At Their Nest – oil on canvas laid down on board – 12¾ x 11in.
(Christie's) **$176,000** **£123,728**

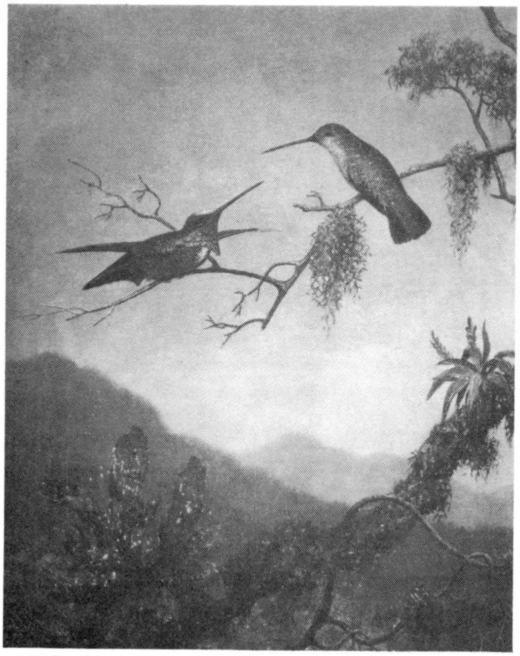

MARTIN JOHNSON HEADE – Amethyst Hummingbirds – oil on canvas laid down on board – 12¾ x 11in.
(Christie's) **$55,000** **£38,665**

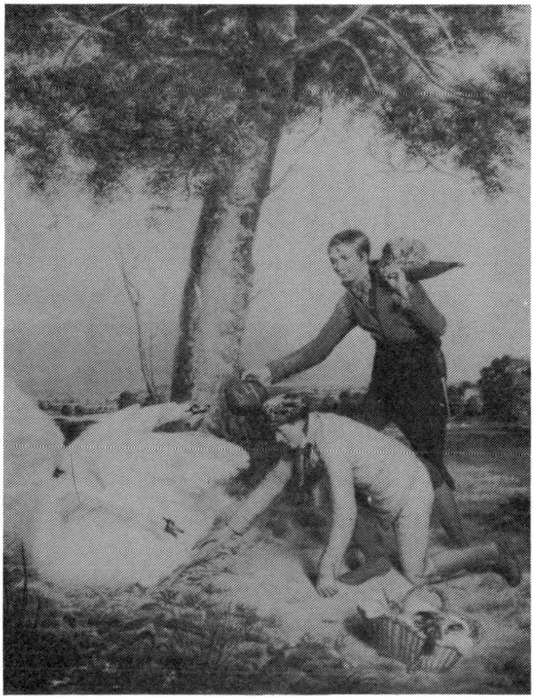

THOMAS HEAPHY – Two Servant Boys Taunting Swans – pencil and watercolour – 25¼ x 19¾in.
(Christie's) **$5,670 £3,780**

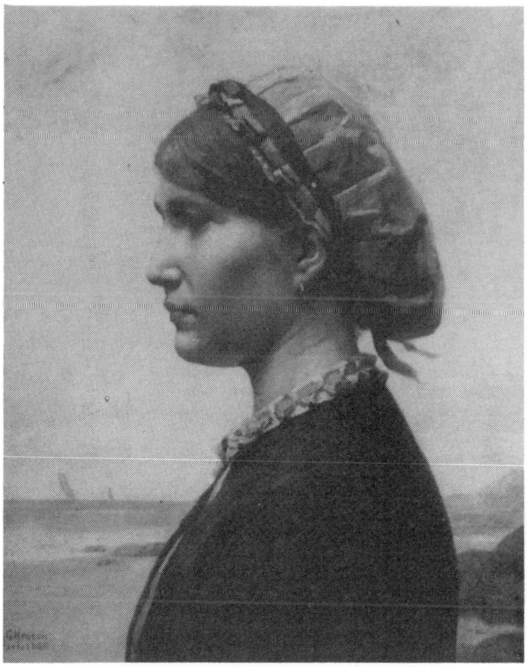

AUGUSTUS GEORGE HEATON – Near The Sea – signed and dated 1880 – oil on canvas – 21¾ x 17½in.
(Christie's) **$1,650 £1.028**

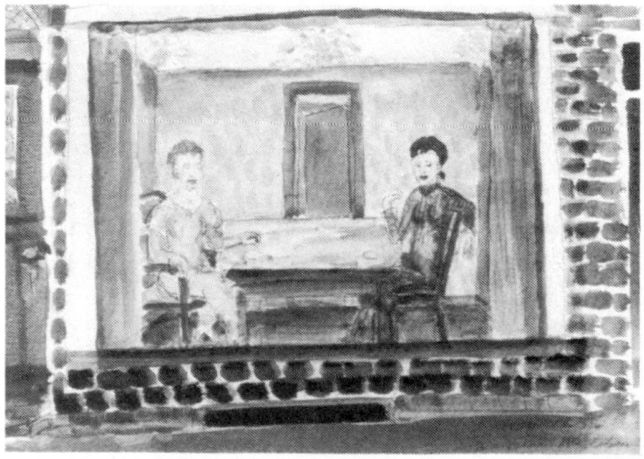

ERICH HECKEL – Wartende Madchen – signed, inscribed and dated '56 – watercolour and pencil on paper – 12¼ x 16½in.
(Christie's) **$3,168 £2,200**

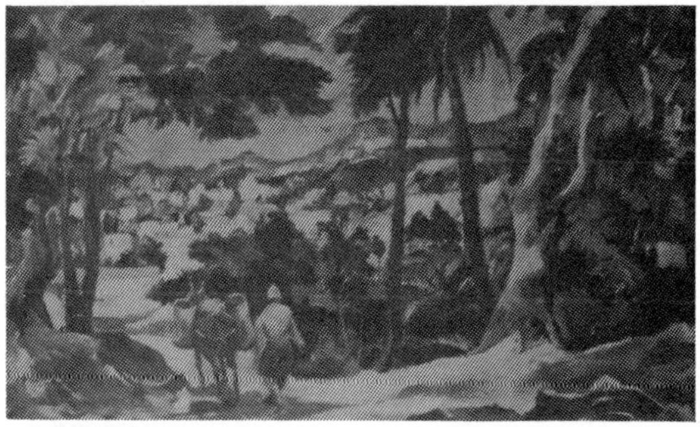

FRANZ HECKENDORF – Spanische Landschaft – signed and dated '25 – oil on canvas – 100.5 x 140cm.
(Phillips) **$6,510 £4,200**

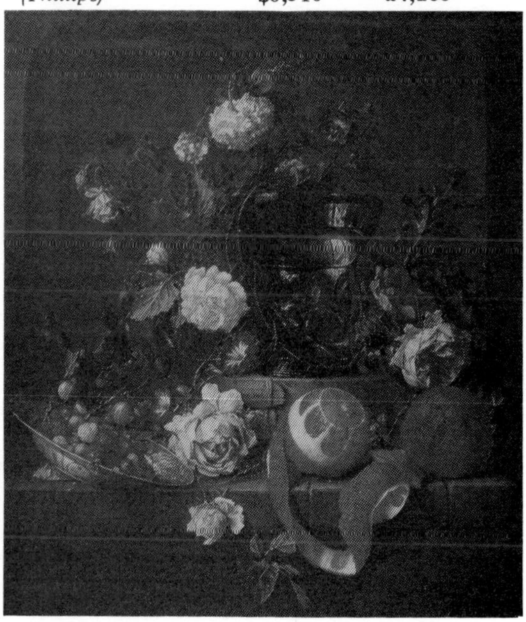

CORNELIS DE HEEM – A Still Life In A Stone Niche – signed – on canvas – 26¼ x 21½in.
(Phillips) **$190,900 £115,000**

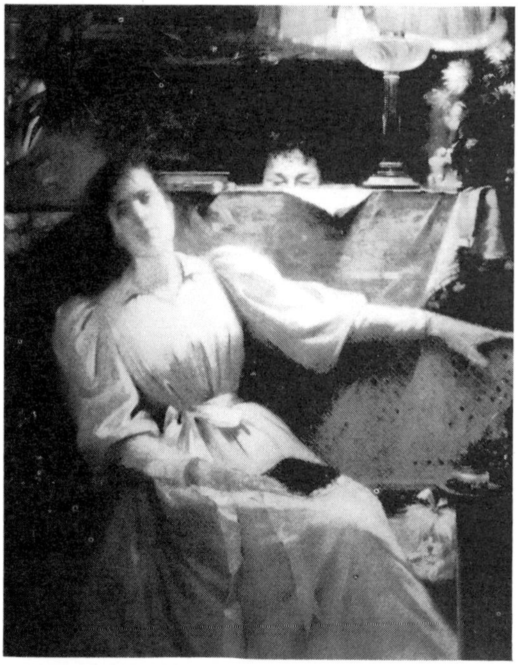

LOUISE DE HEM – A Portrait Of A Lady Seated Three-Quarter Length, In An Interior – 58½ x 46¾in.
(Christie's) **$2,340** **£1,540**

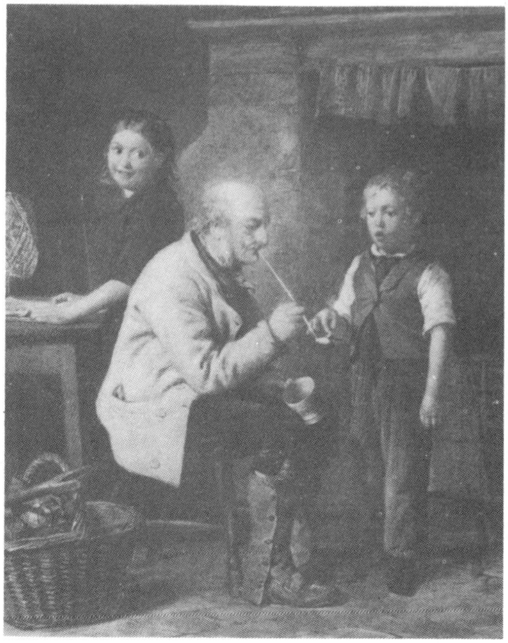

WILLIAM HEMSLEY – Lighting The Pipe – 12 x 10in.
(Christie's) **$1,861** **£1,320**

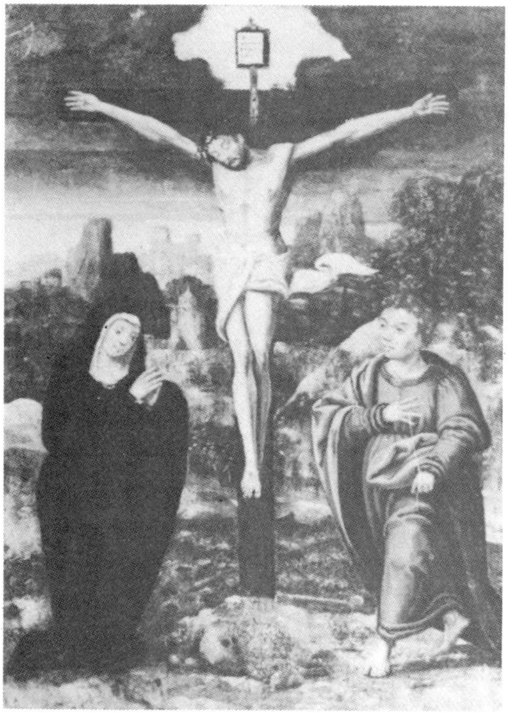

JAN VAN HEMESSEN, Follower of – The Crucifixion – oil on panel – 15 x 11in.
(Phillips) **$987** **£700**

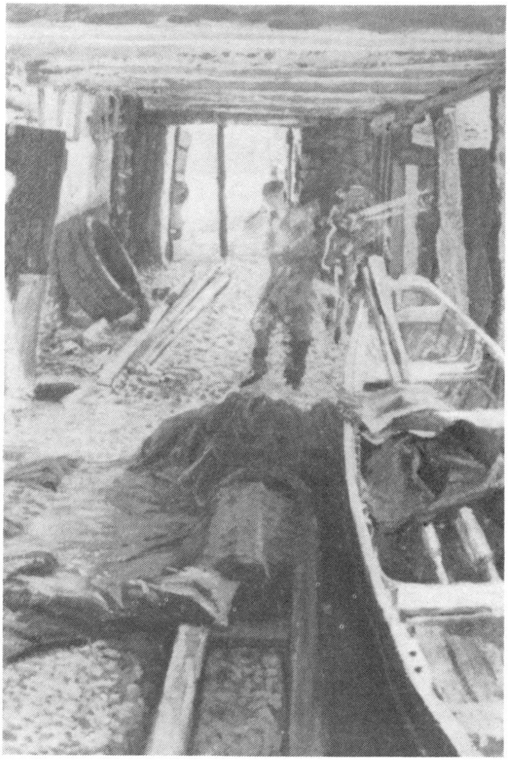

CHARLES NAPIER HEMY – The Boat-House At Mylor Creek – oil on paper – 18½ x 13in.
(Christie's) **$1,887** **£1,320**

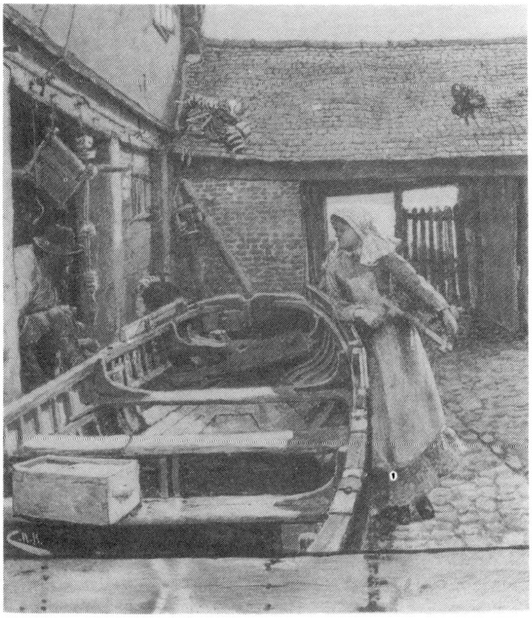

CHARLES NAPIER HEMY – The Fisherman's Daughter, A Cornish Study – signed with initials, and signed and inscribed on the reverse – oil on board – 16¼ x 12½in.
(Christie's) **$1,295** **£825**

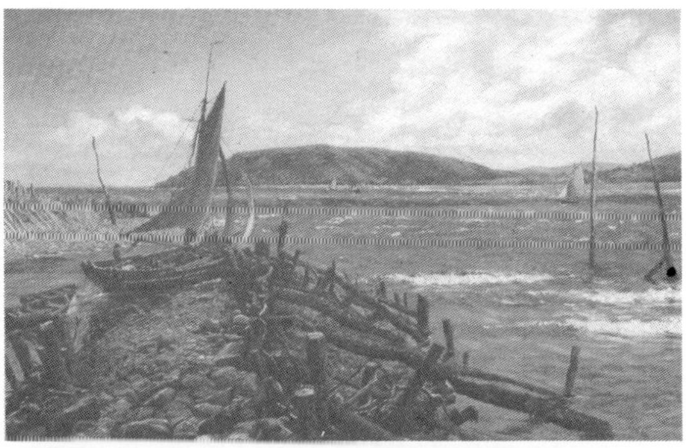

CHARLES NAPIER HEMY – Fishing-Boats In An Estuary – signed – oil on canvas – 21½ x 30in.
(Christie's) **$6,606** **£4,620**

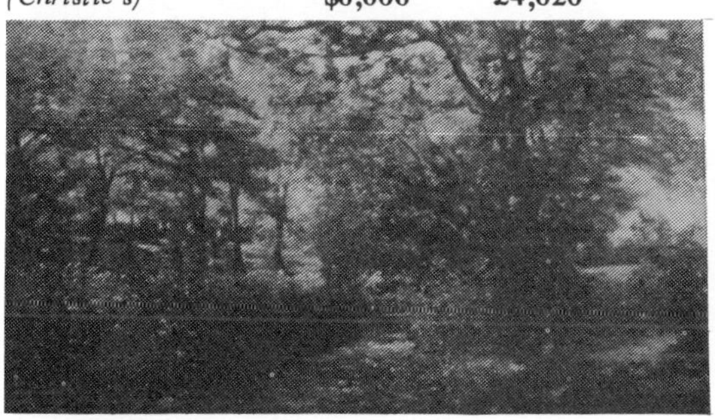

J. MORRIS HENDERSON – Woodland Burn – oil on canvas – 27 x 36in.
(Prudential Fine Art Auctioneers) **$664** **£400**

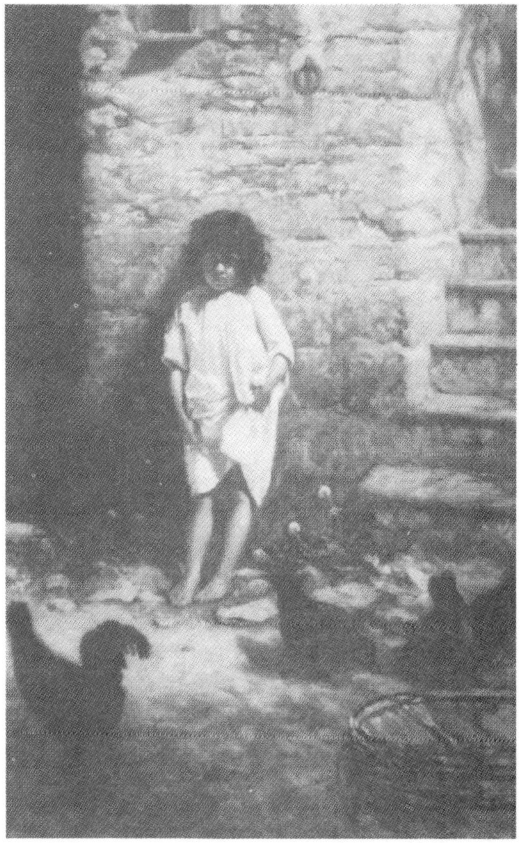

WILLIAM JOHN HENNESSEY – Daydreaming – signed and dated 1892 – oil on canvas – 42¼ x 27¼in.
(Christie's) **$2,860** **£1,989**

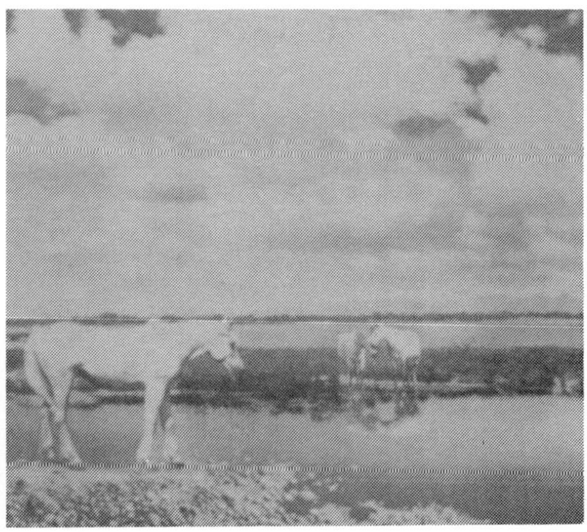

PATRICK HENNESSY – The Twelve Pins, Connemara – signed – oil on canvas – 38¼ x 50in.
(Christie's) **$2,359** **£1,650**

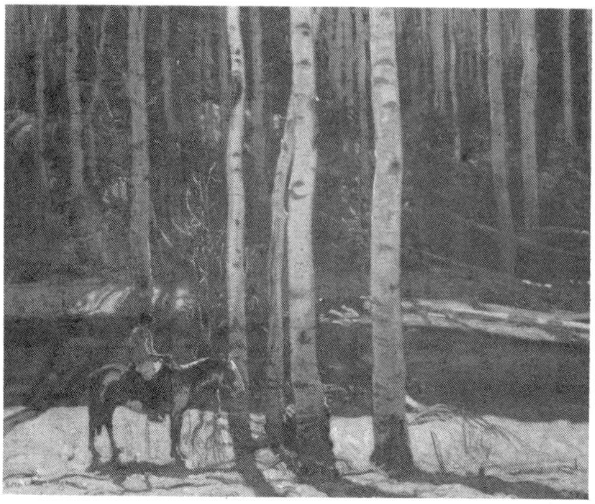

ERNEST MARTIN HENNINGS – Canyon Stream – signed – oil on canvas – 30 x 30in.
(Christie's) **$49,500 £34,798**

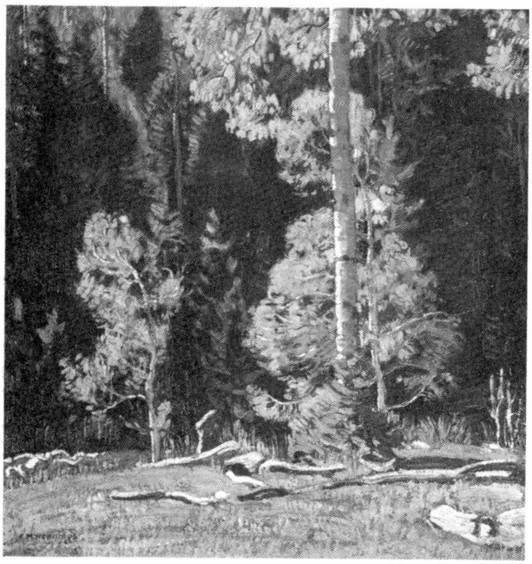

ERNEST MARTIN HENNINGS – Birches – signed – oil on board – 14 x 11¾in.
(Christie's) **$4,180 £2,938**

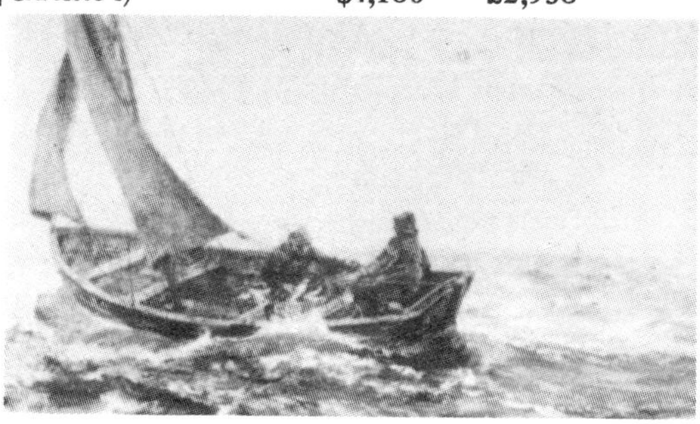

CHARLES NAPIER HENRY – 'At The Fast Of The Cliff, Falmouth' – signed and dated 1908 – oil on canvas – 18 x 27¼in.
(Phillips) **$2,142 £1,400**

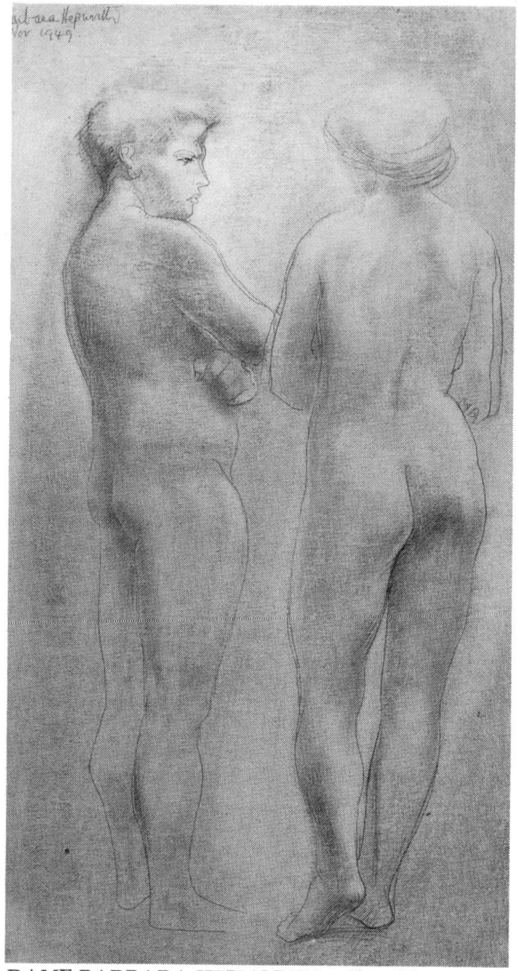

DAME BARBARA HEPWORTH – Two Figures With Folded Arms – signed and dated 1949 – thinned oil and pencil on board – 24 x 13½in.
(Christie's) **$31,086 £19,800**

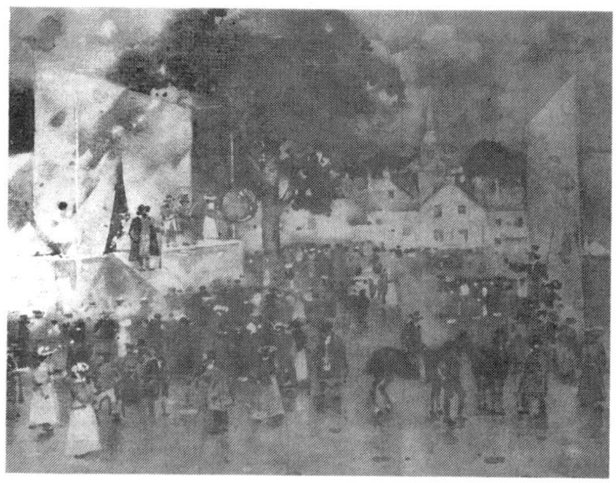

JAMES WATTERSTON HERALD – The Travelling Theatre – signed and dated 1907 – watercolour heightened with bodycolour – 15¾ x 19¾in.
(Christie's) **$6,480 £4,500**

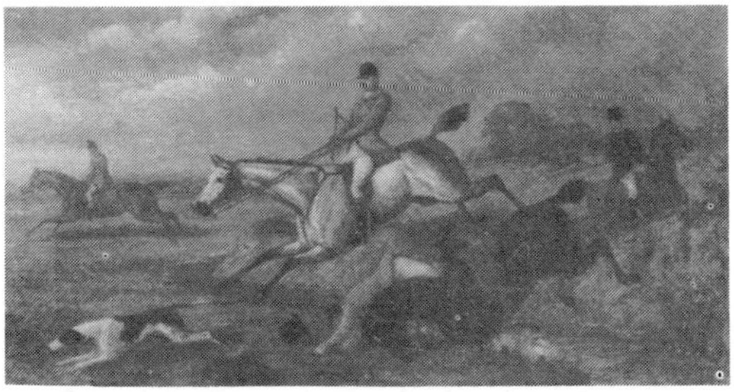

EDWARD BENJAMIN HERBERTE – Over The Ditch; and Over The Fence – signed and dated 1874 – 9¾ x 17¾in.
(Christie's) **$3,702** **£2,420 Pair**

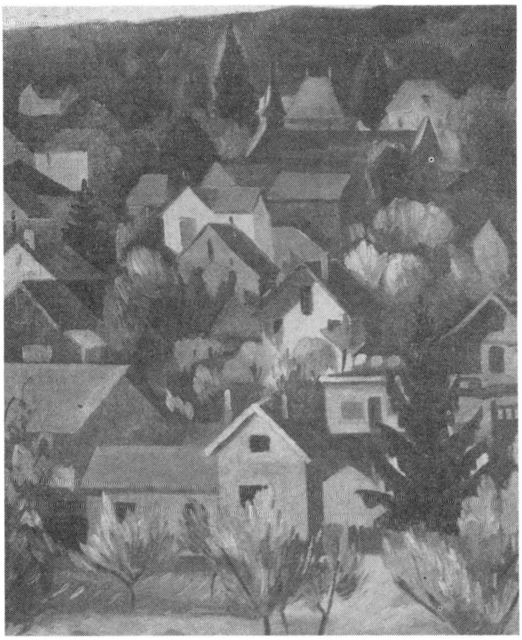

AUGUSTE HERBIN – Le Village cubiste – signed – oil on canvas.
(Christie's) **$20,207** **£12,100**

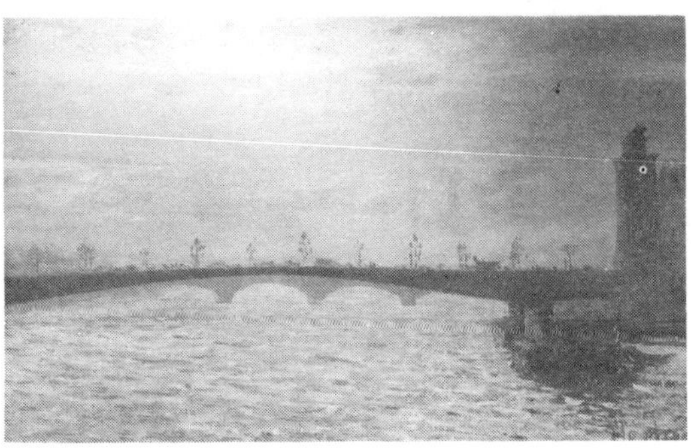

AUGUSTE HERBIN – Paris, Pont Alexandre III, Soleil couchant – signed – oil on canvas – 15 x 24in.
(Christie's) **$12,320** **£7,700**

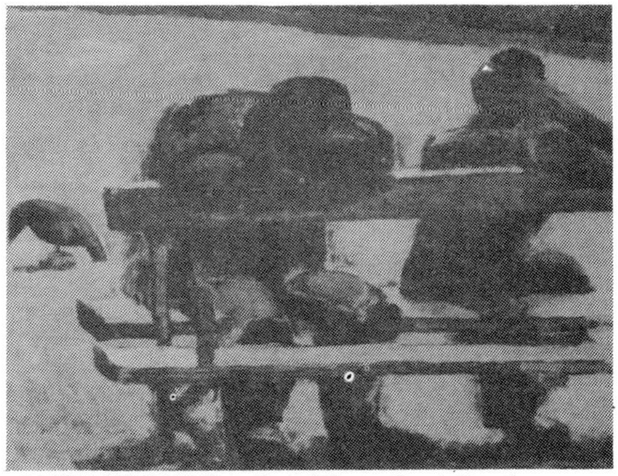

JOSEF HERMAN – Two Miners On A Bench – on canvas board – 16½ x 20½in.
(Lawrence Fine Art) **$1,369** **£825**

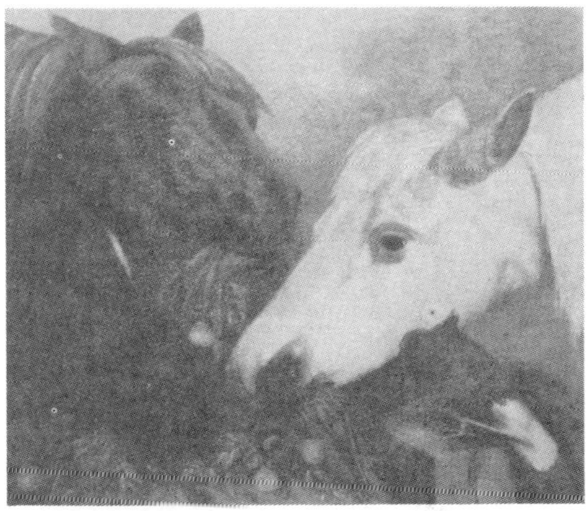

JOHN FREDERICK HERRING, After – Farm Yard Friends – oil on canvas – 22½ x 26½in.
(Christie's) **$760** **£528**

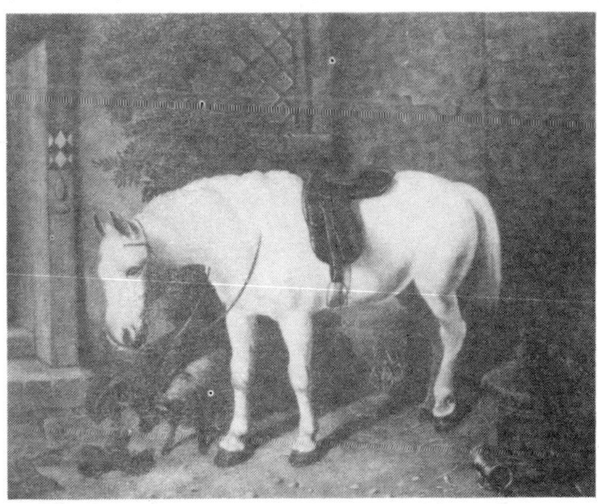

JOHN FREDERICK HERRING, After – A Grey Horse, Saddled Up, Waiting For His Master With The Other Farm Animals – oil on canvas – 24 x 30in.
(Christie's) **$1,477** **£935**

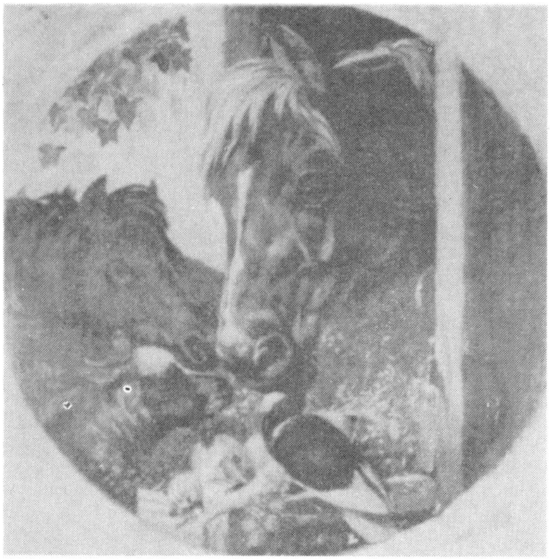

JOHN FREDERICK HERRING, Follower of – Horses Feeding – oil on canvas – 14in. square.
(Christie's) **$537** **£330**

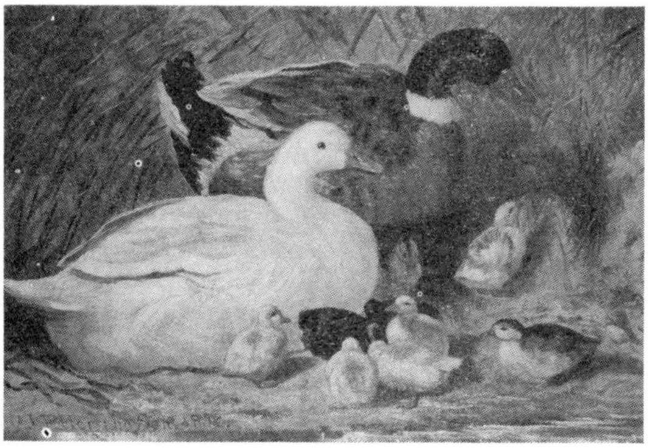

JOHN FREDERICK HERRING, Snr., and assistants – Ducks And Ducklings By A Riverside – signed and dated 1852 – on board – 10 x 11¾in.
(Christie's) **$4,374** **£2,916**

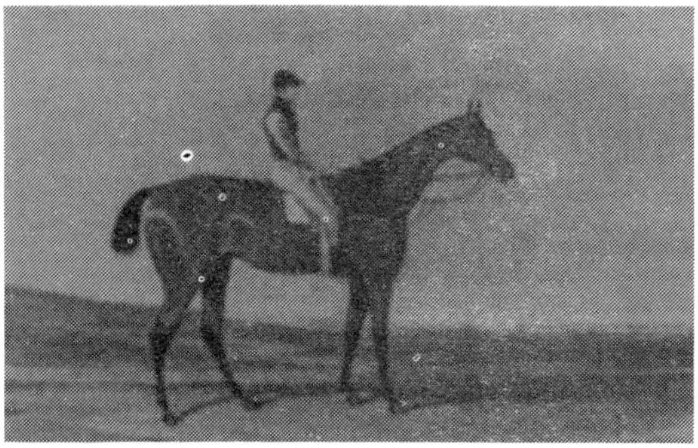

JOHN FREDERICK HERRING, Snr., Follower of – A Bay Racehorse With Jockey Up – oil on canvas – 24 x 20in.
(Phillips) **$1,494** **£900**

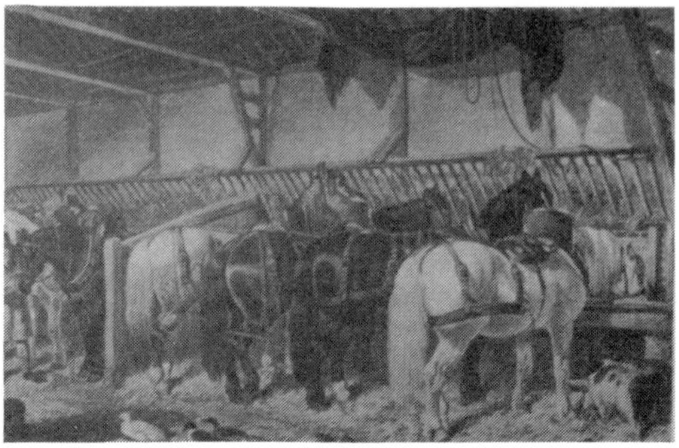

JOHN FREDERICK HERRING, Snr., After – Fores's Stable Scenes – coloured aquatints – 17 x 26in.
(Christie's) **$829** **£580 Four**

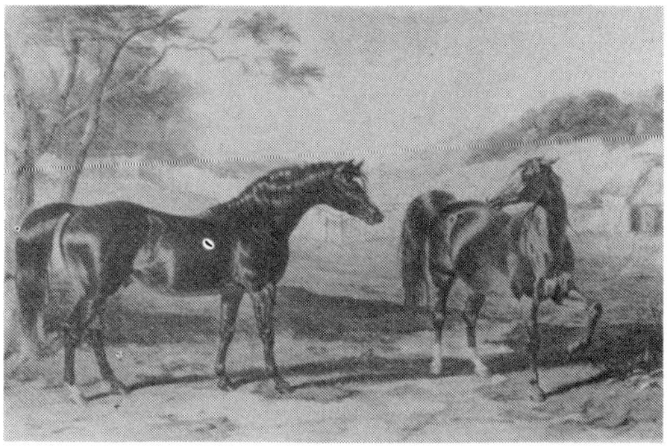

JOHN FREDERICK HERRING, Snr., After – The British Stud, Touchstone And Emma – by J. Harris – coloured aquatint part printed in colours – 22 x 30in.
(Christie's) **$514** **£360**

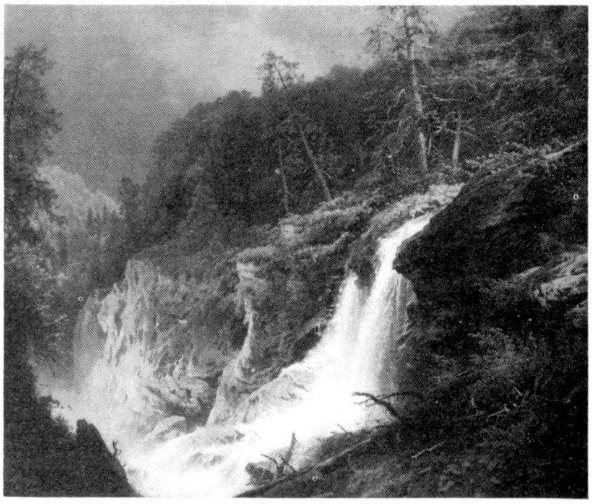

HERMAN HERZOG – Western Waterfall – signed – oil on canvas – 33¼ x 40¼in.
(Christie's) **$44,000** **£30,932**

ARTHUR HEYER – Cats In An Interior – signed – 19¾ x 27¾in.
(Christie's) **$1,254** **£825**

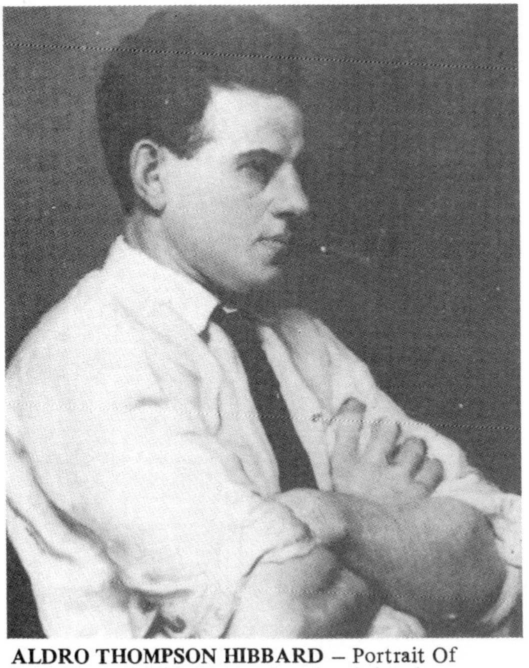

ALDRO THOMPSON HIBBARD – Portrait Of John Howard With Pipe – signed and dated 1910 – oil on canvas – 24 x 20in.
(Robt. W. Skinner Inc.) **$800** **£555**

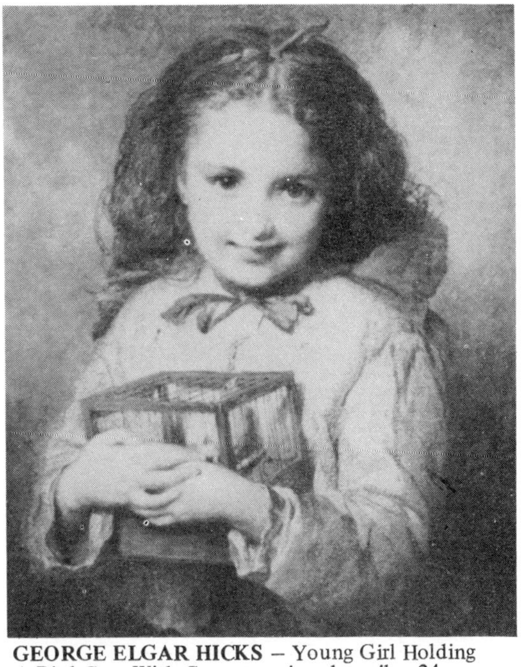

GEORGE ELGAR HICKS – Young Girl Holding A Bird Cage With Canary – signed – oil – 24 x 20in.
(Capes, Dunn & Co.) **$13,040** **£8,000**

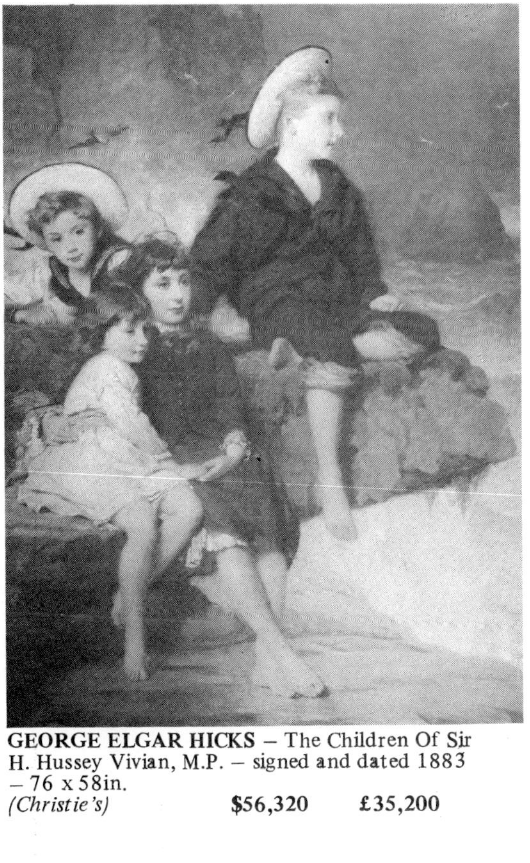

GEORGE ELGAR HICKS – The Children Of Sir H. Hussey Vivian, M.P. – signed and dated 1883 – 76 x 58in.
(Christie's) **$56,320** **£35,200**

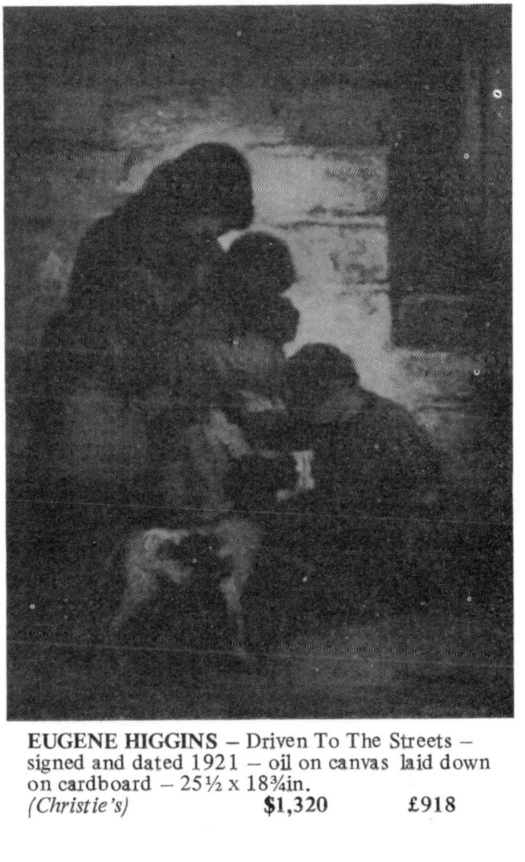

EUGENE HIGGINS – Driven To The Streets – signed and dated 1921 – oil on canvas laid down on cardboard – 25½ x 18¾in.
(Christie's) **$1,320** **£918**

HILDER

ROWLAND HILDER – 'Shoreham Valley' – signed – watercolour – 9.75 x 13.5in.
(Lots Road Chelsea Auction Galleries) **$960** **£600**

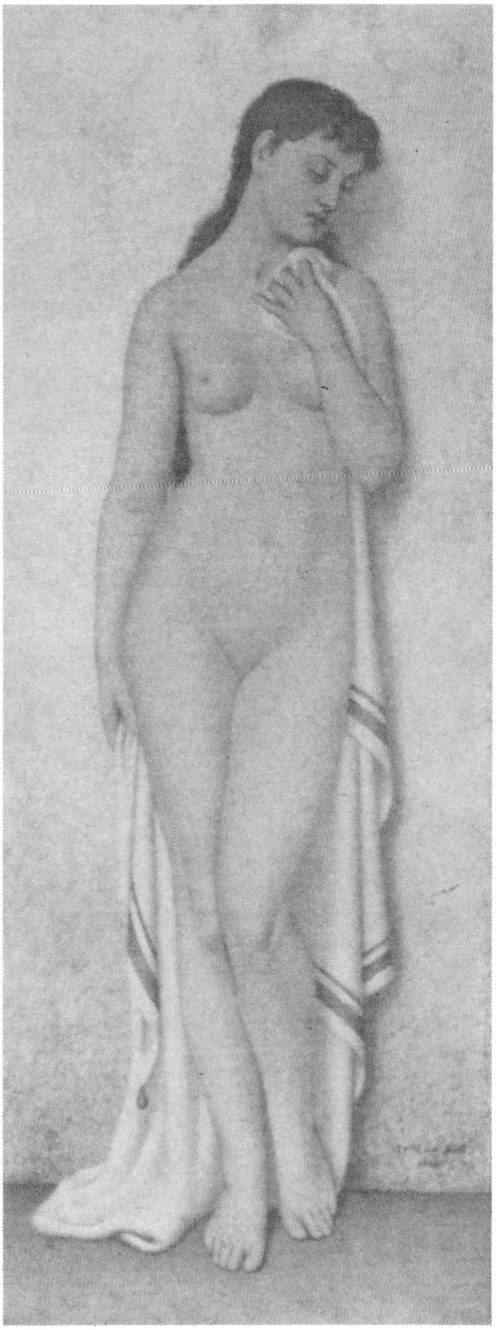

ARTHUR HILL – A Nude, Full Length – signed and dated 1908 – 36 x 13in.
(Christie's) **$1,163** **£825**

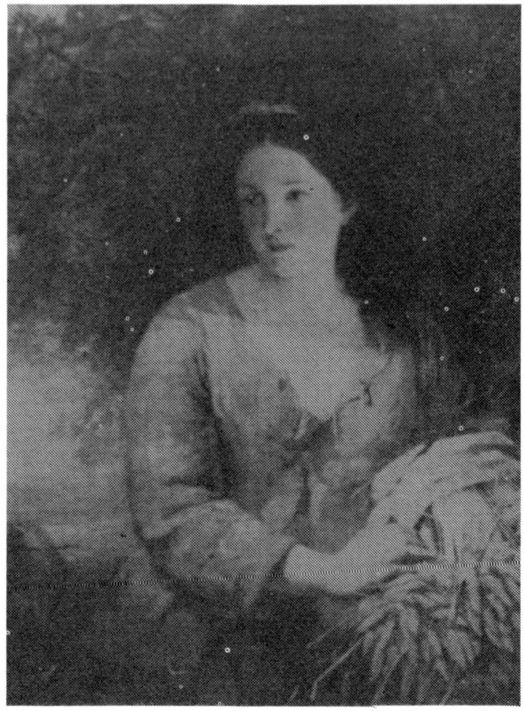

JAMES JOHN HILL – Portrait Of A Young Country Lass Bearing A Sheaf Of Wheat – signed – on board – 36 x 28in.
(Phillips) **$3,059** **£1,900**

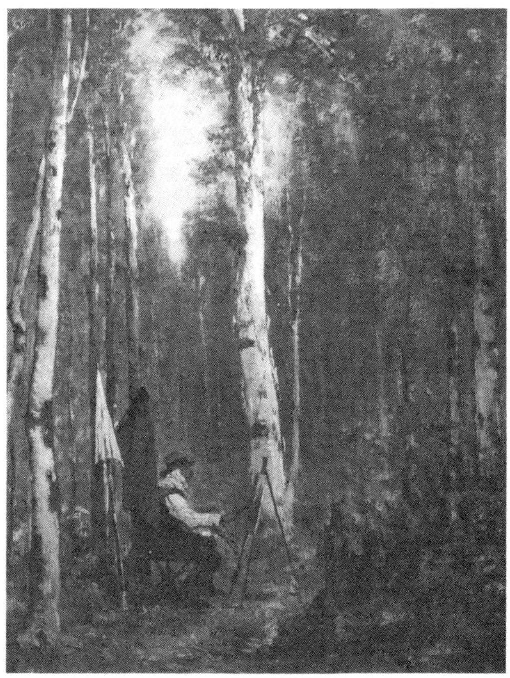

THOMAS HILL – Artist At His Easel In The Woods – signed – oil on panel – 21 x 13¾in.
(Christie's) **$16,500** **£11,479**

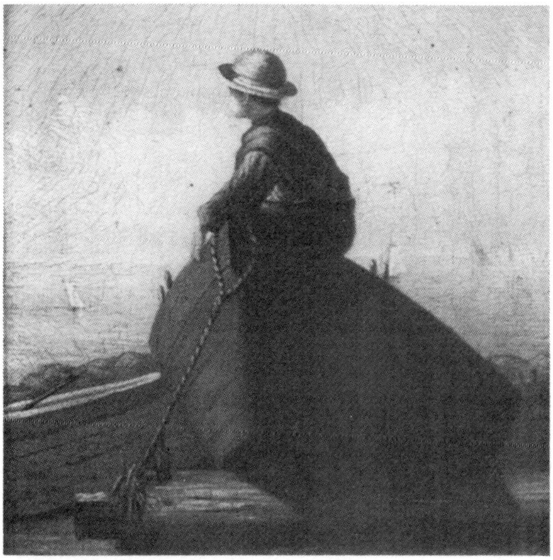

THOMAS HILL – Waiting For Dad – signed – oil on canvas – 9¼ x 7¼in.
(Christie's) **$7,700** **£5,413**

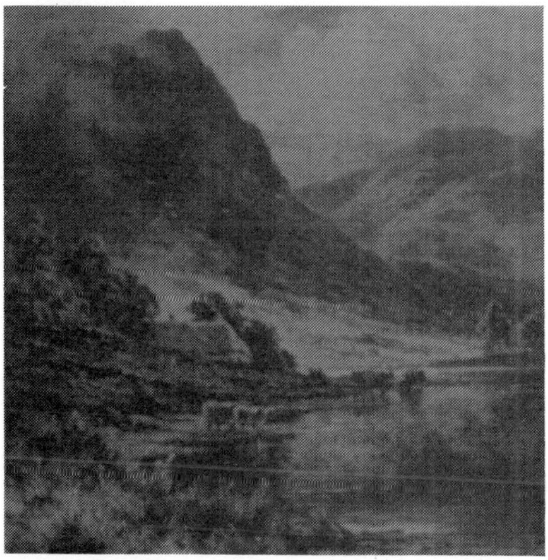

H. D. HILLIER – Loch Maree, Ross-shire – signed, also signed and inscribed on reverse – on canvas – 16 x 14in.
(Phillips) **$1,288** **£800**

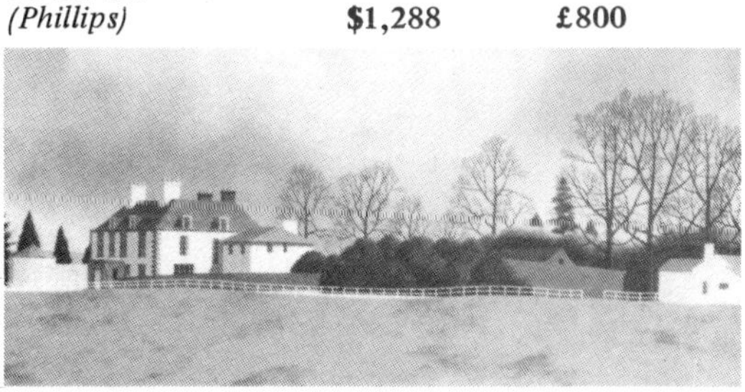

TRISTRAM HILLIER – Red Lynch House – signed and dated '65 – oil on canvas – 15¾ x 25¾in.
(Christie's) **$2,202** **£1,540**

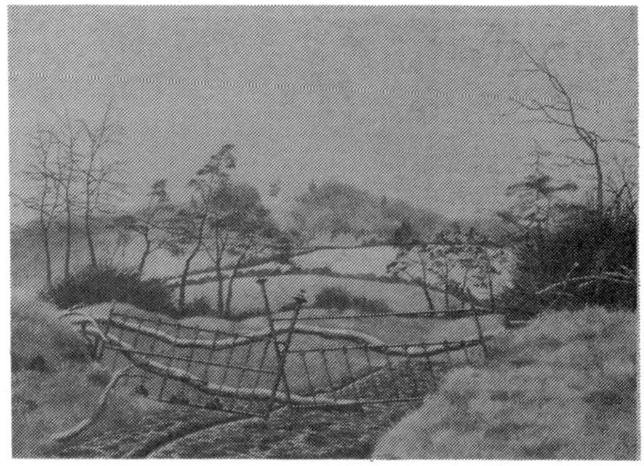

TRISTRAM HILLIER – Snowfall, 1944 – signed – oil on panel – 20.5 x 25.5cm.
(Phillips) **$2,880** **£1,800**

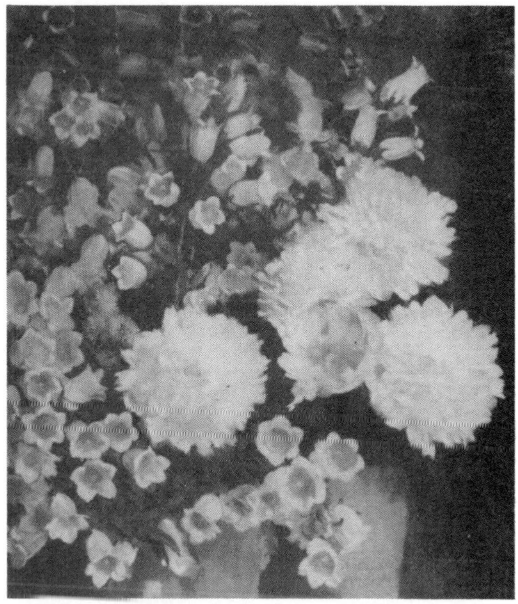

LAURA COOMBS HILLS – Peonies And Canterbury Bells – signed – pastel on board – 28 x 23¼in.
(Robt. W. Skinner Inc.) **$9,500** **£6,597**

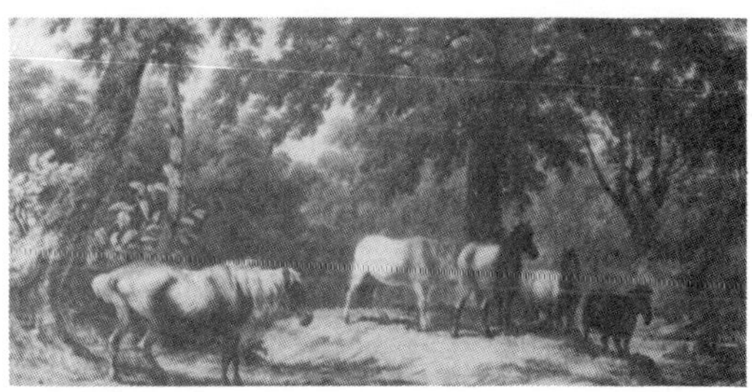

ROBERT HILLS – Horses In A Clearing – signed and dated 1812 – pencil and watercolour – 19¼ x 23½in.
(Christie's) **$4,373** **£3,080**

HINE

HENRY GEORGE HINE – Swanage Bay, Dorset – signed and dated 1864 – pencil and water-colour heightened with white – 8 x 21¼in.
(Christie's) **$2,739** **£1,650**

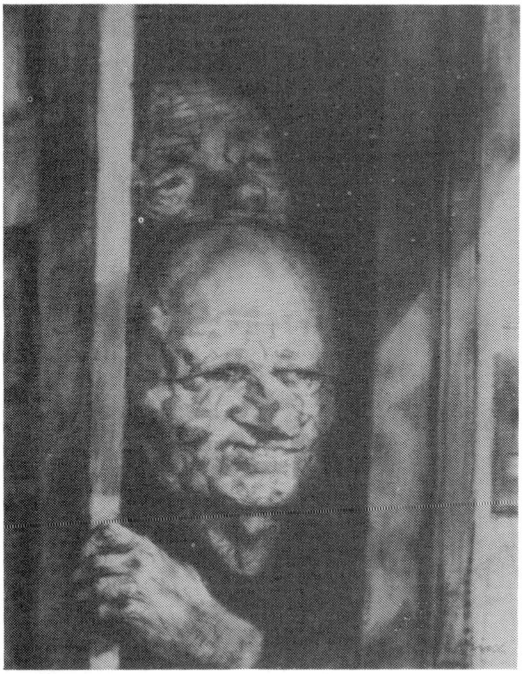

JOSEPH HIRSCH – The Smile – signed – charcoal on paper – 17 x 14½in.
(Christie's) **$440** **£274**

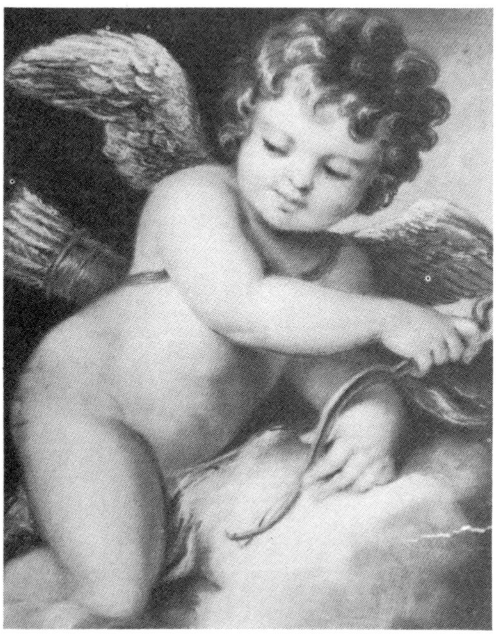

WILLIAM HOARE of Bath – Cupid – pastel on paper laid down on canvas – 24 x 18in.
(Christie's) **$744** **£496**

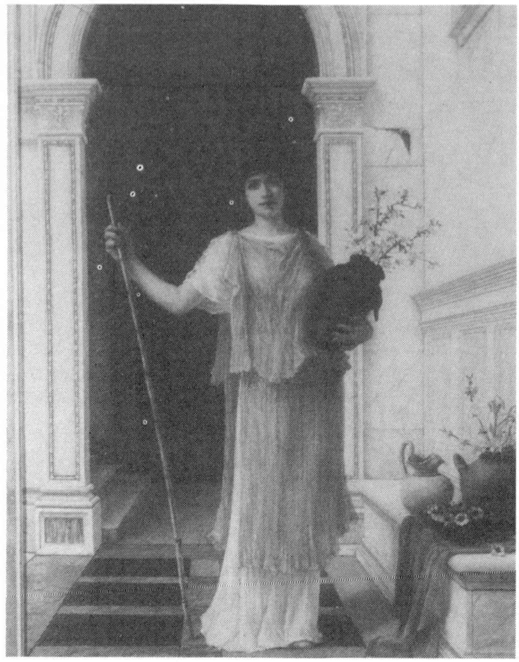

GEORG VON HOESSLIN – Votive Offerings – signed and inscribed – 30 x 19in.
(Christie's) **$3,344** **£2,200**

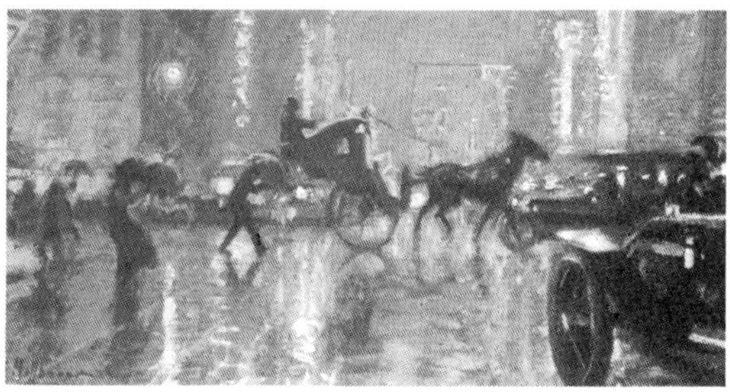

CHARLES HOFFBAUER – A Rainy Day In New York City – signed – oil on canvas – 12 x 16¼in.
(Christie's) **$8,250** **£5,799**

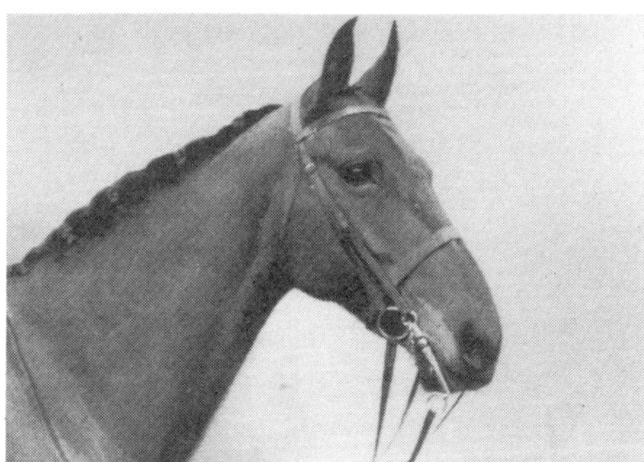

F. MABEL HOLLAMS – Charlotte, A Bay Hunter – signed and inscribed – on board – 13½ x 16½in.
(Christie's) **$1,093** **£715**

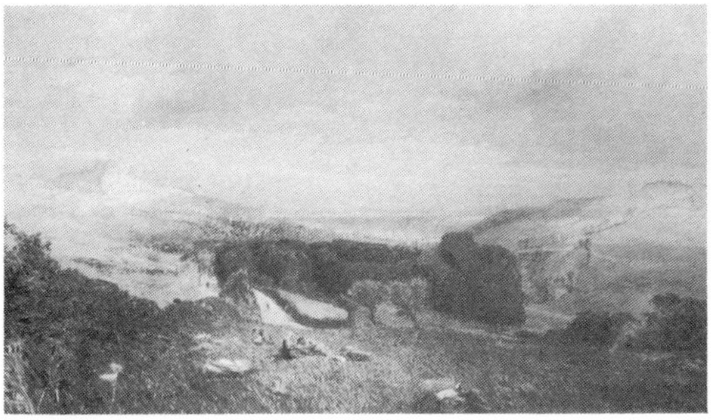

JAMES HOLLAND – Dover From Blacklands – signed and dated 1846 – pencil and watercolour – 14¾ x 21¼in.
(Christie's) **$6,429** **£3,850**

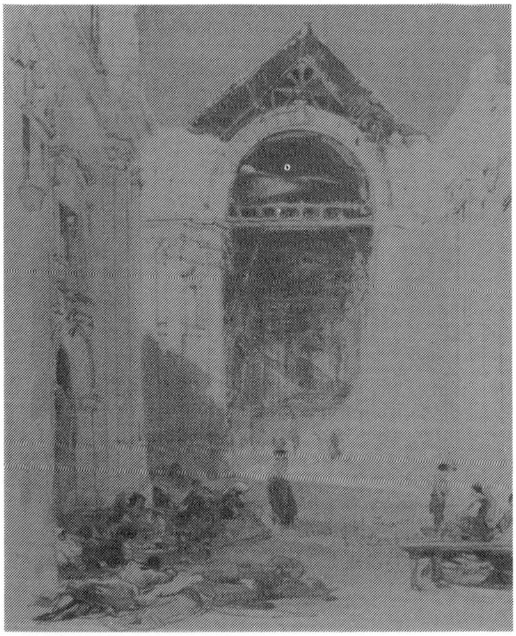

JAMES HOLLAND – Ruins Of St. Francisco, Lisboa – inscribed and dated '37 – bodycolour over pencil – 37 x 20cm.
(Phillips) **$1,630** **£1,000**

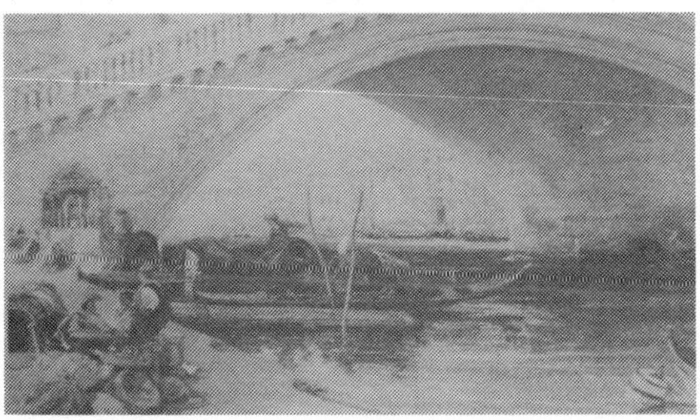

JAMES HOLLAND – The Rialto, Venice – signed with monogram and dated '63 – bodycolour over pencil – 33 x 54cm.
(Phillips) **$2,934** **£1,800**

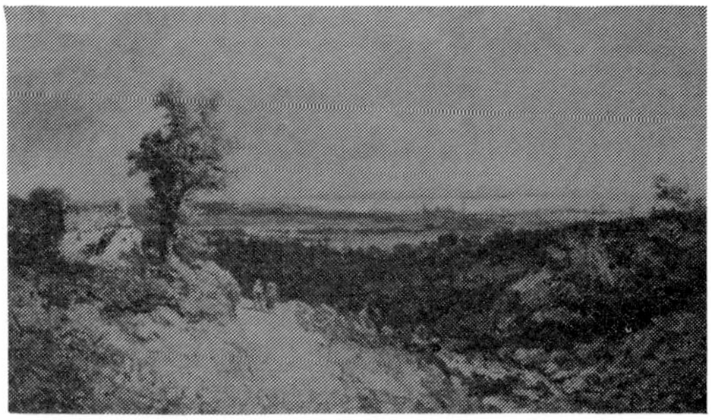

JAMES HOLLAND – An Extensive Landscape With A View Towards A Distant Town – signed – 18 x 24in.
(Lawrence Fine Art) **$1,186** **£715**

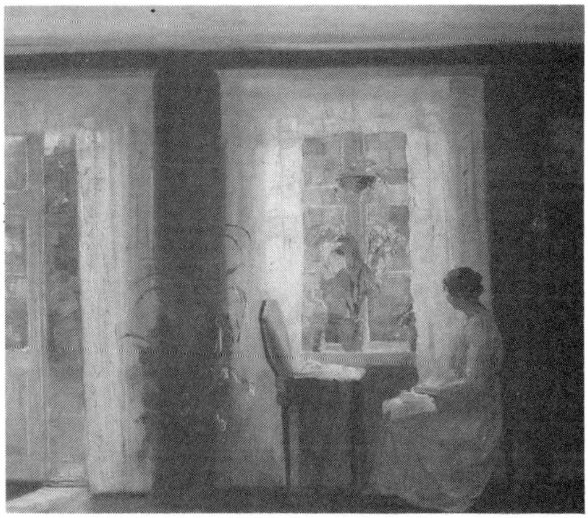

CARL HOLSOE – A Woman At A Sunny Window – signed – 18½ x 19½in.
(Christie's) **$20,064** **£13,200**

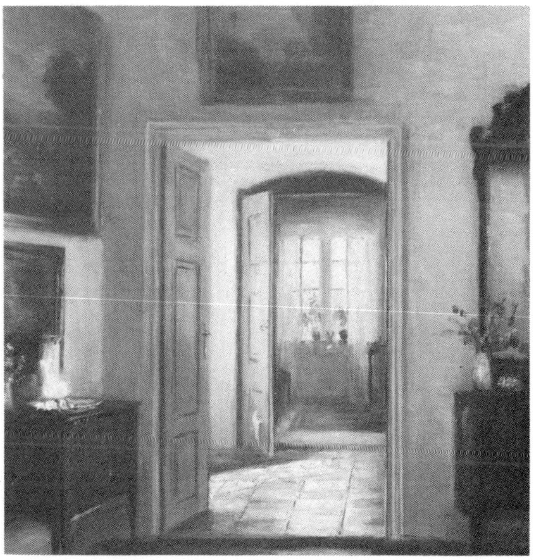

CARL VILHELM HOLSOE – An Interior – signed – 20½ x 19in.
(Christie's) **$19,008** **£13,200**

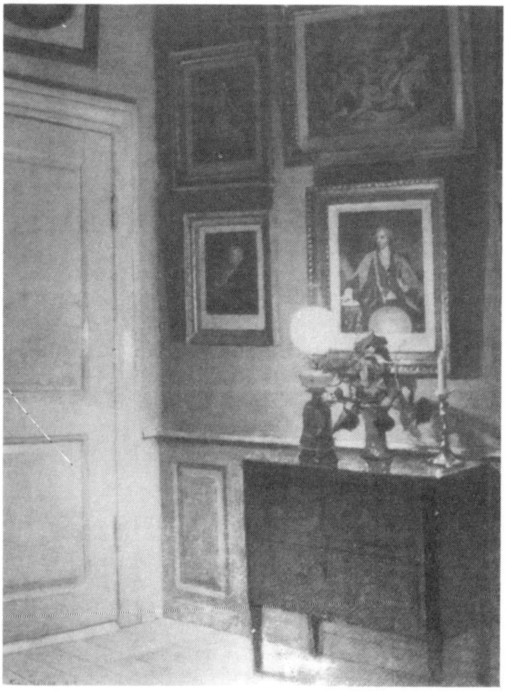

NIELS HOLSOE – An Interior – signed and dated 1914 – 23½ x 18in.
(Christie's) **$2,173** **£1,430**

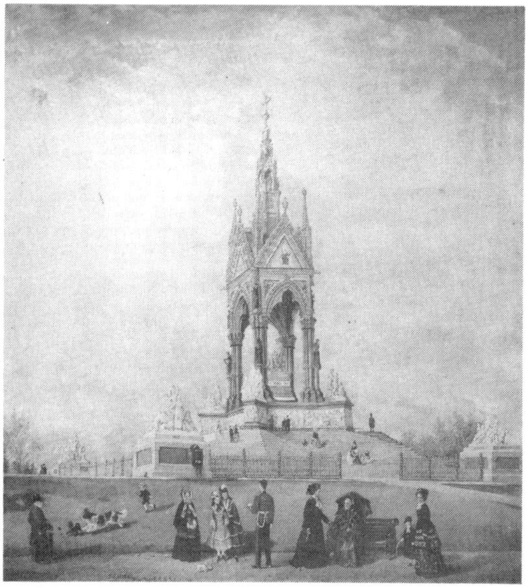

EDWIN FREDERICK HOLT – The Albert Memorial, London – signed, inscribed and dated 1877 – 32 x 30in.
(Christie's) **$18,513** **£12,100**

EDWIN FREDERICK HOLT – Horses Being Collected From Their Stables For The Hunt – signed and dated 1900 – oil on canvas – 16 x 20in.
(Christie's) **$2,112** **£1,320**

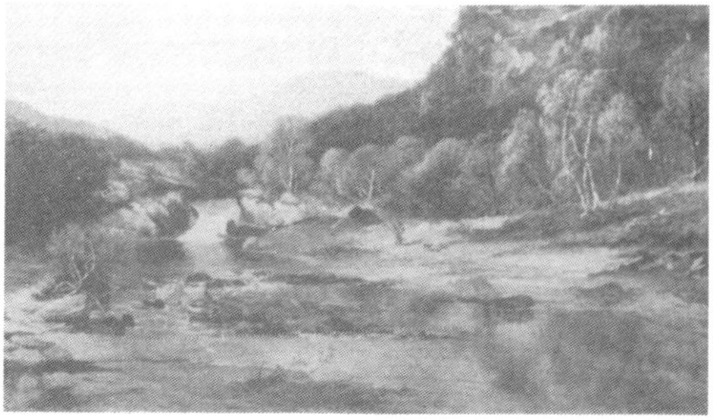

ARTHUR BRANDISH HOLTE – A Rocky River Landscape With A Figure And Dog On A Bank – signed – 24 x 35in.
(Christie's) **$1,500** **£1,000**

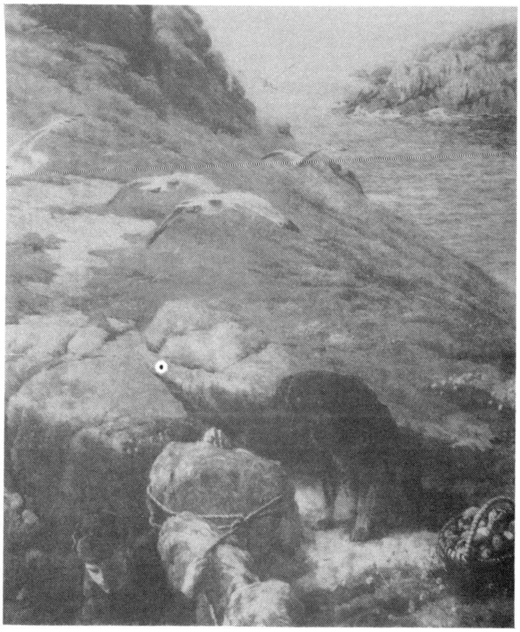

JAMES CLARKE HOOK – A Gull Catcher – signed with monogram and dated 1877 – 47½ x 37in.
(Christie's) **$4,039** **£2,640**

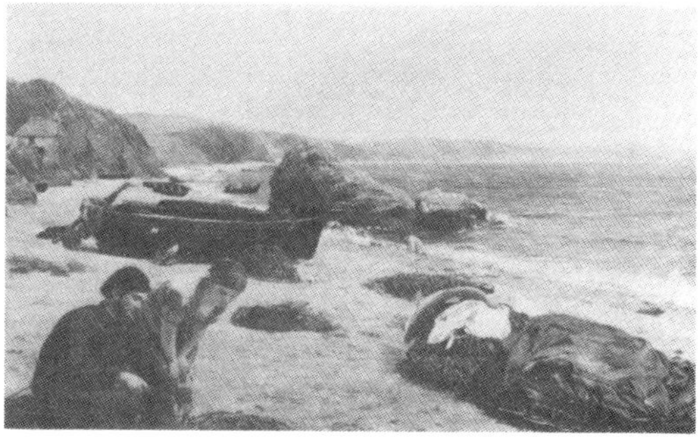

JAMES CLARKE HOOK – A Little Blue Bay – signed with monogram and dated 1876 – oil on canvas – 19½ x 32in.
(Christie's) **$2,448** **£1,600**

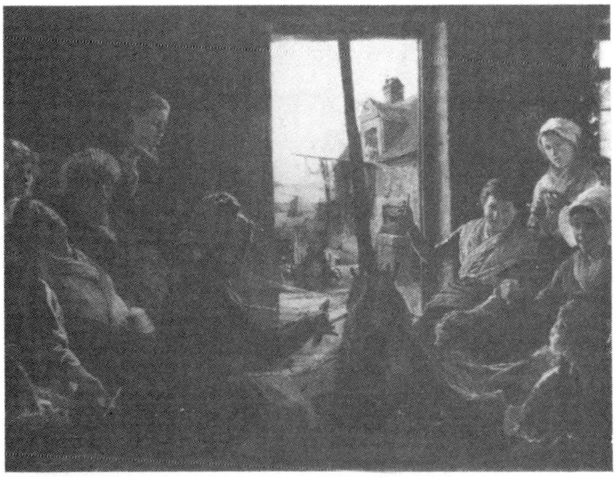

JAMES CLARKE HOOK – Mending The Fisherman's Nets – signed and dated 1876 – oil on canvas – 27½ x 35½in.
(Phillips) **$3,672** **£2,400**

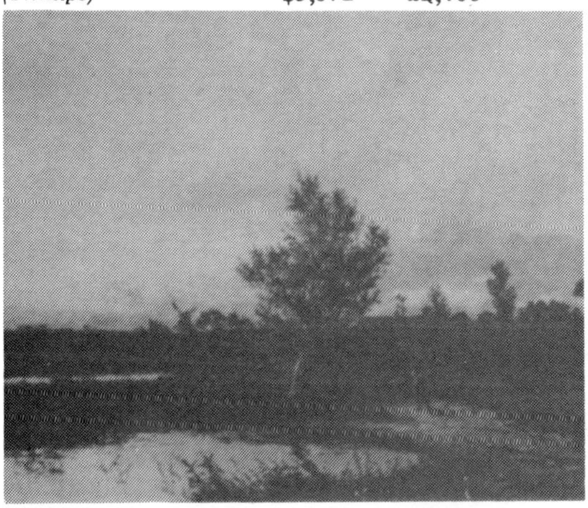

JOHN HORACE HOOPER – Windmill And Figure In Lincolnshire – signed – oil on canvas – 24 x 36in.
(Robt. W. Skinner Inc.) **$400** **£245**

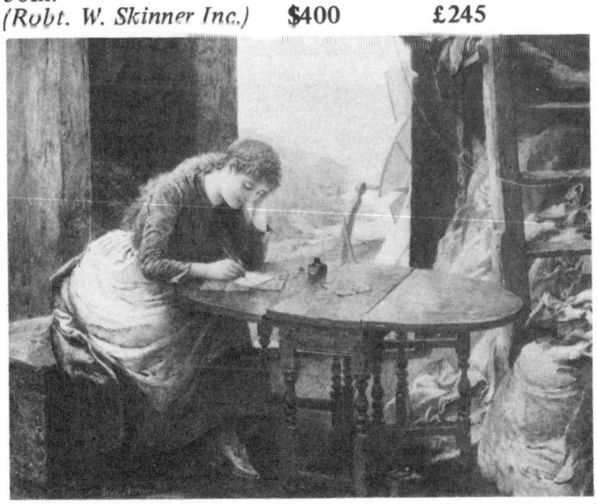

ARTHUR HOPKINS – The First Love Letter – signed and inscribed, and signed again on the reverse – watercolour – 16 x 20in.
(Christie's) **$2,326** **£1,650**

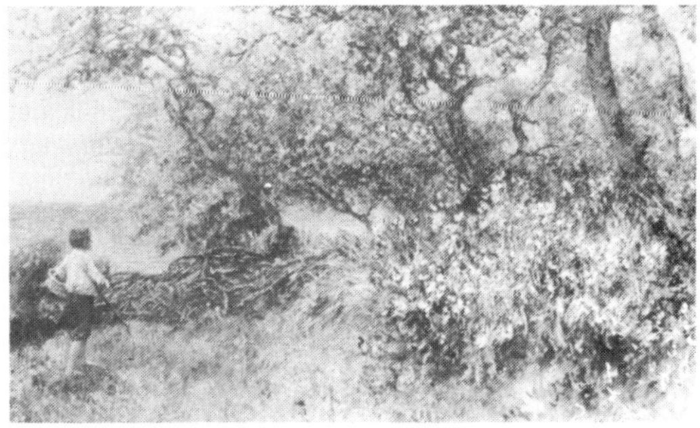

ARTHUR HOPKINS – An Orchard Garden – signed and indistinctly inscribed – watercolour heightened with bodycolour – 10½ x 14½in.
(Christie's) **$2,791** **£1,980**

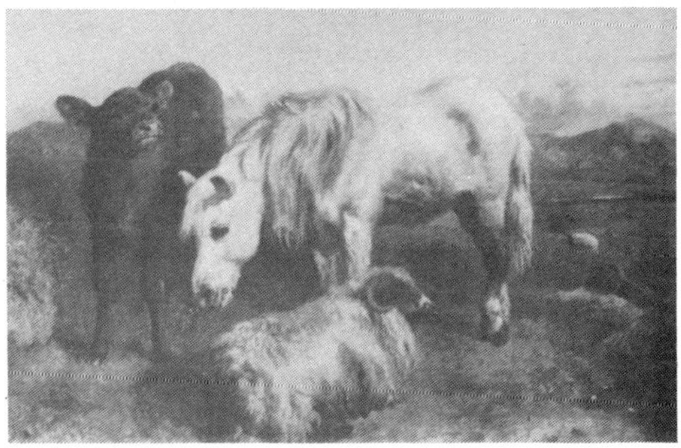

GEORGE W. HORLOR – A Calf, Pony And A Ram In A Landscape – signed and dated 1870 – 16 x 24in.
(Christie's) **$1,861** **£1,320**

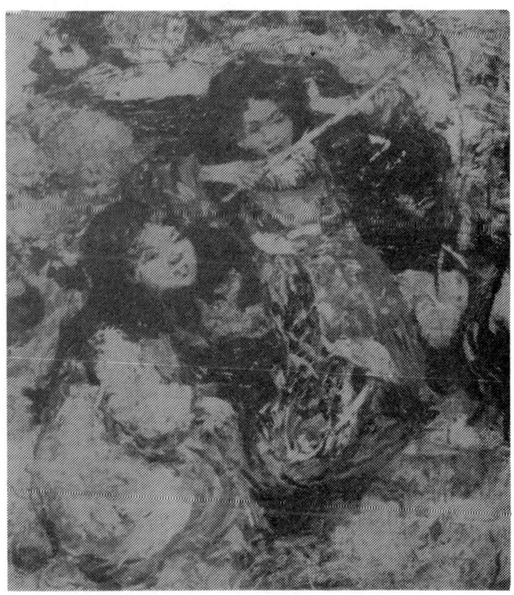

EDWARD ATKINSON HORNEL – Two Japanese Girls – signed and dated '96 – oil on panel – 38 x 32cm.
(Phillips) **$8,800** **£5,500**

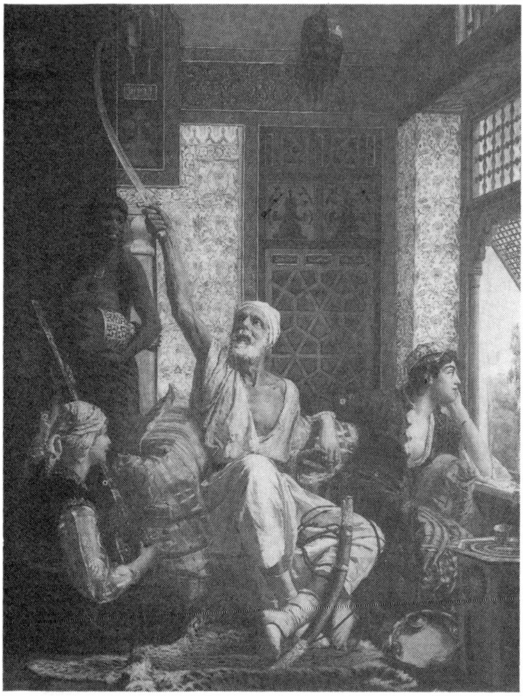

WALTER CHARLES HORSLEY – Fighting His Battles O'er Again – signed and dated 1883 – 48¾ x 38½in.
(Christie's) **$28,160** **£17,600**

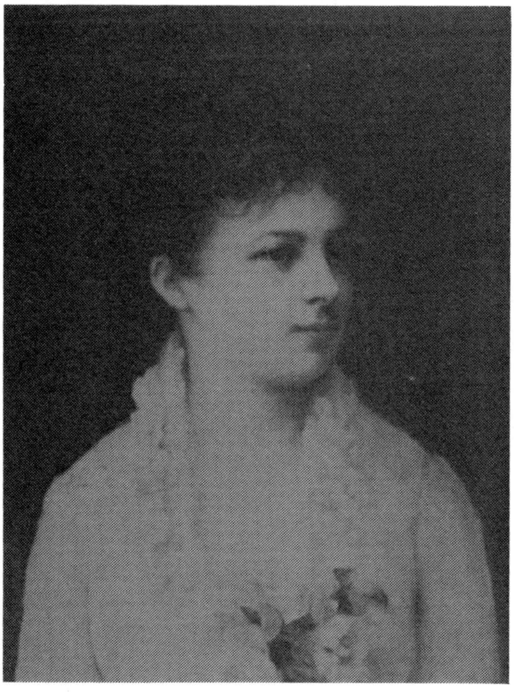

JEAN HOUSSAYE – Portrait De Jeune Fille – signed – oil on panel – 24 x 18.5cm.
(Phillips) **$852** **£550**

MARION HOWARD – 'Trees Of Belgium' – oil on canvas – 20 x 24in.
(Robt. W. Skinner Inc.) **$2,700** **£1,656**

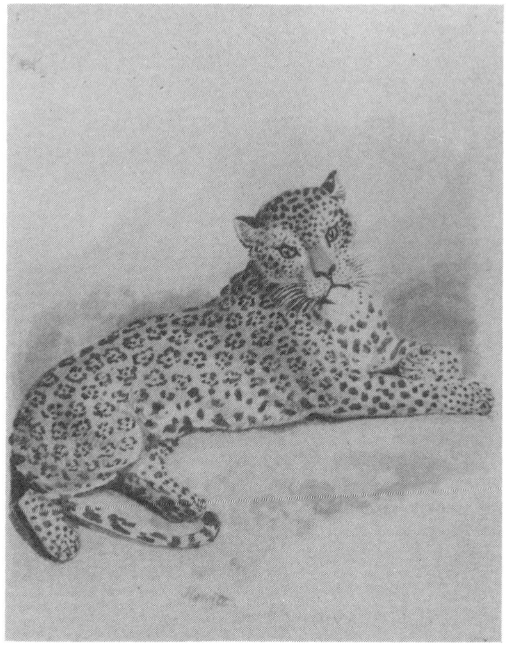

SAMUEL HOWITT – A Leopard Reclining – signed and inscribed – pencil and watercolour – 9½ x 7¼in.
(Christie's) **$2,479** **£1,485**

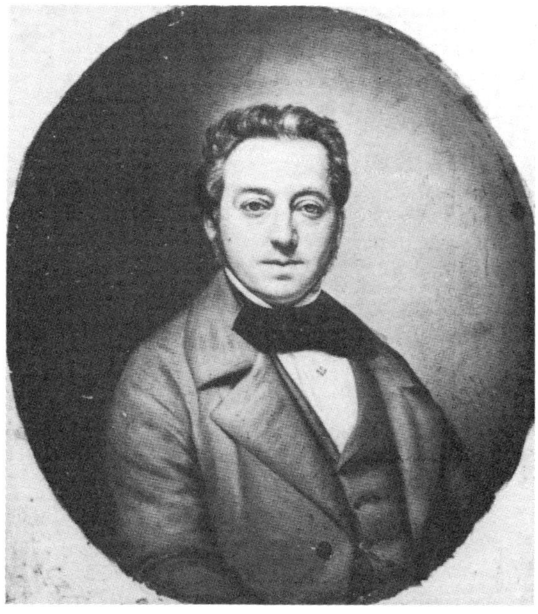

PHILIPP HOYOLL – Portrait Of A Gentleman, Half Length, Seated – signed and dated 6/55, inscribed – on canvas – 41.5 x 35cm.
(Phillips) **$302** **£200**

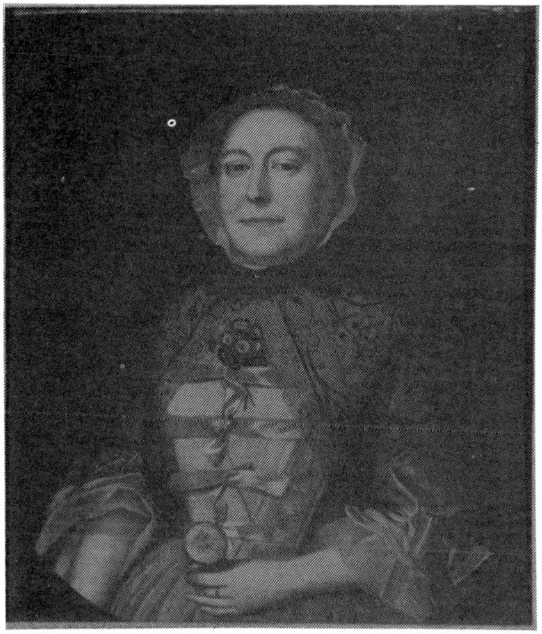

THOMAS HUDSON, Circle of – Portrait Of A Lady Seated Half Length, Wearing A Grey Dress With Bows And A Black Lace Shawl, Holding A Porcelain Encased Watch – 30 x 25½in.
(Christie's) **$1,458** **£972**

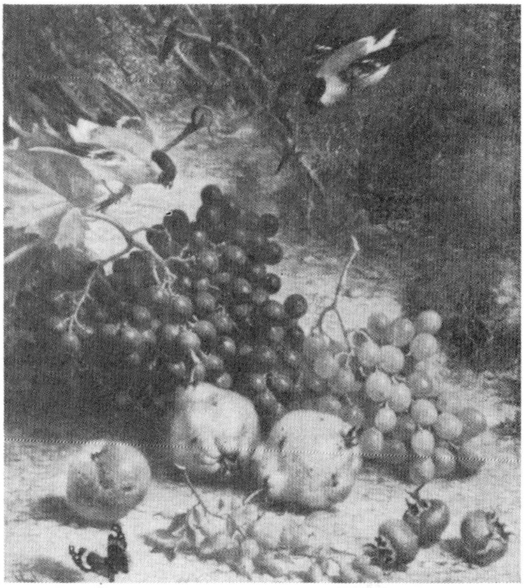

WILLIAM HUGHES – The Bullfinches Banquet – signed and dated '95, and inscribed on the reverse – 23½ x 19½in.
(Christie's) **$4,963** **£3,520**

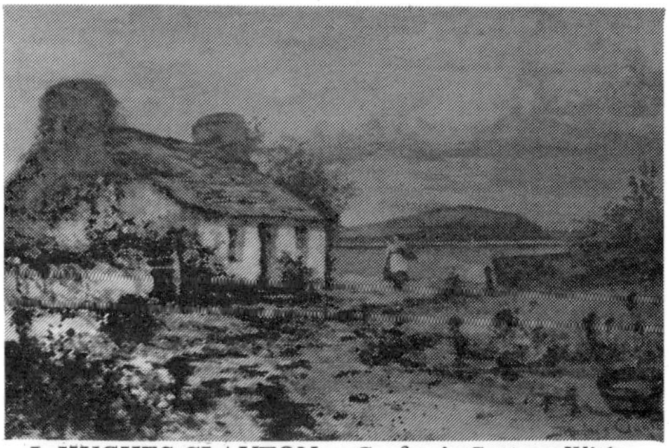

J. HUGHES-CLAYTON – Crofter's Cottage With Figures – signed – watercolour – 7½ x 12in.
(Hobbs & Chambers) **$308** **£200**

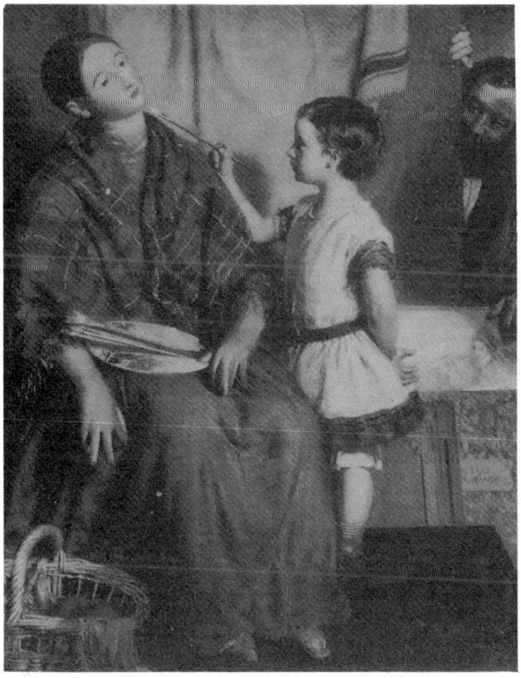

THOMAS JOHN HUGHES – A First Attempt – signed and dated 1860 – 30 x 24in.
(Christie's) **$3,197** **£2,090**

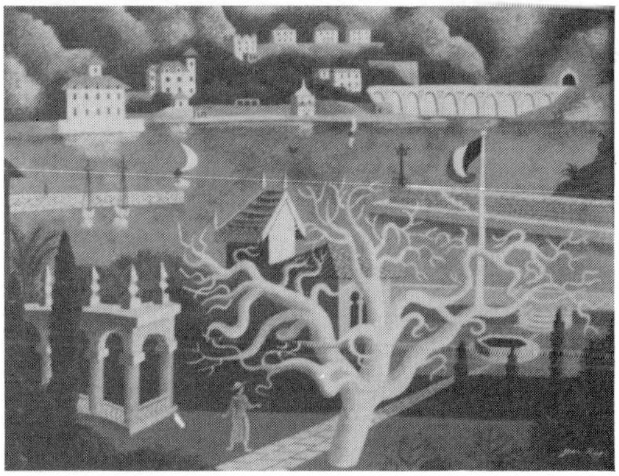

JEAN HUGO – La Baie de Beaulieu – signed – gouache on board – 10 x 12½in.
(Christie's) **$2,640** **£1,650**

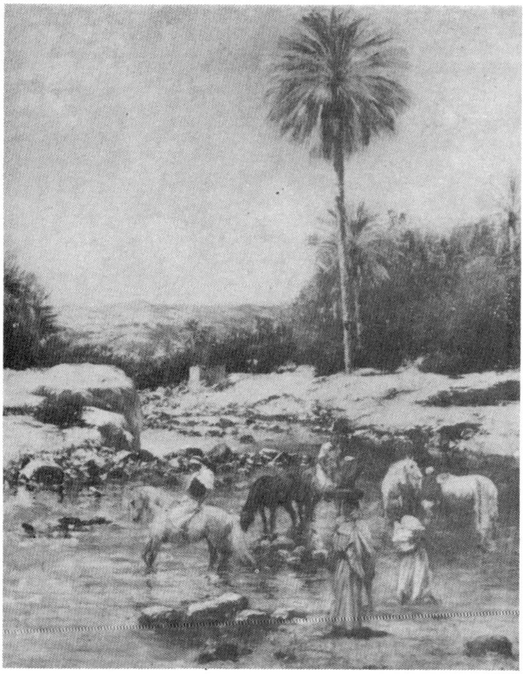

VICTOR PIERRE HUGUET – Arab Horseman Crossing A River – signed – on canvas – 61.5 x 50.5cm.
(Phillips) **$5,285** **£3,500**

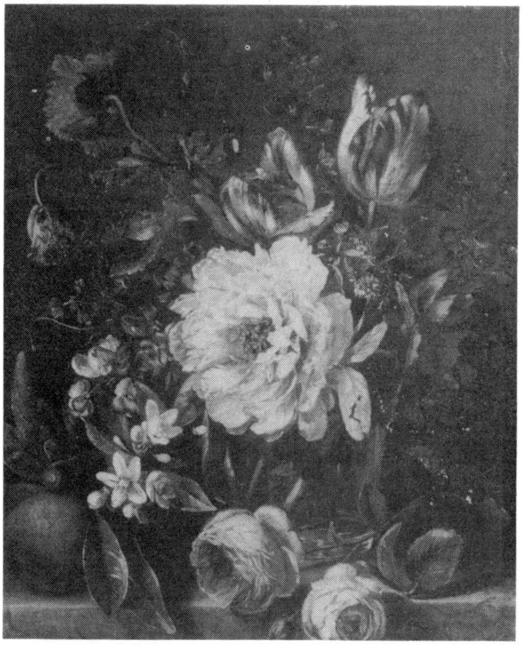

GEERTRUIDA MARGARETHA JACOBA HUIDEKOPER – Peonies, Roses, Tulips And Other Flowers In A Glass Vase With An Orange On A Ledge – signed with initials and dated 1848 – 18¼ x 15in.
(Christie's) **$7,524** **£4,950**

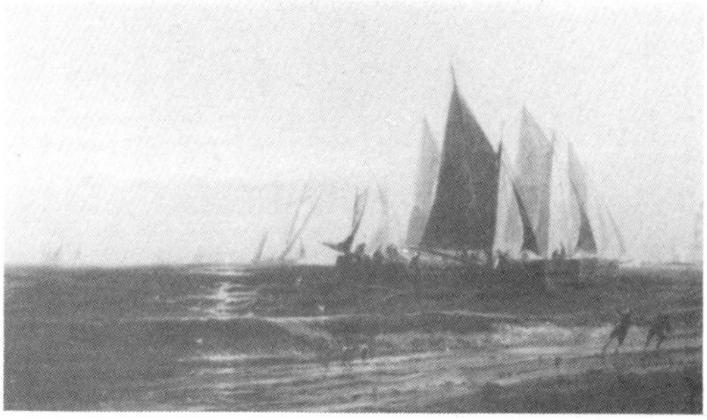

ABRAHAM HULK – Return Of The Herring Fleet, Coast Of Scotland – signed, inscribed on the reverse – oil on canvas – 23½ x 41½in.
(Christie's) **$2,217** **£1,540**

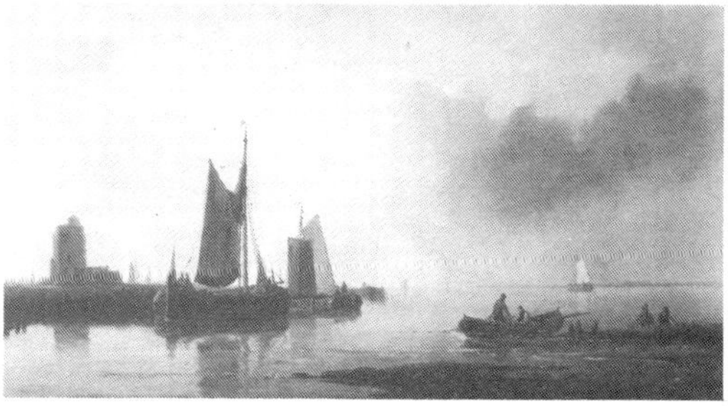

ABRAHAM HULK, Snr. – Fishing Boats In An Estuary – signed – 25½ x 33¾in.
(Christie's) **$7,920** **£5,500**

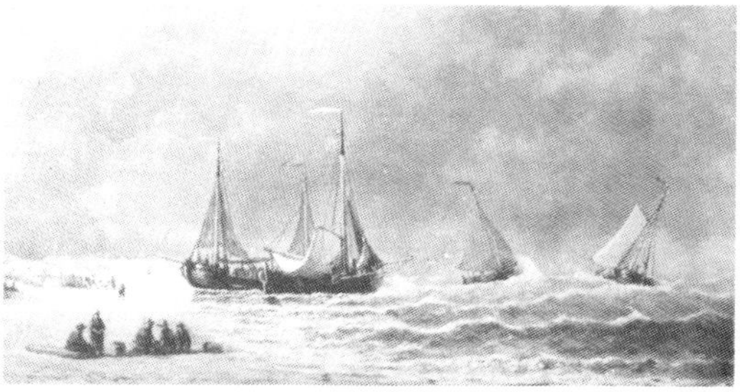

HENDRIK HULK – Shipping Off The Coast Of Normandy – signed – oil on canvas board – 17 x 26in.
(Christie's) **$1,584** **£1,100**

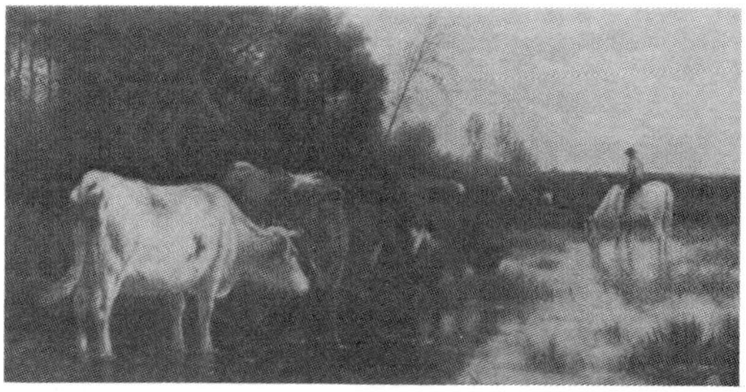

WILLIAM FREDERICK HULK – Abinger Marsh, Surrey; and Shelford Near Guildford – signed, and signed and inscribed on old labels on the reverse – 12 x 20in.
(Christie's) **$1,395** **£990 Pair**

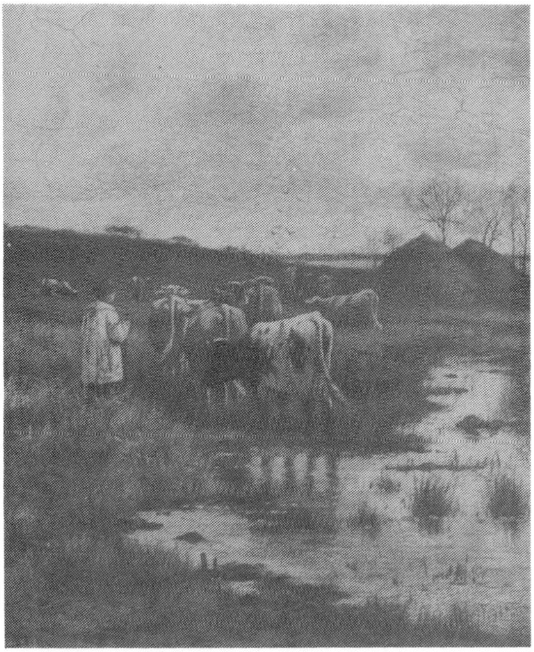

WILLIAM FREDERICK HULK – Near Abinger Hammer, Surrey – signed with initials and signed and inscribed on an old label attached to the stretcher – 13¾ x 12in.
(Christie's) **$810** **£540**

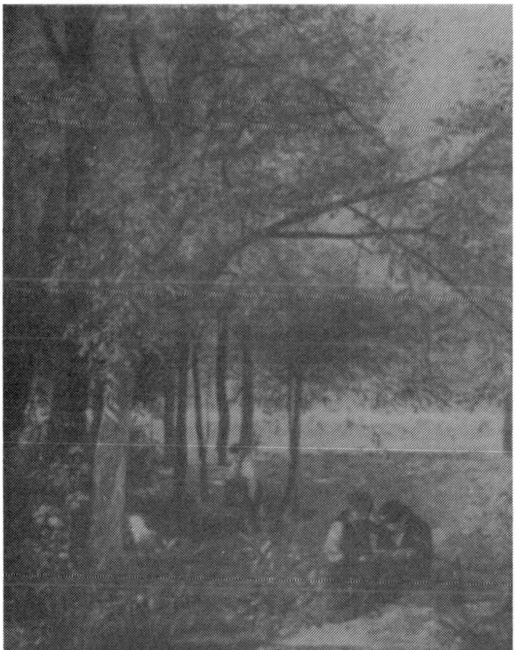

CHARLES HUNT – Landscape, Boys Fishing – signed and dated 1862 – 12 x 10in.
(Lawrence Fine Art) **$3,469** **£2,090**

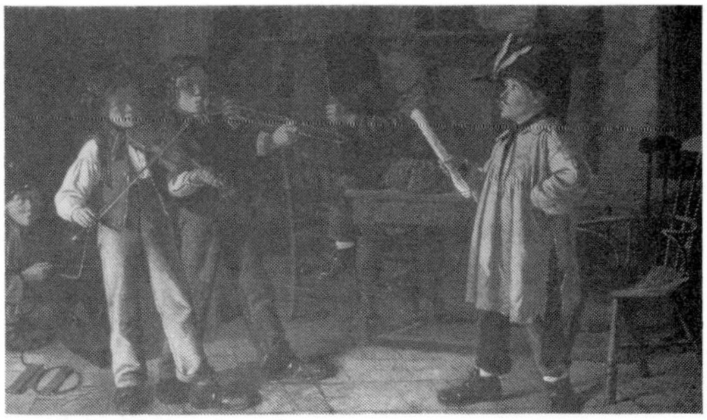

CHARLES HUNT – The Recital – signed and dated 1861 – 11 x 16in.
(Christie's) **$10,098** **£6,600**

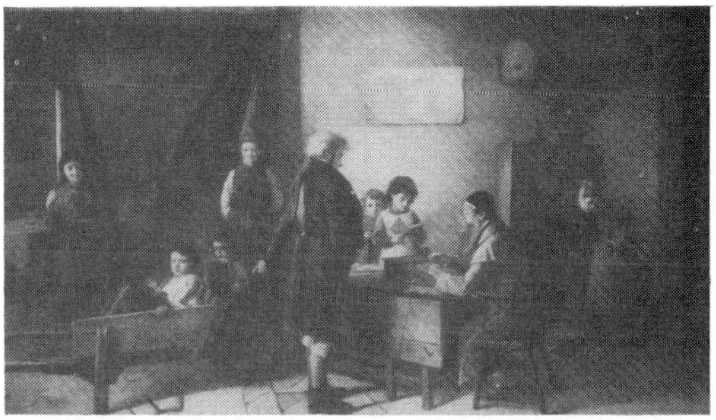

CHARLES HUNT – Catching The Truant – signed and dated 1882 – 40 x 60in.
(Christie's) **$7,573** **£4,950**

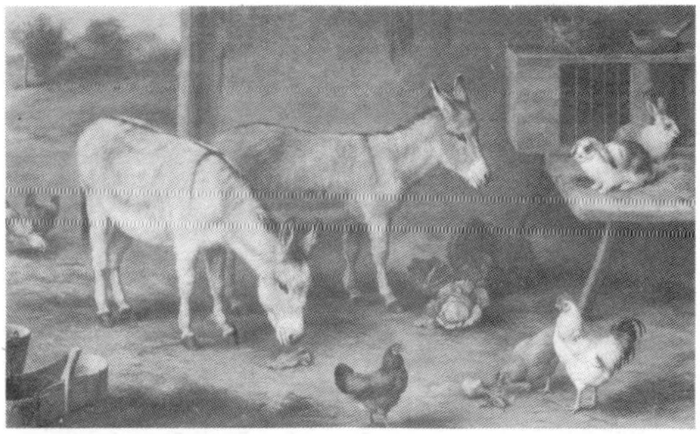

EDGAR HUNT – Donkeys, Chickens And Rabbits In A Barn – signed and dated 1922 – 21 x 29in.
(Christie's) **£24,300** **£16,200**

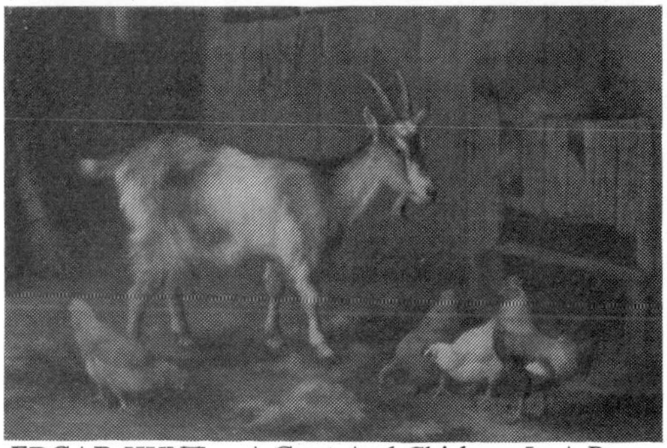

EDGAR HUNT – A Goat And Chickens In A Barn – signed and dated 1921 – 10½ x 14½in.
(Christie's) **$8,910** **£5,940**

HUNT

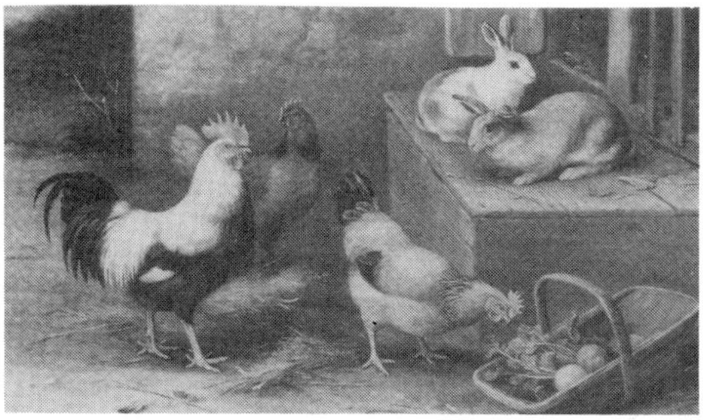

EDGAR HUNT – Chickens And Rabbits – signed and dated 1922 – 11 x 15¼in.
(Christie's) **$11,781** **£7,700**

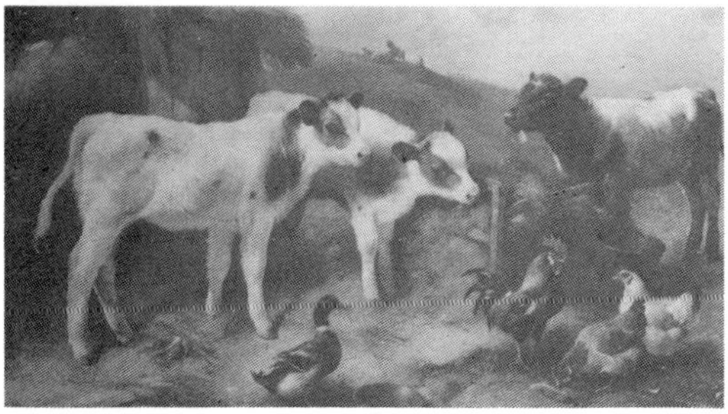

WALTER HUNT – Calves And Poultry By A Barn – signed and dated 1924, and signed and inscribed on the reverse – 19¼ x 30in.
(Christie's) **$17,061** **£12,100**

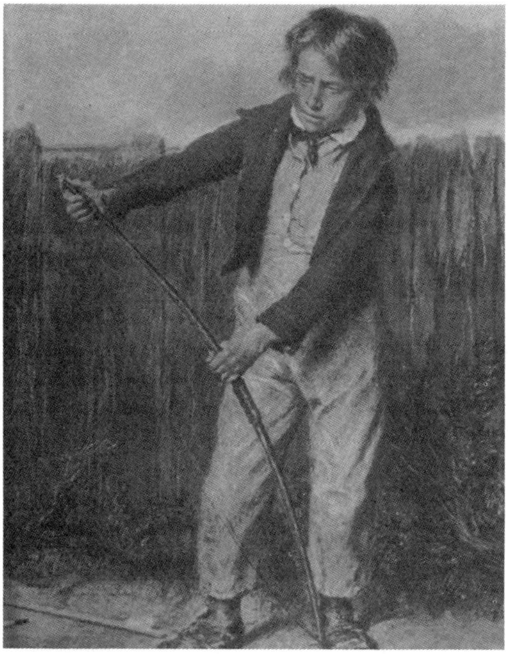

WILLIAM HENRY HUNT – A Young Archer – signed – pencil, watercolour and bodycolour – 15 x 10¾in.
(Christie's) **$1,085** **£770**

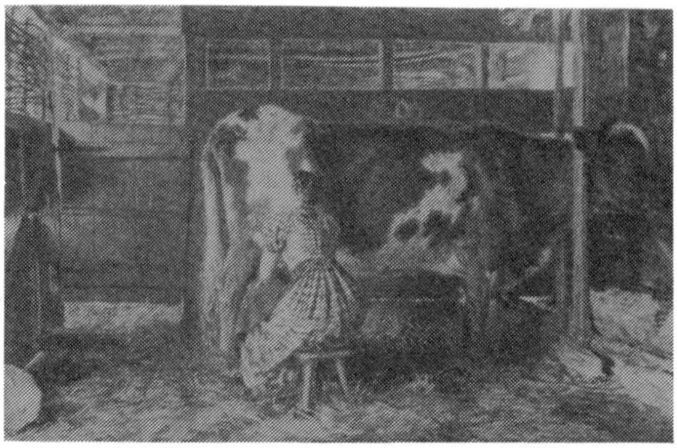

WILLIAM HENRY HUNT – A Young Girl Milking A Cow – watercolour heightened with gum arabic – 45 x 57cm.
(Phillips) **$4,564** **£2,800**

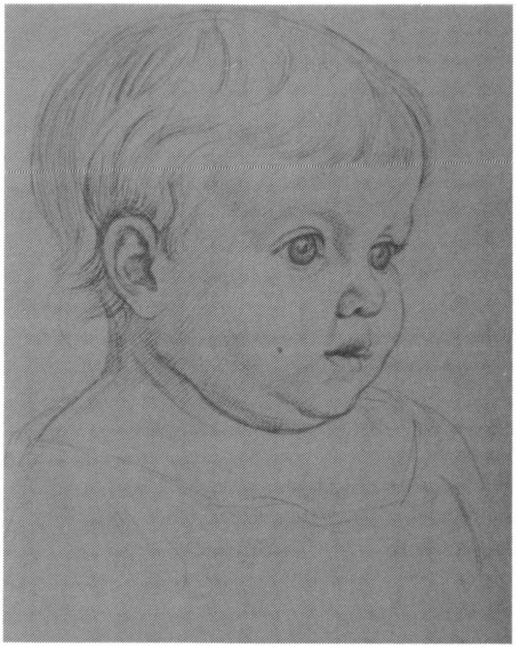

WILLIAM HOLMAN HUNT – Gladys Holman Hunt – signed with monogram, inscribed and dated 1877 – silverpoint – 24 x 18cm.
(Phillips) **$1,173** **£720**

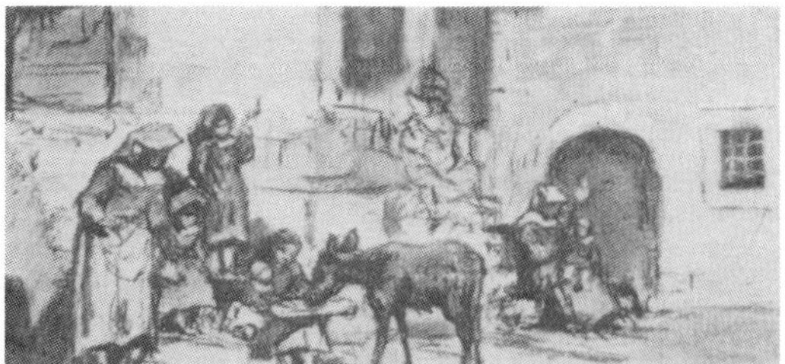

WILLIAM MORRIS HUNT – Spanish Street Scene – signed with monogrammed initials and dated '68 – charcoal on buff paper – 11½ x 17½in.
(Christie's) **$1,045** **£727**

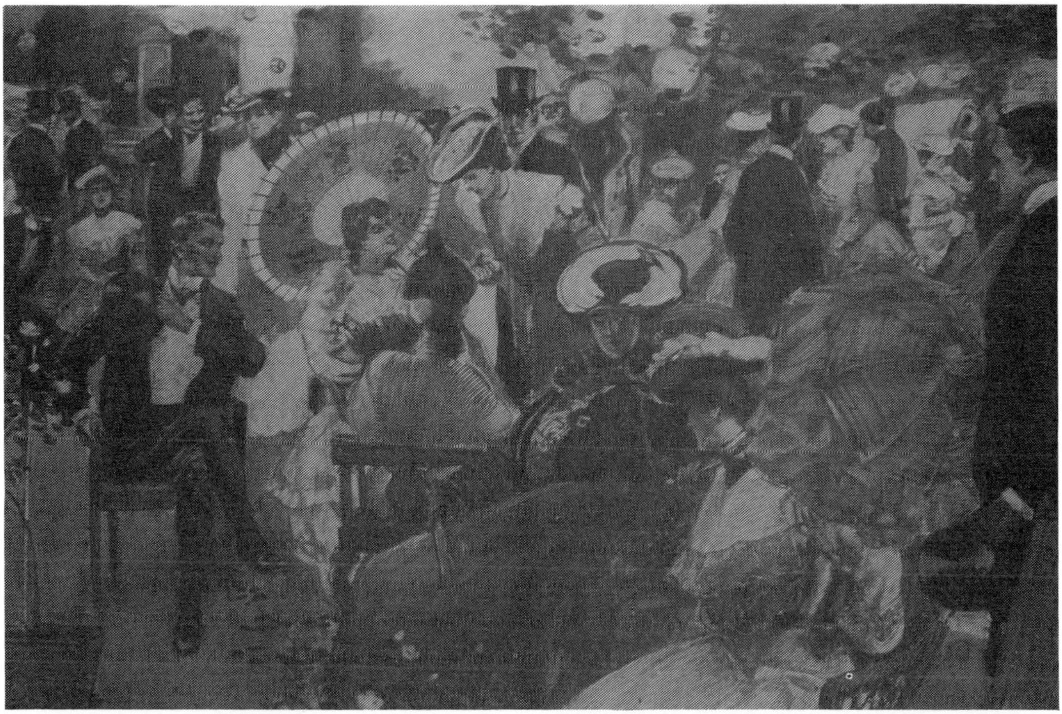

GEORGE LESLIE HUNTER – A Garden Party – signed – watercolour heightened with white – 14½ x 19¾in. *(Christie's)* **$4,320 £3,000**

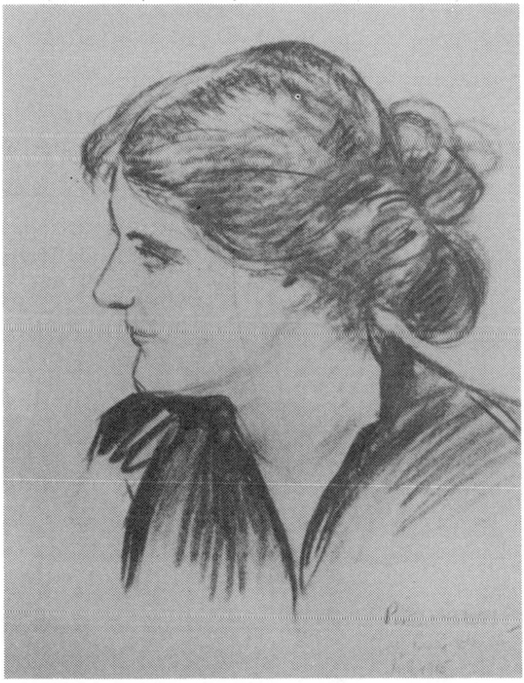

GEORGE LESLIE HUNTER – Portrait Of Minnie, The Artist's Mistress – signed, inscribed and dated 1915 – black chalk and blue crayon on buff paper – 23.5 x 18.5cm.
(Phillips) **$498** **£300**

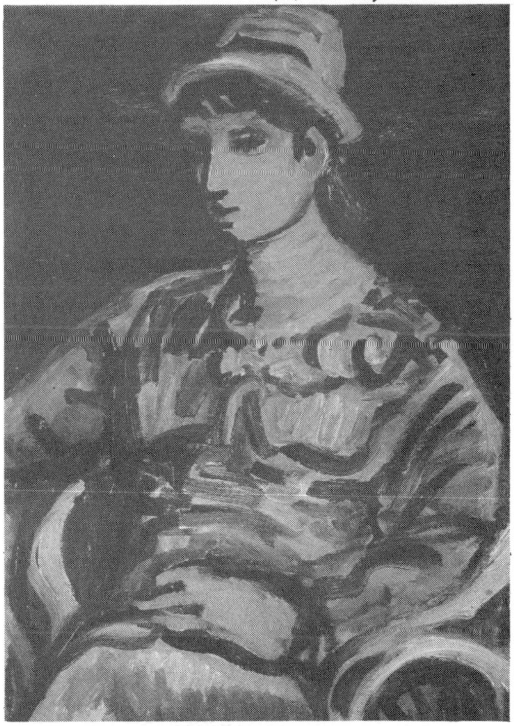

GEORGE LESLIE HUNTER – The Wicker Chair – oil on canvas – 29 x 21in.
(Christie's) **$14,400** **£10,000**

HUNTER

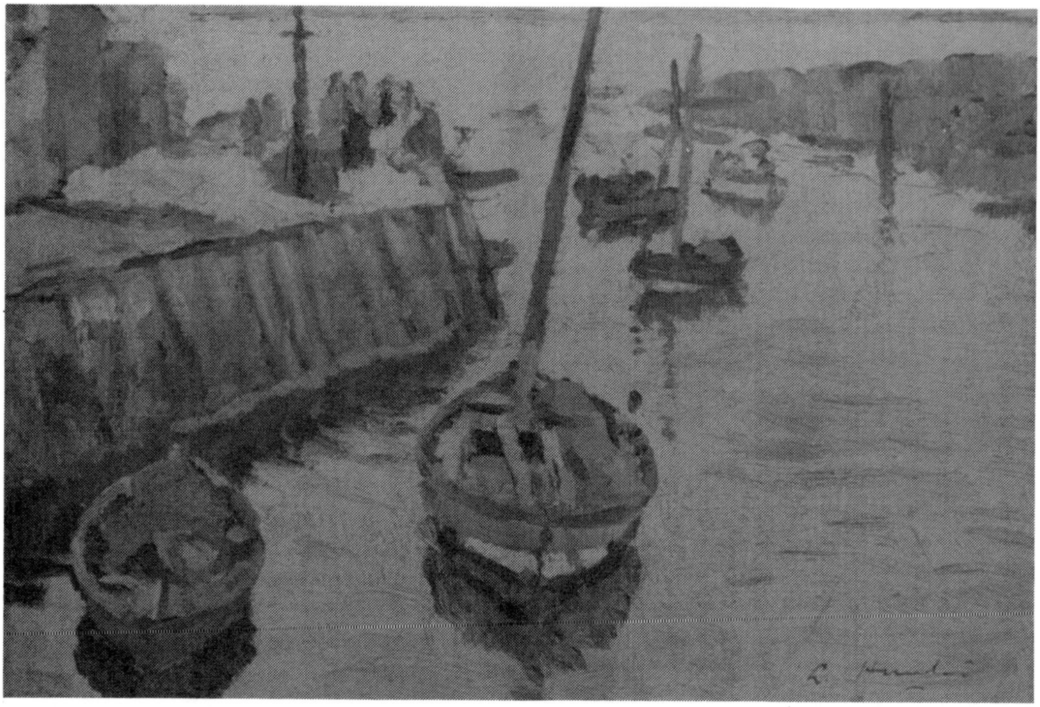

LESLIE HUNTER – The Harbour At Pittenweem – signed – oil on board – 21 x 28cm. *(Phillips)* **$9,280 £5,800**

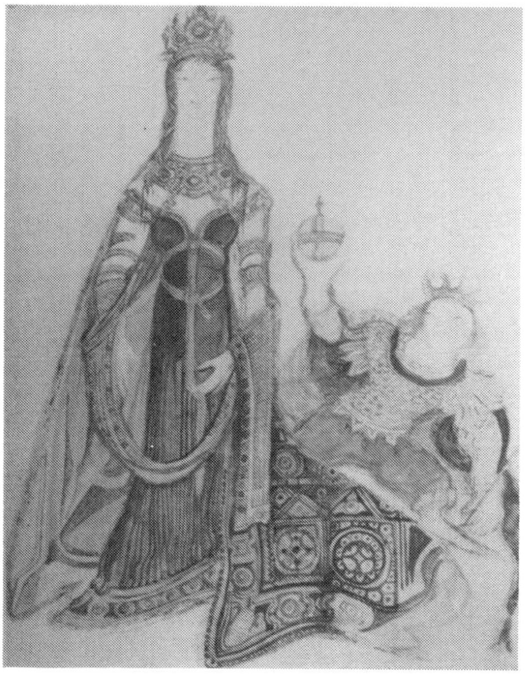

LELSIE HURRY – Costume Design: The Queen, Wife To Cymbeline, And The Dwarf – signed, inscribed and dated 1945 – wax crayons, pen, ink and watercolour – 55 x 43cm.
(Phillips) **$830** **£500**

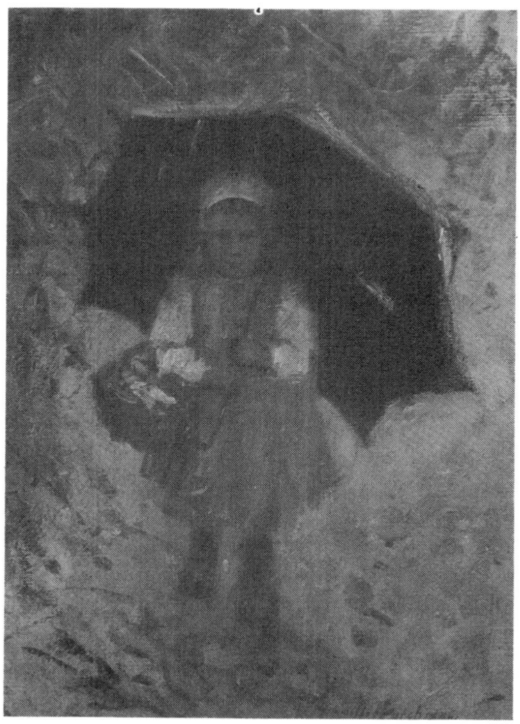

ROBERT GEMMELL HUTCHISON – Caught In The Rain – signed – oil on canvas – 14 x 10in.
(Christie's) **$10,080** **£7,000**

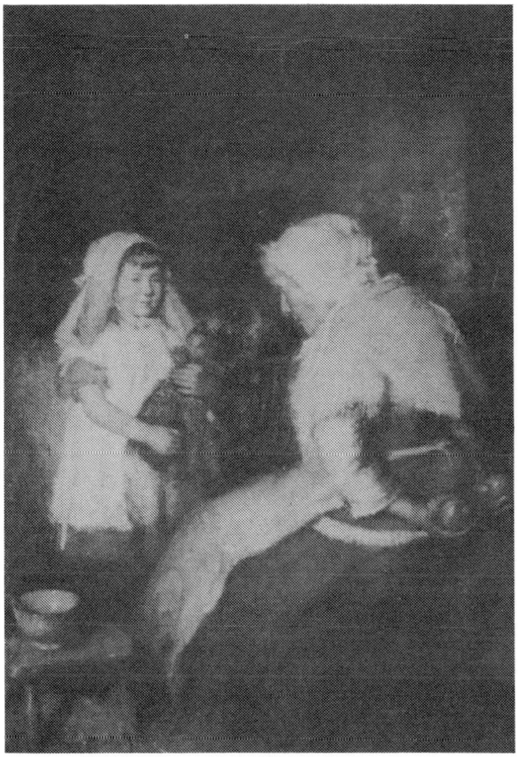

ROBERT GEMMELL HUTCHISON – Hoping For A Reward – signed – 14 x 10in.
(Lawrence Fine Art) **$8,217** **£4,950**

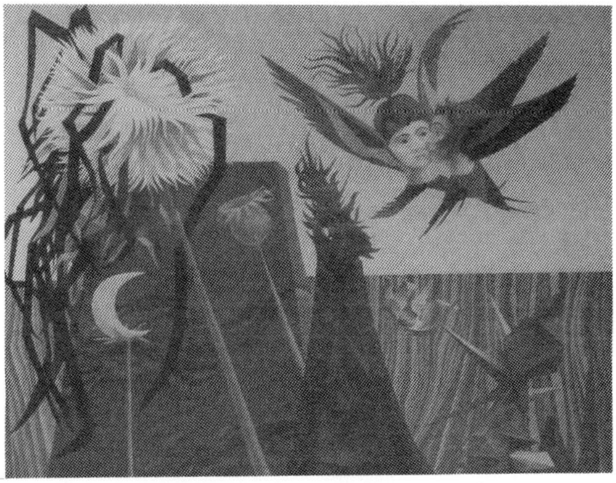

WOLFGANG HUTTER – Fliegende Kopfe – signed and dated 1960 – oil on canvas – 15 x 19in.
(Christie's) **$5,632** **£3,520**

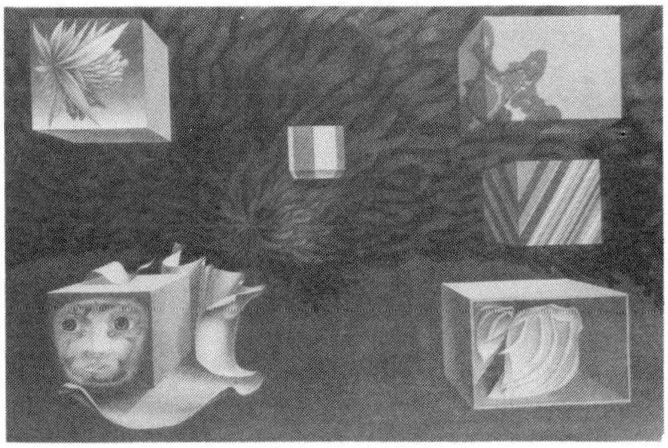

WOLFGANG HUTTER – Mitternacht – signed and dated '68 – oil on board – 11½ x 16½in.
(Christie's) **$2,288** **£1,430**

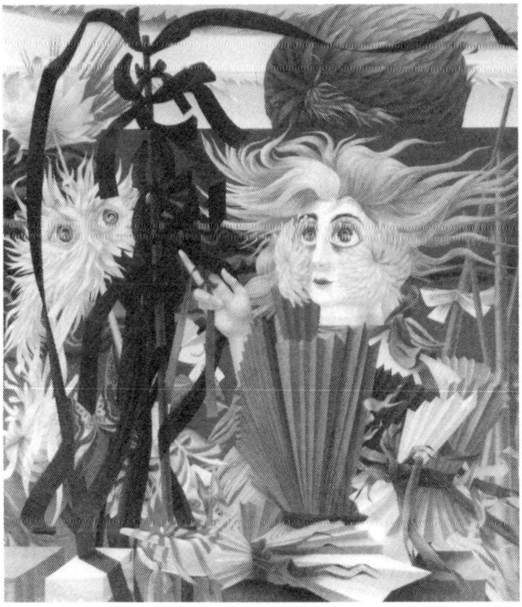

WOLFGANG HUTTER – Zauberin – signed and dated 1963 – oil on canvas – 27¼ x 23¼in.
(Christie's) **$10,296** **£7,150**

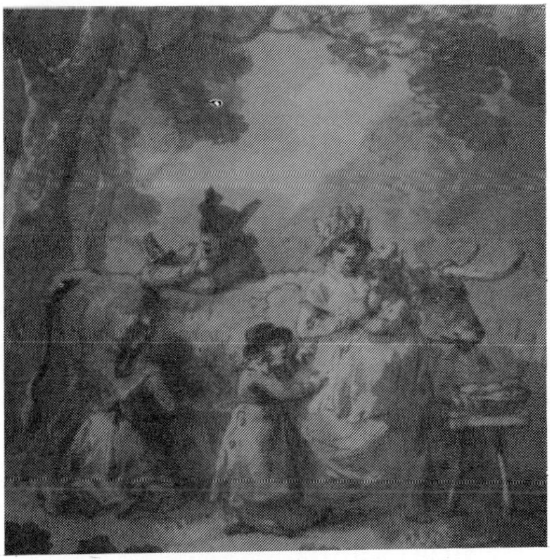

JULIUS CAESAR IBBETSON – Milking Time; and Going To Market – pen and grey ink and watercolour – 4¾ x 4in.
(Christie's) **$4,373** **£3,080 Pair**

ICART

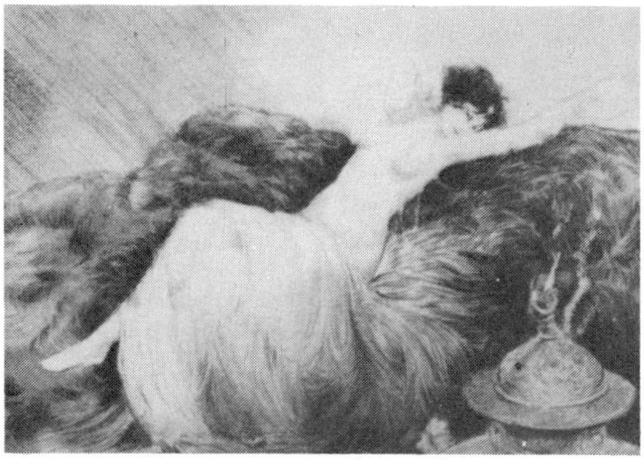

LOUIS ICART – 'Fumette' – signed – watercolour and pencil on paper – 15¼ x 20¾in.
(Robt. W. Skinner Inc.) **$1,500** **£986**

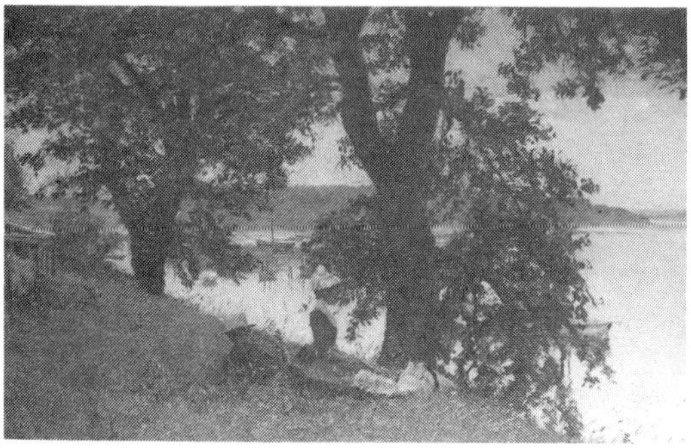

PETER ILSTED – On The Bank – signed and dated 1889 – 16 x 21in.
(Christie's) **$35,200** **£22,000**

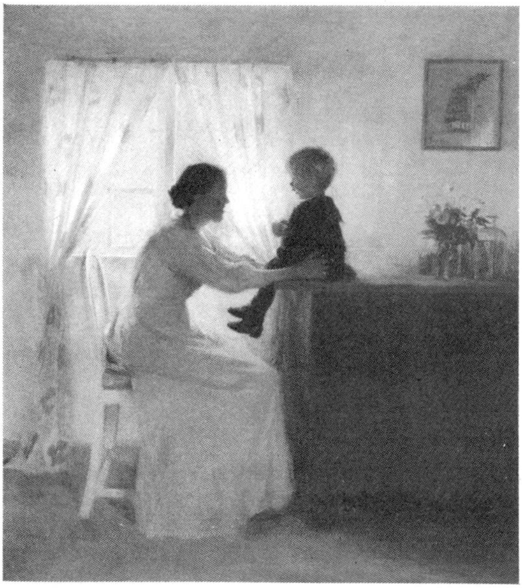

PETER VILHELM ILSTED – A Mother And Child In An Interior – signed with monogram and dated 1898, and signed and inscribed on an old label on the reverse – 24 x 22in.
(Christie's) **$63,360** **£44,000**

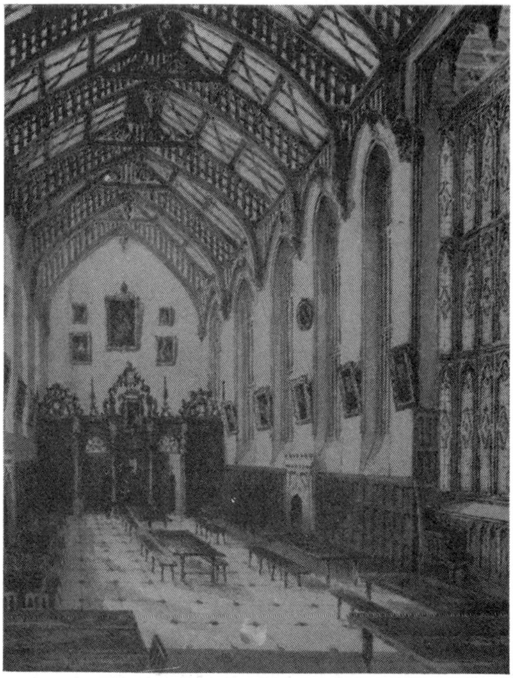

JOSEPH MURRAY INCE – Exeter College, Oxford, The Interior Of The Chapel; and Of The Hall – signed and dated – pencil and watercolour with touches of gum arabic – 10¼ x 7in.
(Christie's) **$1,377** **£825 Pair**

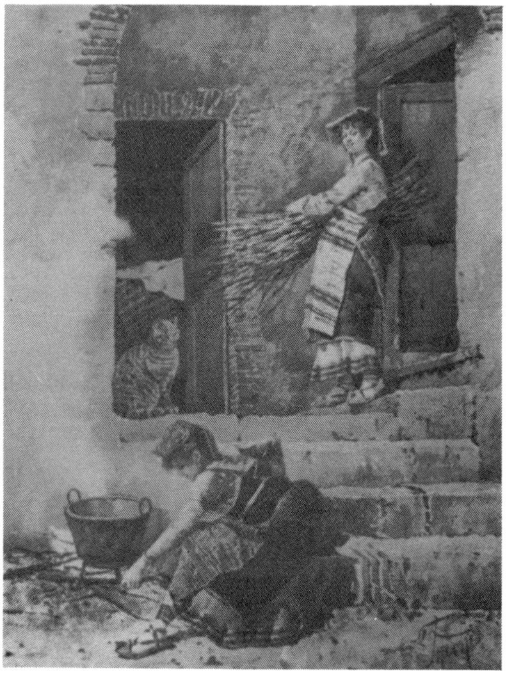

FILIPPO INDONI – Women Preparing A Cooking Fire – signed – pencil and watercolour – 21 x 14in.
(Christie's) **$880** **£550**

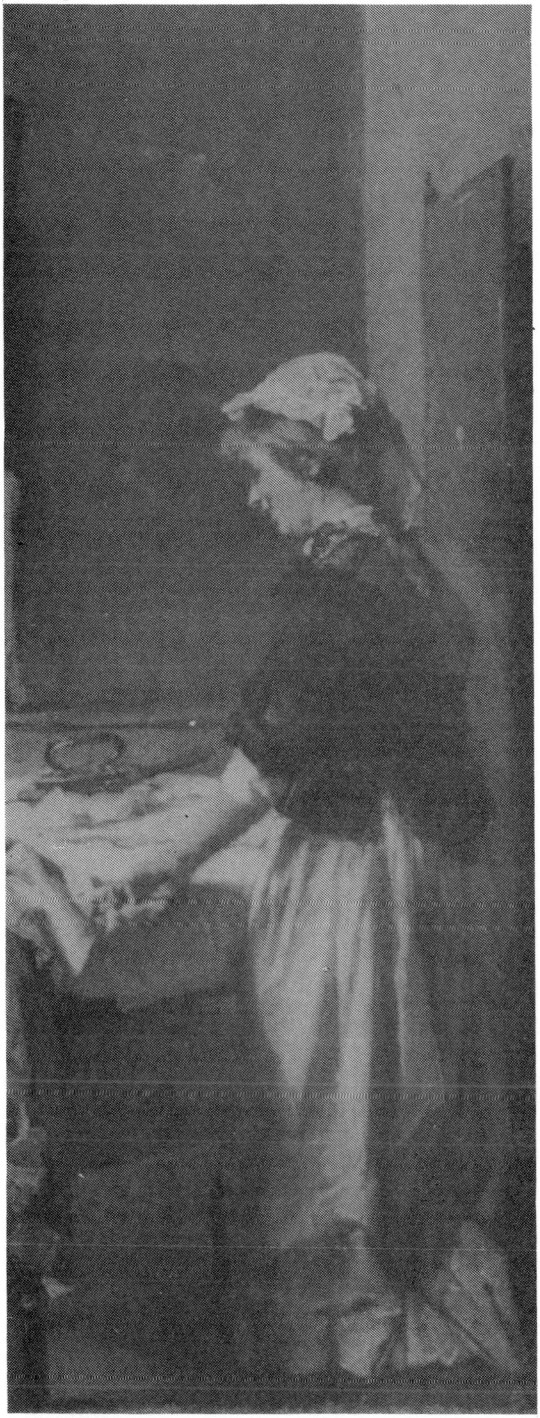

DOMENICO INDUNO, Circle of – Doing The Ironing – 15¾ x 8in.
(Christie's) **$18,260** **£11,000**

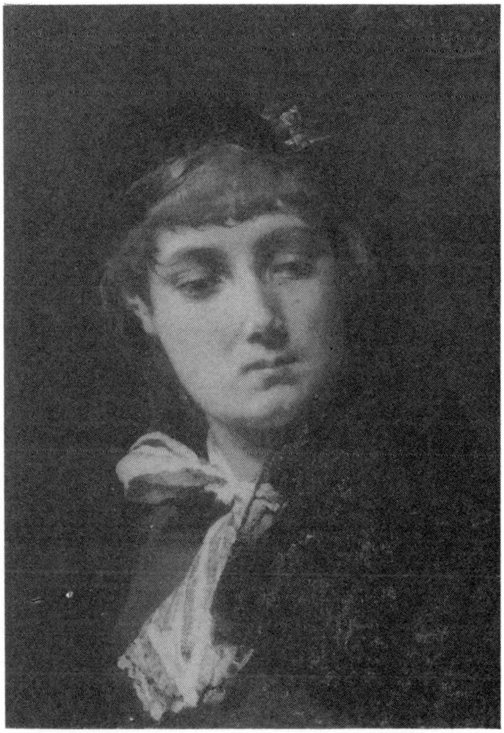

DOMENICO INDUNO – A Lady In Black Lace – signed and dated 1870 – 11 x 8in.
(Christie's) **$10,043** **£6,050**

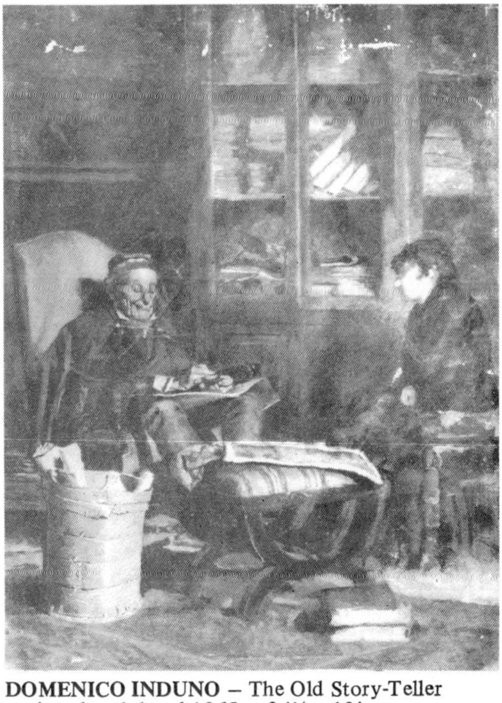

DOMENICO INDUNO – The Old Story-Teller – signed and dated 1865 – 24½ x 18in.
(Christie's) **$7,128** **£4,950**

INDUNO

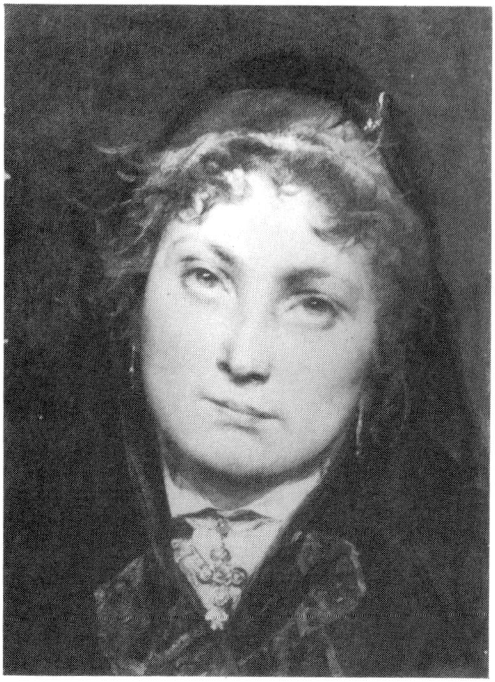

DOMENICO INDUNO – Head Of A Woman; and Figures In An Interior – one signed – 10¼ x 7¼in. and 8¾ x 11¾in.
(Christie's) **$21,912** **£13,200** Two

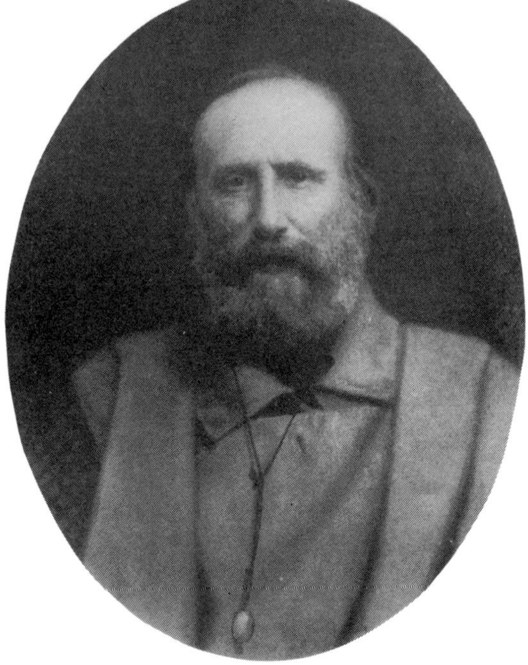

DOMENICO INDUNO, Attributed to – Portrait Of A Bearded Man – with signature and date '62 – on board – 11 x 8¾in.
(Christie's) **$6,938** **£4,180**

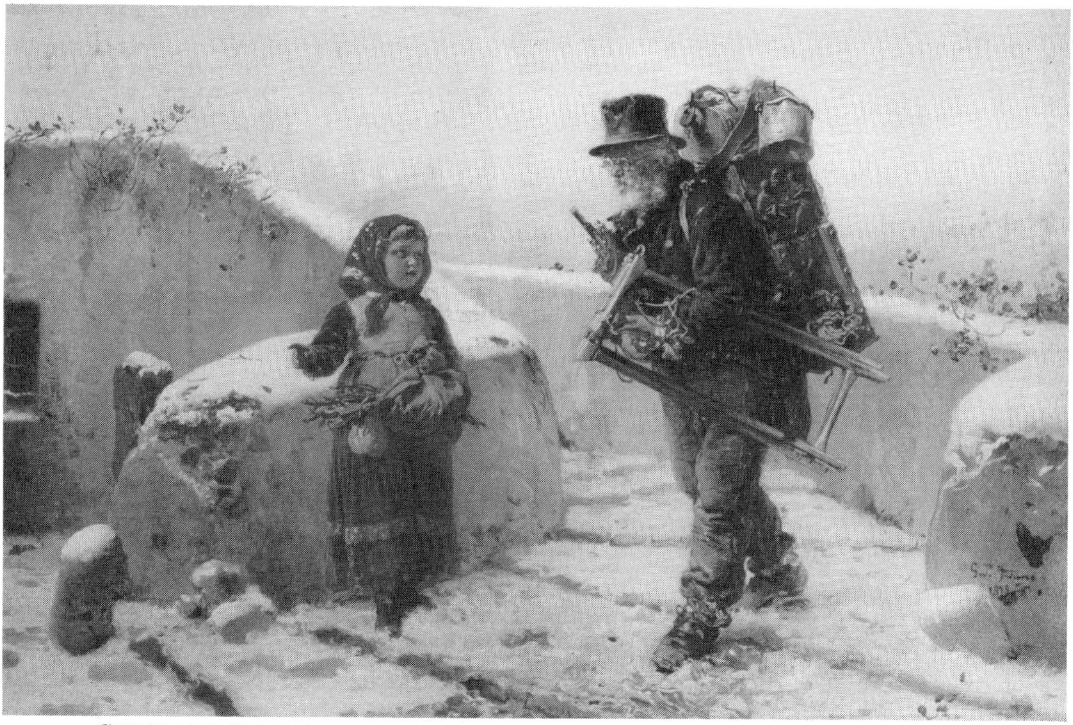

GEROLAMO INDUNO – The Pedlar – signed and dated 1879 – 17¼ x 22½in. *(Christie's)*
$100,430 **£60,500**

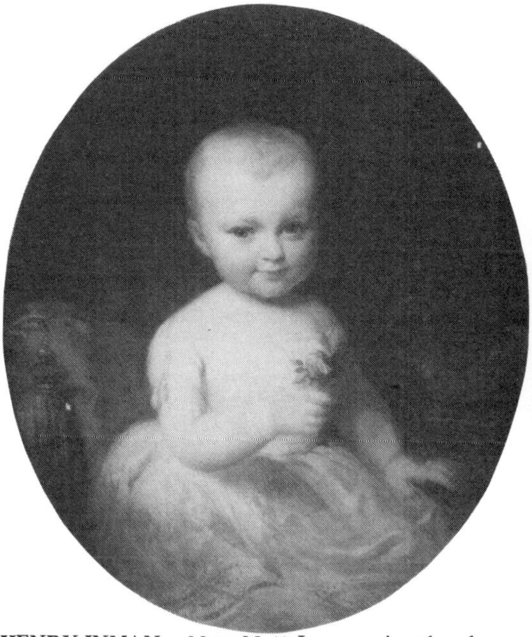

HENRY INMAN – Mary Mott Jones – signed and dated 1845 – oil on canvas – 24 x 19¾in.
(Christie's) **$2,860** **£1,782**

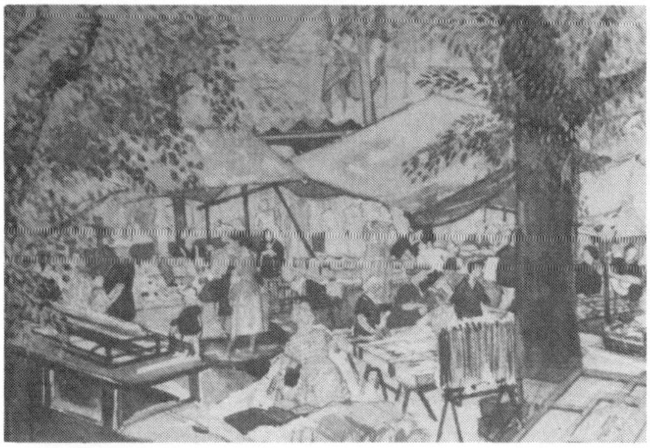

LAURENCE IRVING – The Market, Amboise – signed with monogram – watercolour and body-colour over charcoal – 24 x 34.5cm.
(Phillips) **$535** **£350**

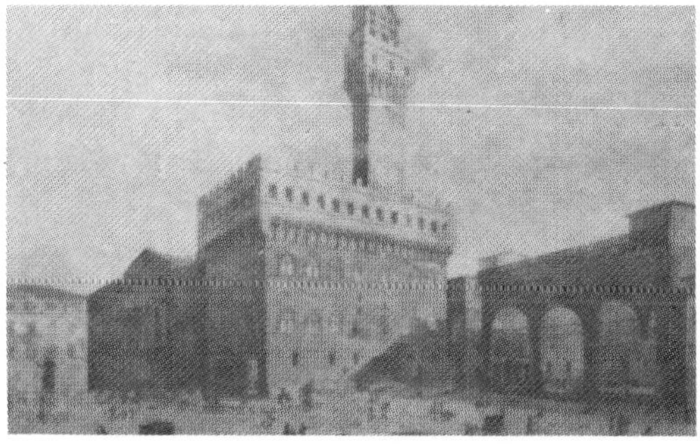

ITALIAN SCHOOL, early 19th century – Florence – oil on panel – 23 x 29in.
(Christie's) **$4,896** **£3,400**

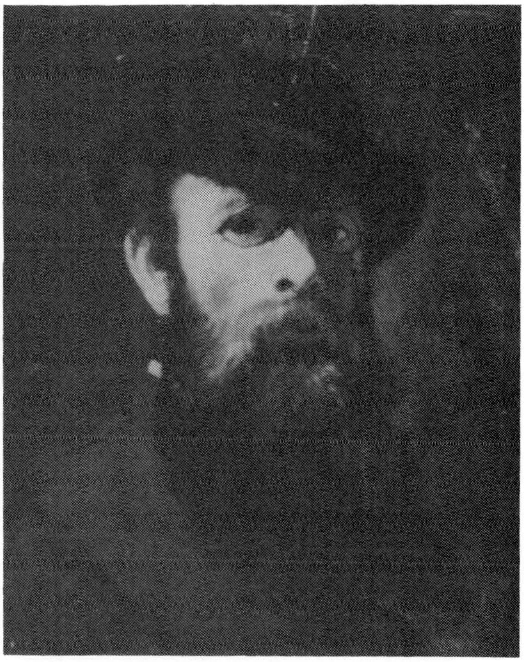

ITALIAN SCHOOL, Circa 1870 – Portrait Of A Man In A Hat, Wearing Pinz-Nez, Bust Length – signed indistinctly and inscribed – on panel – 33 x 27cm.
(Phillips) **$241** **£160**

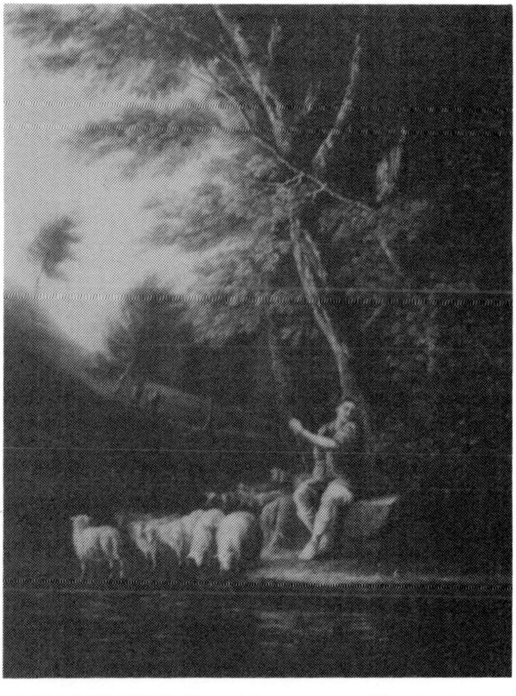

ITALIAN SCHOOL, 19th century – Shepherd With His Flock – oil on canvas – 36 x 28in.
(Christie's) **$1,210** **£789**

JACOB

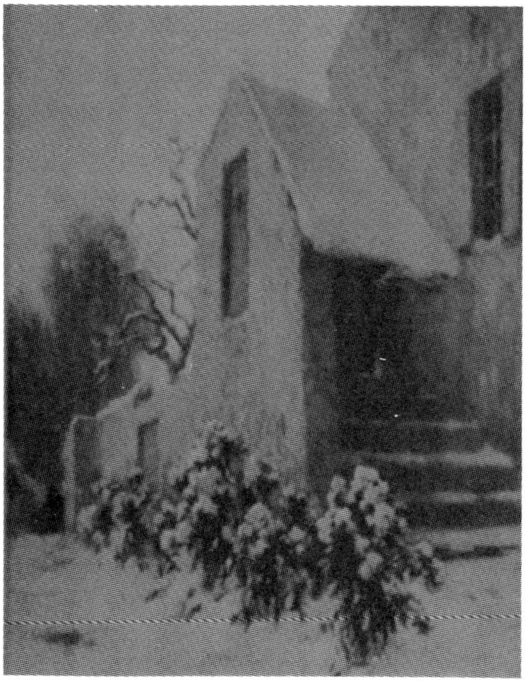

ALEXANDRE JACOB – Snow In The Garden – signed – oil on panel – 46 x 33cm.
(Phillips) **$2,480** **£1,600**

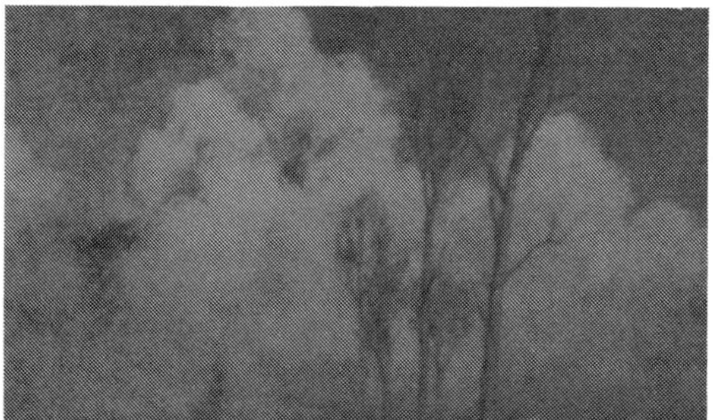

ALEXANDRE JACOB – Chevaux Au Bord Du Marne – oil on panel – 24 x 26cm.
(Phillips) **$1,860** **£1,200**

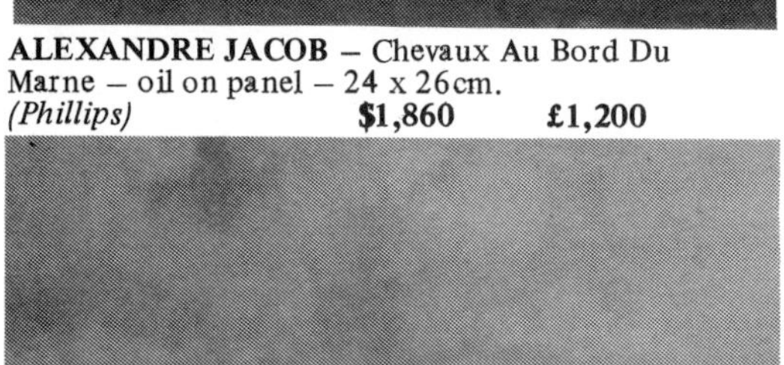

ALEXANDRE JACOB – Ciel Sur La Haute Savoie – signed – oil on linen laid down on board – 17.5 x 23.5cm.
(Phillips) **$1,550** **£1,000**

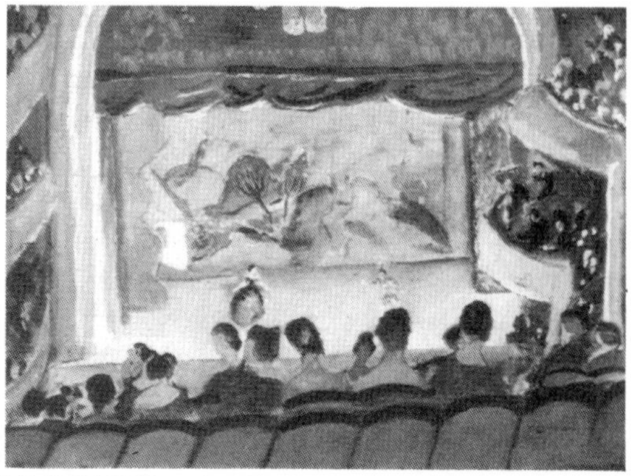

MAX JACOB – Au Theatre – signed – gouache on paper – 10¾ x 13¾in.
(Christie's) **$2,534** **£1,760**

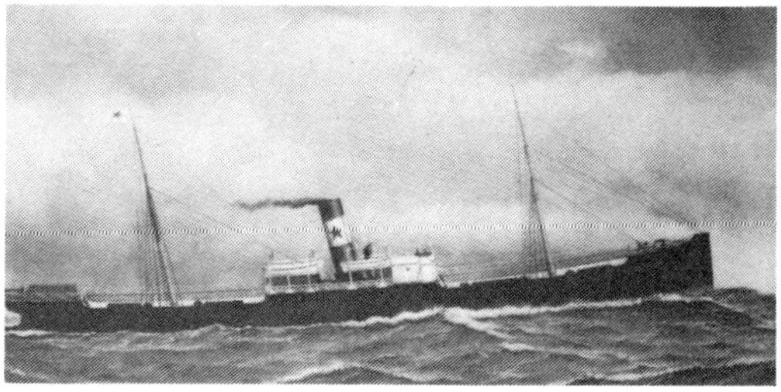

ANTONIO JACOBSEN – The Kansas City – signed and dated 1899 – oil on canvas – 21¾ x 36in.
(Christie's) **$7,700** **£5,356**

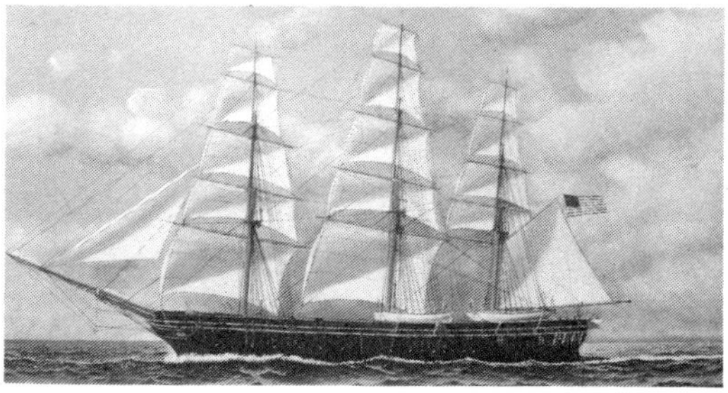

ANTONIO JACOBSEN – A Naval Vessel – signed and dated 1907 – oil on board – 22 x 35¾in.
(Christie's) **$8,800** **£6,122**

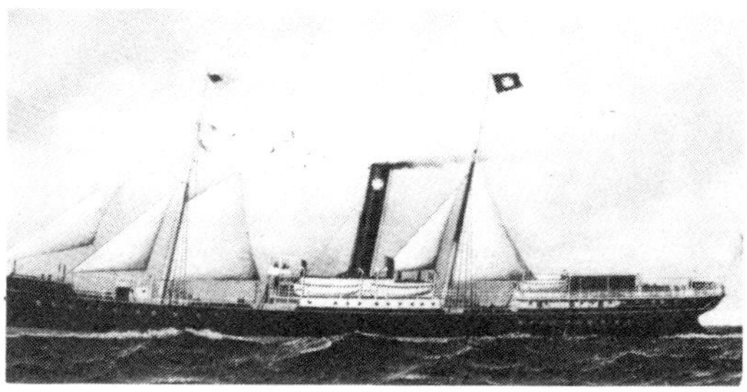

ANTONIO JACOBSEN – Portrait Of The Steamship 'Anslem' – signed and dated 1899, also inscribed – oil on canvas – 22 x 35½in.
(Robt. W. Skinner Inc.) **$6,750** **£4,687**

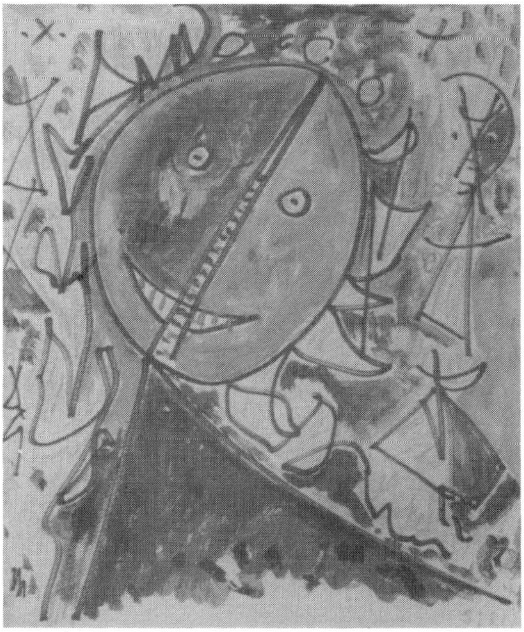

EGILL JACOBSEN – Untitled – signed with initials and dated '81 – felt pen, coloured chalks, watercolour and oil on paper – 18¼ x 15in.
(Christie's) **$1,936** **£1,210**

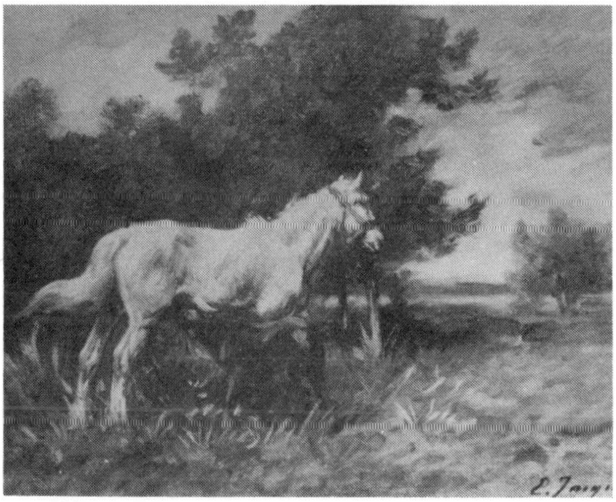

EMILE JACQUE – Mare And Foal In Pasture – signed – oil on canvas – 8½ x 10½in.
(Morphets) **$1,304** **£800**

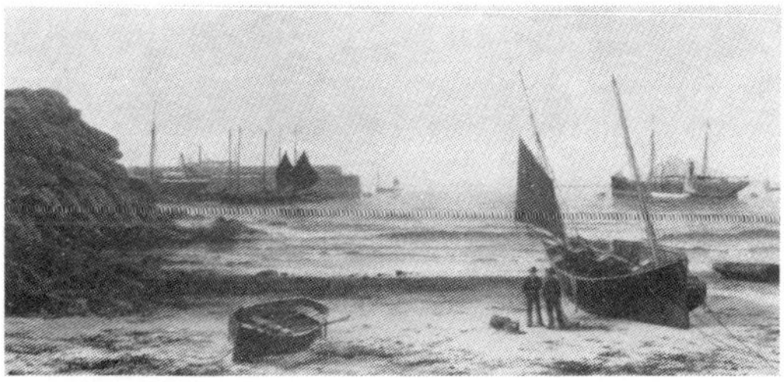

DAVID JAMES – Scilly Isles – signed and dated '86 – 24 x 49in.
(Christie's) **$2,171** **£1,540**

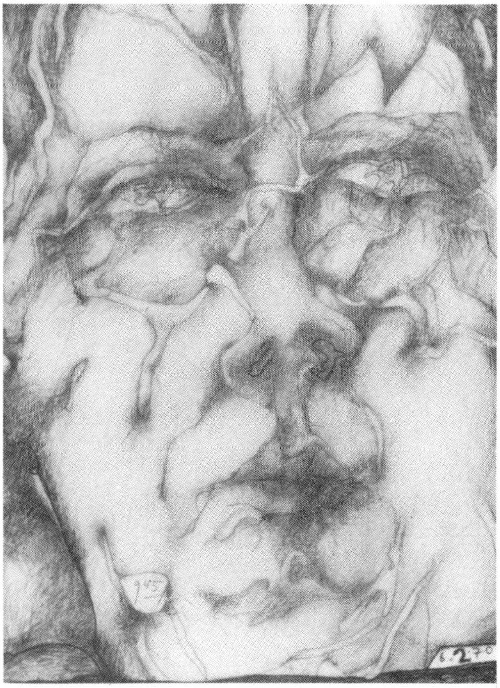

HORST JANSSEN – Selbstportrat – signed and dated '70 – coloured crayons and pencil on paper – 9¼ x 6½in.
(Christie's) **$10,296** **£7,150**

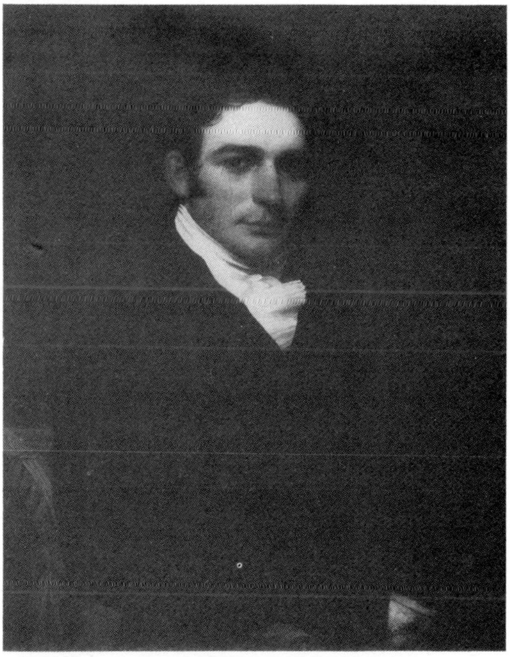

JOHN WESLEY JARVIS – Portrait Of Major Richard Wisner Thorne Of New York City – oil on canvas – 29¾ x 25in.
(Christie's) **$2,860** **£2,010**

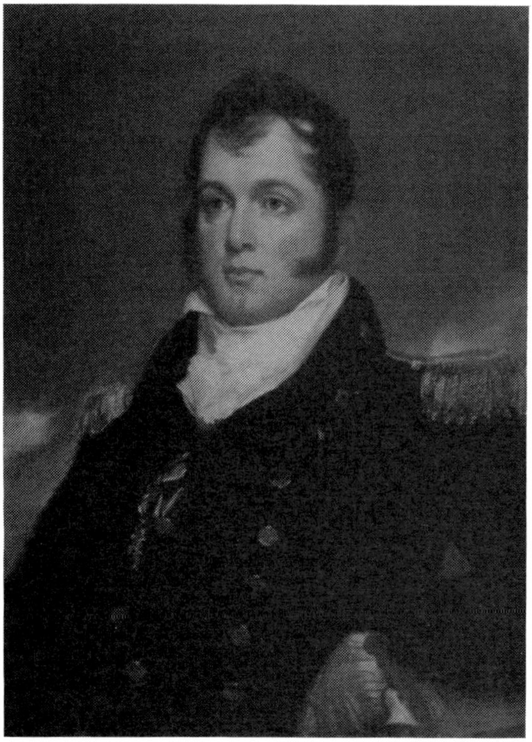

JOHN WESLEY JARVIS – Portrait Of Commodore Oliver Hazard Perry – oil on panel – 29 x 21in.
(Christie's) **$71,500** **£46,668**

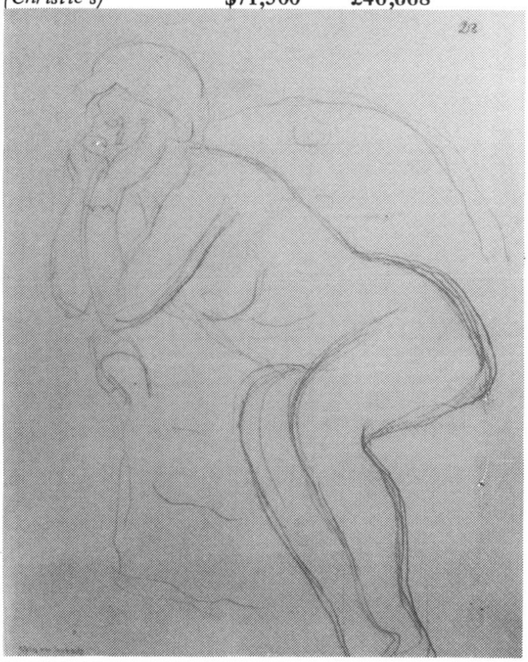

ALEXEJ JAWLENSKY – Akt im Sofa – soft pencil on paper – 11¾ x 9½in.
(Christie's) **$5,280** **£3,300**

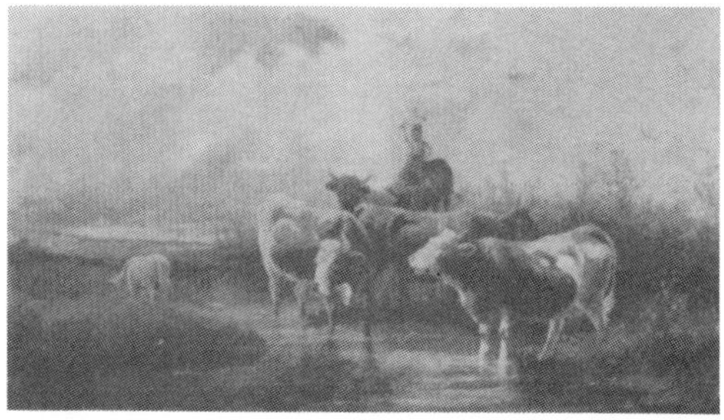

J. C. JEAN – A Drover And Cattle Fording A Stream – signed – oil on canvas – 19 x 31in.
(Christie's) **$336** **£220**

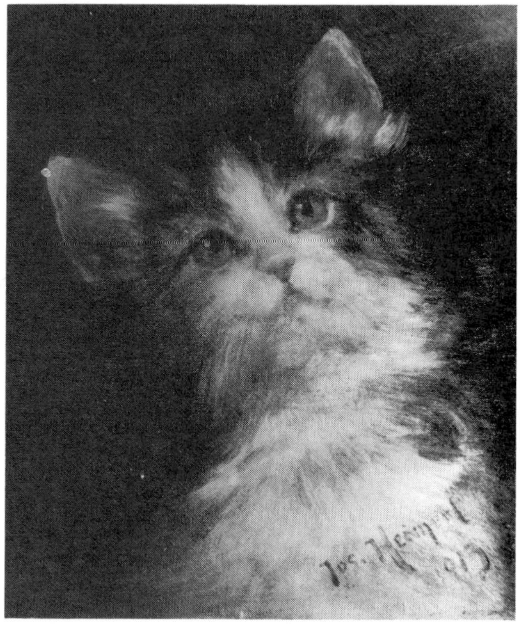

JOSEF JEIMERL – A Kitten – signed and dated 1913 – on panel – 5½ x 4½in.
(Christie's) **$1,504** **£990**

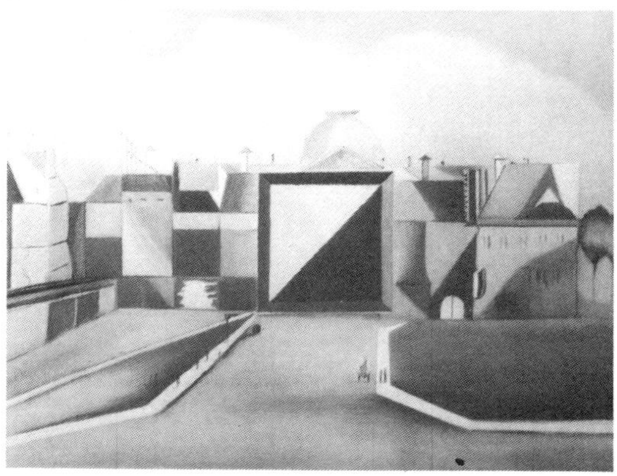

HUMPHREY JENNINGS – Tableaux Parisien – signed and dated 1938-9 – oil on canvas – 20 x 24in.
(Christie's) **$1,415** **£990**

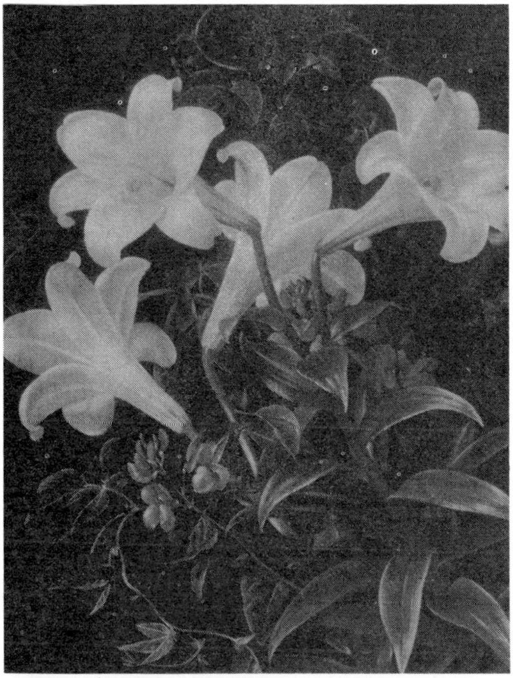

JOHAN LAURENTS JENSEN – Lilies – signed and dated 1843 – on panel – 17¾ x 13in.
(Christie's) **$14,212** **£9,350**

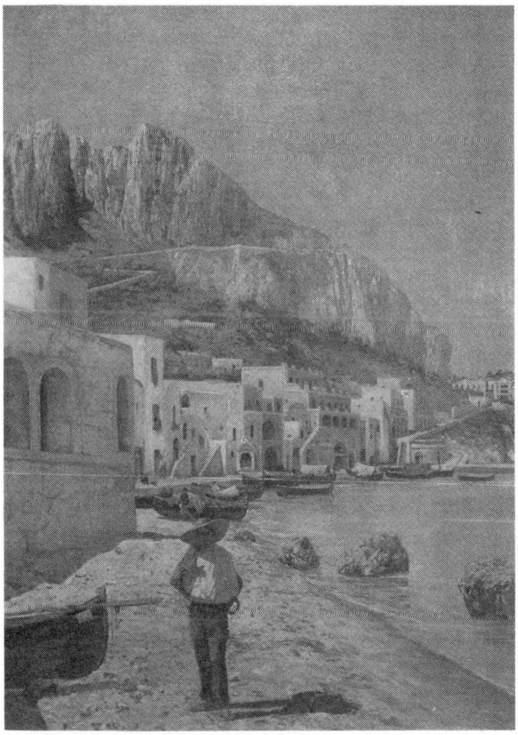

HOLGER HVITFELD JERICHAU – Capri – signed – 41½ x 28in.
(Christie's) **$12,540** **£8,250**

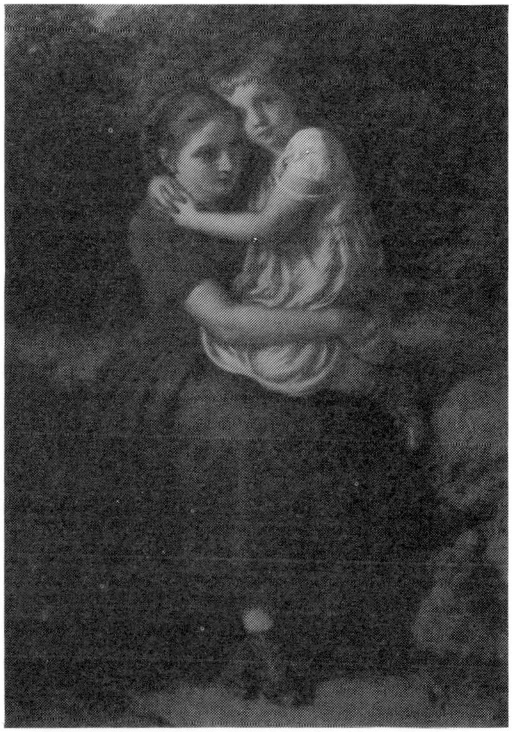

HENRY LE JEUNE – The Sisters – signed with monogram and dated 1868 – on panel – 19 x 13½in.
(Christie's) **$8,751** **£5,720**

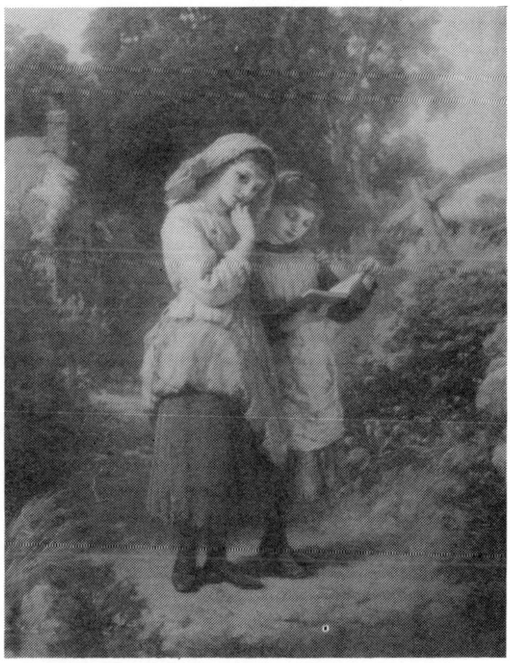

HENRY LE JEUNE – A Good Book – signed with monogram and dated 1876 – 27 x 29½in.
(Christie's) **$15,510** **£11,000**

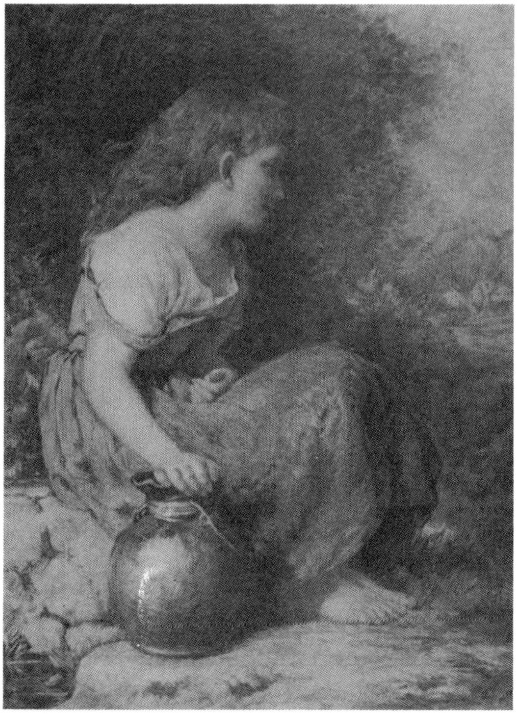

HENRY L. LE JEUNE – The Water Carrier – signed with monogram and dated 1866 – pencil and watercolour – 16 x 12in.
(Christie's) **$930** **£660**

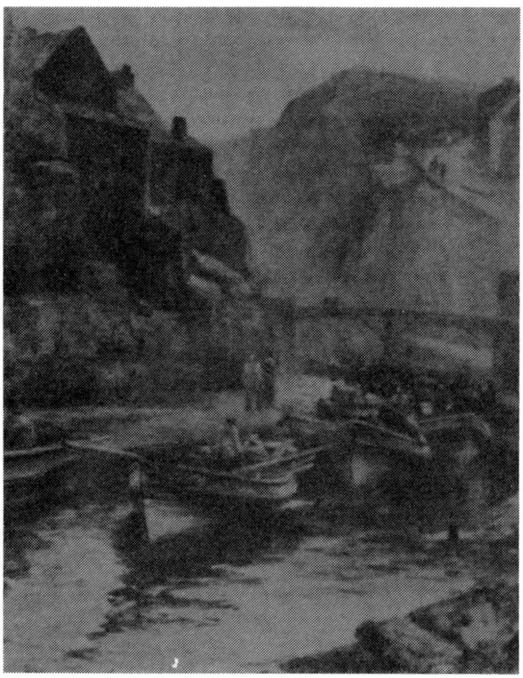

ROBERT JOBLING – A River Convoy – signed and dated 1906 – on canvas – 36 x 28in.
(Phillips) **$1,932** **£1,200**

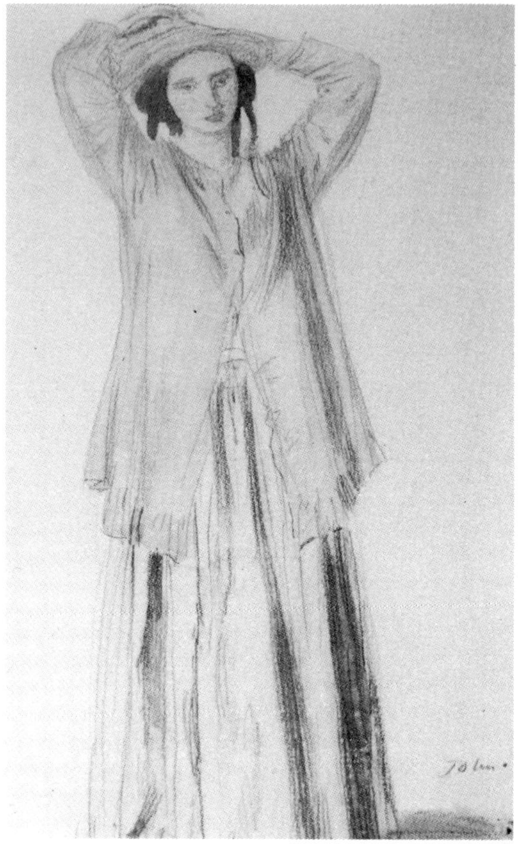

AUGUSTUS JOHN – Dorelia, Standing, In A Blue Smock – signed – watercolour and pencil on paper – 11½ x 6½in.
(Christie's) **$14,256** **£9,900**

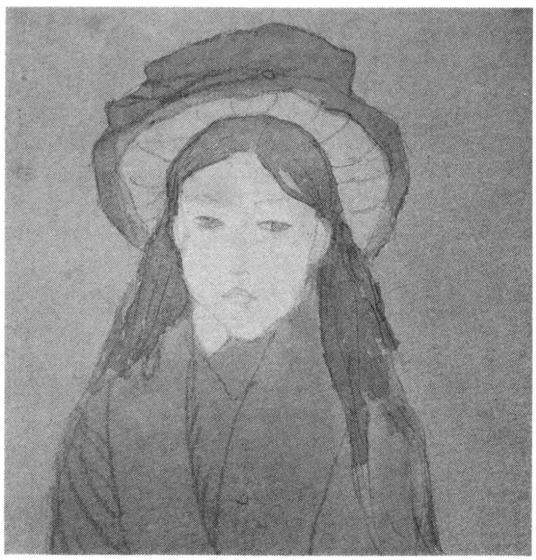

GWEN JOHN – Little Girl – watercolour, bodycolour and pencil on beige paper – 8¼ x 6¾in.
(Christie's) **$20,449** **£14,300**

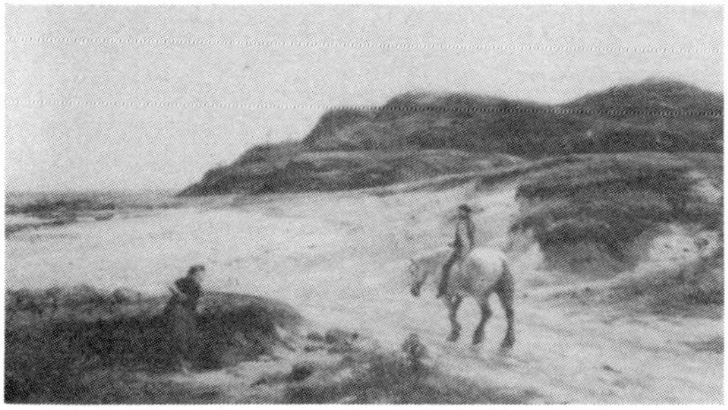

CHARLES EDWARD JOHNSON – On The Shore Road, Iona – signed and dated 1881 – 25 x 35in.
(Christie's) **$669** **£462**

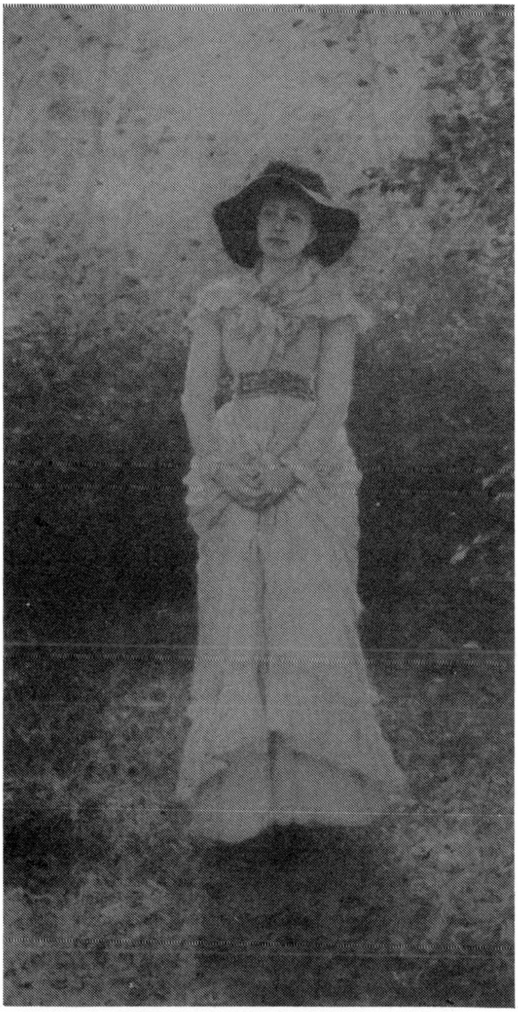

EDWARD KILLINGWORTH JOHNSON – The Reverie – signed and dated 1882 – pencil and watercolour heightened with white – 21½ x 11¾in.
(Christie's) **$5,112** **£3,080**

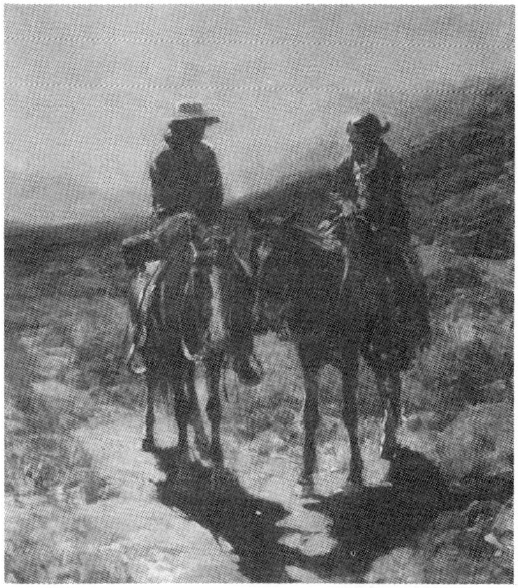

FRANK TENNEY JOHNSON – Lovers Of The Desert – signed – oil on canvas – 36 x 28in.
(Christie's) **$37,400** **£26,292**

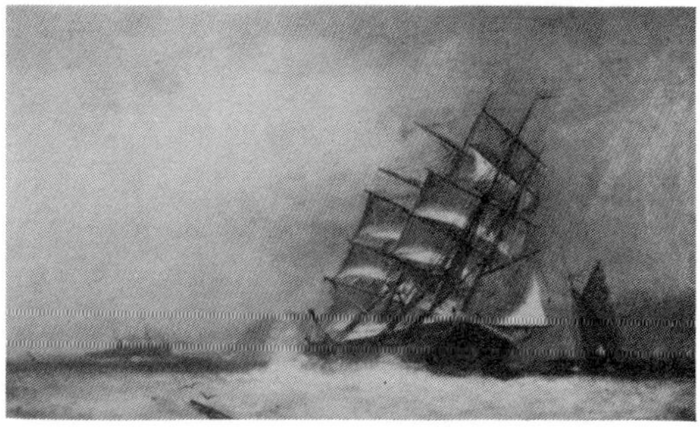

MARSHALL JOHNSON – Clipper Ship On A Coastal Route – signed – oil on canvas – 18 x 24in.
(Robt. W. Skinner Inc.) **$2,000** **£1,388**

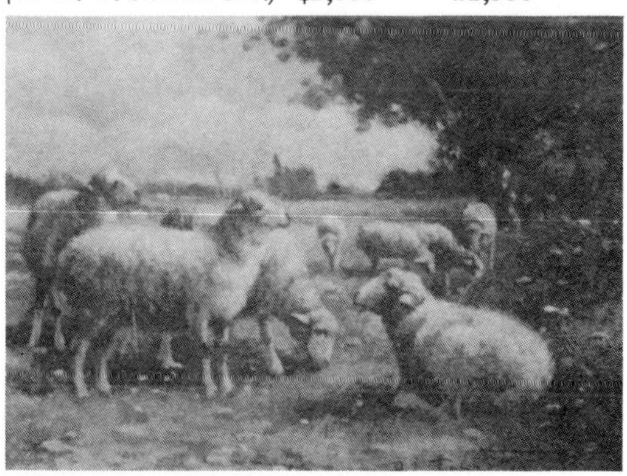

REUBEN LE GRAND JOHNSON – Sheep Resting In A Landscape – signed – oil on panel – 6 x 8in.
(Christie's) **$574** **£396**

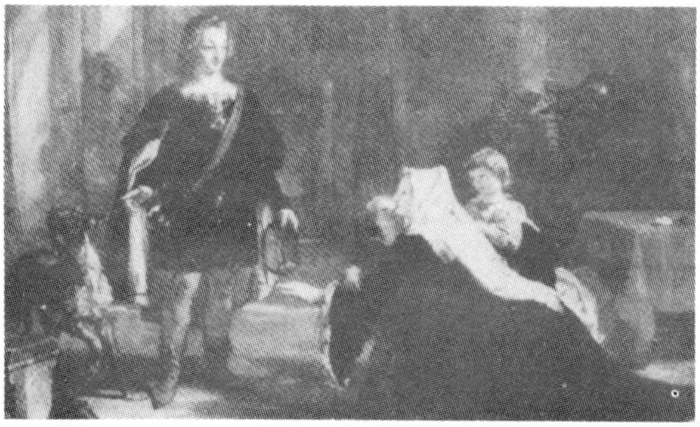

ALEXANDER JOHNSTON – Returned From The Hunt – signed and dated 1853 – oil on canvas – 11 x 15½in.
(Christie's) **$633** **£440**

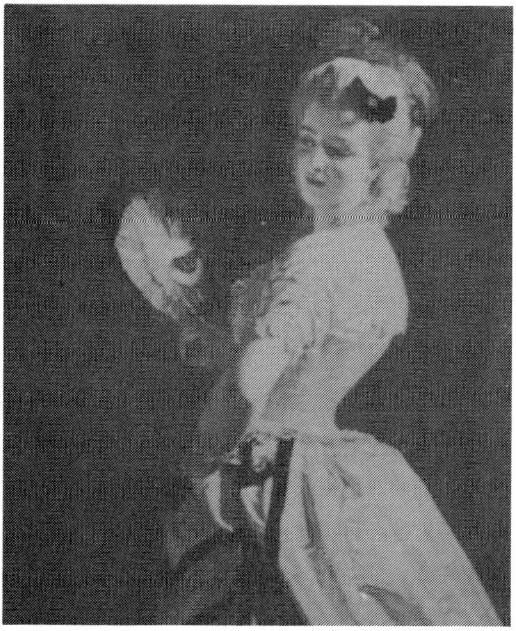

ALEXANDER JOHNSTON – The Flirt – signed – on canvas – 37 x 28¼in.
(Phillips) **$1,932** **£1,200**

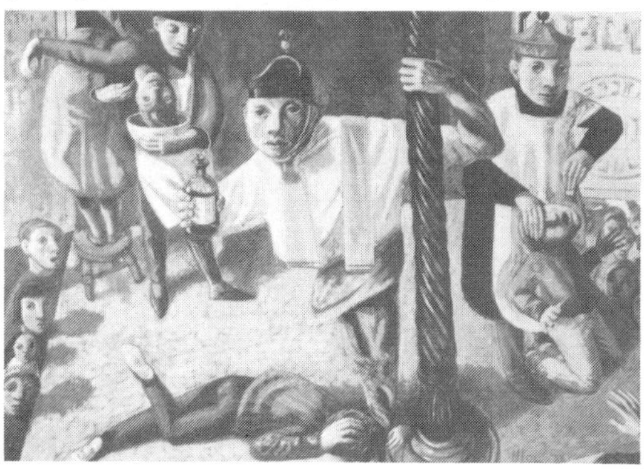

NICHOLAS JOLLY – Travelling Performers – signed and dated '86 – oil on canvas – 60 x 70in.
(Christie's) **$2,245** **£1,430**

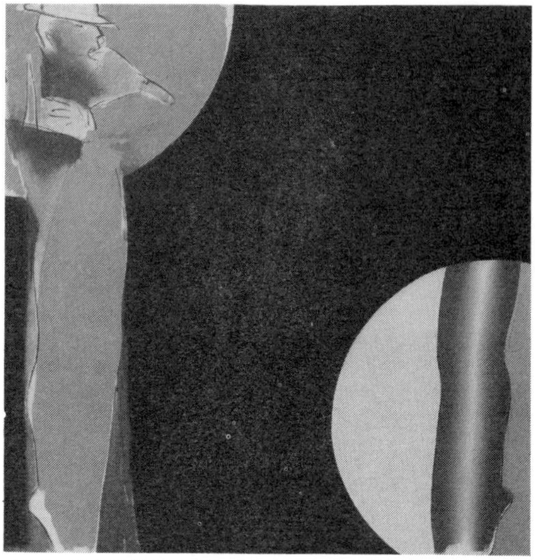

ALLEN JONES – Untitled – oil and charcoal on canvas – 60 x 60in.
(Christie's) **$7,920** **£4,950**

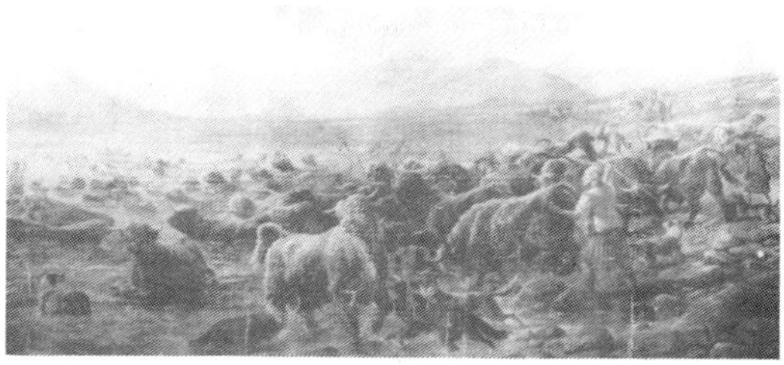

CHARLES JONES – Highland Cattle Being Driven Across A Loch – signed with monogram and dated 1873, and signed and dated on the reverse – 47½ x 95in.
(Christie's) **$7,200** **£5,000**

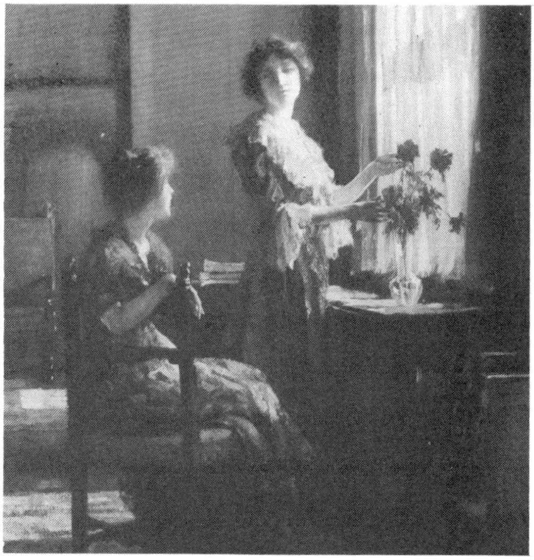

FRANCIS COATES JONES – Sunny Window – signed – oil on canvas – 27¼ x 22¼in.
(Christie's) **$22,000** **£13,708**

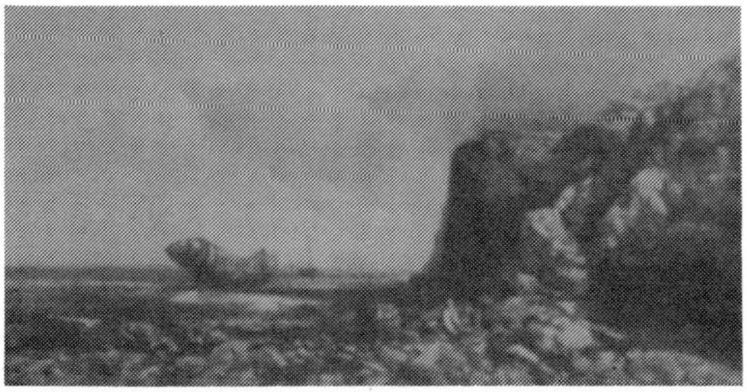

WILLIAM E. JONES – Samphire Gatherers – signed, also signed, inscribed and dated 1855 on a label on the reverse – on panel – 11 x 19in.
(Phillips) **$1,932** **£1,200**

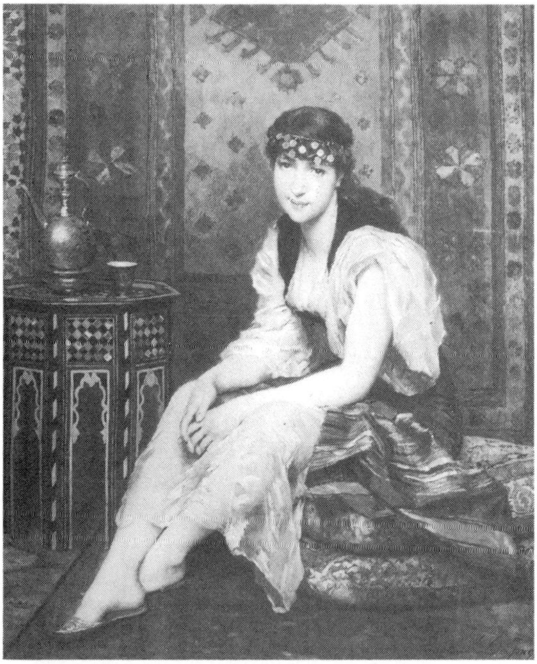

GUSTAVE DE JONGHE – An Eastern Beauty – signed – on panel – 18 x 14¾in.
(Christie's) **$9,680** **£6,050**

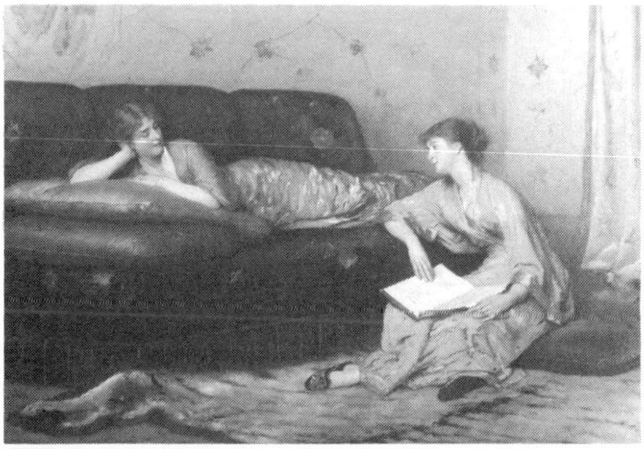

GUSTAV LEONHARD DE JONGHE – In The Boudoir – signed – on panel – 23¼ x 29in.
(Christie's) **$15,840** **£11,000**

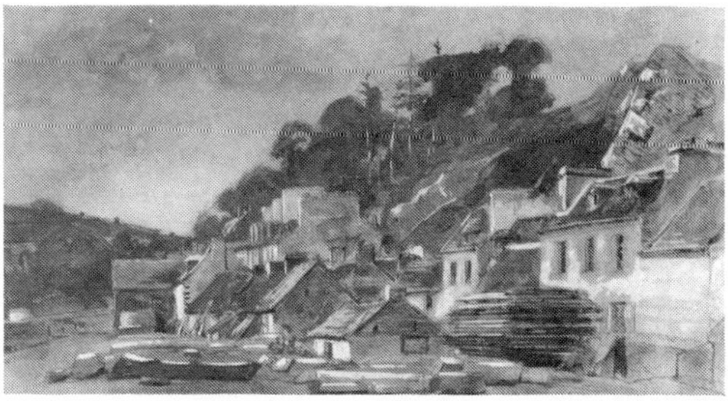

JOHAN BARTHOLD JONGKIND – Vue de Chateaulin – signed and dated '51 – watercolour and pencil on paper – 9½ x 14¼in.
(Christie's) **$13,464** **£9,350**

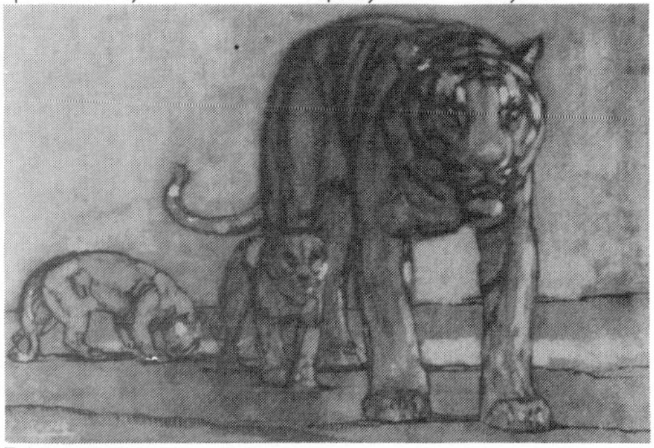

PAUL JOUVE – Tigresse avec ses Petits – signed – oil, brush and ink on board – 19¼ x 20¼in.
(Christie's) **$3,168** **£1,980**

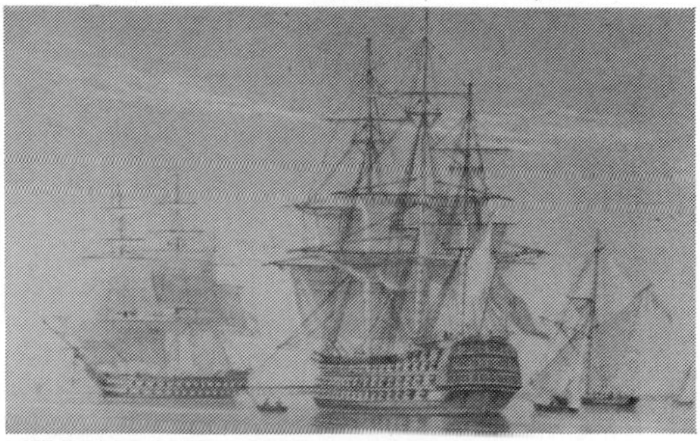

WILLIAM AND JOHN CANTILOE JOY – Shipping On A Calm Sea – watercolour – 21 x 31cm.
(Phillips) **$1,597** **£980**

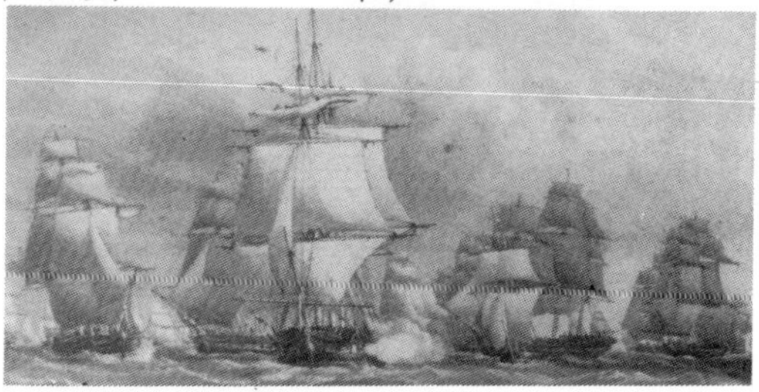

WILLIAM AND JOHN CANTILOE JOY – **A** Fleet At Sea In A Stiff Breeze – watercolour heightened with white – 11¼ x 15¾in.
(Christie's) **$2,967** **£2,090**

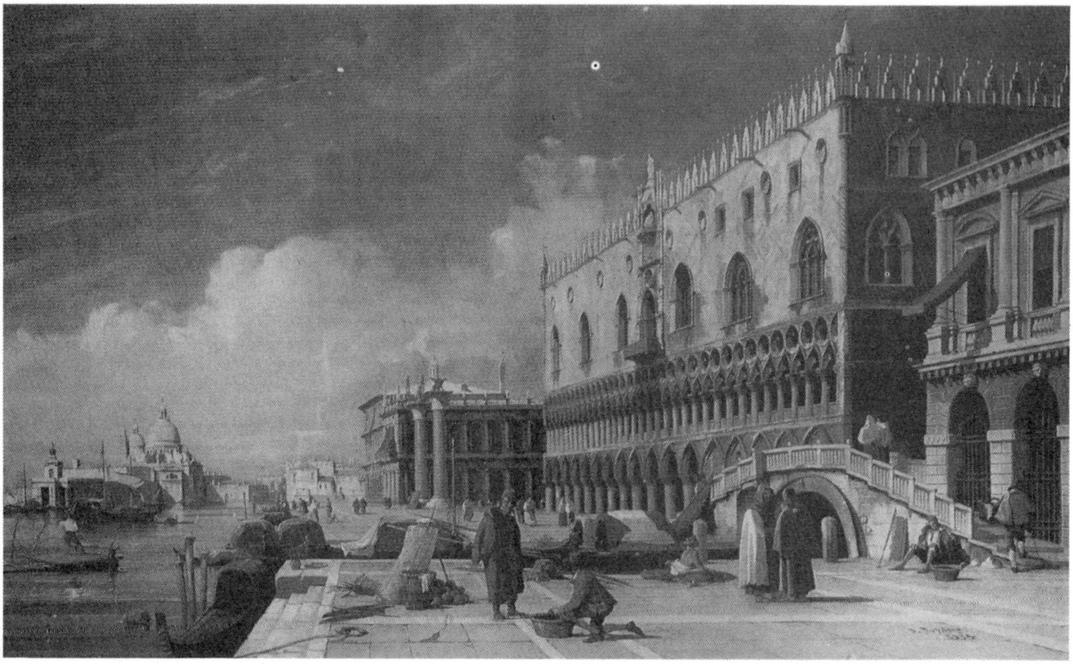

JULES ROMAIN JOYANT – Figures Before The Doge's Palace, Santa Maria Della Salute Beyond – signed and dated 1834 – oil on canvas – 104 x 165 cm. *(Phillips)* **$13,680 £9,500**

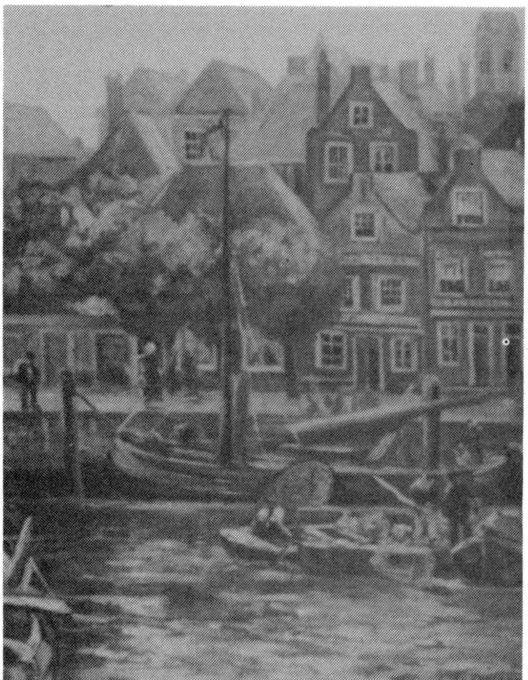

ALFRED JUERGENS – Port Scene – signed, inscribed and dated 1894 – oil on board – 18½ x 15¾in.
(Robt. W. Skinner Inc.) **$750** **£493**

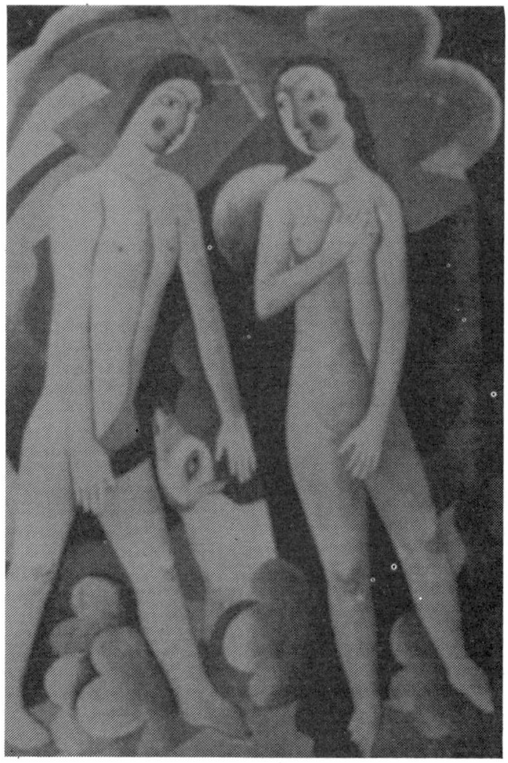

BELA KADAR – Adam And Eve – signed – watercolour on paper laid down – 87 x 59.5 cm.
(Phillips) **$4,185** **£2,700**

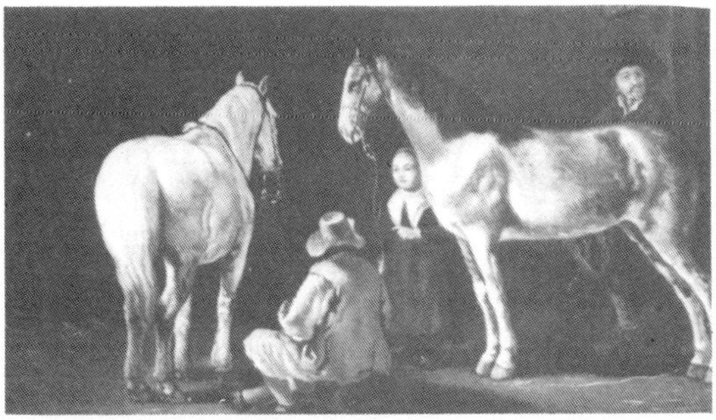

ABRAHAM KALRAET – Two Stable Hands Tending Their Horses In A Stall, Accompanied By A Girl – oil on panel – 11½ x 17¾in.
(Phillips) **$2,256** **£1,600**

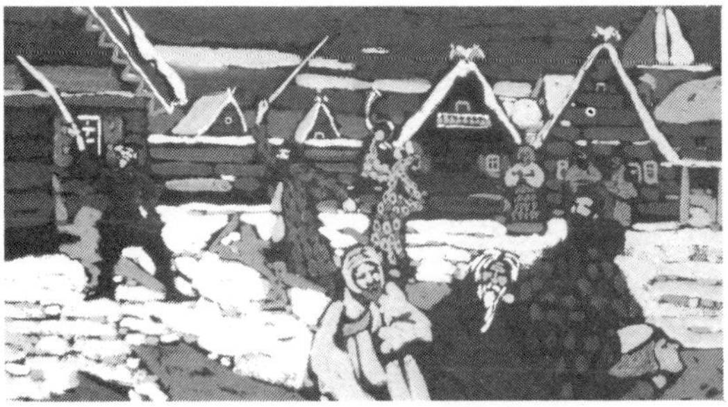

WASSILY KANDINSKY – Szene – signed – gouache on black paper – 11¼ x 19in.
(Christie's) **$110,880** **£77,000**

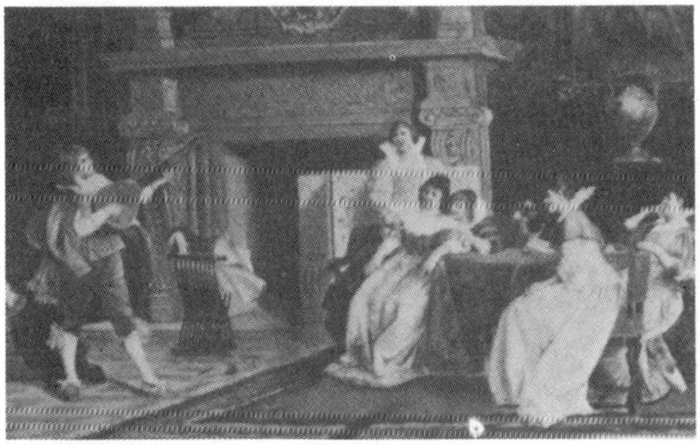

P. KARLY – A Musical Evening; and The Proposal – signed – on panel – 31 x 40cm.
(Phillips) **$2,265** **£1,500 Pair**

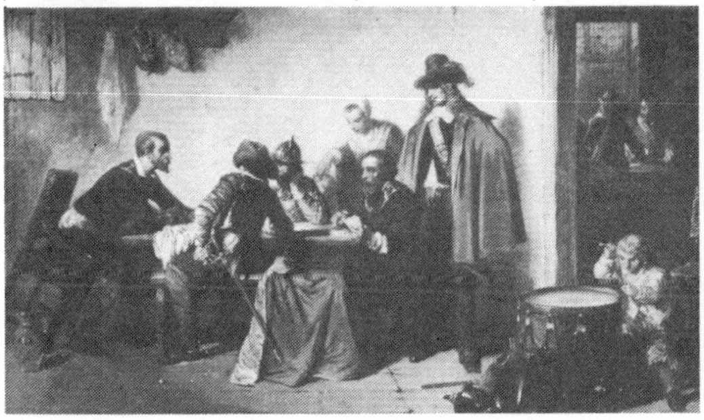

HERMAN TEN KATE – A Winning Hand – signed and dated '49 – on canvas – 31 x 47cm.
(Phillips) **$3,020** **£2,000**

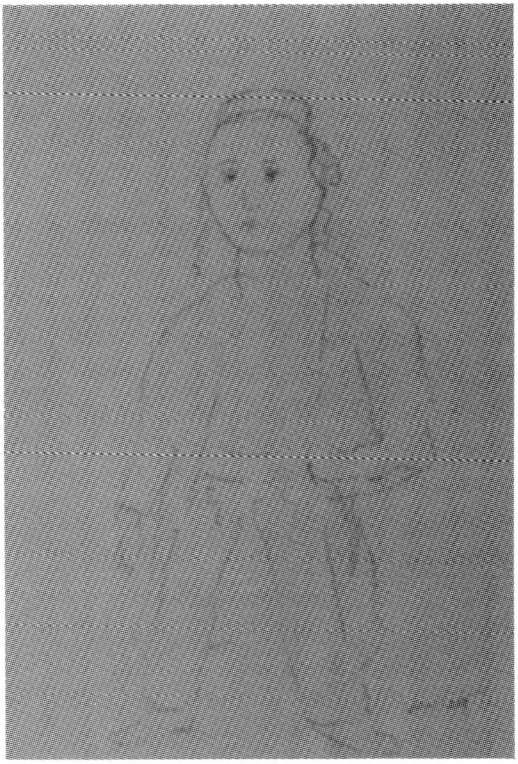

MANE KATZ – Yeshiva Boy – signed – pen and ink – 47 x 68cm.
(Phillips) **$2,015** **£1,300**

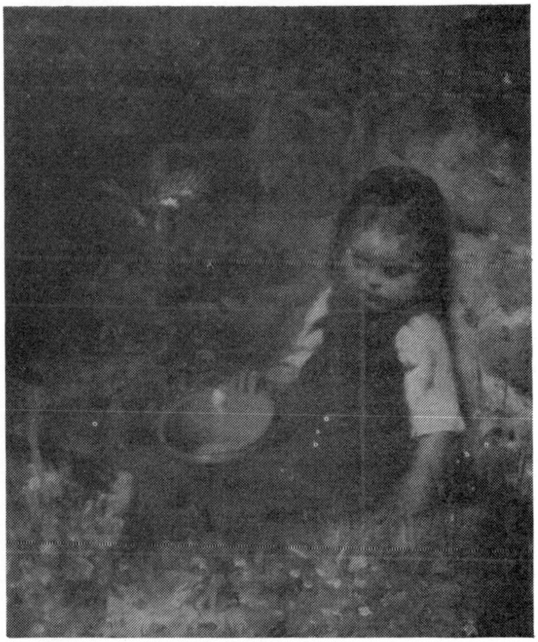

HERMANN KAULBACH – Asleep – signed – on panel – 7¼ x 5½in.
(Christie's) **$15,840** **£11,000**

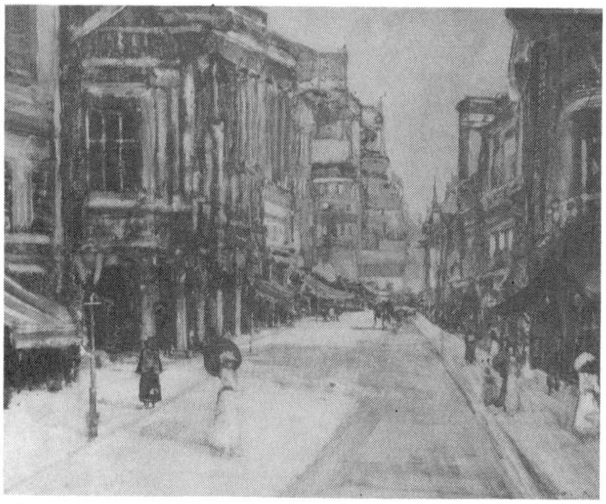

JAMES KAY – A Girl In A White Dress With A Red Parasol Standing In A Paris Street – signed – watercolour – 19 x 24in.
(Christie's) **$9,360** **£6,500**

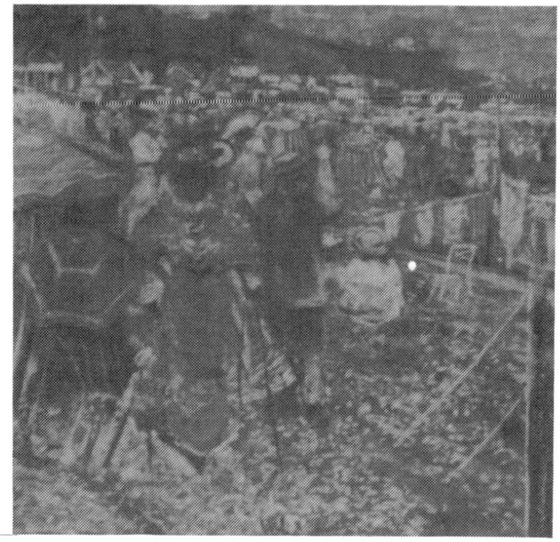

JAMES KAY – On The Beach, Bank Holiday – signed – pastel on brown paper – 49 x 59cm.
(Phillips) **$2,324** **£1,400**

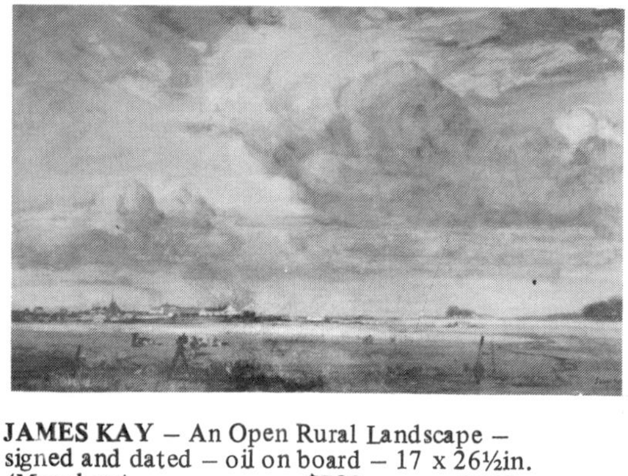

JAMES KAY – An Open Rural Landscape – signed and dated – oil on board – 17 x 26½in.
(Morphets) **$782** **£480**

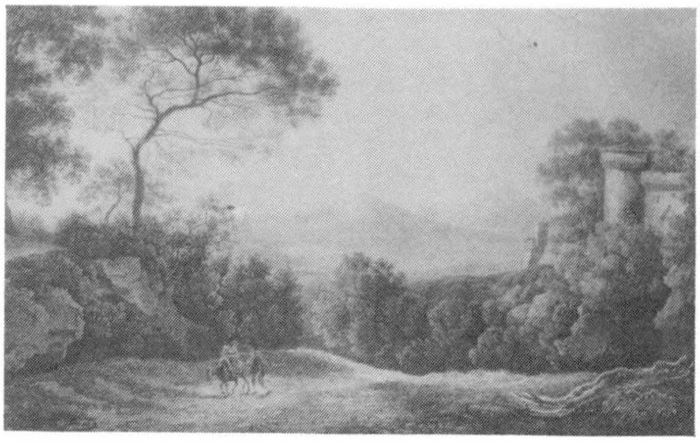

FRANZ KEISERMAN – Vue d'apres nature a Tivoli au soleil couchant – signed and dated 1813, and inscribed on the mount – pencil and watercolour – 15¾ x 22½in.
(Christie's) **$5,280** **£3,300**

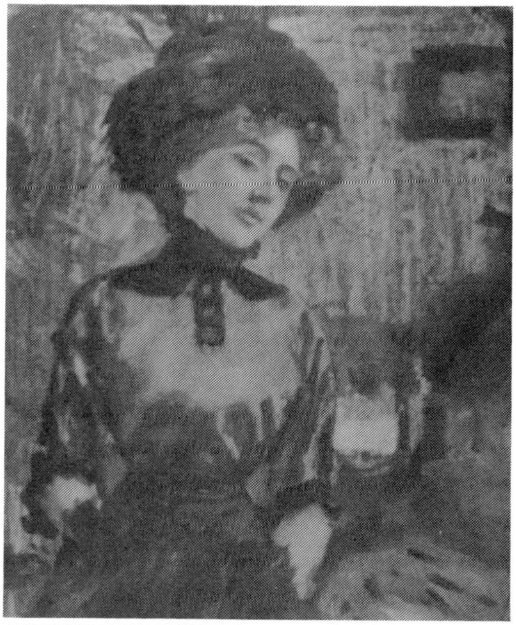

ALBERT VON KELLER – Portrait Of A Woman Stylishly Dressed – signed and dated 1911 – oil on panel – 13½ x 9¾in.
(Robt. W. Skinner Inc.) **$2,100** **£1,288**

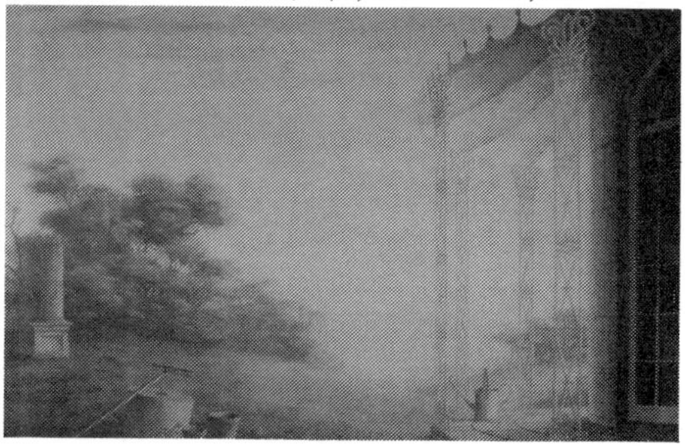

FELIX KELLY – The Pavilion – signed and dated '50 – oil on board – 41 x 36cm.
(Phillips) **$2,160** **£1,350**

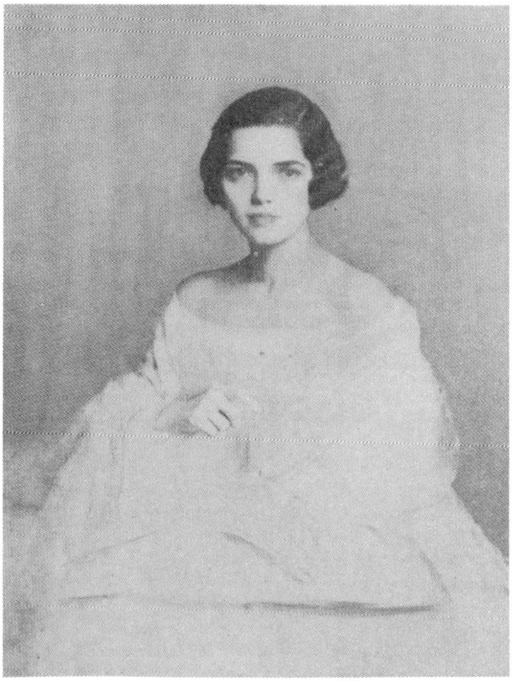

SIR GERALD KELLY – Portrait Of Frances MacGreggor, Half Length – oil on canvas – 40 x 30in.
(Christie's) **$1,573** **£1,100**

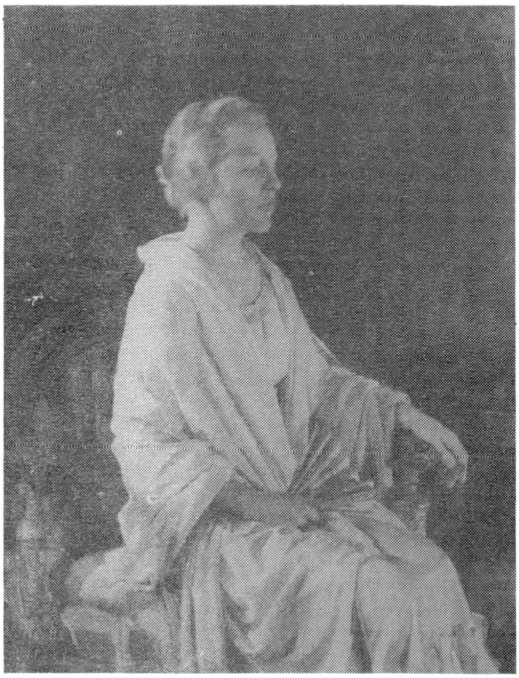

SIR GERALD KELLY – Jane XLVI (c) – inscribed – oil on canvas – 122 x 89cm.
(Phillips) **$6,080** **£3,800**

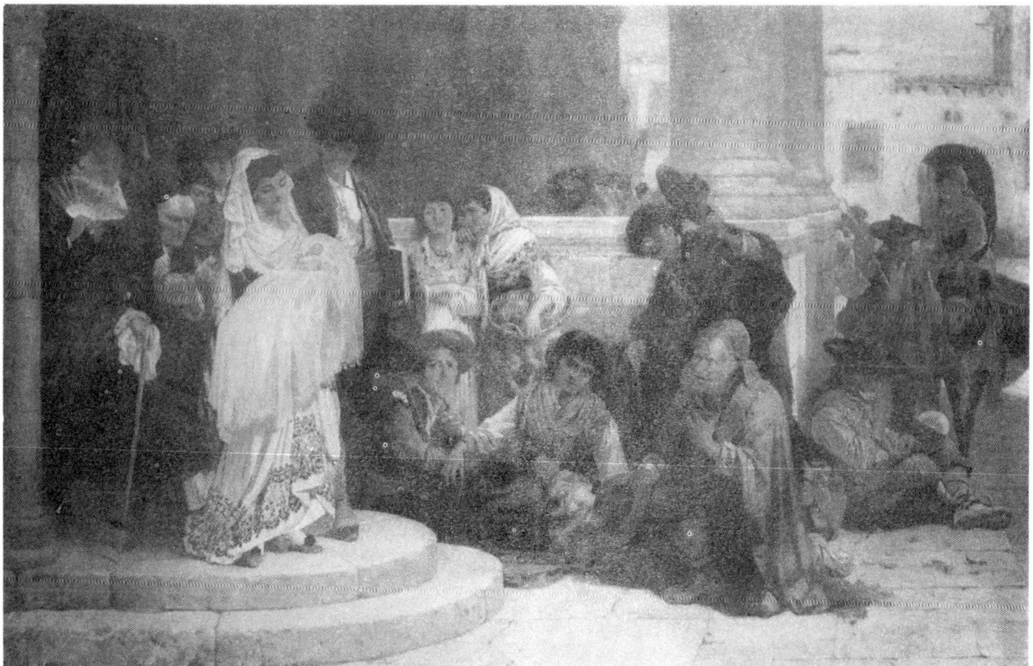

ROBERT KEMM – 'The Christening' – signed – oil on canvas – 42¼ x 60¼in. *(Phillips)*
$9,180 **£6,000**

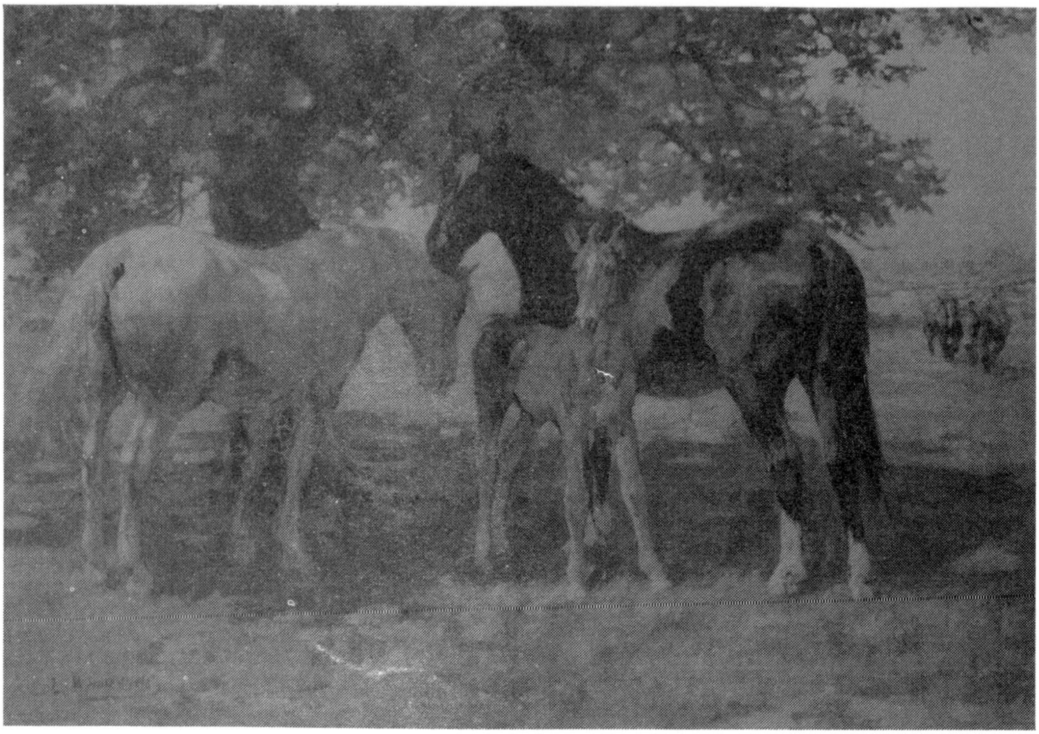

LUCY KEMP-WELCH – Mare And Foal In The Shade Of An Oak – signed – oil on canvas – 46 x 61cm.
(Phillips) **$20,000 £12,500**

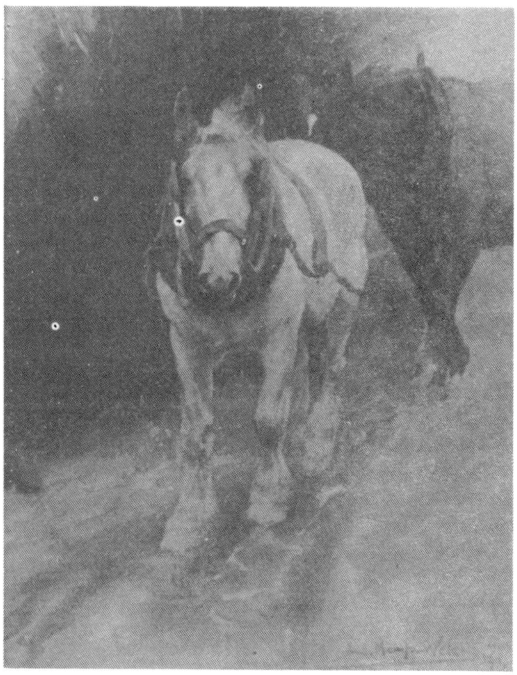

LUCY KEMP-WELCH – Two Shire Horses In Country Lane – signed and dated 1911 – watercolour – 11 x 8½in.
(Hobbs & Chambers) **$1,920 £1,200**

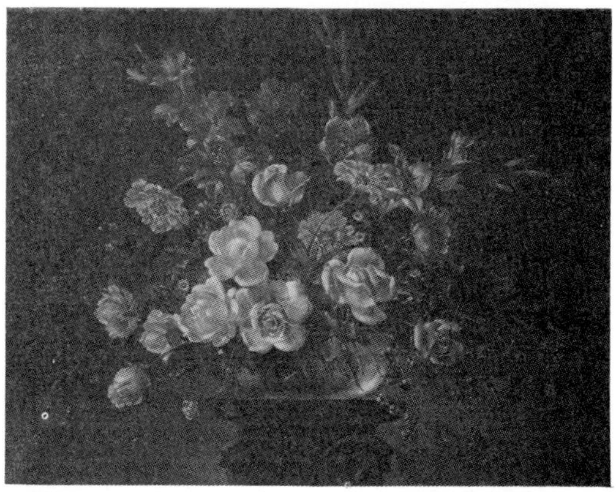

CECIL KENNEDY – Roses And Irises In A Bowl – signed – oil on canvas – 25 x 30in.
(Christie's) **$10,224 £7,150**

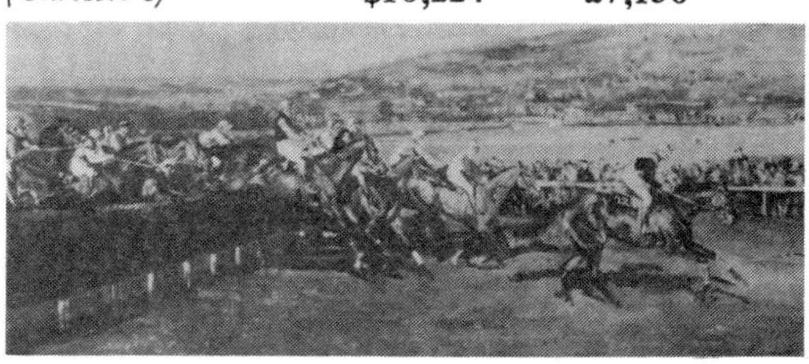

JOHN T. KENNEY – The Steeplechase – signed and dated '66 – oil on canvas – 51 x 91cm.
(Phillips) **$3,486 £2,100**

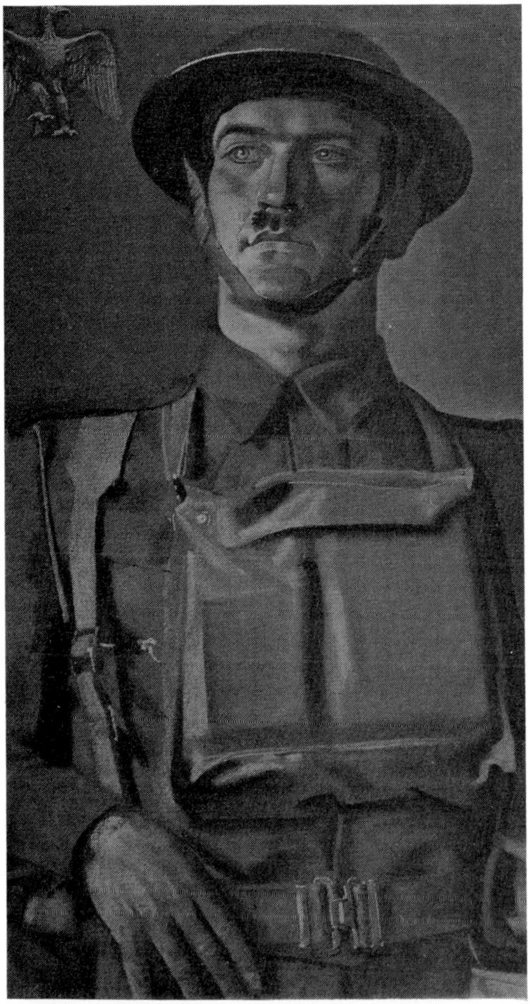

ERIC KENNINGTON – Sergeant-Major A. F. Sutton, D.C.M., The Essex Regiment – signed with initials and dated '42 – pastel – 30 x 20½in.
(Christie's) **$4,317** **£2,750**

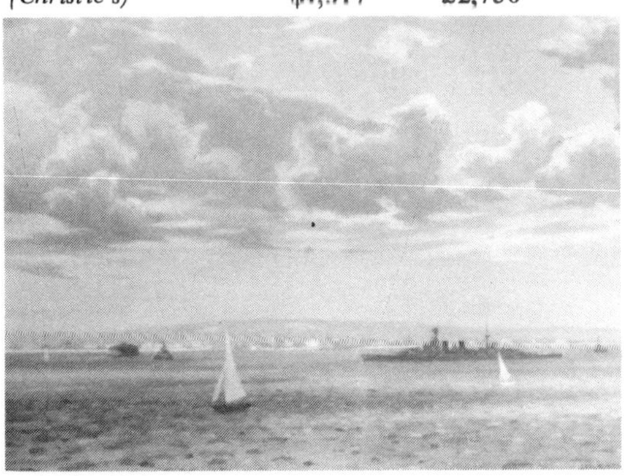

LESLIE KENT – Battleship Off Shore At Malta – signed – oil on board – 25 x 30in.
(Morphets) **$1,222** **£750**

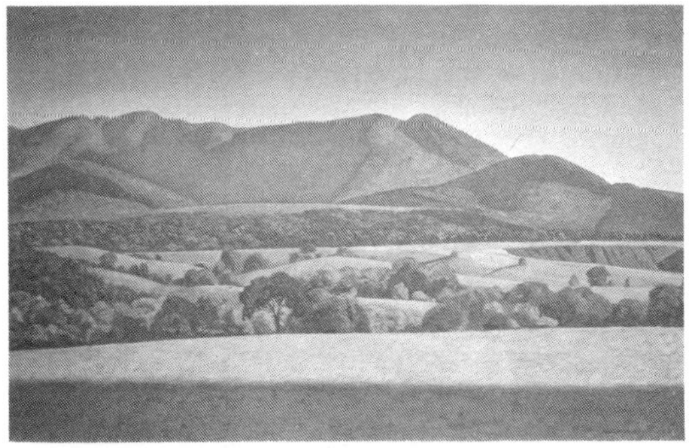

ROCKWELL KENT – Kelly's Basin, Jay Mountain – signed – oil on canvas – 27¾ x 44in.
(Christie's) **$46,200** **£32,478**

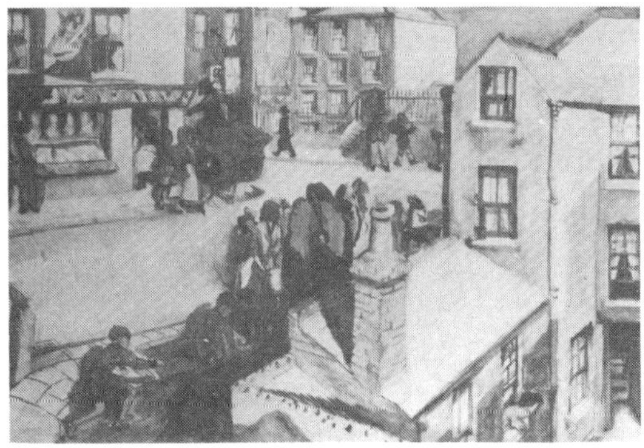

HARRY AARON KERNOFF – Irish Street Scene – pencil and black chalk over watercolour – 51 x 71cm.
(Phillips) **$795** **£520**

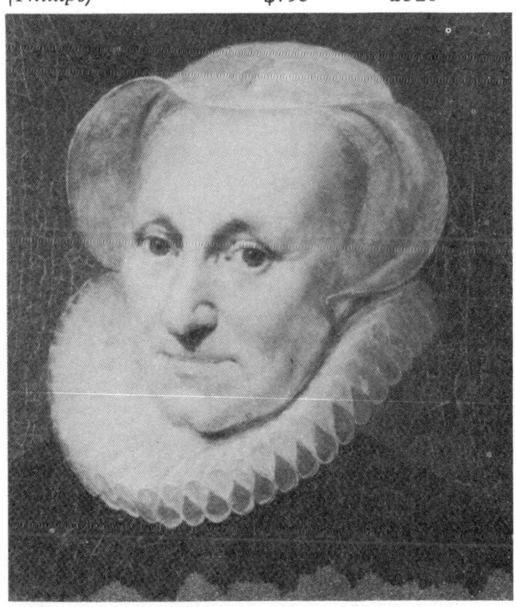

ADRIAEN THOMAS KEY, Circle of – Portrait Of A Woman, Bust Length, Wearing A Lace Cap – oil on panel – 15¾ x 11¾in.
(Phillips) **$874** **£620**

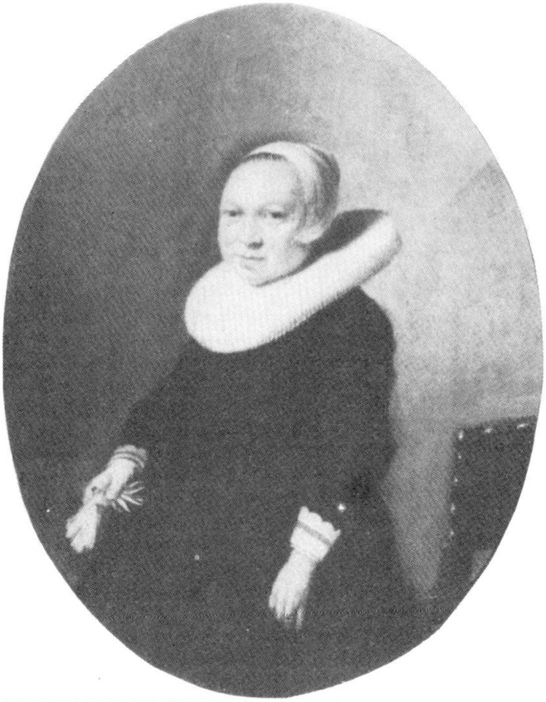

THOMAS DE KEYSER, Attributed to – Portrait Of A Woman, Three-Quarter Length, Standing Beside A Chair, Holding A Pair Of Gloves – oil on panel – 12 x 9½in.
(Phillips) **$1,410** **£1,000**

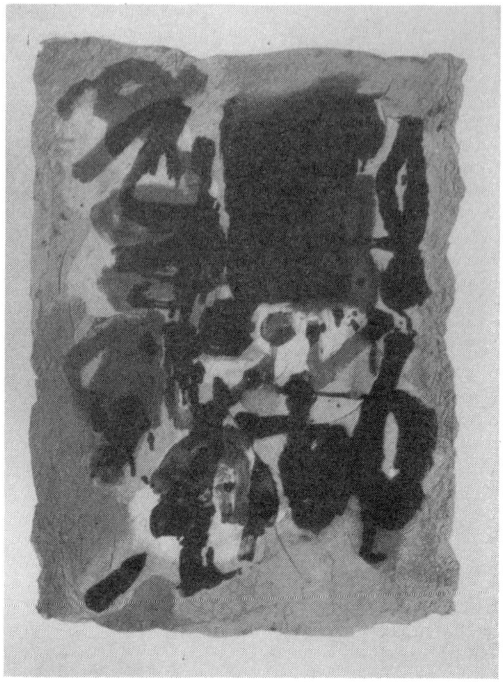

LADISLAS KIJNO – Untitled – signed – tempera, black ink and coloured inks on brown crumpled paper mounted on paper – 22 x 15½in.
(Christie's) **$563** **£352**

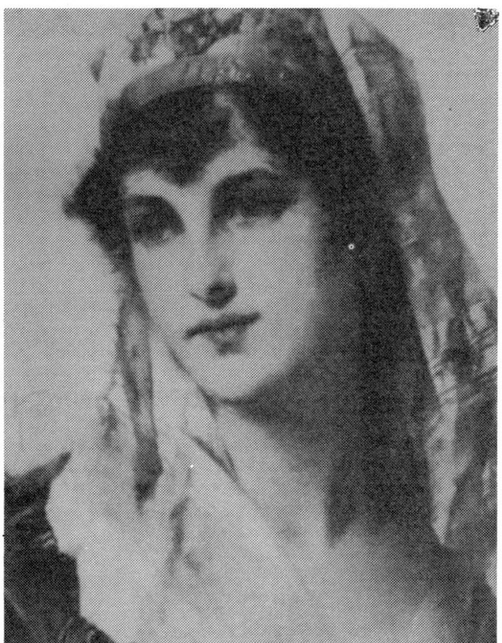

CONRAD KIESEL – The Favourite – signed – oil on panel – 33 x 25cm.
(Phillips) **$2,672** **£1,600**

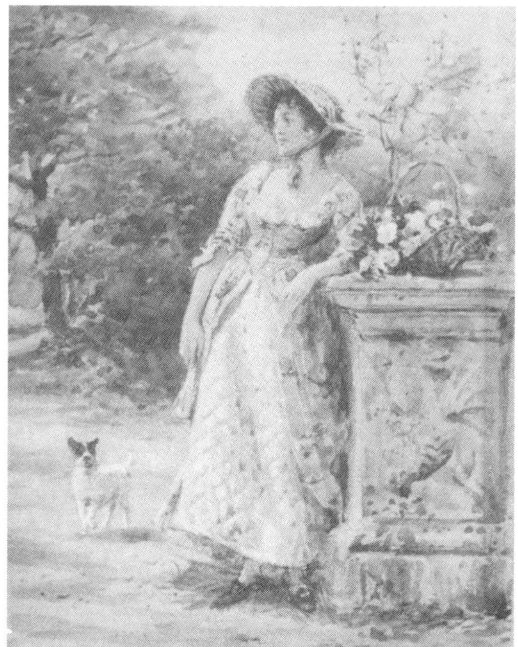

GEORGE GOODWIN KILBURNE – Gathering Flowers – signed – watercolour heightened with bodycolour on brown paper – 6½ x 4¾in.
(Christie's) **$1,296** **£864**

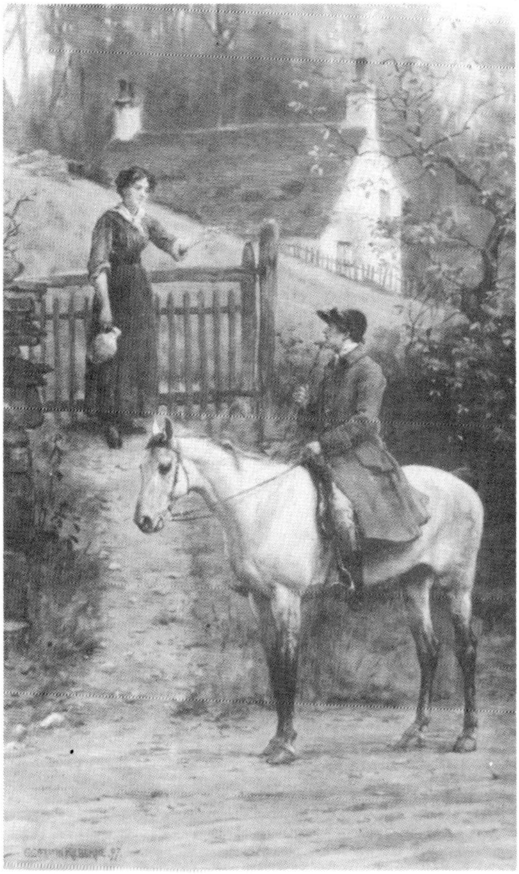

GEORGE GOODWIN KILBURNE – 'Where Are The Hounds?' – signed and dated '97 – oil on canvas – 12¼ x 7½in.
(Phillips) **$2,907** **£1,900**

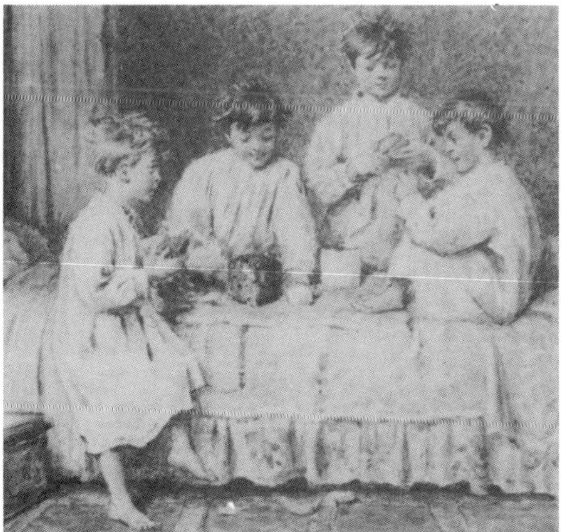

GEORGE GOODWIN KILBURNE – The Midnight Feast – pencil and watercolour – 3¼ x 3¼in.
(Christie's) **$4,032** **£2,860**

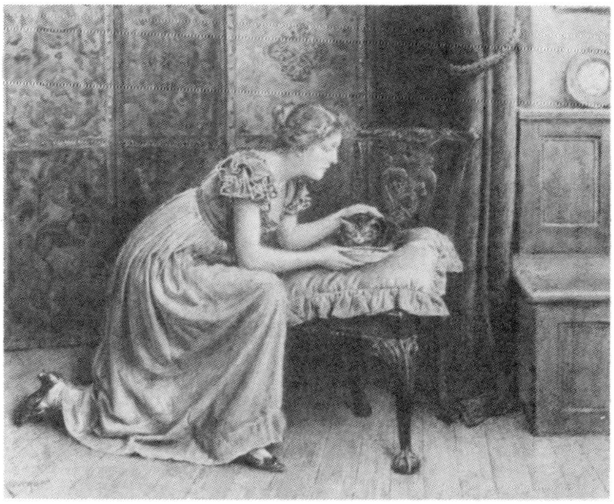

GEORGE GOODWIN KILBURNE – The Invalid – signed, and inscribed on the reverse – watercolour on card – 10¼ x 13½in.
(Christie's) **$891** **£594**

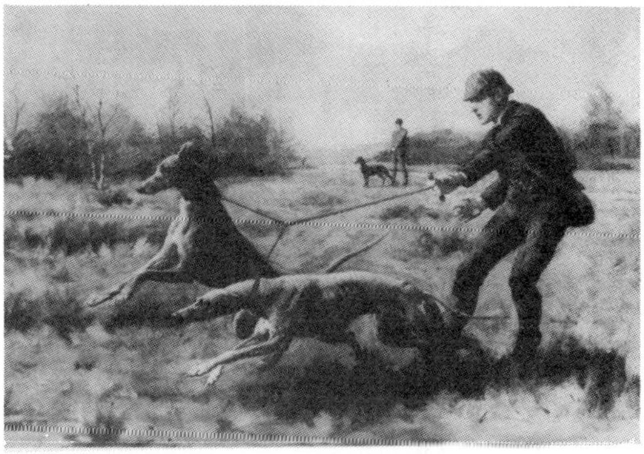

GEORGE GOODWIN KILBURNE – Greyhounds On The Leash – signed and dated – oil – 20 x 30in.
(Woolley & Wallis) **$4,371** **£3,100**

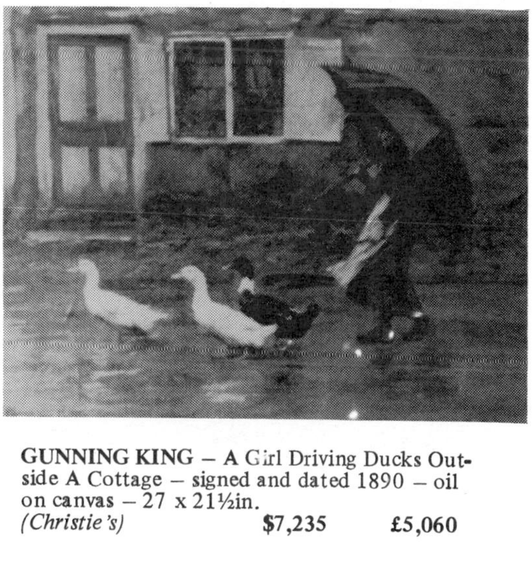

GUNNING KING – A Girl Driving Ducks Outside A Cottage – signed and dated 1890 – oil on canvas – 27 x 21½in.
(Christie's) **$7,235** **£5,060**

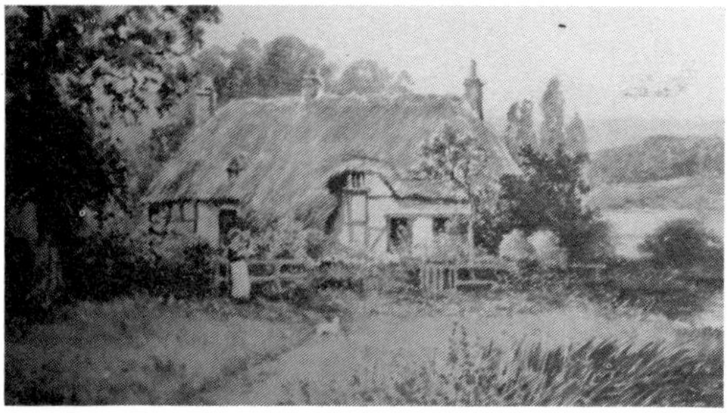

HENRY JOHN YEEND KING – A Woman And Child Beside A Country Cottage; and Farmer On A Country Lane Beside A Cottage – signed – pencil and watercolour, the second heightened with white – 9¼ x 14¼in.
(Christie's) **$1,551** **£1,100 Pair**

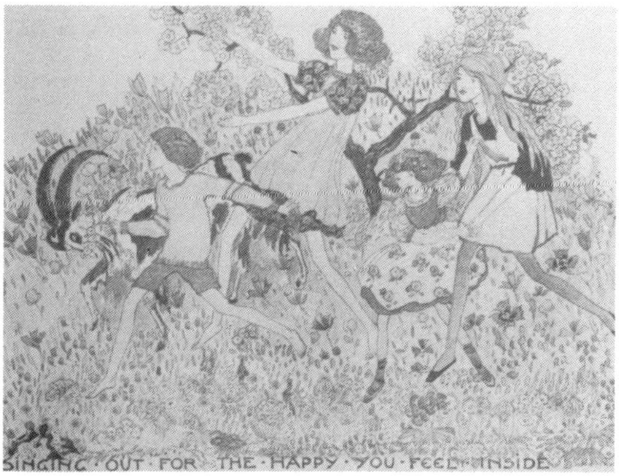

JESSIE MARION KING – Singing Out For The Happy You Feel Inside – signed and inscribed – pen and black ink and watercolour on vellum – 12 x 14in.
(Christie's) **$1,368** **£950**

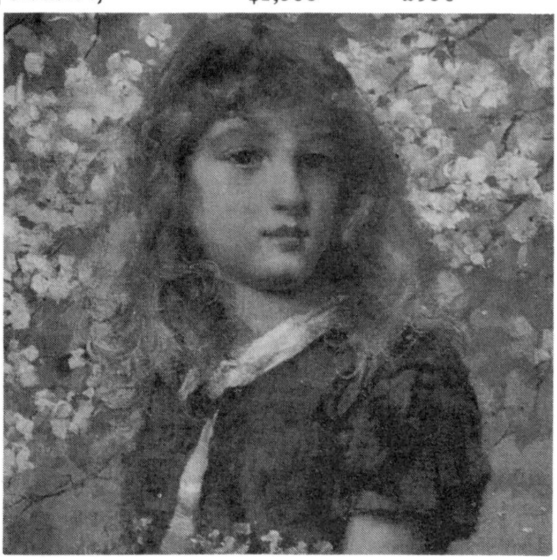

JOHN YEEND KING – Springtime – signed – oil on canvas – 18 x 14½in.
(Christie's) **$3,454** **£2,200**

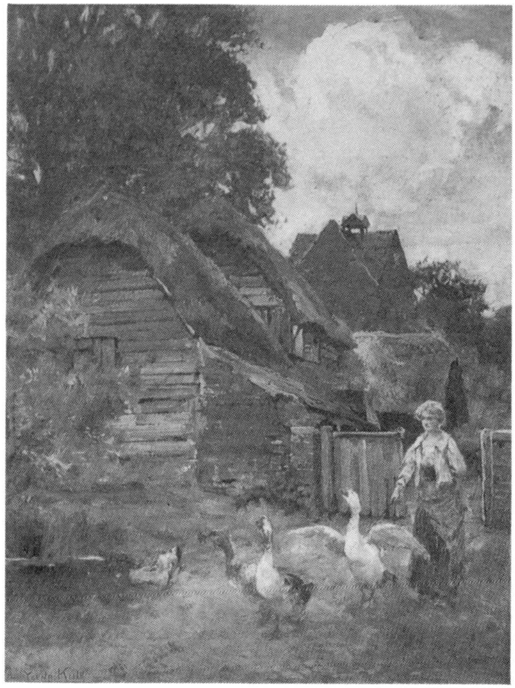

JOHN YEEND KING – Intruders – signed – oil on board – 24 x 18in.
(Christie's) **$2,044** **£1,430**

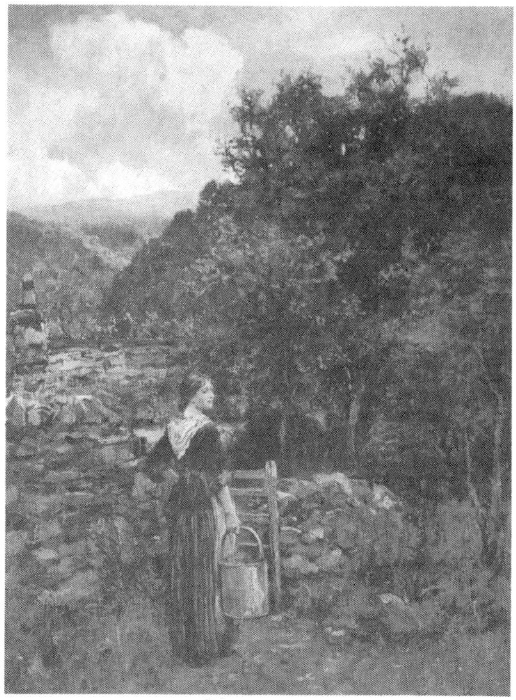

JOHN YEEND KING – A Young Girl Standing Outside A Cottage Holding A Pail – signed – oil on canvas – 23½ x 17½in.
(Christie's) **$2,359** **£1,650**

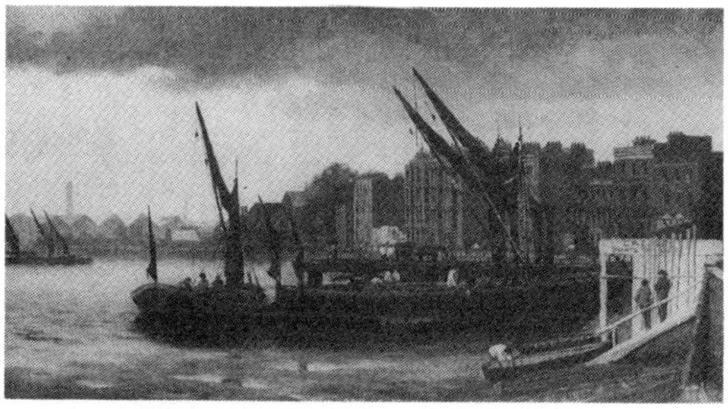

WILLIAM GUNNING KING – The Chelsea Ferry – signed with monogram and dated '78 – 9 x 14in.
(Christie's) **$3,564** **£2,376**

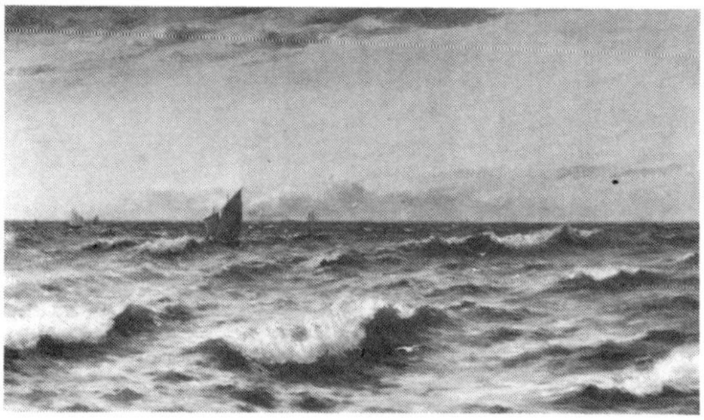

WILLIAM J. KING – 'Evening, North Sea' – signed – oil on canvas – 20 x 30in.
(Biddle & Webb) **$749** **£460**

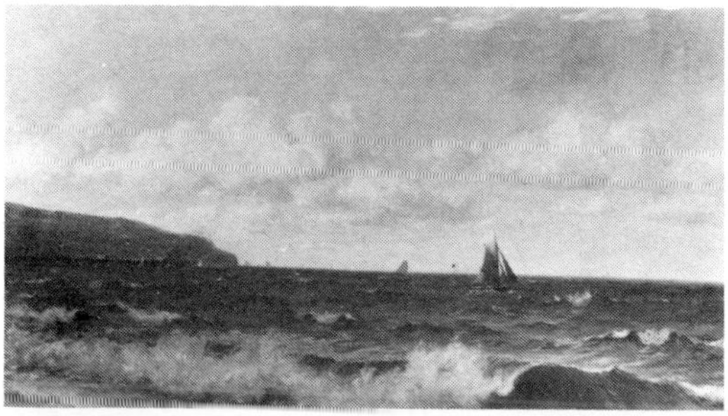

WILLIAM J. KING – 'Great Orme, Llandudno' – signed – oil on canvas – 24 x 34in.
(Biddle & Webb) **$1,222** **£750**

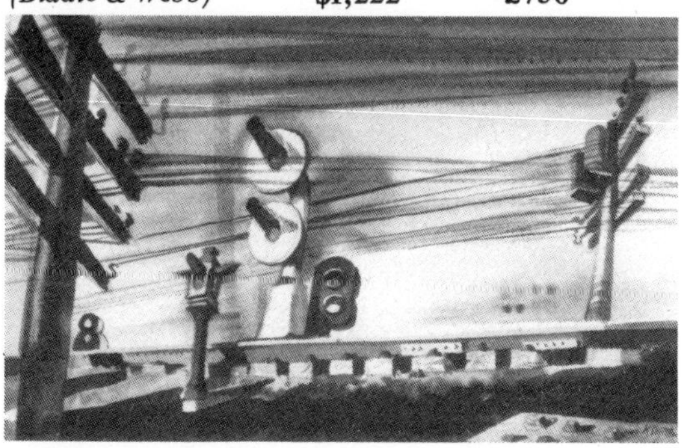

DONG KINGMAN – Train Tracks – signed – watercolour on paper – 19¾ x 29¾in.
(Christie's) **$1,430** **£1,005**

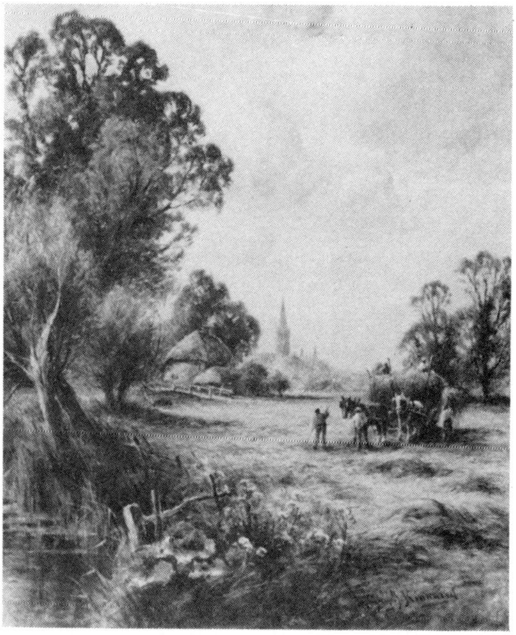

HENRY JOHN KINNAIRD – Near Salisbury: Haymakers In A Field Near A River – signed – watercolour heightened with white – 20 x 14¾in.
(Christie's) **$3,102** **£2,200**

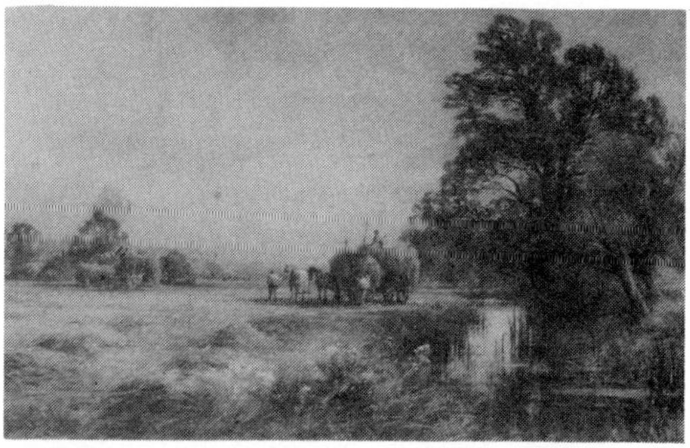

HENRY JOHN KINNAIRD – A Hayfield Near Bury, Sussex – signed and inscribed – watercolour heightened with white – 13½ x 20½in.
(Christie's) **$3,286** **£1,980**

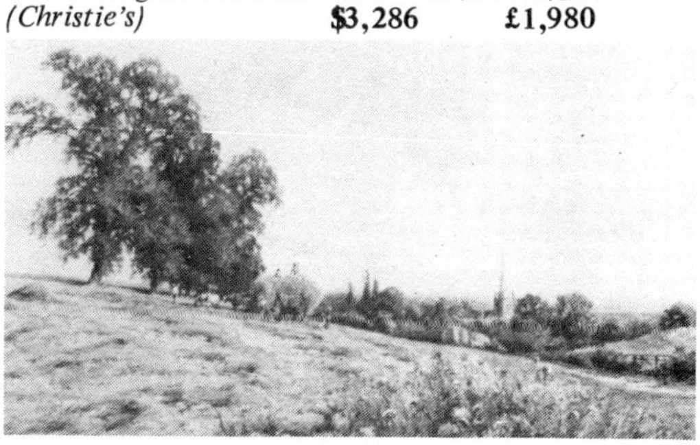

HENRY JOHN KINNAIRD – A Hayfield In Essex – signed and inscribed – watercolour heightened with white – 13½ x 21½in.
(Christie's) **$2,481** **£1,760**

KIRCHNER

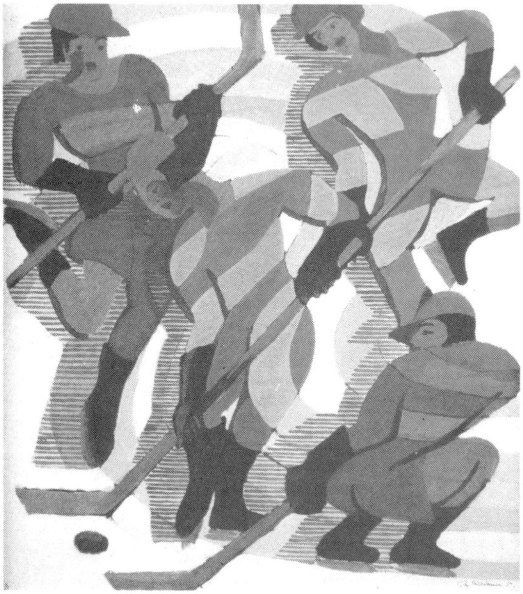

ERNST LUDWIG KIRCHNER – Eishockeyspieler – signed and dated '34 – oil on canvas – 31½ x 27½in.
(Christie's) **$38,016 £26,400**

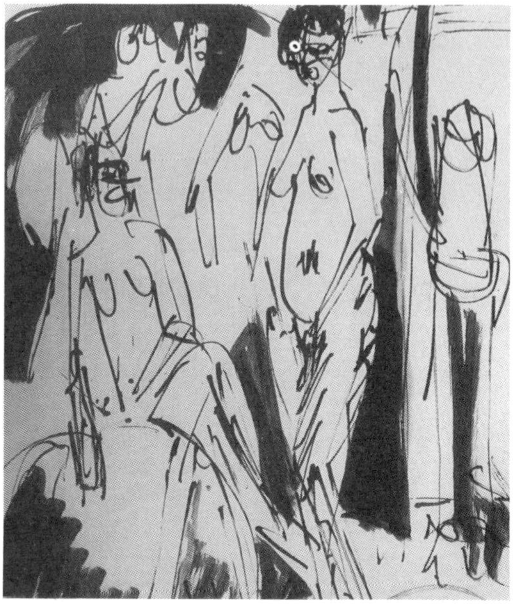

ERNST LUDWIG KIRCHNER – Drei Frauenakte – brush, pen and black ink on paper – 19½ x 14¼in.
(Christie's) **$14,256 £9,900**

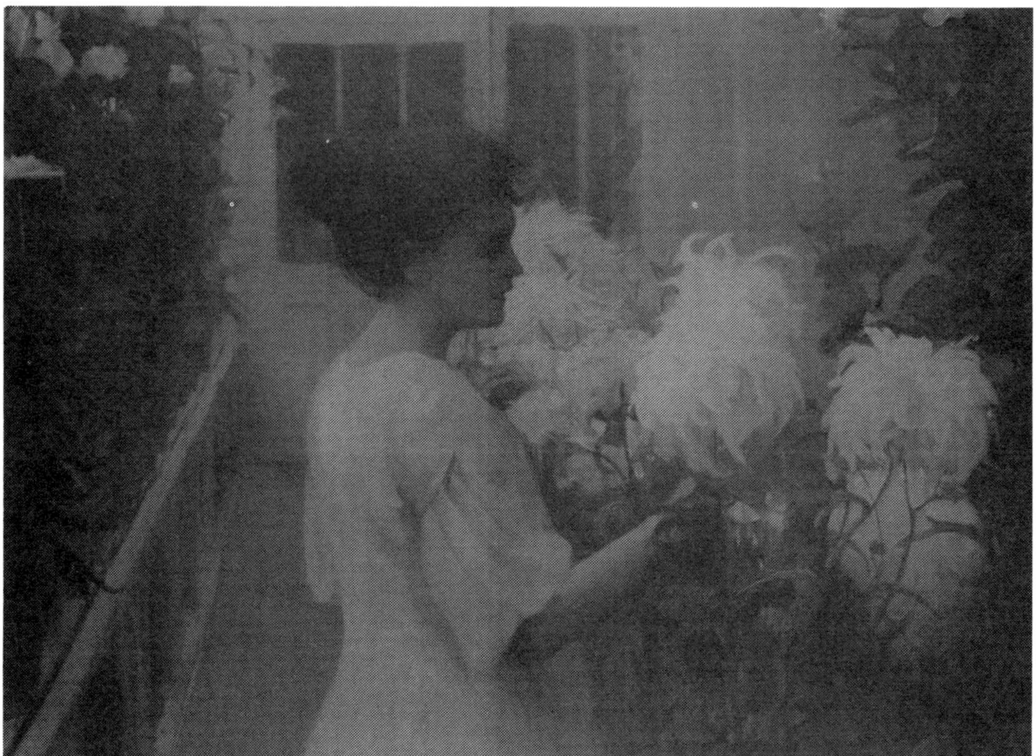

ETHEL KIRKPATRICK – Chrysanthemums – signed – oil on canvas – 43 x 56cm. *(Phillips)*
$6,400 £4,000

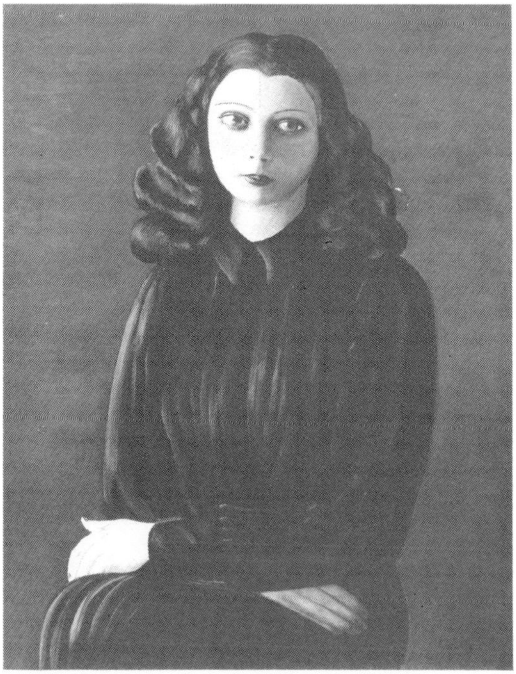

MOISE KISLING – Portrait de jeune Femme brune – signed – oil on canvas – 36½ x 27½in.
(Christie's) **$110,880** **£77,000**

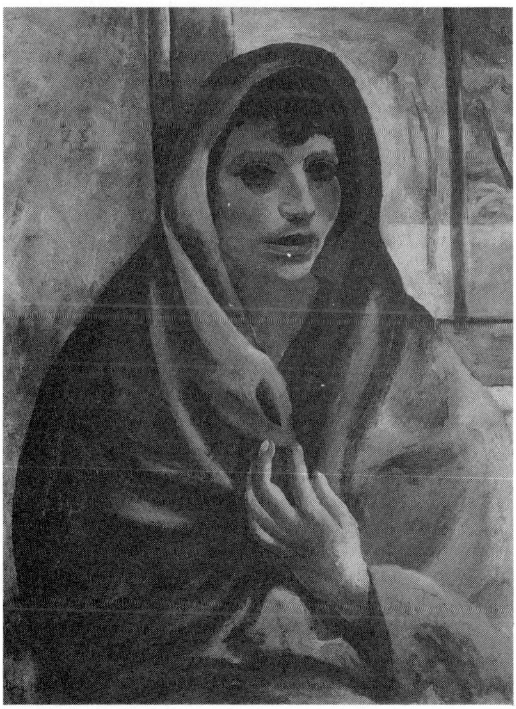

MOISE KISLING – La Fille au Chale vert – signed and dated 1919 – oil on canvas – 32 x 25¾in.
(Christie's) **$67,969** **£40,700**

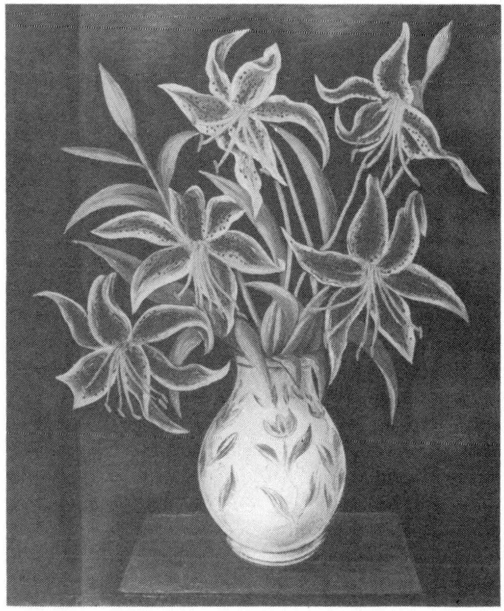

MOISE KISLING – Vase de Lis – signed – oil on canvas – 25½ x 21in.
(Christie's) **$101,035** **£60,500**

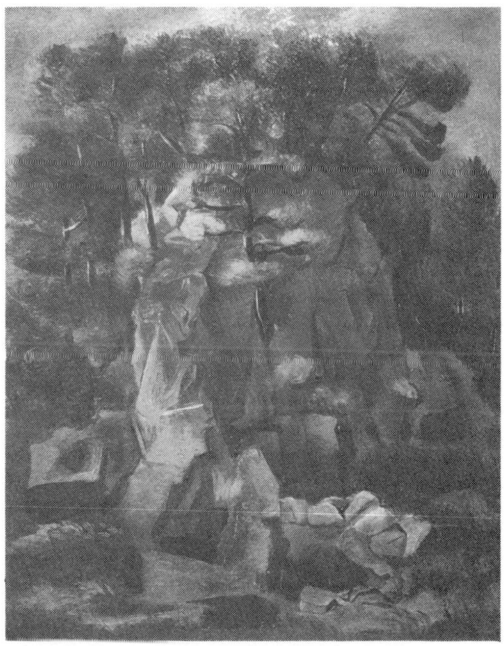

MOISE KISLING – Rochers rouges a Sanary – signed – oil on canvas – 21¾ x 18in.
(Christie's) **$24,640** **£15,400**

MOISE KISLING – Nu sur le Divan – signed – oil on canvas – 15 x 21½in.
(Christie's) **$55,110** **£33,000**

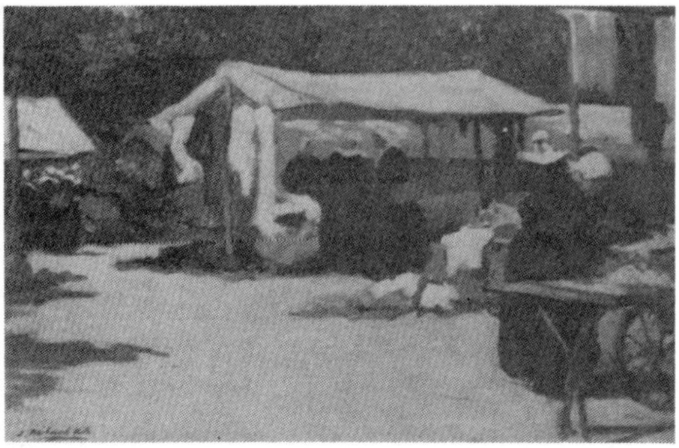

JOSEPH MILNER KITE – A Breton Market – signed – oil on canvas – 10½ x 16in.
(Christie's) **$1,415** **£990**

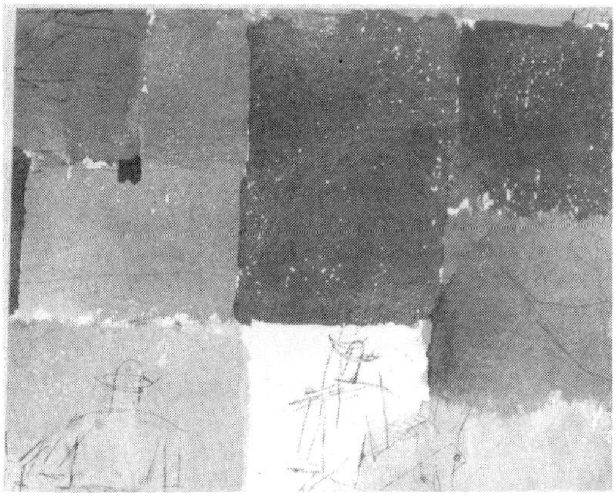

PAUL KLEE – Composition With Figures – signed, dated 1915 – watercolour, pen and ink on paper – 4¼ x 5¼in.
(Christie's) **$42,240** **£26,400**

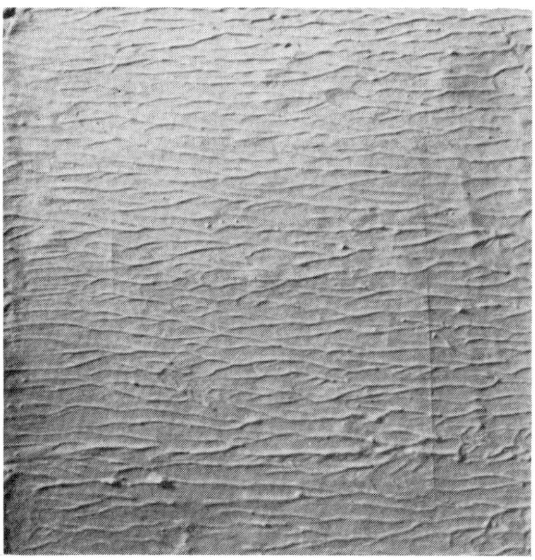

YVES KLEIN – Monochrome – IKB on paper mounted on paperboard – 8¼ x 7in.
(Christie's) **$28,160** **£17,600**

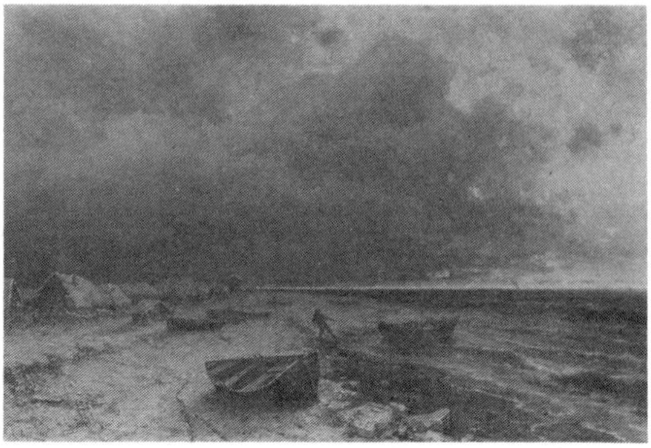

JULIUS VON KLEVER – The Isle Of Nargoe, Finland – signed and dated 1912 – on canvas – 90 x 135 cm.
(Phillips) **$6,946** **£4,600**

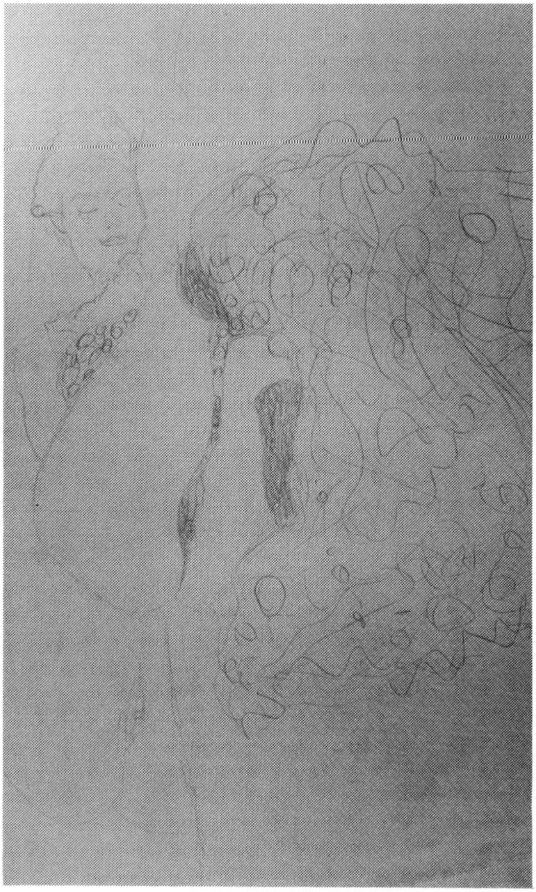

GUSTAV KLIMT – Liegender Halbakt – signed – pencil on paper – 14½ x 22in.
(Christie's) **$39,600** **£27,500**

JOHANN BERNARD KLOMBECK – A Wooded River Landscape With Figures And Cattle On A Path – signed and dated 1859 – 29¼ x 35in.
(Christie's) **$15,840** **£11,000**

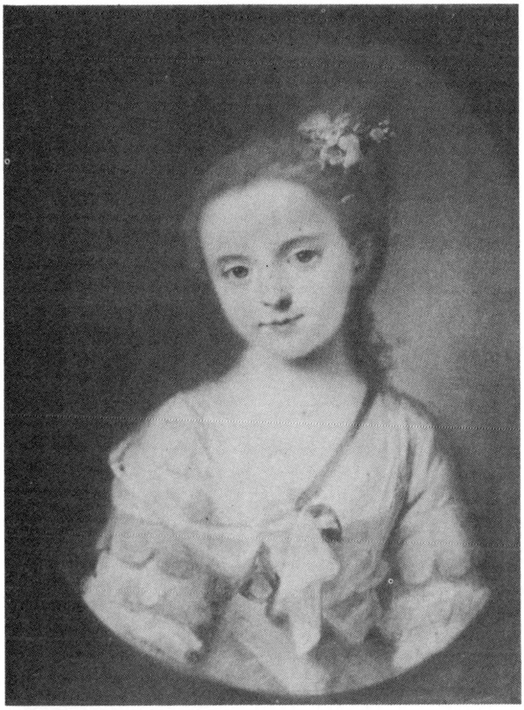

GEORGE KNAPTON, Attributed to – Portrait Of A Girl, Half Length, In White Dress; and Portrait Of A Boy, Half Length, In Blue Coat And Lilac Waistcoat – pastel – 23½ x 17½in.
(Christie's) **$7,452** **£4,968 Pair**

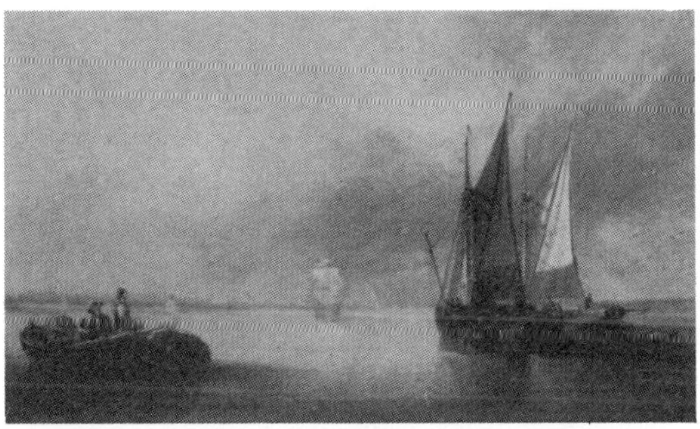

WILLIAM ADOLPHUS KNELL – Shipping Off-Shore In A Calm – signed with initials and dated 1848 – oil on panel – 9¾ x 14in.
(Christie's) **$6,514** **£4,620**

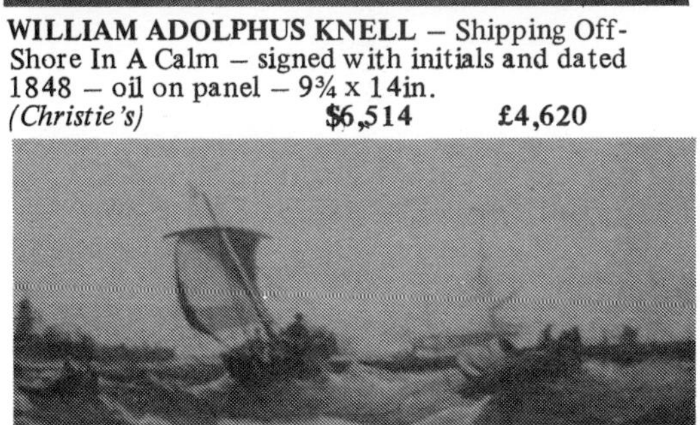

WILLIAM CALCOTT KNELL – Off The Kentish Coast – signed – oil on canvas – 21½ x 37½in.
(Christie's) **$1,972** **£1,210**

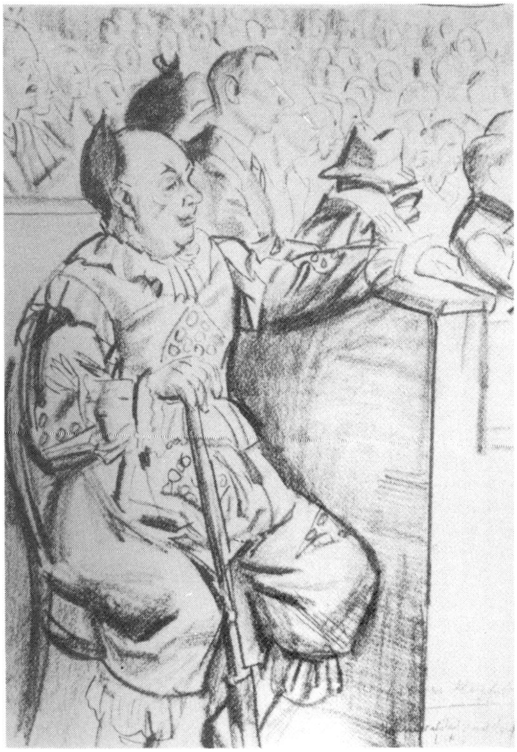

DAME LAURA KNIGHT – Whimsical's Last Year At Olympia – signed, signed with initials and inscribed – black chalk – 35.5 x 26cm.
(Phillips) **$2,754** **£1,800**

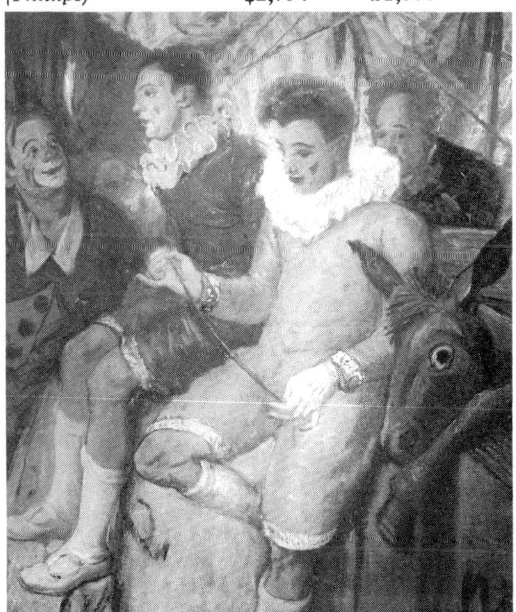

DAME LAURA KNIGHT – Circus Clowns – signed and dated '34 – oil on canvas – 32 x 27in.
(Christie's) **$20,724** **£13,200**

KNIGHT

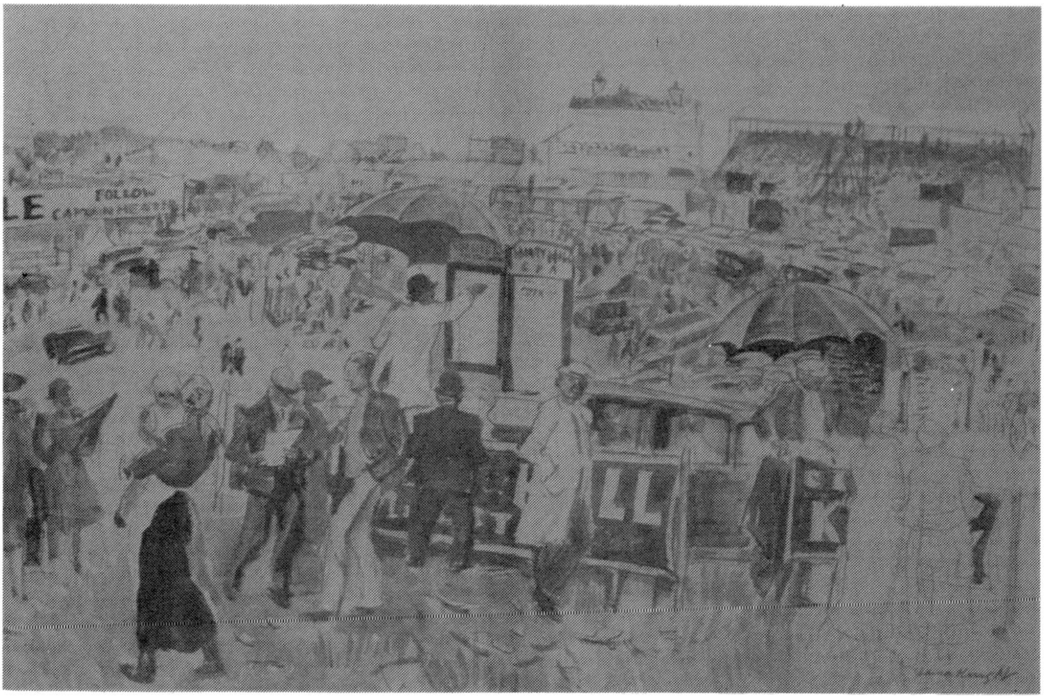

DAME LAURA KNIGHT – Between Races At Epsom – signed – pencil and watercolour – 34 x 48cm.
(Phillips) **$11,200 £7,000**

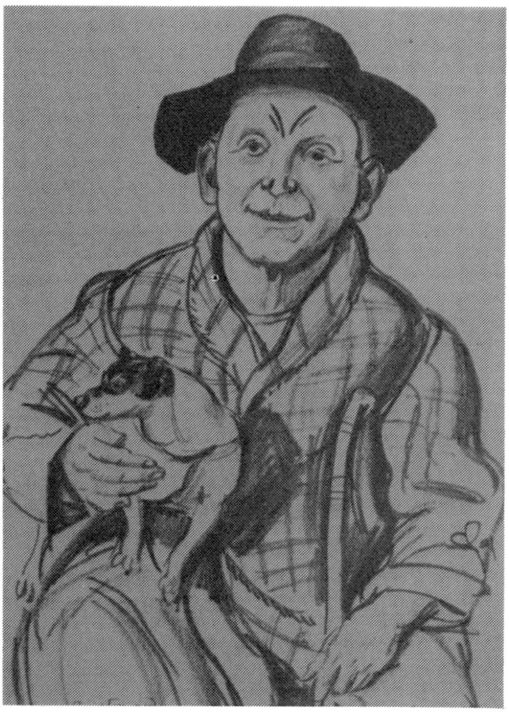

DAME LAURA KNIGHT – Joe Craston And His 'Buffer' – signed and inscribed – black chalk – 36 x 26cm.
(Phillips) **$3,486 £2,100**

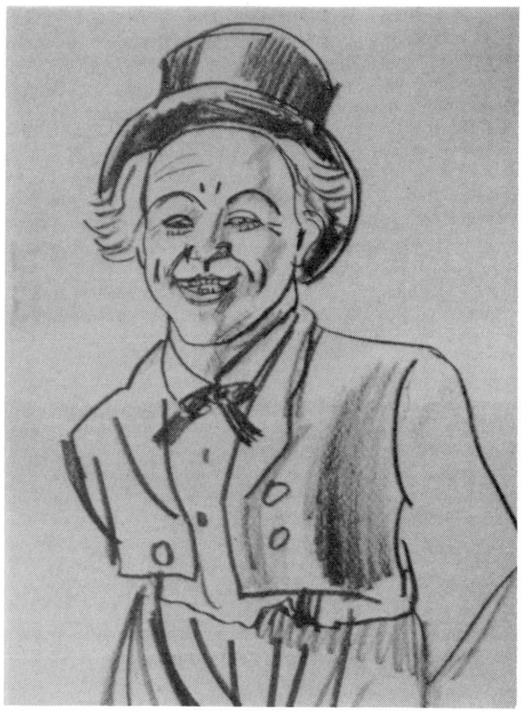

DAME LAURA KNIGHT – The Clown – signed – black chalk – 35 x 25cm.
(Phillips) **$535 £350**

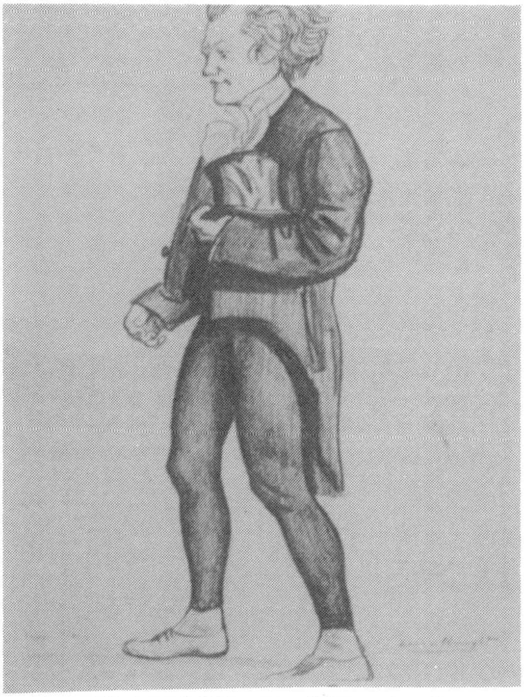

DAME LAURA KNIGHT – Max Wall – signed and inscribed – black chalk – 36.5 x 26cm.
(Phillips) **$459** **£300**

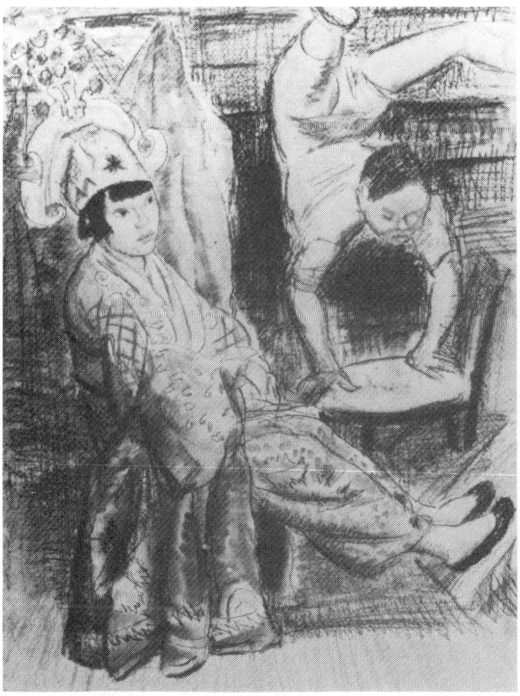

DAME LAURA KNIGHT – A Last Minute Practice – signed and dated 1960 – black chalk and watercolour – 58 x 38cm.
(Phillips) **$2,142** **£1,400**

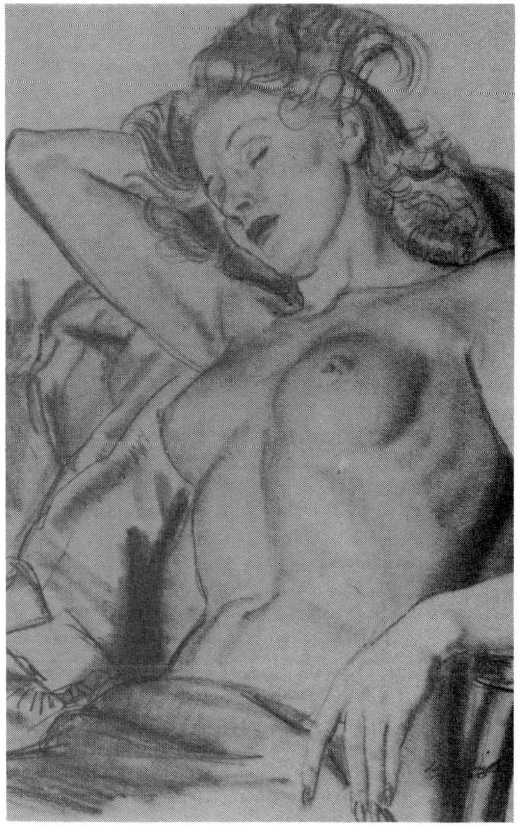

DAME LAURA KNIGHT – Sleeping Nude – signed – black crayon – 22½ x 15¼in.
(Christie's) **$6,562** **£4,180**

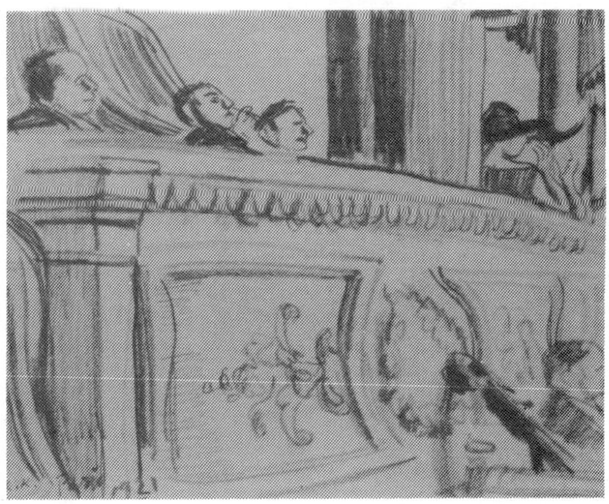

DAME LAURA KNIGHT – Folies Bergeres – signed with initials, inscribed and dated 1921 – black crayon – 20 x 26cm.
(Phillips) **$3,213** **£2,100**

DAME LAURA KNIGHT – Circus Horses And Attendant – signed – black chalk – 35 x 25cm.
(Phillips) **$489** **£320**

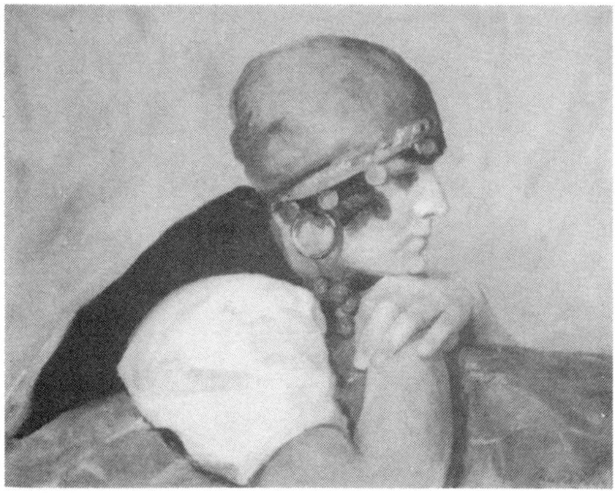

DAME LAURA KNIGHT – Head And Shoulders Portrait Of A Gypsy Lady In Red Scarf And Earrings Resting Her Chin On Crossed Hands – signed – oil on canvas – 40 x 51cm.
(W. H. Lane & Son) **$4,980 £3,000**

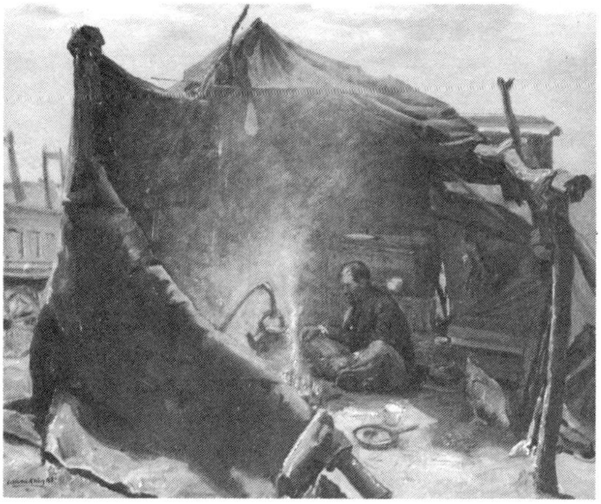

DAME LAURA KNIGHT – His Only Home – signed – oil on canvas – 25 x 30in.
(Christie's) **$6,292 £4,400**

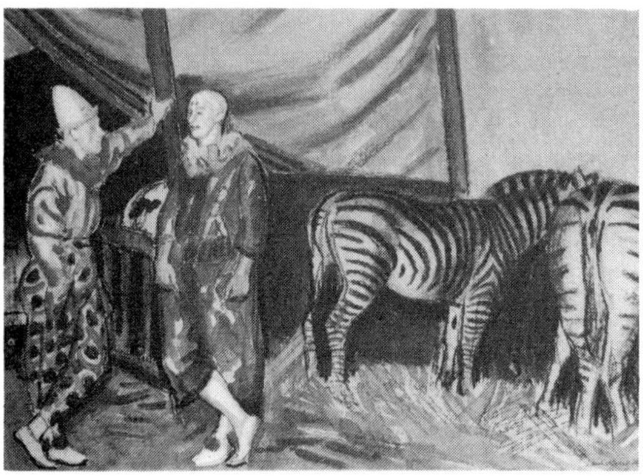

DAME LAURA KNIGHT – Two Clowns And Two Zebras – signed – black chalk and watercolour heightened with white – 38 x 56cm.
(Phillips) **$8,520 £6,000**

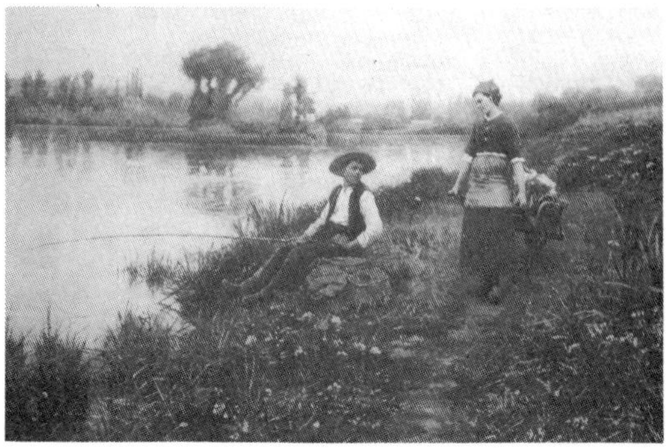

DANIEL RIDGWAY KNIGHT – A Passing Conversation – signed and dated '85 – oil on canvas – 25¾ x 32in.
(Christie's) **$28,600 £20,105**

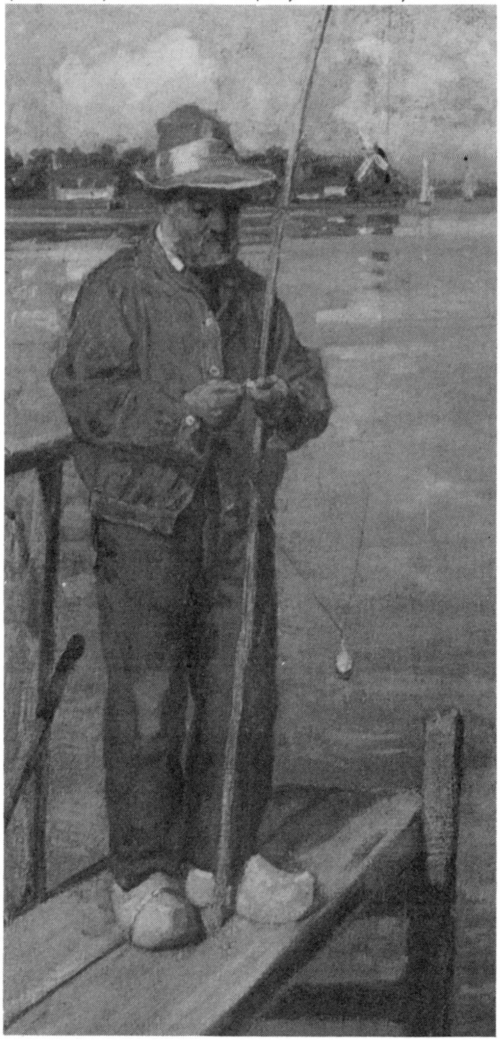

HAROLD KNIGHT – The Dutch Fisherman – signed and dated '95 – oil on canvas – 93 x 42cm.
(Phillips) **$3,976 £2,800**

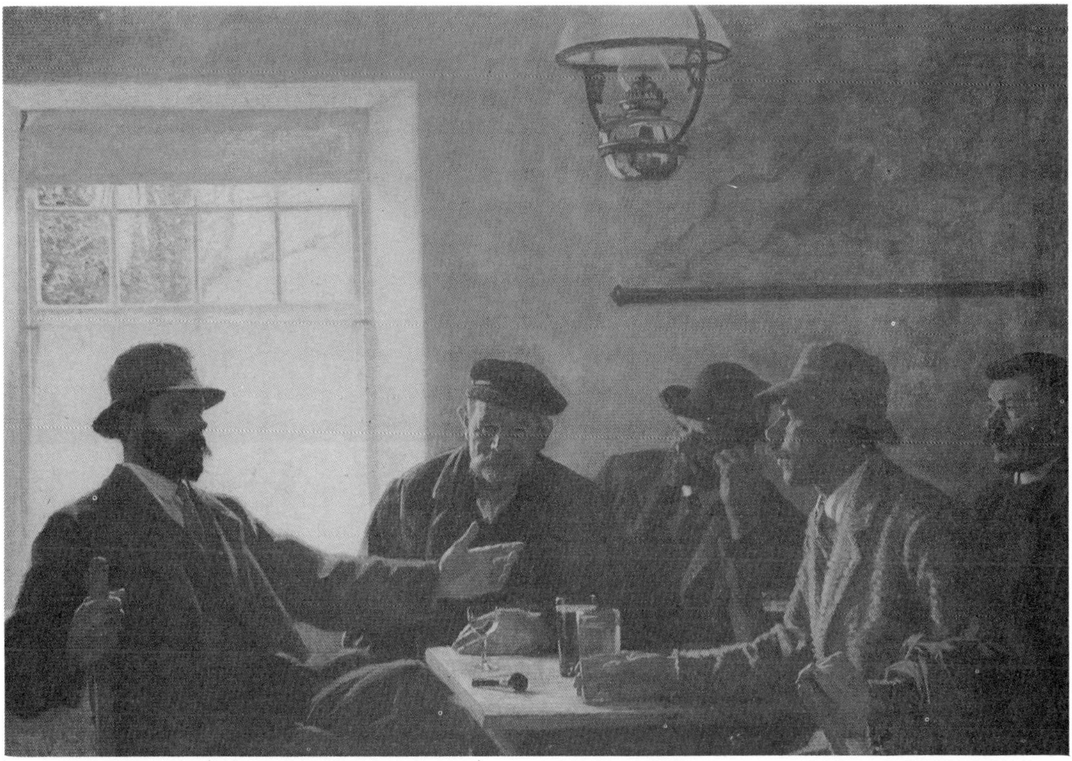

HAROLD KNIGHT – The Council, Portrait Group 1916 – signed – oil on canvas – 150 x 183cm.
(Phillips) **$78,100 £55,000**

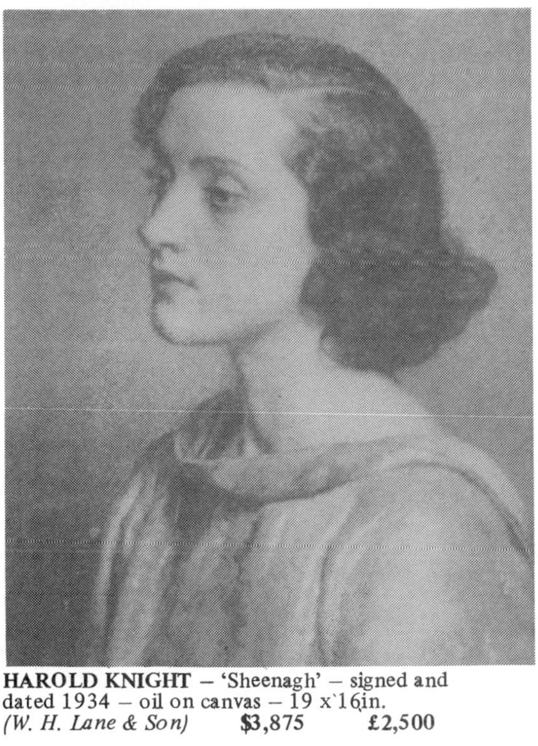

HAROLD KNIGHT – 'Sheenagh' – signed and dated 1934 – oil on canvas – 19 x 16in.
(W. H. Lane & Son) **$3,875 £2,500**

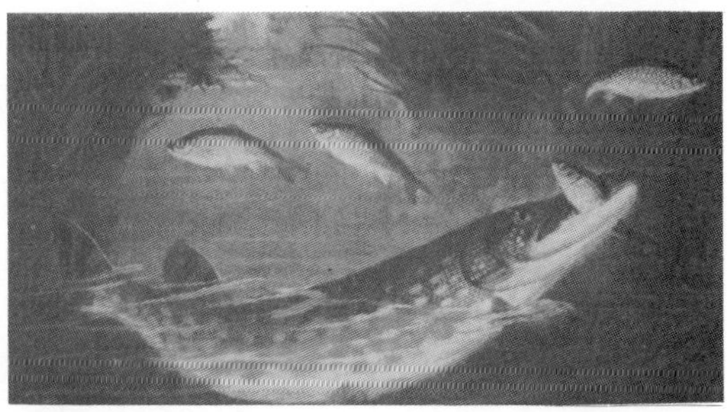

ROLAND KNIGHT – A Pike Attacking Perch; and Trout On A Rocky Bank – signed – 15½ x 23½in.
(Christie's) **$1,861 £1,320 Pair**

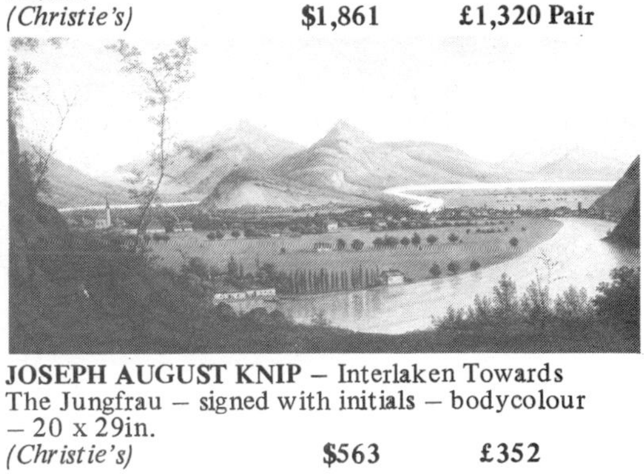

JOSEPH AUGUST KNIP – Interlaken Towards The Jungfrau – signed with initials – bodycolour – 20 x 29in.
(Christie's) **$563 £352**

KNOWLES

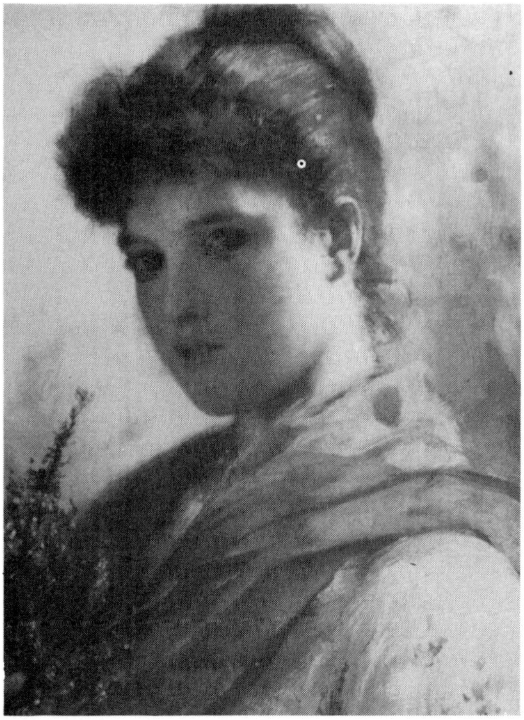

DAVIDSON KNOWLES – Portrait Of A Girl, Half Length, Holding A Sprig Of Heather – signed – 20 x 13in.
(Christie's) **$1,009** **£660**

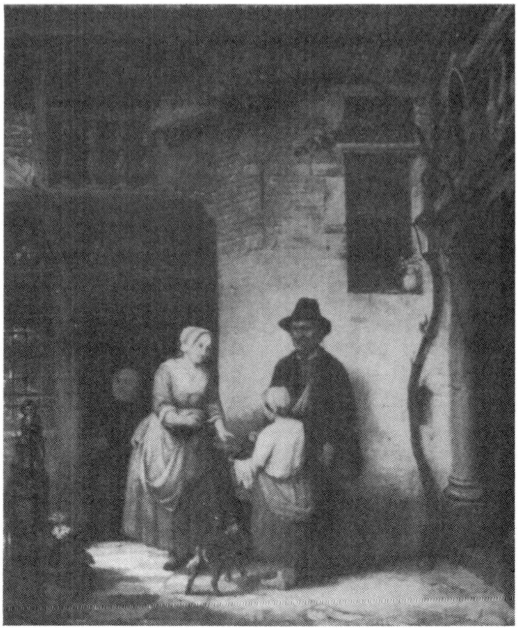

E. KNUDEN – Hawkers At The Door – signed and dated 1858 – oil on panel – 37 x 33cm.
(Phillips) **$1,224** **£850**

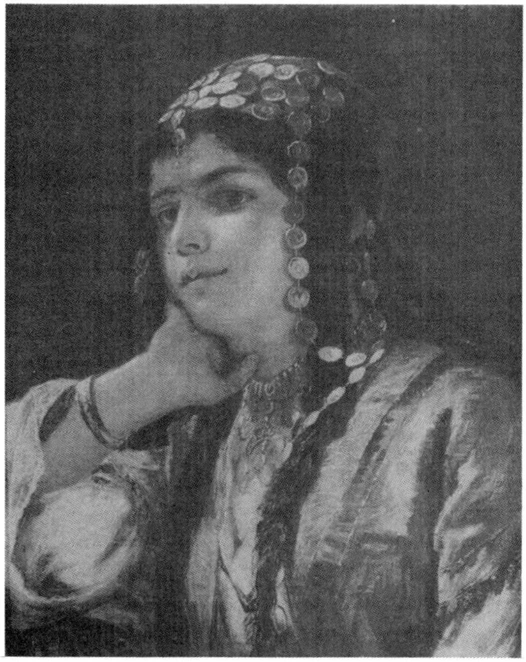

DAVIDSON KNOWLES – The Belle Of The Harem – on panel – 17¾ x 13½in.
(Christie's) **$567** **£378**

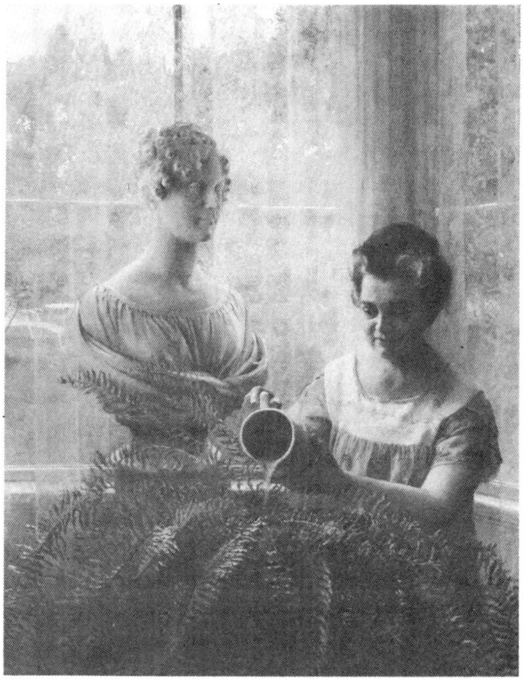

JOHN KOCH – Dora, Summer Light – signed and dated '74 – oil on canvas – 50 x 40in.
(Christie's) **$12,100** **£8,506**

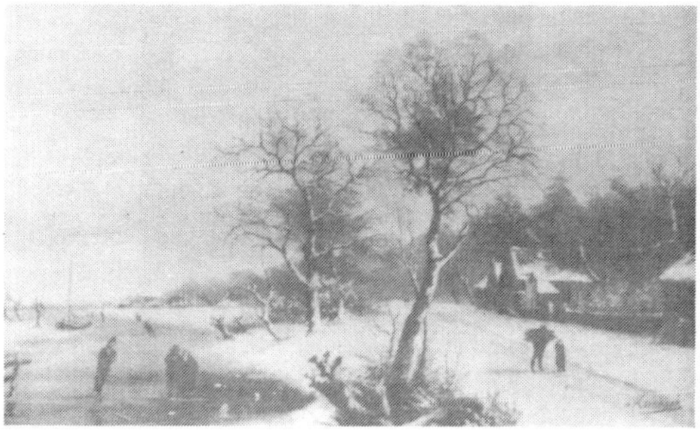

KOEKKOEK – Landscape In Winter With Figures On A Frozen Pond Beside A Snow Covered Road With Trees And Houses – signed – oil on canvas – 14 x 20in.
(W. H. Lane & Son) **$1,550** **£1,000**

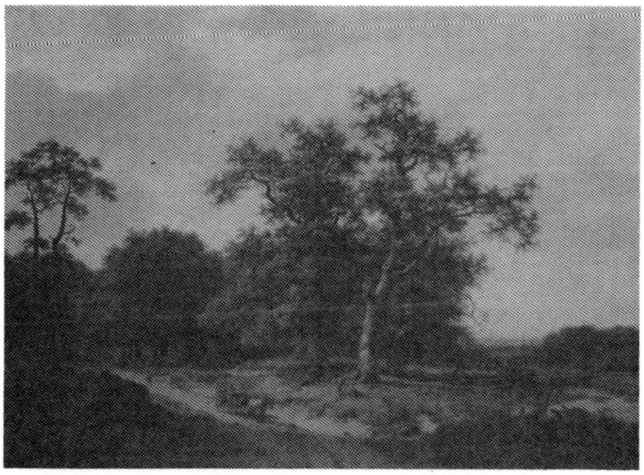

MARINUS ADRIANUS KOEKKOEK – An Extensive Wooded Landscape With Peasants In A Horse-Drawn Cart – signed and dated 1855 – 25½ x 36in.
(Christie's) **$15,840** **£11,000**

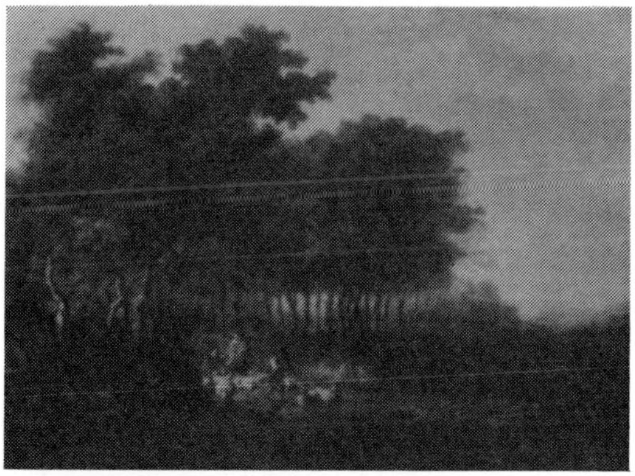

MARIANUS ADRIANUS KOEKKOEK, Attributed to – Travellers On A Country Path – oil on panel – 32.5 x 43cm.
(Phillips) **$3,173** **£1,900**

WILLEM KOEKKOEK – A Canal Running Through A Town With Figures Unloading A Barge – signed – 23 x 34in.
(Christie's) **$28,160** **£17,600**

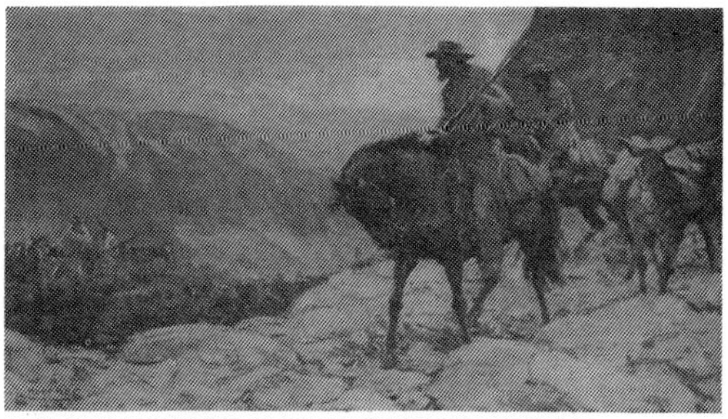

WILLIAM HENRY DETHLEF KOERNER – Hunters And Packmules – signed and dated 1922 – oil on canvas – 22 x 36in.
(Christie's) **$11,000** **£7,733**

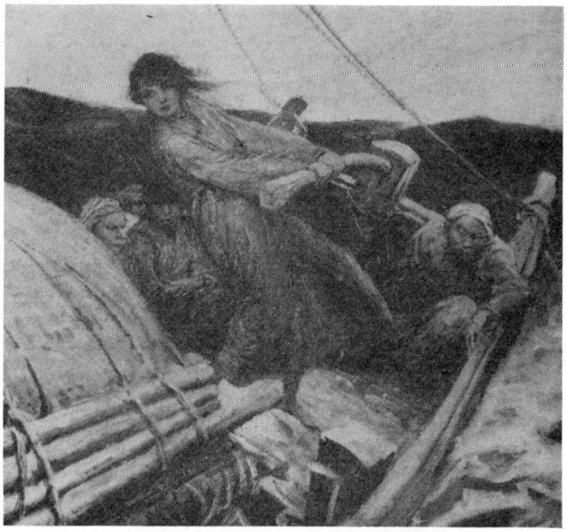

WILLIAM HENRY DETHLEF KOERNER – Trial By Water – inscribed – oil on canvas – 30¼ x 24in.
(Christie's) **$3,300** **£2,056**

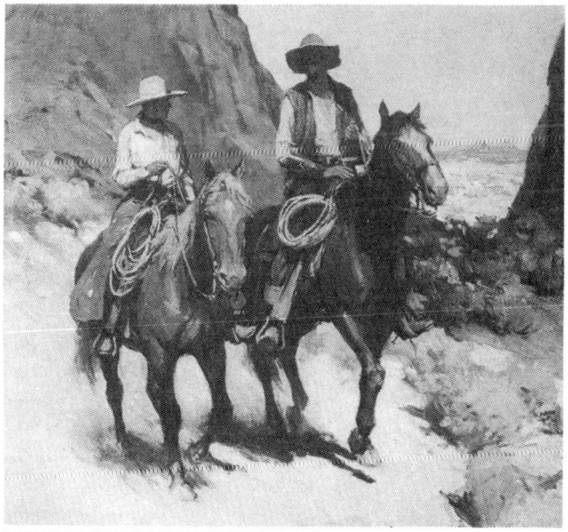

WILLIAM HENRY DETHLEF KOERNER – Illustration For The Trusty Knaves – signed and dated 1931 and inscribed – oil on canvas – 36¼ x 30in.
(Christie's) **$13,200** **£9,279**

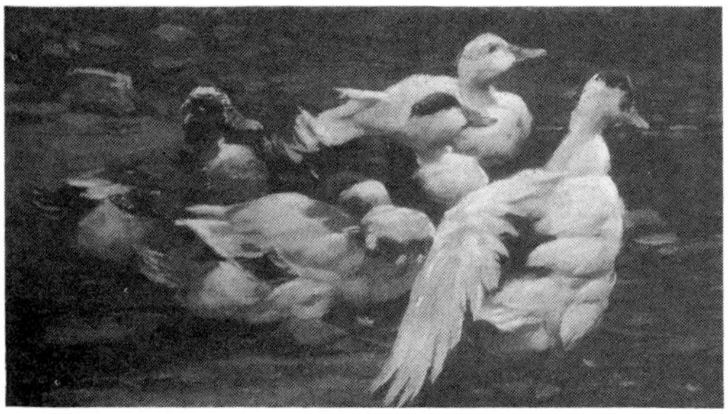

ALEXANDER KOESTER – Ducks On A Pond – signed – pastel – 13 x 19¾in.
(Christie's) **$7,920** **£4,950**

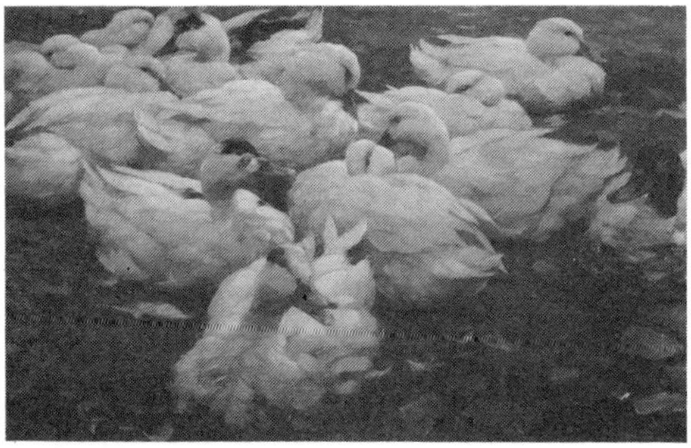

ALEXANDER KOESTER – Ducks On A River – signed – 20½ x 32in.
(Christie's) **$73,920** **£46,200**

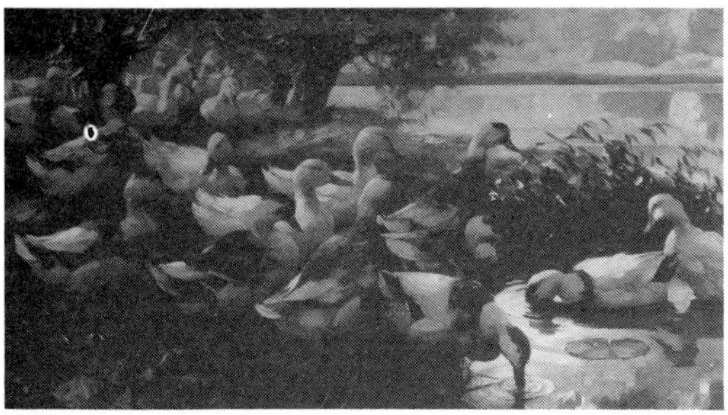

ALEXANDER KOESTER – Ducks On A River Bank – signed – 31 x 51in.
(Christie's) **$123,200** **£77,000**

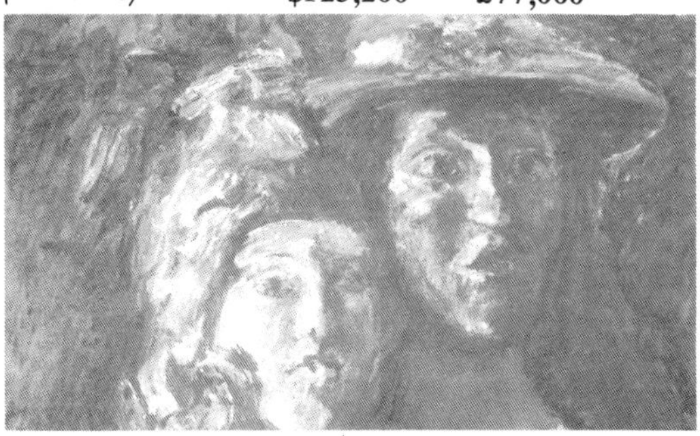

OSKAR KOKOSCHKA – Zwei Madchen – signed, inscribed on the reverse and dated 1934 – oil on canvas – 19¾ x 24in.
(Christie's) **$63,360** **£44,000**

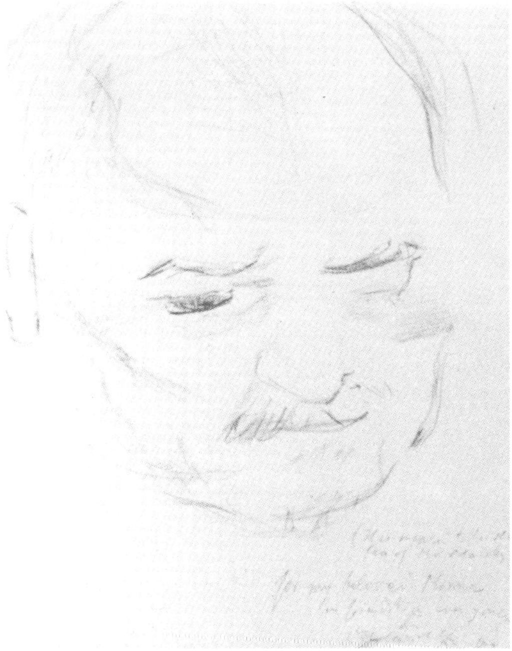

OSKAR KOKOSCHKA – Portrait Of Maisky – signed, inscribed and dated '42 – coloured crayons on paper – 11¾ x 9¼in.
(Christie's) **$5,068** **£3,520**

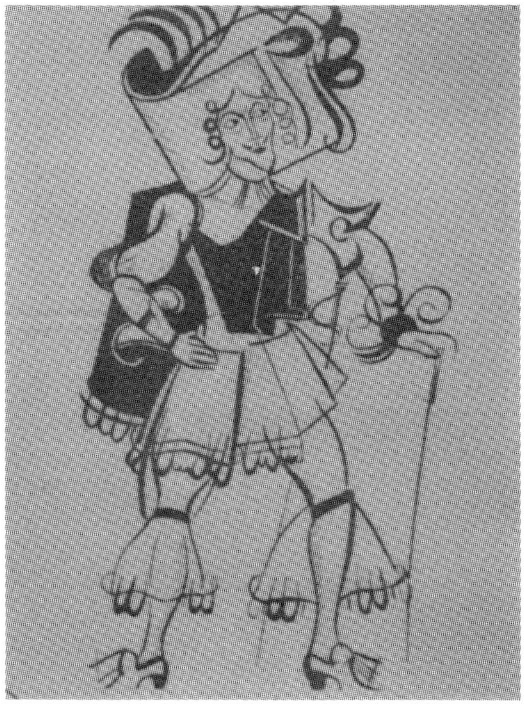

VASSILI KOMARDENKOV – Portrait Of The Actor Scirsku In The Role Of Salvador Rosa – ink on paper – 16 x 24cm.
(Phillips) **$387** **£250**

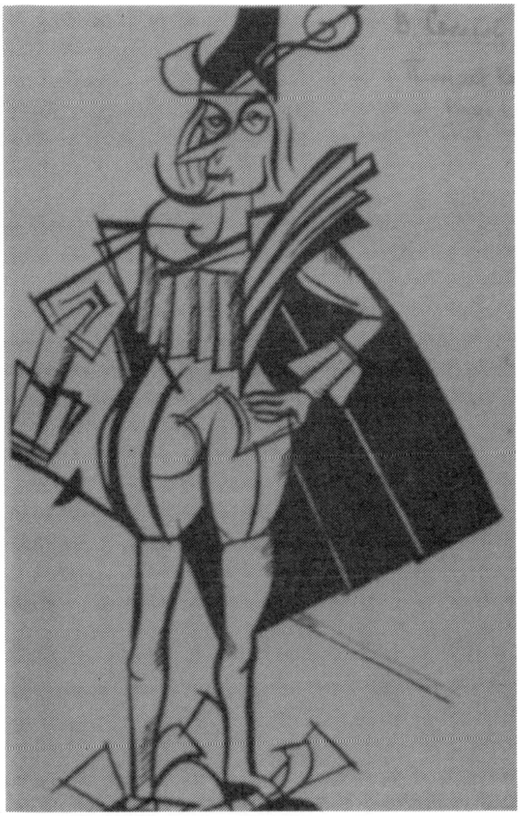

VASSILI KOMARDENKOV – Portrait Of The Actor Sokolov In The Role Of Pasquale Capuzzi – ink on paper – 16 x 24cm.
(Phillips) **$387** **£250**

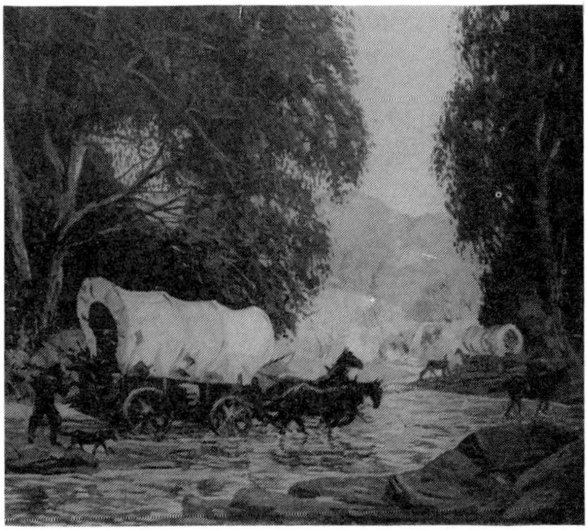

CARL R. KRAFFT – Fording The Stream – signed – oil on canvas – 24 x 27in.
(Christie's) **$1,870** **£1,165**

CARL R. KRAFFT – Sundown – signed, and signed and dated 1923/24 on verso – oil on canvas – 39¾ x 51½in.
(Robt. W. Skinner Inc.) **$3,600** **£2,500**

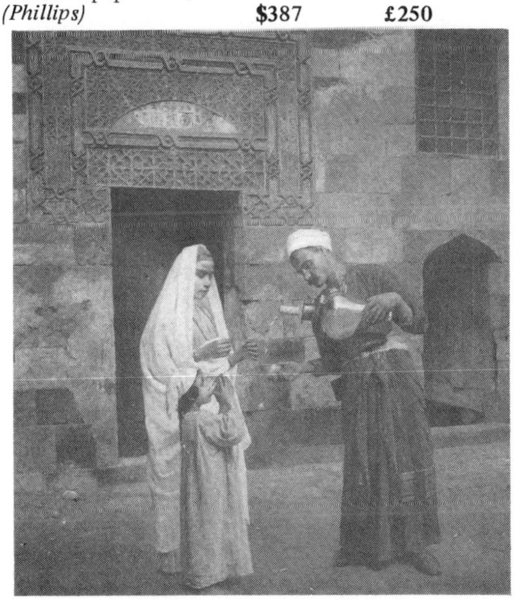

FRANZ XAVIER KOSLER – The Waterseller – signed and dated 1902 – 24½ x 17¾in.
(Christie's) **$12,320** **£7,700**

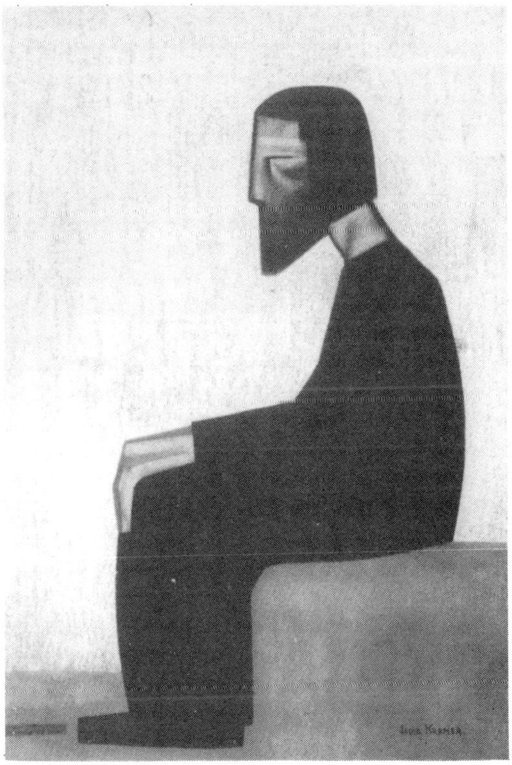

JACOB KRAMER – Study For 'The Jew' – signed – pastel – 19 x 13½in.
(Christie's) **$6,606** **£4,620**

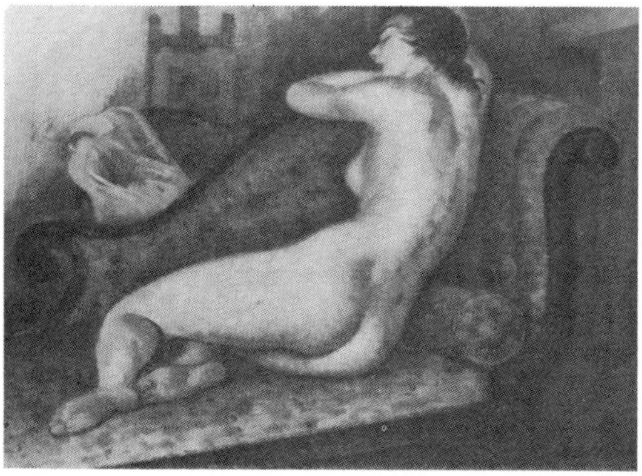

LEON KROLL – Asleep On The Chaise – signed – oil on paper – 13 x 16½in.
(Christie's) **$2,420** **£1,683**

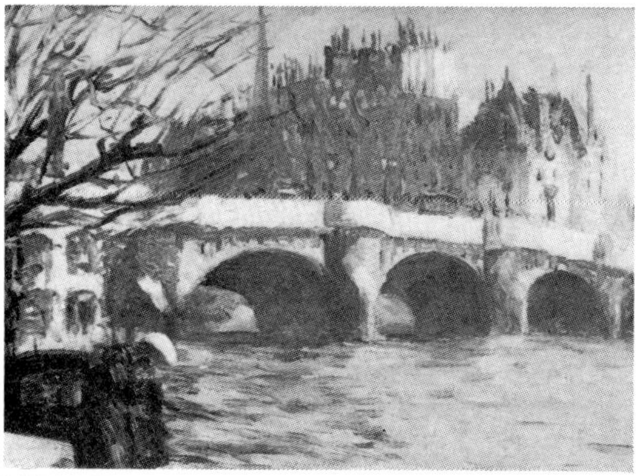

LEON KROLL – Pont Neuf From The Right Bank Of The Seine – oil on canvas – 12½ x 16¼in.
(Christie's) **$3,850** **£2,706**

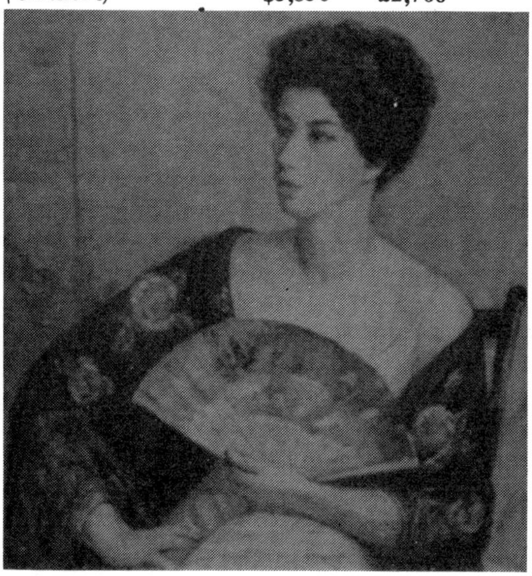

LOUIS KRONBERG – Spanish Dancer With Fan – signed, also signed and dated 1958 on the stretcher – oil on canvas – 32 x 26in.
(Robt. W. Skinner Inc.) **$800** **£490**

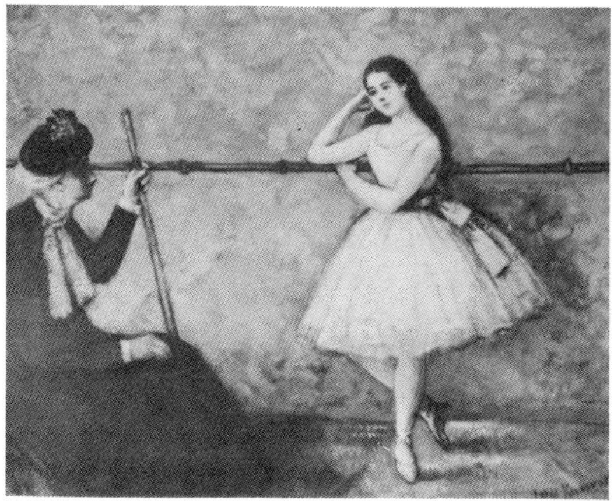

LOUIS KRONBERG – Teacher And Pupil – signed – oil on canvas – 26 x 32in.
(Robt. W. Skinner Inc.) **$1,400** **£972**

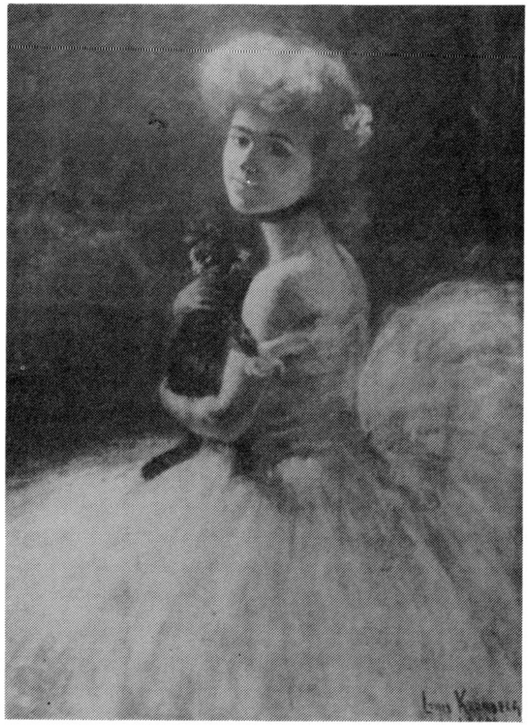

LOUIS KRONBERG – Ballerina Holding A Kitten – signed and dated 1904 – oil on canvas – 17¾ x 13¾in.
(Robt. W. Skinner Inc.) **$2,200** **£1,447**

FREDERICK MARIANUS KRUSEMAN – Skaters In A Dutch Winter Landscape – signed – on panel – 59 x 77cm.
(Phillips) **$18,000** **£12,500**

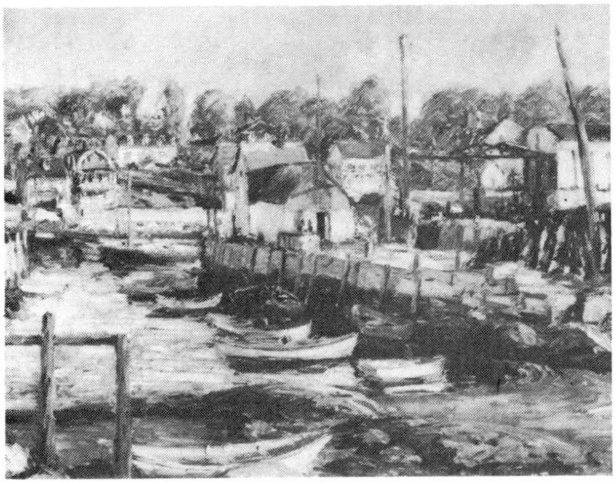

MAX KUEHNE – The Harbour, Rockport – signed – oil on canvas – 24¼ x 30¼in.
(Christie's) **$7,150** **£4,974**

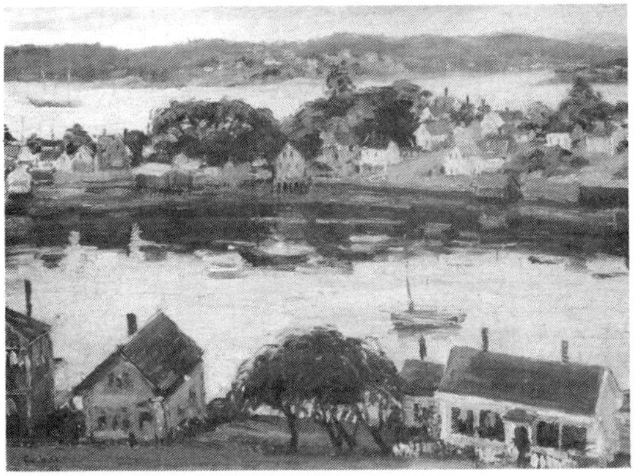

MAX KUEHNE – Rocky Neck, Gloucester – signed and dated '18, and signed and dated on the reverse – oil on canvas laid down on board – 20 x 24in.
(Christie's) **$12,100** **£8,417**

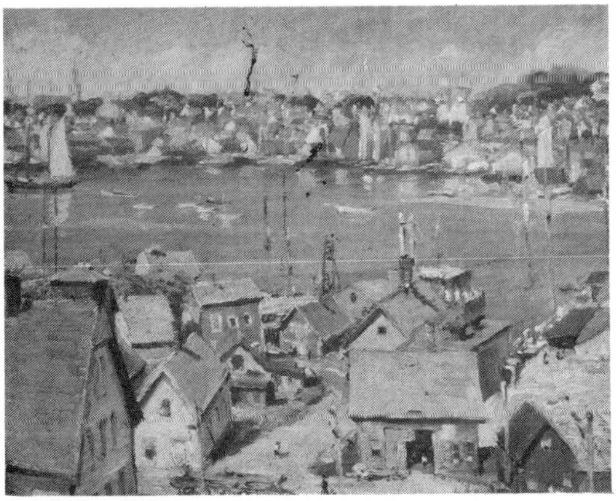

MAX KUEHNE – The Harbour, Gloucester – signed and dated '16 – oil on canvas laid down on board – 20 x 24in.
(Christie's) **$20,900** **£14,540**

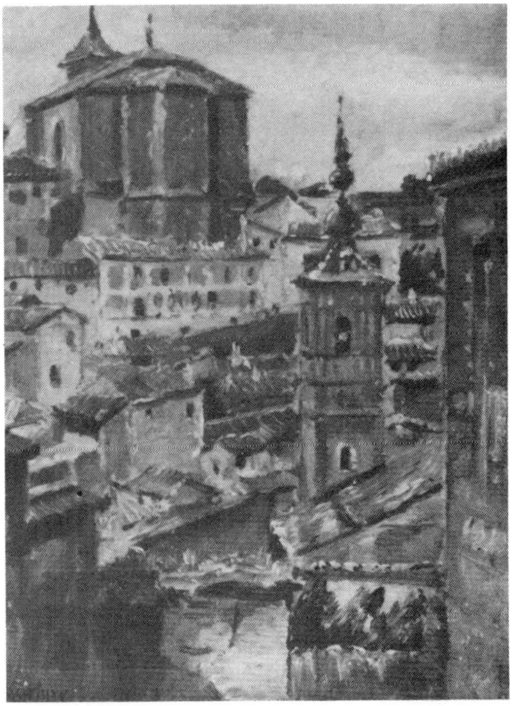

MAX KUEHNE – Spanish City – signed – oil on panel – 7¾ x 6¼in.
(Christie's) **$880** **£612**

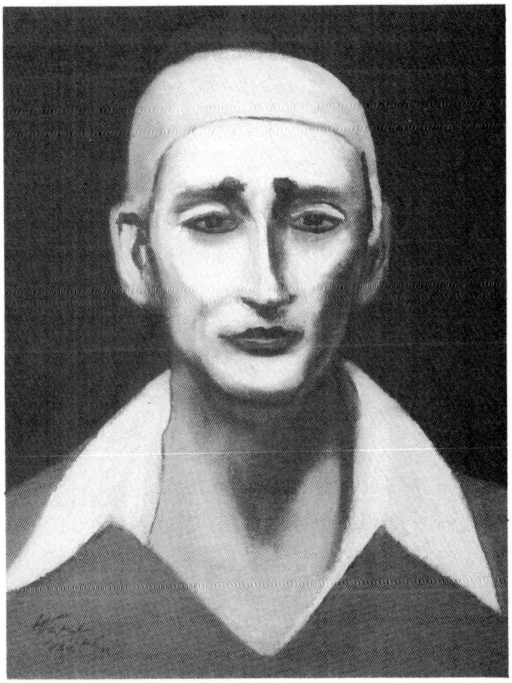

WALT KUHN – Clown, signed and dated 1934 – oil on canvas – 15 x 12in.
(Christie's) **$30,800** **£21,652**

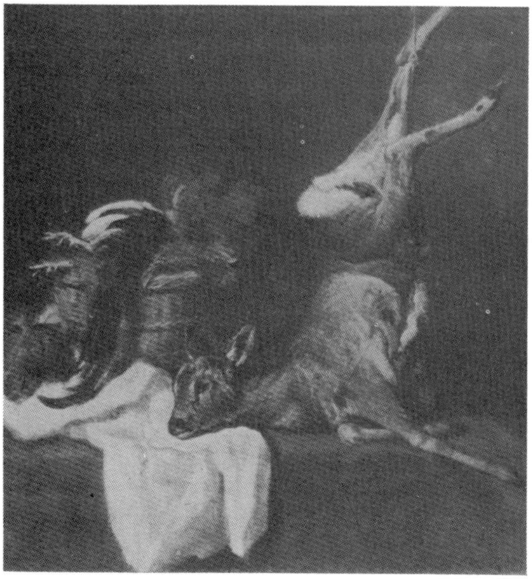

LUDWIG ADAM KUNZ – A Still Life Of Dead Game On A Table – signed and dated 1916 – oil on canvas – 71 x 70cm.
(Phillips) **$576** **£400**

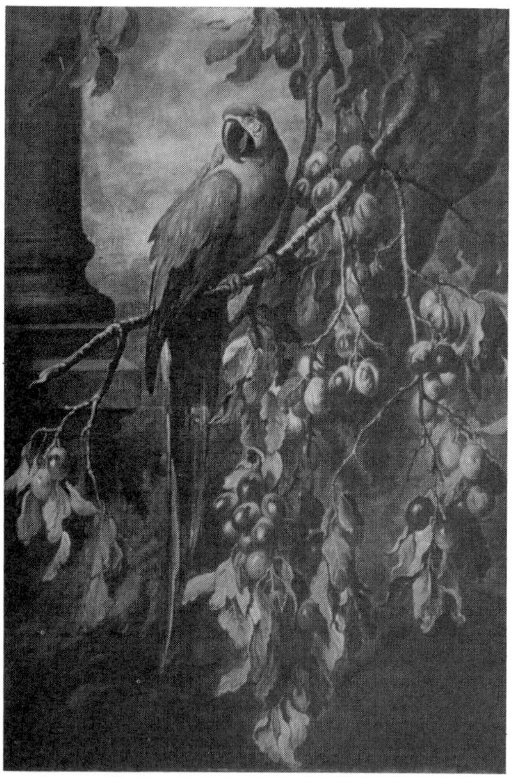

LUDWIG ADAM KUNZ – A Parrot In A Plum Tree By A Classical Column – signed and dated 1919 – on canvas – 121 x 84cm.
(Phillips) **$3,888** **£2,700**

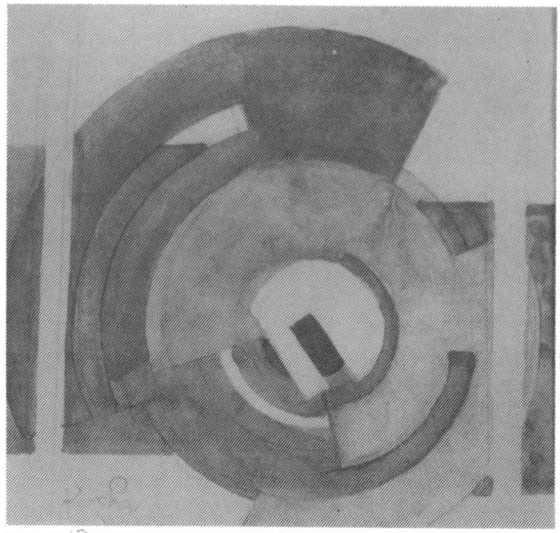

FRANTISEK KUPKA – Rythme Circulaire – signed – watercolour, coloured crayons and pencil on paper – 8½ x 8½in.
(Christie's) **$8,800** **£5,500**

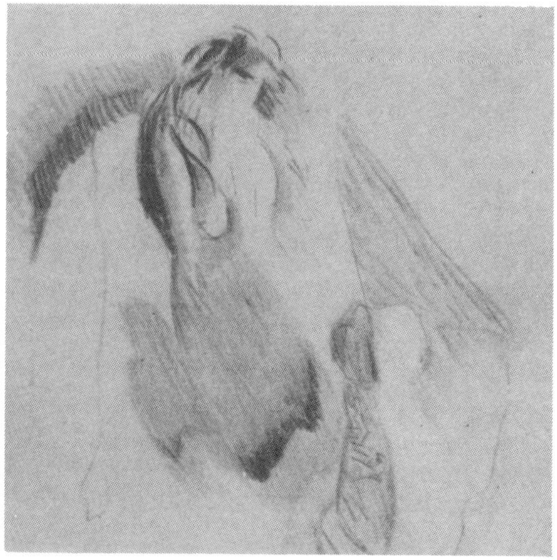

FRANTISEK KUPKA – Composition – coloured crayons on paper – 8¼ x 7¼in.
(Christie's) **$1,584** **£990**

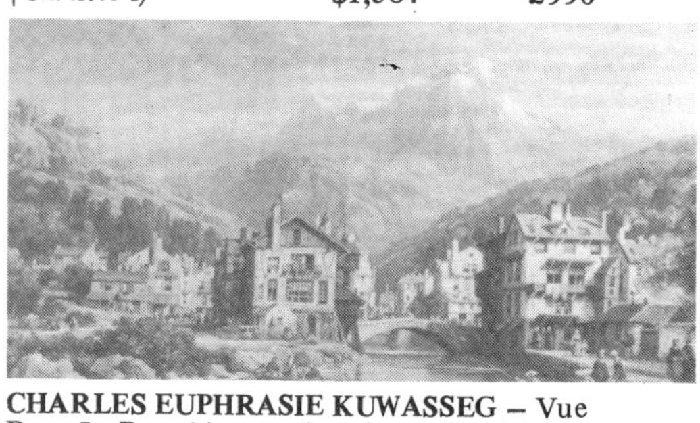

CHARLES EUPHRASIE KUWASSEG – Vue Dans La Dauphinee – signed and dated 1876, also signed and inscribed on the reverse – oil on canvas – 38 x 62cm.
(Phillips) **$5,472** **£3,800**

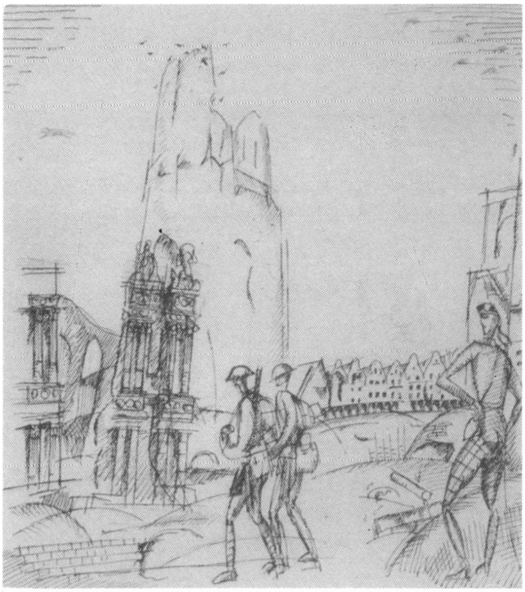

JEAN EMILE LABOUREUR – Souvenir d'Arras – inscribed – black ink and pencil on paper – 8 x 7¼in.
(Christie's) **$352** **£220**

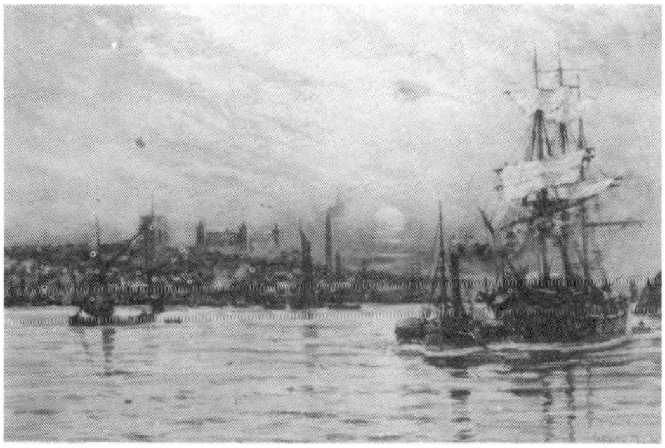

CHARLES J. DE LACY – A Ship Under Tow Passing The Towers Of London – signed – watercolour – 12½ x 18in.
(Anderson & Garland) **$829** **£580**

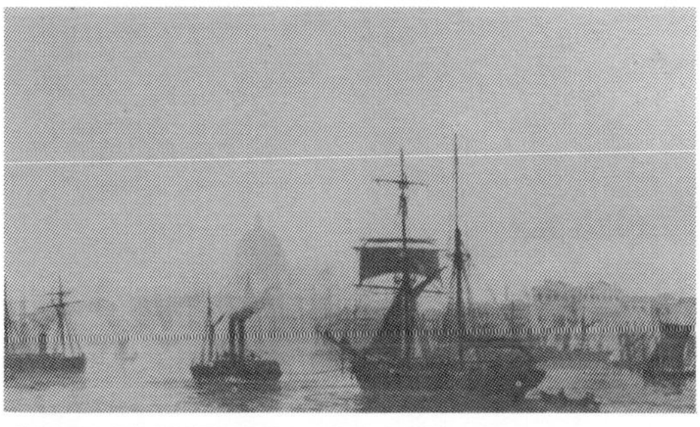

CHARLES JOHN DE LACY – Shipping In The Pool Of London At Day Break – signed – on canvas – 20 x 30in.
(Phillips) **$5,706** **£3,600**

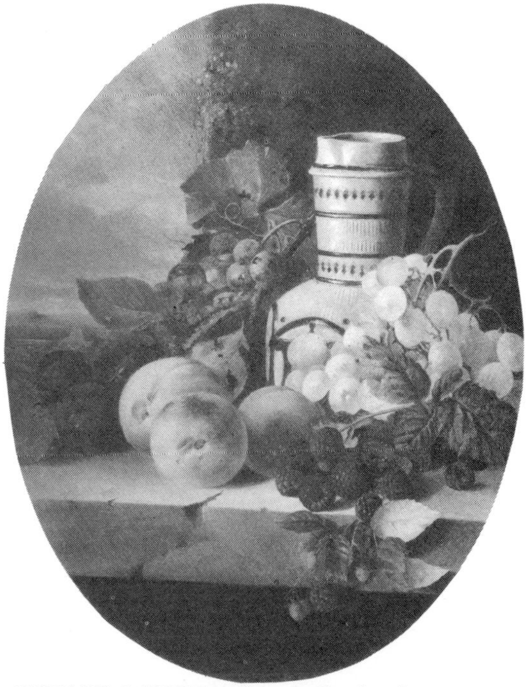

EDWARD LADELL – Grapes, Raspberries, Peaches, Plums And A Stoneware Jug On A Stone Ledge With A Landscape Beyond – signed with monogram and dated 1858 – 17¾ x 13¾in.
(Christie's) **$12,320** **£7,700**

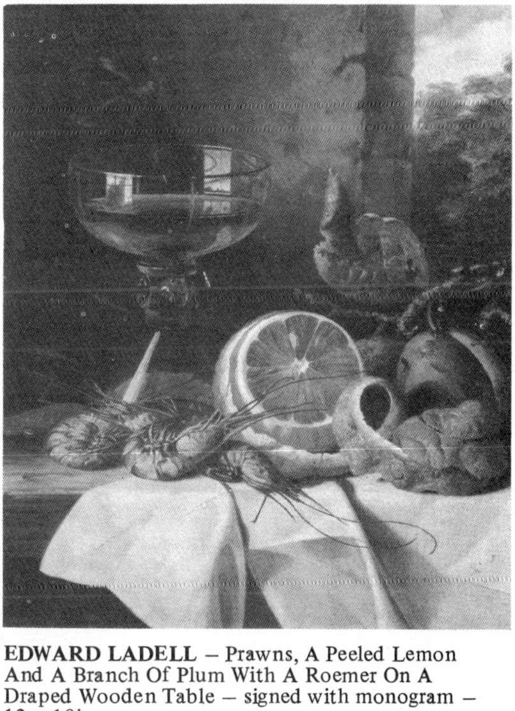

EDWARD LADELL – Prawns, A Peeled Lemon And A Branch Of Plum With A Roemer On A Draped Wooden Table – signed with monogram – 12 x 10in.
(Christie's) **$7,128** **£4,950**

LAGYE

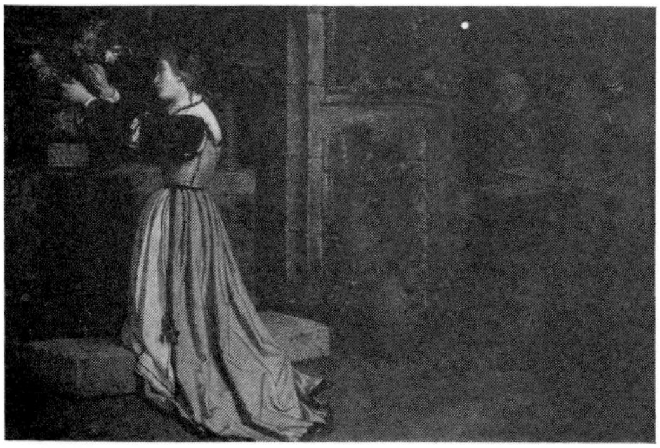

VICTOR LAGYE – Faust And Marguerite – signed and dated 1868 and inscribed – 66.5 x 83cm.
(Phillips) **$2,880** **£2,000**

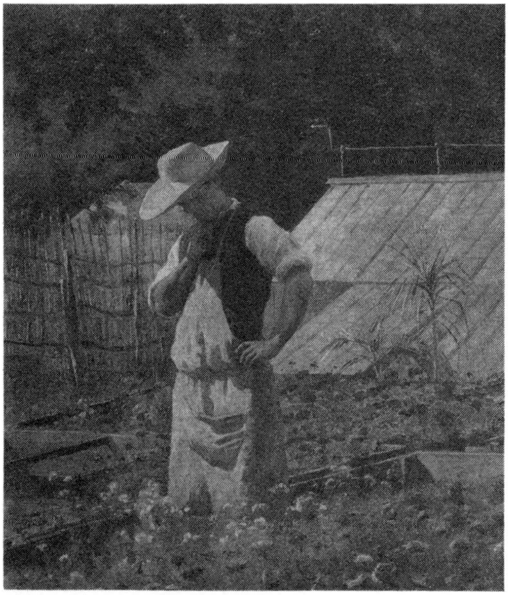

HENRI ADOLPHE LAISSEMENT – Un coin de la roseraie a Bagatelle – signed – 10¾ x 8½in.
(Christie's) **$24,640** **£15,400**

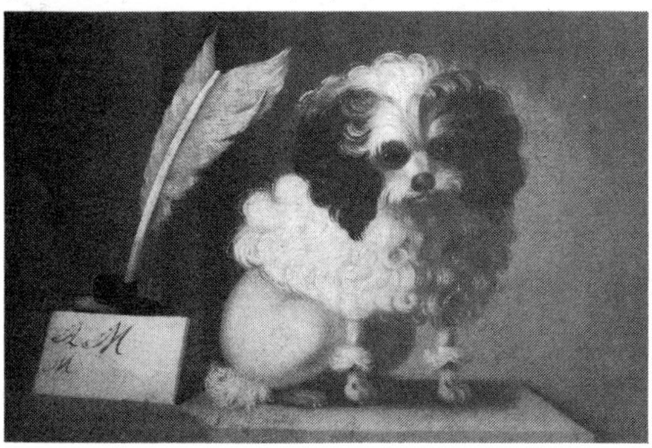

DE LAMARRE – A Lowchen Seated By A Quill – signed – oil – 9½ x 12½in.
(Bonhams) **$7,750** **£5,000**

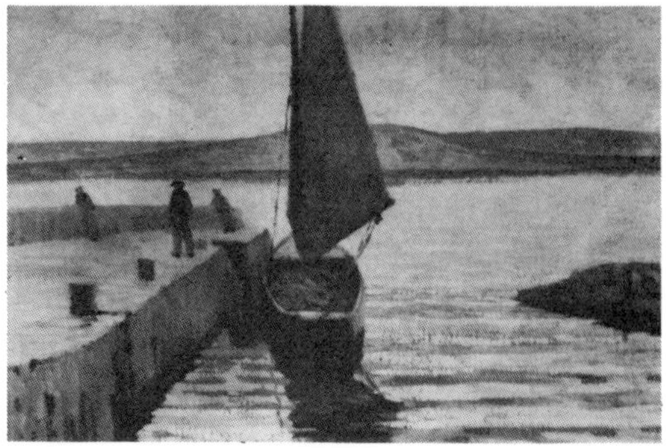

HENRY LAMB – Sailing Boat At A Quayside – signed – oil – 16 x 20in.
(Woolley & Wallis) **$366** **£260**

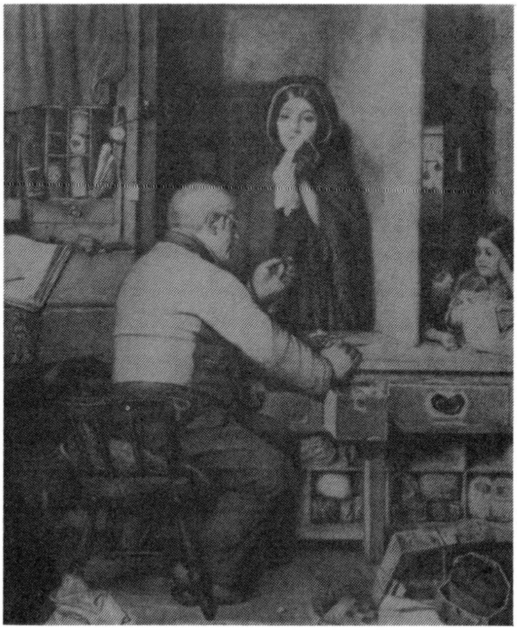

THOMAS REYNOLDS LAMONT – A Widow's Pledge – signed – watercolour over pencil – 76 x 62cm.
(Phillips) **$2,574** **£1,800**

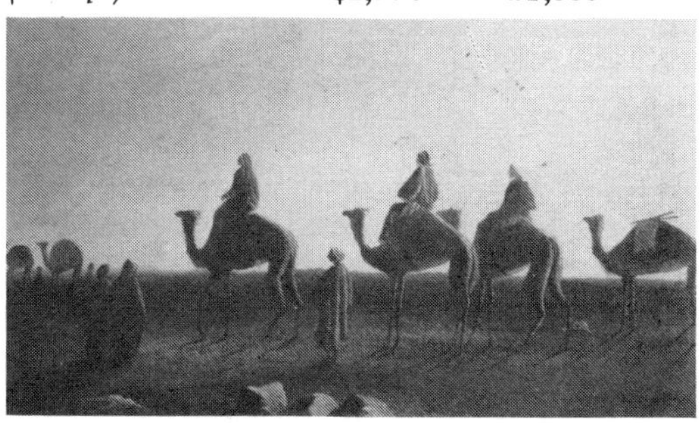

A. E. LAMPLOUGH – Camels And Figures – oil – 15½ x 26½in.
(Michael G. Matthews) **$144** **£90**

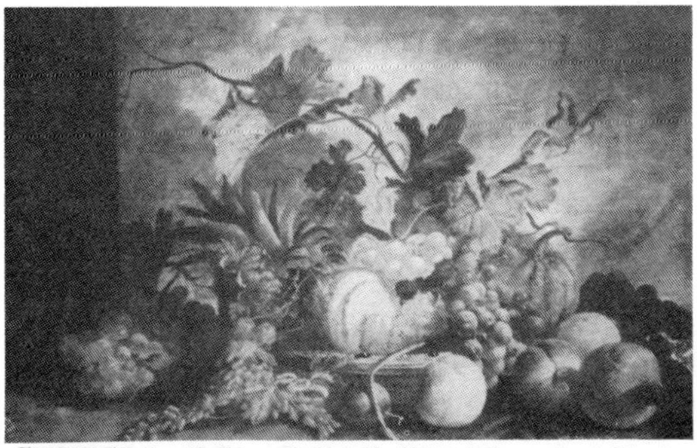

GEORGE LANCE – Still Life With Vines And Fruit On A Ledge – signed – oil on canvas – 24 x 36in.
(Phillips) **$2,448** **£1,600**

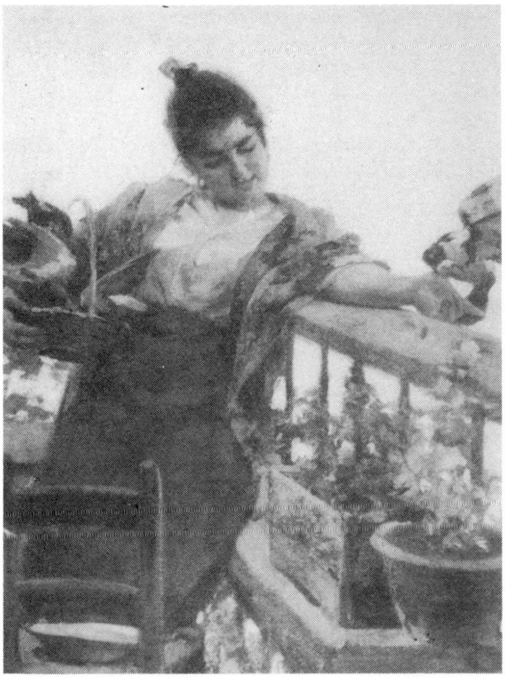

EGISTO LANCEROTTO – Feeding The Doves – signed – on canvas – 27 x 19in.
(Christie's) **$6,938** **£4,180**

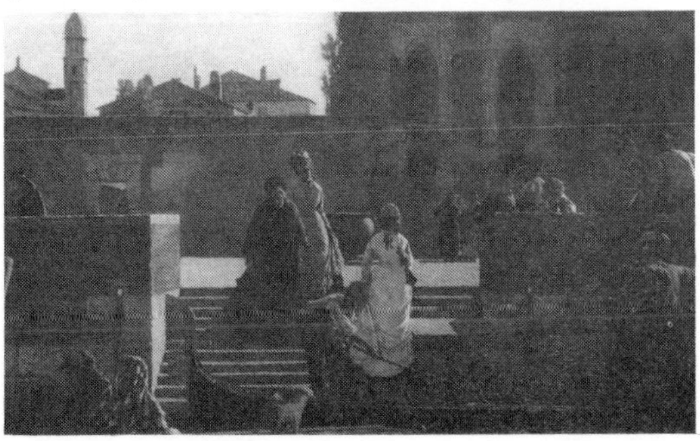

EGISTO LANCEROTTO – A Venetian Canal With Landies Embarking – signed – 24 x 36in.
(Christie's) **$21,120** **£13,200**

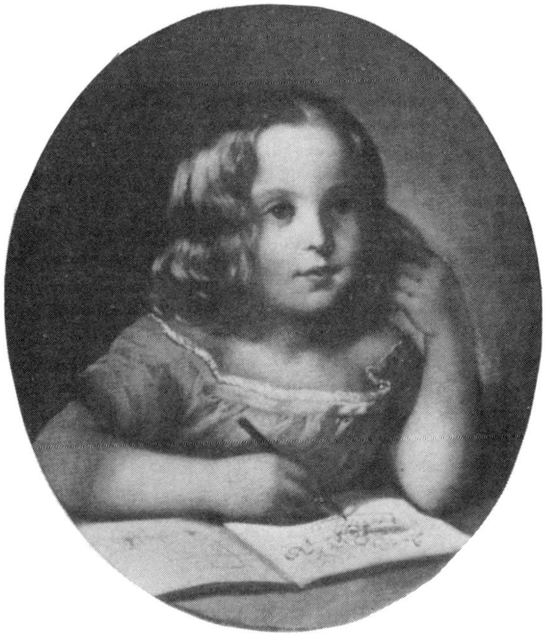

CHARLES LANDSEER – The Drawing Lesson – signed with monogram and dated 1854 – 19¼ x 16¾in.
(Christie's) **$744** **£528**

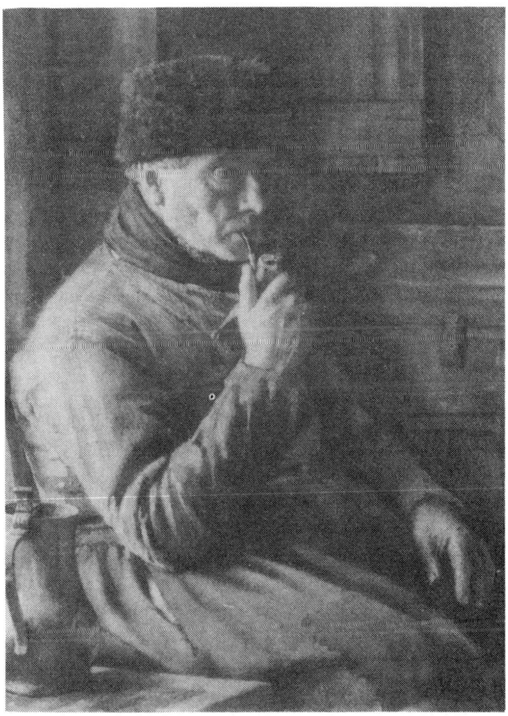

WALTER LANGLEY – A Quiet Pipe – signed and dated '05 – watercolour – 14½ x 11in.
(Christie's) **$2,763** **£1,760**

LANGLEY

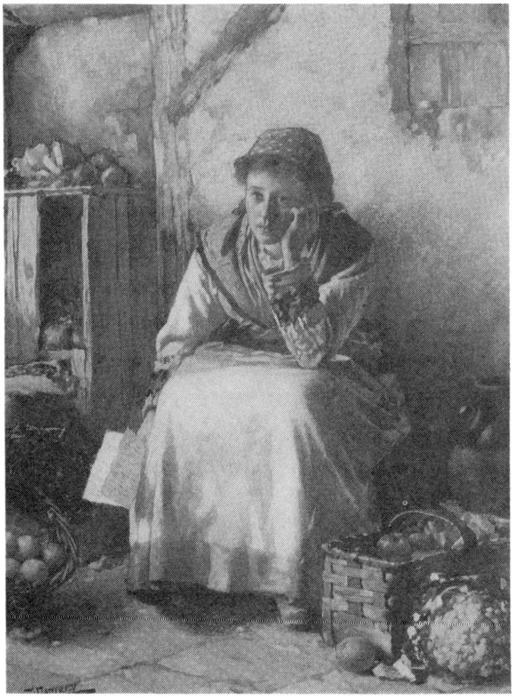

WALTER LANGLEY – News From Afar – signed – watercolour over traces of pencil – 48.5 x 38cm.
(Phillips) **$3,266** **£2,300**

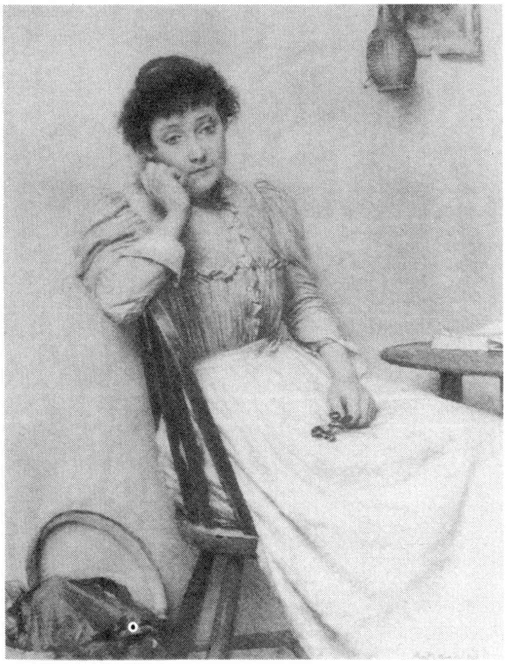

WALTER LANGLEY – Far Away Thoughts – signed – watercolour heightened with white – 15¾ x 12½in.
(Christie's) **$3,702** **£2,420**

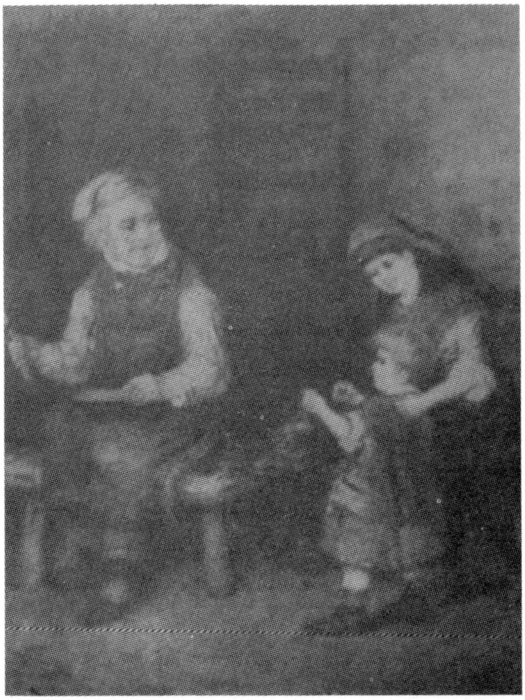

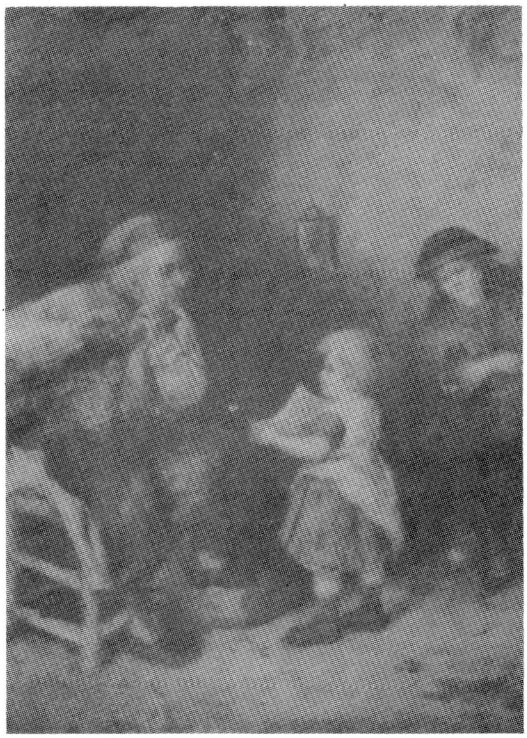

MARK W. LANGLOIS – At The Cobblers; and The Flute Player – signed – oil on canvas – 30 x 25in.
(Christie's) **$1,683** **£1,100 Pair**

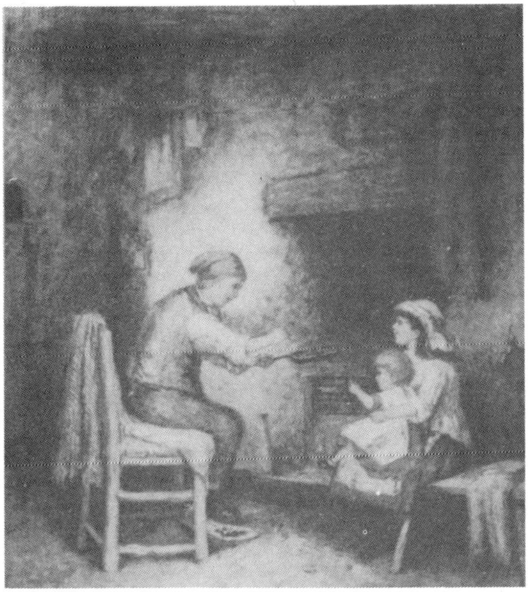

MARK W. LANGLOIS – Roast Chestnuts; and An Attentive Audience – signed – oil on canvas – 20½ x 16¼in.
(Christie's) **$1,300** **£850 Pair**

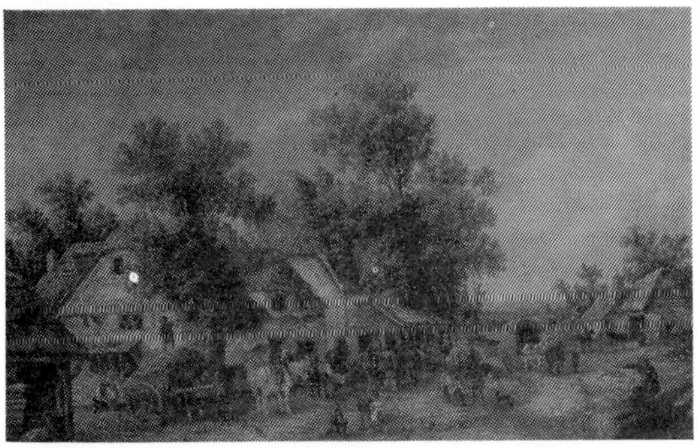

GEORGE LARA – The Wayside Inn – bears a false signature – 20 x 30in.
(Phillips) **$3,059** **£1,900**

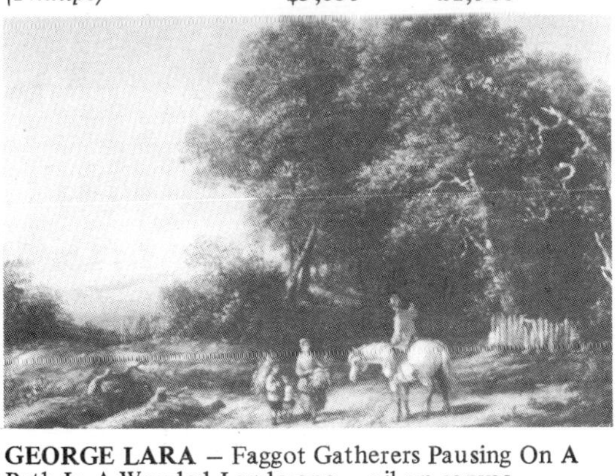

GEORGE LARA – Faggot Gatherers Pausing On A Path In A Wooded Landscape – oil on canvas – 10 x 12in.
(Phillips) **$2,295** **£1,500**

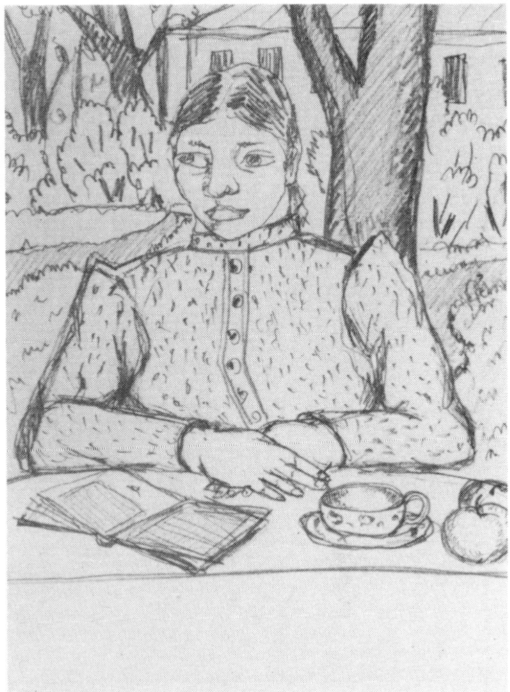

MIKHAIL LARIONOV – Gontcharova a Table – pencil on paper – 10¼ x 7½in.
(Christie's) **$1,320** **£825**

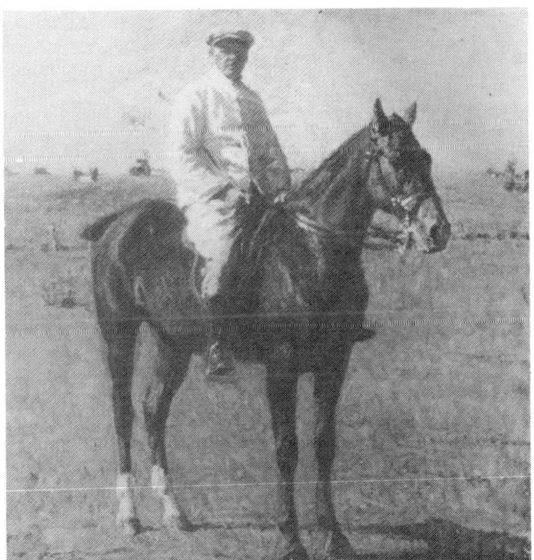

HUGO VALDEMAR LARSEN – Portrait Of A Man Mounted On A Chestnut Horse – signed and dated 1918 – oil on canvas – 105 x 101cm.
(Phillips) **$3,168** **£2,200**

CHARLES JAMES LAUDER – King William Street, St. Magnus The Martyr And Monument Beyond – signed – oil on canvas – 23¼ x 35¾in.
(Christie's) **$1,887** **£1,320**

LAURENCIN

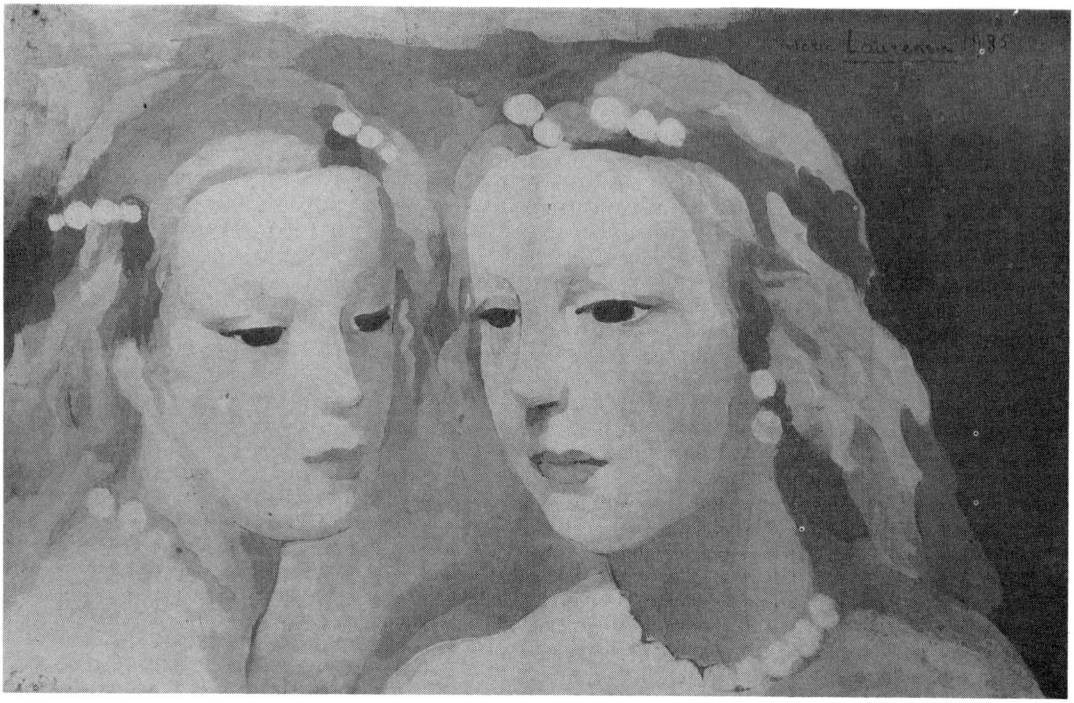

MARIE LAURENCIN – Deux Tetes de Femme – signed and dated 1935 – oil on canvas – 10¾ x 16in.
(Christie's) **$174,515 £104,500**

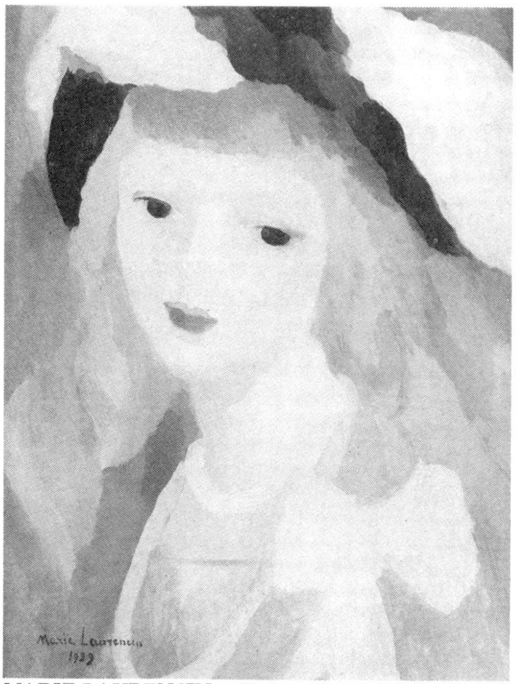

MARIE LAURENCIN – Femme au Chapeau – signed and dated 1929 – oil on canvas – 18 x 15in.
(Christie's) **$142,560 £99,000**

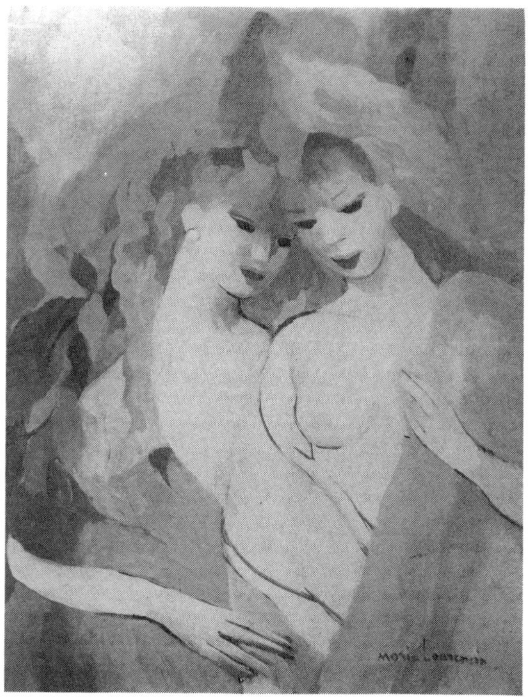

MARIE LAURENCIN – Les Deux Femmes – signed – oil on canvas – 24 x 19¾in.
(Christie's) **$275,550 £165,000**

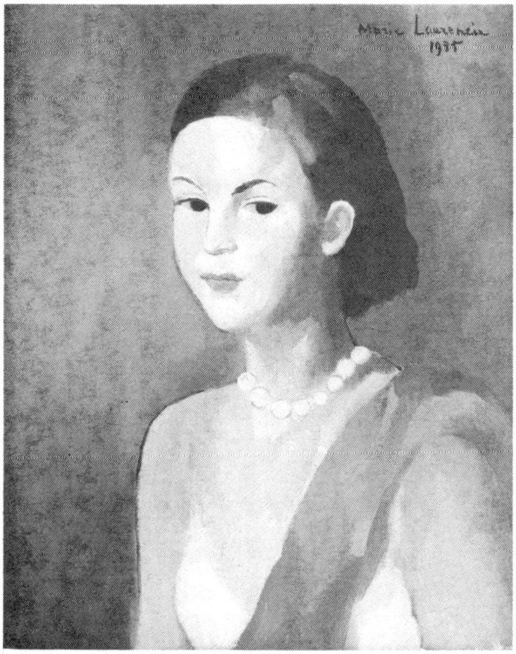

MARIE LAURENCIN – Mademoiselle O – signed and dated 1935 – oil on canvas – 18¼ x 15in.
(Christie's) **$95,040 £66,000**

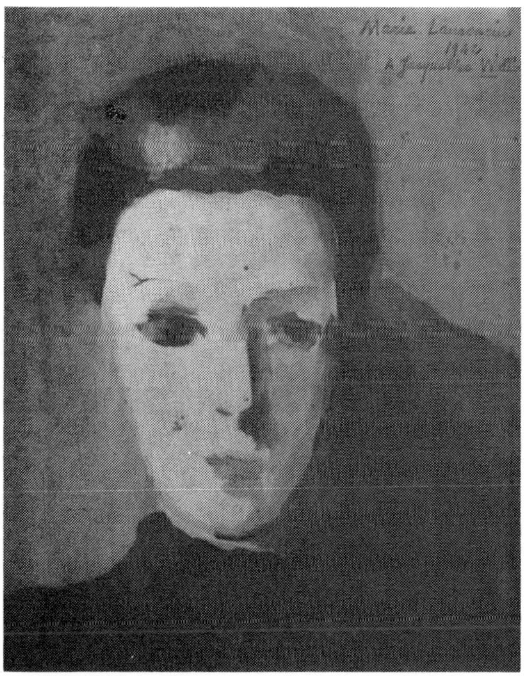

MARIE LAURENCIN – Portrait de Jacqueline Wallard – signed and dated 1942 – oil on panel – 10½ x 8½in.
(Christie's) **$31,229 £18,700**

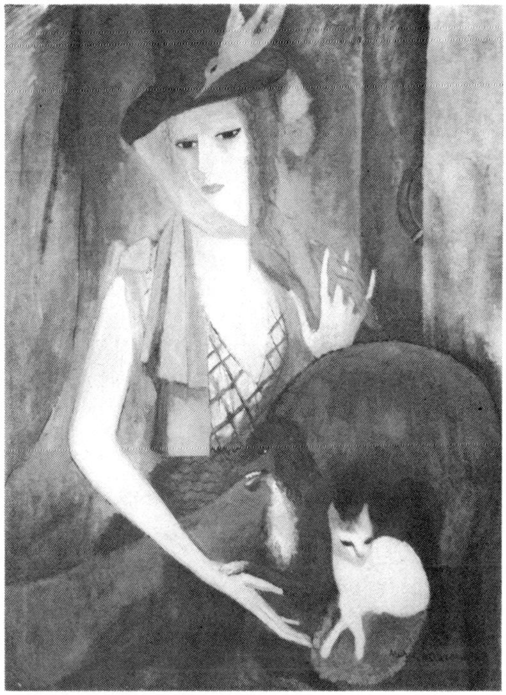

MARIE LAURENCIN – Femme au Chat et au Chien – signed – oil on canvas – 39½ x 28¾in.
(Christie's) **$316,800 £220,000**

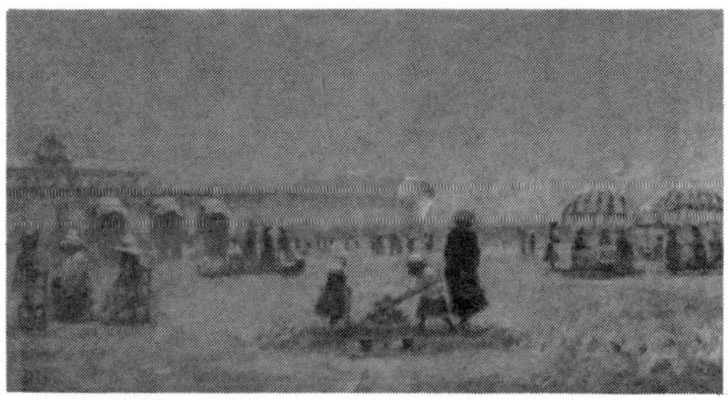

JEAN LAURENT – Victorian Figures On Beach Before A Pier – signed – oil on canvas – 39 x 54cm.
(W. H. Lane & Son) **$3,652 £2,200**

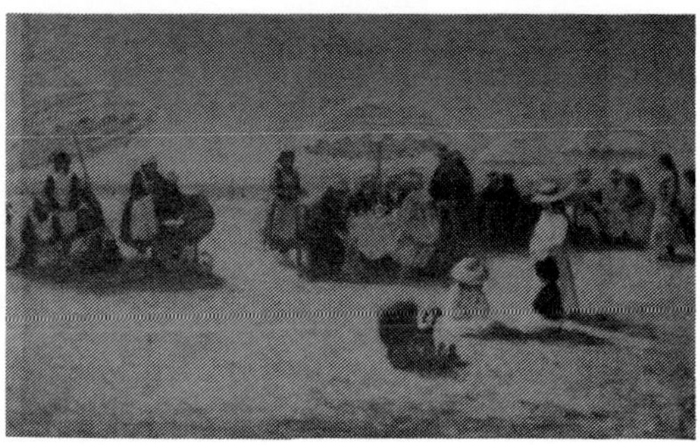

JEAN LAURENT – Les Parasols – signed – oil on canvas – 77 x 122cm.
(Phillips) **$4,650 £3,000**

LAVERY

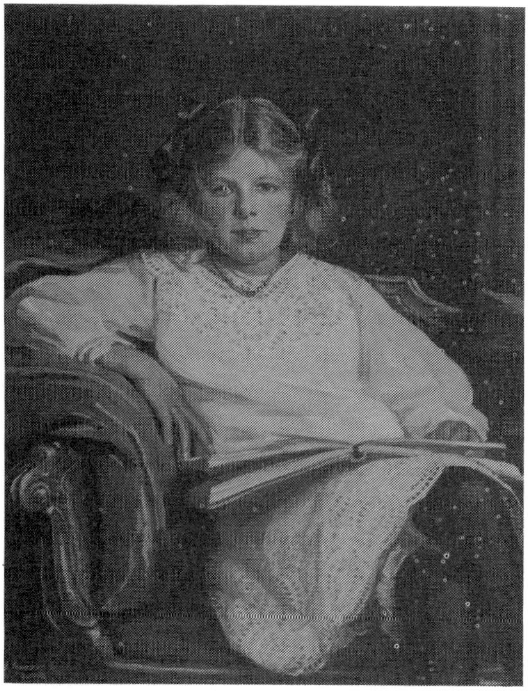

SIR JOHN LAVERY – Portrait Of Betty, Reading A Book – signed, and signed, inscribed and dated 1915 on the reverse – oil on canvas – 34 x 27in.
(Christie's) **$13,816** **£8,800**

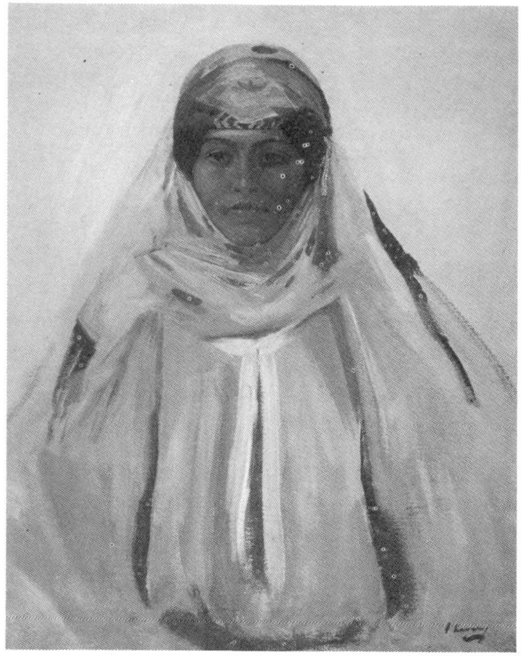

SIR JOHN LAVERY – Fatima Farghe – signed, and signed and inscribed on the reverse – oil on canvas – 30 x 25in.
(Christie's) **$10,224** **£7,150**

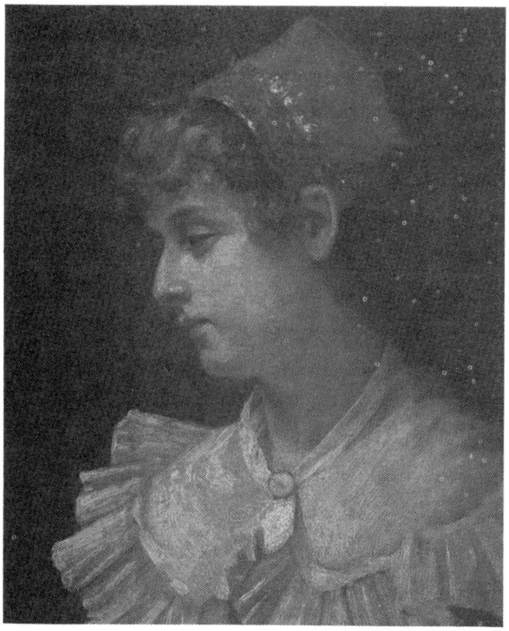

SIR JOHN LAVERY – Gretchen – signed and dated '80, and signed, inscribed and dated on a label – oil on canvas – 12 x 10in.
(Christie's) **$4,719** **£3,300**

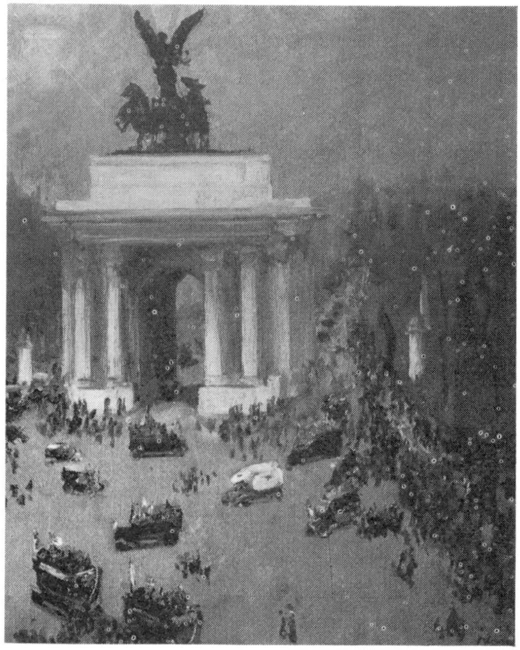

SIR JOHN LAVERY – Armistice Day, London – signed, also signed, inscribed and dated 1918 on the reverse – oil on canvas – 76 x 64cm.
(Phillips) **$14,200** **£10,000**

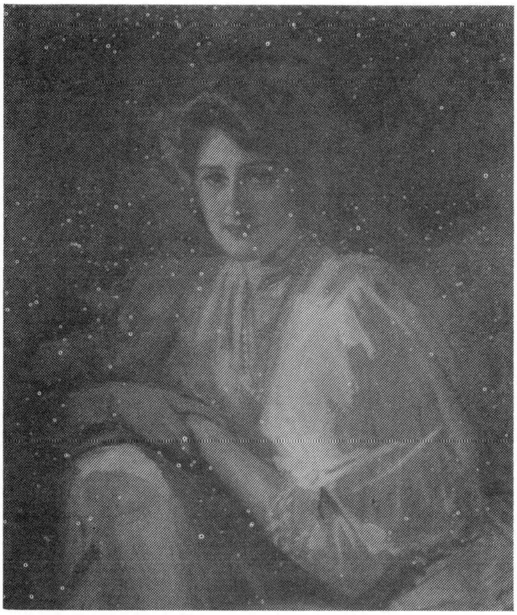

SIR JOHN LAVERY – Portrait Of 'Phyllis', Half Length In A White Dress – signed, and signed and inscribed on the reverse – oil on canvas – 29¾ x 24½in.
(Christie's) **$10,224** **£7,150**

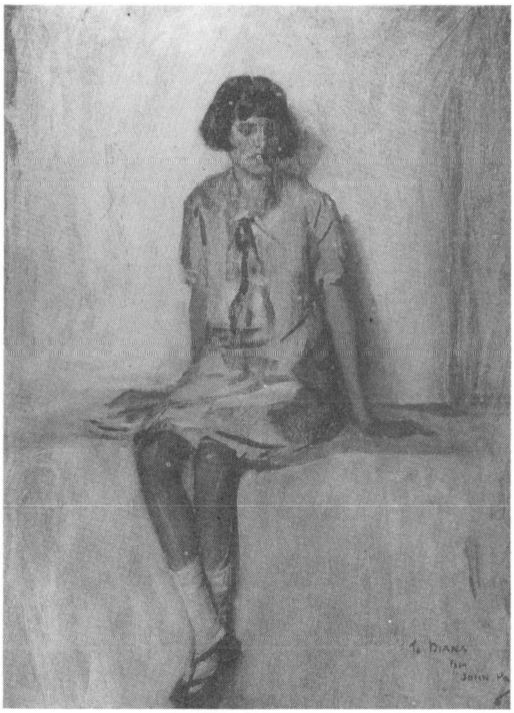

SIR JOHN LAVERY – Portrait Of Lady Diana Semphill – inscribed – oil on board – 60.5 x 46cm.
(Phillips) **$4,260** **£3,000**

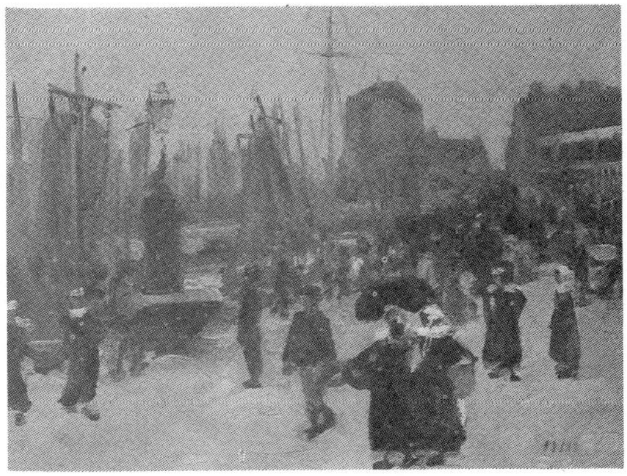

SIR JOHN LAVERY – A Wet Day, Concarneau – signed – oil on canvas – 11 x 13in.
(Christie's) **$12,584** **£8,800**

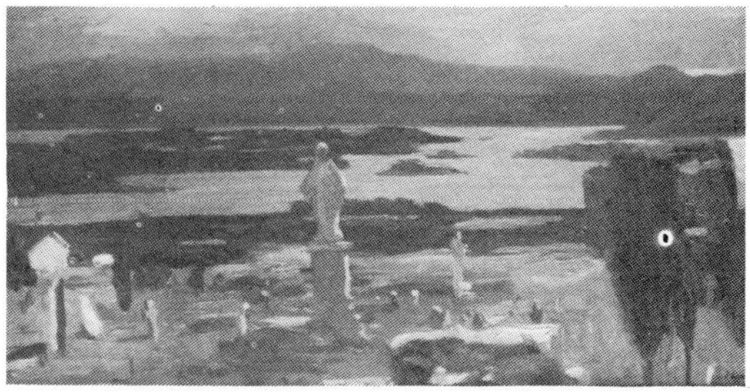

SIR JOHN LAVERY – The Madonna Of The Lakes, The Lakes Of Killarney – signed, and signed, inscribed and dated 1913 on the reverse – oil on canvas – 16 x 30in.
(Christie's) **$3,460** **£2,420**

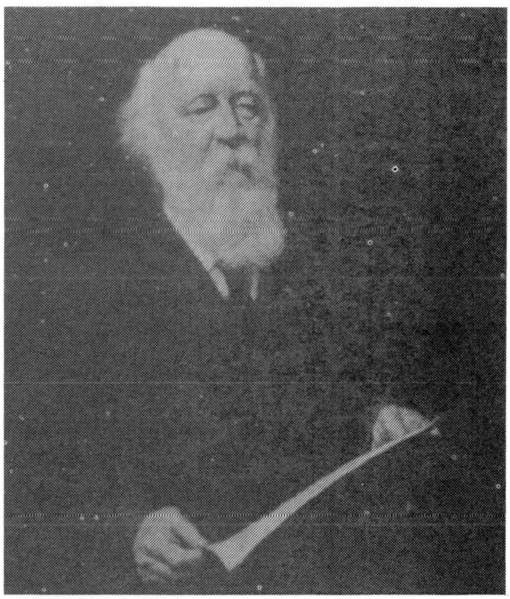

GEORGE WARREN LAWLOR – Portrait Of Darius Cobb – signed and dated 1915, inscribed on the reverse – oil on canvas – 40¼ x 30in.
(Robt. W. Skinner Inc.) **$850** **£521**

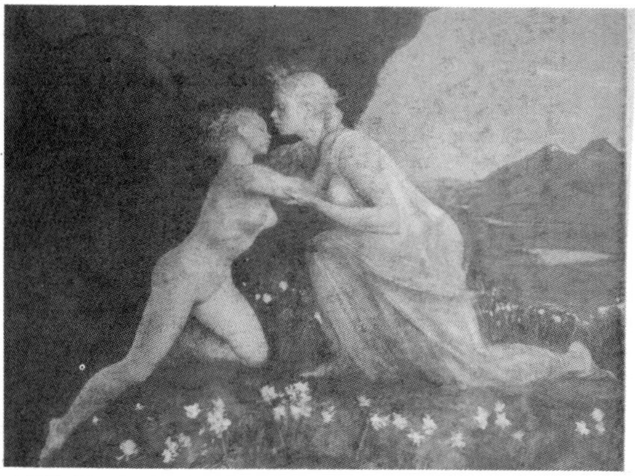

ALFRED KINGSLEY LAWRENCE – The Return Of Persephone – oil on canvas laid down on panel – 49½ x 60in.
(Christie's) **$3,932** **£2,750**

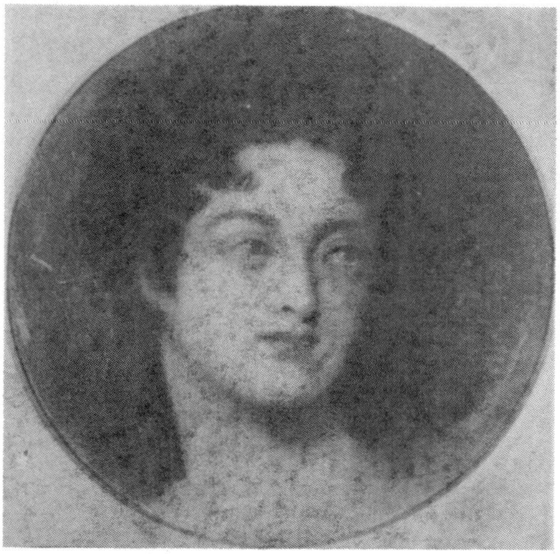

SIR THOMAS LAWRENCE, Circle of – Portrait Of A Young Beauty, Head And Shoulders – oil on canvas – 12½in. diam.
(Christie's) **$466** **£286**

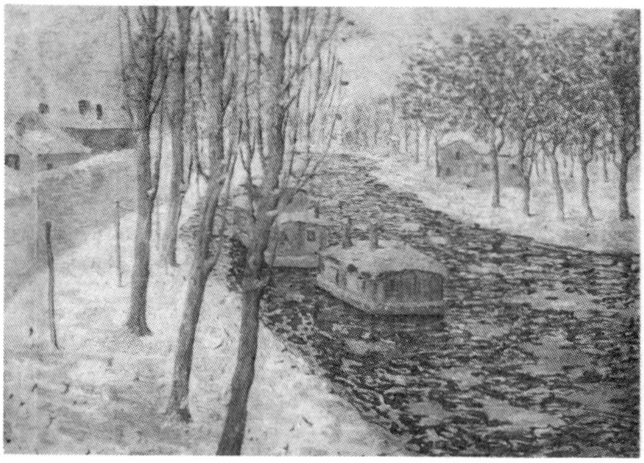

ERNEST LAWSON – Canal Scene In Winter – signed and dated '98 – oil on canvas – 22 x 26in.
(Christie's) **$82,500** **£57,997**

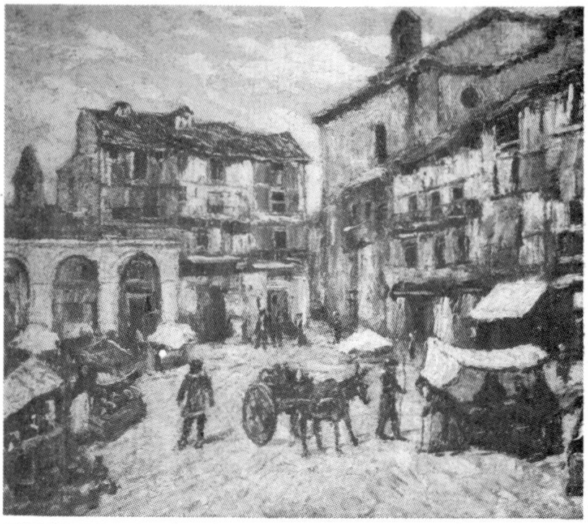

ERNEST LAWSON – Marketplace, Segovia – signed – oil on canvas – 25 x 30in.
(Christie's) **$6,050** **£4,253**

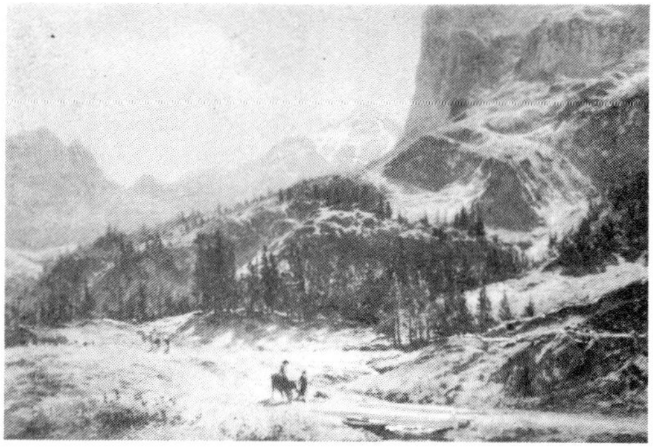

BENJAMIN WILLIAMS LEADER – At Rosenlaui, Switzerland – signed and dated 1873, and signed and inscribed on the reverse – oil on board – 15 x 23in.
(Christie's) **$2,946** **£2,090**

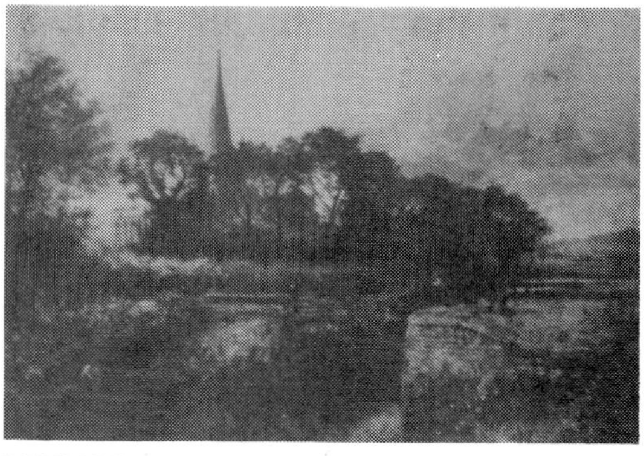

BENJAMIN WILLIAMS LEADER – The Lock And Church, Stratford On Avon – signed and dated 1870 and 1900, and signed and inscribed on the reverse – oil on board – 15½ x 23¾in.
(Christie's) **$4,963** **£3,520**

BENJAMIN WILLIAMS LEADER – A Summer's Day – signed and dated 1879 – 26 x 42in.
(Christie's) **$40,326** **£28,600**

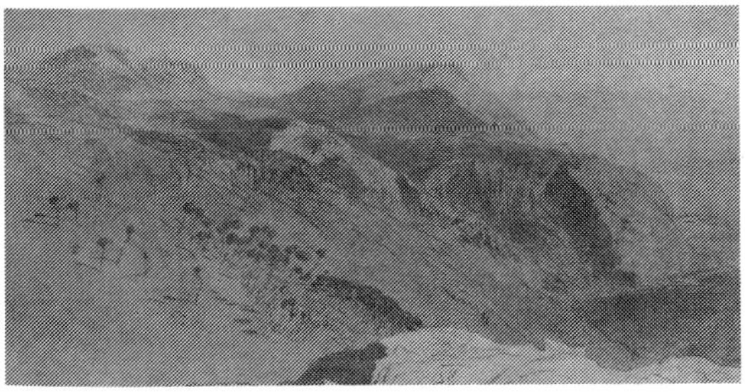

EDWARD LEAR – 'Eze' – inscribed and dated 1864 – pen and ink and watercolour heightened with white – 33 x 52cm.
(Phillips) **$13,692** **£8,400**

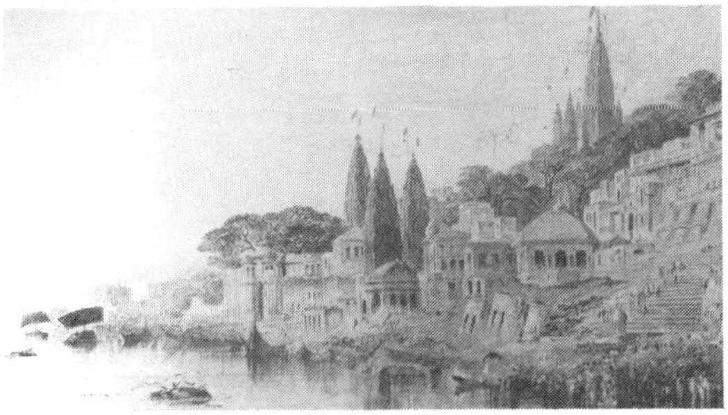

EDWARD LEAR – Scindia Ghat, Benares – signed with monogram and dated 1875, inscribed on the reverse – watercolour heightened with white – 10 x 15½in.
(Christie's) **$18,370** **£11,000**

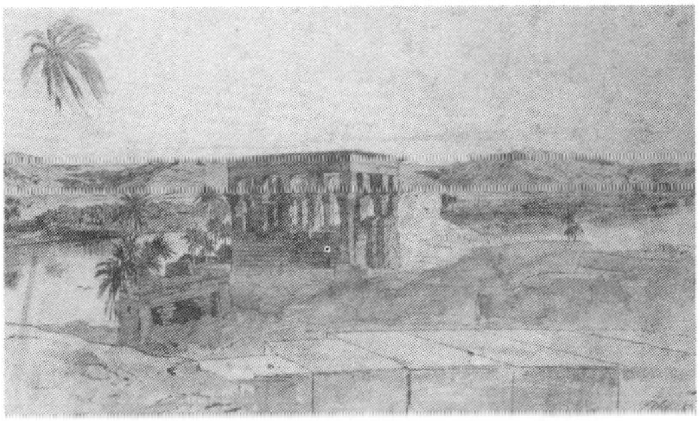

EDWARD LEAR – Philac – inscribed and dated 1854 – pencil, pen and brown ink and watercolour – 13¼ x 19¼in.
(Christie's) **$34,903** **£20,900**

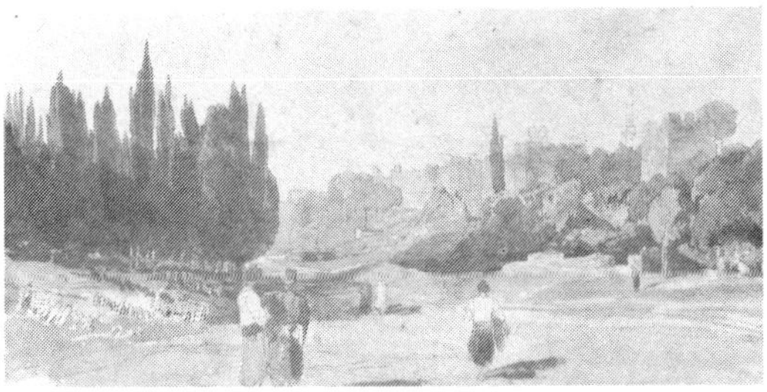

EDWARD LEAR – The Walls Of Constantinople – inscribed and dated 1848 – pencil, pen and brown ink and watercolour – 7 x 12½in.
(Christie's) **$11,940** **£7,150**

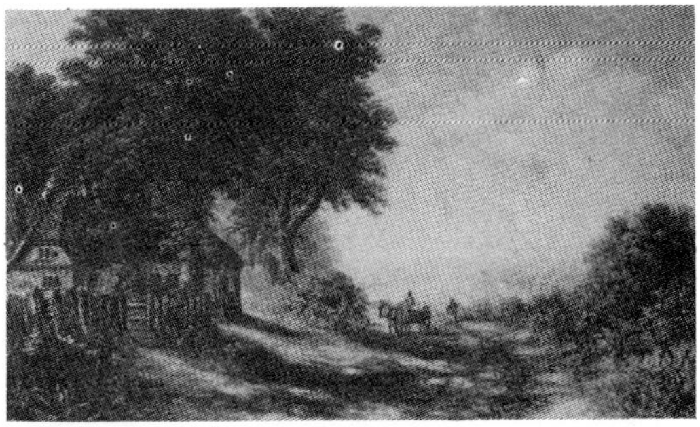

CHARLES LEAVER – Near Harding, Berkshire; and Near Alton, Hampshire – signed and dated 1865 – 12 x 18½in.
(Christie's) **$2,326** **£1,650 Pair**

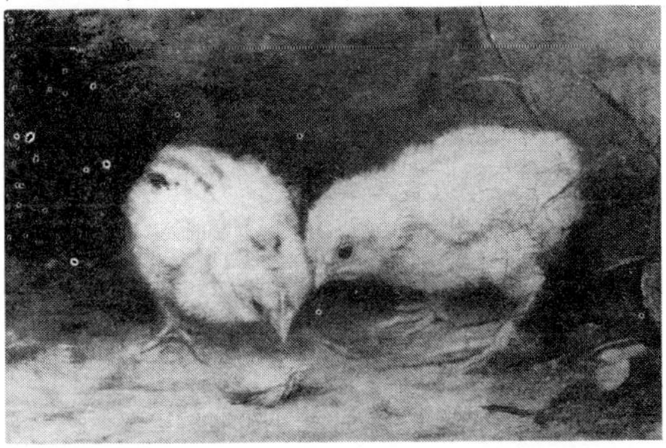

LUCY A. LEAVERS – At Play – signed with initials, and signed and inscribed on an old label on the reverse – 6¼ x 9in.
(Christie's) **$5,049** **£3,300**

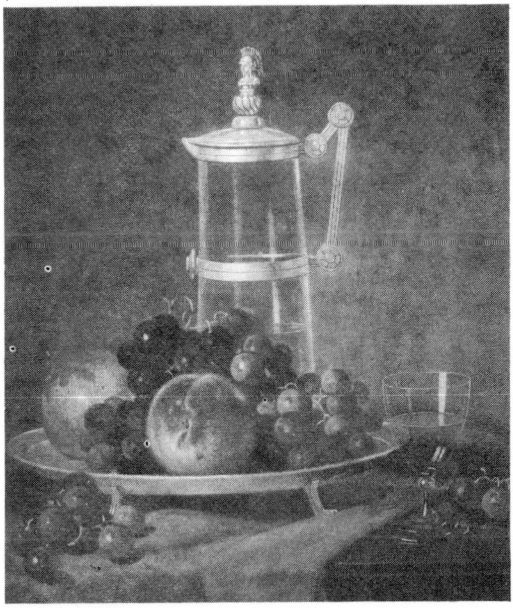

EDWARD CHALMERS LEAVITT – Tabletop Still Life – signed and dated 1876 – oil on canvas – 20¼ x 16¼in.
(Christie's) **$6,600** **£4,112**

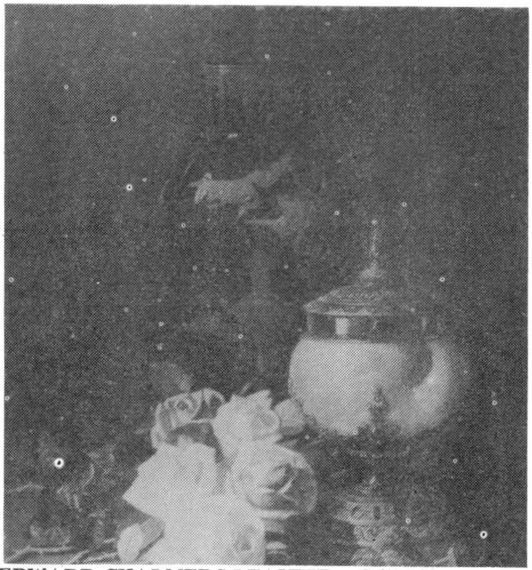

EDWARD CHALMERS LEAVITT – Still Life With Japanese Vase – signed and dated 1884 – oil on canvas – 30 x 20in.
(Robt. W. Skinner Inc.) **$3,250** **£2,256**

EDWARD CHALMERS LEAVITT – Still Life With Fruit And Venetian Glass – signed and dated 1881 – oil on canvas – 24 x 36in.
(Robt. W. Skinner Inc.) **$3,250** **£2,256**

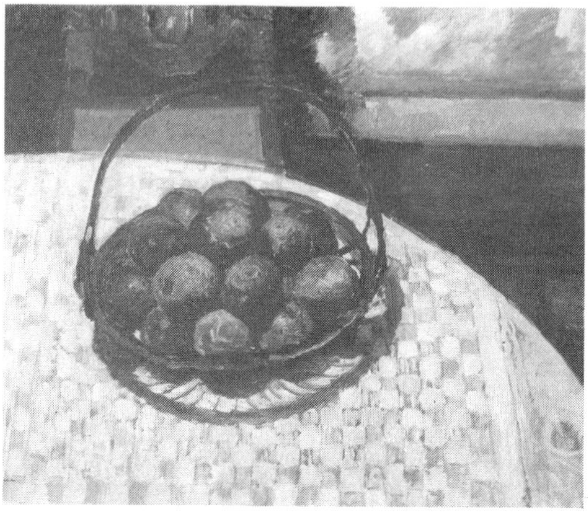

HENRI LEBASQUE – La Corbeille de Fruits – signed – oil on canvas – 26 x 32in.
(Christie's) **$58,784** **£35,200**

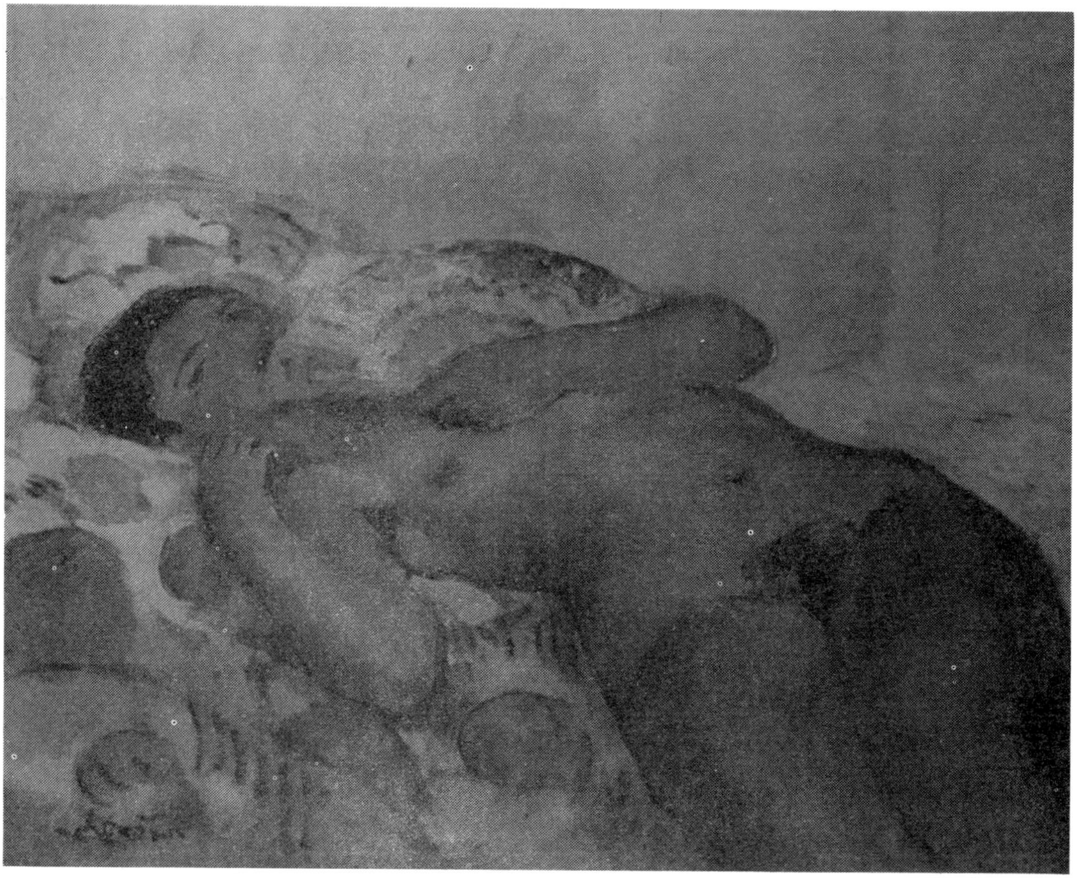

HENRI LEBASQUE – Nu A l'Eventail – signed – oil on canvas – 33 x 41cm. *(Phillips)* **$9,300** **£6,000**

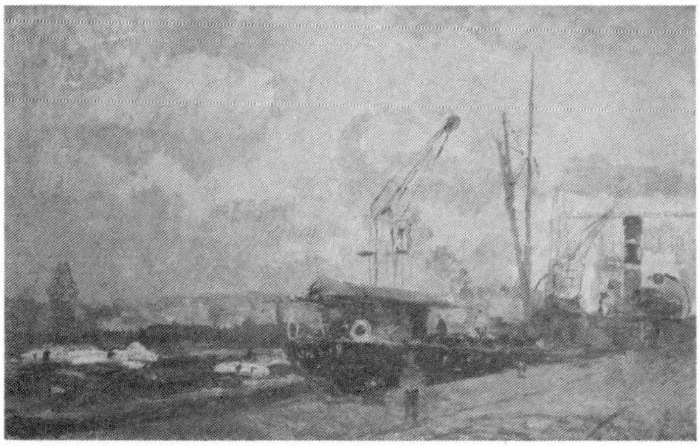

ALBERT LEBOURG – Steamers et Chalands dans le Port de Rouen, Effet de Soleil couchant – signed and dated 1907 – oil on canvas – 22¾ x 35½in.
(Christie's) **$27,555** **£16,500**

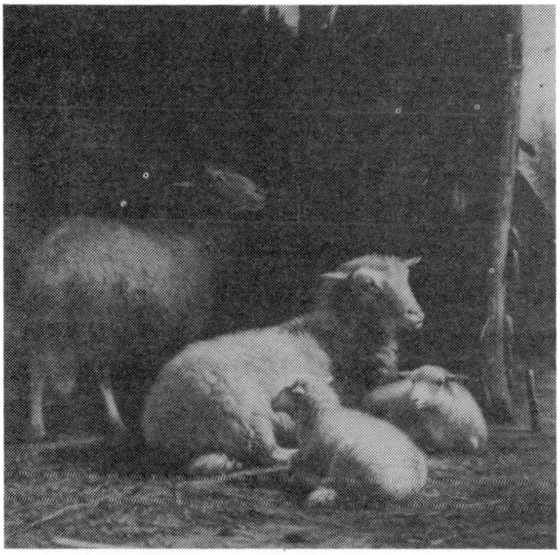

FRANS LEBRET – Ewes And Lambs Nestled In A Shed – signed – oil on canvas – 29½ x 39½in.
(Robt. W. Skinner Inc.) **$1,900** **£1,319**

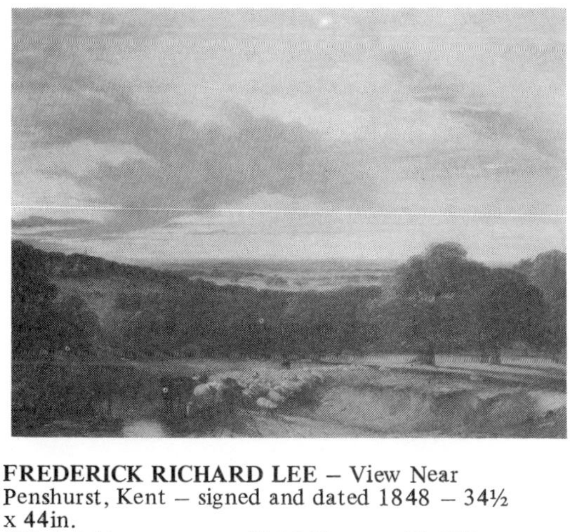

FREDERICK RICHARD LEE – View Near Penshurst, Kent – signed and dated 1848 – 34½ x 44in.
(Christie's) **$14,960** **£9,350**

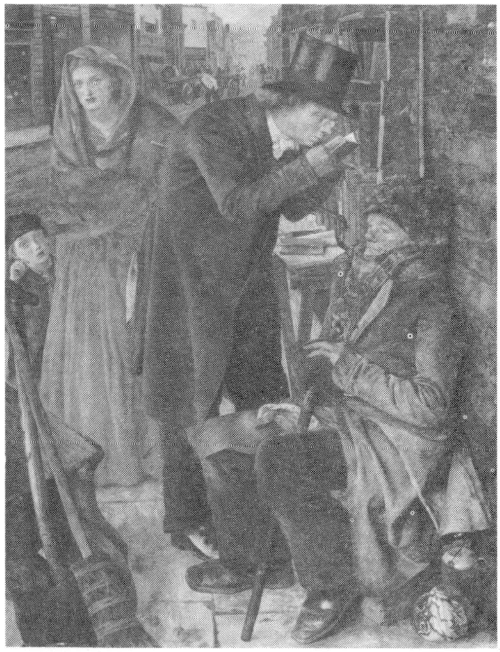

JOHN J. LEE – The Bookstall – signed and dated 1863 – 40 x 32in.
(Christie's) **$105,600** **£66,000**

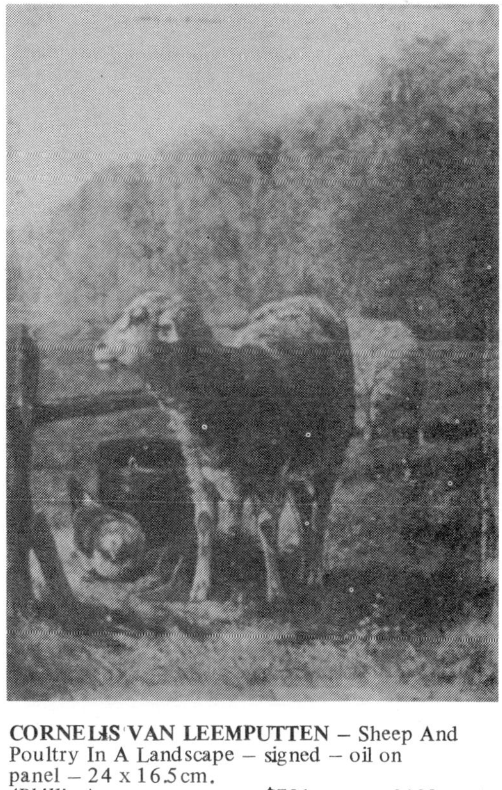

CORNELIS VAN LEEMPUTTEN – Sheep And Poultry In A Landscape – signed – oil on panel – 24 x 16.5cm.
(Phillips) **$701** **£420**

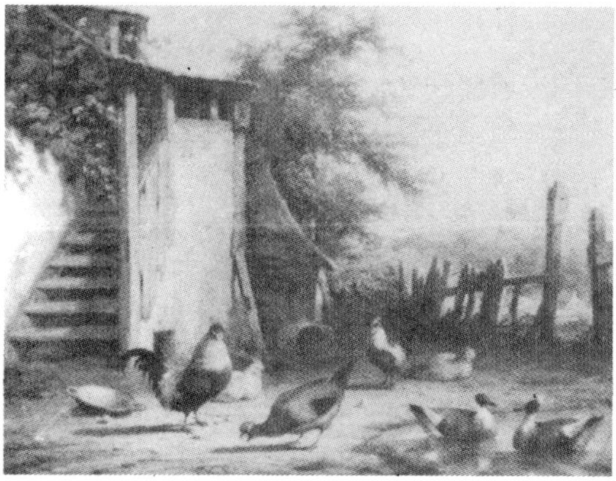

CORNELIS VAN LEEMPUTTEN – Poultry And Ducks In A Farmyard – signed – on panel – 8½ x 11in.
(Christie's) **$1,650** **£1,100**

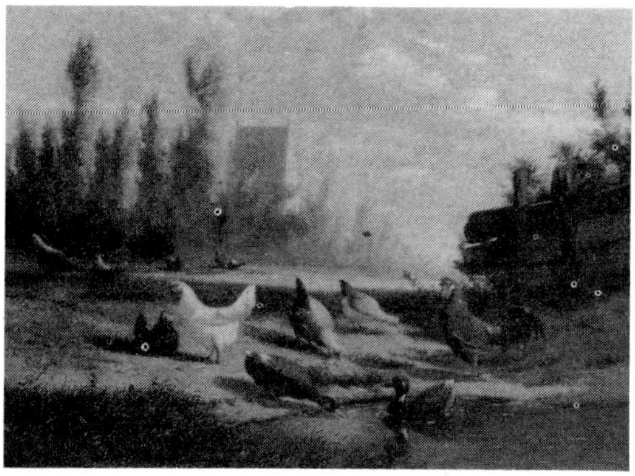

JEFF LOUIS VAN LEEMPUTTEN – Poultry By A Pond – signed and dated 1874 – on panel – 9¼ x 13¾in.
(Christie's) **$1,504** **£990**

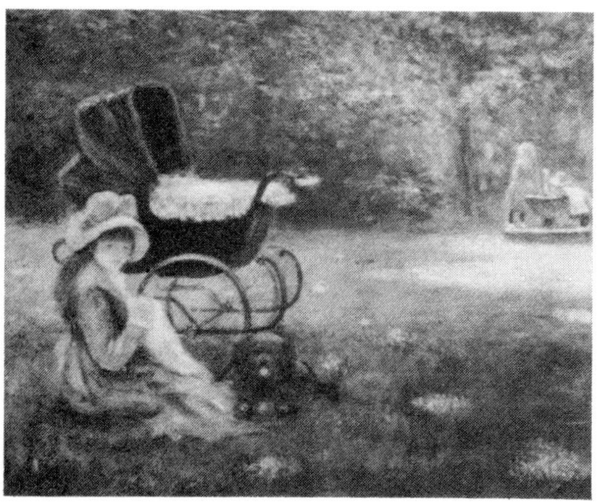

MARIE LEFEVRE – Victorian Children In The Park With Dog And Pram – signed – oil on canvas – 35 x 40cm.
(W. H. Lane & Son) **$1,162** **£700**

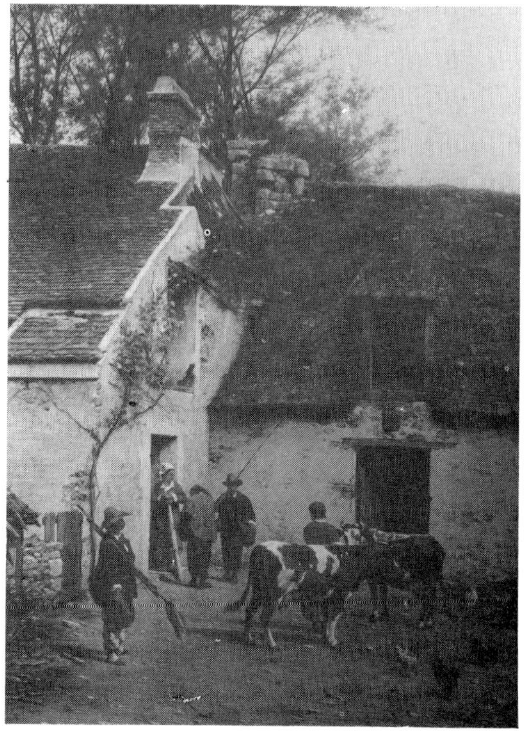

LEON LEGAT – 'Off To The Fishing' – signed – on canvas – 117 x 90cm.
(Phillips) **$11,520** **£8,000**

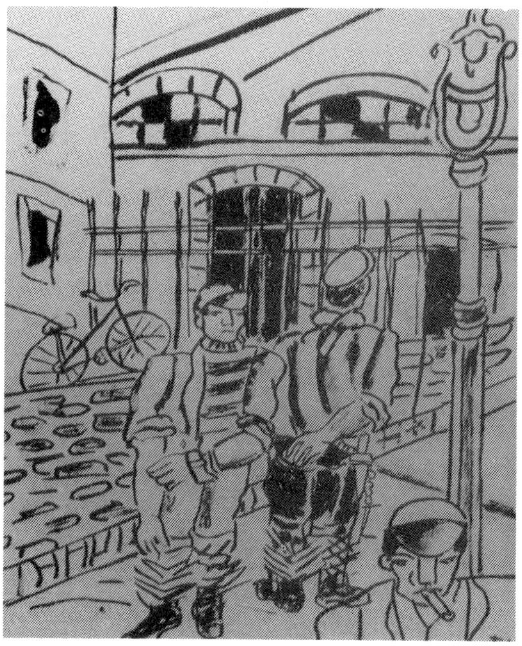

FERNAND LEGER – Vaugirard, les Abattoirs (etude pour 'La Ville') – signed – brush and black ink on paper – 16½ x 12½in.
(Christie's) **$12,672** **£8,800**

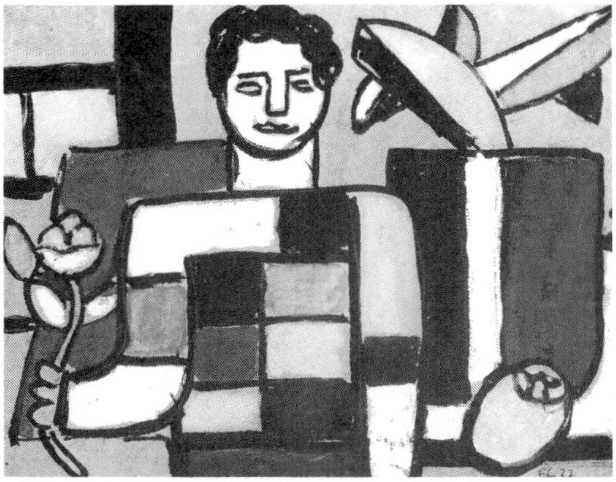

FERNAND LEGER – Jeune Homme aux Fleurs – signed and dated '31 – gouache on paper – 9¾ x 12¾in.
(Christie's) **$38,016** **£26,400**

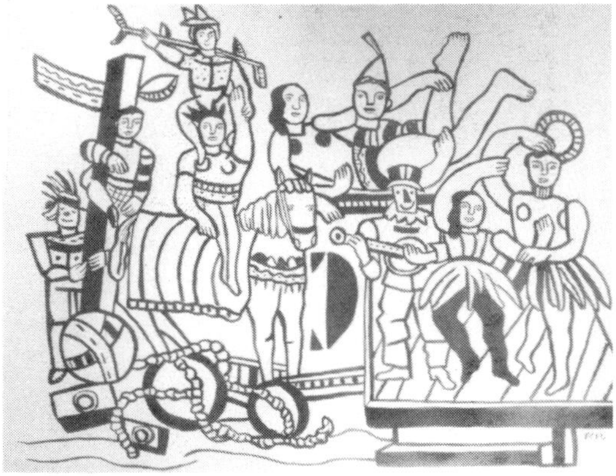

FERNAND LEGER – Study For 'La Grande Parade' – signed and dated – brush and black ink on paper – 24½ x 31½in.
(Christie's) **$87,120** **£60,500**

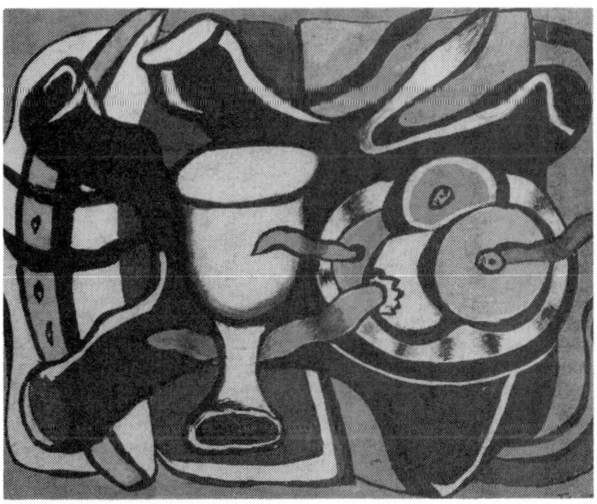

FERNAND LEGER – Nature morte aux Pommes – signed and dated '48 – gouache on paper – 10 x 13in.
(Christie's) **$38,720** **£24,200**

RENE LEGRAND – Extensive Beach Scene With Edwardian Woman And Children Building Sand Castles And Paddling – signed – oil on canvas – 50 x 76cm.
(W. H. Lane & Son) **$3,984** **£2,400**

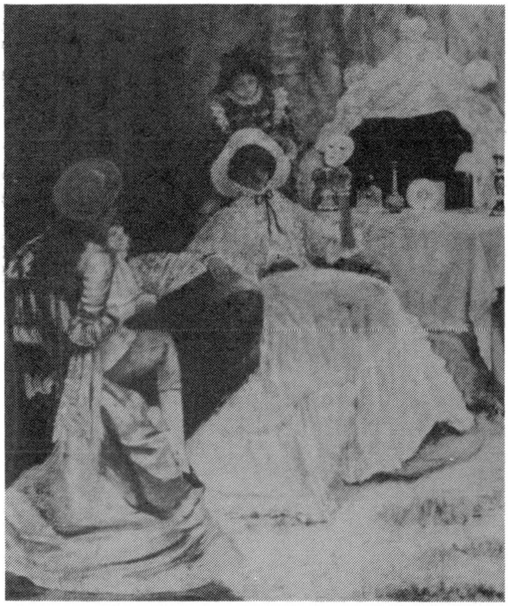

RENE LEGRAND – Columbine Supreme – signed and inscribed on the reverse – oil on canvas – 51 x 41cm.
(Phillips) **$1,860** **£1,200**

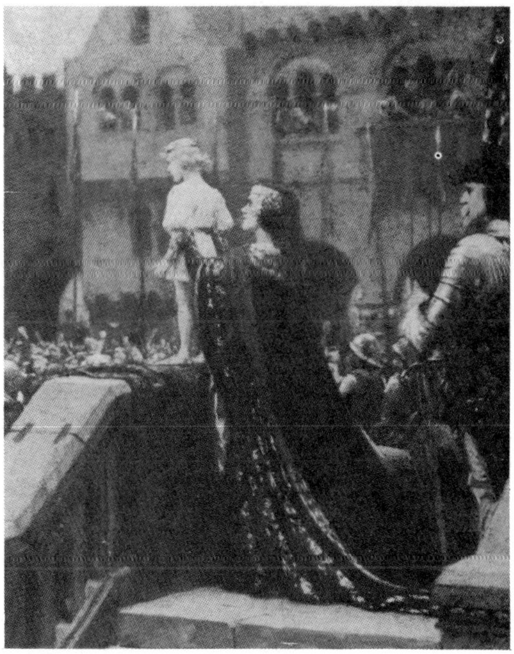

EDMUND BLAIR LEIGHTON – 'Vox Populi' – signed – oil on panel – 9 x 7¼in.
(Phillips) **$459** **£300**

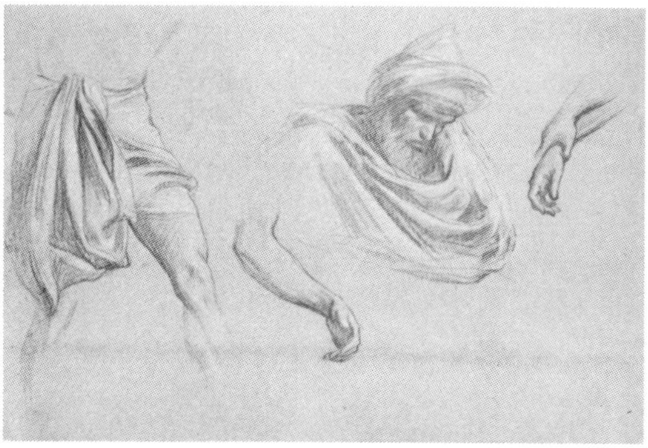

FREDERIC LORD LEIGHTON – A Sheet Of Studies For Jezebel And Ahab – black and white chalk on blue paper – 10¾ x 15½in.
(Christie's) **$1,053** **£702**

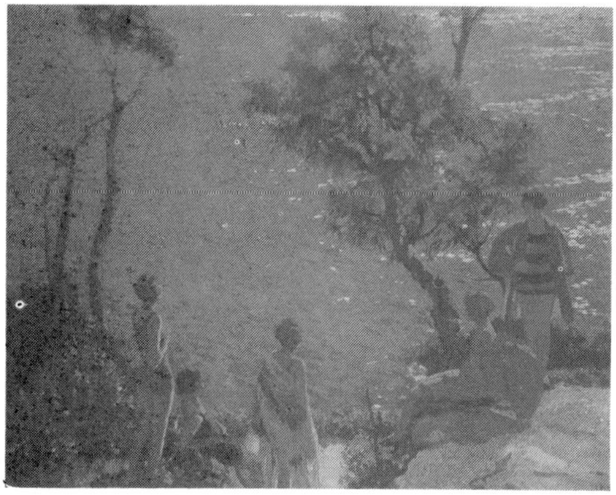

FRED LEIST – A Bathing Party, Sydney Harbour – signed – oil on board – 71 x 91cm.
(Phillips) **$24,140** **£17,000**

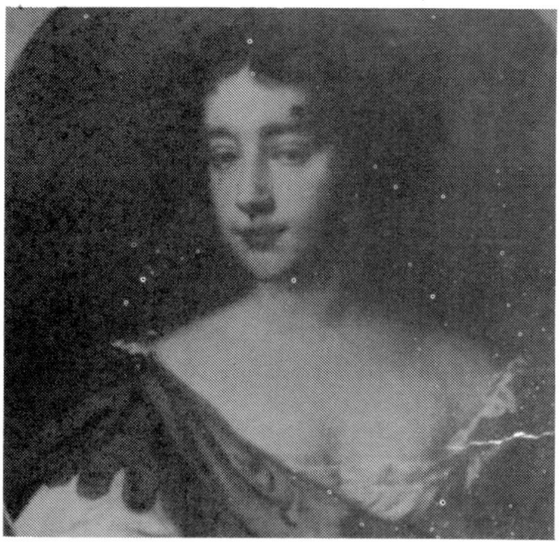

PETER LELY, After – A Portrait Of Nell Gwynn, Bust Length, Wearing A Brown Dress And Blue Cape – oil on canvas – 24 x 20in.
(Phillips) **$796** **£480**

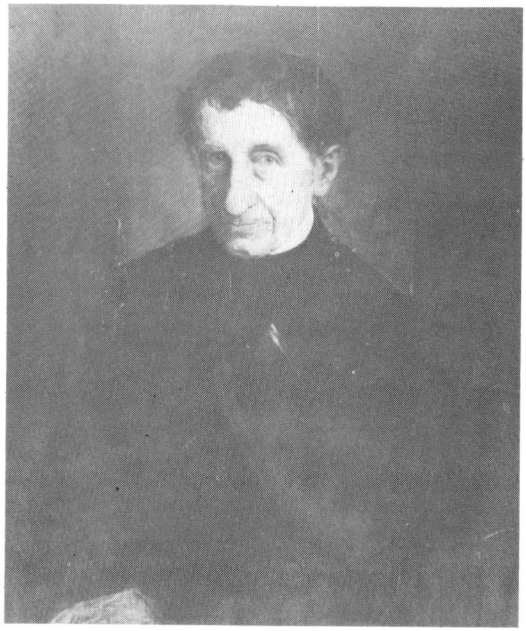

FRANZ SERAPH VON LENBACH – Portrait Of Doctor Dollinger – signed and dated '78 – on panel – 87 x 69cm.
(Phillips) **$2,448** **£1,700**

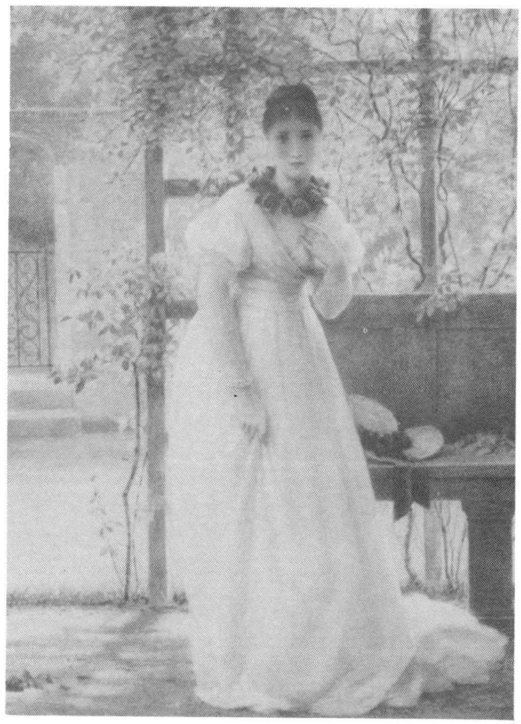

GEORGE DUNLOP LESLIE – In The Walled Garden – signed and dated 1869 – watercolour heightened with white – 25 x 18in.
(Christie's) **$5,890** **£3,850**

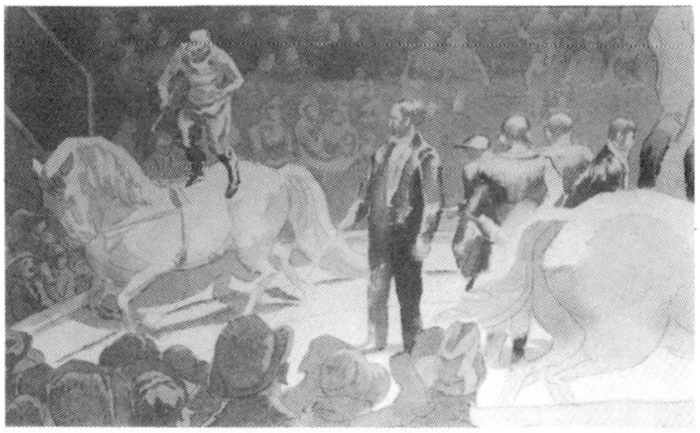

THERESE LESSORE – Equestrian Circus Acts – signed and dated 1928 – watercolour – 7½ x 12¼in.
(Geering & Colyer) **$1,694** **£1,100 Pair**

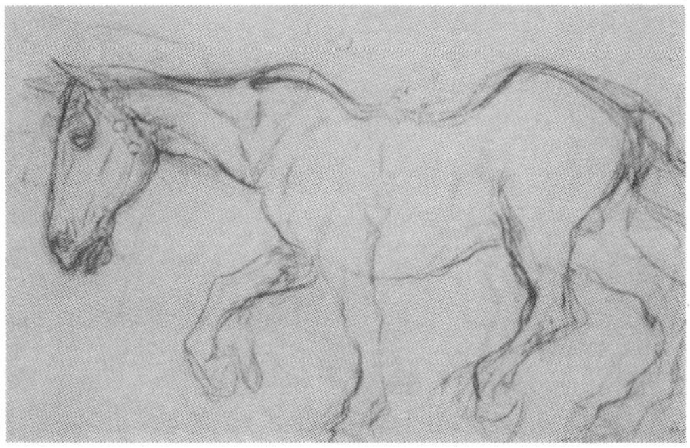

JACK LEVINE – Horse – signed – charcoal and brown ink on buff paper – 19½ x 30¾in.
(Christie's) **$1,210** **£841**

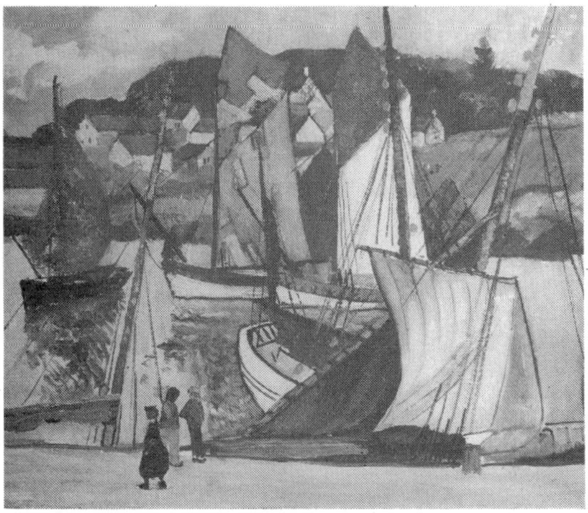

RICHARD HAYLEY LEVER – Sailboats In Cornwall – signed – oil on canvas – 20¼ x 24¼in.
(Christie's) **$12,100** **£7,539**

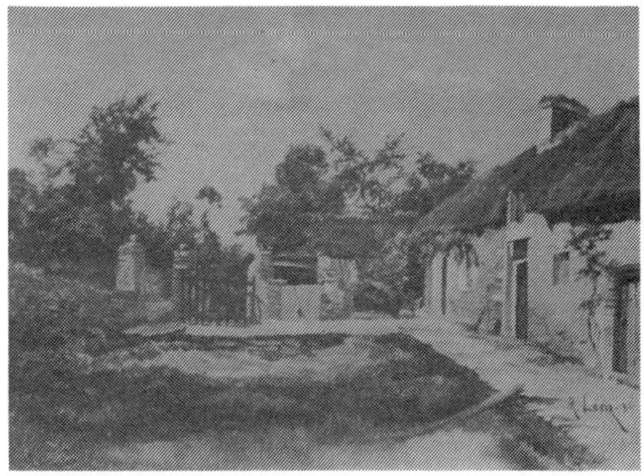

MAURICE LEVIS – Figures Outside A Thatched Cottage – signed and dated '91 – on panel – 16 x 21.5cm.
(Phillips) **$1,283** **£850**

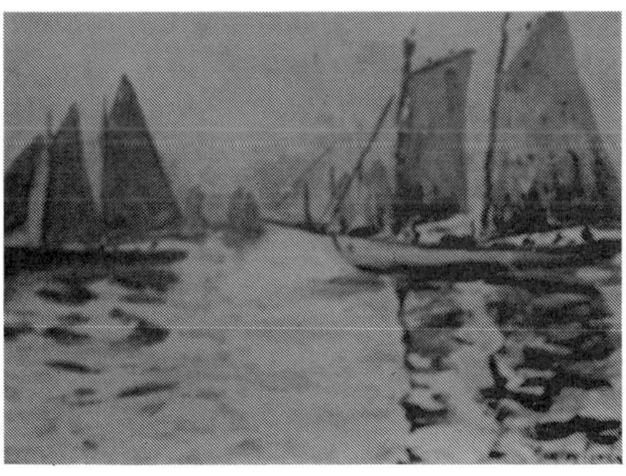

RICHARD HAYLEY LEVER – Sunset In The Harbour – signed – oil on board – 12 x 16in.
(Robt. W. Skinner Inc.) **$2,000** **£1,226**

RICHARD HAYLEY LEVER – Boat House, Marblehead – signed and inscribed – watercolour on paper – 14¼ x 22¼in.
(Christie's) **$1,540** **£1,071**

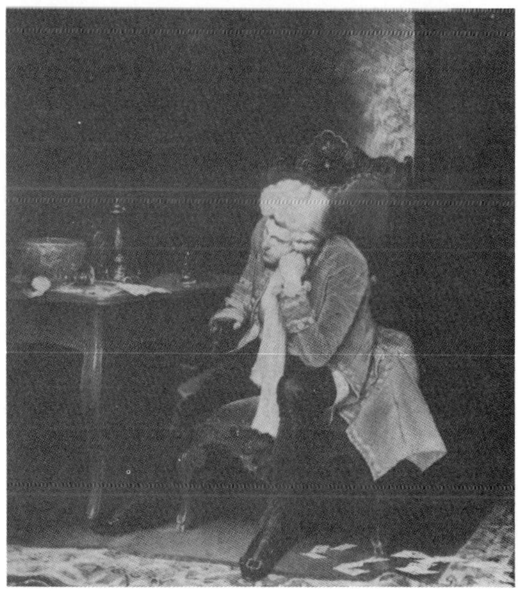

STEPHEN LEWIN – The Loser – signed and dated '85 – 42 x 31½in.
(Christie's) **$2,481** **£1,760**

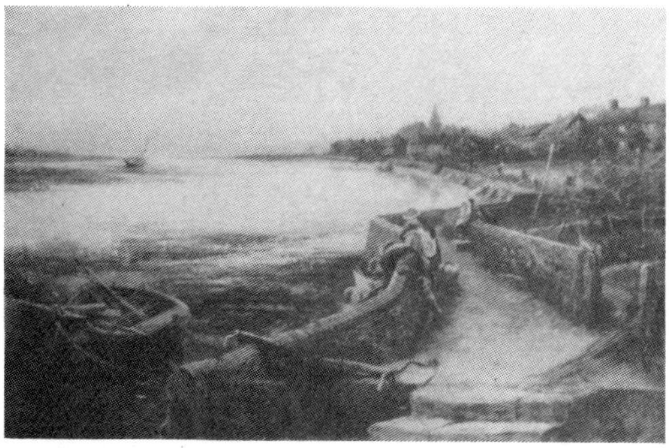

CHARLES JAMES LEWIS – A Village Near Chichester – signed, and signed and inscribed on a label on the stretcher – 22 x 32½in.
(Christie's) **$1,861** **£1,320**

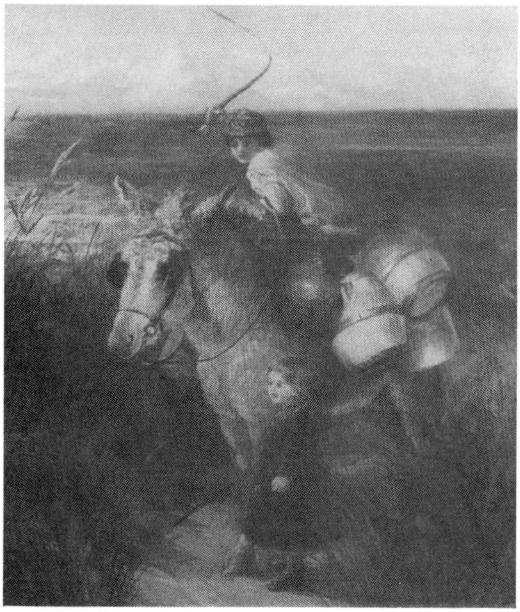

CHARLES JAMES LEWIS – In The Dunes – signed and indistinctly dated – 16½ x 12¾in.
(Christie's) **$1,053** **£702**

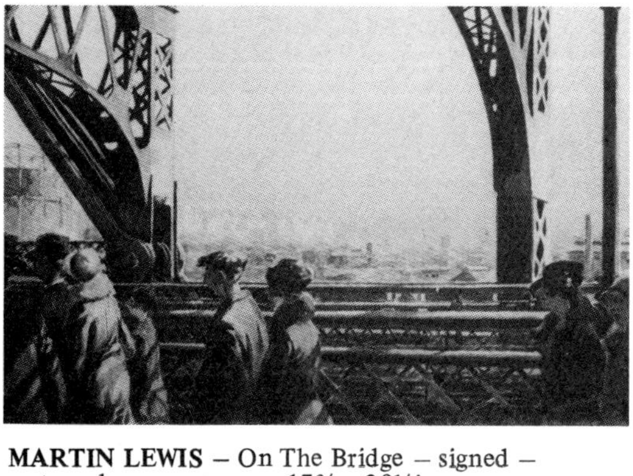

MARTIN LEWIS – On The Bridge – signed – watercolour on paper – 17¾ x 20½in.
(Christie's) **$7,150** **£4,974**

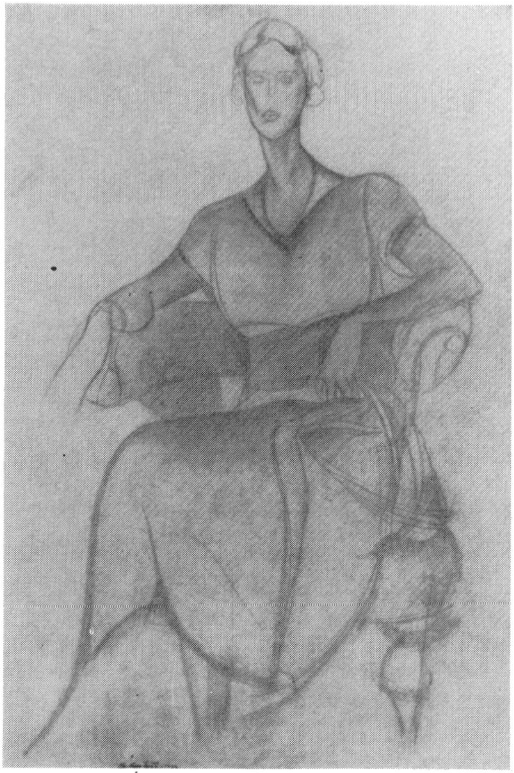

PERCY WYNDHAM LEWIS – Portrait Of A Lady, Full Length, Seated In A Chair – signed and dated 1922 – pencil and brown wash – 18 x 12¾in.
(Christie's) **$5,181** **£3,300**

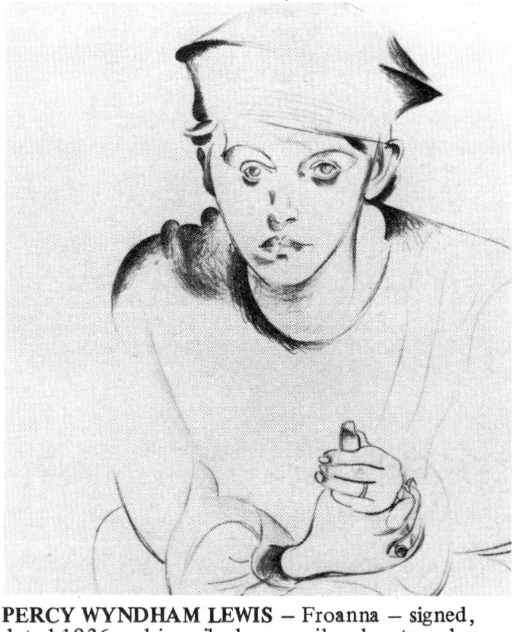

PERCY WYNDHAM LEWIS – Froanna – signed, dated 1936 and inscribed – pencil and watercolour on paper – 19½ x 10½in.
(Christie's) **$6,336** **£4,400**

LUCAS VAN LEYDEN, Manner of – The Card Players – oil on copper – 13½ x 18½in.
(Phillips) **$3,384** **£2,400**

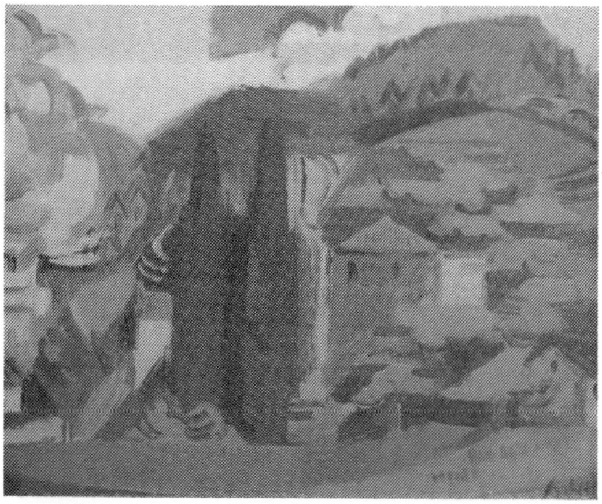

ANDRE LHOTE – Paysage du Midi – signed – oil on board – 10½ x 13½in.
(Christie's) **$7,920** **£4,950**

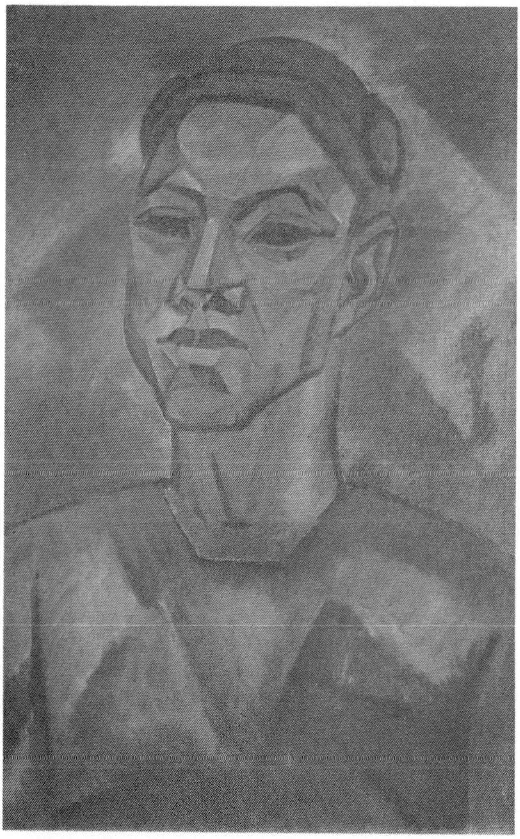

ANDRE LHOTE – Le Negre – signed, and inscribed and dated 1912 on the reverse – oil on canvas – 29½ x 19½in.
(Christie's) **$13,464** **£9,350**

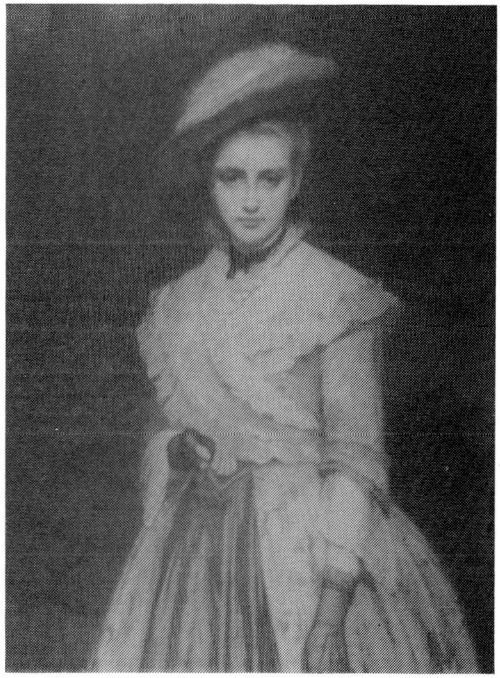

CHARLES SILLEM LIDDERDALE – The Squire's Daughter – signed with monogram and dated '78 – 30 x 21in.
(Christie's) **$3,197** **£2,090**

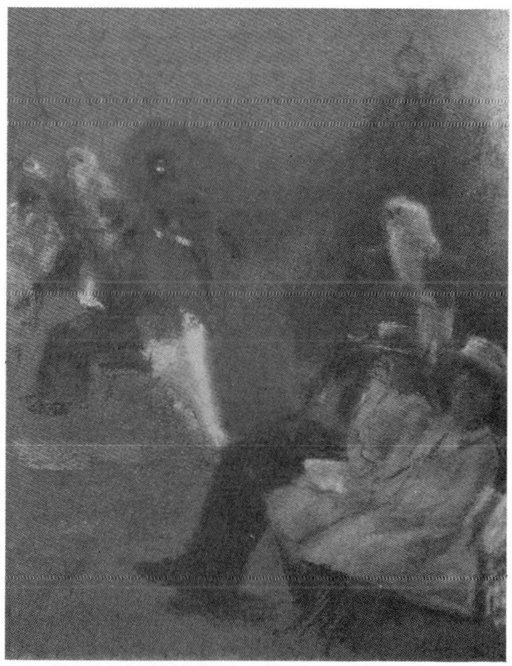

MAX LIEBERMANN – Entwurf fur 'Papageienallee' – signed – pastel and charcoal on grey paper – 18½ x 14½in.
(Christie's) **$50,688** **£35,200**

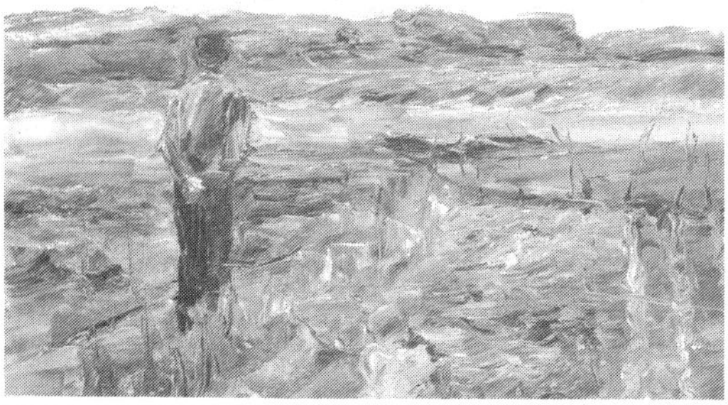

MAX LIEBERMANN – Im Krautergarten – signed and dated 1912 – oil on canvas – 19½ x 26¾in.
(Christie's) **$60,192 £41,800**

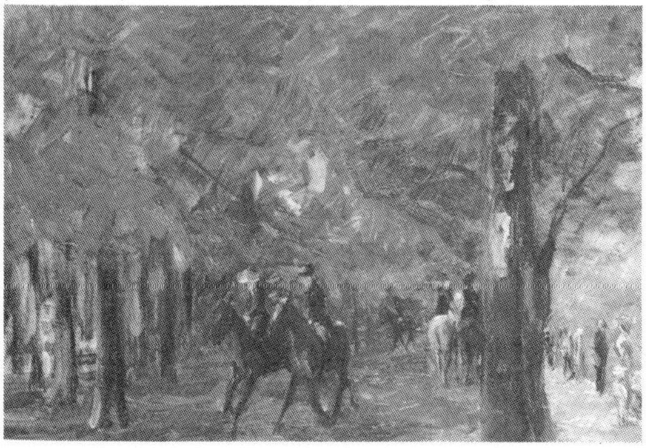

MAX LIEBERMANN – Reiter im Tiergarten, Berlin – signed – oil on panel – 12½ x 16in.
(Christie's) **$158,400 £110,000**

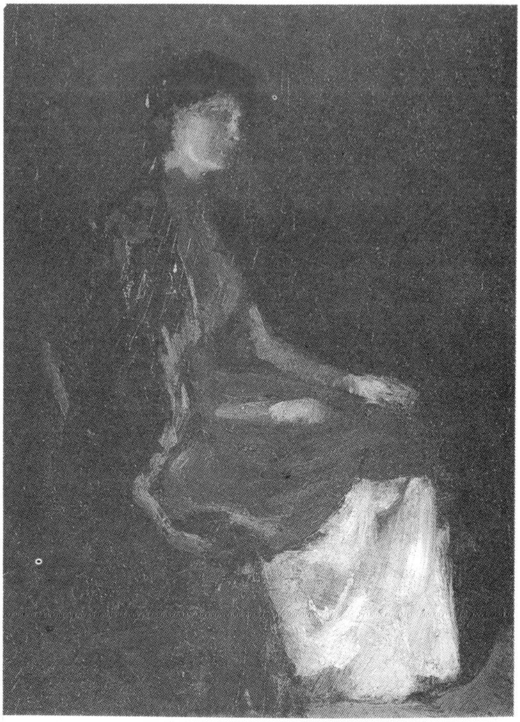

MAX LIEBERMANN – Sitzendes Modell – signed – oil on panel – 16½ x 11in.
(Christie's) **$13,464 £9,350**

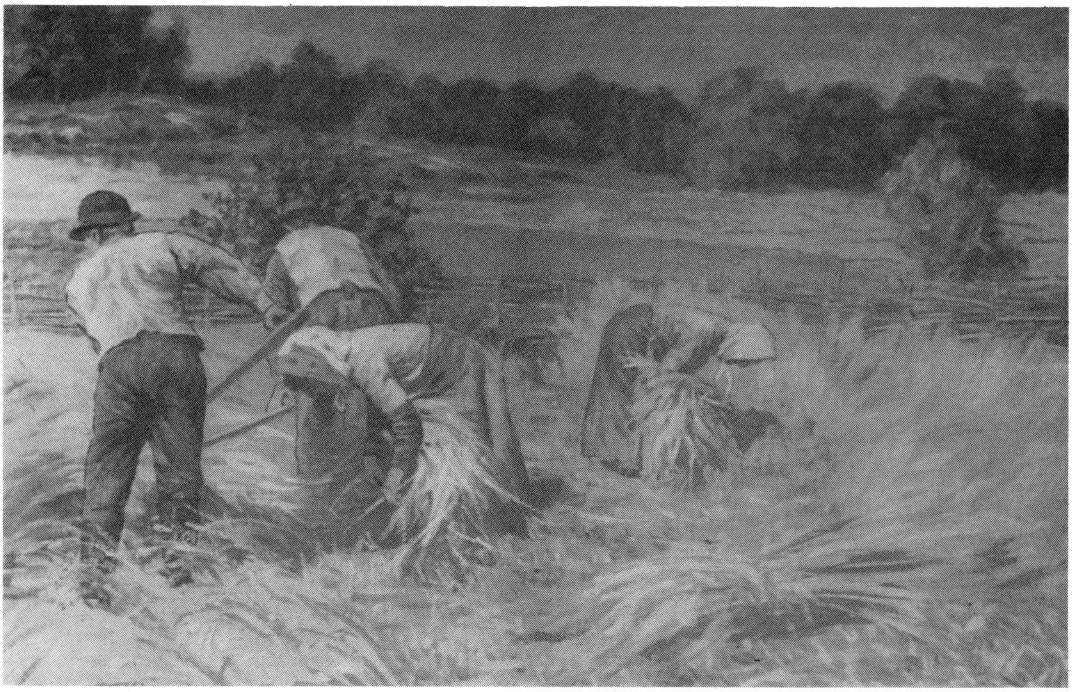

EMIL LINDGREN – Harvesters In A Landscape – signed, dated 1923 and inscribed – oil on canvas – 27 x 36in. *(Christie's)* **$4,576 £2,860**

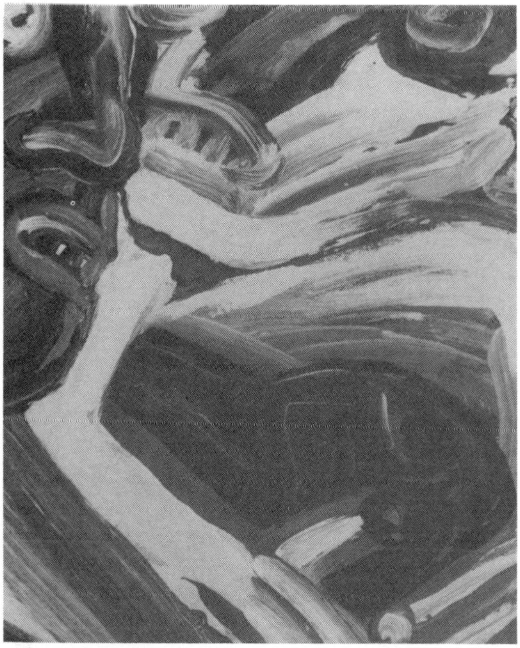

BENGT LINDSTROM – Untitled – signed – gouache on paperboard mounted on canvas – 29 x 22in.
(Christie's) **$1,320** **£825**

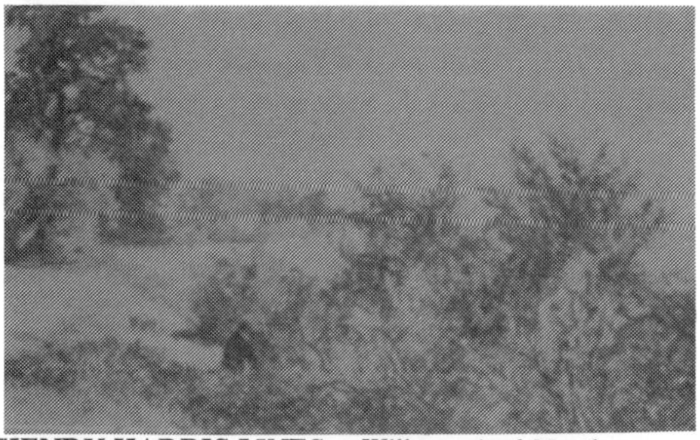

HENRY HARRIS LINES – Willows And Nettles – signed and dated 1856, also signed and inscribed on the reverse – on board – 10 x 14in.
(Phillips) **$611** **£380**

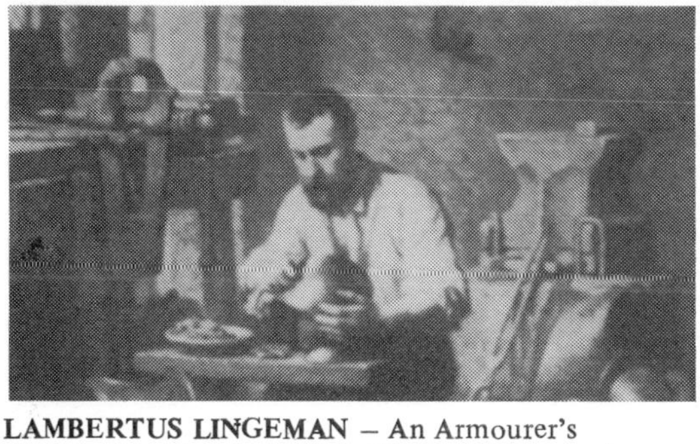

LAMBERTUS LINGEMAN – An Armourer's Workshop – signed and dated '77 – oil on panel – 24 x 30cm.
(Phillips) **$1,753** **£1,050**

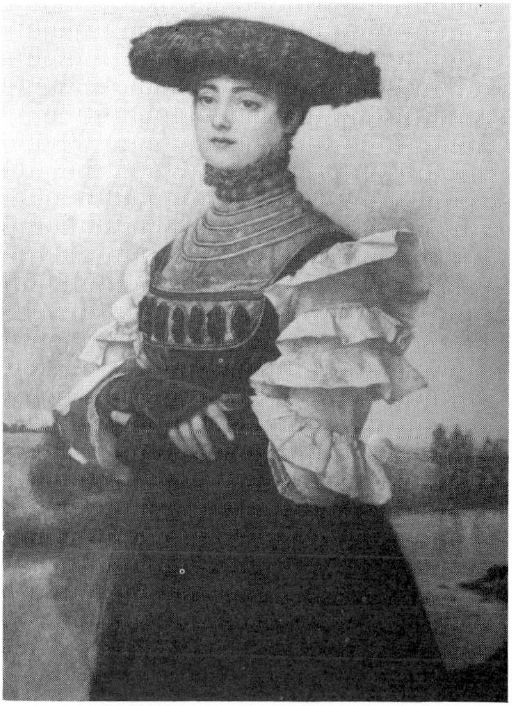

JAMES D. LINTON – Portrait Study Of A Young Lady Near A River – signed with monogram and dated '88 – watercolour – 18 x 13in.
(Biddle & Webb) **$1,501** **£950**

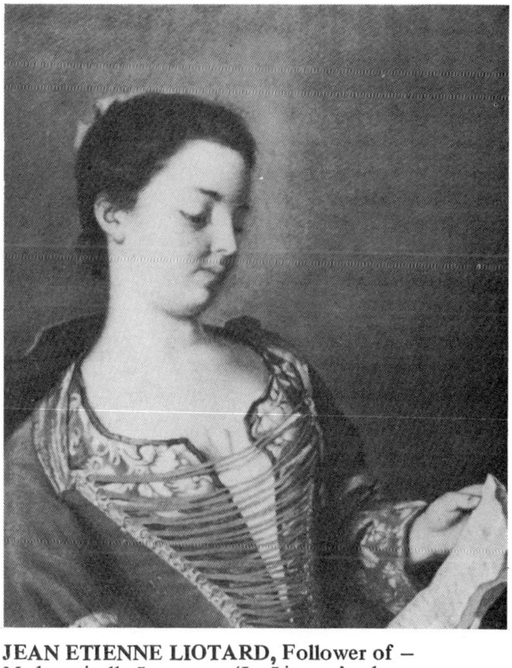

JEAN ETIENNE LIOTARD, Follower of – Mademoiselle Lavergne, 'La Liseuse' – bears monogram – oil on canvas – 13¾ x 11½in.
(Phillips) **$1,339** **£950**

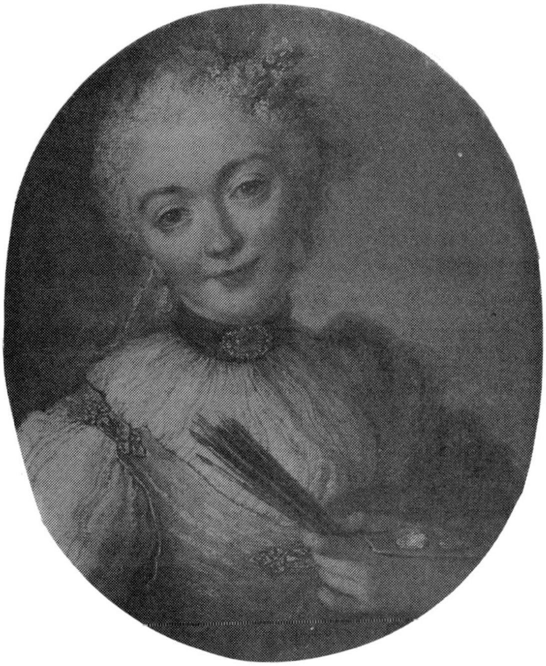

ANNA DOROTHEA THERBUSCH LISIEWSKA – A Portrait Of A Painter – on canvas – 19¾ x 16¼in.
(Phillips) **$7,968** **£4,800**

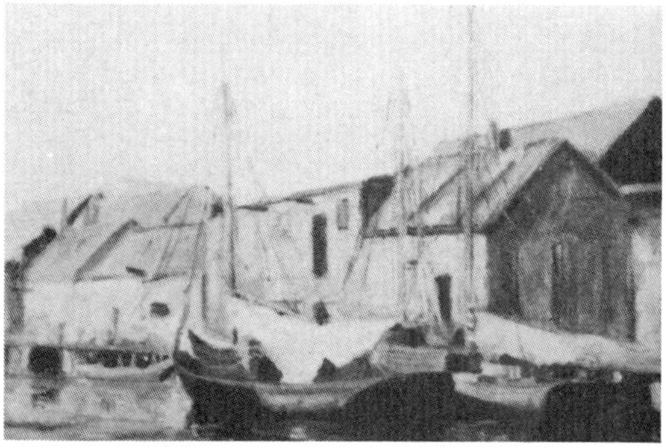

PHILIP LITTLE – Sailboats Along The Wharf – signed – oil on canvas – oil on canvas – 20 x 26¼in.
(Robt. W. Skinner Inc.) **$3,400** **£2,361**

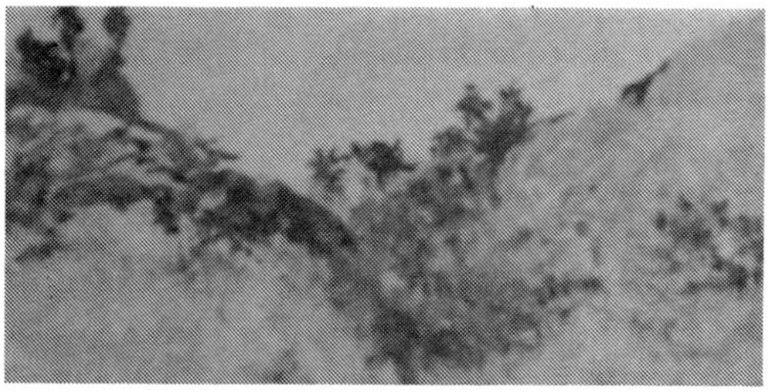

PHILIP LITTLE – Autumn Landscape – signed and dated 1933 – watercolour on paper – 9 x 13½in.
(Robt. W. Skinner Inc.) **$200** **£122**

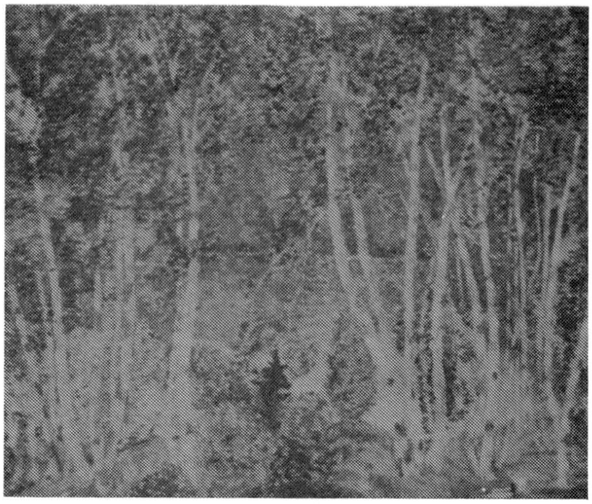

DOROTHEA M. LITZINGER – Lake Landscape With White Birch – oil on canvas – 40 x 45in.
(Robt. W. Skinner Inc.) **$5,500** **£3,374**

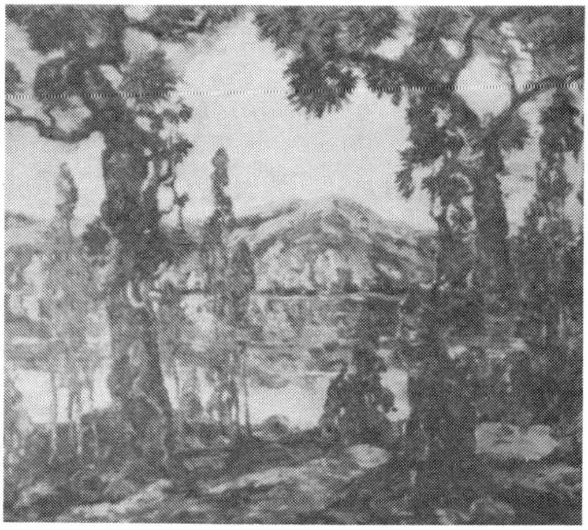

DOROTHEA M. LITZINGER – Lake Landscape – oil on canvas – 40 x 42in.
(Robt. W. Skinner Inc.) **$2,800** **£1,717**

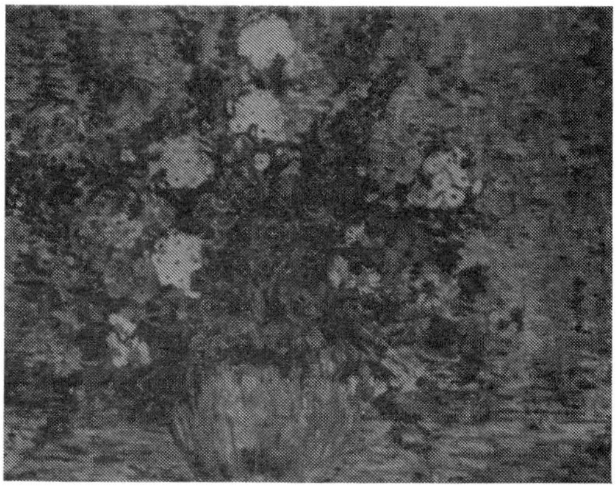

DOROTHEA M. LITZINGER – Flowers – oil on canvas – 34 x 40in.
(Robt. W. Skinner Inc.) **$6,500** **$3,987**

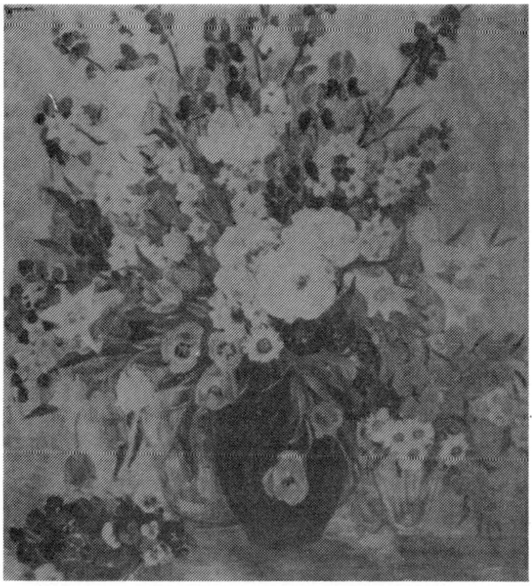

DOROTHEA M. LITZINGER – Floral Still Life – signed – oil on canvas – 50 x 45in.
(Robt. W. Skinner Inc.) **$4,750** **£2,914**

DOROTHEA M. LITZINGER – Floral Still Life – signed – oil on canvas – 54 x 48in.
(Robt. W. Skinner Inc.) **$3,500** **£2,430**

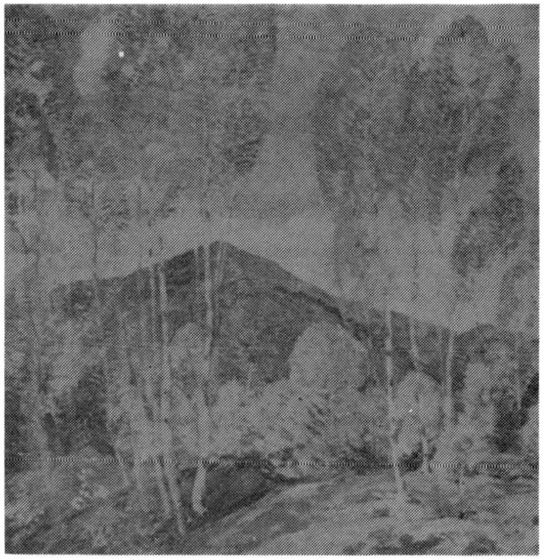

DOROTHEA M. LITZINGER – Hilltop Landscape With Birch Trees – oil-on canvas – 36 x 36in.
(Robt. W. Skinner Inc.) **$5,000** **£3,067**

HENRY LIVENS – Still Life, Flowers With Bird's Eggs And Nest – signed and dated – oil on canvas – 20 x 24in.
(Morphets) **$1,046** **£675**

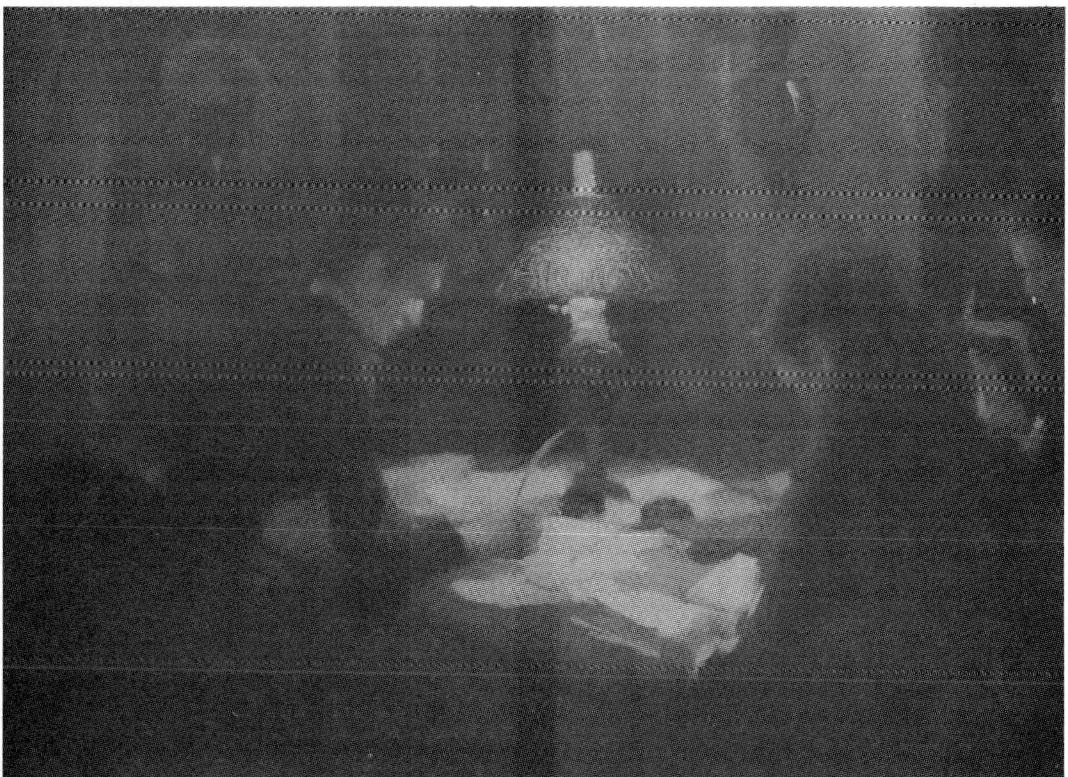

SIR WILLIAM LLEWELLYN – Lamplit Interior – signed and dated '87, also signed on the reverse – oil on panel – 28 x 40cm. *(Phillips)* **$4,800** **£3,000**

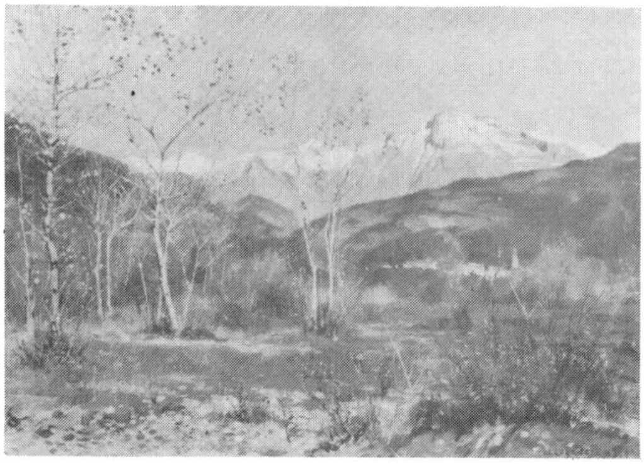

WILLIAM LOGSDAIL – The Col De Tenda From Ventimeglia – signed and dated '91 – oil on canvas board – 25.5 x 35.5cm.
(Phillips) **$1,101** **£720**

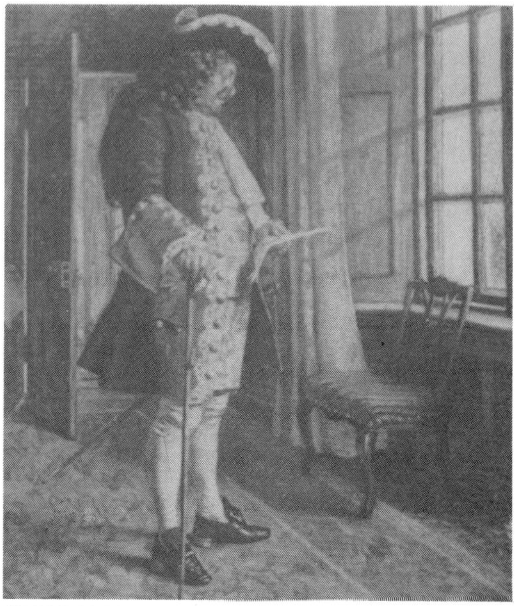

JOHN ARTHUR LOMAX, Circle of – The Letter – paper laid on panel – 14 x 12in.
(Christie's) **$466** **£286**

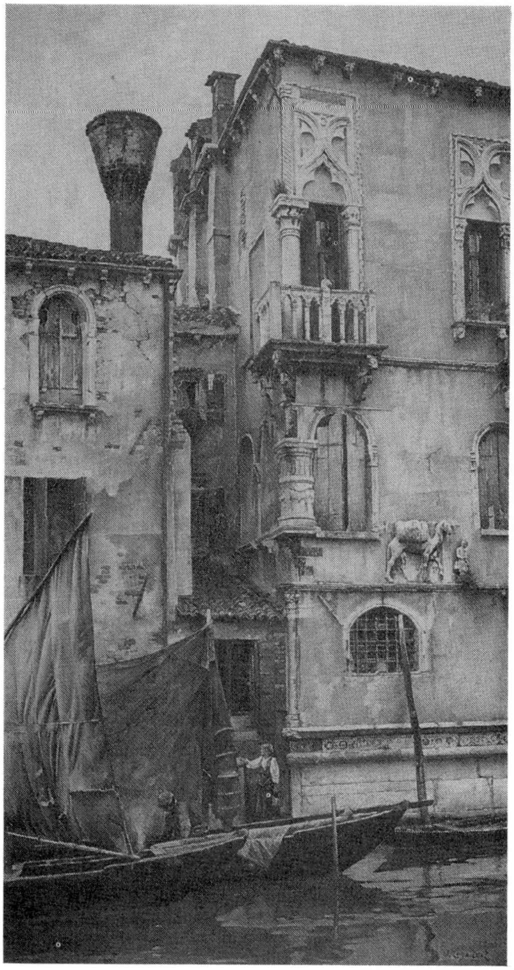

WILLIAM LOGSDAIL – A Venetian Backwater – signed – 40 x 22in.
(Christie's) **$7,573** **£4,950**

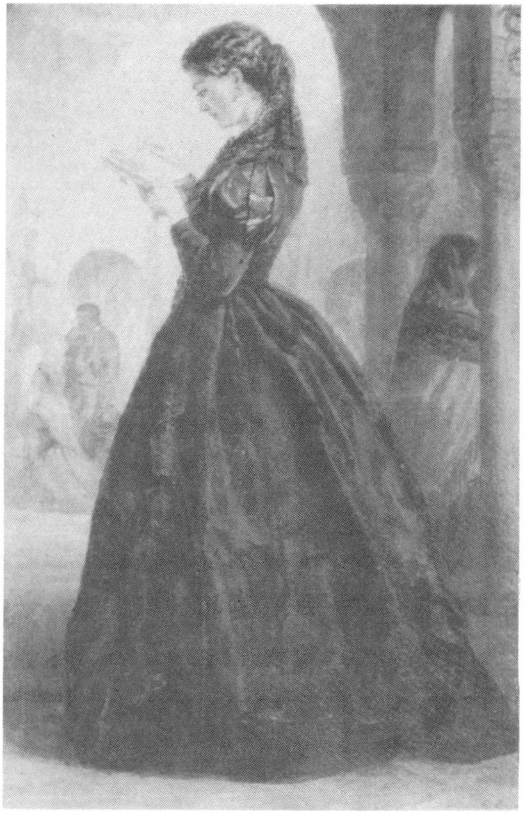

EDWIN LONG – At Mass – signed – 32 x 19¼in.
(Christie's) **$1,215** **£810**

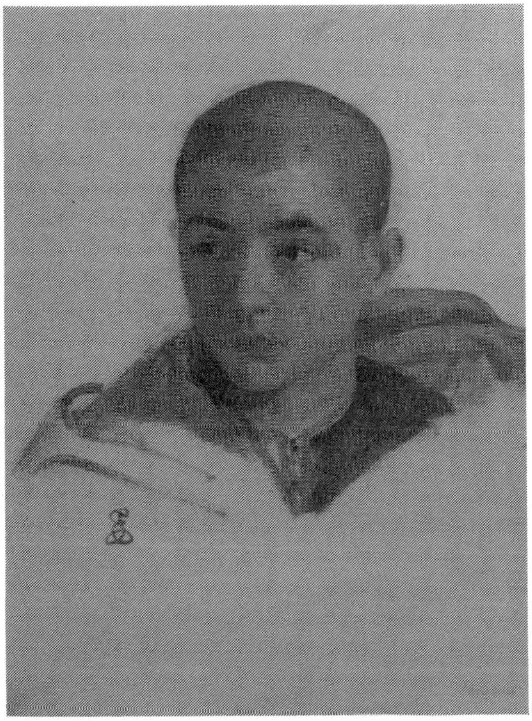

EDWIN LONG – Portrait Of A Young Man, Head And Shoulders, In Middle Eastern Costume – signed with monogram, inscribed and dated '73 – on canvas – 17¾ x 13in.
(Phillips) **$2,093** **£1,300**

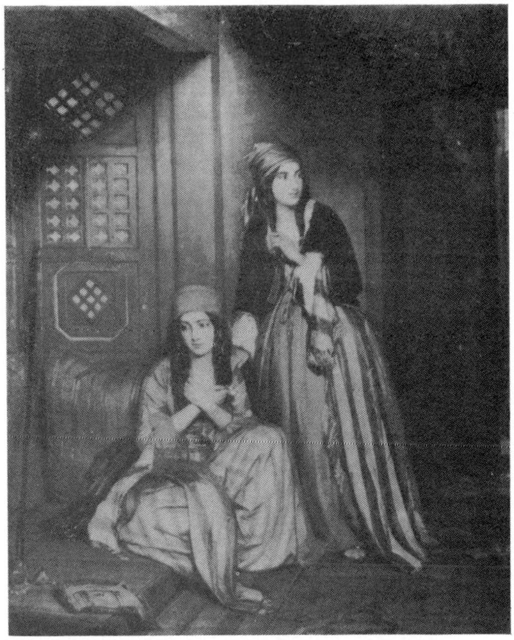

EDWIN LONG, Attributed to – The Sisters – with Goodall signature and the date 1858 – 36 x 28in.
(Christie's) **$1,861** **£1,320**

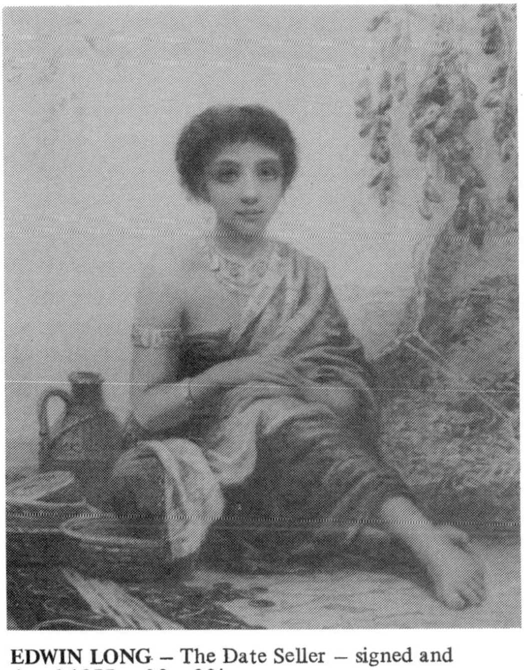

EDWIN LONG – The Date Seller – signed and dated 1877 – 29 x 22in.
(Christie's) **$4,860** **£3,240**

ALLESSANDRO LONGHI, Circle of – Portrait Of A Young Woman – on canvas – 30 x 25in.
(Phillips) **$4,648** **£2,800**

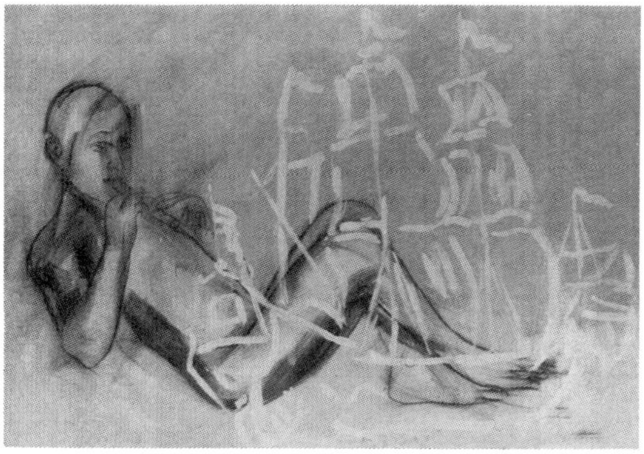

NINO LONGOBARDI – Untitled – tempera and crayon on canvas – 55¼ x 78¾in.
(Christie's) **$12,672** **£8,800**

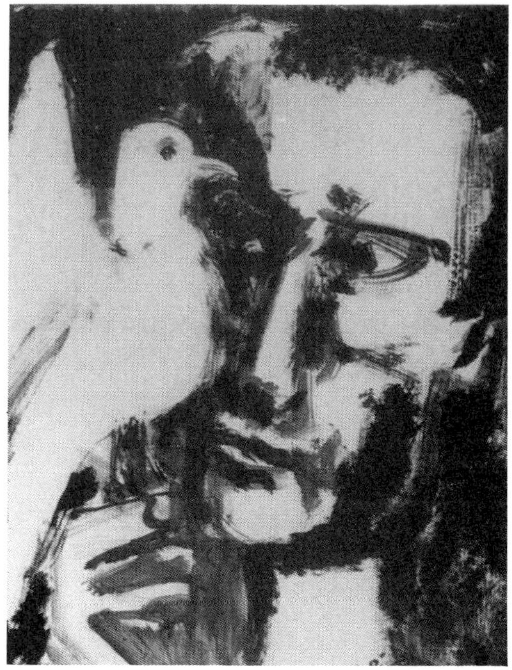

BERNARD LORJOU – Portrait a la Colombe – signed – mixed media on board – 25 x 18¾in.
(Christie's) **$1,298** **£902**

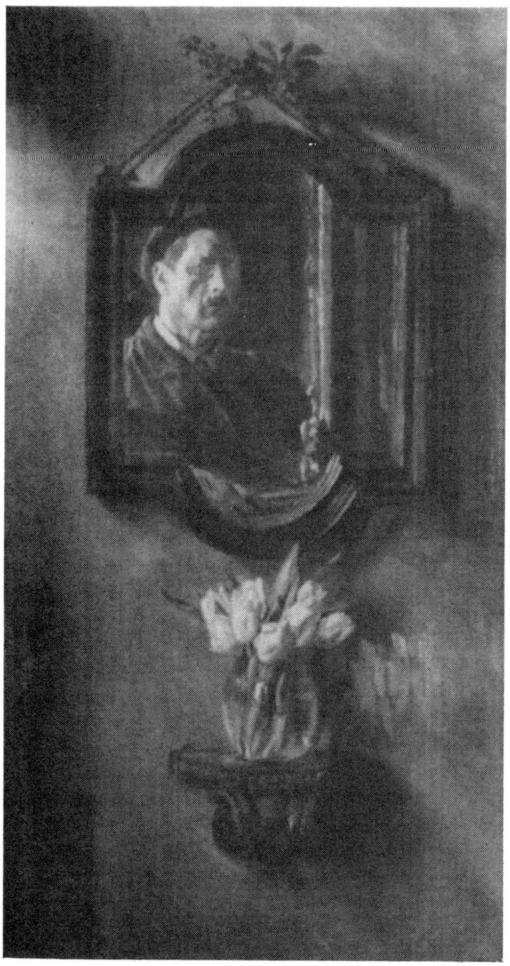

JOHN HENRY LORIMER – Self Portrait Of The Artist Reflected In A Mirror, With A Vase Of Tulips Below – signed – oil on canvas – 36½ x 21in.
(Christie's) **$2,072** **£1,320**

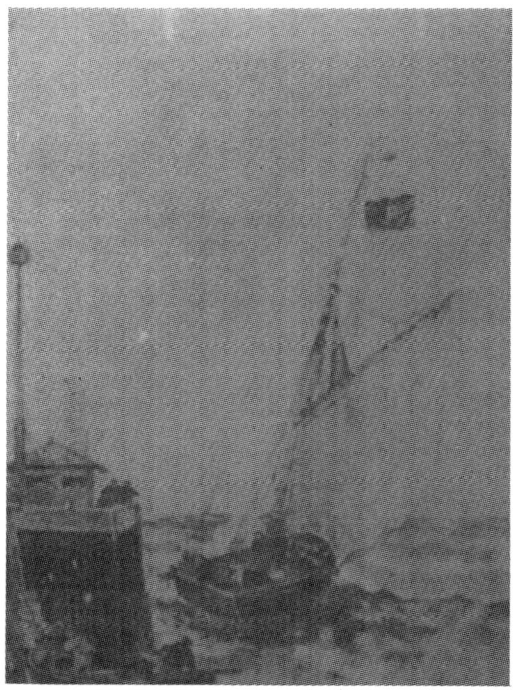

M. A. LOSSCHER – French Pilot Boat Off A Pier With Figures Leaving A Rowing Boat, On Choppy Seas – signed and dated 1909 – oil on canvas – 19½ x 13½in.
(W. H. Lane & Son) **$85** **£60**

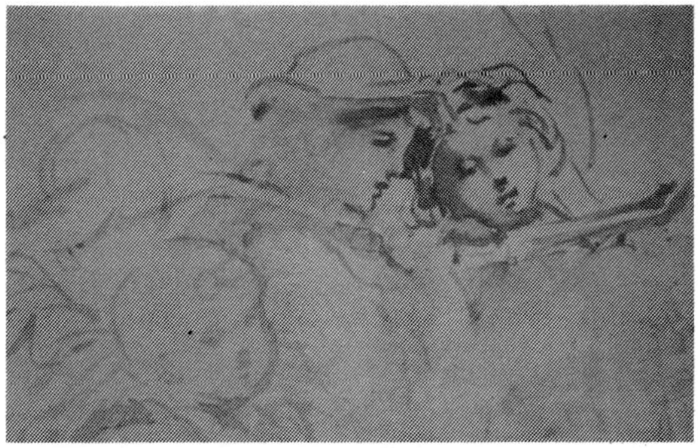

LOUISA, Marchioness of Waterford – Carol Singing – pencil and brown wash – 7 x 10¼in. – seventeen.
(Lawrence Fine Art) **$1,278** **£770**

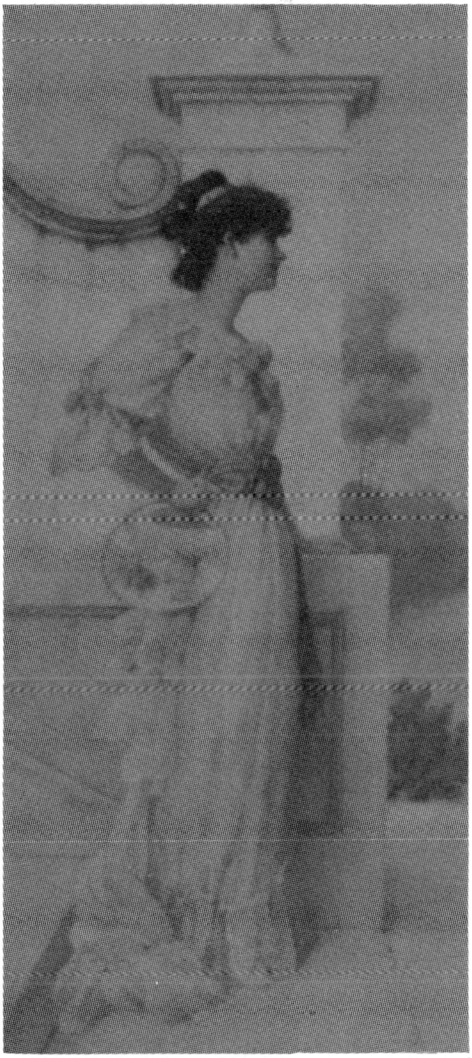

CHARLES FREDERICK LOWCOCK – 'Expectation' – signed – on board – 18 x 8in.
(Phillips) **$3,542** **£2,200**

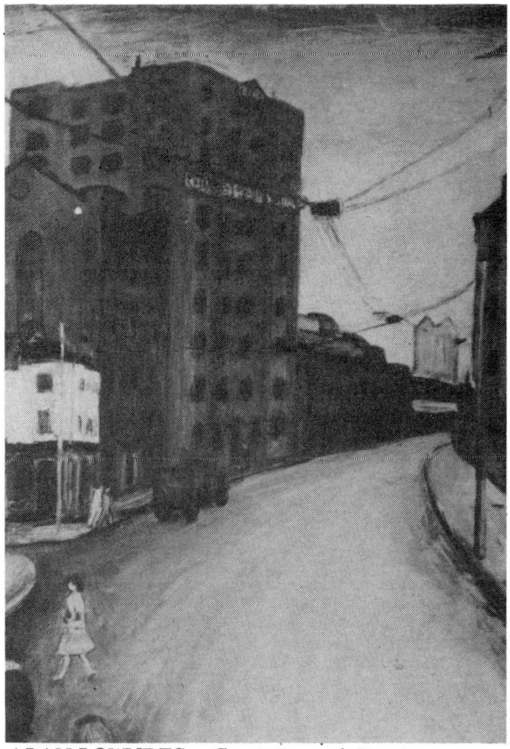

ALAN LOWNDES – Great Howard Street, Liverpool – signed and dated 1960. and inscribed and dated on the reverse – oil on canvas – 30 x 20in.
(Christie's) **$2,245** **£1,430**

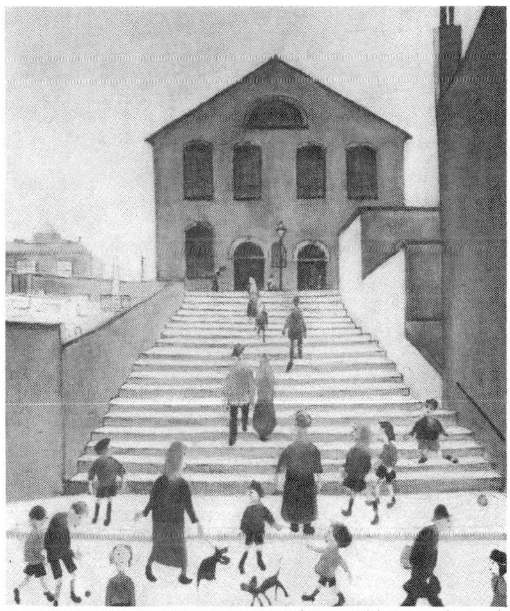

LAURENCE STEPHEN LOWRY – Old Church And Steps – signed and dated 1960 – oil on canvas – 24 x 20in.
(Christie's) **$31,680** **£22,000**

LOWRY

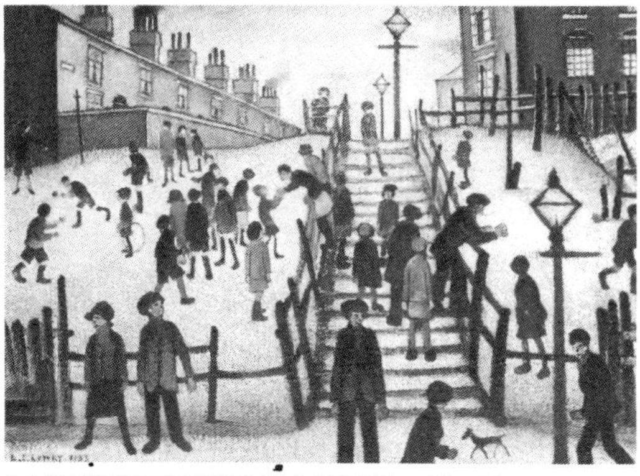

LAURENCE STEPHEN LOWRY – The Playground – signed and dated 1935 – oil on panel – 15¼ x 20¾in.
(Christie's) **$40,898** **£28,600**

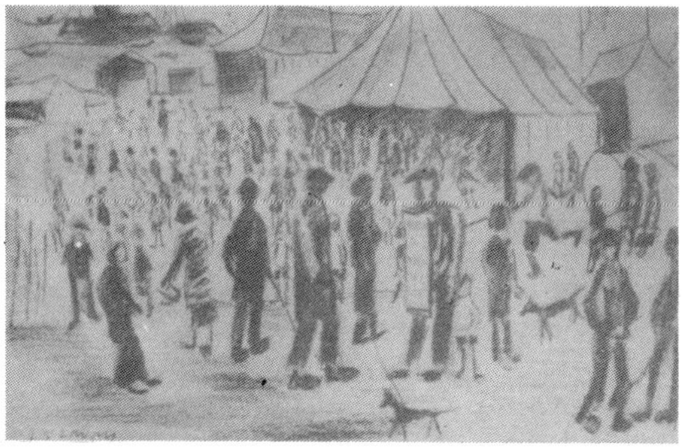

LAURENCE STEPHEN LOWRY – A Fairground With Many Figures Before Tents And A Sandwich Board Man 'Prepare To Meet Thy God' – signed – charcoal and pencil – 10¼ x 14½in.
(W. H. Lane & Son) **$943** **£660**

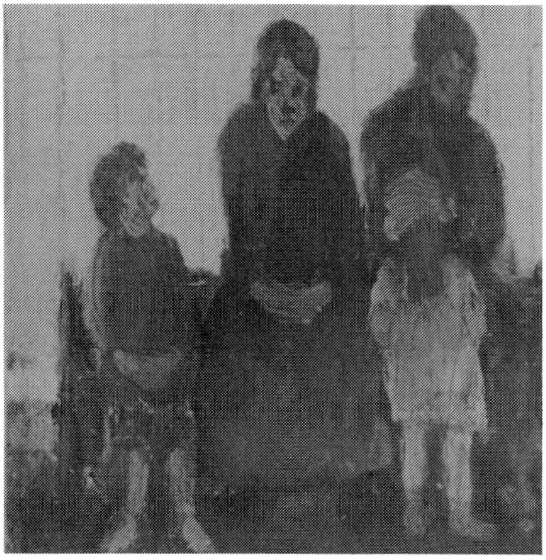

LAURENCE STEPHEN LOWRY – Two Women And Two Children – recto – signed and dated 1967 – oil on board – 22 x 16.5cm., Interior With Figures – verso.
(Phillips) **$4,648** **£2,800**

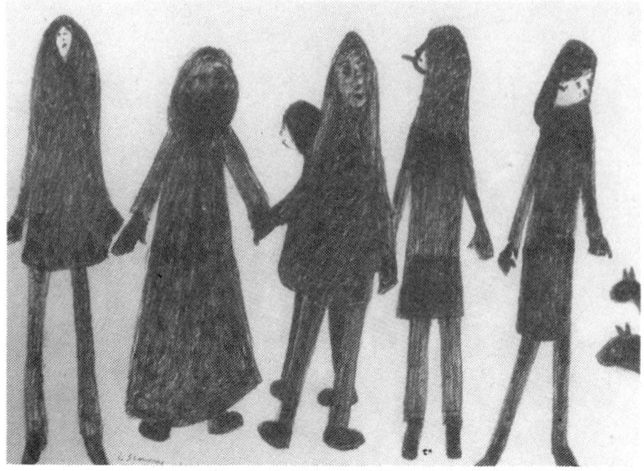

LAURENCE STEPHEN LOWRY – A Group Of People – signed and dated 1974 – black crayon, felt tip and soft pencil – 11¼ x 15¾in.
(Christie's) **$1,887** **£1,320**

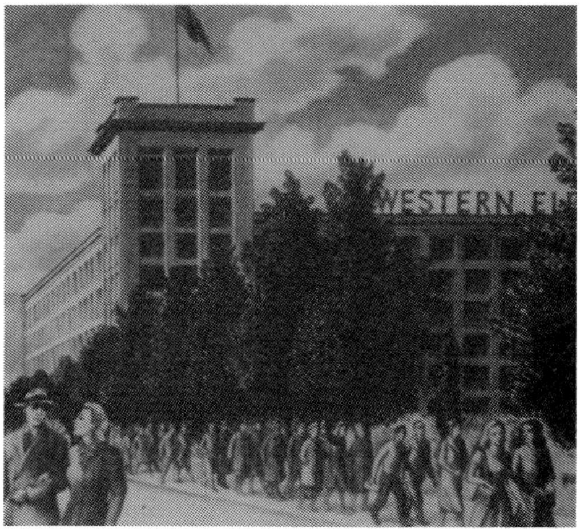

LOUIS LOZOWICK – Western Electric – charcoal and pencil on paper – 18¼ x 19¾in.
(Christie's) **$2,640** **£1,644**

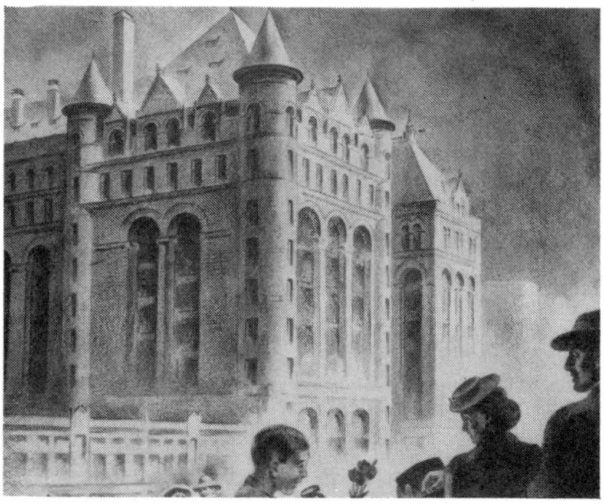

LOUIS LOZOWICK – Flower Seller – signed – brush and black ink, ink wash and charcoal on board – 13½ x 15¾in.
(Christie's) **$2,640** **£1,644**

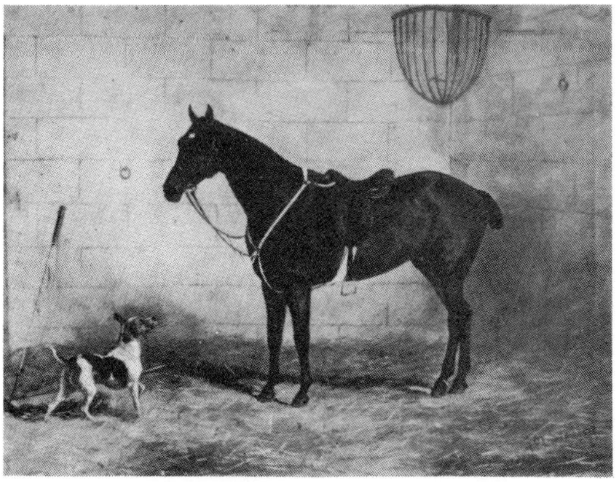

HENRY FREDRICK LUCAS LUCAS – 'Kate', A Bay Polo Pony, Saddled Up, Standing In A Loose Box With 'Myrtle', A Hound – signed and dated 1884, and inscribed on the reverse – 13¼ x 18¼in.
(Christie's) **$2,916** **£1,944**

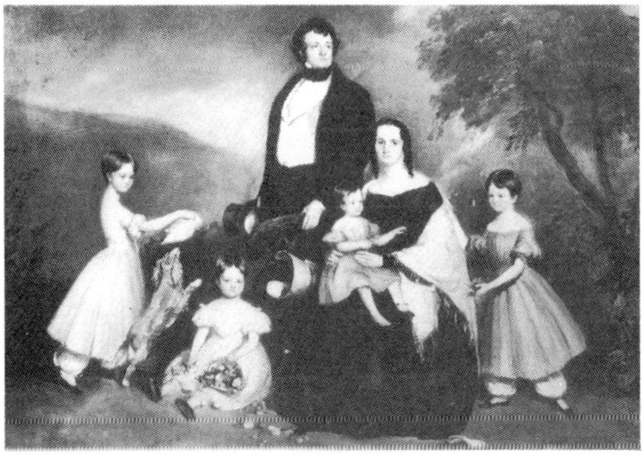

JOHN LUCAS, Circle of – A Family Group: A Gentleman, Standing Behind His Wife, Holding Their Daughter, A Young Girl With Her Two Sisters, In A Hilly Landscape – 25 x 36in.
(Christie's) **$6,804** **£4,536**

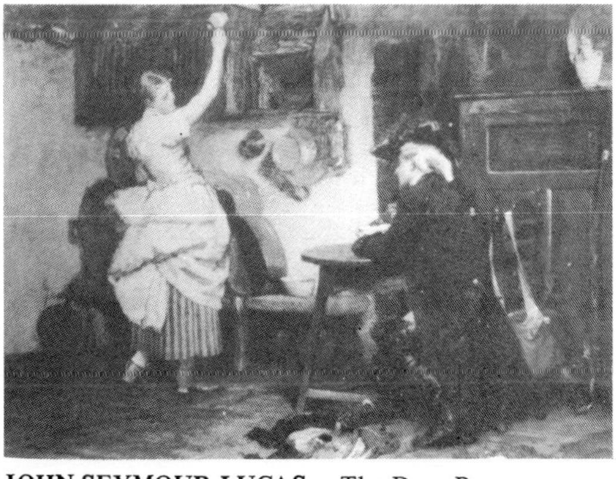

JOHN SEYMOUR LUCAS – The Days Bag – signed and dated 1885 – oil on canvas – 21 x 27in.
(Christie's) **$2,851** **£1,980**

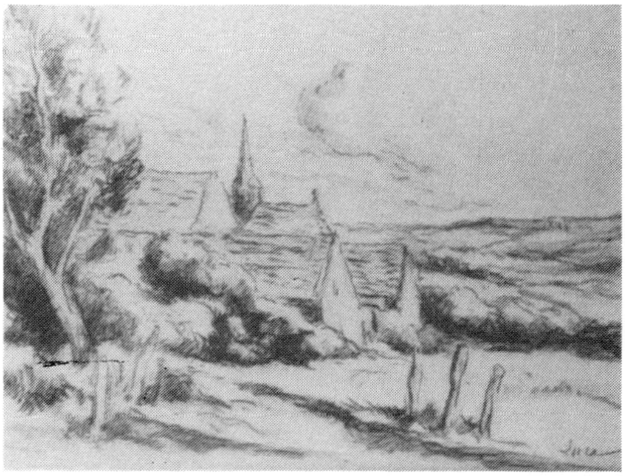

MAXIMILIEN LUCE – Eglise dans un Paysage – signed – soft pencil, pen and ink on paper – 11 x 15in.
(Christie's) **$3,344** **£2,090**

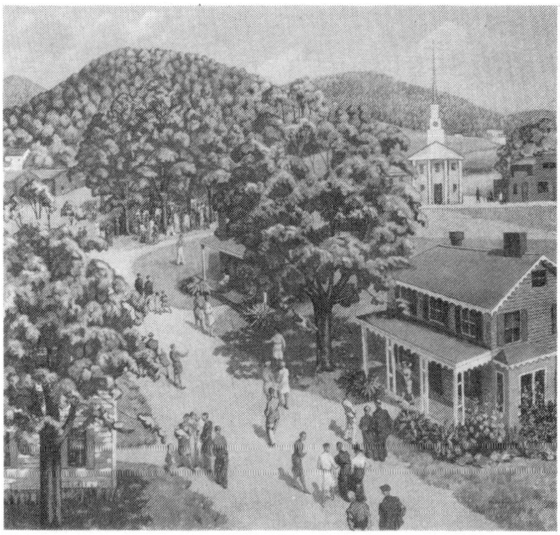

MOLLY LUCE – Concert In The Park – signed and dated '29 – oil on canvas – 33 x 36in.
(Christie's) **$11,000** **£7,179**

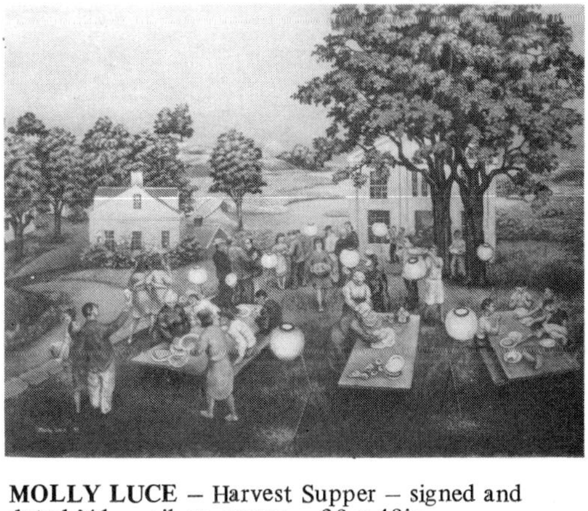

MOLLY LUCE – Harvest Supper – signed and dated '41 – oil on canvas – 30 x 40in.
(Christie's) **$8,250** **£5,384**

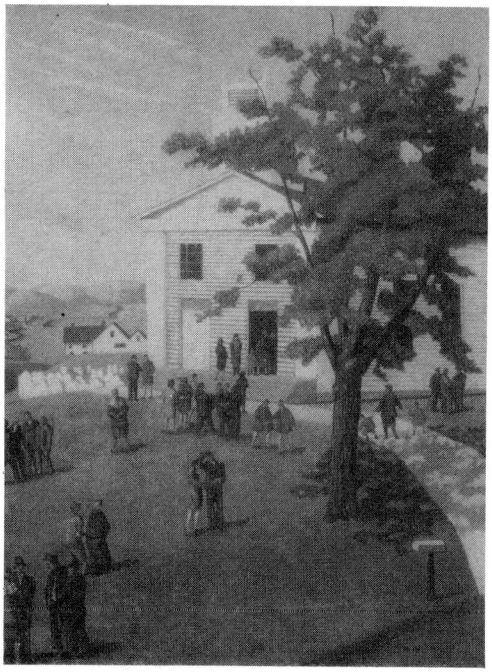

MOLLY LUCE – Church At South Ridge – signed and dated 1928 – oil on canvas – 24 x 18in.
(Christie's) **$7,150** **£4,666**

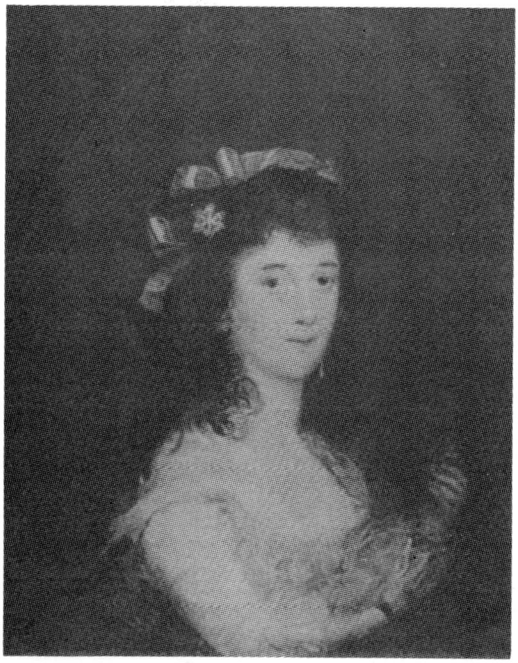

FRANCESCO JOSE DE GOYA Y LUCIENTES, Follower of – Portrait Of A Lady, Long Bust Length, Wearing A Ribboned Headdress – oil on canvas – 12 x 10in.
(Phillips) **$451** **£320**

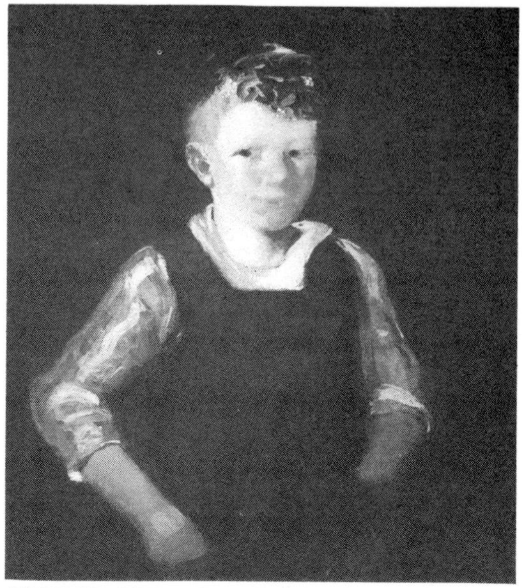

GEORGE LUKS – Patsy The Cobbler – signed – oil on canvas – 30¼ x 25¼in.
(Christie's) **$4,400** **£3,093**

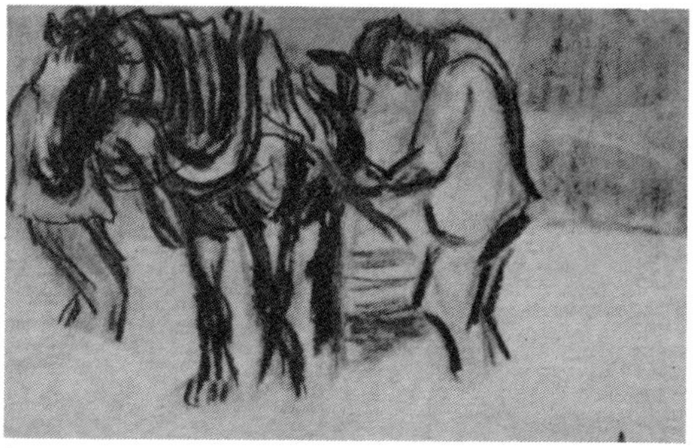

GEORGE BENJAMIN LUKS – The Draymen; and Horse And Wagon – signed – charcoal and white chalk and wash on buff paper – 5¼ x 7¼in.
(Christie's) **$1,870** **£1,300 Two**

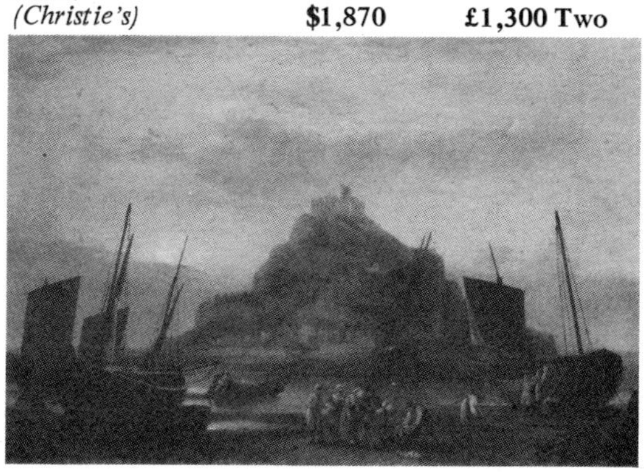

THOMAS LUNY – A View Of St. Michael's Mount With Fisherfolk – signed and dated 1831 – 20 x 27in.
(Christie's) **$2,430** **£1,620**

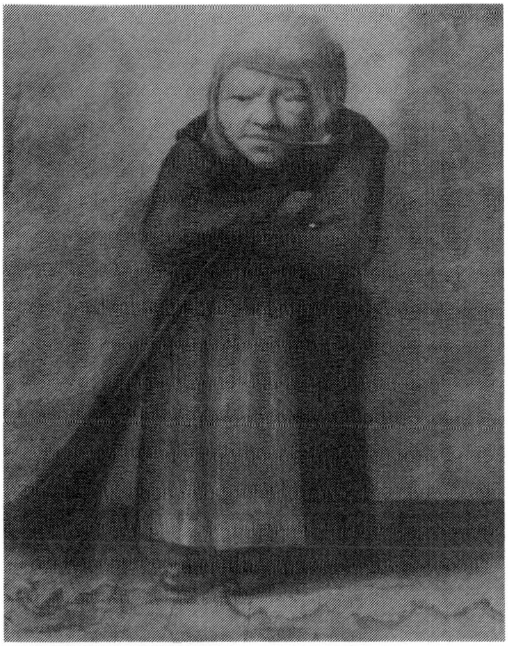

EDWARD LUTTERELL – An Irish Street Sweeper At The Crossing, Clargis Street – signed and dated 1674 – pastel – 13¼ x 10¾in.
(Christie's) **$1,215** **£810**

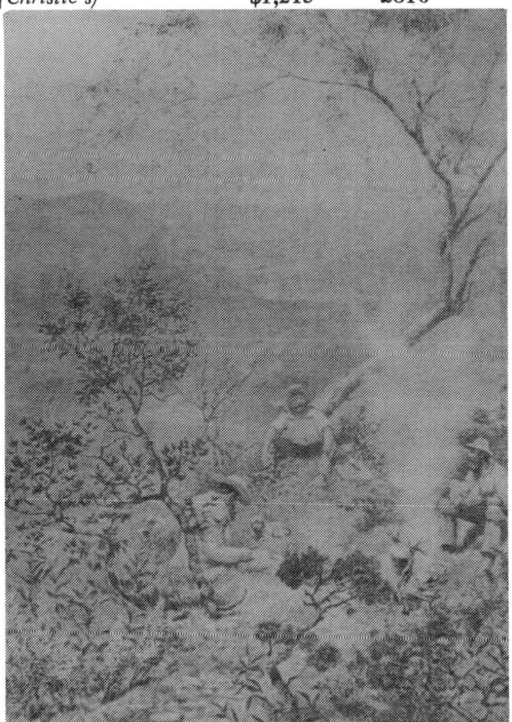

JAMES MACBETH – 'The Bush Clearers, National Park, Near Sydney' – signed, inscribed and dated 1888 – watercolour – 72 x 50cm.
(Phillips) **$3,260** **£2,000**

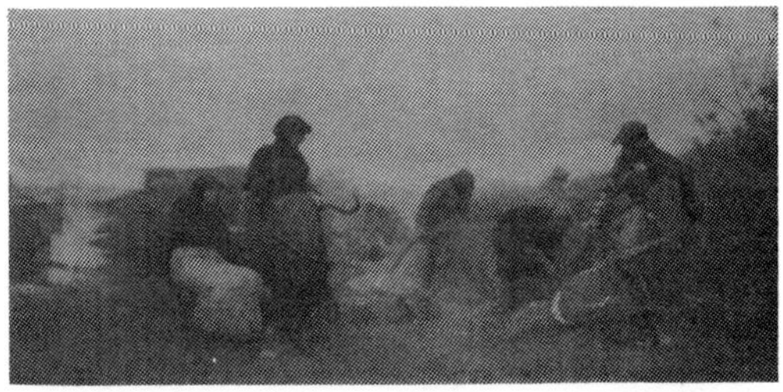

ROBERT WALKER MacBETH – Sedge Cutting In Wicken Fen, Cambridgeshire, Early Morning – signed with initials and dated '78 – 39¼ x 78½in.
(Christie's) **$9,720** **£6,480**

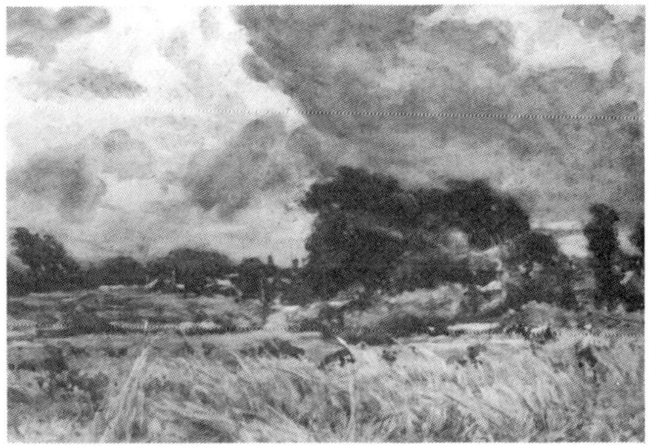

A. D. McCORMACK – 'In Surrey', Stormy Landscape With Figure – signed with initials – watercolour – 14.5 x 19.5in.
(Biddle & Webb) **$518** **£360**

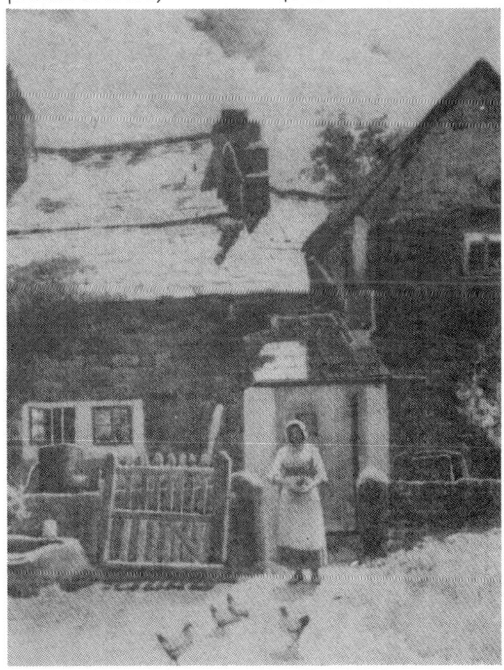

JOHN McDOUGAL – A Bit Of Old Bidslow? – A Woman Feeding Chickens Before A Farmhouse – signed – watercolour – 20 x 15in.
(W. H. Lane & Son) **$429** **£300**

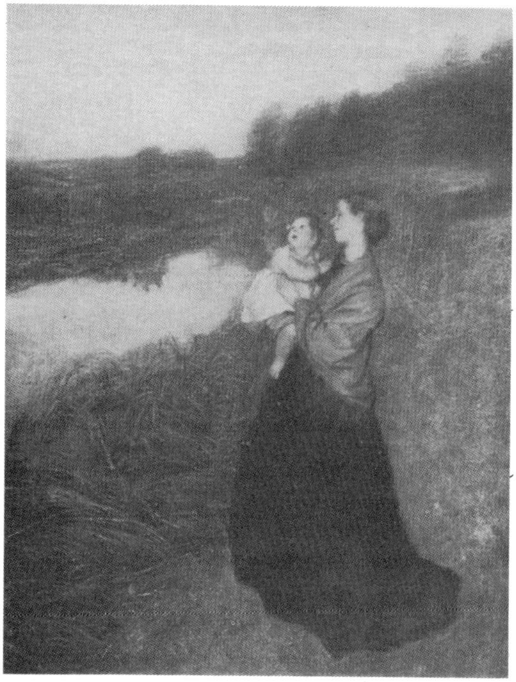

AMBROSE McEVOY – The Lark – oil on canvas – 28¼ x 23in.
(Christie's) **$2,359** **£1,650**

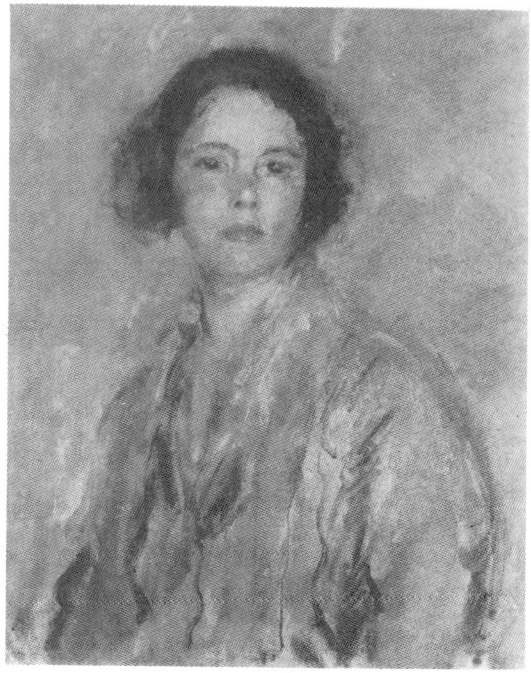

AMBROSE McEVOY – Portrait Of A Lady, Half Length – oil on canvas – 26¾ x 21½in.
(Christie's) **$1,573** **£1,100**

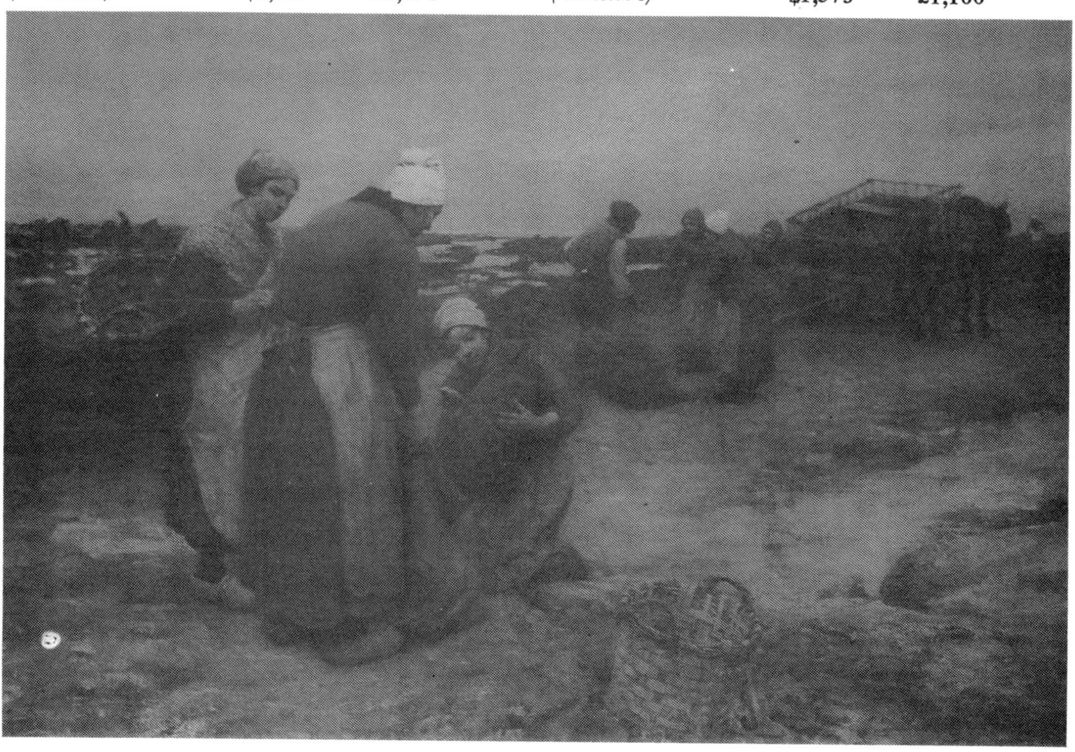

ROBERT McGREGOR – The Mussel Gatherers, France – signed, and indistinctly inscribed and signed on a label verso – oil on canvas – 34 x 44in. *(Christie's)* **$18,000** **£12,500**

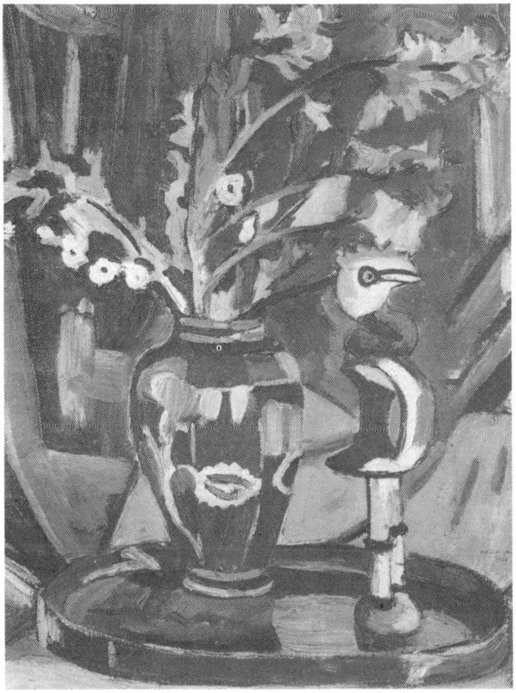

HELMUTH MACKE – Stilleben mit Blumen – signed and dated 1920, also signed and dated on the reverse – oil on canvas – 26½ x 21in.
(Christie's) **$10,296 £7,150**

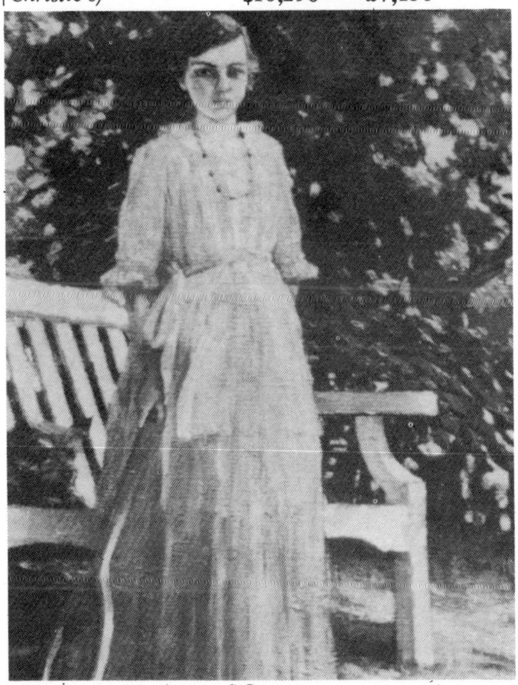

JAMES HAMILTON McKENZIE – Portrait Of A Young Girl, Full Length, Holding A Racquet – signed – oil on canvas – 30 x 18in.
(Christie's) **$1,415 £990**

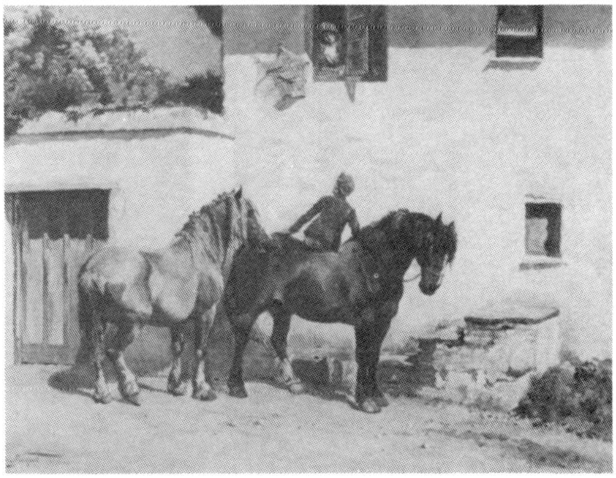

PERCY MACQUOID – 'A Secret Word' – signed and dated 1889 – oil on panel – 17½ x 24½in.
(Phillips) **$1,530 £1,000**

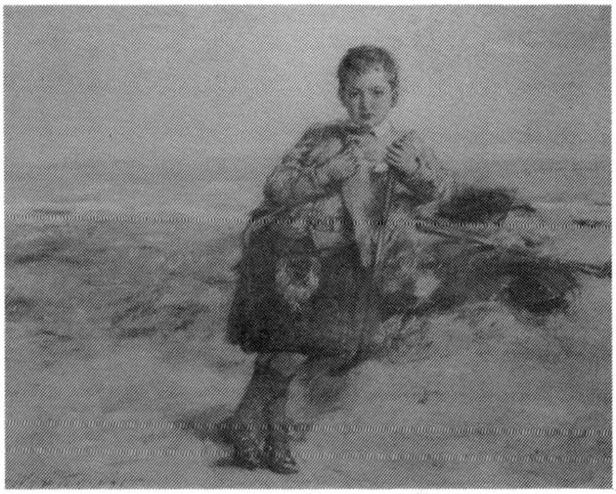

WILLIAM McTAGGART – The Golfer, A Portrait Of Master Stephen, The Son Of W. Stephen Esq. – signed – oil on canvas – 19 x 25in.
(Christie's) **$9,360 £6,500**

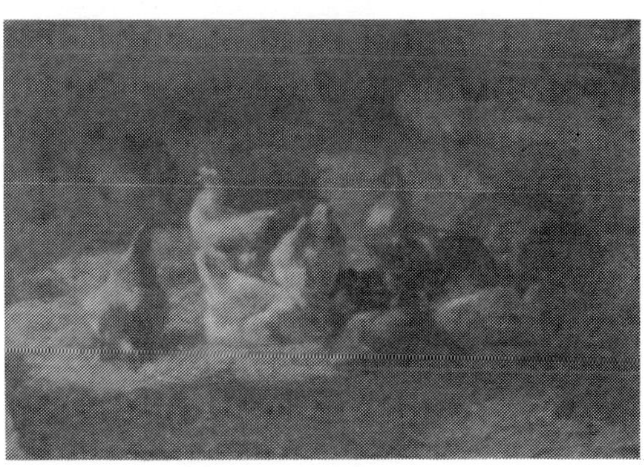

EUGENE REMY MAES – Poultry In A Barn – signed – oil on panel – 17 x 24cm.
(Phillips) **$2,171 £1,300 Pair**

MAGRITTE

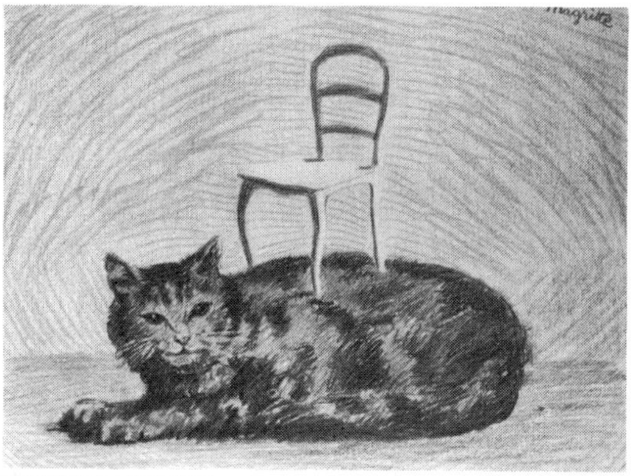

RENE MAGRITTE – La Vocation – signed, inscribed and dated 1964 – coloured crayons on paper – 8¾ x 11½in.
(Christie's) **$20,592 £14,300**

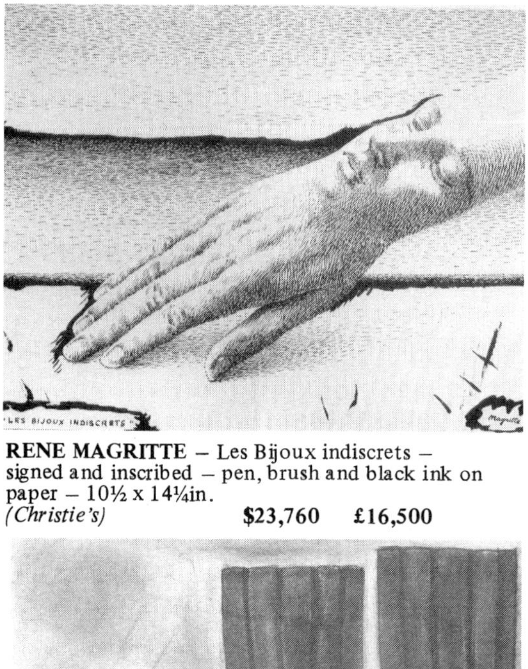

RENE MAGRITTE – Les Bijoux indiscrets – signed and inscribed – pen, brush and black ink on paper – 10½ x 14¼in.
(Christie's) **$23,760 £16,500**

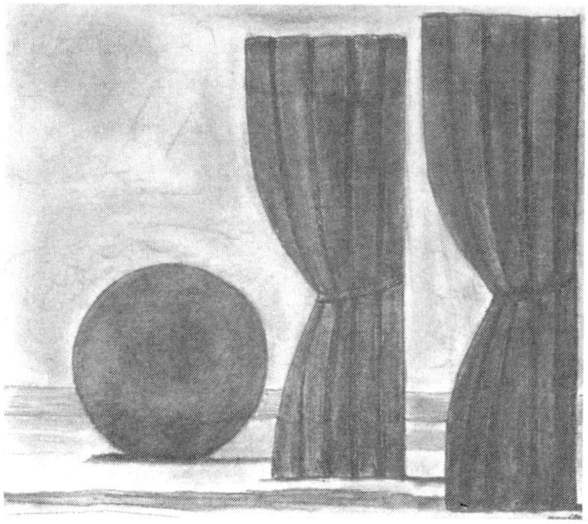

RENE MAGRITTE – Le Monde eveille – signed – brown crayon on paper – 17 x 21in.
(Christie's) **$17,600 £11,000**

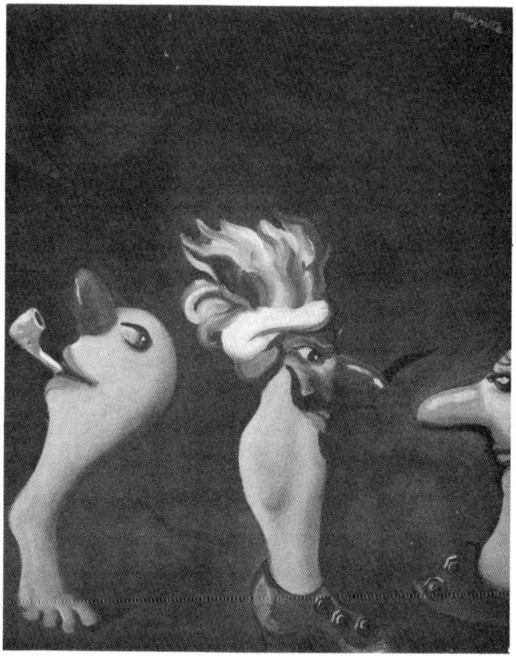

RENE MAGRITTE – La Marche Triomphale – signed, and inscribed and dated 1947 on the reverse – oil on canvas – 25 x 21in.
(Christie's) **$28,512 £19,800**

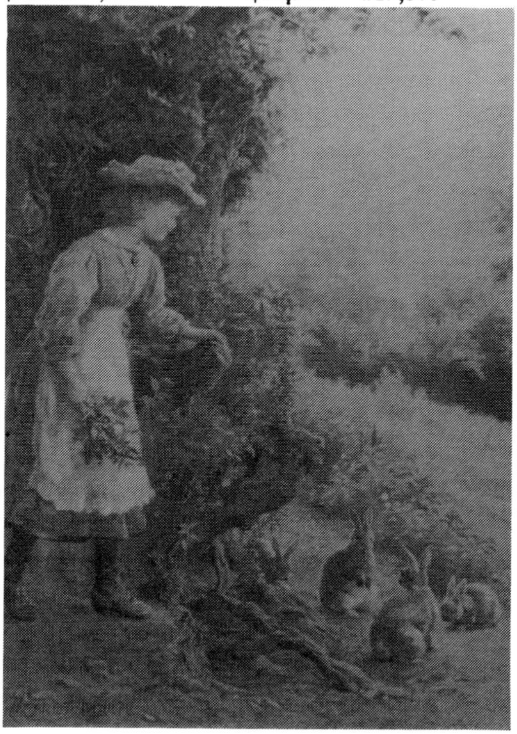

HELENA MAGUIRE – Discovered! – signed – watercolour – 47 x 33cm.
(Phillips) **$1,956 £1,200**

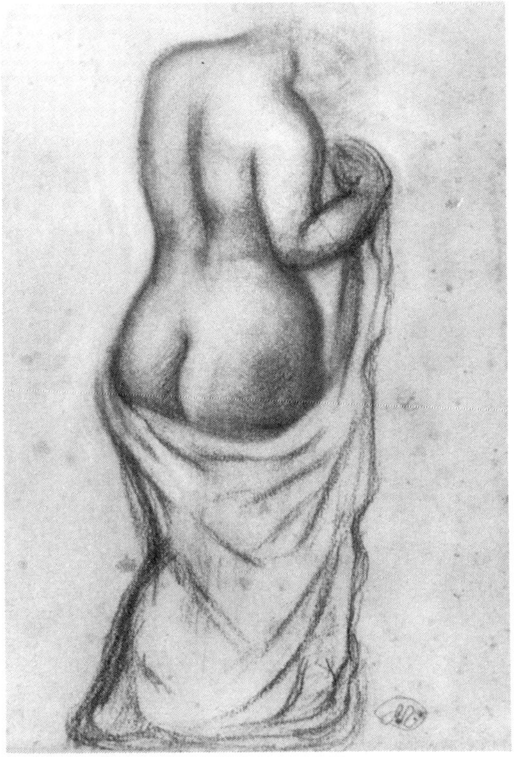

ARISTIDE MAILLOL – Nu drape – signed – red chalk heightened with white on paper – 14 x 10½in.
(Christie's) **$5,068** **£3,520**

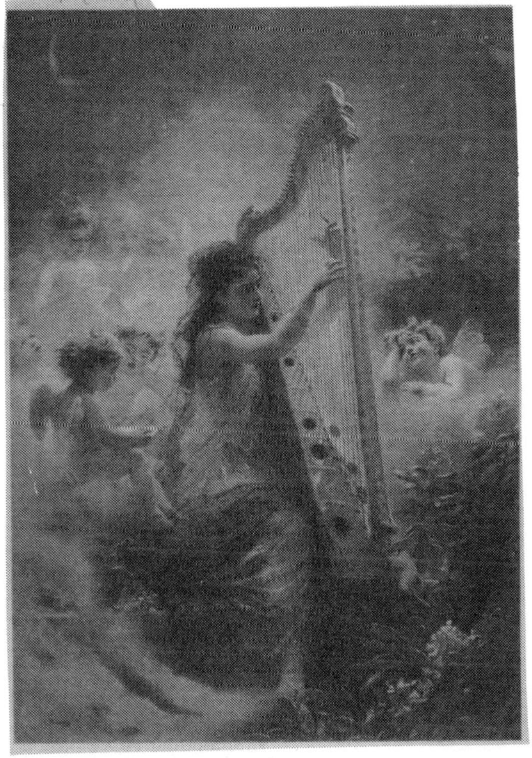

CONSTANTIN MAKOWSKY – The Food Of Love – signed – 92 x 63¼in.
(Christie's) **$33,440** **£22,000**

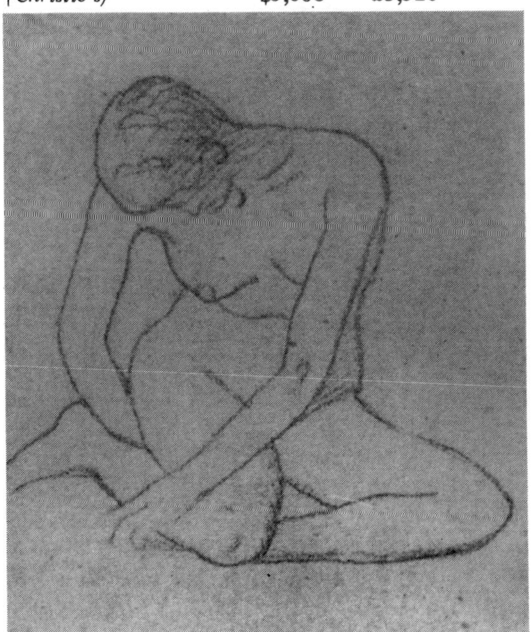

ARISTIDE MAILLOL – Nu assis – signed with monogram – pencil on paper – 11½ x 7¾in.
(Christie's) **$1,742** **£1,210**

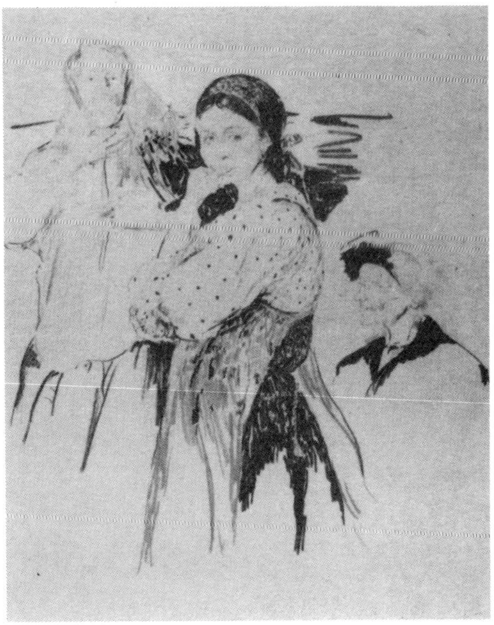

PHILIPPE MALIAVINE – Three Peasant Women – signed in pencil – pencil and crayon on paper – 17 x 12½in.
(Robt. W. Skinner Inc.) **$100** **£69**

MANET

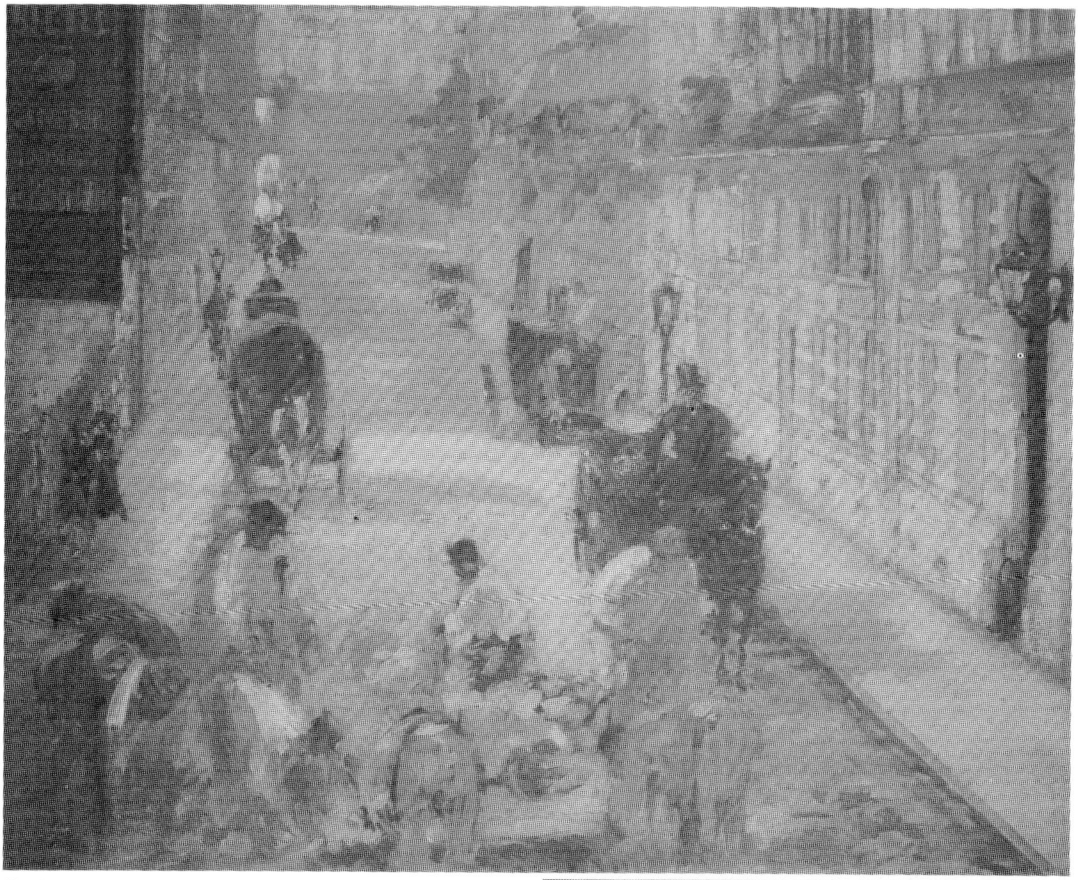

EDOUARD MANET – La rue Mosnier aux Paveurs – signed – oil on canvas – 25¾ x 32¼in.
(Christie's) **$11,088,000 £7,700,000**

WILLIAM MANNERS – A River Landscape With Cottages, A Stone Bridge And A Cart And Donkey On A Path – signed and dated 1885 – 9½ x 13½in.
(Christie's) **$585 £380**

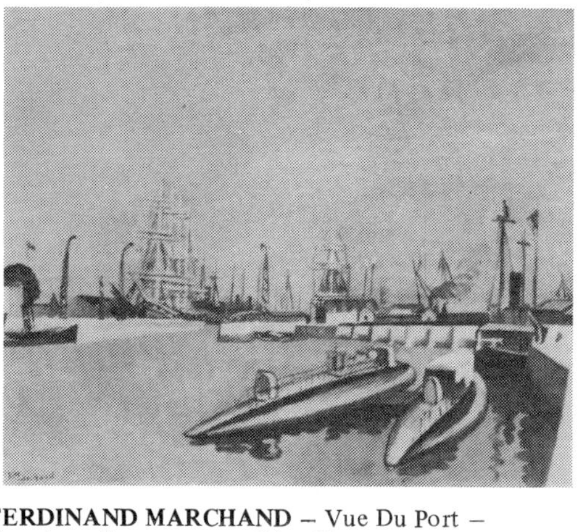

FERDINAND MARCHAND – Vue Du Port – signed – oil on canvas – 54 x 65cm.
(Phillips) **$496 £320**

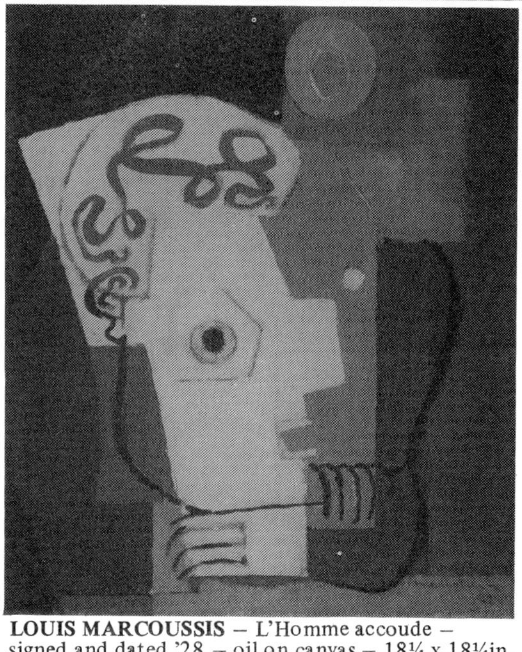

LOUIS MARCOUSSIS – L'Homme accoude – signed and dated '28 – oil on canvas – 18¼ x 18¼in.
(Christie's) **$44,088 £26,400**

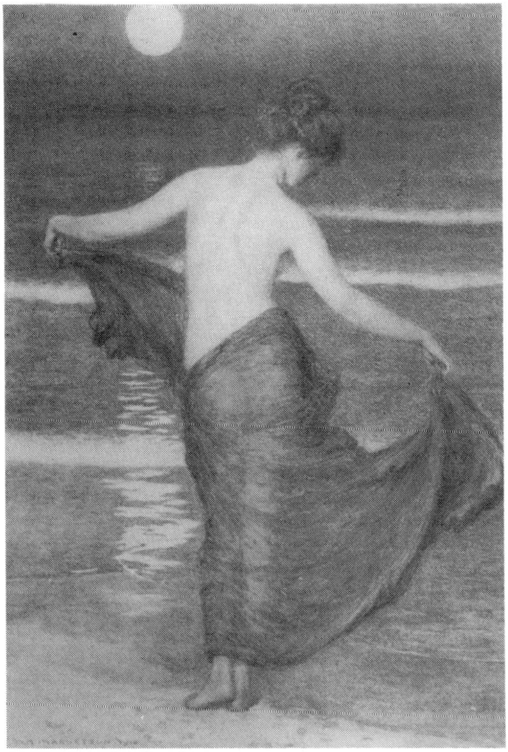

WILLIAM HENRY MARGETSON – The Passing Of Summer – signed and dated 1910 – pencil and watercolour – 20½ x 14½in.
(Christie's) **$3,702** **£2,420**

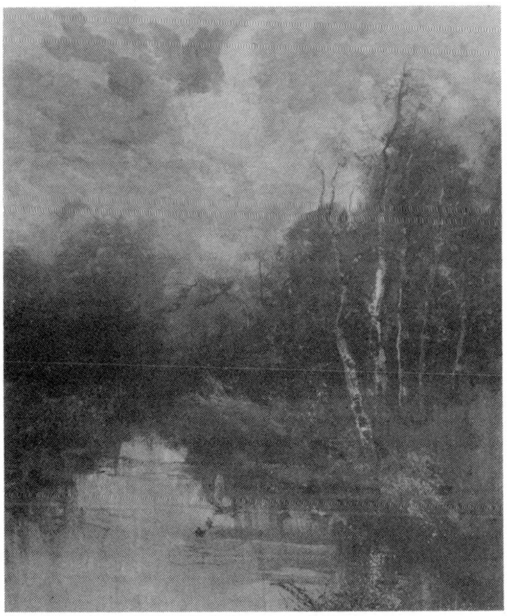

POMPEO MARIANI – River Landscapes – all signed, one inscribed – on board – 13¾ x 10¼in.
(Christie's) **$5,843** **£3,520 Three**

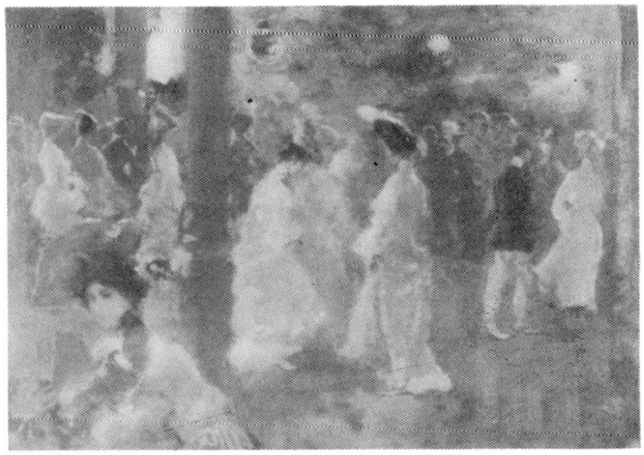

POMPEO MARIANI – An Elegant Gathering; and Elegant Figures In A Park – signed – on board – 16 x 22½in.
(Christie's) **$11,869** **£7,150**

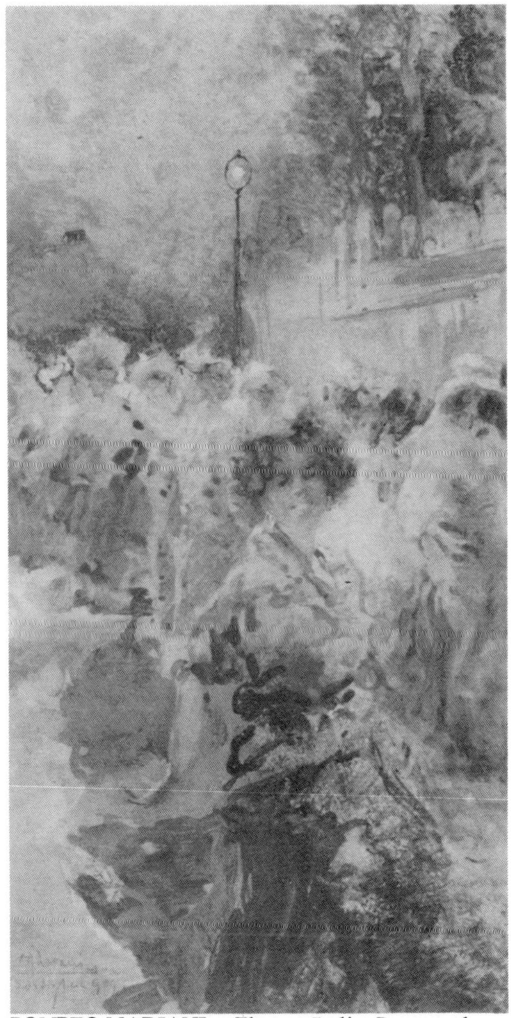

POMPEO MARIANI – Elegant Ladies Promenading – signed and dated '909 – oil on card – 14 x 6¾in. – and a watercolour.
(Christie's) **$9,130** **£5,500 Two**

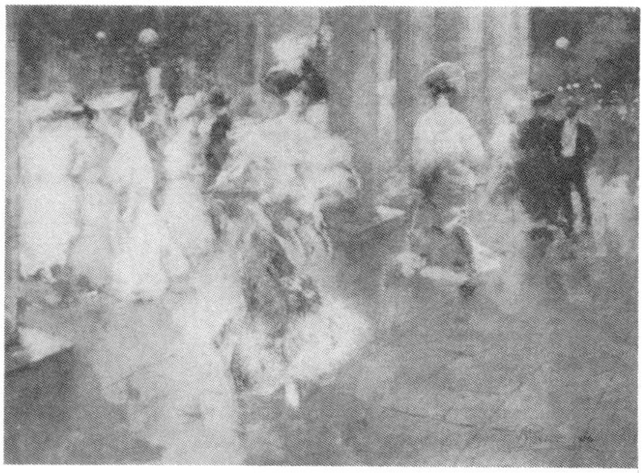

POMPEO MARIANI – Elegant Figures, Monte Carlo – signed and dated 1906 – oil and bodycolour on card – 17¾ x 23½in.
(Christie's) **$21,912** **£13,200** Two

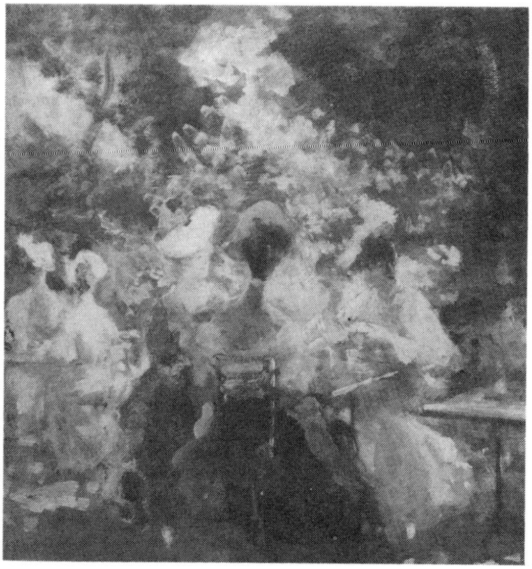

POMPEO MARIANI – An Elegant Teaparty – signed – on board – 24 x 17¾in.
(Christie's) **$25,564** **£15,400**

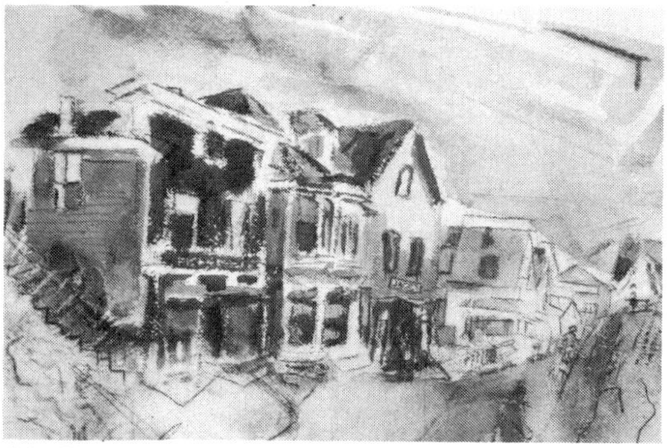

JOHN MARIN – A Bit Of Stonington – signed and dated '26 – watercolour and charcoal on paper – 13½ x 17¼in.
(Christie's) **$22,000** **£15,466**

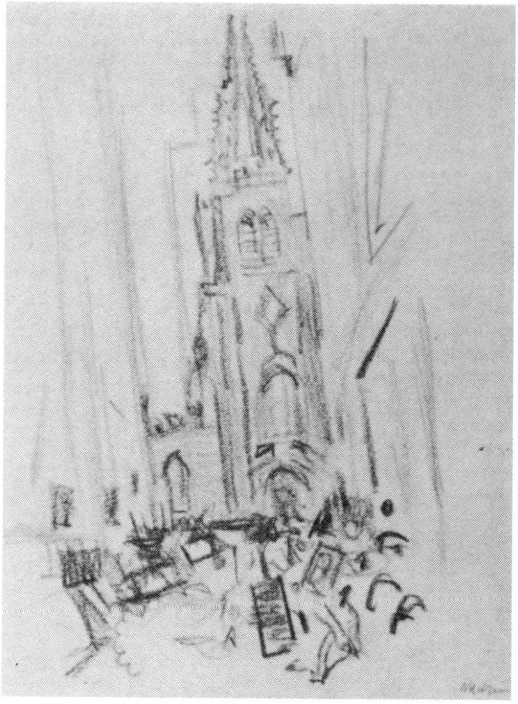

JOHN MARIN – Trinity Church, New York – signed and dated 10/36 – pencil and crayon on paper laid down on board – 6¾ x 5in.
(Christie's) **$1,760** **£1,224**

R, MARIN – The Departure – signed and dated 1886 – 33 x 48½in.
(Christie's) **$3,009** **£1,980**

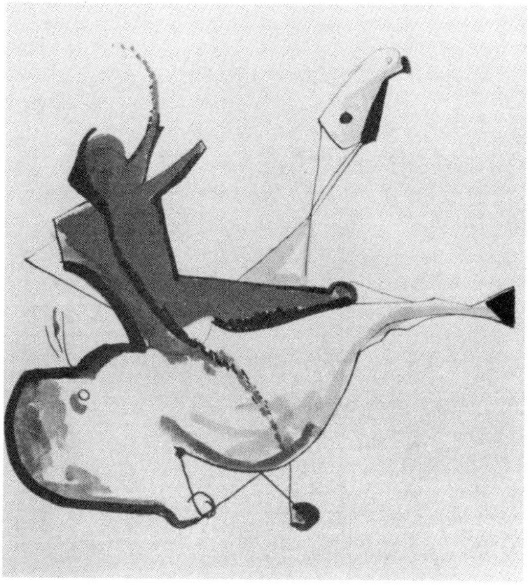

MARINO MARINI – Cavaliere – signed – red gouache, pen, black ink and grey wash on paper – 15¾ x 14½in.
(Christie's) **$12,672** **£8,800**

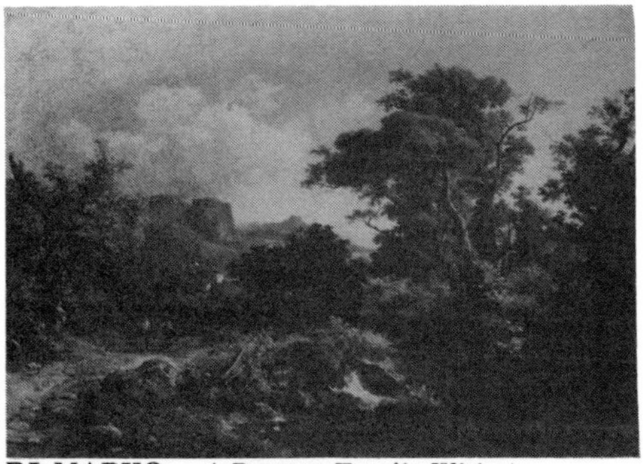

KARL MARKO – A Peasant Family With A Donkey In A Campagna Landscape – signed and dated 1849 – oil on panel – 87 x 117cm.
(Phillips) **$7,682** **£4,600**

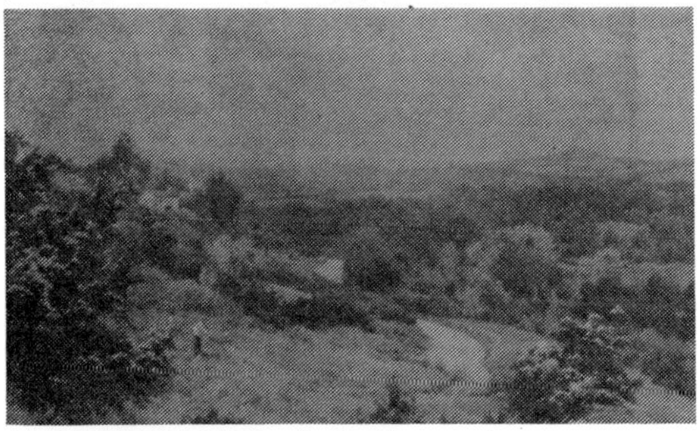

GEORGE MARKS – Springtime – signed – watercolour – 18.5 x 26cm.
(Phillips) **$2,282** **£1,400**

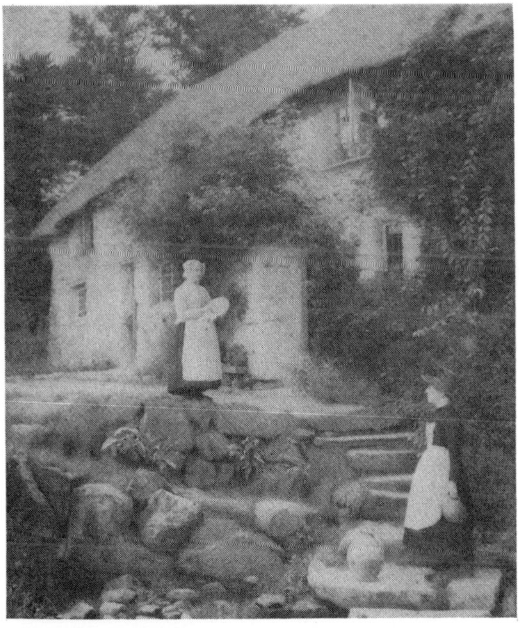

GEORGE MARKS – A Morning Chat – signed, and signed and inscribed on the artist's label – pencil and watercolour heightened with white – 27½ x 20½in.
(Christie's) **$2,356** **£1,540**

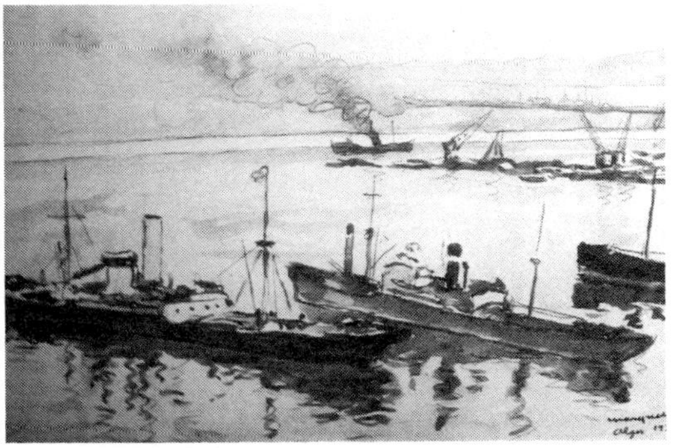

ALBERT MARQUET – Le Port d'Alger – signed, dated and inscribed 1934 – watercolour and pencil on paper – 6½ x 9¾in.
(Christie's) **$13,464** **£9,350**

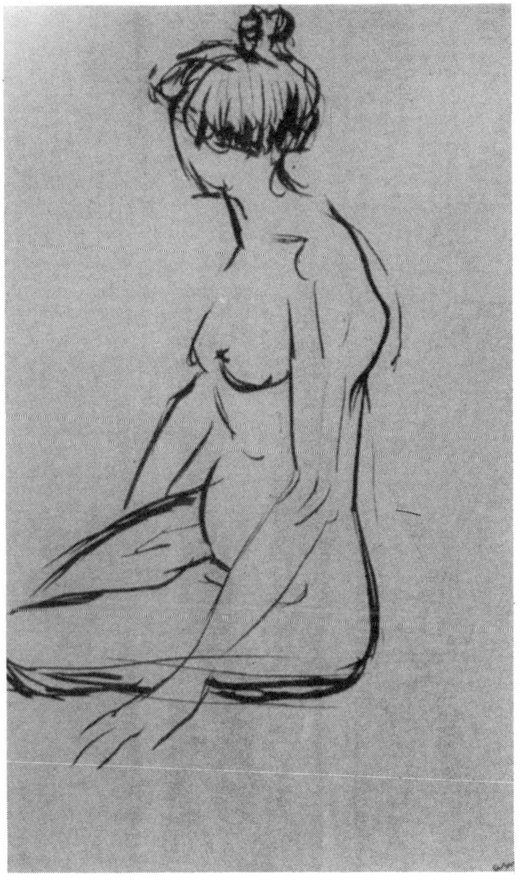

ALBERT MARQUET – Nu assis – signed with initials – brush and ink on paper – 10¾ x 6¾in.
(Christie's) **$1,232** **£770**

ALBERT MARQUET – Les Voiliers, Audierne, Bretagne – signed – watercolour on paper – 6½ x 9½in.
(Christie's) **$10,560** **£6,600**

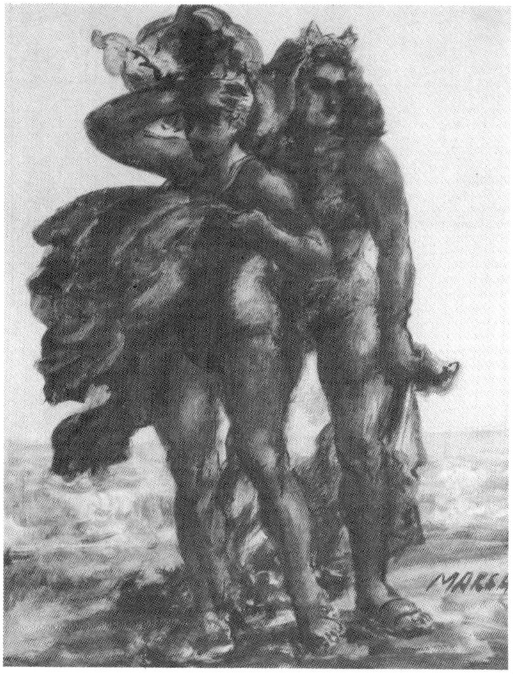

REGINALD MARSH – Muscle Women – signed – watercolour on paper – 26 x 20½in.
(Christie's) **$7,700 £5,413**

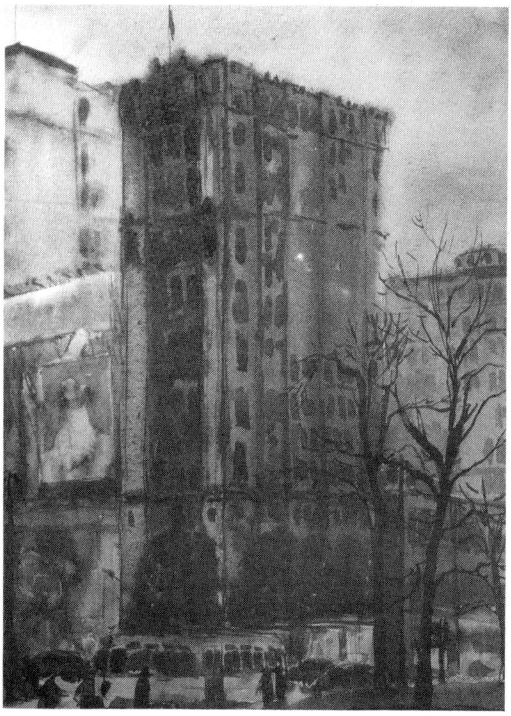

REGINALD MARSH – A Rainy Day In New York – signed – watercolour and pencil on paper – 22½ x 15¼in.
(Christie's) **$12,100 £7,539**

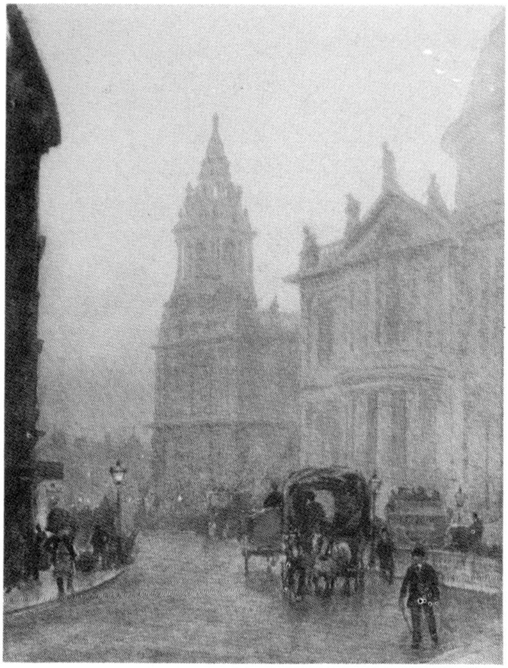

HERBERT MENZIES MARSHALL – The South Front Of St. Paul's Cathedral, At Evening – signed and dated 1895, inscribed on the reverse – watercolour on card – 12¼ x 8¼in.
(Christie's) **$3,078 £2,052**

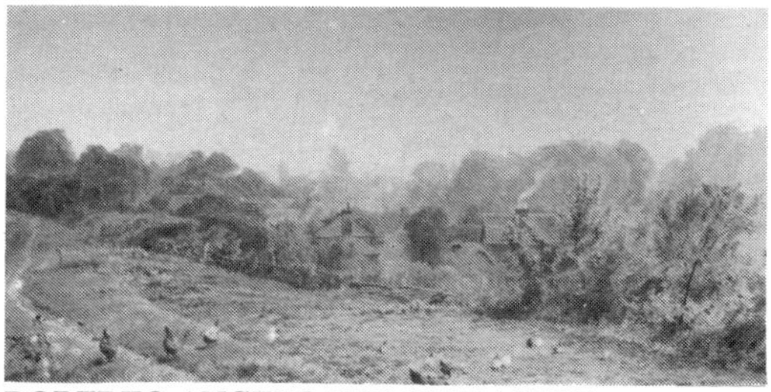

ROBERTO ANGELO KITTERMASTER MARSHALL – Rural Landscape With Village And Poultry – signed – 12¾ x 20¾in.
(Dacre, Son & Hartley) **$2,092 £1,350**

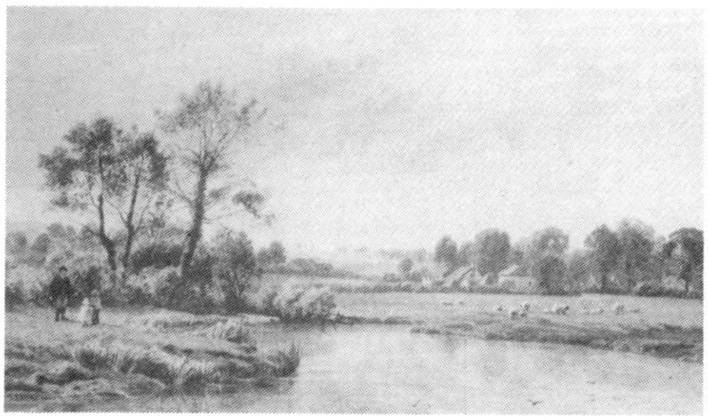

ROBERT ANGELO KITTERMASTER MARSHALL – Figures By A River In Summer, A Village In The Distance – signed – watercolour – 9 x 14in.
(Christie's) **$2,016 £1,430**

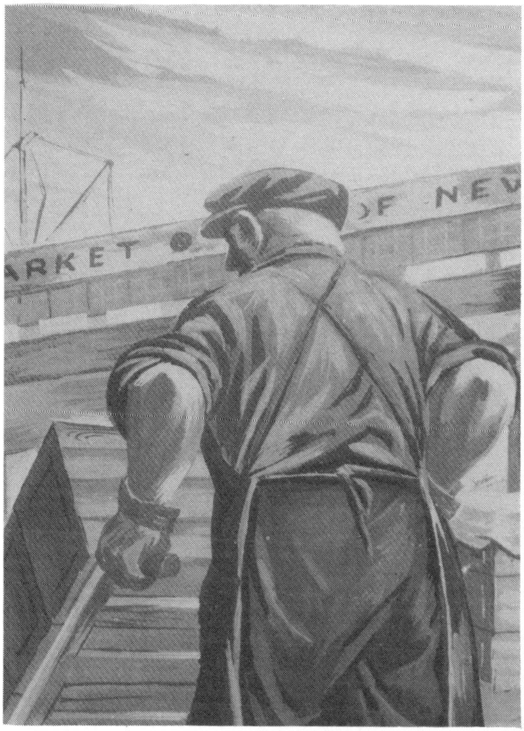

FLETCHER MARTIN – Fish Market Worker – signed with initials – gouache on paper – 15 x 10½in.
(Christie's) **$3,850** **£2,398**

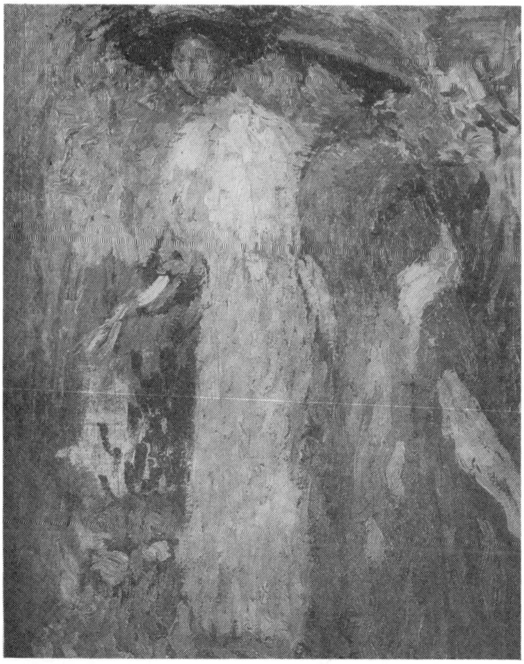

HENRI MARTIN – La Promenade – signed – oil on panel – 18 x 14½in.
(Christie's) **$34,903** **£20,900**

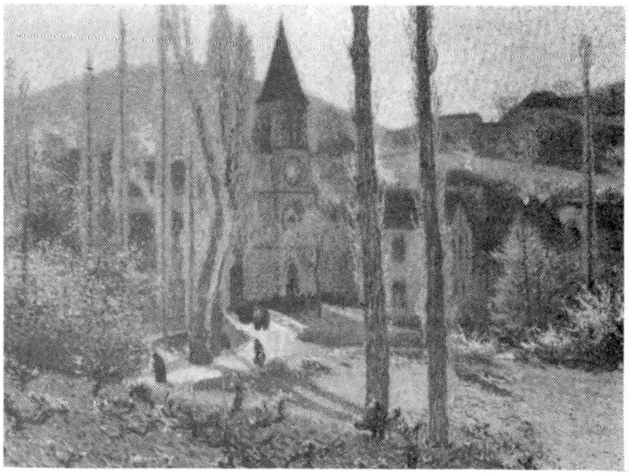

HENRI MARTIN – Vue de La Bastide-du-Vent, Lot – signed – oil on canvas – 40½ x 55¼in.
(Christie's) **$79,200** **£55,000**

HENRI MARTIN – Fishing Boats Moored Before The Slip At Newlyn – signed – 25 x 36cm.
(W. H. Lane & Son) **$1,162** **£700**

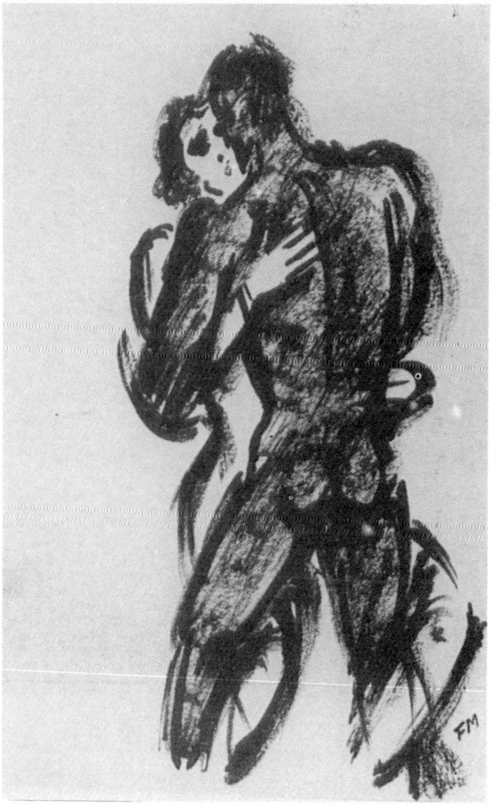

FRANZ MASEREEL – An album, bound in tooled brown leather, of 46 pages, containing 55 drawings, 34 signed with initials, three dated 1958, 41 of which are brush and black ink on paper, twelve pen and ink and two coloured crayons on paper, the measurements varying between 6¾ x 4¼in. and 3½ x 3in., the album 8½ x 11¾in.
(Christie's) **$2,059** **£1,430**

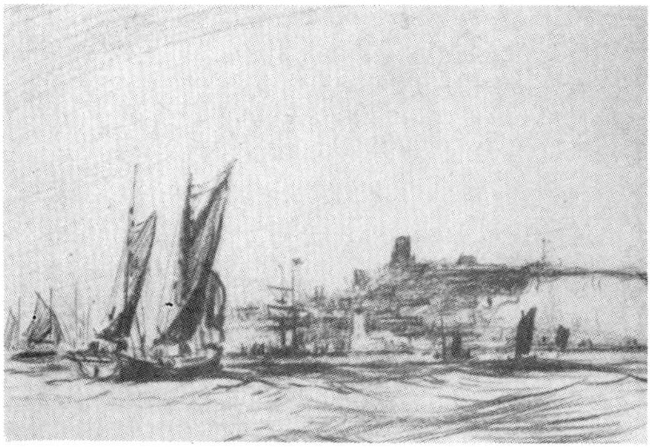

FRANK HENRY MASON – A Large Collection Of Sketch Books, Including Views Of Scarborough, Portsmouth, Barnard Castle, On The Continent And Elsewhere, The Majority Marine Studies – some inscribed – the majority pencil, a few with watercolour – 13 x 10in. and smaller, 54 in all.
(Christie's) **$620** **£440**

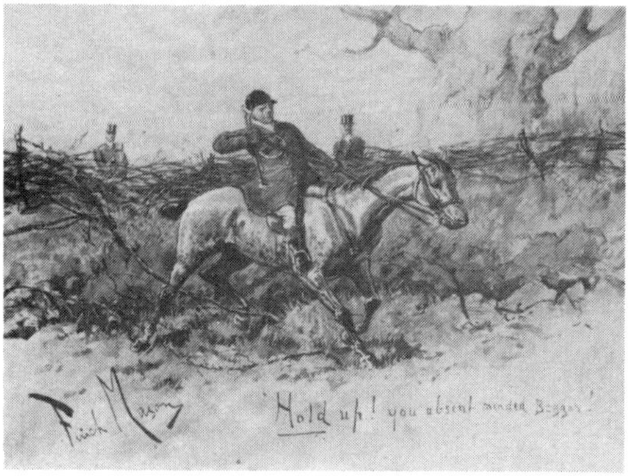

GEORGE FINCH MASON – 'Hold Up! you absent minded Beggar' – signed and inscribed – pencil and watercolour heightened with white – 10½ x 14¼in.
(Christie's) **$673** **£440**

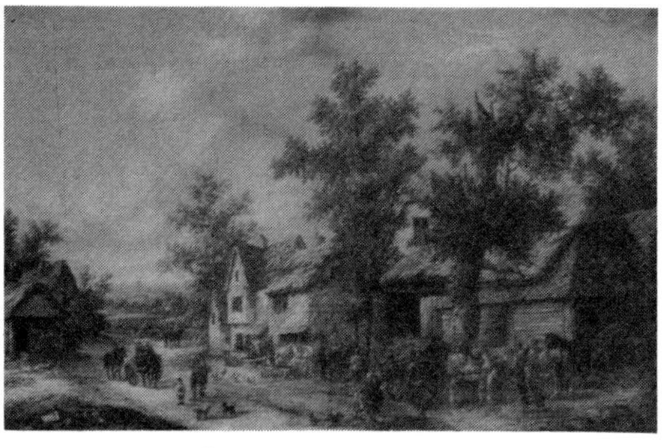

THOMAS MASTERS – The Half-Way House, Hillingham – signed with initials – 20 x 30in.
(Christie's) **$3,366** **£2,200**

CAMILLE MATISSE – Fleurs Dans Un Vase – signed – oil on panel – 34 x 29cm.
(Phillips) **$1,240** **£800**

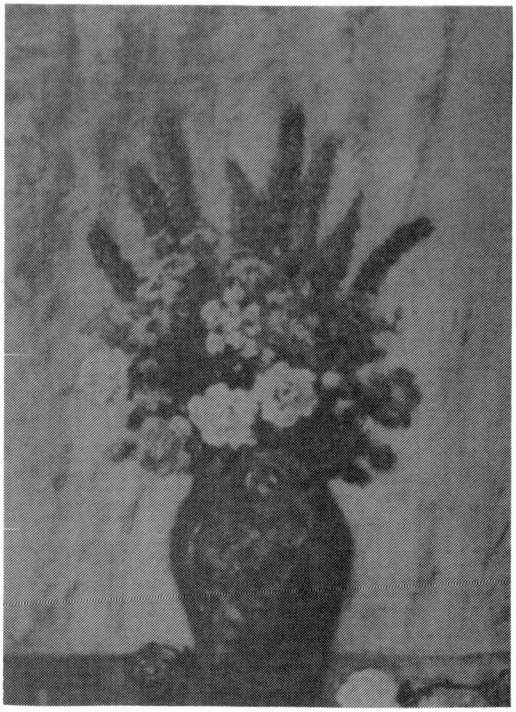

CAMILLE MATISSE – Fleurs d'Ete – signed – oil on canvas – 70 x 50.5cm.
(Phillips) **$1,364** **£880**

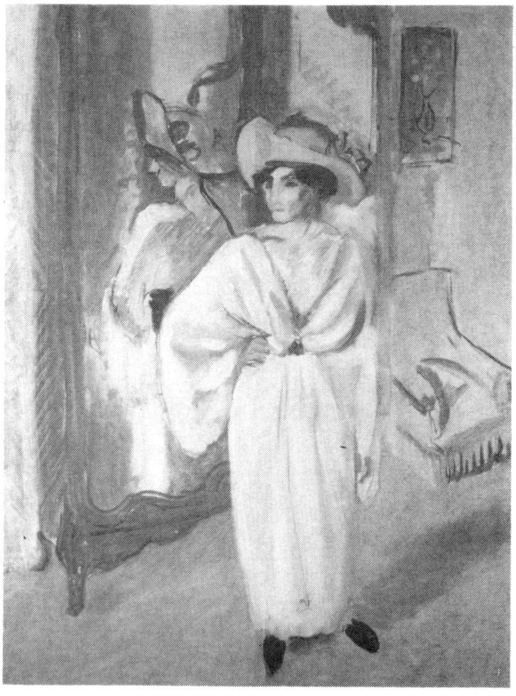

HENRI MATISSE – Femme en Blanc – signed – oil on canvas – 29 x 21½in.
(Christie's) **$1,010,350** **£605,000**

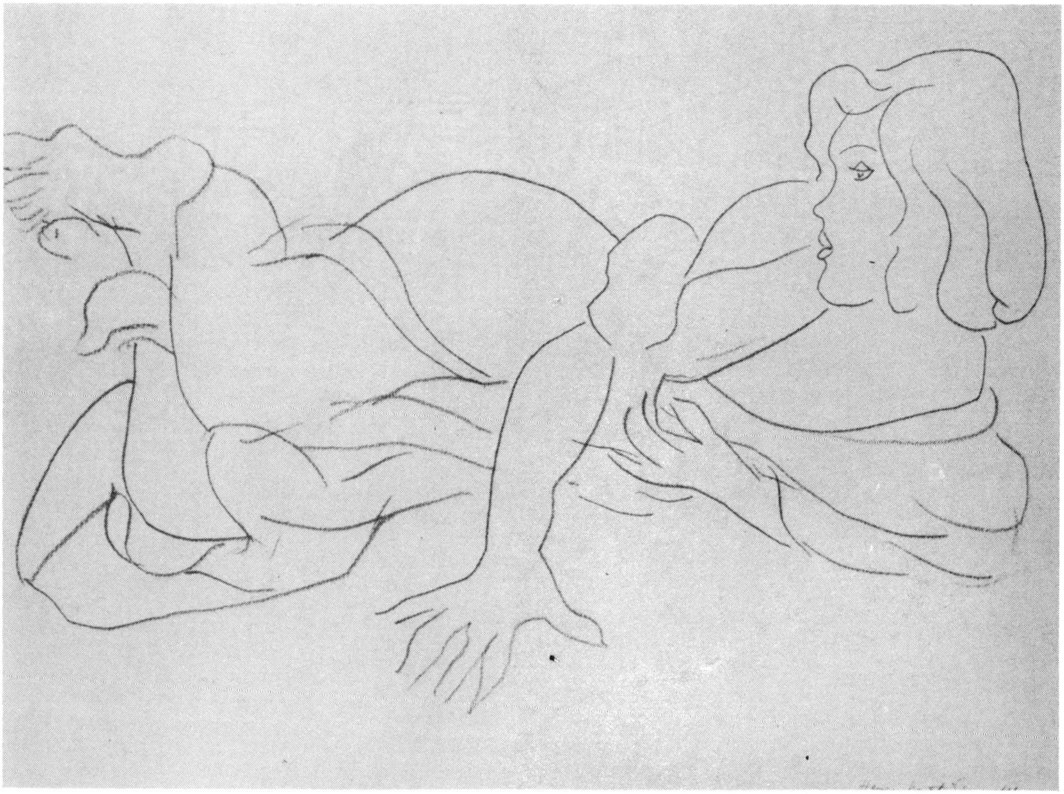

HENRI MATISSE – Jeune Femme allongee – signed and dated '41 – soft pencil on paper – 12½ x 17in.
(Christie's) **$79,200** **£49,500**

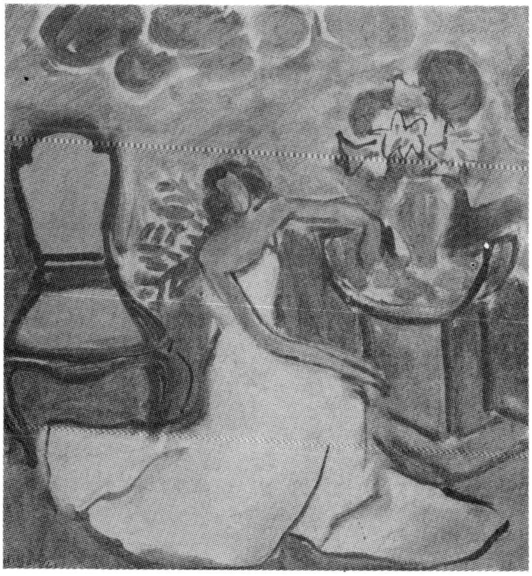

HENRI MATISSE – Jeune Fille en Robe blanche – signed and dated '41 – oil on canvas – 15 x 18in.
(Christie's) **$617,760** **£429,000**

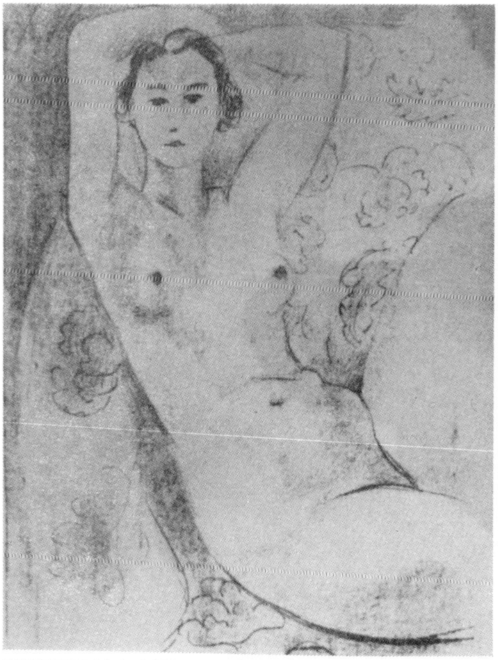

HENRI MATISSE – Nude Lady – signed – pencil – limited edition print 25/250 – 21 x 14in.
(Chancellors Hollingsworths) **$1,043** **£700**

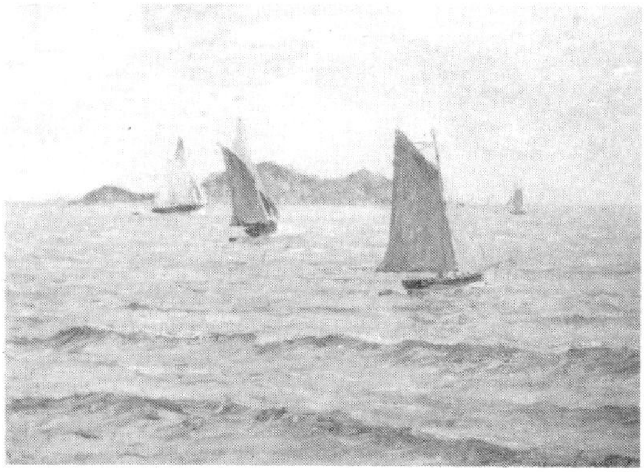

MAXIME MAUFRA – Les Voiliers – signed – oil on canvas – 13 x 18in.
(Christie's) **$2,534** **£1,760**

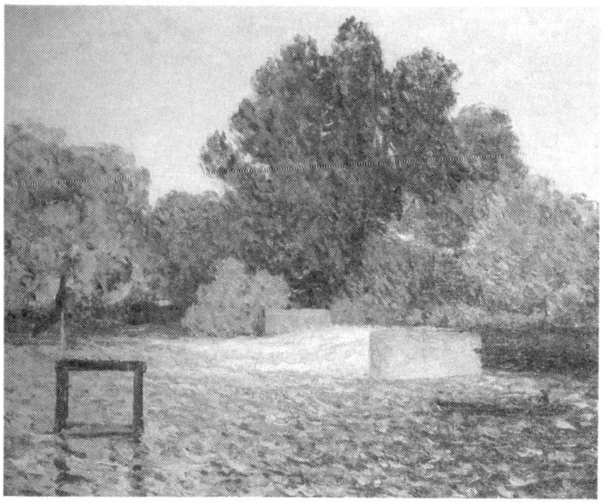

MAXIME MAUFRA – Le Barrage a Pontoise – signed and dated 1900 – oil on canvas – 18 x 21in.
(Christie's) **$11,088** **£7,700**

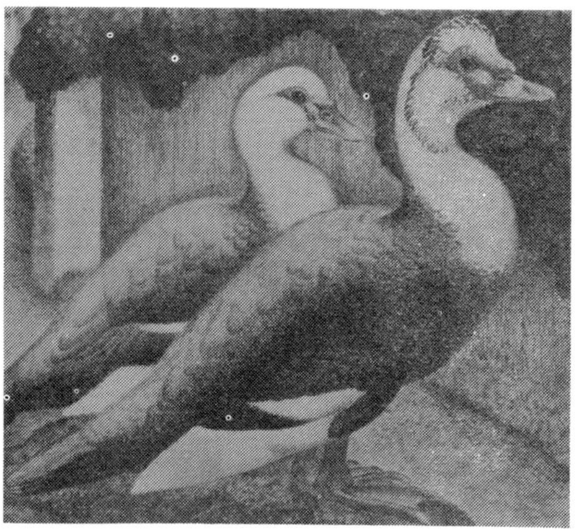

EILEEN MAYO – Muscovy Ducks – signed – pen and ink and watercolour over traces of pencil – 34 x 38cm.
(Phillips) **$697** **£420**

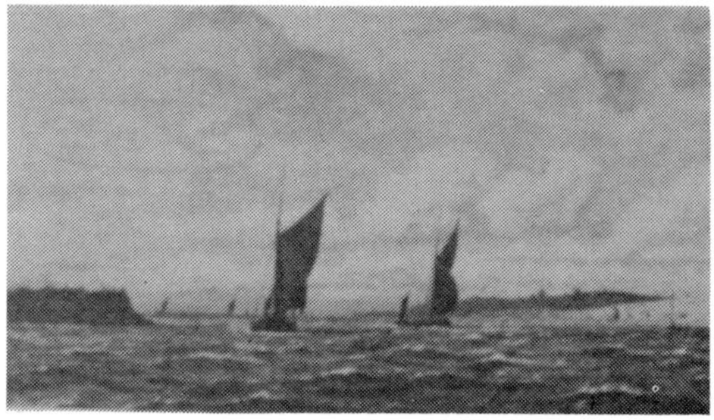

FREDERICK W. MAYOR – Fishing Barges At The Mouth Of A Harbour; and Yacht In A Gale – signed with monogram – on canvas – 14 x 24in.
(Phillips) **$885** **£550 Pair**

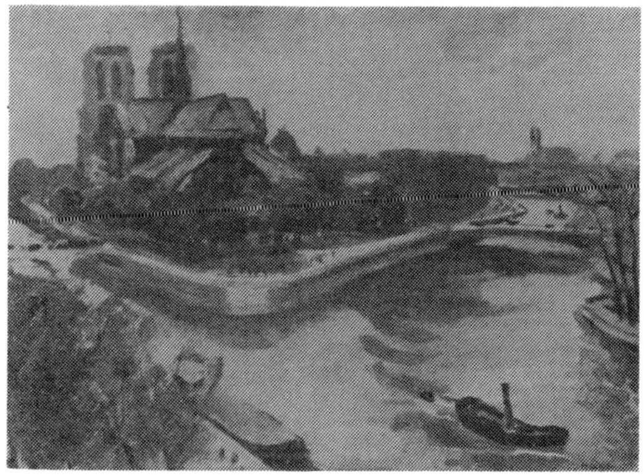

PAUL MAZE – Notre Dame – signed – oil on canvas – 33 x 46cm.
(Phillips) **$1,562** **£1,100**

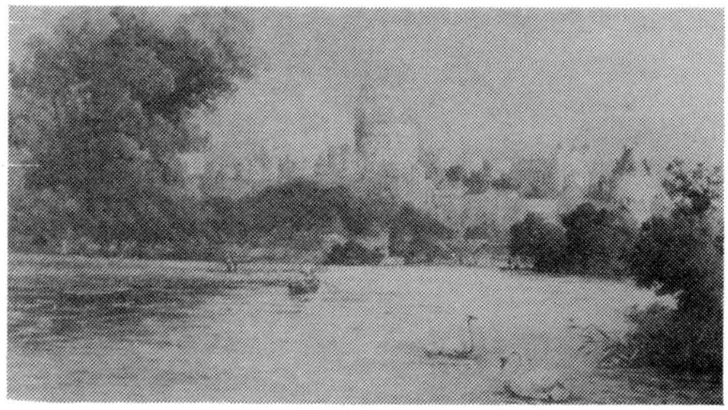

ARTHUR MEADOWS – Windsor From The River – signed and dated 1887 – watercolour – 36 x 51cm.; and A Lane At Cookham.
(Phillips) **$1,141** **£700 Two**

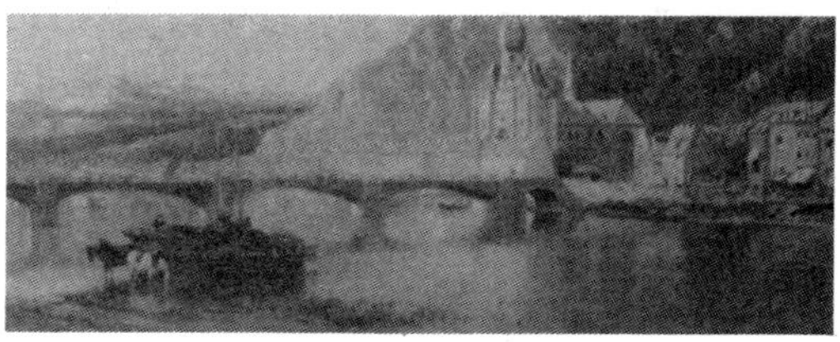

ARTHUR JOSEPH MEADOWS – Dinant On The Meuse, Sunset – signed and dated 1898 – 11½ x 19¾in.
(Christie's) **$1,240** **£880**

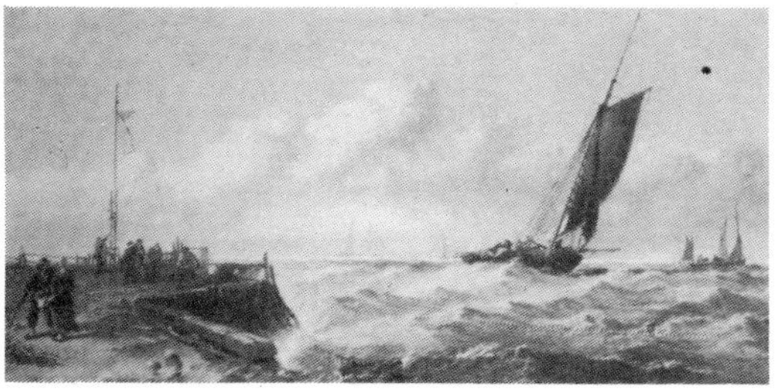

ARTHUR JOSEPH MEADOWS – Shipping Off Yarmouth – signed and dated 1873 – 15½ x 25½in.
(Christie's) **$9,720** **£6,480**

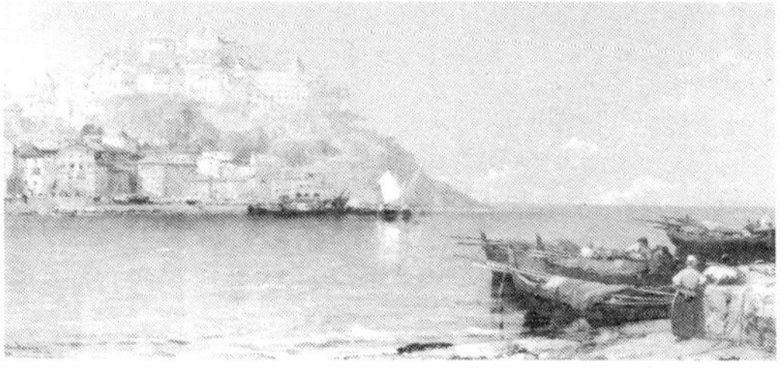

ARTHUR JOSEPH MEADOWS – 'Port Maurizio – On The Riviera' – signed and dated 1891, also signed, dated and inscribed on the reverse – oil on canvas – 20 x 30in.
(Phillips) **$13,464** **£8,800**

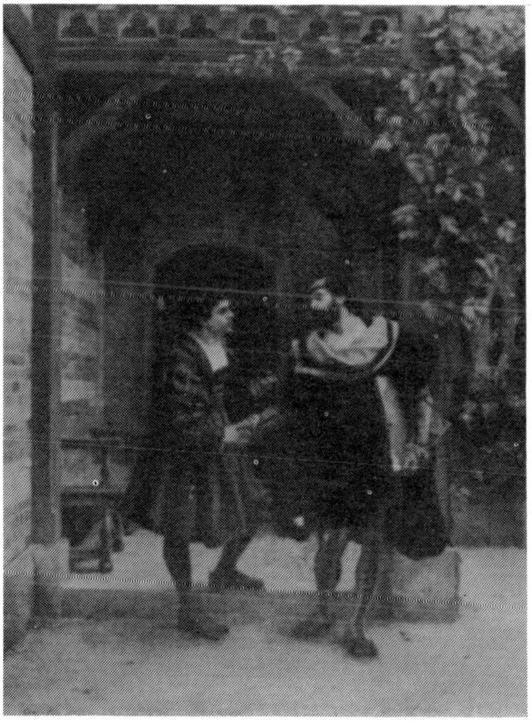

JEAN CHARLES MEISSONIER – An Artist And A Gentleman – signed and dated 1880 – oil on canvas – 26 x 20in.
(Robt. W. Skinner Inc.) **$1,600** **£981**

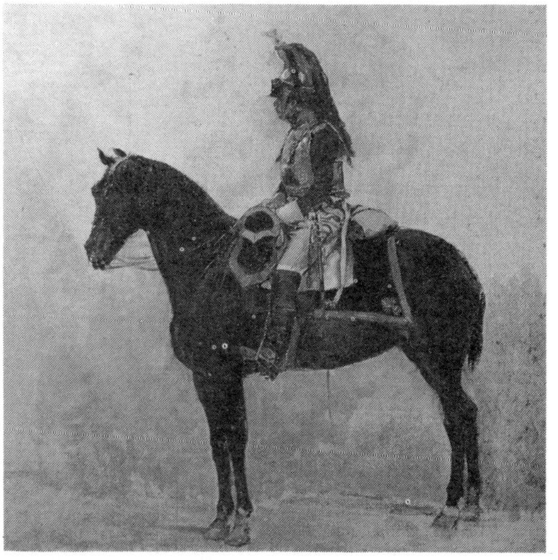

JEAN LOUIS ERNEST MEISSONIER – Le Cuirassier – 9½ x 10in.
(Christie's) **$14,080** **£8,800**

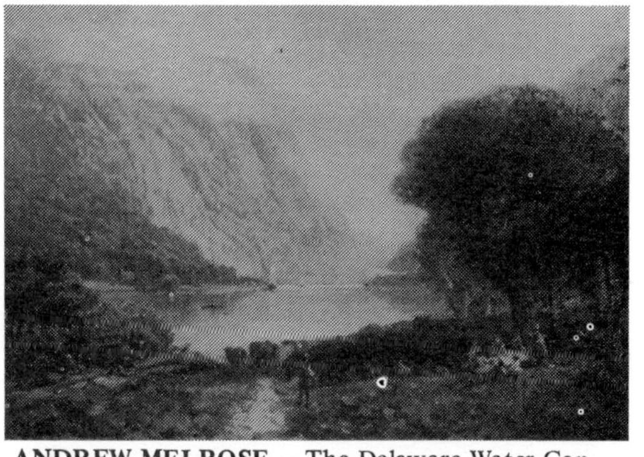

ANDREW MELROSE – The Delaware Water Gap – signed and inscribed, and inscribed on the reverse – oil on canvas – 15 x 20¼in.
(Christie's) **$18,700** **£13,146**

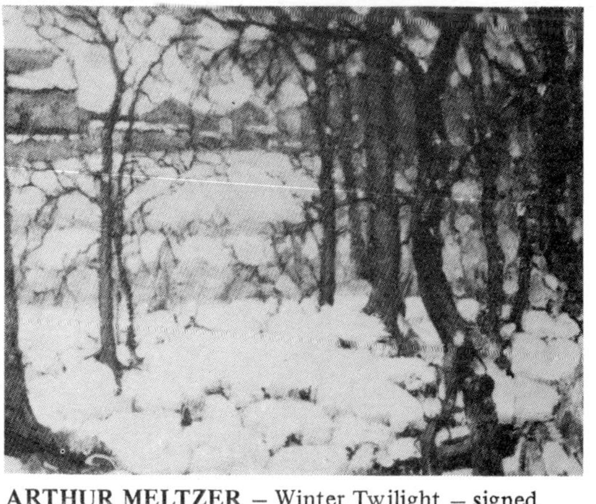

ARTHUR MELTZER – Winter Twilight – signed – oil on canvas – 12 x 14in.
(Robt. W. Skinner Inc.) **$1,200** **£833**

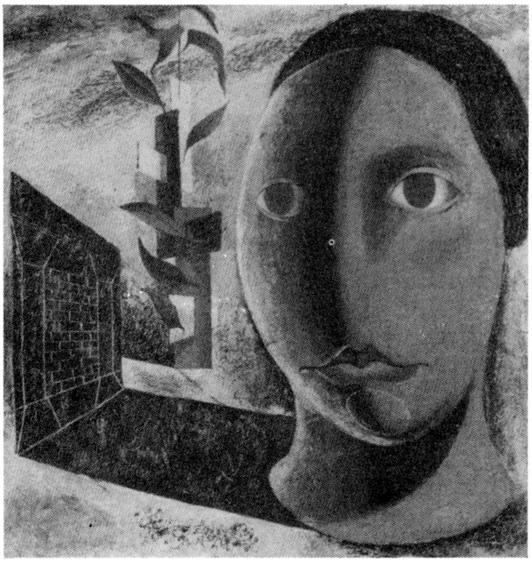

JOHN MELVILLE – Tete De Femme – indistinctly signed, and signed and inscribed on the reverse – oil on canvas – 20 x 20in.
(Christie's) **$2,516** **£1,760**

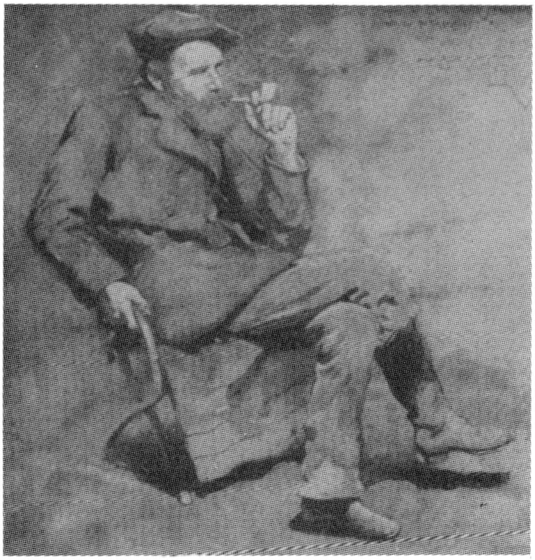

WILLARD LEROY METCALF – A Quiet Pipe – signed, dated '83 and inscribed – gouache en grisaille on paper laid down on board – 9 x 10in.
(Christie's) **$3,850** **£2,398**

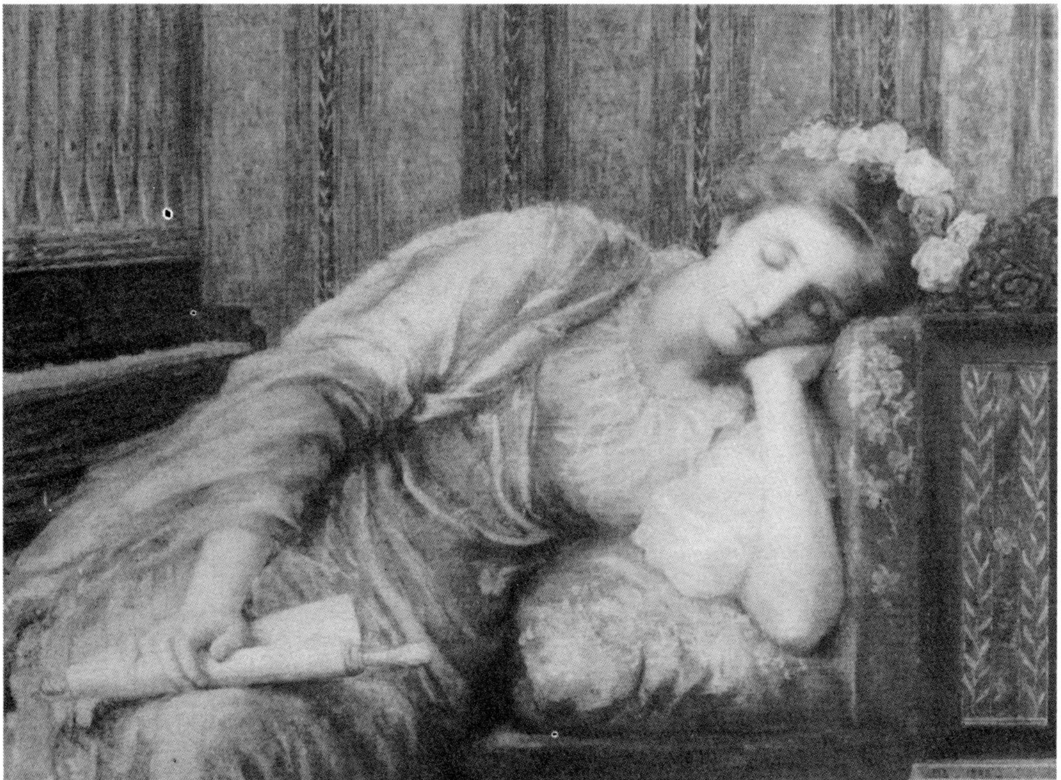

ANNA LEA MERRITT – Saint Cecila, From Tennyson – signed with monogram and dated 1886 – oil on canvas – 18 x 24in. *(Phillips)* **$4,896** **£3,200**

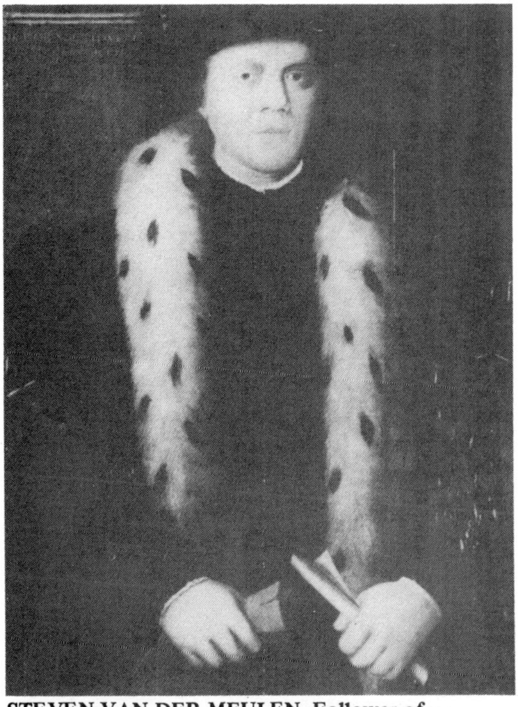

STEVEN VAN DER MEULEN, Follower of – Portrait Of Sir Robert Southwell Of Mereworth – inscribed – on panel – 36 x 26½in.
(Christie's) **$972** **£648**

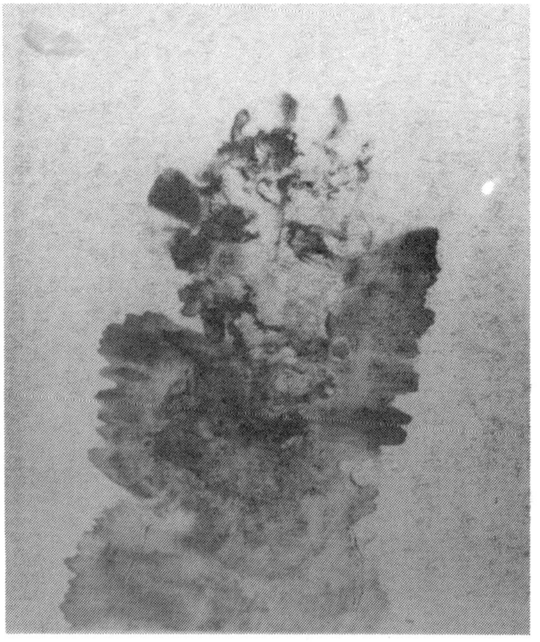

HENRI MICHAUX – Tete – signed with initials – watercolour on rice paper – 21 x 17¼in.
(Christie's) **$7,040** **£4,400**

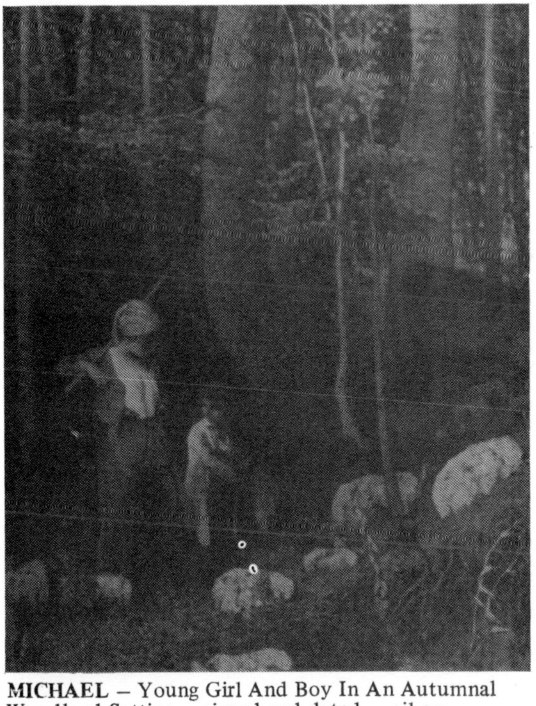

MICHAEL – Young Girl And Boy In An Autumnal Woodland Setting – signed and dated – oil on canvas – 33 x 23in.
(Morphets) **$7,440** **£4,800**

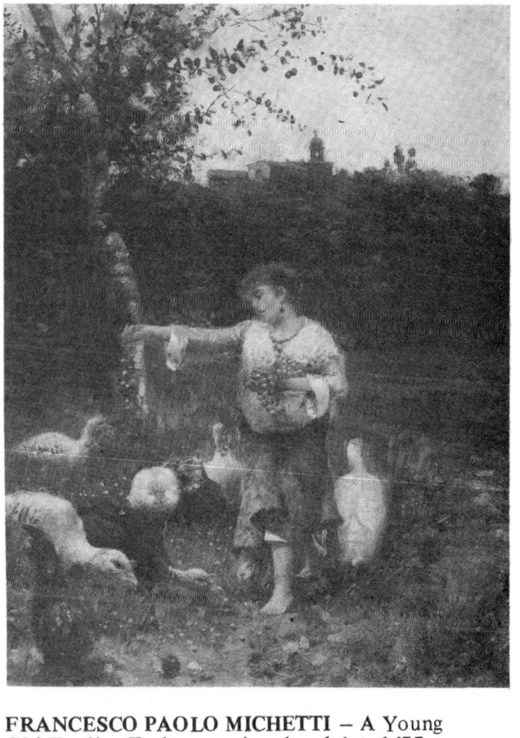

FRANCESCO PAOLO MICHETTI – A Young Girl Feeding Turkeys – signed and dated '77 – on panel – 16 x 13in.
(Christie's) **$26,400** **£16,500**

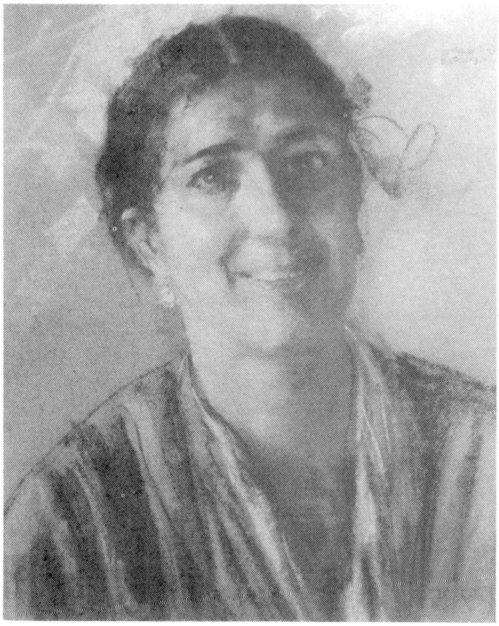

FRANCESCO PAOLO MICHETTI – Head Of A Woman – signed – pastel – 16 x 13¼in. – and a charcoal drawing.
(Christie's) **$8,217** **£4,950 Two**

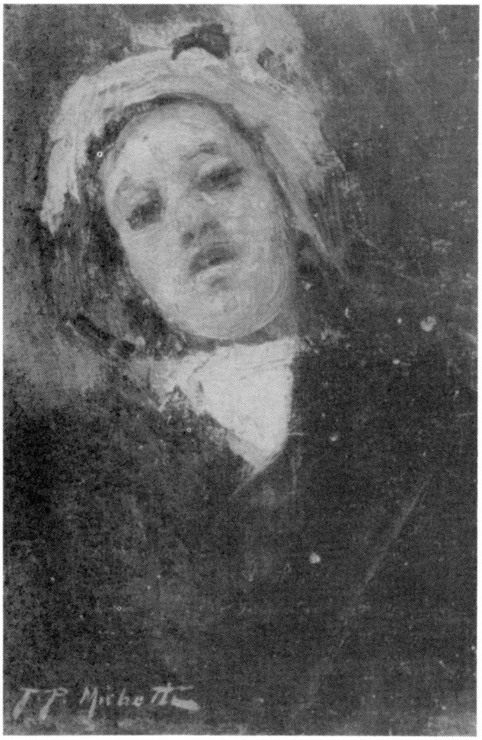

FRANCESCO PAOLO MICHETTI – Studies Of Girls' Heads – signed – on panel – 4 x 2¾in. and smaller.
(Christie's) **$4,565** **£2,750 Two**

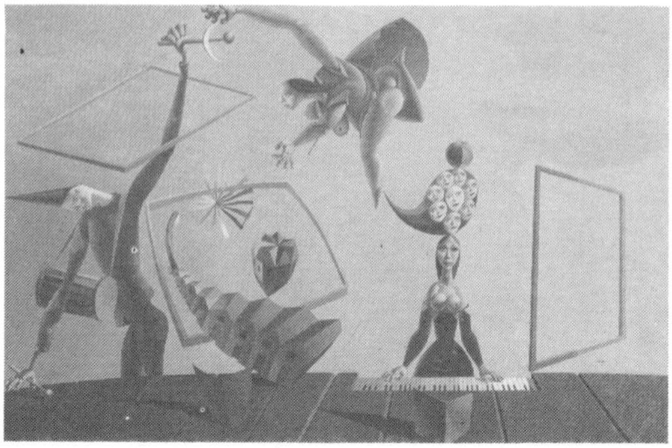

COLIN MIDDLETON – The Toy-Box – signed, signed, inscribed and dated 1948 on the reverse – oil on canvas – 51 x 76cm.
(Phillips) **$12,780** **£9,000**

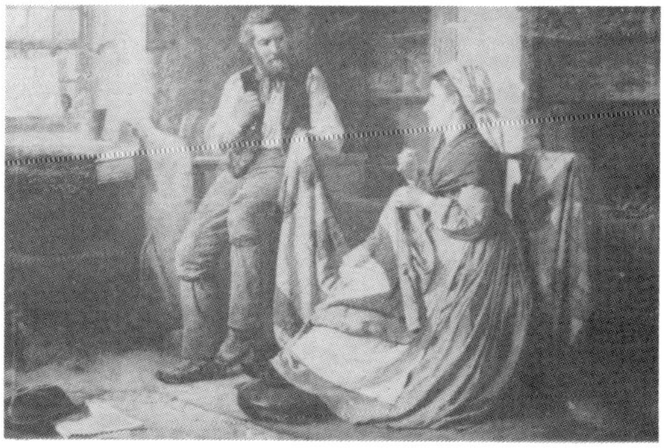

WILLIAM HENRY MIDWOOD – The Patchwork Quilt – signed and dated 1876 – oil on canvas – 28 x 36in.
(Christie's) **$4,032** **£2,800**

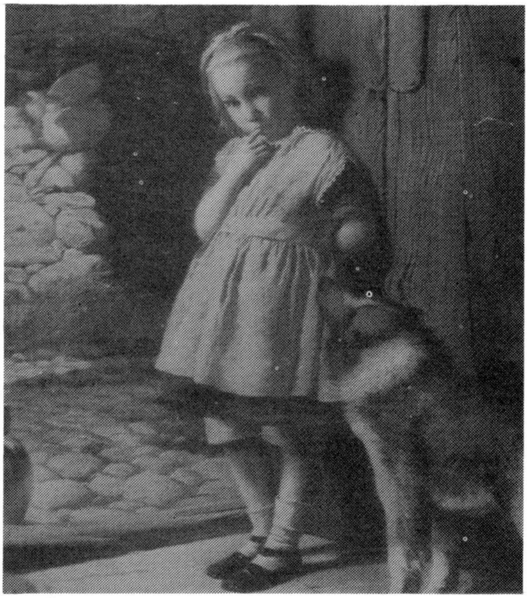

WILLIAM HENRY MIDWOOD – On The Door-Step – signed – on board – 15½ x 12in.
(Christie's) **$3,029** **£1,980**

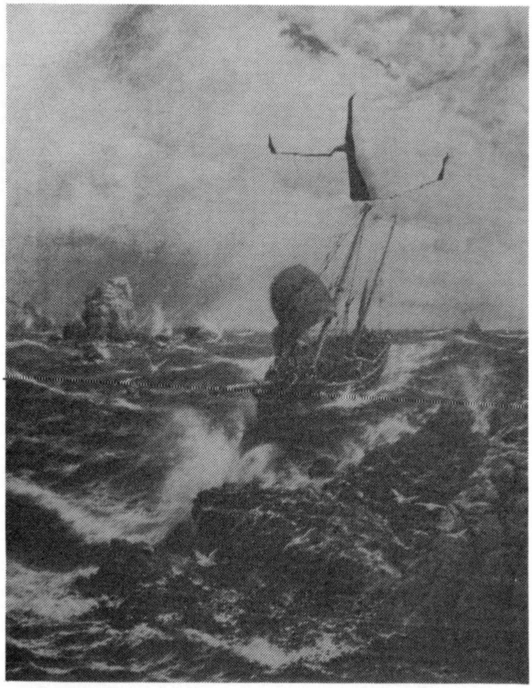

THOMAS ROSE MILES – The Channel Through The Reef – signed, and signed and inscribed on the reverse – 40 x 30in.
(Christie's) **$1,134** **£756**

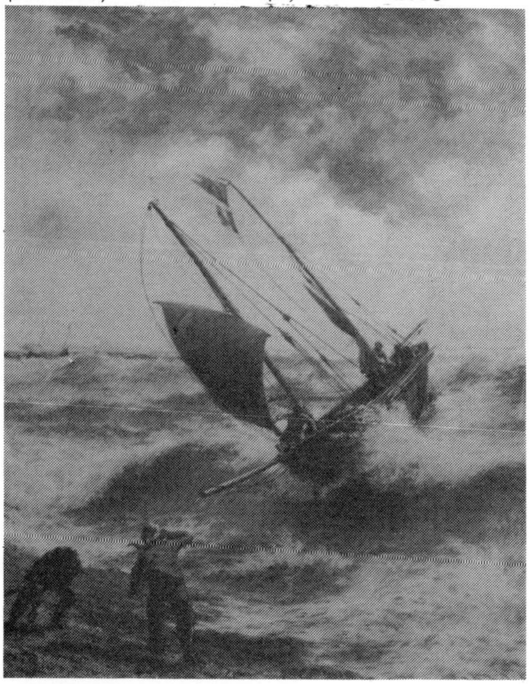

THOMAS ROSE MILES – After A Stormy Night, Hastings – signed, and signed and inscribed on the reverse – 36¼ x 28in.
(Christie's) **$1,296** **£864**

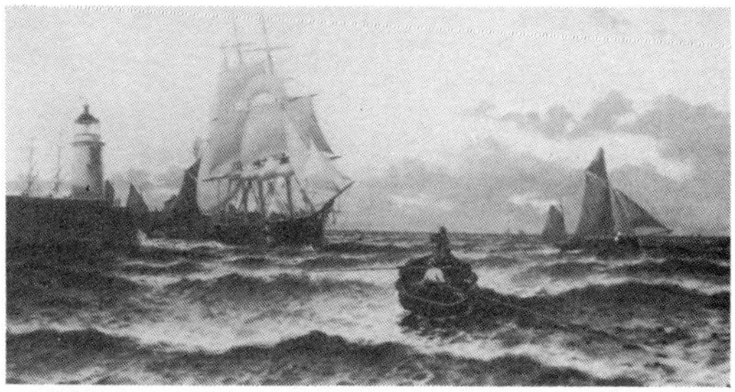

THOMAS ROSE MILES – In The Mouth Of The Harbour – signed – 30 x 50in.
(Christie's) **$3,888** **£2,592**

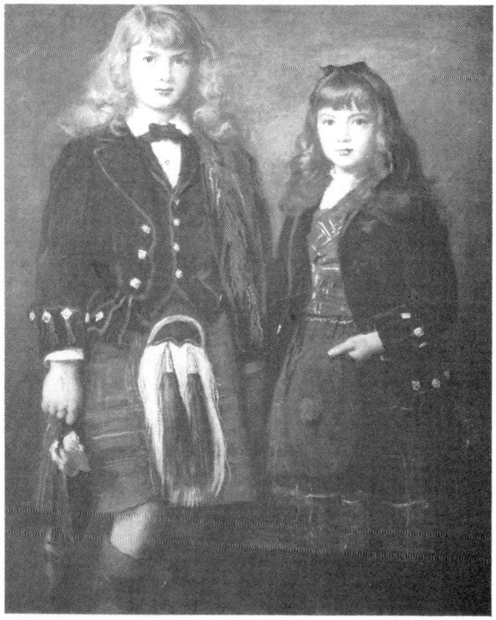

SIR JOHN EVERETT MILLAIS – Twa Bairns, A Group Portrait Of Frederick And Mary Stewart Phillips In Highland Dress – signed with monogram and dated 1888 – 53 x 40in.
(Christie's) **$126,720** **£88,000**

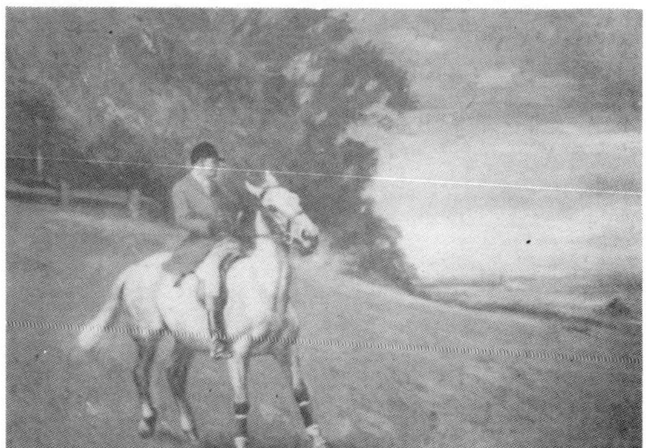

RAOUL MILLAIS – Huntsman On Grey Hunter, The Fox Fleeing Downhill – signed and dated '30 – oil – 19½ x 23½in.
(Hobbs & Chambers) **$2,618** **£1,700**

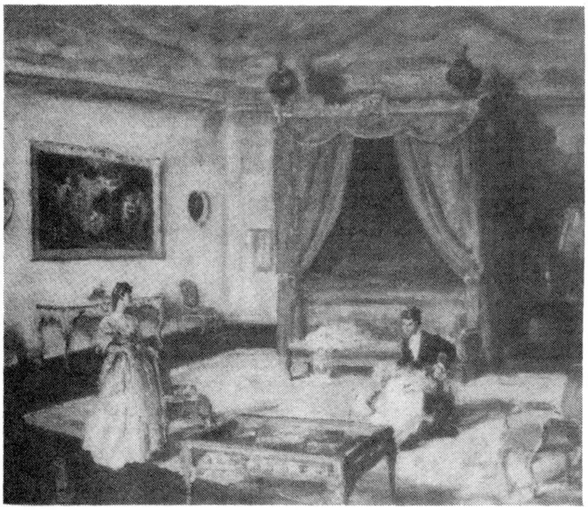

RAOUL MILLAIS – In A Bedroom – signed – oil on canvas – 20 x 24in.
(Christie's) **$1,295** **£825**

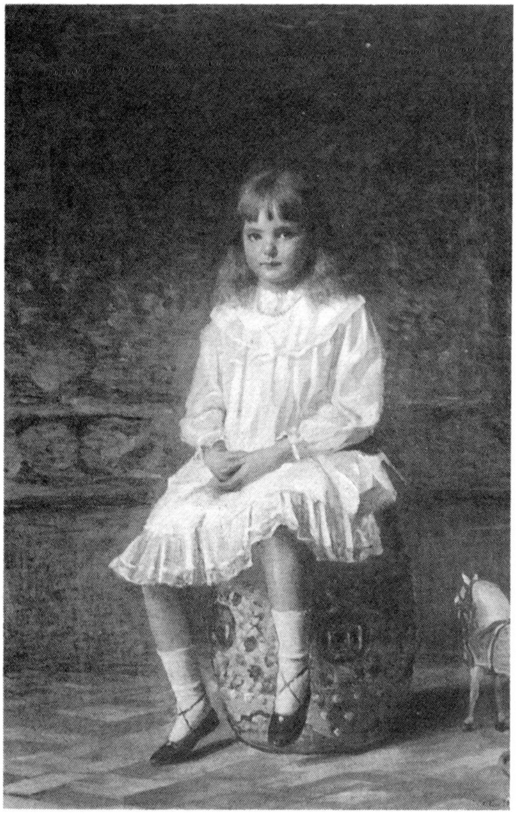

WILLIAM E. MILLER – Portrait Of A Young Girl Sitting On A Chinese Garden Seat – signed and dated 1905 – oil on canvas – 60 x 40½in.
(Christie's) **$5,033** **£3,520**

J. W. MILLIKEN – 'A Market Day, Bruges'; and 'Place Memlinck, Bruges' – signed – watercolour – 10 x 14in.
(Biddle & Webb) **$923** **£620 Pair**

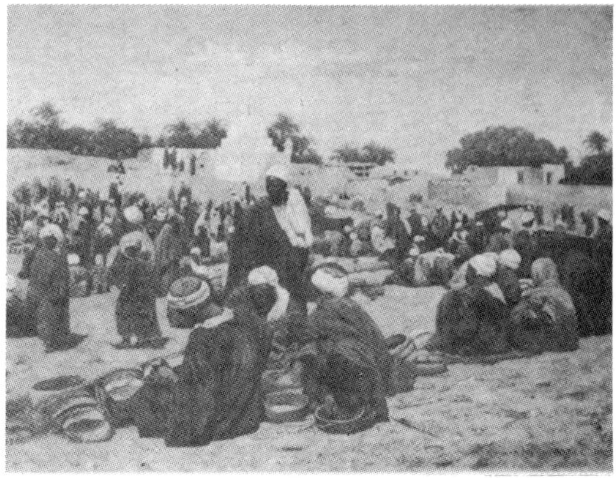

EDWARD MILLS – Luxor Market – signed and dated 1890, and signed and inscribed on an old label on the reverse – 17½ x 23¾in.
(Christie's) **$3,888** **£2,592**

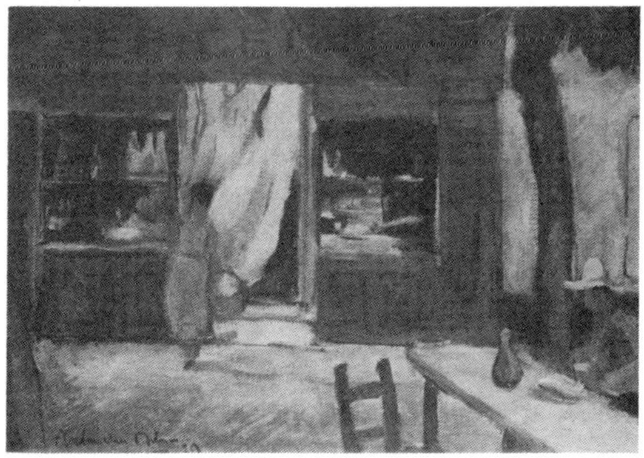

JOHN MacLAUGHLAN MILNE – L'Epicerie – signed and dated 1929 – oil on canvas – 15 x 21¾in.
(Christie's) **$9,360** **£6,500**

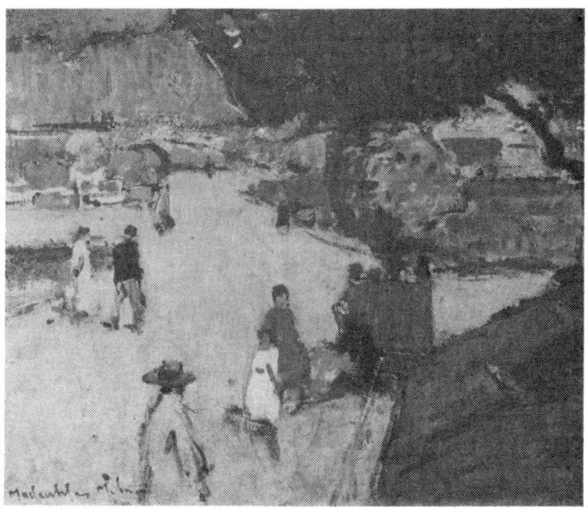

JOHN MacLAUGHLAN MILNE – Jardin de Luxembourg, Paris – signed – oil on board – 15 x 18in.
(Christie's) **$9,360** **£6,500**

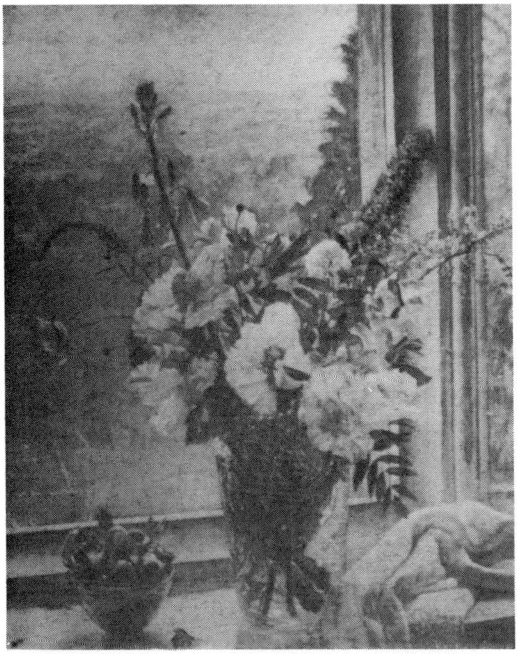

MALCOLM MILNE – Vase Of Flowers, And A Bowl Of Conkers On A Window Ledge – signed and dated '24 – oil on canvas – 29¼ x 24in.
(Christie's) **$6,908** **£4,400**

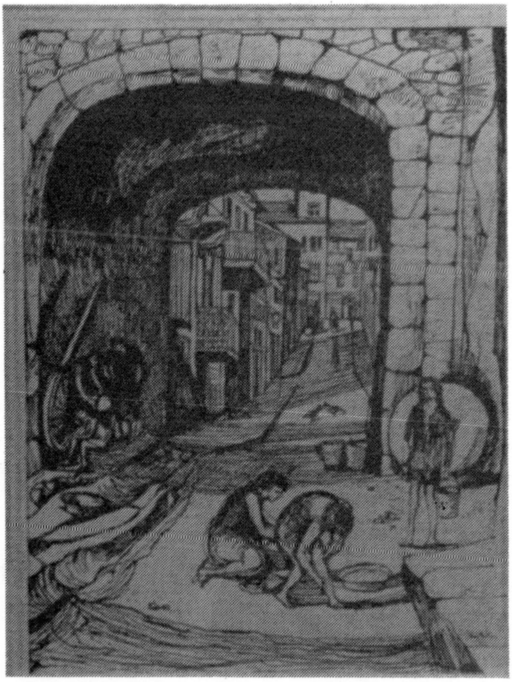

JOHN MINTON – La Porte Genoise, Porto Vecchio, Corsica – signed and dated 1947 – pen and ink on buff paper – 37.5 x 28cm.
(Phillips) **$1,760** **£1,100**

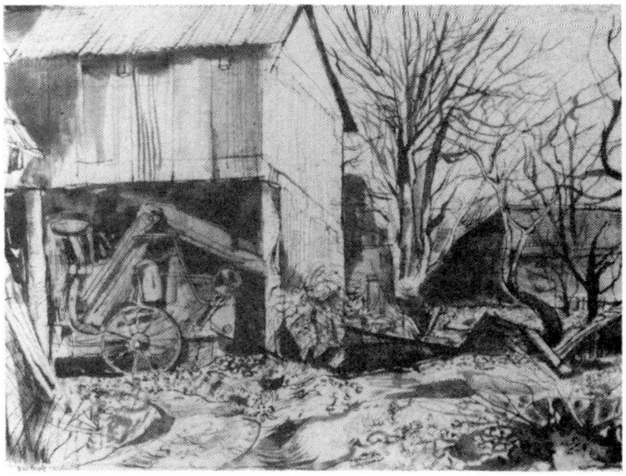

JOHN MINTON – Farmyard Scene – signed and dated 1945 – pen, ink and grey wash – 11 x 14½in.
(Christie's) **$2,202** **£1,540**

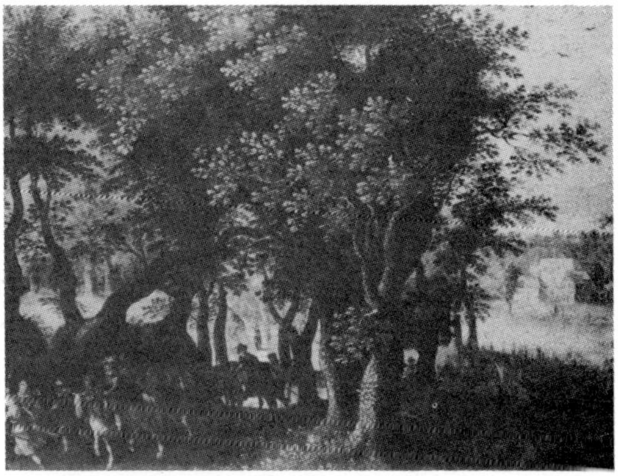

ANTON MIROU, Attributed to – A Wooded Landscape With A Band Of Soldiers On A Track; and A View Across A River To A Village Beyond – on panel – 21 x 26in.
(Lawrence Fine Art) **$5,843** **£3,520 Pair**

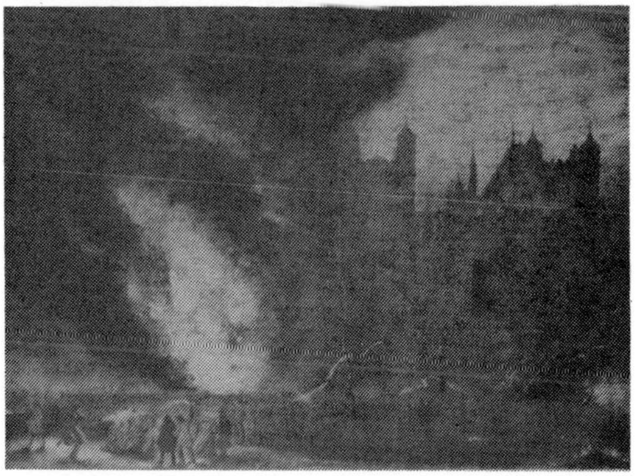

A. L. MITCHELL – Guy Fawkes Celebrations, The Cathedral Yard, Exeter – signed and dated 1848 – watercolour – 20½ x 29½in.
(Lawrence Fine Art) **$693** **£418**

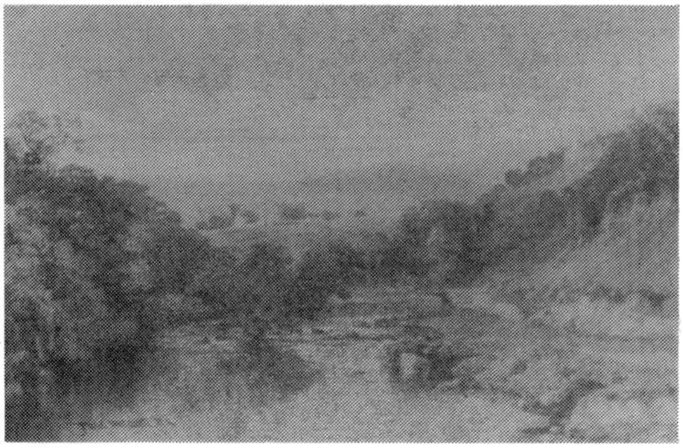

PHILIP MITCHELL – An Angler On The Banks Of A River – signed – pencil and watercolour – 11¾ x 18½in.
(Christie's) **$639** **£385**

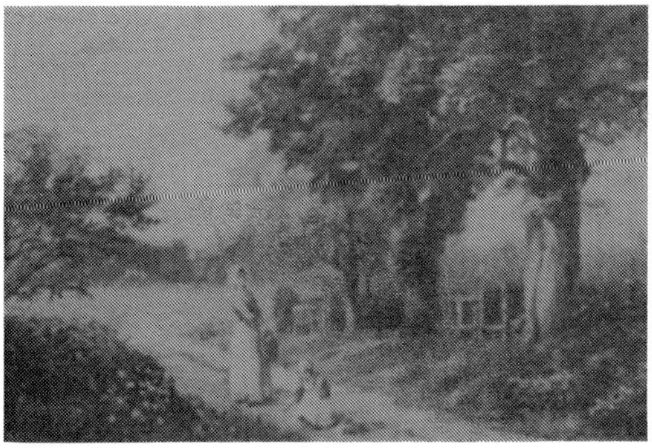

JANE MOBERLEY – Picking Wild Summer Flowers – signed with monogram – on canvas – 12¼ x 18in.
(Phillips) **$1,771** **£1,100**

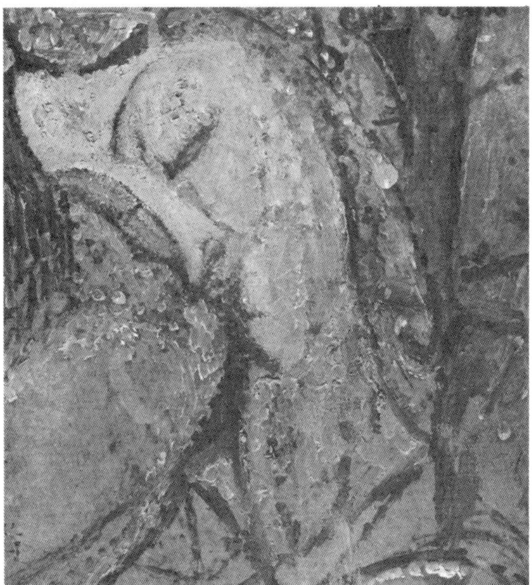

AMEDEO MODIGLIANI – Cherubin – inscribed – oil on green paper laid on board – 12¼ x 9¼in.
(Christie's) **$39,600** **£27,500**

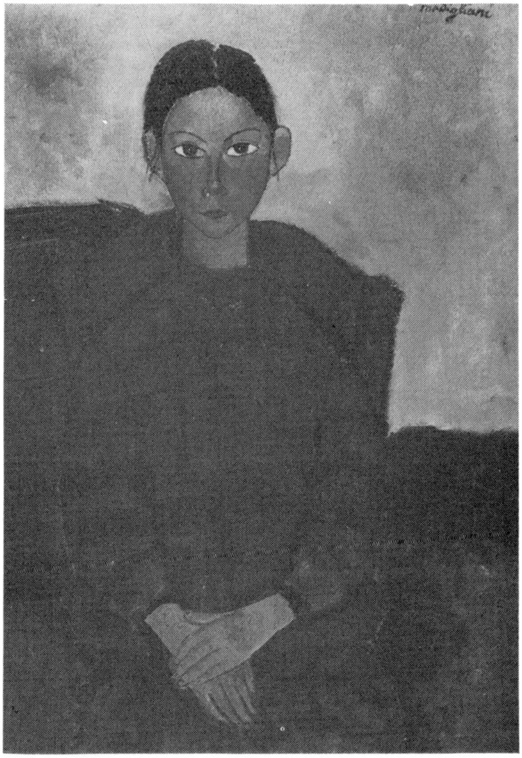

AMEDEO MODIGLIANI – Fillette au Tablier noir – signed – oil on canvas – 36¼ x 23¾in.
(Christie's) **$4,408,800** **£2,640,000**

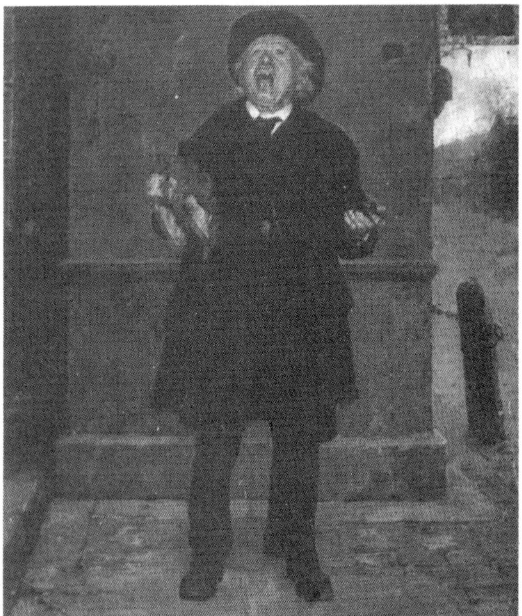

LOUIS CHARLES MOELLER – Sneezing – signed – oil on paper laid down on board – 9¾ x 8in.
(Christie's) **$3,300** **£2,319**

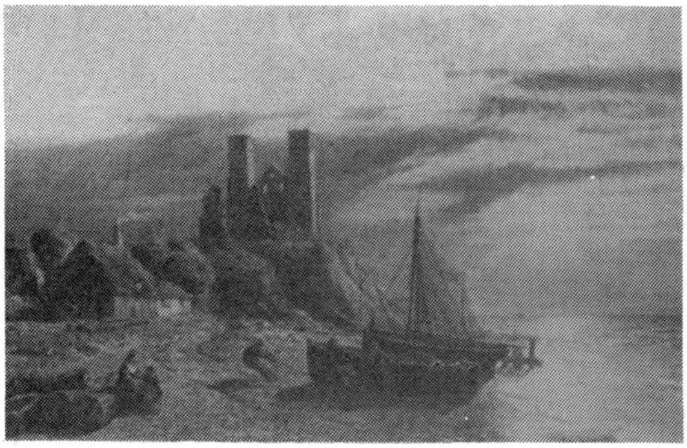

JOHN MOGFORD – The Reculvers, Kent – signed – watercolour heightened with white – 12¾ x 20½in.
(Christie's) **$4,032** **£2,860**

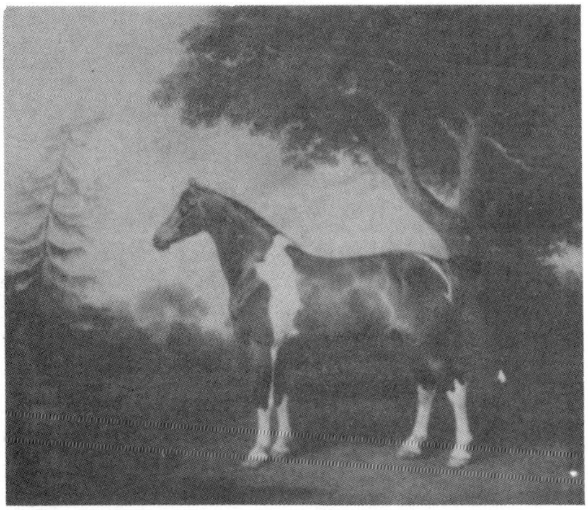

THOMAS MOGFORD – A Horse Standing In An Extensive Parkland – signed and dated 1836 – 24½ x 30in.
(Christie's) **$4,312** **£2,800**

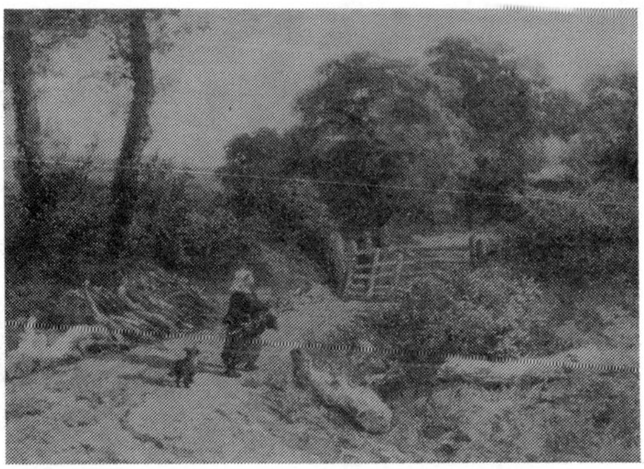

JOHN HENRY MOLE – A Woman Carrying Faggots In A Lane – signed and dated 1872 – pencil and watercolour heightened with white – 6½ x 9½in.
(Christie's) **$1,460** **£880**

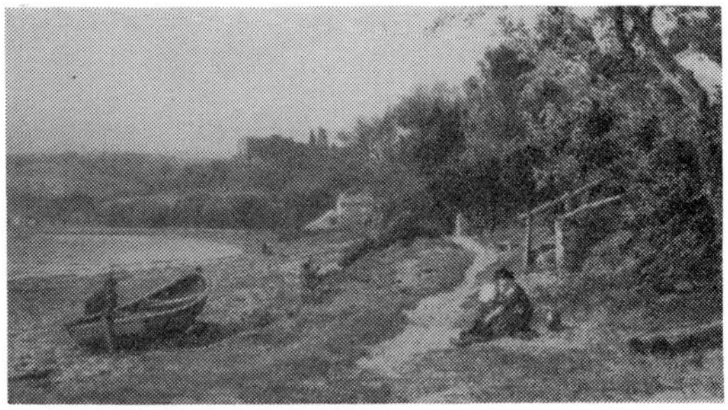

JOHN HENRY MOLE – A Mother And Child On A Foreshore, Castle Ruins Beyond – signed and dated 1868 – watercolour and bodycolour over traces of pencil – 20 x 33cm.
(Phillips) **$1,711** **£1,050**

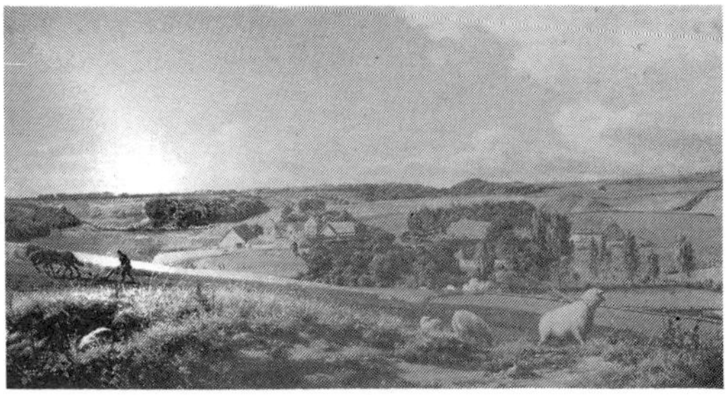

JOHANN PETER CHRISTOFFER MOLLER – A Wooded Landscape With A Farmhouse And A Man Ploughing – signed and dated 1881 – 28 x 41½in.
(Christie's) **$4,928** **£3,080**

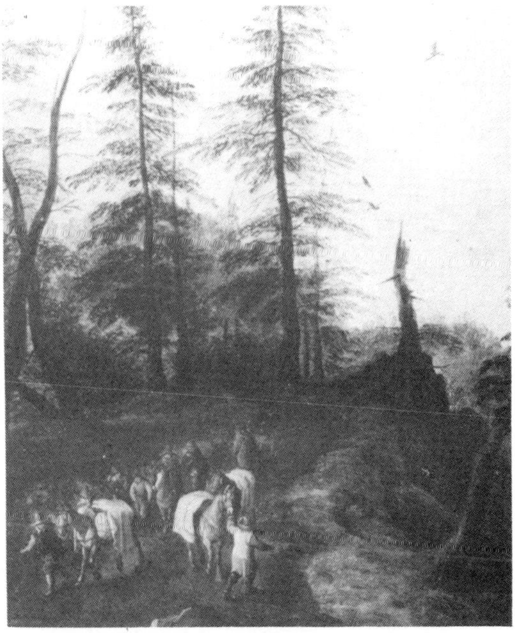

JOOS DE MOMPER, Attributed to – Travellers With Pack Horses Riding Along A Path, In A Wooded Landscape – oil on panel – 15¾ x 12½in.
(Phillips) **$3,948** **£2,800**

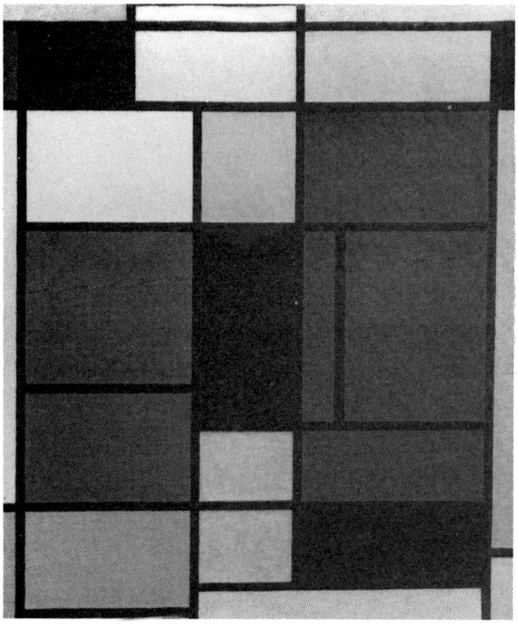

PIET MONDRIAN – Tableau No. 1 – signed with initials and dated '21-25 – oil on canvas – 29½ x 25½in.
(Christie's) **$2,204,400 £1,320,000**

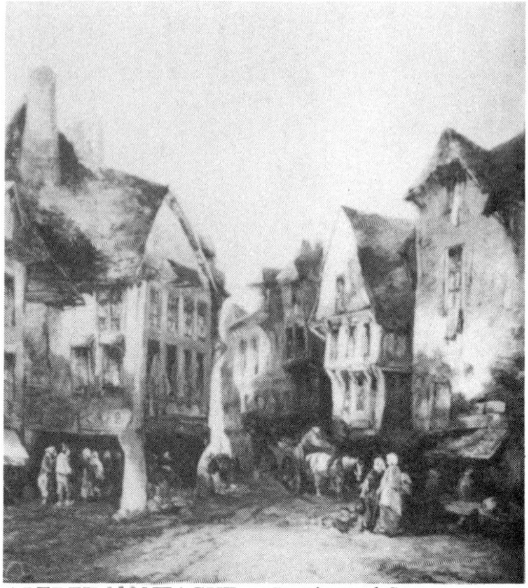

ALFRED MONTAGUE – Continental Street Scene With Market Stalls, Figures, Horse Drawn Cart And Church Spire In Background – signed and dated 1879 – oil – 14 x 12in.
(Capes, Dunn & Co.) **$1,467 £900**

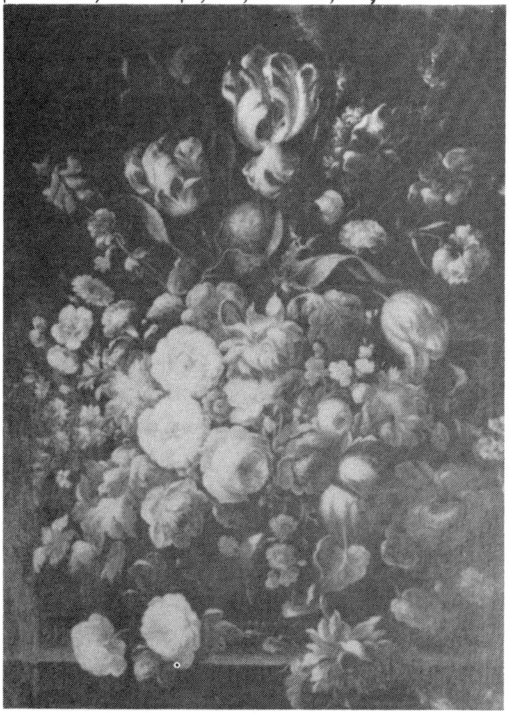

JEAN-BAPTISTE MONNOYER, Manner of – Still Life Of Mixed Flowers In A Glass Bowl On A Ledge – initials A.M. – oil on canvas – 41½ x 29½in.
(Christie's) **$3,406 £2,090**

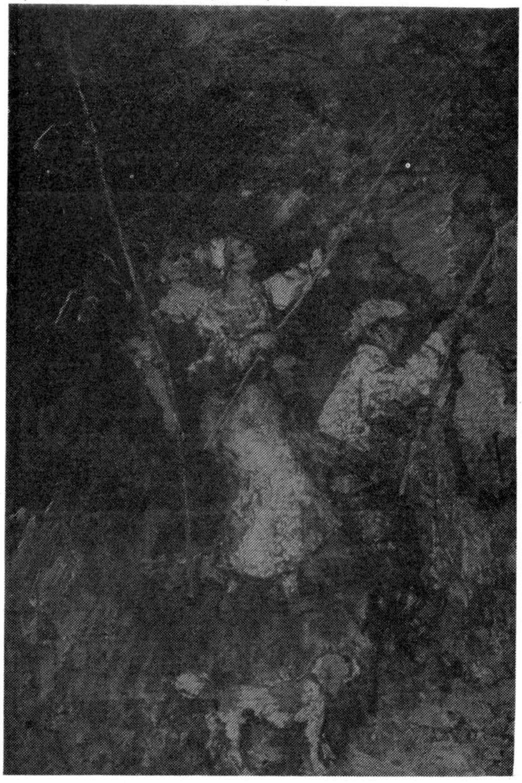

ADOLPHE JOSEPH THOMAS MONTICELLI – Les Ceuilleurs de Pommes – signed – oil on panel – 14¼ x 8¼in.
(Christie's) **$15,048 £10,450**

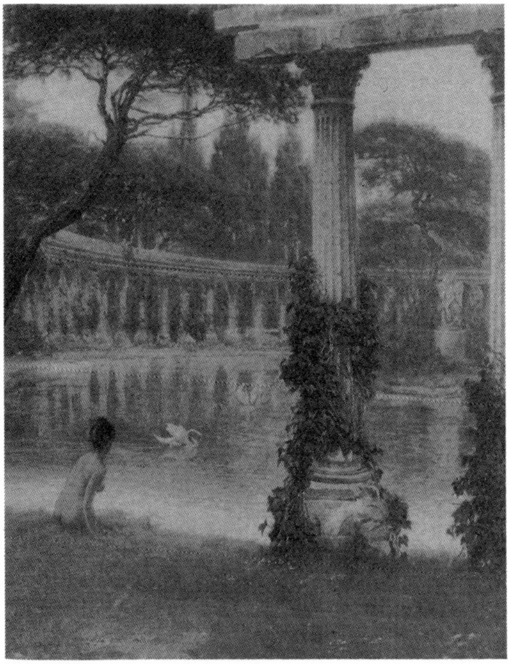

EDGARD DE SAINT-PIERRE DE MONTZAIGLE – Bather By A Classical Pool – signed – on panel – 24½ x 18in.
(Christie's) **$3,344** **£2,200**

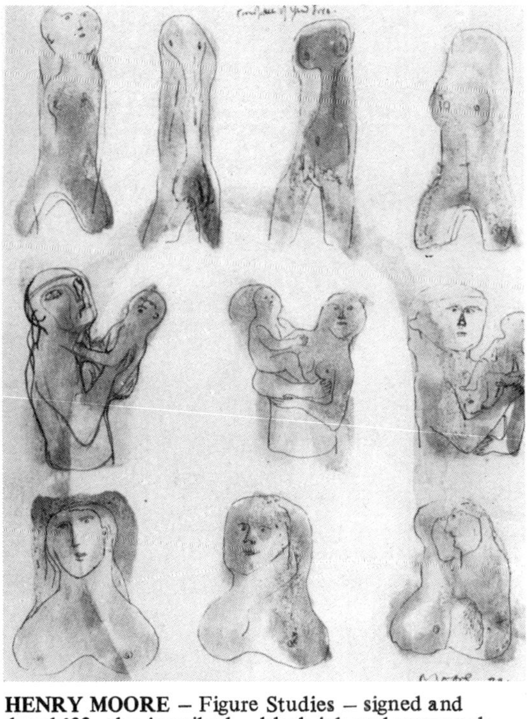

HENRY MOORE – Figure Studies – signed and dated '32, also inscribed – black ink and grey wash on paper – 10 x 7½in.
(Christie's) **$6,336** **£4,400**

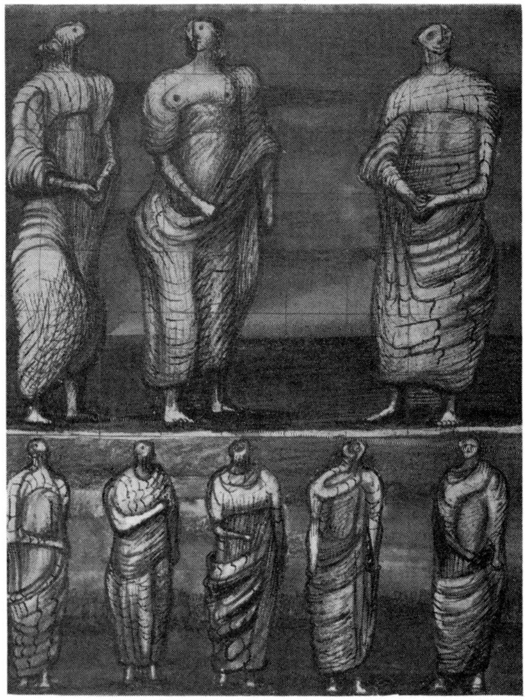

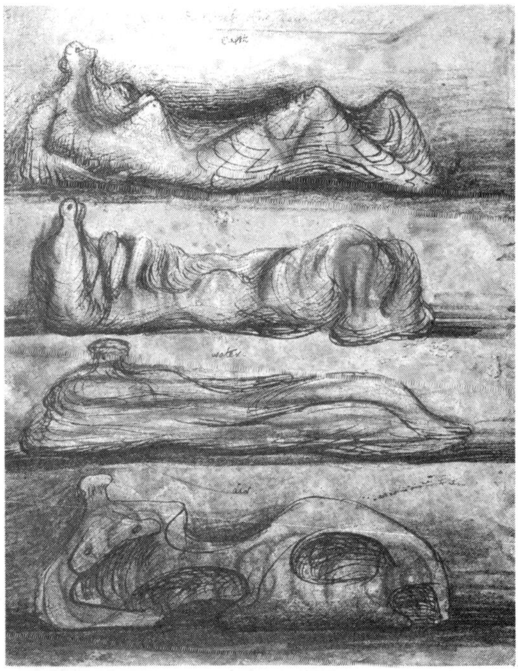

HENRY MOORE – Standing Figures, recto – signed and dated '48 – watercolour, pen and black ink, charcoal and white chalk on squared paper; Reclining Figures, verso – inscribed – watercolour, pen and black ink, pastel and charcoal on paper – 11 x 9in.
(Christie's) **$88,000** **£55,000**

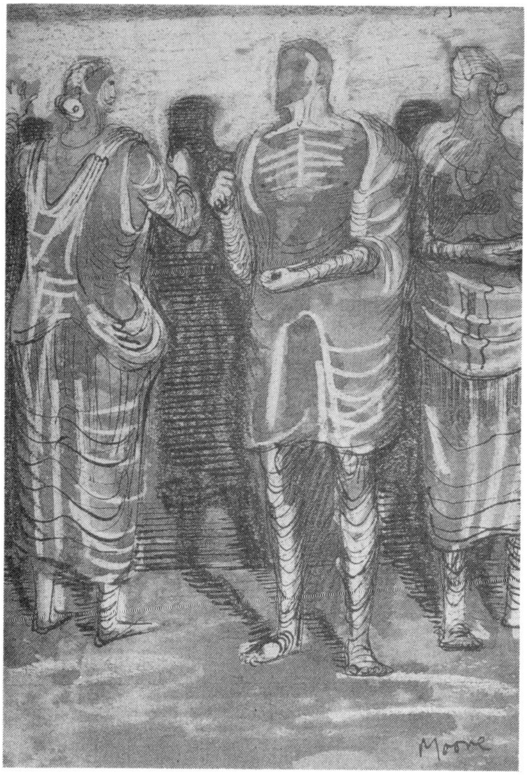

HENRY MOORE – Family Group, Euryclea Holding Telemachus – signed – watercolour, pen and ink heightened with white gouache on paper – 8½ x 5½in.
(Christie's) **$21,120** **£13,200**

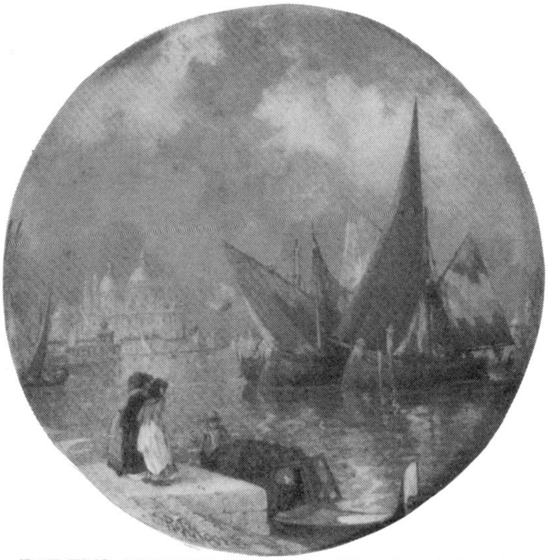

RUBENS ARTHUR MOORE – The Grand Canal Venice; and Burano – signed – on board – 8in. diam.
(Christie's) **$2,187** **£1,430 Pair**

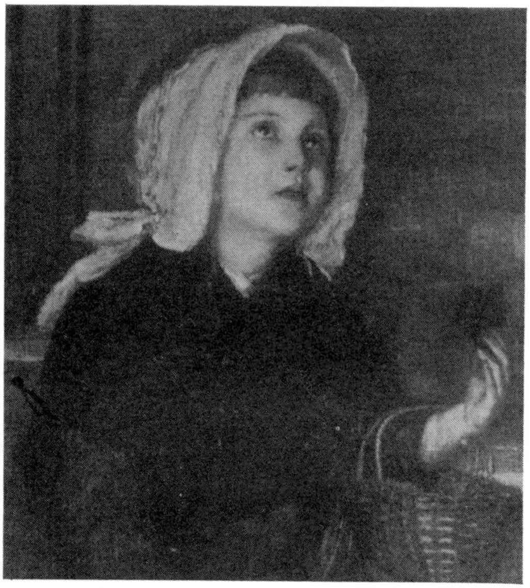

JAMES MOORE – Street Violets – signed with initials and dated 1885, and signed and inscribed on an old label – 24 x 19¾in.
(Christie's) **$1,851** **£1,210**

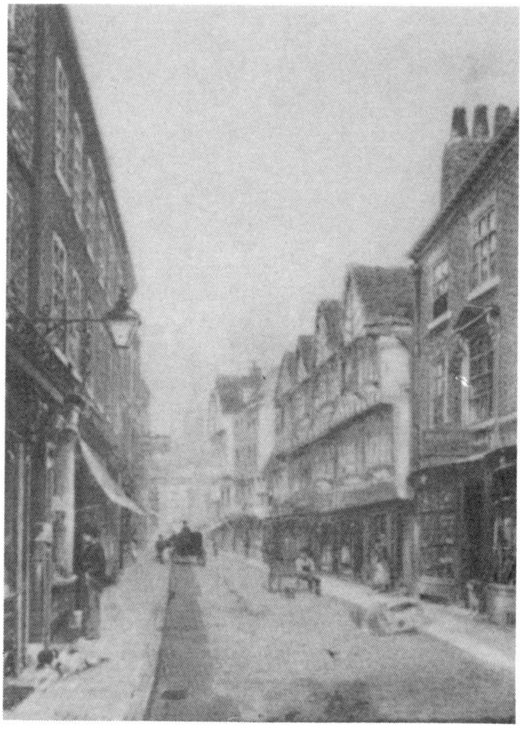

RUBENS ARTHUR MOORE – Stone Gate, York – oil on canvas – 10 x 7¼in.
(Christie's) **$797** **£550**

FRANCIS LUIS MORA – Betty And Rosemary – signed and inscribed – watercolour on paper – 11¾ x 18in.
(Christie's) **$6,600** **£4,639**

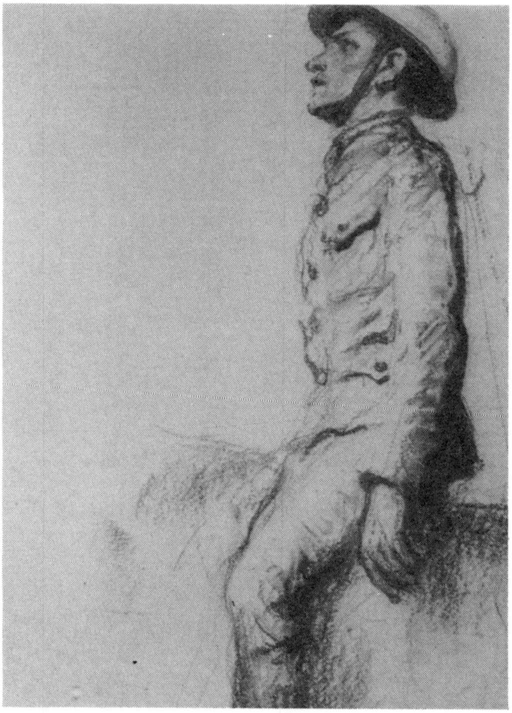

FRANCIS LUIS MORA – Soldier, World War I – charcoal on paper – 18½ x 13¾in.
(Christie's) **$550** **£342**

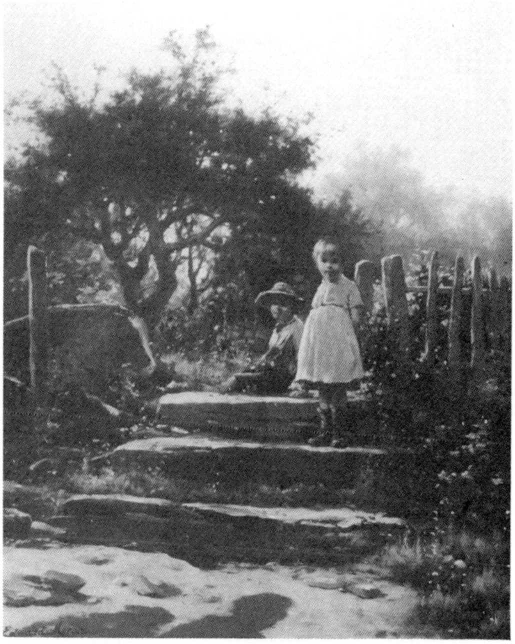

EDWARD MORAN – Good Morning – signed – oil on canvas – 26¼ x 21¾in.
(Christie's) **$11,000** **£7,733**

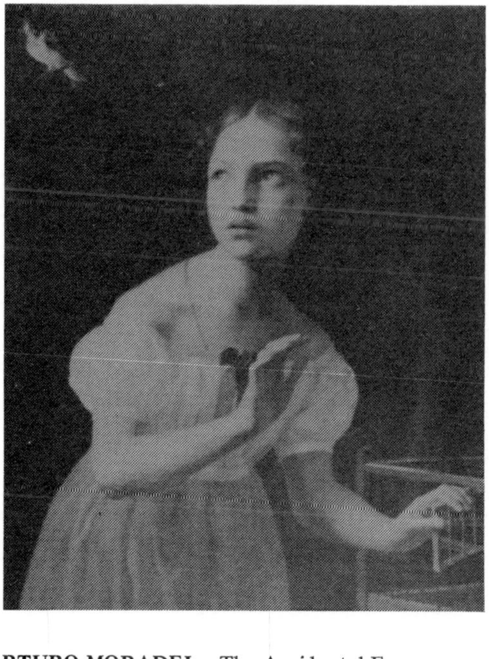

ARTURO MORADEI – The Accidental Escape – signed – oil on canvas – 31 x 25in.
(Robt. W. Skinner Inc.) **$500** **£306**

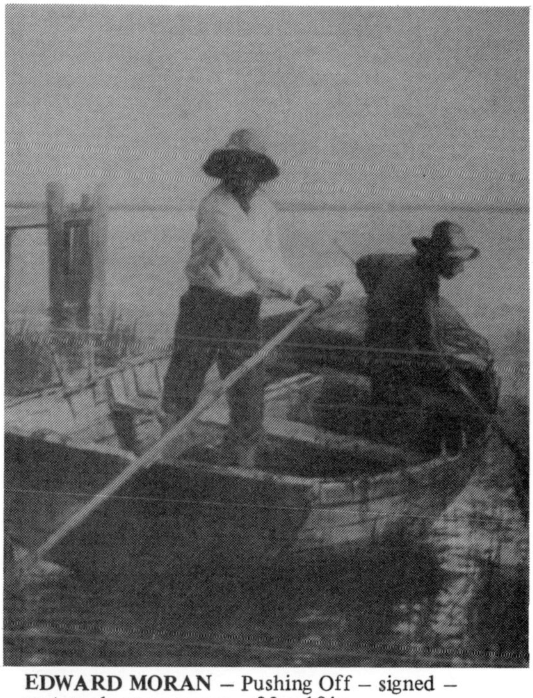

EDWARD MORAN – Pushing Off – signed – watercolour on paper – 22 x 19in.
(Christie's) **$8,800** **£6,186**

EDWARD MORAN – Ships At Night – signed – oil on canvas – 18 x 24in.
(Christie's) **$18,700** **£13,146**

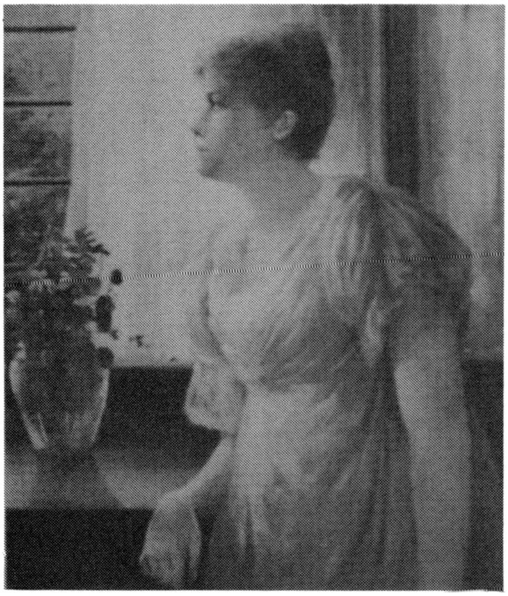

PAUL NIMMO MORAN – Girl In White By A Window – signed – oil on canvas – 13½ x 10in.
(Robt. W. Skinner Inc.) **$800** **£490**

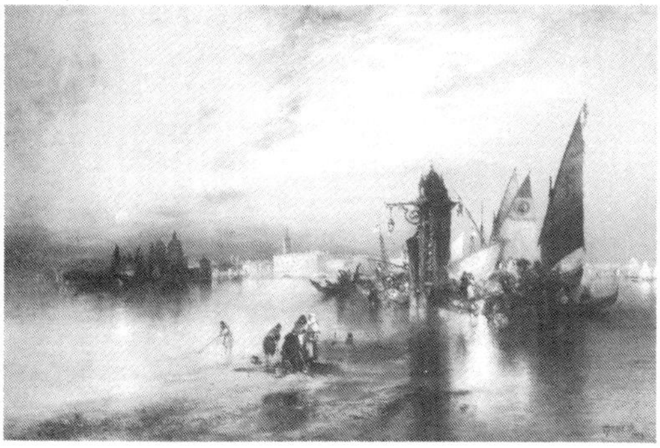

THOMAS MORAN – Venice – signed with initials in monogram and dated 1898 – oil on canvas – 20½ x 30in.
(Christie's) **$60,500** **£42,531**

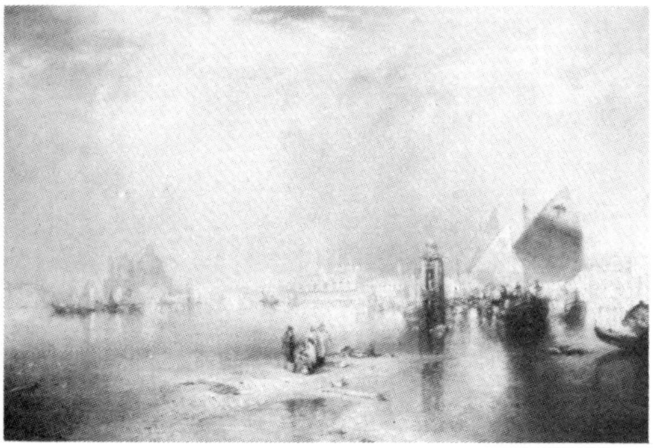

THOMAS MORAN – Grand Canal, Venice – signed with initials conjoined and dated 1906 – oil on canvas – 20 x 30¼in.
(Christie's) **$44,000** **£30,932**

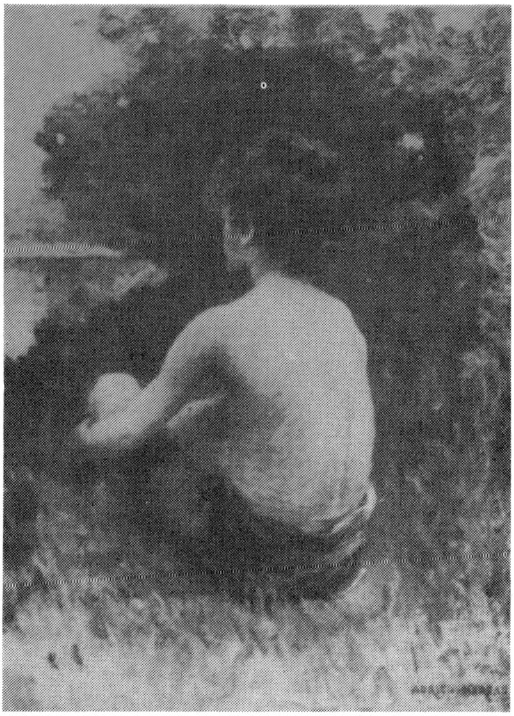

ADRIEN MOREAU – Portrait D'un Garcon – signed – oil on canvas – 31 x 24cm.
(Phillips) **$1,116** **£720**

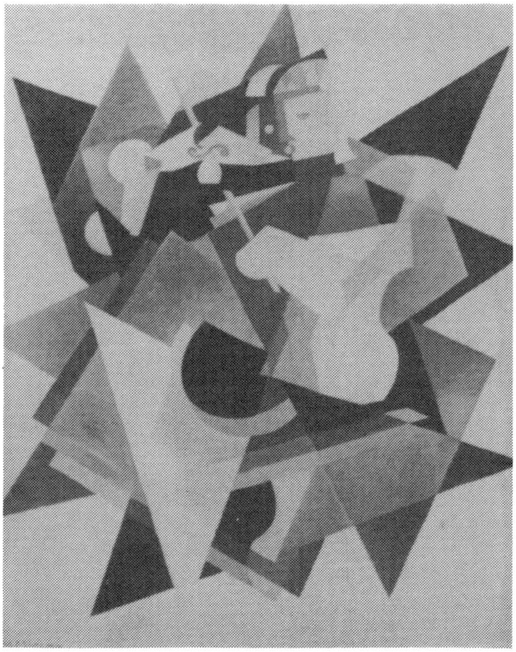

MICHEL MORENO – Pierrot Au Violon – signed, inscribed on the reverse – oil on canvas – 81 x 65cm.
(Phillips) **$930** **£600**

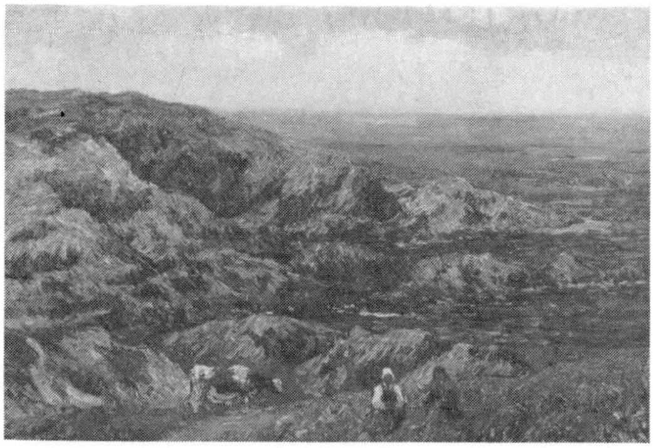

HENRY MORET – Bords de Mer – signed – oil on canvas – 19½ x 23½in.
(Christie's) **$55,110** **£33,000**

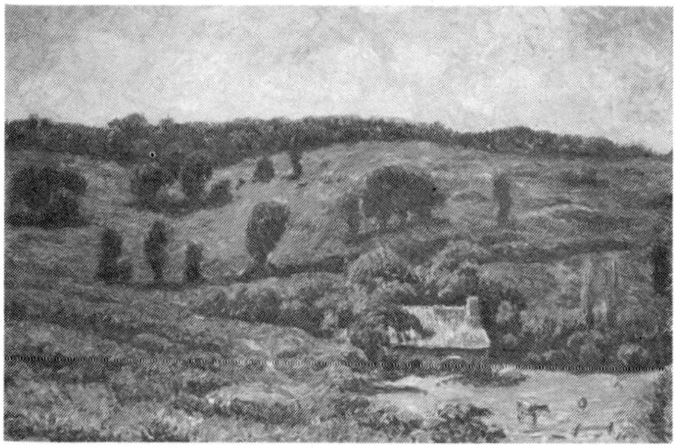

HENRY MORET – Un Moulin en Riec, Finistere – signed and dated '09 – oil on canvas – 28¾ x 36¼in.
(Christie's) **$98,208** **£68,200**

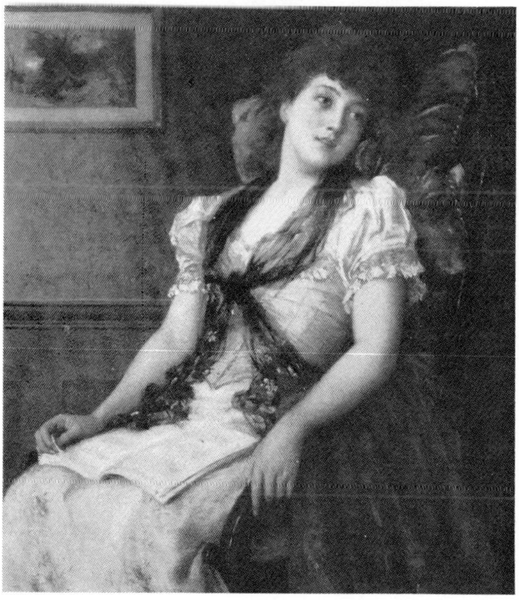

JOHN MORGAN, Attributed to – 'The Afternoon Rest' – oil on canvas – 36 x 28in.
(Phillips) **$3,672** **£2,400**

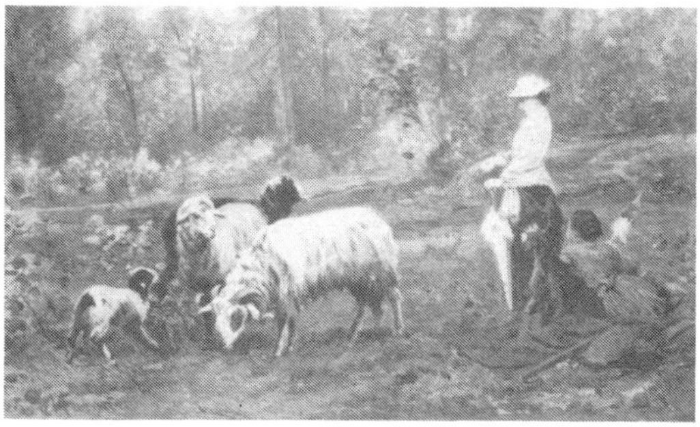

PIETRO MORGARI – Picnic Visitors – signed – oil on panel – 17.5 x 28cm.
(Phillips) **$2,160** **£1,500**

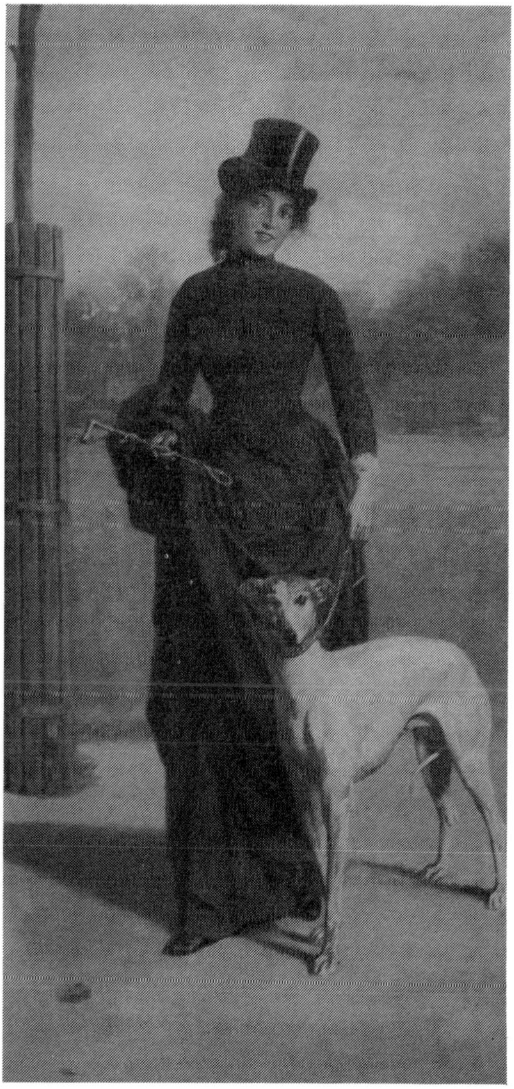

RODOLFO MORGARI – The Morning Walk – 66 x 33in.
(Christie's) **$12,672** **£8,800**

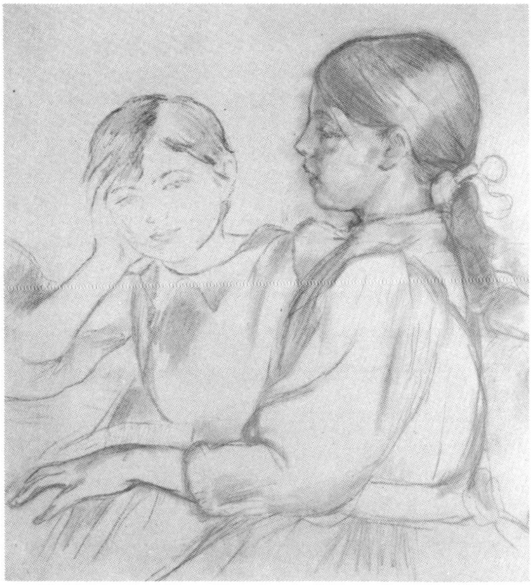

BERTHE MORISOT – Julie Manet et Jeannie Gobillard au Piano – red chalk and soft pencil on tracing paper – 23 x 21½in.
(Christie's) **$87,120 £60,500**

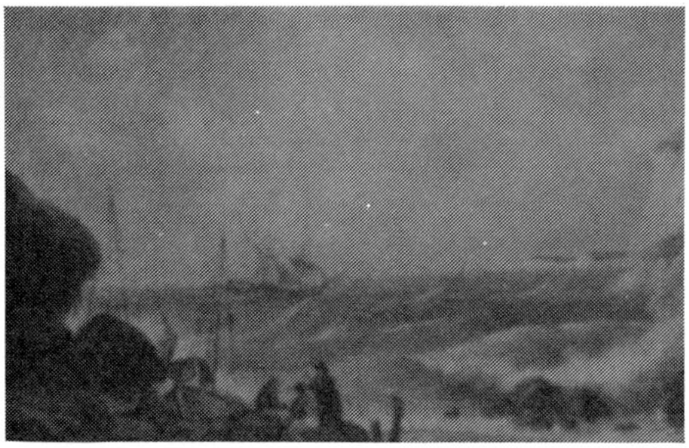

GEORGE MORLAND – Fishermen On A Shore, A Barque At Sea Beyond In A Coastal Landscape – signed – oil on canvas – 11 x 14½in.
(Phillips) **$2,324 £1,400**

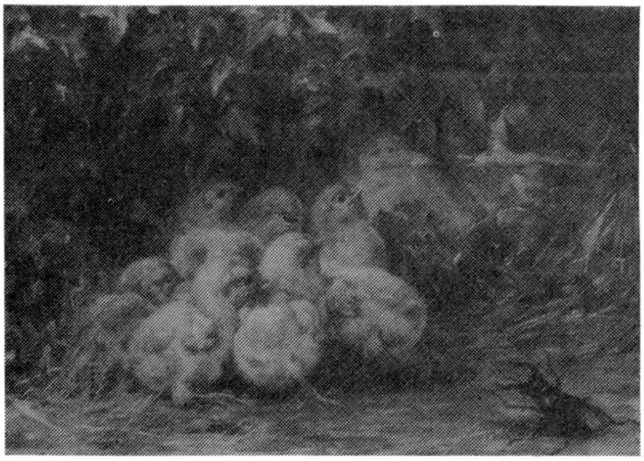

ROBERT MORLEY – Union Is Strength – signed – on panel – 10½ x 15in.
(Christie's) **$10,098 £6,600**

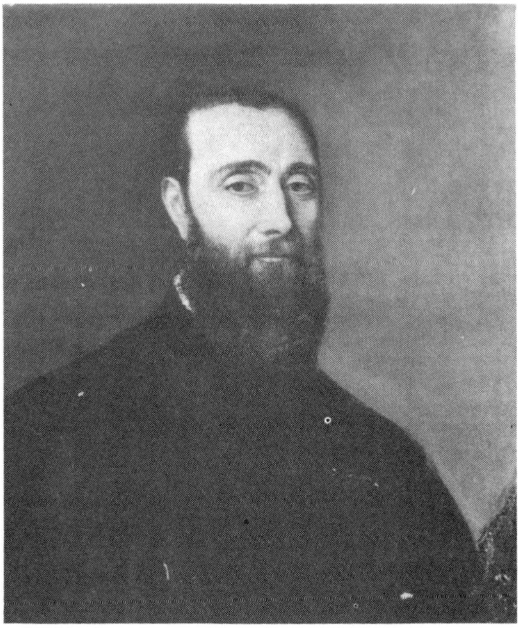

GIOVANNI BATTISTA MORONI, Attributed to – Portrait Of A Gentleman, Long Bust Length, Said To Be Garcilasso De La Vega – oil on canvas – 25¾ x 22¼in.
(Phillips) **$2,115 £1,500**

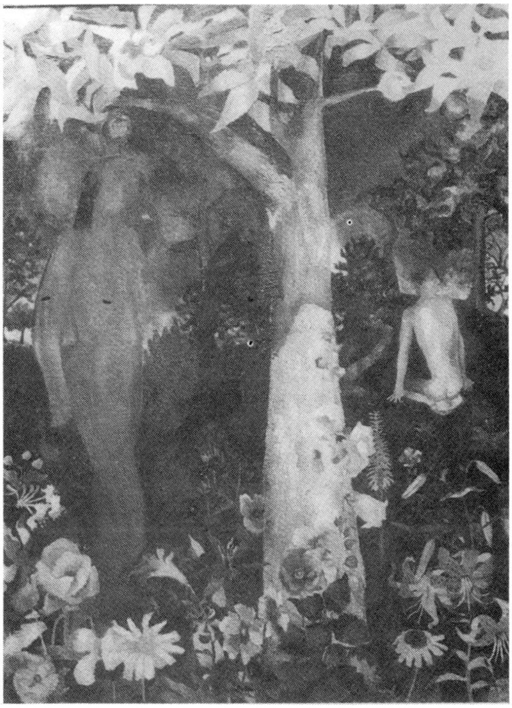

SIR CEDRIC MORRIS – Adam And Eve In The Garden Of Eden – oil on canvas – 48 x 36in.
(Christie's) **$2,831 £1,980**

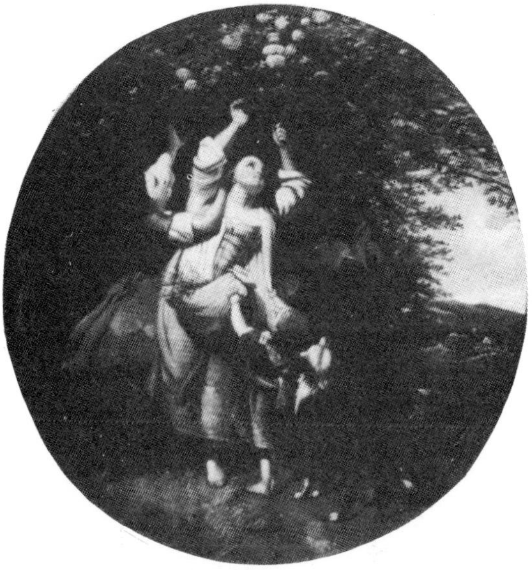

WILLIAM WALKER MORRIS – Picking Blossom – signed and dated 1861 – oil on canvas laid down on board – 32 x 28½in.
(Phillips) **$1,836** **£1,200**

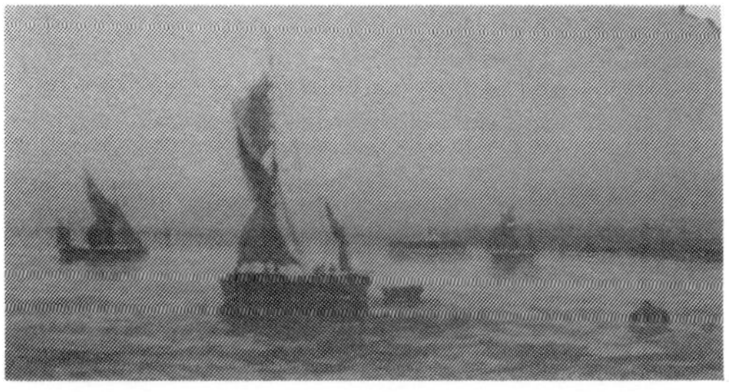

T. MORTIMER – Fishing Boats Under Sail And A Steamer Off A Port – signed – watercolour – 9½ x 20½in.
(W. H. Lane & Son) **$200** **£140**

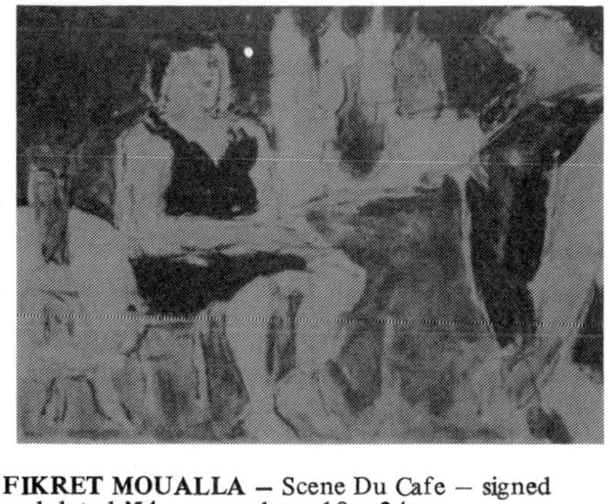

FIKRET MOUALLA – Scene Du Cafe – signed and dated '54 – gouache – 18 x 24cm.
(Phillips) **$465** **£300**

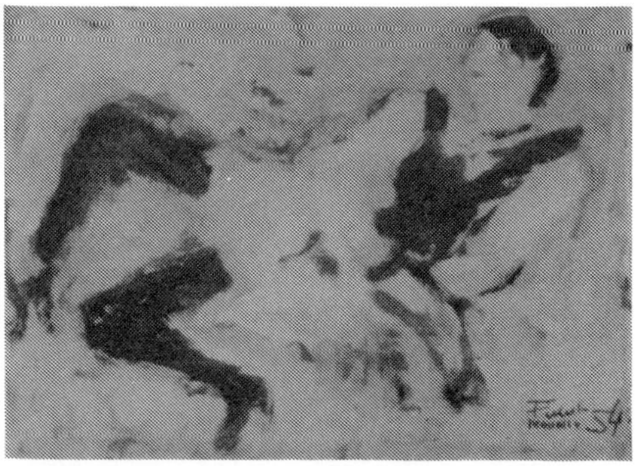

FIKRET MOUALLA – Maison Close – signed and dated '54 – gouache – 18 x 24cm.
(Phillips) **$310** **£200**

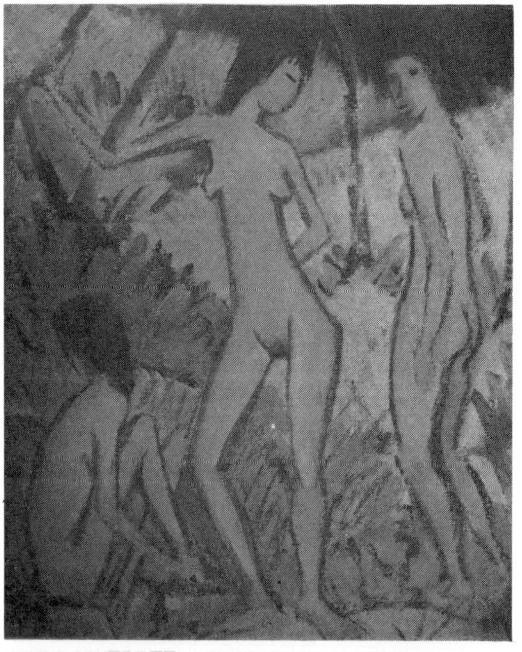

OTTO MUELLER – Drei Akte in Landschaft – signed – leimfarbe on burlap – 47 x 37¼in.
(Christie's) **$367,400** **£220,000**

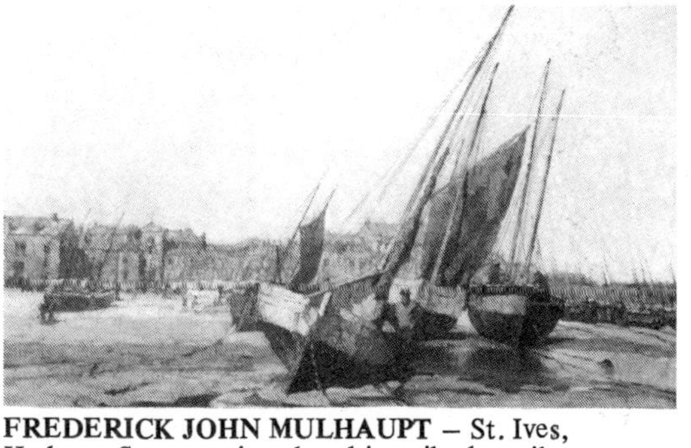

FREDERICK JOHN MULHAUPT – St. Ives, Harbour Scene – signed and inscribed – oil on canvas – 20¾ x 25¾in.
(Christie's) **$11,000** **£7,733**

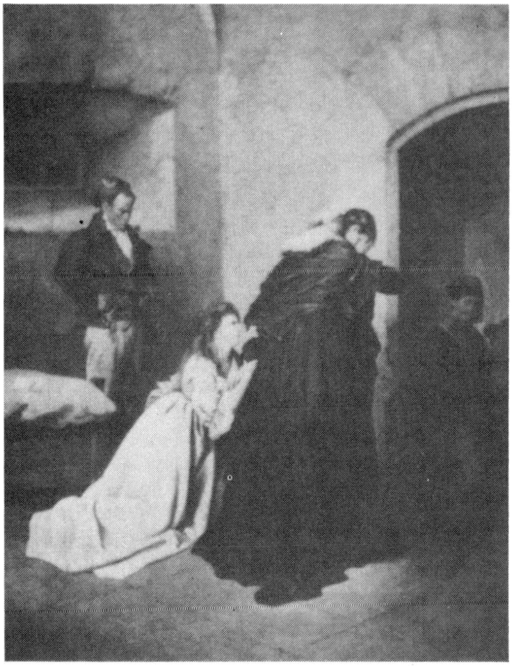

CHARLES LOUIS MULLER, Attributed to – Marie Antoinette And Maria Theresa – oil on canvas – 26½ x 20in.
(Christie's) **$1,224** **£800**

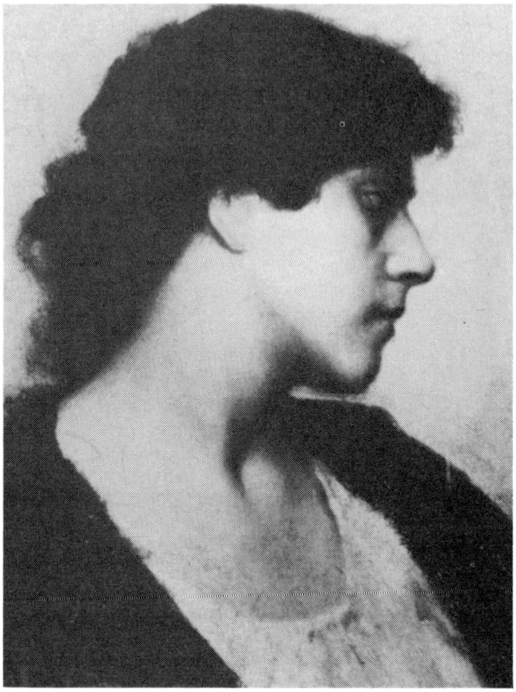

LEOPOLD CARL MULLER – A Portrait Of A Young Dark Haired Lady – signed and dated 1876, and inscribed on a label verso – oil on panel – 21 x 13cm.
(Phillips) **$936** **£650**

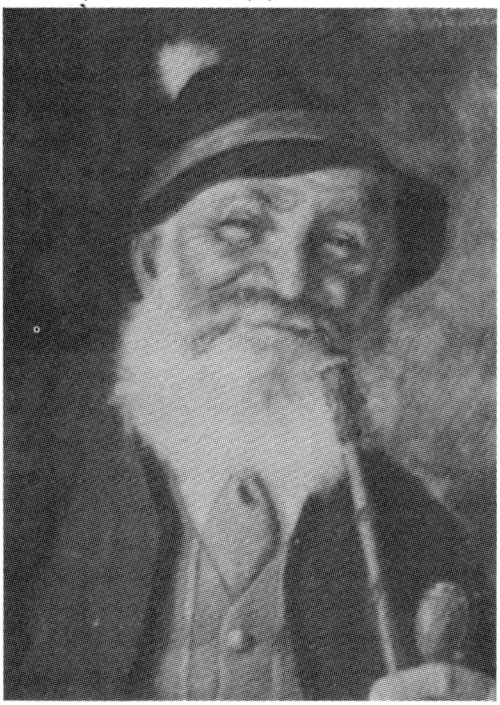

FRITZ MULLER – A Bavarian Smoking A Pipe – signed and inscribed – oil on board – 11½ x 9¼in.
(Christie's) **$1,178** **£770**

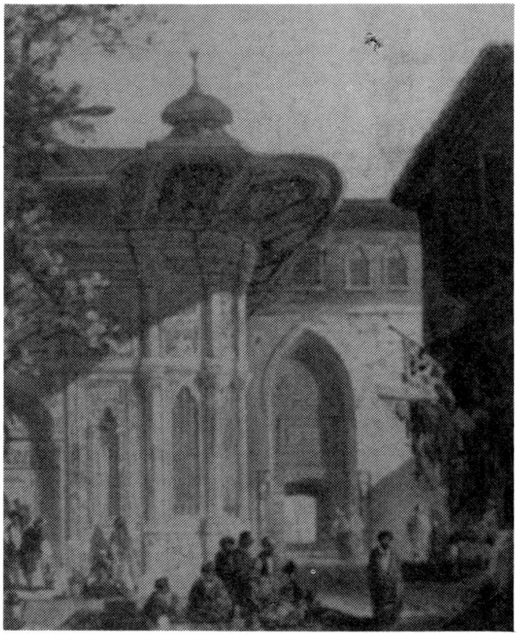

WILLIAM JAMES MULLER, Attributed to – A Market Scene Thought To Be The Fountain, Toasoon Pasha, Cairo – bears signature – oil on canvas – 14¼ x 10¼in.
(Phillips) **$664** **£400**

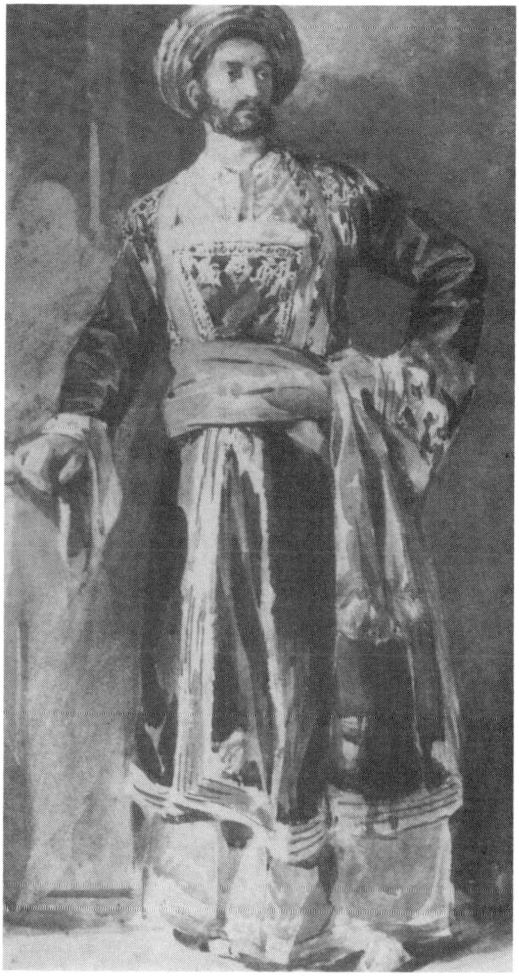

WILLIAM JAMES MULLER – Study Of A Turkish Pasha(?) In Ceremonial Costume – pencil and watercolour – 17¼ x 8¼in.
(Christie's) **$7,348** **£4,400**

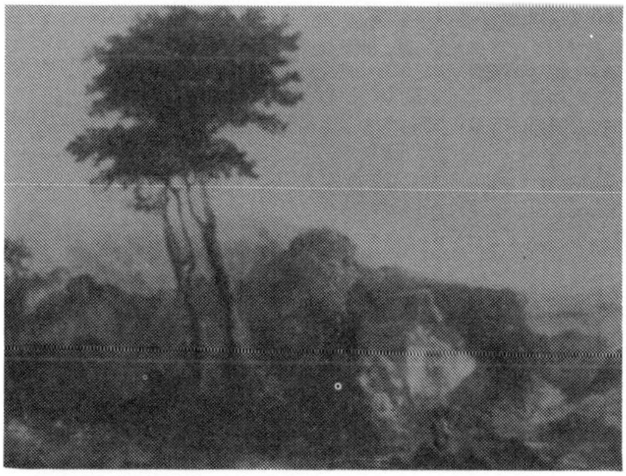

WILLIAM JAMES MULLER – Figure Before A Cottage Before A Wooded Landscape – signed – oil on canvas – 18½ x 24in.
(Phillips) **$464** **£280**

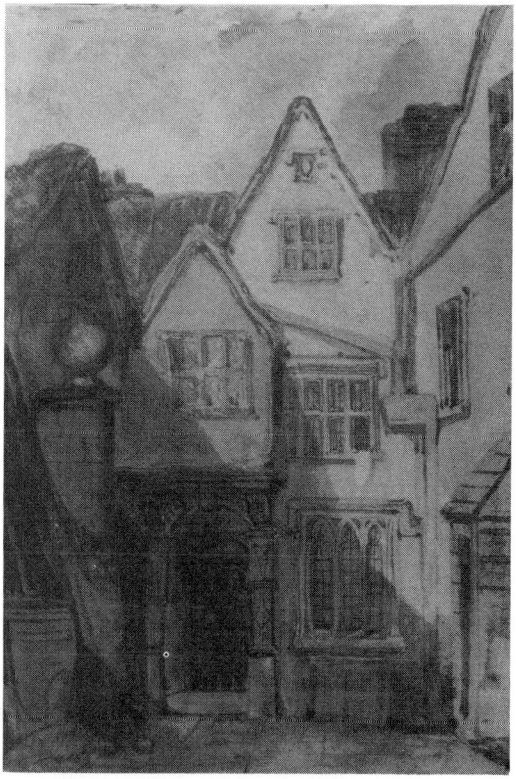

WILLIAM JAMES MULLER – Alderman Whitson's House, St. James's, Bristol – signed with initials and dated 1832 – pencil and watercolour heightened with white – 7 x 4¾in.
(Christie's) **$1,377** **£825**

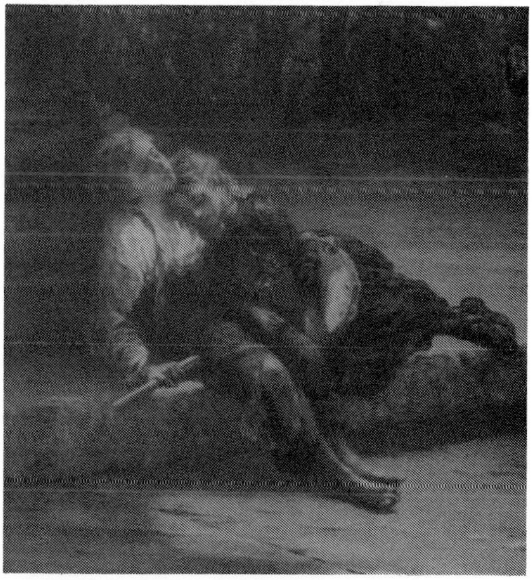

AUGUSTUS E. MULREADY – Wandering Minstrels – signed and dated 1876, and signed, inscribed and dated on the reverse – 28½ x 36½in.
(Christie's) **$15,390** **£10,260**

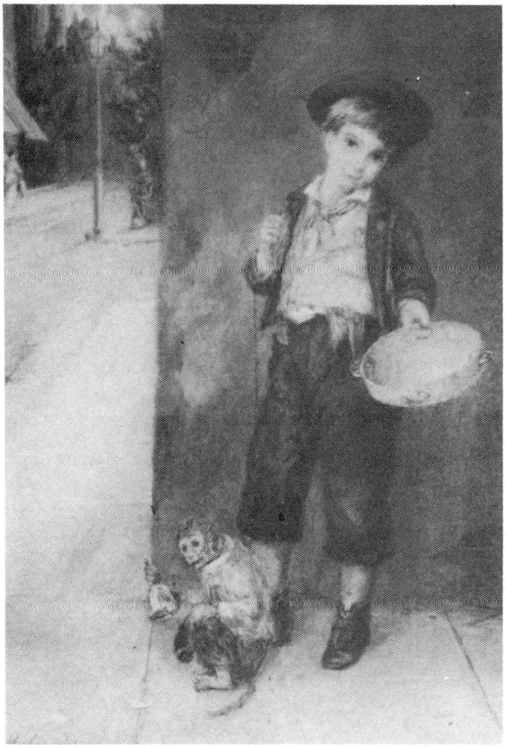

AUGUSTUS E. MULREADY – A Street Urchin With A Monkey – signed and dated 1881 – oil on board – 8 x 6in.
(Christie's) **$2,171 £1,540**

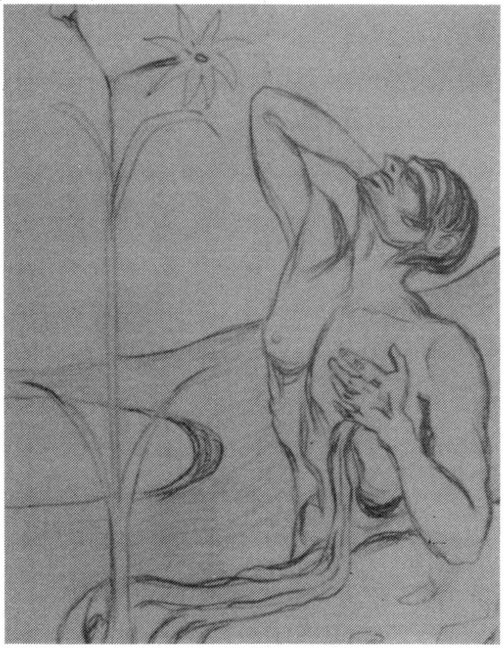

EDVARD MUNCH – The Flower Of Pain – charcoal on tracing paper – 15¾ x 12¼in.
(Christie's) **$28,512 £19,800**

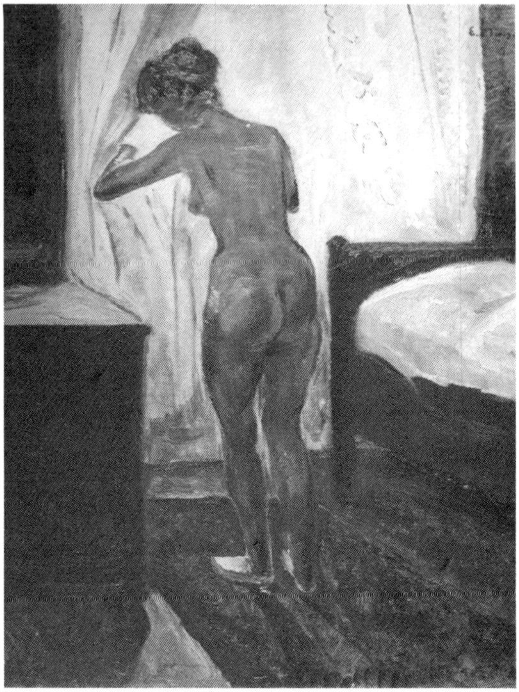

EDVARD MUNCH – Nude Woman At A Window – signed – oil on canvas – 31¾ x 25½in.
(Christie's) **$443,520 £308,000**

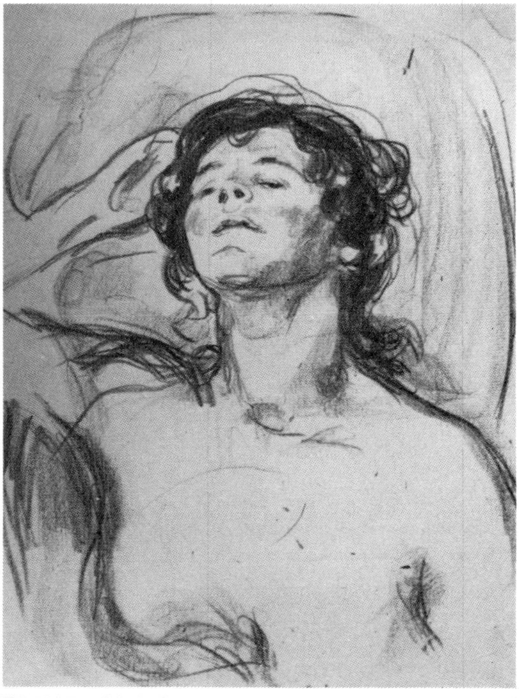

EDVARD MUNCH – Ruhende Frau (Halbakt) – lithographic crayon on Japan paper – 24¼ x 18¾in.
(Christie's) **$31,680 £22,000**

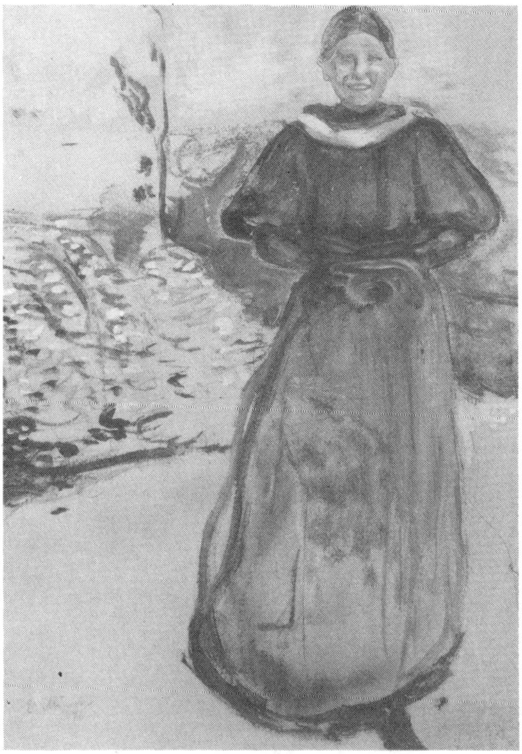

EDVARD MUNCH – Girl In A Red Dress (Inger Munch) – signed and dated 1896 – oil and crayon on board – 38¼ x 24in.
(Christie's) **$119,405** **£71,500**

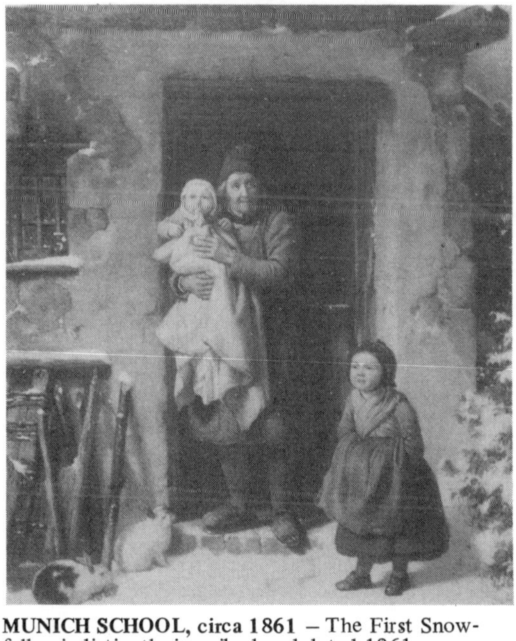

MUNICH SCHOOL, circa 1861 – The First Snowfall – indistinctly inscribed and dated 1861 on the reverse – 26 x 20¾in.
(Christie's) **$4,012** **£2,640**

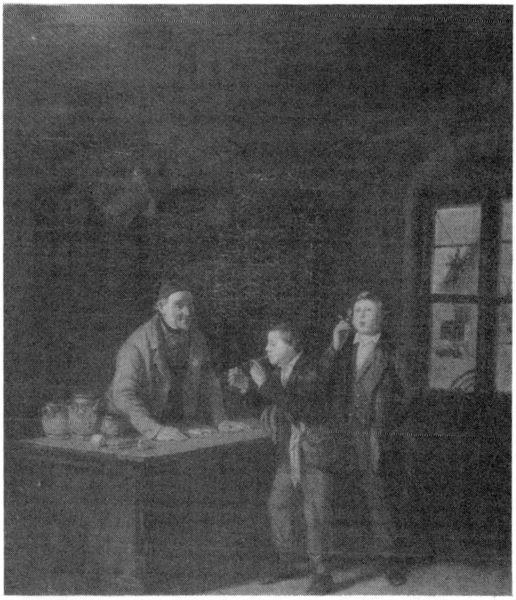

MUNICH SCHOOL, circa 1860 – The First Smoke – indistinctly inscribed on the reverse – 26 x 20½in.
(Christie's) **$1,254** **£825**

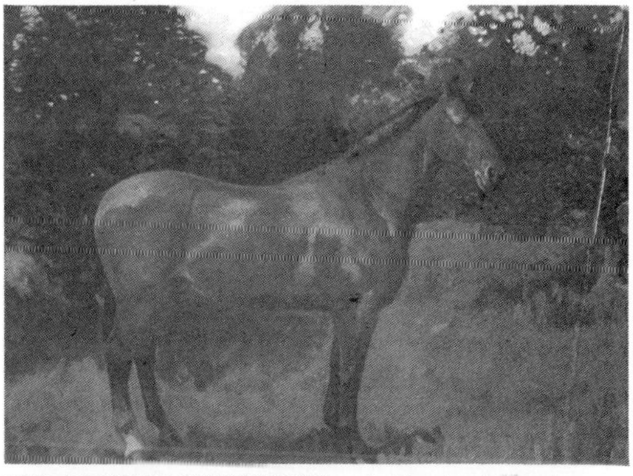

SIR ALFRED MUNNINGS – A Chestnut Hunter In A Meadow – signed and dated 1906 – oil on canvas – 20 x 25in.
(Christie's) **$11,011** **£7,700**

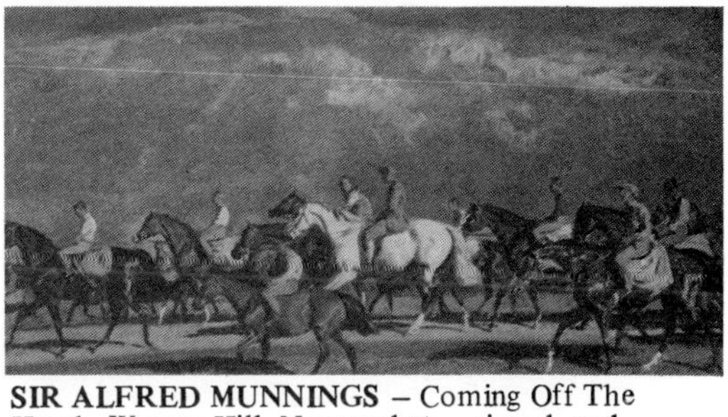

SIR ALFRED MUNNINGS – Coming Off The Heath, Warren Hill, Newmarket – signed, and inscribed on the reverse – oil on panel – 17 x 32¼in.
(Christie's) **$165,165** **£115,500**

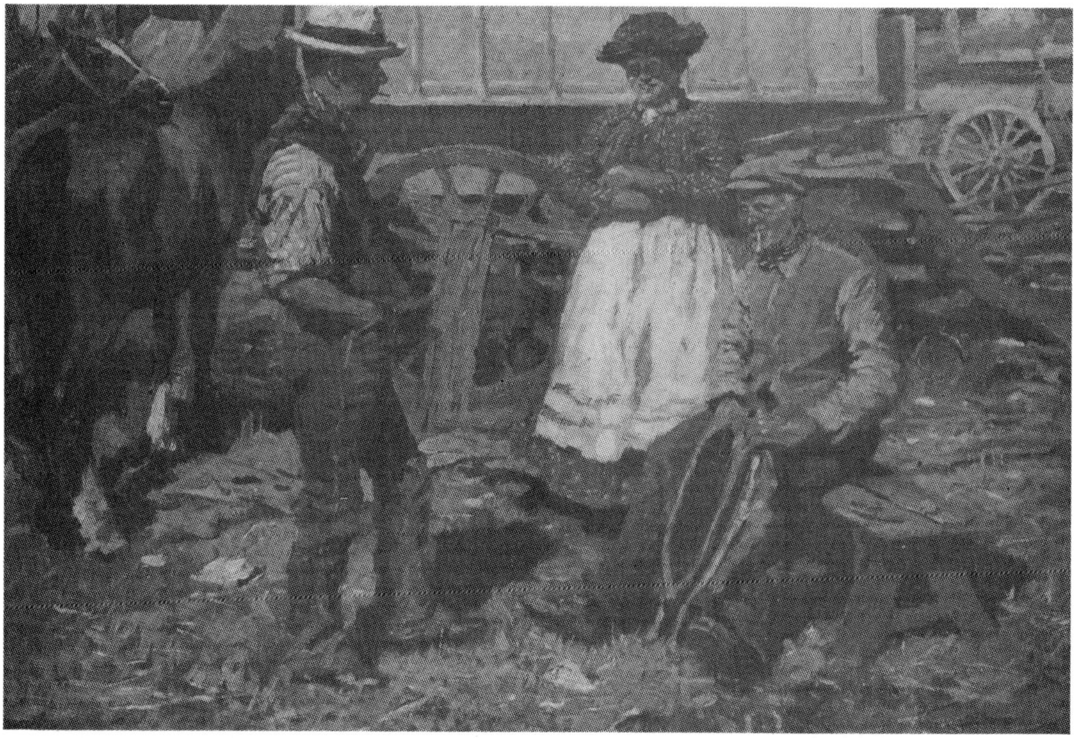

SIR ALFRED MUNNINGS – The Caravanners – signed – oil on canvas – 46 x 59cm. *(Phillips)* **$113,600 £80,000**

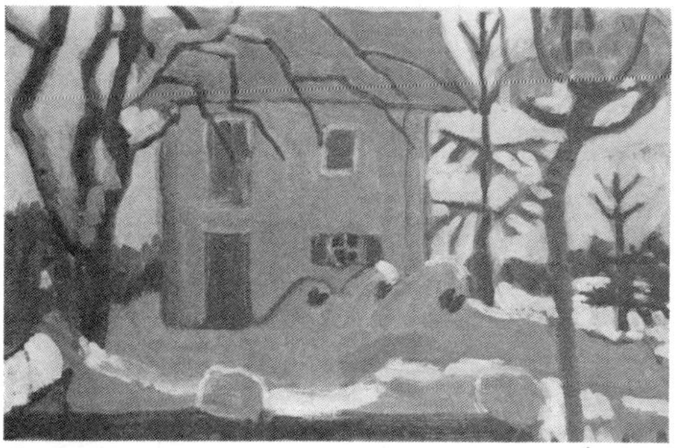

GABRIELE MUNTER – Haus in der Wintersonne – signed – oil on board – 13 x 16in.
(Christie's) **$40,414 £24,200**

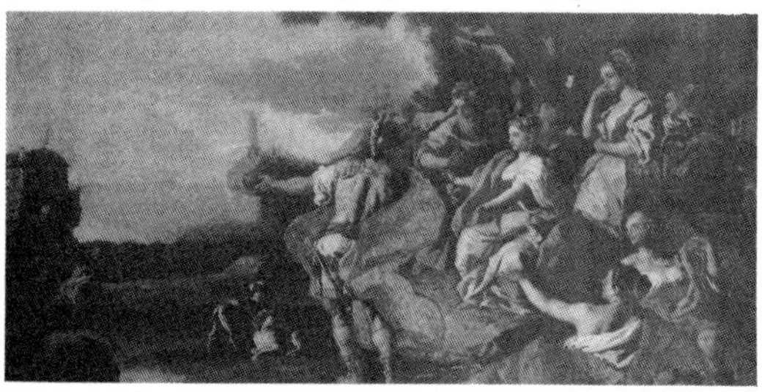

FRANCESCO DE MURA, Studio of – The Departure Of Aeneas – oil on canvas – 39½ x 60¾in.
(Phillips) **$7,332 £5,200**

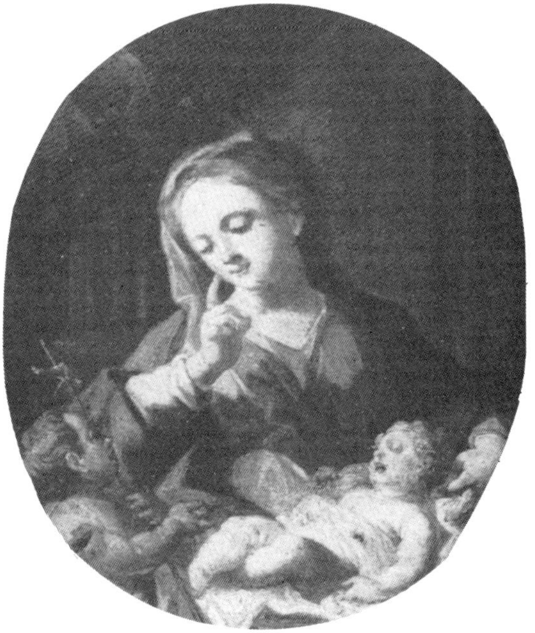

FRANCESCO DE MURA, Circle of – The Madonna And Child With St. John – oil on panel – 17½ x 13in.
(Phillips) **$1,339 £950**

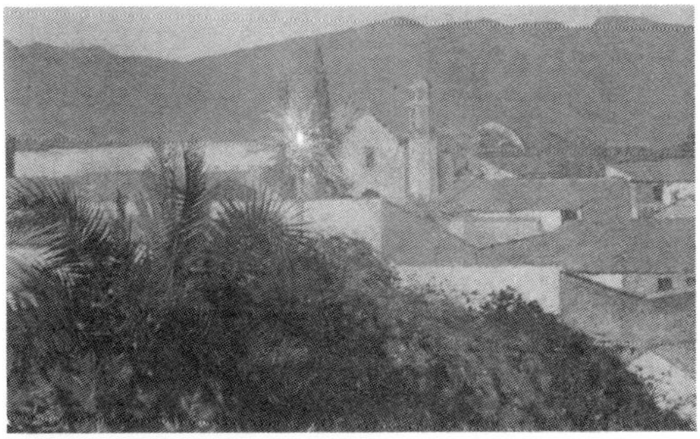

HERMAN DUDLEY MURPHY – Tepetate – signed, also signed, dated 1932 and inscribed on the reverse – oil on canvas – 25¼ x 30¼in.
(Christie's) **$4,400** **£3,061**

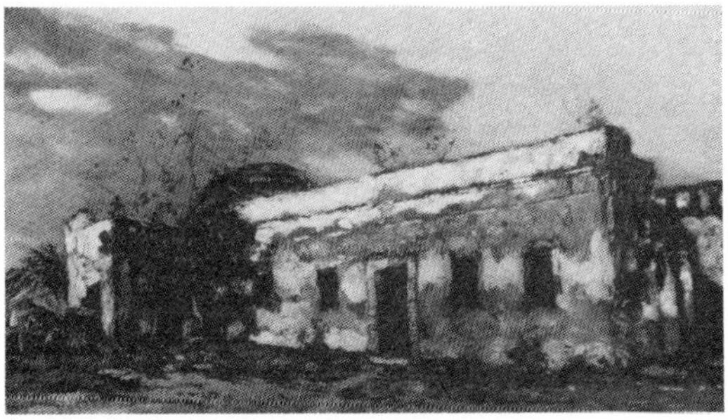

HERMAN DUDLEY MURPHY – 'The Old Church' – signed and monogrammed, also signed and inscribed on verso – oil on artist board – 11½ x 15¼in.
(Robt. W. Skinner Inc.) **$1,500** **£1,041**

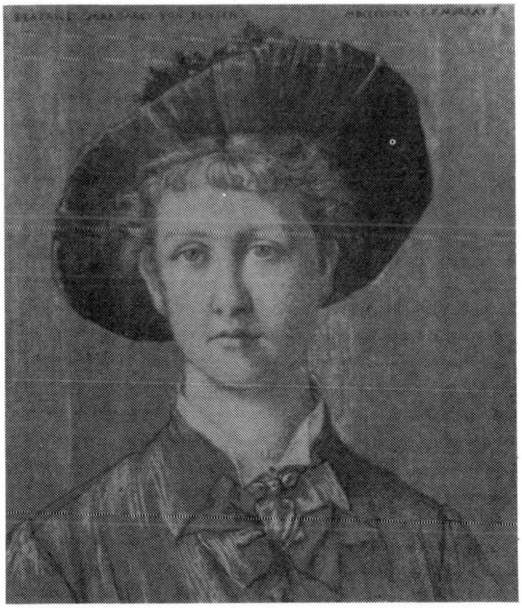

CHARLES FAIRFAX MURRAY – Portrait Of Beatrice Margaret Von Bunsen – signed, inscribed and dated 1879 – brown wash heightened with white and gold – 36 x 28cm.
(Phillips) **$684** **£420**

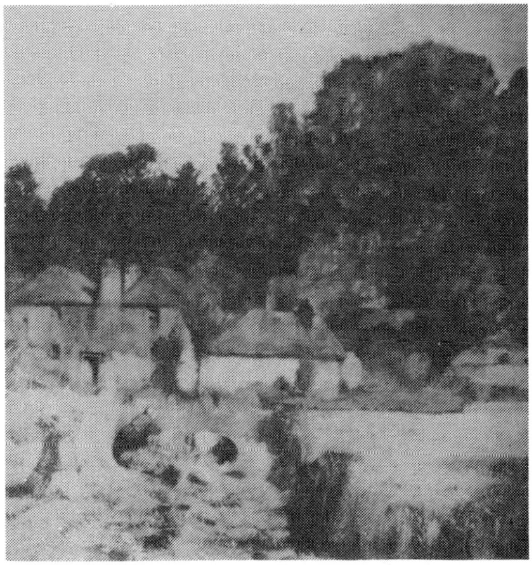

SIR DAVID MURRAY – Harvest Time – signed and dated 1909 – oil on canvas laid down on board – 11½ x 11½in.
(Christie's) **$5,472** **£3,800**

JEROME MYERS – Village Market – bears signature and initialled – oil on canvas – 16¼ x 20in.
(Christie's) **$2,420** **£1,683**

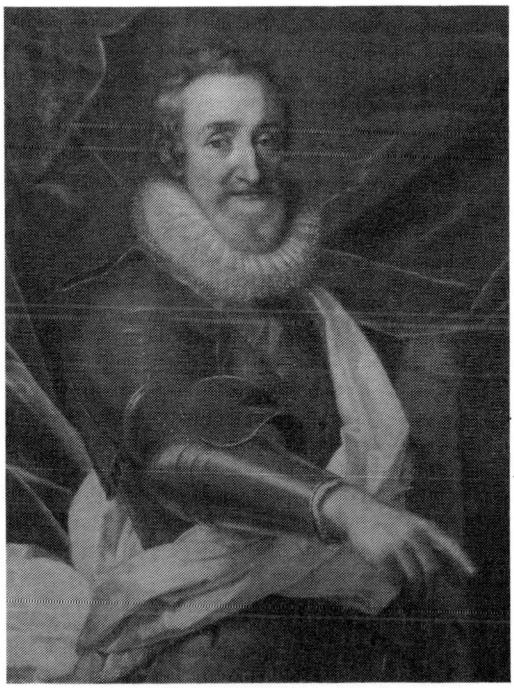

DANIEL MYTENS, The Elder, Circle of – Portrait Of A Nobleman In Armour – on canvas – 36¼ x 29¾in.
(Phillips) **$3,652** **£2,200**

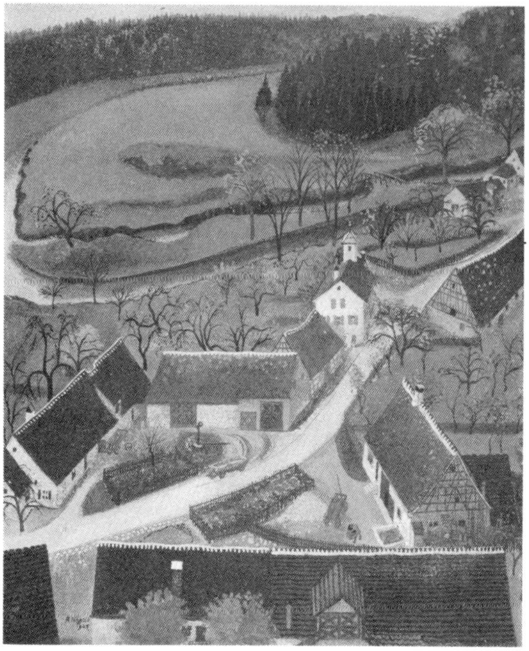

REINHOLD NAGELE – Landschaft in Schwaben – signed and dated 1925 – oil on canvas – 17¼ x 15¼in.
(Christie's) **$17,424 £12,100**

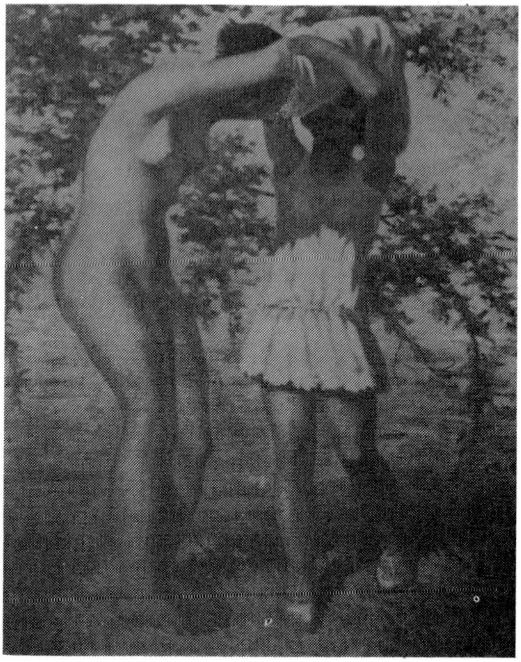

CHARLES NAILLOD – La Chemise Enlevee – signed and dated 1927 – oil on canvas – 81 x 65cm.
(Phillips) **$1,007 £650**

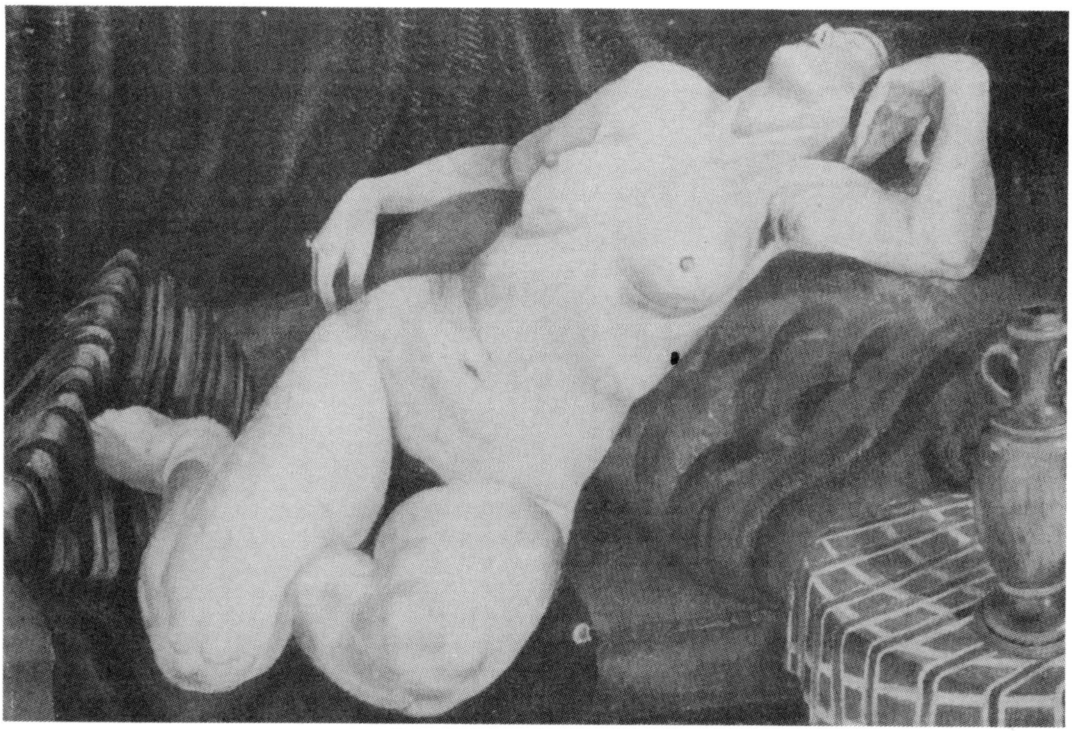

JOHN NASH – Reclining Nude Girl On A Divan – signed – oil on canvas – 18 x 24in. *(Christie's)*
$2,044 £1,430

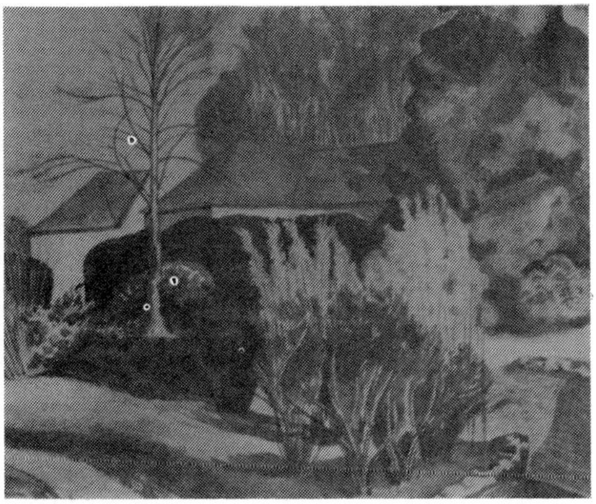

JOHN NASH – Garden Scene – signed twice and inscribed – pencil and watercolour – 38 x 55cm.
(Phillips) **$2,656** **£1,600**

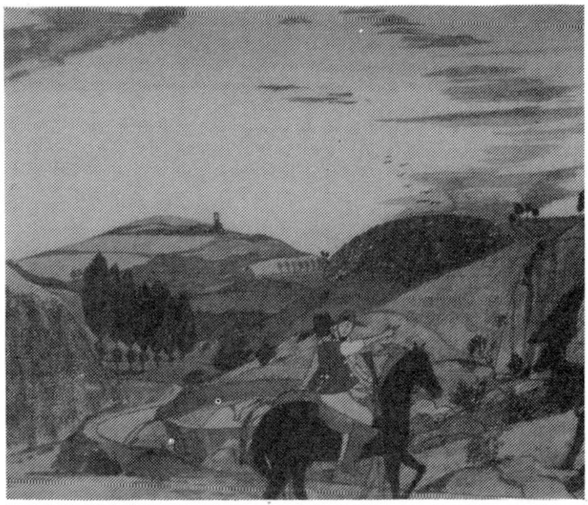

JOHN NASH – George Barrow In Spain – signed – watercolour, coloured crayons, pen, black ink and pencil – 11¼ x 15¼in.
(Christie's) **$1,730** **£1,210**

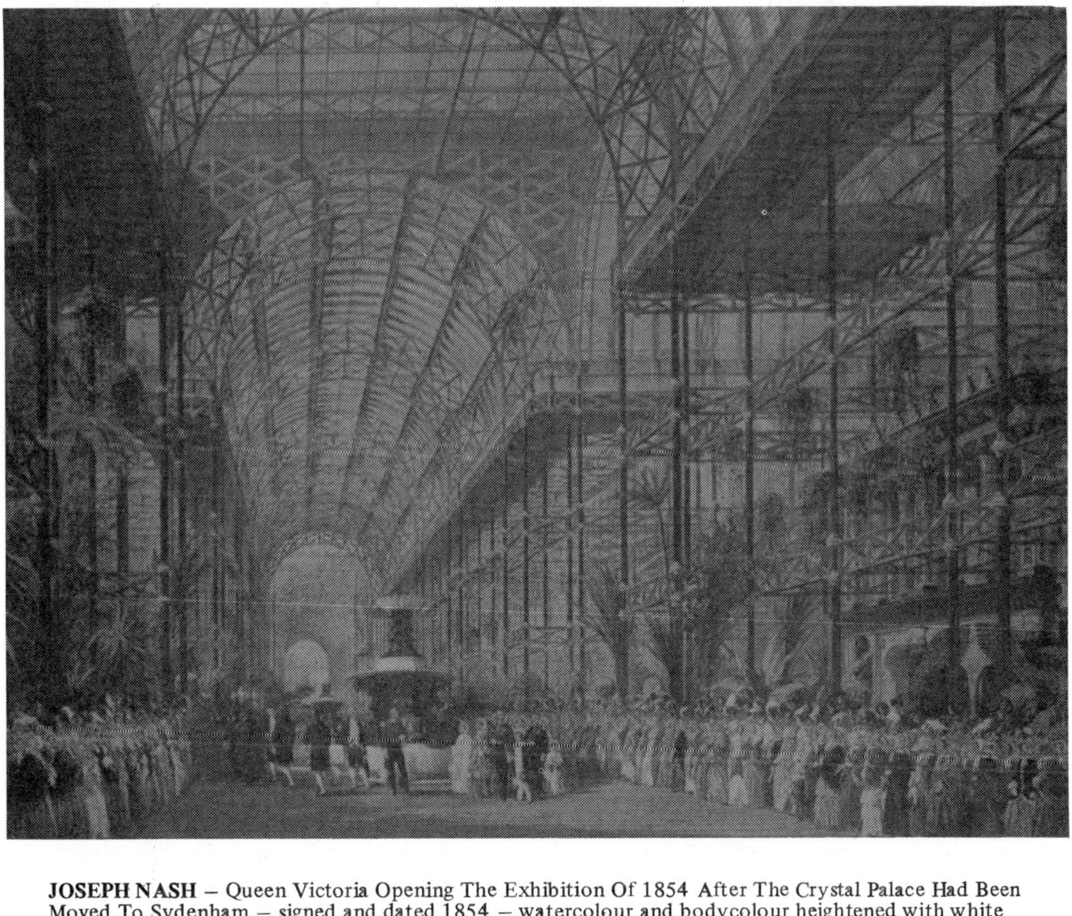

JOSEPH NASH – Queen Victoria Opening The Exhibition Of 1854 After The Crystal Palace Had Been Moved To Sydenham – signed and dated 1854 – watercolour and bodycolour heightened with white on paper laid on linen – 59 x 76cm. *(Phillips)* **$31,785** **£19,500**

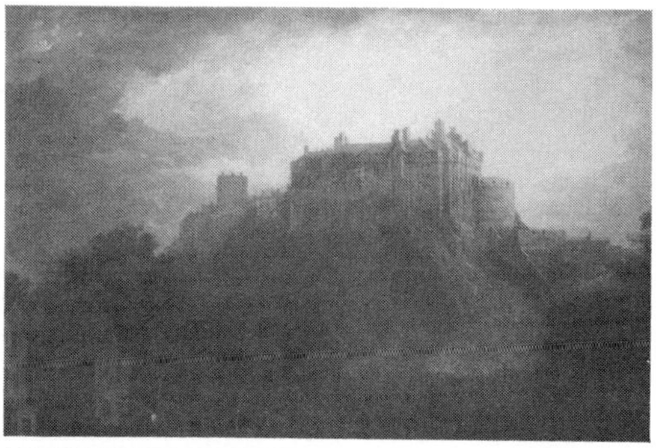

ALEXANDER NASMYTH – Edinburgh Castle From The West, With Figures In The Foreground And Houses Beyond – oil on canvas – 18 x 24in.
(Christie's) **\$9,360** **£6,500**

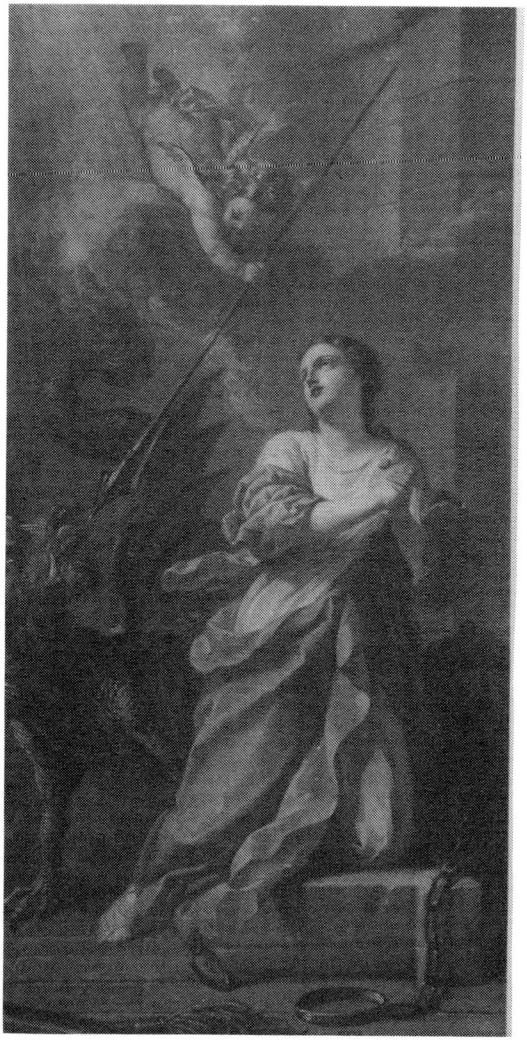

CHARLES JOSEPH NATOIRE – Saint Margaret Of Antioch – on canvas – 77 x 37in.
(Phillips) **\$6,640** **£4,000**

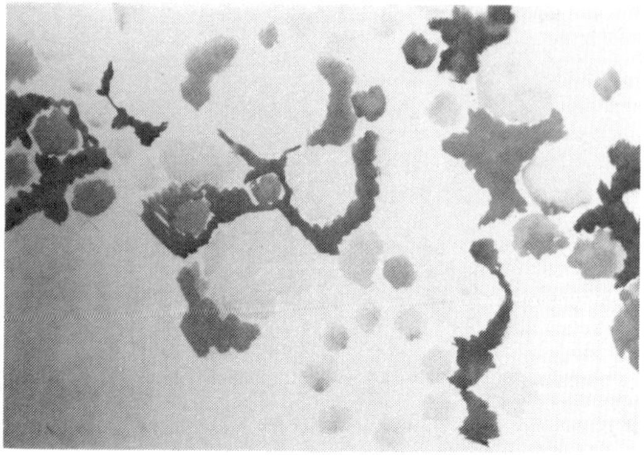

ERNST WILHELM NAY – Accompanied By Red – signed and dated '55 – watercolour on paper – 16¼ x 23¾in.
(Christie's) **\$14,960** **£9,350**

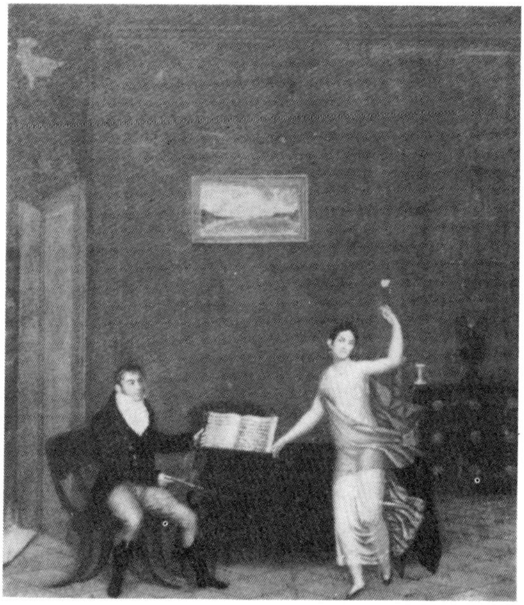

NEAPOLITAN SCHOOL, Circa 1820 – A Lady Dancing To A Fiddler's Tune, In An Elegant Interior – oil on canvas – 23 x 18½in.
(Phillips) **\$2,961** **£2,100**

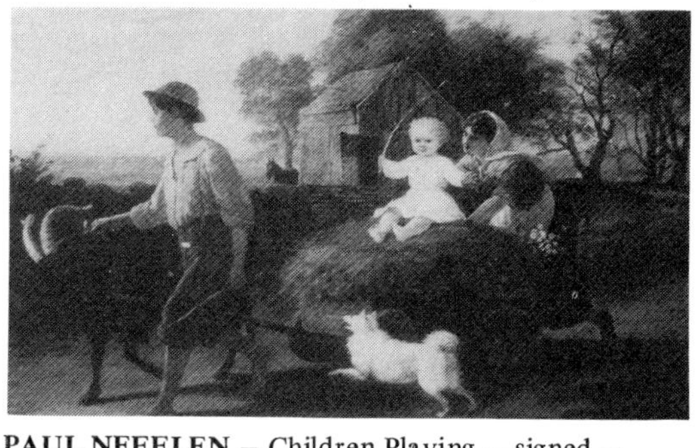

PAUL NEFFLEN – Children Playing – signed – oil on canvas – 16 x 20in.
(Christie's) **\$1,760** **£1,148**

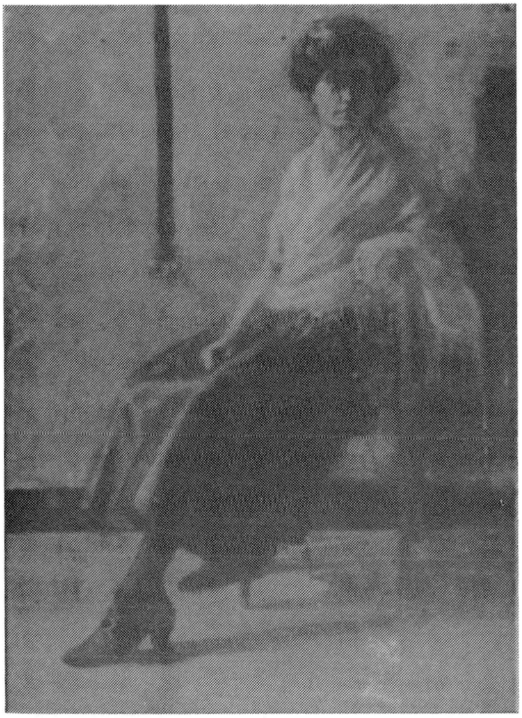

NEWLYN SCHOOL – Study Of A Young Woman In A Shawl, Seated On A Chair – oil on canvas – 18½ x 13in.
(W. H. Lane & Son) **$155** **£100**

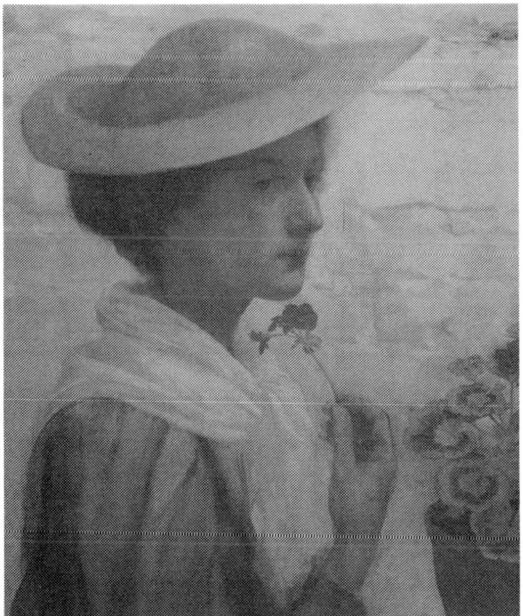

NEWLYN SCHOOL – Girl In A Straw Hat – oil on canvas – 61.5 x 51.5cm.
(Phillips) **$2,400** **£1,500**

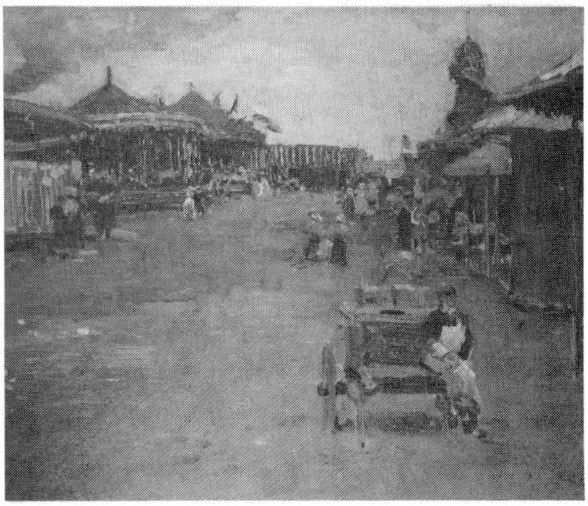

NEWLYN SCHOOL – At The Fair – oil on canvas – 41 x 51cm.
(Phillips) **$5,964** **£4,200**

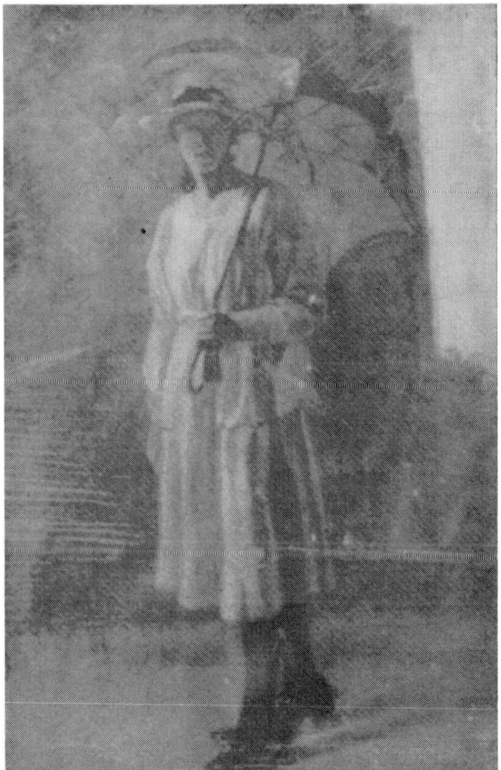

NEWLYN SCHOOL – Portrait Of A Lady With White Dress And Red Umbrella – oil on canvas – 21½ x 14in.
(W. H. Lane & Son) **$255** **£165**

ALGERNON NEWTON – Rooftops In Hampstead: Misty Dawn – signed and inscribed on the reverse – oil on canvas – 33 x 66cm.
(Phillips) **$1,660** **£1,000**

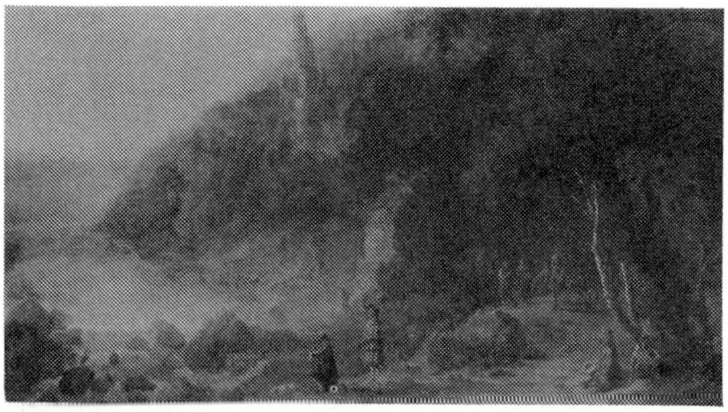

GILLIS NEYTS – Hunters In A Landscape – signed and dated 1662 – on copper – 16¼ x 22in.
(Phillips) **$6,640** **£4,000**

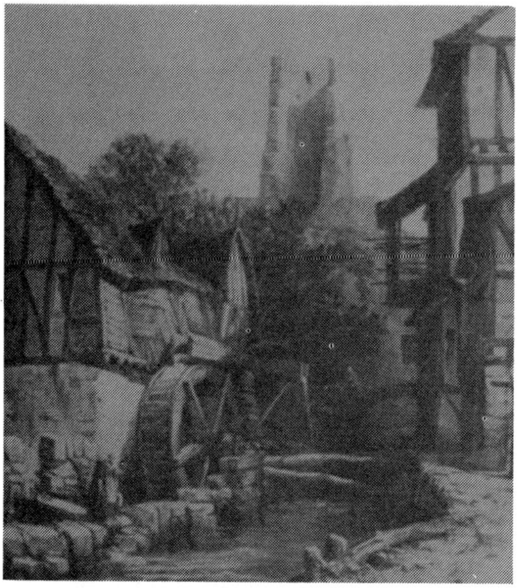

RICHARD HENRY NIBBS – The Old Watermill – signed – on canvas – 30 x 25in.
(Phillips) **$2,415** **£1,500**

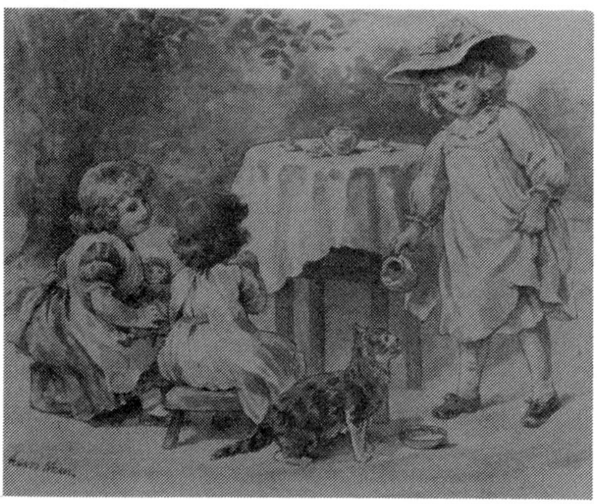

AGNES NICHOLL (nee Bouvier) – A Tea Party – signed – pencil, pen and brown ink and watercolour – 8 x 10¼in.
(Christie's) **$474** **£286**

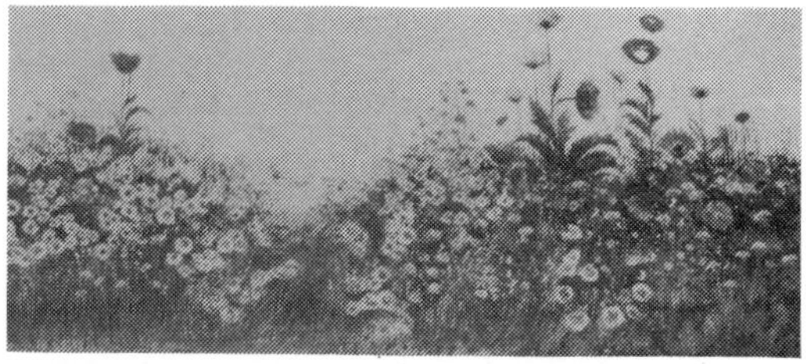

ANDREW NICHOLL – Figures And Boats On A Beach, Seen Through A Bank Of Flowers – signed – watercolour heightened with white and scratching out – 30 x 50cm.
(Phillips) **$3,749** **£2,300**

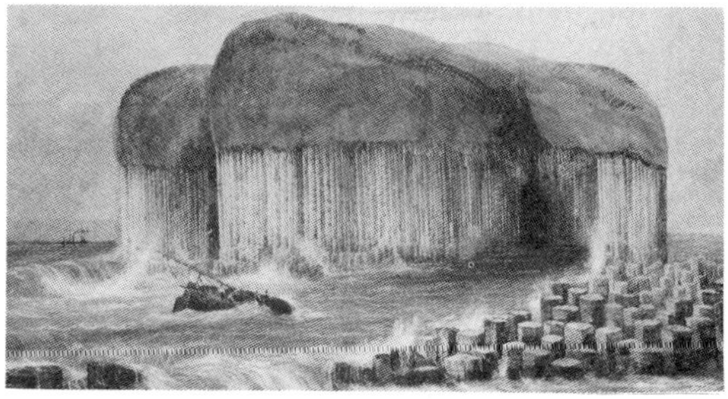

ANDREW NICHOLL – Fingal's Cave, Staffa – signed – pencil and watercolour heightened with white – 19½ x 28in.
(Christie's) **$2,016** **£1,430**

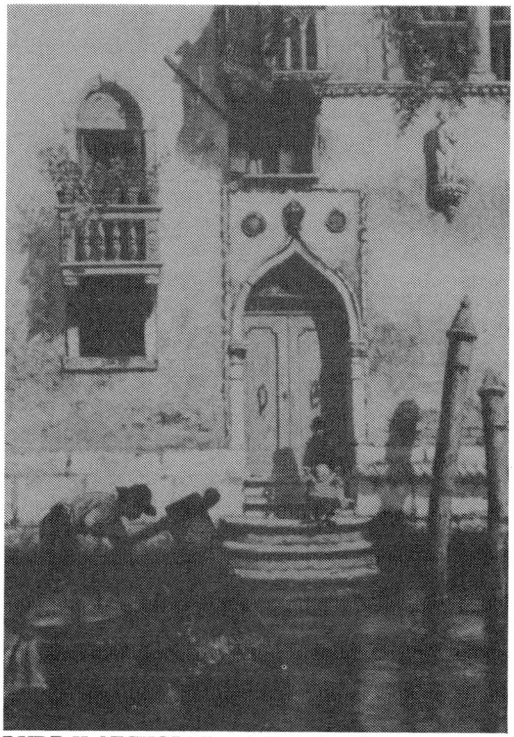

BURR H. NICHOLLS – A Venetian Waterway – signed, inscribed and dated 1883 – oil on canvas – 81 x 53cm.
(Phillips) **$3,168** **£2,200**

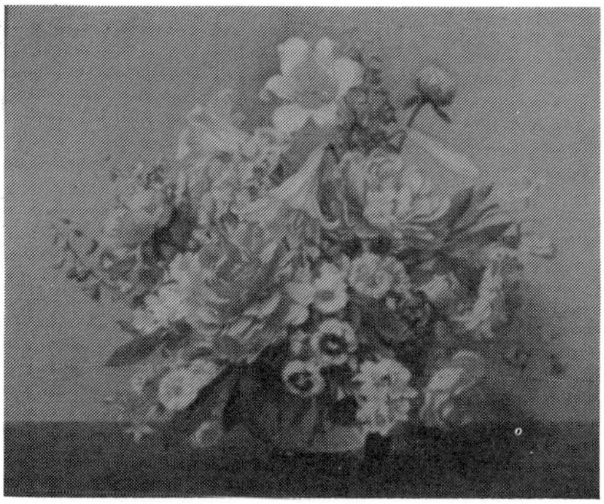

JOHN E. NICHOLLS – Still Life Peonies, Lillies And Roses – signed and dated 1953 – oil on panel.
(Prudential Fine Art Auctioneers) **$1,079** **£650**

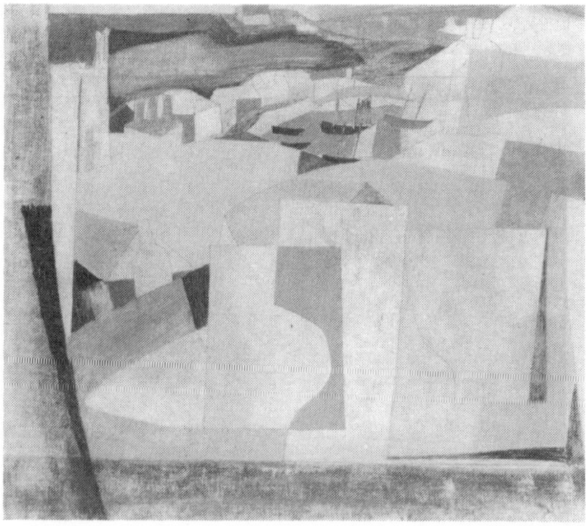

BEN NICHOLSON – St. Ives Harbour – signed, dated and inscribed on the reverse – oil on canvas laid on board – 13¾ x 15¾in.
(Christie's) **$190,080** **£132,000**

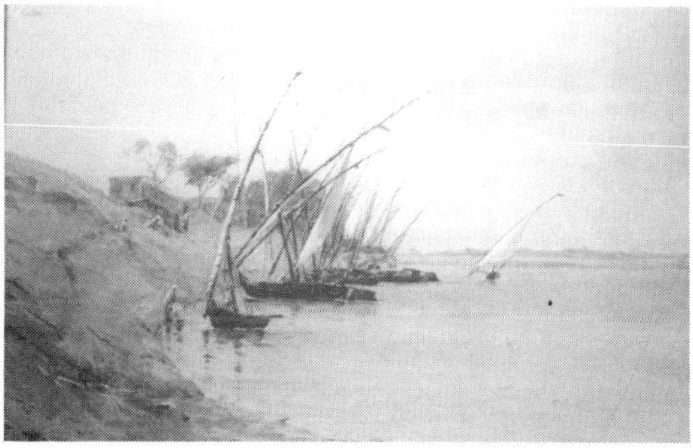

ERSKINE D. NICOL – Figures And Feluccas By The Banks Of The Nile – signed and dated 1901 – watercolour – 11 x 15in.
(Geering & Colyer) **$624** **£390**

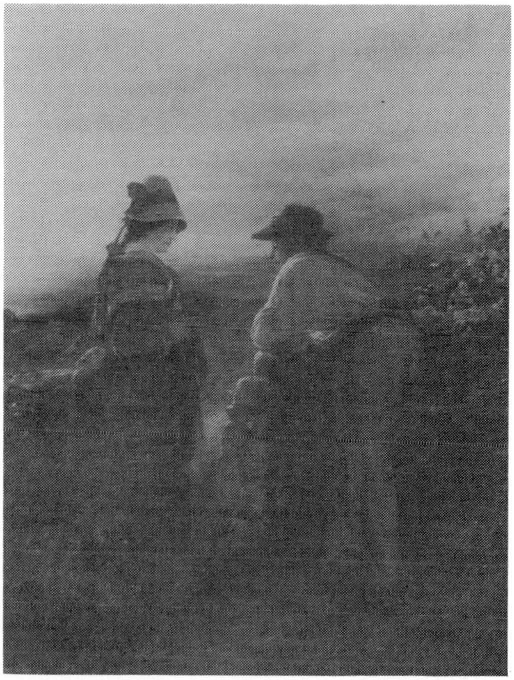

ERSKINE NICOL – Country Gossips – signed and dated 1861 – 23½ x 17in.
(Christie's) **$1,296** **£864**

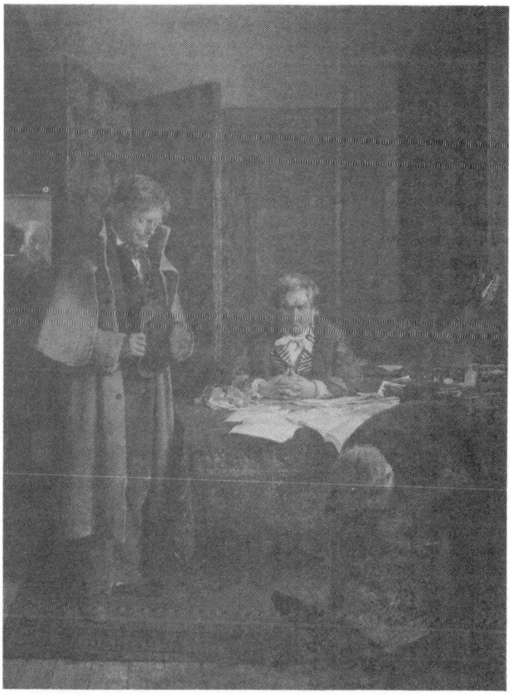

ERSKINE NICOL – Renewal Of The Lease Refused – signed and dated 1868, and inscribed on label on verso – oil on canvas – 36¾ x 28½in.
(Christie's) **$30,240** **£21,000**

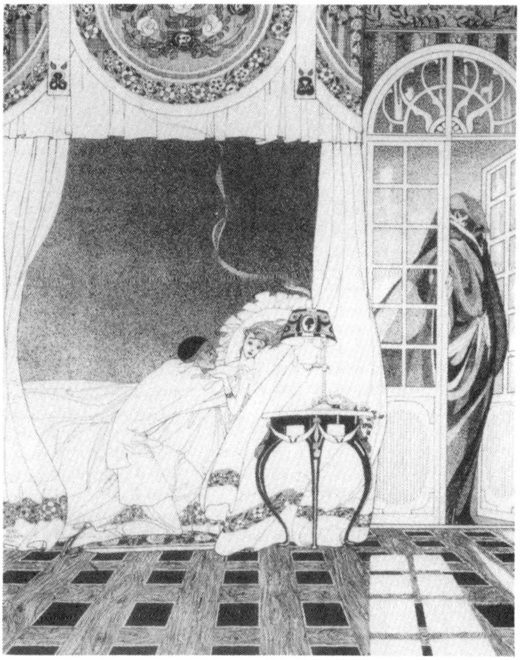

KAY NIELSEN – The Inevitable – signed and dated 1910 – pencil, pen and black ink on paper – 12½ x 9½in.
(Christie's) **$7,603** **£5,280**

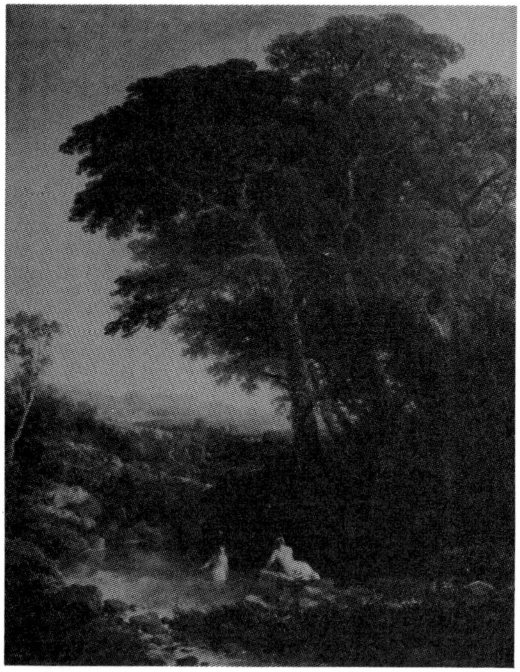

EDMUND JOHN NIEMANN – Bathers In A Wooded Landscape – signed and dated 1861 – 18 x 14in.
(Christie's) **$1,008** **£715**

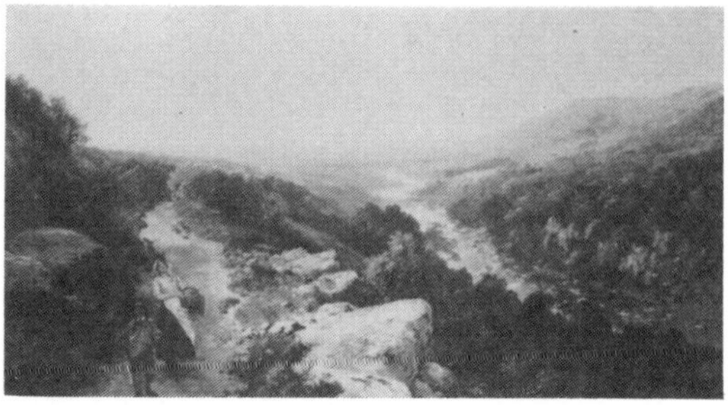

EDMUND JOHN NIEMANN – An Extensive River Landscape – signed – 34½ x 58¼in.
(Christie's) **$4,963** **£3,520**

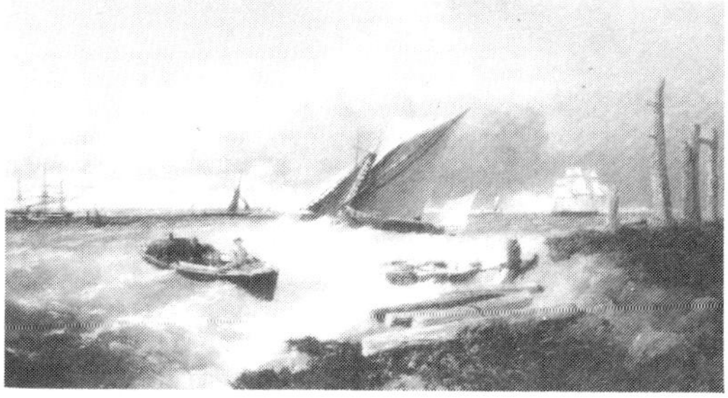

EDMUND JOHN NIEMANN – A Schooner And Other Shipping Offshore In Choppy Seas – signed and dated '59 – 24½ x 44½in.
(Christie's) **$3,702** **£2,420**

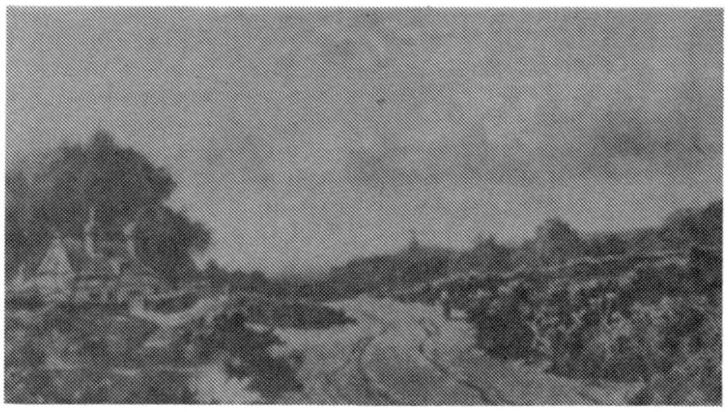

EDMUND JOHN NIEMANN – An Extensive Summer Landscape – signed – on panel – 11½ x 17½in.
(Phillips) **$1,610** **£1,000**

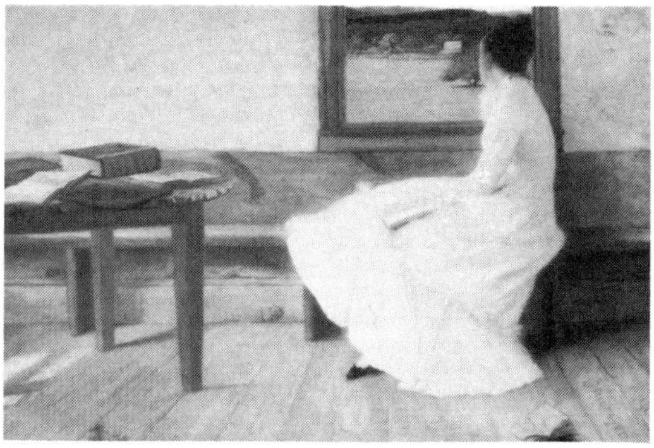

JOHN HENRY NIEMEYER – Wistful – signed and dated 1881 – oil on canvas – 24 x 29¾in.
(Christie's) **$14,300** **£10,052**

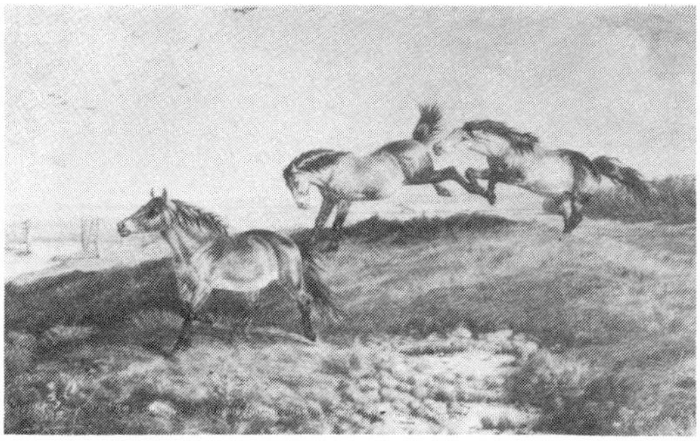

BASIL NIGHTINGALE – Horses In A Meadow – signed and dated 1888 – watercolour – 15¼ x 22½in.
(Christie's) **$949** **£605**

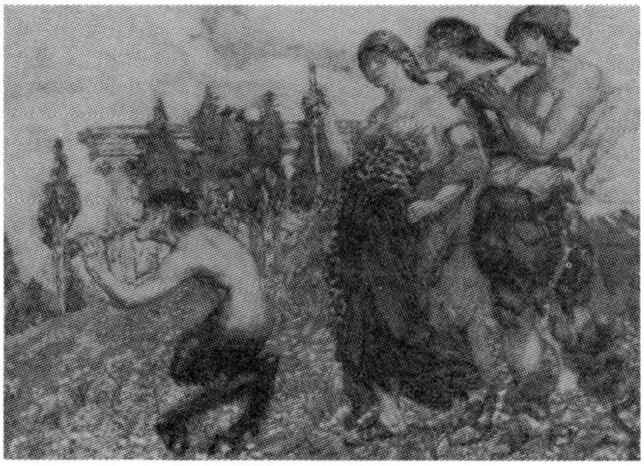

NOEL LAURA NISBET – Spring – signed, inscribed on the reverse – watercolour and bodycolour – 20 x 25¼in.
(Christie's) **$1,415** **£990**

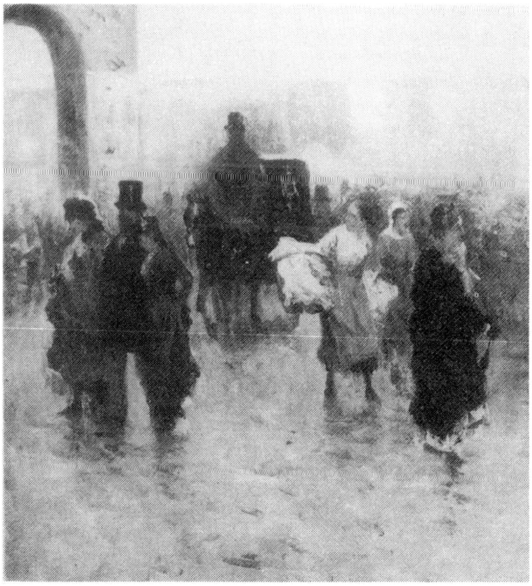

GIUSEPPE DE NITTIS, Attributed to – A Street Scene, Paris – with signature – on board – 8½ x 7¼in.
(Christie's) **$4,012** **£2,640**

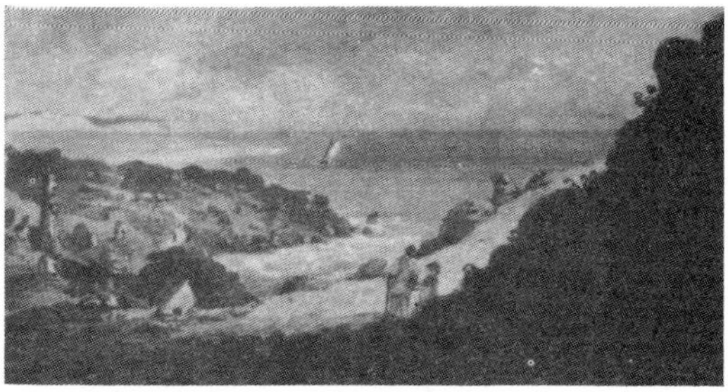

JOHN NIXON – Portland Island And Ruins, Figures In Foreground – signed and dated 1803 – watercolour – 4½ x 8½in.
(Hobbs & Chambers) **$261** **£170**

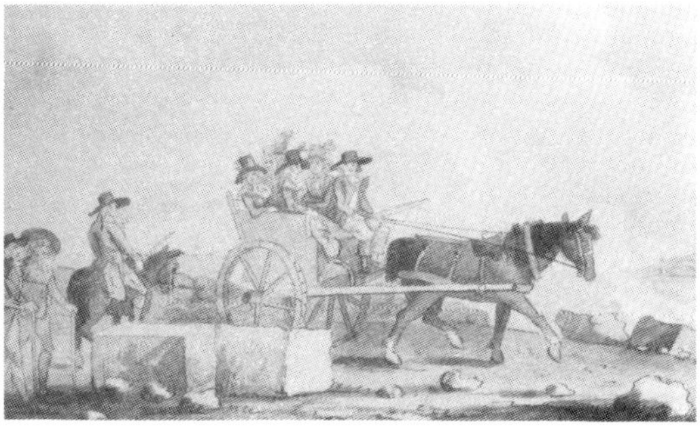

JOHN NIXON – The Grand Tour Of Portland – signed, inscribed and dated 1789 – pen and grey ink and watercolour – 6¾ x 10¾in.
(Christie's) **$1,874** **£1,320**

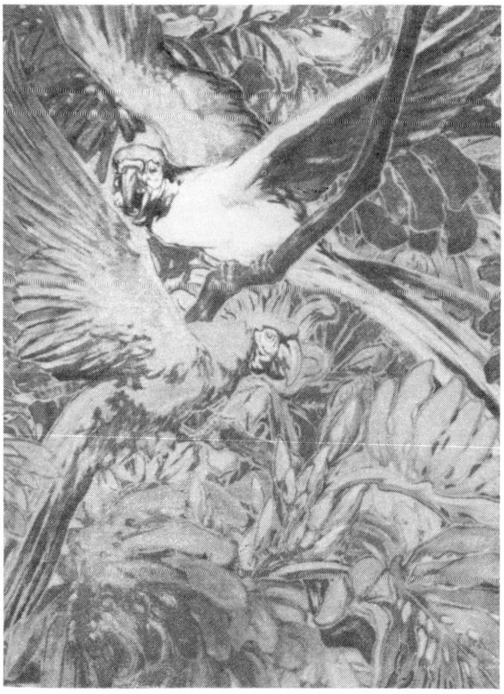

KATE NIXON – Two Parrots – signed – oil on canvas – 29 x 21in.
(Christie's) **$725** **£462**

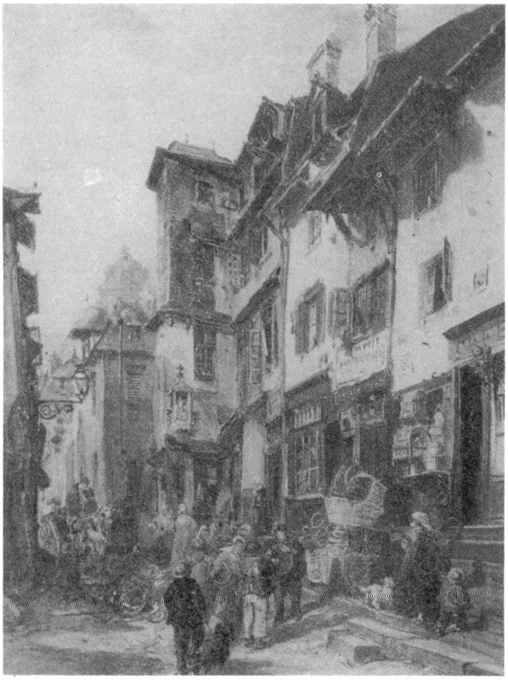

JULES NOEL – A Crowded Street Scene, Northern France – signed – 21½ x 15in.
(Christie's) **$5,350 £3,520**

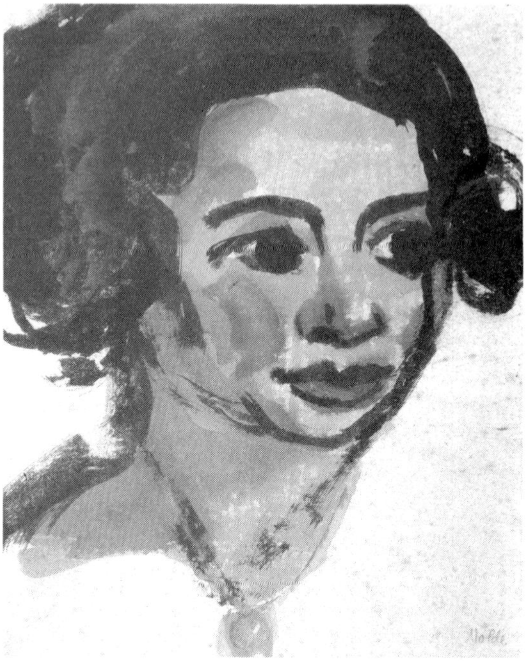

EMIL NOLDE – Kopf einer jungen Frau – signed – watercolour on Japan paper – 18 x 13½in.
(Christie's) **$60,193 £41,800**

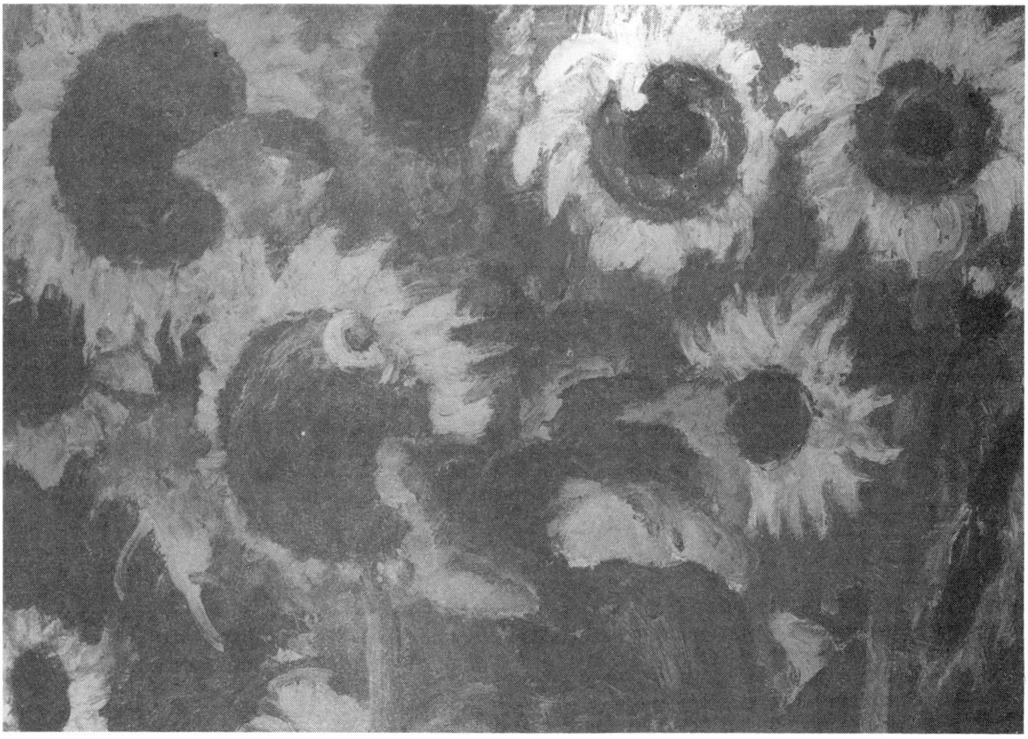

EMIL NOLDE – Sonnenblumen II – signed, and signed and inscribed on the reverse – oil on panel – 28¾ x 34½in. *(Christie's)* **$404,140 £242,000**

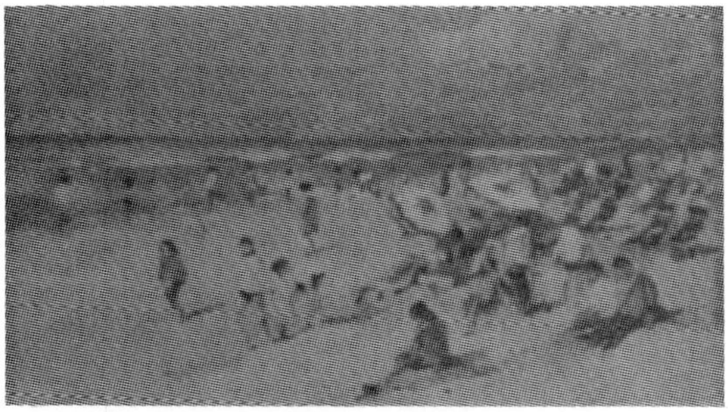

ADRIANUS CORNELIS VAN NOORT – Beach Scene With Children – signed – oil on canvas – 12 x 15¾in.
(Robt. W. Skinner Inc.) **$1,300** **£797**

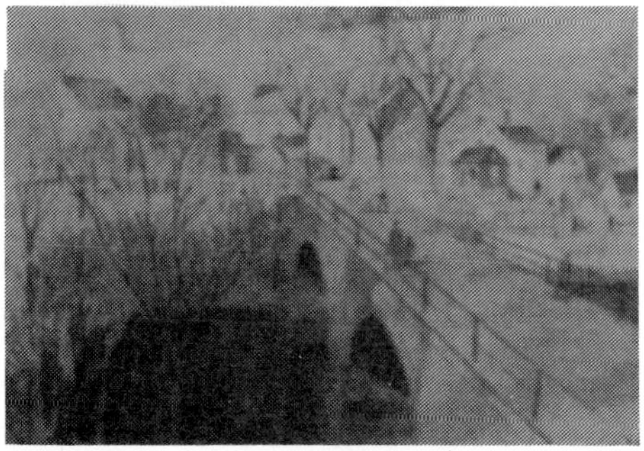

CARL HAROLD NORDSTROM – Bridge At Ipswich – signed – watercolour on paper – 11¼ x 17¼in.
(Robt. W. Skinner Inc.) **$450** **£276**

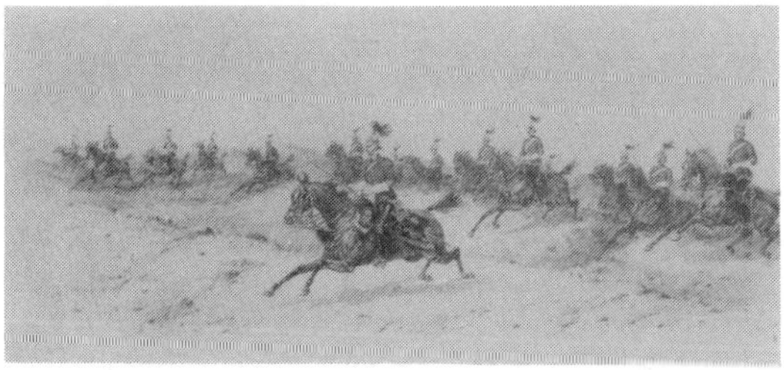

ORLANDO NORIE – A Mounted Troop Of The 1st Dragoons – signed – pencil and watercolour heightened with white – 7¾ x 17¾in.
(Christie's) **$1,369** **£825 Pair**

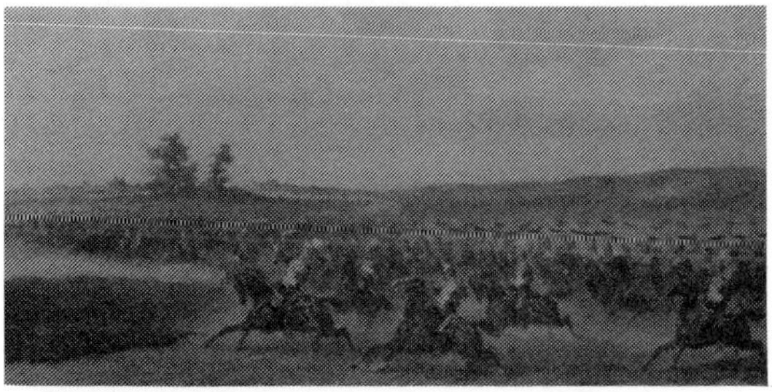

ORLANDO NORIE – Charge Of The 17th Lancers – signed – watercolour heightened with bodycolour – 40 x 71cm.
(Phillips) **$1,336** **£820**

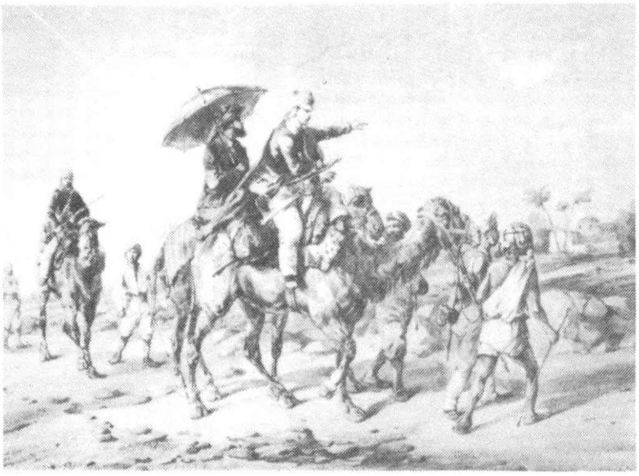

ORLANDO NORIE – Livingstone And Stanley Travelling On Camels – signed – pencil and watercolour – 13¼ x 18¾in.
(Christie's) **$1,262** **£825**

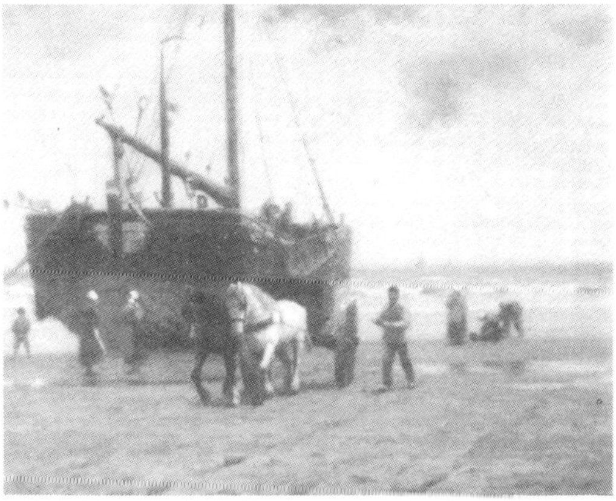

WILLIAM EDWARD NORTON – Dutch Coast – signed, and signed and inscribed on the reverse – oil on canvas – 16¼ x 20in.
(Christie's) **$2,200** **£1,546**

NORWICH SCHOOL – River Sunset With Windmill – oil on panel – 6½ x 8in.
(Michael G. Matthews) **$72** **£45**

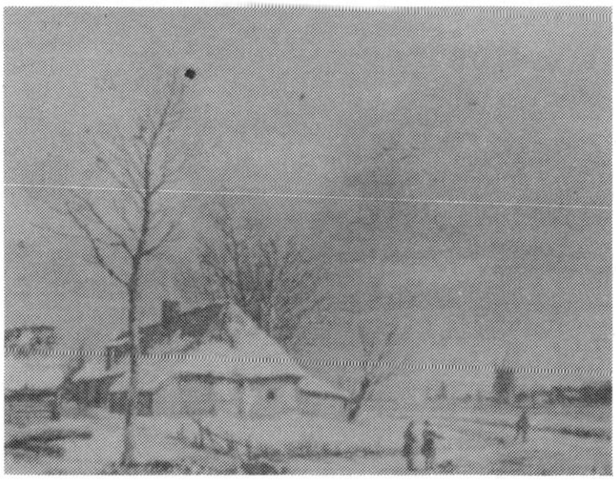

PIETER FRANS DE NOTER – Figures In A Frozen Dutch Landscape – signed and dated 1834 – oil on panel – 15.5 x 19cm.
(Phillips) **$3,006** **£1,800**

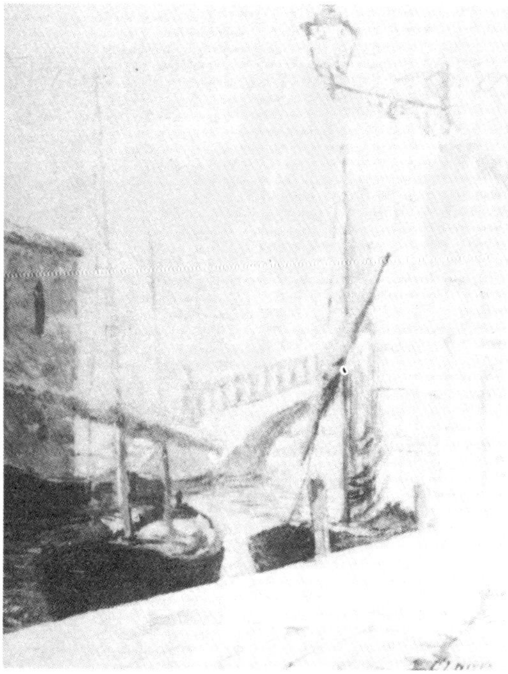

GEORGE LOFTUS NOYES – View Of A Venetian Canal – signed – oil on canvas – 15¼ x 11½in.
(Robt. W. Skinner Inc.) **$1,500** **£1,041**

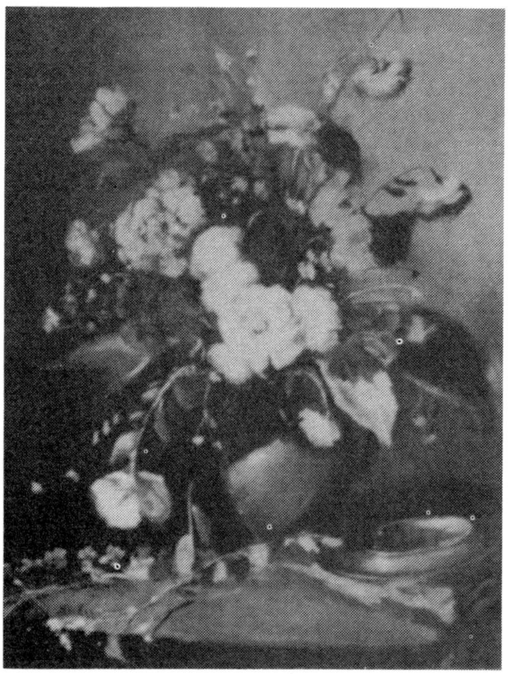

FRANS OERDER – Floral Still Life – signed – oil on canvas – 22 x 18in.
(Robt. W. Skinner Inc.) **$1,500** **£920**

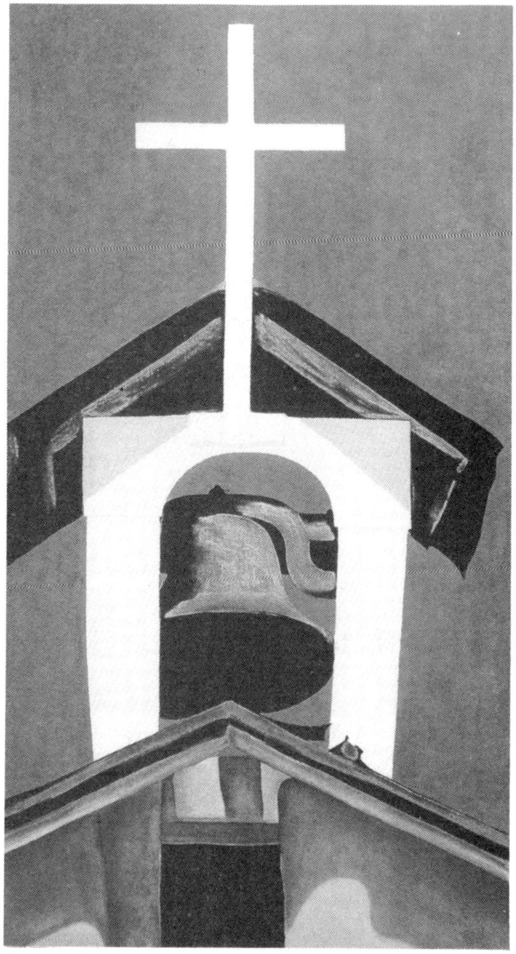

GEORGIA O'KEEFFE – Bell-Cross-Ranchos Church, New Mexico, 1930 – inscribed and dated 1930 on an old label – oil on canvas – 30 x 16in.
(Christie's) **$418,000** **£293,854**

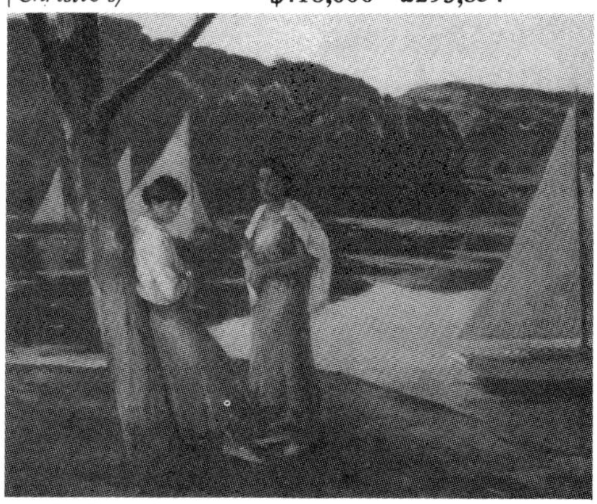

IVAN G. OLINSKY – Hamburg Cove – signed, inscribed on the reverse – oil on canvas – 30 x 36¼in.
(Christie's) **$5,500** **£3,826**

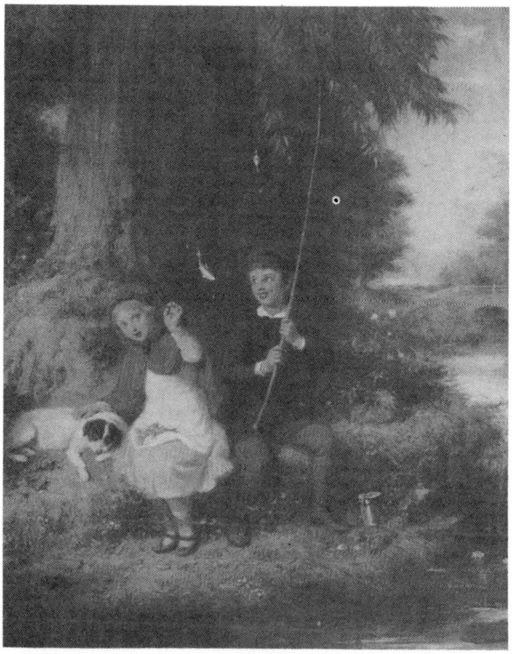

GEORGE BERNARD O'NEILL – The First Catch Of The Day – signed – 12¼ x 10in.
(Christie's) **$6,979** **£4,950**

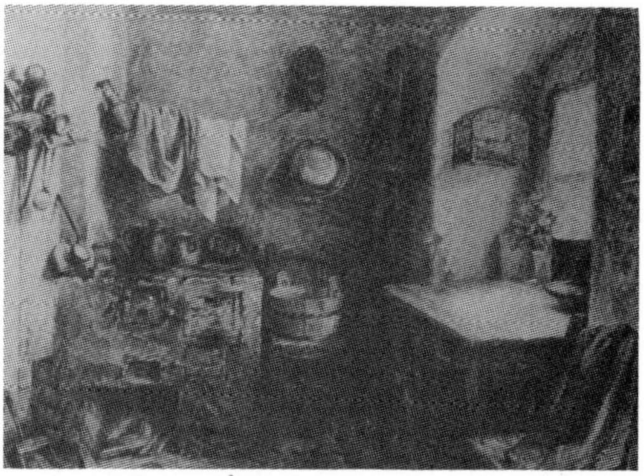

M. ONKEN-PALMÈ – The Sunlit Interior Of A Cottage Kitchen – signed – on canvas – 35 x 40cm.
(Phillips) **$679** **£450**

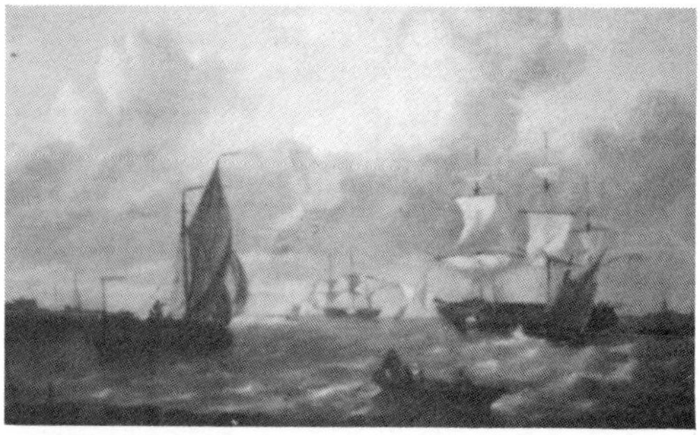

G. W. OPDENHOFF – Dutch Coastal Marine Scene – oil on canvas – 36 x 24in.
(R. R. Leonard & Son) **$3,750** **£2,500**

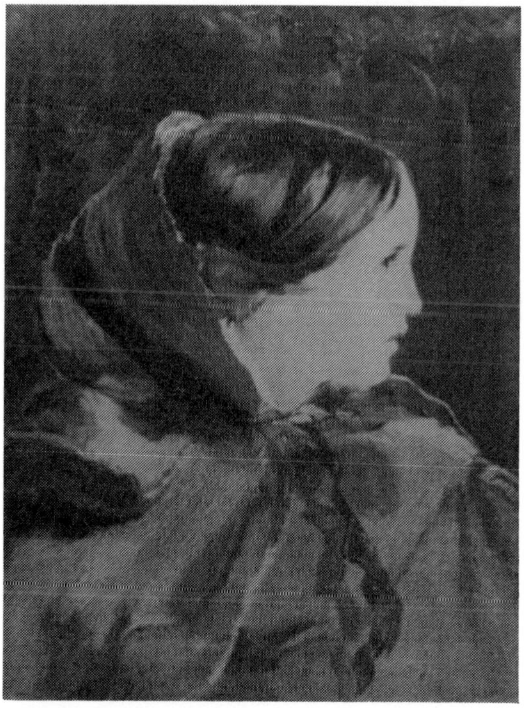

HENRY O'NEILL, Attributed to – Study Of A Young Girl Bonneted, Wearing A Red Cape – on panel – 9¼ x 7in.
(Phillips) **$418** **£260**

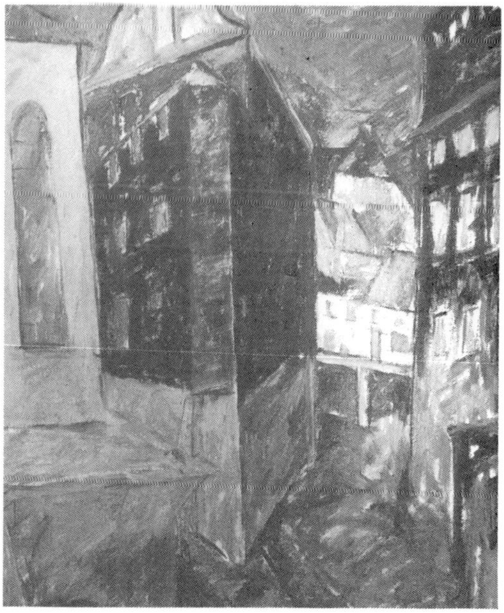

WALTER OPHEY – Rote Hauser in einer Stadt – dated 1921 – oil on canvas – 25¼ x 19½in.
(Christie's) **$15,048** **£10,450**

ORPEN

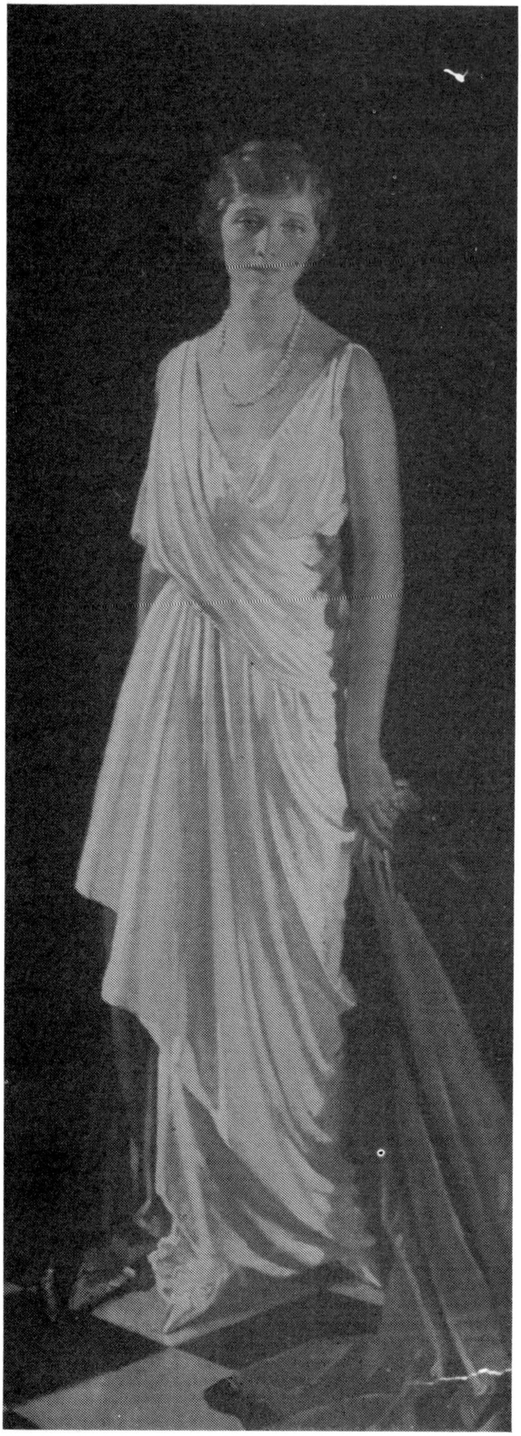

SIR WILLIAM ORPEN – Portrait Of Mrs. Lewisohn, Full Length – signed – oil on canvas – 79½ x 36in.
(Christie's) **$22,451** **£14,300**

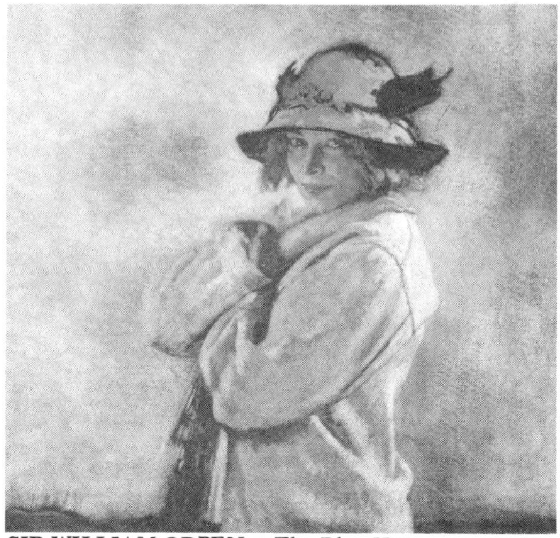

SIR WILLIAM ORPEN – The Blue Hat – signed – oil on canvas – 37 x 34¼in.
(Christie's) **$180,895** **£126,500**

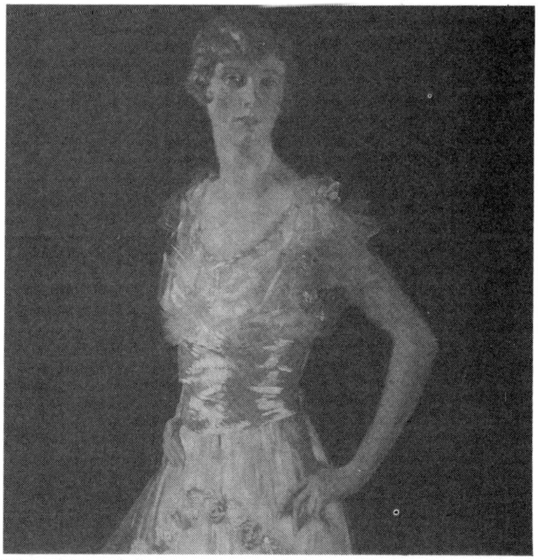

WILLIAM ORPEN – Portrait Of Gardenia, Three-Quarter Length – signed – oil on canvas – 50½ x 40¼in.
(Christie's) **$27,632** **£17,600**

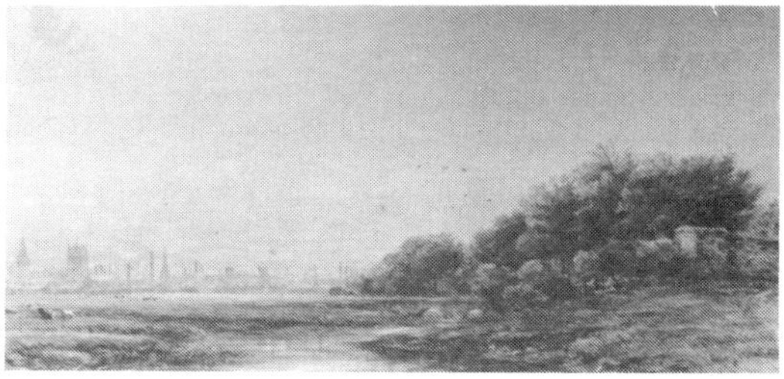

JAMES ORROCK – Rural River Scene With Town In Background And Cattle Grazing To The Fore – signed – watercolour – 12 x 19in.
(Biddle & Webb) **$945** **£580**

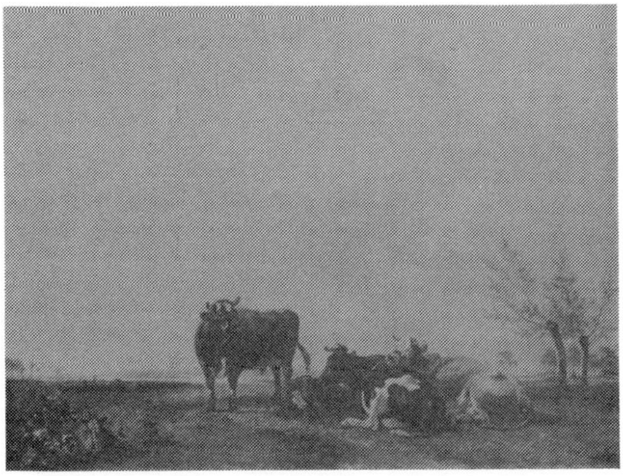

PIETER GERARDUS VAN OS – Cattle And Sheep Resting In An Extensive Dutch Landscape – signed and dated 1836 – on canvas – 61 x 74cm.
(Phillips) **$2,265** **£1,500**

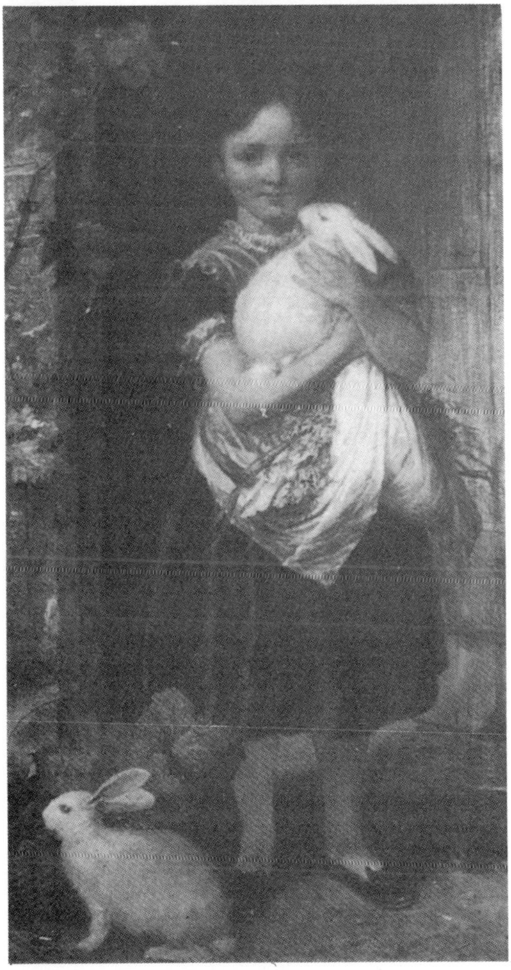

EMILY MARY OSBORN, Attributed to – The Pet Rabbits – signed with a monogram – 53½ x 28½in.
(Christie's) **$2,430** **£1,620**

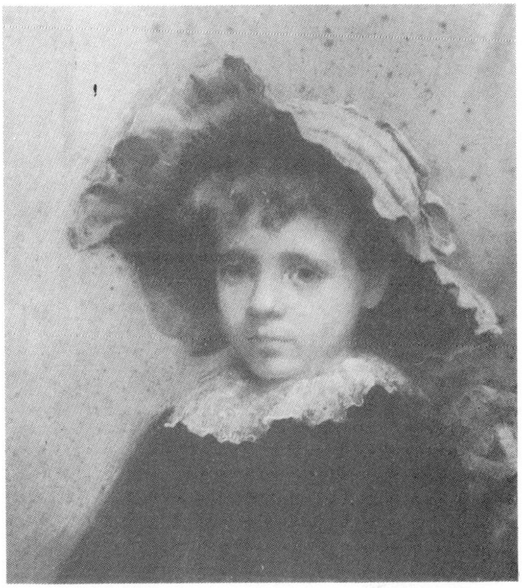

WALTER OSBORNE – Portrait Of A Young Boy, Possibly Hugh Lane, Wearing A Green Hat – signed and dated '91 – pastel – 17¾ x 14¼in.
(Christie's) **$5,977** **£4,180**

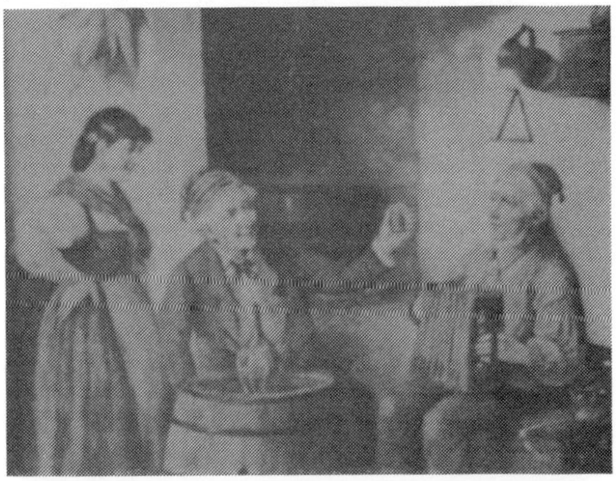

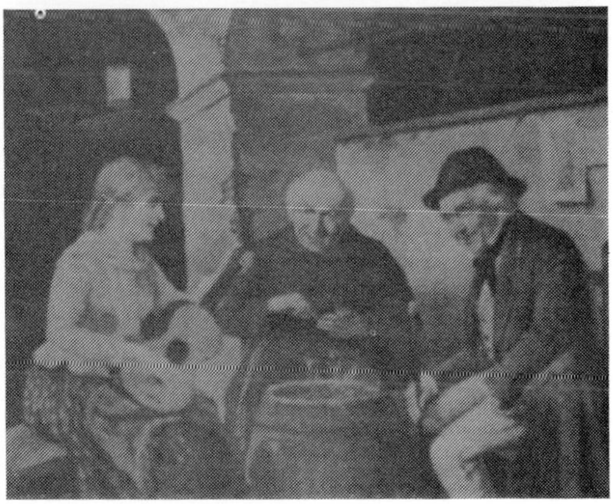

CARL OSTERSETZER – Tavern Entertainment – signed – oil on panel – 21 x 26cm.
(Phillips) **$2,004** **£1,200 Pair**

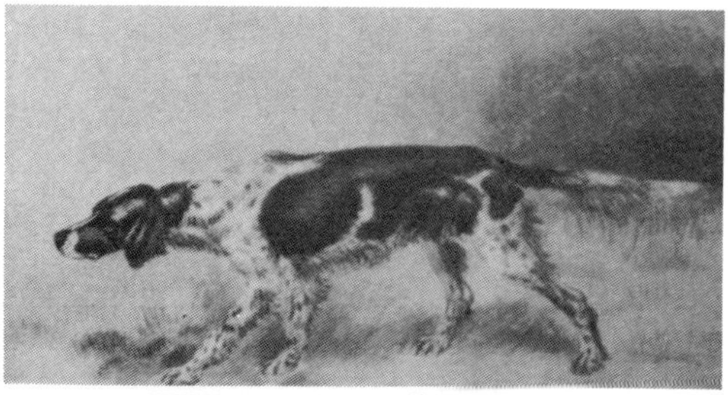

EDMUND HENRY OSTHAUS – An English Setter – signed and dated '92 – watercolour on paper laid down on cardboard – 5¾ x 9in.
(Christie's) **$1,540** **£1,071**

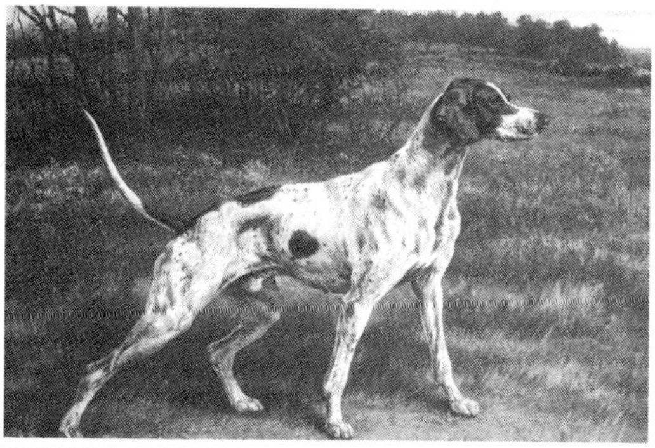

EDMUND HENRY OSTHAUS – On The Point – signed – oil on canvas – 24 x 30in.
(Christie's) **$10,450** **£7,346**

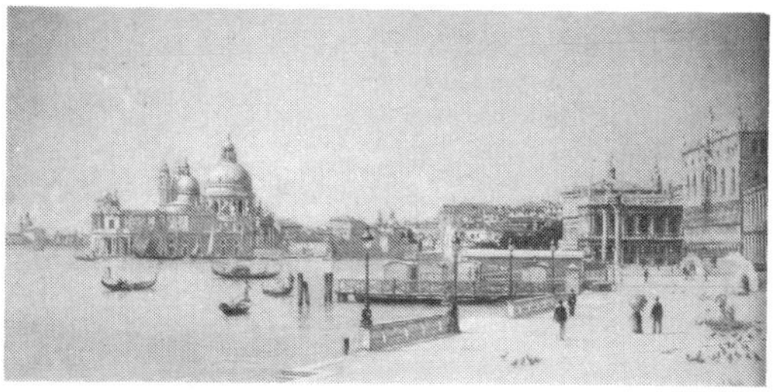

MANUEL MUNOZ OTERO – La Riva degli Schiavoni, Venice – signed, and signed and inscribed on the reverse – 10 x 20in.
(Christie's) **$21,120** **£13,200**

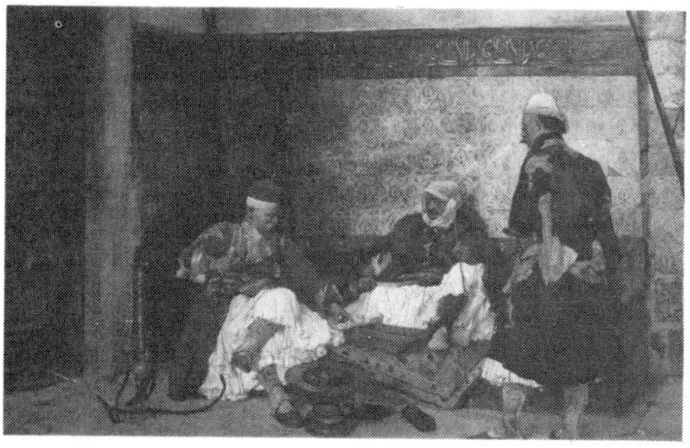

RUDOLPH VAN OTTENFELD – Backgammon – signed and dated 1890 – on panel – 10½ x 13in.
(Christie's) **$12,320** **£7,700**

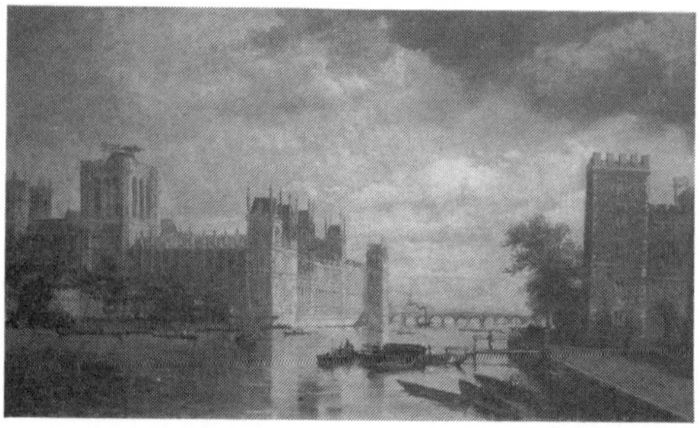

PIERRE JUSTIN OUVRIE – A View Of The Thames With The Palaces Of Westminster And Lambeth – signed – 17 x 28in.
(Christie's) **$15,840** **£9,900**

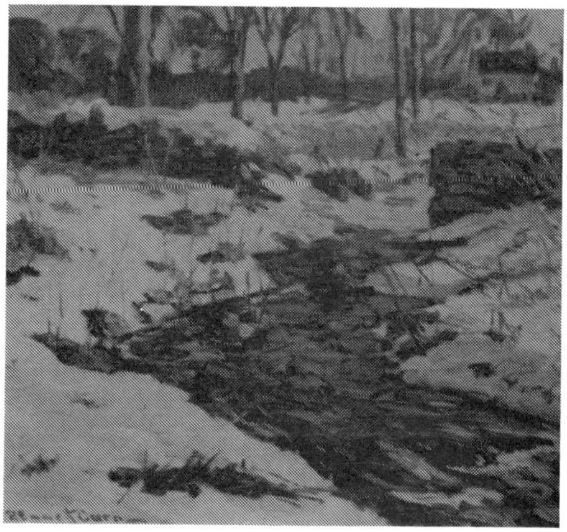

ROBERT EMMETT OWEN – 'Stream On A Winter Afternoon' – signed – oil on canvas – 18 x 20in.
(Robt. W. Skinner Inc.) **$2,600** **£1,595**

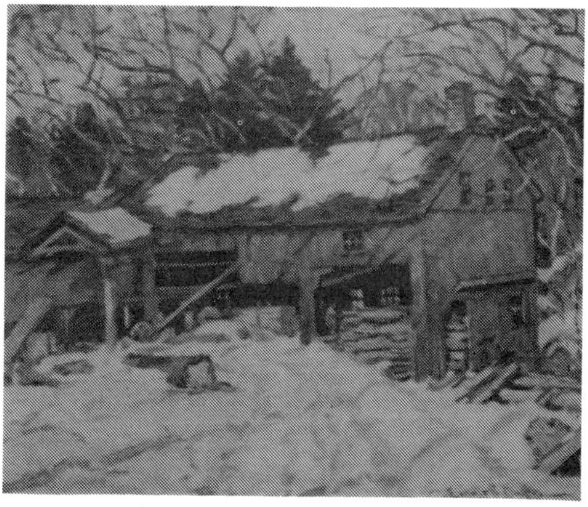

ROBERT EMMETT OWEN – 'Old Red Mill, Silvermine, Connecticut' – signed – oil on canvas – 20½ x 24½in.
(Robt. W. Skinner Inc.) **$3,000** **£1,840**

ROBERT EMMETT OWEN – House In Springtime – signed – oil on board – 14 x 18in.
(Robt. W. Skinner Inc.) **$425** **£260**

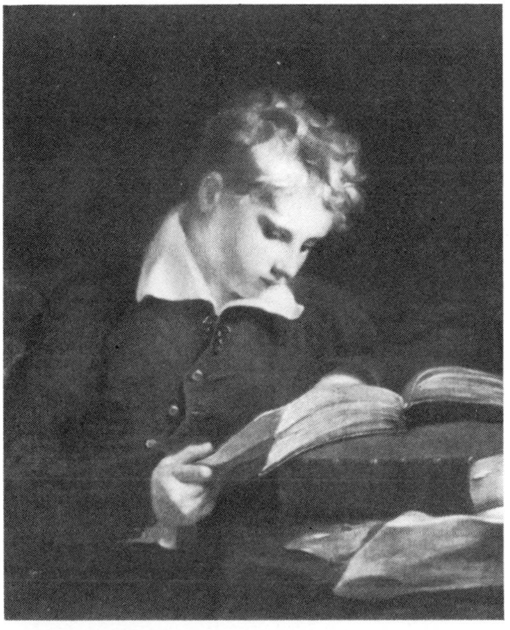

WILLIAM OWEN, Circle of – Portrait Of A Boy, Seated Half Length, Wearing A Green Jacket, Reading A Book – 30 x 25in.
(Christie's) **$1,620** **£1,080**

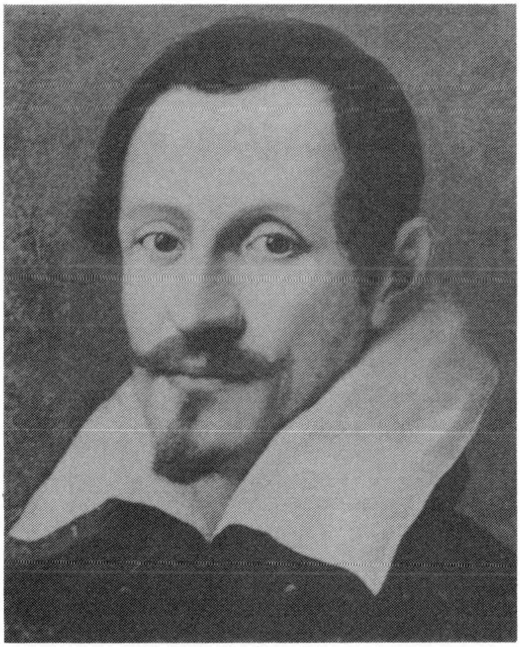

FRANCISCO PACHECO, Circle of – Portrait Of A Man, Bust Length, With A Moustache And Goatee Beard – oil on canvas – 15½ x 11½in.
(Phillips) **$846** **£600**

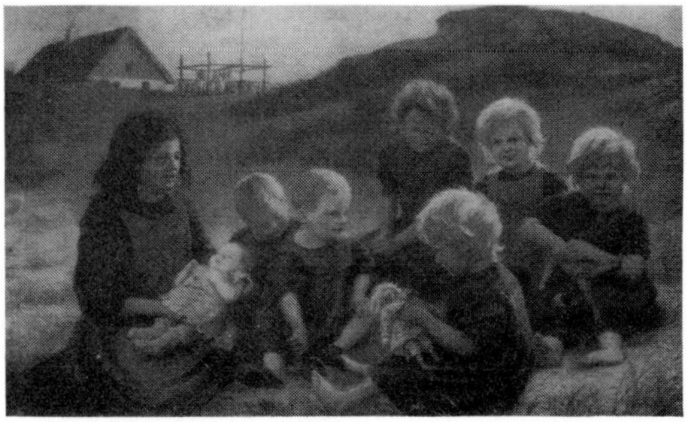

WILHELM PACHT – Children Playing In The Dunes – signed – 24½ x 30½in.
(Christie's) **$1,504** **£990**

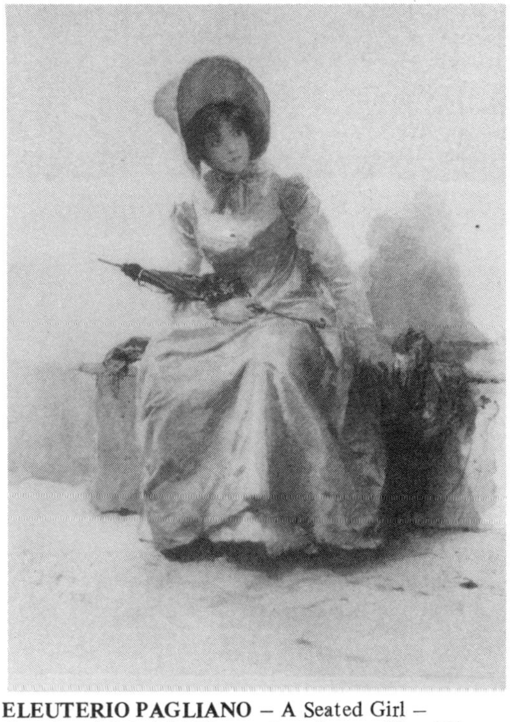

ELEUTERIO PAGLIANO – A Seated Girl – signed and dated 1892 – watercolour – 17 x 13in.
(Christie's) **$6,391** **£3,850**

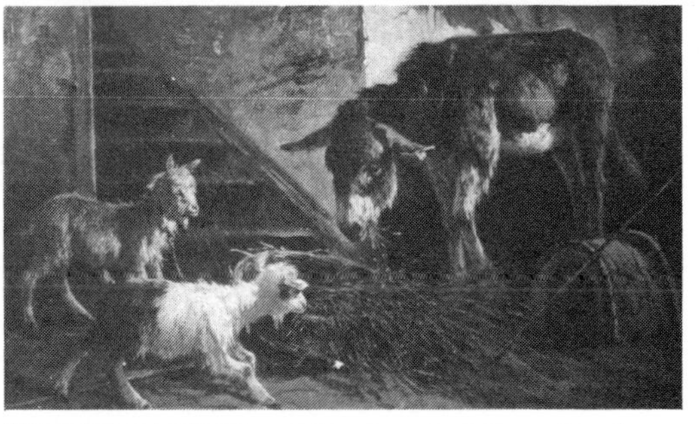

FILIPPO PALIZZI – A Donkey And Goats Feeding From A Basket – signed – 15½ x 20½in.
(Christie's) **$22,880** **£14,300**

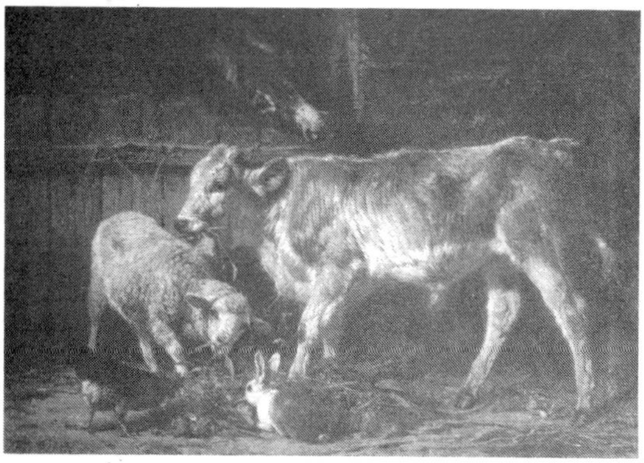

FILIPPO PALIZZI – A Chicken, A Rabbit, Sheep And A Calf In A Stable With A Donkey Looking On – signed and dated 1872 – 15½ x 21¾in.
(Christie's) **$34,848 £24,200**

ANNA PALM – View Of Stockholm – signed and inscribed – watercolour and gouache on paper – 6½ x 12¼in.
(Robt. W. Skinner Inc.) **$2,500 £1,736**

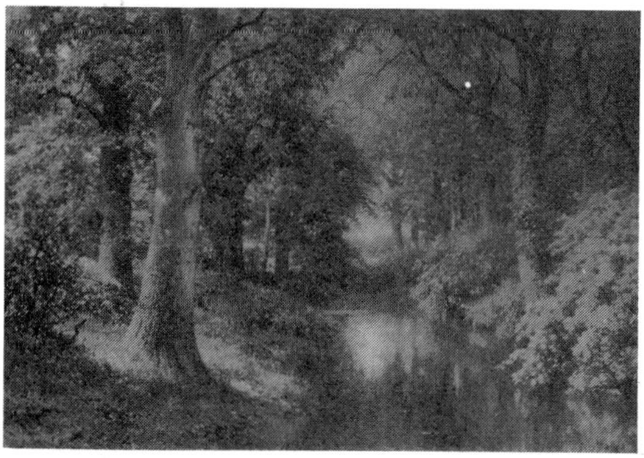

HARRY SUTTON PALMER – Nature's Mirror: Bluebells By A Stream In A Wood – signed – pencil and watercolour – 18¼ x 25¼in.
(Christie's) **$6,938 £4,180**

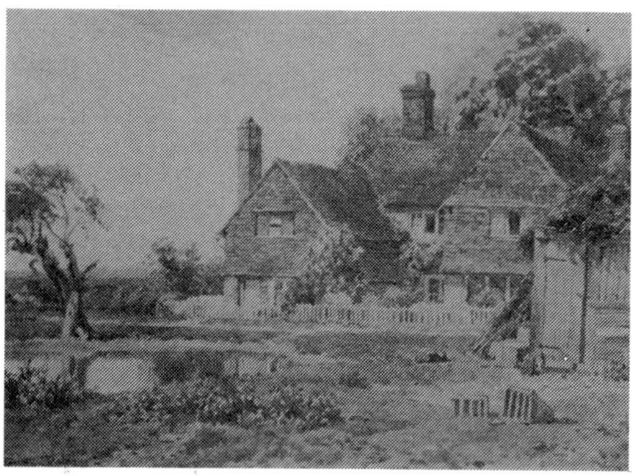

HARRY SUTTON PALMER – A House By A Pond – signed – watercolour – 27 x 36cm.
(Phillips) **$1,467 £900**

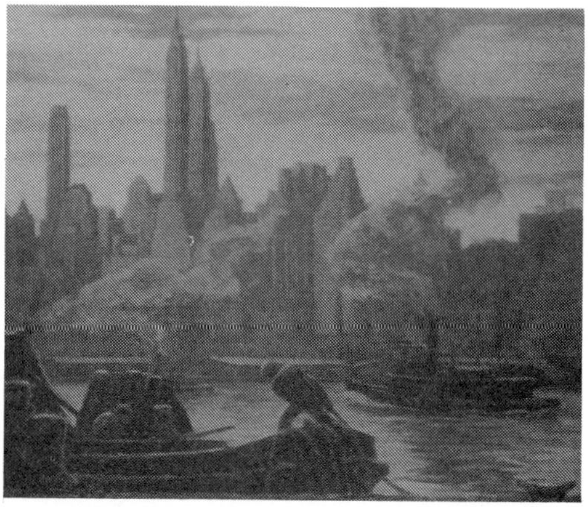

ALPHONSE PALUMBO – Tugboats On The East River – signed – oil on canvas – 30½ x 34in.
(Christie's) **$5,500 £3,427**

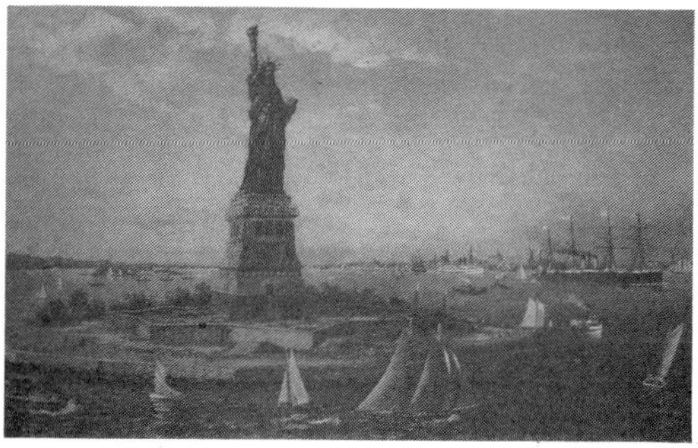

FRED PANSING – Liberty Island, New York Harbour – signed and dated 1833 – oil on canvas – 28 x 40¼in.
(Christie's) **$44,000 £30,610**

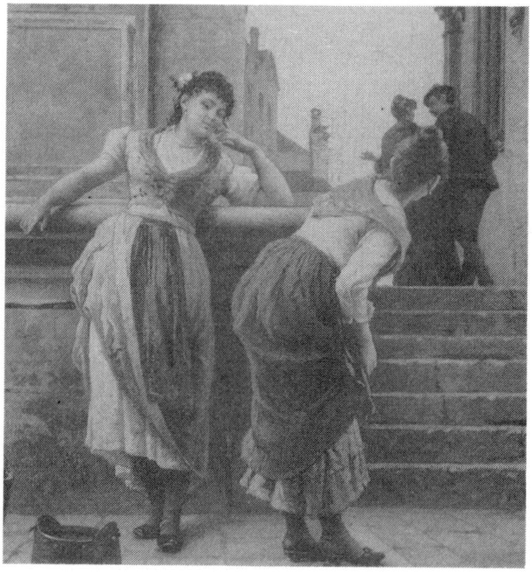

ANTONIO PAOLETTI – Eavesdropping – signed and inscribed – on panel – 12 x 9in.
(Christie's) **$2,508 £1,650**

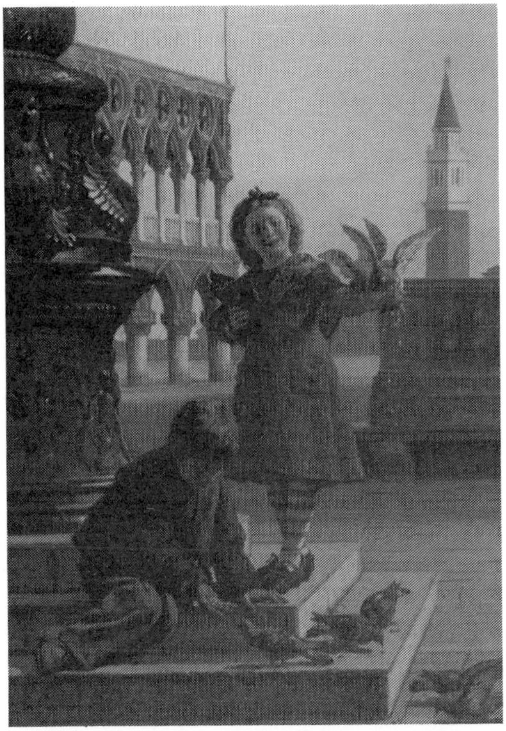

ANTONIO PAOLETTI – Feeding The Pigeons In Piazza San Marco; and A Helping Hand – signed and inscribed – 13 x 9¼in.
(Christie's) **$10,032** **£6,600 Pair**

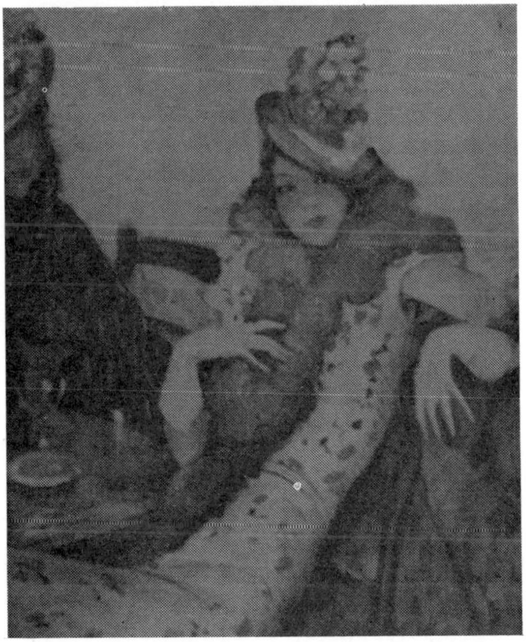

MARCEL DE PAREDES – Tete A Tete – signed – oil on canvas – 61 x 51cm.
(Phillips) **$1,550** **£1,000**

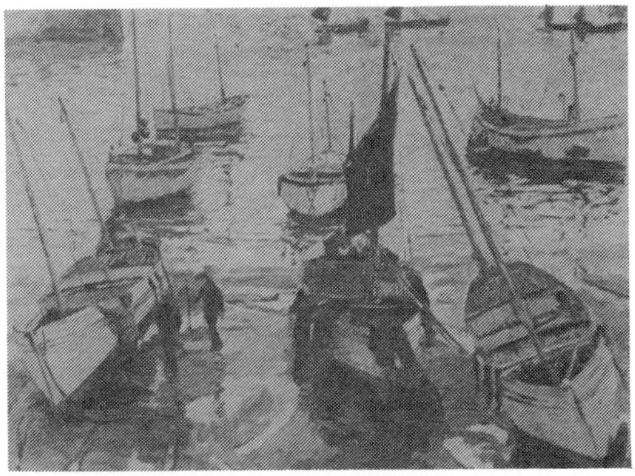

JOHN ANTHONY PARK – Beached Boats, St. Ives – signed – oil on canvas – 71 x 92cm.
(Phillips) **$5,440** **£3,400**

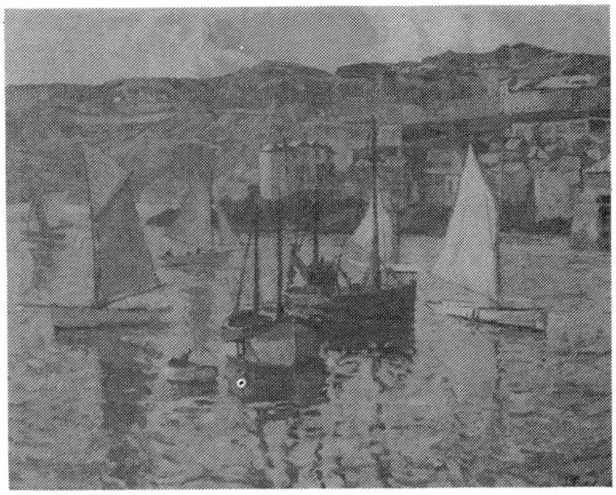

JOHN ANTHONY PARK – Sailing Boats, St. Ives – signed, also traces of signature on a label on the reverse – oil on canvas – 61 x 76cm.
(Phillips) **$6,080** **£3,800**

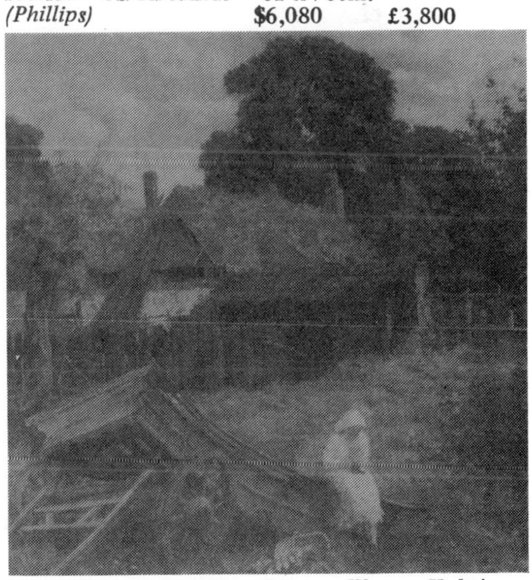

HENRY H. PARKER – A Young Woman Knitting Seated On A Cart By A Farm – signed – 24 x 20in.
(Christie's) **$2,019** **£1,320**

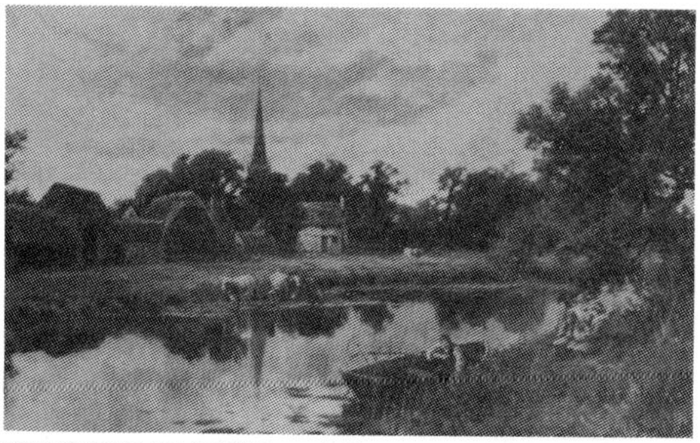

HENRY H. PARKER – A Farmstead With Cattle And Figures By A River In A Wooded Landscape – signed – 16¼ x 24in.
(Christie's) **$3,564** **£2,376**

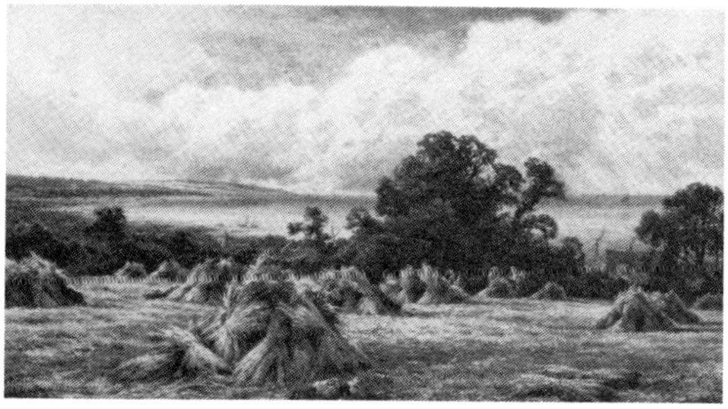

HENRY H. PARKER – Harvesting On The Sussex Coast, Littlehampton – signed, and signed and inscribed on the reverse – 20 x 30¼in.
(Christie's) **$8,530** **£6,050**

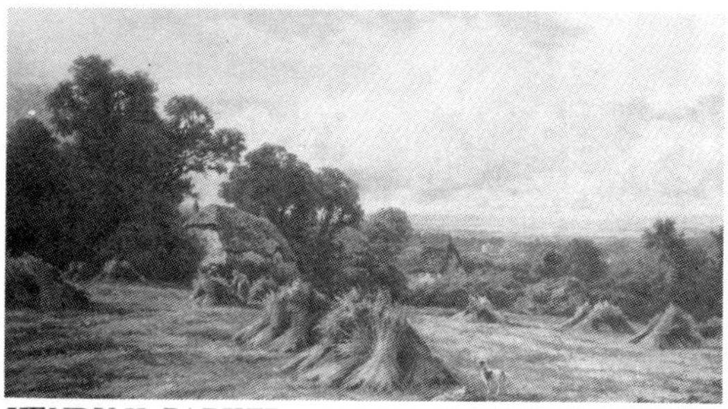

HENRY H. PARKER – Harvest Time Near Haselmere, Surrey – signed, and signed and inscribed on the reverse – 20 x 30in.
(Christie's) **$16,200** **£10,800**

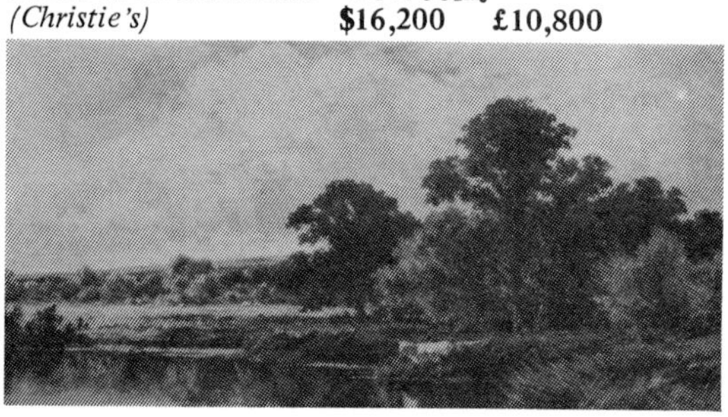

HENRY H. PARKER – On The Way, Elstead, Surrey – signed, also signed and inscribed on the reverse – 12 x 18in.
(Phillips) **$2,737** **£1,700**

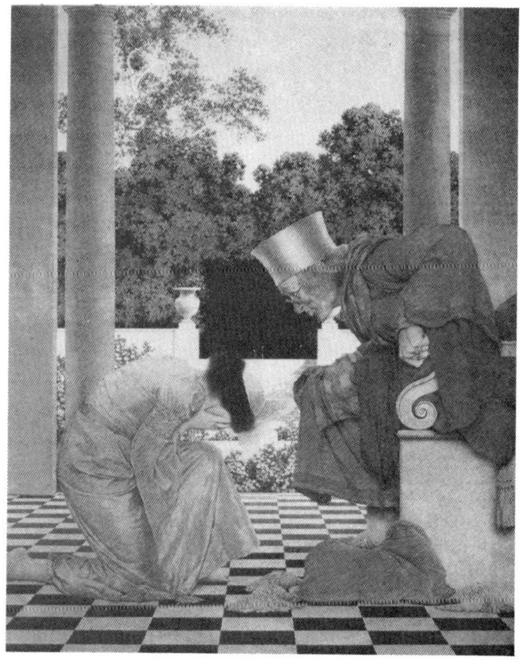

MAXFIELD PARRISH – Lady Ursula Informs The King – signed with initials, inscribed on the reverse – oil on board – 20 x 16¼in.
(Christie's) **$44,000** **£30,932**

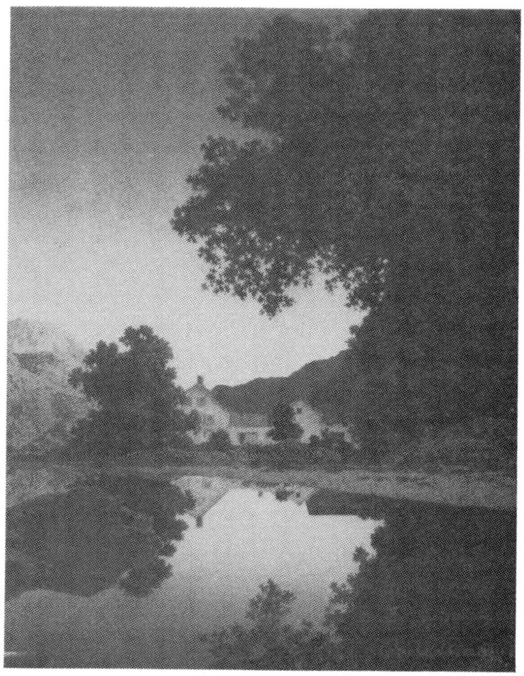

MAXFIELD PARRISH – The Hills Of New Hampshire – signed and dated 1950 – oil on panel – 10¾ x 8¾in.
(Christie's) **$22,000** **£13,708**

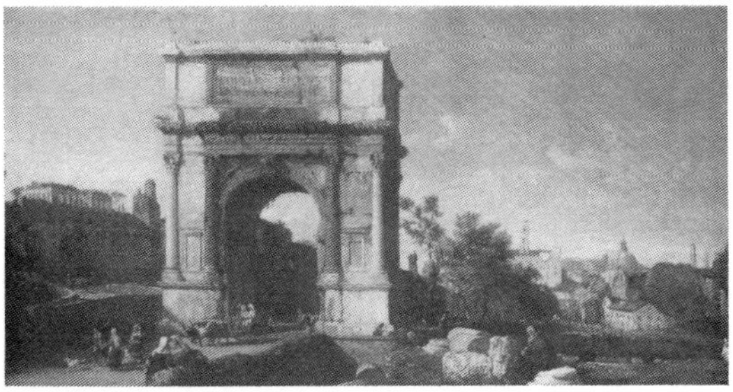

WILLIAM PARROTT – Views Of The Forum, Rome – one signed and dated 1848 – 30¼ x 57¼in.
(Christie's) **$22,680** **£15,120 Two**

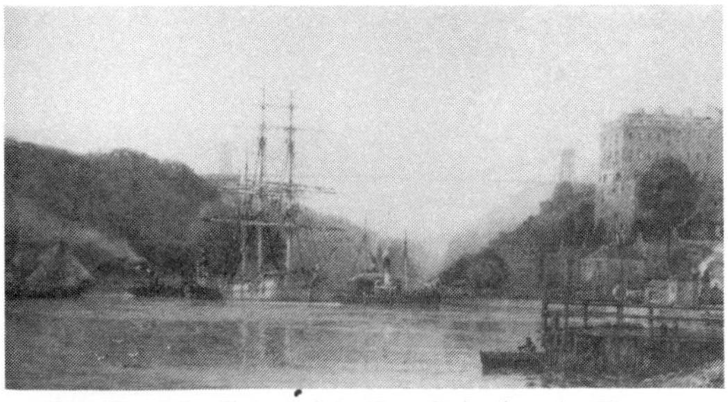

ARTHUR WILDE PARSONS – Shipping At The Entrance Of The Avon Gorge Below The Clifton Suspension Bridge – signed and dated 1912 – pencil and watercolour – 23¼ x 39in.
(Christie's) **$5,478** **£3,300**

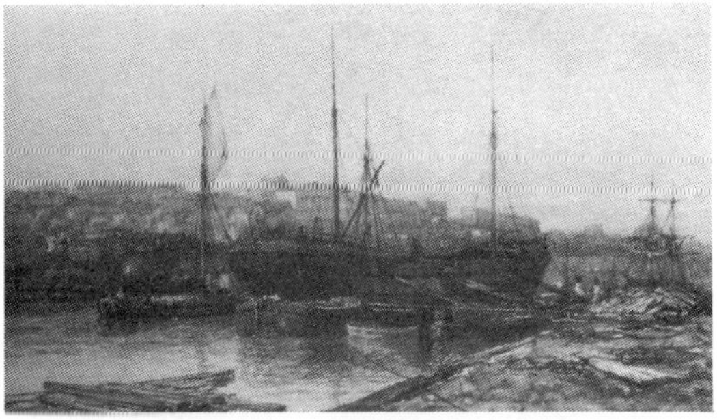

ARTHUR WILDE PARSONS – Bristol Docks – signed and dated '96 – watercolour – 19¾ x 29¾in.
(Christie's) **$1,458** **£972**

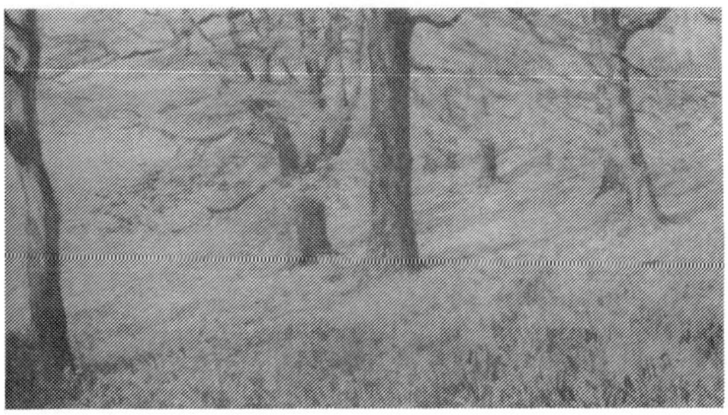

BEATRICE PARSONS – Bluebell Wood – signed – watercolour – 15 x 24cm.
(Phillips) **$815** **£500**

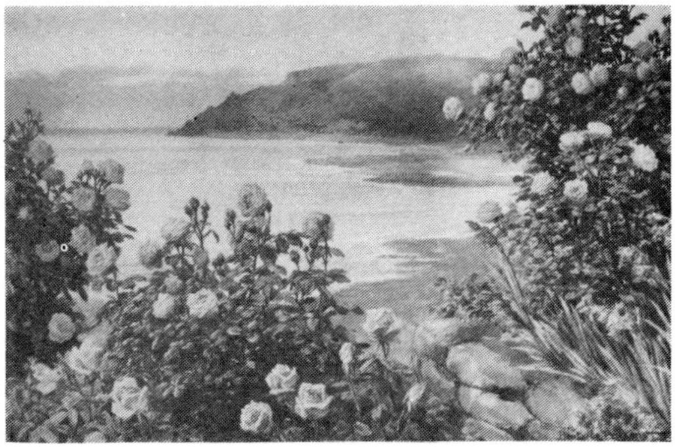

BEATRICE PARSONS – Rose Garden, Porlock Bay, Somerset – signed, and inscribed on the reverse – watercolour – 9 x 12in.
(Christie's) **$2,481** **£1,760**

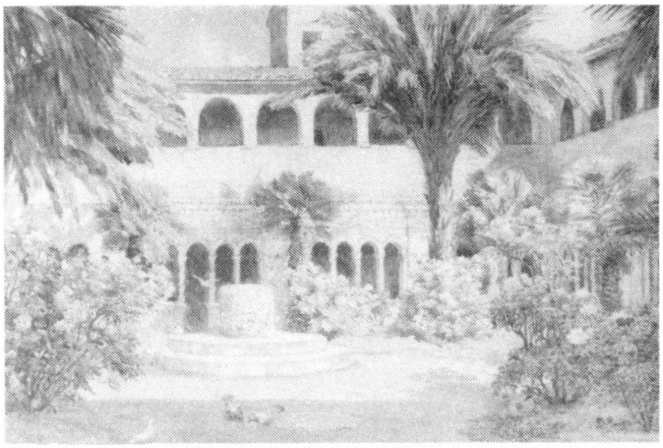

BEATRICE PARSONS – Roses In The Cloisters Of St. John Lateran, Rome – signed and inscribed – pencil and watercolour heightened with white, on board – 9¼ x 12in.
(Christie's) **$2,217** **£1,540**

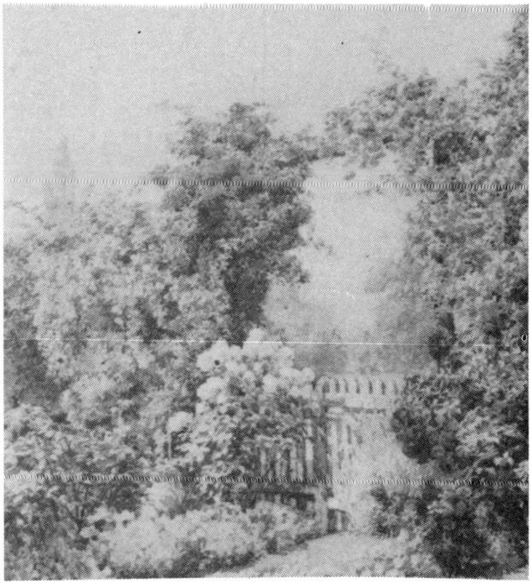

BEATRICE PARSONS – The Garden Gate – signed – watercolour – 11¼ x 8¾in.
(Christie's) **$2,636** **£1,870**

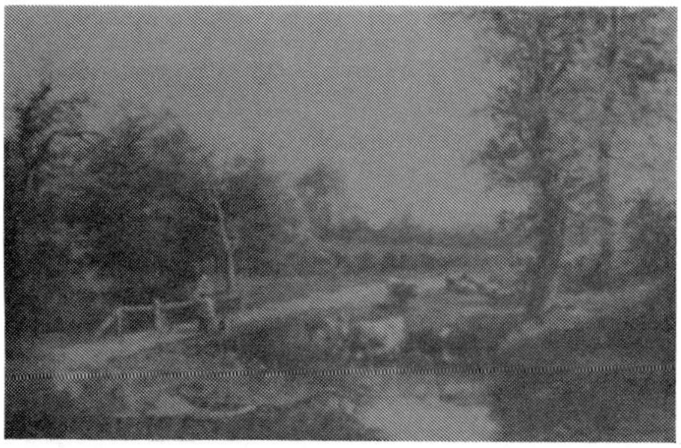

GEORGE PARSONS-NORMAN – Figure Beneath Trees Beside A River In A Sunset Landscape – signed – on canvas – 17 x 14¾in.
(Phillips) **$1,046** **£650**

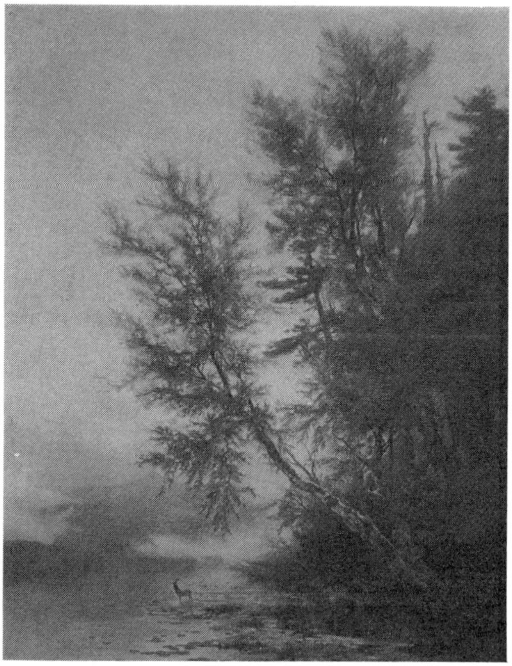

ARTHUR PARTON – On The Delaware, Near Milford, Pennsylvania – signed and dated 1879 – oil on canvas – 45 x 32¼in.
(Christie's) **$6,050** **£3,948**

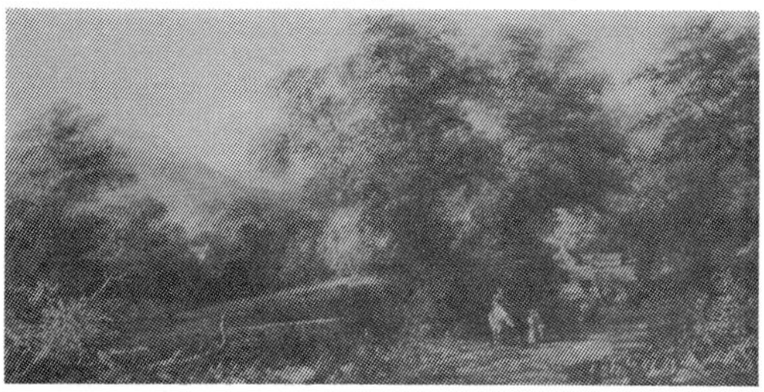

EDWARD PARTRIDGE – Figures And Cattle On A Path In A Lakeland Landscape Between Penrith And Ullswater – signed – on canvas – 10 x 20in.
(Phillips) **$1,416** **£880**

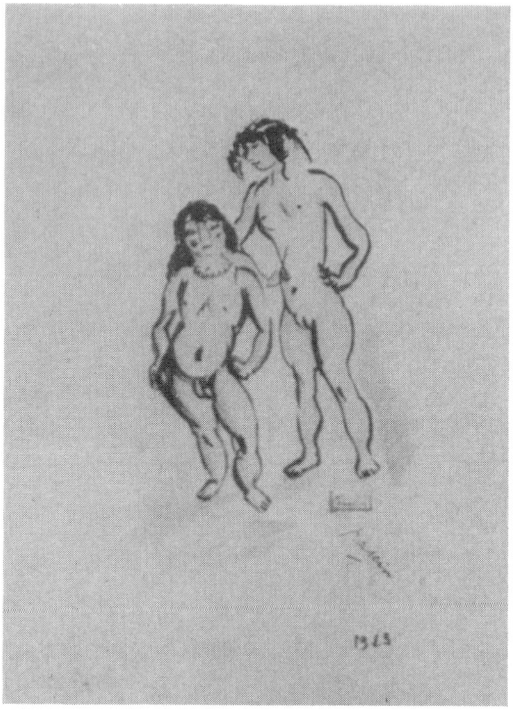

JULES PASCIN – Deux Nus – wash on paper – 10¼ x 7½in.
(Christie's) **$880** **£550**

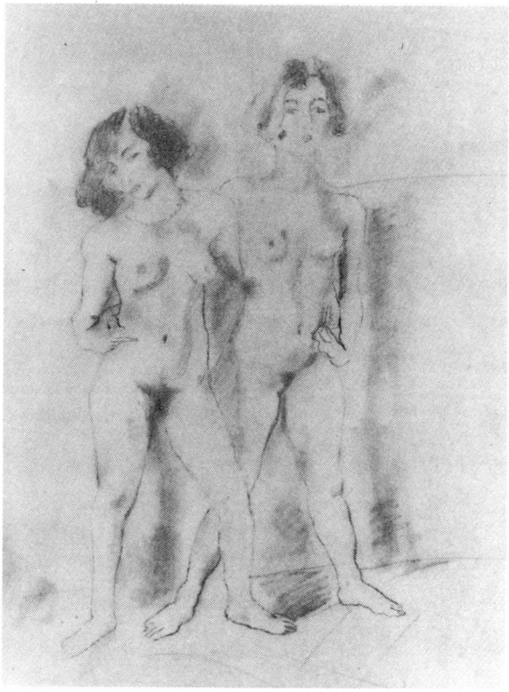

JULES PASCIN – Deux jeunes Filles – signed – pastel and soft pencil on paper – 23½ x 17¼in.
(Christie's) **$20,592** **£14,300**

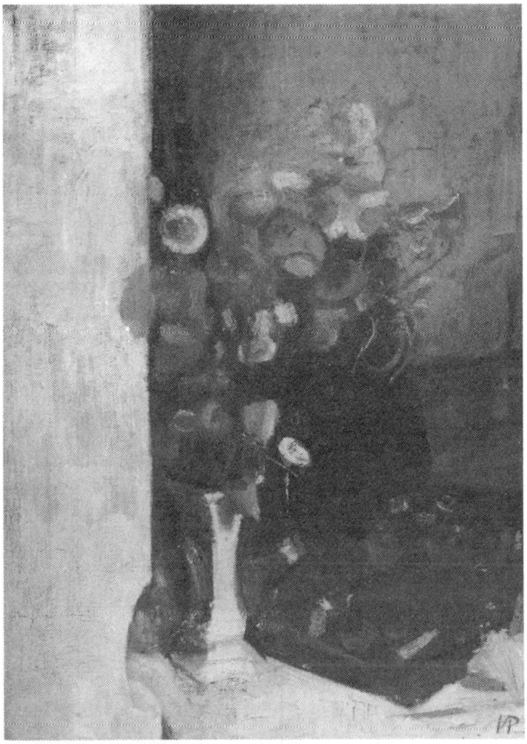

VICTOR PASMORE – Everlasting Flowers – signed with initials – oil on canvas – 24 x 18in.
(Christie's) **$14,943** **£10,450**

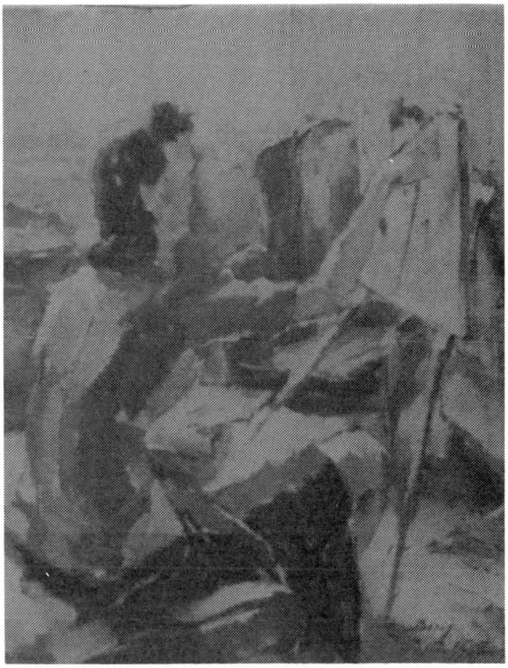

BORIS PASTOUKHOFF – In The Studio – signed and inscribed – oil on canvas – 73 x 60cm.
(Phillips) **$496** **£320**

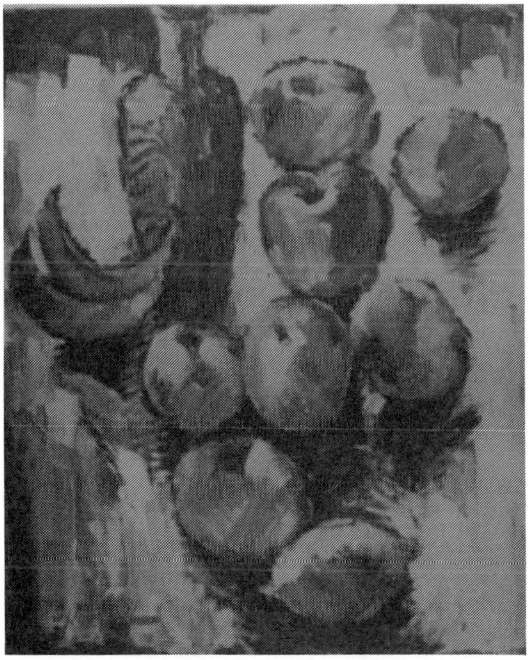

BORIS PASTOUKHOFF – Still Life With Apples – signed – oil on canvas – 65 x 54cm.
(Phillips) **$697** **£450**

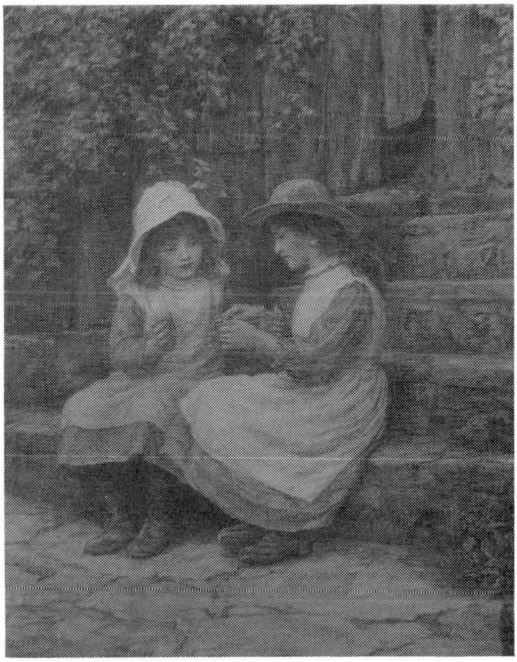

CAROLINE PATERSON – Cat's Cradle – signed – watercolour – 40 x 35cm.
(Phillips) **$13,692** **£8,400**

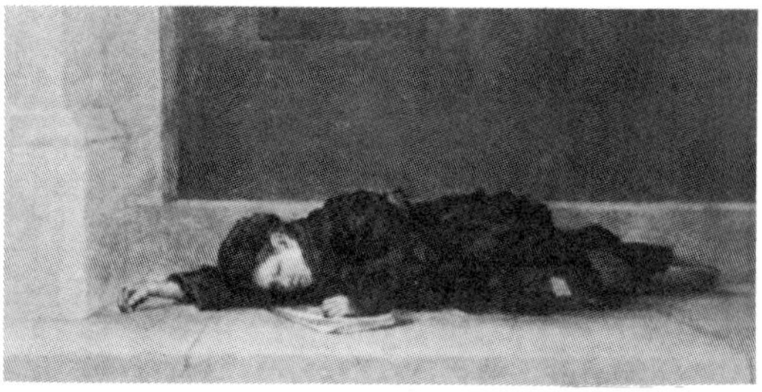

DAVID PATON – 'The Sleeping Urchin' – signed and dated 1885 – oil on canvas – 30 x 50in.
(Phillips) **$1,836 £1,200**

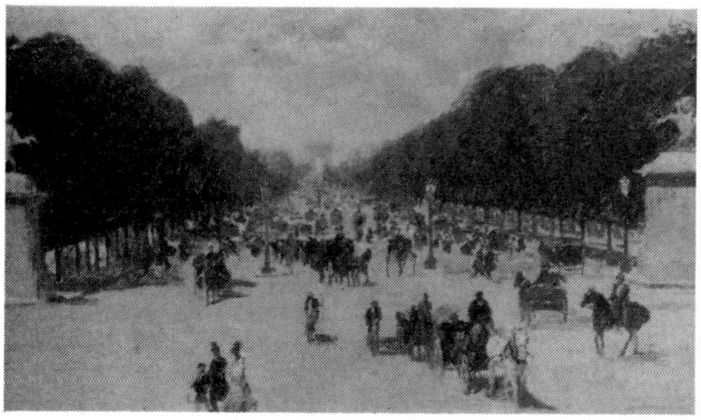

ELIE ANATOLE PAVIL – The Champs Elysees, Paris – signed – on panel – 8¾ x 10¾in.
(Christie's) **$2,173 £1,430**

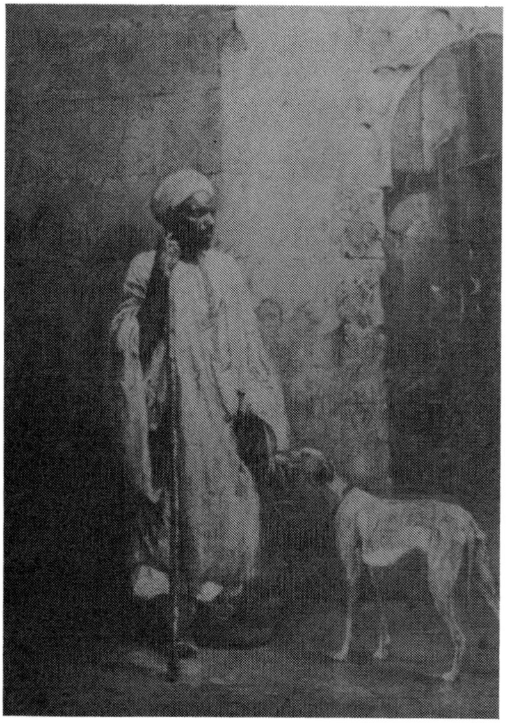

EUGENE PAVY – A Moorish Warrior And His Dog By A Street Corner – signed and dated 1882 – on panel – 25 x 18cm.
(Phillips) **$1,584 £1,100**

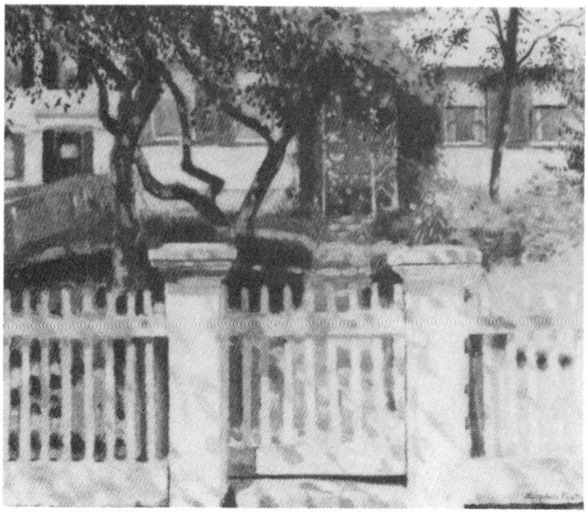

ELIZABETH VAUGHN OKIE PAXTON – Provincetown Doorway – signed – oil on academy board – 18 x 21¾in.
(Robt. W. Skinner Inc.) **$6,250 £4,340**

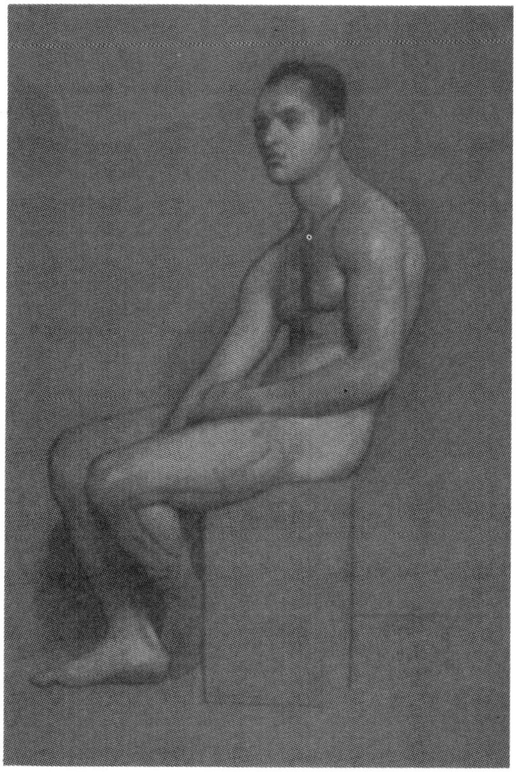

WILLIAM McGREGOR PAXTON – Study Of A Seated Male Nude – signed and dated 1936 – charcoal and white chalk on green paper; Study Of Hands And Foot – signed – charcoal, conte crayon and white chalk on brown paper; and Study Of Arms – signed and dated 1933 – charcoal and white chalk on grey paper – 15 x 10¾in.; 12 x 8½in. and 11¾ x 8¾in.
(Christie's) **$4,400 £2,741 Three**

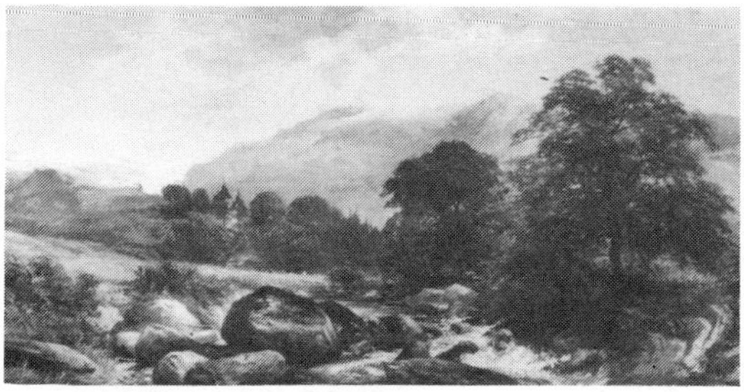

DAVID PAYNE – River Scene – signed – oil on canvas – 18 x 30in.
(Biddle & Webb) **$1,137** **£720**

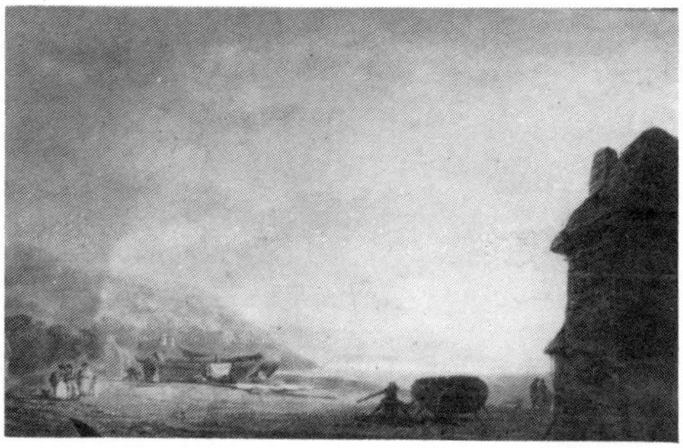

WILLIAM PAYNE – Beach Scene With Fishing Boats, Figures And Cottage – signed – watercolour – 11½ x 16in.
(Chancellors Hollingsworths) **$1,110** **£740**

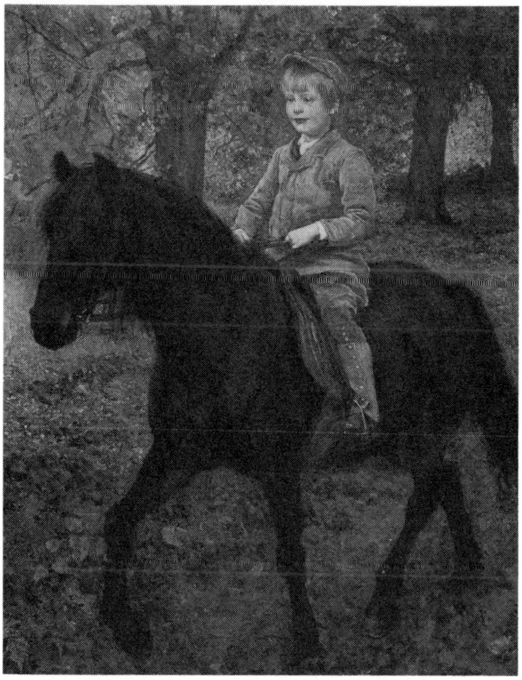

RALPH PEACOCK – The Morning Ride – signed – oil on canvas – 48 x 36in.
(Christie's) **$11,225** **£7,150**

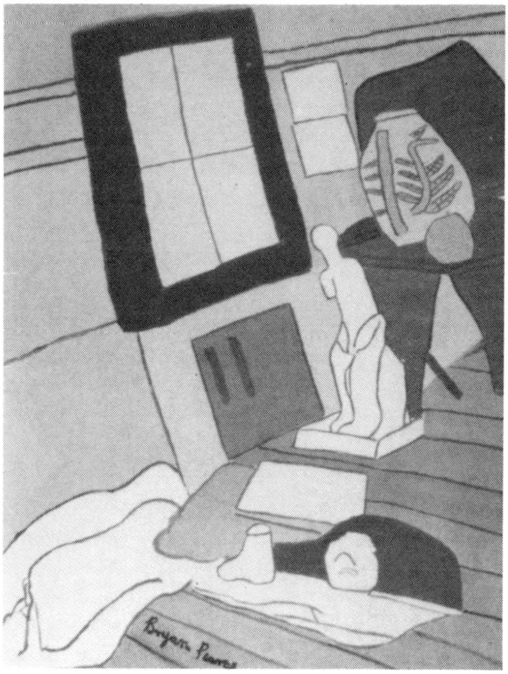

BRYAN PEARCE – 'Studio Window' – signed and dated 1955 on verso – oil on board – 60 x 50cm.
(W. H. Lane & Son) **$697** **£420**

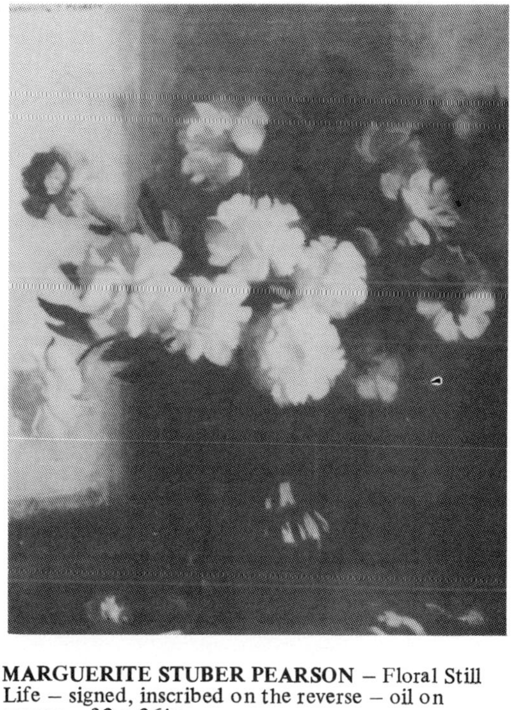

MARGUERITE STUBER PEARSON – Floral Still Life – signed, inscribed on the reverse – oil on canvas – 32 x 26in.
(Robt. W. Skinner Inc.) **$1,800** **£1,184**

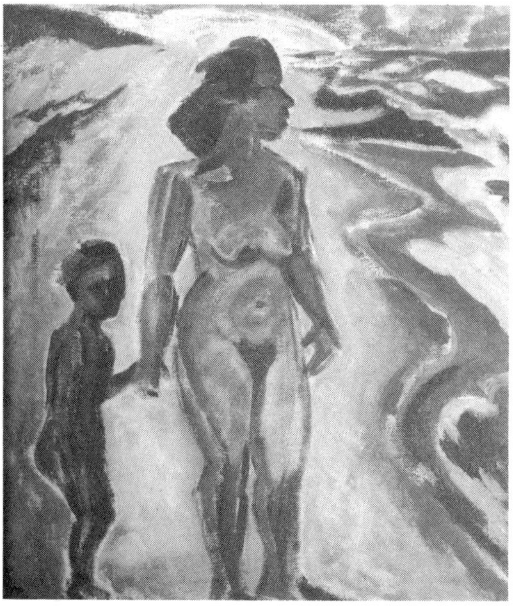

MAX PECHSTEIN – Vor dem Bad – signed with monogram and dated 1919, inscribed on the reverse – oil on canvas – 32 x 27¾in.
(Christie's) **$71,280** **£49,500**

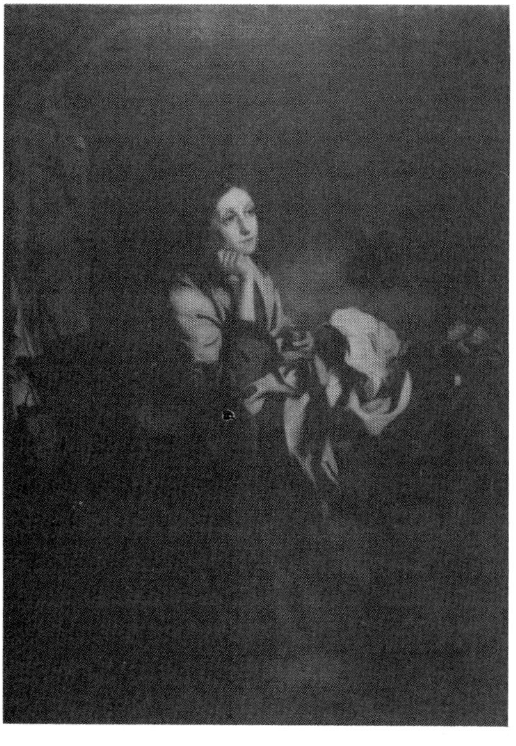

JOHN THOMAS PEELE – 'Song Of The Shirt' – oil on canvas – 30¼ x 23in.
(Robt. W. Skinner Inc.) **$800** **£555**

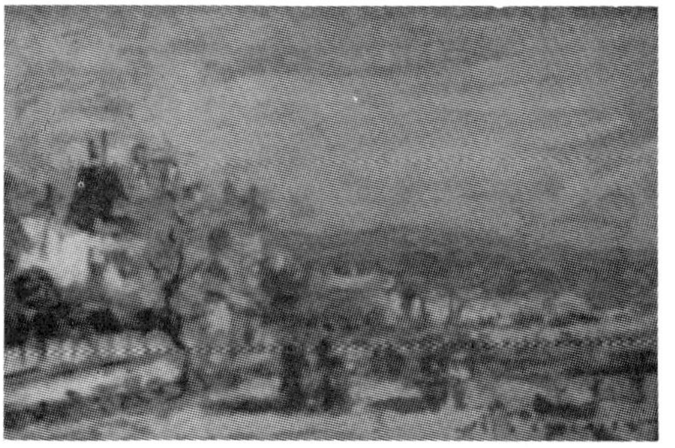

AUGUSTE PEGURIER – La Promenade des Anglais and Nice – inscribed on label verso – oil on panel – 6¼ x 9½in.
(Prudential Fine Art Auctioneers) **$597** **£360**

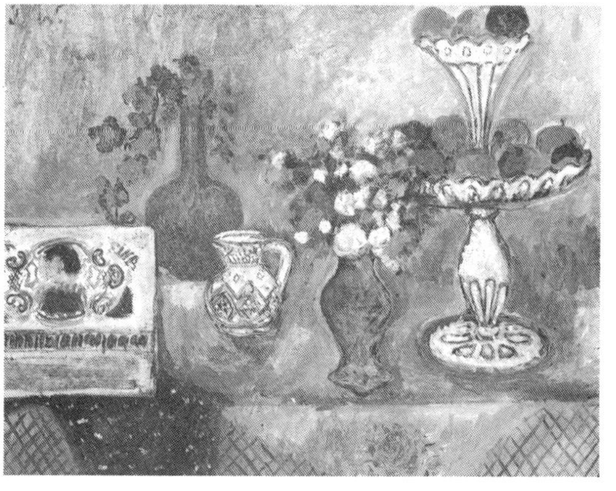

MAX PEIFFER-WATENPHUL – Stilleben auf einen Tisch – signed and dated '32 – oil on canvas – 25½ x 31½in.
(Christie's) **$14,256** **£9,900**

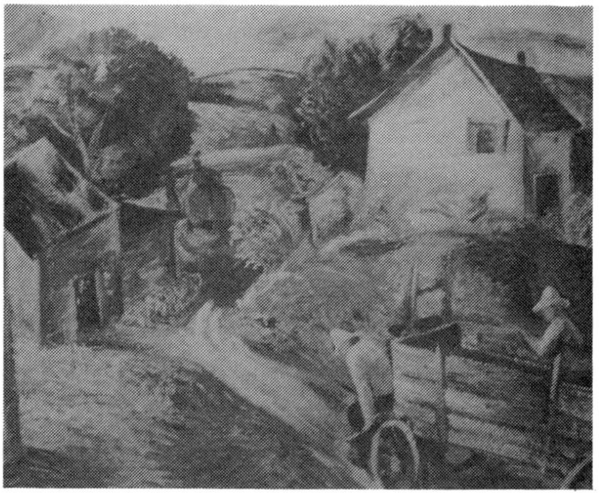

WALDO PEIRCE – The Farm – signed with conjoined initials – oil on canvas – 30 x 24¼in.
(Christie's) **$4,180** **£2,908**

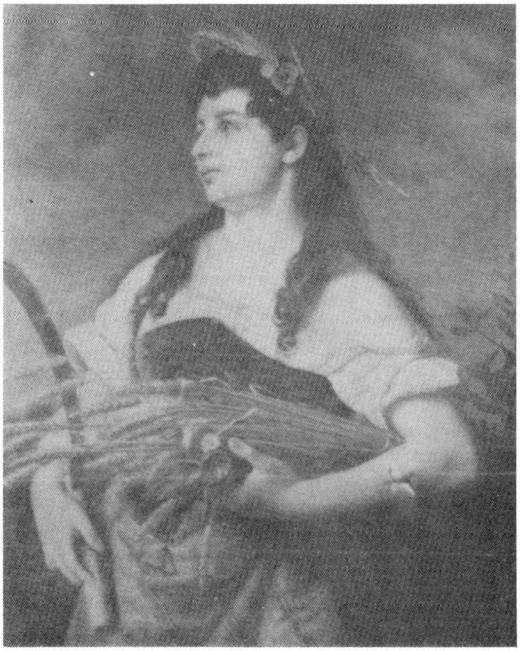

THOMAS KENT PELHAM, Attributed to – A Girl With Sickle And A Sheaf Of Barley – oil on canvas – 32 x 26½in.
(Christie's) **$720** **£500**

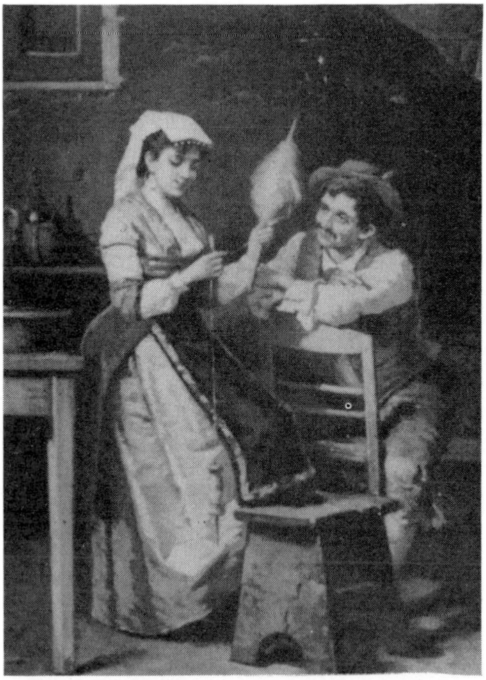

FRANCESCO PELUSO – A Courting Couple – signed – oil on canvas – 15½ x 10½in.
(Robt. W. Skinner Inc.) **$425** **£279**

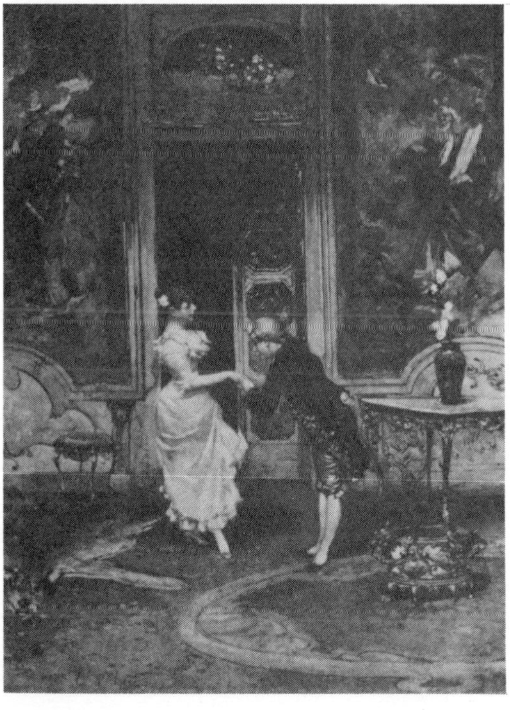

RICCARDO PELLEGRINI – Request For The Next Dance – signed and dated 1894 – on canvas – 65 x 50cm.
(Phillips) **$1,359** **£900**

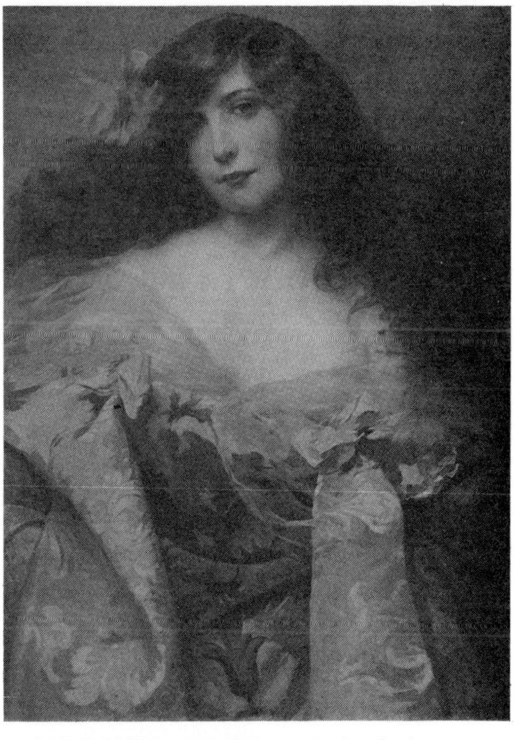

ALBERT JOSEPH PENOT – A Red-Haired Beauty – signed – 39½ x 25in.
(Christie's) **$4,928** **£3,080**

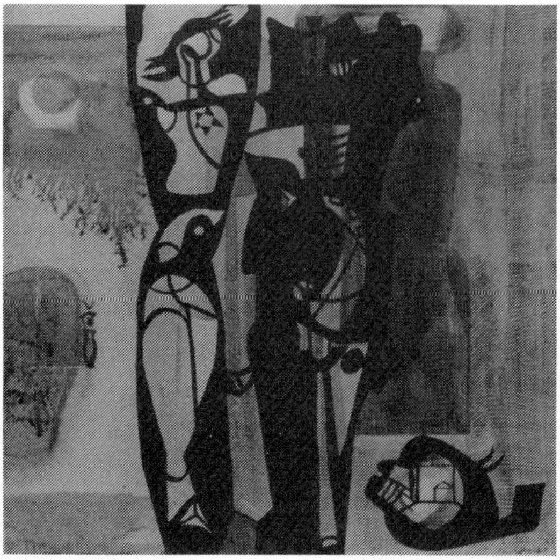

SIR ROLAND PENROSE – Composition – signed and dated '46 – brush, indian ink and watercolour over traces of pencil – 29.5 x 29.5cm.
(Phillips) **$1,494** **£900**

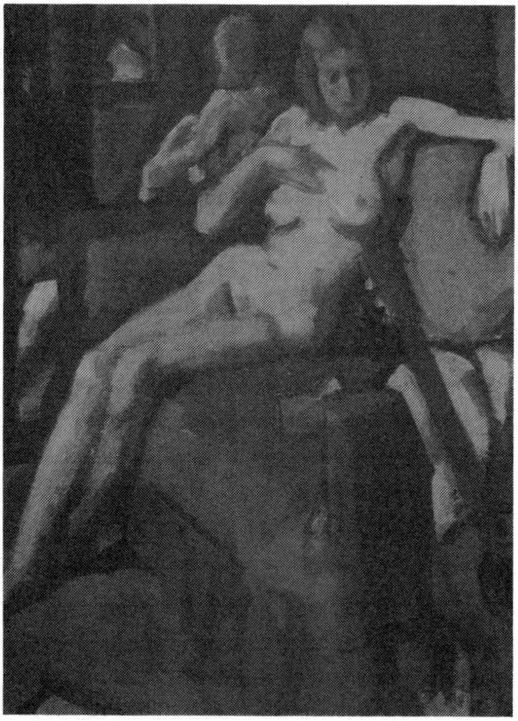

SAMUEL JOHN PEPLOE – Nude In An Interior With A Guitar – signed, and signed verso, circa 1930 – oil on canvas – 40 x 30in.
(Christie's) **$6,912** **£4,800**

PAUL EMMANUEL PERAIRE – L'Artiste au Bord d'une Riviere – signed – oil on canvas – 12¾ x 18in.
(Christie's) **$3,520** **£2,200**

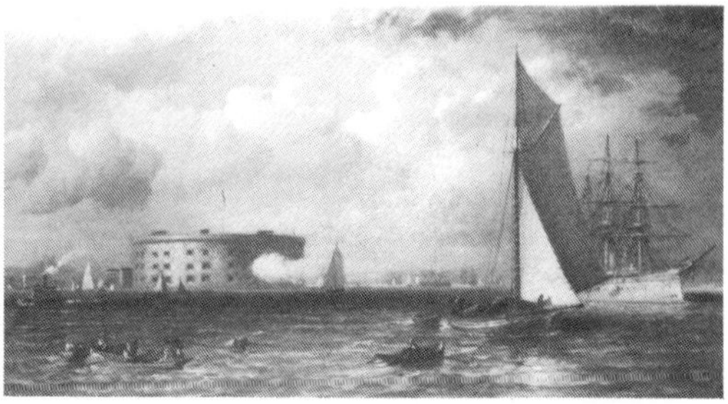

GRANVILLE PERKINS – Ships Near The Battery – signed with initials, and signed and dated on the reverse – oil on canvas – 12 x 22in.
(Christie's) **$11,000** **£7,733**

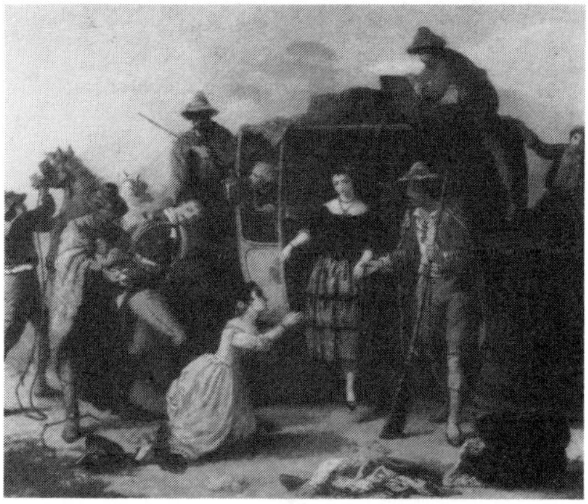

WILLIAM PERRY – The Brigands' Ransom – signed and indistinctly dated – 43 x 52½in.
(Christie's) **$2,019** **£1,320**

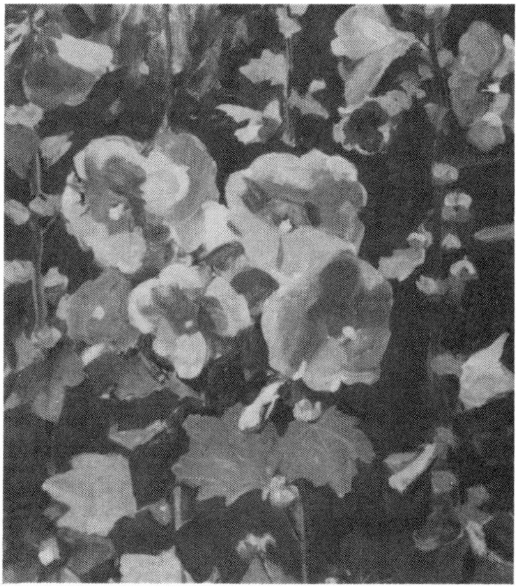

JANE PETERSON – Hollyhocks – signed on the reverse – oil on canvas – 30 x 25in.
(Christie's) **$1,870** **£1,300**

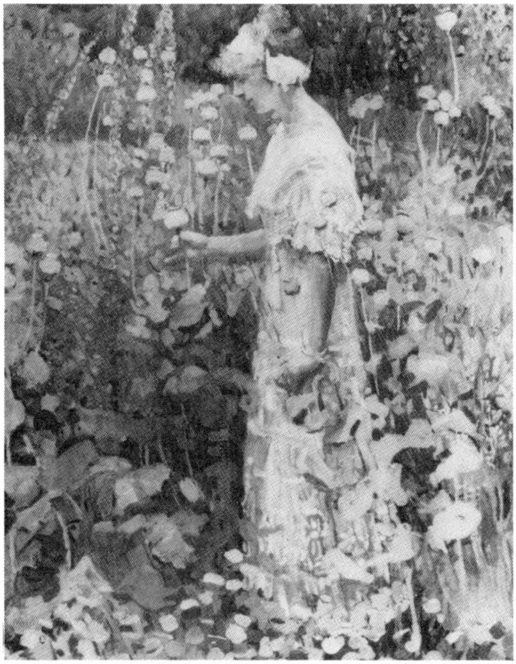

JANE PETERSON – Hollyhock Garden – signed – oil on canvas – 40 x 30in.
(Robt. W. Skinner Inc.) **$33,000** **£22,916**

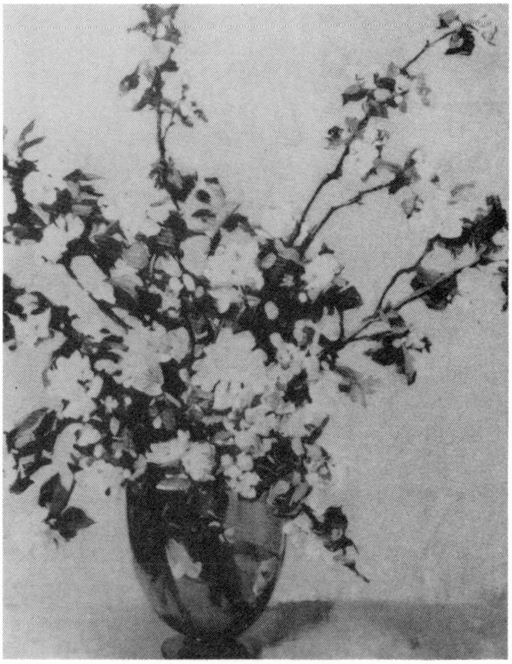

JANE PETERSON – Still Life With Dogwood – signed – oil on canvas – 40 x 30in.
(Robt. W. Skinner Inc.) **$2,200** **£1,527**

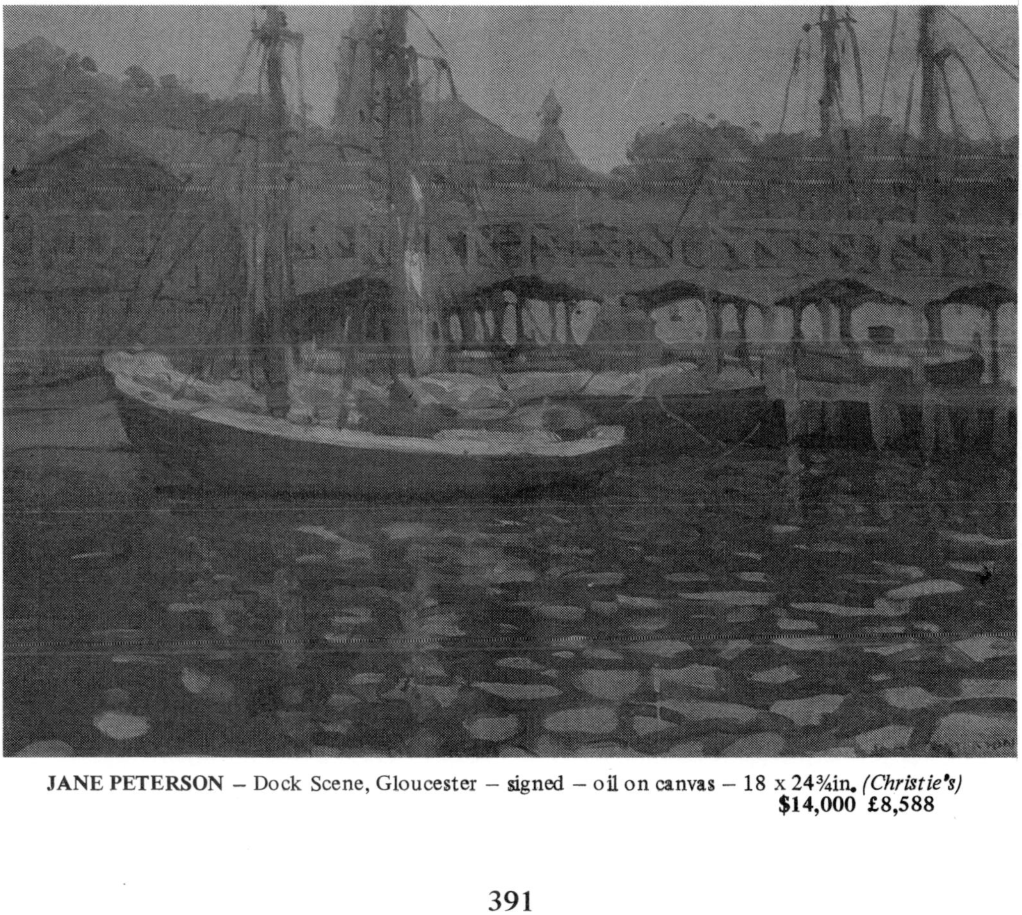

JANE PETERSON – Dock Scene, Gloucester – signed – oil on canvas – 18 x 24¾in. *(Christie's)*
$14,000 **£8,588**

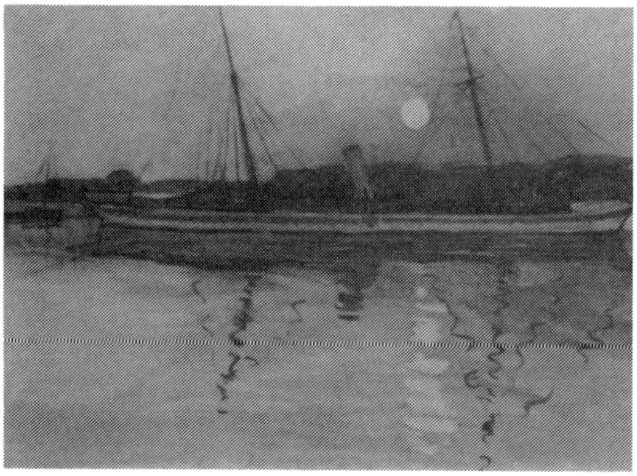

JANE PETERSON – Moonlit Yacht – signed – gouache on paper – 17½ x 23½in.
(Robt. W. Skinner Inc.) **$1,600** **£1,052**

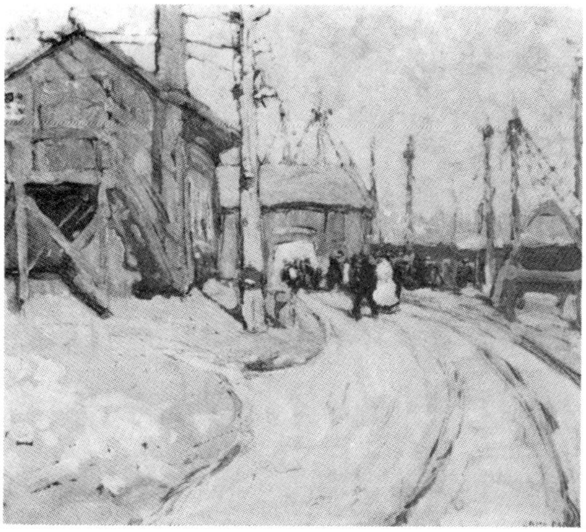

JANE PETERSON – Dock Scene – signed – oil on canvas – 15 x 18¼in.
(Robt. W. Skinner Inc.) **$10,000** **£6,944**

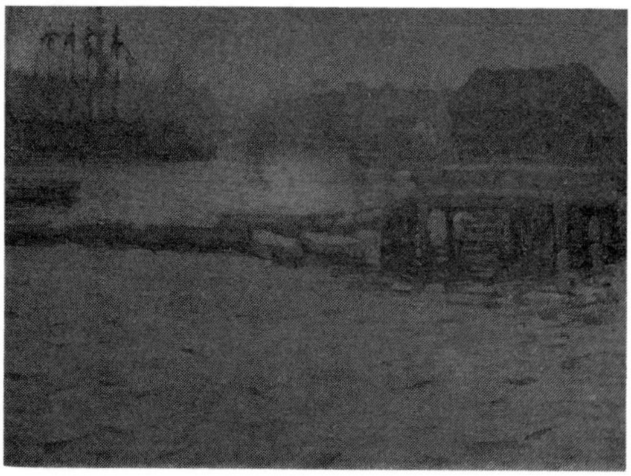

JANE PETERSON – 'Rocky Neck, Gloucester Harbour – Evening Light' – signed indistinctly – oil on canvas – 18¼ x 24¼in.
(Robt. W. Skinner Inc.) **$15,000** **£9,202**

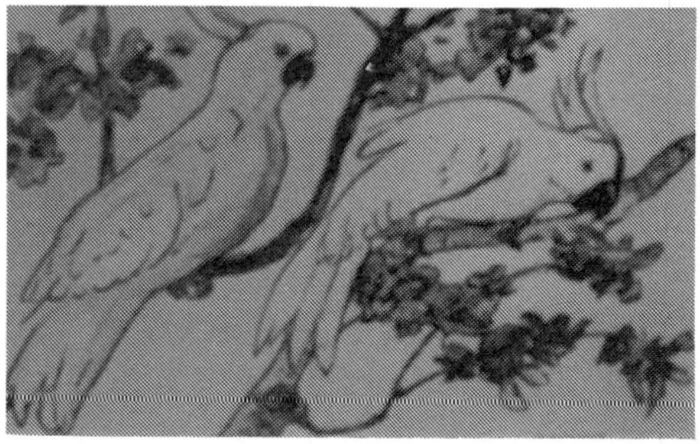

JANE PETERSON – A Pair Of White Cockatoos On A Branch – signed – gouache on paper – 13 x 20½in.
(Robt. W. Skinner Inc.) **$500** **£306**

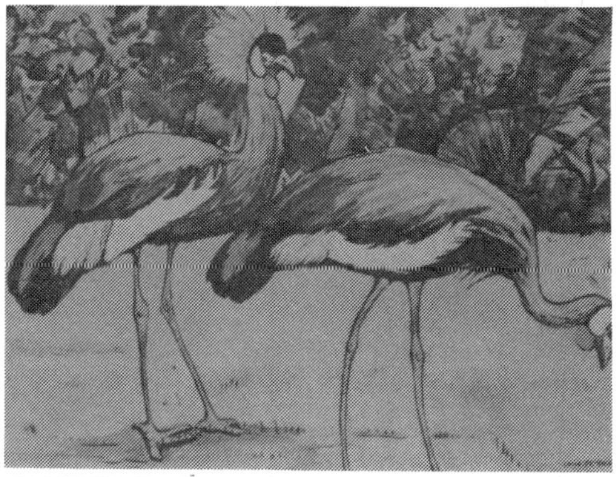

JANE PETERSON – Cranes In A Tropical Setting – signed – gouache on board – 20 x 26¾in.
(Robt. W. Skinner Inc.) **$800** **£490**

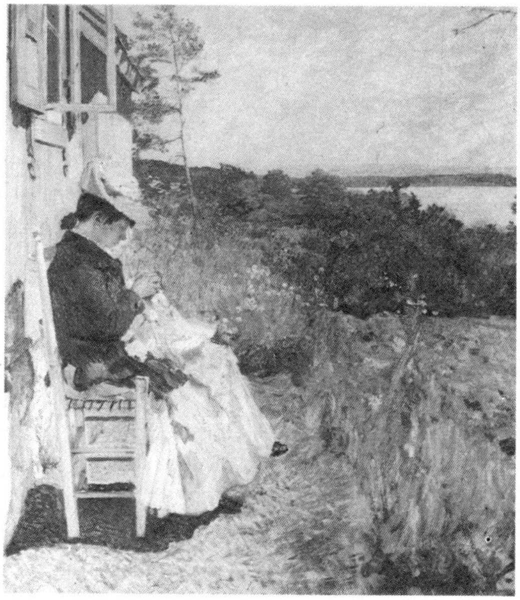

EILIF PETERSSEN – A Young Woman Sewing Seated Outside A House, A Bay Beyond – signed and dated '91 – 38 x 29½in.
(Christie's) **$126,720** **£88,000**

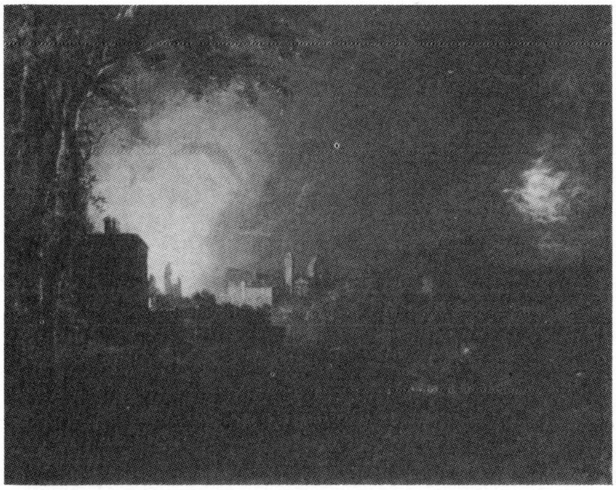

SEBASTIAN PETHER, Attributed to – Figures By A Burning House, Outside A Town – 21 x 25½in.
(Christie's) **$1,318** **£935**

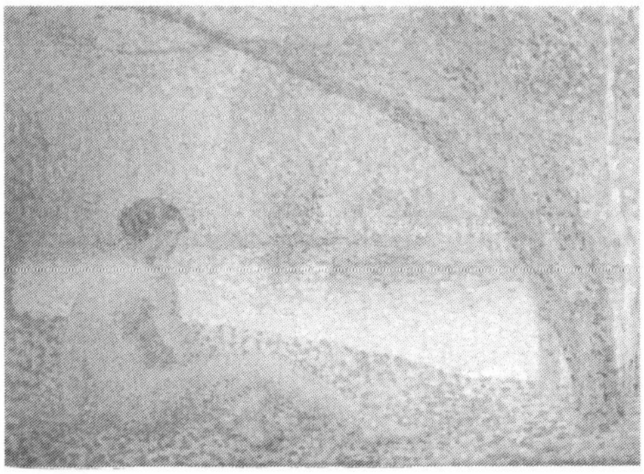

HIPPOLYTE PETITJEAN – Femme au Bord de l'Eau – signed – oil on canvas – 17¼ x 19¼in.
(Christie's) **$56,947** **£34,100**

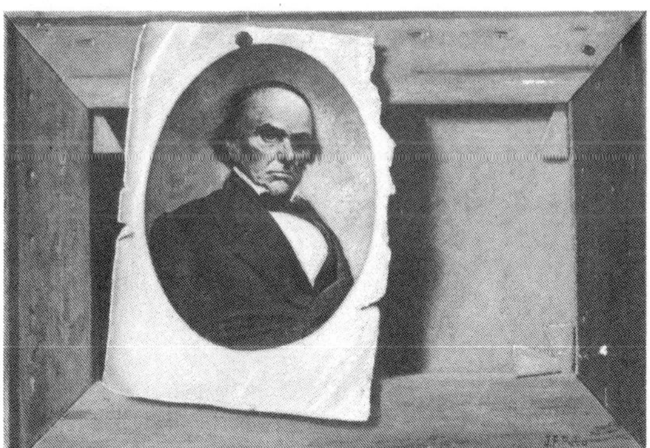

JOHN FREDERICK PETO – The Great Orator – signed and dated 1904, and signed and dated on the reverse – oil on canvas – 10 x 14in.
(Christie's) **$41,800** **£29,385**

GEORGE PETTITT – 'Wytheburn', Mountainous Landscape With Two Figures In Foreground, Distant Drover And Cattle – oil – 15 x 20in.
(Capes, Dunn & Co.) **$1,059** **£650**

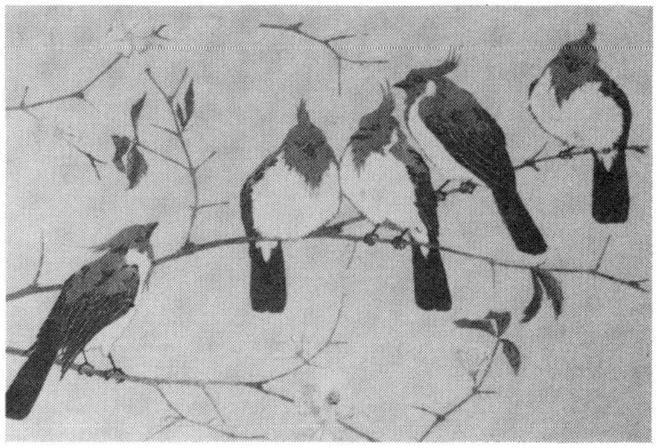

M. PHILIPP – Weaver Birds; and Carminals – signed – woodcuts, printed in colours – 11 x 15in.
(Christie's) **$135** **£95 Pair**

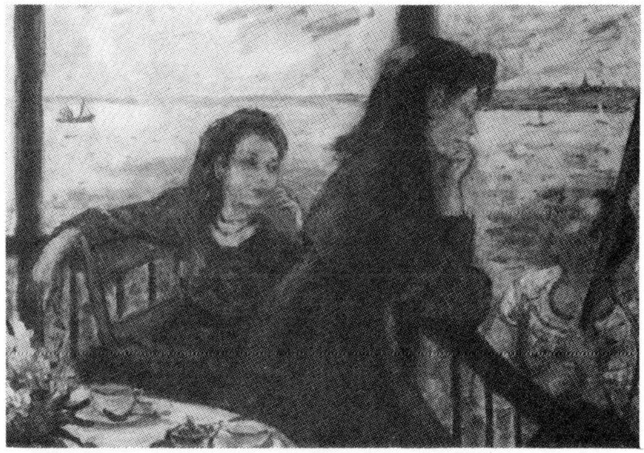

ROBERT PHILIPP – Tea At The Harbour – signed, signed and dated 1967 on the reverse – 30¼ x 25in.
(Christie's) **$6,050** **£4,208**

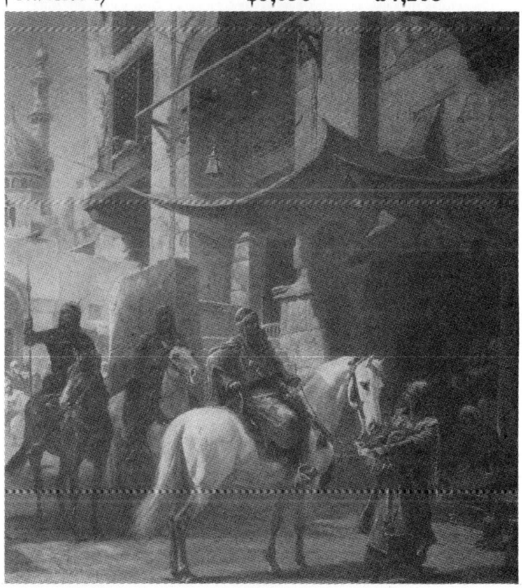

PAUL DOMINIQUE PHILIPPOTEAUX – Arab Warriors In A Street – signed – 24¼ x 20½in.
(Christie's) **$14,960** **£9,350**

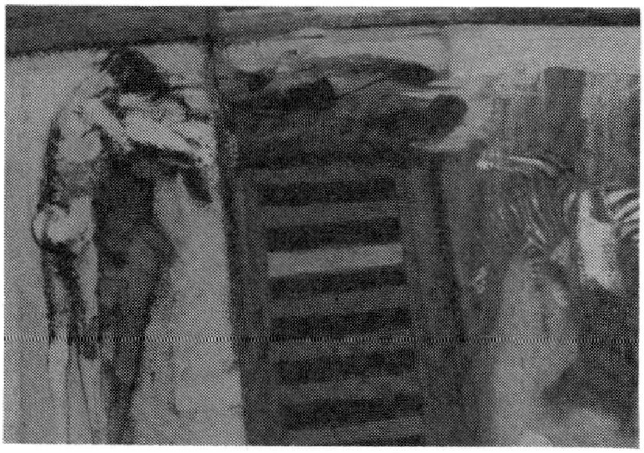

SIR ROBIN PHILIPSON – The Meeting – signed on the reverse – oil on canvas – 51 x 61cm.
(Phillips) **$2,656** **£1,600**

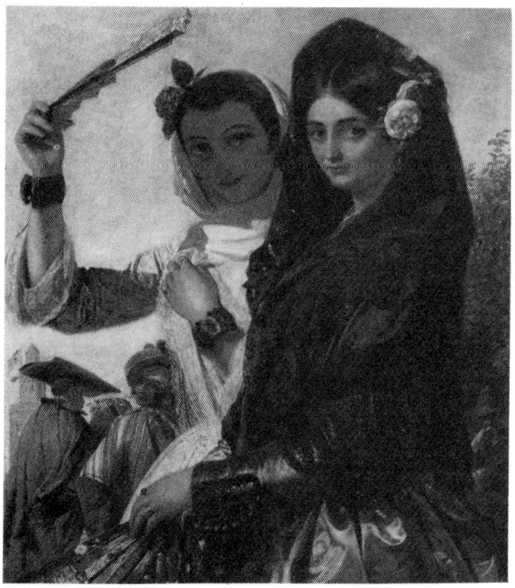

JOHN PHILLIP – 'Daughters Of The Alambra' – signed – oil on canvas – 24 x 17¾in.
(Phillips) **$4,284** **£2,800**

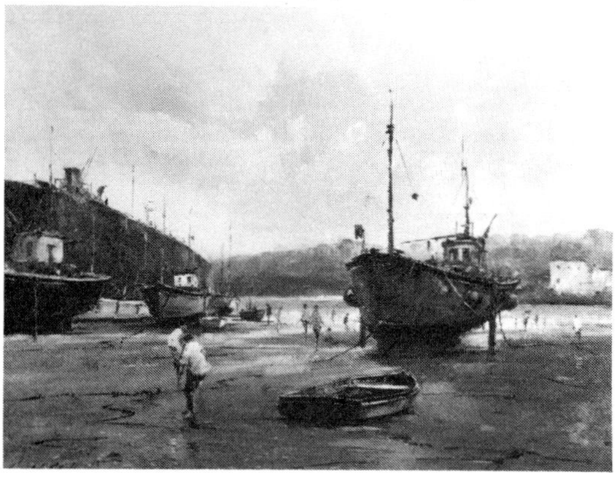

GERALD PHILLIPS – 'Low Tide, The Harbour, St. Ives, Cornwall' – signed – 20 x 24in.
(Biddle & Webb) **$304** **£200**

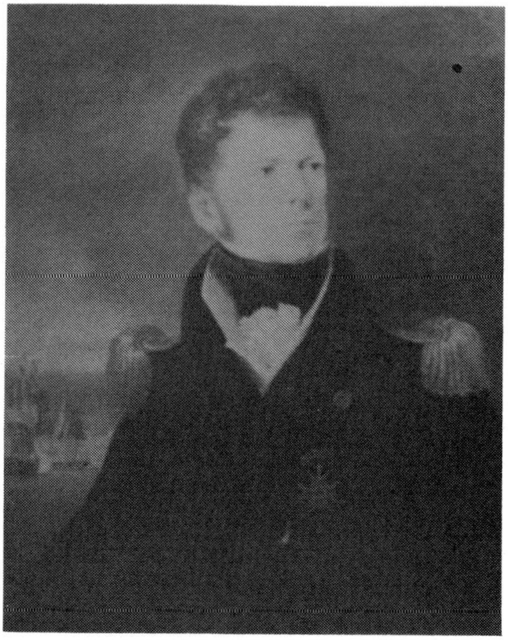

THOMAS PHILLIPS, Circle of – A Portrait Of Capt. Peter Rainier, C.B., A.D.C., Commander Of H.M.S. Caroline And H.M.S. Britannia – oil on canvas – 30 x 25in.
(Phillips) **$1,328** **£800**

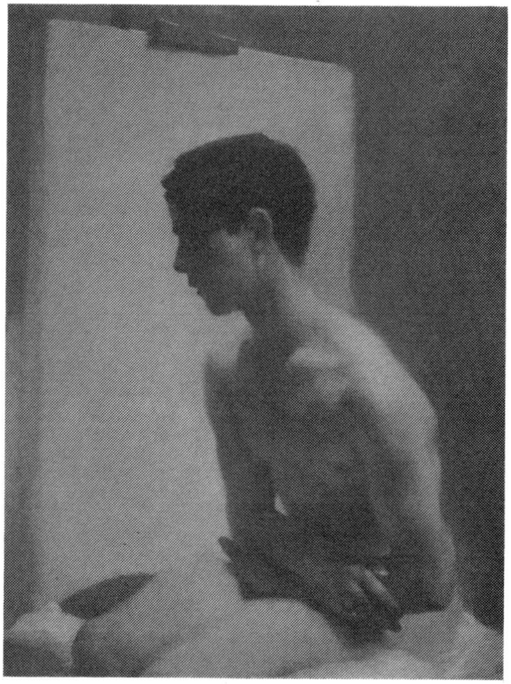

GLYN PHILPOT – The Little Model – signed with initials – oil on canvas – 91 x 71cm.
(Phillips) **$35,500** **£25,000**

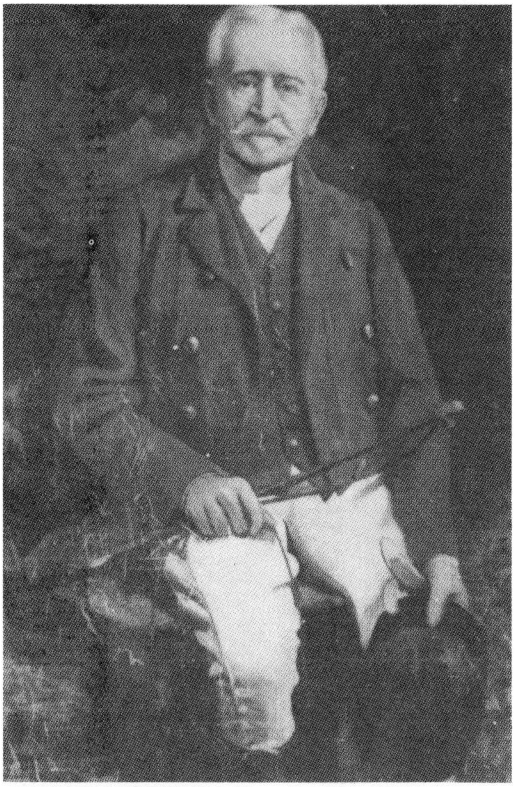

GEORGE PHOENIX – Portrait Of An Elderly Huntsman, Seated Three-Quarter Length, Wearing A Scarlet Frock Coat And Holding A Hat And Crop – signed – oil on canvas – 50 x 30in.
(Christie's) **$1,584** **£1,100**

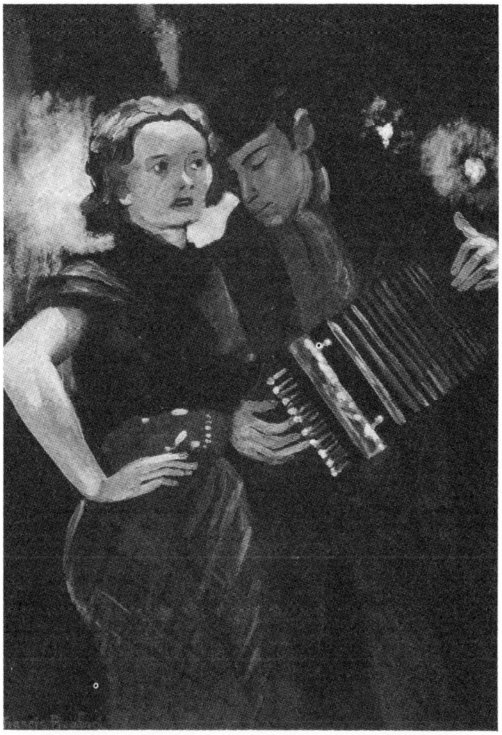

FRANCIS PICABIA – L'Accordeoniste – signed – oil on canvas – 41¾ x 29¾in.
(Christie's) **$17,424** **£12,100**

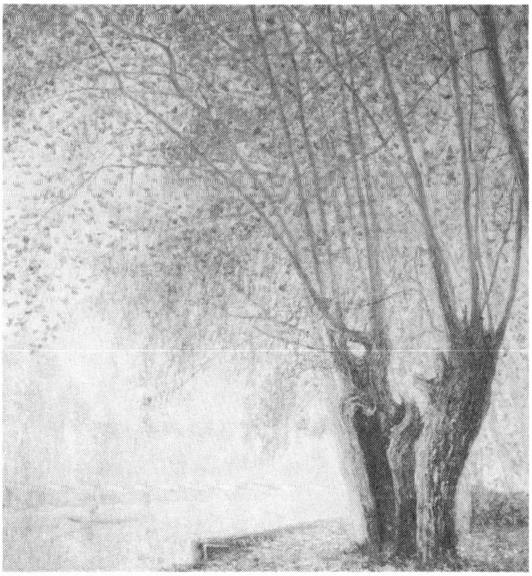

FRANCIS PICABIA – Les Saules, Effet de Soleil d'Automne – signed and dated 1904 – oil on canvas – 36¼ x 28¾in.
(Christie's) **$101,035** **£60,500**

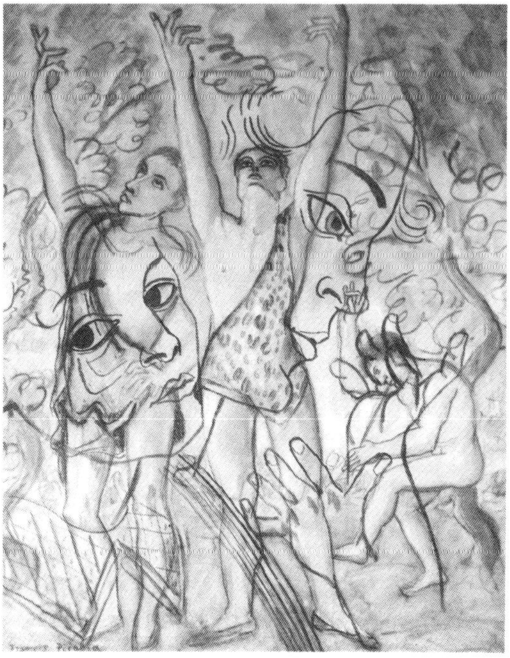

FRANCIS PICABIA – Janiria – signed – oil on canvas – 36¼ x 28¾in.
(Christie's) **$50,688** **£35,200**

PICASSO

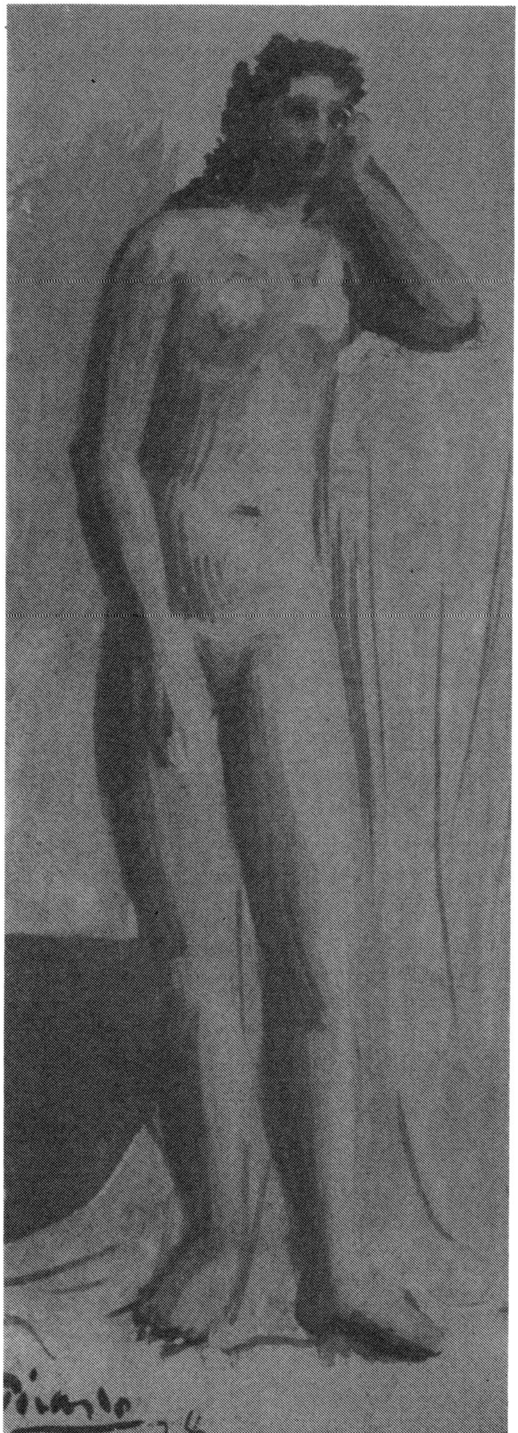

PABLO PICASSO – Femme nue accoudee – signed and dated '24 – oil on canvas – 8¾ x 4in.
(Christie's) **$118,800 £82,500**

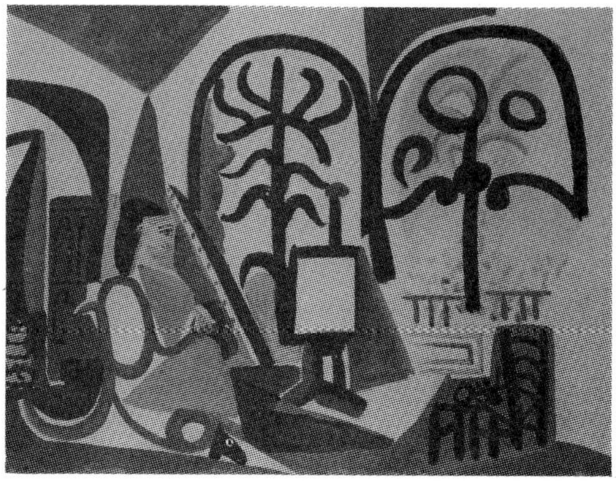

PABLO PICASSO – Femme dans l'Atelier – signed – oil on canvas – 35 x 45½in.
(Christie's) **$348,480 £242,000**

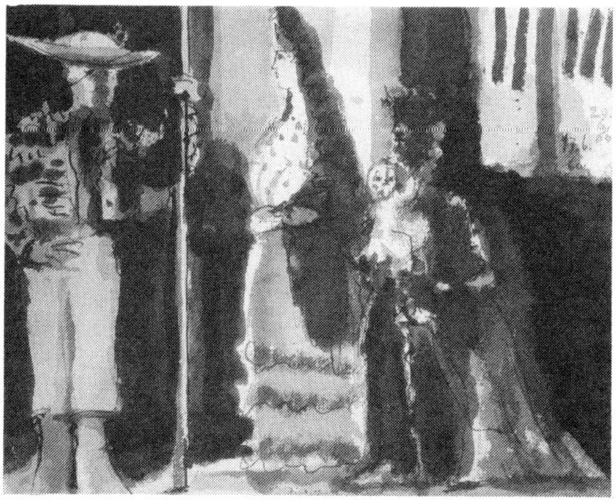

PABLO PICASSO – Picador et Personnages – signed and dated '60 – pen and black ink, black and grey wash on paper – 19½ x 25½in.
(Christie's) **$118,800 £82,500**

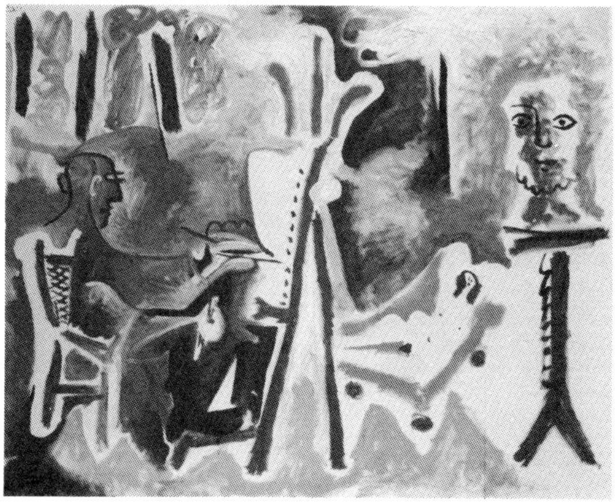

PABLO PICASSO – Le Peintre et son Modele – signed, dated on the reverse '63 – oil on canvas – 51¼ x 63¾in.
(Christie's) **$633,600 £440,000**

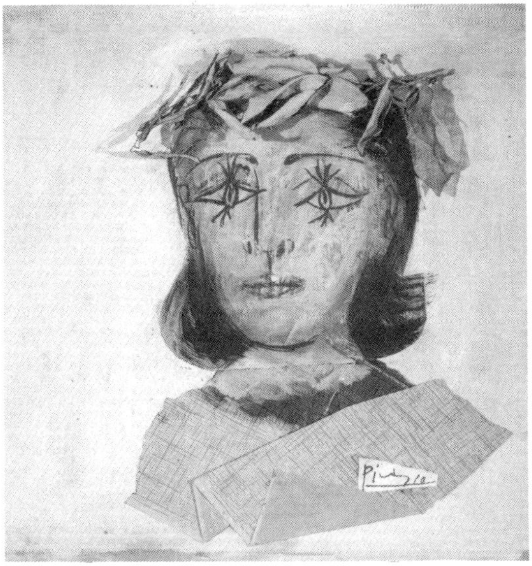

PABLO PICASSO – Tete de Dora Maar – signed – paper and leaf collage and gouache on corrugated paper – 15¾ x 15¼in.
(Christie's) **$221,760 £154,000**

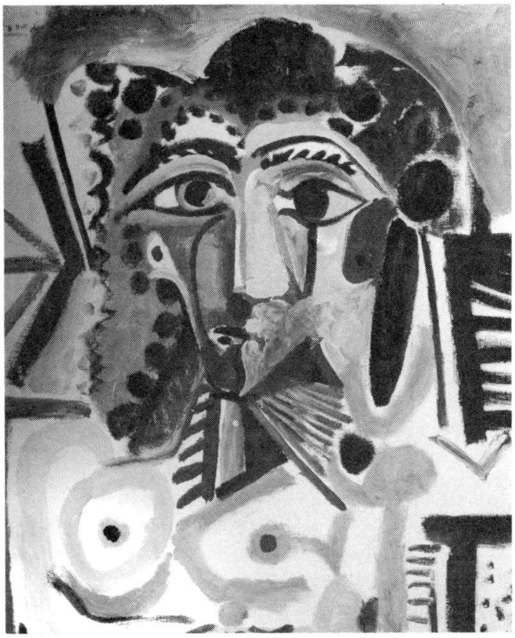

PABLO PICASSO – Buste de Femme – signed, and signed and dated on the reverse '65 – oil on canvas – 39¼ x 31¾in.
(Christie's) **$514,360 £308,000**

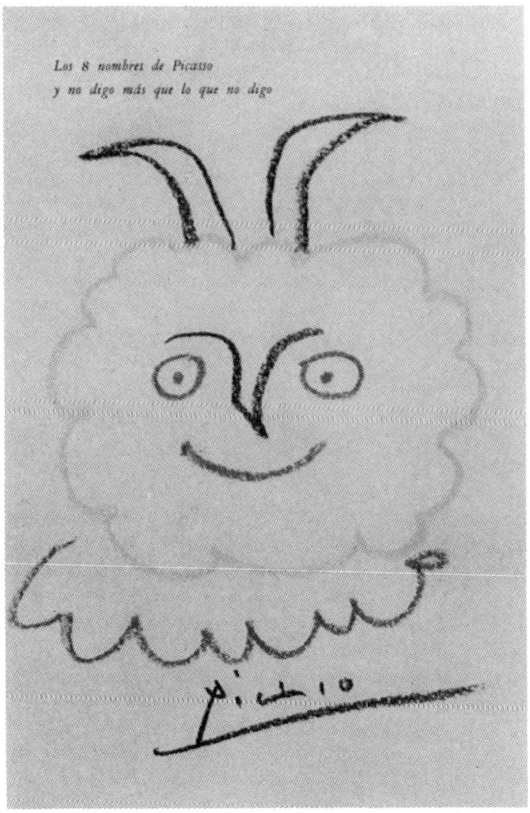

PABLO PICASSO – Tete de Femme souriant – signed – blue, red and yellow wax crayons on paper – 9½ x 6¾in.
(Christie's) **$8,236 £5,720**

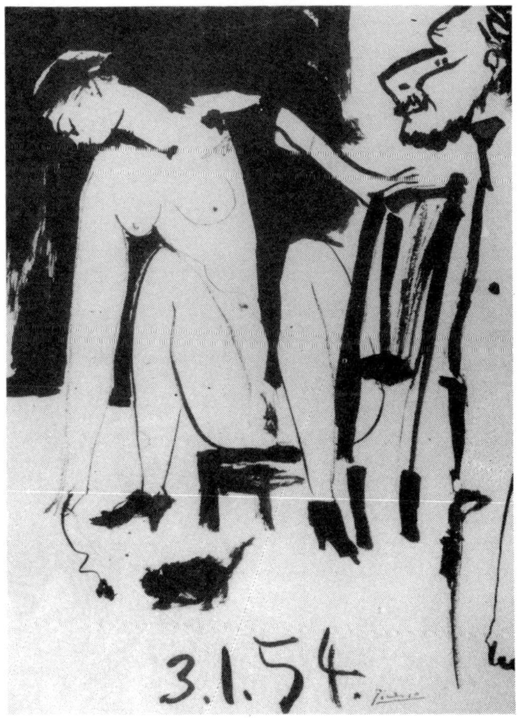

PABLO PICASSO – Femme Jouant avec un Chat – signed and dated '54 – brush and black ink on paper – 12¼ x 9¼in.
(Christie's) **$29,920 £18,700**

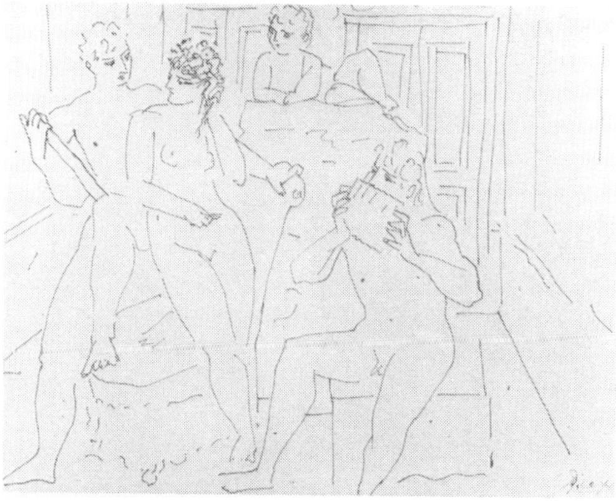

PABLO PICASSO – Jeune Homme au Miroir, Nu, Joueur de Flute de Pan, et Enfant – signed – pen and ink on paper – 9¾ x 12½in.
(Christie's) **$66,528 £46,200**

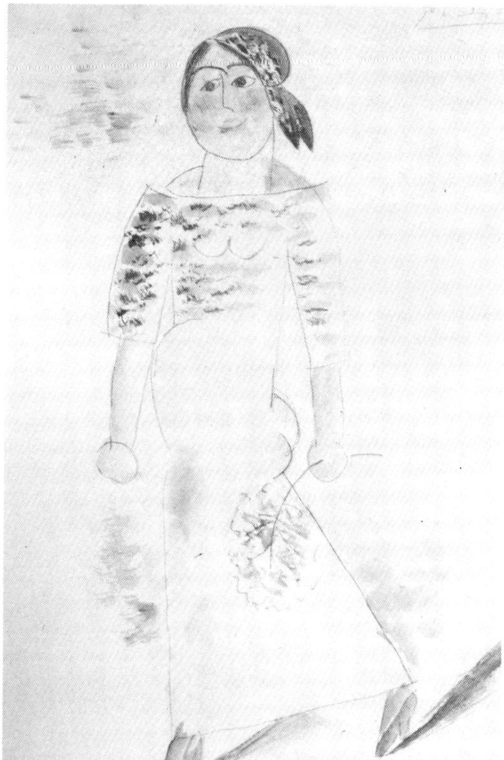

PABLO PICASSO – Catalane – signed – watercolour and pencil on paper – 13¾ x 9¾in.
(Christie's) **$79,200 £55,000**

PABLO PICASSO – Le Dejeuner – signed and dated '62 – coloured crayons and pencil on paper – 8½ x 12¾in.
(Christie's) **$47,520 £33,000**

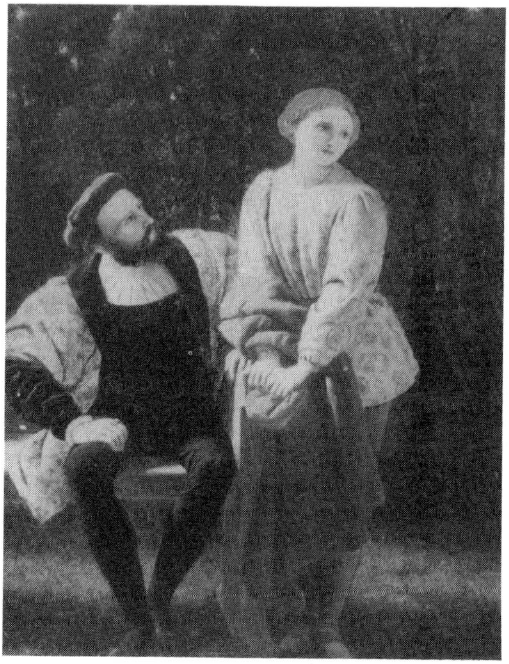

FREDERICK RICHARD PICKERSGILL – The Duke Orsino And Viola, Twelfth Night Act II, Scene 4 – signed with initials – on panel – 18 x 14in.
(Christie's) **$2,019 £1,320**

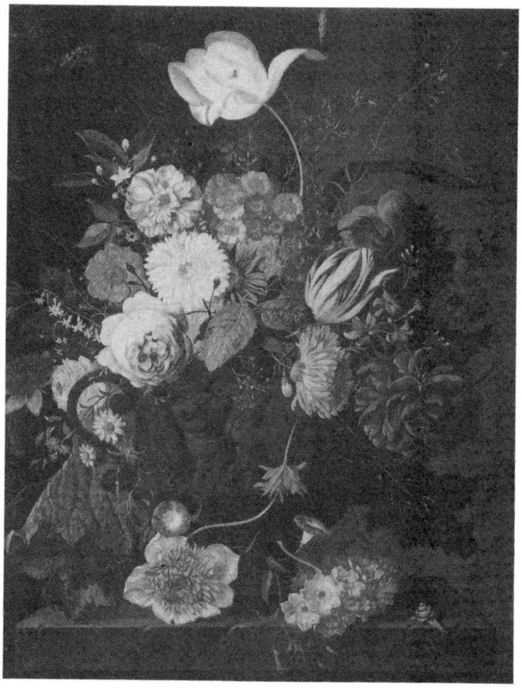

FRANZ XAVIER PIELER – Still Life Of Flowers In A Classical Vase On A Stone Ledge – signed indistinctly – oil on panel – 53 x 42cm.
(Phillips) **$12,960 £9,000**

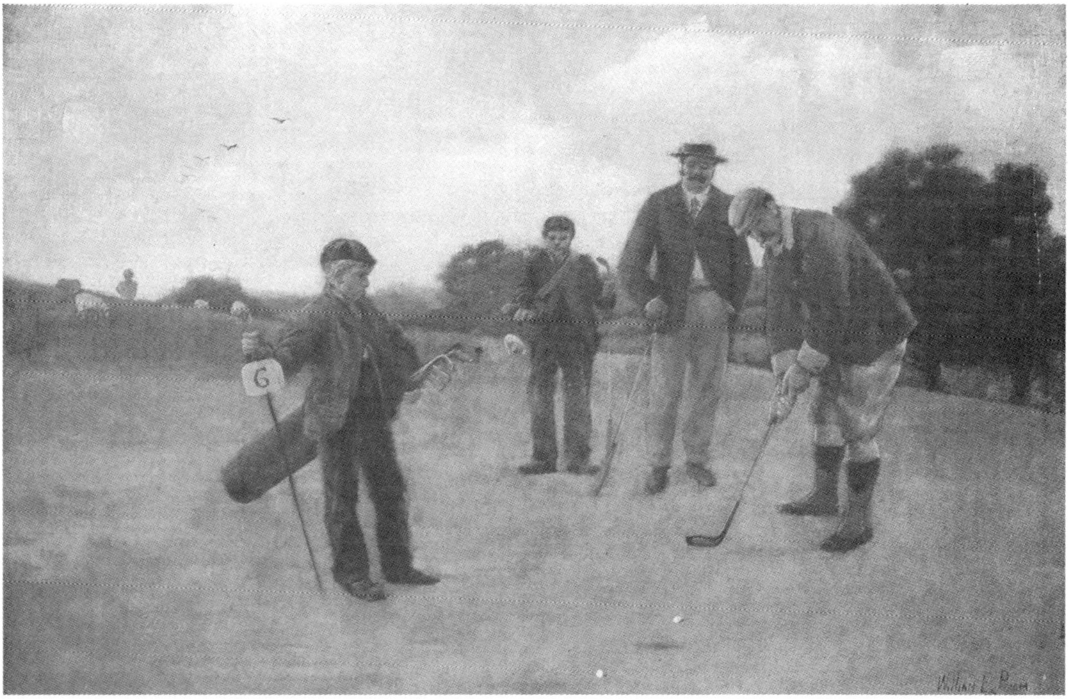

WILLIAM E. PIMM – Putting On The Sixth Green – signed – oil on canvas – 15¾ x 23½in.
(Christie's) **$25,168 £17,600**

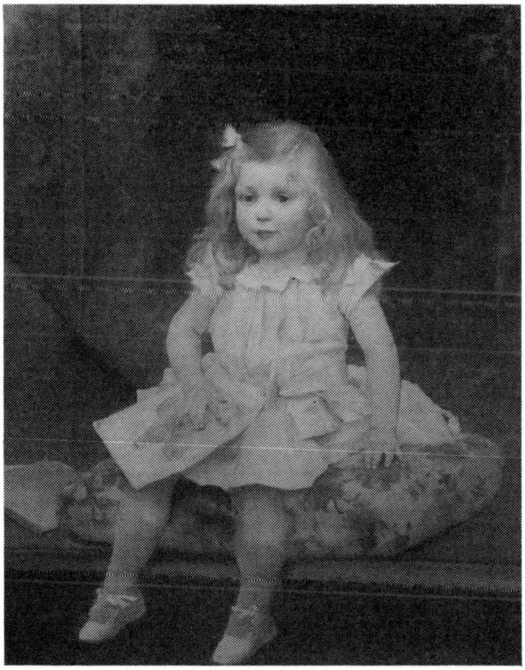

EMILE AUGUSTE PINCHART – A Portrait Of A Little Girl Seated On A Cushion – signed – oil on canvas – 92 x 73cm.
(Phillips) **$2,736 £1,900**

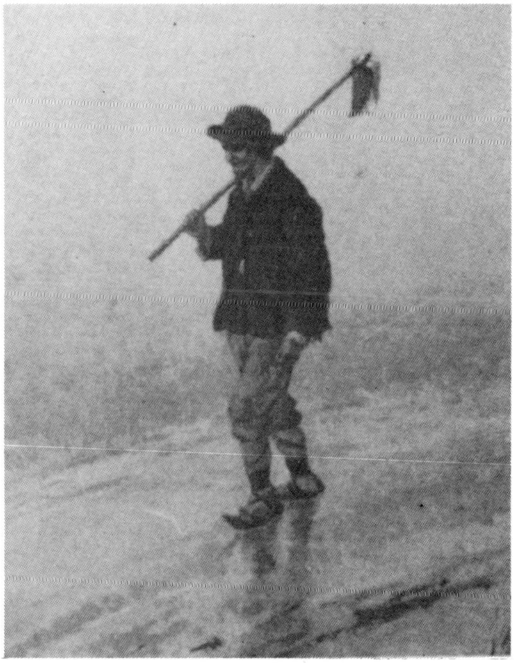

E. PINTO – The Labourer; and The Wood Carrier – signed, inscribed on the reverse – oil on panel – 10½ x 5½in.
(Christie's) **$168 £110 Pair**

PISSARRO

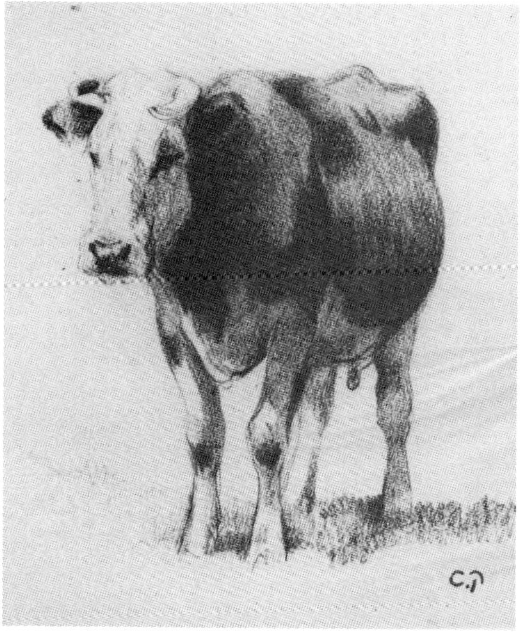

CAMILLE PISSARRO – Le Taureau – soft pencil on paper – 9 x 8in.
(Christie's) **$5,632** **£3,520**

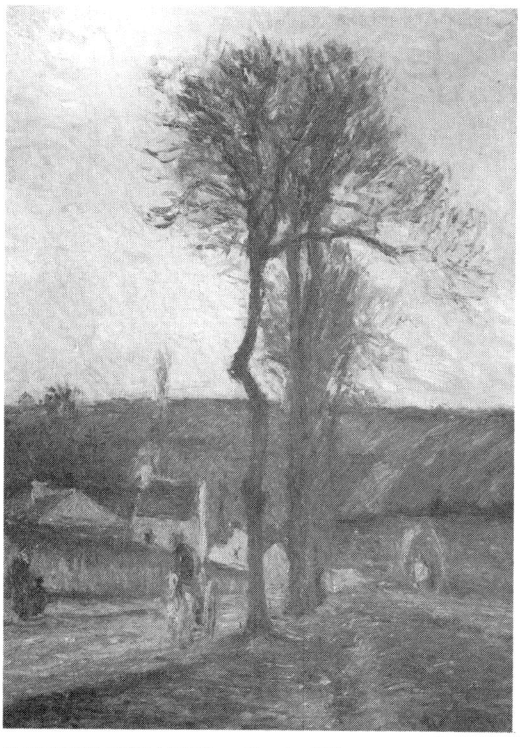

CAMILLE PISSARRO – Route d'Ennery a l'Hermitage, Environs de Pontoise – signed and dated '78 – oil on canvas – 18 x 15in.
(Christie's) **$220,440** **£132,000**

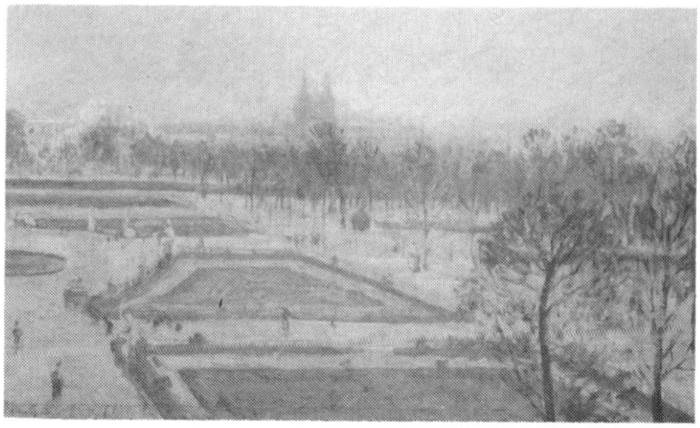

CAMILLE PISSARRO – Le Bassin des Tuileries, Brume – signed and dated 1900 – oil on canvas – 21¼ x 25¾in.
(Christie's) **$514,360** **£308,000**

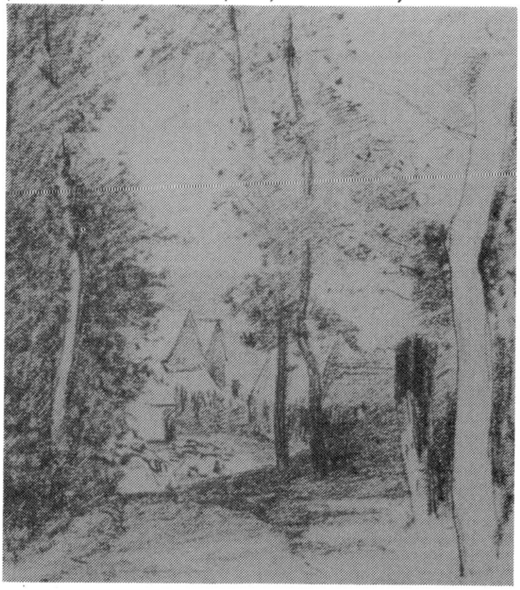

CAMILLE PISSARRO – Maisons en Foret – signed – soft pencil on brown paper – 12 x 9¼in.
(Christie's) **$11,440** **£7,150**

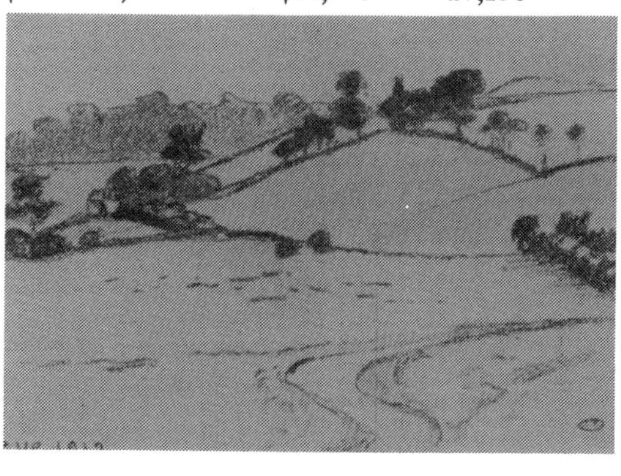

LUCIEN PISSARRO – Landscape Near Rye – signed with monogram, inscribed and dated 1912 – coloured chalks – 11 x 15cm.
(Phillips) **$1,494** **£900**

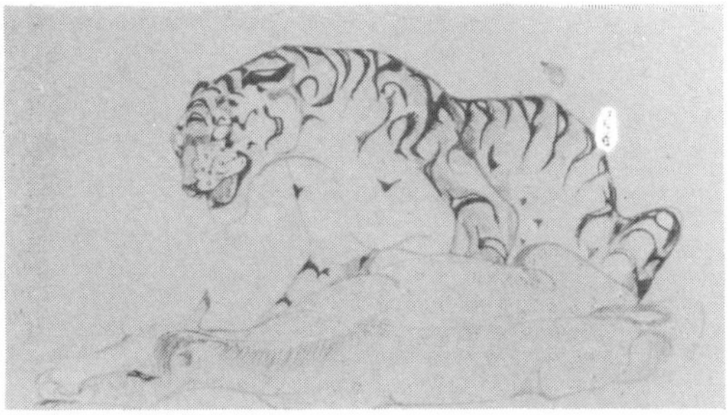

OROVIDA PISSARRO – A Tiger And His Prey – signed and dated 1930 – watercolour on buff paper – 16 x 23.5cm.
(Phillips) **$1,494** **£900**

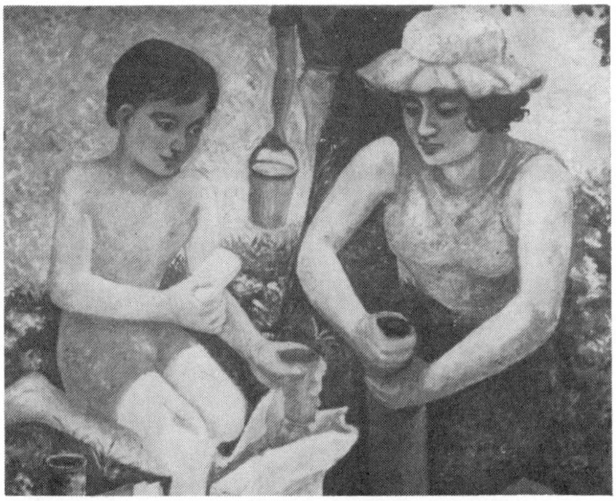

OROVIDA PISSARRO – The Picnic – signed – oil on board – 27 x 29¾in.
(Christie's) **$2,072** **£1,320**

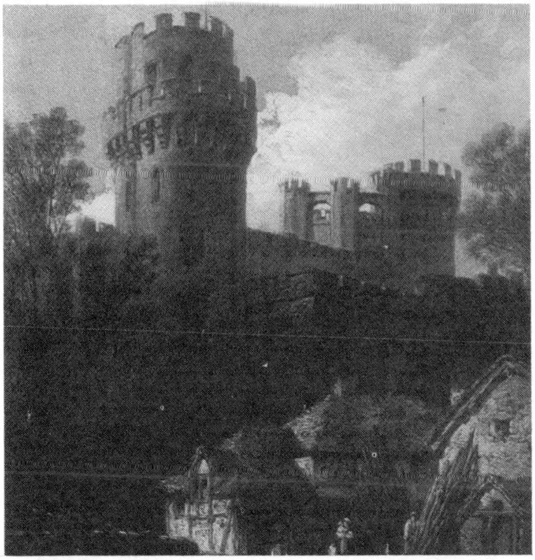

WILLIAM PITT – Caesar's Tower, Warwick Castle; and The Eagle Tower, Carnarvon Castle – signed with monogram and dated 1872, signed and dated on the reverse – 13½ x 11½in.
(Christie's) **$972** **£648 Two**

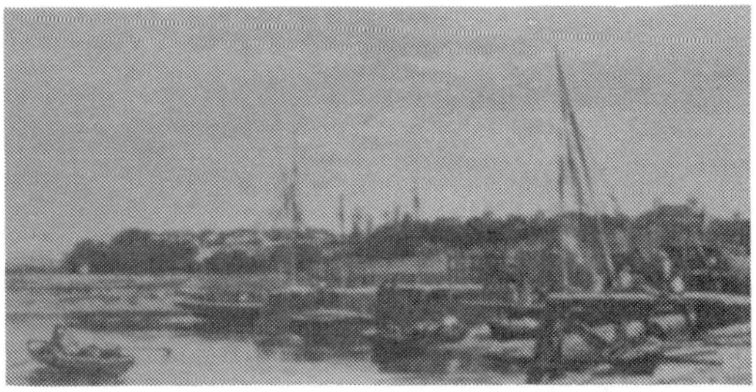

WILLIAM PITT – Rouedge On The Colne, Essex – signed, inscribed and dated 1866 on reverse – on canvas – 9¼ x 15in.
(Phillips) **$1,127** **£700**

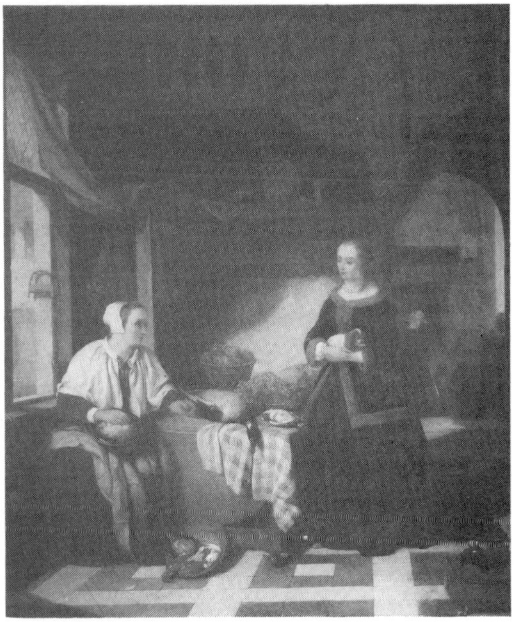

JEAN PLATTEELS – In The Kitchen – signed and dated 1860 – on panel – 29 x 25in.
(Christie's) **$5,350** **£3,520**

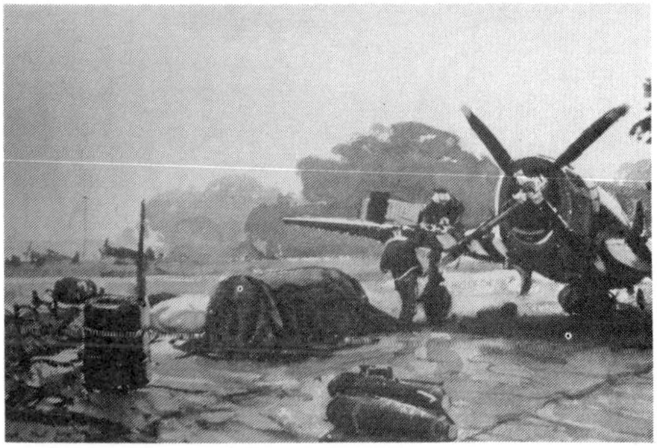

OGDEN MINTON PLEISSNER – Preparing The Mission – signed and dated 1944 – watercolour on paper – 11¾ x 17¾in.
(Christie's) **$4,400** **£3,061**

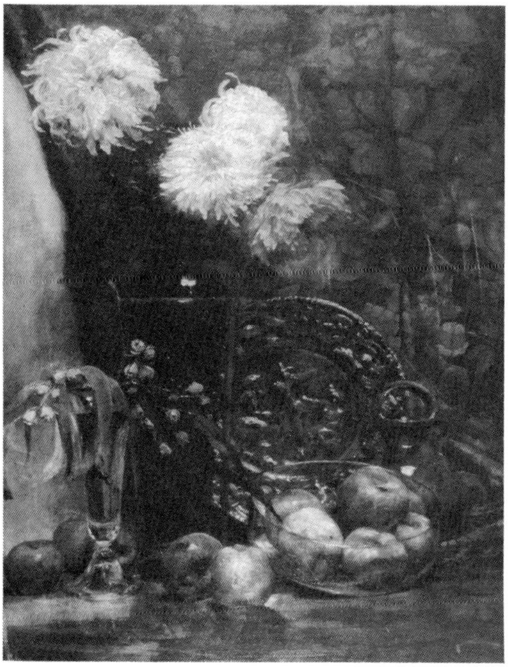

G. PLOQUIN – Chrysanthemums In A Vase With Apples In A Bowl On A Table – signed – 46 x 35¼in.
(Christie's) **$6,652** **£4,620**

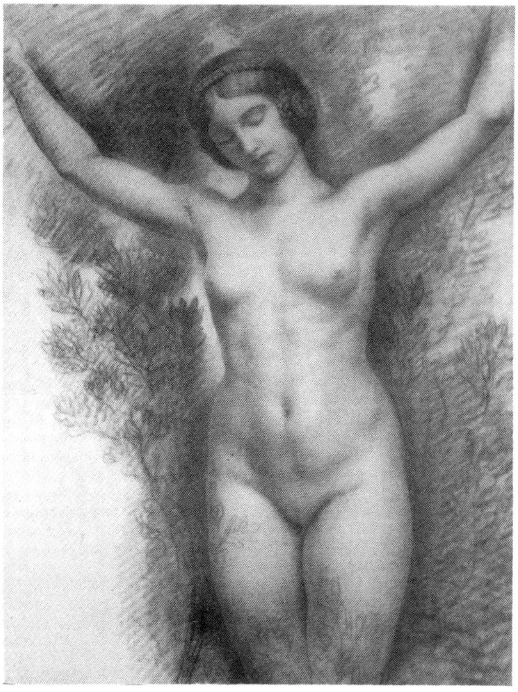

ARMAND POINT – La Nymphe Daphne se metamorphose en Laurier – red chalk on buff paper – 25 x 18½in.
(Christie's) **$4,118** **£2,860**

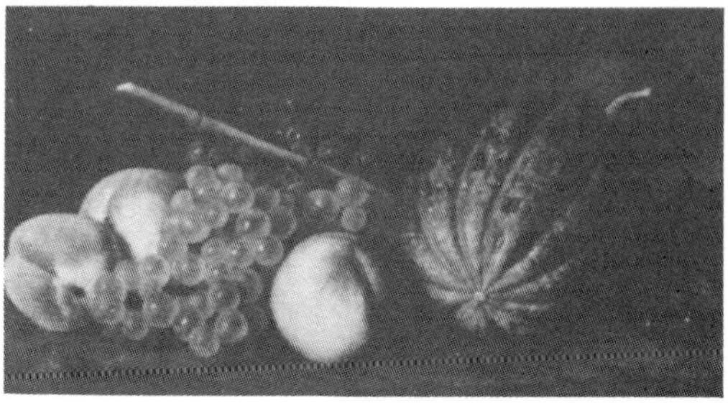

CHRISTIAEN VAN POL – Still Life With Peaches, Gourd And Grapes – signed – oil on canvas – 10¼ x 18½in.
(Robt. W. Skinner Inc.) **$2,500** **£1,736**

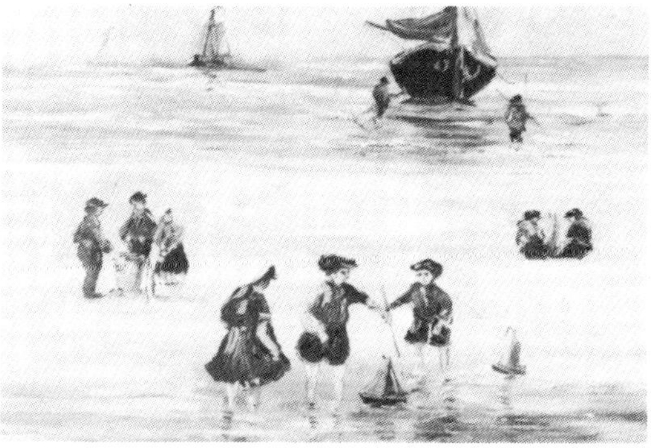

LOUS VAN DER POL – Children Playing At The Shore – signed – oil on panel – 19½ x 23½in.
(Robt. W. Skinner Inc.) **$400** **£277**

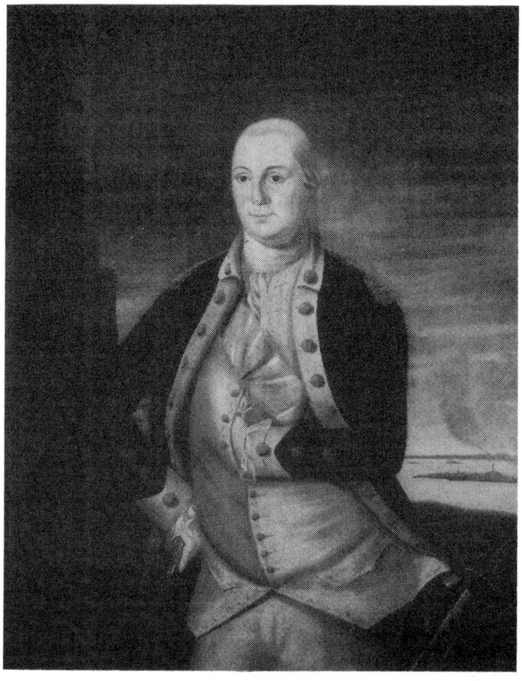

CHARLES PEALE POLK – Portrait Of George Washington – oil on canvas – 46½ x 38in.
(Christie's) **$9,350** **£6,102**

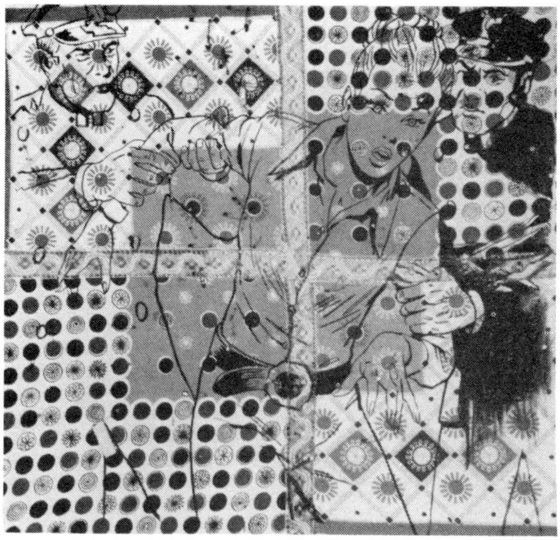

SIGMAR POLKE – Tischdecke, Sicherheitsverwahrung – signed with initials, also signed and dated '78 on the stretcher – dispersion on fabric – 51¼ x 43¼in.
(Christie's) **$38,016 £26,400**

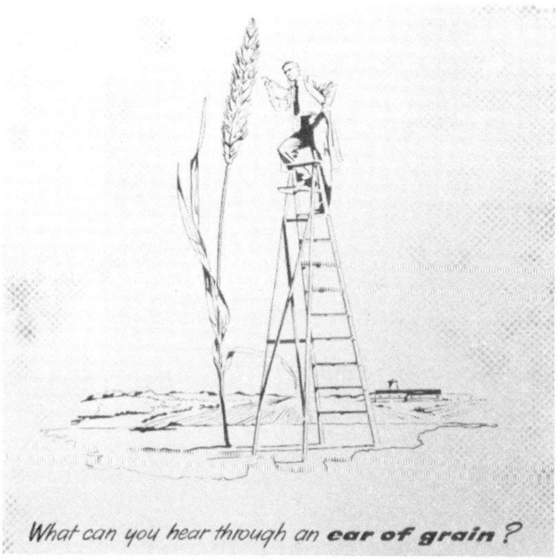

SIGMAR POLKE – What Can You Hear Through An Ear Of Grain? – signed and dated '76 – oil on canvas – 43¼ x 43¼in.
(Christie's) **$31,680 £22,000**

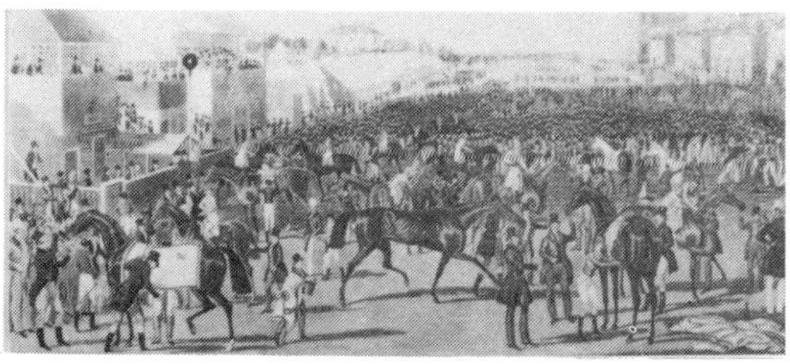

JAMES POLLARD, After – Epsom, The Race Over – coloured aquatint – 15 x 21½in.
(Christie's) **$135 £95**

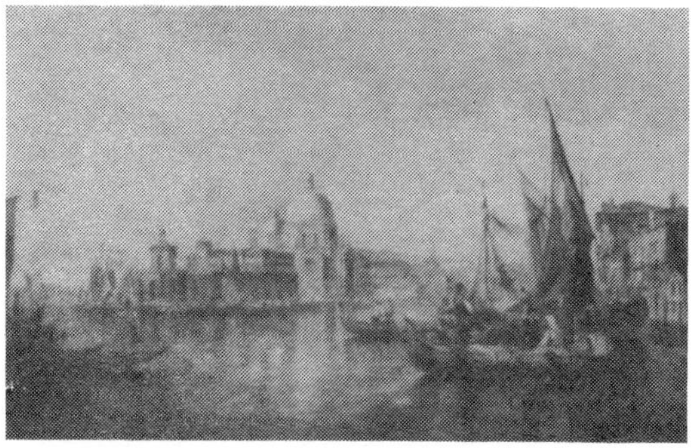

ALFRED POLLENTINE, Follower of – The Grand Canal, Venice – with signature David Roberts – oil on canvas – 23½ x 41½in.
(Christie's) **$2,921 £1,760**

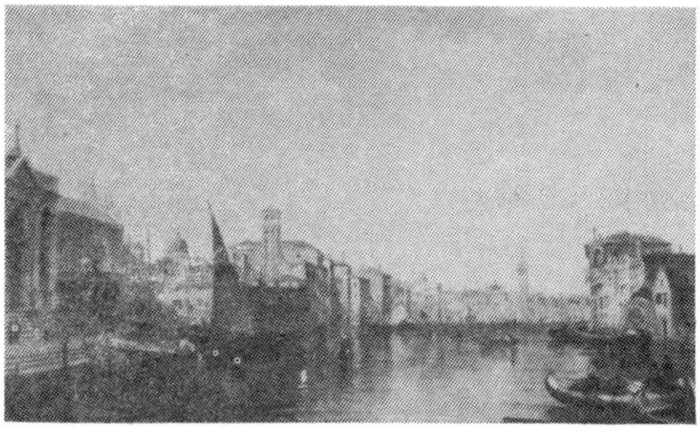

ALFRED POLLENTINE – The Grand Canal, Venice; and The Ducal Palace, Venice – one signed, also signed and inscribed on the reverse, the other signed on canvas – 12 x 20in.
(Phillips) **$2,415 £1,500 Pair**

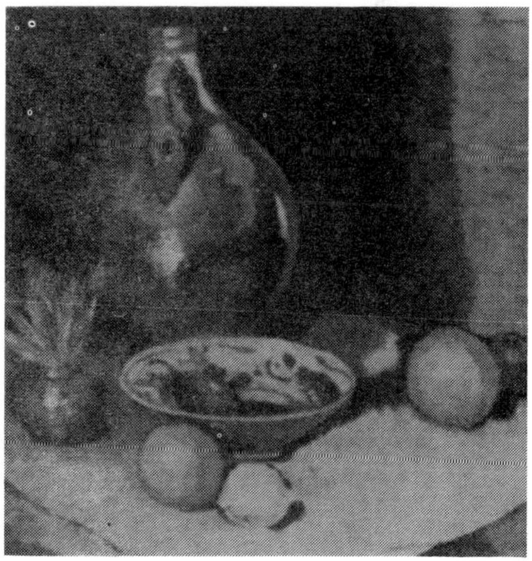

JAN POORTENAAR – Stilleven Mit Kruik – signed – oil on canvas – 60.5 x 60.5cm.
(Phillips) **$620 £400**

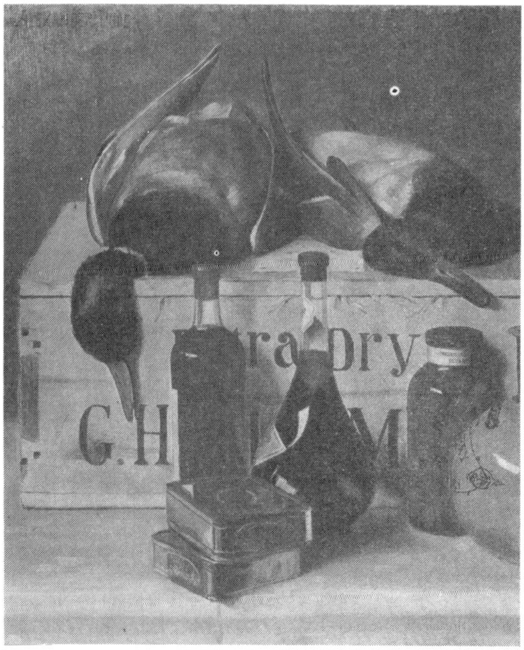

ALEXANDER POPE – Still Life With Mallards – signed – oil on canvas – 24¼ x 20in.
(Christie's) **$13,200** **£8,224**

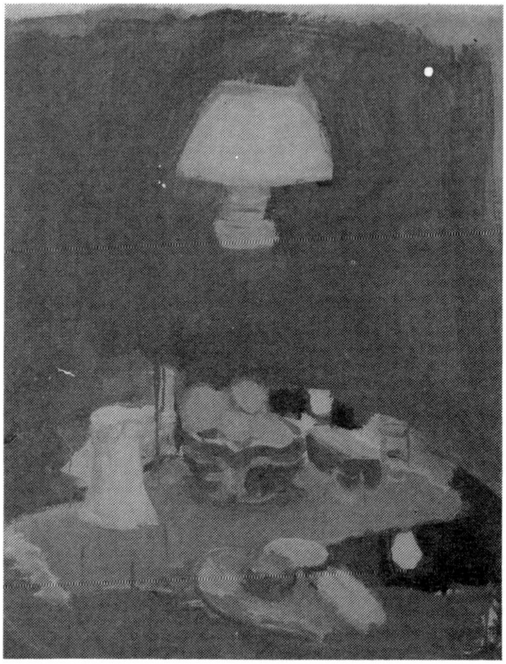

FAIRFIELD PORTER – Still Life With Suspended Lamp – oil on canvas laid down on canvas – 20 x 16in.
(Robt. W. Skinner Inc.) **$5,750** **£3,527**

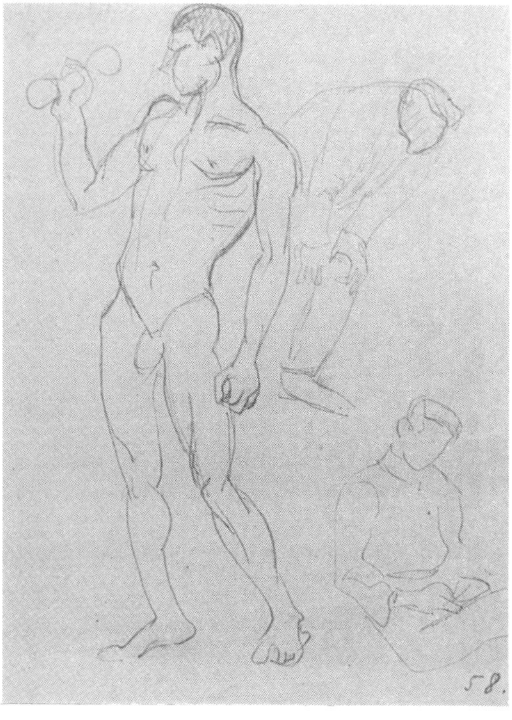

LIUBOV POPOVA – Studies Of Male Figures – pencil on paper – 10½ x 8¼in.
(Christie's) **$411** **£286**

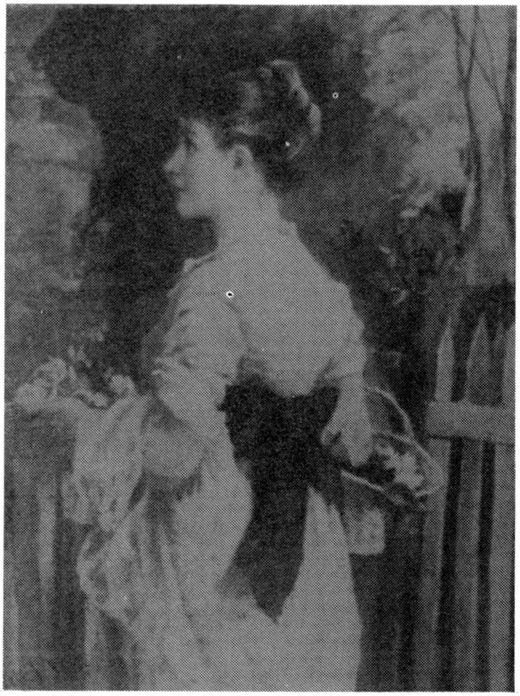

LASLETT JOHN POTT – The Flower Girl – signed – on panel – 8¾ x 6¾in.
(Phillips) **$1,046** **£650**

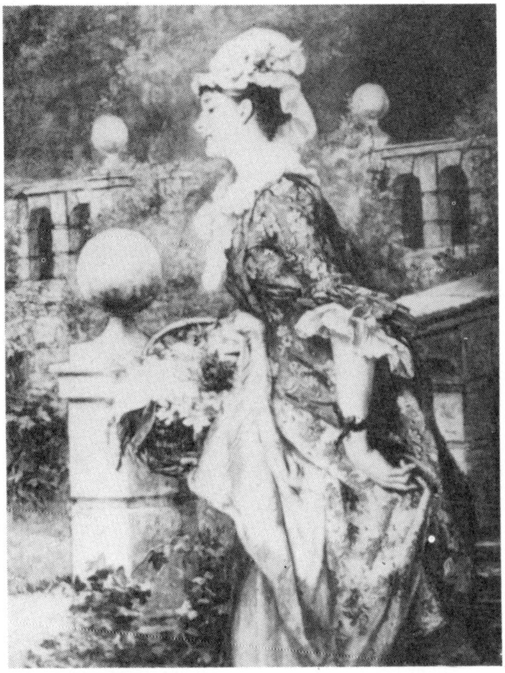

LASLETT JOHN POTT – 'Flowers For My Lady', Lady On A Terrace Carrying A Basket – signed and dated – oil – 30 x 20in.
(Capes, Dunn & Co.) **$5,868** **£3,600**

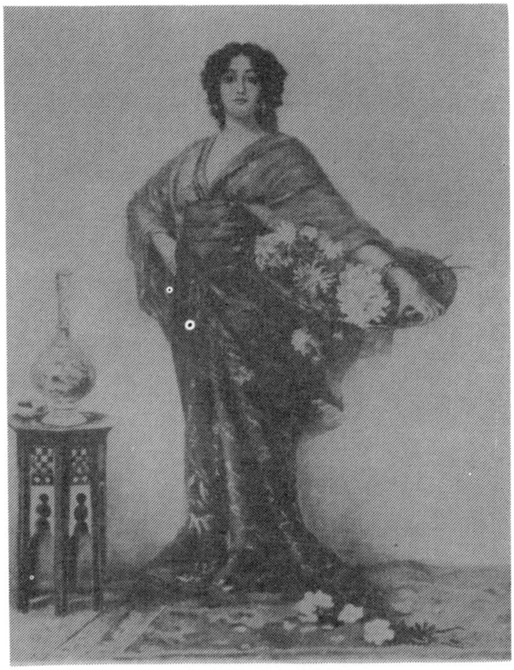

FRANK HUDDLESTONE POTTER – A Girl In An Interior With A Basket Of Flowers – signed and dated – oil on board – 21 x 16in.
(Woolley & Wallis) **$338** **£240**

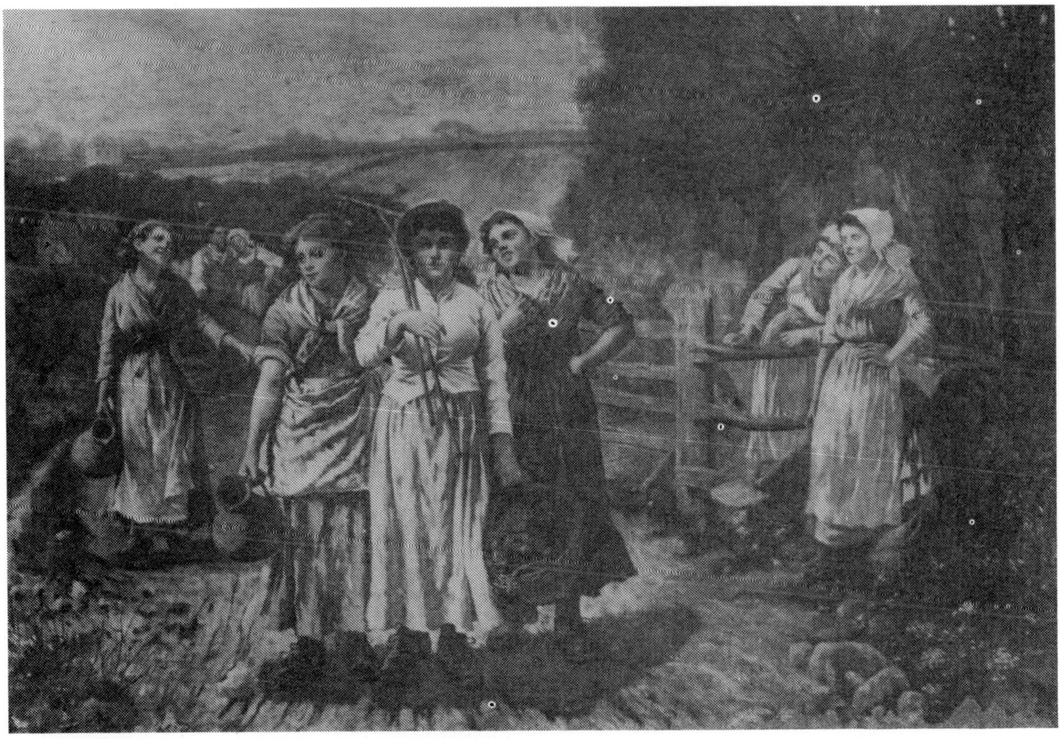

POTTER – Study Of Maids Near A Field Gateway – signed – oil on canvas – 40 x 52in. *(Biddle & Webb)* **$896** **£550**

POTTHAST

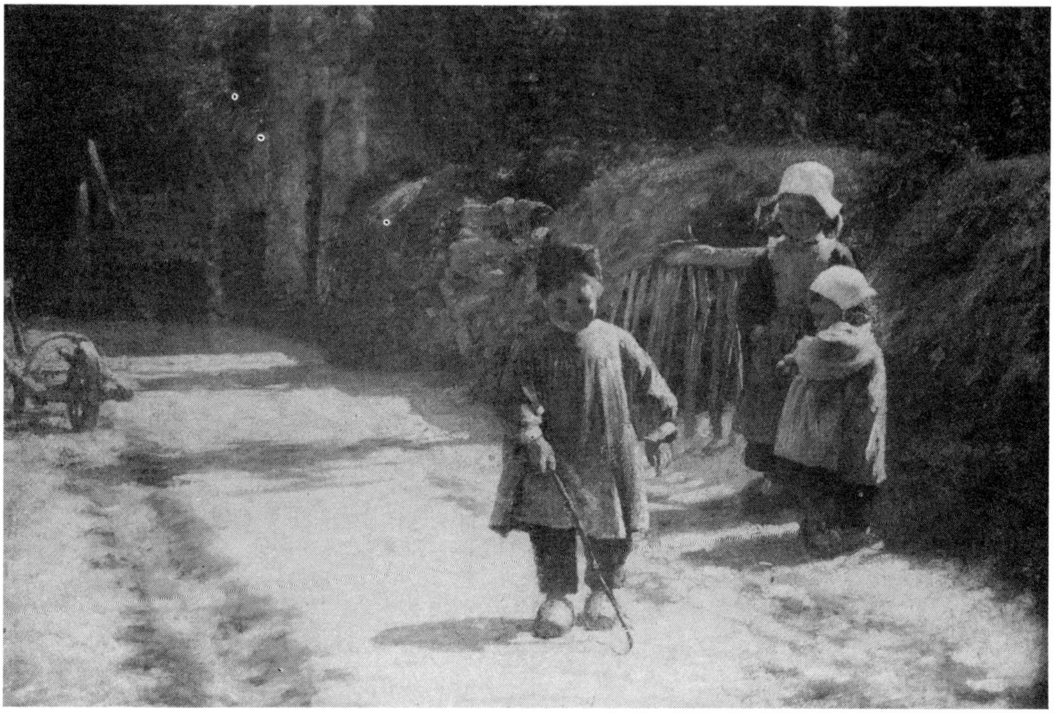

EDWARD HENRY POTTHAST – Children In Brittany – signed – oil on canvas – 16 x 22¾in.
(Christie's) **$52,800 £32,899**

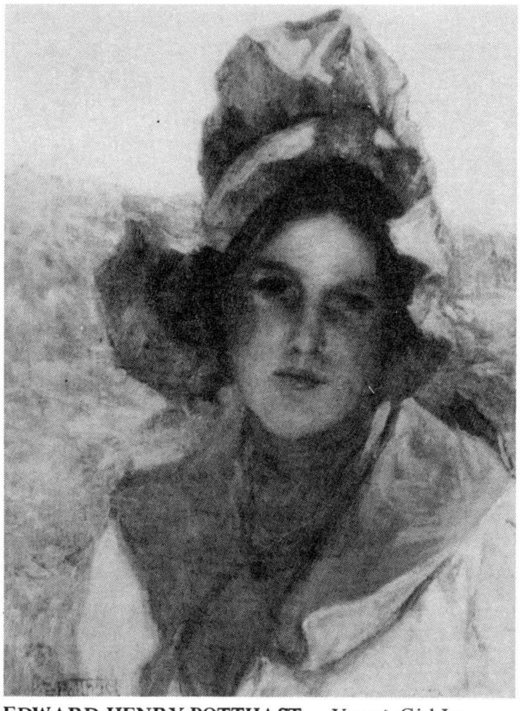

EDWARD HENRY POTTHAST – Young Girl In A Red Bonnet – signed – oil on canvas – 20 x 15in.
(Robt. W. Skinner Inc.) **$31,000 £21,527**

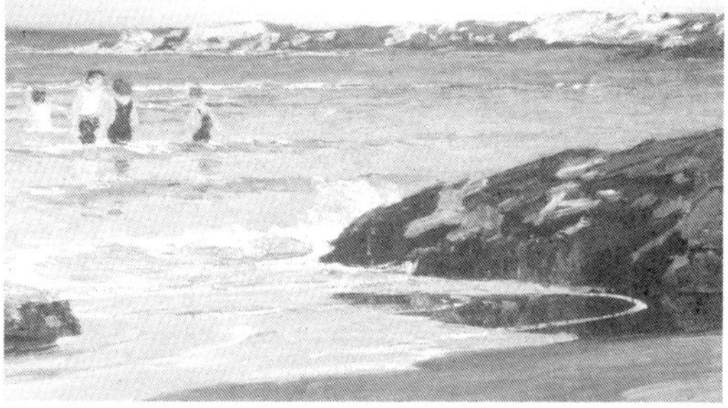

EDWARD HENRY POTTHAST – Low Tide – signed, also signed on the reverse – oil on board – 12 x 16in.
(Christie's) **$38,500 £27,065**

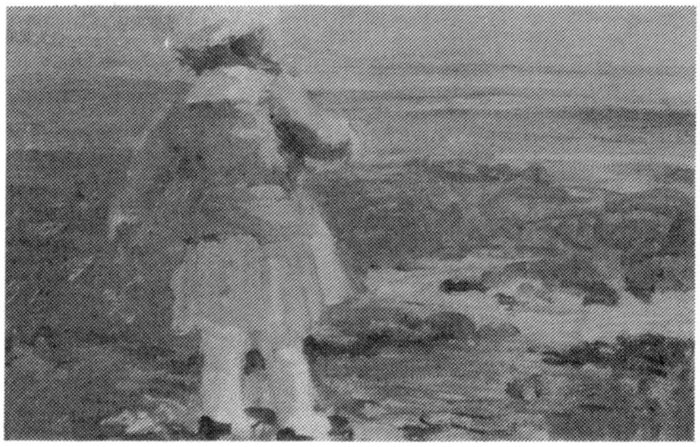

EDWARD HENRY POTTHAST – Gazing Out To Sea – oil on board – 7¼ x 9¼in.
(Christie's) **$19,800 £12,337**

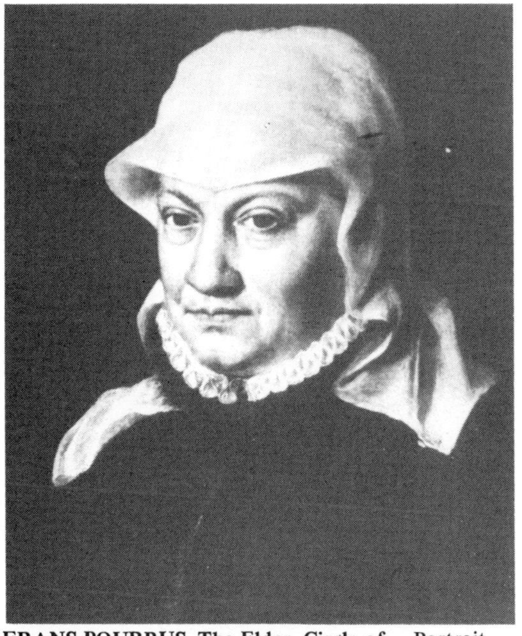

FRANS POURBUS, The Elder, Circle of – Portrait Of A Lady, Bust Length, wearing a linen cap – oil on canvas – 16½ x 14in.
(Phillips) **$1,015** **£725**

GASPARD POUSSIN, Circle of, Called Gaspard Dughet – The Finding Of Moses – on canvas – 38 x 34½in.
(Phillips) **$28,220** **£17,000**

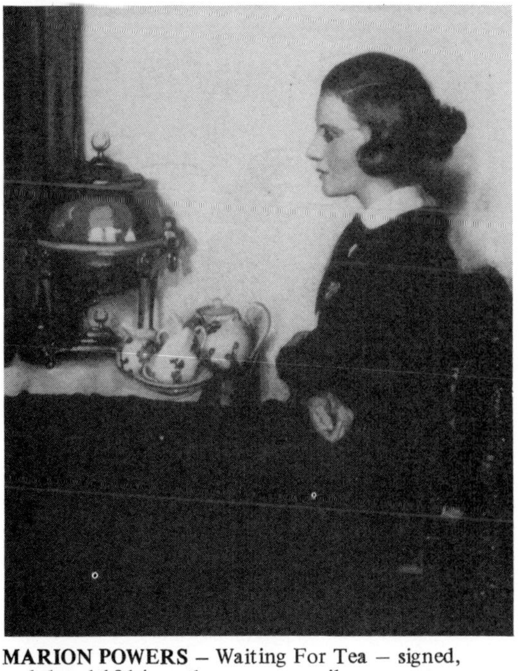

MARION POWERS – Waiting For Tea – signed, and dated 1914 on the reverse – oil on canvas – 36 x 29in.
(Christie's) **$3,300** **£2,056**

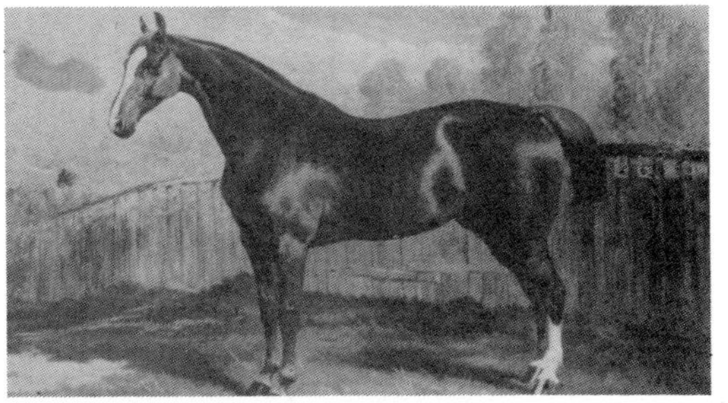

A. F. DE PRADES – A Chestnut Hunter; and A Bay Hunter – signed, and one dated 1871 – on board – 18¾ x 24¾in.
(Christie's) **$4,653** **£3,300 Pair**

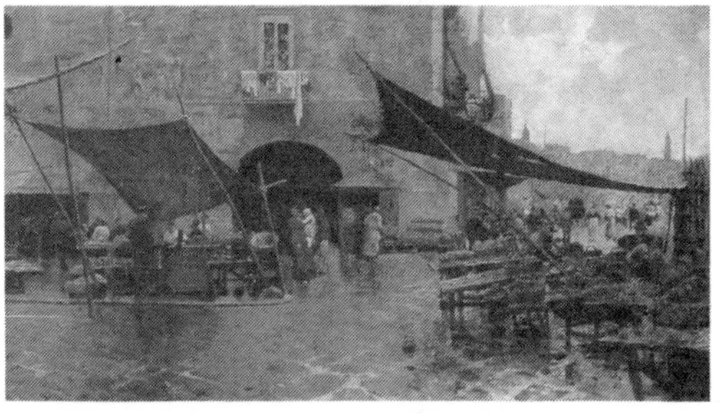

ATTILIO PRATELLA – A Market Scene, Messina – signed – 11¾ x 23½in.
(Christie's) **$24,640** **£15,400**

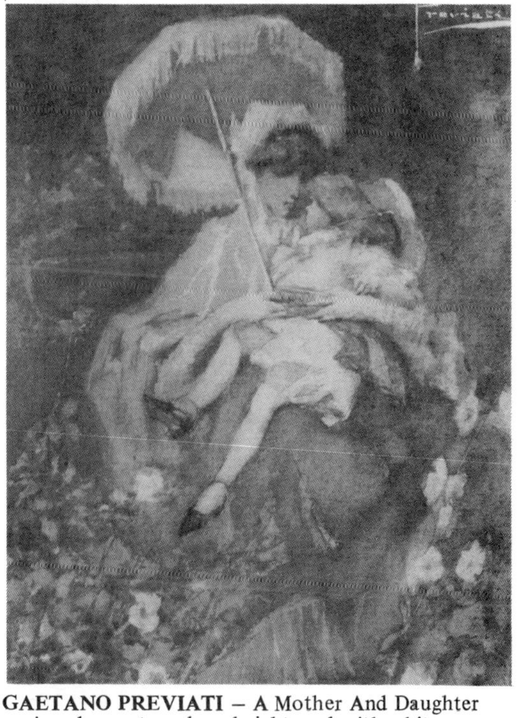

GAETANO PREVIATI – A Mother And Daughter – signed – watercolour heightened with white – 16½ x 11in.
(Christie's) **$4,565** **£2,750**

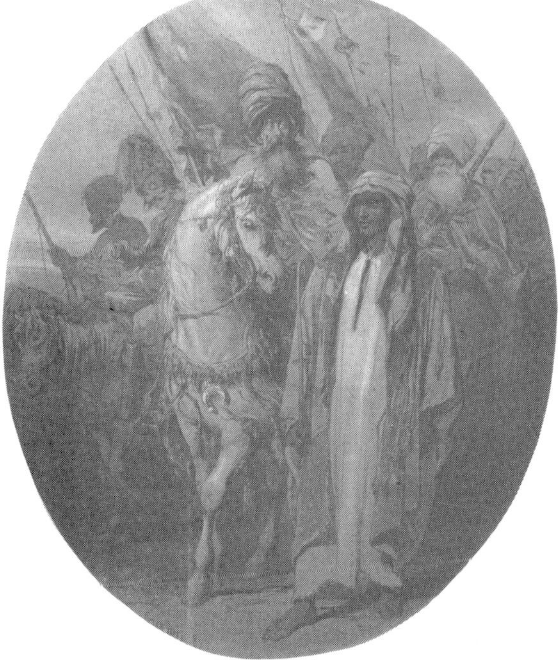

AMADEO, COUNT PREZIOSI – Arab Warriors Advancing – signed and dated 1855 – black chalk and watercolour – 20 x 16in.
(Christie's) **$8,800** **£5,500**

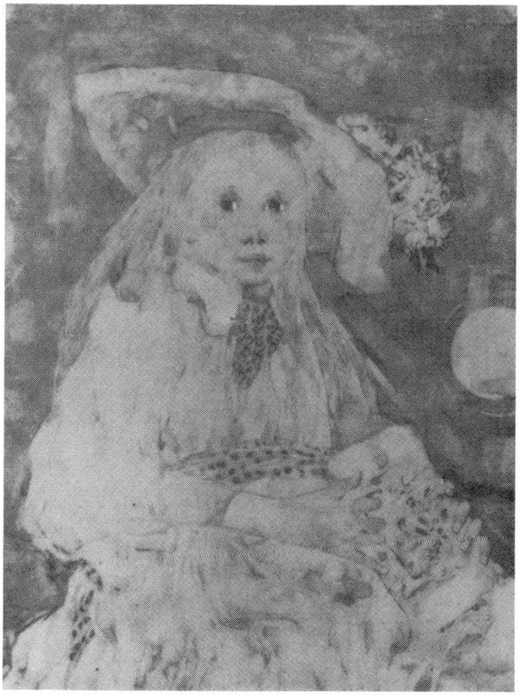

JOHN QUINTON PRINGLE – Three-Quarter Length Portrait Of A Girl Wearing A Light Blue Dress And Green Bonnet – circa 1898 – watercolour on ivorine – 3¼ x 2¾in.
(Christie's) **$5,760** **£4,000**

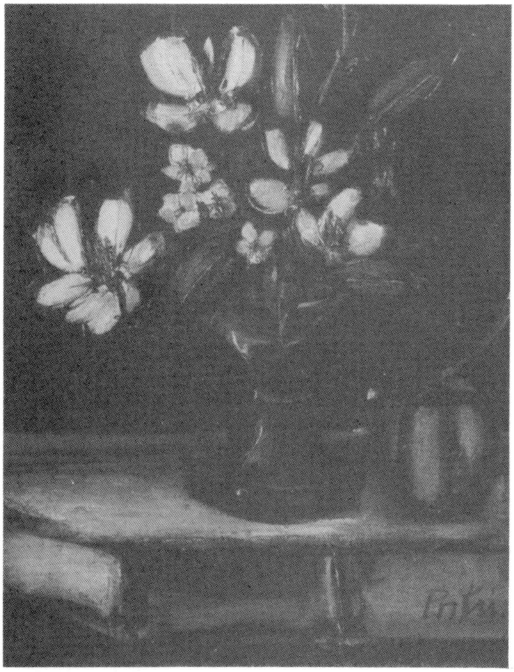

FRANZ PRIKING – Bouquet de Fleurs et Fruit – signed and dated '57 – oil on canvas – 25½ x 21½in.
(Christie's) **$1,144** **£715**

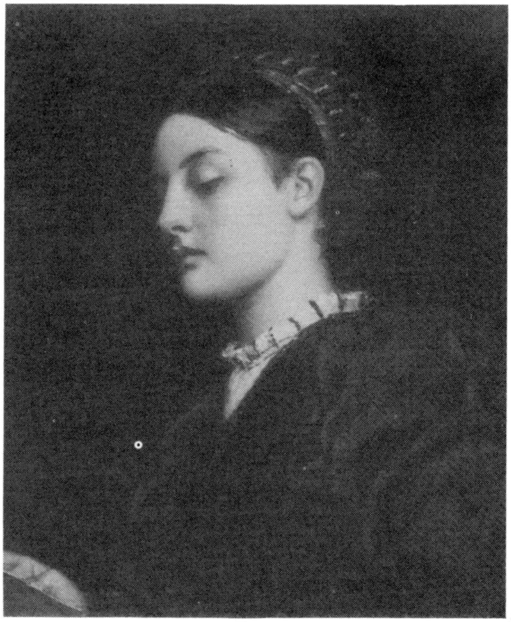

VALENTINE CAMERON PRINSEP – Reading The Letter – 13½ x 11½in.
(Christie's) **$4,375** **£2,860**

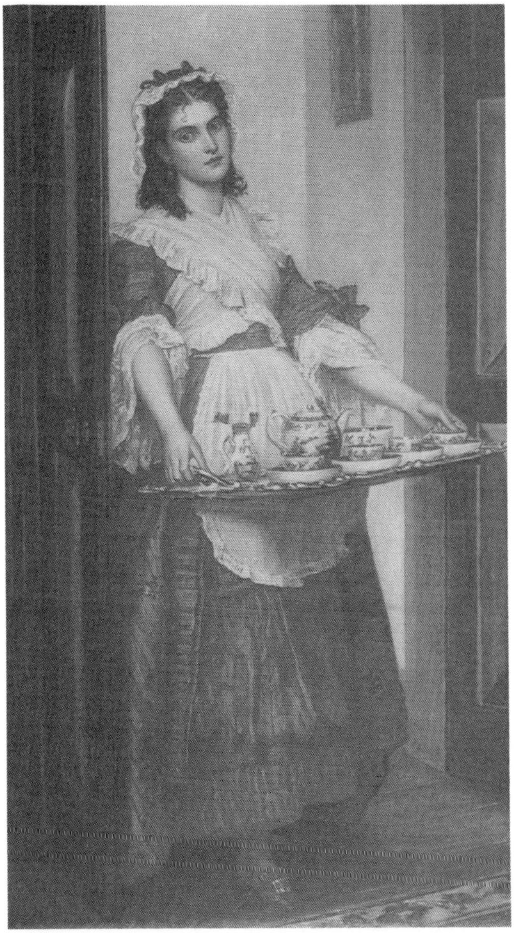

VALENTINE CAMERON PRINSEP – The Dish Of Tea – 37½ x 21in.
(Christie's) **$12,320** **£7,700**

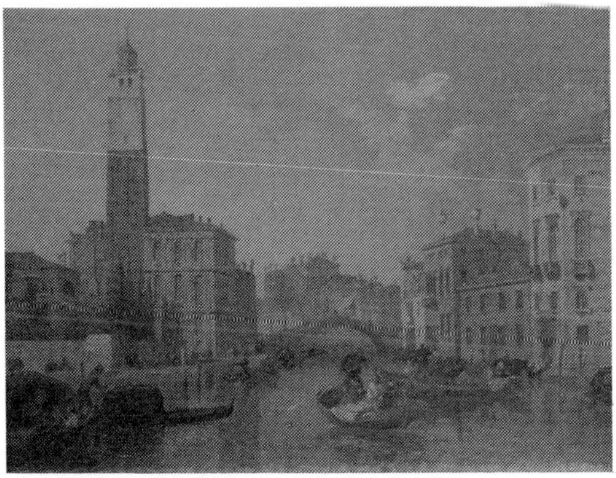

EDWARD PRITCHETT – The Grand Canal With San Geremia, Venice – signed – 17 x 25in.
(Christie's) **$18,216** **£12,650**

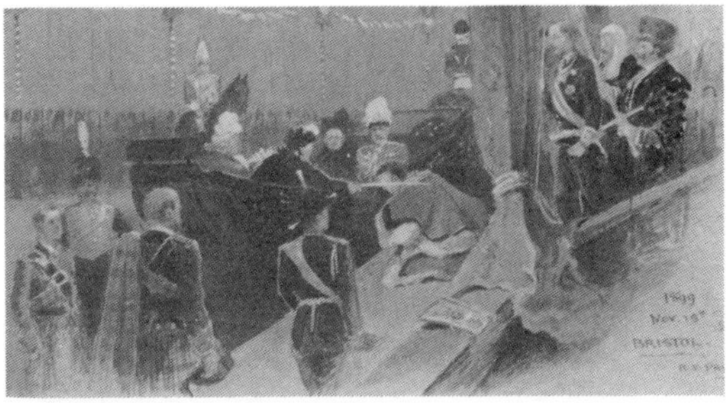

ROBERT TAYLOR PRITCHETT – Queen Victoria Conferring A Knighthood In Bristol – signed with monogram and dated 1899 – pencil and watercolour heightened with white on grey paper – 6½ x 9½in.
(Christie's) **$615** **£410**

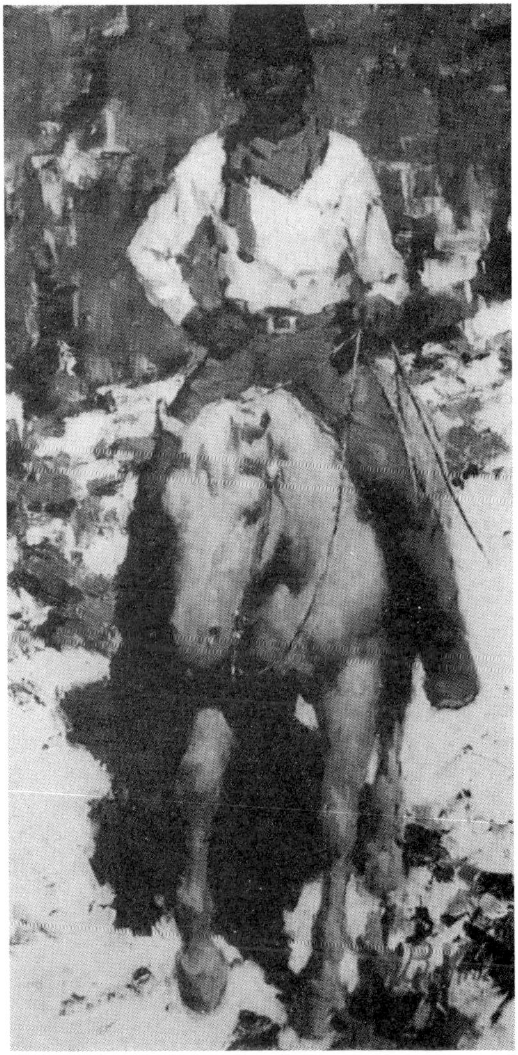

BURT PROCTOR – Indian On Horseback – signed – oil on masonite – 36 x 18in.
(Christie's) **$4,400** **£3,093**

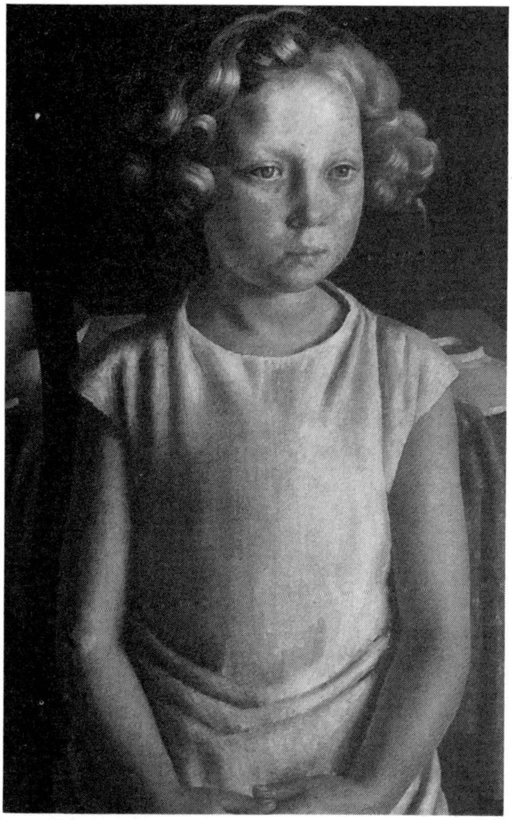

DOD PROCTER – The Little Girl – signed and dated 1928 – oil on canvas – 71 x 43cm.
(Phillips) **$13,490** **£9,500**

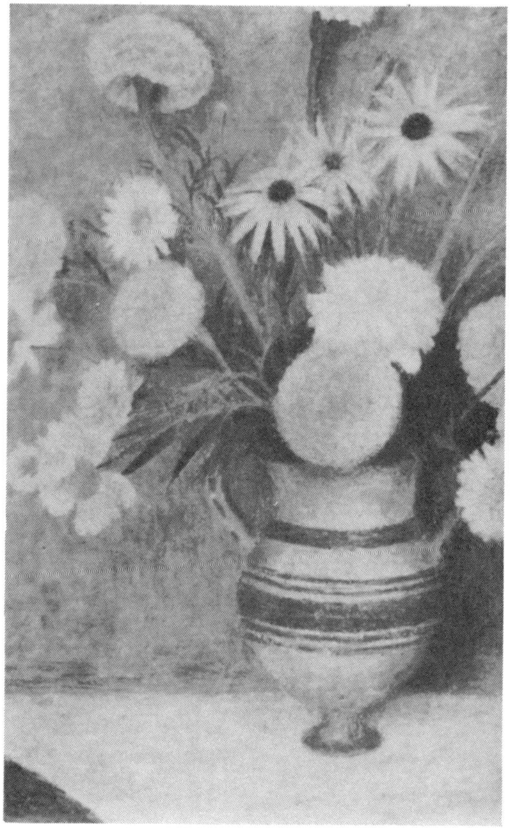

DOD PROCTER – Vase Of Marigolds – oil on board – 62 x 32cm.
(W. H. Lane & Son) **$1,494** **£900**

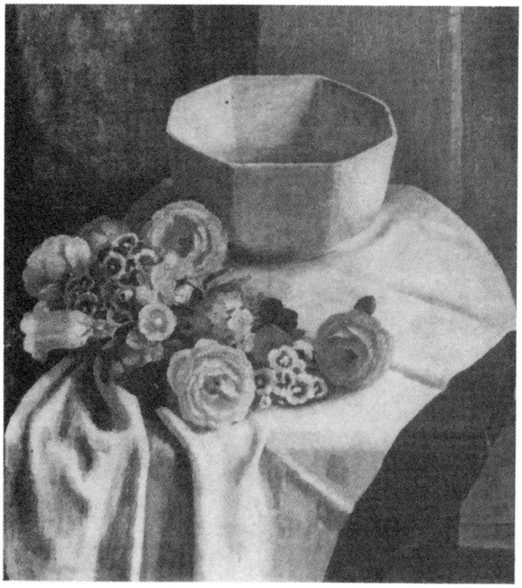

DOD PROCTER – Mixed Flowers And A Bowl On A Table – signed and dated '26 – oil on canvas – 20 x 18in.
(Christie's) **$3,932** **£2,750**

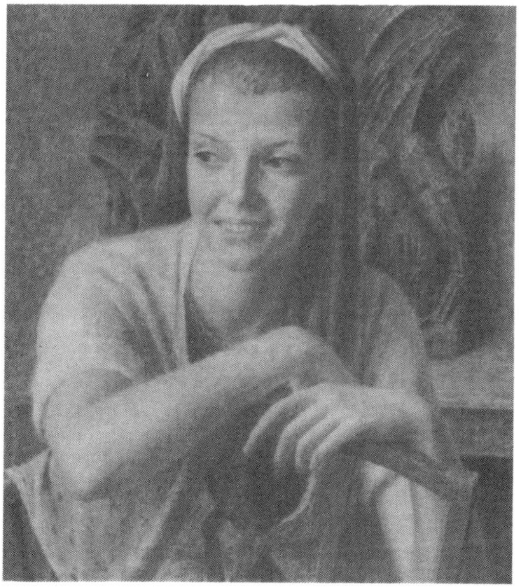

DOD PROCTER – Smiling Girl – oil on board – 24¼ x 22¼in.
(Christie's) **$2,674** **£1,870**

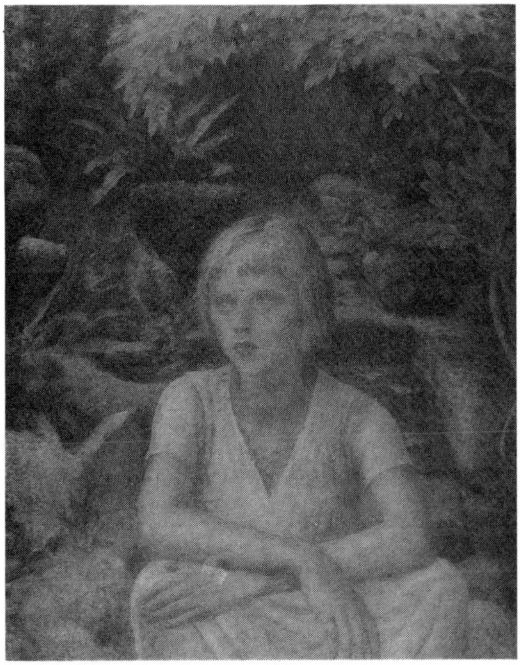

DOD PROCTER – In The Rock Garden – signed – oil on canvas – 91 x 71cm.
(Phillips) **$21,300** **£15,000**

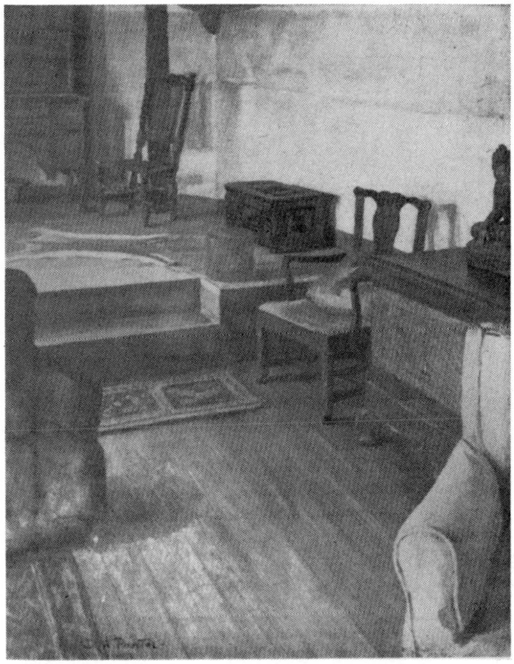

DOD PROCTER – The Sitting Room – signed – oil on canvas – 20 x 16in.
(Christie's) **$1,887** **£1,320**

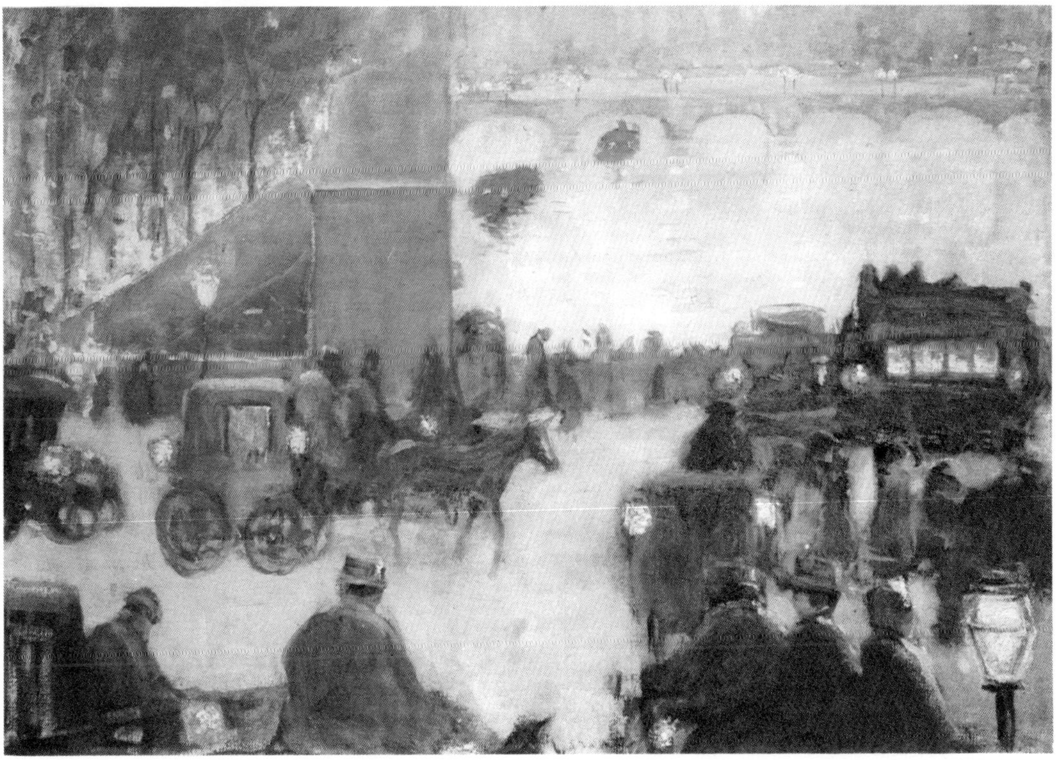

IDA SEDGWICK PROPER – Paris At Night – signed – oil on canvas – 23½ x 28½in. *(Christie's)*
$15,400 **£10,826**

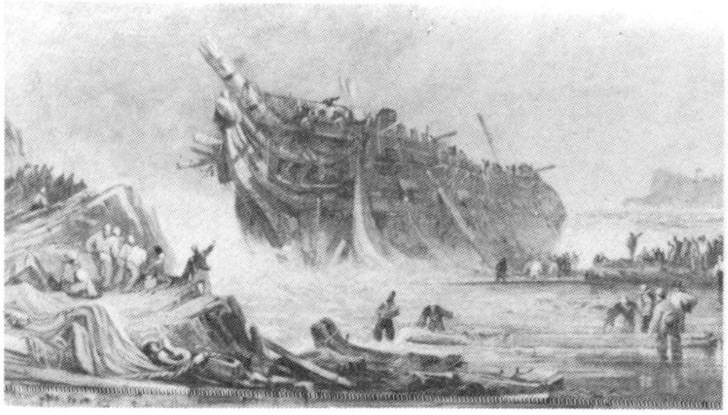

SAMUEL PROUT – The Shipwreck – signed – pencil and watercolour heightened with white and touches of bodycolour – 11¼ x 18¾in.
(Christie's) **$2,430** **£1,620**

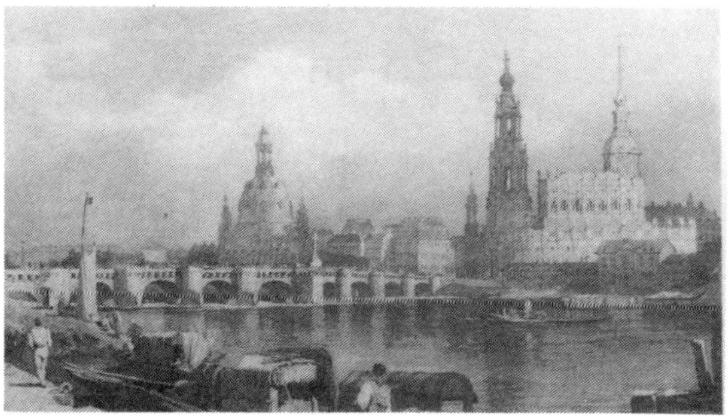

SAMUEL PROUT – Dresden – signed with monogram – pen and brown ink and watercolour – 10¼ x 16in.
(Christie's) **$7,348** **£4,400**

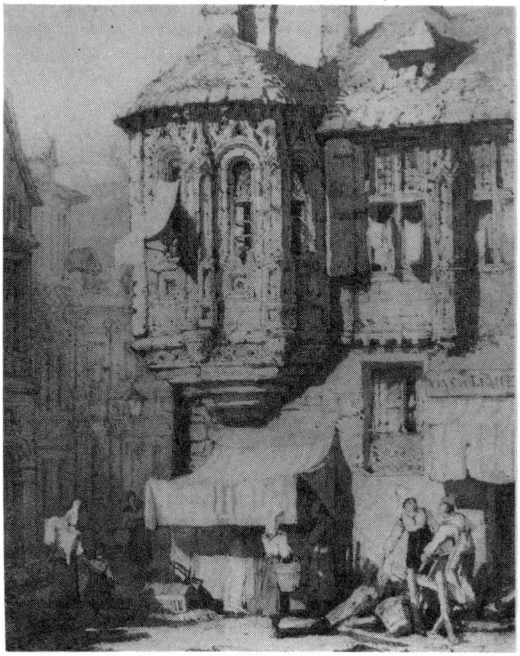

SAMUEL PROUT – Joan Of Arc's House, Rouen – signed – pen and brown ink and watercolour – 11½ x 8¼in.
(Christie's) **$1,469** **£880**

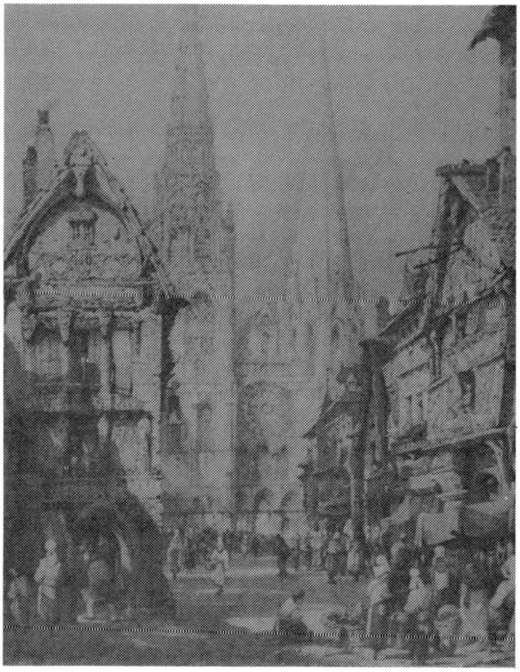

SAMUEL GILLESPIE PROUT – Chartres Cathedral – signed – watercolour over traces of pencil – 58 x 43cm.
(Phillips) **$3,260** **£2,000**

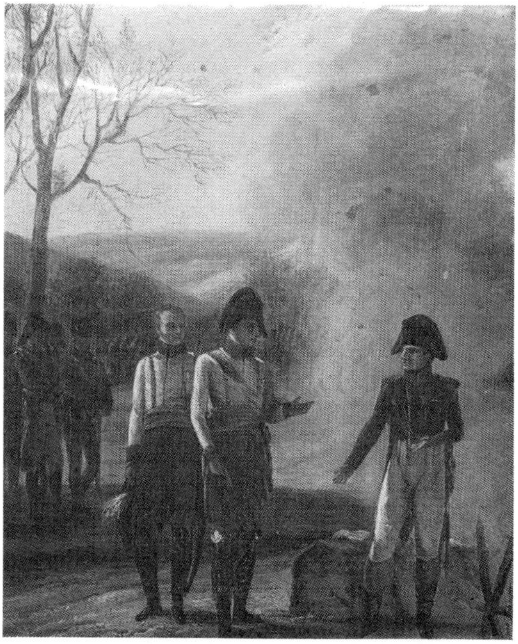

PIERRE PAUL PRUD'HON – The Meeting Of Napoleon And Francois II, Emperor Of Austria, With The Prince Of Liechtenstein At Sarutschitz, Moravie, After The Battle Of Austerlitz On The 4th December 1805 – 12½ x 9½in.
(Christie's) **$22,176** **£15,400**

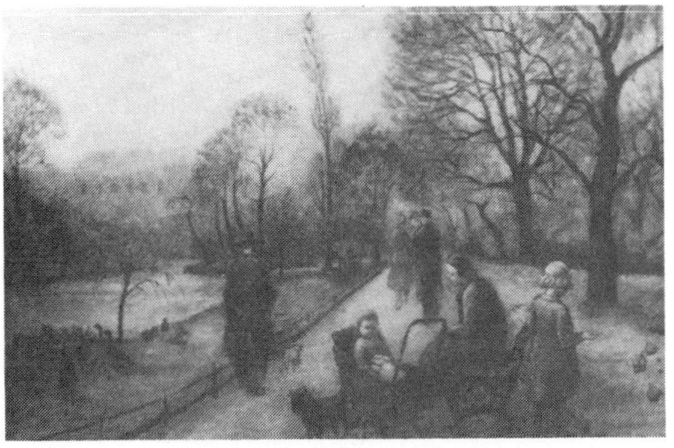

MARGARET PRYOR – In The Park, St. James – signed – oil on canvas – 22¼ x 30¼in.
(Christie's) **$2,417** **£1,540**

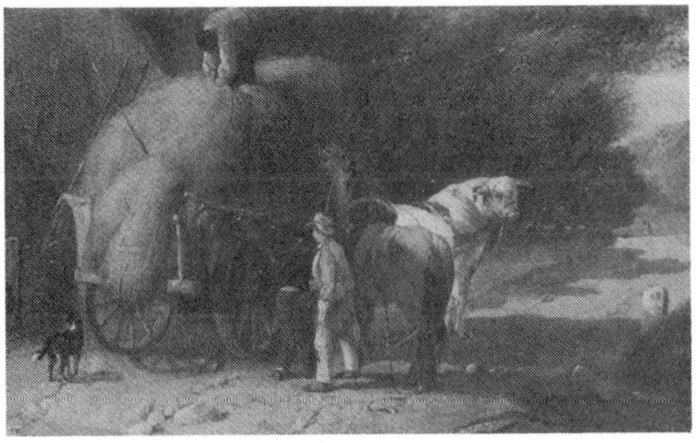

JOHN ANTHONY PULLER, Attributed to – The Hay Cart; and Children Playing – signed with initials – 8½ x 11½in.
(Christie's) **$3,564** **£2,376 Pair**

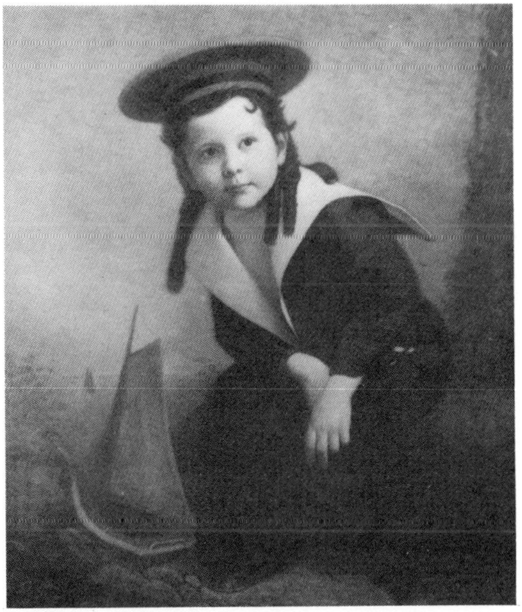

ALBERT J. PURDY – Portrait Of A Young Boy In A Sailor Suit – signed and dated 1899 – oil on canvas – 42 x 32in.
(Robt. W. Skinner Inc.) **$2,400** **£1,666**

WILLIAM PURSER – In The Harbour, Genoa – signed – pencil and watercolour – 5¼ x 7½in.
(Christie's) **$593** **£418**

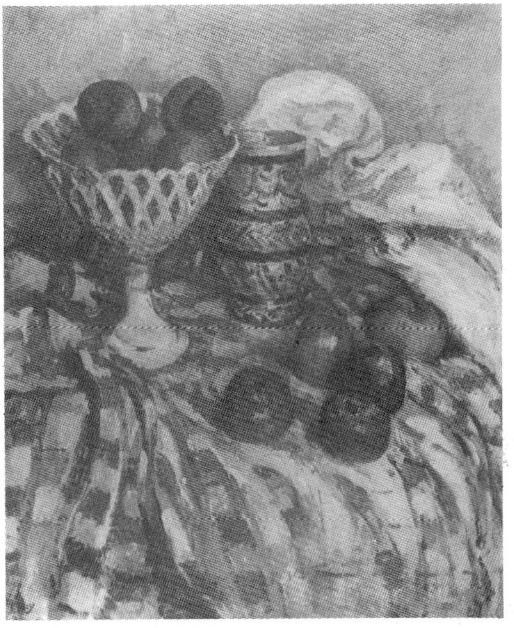

JEAN PUY – Nature morte – signed, and signed on the reverse – oil on canvas – 28¾ x 23½in.
(Christie's) **$8,800** **£5,500**

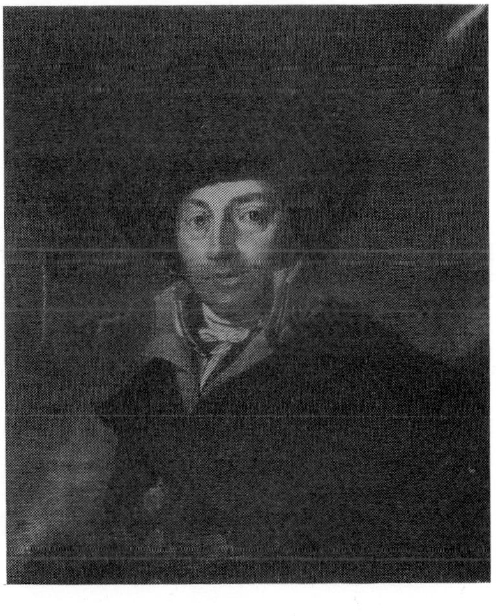

GERARD VAN DER PUYL – Portrait Of A Gentleman, Bust Length, Wearing A Blue Coat With A Red Collar, And A Hat – signed – 25 x 21in.
(Christie's) **$567** **£378**

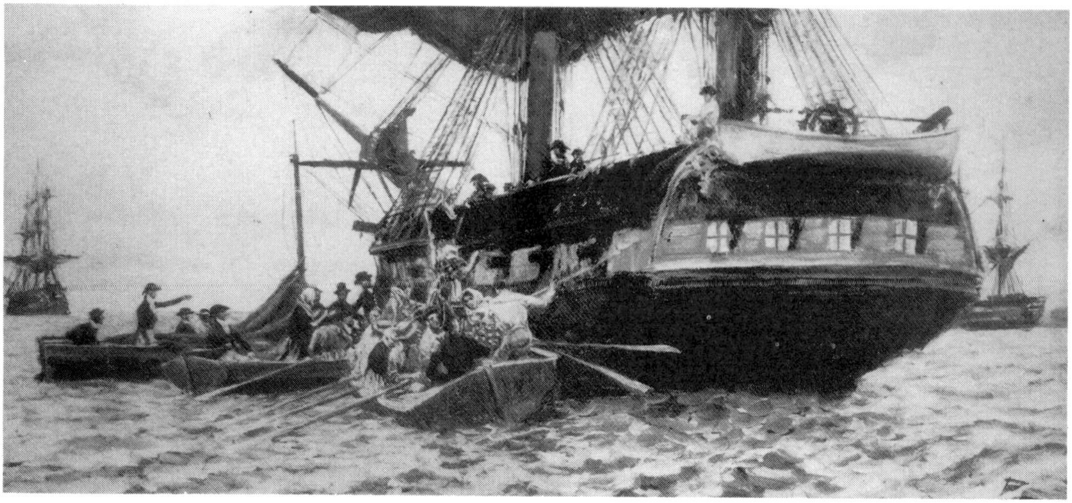

HOWARD PYLE – Going Ashore – signed – gouache en grisaille on paper laid down on board – 5¼ x 11¾in. *(Christie's)* **$13,200 £8,224**

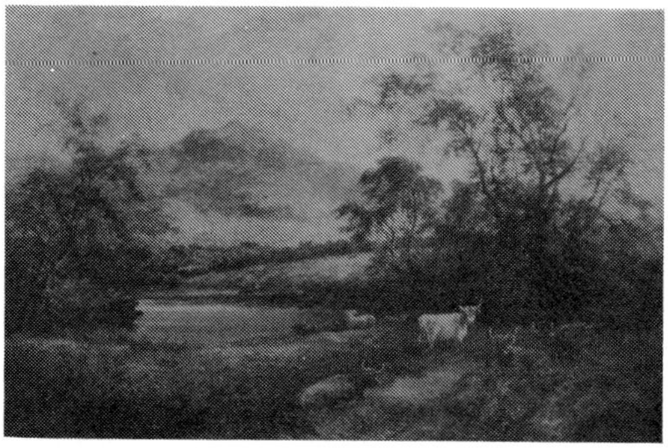

DAVID PYNE – Scene Near Loch Long – signed, and signed and inscribed on the reverse – 24 x 36in.
(Christie's) **$1,460 £880**

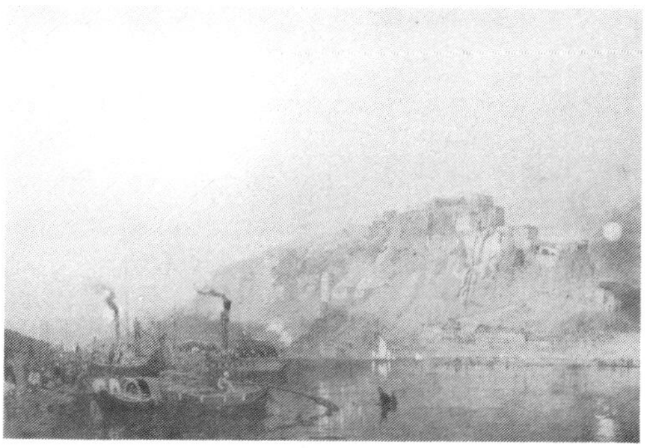

JAMES BAKER PYNE – Ehrenbreitstein On The Rhine – pencil, watercolour and bodycolour, watermark E & S 1819 – 13¼ x 19¼in.
(Christie's) **$5,511 £3,300**

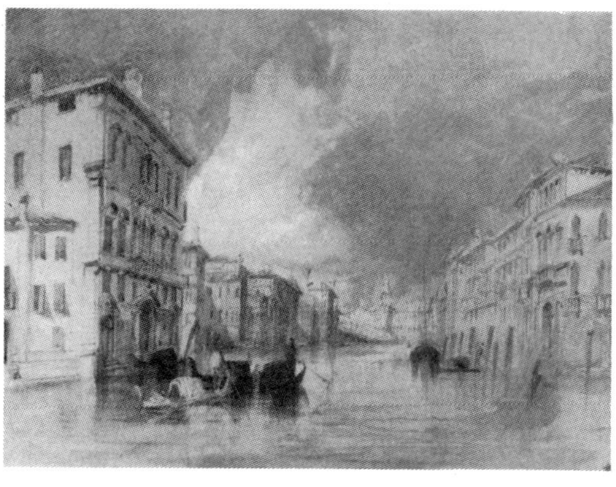

JAMES BAKER PYNE – The Grand Canal, Venice – pencil and watercolour heightened with white – 10 x 13¾in.
(Christie's) **$3,748 £2,640**

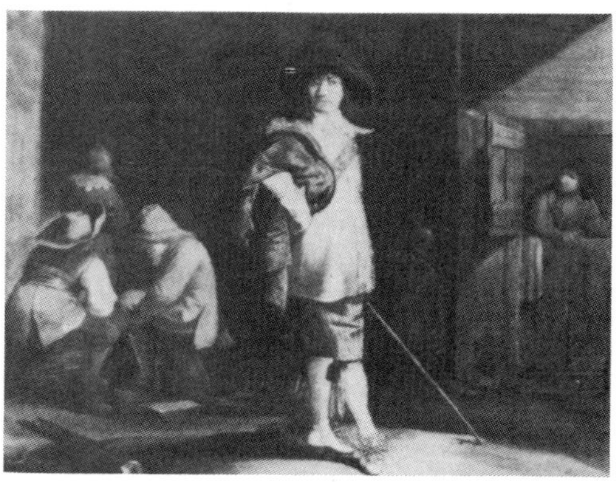

PIETER QUAST – A Cavalier Standing In An Inn, Beyond Three Figures Gather Round A Fire – signed with monogram – oil on panel – 15¼ x 19¼in.
(Phillips) **$2,679 £1,900**

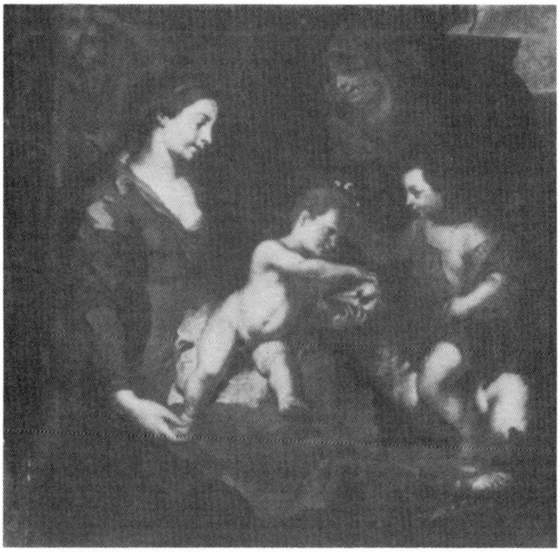

ERASMUS QUELLINUS, Circle of – The Holy Family With St. Elizabeth And St. John – oil on panel – 36¼ x 28½in.
(Phillips) **$2,115** **£1,500**

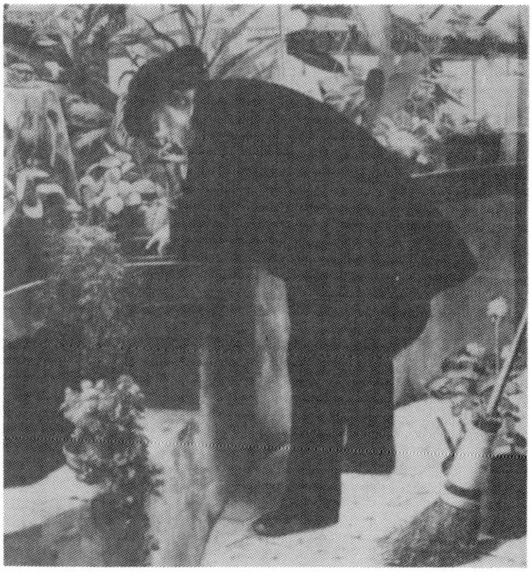

EDUARD QUITTON – The Botanist – signed and dated 1879 – 25.5 x 20.5cm.
(Phillips) **$3,456** **£2,400**

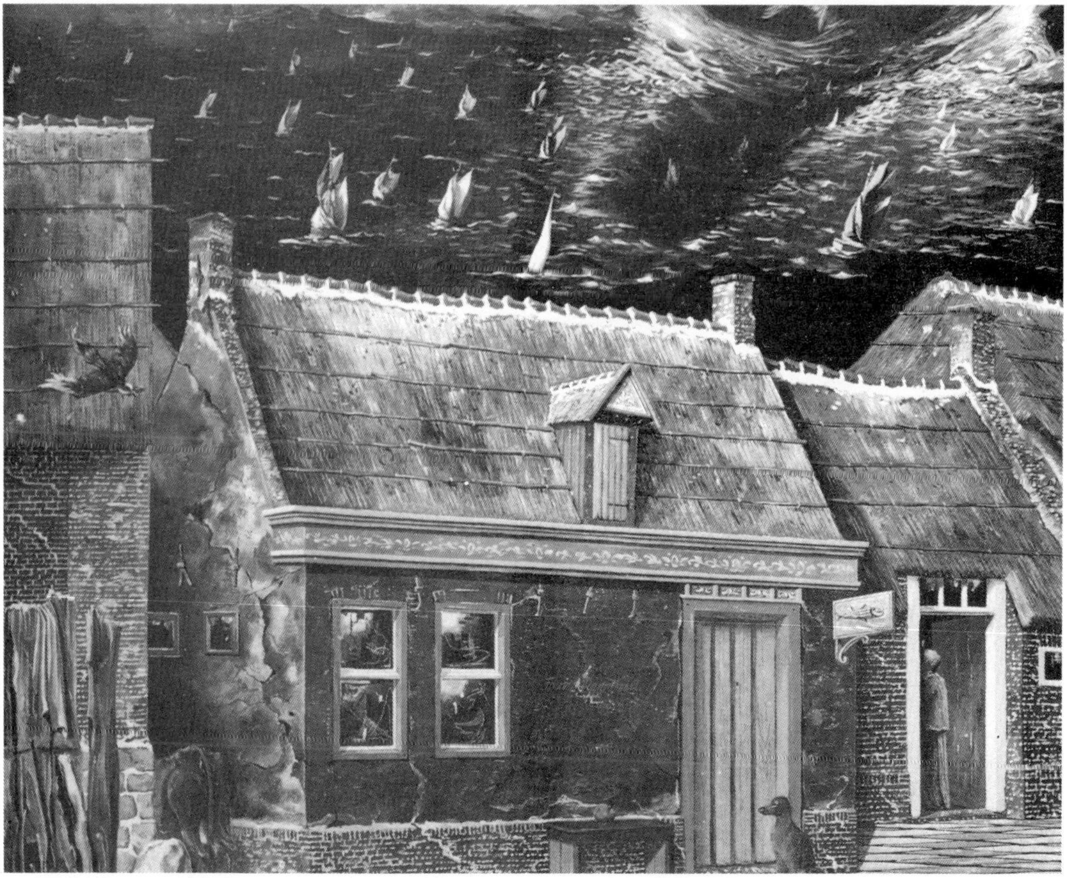

FRANZ RADZIWILL – Visionare Landschaft – signed – oil on canvas laid on panel – 38¼ x 41¼in.
(Christie's) **$41,184** **£28,600**

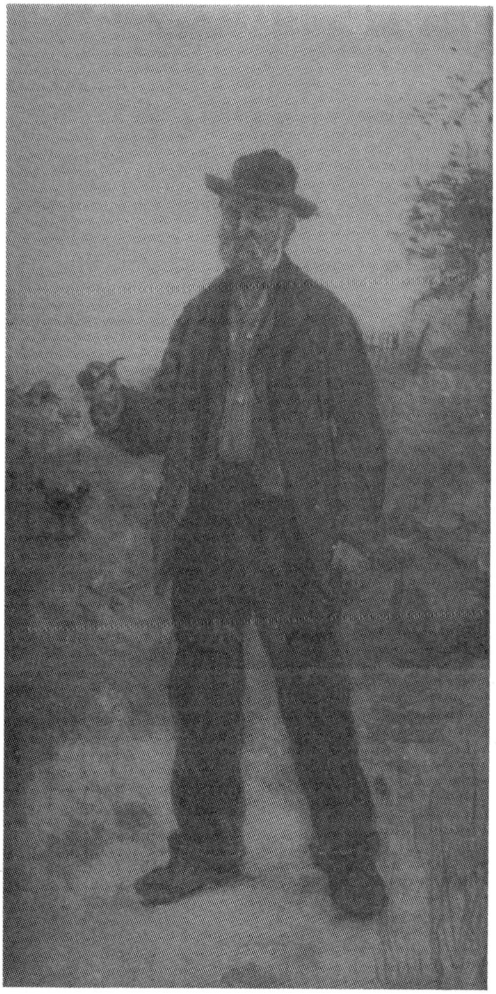

JEAN FRANCOIS RAFFAELLI – Peasant In A Field – signed – oil on panel – 9¾ x 4¼in.
(Christie's) **$4,400** **£2,871**

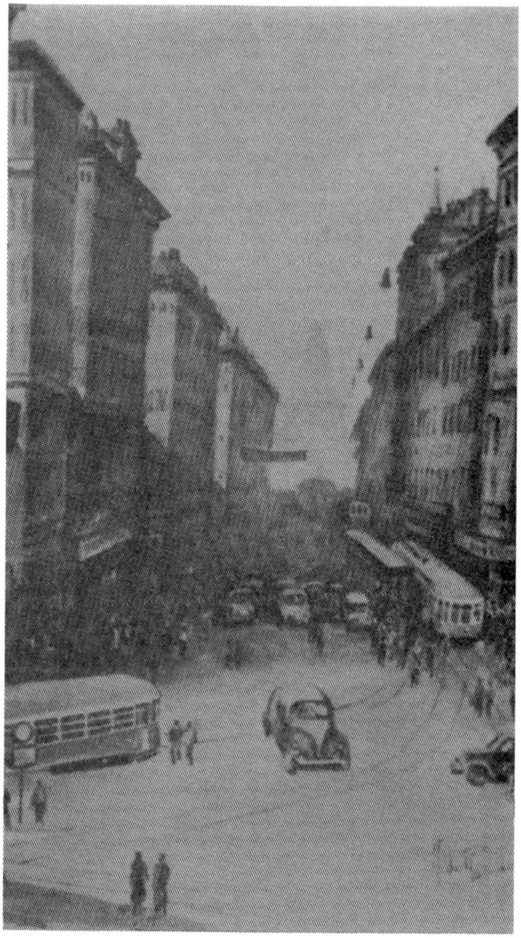

ALDO RAIMONDI – Via Verso Il Castello Sforzesco-Milano – signed and dated 1952 – watercolour on paper laid down – 62 x 41cm.
(Phillips) **$155** **£100**

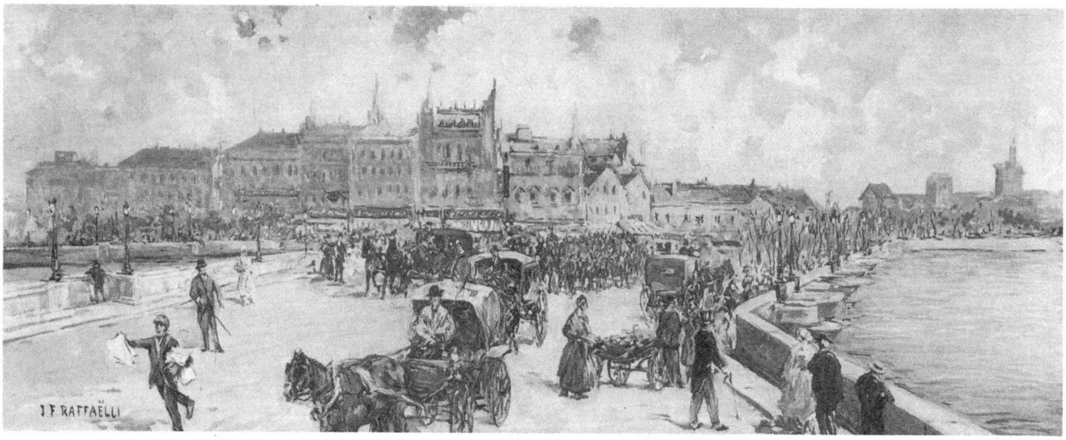

JEAN FRANCOIS RAFFAELLI – Le Pont Neuf, Paris – signed – oil on panel – 7 x 16in.
(Christie's) **$14,256** **£9,900**

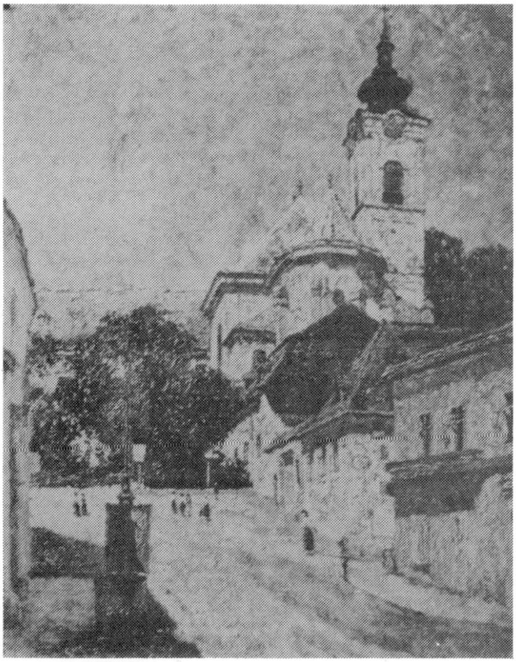

HANS RANZONI – The Road To Church – signed and dated 1923 – oil on board – 29.5 x 24cm.
(Phillips) **$744** **£480**

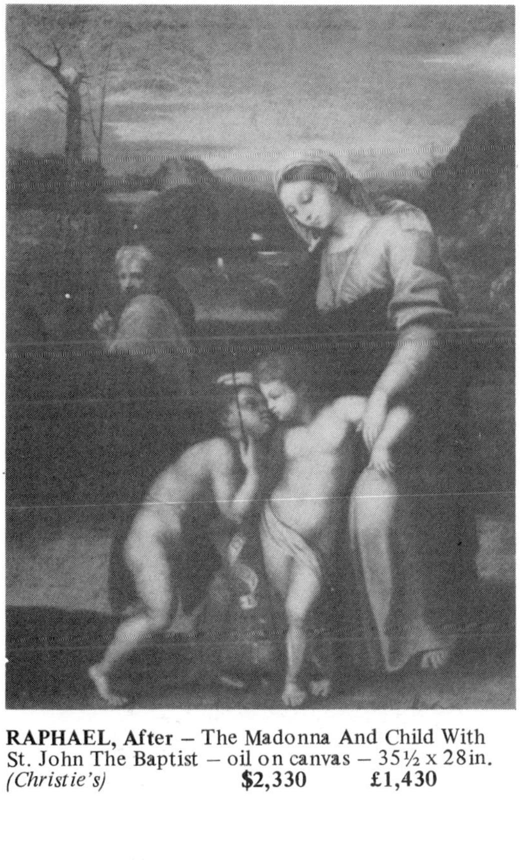

RAPHAEL, After – The Madonna And Child With St. John The Baptist – oil on canvas – 35½ x 28in.
(Christie's) **$2,330** **£1,430**

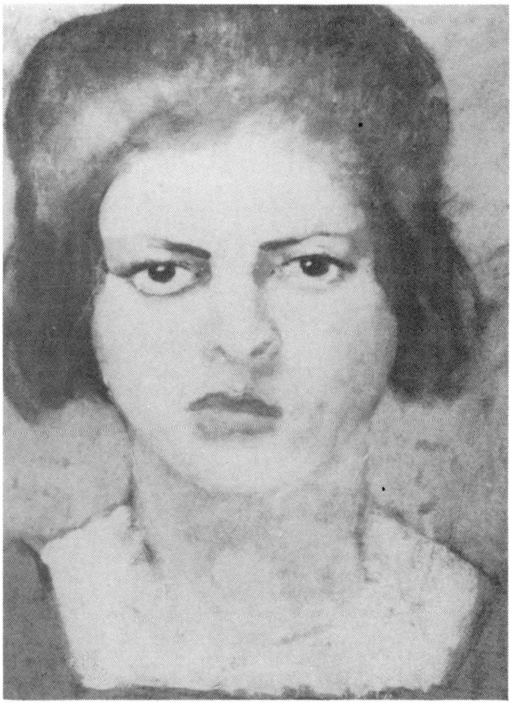

ARMAND RASSENFOSSE – Fille a la Robe bleue – oil on panel – 13¾ x 9¼in.
(Christie's) **$2,112** **£1,320**

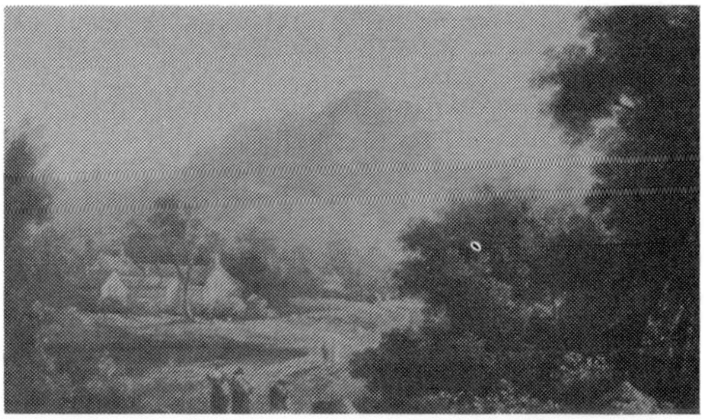

JOHN RATHBONE – A Wooded Landscape With Figures On A Track By A Cottage; and A Wooded River Landscape With Figures – on panel – 8 x 11in.
(Lawrence Fine Art) **$1,369** **£825 Pair**

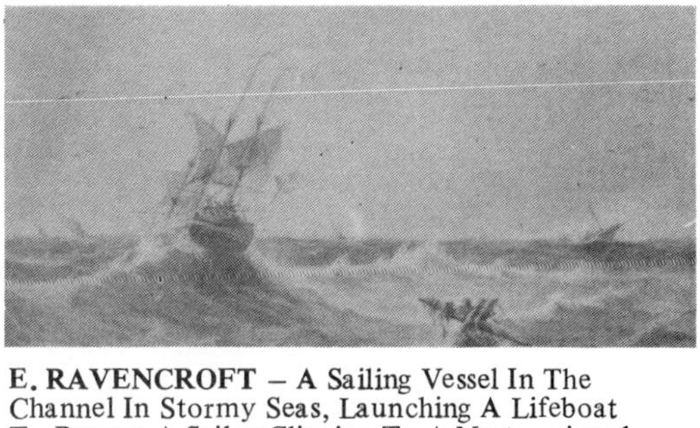

E. RAVENCROFT – A Sailing Vessel In The Channel In Stormy Seas, Launching A Lifeboat To Rescue A Sailor Clinging To A Mast – signed – watercolour – 17 x 26in.
(W. H. Lane & Son) **$343** **£240**

RAYMOND

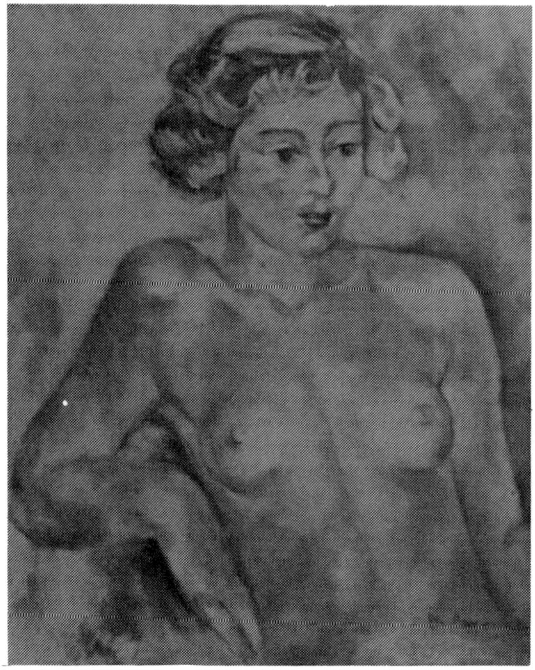

MARIE RAYMOND – Portrait D'Une Femme Nue – signed – oil on canvas – 61 x 49.5 cm.
(Phillips) **$1,365 £900**

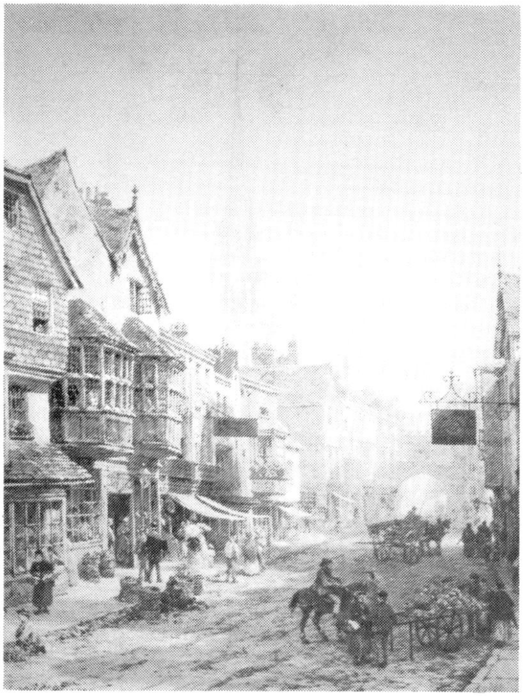

LOUISE RAYNER – The High Street, Salisbury – signed – watercolour heightened with bodycolour – 13¾ x 11in.
(Christie's) **$12,636 £8,424**

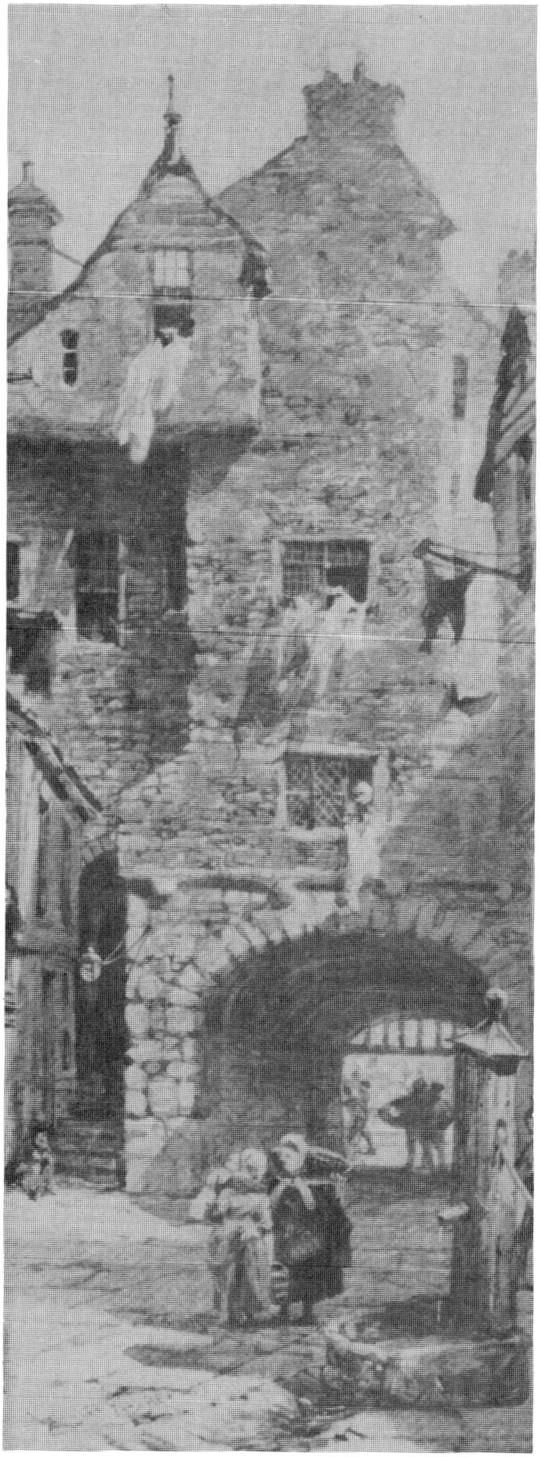

LOUISE RAYNER – Edinburgh: The Marquess Of Huntley Close – signed – watercolour and bodycolour – 10 x 4¾in.
(Christie's) **$1,706 £1,210**

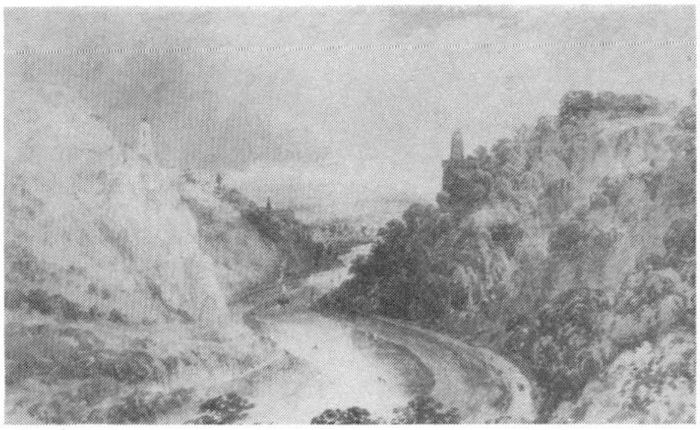

SAMUEL READ – The Avon Gorge Looking Southward, Showing The Clifton Suspension Bridge Partially Constructed – signed – pencil and watercolour heightened with white – 12¼ x 18¾in.
(Christie's) **$1,278** **£770**

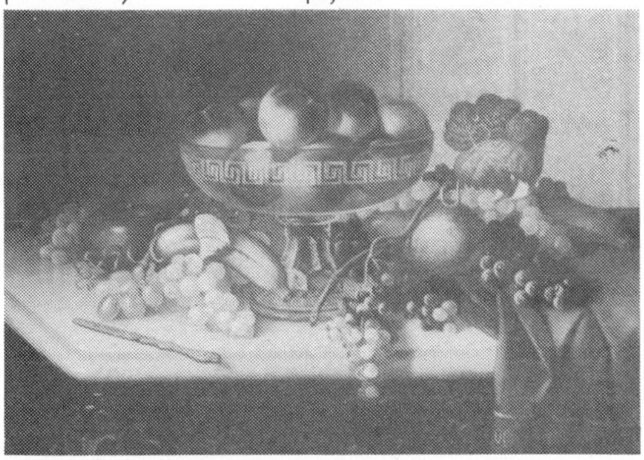

CARDUCIUS PLANTAGENET REAM – Still Life, Fruit And Knife – signed – oil on canvas – 22 x 28in.
(Christie's) **$11,000** **£7,733**

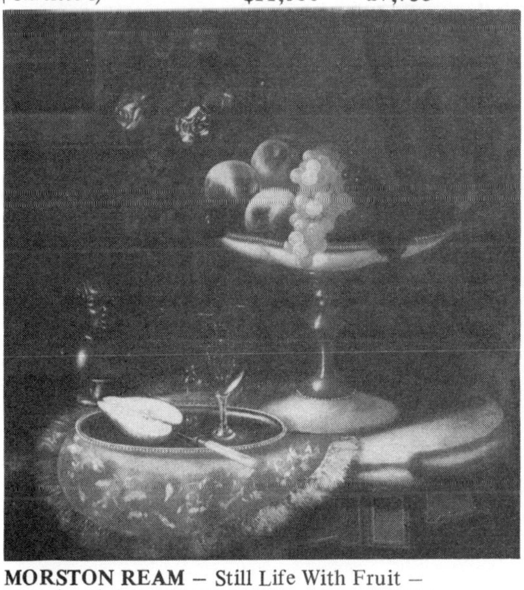

MORSTON REAM – Still Life With Fruit – signed and dated 1875 – oil on canvas – 31¾ x 26in.
(Christie's) **$10,450** **£6,511**

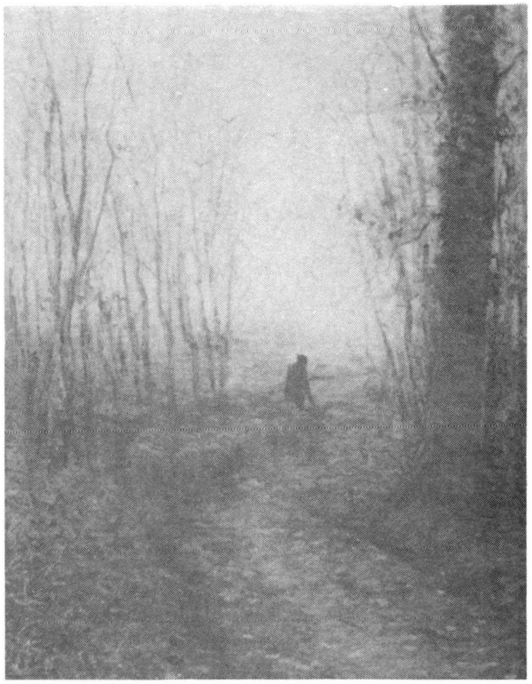

EDWARD WILLIS REDFIELD – The Shepherd – signed and dated '93 – oil on canvas – 29 x 21¼in.
(Christie's) **$6,600** **£4,591**

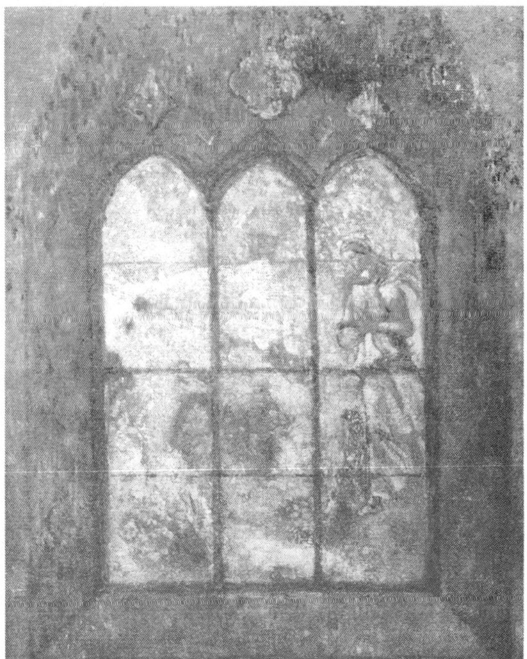

ODILON REDON – Le Vitrail – signed – oil on canvas – 26¾ x 19½in.
(Christie's) **$79,200** **£55,000**

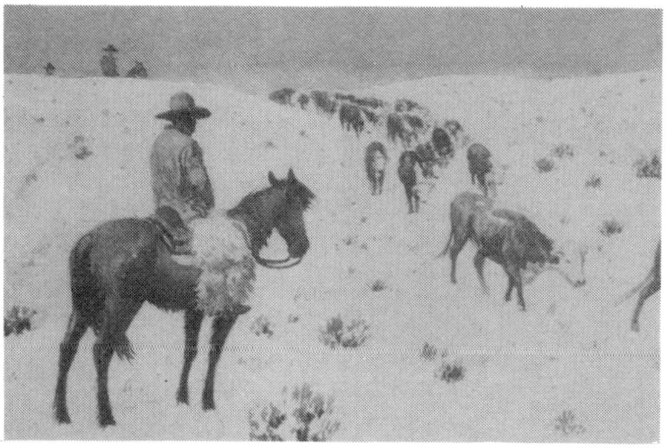

LEONARD HOWARD REEDY – White Faces; and Wolves And Range Horses – signed and inscribed – watercolour and pencil on paper laid down on board – one 22.7 x 30.5 cm., the other 22.3 x 30.5 cm.
(Christie's) **$770** **£479 Two**

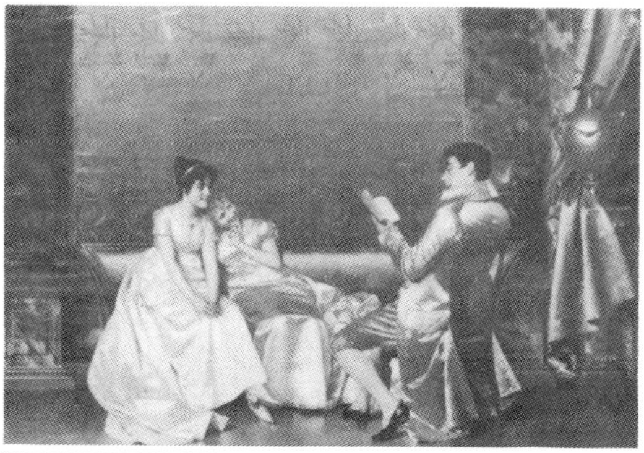

VITTORIO REGGIANINI – The Love Poem – signed – oil on canvas – 21½ x 28in.
(Christie's) **$11,088** **£7,700**

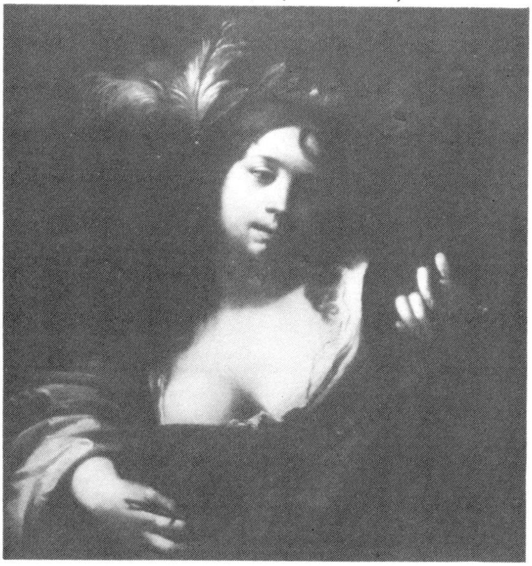

NICOLAS REGNIER, Circle of – The Cittern Player – oil on canvas – 34½ x 24¼in.
(Phillips) **$4,230** **£3,000**

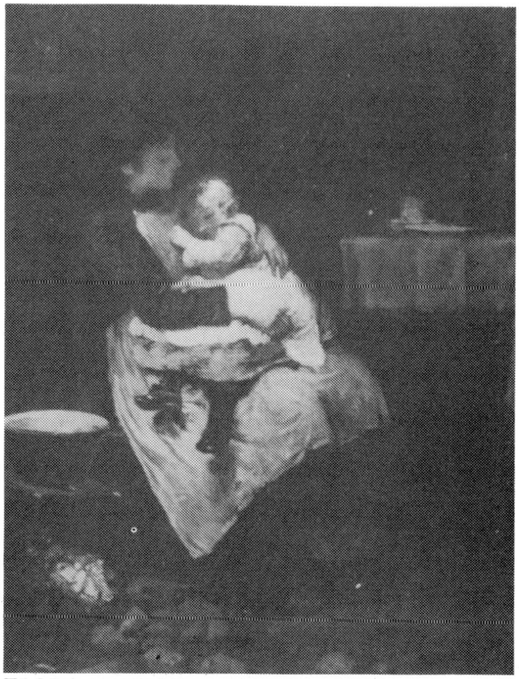

FLORA MACDONALD REID – Hush – signed and dated '90-1 – 24 x 18in.
(Christie's) **$2,016** **£1,430**

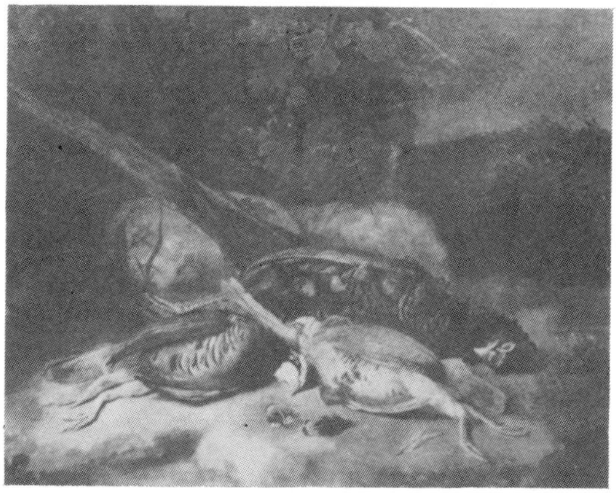

PHILIP REINAGLE – Still Life Of Game In A Landscape – oil on canvas – 25 x 30in.
(Christie's) **$1,267** **£880**

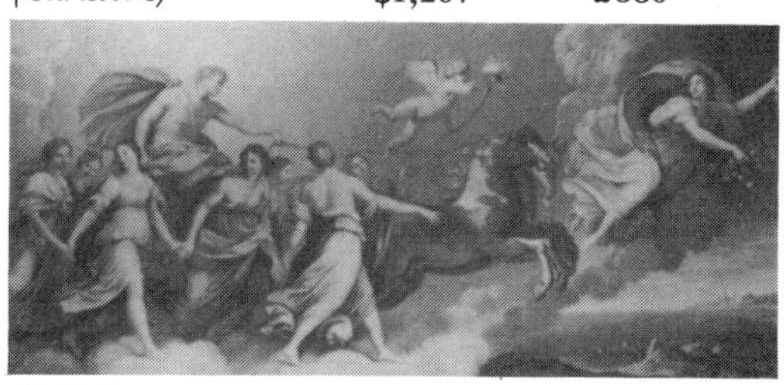

GUIDO RENI, After – Aurora; and Flora – bodycolour – 13½ x 26½in.
(Christie's) **$2,112** **£1,320 Pair**

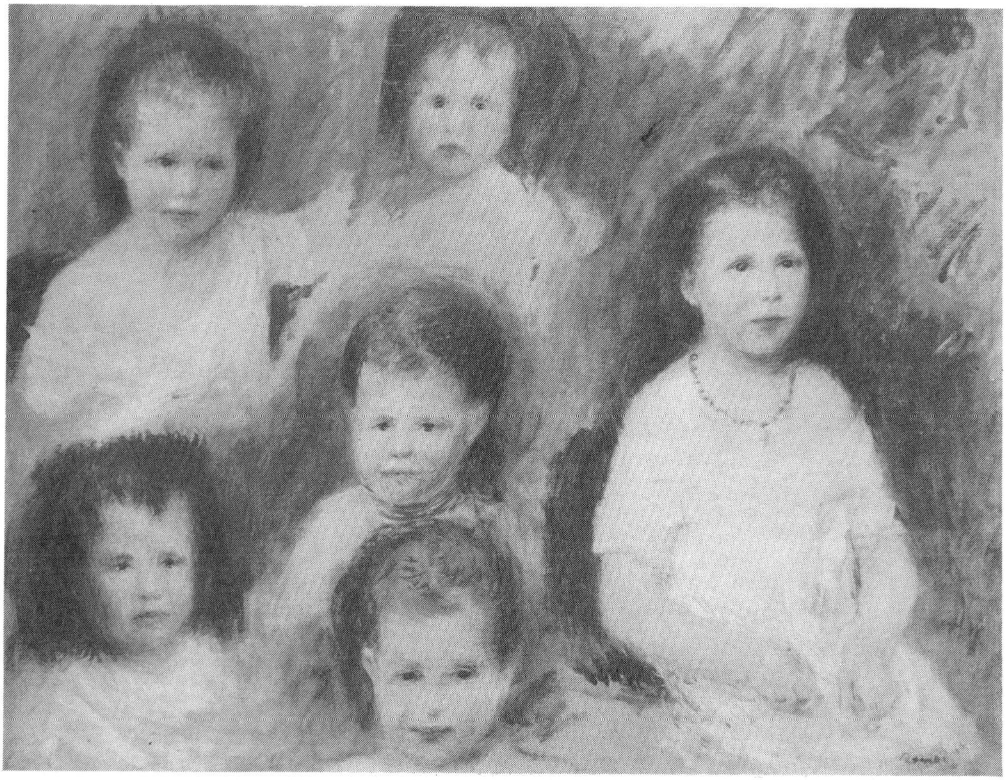

PIERRE AUGUSTE RENOIR – Les Petits – signed – oil on canvas – 15½ x 18¾in. *(Christie's)* **$477,620 £286,000**

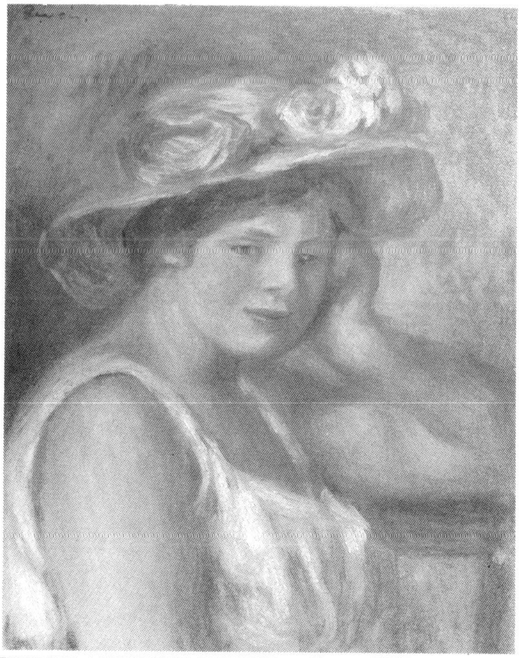

PIERRE AUGUSTE RENOIR – Jeune Fille au Chapeau – signed – oil on canvas – 20½ x 15½in. *(Christie's)* **$792,000 £550,000**

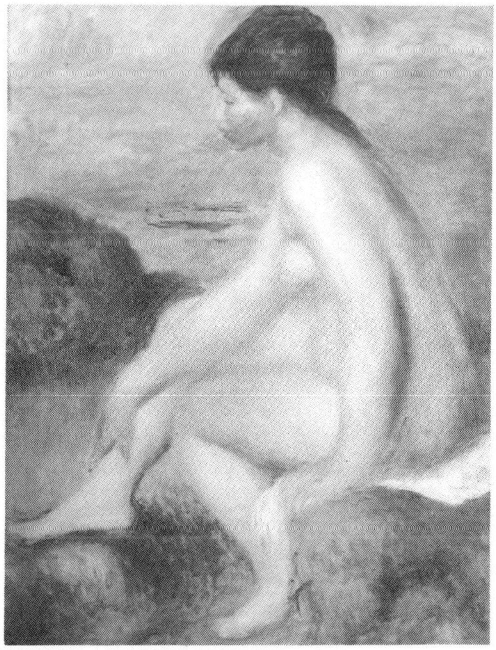

PIERRE AUGUSTE RENOIR – Baigneuse – signed – oil on canvas – 21 x 15in. *(Christie's)* **$1,504,800 £1,045,000**

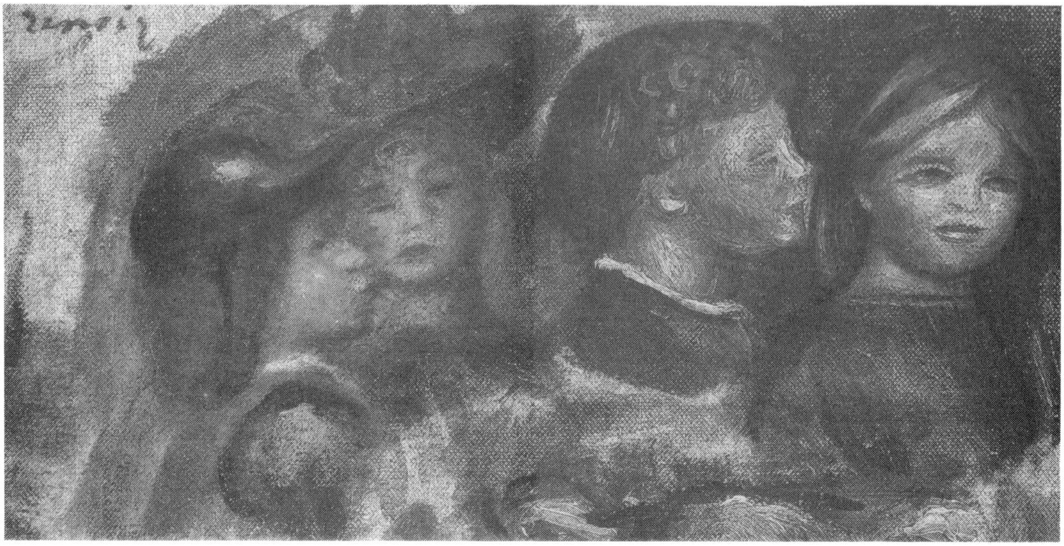

PIERRE AUGUSTE RENOIR – Etudes de jeunes Filles – signed – oil on canvas – 4½ x 8½in.
(Christie's) **$128,500 £77,000**

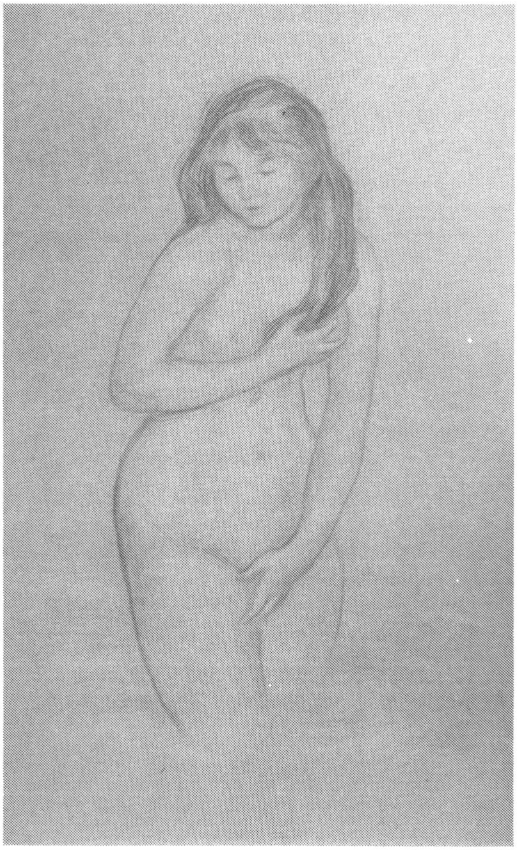

PIERRE AUGUSTE RENOIR – Jeune Femme se baignant – signed – red chalk heightened with white on buff paper – 13 x 10in.
(Christie's) **$66,528 £46,200**

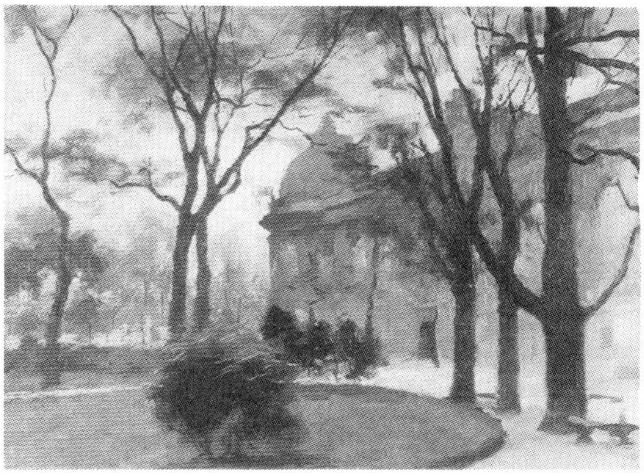

JULES ERNEST RENOUX – Derriere le Petit Palais – signed and inscribed – oil on canvas – 15 x 18in.
(Christie's) **$871 £605**

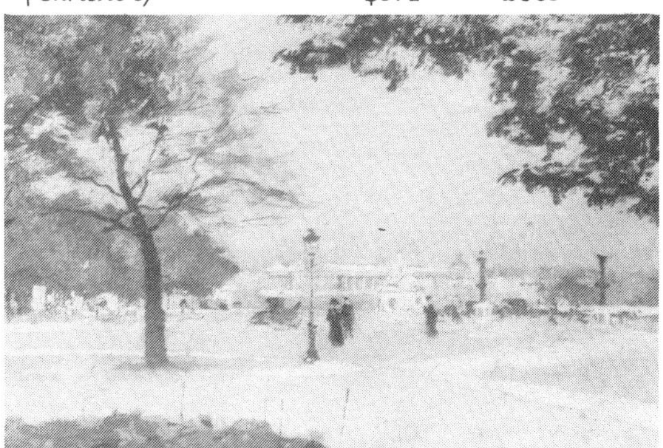

JULES ERNEST RENOUX – Place de la Concorde – signed – oil on canvas – 15 x 18in.
(Christie's) **$4,576 £2,860**

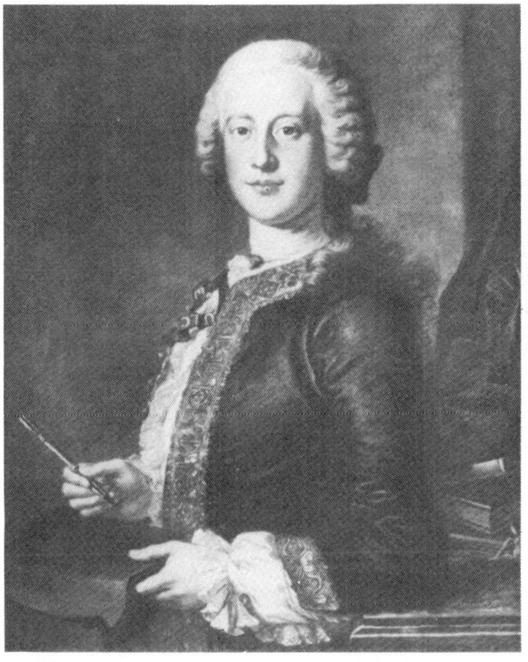

JAN VAN REYSSCHOOT – Portrait Of An Artist, Said To Be Sir John Cotton, 6th Bt. Of Conington – oil on canvas – 32¼ x 26in.
(Phillips) **$2,256** **£1,600**

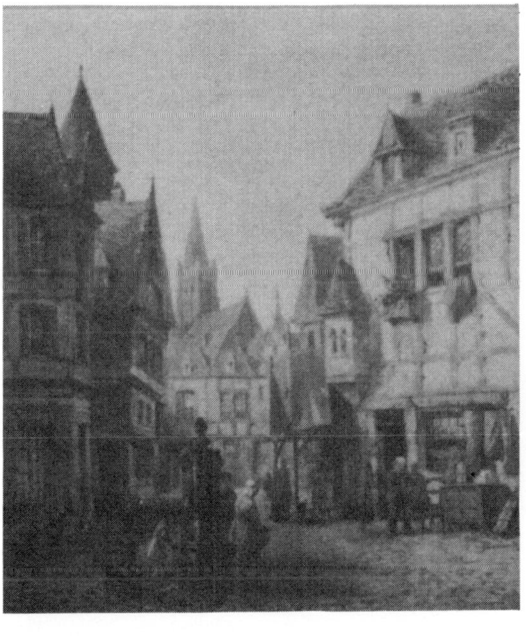

FELICIA A. REZIA – Ancient Architecture – signed, indistinctly dated, signed and inscribed on a label on the reverse – oil on canvas – 13½ x 11½in.
(Christie's) **$847** **£550**

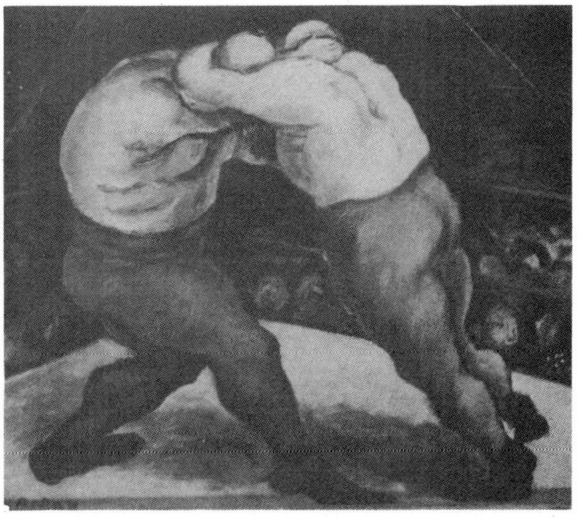

LOUIS RIBAK – Wrestlers – signed – oil on panel – 9 x 10¾in.
(Christie's) **$2,420** **£1,683**

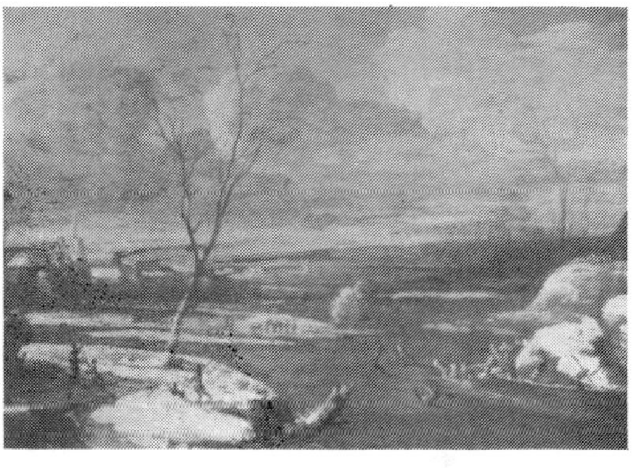

MARCO RICCI, Follower of – A Winter Landscape; and A Southern Coast In Summer – watercolour and gouache – on paper – 5½ x 8in.
(Lawrence Fine Art) **$1,643** **£990 Pair**

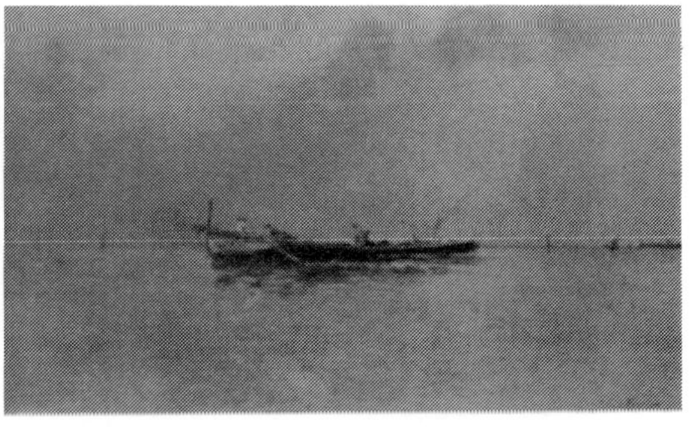

OSCAR RICCIARDI – Fishermen By The Bay – signed – oil on canvas – 28.25 x 47.5cm.
(Phillips) **$1,472** **£950**

OSCAR RICCIARDI – Fishermen Mending Their Nets – signed – oil on canvas – 29.25 x 49.5cm.
(Phillips) **$1,317** **£850**

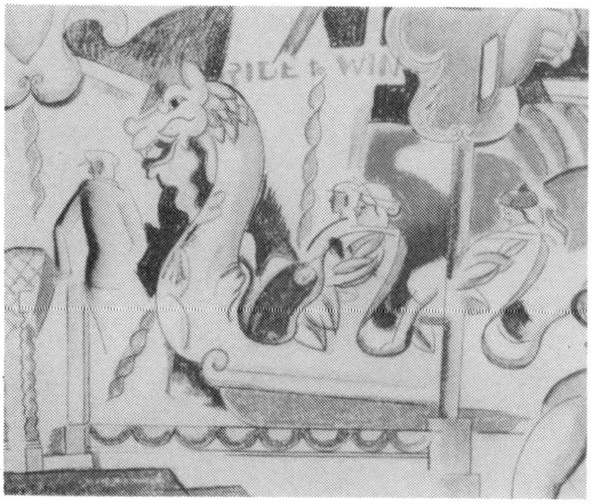

ANNE ESTELLE RICE – Ride To Win – signed and dated '34 – pastel and black crayon – 12½ x 16¼in.
(Christie's) **$1,415** **£990**

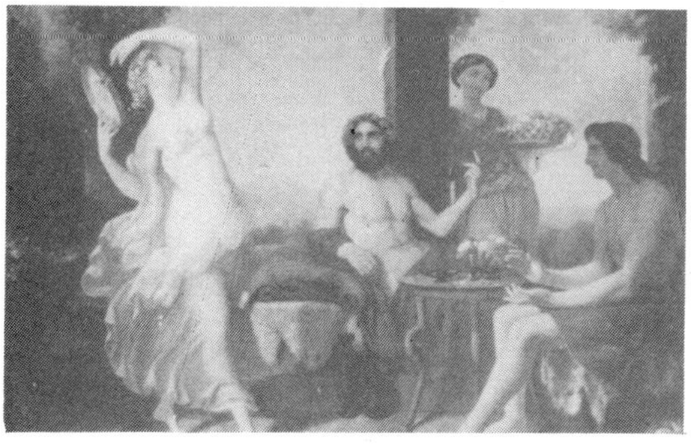

CHARLOTTE RICHARD – Dancing For The King – signed and dated 1847 – oil on canvas laid on board – 18½ x 27½in.
(Christie's) **$986** **£605**

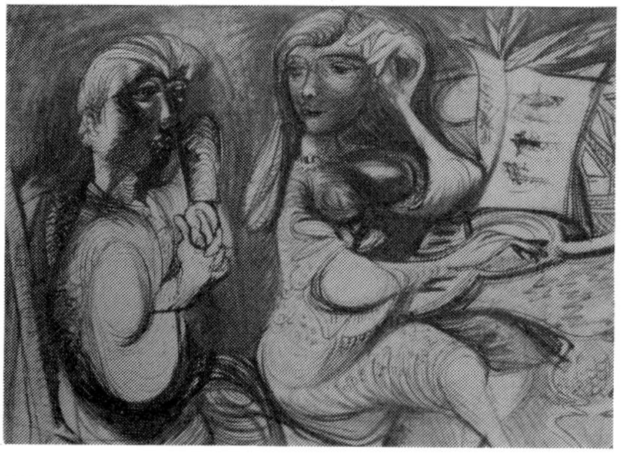

CERI RICHARDS – Two Women – signed and dated 1946 – pen and indian ink, watercolour, charcoal and pastel – 36 x 52cm.
(Phillips) **$4,800** **£3,000**

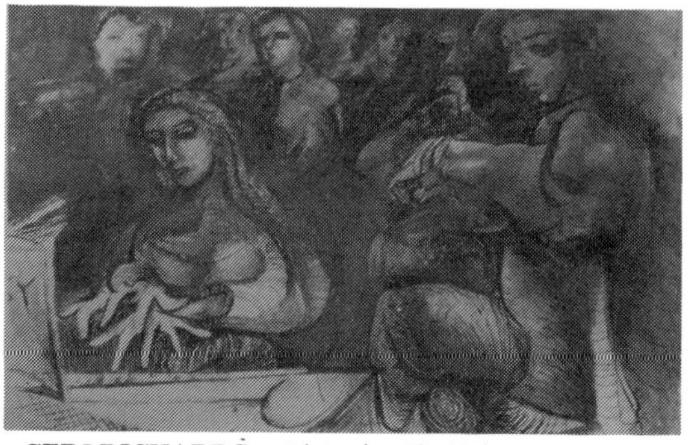

CERI RICHARDS – Listening To Debussy – signed and dated 1945 – pen and indian ink and wax crayon – 38 x 56cm.
(Phillips) **$1,680** **£1,050**

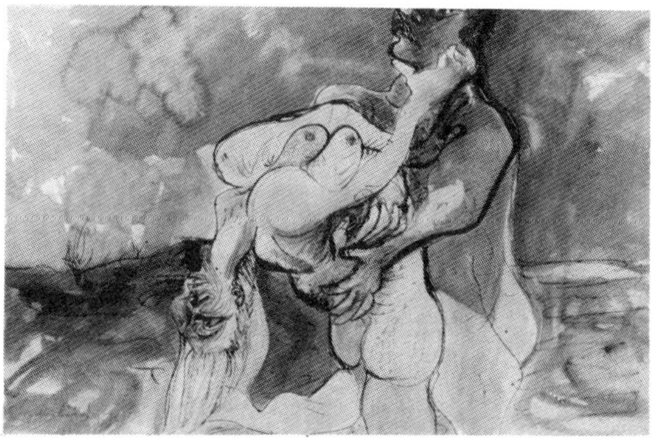

CERI RICHARDS – The Rape Of The Sabine – signed and dated '47 – watercolour, gouache, pen, brush and black ink – 14¾ x 22in.
(Christie's) **$1,887** **£1,320**

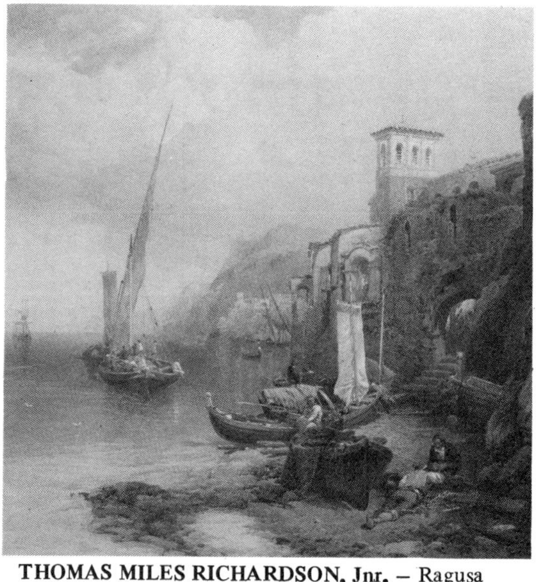

THOMAS MILES RICHARDSON, Jnr. – Ragusa On The Adriatic – signed and dated 1867 – pencil, pen and ink and watercolour heightened with white – 29¾ x 25¾in.
(Christie's) **$5,670** **£3,780**

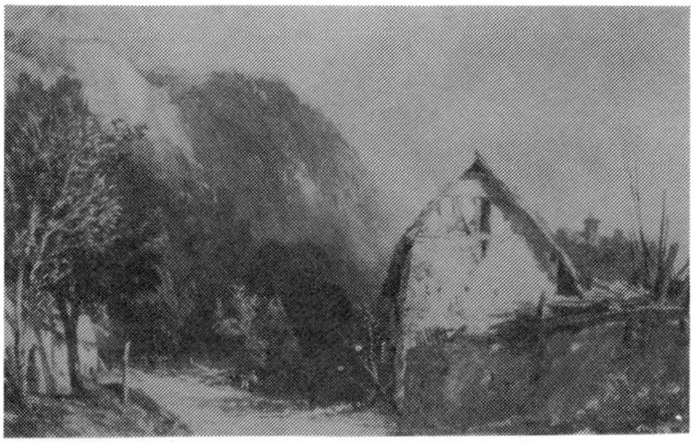

THOMAS MILES RICHARDSON, Jnr. – The Village Of Sayn, Prussia – signed, and inscribed and dated 1848 on the reverse – pencil and watercolour – 9¾ x 14¼in.
(Christie's) **$876** **£528**

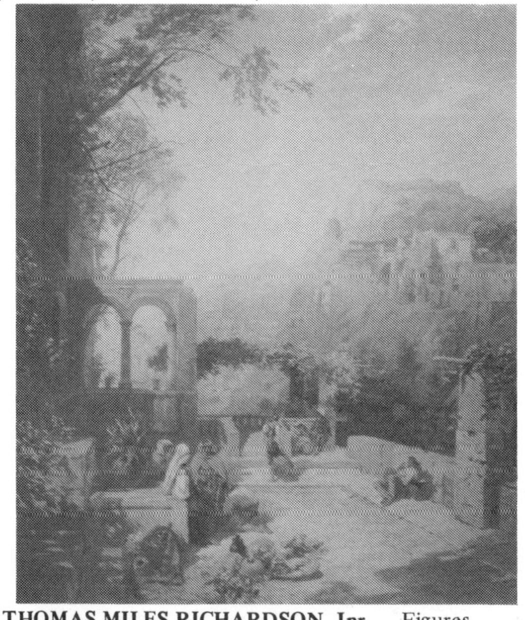

THOMAS MILES RICHARDSON, Jnr. – Figures In A Courtyard, Amalfi – signed and dated 1862 – – pencil and watercolour heightened with white – 29¼ x 25½in.
(Christie's) **$8,817** **£5,280**

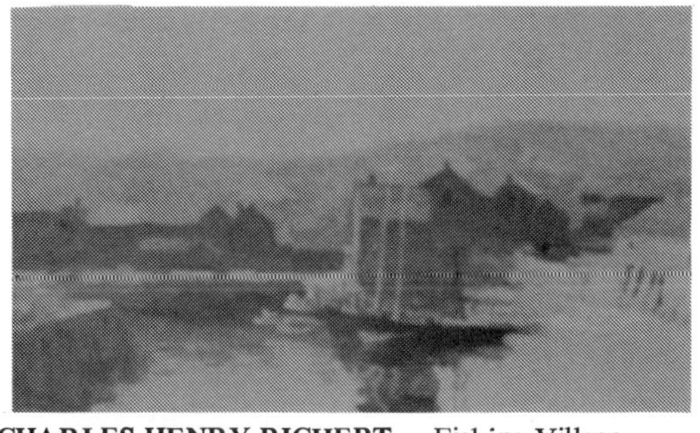

CHARLES HENRY RICHERT – Fishing Village – – signed – oil on board – 14 x 18in.
(Robt. W. Skinner Inc.) **$700** **£429**

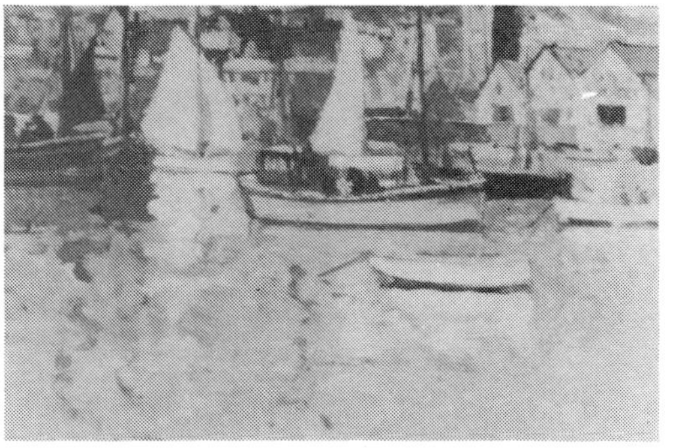

LEONARD RICHMOND – 'The Harbour, St. Ives, Cornwall' – signed – oil on board – 30 x 40cm.
(W. H. Lane & Son) **$1,460** **£880**

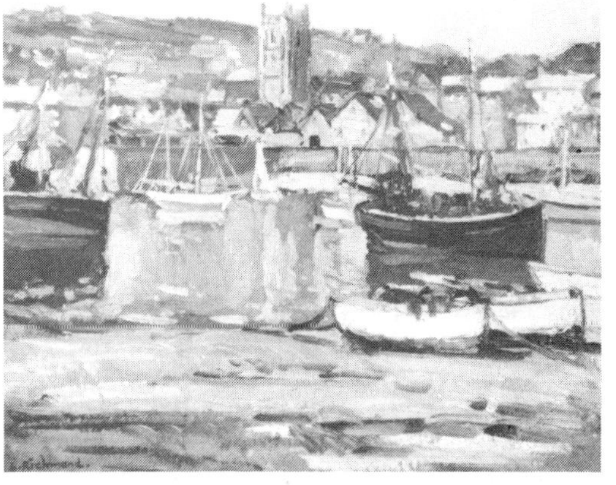

LEONARD RICHMOND – Low Tide In St. Ives Harbour signed oil on board – 34 x 40cm.
(W. H. Lane & Son) **$1,826** **£1,100**

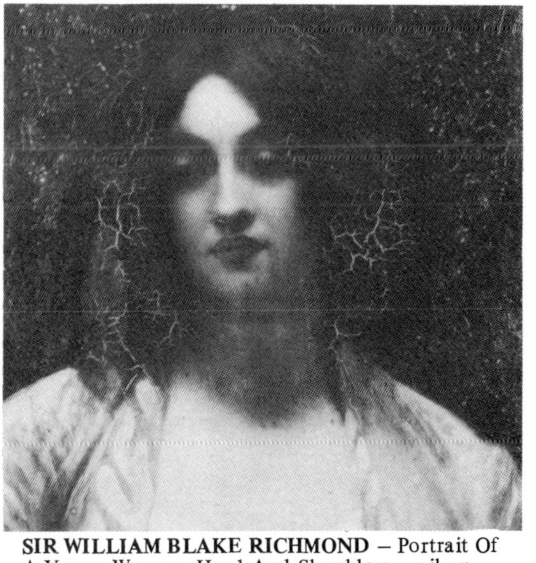

SIR WILLIAM BLAKE RICHMOND – Portrait Of A Young Woman, Head And Shoulders – oil on panel – 18¼ x 15½in.
(Phillips) **$2,754** **£1,800**

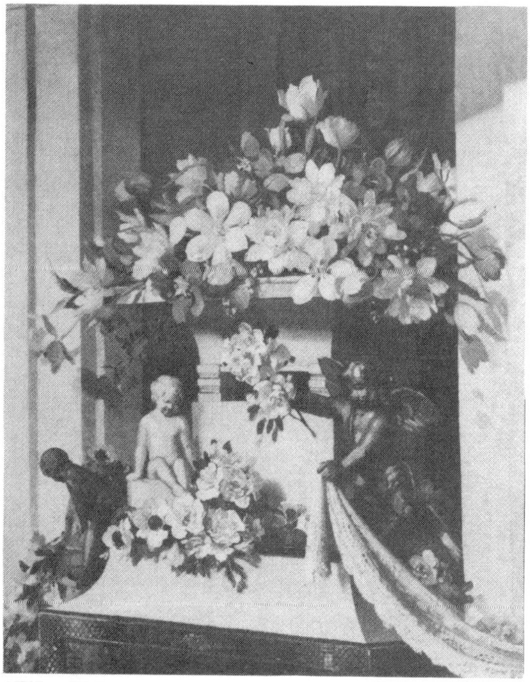

HERBERT DAVIS RICHTER – Still Life With Spring Flowers And Cherubs – signed – oil on canvas – 126 x 102cm.
(Phillips) **$1,254** **£820**

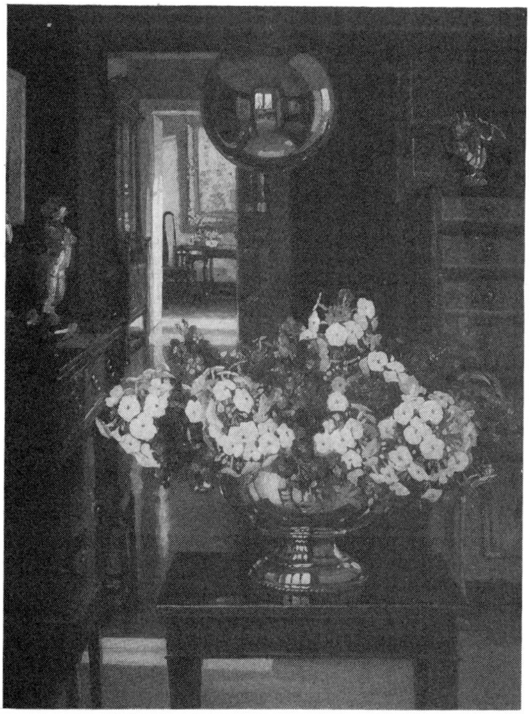

HERBERT DAVIS RICHTER – Household Gods – signed – oil on canvas – 40 x 36in.
(Christie's) **$8,289** **£5,280**

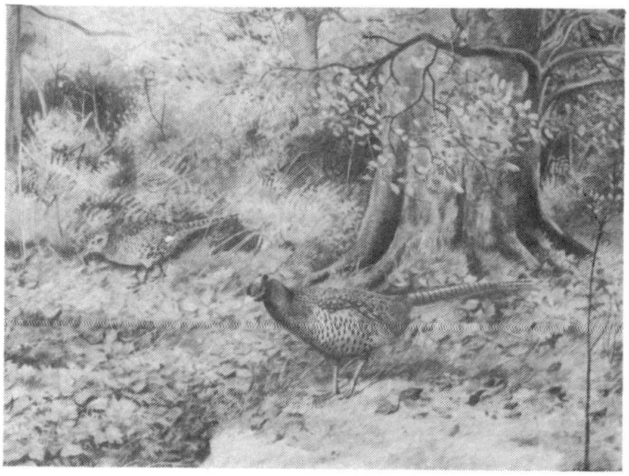

PHILIP RICKMAN – Autumn: A Cock And A Hen Pheasant In A Beech Wood – signed and dated 1972 – watercolour and bodycolour – 21½ x 29¾in.
(Christie's) **$4,653** **£3,300**

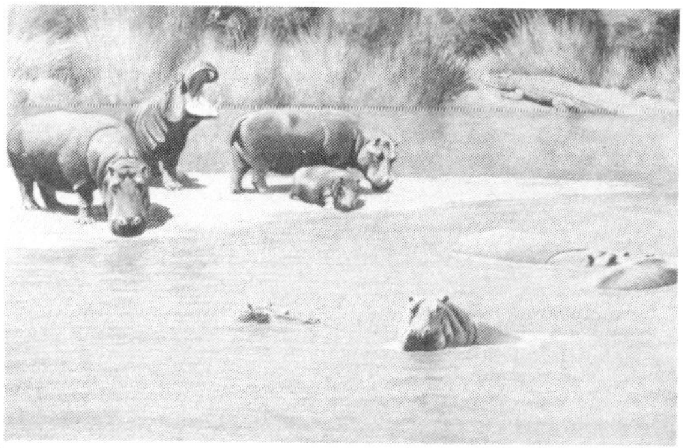

W. H. RIDDELL – Hippopotami; Buffalo And Cranes; Gazelle, Giraffes And An Ostrich; and Rhinoceri and Elephants – signed – bodycolour – 13½ x 20½in.
(Christie's) **$2,946** **£2,090 Four**

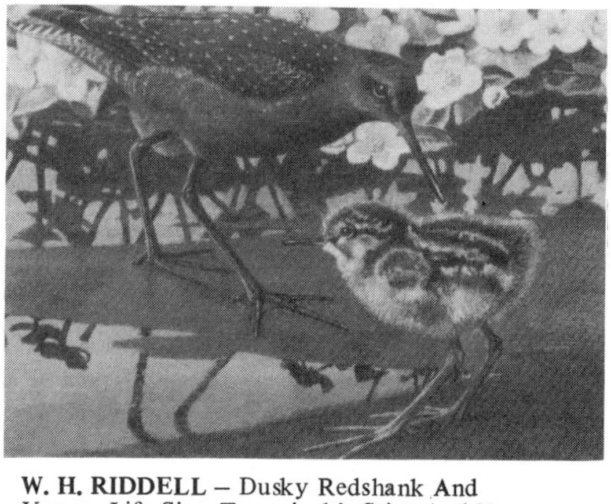

W. H. RIDDELL – Dusky Redshank And Young, Life Size; Temminck's Stint And Young, and Wood Sandpiper And Young; Ruff And Young; and Bar-tailed Godwit and Young – signed and inscribed on the reverse – watercolour and bodycolour – 6 x 8in.
(Christie's) **$2,019** **£1,320 Four**

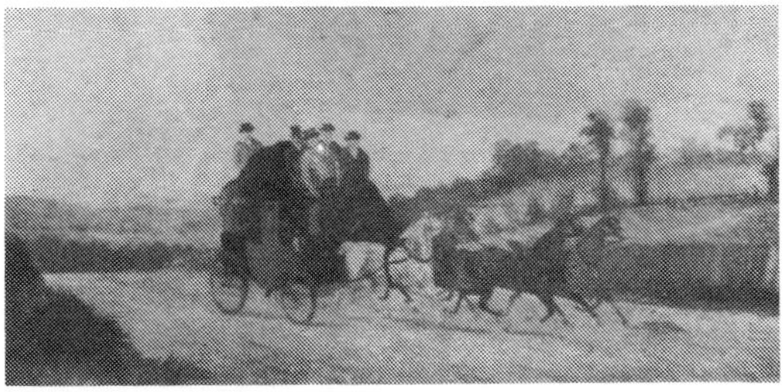

PHILIP H. RIDEOUT – Coaching Scenes – signed and dated 1886 – 9½ x 13½in.
(Christie's) **$4,375** **£2,860** Four

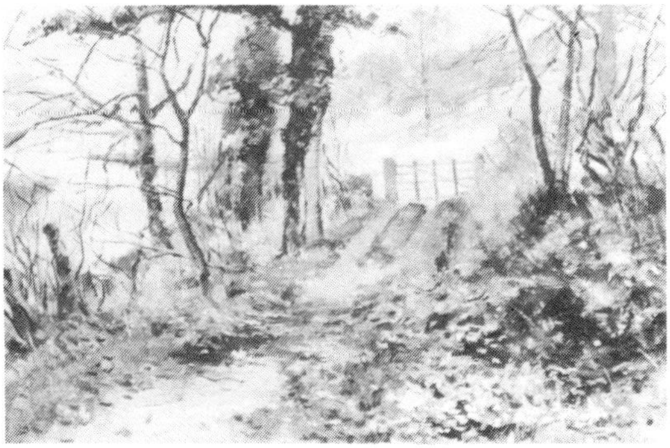

ARTHUR H. RIGG – Woodland Path By River – signed – oil – 12 x 16in.
(Capes, Dunn & Co.) **$179** **£110**

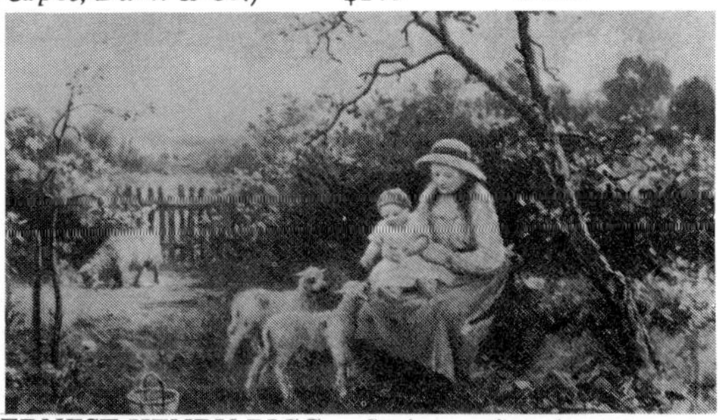

ERNEST HENRY RIGG – Spring – signed – 15¾ x 23½in.
(Christie's) **$3,702** **£2,420**

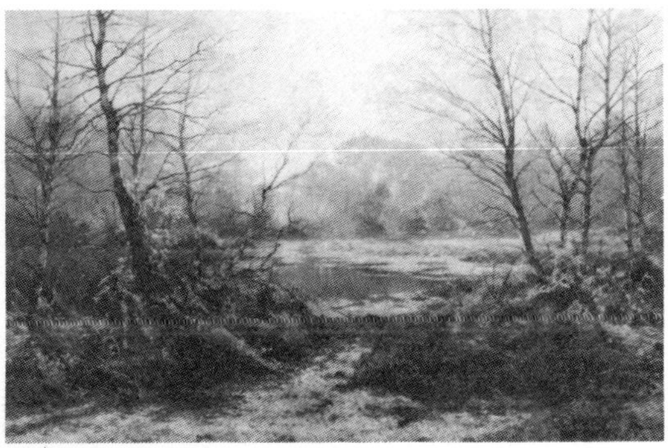

ALBERT GABRIEL RIGOLOT – Extensive Autumn Landscape – signed – oil on canvas – 25¾ x 40in.
(Robt. W. Skinner Inc.) **$4,500** **£3,125**

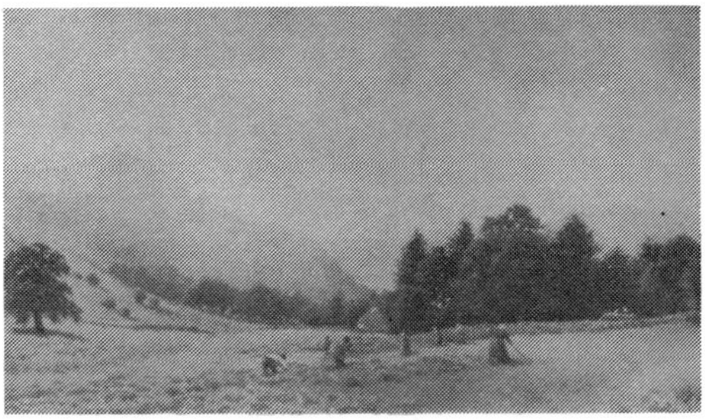

M. L. RILEY – 'Fine Hay Weather' – signed and dated 1902, also inscribed on old exhibition label verso – watercolour – 33 x 50cm.
(Phillips) **$782** **£480**

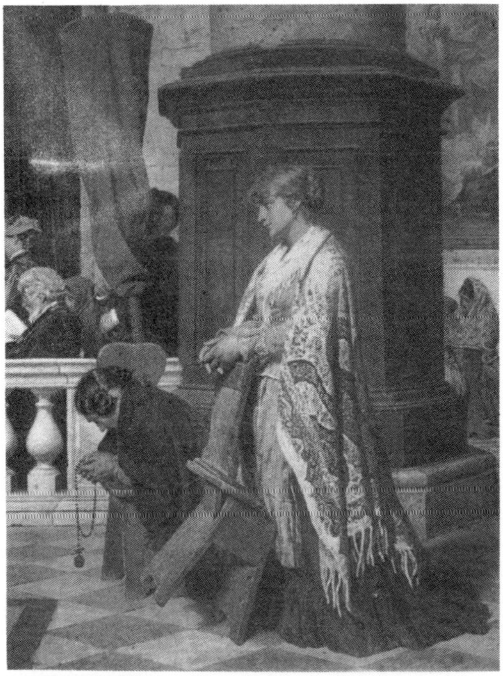

LUIGI DA RIOS – Temptation In The House Of God – signed and dated 1881 – watercolour – 21½ x 15¼in.
(Christie's) **$4,224** **£2,640**

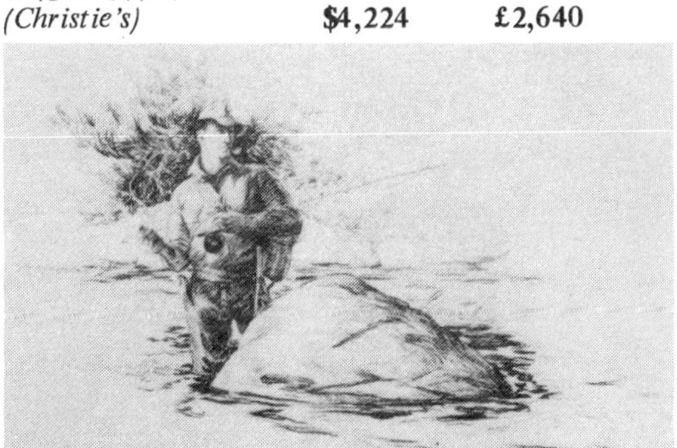

AIDEN LASSELL RIPLEY – Fly Fishermen – signed – graphite on paper – 8¾ x 13¼in.
(Robt. W. Skinner Inc.) **$450** **£296**

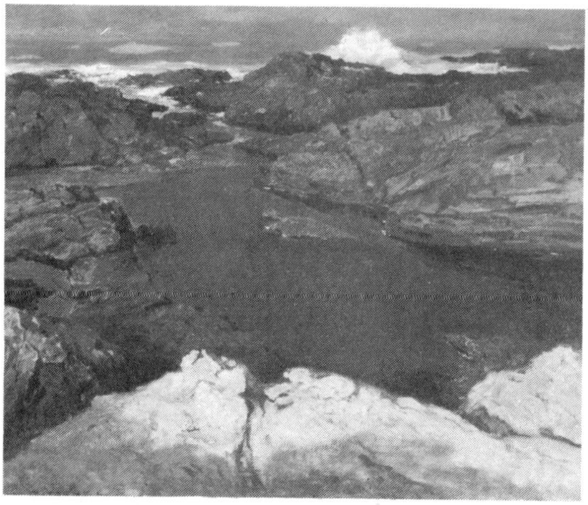

WILLIAM RITSCHEL – Seascape, Carmel – signed – oil on canvas – 34¼ x 40¼in,
(Christie's) **$18,700** **£13,009**

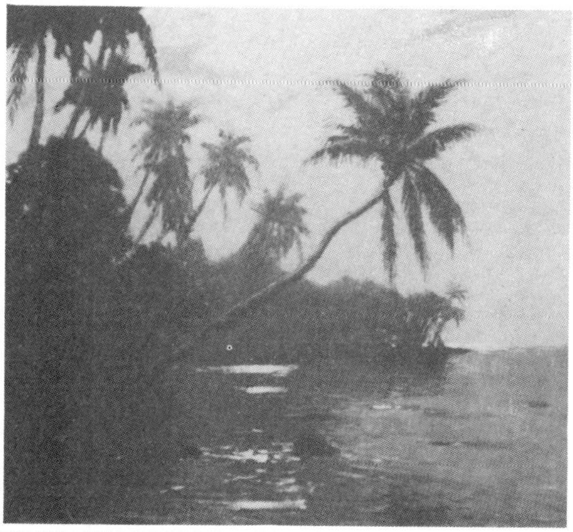

WILLIAM RITSCHEL – Moonbeams Of Tahiti – signed, signed and inscribed on the reverse – oil on canvas – 30¼ x 30¼in.
(Christie's) **$3,300** **£2,295**

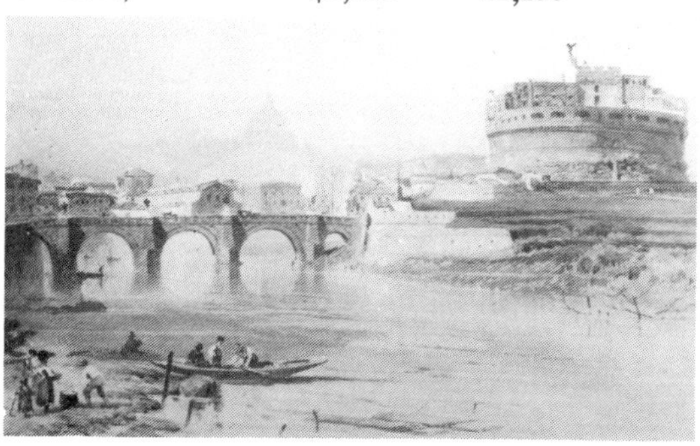

HENRY PARSONS RIVIERE – Rome: The Castel San Angelo With St. Peter's In The Distance – signed – pencil and watercolour heightened with white – 18¾ x 27¼in.
(Christie's) **$1,551** **£1,100**

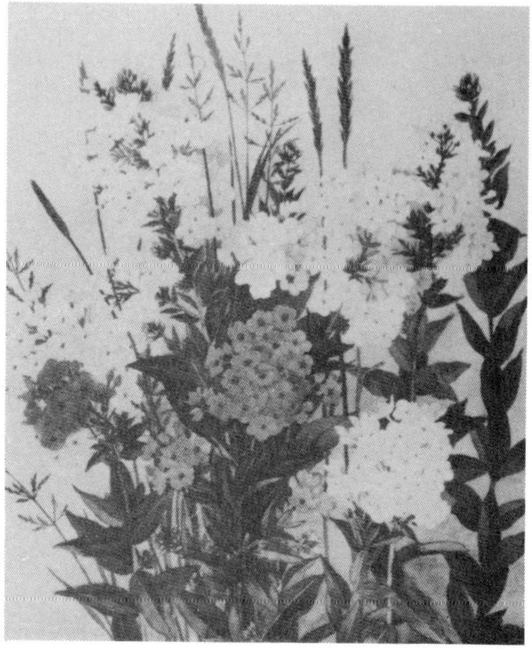

ELLEN ROBBINS – Still Life With Wild Flowers – signed and dated 1884 – watercolour on paper – 25 x 21in.
(Robt. W. Skinner Inc.) **$650** **£427**

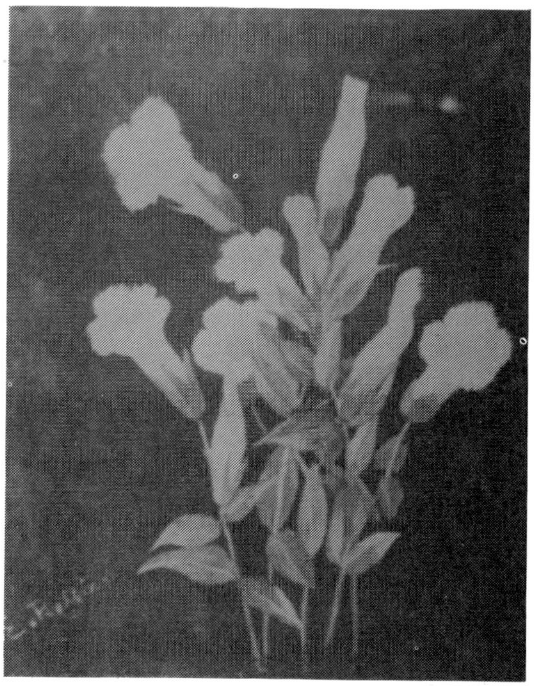

ELLEN ROBBINS – White Fringed Gentian – signed – watercolour on paper – 8 x 6in.
(Robt. W. Skinner Inc.) **$200** **£122**

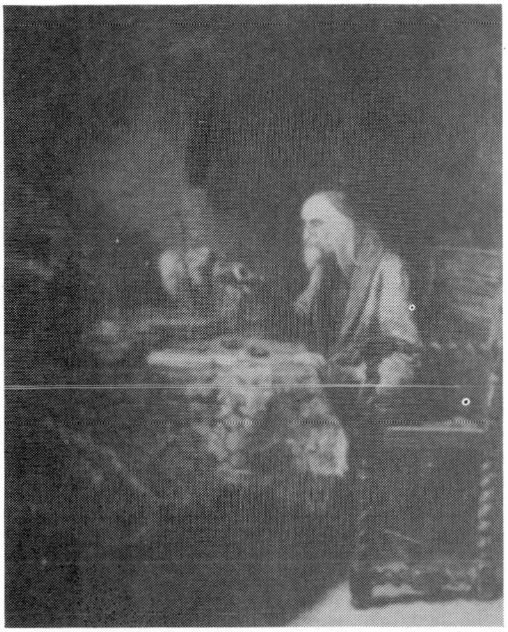

TONY ROBERT-FLEURY – The Miser – signed – 26 x 22in.
(Christie's) **$1,078** **£700**

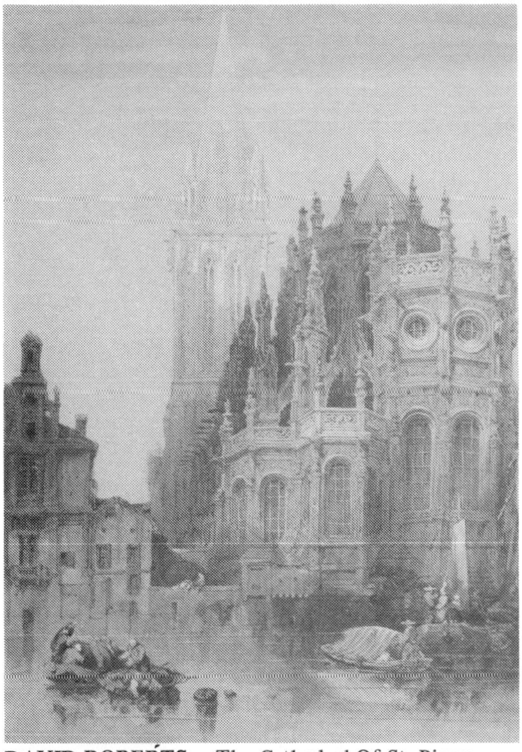

DAVID ROBERTS – The Cathedral Of St. Pierre, Caen – signed and dated 1830(?) – pencil, pen and brown ink and watercolour heightened with white and touches of gum arabic – 13½ x 9½in.
(Christie's) **$8,817** **£5,280**

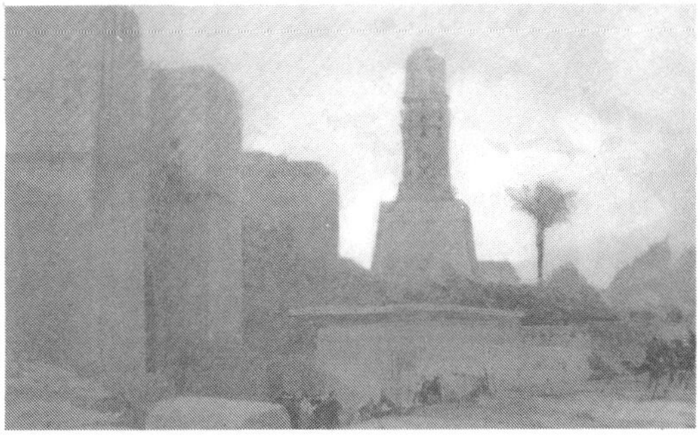

DAVID ROBERTS – Bab el Nazar or Gate Of Victory, Cairo – signed, inscribed and dated 1839 – pencil and watercolour heightened with white on buff paper – 9¼ x 13¼in.
(Christie's) **$9,372** **£6,600**

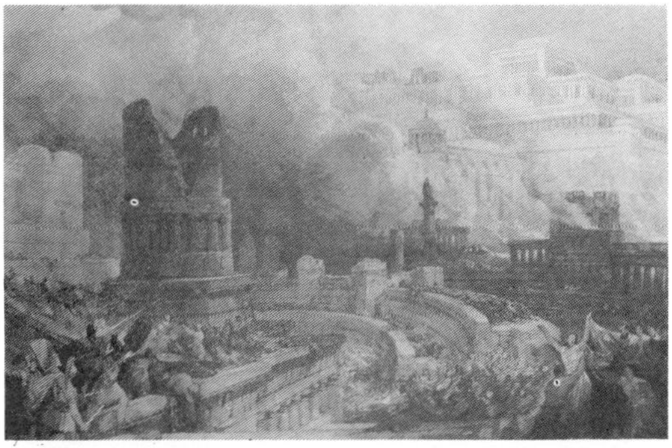

DAVID ROBERTS – The Destruction Of A City – signed and dated 1832 – pencil and watercolour heightened with white and gum arabic – 8¼ x 12¼in.
(Christie's) **$11,022** **£6,600**

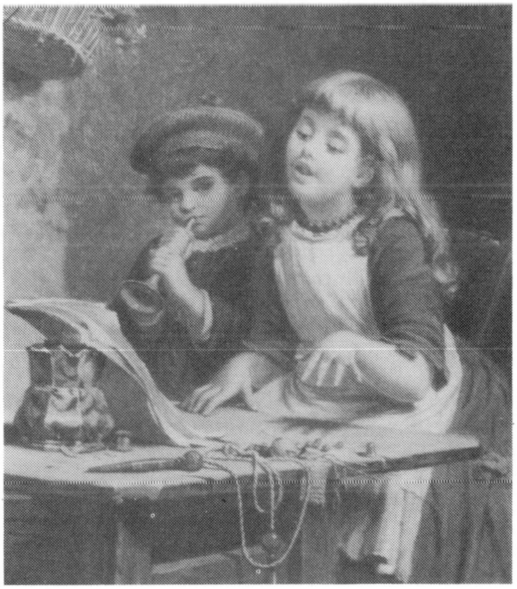

EDWIN ROBERTS – The Duet; and Shop – signed – 16 x 12in.
(Christie's) **$6,732** **£4,400 Pair**

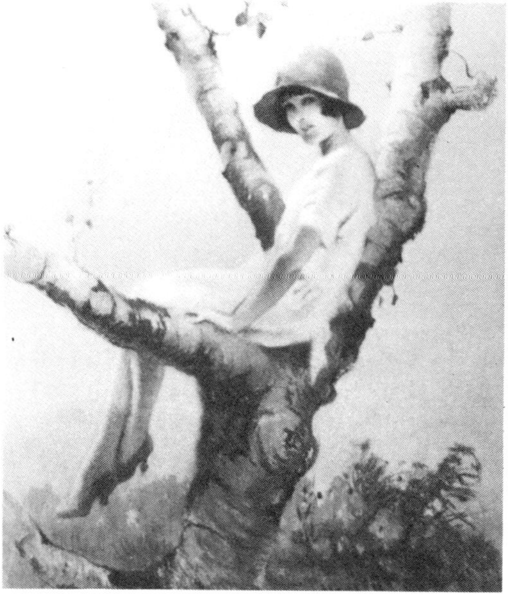

LANCELOT ROBERTS – 'Wendy', Young Woman Seated In A Tree – signed – pastel drawing – 22 x 17in.
(Capes, Dunn & Co.) **$5,216** **£3,200**

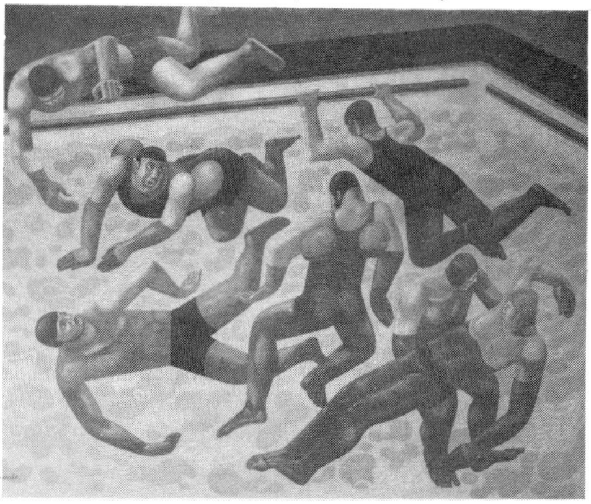

WILLIAM ROBERTS – Water Polo – signed – oil on canvas – 16 x 20in.
(Christie's) **$17,270** **£11,000**

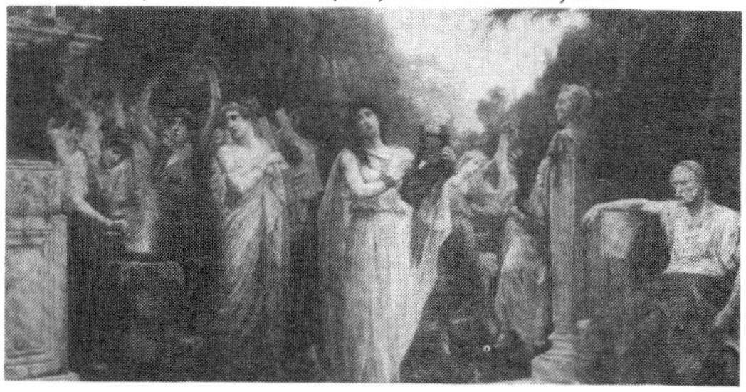

GEORGE EDWARD ROBERTSON – A Classical Sacrifice – signed – 57 x 96in.
(Christie's) **$11,781** **£7,700**

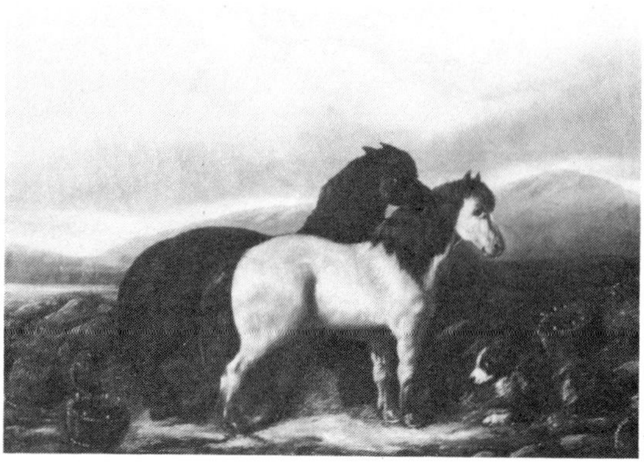

J. ROBERTSON – Ponies In A Highland Landscape – signed – oil on canvas – 18 x 26in.
(Biddle & Webb) **$505** **£320**

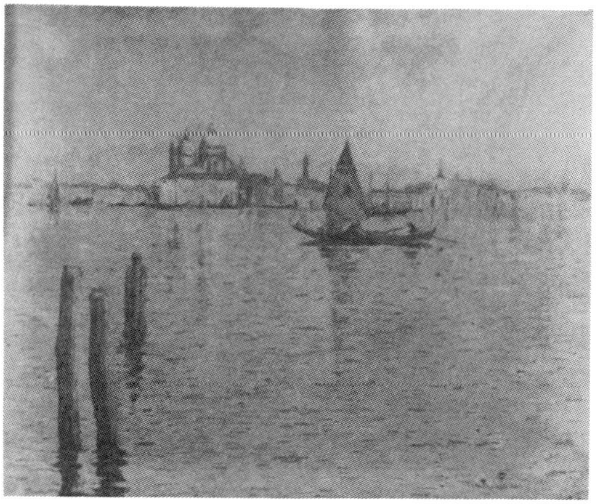

TOM ROBERTSON – Venice From The Lagoon – signed – 24½ x 29½in.
(Christie's) **$3,722** **£2,640**

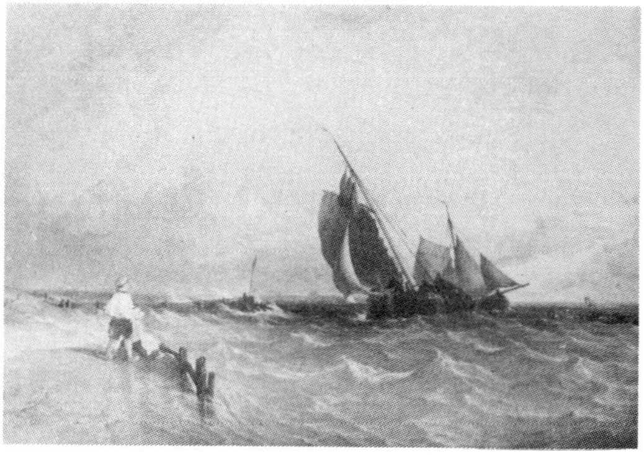

THOMAS SEWELL ROBINS – Dutch Fishing Boats Entering An Estuary In A Strong Breeze – signed with initials and dated '58, and inscribed on the artist's label – pencil and watercolour – 16½ x 23½in.
(Christie's) **$4,342** **£3,080**

THOMAS SEWELL ROBINS – Shipping Off The Pier, Calais, In A Storm – signed with initials and dated '61 – pencil and watercolour – 12¼ x 18½in.
(Christie's) **$3,104** **£1,870**

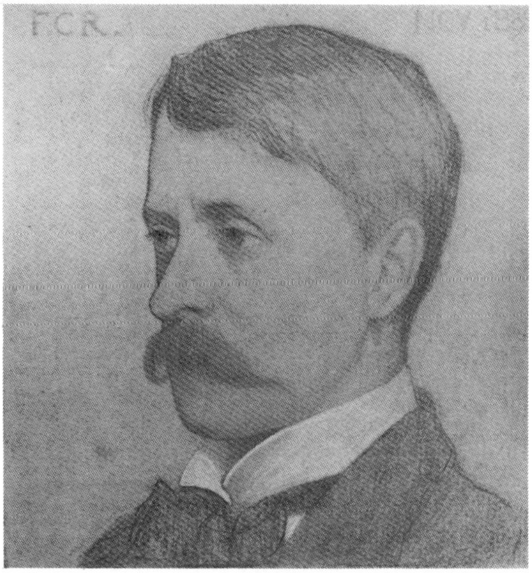

FREDERICK CAYLEY ROBINSON – Self Portrait – signed with initials and dated 1898 – coloured chalks on buff paper – 22 x 20cm.
(Phillips) **$2,130** **£1,500**

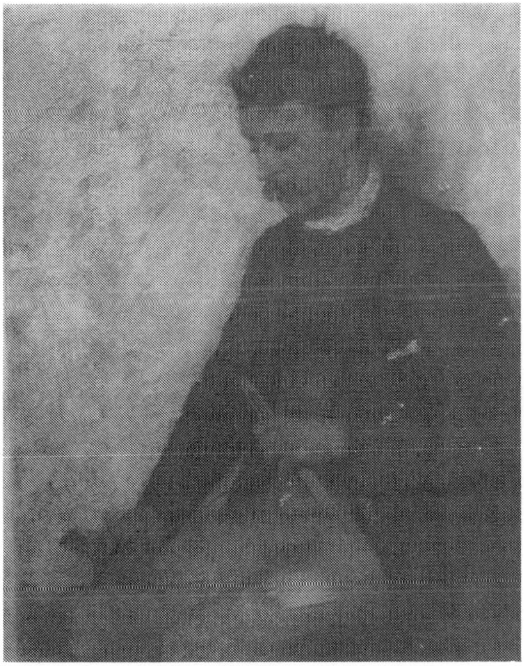

FREDERICK CAYLEY ROBINSON – Portrait Of The Artist – oil on board – 27.5 x 22cm.
(Phillips) **$2,556** **£1,800**

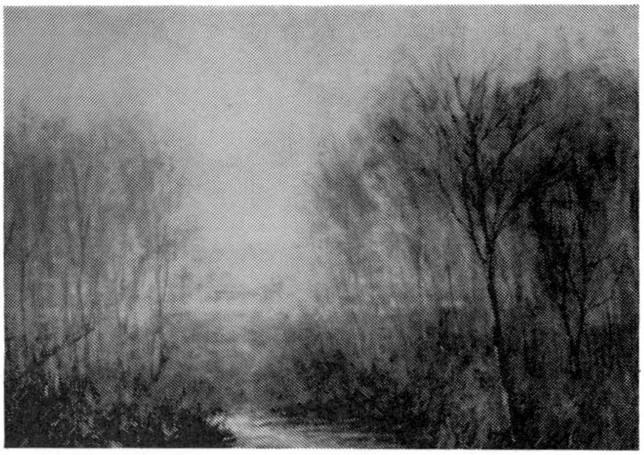

HAL ROBINSON – Twilight River Landscape – signed – oil on canvas – 30 x 36in.
(Robt. W. Skinner Inc.) **$800** **£490**

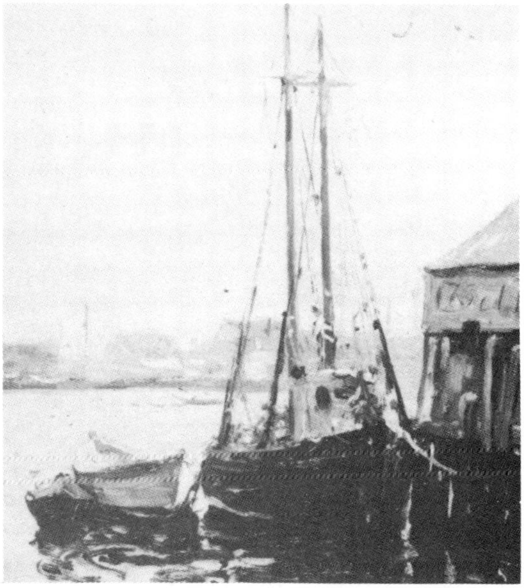

WILLIAM S. ROBINSON – 'Home Port' – signed, also inscribed and dated 1929 on verso – oil on artist's board – 10 x 8in.
(Robt. W. Skinner Inc.) **$1,100** **£763**

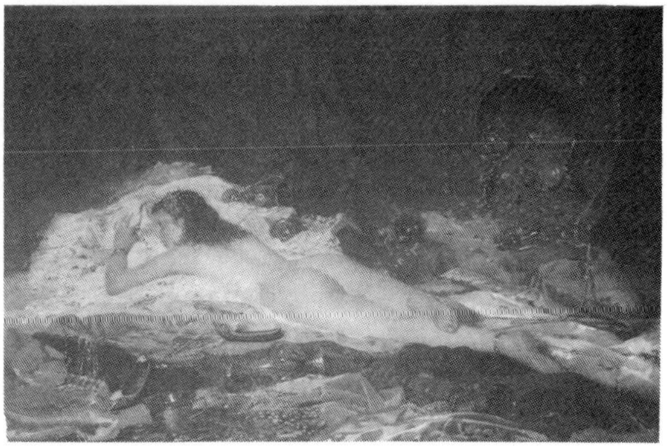

DELLA ROCCA – Embarras de Richesse – signed – 28½ x 36in.
(Christie's) **$19,008** **£13,200**

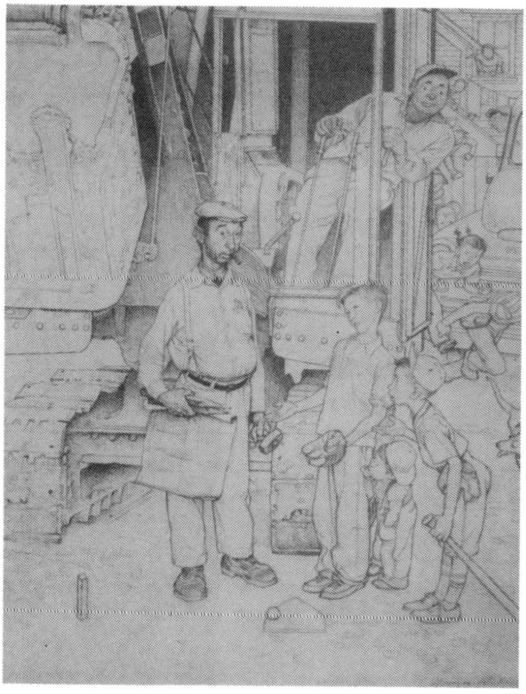

NORMAN ROCKWELL – Don't Take Our Playground – Please! – signed – oil on canvas – 17½ x 16½in.
(Christie's) **$14,300 £10,052**

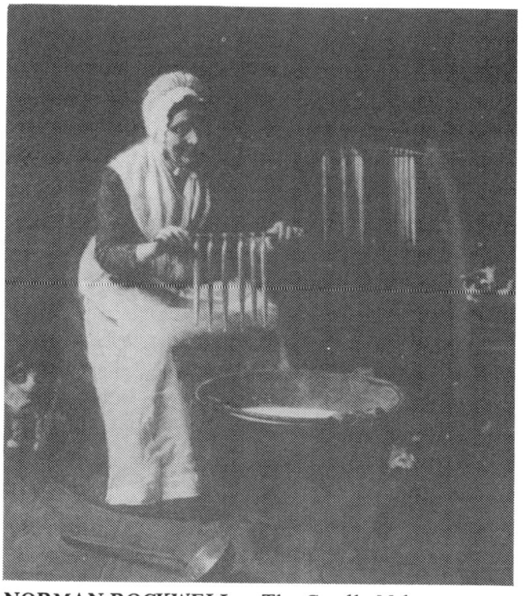

NORMAN ROCKWELL – The Candle Maker – signed and dated '25 – oil on canvas – 29 x 25¾in.
(Christie's) **$41,800 £29,385**

ROBERT HENRY ROE – Red Deer In A Mountainous Landscape – signed and dated 1880 – 32 x 50¼in.
(Christie's) **$1,861 £1,320**

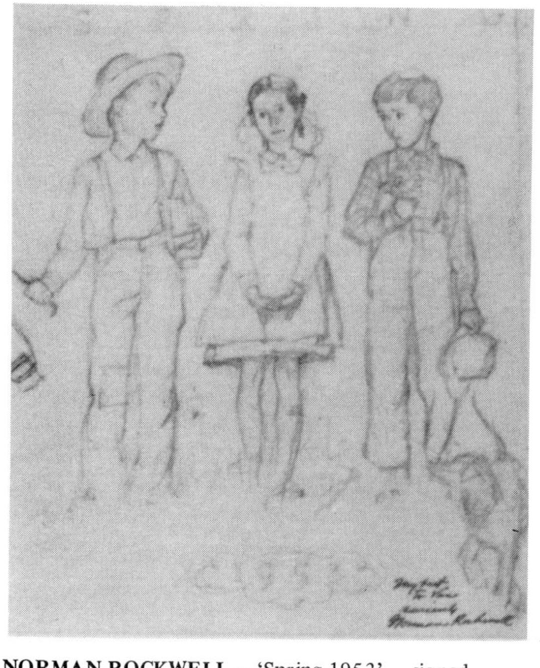

NORMAN ROCKWELL – 'Spring 1953' – signed and inscribed – pencil on paper – 13 x 11in.
(Robt. W. Skinner Inc.) **$1,700 £1,118**

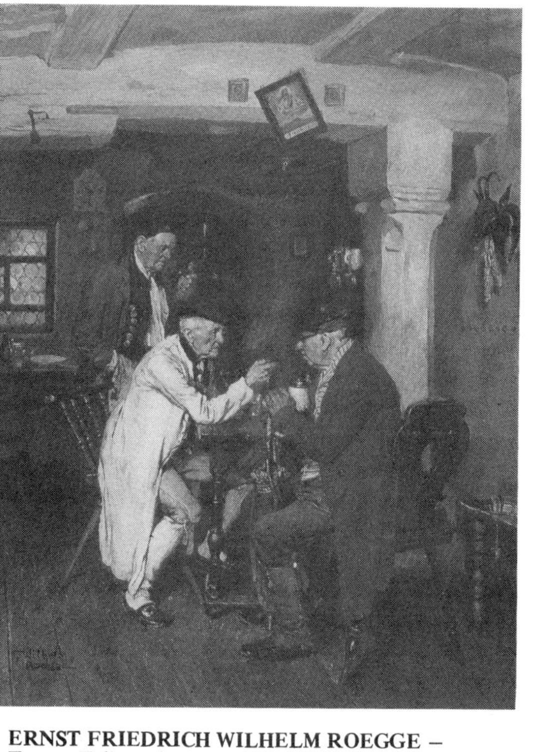

ERNST FRIEDRICH WILHELM ROEGGE – Tavern Talk – signed – on panel – 35 x 26cm.
(Phillips) **$6,480 £4,500**

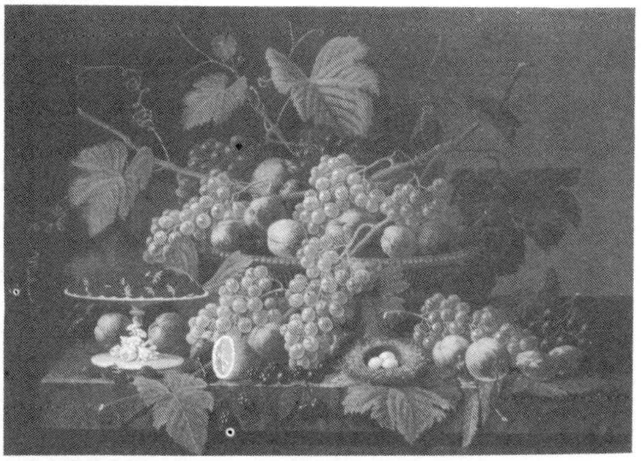

SEVERIN ROESEN – Still Life With Fruit – signed and dated 1854 – oil on canvas – 30 x 40in.
(Christie's) **$30,800 £21,652**

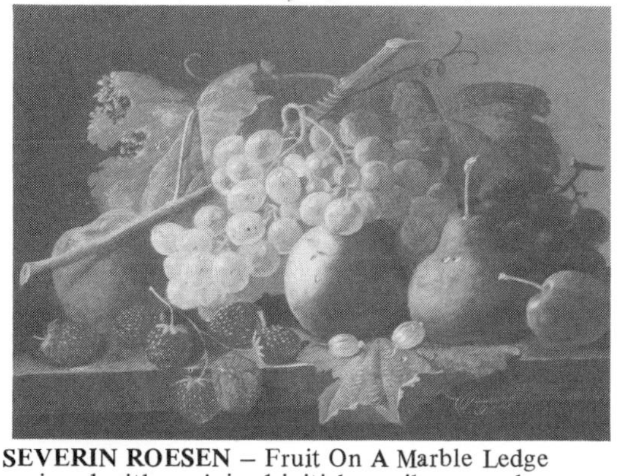

SEVERIN ROESEN – Fruit On A Marble Ledge – signed with conjoined initials – oil on panel – 10¾ x 15in.
(Christie's) **$20,900 £13,641**

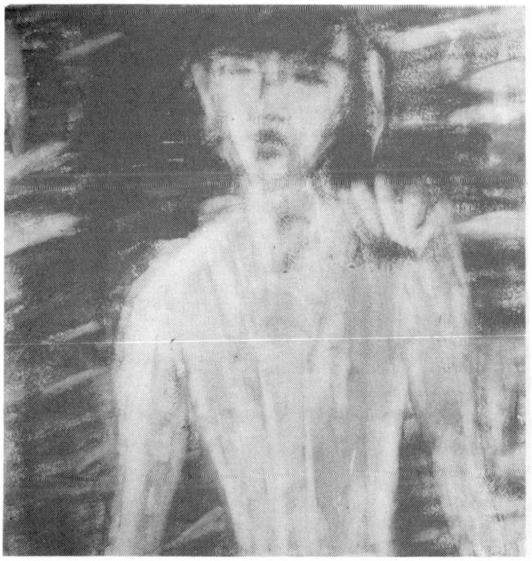

CHRISTIAN ROHLFS – Junges Madchen sitzend – signed and dated '29 – tempera on paper – 24 x 19¾in.
(Christie's) **$26,400 £16,500**

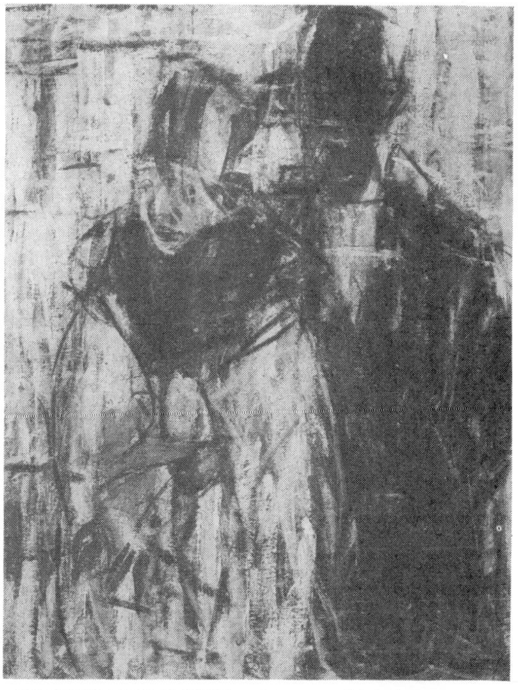

CHRISTIAN ROHLFS – Mann und Madchen – signed with initials and dated '17 – oil on canvas – 31½ x 23¾in.
(Christie's) **$51,436 £30,800**

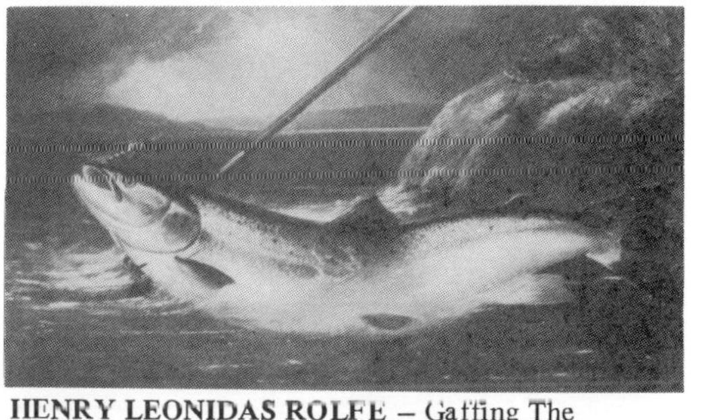

HENRY LEONIDAS ROLFE – Gaffing The Salmon – signed and dated 1874 – 22¾ x 34¾in.
(Christie's) **$1,706 £1,210**

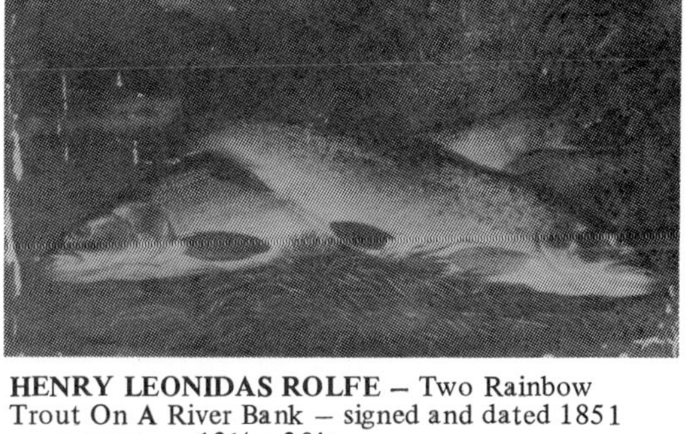

HENRY LEONIDAS ROLFE – Two Rainbow Trout On A River Bank – signed and dated 1851 – on canvas – 12½ x 20in.
(Phillips) **$1,207 £750**

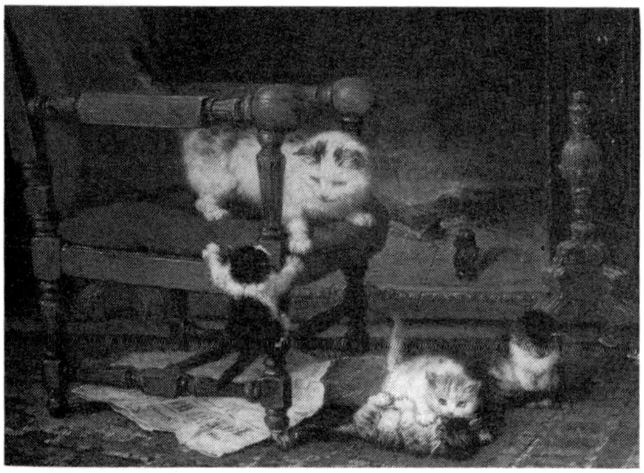

HENRIETTE RONNER-KNIP – Playing By The Fire; and The Proud Mother – signed – on panel – 12¼ x 17¼in.
(Christie's) **$38,720** **£24,200 Pair**

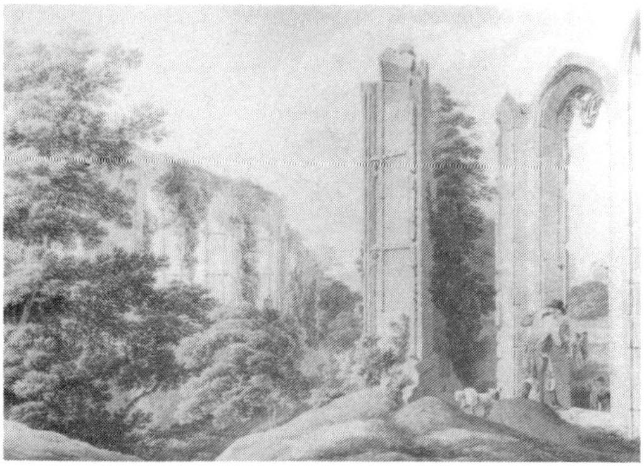

MICHAEL 'ANGELO' ROOKER – The Hall Of Kenilworth Castle – signed – pencil and grey wash – 10¾ x 14¾in.
(Christie's) **$3,306** **£1,980**

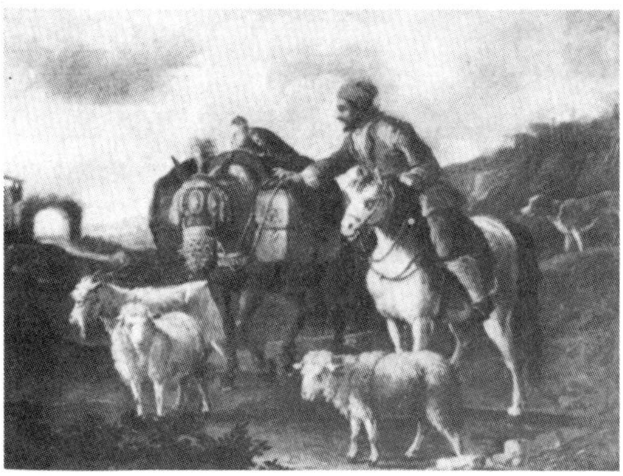

PHILLIP PETER ROOS, Called Rosa Da Tivoli – A Traveller With A Packmule – oil on canvas – 26 x 35½in.
(Phillips) **$2,961** **£2,100**

ALBERTO ROSATI – The Orange Girl – signed – watercolour heightened with white – 21¼ x 14¾in.
(Christie's) **$3,344** **£2,090**

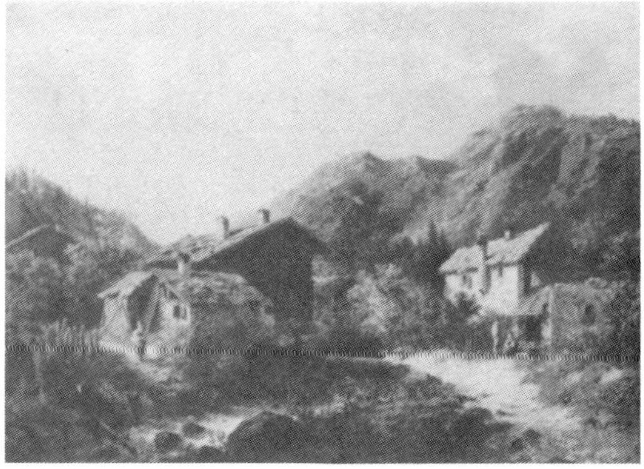

KARL JULIUS ROSE – Figures By A Mill In An Alpine Landscape – signed and dated 1880 – on canvas; other dated '79.
(Phillips) **$1,479** **£980 Pair**

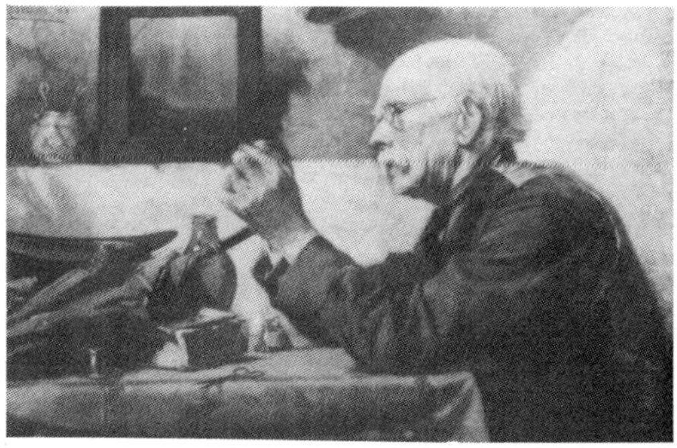

HARRY ROSELAND – 'A Stitch In Time' – signed and dated '93 – oil on canvas – 10 x 14in.
(Robt. W. Skinner Inc.) **$7,200** **£5,000**

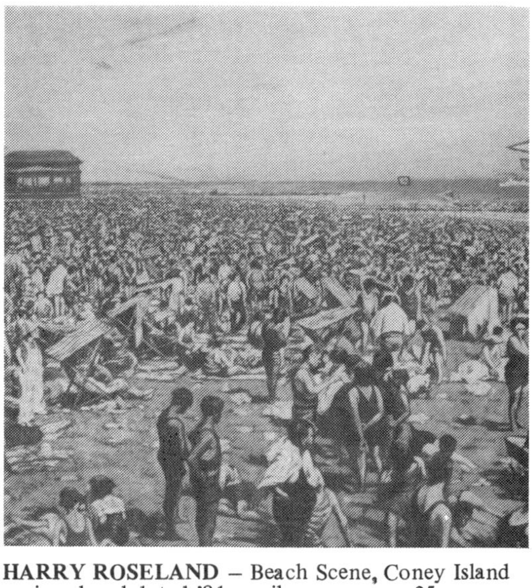

HARRY ROSELAND – Beach Scene, Coney Island – signed and dated '91 – oil on canvas – 35 x 45¼in.
(Christie's) **$66,000** **£46,398**

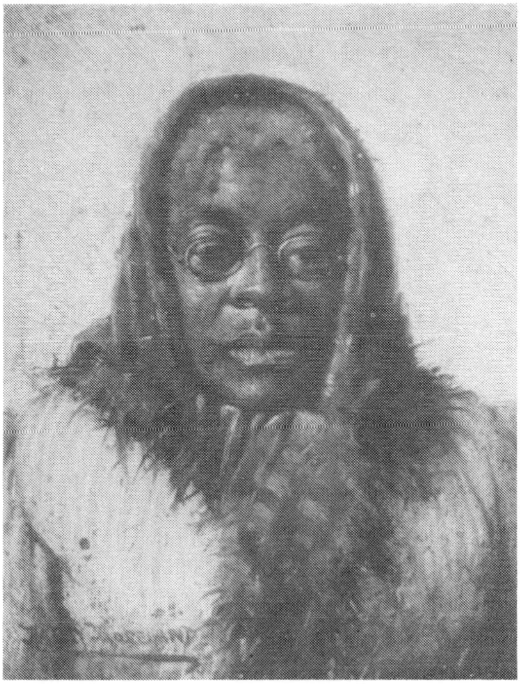

HENRY ROSELAND – Character Study – signed – oil on board – 8 x 6¼in.
(Christie's) **$2,420** **£1,701**

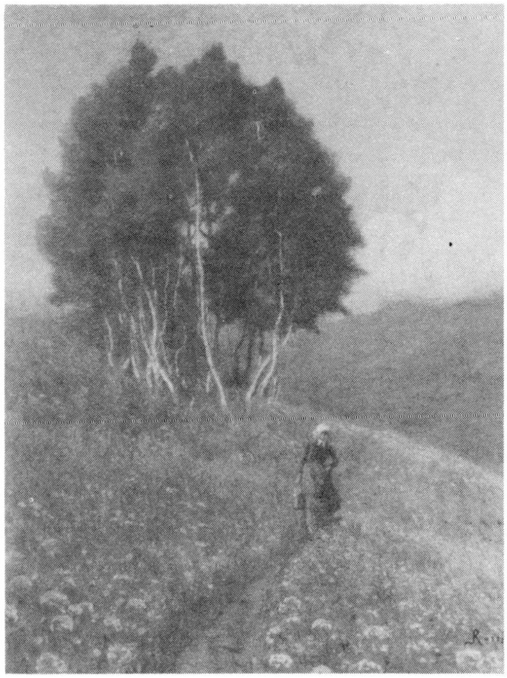

LUIGI ROSSI – A Woman On A Path – signed – on panel – 13¾ x 10½in. – and A Study Of Poultry.
(Christie's) **$8,217** **£4,950 Two**

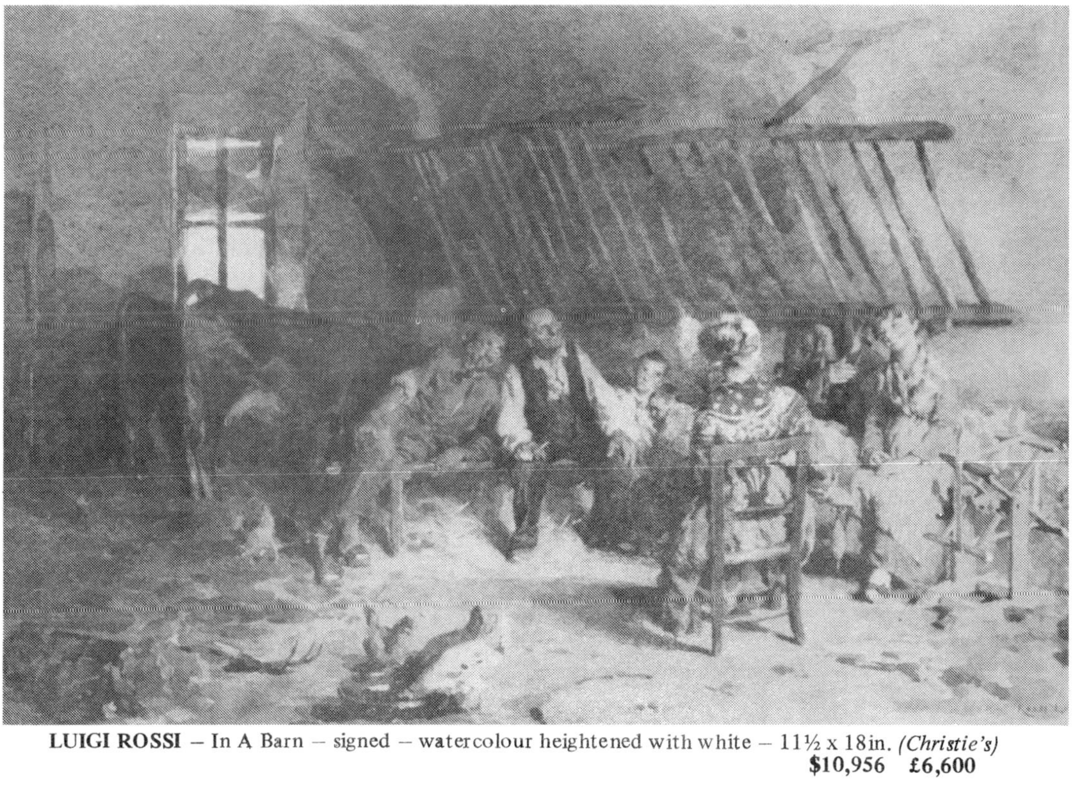

LUIGI ROSSI – In A Barn – signed – watercolour heightened with white – 11½ x 18in. *(Christie's)*
$10,956 **£6,600**

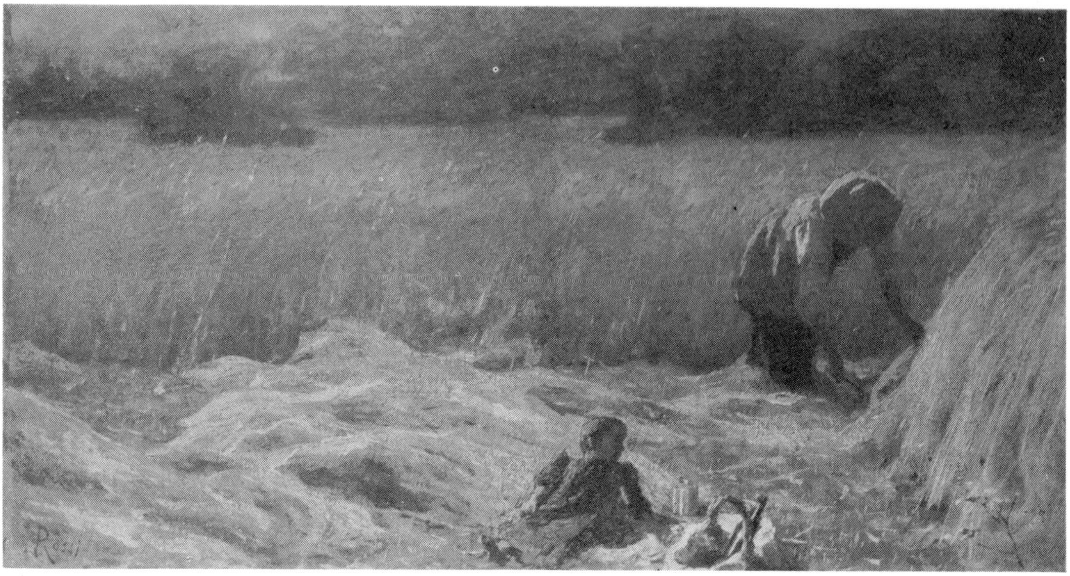

LUIGI ROSSI – Harvesters – signed – 9½ x 17¼in. *(Christie's)* **$36,520 £22,000**

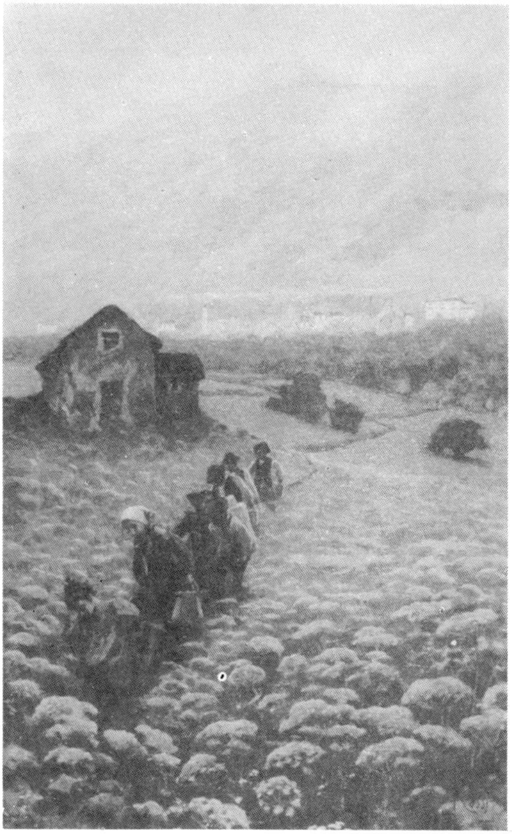

LUIGI ROSSI – Peasants Going To Work Through A Field – signed – watercolour heightened with white – 21¼ x 17in.
(Christie's) **$12,466** £7,510

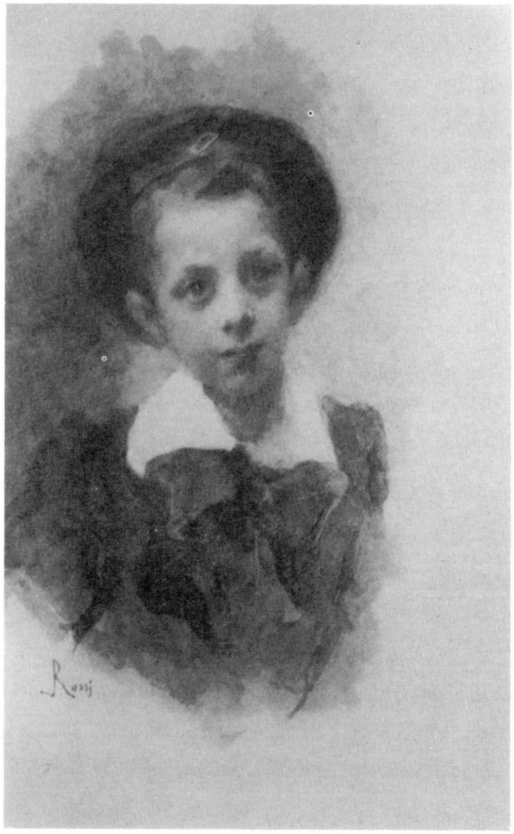

LUIGI ROSSI – Portrait Of A Boy – signed – watercolour heightened with white – 15 x 9½in. – and another watercolour.
(Christie's) **$5,112** **£3,080** Two

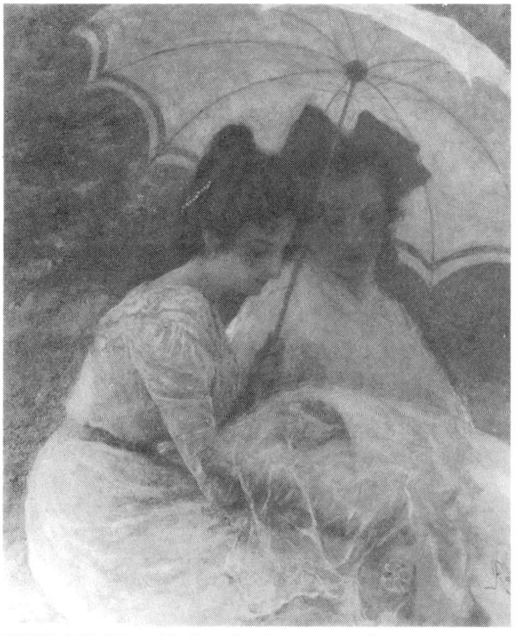

LUIGI ROSSI – Under The Parasol – signed – 21¾ x 18in.
(Christie's) **$47,476** **£28,600**

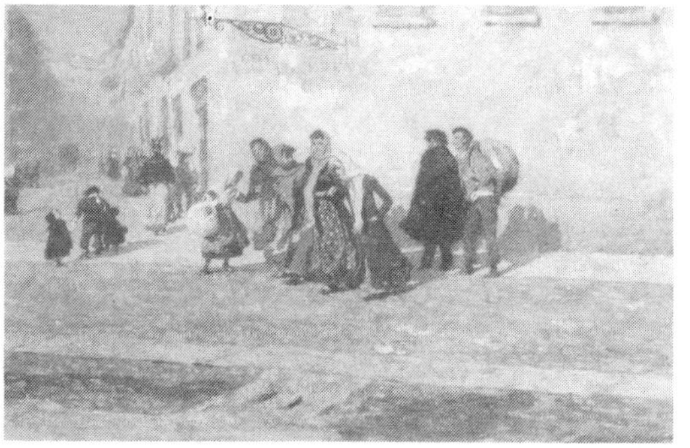

LUIGI ROSSI – Going To The Fair – signed – 17¼ x 29in.
(Christie's) **$47,476** **£28,600**

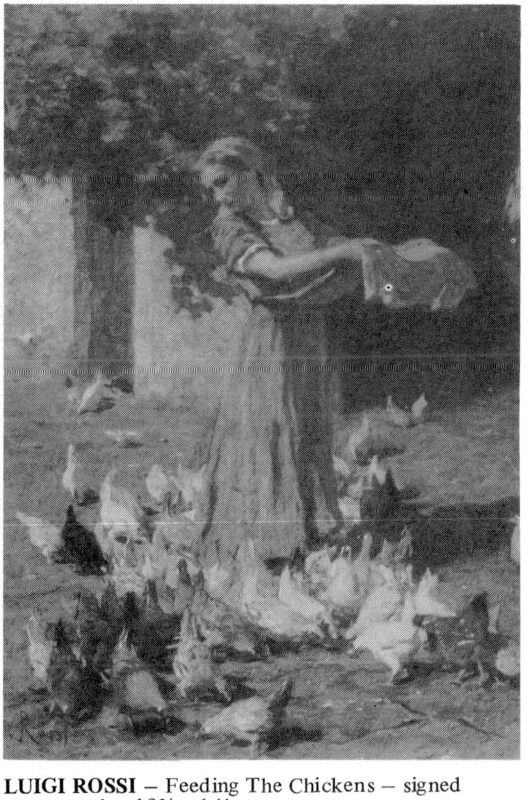

LUIGI ROSSI – Feeding The Chickens – signed – on panel – 19¾ x 14in.
(Christie's) **$31,042** **£18,700**

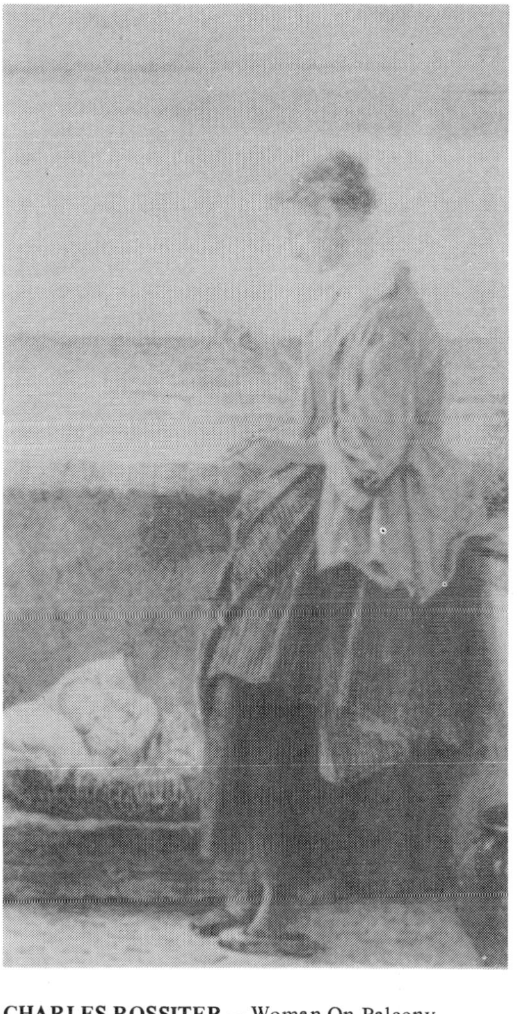

CHARLES ROSSITER – Woman On Balcony, Mending Nets, Child At Her Feet – initialled – watercolour – 8 x 5in.
(Capes, Dunn & Co.) **$261** **£180**

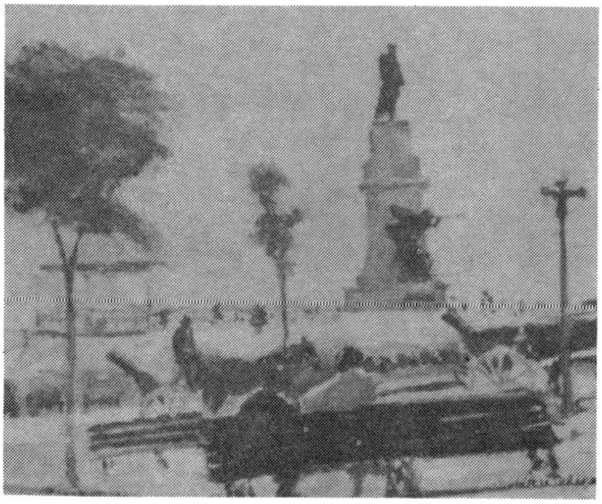

HAROLD ROTENBERG – Park Scene With Figures – signed – oil on board – 9¾ x 11¾in.
(Robt. W. Skinner Inc.) **$800** **£490**

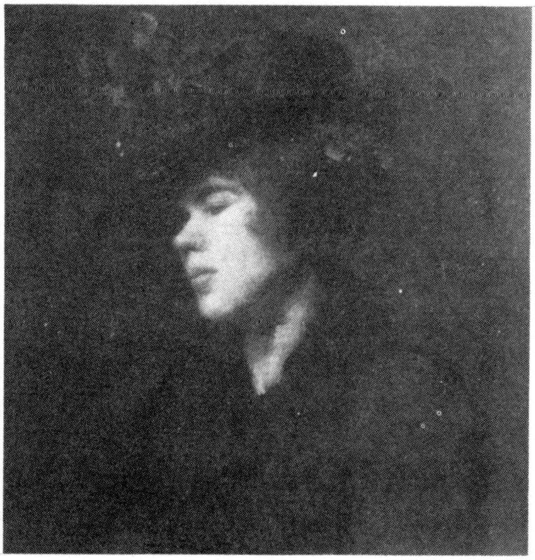

SIR WILLIAM ROTHENSTEIN – Portrait Of Ida Nettleship, Half Length, Dressed In Black – oil on canvas – 24 x 20in.
(Christie's) **$1,887** **£1,320**

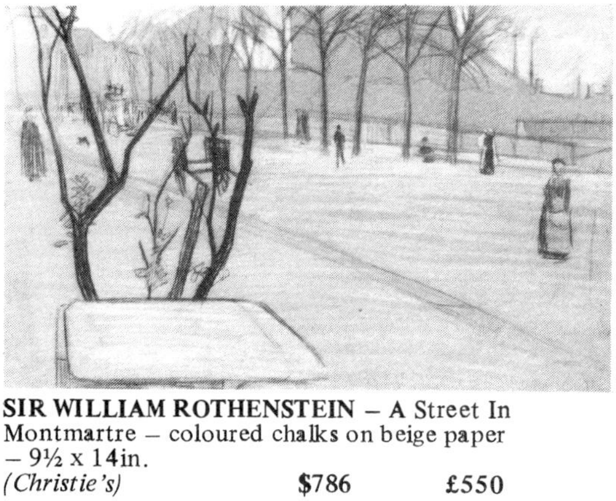

SIR WILLIAM ROTHENSTEIN – A Street In Montmartre – coloured chalks on beige paper – 9½ x 14in.
(Christie's) **$786** **£550**

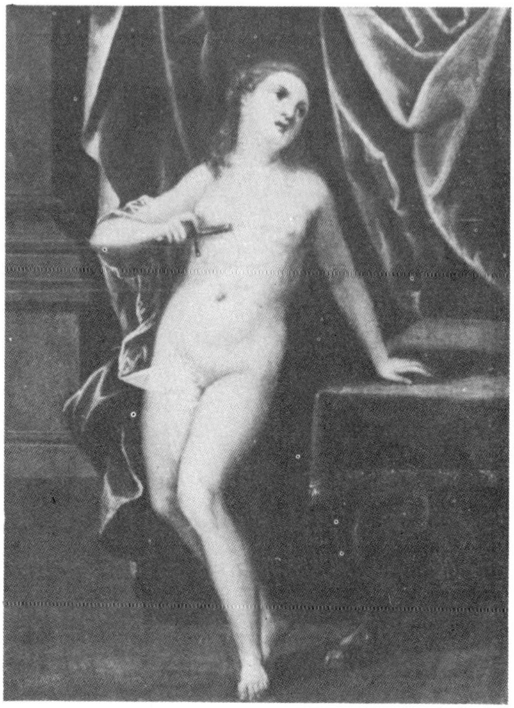

JOHANN ROTTENHAMMER, Attributed to – Lucretia – oil on copper – 8¾ x 6¼in.
(Phillips) **$183** **£130**

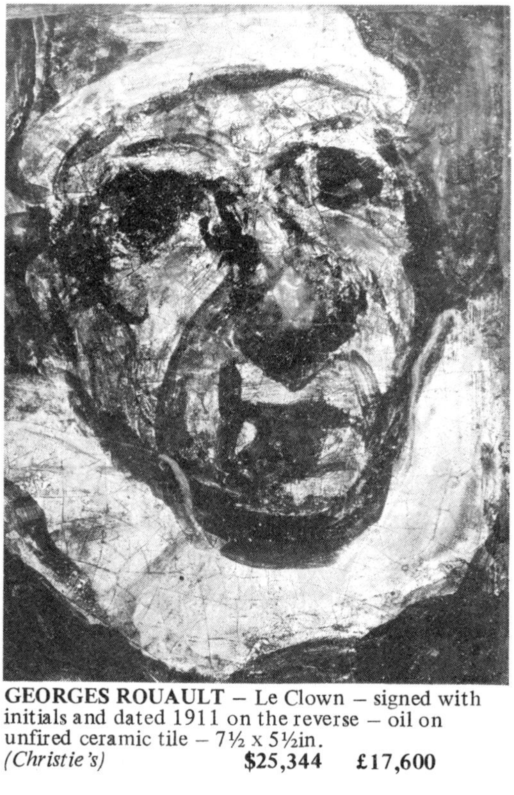

GEORGES ROUAULT – Le Clown – signed with initials and dated 1911 on the reverse – oil on unfired ceramic tile – 7½ x 5½in.
(Christie's) **$25,344** **£17,600**

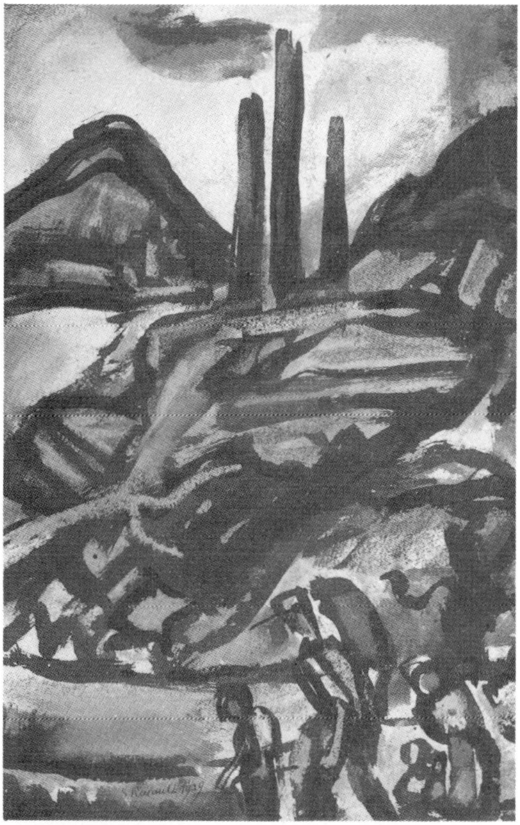

GEORGES ROUAULT – La Route est longue – signed and dated 1929 – watercolour and pastel on paper – 18¾ x 13in.
(Christie's) **$25,344** **£17,600**

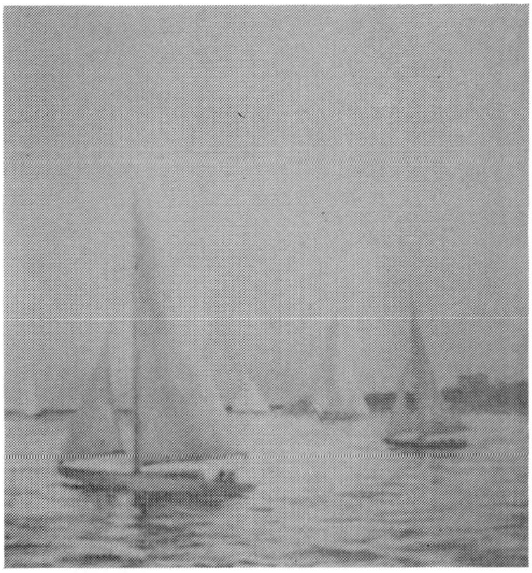

ORLANDO ROULAND – 'A Light Breeze' – signed – oil on canvas – 16 x 12in.
(Robt. W. Skinner Inc.) **$700** **£429**

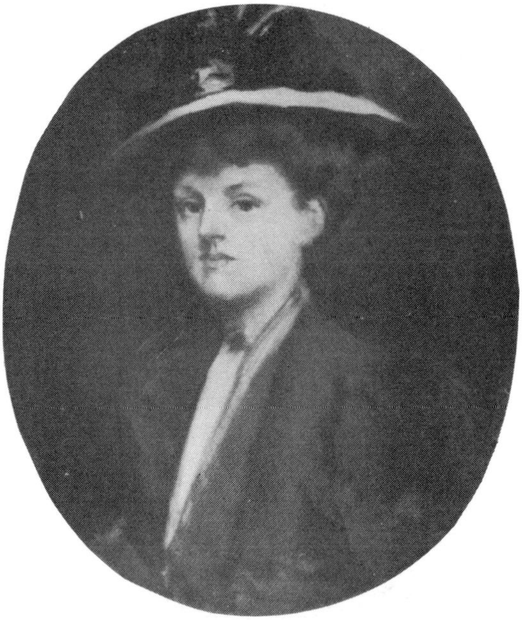

THEODORE ROUSSEL – Portrait Of A Lady, Bust Length Wearing A Blue Coat – oil on canvas – 28½ x 24in.
(Christie's) **$1,036** **£660**

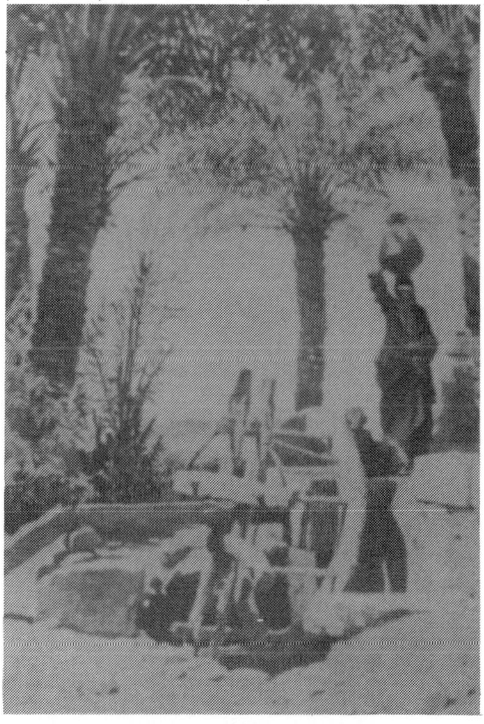

ALEXANDRE NICOLAIEVITCH ROUSSOFF – By The Well, The Pyramid Of Chephren – signed, inscribed and dated 1891 – watercolour – 40 x 21cm.
(Phillips) **$1,467** **£900**

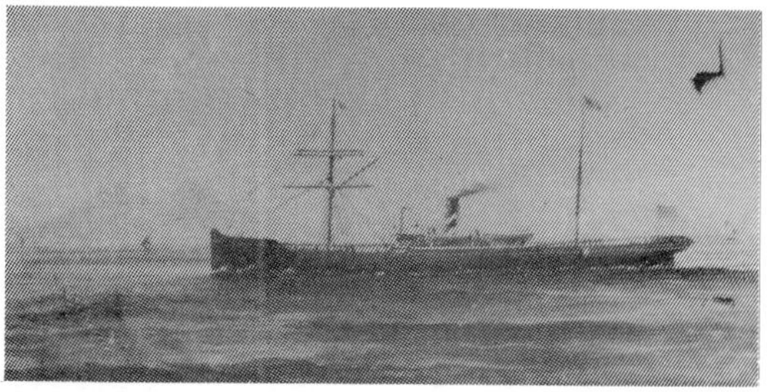

LOUIS ROUX, Attributed to – The Two-Masted Tramp Steamer 'Advance', Vesuvius And Naples Beyond – on canvas – 19¾ x 30in.
(Phillips) **$1,771** **£1,100**

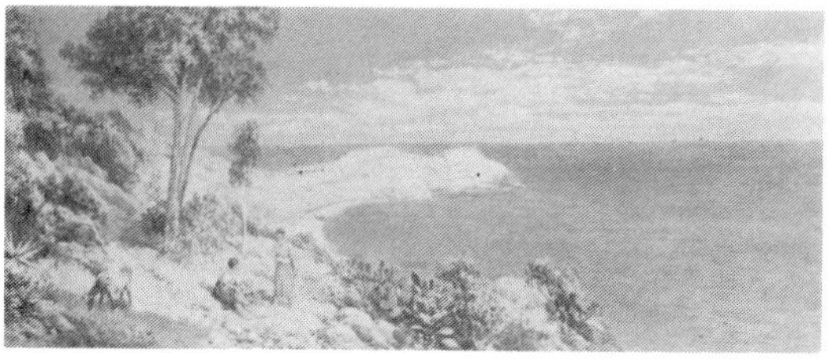

CHARLES ROWBOTHAM – At Taormina, Sicily; and Near Castel-A-Mare, Bay Of Naples – signed, and inscribed on the reverse – watercolour and bodycolour on card – 9½ x 20¼in.
(Christie's) **$1,861** **£1,320 Pair**

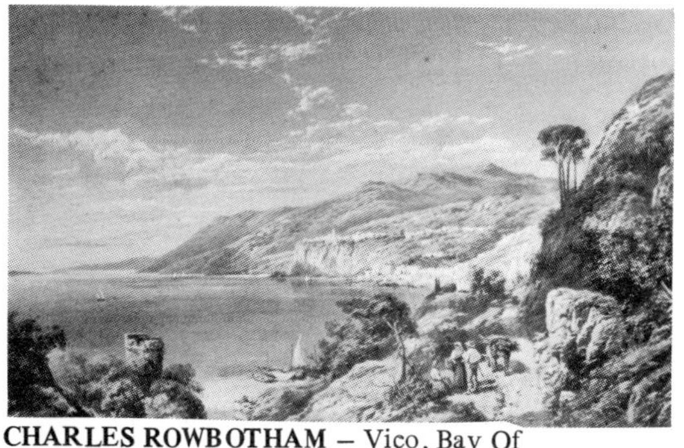

CHARLES ROWBOTHAM – Vico, Bay Of Naples – signed and dated 1895 – watercolour heightened with bodycolour – 25¾ x 36in.
(Christie's) **$2,592** **£1,728**

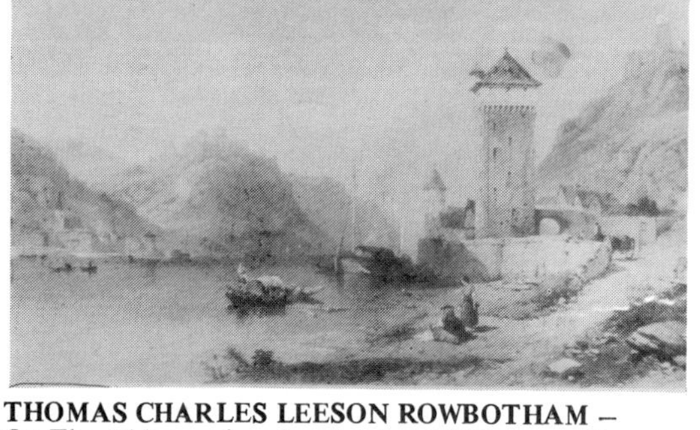

THOMAS CHARLES LEESON ROWBOTHAM – On The Rhine – signed and dated 1860 – pencil and watercolour heightened with white – 16¾ x 25¼in.
(Christie's) **$4,747** **£2,860**

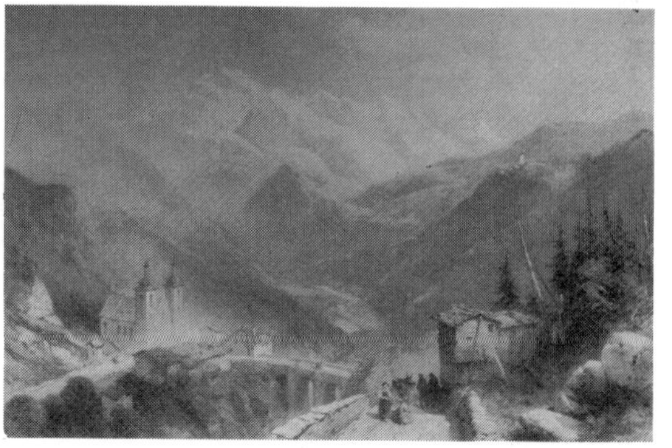

THOMAS CHARLES LEESON ROWBOTHAM – Figures On A Path Above A Bridge Leading To An Alpine Village – signed and dated 1860 – pencil and watercolour heightened with white – 16½ x 24¾in.
(Christie's) **$4,017** **£2,420**

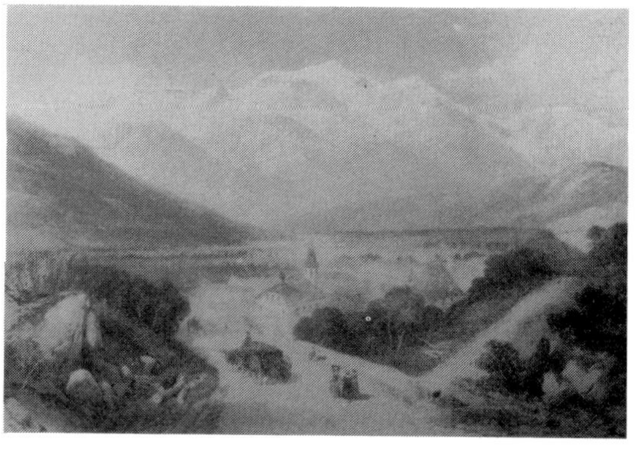

THOMAS CHARLES LEESON ROWBOTHAM – Figures And A Horse-Drawn Cart On A Road Above An Alpine Town – signed and dated 1865 – pencil and watercolour heightened with white – 19¾ x 30½in.
(Christie's) **$1,826** **£1,100**

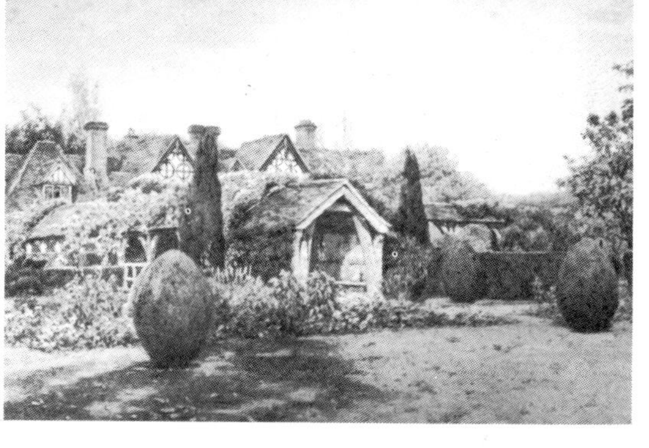

ERNEST ARTHUR ROWE – The Gardens At Great Tangley Manor, Near Guildford, Surrey – signed, and inscribed on the reverse of the mount – watercolour – 10 x 14in.
(Christie's) **$1,085** **£770**

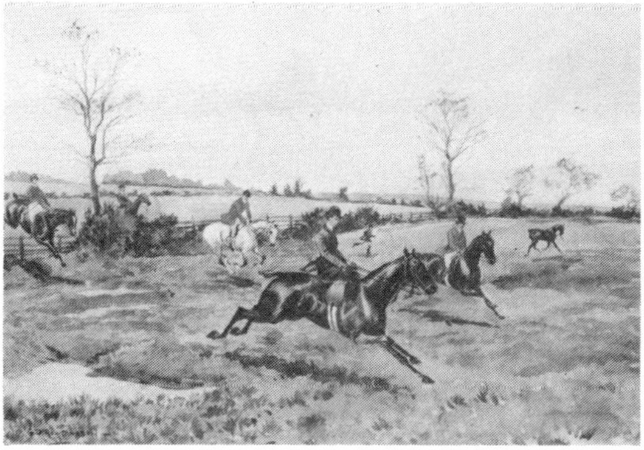

GEORGE DERVILLE ROWLANDSON – Hunting Scenes: Going To The Meet; Full Cry; Fording A River; and A Fall At The Water – signed – pencil and watercolour heightened with white – 10 x 14in.
(Christie's) **$1,551** **£1,100** **Four**

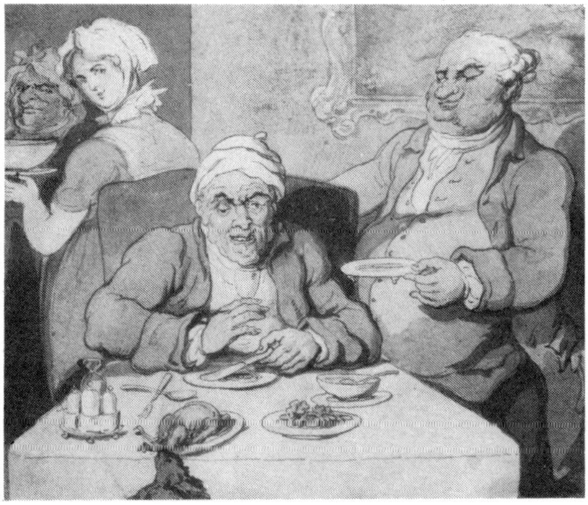

THOMAS ROWLANDSON – The Sensualist – inscribed – pencil, pen and brown ink and watercolour – 7¼ x 8¼in.
(Christie's) **$1,502** **£1,100**

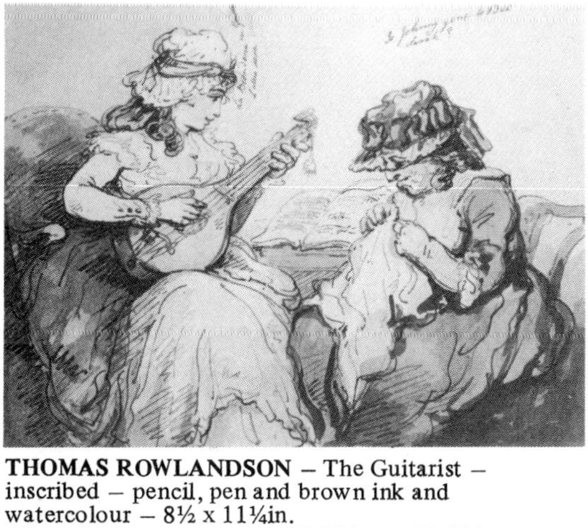

THOMAS ROWLANDSON – The Guitarist – inscribed – pencil, pen and brown ink and watercolour – 8½ x 11¼in.
(Christie's) **$3,726** **£2,484**

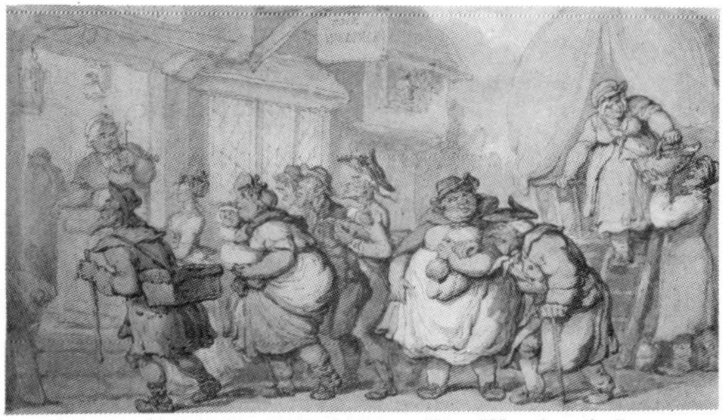

THOMAS ROWLANDSON – The Woolpack Inn: Arrival Of 'The Flying Waggon' – pencil, pen and brown ink and watercolour – 9½ x 15in.
(Christie's) **$5,935** **£4,180**

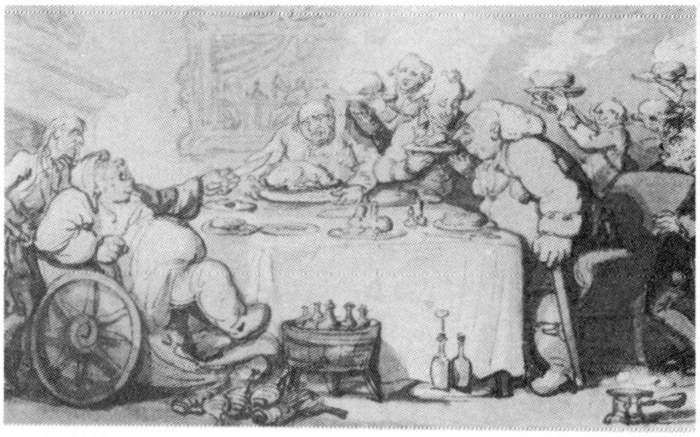

THOMAS ROWLANDSON – The Comforts Of Bath: The Feast – pencil, pen and grey ink and watercolour – 4½ x 7¼in.
(Christie's) **$4,536** **£3,024**

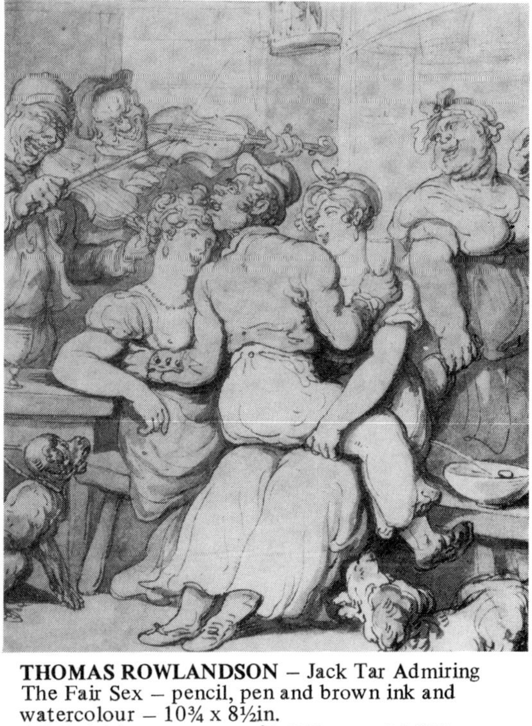

THOMAS ROWLANDSON – Jack Tar Admiring The Fair Sex – pencil, pen and brown ink and watercolour – 10¾ x 8½in.
(Christie's) **$4,959** **£2,970**

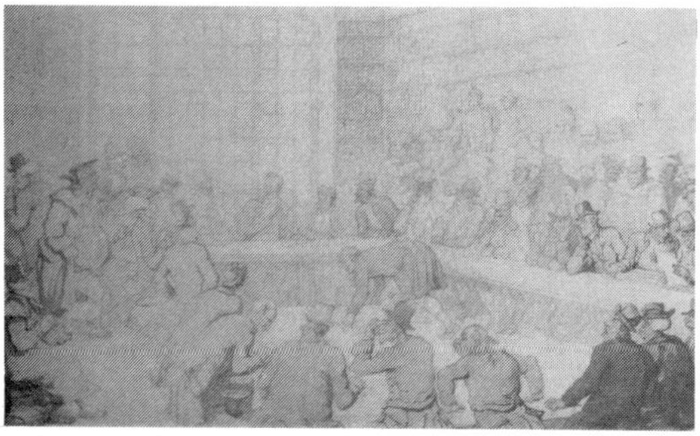

THOMAS ROWLANDSON – Dr. Syntax At An Auction – pencil, pen and ink and watercolour – 10½ x 16½in.
(Christie's) **$6,429** **£3,850**

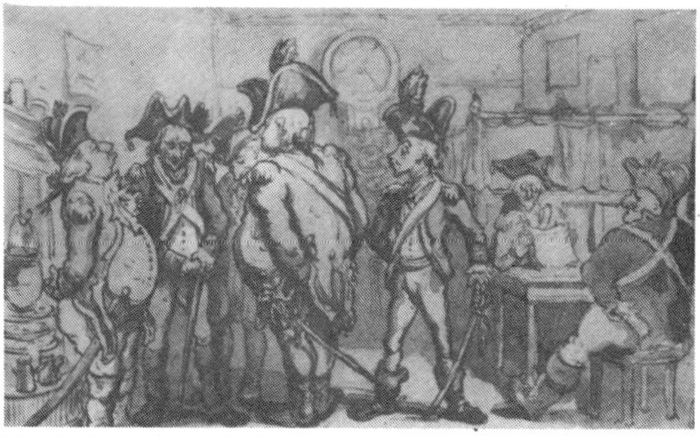

THOMAS ROWLANDSON – Militia Men At An Inn – signed – watercolour – 5 x 7.5in.
(Woolley & Wallis) **$685** **£486**

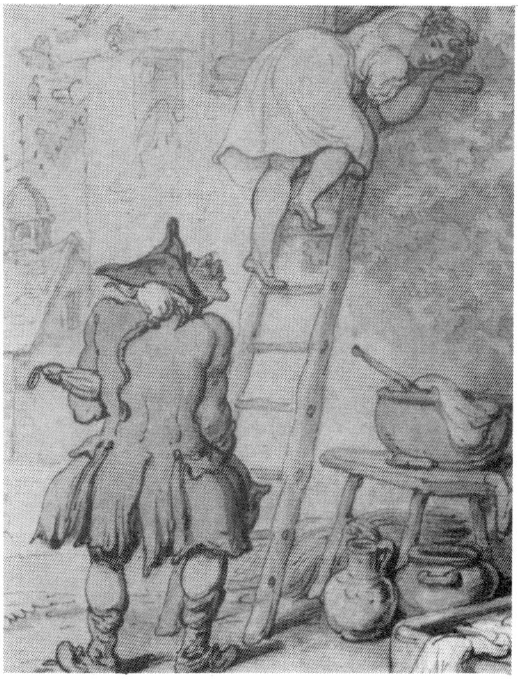

THOMAS ROWLANDSON – The Ogler – pen and brown and red ink and watercolour – 5¾ x 4¼in.
(Christie's) **$2,655** **£1,870**

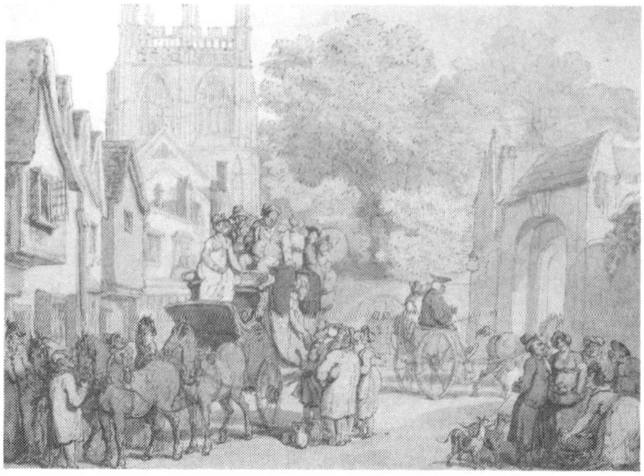

THOMAS ROWLANDSON – Merton College, Oxford – pen and ink and watercolour – 24 x 32.5cm.
(Phillips) **$22,880** **£16,000**

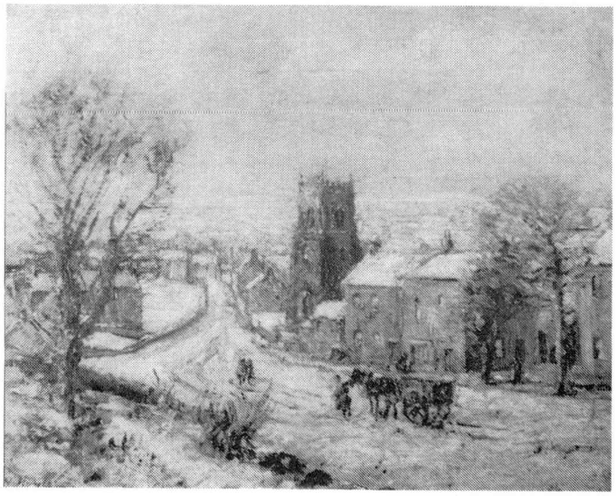

HERBERT ROYLE – A Village On The Wolds – signed – 8 x 10in.
(Dacre, Son & Hartley) **$1,162** **£750**

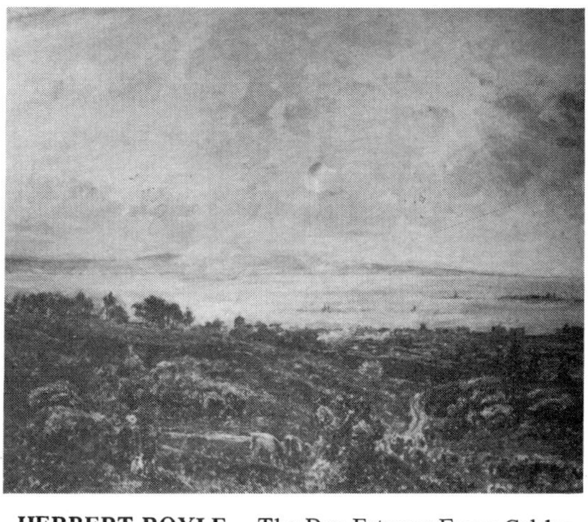

HERBERT ROYLE – The Dee Estuary From Calsby Hill, Wirral – signed and inscribed on the reverse – 25 x 30in.
(Dacre, Son & Hartley) **$1,627** **£1,050**

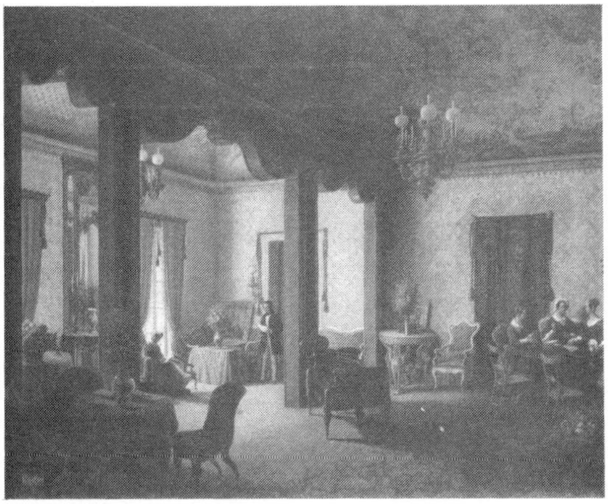

CARL LUDWIG RUNDT – The Interior Of The Salon Of Tsarina Alexandra, In The Villa Des Herzogs Serradifalco, Palermo – signed with monogram and dated 1856 – 30½ x 39½in.
(Christie's) **$26,400** **£16,500**

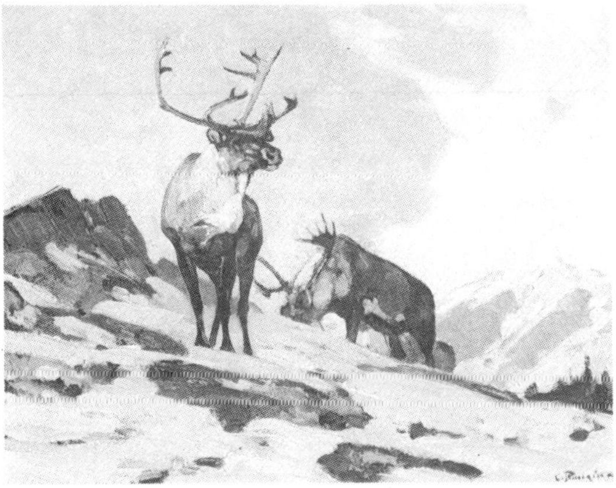

CARL RUNGIUS – King Of The Mountain – signed – oil on canvas – 16¼ x 20¼in.
(Christie's) **$15,400** **£10,826**

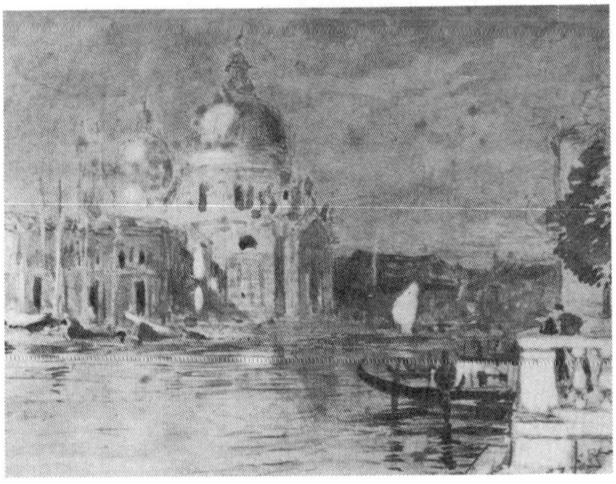

JOHN RUSKIN – Santa Maria della Salute, Venice – signed with initials – pencil and watercolour heightened with white – 5 x 6½in.
(Christie's) **$2,811** **£1,980**

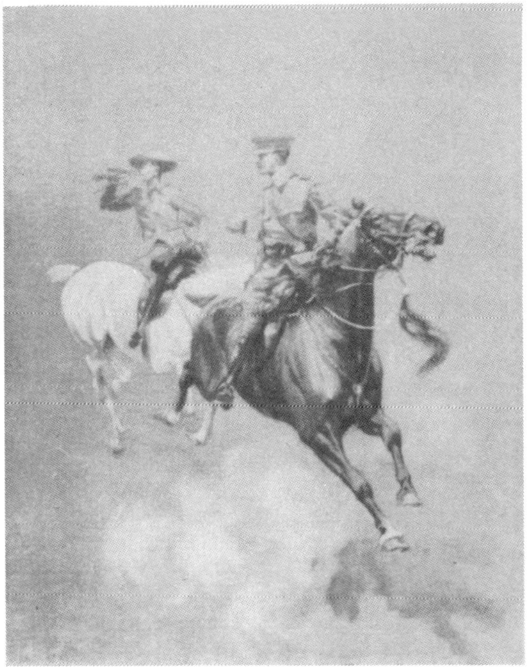

GEORGE WILLIAM RUSSELL – Sounding The Charge – signed – oil on linen – 21 x 16in.
(Robt. W. Skinner Inc.) **$550** **£381**

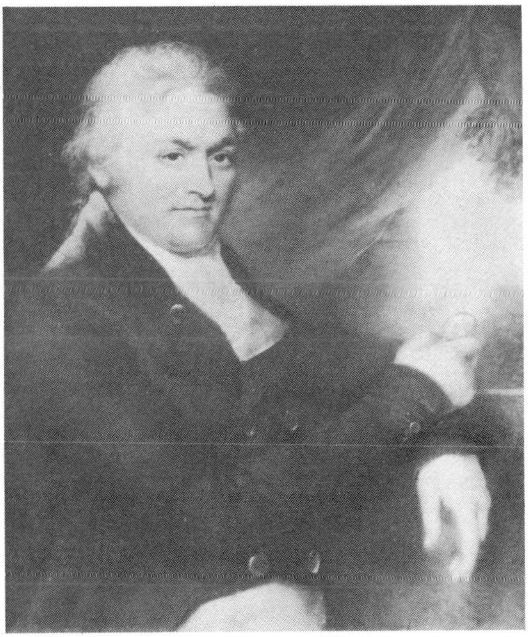

JOHN RUSSELL – Portrait Of Wade Brown, Half Length, In Blue Coat And White Stock, Leaning On A Plinth – signed and dated 1800 – pastel – 30 x 25in.
(Christie's) **$1,053** **£702**

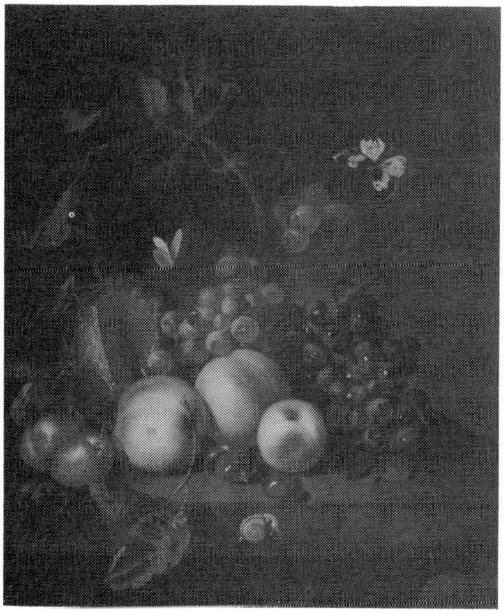

RACHEL RUYSCH – A Still Life On A Marble Ledge – on canvas – 19¼ x 15½in.
(Phillips) **$17,430** **£10,500**

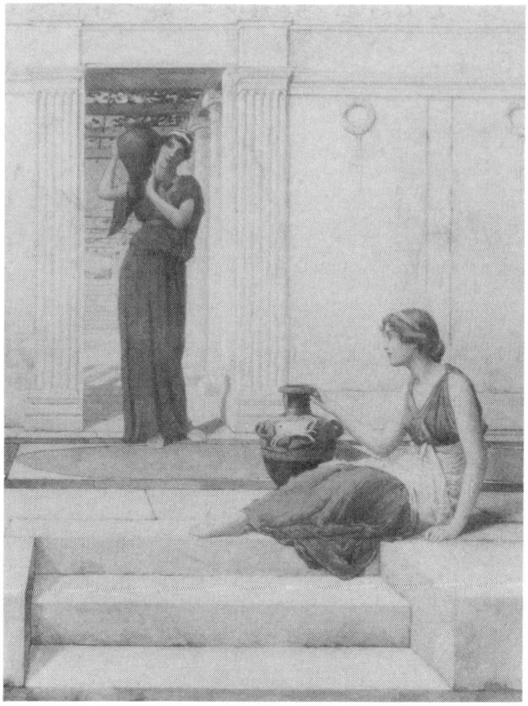

HENRY RYLAND – Classical Maidens By A Pool – signed – pencil and watercolour on card – 21¼ x 15¼in.
(Christie's) **$2,524** **£1,650**

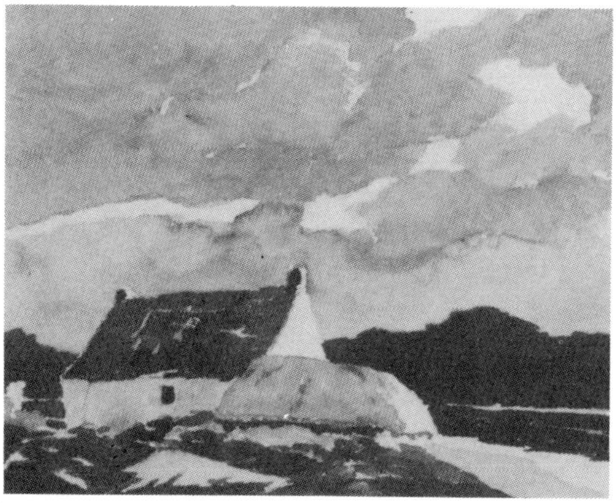

CHAUNCEY FOSTER RYDER – 'Loch Eve, Ross-shire, Scotland' – signed – watercolour on paper – 9½ x 11¼in.
(Robt. W. Skinner Inc.) **$475** **£329**

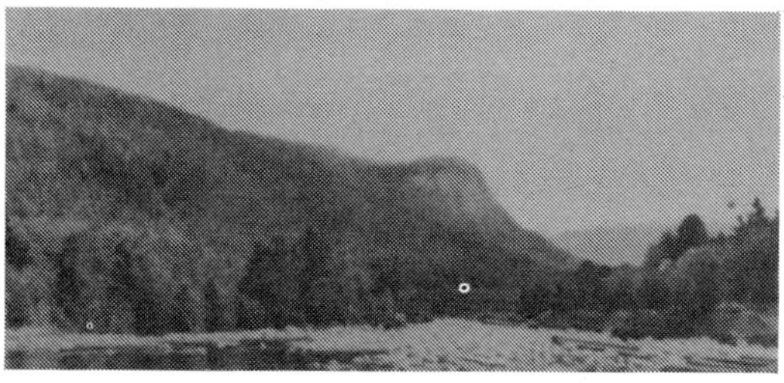

HENRY ORNE RYDER – River Landscape With Covered Bridge – signed – oil on canvas – 27 x 45in.
(Robt. W. Skinner Inc.) **$950** **£582**

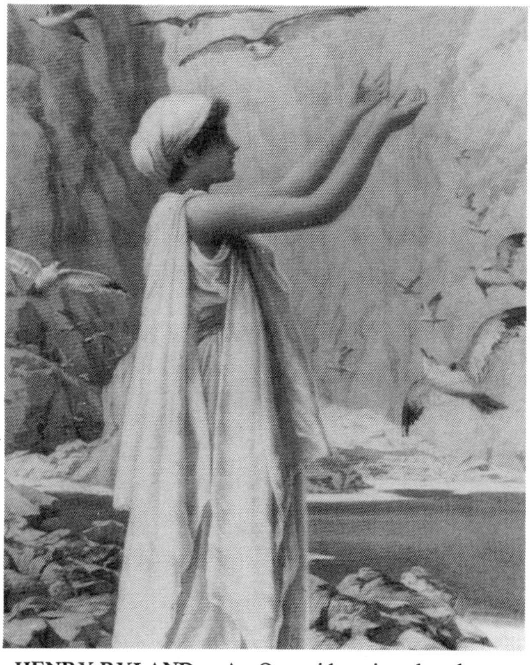

HENRY RYLAND – An Oceanid – signed and dated 1899 – pencil and watercolour heightened with white – 28¾ x 21in.
(Christie's) **$3,168** **£2,200**

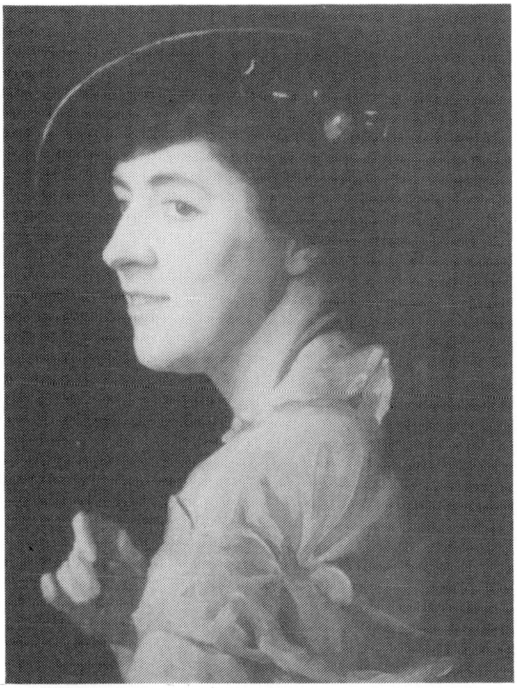

ROBERT KNIGHT RYLAND – Portrait Of Irene Dobson – signed and dated 1914 – oil on canvas – 20 x 14¼in.
(Christie's) **$1,650** **£1,028**

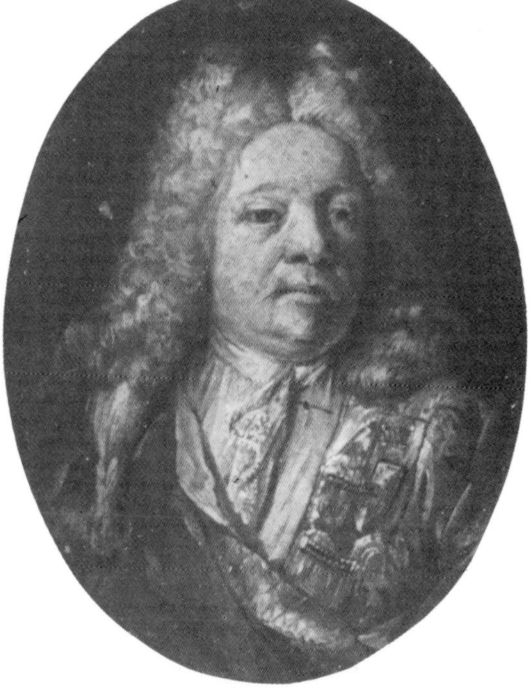

LUDOVIC RYSBRACK – Portrait Of A Gentleman, Long Bust Length, Wearing A Blue Cape – signed and dated 1717 – oil on copper – 3½ x 2¾in.
(Phillips) **$916** **£650**

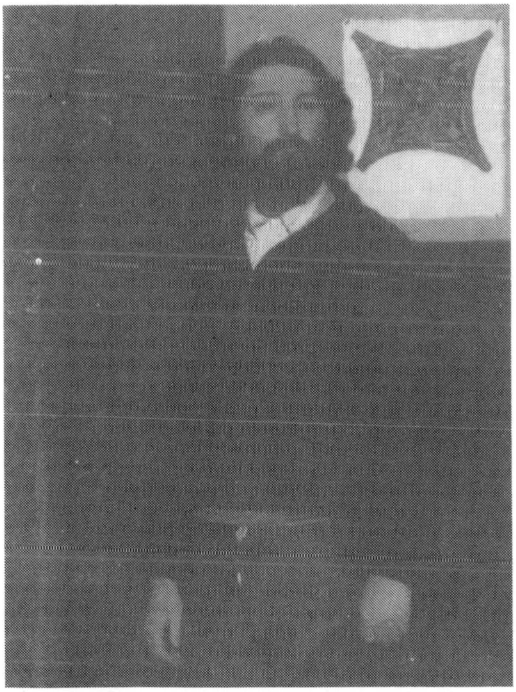

ROBERT KNIGHT RYLAND – The Bearded Man – oil on canvas – 13 x 21in.
(Christie's) **$2,200** **£1,370**

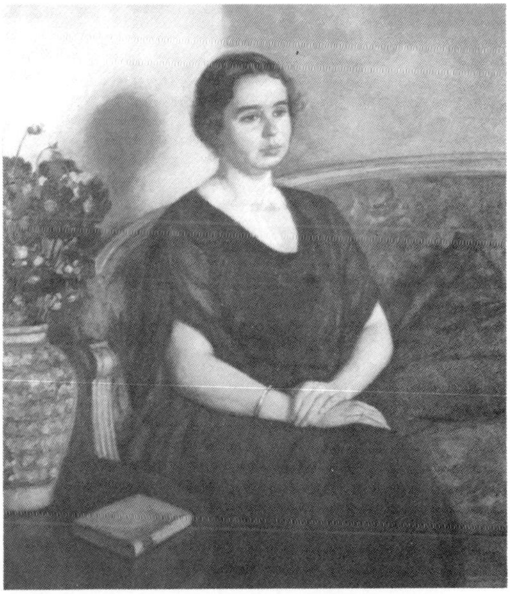

THEO VAN RYSSELBERGHE – Portrait De Madame Dubois – signed with monogram and dated 1922 – oil on canvas – 43¼ x 33in.
(Christie's) **$7,920** **£5,500**

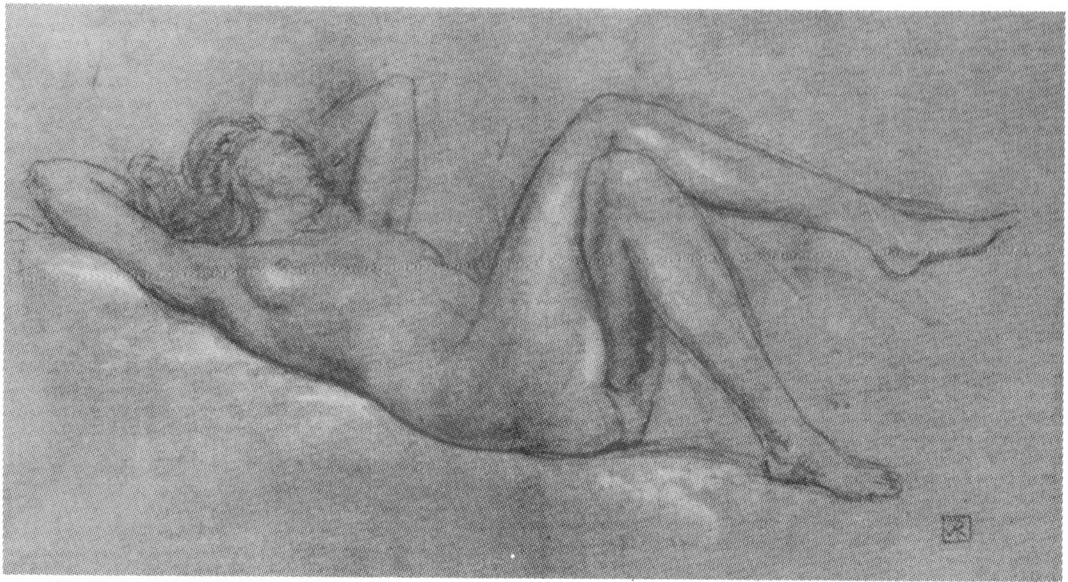

THEO VAN RYSSELBERGHE – Femme nue allongee – signed – sanguine and white chalk on paper – 15 x 22¾in. *(Christie's)* **$2,640 £1,650**

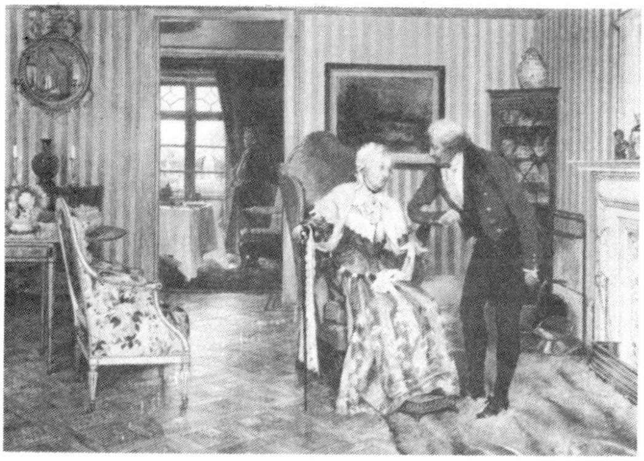

WALTER DENDY SADLER – For Fifty Years – signed – 26 x 34in.
(Christie's) **$4,963 £3,520**

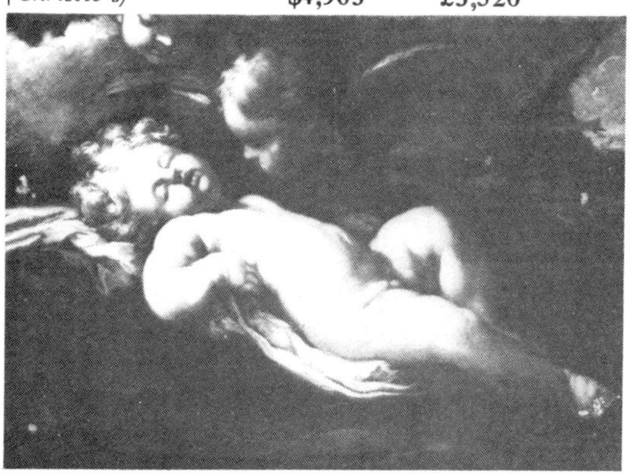

GIOVANNI CAMILLO SAGRESTANI, Attributed to – A Child Sleeping Being Watched Over By Cherubs – oil on canvas – 20 x 26¼in.
(Phillips) **$1,551 £1,100**

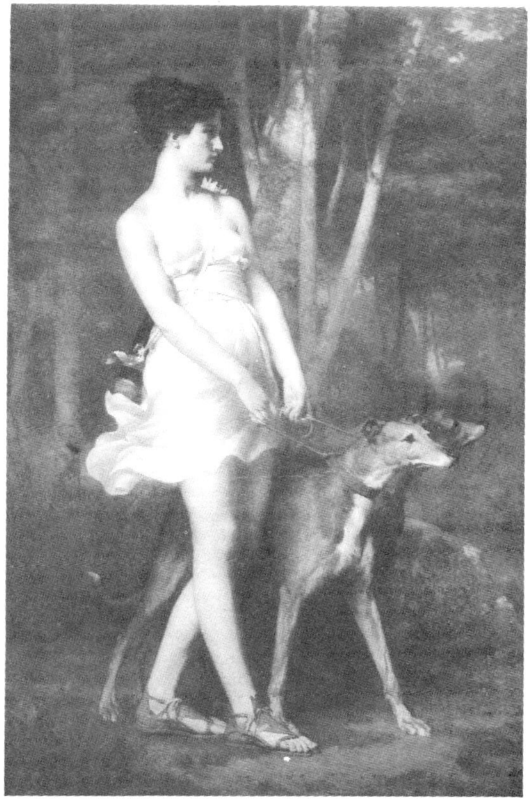

GASTON CASIMIR SAINTPIERRE – Diana, The Huntress – signed – 77¼ x 51in.
(Christie's) **$49,104 £34,100**

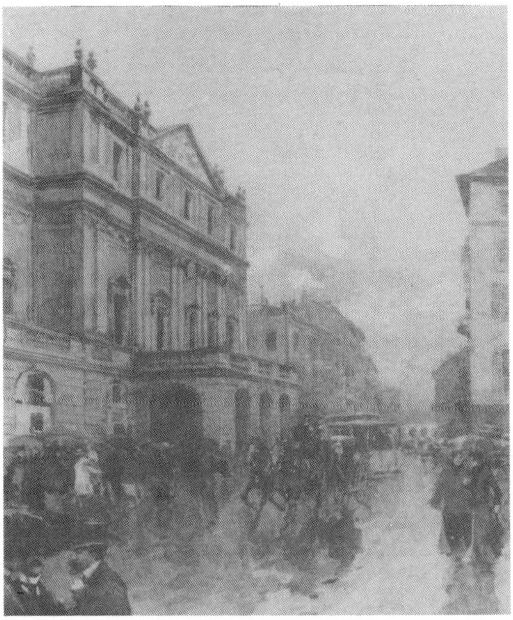

PAOLO SALA – A Street Scene – signed – watercolour heightened with white – 13½ x 10¼in. – and A Market Scene.
(Christie's) **$15,521** **£9,350 Two**

PAOLO SALA – Broad Sanctuary, Westminster, London – signed and inscribed – on panel – 10½ x 8in.
(Christie's) **$11,869** **£7,150**

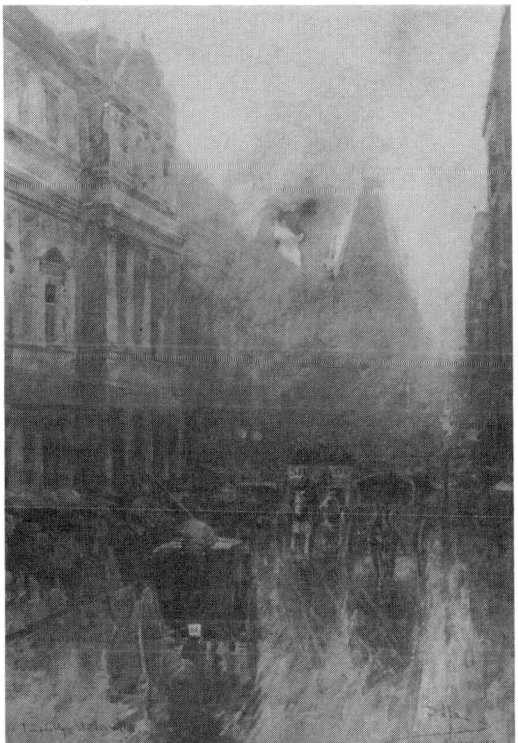

PAOLO SALA – Piccadilly – signed, inscribed and dated '900 – watercolour – 20½ x 13¾in.
(Christie's) **$7,669** **£4,620**

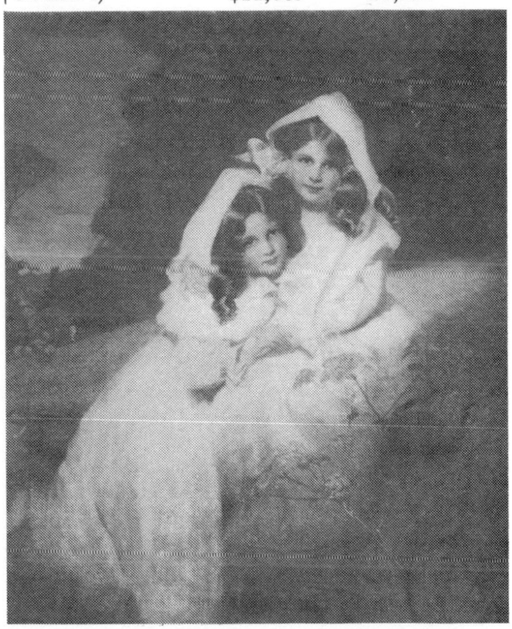

FRANK O. SALISBURY – The Field Mice Nutbrown Maidens, The Twins – signed and dated 1910, inscribed and dated on the reverse – oil on canvas – 64 x 49in.
(Christie's) **$9,498** **£6,050**

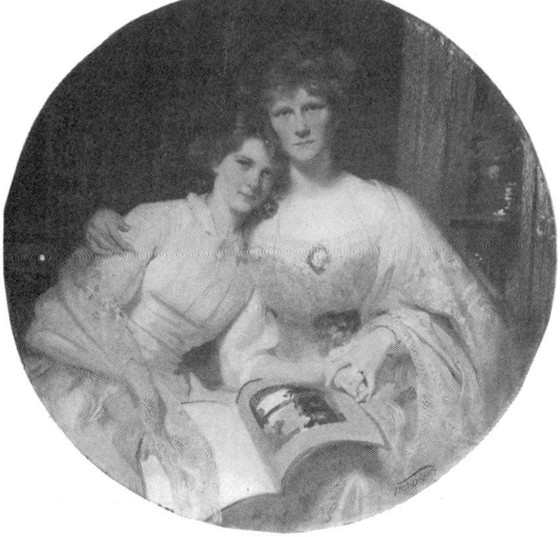

FRANK O. SALISBURY – Portrait Of A Mother With Her Daughter, Half Length, Holding A Book – signed – oil on canvas – 47in. diam.
(Christie's) **$5,977** **£4,180**

FRANK O. SALISBURY – 'The Pause' – signed – on canvas – 24½in. diam.
(Phillips) **$4,830** **£3,000**

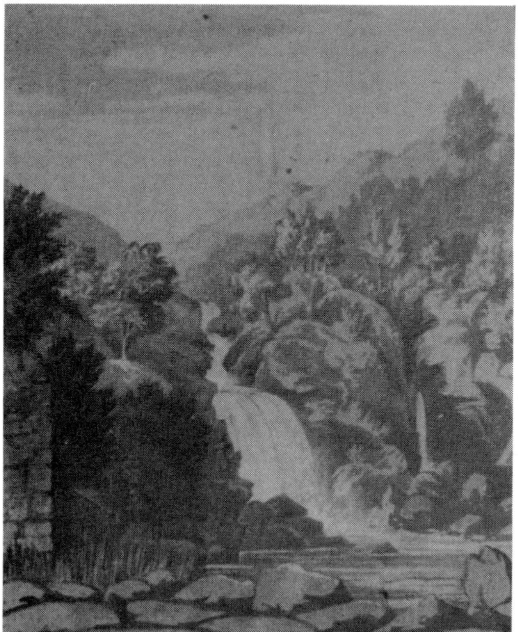

P. SANDBY – Waterfalls In Mountain Scene – 10½ x 8in.
(Michael G. Matthews) **$160** **£100**

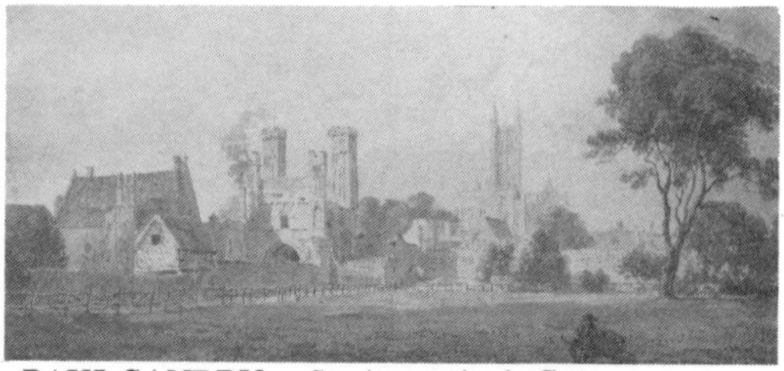

PAUL SANDBY – St. Augustine's Gate, Canterbury Cathedral Beyond – inscribed – pencil and watercolour – 10½ x 17½in.
(Christie's) **$13,777** **£8,250**

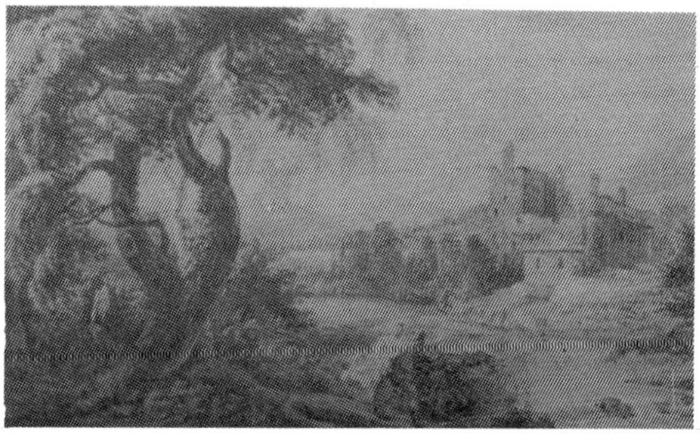

PAUL SANDBY – Figures Before A Ruined Castle – signed and dated 1786 – watercolour over pencil – 37 x 51cm.
(Phillips) **$8,476** **£5,200**

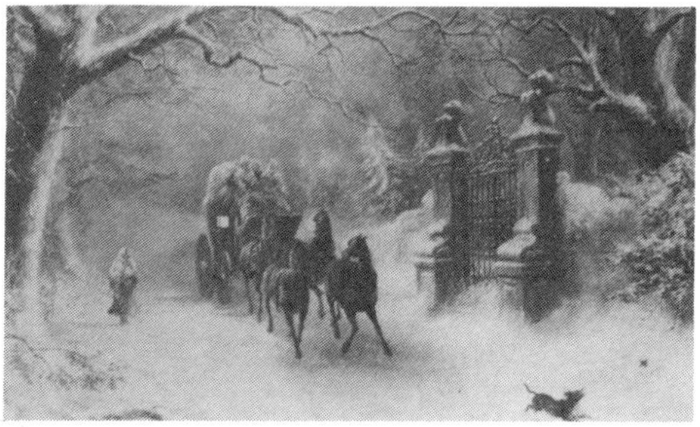

ROBERT SANDERSON, Attributed to – A Coach And Four In A Winter Landscape – signed – 23½ x 35in.
(Christie's) **$2,592** **£1,728**

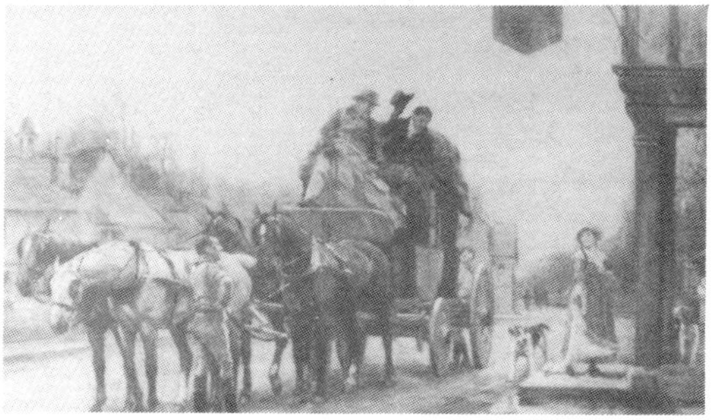

JOHN SANDERSON-WELLS – A Halt At The Bell Inn; and Setting Out – signed – oil on canvas – 16½ x 24½in.
(Christie's) **$7,920** **£5,500 Pair**

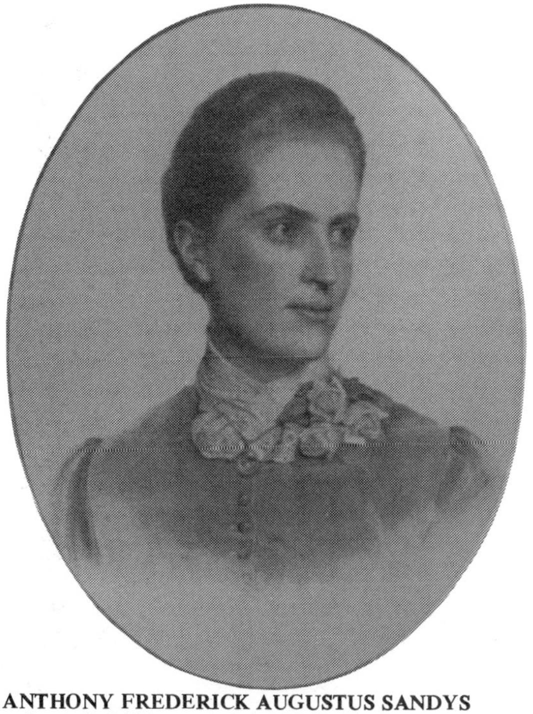

ANTHONY FREDERICK AUGUSTUS SANDYS – Portrait Of Margaret Helen Macmillan – signed, inscribed and dated 1884 – pencil and coloured chalks – 70 x 53cm.
(Phillips) **$2,119** **£1,300**

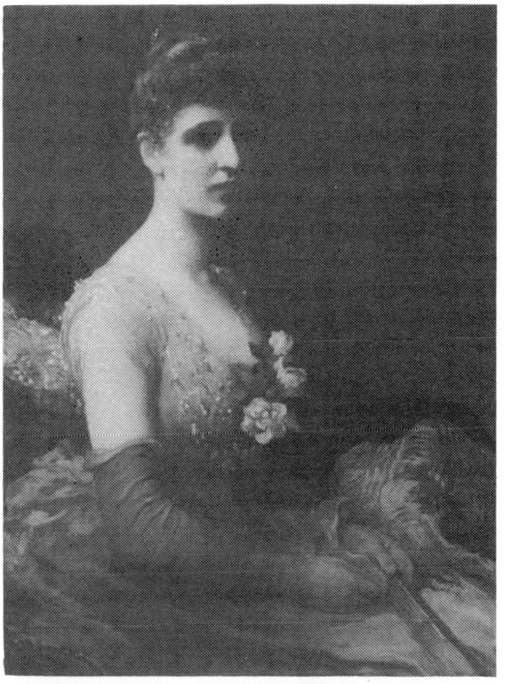

JAMES SANT – Portrait Of Lady Dixon Of Rheda Wearing A Yellow Dress, Holding A Fan – signed with monogram – oil on canvas – 35½ x 27½in.
(Christie's) **$6,044** **£3,850**

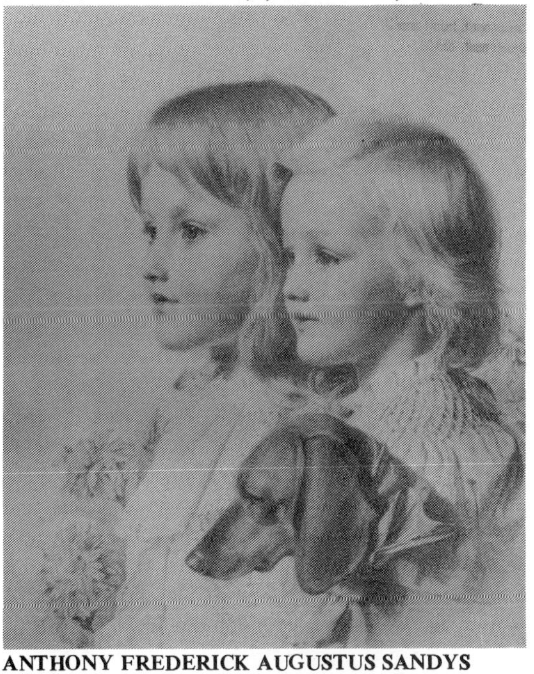

ANTHONY FREDERICK AUGUSTUS SANDYS – A Double Portrait Of Conrad Herbert Flower And Violet Flower – signed, inscribed and dated 1885 – pencil and coloured chalks – 68 x 51cm.
(Phillips) **$11,736** **£7,200**

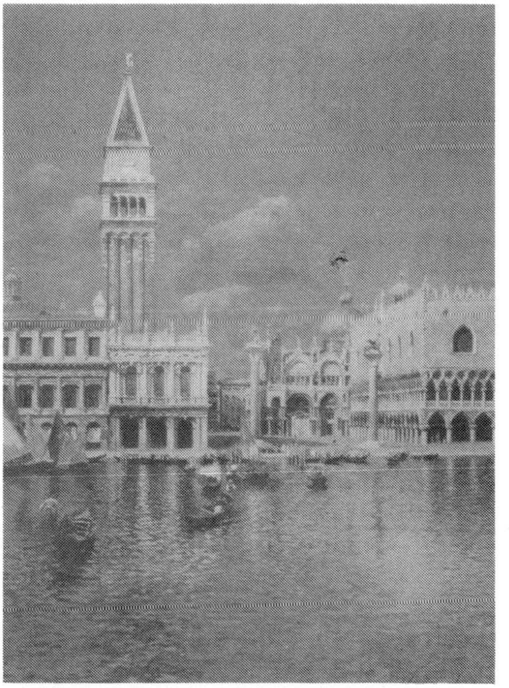

RUBENS SANTORO – A View Of St. Marks From The Lagoon – signed – oil on canvas – 49.5 x 37cm.
(Phillips) **$23,040** **£16,000**

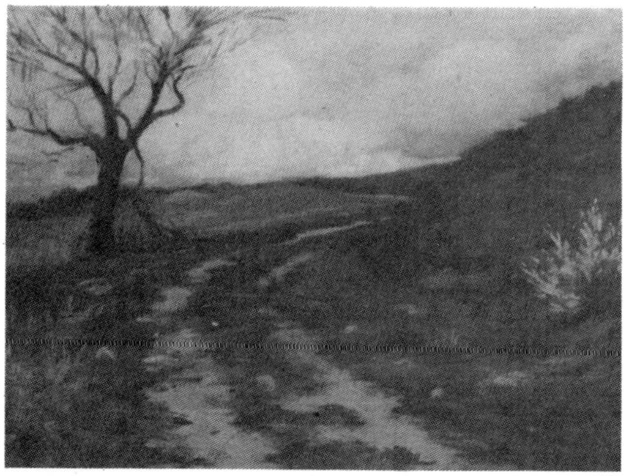

DANIEL SANTRY – French Country Landscape With Winding Road – signed – oil on canvas – 18 x 24in.
(Robt. W. Skinner Inc.) **$500** **£347**

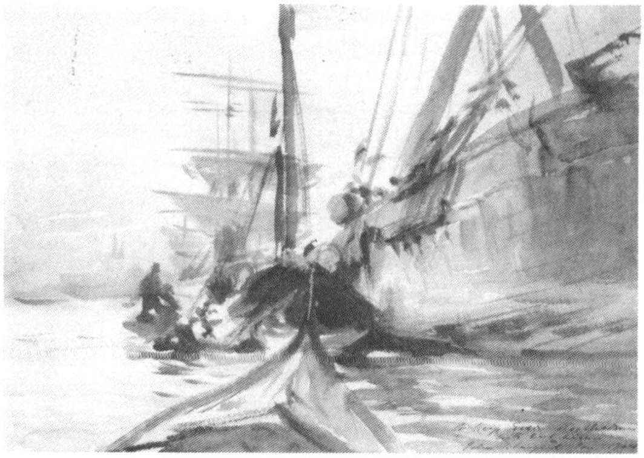

JOHN SINGER SARGENT – Unloading Boats – signed and dated 1904 – watercolour – 9¾ x 13¾in.
(Christie's) **$78,650** **£55,000**

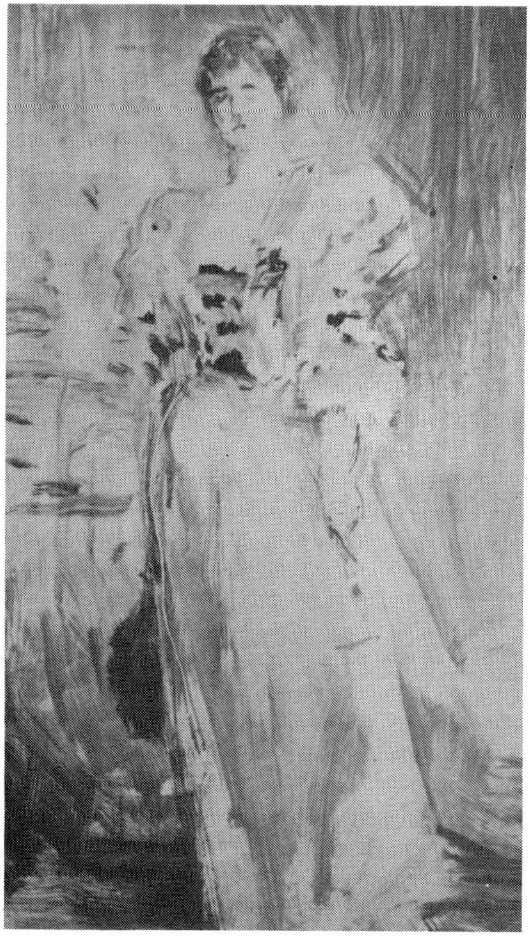

JOHN SINGER SARGENT – Portrait Of Edith, Lady Londonderry – oil sketch – on board – 11½ x 8¼in.
(Lawrence Fine Art) **$31,042** **£18,700**

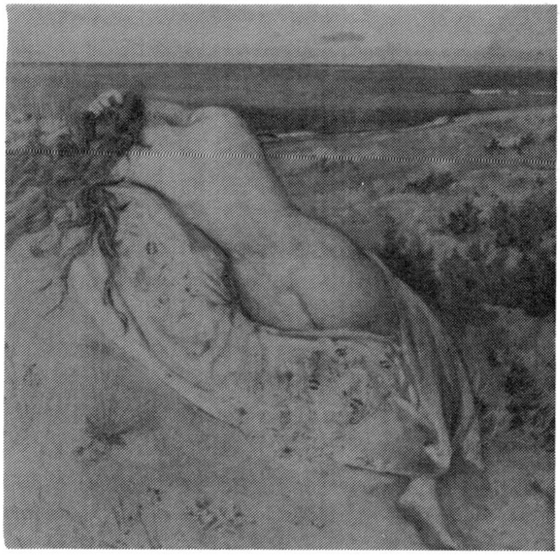

GIULIO ARISTIDE SARTORIO – Reclining Nude On A Beach – signed – oil on board – 15¾ x 14¼in.
(Robt. W. Skinner Inc.) **$4,000** **£2,453**

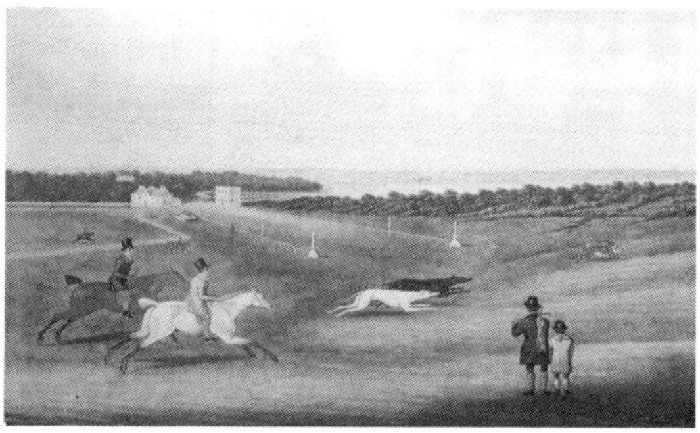

JOHN NOTT SARTORIUS, Manner of – Two Gentlemen On A Bay And A Grey With Two Greyhounds Coursing A Hare By A Racehorse, In An Extensive Landscape – 18 x 23½in.
(Christie's) **$2,592** **£1,728**

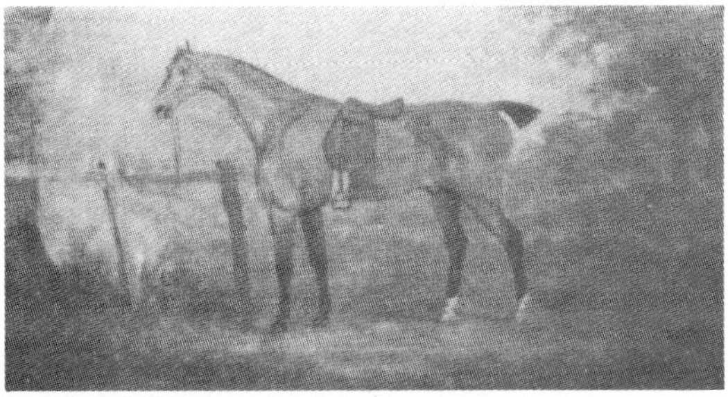

JOHN NOTT SARTORIUS, Attributed to – A Wooded Landscape With A Saddles Bay Cob Tethered To A Rail – with signature and date 1819 – oil on canvas – 17 x 21in.
(Christie's) **$2,392** **£1,650**

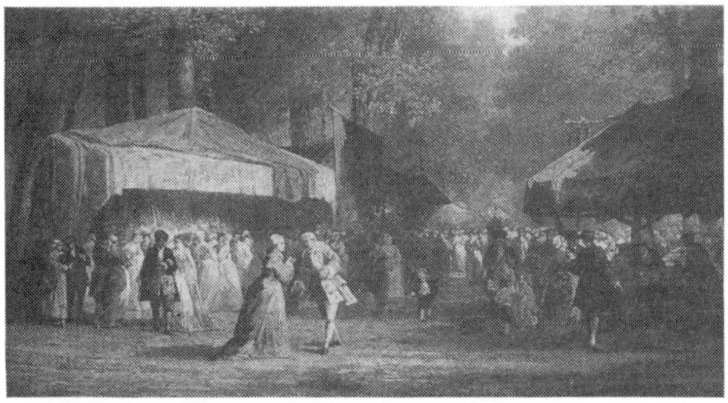

LEONARD SAURFELT – In The Pleasure Gardens – signed and dated 1886 – 16 x 24¾in.
(Christie's) **$6,019** **£3,960**

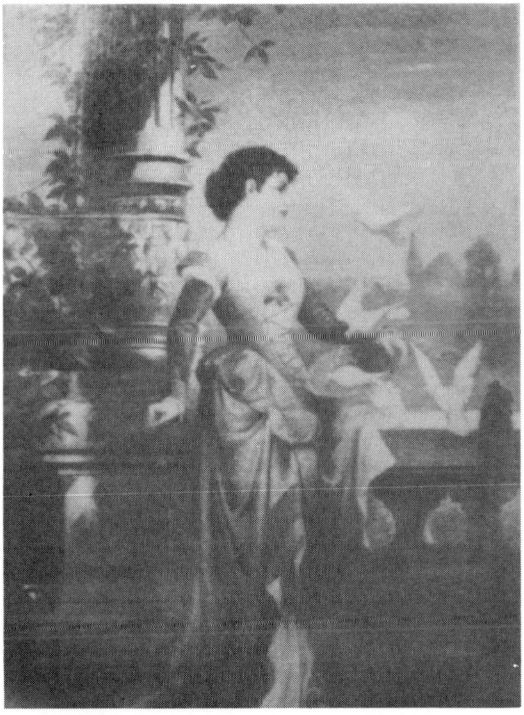

C. SAVINE – Feeding The Doves – signed – oil on canvas – 31 x 20in.
(Christie's) **$1,144** **£715**

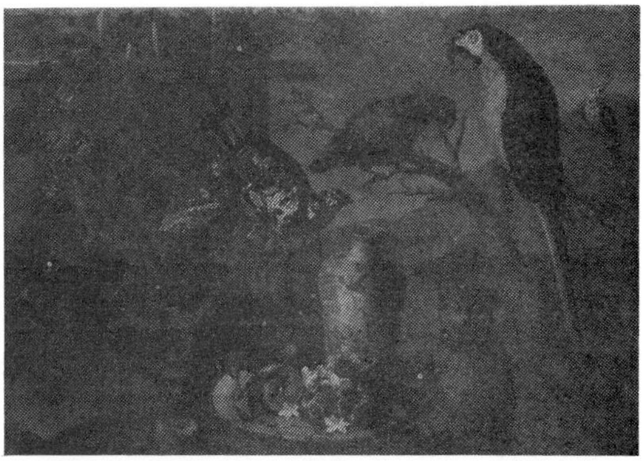

PIETRO NERI SCACCIATI – Exotic Birds In A Landscape – on canvas – 33½ x 45½in.
(Phillips) **$22,410** **£13,500**

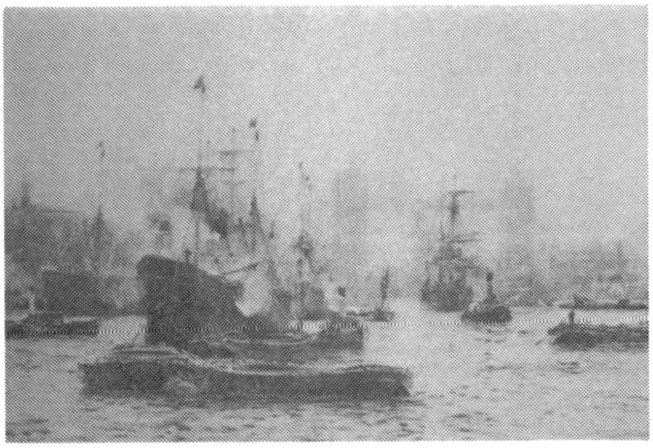

FREDERICK WILLIAM SCARBROUGH – The Pool Of London With Tower Bridge – signed and inscribed – watercolour heightened with white – 13¾ x 21in.
(Christie's) **$5,068** **£3,520**

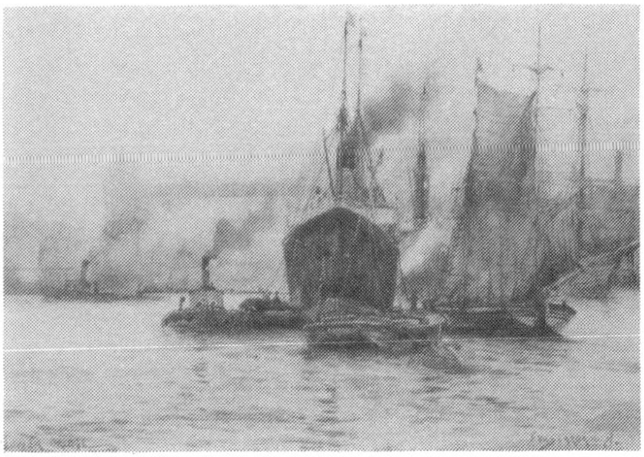

FREDERICK WILLIAM SCARBROUGH – Tower Bridge, London – signed and inscribed – watercolour heightened with white – 9¾ x 13¾in.
(Christie's) **$2,187** **£1,430**

FREDERICK W. SCARBROUGH – 'The Upper Pool', London – signed and inscribed – watercolour heightened with white – 34 x 52cm.
(Phillips) **$2,934** **£1,800**

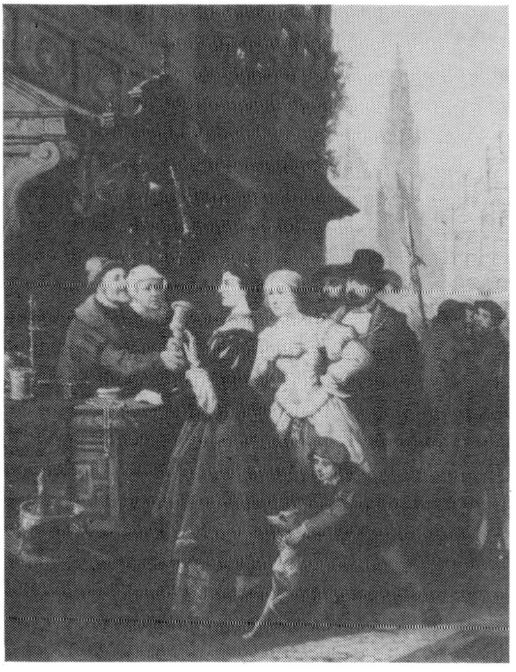

HENDRIK FRANS SCHAEFELS – Elegant Ladies At An Antiquarian's Shop In A Continental Street – signed and dated 1862 – oil on panel – 68 x 53.5 cm.
(Phillips) **$4,676** **£2,800**

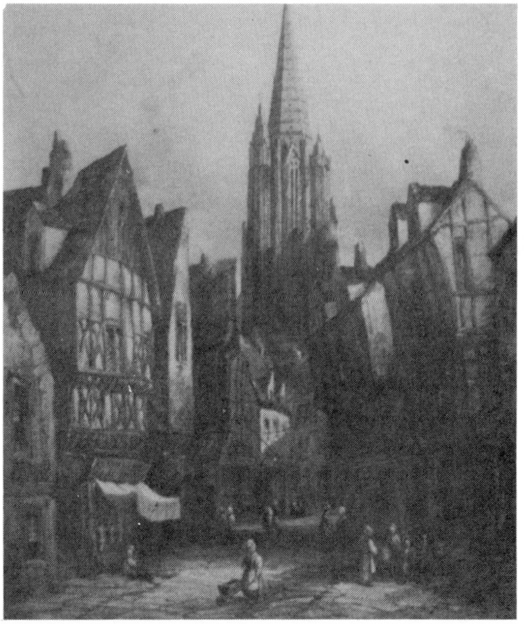

HENRY SCHAFER – Oudeel S. Seine, France; and Felamp, Normandy – signed and dated 1871, also signed and inscribed on the reverse – oil on canvas – 15½ x 11¾in.
(Christie's) **$2,861** **£1,870 Pair**

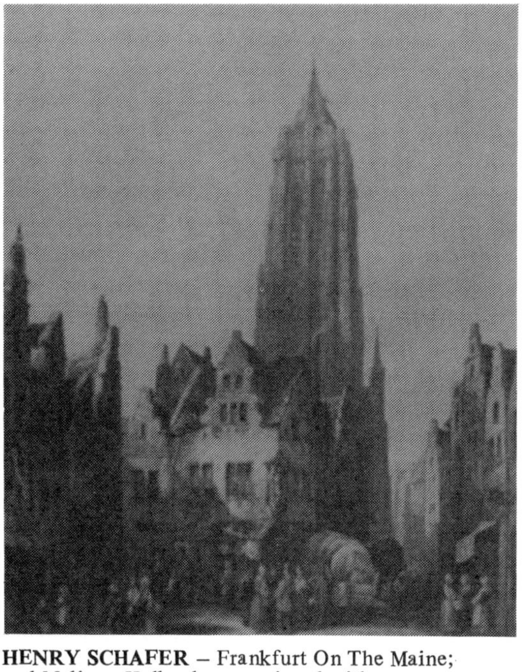

HENRY SCHAFER – Frankfurt On The Maine; and Malines, Holland – one signed with monogram and dated 1883, also signed and inscribed on the reverse, the other signed – on canvas – 16 x 12in.
(Phillips) **$2,898** **£1,800 Pair**

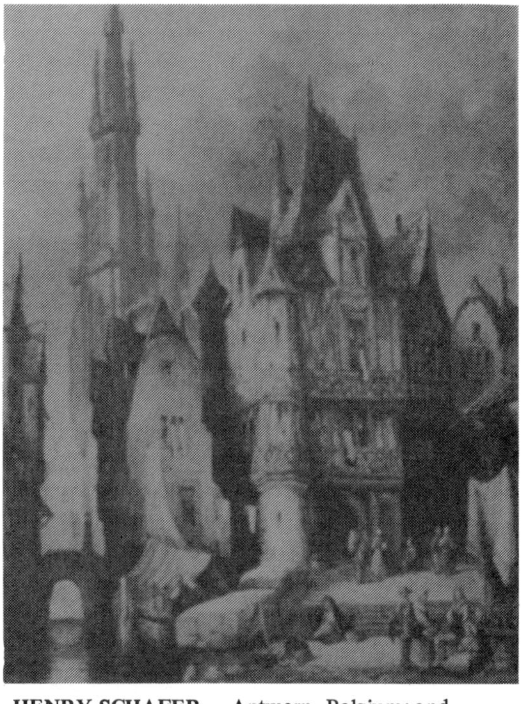

HENRY SCHAFER – Antwerp, Belgium; and Morlaix, Brittany – one signed with monogram and dated 1886, the other signed – on canvas – 16 x 12in.
(Phillips) **$2,576** **£1,600 Pair**

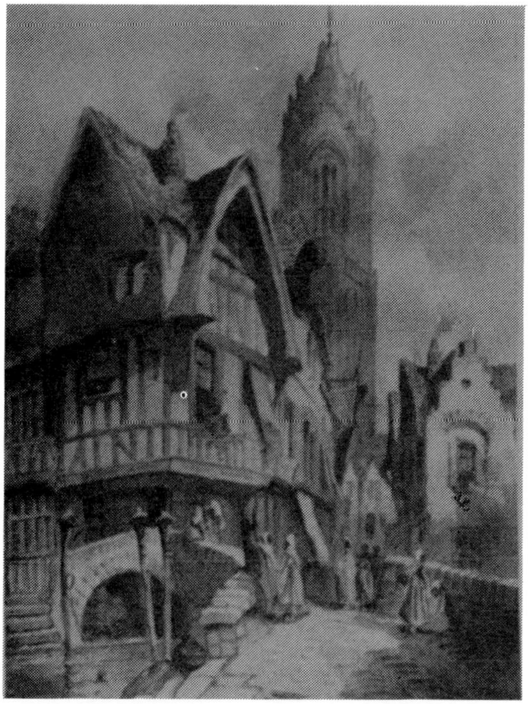

HERMAN SCHAFER – St. Michael's Church – Hamburg – signed and dated 1890 – watercolour and graphite on paper – 14 x 10¼in.
(Robt. W. Skinner Inc.) **$300** **£184**

HUGO SCHEIBER – Der Hafen – signed – oil on board – 28 x 40¼in.
(Christie's) **$11,088** **£7,700**

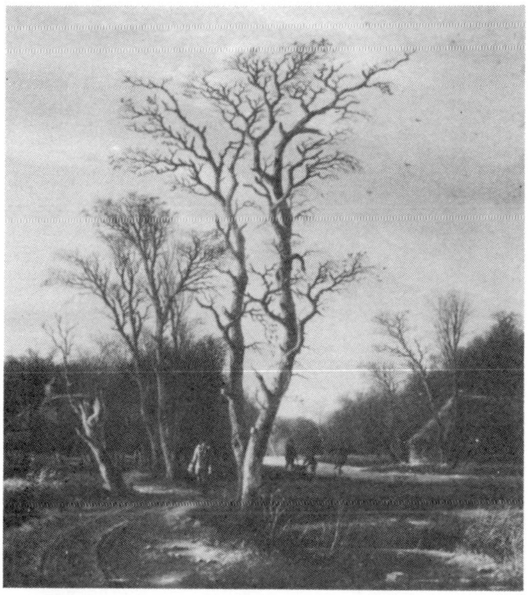

ANDREAS SCHELFHOUT – Skaters On A Woodland River At Evening – signed and indistinctly dated – on panel – 38 x 34cm.
(Phillips) **$1,661** **£1,100**

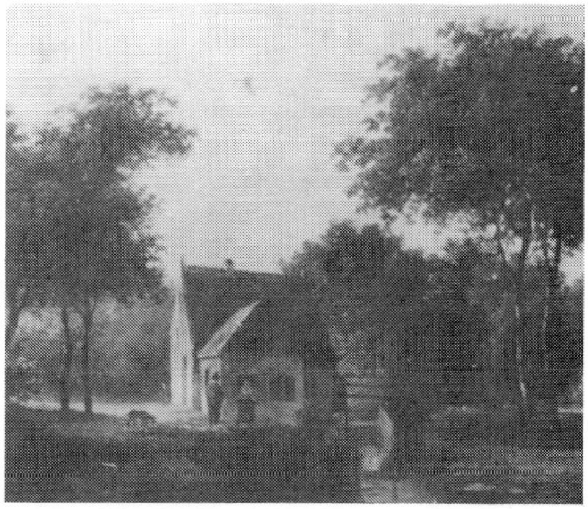

ANDREAS SCHELFHOUT – Figures By A Riverside Cottage – signed and dated '59(?) – oil on panel – 24 x 31cm.
(Phillips) **$1,670** **£1,000**

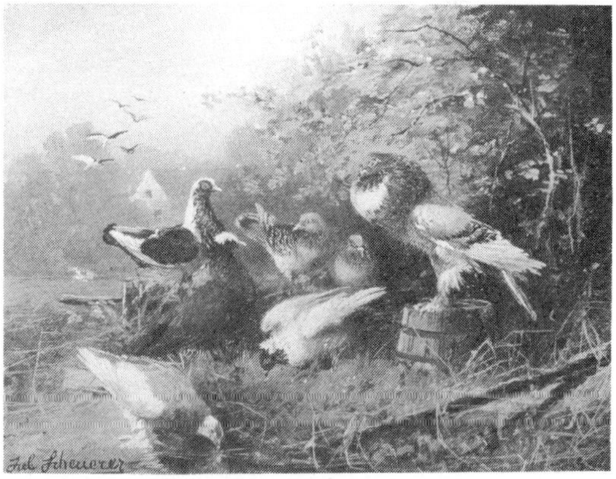

JULIUS SCHEUERER – Doves By A Farmyard Pond – signed – oil on panel – 7 x 9cm.
(Phillips) **$5,472** **£3,800**

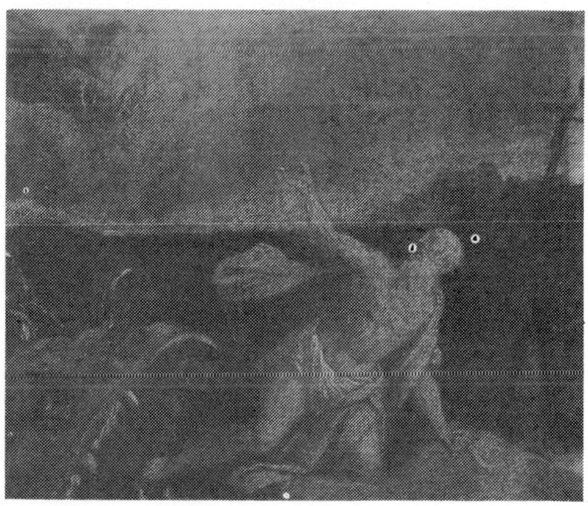

ANDREA SCHIAVONE, Called Andrea Meldolla – Jonah And The Whale – on canvas – 7¾ x 7¾in.
(Phillips) **$4,316** **£2,600**

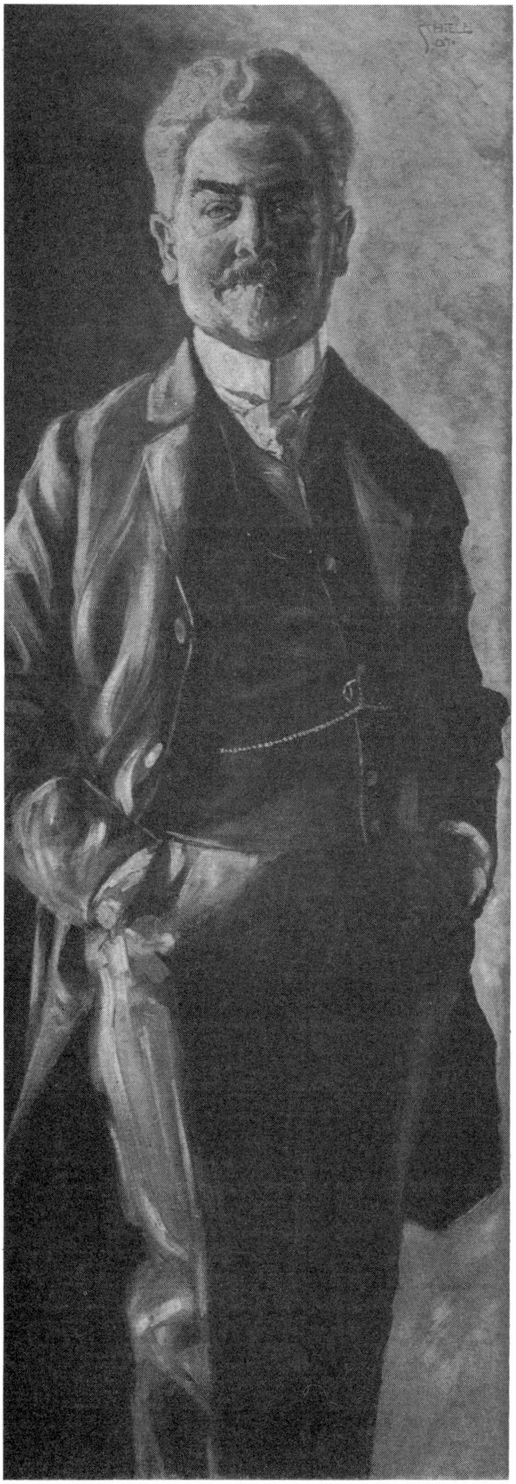

EGON SCHIELE – Bildnis Leopold Czihaczek – signed and dated '07 – oil on canvas – 59 x 19½in.
(Christie's) **$137,775** **£82,500**

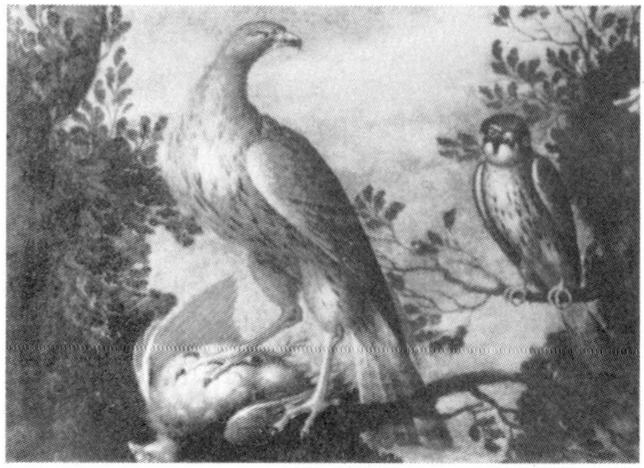

JOHAN MATHIEU SCHILDT, Circle of – A Sparrowhawk Stands Over His Kill, A Partridge, A Peregrine Falcon Looks On – oil on canvas – 20½ x 26¾in.
(Phillips) **$1,410** **£1,000**

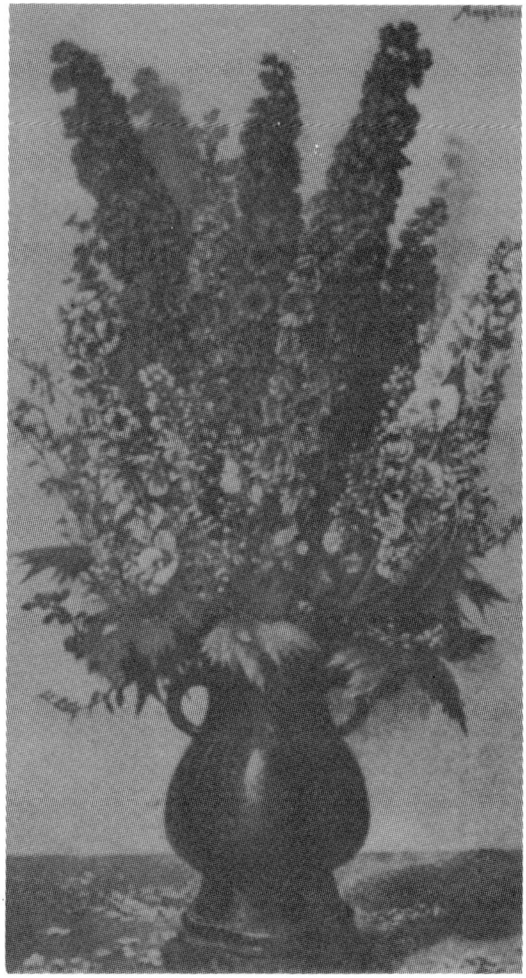

HERBERT GUSTAVE SCHMALZ – Delphiniums – signed – oil on canvas – 118 x 65.5cm.
(Phillips) **$806** **£520**

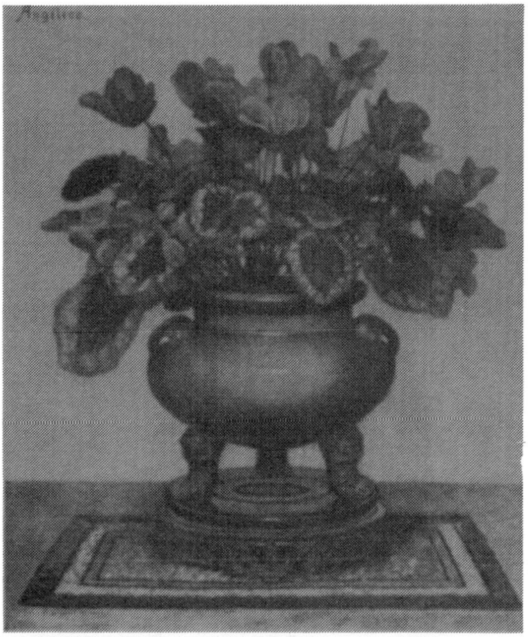

HERBERT GUSTAVE SCHMALZ – Cyclamens In Oriental Vase – signed – oil on canvas – 67 x 58cm.
(Phillips) **$465** **£300**

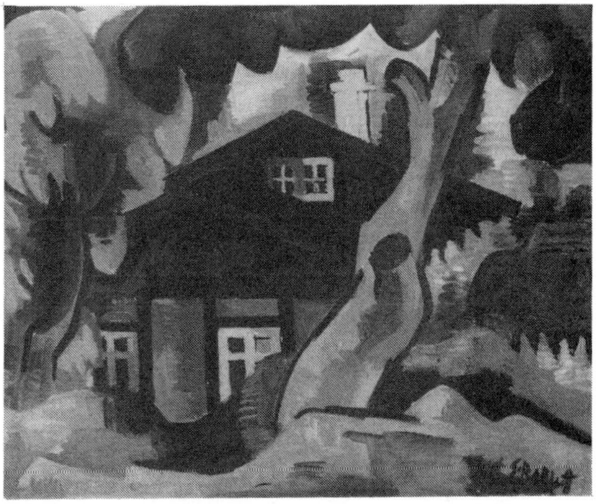

KARL SCHMIDT-ROTTLUFF – Bauernhaus – signed – oil on canvas – 30 x 39¾in.
(Christie's) **$156,145** **£93,500**

KERSHAW SCHOFIELD – View Of A Garden Terrace – signed – oil on canvas – 34 x 44in.
(Morphets) **$1,162** **£750**

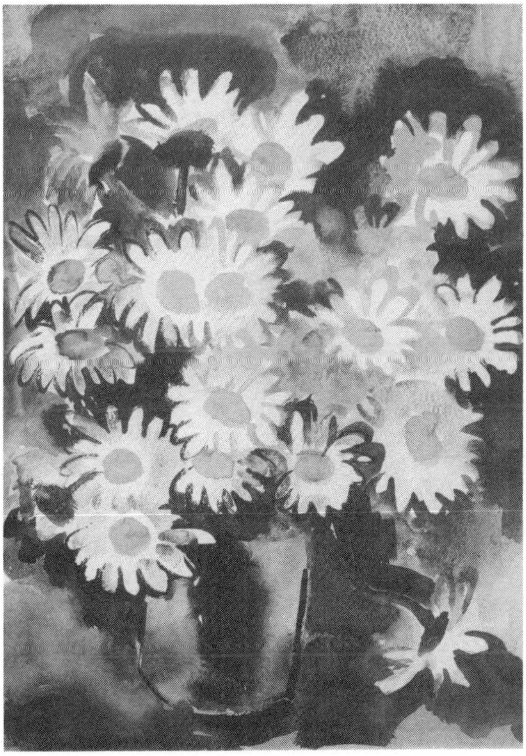

KARL SCHMIDT-ROTTLUFF – Blumenstilleben – signed – watercolour on paper – 27 x 19¾in.
(Christie's) **$45,760** **£28,600**

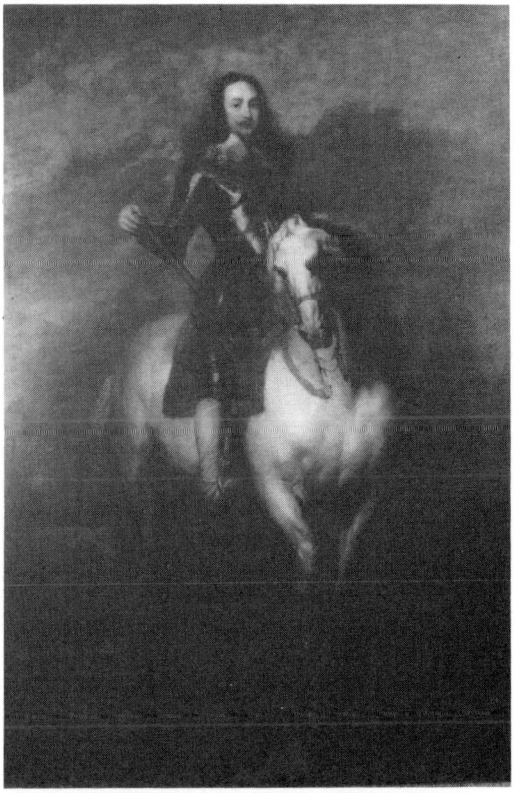

SCHOOL OF VAN DYCK – An Equestrian Portrait Of Charles I – inscribed – oil on canvas – 70¼ x 47½in.
(Geering & Colyer) **$4,640** **£2,900**

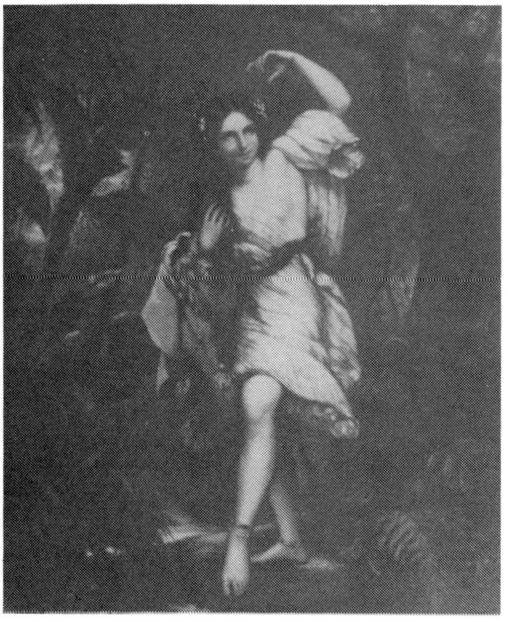

FREDERIC HENRI SCHOPIN, Attributed to – A Nymph In An Exotic Forest – oil on copper – 53 x 43cm.
(Phillips) **$720** **£500**

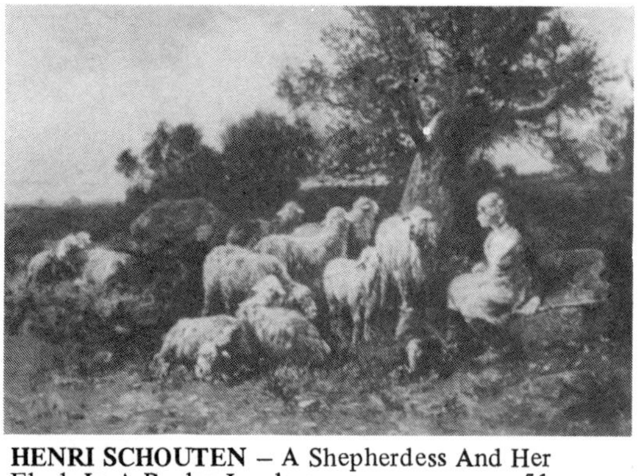

HENRI SCHOUTEN – A Shepherdess And Her Flock In A Rocky Landscape – on canvas – 51 x 76cm.
(Phillips) **$1,434** **£950**

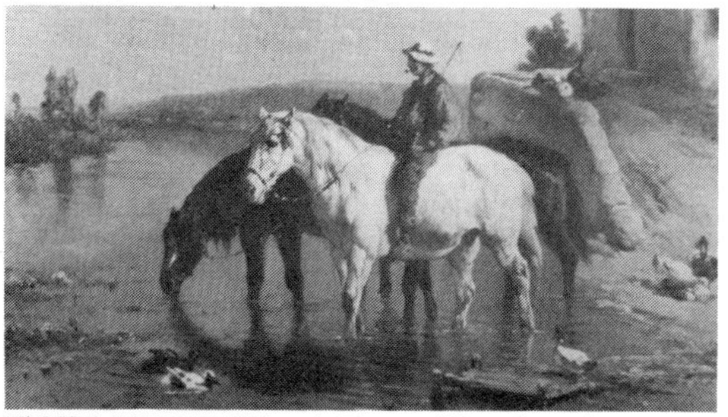

HENRI SCHOUTEN – A Farmer Watering His Horses On The Edge Of A River – signed – on canvas – 36 x 51cm.
(Phillips) **$1,434** **£950**

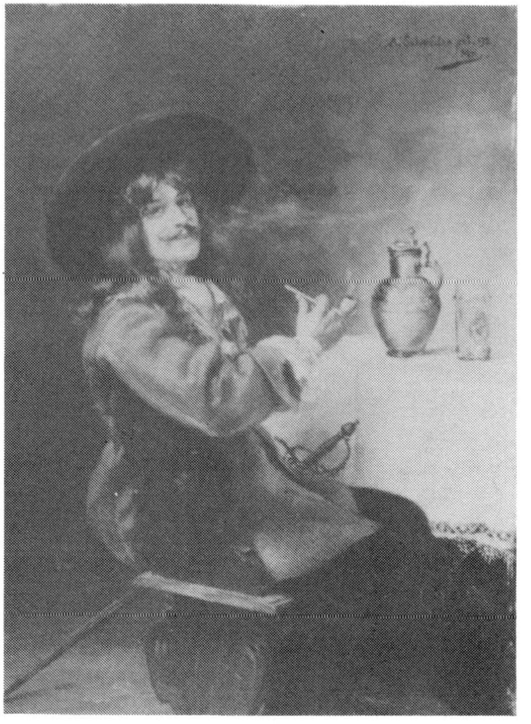

ALBERT FRIEDRICH SCHRODER – A Cavalier's Refreshment – signed and inscribed, dated '92 – on panel – 32 x 24cm.
(Phillips) **$1,584** **£1,100**

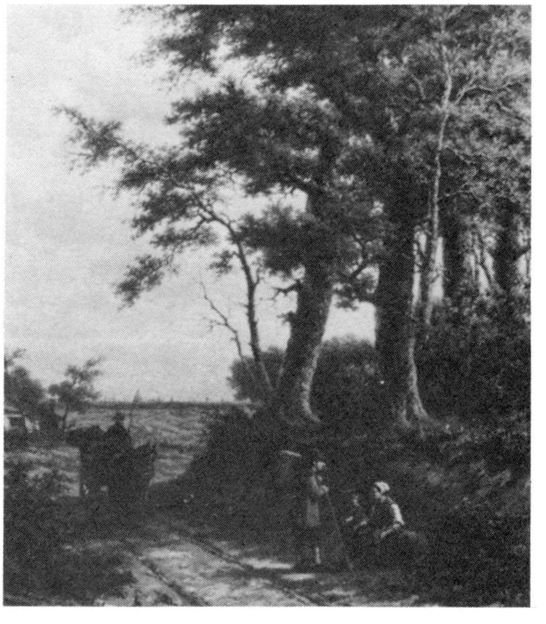

LION SCHULMAN – Rustics And A Cart On A Wooded Country Lane – signed – on canvas – 67 x 60cm.
(Phillips) **$1,057** **£700**

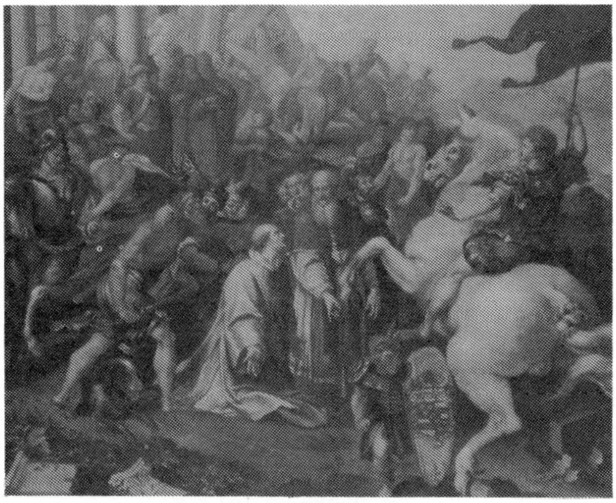

CHRISTOPH SCHWARZ, Circle of – The Arrest Of Two Saints – on copper – 15¼ x 15¾in.
(Phillips) **$9,130** **£5,500**

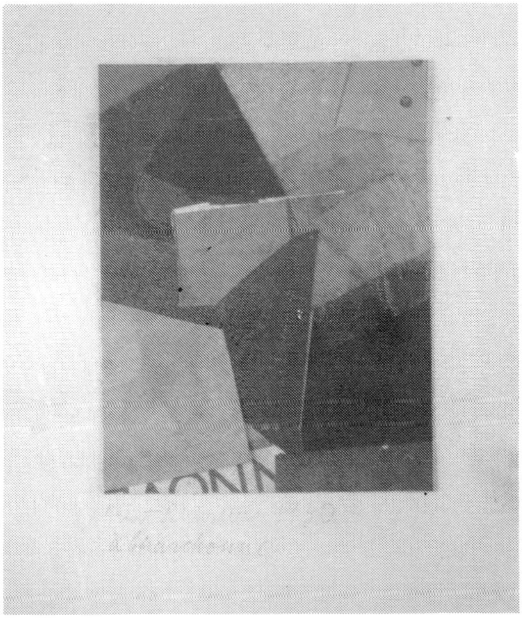

KURT SCHWITTERS – Composition – signed and dated 1930 – collage – 3¼ x 2¼in.
(Christie's) **$21,120** **£13,200**

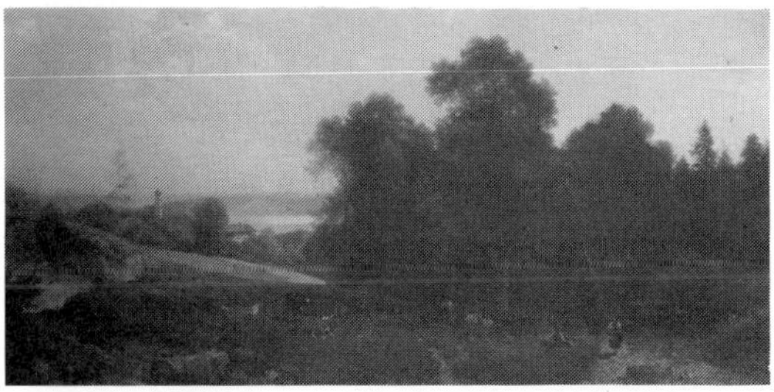

LUDWIG SCKELL – A Wooded Landscape With Shepherds, Sheep And Cattle – signed and inscribed – 19½ x 33½in.
(Christie's) **$17,600** **£11,000**

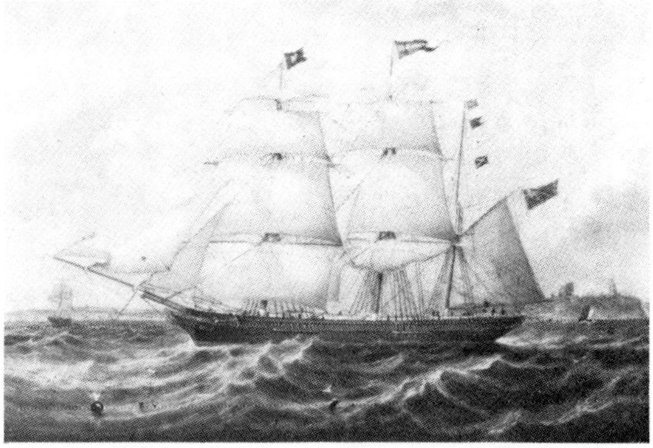

JOHN SCOTT – St. Oswin, A Sailing Ship Off The Tyne – signed and dated 1866 – 17¼ x 26in.
(Christie's) **$6,979** **£4,950**

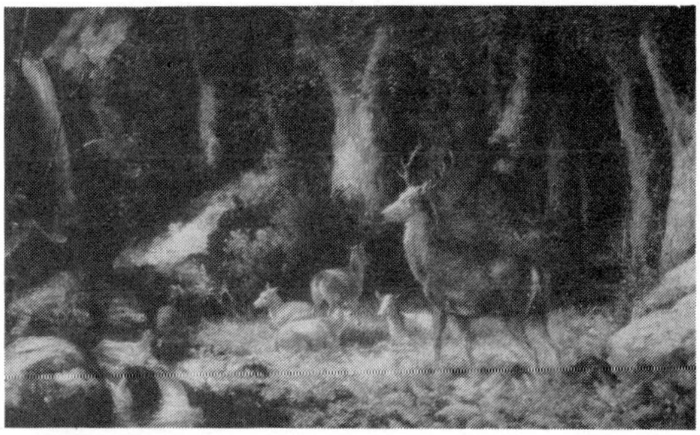

JOHN WHITE ALLEN SCOTT – Deer By A Stream – signed and dated '72 – oil on canvas – 12 x 20¼in.
(Christie's) **$1,760** **£1,148**

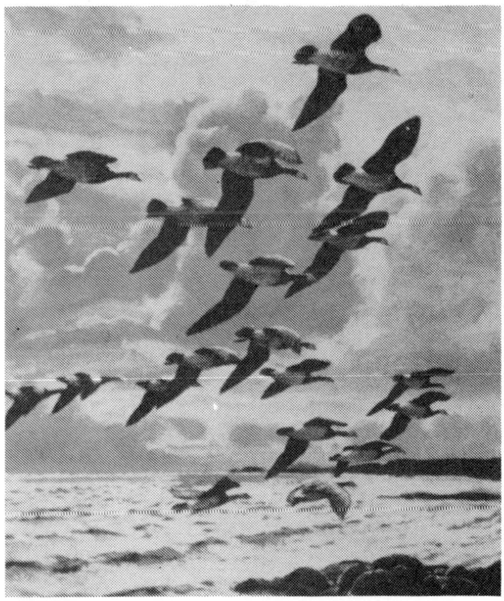

SIR PETER SCOTT – Barnacle Geese Low Over The Sea – signed and dated 1956 – oil on board – 29½ x 23½in.
(Christie's) **$3,460** **£2,420**

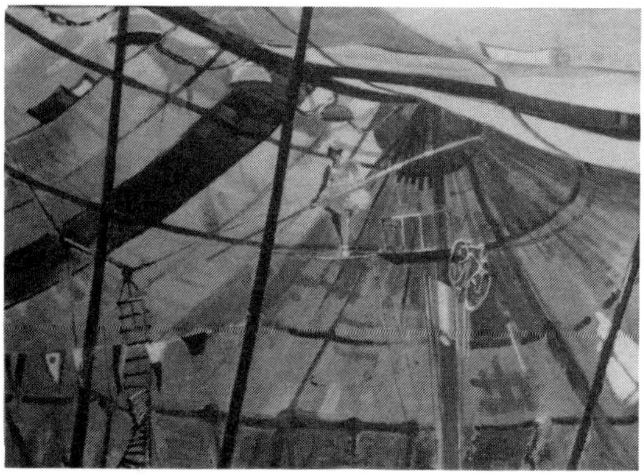

EDWARD SEAGO – 'The Big Top' – signed – oil – 17½ x 23½in.
(Geering & Colyer) **$6,048** **£4,200**

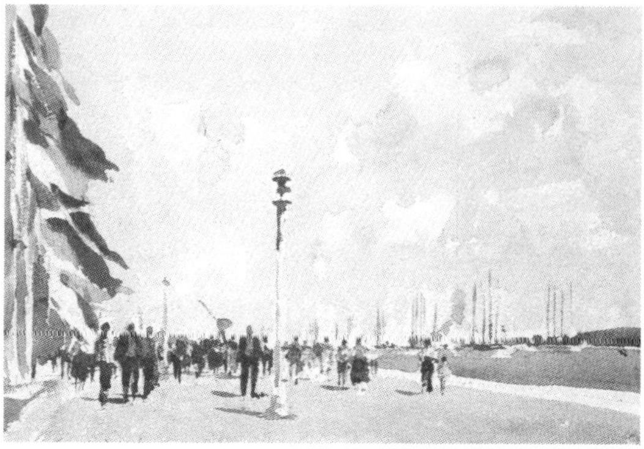

EDWARD SEAGO – Blessing Of The Schooner Fleet At Belem, Portugal – signed – watercolour – 10¼ x 14½in.
(Christie's) **$5,977** **£4,180**

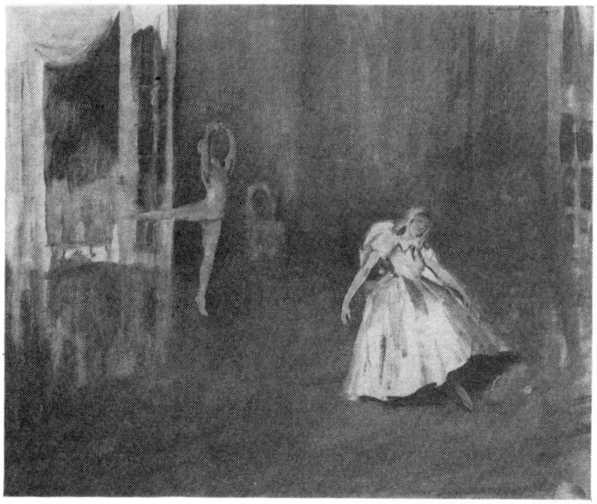

EDWARD SEAGO – Spectra De La Rose – signed and dated '38 – oil on canvas – 25 x 30in.
(Christie's) **$5,181** **£3,300**

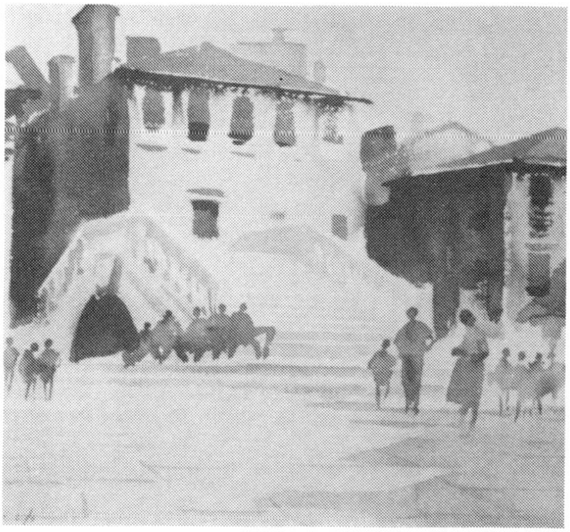

EDWARD SEAGO – The Square, Chioggia – signed – watercolour – 10¼ x 14¼in.
(Christie's) **$2,202** **£1,540**

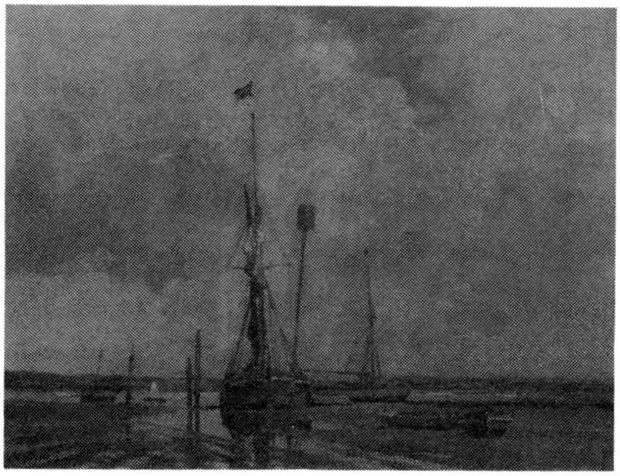

EDWARD SEAGO – The Red Can Marker – signed – oil on canvas – 51 x 66cm.
(Phillips) **$12,800** **£8,000**

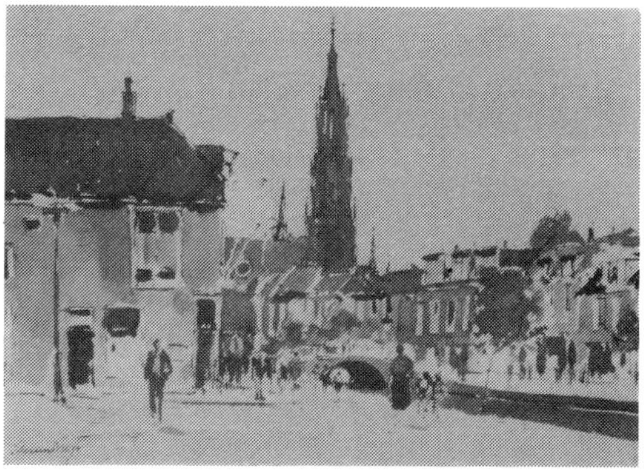

EDWARD SEAGO – The Cathedral Town, Delft – signed – pen, ink and watercolour – 26.5 x 37.5cm.
(Phillips) **$1,328** **£800**

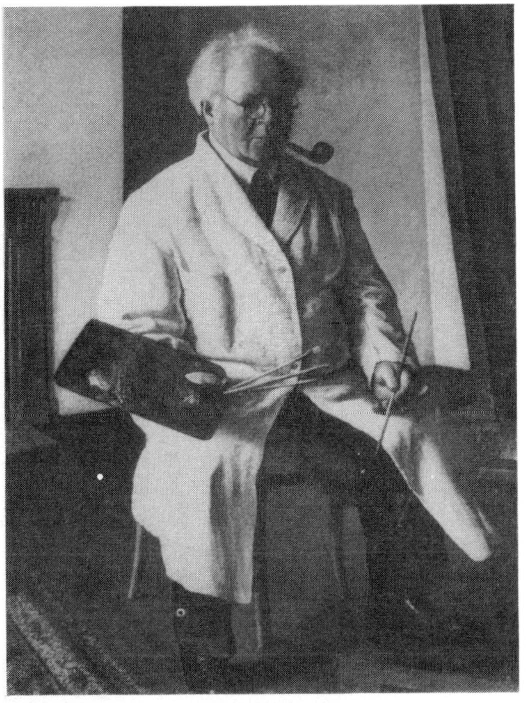

ARTHUR SEGAL – Selbstportrat mit Palette und Pfeife – oil on board – 32 x 29½in.
(Christie's) **$3,168** **£1,980**

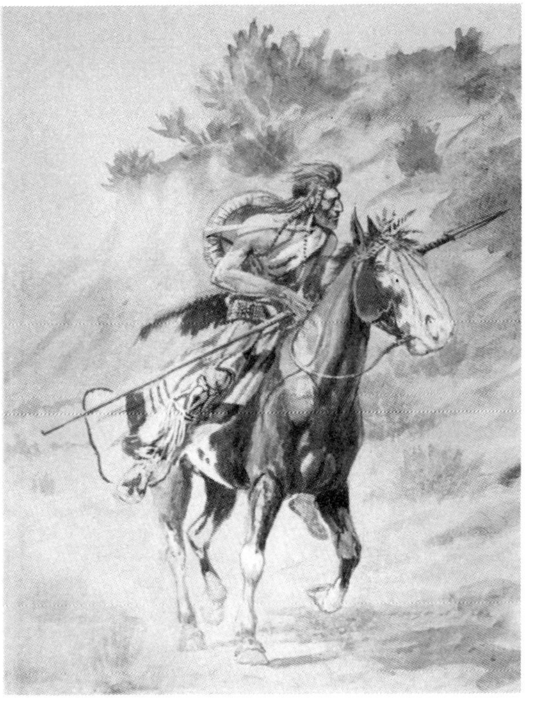

OLAF CARL SELTZER – Indian On Horseback – watercolour on board – 12 x 9in.
(Christie's) **$2,750** **£1,933**

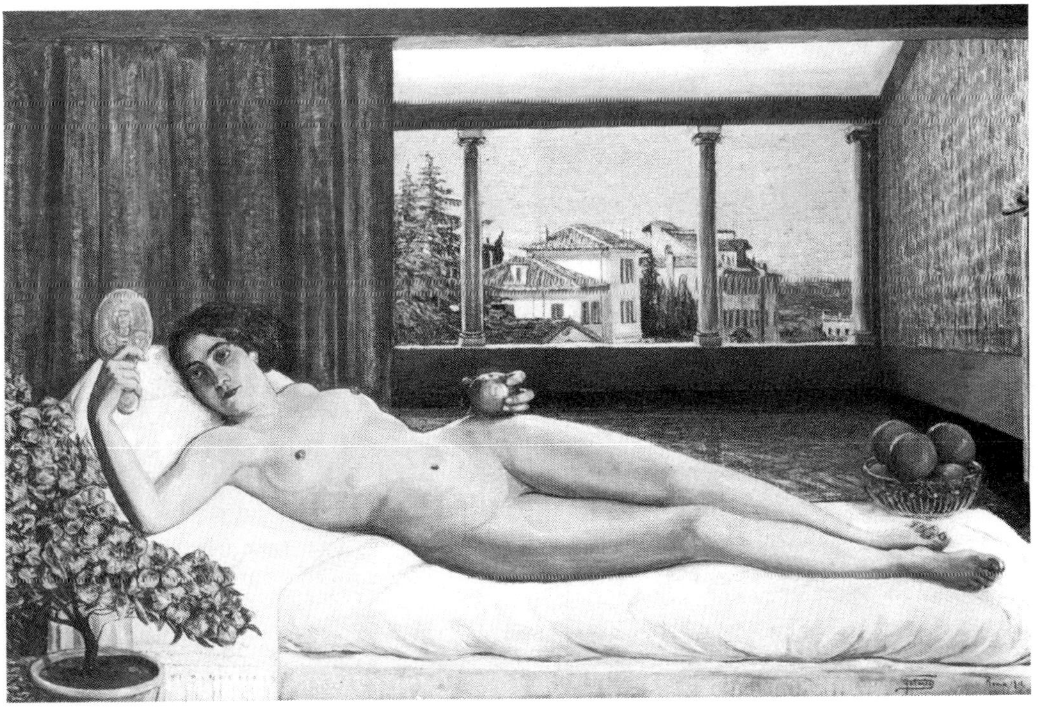

GOTTARDO SEGANTINI – Venere Eterna – signed and dated 1912 – oil on canvas – 41¾ x 61in.
(Christie's) **$11,880** **£8,250**

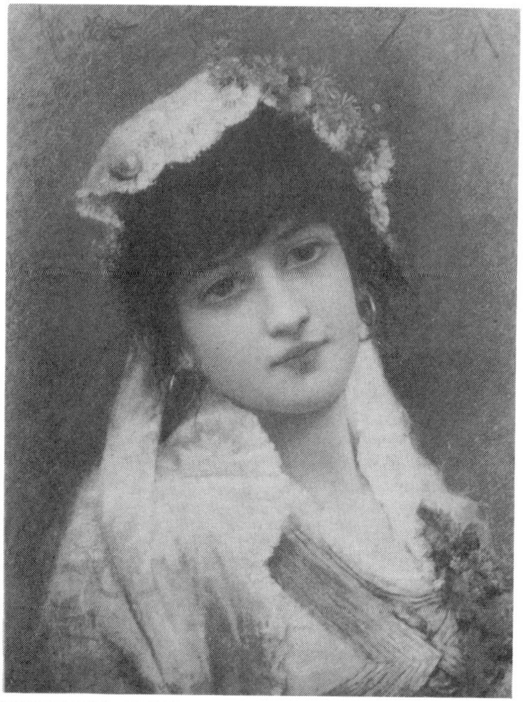

EMILE EISMAN SEMENOWSKY – The Flower Girl – signed and dated 1882 – on panel – 12¾ x 9½in.
(Christie's) **$5,852** **£3,850**

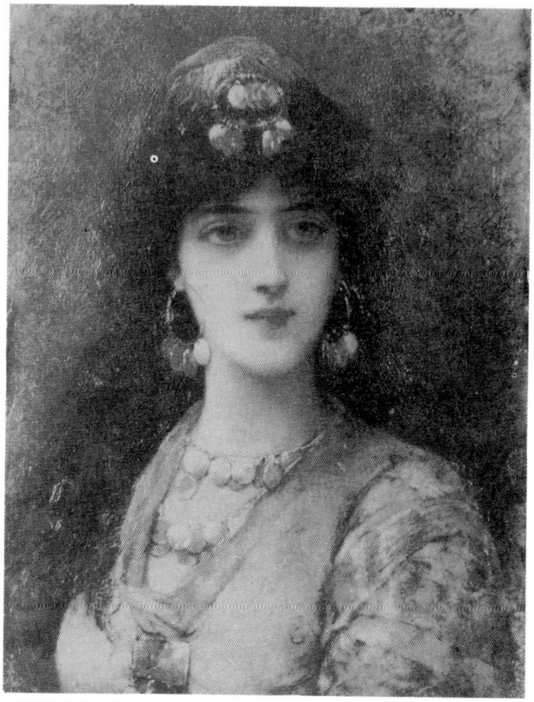

EMILE EISMAN SEMENOWSKY – A Dark Gypsy Beauty – signed and inscribed – on panel – 13 x 9½in.
(Christie's) **$2,508** **£1,650**

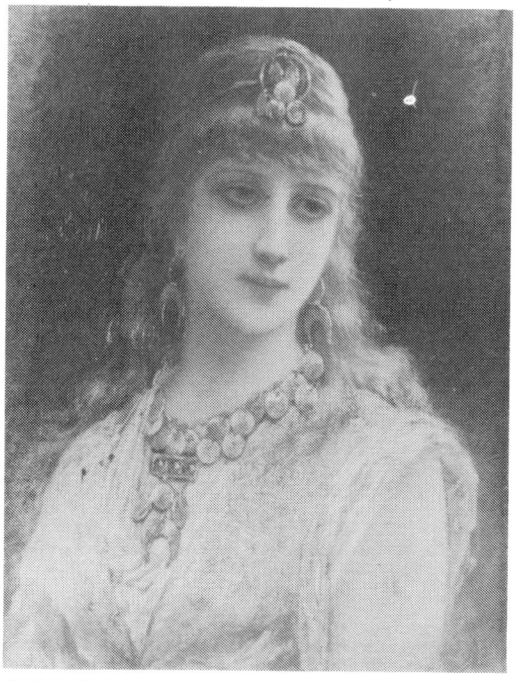

EMILE EISMAN SEMENOWSKY – A Fair Gypsy Beauty – signed and inscribed – on panel – 13 x 9½in.
(Christie's) **$2,340** **£1,540**

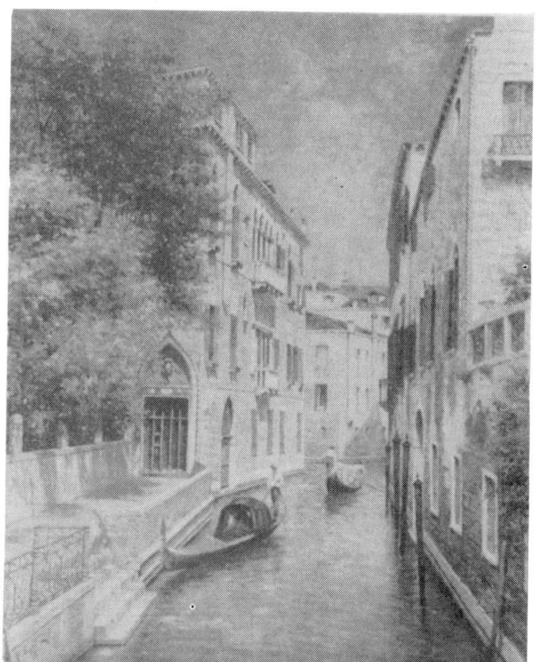

RAFAEL SENET – A Venetian Backwater – signed – 32¼ x 26in.
(Christie's) **$8,025** **£5,280**

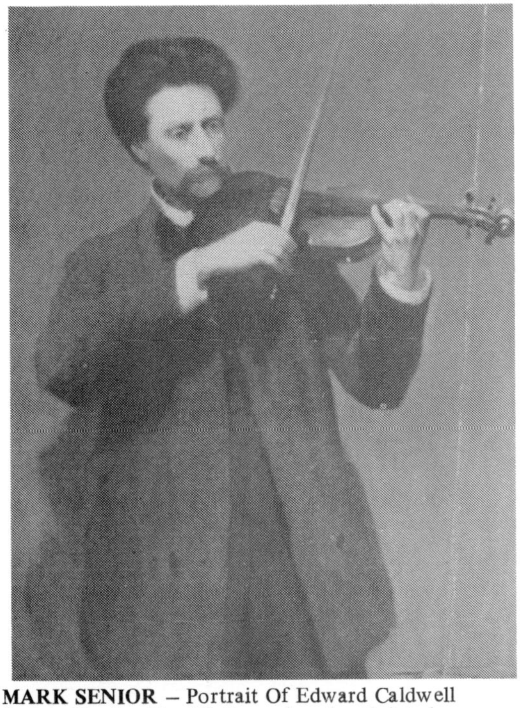

MARK SENIOR – Portrait Of Edward Caldwell Spruce Playing The Violin – signed and dated 1898 – oil on canvas – 47 x 34in.
(Christie's) **$1,887** **£1,320**

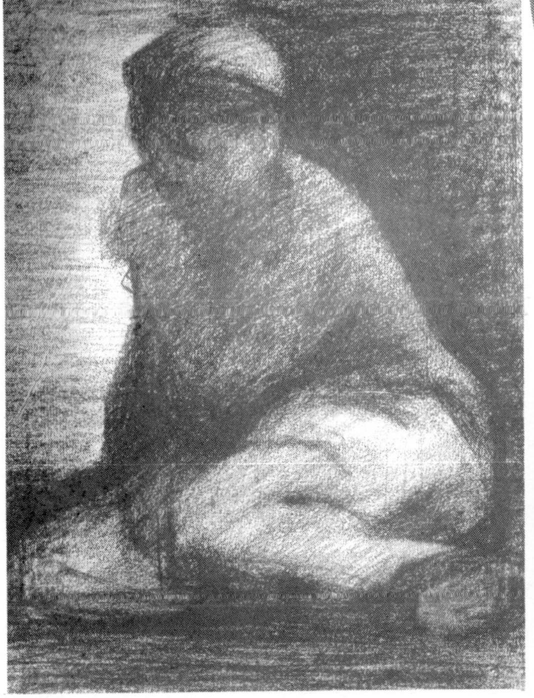

GEORGE SEURAT – Jeune Gardon accroupi – conte crayon on paper – 12½ x 9¾in.
(Christie's) **$245,520** **£170,500**

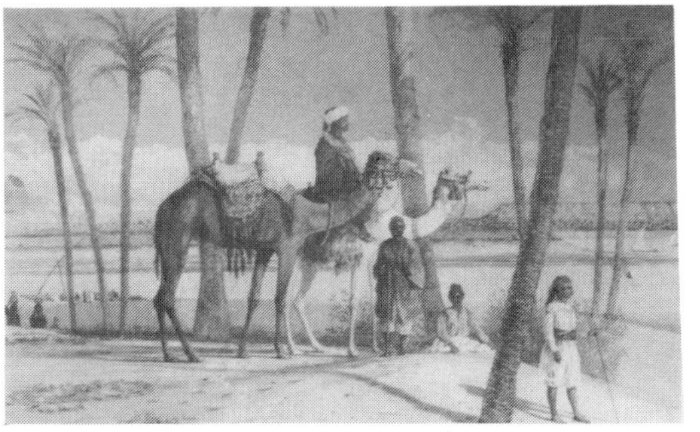

WALTER SEVERN – Dromedaries, Upper Egypt – signed, inscribed and dated 1873 – pencil and watercolour heightened with white – 20¼ x 29½in.
(Christie's) **$1,643** **£990**

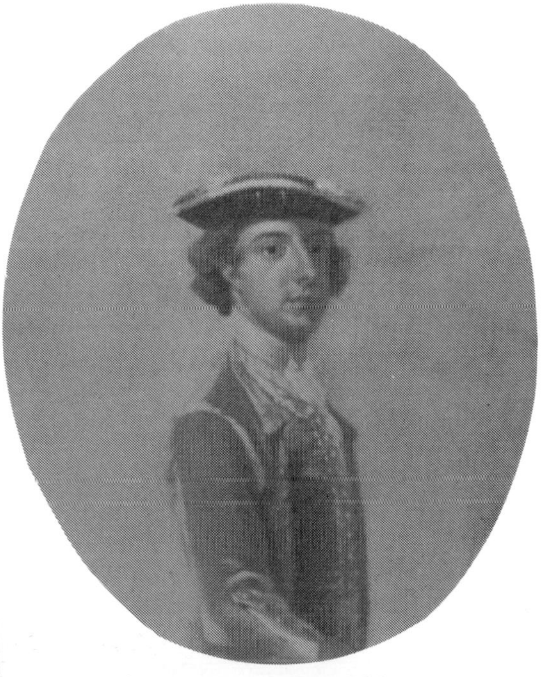

JAMES SEYMOUR – A Portrait Of A Huntsman, Half-Length – oil on canvas – 19¾ x 16in.
(Phillips) **$1,660** **£1,000**

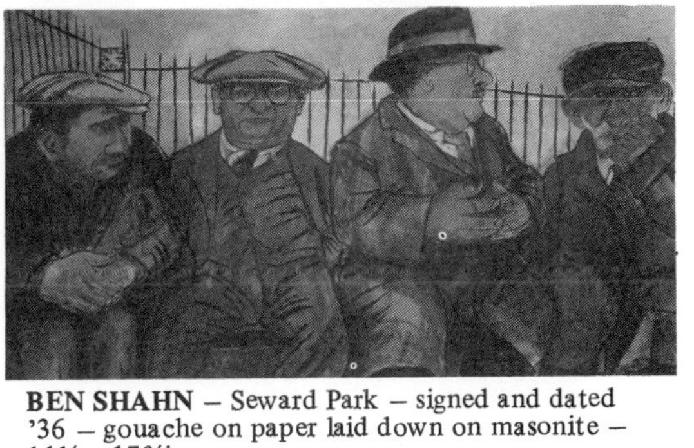

BEN SHAHN – Seward Park – signed and dated '36 – gouache on paper laid down on masonite – 11¼ x 17¾in.
(Christie's) **$20,900** **£14,540**

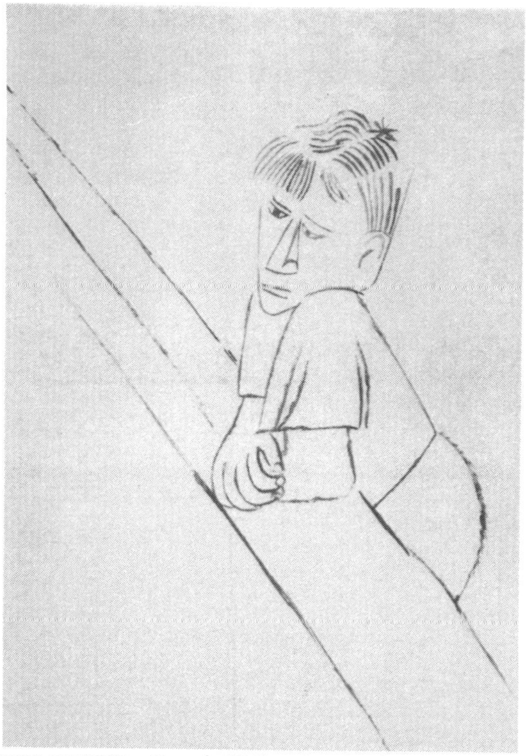

BEN SHAHN – Boy At Wall – signed – brush and brown ink on paper – 19 x 12½in.
(Christie's) **$1,760** **£1,224**

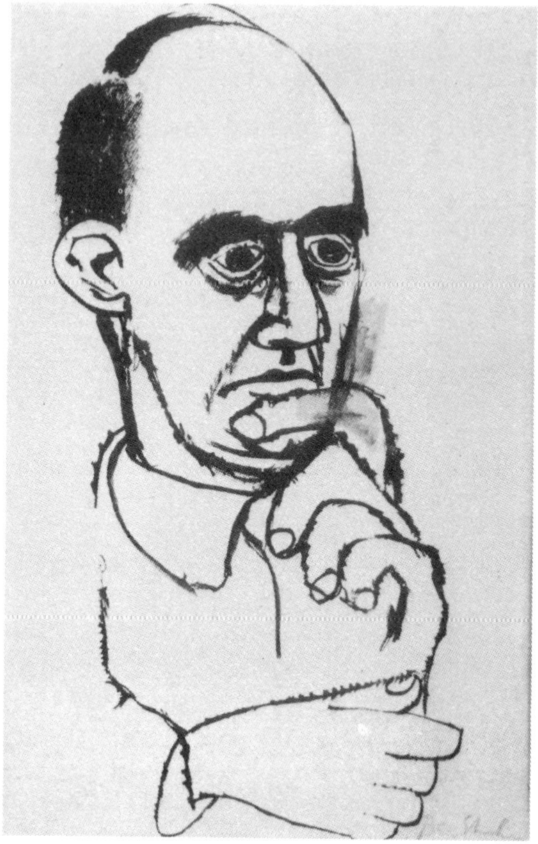

BEN SHAHN – Stevenson – signed – brush and black ink on brown paper – 22¾ x 14¼in.
(Christie's) **$4,400** **£3,093**

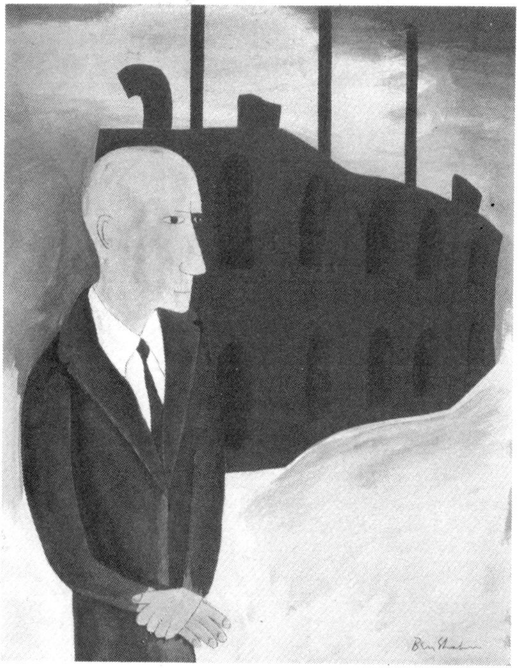

BEN SHAHN – A Corporate Portrait – signed – gouache on board – 25¼ x 19¼in.
(Christie's) **$17,600** **£12,372**

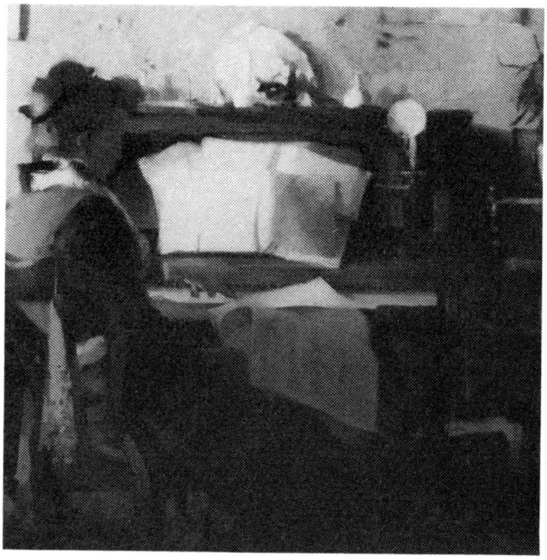

WILLIAM SOMERVILLE SHANKS – The Piano – signed – oil on canvas – 51 x 66cm.
(Phillips) **$11,360** **£8,000**

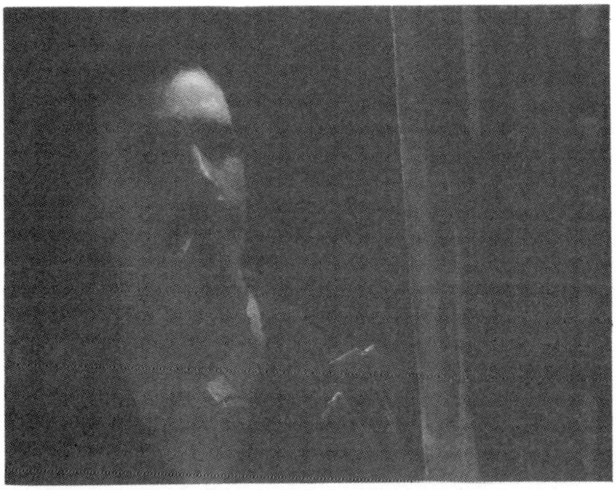

JAMES JEBUSA SHANNON – Self Portrait – signed and dated 1884 – oil on canvas – 16¼ x 20¼in.
(Christie's) **$11,000** **£7,652**

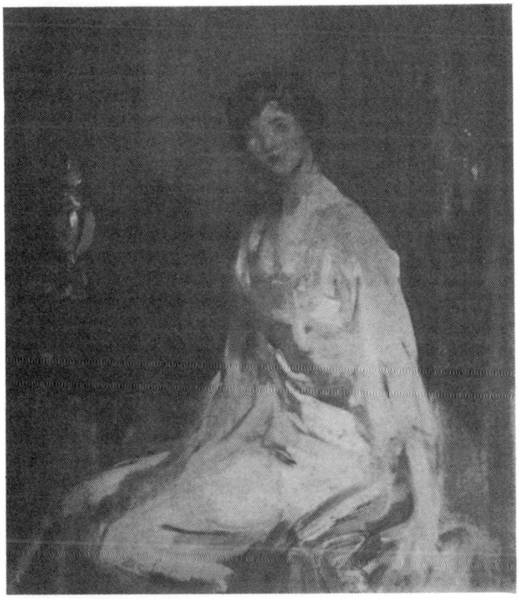

SIR JAMES JEBUSA SHANNON – Portrait Of Lady Patricia Ramsay – oil on board – 17 x 14½in.
(Christie's) **$1,122** **£715**

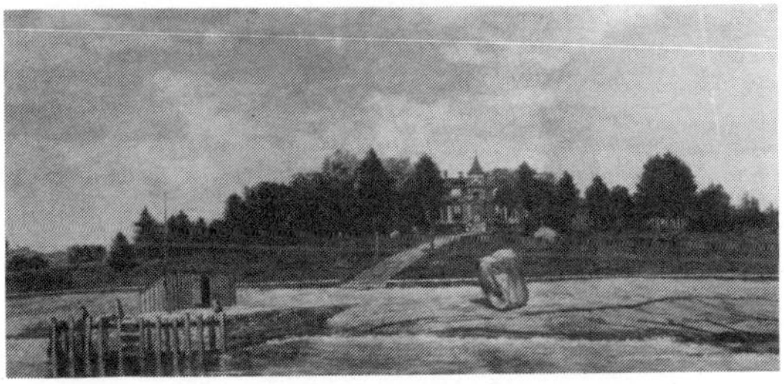

FRANK HENRY SHAPLEIGH – House On A Hill With Seaside Rock – signed and dated 1888 – oil on canvas – 26 x 42in.
(Robt. W. Skinner Inc.) **$3,000** **£1,840**

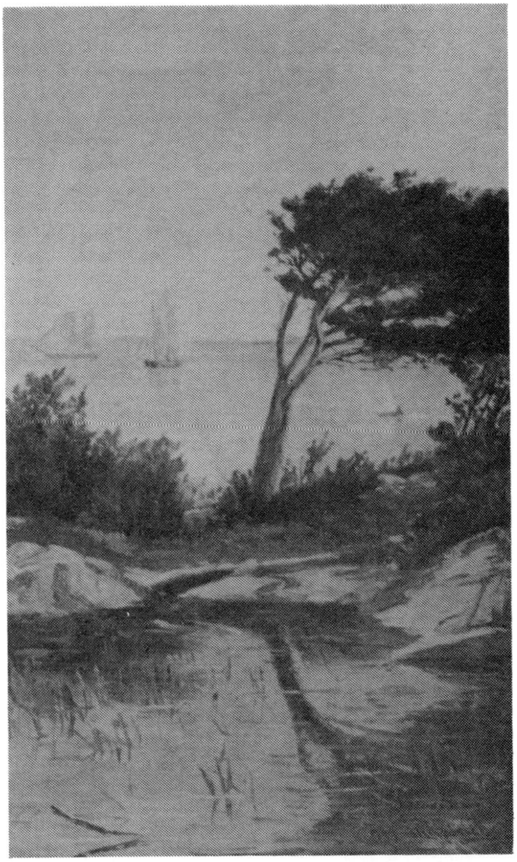

FRANK HENRY SHAPLEIGH – 'Old Cedar At Cohasset' – signed, also signed on the reverse – oil on panel – 12 x 7¼in.
(Robt. W. Skinner Inc.) **$1,500** **£920**

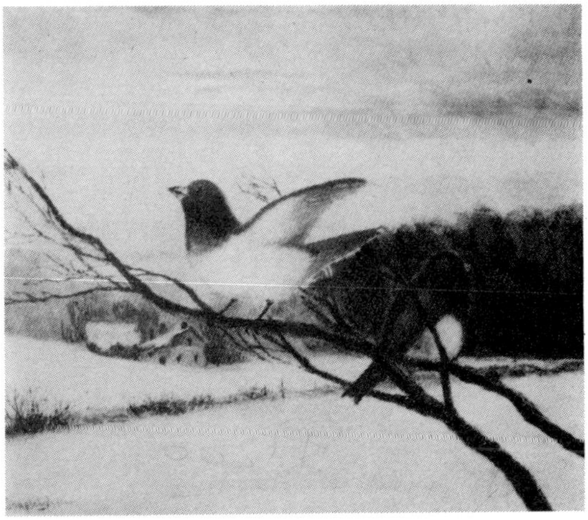

FRANK HENRY SHAPLEIGH – Winter Landscape With Birds – signed and dated 1866 – oil on artist board – 7 x 8½in.
(Robt. W. Skinner Inc.) **$1,000** **£694**

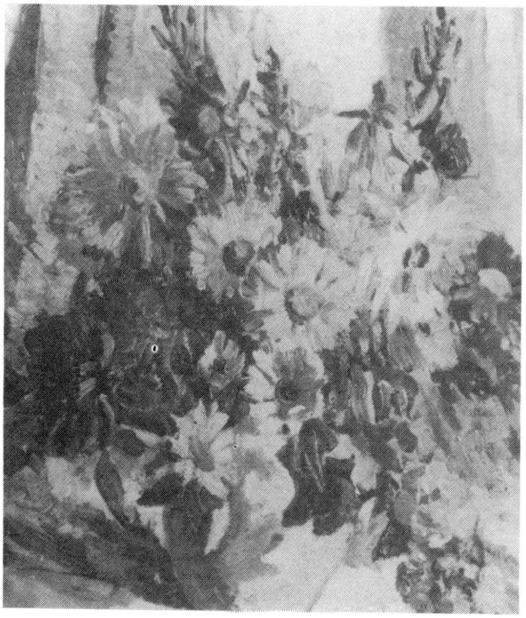

DOROTHEA SHARP – Summer Flowers In A Vase – signed – oil on board – 46 x 38cm.
(Phillips) **$3,672** **£2,400**

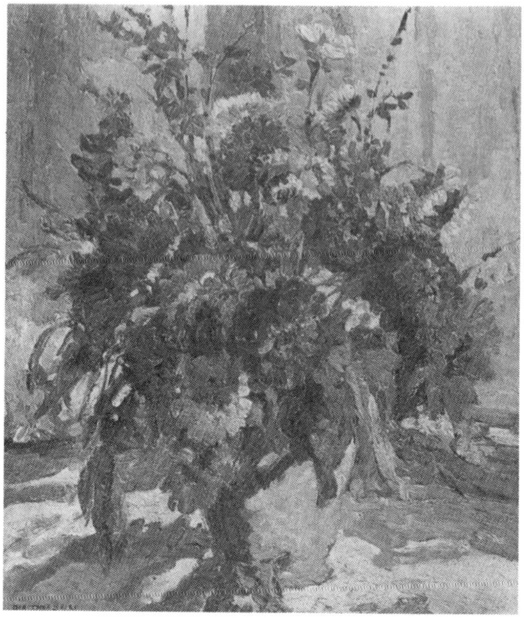

DOROTHEA SHARP – Still Life Of A Vase Of Flowers – signed – oil on board – 23¼ x 19¼in.
(Christie's) **$6,292** **£4,400**

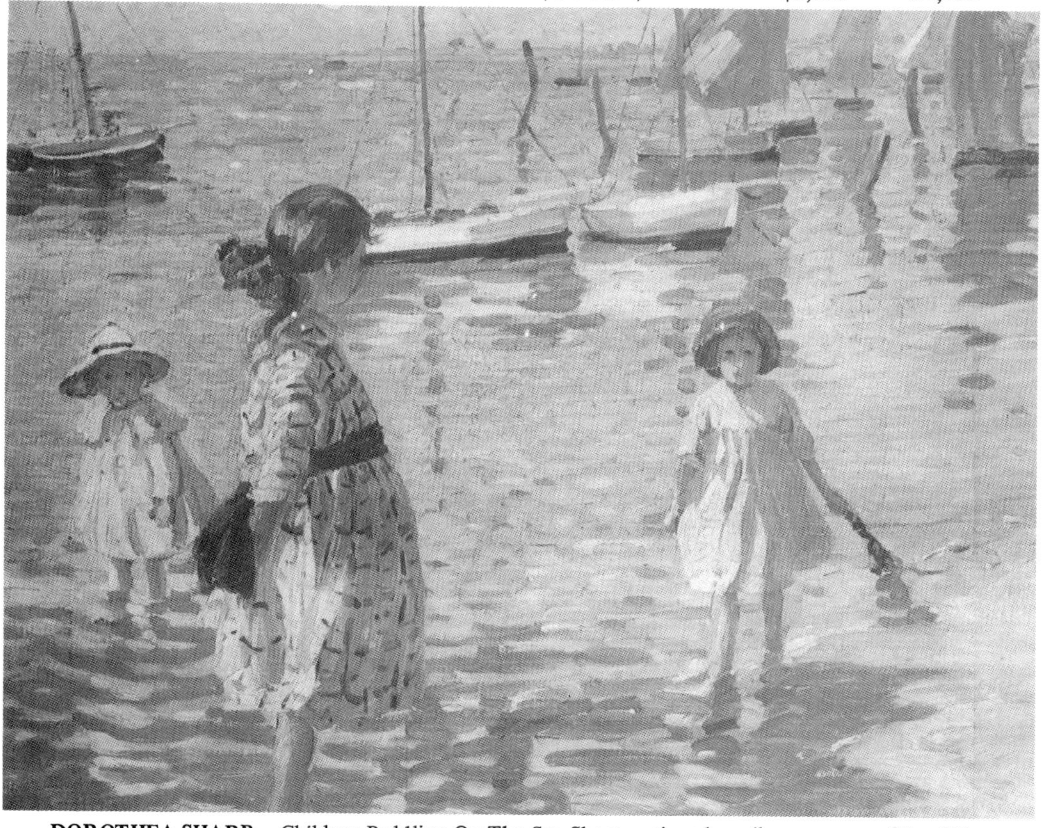

DOROTHEA SHARP – Children Paddling On The Sea-Shore – signed – oil on canvas – 25 x 30in.
(Christie's) **$42,471** **£29,700**

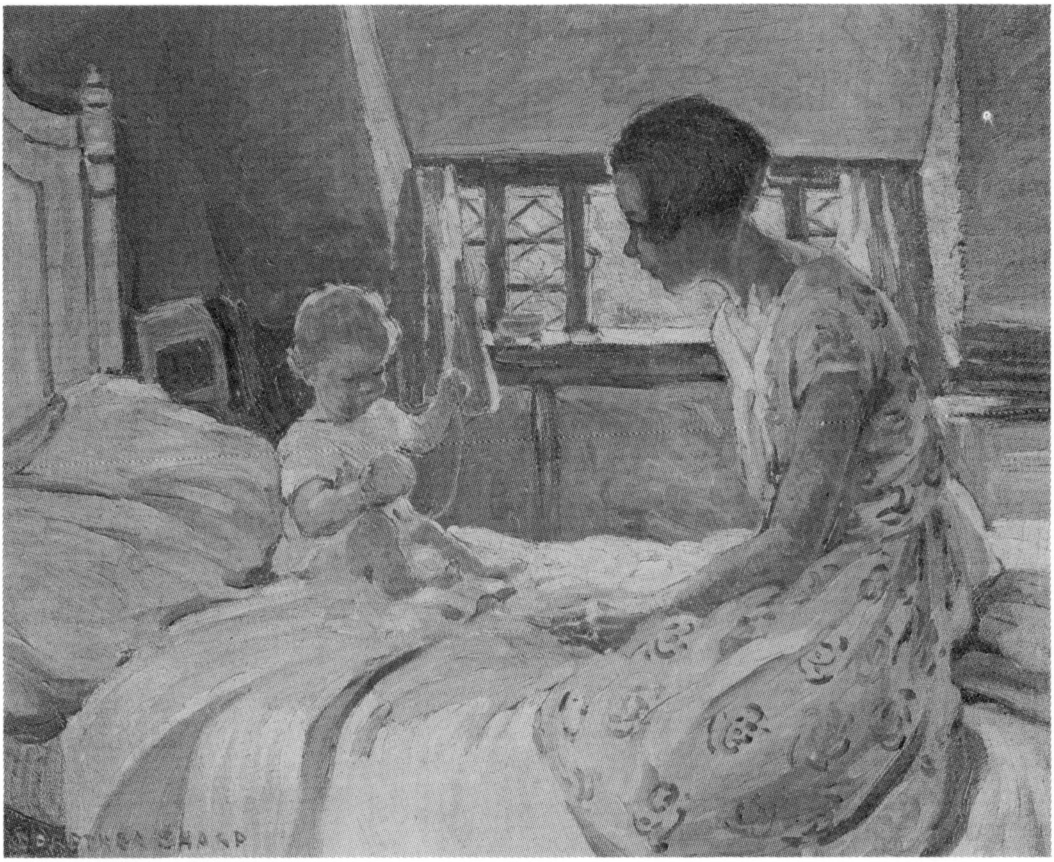

DOROTHEA SHARP – The Ball Of Wool – signed – oil on canvas – 25 x 30in. *(Christie's)* **$27,632 £17,600**

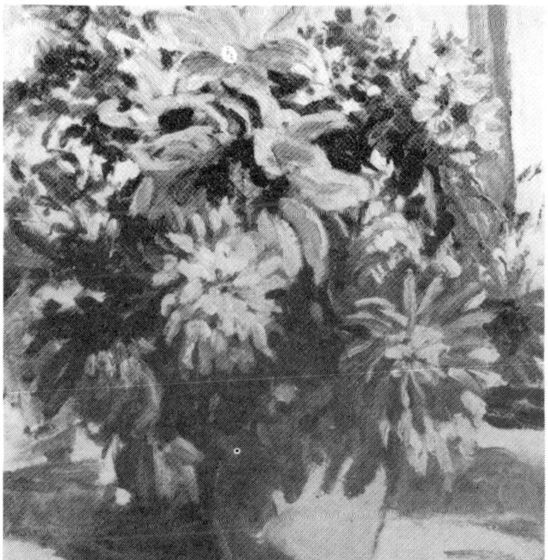

DOROTHEA SHARP – Dahlias And Mixed Summer Flowers In A Vase – signed – oil on board – 46 x 38cm.
(Phillips) **$3,672 £2,400**

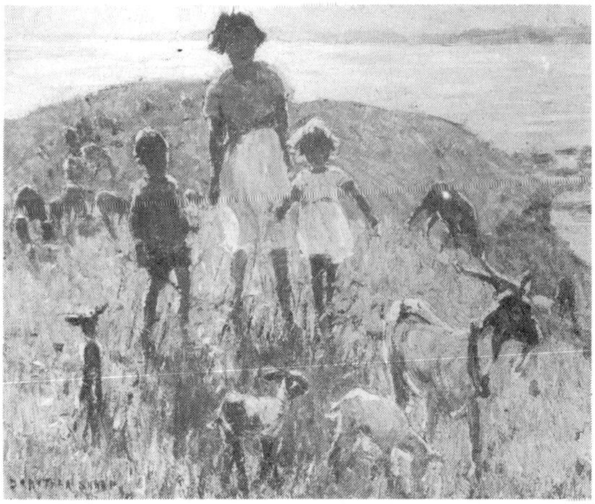

DOROTHEA SHARP – The Young Goatherds – signed – oil on canvas – 25¼ x 30¼in.
(Christie's) **$24,178 £15,400**

DOROTHEA SHARP – Resting On The Rocks – recto; and By The Sea – verso – oil on board – 31 x 41cm.
(Phillips) **$4,480 £2,800**

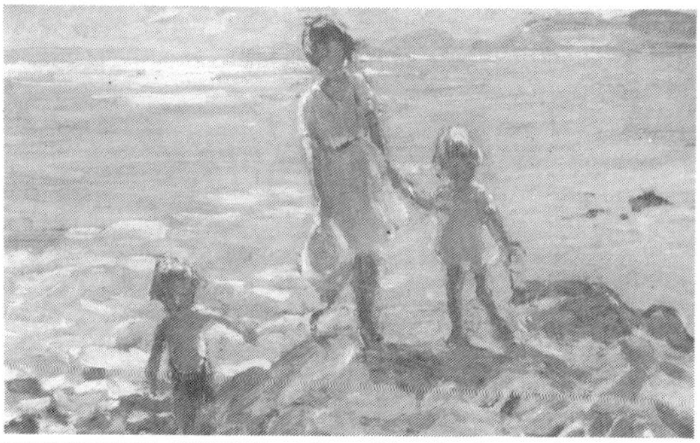

DOROTHEA SHARP – Over The Rocks – signed with initials – oil on panel – 11½ x 15½in.
(Christie's) **$8,651** **£6,050**

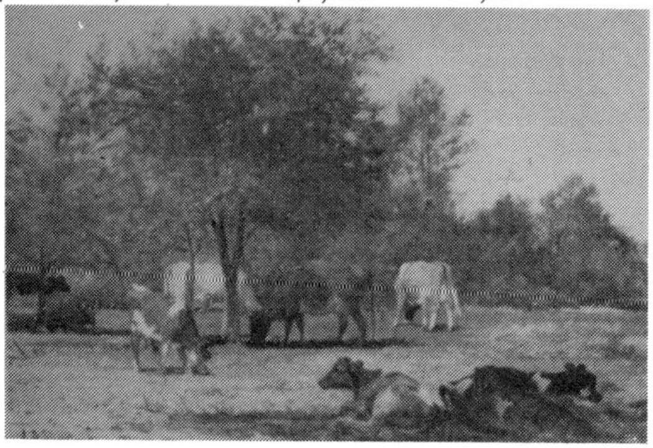

AARON DRAPER SHATTUCK, Attributed to – Cows In A Landscape – signed and dated '74 – oil on board – 12¼ x 18in.
(Robt. W. Skinner Inc.) **$300** **£184**

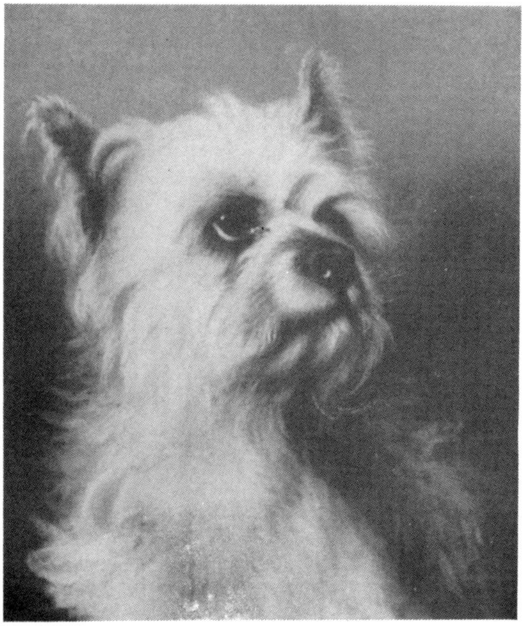

HUGH GEORGE SHAW – A Cairn – signed and dated 1871 – 12 x 10in.
(Christie's) **$853** **£605**

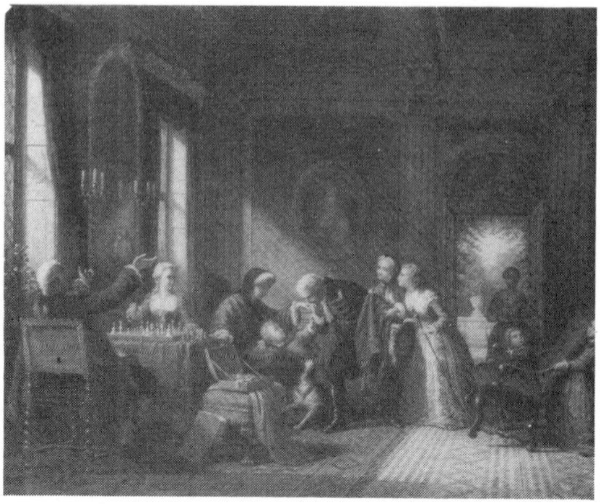

ANDREW SHEERBOOM – The Gallant's Arrival – signed and dated 1868 – 20 x 23¾in.
(Christie's) **$3,702** **£2,420**

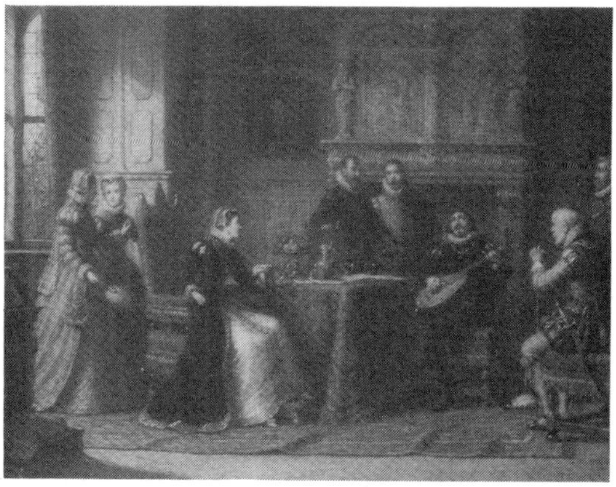

ANDREW SHEERBOOM – Queen Mary And Rizzio – signed – 17¼ x 21in.
(Christie's) **$4,375** **£2,860**

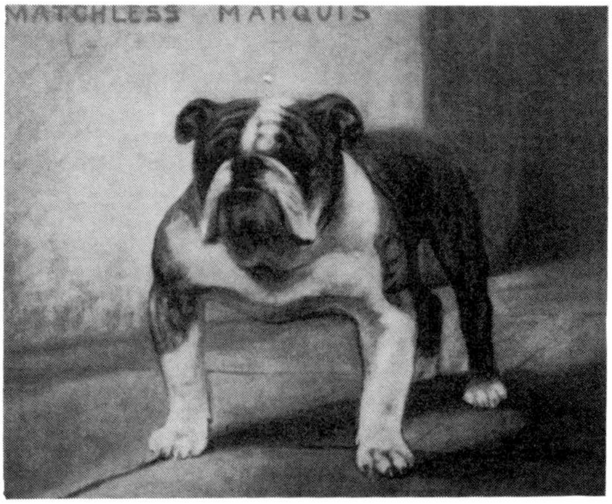

A. SHENTON – Matchless Marquis, An English Bulldog – signed – oil – 13 x 16in.
(Bonhams) **$341** **£220**

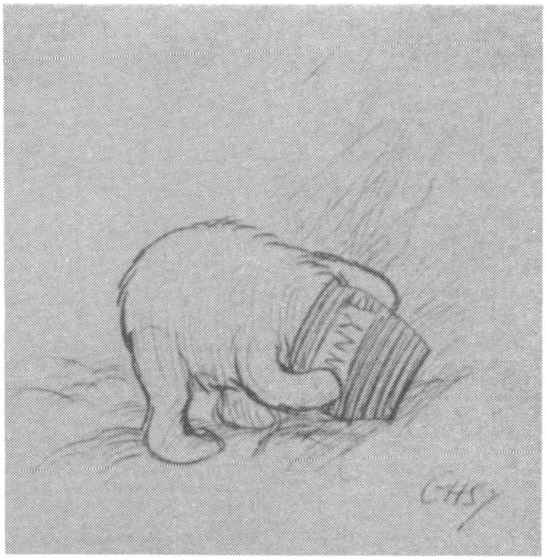

ERNEST HOWARD SHEPARD – Pooh And The Honeypot – signed with initials – pen and ink – 8 x 7.5cm.
(Phillips) **$3,015** **£1,850**

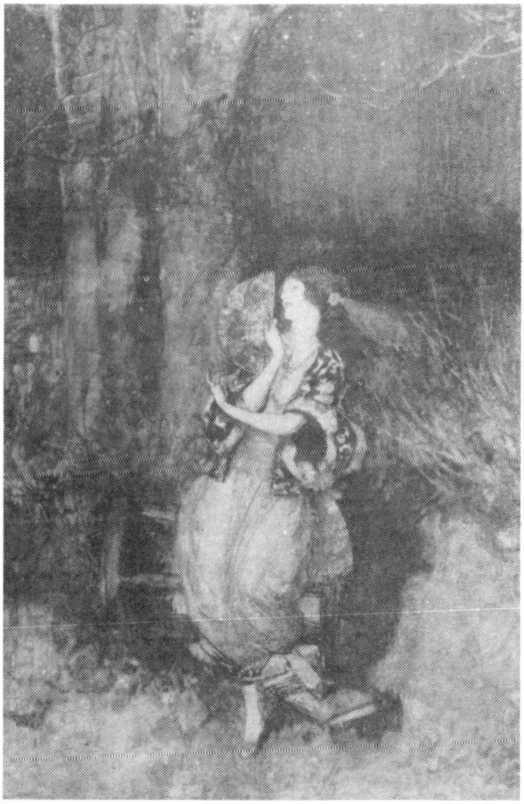

ERNEST HOWARD SHEPARD – Full Moon – signed and dated 1928 – pencil, pen and black ink, watercolour and bodycolour – 13 x 9½in.
(Christie's) **$3,240** **£2,160**

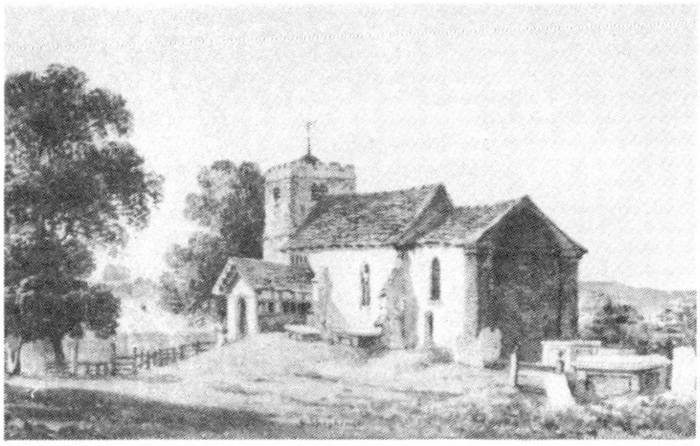

GEORGE SHEPHERD – St. Margaret's Church, Ockley, Surrey – watercolour – 3¾ x 6in.
(Christie's) **$930** **£660**

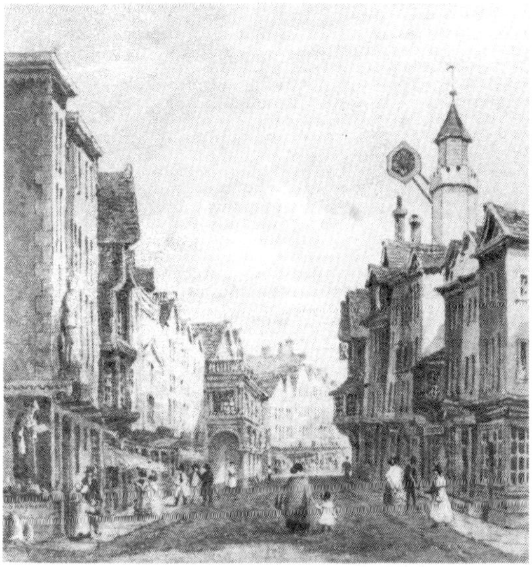

GEORGE SHEPHERD – Fore Street, Exeter – signed and dated 1826 – pen and brown ink and watercolour – 6¼ x 6in.
(Christie's) **$1,249** **£880**

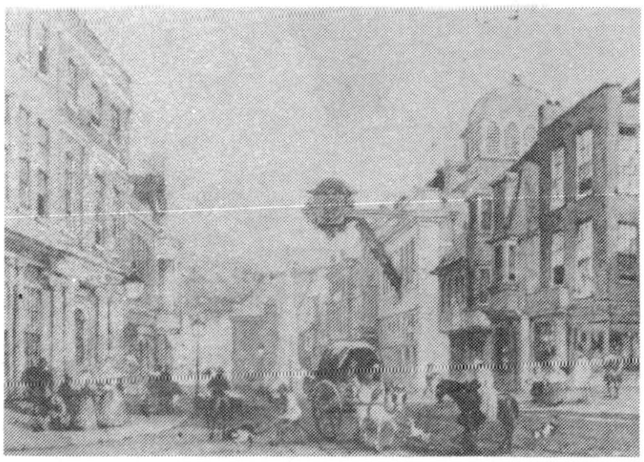

GEORGE SIDNEY SHEPHERD – The Buttercross, Winchester – signed – watercolour and bodycolour over pencil heightened with gum arabic – 17 x 24cm.
(Phillips) **$4,147** **£2,900**

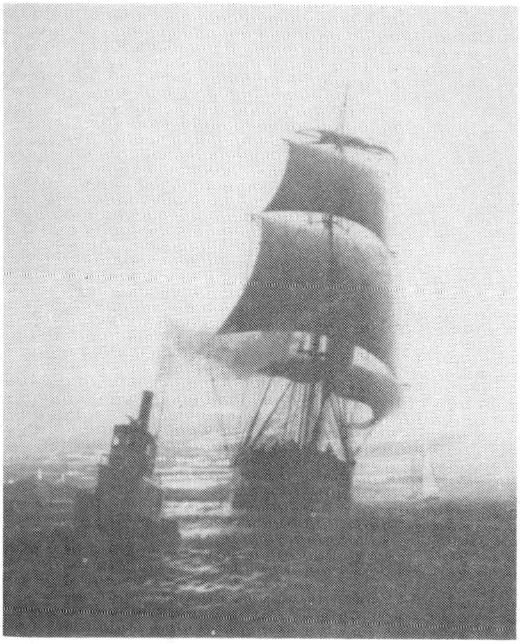

WARREN SHEPPARD – Towing A Ship Off Port – signed and dated '82 – oil on canvas – 26¼ x 21¾in.
(Christie's) **$5,280** **£3,673**

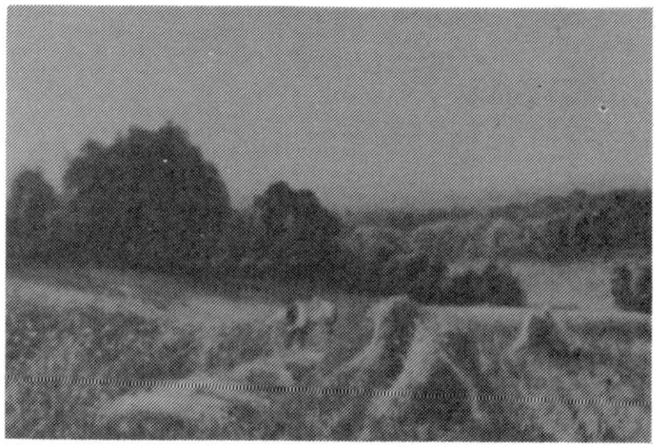

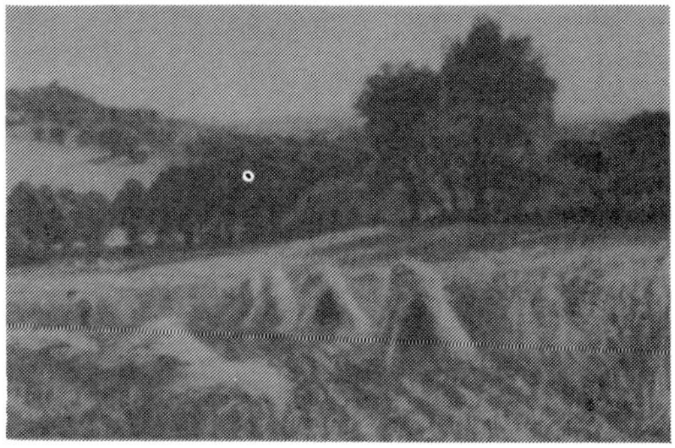

DANIEL SHERRIN – Harvesting The Wheat – signed – on canvas – 20 x 30in., also a companion.
(Phillips) **$2,576** **£1,600 Pair**

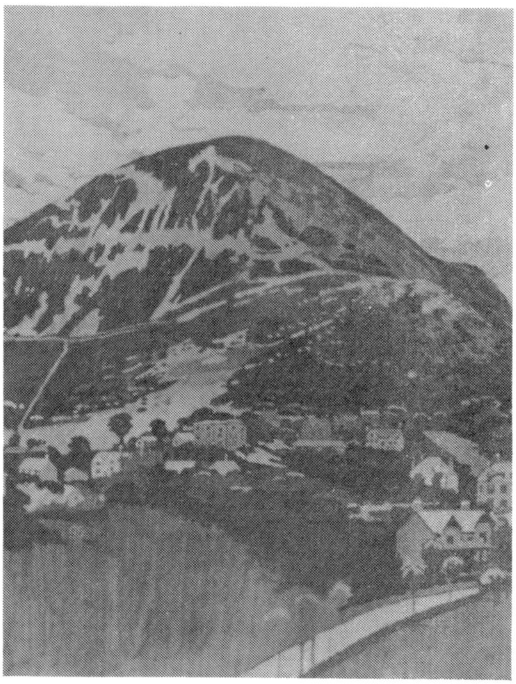

GEORGE SHERINGHAM – Moel Lys – signed on the reverse – pencil and oil on board – 40.5 x 32.5cm.
(Phillips) **$1,079** **£650**

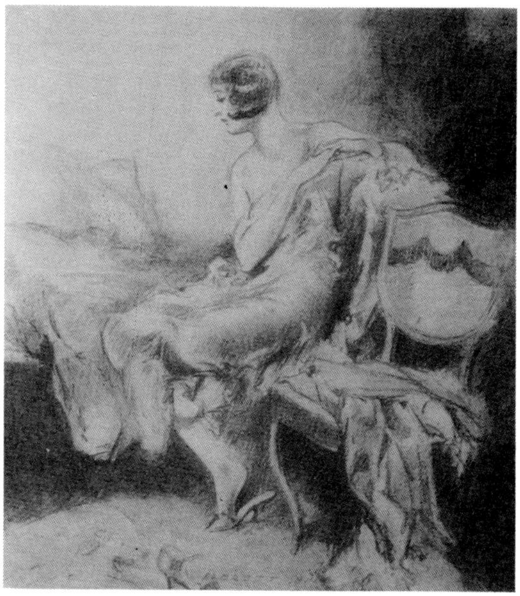

EVERETT SHINN – Lady In Her Boudoir – signed and dated 1925 – charcoal, red chalk and watercolour on board – 20¾ x 19¼in.
(Christie's) **$3,850** **£2,398**

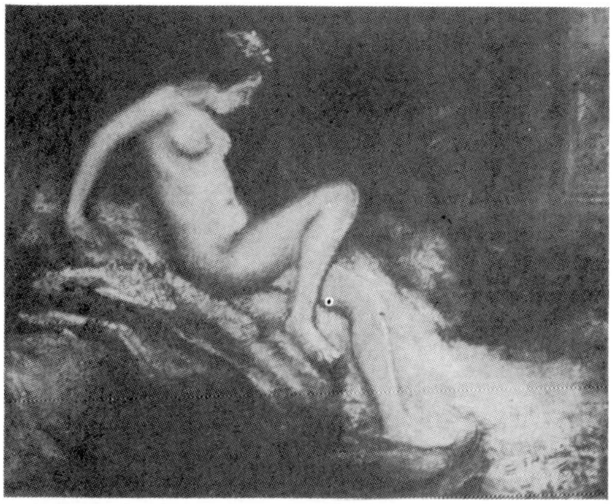

EVERETT SHINN – Nymph On The Rocks – signed and dated 1900 – pastel and pen and black ink on board – 7¾ x 10in.
(Christie's) **$1,100** **£765**

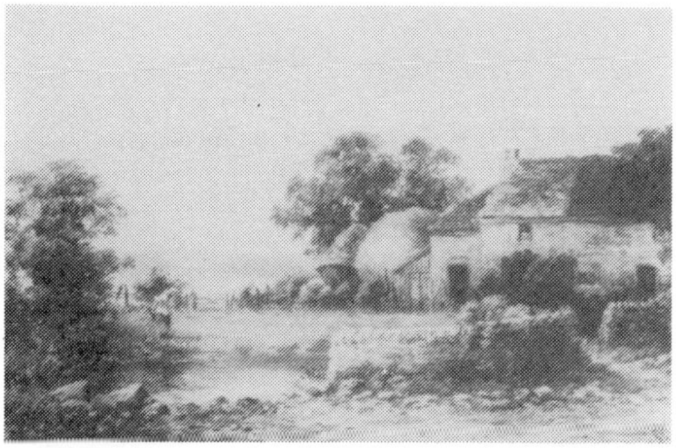

WALTER SHIRLAW – At Caythorpe, Nottinghamshire, A Summer Farm Landscape With A Girl And Chickens – signed with monogram and dated '77 – oil on canvas – 6 x 9in.
(Geering & Colyer) **$862** **£560**

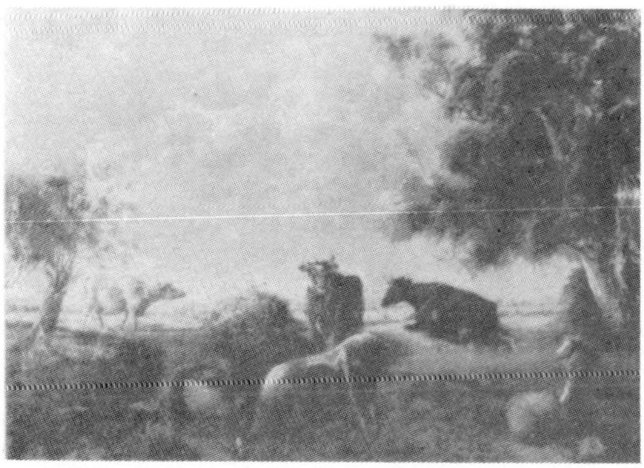

D. SHOUSMITH? – Cattle In An Extensive Landscape – indistinctly signed – oil on canvas – 27½ x 35½in.
(Christie's) **$459** **£300**

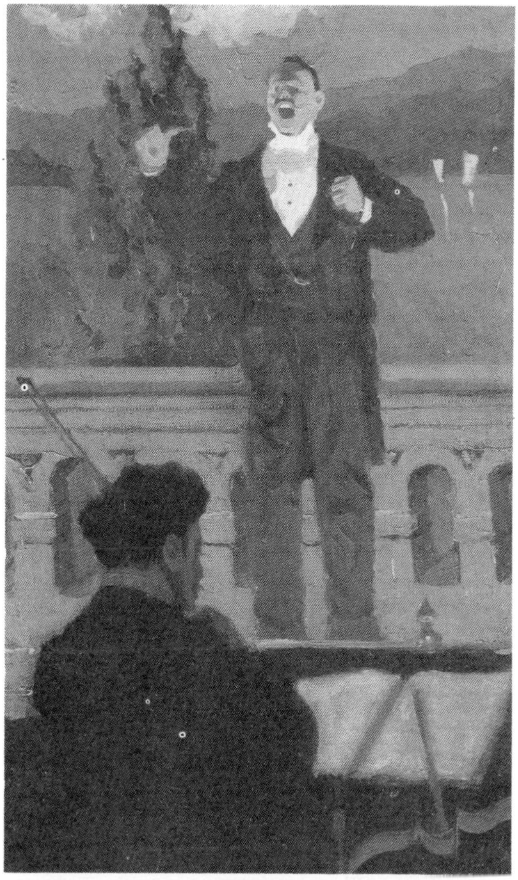

WALTER RICHARD SICKERT – The Lion Comique – signed – oil on canvas – 19¾ x 11¾in.
(Christie's) **$102,245** **£71,500**

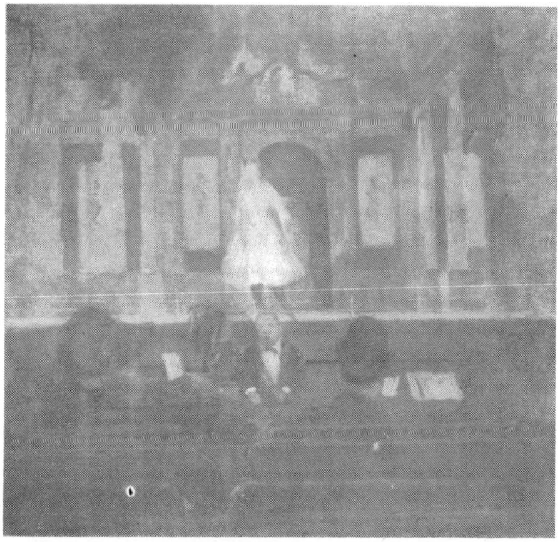

WALTER RICHARD SICKERT – Queenie Lawrence On The Stage At Gatti's – signed and inscribed – oil on canvas – 24 x 24in.
(Christie's) **$60,192** **£41,800**

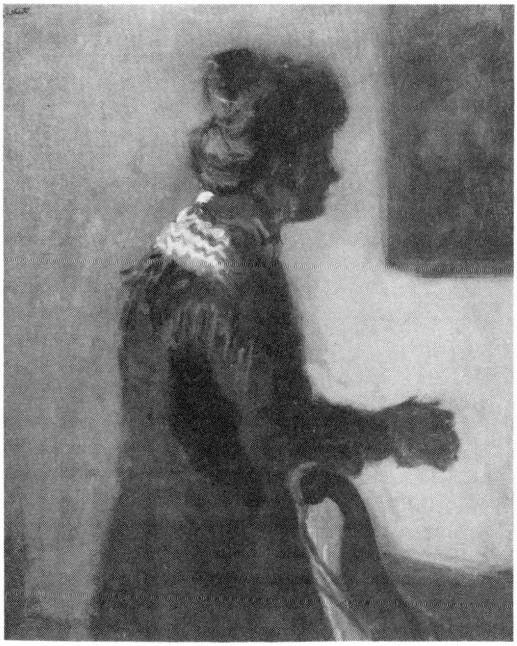

WALTER RICHÁRD SICKERT – Carolina dell 'Acqua In A Red Dress – signed – oil on canvas – 18¼ x 15in.
(Christie's) **$31,680 £22,000**

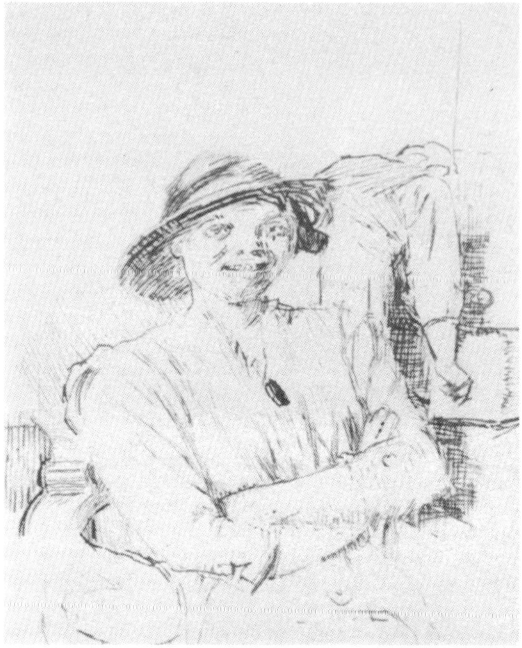

WALTER RICHARD SICKERT – Chicken – signed and inscribed – pen, brown ink and pencil – 14¼ x 9¼in.
(Christie's) **$2,674 £1,870**

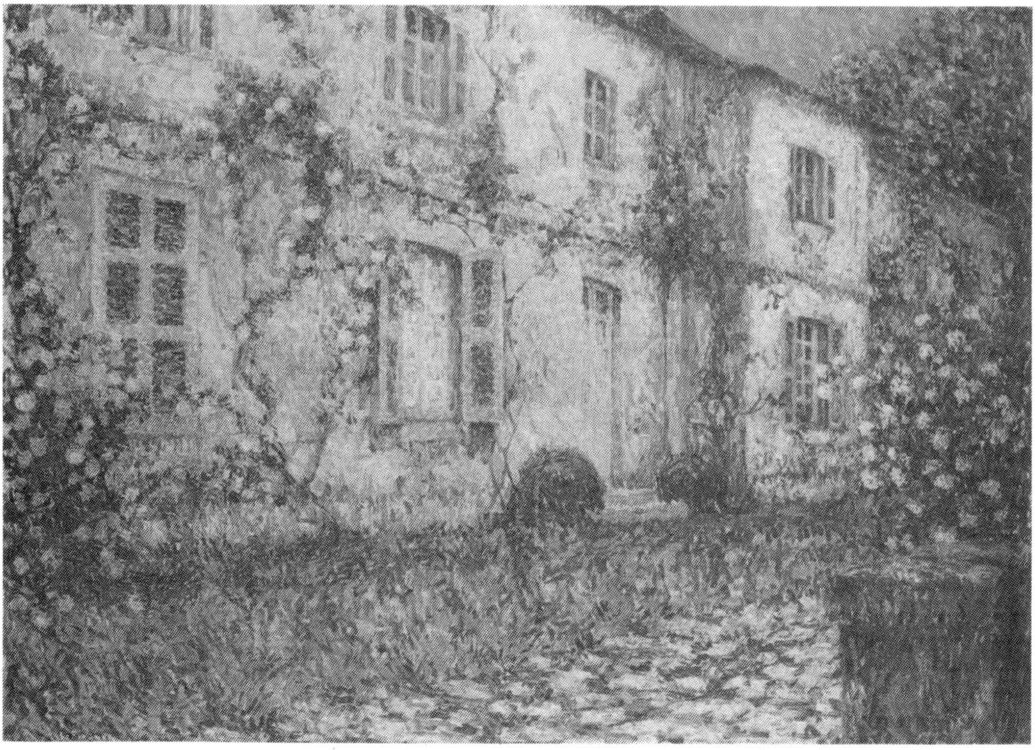

HENRI LE SIDANER – La Maison d'Ete – signed – oil on canvas – 29 x 36in. *(Christie's)*
$165,330 £99,000

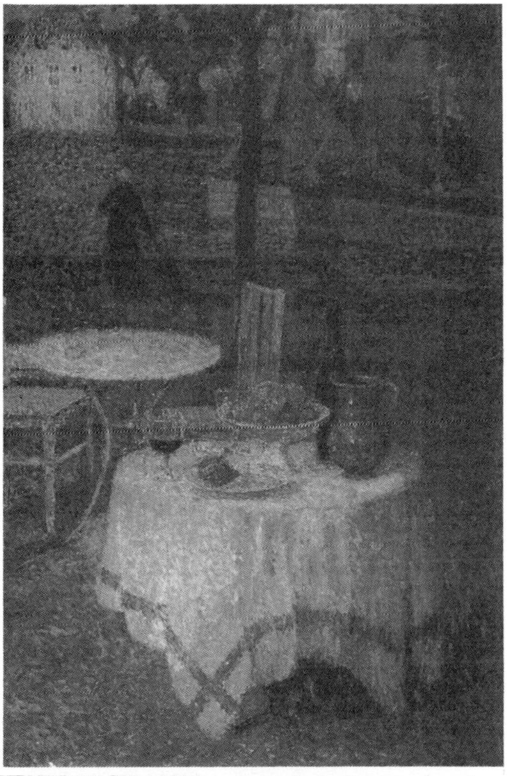

HENRI LE SIDANER – Le Cafe du Port – signed – oil on canvas – 55 x 36¾in.
(Christie's) **$95,040** **£66,000**

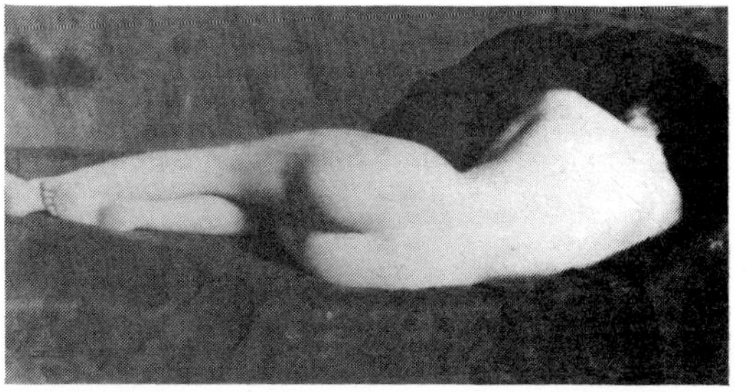

PAUL SIEFFERT – 'Nu Allonge' – signed, also signed on verso – oil on canvas – 46 x 87 cm.
(Phillips) **$2,505** **£1,500**

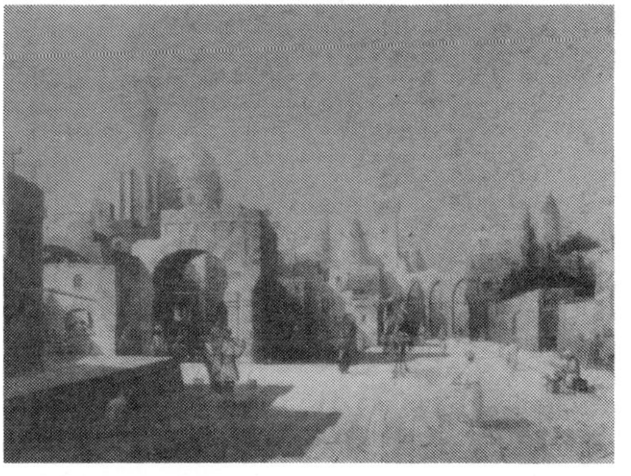

AUGUST SIEGEN – An Arab Street Scene – signed – 29 x 39½in.
(Christie's) **$6,688** **£4,400**

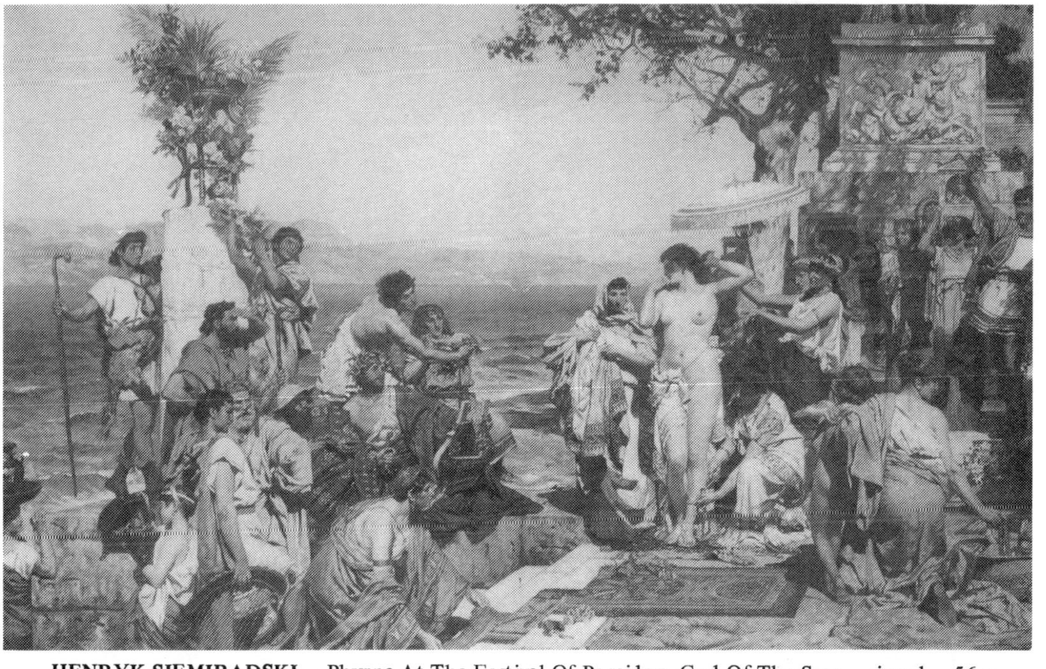

HENRYK SIEMIRADSKI – Phyrne At The Festival Of Poseidon, God Of The Seas – signed – 56 x 84½in. *(Christie's)* **$29,920** **£18,700**

SIENESE

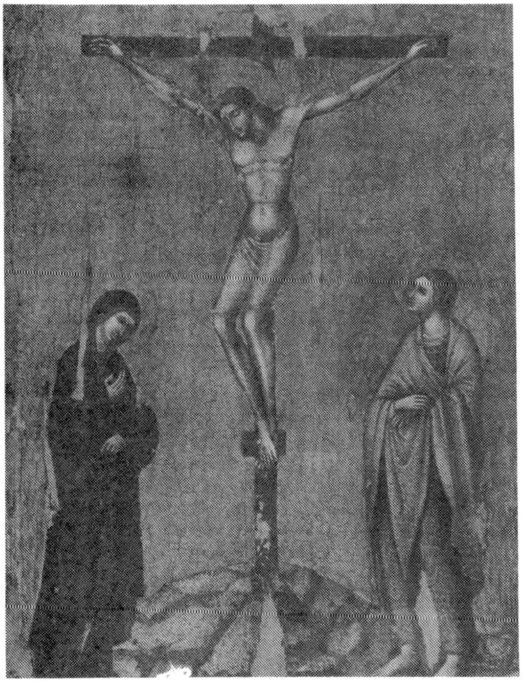

SIENESE SCHOOL, 14th century – The Crucifixion – on panel – 14½ x 10½in.
(Phillips) **$21,580 £13,000**

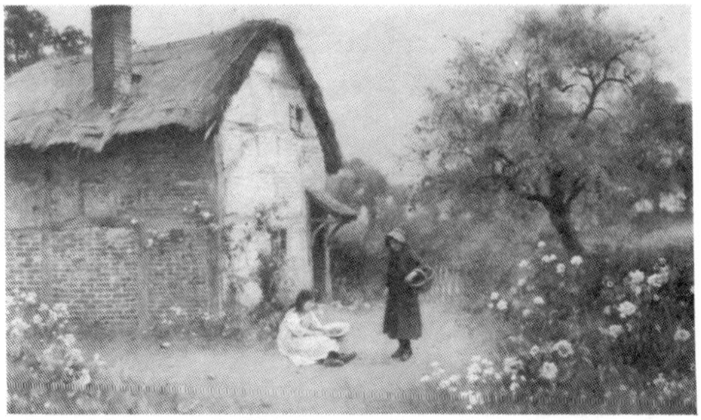

BENJAMIN D. SIGMUND – Two Girls Outside A Thatched Cottage – signed – watercolour heightened with white, on card – 10½ x 14½in.
(Christie's) **$2,268 £1,512**

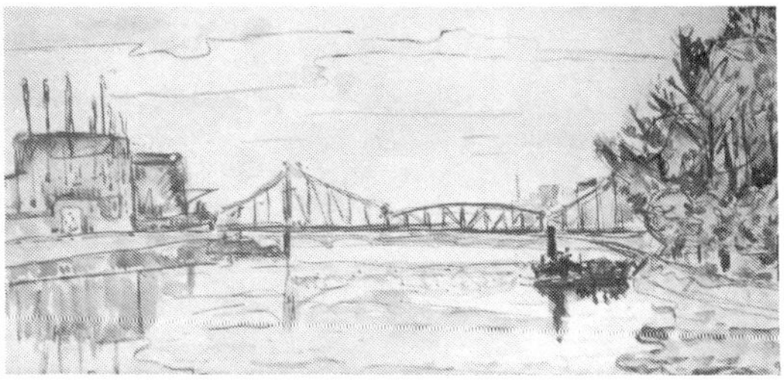

PAUL SIGNAC – Maisons a Alfort – signed and inscribed – watercolour and pencil on paper – 7 x 15in.
(Christie's) **$15,840 £9,900**

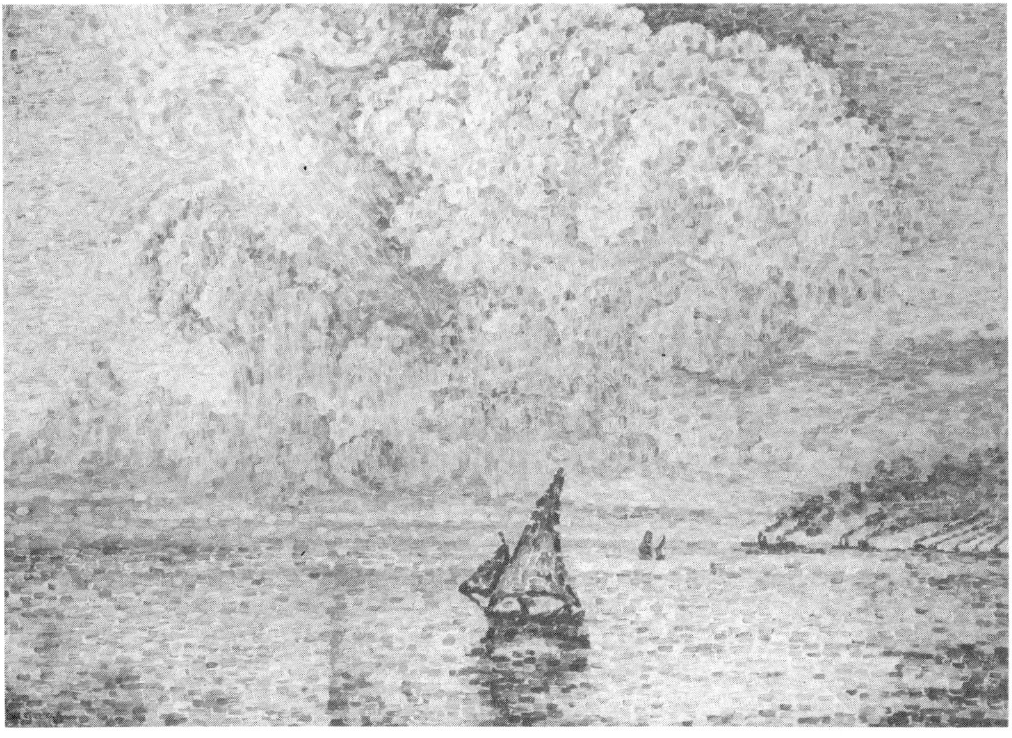

PAUL SIGNAC – Antibes, le Nuage rose – signed and dated 1916 – oil on canvas – 28¾ x 36¼in.
(Christie's) **$955,240 £572,000**

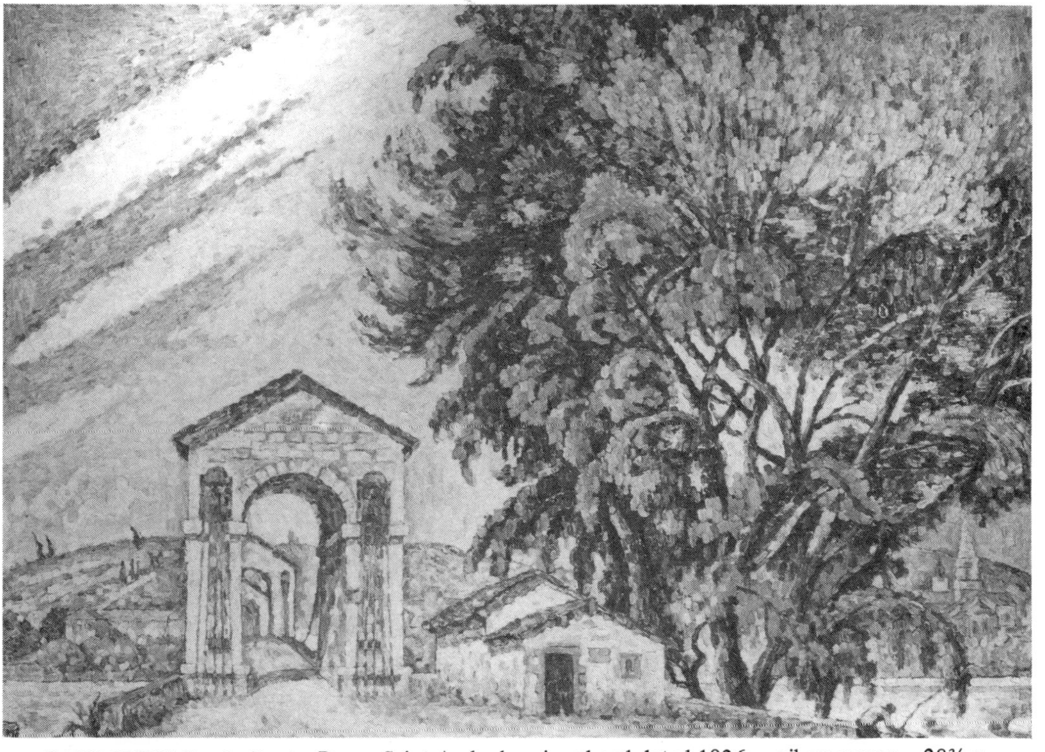

PAUL SIGNAC – Le Pont a Bourg-Saint-Andeol – signed and dated 1926 – oil on canvas – 28¾ x 36¼in. *(Christie's)* **$624,580 £374,000**

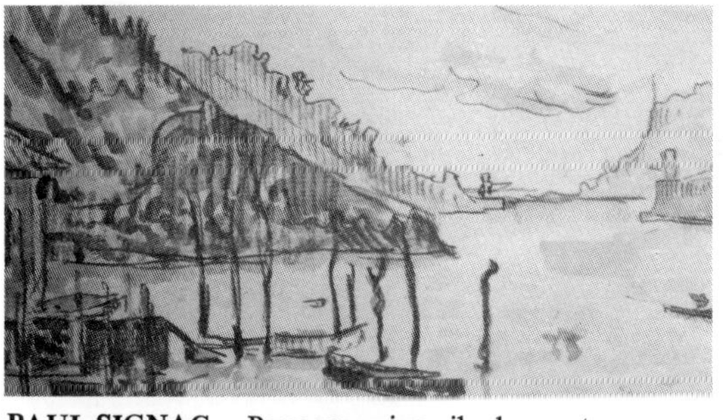

PAUL SIGNAC – Passages – inscribed – watercolour and soft pencil on paper – 7 x 9½in.
(Christie's) **$6,336 £4,400**

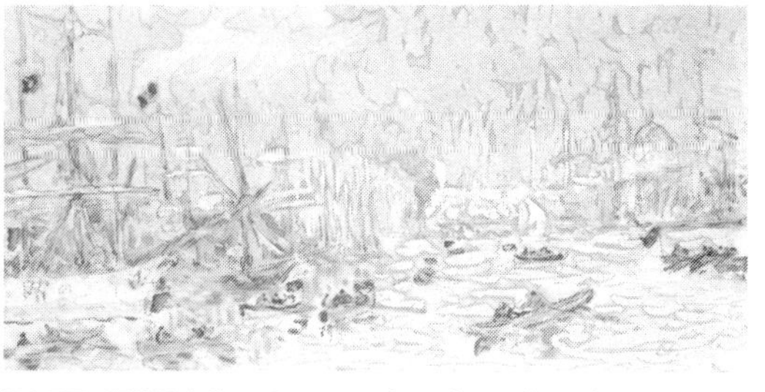

PAUL SIGNAC – Constantinople – signed, inscribed and dated '15 – watercolour and pencil on paper – 11¾ x 16¼in.
(Christie's) **$35,200 £22,000**

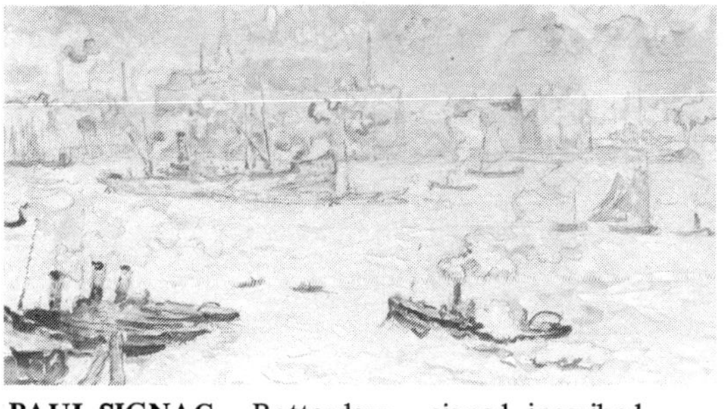

PAUL SIGNAC – Rotterdam – signed, inscribed and dated 1906 – watercolour and pencil on paper – 10 x 16in.
(Christie's) **$24,640 £15,400**

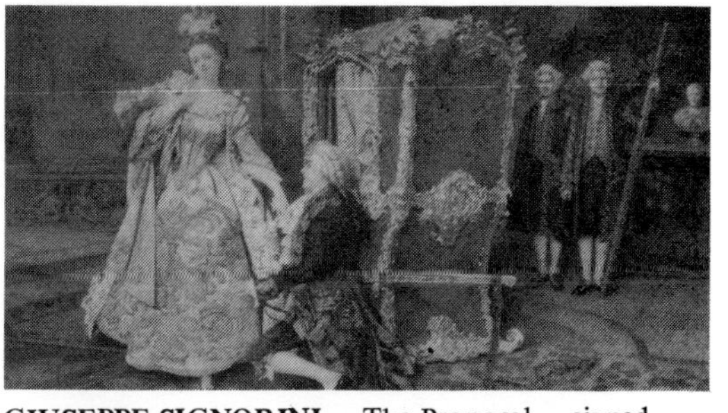

GIUSEPPE SIGNORINI – The Proposal – signed and inscribed – watercolour and bodycolour – 17¾ x 23½in.
(Christie's) **$4,928 £3,080**

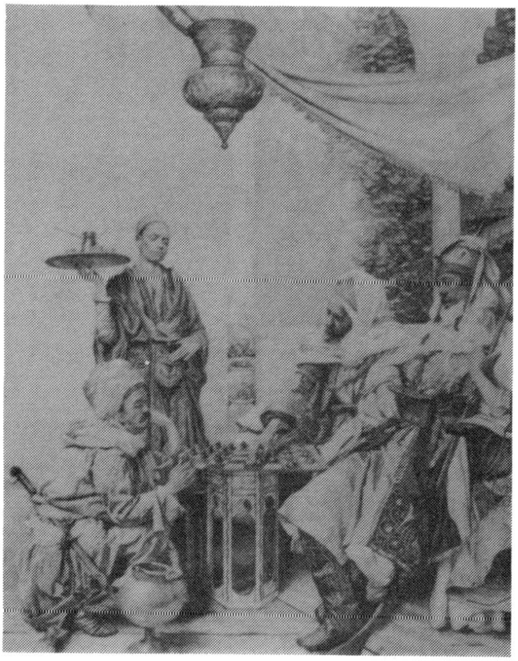

GIUSEPPE SIGNORINI – Chess Players – signed and inscribed – watercolour on paper – 33¼ x 22¼in.
(Robt. W. Skinner Inc.) **$2,900** **£1,779**

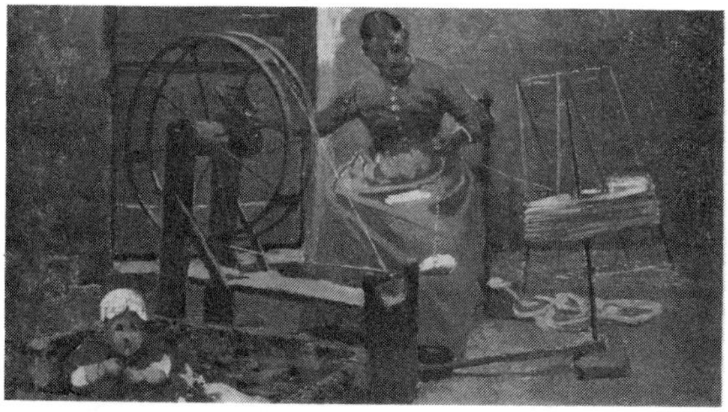

TELEMACO SIGNORINI – A Woman Spinning Wool – signed – on panel – 3¾ x 4¾in.
(Christie's) **$20,086** **£12,100**

MARIA ELENA VIEIRA DA SILVA – Untitled – signed – watercolour on paper – 8½ x 10½in.
(Christie's) **$11,968** **£7,480**

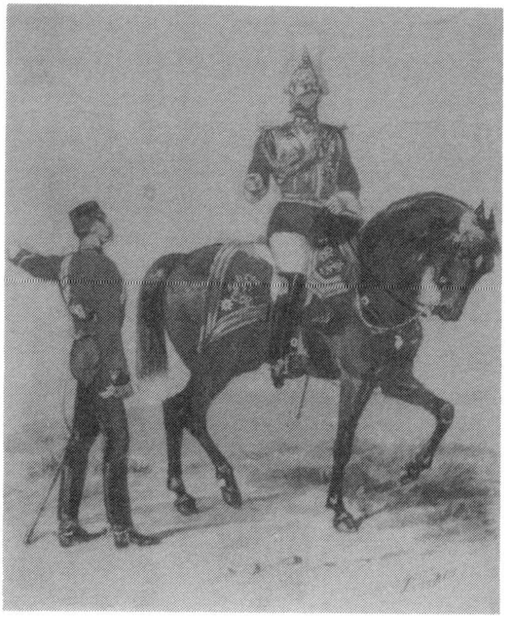

RICHARD SIMKIN – A Mounted Officer Of The 1st Life Guards And An Officer In Stable Dress; and A Mounted Officer Of The 4th Dragoon Guards – signed and dated '77 – pencil and watercolour heightened with white – 7¼ x 5¾in. and 7¼ x 5½in.
(Christie's) **$547** **£330 Two**

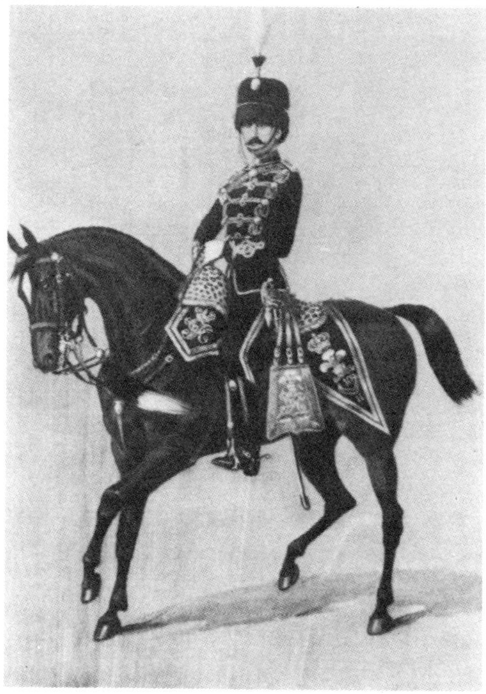

RICHARD SIMKIN – A Mounted Officer Of The 10th Hussars; and A Mounted Officer Of The 17th Lancers – signed – oil on panel – 14 x 10in.
(Phillips) **$1,912** **£1,250 Pair**

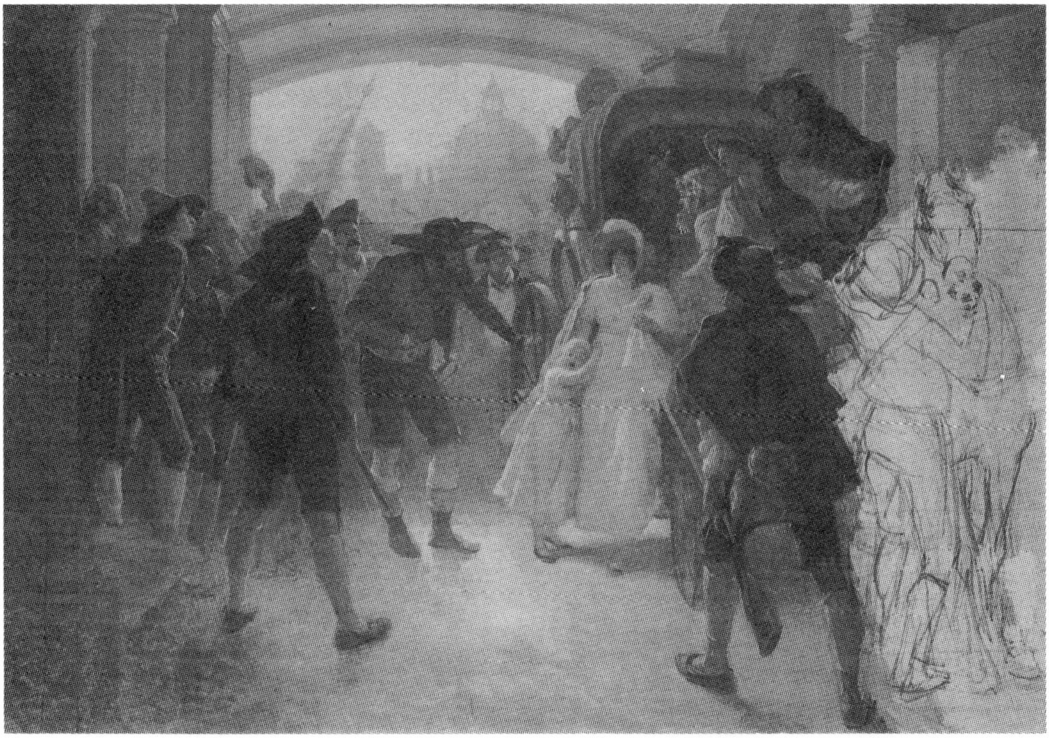

FRANZ XAVER SIMM – Safe Conduct – oil on panel – 64 x 81cm. *(Phillips)* **$5,184 £3,600**

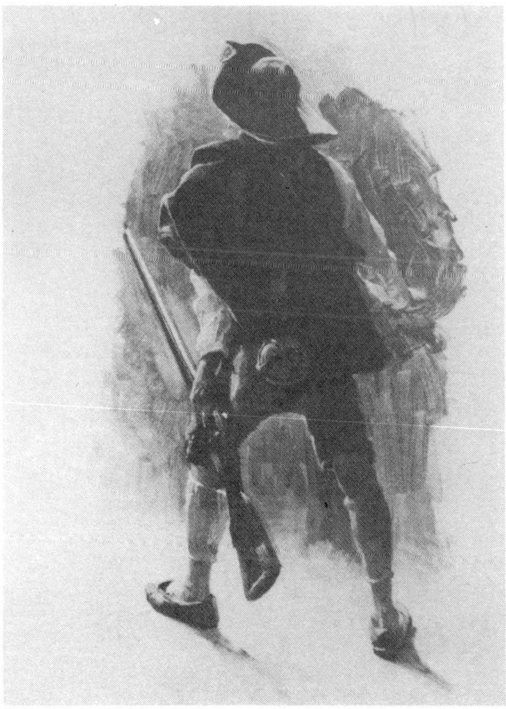

FRANZ XAVER SIMM – A Study Of A Soldier – oil on board – 43 x 22cm.
(Phillips) **$576 £400**

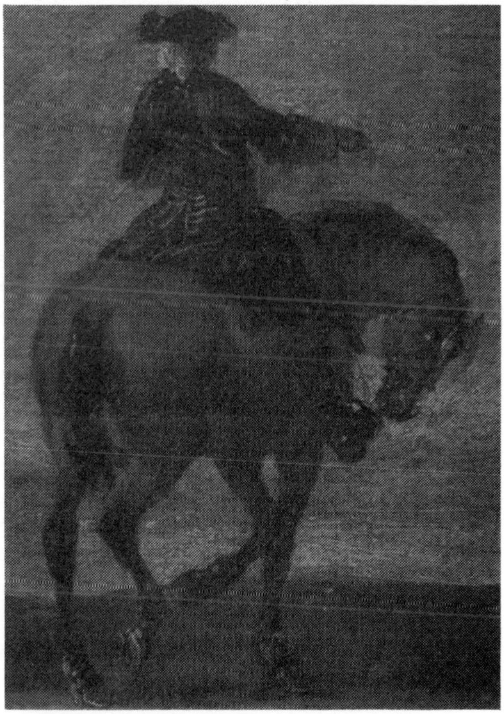

FRANCESCO SIMONINI – A Mounted Officer – on canvas – 10 x 7in.
(Phillips) **$2,490 £1,500**

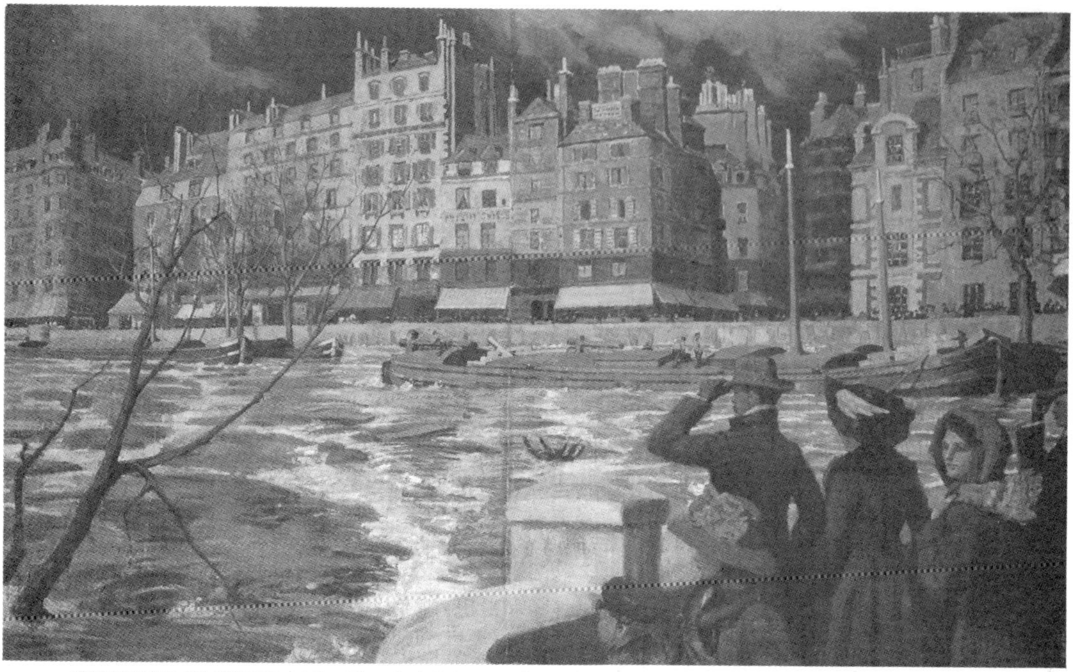

CHARLES SIMPSON – The Flooded Seine, Paris – signed, inscribed and dated 1910, and signed, inscribed and dated on the reverse – oil on canvas – 70 x 96in.
(Christie's) **$7,078 £4,950**

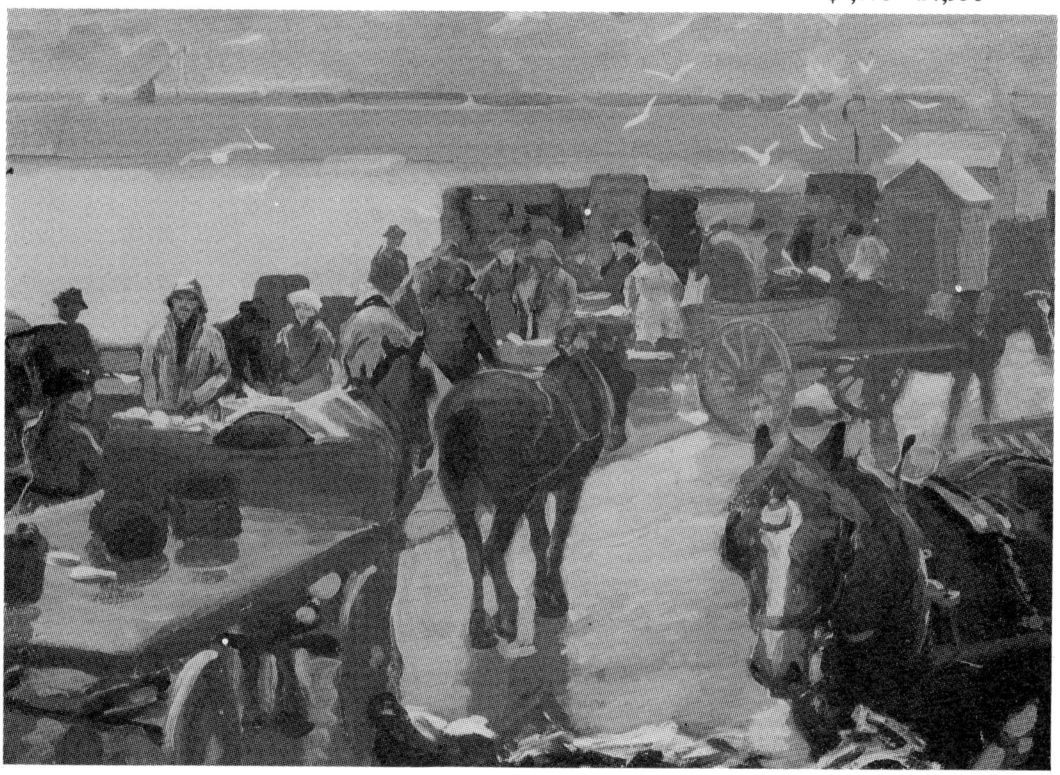

CHARLES SIMPSON – The Fish Market, Newlyn – signed – gouache – 64 x 76cm. *(Phillips)*
$5,680 £4,000

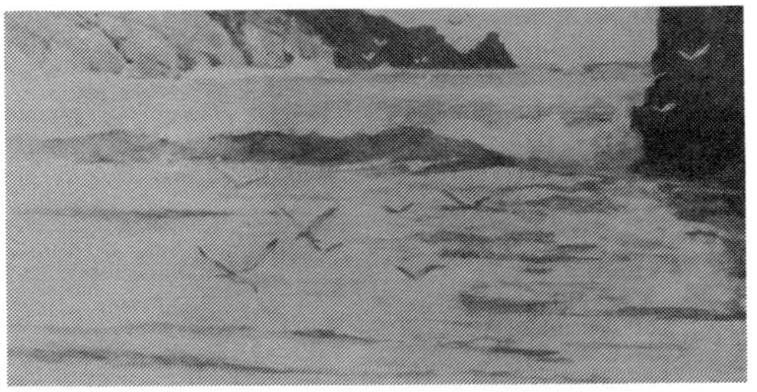

CHARLES SIMPSON – Gulls Around A Cove – signed – bodycolour and gouache – 53 x 72cm.
(Phillips) **$1,195** **£720**

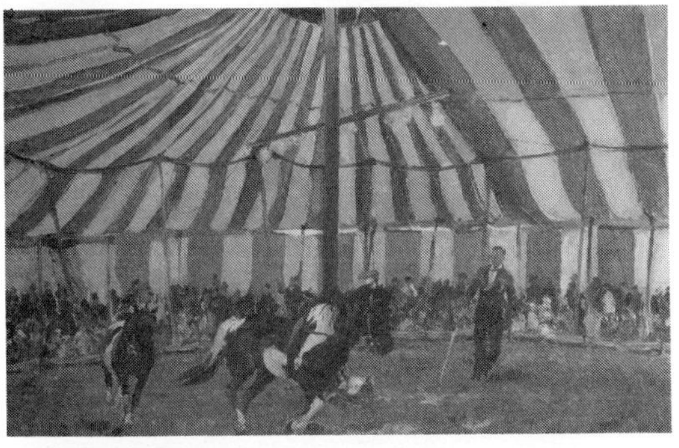

CHARLES SIMPSON – The Big Top – signed – oil on canvas – 51 x 61cm.
(Phillips) **$11,360** **£8,000**

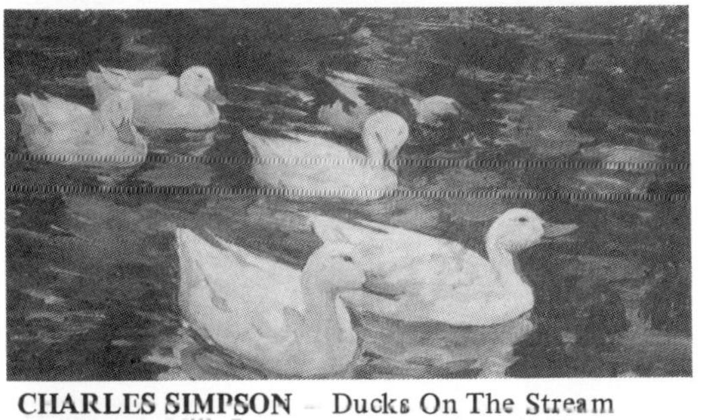

CHARLES SIMPSON – Ducks On The Stream At Clapper Mill, Lamorna – signed – oil on canvas – 21 x 31¼in.
(Christie's) **$11,011** **£7,700**

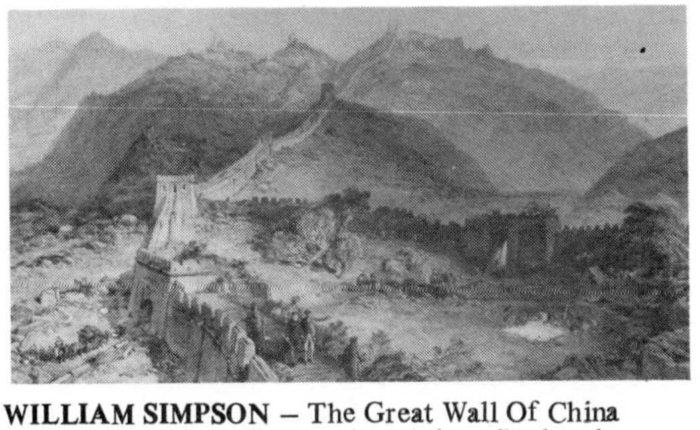

WILLIAM SIMPSON – The Great Wall Of China At The Nan-Chow Gate – signed, inscribed and dated 1886 – watercolour and bodycolour over pencil – 52 x 79cm.
(Phillips) **$27,170** **£19,000**

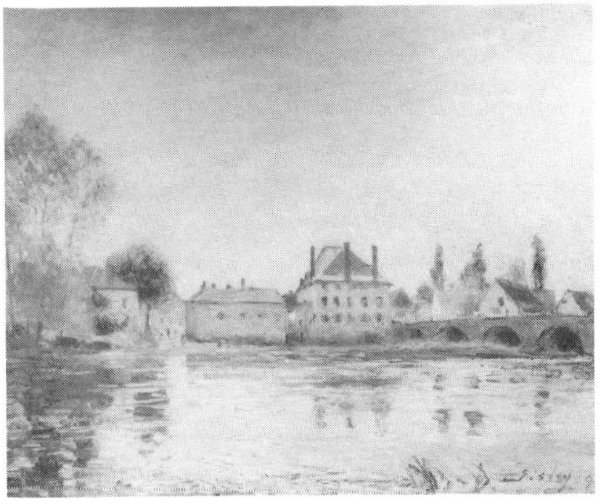

ALFRED SISLEY – Le Pont de Moret – signed and dated '90 – oil on canvas – 15 x 18in.
(Christie's) **$551,100** **£330,000**

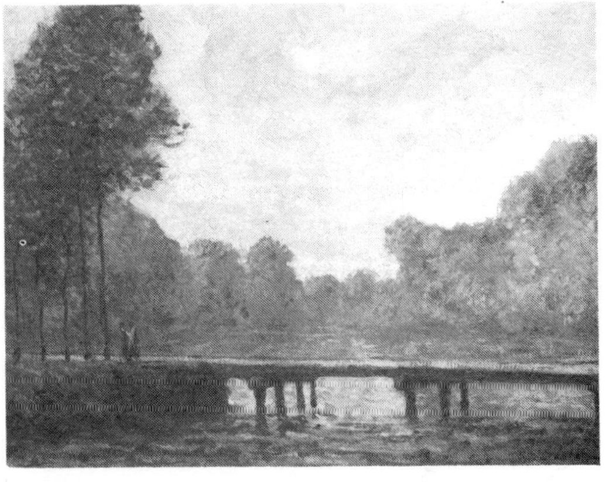

ALFRED SISLEY – Petit Pont sur l'Orvanne – signed and dated '90 – oil on canvas – 15 x 21½in.
(Christie's) **$312,290** **£187,000**

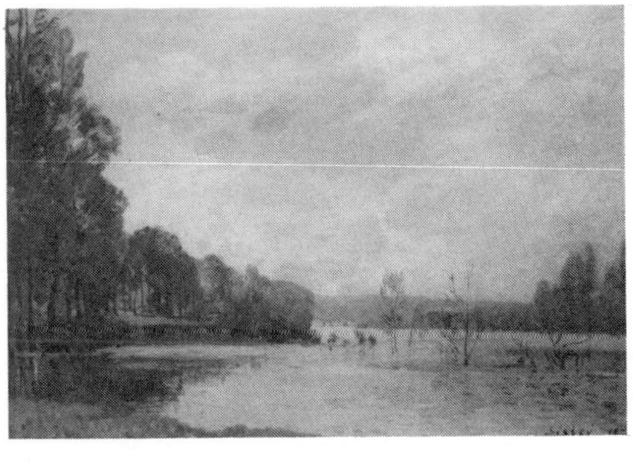

ALFRED SISLEY – L'Inondation – signed and dated 1872 – oil on canvas – 20¼ x 29in.
(Christie's) **$330,660** **£198,000**

SITZENS –Five Winged Cherubs Catching Doves – signed – oil – 23 x 41in.
(Chancellors Hollingsworths) **$725** **£500**

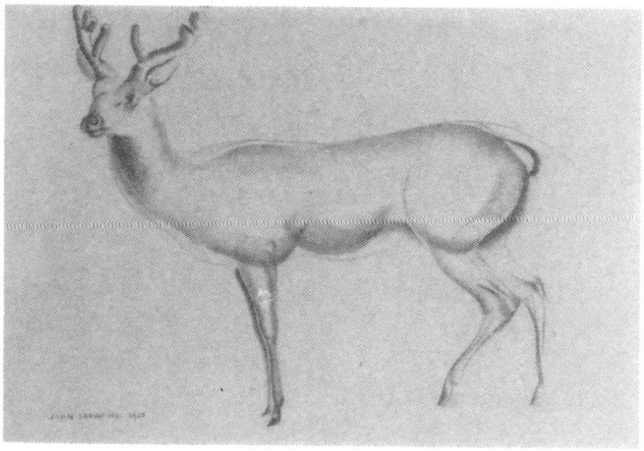

JOHN SKEAPING – A Deer; A Bison; and A Calf – two signed and dated 1928, the other signed and dated '29 – two crayon, the other black ink, brown and black crayon – 9¼ x 13½in.; 8¼ x 12½in.; and 8¾ x 12¾in.
(Christie's) **$3,775** **£2,640 Three**

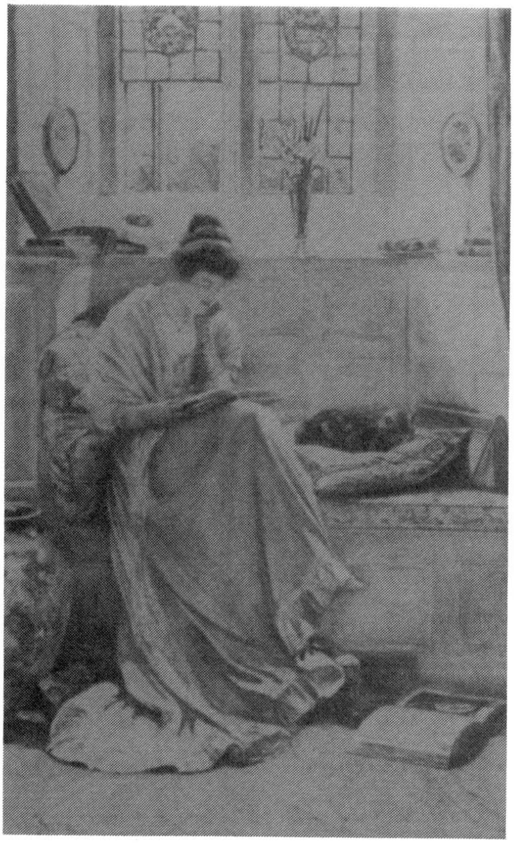

JOSEPH RATCLIFFE SKELTON – An Absorbing Story – signed – watercolour – 47 x 25cm.
(Phillips) **$978** **£600**

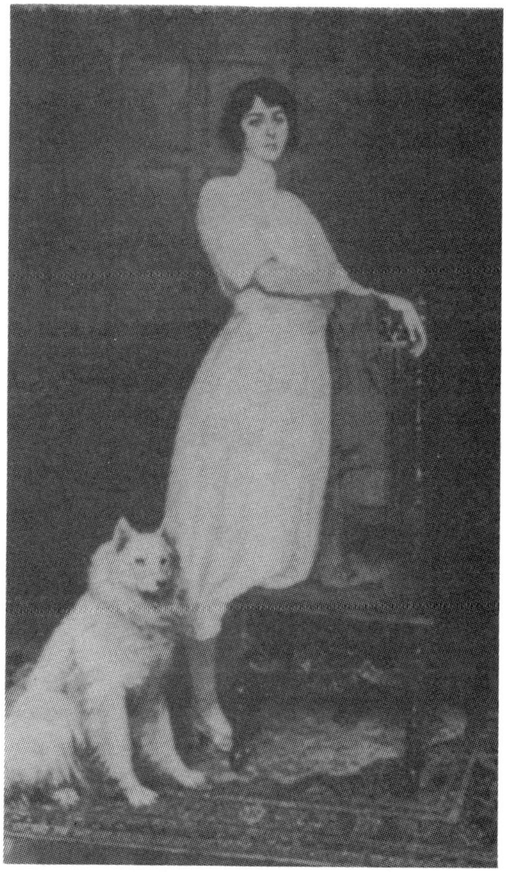

EDWARD F. SKINNER – Waiting Expectantly – signed and dated 1923 – on canvas – 30¼ x 18in.
(Phillips) **$1,690** **£1,050**

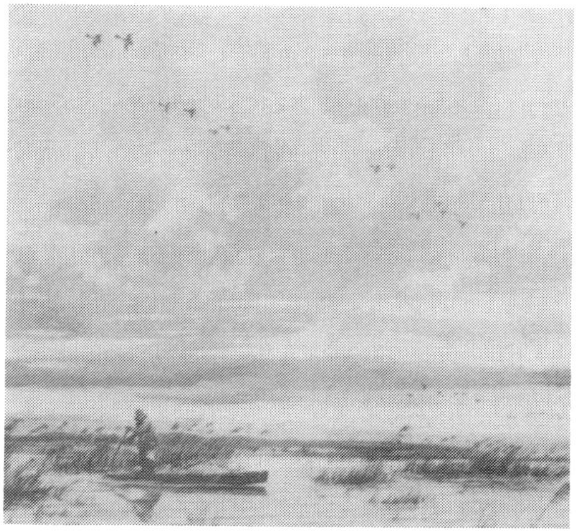

ERIC SLOANE – 'Poling Out' – signed, also inscribed and signed on the backing – oil on canvas board – 20 x 24in.
(Robt. W. Skinner Inc.) **$1,700** **£1,180**

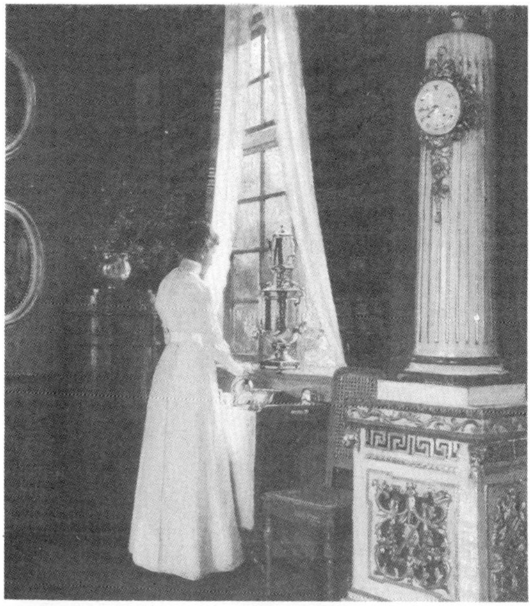

HARALD SLOTT-MOLLER – An Interior With A Lady At A Window – signed – 33½ x 27¼in.
(Christie's) **$21,384 £14,850**

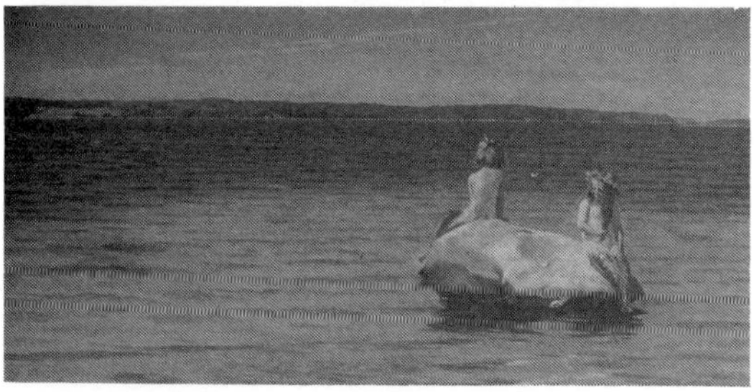

HARALD SLOTT-MOLLER – Mermaids – signed, and signed and inscribed on a label on the reverse – 16½ x 31in.
(Christie's) **$10,560 £6,600**

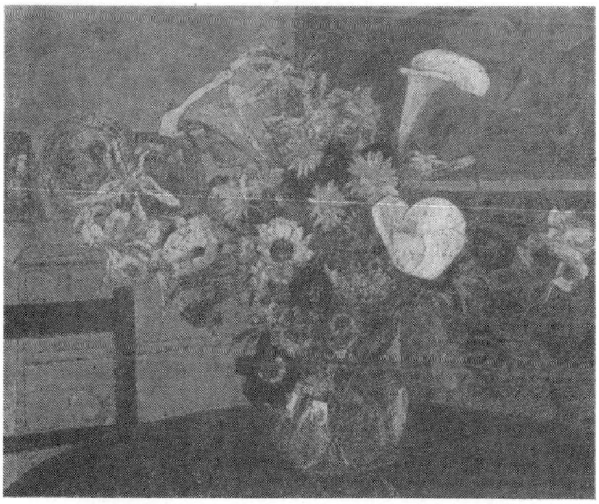

LEON DE SMET – Bouquet de Fleurs – signed and dated 1925 – oil on canvas – 28½ x 32¼in.
(Christie's) **$47,520 £33,000**

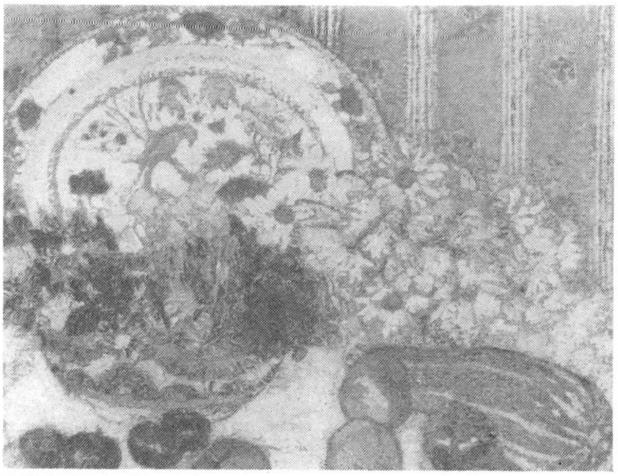

LEON DE SMET – Nature morte – signed and dated 1917 – oil on canvas – 25¼ x 30¼in.
(Christie's) **$36,740 £22,000**

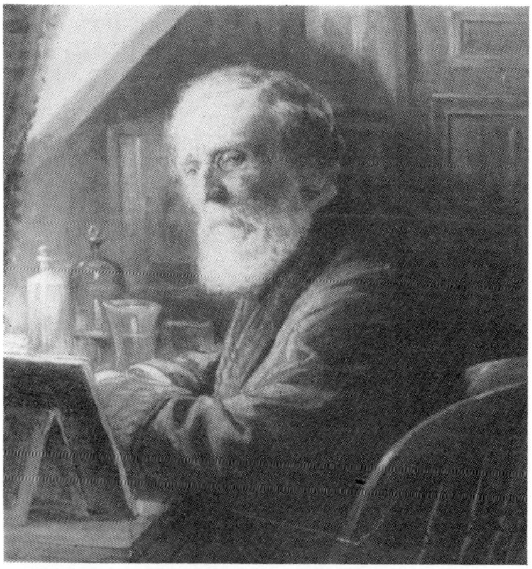

JAMES DAVID SMILLIE – Self-Portrait – signed and dated '03, also signed and inscribed on the reverse – oil en grisaille on board – 12¼ x 9¼in.
(Christie's) **$4,400 £3,093**

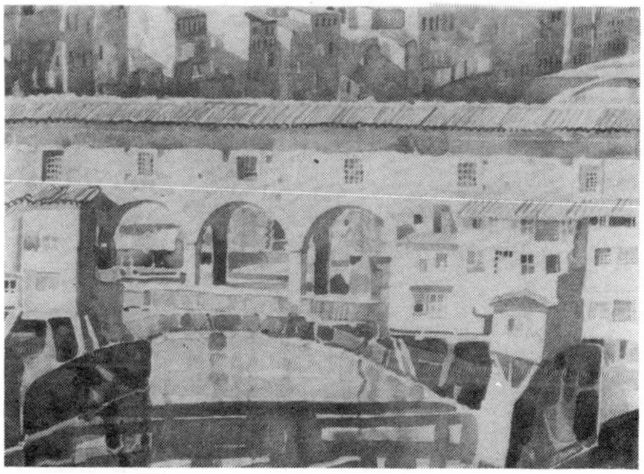

BORIS SMIRNOFF – Ponte Vecchio, Firenze – signed – watercolour and pencil on paper – 18½ x 23¾in.
(Christie's) **$880 £550**

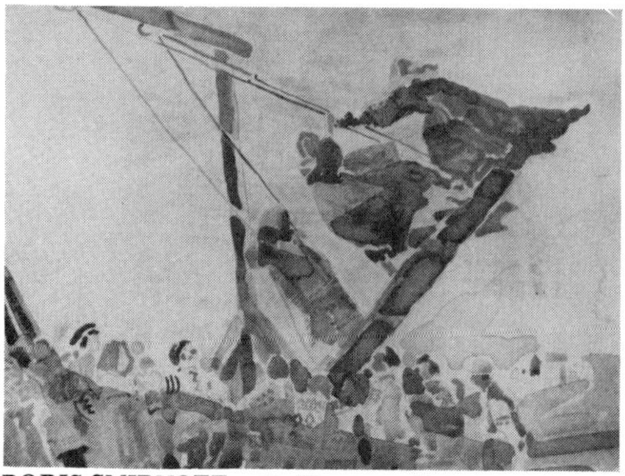

BORIS SMIRNOFF – La Kermesse Russe – signed – watercolour and pencil on paper – 18¾ x 21½in.
(Christie's) **$1,936** **£1,210**

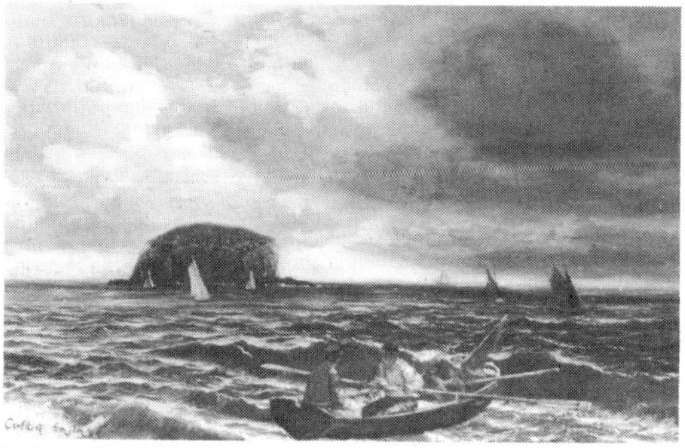

CARLTON SMITH – 'A Breezy Day Off Weston-Super-Mare' – signed and dated '85 – oil on canvas – 12 x 20in.
(Biddle & Webb) **$733** **£450**

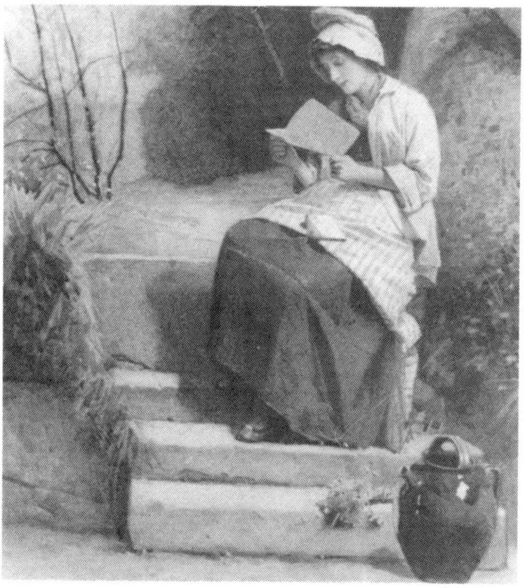

CARLTON A. SMITH – Lady Reading A Letter – watercolour – 17¼ x 13in.
(Michael G. Matthews) **$2,180** **£1,425**

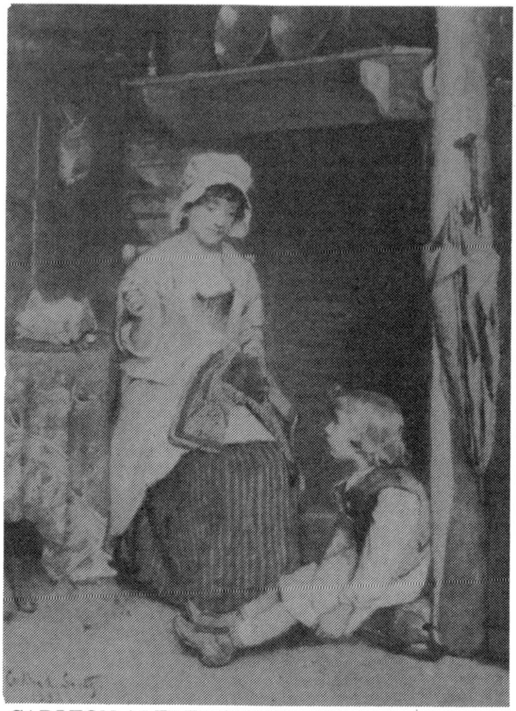

CARLTON ALFRED SMITH – 'His only pair' – signed and dated 1882 – watercolour – 36 x 25cm.
(Phillips) **$3,015** **£1,850**

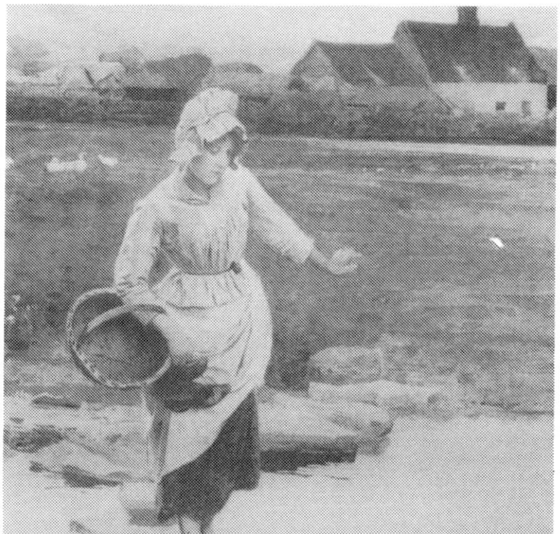

CARLTON ALFRED SMITH – The Stepping Stones – signed and dated 1902 – watercolour – 14½ x 10in.
(Christie's) **$1,944** **£1,296**

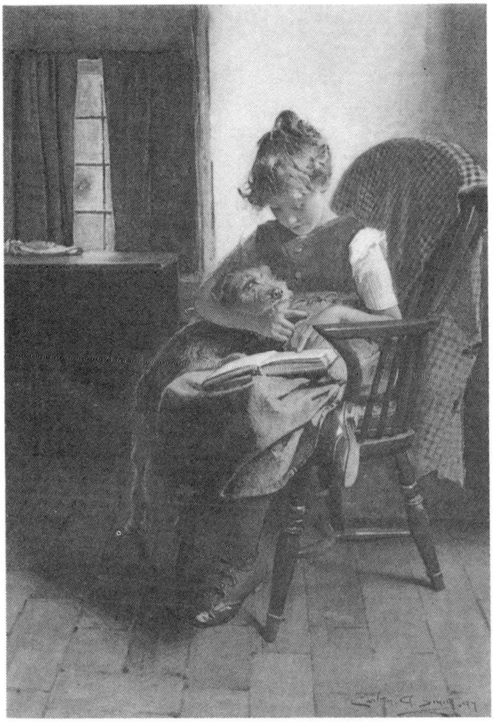

CARLTON ALFRED SMITH – The First Lesson – signed and dated '97, and inscribed on the reverse – watercolour heightened with white, on card – 21½ x 14¾in.
(Christie's) **$11,088** **£7,700**

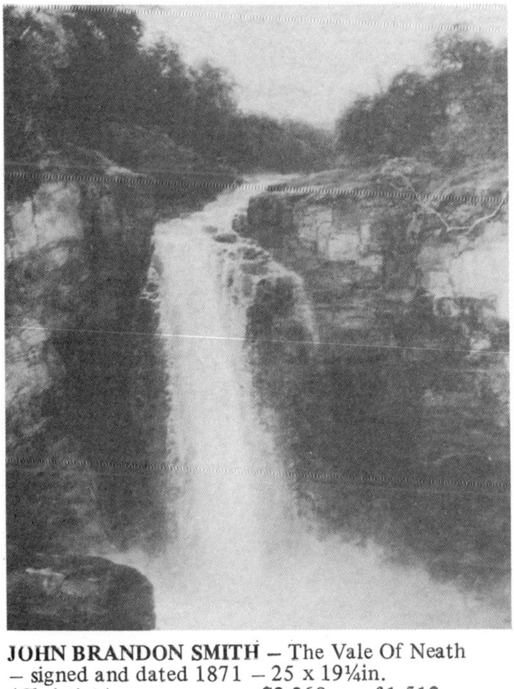

JOHN BRANDON SMITH – The Vale Of Neath – signed and dated 1871 – 25 x 19¼in.
(Christie's) **$2,268** **£1,512**

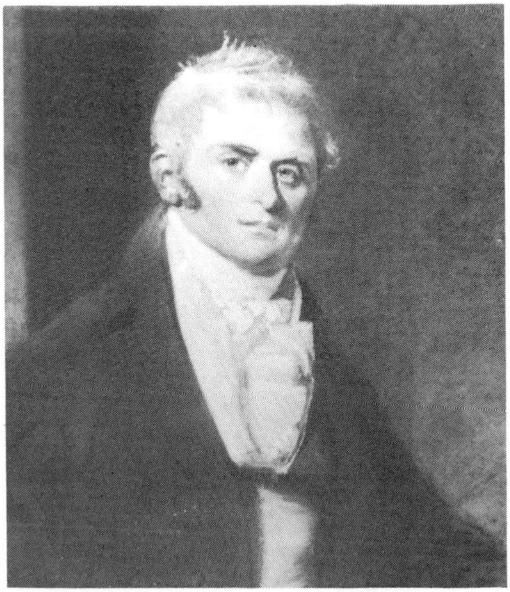

JOHN RAPHAEL SMITH – Portrait Of A Gentleman; and Portrait Of His Wife – pastel – 10 x 8¼in.
(Christie's) **$517** **£345 Pair**

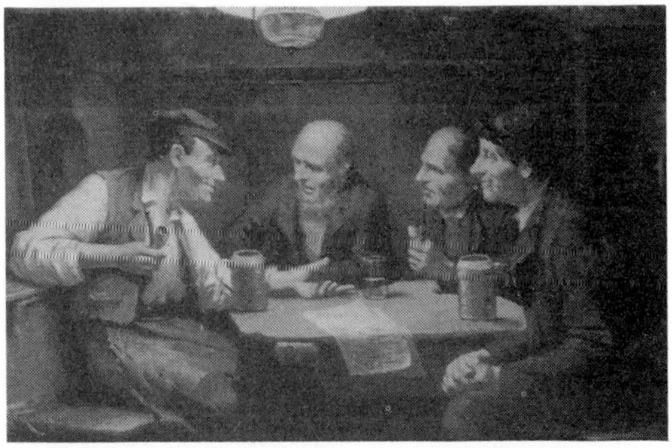

LUDVIG AUGUST SMITH – A Debatable Point – signed – on panel – 8¼ x 12½in.
(Christie's) **$2,173** **£1,430**

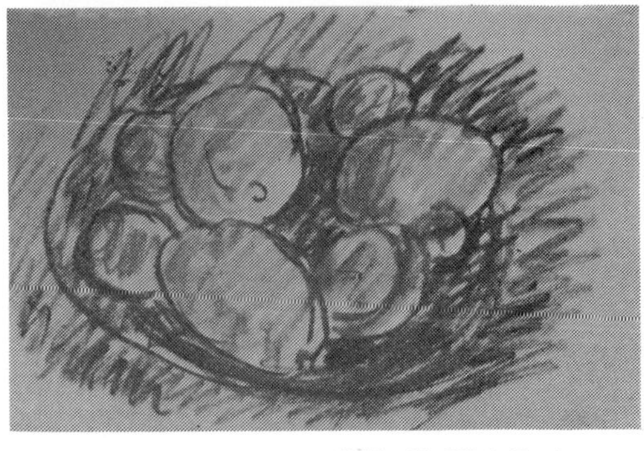

SIR MATTHEW SMITH – Still Life With Fruit – signed with initials – charcoal and pastel – 25 x 39cm.
(Phillips) **$830** **£500**

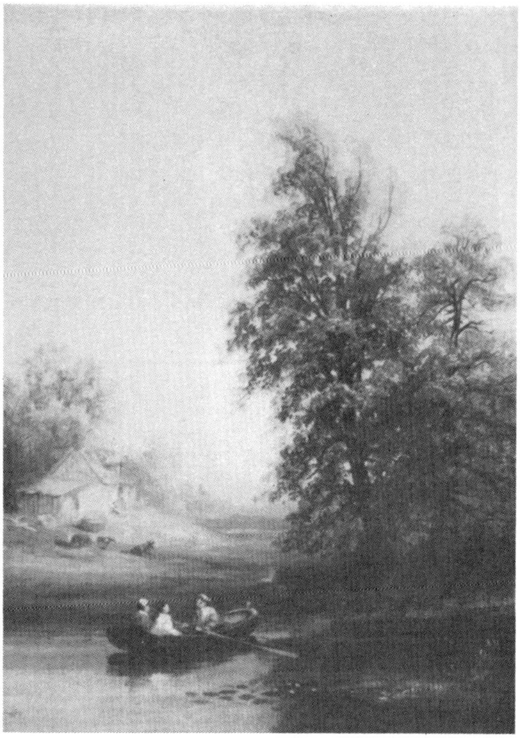

XANTHUS RUSSELL SMITH – On The Tacony – signed and dated 1885 – oil on canvas – 12 x 9in.
(Christie's) **$1,650** **£1,147**

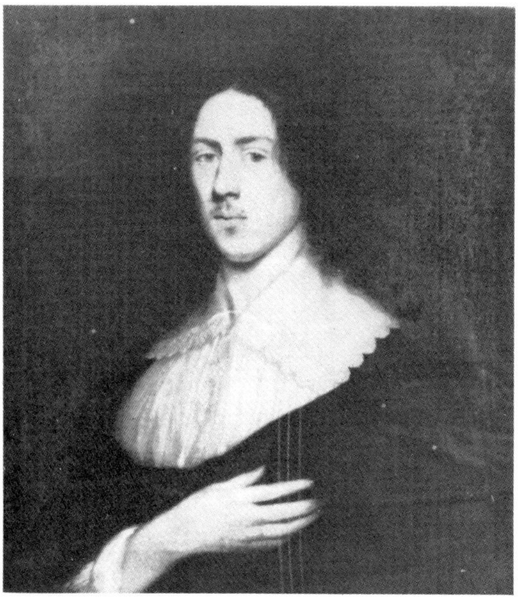

GERARD SOEST, Circle of – Portrait Of A Gentleman, Half Length, Said To Be Roger Abdy – oil on canvas – 28½ x 25½in.
(Phillips) **$1,339** **£950**

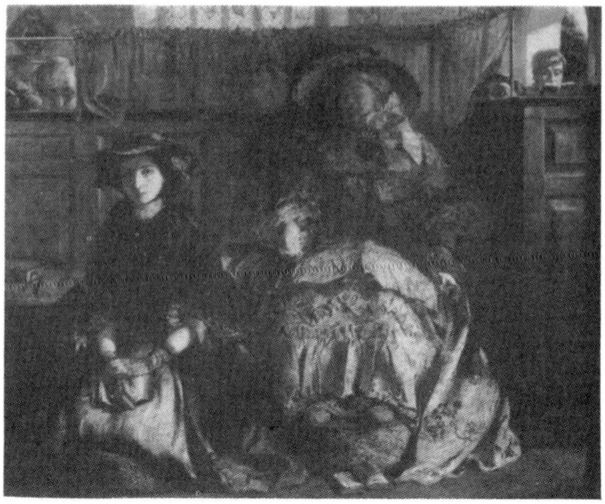

ABRAHAM SOLOMON – Mad Blaiz – signed and dated 1857 – 20 x 24in.
(Christie's) **$4,653** **£3,300**

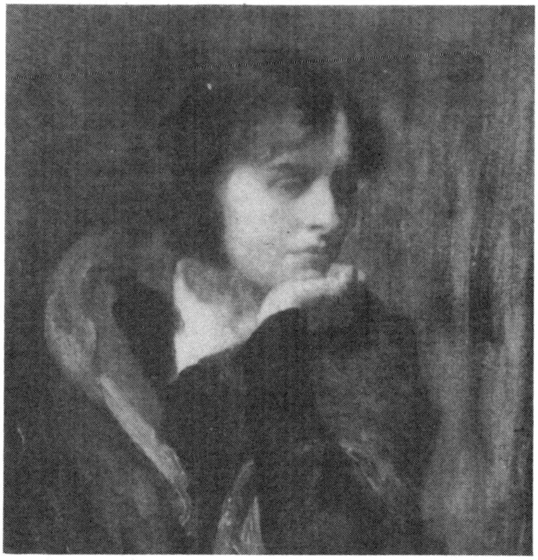

SOLOMON JOSEPH SOLOMON – Portrait Of A Young Lady, Half Length – signed with monogram – oil on canvas – 23¼ x 19¼in.
(Christie's) **$2,590** **£1,650**

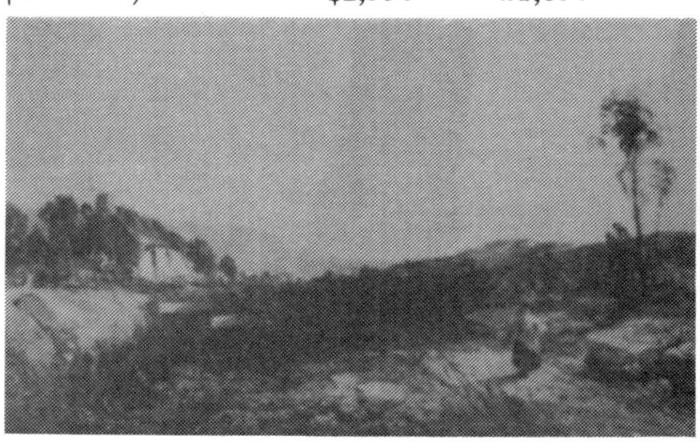

THOMAS JAMES SOPER – Figure On A Path In A Coastal Landscape – signed and dated 1849 – on canvas – 12 x 16in.
(Phillips) **$998** **£620**

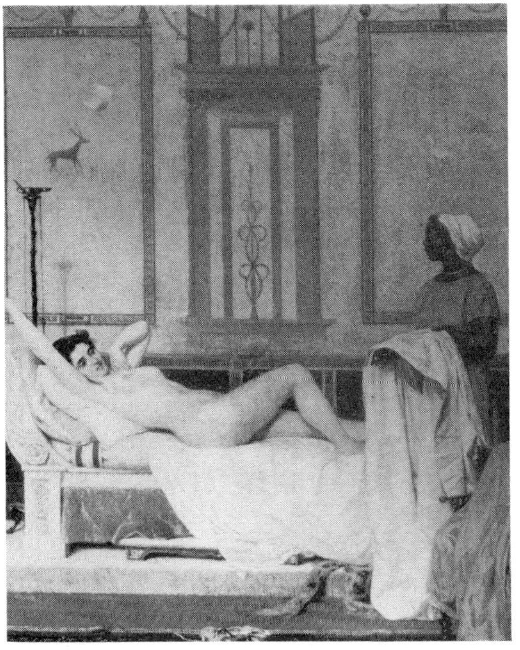

RAFFAELO SORBI – Preparing For The Bath; and Feeding The Doves – signed and dated 1868, and one inscribed on a label on the reverse – 23 x 17in.
(Christie's) **$25,080** **£16,500 Pair**

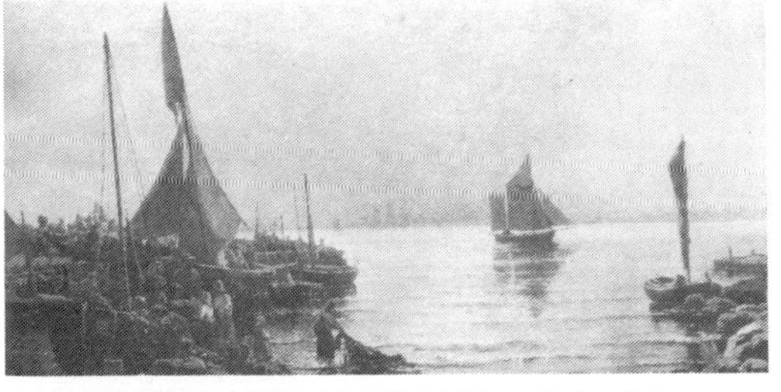

CARL FREDERICK SORENSEN – Fisherfolk Hauling In The Nets By A Jetty – signed and dated 1871 – 29½ x 42½in.
(Christie's) **$9,196** **£6,050**

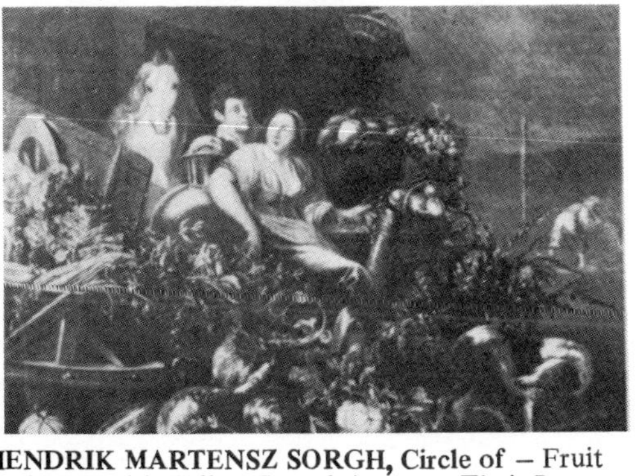

HENDRIK MARTENSZ SORGH, Circle of – Fruit And Vegetable Sellers Seated Amongst Their Produce Before A Horse And Cart – oil on canvas – 20 x 23¾in.
(Phillips) **$1,240** **£880**

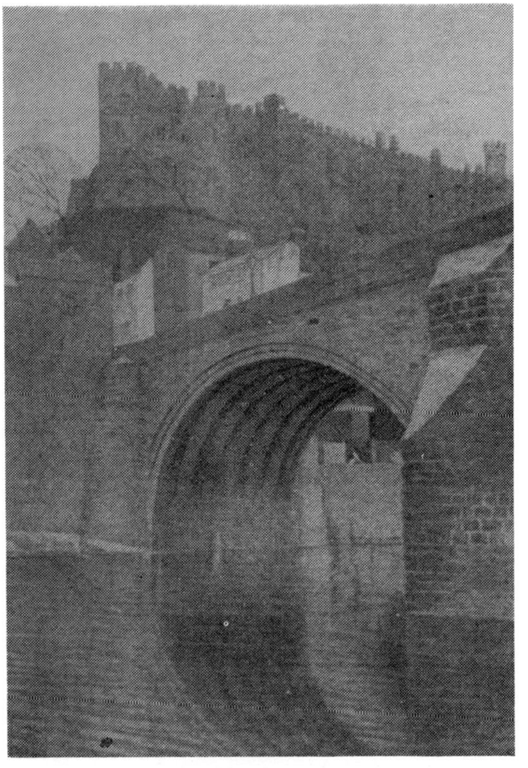

JOSEPH EDWARD SOUTHALL – The Castle And Bridge, Durham – signed with monogram and dated 1926 – pencil and watercolour – 30 x 20cm.
(Phillips) **$1,460** **£880**

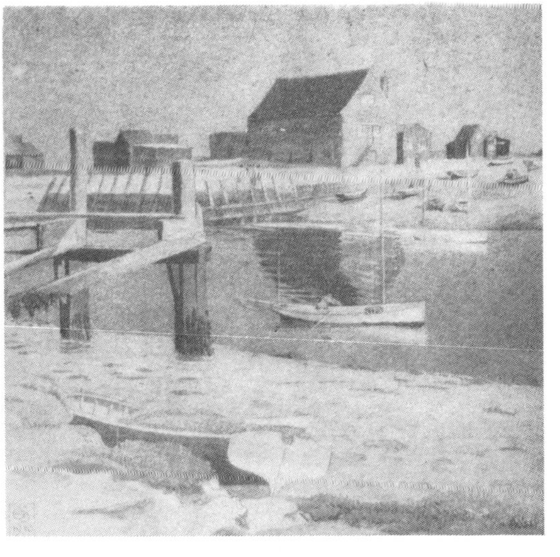

JOSEPH EDWARD SOUTHALL – Sailing Vessels In An Inlet – signed with monogram and dated 1924 and 1930 – pencil and watercolour on paper laid down on card – 12 x 11¾in.
(Christie's) **$2,044** **£1,430**

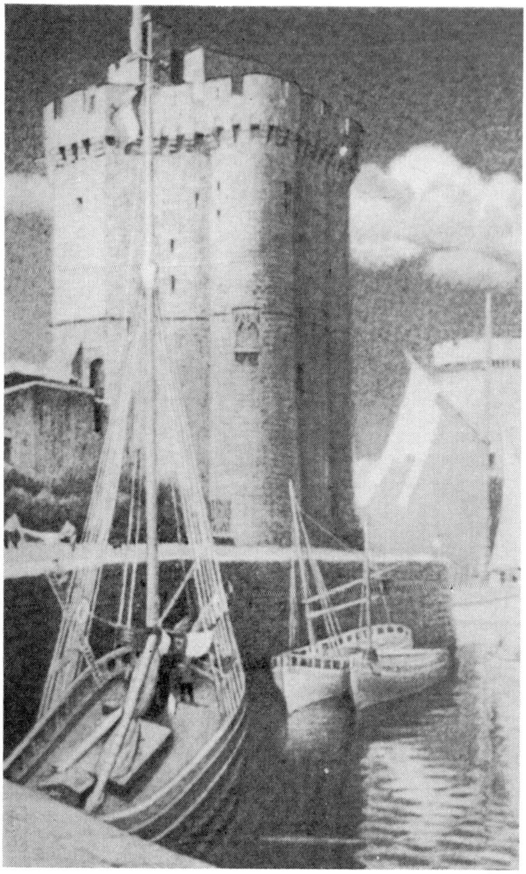

JOSEPH EDWARD SOUTHALL – The Tower Of St. Nicholas, La Rochelle – signed with monogram and dated 1933, inscribed on the reverse – watercolour and pencil – 12½ x 8¼in.
(Christie's) **$4,490** **£2,860**

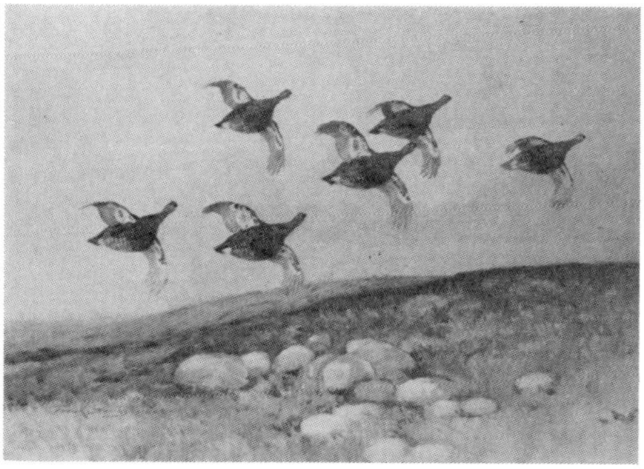

FRANK SOUTHGATE – 'Turning off from the Flankers': A Covey Of Grouse In Flight – signed, and inscribed on the reverse – watercolour and bodycolour – 15½ x 22in.
(Christie's) **$1,085** **£770**

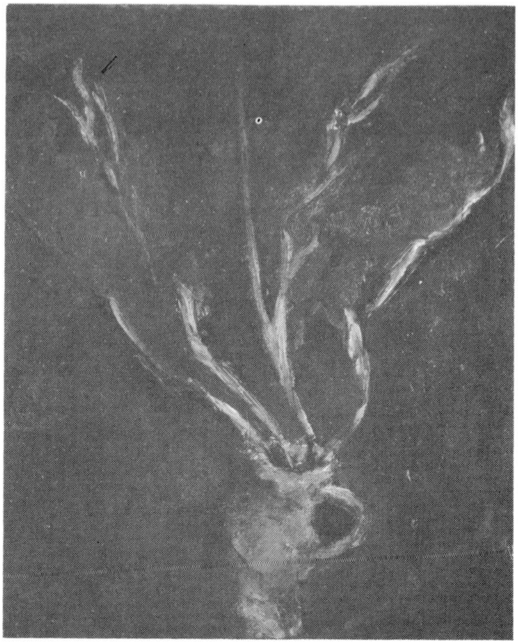

CHAIM SOUTINE – Les Glaieuls rouges – signed – oil on canvas – 26 x 22¾in.
(Christie's) **$220,440** **£132,000**

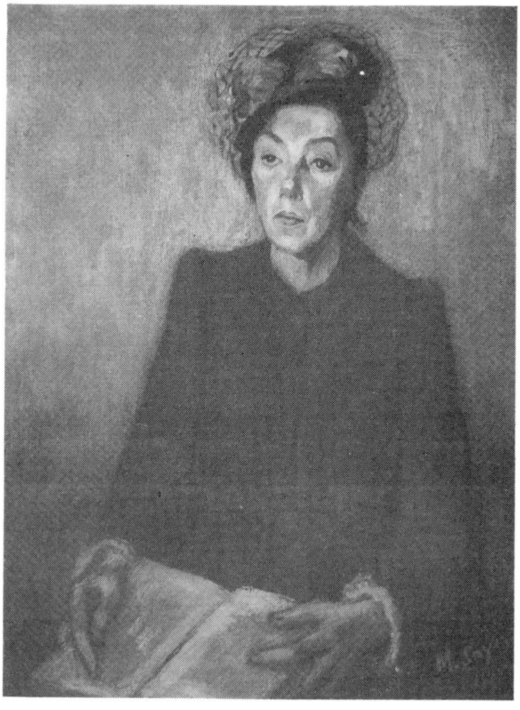

MOSES SOYER – Woman In Red – signed and dated 1943 – oil on canvas – 26 x 20in.
(Christie's) **$3,300** **£2,056**

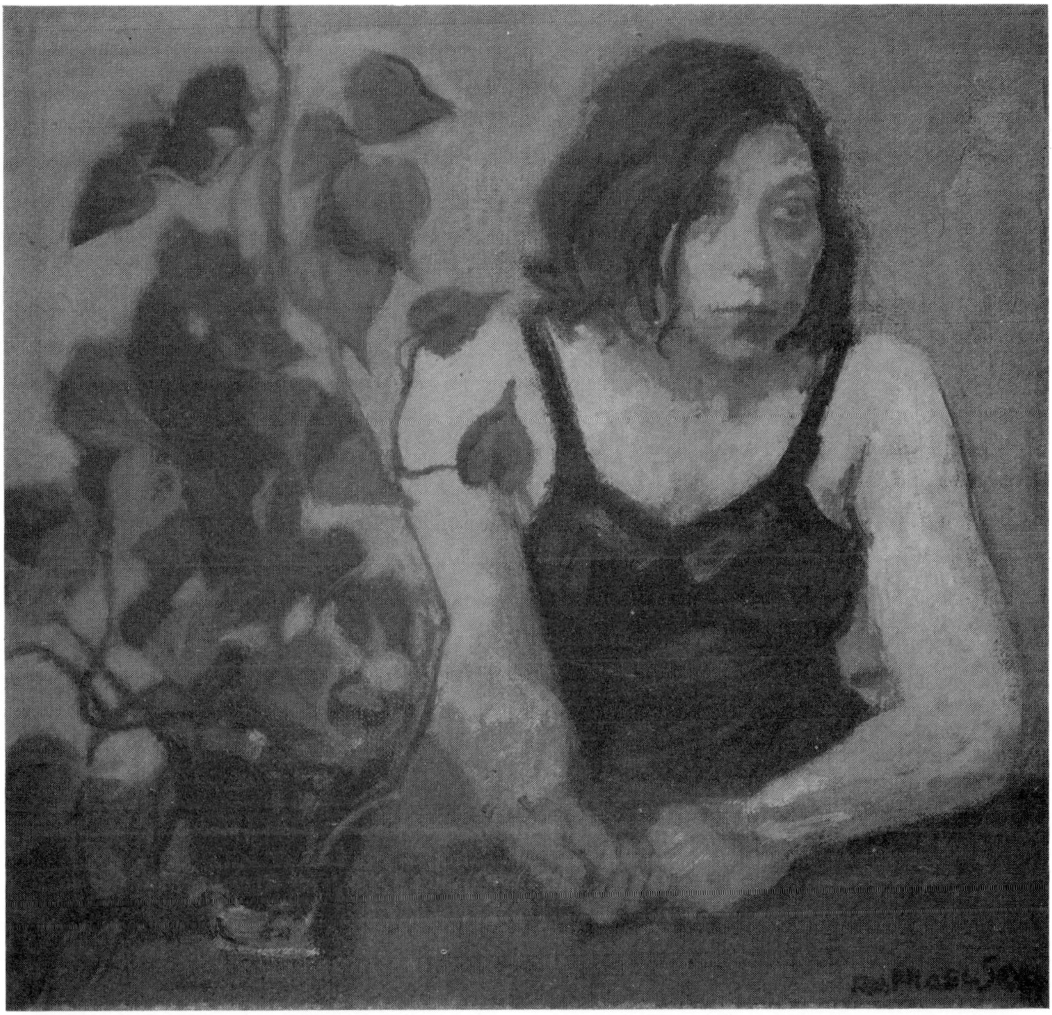

RAPHAEL SOYER – The Ivy Plant – signed – oil on canvas – 12 x 12¼in. *(Christie's)* **$4,400 £2,742**

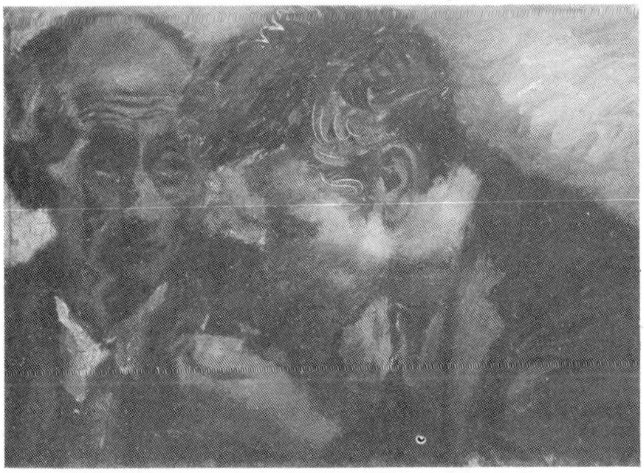

RAPHAEL SOYER – Two Men Talking – signed – oil on panel – 8¾ x 11¼in.
(Christie's) **$9,900 £6,959**

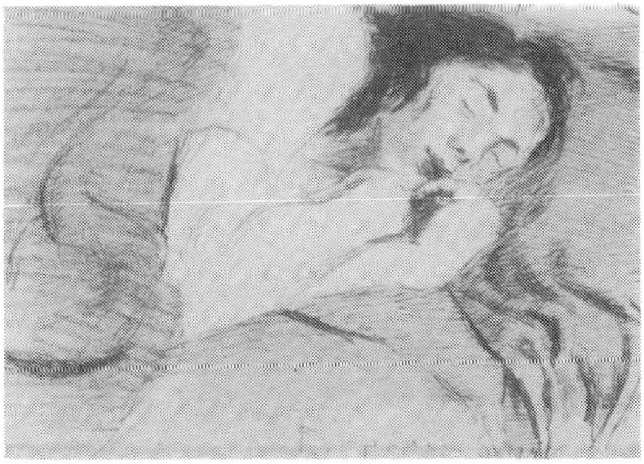

RAPHAEL SOYER – Sleeping Lady – signed – pen and black ink and crayon on paper – 7½ x 12¼in.
(Christie's) **$1,760 £1,224**

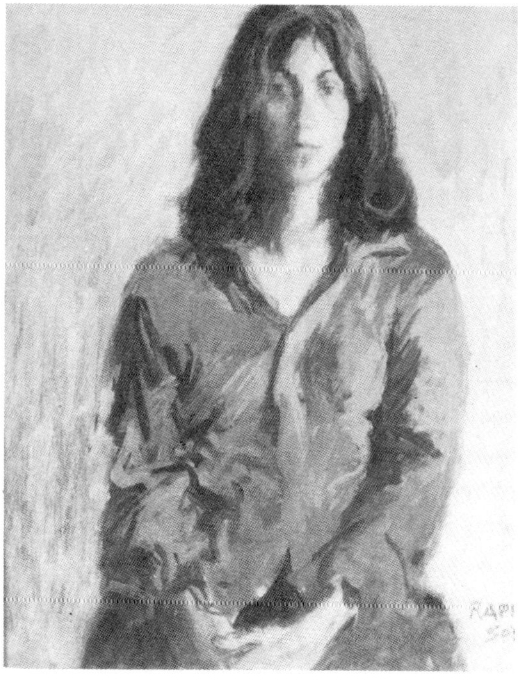

RAPHAEL SOYER – Model – signed – oil on canvas – 20 x 16in.
(Christie's) **$6,050** **£4,253**

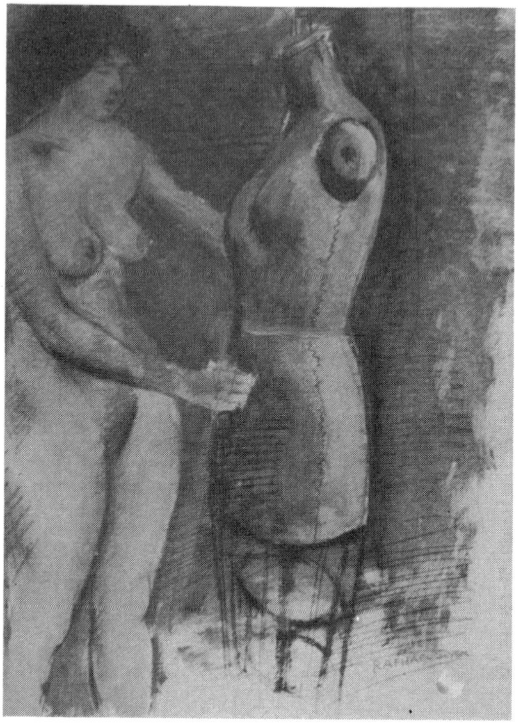

RAPHAEL SOYER – Nude And Dress Form – signed – watercolour, charcoal and pen and black ink on paper – 15¼ x 11¼in.
(Christie's) **$2,200** **£1,370**

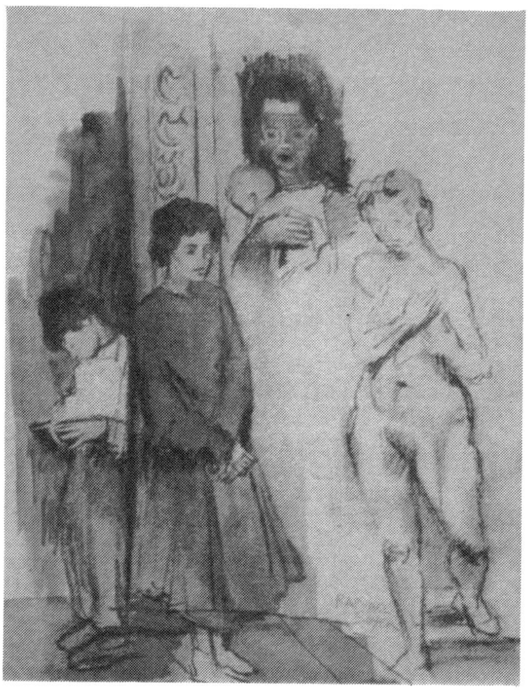

RAPHAEL SOYER – Study For 'City Children' – signed – watercolour, charcoal and pencil on paper – 16¾ x 13¾in.
(Christie's) **$2,420** **£1,507**

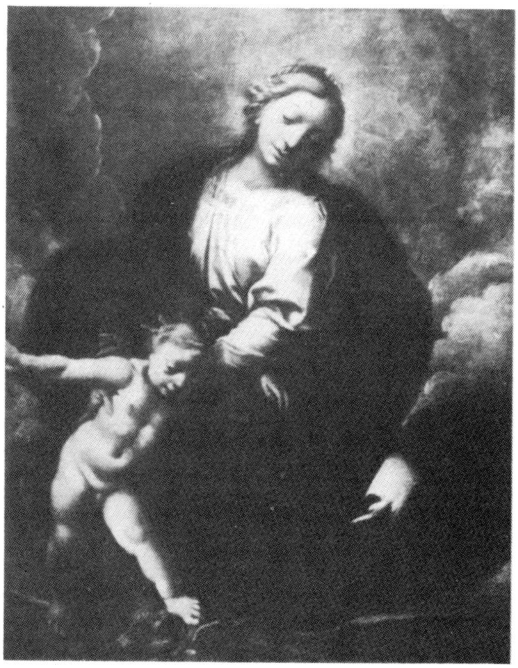

SPANISH SCHOOL, 17th century – Madonna And Child – oil on canvas – 40½ x 32¾in.
(Phillips) **$1,339** **£950**

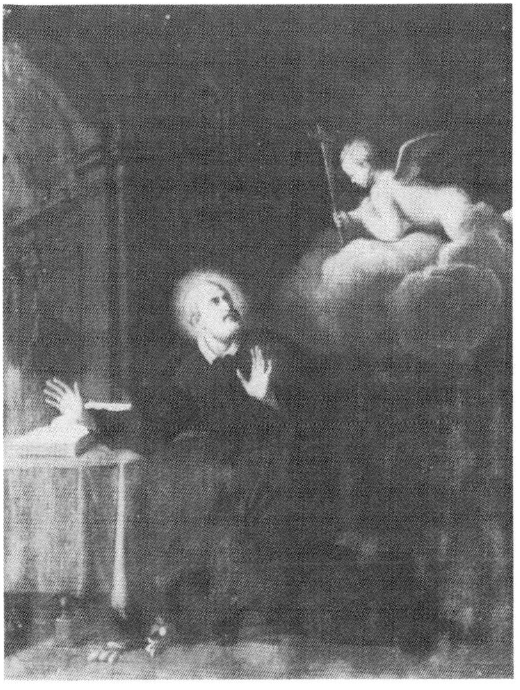

SPANISH SCHOOL, 17th century – A Cherub Holding Up A Crucifix Before A Kneeling Saint – oil on canvas – 37¼ x 28¾in.
(Phillips) **$310** **£220**

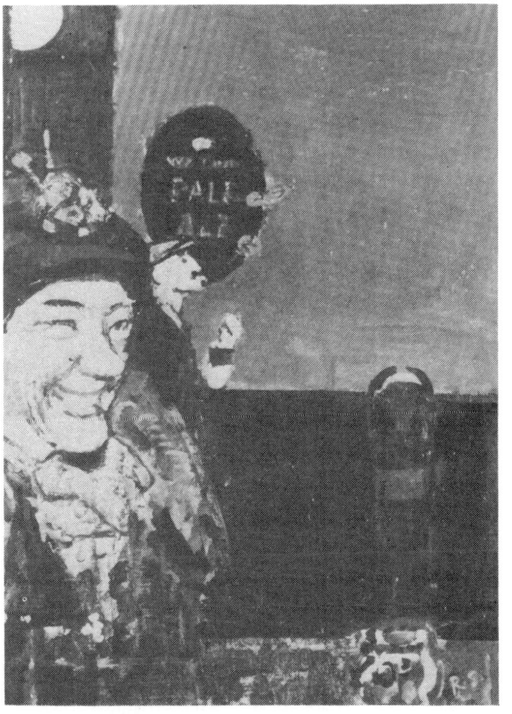

RUSKIN SPEAR – Pale Ale – signed with initials – oil on board – 19¾ x 15½in.
(Christie's) **$4,835** **£3,080**

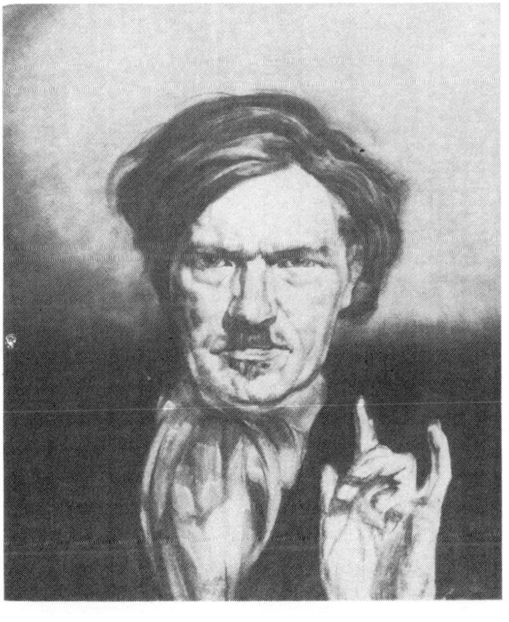

AUSTIN OSMAN SPARE – The Esoteric Brotherhood – signed with initials and dated '38 – coloured chalk – 58 x 46cm.
(Phillips) **$918** **£600**

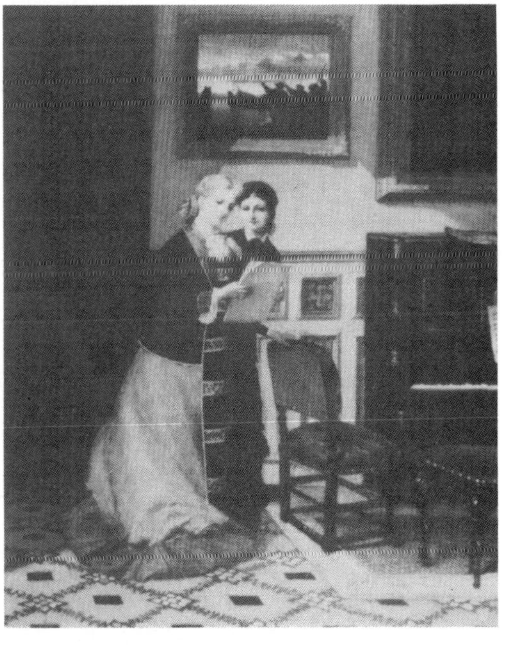

THOMAS TRUMAN SPEAR – 'New Music' – inscribed and dated 1875 – oil on canvas – 36 x 29¼in.
(Robt. W. Skinner Inc.) **$900** **£625**

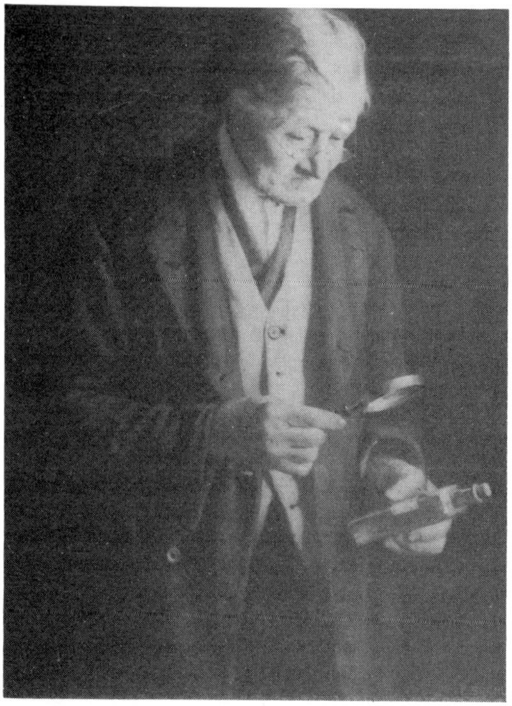

CHARLES SPENCELAYH – An Old Remedy – signed – 20 x 14in.
(Christie's) **$5,385** **£3,520**

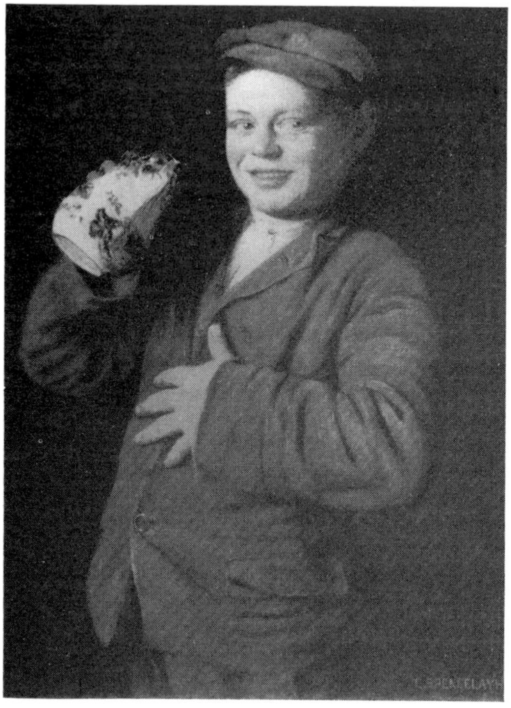

CHARLES SPENCELAYH – A Warming Drink – signed – 13 x 9in.
(Christie's) **$3,029** **£1,980**

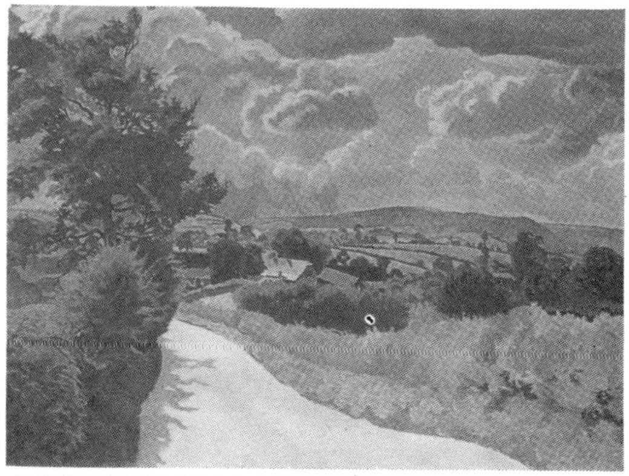

GILBERT SPENCER – Twyford, Dorset – signed – oil on canvas – 26 x 35in.
(Christie's) **$7,864** **£5,500**

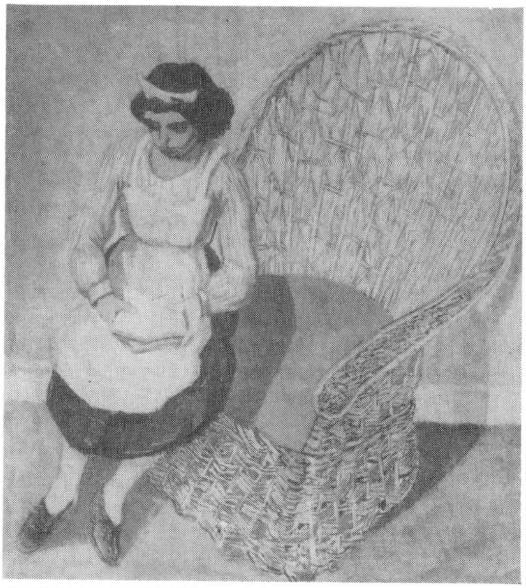

GILBERT SPENCER – A Woman Reading – signed – oil on canvas – 18 x 15¾in.
(Christie's) **$1,554** **£990**

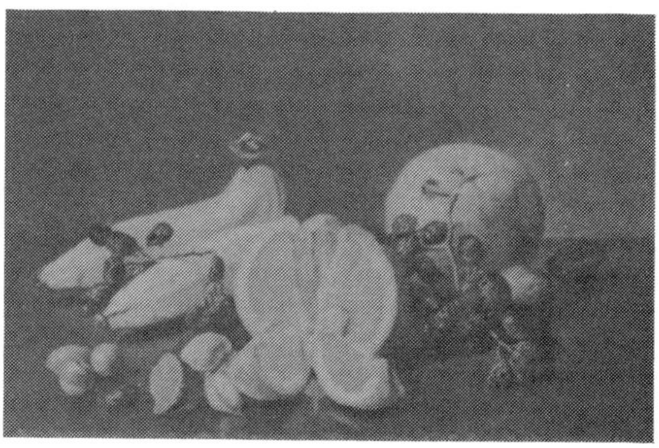

J. C. SPENCER – Still Life With Fruit And Nuts – signed and dated 1897 – oil on canvas – 12 x 18in.
(Robt. W. Skinner Inc.) **$1,600** **£981**

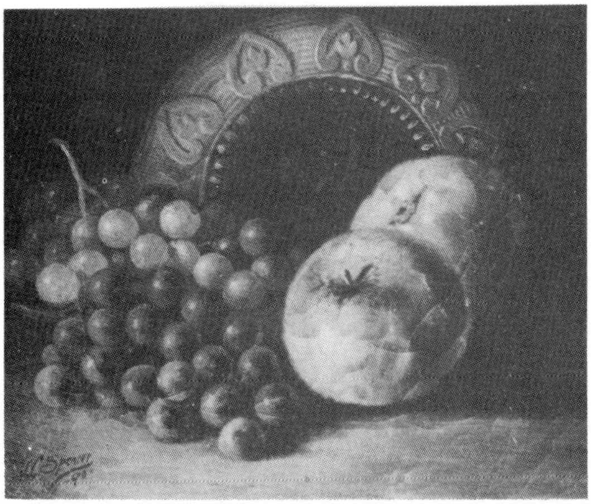

J. C. SPENCER – Still Life With Fruit – signed and dated '90 – oil on canvas – 10 x 12in.
(Robt. W. Skinner Inc.) **$600** **£416**

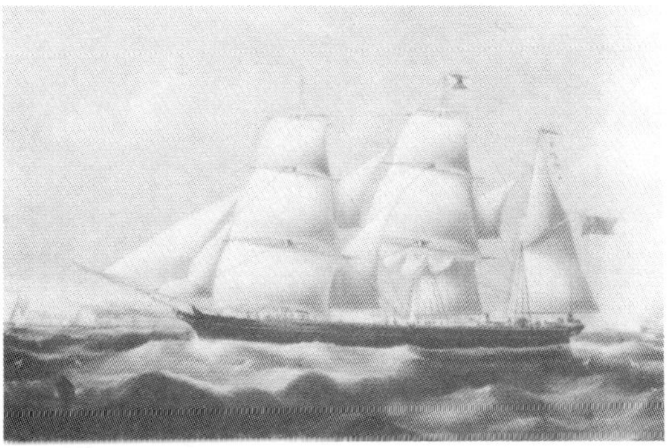

R. B. SPENCER – A Portrait Of A Barque Underway Off Dover – signed – oil – 23 x 35in.
(Anderson & Garland) **$7,579** **£5,300**

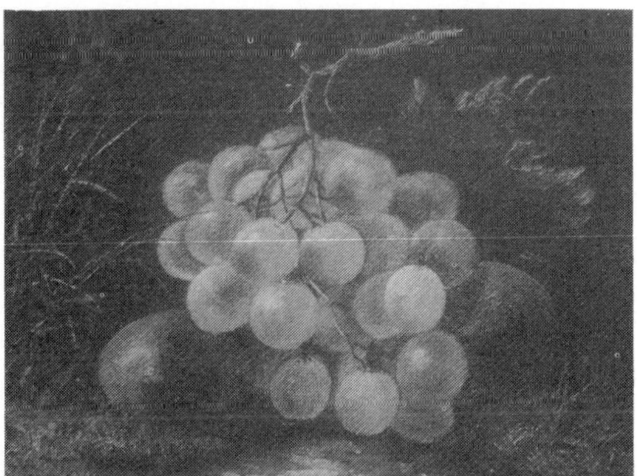

W. CLYDE SPENCER – Still Life With Grapes And Plums – signed – oil on canvas – 8 x 10in.
(Christie's) **$1,100** **£717**

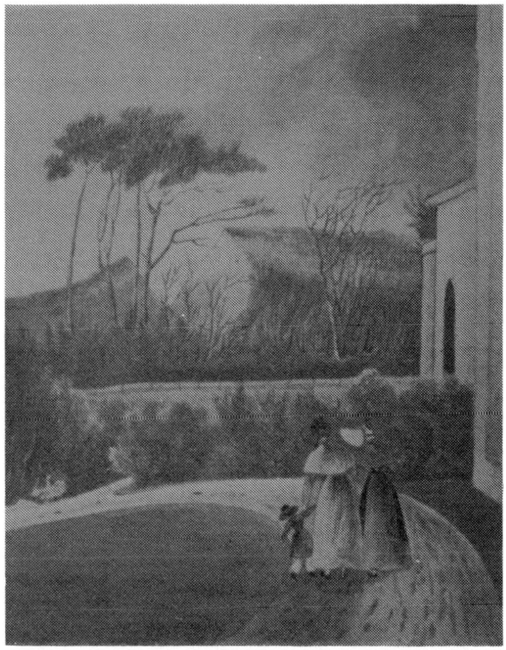

DIANA SPERLING – Album Depicting Ford Abbey, Hedingham Castle, Holy Head, Park Place, Norbury Park etc. – drawings and watercolours – most inscribed and one dated 1833 – 22 x 17.5cm.
(Phillips) **$749** **£460**

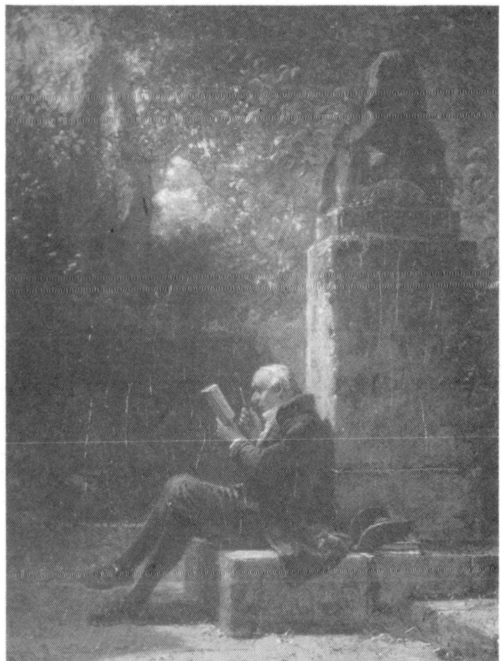

CARL SPITZWEG – Der Philosoph (Der Leser Im Park) – signed with monogram – 14½ x 11in.
(Christie's) **$174,240** **£121,000**

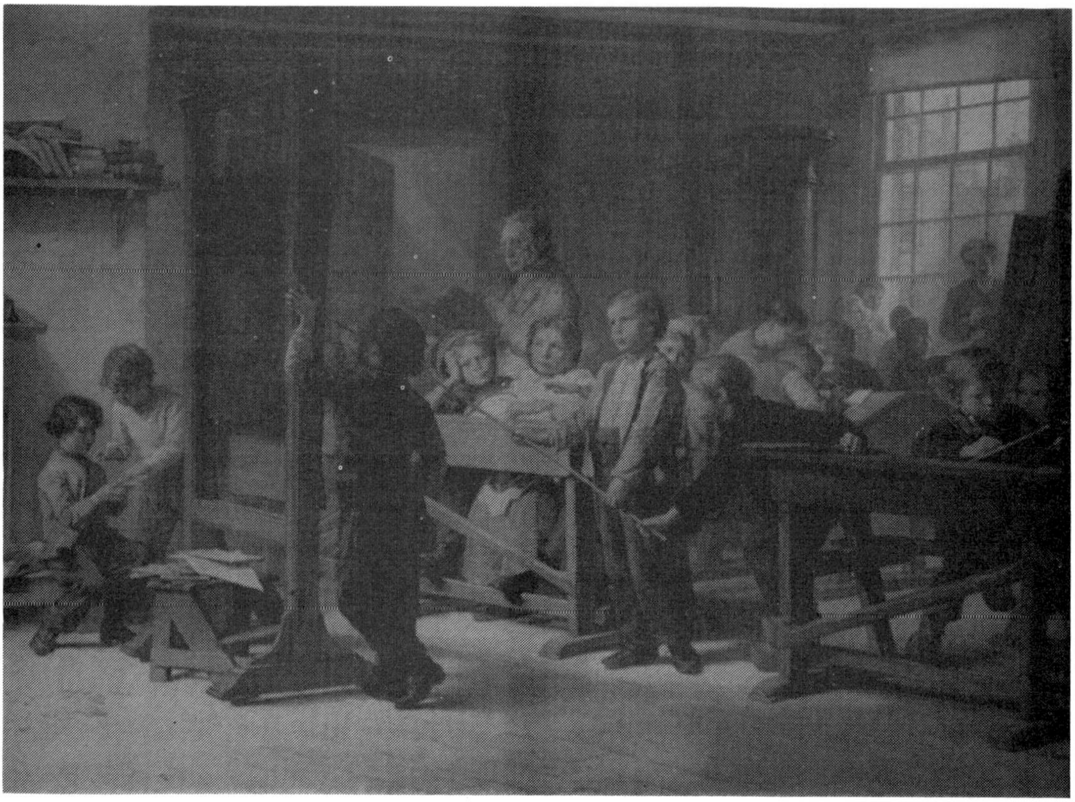

JACOB SPOEL – 'Divided Attention' – signed – oil on canvas – 66 x 86cm. *(Phillips)* **$14,195 £8,500**

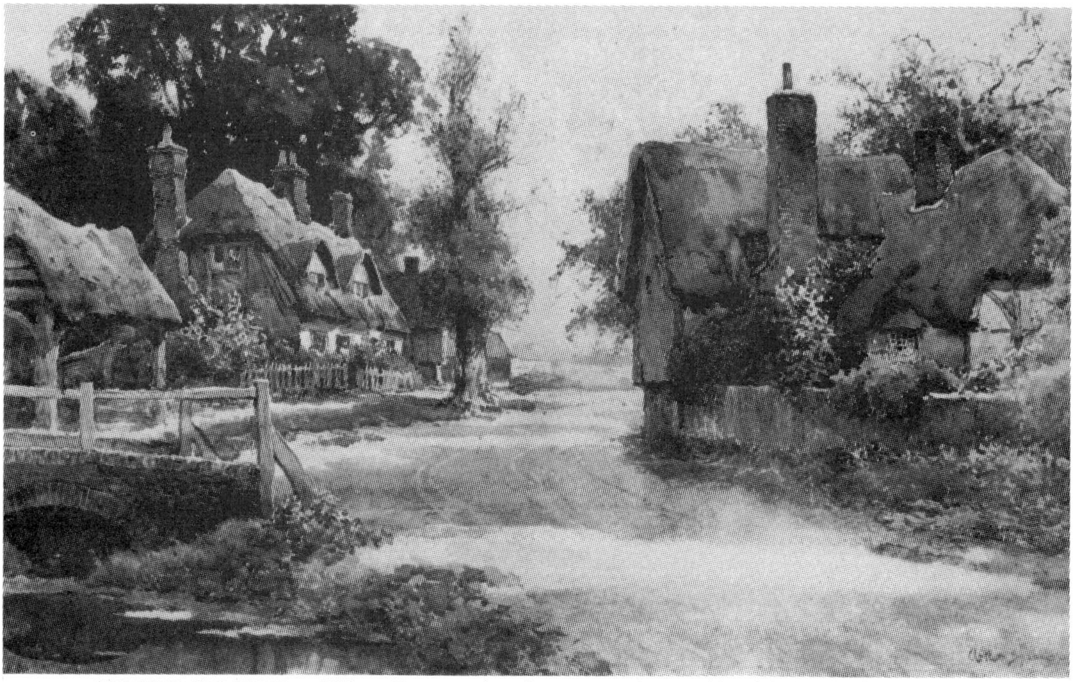

ARTHUR SPOONER – Village Scene – signed – watercolour – 17 x 27.5in. *(Biddle Webb)* **$1,453 £920**

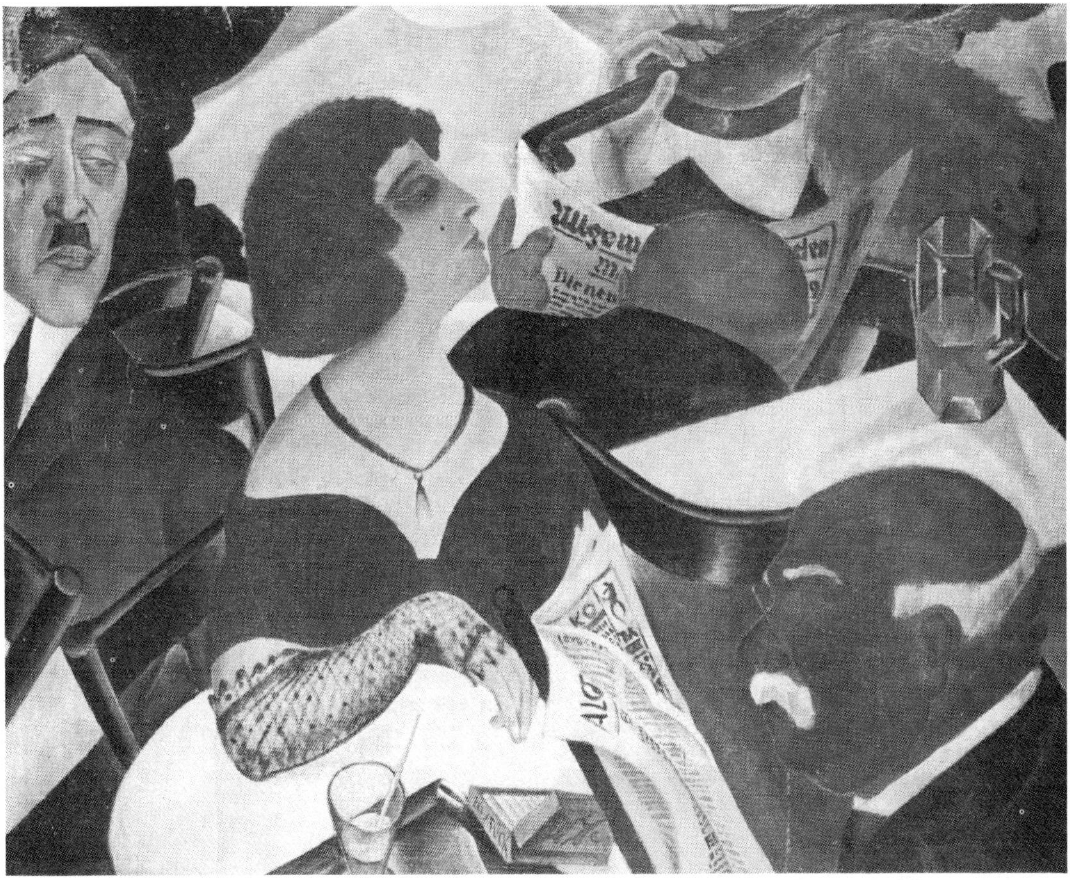

RICHARD SPRICK – Das Kaffeehaus – signed and dated '22 – oil on canvas – 33¼ x 38¼in. *(Christie's)* **$28,512 £19,800**

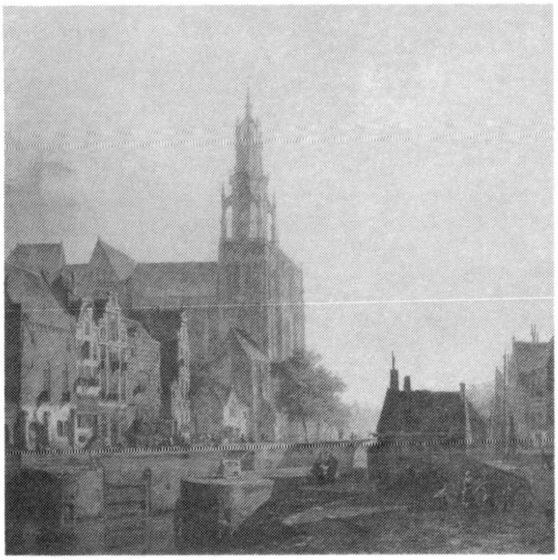

CORNELIS SPRINGER – A Capriccio View Of Antwerp – signed and dated 1841 – 29 x 36in. *(Christie's)* **$47,520 £33,000**

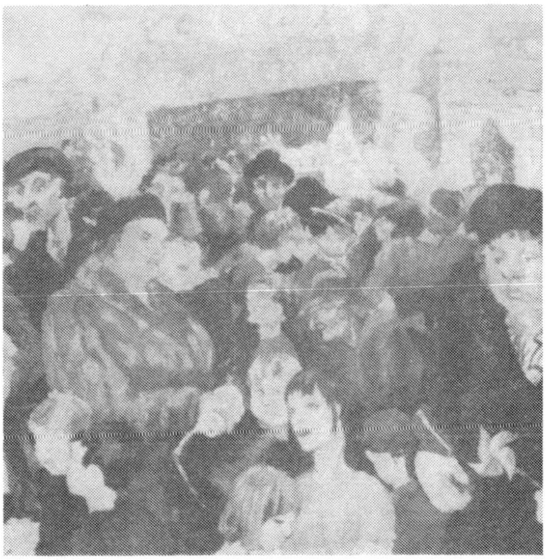

STEVEN SPURRIER – At The Fair – oil on canvas – 38 x 51cm. *(Phillips)* **$2,907 £1,900**

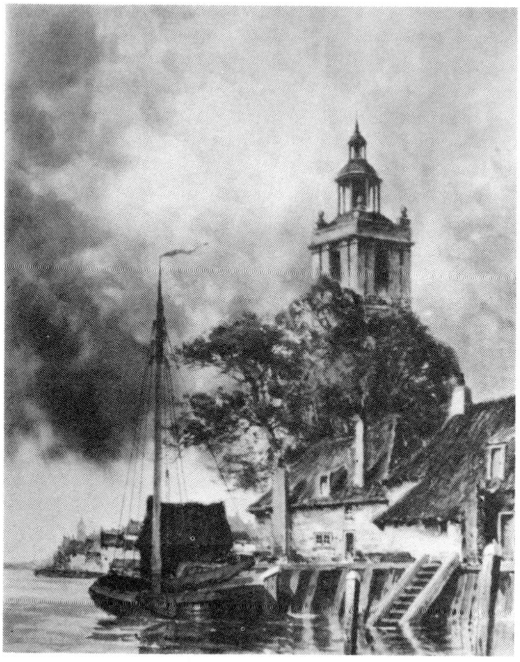

LOUIS VAN STAATEN – Dutch Canal Scene With Church; and Dutch Canal Scene With Windmill – signed – watercolour – 23 x 15in.
(Worsfolds) **$725** **£500 Pair**

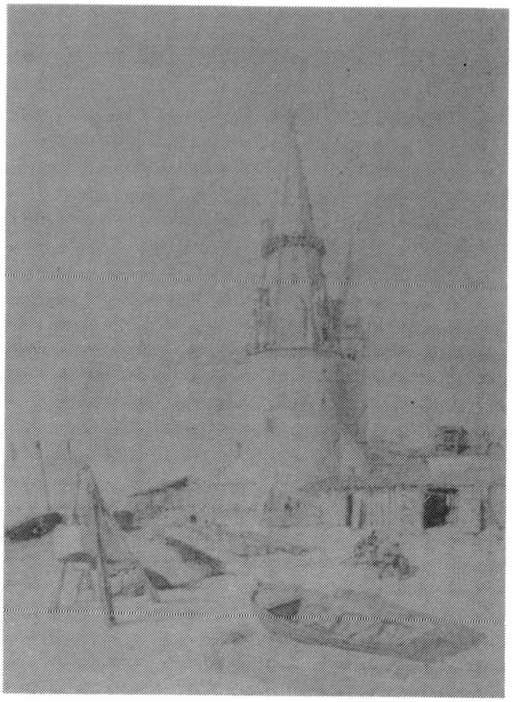

CLARKSON STANFIELD – On The Shore, La Rochelle – signed with monogram and inscribed and dated 1851 – watercolour over pencil – 48 x 33.5cm.
(Phillips) **$586** **£360**

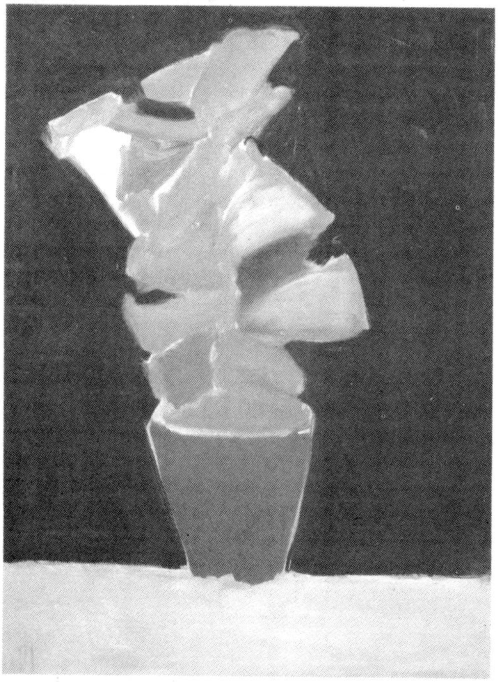

NICOLAS DE STAEL – Fleurs a Fontenay – signed, and signed, dated 1954 and inscribed on the reverse – oil on canvas – 39¼ x 28¾in.
(Christie's) **$205,920** **£143,000**

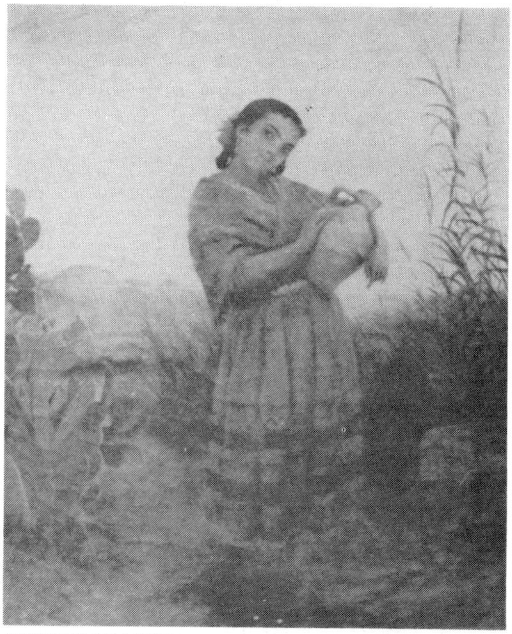

HENRY STANIER – Una Gitana – signed, inscribed and dated 1854, also signed and inscribed on the reverse – oil on canvas – 22 x 17½in.
(Christie's) **$1,075** **£660**

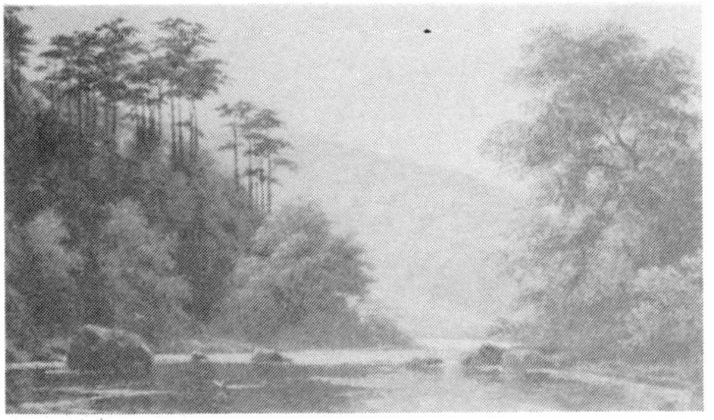

J. STANLEY – 'In The Eden Valley' – signed and inscribed – oil on canvas – 20 x 30in.
(Christie's) **$466** **£286**

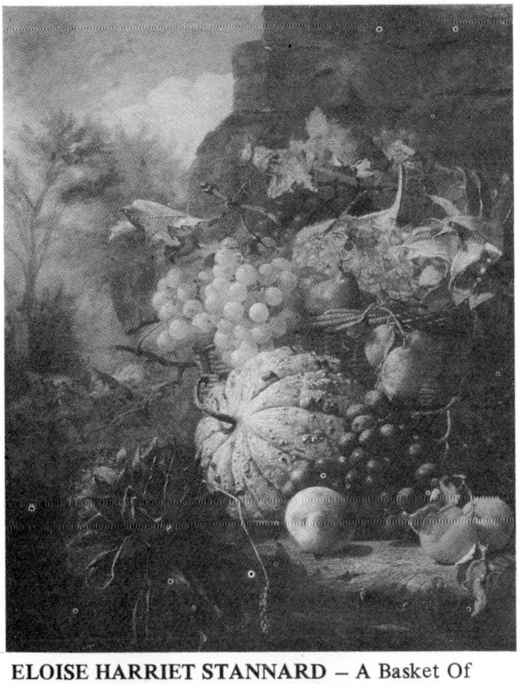

ELOISE HARRIET STANNARD – A Basket Of Grapes, A Pineapple, A Pear And Plums On A Bough, With A Melon And Peaches – signed, and signed and inscribed on a label on the reverse – 30½ x 24in.
(Christie's) **$8,530** **£6,050**

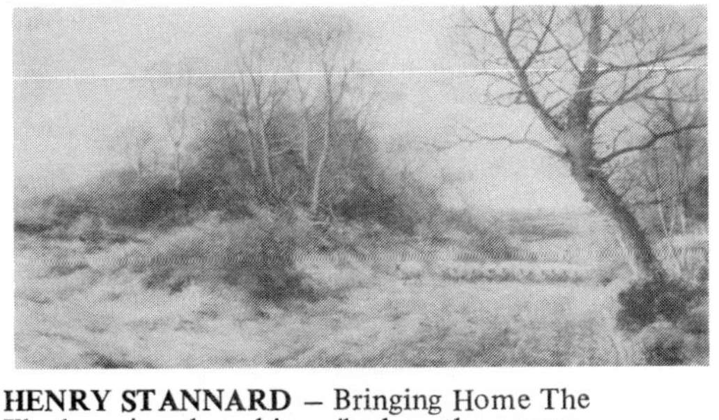

HENRY STANNARD – Bringing Home The Flock – signed, and inscribed on the reverse – watercolour – 14½ x 26¼in.
(Christie's) **$1,460** **£880**

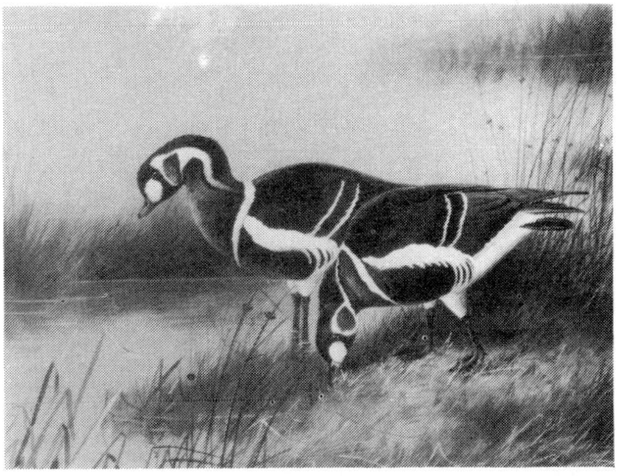

HENRY STANNARD – Partridges In Mid Winter – signed – pencil and watercolour heightened with white – 13¼ x 19¼in.
(Christie's) **$821** **£495**

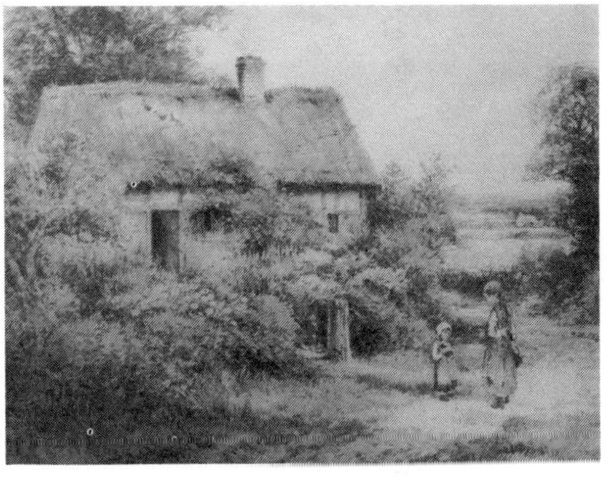

HENRY JOHN SYLVESTER STANNARD – Two Children On A Path Outside A Cottage – signed – watercolour – 10½ x 14½in.
(Christie's) **$5,843** **£3,520**

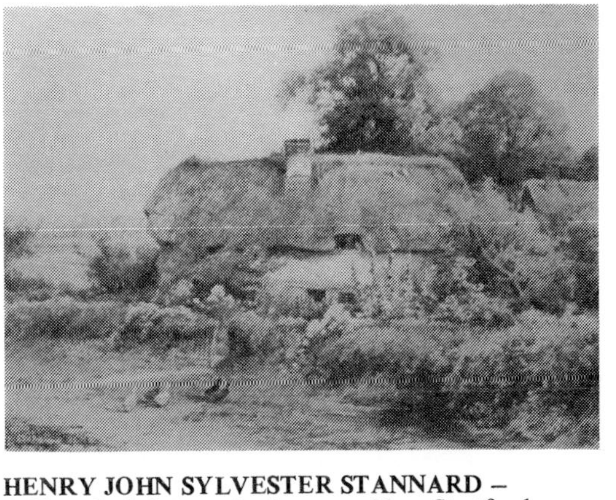

HENRY JOHN SYLVESTER STANNARD – A Thatched Cottage In Summer, Near Stratford-on-Avon – signed – watercolour and bodycolour – 24 x 34.5cm.
(Phillips) **$3,912** **£2,400**

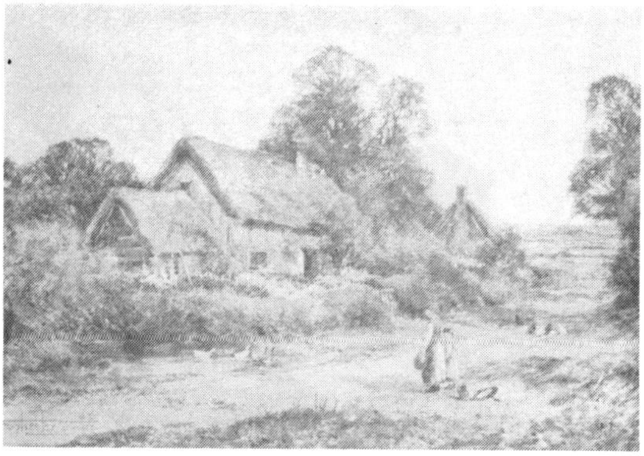

HENRY JOHN SYLVESTER STANNARD –
Roadside Cottages Near Woburn, Bedfordshire – signed, and inscribed on the reverse – pencil and watercolour heightened with white on board – 14½ x 21in.
(Christie's) **$7,068** **£4,620**

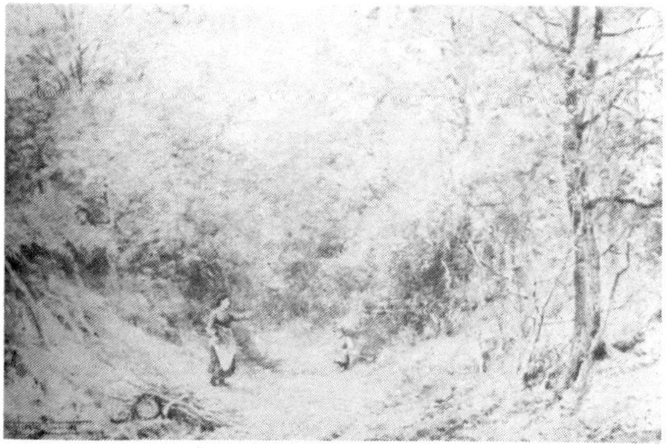

HENRY JOHN SYLVESTER STANNARD –
Autumn Tints: Gathering Brushwood – signed – watercolour – 13 x 20in.
(Christie's) **$651** **£462**

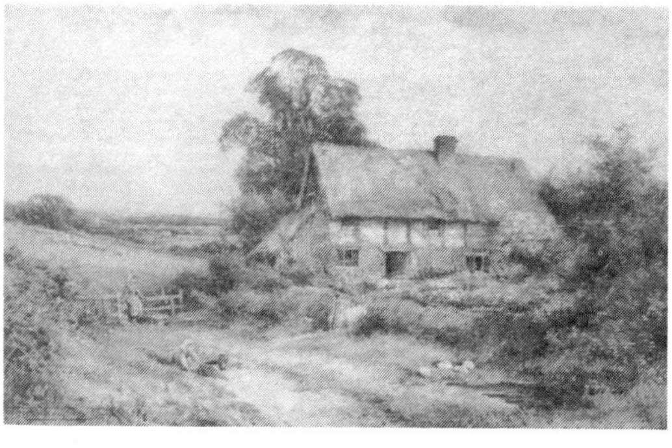

HENRY JOHN SYLVESTER STANNARD –
By The Shepherd's Cottage, Maulden, Bedfordshire – signed, and inscribed on the reverse – watercolour – 16¼ x 26½in.
(Christie's) **$9,130** **£5,500**

HENRY JOHN SYLVESTER STANNARD –
Going Out To Pasture, Flitwick Moor – signed – watercolour – 12¾ x 21¼in.
(Christie's) **$3,722** **£2,640**

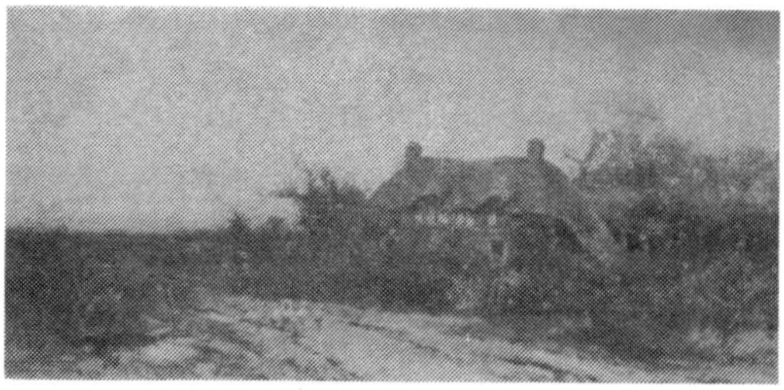

HENRY JOHN SYLVESTER STANNARD –
A Bedfordshire Cottage At Dusk – signed – watercolour – 34 x 63cm.
(Phillips) **$2,934** **£1,800**

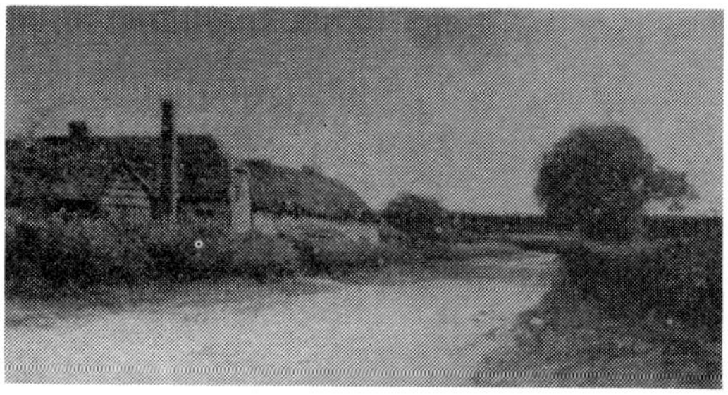

HENRY JOHN SYLVESTER STANNARD –
Cottages By A Country Lane – signed – watercolour – 35 x 63cm.
(Phillips) **$3,260** **£2,000**

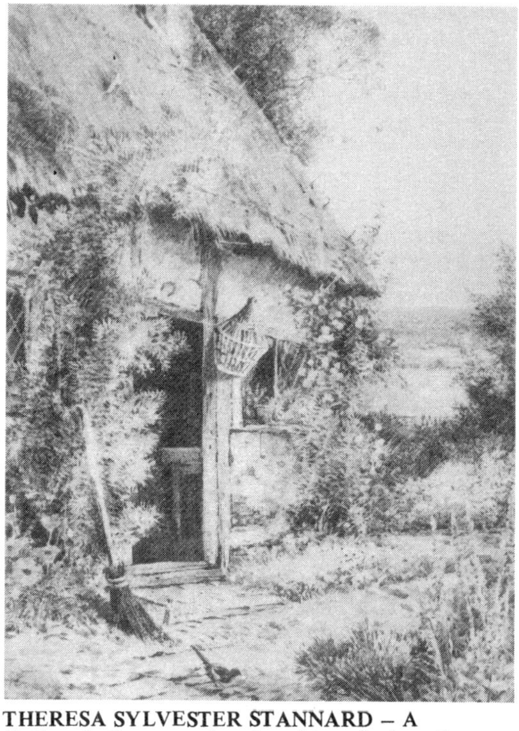

THERESA SYLVESTER STANNARD – A
Cottage In Sussex – signed, and inscribed on the reverse – pencil and watercolour heightened with white on board – 13½ x 9½in.
(Christie's) **$2,524** **£1,650**

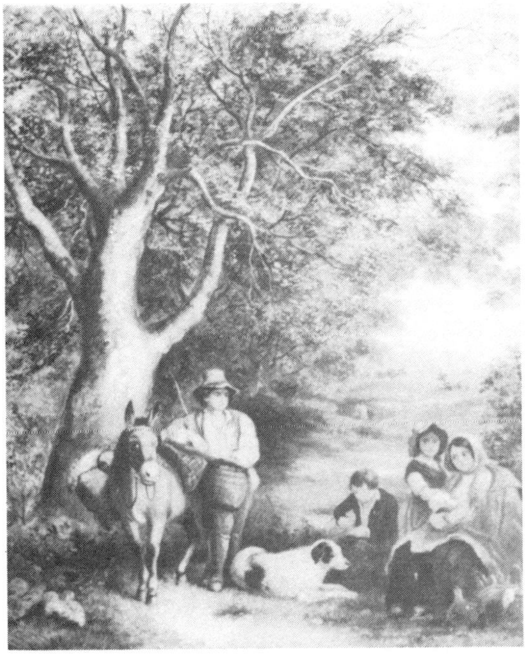

ARTHUR JAMES STARK – Travellers Resting In A Wooded Landscape – signed – 24 x 20¼in.
(Christie's) **$1,551** **£1,100**

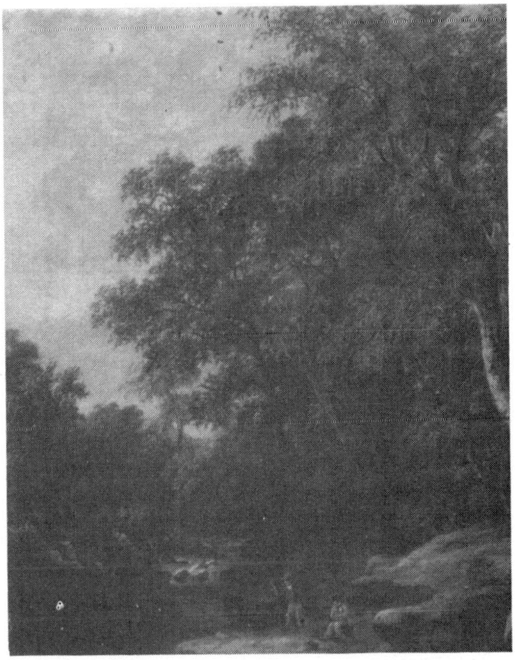

JAMES STARK – Fishermen In River Landscape – oil on canvas – 29½ x 23in.
(Michael G. Matthews) **$7,680** **£4,800**

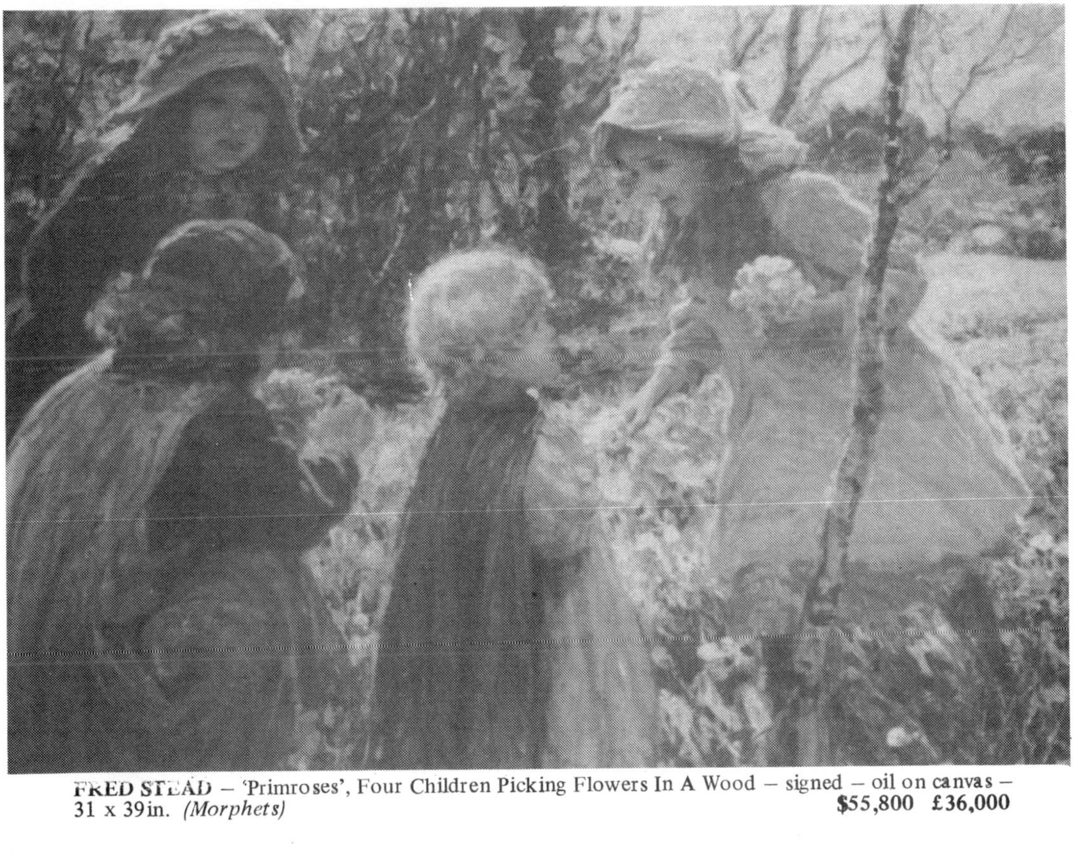

FRED STEAD – 'Primroses', Four Children Picking Flowers In A Wood – signed – oil on canvas – 31 x 39in. *(Morphets)* **$55,800** **£36,000**

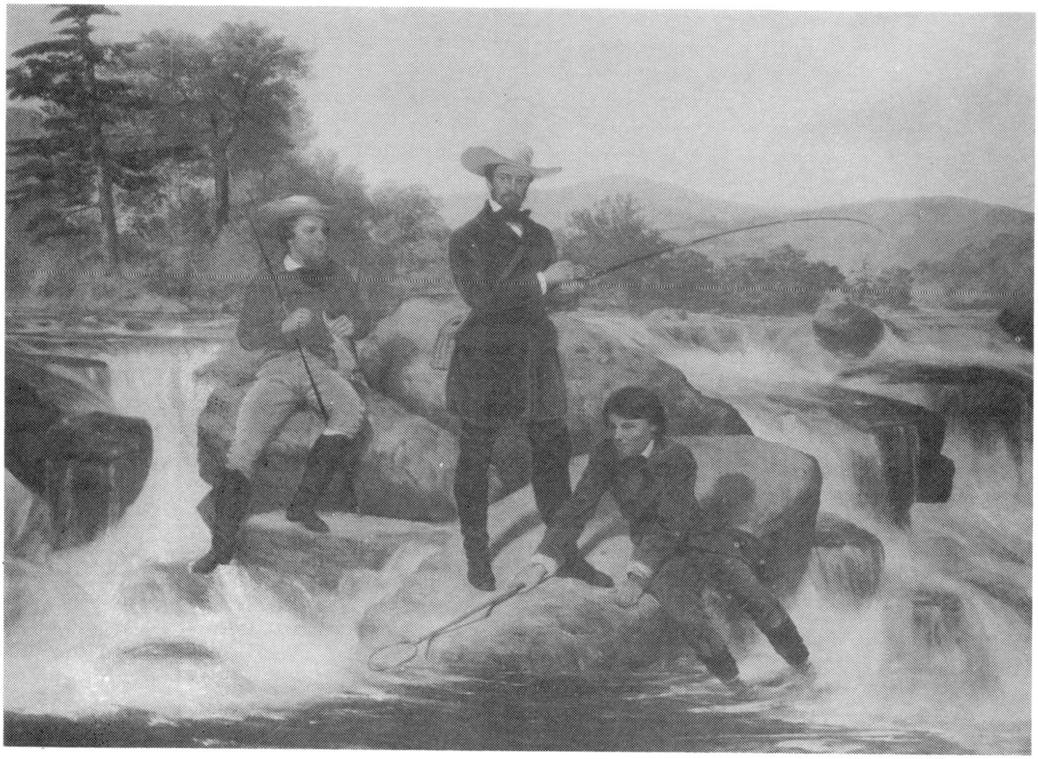

JULIUS BRUTUS STEARNS – Trout Fishing – signed and dated 1853 – oil on canvas – 37¼ x 50¼in.
(Christie's) **$66,000 £43,078**

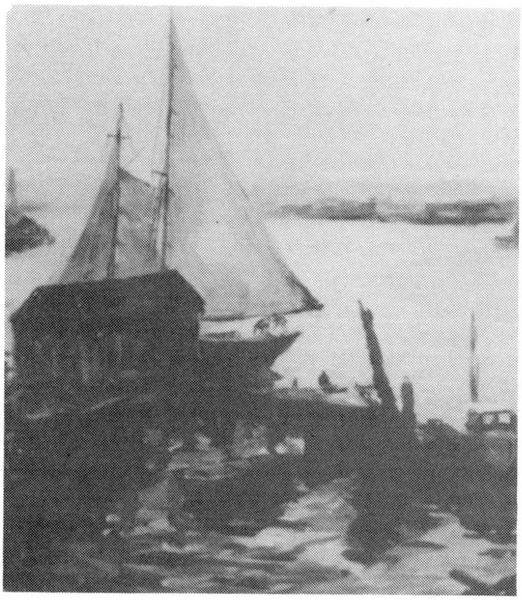

MARIAN WILLIAMS STEELE – Sunset Harbour View – signed – oil on canvas – 25 x 30in.
(Robt. W. Skinner Inc.) **$800 £555**

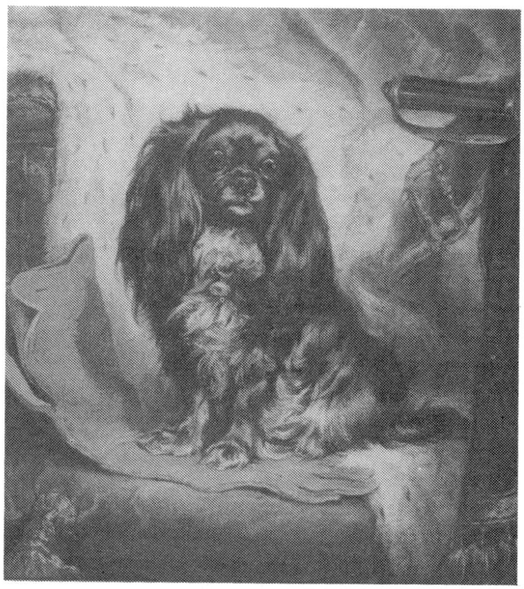

GOURLAY STEELL – Jeannie, Queen Victoria's Favourite Spaniel – signed and dated 1858 – gouache – 19¾ x 20¾in.
(Bonhams) **$5,890 £3,800**

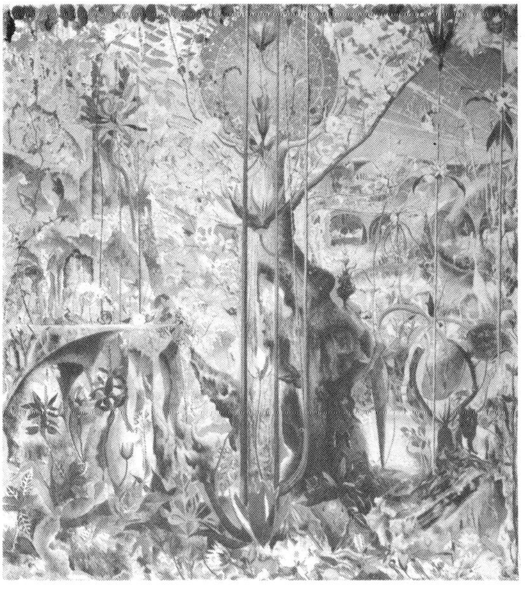

JOSEPH STELLA – Tree Of My Life, 1919 – signed – oil on canvas – 83½ x 75½in.
(Christie's) **$2,200,000 £1,546,600**

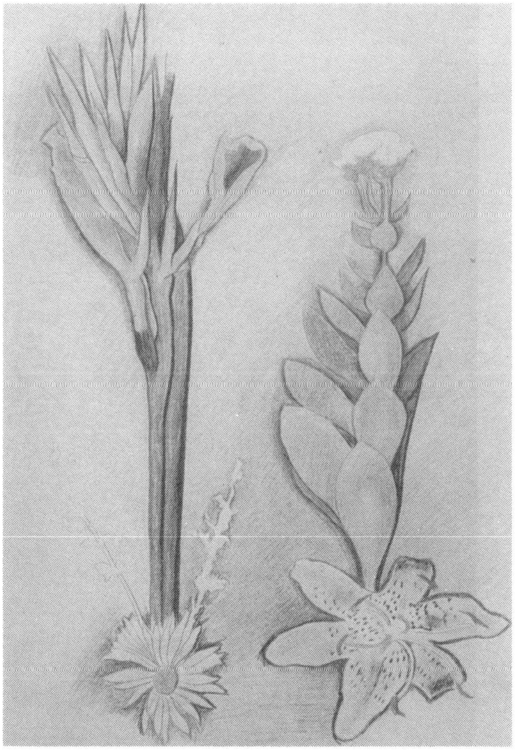

JOSEPH STELLA – Floral Still Life – signed and dated 1919 – silverpoint and crayon on paper – 19 x 13¼in.
(Christie's) **$2,860 £1,782**

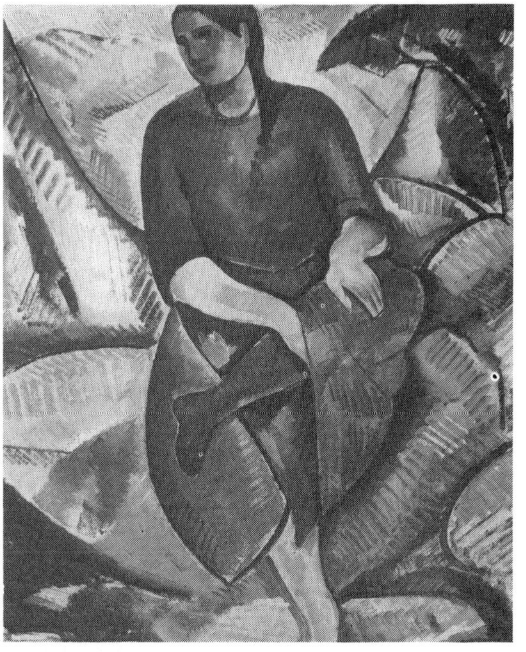

MAURICE STERNE – Angelina Toppoli – signed – oil on canvas – 32 x 25¾in.
(Christie's) **$10,450 £6,511**

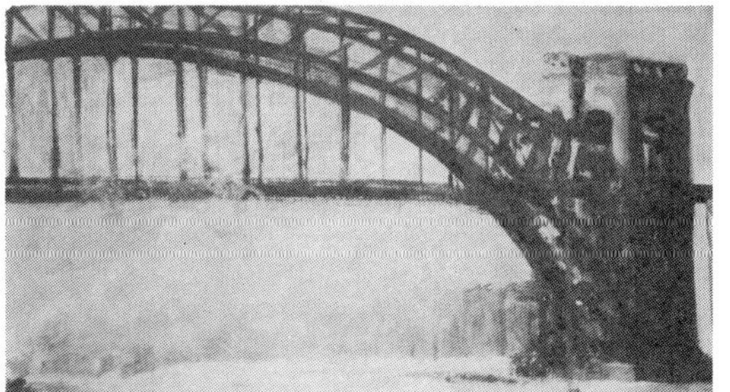

ALBERT STERNER – Hellgate Bridge, Winter – signed and dated 1934, also dated and inscribed on the reverse – oil on board – 20 x 24in.
(Christie's) **$2,860 £1,989**

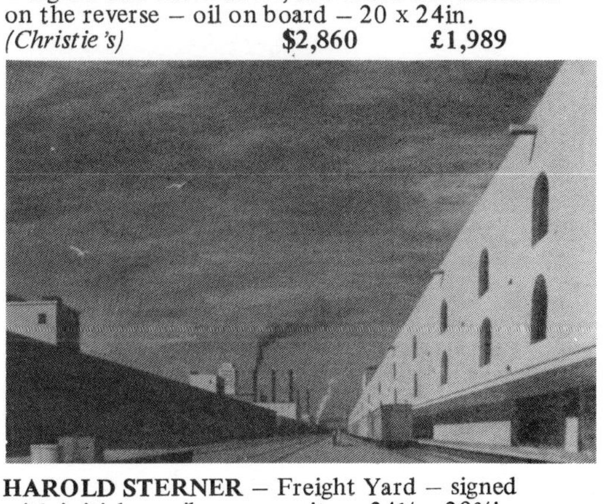

HAROLD STERNER – Freight Yard – signed with initials – oil on masonite – 24¼ x 29¾in.
(Christie's) **$1,210 £841**

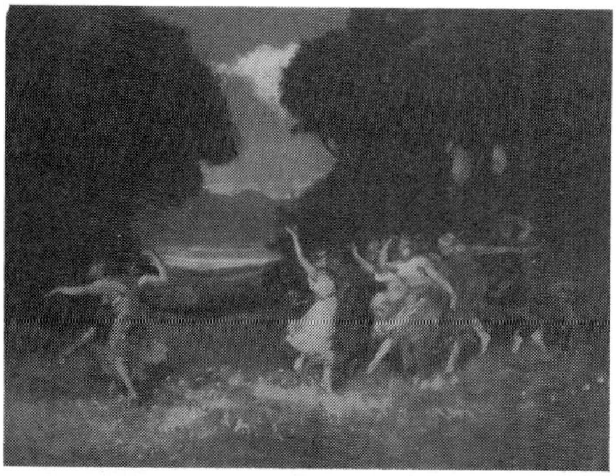

CHARLES WALTER STETSON – Summer Joy – signed and dated 1901, also dated and inscribed on the reverse – oil on canvas – 18¼ x 24¼in.
(Christie's) **$6,050** **£3,769**

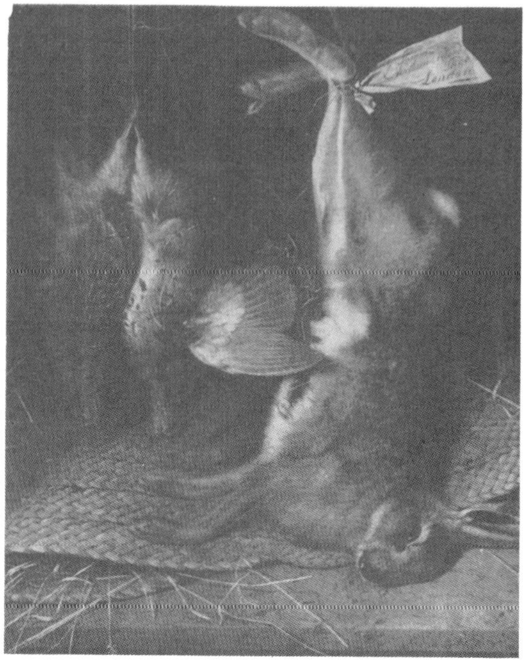

GEORGE STEVENS – Still Life Of A Hare And A Brace Of Partridges – signed and inscribed – 30¼ x 25¼in.
(Christie's) **$2,268** **£1,512**

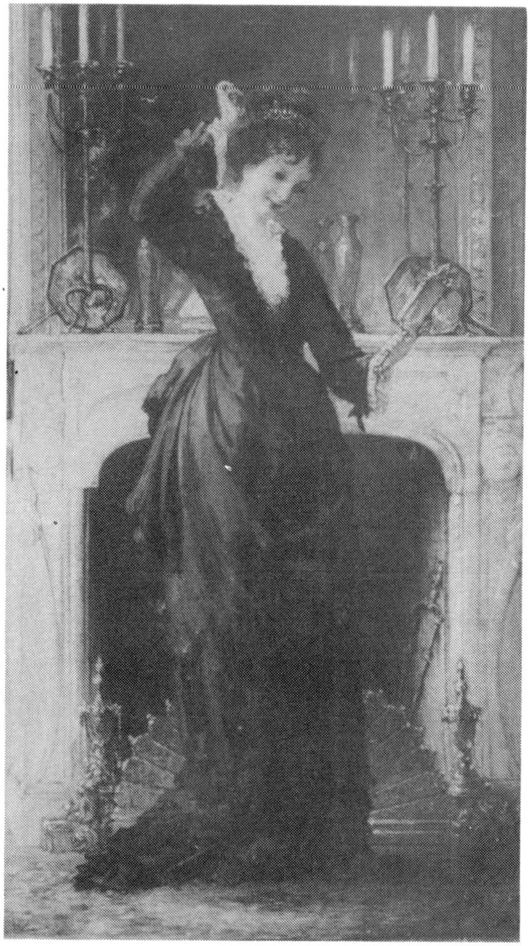

ALFRED STEVENS – In The Boudoir – signed – 12¾ x 8¼in.
(Christie's) **$15,840** **£11,000**

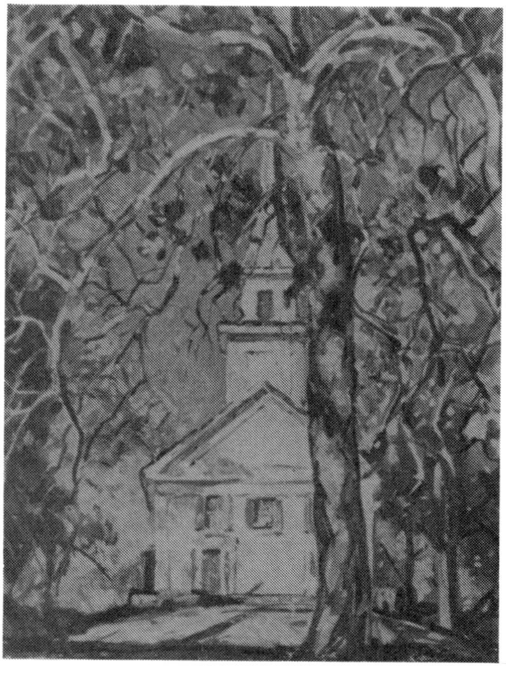

WILLIAM LESTER STEVENS – New England Church – signed – oil on canvas – 26 x 20in.
(Robt. W. Skinner Inc.) **$950** **£582**

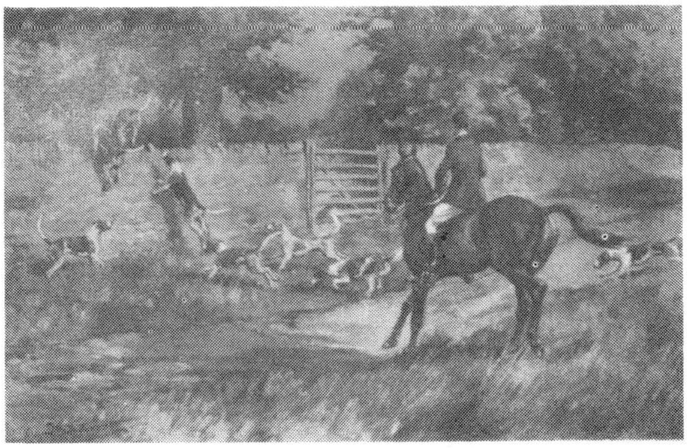

F. A. STEWART – Duke Of Beaufort Hunting With Hounds – signed – watercolour – 8¾ x 14in.
(Hobbs & Chambers) **$3,680** **£2,300**

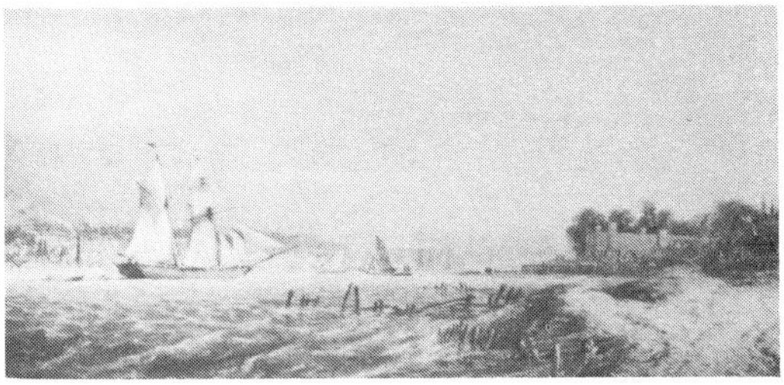

FRANK ALGERNON STEWART – 'In The Making' – signed, inscribed and dated '21 – pencil and watercolour heightened with white – 9¼ x 9¼in.
(Christie's) **$3,366** **£2,200**

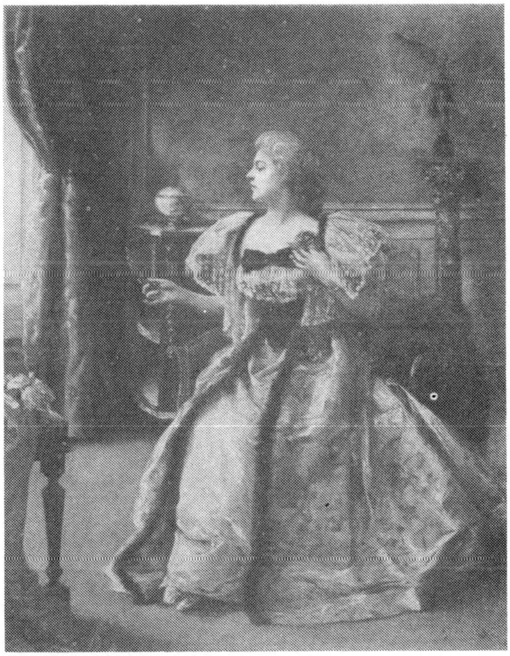

JULIUS L. STEWART – Lady With A Mirror – signed and dated '90 – oil on panel – 17¾ x 23¾in.
(Christie's) **$4,400** **£3,093**

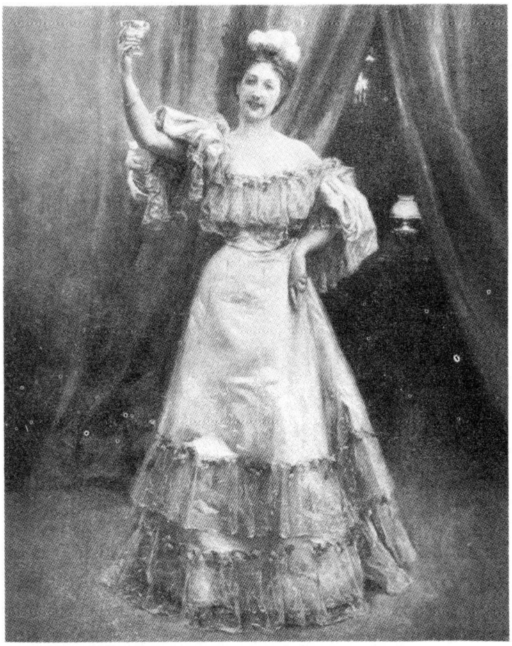

JULIUS L. STEWART – A Toast – signed and dated '96 – oil on canvas – 31½ x 22½in.
(Christie's) **$7,700** **£5,413**

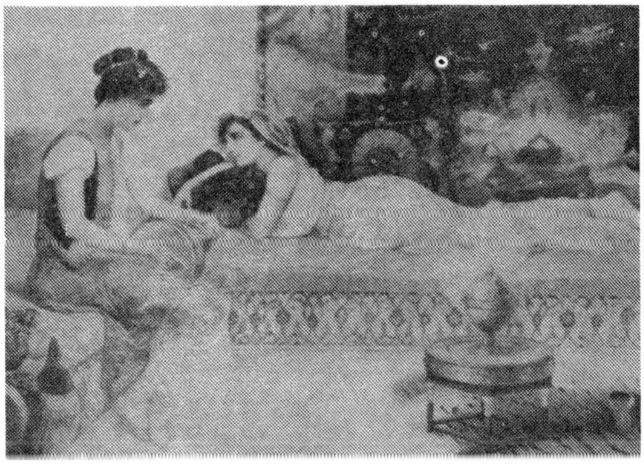

VINCENT G. STIEPEVICH – Music In The Harem – signed – oil on canvas – 20 x 30in.
(Robt. W. Skinner Inc.) **$6,500** **£3,987**

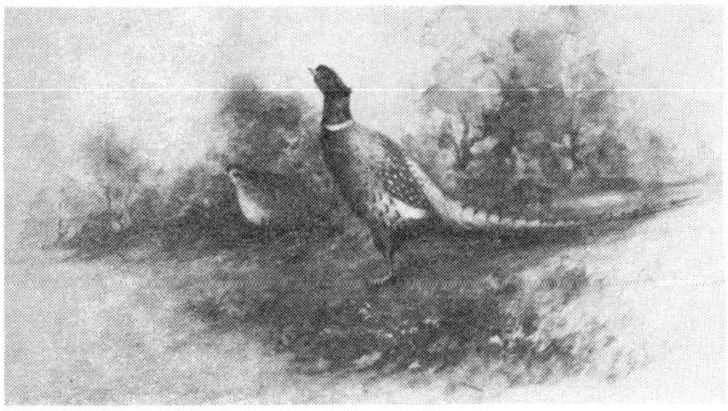

JAMES STINTON – A Cock And Hen Pheasant By The Edge Of A Wood – signed – watercolour heightened with white – 6¼ x 10¾in.
(Christie's) **$730** **£440**

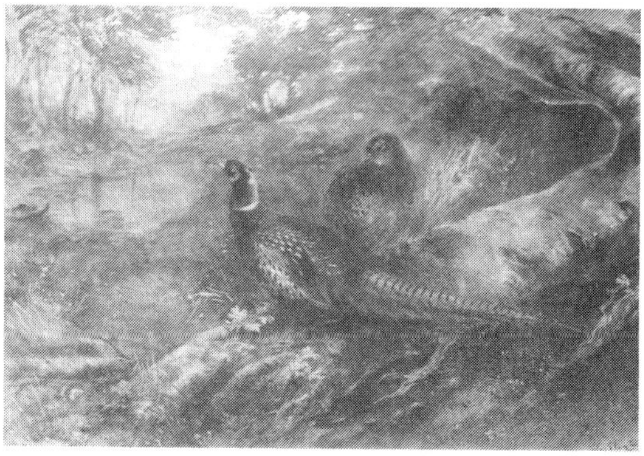

JAMES STINTON – Pheasants In A Wood – signed – watercolour heightened with white – 9½ x 14½in.
(Christie's) **$1,430** **£935**

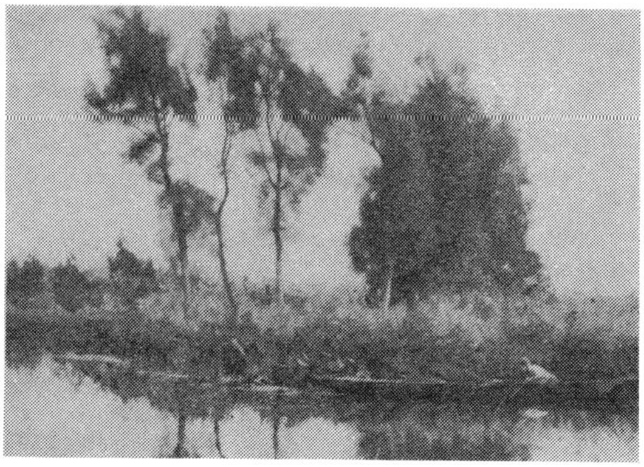

ADRIAN STOKES – Evening On The Kennet – signed – oil on canvas – 51 x 69cm.
(Phillips) **$4,482** **£2,700**

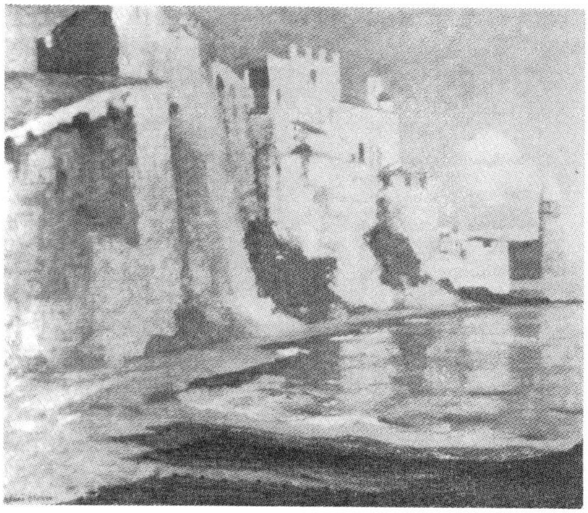

ADRIAN STOKES – Collioure, The Net-Mender – signed, and signed and inscribed on a label – oil on canvas – 25 x 30in.
(Christie's) **$2,674** **£1,870**

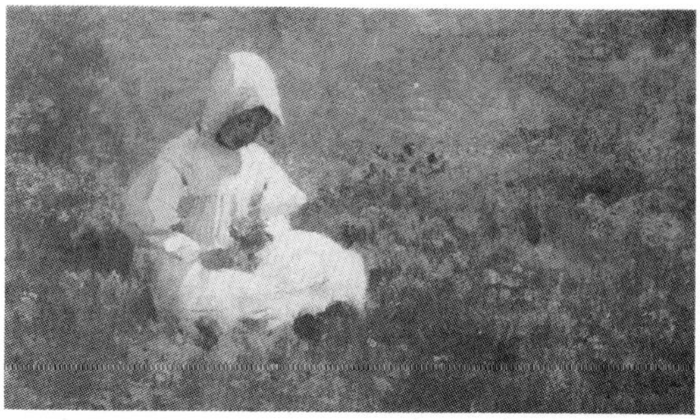

MARIANNE STOKES – A Young Girl Picking Flowers – signed – 13¾ x 18in.
(Christie's) **$4,719** **£3,300**

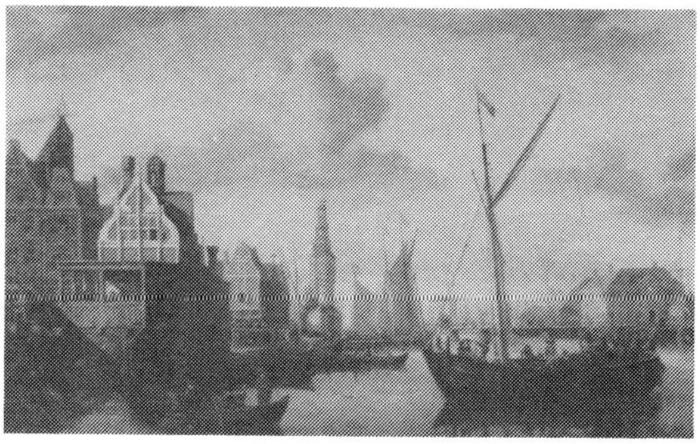

ABRAHAM STORCK – The Port Of Amsterdam – signed – oil – 34 x 48in.
(Woolley & Wallis) **$42,300** **£30,000**

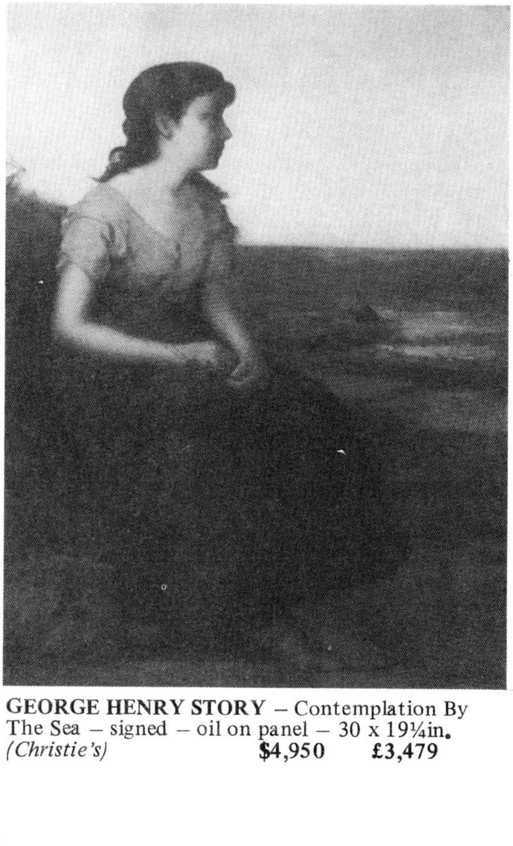

GEORGE HENRY STORY – Contemplation By The Sea – signed – oil on panel – 30 x 19¼in.
(Christie's) **$4,950** **£3,479**

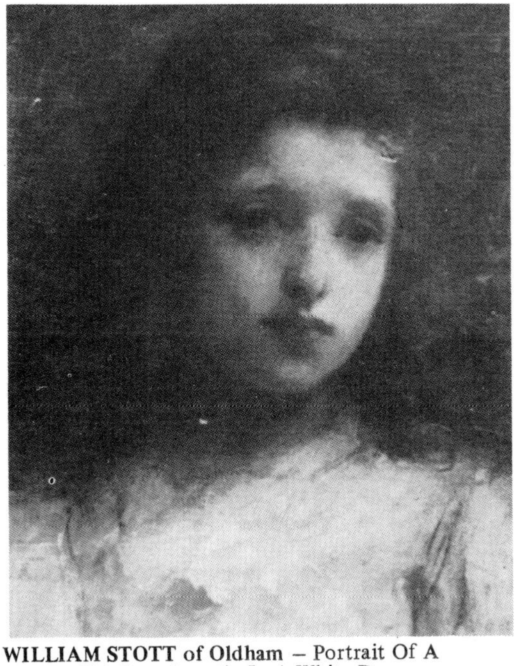

WILLIAM STOTT of Oldham – Portrait Of A Young Girl, Bust Length, In A White Dress – signed – oil on canvas – 17 x 13in.
(Christie's) **$3,460** **£2,420**

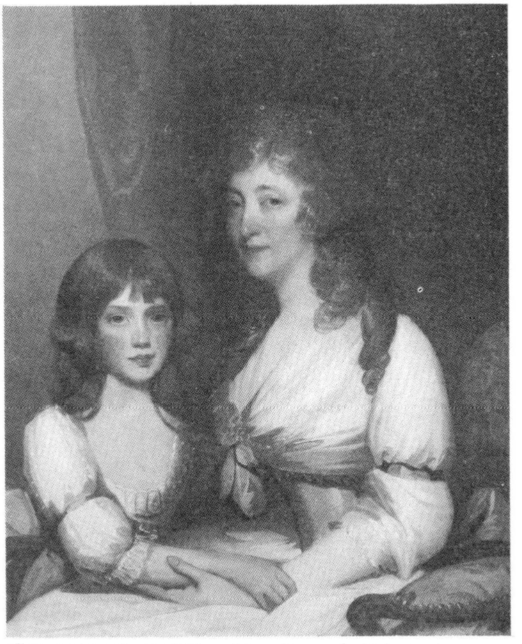

GILBERT STUART – Mrs. Samuel Dick And Daughter Charlotte Anna – oil on canvas – 36 x 29½in.
(Christie's) **$16,500** **£11,599**

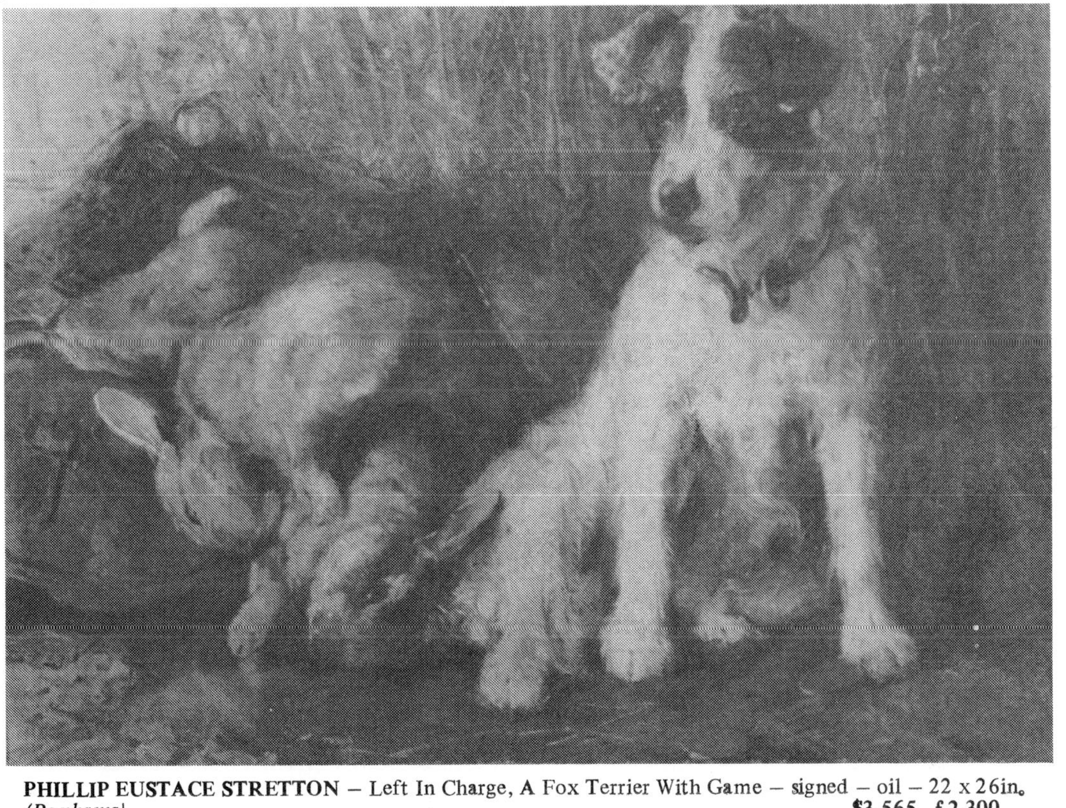

PHILLIP EUSTACE STRETTON – Left In Charge, A Fox Terrier With Game – signed – oil – 22 x 26in.
(Bonhams) **$3,565** **£2,300**

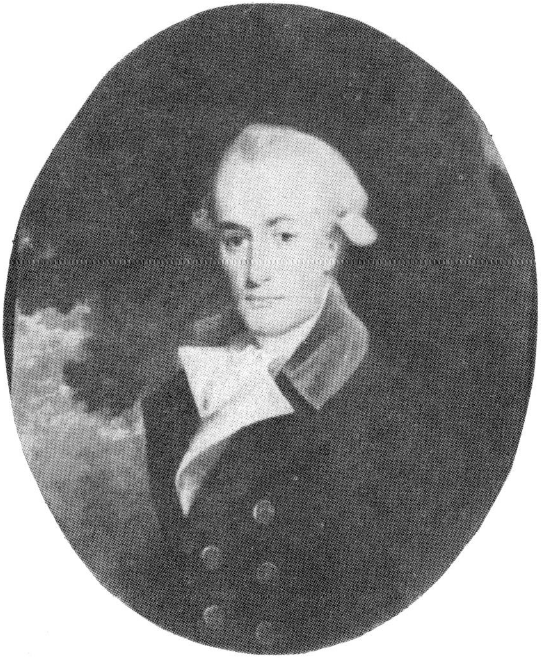

GILBERT STUART, Circle of – Portrait Of A Gentleman, Bust Length, In A Grey Coat, With Red Collar, And White Shirt, In A Landscape – 30 x 25in.
(Christie's) **$1,944** **£1,296**

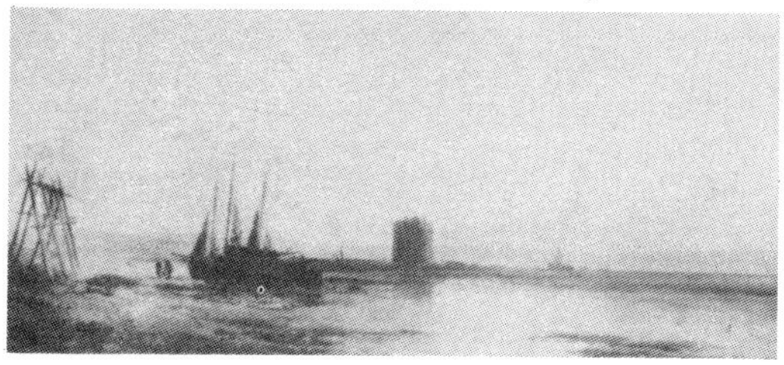

RALPH STUBBS – A Coastal Landscape With Fishing Smacks And A Tower At Low Tide – signed and dated 1861 – oil on canvas – 15½ x 31in.
(Christie's) **$1,147** **£750**

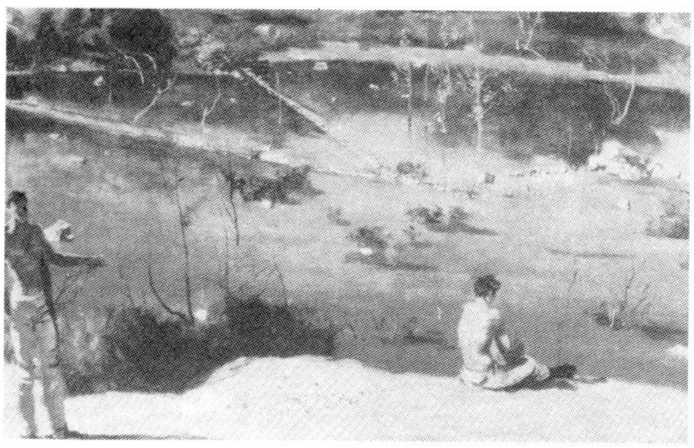

WALTER J. STUEMPFIG – Bathers – signed – oil on canvas – 25 x 35in.
(Christie's) **$5,280** **£3,711**

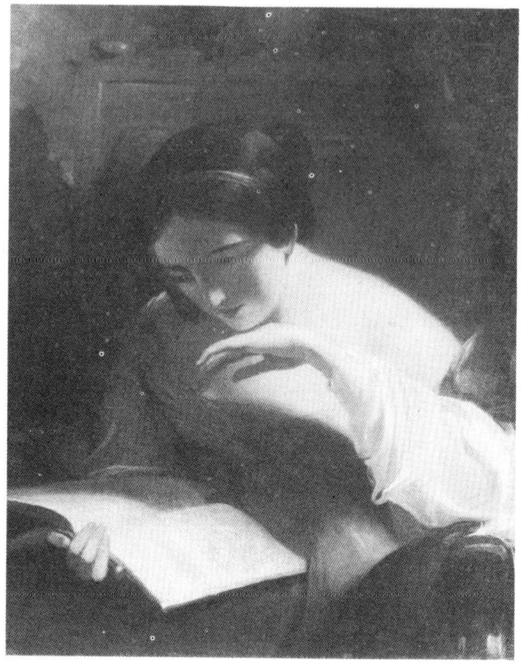

THOMAS SULLY – Portrait Of A Girl Reading – oil on canvas – 29½ x 24½in.
(Christie's) **$28,600** **£20,105**

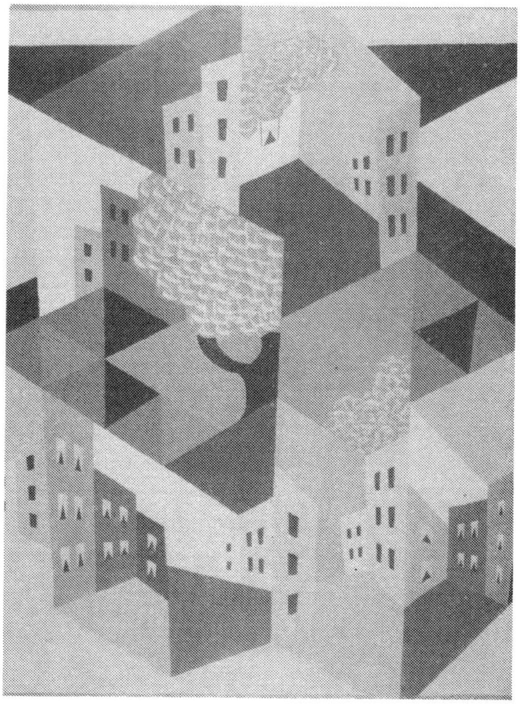

LEOPOLD SURVAGE – La Cite – signed – oil on canvas – 25½ x 20in.
(Christie's) **$34,903** **£20,900**

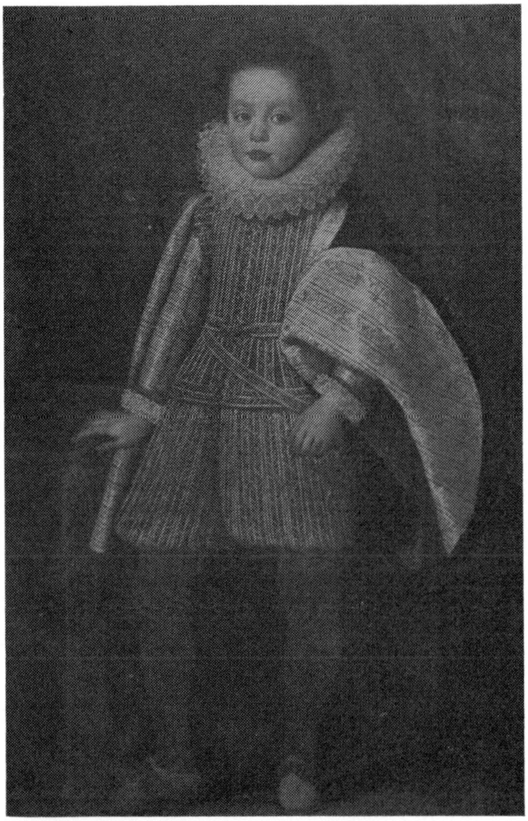

JUSTUS SUSTERMANS – Portrait Of A Young Nobleman – on canvas – 50¼ x 31¼in.
(Phillips) **$23,240** **£14,000**

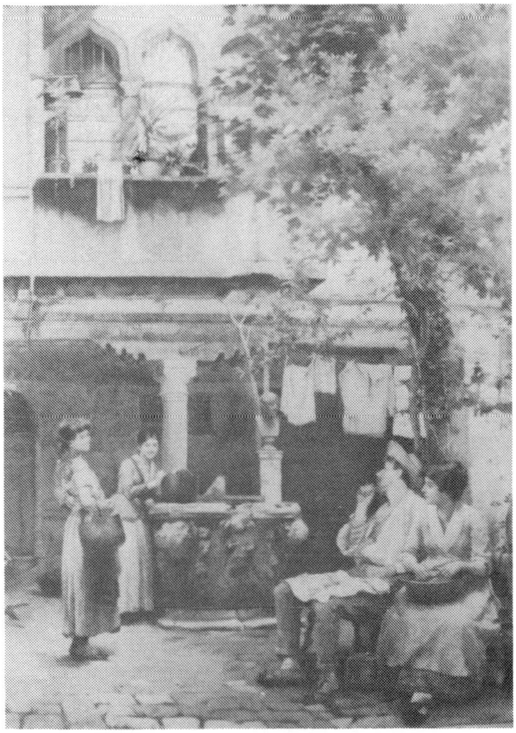

LEGHE SUTHERS – An Italian Courtyard – signed – oil on canvas – 91 x 65cm.
(Phillips) **$4,970** **£3,500**

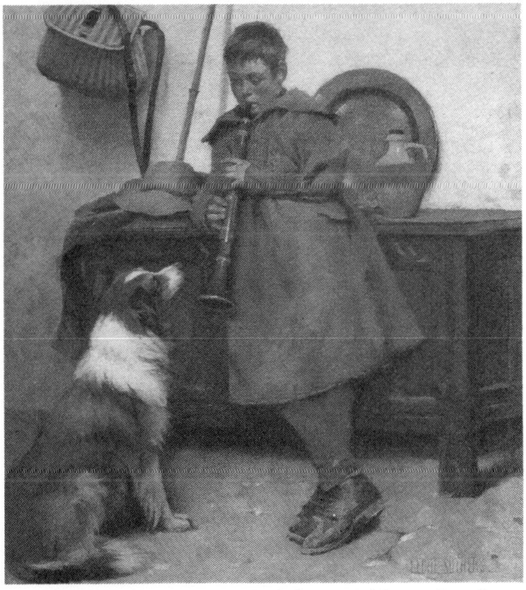

LEGHE SUTHERS – An Indulgent Critic – signed – oil on canvas – 31 x 24¾in.
(Christie's) **$34,606** **£24,200**

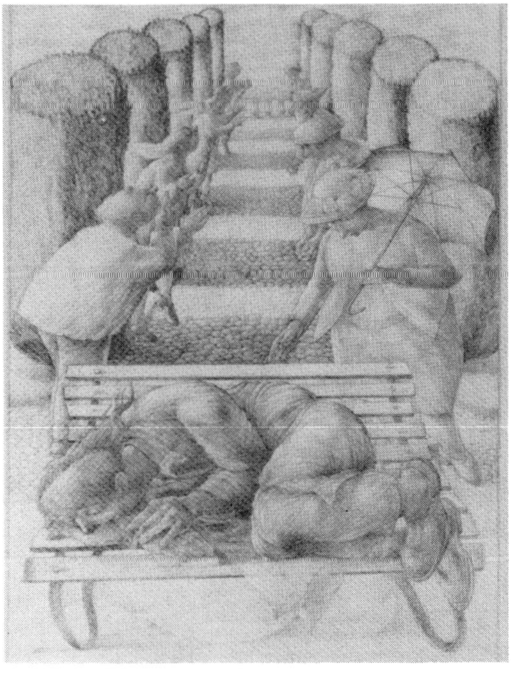

BETTY SWANWICK – The Dream – pencil – 74 x 55cm.
(Phillips) **$918** **£606**

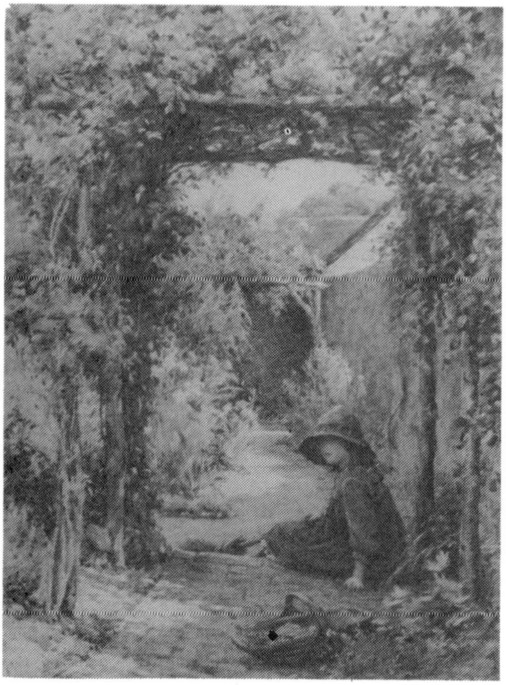

HAROLD SWANWICK – The Little Gardener – signed, also inscribed verso – watercolour – 35 x 26cm.
(Phillips) **$9,128** **£5,600**

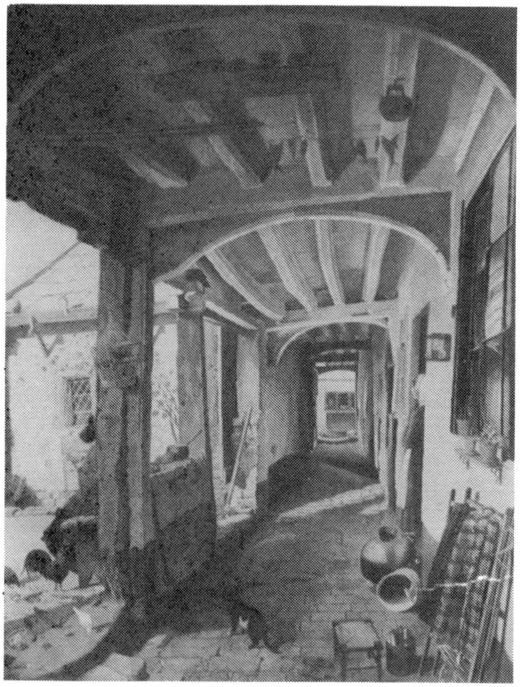

SAMUEL DUNKINFIELD SWARBRECK – In The Yard – signed and dated 1853 – 30½ x 25in.
(Christie's) **$5,890** **£3,850**

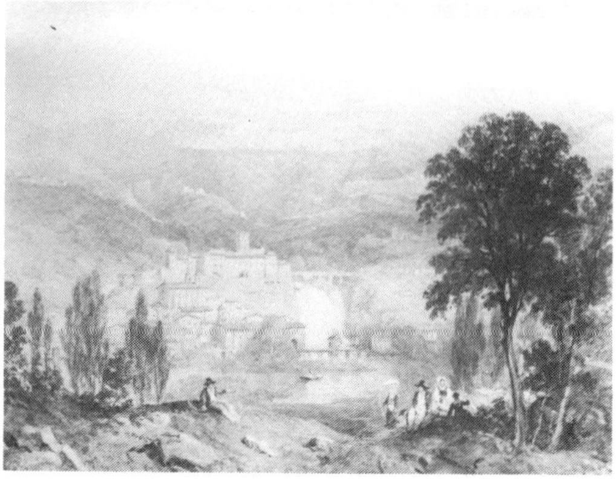

EDWARD SWINBURNE – Isola Farnese, Italy – signed – pencil and watercolour – 13¼ x 17¾in.
(Christie's) **$1,240** **£880**

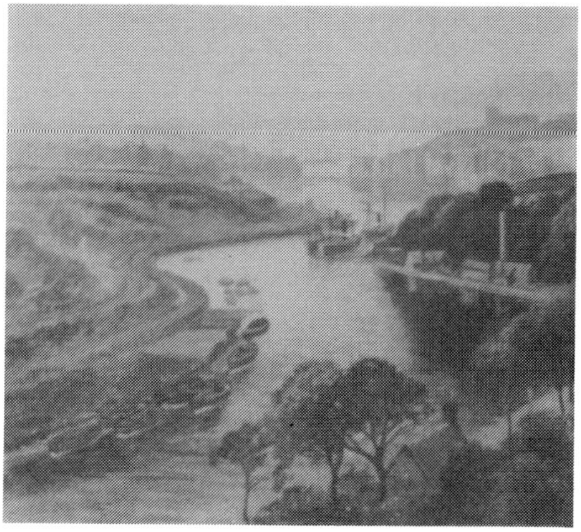

JOHN SYER – Whitby Harbour With The Abbey Ruins In The Distance – signed with indistinct inscription on the reverse – oil on board – 12 x 18in.
(Christie's) **$638** **£440**

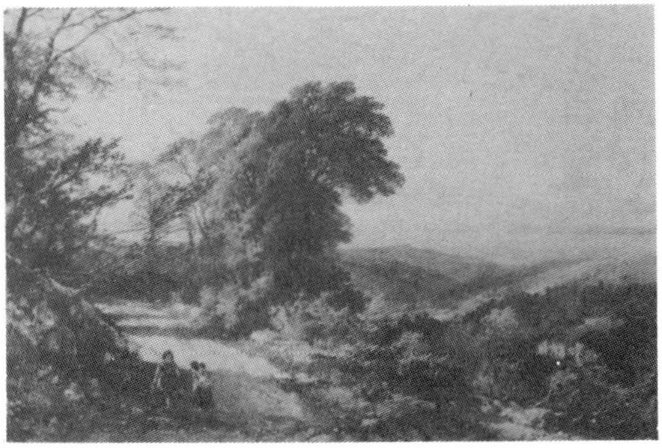

JOHN SYER – A Country Landscape With Figures On A Track Crossing A Stream – signed – 18½ x 29in.
(Christie's) **$1,800** **£1,200**

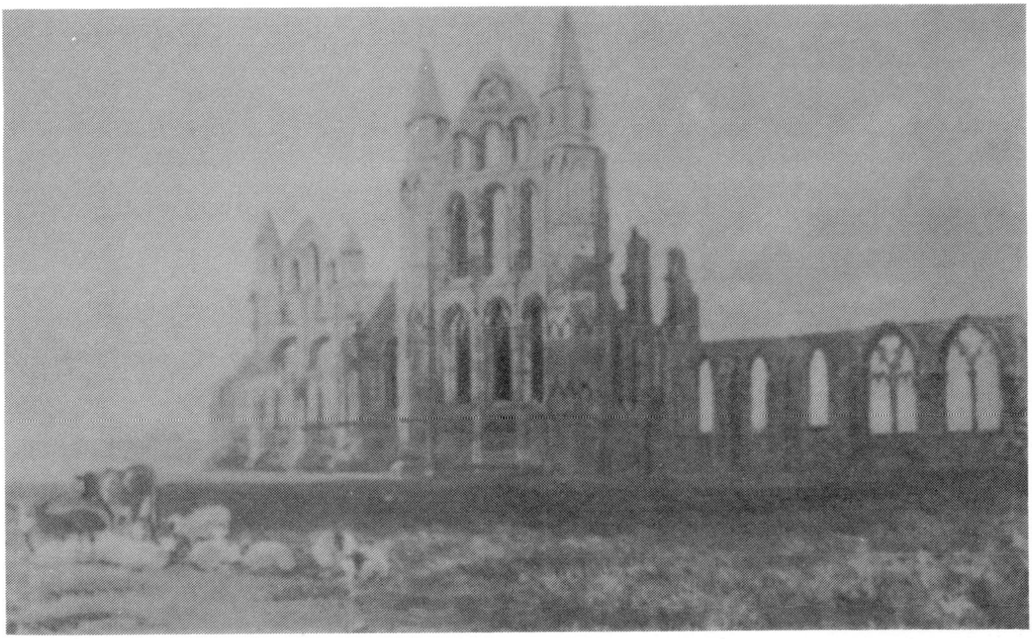

JOHN SYER – Whitby Abbey – signed, inscribed on the reverse – oil on board – 12 x 18in. *(Christie's)*
$478 £330

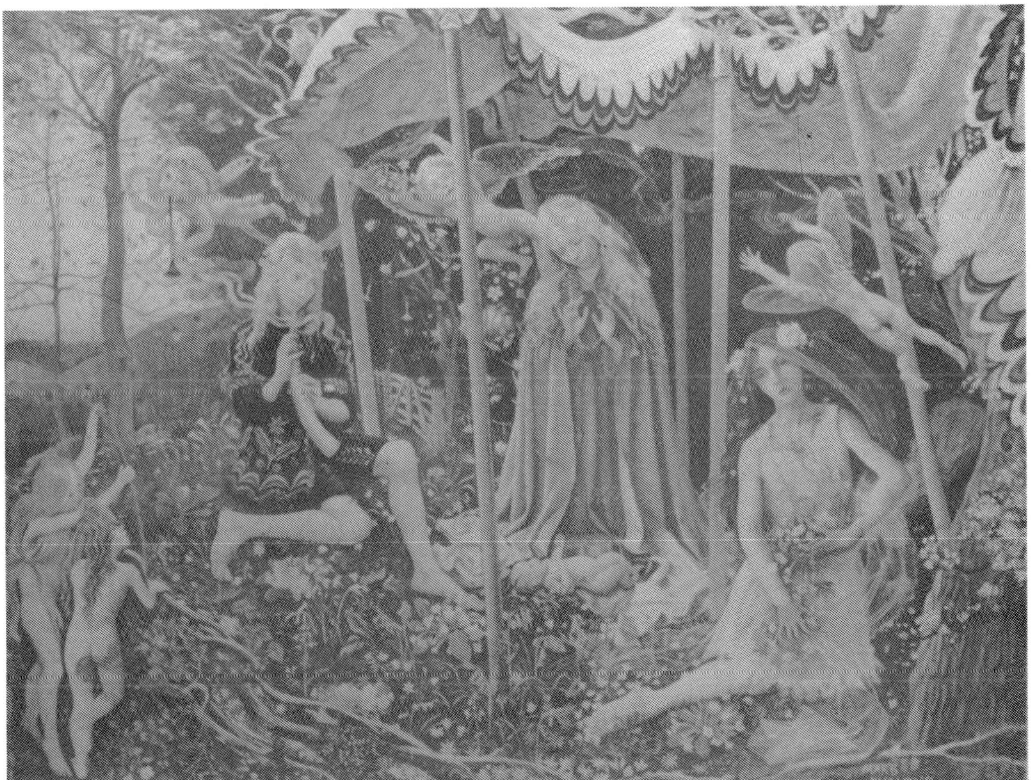

MARK LANCELOT SYMONS – The Nativity – signed – oil on panel – 101 x 127cm. *(Phillips)*
$14,200 £10,000

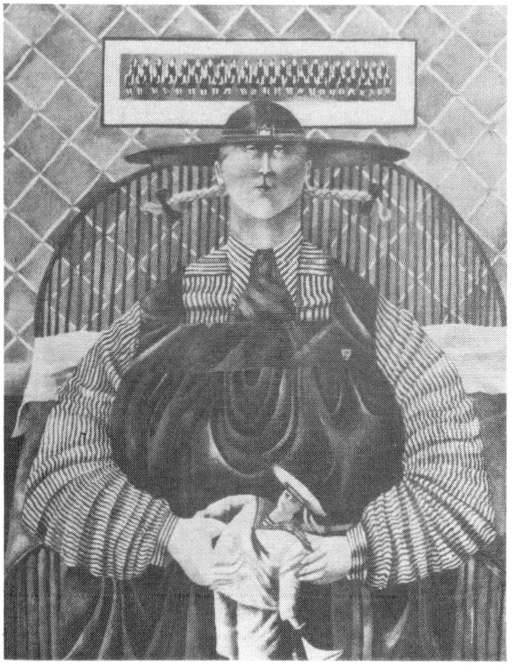

ELIZABETH TAGGART – The Schoolgirl – signed and signed and dated '75 on the reverse – oil on canvas – 45.5 x 35.5cm.
(Phillips) **$459** **£300**

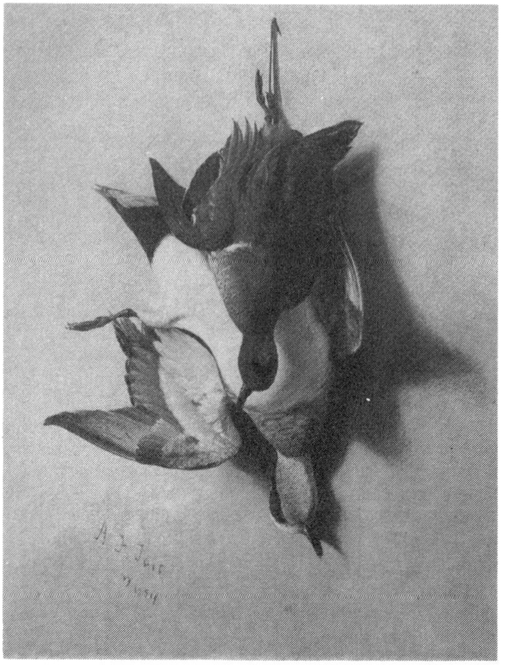

ARTHUR FITZWILLIAM TAIT – Dead Game – signed and dated 1854 – oil on panel – 16½ x 12½in.
(Christie's) **$12,100** **£7,897**

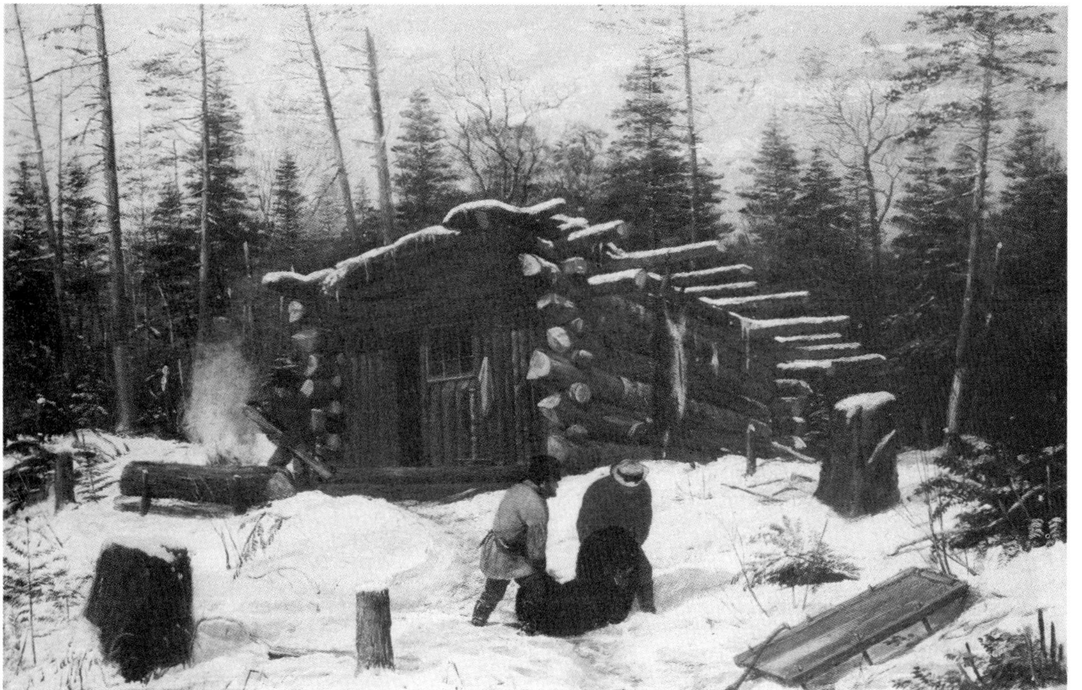

ARTHUR FITZWILLIAM TAIT – Bringing Home Game: Winter Shanty At Ragged Lake – signed and dated 1856 – oil on canvas – 17 x 24in. *(Christie's)* **$220,000 £154,660**

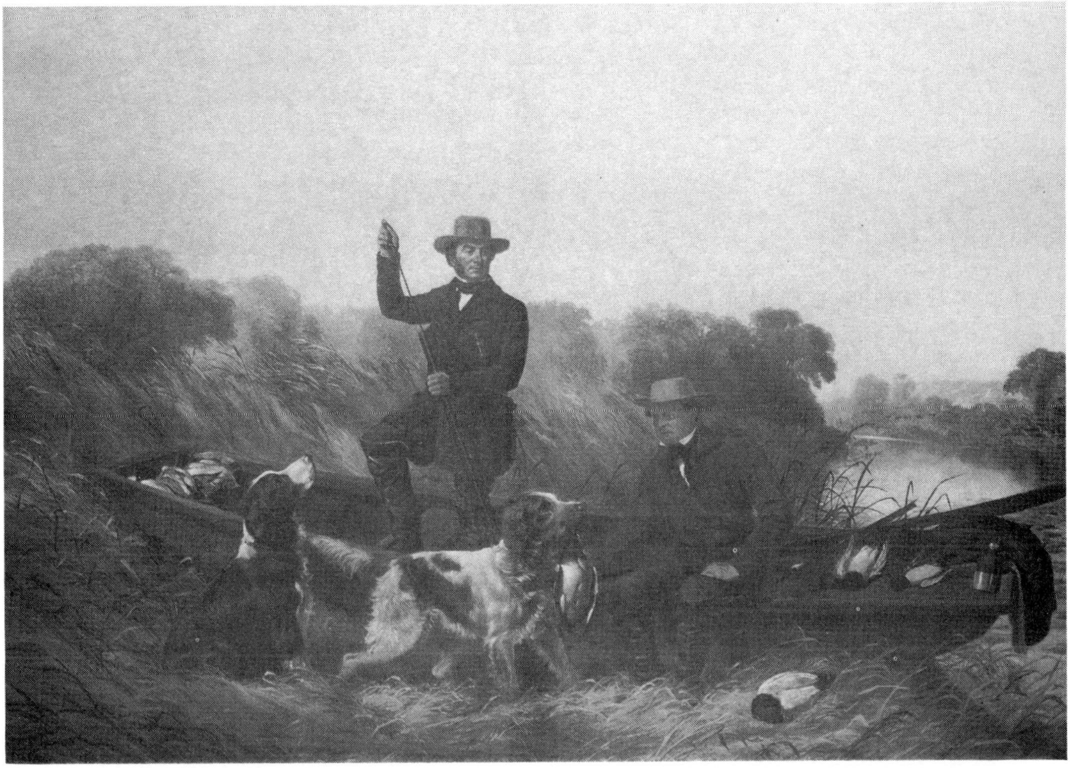

ARTHUR FITZWILLIAM TAIT – Duck Shooting – oil on canvas – 38 x 50in. *(Christie's)*
\$418,000 £272,828

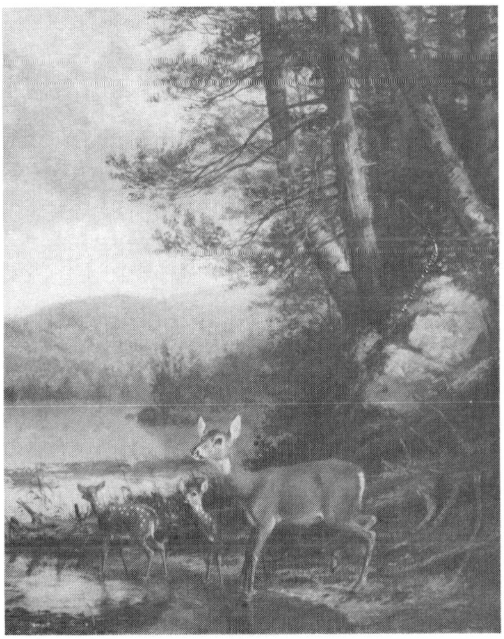

ARTHUR FITZWILLIAM TAIT – Doe And Two Fawns – signed and dated '72, also signed and dated on the reverse – oil on panel – 20 x 15½in.
(Christie's) **\$18,700 £12,205**

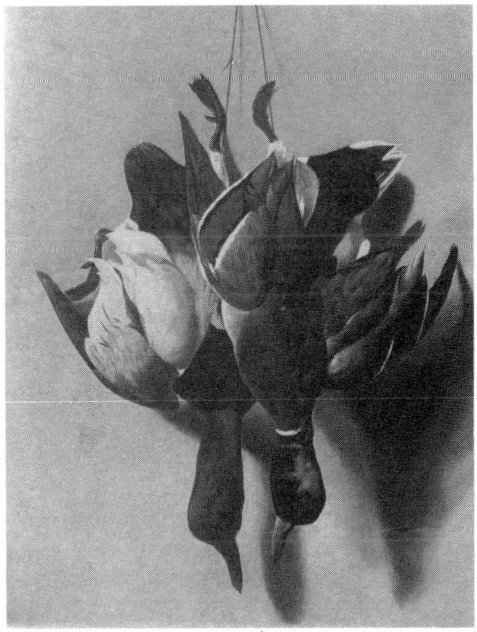

ARTHUR FITZWILLIAM TAIT – Ducks, Mallard And Canvasback – signed and dated 1854 – oil on panel – 16½ x 12½in.
(Christie's) **\$13,200 £8,615**

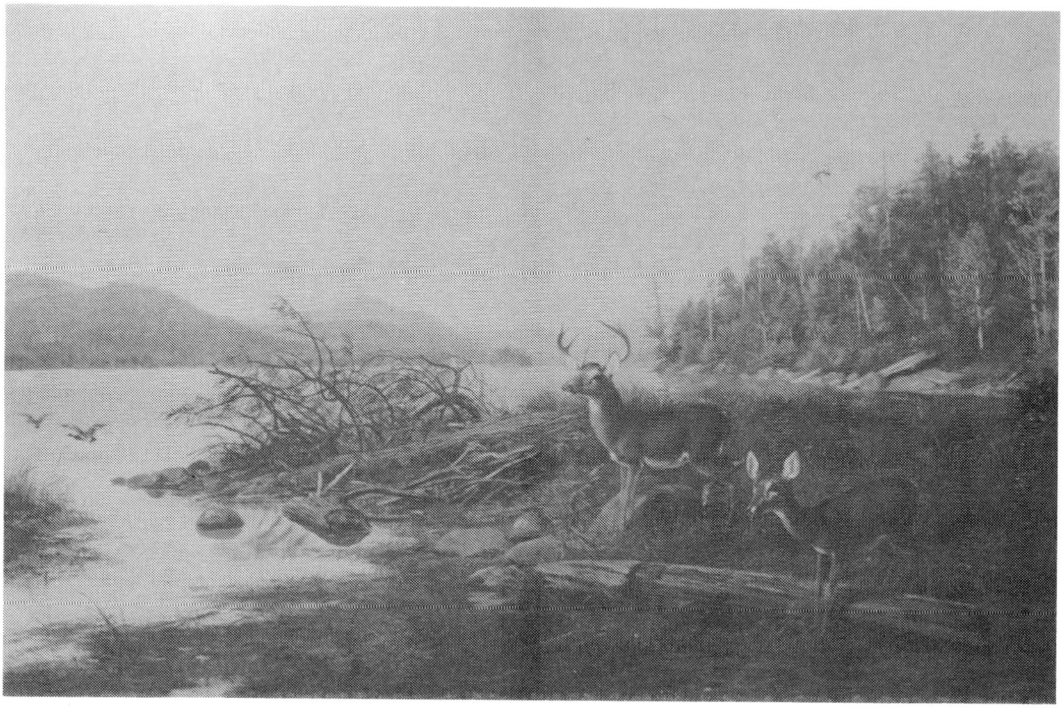

ARTHUR FITZWILLIAM TAIT – View On Long Lake – signed and dated 1881 – oil on canvas – 20 x 30in.
(Christie's) **$26,400 £17,231**

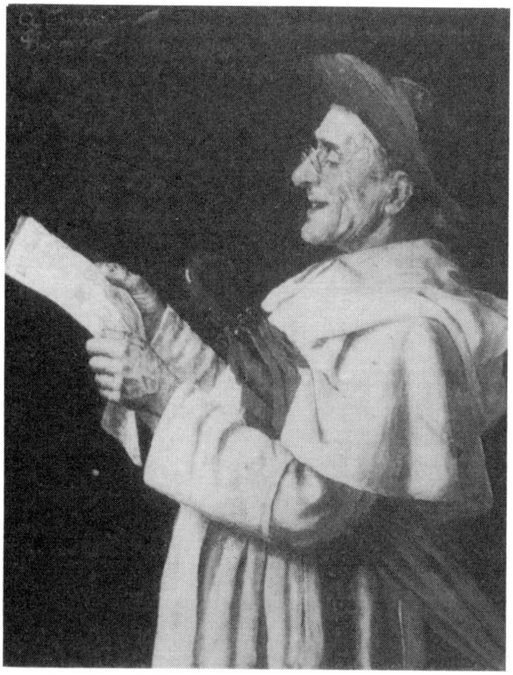

ARNALDO TAMBURINI – An Amusing Read – signed and inscribed – 12¼ x 10in.
(Christie's) **$2,173** **£1,430**

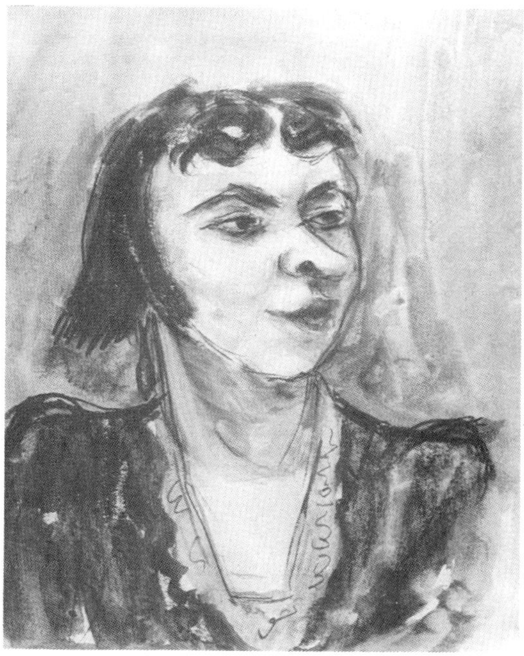

GEORG TAPPERT – Frauenkopf – watercolour and charcoal on paper – 17¼ x 14in.
(Christie's) **$3,009** **£2,090**

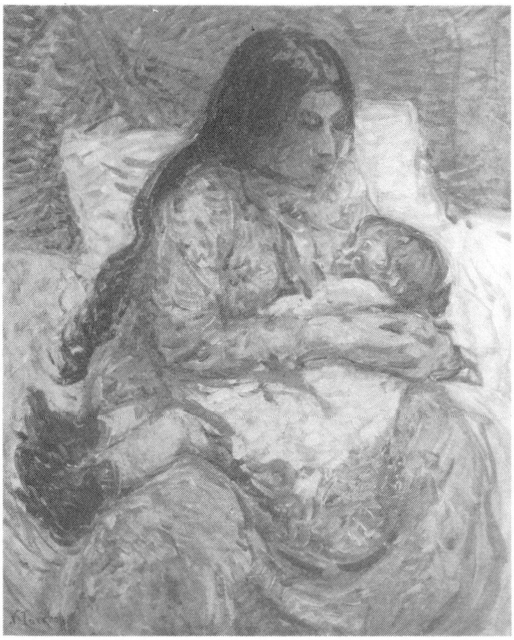

NICOLAI TARKOFF – Maternite – signed – oil on canvas – 25½ x 17¾in.
(Christie's) **$12,320** **£7,700**

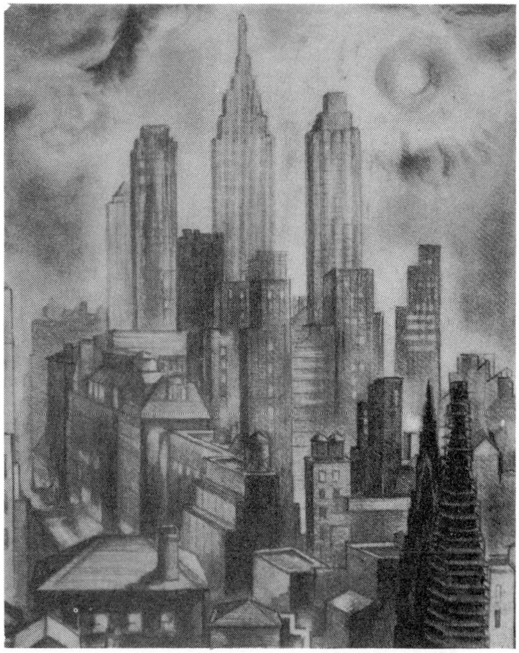

FREDERICK TAUBES – Lower Manhattan Skyline – pencil on paper – 13 x 10½in.
(Christie's) **$495** **£308**

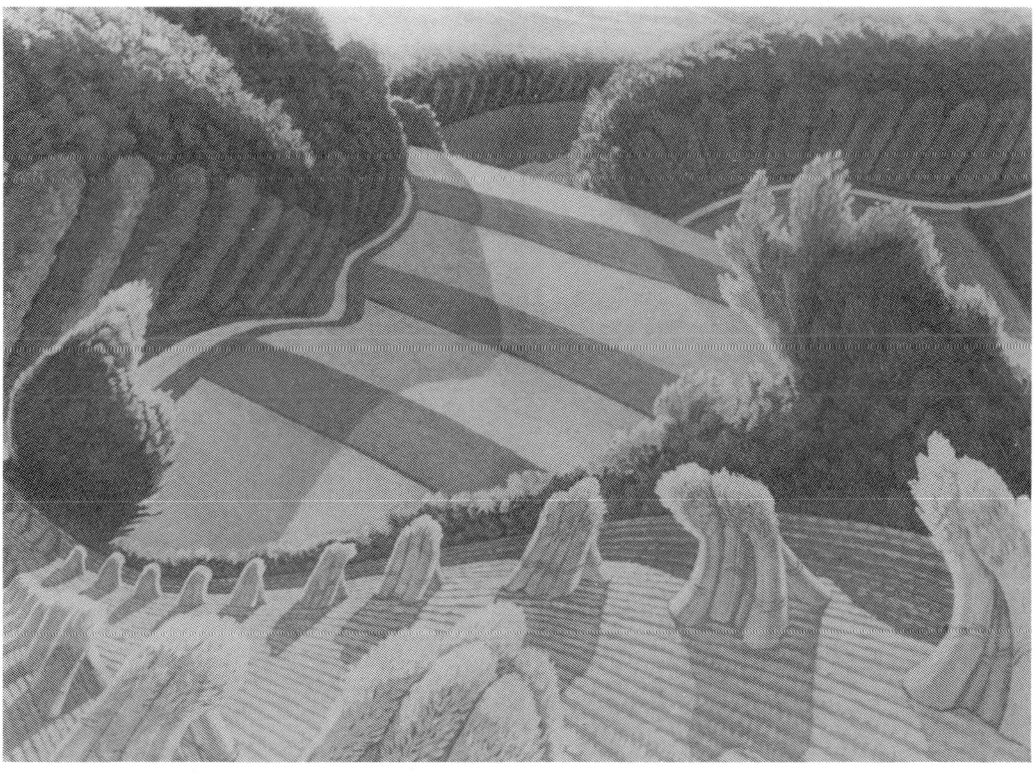

JAMES C. TARR – Corn In Buckinghamshire – signed and inscribed on a label on the backboard – oil on board – 63 x 76cm. *(Phillips)* **$1,992** **£1,200**

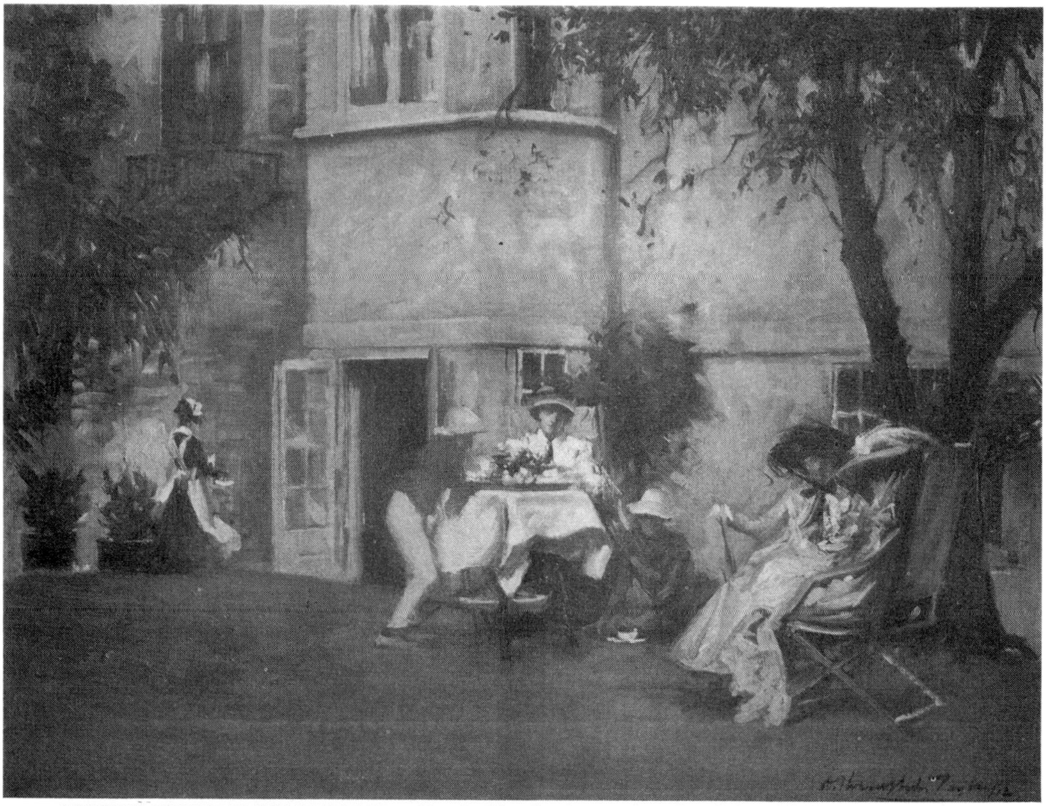

ALBERT CHEVALLIER TAYLER – Tea In The Garden – signed and dated '18 – oil on canvas – 15½ x 19¾in. *(Christie's)* **$34,540 £22,000**

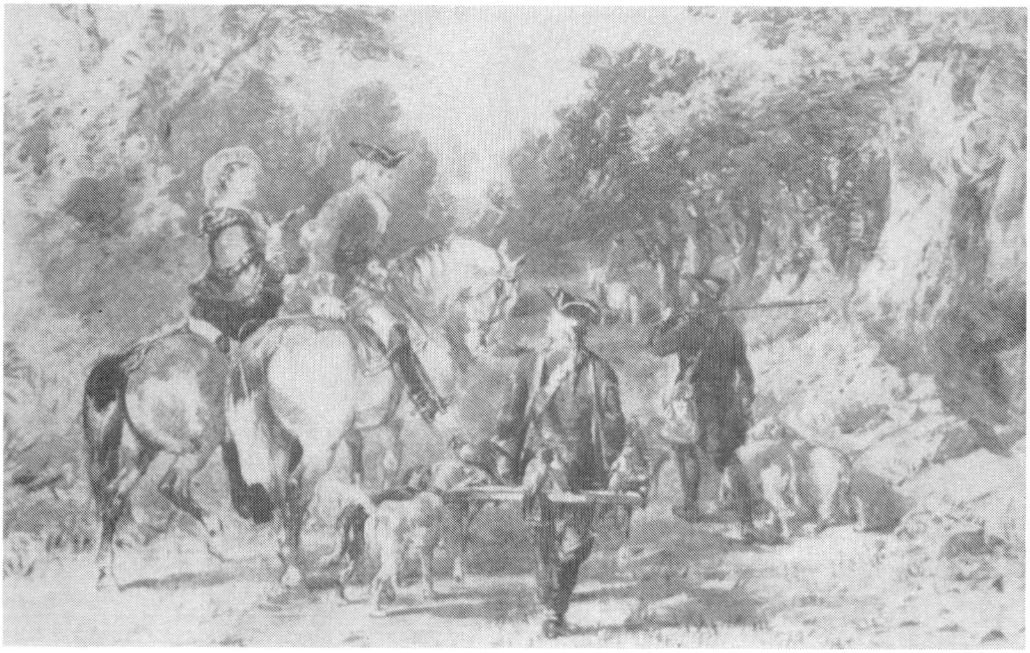

JOHN FREDERICK TAYLER – A Hawking Party Setting Out – signed and dated 1850 – pencil and watercolour heightened with white – 11¼ x 15¼in. *(Christie's)* **$1,460 £880**

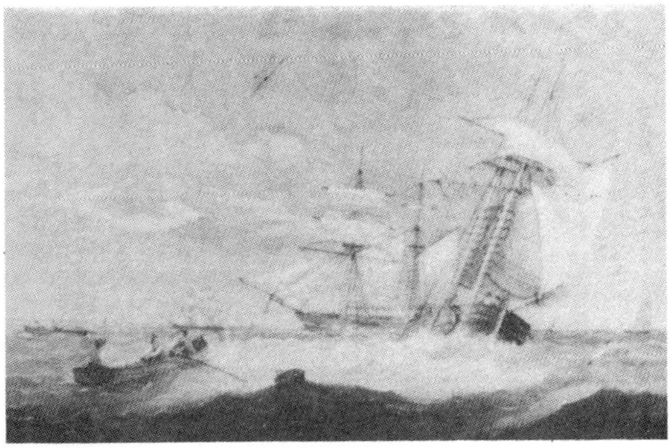

CHARLES TAYLOR, Jnr. – Harbour Passage – signed and dated 1863 – watercolour on paper – 13 x 20in.
(Robt. W. Skinner Inc.) **$500** **£347**

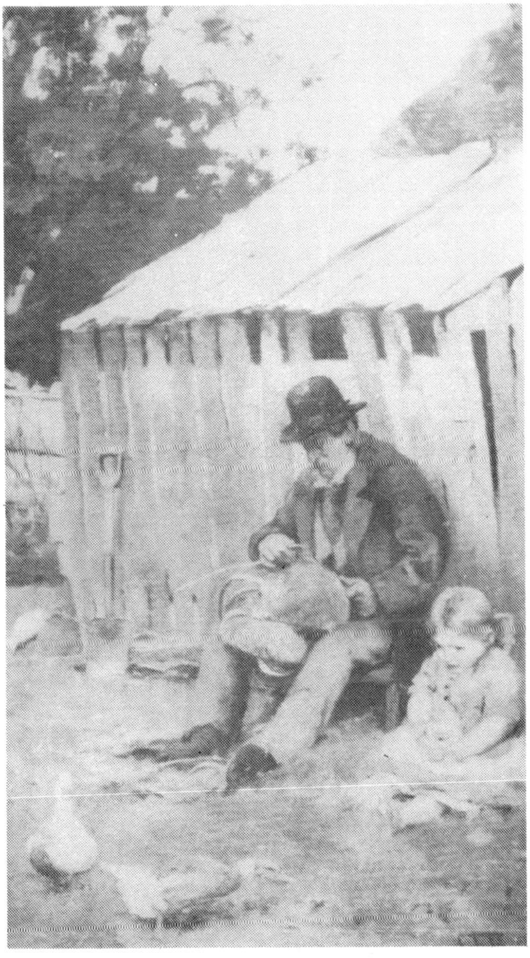

JAMES FRASER TAYLOR – Basket-Making, A Man And Young Girl Seated Before A Shed With Geese – signed and dated 1880 – oil on canvas – 60 x 70cm.
(W. H. Lane & Son) **$2,490** **£1,500**

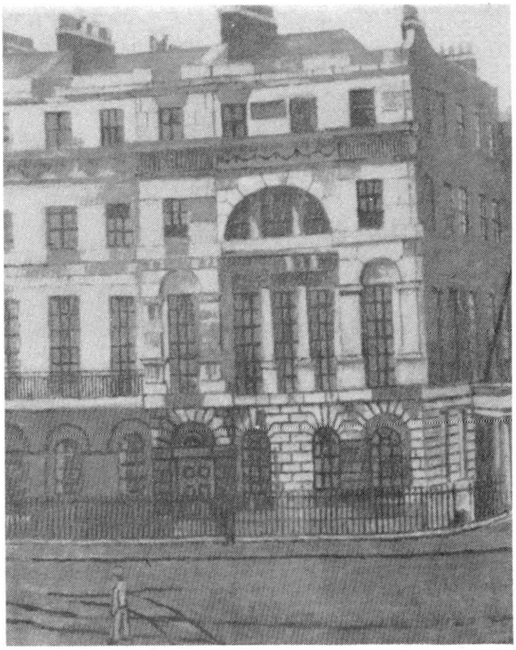

WALTER TAYLOR – A London Street Corner, Possibly Fitzroy Square – oil on canvas – 26¾ x 21¾in.
(Christie's) **$1,022** **£715**

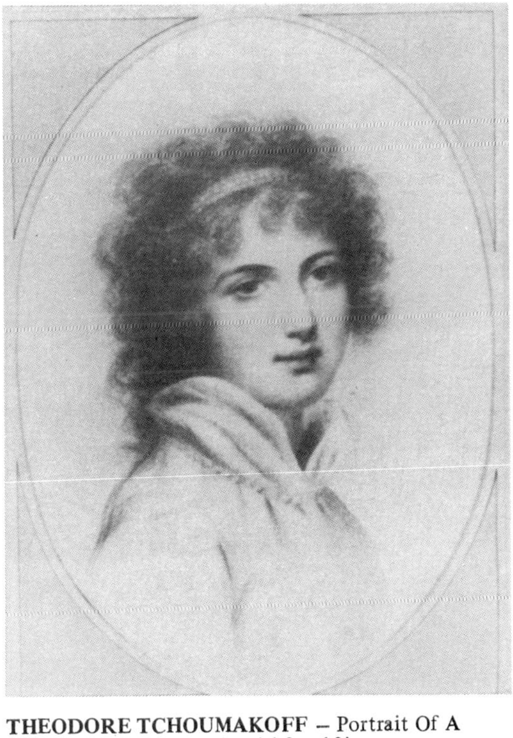

THEODORE TCHOUMAKOFF – Portrait Of A Lady – signed – pastel – 14.2 x 10in.
(Woolley & Wallis) **$296** **£210**

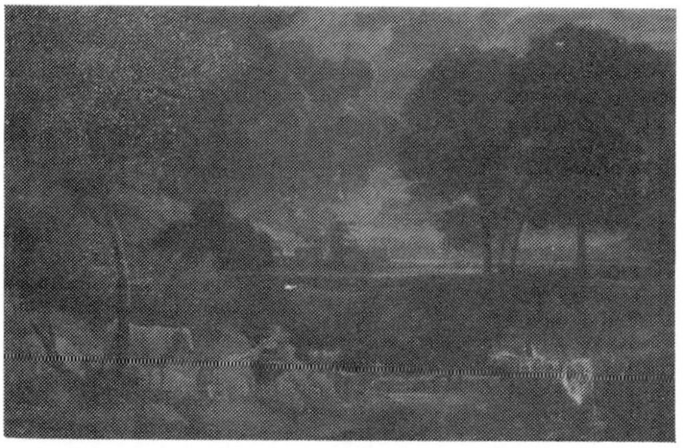

CAVALIERE PIETRO TEMPESTA, Called Pieter Mulier The Younger – A Pastoral Landscape – on canvas – 29½ x 43in.
(Phillips) **$7,470** **£4,500**

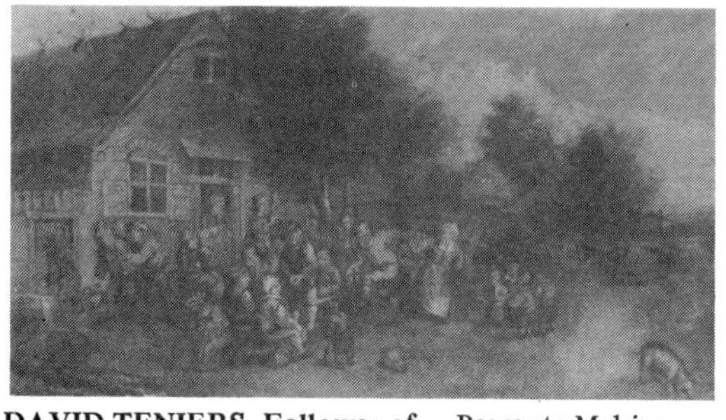

DAVID TENIERS, Follower of – Peasants Making Merry Outside A House – oil on copper – 9 x 12in.
(Biddle & Webb) **$1,086** **£715**

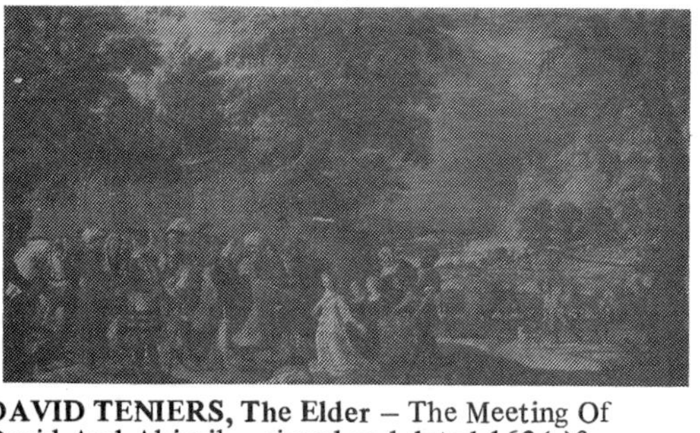

DAVID TENIERS, The Elder – The Meeting Of David And Abigail – signed and dated 162(a)?, and inscribed – on panel – 21¾ x 33½in.
(Phillips) **$36,520** **£22,000**

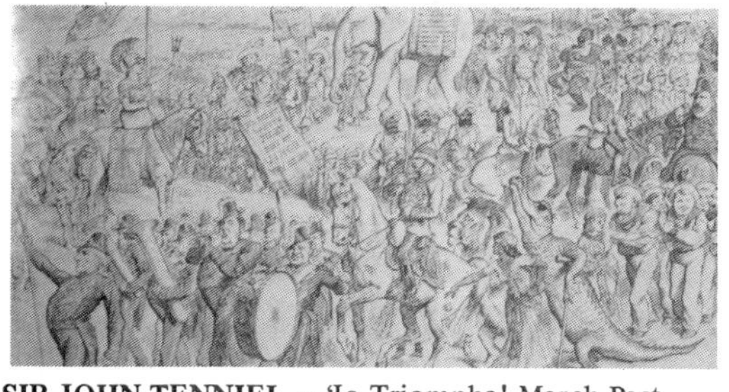

SIR JOHN TENNIEL – 'Io Triomphe! March Past Of The Old Year' – signed with monogram and dated 1883 – pen and grey ink – 10¾ x 19in.
(Christie's) **$542** **£385**

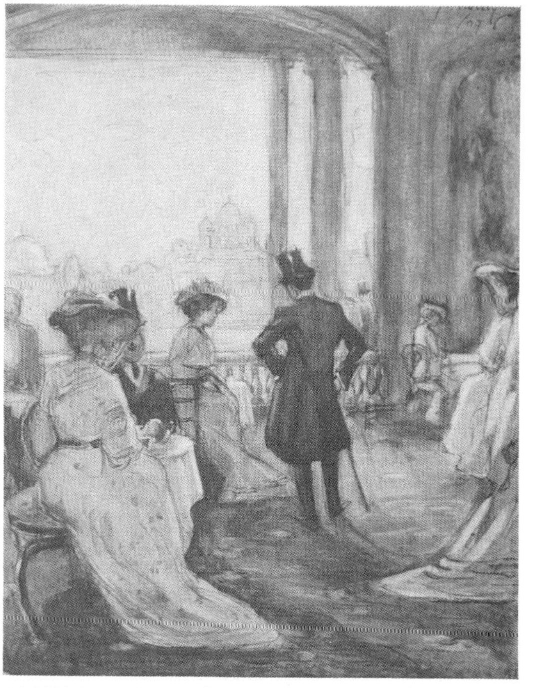

JOSEPH ALFRED TERRY – Figures Taking Tea In An Interior – signed and dated '09 – watercolour and bodycolour heightened with white – 11 x 8½in.
(Christie's) **$255** **£170**

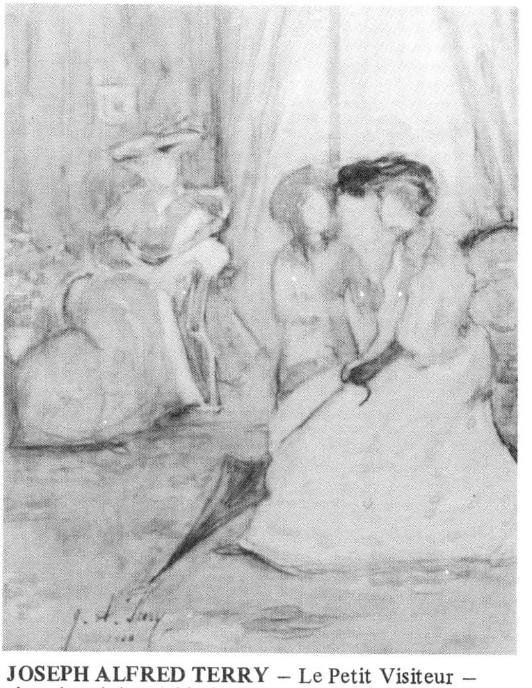

JOSEPH ALFRED TERRY – Le Petit Visiteur – signed and dated 1908 – watercolour, pencil and bodycolour. heightened with white – 11 x 8½in.
(Christie's) **$1,125** **£750**

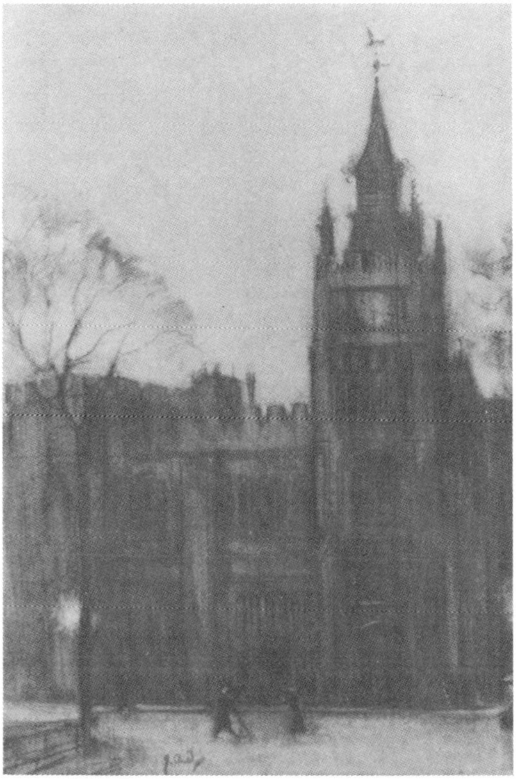

JOSEPH ALFRED TERRY – The Inner Temple – signed with initials – pencil, charcoal and water-colour, heightened with white – 20¾ x 14¼in.
(Christie's) **$195** **£130**

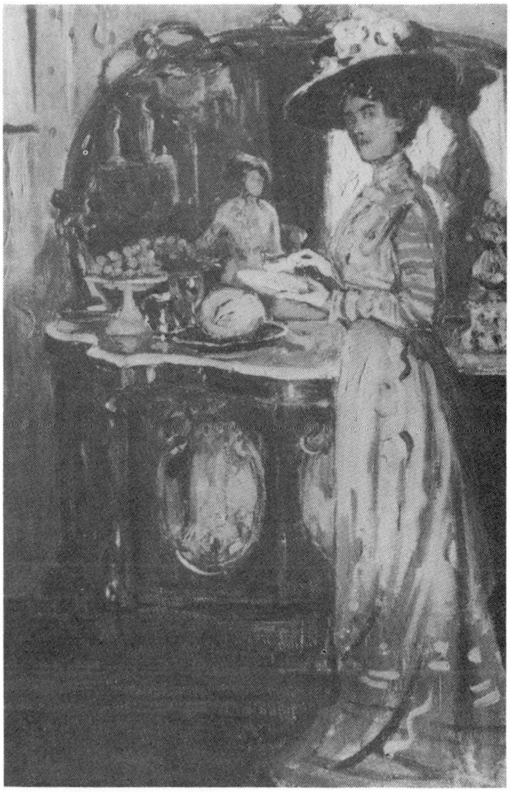

JOSEPH ALFRED TERRY – A Young Lady Taking A Slice Of Melon – signed – oil on canvas – 20 x 13in.
(Christie's) **$2,250** **£1,500**

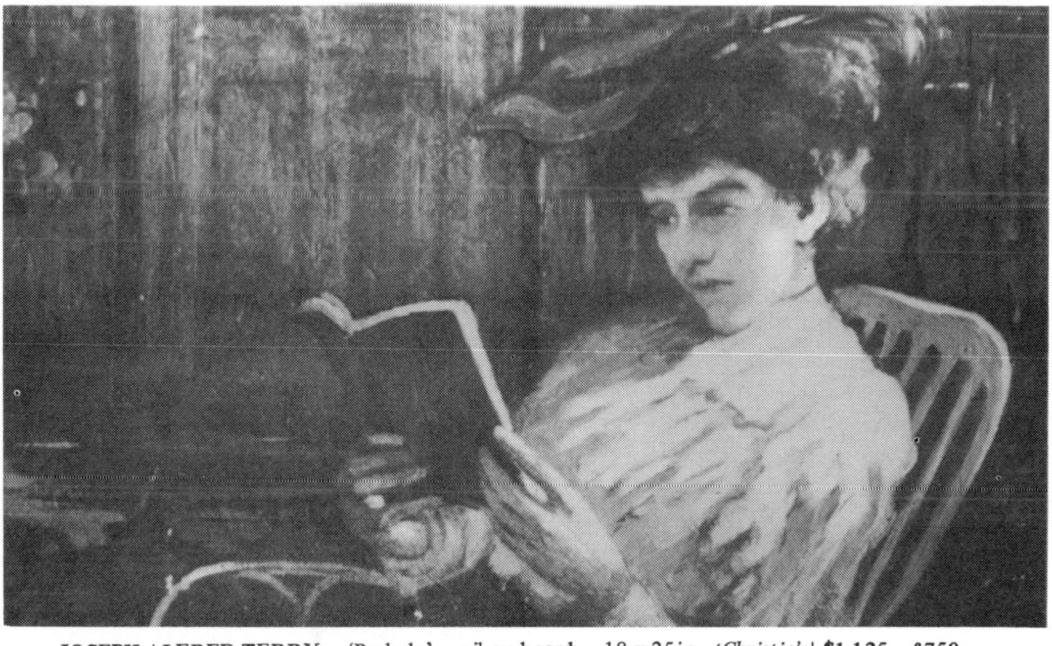

JOSEPH ALFRED TERRY – 'Prelude' – oil on board – 18 x 25in. *(Christie's)* **$1,125** **£750**

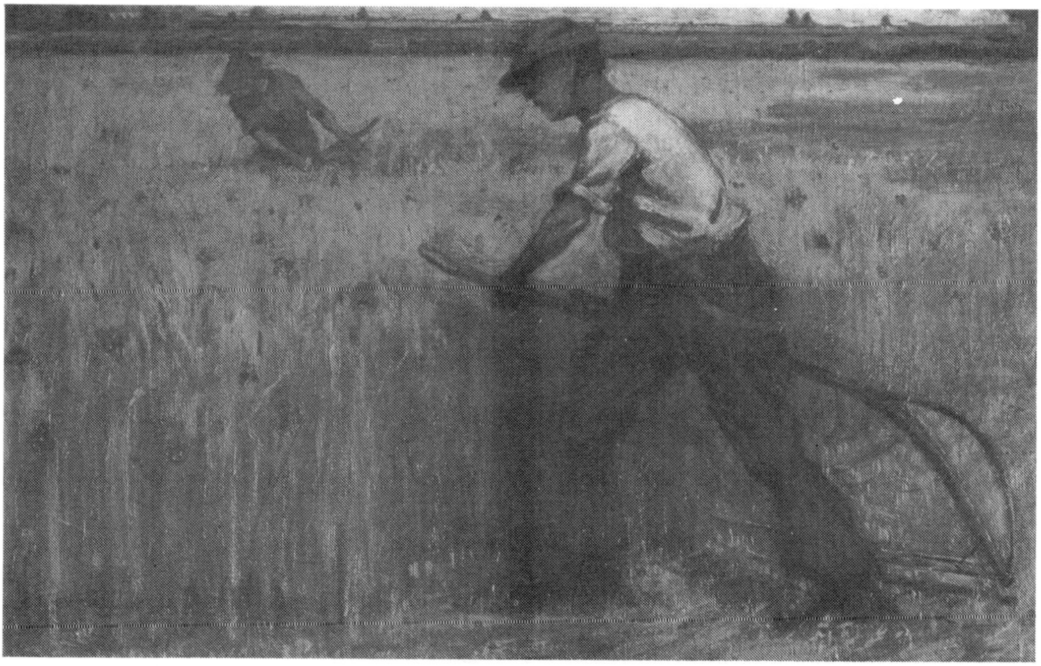

JOSEPH ALFRED TERRY – The Mower – signed, signed and inscribed on a label on the reverse – oil on canvas – 26½ x 36½in. *(Christie's)* **$13,500 £9,000**

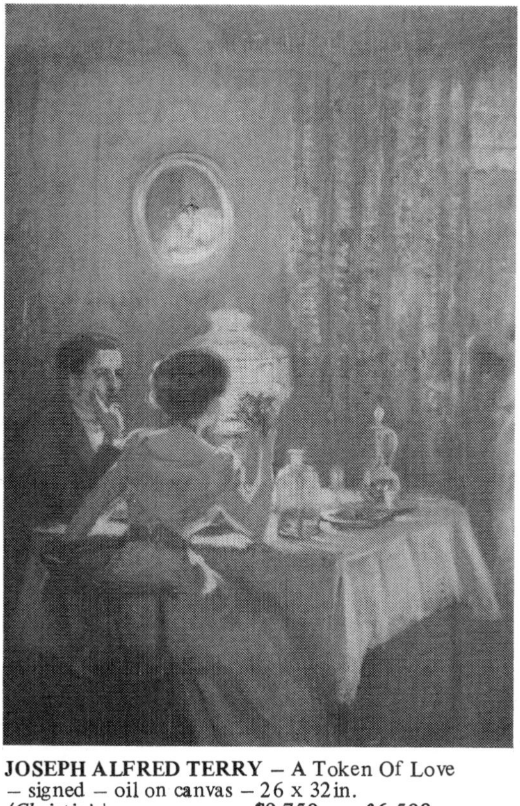

JOSEPH ALFRED TERRY – A Token Of Love – signed – oil on canvas – 26 x 32in.
(Christie's) **$9,750 £6,500**

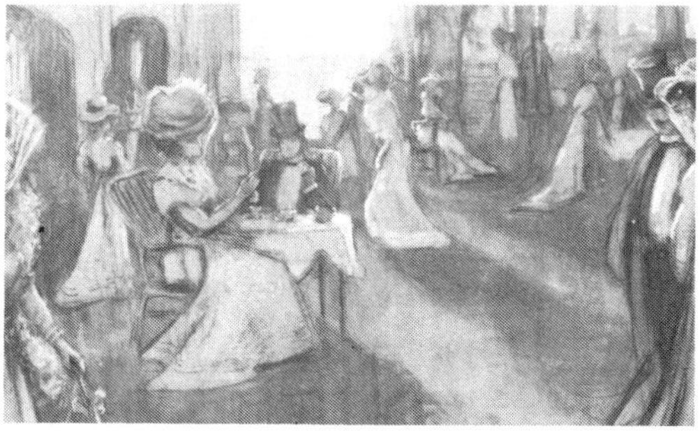

JOSEPH ALFRED TERRY – 'The En Plein Air', With Figures In Conversation – signed – watercolour, pencil and bodycolour heightened with white – 12½ x 15½in.
(Christie's) **$2,700 £1,800**

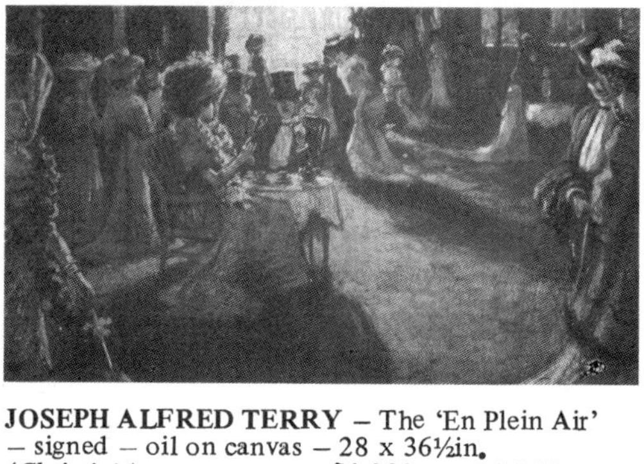

JOSEPH ALFRED TERRY – The 'En Plein Air' – signed – oil on canvas – 28 x 36½in.
(Christie's) **$4,800 £3,200**

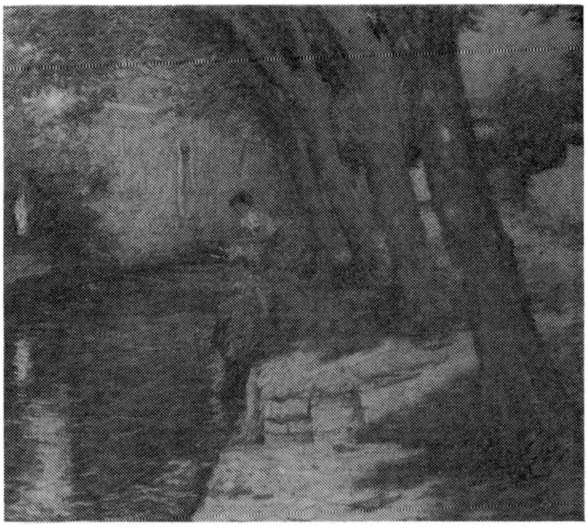

HENRY HERBERT LA THANGUE – A Provencal Road – signed – oil on canvas – 65 x 75cm.
(Phillips) **$38,400** **£24,000**

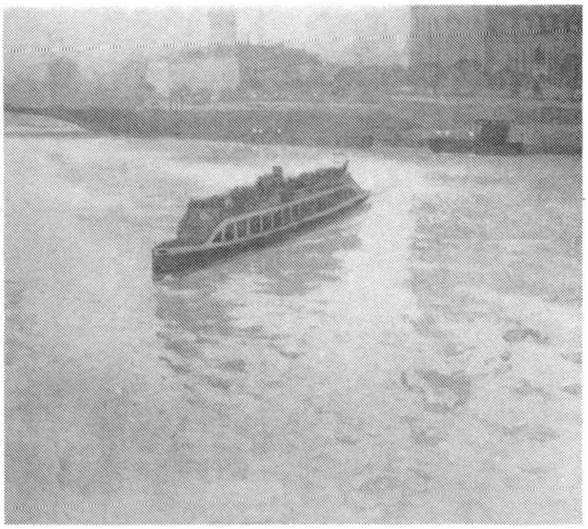

FRITZ THAULOW – A View Of Paris From The River Seine – signed and dated 1893 – 29 x 45½in.
(Christie's) **$22,880** **£14,300**

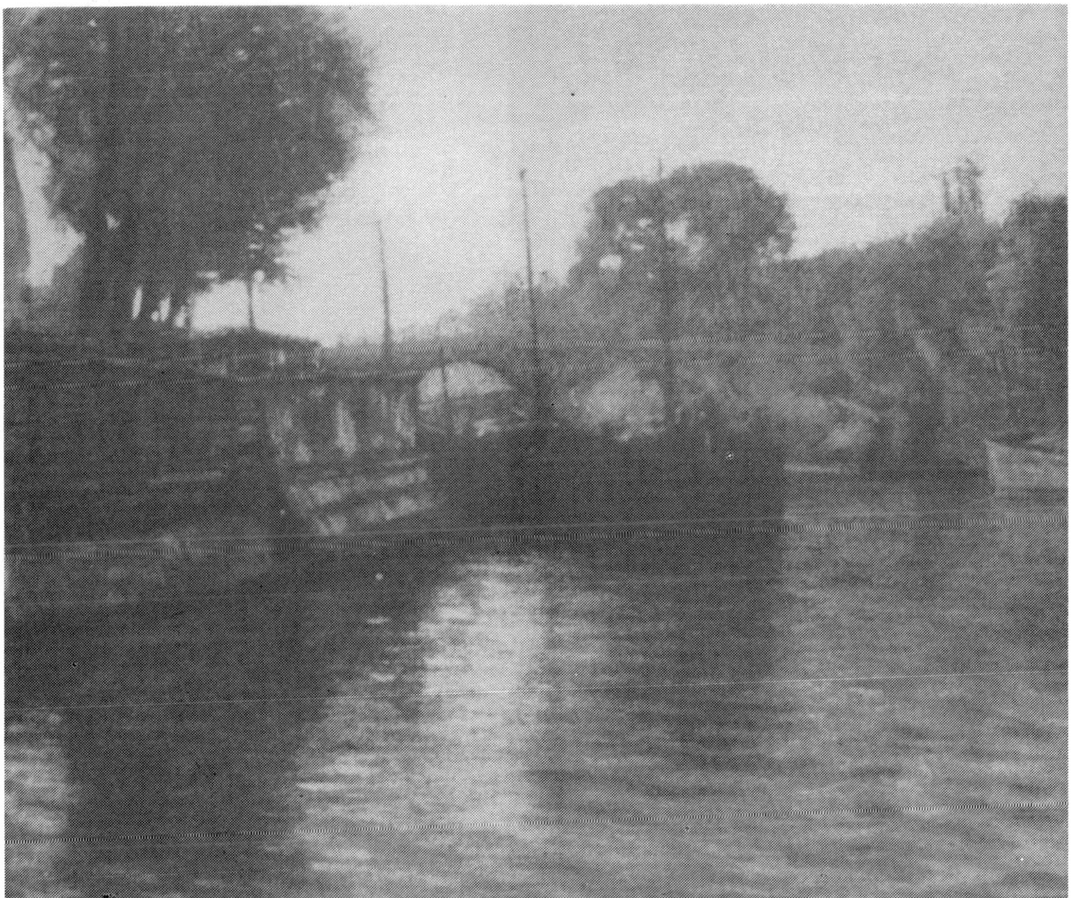

FRITZ THAULOW – La Seine – signed – pastel on canvas – 38 x 46cm. *(Phillips)* **$7,750** **£5,000**

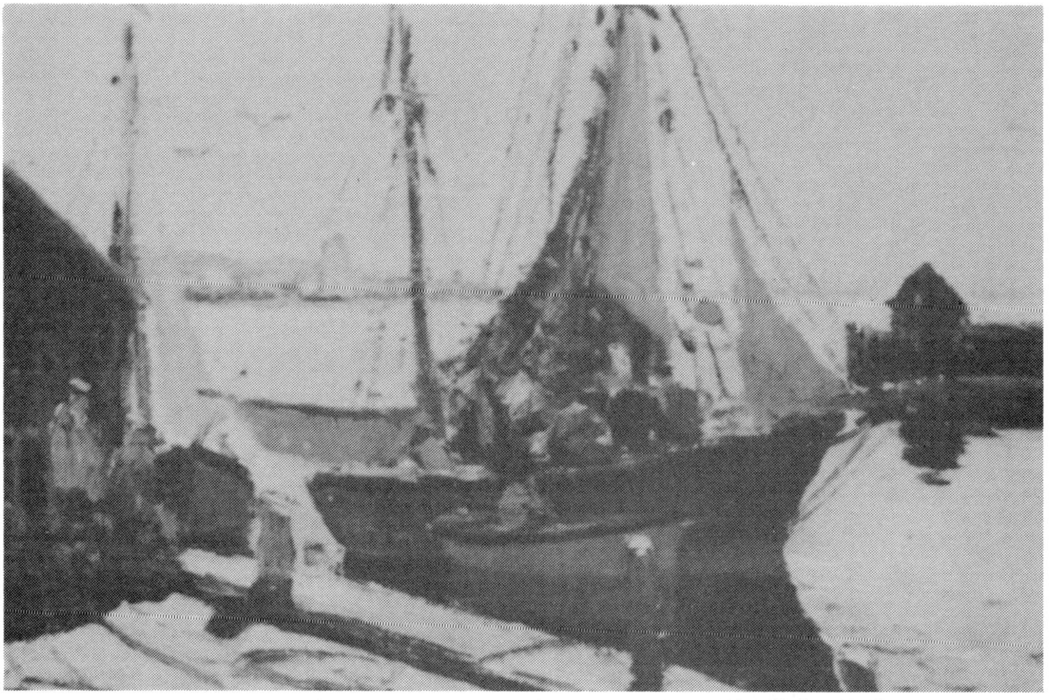

ANTHONY THIEME – Morning Light – signed – oil on board – 12 x 16in. *(Robt. W. Skinner Inc.)* **$1,600 £981**

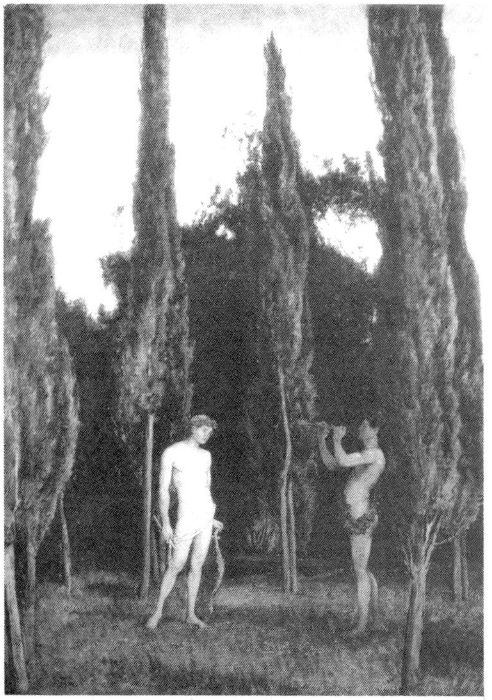

HANS THOMA – Apollo And Marsyas – signed with monogram and dated 1888 – on board – 38¾ x 28¼in.
(Christie's) **$39,600 £27,500**

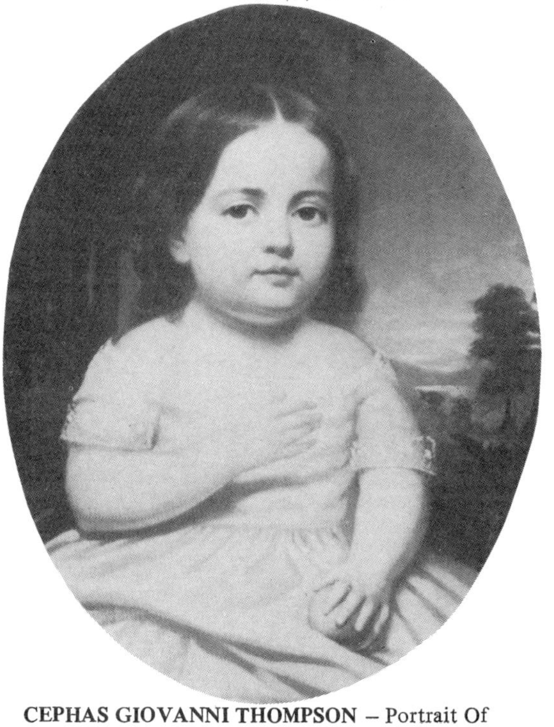

CEPHAS GIOVANNI THOMPSON – Portrait Of A Girl With A Ball – signed with monogrammed initials and dated 1850 – oil on canvas – 22½ x 18¼in.
(Christie's) **$2,200 £1,530**

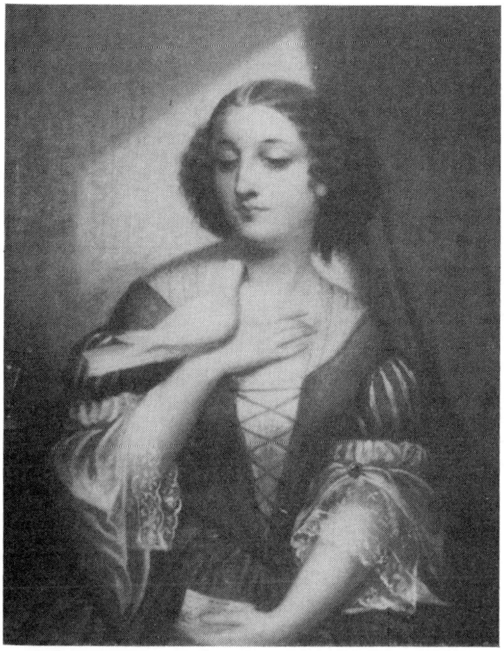

CEPHUS GIOVANNI THOMPSON – Pet Dove – signed with monogrammed initials and dated 1862 – oil on canvas – 12¼ x 10¼in.
(Christie's) **$1,100** **£685**

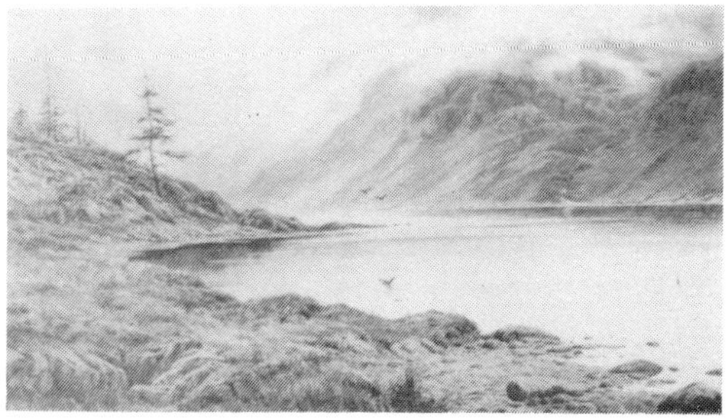

EDWARD H. THOMPSON – 'Wreathing Mists', The Head Of Buttermere And High Style – signed and dated 1924 – oil – 14 x 20in.
(Capes, Dunn & Co.) **$652** **£400**

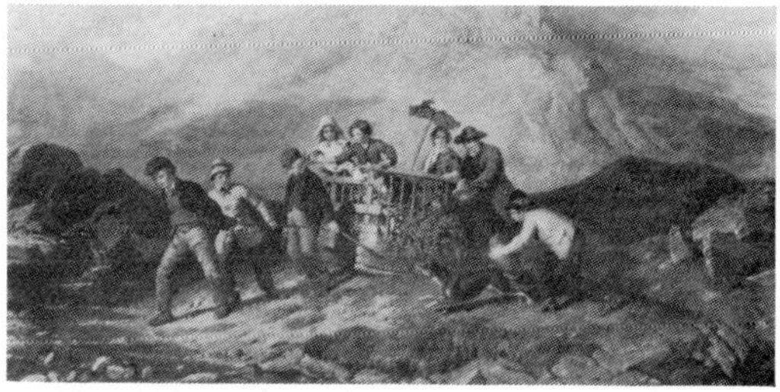

JACOB THOMPSON – The Height Of Ambition, A Scene In The Mardale Mountains – signed and dated 1864 – 25¼ x 38¾in.
(Christie's) **$9,306** **£6,600**

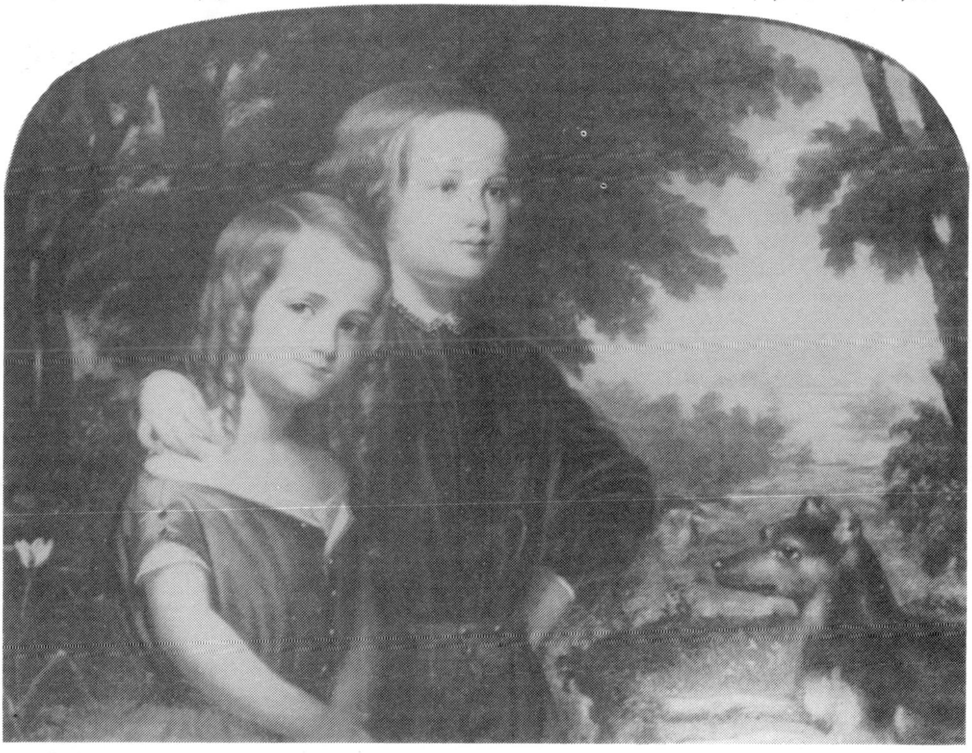

CEPHUS GIOVANNI THOMPSON – Brother And Sister – signed with monogrammed initials and dated 1851 – oil on canvas – 29¼ x 36in. *(Christie's)* **$4,960** **£3,084**

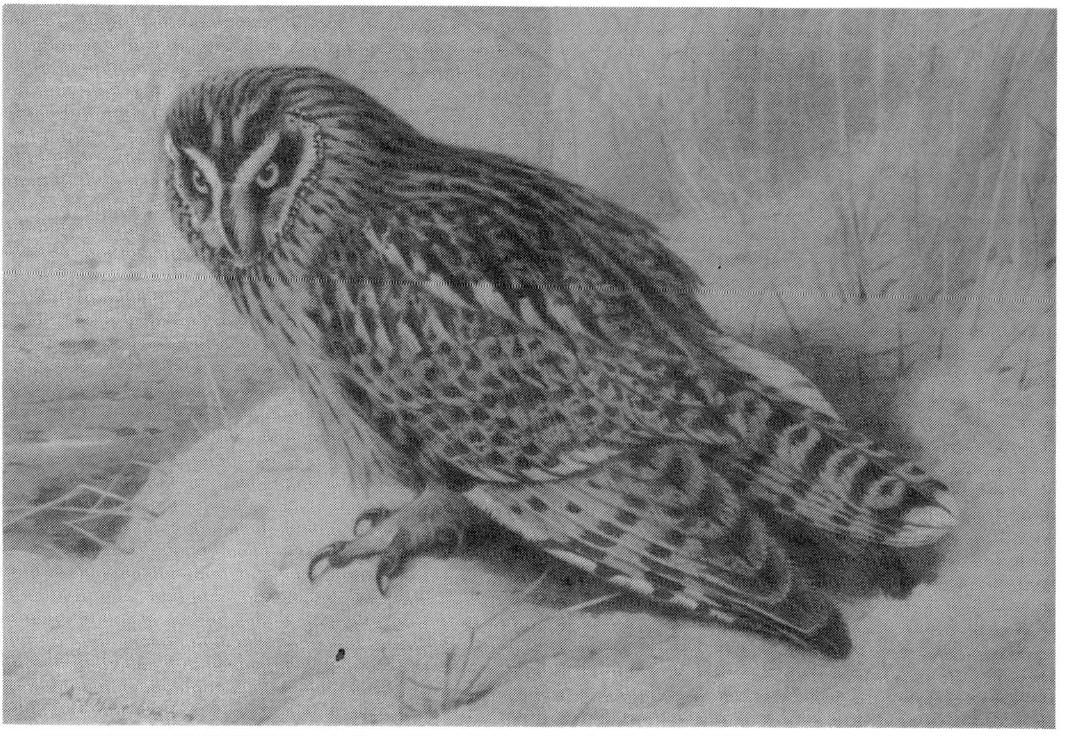

ARCHIBALD THORBURN – A Short-Eared Owl – signed and dated 1925 – watercolour heightened with white on light-brown paper – 7¼ x 10½in. *(Christie's)* **$8,764 £5,280**

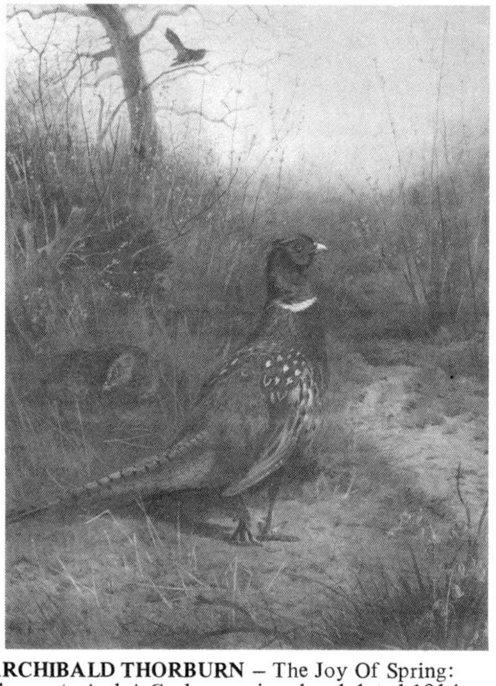

ARCHIBALD THORBURN – The Joy Of Spring: Pheasants And A Cuckoo – signed and dated 1914 – watercolour heightened with bodycolour – 30¾ x 22¼in.
(Christie's) **$38,016 £26,400**

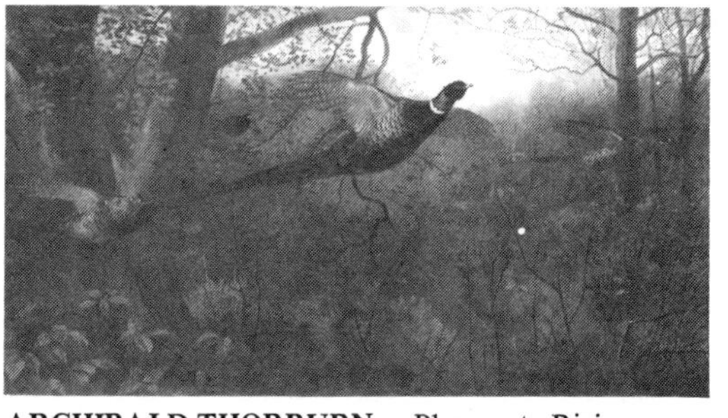

ARCHIBALD THORBURN – Pheasants Rising From A Wood – signed and dated 1900 – watercolour and bodycolour – 16¾ x 30in.
(Christie's) **$24,816 £17,600**

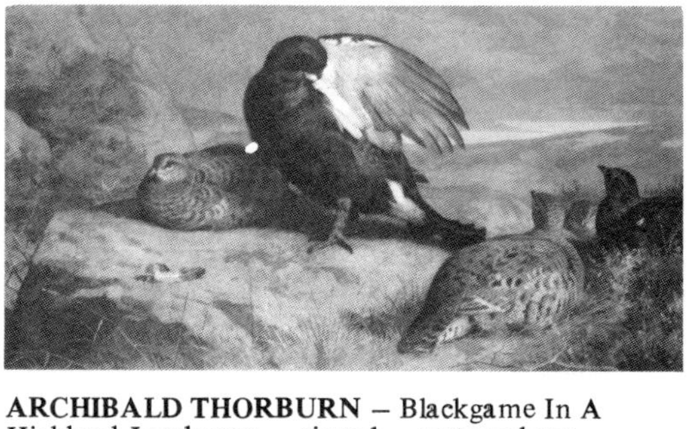

ARCHIBALD THORBURN – Blackgame In A Highland Landscape – signed – watercolour heightened with bodycolour – 18 x 27¼in.
(Christie's) **$29,160 £19,440**

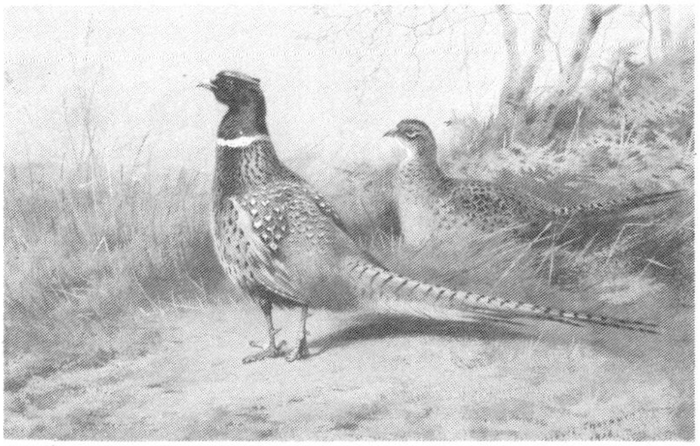

ARCHIBALD THORBURN – A Cock And A Hen Pheasant – signed and dated 1916 – watercolour and bodycolour on grey paper – 7¼ x 10¼in.
(Christie's) **$10,081** **£7,150**

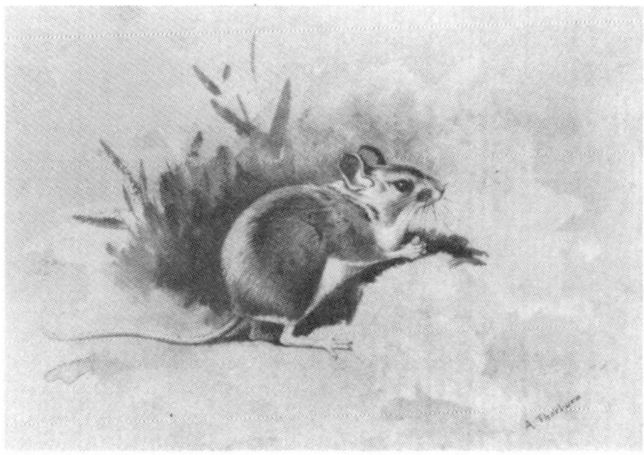

ARCHIBALD THORBURN – Common Field Mouse – signed – watercolour – 6 x 8in.
(Woolley & Wallis) **$817** **£580**

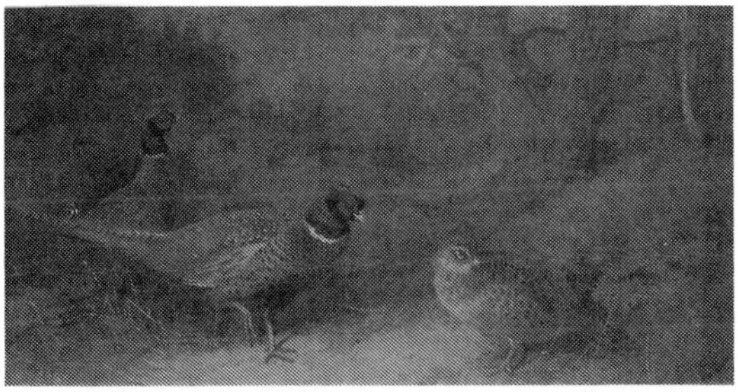

ARCHIBALD THORBURN – A Hen And Two Cock Pheasants In A Woodland – signed and dated 1922 – watercolour and bodycolour – 10½ x 14½in.
(Christie's) **$19,920** **£12,000**

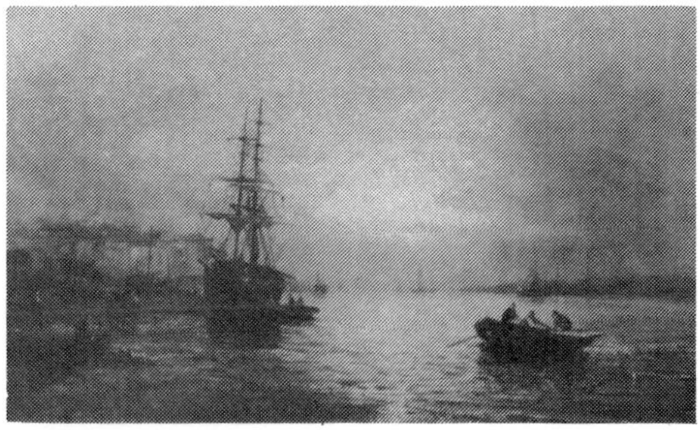

WILLIAM THORNLEY – Estuary Scene, Evening – signed – on canvas – 9¾ x 15¾in.
(Phillips) **$2,093** **£1,300**

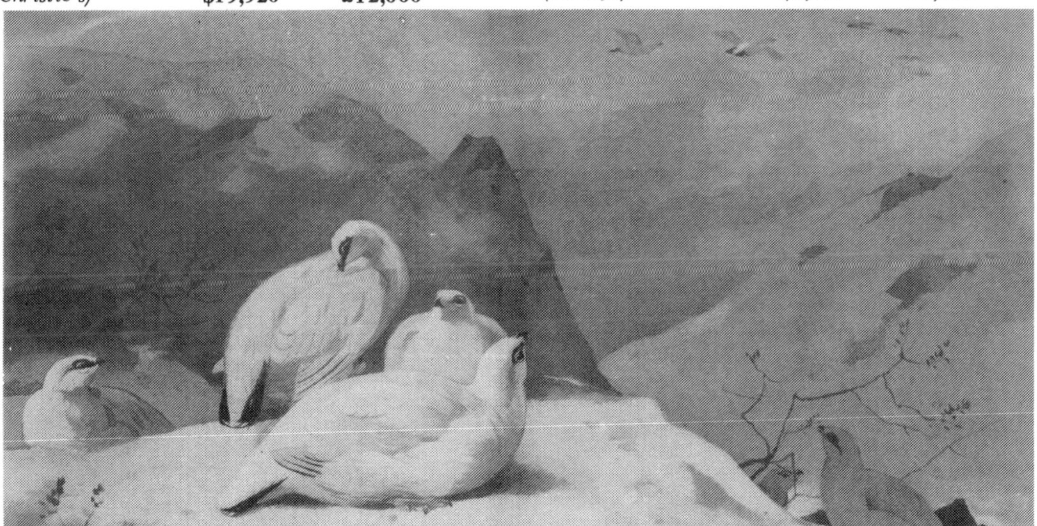

ARCHIBALD THORBURN – Ptarmigan In A Snowy Highland Landscape – signed – pencil and watercolour heightened with white on grey paper – 8¾ x 12¾in. *(Christie's)* **$4,747** **£2,860**

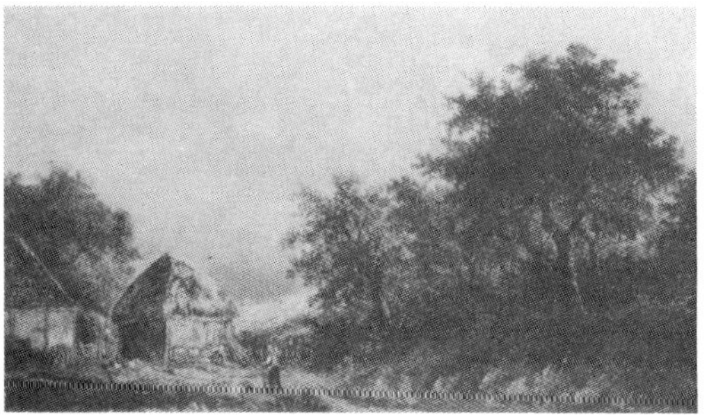

JOSEPH THORS – A Wooded Landscape With A Man On A Path By A Pond – signed – oil on panel – 9½ x 13¾in.
(Christie's) **$1,318** **£935**

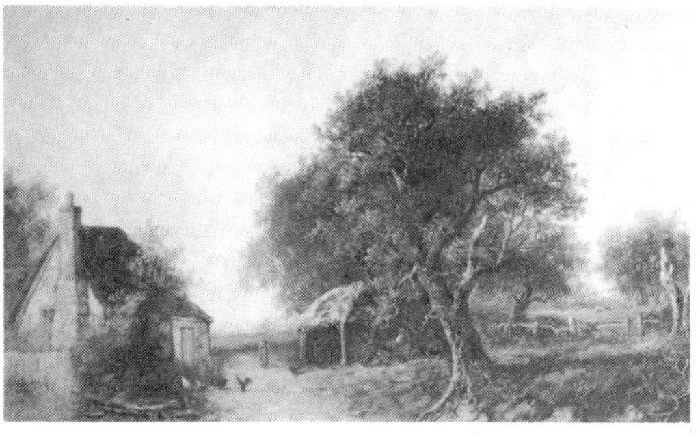

JOSEPH THORS – Landscape With A Cottage, Farm Building And Hens – signed – oil – 16 x 24in.
(Woolley & Wallis) **$2,538** **£1,800**

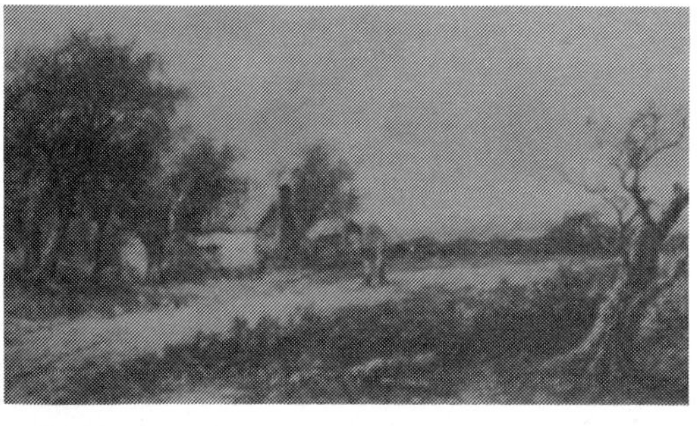

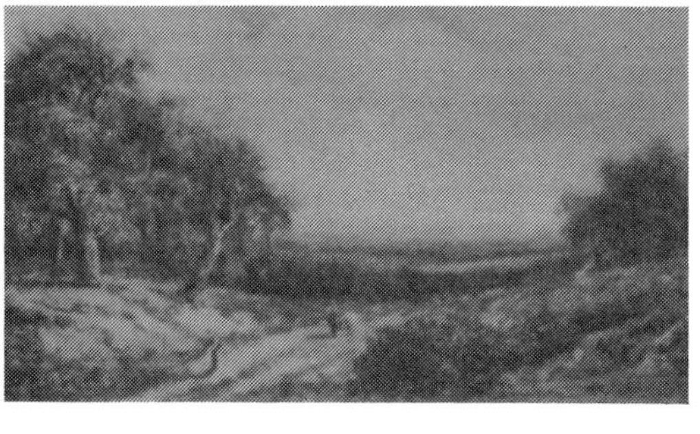

JOSEPH THORS – Figures On A Path Before Cottages; and Figures On A Moorland Path – signed – on panel – 7¾ x 12in.
(Phillips) **$4,025** **£2,500 Pair**

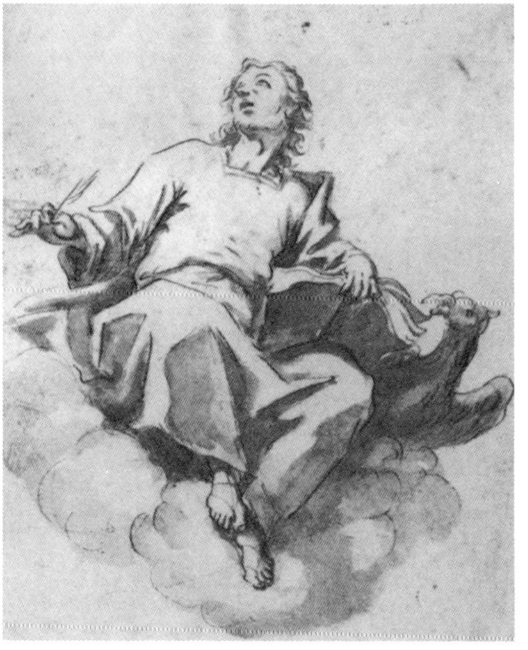

GIOVANNI BATTISTA TIEPOLO, Circle of – St. John The Evangelist – pen and ink with wash – 9½ x 7¼in.
(Phillips) **$267** **£190**

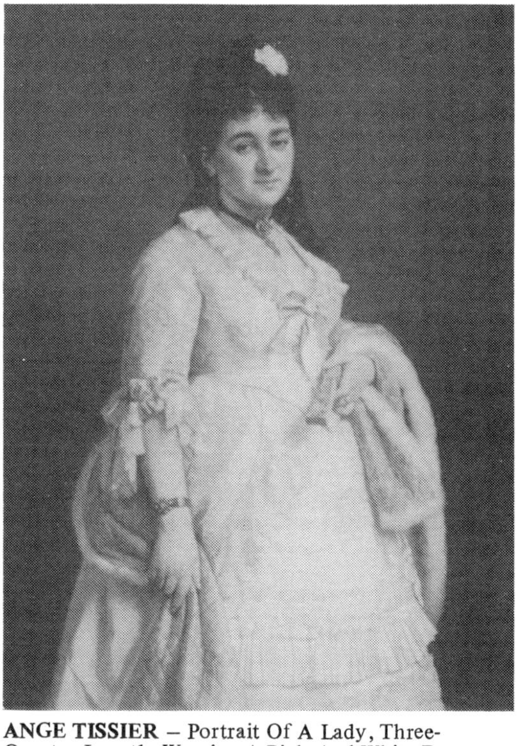

ANGE TISSIER – Portrait Of A Lady, Three-Quarter Length, Wearing A Pink And White Dress – signed – 50 x 35in.
(Christie's) **$1,504** **£990**

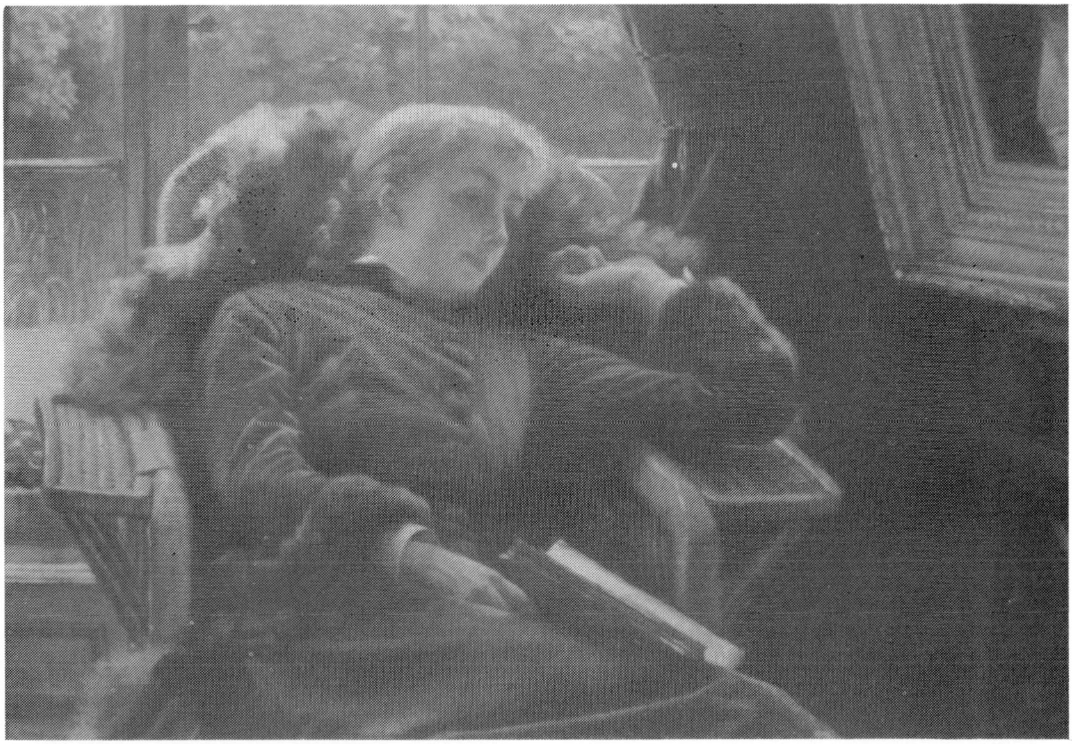

JAMES JACQUES JOSEPH TISSOT – Kathleen In An Armchair – signed and dated 1878 – oil on panel – 12¼ x 17in. *(Robt. W. Skinner Inc.)* **$160,000 £98,159**

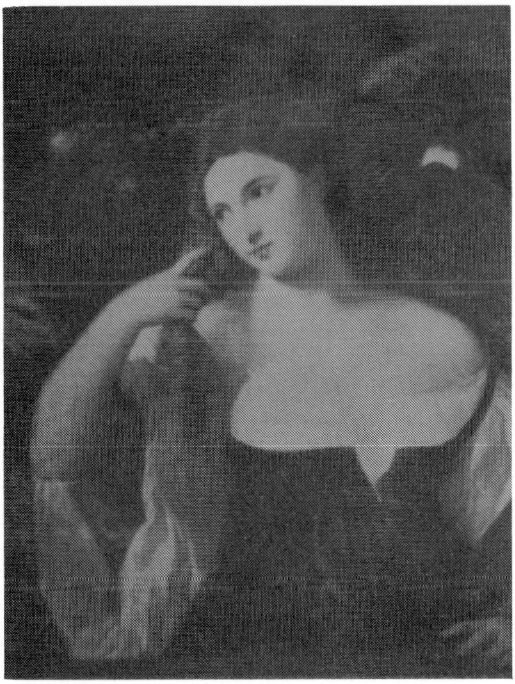

TITIAN, After – **A** Woman At A Mirror – 38½ x 28½in.
(Lawrence Fine Art) **$876 £528**

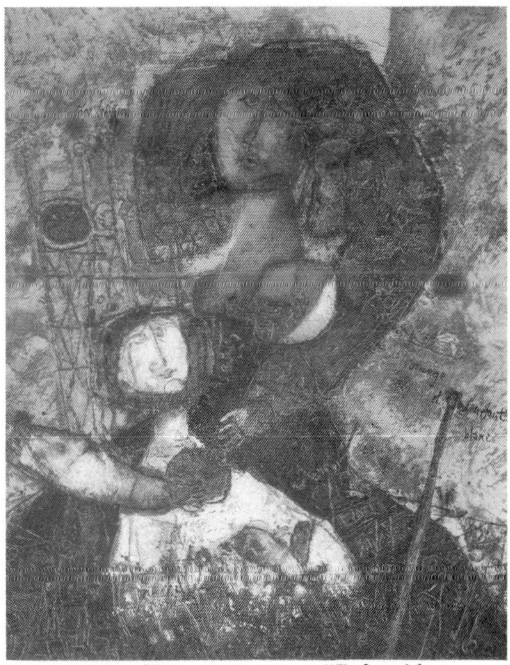

THEO TOBIASSE – L'Orange et l'Enfant blanc – signed, inscribed and dated '63 – oil on canvas – 32 x 25¾in.
(Christie's) **$9,187 £6,380**

TOBIASSE

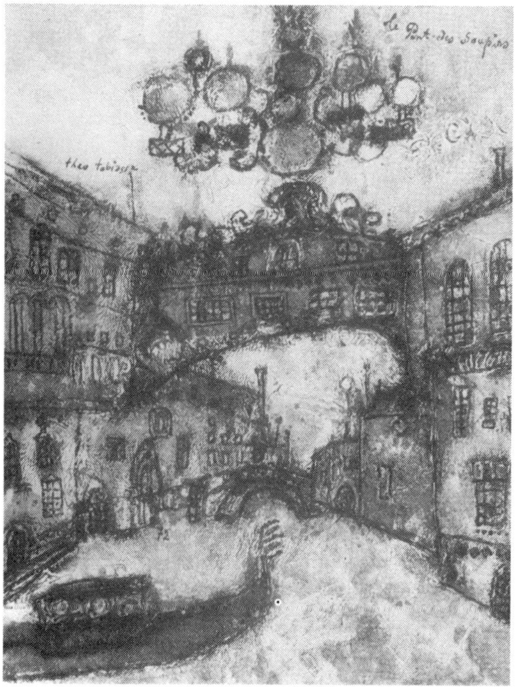

THEO TOBIASSE – Le Pont des Soupirs – signed, dated '72 and inscribed – oil on canvas – 21¾ x 18¼in.
(Christie's) **$6,160** **£3,850**

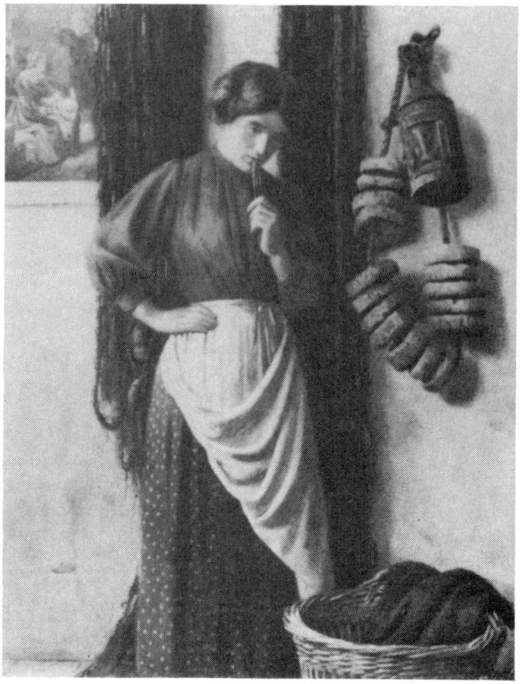

RALPH TODD – A Cornish Fisher-Girl – signed – watercolour – 14¾ x 10¼in.
(Christie's) **$1,208** **£770**

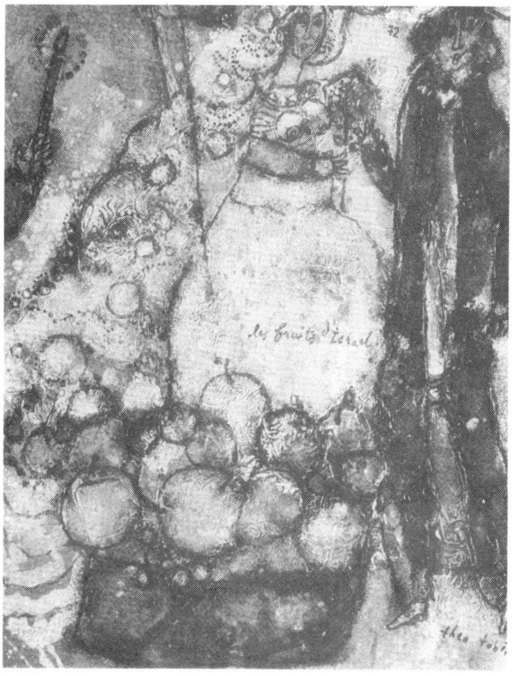

THEO TOBIASSE – Les Fruits d'Israel – signed, dated '72 and inscribed – oil on canvas – 21¾ x 18¼in.
(Christie's) **$6,160** **£3,850**

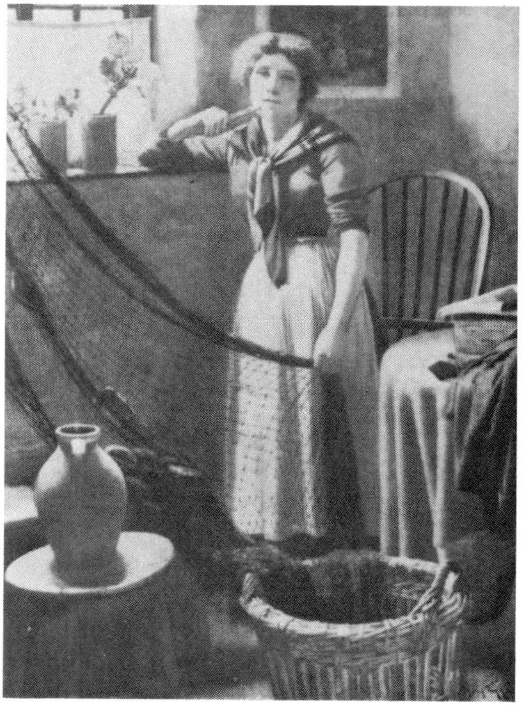

RALPH TODD – Mending The Nets – signed – watercolour – 20¼ x 14¼in.
(Christie's) **$943** **£660**

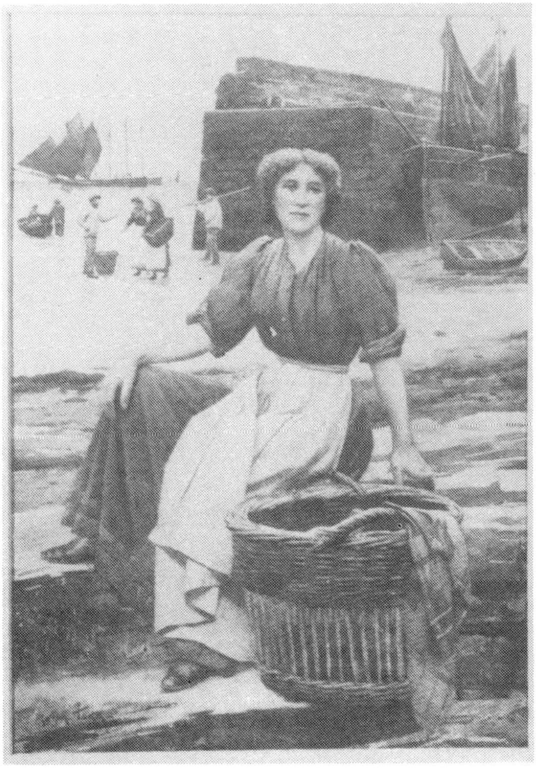

RALPH TODD – A Cornish Fishergirl – signed – watercolour – 38 x 27 cm.
(Phillips) **$1,606** **£1,050**

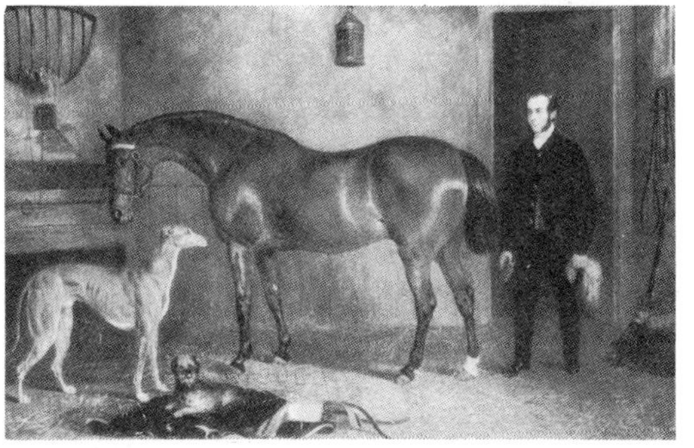

EDWARD TOLLEY – A Bay Hunter In A Loose-box With A Groom, A Greyhound And A Terrier – signed and dated 1861 – 24¾ x 33in.
(Christie's) **$4,860** **£3,240**

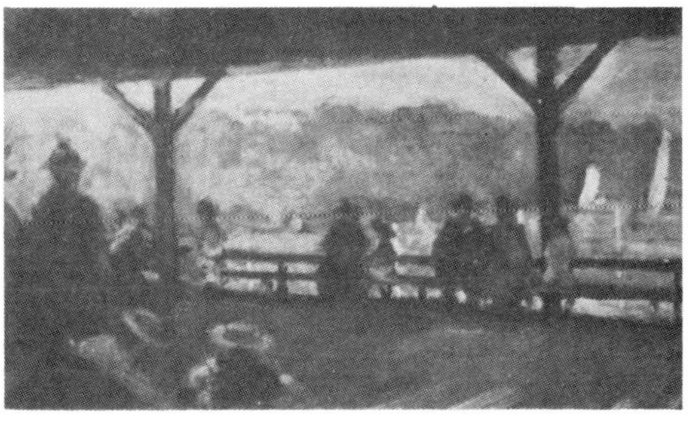

FRANK HECTOR TOMPKINS – Autumn Evening – signed – oil on board – 12 x 16in.
(Christie's) **$1,320** **£918**

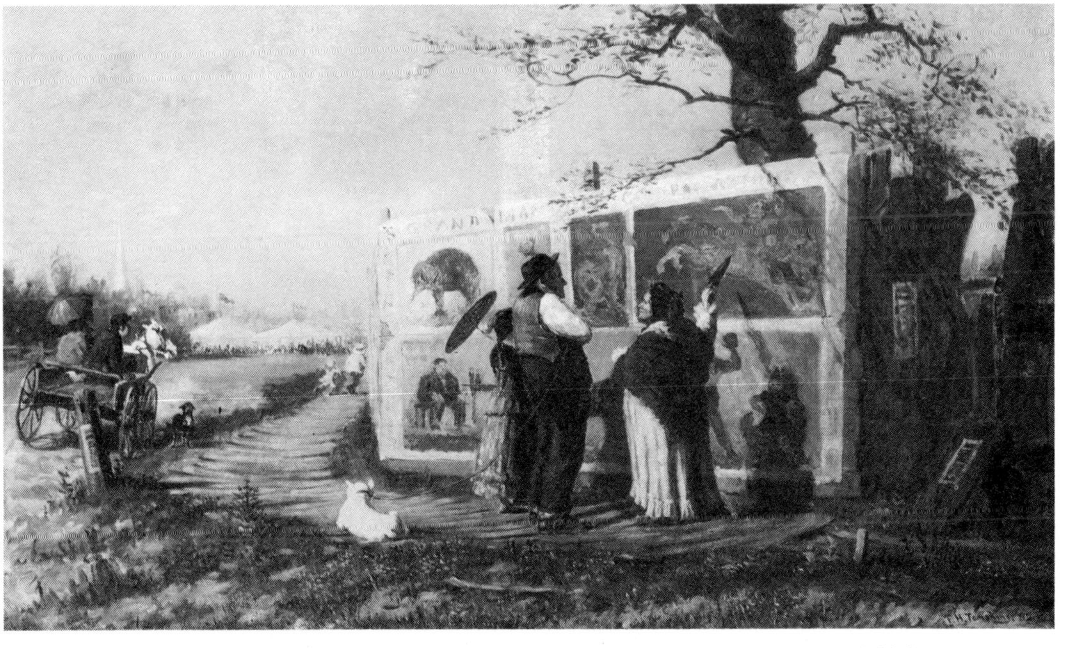

FRANK HECTOR TOMKINS – Circus Time – signed and dated '82 – oil on canvas laid down on masonite – 22 x 36in. *(Christie's)* **$16,500** **£11,599**

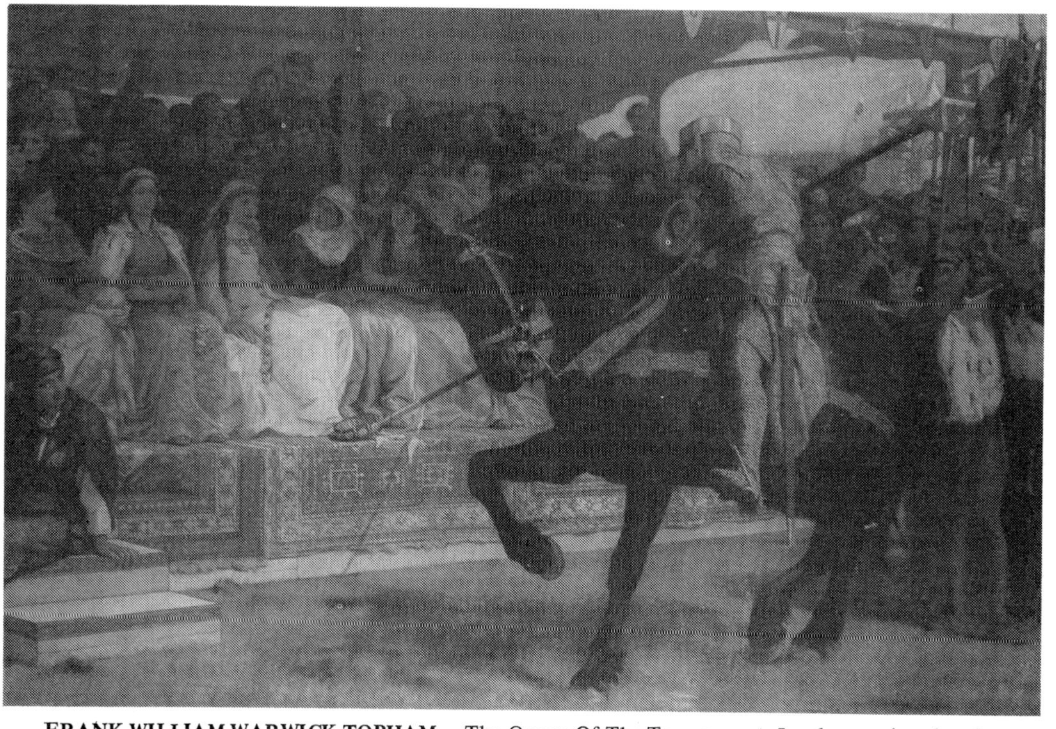

FRANK WILLIAM WARWICK TOPHAM – The Queen Of The Tournament, Ivanhoe – signed and dated 1885 – 60½ x 88in. *(Christie's)* **$18,513 £12,100**

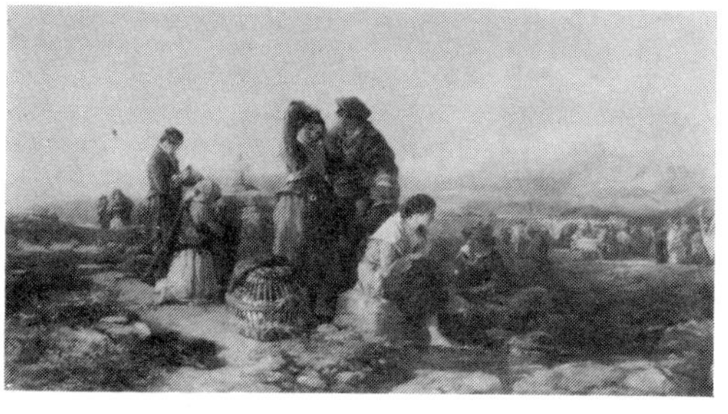

FRANCIS WILLIAM TOPHAM – Ballinasloe Fair – signed and dated 1852 – pencil and water-colour heightened with white – 21¾ x 39½in. *(Christie's)* **$8,764 £5,280**

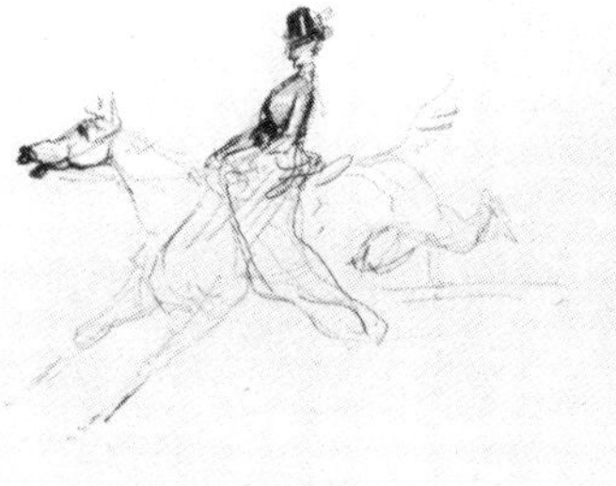

HENRI DE TOULOUSE-LAUTREC – Amazone sautant – recto; Danse paysanne – verso – pencil on paper – 5 x 8in. *(Christie's)* **$19,008 £13,200**

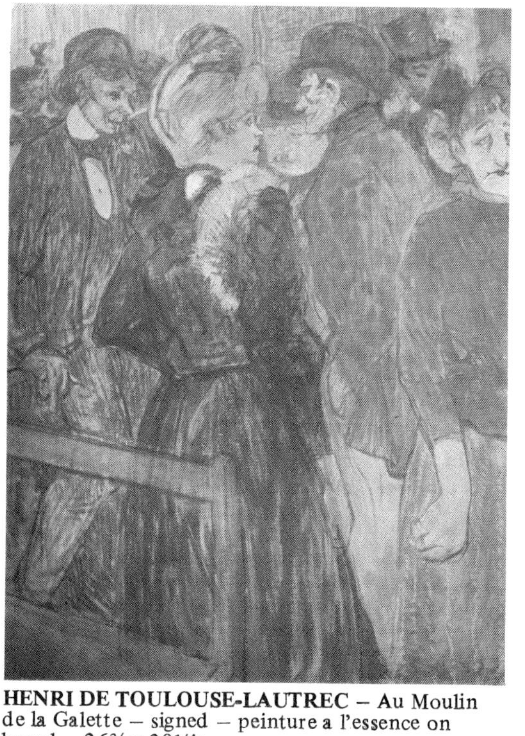

HENRI DE TOULOUSE-LAUTREC – Au Moulin de la Galette – signed – peinture a l'essence on board – 26¾ x 20½in. *(Christie's)* **$2,534,400 £1,760,000**

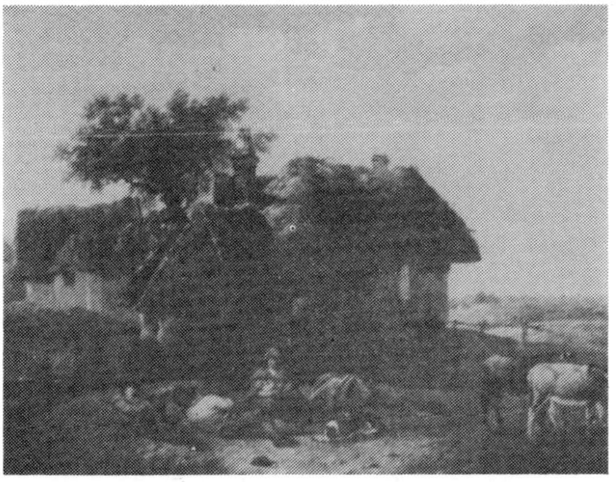

CHARLES TOWNE – A Peasant Family Outside A Cottage In An Extensive Landscape – oil on canvas – 12 x 15in.
(Christie's) **$1,826** **£1,100**

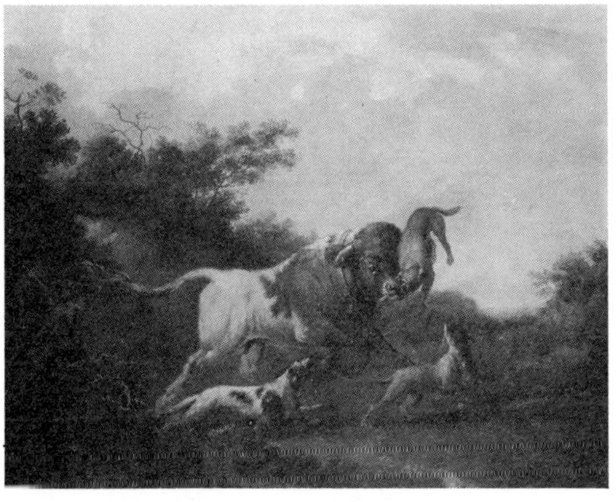

CHARLES TOWNE – Bull Baiting – indistinctly signed – 24¾ x 30in.
(Christie's) **$6,156** **£4,104**

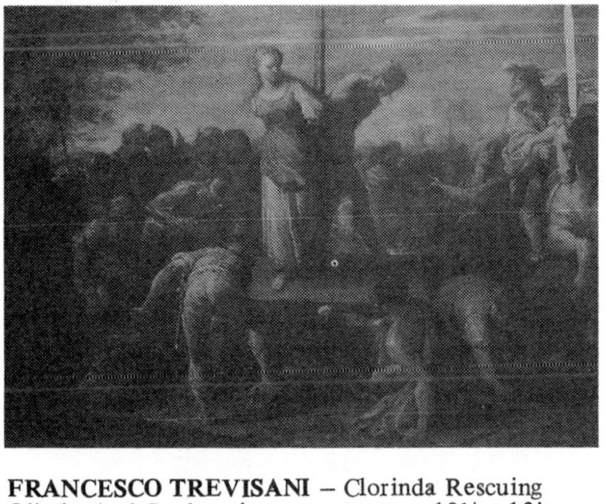

FRANCESCO TREVISANI – Clorinda Rescuing Olindo And Sophronia – on copper – 10¼ x 13in.
(Phillips) **$27,390** **£16,500**

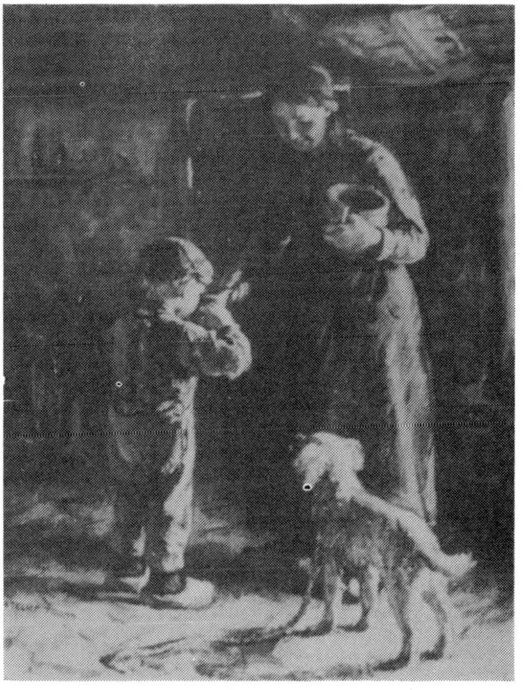

JAN ZOETELIEF TROMP – A Morsel From The Cook – signed – oil on canvas – 46 x 38.5cm.
(Phillips) **$3,340** **£2,000**

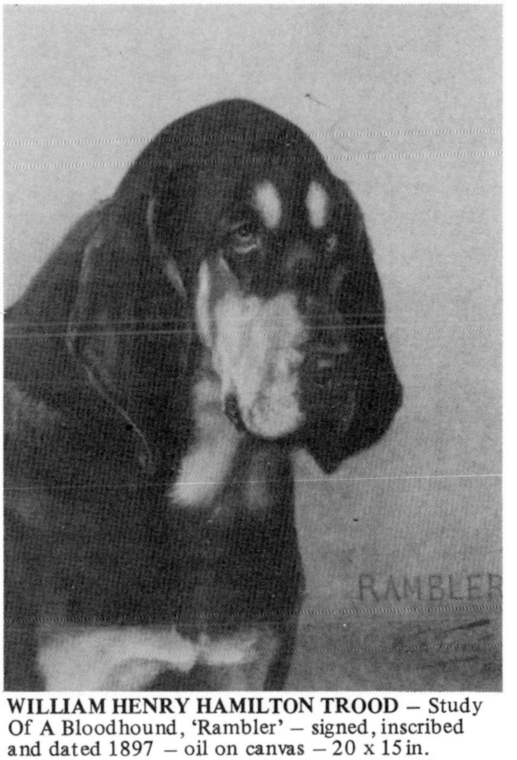

WILLIAM HENRY HAMILTON TROOD – Study Of A Bloodhound, 'Rambler' – signed, inscribed and dated 1897 – oil on canvas – 20 x 15in.
(Phillips) **$1,530** **£1,000**

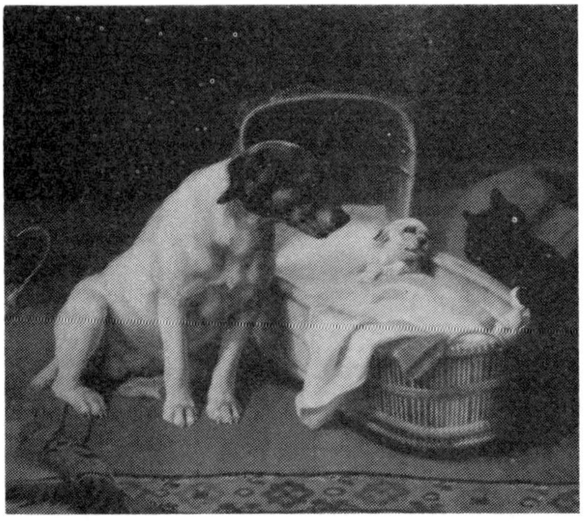

WILLIAM HENRY HAMILTON TROOD – Study Of A Terrier, Puppy In A Wicker Cradle And A Black Cat – signed and dated – oil on canvas – 16 x 22in.
(Morphets) **$13,020** **£8,400**

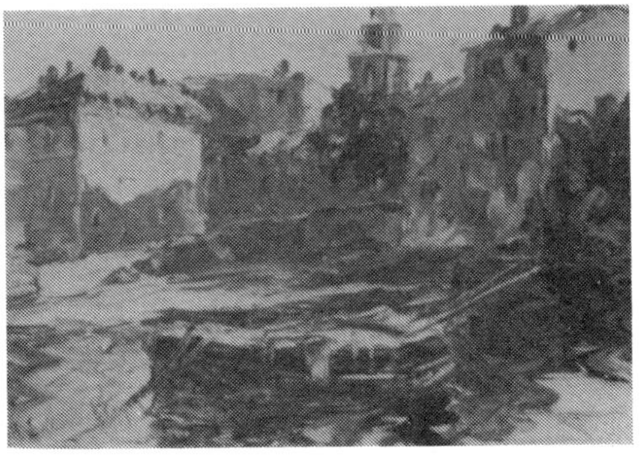

A. SALOMON LE TROPEZIEN – Vue Du Port De St. Tropez – signed – oil on panel – 25 x 35cm.
(Phillips) **$279** **£180**

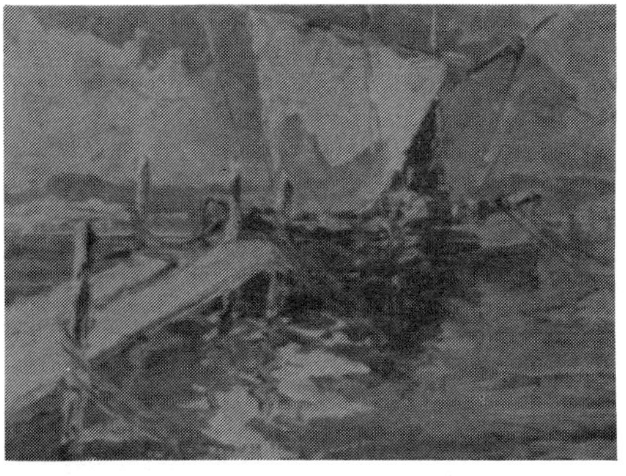

A. SALOMON LE TROPEZIEN – Bateaux En Voiles, Saint Maxime – signed – oil on panel – 25 x 35cm.
(Phillips) **$279** **£180**

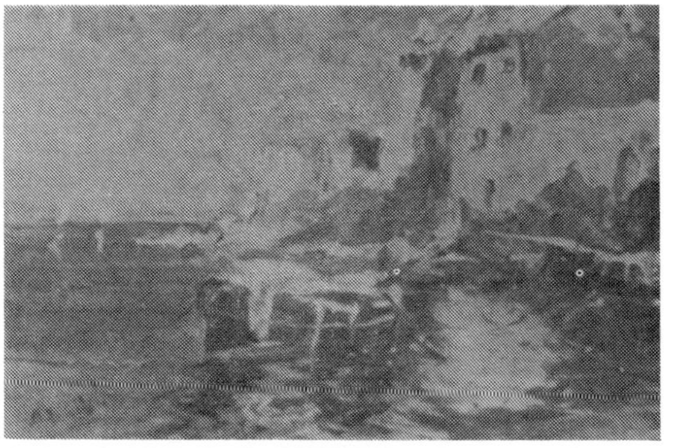

A. SALOMON LE TROPEZIEN – Bateaux A St. Tropez – signed – oil on panel – 25.5 x 35cm.
(Phillips) **$279** **£180**

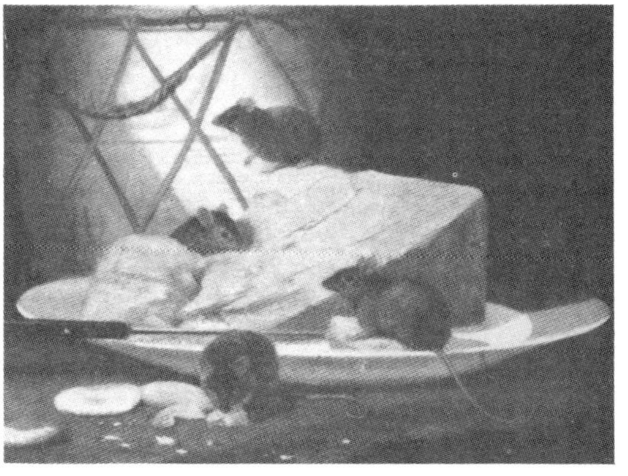

NEWBOLD HOUGH TROTTER – Uninvited Guests – signed and dated 1875 – oil on panel – 9 x 12in.
(Christie's) **$3,300** **£2,295**

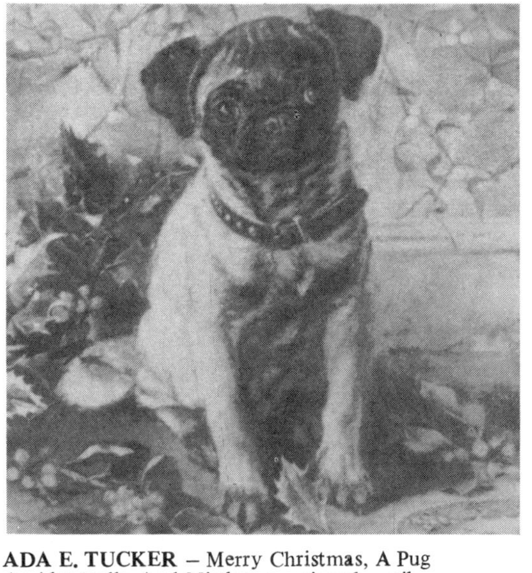

ADA E. TUCKER – Merry Christmas, A Pug Amidst Holly And Mistletoe – signed – oil – 17 x 13in.
(Bonhams) **$1,860** **£1,200**

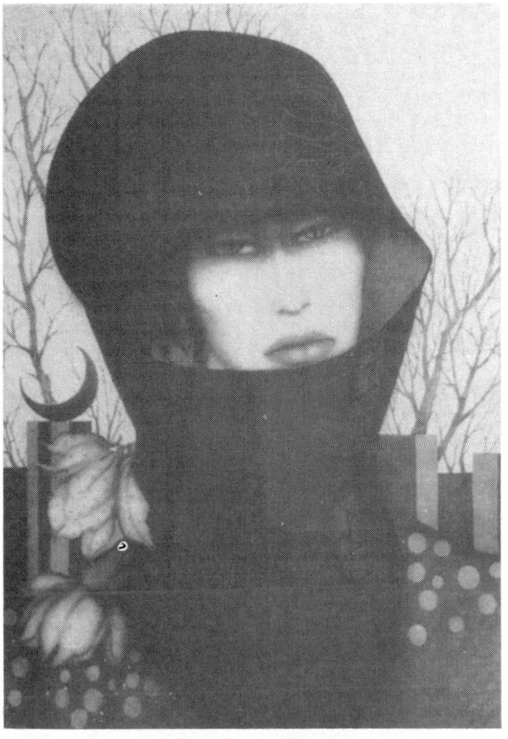

JEF VAN TUERENHOUT – Bosbloemen – signed and inscribed – gouache, black ink, coloured chalks and charcoal on paper mounted on board – 38¾ x 27¼in.
(Christie's) **$5,280** **£3,300**

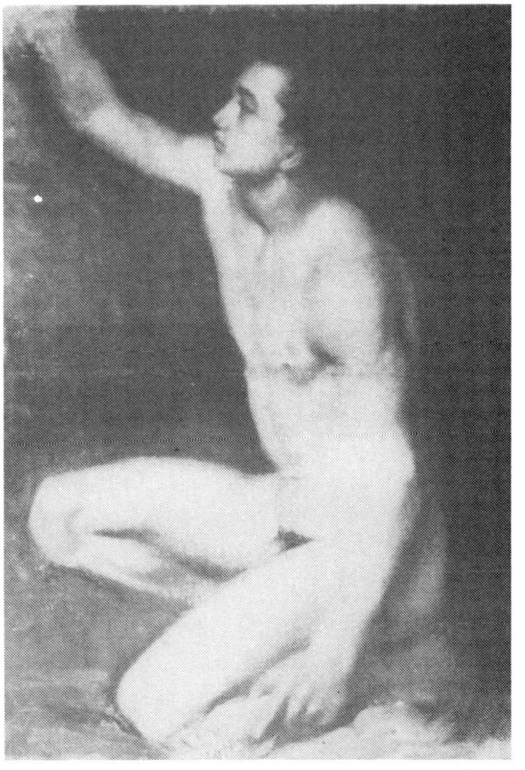

HENRY SCOTT TUKE – Study Of A Young Nude Man – oil on canvas laid on board – 61 x 44cm.
(W. H. Lane & Son) **$1,826** **£1,100**

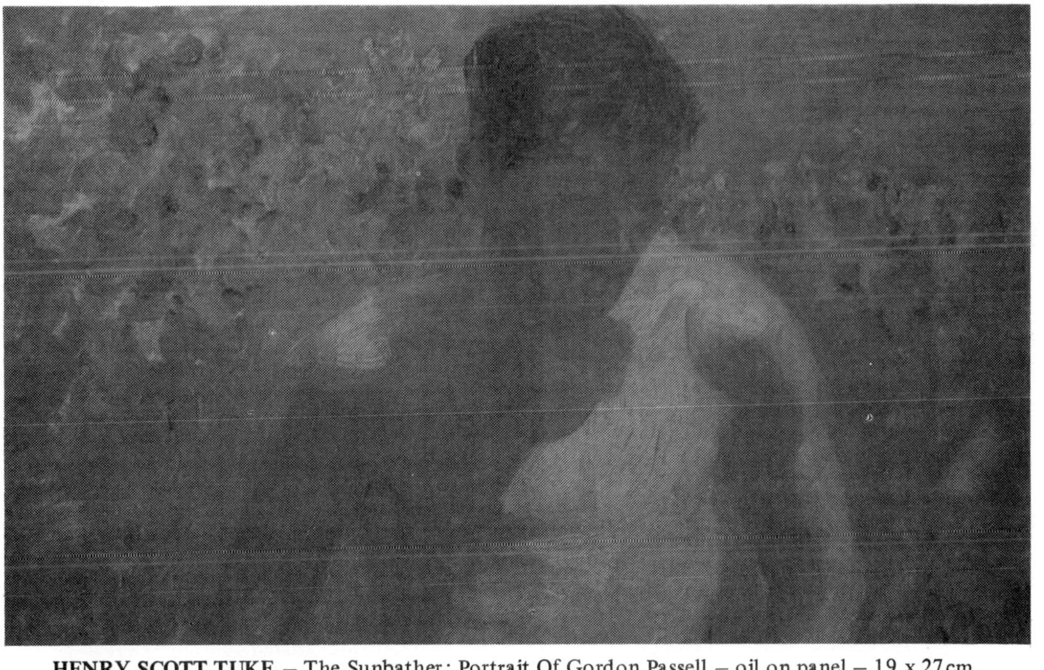

HENRY SCOTT TUKE – The Sunbather: Portrait Of Gordon Passell – oil on panel – 19 x 27cm.
(Phillips) **$2,800** **£1,800**

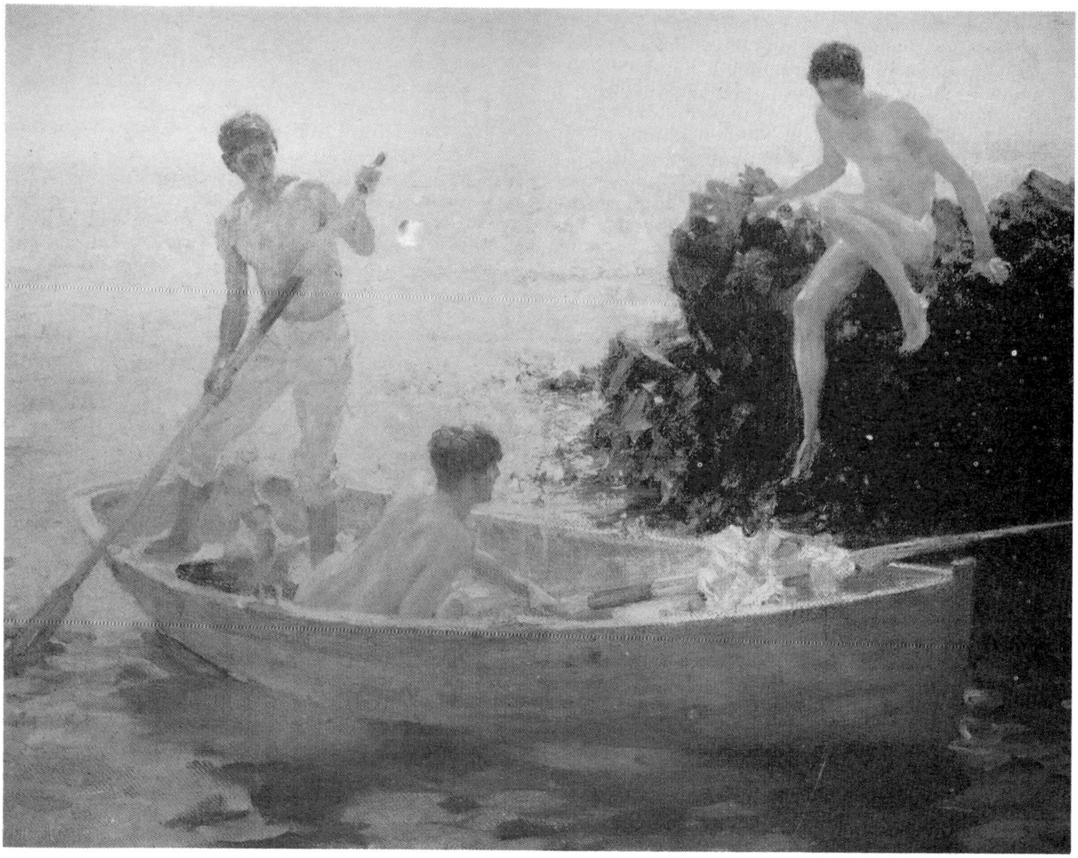

HENRY SCOTT TUKE – The Bathing Cove – signed and dated 1912 – 51 x 61cm. *(Phillips)*
$49,700 £35,000

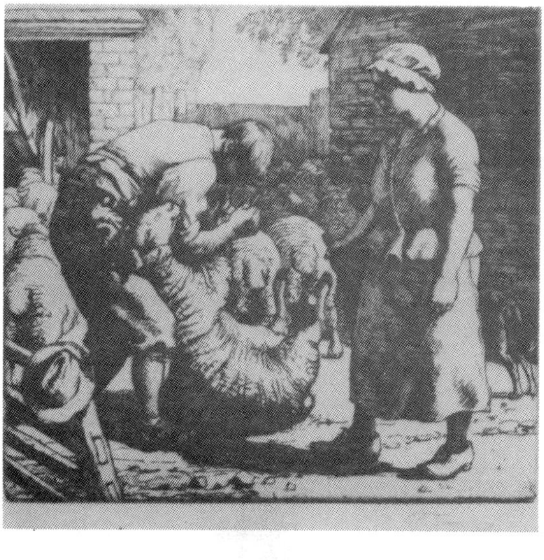

CHARLES FREDERICK TUNNICLIFFE – The Sheep Doctor – signed – etching – 6.7 x 7.5in.
(Woolley & Wallis) **$408** **£290**

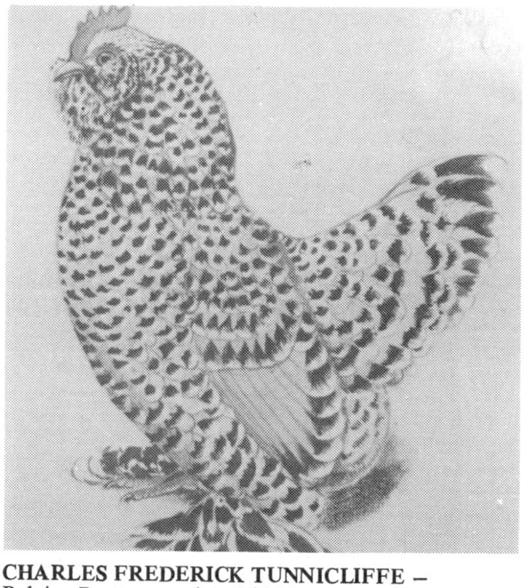

CHARLES FREDERICK TUNNICLIFFE –
Belgian Bantams – dated 1980 on the reverse – watercolour, bodycolour and pencil – 11 x 9½in.
(Christie's) **$2,988** **£2,090 Two**

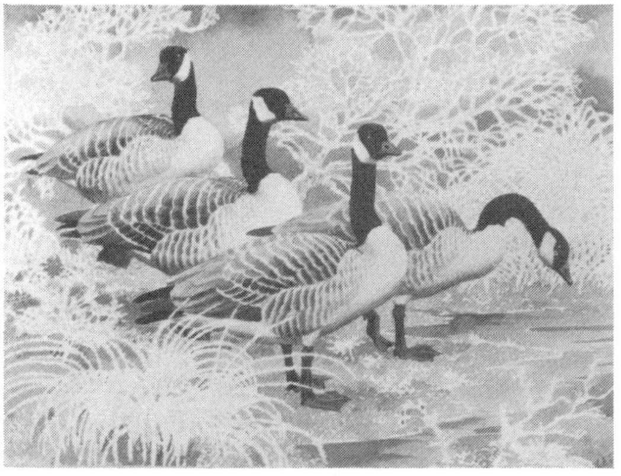

CHARLES FREDERICK TUNNICLIFFE – Canada Geese – signed – watercolour and pencil – 13½ x 18½in.
(Christie's) **$3,799** **£2,420**

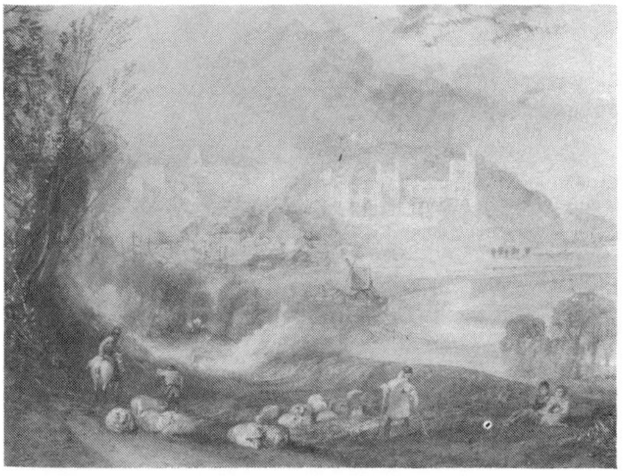

JOSEPH MALLORD WILLIAM TURNER – Arundel Castle And Town – watercolour heightened with touches of bodycolour and gum arabic – 11½ x 17¼in.
(Christie's) **$293,920** **£176,000**

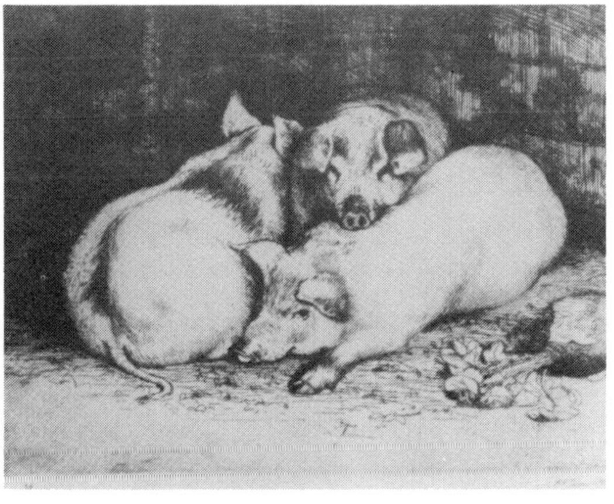

CHARLES FREDERICK TUNNICLIFFE – Porkers – signed – etching – 6.7 x 7.7in.
(Woolley & Wallis) **$870** **£580**

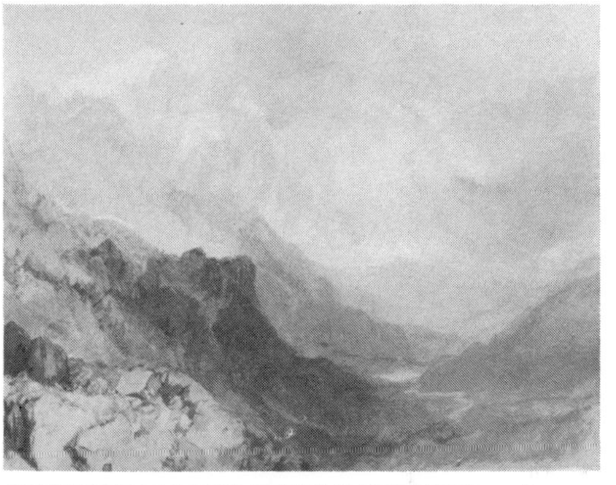

JOSEPH MALLORD WILLIAM TURNER – An Alpine Valley, Probably The Val d'Aosta – watercolour – 9½ x 13¼in.
(Christie's) **$165,330** **£99,000**

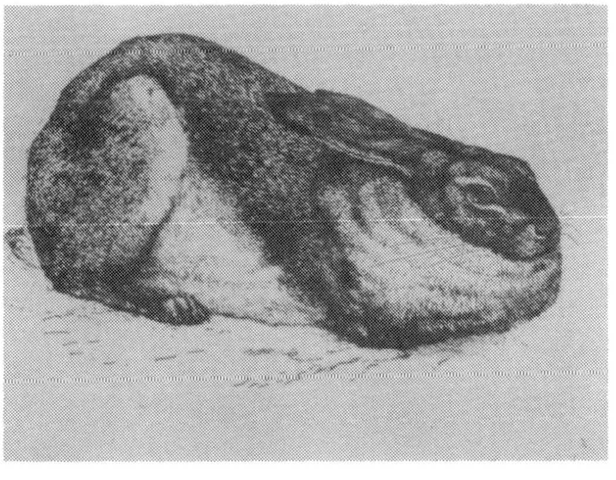

CHARLES FREDERICK TUNNICLIFFE – Sitting Hare – signed – etching – 5.2 x 7.2in.
(Woolley & Wallis) **$1,050** **£700**

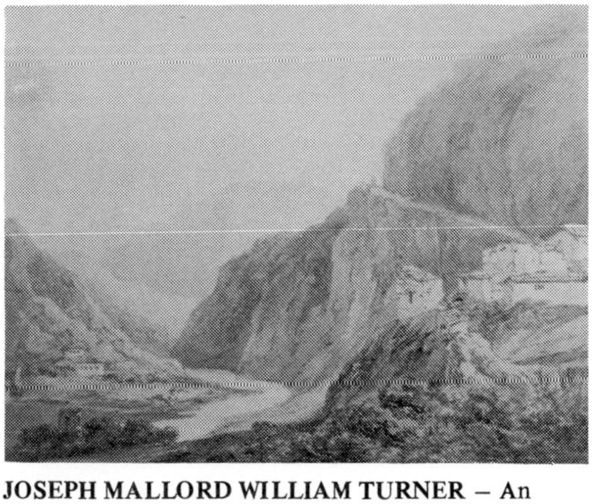

JOSEPH MALLORD WILLIAM TURNER – An Italianate Gorge River Landscape – watercolour over pencil – 19 x 25cm.
(Phillips) **$5,216** **£3,200**

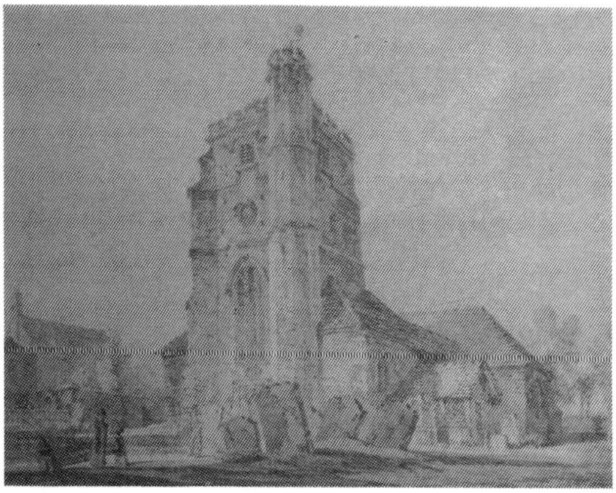

JOSEPH MALLORD WILLIAM TURNER – View Of Hadley Church, Hertfordshire – signed and dated 1793 – watercolour over pencil – 28.5 x 36.5cm.
(Phillips) **$14,344** **£8,800**

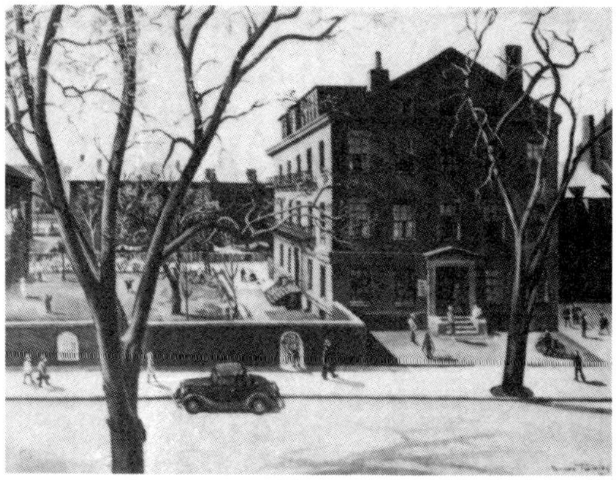

YVONNE TWINING – View In The South End, Boston – signed and dated '37 – oil on canvas – 22¼ x 30in.
(Robt. W. Skinner Inc.) **$2,100** **£1,458**

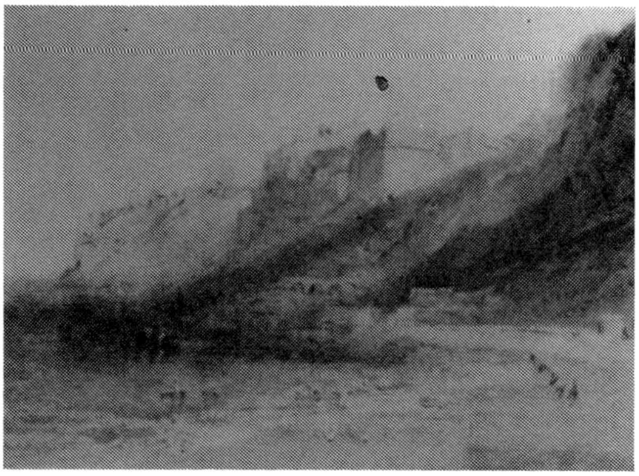

JOSEPH MALLORD WILLIAM TURNER, Attributed to – 'Sorrento' – inscribed on the reverse – watercolour on paper – 8 x 9¼in.
(Robt. W. Skinner Inc.) **$400** **£245**

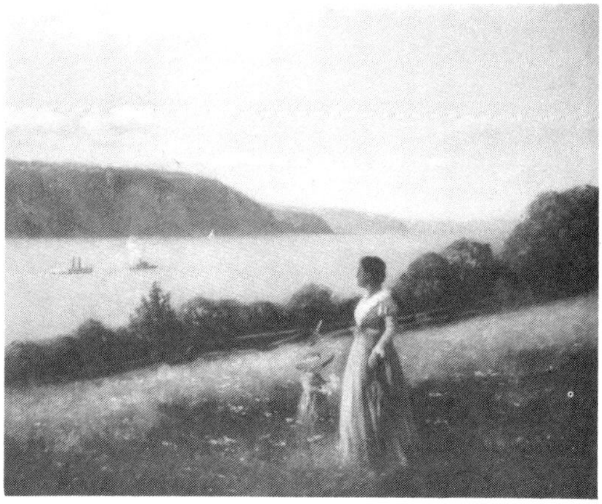

BAYARD HENRY TYLER – Woman Looking Out Over A River – signed and dated 1890, also inscribed – 25 x 30in.
(Christie's) **$5,500** **£3,826**

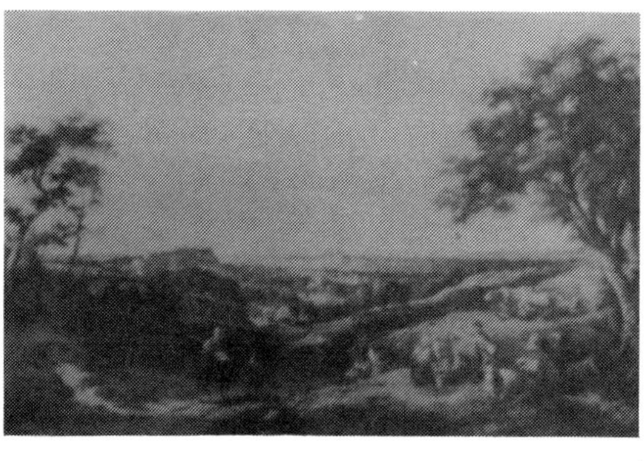

WILLIAM TURNER, Circle of – St. Helier, Jersey – oil on canvas – 24 x 36in.
(Phillips) **$3,486** **£2,100**

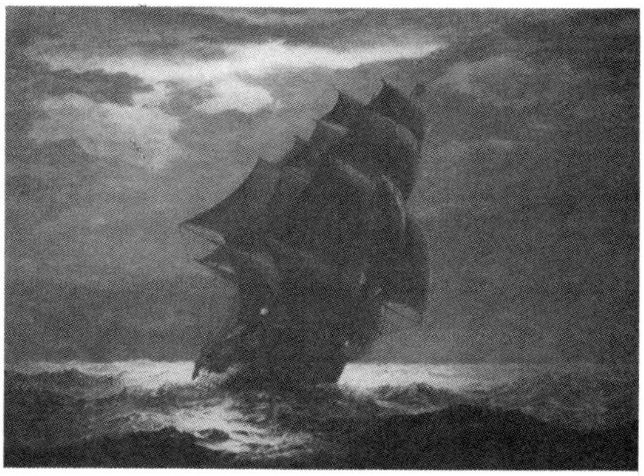

JAMES GALE TYLER – A Wind That Follows Fast – signed – oil on canvas – 30¼ x 42in.
(Christie's) **$4,180** **£2,908**

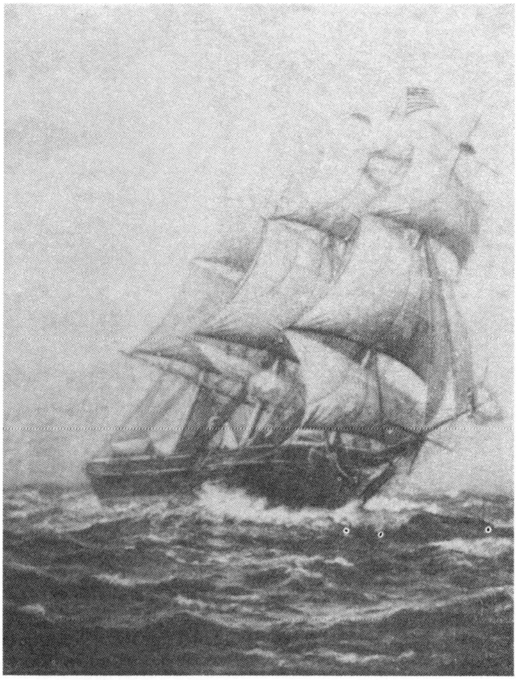

JAMES GALE TYLER – A Favouring Wind – signed – oil on canvas – 30 x 24¼in.
(Christie's) **$1,650** **£1,145**

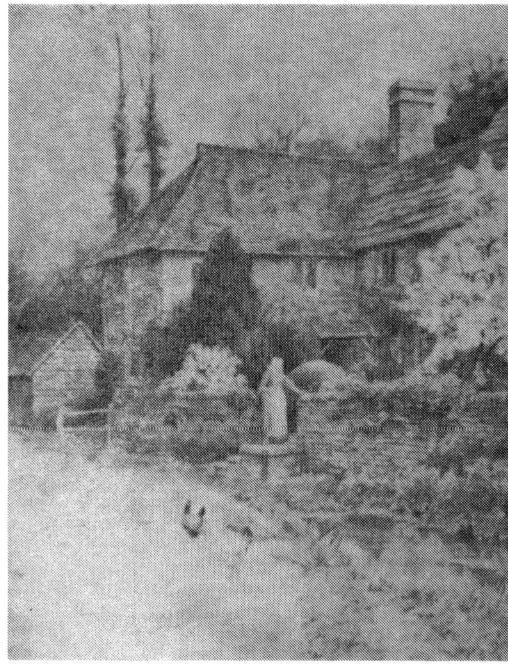

THOMAS NICHOLSON TYNDALE – A Woman Outside A Country Cottage, Near Ockley, Surrey – signed – watercolour – 34 x 26cm.
(Phillips) **$1,385** **£850**

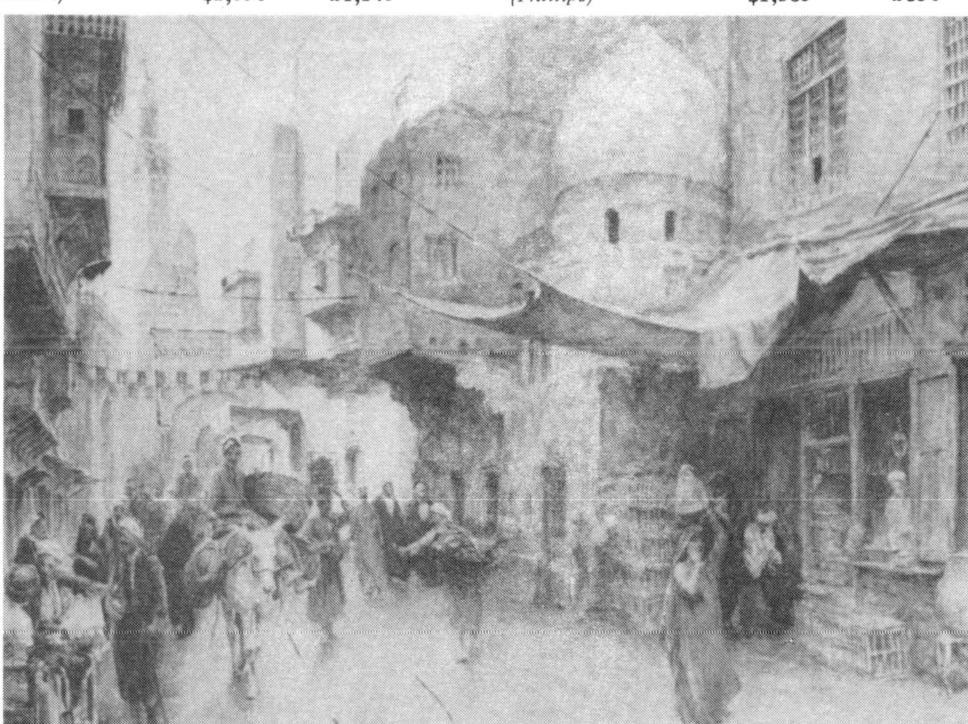

WALTER FREDERICK ROOFE TYNDALE – A Street In Cairo – signed – watercolour with touches of bodycolour – 11¼ x 15¼in. *(Christie's)* **$3,726** **£2,484**

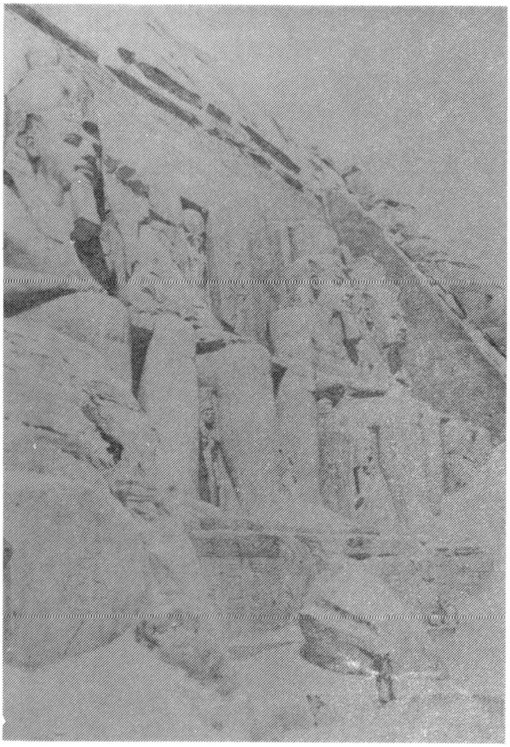

WALTER FREDERICK ROOFE TYNDALE – Abu Simbel, Upper Nile – signed – watercolour – 45.5 x 33cm.
(Phillips) **$5,379 £3,300**

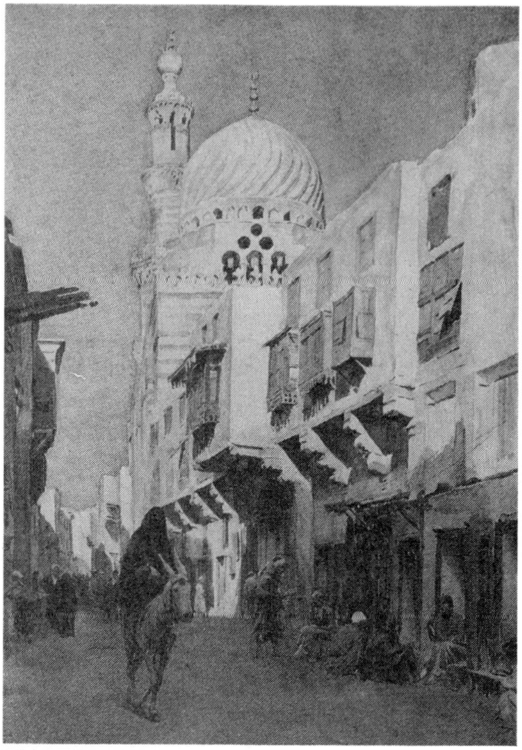

WALTER FREDERICK ROOFE TYNDALE – Figures In An Arabian Street – signed and dated '97 – watercolour over traces of pencil – 34 x 23.5cm.
(Phillips) **$2,431 £1,700**

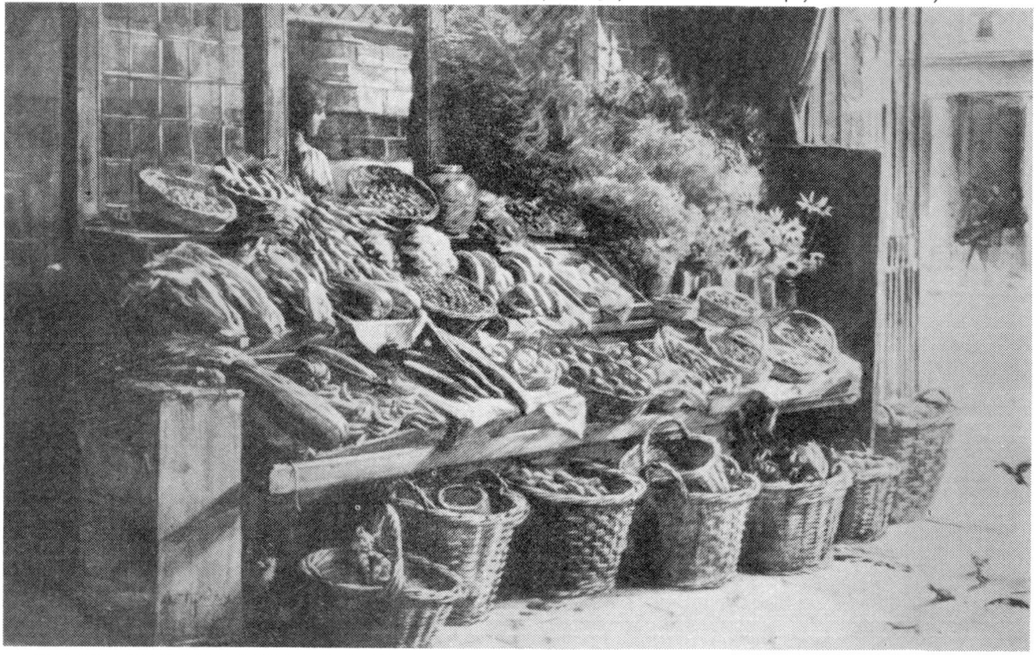

WALTER FREDERICK ROOFE TYNDALE – Miss Lydiard's Stall, Bath – signed, and inscribed on the reverse – watercolour heightened with white – 10¼ x 14¼in. *(Christie's)* **$2,916 £1,944**

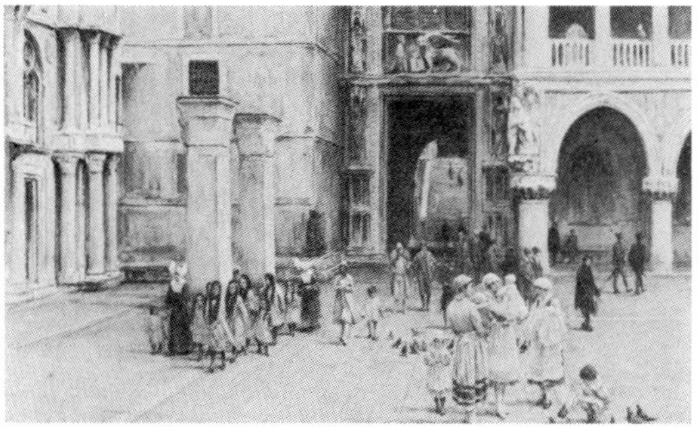

WALTER FREDERICK ROOFE TYNDALE – Figures Near The Porta Della Carta, Venice – signed – watercolour heightened with white – 9¼ x 13¼in.
(Christie's) **$1,620** **£1,080**

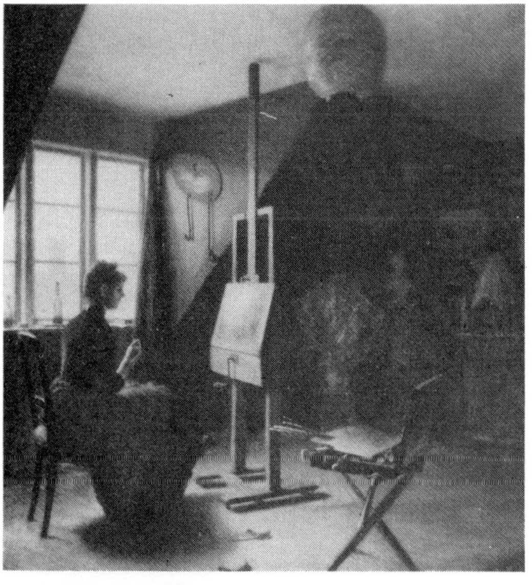

ULLNER-LARSEN – An Artist In Her Studio – signed and dated '88, and signed and inscribed on an old label on the reverse – 30 x 24¾in.
(Christie's) **$2,006** **£1,320**

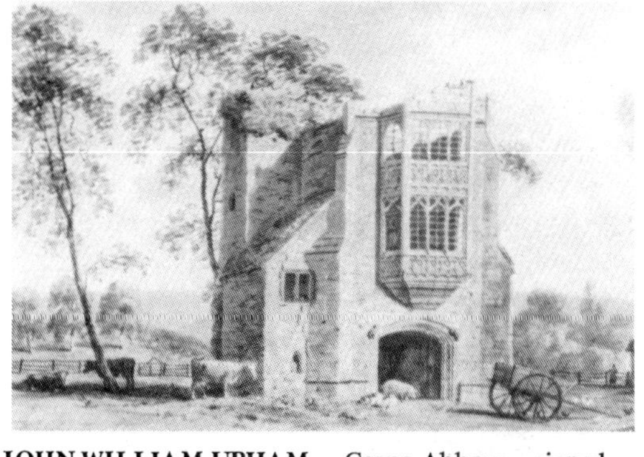

JOHN WILLIAM UPHAM – Cerne Abbey – signed and dated 1802, and inscribed on the reverse – pencil and watercolour – 12½ x 14¾in.
(Christie's) **$1,562** **£1,100**

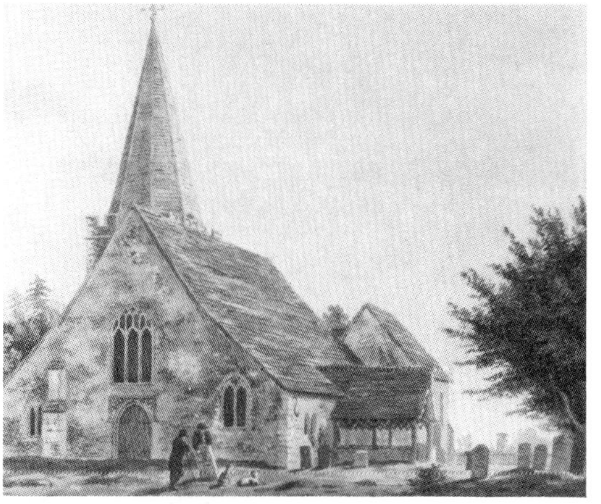

JOHN WILLIAM UPHAM – West View Of Stoke Poges Church, Buckinghamshire With Gray's Monument – signed and dated 1802 – pencil and watercolour – 9¾ x 12¼in.
(Christie's) **$750** **£528**

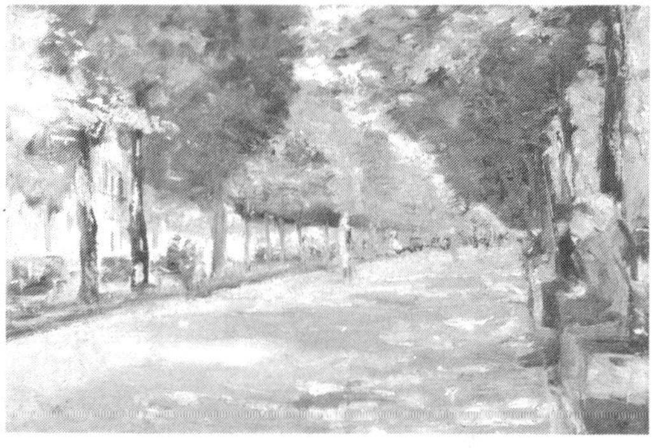

LESSER URY – Im Tiergarten, Berlin – oil on canvas – 13¾ x 19½in.
(Christie's) **$28,512** **£19,800**

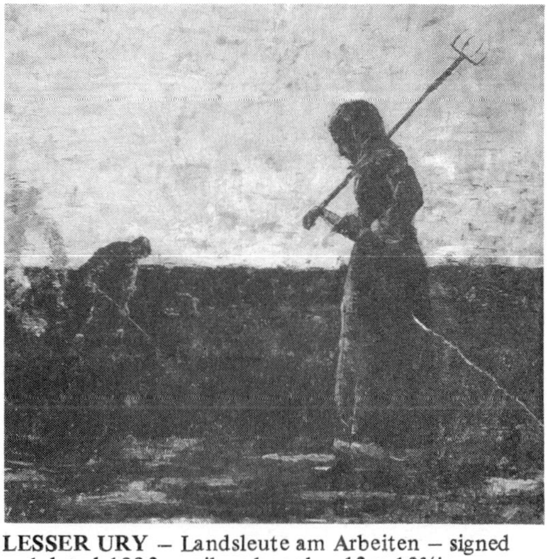

LESSER URY – Landsleute am Arbeiten – signed and dated 1883 – oil on board – 12 x 13¾in.
(Christie's) **$11,022** **£6,600**

UTRILLO

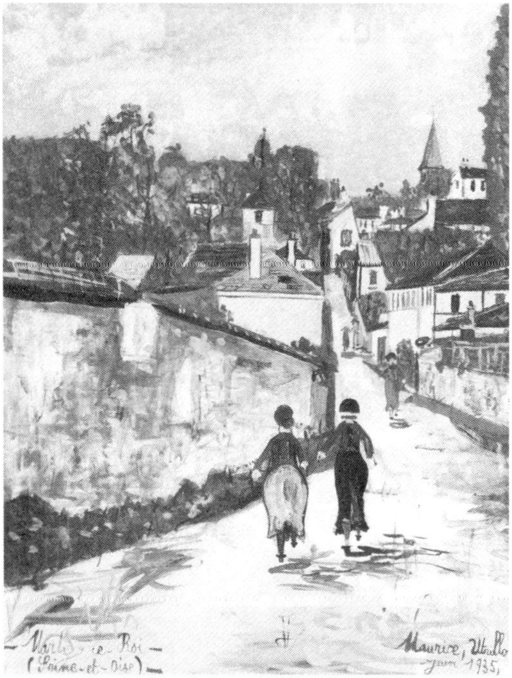

MAURICE UTRILLO – Promenade a Marly-Le-Roi (Yvelines) – signed and dated 1935 and inscribed – gouache on paper – 25 x 19¼in.
(Christie's) **$63,360 £44,000**

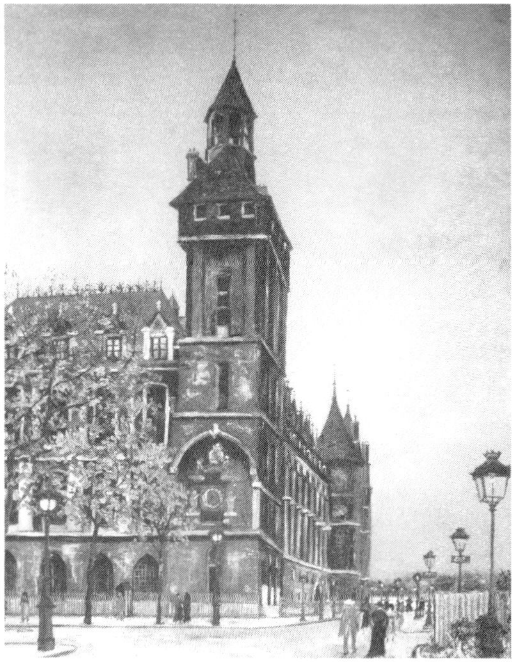

MAURICE UTRILLO – La Conciergerie du Quai de l'Horloge, Paris – signed, and signed and inscribed on the reverse – oil on canvas – 25½ x 19¾in.
(Christie's) **$190,080 £132,000**

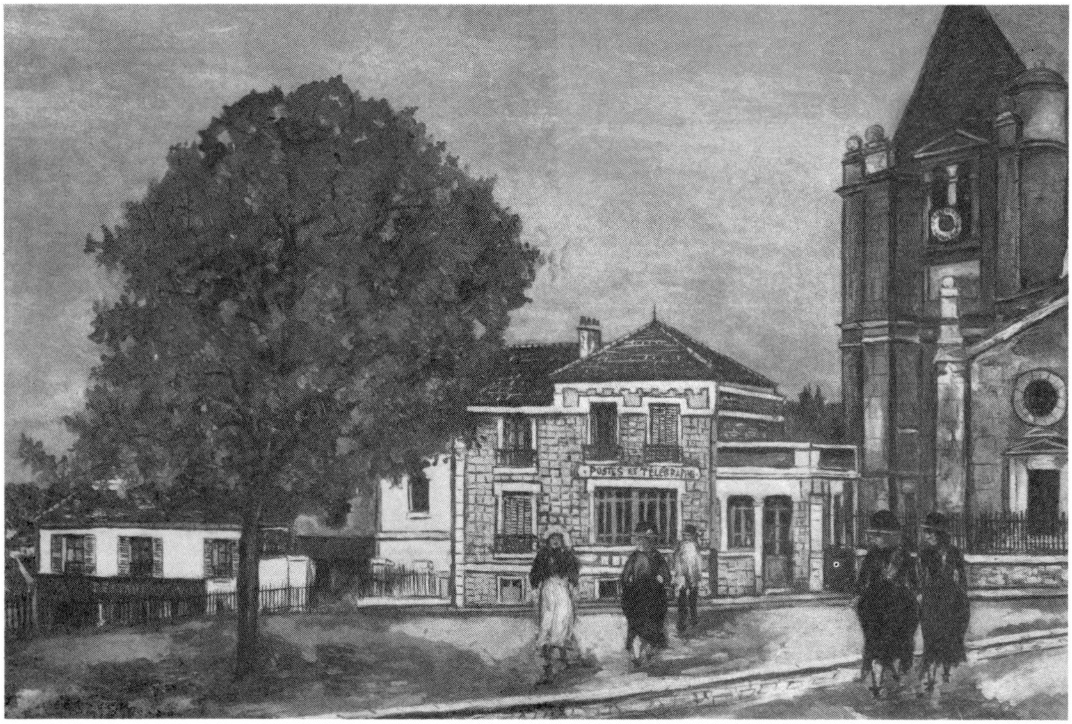

MAURICE UTRILLO – L'Eglise et le Bureau de Poste d'Ecouen – signed and dated 1924 – oil on canvas – 23 x 31in. *(Christie's)* **$202,070 £121,000**

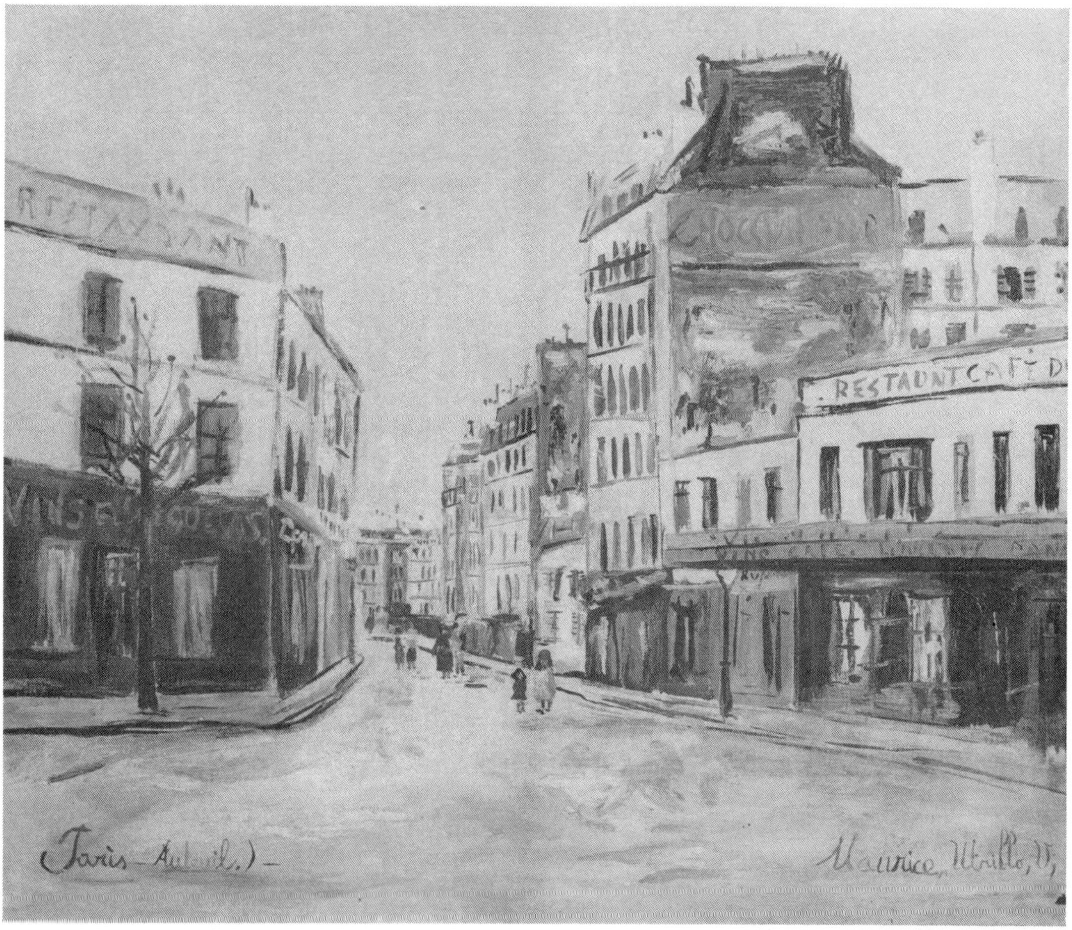

MAURICE UTRILLO – Paris, Auteuil – signed and inscribed – oil on canvas – 21½ x 25½in.
(Christie's) **$165,330** **£99,000**

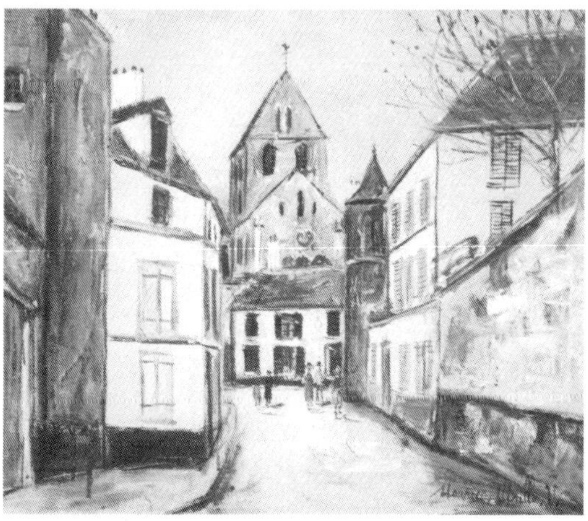

MAURICE UTRILLO – L'Eglise d'Auvers-sur-Oise – signed – oil on canvas – 20 x 23¾in.
(Christie's) **$82,368** **£57,200**

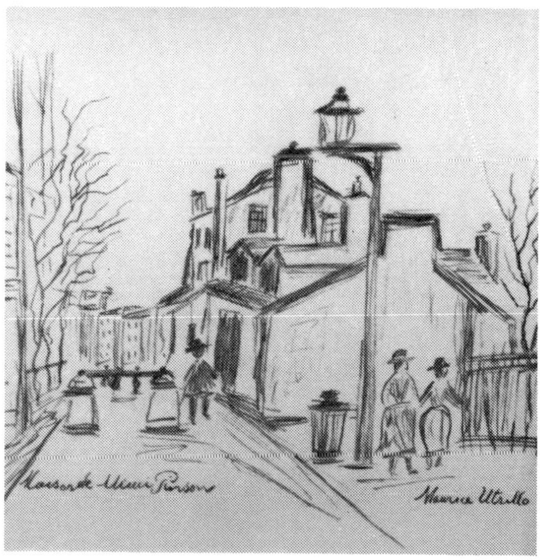

MAURICE UTRILLO – La Maison de Mimi Pinson – signed, inscribed – charcoal on paper – 17¾ x 18¾in.
(Christie's) **$13,728** **£8,580**

UTRILLO

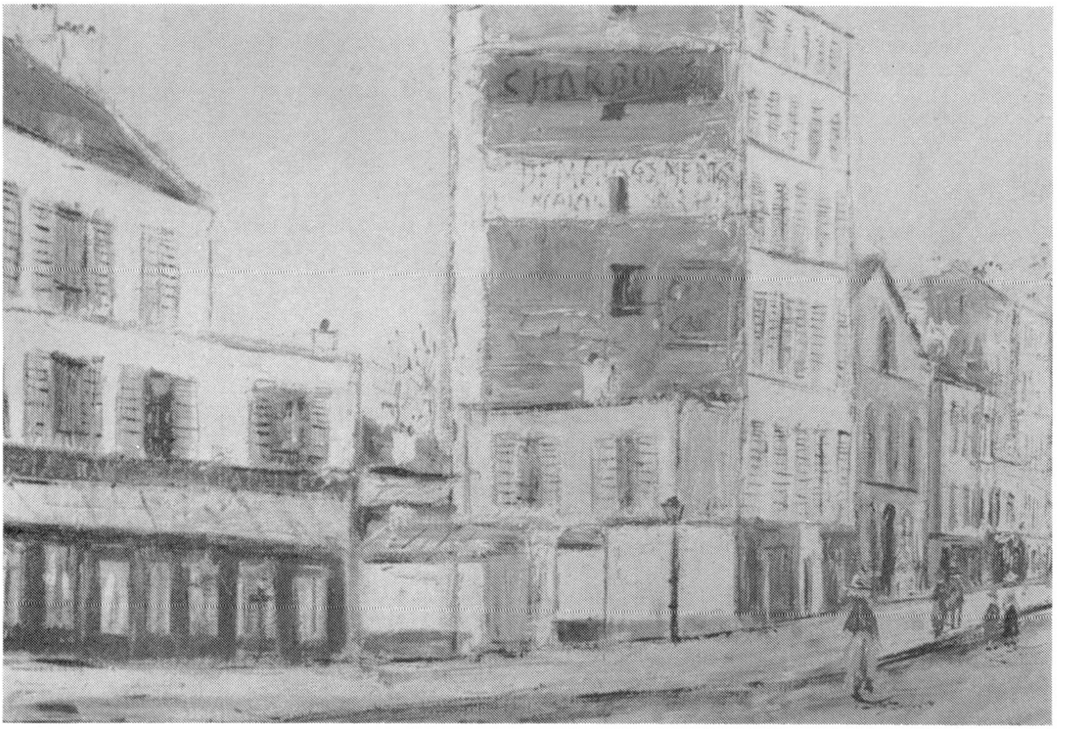

MAURICE UTRILLO – Le Mur rouge – signed and inscribed – oil on canvas – 18 x 55½in. *(Christie's)*
$95,524 £57,200

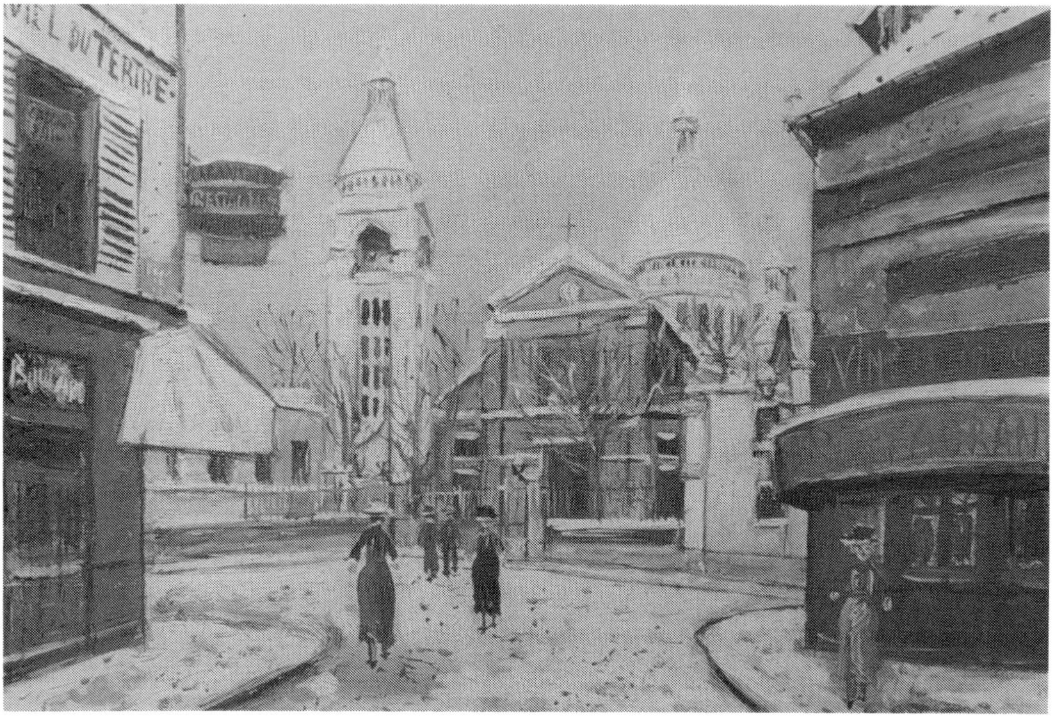

MAURICE UTRILLO – Eglise de St. Pierre et le Sacre Coeur de Montmartre – signed and dated 1937 – oil on canvas – 13 x 16in. *(Christie's)* **$106,546 £63,800**

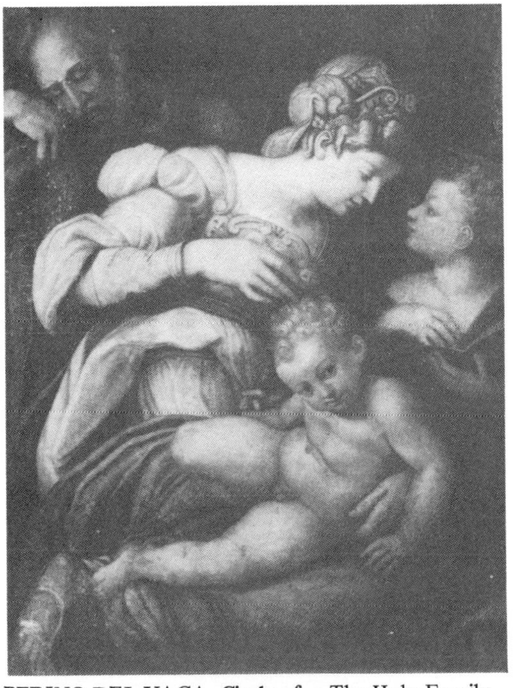

PERINO DEL VAGA, Circle of – The Holy Family With St. John – oil on panel – 42 x 31½in.
(Phillips) **$9,024 £6,400**

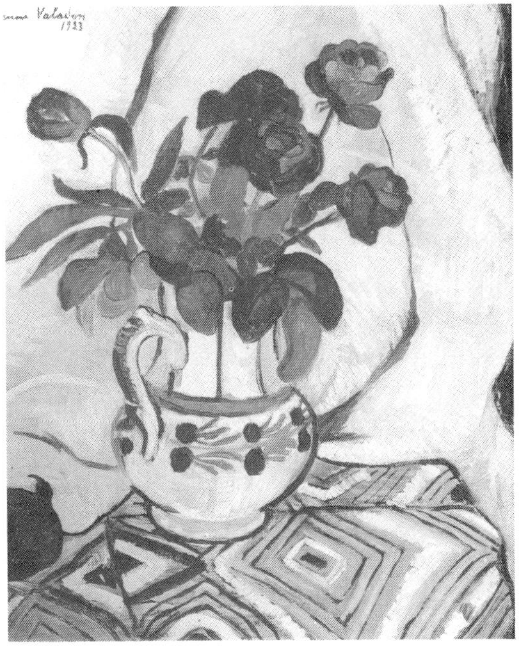

SUZANNE VALADON – Le Bouquet de Roses – signed and dated 1923 – oil on canvas – 21¾ x 18in.
(Christie's) **$31,680 £22,000**

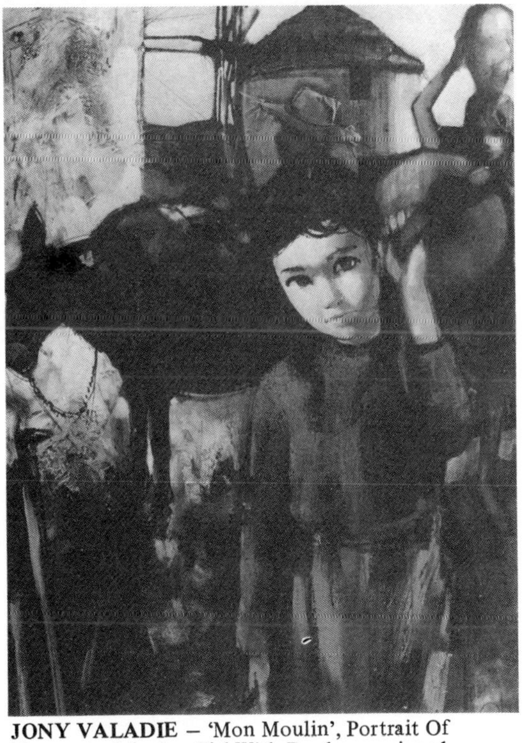

JONY VALADIE – 'Mon Moulin', Portrait Of Young Andalusian Girl With Donkey – signed – oil on canvas – 29 x 21in.
(Worsfolds) **$798 £550**

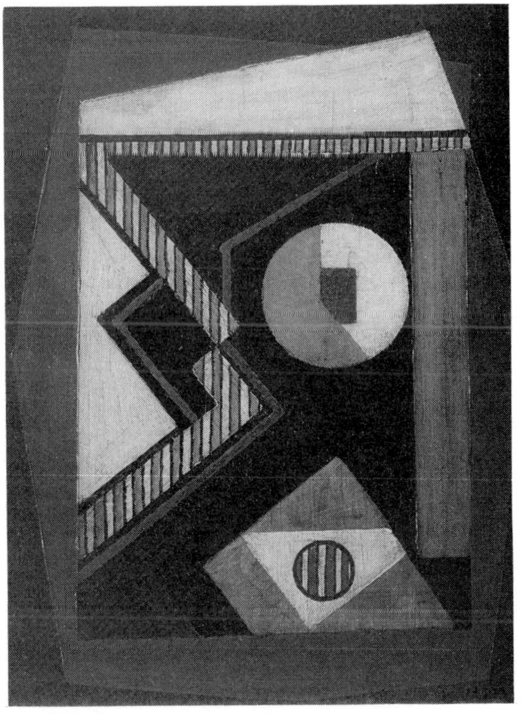

GEORGES VALMIER – Composition abstraite – signed – oil on panel – 10½ x 9¼in.
(Christie's) **$16,533 £9,900**

VALMIER

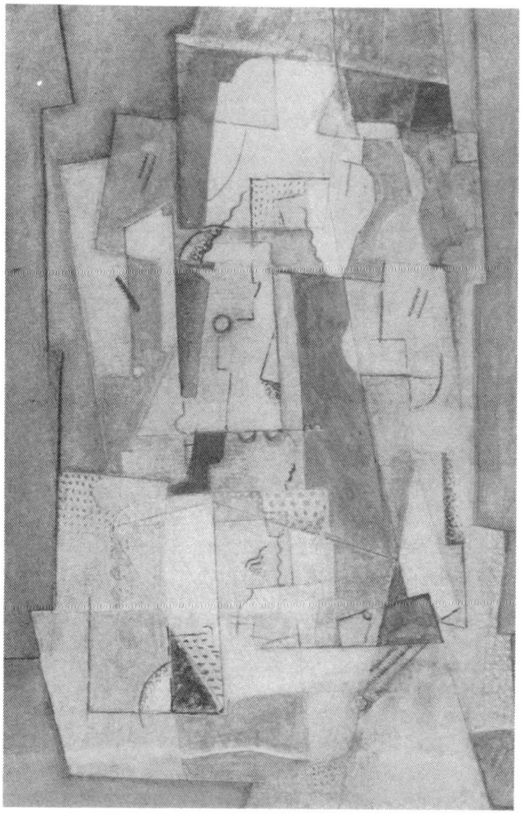

GEORGES VALMIER – Composition cubiste – signed – watercolour, pen and ink on paper – 6¾ x 4¼in.
(Christie's) **$15,840** **£9,900**

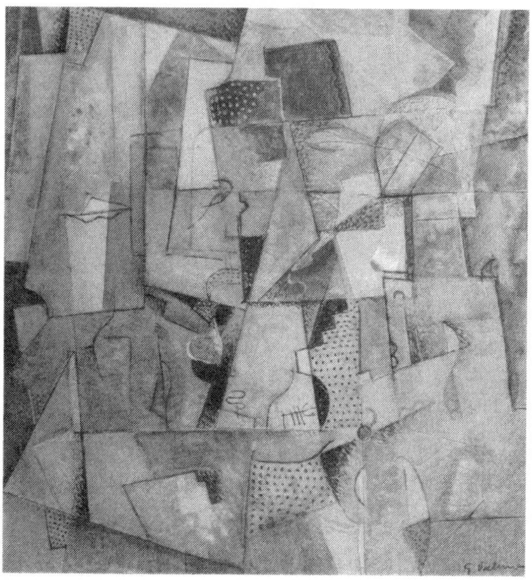

GEORGES VALMIER – Composition cubiste – signed – watercolour, pen and ink on paper – 5¼ x 4¾in.
(Christie's) **$12,320** **£7,700**

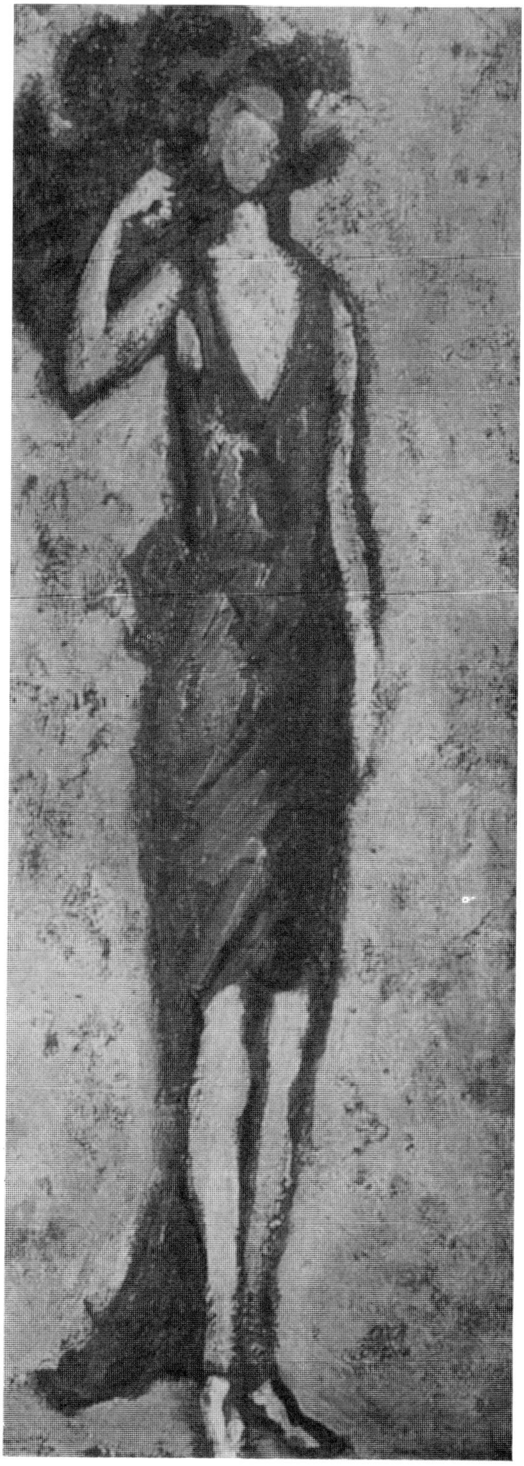

LOUIS VALTAT – Femme dans une Robe bleue – oil on canvas – 15¼ x 6½in.
(Christie's) **$7,348** **£4,400**

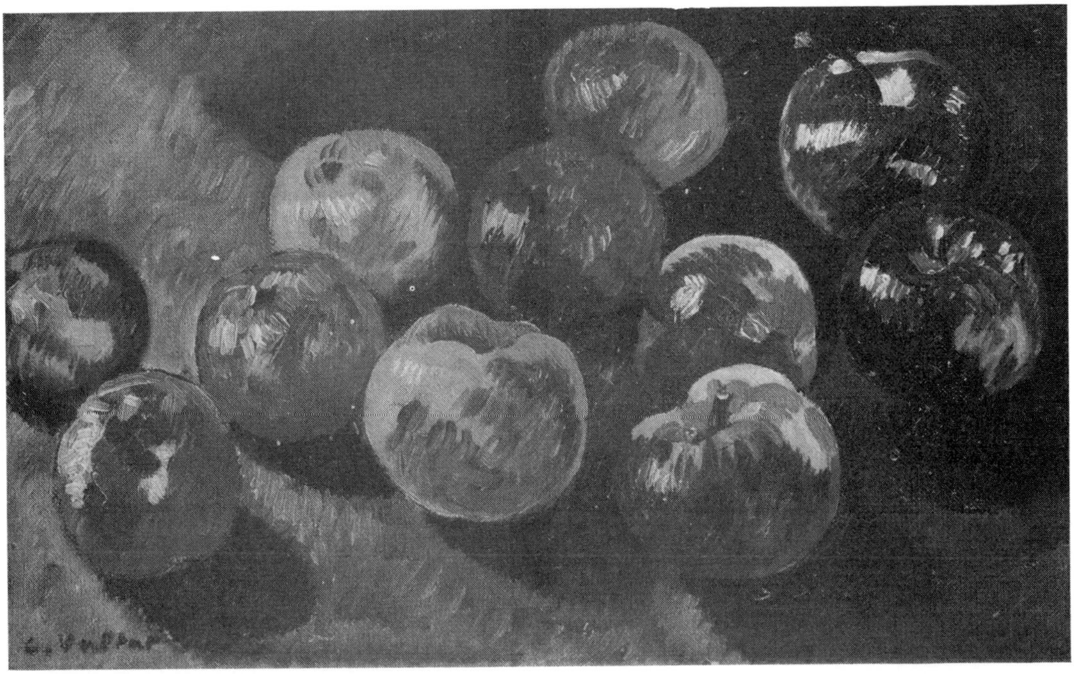

LOUIS VALTAT – Nature morte aux Pommes – signed – oil on canvas – 10¾ x 16¼in. *(Christie's)*
$11,022 £6,600

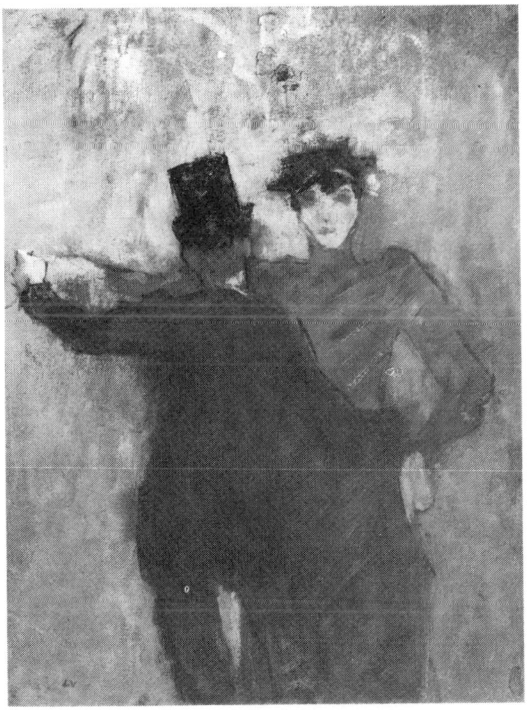

LOUIS VALTAT – Les Danseurs – signed with initials – oil on canvas – 22½ x 17in.
(Christie's) **$20,207 £12,100**

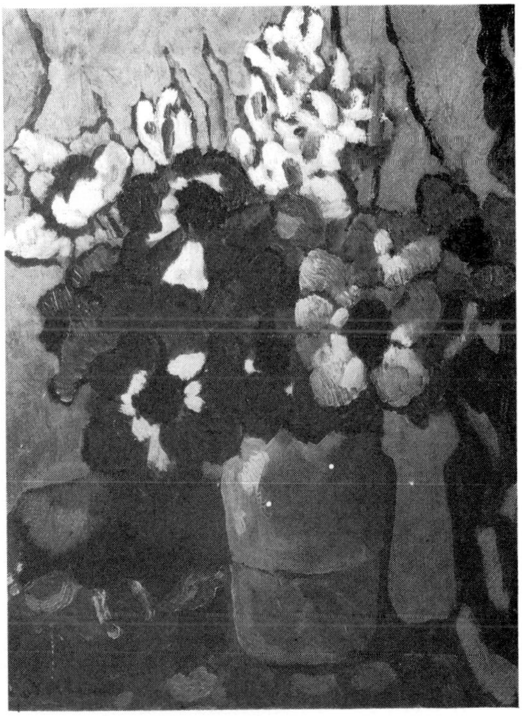

LOUIS VALTAT – Bouquet de Fleurs – signed – oil on canvas – 16½ x 13¼in.
(Christie's) **$27,555 £16,500**

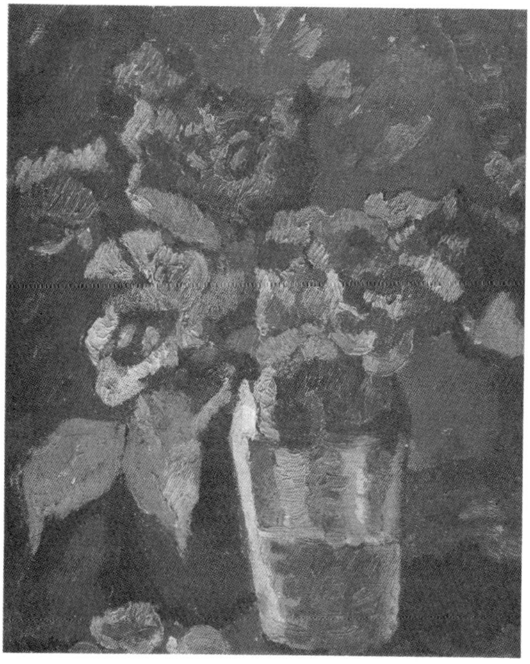

LOUIS VALTAT – Bouquet de Fleurs – signed – oil on canvas – 18¼ x 15in.
(Christie's) **$17,424 £12,100**

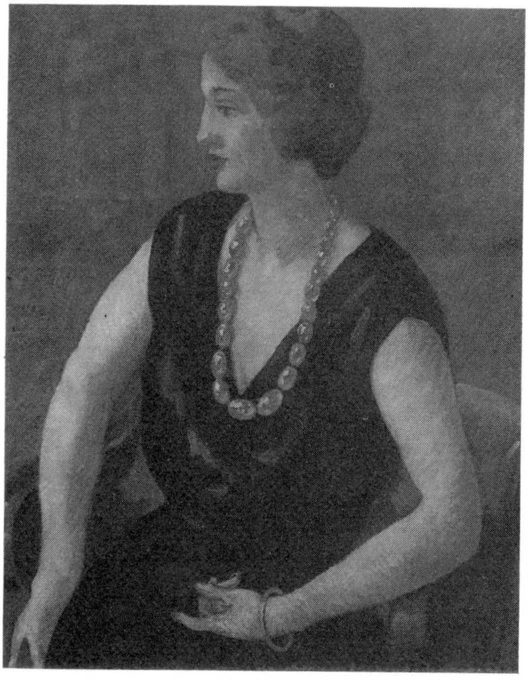

LOUIS VALTAT – Femme au Collier jaune, Mme. Mead, Chanteuse de l'Opera – signed – oil on canvas – 31¾ x 25½in.
(Christie's) **$18,370 £11,000**

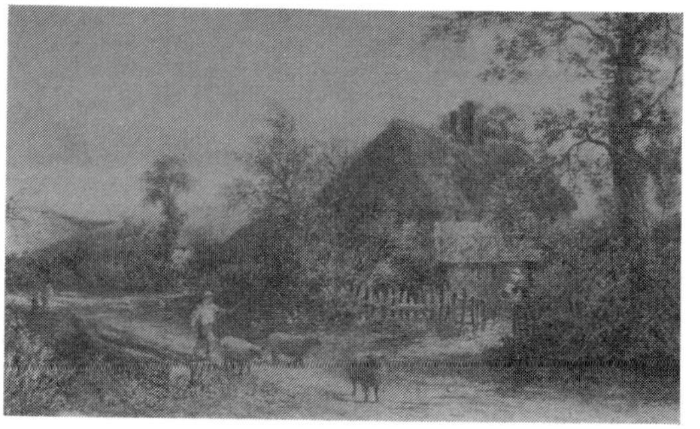

EDGAR JOHN VARLEY – A Sussex Lane With A Shepherd Driving Sheep – signed, and signed again and inscribed on the reverse – watercolour heightened with white – 7¼ x 11½in.
(Christie's) **$2,008 £1,210**

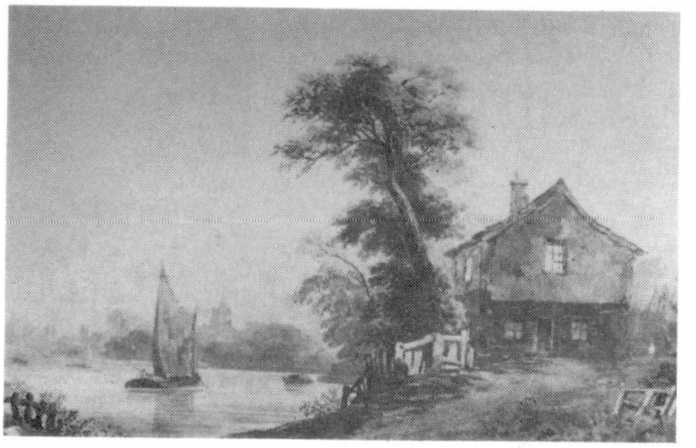

JOHN VARLEY – View Of The Thames At Chiswick – watercolour – 26 x 37cm.
(Phillips) **$1,859 £1,300**

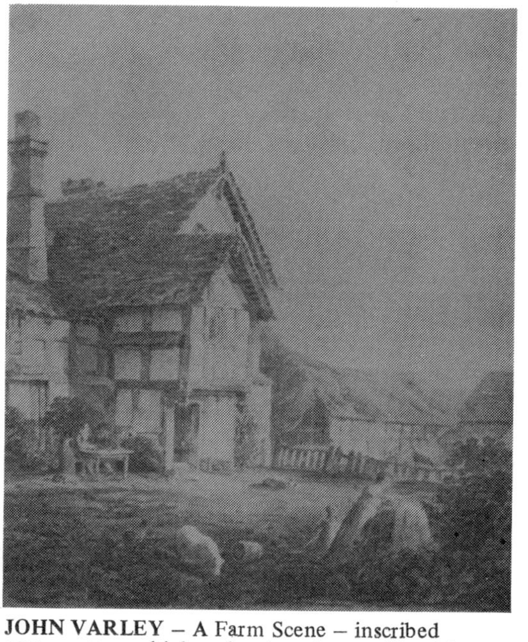

JOHN VARLEY – A Farm Scene – inscribed verso – pen and ink and watercolour – 27 x 25cm.
(Phillips) **$815 £500**

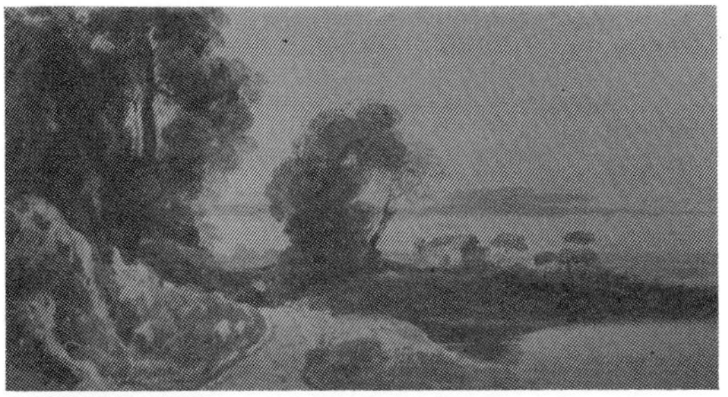

JOHN VARLEY – Figures In A Wooded River Landscape – signed – watercolour – 21 x 32cm.
(Phillips) **$1,630** **£1,000**

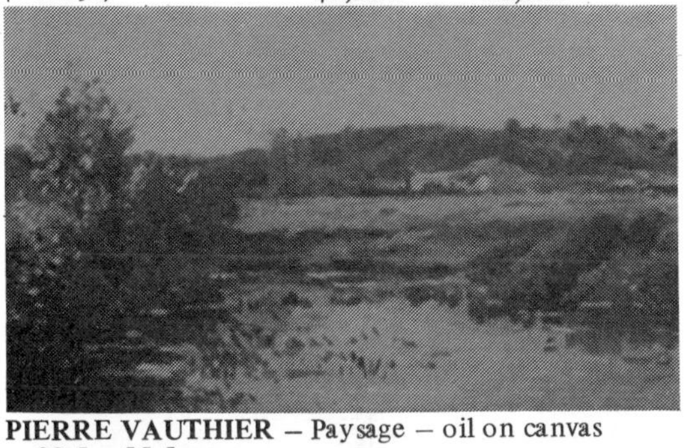

PIERRE VAUTHIER – Paysage – oil on canvas – 38.5 x 55.5cm.
(Phillips) **$775** **£500**

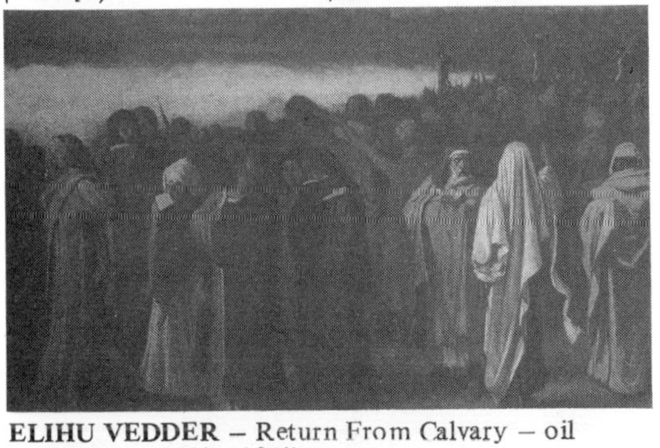

ELIHU VEDDER – Return From Calvary – oil on canvas – 13¾ x 19¾in.
(Christie's) **$6,600** **£4,112**

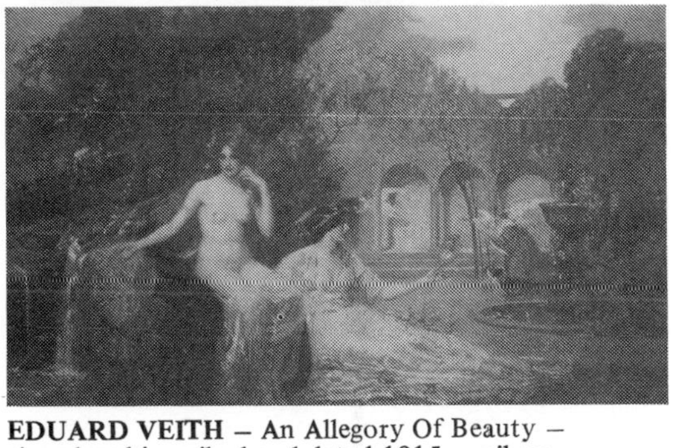

EDUARD VEITH – An Allegory Of Beauty – signed and inscribed and dated 1915 – oil on canvas – 115 x 179cm.
(Phillips) **$15,030** **£9,000**

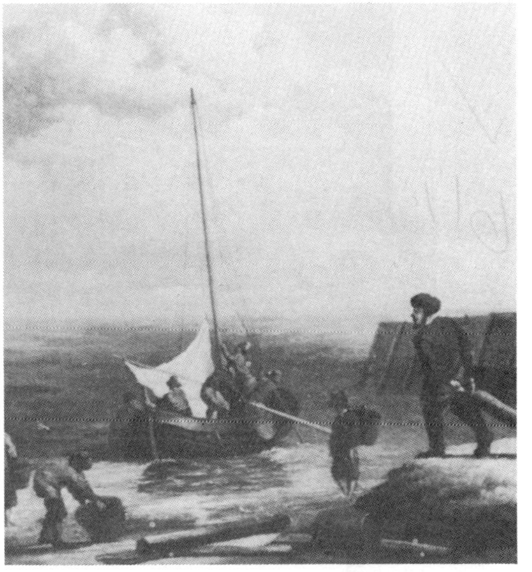

WILLIAM VAN DER VELDE, Studio of – Figures Beside A Quay From Which A Fishing Vessel Sets Sail – oil on canvas – 14½ x 11in.
(Phillips) **$1,269** **£900**

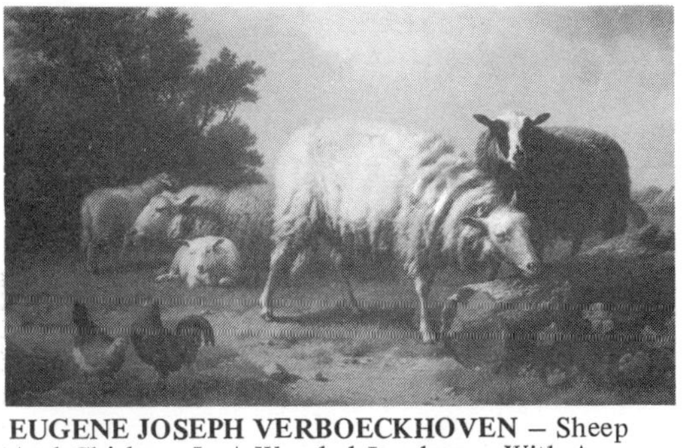

EUGENE JOSEPH VERBOECKHOVEN – Sheep And Chickens In A Wooded Landscape With A Farmstead Beyond – signed and dated 1869 – 22 x 29in.
(Christie's) **$14,080** **£8,800**

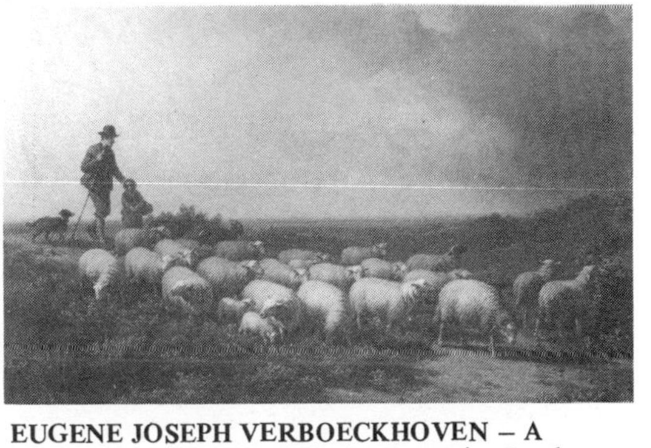

EUGENE JOSEPH VERBOECKHOVEN – A Shepherd And His Flock In An Extensive Landscape – signed and dated 1875, and signed and authenticated on an old label on the reverse – on panel – 16 x 24in.
(Christie's) **$16,720** **£10,450**

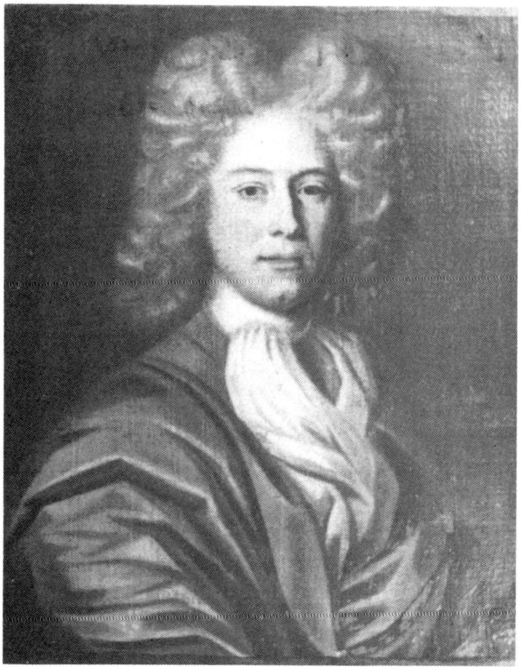

JOHANNES VERELST – Portrait Of A Gentleman With White Cravat – signed and dated – oil – 28 x 23in.
(Christie's) **$725** **£500**

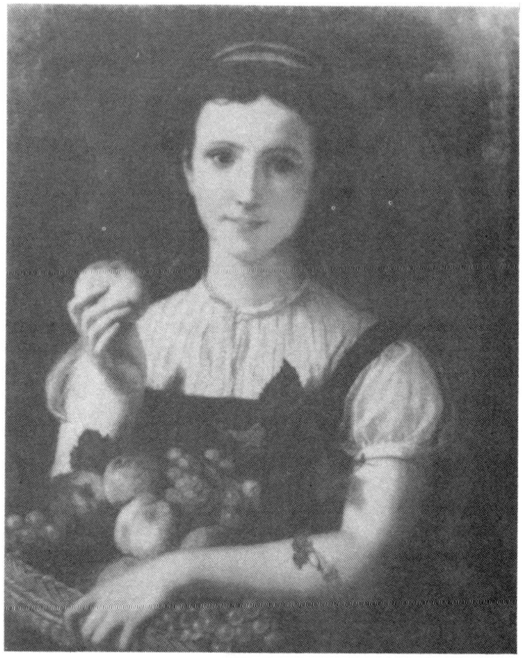

CHARLES MICHEL MARIA VERLAT – The Fruit Seller – signed and dated 1867 – oil on panel – 28¾ x 23in.
(Christie's) **$1,900** **£1,320**

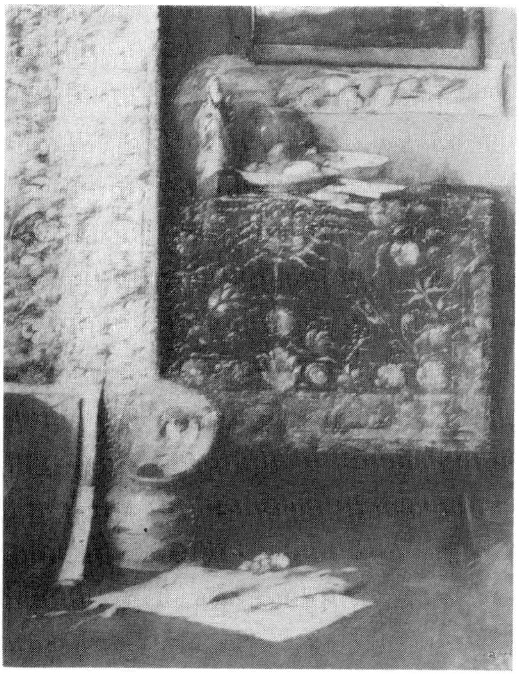

ALFRED VERHAEREN – Interieur Japonais – signed with initials – on panel – 26½ x 21½in.
(Christie's) **$3,009** **£1,980**

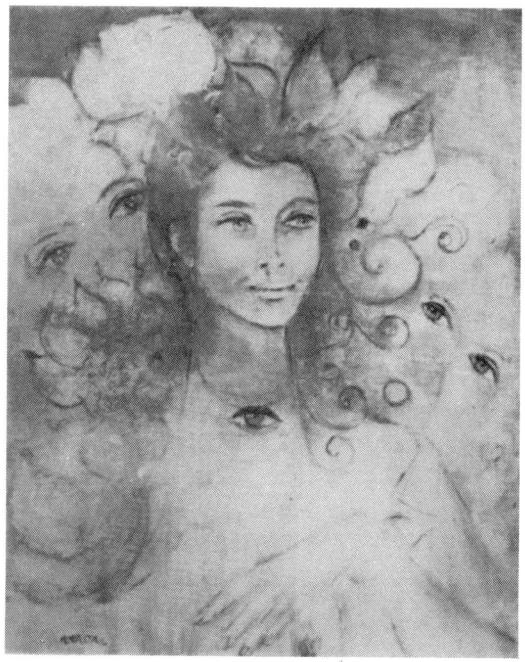

VERONE – Indifferent – signed – oil on canvas – 21¾ x 18in.
(Christie's) **$1,408** **£ £880**

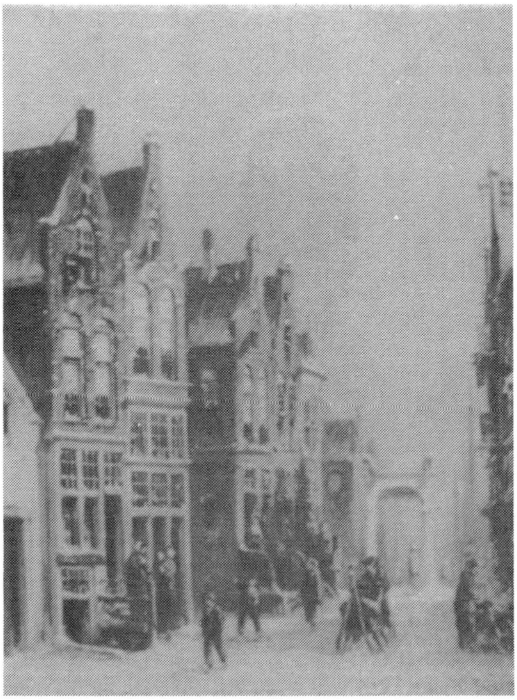

PETRUS GERARDUS VERTIN – Figures In A Snowy Dutch Street – signed and dated '06 – oil on panel – 24.5 x 18.5cm.
(Phillips) **$3,006** **£1,800**

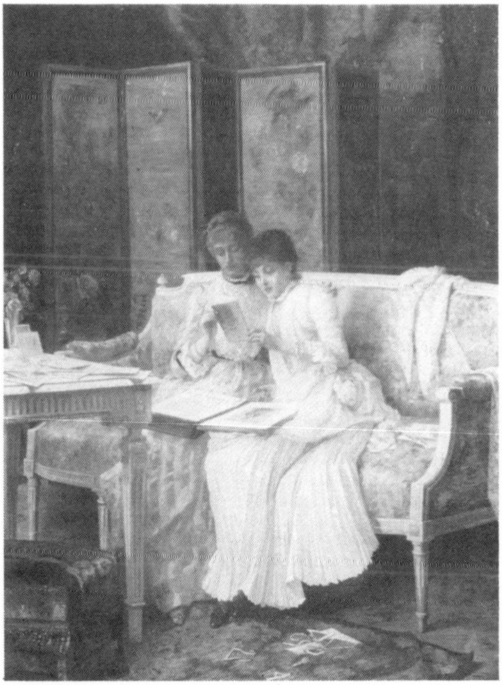

ALBERTO VIANELLI – A Jury – signed and inscribed – 46 x 31½in.
(Christie's) **$15,840** **£11,000**

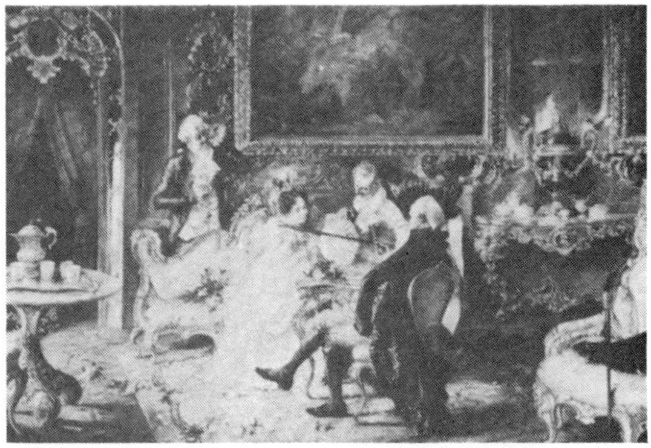

G. VIDAL – The Intimates – signed and dated '902 – on canvas – 43 x 63cm.
(Phillips) **$1,087** **£720**

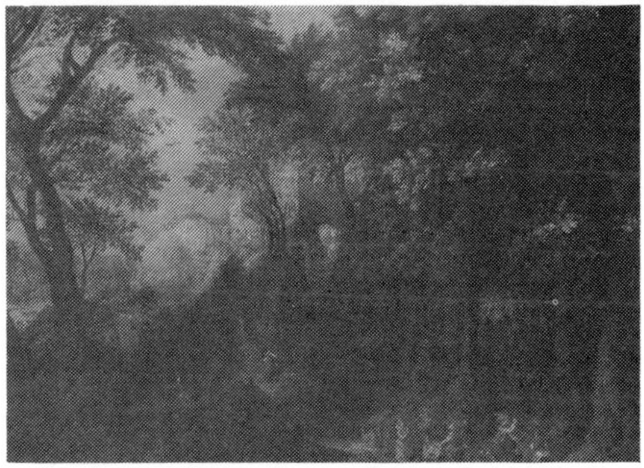

DAVID VINCKBOONS – A Wooded Landscape – on canvas – 33½ x 41¼in.
(Phillips) **$9,628** **£5,800**

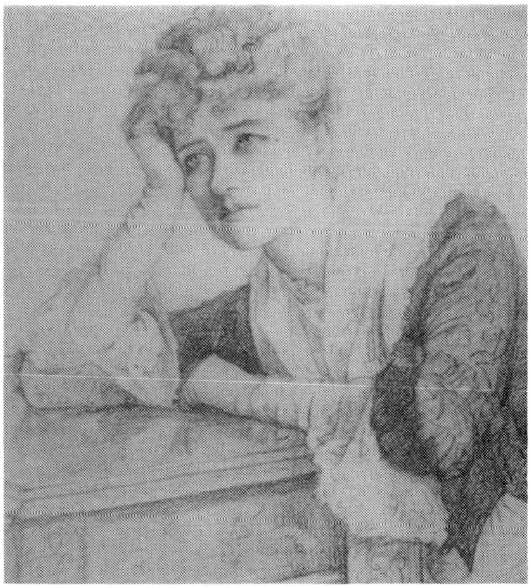

VIOLET, DUCHESS OF RUTLAND – Portrait Of Ellen Terry In The Role Of 'Olivia', Waist Length, Leaning On A Cabinet – signed with monogram and dated 1878 – pencil – 9¼ x 7 in.
(Christie's) **$1,278** **£770**

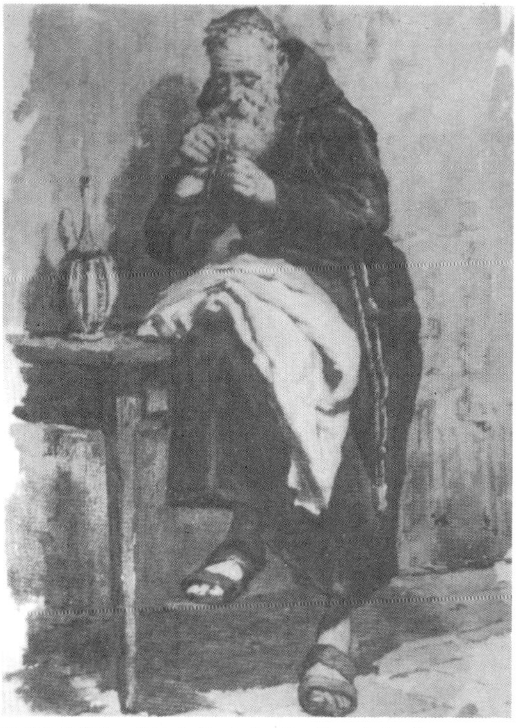

E. VITALE – Monk Seated, Mending A Sock – signed – watercolour – 12½ x 6in.
(W. H. Lane & Son) **$195** **£130**

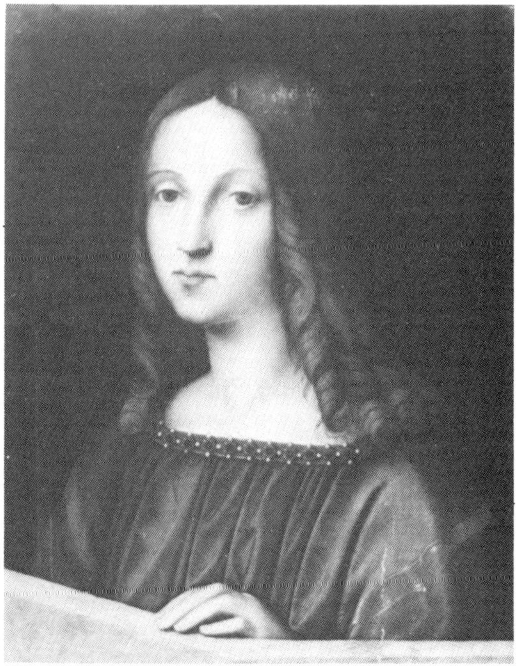

ANTONIO VIVARINI, Circle of – St. John The Evangelist – oil on panel – 17½ x 13½in.
(Phillips) **$3,384** **£2,400**

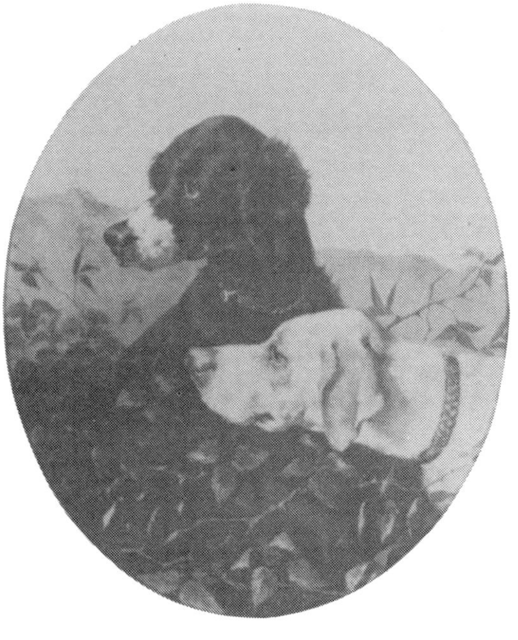

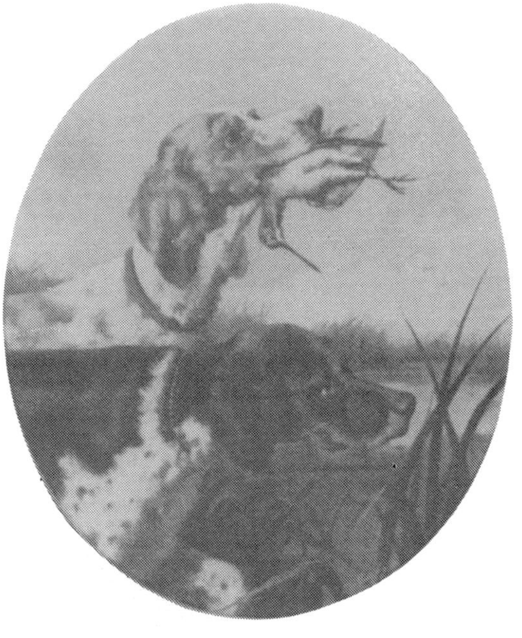

DE VIVO – The Chevalier Bracco Italiano In A Landscape; and In A Marsh – signed – oil – 26½ x 22in. *(Christie's)* **$2,557** **£1,650 Pair**

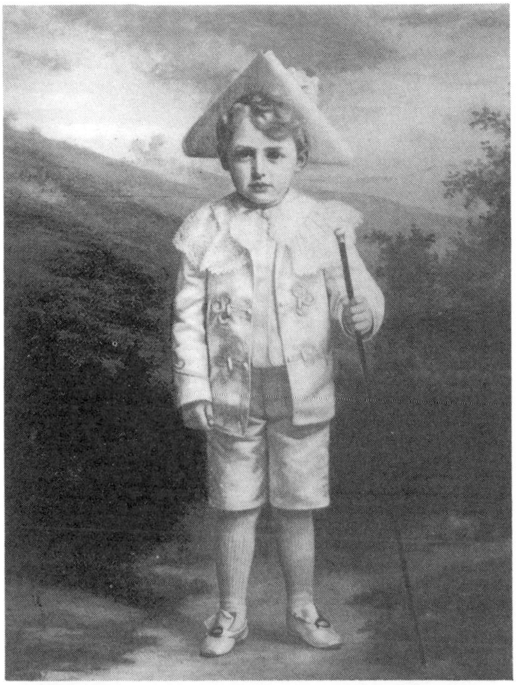

W. VIZARD – Portrait Of A Young Boy, Standing Full Length, In A Landscape – signed and dated 1901 – 36 x 28in.
(Christie's) **$4,375** **£2,860**

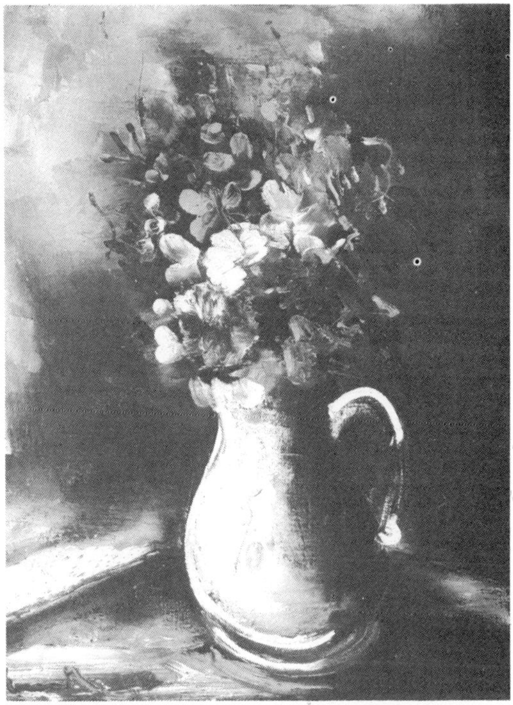

MAURICE DE VLAMINCK – Bouquet de Fleurs – signed – oil on canvas – 24¼ x 18¼in.
(Christie's) **$66,528** **£46,200**

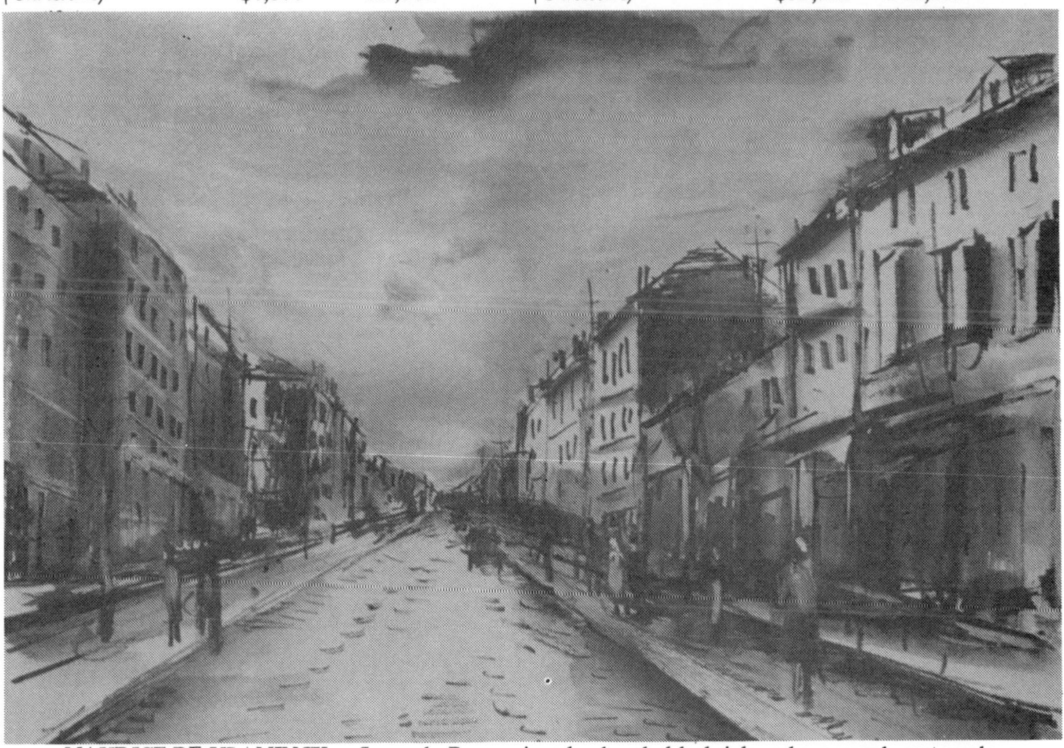

MAURICE DE VLAMINCK – Scene de Rue – signed – brush, black ink and grey wash, watercolour and gouache on paper – 18 x 21½in. *(Christie's)* **$22,000** **£13,750**

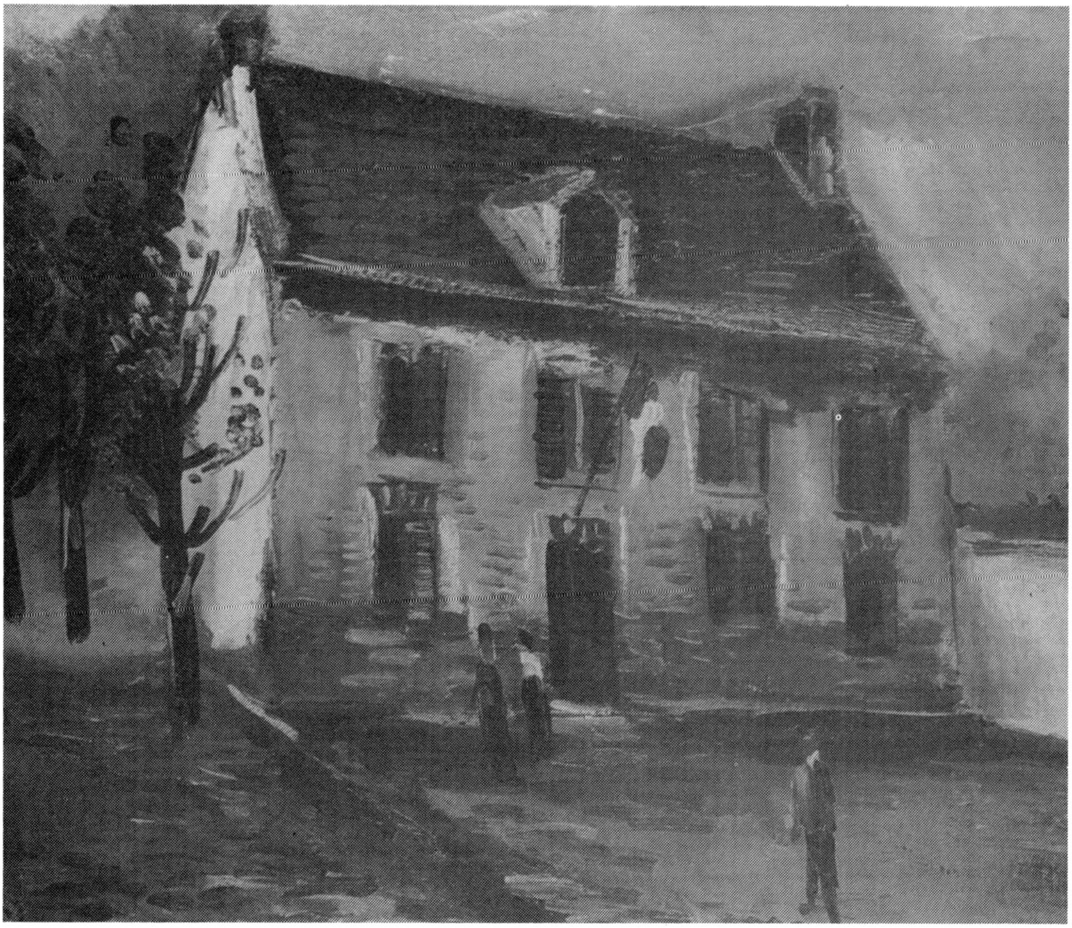

MAURICE DE VLAMINCK – La Mairie – signed – oil on canvas – 15 x 18¼in. *(Christie's)*
$44,352 £30,800

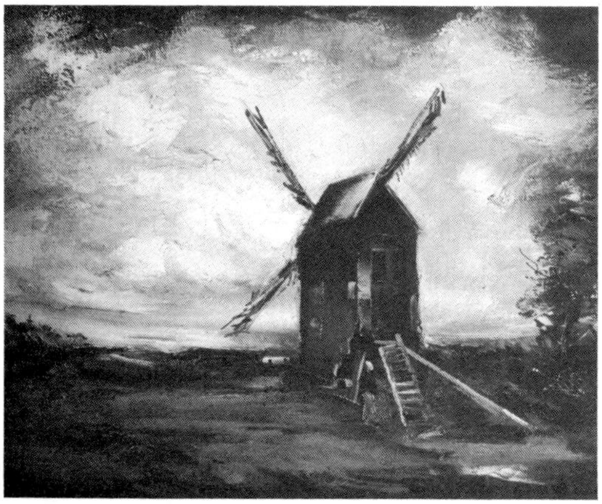

MAURICE DE VLAMINCK – Moulin-a-Vent, Paysage orageux – signed – oil on canvas – 21½ x 25in.
(Christie's) **$44,352 £30,800**

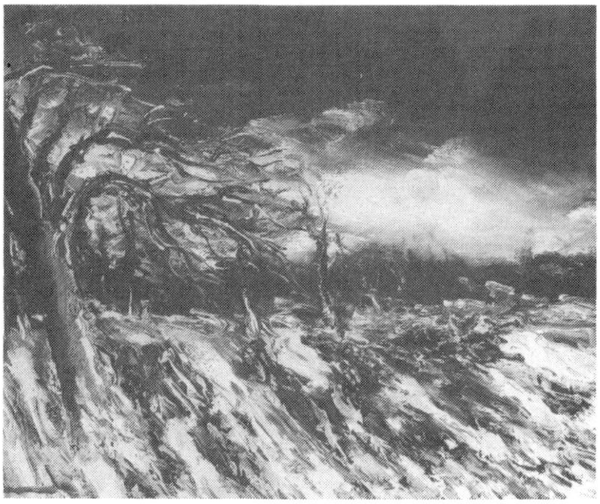

MAURICE DE VLAMINCK – Paysage de Neige – signed – oil on canvas – 21¼ x 25½in.
(Christie's) **$62,458 £37,400**

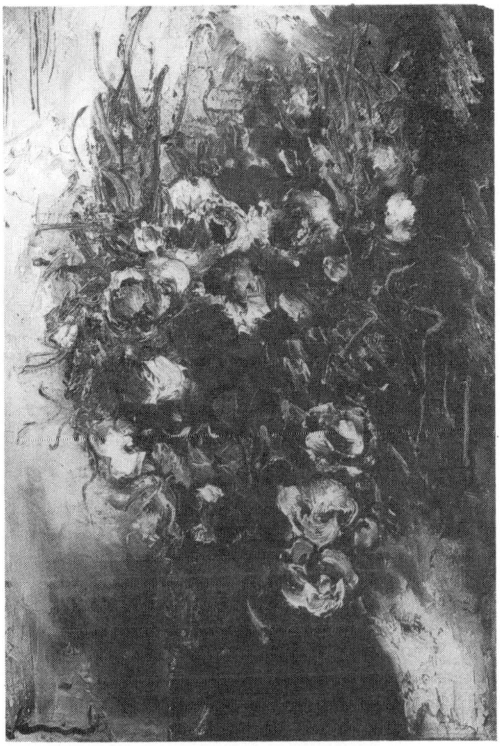

MAURICE DE VLAMINCK – Bouquet de Fleurs – signed – oil on canvas – 22 x 15¼in.
(Christie's) **$66,132 £39,600**

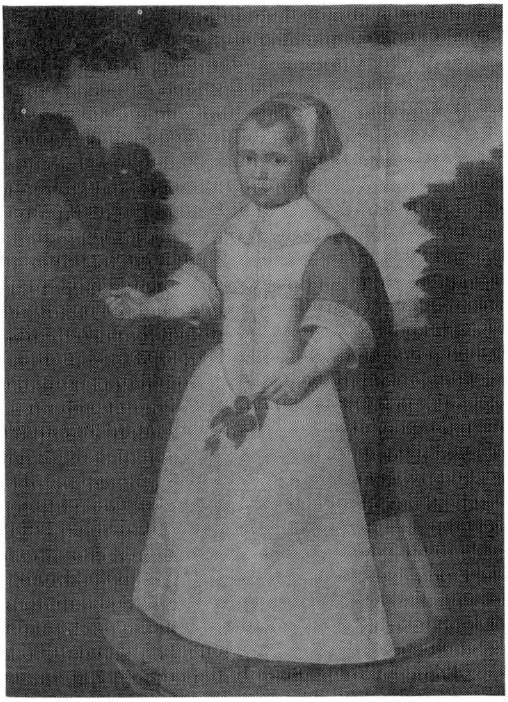

WILLEM WILLEMSZN VAN VLIET, Circle of – Portrait Of A Young Girl – inscribed and dated 1609 – on panel – 40 x 32¾in.
(Phillips) **$49,800 £30,000**

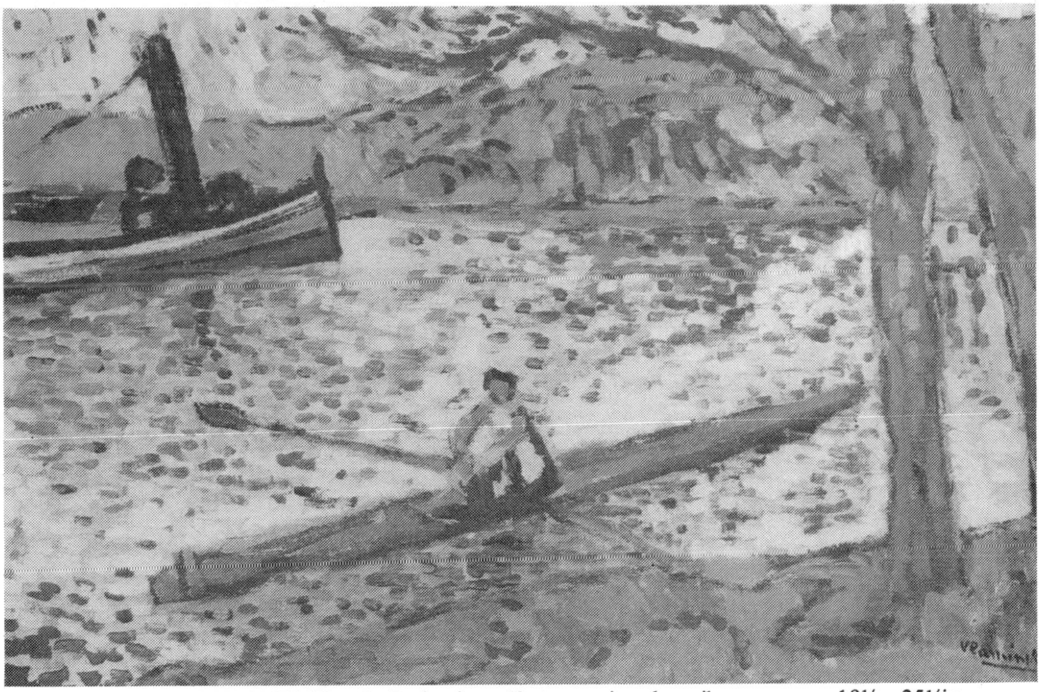

MAURICE DE VLAMINCK – La Perissoire a Chatou – signed – oil on canvas – 19¼ x 25½in.
(Christie's) **$696,960 £484,000**

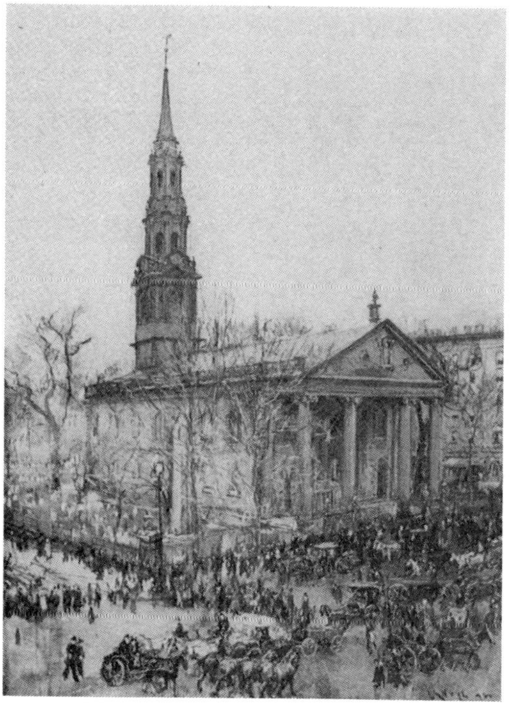

LOUIS CHARLES VOGT – St. Paul's Church, New York – signed and dated '92 – gouache and pen and black ink on paper – 13½ x 10½in.
(Christie's) **$4,950 £3,479**

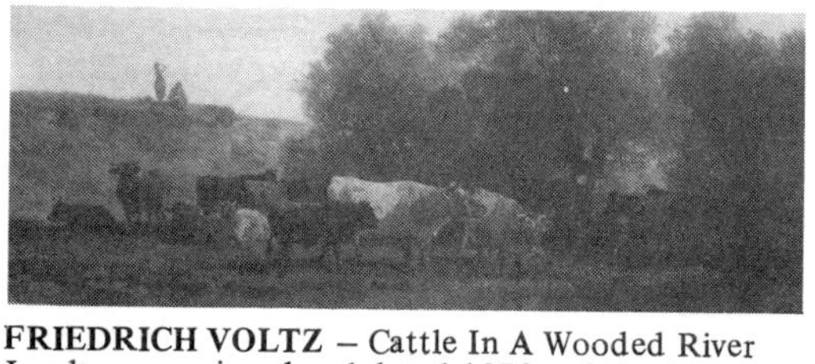

FRIEDRICH VOLTZ – Cattle In A Wooded River Landscape – signed and dated 1872 – 9½ x 24in.
(Christie's) **$26,400 £16,500**

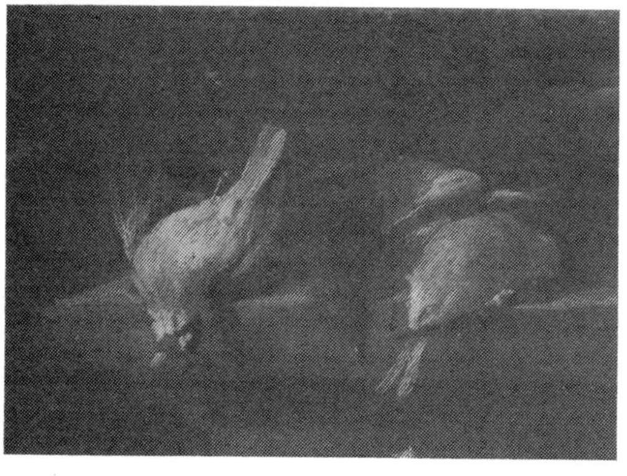

JAN VONCK – A Still Life, A Bullfinch, Goldfinch And A Starling Lay On A Stone Ledge – signed – on panel – 10½ x 25½in.
(Phillips) **$5,312 £3,200**

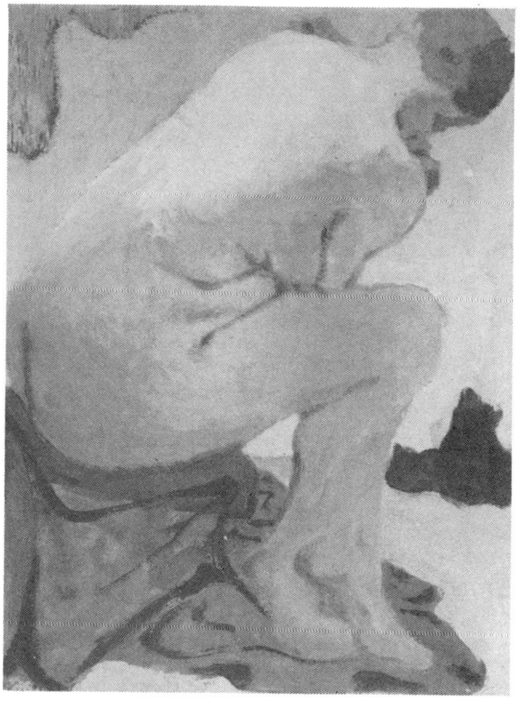

EDOUARD VUILLARD – Nu assis – oil on board – 11¾ x 8¾in.
(Christie's) **$63,360 £44,000**

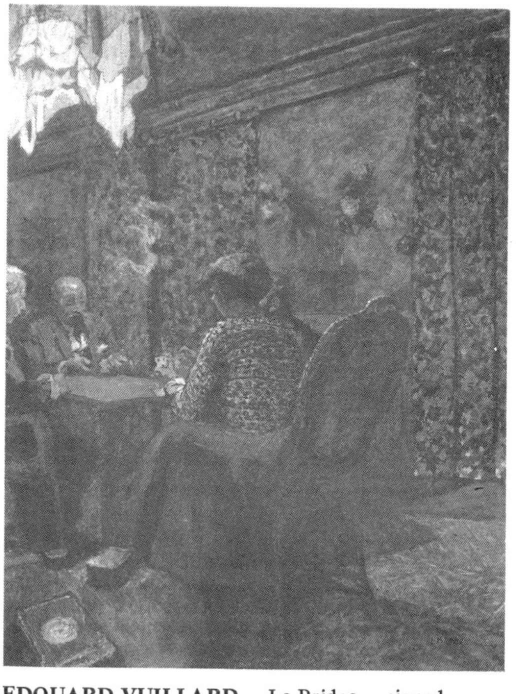

EDOUARD VUILLARD – Le Bridge – signed – peinture a la colle on paper laid on canvas – 39¼ x 29¾in.
(Christie's) **$253,440 £176,000**

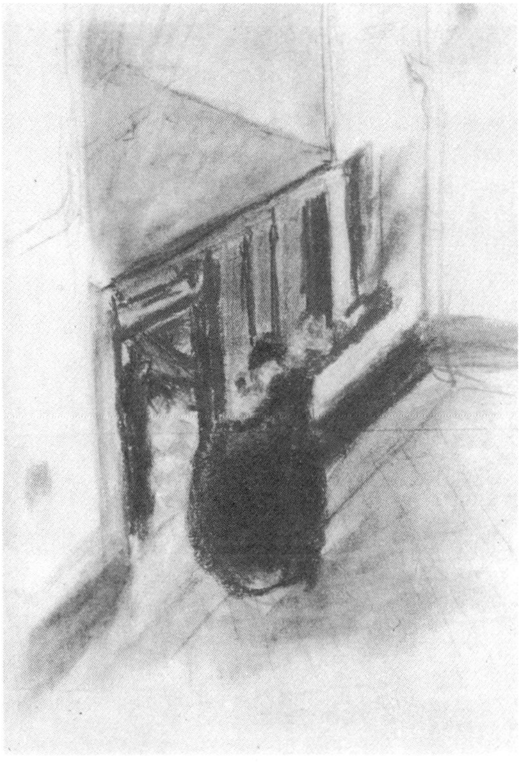

EDOUARD VUILLARD – La Cour de la Rue des Batignolles – pastel on Chine volant paper – recto; La Partie de Dames, from 'Paysages et Interieurs' – lithograph printed in colours, on Chine volant – verso – 14 x 10in.
(Christie's) **$31,680** **£22,000**

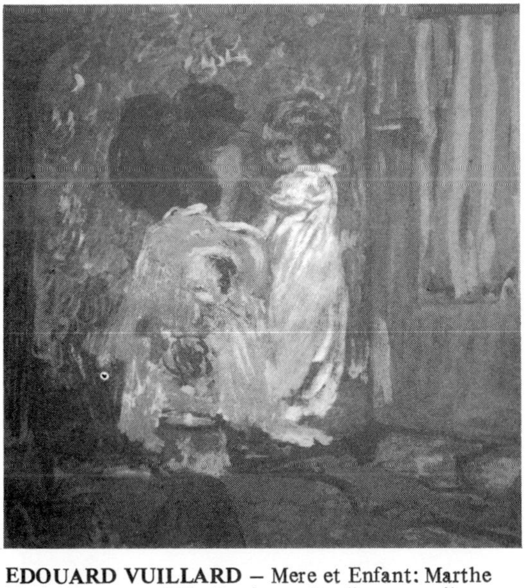

EDOUARD VUILLARD – Mere et Enfant: Marthe Nathanson et sa Fille Denise au Pouilguen – oil on board – 30¼ x 29¼in.
(Christie's) **$126,720** **£88,000**

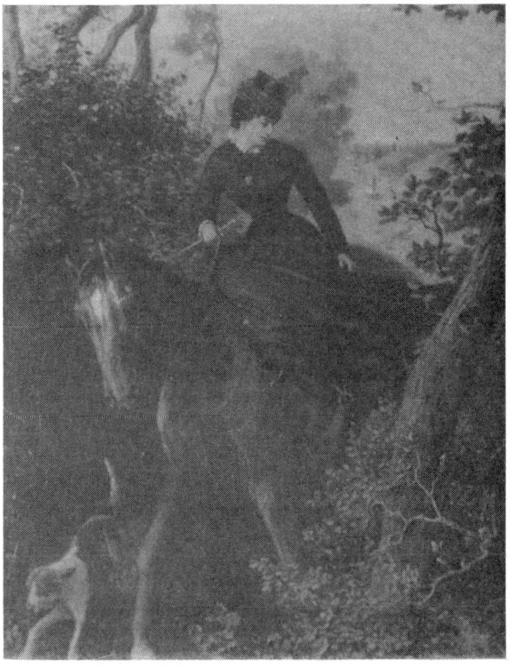

W.B. – An Awkward Moment – indistinctly signed – 25½ x 20¼in.
(Christie's) **$1,254** **£825**

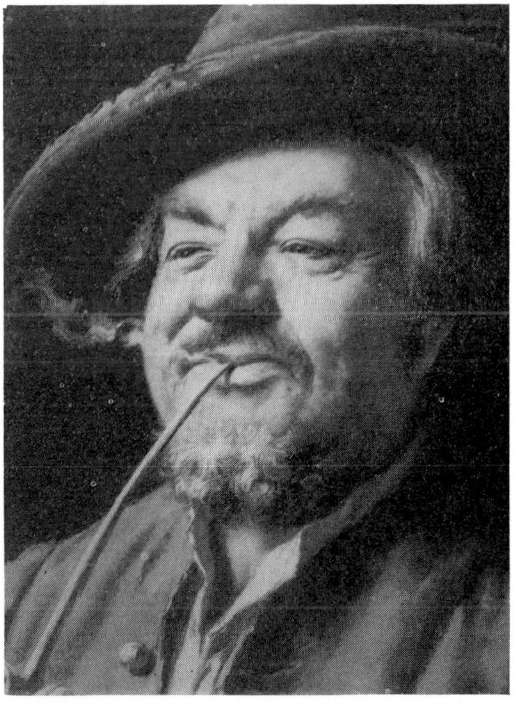

FRITZ WAGNER – A Smoking Cavalier – signed – 9 x 7in.
(Christie's) **$836** **£550**

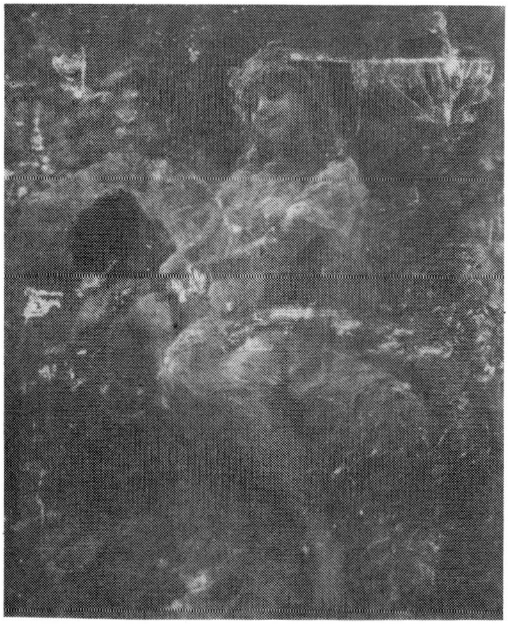

PAUL WAGNER – Young Love – signed and inscribed – on canvas – 151 x 101cm.
(Phillips) **$3,171** **£2,100**

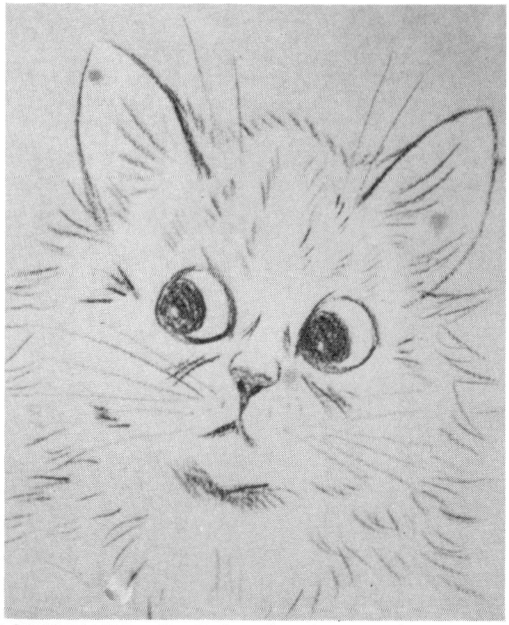

LOUIS WAIN – Startled – signed – sanguine chalk and yellow wash – 7½ x 6¼in.
(Bonhams) **$403** **£260**

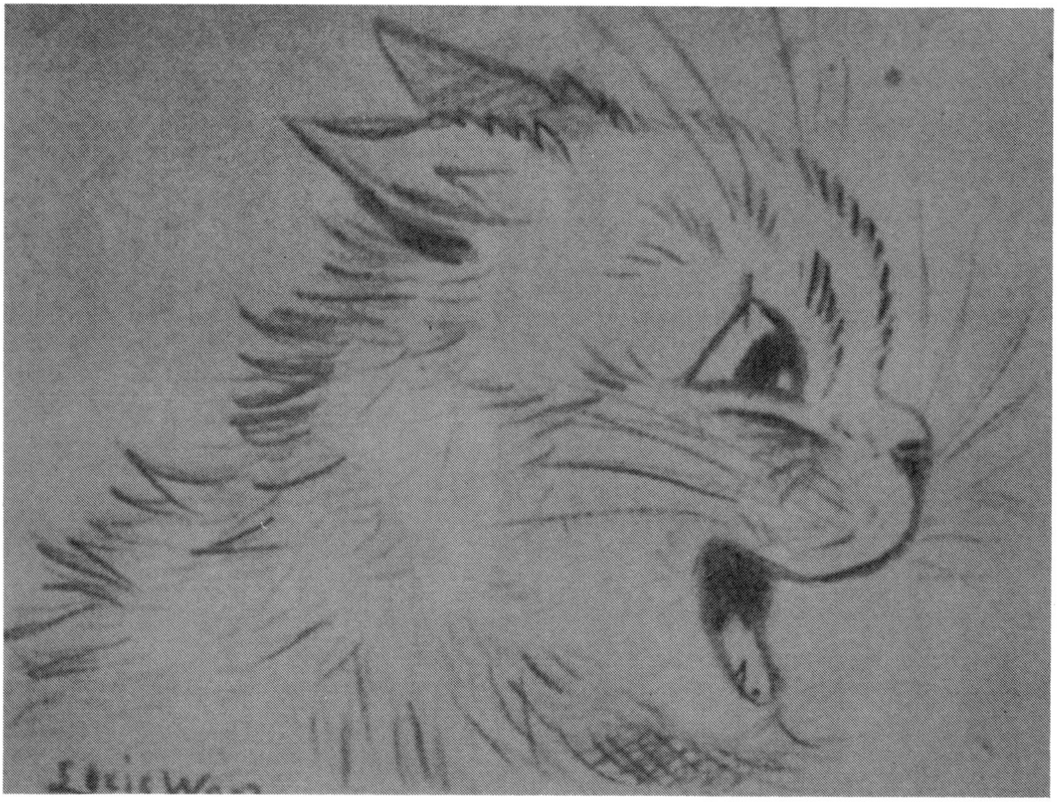

LOUIS WAIN – Great Amusement – signed – coloured chalks – 6½ x 8in. *(Bonhams)*
$232 **£150**

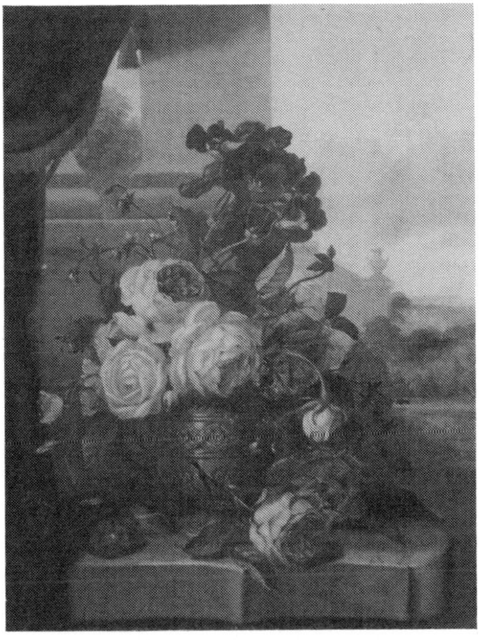

JOHN WAINWRIGHT – Roses, Begonia, Convulvulus And Speedwell In A Bronze Urn On A Ledge, A Landscape Beyond – signed and dated 1866 – 18 x 14in.
(Christie's) **$7,128** **£4,950**

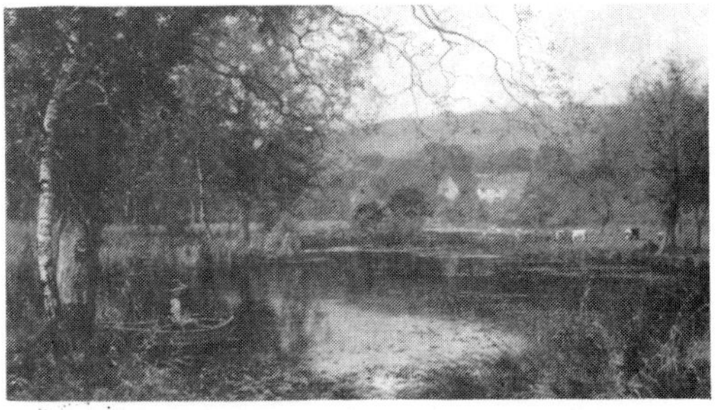

EDWARD WILKINS WAITE – An Autumn Landscape, With A Man In A Rowing Boat On A Pond, Cattle, A Watermill And A Wooded Hill Beyond – signed – oil on canvas – 27½ x 41½in.
(Geering & Colyer) **$14,000** **£8,750**

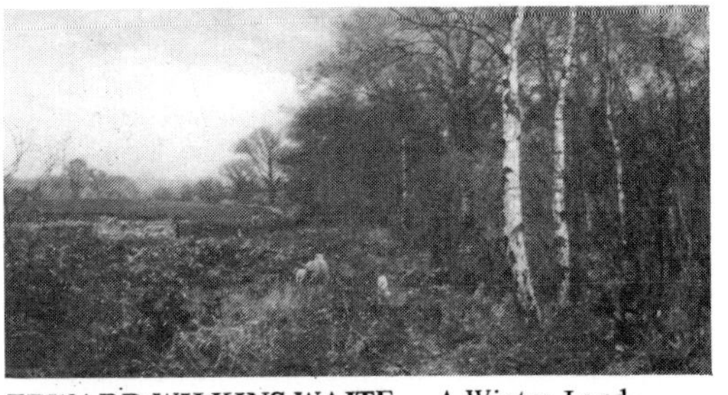

EDWARD WILKINS WAITE – A Winter Landscape With A Shepherd, Sheepdog And Sheep – signed – oil on canvas – 23¾ x 35¾in.
(Geering & Colyer) **$9,600** **£6,000**

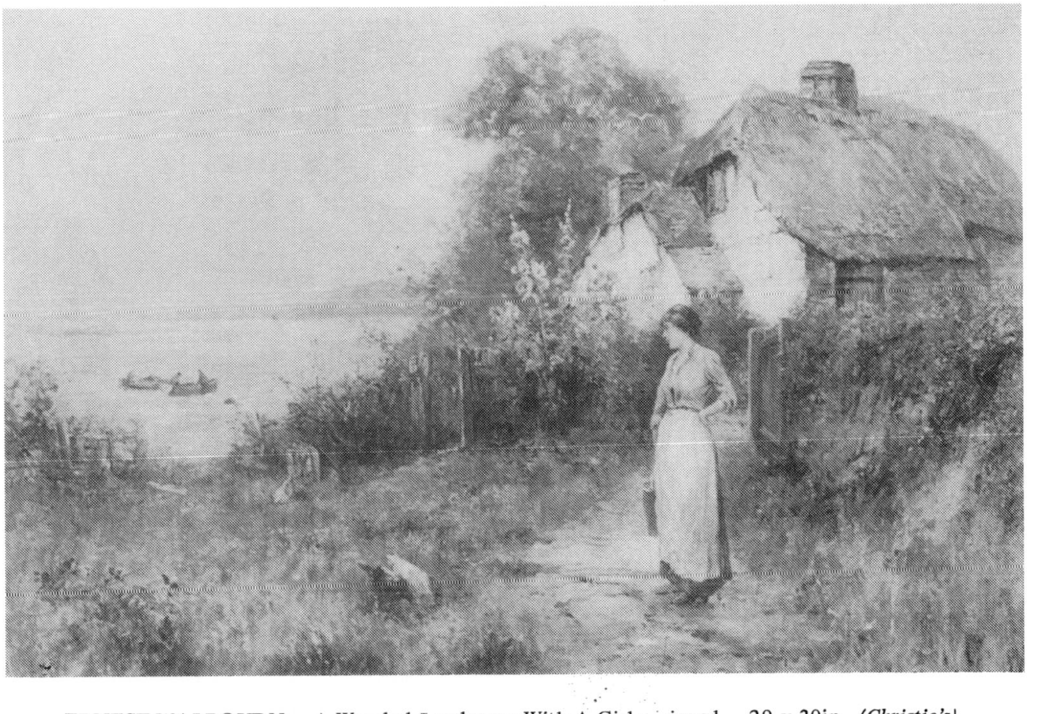

ERNEST WALBOURN – A Wooded Landscape With A Girl – signed – 20 x 30in. *(Christie's)*
$6,204 **£4,400**

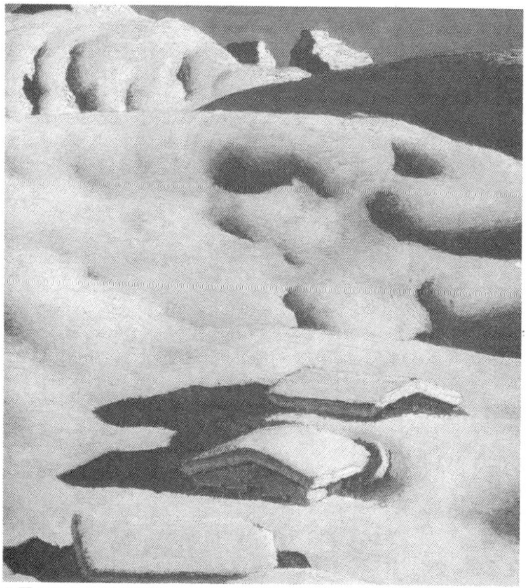

ALFONS WALDE – Almen im Schnee – signed, also inscribed and dated on a label on the reverse – oil on board – 22 x 18in.
(Christie's) $28,512 £19,800

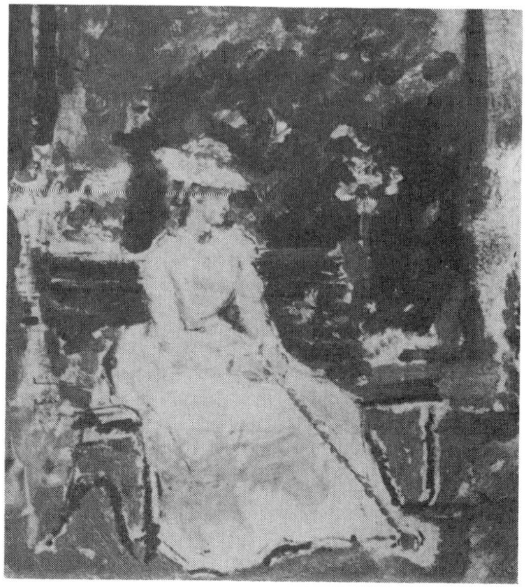

DAME ETHEL WALKER – The Garden Bench – oil on board – 13¼ x 9½in.
(Christie's) $4,835 £3,080

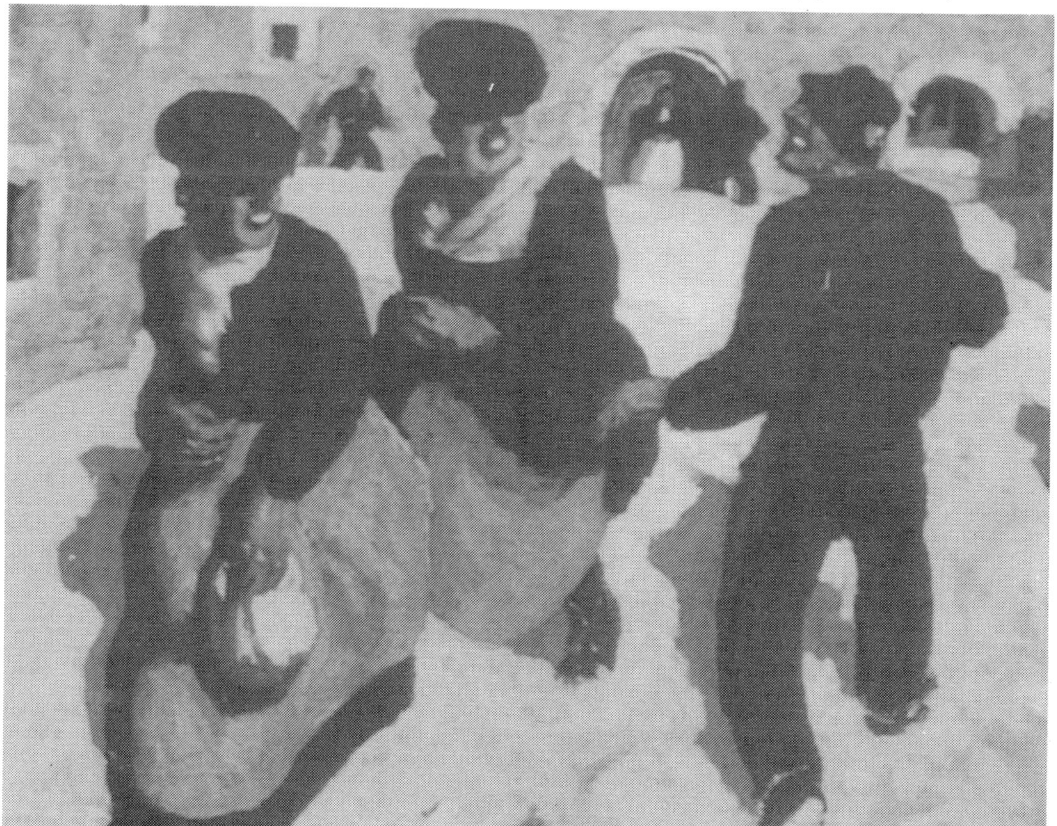

ALFONS WALDE – Begegnung – signed and inscribed – oil with gouache on thick paper – 6½ x 7½in.
(Christie's) $12,672 £8,800

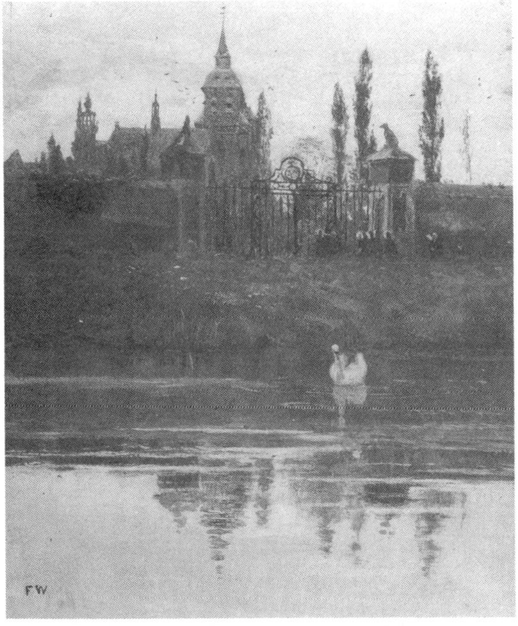

FREDERICK WALKER – The Abbey Gates – signed with initials – on paper – 8¼ x 7in.
(Christie's) **$1,458** **£972**

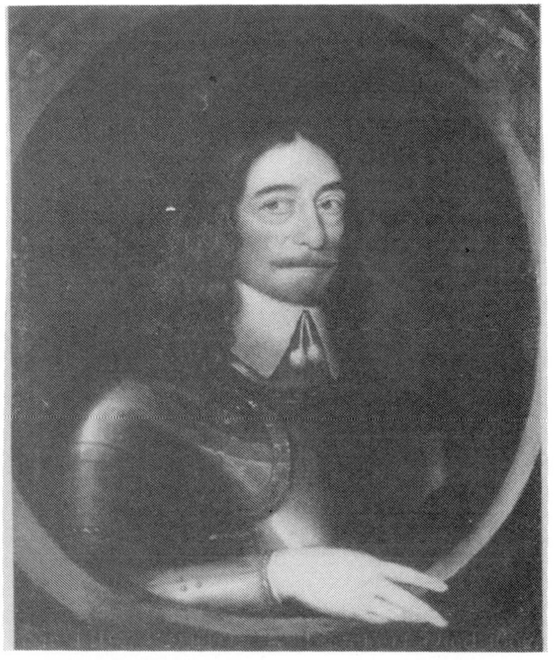

ROBERT WALKER, Circle of – Portrait Of Sir Thomas Cotton, Bust Length, In Armour – inscribed – 30 x 24½in.
(Christie's) **$486** **£324**

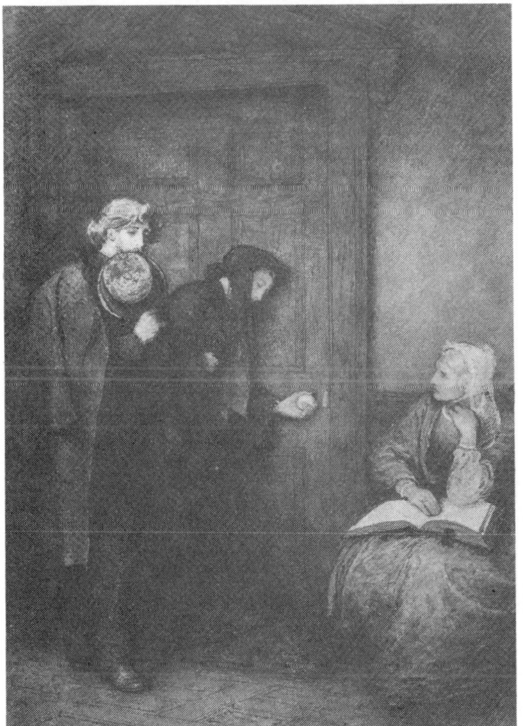

FREDERICK WALKER – At The Sick Man's Door – signed with initials – watercolour heightened with bodycolour – 7¼ x 5¼in.
(Christie's) **$5,049** **£3,300**

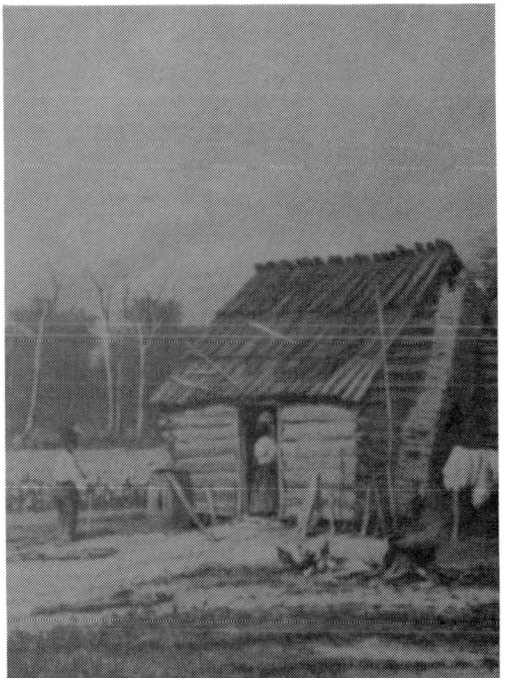

WILLIAM AIKEN WALKER – Cabin Scene – signed with conjoined initials – oil on academy board – 12¼ x 9¼in.
(Robt. W. Skinner Inc.) **$7,000** **£4,204**

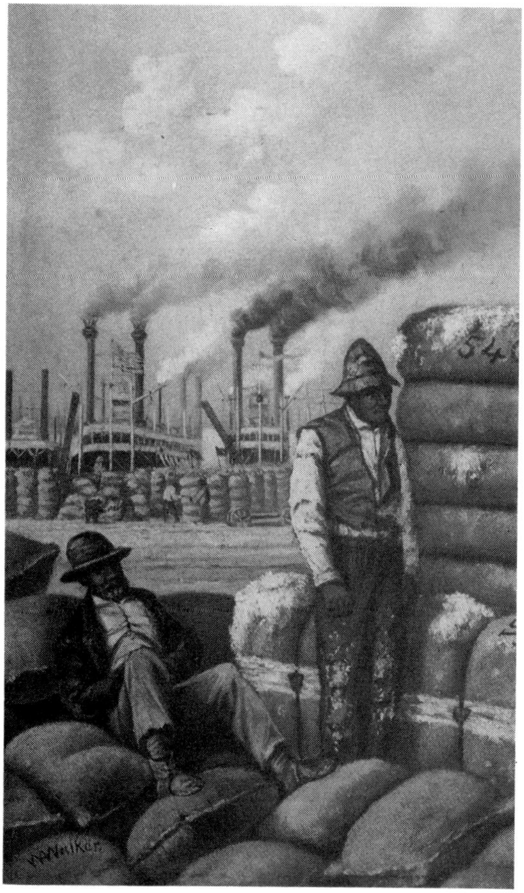

WILLIAM AIKEN WALKER – Cotton For Market – signed with initials – oil on canvas laid down on board – 14 x 7¾in.
(Christie's) **$18,700** **£11,651**

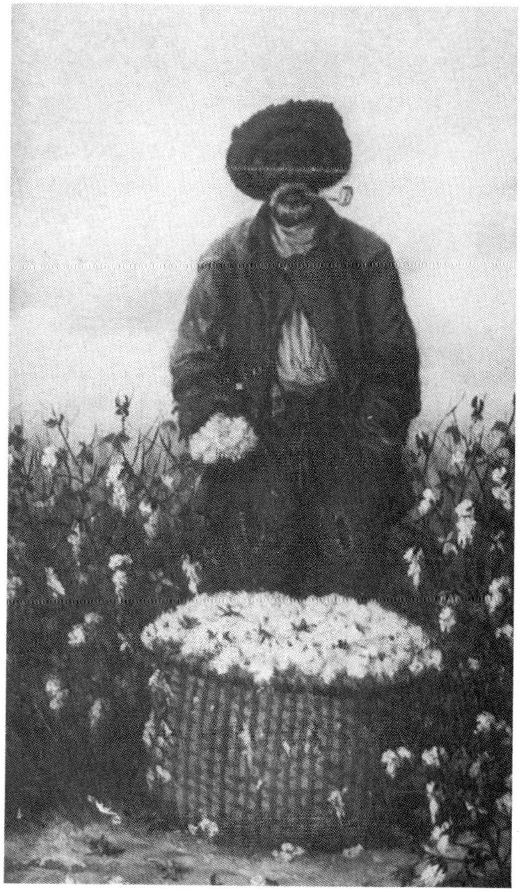

WILLIAM AIKEN WALKER – A Day's Work – signed with initials conjoined – oil on board – 11½ x 5¾in.
(Christie's) **$2,200** **£1,546**

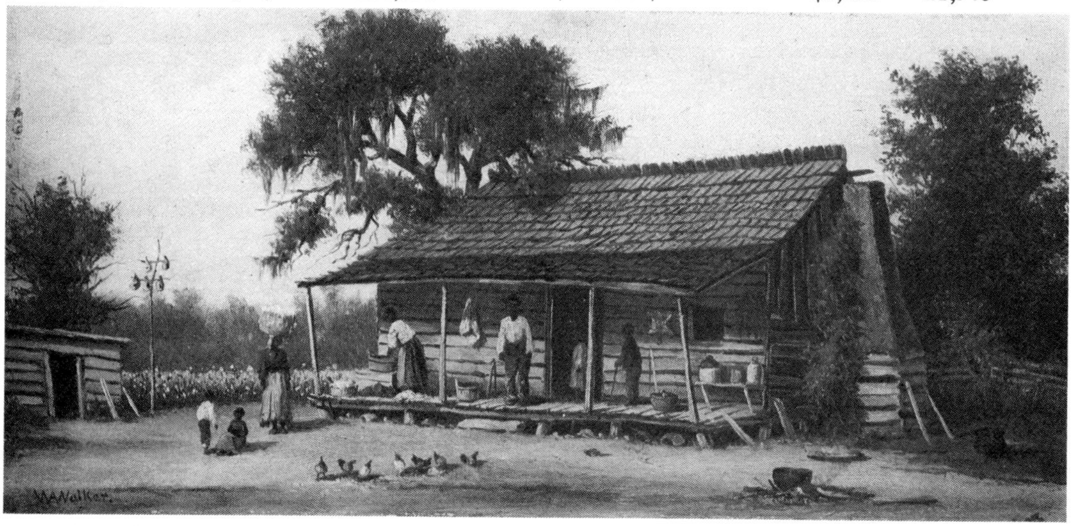

WILLIAM AIKEN WALKER – Cabin – signed with initials conjoined – oil on board – 6¼ x 12¼in.
(Christie's) **$8,800** **£6,186**

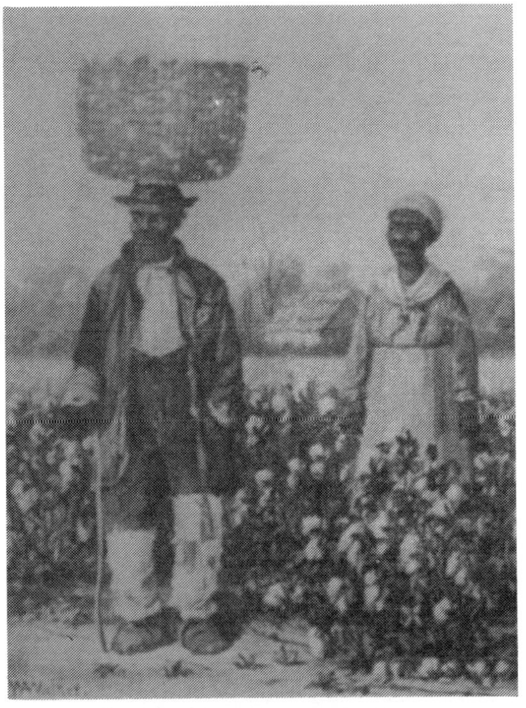

WILLIAM AIKEN WALKER – Cotton Pickers – signed with conjoined initials – oil on academy board – 12¼ x 9¼in.
(Robt. W. Skinner Inc.) **$6,750 £4,141**

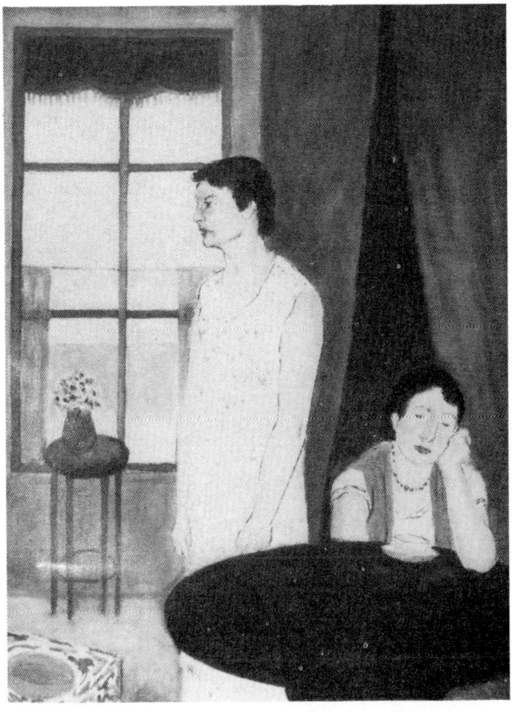

ABRAHAM WALKOWITZ – Figures In An Interior – signed – oil on canvas laid down on board – 24 x 18in.
(Christie's) **$5,500 £3,866**

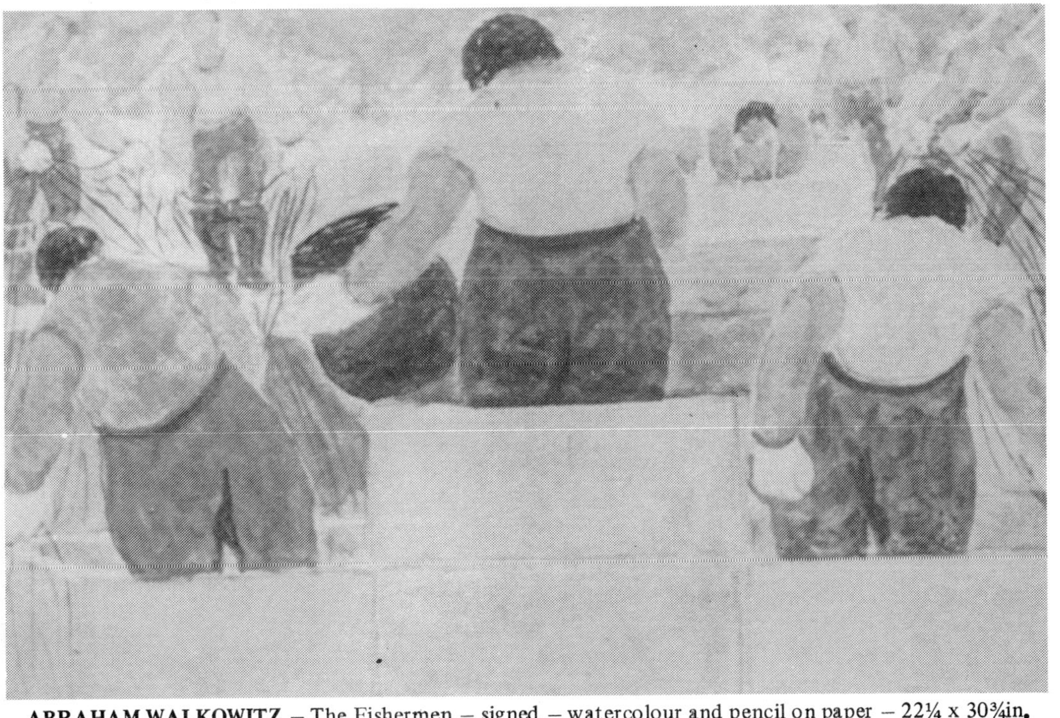

ABRAHAM WALKOWITZ – The Fishermen – signed – watercolour and pencil on paper – 22¼ x 30¾in.
(Christie's) **$2,420 £1,683**

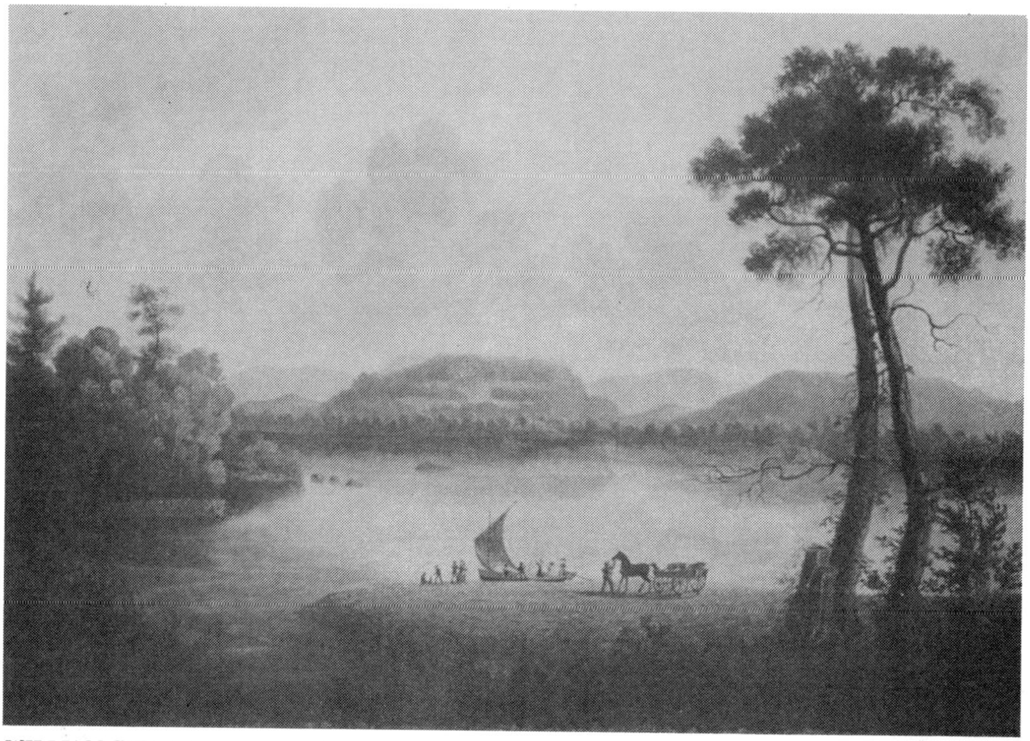

WILLIAM GUY WALL – Farewells On The Hudson – signed – oil on canvas – 22¼ x 27in. *(Christie's)*
$11,000 £7,733

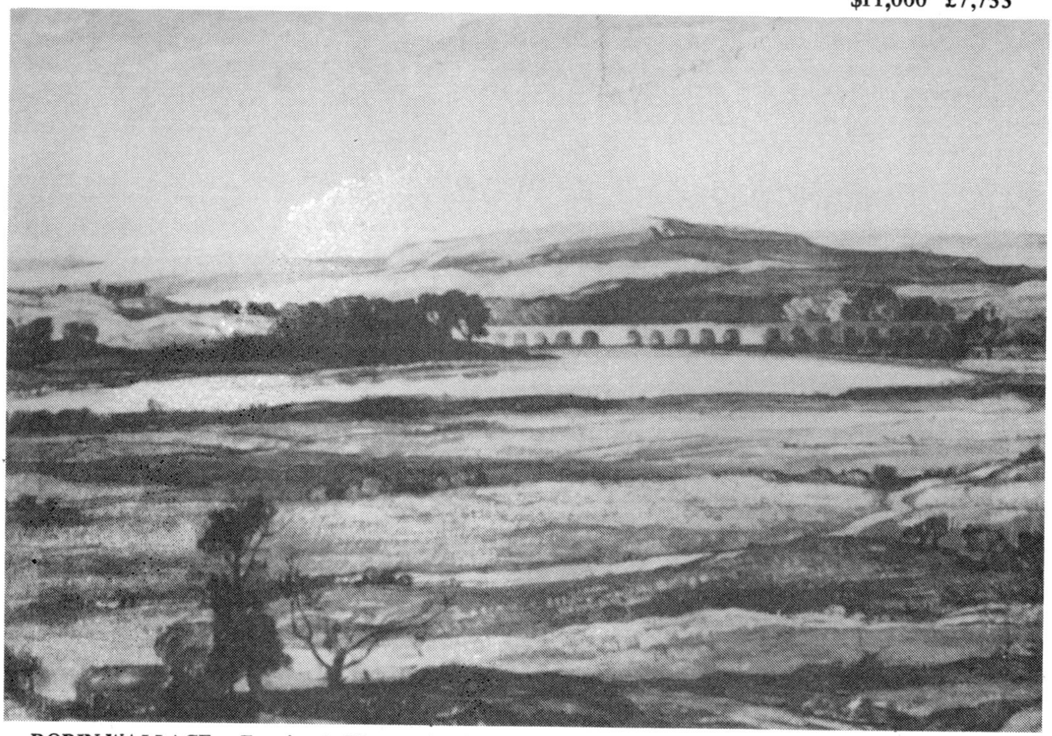

ROBIN WALLACE – Evening In Westmorland – signed and dated 1927 – oil on canvas – 63.5 x 76cm. *(Christie's)*
$306 £200

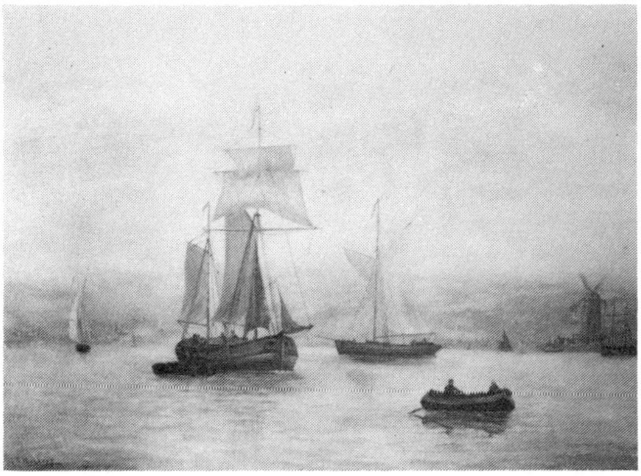

G. S. WALTERS – Shipping Off A Dutch Coastline – signed – oil on canvas.
(Biddle & Webb) **$600** **£380**

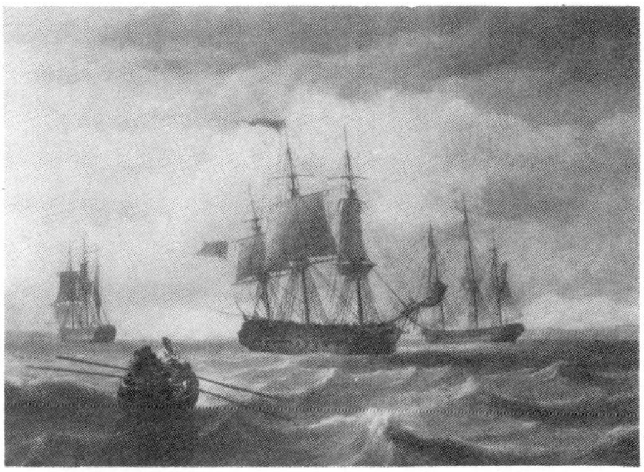

JOSEPH WALTERS – A West Indiaman Hove To In The Bristol Channel, With A Boat Going Out To Her, And Two Merchantmen Beyond – signed – 16¼ x 22¼in.
(Christie's) **$2,106** **£1,404**

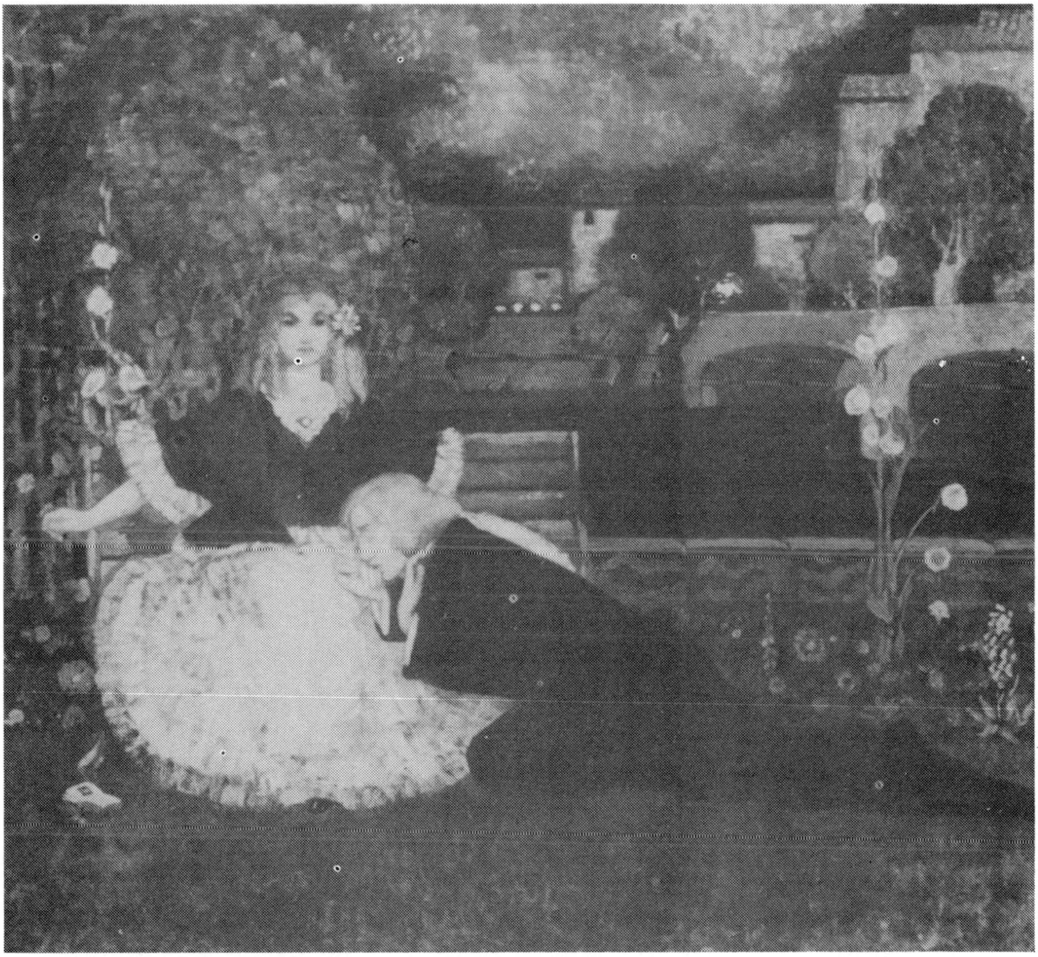

CECILE WALTON – La Belle Dame Sans Merci – signed – oil on canvas – 60 x 63.5cm. *(Phillips)*
$1,300 **£850**

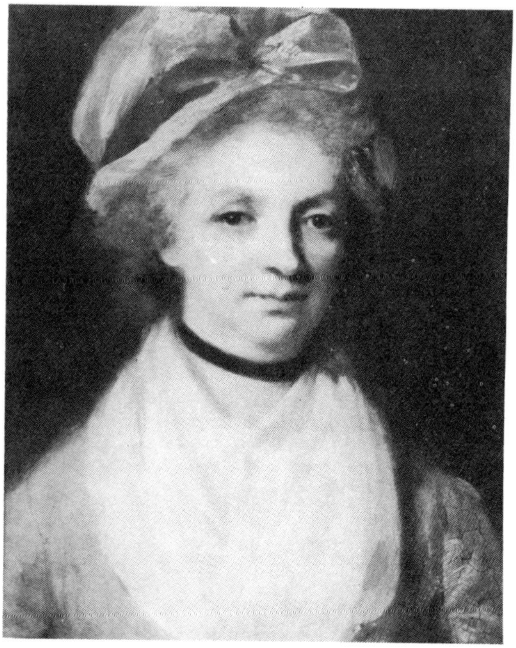

HENRY WALTON, Circle of – Portrait Of A Lady, Small Bust Length, Wearing A Grey Dress With A White Collar And Bonnet – on copper – 10¼ x 8½in.
(Christie's) **$517** **£345**

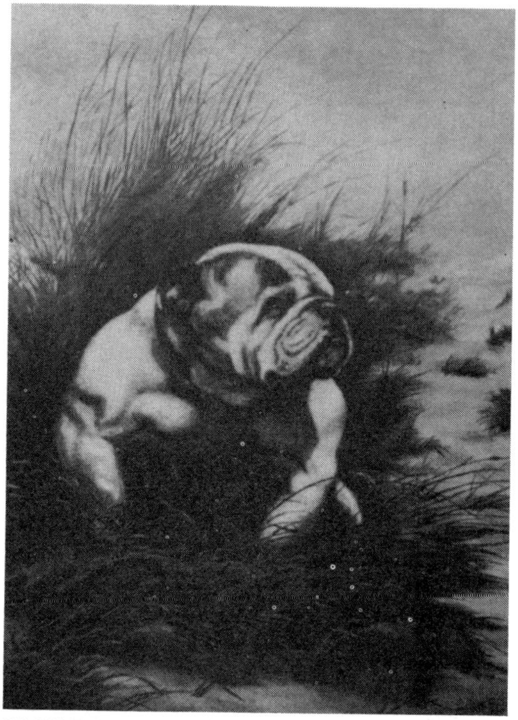

W. WARD – An English Bulldog Amidst Dunes – signed – oil – 19 x 13in.
(Bonhams) **$434** **£280**

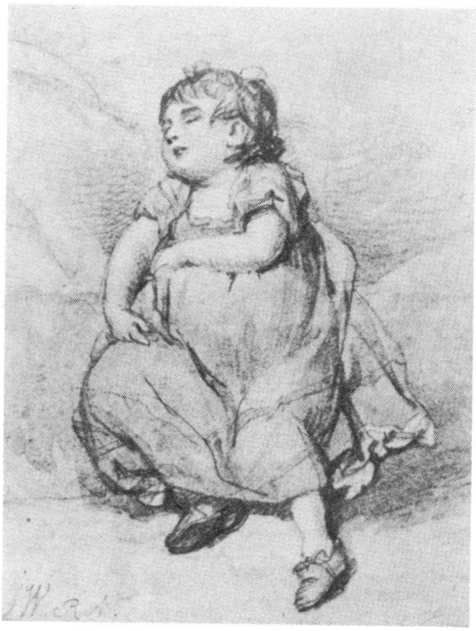

JAMES WARD – A Sleeping Child – signed with initials and indistinctly inscribed – pencil and watercolour – 6 x 4½in.
(Christie's) **$729** **£486**

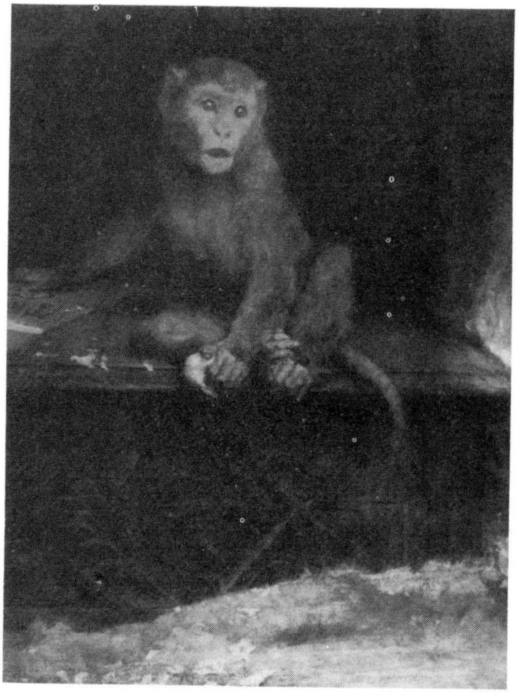

ARTHUR WARDLE – Monkey Business – signed – 24 x 20in.
(Christie's) **$1,514** **£990**

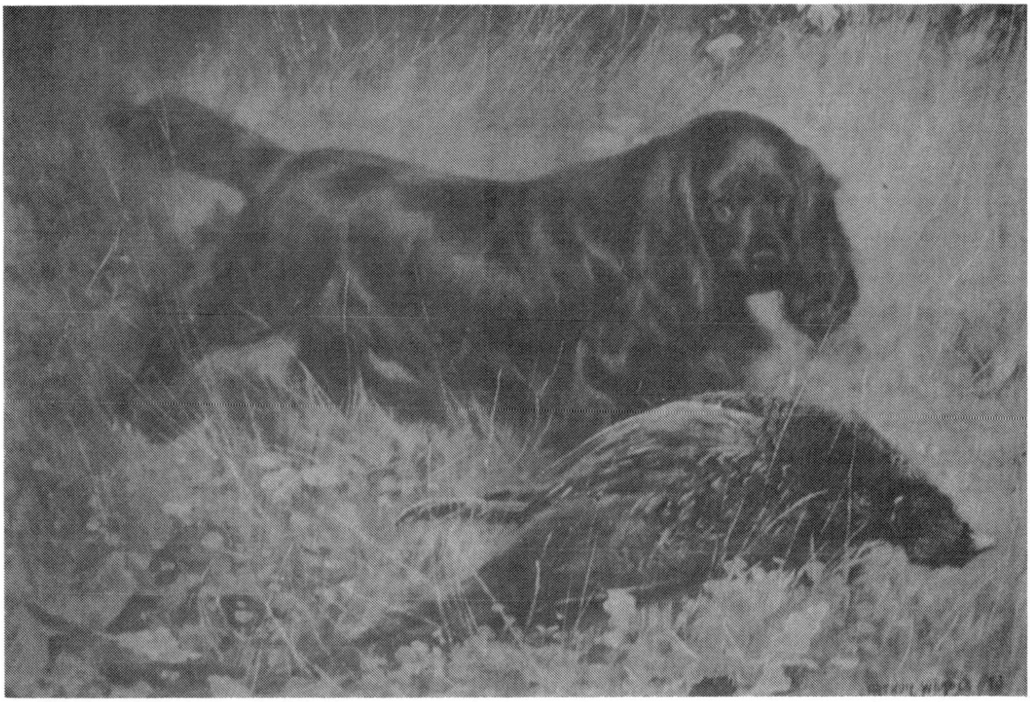

ARTHUR WARDLE – A Spaniel About To Retrieve A Pheasant – signed and dated '93 – oil on board – 19½ x 23¾in. *(Warners)* **$16,320 £10,200**

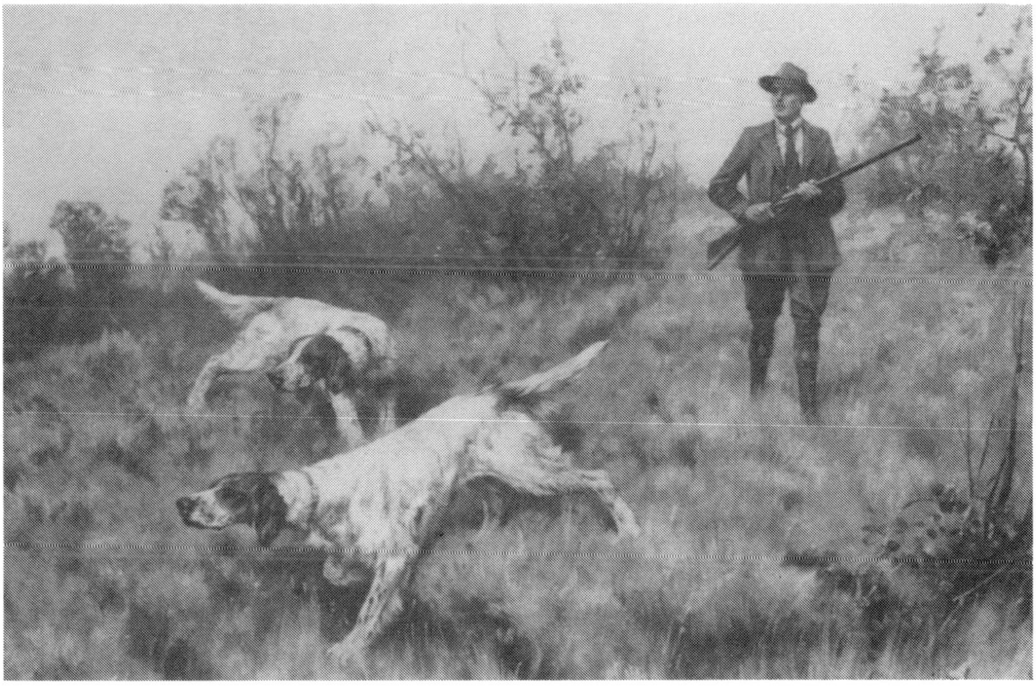

ARTHUR WARDLE – Walking Up – signed – 15 x 21in. *(Christie's)* **$6,732 £4,400**

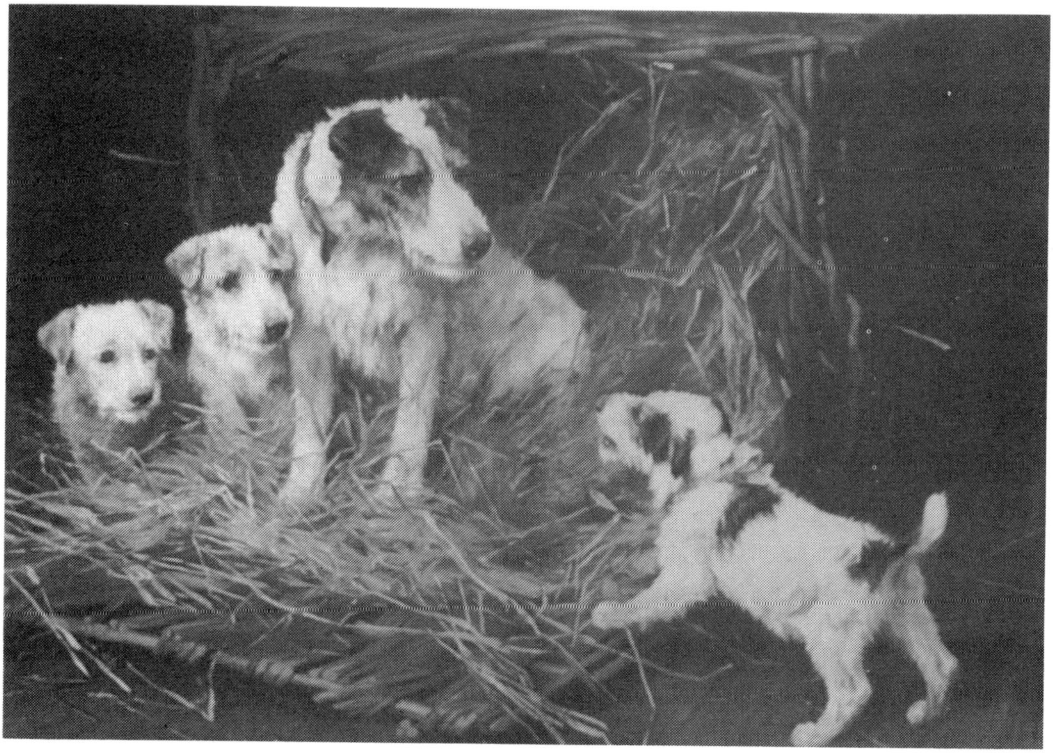

ARTHUR WARDLE – A Proud Mother – signed – 23¼ x 29¼in. *(Christie's)* **$10,081 £7,150**

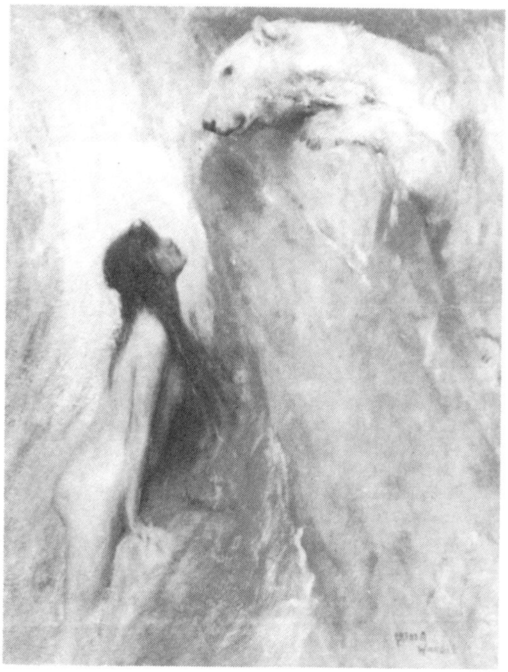

ARTHUR WARDLE – An Arctic Encounter – signed – on panel – 13 x 9¾in.
(Christie's) **$2,791 £1,980**

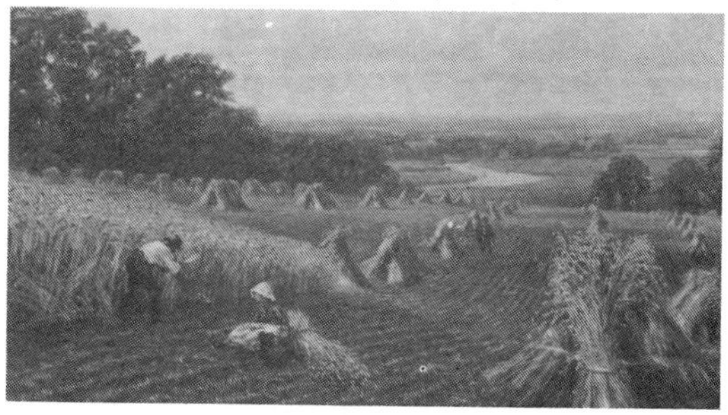

HENRY CLIFFORD WARREN – Harvesting On The Banks Of The Thames Near Shepperton – signed and dated 1881 – watercolour – 18¼ x 26¼in.
(Anderson & Garland) **$286 £200**

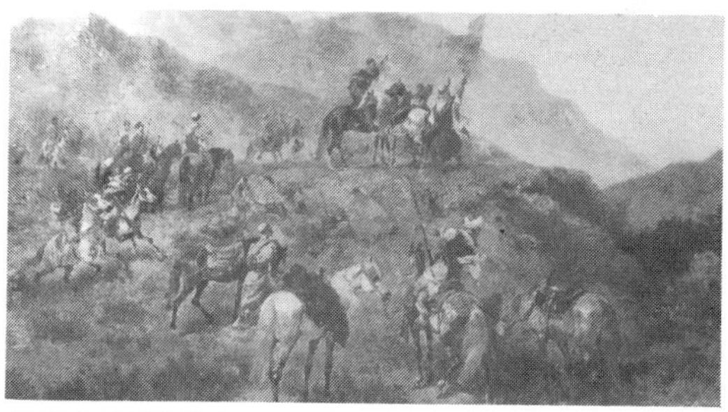

GEORGES WASHINGTON – Warriors In A Rocky Landscape – signed – 18 x 23in.
(Christie's) **$11,440 £7,150**

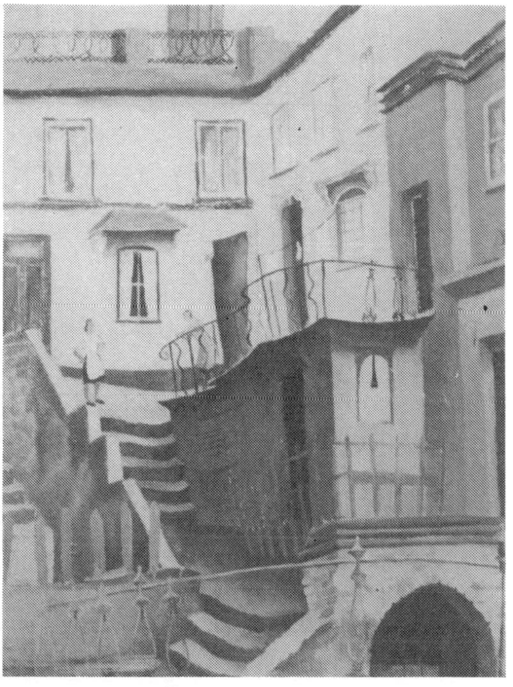

BILLIE WATERS – Quayside Houses, St. Ives – signed – oil on board – 45 x 35.5cm.
(Phillips) **$1,494** **£900**

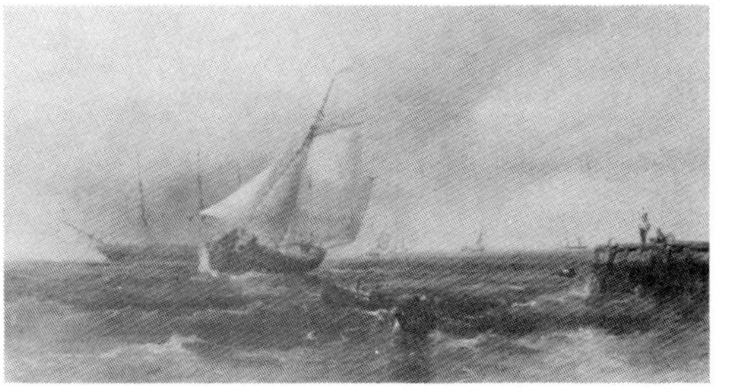

ROBERT WATSON – Off The Tyne – signed and dated 1865 – 15½ x 23½in.
(Christie's) **$2,946** **£2,090**

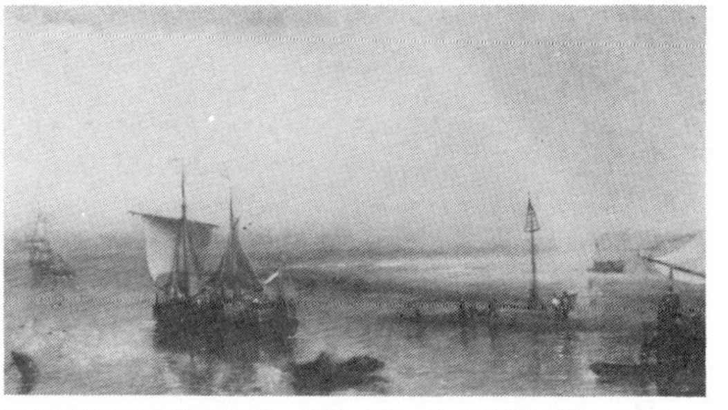

ROBERT WATSON – The Mouth Of The Tyne, With A Rainbow – signed and dated 1855, and signed and inscribed on the reverse – 23 x 35in.
(Christie's) **$4,342** **£3,080**

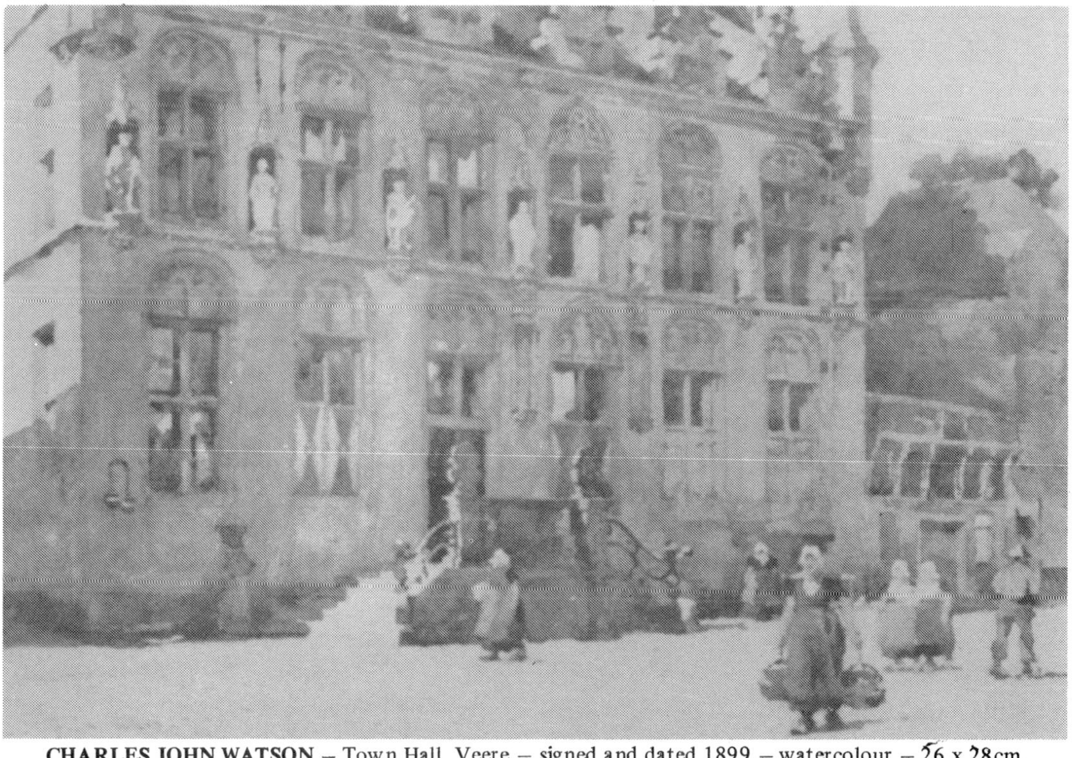

CHARLES JOHN WATSON – Town Hall, Veere – signed and dated 1899 – watercolour – 26 x 28cm.
(Phillips) **$521** **£320**

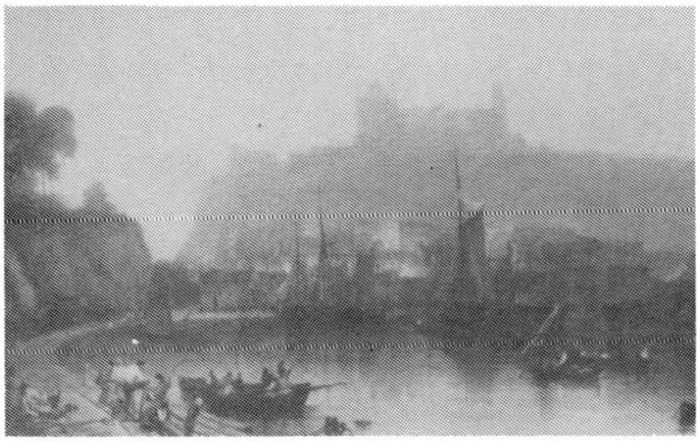

ROBERT WATSON, Circle of – Shipping At Whitby – 19¼ x 29½in.
(Christie's) **$1,861 £1,320**

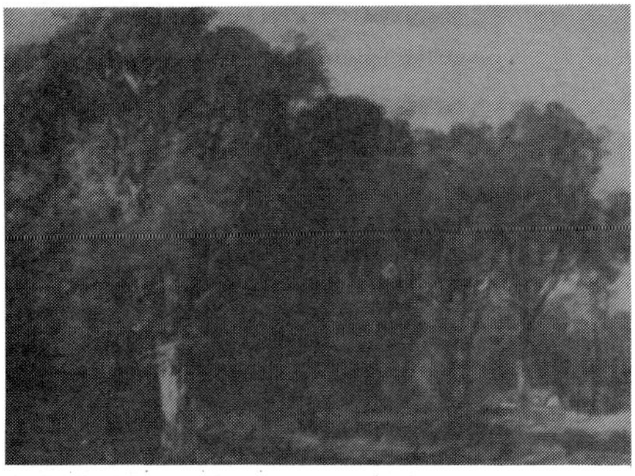

FREDERICK WATERS WATTS' Attributed to – Figures By A Fallen Tree In A Glade, A Cottage Beyond – oil on board – 13¾ x 17¼in. *(Phillips)*
$830 £500

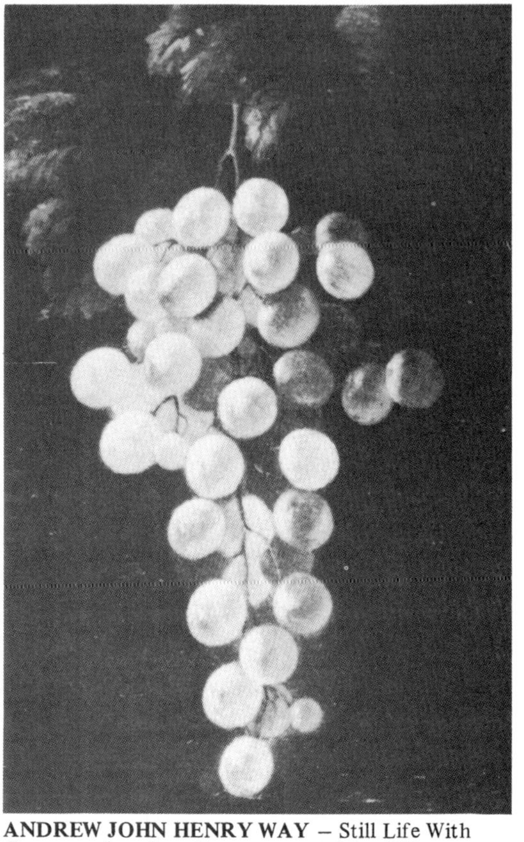

ANDREW JOHN HENRY WAY – Still Life With Grapes – signed – oil on canvas – 12 x 8¼in.
(Robt. W. Skinner Inc.) **$1,800 £1,250**

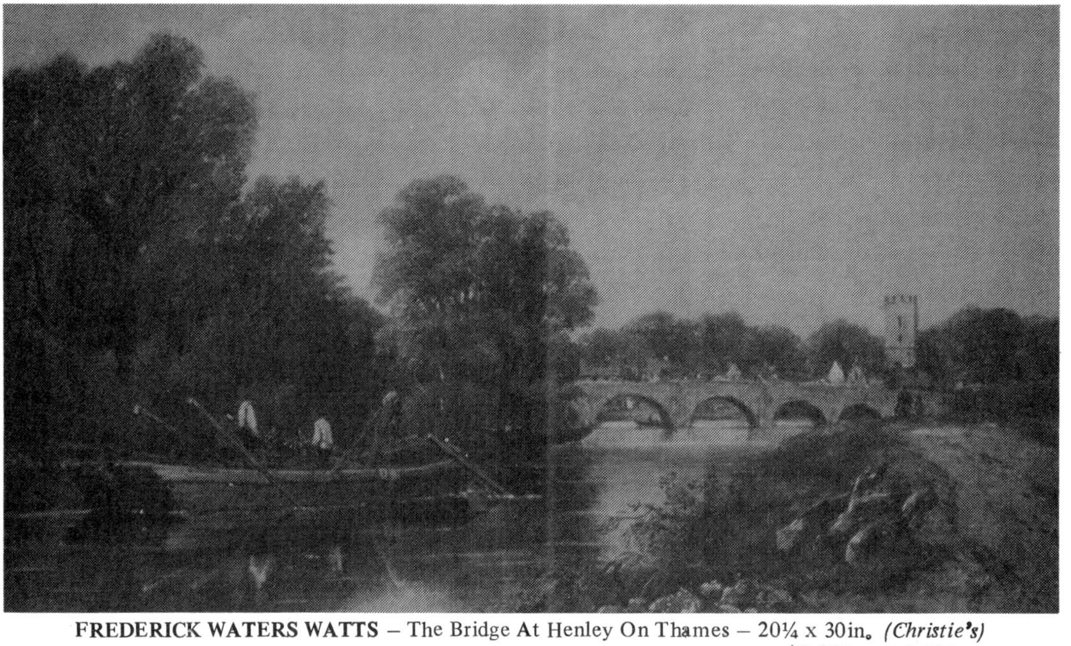

FREDERICK WATERS WATTS – The Bridge At Henley On Thames – 20¼ x 30in. *(Christie's)*
$9,306 £6,600

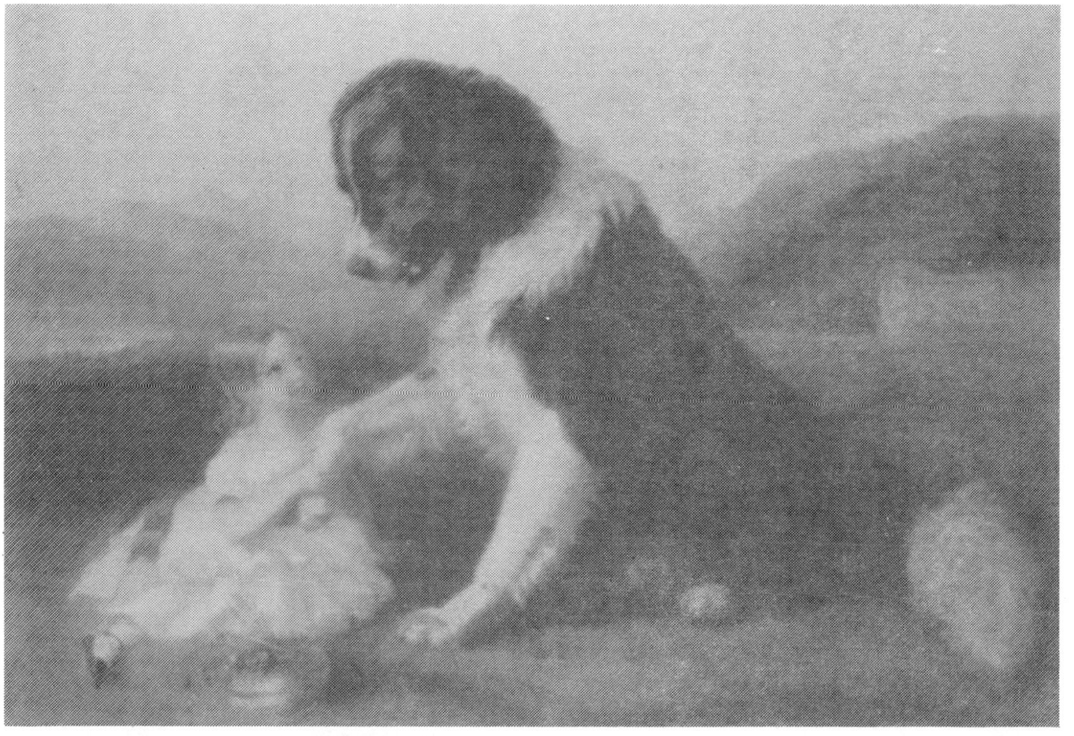

BYRON WEBB – A Newfoundland Proffering A Paw To An Elegant Young Lady In A Highland Landscape – signed – oil – 30 x 36in. *(Bonhams)* **$8,990 £5,800**

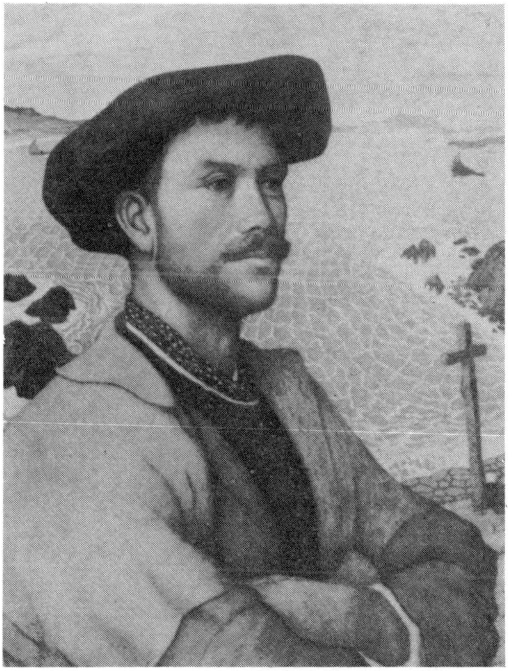

CECIL J. WEBB – A Breton Fisherman – signed – tempera on panel – 23¾ x 18in.
(Christie's) **$4,835 £3,080**

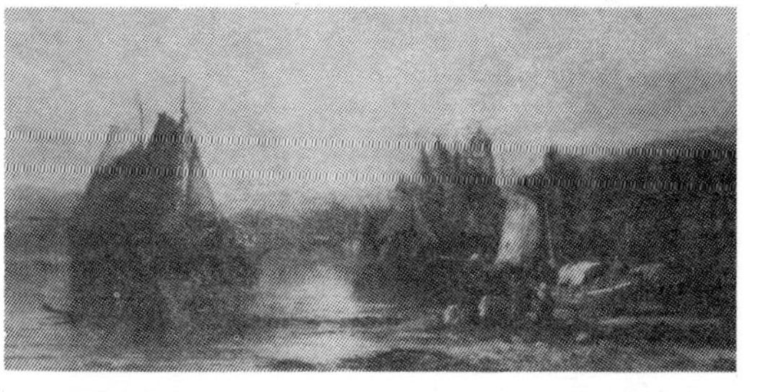

JAMES WEBB – Elfeld, On The Rhine – signed, inscribed and dated '85 – on canvas – 30 x 51¼in.
(Phillips) **$4,830 £3,000**

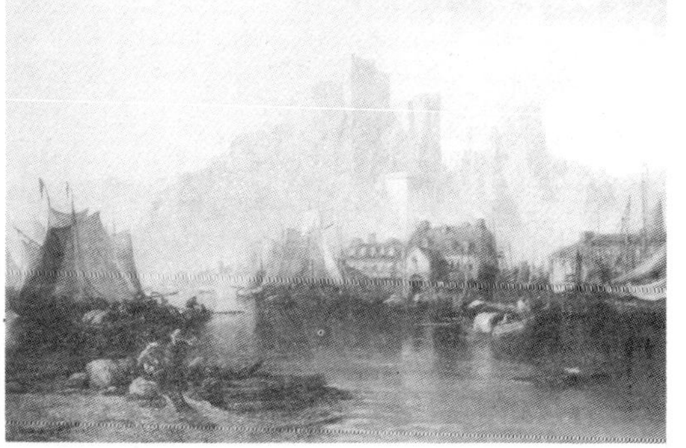

JAMES WEBB – A Castle On The Rhine – signed and dated '61 – 40 x 60½in.
(Christie's) **$9,720 £6,480**

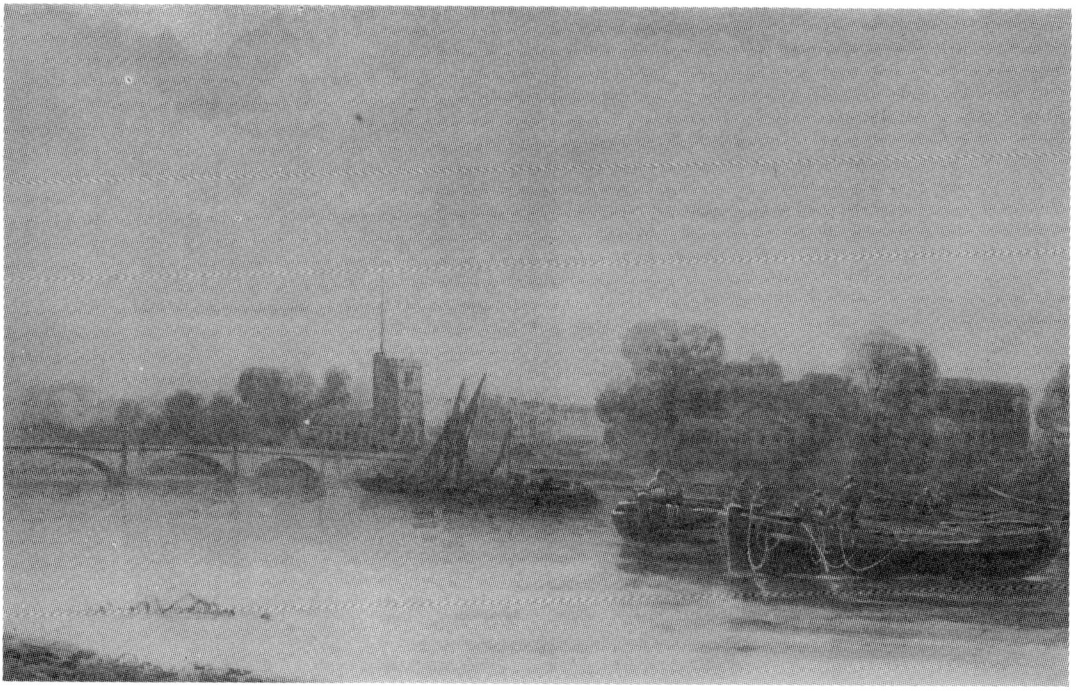

JAMES WEBB – Barges On The Thames Near Putney Bridge – signed – pencil and watercolour heightened with white – 14½ x 22¾in. *(Christie's)* **$821 £495**

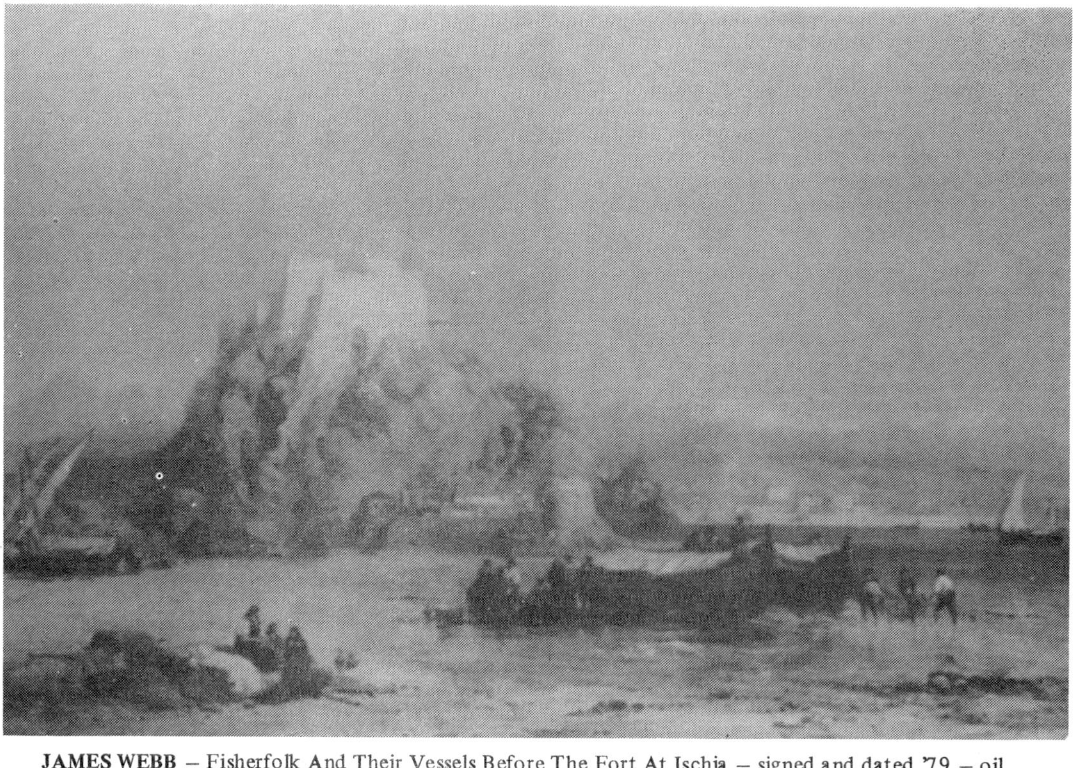

JAMES WEBB – Fisherfolk And Their Vessels Before The Fort At Ischia – signed and dated '79 – oil on canvas – 30 x 50¼in. *(Phillips)* **$5,202 £3,400**

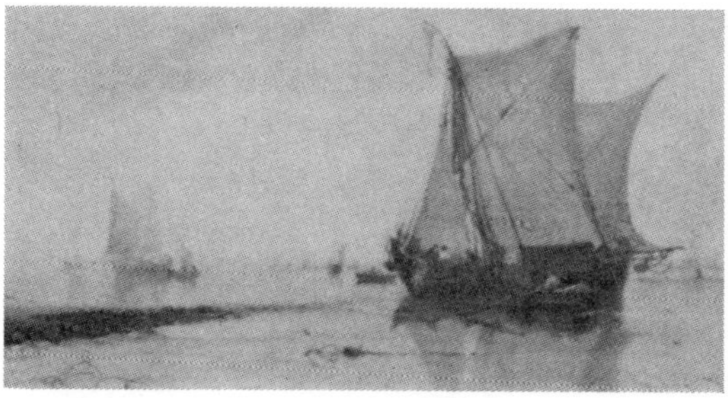

JAMES WEBB – 'On The Scheldt'; and 'On The French Coast' – signed – oil on canvas – 8 x 12in.
(Christie's) **$2,376** **£1,650 Pair**

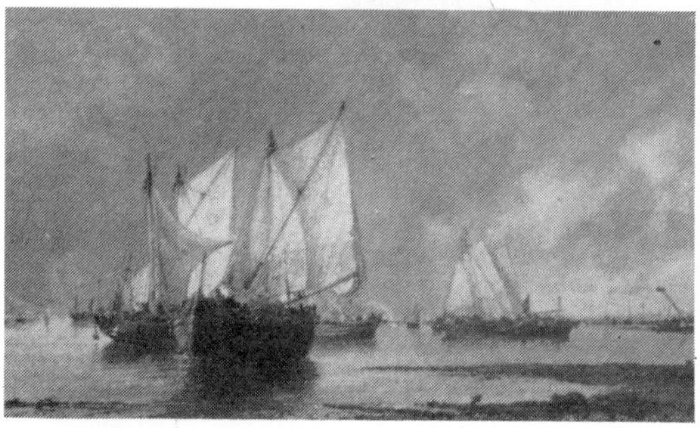

JAMES WEBB – A Coastal Landscape With Becalmed Fishing Boats – signed and dated 1874 – 10¼ x 16in.
(Christie's) **$2,019** **£1,320**

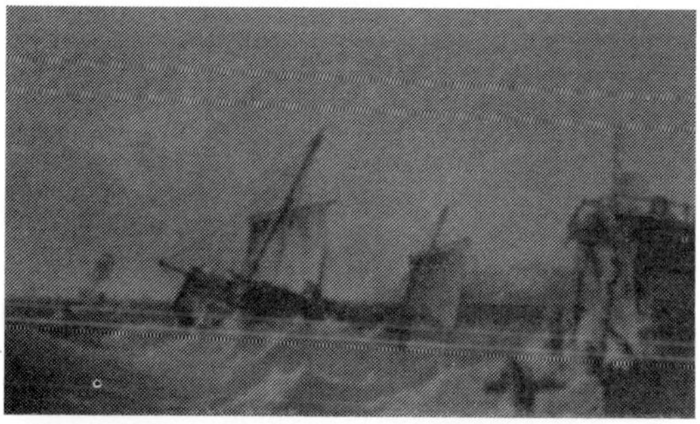

JAMES WEBB – Figures In A Fishing Boat In A Swell, Near A Jetty – signed and dated 1858 – on canvas – 18 x 30in.
(Phillips) **$2,817** **£1,750**

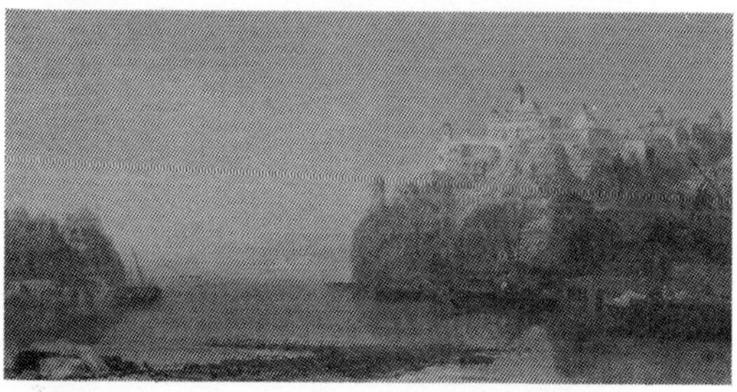

JAMES WEBB – A View Of Constantinople On The Bosphorus – signed – on canvas – 14¼ x 24¼in.
(Phillips) **$5,635** **£3,500**

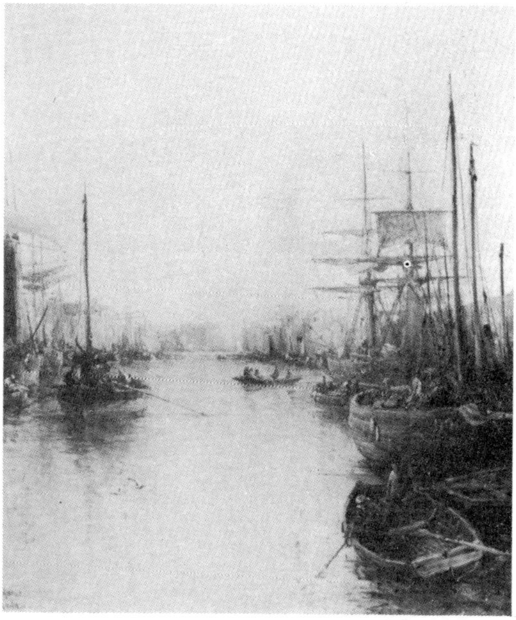

WILLIAM EDWARD WEBB – 'Morning – Douglas Harbour' – signed and inscribed – oil on canvas – 20 x 16in.
(Phillips) **$3,519** **£2,300**

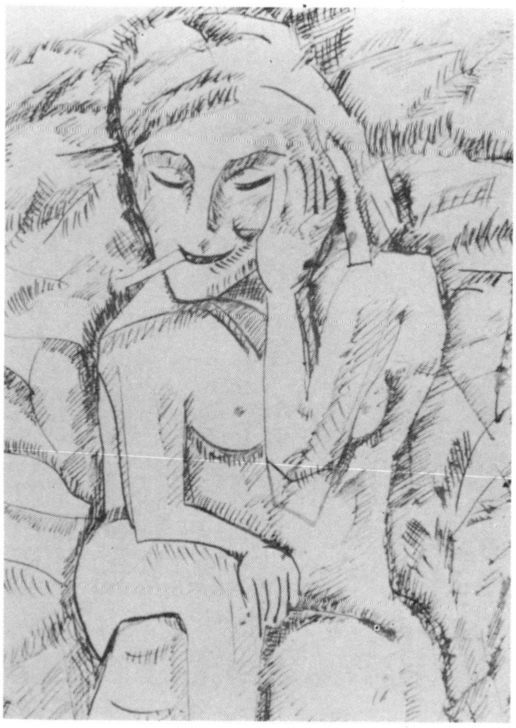

MAX WEBBER – Anna – signed and dated '12 – pen and ink on paper – 18¼ x 12in.
(Christie's) **$1,760** **£1,224**

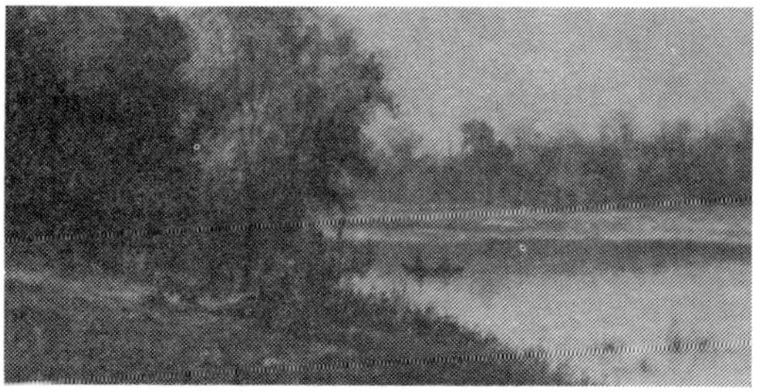

WESLEY WEBBER – Autumn Scene By A Pond – signed – oil on canvas – 12 x 18in.
(Robt. W. Skinner Inc.) **$500** **£306**

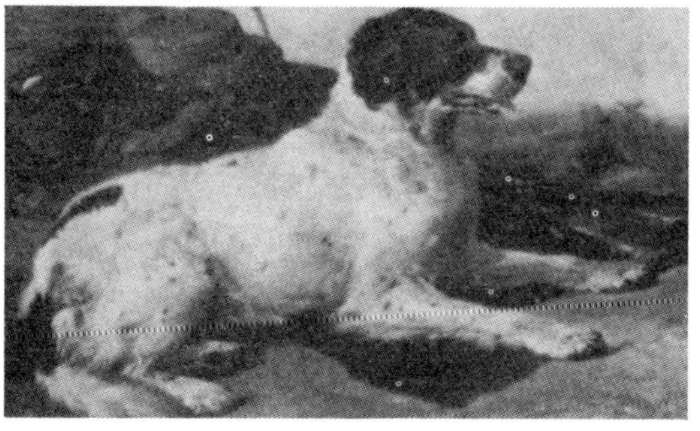

HENRY WEEKES – Waiting For Master – signed – oil on canvas – 11 x 15½in.
(Christie's) **$2,692** **£1,870**

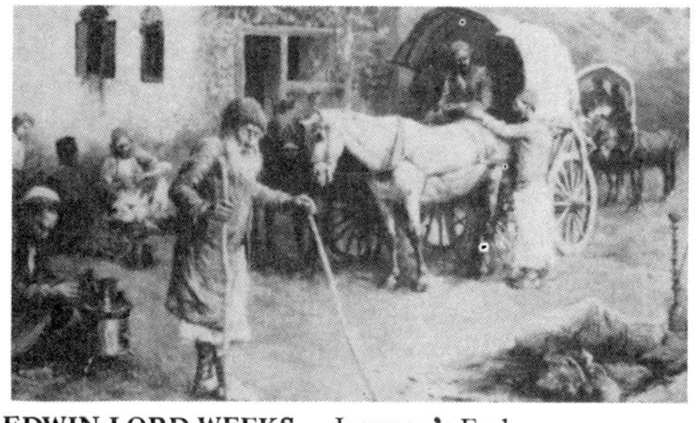

EDWIN LORD WEEKS – Journey's End – signed – oil en grisaille on canvas – 16 x 23¾in.
(Christie's) **$1,320** **£918**

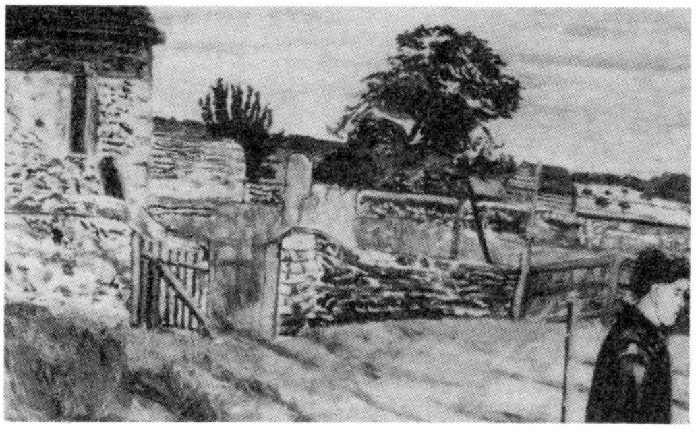

CAREL WEIGHT – Greatham Church, Sussex – signed, inscribed on the reverse – oil on board – 11½ x 15½in.
(Christie's) **$1,022** **£715**

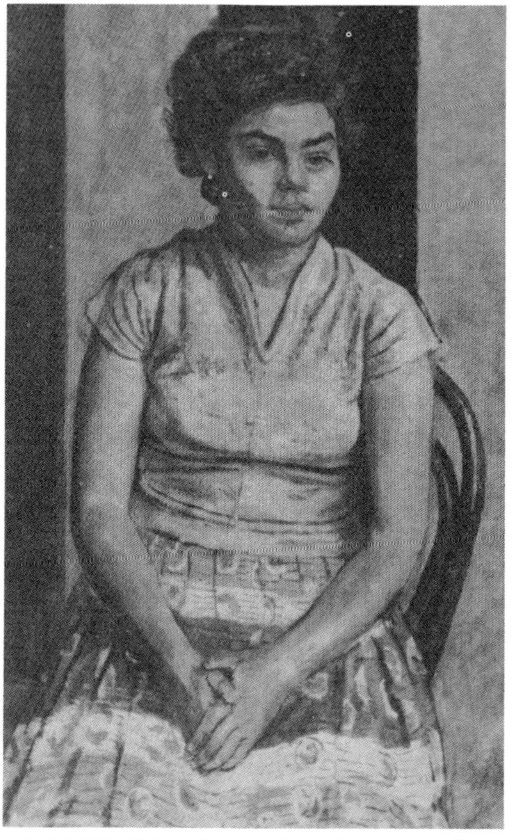

CAREL WEIGHT – Woman In A Chair – signed – oil on canvas – 55 x 31cm.
(Phillips) **$852** **£600**

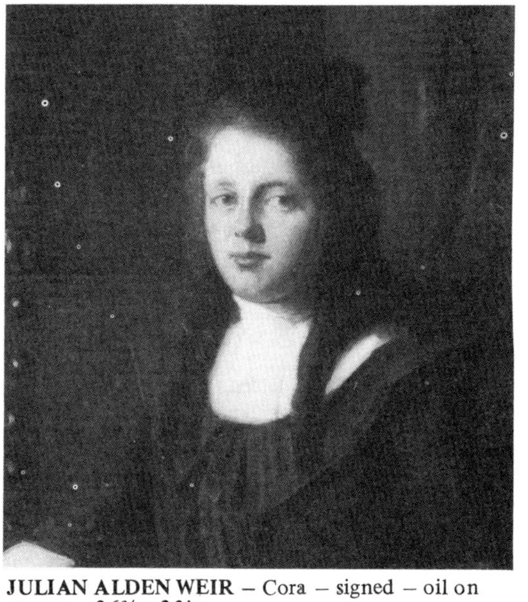

JULIAN ALDEN WEIR – Cora – signed – oil on canvas – 26¾ x 23in.
(Christie's) **$16,500** **£11,599**

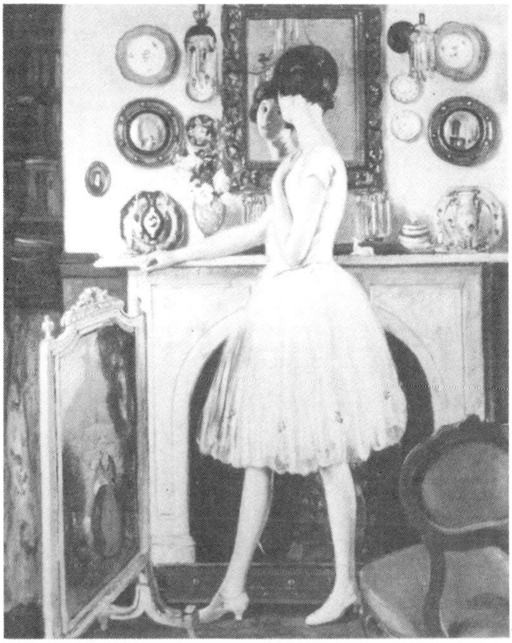

DENYS GEORGE WELLS – A Young Girl Before A Fire-Place, Looking At Her Reflection In The Mirror – oil on canvas – 30 x 25in.
(Christie's) **$3,460** **£2,420**

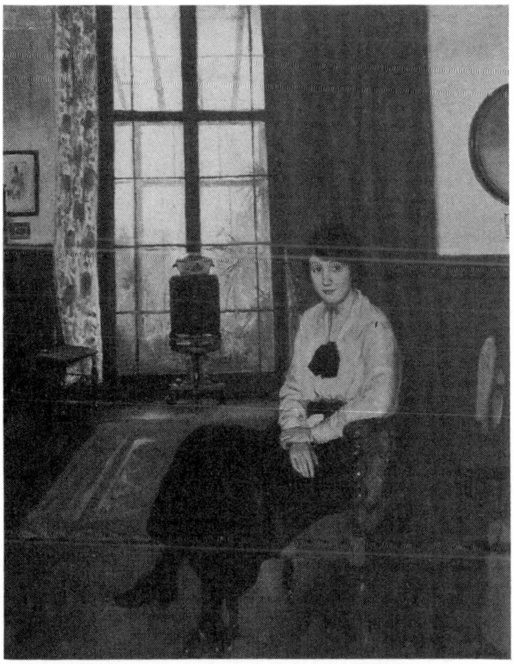

DENYS GEORGE WELLS – The Pink Blouse – signed dated '14 – oil on panel – 24 x 20in.
(Christie's) **$3,108** **£1,980**

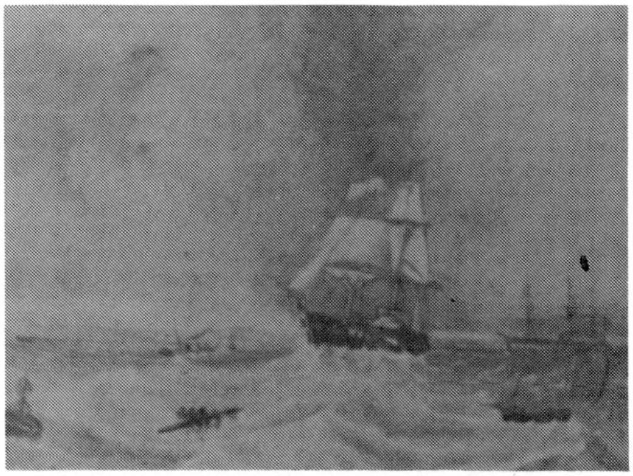

J. H. WELLS – A Paddle-Steamer Packet And Other Shipping – indistinctly signed and dated – oil on canvas – 16 x 22in.
(Phillips) **$581** **£350**

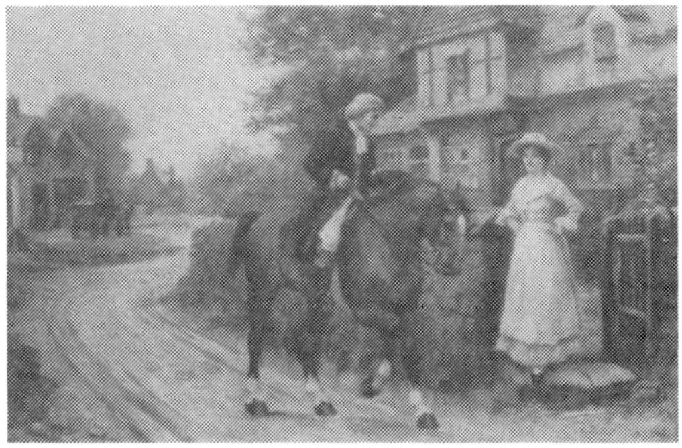

JOHN SANDERSON WELLS – A Cordial Greeting – signed – on panel – 7 x 10in.
(Christie's) **$1,093** **£715**

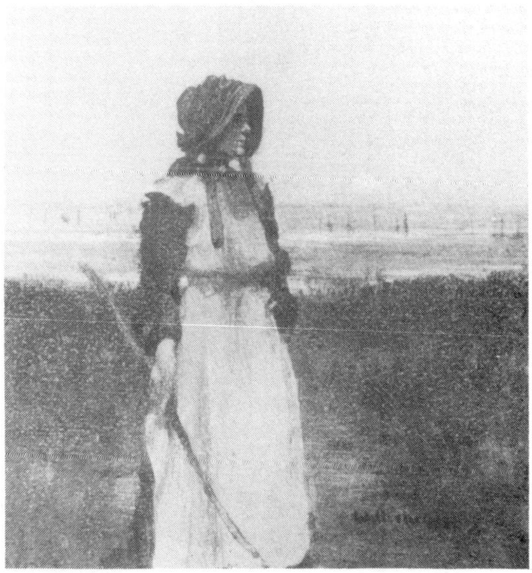

WILLIAM PAGE ATKINSON WELLS – The Goosegirl – signed – watercolour heightened with gum arabic – 7½ x 7in.
(Christie's) **$691** **£480**

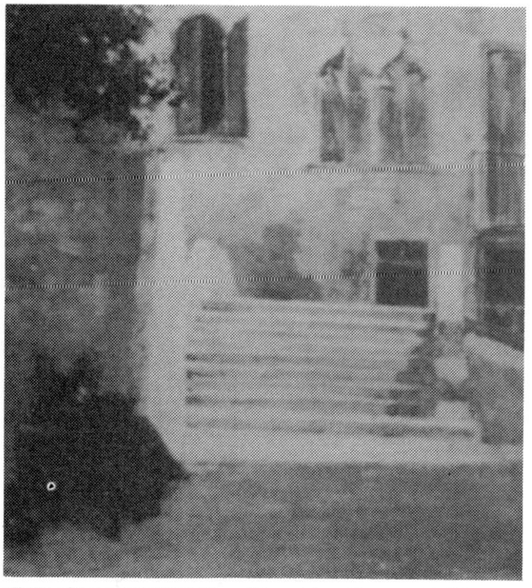

THEODORE WENDEL – Venetian Passage With Figure – signed and dated '82 – oil on panel – 9 x 7¼in.
(Robt. W. Skinner Inc.) **$3,300** **£2,024**

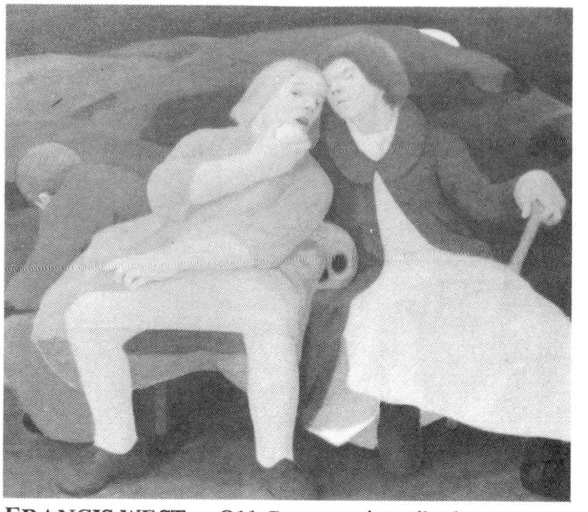

FRANCIS WEST – Old Crones – inscribed on the reverse – oil on canvas – 35½ x 37½in.
(Christie's) **$1,101** **£770**

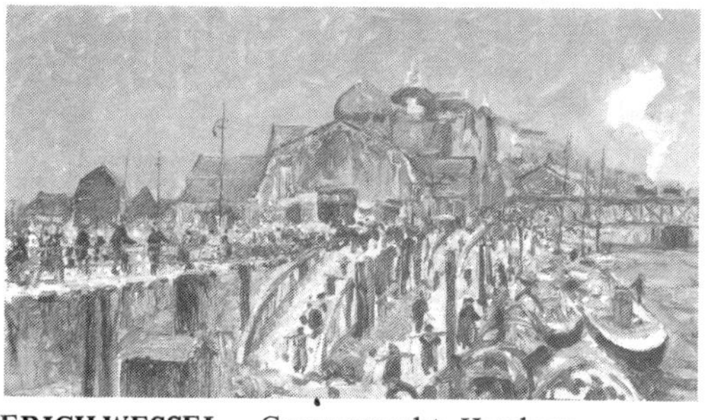

ERICH WESSEL – Gemusemarkt, Hamburg – signed and dated '32 – oil on canvas – 22¾ x 34¼in.
(Christie's) **$5,544** **£3,850**

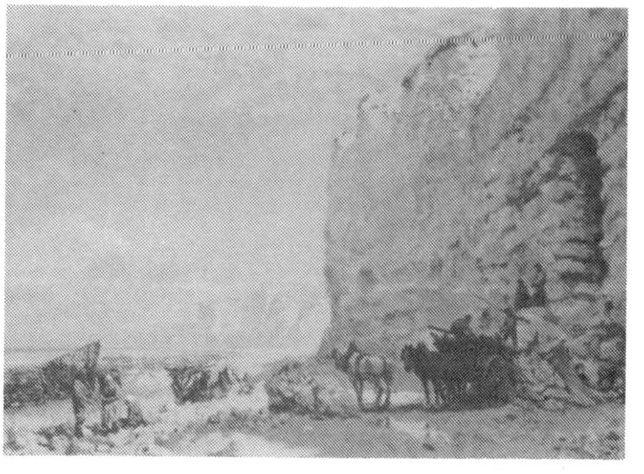

RICHARD WHATELY WEST – 'On The Norman Coast' – signed and dated 1887 – oil – 29½ x 44½in.
(Geering & Colyer) **$1,296** **£900**

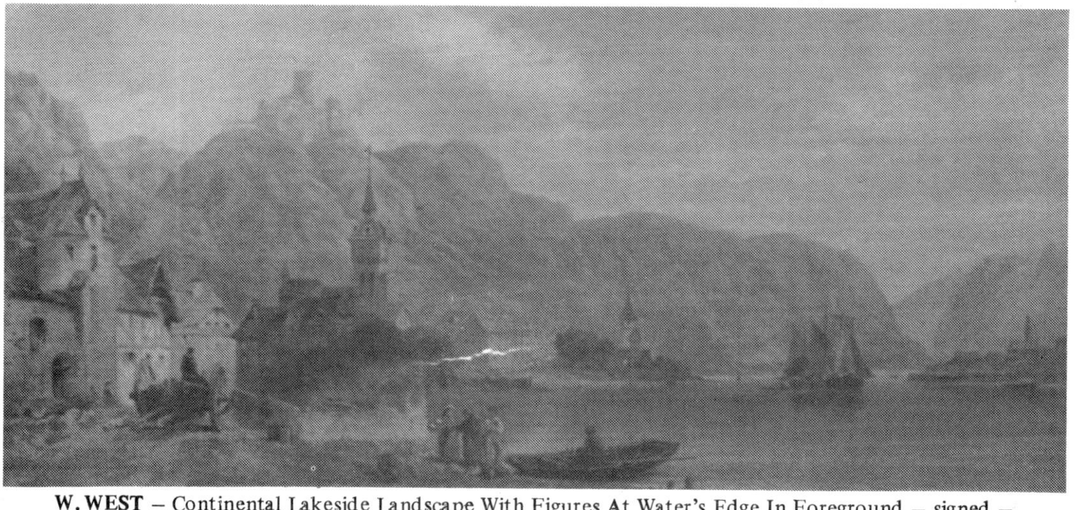

W. WEST – Continental Lakeside Landscape With Figures At Water's Edge In Foreground – signed – oil. *(Hobbs & Chambers)* **$646** **£420**

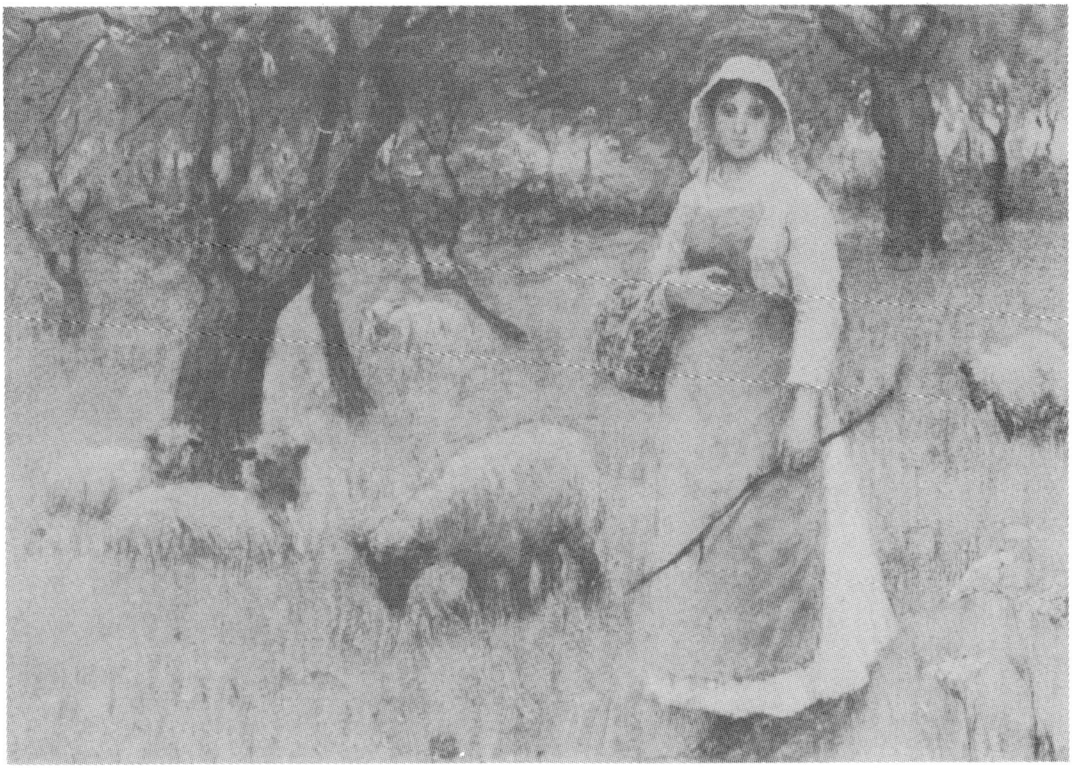

GEORGE FALKENER WETHERBEE – 'Through The Orchard' – signed, also inscribed on an old label on backboard – watercolour with scratching out – 24 x 33cm. *(Phillips)* **$1,716 £1,200**

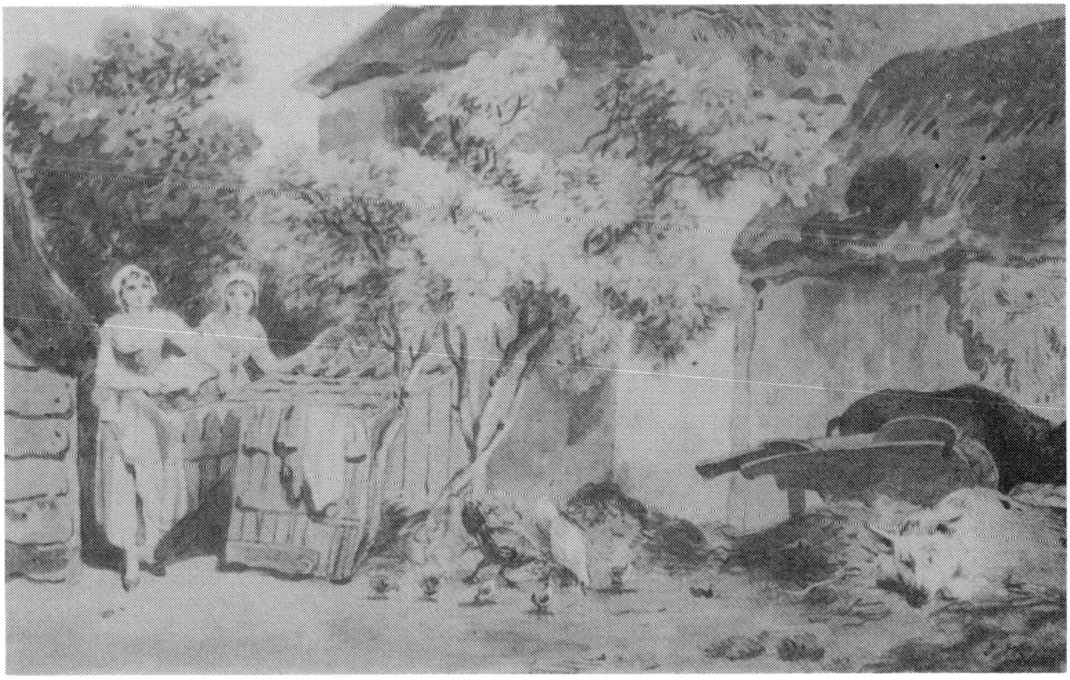

FRANCIS WHEATLEY – Washerwomen Entering A Farmyard – signed with initials, pencil and watercolour heightened with white – 5¼ x 8in. *(Christie's)* **$1,458 £972**

WHEELER

ALFRED WHEELER – A Pair Of Cairns With Blue Collars – signed – on board – 6½ x 12¼in.
(Christie's) **$775** **£550**

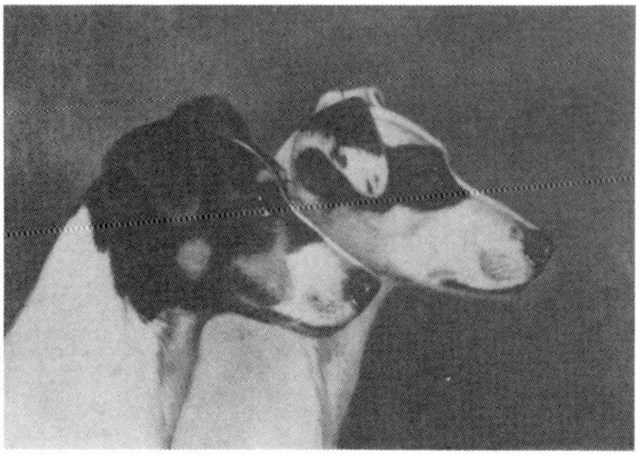

JOHN ALFRED WHEELER – Two Smooth-Haired Fox Terriers – signed – on board – 9 x 12½in.
(Christie's) **$1,240** **£880**

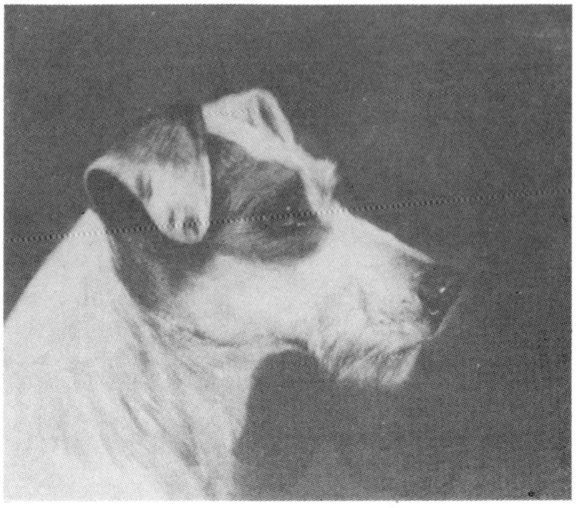

JOHN ALFRED WHEELER – A Wire-Haired Fox Terrier – signed – on board – 8 x 9½in.
(Christie's) **$775** **£550**

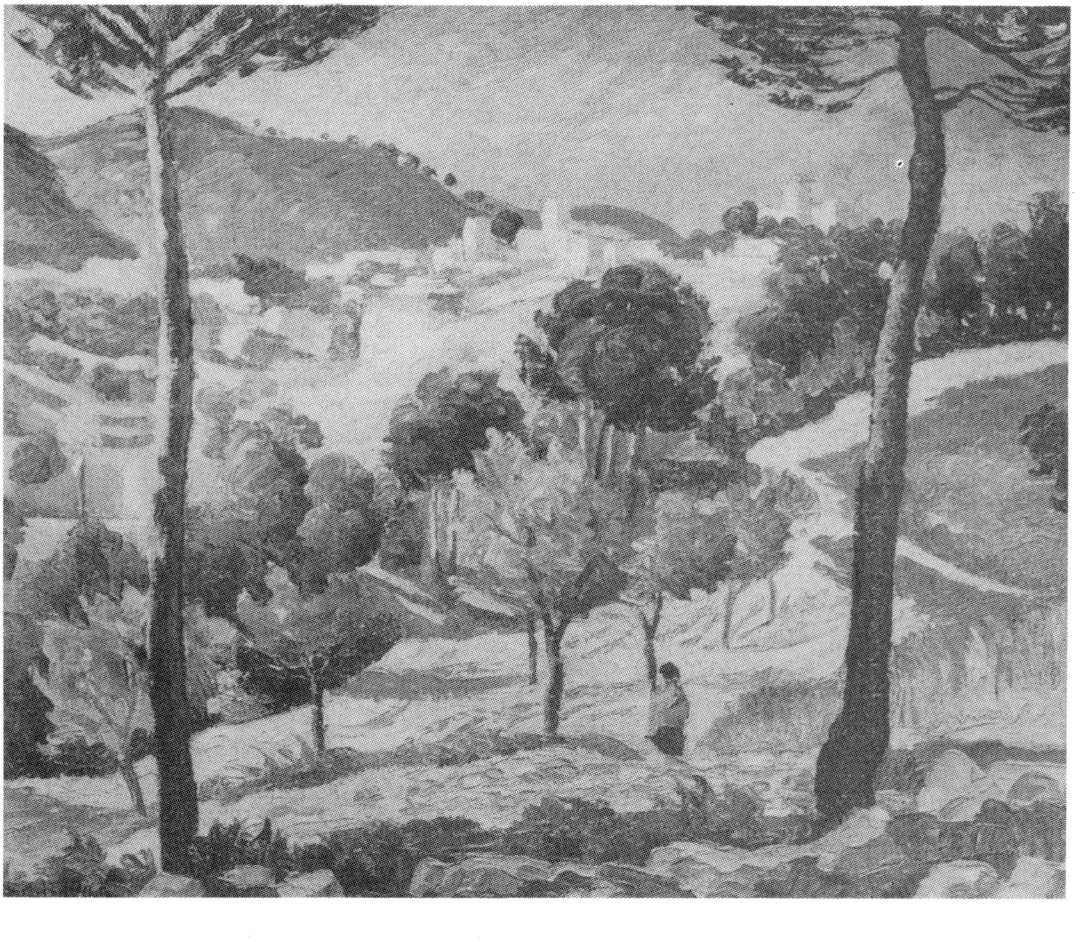

ETHELBERT WHITE – Genova, Mallorca – signed, inscribed on the reverse – oil on canvas – 18¼ x 22in. *(Christie's)* **$2,388** **£1,430**

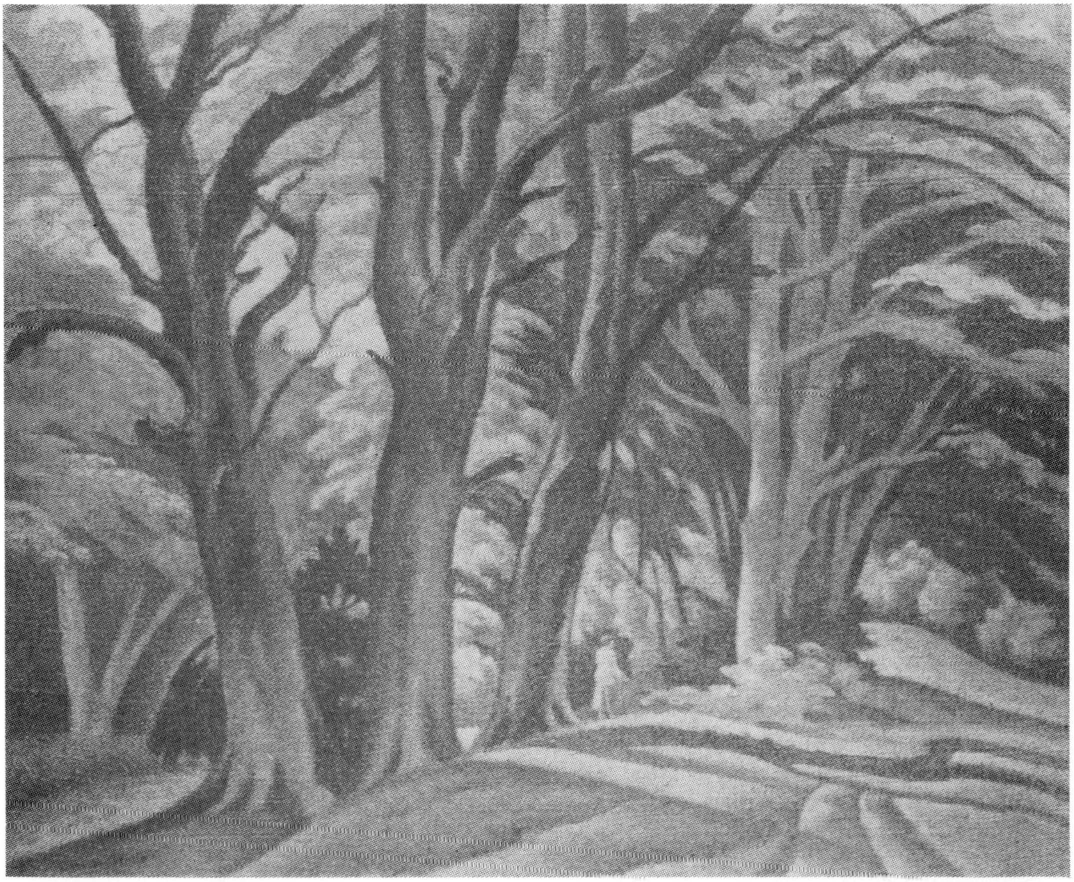

ETHELBERT WHITE – The Beechwood – signed – oil on canvas – 20 x 24in.
(Christie's) **$1,837** **£1,100**

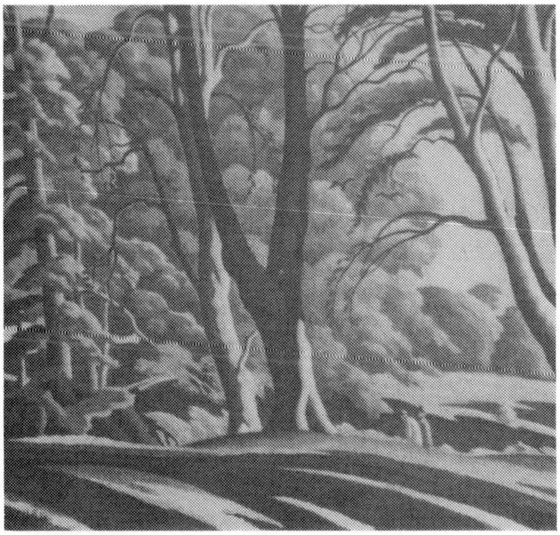

ETHELBERT WHITE – Wooded Landscape With Figures – signed – oil on canvas – 13½ x 17½in.
(Christie's) **$1,573** **£1,100**

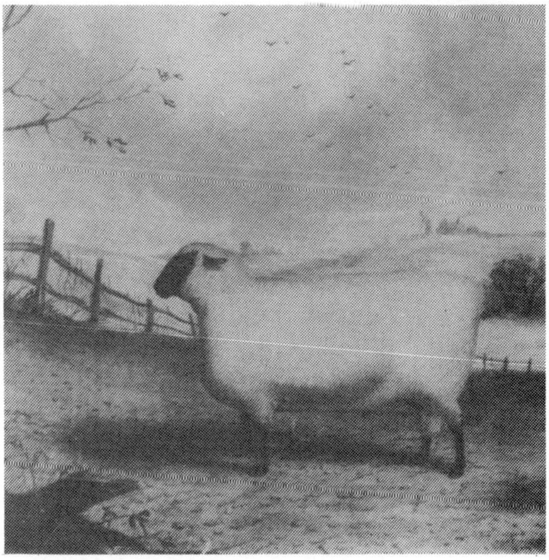

ROBERT WHITFORD – Shearling Hampshire Down Ram, Bred By And The Property Of Frank R. Moore Of Littlecott, Champion Prize Winner At The Marlborough And Pewsey Vale Show, 1884 – signed and dated – oil – 20 x 24in.
(Woolley & Wallis) **$3,000** **£2,000**

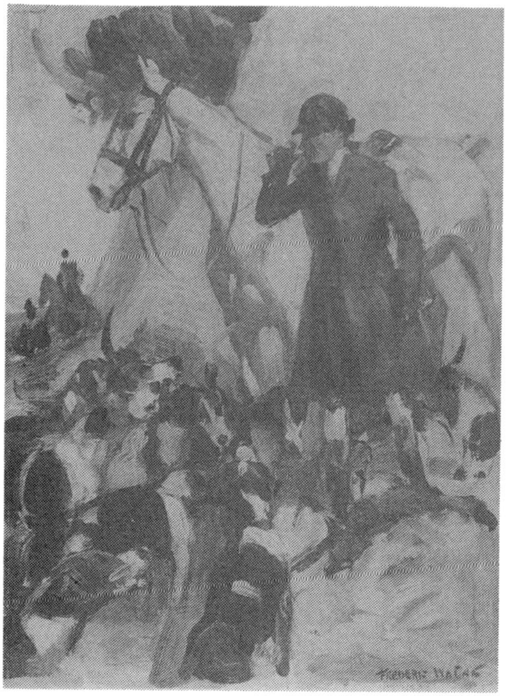

FREDRIC WHITING – The Chalk Pit, A Sketch – signed – oil on board – 30.5 x 22.5cm.
(Phillips) **$1,360** **£850**

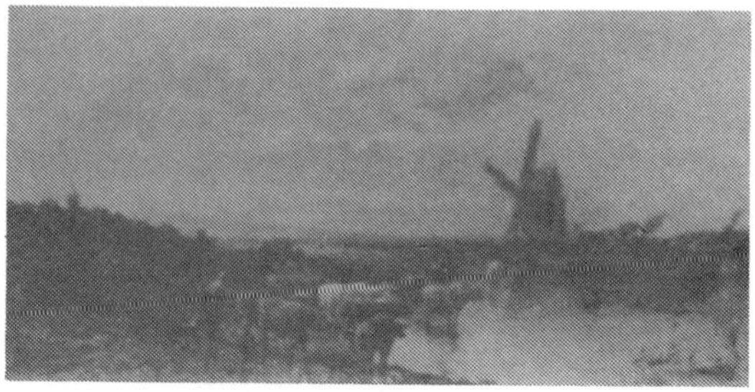

THOMAS WHITTLE – 'Sunset, After A Shower' – signed and dated 1870, also signed, inscribed and dated on the reverse – on canvas – 16 x 24in.
(Phillips) **$772** **£480**

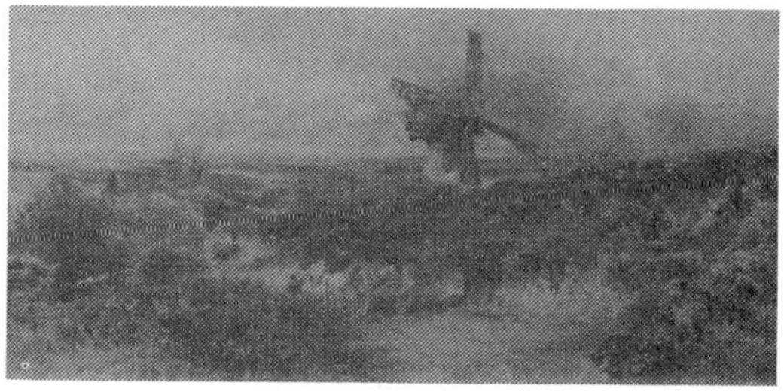

JOSIAH WOOD WHYMPER – Cart And Figures Before A Windmill In An Open Landscape – signed and dated 1870 – watercolour – 48 x 70cm.
(Phillips) **$3,015** **£1,850**

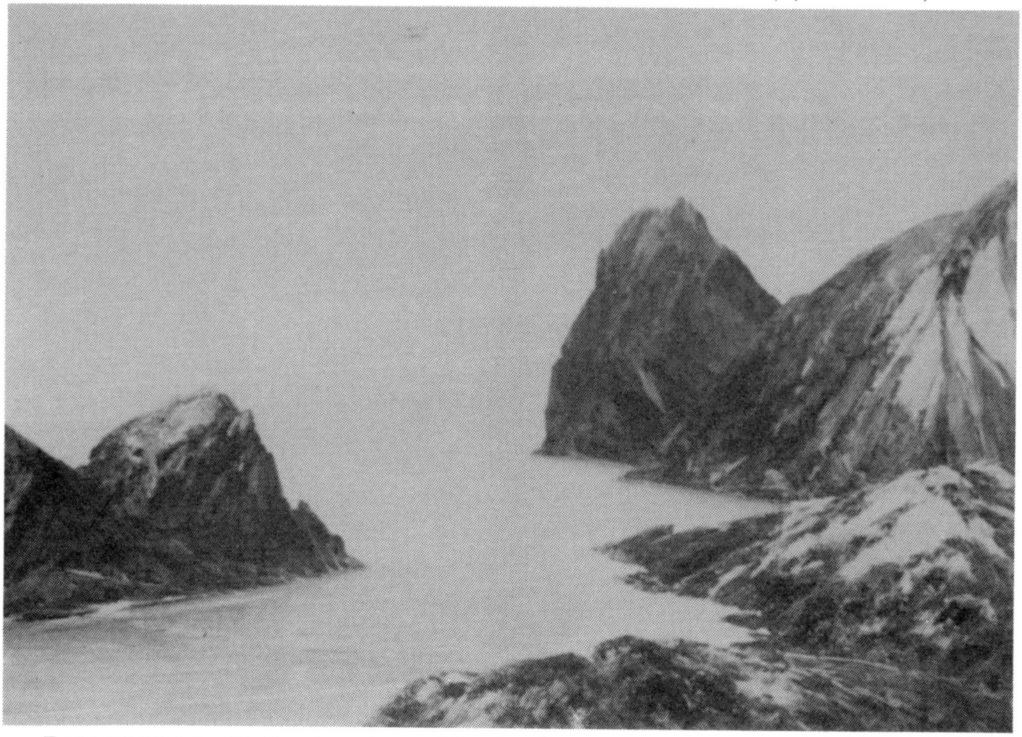

F. T. WIDGERY – 'Mullion Cove, Cornwall' – signed – gouache and watercolour – 17½ x 23½in.
(Capes, Dunn & Co.) **$293** **£180**

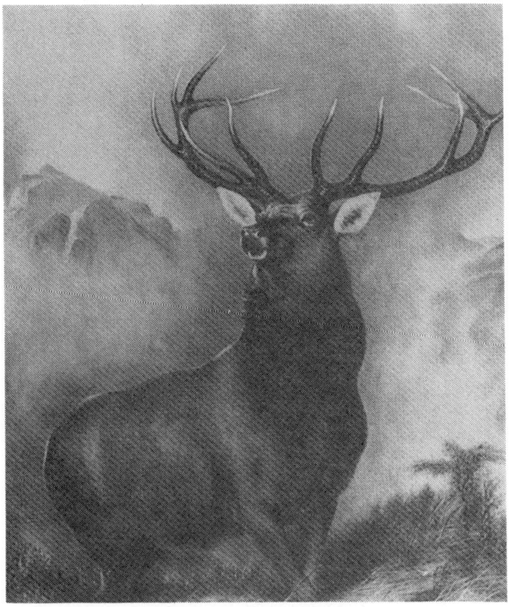

WILLIAM WIDGERY, After Sir Edwin Landseer – The Monarch Of The Glen – signed and dated 1857 – 50 x 56in.
(Christie's) **$4,375** **£2,860**

WILLIAM WIDGERY – A Wooded River Landscape With Ponies – signed – 10 x 45in.
(Christie's) **$1,293** **£770**

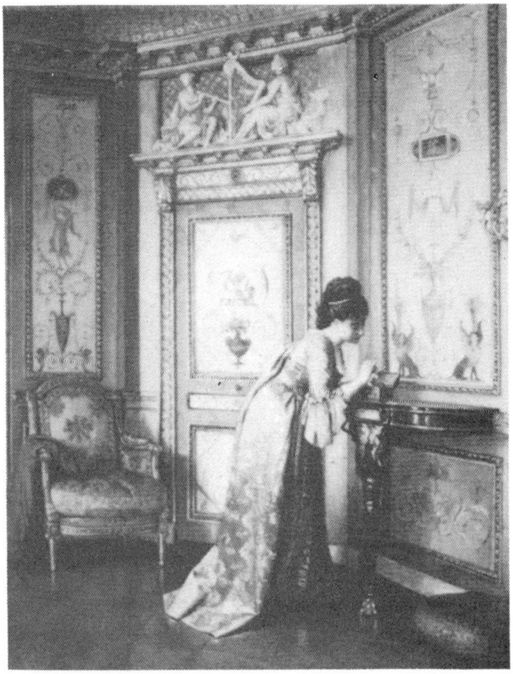

MOSES WIGHT – Marie Antoinette – signed and inscribed, also inscribed on the reverse – oil on canvas – 22¼ x 18¼in.
(Christie's) **$4,400** **£3,061**

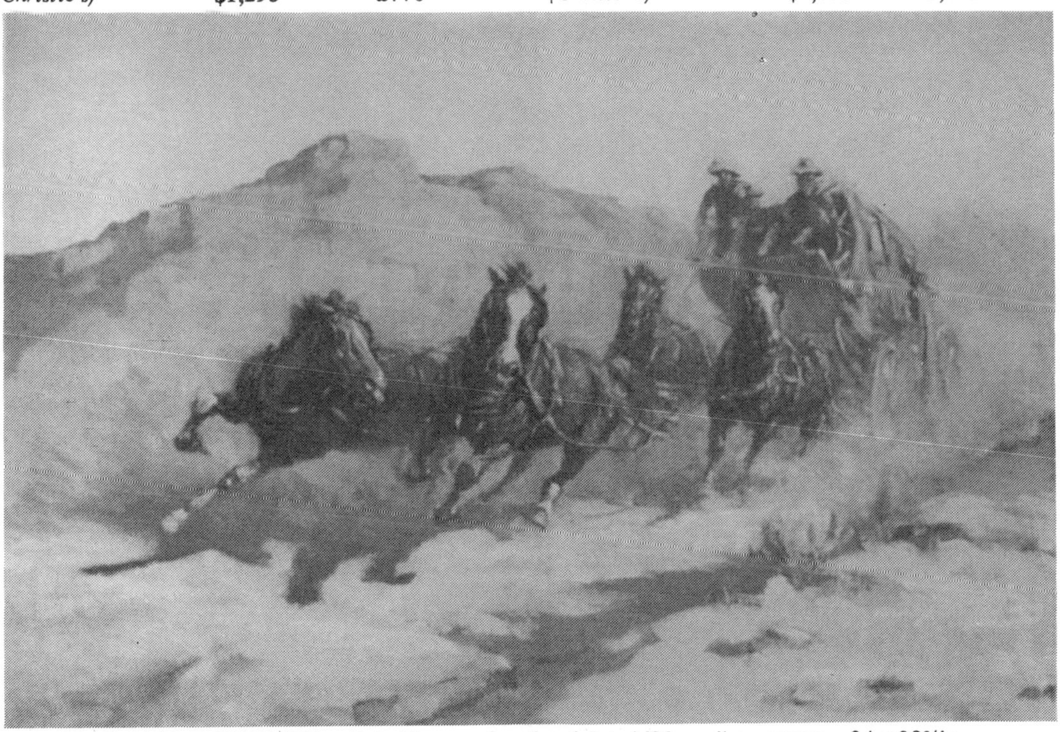

OLAF CARL WIEGHORST – Late Stage – signed and dated '20 – oil on canvas – 24 x 29¾in.
(Christie's) **$12,100** **£8,506**

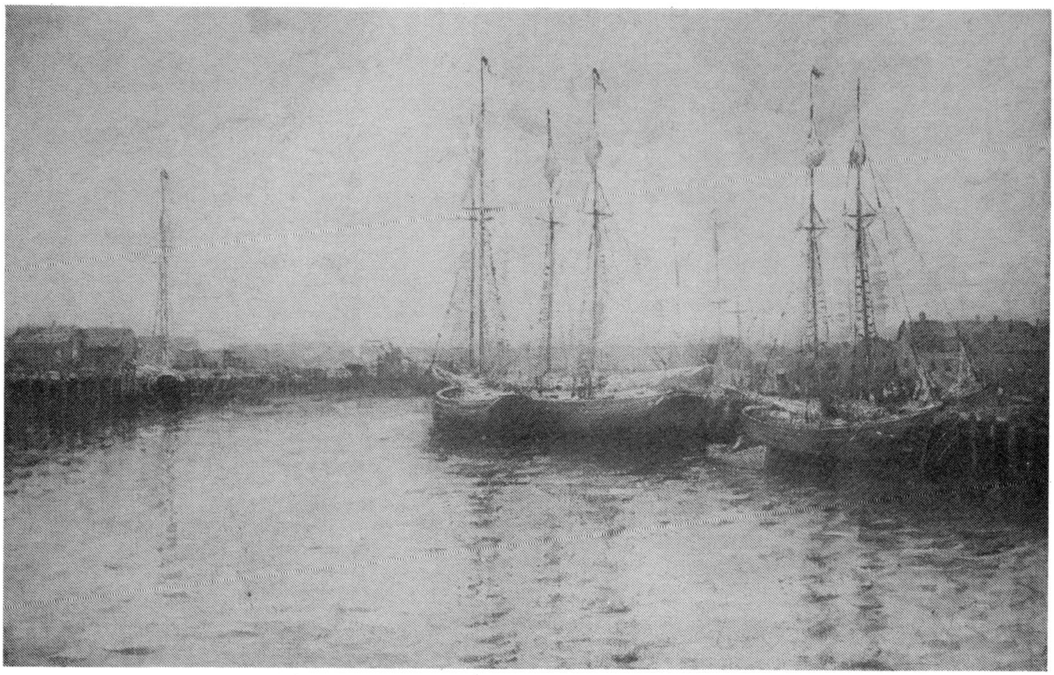

GUY CARLETON WIGGINS – Ships At Dock – signed, also signed and dated 1913 on the reverse – oil on canvas – 40¼ x 50in. *(Christie's)* **$46,200 £28,306**

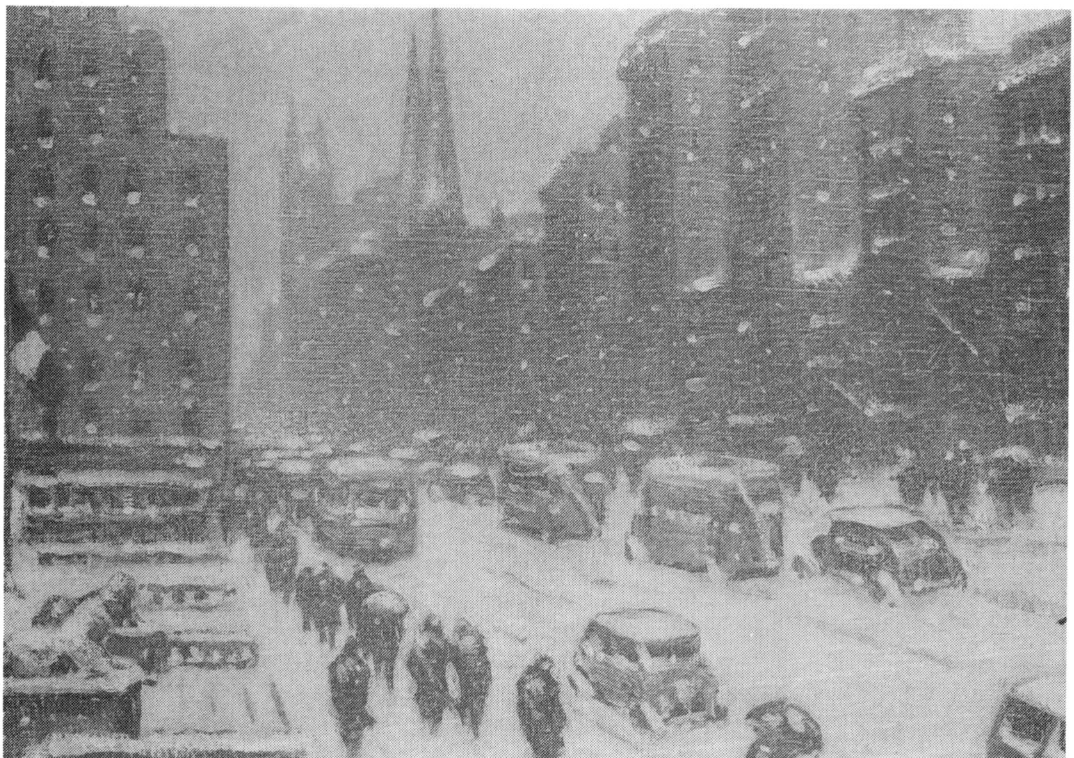

GUY CARLETON WIGGINS – Fifth Avenue At The Library – signed, also signed and inscribed on the reverse – oil on canvas – 17¾ x 20in. *(Christie's)* **$26,400 £16,175**

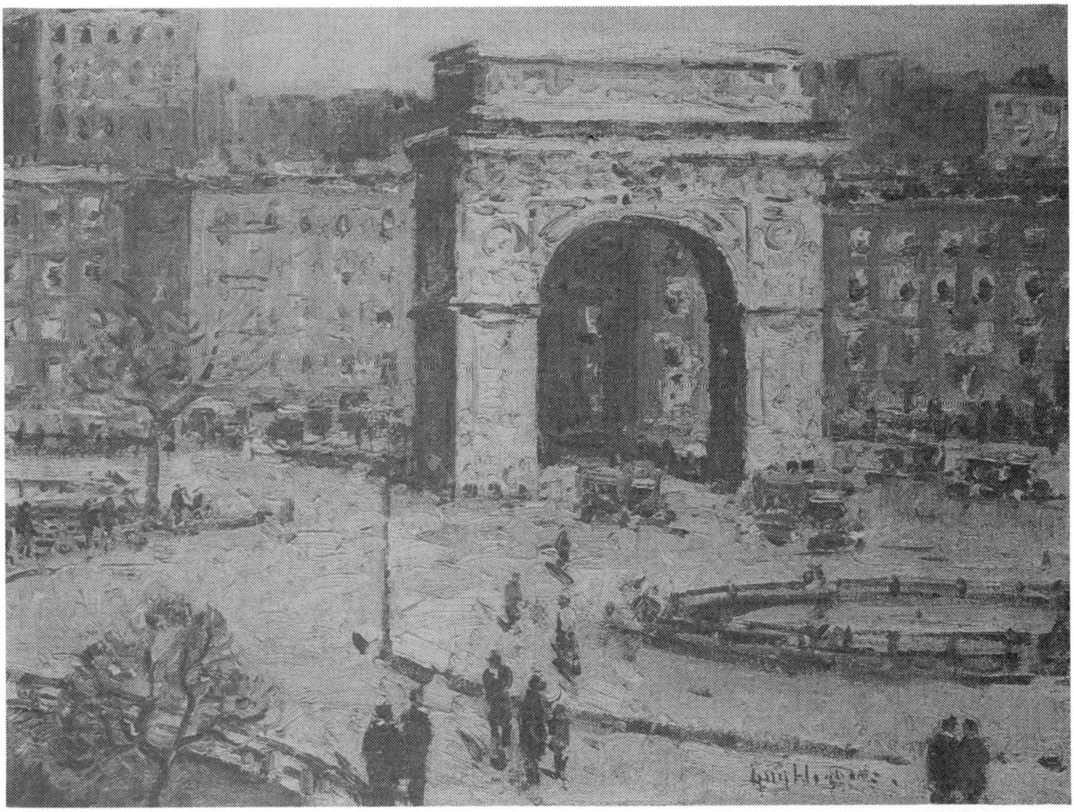

GUY CARLETON WIGGINS – Washington Square – signed – oil on canvas – 12 x 16in.
(Christie's) **$28,600** **£17,523**

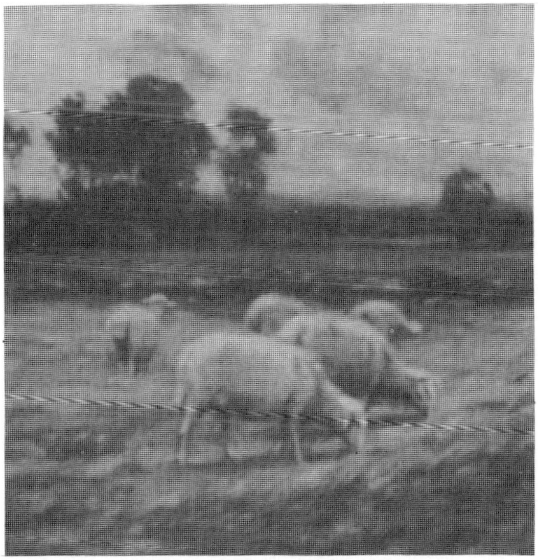

CARLETON WIGGINS – Sheep And Landscape – signed and dated 1917, also signed on verso – oil on canvas – 16¼ x 20in.
(Robt. W. Skinner Inc.) **$600** **£416**

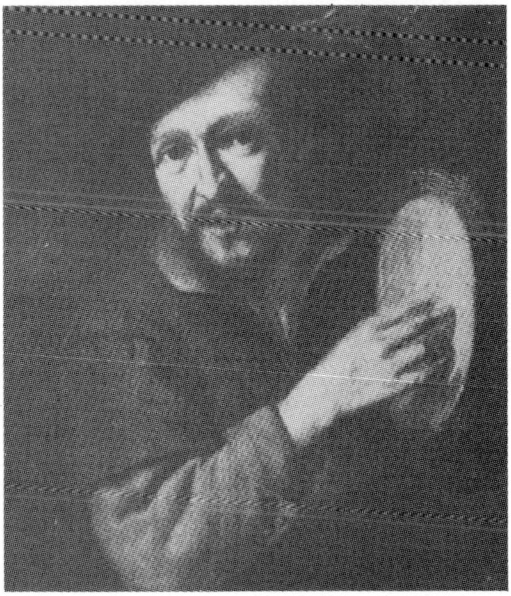

MATTHIJS WIJTMANS, Circle of – The Tambourine Player – oil on panel – 5½ x 4¼in.
(Phillips) **$465** **£300**

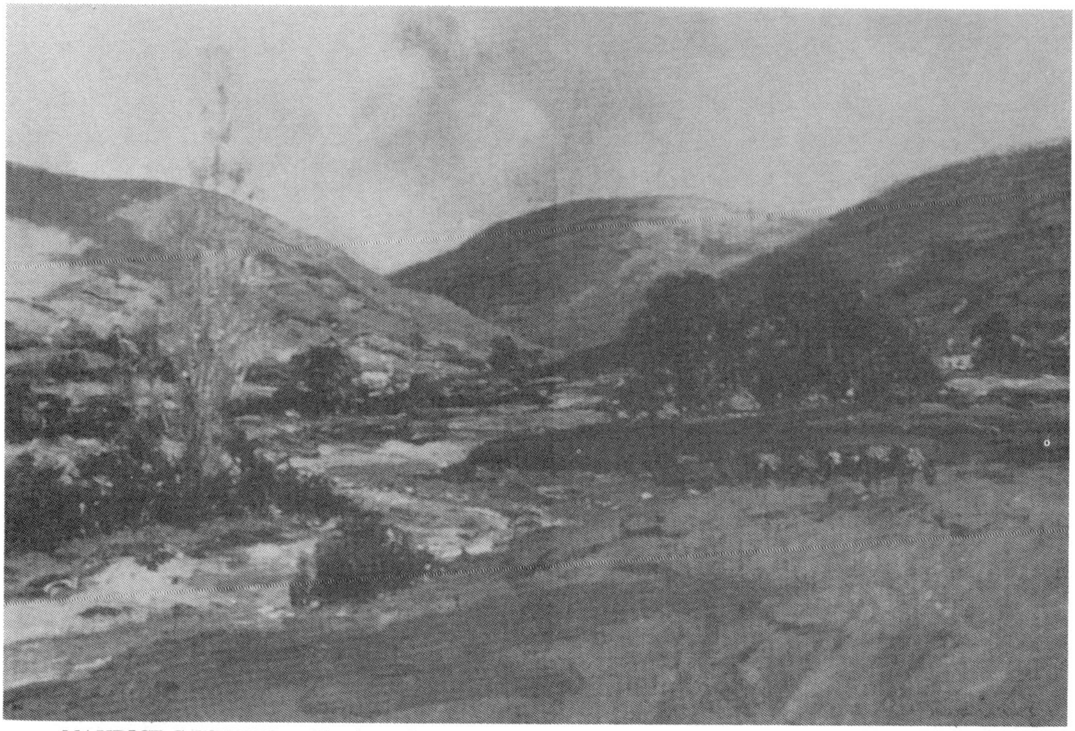

MAURICE C. WILKES – Glendon River, County Antrim – signed – oil on board – 19 x 25¼in.
(Christie's) **$2,204 £1,320**

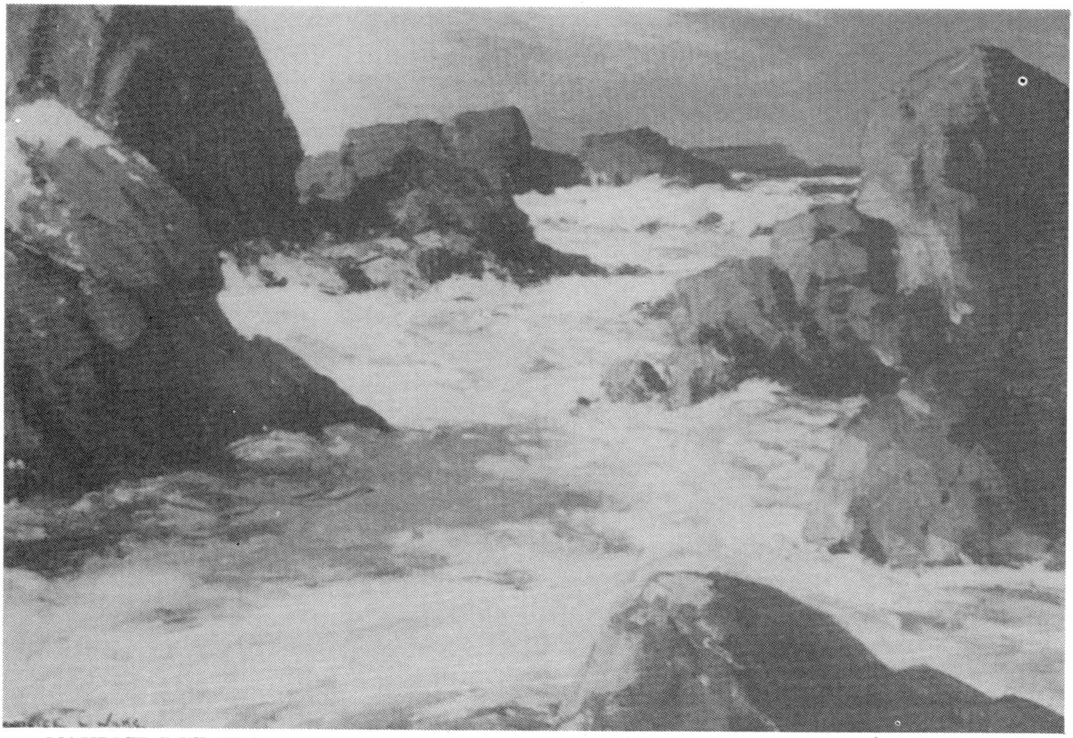

MAURICE C. WILKES – Rocks And Sea, Ballintoy, County Antrim – signed, inscribed on the reverse – oil on canvas – 20¼ x 14¼in. *(Christie's)* **$1,337 £825**

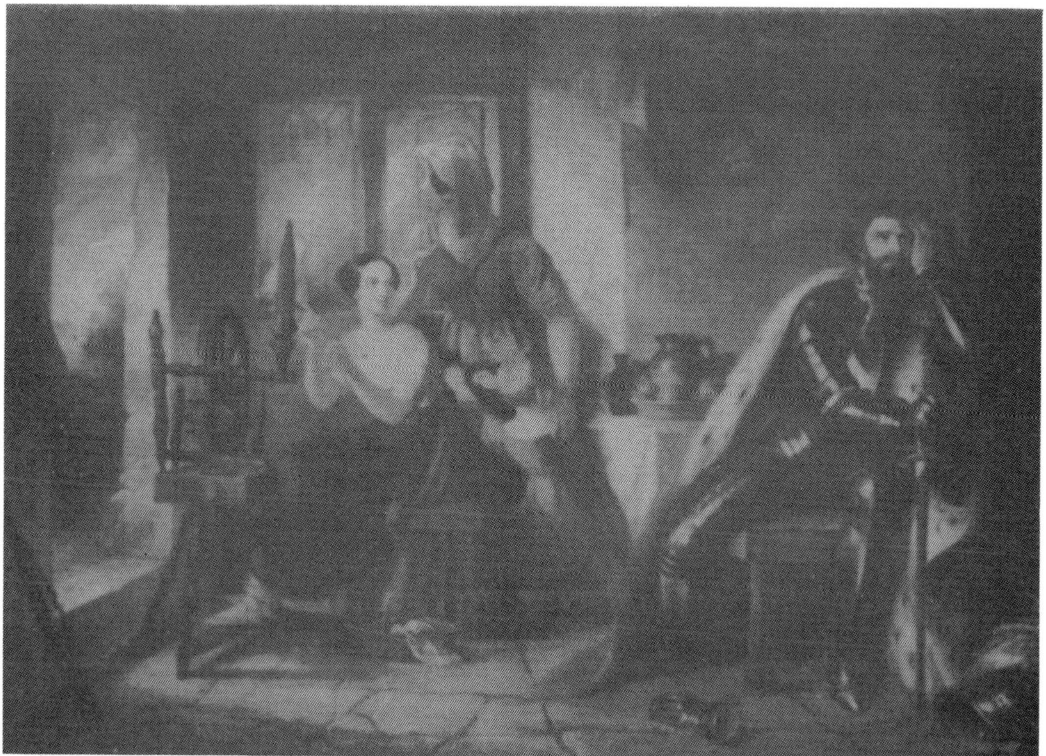

SIR DAVID WILKIE, Follower of – Robert The Bruce In A Cottage – oil on canvas – 33 x 44in.
(Christie's) **$1,911 £1,210**

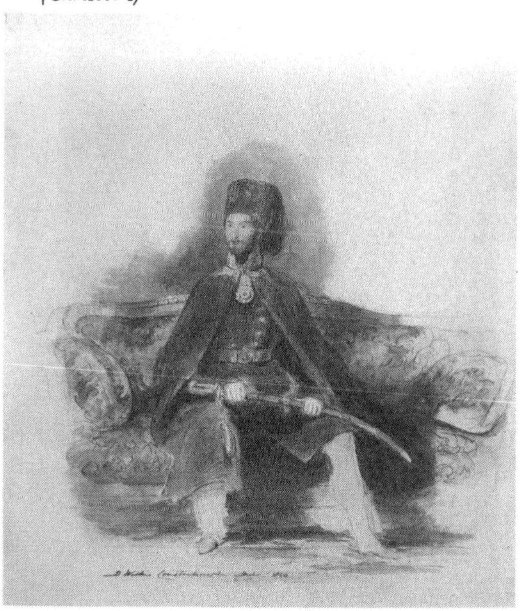

SIR DAVID WILKIE – Portrait Of Abd-Ul-Mejid, Sultan Of Turkey – signed, inscribed and dated 1840 – pencil, black and red chalk and water-colour heightened with white and gold body-colour on stone-coloured paper – 15¼ x 13in.
(Christie's) **$24,300 £16,200**

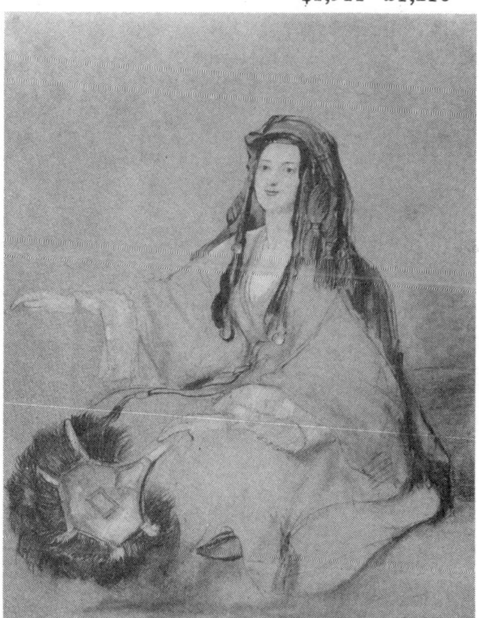

SIR DAVID WILKIE – Portrait Of Mrs. Moore – signed and dated 1841 – pencil, black and red chalk and watercolour heightened with white on stone-coloured paper – 18½ x 12½in.
(Christie's) **$10,530 £7,020**

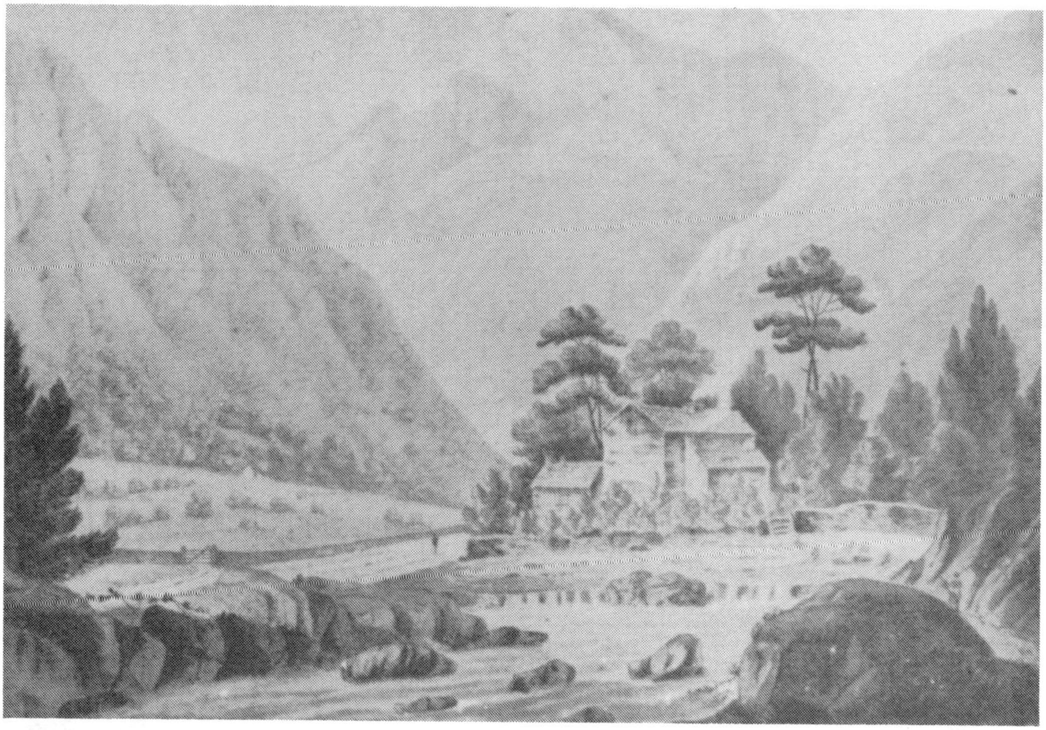

JOSEPH WILKINSON – Cottage In The Vale Of Newlands, Near Keswick, Cumberland – signed with monogram and inscribed verso – watercolour over pencil – 39 x 54cm. *(Phillips)* **$391 £240**

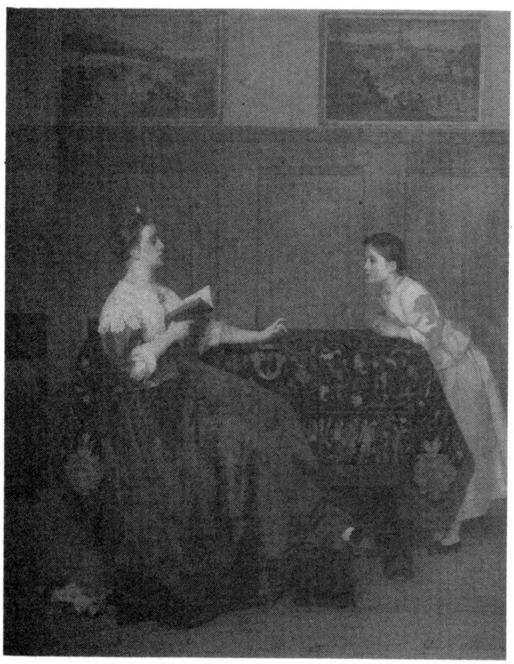

FLORENT WILLEMS – The Morning Lesson – signed and dated '58 – on panel – 74.7 x 60.5cm. *(Phillips)* **$11,325 £7,500**

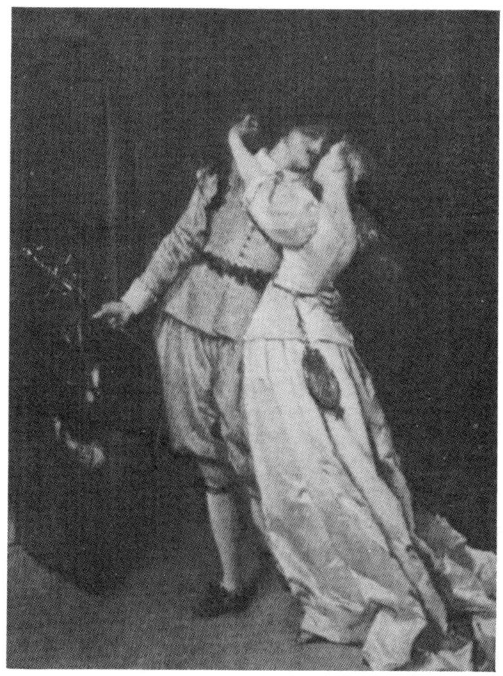

FLORENT WILLEMS – 'Les Adieux' – signed and dated '58 – on panel – 14 x 9cm. *(Phillips)* **$1,132 £750**

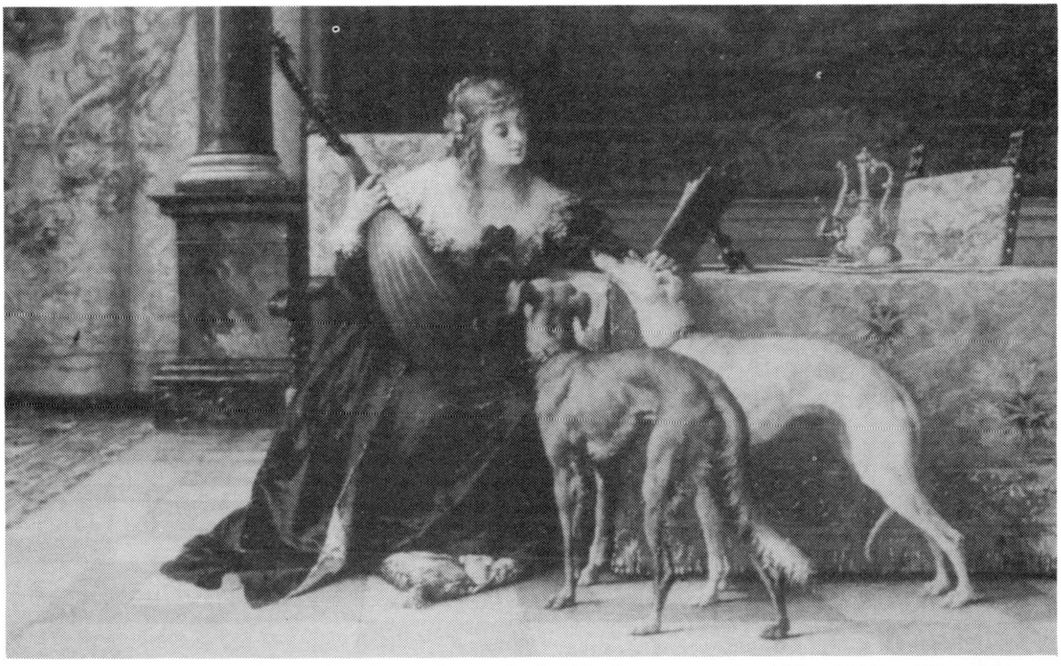

FLORENT WILLEMS, Attributed to – Sympathetic Friends – on panel – 12½ x 16¾in. *(Christie's)* **$5,350 £3,520**

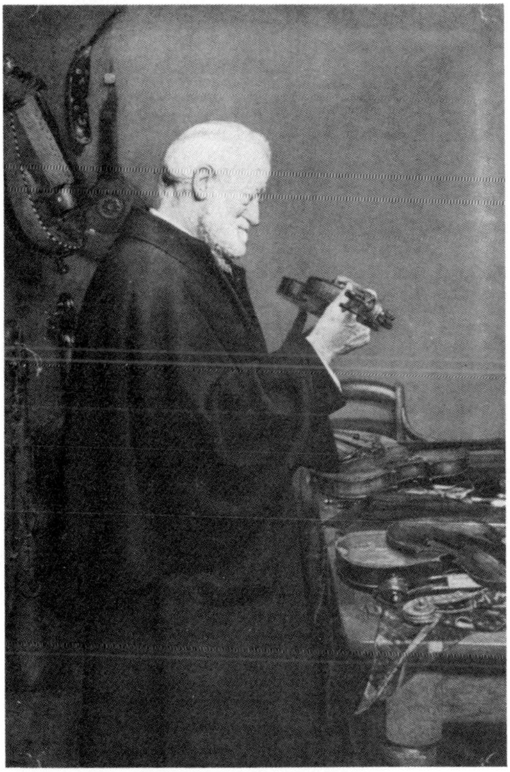

BENJAMIN WILLIAMS – Maker Unknown – pencil and watercolour – 40½ x 26¾in.
(Christie's) **$2,692 £1,870**

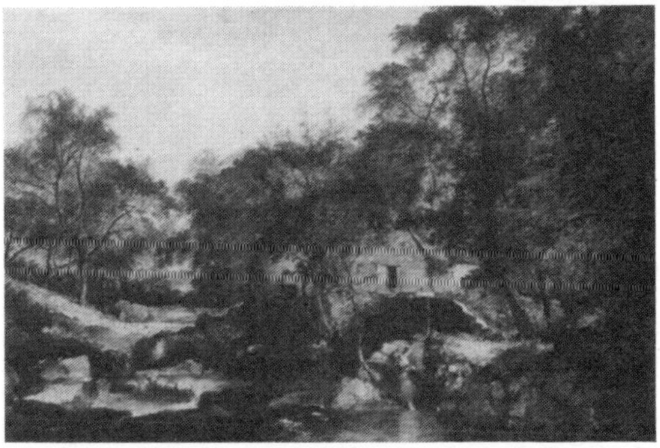

EDWARD CHARLES WILLIAMS – A Wooded River Landscape With Figures By A Mill – signed with initials – 39 x 59in.
(Christie's) **$4,032 £2,860**

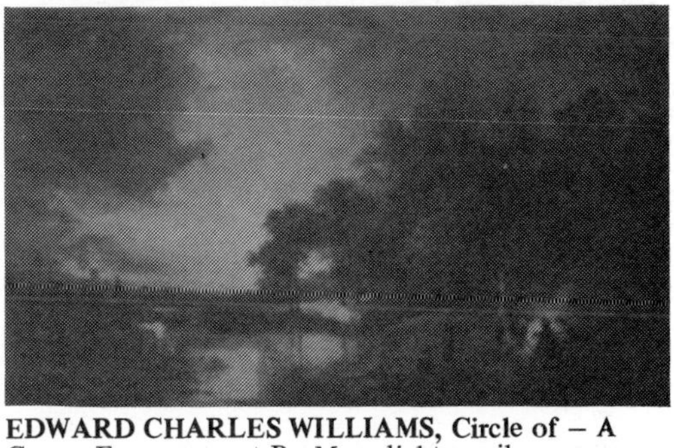

EDWARD CHARLES WILLIAMS, Circle of – A Gypsy Encampment By Moonlight – oil on canvas – 31¼ x 41¼in.
(Phillips) **$1,195 £720**

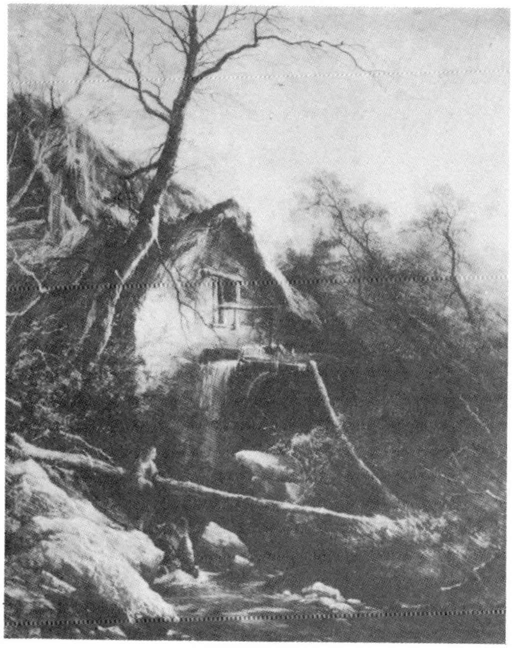

GEORGE AUGUSTUS WILLIAMS – Figures By A Mill In A Wooded River Landscape – signed with monogram – 20 x 16in.
(Christie's) **$1,134** **£756**

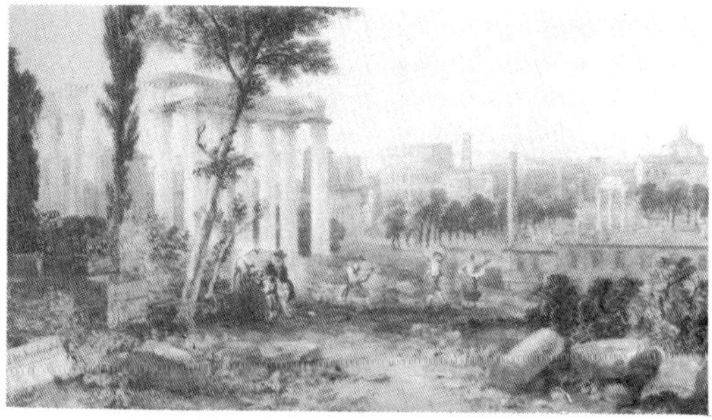

HUGH WILLIAM 'GRECIAN' WILLIAMS – The Roman Forum – pencil and watercolour heightened with white – 15¼ x 23¼in.
(Christie's) **$1,093** **£770**

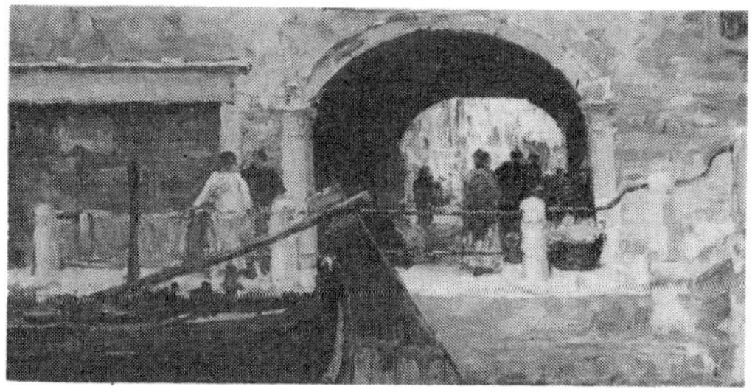

TERRICK WILLIAMS – A Venetian Archway – signed, and signed, inscribed and dated 1893 on the reverse – oil on canvas – 12 x 18in.
(Christie's) **$3,799** **£2,420**

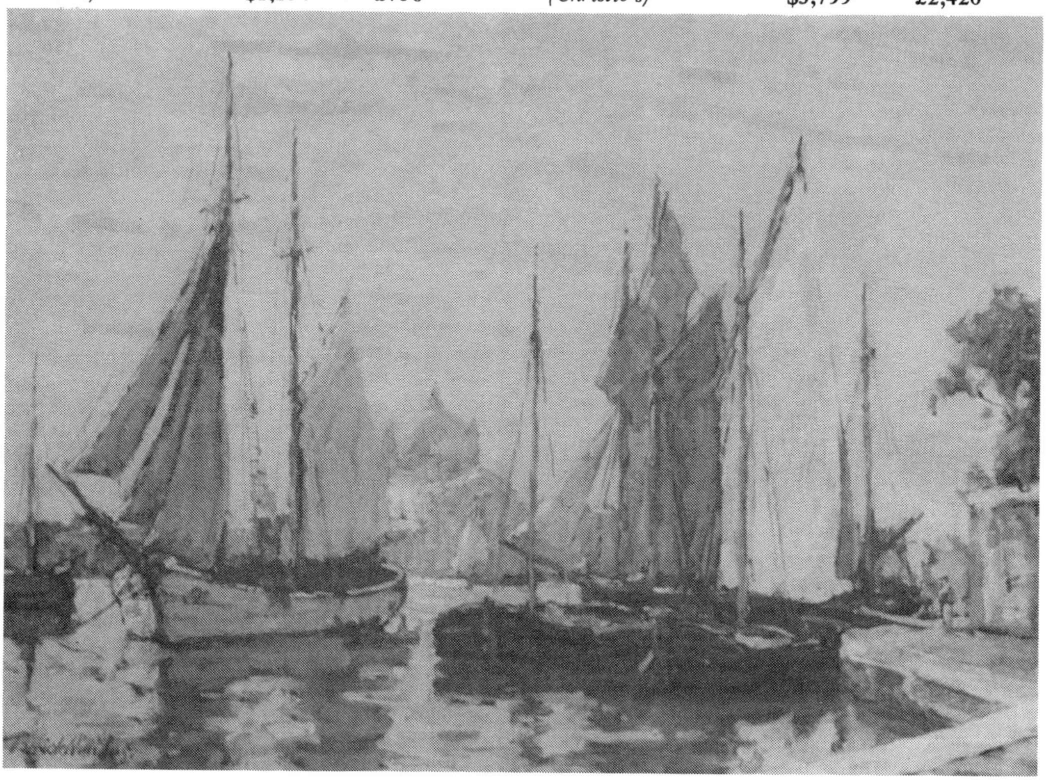

TERRICK WILLIAMS – Venice – signed – oil on board – 15¼ x 20¾in. *(Christie's)* **$6,908** **£4,400**

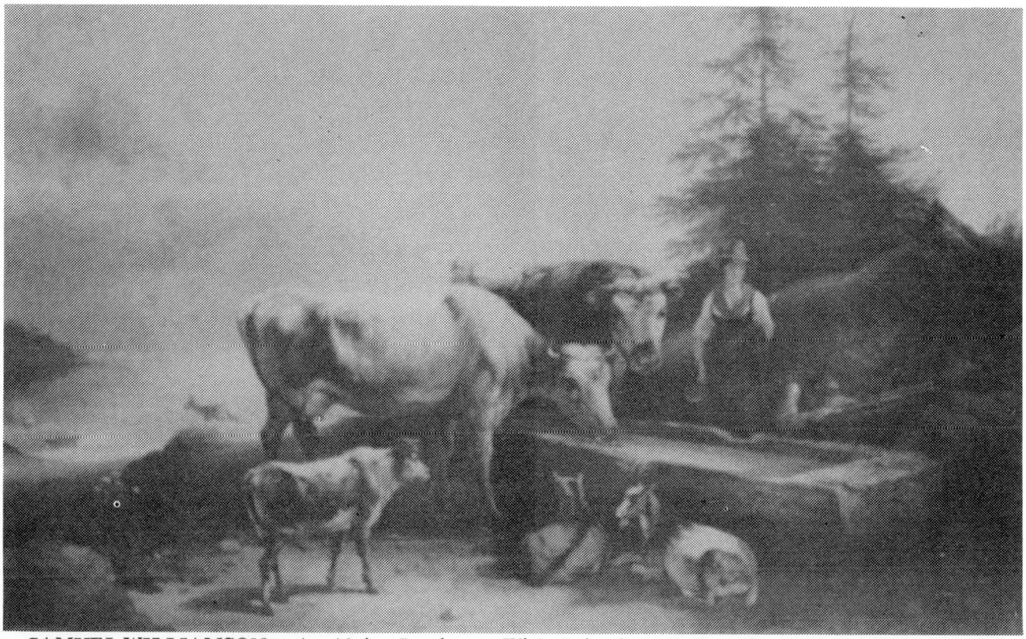

SAMUEL WILLIAMSON – An Alpine Landscape With Animals At A Trough – signed and dated 1827 – 15½ x 19½in. *(Christie's)* **$775 £550**

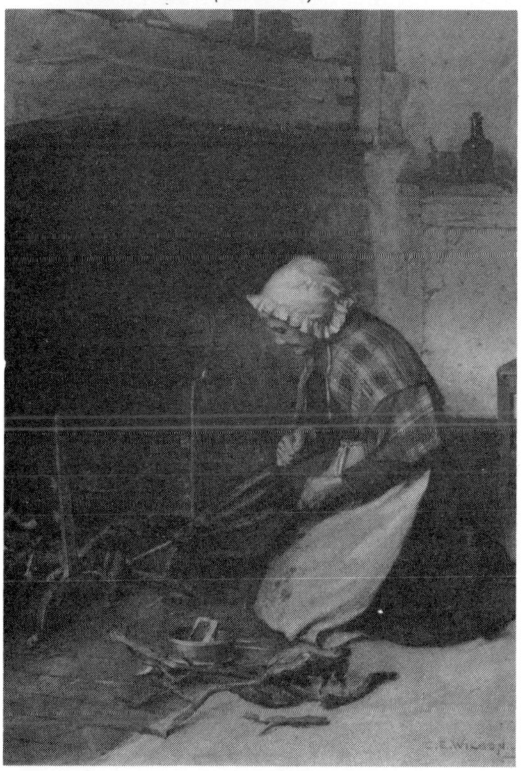

CHARLES EDWARD WILSON – 'In The Days Of The Tinderbox' – signed – watercolour – 15½ x 11¼in.
(Geering & Colyer) **$2,880 £2,000**

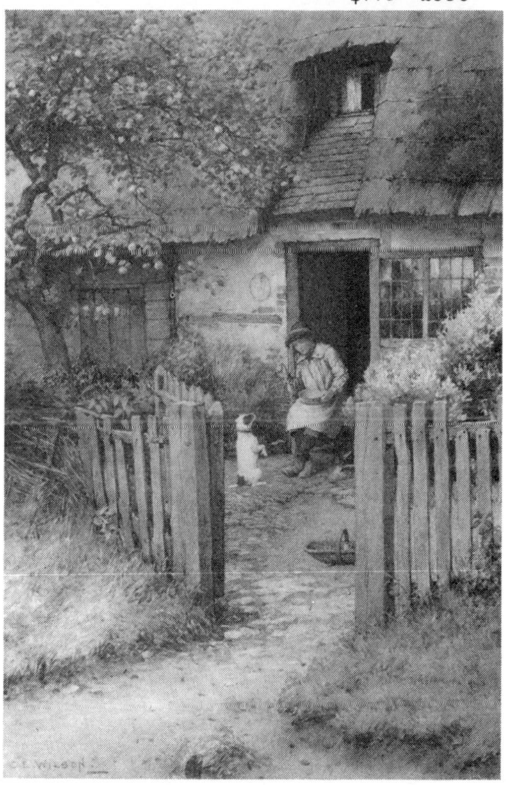

CHARLES EDWARD WILSON – A Mute Appeal – signed – watercolour – 14¾ x 10in.
(Christie's) **$4,536 £3,024**

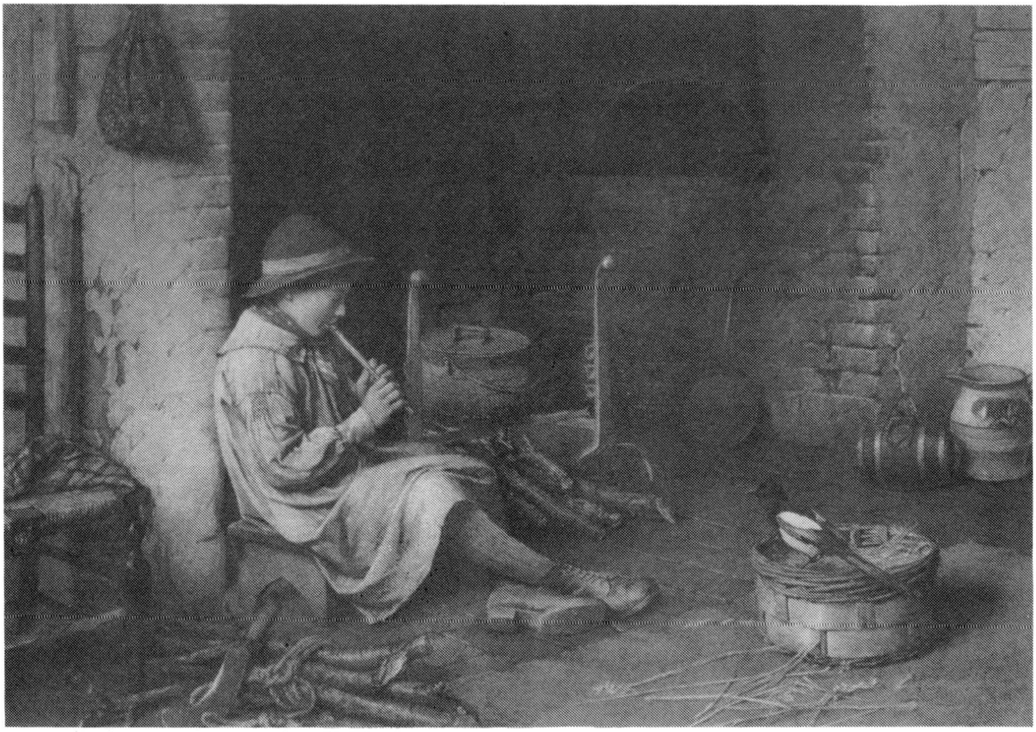

CHARLES EDWARD WILSON – Idle Moments – signed – pencil and watercolour heightened with white – 14½ x 21¼in. *(Christie's)* **$7,573 £4,950**

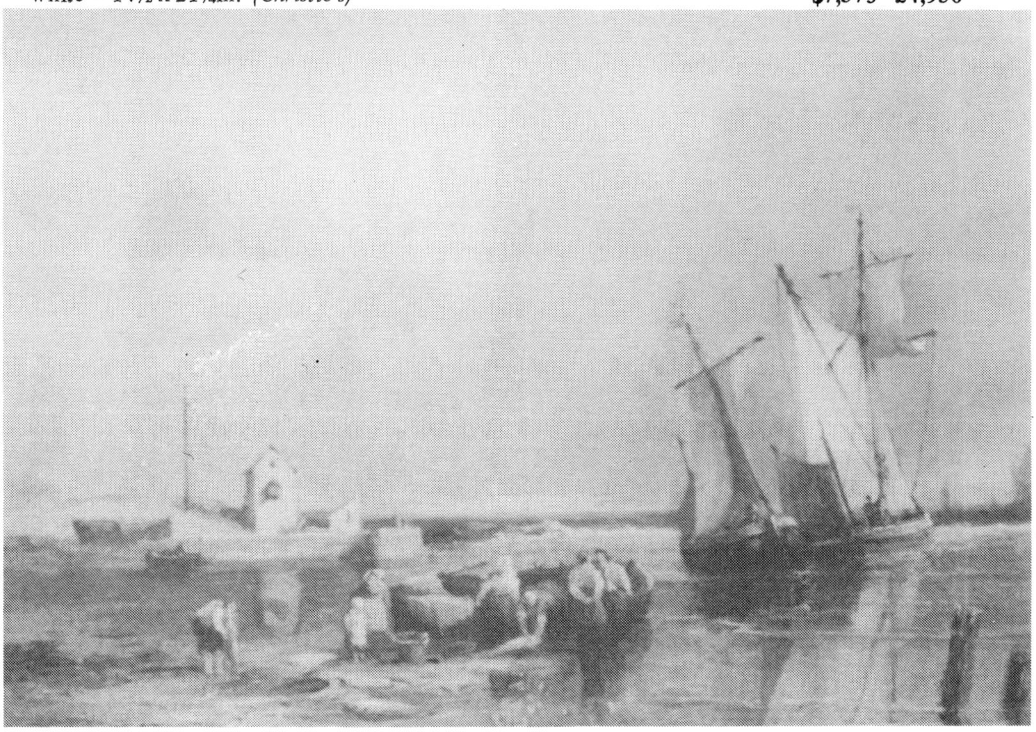

JOHN WILSON – Ely Harbour, Fifeshire – signed, and signed and inscribed on a label on the reverse – oil on panel – 8½ x 11½in. *(Christie's)* **$1,470 £902**

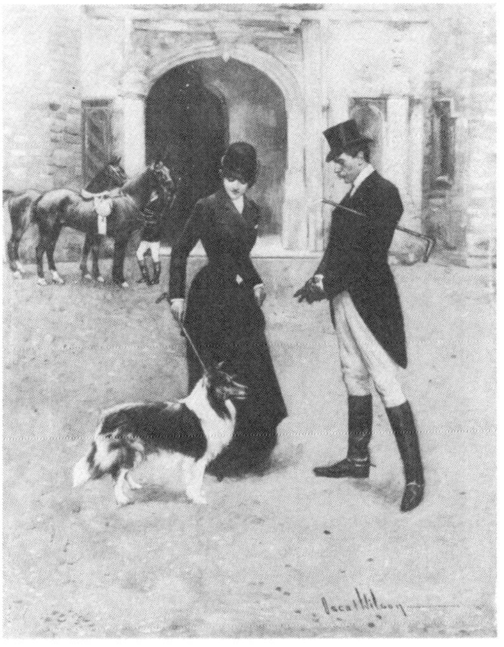

OSCAR WILSON – 'Off To The Meet' – signed – oil on board, en grisaille – 18½ x 14½in.
(Phillips) **$1,147** **£750**

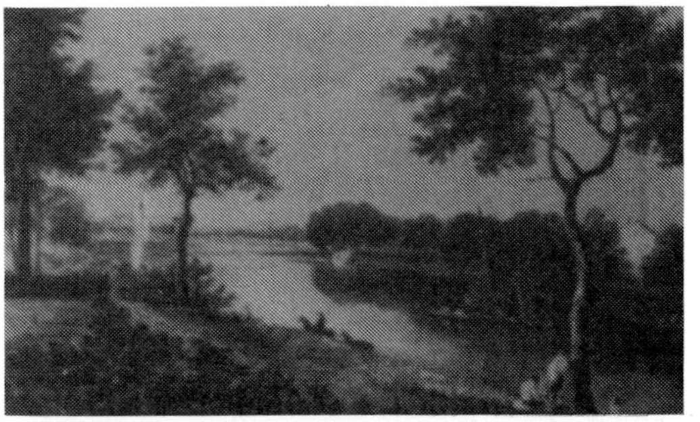

RICHARD WILSON, After – The Thames Near Marble Hill – oil on canvas – 14 x 18¾in.
(Phillips) **$664** **£400**

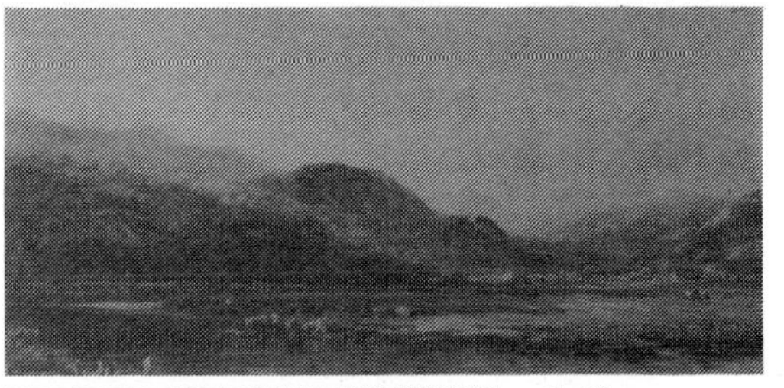

EDMUND MORISON WIMPERIS – Cattle Watering At A Highland Lake – signed with initials and dated '92 – watercolour – 36 x 61cm.
(Phillips) **$1,467** **£900**

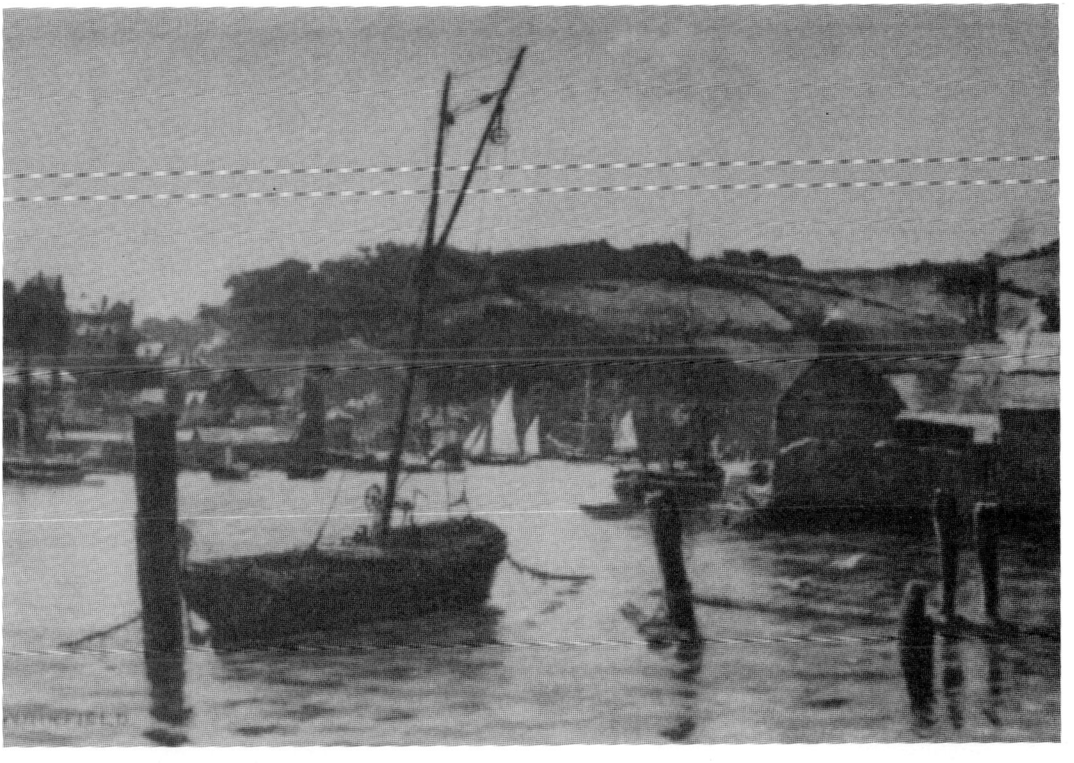

FREDERICK A. WINKFIELD – Boats In Dartmouth Harbour – signed – oil on board – 20 x 30cm.
(W. H. Lane & Son) **$830** **£500**

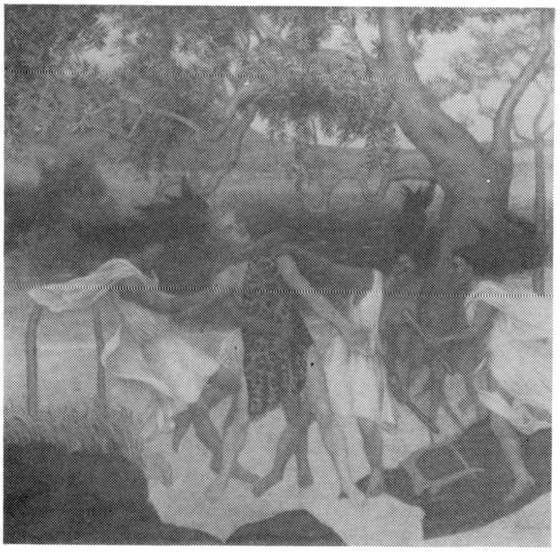

HENRY WINSLOW – Death Of Orpheus – signed, also inscribed on a label on the reverse – tempera on board – 61 x 61cm.
(Phillips) **$996** **£600**

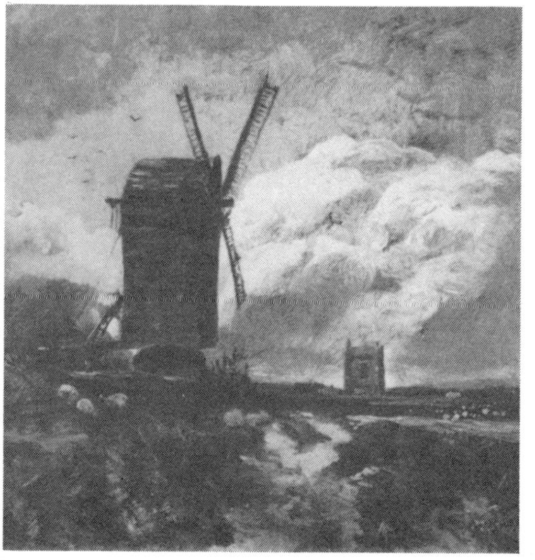

PETER DE WINT, Attributed to – An Extensive Landscape With A Village On The Horizon And A Windmill – oil on board – 11 x 9in.
(Christie's) **$1,095** **£660**

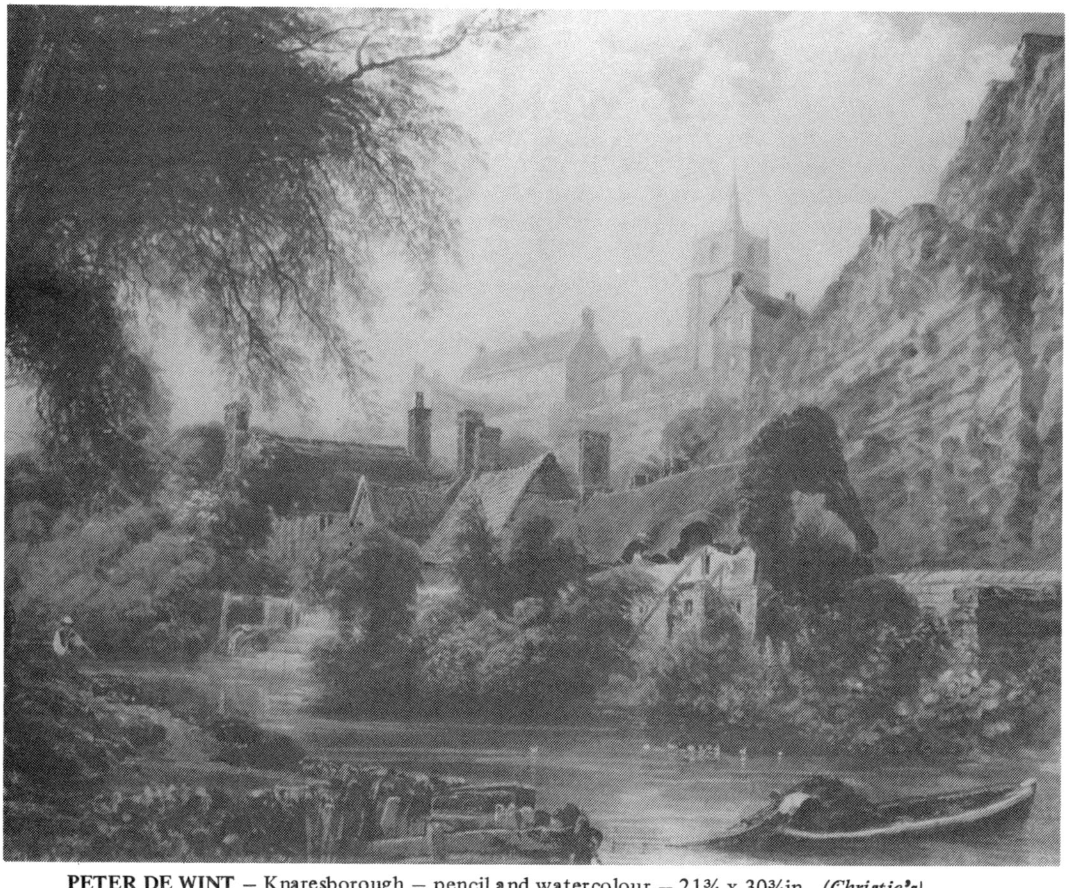

PETER DE WINT – Knaresborough – pencil and watercolour – 21¾ x 30¾in. *(Christie's)*
$27,540 **£18,360**

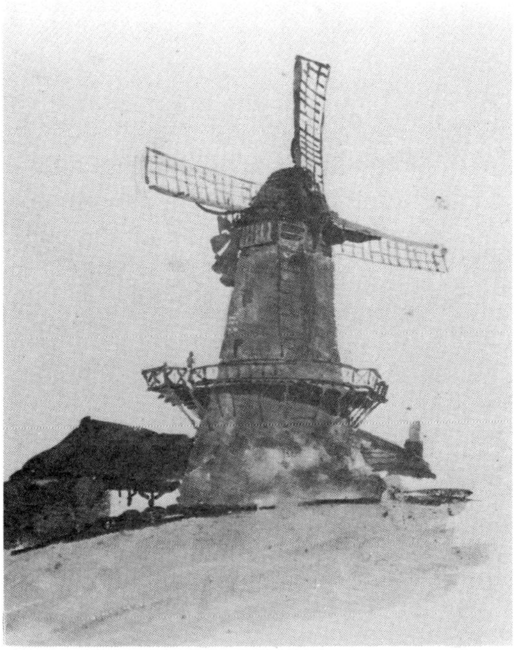

PETER DE WINT – **A** Windmill And Farm Buildings – pencil and watercolour on oatmeal paper – 12¼ x 9¼in.
(Christie's) **$4,536** **£3,024**

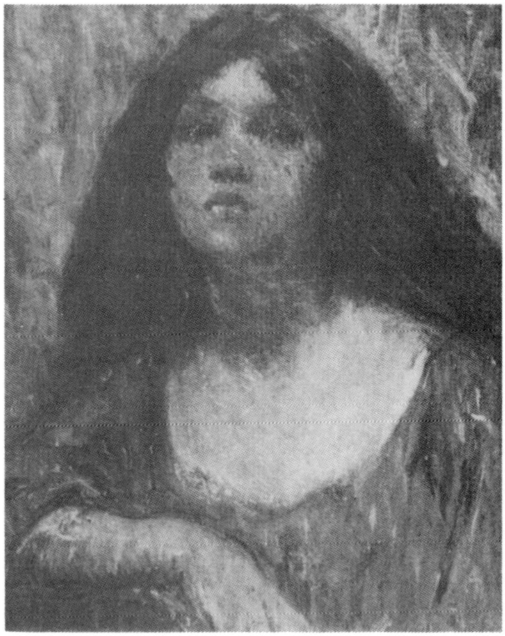

CHARLES ALLEN WINTER – **A** Red-Haired Girl – oil on academy board – 11¾ x 9¾in.
(Robt. W. Skinner Inc.) **$600** **£416**

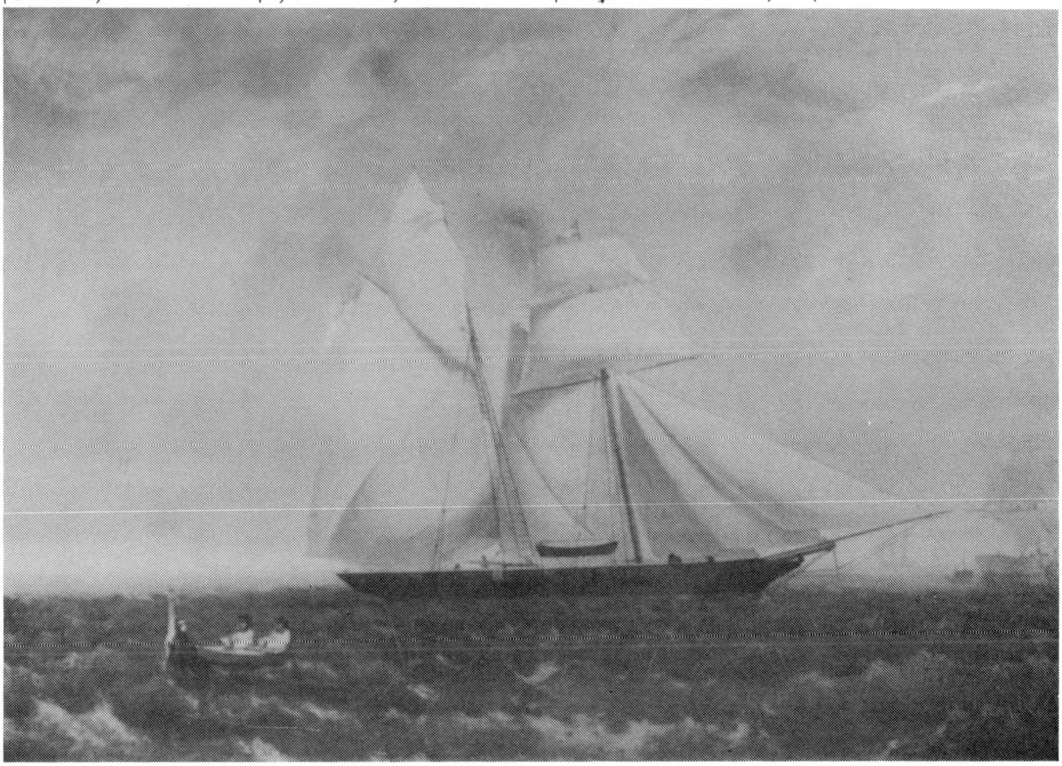

H. L. WITTLEY – An Armed Schooner Yacht And Other Shipping Off A Coast – signed – 31½ x 47½in. *(Christie's)* **$3,240** **£2,160**

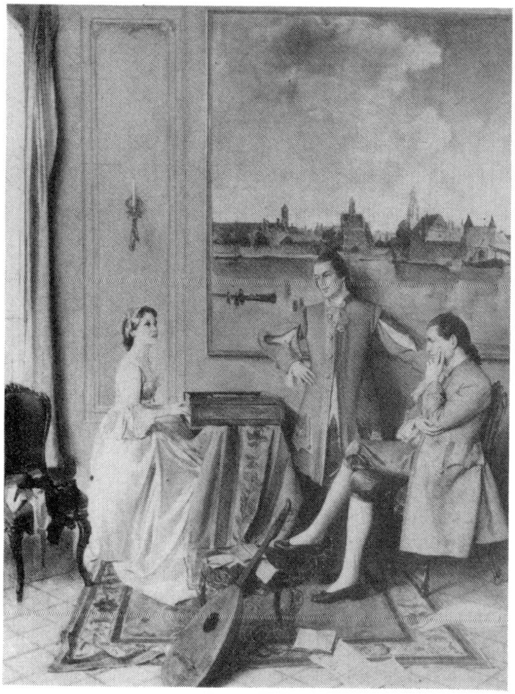

FRANZ XAVIER WOLF – The Rehearsal – signed – on panel – 24½ x 19in.
(Christie's) **$5,852** **£3,850**

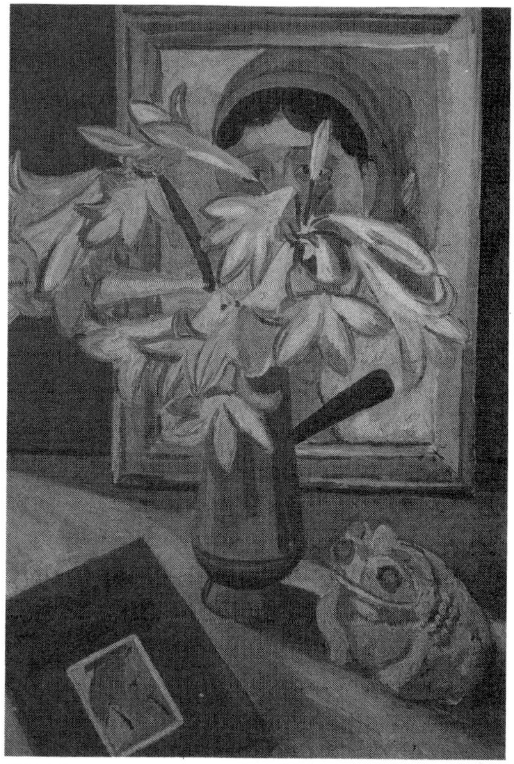

EDWARD WOLFE – Mexican Flowerpiece – oil on canvas – 81 x 56cm.
(Phillips) **$2,840** **£2,000**

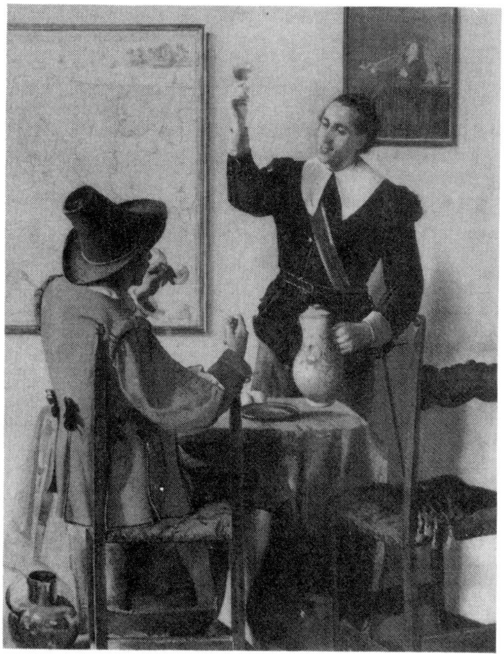

FRANZ XAVIER WOLF – The Toast – signed – on panel – 16 x 13in.
(Christie's) **$2,508** **£1,650**

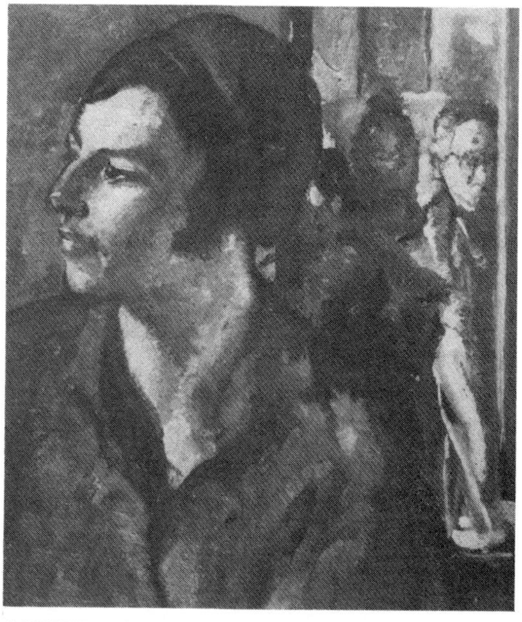

ALFRED WOLMARK – Woman In Red With Self Portrait – signed, also signed and dated 1932 on the reverse – oil on board – 46 x 40cm.
(Phillips) **$3,124** **£2,200**

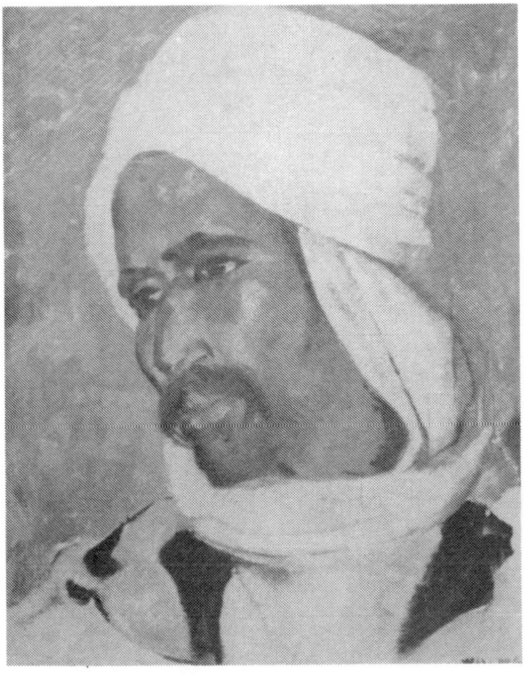

ALFRED WOLMARK – Head Of An Arab – signed, also signed and inscribed on the reverse – oil on board – 41 x 33cm.
(Phillips) **$1,128** **£680**

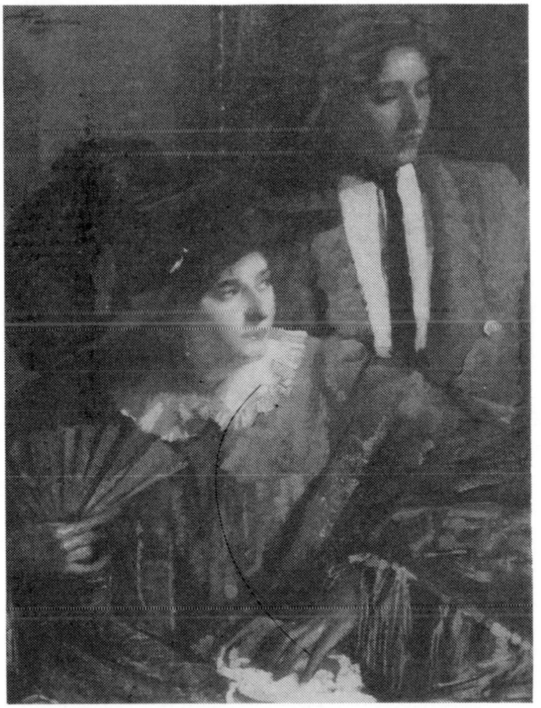

ALFRED WOLMARK – In Costume – Sarah And Gitel – signed – oil on canvas – 36 x 28in.
(Christie's) **$32,813** **£20,900**

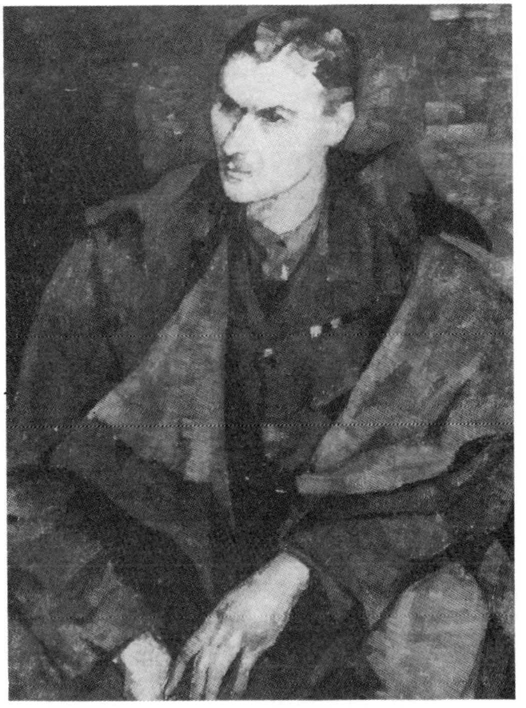

ALFRED WOLMARK – Portrait Of Captain F. H. E. Townsend, M.C., R.A. – signed with initial – oil on canvas – 36¼ x 28in.
(Christie's) **$1,258** **£880**

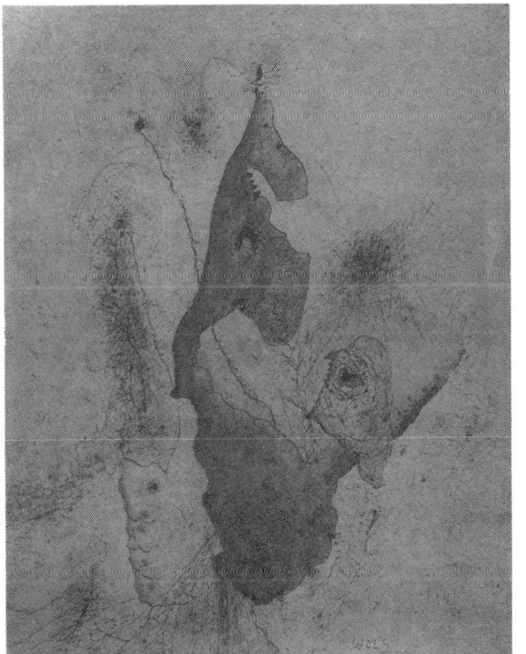

WOLS – Composition – signed – watercolour, pen and ink on paper – 10½ x 7¼in.
(Christie's) **$28,160** **£17,600**

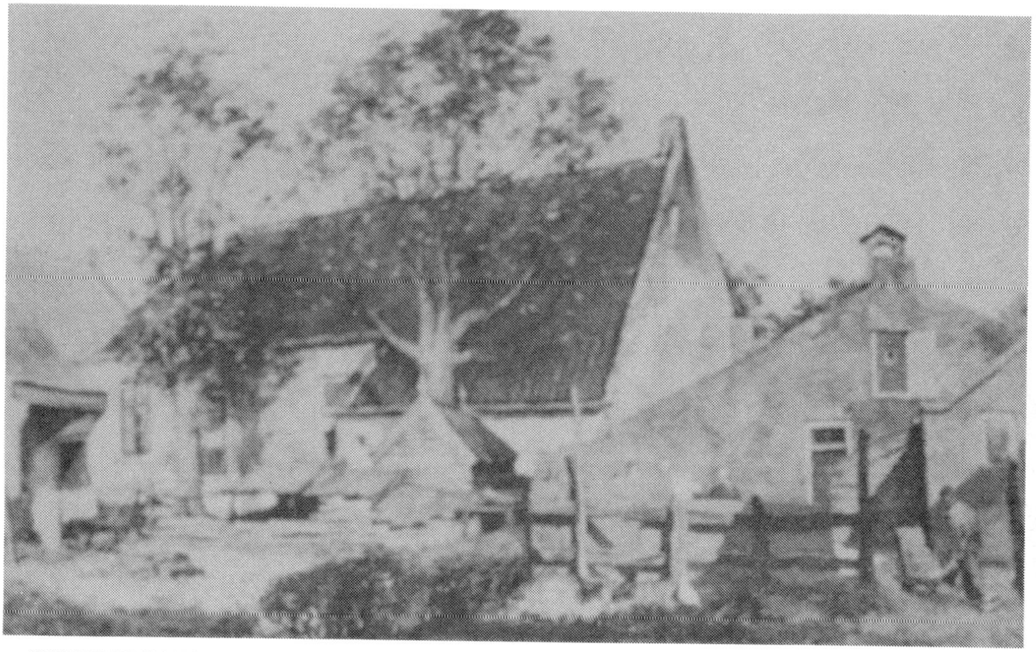

HENDRIK HAN WOLTER – Figures Before Farm Buildings – signed – oil on panel – 42 x 66cm.
(Phillips)
$701 £420

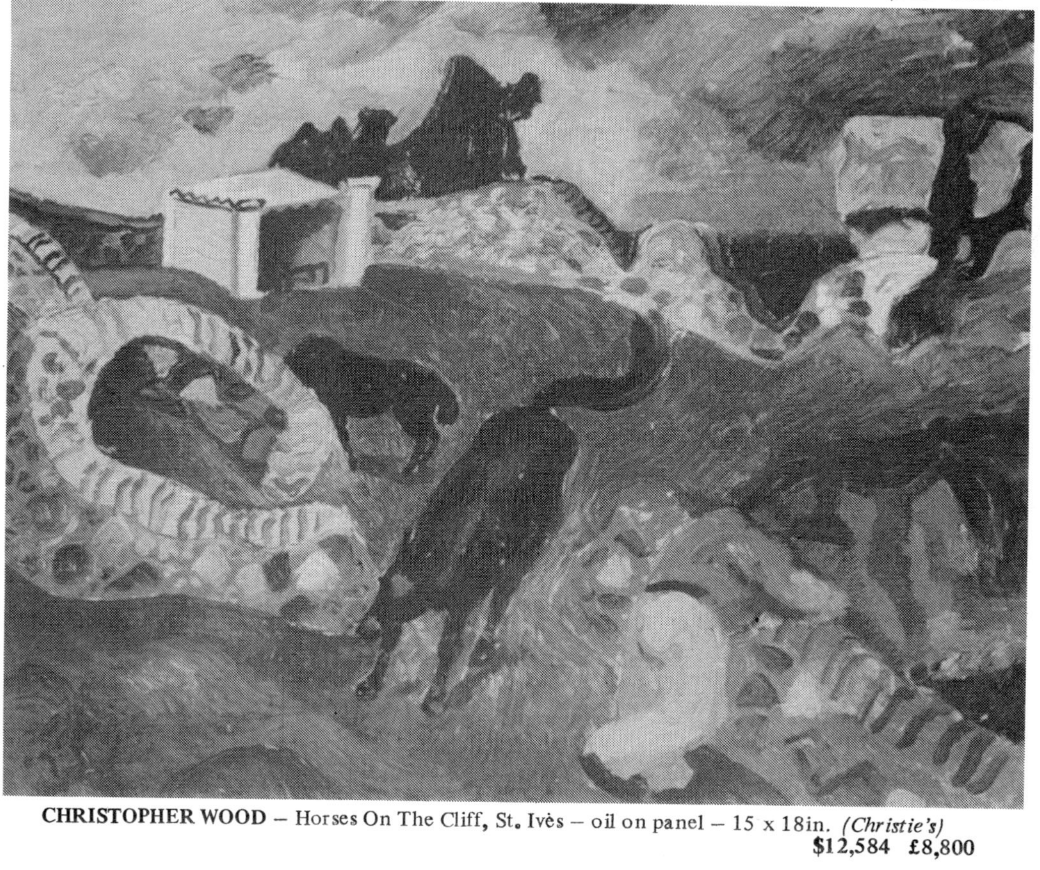

CHRISTOPHER WOOD – Horses On The Cliff, St. Ivès – oil on panel – 15 x 18in. *(Christie's)*
$12,584 £8,800

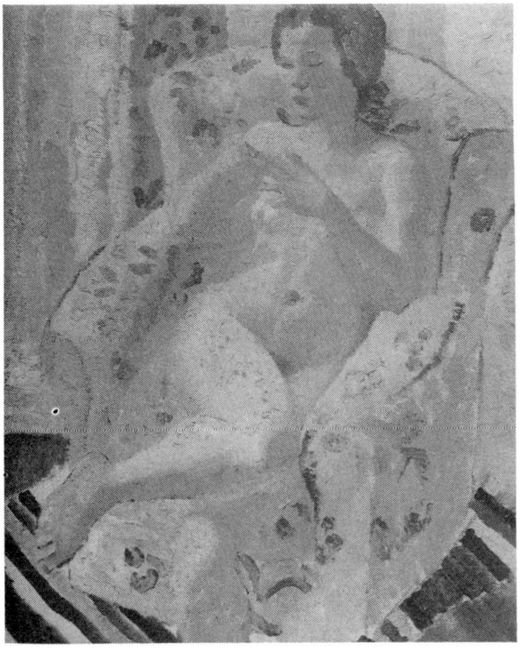

CHRISTOPHER WOOD – Seated Nude Girl In An Interior – oil on canvas – 21½ x 18in.
(Christie's) **$12,584** **£8,800**

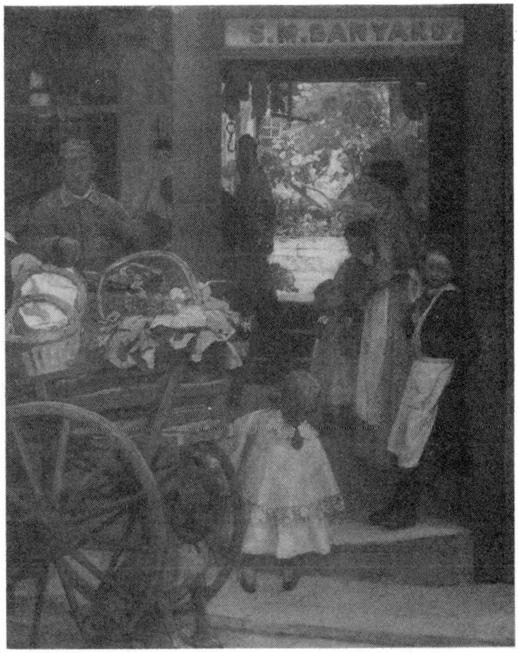

URSULA WOOD – The Market Stall – signed and dated 1895 – oil on canvas – 23½ x 17½in.
(Christie's) **$22,451** **£14,300**

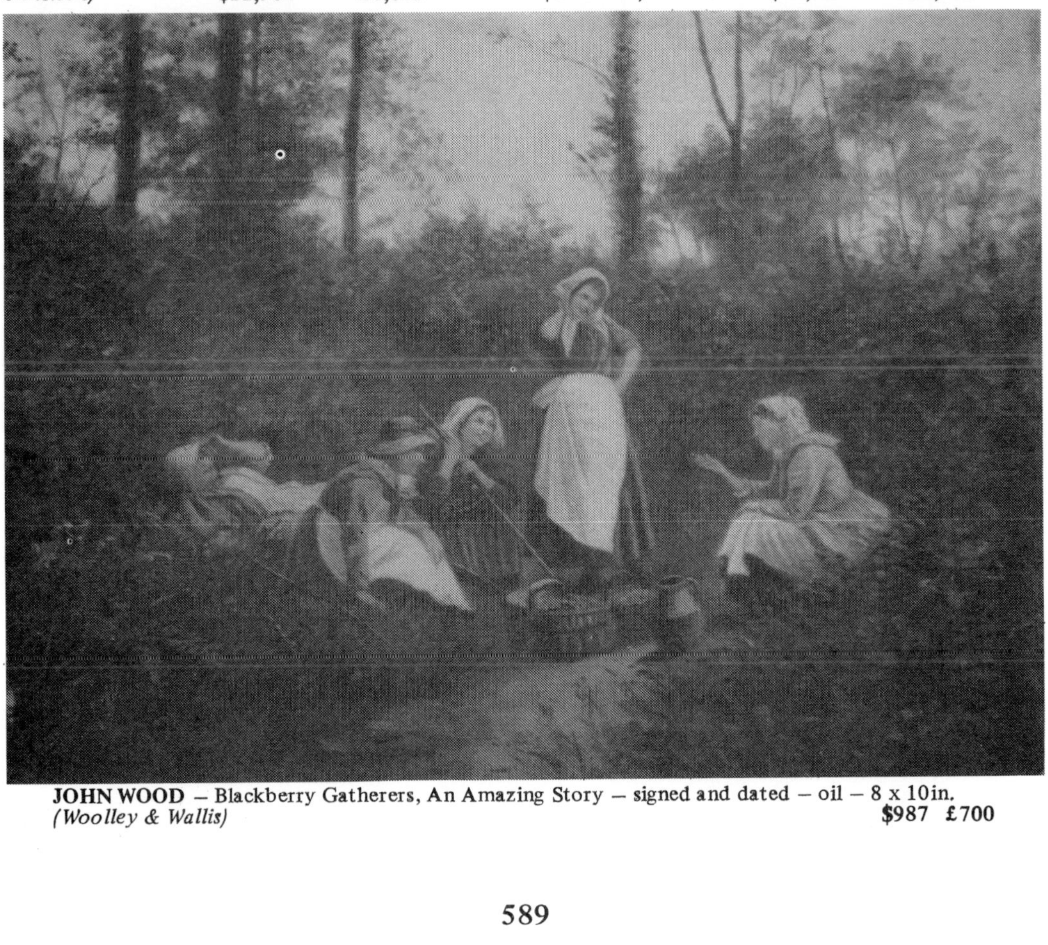

JOHN WOOD – Blackberry Gatherers, An Amazing Story – signed and dated – oil – 8 x 10in.
(Woolley & Wallis) **$987** **£700**

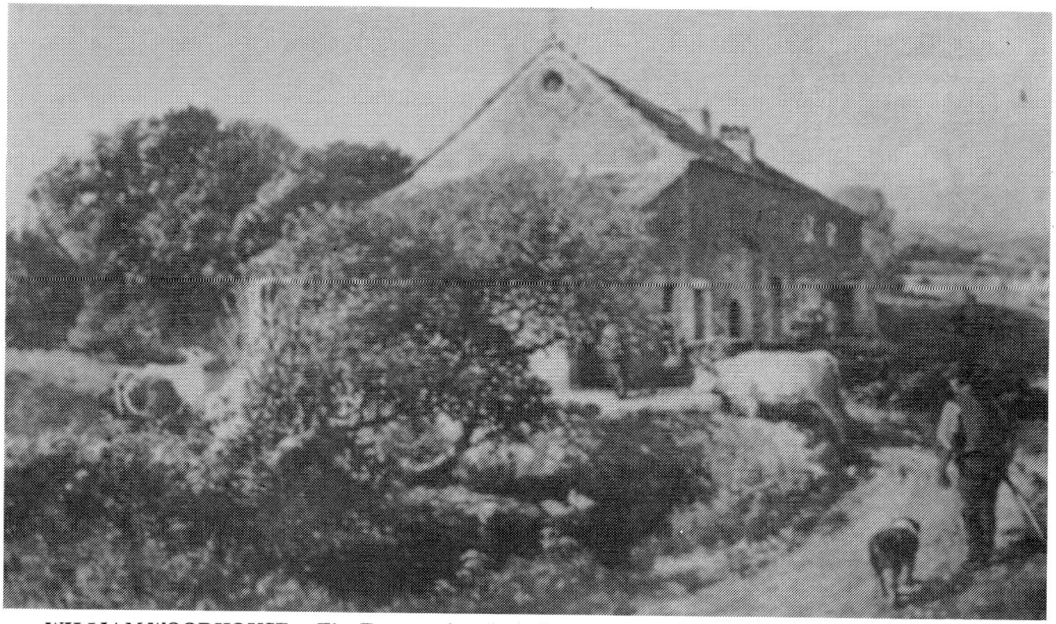

WILLIAM WOODHOUSE – The Farm – signed – oil on canvas – 20 x 30in. *(Christie's)*
$3,799 £2,420

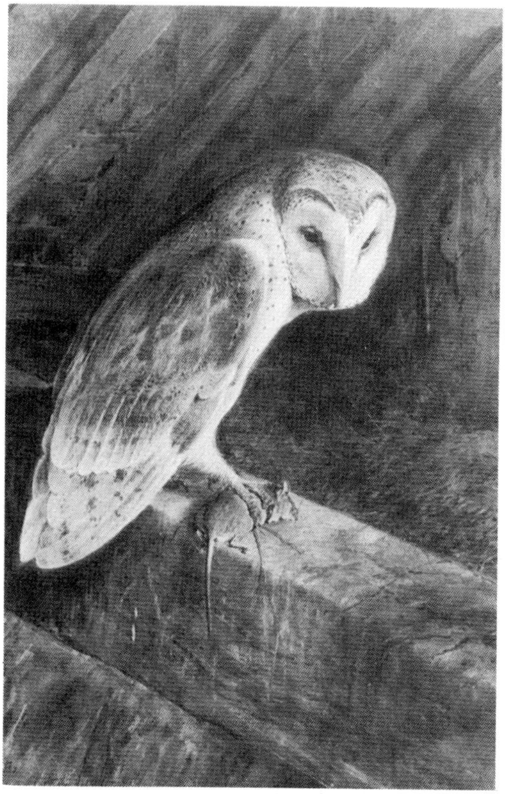

WILLIAM WOODHOUSE – A Light-Breasted Barn Owl, Clutching A Dead Mouse – signed – watercolour heightened with white – 20½ x 14½in.
(Christie's) **$1,267 £880**

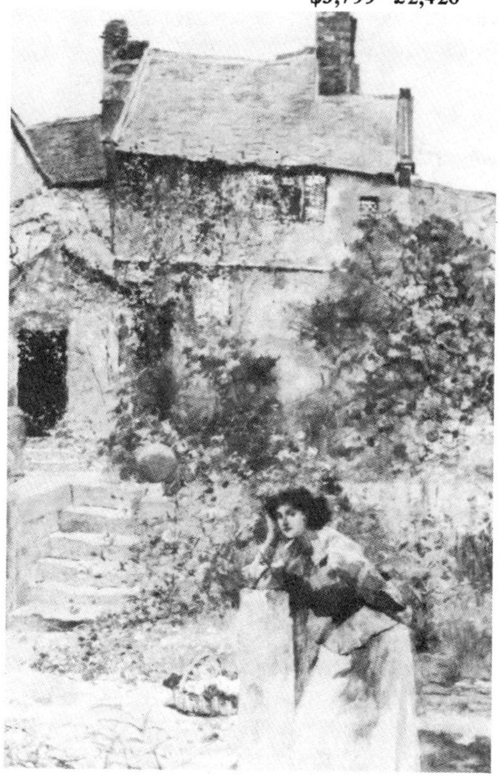

DAVID WOODLOCK – A Young Woman Leaning On A Post Beside A Basket Of Flowers Before A Cottage – signed and dated '96 – oil on canvas – 16 x 10in.
(Phillips) **$1,377 £900**

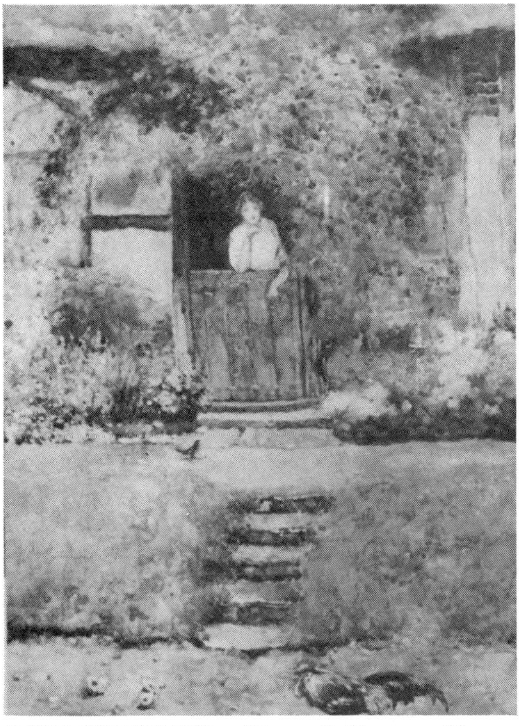

DAVID WOODLOCK – Woman In Doorway Of Cottage, Adorned With Flowers – watercolour – 11½ x 7¾in.
(Capes, Dunn & Co.) **$870** **£600**

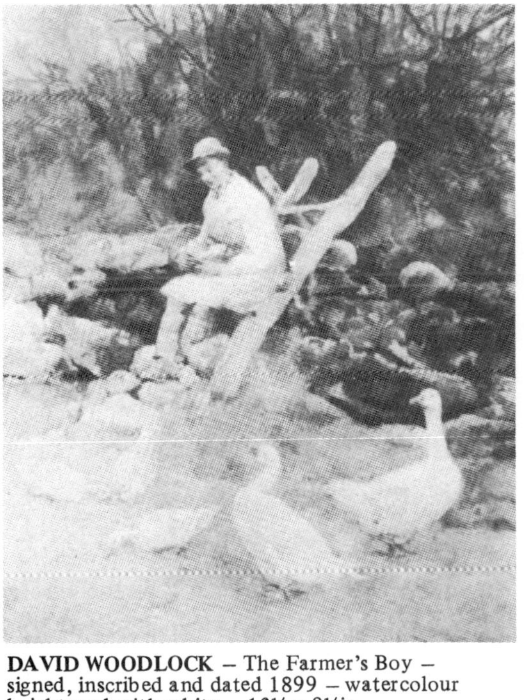

DAVID WOODLOCK – The Farmer's Boy – signed, inscribed and dated 1899 – watercolour heightened with white – 13½ x 9½in.
(Christie's) **$2,016** **£1,430**

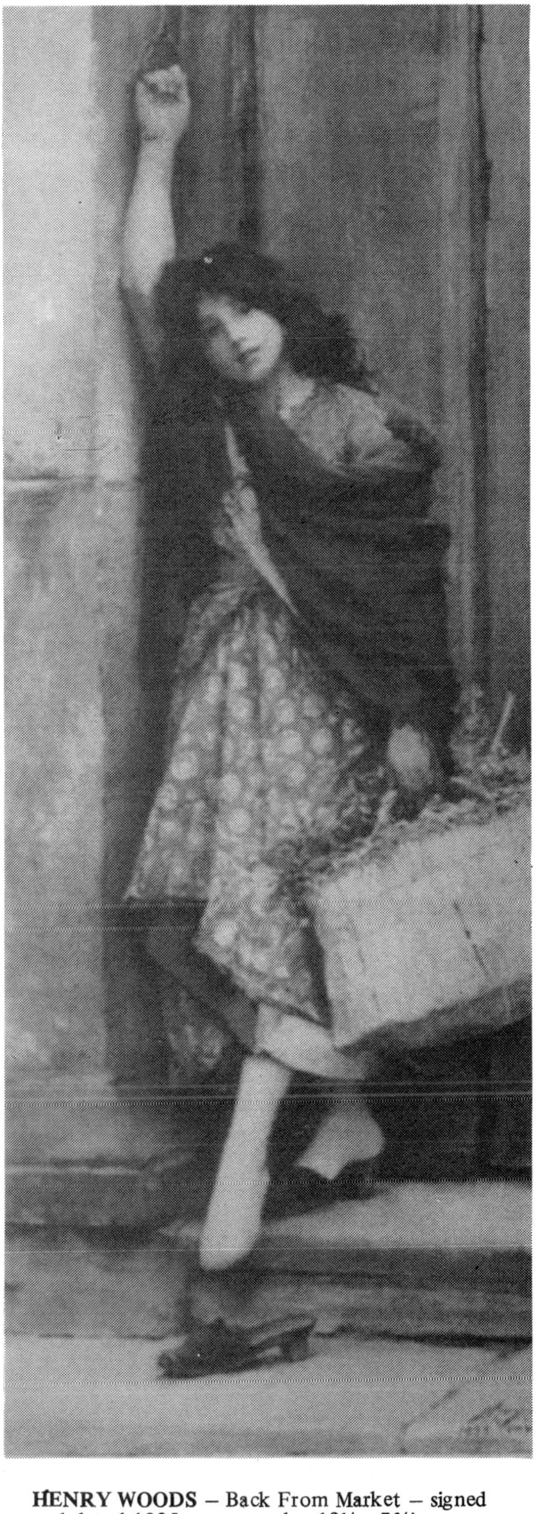

HENRY WOODS – Back From Market – signed and dated 1885 – on panel – 19½ x 7¾in.
(Christie's) **$1,620** **£1,080**

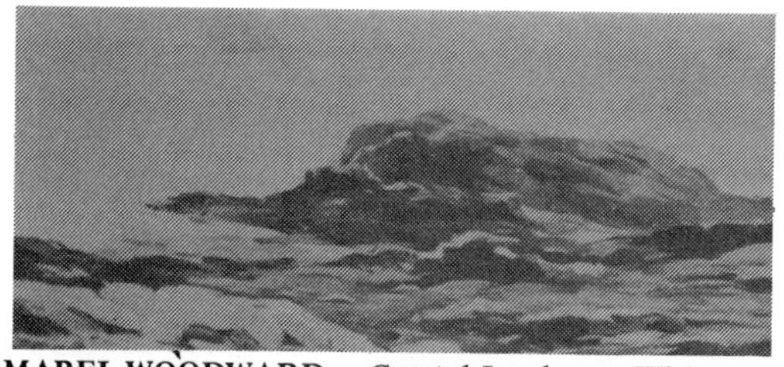

MABEL WOODWARD – Coastal Landscape With Sailboats – signed – oil on board – 10 x 13in.
(Robt. W. Skinner Inc.) **$900** **£552**

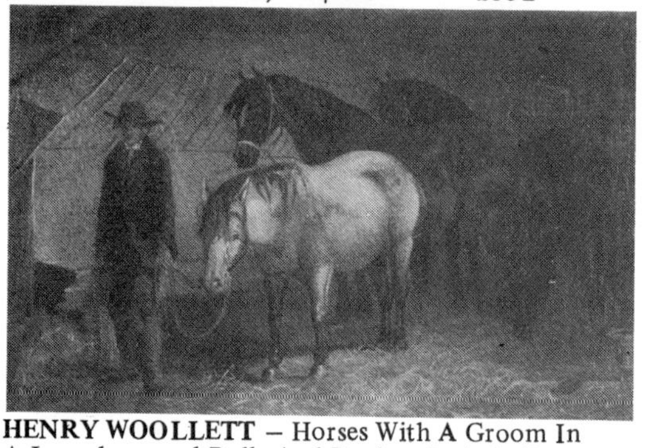

HENRY WOOLLETT – Horses With A Groom In A Loosebox; and Bulls And Poultry In A Stall – signed – 6¾ x 10¼in.
(Christie's) **$1,782** **£1,188 Pair**

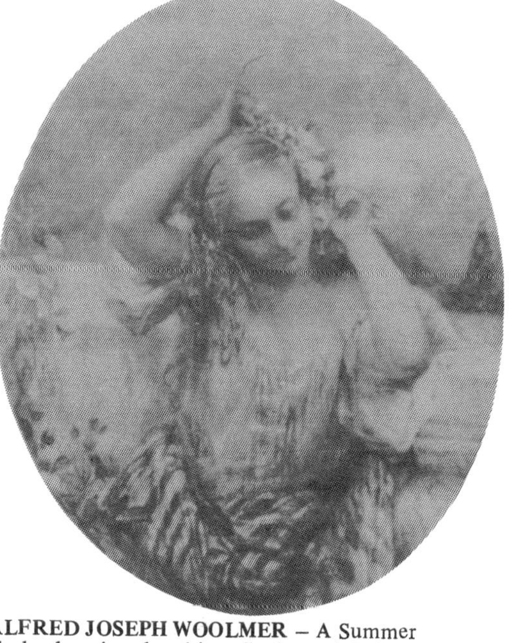

ALFRED JOSEPH WOOLMER – A Summer Garland – signed and inscribed on a label on the reverse – oil on board – 10 x 8in.
(Christie's) **$797** **£550**

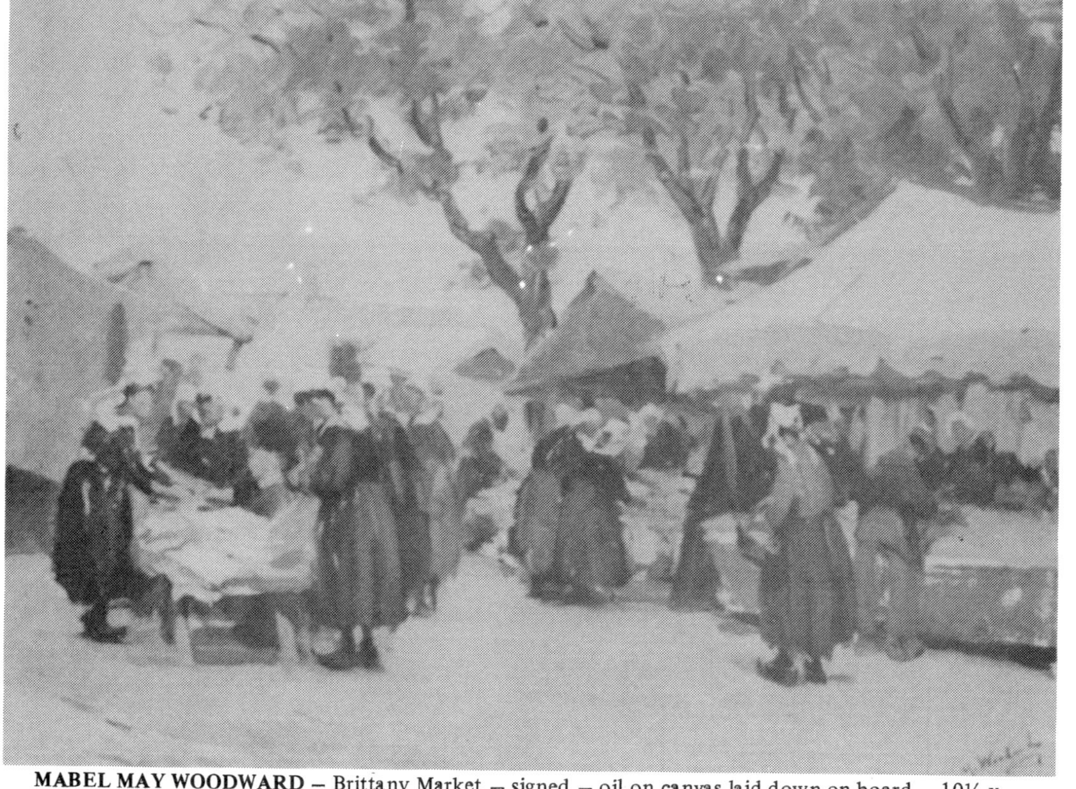

MABEL MAY WOODWARD – Brittany Market – signed – oil on canvas laid down on board – 10¼ x 13in. *(Christie's)*
$1,760 **£1,224**

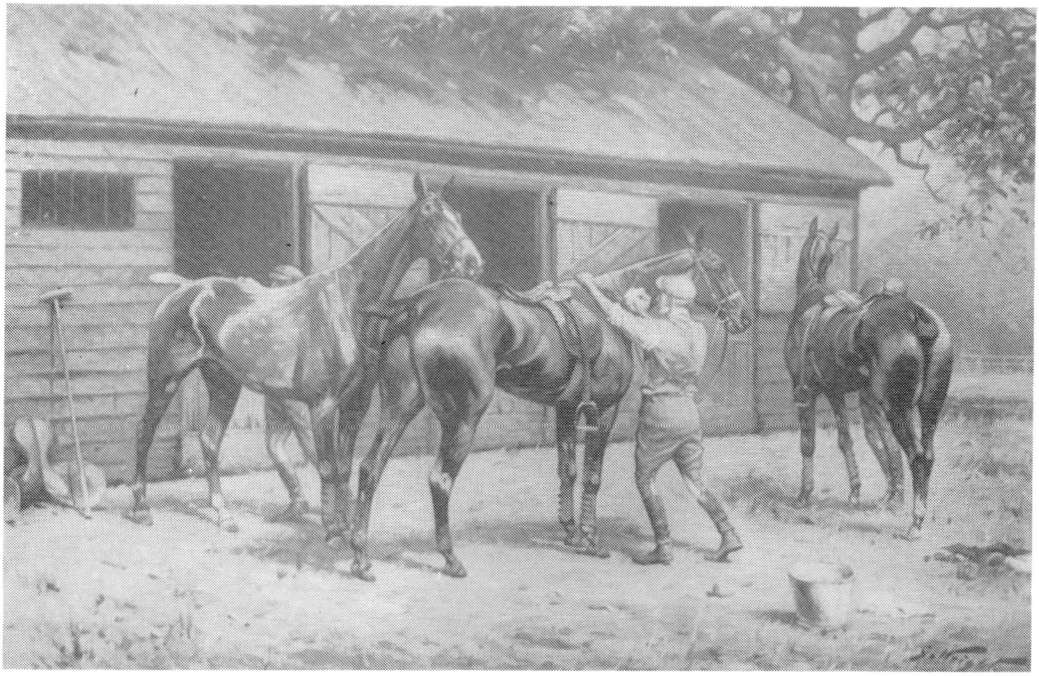

GEORGE WRIGHT – At The Stable – signed – grisaille – 12 x 18in. *(Christie's)* **$2,592 £1,728**

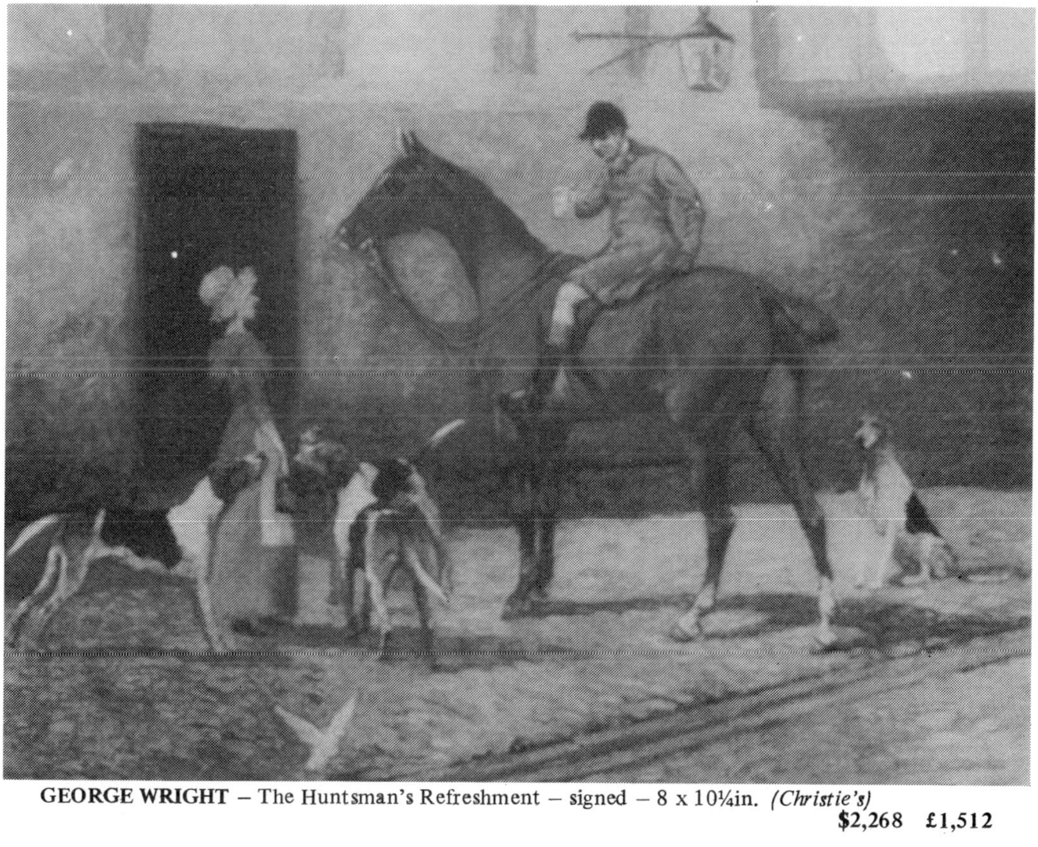

GEORGE WRIGHT – The Huntsman's Refreshment – signed – 8 x 10¼in. *(Christie's)* **$2,268 £1,512**

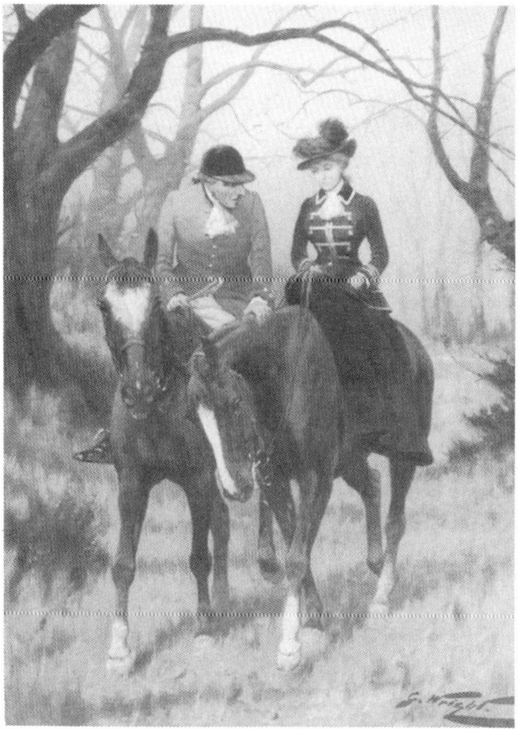

GEORGE WRIGHT – Hunting Trysts – signed – 17 x 13in.
(Christie's) **$4,212 £2,808**

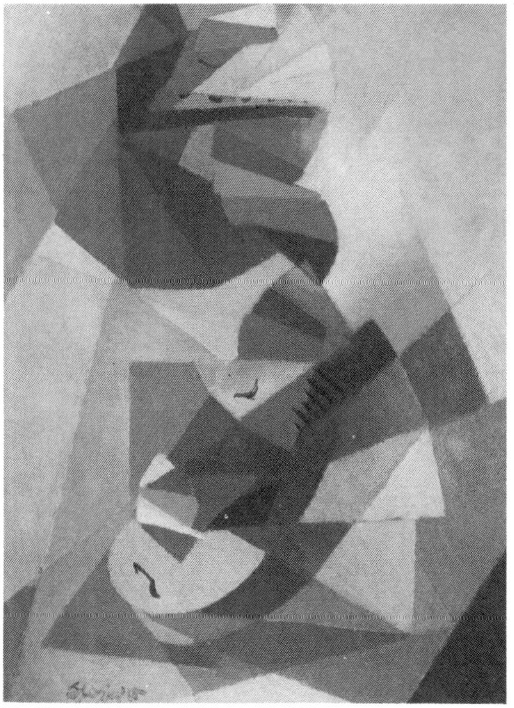

STANTON MACDONALD WRIGHT – Deux Musiciennes – signed, also signed, inscribed and dated 1954 on the reverse – oil on canvas – 30¼ x 20in.
(Christie's) **$17,600 £12,372**

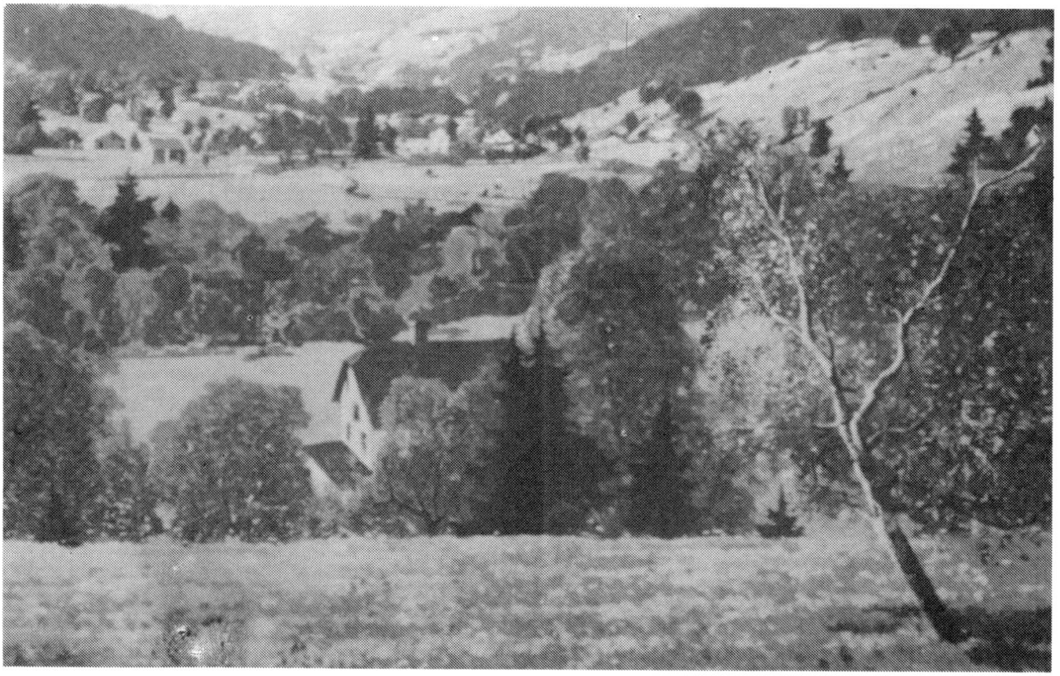

CARL WUERNER – A Quiet Summer Day – signed and dated '26 – oil on canvas – 28 x 30in.
(Christie's) **$6,600 £4,591**

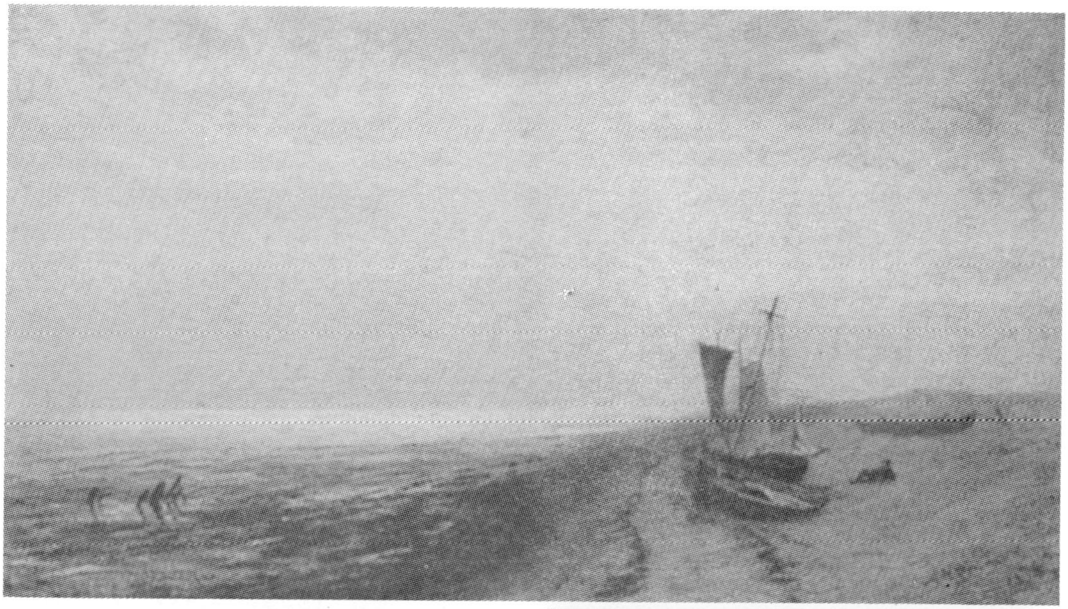

ALEXANDER HELWIG WYANT – Resting On The Shore – signed and dated 1873, also signed and dated on the reverse – oil on canvas – 9¼ x 14¼in.
(Christie's) **$7,700** **£4,717**

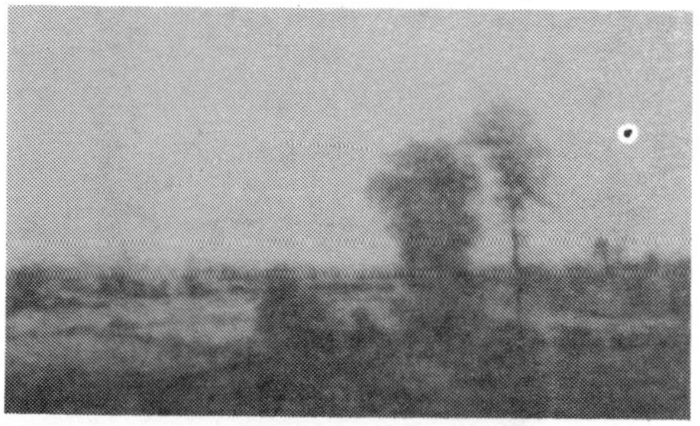

ALEXANDER H. WYANT – Extensive Landscape At Twilight – signed – oil on canvas – 13 x 20in.
(Robt. W. Skinner Inc.) **$2,200** **£1,349**

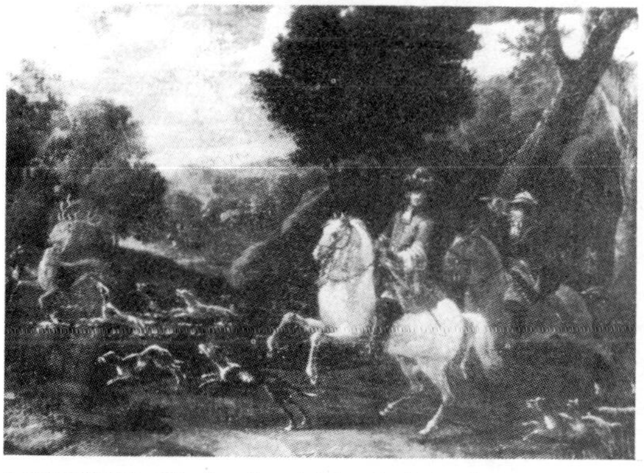

JAN WYCK, Circle of – **A** Wooded Landscape With A Stag Hunt – 12¾ x 15¾in.
(Christie's) **$679** **£453**

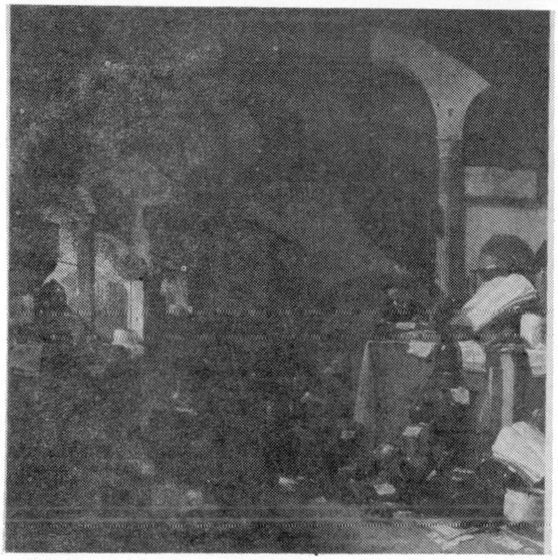

THOMAS WYCK – The Alchemist – signed – on canvas – 48½ x 44¼in.
(Phillips) **$69,720** **£42,000**

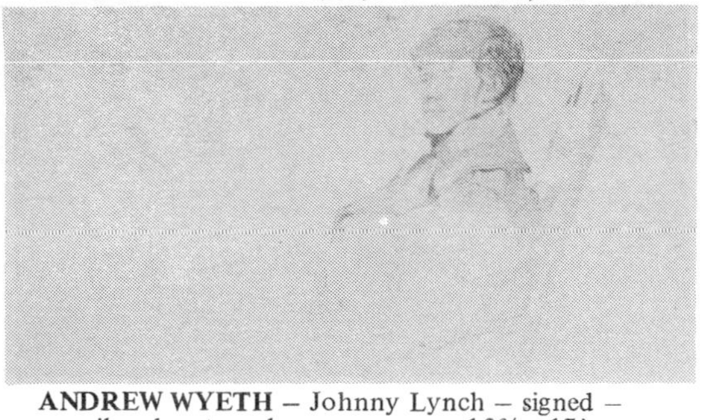

ANDREW WYETH – Johnny Lynch – signed – pencil and watercolour on paper – 13¾ x 17in.
(Christie's) **$17,600** **£10,783**

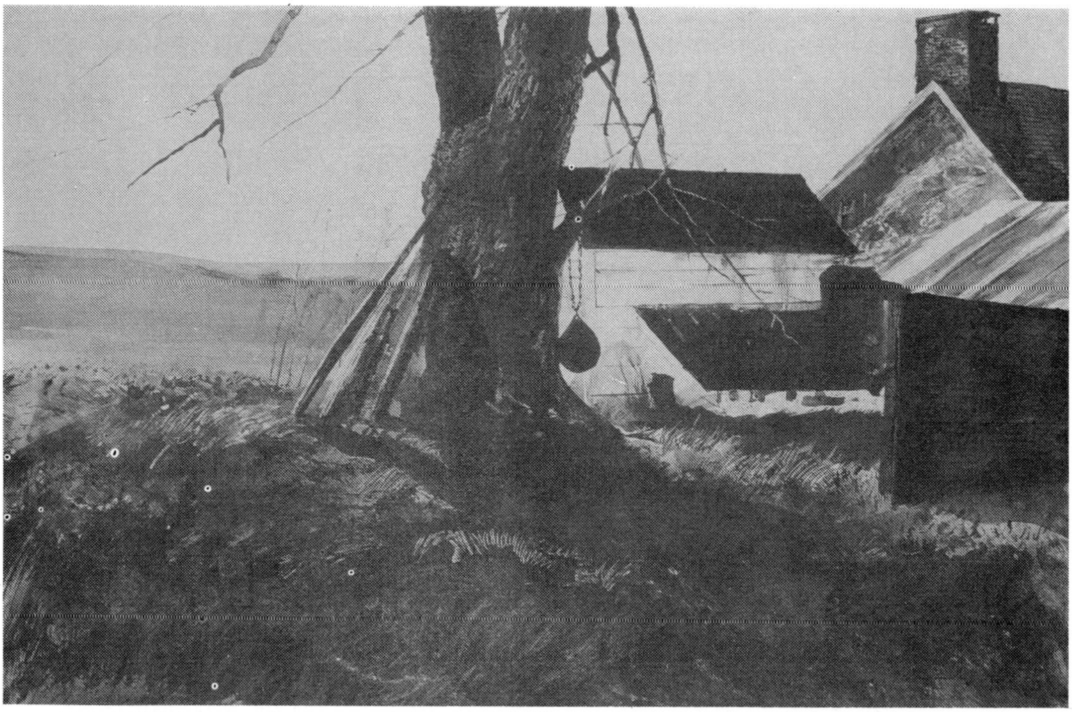

ANDREW WYETH – The Gong – signed – watercolour and gouache on paper laid down on board – 14¼ x 21¼in. *(Christie's)* **$44,000 £26,958**

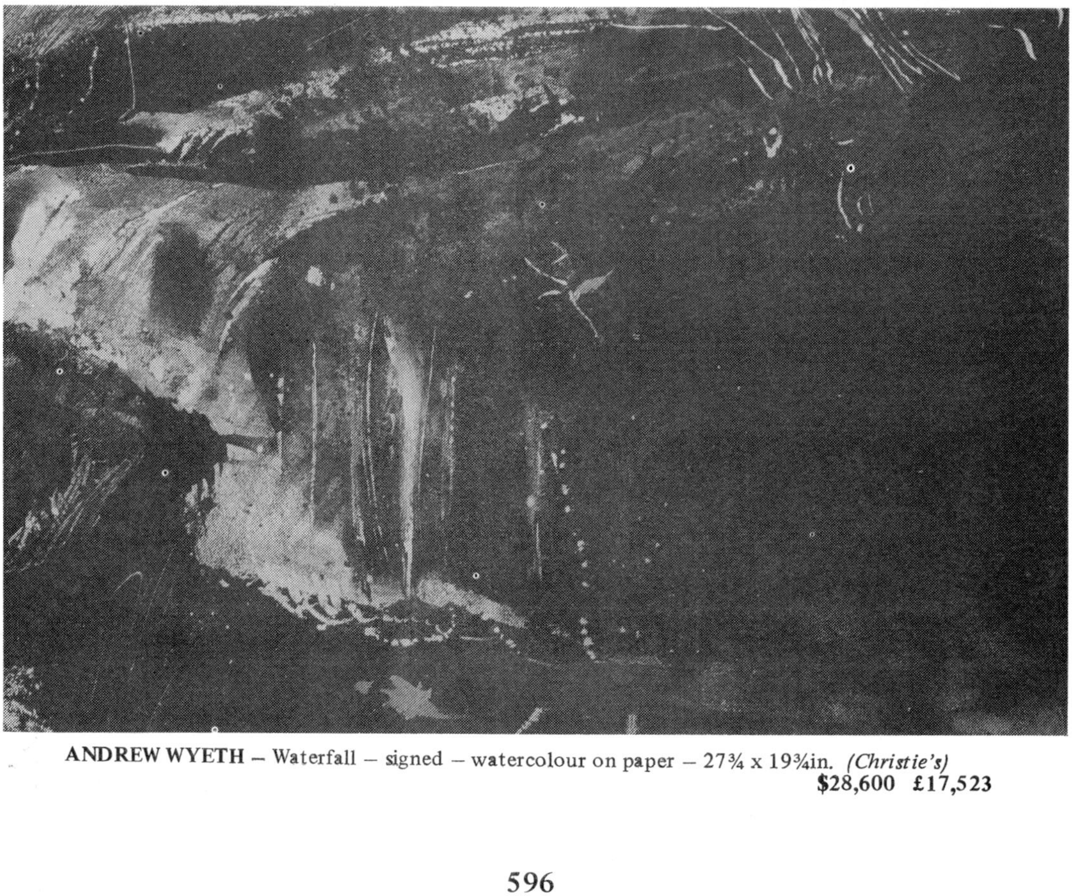

ANDREW WYETH – Waterfall – signed – watercolour on paper – 27¾ x 19¾in. *(Christie's)* **$28,600 £17,523**

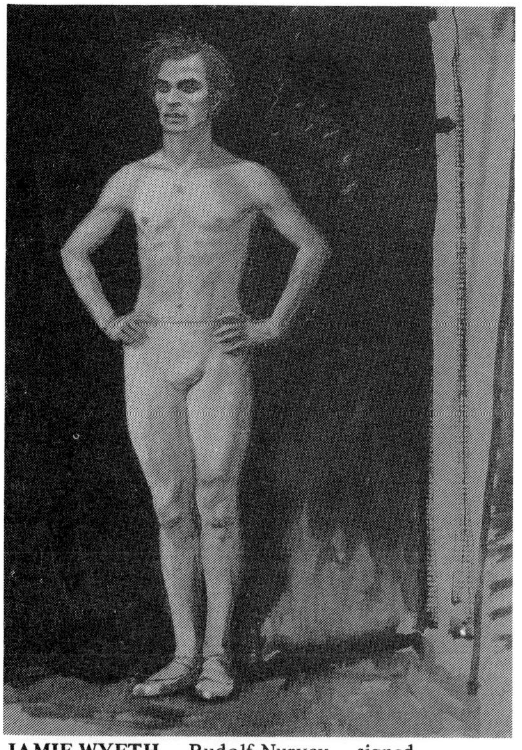

JAMIE WYETH – Rudolf Nuryev – signed – charcoal, chalk and watercolour on cardboard – 45¾ x 34¾in.
(Christie's) **$12,100** **£7,413**

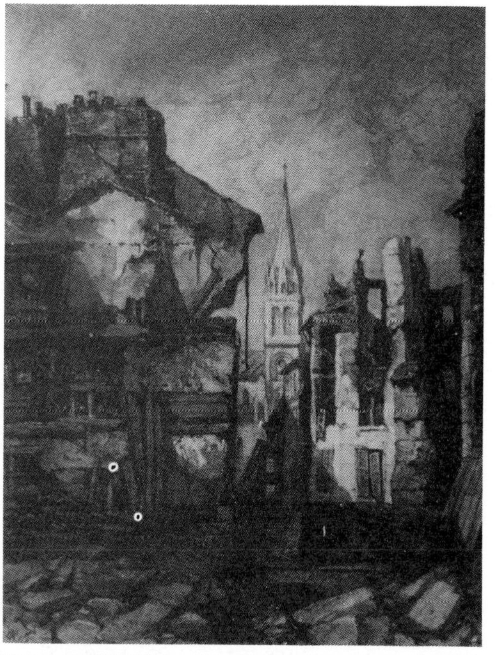

WILLIAM WYLD – The Palace, St. Cloud: Inside The Ruins; and A Street At St. Cloud With Demolished Houses – pencil and watercolour, the second with red chalk and heightened with white – 13¼ x 9¼in.
(Christie's) **$1,562** **£1,100** **Two**

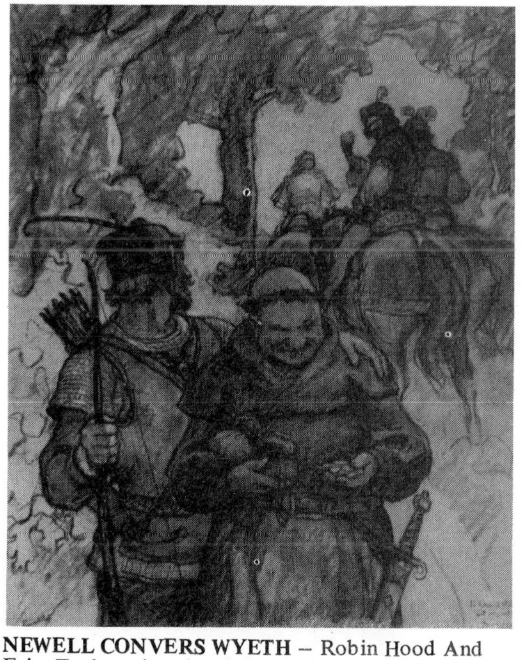

NEWELL CONVERS WYETH – Robin Hood And Friar Tuck – signed and dated 1937 – charcoal on brown paper – 34½ x 28in.
(Christie's) **$7,700** **£4,797**

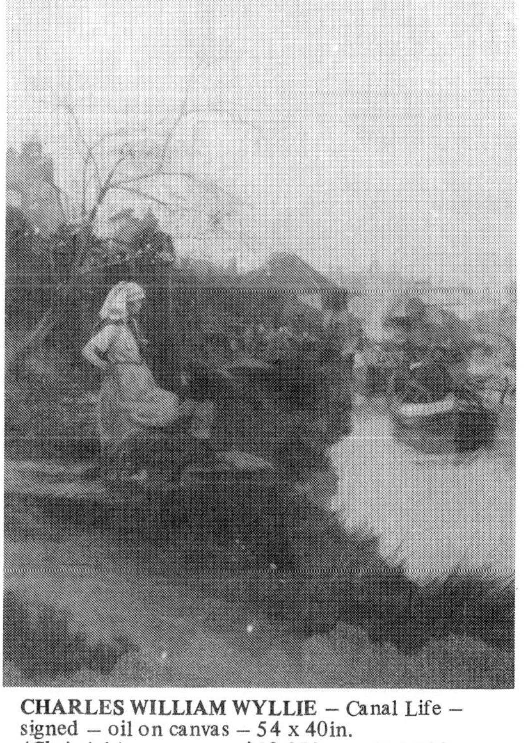

CHARLES WILLIAM WYLLIE – Canal Life – signed – oil on canvas – 54 x 40in.
(Christie's) **$29,359** **£18,700**

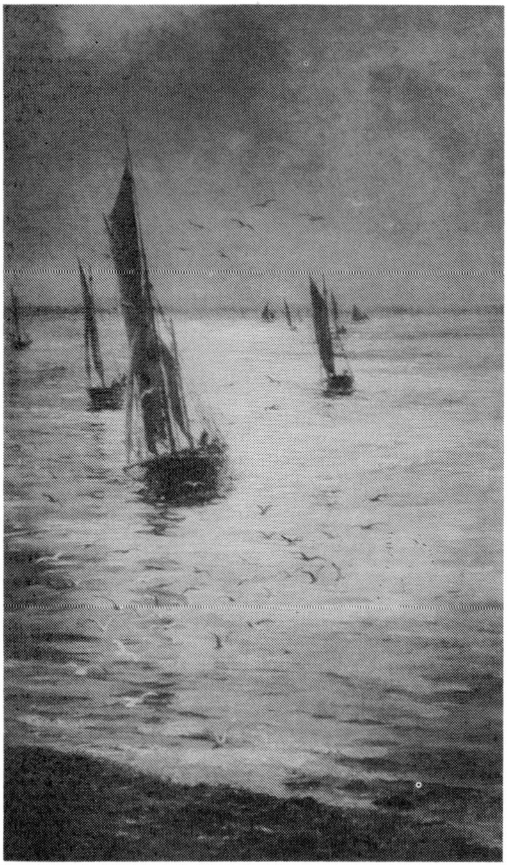

WILLIAM LIONEL WYLLIE – Homeward Bound – signed – oil on canvas laid down on board – 30 x 18¼in.
(Christie's) **$6,613** **£3,960**

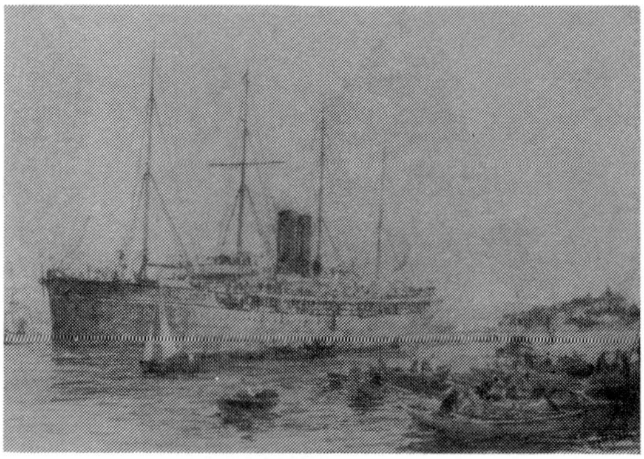

WILLIAM LIONEL WYLLIE – A Steamer Arriving In Port – signed – pencil and watercolour – 9 x 12¾in.
(Christie's) **$1,278** **£770**

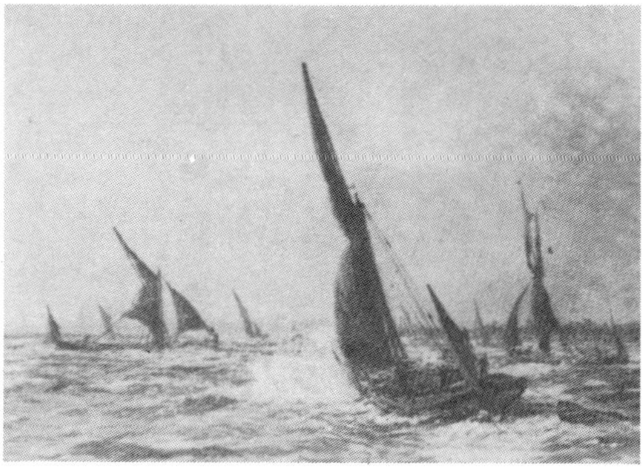

WILLIAM LIONEL WYLLIE – Fishing Boats Off The Coast – signed – oil on canvas – 14 x 20in.
(Christie's) **$5,977** **£4,180**

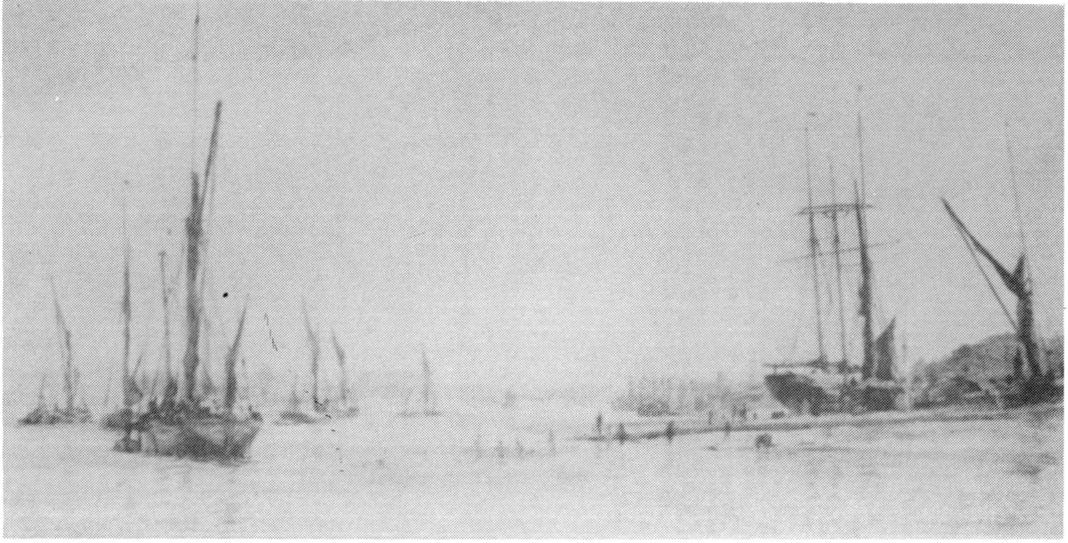

WILLIAM LIONEL WYLLIE – Waiting For Flood Tide, North Woolwich – signed and inscribed – pencil and watercolour – 10 x 17in. *(Christie's)* **$3,412** **£2,420**

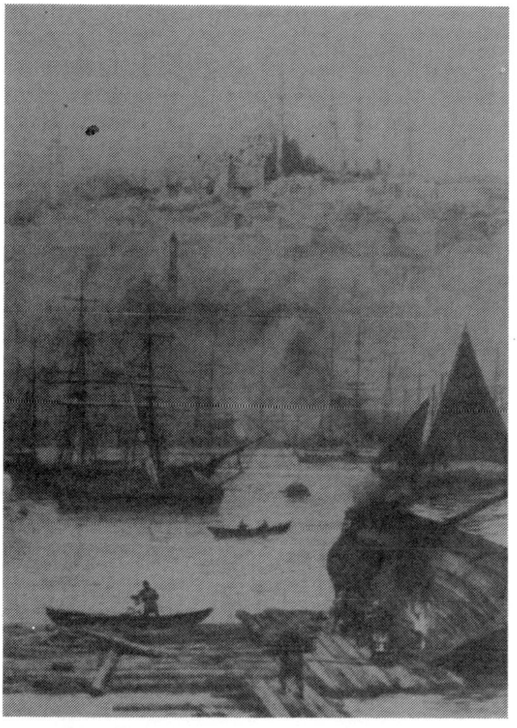

WILLIAM LIONEL WYLLIE – The Golden Horn – signed and dated 1896 – watercolour over pencil – 51 x 37cm.
(Phillips) **$3,749** **£2,300**

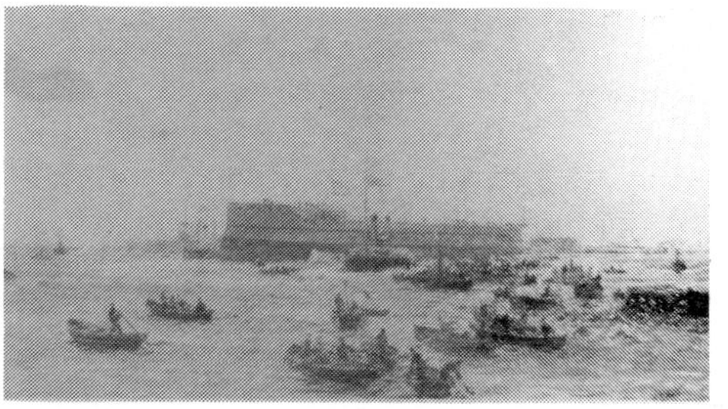

WILLIAM LIONEL WYLLIE – Launching The Ship – signed – watercolour over pencil – 18 x 33cm.
(Phillips) **$3,097** **£1,900**

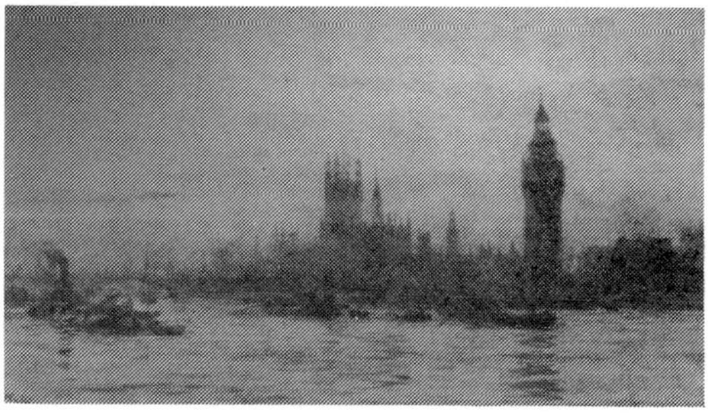

WILLIAM LIONEL WYLLIE – The Thames At Westminster, Sunset – signed – watercolour over pencil – 18.5 x 31cm.
(Phillips) **$2,771** **£1,700**

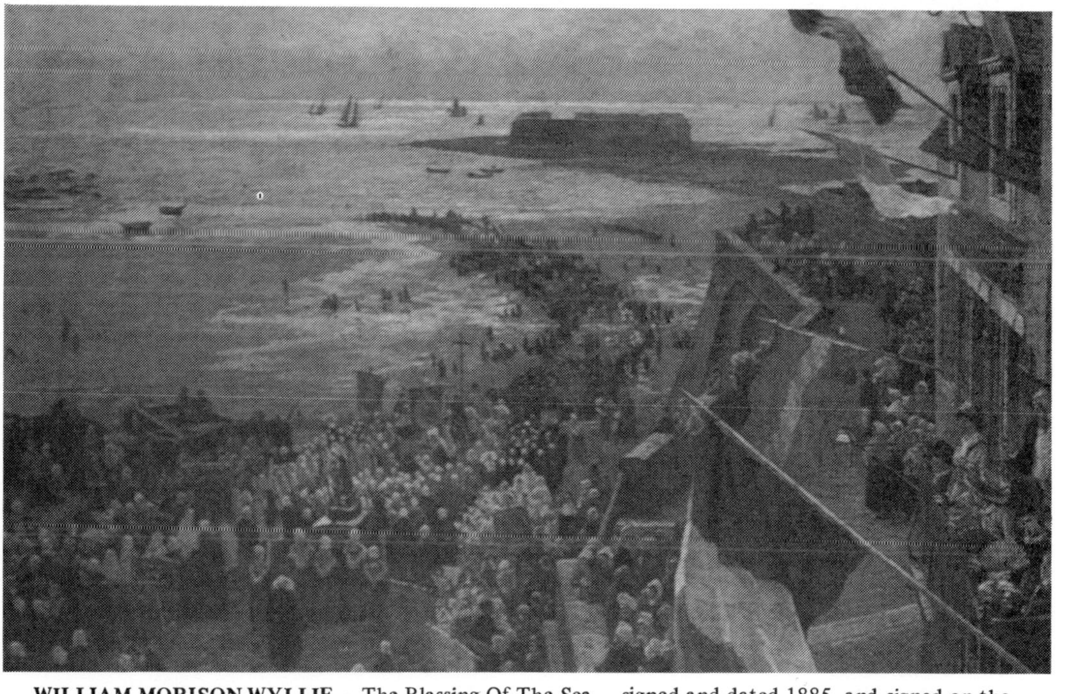

WILLIAM MORISON WYLLIE – The Blessing Of The Sea – signed and dated 1885, and signed on the reverse – oil on canvas – 39 x 50½in. *(Christie's)* **$10,224** **£7,150**

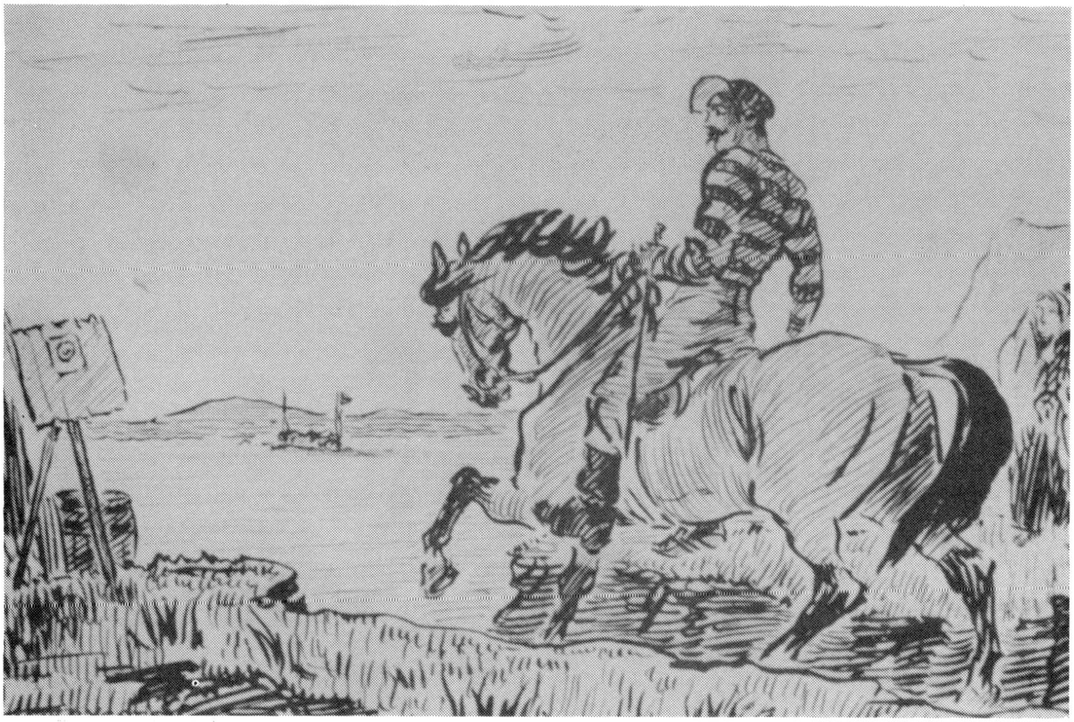

JACK BUTLER YEATS – Country Jockey – signed – watercolour, pen and ink on paper – 6¾ x 11½in. *(Christie's)* **$6,336 £4,400**

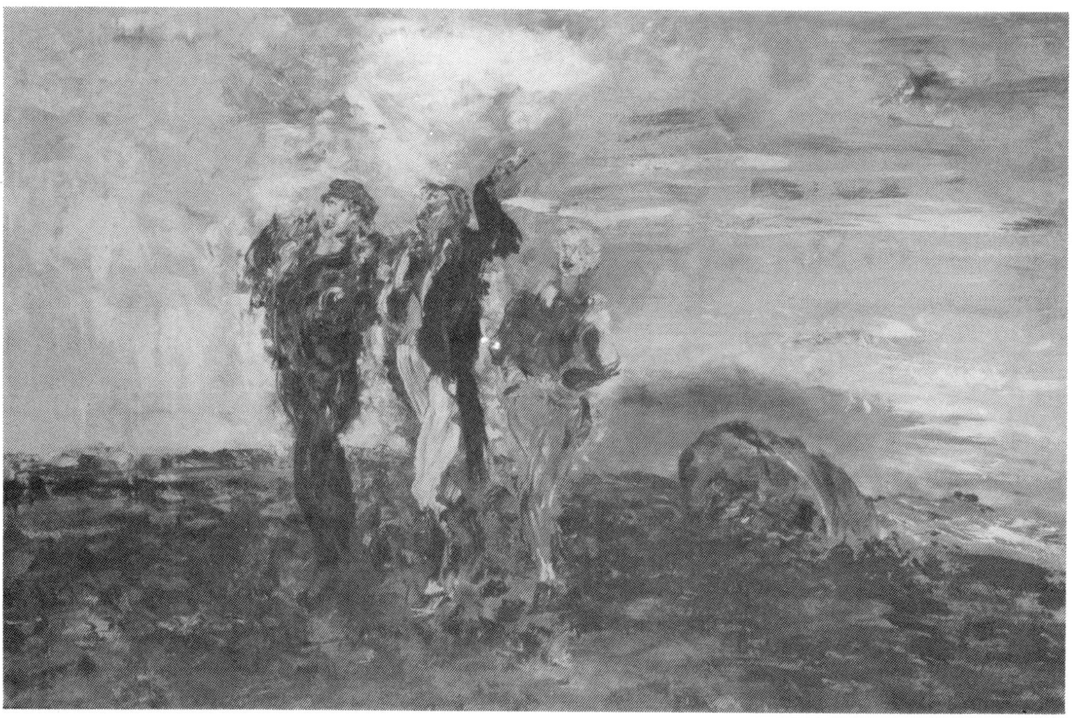

JACK BUTLER YEATS – Shouting – signed – oil on canvas – 40 x 60in. *(Christie's)* **$110,880 £77,000**

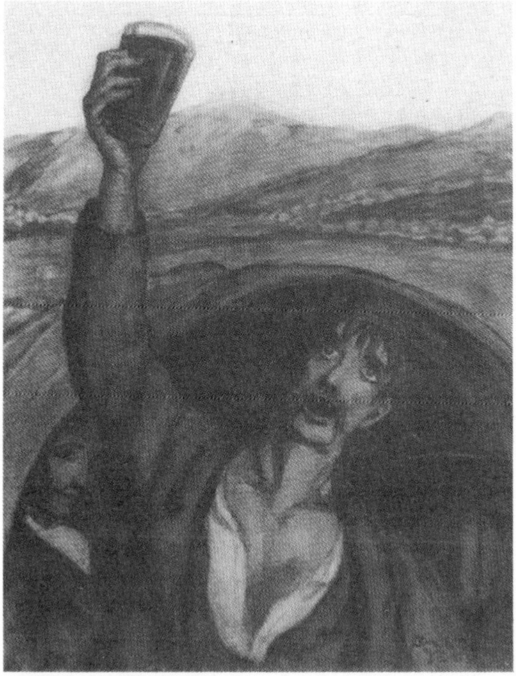

JACK BUTLER YEATS – Tinkers Drinking In A Covered Wagon – signed – watercolour and pencil – 11¾ x 9¼in.
(Christie's) **$4,719** **£3,300**

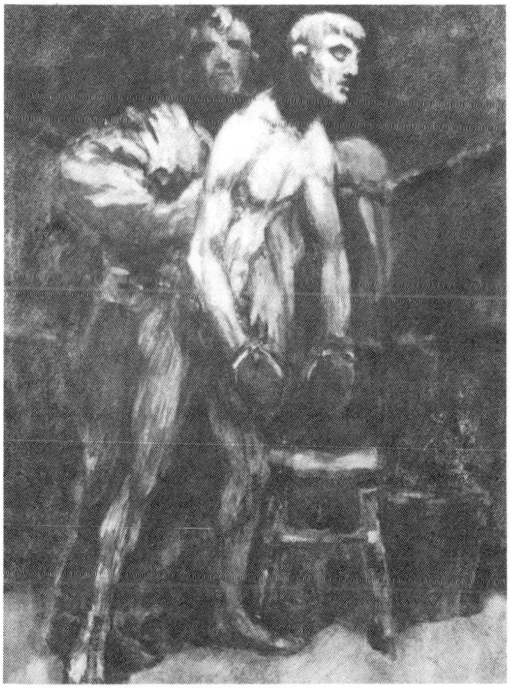

JACK BUTLER YEATS – The End Of A Round – signed – watercolour and pencil on paper – 9¾ x 6¾in.
(Christie's) **$10,296** **£7,150**

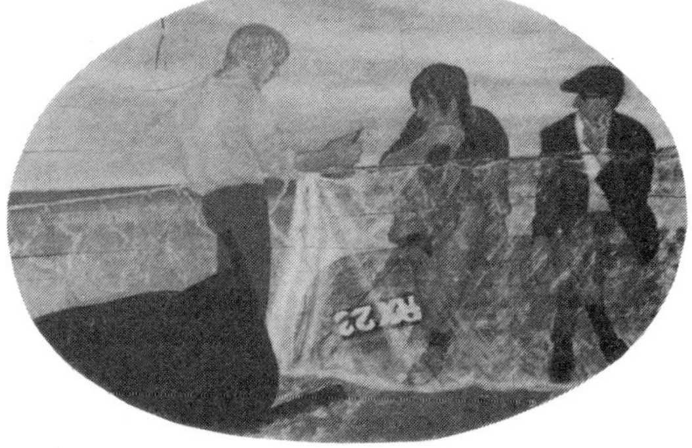

LAETITIA YHAP – Basin & Oxo Watching Paul Fitting Up A Net – signed, inscribed and dated 1978/79 on the reverse – oil on panel – 8¼ x 12in.
(Christie's) **$1,295** **£825**

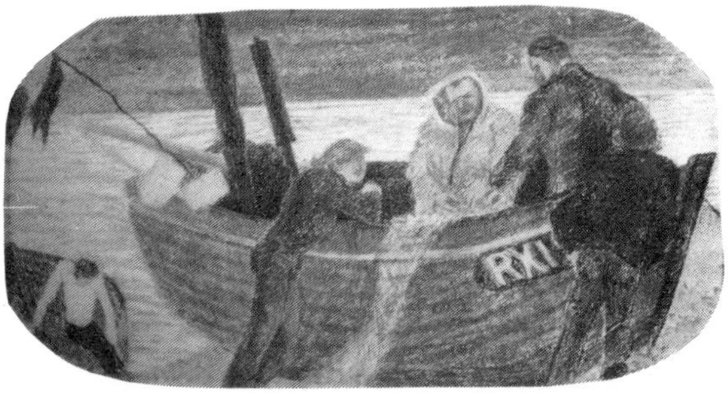

LAETITIA YHAP – Corky Leaning And Chatting; and Stu In Summer 1976 – signed, inscribed and dated 1976 – oil pastel on Japanese paper – 7¼ x 7½in. and 6¾ x 7¾in.
(Christie's) **$471** **£330 Two**

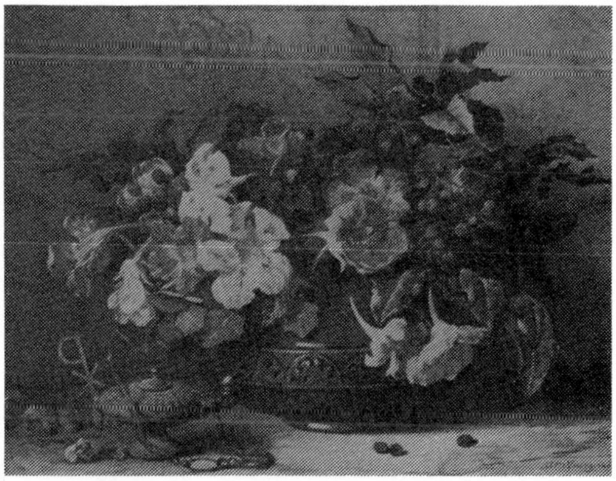

ANNIE MARY YOUNGMAN – An Oil Lamp By A Bowl Of Elderberries And Nasturtiums – signed – pencil and watercolour – 10½ x 13¾in.
(Christie's) **$1,643** **£990**

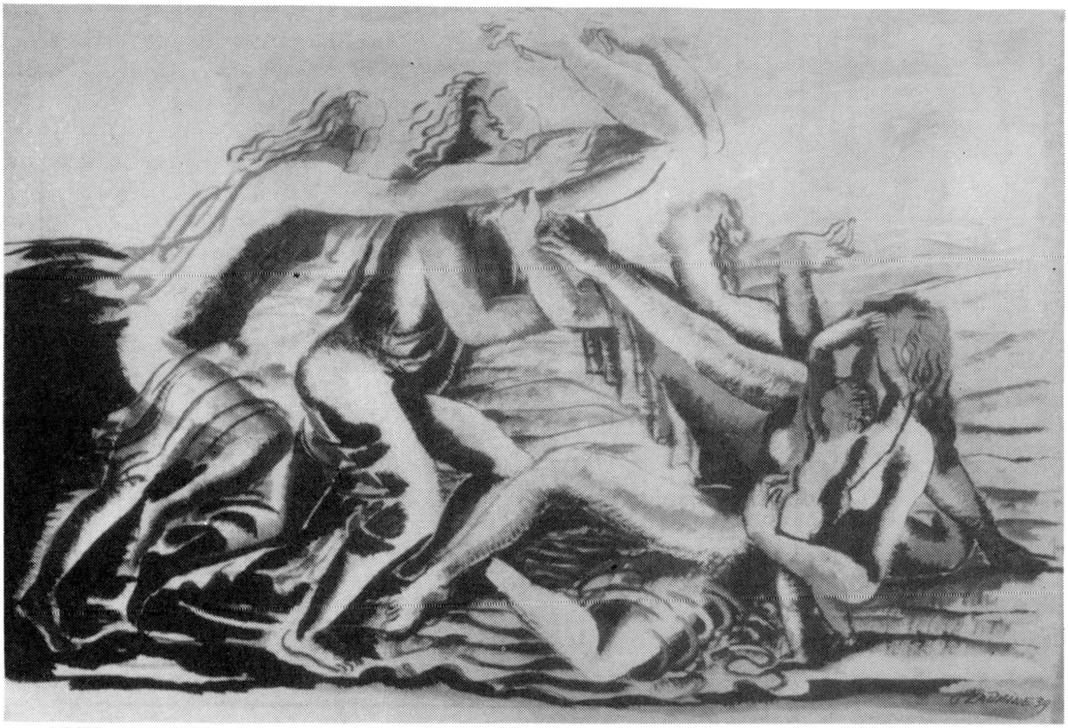

OSSIP ZADKINE – La mauvaise Nouvelle – signed and dated '39 – gouache, brush and black ink on paper – 19¼ x 27in. *(Christie's)* **$7,920 £4,950**

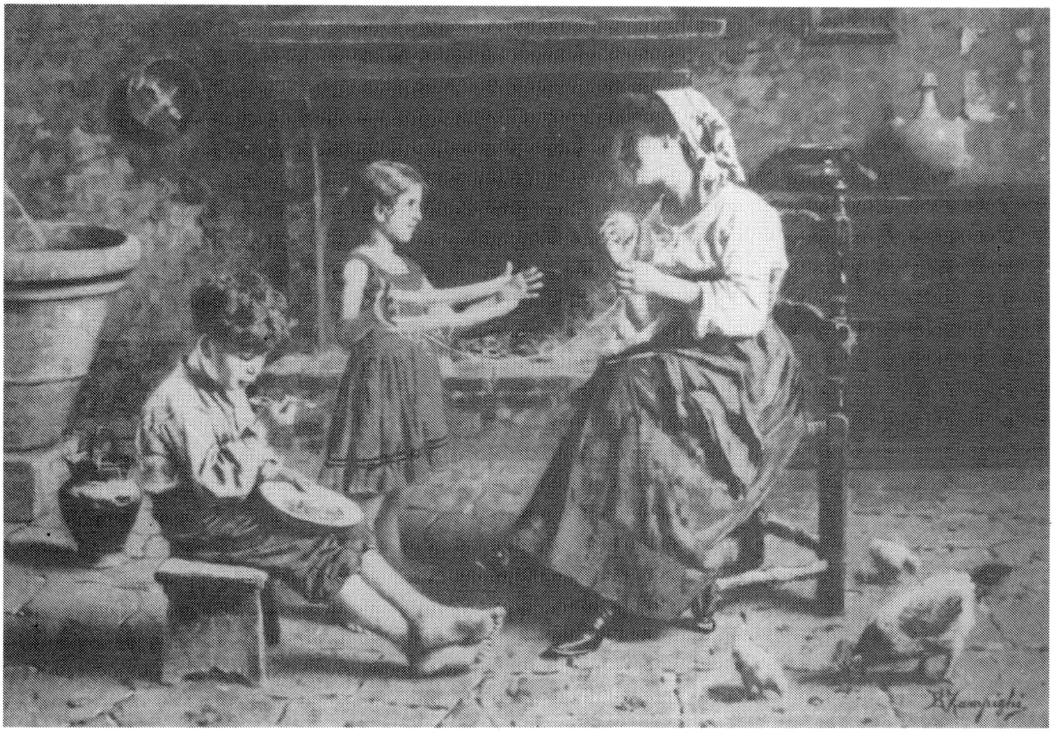

EUGENIO ZAMPIGHI – Winding The Wool; and Learning To Walk – signed – 9½ x 13½in. *(Lawrence Fine Art)* **$6,391 £3,850 Pair**

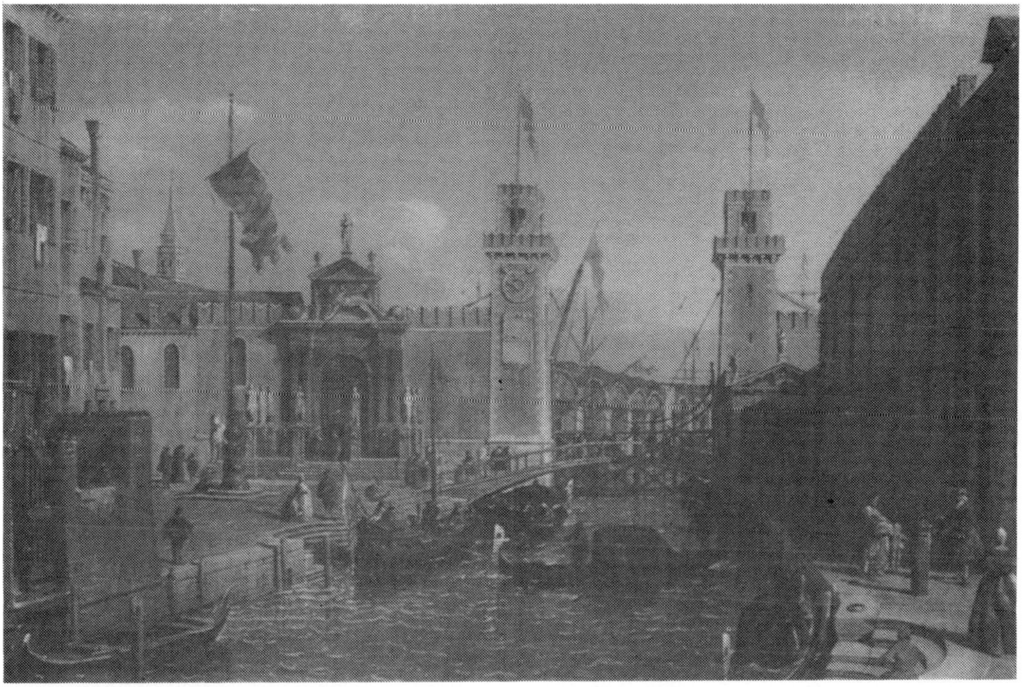

FRANCESCO ZANIN – The Arsenale, Venice; and S.S. Giovanni e Paolo, Venice – signed and one dated 1865 – 17½ x 25½in. *(Christie's)* **$9,504 £6,600 Pair**

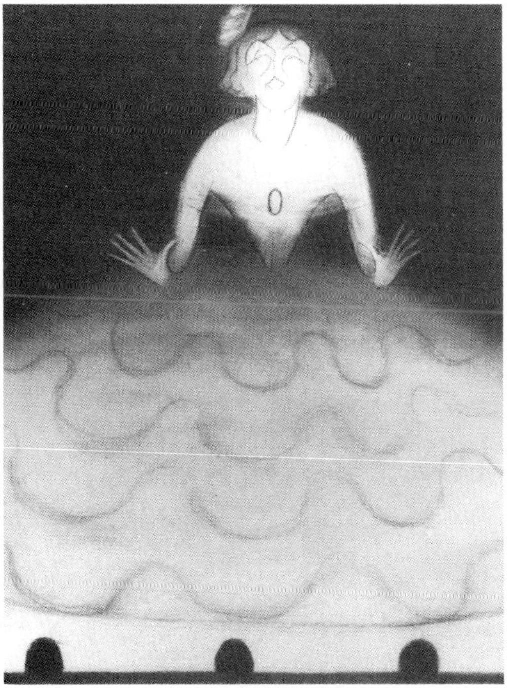

MARIUS DE ZAYAS – Female Entertainer In Front Of The Footlights – charcoal on paper – 23½ x 17¼in.
(Christie's) **$2,217 £1,540**

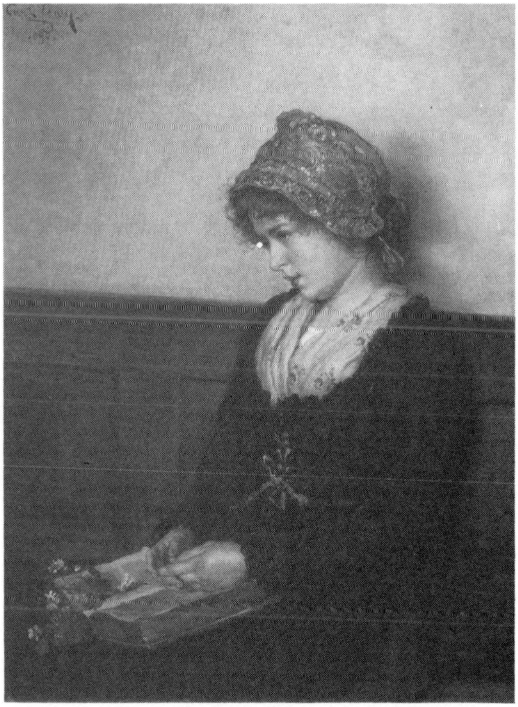

KARL ZEWY – Distracted By A Posy – signed and dated 1896 – oil on panel – 33 x 24.5cm.
(Phillips) **$11,520 £8,000**

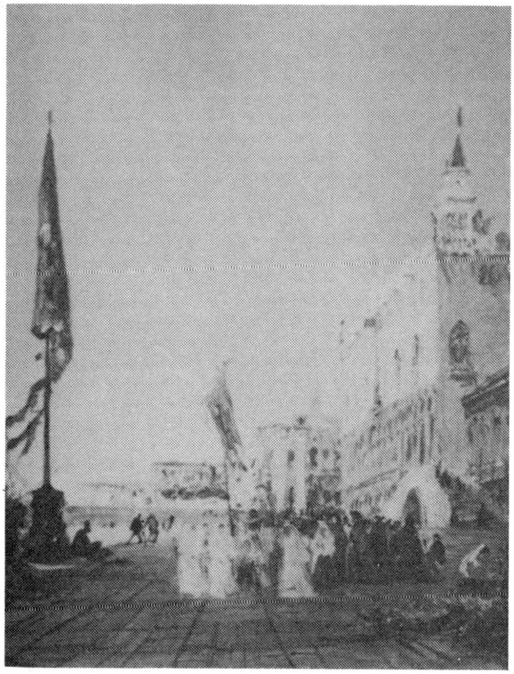

FELIX ZIEM – A Procession On The Riva Degli Schiavoni, Venice – signed – on panel – 25½ x 19¾in.
(Christie's) **$5,346** **£3,300**

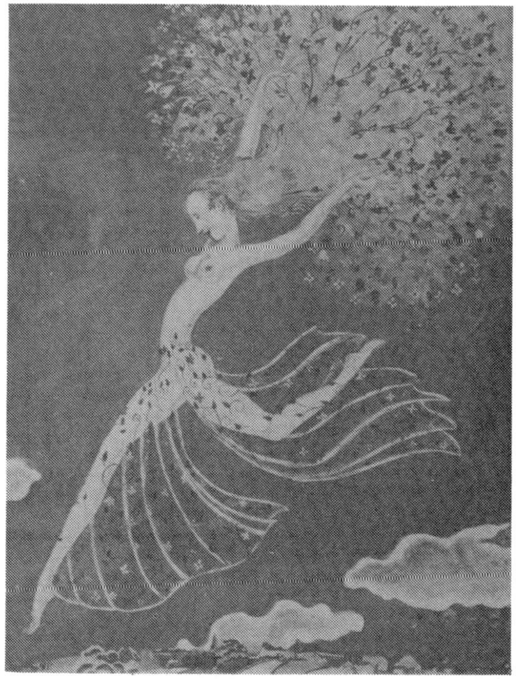

ANNA ZINKEISEN – Maytime – signed – gouache – 37.5 x 29cm.
(Phillips) **$697** **£420**

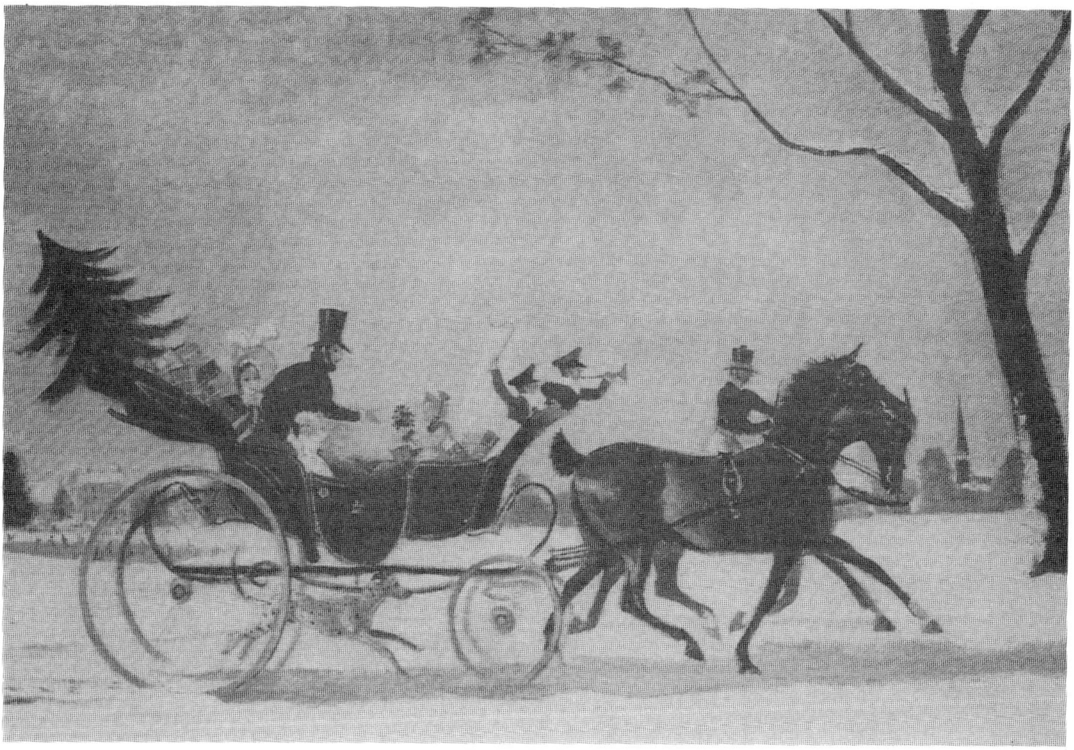

DORIS ZINKEISEN – Christmas Time – signed – oil on canvas – 25 x 30in. *(Christie's)* **$1,745** **£1,045**

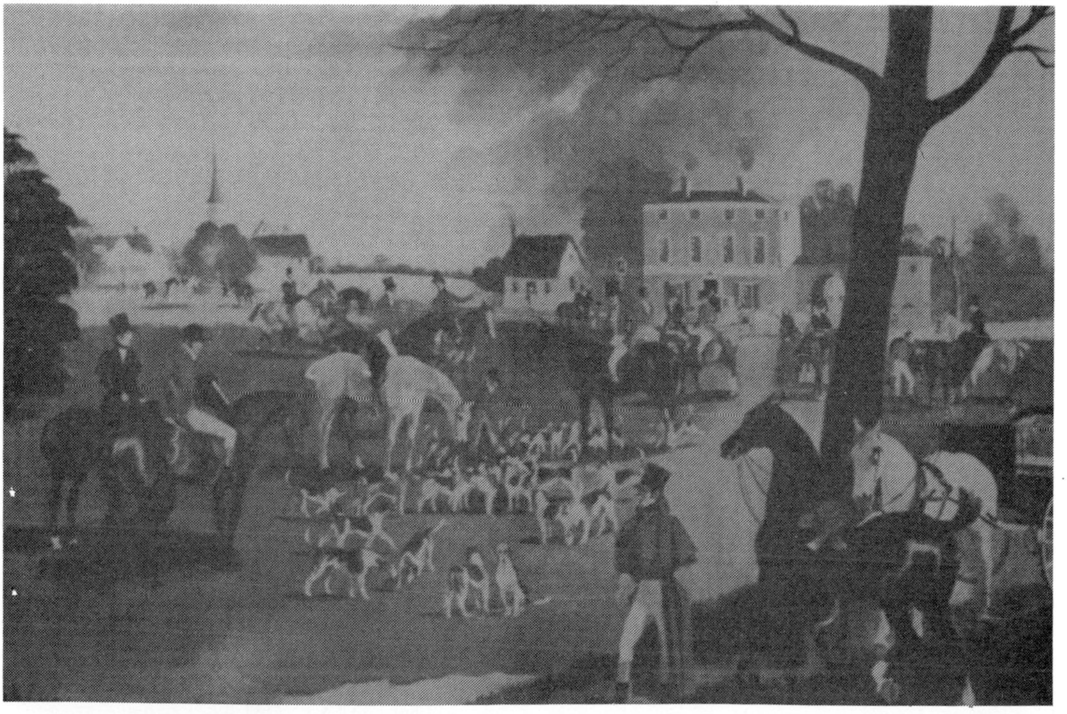

DORIS ZINKEISEN – The Meet – signed – oil on canvas – 61 x 71cm. *(Phillips)* **$1,494 £900**

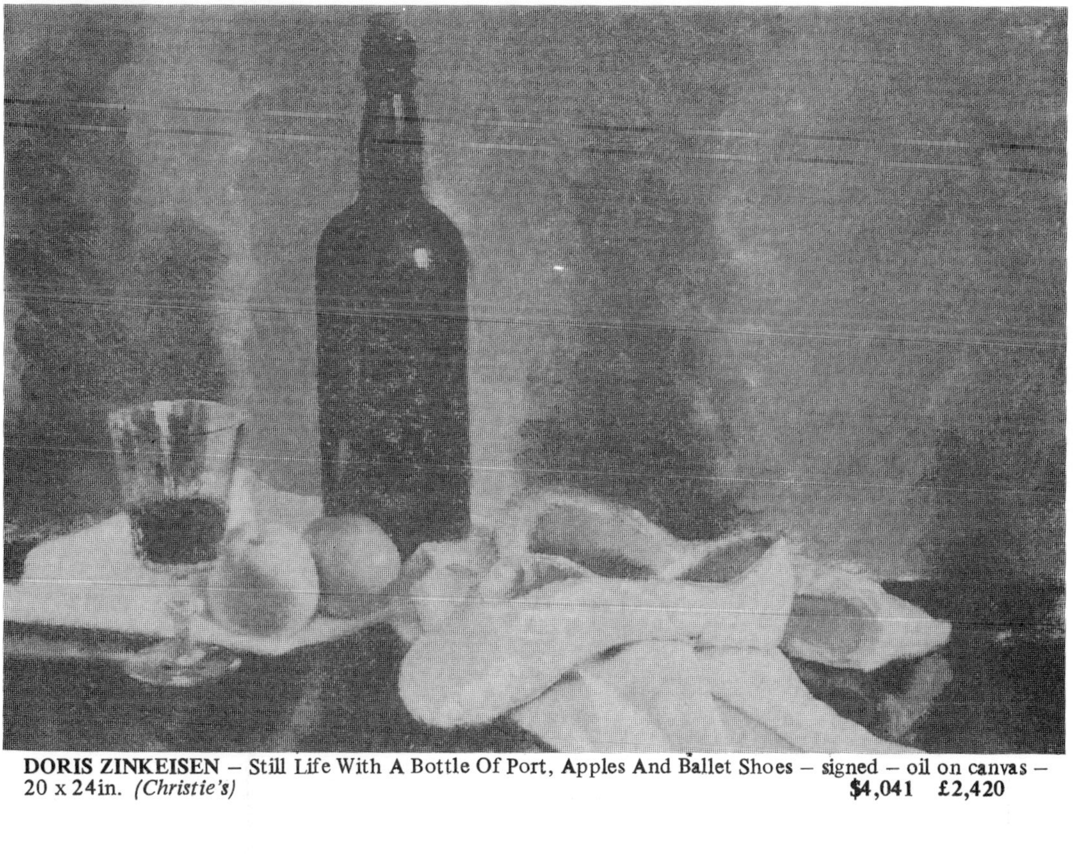

DORIS ZINKEISEN – Still Life With A Bottle Of Port, Apples And Ballet Shoes – signed – oil on canvas – 20 x 24in. *(Christie's)* **$4,041 £2,420**

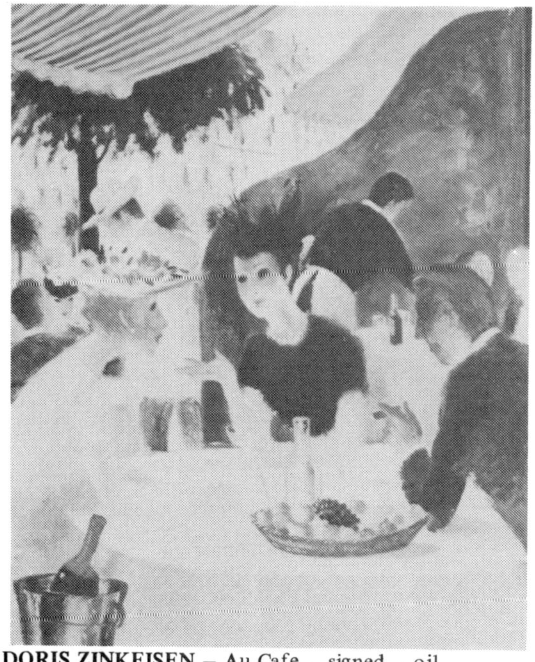

DORIS ZINKEISEN – Au Cafe – signed – oil on canvas – 61 x 51cm.
(Phillips) **$2,490** **£1,500**

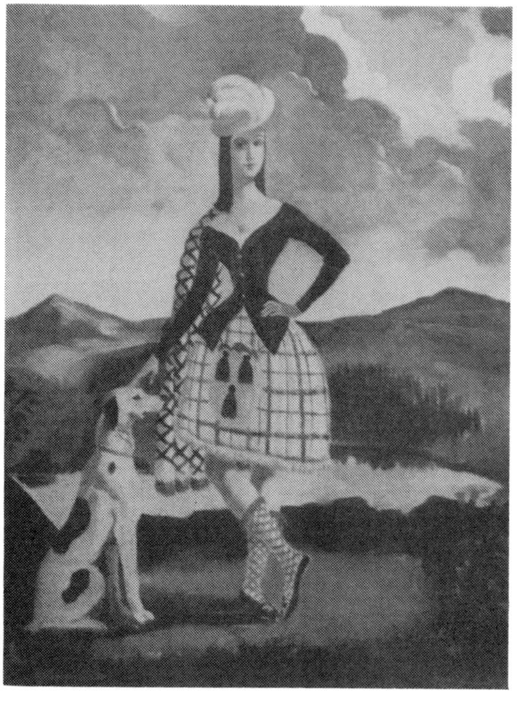

DORIS ZINKEISEN – A Highland Lass – signed – oil on canvas – 20 x 16in.
(Christie's) **$1,653** **£990**

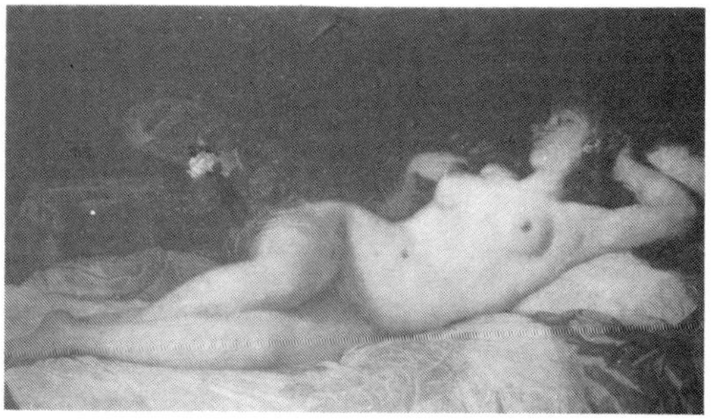

ANTONIO ZONA – A Reclining Nude – signed and inscribed – 39½ x 55½in.
(Christie's) **$6,336** **£4,400**

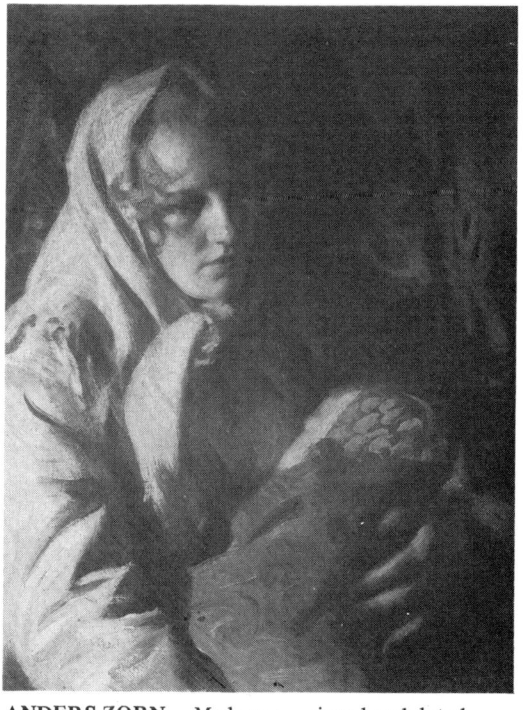

ANDERS ZORN – Madonna – signed and dated '99? – 29 x 22¾in.
(Christie's) **$114,400** **£71,500**

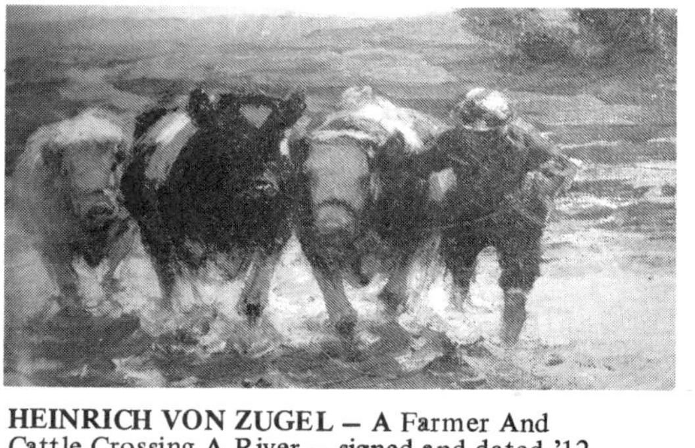

HEINRICH VON ZUGEL – A Farmer And Cattle Crossing A River – signed and dated '12 – on canvas – 35 x 46cm.
(Phillips) **$24,480** **£17,000**